Department of International Economic and Social Affairs, Statistical Office of the United Nations
Département des affaires économiques et sociales internationales, Bureau de statistique des Nations Unies

Industrial Statistics Yearbook 1985
Annuaire de statistiques industrielles 1985

Volume II

Commodity Production Statistics
1976 - 1985

Statistiques de production (par produit)
1976 - 1985

United Nations / Nations Unies
New York, 1987

NOTE

Symbols of United Nations documents are composed of capital letters combined with figures. Mention of such a symbol indicates a reference to a United Nations document.

General disclaimer

The designations employed and the presentation of material in this publication do not imply the expression of any opinion whatsoever on the part of the Secretariat of the United Nations concerning the legal status of any country, territory, city or area, or of its authorities, or concerning the delimitation of its frontiers or boundaries.

Where the designation "country or area" appears in the headings of tables, it covers countries, territories, cities or areas. In prior issues of this publication, where the designation "country" appears in the headings of tables, it should be interpreted to cover countries, territories, cities or areas.

In some tables, the designation "developed" and "developing" economies is intended for statistical convenience and does not necessarily express a judgement about the stage reached by a particular country or area in the development process.

NOTE

Les cotes des documents de l'Organisation des Nations Unies se composent de lettres majuscules et de chiffres. La simple mention d'une cote dans un texte signifie qu'il s'agit d'un document de l'Organisation.

Déni de responsabilité

Les appellations employées dans cette publication et la présentation des données qui y figurent n'impliquent de la part du Secrétariat de l'Organisation des Nations Unies aucune prise de position quant au statut juridique des pays, territoires, villes ou zones, ou de leurs autorités, ni quant au tracé de leurs frontières ou limites.

L'appellation "pays ou zone" figurant dans les titres des rubriques des tableaux désigne des pays, des territoires, des villes ou des zones. L'appellation "pays" figurant dans certaines rubriques des tableaux de numéros antérieurs de cette publication doit être interprétée comme désignant des pays, des territoires, des villes ou des zones.

Les appellations économies "développées" et économies "en voie de développement" qui figurent dans certains tableaux sont utilisées pour plus de commodité dans la présentation des statistiques et n'impliquent pas nécessairement un jugement quant au stade de développement auquel sont parvenus un pays ou une zone donnés.

ST/ESA/STAT/SER.P/24(Vol.II)

UNITED NATIONS PUBLICATION

Sales No. E/F.87.XVII.9

05000H

(only hardbound edition for sale)

PUBLICATION DES NATIONS UNIES

Numéro de vente : E/F.87.XVII.9

05000H

(édition reliée toile en vente seulement)

ISBN 92-1-061121-7

ISBN 92-1-161289-6 (vols.I and II the set)

Inquiries should be directed to:

PUBLISHING DIVISION

UNITED NATIONS

NEW YORK, N.Y. 10017

Adresser toutes demandes de renseignements à la :

DIVISION DES PUBLICATIONS

NATIONS UNIES

NEW YORK, N.Y. 10017

Manufactured in United States of America—Imprimé aux Etats-Unis d'Amérique

TABLE OF CONTENTS - TABLE DES MATIERES

INTRODUCTION

This is the nineteenth in a series of annual compilations of statistics on world industry designed to meet both the general demand for information of this kind and the special requirements of the United Nations, particularly the United Nations Industrial Development Organization (UNIDO), and related international bodies. Beginning with the 1982 edition, the title of the publication was changed to *Industrial Statistics Yearbook* as the result of a decision to standardize the titles of recurrent publications issued by the Statistical Office. The previous title, *Yearbook of Industrial Statistics*, was introduced in the 1974 edition. The first seven editions in this series were published under the title *The Growth of World Industry*.

The *Industrial Statistics Yearbook* comprises two volumes. Volume I contains general industrial statistics providing the basic country data as well as a selection of indicators showing the global and regional trends in industrial activity.

This volume, on the other hand, deals specifically with the annual statistics of production of industrial commodities. This information at the commodity level supplements the data presented on an industry basis in Volume I and provides a more specific indication of the nature and importance of the industrial activities undertaken in each country.

The current issue of Volume II contains production statistics on 553 industrial commodities (582 statistical series) and provides information on about 200 countries or areas. Most of the statistics in the present edition refer to the ten-year period 1976-1985.

Presentation of statistics

In principle, the data in this volume refer to the total industrial production of each commodity during the years indicated and within the national boundaries of each country. The data should thus include: (a) the production of industrial establishments for which the commodity is a primary product; (b) the production of industrial establishments for which it is a secondary product; (c) for products, the production of industrial establishments for which it is an intermediate product. Unless otherwise stated in the foot-notes, production by non-industrial establishments, such as farm production of dairy products, is excluded.

Selection, ordering and coding of commodities

The selection of industrial commodities is based on a comprehensive list of products and materials [1] prepared by the Statistical Office of the United Nations for the 1973 World Programme of Industrial Statistics. A complete enumeration of the commodities contained in this publication is given in the index shown at the end of the volume. Definitions of commodities are also provided at the end of each relevant table. These definitions are based largely on the description of related items of the Brussels Tariff Nomenclature (BTN). [2]

1 *Recommendations for the 1973 World Programme of Industrial Statistics, part II, List of Selected Products and Materials*, Statistical Papers, Series M, No. 54 (part II) (United Nations publication, Sales No. E.71.XVII.16).

2 Customs Co-operation Council, Explanatory Notes to the Brussels Nomenclature (Brussels, 1955).

Ce recueil de statistiques annuel sur l'industrie mondiale est le dix-neuvième d'une série qui vise à répondre tant à la demande générale d'information dans ce domaine qu'aux besoins spécifiques de l'Organisation des Nations Unies, et en particulier de l'Organisation des Nations Unies pour le développement industriel (ONUDI), ainsi que des organismes internationaux qui lui sont reliés. A partir de 1982 publié sous le titre *Annuaire de statistiques industrielles (Industrial Statistics Yearbook)*, il fait suite à ceux qui avaient paru dans la série *Croissance de l'industrie mondiale*, puis, à partir de 1974, en anglais seulement, sous le titre *Yearbook of Industrial Statistics*.

L'*Annuaire de statistiques industrielles* comprend deux volumes. Le volume I regroupe les statistiques industrielles générales, où l'on trouve les données de base par pays ainsi qu'un choix d'indicateurs des tendances mondiales et régionales de l'activité industrielle.

Le volume II est consacré aux statistiques annuelles de production des produits industriels. Ces données complètent les statistiques relatives aux industries que l'on trouve dans le volume I et fournissent des indications plus précises quant à la nature et à l'importance des activités industrielles dans chaque pays.

Les statistiques de production figurant dans la présente édition du volume II portent sur 553 produits de base industriels (582 séries statistiques) et quelque 200 pays ou zones. La plupart couvrent la décennie 1976-1985.

Présentation des statistiques

En principe, les données présentées dans ce volume portent sur la production industrielle totale de chaque produit pendant les années indiquées et dans les frontières nationales de chaque pays. Elles devraient donc indiquer, pour chacun de ces produits: (a) la production des établissements industriels pour lesquels il s'agit d'un produit primaire; (b) la production des établissements industriels pour lesquels il s'agit d'un produit secondaire; (c) pour certains produits la production des établissements industriels pour lesquels il s'agit d'un produit intermédiaire. Sauf indication contraire figurant en note, les données s'entendent à l'exclusion de la production des établissements non industriels, telle que la production agricole de produits laitiers.

Choix, classement et codage des produits de base

Le choix des produits de base industriels repose sur une liste exhaustive de produits et matières [1] établie par le Bureau de statistique de l'Organisation des Nations Unies en vue du Programme mondial de statistiques de l'industrie de 1973. On trouvera une liste complète des produits cités dans la présente publication en consultant l'annexe qui figure à la fin du volume. Les définitions des produits sont également indiquées à la fin des tableaux correspondants. Elles s'inspirent en grande partie de la description des éléments correspondants de la Nomenclature douanière de Bruxelles (NDB). [2]

1 *Recommandations pour le Programme mondial de statistiques industrielles de 1973, Deuxième partie, Liste partielle de produits et matières, Etudes statistiques*, Série M, No. 54 (deuxième partie) (Publication des Nations Unies, numéro de vente: F.71.XVII.I6).

2 Conseil de coopération douanière, notes explicatives de la Nomenclature douanière de Bruxelles (Bruxelles, 1955).

The coding of the commodities has been based on the codes of the *International Standard Industrial Classification of All Economic Activities* (ISIC). [3] The first four digits of the six-digit code number relate to the pertinent ISIC industry group of which the commodity is a principal product.

The remaining two digits indicate the position of the item within the set of commodities pertaining to this industry group. In a few cases, however, a seventh digit has been introduced to provide more detail for a given commodity than the afore mentioned "list of selected products and materials" would allow. As a result, the data previously shown under refined copper, for example, have now been broken down to supply additional useful information on the production of primary and secondary refined copper separately. As a rule, where two or more units of measurement are recommended, the series are differentiated by the use of capital letters "A", "B" etc. following the basic code. In a few cases, however, these letters also relate to the components of a given item. Where the codes for a commodity are identified by the letter "M", the data are shown in terms of metal content of metal-bearing ores and concentrates.

The position of the commodity in the *Standard International Trade Classification* Revised (SITC) [4] is shown on the right-hand side of the definition. In this case, also, a six-digit code number is used, the first five digits being the code number of the most closely related SITC item and the sixth digit indicating whether the item is the equivalent of the SITC item (use of zero in the sixth place) or only part of it (use of 1, 2 etc. in the sixth place). Where the item in the list corresponds to more than one SITC item, a plus sign is added to the code number given which corresponds to the first (lower digit) SITC reference. A further indication of the SITC equivalent in such cases is normally given at the end of the commodity description.

Comparability of the data

The metric system of weights and measures has been used throughout the volume. While efforts have been made to ensure the comparability of the series published for each commodity through the use of standard definitions and units of measurements, the compilation of the data in standard form has occasionally presented difficulties. In some cases, for example, units of measurement other than the recommended units have been used in reporting and, in these cases, the data have been converted into the recommended units either by the use of standard conversion factors or by *ad hoc* conversion factors. The latter have been utilized in the compilation of certain tables in the publication; some of these factors are only of an approximate character and have been employed solely to obtain a reasonable measure of international comparability on the tables. A list of conversion factors is given following the introduction. In other cases, however, the data could not be converted into the recommended units for lack of appropriate conversion factors.

[3] Statistical Papers, Series M, No. 4, Rev. 2 (United Nations publication, Sales No. E.68.XVII.8).

[4] Statistical Papers, Series M, No. 34 (United Nations publication, Sales No. E.61.XVII.6).

Le codage des produits a été établi d'après celui de la *Classification internationale type, par industrie, de toutes les branches d'activité économique* (CITI). [3] Des six chiffres que comprend l'indicatif, les quatre premiers correspondent au groupe de la CITI dont le produit considéré est la principale production.

Les deux autres chiffres correspondent au numéro de série (position) du produit considéré à l'intérieur du groupe. Dans certains cas, on a ajouté un septième chiffre pour fournir des indications plus détaillées sur un produit donné que la "Liste partielle de produits et matières" susmentionnée. C'est ainsi que l'on a dissocié les données antérieurement fournies sous la rubrique "Cuivre affiné" pour présenter des informations complémentaires sur la production primaire et la production secondaire de cuivre affiné. En règle générale, lorsque deux unités de mesure ou plus sont recommandées, les séries sont différenciées par l'utilisation de lettres majuscules "A", "B", etc., à la suite de l'indicatif principal. Dans un petit nombre de cas, toutefois, ces lettres correspondent aussi aux éléments d'une position donnée. Lorsque l'indicatif d'un produit contient la lettre "M", les données sont fournies en poids de métal contenu dans les minerais métalliques et les concentrés.

La position de l'article dans la *Classification type pour le commerce international* (CTCI) [4] révisée est indiquée à droite de la définition. Dans ce cas aussi on utilise un indicatif à six chiffres: les cinq premiers correspondent à celui de la position de la CTCI la plus proche et le sixième précisant s'il y a identité (auquel cas ce chiffre est un zéro) ou correspondance partielle seulement (ce chiffre étant alors 1, 2 et aussi de suite). Lorsque le poste de la liste correspond à plus d'une position de la CTCI, l'indicatif retenu est celui de la première rubrique de la CTCI (par ordre numérique croissant) où il en est question, affecté du signe plus. En pareil cas, l'équivalence par rapport à la CTCI est généralement indiquée à la fin de la description.

Comparabilité des données

Le système métrique de poids et mesures a été utilisé tout au long du présent volume. Malgré les efforts faits pour assurer la comparabilité des séries publiées pour chaque article par l'application de définitions et d'unités de mesure normalisées, la collecte des données sous une forme normalisée n'est pas toujours allée sans mal. Dans les cas, par exemple, où elles ont été fournies dans des unités de mesure autres que les unités recommandées, elles ont eté converties dans les unités recommandées à l'aide soit de facteurs de conversion normalisés, soit, pour l'établissement de certains tableaux, de facteurs de conversion spéciaux dont quelques-uns n'ont qu'un caractère d'approximation et n'ont été employés que pour assurer des possibilités raisonnables de comparaison des tableaux entre les divers pays. On trouvera une liste des facteurs de conversion utilisés à la suite de l'introduction. Il y a cependant des cas où les données n'ont pu être converties dans les unités recommandées, faute de facteurs de conversion appropriés.

[3] Etudes Statistiques, Série M, No. 4, Rev. 2 (Publication des Nations Unies, numéro de vente: F.68.XVII.8).

[4] Etudes statistiques, Série M, No. 34 (Publication des Nations Unies, numéro de vente: F.61.XVII.6).

Aggregates and estimation of missing data

Most of the tables in the publication contain aggregate figures described as total. The aggregates of data are shown for commodities for which it is believed a satisfactory degree of comparability exists in the series for the different countries. They represent the summation of the country data shown in the tables and also make provision for including estimates of the missing data. The data relating to the Byelorussian SSR and the Ukrainian SSR, however, are not included in the summation of the country data since they make up part of the total production for the USSR.

In providing the estimates of the missing data for a given country and commodity, the following methods have been utilized:

(a) When the available data is limited to a single year, this figure is repeated for the remaining years;

(b) When data are available for less than five years of the period shown, the average of the years is used for the missing data;

(c) When data are available for five or more years of the period shown, estimates for the missing data are derived from a regression straight line, using the least squares method, applied to the reported data.

When some data in a given table are shown in units of measurement other than the unit indicated for that table and conversion of such data to the standard unit is not possible, aggregate figures are not published.

Sources

Like the previous issues, the *Industrial Statistics Yearbook* has been prepared by the Statistical Office of the United Nations with the generous co-operation of the national statistical authorities.

Acknowledgement is also due to the following specialized agencies and intergovernmental bodies whose publications have been utilized in updating our statistics: Food and Agriculture Organization of the United Nations (Rome), secretariat of the Commission of the European Economic Communities (Brussels), International Atomic Energy Agency (Vienna), International Coffee Organization (London), International Monetary Fund (Washington, D.C.), secretariat of the International Rubber Study Group (London), International Sugar Organization (London), International Tin Council (London), International Wheat Council (London) and International Superphosphate and Compound Manufacturers' Association (London), Nuclear Energy Agency of the Organisation for Economic Co-operation and Development (Paris), Organisation for Economic Co-operation and Development (Paris), Organization of American States (Washington, D.C.) and Organization of the Petroleum Exporting Countries (Vienna).

Agrégats et estimation des données manquantes

La plupart des tableaux présentés font apparaître des agrégats, qualifiés de totaux. Ces agrégats sont fournis dans le cas des produits pour lesquels les séries nationales disponibles sont aisément comparables. Ils représentent la somme des données nationales figurant dans les tableaux, complétées, le cas échéant, par des estimations des grandeurs manquantes. Toutefois, les données relatives aux RSS de Biélorussie et d'Ukraine ne sont pas incluses dans la somme des données par pays, dans la mesure où elles constituent une partie de la production totale de l'URSS.

Les estimations correspondant aux données manquantes pour un pays et un produit donnés sont établies de la façon suivante:

(a) lorsque les données disponibles ne portent que sur une seule année, le chiffre correspondant est repris pour les autres années;

(b) lorsque les données disponibles portent sur moins de cinq années de la période considérée, on utilise, pour les données manquantes, la moyenne des années disponibles;

(c) lorsque les données disponibles pour la période considérée portent sur cinq ans ou davantage, les estimations correspondant aux données manquantes sont obtenues par régression linéaire, suivant la méthode des moindres carrés appliquée aux données existantes.

Lorsque, dans un tableau, certaines données sont fournies dans des unités de mesure autres que l'unité indiquée pour ce tableau et qu'elles ne peuvent être converties dans l'unité normalisée, aucun agrégat n'est donné.

Sources

Comme pour les éditions précédentes, l'*Annuaire de statistiques industrielles* a été établi par le Bureau de statistique de l'Organisation des Nations Unies, auquel les services statistiques nationaux ont largement prêté leur concours.

Le Bureau de statistique se doit aussi de remercier les institutions spécialisées et les organes intergouvernementaux dont il a utilisé les publications pour mettre à jour les statistiques, à savoir: l'Organisation des Nations Unies pour l'âlimentation et l'agriculture (FAO) (Rome), le Secrétariat de la Commission des Communautés européennes (Bruxelles), l'Agence internationale de l'énergie atomique (Vienne), le Fonds monétaire international (Washington, D.C.), le Secrétariat du Groupe international d'étude du caoutchouc (Londres), l'Organisation internationale du sucre (Londres), le Conseil international de l'étain (Londres), le Conseil international du blé (Londres), et l'Association internationale des fabricants de superphosphates et d'engrais composés (Londres), l'Agence pour l'énergie nucléaire de l'Organisation de coopération et de développement économiques (Paris), l'Organisation de coopération et de développement économiques (Paris), l'Organisation des Etats américains (Washington, D.C.) et l'Organisation des pays exportateurs de pétrole (Vienne).

Governmental agencies, private institutes and associations and others to whom credit is also due for the valuable information used in this publication are as follows: Agency for International Development (Washington, D.C.), American Bureau of Metal Statistics (New York), Lloyd's Register of Shipping (London), Billboard Publications, Inc. (New York), Instituto Latinoamericano del Fierro y el Acero (ILAFA) (Buenos Aires), Institute of Geological Sciences, Natural Environment Research Council (London), Metallgesellschaft Aktiengesellschaft (Frankfurt), Textile Economics Bureau (New York), United States Bureau of Mines (Washington, D.C.), United States Department of Agriculture (Washington, D.C.) and World Bureau of Metal Statistics (London).

Pour la présente publication, le Bureau de statistique est en outre redevable d'informations utiles aux services nationaux, instituts et associations privées et autres organismes suivants: Agency for International Development (Washington, D.C.), American Bureau of Metal Statistics (New York), Registre des transports maritimes de la Lloyd's (Londres), Billboard Publications, Inc. (New York), Instituto Latinoamericano del Fierro y el Acero (ILAFA) (Buenos Aires), Institute of Geological Sciences, Natural Environment Research Council (Londres), Metallgesellschaft Aktiengesellschaft (Francfort), Textile Economics Bureau (New York), Office des Mines des Etats-Unis (Washington, D.C.), Ministère américain de l'agriculture (Washington, D.C.) et World Bureau of Metal Statistics (Londres).

Country order and nomenclature

A complete listing, in alphabetical order, of countries and territories is provided in the country index at the end of this publication.

In the tables, however, the countries are arranged in continental and regional order irrespective of their political status. The order followed for the continental division is as follows: Africa; America, North; America, South; Asia, excluding the USSR; Europe, excluding the USSR; USSR; and Oceania. Within Europe, they are further arranged in regional order as follows: European Economic Community (EEC), European Free Trade Association (EFTA), Eastern Europe; and Other.

Data relating to the People's Republic of China generally include those for Taiwan Province in the field of statistics relating to population, area, natural resources, natural conditions, such as climate etc. In other fields of statistics, they do not include Taiwan Province unless otherwise stated. Therefore, in this publication, the data published under the heading "China" exclude those for Taiwan province.

The data which relate to the Federal Republic of Germany and the German Democratic Republic include the relevant data relating to Berlin, for which separate data have not been supplied. This is without prejudice to any question of status which may be involved.

For reasons of space or geographical clarity, some country names have been abbreviated. These abbreviated country names are, of course, intended to be of purely geographical significance to the reader and to convey no political implications whatsoever.

Since the 1970 edition of the publication, the following changes in designation have been made:

Data formerly given under Antigua are now shown under *Antigua and Barbuda*;

Bangladesh, formerly East Pakistan, became independent on 26 March 1971;

Data formerly given under British Honduras are now shown under *Belize*;

Data formerly given under Dahomey are now shown under *Benin*;

Data formerly given under Brunei are now shown under *Brunei Darussalam;*

Classement par pays et nomenclature

L'index par pays que l'on trouvera à la fin de ce volume offre une liste alphabétique complète des pays et territoires.

Dans les tableaux, en revanche, les pays sont classés par continent et par région, indépendamment de leur status politique. Le classement adopté pour la répartition par continent est le suivant: Afrique; Amérique du Nord; Amérique du Sud; Asie, sans l'URSS; Europe, sans l'URSS; Océanie. Pour l'Europe, on a adopté le classement régional suivant: Communauté économique européenne (CEE), Association européenne de libre échange (AELE), Europe orientale; autres.

Les statistiques relatives à la République populaire de Chine englobent généralement la province de Taïwan lorsqu'il s'agit de population, superficie, ressources naturelles et données physiques comme le climat, notamment. Dans les statistiques relatives aux autres domaines, la province de Taïwan n'est pas comprise, sauf indication contraire. Dans la présente publication, la rubrique "Chine" s'entend donc à l'exclusion de la province de Taïwan.

Les statistiques concernant la République fédérale d'Allemagne et la République démocratique allemande englobent la ville de Berlin, pour laquelle des données distinctes n'ont pas été fournies, ce qui ne préjuge en rien l'eventuelle question de son statut.

Pour des raisons de place ou de clarté géographique, certains noms de pays ont été abrégés. Il est bien entendu que ces abréviations n'ont de valeur que purement géographique pour le lecteur et qu'elles n'impliquent aucune prise de position politique.

Depuis l'édition 1970 de cet Annuaire, un certain nombre de changements d'appellation sont intervenus:

Les données figurant auparavant sous la rubrique Antigua sont présentées sous la rubrique *Antigua-et-Barbuda*;

Le *Bangladesh*, ex-Pakistan oriental, a accédé à l'indépendance le 26 mars 1971;

Les données figurant auparavant sous la rubrique Honduras britannique sont présentées sous la rubrique *Belize*;

Les données figurant auparavant sous la rubrique Dahomey sont présentées sous la rubrique *Bénin*;

Les données figurant auparavant sous la rubrique Brunéi sont présentées sous la rubrique *Brunéi Darussalam*;

Data formerly given under Upper Volta are now shown under *Burkina Faso;*

Data variously shown under Cameroon and United Republic of Cameroon are now listed under *Cameroon*;

Data formerly given under Cape Verde Islands are now shown under *Cape Verde*;

Data variously shown under Central African Republic and Central African Empire are now listed under *Central African Republic*;

Data formerly given under Comoro Islands are now shown under *Comoros*;

Data formerly shown under Ivory Coast are now shown under *Côte d'Ivoire*;

Data variously shown under Khmer Republic and Cambodia in previous editions, are now listed under *Democratic Kampuchea*;

Data initially given under Yemen, People's Democratic Republic of and listed later under Yemen, Democratic are now shown under *Democratic Yemen*;

Data formerly given under Territory of Afars and Issas are now shown under *Djibouti*;

Data formerly given under Portuguese Timor are now shown under *East Timor*;

Data formerly given Gilbert Islands are now shown under *Kiribati*;

Data formerly given under Portuguese Guinea are now shown under *Guinea-Bissau*;

Data formerly given under Iran are now shown under *Iran (Islamic Republic of)*;

Data formerly given under Laos are now shown under *Lao People's Democratic Republic*;

Data formerly given under Libyan Arab Republic are now shown under *Libyan Arab Jamahiriya*;

Data formerly given under Panama Canal Zone are now shown under *Former Canal Zone*;

Data formerly given under Papua and New Guinea separately are now shown under *Papua New Guinea*;

Data formerly given under St. Lucia are now shown under *Saint Lucia*;

Data formerly given under St. Kitts-Nevis are now shown under *Saint Christopher and Nevis*;

Les données figurant auparavant sous la rubrique Haute Volta sont présentées sous la rubrique *Burkina Faso;*

Les données figurant auparavant soit sous la rubrique Cameroun, soit sous la rubrique République-Unie du Cameroun, sont présentées sous la rubrique *Cameroun*;

Les données figurant auparavant sous la rubrique îles du Cap-Vert sont présentées sous la rubrique *Cap-Vert*;

Les données figurant auparavant soit sous la rubrique République centrafricaine, soit sous la rubrique Empire centrafricain sont présentées sous la rubrique *République centrafricaine*;

Les données figurant auparavant sous la rubrique îles Comores sont présentées sous la rubrique *Comores*;

Les données figurant auparavant sous la rubrique Ivory Coast sont présentées sous la rubrique *Côte d'Ivoire*;

Les données figurant auparavant soit sous la rubrique République khmère, soit sous la rubrique Cambodge, sont présentées sous la rubrique *Kampuchea démocratique*;

Les données figurant initialement sous la rubrique Yémen, République populaire démocratique du, et par la suite sous la rubrique Yémen (démocratique), sont présentées sous la rubrique *Yémen démocratique*;

Les données figurant auparavant sous la rubrique Territoire des Afars et des Issas sont présentées sous la rubrique *Djibouti*;

Les données figurant auparavant sous la rubrique Timor portugais sont présentées sous la rubrique *Timor oriental*;

Les données figurant auparavant sous la rubrique îles Gilbert sont présentées sous la rubrique *Kiribati*;

Les données figurant auparavant sous la rubrique Guinée portugaise sont présentées sous la rubrique *Guinée-Bissau*;

Les données figurant auparavant sous la rubrique Iran sont présentées sous la rubrique *Iran (République islamique d')*;

Les données figurant auparavant sous la rubrique Laos sont présentées sous la rubrique *République démocratique populaire lao*;

Les données figurant auparavant sous la rubrique République arabe libyenne sont présentées sous la rubrique *Jamahiriya arabe libyenne*;

Les données figurant auparavant sous la rubrique Zone du canal de Panama sont présentées sous la rubrique *ancienne Zone du Canal*;

Les données figurant auparavant sous les rubriques distinctes de Papouasie et Nouvelle-Guinée sont présentées sous la rubrique *Papouasie-Nouvelle-Guinée*;

Les données figurant auparavant sous la rubrique Ste Lucie sont présentées sous la rubrique *Sainte-Lucie*;

Les données figurant auparavant sous la rubrique Saint-Kitts-et-Nevis sont présentées sous la rubrique *Saint-Christophe-et-Nevis*;

Data formerly given under St. Vincent are now shown under *Saint Vincent and the Grenadines*;

Data formerly given under Western Samoa are now shown under *Samoa*;

Data formerly given under British Solomon Islands are now shown under *Solomon Islands*;

Data formerly given under Ceylon are now shown under *Sri Lanka*;

Data formerly given under Surinam are now shown under *Suriname*;

Data formerly given under Ellice Islands are now shown under *Tuvalu*;

Data formerly given under New Hebrides are now shown under *Vanuatu*;

Data initially given under Democratic Republic of Viet-Nam and Republic of South Viet-Nam separately and listed later under Socialist Republic of Viet Nam are now shown under *Viet Nam*;

Data formerly given under Spanish Sahara are now shown under *Western Sahara*;

Data formerly given under Southern Rhodesia are now shown under *Zimbabwe*.

Explanation of symbols

The following symbols have been employed in making entries in the tables:

...	Data not available
0	Magnitude nil or less than half of the unit of measurement employed
.	Not applicable
c	Data are confidential
*	Provisional or estimated figure
o	FAO estimate
#	A marked break in the series, data prior to the sign not comparable

Decimal figures are always preceded by a period (.)

Figures not included in totals and sub-totals are given in parentheses.

Les données figurant auparavant sous la rubrique St. Vincent sont présentées sous la rubrique *Saint-Vincent-et-Grenadines*;

Les données figurant auparavant sous la rubrique Samoa-Occidental sont présentées sous la rubrique *Samoa*;

Les données figurant auparavant sous la rubrique îles Salomon britanniques sont présentées sous la rubrique *Iles Salomon*;

Les données figurant auparavant sous la rubrique Ceylan sont présentées sous la rubrique *Sri Lanka*;

Les données figurant auparavant sous la rubrique Surinam sont présentées sous la rubrique *Suriname*;

Les données figurant auparavant sous la rubrique îles Ellice sont présentées sous la rubrique *Tuvalu*;

Les données figurant auparavant sous la rubrique Nouvelles-Hébrides sont présentées sous la rubrique *Vanuatu*;

Les données figurant originairement sous les rubriques République démocratique du Viet Nam et République du Sud Viet Nam et classées par la suite sous la rubrique République socialiste du Viet Nam sont présentées sous la rubrique *Viet Nam*;

Les données figurant auparavant sous la rubrique Sahara espagnol sont présentées sous la rubrique *Sahara occidental*;

Les données figurant auparavant sous la rubrique Rhodésie du Sud sont présentées sous la rubrique *Zimbabwe*.

Explication des symboles

Les symboles employés dans les tableaux sont les suivants:

...	Données non disponibles
0	Grandeur nulle ou inférieure à la moitié de l'unité de mesure utilisée
.	Ne s'applique pas
c	Données à caractère confidentiel
*	Chiffre provisoire ou estimatif
o	Estimation de la FAO
#	Marque une interruption dans la série et la non-comparabilité des données précédant le symbole

Les décimales sont toujours précédées d'un point (.)

Les chiffres non inclus dans les totaux et les totaux partiels sont indiqués entre parenthèses.

CONVERSION COEFFICIENTS AND FACTORS - COEFFICIENTS ET FACTEURS DE CONVERSION

Note. The metric system of weights and measures has been employed in the *Industrial Statistics Yearbook*. In this system, the relationship between units of volume and capacity is: 1 litre = 1 cubic decimetre exactly (as decided by the 12th International Conference of Weights and Measures, New Delhi, November 1964).

Section A shows the equivalents of the basic metric, British imperial and United States units of measurement. According to an agreement between the national standard institutions of English-speaking nations, the British and United States units of length, area and volume are now identical, and based on the yard = 0.9144 metre exactly. The weight measures in both systems are based on the pound = 0.45359237 kilogram exactly. (Reference: *Weights and Measures Act 1963* (London), and Federal Register announcement of 1 July 1959: *Refinement of Values for the Yard and Pound* (Washington D.C.).)

Section B shows various derived or conventional conversion coefficients and equivalents.

Section C shows other conversion coefficients or factors which have been utilized in the compilation of certain tables in the *Industrial Statistics Yearbook*. Some of these are only of an approximate character and have been employed solely to obtain a reasonable measure of international comparability on the tables.

For a comprehensive survey of international and national systems of weights and measures and of units weights for a large number of commodities in different countries, see *World Weights and Measures*, Statistical Papers, Series M. No. 21, Rev. 1 (United Nations publication, Sales No. 66.XVII.3).

Remarque. *L'Annuaire de statistiques industrielles* utilise le système métrique pour les poids et mesures. La relation entre unités métriques de volume et de capacité est: 1 litre = 1 décimètre cube (dm^3) exactement (comme ce fut décidé à la Conférence internationale de poids et mesures, New Delhi, novembre 1964).

La section A fournit les équivalents principaux des systèmes de mesure métrique, britannique et américain. Suivant un accord entre les institutions de normalisation nationales des pays de langue anglaise, les mesures britanniques et américaines de longueur, superficie et volume sont désormais identiques, et sont basées sur le yard = 0.9144 mètre exactement. Les mesures de poids se rapportent, dans les deux systèmes, à la pound (livre) = 0.45359237 kilogramme exactement. (Référence: *Weights and Measures Act 1963 (Londres)*, et *Federal Register Announcement of 1 July 1959: Refinement of Values for the Yard and Pound* (Washington, D.C.).).

La section B fournit divers coeficients et facteurs de conversion conventionnels ou dérivés.

La section C fournit d'autres coefficients ou facteurs de conversion utilisés dans l'élaboration de certains tableaux de l'*Annuaire de statistiques industrielles.* D'aucuns ne sont que des approximations et n'ont été utilisés que pour obtenir un degré raisonnable de comparabilité sur le plan international.

Pour une étude d'ensemble des systèmes internationaux et nationaux de poids et mesures, et d'unités de poids pour un grand nombre de produits dans différents pays, voir *World Weights and Measures,* Etudes statistiques, Série M., No. 21, Rev. 1 (publication des Nations Unies, numéro de vente: 66.XVII.3).

A. Equivalents of metric, British imperial and United States units of measure
Equivalents des unités métriques, britanniques et américaines

Metric units Unités métriques	British imperial and U.S. equivalents Equivalents en mesures britanniques et des Etats-Unis	British imperial and U.S. units Unités britannniques et des Etats-Unis	Metric equivalents Equivalents en mesures métriques	
Length-Longeur:				
1 centimetre-centimètre (cm)	0.3937008 inch	1 inch	2.540	cm
1 metre-mètre (m)	(3.280840 feet	1 foot	30.480	cm
	(1.093613 yard	1 yard	0.9144	m
1 kilometre - kilomètre (km)	(0.6213712 mile	1 mile	1609.344	m
	(0.5399568 int. naut. mile	1 international nautical mile	1852.000	m
Area - Superficie:				
1 square centimetre - cm^2	0.1550003 square inch	1 square inch	6.45160	cm^2
1 square metre - m^2	(10.763910 square feet	1 square foot	9.290304	dm^2
	(1.195990 square yards	1 square yard	0.83612736	m^2
1 hectare - ha	2.471054 acres	1 acre	0.4046856	ha^2
1 square kilometre - km^2	0.3861022 square mile	1 square mile	2.589988	km^2
Volume:				
1 cubic centimetre - cm^3	0.06102374 cubic inch	1 cubic inch	16.38706	cm^3
1 cubic metre - m^3	(35.31467 cubic feet	1 cubic foot	28.316847	dm^3
	(1.307951 cubic yards	1 cubic yard	0.76455486	m^3
Capacity - Capacité:				
	(0.8798766 imp. quart	1 British imperial quart	1.136523	l
1 litre (l)	(1.056688 U.S. liq. quart	1 U.S. liquid quart	0.9463529	l
	(0.908083 U.S. dry quart	1 U.S. dry quart	1.1012208	l
	(21.99692 imp. gallons	1 imperial gallon	4.546092	l
1 hectolitre (hl)	(26.417200 U.S. gallons	1 U.S. gallon	3.785412	l
	(2.749614 imp. bushels	1 imperial bushel	36.368735	l
	(2.837760 U.S. bushels	1 U.S. bushel	35.239067	l
Weight or mass - Poids				
	(35.27396 av. ounces	1 av. ounce	28.349523	g
1 kilogram (kg)	(32.15075 troy ounces	1 troy ounce	31.10348	g
	(2.204623 av. pounds	1 av. pound	453.59237	g
		1 cental (100 lb.)	45.359237	kg
		1 hundredweight (112 lb.)	50.802345	kg
1 ton - tonne (t)	(1.1023113 short tons	1 short ton (2 000 lb.)	0.9071847	t
	(0.9842065 long tons	1 long ton (2 240 lb.)	1.0160469	t

Conversion coefficients and factors (continued) - Coefficients et facteurs de conversion (suite)

B. Various conventional or derived coefficients - Divers coefficients conventionnels ou dérivés

FOREST PRODUCTS – PRODUITS FORESTIERS

Sawnwood, coniferous		
1 metric ton	=	1.82 cubic metres
1 standard (Petrograd)	=	4.672 cubic metres
10^3 board feet	=	2.3597 cubic metres
1 cubic metre	=	0.550 metric ton
Sawnwood, broadleaved		
1 metric ton	=	1.43 cubic metres
1 standard (Petrograd)	=	4.672 cubic metres
10^3 board feet	=	2.3597 cubic metres
1 cubic metre	=	0.700 metric ton
Railway sleepers		
1 metric ton	=	1.28 cubic metres
1 cubic metre	=	0.780 metric ton
Plywood		
1 metric ton	=	1.54 cubic metres
10^3 square metres (1 mm thickness)	=	1 cubic metre
10^3 square feet (1/8 inch thickness)	=	0.295 cubic metre
1 cubic metre	=	0.650 metric ton
Veneer sheets		
1 metric ton	=	1.33 cubic metres
10^3 square metres (1 mm thickness)	=	1 cubic metre
10^3 square feet (1/8 inch thickness)	=	0.295 cubic metre
1 cubic metre	=	0.750 metric ton
Particle board		
1 metric ton	=	1.54 cubic metres
1 cubic metre	=	0.650 metric ton
10^3 square metres (1 mm thickness)	=	1 cubic metre
10^3 square feet (1/8 inch thickness)	=	0.295 cubic metre
Fibreboard, compressed		
1 metric ton	=	1.053 cubic metres
1 cubic metre	=	0.950 metric ton
10^3 square metres (1 mm thickness)	=	1 cubic metre
10^3 square feet (1/8 inch thickness)	=	0.295 cubic metre
Fibreboard, non-compressed		
1 metric ton	=	4 cubic metres
1 cubic metre	=	0.250 metric ton
10^3 square metres (1 mm thickness)	=	1 cubic metre
10^3 square feet (1/8 inch thickness)	=	0.295 cubic metre

Sciages, conifères		
1 tonne métrique	=	1.82 mètres cubes
1 standard (Petrograd)	=	4.672 mètres cubes
10^3 pieds superficiels	=	2.3597 mètres cubes
1 mètre cube	=	0.550 tonne métrique
Sciages, non-conifères		
1 tonne métrique	=	1.43 mètres cubes
1 standard (Petrograd)	=	4.672 mètres cubes
10^3 pieds superficiels	=	2.3597 mètres cubes
1 mètre cube	=	0.700 tonne métrique
Traverses pour voies ferrées		
1 tonne métrique	=	1.28 mètres cubes
1 mètre cube	=	0.780 tonne métrique
Contreplaqués		
1 tonne métrique	=	1.54 mètres cubes
10^3 mètres carrés (1 mm d'épaisseur)	=	1 mètre cube
10^3 pieds carrés (1/8 de pouce d'épaisseur)	=	0.295 mètre cube
1 mètre cube	=	0.650 tonne métrique
Feuilles de placages		
1 tonne métrique	=	1.33 mètres cubes
10^3 mètres carrés (1 mm d'épaisseur)	=	1 mètre cube
10^3 pieds carrés (1/8 de pouce d'épaisseur)	=	0.295 mètre cube
1 mètre cube	=	0.750 tonne métrique
Panneaux de particules		
1 tonne métrique	=	1.54 mètres cubes
1 mètre cube	=	0.650 tonne métrique
10^3 mètres carrés (1 mm d'épaisseur)	=	1 mètre cube
10^3 pieds carrés (1/8 de pouce d'épaisseur)	=	0.295 mètre cube
Panneaux de fibres, durs		
1 tonne métrique	=	1.053 mètres cubes
1 mètre cube	=	0.950 tonne métrique
10^3 mètres carrés (1 mm d'épaisseur)	=	1 mètre cube
10^3 pieds carrés (1/8 de pouce d'épaisseur)	=	0.295 mètre cube
Panneaux de fibres, isolants		
1 tonne métrique	=	4 mètres cubes
1 mètre cube	=	0.250 tonne métrique
10^3 mètres carrés (1 mm d'épaisseur)	=	1 mètre cube
10^3 pieds carrés (1/8 de pouce d'épaisseur)	=	0.295 mètre cube

B. Various conventional or derived coefficients (continued) – Divers coefficients conventionnels ou dérivés (suite)

MISCELLANEOUS ITEMS — FACTEURS DIVERS

Ship tonnage – Tonnage de navire

1 register ton (100 cubic feet) – tonne de jauge = 2.83 m^3
1 British shipping ton (42 cubic feet) = 1.19 m^3
1 U.S. shipping ton (40 cubic feet) = 1.13 m^3

1 cubic metre – m^3 = (0.353 register ton – tonne de jauge
(0.841 British shipping ton
(0.885 U.S. shipping ton

1 deadweight ton (dwt ton = long ton) = 1.016047 metric ton – tonne métrique

1 metric ton – tonne métrique – 0.984 dwt ton

Electric energy – Energie électrique

1 Kilowatt (kW) = (1.34102 British horsepower (hp)
(1.35962 cheval vapeur (cv)

1 British horsepower (hp) = 0.7457 kW
1 cheval vapeur (cv) = 0.735499 kW

Alcohol – Alcool

1 Imperial proof gallon = 0.57 Imperial gallon of pure alcohol at 51°F = 2.59 litres d'alcool pur à 10.6°C
1 U.S. proof gallon = 0.5 U.S. gallon of pure alcohol at 60°F = 1.893 litre d'alcool pur à 15.6°C
1 litre of pure alcohol – litre d'alcool pur = 0.386 Imperial proof gallon = 0.528 U.S. proof gallon.

Salted fish

A coefficient of 0.66 was employed to convert quantities reported as wet salted to a dried salted basis.

Poisson salé

Un coefficient de 0.66 a été utilisé pour exprimer en salé sec les données relevées en salé humide.

Sugar

1 metric ton raw sugar = 0.9 metric ton refined sugar.
For the United States and its possessions:
1 metric ton refined sugar = 1.07 metric tons raw sugar.

Sucre

1 tonne métrique de sucre brut = 0.9 tonne métrique de sucre raffiné.
Pour les Etates-Unis et leurs possessions:
1 tonne métrique de sucre raffiné = 1.07 t.m. de sucre brut.

C. Other coefficients or conversion factors employed in Industrial Statistics Yearbook tables
Autres coefficients ou facteurs de conversion utilisés dans les tableaux de l'Annuaire de statistiques industrielles

MINERALS – PRODUITS MINERAUX

Molybdenum

1 ton of molybdenite (MoS_2)	=	0.5995 ton of molybdenum (Mo)
1 ton of molybdenum (Mo)	=	1.668 tons of molybdenite (MoS_2)

Vanadium

1 ton of vanadium pentoxide (V_2O_5)	=	0.560199 ton of vanadium (V)
1 ton of vanadium (V)	=	1.78508 tons of vanadium pentoxide (V_2O_5)

Tungsten

1 ton tungsten (W)	=	1.26098 tons of tungsten trioxide (WO_3)
1 ton tungsten trioxide (WO_3)	=	0.79303 ton of tungsten (W)

Chromium

1 ton of chromic oxide (Cr_2O_3)	=	0.68425 ton of chromium (Cr)
1 ton of chromium (Cr)	=	1.46145 tons of chromic oxide (Cr_2O_3)

Minerais de molybdène

1 tonne de molybdénite (MoS_2)	=	0.5995 tonne de molybdène (Mo)
1 tonne de molybdène (Mo)	=	1.668 tonnes de molybdénite (MoS_2)

Minerais de vanadium

1 tonne de pentoxyde de vanadium (V_2O_5)	=	0.560199 tonne de vanadium (V)
1 tonne de vanadium pentoxyde (V)	=	1.78508 tonnes de de vanadium (V_2O_5)

Minerais de tungstène

1 tonne de tungstène (W)	=	1.26098 tonnes de tungstène trioxyde (WO_3)
1 tonne de tungstène trioxyde (WO_3)	=	0.79303 tonne de tungstène (W)

Minerais de chrome

1 tonne d'oxyde de chrome (Cr_2O_3)	=	0.68425 tonne de chrome (Cr)
1 tonne de chrome (Cr)	=	1.46145 tonnes d'oxyde de chrome (Cr_2O_3)

C. Other coefficients or conversion factors employed in Industrial Statistics Yearbook tables (continued)

Autres coefficients ou facteurs de conversion utilisés dans les tableaux de l'Annuaire de statistiques industrielles (suite)

TEXTILES

Cotton fabrics

1 metric ton	=	7194.24 square metres
10^3 metres	=	1195 square metres

Linen fabrics

1 metric ton	=	2721.088 square metres
10^3 metres	=	928 square metres

Woollen fabrics

1 metric ton	=	2806.624 square metres
10^3 metres	=	1650 square metres

Silk and synthetic fabrics

1 metric ton	=	9017.133 square metres
10^3 metres	=	1370 square metres

Jute fabrics

1 metric ton	=	2108.07 square metres

Tissus de coton

1 tonne métrique	=	7194.24 mètres carrés
10^3 mètres	=	1195 mètres carrés

Tissus de lin

1 tonne métrique	=	2721.088 mètres carrés
10^3 mètres	=	928 mètres carrés

Tissus de laine

1 tonne métrique	=	2806.624 mètres carrés
10^3 mètres	=	1650 mètres carrés

Tissus de soie et de fibres synthétiques

1 tonne métrique	=	9017.133 mètres carrés
10^3 mètres	=	1370 mètres carrés

Tissus de jute

1 tonne métrique	=	2108.07 mètres carrés

CHEMICALS — PRODUITS CHIMIQUES

Sulphuric acid, hydrochloric acid and nitric acid

Sulphuric acid production reported by countries at 66°Baumé is published without adjustment. The production of all other countries is converted to 100% H_2SO_4according to the percentages given in the following table:

Acide sulfurique, acide chlorhydrique et acide nitrique

La production d'acide sulfurique indiquée pour les pays à 66° Baumé est publiée sans ajustement. La production de tous les autres pays est convertie en 100% de SO_4H_2 suivant les pourcentages donnés dans le tableau suivant:

Sulphuric acid - Acide sulfurique		Hydrochloric acid - Acide chlorhydrique		Nitric acid - Acide nitrique	
°Bé	%H_2SO_4	°Bé	%HCl	°Bé	%HNO_3
50.3	63	18	28.5	34.3	50
53.0	67	20	32.2	38.9	60
55.0	70	21	34.0	42.4	70
60.5	79	22	36.0	45.1	80
65.1	90	23	38.0	47.2	90
65.5	92	24	40.0	49.2	100

Sulphur trioxide (SO_3) has been converted into H_2SO_4 by the addition of 22.5%, representing the proportion of water in the acid (81.6% SO_3 and 18.4% H_2O), that is, applying a coefficient of 122.5% to the original figure of SO_3 Oleum or "fuming" at 20% is converted at 105% H_2SO_4.

Le trioxide sulfurique (SO_3) a été converti en SO_4H_2 en ajoutant 22.5% représentant la proportion de l'eau dans l'acide (81.6% SO_3 et 11.4% H_2O), c'est-à-dire en appliquant un coefficient de 122.5% au chiffre original de SO_3. L'oleum ou "fuming" à 20% est converti en 105% de SO_4H_2.

Acetylene

1 cubic metre = 1.105 kilograms.

Ethyl alcohol

1 quintal = 1.2674 hectolitres.

Acétylène

1 mètre cube = 1.105 kilogrammes.

Alcool éthylique

1 quintal = 1.2674 hectolitres.

Conversion coefficients and factors (continued) - Coefficients et facteurs de conversion (suite)

C. Other coefficients or conversion factors employed in *Industrial Statistics Yearbook* tables (continued)

Autres coefficients ou facteurs de conversion utilisés dans les tableaux de l'*Annuaire de statistiques industrielles* (suite)

SELECTED ENERGY CONVERSION FACTORS - FACTEURS DE CONVERSION POUR CERTAINS PRODUITS EN MATIERE D'ENERGIE

Crude petroleum

1 barrel = 42 U.S. gallons = 34.97 imperial gallons = 158.99 litres = 0.15899 cubic metres.
1 cubic metre = 6.2898 barrels.
The equivalent of barrels in metric tons depends on the specific gravity of the petroleum which varies from country to country. The average specific gravity for each producing country is indicated in the table on the production of crude petroleum in the Energy Statistics Yearbook.

Natural Gas and Manufactured Gas (Gasworks Gas and Coke-oven Gas)

Data for all gases are presented in terajoules. For comparison with earlier years, multiply teracalories with a factor of 4.1868 to obtain terajoules.

Petroleum products.

The following approximate coefficients have been used to convert original data, expressed in capacity or volume, into metric tons:

Pétrole brut

1 baril = 42 gallons E.U. = 34.97 gallons britanniques = 158.99 litres = 0.15899 m^3.
1m^3 = 6.2898 barils.
L'équivalent du baril en tonnes métriques dépend du poids spécifique du pétrole qui varie d'un pays à l'autre. Le poids spécifique moyen utilisé pour chaque pays producteur se trouve dans l'Annuaire des statistiques de l'énergie dans le tableau relatif à la production de pétrole brut.

Gaz naturel et gaz manufacturé (Gaz d'usines et de cokeries)

Les données pour tous les gaz sont présentées en terajoules. Pour permettre la comparaison avec les éditions antérieures, il faut multiplier les téracalories par un facteur de 4.1868 afin d'obtenir des terajoules.

Dérivés du pétrole

Les coefficients approximatifs suivants ont été utilisés pour convertir en tonnes métriques les données de base, exprimées en capacité ou en volume:

Product	Kilolitres = m^3	000 gallons imperial britanniques	000 gallons U.S. - E.U.	U.S. barrels Barils E.U.	Produit
Liquefied petroleum gas	0.54	2.4549	2.0441	0.08585	Gaz de pétrole liquéfié
Naptha	0.72	3.2731	2.7255	0.1145	Naphta
Motor spirit	0.74	3.3641	2.8012	0.1177	Essence
Aviation spirit	0.73	3.3186	2.7633	0.1161	Essence avion
Kerosene, white spirit and jet fuel	0.81	3.6823	3.0662	0.1288	Pétrole lampant, white-spirit carburéacteur
Distillate fuel oils	0.87	3.9551	3.2933	0.1383	Huiles légères
Residual fuel oils	0.95	4.3188	3.5961	0.1510	Huiles lourdes
Lubricating oils	0.90	4.0915	3.4069	0.1431	Huiles de graissage
Bitumen (asphalt)	1.04	4.7279	3.9368	0.1653	Bitume (asphalte)
Paraffin wax	0.80	3.6369	3.0283	0.1272	Paraffine
Petroleum coke	1.14	5.1825	4.3154	0.1812	Coke de pétrole
Natural gasolene	0.63	2.8640	2.3848	0.1002	Gazoline naturelle
Plant condensates	0.70	3.1822	2.6498	0.1113	Le condensat de raffinerie
Fuel oils n.o.s.	0.91	4.1369	3.4447	0.1447	Huiles légères et lourdes non spécifiées

Coal equivalent [1] (metric tons unless otherwise indicated):

Coal, anthracite and bituminous	1.0
Coal briquettes	1.0
Cokes of coal	0.9
Brown coal and lignite	0.385
Cokes of brown coal or lignite	0.67
Briquettes of brown coal and lignite	0.67
Peat for fuel	0.325
Peat briquettes	0.5
Crude petroleum	1.454
Natural gas liquids (weighted average)	1.542
Liquefied petroleum gases	1.554
Natural gasolene	1.532
Condensate and other	1.512
Motor spirit	1.5
Kerosene and jet fuel	1.474
Gas-diesel oils	1.45
Residual fuel oils	1.416
Natural gas (terajoules[2])	34.131
Manufactured gas (terajoules[2])	34.131

Coal equivalent (metric tons) of hydro, nuclear and geothermal electricity:
1000 kWh = 0.123

[1] It should be noted that the base used for coal equivalency comprises 7000 calories/gramme.
[2] Under standard conditions of I5ºC, 1013.25 mbar, dry.

Equivalent en houille[1] (tonnes métriques sauf indication contraire):

Charbon, anthracite et la houille bitumineuse	1.0
Briquettes de charbon	1.0
Cokes de charbon	0.9
Charbon brun et lignite	0.385
Cokes de charbon brun ou de lignite	0.67
Briquettes de charbon brun ou de lignite	0.67
Tourbe pour combustible	0.325
Briquettes de tourbe	0.5
Pétrole brut	1.454
Condensats provenant du gaz naturel (moyenne pondéré)	1.542
Gaz de pétrole liquéfié	1.554
Gazoline naturelle	1.532
Condensat et autres	1.512
Essence	1.5
Pétrole lampant et carburéacteur	1.474
Gaz oil fuel oil fluides	1.45
Huile lourde	1.416
Gaz naturel (terajoules[2])	34.131
Gaz d'usine (terajoules[2])	34.131

Equivalent en houille (tonnes métriques) d'électricitè, hydraulique, nucléaire et géothermique:
1000 kWh = 0.123

[1] Veuillez noter que l'équivalence en houille est faite sur la base de 7000 calories/gramme.
[2] En volume standard (à 15ºC, 1013.25 mbar, gaz sec).

Hard Coal – Houille

Unit : Thousand metric tons

Unité : Milliers de tonnes métriques

Country or area	1976	1977	1978	1979	1980	1981	1982	1983	1984	1985	Pays ou zone
Africa	**81 769**	**92 233**	**95 380**	**110 464**	**121 356**	**137 527**	**141 841**	**147 947**	**167 734**	**178 119**	**Afrique**
Algeria	8	7	7	7	7	7	* 7	* 7	* 7	* 8	Algérie
Botswana	224	294	314	355	371	380	414	395	393	437	Botswana
Cameroon	* 0	0	0	* 0	* 0	* 0	* 0	* 0	* 0	* 1	Cameroun
Morocco	702	707	720	710	680	704	735	751	838	* 900	Maroc
Mozambique	553	310	118	320	* 400	350	* 380	* 380	* 390	* 380	Mozambique
Niger	...	...	...	...	* 20	* 30	* 45	130	* 55	* 61	Niger
Nigeria	312	265	264	172	176	104	57	54	* 50	* 50	Nigéria
South Africa	76 044	87 084	90 552	105 480	116 040	132 778	136 908	143 123	162 909	173 131	Afrique du Sud
Swaziland	126	129	166	168	176	164	164	* 150	* 155	* 160	Swaziland
United Rep. Tanzania	3	3	* 4	1	1	* 1	* 1	* 1	* 1	* 1	Rép.Unie de Tanzanie
Zaire	109	128	107	* 100	138	* 140	123	113	* 125	* 130	Zaïre
Zambia	762	708	615	* 599	579	507	604	452	511	510	Zambie
Zimbabwe*	2 926	2 598	2 513	2 552	2 768	2 362	2 403	2 391	2 300	2 350	Zimbabwe*
America, North	**618 280**	**629 117**	**590 543**	**696 450**	**737 567**	**730 681**	**742 790**	**688 082**	**790 712**	**784 219**	**Amérique du Nord**
Canada	14 389	15 317	17 141	18 610	20 173	21 739	22 379	22 563	32 063	34 310	Canada
Mexico	5 650	6 610	6 756	7 357	7 010	8 097	7 634	8 951	8 387	* 8 600	Mexique
United States	598 241	607 190	566 646	670 483	710 384	700 845	712 777	656 568	750 262	741 309	Etats–Unis
America, South	**9 003**	**9 808**	**10 271**	**11 382**	**11 175**	**11 989**	**13 001**	**14 344**	**15 368**	**15 946**	**Amérique du Sud**
Argentina	615	533	434	727	390	498	515	486	509	400	Argentine
Brazil	3 391	4 009	4 582	5 028	5 242	5 689	6 346	6 737	7 519	7 712	Brésil
Chile	1 261	1 306	1 129	926	968	1 099	985	990	1 184	1 183	Chili
Colombia	3 629	3 814	4 019	4 618	4 487	4 563	* 5 035	* 6 000	* 6 000	* 6 500	Colombie
Peru	20	25	26	28	44	94	73	92	105	* 110	Pérou
Venezuela	87	121	81	55	44	46	47	39	51	41	Venezuela
Asia	**667 815**	**713 431**	**783 155**	**800 191**	**792 739**	**810 770**	**860 739**	**913 848**	**996 196**	**1 054 925**	**Asie**
Afghanistan	160	170	218	132	119	125	145	145	148	151	Afghanistan
Burma	13	18	28	12	11	18	29	36	44	43	Birmanie
China	483 000	527 000	593 000	610 350	595 840	598 250	641 360	687 630	759 120	* 810 000	Chine
India	100 876	100 297	101 549	103 364	109 152	123 104	128 504	134 782	144 870	149 710	Inde
Indonesia	193	231	264	279	304	350	481	486	1 085	1 492	Indonésie
Iran(Islamic Rep.of)*	900	900	900	900	900	700	800	800	850	900	Iran(Rép.islamique)*
Japan	18 396	18 246	18 992	17 644	18 027	17 687	17 606	17 062	16 644	16 382	Japon
Korea,Dem.Ppl's.Rep.*	33 000	34 000	35 000	35 000	36 000	36 000	36 500	38 000	38 000	39 000	Corée,Rép.pop.dém.de*
Korea, Republic of	16 428	17 233	18 054	18 208	18 624	19 865	20 116	19 861	21 370	22 543	Corée, République de
Mongolia	205	279	320	380	392	346	401	408	458	480	Mongolie
Pakistan	1 055	1 200	1 251	1 387	1 568	1 576	1 765	1 609	1 869	2 238	Pakistan
Philippines	121	285	255	263	325	331	538	1 020	1 195	1 223	Philippines
Thailand	0	0	0	1	1	2	2	0	0	0	Thaïlande
Turkey	4 632	4 416	4 440	4 051	3 602	3 970	4 008	3 538	3 632	3 605	Turquie
Viet Nam	5 600	6 200	6 000	5 500	5 300	6 000	6 100	6 235	4 900	* 5 300	Viet Nam
Europe	**481 206**	**480 789**	**484 620**	**494 672**	**498 004**	**467 622**	**490 318**	**479 075**	**406 780**	**452 664**	**Europe**
EEC	***250 715***	***243 578***	***239 550***	***240 764***	***251 166***	***249 702***	***246 386***	***233 695***	***160 838***	***206 032***	***CEE***
Belgium	7 238	7 068	6 590	6 125	6 324	6 136	6 539	6 097	6 298	6 211	Belgique
France incl. Monaco	23 300	22 996	21 140	20 627	20 194	20 303	18 756	18 649	18 278	17 103	France y comp.Monaco
Germany, Fed. Rep.	96 325	91 310	90 104	93 312	94 492	95 545	96 318	89 620	84 868	88 489	Allemagne, Rép. féd.
Ireland	58	54	21	63	60	69	62	75	70	57	Irlande
Netherlands	0	0	0	0	0	0	0	0	142	126	Pays–Bas
United Kingdom	123 794	122 150	121 695	120 637	130 096	127 649	124 711	119 254	51 182	94 046	Royaume–Uni
EFTA	***724***	***652***	***574***	***452***	***483***	***622***	***631***	***702***	***658***	***757***	***AELE***
Norway,Svlbd,J.Myn I.	519	455	378	259	288	410	440	504	451	507	Norvège,Svalbd,J.May
Portugal	193	195	180	179	177	184	178	185	194	238	Portugal
Sweden	12	2	16	14	18	28	13	13	13	12	Suède
East Europe	***218 663***	***224 174***	***232 502***	***241 169***	***232 820***	***202 242***	***227 245***	***228 870***	***229 267***	***229 384***	***Europe de l'est***
Bulgaria	295	287	273	274	267	246	241	243	223	223	Bulgarie
Czechoslovakia	28 562	27 354	29 150	28 781	28 307	27 622	27 463	26 915	26 421	26 223	Tchécoslovaquie
German Dem. Rep.	458	349	85	0	0	0	0	0	0	0	Rép. dém. allemande
Hungary	2 934	2 925	2 954	3 002	3 065	3 066	3 039	2 827	2 573	2 639	Hongrie
Poland	179 303	186 112	192 622	201 004	193 121	163 022	189 314	191 092	191 592	191 642	Pologne
Romania	7 111	7 147	7 418	8 108	8 060	8 286	7 188	7 793	8 458	8 657	Roumanie

For general note and footnotes, see end of table.

Voir la fin du tableau pour la remarque générale et les notes.

Hard Coal (continued) – Houille (suite)

Unit : Thousand metric tons

Unité : Milliers de tonnes métriques

Country or area	1976	1977	1978	1979	1980	1981	1982	1983	1984	1985	Pays ou zone
Other Europe	***11 104***	***12 385***	***11 994***	***12 287***	***13 535***	***15 056***	***16 056***	***15 808***	***16 017***	***16 491***	***Autre Europe***
Spain	10 517	11 874	11 523	11 853	13 147	14 672	15 668	15 416	15 629	16 091	Espagne
Yugoslavia	587	511	471	434	388	384	388	392	388	400	Yougoslavie
USSR	**494 377**	**499 768**	**501 536**	**496 486**	**492 920**	**481 324**	**488 022**	**486 812**	**483 279**	**494 397**	**URSS**
Oceania	**64 713**	**71 882**	**71 960**	**73 808**	**74 449**	**87 840**	**91 644**	**100 009**	**106 512**	**119 686**	**Océanie**
Australia	62 396	69 655	69 928	72 069	72 496	85 855	89 536	97 754	104 205	117 504	Australie
New Zealand	2 317	2 227	2 032	1 739	1 953	1 985	2 108	2 255	2 307	2 182	Nouvelle–Zélande
Total	**2 417 163**	**2 497 028**	**2 537 465**	**2 683 453**	**2 728 210**	**2 727 753**	**2 828 355**	**2 830 117**	**2 966 581**	**3 099 956**	**Total**

General note.
Anthracite, bituminous and semi–bituminous coal with a gross calorific value over 5700 calories/gramme on the ash–free and moist basis. Fresh produced breeze, middlings and slurries are included. Production comprises the sum of sales, mine consumption, issues to miners and issues to coking, briquetting and other ancillary, plants at mines. (SITC 32140–0).

Asia
China: Prior to 1977, including brown coal.

Europe
Czechoslovakia: Beginning 1978, including recovered slurries.

France incl. Monaco: Including recovered slurries.

Hungary: Including recovered slurries.

Spain: Including recovered slurries.

United Kingdom: Including recovered slurries.

Remarque générale.
Anthracite, charbon bitumineux et semi–bitumineux d'un pouvoir calorifique brut supérieur à 5700 cal/g sur produit humide exempt de cendres, y compris les pousiers, les mixtes et les schlamms. La production représente le tonnage vendu, compte non tenu de la consommation des mines, des livraisonsaux mineurs et des livraisons aux cokeries, aux usines d'agglomération et aux autres usines annexes des mines. (CTCI 32140–0).

Asie
Chine: Avant 1977, y compris le lignite.

Europe
Tchécoslovaquie: Avant 1977, y compris les schlamms récupérés.

France y comp. Monaco: y compris les schlamms récupérés.

Hongrie: Y compris les schlamms récupérés.

Espagne: Y compris les schlamms récupérés.

Royaume–Uni: Y compris les schlamms récupérés.

Brown coal, including lignite – Charbon brun et lignite

Unit : Thousand metric tons

Unité : Milliers de tonnes métriques

Country or area	1976	1977	1978	1979	1980	1981	1982	1983	1984	1985	Pays ou zone
America, North	**34 187**	**39 720**	**45 661**	**52 600**	**58 821**	**64 820**	**68 470**	**75 157**	**82 601**	**89 084**	**Amérique du Nord**
Canada	11 086	13 203	13 343	14 587	16 514	18 349	20 528	22 224	25 339	26 543	Canada
United States	23 101	26 517	32 318	38 013	42 307	46 471	47 942	52 933	57 262	62 541	Etats–Unis
America, South	**28**	**30**	**30**	**35**	**40**	**36**	**40**	**40**	**40**	**35**	**Amérique du Sud**
Chile	28	* 30	30	* 35	40	36	* 40	40	* 40	* 35	Chili
Asia	**24 521**	**48 117**	**50 811**	**58 149**	**58 838**	**61 497**	**66 638**	**72 119**	**82 199**	**101 539**	**Asie**
Burma	0	0	3	36	27	38	38	35	43	43	Birmanie
China	...	23 310	24 850	25 250	24 310	23 390	24 970	26 900	30 110	* 35 000	Chine
India	3 900	3 632	3 613	3 264	4 548	5 964	6 672	7 347	7 649	7 775	Inde
Japan	53	57	39	32	25	0	0	0	0	0	Japon
Korea,Dem.Ppl's.Rep.*	9 000	9 000	9 000	9 500	10 000	10 000	10 500	11 000	11 000	12 000	Corée,Rép.pop.dém.de*
Mongolia	2 716	3 045	3 478	3 735	3 985	3 957	4 520	4 566	4 973	6 038	Mongolie
Nepal	...	...	6	6	6	6	6	6	* 6	* 6	Népal
Thailand	600	516	632	1 362	1 468	1 666	2 113	1 997	2 362	5 188	Thaïlande
Turkey	8 252	8 557	9 190	14 964	14 469	16 476	17 819	20 268	26 056	35 489	Turquie
Europe	**647 931**	**652 082**	**660 908**	**681 750**	**693 524**	**717 275**	**738 596**	**759 775**	**797 072**	**817 326**	**Europe**
EEC	***161 498***	***150 680***	***149 908***	***158 757***	***157 552***	***162 123***	***159 073***	***159 267***	***163 381***	***160 367***	***CEE***
France incl. Monaco	3 188	3 080	2 732	2 454	2 558	2 945	3 065	2 606	2 426	1 861	France y comp.Monaco
Germany, Fed. Rep.	134 535	122 948	123 587	130 608	129 862	130 649	127 352	124 365	126 703	120 718	Allemagne, Rép. féd.
Greece	22 569	23 572	21 677	23 573	23 198	27 315	27 399	30 594	32 502	35 888	Grèce
Italy and San Marino	1 206	1 080	1 912	2 122	1 934	1 214	1 257	1 702	1 750	* 1 900	Italie y comp. S.Mrn
EFTA	***3 215***	***3 128***	***3 076***	***2 741***	***2 865***	***3 061***	***3 297***	***3 041***	***2 901***	***3 081***	***AELE***
Austria	3 215	3 128	3 076	2 741	2 865	3 061	3 297	3 041	2 901	3 081	Autriche
East Europe	***442 808***	***455 718***	***460 440***	***467 041***	***471 038***	***479 666***	***498 068***	***513 933***	***541 783***	***562 063***	***Europe de l'est***
Albania*	900	950	1 200	1 400	1 500	1 600	1 600	1 700	1 775	1 790	Albanie*
Bulgaria	25 184	24 887	25 531	27 955	29 946	28 995	31 974	32 147	32 136	30 657	Bulgarie
Czechoslovakia	89 468	93 236	94 879	96 227	94 890	95 282	97 097	100 470	102 857	100 387	Tchécoslovaquie
German Dem. Rep.	246 897	253 705	253 264	256 063	258 097	266 734	276 038	277 968	296 341	312 156	Rép. dém. allemande
Hungary	22 323	22 529	22 716	22 657	22 635	22 876	23 040	22 386	22 474	21 403	Hongrie
Poland	39 305	40 780	41 005	38 083	36 866	35 538	37 649	42 532	50 378	57 746	Pologne
Romania	18 731	19 631	21 845	24 656	27 104	28 641	30 670	36 730	35 822	37 924	Roumanie
Other Europe	***40 410***	***42 556***	***47 484***	***53 211***	***62 069***	***72 425***	***78 158***	***83 534***	***89 007***	***91 815***	***Autre Europe***
Spain	4 151	5 804	8 271	10 696	15 455	20 886	23 882	24 534	24 323	23 752	Espagne
Yugoslavia	36 259	36 752	39 213	42 515	46 614	51 539	54 276	59 000	64 684	68 063	Yougoslavie
USSR	**160 031**	**163 513**	**162 871**	**161 145**	**159 940**	**156 493**	**159 325**	**154 774**	**152 297**	**153 306**	**URSS**
Oceania	**29 383**	**31 160**	**30 624**	**32 310**	**33 102**	**32 314**	**37 789**	**34 915**	**34 725**	**38 607**	**Océanie**
Australia	29 212	30 994	30 473	32 101	32 894	32 102	37 567	34 686	34 499	38 380	Australie
New Zealand	171	166	151	209	208	212	222	229	226	227	Nouvelle–Zélande
Total	**896 081**	**934 622**	**950 905**	**985 989**	**1 004 265**	**1 032 435**	**1 070 858**	**1 096 780**	**1 148 934**	**1 199 897**	**Total**

General note.
Brown coal is a fuel intermediate between hard coal and peat. The dividing line between brown coal and hard coal is drawn on the basis of a gross calorific value of 5700 calories/gramme on the moist, ash–free basis. Lignite, which is a variety of brown coal of a lower calorific value, is included. (SITC 32160–1).

Remarque générale.
Le lignite est un combustible intermédiaire entre la houille et la tourbe. La ligne de démarcation entre le lignite et la houille est le pouvoir calorifique brut de 5700 cal/kg sur produit humide exempt de cendres. Cette rubrique comprend le lignite commun qui est une variété de lignite à faible pouvoir calorifique. (CTCI 32160–1).

USSR: Including oil shale.

URSS: Y compris le schiste bitumineux.

Crude petroleum – Pétrole brut

Unit : Thousand metric tons

Unité : Milliers de tonnes métriques

Country or area	1976	1977	1978	1979	1980	1981	1982	1983	1984	1985	Pays ou zone
Africa	**287 367**	**303 867**	**295 134**	**323 489**	**298 462**	**226 352**	**216 440**	**216 959**	**225 705**	**237 164**	**Afrique**
Algeria	* 47 810	51 700	54 043	53 698	47 358	36 943	33 542	31 292	29 700	29 357	Algérie
Angola	7 564	7 062	6 469	* 7 200	* 7 428	* 7 158	* 6 410	* 8 304	* 10 292	* 11 427	Angola
Benin	...	...	...	...	...	* 0	* 0	1	* 1	* 1	Bénin
Cameroon	0	* 38	* 505	2 004	2 700	4 340	5 331	5 689	* 6 475	* 6 705	Cameroun
Congo	2 010	1 801	2 570	2 784	3 295	4 283	4 481	5 365	6 007	* 5 830	Congo
Côte d'Ivoire	...	...	...	* 350	* 120	* 389	757	* 1 158	* 1 368	* 1 410	Côte d'Ivoire
Egypt	16 756	24 075	24 417	25 078	29 400	29 405	32 772	35 957	41 217	44 312	Egypte
Gabon	11 326	11 267	10 600	10 316	8 895	7 652	7 792	* 7 842	* 8 725	* 8 201	Gabon
Ghana	...	* 0	39	75	88	63	* 39	* 70	* 92	* 94	Ghana
Libyan Arab Jamah	93 452	99 503	95 606	100 879	88 324	58 726	55 380	53 258	46 255	49 937	Jamah.arabe libyenne
Morocco	9	22	24	19	14	18	15	18	17	18	Maroc
Nigeria	103 479	102 969	94 760	114 500	104 190	70 920	63 630	61 325	68 731	73 194	Nigéria
Tunisia	3 710	4 304	4 956	5 536	5 627	5 407	5 146	5 532	5 480	5 408	Tunisie
Zaire	1 251	1 126	1 145	1 050	1 023	1 048	1 145	* 1 148	1 345	* 1 270	Zaïre
America, North	**518 368**	**531 795**	**567 378**	**581 035**	**606 041**	**615 205**	**640 574**	**643 083**	**658 593**	**659 690**	**Amérique du Nord**
Barbados	20	17	37	39	42	29	35	55	87	93	Barbade
Canada	64 523	64 668	64 333	73 279	70 405	62 928	62 163	66 408	70 668	72 206	Canada
Cuba	234	256	288	288	274	253	541	742	770	868	Cuba
Guatemala	13	7	30	78	203	208	317	350	237	184	Guatemala
Mexico	41 336	49 303	62 346	75 461	99 938	120 203	142 783	139 758	139 946	135 674	Mexique
Trinidad and Tobago	10 990	11 832	11 854	11 072	10 983	9 780	9 144	8 255	8 758	9 186	Trinité–et–Tobago
United States	401 252	405 712	428 490	420 818	424 196	421 804	425 591	427 515	438 127	441 479	Etats–Unis
America, South	**172 972**	**170 881**	**171 658**	**185 648**	**178 445**	**177 891**	**169 525**	**167 584**	**176 694**	**174 591**	**Amérique du Sud**
Argentina	20 810	22 167	23 236	24 279	25 281	25 534	25 196	25 200	24 637	23 634	Argentine
Bolivia	1 890	1 612	1 506	1 294	1 107	1 029	1 134	1 030	969	917	Bolivie
Brazil	8 344	8 025	8 002	8 262	9 083	10 675	12 984	16 595	23 269	27 492	Brésil
Chile	938	928	780	1 010	1 604	1 950	2 003	1 919	1 879	1 591	Chili
Colombia	7 553	7 106	6 755	6 410	6 501	6 912	7 325	7 675	8 606	9 107	Colombie
Ecuador	9 488	9 283	10 223	10 874	10 417	10 745	10 746	12 088	13 088	14 279	Equateur
Peru	3 779	4 571	7 528	9 413	9 664	9 358	9 729	8 589	9 358	9 296	Pérou
Suriname	0	0	0	0	0	0	* 17	* 18	* 38	* 89	Suriname
Venezuela	120 170	117 189	113 628	124 106	114 788	111 688	100 391	94 470	94 850	88 186	Venezuela
Asia	**1 296 948**	**1 311 380**	**1 229 228**	**1 313 973**	**1 137 820**	**1 003 981**	**854 944**	**801 595**	**808 604**	**768 456**	**Asie**
Bahrain	2 902	2 895	2 754	2 556	2 414	2 335	2 225	2 113	2 022	2 024	Bahreïn
Bangladesh	7	7	6	7	6	6	9	* 11	20	22	Bangladesh
Brunei Darussalam	9 959	10 540	11 146	12 531	11 881	7 933	8 098	8 070	7 597	* 7 901	Brunéi Darussalam
Burma	1 159	1 343	1 352	1 415	1 559	1 478	1 385	1 438	1 664	1 599	Birmanie
China	87 160	93 640	104 052	106 152	105 946	101 221	102 123	106 068	114 613	124 895	Chine
India	8 659	10 185	11 271	12 839	9 399	14 925	19 734	25 148	27 933	29 860	Inde
Indonesia	74 195	82 931	80 258	78 072	77 610	78 848	65 818	66 128	68 518	67 710	Indonésie
Iran(Islamic Rep.of)	295 084	278 797	212 217	171 341	72 667	72 020	120 450	122 989	109 186	108 948	Iran(Rép.islamique)
Iraq	118 905	115 145	125 629	170 493	130 123	43 949	49 629	46 760	58 741	69 891	Iraq
Israel	36	29	24	21	20	16	12	* 12	9	9	Israël
Japan	580	586	535	482	428	387	397	418	405	530	Japon
Kuwait,part Ntl.Zone	113 710	99 325	112 321	125 629	84 116	56 931	41 626	53 291	58 947	53 771	Koweït et prt.Zne.N.
Malaysia	8 026	8 981	10 706	13 838	13 438	12 563	14 752	18 673	21 371	21 246	Malaisie
Oman	18 290	16 968	15 696	14 637	14 030	16 274	16 679	19 301	20 746	24 709	Oman
Pakistan	335	499	472	495	476	474	529	632	651	1 278	Pakistan
Philippines	0	0	0	1 096	535	212	463	731	552	561	Philippines
Qatar	24 018	21 414	23 555	24 500	22 768	20 070	16 038	12 983	19 455	14 286	Qatar
S.Arabia,pt.Ntrl.Zn.	425 804	458 596	414 757	476 286	495 898	489 439	323 345	248 656	228 250	168 418	Arab.saoud,p.Zn.neut
Syrian Arab Republic	10 041	9 117	9 924	8 701	9 198	9 493	8 191	9 359	9 417	9 236	Rép. arabe syrienne
Thailand	8	8	8	9	8	17	16	351	788	1 158	Thaïlande
Turkey	2 595	2 604	2 731	2 831	2 330	2 363	2 333	2 203	2 087	2 110	Turquie
United Arab Emirates	95 265	97 555	89 605	89 846	82 791	72 872	60 974	56 146	55 517	58 194	Emirats arabes unis
Europe	**61 504**	**86 409**	**104 983**	**129 074**	**137 268**	**145 415**	**162 544**	**182 968**	**196 760**	**202 255**	**Europe**
EEC	***20 624***	***46 824***	***62 364***	***85 917***	***88 693***	***98 391***	***112 898***	***125 848***	***137 871***	***140 943***	***CEE***
Denmark	194	503	432	432	298	758	1 686	2 152	2 314	2 892	Danemark
France incl. Monaco	1 057	1 037	1 117	1 197	1 196	1 676	1 646	1 661	2 065	2 642	France y comp.Monaco
Germany, Fed. Rep.	5 524	5 399	5 059	4 739	5 202	5 031	4 905	5 223	5 719	5 658	Allemagne, Rép. féd.
Greece	0	0	0	0	0	196	986	1 176	1 251	1 250	Grèce
Italy and San Marino	1 102	1 083	1 422	1 637	1 800	1 436	1 727	2 208	2 240	2 352	Italie y comp. S.Mrn
Netherlands	1 371	1 382	1 402	1 316	1 280	1 348	1 637	2 589	3 102	3 728	Pays–Bas

For general note and footnotes, see end of table.

Voir la fin du tableau pour la remarque générale et les notes.

Unit : Thousand metric tons — Unité : Milliers de tonnes métriques

Country or area	1976	1977	1978	1979	1980	1981	1982	1983	1984	1985	Pays ou zone
United Kingdom	11 376	37 420	52 932	76 596	78 917	87 946	100 311	110 839	121 180	122 421	Royaume–Uni
EFTA	***15 730***	***15 316***	***18 749***	***20 546***	***26 051***	***24 794***	***25 819***	***31 775***	***35 038***	***38 177***	***AELE***
Austria	1 931	1 762	1 791	1 726	1 475	1 338	1 290	1 269	1 245	1 155	Autriche
Norway,Svlbd,J.Myn I.	13 799	13 554	16 957	18 819	24 551	23 450	24 515	30 483	33 780	37 014	Norvège,Svalbd,J.May
Sweden	0	0	1	1	25	6	14	23	13	8	Suède
East Europe	***19 498***	***19 474***	***18 814***	***17 310***	***16 693***	***16 626***	***17 956***	***18 243***	***17 492***	***16 803***	***Europe de l'est***
Albania*	1 900	1 950	2 100	2 200	2 400	2 200	3 500	3 990	3 410	3 415	Albanie*
Bulgaria	117	129	246	* 260	* 275	* 300	* 300	* 300	* 300	* 300	Bulgarie
Czechoslovakia	131	123	117	109	93	89	89	93	91	123	Tchécoslovaquie
German Dem. Rep.	53	67	66	60	54	54	57	53	42	40	Rép. dém. allemande
Hungary	2 142	2 191	2 198	2 027	2 031	2 024	2 027	2 004	2 007	2 012	Hongrie
Poland	455	364	363	331	329	315	241	210	189	195	Pologne
Romania	14 700	14 650	13 724	12 323	11 511	11 644	11 742	11 593	11 453	10 718	Roumanie
Other Europe	***5 652***	***4 795***	***5 056***	***5 301***	***5 831***	***5 604***	***5 871***	***7 102***	***6 359***	***6 332***	***Autre Europe***
Spain	1 772	844	980	1 158	1 602	1 229	1 531	2 977	2 315	2 183	Espagne
Yugoslavia	3 880	3 951	4 076	4 143	4 229	4 375	4 340	4 125	4 044	4 149	Yougoslavie
USSR	**519 677**	**545 799**	**571 531**	**585 571**	**603 207**	**608 820**	**612 551**	**616 343**	**612 710**	**595 000**	**URSS**
Oceania	**19 452**	**20 226**	**20 725**	**20 154**	**20 070**	**18 761**	**18 682**	**18 292**	**21 397**	**25 422**	**Océanie**
Australia	18 975	19 552	20 160	19 781	* 19 755	18 349	18 034	17 655	20 586	24 579	Australie
New Zealand	477	674	565	373	315	412	648	637	811	* 843	Nouvelle–Zélande
Total	**2 876 288**	**2 970 357**	**2 960 637**	**3 138 944**	**2 981 313**	**2 796 425**	**2 675 260**	**2 646 824**	**2 700 463**	**2 662 578**	**Total**

General note.
Liquid product obtained from oil wells and consisting predominantly of non–aromatic hydrocarbons (paraffinic, cyclanic etc.), provided that they have been subjected to no further processes other than those of decantation, dehydration or stabilization (removal of certain dissolved hydrocarbon gases for convenience of transport), or to which have been added only hydrocarbons previously recovered by physical methods during the course of the above–mentioned processes. Shale oils, natural gasolene and oils obtained from the distillation of hard coal, brown coal and their derivatives are excluded. (SITC 33101–1A).

Remarque générale.
Produits liquides qui proviennent des gisements de pétrole, et qui sont constitués principalement par des hydrocarbures non aromatiques (paraffiniques, cyclaniques etc.) à condition qu'ils n'aient pas subi d'autres traitements que la décantation, la déshydratation ou la stabilisation (la stabilisation consiste à ôter des huiles brutes, pour faciliter leur transport, certains hydrocarbures gazeux qui y sont dissous) et pour autant qu'on ne leur a pas ajouté d'autres hydrocarbures naturels que ceux précédemment récupérés par des méthodes physiques au cours des traitements précités. L'huile de schiste, la gazoline naturelle et les huiles obtenues par distillation de la houille, du lignite et de leurs dérivés ne sont pas comprises dans cette rubrique. (CTCI 33101–1A).

Natural gasolene – Gazoline naturelle

Unit : Thousand metric tons — Unité : Milliers de tonnes métriques

Country or area	1976	1977	1978	1979	1980	1981	1982	1983	1984	1985	Pays ou zone
America, North	**19 777**	**20 118**	**19 269**	**17 670**	**18 161**	**20 736**	**19 285**	**17 057**	**20 516**	**20 594**	**Amérique du Nord**
Canada	4 790	4 749	4 241	4 202	3 809	3 649	3 568	3 337	3 452	3 644	Canada
Mexico	* 1 705	* 2 060	* 2 383	* 2 881	* 3 484	6 430	6 539	6 530	6 363	6 651	Mexique
Trinidad and Tobago	6	6	9	* 8	* 9	* 10	* 10	* 10	* 10	* 10	Trinité–et–Tobago
United States	13 276	13 303	12 636	10 579	10 859	10 647	9 168	7 180	10 691	10 289	Etats–Unis
America, South	**1 034**	**1 010**	**879**	**1 042**	**987**	**1 028**	**1 103**	**953**	**970**	**1 175**	**Amérique du Sud**
Argentina	42	53	51	113	* 115	182	* 227	218	237	225	Argentine
Bolivia	4	4	4	33	77	77	71	73	* 60	56	Bolivie
Chile	* 95	102	* 92	* 120	93	104	108	94	96	71	Chili
Colombia	70	70	101	* 82	79	76	65	* 80	* 70	* 70	Colombie
Ecuador	12	11	8	7	8	5	4	11	16	23	Equateur
Peru	56	54	58	50	37	36	34	6	20	* 25	Pérou
Venezuela	755	716	565	637	578	548	594	471	* 471	705	Venezuela
Asia	**3 559**	**4 211**	**4 336**	**7 506**	**5 371**	**5 271**	**5 148**	**5 020**	**5 153**	**4 668**	**Asie**
Bahrain	...	...	...	...	95	117	115	128	113	182	Bahreïn
Brunei Darussalam	59	83	90	80	77	23	34	47	73	* 79	Brunéi Darussalam
Burma*	1	1	1	1	1	1	1	1	1	1	Birmanie*
India	0	0	0	0	0	16	49	57	84	76	Inde
Indonesia	6	* 6	* 7	* 7	* 6	* 5	* 3	* 4	* 4	* 5	Indonésie
Iran(Islamic Rep.of)*	650	700	800	650	200	150	200	250	200	250	Iran(Rép.islamique)*
Iraq*	92	120	120	120	120	60	70	60	70	80	Iraq*
Japan	4	4	4	4	4	4	4	5	5	6	Japon
Kuwait,part Ntl.Zone	553	587	564	1 027	773	578	409	504	539	553	Koweït et prt.Zne.N.
Oman	...	...	...	...	...	* 10	73	* 90	* 150	* 160	Oman
Qatar	* 73	* 20	* 0	* 0	46	132	148	184	225	* 250	Qatar
S.Arabia,pt.Ntrl.Zn.	* 2 100	* 2 690	* 2 670	* 5 500	3 910	4 055	2 998	2 639	2 719	1 940	Arab.saoud,p.Zn.neut
Thailand	...	...	...	...	...	...	...	...	...	86	Thaïlande
United Arab Emirates	0	0	80	117	139	120	1 044	1 051	970	* 1 000	Emirats arabes unis
Europe	**683**	**765**	**937**	**1 118**	**1 163**	**1 160**	**1 310**	**1 427**	**1 511**	**1 596**	**Europe**
EEC	***29***	***79***	***128***	***131***	***161***	***149***	***253***	***397***	***430***	***460***	***CEE***
United Kingdom	29	79	128	131	161	149	253	397	430	460	Royaume–Uni
East Europe	***637***	***674***	***799***	***977***	***992***	***1 001***	***1 047***	***1 018***	***1 069***	***1 121***	***Europe de l'est***
Czechoslovakia	3	* 3	* 3	* 3	* 3	* 3	* 3	* 3	* 3	* 3	Tchécoslovaquie
Hungary	153	196	316	484	479	478	518	490	541	593	Hongrie
Poland	21	10	15	15	20	* 20	26	* 25	* 25	* 25	Pologne
Romania*	460	465	465	475	490	500	500	500	500	500	Roumanie*
Other Europe	***17***	***12***	***10***	***10***	***10***	***10***	***10***	***12***	***12***	***15***	***Autre Europe***
Yugoslavia	17	12	* 10	* 10	* 10	* 10	* 10	* 12	* 12	* 15	Yougoslavie
Oceania	**4**	**5**	**6**	**6**	**6**	**5**	**6**	**6**	**7**	**7**	**Océanie**
New Zealand	4	5	6	* 6	* 6	5	6	* 6	7	* 7	Nouvelle–Zélande
Total	**25 057**	**26 109**	**25 427**	**27 342**	**25 688**	**28 200**	**26 852**	**24 463**	**28 157**	**28 040**	**Total**

General note.
Light spirit extracted from the natural gas associated with crude petroleum. (SITC 33210–1A).

America, North:
United States: Beginning 1984, including condensate production.

Remarque générale.
Essence légère extraite du gaz naturel associé au pétrole brut. (CTCI 33210–1A).

Amérique du Nord
Etats–Unis: A partir de 1984, y compris la production des condensats d'usine.

Natural gas – Gaz naturel

Unit : Petajoules

Unité : Petajoules

Country or area	1976	1977	1978	1979	1980	1981	1982	1983	1984	1985	Pays ou zone
Africa	**527**	**590**	**1 110**	**981**	**1 036**	**917**	**920**	**1 327**	**1 450**	**1 578**	**Afrique**
Algeria	317	229	737	608	759	505	518	873	936	1 029	Algérie
Angola	2	3	3	3	3	4	4	4	5	5	Angola
Congo	1	0	0	0	0	0	0	0	0	0	Congo
Egypt	15	43	63	112	63	74	83	85	109	140	Egypte
Gabon	6	7	6	6	6	8	8	8	8	8	Gabon
Libyan Arab Jamah	149	152	184	183	134	105	85	115	150	156	Jamah.arabe libyenne
Morocco	3	3	3	3	3	4	3	3	3	3	Maroc
Nigeria	25	144	101	51	52	200	200	220	221	220	Nigéria
Tunisia	10	11	13	15	17	17	20	19	19	17	Tunisie
America, North	**23 969**	**22 549**	**22 518**	**23 418**	**23 230**	**22 963**	**21 680**	**19 887**	**21 390**	**20 575**	**Amérique du Nord**
Barbados	0	0	0	0	1	0	0	0	1	1	Barbade
Canada	2 820	2 962	2 856	3 041	2 790	2 748	2 825	2 740	2 972	3 194	Canada
Cuba	1	1	0	1	1	0	0	0	0	0	Cuba
Mexico	520	573	701	832	1 036	1 033	1 075	1 040	962	891	Mexique
Trinidad and Tobago	77	92	114	128	146	125	125	120	115	110	Trinité–et–Tobago
United States	20 552	18 921	18 846	19 415	19 256	19 057	17 655	15 986	17 341	16 380	Etats–Unis
America, South	**946**	**1 045**	**1 078**	**1 205**	**1 285**	**1 324**	**1 435**	**1 502**	**1 613**	**1 744**	**Amérique du Sud**
Argentina	268	270	255	303	327	340	393	457	478	570	Argentine
Bolivia	61	64	68	74	84	90	93	90	86	83	Bolivie
Brazil	20	40	32	35	41	37	43	63	77	97	Brésil
Chile	46	54	59	41	27	33	34	37	37	38	Chili
Colombia	75	85	113	121	140	149	159	165	166	174	Colombie
Ecuador	2	2	2	2	2	3	4	4	4	7	Equateur
Peru	21	19	20	19	21	25	26	19	24	45	Pérou
Venezuela	453	510	528	611	643	647	682	668	741	731	Venezuela
Asia	**2 522**	**2 701**	**2 945**	**3 428**	**3 361**	**3 449**	**3 268**	**3 662**	**4 191**	**4 376**	**Asie**
Afghanistan	93	93	90	85	102	98	95	99	106	111	Afghanistan
Bahrain	85	92	101	110	114	115	126	131	140	139	Bahreïn
Bangladesh	27	32	34	39	45	50	64	72	91	103	Bangladesh
Brunei Darussalam	295	340	351	356	352	335	335	339	353	349	Brunéi Darussalam
Burma	10	9	11	11	13	16	19	20	27	36	Birmanie
China	394	472	534	565	555	496	464	475	484	504	Chine
India	47	50	56	62	51	59	89	107	125	151	Inde
Indonesia	115	162	353	518	607	652	646	773	940	937	Indonésie
Iran(Islamic Rep.of)	788	743	668	700	279	247	257	326	327	324	Iran(Rép.islamique)
Iraq	70	46	48	68	50	13	14	13	19	23	Iraq
Israel	2	2	2	3	6	6	3	2	2	2	Israël
Japan	114	119	112	102	85	92	90	87	92	95	Japon
Kuwait,part Ntl.Zone	131	143	161	134	284	234	179	196	213	211	Koweït et prt.Zne.N.
Malaysia	14	13	3	3	3	4	4	116	226	306	Malaisie
Oman	...	...	...	10	29	120	109	153	226	231	Oman
Pakistan	162	180	185	198	234	272	281	296	297	315	Pakistan
Qatar	58	63	58	170	176	194	180	152	163	168	Qatar
S.Arabia,pt.Ntrl.Zn	23	24	24	25	49	40	50	50	74	59	Arab.saoud,p.Zn.neut
Syrian Arab Republic	5	1	1	1	2	2	2	3	5	6	Rép. arabe syrienne
Thailand	0	0	0	0	0	11	50	60	90	116	Thaïlande
Turkey	...	...	1	0	1	1	2	0	1	3	Turquie
United Arab Emirates	34	55	92	212	268	342	169	149	149	150	Emirats arabes unis
Europe	**8 601**	**8 826**	**9 087**	**9 341**	**9 275**	**9 163**	**8 776**	**8 934**	**8 614**	**8 887**	**Europe**
EEC	***6 441***	***6 443***	***6 143***	***6 300***	***6 054***	***5 888***	***5 519***	***5 692***	***5 252***	***5 525***	***CEE***
Belgium	1	1	1	1	2	1	1	1	1	2	Belgique
Denmark	...	...	...	...	...	...	0	0	9	45	Danemark
France incl. Monaco	278	299	307	303	289	277	257	260	247	211	France y comp.Monaco
Germany, Fed. Rep.	676	673	720	729	668	673	580	635	617	584	Allemagne, Rép. féd.
Greece	...	...	...	...	0	0	4	3	4	3	Grèce
Ireland	...	...	0	21	34	52	77	83	88	90	Irlande
Italy and San Marino	600	526	536	482	477	535	583	493	522	537	Italie y comp. S.Mrn
Netherlands	3 421	3 407	3 120	3 293	3 205	2 975	2 533	2 691	2 270	2 388	Pays–Bas
United Kingdom	1 465	1 536	1 458	1 470	1 379	1 374	1 483	1 527	1 494	1 665	Royaume–Uni
EFTA	***101***	***221***	***756***	***985***	***1 143***	***1 116***	***1 082***	***1 081***	***1 148***	***1 114***	***AELE***
Austria	88	98	99	95	78	58	53	49	51	47	Autriche

For general note, see end of table.

Voir la fin du tableau pour la remarque générale.

Natural gas (continued) – Gaz naturel (suite)

Unit : Petajoules

Unité : Petajoules

Country or area	1976	1977	1978	1979	1980	1981	1982	1983	1984	1985	Pays ou zone
Norway,Svlbd,J.Myn I..	14	123	658	890	1 065	1 058	1 029	1 032	1 097	1 067	Norvège,Svalbd,J.May
Switzrld,Liechtenst.........	...	...	...	...	...	...	0	0	0	1	Suisse,Liechtenstein
East Europe................	***1 987***	***2 083***	***2 108***	***1 980***	***2 004***	***2 081***	***2 098***	***2 093***	***2 099***	***2 104***	***Europe de l'est***
Albania.........................	14	14	14	14	15	15	16	16	17	17	Albanie
Bulgaria........................	1	0	1	5	11	8	6	6	6	5	Bulgarie
Czechoslovakia.............	30	32	40	29	21	23	21	19	24	23	Tchécoslovaquie
German Dem. Rep.........	113	111	91	82	72	84	84	100	105	100	Rép. dém. allemande
Hungary........................	203	219	244	216	237	232	255	249	255	274	Hongrie
Poland..........................	243	242	243	224	193	187	167	166	167	162	Pologne
Romania.......................	1 383	1 465	1 475	1 409	1 455	1 532	1 549	1 537	1 526	1 522	Roumanie
Other Europe..............	***72***	***79***	***80***	***77***	***75***	***79***	***77***	***68***	***114***	***145***	***Autre Europe***
Spain............................	0	0	0	0	0	0	0	0	7	11	Espagne
Yugoslavia....................	72	79	80	77	75	79	77	68	107	134	Yougoslavie
USSR...........................	**11 170**	**12 046**	**12 967**	**14 160**	**15 149**	**16 165**	**17 418**	**18 638**	**20 469**	**22 149**	**URSS**
Oceania.......................	**222**	**280**	**335**	**351**	**398**	**458**	**537**	**549**	**603**	**646**	**Océanie**
Australia......................	188	225	281	311	359	414	458	463	489	523	Australie
New Zealand...............	34	56	55	41	39	44	79	85	114	123	Nouvelle–Zélande
Total...........................	**47 958**	**48 037**	**50 041**	**52 885**	**53 735**	**54 439**	**54 035**	**54 499**	**58 329**	**59 957**	**Total**

General note.
Natural gas from underground sources (whether or not in association with crude petroleum), gas recovered from coal mines and sewage gas measured at 15 degrees centigrade and standard sea–level atmospheric pressure (760 mm Hg). Production should be confined to gas of these types which is actually collected and used as fuel or raw material. It should therefore exclude gas used for repressuring and gas flared, vented or otherwise wasted, whether or not such gas has first been processed for the extraction of natural gasolene. (SITC 34110–1B).

Remarque générale.
Gaz naturel provenant de gisements souterrains (associés ou non au pétrole brut), gaz récupérés dans les charbonnages ou provenant de la fermentation des boues d'égouts mesurés à la température de 15° C et à la pression atmosphérique normale au niveau de la mer (760 mm de mercure). Le chiffre indiqué doit se rapporter uniquement aux gaz de ces types qui sont effectivement collectés et utilisés comme combustibles ou matières premières. La rubrique ne comprend donc pas le gaz utilisé pour la remise en pression des gisements, le gaz brûlé aux torches, éventé ou autrement perdu, qu'il ait été d'abord traité ou non pour l'extraction de la gazoline naturelle. (CTCI 34110–1B).

Unit : Thousand metric tons — Unité : Milliers de tonnes métriques

Country or area	1976	1977	1978	1979	1980	1981	1982	1983	1984	1985	Pays ou zone
Africa	**35 834**	**38 350**	**34 207**	**41 976**	**37 760**	**38 967**	**35 256**	**28 357**	**34 267**	**33 722**	**Afrique**
Algeria	1 507	1 721	1 487	1 548	1 867	1 850	2 103	* 1 991	* 1 980	* 1 825	Algérie
Egypt	621	704	765	717	888	972	1 070	1 033	947	1 061	Egypte
Liberia	15 154	10 991	10 810	12 858	11 972	12 259	11 177	9 671	9 211	8 909	Libéria
Mauritania[1]	6 233	6 317	4 299	5 812	5 332	* 5 243	* 4 750	* 4 250	* 5 754	* 5 600	Mauritanie[1]
Morocco	202	240	36	36	46	43	132	102	96	106	Maroc
Sierra Leone	0	0	0	0	0	0	6	192	* 224	* 190	Sierra Leone
South Africa	9 800	16 576	15 153	19 760	16 471	17 728	15 371	10 395	15 334	15 206	Afrique du Sud
Swaziland	1 229	915	798	311	0	0	0	0	0	0	Swaziland
Tunisia	276	180	185	213	211	212	147	169	166	165	Tunisie
Zimbabwe	[1] 812	[1] 706	[1] 674	[1] 721	[1] 973	[1] 660	[1] 500	[1] 554	[1] 555	* 660	Zimbabwe
America, North	**87 879**	**71 607**	**81 538**	**95 205**	**79 856**	**83 689**	**48 888**	**49 962**	**63 486**	**60 462**	**Amérique du Nord**
Canada[2]	34 081	32 977	26 403	36 664	30 177	30 654	20 501	20 105	24 357	24 096	Canada[2]
Mexico	3 644	3 587	3 556	4 041	5 087	5 749	5 382	5 306	5 489	5 161	Mexique
United States[3]	50 154	35 043	51 579	54 500	44 592	47 286	23 005	24 551	33 640	31 205	Etats–Unis[3]
America, South	**93 877**	**87 121**	**88 070**	**98 853**	**114 914**	**103 063**	**97 227**	**90 899**	**113 831**	**98 731**	**Amérique du Sud**
Argentina	273	544	483	396	275	249	389	390	346	367	Argentine
Bolivia	5	4	35	16	4	4	5	* 7	0	0	Bolivie
Brazil	73 027	68 556	70 649	79 901	94 993	83 442	81 559	77 649	97 813	* 81 600	Brésil
Chile	6 186	4 941	4 769	4 978	5 344	5 190	3 874	3 602	4 250	3 930	Chili
Colombia	229	212	209	174	226	189	205	201	207	200	Colombie
Peru	2 199	4 107	3 275	3 622	3 767	4 051	3 715	3 101	2 865	3 209	Pérou
Uruguay	0	0	0	0	1	3	4	0	0	...	Uruguay
Venezuela	11 958	8 757	8 650	9 766	10 304	9 935	7 476	5 949	8 350	9 423	Venezuela
Asia	**79 195**	**80 358**	**90 988**	**89 929**	**88 611**	**84 689**	**86 668**	**86 747**	**96 559**	**103 035**	**Asie**
China	44 850	46 920	58 895	59 380	56 295	52 295	53 660	56 695	63 350	69 095	Chine
Hong Kong	19	0	0	0	0	0	0	0	0	0	Hong–kong
India	27 430	26 759	24 776	25 066	26 378	26 219	26 887	23 693	26 620	27 837	Inde
Indonesia[4]	166	178	124	46	36	49	78	76	47	75	Indonésie[4]
Iran(Islamic Rep.of)[1 5]	653	671	952	* 371	* 370	* 370	* 400	* 450	* 450	* 450	Iran(Rép.islamique)[1 5]
Japan[6]	450	487	361	383	294	275	227	185	202	212	Japon[6]
Korea,Dem.Ppl's.Rep.* [1]	2 740	2 850	2 950	3 050	3 250	3 250	3 250	3 250	3 250	3 250	Corée,Rép.pop.dém.de* [1]
Korea, Republic of	358	365	329	257	305	311	310	331	310	304	Corée, République de
Malaysia	172	185	320	202	208	298	191	64	109	102	Malaisie
Philippines	354	* 1	1	4	0	4	4	2	0	0	Philippines
Thailand	14	36	50	59	48	31	15	23	35	54	Thaïlande
Turkey	1 989	1 906	2 230	1 111	1 427	1 587	1 646	1 978	2 186	1 656	Turquie
Europe	**49 207**	**42 524**	**38 649**	**41 176**	**39 674**	**34 264**	**26 619**	**25 294**	**28 585**	**29 057**	**Europe**
EEC	***17 536***	***14 329***	***13 080***	***12 536***	***10 828***	***8 185***	***6 916***	***6 111***	***5 864***	***5 715***	***CEE***
Belgium	20	14	13	0	0	0	0	0	0	0	Belgique
Denmark	3	2	0	2	3	* 3	* 3	0	0	0	Danemark
France	13 792	11 050	10 310	9 800	9 100	6 800	6 200	5 174	4 679	4 536	France
Germany, Fed. Rep.	750	816	510	526	597	477	387	280	293	319	Allemagne, Rép. féd.
Greece	949	881	725	789	625	551	221	572	810	800	Grèce
Italy	216	201	148	96	76	50	2	0	0	0	Italie
Luxembourg	615	466	272	213	189	146	0	0	0	0	Luxembourg
United Kingdom	1 191	899	1 102	1 110	238	158	103	85	82	60	Royaume–Uni
EFTA	***23 708***	***20 334***	***17 779***	***20 972***	***21 217***	***18 976***	***12 685***	***12 423***	***15 627***	***16 992***	***AELE***
Austria	1 165	1 069	866	999	986	948	1 045	1 107	1 138	1 019	Autriche
Finland	444	658	717	593	523	554	562	555	597	508	Finlande
Norway	2 565	2 339	2 440	2 616	2 480	2 670	1 648	2 307	2 500	2 321	Norvège
Portugal	28	27	26	29	25	* 13	9	12	14	29	Portugal
Sweden	19 506	16 241	13 730	16 735	17 203	14 791	9 421	8 442	11 378	13 115	Suède
East Europe	***2 375***	***2 225***	***2 263***	***2 055***	***1 844***	***1 777***	***1 648***	***1 679***	***1 700***	***1 762***	***Europe de l'est***
Bulgaria	748	707	762	651	590	537	474	554	622	607	Bulgarie
Czechoslovakia	522	551	558	548	525	520	499	507	494	489	Tchécoslovaquie
German Dem. Rep.	21	20	20	13	12	* 9	* 9	9	8	* 9	Rép. dém. allemande
Hungary	142	116	120	121	90	88	101	96	82	68	Hongrie
Poland	215	198	159	75	31	32	15	3	3	3	Pologne

For general note and footnotes, see end of table. — Voir la fin du tableau pour la remarque générale et les notes.

Unit : Thousand metric tons

Unité : Milliers de tonnes métriques

Country or area	1976	1977	1978	1979	1980	1981	1982	1983	1984	1985	Pays ou zone
Romania	727	633	644	647	596	591	550	510	491	586	Roumanie
Other Europe	***5 588***	***5 636***	***5 527***	***5 613***	***5 785***	***5 326***	***5 370***	***5 081***	***5 394***	***4 588***	***Autre Europe***
Spain	4 089	4 122	3 906	3 994	4 372	3 816	3 690	3 552	3 557	2 903	Espagne
Yugoslavia	1 499	1 514	1 621	1 619	1 413	1 510	1 680	1 529	1 837	1 685	Yougoslavie
USSR	**131 408**	**132 019**	**134 369**	**131 453**	**132 885**	**131 071**	**132 055**	**133 563**	**134 809**	**135 633**	**URSS**
Ukrainian SSR	*69 804*	*69 777*	*70 324*	*69 399*	*68 916*	*68 714*	*68 793*	*68 395*	*67 701*	*66 208*	*RSS d'Ukraine*
Oceania	**58 263**	**60 164**	**54 739**	**53 248**	**61 319**	**59 064**	**54 886**	**45 302**	**56 817**	**63 500**	**Océanie**
Australia[7]	58 263	60 164	54 739	53 248	61 319	59 064	54 886	[1] 45 302	[1] 56 817	[1] 63 500	Australie[7]
Total	**535 663**	**512 143**	**522 560**	**551 840**	**555 019**	**534 807**	**481 599**	**460 124**	**528 354**	**524 140**	**Total**

General note.
Fe content of iron ores and concentrates and all other iron–bearing ores and concentrates intended for treatment for iron recovery. (SITC 28130–1M).

[1] Source: U. S. Bureau of Mines, (Washington, D. C.).
[2] Shipments.
[3] Including metal content of by–product ore.
[4] Content of iron sand concentrate.
[5] Twelve months beginning 21 March of year stated.
[6] Including iron content of iron sand and pyrites.
[7] Twelve months ending 30 June of year stated.

Remarque générale.
Fe contenu des minerais de fer et concentrés et tous autres minerais ferrifères et concentrés, destinés à être traités en vue de l'extraction du fer. (CTCI 28130–1M).

[1] Source: U.S. Bureau of Mines, (Washington, D.C.).
[2] Expéditions.
[3] Y compris la teneur en métal des minerais de récupération
[4] La teneur en fer des concentrés de sables ferrugineux.
[5] Période de douze mois commençant le 21 mars de l'année indiquée.
[6] Y compris la teneur en fer des sables ferrugineux et des pyrites.
[7] Période de douze mois finissant le 30 juin de l'année indiquée.

Copper-bearing ores – Minerais cuprifères

Unit : Thousand metric tons — Unité : Milliers de tonnes métriques

Country or area	1976	1977	1978	1979	1980	1981	1982	1983	1984	1985	Pays ou zone
Africa	**1 618.2**	**1 626.9**	**1 492.4**	**1 412.0**	**1 463.9**	**1 495.8**	**1 470.8**	**1 475.3**	**1 447.2**	**1 380.6**	**Afrique**
Algeria[1]	0.4	0.3	0.2	0.2	0.2	0.2	0.2	* 0.1	* 0.1	* 0.0	Algérie[1]
Botswana	12.5	11.8	14.6	14.6	15.6	17.8	18.4	20.3	21.5	21.7	Botswana
Congo	7.1	6.6	1.6	2.9	2.6	6.3	3.4	3.9	2.5	2.9	Congo
Mauritania[2]	9.4	7.6	1.8	0.0	0.0	...	...	...	...	...	Mauritanie[2]
Morocco[1]	4.6	3.4	3.4	6.6	5.7	6.3	17.6	19.5	18.1	16.7	Maroc[1]
Mozambique[3]	2.0	3.0	0.3	0.2	0.0	0.0	0.0	0.0	0.0	0.0	Mozambique[3]
Namibia[3 4]	43.5	49.2	37.7	41.9	39.2	44.3	48.8	52.1	50.0	47.0	Namibie[3 4]
South Africa[4]	196.9	205.4	205.7	190.6	200.7	199.4	188.7	205.0	198.2	202.3	Afrique du Sud[4]
Uganda[3]	7.0	4.0	1.3	0.0	0.0	0.0	0.0	0.0	0.0	0.0	Ouganda[3]
Zaire[4 5]	443.9	481.6	425.4	401.4	459.3	504.8	494.8	502.2	500.7	502.1	Zaïre[4 5]
Zambia	849.6	819.2	766.6	724.0	713.8	689.8	672.8	649.9	633.4	565.7	Zambie
Zimbabwe[4]	41.3	34.8	33.8	29.7	26.9	24.6	24.7	21.6	22.7	20.4	Zimbabwe[4]
America, North	**2 283.2**	**2 219.1**	**2 109.1**	**2 194.7**	**2 077.1**	**2 490.4**	**2 001.9**	**1 899.9**	**2 004.9**	**2 018.1**	**Amérique du Nord**
Canada[4]	730.9	759.4	659.4	636.4	716.4	718.1	612.5	653.0	721.8	730.3	Canada[4]
Cuba	2.8	2.6	2.8	2.9	3.4	3.0	2.7	2.7	2.7	3.1	Cuba
Guatemala[2]	...	2.5	2.1	1.8	0.8	0.7	* 0.7	0.0	0.0	0.0	Guatemala[2]
Mexico[4]	89.0	89.7	87.2	107.1	175.4	230.5	239.1	206.1	189.1	178.9	Mexique[4]
Nicaragua[1 2]	1.3	0.5	* 0.1	0.0	0.0	0.0	0.0	0.0	0.0	0.0	Nicaragua[1 2]
United States[6]	1 456.6	1 364.4	1 357.6	1 446.6	1 181.1	1 538.2	1 147.0	1 038.1	1 091.3	1 105.8	Etats-Unis[6]
America, South	**1 247.3**	**1 385.3**	**1 410.3**	**1 468.4**	**1 433.1**	**1 462.9**	**1 651.4**	**1 633.0**	**1 729.0**	**1 800.3**	**Amérique du Sud**
Argentina	0.3	0.2	0.3	0.1	0.2	0.1	0.0	0.0	0.2	0.4	Argentine
Bolivia[4]	5.1	3.2	3.3	1.8	1.9	2.6	2.3	2.0	1.6	1.7	Bolivie[4]
Brazil	0.0	0.0	0.0	0.0	0.4	11.8	24.5	40.0	44.4	* 36.3	Brésil
Chile[4]	1 013.2	1 053.5	1 029.5	1 067.8	1 063.0	1 105.5	1 255.1	1 255.4	1 307.5	1 359.8	Chili[4]
Ecuador[2]	0.3	1.0	0.8	1.2	0.9	0.8	0.0	0.0	* 0.2	* 0.1	Equateur[2]
Peru	228.4	327.4	376.4	397.4	366.7	342.1	369.5	335.6	375.1	402.0	Pérou
Asia	**603.8**	**645.0**	**616.0**	**635.1**	**623.8**	**692.7**	**744.4**	**743.5**	**716.7**	**720.4**	**Asie**
Burma[7]	[2] 0.1	[2] 0.0	[2] 0.1	[2] 0.1	[2] 0.1	# 0.3	0.2	0.3	0.3	0.2	Birmanie[7]
China* [2]	105.0	110.0	115.0	115.0	115.0	170.0	175.0	175.0	180.0	185.0	Chine* [2]
Cyprus[4 8]	7.9	7.0	5.2	1.2	...	0.2	0.8	1.1	1.3	1.1	Chypre[4 8]
India	29.1	29.0	26.6	27.7	24.5	25.6	30.4	46.6	52.2	50.3	Inde
Indonesia	69.1	57.1	58.9	60.2	59.7	60.1	70.5	65.4	60.7	74.3	Indonésie
Iran(Islamic Rep.of)* [2 9]	6.0	13.5	6.0	3.0	1.0	2.0	43.0	65.0	60.0	60.0	Iran(Rép.islamique)* [2 9]
Israel	2.1	0.0	0.0	0.0	0.4	* 4.4	[2] 3.5	[2] 3.5	[2] 2.9	[2] 0.0	Israël
Japan[1]	81.6	81.4	72.0	59.1	52.6	51.5	50.7	46.0	43.3	43.2	Japon[1]
Korea,Dem.Ppl's.Rep.* [2]	15.0	15.0	15.0	15.0	15.0	15.0	15.0	15.0	15.0	15.0	Corée,Rép.pop.dém.de* [2]
Korea, Republic of	2.3	1.7	0.7	0.5	0.4	0.5	0.3	0.4	0.3	0.2	Corée, République de
Malaysia[10 11]	18.2	24.0	25.9	24.5	27.0	28.6	30.1	29.0	28.9	30.5	Malaisie[10 11]
Philippines	237.6	272.8	263.4	298.3	304.5	302.3	292.1	271.4	233.4	* 226.2	Philippines
Turkey	29.9	33.4	27.2	30.5	20.5	32.1	32.8	24.8	38.6	34.5	Turquie
Europe	**675.4**	**686.8**	**727.9**	**739.9**	**759.0**	**723.6**	**788.6**	**850.2**	**886.2**	**883.0**	**Europe**
EEC	***7.6***	***7.6***	***7.0***	***6.7***	***6.9***	***6.5***	***3.7***	***3.7***	***2.8***	***1.7***	***CEE***
France	[12] 0.2	[12] 0.1	[12] 0.2	[12] 0.1	[12] 0.1	[12] 0.1	# 0.1	0.2	0.2	0.1	France
Germany, Fed. Rep.	1.6	1.2	0.8	0.9	[1 2] 1.3	[1 2] 1.4	[1 2] 1.3	[1 2] 1.2	[1 2] 1.0	[1 2] 0.9	Allemagne, Rép. féd.
Ireland[1]	4.1	4.8	4.8	4.8	4.2	3.5	1.6	0.0	0.0	0.0	Irlande[1]
Italy[1]	1.0	0.7	0.5	0.3	0.6	0.8	0.1	1.6	0.9	0.1	Italie[1]
United Kingdom	...	...	...	...	...	0.7	0.6	0.7	0.7	0.6	Royaume-Uni
EFTA	***121.5***	***120.9***	***123.6***	***116.0***	***110.4***	***120.7***	***119.2***	***136.0***	***145.3***	***138.3***	***AELE***
Austria	1.2	0.0	0.0	0.0	0.0	0.0	0.0	0.0	0.0	0.0	Autriche
Finland	44.0	46.7	46.8	41.1	36.8	38.2	38.1	37.7	29.5	26.6	Finlande
Norway[1]	31.1	29.1	29.1	28.7	28.9	28.1	27.9	22.6	25.0	19.3	Norvège[1]
Portugal[13]	0.4	0.3	0.3	0.5	0.7	0.6	0.5	0.4	0.4	0.3	Portugal[13]
Sweden[1]	44.9	44.8	47.4	45.8	44.0	53.8	52.7	75.3	90.4	92.2	Suède[1]
East Europe	***390.6***	***406.1***	***437.0***	***469.7***	***484.4***	***434.6***	***498.7***	***526.2***	***537.4***	***543.6***	***Europe de l'est***
Albania[14]	* 10.0	* 10.0	11.5	9.7	10.8	11.5	14.0	15.0	14.1	15.0	Albanie[14]
Bulgaria[14]	* 57.0	* 57.0	58.0	60.0	62.0	62.0	65.0	68.0	73.0	78.0	Bulgarie[14]
Czechoslovakia	10.1	9.9	9.1	10.4	11.4	9.5	10.0	10.0	10.0	10.1	Tchécoslovaquie
German Dem. Rep.* [14]	16.0	17.0	15.0	14.0	11.8	12.0	13.0	12.0	12.0	12.0	Rép. dém. allemande* [14]

For general note and footnotes, see end of table.

Voir la fin du tableau pour la remarque générale et les notes.

Unit : Thousand metric tons

Unité : Milliers de tonnes métriques

Country or area	1976	1977	1978	1979	1980	1981	1982	1983	1984	1985	Pays ou zone
Poland	267.0	284.9	316.2	346.5	360.4	309.6	366.7	393.2	398.3	398.5	Pologne
Romania* [14]	30.0	27.0	27.0	29.0	28.0	30.0	30.0	28.0	30.0	30.0	Roumanie* [14]
Other Europe	***155.7***	***152.2***	***160.3***	***147.4***	***157.3***	***161.9***	***166.9***	***184.3***	***200.7***	***199.4***	***Autre Europe***
Spain	35.6	36.0	36.9	36.0	42.5	50.9	47.6	54.8	63.1	56.9	Espagne
Yugoslavia	120.1	116.2	123.3	111.4	114.8	111.0	119.3	129.5	137.6	142.5	Yougoslavie
USSR* [14]	**980.0**	**980.0**	**970.0**	**970.0**	**980.0**	**1 000.0**	**1 010.0**	**1 020.0**	**1 020.0**	**1 030.0**	**URSS* [14]**
Oceania	**394.8**	**399.5**	**415.7**	**409.5**	**381.9**	**411.8**	**429.7**	**436.5**	**413.7**	**426.8**	**Océanie**
Australia [15]	218.3	217.2	217.1	238.7	235.1	246.4	259.7	235.3	249.3	251.8	Australie [15]
Papua New Guinea	176.5	182.3	198.6	170.8	146.8	165.4	170.0	201.2	164.4	175.0	Papouasie–Nvl–Guinée
Total	**7 802.7**	**7 942.6**	**7 741.5**	**7 829.6**	**7 715.4**	**8 277.3**	**8 096.7**	**8 058.3**	**8 217.7**	**8 259.2**	**Total**

General note.
Cu content of copper ores and concentrates and all other copper–bearing ores and concentrates intended for treatment for copper recovery. (SITC 28311–1M+).

[1] Content of concentrates.
[2] Source: U. S. Bureau of Mines, (Washington, D. C.).
[3] Source: World Metal Statistics, (London).
[4] Content of all copper–bearing materials in the form they are to be used or exported.
[5] Source: Banque du Zaire, (Kinshasa).
[6] Copper content calculated as recoverable.
[7] Content of matte.
[8] Excluding copper content of iron pyrites.
[9] Twelve months beginning 21 March of year stated.
[10] Exports.
[11] Data refer to Peninsular Malaysia only.
[12] Source: Mineral Industrial Statistics, Ministry of Industrial and Scientific Development, (Paris).
[13] Excluding copper sediments obtained from copper–bearing pyrites.
[14] Source: Metallgesellschaft Aktiengesellschaft, (Frankfurt).
[15] Twelve months ending 30 June of year stated.

Remarque générale.
Cu contenu des minerais de cuivre et concentrés et tous autres minerais cuprifères et concentrés, destinés à être traités en vue de l'extraction du cuivre. (CTCI 28311–1M+).

[1] Teneur des concentrés.
[2] Source: U.S. Bureau of Mines, (Washington, D.C.).
[3] Source: World Metal Statistics, (Londres).
[4] Teneur en cuivre de tous les matériaux prêts à être utilisés ou exportés.
[5] Source: Banque du Zaire, (Kinshasa).
[6] Teneur en cuivre considérée récupérable.
[7] Teneur des mattes.
[8] Non compris la teneur en cuivre des pyrites de fer.
[9] Période de douze mois commençant le 21 mars de l'année indiquée.
[10] Exportations.
[11] Données se rapportant à la Malaisie péninsulaire seulement.
[12] Source: Statistiques de l'industrie minérale, Ministère du développement industrielle et scientifique, (Paris).
[13] Non compris les sédiments cuivreux obtenus à partir de pyrites cuprifères.
[14] Source: Metallgesellschaft Aktiengesellschaft, (Francfort).
[15] Période de douze mois finissant le 30 juin de l'année indiquée.

Unit : Metric tons | Unité : Tonnes métriques

Country or area	1976	1977	1978	1979	1980	1981	1982	1983	1984	1985	Pays ou zone
Africa	**49 696**	**50 885**	**60 620**	**61 164**	**56 350**	**57 828**	**53 199**	**48 861**	**53 855**	**54 462**	**Afrique**
Botswana	12 581	12 099	16 049	16 173	15 442	18 279	17 763	18 214	18 604	19 565	Botswana
Morocco[1]	* 140	*[2] 160	*[2] 170	*[2] 160	[2] 134	[2] 131	[2] 127	[2] 0	[2] 0	[2] 0	Maroc[1]
South Africa[3]	22 371	21 955	[2] 28 700	[2] 30 240	[2] 25 700	[2] 26 400	*[2] 22 000	*[2] 20 500	*[2] 25 000	*[2] 25 000	Afrique du Sud[3]
Zimbabwe	14 604	16 671	15 701	14 591	15 074	13 018	13 309	10 147	10 251	9 897	Zimbabwe
America, North	**317 840**	**307 508**	**190 755**	**203 785**	**259 592**	**225 433**	**134 758**	**184 523**	**244 453**	**240 914**	**Amérique du Nord**
Canada[4]	240 824	232 512	128 310	126 482	184 802	155 175	88 581	125 022	173 725	175 570	Canada[4]
Cuba	37 021	36 750	34 787	32 324	38 207	40 260	37 603	39 257	33 227	33 577	Cuba
Dominican Republic	24 999	24 899	14 302	25 112	16 350	19 022	5 668	20 244	24 311	25 366	Rép. dominicaine
Guatemala[2]	0	298	1 079	6 199	6 940	0	0	0	0	...	Guatemala[2]
Mexico	56	34	22	1	0	0	0	0	0	...	Mexique
United States[5]	14 940	13 015	12 255	13 667	13 293	10 976	2 906	0	13 190	5 558	Etats–Unis[5]
America, South	**5 273**	**4 241**	**3 600**	**2 964**	**5 838**	**6 567**	**14 451**	**15 561**	**23 532**	**24 000**	**Amérique du Sud**
Brazil	5 273	4 241	3 600	2 964	5 838	6 567	14 451	15 561	23 532	* 24 000	Brésil
Asia	**41 712**	**68 058**	**59 714**	**58 760**	**62 318**	**58 398**	**50 625**	**36 790**	**29 151**	**50 607**	**Asie**
Burma[6]	*[2] 24	*[2] 17	*[2] 18	*[2] 18	*[2] 14	20	20	20	20	* 20	Birmanie[6]
Indonesia[7]	26 449	31 260	30 168	37 264	36 923	36 893	39 382	30 673	25 603	22 934	Indonésie[7]
Philippines	15 239	36 781	29 528	21 478	25 381	21 485	11 223	6 097	3 528	* 27 653	Philippines
Europe	**34 183**	**27 340**	**31 765**	**33 232**	**33 180**	**30 760**	**23 813**	**30 300**	**35 323**	**37 500**	**Europe**
EEC	***16 450***	***9 630***	***14 888***	***14 632***	***13 880***	***10 860***	***4 778***	***13 000***	***16 700***	***17 000***	*CEE*
Greece	16 450	9 630	14 888	14 632	13 880	10 860	4 778	* 13 000	* 16 700	* 17 000	Grèce
EFTA	***6 833***	***6 310***	***4 877***	***6 400***	***7 000***	***7 400***	***6 835***	***5 800***	***6 923***	***8 500***	*AELE*
Finland	6 433	5 810	4 377	5 800	6 400	6 900	6 335	5 300	6 323	7 900	Finlande
Norway[8]	400	500	500	600	600	500	500	500	600	600	Norvège[8]
East Europe	***10 900***	***11 400***	***12 000***	***12 200***	***12 300***	***12 500***	***12 200***	***11 500***	***11 700***	***12 000***	*Europe de l'est*
Albania[8]	7 000	7 500	8 000	8 500	8 500	8 800	9 000	9 000	9 700	10 000	Albanie[8]
German Dem. Rep.[8]	2 500	2 500	2 700	2 500	2 700	2 700	2 500	2 200	2 000	2 000	Rép. dém. allemande[8]
Poland* [8]	1 400	1 400	1 300	1 200	1 100	1 000	700	300	0	0	Pologne* [8]
USSR* [2]	**141 000**	**147 000**	**149 000**	**151 000**	**154 000**	**158 000**	**165 000**	**170 000**	**175 000**	**180 000**	**URSS* [2]**
Oceania	**200 636**	**197 894**	**154 147**	**160 379**	**150 985**	**151 457**	**141 525**	**129 107**	**134 096**	**154 628**	**Océanie**
Australia[9]	80 953	81 099	86 991	80 385	64 393	73 367	81 424	82 945	75 770	82 267	Australie[9]
New Caledonia	119 683	116 795	67 156	79 994	86 592	78 090	60 101	46 162	58 326	72 361	Nouvelle–Calédonie
Total	**790 340**	**802 926**	**649 601**	**671 284**	**722 263**	**688 443**	**583 371**	**615 142**	**695 410**	**742 111**	**Total**

General note.
Ni content of nickel ores and concentrates and all other nickel–bearing ores and concentrates intended for treatment for nickel recovery. (SITC 28321–1M+).

[1] Content of cobalt ore.
[2] Source: U. S. Bureau of Mines, (Washington, D. C.).
[3] Content of matte and refined nickel.
[4] Refined nickel in oxides and salts sold, nickel in matte exported and recoverable nickel in concentrates shipped to smelters.
[5] Shipments.
[6] Content of speiss.
[7] Including small amount of cobalt not reported separately.
[8] Source: Metallgesellschaft Aktiengesellschaft, (Frankfurt).
[9] Twelve months ending 30 June of year stated.

Remarque générale.
Ni contenu des minerais de nickel et concentrés et tous autres minerais nickelifères et concentrés, destinés à être traités en vue de l'extraction du nickel. (CTCI 28321–1M+).

[1] Teneur du minerai de cobalt.
[2] Source: U.S. Bureau of Mines, (Washington, D.C.).
[3] Teneur des mattes et du nickel affiné.
[4] Teneur en nickel affiné des oxydes et sels vendus, teneur en nickel des mattes exportées et nickel récupérable dans les concentrés livrés aux fonderies.
[5] Expéditions.
[6] Teneur du speiss.
[7] Y compris de petites quantités de cobalt dont la production n'est pas indiquée séparement.
[8] Source: Metallgesellschaft Aktiengesellschaft, (Francfort).
[9] Période de douze mois finissant le 30 juin de l'année indiquée.

Bauxite

Unit : Thousand metric tons — Unité : Milliers de tonnes métriques

Country or area	1976	1977	1978	1979	1980	1981	1982	1983	1984	1985	Pays ou zone
Africa	**12 275**	**11 892**	**12 766**	**14 306**	**14 887**	**13 614**	**12 531**	**13 864**	**15 851**	**16 074**	**Afrique**
Ghana	292	279	328	235	225	181	64	70	48	170	Ghana
Guinea[1]	11 316	10 871	11 648	13 379	13 911	12 822	11 827	12 986	14 738	14 738	Guinée[1]
Mozambique[2]	2	2	0	0	0	0	0	0	0	0	Mozambique[2]
Sierra Leone	662	737	785	687	747	606	632	785	1 042	1 145	Sierra Leone
Zimbabwe	*[2] 3	*[2] 3	5	5	4	5	8	23	23	21	Zimbabwe
America, North	**14 247**	**15 114**	**14 995**	**14 730**	**14 905**	**14 423**	**9 637**	**8 551**	**9 461**	**6 893**	**Amérique du Nord**
Dominican Republic[3]	621	576	558	524	510	405	152	0	0	0	Rép. dominicaine[3]
Haiti	733	685	639	518	477	488	431	0	0	0	Haïti
Jamaica[3]	10 473	11 417	11 732	11 502	12 049	11 683	8 158	7 725	8 605	6 219	Jamaïque[3]
United States	2 420	2 436	2 066	2 186	1 869	1 847	896	826	856	674	Etats–Unis
America, South	**8 788**	**9 552**	**9 440**	**10 516**	**14 297**	**12 686**	**11 132**	**11 317**	**15 063**	**11 846**	**Amérique du Sud**
Brazil	998	1 352	1 401	2 884	6 688	6 969	6 290	7 199	10 355	* 6 433	Brésil
Guyana	3 203	3 344	3 014	2 863	2 716	1 592	1 782	1 325	* 1 333	* 1 675	Guyana
Suriname	4 587	4 856	5 025	4 769	4 893	4 125	3 060	2 793	3 375	3 738	Suriname
Asia	**4 807**	**5 503**	**5 236**	**5 048**	**6 003**	**5 951**	**5 398**	**5 165**	**5 496**	**5 472**	**Asie**
China* [4 5]	1 300	1 500	1 500	1 500	1 500	1 500	1 600	1 600	1 600	1 650	Chine* [4 5]
India	1 449	1 519	1 663	1 952	1 785	1 955	1 998	1 976	2 078	2 268	Inde
Indonesia[3]	940	1 301	1 008	1 052	1 249	1 203	700	778	1 003	830	Indonésie[3]
Malaysia[6]	660	616	615	387	920	701	589	502	680	492	Malaisie[6]
Pakistan[7]	0	0	1	2	2	2	3	3	4	2	Pakistan[7]
Turkey	458	567	449	155	547	590	508	306	131	230	Turquie
Europe	**10 555**	**10 679**	**10 811**	**11 223**	**11 751**	**11 689**	**11 227**	**10 899**	**10 634**	**10 485**	**Europe**
EEC	***4 911***	***4 974***	***4 633***	***4 718***	***5 203***	***5 117***	***4 545***	***4 057***	***3 826***	***3 913***	***CEE***
Denmark	0	0	0	0	0	25	23	14	...	0	Danemark
France	2 330	2 059	1 978	1 969	1 921	1 824	1 610	1 595	1 527	1 452	France
Greece	2 557	2 880	2 631	2 723	3 259	3 249	2 888	2 435	2 286	2 461	Grèce
Italy	24	35	24	26	23	19	24	13	0	0	Italie
East Europe	***3 598***	***3 651***	***3 607***	***3 476***	***3 400***	***3 314***	***3 007***	***3 337***	***3 454***	***3 315***	***Europe de l'est***
Hungary	2 918	2 949	2 899	2 976	2 950	2 914	2 627	2 917	2 994	2 815	Hongrie
Romania[8]	680	702	708	500	450	400	380	420	460	500	Roumanie[8]
Other Europe	***2 046***	***2 054***	***2 571***	***3 029***	***3 148***	***3 258***	***3 675***	***3 505***	***3 354***	***3 257***	***Autre Europe***
Spain	13	* 10	6	17	10	9	7	5	7	7	Espagne
Yugoslavia	2 033	2 044	2 565	3 012	3 138	3 249	3 668	3 500	3 347	3 250	Yougoslavie
USSR* [2]	**4 500**	**4 600**	**4 600**	**4 600**	**4 600**	**4 600**	**4 600**	**4 600**	**4 600**	**4 600**	**URSS* [2]**
Oceania	**19 755**	**22 806**	**24 642**	**25 541**	**27 629**	**25 450**	**24 690**	**24 372**	**32 182**	**32 400**	**Océanie**
Australia[7]	19 755	22 806	24 642	25 541	27 629	25 450	24 690	[2] 24 372	[2] 32 182	[2] 32 400	Australie[7]
Total	**74 927**	**80 146**	**82 490**	**85 964**	**94 072**	**88 413**	**79 215**	**78 768**	**93 287**	**87 770**	**Total**

General note.
Gross weight of crude ore mined. (SITC 28330–0).

Remarque générale.
Poids brut du minerai brut naturel. (CTCI 28330–0).

[1] Source: World Metal Statistics, (London).
[2] Source: U. S. Bureau of Mines, (Washington, D. C.).
[3] Dried equivalent of crude ore.
[4] Including an estimated 160000 metric tons annually of production for refractory applications.
[5] Diasporic bauxite for production of aluminium only. Source:U. S. Bureau of Mine, (Washington, D. C.).
[6] Data refer to Peninsular Malaysia only.
[7] Twelve months ending 30 June of year stated.
[8] Source: Metallgesellschaft Aktiengesellschaft, (Frankfurt).

[1] Source: World Metal Statistics, (Londres).
[2] Source: U.S. Bureau of Mines, (Washington, D.C.).
[3] Equivalent desséché de minerai brut.
[4] Une quantité estimative annuelle de 160000 tonnes réservée à la production d'éléments réfractaires.
[5] Bauxite (diaspore) pour la production d'aluminium seulement. Source: U. S. Bureau of Mine, (Washington, D. C.).
[6] Données se rapportant à la Malaisie péninsulaire seulement.
[7] Période de douze mois finissant le 30 juin de l'année indiquée.
[8] Source: Metallgesellschaft Aktiengesellschaft, (Francfort).

Unit : Thousand metric tons | Unité : Milliers de tonnes métriques

Country or area	1976	1977	1978	1979	1980	1981	1982	1983	1984	1985	Pays ou zone
Africa	**145.2**	**175.7**	**180.2**	**186.2**	**278.7**	**291.2**	**260.4**	**252.4**	**265.6**	**269.6**	**Afrique**
Algeria[1]	2.1	0.9	1.8	2.4	1.8	3.3	3.2	* 3.0	* 3.6	* 3.6	Algérie[1]
Congo[1]	2.5	2.4	0.6	1.0	0.9	2.3	1.2	1.4	0.9	1.0	Congo[1]
Morocco[1]	68.1	107.4	115.3	114.1	118.9	116.0	102.1	95.8	99.1	105.5	Maroc[1]
Namibia[1 2]	46.4	41.2	38.6	41.0	47.7	46.5	34.9	33.8	42.6	43.2	Namibie[1 2]
Nigeria* [3]	0.1	0.1	0.0	0.1	0.4	0.2	0.3	0.3	0.3	0.3	Nigéria* [3]
South Africa[1]	0.0	0.0	0.0	0.0	86.1	98.9	90.3	87.5	94.8	98.4	Afrique du Sud[1]
Tunisia[1 4]	10.4	10.2	8.0	10.0	8.8	6.0	5.3	4.9	4.1	2.5	Tunisie[1 4]
Zambia	15.5	13.5	15.9	17.6	14.1	18.0	23.1	25.7	20.3	15.1	Zambie
America, North	**1 029.4**	**1 036.4**	**1 071.9**	**1 061.5**	**995.3**	**918.6**	**976.1**	**932.2**	**821.8**	**925.8**	**Amérique du Nord**
Canada	256.3	281.0	319.8	310.7	251.6	272.9	272.2	272.0	264.3	263.9	Canada
Greenland	31.3	33.7	36.0	35.3	34.3	30.1	30.4	24.3	20.2	20.4	Groënland
Guatemala[5]	0.1	0.1	0.1	0.1	0.1	0.1	0.1	0.2	0.2	0.2	Guatemala[5]
Honduras	23.9	20.6	15.8	[3] 16.4	[3] 13.3	[3] 12.6	[3] 15.1	[3] 19.3	[3] 20.5	20.7	Honduras
Mexico	164.8	163.5	170.5	173.5	145.5	157.4	145.8	167.4	183.3	206.7	Mexique
United States[6]	553.0	537.5	529.7	525.6	550.4	445.5	512.5	449.0	333.2	414.0	Etats–Unis[6]
America, South	**251.6**	**254.0**	**262.9**	**254.9**	**261.6**	**264.3**	**278.3**	**277.3**	**262.5**	**269.8**	**Amérique du Sud**
Argentina[1]	33.0	33.6	30.3	31.8	32.6	32.7	32.8	31.7	28.5	28.6	Argentine[1]
Bolivia	19.2	18.9	18.0	16.0	17.2	16.8	12.4	12.1	7.4	6.2	Bolivie
Brazil	22.6	24.0	31.2	22.4	21.8	21.6	19.4	18.8	16.7	* 19.2	Brésil
Chile	1.8	0.9	0.4	0.3	0.5	0.2	1.6	1.7	4.3	2.5	Chili
Colombia[3]	0.1	0.2	0.1	0.2	0.2	0.1	0.2	0.2	0.1	0.1	Colombie[3]
Ecuador[3]	0.2	0.2	0.2	* 0.2	0.2	0.2	* 0.2	* 0.2	* 0.2	* 0.2	Equateur[3]
Peru	174.7	176.1	182.7	184.0	189.1	192.7	211.7	212.6	205.3	213.0	Pérou
Asia	**370.0**	**391.8**	**387.4**	**397.8**	**400.6**	**405.4**	**396.6**	**387.5**	**424.4**	**430.6**	**Asie**
Burma[1]	* [3] 7.6	* [3] 8.3	* [3] 9.9	* [3] 15.0	* [3] 14.2	16.1	16.0	23.1	21.9	* 21.9	Birmanie[1]
China* [3]	130.0	135.0	145.0	155.0	160.0	160.0	160.0	160.0	160.0	160.0	Chine* [3]
India[1]	12.8	12.9	12.8	16.0	14.5	15.2	17.8	23.1	22.4	26.6	Inde[1]
Iran(Islamic Rep.of)[3 7]	35.0	40.0	* 30.0	* 15.0	* 12.0	* 20.0	* 25.0	* 20.0	* 20.0	* 20.4	Iran(Rép.islamique)[3 7]
Japan[1]	51.7	54.8	56.5	46.9	44.7	46.9	45.9	46.9	48.7	50.0	Japon[1]
Korea, D. P. Rp.* [3]	110.0	110.0	105.0	120.0	125.0	110.0	95.0	75.0	110.0	110.0	Corée, Rp. P. D.* [3]
Korea, Republic of[1]	12.6	16.3	15.2	12.4	10.6	11.4	10.3	10.6	9.9	8.8	Corée, République de[1]
Philippines[1]	[2] 4.5	[2] 3.7	[2] 1.4	[2] 1.9	# 1.8	1.1	0.0	0.0	0.0	0.0	Philippines[1]
Thailand[1]	0.9	0.5	1.6	8.2	9.9	16.3	17.5	19.8	15.7	18.5	Thaïlande[1]
Turkey	4.8	10.3	10.0	7.3	7.8	8.4	9.1	9.1	15.8	* 14.4	Turquie
Europe	**661.2**	**658.7**	**644.6**	**668.6**	**615.1**	**576.2**	**559.5**	**573.1**	**597.3**	**580.6**	**Europe**
EEC	***158.0***	***150.3***	***146.5***	***172.5***	***150.8***	***118.1***	***104.7***	***104.9***	***106.9***	***96.1***	***CEE***
France[1]	28.0	31.5	32.5	29.3	28.4	19.2	5.9	1.5	2.0	1.8	France[1]
Germany, Fed. Rep.[1]	31.7	31.1	22.4	# [3] 25.2	[3] 23.1	[3] 21.6	[3] 23.5	[3] 23.5	[3] 21.0	[3] 20.5	Allemagne, Rép. féd.[1]
Greece[1]	30.3	15.7	17.2	22.0	21.3	18.5	18.9	19.4	21.2	* 20.0	Grèce[1]
Ireland[1]	32.6	41.0	47.8	71.0	59.0	30.5	36.2	33.6	37.2	34.6	Irlande[1]
Italy[1]	23.4	22.9	22.1	22.5	16.7	21.2	16.3	23.1	21.4	15.6	Italie[1]
United Kingdom[1 8]	11.9	8.2	4.6	2.4	2.4	7.0	4.0	3.8	4.0	3.6	Royaume–Uni[1 8]
EFTA	***92.0***	***96.9***	***91.3***	***91.2***	***81.2***	***98.3***	***97.8***	***98.0***	***99.0***	***96.1***	***AELE***
Austria	5.4	5.0	5.5	5.2	5.5	5.7	5.6	5.7	5.3	7.7	Autriche
Finland[9]	1.1	0.6	0.8	1.4	1.1	1.6	1.9	2.1	2.5	2.4	Finlande[9]
Norway[1]	3.9	3.2	3.1	3.0	2.5	3.0	3.6	4.3	4.0	3.6	Norvège[1]
Sweden[1]	81.6	88.1	81.9	81.6	72.1	88.1	86.8	85.8	87.3	82.4	Suède[1]
East Europe	***222.4***	***215.9***	***211.1***	***202.9***	***174.5***	***157.4***	***170.5***	***173.8***	***181.0***	***186.6***	***Europe de l'est***
Bulgaria[5]	110.0	110.0	110.0	108.0	100.0	90.0	95.0	95.0	95.0	97.0	Bulgarie[5]
Czechoslovakia[1]	3.5	3.7	3.5	3.4	2.9	2.7	2.6	2.7	2.6	2.7	Tchécoslovaquie[1]
Hungary[1]	0.9	1.2	1.0	1.0	1.1	0.5	0.6	0.7	0.6	0.6	Hongrie[1]
Poland[5]	72.0	66.0	63.0	57.0	47.5	44.2	45.3	47.0	52.8	51.3	Pologne[5]
Romania* [5]	36.0	35.0	33.5	33.5	23.0	20.0	27.0	28.5	30.0	35.0	Roumanie* [5]
Other Europe	***188.9***	***195.5***	***195.7***	***202.0***	***208.6***	***202.5***	***186.4***	***196.4***	***210.4***	***201.8***	***Autre Europe***
Spain	66.4	65.5	71.3	72.3	87.1	83.9	73.3	82.0	96.7	86.7	Espagne
Yugoslavia	122.5	130.0	124.4	129.8	121.5	118.6	113.1	114.4	113.6	115.1	Yougoslavie
USSR* [3]	**410.0**	**405.0**	**410.0**	**415.0**	**420.0**	**425.0**	**430.0**	**435.0**	**435.0**	**440.0**	**URSS* [3]**

For general note and footnotes, see end of table.

Voir la fin du tableau pour la remarque générale et les notes.

Unit : Thousand metric tons — Unité : Milliers de tonnes métriques

Country or area	1976	1977	1978	1979	1980	1981	1982	1983	1984	1985	Pays ou zone
Oceania	**396.7**	**418.2**	**418.8**	**423.5**	**407.7**	**381.4**	**454.8**	**480.6**	**440.7**	**491.0**	**Océanie**
Australia[10]	396.7	418.2	418.8	423.5	407.7	381.4	454.8	480.6	440.7	491.0	Australie[10]
Total	**3 264.0**	**3 339.8**	**3 375.8**	**3 407.5**	**3 378.9**	**3 262.1**	**3 355.6**	**3 338.1**	**3 247.2**	**3 407.5**	**Total**

General note.
Pb content of lead ores and concentrates and all other lead–bearing ores and concentrates intended for treatment for lead recovery. (SITC 28340–1M+).

[1] Content of concentrates.
[2] Source: World Metal Statistics, (London).
[3] Source: U. S. Bureau of Mines, (Washington, D. C.).
[4] Excluding content of mixed ores or concentrates.
[5] Source: Metallgesellschaft Aktiengesellschaft, (Frankfurt).
[6] Calculated as recoverable.
[7] Twelve months beginning 21 March of year stated.
[8] Including zinc content.
[9] Content of lead concentrates only.
[10] Twelve months ending 30 June of year stated.

Remarque générale.
Pb contenu des minerais de plomb et concentrés et tous autres minerais plombifères et concentrés, destinés à être traités en vue de l'extraction du plomb. (CTCI 28340–1M+).

[1] Teneur des concentrés.
[2] Source: World Metal Statistics, (Londres).
[3] Source: U.S. Bureau of Mines, (Washington, D.C.).
[4] Non compris la teneur des minerais mixtes ou concentrés.
[5] Source: Metallgesellschaft Aktiengesellschaft, (Francfort).
[6] Considéré récupérable.
[7] Période de douze mois commençant le 21 mars de l'année indiquée.
[8] Y compris la teneur en zinc.
[9] Teneur des concentrées de plomb seulement.
[10] Période de douze mois finissant le 30 juin de l'année indiquée.

Zinc –bearing ores – Minerais zincifères

Unit : Thousand metric tons — Unité : Milliers de tonnes métriques

Country or area	1976	1977	1978	1979	1980	1981	1982	1983	1984	1985	Pays ou zone
Africa	**258.6**	**264.0**	**262.3**	**227.4**	**247.9**	**263.4**	**293.2**	**302.0**	**277.5**	**267.2**	**Afrique**
Algeria[1]	7.7	3.1	4.1	4.8	8.4	10.9	11.3	11.4	14.6	12.0	Algérie[1]
Congo[1]	5.1	4.7	1.1	2.0	1.9	4.5	2.4	2.8	1.8	2.1	Congo[1]
Morocco[1]	15.4	11.5	5.4	6.7	11.1	7.7	11.7	7.6	10.5	14.7	Maroc[1]
Namibia[2]	26.9	38.3	36.6	29.0	25.4	36.4	35.7	33.2	30.6	36.0	Namibie[2]
Nigeria[3]	0.0	0.0	0.0	0.0	0.0	* 0.1	* 0.1	* 0.1	* 0.1	* 0.1	Nigéria[3]
South Africa	[4] 77.1	[4] 72.4	[4] 68.7	[4] 56.5	# 87.8	87.2	91.5	110.0	106.1	* 96.9	Afrique du Sud
Tunisia[1]	7.3	7.1	7.4	8.7	9.0	7.8	8.4	7.5	6.7	5.6	Tunisie[1]
Zaire[1 5]	70.3	81.8	88.5	73.0	67.5	66.7	81.0	* 74.7	* 68.4	* 67.9	Zaïre[1 5]
Zambia	48.8	45.0	50.4	46.6	36.9	42.2	51.1	54.6	38.8	31.9	Zambie
America, North	**1 788.5**	**1 848.2**	**1 730.6**	**1 725.8**	**1 541.9**	**1 624.7**	**1 610.3**	**1 641.5**	**1 746.2**	**1 639.6**	**Amérique du Nord**
Canada	982.1	1 070.5	1 066.9	1 099.9	883.7	995.0	965.6	987.7	1 062.7	1 038.5	Canada
Greenland	88.5	83.5	90.0	92.9	86.8	86.4	85.0	83.0	74.2	72.8	Groënland
Guatemala[3 6]	0.5	1.0	0.3	0.3	0.0	3.0	0.0	0.0	0.0	0.0	Guatemala[3 6]
Honduras	18.7	19.8	25.7	[3] 19.8	[3] 16.0	[3] 16.2	[3] 24.6	[3] 38.0	[3] 41.5	51.9	Honduras
Mexico[7]	259.2	265.5	244.9	245.5	238.2	211.6	231.9	257.4	290.2	275.4	Mexique[7]
United States[8]	439.5	407.9	302.7	267.3	317.1	312.4	303.2	275.3	277.5	201.1	Etats–Unis[8]
America, South	**606.2**	**569.0**	**615.6**	**649.8**	**650.9**	**662.7**	**723.0**	**748.8**	**722.4**	**768.9**	**Amérique du Sud**
Argentina[1]	40.6	39.2	36.6	37.5	33.7	35.1	36.6	36.6	34.9	36.4	Argentine[1]
Bolivia[1]	53.0	63.5	59.6	49.6	50.3	47.0	45.7	47.2	37.8	38.1	Bolivie[1]
Brazil[3]	51.3	57.6	58.7	69.0	67.0	71.0	71.0	73.0	72.0	72.0	Brésil[3]
Chile[1]	5.1	3.9	1.8	1.8	1.1	1.5	5.7	6.0	19.2	22.3	Chili[1]
Colombia[3]	0.1	0.0	0.0	0.0	0.2	0.2	0.0	0.0	0.0	* 1.0	Colombie[3]
Ecuador[3]	0.1	2.0	1.3	* 1.0	0.6	0.7	0.0	0.0	* 0.1	* 0.1	Equateur[3]
Peru	456.1	402.8	457.5	490.8	498.0	507.1	564.0	586.0	558.4	599.0	Pérou
Asia	**773.3**	**803.1**	**782.0**	**716.5**	**690.4**	**707.3**	**726.8**	**714.1**	**763.4**	**849.0**	**Asie**
Burma[1 9]	2.1	1.8	2.5	2.9	3.9	3.4	5.1	4.4	5.0	4.2	Birmanie[1 9]
China* [3]	150.0	155.0	160.0	160.0	160.0	160.0	160.0	160.0	160.0	190.0	Chine* [3]
India[1]	27.1	27.4	39.1	42.5	32.0	31.3	32.9	40.9	48.0	53.4	Inde[1]
Iran(Islamic Rep.of)[3 10]	72.0	61.5	* 45.0	* 25.0	* 30.0	* 35.0	* 40.0	* 30.0	* 30.0	* 36.0	Iran(Rép.islamique)[3 10]
Japan[1]	260.0	275.7	274.6	243.4	238.1	242.0	251.4	255.7	252.7	253.0	Japon[1]
Korea,Dem.Ppl's.Rep.* [3]	160.0	150.0	145.0	145.0	140.0	140.0	140.0	140.0	140.0	160.0	Corée,Rép.pop.dém.de* [3]
Korea, Republic of[1]	56.2	68.8	66.3	62.2	56.1	56.5	59.1	56.9	53.1	44.8	Corée, République de[1]
Philippines[1]	11.6	12.4	9.5	9.7	6.8	5.3	3.0	2.3	2.2	* 1.9	Philippines[1]
Thailand[4]	0.0	0.0	0.0	1.0	0.0	2.9	4.0	3.0	41.0	68.3	Thaïlande[4]
Turkey	34.3	50.4	40.0	24.9	23.3	30.8	31.3	20.9	31.5	* 37.4	Turquie
Europe	**1 061.8**	**1 136.9**	**1 229.6**	**1 277.8**	**1 304.6**	**1 180.8**	**1 167.7**	**1 254.6**	**1 342.3**	**1 348.8**	**Europe**
EEC	***327.2***	***368.1***	***392.2***	***442.8***	***453.4***	***346.3***	***378.7***	***407.1***	***426.2***	***422.2***	***CEE***
France[1]	34.7	41.8	39.9	37.0	35.8	37.4	37.0	34.0	36.0	40.3	France[1]
Germany, Fed. Rep.	115.3	115.6	88.9	117.1	[1 3] 120.8	[1 3] 110.7	[1 3] 105.8	[1 3] 113.5	[1 3] 113.0	[1 3] 117.8	Allemagne, Rép. féd.
Greece[1]	28.3	16.6	22.5	22.4	23.5	24.3	19.9	21.4	21.9	* 22.0	Grèce[1]
Ireland[1]	62.8	116.3	176.0	212.0	229.0	120.3	167.2	185.9	205.9	191.6	Irlande[1]
Italy[1]	81.2	70.2	62.3	54.3	39.9	42.7	38.6	43.4	42.3	45.4	Italie[1]
United Kingdom	4.9	7.5	2.7	0.0	4.4	10.9	* 10.2	8.9	7.2	5.0	Royaume–Uni
EFTA	***241.4***	***254.2***	***275.0***	***275.6***	***283.3***	***296.0***	***287.0***	***325.7***	***342.3***	***349.0***	***AELE***
Austria	22.7	22.0	24.8	22.8	21.7	20.5	21.9	22.7	36.3	37.8	Autriche
Finland	61.1	61.3	53.2	54.5	58.4	53.6	54.7	56.3	60.2	60.6	Finlande
Norway[1]	29.3	30.6	29.6	28.4	27.5	29.7	31.8	32.4	28.5	27.4	Norvège[1]
Sweden[1]	128.3	140.2	167.4	169.9	175.8	192.1	178.6	214.4	217.3	223.2	Suède[1]
East Europe	***302.7***	***304.0***	***311.8***	***315.1***	***289.5***	***267.8***	***251.0***	***259.3***	***257.6***	***260.5***	***Europe de l'est***
Bulgaria[4]	85.5	80.0	78.0	75.0	70.0	65.0	66.0	68.0	65.0	68.0	Bulgarie[4]
Hungary[1]	2.2	3.0	2.8	3.1	2.8	1.3	1.5	2.3	1.9	1.6	Hongrie[1]
Poland[4]	215.0	221.0	231.0	237.0	216.7	201.5	183.5	189.0	190.7	190.9	Pologne[4]
Other Europe	***190.4***	***210.7***	***250.6***	***244.4***	***278.4***	***270.7***	***250.9***	***262.5***	***316.1***	***317.1***	***Autre Europe***
Spain	83.7	98.3	146.8	142.7	183.1	182.0	167.1	175.8	230.4	227.8	Espagne
Yugoslavia	106.6	112.4	103.8	101.7	95.3	88.6	83.8	86.8	85.8	89.3	Yougoslavie
USSR* [3]	**720.0**	**735.0**	**770.0**	**770.0**	**785.0**	**790.0**	**800.0**	**805.0**	**810.0**	**810.0**	**URSS* [3]**

For general note and footnotes, see end of table. — Voir la fin du tableau pour la remarque générale et les notes.

Unit : Thousand metric tons

Unité : Milliers de tonnes métriques

Country or area	1976	1977	1978	1979	1980	1981	1982	1983	1984	1985	Pays ou zone
Oceania	**479.3**	**475.3**	**484.4**	**498.5**	**518.0**	**481.9**	**623.9**	**699.0**	**658.7**	**734.0**	**Océanie**
Australia[1 11]	479.3	475.3	484.4	498.5	518.0	481.9	623.9	[3] 699.0	[3] 658.7	[3] 734.0	Australie[1 11]
Total	**5 687.6**	**5 831.5**	**5 874.5**	**5 865.8**	**5 738.7**	**5 710.7**	**5 944.9**	**6 165.0**	**6 320.5**	**6 417.5**	**Total**

General note.
Zn content of zinc ores and concentrates and all other zinc-bearing ores and concentrates intended for treatment for zinc recovery. (SITC 28350-1M+).

[1] Content of concentrates.
[2] Source: World Metal Statistics, (London).
[3] Source: U. S. Bureau of Mines, (Washington, D. C.).
[4] Source: Metallgesellschaft Aktiengesellschaft, (Frankfurt).
[5] Source: Banque du Zaire, (Kinshasa).
[6] Exports.
[7] Content of all zinc-bearing materials in the form they are to be used or exported.
[8] Calculated as recoverable.
[9] Government production only.
[10] Twelve months beginning 21 March of year stated.
[11] Twelve months ending 30 June of year stated.

Remarque générale.
Zn contenu des minerais de zinc et concentrés et tous autres minerais zincifères et concentrés, destinés à être traités en vue de l'extraction du zinc. (CTCI 28350-1M+).

[1] Teneur des concentrés.
[2] Source: World Metal Statistics, (Londres).
[3] Source: U.S. Bureau of Mines, (Washington, D.C.).
[4] Source: Metallgesellschaft Aktiengesellschaft, (Francfort).
[5] Source: Banque du Zaire, (Kinshasa).
[6] Exportations.
[7] Teneur en zinc de tous les matériaux prêts à être utilisés ou exportés.
[8] Considéré récupérable.
[9] Production de l'Etat seulement.
[10] Période de douze mois commençant le 21 mars de l'année indiquée.
[11] Période de douze mois finissant le 30 juin de l'année indiquée.

Tin–bearing ores – Minerais stannifères

Unit : Metric tons — Unité : Tonnes métriques

Country or area	1976	1977	1978	1979	1980	1981	1982	1983	1984	1985	Pays ou zone
Africa	**15 253**	**15 053**	**13 241**	**11 498**	**11 412**	**10 916**	**10 306**	**9 575**	**9 822**	**9 084**	**Afrique**
Burundi	26	* 100	* 100	0	0	0	0	0	0	0	Burundi
Cameroon[1]	19	10	11	20	* 24	* 24	* 24	* 24	* 24	* 24	Cameroun[1]
Namibia* [1]	800	1 000	1 000	1 000	1 000	800	800	800	900	900	Namibie* [1]
Niger	99	88	79	74	78	71	52	64	* 85	* 84	Niger
Nigeria	3 710	[1] 3 267	[1] 3 033	[1] 2 859	[1] 2 664	[1] 2 416	[1] 1 822	[1] 1 560	[1] 1 326	* [1] 858	Nigéria
Rwanda	1 560	1 567	1 497	1 337	1 448	1 251	1 158	1 068	1 092	813	Rwanda
South Africa	2 676	2 876	2 887	2 697	2 913	2 811	3 035	2 668	2 225	2 155	Afrique du Sud
Swaziland	1	1	* 2	* 2	0	10	7	0	0	0	Swaziland
Uganda[1]	* 120	* 120	239	37	67	30	30	* 30	* 30	30	Ouganda[1]
Zaire	5 322	5 094	3 438	2 495	[1] 2 274	[1] 2 346	[1] 2 174	[1] 2 110	[1] 2 928	[1] 3 009	Zaïre
Zambia	0	# [1] 10	* [1] 10	* [1] 10	* [1] 10	[1] 0	* [1] 7	* [1] 16	* [1] 3	* [1] 4	Zambie
Zimbabwe	920	920	945	967	934	1 157	1 197	1 235	1 209	1 207	Zimbabwe
America, North	**906**	**644**	**533**	**460**	**403**	**376**	**262**	**290**	**373**	**593**	**Amérique du Nord**
Canada	275	328	360	337	243	248	135	140	209	113	Canada
Mexico	481	220	73	23	60	28	27	50	64	380	Mexique
United States* [1]	150	96	100	100	100	100	100	100	100	100	Etats–Unis* [1]
America, South	**36 462**	**40 404**	**38 299**	**35 771**	**35 629**	**40 030**	**34 576**	**41 235**	**43 133**	**46 878**	**Amérique du Sud**
Argentina	358	537	362	386	351	413	342	291	274	451	Argentine
Bolivia[2]	30 315	33 740	30 881	27 791	27 271	29 801	24 343	25 278	19 911	16 136	Bolivie[2]
Brazil[1]	5 482	5 761	6 320	6 645	6 930	8 297	8 218	13 275	* 19 957	* 26 514	Brésil[1]
Peru	[1] 307	[1] 366	[1] 736	949	1 077	1 519	1 673	2 391	2 991	3 777	Pérou
Asia	**129 926**	**128 458**	**140 066**	**145 478**	**146 009**	**145 339**	**131 082**	**107 635**	**106 683**	**96 978**	**Asie**
Burma[1]	394	* 400	* 600	* 700	1 237	1 374	1 598	1 573	1 943	* 1 960	Birmanie[1]
China* [3]	20 000	18 000	18 000	17 000	16 000	16 000	16 000	17 000	17 500	18 000	Chine* [3]
Indonesia	24 456	25 926	27 411	29 535	32 527	35 392	33 806	26 553	23 225	22 413	Indonésie
Japan	643	605	603	660	549	561	529	600	485	510	Japon
Korea, Republic of	3	* 13	* 16	26	7	0	0	0	16	18	Corée, République de
Lao Peoples Dem.Rep.* [1]	576	600	600	600	600	600	600	600	600	600	Rép. dém. pop. lao* [1]
Malaysia[4]	63 401	58 709	62 650	62 995	61 404	59 938	52 342	41 367	41 307	36 884	Malaisie[4]
Thailand[1] [5]	20 453	24 205	30 186	33 962	33 685	31 474	26 207	19 942	21 607	16 593	Thaïlande[1] [5]
Europe	**5 805**	**6 265**	**5 487**	**4 809**	**5 671**	**6 546**	**7 101**	**7 117**	**8 621**	**8 943**	**Europe**
EEC	***3 300***	***3 800***	***2 800***	***2 400***	***3 028***	***3 873***	***4 197***	***4 076***	***5 011***	***5 044***	***CEE***
France	0	0	0	0	0	* 4	20	8	0	0	France
United Kingdom[6]	3 300	3 800	2 800	2 400	3 028	3 869	* 4 177	* 4 068	5 011	5 044	Royaume–Uni[6]
EFTA	***332***	***267***	***282***	***240***	***292***	***356***	***411***	***371***	***320***	***263***	***AELE***
Portugal	332	267	282	240	292	356	411	371	320	263	Portugal
East Europe	***1 453***	***1 556***	***1 694***	***1 673***	***1 914***	***1 753***	***1 975***	***2 226***	***2 852***	***3 171***	***Europe de l'est***
Czechoslovakia	153	156	94	73	114	153	175	226	352	371	Tchécoslovaquie
German Dem. Rep.* [3]	1 300	1 400	1 600	1 600	1 800	1 600	1 800	2 000	2 500	2 800	Rép. dém. allemande* [3]
Other Europe	***720***	***642***	***711***	***496***	***437***	***564***	***518***	***444***	***438***	***465***	***Autre Europe***
Spain	720	642	711	496	437	564	518	444	438	465	Espagne
USSR* [3]	**16 000**	**17 000**	**18 000**	**18 000**	**16 000**	**16 000**	**16 000**	**17 000**	**17 000**	**16 000**	**URSS* [3]**
Oceania	**9 685**	**10 325**	**11 771**	**12 011**	**12 379**	**12 690**	**12 750**	**10 692**	**8 688**	**7 215**	**Océanie**
Australia[7]	9 685	10 325	11 771	12 011	12 379	12 690	12 750	10 692	8 688	7 215	Australie[7]
Total	**214 037**	**218 149**	**227 397**	**228 027**	**227 503**	**231 897**	**212 077**	**193 544**	**194 320**	**185 691**	**Total**

General note.
Sn content of tin concentrates and all other tin–bearing ores and concentrates intended for treatment for tin recovery. (SITC 28360–1M+).

Remarque générale.
Sn contenu des minerais d'étain et concentrés et tous autres minerais stannifères et concentrés, destinés à être traités en vue de l'extraction de l'étain. (CTCI 28360–1M+).

For footnotes, see end of table.

Voir la fin du tableau pour les notes.

[1] Source: International Tin Council, (London).
[2] Content of ores plus metal exported.
[3] Source: Metallgesellschaft Aktiengesellschaft, (Frankfurt).
[4] Data refer to Peninsular Malaysia only.
[5] Including tin in tin wolfram concentrates.
[6] Including tungsten ores.
[7] Twelve months ending 30 June of year stated.

[1] Source: Conseil international de l'étain, (Londres).
[2] Teneur des minerais plus métal exporté.
[3] Source: Metallgesellschaft Aktiengesellschaft, (Francfort).
[4] Données se rapportant à la Malaisie péninsulaire seulement.
[5] Y compris les concentrés de l'étain wolfram.
[6] Y compris les minerais de tungstène.
[7] Période de douze mois finissant le 30 juin de l'année indiquée.

Manganese–bearing ores – Minerais manganifères

Unit : Thousand metric tons

Unité : Milliers de tonnes métriques

Country or area	1976	1977	1978	1979	1980	1981	1982	1983	1984	1985	Pays ou zone
Africa	**3 677.0**	**3 335.8**	**2 932.3**	**3 526.1**	**3 585.3**	**2 891.3**	**3 073.0**	**2 271.6**	**2 525.3**	**2 878.1**	**Afrique**
Egypt	1.8	1.6	2.5	0.0	0.0	0.0	0.0	0.0	0.0	0.0	Egypte
Gabon	1 093.9	941.0	872.3	1 173.0	* 1 172.0	758.6	771.3	* 947.1	1 077.6	1 199.2	Gabon
Ghana	152.1	140.4	152.0	121.8	120.0	107.1	76.8	83.1	137.6	151.5	Ghana
Morocco	60.1	58.2	64.7	69.5	66.9	56.2	49.5	37.7	30.3	22.4	Maroc
South Africa	2 274.1	2 173.1	1 840.6	2 161.6	2 222.6	1 959.9	2 175.2	1 203.8	1 271.7	1 501.6	Afrique du Sud
Sudan[1]	0.2	0.2	0.2	* 0.2	* 0.4	* 0.4	* 0.4	* 0.0	* 0.0	* 0.0	Soudan[1]
Zaire	94.7	21.3	0.0	0.0	3.4	9.2	0.0	0.0	8.1	...	Zaïre
America, North	**191.3**	**199.8**	**223.1**	**205.4**	**181.5**	**230.3**	**186.7**	**136.3**	**190.9**	**152.9**	**Amérique du Nord**
Mexico	163.2	175.2	188.3	177.4	161.0	208.2	183.1	133.0	180.9	150.6	Mexique
United States[2]	28.1	24.6	34.7	28.0	20.6	22.1	3.6	3.3	* 10.0	2.3	Etats–Unis[2]
America, South	**1 289.0**	**1 227.5**	**1 220.2**	**1 251.0**	**1 350.2**	**1 402.4**	**1 274.7**	**1 151.4**	**1 548.5**	**1 071.6**	**Amérique du Sud**
Argentina	10.0	13.8	4.0	3.2	1.5	0.5	0.8	1.5	2.2	3.4	Argentine
Bolivia	3.7	2.6	[1] 0.4	[1] 3.1	[1] 0.4	[1] 0.2	[1] 0.1	[1] 0.0	...	...	Bolivie
Brazil	1 267.8	1 204.0	1 207.5	1 236.0	1 339.4	1 393.0	1 268.6	1 141.4	1 537.5	* 1 056.0	Brésil
Chile	7.5	7.0	8.3	8.6	9.0	8.6	5.2	8.5	8.5	11.8	Chili
Peru[1]	...	0.0	0.0	0.0	0.0	0.0	0.0	0.0	0.3	0.3	Pérou[1]
Asia	**1 096.9**	**1 114.2**	**1 070.0**	**1 166.9**	**1 164.3**	**1 086.6**	**1 073.7**	**999.1**	**954.6**	**986.1**	**Asie**
China* [1]	340.0	340.0	380.0	450.0	480.0	480.0	480.0	480.0	480.0	480.0	Chine* [1]
India	666.0	677.0	598.3	658.6	630.5	574.5	559.1	490.0	437.8	481.9	Inde
Indonesia	5.1	3.1	3.1	3.1	2.2	1.3	9.3	4.3	4.7	* 4.0	Indonésie
Iran(Islamic Rep.of)[1 3]	13.0	13.0	10.0	* 7.0	0.0	0.0	0.0	0.0	...	...	Iran(Rép.islamique)[1 3]
Japan[4]	38.7	32.8	28.7	23.2	19.1	21.0	19.9	19.9	16.7	5.6	Japon[4]
Korea, Republic of	0.6	0.3	0.3	0.0	0.0	0.0	0.0	0.0	0.0	0.0	Corée, République de
Pakistan[5]	0.0	0.0	0.0	0.0	0.1	0.0	0.0	0.0	0.0	0.1	Pakistan[5]
Philippines	4.3	7.5	2.2	2.1	* 1.5	* 1.8	* 0.8	* 1.2	* 0.3	* 0.3	Philippines
Thailand	17.6	26.9	25.3	12.4	19.0	3.8	2.7	2.3	3.0	1.5	Thaïlande
Turkey	11.6	13.6	22.2	10.4	11.9	4.1	1.9	* 1.3	9.2	* 11.0	Turquie
Europe	**49.2**	**55.7**	**55.0**	**52.2**	**53.6**	**49.6**	**53.3**	**46.2**	**45.5**	**47.3**	**Europe**
EEC	***5.3***	***6.9***	***5.6***	***5.8***	***5.5***	***5.5***	***5.4***	***4.5***	***5.6***	***5.3***	***CEE***
Greece[4]	4.1	4.4	3.5	2.8	2.8	2.9	2.8	2.3	2.7	* 2.7	Grèce[4]
Italy	1.2	2.5	2.1	2.9	2.7	2.6	2.6	2.2	2.9	2.6	Italie
East Europe	***37.3***	***40.1***	***39.6***	***35.9***	***37.5***	***33.2***	***38.2***	***30.7***	***33.2***	***30.9***	***Europe de l'est***
Bulgaria	11.2	11.4	11.4	12.3	14.2	13.2	13.2	13.1	13.0	11.3	Bulgarie
Czechoslovakia[1]	0.2	0.0	0.0	0.0	0.0	0.0	0.0	0.0	0.0	...	Tchécoslovaquie[1]
Hungary	25.9	28.7	28.2	23.6	23.3	20.0	25.0	17.6	20.1	19.6	Hongrie
Other Europe	***6.5***	***8.7***	***9.8***	***10.5***	***10.6***	***10.9***	***9.6***	***11.1***	***6.7***	***11.1***	***Autre Europe***
Yugoslavia	6.5	8.7	9.8	10.5	10.6	10.9	9.6	11.1	6.7	11.1	Yougoslavie
USSR	**2 991.8**	**2 903.8**	**2 945.1**	**3 161.6**	**3 039.6**	**2 760.8**	**2 957.4**	**2 975.6**	**2 994.4**	**2 927.6**	**URSS**
Ukrainian SSR	*2 327.0*	*2 226.0*	*2 239.0*	*2 380.0*	*2 267.0*	*2 031.0*	*2 247.0*	*2 276.0*	*2 278.0*	*2 231.0*	*RSS d'Ukraine*
Oceania	**789.6**	**822.7**	**643.2**	**666.6**	**1 040.6**	**717.2**	**587.9**	**684.0**	**864.0**	**970.0**	**Océanie**
Australia[5]	771.1	811.4	633.0	662.2	1 039.1	717.2	587.9	684.0	864.0	970.0	Australie[5]
Vanuatu[6 7]	18.5	11.3	10.1	4.4	1.4	0.0	0.0	0.0	0.0	0.0	Vanuatu[6 7]
Total	**10 084.8**	**9 659.6**	**9 088.9**	**10 029.8**	**10 415.2**	**9 138.2**	**9 206.8**	**8 264.2**	**9 123.2**	**9 033.6**	**Total**

General note.
Mn content of manganese ores and concentrates and all other manganese–bearing ores and concentrates intended for treatment for manganese recovery. (SITC 28370–1M+).

[1] Source: U. S. Bureau of Mines, (Washington, D. C.).
[2] Shipments from mines.
[3] Twelve months beginning 21 March of year stated.
[4] Content of concentrates.
[5] Twelve months ending 30 June of year stated.
[6] Exports.
[7] Source: Mineral Industrial Statistics, Ministry of Industrial and Scientific Development, (Paris).

Remarque générale.
Mn contenu des minerais de manganèse et concentrés et tous autres minerais manganifères et concentrés, destinés à être traités en vue de l'extraction du manganèse. (CTCI 28370–1M+).

[1] Source: U.S. Bureau of Mines, (Washington, D.C.).
[2] Expéditions des mines.
[3] Période de douze mois commençant le 21 mars de l'année indiquée.
[4] Teneur des concentrés.
[5] Période de douze mois finissant le 30 juin de l'année indiquée.
[6] Exportations.
[7] Source: Statistiques de l'industrie minérale, Ministère du développement industrielle et scientifique, (Paris).

Chromium–bearing ores – Minerais chromifères

Unit : Thousand metric tons

Unité : Milliers de tonnes métriques

Country or area	1976	1977	1978	1979	1980	1981	1982	1983	1984	1985	Pays ou zone
Africa	**1 096**	**1 275**	**1 145**	**1 217**	**1 307**	**1 117**	**842**	**872**	**1 127**	**1 266**	**Afrique**
Madagascar	60	47	34	36	42	28	13	12	17	36	Madagascar
South Africa	744	999	947	993	1 075	903	681	711	946	1 051	Afrique du Sud
Sudan[1]	8	7	7	10	9	9	* 7	* 7	* 7	* 7	Soudan[1]
Zimbabwe	284	222	157	178	181	176	142	142	157	173	Zimbabwe
America, North	**5**	**5**	**7**	**7**	**7**	**5**	**7**	**8**	**9**	**9**	**Amérique du Nord**
Cuba	5	5	7	7	7	5	7	8	9	9	Cuba
America, South	**233**	**180**	**251**	**234**	**219**	**243**	**176**	**124**	**186**	**187**	**Amérique du Sud**
Brazil	231	178	249	232	217	241	174	122	184	* 185	Brésil
Colombia* [1]	2	...	...	...	...	...	...	...	...	...	Colombie* [1]
Asia	**582**	**611**	**505**	**476**	**415**	**381**	**384**	**337**	**415**	**472**	**Asie**
Cyprus	3	5	5	5	5	3	1	0	0	0	Chypre
India	133	116	85	99	99	105	108	107	139	174	Inde
Iran(Islamic Rep.of)* [1 2]	74	108	92	63	38	14	19	23	23	23	Iran(Rép.islamique)* [1 2]
Japan[3]	5	4	2	3	3	2	2	2	1	3	Japon[3]
Pakistan	4	3	3	2	1	0	1	2	1	1	Pakistan
Philippines[4]	108	137	137	143	126	111	81	68	66	69	Philippines[4]
Turkey	241	225	167	145	134	136	162	135	179	* 199	Turquie
Viet Nam	14	12	13	16	9	9	10	1	5	4	Viet Nam
Europe	**363**	**417**	**425**	**347**	**334**	**325**	**312**	**296**	**322**	**371**	**Europe**
EEC	***11***	***14***	***13***	***15***	***14***	***9***	***10***	***9***	***21***	***22***	***CEE***
Greece	11	14	13	15	14	9	10	9	21	* 22	Grèce
EFTA	***111***	***149***	***128***	***117***	***101***	***112***	***109***	***91***	***92***	***111***	***AELE***
Finland	111	149	128	117	101	112	109	91	92	111	Finlande
East Europe	***239***	***253***	***284***	***216***	***219***	***204***	***194***	***197***	***207***	***237***	***Europe de l'est***
Albania* [1]	239	253	284	216	219	204	194	197	207	237	Albanie* [1]
Other Europe	***0***	***0***	***0***	***0***	***0***	***0***	***0***	***0***	***2***	***2***	***Autre Europe***
Yugoslavia	0	0	0	0	0	0	0	0	2	2	Yougoslavie
USSR* [1]	**830**	**830**	**830**	**830**	**830**	**830**	**840**	**840**	**840**	**850**	**URSS* [1]**
Oceania	**3**	**2**	**3**	**4**	**1**	**0**	**16**	**30**	**30**	**26**	**Océanie**
Australia	...	0	0	0	1	0	0	0	0	0	Australie
New Caledonia	2	2	2	4	1	0	16	30	30	26	Nouvelle–Calédonie
Total	**3 110**	**3 320**	**3 165**	**3 115**	**3 113**	**2 901**	**2 577**	**2 508**	**2 929**	**3 182**	**Total**

General note.

Cr content of chromium ores and concentrates and all other chromium–bearing ores and concentrates intended for treatment for Cr recovery. (SITC 28391–1M).

[1] Source: U. S. Bureau of Mines, (Washington, D. C.).
[2] Twelve months beginning 21 March of year stated.
[3] Content of concentrates.
[4] Twelve months ending 30 June of year stated.

Remarque générale.

Cr contenu des minerais de chrome et concentrés et tous autres minerais chromifères et concentrés destinés à être traités en vue de l'extraction du chrome. (CTCI 28391–1M).

[1] Source: U.S. Bureau of Mines, (Washington, D.C.).
[2] Période de douze mois commençant le 21 mars de l'année indiquée.
[3] Teneur des concentrés.
[4] Période de douze mois finissant le 30 juin de l'année indiquée.

Tungsten–bearing ores – Minerais tungstifères

Unit : Metric tons — Unité : Tonnes métriques

Country or area	1976	1977	1978	1979	1980	1981	1982	1983	1984	1985	Pays ou zone
Africa	**908**	**854**	**837**	**795**	**668**	**376**	**399**	**304**	**331**	**278**	**Afrique**
Burundi	2	2	2	0	0	0	0	0	0	...	Burundi
Namibia[1,2]	* 140	* 150	* 150	* 160	* 150	0	0	0	0	...	Namibie[1,2]
Rwanda	445	450	385	407	377	289	333	238	267	172	Rwanda
South Africa	0	13	13	0	0	0	0	...	...	...	Afrique du Sud
Uganda* [2]	5	5	5	5	1	1	4	4	4	4	Ouganda* [2]
Zaire	288	206	179	136	# [2] 69	[2] 46	[2] 38	[2] 44	[2] 30	[2] 18	Zaïre
Zimbabwe[2,3]	28	28	103	87	71	40	24	9	21	6	Zimbabwe[2,3]
America, North	**4 567**	**4 694**	**5 605**	**5 795**	**6 175**	**5 122**	**4 097**	**2 307**	**4 718**	**4 387**	**Amérique du Nord**
Canada[4]	1 719	1 811	2 289	2 581	3 178	1 377	2 403	1 220	3 328	3 174	Canada[4]
Guatemala[2]	0	0	0	0	48	42	40	0	0	6	Guatemala[2]
Mexico	186	151	186	200	211	158	79	71	217	224	Mexique
United States	2 662	2 732	3 130	3 014	2 738	3 545	1 575	1 016	1 173	983	Etats–Unis
America, South	**4 834**	**4 623**	**4 674**	**4 657**	**4 721**	**6 659**	**6 219**	**5 037**	**4 578**	**4 355**	**Amérique du Sud**
Argentina	62	70	97	59	35	11	17	41	38	12	Argentine
Bolivia	3 132	3 063	3 073	3 114	3 359	3 504	3 195	# [2] 2 449	* [2] 1 893	* [2] 1 643	Bolivie
Brazil	802	964	922	920	903	# 2 550	2 602	1 842	1 892	* 1 900	Brésil
Peru	838	* [2] 526	[2] 582	564	424	594	405	705	755	800	Pérou
Asia	**16 666**	**17 007**	**20 579**	**20 913**	**22 930**	**21 044**	**19 333**	**17 332**	**19 336**	**20 511**	**Asie**
Burma[2]	276	278	471	692	823	825	844	930	1 096	945	Birmanie[2]
China* [2]	8 960	8 960	11 500	13 090	14 990	13 480	12 530	12 530	13 500	15 000	Chine* [2]
India	23	22	21	20	23	20	28	16	20	17	Inde
Japan	814	772	775	746	668	631	604	474	477	568	Japon
Korea, D. P. Rp.* [2]	2 140	2 140	2 140	2 140	2 200	2 200	2 200	500	1 000	1 000	Corée, Rp. P. D.* [2]
Korea, Republic of	2 628	2 786	2 601	2 570	2 570	2 643	2 234	2 294	2 490	2 384	Corée, République de
Malaysia	54	96	71	53	40	35	36	25	12	11	Malaisie
Thailand	1 771	1 953	3 000	1 602	1 616	1 210	857	563	741	586	Thaïlande
Europe	**3 263**	**3 125**	**4 004**	**4 533**	**5 356**	**4 626**	**4 764**	**4 641**	**4 616**	**4 850**	**Europe**
EEC	***981***	***539***	***1 081***	***937***	***917***	***866***	***1 127***	***1 243***	***601***	***620***	***CEE***
France	971	461	1 016	871	849	816	# 1 127	1 243	601	620	France
United Kingdom[2]	* 10	78	65	* 66	* 68	* 50	0	0	0	0	Royaume–Uni[2]
EFTA	***1 954***	***2 279***	***2 565***	***3 202***	***3 992***	***3 323***	***3 092***	***2 882***	***3 449***	***3 700***	***AELE***
Austria[2]	541	1 116	1 179	1 496	2 150	1 616	1 465	1 408	1 632	1 565	Autriche[2]
Portugal	1 259	1 005	1 104	1 387	1 553	1 395	1 359	1 182	1 509	1 765	Portugal
Sweden	154	158	282	319	289	312	268	292	308	370	Suède
Other Europe	***328***	***307***	***358***	***394***	***447***	***437***	***545***	***516***	***566***	***530***	***Autre Europe***
Spain	328	307	358	394	447	437	545	516	566	530	Espagne
USSR* [2]	**8 010**	**8 250**	**8 490**	**8 700**	**8 700**	**8 700**	**9 000**	**9 100**	**9 100**	**9 200**	**URSS* [2]**
Oceania	**1 881**	**2 269**	**2 457**	**2 834**	**3 586**	**3 594**	**3 059**	**2 154**	**1 903**	**1 907**	**Océanie**
Australia[1]	1 870	2 260	2 444	2 822	3 564	3 578	3 048	2 148	1 897	1 902	Australie[1]
New Zealand	11	9	13	12	22	16	11	[2] 6	[2] 6	[2] 5	Nouvelle–Zélande
Total	**40 129**	**40 822**	**46 646**	**48 227**	**52 136**	**50 121**	**46 871**	**40 875**	**44 582**	**45 488**	**Total**

General note.
W content of tungsten concentrates and all other tungsten–bearing ores and concentrates intended for treatment for W recovery. (SITC 28392–1M+).

Remarque générale.
W contenu des minerais concentrés de tungstène et tous autres minerais tungstifères ou concentrés contenant du tungstène, destinés à être traités en vue de l'extraction du tungstène. (CTCI 28392–1M+).

[1] Twelve months ending 30 June of year stated.
[2] Source: U. S. Bureau of Mines, (Washington, D. C.).
[3] Limited coverage. Twelve months ending 30 September of the year.
[4] Shipments from mines.

[1] Période de douze mois finissant le 30 juin de l'année indiquée.
[2] Source: U.S. Bureau of Mines, (Washington, D.C.).
[3] Couverture limitée. Période de douze mois finissant au 30 septembre de l'année indiquée.
[4] Expéditions des mines.

Ilmenite – Ilménite

Unit : Thousand metric tons

Unité : Milliers de tonnes métriques

Country or area	1976	1977	1978	1979	1980	1981	1982	1983	1984	1985	Pays ou zone
America, North	**591.9**	**579.2**	**535.0**	**580.0**	**505.0**	**492.0**	**238.9**	**322.7**	**277.6**	**232.5**	**Amérique du Nord**
United States	591.9	579.2	535.0	580.0	505.0	492.0	238.9	...	...	...	Etats–Unis
America, South	**14.6**	**13.3**	**20.1**	**13.2**	**16.8**	**19.9**	**13.2**	**48.2**	**61.2**	**45.0**	**Amérique du Sud**
Brazil	14.6	13.3	20.1	13.2	16.8	19.9	13.2	48.2	61.2	45.0	Brésil
Asia	**411.3**	**341.8**	**392.4**	**431.2**	**418.1**	**441.6**	**346.6**	**448.2**	**441.2**	**605.0**	**Asie**
India	175.5	154.0	172.5	162.9	184.6	188.8	177.1	144.8	165.3	174.8	Inde
Malaysia[1]	180.0	153.7	186.8	212.8	199.5	172.8	101.2	222.7	235.0	314.7	Malaisie[1]
Sri Lanka	55.8	34.1	33.0	55.4	34.0	80.0	68.3	80.5	40.3	115.0	Sri Lanka
Thailand[2]	...	...	...	...	...	0.0	0.0	0.2	0.5	0.5	Thaïlande[2]
Europe	**889.6**	**953.4**	**899.2**	**939.8**	**987.2**	**819.5**	**720.1**	**720.1**	**819.0**	**789.4**	**Europe**
EFTA	***889.6***	***953.4***	***899.2***	***939.8***	***987.2***	***819.5***	***720.1***	***720.1***	***819.0***	***789.4***	***AELE***
Finland	122.6	124.7	131.9	119.7	159.0	161.5	167.8	163.9	167.0	# 53.3	Finlande
Norway[2]	766.7	828.5	767.0	819.7	827.8	657.6	551.8	555.9	651.8	735.8	Norvège[2]
Portugal	0.4	0.2	* 0.3	0.4	0.4	0.4	0.6	0.3	0.2	0.2	Portugal
USSR* [2]	**381.0**	**400.0**	**410.0**	**410.0**	**420.0**	**426.4**	**430.9**	**435.5**	**440.0**	**445.0**	**URSS* [2]**
Oceania	**929.0**	**990.0**	**1 137.0**	**1 207.0**	**1 336.0**	**1 259.0**	**1 238.0**	**932.0**	**1 017.0**	**1 264.0**	**Océanie**
Australia	* 929.0	990.0	1 137.0	1 207.0	1 336.0	1 259.0	1 238.0	932.0	1 017.0	1 264.0	Australie
Total	**3 217.4**	**3 277.7**	**3 393.7**	**3 581.1**	**3 683.1**	**3 458.4**	**2 987.7**	**2 906.7**	**3 056.0**	**3 380.8**	**Total**

General note.
Gross weight of ilmenite concentrates. (Part of SITC 28393–1).

[1] Exports.
[2] Source: U. S. Bureau of Mines, (Washington, D. C.).

Remarque générale.
Poids brut de concentrés d'ilménite. (Partie de CTCI 28393–1).

[1] Exportations.
[2] Source: U.S. Bureau of Mines, (Washington, D.C.).

Unit : Metric tons

Unité : Tonnes métriques

Country or area	1976	1977	1978	1979	…	Pays ou zone
Africa	**20 736**	**9 065**	**33 211**	**49 2**	**)0**	**Afrique**
Sierra Leone[1]	...	...	...	7 4	00	Sierra Leone[1]
South Africa* [1]	...	4 535	18 100	41 7	00	Afrique du Sud* [1]
America, South	**128**	**128**	**365**	**4**	**00**	**Amérique du Sud**
Brazil	128	128	365	[illegible]	500	Brésil
Asia	**8 044**	**8 038**	**18 604**	**21**	**541**	**Asie**
India	7 005	7 058	7 107	6	936	Inde
Sri Lanka	1 039	980	11 497	14	605	Sri Lanka
USSR* [1]	**27 215**	**9 000**	**9 000**	[illegible]	**000**	**URSS* [1]**
Oceania	**368 000**	**371 000**	**274 000**	**26**	**000**	**Océanie**
Australia	368 000	371 000	274 000	26	1 000	Australie
Total	**424 123**	**397 231**	**335 180**	**34**	**5 041**	**Total**

General note.
Gross weight of rutile concentrates (Part of SITC 28393–1).

1 28393–1)

[1] Source: U. S. Bureau of Mines, (Washington, D. C.).

D.C.).

Molybdenum–bearing ores – Minerais molybdénifères

Unit : Metric tons

Unité : Tonnes métriques

Country or area	1976	1977	1978	1979	1980	1981	1982	1983	1984	1985	Pays ou zone
America, North	**65 996**	**72 093**	**73 757**	**76 526**	**80 314**	**78 042**	**57 425**	**31 297**	**62 631**	**60 502**	**Amérique du Nord**
Canada[1 2]	14 618	16 568	13 943	11 175	11 889	14 134	13 961	10 194	11 556	7 568	Canada[1 2]
Mexico	16	1	11	48	74	451	5 190	5 866	4 054	3 761	Mexique
United States[1]	51 362	55 524	59 803	65 303	68 351	63 457	38 274	15 237	47 021	49 173	Etats–Unis[1]
America, South	**11 749**	**11 394**	**13 926**	**14 756**	**16 356**	**17 848**	**22 941**	**17 892**	**19 940**	**22 217**	**Amérique du Sud**
Chile[1]	10 899	10 938	13 196	13 560	13 668	15 360	20 048	15 264	16 861	18 389	Chili[1]
Peru	850	[3] 456	[3] 730	[3] 1 196	[3] 2 688	[3] 2 488	[3] 2 893	[3] 2 628	[3] 3 079	[3] 3 828	Pérou
Asia	**1 752**	**1 784**	**2 399**	**2 447**	**2 448**	**2 633**	**2 538**	**2 278**	**2 305**	**2 409**	**Asie**
China* [3]	1 500	1 500	2 000	2 000	2 000	2 000	2 000	2 000	2 000	2 000	Chine* [3]
Japan[1]	[3] 132	[3] 182	[3] 123	[3] 117	[3] 56	[3] 74	[3] 97	[3] 97	[3] 147	76	Japon[1]
Korea, Republic of	120	102	221	189	301	465	361	141	158	333	Corée, République de
Philippines[1]	0	0	55	141	91	94	80	40	0	0	Philippines[1]
Europe	**140**	**150**	**150**	**150**	**150**	**150**	**170**	**190**	**190**	**190**	**Europe**
East Europe	***140***	***150***	***150***	***150***	***150***	***150***	***170***	***190***	***190***	***190***	***Europe de l'est***
Bulgaria* [3]	140	150	150	150	150	150	170	190	190	190	Bulgarie* [3]
USSR* [3]	**9 300**	**9 700**	**9 900**	**10 200**	**10 400**	**10 700**	**11 000**	**11 100**	**11 200**	**11 300**	**URSS* [3]**
Oceania	**0**	**0**	**0**	**0**	**25**	**20**	**17**	**10**	**9**	**8**	**Océanie**
Australia[1 4]	0	0	0	0	25	20	17	10	9	8	Australie[1 4]
Total	**88 937**	**95 121**	**100 132**	**104 079**	**109 693**	**109 393**	**94 091**	**62 767**	**96 275**	**96 626**	**Total**

General note.
Mo content of molybdenum ores and concentrates and all other molybdenum–bearing ores and concentrates intended for treatment for molybdenum recovery. (SITC 28393–2M).

[1] Content of concentrates.
[2] Shipments.
[3] Source: U. S. Bureau of Mines, (Washington, D. C.).
[4] Twelve months ending 30 June of year stated.

Remarque générale.
Mo contenu des minerais de molybdène et concentrés et tous autres minerais molybdénifères et concentrés, destinés à être traités en vue de l'extraction du molybdène. (CTCI 28393–2M).

[1] Teneur des concentrés.
[2] Expéditions.
[3] Source: U.S. Bureau of Mines, (Washington, D.C.).
[4] Période de douze mois finissant le 30 juin de l'année indiquée.

Tantalum and Niobium (Columbium) minerals – Minerais de tantale et de niobium (nolombium)

Unit : Metric tons — Unité : Tonnes métriques

Country or area	1976	1977	1978	1979	1980	1981	1982	1983	1984	1985	Pays ou zone
Africa	**913**	**1 146**	**916**	**780**	**811**	**646**	**388**	**215**	**302**	**348**	**Afrique**
Mozambique[1 2 3]	91	78	78	66	...	83	47	37	17	17	Mozambique[1 2 3]
Nigeria[1 2 3]	651	862	667	568	555	379	181	88	121	101	Nigéria[1 2 3]
Rwanda[1 2]	45	64	54	47	60	57	62	50	52	28	Rwanda[1 2]
Uganda[1 2 3]	2	2	2	2	...	...	...	...	...	...	Ouganda[1 2 3]
Zaire[1 2]	83	111	83	68	92	80	60	36	51	160	Zaïre[1 2]
Zimbabwe[1 2 3]	41	29	32	29	41	45	36	2	59	40	Zimbabwe[1 2 3]
America, North	**3 751**	**4 452**	**4 405**	**4 470**	**4 026**	**4 391**	**5 030**	**3 039**	**4 399**	**4 944**	**Amérique du Nord**
Canada[1 2 3]	3 751	4 452	4 405	4 470	4 026	4 391	5 030	3 039	4 399	4 944	Canada[1 2 3]
America, South	**19 004**	**15 613**	**17 900**	**28 911**	**30 700**	**29 886**	**19 593**	**16 828**	**30 087**	**32 180**	**Amérique du Sud**
Argentina[1 2 3]	1	0	0	2	0	0	0	0	0	...	Argentine[1 2 3]
Brazil[4]	19 003	15 613	17 900	28 909	30 700	29 886	19 593	16 828	30 087	32 180	Brésil[4]
Asia	**153**	**119**	**87**	**447**	**389**	**71**	**46**	**616**	**522**	**344**	**Asie**
Malaysia[1 2 3]	46	45	23	40	33	22	7	67	45	76	Malaisie[1 2 3]
Thailand[1 2]	107	74	64	407	356	49	39	549	477	268	Thaïlande[1 2]
Europe	**56**	**53**	**52**	**38**	**55**	**68**	**60**	**50**	**32**	**32**	**Europe**
EFTA	***5***	***3***	***8***	***4***	***4***	***9***	***6***	***3***	***0***	***0***	***AELE***
Portugal[1 2]	5	3	8	4	4	9	6	3	0	0	Portugal[1 2]
Other Europe	***51***	***50***	***44***	***34***	***51***	***59***	***54***	***47***	***32***	***32***	***Autre Europe***
Spain[1 2 3]	...	...	44	34	51	59	54	47	32	32	Espagne[1 2 3]
Oceania	**127**	**157**	**139**	**172**	**202**	**264**	**116**	**117**	**206**	**186**	**Océanie**
Australia[1 2 3]	127	157	139	172	202	264	116	117	206	186	Australie[1 2 3]
Total	**24 004**	**21 540**	**23 499**	**34 818**	**36 183**	**35 326**	**25 233**	**20 865**	**35 548**	**38 034**	**Total**

General note.
Gross weight of tantalum and niobium (colombium) concentrates. (SITC 28393–3).

[1] Excluding columbium and tantalum–bearing tin concentrates and slags.

[2] Concentrates of columbite, tantalite, pyrochlore and microlite.

[3] Source: U. S. Bureau of Mines, (Washington, D. C.).

[4] Concentrates.

Remarque générale.
Poids brut de concentrés de tantale et de niobium (colombium) (CTCI 28393–3).

[1] Non compris les concentrés d'étain et scories stannifères qui comprend colombium et tantale.

[2] Concentrés de colombium, de tantale, de pyrochlore et de microlite.

[3] Source: U.S. Bureau of Mines, (Washington, D.C.).

[4] Concentrés.

Unit : Metric tons | Unité : Tonnes métriques

Country or area	1976	1977	1978	1979	1980	1981	1982	1983	1984	1985	Pays ou zone
Africa	**358**	**402**	**326**	**285**	**301**	**218**	**128**	**75**	**112**	**105**	**Afrique**
Mozambique[1]	6	8	8	6	...	...	...	...	...	...	Mozambique[1]
Nigeria[1]	312	351	293	249	* 244	* 165	* 82	* 39	* 54	* 41	Nigéria[1]
Rwanda[1]	* 13	* 20	* 15	* 16	* 19	* 17	* 18	* 15	* 15	8	Rwanda[1]
Zaire* [1]	22	18	5	9	26	22	16	14	27	43	Zaïre* [1]
Zimbabwe[1]	* 5	* 5	* 5	...	...	7	5	0	9	* 6	Zimbabwe[1]
America, North	**1 047**	**1 754**	**1 729**	**1 756**	**1 730**	**1 916**	**2 154**	**1 256**	**1 987**	**2 223**	**Amérique du Nord**
Canada[1]	* 1 047	* 1 754	* 1 729	* 1 756	* 1 730	1 916	2 154	1 256	1 987	* 2 223	Canada[1]
America, South	**44**	**26**	**38**	**70**	**97**	**63**	**44**	**61**	**39**	**41**	**Amérique du Sud**
Argentina[1]	0	1	0	1	...	...	...	...	...	...	Argentine[1]
Brazil[1]	44	25	38	69	97	* 63	* 44	* 61	* 39	* 41	Brésil[1]
Asia	**49**	**33**	**21**	**105**	**86**	**12**	**8**	**103**	**86**	**56**	**Asie**
Malaysia[1]	20	18	6	10	* 8	* 4	* 1	* 10	4	* 11	Malaisie[1]
Thailand[1]	* 29	15	15	95	78	8	7	93	* 82	* 45	Thaïlande[1]
Europe	**1**	**1**	**7**	**3**	**2**	**5**	**4**	**2**	**0**	**0**	**Europe**
EFTA	***1***	***1***	***7***	***3***	***2***	***5***	***4***	***2***	***0***	***0***	***AELE***
Portugal	1	1	7	* 3	* 2	* 5	* 4	* 2	0	0	Portugal
Oceania	**24**	**31**	**28**	**34**	**41**	**48**	**20**	**20**	**36**	**36**	**Océanie**
Australia[1]	24	31	28	34	* 41	* 48	* 20	* 20	* 36	* 36	Australie[1]
Total	**1 523**	**2 247**	**2 149**	**2 253**	**2 257**	**2 262**	**2 358**	**1 517**	**2 260**	**2 461**	**Total**

General note.
Nb content of niobium (colombium) ores and concentrates. (Part of SITC 28393–3M).

[1] Source: U. S. Bureau of Mines, (Washington, D. C.).

Remarque générale.
Nb contenu de minerais de niobium (colombium) et concentrés. (Partie de CTCI 38393–3M).

[1] Source: U.S. Bureau of Mines, (Washington, D.C.).

Tantalum concentrates – Concentrés de tantale

Unit : Metric tons

Unité : Tonnes métriques

Country or area	1976	1977	1978	1979	1980	1981	1982	1983	1984	1985	Pays ou zone
Africa	**128**	**168**	**100**	**88**	**103**	**110**	**77**	**49**	**72**	**79**	**Afrique**
Mozambique[1]	44	38	36	30	...	35	22	16	5	6	Mozambique[1]
Nigeria[1]	41	80	40	34	* 34	* 23	* 11	* 6	* 8	* 8	Nigéria[1]
Rwanda	11	14	9	9	11	13	14	11	* 11	6	Rwanda
Zaire* [1]	21	25	4	7	20	23	17	15	28	45	Zaïre* [1]
Zimbabwe[1]	* 11	* 11	* 11	* 8	* 10	* 16	* 13	1	20	* 14	Zimbabwe[1]
America, North	**105**	**120**	**126**	**130**	**94**	**23**	**77**	**0**	**0**	**0**	**Amérique du Nord**
Canada[1]	105	120	126	130	94	23	77	0	0	0	Canada[1]
America, South	**58**	**43**	**64**	**118**	**172**	**81**	**59**	**77**	**50**	**53**	**Amérique du Sud**
Brazil[1]	58	43	64	118	172	* 81	* 59	* 77	* 50	* 53	Brésil[1]
Asia	**34**	**24**	**12**	**70**	**121**	**12**	**10**	**131**	**131**	**79**	**Asie**
Malaysia[1]	5	7	2	3	* 4	* 2	* 1	5	2	* 6	Malaisie[1]
Thailand[1]	* 29	17	* 10	67	117	10	9	126	129	* 73	Thaïlande[1]
Europe	**1**	**1**	**2**	**1**	**2**	**5**	**4**	**2**	**0**	**0**	**Europe**
EFTA	***1***	***1***	***2***	***1***	***2***	***5***	***4***	***2***	***0***	***0***	***AELE***
Portugal[1]	1	1	2	1	* 2	* 5	* 4	* 2	0	0	Portugal[1]
Oceania	**39**	**52**	**46**	**57**	**67**	**93**	**41**	**41**	**70**	**64**	**Océanie**
Australia[1]	39	52	46	57	* 67	* 93	* 41	* 41	* 70	* 64	Australie[1]
Total	**365**	**408**	**350**	**464**	**559**	**324**	**268**	**300**	**323**	**275**	**Total**

General note.
Ta content of tantalum bearing ores and concentrates. (Part of SITC 28393-3M).

Remarque générale.
Ta contenu de minerais de tantale et concentrés. (Partie de CTCI 28393-3M).

[1] Source: U. S. Bureau of Mines, (Washington, D. C.).

[1] Source: U.S. Bureau of Mines, (Washington, D.C.).

Vanadium bearing ores Minerais vanadifères

Unit : Metric tons

Unité : Tonnes métriques

Country or area	1976	1977	1978	1979	1980	1981	1982	1983	1984	1985	Pays ou zone
Africa	**10 572**	**11 984**	**11 640**	**12 300**	**14 903**	**12 617**	**11 713**	**8 833**	**12 517**	**14 128**	**Afrique**
Namibia[1]	700	750	440	0	0	0	0	0	0	...	Namibie[1]
South Africa[2]	9 872	11 234	[1] 11 200	* [1] 12 300	* [1] 14 903	* [1] 12 617	* [1] 11 713	* [1] 8 833	* [1] 12 517	* [1] 14 015	Afrique du Sud[2]
America, North	**6 691**	**5 900**	**3 875**	**5 008**	**4 360**	**4 650**	**3 718**	**1 969**	**1 467**	**1 401**	**Amérique du Nord**
United States[3 4]	6 691	5 900	3 875	5 008	4 360	4 650	3 718	1 969	1 467	...	Etats-Unis[3 4]
America, South	**1 090**	**860**	**690**	**460**	**270**	**130**	**0**	**0**	**0**	**0**	**Amérique du Sud**
Chile* [1]	1 090	860	690	460	270	130	0	0	0	0	Chili* [1]
Asia	**2 634**	**2 896**	**2 000**	**3 600**	**4 500**	**4 500**	**4 500**	**4 500**	**4 500**	**4 500**	**Asie**
China* [1]	...	...	2 000	3 600	4 500	4 500	4 500	4 500	4 500	4 500	Chine* [1]
Europe	**2 064**	**2 504**	**3 414**	**3 485**	**3 499**	**3 624**	**3 425**	**3 359**	**3 228**	**2 245**	**Europe**
EFTA	***2 064***	***2 504***	***3 414***	***3 485***	***3 499***	***3 624***	***3 425***	***3 359***	***3 228***	***2 245***	***AELE***
Finland	1 534	1 964	2 954	2 915	3 009	3 279	3 315	3 359	3 228	2 245	Finlande
Norway* [1]	530	540	460	570	490	345	110	0	0	0	Norvège* [1]
USSR* [1 5]	**8 000**	**8 600**	**9 100**	**9 100**	**9 500**	**9 500**	**9 500**	**9 500**	**9 500**	**9 500**	**URSS* [1 5]**
Total	**31 051**	**32 744**	**30 719**	**33 953**	**37 032**	**35 021**	**32 856**	**28 161**	**31 212**	**31 774**	**Total**

General note.
V content or vanadium ores and concentrates and all other vanadium-bearing ores and concentrates intended for treatment for vanadium recovery. (SITC 28393-4M).

[1] Source: U. S. Bureau of Mines, (Washington, D. C.).
[2] Including vanadium content of slag.
[3] Recoverable vanadium contained in uranium and vanadium ores and concentrates received at mills. Including vanadium recovered from ferrophosphorus derived from domestic phosphate rock.
[4] 1985, data are confidential.
[5] Vanadium contained in exported slags. Excluding production for domestic consumption or for export in any form except slag.

Remarque générale.
V contenu des minerais de vanadium et concentrés et tous autres minerais vanadifères ou concentrés, destinés à être traités en vue de l'extraction du vanadium. (CTCI 28393-4M).

[1] Source: U.S. Bureau of Mines, (Washington, D.C.).
[2] Y compris la teneur en vanadium des scories.
[3] Vanadium récupérable contenu dans les minerais et concentrés d'uranium et de vanadium livrés aux usines. Y compris le vanadium extrait des ferrophosphores obtenus à partir des phosphates naturels locaux.
[4] Pour 1985, les données sont confidentielles.
[5] Vanadium contenu dans les scories exportées. Non compris la production destinée à la consommation intérieure ou à l'exportation sous toute forme autre que de scories.

Zirconium ore – Minerais de zirconium

Unit : Metric tons

Unité : Tonnes métriques

Country or area	1976	1977	1978	1979	1980	1981	1982	1983	1984	1985	Pays ou zone
Africa	**11 250**	**16 824**	**36 287**	**81 646**	**79 832**	**100 000**	**120 000**	**162 281**	**153 123**	**160 533**	**Afrique**
South Africa[1]	11 250	16 824	* 36 287	* 81 646	* 79 832	* 100 000	* 120 000	162 281	153 123	* 160 533	Afrique du Sud[1]
America, South	**3 058**	**4 649**	**4 300**	**2 622**	**3 410**	**6 000**	**4 966**	**13 790**	**6 375**	**7 000**	**Amérique du Sud**
Brazil	3 058	4 649	4 300	2 622	3 410	6 000	4 966	13 790	6 375	* 7 000	Brésil
Asia	**22 413**	**21 895**	**24 485**	**25 780**	**32 435**	**32 077**	**33 615**	**34 863**	**38 991**	**46 391**	**Asie**
China* [1]	...	9 071	9 071	10 886	13 970	15 000	15 000	15 000	15 000	15 000	Chine* [1]
India[1]	10 341	10 704	11 166	12 179	14 820	12 400	10 483	11 395	12 000	14 800	Inde[1]
Malaysia[2]	3 128	1 809	927	1 270	552	1 307	2 147	2 548	7 993	11 652	Malaisie[2]
Sri Lanka	9	9	3 296	1 329	3 032	3 266	5 789	5 721	3 708	4 061	Sri Lanka
Thailand	55	302	25	116	61	104	196	199	290	878	Thaïlande
Oceania	**387 000**	**408 000**	**365 000**	**454 000**	**447 000**	**461 000**	**459 000**	**404 000**	**412 000**	**452 000**	**Océanie**
Australia	387 000	408 000	365 000	454 000	447 000	461 000	459 000	404 000	412 000	452 000	Australie
Total	**423 721**	**451 368**	**430 072**	**564 048**	**562 677**	**599 077**	**617 581**	**614 934**	**610 489**	**665 924**	**Total**

General note.
Crude weight of zirconium concentrates. (Part of SITC 28393–5).

[1] Source: U. S. Bureau of Mines, (Washington, D. C.).
[2] Exports.

Remarque générale.
Poids brut de concentrés de zirconium. (Partie de CTCI 28393–5).

[1] Source: U.S. Bureau of Mines, (Washington, D.C.).
[2] Exportations.

Antimony–bearing ores – Minerais stibifères

Unit : Metric tons | Unité : Tonnes métriques

Country or area	1976	1977	1978	1979	1980	1981	1982	1983	1984	1985	Pays ou zone
Africa	**13 623**	**14 397**	**12 816**	**13 652**	**13 805**	**10 598**	**10 435**	**6 925**	**8 680**	**8 389**	**Afrique**
Algeria[1]	60	60	60	60	0	0	0	0	...	...	Algérie[1]
Morocco	1 713	1 544	2 422	920	588	525	925	480	984	805	Maroc
South Africa[2]	11 490	12 493	10 214	12 514	13 067	9 810	[1] 9 135	[1] 6 302	[1] 7 440	[1] 7 390	Afrique du Sud[2]
Zimbabwe[2]	* [3] 360	* [3] 300	# 120	158	150	263	375	143	256	194	Zimbabwe[2]
America, North	**7 347**	**7 402**	**6 494**	**7 187**	**5 427**	**4 586**	**2 485**	**4 146**	**4 597**	**6 707**	**Amérique du Nord**
Canada[4]	[3] 3 324	[3] 3 165	3 005	2 954	2 361	1 670	454	858	837	744	Canada[4]
Guatemala[1]	1 120	916	230	660	556	510	0	0	90	1 057	Guatemala[1]
Honduras	[1] 100	[1] 70	[1] 78	[1] 46	[1] 23	[1] 20	[1] 10	* [1] 10	101	...	Honduras
Mexico[5]	2 546	2 698	2 457	2 872	2 176	1 800	1 565	2 518	3 064	4 266	Mexique[5]
United States[6]	257	553	724	655	311	586	456	760	505	...	Etats–Unis[6]
America, South	**17 658**	**17 525**	**14 355**	**15 039**	**15 837**	**16 003**	**14 332**	**10 519**	**9 954**	**9 303**	**Amérique du Sud**
Argentina	2	0	0	0	0	0	0	0	0	...	Argentine
Bolivia[5]	17 015	16 341	13 336	14 420	15 465	15 296	13 978	9 950	9 281	8 925	Bolivie[5]
Brazil[7]	38	365	274	73	28	24	0	0	0	0	Brésil[7]
Peru[5]	[1] 603	[1] 819	[1] 745	[1] 546	344	683	354	569	673	377	Pérou[5]
Asia	**14 995**	**15 331**	**15 906**	**14 589**	**14 558**	**12 337**	**13 986**	**17 213**	**18 295**	**17 588**	**Asie**
Burma* [1]	460	530	590	680	440	28	1	0	0	0	Birmanie* [1]
China* [1]	8 400	10 000	10 000	10 000	10 000	10 000	12 000	15 000	15 000	15 000	Chine* [1]
Korea, Republic of[1]	10	0	0	0	0	0	0	...	...	...	Corée, République de[1]
Malaysia[1]	250	260	260	307	131	191	139	136	17	26	Malaisie[1]
Pakistan[8]	360	93	103	69	0	39	51	0	0	6	Pakistan[8]
Thailand[5]	3 800	2 527	2 970	3 038	3 019	1 241	689	1 236	2 040	1 283	Thaïlande[5]
Turkey	1 715	1 921	1 983	495	968	838	1 106	834	1 231	* 1 266	Turquie
Europe	**4 260**	**4 618**	**5 399**	**4 957**	**4 524**	**4 515**	**4 067**	**3 216**	**3 325**	**3 689**	**Europe**
EEC	***1 229***	***986***	***951***	***948***	***708***	***1 008***	***647***	***319***	***264***	***515***	***CEE***
France[1 2]	0	0	0	0	0	312	308	299	0	0	France[1 2]
Greece[7]	220	160	20	0	0	0	0	...	...	...	Grèce[7]
Italy	1 009	826	931	948	708	696	339	0	244	495	Italie
EFTA	***568***	***561***	***549***	***655***	***691***	***667***	***711***	***705***	***770***	***729***	***AELE***
Austria	568	561	549	655	691	667	711	705	770	729	Autriche
East Europe	***285***	***492***	***781***	***816***	***820***	***739***	***731***	***753***	***763***	***782***	***Europe de l'est***
Czechoslovakia	285	492	781	816	820	739	731	753	763	782	Tchécoslovaquie
Other Europe	***2 178***	***2 579***	***3 118***	***2 538***	***2 305***	***2 101***	***1 978***	***1 439***	***1 528***	***1 663***	***Autre Europe***
Spain	157	331	442	501	625	646	461	489	583	575	Espagne
Yugoslavia	2 021	2 248	2 676	2 037	1 680	1 455	1 517	950	945	1 088	Yougoslavie
USSR* [1]	**7 700**	**7 900**	**8 100**	**8 200**	**8 200**	**8 600**	**9 000**	**9 200**	**9 300**	**9 400**	**URSS* [1]**
Oceania	**1 875**	**1 526**	**984**	**1 588**	**1 435**	**1 207**	**1 218**	**768**	**719**	**1 409**	**Océanie**
Australia[9]	1 875	1 526	984	1 588	1 435	1 207	1 218	768	719	1 409	Australie[9]
Total	**67 458**	**68 699**	**64 054**	**65 212**	**63 786**	**57 846**	**55 523**	**51 987**	**54 870**	**56 485**	**Total**

General note.
Sb content of antimony ores and concentrates and all other antimony–bearing ores and concentrates intended for treatment for antimony recovery. (SITC 28399–1M+).

1 Source: U. S. Bureau of Mines, (Washington, D. C.).
2 Content of concentrates.
3 Source: World Metal Statistics, (London).
4 Content of smelter products.
5 Content of all antimony–bearing materials in the form they are to be used or exported.
6 1985, data are confidential.
7 Source: Metallgesellschaft Aktiengesellschaft, (Frankfurt).
8 Twelve months ending 30 June of year stated.
9 Content of antimony ore, antimony concentrate and lead concentrate.

Remarque générale.
Sb contenu des minerais d'antimoine et concentrés, ainsi que tous autres minerais stibifères et concentrés destinés à être traités en vue de l'extraction de l'antimoine. (CTCI 28399–1M+).

1 Source: U.S. Bureau of Mines, (Washington, D.C.).
2 Teneur des concentrés.
3 Source: World Metal Statistics, (Londres).
4 Teneur des produits de fonderie.
5 Teneur en antimoine de tous les matériaux prêts à être utilisés ou exportés.
6 Pour 1985, les données sont confidentielles.
7 Source: Metallgesellschaft Aktiengesellschaft, (Francfort).
8 Période de douze mois finissant le 30 juin de l'année indiquée.
9 Teneur du minerai d'antimoine, du concentré d'antimoine et du concentré de plomb.

Cobalt–bearing ores – Minerais cobaltifères

Unit : Metric tons

Unité : Tonnes métriques

Country or area	1976	1977	1978	1979	1980	1981	1982	1983	1984	1985	Pays ou zone
Africa	**13 226**	**12 936**	**15 942**	**18 646**	**18 869**	**14 765**	**9 101**	**14 003**	**21 808**	**24 672**	**Afrique**
Botswana	* [1] 130	* [1] 160	* [1] 260	* [1] 290	226	254	254	223	259	222	Botswana
Morocco	790	858	959	880	737	689	697	0	0	0	Maroc
Zaire	10 686	10 215	13 146	14 000	14 482	11 159	5 608	* 11 300	* 18 000	* 20 000	Zaïre
Zambia[2]	1 620	1 703	1 560	3 271	3 309	2 569	2 444	2 407	3 472	4 359	Zambie[2]
Zimbabwe	0	0	17	205	115	94	98	73	77	91	Zimbabwe
America, North	**2 956**	**3 075**	**2 694**	**2 870**	**3 728**	**3 790**	**2 774**	**3 030**	**3 523**	**4 096**	**Amérique du Nord**
Canada	1 356	1 485	1 234	1 640	2 118	2 080	1 274	1 410	2 123	2 676	Canada
Cuba* [1]	1 600	1 590	1 460	1 230	1 610	1 710	1 500	1 620	1 400	1 420	Cuba* [1]
Asia	**492**	**1 084**	**1 192**	**1 370**	**1 331**	**997**	**466**	**165**	**64**	**911**	**Asie**
Philippines	492	1 084	1 192	1 370	1 331	997	466	165	64	911	Philippines
Europe	**1 279**	**1 227**	**1 236**	**1 070**	**950**	**940**	**1 038**	**930**	**860**	**725**	**Europe**
EFTA	***1 279***	***1 227***	***1 236***	***1 070***	***950***	***940***	***1 038***	***930***	***860***	***725***	***AELE***
Finland[3]	1 279	1 227	1 236	1 070	950	940	1 038	930	860	725	Finlande[3]
USSR* [1]	**1 800**	**1 900**	**1 950**	**2 000**	**2 100**	**2 200**	**2 300**	**2 400**	**2 600**	**2 700**	**URSS* [1]**
Oceania	**2 026**	**2 210**	**2 646**	**3 451**	**3 133**	**3 513**	**3 075**	**2 833**	**1 952**	**2 602**	**Océanie**
Australia[4 5]	2 026	2 210	2 646	3 451	3 133	3 513	3 075	2 833	1 952	2 602	Australie[4 5]
Total	**21 779**	**22 432**	**25 660**	**29 407**	**30 111**	**26 205**	**18 754**	**23 361**	**30 807**	**35 706**	**Total**

General note.
Co content of cobalt ores and concentrates and all other cobalt–bearing ores and concentrates intended for treatment for cobalt recovery. (SITC 28399–2M+).

[1] Source: U. S. Bureau of Mines, (Washington, D. C.).
[2] Metal recovered.
[3] Content of cupriferous pyrites.
[4] Twelve months ending 30 June of year stated.
[5] Content of nickel concentrates.

Remarque générale.
Co contenu des minerais de cobalt et concentrés et tous autres minerais cobaltifères et concentrés destinés à être traités en vue de l'extraction du cobalt. (CTCI 28399–2M+).

[1] Source: U.S. Bureau of Mines, (Washington, D.C.).
[2] Métal récupéré.
[3] Teneur des pyrites cuprifères.
[4] Période de douze mois finissant le 30 juin de l'année indiquée.
[5] Teneur des concentrés de nickel.

Mercury – Mercure

Unit : Metric tons

Unité : Tonnes métriques

Country or area	1976	1977	1978	1979	1980	1981	1982	1983	1984	1985	Pays ou zone
Africa	**1 065**	**1 049**	**1 055**	**508**	**842**	**862**	**379**	**345**	**792**	**861**	**Afrique**
Algeria	1 065	1 049	1 055	508	[1] 842	[1] 862	[1] 379	* [1] 345	* [1] 792	* [1] 861	Algérie
America, North	**1 315**	**1 307**	**909**	**1 086**	**1 202**	**1 202**	**1 183**	**1 085**	**1 041**	**834**	**Amérique du Nord**
Mexico	518	333	76	68	145	240	295	221	384	264	Mexique
United States	797	974	833	1 018	1 057	962	888	864	657	570	Etats–Unis
America, South	**0**	**1**	**0**	**0**	**0**	**0**	**0**	**0**	**0**	**0**	**Amérique du Sud**
Chile	0	1	0	0	0	0	0	0	...	...	Chili
Asia	**769**	**862**	**873**	**863**	**854**	**904**	**946**	**861**	**882**	**933**	**Asie**
China* [1]	600	700	700	700	700	700	700	700	700	700	Chine* [1]
Turkey	169	162	173	163	154	204	246	161	182	233	Turquie
Europe	**3 095**	**1 416**	**1 643**	**1 688**	**2 244**	**2 283**	**2 059**	**1 746**	**1 820**	**1 934**	**Europe**
EEC	***987***	***177***	***191***	***153***	***155***	***350***	***181***	***69***	***0***	***7***	***CEE***
Germany, Fed. Rep.[2]	219	163	188	153	152	148	# 53	69	0	...	Allemagne, Rép. féd.[2]
Italy	768	14	3	0	3	202	128	0	0	0	Italie
EFTA	***13***	***22***	***40***	***47***	***75***	***67***	***71***	***65***	***79***	***130***	***AELE***
Finland[3]	13	22	40	47	75	67	71	65	79	130	Finlande[3]
East Europe	***191***	***183***	***196***	***170***	***159***	***153***	***151***	***144***	***152***	***158***	***Europe de l'est***
Czechoslovakia	191	183	196	170	159	153	151	144	152	158	Tchécoslovaquie
Other Europe	***1 904***	***1 034***	***1 216***	***1 318***	***1 855***	***1 713***	***1 656***	***1 468***	***1 589***	***1 639***	***Autre Europe***
Spain	1 473	926	1 020	1 147	1 696	1 560	1 656	1 416	1 520	1 551	Espagne
Yugoslavia	431	108	196	171	159	153	0	52	* 69	88	Yougoslavie
USSR* [1]	**1 930**	**2 000**	**2 070**	**2 100**	**2 140**	**2 175**	**2 206**	**2 206**	**2 206**	**2 241**	**URSS* [1]**
Total	**8 174**	**6 635**	**6 550**	**6 245**	**7 282**	**7 426**	**6 773**	**6 243**	**6 741**	**6 803**	**Total**

General note.
Total Hg recovered from mercury–bearing ores and concentrates. (SITC 28399–3M).

[1] Source: U. S. Bureau of Mines, (Washington, D. C.).
[2] Beginning 1982, official data are confidential. Data shown are U. S. Bureau of Mines (Washington, D.C.) estimates.

[3] Twelve months ending 30 June of year stated.

Remarque générale.
Poids total du mercure extrait des minerais ou concentrés contenant du mercure. (CTCI 28399–3M).

[1] Source: U.S. Bureau of Mines, (Washington, D.C.).
[2] A partir de 1982, les chiffres sont confidentiels. Les données officielles publiées se rapportent aux estimations du 'U. S. Bureau of Mines' (Washington D.C.).
[3] Période de douze mois finissant le 30 juin de l'année indiquée.

Silver-bearing ores – Minerais argentifères

Unit : Metric tons | Unité : Tonnes métriques

Country or area	1976	1977	1978	1979	1980	1981	1982	1983	1984	1985	Pays ou zone
Africa	**284**	**325**	**363**	**408**	**509**	**519**	**479**	**474**	**543**	**497**	**Afrique**
Algeria* [1]	2	1	2	3	3	3	3	4	4	4	Algérie* [1]
Ghana[1]	* 1	* 1	1	1	* 1	* 1	1	1	* 1	* 1	Ghana[1]
Morocco	21	24	22	37	38	41	53	88	120	* 85	Maroc
Namibia[1]	* 44	55	58	113	105	107	87	110	101	* 106	Namibie[1]
South Africa	88	97	97	101	222	235	* 215	170	215	209	Afrique du Sud
Tunisia	8	7	2	3	7	3	4	3	2	1	Tunisie
Zaire	81	110	114	[2] 92	[2] 79	[2] 80	[2] 59	[2] 40	[2] 47	[2] 47	Zaïre
Zambia[3]	[1] 33	[1] 24	[1] 33	[1] 28	24	22	28	29	25	19	Zambie[3]
Zimbabwe	6	6	34	30	30	27	29	29	28	25	Zimbabwe
America, North	**3 829**	**4 104**	**4 238**	**4 027**	**3 666**	**4 251**	**4 217**	**4 587**	**4 673**	**4 708**	**Amérique du Nord**
Canada	1 281	1 314	1 267	1 147	1 070	1 203	1 291	1 197	1 169	1 197	Canada
Dominican Republic	29	44	59	73	53	64	66	42	38	49	Rép. dominicaine
El Salvador[1]	5	3	6	5	5	4	3	1	* 1	* 1	El Salvador[1]
Honduras	114	88	87	76	54	56	53	83	89	83	Honduras
Mexico	1 326	1 463	1 579	1 537	1 473	1 655	1 550	1 911	1 987	2 153	Mexique
Nicaragua[1]	6	5	15	10	5	4	2	2	2	1	Nicaragua[1]
United States	1 068	1 187	1 225	1 179	1 006	1 265	1 252	1 351	1 387	1 224	Etats-Unis
America, South	**1 689**	**1 697**	**1 874**	**1 924**	**1 915**	**2 137**	**2 307**	**2 462**	**2 421**	**2 676**	**Amérique du Sud**
Argentina	70	76	64	69	73	78	84	78	62	68	Argentine
Bolivia[4]	177	209	198	181	176	204	151	158	80	* 124	Bolivie[4]
Brazil	8	12	16	34	24	19	23	15	26	* 27	Brésil
Chile	228	263	255	272	299	361	382	468	490	517	Chili
Colombia	3	3	3	3	5	4	4	4	5	5	Colombie
Ecuador[1]	1	2	1	1	1	1	0	0	0	0	Equateur[1]
Peru	1 202	1 132	1 337	1 364	1 337	1 470	1 663	1 739	1 758	* 1 935	Pérou
Asia	**517**	**562**	**581**	**601**	**562**	**569**	**599**	**598**	**620**	**639**	**Asie**
Burma[2]	22	25	25	31	30	14	16	17	18	* 18	Birmanie[2]
China* [1]	31	31	47	62	78	78	78	78	78	78	Chine* [1]
India	3	13	12	12	11	17	14	16	25	26	Inde
Indonesia[5]	3	3	3	2	2	2	3	2	2	2	Indonésie[5]
Japan	289	299	301	270	268	280	306	307	324	339	Japon
Korea, D. P. Rp.* [1]	50	50	50	50	50	50	50	50	50	50	Corée, Rp. P. D.* [1]
Korea, Republic of	57	64	64	88	33	41	45	49	52	51	Corée, République de
Malaysia[2]	9	20	21	21	22	15	16	15	15	16	Malaisie[2]
Philippines	46	50	51	57	61	63	62	57	49	52	Philippines
Turkey* [2]	7	7	7	8	7	9	9	7	7	7	Turquie* [2]
Europe	**1 446**	**1 581**	**1 601**	**1 695**	**1 832**	**1 780**	**2 402**	**2 925**	**2 630**	**2 667**	**Europe**
EEC	***285***	***355***	***325***	***383***	***402***	***475***	***1 172***	***1 585***	***1 145***	***1 114***	***CEE***
France	114	220	207	231	248	303	# 1 013	1 403	992	940	France
Germany, Fed. Rep.	[6] 33	[6] 33	[6] 24	# [1] 32	[1] 33	[1] 35	[1] 40	[1] 40	[1] 38	[1] 38	Allemagne, Rép. féd.
Greece[1]	57	* 33	* 42	54	52	60	49	56	* 56	* 53	Grèce[1]
Ireland	[2] 29	27	18	30	24	19	11	10	9	9	Irlande
Italy	48	38	31	33	42	55	56	73	48	72	Italie
United Kingdom	...	...	...	...	...	3	3	3	2	2	Royaume-Uni
EFTA	***169***	***195***	***201***	***209***	***204***	***205***	***223***	***234***	***271***	***282***	***AELE***
Finland[5 7]	24	25	35	32	44	38	37	30	35	31	Finlande[5 7]
Portugal	1	1	1	1	1	1	1	1	1	1	Portugal
Sweden	144	169	165	176	159	166	185	203	235	250	Suède
East Europe	***744***	***793***	***827***	***846***	***901***	***771***	***788***	***805***	***868***	***959***	***Europe de l'est***
Bulgaria* [2]	28	26	28	25	24	23	25	25	26	26	Bulgarie* [2]
Czechoslovakia* [2]	37	37	36	40	35	35	33	30	32	32	Tchécoslovaquie* [2]
German Dem. Rep.* [1]	50	50	50	48	47	45	45	43	40	44	Rép. dém. allemande* [1]
Hungary* [2]	1	1	1	1	1	1	1	1	1	1	Hongrie* [2]
Poland	590	644	680	702	766	640	657	678	744	831	Pologne
Romania[1]	* 38	* 35	* 32	30	28	* 27	* 27	28	25	* 25	Roumanie[1]
Other Europe	***248***	***238***	***248***	***257***	***325***	***329***	***219***	***301***	***346***	***312***	***Autre Europe***
Spain	104	92	89	95	176	191	115	177	218	156	Espagne

For general note and footnotes, see end of table.

Voir la fin du tableau pour la remarque générale et les notes.

Silver bearing ores (continued) – Minerais argentifères (suite)

Unit : Metric tons

Unité : Tonnes métriques

Country or area	1976	1977	1978	1979	1980	1981	1982	1983	1984	1985	Pays ou zone
Yugoslavia[7]	144	146	159	162	149	138	104	124	128	156	Yougoslavie[7]
USSR* [1]	**1 370**	**1 400**	**1 430**	**1 430**	**1 430**	**1 446**	**1 459**	**1 465**	**1 474**	**1 490**	**URSS* [1]**
Oceania	**768**	**887**	**890**	**919**	**829**	**801**	**932**	**1 100**	**1 040**	**1 085**	**Océanie**
Australia[8]	722	840	837	874	792	759	888	* [1] 1 053	* [1] 995	1 038	Australie[8]
Fiji[1]	1	0	0	0	0	0	1	0	0	1	Fidji[1]
Papua New Guinea	45	47	53	45	37	42	43	47	45	46	Papouasie–Nvl–Guinée
Total	**9 903**	**10 556**	**10 977**	**11 004**	**10 743**	**11 503**	**12 395**	**13 611**	**13 401**	**13 762**	**Total**

General note.
Ag content of silver ores and concentrates and all other silver–bearing ores and concentrates intended for treatment for silver recovery. (SITC 28501–2M).

1 Source: U. S. Bureau of Mines, (Washington, D. C.).
2 Source: Metallgesellschaft Aktiengesellschaft, (Frankfurt).
3 Silver recovered.
4 Exports.
5 Silver content of concentrates.
6 Silver refined, including silver recovered as a by–product.
7 Silver refined from copper, lead and zinc ore.
8 Twelve months ending 30 June of year stated.

Remarque générale.
Ag contenu des minerais d'argent et concentrés et tous autres minerais argentifères et concentrés, destinés à être traités en vue de l'extraction de l'argent. (CTCI 28501–2M).

1 Source: U.S. Bureau of Mines, (Washington, D.C.).
2 Source: Metallgesellschaft Aktiengesellschaft, (Francfort).
3 Argent récupéré.
4 Exportations.
5 Teneur en argent des concentrés.
6 Argent affiné, y compris l'argent récupéré comme sous–produit.
7 Argent affiné provenant de minerais de cuivre, plomb et zinc.
8 Période de douze mois finissant le 30 juin de l'année indiquée.

Uranium–bearing ores – Minerais uranifères

Unit : Metric tones — Unité : Tonnes métriques

Country or area	1976	1977	1978	1979	1980	1981	1982	1983	1984	1985	Pays ou zone
Africa	**6 284**	**8 216**	**9 740**	**13 357**	**15 321**	**15 482**	**14 820**	**14 201**	**13 626**	**12 385**	**Afrique**
Gabon	* 1 412	907	1 022	1 100	1 033	1 020	970	1 006	918	940	Gabon
Namibia	654	2 340	2 697	3 840	4 042	3 971	3 776	3 719	* 3 700	3 385	Namibie
Niger	1 460	1 609	2 060	3 620	4 100	4 360	4 259	3 426	3 276	3 180	Niger
South Africa	2 758	3 360	3 961	4 797	6 146	6 131	5 815	6 050	5 732	4 880	Afrique du Sud
America, North	**14 650**	**17 290**	**21 000**	**21 310**	**23 950**	**22 513**	**18 411**	**15 275**	**16 892**	**15 232**	**Amérique du Nord**
Canada	4 850	5 790	6 800	6 820	7 150	7 720	8 080	7 140	11 170	10 880	Canada
Mexico	0	0	0	* 90	...	...	...	...	...	...	Mexique
United States	9 800	11 500	14 200	14 400	16 800	14 793	10 331	8 135	5 722	4 352	Etats–Unis
America, South	**40**	**100**	**126**	**237**	**187**	**127**	**397**	**368**	**246**	**280**	**Amérique du Sud**
Argentina	40	100	126	134	187	123	155	179	129	* 170	Argentine
Brazil	0	0	0	103	0	4	242	189	117	* 110	Brésil
Asia	**2**	**3**	**2**	**2**	**5**	**3**	**5**	**4**	**4**	**107**	**Asie**
India*	...	...	...	...	...	...	...	...	...	100	Inde*
Japan	2	3	2	2	5	3	* 5	4	4	* 7	Japon
Europe	**2 167**	**2 387**	**2 507**	**2 691**	**2 941**	**2 869**	**3 201**	**3 637**	**3 555**	**3 649**	**Europe**
EEC	***1 909***	***2 112***	***2 218***	***2 387***	***2 669***	***2 589***	***2 938***	***3 363***	***3 244***	***3 270***	***CEE***
Belgium	...	...	...	...	...	...	45	45	45	40	Belgique
France incl. Monaco	1 871	2 097	2 183	2 362	2 634	2 553	2 859	3 271	3 168	3 200	France y comp.Monaco
Germany, Fed. Rep.	38	15	35	25	35	36	34	47	31	30	Allemagne, Rép. féd.
EFTA	***88***	***95***	***98***	***114***	***82***	***102***	***113***	***104***	***115***	***119***	***AELE***
Portugal	88	95	98	114	82	102	113	104	115	119	Portugal
Other Europe	***170***	***180***	***191***	***190***	***190***	***178***	***150***	***170***	***196***	***260***	***Autre Europe***
Spain	170	180	191	190	190	178	150	170	196	200	Espagne
Yugoslavia*	...	...	...	...	...	...	...	...	...	60	Yougoslavie*
Oceania	**359**	**356**	**418**	**577**	**689**	**1 903**	**4 422**	**3 211**	**4 390**	**3 252**	**Océanie**
Australia	359	356	418	577	689	1 903	4 422	3 211	* 4 390	3 252	Australie
Total	**23 502**	**28 352**	**33 793**	**38 174**	**43 093**	**42 897**	**41 256**	**36 696**	**38 713**	**34 905**	**Total**

General note.
U content of uranium ores and concentrates and all other uranium–bearing ores and concentrates intended for treatment for uranium recovery. (SITC 28600–2M).

Remarque générale.
U contenu des minerais d'uranium et concentrés et tous autres minerais uranifères et concentrés, destinés à être traités en vue de l'extraction de l'uranium. (CTCI 28600–2M).

Unit : Kilogrammes

Unité : Kilogrammes

Country or area	1976	1977	1978	1979	1980	1981	1982	1983	1984	1985	Pays ou zone
Africa	**746 423**	**730 939**	**732 718**	**729 930**	**697 961**	**682 065**	**689 977**	**705 693**	**710 437**	**692 963**	**Afrique**
Botswana	[1] 0	[1] 0	[1] 0	[1] 0	0	10	15	11	18	13	Botswana
Burundi	[2] 13	[2] 14	[2] 14	[2] 4	[2] 4	[2] 3	[2] 3	* [2] 9	* 35	25	Burundi
Cameroon	[1] 8	[1] 6	[1] 6	[1] 5	[1] 2	[1] 2	[2] 4	[2] 8	* [2] 8	* [2] 8	Cameroun
Central African Rep.[2]	* 8	* 3	* 30	68	62	43	44	78	* 216	240	Rép. centrafricaine[2]
Congo	[1] 8	21	11	4	2	2	3	8	* 3	* 5	Congo
Ethiopia[1 3]	933	311	249	248	289	386	373	435	* 467	* 467	Ethiopie[1 3]
Gabon[2]	96	80	30	30	17	* 17	* 17	* 17	* 41	* 31	Gabon[2]
Ghana	16 494	14 957	12 505	11 094	10 981	10 596	10 280	8 602	8 923	9 311	Ghana
Kenya	1	4	6	7	4	1	1	5	1	1	Kenya
Liberia	* [1] 140	[1] 93	[1] 93	[1] 34	[1] 225	478	359	440	294	134	Libéria
Madagascar	[1] 5	[1] 2	[1] 4	4	4	1	3	3	3	4	Madagascar
Mali* [2]	28	29	30	156	311	498	404	404	500	498	Mali* [2]
Namibia* [2 4]	...	...	...	202	187	187	230	232	196	194	Namibie* [2 4]
Rwanda	[2] 29	[2] 58	[2] 36	14	27	46	15	39	8	1	Rwanda
South Africa	713 390	699 887	704 449	703 473	672 786	655 728	662 628	674 944	680 696	664 630	Afrique du Sud
Sudan* [2]	9	9	9	9	9	9	12	16	47	47	Soudan* [2]
Swaziland	2	6	0	0	0	0	0	0	0	0	Swaziland
United Rep. Tanzania	0	1	4	10	8	* [2] 12	* [2] 19	* [2] 25	* [2] 83	* [2] 84	Rép.Unie de Tanzanie
Zaire	[1] 2 686	[1] 2 540	[1] 2 375	[1] 2 315	[1] 1 271	[1] 2 027	[2] 1 889	[2] 6 000	* [2] 3 642	* [2] 2 333	Zaïre
Zambia[5]	341	217	259	247	329	328	311	316	379	246	Zambie[5]
Zimbabwe	12 037	12 504	12 410	12 006	11 443	11 691	13 367	14 101	14 877	14 691	Zimbabwe
America, North	**105 956**	**108 338**	**101 634**	**100 041**	**101 160**	**114 237**	**130 888**	**156 447**	**162 036**	**184 209**	**Amérique du Nord**
Canada	52 621	53 921	53 967	51 142	50 620	49 500	64 733	73 513	77 407	87 562	Canada
Costa Rica*	299	379	495	520	[2] 560	[2] 622	[2] 840	[2] 933	[2] 1 089	[2] 1 089	Costa Rica*
Dominican Republic	13 304	11 204	7 589	11 310	11 926	12 846	11 776	11 240	10 448	10 204	Rép. dominicaine
El Salvador[2]	94	67	113	85	78	121	103	20	* 9	* 9	El Salvador[2]
Honduras	[1] 25	[1] 22	[1] 25	[1] 17	[1] 15	[1] 11	[2] 53	[2] 67	[2] 87	[2] 78	Honduras
Mexico	5 064	6 616	6 283	5 911	6 096	6 319	6 104	6 930	7 058	7 524	Mexique
Nicaragua	[1] 1 951	[1] 1 904	[1] 2 095	[1] 1 060	[1] 1 701	[2] 1 926	[2] 1 691	[2] 1 444	[2] 1 088	[2] 762	Nicaragua
United States	32 598	34 225	31 067	29 996	30 164	42 892	45 588	62 300	64 850	76 981	Etats–Unis
America, South	**23 466**	**22 463**	**25 363**	**23 036**	**43 190**	**54 886**	**64 305**	**93 289**	**86 271**	**92 044**	**Amérique du Sud**
Argentina	[1] 181	[1] 171	[1] 174	[1] 315	[1] 341	459	632	727	688	882	Argentine
Bolivia	1 292	756	767	943	* 1 620	2 064	1 249	1 531	1 270	561	Bolivie
Brazil[6]	4 922	5 355	9 359	4 460	13 752	17 276	25 517	53 684	37 218	29 000	Brésil[6]
Chile	4 018	3 620	3 182	3 465	6 836	12 456	16 907	17 759	16 829	17 240	Chili
Colombia	[1] 9 454	[1] 7 997	[1] 7 596	[1] 8 493	[1] 15 790	[1] 16 069	[1] 14 294	[2] 13 266	[2] 22 726	[2] 35 532	Colombie
Ecuador	[1] 343	[1] 244	[1] 85	[1] 92	[1] 104	[1] 73	[2] 50	[2] 19	* [2] 31	* [2] 31	Equateur
French Guiana	84	150	90	62	92	167	162	249	315	407	Guyane française
Guyana	187	370	479	329	342	599	269	143	* 346	321	Guyana
Peru	2 470	3 247	3 206	4 406	3 870	4 821	4 306	4 815	* 5 100	* 5 856	Pérou
Suriname[1]	2	12	9	5	12	25	17	12	8	4	Suriname[1]
Venezuela	[1] 513	[1] 541	[1] 416	[1] 466	431	877	902	1 084	1 740	2 210	Venezuela
Asia	**31 527**	**34 150**	**36 485**	**35 589**	**39 344**	**88 598**	**94 561**	**95 917**	**96 716**	**107 314**	**Asie**
China[2]	* 2 488	* 3 110	* 4 666	* 6 221	* 6 998	# 52 876	* 55 986	* 57 541	* 59 097	* 59 097	Chine[2]
India	3 152	3 014	2 774	2 637	2 452	2 495	2 244	2 154	1 989	1 850	Inde
Indonesia	[1] 355	[1] 256	[1] 254	[1] 170	248	183	223	259	239	* 235	Indonésie
Japan	4 282	4 635	4 517	3 970	3 183	3 087	3 239	3 139	3 220	5 309	Japon
Korea, D. P. Rp.* [2]	5 000	5 000	5 000	5 000	5 000	5 000	5 000	5 000	5 000	5 000	Corée, Rp. P. D.* [2]
Korea, Republic of	521	631	828	749	1 282	1 342	1 734	2 242	2 462	2 403	Corée, République de
Malaysia[7]	138	140	201	197	156	180	181	185	234	357	Malaisie[7]
Philippines	15 591	17 364	18 245	16 645	20 025	23 435	25 954	25 397	24 475	33 063	Philippines
Europe	**27 891**	**26 499**	**26 112**	**23 797**	**22 571**	**22 786**	**20 603**	**22 249**	**21 644**	**21 549**	**Europe**
EEC	***12 687***	***11 516***	***12 314***	***10 823***	***10 459***	***10 621***	***7 290***	***8 654***	***7 086***	***7 050***	***CEE***
France	1 898	1 569	1 855	1 683	1 163	1 131	# 1 651	2 744	2 416	2 380	France
Germany, Fed. Rep.[8 9]	10 789	9 947	10 459	9 140	9 296	* 9 490	* 5 639	* 5 910	* 4 670	* 4 670	Allemagne, Rép. féd.[8 9]
EFTA	***3 063***	***3 240***	***3 562***	***3 509***	***3 544***	***3 275***	***3 802***	***4 352***	***5 471***	***5 529***	***AELE***
Finland[10]	817	852	905	881	1 301	992	1 144	784	870	590	Finlande[10]
Portugal	312	275	284	320	216	244	211	199	193	229	Portugal
Sweden	1 934	2 113	2 373	2 308	2 027	2 039	2 447	3 369	4 408	4 710	Suède
East Europe	***3 292***	***2 978***	***2 665***	***2 351***	***1 900***	***1 900***	***1 600***	***900***	***600***	***622***	***Europe de l'est***

For general note and footnotes, see end of table.

Voir la fin du tableau pour la remarque générale et les notes.

Gold–bearing ores (continued) – Minerais aurifères (suite)

Unit : Kilogrammes

Unité : Kilogrammes

Country or area	1976	1977	1978	1979	1980	1981	1982	1983	1984	1985	Pays ou zone
Hungary[11]	...	...	...	...	1 900	1 900	1 600	900	600	622	Hongrie[11]
Other Europe	***8 849***	***8 765***	***7 571***	***7 114***	***6 668***	***6 990***	***7 911***	***8 343***	***8 487***	***8 348***	***Autre Europe***
Spain	3 963	3 657	3 137	2 791	3 364	3 408	3 700	4 105	4 595	3 888	Espagne
Yugoslavia[12]	[1] 4 886	[1] 5 108	[1] 4 434	[1] 4 323	[1] 3 304	3 582	4 211	4 238	3 892	4 460	Yougoslavie[12]
USSR* [2]	**239 500**	**244 200**	**248 830**	**253 800**	**258 160**	**262 050**	**265 930**	**267 460**	**269 045**	**270 600**	**URSS* [2]**
Oceania	**39 301**	**39 782**	**45 518**	**40 369**	**33 324**	**34 012**	**41 570**	**45 491**	**53 292**	**91 382**	**Océanie**
Australia[13]	16 901	15 666	21 047	19 584	18 273	15 991	22 328	25 825	33 881	48 853	Australie[13]
Fiji	2 046	1 535	873	923	774	960	1 423	1 248	1 509	1 865	Fidji
New Zealand	[1] 102	[1] 223	[1] 219	[1] 218	[2] 200	[2] 189	[2] 242	[2] 301	[2] 672	[2] 1 400	Nouvelle–Zélande
Papua New Guinea	[1] 20 233	[1] 22 346	[1] 23 367	[1] 19 611	[1] 14 050	16 830	17 540	18 067	17 169	39 235	Papouasie–Nvl–Guinée
Solomon Islands	*[2] 19	*[2] 12	*[2] 12	33	27	42	37	50	61	29	Iles Salomon
Total	**1 214 064**	**1 206 371**	**1 216 660**	**1 206 562**	**1 195 710**	**1 258 634**	**1 307 834**	**1 386 546**	**1 399 441**	**1 460 061**	**Total**

General note.
Au content of gold ores and concentrates and all other gold–bearing ores and concentrates intended for treatment for gold recovery.

[1] Source: International Monetary Fund (IMF), (Washington, D. C.).
[2] Source: U. S. Bureau of Mines, (Washington, D. C.).
[3] Twelve months ending 10 September of year stated.
[4] Data refer to smelter production.
[5] Recovered from refinery sludges.
[6] Gold refined from domestic ores.
[7] Data refer to Peninsular Malaysia and Sarawak only.
[8] Gold refined, including gold recovered as a by–product.
[9] Beginning 1981, official data are confidential. Data shown are U. S. Bureau of Mines (Washington, D.C.) estimates.
[10] Gold content of concentrates.
[11] Source: World Metal Statistics, (London).
[12] Gold refined from copper, lead and zinc ores.
[13] Twelve months ending 30 June of year stated.

Remarque générale.
Au contenu des minerais d'or et concentrés et tous autres minerais aurifères et concentrés, destinés à être traités en vue de l'extraction de l'or.

[1] Source: Fonds monétaire international (FMI), (Washington, D.C.).
[2] Source: U.S. Bureau of Mines, (Washington, D.C.).
[3] Période de douze mois finissant le 10 septembre de l'année indiquée.
[4] Données se rapportant à la production des fonderies.
[5] Récupéré dans les boues des raffineries.
[6] Or affiné provenant de minerais indigène.
[7] Données se rapportant à la Malaisie péninsulaire et au Sarawak seulement.
[8] Or affiné, y compris l'or récupéré comme sous produit.
[9] A partir de 1981, les chiffres sont confidentiels. Les données officielles publiées se rapportent aux estimations du 'U. S. Bureau of Mines' (Washington D.C.).
[10] Teneur en or des concentrés.
[11] Source: World Metal Statistics, (Londres).
[12] Or affiné provenant de minerais de cuivre, plomb et zinc.
[13] Période de douze mois finissant le 30 juin de l'année indiquée.

Slate – Ardoise

Unit : Thousand metric tons

Unité : Milliers de tonnes métriques

Country or area	1976	1977	1978	1979	1980	1981	1982	1983	1984	1985	Pays ou zone
Africa	**824**	**817**	**821**	**750**	**750**	**880**	**905**	**821**	**821**	**821**	**Afrique**
Egypt	...	...	...	728	728	858	883	...	...	...	Egypte
South Africa	25	18	22	...	...	...	...	...	...	...	Afrique du Sud
America, North	**53**	**52**	**48**	**79**	**82**	**109**	**37**	**46**	**42**	**37**	**Amérique du Nord**
United States[1]	53	52	48	79	82	109	37	46	42	37	Etats-Unis[1]
America, South	**20**	**35**	**212**	**54**	**27**	**38**	**22**	**116**	**79**	**93**	**Amérique du Sud**
Brazil[2,3]	1	5	187	35	8	19	4	98	61	* 75	Brésil[2,3]
Peru[2]	19	30	25	19	19	* 19	* 18	* 18	* 18	* 18	Pérou[2]
Asia	**21**	**22**	**14**	**19**	**15**	**13**	**7**	**6**	**3**	**6**	**Asie**
India	21	22	14	19	15	13	7	6	3	6	Inde
Europe	**1 911**	**1 963**	**2 512**	**2 680**	**2 706**	**3 694**	**3 454**	**3 041**	**2 996**	**3 188**	**Europe**
EEC	***324***	***312***	***952***	***1 010***	***1 297***	***1 592***	***1 921***	***1 768***	***1 550***	***1 697***	***CEE***
France	89	88	86	86	95	89	70	52	64	58	France
Germany, Fed. Rep.	2	2	3	4	[2] 50	[2] 52	[2] 53	[2] 62	[2] 23	[2] 28	Allemagne, Rép. féd.
Italy	98	* [2] 100	* [2] 100	...	# [2] 1 021	* [2] 1 100	...	...	...	...	Italie
Luxembourg	1	...	...	...	...	...	...	...	...	...	Luxembourg
United Kingdom[4]	134	121	762	347	130	350	785	494	157	158	Royaume-Uni[4]
EFTA	***223***	***201***	***184***	***168***	***164***	***153***	***155***	***117***	***122***	***113***	***AELE***
Norway[2]	52	59	52	...	...	...	...	...	...	...	Norvège[2]
Portugal	38	50	59	46	45	33	42	35	46	...	Portugal
Sweden	133	92	73	68	65	66	59	28	22	20	Suède
East Europe	***230***	***243***	***220***	***180***	***205***	***189***	***153***	***162***	***159***	***151***	***Europe de l'est***
Poland	230	243	220	180	205	189	153	162	159	151	Pologne
Other Europe	***1 134***	***1 207***	***1 156***	***1 322***	***1 040***	***1 760***	***1 225***	***994***	***1 164***	***1 227***	***Autre Europe***
Spain	1 134	1 207	1 156	1 322	1 040	1 760	1 225	994	1 164	...	Espagne
USSR	**35 089**	**35 921**	**36 483**	**37 129**	**37 389**	**36 928**	**35 236**	**33 256**	**33 204**	**32 076**	**URSS**
Oceania	**169**	**87**	**91**	**147**	**123**	**125**	**129**	**175**	**148**	**152**	**Océanie**
Australia[5,6,7]	169	87	91	147	123	125	129	175	...	...	Australie[5,6,7]
Total	**38 087**	**38 897**	**40 181**	**40 858**	**41 092**	**41 787**	**39 790**	**37 461**	**37 293**	**36 374**	**Total**

General note.
Slate including slate not further worked than roughly split, roughly squared or squared by sawing. Roofing slate and mosaic cubes are excluded. (SITC 27311-0).

1 Sold or used by producers.
2 Source: U. S. Bureau of Mines, (Washington, D. C.).
3 Gross weight only.
4 Including waste used for constructional fill and powder and granules used in manufacturing.
5 Incomplete coverage.
6 Twelve months ending 30 June of year stated.
7 Including marble, travertines, granite, porphyry, sandstone etc.

Remarque générale.
Ardoise, y compris l'ardoise brute, refendue, dégrossie ou simplement débitée par sciage, à l'exclusion de l'ardoise de couverture et des cubes pour mosaïques. (CTCI 27311-0).

1 Vendu ou utilisé par les producteurs.
2 Source: U.S. Bureau of Mines, (Washington, D.C.).
3 Poids brut seulement.
4 Y compris les déchets utilisés pour le remblayage ainsi que les poudres et granules employées en manufacture.
5 Couverture incomplète.
6 Période de douze mois finissant le 30 juin de l'année indiquée.
7 Y compris le marbre, les travertins, le granit, le porphyre, le grès etc.

Marble, travertines etc. – Marbre, travertins etc.

Unit : Thousand cubic metres — Unité : Milliers de mètres cubes

Country or area	1976	1977	1978	1979	1980	1981	1982	1983	1984	1985	Pays ou zone
Africa											**Afrique**
Algeria	9	9	12	15	...	...	...	...	...	...	Algérie
Cameroon[1,2]	2	3	* 1	1	...	...	...	...	...	...	Cameroun[1,2]
Egypt	12	12	23	26	32	* [3] 47	* [3] 19	* [3] 16	* [3] 18	* [3] 43	Egypte
Madagascar[1,3]	30	12	2	4	* 1	...	0	* 4	0	0	Madagascar[1,3]
Nigeria[1,3]	11	6	9	1	0	4	3	3	1	1	Nigéria[1,3]
South Africa[1,2,3]	16	9	6	8	6	6	7	5	1	1	Afrique du Sud[1,2,3]
Tunisia	1	1	2	0	1	1	...	...	...	...	Tunisie
America, North											**Amérique du Nord**
Cuba[4]	5	7	7	10	9	8	10	14	14	19	Cuba[4]
Dominican Republic	1	1	0	0	1	1	2	1	2	...	Rép. dominicaine
Mexico[1]	[3] 2	[3] 1	[3] 145	[3] 156	[3] 164	[3] 171	[3] 120	[3] 149	149	263	Mexique[1]
United States[1,5]	426	490	490	354	323	311	...	...	...	...	Etats–Unis[1,5]
America, South											**Amérique du Sud**
Argentina[1]	120	103	101	157	153	114	80	101	113	117	Argentine[1]
Brazil[2]	54	59	66	66	68	67	122	141	175	* 170	Brésil[2]
Chile[1,2]	0	1	8	4	3	2	1	1	1	...	Chili[1,2]
Colombia[1,3]	...	9	12	17	17	17	17	16	15	17	Colombie[1,3]
Ecuador[1,2]	[3] 0	[3] 3	[3] 3	* 3	0	2	0	6	* 5	* 4	Equateur[1,2]
Peru[1,2,3]	15	2	7	12	12	3	3	3	3	3	Pérou[1,2,3]
Uruguay[1,2]	4	4	5	5	8	4	5	4	4	4	Uruguay[1,2]
Asia											**Asie**
Cyprus[1]	28	42	48	53	66	56	75	90	88	80	Chypre[1]
Indonesia[6]	26	35	33	25	25	29	29	24	* 16	* 10	Indonésie[6]
Iran(Islamic Rep.of)[1,3]	720	597	800	...	...	200	200	* 220	* 200	200	Iran(Rép.islamique)[1,3]
Pakistan[1,7]	65	46	71	119	92	114	95	121	* 100	...	Pakistan[1,7]
Philippines[8]	[1,3] 11	[1,3] 12	[3] 18	[3] 12	[3] 9	[3] 7	[3] 7	[3] 6	[3] 5	4	Philippines[8]
Thailand[1,2]	...	...	...	5	6	8	9	26	38	21	Thaïlande[1,2]
Turkey	2	2	9	5	[1,3] 16	[1,3] 37	[1,3] 24	[1,3] 39	[1,3] 40	[1,3] 40	Turquie
United Arab Emirates* [6]	...	26	39	26	...	...	...	...	...	...	Emirats arabes unis* [6]
Europe											**Europe**
EEC											***CEE***
Belgium[4]	2	3	4	4	4	6	8	1	4	1	Belgique[4]
France[2]	...	* [1] 15	...	[1] 22	7	6	5	6	5	4	France[2]
Germany, Fed. Rep.	20	21	25	40	37	36	32	33	51	51	Allemagne, Rép. féd.
Greece	[2] 165	[2] 145	[2] 154	210	212	216	211	207	230	280	Grèce
Italy* [1,4]	3 050	3 280	3 280	...	2 200	2 100	2 000	1 900	2 000	2 100	Italie* [1,4]
EFTA											***AELE***
Austria[9]	51	71	34	44	[1] 18	[1] 13	[1] 11	[1] 13	[1] 11	[1] 11	Autriche[9]
Norway	...	78	68	...	...	...	...	...	...	...	Norvège
Portugal[2]	[1] 253	[1] 267	[1] 303	* [1] 329	[1] 371	* 137	* 144	* 148	* 158	...	Portugal[2]
Sweden	13	11	9	5	4	3	* 4	6	6	7	Suède
Other Europe											***Autre Europe***
Spain	289	311	292	333	[1] 753	[1] 694	[1] 665	[1] 865	[1] 623	...	Espagne
Yugoslavia	136	144	133	267	235	205	157	145	99	138	Yougoslavie

General note.
Marble, travertines, ecaussine and other similar hard calcareous monumental and building stone and alabaster, provided that their apparent specific gravity is 2.5 or more (that is, effective weight in kg/1000 cubic cm), presented in the mass or in form of blocks, slabs or sheets. Stones identifiable as mosaic cubes or as paving flagstones are excluded. (SITC 27312–0).

Remarque générale.
Marbre, travertin, écaussine et autres pierres calcaires dures analogues de taille ou de construction, d'une densité moyenne apparente égale ou supérieure à 2,5 (poids en kg/dm³), à l'état brut ou sous forme de blocs, moëllons ou plaques, à l'exclusion des cubes pour mosaïques et des dalles de pavage. (CTCI 27312–0).

[1] In thousand metric tons.
[2] Marble only.
[3] Source: U. S. Bureau of Mines, (Washington, D. C.).
[4] Marble in blocks only.
[5] Shipped or used by producers.
[6] In thousand square metres.
[7] Twelve months ending 30 June of year stated.
[8] Including finished and unfinished marble.
[9] Including granite, porphyry, sandstone etc.

[1] En milliers de tonnes métriques.
[2] Marbre seulement.
[3] Source: U.S. Bureau of Mines, (Washington, D.C.).
[4] Marbre en blocs seulement.
[5] Expedié ou utilisé par les producteurs.
[6] En milliers de mètres carrés.
[7] Période de douze mois finissant le 30 juin de l'année indiquée.
[8] Y compris le marbre taillé et brut.
[9] Y compris le granite, le porphyre, le grès, etc.

Granite, porphyry, sandstone etc. – Granite, porphyre, grès etc.

Unit : Thousand metric tons | Unité : Milliers de tonnes métriques

Country or area	1976	1977	1978	1979	1980	1981	1982	1983	1984	1985	Pays ou zone
Africa											**Afrique**
Egypt[1]	[2] 120	[2] 120	[2] 111	[3] 875	[3] 134	[3] 141	[3] 880	[3] 613	[3] 814	[3] 1 210	Egypte[1]
South Africa[3 4 5]	296	413	213	214	210	206	173	161	210	327	Afrique du Sud[3 4 5]
America, North											**Amérique du Nord**
United States[6]	791	744	777	569	600	618	595	545	* 579	* 546	Etats–Unis[6]
America, South											**Amérique du Sud**
Argentina[7]	25	26	29	39	41	47	33	42	26	31	Argentine[7]
Brazil[1 3 4]	56 077	51 815	37 842	42 684	47 515	49 663	44 050	35 415	38 815	40 000	Brésil[1 3 4]
Uruguay[4]	...	...	...	6	6	4	4	2	...	...	Uruguay[4]
Venezuela	...	...	...	...	...	1 034	1 388	748	326	159	Venezuela
Asia											**Asie**
Cyprus[8]	45	46	63	87	105	760	980	500	450	343	Chypre[8]
Indonesia[4]	804	722	495	678	926	1 811	2 130	* 2 405	* 1 583	* 1 534	Indonésie[4]
Korea, Republic of	...	...	...	...	245	268	191	217	257	318	Corée, République de
Pakistan	2	12	1	3	1	0	1	0	...	...	Pakistan
Philippines	[1] 205	[1] 193	[1] 209	[2 3] 91	[2 3] 57	[2 3] 37	[2 3] 33	[2 3] 47	[2 3] 5	[2 3] 40	Philippines
Singapore[1 4]	2 524	2 572	2 235	2 507	3 185	4 484	5 947	7 569	7 422	6 743	Singapour[1 4]
Europe											**Europe**
EEC											***CEE***
Belgium[4]	2 562	2 300	2 217	2 321	2 914	2 645	2 057	1 749	2 189	1 833	Belgique[4]
Denmark[1]	35	39	46	39	69	...	...	110	153	156	Danemark[1]
France	637	644	558	620	589	566	515	521	453	456	France
Germany, Fed. Rep.[1]	9	9	7	15	2	3	5	4	5	3	Allemagne, Rép. féd.[1]
Italy	1 448	* 2 010	* 2 010	...	* 2 750	* 3 150	...	...	...	...	Italie
United Kingdom[9]	50 736	47 854	48 657	49 739	# 38 285	34 934	40 790	42 932	42 498	42 590	Royaume–Uni[9]
EFTA											***AELE***
Finland	16	21	27	36	42	41	53	53	63	...	Finlande
Norway[3 4]	...	...	...	...	10	9	7	8	8	...	Norvège[3 4]
Portugal	3 243	3 625	6 779	5 196	5 535	5 967	5 622	5 217	4 209	...	Portugal
Sweden	132	120	117	123	110	131	120	125	139	133	Suède
East Europe											***Europe de l'est***
Hungary	215	182	133	196	198	211	181	203	209	186	Hongrie
Poland	7 468	9 020	9 132	8 477	7 756	7 398	6 324	6 289	6 392	6 501	Pologne
Other Europe											***Autre Europe***
Spain	[1] 13 984	...	...	...	9 777	12 892	12 713	12 019	13 915	...	Espagne

General note.
Monumental and building stones, including such stone not further worked than roughly split, roughly squared or squared by sawing, such as granite, porphyry, basalt, sandstone and other hard indigenous rocks. (SITC 27313–0).

[1] In thousand cubic metres.
[2] Sandstone only.
[3] Source: U. S. Bureau of Mines, (Washington, D. C.).
[4] Granite only.
[5] Domestic sales plus exports.
[6] Sold or used by producers.
[7] Granite in blocks only.
[8] Building stone only.
[9] Sandstone and igneous rocks only.

Remarque générale.
Pierres de taille et de construction, telles que le granit, le porphyre, le basalte, le grès et d'autres roches dures naturelles, brutes, dégrossies ou simplement débitées par sciage. (CTCI 27313–0).

[1] En milliers de mètres cubes.
[2] Grès seulement.
[3] Source: U.S. Bureau of Mines, (Washington, D.C.).
[4] Granite seulement.
[5] Ventes nationales plus exportations.
[6] Vendu ou utilisé par les producteurs.
[7] Granite en blocs seulement.
[8] Pierre de construction seulement.
[9] Grès et roches ignées seulement.

Limestone flux and calcareous stone – Castine et pierres à chaux et à ciment

Unit : Thousand metric tons

Unité : Milliers de tonnes métriques

Country or area	1976	1977	1978	1979	1980	1981	1982	1983	1984	1985	Pays ou zone
Africa											**Afrique**
Cameroonl [1]	60	91	79	80	40	67	83	51	...	79	Camerounl [1]
Egypt[2]	5 400	5 500	5 667	5 845	5 196	5 535	7 037	[1] 9 276	[1] 10 000	[1] 12 059	Egypte[2]
Ethiopia* [1 3]	8	8	7	7	2	5	5	5	5	5	Ethiopie* [1 3]
Kenya	32	78	19	31	[1] 1 541	[1] 1 500	...	[1] 1 580	[1] 1 444	[1] 25	Kenya
Malawi[1 3]	149	117	155	169	123	116	80	* 109	* 100	* 100	Malawi[1 3]
Mali[1 3]	...	0	1	1	5	5	...	...	...	...	Mali[1 3]
Nigeria[1 3]	1 553	1 243	1 200	2 006	2 336	1 509	920	1 400	1 890	1 800	Nigéria[1 3]
South Africa	18 543	17 274	19 634	19 127	22 053	23 373	22 518	20 288	21 084	18 943	Afrique du Sud
United Rep. Tanzania	2	8	20	9	11	12	...	...	...	...	Rép.Unie de Tanzanie
Zambia	565	414	486	580	515	499	427	511	916	590	Zambie
Zimbabwe[1 3]	...	1 299	1 087	1 057	1 218	1 409	1 270	1 305	1 152	1 325	Zimbabwe[1 3]
America, North											**Amérique du Nord**
Bahamas[1 3]	...	...	524	508	550	532	...	...	...	...	Bahamas[1 3]
Belize[1 3]	...	198	348	364	337	480	356	609	* 600	* 600	Belize[1 3]
Cuba[2]	4 323	4 233	4 678	4 497	4 003	4 700	4 652	5 118	5 461	5 637	Cuba[2]
Dominican Republic[2 3]	272	302	353	405	446	406	420	444	324	357	Rép. dominicaine[2 3]
Jamaica[1]	...	717	614	370	403	* 400	...	...	83	* 100	Jamaïque[1]
Mexico	[4] 4 763	[4] 4 750	# 22 565	24 086	31 173	39 046	40 880	35 276	29 055	30 840	Mexique
Trinidad and Tobago[3]	533	569	477	742	622	687	774	...	...	...	Trinité–et–Tobago[3]
United States[5]	23 477	21 904	23 580	21 701	17 265	16 050	...	...	...	...	Etats–Unis[5]
America, South											**Amérique du Sud**
Argentina	13 608	14 081	15 956	15 238	14 322	14 491	12 651	12 318	11 167	8 849	Argentine
Brazil[3]	34 883	39 303	46 283	44 664	50 170	52 066	49 027	44 918	45 758	* 45 000	Brésil[3]
Chile	1 794	1 918	2 188	2 297	2 766	2 923	1 667	2 142	2 326	2 470	Chili
Colombia[1 3]	7 800	8 112	9 431	9 700	9 760	10 053	10 620	10 685	11 565	11 756	Colombie[1 3]
Ecuador[1 3]	880	1 061	1 410	1 300	1 738	2 391	1 200	1 500	1 600	* 3 000	Equateur[1 3]
Peru[1 3]	...	...	...	...	3 175	3 800	2 590	2 500	2 500	* 2 500	Pérou[1 3]
Uruguay[1 3]	859	1 192	1 190	* 1 100	1 335	* 1 250	* 1 098	757	666	* 700	Uruguay[1 3]
Venezuela[1 3]	21 515	18 995	32 736	19 872	19 074	31 690	5 760	27 302	10 847	12 000	Venezuela[1 3]
Asia											**Asie**
Bangladesh[6]	62	62	61	58	45	39	45	32	34	36	Bangladesh[6]
Burma[1 3]	645	1 159	1 437	1 259	1 151	1 219	1 221	1 247	1 210	1 541	Birmanie[1 3]
Cyprus	24 000	25 000	19 376	20 993	15 057	12 359	11 000	9 000	7 000	8 000	Chypre
India	31 243	31 636	32 341	32 471	30 088	33 276	35 530	39 772	46 782	49 353	Inde
Indonesia[3]	2 121	3 724	4 699	6 107	7 605	8 749	11 002	* 12 073	* 11 314	* 12 059	Indonésie[3]
Iran(Islamic Rep.of)[1 3]	8 000	9 000	15 000	...	11 000	11 000	14 000	12 000	12 000	12 000	Iran(Rép.islamique)[1 3]
Japan	147 530	154 121	172 543	182 781	184 780	176 702	168 259	169 780	169 825	164 156	Japon
Jordan[1 3]	...	...	6	6	4	7	7	7	7	7	Jordanie[1 3]
Korea, Republic of	18 004	21 371	23 468	25 430	26 704	27 584	29 332	31 347	31 171	31 037	Corée, République de
Pakistan[6]	2 968	3 888	4 029	3 298	2 798	3 464	3 682	4 232	5 184	* 5 280	Pakistan[6]
Philippines[7]	6 943	6 334	9 231	10 152	10 100	10 676	7 208	6 686	* 4 024	3 521	Philippines[7]
Qatar[1 3]	...	...	...	...	2 036	2 300	2 185	1 600	1 500	1 100	Qatar[1 3]
Sri Lanka	594	535	962	# [1] 1 132	[1] 1 261	[1] 1 812	[1] 1 616	[1] 947	* [1] 1 000	* [1] 1 000	Sri Lanka
Thailand	493	706	2 631	2 964	3 958	5 486	6 372	8 944	9 236	9 877	Thaïlande
Turkey* [1]	139	123	179	435	90	467	838	343	350	350	Turquie* [1]
Europe											**Europe**
EEC											***CEE***
Belgium	24 155	29 092	27 052	27 462	29 659	27 584	24 665	22 046	20 517	20 502	Belgique
Denmark[8]	2 165	1 972	2 008	2 332	1 738	1 811	2 290	2 169	2 163	2 058	Danemark[8]
France	7 026	7 080	6 495	6 606	6 603	5 974	5 854	6 625	6 700	5 983	France
Germany, Fed. Rep.	57 372	51 362	53 418	57 187	55 761	50 105	43 977	45 348	44 683	41 677	Allemagne, Rép. féd.
Ireland[1 3]	7 292	8 755	11 147	11 101	11 945	9 721	11 831	* 11 000	* 10 598	* 9 337	Irlande[1 3]
Italy	37 412	* 39 000	* 39 000	* 40 000	* 54 000	* 54 000	...	...	...	...	Italie
United Kingdom[9]	89 253	86 372	88 819	92 194	# 72 423	73 701	80 298	87 653	86 080	89 338	Royaume–Uni[9]
EFTA											***AELE***
Finland	1 054	2 819	3 325	2 545	2 534	2 416	2 446	2 609	2 300	* 4 366	Finlande
Norway	5 189	4 607	4 390	5 254	4 146	3 832	4 515	4 303	* 3 995	* 3 827	Norvège
Portugal	6 518	7 350	8 887	10 542	9 738	12 598	13 744	13 447	10 985	...	Portugal
Sweden	6 816	7 299	6 791	6 893	7 187	6 692	6 462	6 630	6 542	7 465	Suède
East Europe											***Europe de l'est***

For general note and footnotes, see end of table.

Voir la fin du tableau pour la remarque générale et les notes.

Unit : Thousand metric tons | Unité : Milliers de tonnes métriques

Country or area	1976	1977	1978	1979	1980	1981	1982	1983	1984	1985	Pays ou zone
Bulgaria	5 274	6 503	7 067	7 336	7 696	7 194	6 861	6 583	6 497	6 126	Bulgarie
Czechoslovakia	22 312	22 586	23 174	23 209	24 213	24 499	23 818	23 519	23 684	23 252	Tchécoslovaquie
Hungary	10 358	10 928	11 470	11 370	11 048	11 101	11 064	10 635	10 336	9 754	Hongrie
Poland	9 215	12 314	12 995	13 087	12 964	11 271	13 478	15 962	17 122	16 278	Pologne
Other Europe											***Autre Europe***
Malta[3]	...	[1] 802	[1 2] 386	[1 2] 400	[1 2] 400	[2] 465	[2] 402	[2] 808	[2] 808	[2] 800	Malte[3]
Spain	84 425	89 661	90 520	85 379	81 233	78 673	83 832	84 080	77 467	...	Espagne
Yugoslavia[1 3]	2 800	3 149	3 778	4 125	4 061	4 081	4 872	...	...	...	Yougoslavie[1 3]
Oceania											**Océanie**
Australia[6]	10 185	10 528	10 750	10 813	11 521	11 894	12 790	* 12 300	10 333	11 811	Australie[6]
New Zealand[1 10]	165	170	159	289	172	178	184	207	214	215	Nouvelle–Zélande[1 10]

General note.
Limestone flux and limestone and calcareous rocks commonly used for the manufacture of lime or cement, excluding building or monumental stone. Those materials in powdered form for soil improvement are included. Dolomite and chalk are excluded. (SITC 27322–0).

1 Source: U. S. Bureau of Mines, (Washington, D. C.).
2 In thousand cubic metres.
3 Limestone only.
4 Incomplete coverage.
5 Sales of fluxing limestone and calcareous marl.
6 Twelve months ending 30 June of year stated.
7 Production for the manufacture of cement and agricultural use.
8 Sales.
9 Including small quantities of dolomite.
10 Limestone for industrial use only.

Remarque générale.
Castine et pierres à chaux et à ciment proprement dites, à l'exclusion des pierres de taille et de construction. Cette position comprend la pierre utilisée sous forme de poudre pour l'amendement des terres. Elle ne comprend pas la dolomie et la craie. (CTCI 27322–0).

1 Source: U.S. Bureau of Mines, (Washington, D.C.).
2 En milliers de mètres cubes.
3 Calcaire seulement.
4 Couverture incomplète.
5 Ventes de castine et de marnes calcaires.
6 Période de douze mois finissant le 30 juin de l'année indiquée.
7 Production destinée à la fabrication du ciment et aux usages agricoles.
8 Ventes.
9 Y compris de petites quantités de dolomite.
10 Calcaire pour usage industriels seulement.

Sand, silica and quartz – Sables, siliceux et quartzeux

Unit : Thousand metric tons — Unité : Milliers de tonnes métriques

Country or area	1976	1977	1978	1979	1980	1981	1982	1983	1984	1985	Pays ou zone
Africa											**Afrique**
Egypt[1,2]	3 535	6 000	7 000	6 147	6 000	6 200	6 874	166	1 500	12 677	Egypte[1,2]
Ethiopia[1,2,3]	...	219	90	97	407	655	650	650	650	650	Ethiopie[1,2,3]
Kenya	17	18	24	13	1	25	0	74	95	100	Kenya
Niger[1,2,3]	6	6	6	6	6	6	...	...	...	...	Niger[1,2,3]
South Africa[4]	1 125	1 017	1 013	1 376	1 617	* 1 385	1 276	1 184	1 471	1 510	Afrique du Sud[4]
United Rep. Tanzania[2,5]	28	28	28	* 30	30	30	...	...	...	...	Rép.Unie de Tanzanie[2,5]
Zambia[3]	282	478	292	[2] 195	[2] 20	[2] 277	[2] 365	[2] 183	[2] 53	[2] 39	Zambie[3]
America, North											**Amérique du Nord**
Belize[2,6]	...	666	734	715	625	589	521	554	* 500	* 500	Belize[2,6]
Canada[7]	2 520	2 317	2 165	2 368	2 525	2 238	1 703	2 303	2 659	* 2 538	Canada[7]
Cuba[8]	121	127	136	208	235	200	320	302	310	293	Cuba[8]
Jamaica[6]	...	9 586	9 572	11 011	6 856	[2] 6 200	[2] 6 500	[2] 9 135	[2] 8 625	[2] 8 500	Jamaïque[6]
Martinique[2,3]	...	261	149	228	306	* 300	...	...	...	...	Martinique[2,3]
Mexico[9]	509	627	532	537	893	1 009	828	929	937	976	Mexique[9]
United States	406 567	425 479	473 197	443 169	336 938	...	222 400	...	...	...	Etats–Unis
America, South											**Amérique du Sud**
Argentina	15 279	16 565	15 168	15 774	17 295	15 718	14 600	12 920	11 802	10 702	Argentine
Brazil[1,10]	1 631	2 067	12 397	17 959	22 014	35 876	40 088	24 450	24 958	* 36 000	Brésil[1,10]
Chile[11]	158	170	194	141	163	165	186	222	293	268	Chili[11]
Colombia[2,3]	398	429	440	480	492	502	497	507	522	512	Colombie[2,3]
Ecuador[2,4]	...	11	17	* 13	18	41	13	* 7	* 7	* 10	Equateur[2,4]
Peru[2,6]	3 547	3 291	2 887	2 377	3 596	2 538	2 850	* 2 800	* 2 800	* 2 800	Pérou[2,6]
Suriname[2,3]	...	...	160	150	155	* 150	* 150	* 150	* 150	...	Suriname[2,3]
Uruguay[12]	* 1 649	* 1 887	* 2 079	* 2 200	2 964	* 2 000	2 042	1 598	* 1 391	* 1 500	Uruguay[12]
Venezuela	[2,6] 14 499	[2,6] 23 238	[2,6] 21 667	[2,6] 19 231	[2,6] 12 248	[8] 8 648	[8] 7 333	[8] 5 673	[8] 6 144	[8] 5 323	Venezuela
Asia											**Asie**
Brunei Darussalam	25	...	...	...	11	19	23	51	...	...	Brunéi Darussalam
Hong Kong[11]	1	2	1	0	0	0	0	0	0	0	Hong–kong[11]
India	1 950	1 876	1 887	1 842	2 047	2 418	2 329	2 982	13 453	3 304	Inde
Indonesia[2,11]	221	269	307	127	260	156	977	372	542	* 679	Indonésie[2,11]
Iran(Islamic Rep.of)[2,4]	300	300	...	...	...	200	* 200	* 220	* 200	* 200	Iran(Rép.islamique)[2,4]
Israel[13,14]	69	72	80	73	64	83	63	65	69	71	Israël[13,14]
Korea, Republic of[1,3]	...	1 742	1 876	1 293	1 863	2 536	1 606	3 414	4 242	4 170	Corée, République de[1,3]
Pakistan[15]	43	51	93	84	104	84	99	141	* 280	* 196	Pakistan[15]
Philippines[2,8]	391	...	419	407	478	472	480	408	413	411	Philippines[2,8]
Sri Lanka	57	35	48	71	45	97	76	84	...	...	Sri Lanka
Syrian Arab Republic[1,6]	4 341	4 567	6 495	7 870	7 787	8 536	15 903	15 795	14 283	14 077	Rép. arabe syrienne[1,6]
Thailand	56	747	192	179	179	76	90	* 131	187	179	Thaïlande
Turkey[2]	220	262	354	320	300	312	310	349	350	429	Turquie[2]
Europe											**Europe**
EEC											***CEE***
Belgium[12]	14 976	13 815	12 856	13 184	12 312	10 558	10 478	11 085	10 728	10 676	Belgique[12]
Denmark[1]	1 921	1 787	2 115	2 462	1 779	1 249	1 352	1 299	1 707	2 140	Danemark[1]
France[16]	93 502	91 955	91 405	91 997	93 654	89 708	83 524	79 234	72 423	72 503	France[16]
Germany, Fed. Rep.	152 850	159 943	172 419	185 389	175 643	152 471	143 949	139 938	139 144	127 884	Allemagne, Rép. féd.
Greece[2,4]	17	25	26	* 27	* 28	* 28	* 28	* 2	* 39	* 38	Grèce[2,4]
Italy[17]	129 178	...	...	...	...	...	...	...	...	...	Italie[17]
Luxembourg[3]	729	638	615	747	710	713	783	703	661	570	Luxembourg[3]
Netherlands[18]	24 400	25 600	23 500	23 030	24 600	20 030	17 360	18 750	19 400	19 000	Pays–Bas[18]
United Kingdom[19]	113 840	# 99 229	102 100	102 495	96 158	89 453	91 206	100 799	99 675	101 605	Royaume–Uni[19]
EFTA											***AELE***
Austria	18 313	18 839	17 154	17 264	17 588	17 614	15 535	15 614	15 672	14 875	Autriche
Finland	158	148	121	159	283	508	1 158	1 019	262	* 223	Finlande
Portugal	5 417	7 182	5 610	5 745	6 015	6 463	5 388	5 086	...	...	Portugal
East Europe											***Europe de l'est***
Bulgaria[1,20]	25 179	27 442	29 862	29 503	36 136	31 180	29 929	29 056	28 408	27 292	Bulgarie[1,20]
Hungary	2 349	2 359	2 731	2 964	2 892	2 935	2 870	2 585	2 798	2 586	Hongrie
Poland[11]	82	70	70	51	44	13	22	22	36	47	Pologne[11]
Romania[2,3]	...	...	* 1 367	2 388	2 716	* 2 800	* 2 900	* 2 500	* 2 500	* 2 500	Roumanie[2,3]

For general note and footnotes, see end of table. — Voir la fin du tableau pour la remarque générale et les notes.

Unit : Thousand metric tons — Unité : Milliers de tonnes métriques

Country or area	1976	1977	1978	1979	1980	1981	1982	1983	1984	1985	Pays ou zone
Other Europe											***Autre Europe***
Spain	[17] 28 369	...	...	...	[2 6] 2 425	[2 6] 1 832	[2 6] 1 611	[2 6] 2 100	[2 6] 2 267	* [2 6] 2 300	Espagne
Yugoslavia	568	860	643	874	1 327	1 105	1 200	620	645	743	Yougoslavie
USSR											**URSS**
Oceania											**Océanie**
Australia[15]	24 394	26 356	25 659	25 473	28 125	29 113	30 607	28 000	26 820	...	Australie[15]
New Caledonia[1 21]	92	111	...	60	65	73	52	37	32	33	Nouvelle–Calédonie[1 21]
New Zealand	232	222	200	220	252	[2] 493	[2] 405	[2] 383	* [2] 520	* [2] 400	Nouvelle–Zélande

General note.
Commercially–extracted sand used in building, in glass industry, for cleaning metals etc. (SITC 27330–1).

1 In thousand cubic metres.
2 Source: U. S. Bureau of Mines, (Washington, D. C.).
3 Sand only.
4 Silica only.
5 Glass sand only.
6 Sand and gravel.
7 Silica and quartz only.
8 Silica and sand only.
9 Quartz and glass sand only.
10 Washed sand only.
11 Quartz only.
12 Sand and quartz only.
13 Excluding silica.
14 Marketed local production.
15 Twelve months ending 30 June of year stated.
16 Industrial sand from quarries and alluvial sand. Excluding crushed sand.
17 Including gravel.
18 Industrial sand only.
19 Including gravel, excluding quartz and silica.
20 Including gravel and crushed stone.
21 Calcareous sand of coral origin.

Remarque générale.
Sables provenant d'exploitations commerciales, utilisés dans la construction, la verrerie, le décapage des métaux etc. (CTCI 27330–1).

1 En milliers de mètres cubes.
2 Source: U.S. Bureau of Mines, (Washington, D.C.).
3 Sable seulement.
4 Silice seulement.
5 Sable utilisé dans la verrerie seulement.
6 Sable et gravier.
7 Siliceux et quartzeux seulement.
8 Silice et sable seulement.
9 Quartzeux et sable utilisé dans la verrerie seulement.
10 Sable délavé seulement.
11 Quartz seulement.
12 Sables et quartz seulement.
13 Non compris la silice.
14 Production locale commercialisée.
15 Période de douze mois finissant le 30 juin de l'année indiquée.
16 Sables industriels de carrières et sables d'alluvions. Les sables de concassage sont exclus.
17 Y compris les graviers.
18 Sables industriels seulement.
19 Y compris les graviers. Non compris le quartz et la silice.
20 Y compris les graviers et les pierres concassées.
21 Sable calcaire d'origine corallienne.

Gravel and crushed stone – Graviers et pierres concassées

Unit : Thousand metric tons

Unité : Milliers de tonnes métriques

Country or area	1976	1977	1978	1979	1980	1981	1982	1983	1984	1985	Pays ou zone
Africa											**Afrique**
Algeria[1,2]	2 605	5 227	6 520	6 800	7 871	8 306	5 860	...	...	...	Algérie[1,2]
Benin[3,4]	16	18	20	21	22	22	...	...	...	...	Bénin[3,4]
Botswana[1,2]	252	264	275	458	424	341	323	577	625	235	Botswana[1,2]
Egypt[1,3,4]	1 500	1 900	2 090	3 000	3 400	3 400	6 480	7 000	7 500	10 736	Egypte[1,3,4]
Niger[1,3,4]	179	180	180	180	180	180	...	...	...	...	Niger[1,3,4]
Swaziland[1]	57	93	452	247	74	82	82	151	98	84	Swaziland[1]
Zambia	565	534	523	252	431	539	...	...	...	...	Zambie
America, North											**Amérique du Nord**
Antigua and Barbuda[3]	...	...	...	...	...	40	44	49	...	...	Antigua-et-Barbuda[3]
Canada[5]	87 876	120 163	122 144	109 719	103 366	85 041	61 929	74 466	78 315	77 930	Canada[5]
Cuba	[1] 9 512	[1] 9 683	[1] 9 985	[1] 15 443	[1] 14 746	[1] 9 717	[1] 8 887	[1] 9 849	[1] 10 681	17 328	Cuba
Dominican Republic[1,2]	1 250	1 326	1 287	* 2 087	* 2 319	* 2 519	2 139	2 012	1 406	1 425	Rép. dominicaine[1,2]
Guadeloupe* [4,5]	...	1 300	700	700	450	451	450	...	...	...	Guadeloupe* [4,5]
Martinique[4]	...	[1] 349	[1] 471	[1] 396	[1] 565	* 600	* 600	...	...	...	Martinique[4]
Trinidad and Tobago[1,6]	465	642	480	1 293	305	770	1 263	...	...	...	Trinité-et-Tobago[1,6]
United States[7]	1 212 910	1 265 570	1 383 000	1 440 800	1 243 900	791 610	* 716 703	781 631	* 867 269	907 911	Etats-Unis[7]
America, South											**Amérique du Sud**
Argentina	5 990	9 214	11 320	11 796	10 657	9 522	8 240	5 878	4 301	4 343	Argentine
Brazil[1]	...	57 360	45 284	47 067	63 474	39 885	...	...	...	...	Brésil[1]
French Guiana[2]	...	...	...	...	...	296	346	392	407	384	Guyane française[2]
Suriname[2]	202	170	115	118	147	122	120	70	66	...	Suriname[2]
Uruguay[3,4]	864	* 865	341	* 400	410	* 350	* 506	439	* 237	* 500	Uruguay[3,4]
Venezuela[6]	...	...	...	...	...	6 763	7 004	5 369	8 189	7 032	Venezuela[6]
Asia											**Asie**
Brunei Darussalam	21	...	...	...	295	85	33	523	...	...	Brunéi Darussalam
Cyprus[2]	2 134	3 267	4 322	5 075	4 709	3 897	3 973	4 100	4 075	3 850	Chypre[2]
Israel[1,4,5]	...	...	...	12	5	5	6	5	6	6	Israël[1,4,5]
Korea, Republic of[1,3]	...	2 928	3 429	3 012	3 181	5 716	4 261	6 125	5 846	6 828	Corée, République de[1,3]
Pakistan[8]	46	40	106	113	114	26	14	418	74	* 23	Pakistan[8]
Philippines[1,9]	494	[4] 1 572	[4] 4 066	[4] 1 908	[4] 1 687	[4] 1 489	[4] 1 031	[4] 1 857	[4] 590	[4] 1 000	Philippines[1,9]
Syrian Arab Republic[1,5]	748	985	1 585	2 013	1 991	1 194	896	650	496	576	Rép. arabe syrienne[1,5]
Europe											**Europe**
EEC											***CEE***
Belgium	15 174	15 210	13 167	11 923	12 229	11 258	10 981	10 870	11 170	11 223	Belgique
Denmark[1]	10 810	10 246	10 734	11 388	9 330	...	...	...	8 311	9 336	Danemark[1]
France	94 800	95 410	100 080	107 500	113 700	111 060	110 770	106 400	96 340	115 088	France
Germany, Fed. Rep.[10]	118 078	126 209	138 801	149 048	141 502	122 713	...	...	...	...	Allemagne, Rép. féd.[10]
Ireland[2,4]	5 770	5 464	5 726	7 168	5 376	5 400	6 497	* 6 500	* 6 714	* 6 749	Irlande[2,4]
Luxembourg[11]	208	183	213	229	216	191	203	129	135	80	Luxembourg[11]
Netherlands	...	...	...	13 650	15 230	12 030	9 790	9 300	9 200	9 100	Pays-Bas
EFTA											***AELE***
Austria	12 536	14 967	15 564	16 585	16 905	16 344	13 669	14 305	14 667	13 755	Autriche
Finland	7 062	15 719	15 905	20 555	21 993	22 051	23 562	25 895	26 992	...	Finlande
Iceland	28	30	28	25	24	21	20	20	20	20	Islande
Norway	6 438	8 418	8 578	8 160	8 670	7 826	...	...	...	...	Norvège
Portugal	325	153	464	396	107	435	394	201	...	...	Portugal
Sweden	13 435	12 333	10 855	11 727	11 699	11 734	12 612	11 995	12 127	9 541	Suède
East Europe											***Europe de l'est***
Czechoslovakia	49 653	50 502	[12] 37 456	[12] 35 874	53 483	54 155	53 232	52 819	53 575	53 719	Tchécoslovaquie
German Dem. Rep.[2]	22 054	22 920	23 043	24 387	23 912	87 698	78 479	75 086	74 039	71 287	Rép. dém. allemande[2]
Hungary	29 323	30 043	32 087	31 338	27 389	27 822	25 918	24 124	16 191	19 364	Hongrie
Poland	43 059	40 936	43 281	47 568	46 577	33 485	26 951	21 581	27 071	26 122	Pologne
Other Europe											***Autre Europe***
Malta[1]	454	343	293	333	317	275	378	280	271	...	Malte[1]
Yugoslavia	2 330	2 575	2 246	2 650	2 437	2 476	2 635	3 508	2 766	2 544	Yougoslavie
USSR											**URSS**

For general note and footnotes, see end of table.

Voir la fin du tableau pour la remarque générale et les notes.

Gravel and crushed stone (continued) – Graviers et pierres concassées (suite)

Unit : Thousand metric tons

Unité : Milliers de tonnes métriques

Country or area	1976	1977	1978	1979	1980	1981	1982	1983	1984	1985	Pays ou zone
Oceania											**Océanie**
Australia[8]	69 125	68 083	74 970	68 181	71 121	68 229	74 566	63 859	70 019	82 524	Australie[8]
Fiji[1]	1 034	806	436	204	* [4] 274	* [4] 210	* [4] 230	* [4] 225	* [4] 225	* [4] 105	Fidji[1]
New Caledonia[1]	108	115	...	151	160	141	154	105	130	107	Nouvelle-Calédonie[1]
New Zealand	20 785	21 402	20 133	17 841	17 846	[4] 17 632	[4] 18 323	[4] 19 858	[4] 21 530	* [4] 20 000	Nouvelle-Zélande

General note.
Pebbles and crushed or broken stone, gravel, macadam and tarred macadam of a kind commonly used for concrete aggregates, for road metalling or for railway or other ballast. Flint and shingle are included. (SITC 27340-0).

Remarque générale.
Cailloux et pierres broyées ou concassées, graviers, macadam avec ou sans enrobement, du type communément utilisé comme granulats pour le béton, comme matériel d'empierrement des routes et comme ballast pour les voies de chemin de fer ou ailleurs, y compris les silex et les galets. (CTCI 27340-0).

[1] In thousand cubic metres.
[2] Including sand.
[3] Gravel only.
[4] Source: U. S. Bureau of Mines, (Washington, D. C.).
[5] Stone only.
[6] Sand and gravel.
[7] Gravel and crushed stone sold or used by producers.
[8] Twelve months ending 30 June of year stated.
[9] Excluding gravel.
[10] Beginning 1982, series discontinued.
[11] Excluding crushed stone.
[12] Incomplete coverage.

[1] En milliers de mètres cubes.
[2] Y compris le sable.
[3] Graviers seulement.
[4] Source: U.S. Bureau of Mines, (Washington, D.C.).
[5] Pierres seulement.
[6] Sable et gravier.
[7] Graviers et pierres concassées vendus ou utilisés par les producteurs.
[8] Période de douze mois finissant le 30 juin de l'année indiquée.
[9] Non compris les graviers.
[10] A partir de 1982, la série a été abandonnée.
[11] Non compris les pierres concassées.
[12] Couverture incomplète.

Clay (total production) – Argile (production totale)

Unit : Thousand metric tons

Unité : Milliers de tonnes métriques

Country or area	1976	1977	1978	1979	1980	1981	1982	1983	1984	1985	Pays ou zone
Africa	**2 047**	**1 968**	**2 075**	**2 170**	**2 193**	**2 333**	**2 316**	**1 329**	**1 461**	**1 461**	**Afrique**
Algeria* [1]	72	39	58	49	48	59	55	52	36	50	Algérie* [1]
Burundi* [1]	3	3	3	2	2	2	2	4	2	4	Burundi* [1]
Egypt[1]	1 000	986	1 085	950	993	1 032	1 030	* 308	* 368	* 362	Egypte[1]
Ethiopia[1 2]	50	41	32	30	55	* 10	* 10	* 10	...	...	Ethiopie[1 2]
Kenya[2]	[1] 0	[1] 1	[1] 2	* [1] 2	2	2	1	1	0	0	Kenya[2]
Madagascar[1 2]	25	2	3	2	3	3	3	* 4	* 3	* 3	Madagascar[1 2]
Morocco[1]	40	26	13	15	20	23	30	31	36	27	Maroc[1]
Mozambique[1]	16	3	2	2	2	2	5	3	1	1	Mozambique[1]
Nigeria	21	31	20	[1] 35	[1] 58	[1] 40	[1] 22	[1] 21	[1] 20	[1] 20	Nigéria
Senegal	5	4	7	13	4	33	* 99	* 100	* 115	* 96	Sénégal
South Africa[1]	438	487	552	691	508	659	586	362	439	* 470	Afrique du Sud[1]
Swaziland[1 3]	1	1	0	0	0	0	0	0	0	0	Swaziland[1 3]
Tunisia[1]	195	200	210	280	300	352	* 350	* 350	* 350	* 350	Tunisie[1]
United Rep. Tanzania* [1 2]	1	1	1	1	1	1	1	1	2	2	Rép.Unie de Tanzanie* [1 2]
Zambia	102	66	20	24	106	28	27	9	* 0	* 2	Zambie
Zimbabwe[1]	...	77	67	74	91	87	95	73	* 81	* 71	Zimbabwe[1]
America, North	**48 149**	**49 111**	**52 478**	**50 099**	**45 454**	**41 448**	**33 265**	**38 177**	**40 773**	**41 891**	**Amérique du Nord**
Costa Rica* [1 2]	1	1	1	0	1	1	1	1	1	1	Costa Rica* [1 2]
Cuba	...	17	34	32	42	39	44	44	50	45	Cuba
Guatemala[1]	...	105	128	131	172	* 168	162	* 146	* 153	* 178	Guatemala[1]
Haiti* [1]	...	67	60	65	70	70	70	70	70	...	Haïti* [1]
Jamaica[1]	...	160	99	99	94	90	...	...	...	...	Jamaïque[1]
Mexico[1 4]	148	368	473	445	657	772	649	644	656	608	Mexique[1 4]
Trinidad and Tobago* [5]	118	134	135	164	156	48	210	...	...	...	Trinité-et-Tobago* [5]
United States[6]	47 527	48 259	51 548	49 163	44 262	40 260	32 064	37 066	39 646	40 800	Etats-Unis[6]
America, South	**6 790**	**7 905**	**9 185**	**8 709**	**10 156**	**28 098**	**27 941**	**27 869**	**28 681**	**28 562**	**Amérique du Sud**
Argentina	2 146	2 789	3 163	2 913	2 829	2 199	1 847	2 393	2 608	1 650	Argentine
Brazil[7]	3 229	3 514	4 457	3 900	5 582	21 601	22 160	21 784	22 477	* 23 000	Brésil[7]
Chile	108	129	127	189	214	234	55	73	68	49	Chili
Colombia[1 2]	761	790	783	819	787	810	856	1 011	938	1 041	Colombie[1 2]
Ecuador[1 2]	3	5	4	4	4	4	5	1	1	2	Equateur[1 2]
Paraguay[1 2]	14	22	35	40	50	70	55	45	50	50	Paraguay[1 2]
Peru[1]	...	316	253	472	347	* 799	* 795	* 795	* 797	* 797	Pérou[1]
Uruguay* [1]	310	330	340	350	321	300	279	152	71	150	Uruguay* [1]
Venezuela[1]	[2] 10	[2] 10	[2] 23	[2] 22	[2] 22	2 081	1 889	1 615	1 671	1 823	Venezuela[1]
Asia	**3 686**	**3 479**	**4 218**	**4 700**	**4 390**	**3 904**	**3 976**	**3 787**	**4 007**	**4 295**	**Asie**
Bangladesh[2]	4	5	6	7	11	10	6	5	3	4	Bangladesh[2]
Burma	* [1] 13	[1] 14	[1] 13	[1] 17	[1] 15	[1] 6	[1] 4	3	3	4	Birmanie
Cyprus	102	214	250	371	380	165	188	230	220	212	Chypre
Hong Kong[8]	1	2	89	3	1	8	31	52	92	92	Hong-kong[8]
India	1 403	1 289	1 320	1 493	1 667	1 550	1 606	1 541	1 677	1 777	Inde
Indonesia[2]	29	38	37	59	75	81	77	60	* 84	* 90	Indonésie[2]
Iran(Islamic Rep.of)[1]	[9] 249	[9] 135	# 290	* 250	220	150	171	* 155	* 155	* 155	Iran(Rép.islamique)[1]
Israel	49	[1] 45	[1] 58	[1] 66	[1] 74	[1] 62	[1] 84	[1] 61	* [1] 67	84	Israël
Japan	625	* 625	* 626	* 617	777	722	682	671	635	684	Japon
Jordan[1]	...	...	9	25	30	20	14	8	26	26	Jordanie[1]
Korea, Republic of[2]	470	357	367	374	273	223	175	232	212	207	Corée, République de[2]
Malaysia[2 10]	26	32	31	33	46	44	44	57	72	83	Malaisie[2 10]
Pakistan[11]	65	63	104	103	108	120	124	140	* 126	* 102	Pakistan[11]
Philippines	499	519	523	859	505	601	591	419	418	376	Philippines
Sri Lanka[3]	5	5	6	6	7	7	8	8	2	6	Sri Lanka[3]
Thailand[2]	24	25	34	43	20	14	18	36	59	107	Thaïlande[2]
Turkey	[12] 105	* [1] 93	* [1] 454	* [1] 373	* [1] 180	* [1] 120	* [1] 152	* [1] 108	* [1] 155	* [1] 285	Turquie
Viet Nam* [1 2]	...	1	1	1	1	1	1	1	1	1	Viet Nam* [1 2]
Europe	**56 009**	**55 540**	**61 484**	**57 945**	**55 402**	**58 323**	**58 465**	**60 092**	**52 620**	**51 578**	**Europe**
EEC	***39 131***	***37 663***	***39 753***	***36 409***	***33 687***	***31 333***	***31 767***	***34 427***	***30 560***	***31 842***	***CEE***
Belgium[2]	106	109	154	65	61	54	53	59	69	37	Belgique[2]
Denmark[2]	* [1] 5	* [1] 5	* [1] 5	* [1] 20	* [1] 20	* [1] 20	* [1] 20	* [1] 20	* [1] 20	19	Danemark[2]
France	324	329	311	361	371	364	392	* 395	* 321	* 367	France
Germany, Fed. Rep.	6 405	6 659	6 858	6 823	6 877	6 358	5 394	6 047	6 443	6 231	Allemagne, Rép. féd.
Greece[9]	[1] 365	598	456	528	538	329	450	452	...	...	Grèce[9]
Italy	602	648	675	643	651	704	684	749	779	819	Italie

For general note and footnotes, see end of table.

Voir la fin du tableau pour la remarque générale et les notes.

Clay (total production) (continued) – Argile (production totale) (suite)

Unit : Thousand metric tons — Unité : Milliers de tonnes métriques

Country or area	1976	1977	1978	1979	1980	1981	1982	1983	1984	1985	Pays ou zone
United Kingdom	31 324	29 315	31 294	27 969	25 169	23 504	24 774	26 705	22 467	23 794	Royaume–Uni
EFTA	***885***	***855***	***4 588***	***4 765***	***6 143***	***5 178***	***4 756***	***4 782***	***3 096***	***5 629***	***AELE***
Austria	313	340	309	376	402	368	367	436	474	550	Autriche
Finland	33	38	45	51	62	61	57	45	49	...	Finlande
Portugal	149	179	3 890	4 011	5 322	4 460	4 027	3 996	2 377	...	Portugal
Sweden[2]	...	298	344	327	357	289	305	305	196	106	Suède[2]
East Europe	***2 486***	***2 604***	***2 880***	***2 982***	***3 004***	***3 271***	***3 055***	***3 092***	***2 982***	***2 913***	***Europe de l'est***
Bulgaria[2]	194	194	199	202	208	458	389	402	409	403	Bulgarie[2]
Czechoslovakia	[3] 545	[3] 580	[3] 499	654	660	652	648	662	668	675	Tchécoslovaquie
German Dem. Rep.[1 2]	...	...	...	[13] 190	[13] 200	[13] 200	[13] 210	[13] 200	* 175	* 175	Rép. dém. allemande[1 2]
Hungary[9]	143	158	157	136	130	133	130	117	103	90	Hongrie[9]
Poland	1 236	1 307	1 300	1 257	1 226	1 242	1 093	1 124	1 037	980	Pologne
Romania* [1 9]	155	155	519	543	580	586	585	587	590	590	Roumanie* [1 9]
Other Europe	***13 507***	***14 418***	***14 263***	***13 789***	***12 568***	***18 541***	***18 887***	***17 791***	***15 982***	***11 194***	***Autre Europe***
Spain	13 175	14 113	13 908	13 398	12 225	18 166	18 550	17 447	15 732	* 10 967	Espagne
Yugoslavia	332	305	355	391	343	375	337	344	250	227	Yougoslavie
USSR* [1 14]	**2 177**	**2 268**	**2 359**	**2 540**	**2 540**	**2 500**	**2 500**	**2 600**	**2 800**	**2 900**	**URSS* [1 14]**
Oceania	**10 378**	**10 027**	**10 056**	**9 326**	**10 289**	**9 502**	**9 208**	**6 838**	**7 429**	**10 791**	**Océanie**
Australia[11]	10 058	9 759	9 904	9 190	10 112	9 320	9 048	6 714	7 251	* 10 615	Australie[11]
New Zealand[1]	320	268	152	136	177	182	160	124	* 178	* 176	Nouvelle–Zélande[1]
Total	**129 236**	**130 298**	**141 855**	**135 489**	**130 424**	**146 108**	**137 671**	**140 692**	**137 771**	**141 478**	**Total**

General note.
All natural crude clayey substances consisting of earth or rocks of sedimentation origin with basis of aluminium silicates such as kaolin, bentonite, andalusite etc. Expanded clays are excluded. (SITC 27621–0).

1 Source: U. S. Bureau of Mines, (Washington, D. C.).
2 Kaolin only.
3 Data refer to kaolin.
4 Beginning 1977, scope of series revised.
5 Estimated data.
6 Sold or used by producers.
7 Gross weight only.
8 Data refer to kaolin except for 1978 which includes 63805 tons of crude clay.
9 Data refer to kaolin and bentonite.
10 Data refer to Peninsular Malaysia only.
11 Twelve months ending 30 June of year stated.
12 Limited coverage.
13 Marketable production.
14 Kaolin including china clay.

Remarque générale.
Toutes substances argileuses naturelles à l'état brut, constituées de roches ou terres sédimentaires à base silico–alumineuse telles que le kaolin, la bentonite, l'andalousite etc., à l'exclusion des argiles expansées. (CTCI 27621–0).

1 Source: U.S. Bureau of Mines, (Washington, D.C.).
2 Kaolin seulement.
3 Données se rapportant au kaolin.
4 A partir de 1977, portée de la série révisée.
5 Données estimatives.
6 Vendu ou utilisé par les producteurs.
7 Poids brut seulement.
8 Données se rapportant au kaolin, sauf pour 1978. La production de 1978 comprend 63805 tonnes d'argile brute.
9 Données se rapportant au kaolin et à la bentonite.
10 Données se rapportant à la Malaisie péninsulaire seulement.
11 Période de douze mois finissant le 30 juin de l'année indiquée.
12 Couverture limitée.
13 Production commercialisable.
14 Kaolin, y compris l'argile à porcelaine.

Bentonite

Unit : Thousand metric tons — Unité : Milliers de tonnes métriques

Country or area	1976	1977	1978	1979	1980	1981	1982	1983	1984	1985	Pays ou zone
Africa	**182**	**152**	**159**	**163**	**162**	**165**	**162**	**139**	**142**	**151**	**Afrique**
Algeria* [1]	39	24	36	35	35	35	35	30	24	33	Algérie* [1]
Egypt	...	4	3	2	3	3	3	2	3	3	Egypte
Morocco	3	5	5	1	3	3	5	4	2	* 3	Maroc
Mozambique	16	3	2	2	2	2	2	0	1	0	Mozambique
South Africa	40	37	35	46	50	44	31	40	42	42	Afrique du Sud
Zimbabwe	...	...	...	...	69	78	86	63	70	70	Zimbabwe
America, North	**3 666**	**3 461**	**4 199**	**4 189**	**3 982**	**4 719**	**3 139**	**2 860**	**3 150**	**3 183**	**Amérique du Nord**
Cuba	...	...	...	...	7	7	7	7	12	13	Cuba
Guatemala [1]	0	...	3	* 3	3	* 3	3	* 8	* 9	* 3	Guatemala [1]
Mexico	[1] 56	[1] 59	[1] 140	[1] 170	[1] 176	[1] 221	[1] 185	[1] 226	[1] 267	268	Mexique
United States	3 610	3 399	4 053	4 012	3 796	4 488	2 944	2 619	2 862	2 899	Etats–Unis
America, South	**316**	**254**	**294**	**388**	**397**	**320**	**318**	**295**	**295**	**391**	**Amérique du Sud**
Argentina	132	115	107	157	131	123	123	135	62	159	Argentine
Brazil	143	108	168	213	248	166	164	129	201	* 200	Brésil
Colombia [1]	* 1	0	0	0	...	...	...	...	...	...	Colombie [1]
Peru [1]	40	31	19	18	18	31	31	* 31	32	* 32	Pérou [1]
Asia	**648**	**602**	**621**	**598**	**797**	**762**	**699**	**618**	**625**	**750**	**Asie**
Burma	0	1	2	1	2	3	3	1	1	1	Birmanie
Cyprus	3	13	9	7	24	47	13	32	32	52	Chypre
India	138	151	153	147	159	144	142	95	127	139	Inde
Iran(Islamic Rep.of)* [1]	50	23	40	20	20	10	11	10	10	10	Iran(Rép.islamique)* [1]
Israel [1,2]	15	8	7	6	18	13	12	7	* 12	* 12	Israël [1,2]
Japan	[1] 399	* [1] 399	* [1] 399	* [1] 399	548	512	484	441	410	462	Japon
Pakistan	1	1	1	1	1	1	1	1	* 2	* 2	Pakistan
Philippines [1]	2	2	2	3	5	6	5	1	* 3	25	Philippines [1]
Turkey* [1]	40	4	8	14	20	...	...	...	28	47	Turquie* [1]
Europe	**1 145**	**1 328**	**1 331**	**1 520**	**1 565**	**1 340**	**1 410**	**1 443**	**1 445**	**1 442**	**Europe**
EEC	***716***	***881***	***789***	***955***	***987***	***751***	***807***	***872***	***899***	***898***	***CEE***
France [1]	* 14	8	* 16	16	* 3	* 3	* 3	* 3	* 4	* 3	France [1]
Germany, Fed. Rep.	...	...	...	...	...	...	...	...	154	169	Allemagne, Rép. féd.
Greece	305	431	376	495	499	297	405	410	...	...	Grèce
Italy	235	280	235	282	323	289	237	297	319	299	Italie
East Europe	***321***	***332***	***434***	***444***	***481***	***471***	***491***	***488***	***473***	***471***	***Europe de l'est***
Bulgaria	...	...	...	...	...	137	152	160	153	146	Bulgarie
Hungary	71	80	82	72	78	81	85	80	64	60	Hongrie
Poland	* [1] 50	* [1] 50	* [1] 50	* [1] 50	82	77	79	71	76	85	Pologne
Romania [1]	64	64	162	180	177	176	175	177	180	* 180	Roumanie [1]
Other Europe	***108***	***115***	***108***	***121***	***98***	***118***	***112***	***83***	***73***	***73***	***Autre Europe***
Spain	108	115	108	121	98	118	112	83	73	* 73	Espagne
Oceania	**6**	**9**	**15**	**12**	**14**	**18**	**35**	**32**	**39**	**36**	**Océanie**
Australia	...	[1] 6	[1] 5	[1] 7	[1] 11	[1] 16	[1] 29	* [1] 30	32	30	Australie
New Zealand [1,3,4]	1	3	10	5	3	2	6	2	7	6	Nouvelle–Zélande [1,3,4]
Total	**5 963**	**5 806**	**6 619**	**6 870**	**6 918**	**7 323**	**5 763**	**5 387**	**5 696**	**5 953**	**Total**

General note.
Bentonite is a clay derived from volcanic ash, largely used as an ingredient of moulding sand, as a filtering and de–colourizing agent in oil refining, and for de–greasing of textiles. (SITC 27621–1).

[1] Source: U. S. Bureau of Mines, (Washington, D. C.).
[2] Metabentonite only.
[3] Processed bentonite.
[4] Including unprocessed bentonite.

Remarque générale.
La bentonite, matière argileuse provenant de cendres d'origine volcanique, principalement utilisée dans la préparation du sable de moulage, comme élément filtrant et décolorant dans la raffinage des huiles et pour le dégraissage des draps. (CTCI 27621–1).

[1] Source: U.S. Bureau of Mines, (Washington, D.C.).
[2] Metabentonite seulement.
[3] Bentonite façonnée.
[4] Y compris la bentonite non traitée.

Fuller's earth – Terre à foulon

Unit : Thousand metric tons

Unité : Milliers de tonnes métriques

Country or area	1976	1977	1978	1979	1980	1981	1982	1983	1984	1985	Pays ou zone
Africa	**65**	**29**	**20**	**33**	**27**	**59**	**129**	**132**	**153**	**124**	**Afrique**
Algeria* [1 2]	22	4	5	5	5	5	5	5	4	4	Algérie* [1 2]
Morocco[3]	37	21	8	14	17	20	25	27	34	24	Maroc[3]
Senegal[1 2]	5	3	7	13	4	33	99	100	115	96	Sénégal[1 2]
South Africa[2]	...	...	0	1	1	1	0	0	0	0	Afrique du Sud[2]
America, North	**1 237**	**1 357**	**1 429**	**1 472**	**1 448**	**1 567**	**1 569**	**1 776**	**1 769**	**1 926**	**Amérique du Nord**
Mexico	[2] 20	[2] 61	[2] 41	[2] 49	[2] 57	[2] 65	[2] 43	[2] 42	[2] 46	58	Mexique
United States[4]	1 217	1 296	1 388	1 423	1 391	1 502	1 526	1 734	1 723	1 868	Etats-Unis[4]
America, South	**0**	**4**	**3**	**5**	**5**	**5**	**12**	**7**	**4**	**5**	**Amérique du Sud**
Argentina[2]	0	4	3	5	5	5	12	7	4	* 5	Argentine[2]
Asia	**35**	**32**	**33**	**51**	**60**	**47**	**41**	**56**	**38**	**49**	**Asie**
India	16	14	15	17	33	26	26	35	20	...	Inde
Pakistan	19	18	18	34	27	21	15	21	* 18	* 17	Pakistan
Europe	**1 096**	**1 112**	**1 184**	**1 140**	**1 159**	**1 269**	**1 431**	**1 321**	**1 326**	**1 403**	**Europe**
EEC	***967***	***970***	***963***	***913***	***908***	***951***	***1 071***	***1 053***	***990***	***1 023***	***CEE***
Germany, Fed. Rep.	...	...	...	...	...	...	821	766	674	701	Allemagne, Rép. féd.
Italy[2]	25	6	* 4	* 1	4	5	7	20	* 30	* 30	Italie[2]
United Kingdom[5]	201	223	218	171	163	205	243	267	286	292	Royaume-Uni[5]
EFTA	***85***	***106***	***182***	***165***	***203***	***276***	***318***	***223***	***292***	***336***	***AELE***
Portugal	85	106	182	165	203	276	318	223	292	...	Portugal
Other Europe	***44***	***36***	***39***	***62***	***48***	***42***	***42***	***45***	***44***	***44***	***Autre Europe***
Spain[2]	...	* 36	39	62	48	42	42	45	44	* 44	Espagne[2]
Oceania	**15**	**15**	**15**	**15**	**15**	**15**	**15**	**15**	**15**	**15**	**Océanie**
Australia[2]	...	...	...	...	...	...	15	* 15	* 15	* 15	Australie[2]
Total	**2 448**	**2 548**	**2 684**	**2 716**	**2 714**	**2 962**	**3 197**	**3 307**	**3 305**	**3 521**	**Total**

General note.
Fuller's earth is a natural earthy material extensively used to decolourize and deodorize vegetable and mineral oils, fats and waxes. (SITC 27621-2).

[1] Attapulgite.
[2] Source: U. S. Bureau of Mines, (Washington, D. C.).
[3] Smectite only.
[4] Sold or used by producers.
[5] Including bentonite.

Remarque générale.
La terre à foulon, une matérielle terreux naturelle très employée pour décolorer et désodoriser les huiles, les graisses et les cires végétales et minérales. (CTCI 27621-2).

[1] Attapulgite.
[2] Source: U.S. Bureau of Mines, (Washington, D.C.).
[3] Smectite seulement.
[4] Vendu ou utilisé par les producteurs.
[5] Y compris la bentonite.

Kaolin

Unit : Thousand metric tons — Unité : Millers de tonnes métriques

Country or area	1976	1977	1978	1979	1980	1981	1982	1983	1984	1985	Pays ou zone
Africa	**190**	**203**	**233**	**245**	**231**	**231**	**214**	**268**	**276**	**272**	**Afrique**
Algeria[1]	* 11	11	17	9	* 8	* 19	* 15	* 17	* 8	* 13	Algérie[1]
Angola[1]	...	1	...	...	...	...	...	...	...	...	Angola[1]
Burundi* [1]	...	...	...	2	2	2	2	4	2	4	Burundi* [1]
Egypt	29	47	46	42	45	32	50	100	120	118	Egypte
Ethiopia[1 2]	* 50	* 41	32	30	55	* 10	* 10	* 10	...	...	Ethiopie[1 2]
Kenya	...	[1]1	[1]2	* [1]2	2	2	1	1	0	0	Kenya
Madagascar	25	2	3	2	3	3	2	4	* 3	* 3	Madagascar
Mozambique	0	0	0	0	0	0	0	3	0	0	Mozambique
Nigeria[1]	...	* 1	1	1	1	1	* 1	* 1	* 0	* 0	Nigéria[1]
South Africa	[1]60	[1]89	[1]122	[1]149	[1]108	155	128	* 125	* 132	128	Afrique du Sud
Swaziland[1]	1	1	0	0	0	0	0	0	0	0	Swaziland[1]
United Rep. Tanzania* [1]	1	1	1	1	1	1	1	1	0	0	Rép.Unie de Tanzanie* [1]
Zimbabwe	...	...	...	...	5	5	3	1	2	2	Zimbabwe
America, North	**5 655**	**6 101**	**6 542**	**7 153**	**7 455**	**7 190**	**5 982**	**6 734**	**7 384**	**7 385**	**Amérique du Nord**
Costa Rica* [1]	...	1	1	1	1	1	1	1	1	...	Costa Rica* [1]
Cuba	...	...	...	...	35	32	37	37	38	32	Cuba
Mexico	[1]72	[1]178	[1]180	[1]77	[1]271	[1]208	[1]172	[1]162	[1]130	282	Mexique
United States[3]	5 547	5 887	6 326	7 040	7 148	6 949	5 772	6 534	7 215	7 070	Etats–Unis[3]
America, South	**552**	**1 220**	**1 237**	**1 431**	**1 430**	**1 517**	**1 524**	**1 685**	**1 634**	**1 767**	**Amérique du Sud**
Argentina	84	74	46	132	92	67	72	145	91	100	Argentine
Brazil	210	260	294	349	410	470	493	420	486	* 500	Brésil
Chile	67	56	48	59	59	57	21	41	49	49	Chili
Colombia[1]	150	790	783	819	787	810	856	1 011	938	* 1 041	Colombie[1]
Ecuador[1]	* 3	5	4	* 4	4	3	5	1	1	* 2	Equateur[1]
Paraguay[1]	* 14	* 22	35	40	50	70	* 55	45	50	50	Paraguay[1]
Peru[1]	14	3	4	6	6	* 6	* 6	* 6	* 6	* 6	Pérou[1]
Venezuela	10	10	23	22	22	34	16	16	13	19	Venezuela
Asia	**1 301**	**1 280**	**1 409**	**1 505**	**1 375**	**1 336**	**1 306**	**1 426**	**1 508**	**1 695**	**Asie**
Bangladesh[4]	[1]4	[1]5	[1]5	[1]7	[1]11	[1]10	[1]6	[1]5	3	4	Bangladesh[4]
Hong Kong	1	2	26	3	1	8	0	1	0	10	Hong–kong
India	391	395	416	489	460	504	555	595	641	758	Inde
Indonesia	29	38	37	59	75	81	77	60	* 84	* 90	Indonésie
Iran(Islamic Rep.of)[1]	127	112	* 180	160	* 150	* 100	* 110	* 100	* 100	* 100	Iran(Rép.islamique)[1]
Israel[1]	10	5	6	23	10	37	12	27	* 27	* 27	Israël[1]
Japan	226	226	227	218	229	210	198	230	225	222	Japon
Korea, Republic of	380	357	367	374	273	223	175	232	212	207	Corée, République de
Malaysia	[1]26	32	31	33	46	44	44	57	72	83	Malaisie
Pakistan[1]	1	1	14	15	27	41	45	13	18	5	Pakistan[1]
Philippines	...	...	...	...	15	11	7	11	9	6	Philippines
Sri Lanka	5	5	5	6	7	7	8	8	2	6	Sri Lanka
Thailand	16	25	34	43	20	14	18	36	59	107	Thaïlande
Turkey* [1]	65	59	44	59	50	45	50	50	55	69	Turquie* [1]
Viet Nam* [1]	...	...	1	1	1	1	1	1	1	1	Viet Nam* [1]
Europe	**8 234**	**8 792**	**8 917**	**9 260**	**9 369**	**8 744**	**7 913**	**8 652**	**10 296**	**9 860**	**Europe**
EEC	***5 905***	***6 493***	***6 387***	***6 721***	***6 727***	***6 105***	***5 217***	***5 860***	***6 694***	***6 709***	***CEE***
Belgium	* 100	* 118	* 118	65	61	54	53	59	69	37	Belgique
Denmark	...	...	...	0	0	0	5	* 20	* 20	14	Danemark
France[5]	300	294	265	315	338	331	347	349	265	314	France[5]
Germany, Fed. Rep.[6]	...	...	...	...	2 232	2 075	1 326	1 969	2 580	2 473	Allemagne, Rép. féd.[6]
Greece	60	55	52	31	39	32	45	42	75	...	Grèce
Italy	108	101	73	93	93	105	83	75	78	60	Italie
United Kingdom[7]	3 847	4 343	4 199	4 444	3 964	3 508	3 358	3 346	3 607	3 762	Royaume–Uni[7]
EFTA	***727***	***645***	***697***	***740***	***785***	***718***	***754***	***815***	***1 560***	***1 081***	***AELE***
Austria[8]	271	272	276	330	341	316	351	403	456	501	Autriche[8]
Finland	2	2	3	3	* 4	* 5	* 4	4	4	...	Finlande
Portugal	64	73	74	80	83	108	94	103	904	...	Portugal
Sweden	...	298	344	327	357	289	305	305	196	106	Suède
East Europe	***1 209***	***1 244***	***1 402***	***1 381***	***1 432***	***1 434***	***1 483***	***1 482***	***1 473***	***1 475***	***Europe de l'est***
Bulgaria	194	194	199	202	208	221	237	242	256	257	Bulgarie

For general note and footnotes, see end of table.
Voir la fin du tableau pour la remarque générale et les notes.

Unit : Thousand metric tons

Unité : Millers de tonnes métriques

Country or area	1976	1977	1978	1979	1980	1981	1982	1983	1984	1985	Pays ou zone
Czechoslovakia	545	580	499	513	518	508	529	539	540	548	Tchécoslovaquie
German Dem. Rep.* [1]	...	...	...	190	200	200	210	200	175	175	Rép. dém. allemande* [1]
Hungary	72	78	75	64	52	52	45	37	39	30	Hongrie
Poland	[1] 94	[1] 91	[1] 66	[1] 49	51	43	52	54	53	55	Pologne
Romania [1]	91	* 91	* 357	* 363	403	* 410	* 410	* 410	* 410	* 410	Roumanie [1]
Other Europe	***393***	***410***	***431***	***418***	***425***	***487***	***459***	***495***	***569***	***595***	***Autre Europe***
Spain	262	299	251	240	228	262	239	255	319	350	Espagne
Yugoslavia	...	111	180	178	197	225	220	240	* 250	245	Yougoslavie
USSR* [1]	**2 177**	**2 268**	**2 359**	**2 540**	**2 540**	**2 500**	**2 500**	**2 600**	**2 800**	**2 900**	**URSS* [1]**
Oceania	**102**	**174**	**125**	**132**	**172**	**183**	**158**	**145**	**185**	**160**	**Océanie**
Australia	* 75	80	91	107	126	134	134	121	160	135	Australie
New Zealand [1]	27	94	34	25	46	49	24	24	* 25	* 25	Nouvelle–Zélande [1]
Total	**18 210**	**20 038**	**20 822**	**22 265**	**22 572**	**21 701**	**19 597**	**21 510**	**24 083**	**24 038**	**Total**

General note.
Kaolin, a high grade, white or nearly white plastic clay used in the porcelain and paper making industries. Kaolin–bearing sands are excluded. (SITC 27621–3).

Remarque générale.
Le kaolin est une argile plastique blanche, ou presque blanche, de première qualité, servant de matière première dans l'industrie de la porcelaine et de matière de charge dans la fabrication du papier. Les sables kaoliniques ne sont pas compris. (CTCI 27621–3).

[1] Source: U. S. Bureau of Mines, (Washington, D. C.).
[2] Including Eritrea.
[3] Kaolin sold or used by producers.
[4] Twelve months ending 30 June of year stated.
[5] Including kaolinitic clay.
[6] Prior to 1980, data are confidential.
[7] Data refer to china clay and ball clay.
[8] Including bleaching earths.

[1] Source: U.S. Bureau of Mines, (Washington, D.C.).
[2] Y compris l'Erythrée.
[3] Argiles kaoliniques vendues ou utilitisées par les producteurs.
[4] Période de douze mois finissant le 30 juin de l'année indiquée.
[5] Y compris les argiles kaoliniques.
[6] Avant 1980, les données sont confidentielles.
[7] Données se rapportant à l'argile à porcelaine et à l'argile figurine.
[8] Y compris les terres décolorantes.

Andalusite, kyanite and sillimanite – Andalousite, cyanite et sillimanite

Unit : Thousand metric tons

Unité : Milliers de tonnes métriques

Country or area	1976	1977	1978	1979	1980	1981	1982	1983	1984	1985	Pays ou zone
Africa	**103.2**	**128.5**	**121.6**	**153.8**	**212.7**	**196.8**	**165.8**	**117.4**	**144.6**	**187.0**	**Afrique**
South Africa[1 2]	103.2	128.5	121.6	153.8	212.7	196.8	165.8	117.4	144.6	187.0	Afrique du Sud[1 2]
America, North	**38.3**	**36.5**	**34.5**	**36.9**	**36.8**	**38.1**	**24.5**	**20.9**	**24.5**	**24.5**	**Amérique du Nord**
United States[3]	38.3	36.5	34.5	36.9	36.8	38.1	24.5	20.9	24.5	24.5	Etats-Unis[3]
America, South	**0.1**	**0.0**	**1.4**	**1.3**	**4.1**	**1.6**	**0.4**	**0.4**	**1.3**	**1.2**	**Amérique du Sud**
Brazil[4]	0.1	0.0	1.4	1.3	4.1	1.6	0.4	0.4	1.3	* 1.2	Brésil[4]
Asia	**62.8**	**57.6**	**44.7**	**56.9**	**63.7**	**49.1**	**50.8**	**53.7**	**54.7**	**48.4**	**Asie**
India[5]	62.3	57.5	44.6	56.8	63.6	49.0	50.8	53.4	54.5	48.2	Inde[5]
Korea, Republic of[1 6]	0.5	0.1	0.1	0.1	0.1	0.1	0.0	0.3	0.2	0.2	Corée, République de[1 6]
Europe	**1 127.0**	**1 100.2**	**1 064.4**	**1 023.5**	**983.6**	**1 028.5**	**898.0**	**737.9**	**812.0**	**884.5**	**Europe**
EEC	***1 121.5***	***1 097.2***	***1 059.3***	***1 018.2***	***977.1***	***1 022.0***	***892.0***	***732.0***	***809.0***	***881.0***	***CEE***
France* [1]	10.0	26.8	30.0	30.0	30.0	30.0	42.0	43.0	52.0	50.0	France* [1]
United Kingdom[7]	...	...	...	...	...	992.0	850.0	689.0	757.0	831.0	Royaume-Uni[7]
Other Europe	***5.5***	***3.0***	***5.1***	***5.4***	***6.5***	***6.5***	***6.0***	***5.9***	***3.0***	***3.5***	***Autre Europe***
Spain	5.5	3.0	5.1	5.4	6.5	6.5	6.0	5.9	3.0	3.5	Espagne
Oceania	**0.6**	**0.7**	**0.6**	**0.5**	**0.5**	**0.6**	**0.6**	**0.4**	**0.3**	**0.5**	**Océanie**
Australia[8]	0.6	0.7	0.6	0.5	0.5	0.6	0.6	0.4	0.3	* 0.5	Australie[8]
Total	**1 331.9**	**1 323.6**	**1 267.1**	**1 272.9**	**1 301.4**	**1 314.7**	**1 140.1**	**930.6**	**1 037.4**	**1 146.1**	**Total**

General note.
Andalusite, Kyanite (or disthene) and sillimanite are natural anhydrous aluminium silicates used as refractories. (SITC 27621-4).

[1] Source: U. S. Bureau of Mines, (Washington, D. C.).
[2] Andalusite and sillimanite.
[3] Synthetic mullite only.
[4] Kyanite.
[5] Kyanite and sillimanite.
[6] Andalusite.
[7] Fire clay only.
[8] Sillimanite.

Remarque générale.
L'andalousite, la cyanite (ou disthène) et la sillimanite sont des silicates d'aluminium naturels anhydres, utilisés comme produits réfractaires. (CTCI 27621-4).

[1] Source: U.S. Bureau of Mines, (Washington, D.C.).
[2] Andalousite et sillimanite.
[3] Mullite synthétique seulement.
[4] Cyanite.
[5] Cyanite et sillimanite.
[6] Andalousite.
[7] Argile réfractaire seulement.
[8] Sillimanite.

Magnesite – Magnésite

Unit : Thousand metric tons

Unité : Milliers de tonnes métriques

Country or area	1976	1977	1978	1979	1980	1981	1982	1983	1984	1985	Pays ou zone
Africa	**133.8**	**128.1**	**107.2**	**153.8**	**157.0**	**116.8**	**92.6**	**210.8**	**366.0**	**348.3**	**Afrique**
Kenya[1]	1.0	3.6	4.0	4.0	0.0	0.0	0.0	...	* 311.3	300.0	Kenya[1]
South Africa	62.9	49.2	37.4	65.3	* 78.8	56.6	* 31.9	* 22.6	33.1	28.9	Afrique du Sud
Zimbabwe	69.9	75.3	65.8	84.5	78.2	60.2	60.7	24.1	21.6	19.4	Zimbabwe
America, North	**40.8**	**24.4**	**47.2**	**42.9**	**47.0**	**44.1**	**64.3**	**66.5**	**70.9**	**64.2**	**Amérique du Nord**
Cuba	...	...	...	24.9	31.2	32.0	41.9	43.3	40.5	44.9	Cuba
Mexico	23.2	3.5	23.1	18.0	15.9	12.1	22.5	23.2	30.4	19.3	Mexique
America, South	**416.4**	**482.9**	**411.3**	**591.8**	**789.6**	**619.9**	**507.0**	**488.1**	**726.0**	**501.7**	**Amérique du Sud**
Bolivia	0.1	0.0	0.0	0.0	0.0	0.0	0.0	...	...	...	Bolivie
Brazil[2]	414.6	481.2	409.9	590.2	788.0	618.3	505.4	486.4	724.3	* 500.0	Brésil[2]
Colombia* [1]	1.7	1.8	1.4	1.6	1.6	1.6	1.6	1.6	1.6	1.6	Colombie* [1]
Asia	**3 256.3**	**3 893.6**	**4 203.7**	**4 959.7**	**5 118.9**	**5 158.0**	**5 262.5**	**5 081.3**	**5 067.6**	**5 548.5**	**Asie**
China* [1]	1 000.0	1 500.0	1 800.0	2 000.0	2 000.0	2 000.0	2 000.0	2 000.0	2 000.0	2 000.0	Chine* [1]
India	329.7	402.0	414.2	396.2	380.1	462.5	418.9	438.9	419.6	421.4	Inde
Iran(Islamic Rep.of)* [1 3]	5.0	5.0	5.0	5.0	4.0	4.0	5.0	5.0	5.0	5.0	Iran(Rép.islamique)* [1 3]
Korea, D. P. Rp.* [1]	1 500.0	1 465.0	1 560.0	1 823.0	1 900.6	1 900.6	1 900.6	1 900.6	1 900.6	1 900.6	Corée, Rp. P. D.* [1]
Nepal	...	...	...	0.1	3.3	5.0	15.0	15.0	* 15.0	* 15.0	Népal
Pakistan	8.1	1.6	2.3	3.0	1.6	0.4	1.7	1.7	3.5	5.0	Pakistan
Philippines	...	...	...	...	3.4	1.5	...	0.6	0.6	0.7	Philippines
Turkey	409.3	516.2	418.0	729.4	825.9	784.0	919.6	719.5	723.3	1 200.8	Turquie
Europe	**3 636.4**	**3 537.3**	**3 282.2**	**4 138.4**	**4 274.7**	**3 450.1**	**3 484.5**	**3 443.9**	**3 844.8**	**4 100.7**	**Europe**
EEC	***1 284.3***	***1 082.8***	***975.3***	***1 677.7***	***1 500.5***	***817.4***	***902.0***	***858.8***	***1 057.0***	***1 088.6***	***CEE***
Greece	1 284.3	1 082.8	975.3	1 677.7	1 500.5	817.4	902.0	858.8	1 057.0	1 088.6	Grèce
EFTA	***926.5***	***1 003.0***	***982.3***	***1 103.6***	***1 318.2***	***1 158.9***	***1 031.4***	***1 005.8***	***1 089.5***	***1 255.0***	***AELE***
Austria	926.5	1 003.0	982.3	1 103.6	1 318.2	1 158.9	1 031.4	1 005.8	1 089.5	1 255.0	Autriche
East Europe	***685.8***	***685.6***	***684.8***	***681.9***	***679.6***	***675.3***	***689.0***	***678.1***	***680.6***	***689.2***	***Europe de l'est***
Czechoslovakia[1]	...	...	...	...	660.0	664.0	672.0	662.0	* 660.0	* 670.0	Tchécoslovaquie[1]
Poland	26.3	25.4	23.7	20.0	19.6	11.3	17.0	16.1	20.6	19.2	Pologne
Other Europe	***739.8***	***765.9***	***639.8***	***675.2***	***776.4***	***798.6***	***862.0***	***901.1***	***1 017.6***	***1 067.9***	***Autre Europe***
Spain	348.8	421.2	306.5	381.9	514.6	* 498.9	533.6	597.1	691.5	650.5	Espagne
Yugoslavia	391.0	344.6	333.2	293.3	261.8	299.7	328.4	304.0	326.1	417.4	Yougoslavie
USSR* [1]	**1 800.0**	**1 850.0**	**1 900.0**	**2 300.0**	**1 995.8**	**2 400.0**	**2 450.0**	**2 500.0**	**2 500.0**	**2 500.0**	**URSS* [1]**
Oceania	**21.5**	**17.4**	**19.0**	**26.6**	**29.0**	**29.2**	**27.3**	**28.3**	**22.9**	**25.5**	**Océanie**
Australia[4]	...	16.9	18.1	26.6	29.0	28.9	27.0	28.1	* 22.7	* 25.4	Australie[4]
New Zealand	0.8	0.6	0.8	0.0	0.0	0.3	...	...	...	...	Nouvelle–Zélande
Total	**9 305.3**	**9 933.8**	**9 970.6**	**12 213.2**	**12 412.1**	**11 818.1**	**11 888.2**	**11 818.9**	**12 598.2**	**13 089.0**	**Total**

General note.
Natural magnesium carbonate, whether or not calcined, other than purified magnesium oxide. (SITC 27624–0).

[1] Source: U. S. Bureau of Mines, (Washington, D. C.).
[2] Gross weight only.
[3] Twelve months ending 21 March of year stated.
[4] Twelve months ending 30 June of year stated.

Remarque générale.
Carbonate de magnésium naturel, calciné ou non, à l'exclusion de l'oxyde de magnésium purifié. (CTCI 27624–0).

[1] Source: U.S. Bureau of Mines, (Washington, D.C.).
[2] Poids brut seulement.
[3] Période de douze mois finissant le 21 mars de l'année indiquée.
[4] Période de douze mois finissant le 30 juin de l'année indiquée.

Chalk – Craie

Unit : Thousand metric tons — Unité : Milliers de tonnes métriques

Country or area	1976	1977	1978	1979	1980	1981	1982	1983	1984	1985	Pays ou zone
America, South	**289**	**416**	**277**	**375**	**518**	**480**	**488**	**478**	**470**	**470**	**Amérique du Sud**
Argentina	40	53	7	13	33	5	18	8	0	0	Argentine
Peru[1]	249	363	270	362	485	475	* 470	* 470	* 470	* 470	Pérou[1]
Asia	**62**	**62**	**76**	**81**	**90**	**87**	**92**	**96**	**106**	**122**	**Asie**
India	61	61	75	80	87	86	90	94	104	120	Inde
Pakistan[2]	1	1	1	1	3	1	2	2	* 2	* 2	Pakistan[2]
Europe	**21 529**	**21 667**	**21 724**	**21 708**	**19 119**	**17 024**	**17 073**	**17 889**	**17 710**	**17 778**	**Europe**
EEC	***20 936***	***20 951***	***21 008***	***20 962***	***18 368***	***16 306***	***16 266***	***17 070***	***16 882***	***16 918***	***CEE***
Belgium	351	441	427	400	327	273	328	260	409	446	Belgique
Denmark	90	124	111	123	115	112	154	183	220	203	Danemark
Germany, Fed. Rep.	232	208	224	249	269	240	243	272	306	321	Allemagne, Rép. féd.
Italy	3 925	...	...	...	...	...	...	...	...	...	Italie
United Kingdom	16 338	16 253	16 321	16 265	13 732	11 756	11 616	12 430	12 022	12 023	Royaume–Uni
EFTA	***126***	***132***	***176***	***163***	***157***	***134***	***159***	***165***	***172***	***173***	***AELE***
Austria	21	21	21	20	21	21	20	19	20	18	Autriche
Norway	67	75	123	107	102	79	...	...	...	...	Norvège
Sweden	38	36	32	36	34	34	34	38	40	40	Suède
East Europe	***259***	***252***	***256***	***291***	***303***	***289***	***233***	***253***	***265***	***264***	***Europe de l'est***
Poland	259	252	256	291	303	289	233	253	265	264	Pologne
Other Europe	***208***	***332***	***284***	***292***	***291***	***295***	***415***	***401***	***391***	***423***	***Autre Europe***
Spain	202	324	277	282	278	278	398	377	362	...	Espagne
Yugoslavia	6	8	7	10	13	17	17	24	29	28	Yougoslavie
Total	**21 880**	**22 145**	**22 077**	**22 164**	**19 727**	**17 591**	**17 653**	**18 463**	**18 286**	**18 370**	**Total**

General note.
Natural calcium carbonate. Phosphatic chalk, steatite and powder chalk prepared are excluded. (SITC 27691–0).

[1] Source: U. S. Bureau of Mines, (Washington, D. C.).
[2] Twelve months ending 30 June of year stated.

Remarque générale.
Carbonate de calcium naturel, à l'exclusion de la craie phosphatée, de la stéatite et de la poudre de craie préparée. (CTCI 27691–0).

[1] Source: U.S. Bureau of Mines, (Washington, D.C.).
[2] Période de douze mois finissant le 30 juin de l'année indiquée.

Guano

Unit : Metric tons — Unité : Tonnes métriques

Country or area	1976	1977	1978	1979	1980	1981	1982	1983	1984	1985	Pays ou zone
Africa	**5 889**	**5 332**	**6 177**	**6 383**	**4 335**	**1 490**	**0**	**7**	**6**	**6**	**Afrique**
Kenya[1]	219	55	...	0	50	50	0	...	6	6	Kenya[1]
Seychelles[2]	5 670	5 277	6 089	6 383	4 285	1 440	0	0	0	0	Seychelles[2]
America, South	**17 907**	**7 017**	**240**	**5**	**14**	**1 198**	**79**	**132**	**3**	**3 153**	**Amérique du Sud**
Chile	16 107	7 017	240	0	0	1 100	50	129	0	3 150	Chili
Peru[1]	1 800	0	0	5	14	98	* 29	* 3	...	...	Pérou[1]
Asia	**1 763**	**162**	**821**	**3 158**	**24 836**	**2 055**	**15 259**	**610**	**508**	**1 228**	**Asie**
Philippines	1 763	162	821	3 158	24 836	2 055	15 259	610	508	1 228	Philippines
Total	**25 559**	**12 511**	**7 238**	**9 546**	**29 185**	**4 743**	**15 338**	**749**	**517**	**4 387**	**Total**

General note.
Natural animal fertilizer whether or not dehydrated but not chemically treated. (SITC 27110–1).

[1] Source: U. S. Bureau of Mines, (Washington, D. C.).
[2] Exports.

Remarque générale.
Engrais naturel d'origine animale, déshydraté ou non, mais non traité chimiquement. (CTCI 27110–1).

[1] Source: U.S. Bureau of Mines, (Washington, D.C.).
[2] Exportations.

Natural phosphates, gross weight – Phosphates naturels, poids brut

Unit : Thousand metric tons — Unité : Milliers de tonnes métriques

Country or area	1976	1977	1978	1979	1980	1981	1982	1983	1984	1985	Pays ou zone
Africa	**25 858**	**30 125**	**32 382**	**33 997**	**33 485**	**33 884**	**30 971**	**34 224**	**36 299**	**35 058**	**Afrique**
Algeria	742	1 173	1 124	1 082	1 025	915	965	* [1] 893	* [1] 1 000	* [1] 1 207	Algérie
Egypt	519	567	639	623	679	737	691	783	* 1 043	* 1 074	Egypte
Morocco	15 656	17 572	19 273	20 031	19 341	20 150	17 835	19 842	21 351	20 779	Maroc
Senegal	1 601	1 596	1 556	1 651	1 408	1 792	1 179	1 397	1 893	2 198	Sénégal
South Africa	[2] 1 731	[2] 2 403	[2] 2 699	[1] 3 221	[1] 3 185	[1] 2 718	[1] 3 161	[1] 2 887	[1] 2 585	[1] 2 421	Afrique du Sud
Togo	2 009	2 857	2 827	2 920	2 933	2 244	2 007	2 081	2 696	2 456	Togo
Tunisia	3 301	3 615	3 712	4 057	4 502	4 924	4 729	5 924	5 313	4 505	Tunisie
Uganda[1]	* 15	* 5	* 5	0	0	0	0	...	...	...	Ouganda[1]
Western Sahara[2]	173	* 232	* 440	...	...	...	...	...	...	...	Sahara occidental[2]
Zimbabwe	111	105	107	130	130	122	122	133	134	135	Zimbabwe
America, North	**44 963**	**47 616**	**50 436**	**51 827**	**54 716**	**53 955**	**37 926**	**43 071**	**49 733**	**51 498**	**Amérique du Nord**
Mexico	224	285	322	171	283	331	512	498	518	645	Mexique
Neth.Antil and Aruba[2] [3]	77	75	77	45	18	0	0	0	...	...	Antill.néer.et Aruba[2] [3]
United States	44 662	47 256	50 037	51 611	54 415	53 624	37 414	42 573	49 197	50 835	Etats–Unis
America, South	**593**	**806**	**1 145**	**1 600**	**2 582**	**2 687**	**2 816**	**3 283**	**3 888**	**4 293**	**Amérique du Sud**
Brazil	490	650	1 023	1 589	2 562	2 658	2 767	3 208	3 798	* 4 214	Brésil
Colombia[1]	13	6	2	6	6	17	20	17	* 28	* 23	Colombie[1]
Peru[1]	...	...	...	5	14	12	29	3	13	12	Pérou[1]
Venezuela[2]	80	139	109	0	0	0	0	...	...	...	Venezuela[2]
Asia	**9 581**	**10 247**	**12 621**	**16 084**	**19 504**	**20 344**	**21 008**	**21 999**	**25 609**	**23 263**	**Asie**
China* [1]	4 000	4 000	4 695	8 517	10 726	11 500	11 720	12 500	14 210	12 000	Chine* [1]
India	682	740	789	681	543	565	633	790	889	925	Inde
Indonesia[1]	7	4	6	* 5	11	8	5	6	* 2	* 3	Indonésie[1]
Israel	639	1 228	1 723	2 086	2 307	1 919	2 148	1 966	2 065	2 195	Israël
Jordan	1 702	1 769	2 320	2 828	3 911	4 244	4 390	4 746	6 120	6 067	Jordanie
Korea,Dem.Ppl's.Rep.[1]	450	500	500	550	* 550	* 550	* 500	* 500	* 500	* 500	Corée,Rép.pop.dém.de[1]
Pakistan	4	3	5	2	2	4	4	1	...	...	Pakistan
Philippines	12	10	1	2	18	8	6	4	7	6	Philippines
Syrian Arab Republic	511	425	747	1 170	1 319	1 319	1 462	1 231	1 515	1 224	Rép. arabe syrienne
Thailand	[1] 7	[1] 3	[1] 3	[1] 5	6	3	4	5	3	4	Thaïlande
Turkey	67	65	32	38	21	43	26	50	96	* 37	Turquie
Viet Nam[1]	* 1 500	* 1 500	* 1 800	# 200	* 90	* 181	* 110	* 200	* 200	* 300	Viet Nam[1]
Europe	**138**	**134**	**112**	**73**	**240**	**337**	**375**	**544**	**654**	**744**	**Europe**
EEC	***113***	***84***	***25***	***12***	***14***	***12***	***11***	***56***	***49***	***45***	***CEE***
France	28	19	25	12	14	12	11	13	...	...	France
Germany, Fed. Rep.[2]	* 85	* 65	0	0	0	0	0	...	...	...	Allemagne, Rép. féd.[2]
EFTA	***25***	***50***	***87***	***61***	***226***	***325***	***364***	***488***	***605***	***699***	***AELE***
Finland[1]	0	0	4	3	138	201	233	381	477	* 512	Finlande[1]
Sweden[1]	25	50	83	58	88	124	131	107	* 128	* 187	Suède[1]
USSR* [1]	**23 900**	**26 925**	**23 900**	**24 400**	**30 300**	**30 700**	**31 300**	**31 600**	**31 900**	**32 200**	**URSS* [1]**
Oceania	**2 536**	**3 272**	**4 281**	**3 640**	**3 807**	**2 938**	**2 837**	**2 905**	**2 628**	**2 742**	**Océanie**
Australia[4]	169	456	397	7	7	35	150	127	11	* 34	Australie[4]
Christmas Isl.(Aust)[1] [3]	1 185	1 251	1 391	1 367	1 713	1 423	1 328	1 094	1 259	1 200	Ile Christmas (Aust)[1] [3]
Kiribati[3] [5]	427	419	494	446	0	0	0	0	0	0	Kiribati[3] [5]
Nauru[1]	755	1 146	1 999	1 820	2 087	1 480	1 359	1 684	1 358	1 508	Nauru[1]
Total	**107 569**	**119 125**	**124 877**	**131 621**	**144 634**	**144 845**	**127 233**	**137 626**	**150 711**	**149 797**	**Total**

General note.
Natural calcium phosphates, natural aluminium calcium phosphates, apatite and phosphatic chalk. Guano is excluded. (SITC 27130–0).

[1] Source: U. S. Bureau of Mines, (Washington, D. C.).
[2] Source: International Superphosphate Manufacturers' Association, (London).
[3] Exports.
[4] Twelve months ending 30 June of year stated.
[5] Including data for Tuvalu (previously known as Ellice Islands). Production ceased after 1979.

Remarque générale.
Phosphates de calcium naturels, les phosphates alumino–calciques naturels, l'apatite et les craies phosphatées, à l'exclusion du guano. (CTCI 27130–0).

[1] Source: U.S. Bureau of Mines, (Washington, D.C.).
[2] Source: Association internationale des fabricants de superphosphates et d'engrais composés, (Londres).
[3] Exportations.
[4] Période de douze mois finissant le 30 juin de l'année indiquée.
[5] Y compris les données relatives à Tuvalu (anciennement îles Ellice).

Unit : Thousand metric tons — Unité : Milliers de tonnes métriques

Country or area	1976	1977	1978	1979	1980	1981	1982	1983	1984	1985	Pays ou zone
Africa	**9 045**	**10 522**	**10 208**	**10 730**	**10 369**	**10 020**	**9 950**	**10 810**	**11 423**	**10 936**	**Afrique**
Algeria[1]	287	411	313	337	317	262	289	272	309	381	Algérie[1]
Egypt[1]	* 155	* 165	177	182	184	203	200	205	* 253	* 246	Egypte[1]
Morocco[1 2]	5 479	6 150	6 111	6 210	5 835	5 958	5 700	6 400	6 762	6 574	Maroc[1 2]
Senegal* [1]	629	654	537	562	497	518	352	436	583	617	Sénégal* [1]
South Africa* [1]	595	841	972	1 171	1 147	942	1 149	996	939	880	Afrique du Sud* [1]
Togo[1]	* 703	* 1 000	1 039	1 056	1 061	806	1 005	755	* 979	* 890	Togo[1]
Tunisia[1 3]	* 1 152	* 1 265	1 022	1 164	1 283	1 287	1 213	1 700	1 554	* 1 303	Tunisie[1 3]
Zimbabwe[1]	45	36	37	48	45	44	42	46	44	45	Zimbabwe[1]
America, North	**15 709**	**16 638**	**15 429**	**15 925**	**16 829**	**16 515**	**11 699**	**13 202**	**14 999**	**15 741**	**Amérique du Nord**
Mexico[1]	* 78	* 99	97	82	118	150	195	114	110	107	Mexique[1]
United States	15 631	16 539	15 332	15 843	16 711	16 365	11 504	13 088	14 889	15 634	Etats–Unis
America, South	**529**	**707**	**416**	**639**	**1 538**	**1 133**	**942**	**1 116**	**1 358**	**1 352**	**Amérique du Sud**
Brazil	490	650	358	589	1 489	1 083	887	1 069	1 305	* 1 300	Brésil
Colombia	* 3	* 2	* 2	2	1	4	4	4	* 7	* 6	Colombie
Peru	...	...	...	...	...	4	9	1	4	4	Pérou
Venezuela	* 28	* 48	49	...	...	...	...	...	...	...	Venezuela
Asia	**3 354**	**3 664**	**3 731**	**4 364**	**5 246**	**5 438**	**5 638**	**7 135**	**8 225**	**7 711**	**Asie**
China* [1]	1 312	1 400	1 033	1 874	2 360	2 530	2 580	3 750	4 260	3 600	Chine* [1]
India	* 238	* 259	246	210	167	173	192	227	262	266	Inde
Indonesia	7	4	6	5	11	8	5	8	* 1	* 1	Indonésie
Iraq	...	...	...	...	...	...	81	80	* 86	...	Iraq
Israel	* 223	* 429	561	[1] 678	[1] 750	[1] 624	[1] 698	[1] 892	* [1] 995	* [1] 1 210	Israël
Jordan[1]	* 600	* 624	749	919	1 271	1 380	1 427	1 544	1 899	1 881	Jordanie[1]
Korea, D. P. Rp.* [1]	157	150	150	150	150	150	150	160	160	160	Corée, Rp. P. D.* [1]
Philippines	* 4	* 3	* 3	* 3	4	2	2	1	0	...	Philippines
Sri Lanka	...	...	...	9	14	15	14	16	* 5	* 6	Sri Lanka
Syrian Arab Republic	* 178	* 149	* 248	356	402	402	443	375	461	386	Rép. arabe syrienne
Thailand[1]	...	1	1	2	2	1	1	1	1	* 1	Thaïlande[1]
Turkey	...	* 22	7	6	6	11	9	* 15	* 29	* 12	Turquie
Viet Nam	* 525	* 525	* 630	* 70	* 27	* 60	* 36	* 66	* 66	105	Viet Nam
Europe	**15**	**27**	**35**	**25**	**85**	**121**	**134**	**183**	**226**	**262**	**Europe**
EEC	***6***	***8***	***2***	***1***	***1***	***1***	***1***	***1***	***1***	***1***	***CEE***
France	* 6	* 8	2	1	1	1	1	1	...	...	France
EFTA	***9***	***19***	***33***	***24***	***84***	***120***	***133***	***182***	***225***	***261***	***AELE***
Finland[1]	...	...	1	1	50	72	83	141	176	* 189	Finlande[1]
Sweden[1]	* 8	* 18	32	23	34	48	50	41	* 49	72	Suède[1]
USSR* [1]	**8 470**	**9 423**	**8 300**	**8 400**	**9 600**	**9 700**	**9 800**	**10 000**	**10 100**	**10 004**	**URSS* [1]**
Oceania	**896**	**1 129**	**1 537**	**1 357**	**1 407**	**1 075**	**1 048**	**1 033**	**970**	**1 010**	**Océanie**
Australia	* 90	* 157	* 79	[1] 2	[1] 2	[1] 6	[1] 59	[1] 1	[1] 4	[1] 8	Australie
Christmas Isl.(Aust)	* 361	* 415	511	491	602	499	466	384	443	421	Ile Christmas (Aust)
Kiribati[4]	...	...	[5] 177	[5] 160	0	0	0	0	0	0	Kiribati[4]
Nauru	* 264	* 401	770	704	803	570	523	648	523	* 581	Nauru
Total	**38 018**	**42 111**	**39 656**	**41 440**	**45 074**	**44 002**	**39 211**	**43 479**	**47 301**	**47 015**	**Total**

General note.
P2O5 content of natural calcium phosphate, natural aluminium calcium phosphates, apatite and phosphatic chalk. Guano is excluded. (SITC 27130–0).

Remarque générale.
Poids de P2O5 contenu dans les phosphates de calcium naturels, les phosphates alumino–calciques naturels, l'apatite et les craies phosphatées, à l'exclusion du guano. (CTCI 27130–0).

[1] Source: U. S. Bureau of Mines, (Washington, D. C.).
[2] Including production for Western Sahara.
[3] Content of concentrates.
[4] Including data for Tuvalu (previously known as Ellice Islands). Production ceased after 1979.
[5] Exports.

[1] Source: U.S. Bureau of Mines, (Washington, D.C.).
[2] Y compris les données relatives Sahara Occidental.
[3] Teneur des concentrés.
[4] Y compris les données relatives à Tuvalu (anciennement îles Ellice).
[5] Exportations.

Potash salts, crude – Sels de potasse bruts

Unit : Thousand metric tons — Unité : Milliers de tonnes métriques

Country or area	1976	1977	1978	1979	1980	1981	1982	1983	1984	1985	Pays ou zone
Africa	**254**	**136**	**0**	**0**	**0**	**0**	**0**	**0**	**63**	**53**	**Afrique**
Congo[1]	254	136	0	0	0	0	0	0	...	...	Congo[1]
America, North	**7 392**	**7 993**	**8 597**	**9 299**	**9 440**	**8 705**	**7 079**	**7 723**	**9 048**	**7 957**	**Amérique du Nord**
Canada	5 215	5 764	6 344	7 074	7 201	6 549	5 295	6 294	7 484	6 661	Canada
United States	2 177	2 229	2 253	2 225	2 239	2 156	1 784	1 429	1 564	1 296	Etats–Unis
America, South	**17**	**11**	**17**	**22**	**25**	**21**	**21**	**21**	**18**	**19**	**Amérique du Sud**
Chile[1]	17	11	* 17	22	25	21	21	21	18	* 19	Chili[1]
Asia	**692**	**725**	**765**	**753**	**809**	**859**	**1 030**	**1 029**	**1 140**	**1 140**	**Asie**
China* [1]	12	18	21	16	12	20	26	29	40	40	Chine* [1]
Israel[1 2]	680	707	744	737	797	839	1 004	1 000	* 1 100	* 1 100	Israël[1 2]
Europe	**8 224**	**8 751**	**9 276**	**9 889**	**10 029**	**9 878**	**8 989**	**9 337**	**9 893**	**9 751**	**Europe**
EEC	***4 433***	***4 828***	***5 231***	***5 713***	***5 816***	***5 557***	***4 732***	***5 133***	***5 637***	***5 636***	***CEE***
Belgium	5	5	5	8	6	5	5	5	6	7	Belgique
France[3]	1 738	1 719	1 928	2 075	2 039	1 969	1 824	1 651	1 873	1 884	France[3]
Germany, Fed. Rep.	2 441	2 798	2 952	3 170	3 307	3 142	2 497	2 985	3 271	3 215	Allemagne, Rép. féd.
Italy	203	225	196	183	143	156	161	184	163	187	Italie
United Kingdom[1]	46	81	150	277	321	285	245	308	324	343	Royaume–Uni[1]
East Europe	***3 161***	***3 229***	***3 323***	***3 395***	***3 422***	***3 460***	***3 434***	***3 431***	***3 465***	***3 465***	***Europe de l'est***
German Dem. Rep.	3 161	3 229	3 323	3 395	3 422	3 460	3 434	3 431	3 465	3 465	Rép. dém. allemande
Other Europe	***630***	***694***	***722***	***781***	***791***	***861***	***823***	***773***	***791***	***650***	***Autre Europe***
Spain	630	694	722	781	791	861	823	773	791	* 650	Espagne
USSR* [1]	**8 310**	**8 350**	**8 200**	**6 635**	**8 064**	**8 449**	**8 079**	**9 300**	**9 776**	**10 000**	**URSS* [1]**
Total	**24 889**	**25 966**	**26 855**	**26 598**	**28 367**	**27 912**	**25 198**	**27 410**	**29 938**	**28 920**	**Total**

General note.
K20 content or equivalent of various mined potash salts. Manufactured fertilizers are not included. (SITC 27140–0).

[1] Source: U. S. Bureau of Mines, (Washington, D. C.).
[2] Twelve months beginning 1 April of year stated.
[3] Recovered quantities of K2O.

Remarque générale.
Equivalent en K20 des divers sels de potasse d'extraction. Cette rubrique ne comprend pas les engrais artificiels. (CTCI 27140–0).

[1] Source: U.S. Bureau of Mines, (Washington, D.C.).
[2] Période de douze mois commençant le 1er avril de l'année indiquée.
[3] Quantités de K2O récupérées.

Sulphur, native – Soufre natif

Unit : Thousand metric tons

Unité : Milliers de tonnes métriques

Country or area	1976	1977	1978	1979	1980	1981	1982	1983	1984	1985	Pays ou zone
America, North	**8 516**	**7 771**	**7 466**	**8 382**	**8 493**	**8 425**	**6 025**	**4 804**	**6 019**	**7 032**	**Amérique du Nord**
Cuba	1	0	0	0	0	0	0	0	0	...	Cuba
Mexico	2 150	1 856	1 818	2 025	2 102	2 077	1 815	1 602	1 826	2 020	Mexique
United States	6 365	5 915	5 648	6 357	6 391	6 348	4 210	3 202	4 193	5 011	Etats–Unis
America, South	**110**	**141**	**161**	**205**	**259**	**265**	**295**	**332**	**313**	**347**	**Amérique du Sud**
Argentina	20	27	18	0	0	* 10	0	0	0	0	Argentine
Bolivia[1]	[2] 14	[2] 6	[2] 14	[2] 15	11	10	6	4	2	2	Bolivie[1]
Brazil	30	44	57	92	131	102	146	193	216	...	Brésil
Chile[2]	18	32	32	77	87	115	105	99	54	79	Chili[2]
Colombia[2]	24	27	35	16	26	26	33	31	* 36	* 35	Colombie[2]
Ecuador* [2]	4	5	5	5	4	2	5	5	5	4	Equateur* [2]
Asia	**948**	**1 033**	**975**	**867**	**1 015**	**500**	**571**	**584**	**803**	**818**	**Asie**
China* [2]	150	200	200	200	200	200	200	200	200	200	Chine* [2]
Indonesia* [2]	3	2	2	2	2	1	1	3	5	5	Indonésie* [2]
Iran(Islamic Rep.of)* [2 3]	188	188	150	75	70	50	10	20	30	30	Iran(Rép.islamique)* [2 3]
Iraq[2]	582	620	600	550	700	200	* 300	* 300	* 500	* 500	Iraq[2]
Pakistan[4]	2	1	1	1	0	0	1	1	1	1	Pakistan[4]
Saudi Arabia	1	1	1	9	11	10	14	14	15	...	Arabie saoudite
Turkey	21	20	20	21	21	29	31	32	37	* 45	Turquie
Europe	**4 943**	**4 833**	**5 082**	**4 867**	**5 209**	**4 825**	**4 986**	**5 044**	**5 042**	**4 926**	**Europe**
EEC	***40***	***54***	***16***	***20***	***27***	***28***	***27***	***15***	***16***	***8***	***CEE***
Denmark	0	0	0	...	...	6	7	7	11	7	Danemark
Italy	40	54	16	17	23	22	20	8	5	1	Italie
East Europe	***4 903***	***4 779***	***5 066***	***4 847***	***5 182***	***4 797***	***4 959***	***5 029***	***5 026***	***4 918***	***Europe de l'est***
Czechoslovakia	12	14	15	17	18	24	24	30	36	42	Tchécoslovaquie
Poland	4 891	4 765	5 051	4 830	5 164	4 773	4 935	4 999	4 990	4 876	Pologne
USSR* [2]	**2 700**	**2 900**	**1 900**	**1 900**	**2 000**	**1 800**	**1 800**	**1 800**	**1 800**	**1 700**	**URSS* [2]**
Total	**17 217**	**16 678**	**15 584**	**16 221**	**16 976**	**15 815**	**13 677**	**12 564**	**13 977**	**14 823**	**Total**

General note.
Unrefined sulphur extracted by melting or otherwise from mineral sulphur occurring in the free state. Sulphur obtained from Frasch–process mines is included. Sublimed sulphur, precipitated sulphur and colloidal sulphur are excluded. (SITC 27410–1).

[1] Exports.
[2] Source: U. S. Bureau of Mines, (Washington, D. C.).
[3] Twelve months beginning 21 March of year stated.
[4] Native sulphur, other than frasch.

Remarque générale.
Soufre non raffiné, obtenu par fusion ou autrement du soufre minéral brut à l'état naturel (soufre natif). Cette position comprend le soufre extrait par le procédé Frasch mais non le soufre sublimé, le soufre précipité, ni le soufre colloïdal. (CTCI 27410–1).

[1] Exportations.
[2] Source: U.S. Bureau of Mines, (Washington, D.C.).
[3] Période de douze mois commençant le 21 mars de l'année indiquée.
[4] Soufre natif, autre que celui extrait par le procédé Frasch.

Iron pyrites, unroasted – Pyrites de fer non grillées

Unit : Thousand metric tons — Unité : Milliers de tonnes métriques

Country or area	1976	1977	1978	1979	1980	1981	1982	1983	1984	1985	Pays ou zone
Africa	**1 032**	**1 110**	**1 015**	**1 284**	**1 666**	**1 666**	**1 838**	**1 883**	**919**	**871**	**Afrique**
Morocco[1]	137	149	177	286	* 125	79	...	...	...	...	Maroc[1]
Namibia* [2]	10	10	8	10	10	20	145	202	260	174	Namibie* [2]
South Africa[2]	735	830	765	911	1 450	1 475	* 1 500	* 1 500	465	* 500	Afrique du Sud[2]
Zambia	99	* 68	9	11	13	...	1	26	18	28	Zambie
Zimbabwe	51	53	56	66	68	65	58	29	57	57	Zimbabwe
America, North	**857**	**548**	**854**	**1 109**	**932**	**841**	**743**	**857**	**862**	**881**	**Amérique du Nord**
Canada	31	24	9	31	32	11	19	* 5	* 5	* 6	Canada
Cuba	64	82	54	29	53	33	48	13	0	0	Cuba
United States	762	442	791	1 049	847	797	676	...	...	...	Etats–Unis
Asia	**4 104**	**4 537**	**5 233**	**5 149**	**5 341**	**7 252**	**5 293**	**6 368**	**5 805**	**6 952**	**Asie**
China* [2]	2 050	2 800	3 600	3 700	3 800	5 900	4 100	5 200	4 700	...	Chine* [2]
Cyprus	195	146	123	46	62	16	56	47	23	70	Chypre
India	48	31	64	67	83	72	56	53	37	17	Inde
Japan[3]	958	798	670	617	637	598	561	551	530	514	Japon[3]
Korea,Dem.Ppl's.Rep.[2]	600	615	625	562	560	500	450	450	450	450	Corée,Rép.pop.dém.de[2]
Korea, Republic of[2]	2	0	0	0	0	0	0	0	0	...	Corée, République de[2]
Philippines	166	109	111	120	122	98	65	* 63	* 65	167	Philippines
Turkey	85	38	40	37	77	68	5	4	0	...	Turquie
Europe	**7 744**	**7 442**	**7 153**	**7 319**	**7 665**	**7 716**	**7 611**	**7 702**	**7 950**	**7 631**	**Europe**
EEC	***1 658***	***1 607***	***1 478***	***1 444***	***1 533***	***1 351***	***1 306***	***1 358***	***1 116***	***1 257***	***CEE***
Germany, Fed. Rep.[2]	523	531	502	460	# 502	483	508	554	* 500	* 400	Allemagne, Rép. féd.[2]
Greece[3]	216	169	147	151	147	162	117	144	165	* 165	Grèce[3]
Ireland[2]	65	47	* 42	* 29	* 25	* 25	14	...	...	...	Irlande[2]
Italy	854	860	787	804	859	681	667	* 646	443	690	Italie
EFTA	***1 682***	***1 365***	***1 307***	***1 380***	***1 526***	***1 759***	***1 513***	***1 567***	***1 700***	***1 651***	***AELE***
Finland	494	295	216	[2] 342	[2] 322	[2] 640	[2] 400	[2] 500	[2] 520	[2] 493	Finlande
Norway	[2] 368	308	293	241	421	413	425	357	428	395	Norvège
Portugal	416	360	314	349	387	287	262	280	334	356	Portugal
Sweden	404	402	484	448	396	419	426	* 430	418	407	Suède
East Europe	***1 553***	***1 653***	***1 670***	***1 677***	***1 642***	***1 782***	***1 777***	***1 777***	***1 757***	***1 757***	***Europe de l'est***
Bulgaria[2]	* 636	* 693	* 705	* 715	* 680	* 680	* 680	* 680	* 680	680	Bulgarie[2]
Czechoslovakia	15	13	3	0	0	* [2] 140	* [2] 140	* [2] 140	* [2] 140	* [2] 140	Tchécoslovaquie
German Dem. Rep.* [2]	25	25	25	25	25	25	20	20	0	0	Rép. dém. allemande* [2]
Hungary* [2]	7	7	7	7	7	7	7	7	7	7	Hongrie* [2]
Romania* [2]	870	915	930	930	930	930	930	930	930	930	Roumanie* [2]
Other Europe	***2 851***	***2 817***	***2 698***	***2 818***	***2 964***	***2 824***	***3 015***	***3 000***	***3 377***	***2 966***	***Autre Europe***
Spain	2 411	2 423	2 292	2 366	2 514	2 424	2 205	2 306	2 769	* 2 459	Espagne
Yugoslavia[3]	440	394	406	452	450	400	810	694	608	507	Yougoslavie[3]
USSR* [2]	**7 400**	**7 800**	**7 800**	**7 800**	**7 900**	**8 000**	**7 800**	**7 600**	**7 300**	**7 600**	**URSS* [2]**
Oceania	**213**	**228**	**252**	**111**	**16**	**74**	**43**	**12**	**16**	**16**	**Océanie**
Australia[4]	213	228	252	111	16	...	...	...	...	...	Australie[4]
Total	**21 350**	**21 665**	**22 307**	**22 772**	**23 520**	**25 549**	**23 327**	**24 422**	**22 852**	**23 951**	**Total**

General note.
All unroasted iron pyrites and unroasted cupreous pyrites. Chalco–pyrite and gem marcasite are excluded. (SITC 27420–0).

1 Pyrrhotite.
2 Source: U. S. Bureau of Mines, (Washington, D. C.).
3 Concentrates.
4 Twelve months ending 30 June of year stated.

Remarque générale.
Toutes les pyrites de fer non grillées, y compris les pyrites cuivreuses non grillées, mais à l'exclusion de la chalcopyrite et de la marcassite utilisée en bijouterie. (CTCI 27420–0).

1 Pyrrhotine.
2 Source: U.S. Bureau of Mines, (Washington, D.C.).
3 Concentrés.
4 Période de douze mois finissant le 30 juin de l'année indiquée.

Fluorspar, excluding precious stones – Spath fluor, non compris les pierres precieuses

Unit : Thousand metric tons — Unité : Milliers de tonnes métriques

Country or area	1976	1977	1978	1979	1980	1981	1982	1983	1984	1985	Pays ou zone
Africa	**453.0**	**545.5**	**588.4**	**625.9**	**722.1**	**689.5**	**506.4**	**426.4**	**480.7**	**524.3**	**Afrique**
Egypt[1]	1.0	1.4	0.7	0.3	1.8	1.0	0.1	0.0	0.0	0.0	Egypte[1]
Kenya[2]	[3] 75.0	[3] 124.0	[3] 106.6	* [3] 77.1	93.4	90.1	88.7	59.1	50.9	58.2	Kenya[2]
Morocco[4]	51.4	40.0	54.2	63.2	64.4	66.7	50.2	60.3	65.9	74.3	Maroc[4]
South Africa[5]	[3] 290.7	[3] 350.7	[3] 393.3	[3] 451.1	522.7	496.5	330.8	268.0	319.0	349.2	Afrique du Sud[5]
Tunisia[4]	34.6	28.9	33.3	33.8	39.4	34.8	36.2	38.6	44.5	42.2	Tunisie[4]
Zambia[1,3]	0.0	* 0.0	0.1	...	...	...	...	...	...	...	Zambie[1,3]
Zimbabwe[3,6]	0.2	0.5	0.3	...	...	...	...	...	...	...	Zimbabwe[3,6]
America, North	**1 238.4**	**873.4**	**1 138.9**	**1 036.1**	**1 062.2**	**1 091.3**	**763.0**	**722.2**	**754.3**	**819.0**	**Amérique du Nord**
Canada* [3,4]	64.0	59.5	...	...	...	...	...	...	...	...	Canada* [3,4]
Mexico[3]	1 003.7	660.1	959.8	875.2	916.5	924.9	631.4	* 605.1	627.4	697.4	Mexique[3]
United States[2,7]	170.8	153.8	117.4	99.2	84.0	104.7	69.9	* 55.4	* 65.1	59.9	Etats–Unis[2,7]
America, South	**71.2**	**97.3**	**87.7**	**113.1**	**70.5**	**77.0**	**80.8**	**98.2**	**96.7**	**146.5**	**Amérique du Sud**
Argentina[2]	* 40.1	* 43.8	26.7	38.1	15.5	20.8	23.7	29.0	23.2	32.5	Argentine[2]
Brazil	31.1	53.5	61.0	75.0	55.0	56.2	57.0	69.2	73.6	* 114.0	Brésil
Asia	**922.5**	**1 090.6**	**1 194.9**	**1 331.9**	**1 390.8**	**1 357.9**	**1 474.4**	**1 484.5**	**1 756.1**	**1 835.7**	**Asie**
China* [2,3]	349.3	434.2	439.1	459.0	479.0	479.0	479.0	499.0	650.0	650.0	Chine* [2,3]
India[2]	17.6	18.8	17.5	21.5	21.3	23.0	25.2	22.3	22.1	20.3	Inde[2]
Korea,Dem.Ppl's.Rep.[3,6]	29.9	39.9	39.9	40.0	40.0	40.0	40.0	40.0	* 40.0	* 40.0	Corée,Rép.pop.dém.de[3,6]
Korea, Republic of[3,6]	20.3	13.0	11.4	8.4	6.9	6.5	3.7	6.4	4.7	* 5.0	Corée, République de[3,6]
Mongolia[6]	322.3	334.9	454.9	567.0	603.5	595.0	666.6	707.9	747.3	786.8	Mongolie[6]
Pakistan[1,3]	0.0	...	0.3	0.4	1.2	* 0.0	* 0.8	* 0.3	* 2.7	* 32.7	Pakistan[1,3]
Thailand[2,3]	181.8	248.1	230.5	234.3	232.9	212.5	257.1	206.6	287.4	298.9	Thaïlande[2,3]
Turkey[3,6]	1.3	1.7	1.3	1.2	* 6.0	* 2.0	* 2.0	* 2.0	* 2.0	* 2.0	Turquie[3,6]
Europe	**1 307.1**	**1 263.2**	**1 229.6**	**1 073.0**	**1 145.0**	**1 318.9**	**1 183.7**	**1 058.0**	**1 115.2**	**1 116.6**	**Europe**
EEC	***801.9***	***734.3***	***709.4***	***661.2***	***671.4***	***797.3***	***723.2***	***607.7***	***600.1***	***590.7***	***CEE***
France[5]	* 305.7	* 286.0	264.0	248.0	260.7	294.0	277.3	222.2	185.6	196.0	France[5]
Germany, Fed. Rep.	67.3	68.0	84.7	76.1	87.3	82.8	77.6	76.5	88.9	92.2	Allemagne, Rép. féd.
Greece[1,3]	* 1.0	0.5	0.6	0.4	0.4	0.3	* 0.3	* 0.3	* 0.3	* 0.3	Grèce[1,3]
Italy[3,5]	210.8	185.7	171.1	182.8	152.0	164.2	166.9	177.7	* 188.3	* 152.2	Italie[3,5]
United Kingdom[2,3]	217.0	194.0	189.0	154.0	171.0	256.0	201.0	131.0	137.0	* 150.0	Royaume–Uni[2,3]
EFTA	***3.3***	***2.4***	***2.8***	***2.9***	***2.9***	***2.9***	***2.9***	***2.0***	***3.5***	***3.2***	***AELE***
Sweden* [2,3]	3.3	2.4	...	...	...	...	...	2.0	3.5	3.2	Suède* [2,3]
East Europe	***208.4***	***216.0***	***216.0***	***216.0***	***226.0***	***216.0***	***216.0***	***216.0***	***216.0***	***216.0***	***Europe de l'est***
Czechoslovakia* [2,3]	93.4	96.0	96.0	96.0	106.0	96.0	96.0	96.0	96.0	96.0	Tchécoslovaquie* [2,3]
German Dem. Rep.* [2,3].	...	100.0	100.0	100.0	100.0	100.0	100.0	100.0	100.0	100.0	Rép. dém. allemande* [2,3]
Romania* [3,6]	15.0	20.0	20.0	20.0	20.0	20.0	20.0	20.0	20.0	20.0	Roumanie* [3,6]
Other Europe	***293.5***	***310.5***	***301.3***	***192.9***	***244.7***	***302.8***	***241.6***	***232.3***	***295.7***	***306.8***	***Autre Europe***
Spain[2]	293.5	310.5	301.3	192.9	244.7	302.8	241.6	232.3	295.7	* 306.8	Espagne[2]
USSR* [2,3]	**...**	**500.8**	**510.0**	**520.0**	**520.0**	**530.0**	**540.0**	**540.0**	**550.0**	**560.0**	**URSS* [2,3]**
Total	**4 487.5**	**4 370.7**	**4 749.6**	**4 700.0**	**4 910.6**	**5 064.6**	**4 548.3**	**4 329.3**	**4 753.1**	**5 002.2**	**Total**

General note.
Fluorspar (or fluorite) is natural calcium floride occurring as solid masses streaked with varied colours, or in agglomerated crystals of various colours. Fluorspar in the form of precious stones is excluded. (SITC 27654–1).

[1] Grade unspecified.
[2] Acid and metallurgical grade.
[3] Source: U. S. Bureau of Mines, (Washington, D. C.).
[4] Acid grade.
[5] Acid, metallurgical amd ceramic grade.
[6] Metallurgical grade.
[7] Shipments.

Remarque générale.
Le spath fluor (ou fluorine) est un fluorure de calcium qui se présente, dans la nature, soit en masses compactes comportant des zones diversement colorées, soit en cristaux agglomérés de couleur variable. Le spath fluor ayant le caractère de pierres gemmes n'est pas compris. (CTCI 27654–1).

[1] La teneur du minerai non spécifiée.
[2] Grade de métallurgique et d'acide.
[3] Source: U.S. Bureau of Mines, (Washington, D.C.).
[4] Grade d'acide.
[5] Grade de céramique, de métallurgique et d'acide.
[6] Grade metallurgique.
[7] Expéditions.

Barytes, whether or not calcined – Barytine même calciné

Unit : Thousand metric tons

Unité : Milliers de Tonnes métriques

Country or area	1976	1977	1978	1979	1980	1981	1982	1983	1984	1985	Pays ou zone
Africa	**233**	**220**	**271**	**398**	**491**	**590**	**658**	**432**	**670**	**564**	**Afrique**
Algeria[1,2]	75	48	73	90	91	89	102	109	88	91	Algérie[1,2]
Egypt	0	1	1	2	5	2	3	4	* 4	* 4	Egypte
Kenya[1]	0	0	0	0	6	* 6	0	0	0	0	Kenya[1]
Morocco	131	150	177	287	358	466	516	288	561	463	Maroc
South Africa	[1] 2	[1] 3	[1] 3	[1] 3	[1] 3	2	3	7	4	3	Afrique du Sud
Tunisia	24	16	16	16	27	25	34	23	12	2	Tunisie
Zimbabwe[1]	* 1	* 3	* 1	* 0	* 0	0	1	1	1	* 1	Zimbabwe[1]
America, North	**1 460**	**1 747**	**518**	**2 146**	**2 405**	**2 993**	**2 028**	**1 087**	**1 193**	**1 210**	**Amérique du Nord**
Canada[1]	65	117	88	75	94	86	28	46	64	70	Canada[1]
Guatemala[1]	...	...	1	4	5	5	* 2	0	0	1	Guatemala[1]
Mexico	[1] 270	271	232	151	269	318	324	357	426	468	Mexique
United States[3]	1 119	1 355	197	1 916	2 037	2 585	1 674	684	703	671	Etats-Unis[3]
America, South	**421**	**575**	**720**	**805**	**765**	**821**	**830**	**443**	**335**	**371**	**Amérique du Sud**
Argentina	41	31	46	55	50	49	37	61	44	51	Argentine
Bolivia[4]	...	[1] 2	[1] 3	[1] 2	9	2	1	1	1	1	Bolivie[4]
Brazil	26	39	87	73	62	99	122	100	105	* 110	Brésil
Chile	[1] 17	[1] 65	[1] 185	* [1] 227	[1] 226	[1] 259	[1] 292	[1] 114	22	54	Chili
Colombia[1]	3	4	4	4	4	3	4	4	3	* 5	Colombie[1]
Peru[1]	331	435	396	445	415	409	375	* 163	* 160	* 150	Pérou[1]
Asia	**1 067**	**1 373**	**1 559**	**1 881**	**1 901**	**1 988**	**1 925**	**1 863**	**2 138**	**2 299**	**Asie**
Afghanistan[1,5]	5	12	13	* 3	3	1	2	* 2	* 2	* 2	Afghanistan[1,5]
Burma	17	20	41	24	3	7	17	15	16	9	Birmanie
China[1]	272	349	399	* 500	* 680	* 800	* 900	* 1 000	* 1 000	* 1 000	Chine[1]
India	236	331	389	491	442	405	364	381	455	575	Inde
Iran(Islamic Rep.of)[1,5]	172	185	200	* 180	* 150	* 75	* 80	* 85	* 91	* 91	Iran(Rép.islamique)[1,5]
Israel	...	...	...	...	1	...	...	...	...	...	Israël
Japan	[1] 54	[1] 58	[1] 71	* [1] 55	56	56	59	70	66	77	Japon
Korea,Dem.Ppl's.Rep.[1]	118	118	109	109	109	109	0	0	...	...	Corée,Rép.pop.dém.de[1]
Korea, Republic of[1]	4	3	1	1	0	0	0	1	3	* 2	Corée, République de[1]
Malaysia	6	11	5	1	0	* 19	25	21	23	23	Malaisie
Pakistan	5	18	19	32	19	21	30	20	30	36	Pakistan
Philippines[1]	4	5	5	6	5	2	9	3	0	...	Philippines[1]
Thailand	[1] 151	[1] 119	[1] 275	[1] 378	305	307	331	187	174	231	Thaïlande
Turkey	[1] 20	[1] 143	[1] 32	[1] 100	127	185	107	77	198	176	Turquie
Europe	**1 448**	**1 583**	**1 509**	**1 413**	**1 393**	**1 327**	**1 294**	**1 128**	**1 127**	**1 124**	**Europe**
EEC	***1 053***	***1 170***	***1 110***	***1 001***	***1 003***	***961***	***925***	***777***	***747***	***755***	***CEE***
Belgium* [1]	...	...	...	...	30	40	40	40	40	40	Belgique* [1]
France	150	211	225	* 170	* 237	* 191	* 156	169	145	116	France
Germany, Fed. Rep.	262	266	169	162	175	165	166	164	167	171	Allemagne, Rép. féd.
Greece[6]	61	87	44	* 48	43	43	39	30	5	* 17	Grèce[6]
Ireland[1]	323	373	349	* 328	260	274	266	199	* 220	* 214	Irlande[1]
Italy	[1] 179	[1] 152	[1] 237	[1] 215	203	185	178	139	107	127	Italie
United Kingdom[1]	50	50	54	45	54	63	81	36	63	* 70	Royaume-Uni[1]
EFTA	***8***	***8***	***8***	***8***	***9***	***9***	***8***	***5***	***9***	***9***	***AELE***
Finland	...	...	...	...	...	...	...	4	9	* 9	Finlande
Portugal[1]	0	* 1	* 1	* 1	* 1	* 1	1	1	0	0	Portugal[1]
East Europe	***235***	***268***	***277***	***282***	***273***	***260***	***265***	***254***	***261***	***260***	***Europe de l'est***
Czechoslovakia* [1]	7	64	64	68	61	61	61	60	60	60	Tchécoslovaquie* [1]
German Dem. Rep.* [1]	31	31	35	36	36	35	35	35	35	34	Rép. dém. allemande* [1]
Poland[1]	81	89	91	96	96	85	91	81	* 91	* 91	Pologne[1]
Romania* [1]	116	85	87	82	80	79	78	78	75	75	Roumanie* [1]
Other Europe	***152***	***137***	***114***	***121***	***108***	***97***	***95***	***92***	***110***	***100***	***Autre Europe***
Spain	91	84	71	74	60	53	50	52	69	* 65	Espagne
Yugoslavia	61	53	43	46	48	45	* 45	* 40	41	35	Yougoslavie
USSR* [1]	**399**	**454**	**476**	**500**	**510**	**510**	**520**	**520**	**530**	**540**	**URSS* [1]**
Oceania	**59**	**54**	**49**	**44**	**39**	**41**	**28**	**12**	**20**	**20**	**Océanie**

For general note and footnotes, see end of table.

Voir la fin du tableau pour la remarque générale et les notes.

Barytes, whether or not calcined (continued) – Barytine même calciné (suite)

Unit : Thousand metric tons

Unité : Milliers de Tonnes métriques

Country or area	1976	1977	1978	1979	1980	1981	1982	1983	1984	1985	Pays ou zone
Australia[1].....................	...	...	...	...	...	41	28	12	* 20	* 20	Australie[1]
Total...........................	**5 087**	**6 007**	**5 103**	**7 187**	**7 503**	**8 271**	**7 284**	**5 485**	**6 013**	**6 129**	**Total**

General note.
Naturally occurring barium sulphate (barytes – sometimes known as heavy spar) and barium carbonate (witherite). Refined or chemically produced barium sulphate and barium carbonate are excluded. Including calcined witherite, which consists largely of impure barium oxide. (SITC 27693–0).

[1] Source: U. S. Bureau of Mines, (Washington, D. C.).
[2] Ground barite only.
[3] Sold or used by producers.
[4] Exports.
[5] Twelve months beginning 21 March of year stated.
[6] Barite concentrates.

Remarque générale.
Le sulfate de baryum naturel, également nommé barytine et, dans certains pays, spath pesant, et le carbonate de baryum naturel ou withérite. Le sulfate de baryum et le carbonate de baryum, raffinés ou obtenus par voie chimique, sont exclus. Y compris la withérite calcinée, qui est essentiellement constituée par de l'oxyde de baryum impur. (CTCI 27693–0).

[1] Source: U.S. Bureau of Mines, (Washington, D.C.).
[2] Barytine moulue seulement.
[3] Vendu ou utilisé par les producteurs.
[4] Exportations.
[5] Période de douze mois commençant le 21 mars de l'année indiquée.
[6] Concentrés de barytine.

ISIC–BASED CODE
2902–22

Borate minerals, crude – Minéraux boratés bruts

CODE BASE CITI
2902–22

Unit : Thousand metric tons

Unité : Milliers de tonnes métriques

Country or area	1976	1977	1978	1979	1980	1981	1982	1983	1984	1985	Pays ou zone
America, North	**1 130.4**	**1 332.7**	**1 409.8**	**1 442.4**	**1 401.6**	**1 343.5**	**1 119.5**	**1 182.1**	**1 240.1**	**1 151.2**	**Amérique du Nord**
United States[1]	1 130.4	1 332.7	1 409.8	1 442.4	1 401.6	1 343.5	1 119.5	1 182.1	1 240.1	1 151.2	Etats–Unis[1]
America, South	**93.4**	**105.4**	**160.1**	**146.9**	**180.5**	**145.1**	**137.0**	**152.2**	**156.5**	**165.0**	**Amérique du Sud**
Argentina	80.9	83.1	127.2	132.4	156.0	125.2	123.4	138.5	142.9	151.4	Argentine
Chile[2]	3.4	4.2	26.5	2.7	3.6	3.6	0.0	1.0	* 3.6	* 3.6	Chili[2]
Peru[2]	* 9.1	18.1	* 6.3	* 11.8	* 20.9	* 16.3	* 13.6	* 12.7	* 10.0	* 10.0	Pérou[2]
Asia	**940.2**	**1 126.2**	**893.2**	**730.2**	**1 361.2**	**1 555.2**	**1 426.2**	**1 240.2**	**1 440.2**	**1 564.2**	**Asie**
China* [2]	...	...	...	27.2	27.2	27.2	27.2	27.2	27.2	27.2	Chine* [2]
Turkey	[2] 913.0	[2] 1 099.0	[2] 866.0	[2] 703.0	1 334.0	1 528.0	1 399.0	1 213.0	1 413.0	* 1 537.0	Turquie
Europe	**143.0**	**143.0**	**143.1**	**143.2**	**142.4**	**143.3**	**138.2**	**137.0**	**144.9**	**152.0**	**Europe**
EEC	***139.0***	***139.0***	***139.0***	***139.0***	***139.0***	***139.0***	***134.0***	***133.0***	***140.9***	***148.0***	***CEE***
Germany, Fed. Rep.	...	...	...	...	...	...	134.0	133.0	140.9	148.0	Allemagne, Rép. féd.
East Europe	***4.0***	***4.0***	***4.1***	***4.2***	***3.4***	***4.3***	***4.2***	***4.0***	***4.0***	***4.0***	***Europe de l'est***
German Dem. Rep.[2 3]	4.0	* 4.0	4.1	4.2	3.4	4.3	4.2	4.0	4.0	* 4.0	Rép. dém. allemande[2 3]
USSR* [2]	**200.0**	**200.0**	**250.0**	**200.0**	**200.0**	**200.0**	**200.0**	**200.0**	**200.0**	**200.0**	**URSS* [2]**
Total	**2 506.8**	**2 907.3**	**2 856.1**	**2 662.7**	**3 285.7**	**3 387.1**	**3 020.9**	**2 911.5**	**3 181.8**	**3 232.4**	**Total**

General note.
Crude natural borate minerals as extracted, concentrates (whether or not calcined) of such materials, and crude natural boric acid as obtained by evaporation of the water left after the condensation of the natural vapours escaping from the earth in certain regions, or by evaporating water drawn from underground sources in those regions. Excluding boric acid containing more than 85 per cent H3BO3 calculated on the dry weight. (SITC 27697–0).

[1] Sold or used by producers.
[2] Source: U. S. Bureau of Mines, (Washington, D. C.).
[3] Processed borax, Na2B4O7, 10H2O content.

Remarque générale.
Les minéraux boratés naturels impurs, dans l'état où ils sont extraits ou obtenus sous forme de concentrés (calcinés ou non), ainsi que l'acide borique naturel brut, tel qu'il provient de l'évaporation des eaux de condensation des vapeurs naturelles issues du sol de certaines régions, ou des eaux captées daus les nappes sousterraines de ces régions. Non compris l'acide borique contenant plus de 85 pour cent de BO3H3 sur produit sec. (CTCI 27697–0).

[1] Vendu ou utilisé par les producteurs.
[2] Source: U.S. Bureau of Mines, (Washington, D.C.).
[3] Borax travaillé, Na2B4O7, 10H2O contenu.

Arsenic (Arsenic trioxide) – Arsenic (Trioxyde d'arsenic)

Unit : Metric tons

Unité : Tonnes métriques

Country or area	1976	1977	1978	1979	1980	1981	1982	1983	1984	1985	Pays ou zone
Africa	**6 985**	**2 614**	**2 401**	**2 220**	**1 288**	**1 370**	**1 895**	**1 126**	**2 504**	**2 471**	**Afrique**
Namibia[1 2]	6 985	2 614	2 401	2 220	1 288	1 370	1 895	1 126	2 504	2 471	Namibie[1 2]
America, North	**4 164**	**5 744**	**6 245**	**6 537**	**6 932**	**6 517**	**4 740**	**4 557**	**5 496**	**6 312**	**Amérique du Nord**
Mexico[1 2]	4 164	5 744	6 245	6 537	6 932	6 517	4 740	4 557	5 496	* 6 312	Mexique[1 2]
America, South	**4 539**	**5 117**	**5 071**	**5 165**	**6 177**	**5 080**	**5 076**	**4 821**	**4 539**	**5 247**	**Amérique du Sud**
Chile* [1]	...	...	...	...	...	...	...	...	3 500	4 000	Chili* [1]
Peru[2]	[1] 789	[1] 1 367	[1] 1 321	[1] 1 415	2 427	...	...	1 071	* 1 039	* 1 247	Pérou[2]
Asia	**768**	**764**	**637**	**772**	**760**	**265**	**406**	**860**	**787**	**739**	**Asie**
Japan[1 2]	59	118	90	182	284	95	* 100	* 300	* 500	* 500	Japon[1 2]
Korea, Republic of[1 2]	709	646	547	590	...	170	306	560	...	...	Corée, République de[1 2]
Europe	**16 093**	**12 625**	**12 589**	**11 153**	**12 345**	**13 756**	**13 517**	**12 250**	**11 832**	**13 689**	**Europe**
EEC	***8 563***	***6 404***	***6 258***	***5 918***	***5 660***	***5 560***	***6 360***	***5 087***	***4 188***	***5 985***	***CEE***
France[2]	* [1] 8 164	* [1] 6 042	* [1] 5 896	* [1] 5 550	* [1] 5 300	5 200	6 000	4 727	3 828	5 625	France[2]
Germany, Fed. Rep.* [1 2]	399	362	362	...	360	360	360	360	360	360	Allemagne, Rép. féd.* [1 2]
EFTA	***7 530***	***6 221***	***6 331***	***5 235***	***6 685***	***8 196***	***7 157***	***7 163***	***7 644***	***7 704***	***AELE***
Portugal[2]	[1] 278	[1] 222	[1] 253	[1] 155	185	196	157	163	144	204	Portugal[2]
Sweden	[3] 7 252	[3] 5 999	[3] 6 078	[3] 5 080	[3] 6 500	* [1 2] 8 000	* [1 2] 7 000	* [1 2] 7 000	* [1 2] 7 500	* [1 2] 7 500	Suède
USSR* [1 2]	**7 402**	**7 529**	**7 620**	**7 700**	**7 700**	**7 750**	**7 800**	**7 900**	**8 000**	**8 100**	**URSS* [1 2]**
Total	**39 951**	**34 393**	**34 563**	**33 547**	**35 202**	**34 738**	**33 434**	**31 514**	**33 158**	**36 558**	**Total**

General note.
Arsenic trioxide (As2O3) (arsenous oxide, white arsenic), obtained by roasting arseniferous ores of nickel and silver or arsenical pyrites. It may sometimes contain impurities (arsenic sulphide, sulphur, antimonous oxide etc.). (SITC 51336–1).

[1] Source: U. S. Bureau of Mines, (Washington, D. C.).
[2] Including calculated arsenic trioxide equivalent of output of elemental arsenic and arsenic compounds other than trioxide.
[3] Arsenic trioxide for sale plus arsenic trioxide equivalent of the output of metallic arsenic for sale.

Remarque générale.
Anhydride arsénieux (As2O3) (trioxyde d'arsenic, oxyde arsénieux, arsenic blanc). On l'obtient par grillage de minerais arsenifères de nickel et d'argent ou de pyrites arsenicales. Il peut contenir des impuretés: sulfure d'arsenic, soufre, oxyde antimonieux etc. (CTCI 51336–1).

[1] Source: U.S. Bureau of Mines, (Washington, D.C.).
[2] Y compris l'equivalent en arsénique trioxide dans la production d'arsénique élémentaire et composés d'arsénique autre que l'arsénique trioxide.
[3] Trioxyde d'arsenic pour la vente et l'equivalent en trioxyde d'arsenic de la production de l'arsenic metallique destiné à la vente.

Salt, unrefined – Sel, non raffiné

Unit : Thousand metric tons

Unité : Milliers de tonnes métriques

Country or area	1976	1977	1978	1979	1980	1981	1982	1983	1984	1985	Pays ou zone
Africa	**2 087**	**2 404**	**2 647**	**2 743**	**2 936**	**2 925**	**2 955**	**3 056**	**3 066**	**3 142**	**Afrique**
Algeria	136	147	171	* 165	172	125	145	[1] 150	[1] 150	[1] 182	Algérie
Angola* [1]	50	50	50	50	50	50	59	55	50	10	Angola* [1]
Cape Verde	14	31	17	17	22	6	3	10	9	6	Cap-Vert
Egypt	591	741	755	728	728	858	883	918	998	* 988	Egypte
Ethiopia	106	# [1,2] 82	* [1,2] 60	* [1,2] 108	* [1,2] 115	* [1,2] 125	* [1,2] 124	* [1,2] 124	[1,2] 133	* [1,2] 133	Ethiopie
Ghana* [1]	52	50	50	50	50	50	50	50	50	50	Ghana* [1]
Kenya	50	40	20	16	49	28	27	83	101	34	Kenya
Libyan Arab Jamah.* [1]	10	10	15	10	10	10	10	12	12	10	Jamah.arabe libyenne* [1]
Madagascar	27	# [1] 26	[1] 30	* [1] 30	* [1] 30	* [1] 30	[1] 30	* [1] 30	* [1] 30	* [1] 30	Madagascar
Mali* [1]	5	5	5	5	5	5	5	6	5	5	Mali* [1]
Mauritius	6	6	6	* 6	6	6	5	6	7	7	Maurice
Morocco	15	12	17	18	67	55	57	70	70	105	Maroc
Mozambique	28	52	51	58	75	86	34	35	19	27	Mozambique
Namibia* [1,3]	220	230	230	230	230	193	184	137	88	152	Namibie* [1,3]
Niger[1]	* 1	* 1	* 1	* 3	* 3	* 3	3	* 3	* 3	* 3	Niger[1]
Senegal	142	140	140	140	140	140	160	170	170	143	Sénégal
Sierra Leone	3	8	4	3	4	19	24	26	36	...	Sierra Leone
Somalia* [1]	2	2	2	# 30	30	27	27	30	30	30	Somalie* [1]
South Africa	224	242	490	539	* 573	540	633	659	589	716	Afrique du Sud
Sudan* [1]	70	92	72	82	80	64	28	73	73	73	Soudan* [1]
Tunisia	288	408	431	417	460	462	421	375	415	380	Tunisie
Uganda* [1]	1	1	1	1	1	6	6	6	6	6	Ouganda* [1]
United Rep. Tanzania[1]	46	28	29	37	36	* 37	* 37	* 28	* 22	* 18	Rép.Unie de Tanzanie[1]
America, North	**52 365**	**52 730**	**53 507**	**55 157**	**51 545**	**51 230**	**49 731**	**47 208**	**52 865**	**51 628**	**Amérique du Nord**
Bahamas[1]	1 353	1 670	1 800	485	754	970	816	862	* 870	* 850	Bahamas[1]
Canada	5 994	6 039	6 452	6 881	7 423	7 239	7 932	8 602	10 190	10 085	Canada
Costa Rica[1]	20	27	34	46	[3] 40	[3] 39	[3] 110	* [3] 109	* [3] 109	* [3] 109	Costa Rica[1]
Cuba	151	130	131	123	131	161	198	180	184	221	Cuba
Dominican Republic	39	68	37	41	43	47	48	50	48	53	Rép. dominicaine
El Salvador* [1]	23	27	27	27	2	2	2	2	2	3	El Salvador* [1]
Guatemala[4]	11	11	11	14	10	14	14	15	* 16	* 17	Guatemala[4]
Honduras[1]	32	32	32	32	* 33	* 30	* 32	* 32	* 32	* 35	Honduras[1]
Mexico	4 391	4 884	5 637	5 507	6 037	7 180	5 886	5 703	5 456	5 451	Mexique
Neth.Antil and Aruba* [1]	211	399	399	399	399	218	272	200	354	354	Antill.néer.et Aruba* [1]
Nicaragua* [1]	15	16	18	18	20	18	18	18	15	16	Nicaragua* [1]
Panama	12	20	15	17	19	15	11	39	18	16	Panama
Puerto Rico[1]	24	24	* 24	* 24	* 27	* 8	* 15	* 32	* 27	* 32	Porto Rico[1]
United States	40 089	39 383	38 890	41 543	* 36 607	35 289	34 377	31 364	35 544	34 386	Etats-Unis
America, South	**5 287**	**5 542**	**5 086**	**5 390**	**6 128**	**5 656**	**5 493**	**6 094**	**6 874**	**7 384**	**Amérique du Sud**
Argentina	660	1 146	699	619	1 003	937	594	677	937	1 341	Argentine
Bolivia* [1]	10	10	10	10	10	10	10	10	10	10	Bolivie* [1]
Brazil	2 473	2 481	2 727	2 866	3 136	2 766	2 888	3 259	3 578	* 3 700	Brésil
Chile	428	424	393	590	441	290	674	715	626	753	Chili
Colombia	1 112	922	751	* 752	838	898	593	694	800	730	Colombie
Peru[1]	304	318	348	399	457	506	485	* 490	* 560	* 500	Pérou[1]
Venezuela	300	241	158	154	243	249	249	249	363	* [1] 350	Venezuela
Asia	**24 966**	**29 604**	**33 646**	**29 872**	**32 103**	**32 789**	**32 110**	**31 085**	**32 264**	**33 478**	**Asie**
Afghanistan[5]	73	78	81	68	37	31	45	52	53	51	Afghanistan[5]
Bangladesh[2]	610	452	823	830	463	269	575	242	672	661	Bangladesh[2]
Burma	126	230	305	258	81	85	75	201	81	44	Birmanie
China	14 010	17 100	19 530	14 770	17 280	18 320	16 380	16 130	16 420	14 790	Chine
Cyprus	3	0	3	6	8	9	10	0	7	10	Chypre
Democratic Kampuchea* [1]	30	30	12	26	30	24	38	40	40	40	Kampuchea démocrat.* [1]
Democratic Yemen* [1]	75	75	75	73	82	73	73	73	73	73	Yémen démocratique* [1]
India[3]	4 076	5 329	6 696	7 032	7 262	7 269	7 308	* 7 008	* 7 656	* 9 876	Inde[3]
Indonesia	560	786	262	706	690	285	800	620	370	950	Indonésie
Iran(Islamic Rep.of)* [1,5]	700	700	700	700	600	600	700	753	753	753	Iran(Rép.islamique)* [1,5]
Iraq* [1]	64	82	82	91	90	80	80	80	80	70	Iraq* [1]
Israel[6]	[1] 86	* [1] 100	142	197	218	215	188	203	276	284	Israël[6]
Japan[7,8]	1 021	1 053	1 073	1 079	1 112	1 002	965	921	951	1 179	Japon[7,8]
Jordan	20	* 20	17	18	31	24	9	34	22	32	Jordanie
Korea, D. P. Rp.* [1]	540	540	540	540	571	571	572	572	572	572	Corée, Rp. P. D.* [1]
Korea, Republic of	640	710	673	446	502	741	976	574	632	642	Corée, République de
Kuwait	15	17	19	20	20	19	19	20	22	21	Koweït
Lebanon* [1]	36	35	12	10	12	16	10	6	6	6	Liban* [1]

For general note and footnotes, see end of table.

Voir la fin du tableau pour la remarque générale et les notes.

Salt, unrefined (continued) – Sel, non raffiné (suite)

Unit : Thousand metric tons

Unité : Milliers de tonnes métriques

Country or area	1976	1977	1978	1979	1980	1981	1982	1983	1984	1985	Pays ou zone
Mongolia	11	13	15	14	9	13	15	14	13	19	Mongolie
Pakistan[2]	427	336	435	486	495	514	534	548	581	571	Pakistan[2]
Philippines	203	200	226	322	346	355	364	382	363	421	Philippines
Sri Lanka	141	47	152	123	114	104	176	128	110	78	Sri Lanka
Syrian Arab Republic	54	48	62	75	90	85	102	88	38	106	Rép. arabe syrienne
Thailand[1]	* 171	* 176	* 175	* 174	* 180	176	176	171	175	178	Thaïlande[1]
Turkey	579	777	929	1 189	1 169	1 397	1 314	1 261	1 290	* 1 190	Turquie
Viet Nam	* [1] 580	* [1] 580	* [1] 530	* [1] 526	[1] 437	[1] 430	[1] 516	[1] 794	[1] 819	670	Viet Nam
Yemen	[1] 100	[1] 73	[1] 58	73	154	64	70	151	167	169	Yémen
Europe	**48 364**	**49 477**	**50 073**	**57 198**	**53 301**	**50 551**	**50 185**	**45 531**	**50 005**	**50 004**	**Europe**
EEC	***32 858***	***33 766***	***33 664***	***40 206***	***34 842***	***30 112***	***30 016***	***26 037***	***29 689***	***29 350***	***CEE***
Denmark	349	314	325	380	347	398	399	452	523	574	Danemark
France	5 890	5 776	6 283	8 057	7 104	6 636	6 694	5 686	7 160	5 690	France
Germany, Fed. Rep.	11 602	12 556	12 961	15 345	12 655	9 048	7 886	6 862	7 825	8 396	Allemagne, Rép. féd.
Greece	141	191	125	163	121	131	105	148	126	* 160	Grèce
Italy[9]	3 844	3 616	3 721	4 490	3 997	3 601	3 604	3 454	3 255	3 176	Italie[9]
Netherlands	3 026	3 111	2 939	3 951	3 464	3 578	3 691	3 124	3 674	4 154	Pays-Bas
United Kingdom	8 006	8 202	7 310	7 820	7 154	6 720	7 637	6 311	7 126	* 7 200	Royaume-Uni
EFTA	***1 437***	***1 398***	***1 409***	***1 627***	***1 717***	***1 865***	***1 704***	***1 486***	***1 753***	***1 785***	***AELE***
Austria	655	533	542	666	713	771	687	530	697	734	Autriche
Portugal	470	499	476	576	626	663	655	639	684	677	Portugal
Switzerland	312	366	391	385	378	431	362	317	372	374	Suisse
East Europe	***10 711***	***11 670***	***12 009***	***12 337***	***12 855***	***14 435***	***14 723***	***14 425***	***14 795***	***15 159***	***Europe de l'est***
Bulgaria[10]	75	87	87	86	82	84	88	87	89	89	Bulgarie[10]
Czechoslovakia[10]	48	49	49	50	56	60	67	77	80	82	Tchécoslovaquie[10]
German Dem. Rep.	2 560	2 642	2 741	3 052	3 128	4 985	5 483	5 339	5 041	5 104	Rép. dém. allemande
Poland	3 818	4 357	4 393	4 429	4 533	4 273	4 329	4 326	4 711	4 865	Pologne
Romania	4 210	4 535	4 739	4 720	5 056	5 033	4 756	4 596	4 874	5 019	Roumanie
Other Europe	***3 358***	***2 643***	***2 991***	***3 028***	***3 887***	***4 139***	***3 742***	***3 583***	***3 768***	***3 710***	***Autre Europe***
Malta[1]	2	1	1	1	1	0	0	0	0	0	Malte[1]
Spain	3 158	2 434	2 692	2 677	3 509	3 721	3 314	3 158	3 388	* 3 300	Espagne
Yugoslavia[11]	198	208	298	350	377	418	428	425	380	410	Yougoslavie[11]
USSR	**14 219**	**14 316**	**14 501**	**14 287**	**14 606**	**15 206**	**15 775**	**16 178**	**16 545**	**16 142**	**URSS**
Ukrainian SSR	*5 922*	*5 753*	*5 942*	*5 848*	*5 968*	*6 611*	*7 162*	*7 410*	*7 724*	*8 018*	*RSS d'Ukraine*
Oceania	**5 391**	**5 076**	**5 475**	**5 394**	**5 390**	**6 772**	**5 055**	**5 251**	**5 047**	**5 050**	**Océanie**
Australia[2]	5 350	5 023	5 410	5 339	5 335	6 716	4 985	* 5 170	* 4 990	* 4 990	Australie[2]
New Zealand	41	53	65	55	[1] 55	[1] 56	[1] 70	[1] 81	[1] 57	* [1] 60	Nouvelle-Zélande
Total	**152 679**	**159 149**	**164 935**	**170 041**	**166 009**	**165 129**	**161 304**	**154 403**	**166 666**	**166 828**	**Total**

General note.
Sodium chloride or common salt (NaCl), irrespective of the source from which it is obtained and the degree of purity or concentration. Refined salt, salt liquors and sea water are excluded. (SITC 27630–1).

1 Source: U. S. Bureau of Mines, (Washington, D. C.).
2 Twelve months ending 30 June of year stated.
3 Sea salt.
4 Data derived from tax paid on sales of salt.
5 Twelve months beginning 21 March of year stated.
6 Marketed quantities.
7 Production in licensed plants only.
8 Twelve months beginning 1 April of year stated.
9 Including brine.
10 Refined salt.
11 Excluding rock salt.

Remarque générale.
Chlorure de sodium ou sel ordinaire (NaCl), sans distinction de provenance ni de degré de pureté ou de concentration, à l'exclusion du sel rafinné, des saumures et de l'eau de mer. (CTCI 27630–1).

1 Source: U.S. Bureau of Mines, (Washington, D.C.).
2 Période de douze mois finissant le 30 juin de l'année indiquée.
3 Sel de marin.
4 Données obtenues à partir des droits prélevés sur les ventes de sel.
5 Période de douze mois commençant le 21 mars de l'année indiquée.
6 Quantités commercialisées.
7 Production des usines agrées seulement.
8 Période de douze mois commençant le 1er avril de l'année indiquée.
9 Y compris la saumure.
10 Sel raffiné.
11 Non compris le sel gemme.

Diamonds, industrial – Diamants industriels

Unit : Thousand carats

Unité : Milliers de carats

Country or area	1976	1977	1978	1979	1980	1981	1982	1983	1984	1985	Pays ou zone
Africa	**20 956**	**21 286**	**20 818**	**19 739**	**20 357**	**17 779**	**19 642**	**21 371**	**27 134**	**28 221**	**Afrique**
Angola[1]	85	88	175	211	* 370	* 350	* 310	* 259	* 202	* 250	Angola[1]
Botswana[1]	2 026	2 287	2 379	3 735	4 336	4 217	6 604	5 902	7 104	7 100	Botswana[1]
Central African Rep.	* [1] 114	[1] 119	[1] 85	[1] 110	115	103	91	65	102	106	Rép. centrafricaine
Côte d'Ivoire	* 16	19	23	32	0	0	0	0	0	...	Côte d'Ivoire
Ghana	[1] 2 055	[1] 1 717	[1] 1 281	[1] 1 128	[1] 1 132	[1] 751	[1] 616	[1] 306	[1] 315	* 585	Ghana
Guinea* [1]	55	55	55	58	26	26	23	17	14	7	Guinée* [1]
Lesotho[1]	1	3	5	4	4	* 11	* 9	...	...	...	Lesotho[1]
Liberia	[1 2] 162	[1 2] 163	[1 2] 180	[1 2] 132	175	204	263	198	239	138	Libéria
Namibia* [1]	85	100	95	83	78	62	51	48	46	45	Namibie* [1]
Sierra Leone[1]	650	538	426	451	275	97	* 87	103	* 105	* 105	Sierra Leone[1]
South Africa[1]	4 165	5 312	5 370	5 198	5 708	6 097	5 812	5 757	5 627	5 660	Afrique du Sud[1]
United Rep. Tanzania[1]	* 219	204	141	157	137	* 107	* 120	* 78	* 78	* 80	Rép.Unie de Tanzanie[1]
Zaire	11 323	10 681	10 603	8 440	8 001	5 754	5 656	8 627	* 13 290	* 14 124	Zaïre
America, South	**1 231**	**1 058**	**1 113**	**956**	**907**	**1 320**	**799**	**689**	**790**	**531**	**Amérique du Sud**
Brazil* [1]	...	...	...	384	414	926	450	450	550	350	Brésil* [1]
Guyana* [1]	8	17	17	16	10	6	7	5	8	7	Guyana* [1]
Venezuela	[1] 654	[1] 483	549	[1] 556	* 483	388	342	234	232	174	Venezuela
Asia	**15**	**15**	**15**	**15**	**15**	**15**	**15**	**25**	**25**	**26**	**Asie**
India	3	3	3	3	3	3	3	3	3	4	Inde
Indonesia* [1]	12	12	12	12	12	12	12	22	22	22	Indonésie* [1]
USSR* [1]	**7 900**	**8 200**	**8 400**	**7 000**	**8 600**	**8 500**	**8 500**	**7 000**	**6 400**	**6 400**	**URSS* [1]**
Total	**30 102**	**30 559**	**30 346**	**27 710**	**29 879**	**27 614**	**28 956**	**29 085**	**34 349**	**35 178**	**Total**

General note.
Mine and alluvial production of rough, uncut and unpolished diamonds for industrial uses. Industrial diamonds comprise all stones the colour, size and texture of which do not permit their use as jewellery, for example, boart, carbonado etc. Diamonds in the form of grit or powder are included. (SITC 27510–0+).

[1] Source: U. S. Bureau of Mines, (Washington, D. C.).
[2] Exports.

Remarque générale.
Production de diamants bruts, non taillés et non polis, en provenance de mines ou d'alluvions, destinés à des usages industriels. Cette rubrique comprend toutes les pierres dont la couleur, la dimension ou la structure interdisent leur emploi en joaillerie, par exemple les borts, les carbonados etc., ainsi que les diamants sous forme d'égrisés et de poudres. (CTCI 27510–0+).

[1] Source: U.S. Bureau of Mines, (Washington, D.C.).
[2] Exportations.

Gypsum, crude – Gypse brut

Unit : Thousand metric tons

Unité : Milliers de tonnes métriques

Country or area	1976	1977	1978	1979	1980	1981	1982	1983	1984	1985	Pays ou zone
Africa	**1 347**	**1 599**	**1 814**	**2 021**	**2 041**	**2 094**	**2 306**	**2 245**	**2 278**	**2 241**	**Afrique**
Algeria* [1]	172	172	172	190	200	200	200	250	250	250	Algérie* [1]
Angola* [1]	20	20	25	25	25	20	20	20	20	20	Angola* [1]
Egypt	200	250	593	796	690	689	845	721	* 726	* 726	Egypte
Ethiopia [1]	...	6	1	1	1	5	5	* 5	* 5	* 5	Ethiopie [1]
Kenya [2]	[1] 0	[1] 0	[1] 0	[1] 0	0	0	0	1	0	48	Kenya [2]
Libyan Arab Jamah.* [1]	59	290	180	164	180	180	175	180	180	180	Jamah.arabe libyenne* [1]
Mauritania [1]	11	10	14	16	12	2	* 5	* 4	* 1	* 6	Mauritanie [1]
Morocco [1]	...	...	...	...	378	* 400	* 420	* 440	* 450	* 450	Maroc [1]
Niger [1]	3	3	3	3	* 3	* 3	* 3	* 3	* 3	* 3	Niger [1]
South Africa	[1] 483	[1] 440	[1] 389	[1] 377	453	* 497	535	* 518	* 535	442	Afrique du Sud
Sudan [1 2]	18	* 15	* 20	* 10	* 10	* 8	* 8	* 8	* 8	* 6	Soudan [1 2]
Tunisia [1]	39	40	40	60	75	* 75	* 75	* 80	* 85	* 90	Tunisie [1]
United Rep. Tanzania [1]	10	8	20	9	11	12	* 12	* 12	* 12	* 12	Rép.Unie de Tanzanie [1]
Zambia [1]	5	5	2	0	...	...	...	...	...	...	Zambie [1]
America, North	**19 527**	**22 160**	**24 590**	**24 547**	**22 365**	**21 241**	**18 972**	**23 432**	**25 022**	**24 438**	**Amérique du Nord**
Barbados	...	547	611	588	933	667	610	...	...	...	Barbade
Canada [2 3]	[1] 6 002	[1] 7 234	[1] 8 075	[1] 8 098	[1] 7 336	7 025	5 987	7 507	7 775	7 761	Canada [2 3]
Cuba	133	202	228	255	246	260	233	178	159	159	Cuba
Dominican Republic	[1] 220	[1] 226	[1] 171	[1] 175	# 251	238	278	147	145	145	Rép. dominicaine
El Salvador [1]	* 6	7	7	7	9	* 6	* 5	* 5	* 5	* 4	El Salvador [1]
Guatemala [1]	* 14	32	38	25	34	29	28	39	26	17	Guatemala [1]
Honduras [1]	10	18	* 23	* 23	* 23	* 20	* 20	* 20	21	23	Honduras [1]
Jamaica	253	215	134	47	95	146	188	136	160	176	Jamaïque
Mexico [1]	1 414	1 496	1 758	2 021	2 171	2 390	2 043	2 958	2 945	2 366	Mexique [1]
Nicaragua [2]	* 30	* 36	* 36	* 36	* 40	* 30	* 20	12	20	8	Nicaragua [2]
United States	10 868	[4] 12 147	[4] 13 509	[4] 13 272	[4] 11 227	[4] 10 430	[4] 9 560	[4] 11 688	[4] 13 000	[4] 12 990	Etats–Unis
America, South	**1 722**	**1 813**	**1 915**	**1 974**	**2 414**	**2 455**	**2 262**	**2 001**	**1 960**	**1 886**	**Amérique du Sud**
Argentina	507	547	611	587	932	671	615	578	567	342	Argentine
Bolivia [1 5]	* 1	* 1	* 1	* 1	1	1	1	* 1	* 1	* 1	Bolivie [1 5]
Brazil	545	543	475	465	606	695	681	556	494	* 550	Brésil
Chile	[1] 122	[1] 147	[1] 174	[1] 169	198	238	90	66	167	196	Chili
Colombia [1]	205	210	255	257	262	270	281	238	* 260	* 250	Colombie [1]
Ecuador [1]	44	42	34	6	6	2	* 2	* 2	* 2	* 2	Equateur [1]
Paraguay [1]	16	14	9	11	12	10	6	4	6	6	Paraguay [1]
Peru [1]	171	142	169	218	280	350	* 350	* 350	* 350	* 350	Pérou [1]
Venezuela	[1] 111	[1] 167	[1] 187	[1] 260	[1] 117	218	236	206	113	189	Venezuela
Asia	**13 503**	**16 373**	**18 252**	**20 178**	**19 933**	**19 610**	**19 036**	**20 364**	**20 688**	**21 659**	**Asie**
Afghanistan	...	...	6	0	0	6	6	10	8	8	Afghanistan
Burma	15	16	19	31	24	14	14	20	17	32	Birmanie
China [1]	* 998	* 998	* 1 542	* 3 629	* 3 266	3 400	3 500	4 300	4 800	5 000	Chine [1]
Cyprus	68	95	61	46	39	26	29	32	22	16	Chypre
India	727	778	888	877	866	957	962	1 022	1 262	1 289	Inde
Iran(Islamic Rep.of)* [1]	6 500	6 900	7 983	6 985	6 985	5 990	4 990	5 440	4 990	4 990	Iran(Rép.islamique)* [1]
Iraq* [1]	163	163	163	163	172	170	170	170	300	300	Iraq* [1]
Israel [1]	200	200	200	73	80	43	42	42	42	42	Israël [1]
Japan [1]	* 3 367	[6] 5 550	[6] 5 794	[6] 6 273	[6] 6 105	[6] 6 137	[6] 6 363	[6] 5 844	* [6] 6 078	* [6] 6 260	Japon [1]
Jordan [1]	21	22	36	36	* 45	53	40	41	110	109	Jordanie [1]
Korea, Republic of [1]	* [7] 499	* 599	* 617	* 617	* 635	* 635	* 726	* 907	506	792	Corée, République de [1]
Lao Peoples Dem.Rep. [1]	...	...	...	0	20	41	60	70	82	* 82	Rép. dém. pop. lao [1]
Lebanon [1]	* 13	15	11	10	* 10	10	* 5	* 5	* 5	* 3	Liban [1]
Mongolia	0	0	0	0	* [1] 30	* [1] 32	* [1] 32	* [1] 32	* [1] 32	* [1] 32	Mongolie
Pakistan	447	283	253	234	368	554	303	341	375	430	Pakistan
Philippines [1]	3	[7] 112	[7] 112	[7] 110	[7] 110	[7] 111	[7] 110	[7] 110	[7] 112	* [7] 112	Philippines [1]
Saudi Arabia [1]	40	42	52	# 300	300	350	363	500	300	* 300	Arabie saoudite [1]
Syrian Arab Republic	* 63	* 85	* 86	[1] 64	[1] 79	[1] 80	[1] 82	* [1] 92	* [1] 93	...	Rép. arabe syrienne
Thailand	268	380	281	352	412	540	753	760	1 110	1 273	Thaïlande
Turkey [1]	33	65	61	* 64	* 72	91	* 91	76	58	78	Turquie [1]
Viet Nam* [1]	10	12	14	14	15	16	27	27	27	27	Viet Nam* [1]
Yemen	...	...	...	* 0	* 0	4	5	23	59	91	Yémen
Europe	**28 024**	**29 249**	**26 030**	**26 586**	**27 005**	**25 947**	**24 689**	**25 509**	**25 307**	**24 289**	**Europe**
EEC	***17 306***	***17 782***	***14 602***	***14 906***	***15 527***	***14 443***	***13 498***	***13 653***	***13 744***	***12 931***	***CEE***
Belgium [1 2]	220	168	183	192	* 174	* 154	0	0	0	...	Belgique [1 2]
France	6 630	6 700	6 071	6 127	6 491	6 147	5 849	5 557	5 435	5 262	France

For general note and footnotes, see end of table.

Voir la fin du tableau pour la remarque générale et les notes.

Gypsum, crude (continued) – Gypse brut (suite)

Unit : Thousand metric tons

Unité : Milliers de tonnes métriques

Country or area	1976	1977	1978	1979	1980	1981	1982	1983	1984	1985	Pays ou zone
Germany, Fed. Rep.	2 282	2 636	2 633	2 878	2 990	2 665	2 545	2 742	2 947	2 148	Allemagne, Rép. féd.
Greece	320	517	507	312	485	629	686	645	583	* 690	Grèce
Ireland[1]	355	342	392	417	381	359	371	352	325	* 304	Irlande[1]
Italy[1]	* 4 173	4 180	1 585	1 479	1 634	1 544	1 335	1 388	* 1 264	* 1 261	Italie[1]
Luxembourg	2	3	1	1	1	1	1	2	2	1	Luxembourg
United Kingdom[2]	3 324	3 236	3 230	* 3 500	3 371	2 944	2 711	2 967	3 188	3 189	Royaume–Uni[2]
EFTA	***1 000***	***1 055***	***1 045***	***1 109***	***1 125***	***1 129***	***1 042***	***1 077***	***1 045***	***1 018***	***AELE***
Austria	770	809	766	798	834	800	728	751	740	694	Autriche
Portugal	* 160	176	209	* 241	236	243	237	249	228	242	Portugal
Switzerland[1]	* 70	* 70	* 70	* 70	* 55	* 86	77	* 77	* 77	* 82	Suisse[1]
East Europe	***4 261***	***4 448***	***4 511***	***4 634***	***4 459***	***4 418***	***4 460***	***4 524***	***4 545***	***4 490***	***Europe de l'est***
Bulgaria	232	295	340	309	311	350	376	386	393	388	Bulgarie
Czechoslovakia	660	682	697	734	757	767	794	848	842	772	Tchécoslovaquie
German Dem. Rep.* [1]	301	340	349	360	360	360	360	360	360	360	Rép. dém. allemande* [1]
Poland* [1]	1 252	1 340	1 350	1 361	1 420	1 311	1 300	1 300	1 300	1 350	Pologne* [1]
Romania* [1]	...	...	1 775	1 870	1 611	1 630	1 630	1 630	1 650	1 620	Roumanie* [1]
Other Europe	***5 457***	***5 964***	***5 872***	***5 937***	***5 894***	***5 957***	***5 689***	***6 255***	***5 973***	***5 850***	***Autre Europe***
Spain	4 909	5 481	5 369	5 369	5 275	5 288	5 049	5 620	5 366	* 5 250	Espagne
Yugoslavia	548	483	503	568	619	669	640	* 635	607	600	Yougoslavie
USSR* [1]	**6 441**	**5 171**	**5 261**	**5 400**	**4 900**	**4 900**	**4 900**	**4 900**	**4 900**	**4 900**	**URSS* [1]**
Oceania	**912**	**992**	**900**	**1 074**	**1 349**	**1 590**	**2 091**	**1 492**	**1 869**	**1 753**	**Océanie**
Australia	* 912	992	900	1 074	1 349	1 590	2 091	1 492	1 869	1 753	Australie
Total	**71 475**	**77 356**	**78 762**	**81 780**	**80 007**	**77 837**	**74 256**	**79 943**	**82 024**	**81 166**	**Total**

General note.
Gypsum is a natural hydrated calcium sulphate generally white and friable. Anhydrite is a natural anhydrous form of calcium sulphate used in the manufacture of sulphuric acid and of certain types of plaster. (SITC 27321–1).

1 Source: U. S. Bureau of Mines, (Washington, D. C.).
2 Including anhydrite.
3 Shipments.
4 Excluding byproduct gypsum.
5 Net exports.
6 Gypsum consumed.
7 Including byproduct gypsum.

Remarque générale.
Le gypse est un sulfate de calcium naturel hydraté, généralement friable et de couleur blanche. L'anhydrite est une forme anhydre du sulfate de calcium naturel, utilisée dans la fabrication de l'acide sulfurique et de certains genres de plâtres. (CTCI 27321–1).

1 Source: U.S. Bureau of Mines, (Washington, D.C.).
2 Y compris l'anhydrite.
3 Expéditions.
4 Non compris le gypse obtenu comme sous–produit.
5 Exportations nettes.
6 Le gypse consommé.
7 Y compris le gypse obtenu comme sous–produit.

Abrasives, natural (pozzolan, pumice etc.) – Abrasifs naturels (pouzzolane, pierre ponce etc.)

Unit : Thousand metric tons — Unité : Milliers de tonnes métriques

Country or area	1976	1977	1978	1979	1980	1981	1982	1983	1984	1985	Pays ou zone
Africa	**33.6**	**33.5**	**33.1**	**48.1**	**54.9**	**63.1**	**60.1**	**69.6**	**76.3**	**83.0**	**Afrique**
Cameroon[1 2]	17.9	* 17.9	17.5	...	...	53.0	50.0	...	...	...	Cameroun[1 2]
Cape Verde* [1 2]	15.4	15.4	15.4	15.4	15.4	10.0	10.0	10.0	10.0	10.0	Cap-Vert* [1 2]
Egypt[2 3]	0.3	* 0.2	* 0.2	0.1	0.1	0.1	0.1	...	...	...	Egypte[2 3]
America, North	**1 237.8**	**1 681.6**	**1 626.7**	**4 614.1**	**3 949.6**	**4 306.1**	**898.6**	**3 492.8**	**970.0**	**995.0**	**Amérique du Nord**
Costa Rica[2]	* 0.9	1.3	1.4	1.3	* 0.9	* 0.9	* 1.8	* 1.8	* 1.8	* 1.8	Costa Rica[2]
Dominica* [2 3]	110.0	109.0	109.0	109.0	109.0	109.0	109.0	109.0	109.0	109.0	Dominique* [2 3]
Guadeloupe* [1 2]	200.0	190.0	200.0	200.0	250.0	240.4	240.4	240.4	240.4	240.4	Guadeloupe* [1 2]
Guatemala	[2] 24.0	[2] 26.0	[2] 54.4	54.6	30.7	20.5	* 16.0	* 15.1	* 13.4	* 33.0	Guatemala
Martinique[3]	* 80.0	286.6	* 166.0	166.0	[2] 153.0	[2] 156.0	[2] 154.0	* [2] 150.0	* [2] 150.0	* [2] 150.0	Martinique[3]
United States[4]	822.9	1 068.7	1 095.9	4 083.2	3 406.0	3 779.3	[5] 377.4	2 976.5	[5] 455.4	[5] 460.8	Etats-Unis[4]
America, South	**156.3**	**223.9**	**204.1**	**266.4**	**286.3**	**302.3**	**225.9**	**242.4**	**226.4**	**219.5**	**Amérique du Sud**
Argentina	57.6	65.0	21.5	46.3	36.5	24.9	53.5	68.6	54.3	13.2	Argentine
Chile[1]	98.7	158.9	182.5	220.1	249.8	277.4	172.4	173.8	172.1	206.3	Chili[1]
Asia	**190.9**	**191.3**	**191.7**	**195.9**	**94.8**	**234.6**	**251.8**	**192.3**	**193.5**	**194.4**	**Asie**
India	2.7	3.1	3.5	7.7	5.2	4.6	6.9	4.2	5.4	6.2	Inde
Turkey[3]	...	...	...	...	89.6	230.0	245.0	...	...	...	Turquie[3]
Europe	**10 223.0**	**13 067.6**	**13 930.0**	**12 635.5**	**11 616.9**	**10 538.6**	**11 015.5**	**10 170.8**	**10 256.7**	**9 396.6**	**Europe**
EEC	***10 069.7***	***12 107.6***	***13 209.0***	***11 809.9***	***10 471.1***	***9 506.4***	***9 942.3***	***9 046.9***	***9 268.0***	***8 415.6***	***CEE***
France[1]	638.0	686.0	653.0	563.0	577.0	470.0	477.0	413.0	489.6	496.1	France[1]
Germany, Fed. Rep.[6 7 8]	2 306.0	3 139.0	3 523.0	2 642.0	2 104.0	1 255.0	...	...	...	...	Allemagne, Rép. féd.[6 7 8]
Greece[1 3]	1 380.2	1 822.6	2 433.0	1 854.9	2 063.1	1 663.3	1 594.1	1 626.6	* 1 535.0	* 1 540.0	Grèce[1 3]
Italy[1 9]	5 745.4	[2] 6 460.0	[2] 6 600.0	[2] 6 750.0	[2] 5 727.0	[2] 6 118.1	[2] 6 300.0	[2] 5 700.0	[2] 6 200.0	[2] 5 600.0	Italie[1 9]
EFTA	***19.9***	***30.0***	***31.0***	***46.5***	***59.4***	***56.3***	***39.4***	***65.9***	***85.9***	***81.0***	***AELE***
Austria	17.7	20.8	21.3	20.9	22.3	21.2	19.5	19.5	21.0	21.9	Autriche
Finland	0.6	1.6	...	...	...	...	...	...	...	...	Finlande
Iceland[3]	1.5	7.6	8.5	24.5	36.0	33.9	18.8	45.3	63.7	58.0	Islande[3]
Other Europe	***133.4***	***930.0***	***690.0***	***779.1***	***1 086.4***	***976.0***	***1 033.8***	***1 057.9***	***902.8***	***900.0***	***Autre Europe***
Spain	133.4	* 930.0	* 690.0	779.1	1 086.4	976.0	1 033.8	1 057.9	902.8	* 900.0	Espagne
Oceania	**93.2**	**29.5**	**43.1**	**27.6**	**16.3**	**36.5**	**50.8**	**18.0**	**16.0**	**21.0**	**Océanie**
American Samoa[2 9]	43.0	1.0	* 3.6	* 1.8	* 2.7	* 2.5	...	...	...	...	Samoa américaines[2 9]
New Zealand[3]	50.2	28.5	39.5	25.8	[2] 13.6	[2] 34.0	[2] 50.0	[2] 17.0	[2] 15.0	* [2] 20.0	Nouvelle-Zélande[3]
Total	**11 934.7**	**15 227.5**	**16 028.7**	**17 787.6**	**16 018.8**	**15 481.2**	**12 502.8**	**14 185.9**	**11 738.9**	**10 909.6**	**Total**

General note.
Data in this table refer to the production of natural abrasives such as pozzolan, pumice and volcanic cinder. Unless otherwise stated, production of other abrasives including emery, natural corundum, tripoli and garnet is not included. Precious or semi-precious stone dust or powder are also excluded. (SITC 27523-1).

1 Pozzolan.
2 Source: U. S. Bureau of Mines, (Washington, D. C.).
3 Pumice.
4 Including pumice for use other than as an abrasive. Also including volcanic cinders used principally for ballast.
5 Excluding volcanic cinder.
6 Marketable production.
7 Including pumice and pumicite for construction purposes.
8 Beginning 1982, series discontinued.
9 Pumice and pumicite.

Remarque générale.
Les données se rapportent à la production des abrasifs naturels (pouzzolane, pierre ponce, lapilli et cendre volcanique). Sauf avis contraire, cette rubrique ne comprend ni les autres abrasifs i.e. émeri, corindon naturel, "tripoli" et grenat, ni les égrisés et les poudres de pierres précieuses et semi-précieuses. (CTCI 27523-1).

1 Pouzzolane.
2 Source: U.S. Bureau of Mines, (Washington, D.C.).
3 Pierre ponce.
4 Y compris la pierre ponce utilisée autrement que comme abrasif. Y compris également les cendres volcaniques utilisées essentiellement comme ballast.
5 Non compris les cendres volcaniques.
6 Production commercialisable.
7 Y compris la pierre ponce et le lapilli utilisés dans la construction.
8 A partir de 1982, la série a été abandonnée.
9 Pierre ponce et lapilli.

Graphite, natural – Graphite naturel

Unit : Metric tons

Unité : Tonnes métriques

Country or area	1976	1977	1978	1979	1980	1981	1982	1983	1984	1985	Pays ou zone
Africa	**22 930**	**21 628**	**22 863**	**20 373**	**17 291**	**27 263**	**23 785**	**33 663**	**26 749**	**25 384**	**Afrique**
Madagascar	[1] 17 410	[1] 15 727	[1] 16 625	[1] 14 242	[1] 9 906	[1] 16 045	# 15 211	13 496	14 155	14 718	Madagascar
South Africa	530	911	583	394	0	0	...	...	...	...	Afrique du Sud
Zimbabwe	* [1] 4 990	* [1] 4 990	# 5 655	5 737	7 385	11 218	8 225	19 862	12 334	10 450	Zimbabwe
America, North	**60 337**	**58 432**	**52 264**	**50 880**	**44 506**	**41 142**	**34 370**	**44 327**	**41 529**	**35 378**	**Amérique du Nord**
Mexico	[1] 60 337	[1] 58 432	[1] 52 264	50 880	44 506	41 142	34 370	44 327	41 529	35 378	Mexique
America, South	**31 540**	**53 688**	**47 870**	**135 987**	**234 888**	**464 091**	**360 003**	**442 830**	**290 022**	**300 000**	**Amérique du Sud**
Argentina	145	85	25	10	5	2	12	20	15	0	Argentine
Brazil	31 395	53 603	47 845	135 977	234 883	464 089	359 991	442 810	290 007	* 300 000	Brésil
Asia	**166 658**	**208 428**	**235 624**	**329 844**	**310 798**	**328 867**	**311 998**	**298 598**	**314 367**	**306 150**	**Asie**
Burma[1,2]	161	96	280	268	199	300	279	200	* 234	* 234	Birmanie[1,2]
China* [1]	50 000	60 000	80 000	182 000	160 000	184 000	185 000	185 000	185 000	185 000	Chine* [1]
India	41 157	48 455	63 784	52 821	54 960	72 796	61 411	43 874	36 923	33 586	Inde
Korea, Dem.Ppl's.Rep.[1]	20 000	20 000	20 000	25 000	25 000	25 000	* 25 400	* 25 400	* 25 400	* 25 400	Corée, Rép.pop.dém.de[1]
Korea, Republic of	41 690	65 955	56 319	56 693	60 586	34 891	26 965	33 266	* 58 563	* 51 890	Corée, République de
Pakistan	...	...	...	...	...	...	150	97	...	...	Pakistan
Sri Lanka	[1] 8 290	[1] 8 875	[1] 10 506	[1] 9 491	[1] 7 656	7 453	8 803	5 870	5 620	7 413	Sri Lanka
Thailand[1]	...	...	...	...	2 074	1 800	630	86	0	0	Thaïlande[1]
Turkey	...	...	...	1 653	200	...	3 360	4 805	...	...	Turquie
Europe	**76 590**	**77 730**	**87 110**	**87 184**	**90 230**	**75 208**	**81 242**	**99 946**	**108 937**	**85 048**	**Europe**
EEC	***13 398***	***12 145***	***10 489***	***7 773***	***9 645***	***11 720***	***14 863***	***12 299***	***14 765***	***13 478***	***CEE***
Germany, Fed. Rep.[1,3]	9 550	8 326	6 381	3 671	# 5 688	8 186	11 653	* 10 000	* 12 000	* 10 900	Allemagne, Rép. féd.[1,3]
Italy	3 848	3 819	4 108	4 102	3 957	3 534	3 210	2 299	...	...	Italie
EFTA	***42 128***	***44 385***	***51 652***	***52 411***	***47 605***	***30 671***	***31 902***	***48 481***	***53 856***	***33 448***	***AELE***
Austria[4]	33 057	35 288	40 501	40 519	37 199	23 807	24 451	40 418	43 789	30 764	Autriche[4]
Norway	9 071	9 097	11 151	11 892	10 406	6 864	7 451	8 063	10 067	2 684	Norvège
East Europe	***21 064***	***21 200***	***24 969***	***27 000***	***32 980***	***32 817***	***34 477***	***39 166***	***40 316***	***38 122***	***Europe de l'est***
Czechoslovakia	15 064	15 200	13 630	14 600	20 480	20 317	21 977	26 666	27 816	25 622	Tchécoslovaquie
Romania* [1]	6 000	6 000	11 339	12 400	12 500	12 500	12 500	12 500	12 500	12 500	Roumanie* [1]
USSR* [1]	**95 000**	**95 000**	**100 000**	**80 000**	**80 000**	**70 000**	**75 000**	**80 000**	**80 000**	**82 000**	**URSS* [1]**
Total	**453 055**	**514 906**	**545 731**	**704 268**	**777 713**	**1 006 571**	**886 398**	**999 364**	**861 604**	**833 960**	**Total**

General note.
Natural graphite (plumbago or black lead) regardless of carbon content. (SITC 27622–0).

[1] Source: U. S. Bureau of Mines, (Washington, D. C.).
[2] Twelve months ending 31 March of year stated.
[3] Marketable production.
[4] Crude production.

Remarque générale.
Graphite naturel (plombagine ou mine de plomb), quelle qu'en soit la teneur en carbone. (CTCI 27622–0).

[1] Source: U.S. Bureau of Mines, (Washington, D.C.).
[2] Période de douze mois finissant le 31 mars de l'année indiquée.
[3] Production commercialisable.
[4] Production brute.

Unit : Thousand metric tons

Unité : Milliers de tonnes métriques

Country or area	1976	1977	1978	1979	1980	1981	1982	1983	1984	1985	Pays ou zone
Africa	**694**	**692**	**544**	**535**	**563**	**523**	**441**	**401**	**359**	**364**	**Afrique**
Egypt[1]	1	1	1	1	1	2	0	0	0	0	Egypte[1]
Mozambique[2]	0	0	0	* 1	* 1	* 2	1	* 1	* 1	* 1	Mozambique[2]
South Africa	370	380	257	249	277	236	212	221	167	164	Afrique du Sud
Swaziland[3]	42	38	37	34	33	35	30	26	26	25	Swaziland[3]
Zimbabwe	281	273	249	250	251	248	198	153	165	174	Zimbabwe
America, North	**1 641**	**1 609**	**1 515**	**1 586**	**1 403**	**1 209**	**901**	**899**	**895**	**808**	**Amérique du Nord**
Canada[4]	1 536	1 517	1 422	1 493	1 323	1 133	837	829	837	750	Canada[4]
United States[5]	105	92	93	93	80	76	64	70	58	58	Etats–Unis[5]
America, South	**96**	**97**	**128**	**144**	**177**	**144**	**152**	**165**	**146**	**161**	**Amérique du Sud**
Argentina	[2] 0	# 1	1	1	* 1	* 1	1	1	1	0	Argentine
Brazil[6]	93	93	123	138	170	138	146	159	135	148	Brésil[6]
Colombia[2]	...	...	...	...	...	5	5	5	10	13	Colombie[2]
Asia	**220**	**288**	**356**	**270**	**226**	**188**	**226**	**268**	**263**	**268**	**Asie**
Afghanistan[2]	13	13	* 13	* 4	0	0	0	...	...	...	Afghanistan[2]
China* [2]	120	200	250	140	132	106	110	160	160	160	Chine* [2]
Cyprus	35	37	34	36	35	26	19	17	7	16	Chypre
India	24	22	23	32	34	28	27	24	27	29	Inde
Indonesia[2]	...	...	...	0	0	* 5	* 25	* 25	* 25	* 25	Indonésie[2]
Japan[7]	8	6	6	4	...	...	...	...	...	...	Japon[7]
Korea, Republic of	5	6	14	15	10	14	16	13	8	5	Corée, République de
Turkey	10	4	13	39	9	3	23	23	30	27	Turquie
Europe	**265**	**248**	**235**	**406**	**215**	**749**	**285**	**2 641**	**3 922**	**3 942**	**Europe**
EEC	***209***	***193***	***179***	***395***	***202***	***736***	***272***	***2 629***	***3 913***	***3 936***	***CEE***
Greece	...	...	...	...	44	599	156	2 490	3 766	* 3 800	Grèce
Italy[2]	165	149	135	144	158	137	116	139	147	* 136	Italie[2]
East Europe	***43***	***46***	***46***	***2***	***2***	***1***	***1***	***1***	***1***	***0***	***Europe de l'est***
Bulgaria[6]	0	1	1	1	1	0	1	1	1	0	Bulgarie[6]
Czechoslovakia	43	45	45	[6] 1	[6] 1	[6] 0	[6] 0	[6] 0	[6] 0	[6] 0	Tchécoslovaquie
Other Europe	***13***	***9***	***10***	***10***	***11***	***12***	***11***	***11***	***7***	***6***	***Autre Europe***
Yugoslavia[8]	13	9	10	10	11	12	11	11	7	6	Yougoslavie[8]
USSR[2]	*** 1 850**	*** 1 900**	*** 1 945**	*** 2 020**	*** 2 150**	**2 479**	**2 700**	**2 800**	**2 850**	*** 2 900**	**URSS[2]**
Oceania	**57**	**56**	**51**	**68**	**91**	**73**	**34**	**12**	**0**	**0**	**Océanie**
Australia[9]	57	56	51	68	91	73	34	12	0	0	Australie[9]
Total	**4 823**	**4 891**	**4 775**	**5 029**	**4 825**	**5 364**	**4 739**	**7 186**	**8 435**	**8 443**	**Total**

General note.
Crude, washed or ground asbestos. (SITC 27640–0).

[1] Including vermiculite.
[2] Source: U. S. Bureau of Mines, (Washington, D. C.).
[3] Exports.
[4] Shipments.
[5] Asbestos sold or used by producers.
[6] Asbestos fibres only.
[7] Beginning 1980, data are confidential.
[8] Excluding asbestos powder.
[9] Twelve months ending 30 June of year stated.

Remarque générale.
Amiante brut, lavé ou broyé. (CTCI 27640–0).

[1] Y compris la vermiculite.
[2] Source: U.S. Bureau of Mines, (Washington, D.C.).
[3] Exportations.
[4] Expéditions.
[5] Amiante vendu ou utilisé par les producteurs.
[6] Fibres d'amiante seulement.
[7] A partir de 1980, les données sont confidentielles.
[8] Non compris l'amiante en poudre.
[9] Période de douze mois finissant le 30 juin de l'année indiquée.

Mica (total production) – Mica (production totale)

Unit : Metric tons — Unité : Tonnes métriques

Country or area	1976	1977	1978	1979	1980	1981	1982	1983	1984	1985	Pays ou zone
Africa	**3 928**	**5 933**	**6 100**	**7 040**	**5 969**	**5 287**	**2 393**	**4 094**	**5 507**	**2 954**	**Afrique**
Egypt[1]	* 10	86	* 86	0	0	0	...	...	...	...	Egypte[1]
Madagascar	81	1 498	1 566	1 167	1 731	588	300	1 096	719	578	Madagascar
Mozambique* [1]	900	800	900	250	200	299	148	309	299	299	Mozambique* [1]
South Africa	[1] 2 380	[1] 3 142	[1] 2 542	[1] 3 617	[1] 2 528	* 2 395	* 1 762	* 2 672	* 4 478	2 057	Afrique du Sud
Sudan* [1]	550	400	1 000	2 000	1 500	2 000	165	10	10	10	Soudan* [1]
United Rep. Tanzania[1]	7	7	6	6	10	5	5	0	0	0	Rép.Unie de Tanzanie[1]
America, North	**112 903**	**117 798**	**126 501**	**121 843**	**108 833**	**122 732**	**96 672**	**128 566**	**147 733**	**126 637**	**Amérique du Nord**
Mexico[1]	1 303	771	401	243	3 600	2 077	510	1 560	1 676	1 446	Mexique[1]
United States	111 600	117 027	126 100	121 600	105 233	120 655	96 162	127 006	146 057	125 191	Etats–Unis
America, South	**5 469**	**4 297**	**7 285**	**5 590**	**5 701**	**1 864**	**1 750**	**4 477**	**4 441**	**4 662**	**Amérique du Sud**
Argentina	2 620	2 142	2 632	1 500	834	503	322	332	290	595	Argentine
Brazil	2 799	1 955	4 553	4 074	4 817	787	878	3 595	3 601	* 3 500	Brésil
Colombia[1]	* 40	* 50	0	0	0	0	0	0	0	...	Colombie[1]
Peru[1]	* 10	150	100	16	50	574	* 550	* 550	* 550	* 550	Pérou[1]
Asia	**14 966**	**19 661**	**26 687**	**19 474**	**18 432**	**18 725**	**29 457**	**22 082**	**30 824**	**20 058**	**Asie**
India	9 494	9 352	9 593	9 073	7 934	8 534	8 775	7 504	6 179	4 880	Inde
Korea, Republic of[1]	5 314	10 133	16 923	10 005	10 330	10 000	20 355	14 402	24 436	* 14 969	Corée, République de[1]
Nepal* [1]	5	5	5	5	5	...	...	...	...	...	Népal* [1]
Pakistan	16	71	...	...	...	4	31	0	...	...	Pakistan
Sri Lanka[1]	137	100	140	369	145	182	291	171	* 200	* 200	Sri Lanka[1]
Europe	**7 060**	**10 065**	**10 714**	**12 547**	**13 925**	**12 854**	**11 657**	**11 890**	**12 065**	**11 646**	**Europe**
EEC	***6 490***	***6 990***	***7 300***	***6 990***	***8 838***	***9 059***	***7 950***	***9 286***	***10 854***	***10 000***	***CEE***
France[1]	* 6 490	* 6 990	* 7 300	* 6 990	8 838	9 059	7 950	9 286	* 10 854	* 10 000	France[1]
EFTA	***2***	***2***	***0***	***0***	***7***	***6***	***7***	***0***	***0***	***2***	***AELE***
Sweden	...	...	0	0	7	6	7	0	0	...	Suède
Other Europe	***568***	***3 073***	***3 414***	***5 557***	***5 080***	***3 789***	***3 700***	***2 604***	***1 211***	***1 644***	***Autre Europe***
Spain	* 500	2 934	3 345	5 169	4 831	3 524	3 428	1 300	990	* 1 000	Espagne
Yugoslavia	68	139	69	388	249	265	272	1 304	221	644	Yougoslavie
USSR* [1]	**43 000**	**44 000**	**45 000**	**46 000**	**46 000**	**47 000**	**48 000**	**49 000**	**49 000**	**50 000**	**URSS* [1]**
Oceania	**161**	**161**	**161**	**161**	**161**	**161**	**161**	**161**	**161**	**161**	**Océanie**
Australia	...	...	...	161	...	...	...	...	...	...	Australie
Total	**187 487**	**201 915**	**222 448**	**212 655**	**199 021**	**208 623**	**190 090**	**220 270**	**249 731**	**216 118**	**Total**

General note.
Mica (muscovite, phlogopite, biotite etc.) constitutes a group of natural complex aluminium silicates characterizedby the fact that they are readily split into glistening, transparent, flexible sheets of varied colour. This item includes crude mica, which consists of mica crystals, of irregular shape, size and thickness, covered with earth (books); mica sheets, obtained by rifting cobbed and trimmed books; mica splittings, obtained by rifting sheet mica; and mica waste and powder. (SITC 27652–0).

[1] Source: U. S. Bureau of Mines, (Washington, D. C.).

Remarque générale.
Les micas (muscovite, phlogopite, biotite etc.) constituent un groupe de silico–aluminates naturels complexes, dont la caractéristique est de se cliver facilement en lamelles flexibles brillantes, transparentes et de teintes diverses. Cette rubrique comprend le mica brut, se présentant sous forme de cristaux de forme, de surface et d'épaisseur irrégulières, encore enrobés de matières terreuses (books); le mica en feuilles, obtenu par clivage de 'books' préalablement dégrossis puis ébarbés; le mica en lamelles, obtenu par simple clivage de feuilles de mica; et les déchets et la poudre de mica. (CTCI 27652–0).

[1] Source: U.S. Bureau of Mines, (Washington, D.C.).

Mica in book form (sheet and splittings) – Mica sous forme feuilletée (en feuilles et en lamelles)

Unit : Metric tons

Unité : Tonnes métriques

Country or area	1976	1977	1978	1979	1980	1981	1982	1983	1984	1985	Pays ou zone
Africa	**3 553**	**4 584**	**4 445**	**3 423**	**3 441**	**2 638**	**503**	**419**	**405**	**402**	**Afrique**
Madagascar	62	* 1 498	1 566	1 167	1 731	334	185	100	96	93	Madagascar
Mozambique* [1 2]	900	800	900	250	200	299	148	309	299	299	Mozambique* [1 2]
Sudan* [2]	...	...	...	2 000	1 500	2 000	165	10	10	10	Soudan* [2]
United Rep. Tanzania[2 3]	7	7	6	6	10	5	5	0	0	0	Rép.Unie de Tanzanie[2 3]
America, South	**3 669**	**3 594**	**3 661**	**4 450**	**5 085**	**1 405**	**1 452**	**4 177**	**4 163**	**4 368**	**Amérique du Sud**
Argentina[3]	329	302	356	360	218	44	24	32	12	318	Argentine[3]
Brazil[4]	...	...	...	4 074	4 817	787	878	3 595	3 601	3 500	Brésil[4]
Peru[2]	...	...	...	16	50	574	* 550	* 550	* 550	* 550	Pérou[2]
Asia	**4 749**	**6 445**	**8 142**	**10 005**	**10 330**	**10 000**	**20 355**	**14 402**	**24 436**	**14 969**	**Asie**
Korea, Republic of[2]	...	...	...	10 005	10 330	10 000	20 355	14 402	24 436	* 14 969	Corée, République de[2]
Europe	**7 739**	**7 056**	**6 374**	**5 507**	**5 080**	**3 789**	**4 831**	**2 246**	**1 942**	**2 000**	**Europe**
Other Europe	***7 739***	***7 056***	***6 374***	***5 507***	***5 080***	***3 789***	***4 831***	***2 246***	***1 942***	***2 000***	***Autre Europe***
Spain	...	...	...	5 169	4 831	3 524	3 428	1 300	990	1 000	Espagne
Yugoslavia[2]	...	...	...	338	249	265	1 403	* 946	* 952	* 1 000	Yougoslavie[2]
Total	**19 710**	**21 679**	**22 622**	**23 385**	**23 936**	**17 832**	**27 141**	**21 244**	**30 946**	**21 739**	**Total**

General note.
Data refer to crude mica, which consists of mica crystals, of irregular shape, size and thickness, covered with earth (books); mica sheets, obtained by rifting cobbed and trimmed books and mica splittings, obtained by rifting sheet mica. (SITC 27652–1).

[1] Including scrap.
[2] Source: U. S. Bureau of Mines, (Washington, D. C.).
[3] Mica sheets only.
[4] Exports.

Remarque générale.
Les données se rapportent au mica brut sous forme de cristaux de forme, de surface et d'épaisseur irregulières, encore enrobés de matières terreuses (books); au mica en feuilles, obtenu par clivage de 'books' préalablement dégrossis puis ébarbés et au mica en lamelles, obtenu par simple clivage de feuilles de mica. (CTCI 27652–1).

[1] Y compris les déchets.
[2] Source: U.S. Bureau of Mines, (Washington, D.C.).
[3] Mica en feuilles seulement.
[4] Exportations.

Mica waste and powder – Déchets et poudre de mica

Unit : Metric tons

Unité : Tonnes métriques

Country or area	1976	1977	1978	1979	1980	1981	1982	1983	1984	1985	Pays ou zone
Africa	**2 392**	**3 196**	**2 670**	**1 923**	**2 805**	**2 649**	**1 877**	**3 668**	**5 101**	**2 543**	**Afrique**
Madagascar[1]	12	...	...	...	...	254	115	* 996	* 623	* 486	Madagascar[1]
South Africa[1]	[2] 2 380	[2] 3 142	[2] 2 542	[2] 1 720	2 528	2 395	* 1 762	2 672	4 478	2 057	Afrique du Sud[1]
America, North	**111 584**	**117 027**	**126 099**	**121 562**	**105 233**	**120 655**	**96 162**	**127 006**	**146 057**	**125 191**	**Amérique du Nord**
United States	111 584	117 027	126 099	121 562	105 233	120 655	96 162	127 006	146 057	125 191	Etats–Unis
America, South	**2 291**	**1 840**	**2 276**	**1 140**	**616**	**459**	**298**	**300**	**278**	**277**	**Amérique du Sud**
Argentina	2 291	1 840	2 276	1 140	616	459	298	300	278	277	Argentine
Asia	**4 443**	**5 419**	**4 821**	**5 476**	**4 538**	**4 638**	**4 865**	**3 933**	**3 524**	**2 807**	**Asie**
India[3]	4 306	5 319	4 681	5 107	4 393	4 456	4 574	3 762	3 324	2 607	Inde[3]
Sri Lanka[1 2]	137	100	140	369	145	182	291	171	200	* 200	Sri Lanka[1 2]
Total	**120 710**	**127 482**	**135 866**	**130 101**	**113 192**	**128 401**	**103 202**	**134 907**	**154 960**	**130 818**	**Total**

General note.
Data refer to mica waste (scrap) and powder. (SITC 27652–2)

[1] Scrap only.
[2] Source: U. S. Bureau of Mines, (Washington, D. C.).
[3] Including domestic consumption.

Remarque générale.
Les données se rapportent aux déchets et au poudre de mica. (CTCI 27652–2).

[1] Déchets seulement.
[2] Source: U.S. Bureau of Mines, (Washington, D.C.).
[3] Y compris la consommation domestique.

Talc, powdered steatite and pyrophyllite – Talc ou stéatite pulverisée et la pyrophyllite

Unit : Thousand metric tons

Unité : Milliers de tonnes métriques

Country or area	1976	1977	1978	1979	1980	1981	1982	1983	1984	1985	Pays ou zone
Africa	**25**	**26**	**25**	**26**	**23**	**27**	**27**	**22**	**31**	**28**	**Afrique**
Egypt	6	7	6	5	4	6	8	5	* 12	* 8	Egypte
South Africa[1]	[2] 13	13	13	15	14	15	14	11	14	* 15	Afrique du Sud[1]
Sudan* [1]	5	...	...	...	...	...	...	...	...	...	Soudan* [1]
Zambia	0	0	0	...	0	1	0	1	0	0	Zambie
Zimbabwe	...	1	1	1	0	0	0	0	0	0	Zimbabwe
America, North	**1 060**	**1 165**	**1 320**	**1 416**	**1 222**	**1 315**	**1 113**	**1 075**	**1 154**	**1 293**	**Amérique du Nord**
Canada[1 3]	69	72	62	90	87	83	71	97	123	132	Canada[1 3]
Mexico[1]	0	0	3	8	10	14	12	11	9	* 10	Mexique[1]
United States	991	1 093	1 255	1 318	1 125	1 218	1 030	967	1 022	1 151	Etats-Unis
America, South	**276**	**313**	**317**	**405**	**458**	**556**	**447**	**440**	**453**	**459**	**Amérique du Sud**
Argentina	45	43	41	25	27	35	26	25	23	16	Argentine
Brazil[1]	[2] 214	254	261	365	413	503	405	397	413	425	Brésil[1]
Chile[1]	0	0	0	1	1	1	0	1	1	0	Chili[1]
Colombia[1]	* 1	3	4	6	* 6	6	6	7	* 7	* 9	Colombie[1]
Peru[1]	[4] 15	11	9	* 6	9	* 9	* 9	* 9	* 8	* 8	Pérou[1]
Uruguay[1]	1	2	2	* 2	2	* 2	* 1	* 1	* 1	* 1	Uruguay[1]
Asia	**2 012**	**2 538**	**2 570**	**2 674**	**3 452**	**3 190**	**3 130**	**3 330**	**3 267**	**3 241**	**Asie**
Afghanistan[1 5]	9	6	2	0	...	...	...	...	...	...	Afghanistan[1 5]
Burma	0	0	0	0	0	0	0	219	55	73	Birmanie
China[1]	* 150	* 150	* 150	* 150	* 920	* 900	950	950	950	950	Chine[1]
India	220	258	327	373	360	367	344	300	345	345	Inde
Japan[1]	[2] 1 345	1 799	1 695	1 709	1 749	1 545	1 492	1 466	1 500	1 434	Japon[1]
Korea,Dem.Ppl's.Rep.* [1]	127	132	150	159	168	168	168	168	168	168	Corée,Rép.pop.dém.de* [1]
Korea, Republic of	[4] 148	[4] 172	[4] 202	237	205	169	125	171	192	194	Corée, République de
Nepal[1 6]	0	1	0	1	2	0	3	15	8	10	Népal[1 6]
Pakistan[1]	[7] 5	9	25	27	30	25	21	16	16	18	Pakistan[1]
Philippines[1]	1	1	4	4	1	0	1	1	* 1	* 1	Philippines[1]
Thailand[1]	[8] 7	10	15	14	12	12	22	20	28	* 44	Thaïlande[1]
Europe	**963**	**1 002**	**1 063**	**1 131**	**1 192**	**1 142**	**1 154**	**1 139**	**1 137**	**1 172**	**Europe**
EEC	***444***	***484***	***495***	***495***	***498***	***512***	***504***	***482***	***443***	***448***	***CEE***
France	[9] 256	286	293	302	302	309	296	289	265	281	France
Germany, Fed. Rep.[10]	...	...	...	...	12	13	22	14	14	15	Allemagne, Rép. féd.[10]
Greece[1]	[9] 6	...	2	5	1	3	3	2	* 2	2	Grèce[1]
Italy	[1] [11] 154	[1] 165	[1] 168	[1] 157	166	169	164	161	143	130	Italie
United Kingdom	15	15	18	17	17	18	19	16	19	20	Royaume-Uni
EFTA	***395***	***382***	***422***	***488***	***542***	***478***	***498***	***504***	***547***	***569***	***AELE***
Austria	106	104	107	114	117	116	117	122	134	131	Autriche
Finland[1]	149	157	195	267	318	308	325	318	310	* 319	Finlande[1]
Norway	118	98	97	87	88	34	33	36	78	100	Norvège
Portugal	2	2	2	2	3	4	5	7	7	5	Portugal
Sweden	[1] 20	[1] 21	[1] 21	[1] 18	[1] 16	16	18	21	18	14	Suède
East Europe	***76***	***76***	***84***	***78***	***78***	***83***	***82***	***83***	***83***	***82***	***Europe de l'est***
Hungary* [1]	16	16	18	18	18	18	17	17	18	17	Hongrie* [1]
Romania[1]	* 60	60	* 66	* 60	* 60	* 65	* 65	* 66	* 65	* 65	Roumanie[1]
Other Europe	***48***	***60***	***62***	***70***	***74***	***69***	***70***	***70***	***64***	***73***	***Autre Europe***
Spain	48	60	62	70	74	69	70	70	64	73	Espagne
USSR* [1]	**440**	**454**	**472**	**480**	**490**	**500**	**510**	**510**	**520**	**520**	**URSS* [1]**
Oceania	**127**	**113**	**147**	**157**	**177**	**108**	**106**	**126**	**176**	**172**	**Océanie**
Australia	...	113	147	157	177	108	106	126	176	172	Australie
Total	**4 903**	**5 611**	**5 914**	**6 289**	**7 014**	**6 838**	**6 488**	**6 642**	**6 739**	**6 885**	**Total**

For general note and footnotes, see end of table.

Voir la fin du tableau pour la remarque générale et les notes.

General note.
Earth materials used chiefly as a source for industrial talcs. The mineral talc is commonly but not necessarily a major constituent. Steatite, i.e. soapstone, French chalk etc. and pyrophyllite are included under this heading. Material that has been ground to size is included. (SITC 27695–0).

1 Source: U. S. Bureau of Mines, (Washington, D. C.).
2 Including talc and pyrophyllite.
3 Shipments.
4 Talc and pyrophyllite only.
5 Twelve months beginning 21 March of year stated.
6 Twelve months beginning 16 July of year stated.
7 Talc and soapstone only.
8 Pyrophyllite only.
9 Ground talc.
10 Prior to 1980, data are confidential.
11 Talc and steatite only.

Remarque générale.
Terres utilisées surtout comme source de talcs industriels. Le talc minéral en est généralement, mais non pas nécessairement, un constituant important. Sont incluses la stéatite (improprement appelée craie de Briançon ou craie d'Espagne) et la pyrophyllite. La matière moulue à la finesse désirée est incluse. (CTCI 27695–0).

1 Source: U.S. Bureau of Mines, (Washington, D.C.).
2 Y compris le talc et la pyrophyllite.
3 Expéditions.
4 Talc et prophyllite seulement.
5 Période de douze mois commençant le 21 mars de l'année indiquée.
6 Période de douze mois commençant le 16 juillet de l'année indiquée.
7 Talc et pierre de savon seulement.
8 Prophyllite seulement.
9 Talc moulu.
10 Avant 1980, les données sont confidentielles.
11 Talc et steatite seulement.

Peat for fuel – Tourbe comme combustible

Unit : Thousand metric tons

Unité : Milliers de tonnes métriques

Country or area	1976	1977	1978	1979	1980	1981	1982	1983	1984	1985	Pays ou zone
Africa	**1**	**1**	**2**	**3**	**9**	**9**	**14**	**13**	**14**	**10**	**Afrique**
Burundi	[1] 1	[1] 1	[1] 2	[1] 3	[1] 9	* [1] 9	14	13	14	10	Burundi
America, North	**7**	**7**	**7**	**7**	**7**	**7**	**7**	**1**	**10**	**10**	**Amérique du Nord**
United States	...	...	...	...	...	...	...	1	10	10	Etats-Unis
America, South	**10**	**10**	**10**	**10**	**10**	**10**	**10**	**10**	**10**	**10**	**Amérique du Sud**
Argentina[1]	10	...	...	...	...	...	...	...	...	...	Argentine[1]
Asia	**70**	**70**	**60**	**60**	**60**	**60**	**60**	**60**	**60**	**60**	**Asie**
Japan* [1]	70	70	60	60	60	60	60	60	60	60	Japon* [1]
Europe	**6 934**	**6 437**	**7 166**	**5 895**	**6 370**	**6 773**	**9 556**	**9 631**	**10 085**	**6 403**	**Europe**
EEC	***6 582***	***6 072***	***5 232***	***4 296***	***5 105***	***6 004***	***5 933***	***5 959***	***6 027***	***3 338***	***CEE***
Germany, Fed. Rep.	227	221	228	230	279	246	253	259	277	284	Allemagne, Rép. féd.
Ireland[1]	5 955	5 451	4 604	3 666	4 426	5 358	5 280	* 5 300	* 5 300	* 2 600	Irlande[1]
Netherlands* [1]	400	400	400	400	400	400	400	400	450	454	Pays-Bas* [1]
EFTA	***319***	***322***	***1 901***	***1 552***	***1 220***	***729***	***3 562***	***3 631***	***4 001***	***3 014***	***AELE***
Finland	286	289	[1] 1 870	[1] 1 551	1 219	728	3 561	3 630	4 000	* 3 000	Finlande
Norway* [1]	1	1	1	1	1	1	1	1	1	1	Norvège* [1]
Sweden	32	32	30	0	0	0	0	0	0	...	Suède
East Europe	***2***	***1***	***1***	***1***	***1***	***1***	***1***	***1***	***1***	***1***	***Europe de l'est***
Poland	2	1	1	...	...	...	...	...	...	...	Pologne
Other Europe	***31***	***42***	***32***	***46***	***44***	***39***	***60***	***40***	***56***	***50***	***Autre Europe***
Spain	31	42	32	46	44	39	60	40	56	* 50	Espagne
USSR* [1]	**60 000**	**60 000**	**60 000**	**60 000**	**60 000**	**60 000**	**60 000**	**60 000**	**60 000**	**60 000**	**URSS* [1]**
Oceania	**5**	**6**	**6**	**14**	**13**	**14**	**10**	**10**	**10**	**10**	**Océanie**
Australia[1]	5	6	6	14	* 13	* 14	* 10	* 10	* 10	* 10	Australie[1]
Total	**67 027**	**66 531**	**67 251**	**65 990**	**66 469**	**66 873**	**69 657**	**69 725**	**70 189**	**66 503**	**Total**

General note.
The data refer to peat used as fuel. Peat is the first stage in the metamorphosis of vegetable matter to coal. It has a high percentage of moisture and a gross calorific value of 3700 to 4000 calories/ gramme. Unless otherwise stated, peat briquettes are excluded. (SITC 32170-1).

[1] Source: U. S. Bureau of Mines, (Washington, D. C.).

Remarque générale.
Les données se rapportent à la tourbe utilisée comme combustible. La tourbe représente la première étape de la transformation de la matière végétale en houille. Elle a une teneur élevée en eau et un pouvoir calorifique brut de 3700 à 4000 cal/g. Sauf indication contraire, les agglomérés de tourbe ne sont pas compris. (CTCI 32170-1).

[1] Source: U.S. Bureau of Mines, (Washington, D.C.).

Peat for agricultural use – Tourbe à usage agricole

Unit : Thousand metric tons — Unité : Milliers de tonnes métriques

Country or area	1976	1977	1978	1979	1980	1981	1982	1983	1984	1985	Pays ou zone
America, North	**1 097**	**1 095**	**1 181**	**1 228**	**1 200**	**1 084**	**1 211**	**1 168**	**1 216**	**1 251**	**Amérique du Nord**
Canada	395	386	435	480	* 488	462	487	529	* 500	* 500	Canada
United States	702	709	746	748	712	622	724	639	716	751	Etats–Unis
America, South	**15**	**15**	**22**	**22**	**23**	**19**	**22**	**23**	**23**	**26**	**Amérique du Sud**
Argentina	[1] 10	[1] 6	[1] 4	4	5	2	4	4	2	4	Argentine
Venezuela* [1]	5	9	18	18	18	...	...	...	...	...	Venezuela* [1]
Asia	**24**	**24**	**24**	**22**	**24**	**24**	**24**	**24**	**24**	**24**	**Asie**
Israel[1]	* 20	* 20	* 20	* 18	* 20	* 20	* 20	20	* 20	* 20	Israël[1]
Korea, Republic of	4	...	...	...	...	...	...	...	...	...	Corée, République de
Europe	**2 414**	**2 664**	**2 780**	**3 238**	**2 639**	**2 552**	**3 028**	**2 741**	**2 544**	**2 457**	**Europe**
EEC	***1 958***	***2 174***	***2 316***	***2 125***	***1 814***	***1 986***	***2 090***	***2 107***	***1 784***	***1 851***	***CEE***
Denmark	39	40	47	45	31	33	33	34	32	39	Danemark
France* [1]	142	140	140	140	140	130	120	110	228	200	France* [1]
Germany, Fed. Rep.[1]	1 706	1 911	2 047	1 849	1 555	1 742	1 842	1 868	1 429	1 516	Allemagne, Rép. féd.[1]
Ireland[1]	* 71	83	82	91	88	81	95	* 95	* 95	* 96	Irlande[1]
EFTA	***347***	***384***	***358***	***1 007***	***712***	***294***	***667***	***364***	***490***	***290***	***AELE***
Finland[1]	198	231	203	773	518	204	577	274	* 400	* 200	Finlande[1]
Norway* [1]	60	60	60	60	60	30	30	30	30	30	Norvège* [1]
Sweden	[1] 89	[1] 93	[1] 95	[1] 174	[1] 134	* 60	* 60	* 60	* 60	* 60	Suède
East Europe	***109***	***106***	***106***	***106***	***113***	***272***	***271***	***270***	***270***	***316***	***Europe de l'est***
Hungary* [1]	73	70	70	70	77	70	70	70	70	...	Hongrie* [1]
Poland[1]	* 36	* 36	* 36	* 36	* 36	# 202	* 201	* 200	* 200	...	Pologne[1]
USSR[1]	*** 132 000**	*** 132 000**	*** 165 000**	*** 200 000**	*** 235 000**	**180 000**	**180 000**	**180 000**	**180 000**	**180 000**	**URSS[1]**
Total	**135 550**	**135 798**	**169 007**	**204 510**	**238 886**	**183 679**	**184 285**	**183 956**	**183 807**	**183 758**	**Total**

General note.
The data refer to peat for agricultural or domestic use. This series includes crushed peat, peat litter etc. used in stables, for soil improvement or for other purposes. It does not include fibres of peat prepared for textile use and flower pots and other articles of peat, including insulating sheets for buildings obtained by cutting or moulding. (SITC 32170–2).

[1] Source: U. S. Bureau of Mines, (Washington, D. C.).

Remarque générale.
Les données se rapportent à la tourbe à usage domestique ou agricole. Cette série comprend la tourbe écrasée et celles qui sont employées pour la litière des animaux, l'amendement du sol ou tous autres usages. La série ne comprend pas toutefois les fibres de tourbe ligneuse traitées en vue de leur utilisation comme textiles et les pots à fleurs et autres articles en tourbe taillée ou moulée, ainsi que les plaques, etc. De tourbe comprimée, employées comme isolants dans la construction. (CTCI 32170–2).

[1] Source: U.S. Bureau of Mines, (Washington, D.C.).

Diamonds, gem – Diamants de joaillerie

Unit : Thousand carats

Unité : Milliers de carats

Country or area	1976	1977	1978	1979	1980	1981	1982	1983	1984	1985	Pays ou zone
Africa	**6 840**	**6 716**	**6 817**	**7 510**	**9 396**	**8 218**	**7 584**	**12 921**	**17 980**	**16 595**	**Afrique**
Angola[1]	255	265	525	630	* 1 110	* 1 050	* 915	* 775	* 700	* 375	Angola[1]
Botswana[1]	354	404	420	659	765	744	1 165	2 420	5 810	5 800	Botswana[1]
Central African Rep.	* 172	178	199	205	227	209	186	230	236	247	Rép. centrafricaine
Côte d'Ivoire[1]	* 22	20	22	5	0	0	0	0	0	...	Côte d'Ivoire[1]
Ghana[1]	228	230	142	125	126	85	68	34	35	65	Ghana[1]
Guinea* [1]	25	25	25	27	12	12	10	23	34	105	Guinée* [1]
Lesotho[1]	4	39	62	48	50	* 49	* 39	...	...	...	Lesotho[1]
Liberia[1]	163	163	128	170	123	132	170	132	* 108	* 66	Libéria[1]
Namibia[1]	* 1 609	1 901	1 803	* 1 570	1 482	1 186	963	915	* 884	* 865	Namibie[1]
Sierra Leone[1]	* 433	423	353	434	317	208	* 203	242	* 240	* 240	Sierra Leone[1]
South Africa[1]	2 858	2 331	2 357	3 186	2 813	3 429	3 342	4 554	4 516	4 543	Afrique du Sud[1]
United Rep. Tanzania[1]	* 219	204	141	157	137	* 110	* 100	* 183	* 186	* 186	Rép.Unie de Tanzanie[1]
Zaire	498	533	640	294	2 234	1 004	423	* 3 355	* 5 169	* 4 032	Zaïre
America, South	**277**	**277**	**364**	**336**	**400**	**242**	**309**	**170**	**169**	**295**	**Amérique du Sud**
Brazil	76	66	86	83	158	136	212	120	123	* 250	Brésil
Guyana* [1]	6	7	7	6	4	4	4	5	6	4	Guyana* [1]
Venezuela	195	204	271	247	238	102	93	45	40	41	Venezuela
Asia	**20**	**18**	**16**	**15**	**15**	**15**	**13**	**16**	**16**	**17**	**Asie**
India	17	15	13	12	12	12	10	11	11	12	Inde
Indonesia* [1]	3	3	3	3	3	3	3	5	5	5	Indonésie* [1]
USSR* [1]	**2 000**	**2 100**	**2 150**	**3 700**	**2 250**	**2 100**	**2 100**	**3 700**	**4 300**	**4 400**	**URSS* [1]**
Total	**9 137**	**9 111**	**9 347**	**11 561**	**12 061**	**10 575**	**10 006**	**16 807**	**22 465**	**21 307**	**Total**

General note.
Mine and alluvial production of rough, uncut and unpolished diamonds intended for gem stones. (SITC 66720–1).

[1] Source: U. S. Bureau of Mines, (Washington, D. C.).

Remarque générale.
Production de diamants bruts, non taillés et non polis, destinés à la joaillerie, en provenance de mines et d'alluvions. (CTCI 66720–1).

[1] Source: U.S. Bureau of Mines, (Washington, D.C.).

Beef and veal, fresh (Total production) – Viande de boeuf ou de veau, non préparée (Production totale)

Unit : Thousand metric tons — Unité : Milliers de tonnes métriques

Country or area	1976	1977	1978	1979	1980	1981	1982	1983	1984	1985	Pays ou zone
Africa	**2 656**	**2 839**	**2 936**	**3 039**	**2 996**	**3 031**	**3 155**	**3 179**	**3 250**	**3 278**	**Afrique**
Algeria	47	50	44	° 45	° 45	° 43	° 50	° 52	° 54	° 55	Algérie
Angola°	45	45	46	48	50	51	52	53	53	54	Angola°
Benin°	10	10	11	11	12	12	12	13	13	13	Bénin°
Botswana°	44	41	30	47	29	43	47	41	41	42	Botswana°
Burkina Faso°	20	21	22	25	22	21	25	24	24	24	Burkina Faso°
Burundi°	11	11	11	11	8	6	6	6	6	7	Burundi°
Cameroon°	45	47	48	48	50	51	48	47	48	50	Cameroun°
Central African Rep.°	22	22	22	19	23	23	24	25	25	25	Rép. centrafricaine°
Chad°	26	27	28	29	28	28	28	26	24	25	Tchad°
Comoros°	2	2	2	2	2	2	2	2	2	2	Comores°
Congo°	1	2	2	2	2	2	2	2	3	3	Congo°
Côte d'Ivoire°	27	32	34	38	42	43	35	42	42	42	Côte d'Ivoire°
Djibouti°	1	1	1	1	1	2	2	2	2	2	Djibouti°
Egypt	229	230	236	239	240	238	255	268	299	° 303	Egypte
Ethiopia	204	° 206	° 212	° 213	° 214	° 214	° 215	° 216	° 214	° 214	Ethiopie
Gambia°	4	4	4	4	4	4	4	4	4	4	Gambie°
Ghana°	12	11	10	11	11	12	12	12	12	12	Ghana°
Guinea°	15	16	16	17	18	18	19	19	19	18	Guinée°
Guinea–Bissau°	2	2	3	3	3	3	3	3	3	3	Guinée–Bissau°
Kenya	° 145	° 189	192	192	193	° 166	° 186	° 197	° 203	° 187	Kenya
Lesotho°	9	9	10	11	11	11	12	12	12	12	Lesotho°
Liberia°	2	3	3	4	3	4	4	4	4	4	Libéria°
Libyan Arab Jamah.	11	° 34	41	41	42	° 42	° 42	° 44	° 44	° 45	Jamah.arabe libyenne
Madagascar°	111	112	115	119	134	134	135	136	136	137	Madagascar°
Malawi°	9	10	11	11	12	17	18	15	18	19	Malawi°
Mali°	42	42	43	38	37	38	40	35	34	36	Mali°
Mauritania°	11	13	16	16	16	16	16	16	16	17	Mauritanie°
Mauritius	1	1	1	2	° 2	° 1	1	1	1	° 1	Maurice
Morocco	* 79	90	95	100	107	131	° 108	° 110	° 120	° 130	Maroc
Mozambique°	34	34	35	35	36	37	36	35	36	37	Mozambique°
Namibia°	31	31	32	32	33	33	34	35	36	37	Namibie°
Niger	° 19	° 31	° 35	34	37	40	35	35	° 37	° 39	Niger
Nigeria°	192	194	216	244	251	254	256	235	225	221	Nigéria°
Réunion	1	1	1	1	1	1	1	1	° 1	° 1	Réunion
Rwanda°	10	11	11	11	12	13	13	13	14	15	Rwanda°
Senegal°	36	36	40	41	32	40	42	43	41	41	Sénégal°
Sierra Leone°	5	5	5	5	5	5	6	6	5	5	Sierra Leone°
Somalia°	45	46	47	44	45	46	46	44	42	42	Somalie°
South Africa	509	544	589	642	585	* 542	* 582	588	620	* 593	Afrique du Sud
Sudan°	189	198	190	193	208	248	293	300	297	330	Soudan°
Swaziland°	15	13	15	17	17	14	15	16	13	14	Swaziland°
Togo°	4	4	4	4	4	5	5	4	5	5	Togo°
Tunisia	34	35	31	20	26	35	28	27	29	° 30	Tunisie
Uganda	82	88	90	° 94	° 94	° 92	° 90	° 90	° 92	° 94	Ouganda
United Rep. Tanzania	° 115	° 128	° 131	131	124	131	140	146	° 150	° 153	Rép.Unie de Tanzanie
Zaire	21	21	21	° 22	° 22	° 22	° 23	° 23	° 23	° 24	Zaïre
Zambia°	28	28	27	28	28	31	33	34	34	35	Zambie°
Zimbabwe°	100	110	106	94	76	66	77	77	76	80	Zimbabwe°
America, North	**14 434**	**14 158**	**13 558**	**12 066**	**12 172**	**12 640**	**12 721**	**13 084**	**13 147**	**13 234**	**Amérique du Nord**
Antigua and Barbuda	0	0	0	0	1	0	0	0	° 0	° 1	Antigua–et–Barbuda
Belize	1	1	1	1	1	1	1	1	1	° 1	Belize
Canada	1 166	1 142	1 063	947	971	1 016	1 032	1 035	997	* 980	Canada
Costa Rica	* 81	* 80	76	84	77	80	66	61	76	* 62	Costa Rica
Cuba	° 125	° 130	° 140	° 145	147	152	150	151	151	° 145	Cuba
Dominican Republic	* 42	39	45	46	49	52	54	56	° 57	° 58	Rép. dominicaine
El Salvador	31	28	33	30	28	* 30	* 30	* 30	32	32	El Salvador
Guadeloupe	3	3	4	4	4	4	4	4	4	° 4	Guadeloupe
Guatemala	66	70	70	76	79	95	* 75	* 63	* 64	* 57	Guatemala
Haiti°	22	22	23	23	24	27	30	32	33	33	Haïti°
Honduras	42	42	54	59	63	60	46	35	* 38	* 39	Honduras
Jamaica	12	12	12	11	12	12	12	14	16	° 16	Jamaïque
Martinique	3	3	2	2	3	3	3	3	4	° 4	Martinique
Mexico	527	588	602	565	590	644	661	706	600	° 665	Mexique
Montserrat°	0	0	0	0	0	0	1	1	1	1	Montserrat°
Neth.Antil and Aruba°	1	1	1	0	0	0	0	0	0	0	Antill.néer.et Aruba°
Nicaragua	73	79	80	77	56	* 43	* 54	* 62	* 59	° 59	Nicaragua
Puerto Rico	21	21	25	28	22	17	17	21	24	24	Porto Rico
Saint Lucia°	0	0	1	1	1	1	1	1	1	1	Sainte–Lucie°
S.Vincent–Grenadines°	0	1	1	1	1	1	1	1	1	1	S.Vincent–Grenadines°
Trinidad and Tobago	1	1	1	2	2	2	2	1	1	° 1	Trinité–et–Tobago

For general note and footnotes, see end of table. — Voir la fin du tableau pour la remarque générale et les notes.

Unit : Thousand metric tons

Unité : Milliers de tonnes métriques

Country or area	1976	1977	1978	1979	1980	1981	1982	1983	1984	1985	Pays ou zone
United States	12 166	11 845	11 282	9 925	9 999	10 353	10 425	10 748	10 928	10 994	Etats–Unis
U.S. Virgin Islands	° 0	1	1	1	1	1	° 1	° 1	° 1	° 1	Iles Vierges amér.
America, South	**6 742**	**7 052**	**7 239**	**6 877**	**6 743**	**7 014**	**6 840**	**6 711**	**6 548**	**6 744**	**Amérique du Sud**
Argentina	2 811	2 914	3 193	3 020	2 839	2 939	2 551	2 384	2 548	* 2 700	Argentine
Bolivia	70	75	77	84	88	° 89	° 90	° 91	° 93	° 94	Bolivie
Brazil	2 176	2 446	2 320	2 114	2 084	2 115	2 397	2 365	2 096	2 136	Brésil
Chile	198	173	165	167	162	185	195	208	197	* 180	Chili
Colombia	* 545	* 540	* 570	597	593	630	596	* 619	* 647	* 643	Colombie
Ecuador	68	74	85	88	92	95	97	92	81	° 115	Equateur
Falkland I(Malvinas)°	0	1	1	1	1	1	1	1	1	1	I Falkland(Malvinas)°
French Guiana	0	° 0	° 0	° 1	° 1	° 1	° 1	° 1	° 1	° 1	Guyane française
Guyana	4	3	3	2	2	2	2	2	2	° 2	Guyana
Paraguay	* 101	* 122	° 114	° 110	° 114	° 116	100	90	* 85	° 100	Paraguay
Peru	87	87	89	87	84	90	91	111	104	101	Pérou
Suriname	1	1	1	* 1	1	1	1	1	1	° 1	Suriname
Uruguay	403	342	314	270	* 336	* 407	* 383	* 412	° 390	° 350	Uruguay
Venezuela	277	274	308	335	346	344	337	335	* 302	* 320	Venezuela
Asia	**2 606**	**2 724**	**2 816**	**2 977**	**2 995**	**3 095**	**3 246**	**3 304**	**3 487**	**3 653**	**Asie**
Afghanistan	62	66	67	71	67	* 68	* 69	° 68	° 68	° 68	Afghanistan
Bahrain°	1	1	1	1	1	1	1	1	1	1	Bahreïn°
Bangladesh	148	151	176	° 159	123	125	126	128	° 129	° 131	Bangladesh
Bhutan°	0	0	0	0	1	1	1	1	1	1	Bhoutan°
Brunei Darussalam°	0	1	1	1	1	1	1	1	1	1	Brunéi Darussalam°
Burma°	90	90	91	92	93	95	96	97	98	99	Birmanie°
China	197	211	205	239	274	255	272	322	380	408	Chine
Cyprus°	3	4	4	4	4	4	4	4	4	4	Chypre°
Dem. Kampuchea°	20	21	20	17	17	18	20	21	22	25	Kampuchea démocrat.°
Democratic Yemen	2	2	1	2	2	3	° 3	° 3	° 3	° 3	Yémen démocratique
Hong Kong	° 29	28	31	32	34	35	37	37	37	38	Hong–kong
India°	161	157	146	152	184	205	210	212	220	224	Inde°
Indonesia	162	166	163	169	154	171	159	154	° 170	° 170	Indonésie
Iran(Islamic Rep.of)	158	168	168	171	180	° 179	° 179	° 175	° 175	° 178	Iran(Rép.islamique)
Iraq	51	° 49	° 53	° 60	° 46	° 43	° 39	° 37	° 43	° 38	Iraq
Israel	23	25	21	19	21	19	20	18	* 18	* 17	Israël
Japan	298	361	403	402	418	471	481	495	536	555	Japon
Jordan°	1	1	1	2	2	2	2	2	2	2	Jordanie°
Korea, D. P. Rp.°	26	27	29	30	31	32	32	35	36	38	Corée, Rp. P. D.°
Korea, Republic of	74	64	74	88	93	99	96	94	123	162	Corée, République de
Kuwait	1	2	3	6	° 6	° 7	° 11	° 14	° 16	° 18	Koweït
Lao Peoples Dem.Rep.°	11	14	17	20	27	29	30	31	33	36	Rép. dém. pop. lao°
Lebanon°	3	3	8	10	12	13	14	15	14	14	Liban°
Macau	1	1	1	1	1	1	1	1	1	° 1	Macao
Malaysia°	15	15	15	16	18	16	19	18	18	19	Malaisie°
Mongolia	68	63	71	75	71	70	66	68	68	66	Mongolie
Nepal	21	22	23	° 24	° 25	° 25	° 26	° 26	° 27	° 28	Népal
Oman°	3	3	4	4	4	3	4	4	4	4	Oman°
Pakistan	329	333	335	340	344	349	448	464	° 470	° 480	Pakistan
Philippines	106	109	* 127	* 124	* 127	122	° 124	90	° 93	° 118	Philippines
Saudi Arabia	9	8	19	19	° 20	° 21	° 22	° 23	° 24	° 25	Arabie saoudite
Sri Lanka	15	13	13	12	12	12	12	13	13	13	Sri Lanka
Syrian Arab Republic	15	15	18	25	26	33	36	° 35	° 30	° 33	Rép. arabe syrienne
Thailand°	196	207	209	226	214	216	218	219	216	225	Thaïlande°
Turkey	202	221	187	249	225	226	235	240	247	251	Turquie
United Arab Emirates°	2	2	2	2	2	2	3	3	3	3	Emirats arabes unis°
Viet Nam	° 86	° 87	° 93	° 100	° 101	° 110	° 116	120	127	° 139	Viet Nam
Yemen	12	11	° 12	° 12	° 13	° 13	° 13	° 14	° 14	° 14	Yémen
Europe	**10 106**	**9 952**	**9 993**	**10 513**	**10 765**	**10 362**	**10 195**	**10 433**	**11 084**	**11 002**	**Europe**
EEC	**6 336**	**6 208**	**6 229**	**6 610**	**6 833**	**6 607**	**6 380**	**6 636**	**7 171**	**7 047**	**CEE**
Denmark	242	243	238	253	245	238	232	241	248	238	Danemark
France	1 800	1 652	1 658	1 823	1 838	1 836	1 745	1 811	1 991	° 1 900	France
Germany, Fed. Rep.	1 376	1 347	1 397	1 478	1 523	1 533	1 477	1 494	1 613	1 576	Allemagne, Rép. féd.
Greece	123	121	118	112	111	94	89	86	85	86	Grèce
Ireland	328	385	389	388	446	316	345	353	389	397	Irlande
Italy	1 018	1 052	1 027	1 106	1 148	1 111	1 107	1 149	1 182	* 1 215	Italie
Netherlands	392	386	375	403	419	437	420	450	515	505	Pays–Bas
United Kingdom	1 057	1 022	1 028	1 047	1 102	1 041	965	1 052	1 148	1 130	Royaume–Uni
EFTA	**744**	**729**	**755**	**790**	**821**	**835**	**848**	**834**	**855**	**860**	**AELE**

For general note and footnotes, see end of table.

Voir la fin du tableau pour la remarque générale et les notes.

Beef and veal, fresh (Total production) (continued) – Viande de boeuf ou de veau, non préparée (Production totale) (suite)

Unit : Thousand metric tons

Unité : Milliers de tonnes métriques

Country or area	1976	1977	1978	1979	1980	1981	1982	1983	1984	1985	Pays ou zone
Austria	183	172	184	193	206	200	200	204	224	235	Autriche
Finland	114	106	106	110	114	122	117	118	124	* 126	Finlande
Iceland	2	2	3	3	2	3	2	º 3	º 2	º 2	Islande
Norway	61	67	69	73	70	76	81	80	* 76	* 78	Norvège
Portugal	86	84	96	99	103	121	127	* 117	º 107	* 89	Portugal
Sweden	149	148	147	152	157	158	161	161	155	158	Suède
Switzerland	149	150	150	161	169	156	160	152	165	171	Suisse
East Europe	**1 990**	**1 968**	**2 001**	**2 086**	**2 042**	**1 859**	**1 920**	**1 905**	**2 003**	**2 056**	**Europe de l'est**
Albania	º 22	* 23	º 25	º 26	º 26	º 26	º 26	* 27	º 27	º 27	Albanie
Bulgaria	100	114	114	118	123	121	127	129	135	º 130	Bulgarie
Czechoslovakia	365	365	371	381	385	373	373	384	406	413	Tchécoslovaquie
German Dem. Rep.	342	* 348	* 389	* 391	* 384	* 412	* 385	* 367	* 369	º 381	Rép. dém. allemande
Hungary	138	134	139	140	153	141	141	127	132	* 147	Hongrie
Poland	* 740	* 676	664	695	667	497	640	610	650	º 670	Pologne
Romania	* 283	* 308	* 300	* 336	* 304	* 289	* 229	* 261	* 285	º 289	Roumanie
Other Europe	**746**	**766**	**732**	**737**	**759**	**743**	**765**	**768**	**737**	**734**	**Autre Europe**
Malta	2	2	2	2	2	2	2	2	º 2	º 2	Malte
Spain	418	431	391	394	422	418	420	422	385	* 382	Espagne
Yugoslavia	326	333	338	341	335	323	343	345	350	º 350	Yougoslavie
USSR	**6 552**	**6 888**	**7 086**	**6 887**	**6 645**	**6 627**	**6 618**	**7 011**	**7 244**	**º 7 400**	**URSS**
Oceania	**2 480**	**2 558**	**2 758**	**2 543**	**2 073**	**1 979**	**2 105**	**2 068**	**1 785**	**1 768**	**Océanie**
Australia	1 840	1 988	2 184	2 018	1 564	1 467	1 576	1 543	1 338	1 267	Australie
Fiji	2	2	3	4	4	3	3	3	3	º 3	Fidji
New Caledonia	2	3	3	3	3	2	3	2	3	º 3	Nouvelle–Calédonie
New Zealand	628	558	562	512	496	498	516	512	433	487	Nouvelle–Zélande
Papua New Guineaº	3	3	2	2	2	2	2	2	2	2	Papouasie–Nvl–Guinéeº
Samoa	0	1	1	1	1	1	1	1	º 1	º 0	Samoa
Solomon Islandsº	1	1	1	1	1	1	1	1	1	1	Iles Salomonº
Vanuatuº	3	2	2	2	2	3	3	3	3	4	Vanuatuº
Total	**45 577**	**46 171**	**46 385**	**44 901**	**44 389**	**44 746**	**44 880**	**45 790**	**46 546**	**47 078**	**Total**

General note.
Fresh, chilled or frozen meat of bovine animals, irrespective of the origin of the animals, expressed in terms of carcass weight, excluding edible offals and tallow. Includes non–industrial production. (SITC 01110–0).
Source: Food and Agriculture Organization of the United Nations (FAO), Rome.

Remarque générale.
Poids net de viande fraîche, réfrigérée ou congelée, provenant de bovins abattus, quelle que soit la provenance de ces animaux, à l'exclusion des abats comestibles et du suif. Y compris production non–industrielle. (CTCI 01110–0).
Source: Organisation des Nations Unies pour l'agriculture(FAO), Rome.

Beef and veal, fresh (Industrial production) – Viande de boeuf ou de veau, non préparée (Production industrielle)

Unit : Thousand metric tons

Unité : Milliers de tonnes métriques

Country or area	1976	1977	1978	1979	1980	1981	1982	1983	1984	1985	Pays ou zone
Africa	**555**	**549**	**542**	**536**	**580**	**459**	**507**	**507**	**538**	**487**	**Afrique**
South Africa	...	...	...	...	580	459	507	507	538	487	Afrique du Sud
America, North	**9 325**	**9 429**	**9 508**	**9 588**	**9 673**	**9 858**	**9 853**	**9 917**	**10 175**	**10 118**	**Amérique du Nord**
Cuba	...	88	83	79	80	138	140	140	137	135	Cuba
United States	...	...	...	...	...	9 720	9 713	9 777	10 038	9 983	Etats–Unis
Asia	**298**	**361**	**403**	**402**	**418**	**471**	**481**	**495**	**536**	**555**	**Asie**
Japan	298	361	403	402	418	471	481	495	536	555	Japon
Europe	**5 313**	**5 257**	**5 382**	**5 621**	**5 655**	**5 513**	**5 515**	**5 607**	**6 071**	**6 030**	**Europe**
EEC	***3 604***	***3 622***	***3 737***	***3 941***	***3 991***	***4 033***	***3 863***	***4 019***	***4 389***	***4 300***	***CEE***
Belgium	281	273	267	281	302	310	274	282	310	317	Belgique
Denmark	248	247	242	258	196	197	192	225	225	215	Danemark
France	...	...	...	1 774	1 766	1 785	1 696	1 764	1 942	1 846	France
Germany, Fed. Rep.[1]	1 337	1 312	1 383	1 466	1 529	1 499	1 440	1 457	1 577	1 541	Allemagne, Rép. féd.[1]
Ireland	...	...	...	...	...	227	249	278	321	367	Irlande
Luxembourg[2]	15	12	13	13	14	15	12	13	14	14	Luxembourg[2]
EFTA	***218***	***172***	***175***	***178***	***218***	***236***	***228***	***222***	***231***	***237***	***AELE***
Finland	157	106	106	107	149	162	152	149	160	...	Finlande
Norway	61	66	69	71	69	74	76	73	* 71	* 74	Norvège
East Europe	***1 255***	***1 208***	***1 210***	***1 267***	***1 227***	***1 020***	***1 190***	***1 150***	***1 215***	***1 276***	***Europe de l'est***
Bulgaria	88	99	99	100	100	101	105	110	111	117	Bulgarie
Czechoslovakia	342	340	350	361	364	347	350	358	377	382	Tchécoslovaquie
Hungary	130	125	125	135	133	122	124	113	117	131	Hongrie
Poland	695	644	636	671	630	450	611	569	610	646	Pologne
Other Europe	***236***	***255***	***260***	***235***	***219***	***224***	***234***	***216***	***236***	***217***	***Autre Europe***
Yugoslavia	236	255	260	235	219	224	234	216	236	217	Yougoslavie
USSR	**4 434**	**4 595**	**4 710**	**4 653**	**4 392**	**4 381**	**4 344**	**4 654**	**4 865**	**4 957**	**URSS**
Byelorussian SSR	*319*	*344*	*356*	*359*	*318*	*284*	*293*	*302*	*328*	*359*	*RSS de Biélorussie*
Ukrainian SSR	*1 019*	*1 070*	*1 159*	*1 179*	*1 111*	*1 103*	*1 085*	*1 123*	*1 174*	*1 264*	*RSS d'Ukraine*
Total	**19 926**	**20 190**	**20 545**	**20 800**	**20 718**	**20 682**	**20 700**	**21 180**	**22 185**	**22 147**	**Total**

General note.
Fresh, chilled or frozen meat of bovine animals, irrespective of the origin of the animals, expressed in terms of carcass weight, excluding edible offals and tallow. Data refer to industrial production only. (SITC 01110–0).

[1] Including edible offals.
[2] Including unrendered fats.

Remarque générale.
Poids net de viande fraîche, réfrigérée ou congelée, provenant de bovins abattus, quelle quesoit la provenance de ces animaux, à l'exclusion des abats comestibles et du suif. Les données se rapportent à la production industrielle seulement. (CTCI 01110–0).

[1] Y compris les abats comestibles.
[2] Y compris les graisses non fondues.

Mutton and lamb, fresh (Total production) – Viande d'ovins et de caprins, non préparée (Production totale)

Unit : Thousand metric tons

Unité : Milliers de tonnes métriques

Country or area	1976	1977	1978	1979	1980	1981	1982	1983	1984	1985	Pays ou zone
Africa	**1 123**	**1 155**	**1 207**	**1 242**	**1 273**	**1 302**	**1 313**	**1 340**	**1 354**	**1 405**	**Afrique**
Algeria	° 60	62	° 65	° 66	° 76	° 78	° 88	° 96	° 99	° 101	Algérie
Angola°	3	3	3	3	3	3	3	3	3	4	Angola°
Benin°	5	5	5	5	6	6	6	6	6	7	Bénin°
Botswana°	3	3	3	4	3	3	3	3	4	4	Botswana°
Burkina Faso°	8	8	8	7	8	8	9	9	9	9	Burkina Faso°
Burundi°	3	3	2	3	3	3	3	3	3	3	Burundi°
Cameroon°	14	15	15	15	15	15	15	14	14	15	Cameroun°
Central African Rep.°	3	3	3	3	3	3	3	4	4	4	Rép. centrafricaine°
Chad°	16	14	14	17	17	16	16	17	15	16	Tchad°
Congo°	0	0	0	0	1	1	1	1	1	1	Congo°
Côte d'Ivoire°	10	10	12	11	11	12	11	12	12	13	Côte d'Ivoire°
Djibouti°	3	3	3	3	3	3	3	3	4	4	Djibouti°
Egypt	44	44	44	43	43	42	45	43	51	° 60	Egypte
Ethiopia	131	° 130	° 132	° 136	° 141	° 144	° 146	° 149	° 151	° 153	Ethiopie
Gabon°	0	1	1	1	1	0	0	0	0	0	Gabon°
Gambia°	1	1	1	1	1	1	1	1	1	1	Gambie°
Ghana°	11	11	11	11	11	11	11	11	11	11	Ghana°
Guinea°	2	2	2	2	2	2	2	2	2	2	Guinée°
Guinea–Bissau°	0	0	0	0	0	0	1	1	1	1	Guinée–Bissau°
Kenya°	32	37	43	43	36	37	38	40	33	45	Kenya°
Lesotho°	4	5	5	5	6	6	6	6	6	6	Lesotho°
Liberia°	1	1	1	1	1	1	1	1	1	1	Libéria°
Libyan Arab Jamah.	34	38	33	49	50	° 53	° 54	° 55	° 56	° 56	Jamah.arabe libyenne
Madagascar°	5	4	5	5	9	11	11	9	8	9	Madagascar°
Malawi°	3	3	3	3	3	3	3	3	3	3	Malawi°
Mali°	34	38	45	45	49	46	44	43	43	45	Mali°
Mauritania°	11	12	12	12	12	12	12	12	12	13	Mauritanie°
Morocco	* 54	61	68	69	71	88	69	° 70	° 70	° 74	Maroc
Mozambique°	2	2	2	2	2	2	2	2	2	2	Mozambique°
Namibia°	20	20	21	22	23	23	24	25	26	26	Namibie°
Niger°	25	34	36	37	41	41	42	44	45	46	Niger°
Nigeria°	149	148	161	163	167	171	174	178	178	178	Nigéria°
Rwanda°	3	3	3	4	4	4	4	4	5	5	Rwanda°
Senegal°	9	9	10	10	10	11	11	11	11	11	Sénégal°
Sierra Leone°	1	1	1	1	1	1	2	2	2	2	Sierra Leone°
Somalia°	62	63	65	64	65	66	67	66	64	64	Somalie°
South Africa	152	148	156	161	161	° 162	° 163	° 164	° 164	° 166	Afrique du Sud
Sudan°	107	109	115	123	126	119	123	125	129	138	Soudan°
Swaziland°	3	3	3	3	3	3	3	3	3	4	Swaziland°
Togo°	3	3	3	4	3	3	3	3	3	4	Togo°
Tunisia	36	34	28	24	27	27	29	32	32	° 33	Tunisie
Uganda	12	15	° 17	° 17	° 13	° 15	° 16	° 16	° 17	° 18	Ouganda
United Rep. Tanzania°	24	25	25	26	26	27	27	28	28	29	Rép.Unie de Tanzanie°
Western Sahara°	0	0	0	0	0	0	0	0	1	1	Sahara occidental°
Zaire	9	9	9	° 9	° 9	° 9	° 10	° 10	° 10	° 10	Zaïre
Zambia°	1	1	1	1	1	1	1	1	1	1	Zambie°
Zimbabwe°	7	8	8	6	4	5	4	4	6	6	Zimbabwe°
America, North	**217**	**210**	**190**	**188**	**200**	**212**	**226**	**234**	**236**	**228**	**Amérique du Nord**
Canada	7	6	5	5	5	7	8	9	9	° 9	Canada
Cuba°	2	2	2	2	2	2	2	2	2	2	Cuba°
Dominican Republic	0	1	° 1	° 1	1	1	1	1	° 1	° 1	Rép. dominicaine
Guatemala°	3	3	3	3	3	4	4	4	4	4	Guatemala°
Haiti°	5	5	4	5	5	5	5	5	5	5	Haïti°
Jamaica	1	1	1	2	2	° 2	2	2	° 2	° 2	Jamaïque
Martinique°	0	0	0	0	0	0	1	1	1	1	Martinique°
Mexico	28	30	31	° 35	° 36	° 36	° 37	° 38	° 38	° 38	Mexique
Trinidad and Tobago°	0	0	1	1	1	1	1	1	1	1	Trinité–et–Tobago°
United States	168	159	140	133	144	153	166	171	172	164	Etats–Unis
America, South	**346**	**346**	**334**	**333**	**310**	**330**	**332**	**333**	**312**	**307**	**Amérique du Sud**
Argentina	135	140	137	137	118	120	117	117	109	104	Argentine
Bolivia	24	25	25	25	26	26	° 27	° 27	° 28	° 28	Bolivie
Brazil°	65	57	48	52	52	52	52	52	52	52	Brésil°
Chile	21	21	20	22	20	20	20	18	17	18	Chili
Colombia	* 9	* 10	* 10	11	11	* 12	* 12	* 13	* 13	13	Colombie
Ecuador°	9	9	9	9	9	10	10	10	10	10	Equateur°
Falkland I(Malvinas)°	1	1	1	1	1	1	1	1	1	1	I Falkland(Malvinas)°
Guyana°	1	1	1	1	1	1	1	1	1	1	Guyana°
Paraguay°	2	2	2	3	3	3	3	3	3	3	Paraguay°

For general note and footnotes, see end of table.

Voir la fin du tableau pour la remarque générale et les notes.

Mutton and lamb, fresh (Total production) (continued) – Viande d'ovins et de caprins, non préparée (Production totale) (suite)

Unit : Thousand metric tons

Unité : Milliers de tonnes métriques

Country or area	1976	1977	1978	1979	1980	1981	1982	1983	1984	1985	Pays ou zone
Peru	31	32	32	32	30	28	30	31	26	25	Pérou
Uruguay	* 38	* 39	* 38	30	° 28	° 47	° 49	° 50	° 41	° 41	Uruguay
Venezuela	10	11	11	° 12	° 12	° 11	° 11	° 12	° 12	° 12	Venezuela
Asia	**2 100**	**2 180**	**2 309**	**2 348**	**2 507**	**2 658**	**2 817**	**2 884**	**2 989**	**3 062**	**Asie**
Afghanistan	142	141	145	142	151	* 158	160	° 159	° 159	° 159	Afghanistan
Bahrain°	1	2	2	3	3	3	4	5	5	5	Bahreïn°
Bangladesh	29	30	45	° 45	47	48	49	50	° 51	° 52	Bangladesh
Burma°	4	4	4	4	4	5	6	7	7	8	Birmanie°
China	292	306	321	378	451	476	526	546	587	647	Chine
Cyprus°	9	10	10	10	10	10	10	10	10	10	Chypre°
Democratic Yemen°	11	11	11	11	11	11	11	12	12	12	Yémen démocratique°
India°	332	336	343	375	387	402	432	436	440	450	Inde°
Indonesia	52	54	57	62	° 57	59	56	59	° 62	° 62	Indonésie
Iran(Islamic Rep.of)	245	* 264	* 267	274	° 277	° 270	° 270	° 275	° 279	° 279	Iran(Rép.islamique)
Iraq	66	° 64	° 62	° 67	° 70	° 58	° 59	° 59	° 67	° 61	Iraq
Israel	4	4	4	° 5	° 4	° 5	° 5	° 5	° 5	° 5	Israël
Jordan°	10	11	11	12	12	14	14	15	16	15	Jordanie°
Korea, D. P. Rp.°	2	2	2	2	3	3	3	3	3	3	Corée, Rp. P. D.°
Korea, Republic of°	1	1	1	2	2	2	2	2	2	2	Corée, République de°
Kuwait	10	13	15	21	° 27	° 29	° 34	° 35	° 37	° 38	Koweït
Lebanon°	6	5	9	11	13	13	13	13	13	13	Liban°
Malaysia°	1	1	1	1	1	1	1	1	1	1	Malaisie°
Mongolia	* 108	* 97	* 121	* 118	* 116	127	132	124	126	115	Mongolie
Nepal	22	23	23	° 23	° 24	° 24	° 24	° 25	° 25	° 26	Népal
Oman°	4	4	4	5	5	6	6	7	7	7	Oman°
Pakistan	225	246	266	288	313	340	389	408	° 420	° 440	Pakistan
Philippines	6	6	6	6	6	° 8	° 7	° 8	° 8	° 8	Philippines
Qatar°	3	3	3	3	3	3	3	3	4	4	Qatar°
Saudi Arabia	30	30	° 45	° 59	° 73	° 87	° 96	° 101	° 104	° 108	Arabie saoudite
Singapore	3	3	° 2	2	2	2	2	2	2	1	Singapour
Sri Lanka	1	1	1	1	1	1	2	1	° 2	° 2	Sri Lanka
Syrian Arab Republic	49	61	65	81	88	90	° 89	° 87	° 97	° 88	Rép. arabe syrienne
Thailand°	0	0	0	1	1	0	0	1	1	1	Thaïlande°
Turkey*	384	397	411	285	292	349	356	370	380	380	Turquie*
United Arab Emirates°	3	4	5	6	6	7	8	9	10	10	Emirats arabes unis°
Viet Nam°	2	2	2	2	2	2	2	2	2	2	Viet Nam°
Yemen°	40	42	42	42	43	44	45	46	47	47	Yémen°
Europe	**1 141**	**1 125**	**1 143**	**1 165**	**1 235**	**1 198**	**1 227**	**1 259**	**1 264**	**1 285**	**Europe**
EEC	**649**	**640**	**653**	**676**	**747**	**711**	**721**	**734**	**742**	**749**	**CEE**
Denmark	0	0	0	0	0	0	0	0	1	° 1	Danemark
France	154	153	156	168	182	* 173	189	179	182	° 185	France
Germany, Fed. Rep.	26	25	26	28	30	28	27	28	28	27	Allemagne, Rép. féd.
Greece	120	121	122	123	123	122	120	121	* 123	° 121	Grèce
Ireland	37	37	41	39	42	44	41	40	* 42	° 44	Irlande
Italy	50	65	63	68	72	69	68	67	71	° 69	Italie
Netherlands	17	16	17	18	21	17	13	11	10	12	Pays-Bas
United Kingdom	245	223	228	231	277	259	264	287	286	290	Royaume-Uni
EFTA	**69**	**72**	**72**	**71**	**71**	**73**	**77**	**78**	**78**	**81**	**AELE**
Austria	2	2	3	3	3	3	3	4	4	° 4	Autriche
Finland	1	1	1	1	1	1	1	° 1	° 1	° 1	Finlande
Iceland	15	15	16	16	14	15	14	14	° 14	° 14	Islande
Norway	16	18	19	19	19	22	24	24	* 25	* 25	Norvège
Portugal	26	26	26	22	24	23	25	26	25	° 27	Portugal
Sweden	5	5	5	5	5	5	5	5	5	5	Suède
Switzerland	4	4	4	4	4	4	4	4	4	5	Suisse
East Europe	**212**	**207**	**208**	**219**	**216**	**210**	**220**	**237**	**241**	**250**	**Europe de l'est**
Albania	° 24	* 23	° 25	° 25	° 26	° 26	° 26	° 26	° 26	° 27	Albanie
Bulgaria	77	64	66	62	64	73	79	81	74	° 84	Bulgarie
Czechoslovakia	7	6	5	6	6	7	8	10	11	11	Tchécoslovaquie
German Dem. Rep.	15	14	15	15	16	15	14	12	16	15	Rép. dém. allemande
Hungary	5	4	6	5	7	8	7	7	8	° 6	Hongrie
Poland	18	18	20	21	19	18	18	18	° 17	° 20	Pologne
Romania	* 67	* 78	* 71	* 85	* 78	* 64	* 68	* 84	* 89	° 86	Roumanie
Other Europe	**206**	**202**	**205**	**193**	**196**	**197**	**201**	**201**	**197**	**198**	**Autre Europe**

For general note and footnotes, see end of table.

Voir la fin du tableau pour la remarque générale et les notes.

Mutton and lamb, fresh (Total production) (continued) – Viande d'ovins et de caprins, non préparée (Production totale) (suite)

Unit : Thousand metric tons

Unité : Milliers de tonnes métriques

Country or area	1976	1977	1978	1979	1980	1981	1982	1983	1984	1985	Pays ou zone
Faeroe Islands°	1	1	0	0	0	0	1	0	0	0	Iles Féroé°
Spain	146	144	142	132	138	140	142	141	138	° 137	Espagne
Yugoslavia	60	57	62	61	58	57	59	60	58	° 60	Yougoslavie
USSR	*** 878**	*** 894**	*** 921**	*** 863**	*** 870**	*** 860**	*** 816**	*** 837**	*** 866**	**° 825**	**URSS**
Oceania	**1 102**	**1 048**	**1 016**	**1 007**	**1 110**	**1 206**	**1 135**	**1 213**	**1 126**	**1 205**	**Océanie**
Australia	588	549	514	491	549	578	511	531	457	475	Australie
New Zealand	514	498	502	515	561	627	624	681	669	730	Nouvelle–Zélande
Total	**6 907**	**6 957**	**7 120**	**7 146**	**7 504**	**7 766**	**7 866**	**8 100**	**8 147**	**8 317**	**Total**

General note.
Fresh, chilled or frozen meat of sheep, lambs, goats and kids, irrespective of the origin of the animals, expressed in terms of carcass weight, excluding edible offals and tallow. Includes non–industrial production. (SITC 01120–0).
Source: Food and Agriculture Organization of the United Nations (FAO), Rome.

Remarque générale.
Poids net de viande fraîche, réfrigérée ou congelée, provenant de moutons, d'agneaux, de chèvres et de chevreaux abattus, quelle que soit la provenance de ces animaux, à l'exclusion des abats comestibles et du suif. Y compris production non–industrielle. (CTCI 01120–0).
Source: Organisation des Nations Unies pour l'agriculture(FAO), Rome.

Mutton and lamb, fresh (Industrial production) – Viande d'ovins et de caprins, non préparée (Production industrielle)

Unit : Thousand metric tons

Unité : Milliers de tonnes métriques

Country or area	1976	1977	1978	1979	1980	1981	1982	1983	1984	1985	Pays ou zone
Africa	**87**	**93**	**99**	**105**	**111**	**111**	**128**	**132**	**137**	**137**	**Afrique**
South Africa	...	...	...	...	...	111	128	132	137	137	Afrique du Sud
America, North	**135**	**138**	**140**	**143**	**146**	**142**	**152**	**162**	**160**	**152**	**Amérique du Nord**
United States	...	...	...	...	146	142	152	162	160	152	Etats–Unis
America, South	**17**	**17**	**16**	**16**	**16**	**15**	**16**	**14**	**11**	**16**	**Amérique du Sud**
Brazil	...	...	...	...	16	15	16	14	11	16	Brésil
Europe	**242**	**240**	**256**	**268**	**283**	**286**	**303**	**298**	**300**	**315**	**Europe**
EEC	***174***	***174***	***181***	***195***	***210***	***212***	***216***	***213***	***211***	***216***	***CEE***
Belgium	4	4	4	5	5	6	6	8	8	8	Belgique
France[1]	145	144	148	159	172	173	179	170	166	166	France[1]
Germany, Fed. Rep.[2]	17	16	17	18	18	14	13	15	16	15	Allemagne, Rép. féd.[2]
Ireland	...	...	...	...	...	19	18	20	21	27	Irlande
EFTA	***16***	***17***	***18***	***19***	***20***	***20***	***25***	***23***	***25***	***25***	***AELE***
Norway	16	17	18	19	20	20	25	23	* 25	* 25	Norvège
East Europe	***37***	***36***	***42***	***43***	***41***	***41***	***49***	***49***	***54***	***63***	***Europe de l'est***
Bulgaria	29	26	30	30	28	30	37	37	42	49	Bulgarie
Czechoslovakia	3	4	4	4	5	5	6	7	8	8	Tchécoslovaquie
Hungary	1	...	...	1	1	1	2	2	1	2	Hongrie
Poland	4	5	7	8	7	5	4	3	3	4	Pologne
Other Europe	***15***	***13***	***15***	***11***	***12***	***13***	***13***	***13***	***10***	***11***	***Autre Europe***
Yugoslavia	15	13	15	11	12	13	* 13	13	10	11	Yougoslavie
USSR	**379**	**396**	**381**	**369**	**346**	**351**	**342**	**372**	**381**	**357**	**URSS**
Byelorussian SSR	*1*	*1*	*1*	*1*	*1*	*1*	*1*	*1*	*2*	*2*	*RSS de Biélorussie*
Ukrainian SSR	*17*	*17*	*16*	*16*	*13*	*11*	*10*	*13*	*13*	*14*	*RSS d'Ukraine*
Total	**860**	**883**	**892**	**901**	**902**	**905**	**941**	**978**	**989**	**977**	**Total**

General note.
Fresh, chilled or frozen meat of sheep, lambs, goats and kids, irrespective of the origin of the animals, expressed in terms of carcass weight, excluding edible offals and tallow. Data refer to industrial production only. (SITC 01120–0).

[1] Meat from indigenous animals, including meat equivalent of exported live animals.
[2] Including edible offals.

Remarque générale.
Poids net de viande fraîche, réfrigérée ou congelée, provenant de moutons, d'agneaux, de chèvres et de chevreaux a battus, guelle que soit la provenance de ces animaux, à l'exclusion des abats comestibles et du suif. Les données se rapportent à la production industrielle seulement. (CTCI 01120–0).

[1] Viande provenant d'animaux élevés dans le pays, y compris l' équivalent en viande des bêtes exportées sur pied.
[2] Y compris les abats comestibles.

Pork, fresh (Total production) – Viande de porc, non préparée (Production totale)

Unit : Thousand metric tons — Unité : Milliers de tonnes métriques

Country or area	1976	1977	1978	1979	1980	1981	1982	1983	1984	1985	Pays ou zone
Africa	**321**	**333**	**336**	**340**	**364**	**385**	**383**	**413**	**418**	**428**	**Afrique**
Angola°	12	12	12	13	13	14	14	15	15	15	Angola°
Benin°	4	4	5	5	5	5	6	6	6	6	Bénin°
Botswana°	1	0	0	0	0	0	0	0	0	0	Botswana°
Burkina Faso°	3	3	4	4	4	5	4	4	4	4	Burkina Faso°
Burundi°	3	2	2	2	3	3	3	3	5	5	Burundi°
Cameroon°	22	24	24	27	29	27	21	15	17	17	Cameroun°
Cape Verde°	1	1	1	1	1	1	1	1	1	1	Cap-Vert°
Central African Rep.°	4	4	4	4	4	4	5	5	5	5	Rép. centrafricaine°
Congo°	1	1	1	1	1	2	2	2	2	2	Congo°
Côte d'Ivoire°	10	11	12	13	13	14	15	16	16	17	Côte d'Ivoire°
Egypt	2	2	2	2	2	3	* 3	° 3	° 3	° 3	Egypte
Ethiopia	1	° 1	° 1	° 1	° 1	° 1	° 1	° 1	° 1	° 1	Ethiopie
Gabon°	2	2	2	2	2	2	2	2	2	2	Gabon°
Ghana°	9	8	8	8	8	9	8	8	8	8	Ghana°
Guinea°	1	1	1	1	1	1	1	1	1	1	Guinée°
Guinea-Bissau°	2	2	3	3	3	4	4	4	4	4	Guinée-Bissau°
Kenya°	3	3	3	6	4	4	4	4	4	4	Kenya°
Lesotho°	3	3	3	3	3	2	3	3	3	3	Lesotho°
Liberia°	3	3	3	3	3	3	4	4	4	4	Libéria°
Madagascar°	21	22	25	25	30	35	31	35	37	38	Madagascar°
Malawi°	8	7	8	7	8	8	8	8	9	9	Malawi°
Mali°	1	1	1	1	2	2	1	2	2	2	Mali°
Mauritius	1	1	° 1	° 1	° 1	° 1	1	1	1	° 1	Maurice
Morocco	* 1	* 1	* 1	* 1	* 1	* 1	° 1	° 1	° 1	° 1	Maroc
Mozambique°	7	7	8	8	8	8	9	9	9	10	Mozambique°
Namibia°	2	3	3	3	3	3	3	3	3	3	Namibie°
Niger°	1	1	1	1	1	1	1	1	1	1	Niger°
Nigeria°	33	35	37	40	42	43	46	48	48	48	Nigéria°
Réunion	4	5	4	5	5	5	5	5	° 5	° 6	Réunion
Rwanda°	2	2	2	2	3	3	3	3	3	3	Rwanda°
Senegal°	6	6	6	7	7	7	7	7	7	7	Sénégal°
Seychelles°	1	0	0	0	0	0	1	1	1	1	Seychelles°
Sierra Leone°	1	1	1	2	2	2	2	2	2	2	Sierra Leone°
South Africa	86	89	85	81	86	* 95	* 100	* 120	* 118	° 120	Afrique du Sud
Swaziland°	0	1	1	1	1	1	1	1	1	1	Swaziland°
Togo°	4	4	4	4	4	3	3	3	3	3	Togo°
Uganda	8	7	° 8	° 8	° 12	° 13	° 13	° 13	° 13	° 14	Ouganda
United Rep. Tanzania°	4	4	4	4	4	5	2	5	5	5	Rép.Unie de Tanzanie°
Zaire	28	27	27	° 27	° 27	° 27	° 27	° 28	° 28	° 29	Zaïre
Zambia°	6	7	7	7	7	8	8	9	9	9	Zambie°
Zimbabwe°	13	13	11	9	9	9	10	12	11	12	Zimbabwe°
America, North	**6 753**	**7 176**	**7 350**	**8 396**	**9 004**	**8 678**	**7 978**	**8 435**	**8 288**	**8 340**	**Amérique du Nord**
Barbados°	5	5	6	5	6	6	6	6	6	6	Barbade°
Belize°	1	1	1	1	1	1	1	1	1	1	Belize°
Canada	533	537	614	737	856	840	833	852	863	* 880	Canada
Costa Rica	9	10	10	* 10	10	10	9	9	° 8	° 8	Costa Rica
Cuba	42	58	62	61	58	68	70	72	82	° 85	Cuba
Dominican Republic	* 21	* 23	* 23	* 23	* 12	* 1	* 0	* 2	* 6	° 39	Rép. dominicaine
El Salvador°	14	14	14	15	16	13	13	13	13	13	El Salvador°
Guadeloupe	1	1	2	2	2	2	2	3	3	° 3	Guadeloupe
Guatemala	12	10	13	18	17	17	17	16	16	16	Guatemala
Haiti	° 30	° 28	° 31	* 29	* 22	* 15	° 8	° 7	° 9	° 9	Haïti
Honduras	9	8	9	10	10	12	11	9	° 10	° 10	Honduras
Jamaica	7	8	8	6	7	7	7	7	7	° 7	Jamaïque
Martinique°	2	1	1	1	1	2	2	2	2	2	Martinique°
Mexico	389	410	425	* 415	* 410	* 438	° 497	° 497	° 500	° 500	Mexique
Neth.Antil and Aruba°	0	0	1	1	1	1	1	0	0	0	Antill.néer.et Aruba°
Nicaragua	19	21	* 20	* 21	* 11	* 13	* 14	° 14	° 14	° 14	Nicaragua
Puerto Rico	19	20	26	23	16	19	20	17	15	18	Porto Rico
Trinidad and Tobago	° 3	3	3	2	2	2	3	4	4	° 4	Trinité-et-Tobago
United States	5 631	6 009	6 075	7 008	7 536	7 201	6 454	6 895	6 719	6 715	Etats-Unis
America, South	**1 477**	**1 514**	**1 528**	**1 624**	**1 730**	**1 739**	**1 711**	**1 692**	**1 649**	**1 696**	**Amérique du Sud**
Argentina	258	241	214	258	263	254	230	207	* 240	° 240	Argentine
Bolivia	26	28	29	30	* 31	° 32	° 33	° 34	° 35	° 35	Bolivie
Brazil*	785	834	850	900	980	980	970	950	860	900	Brésil*
Chile	25	29	34	43	50	56	58	59	59	* 60	Chili
Colombia	100	100	105	95	94	* 105	* 101	* 111	* 113	* 114	Colombie
Ecuador°	42	45	51	57	63	53	57	59	62	65	Equateur°

For general note and footnotes, see end of table.

Voir la fin du tableau pour la remarque générale et les notes.

Pork, fresh (Total production) (continued) – Viande de porc, non préparée (Production totale) (suite)

Unit : Thousand metric tons

Unité : Milliers de tonnes métriques

Country or area	1976	1977	1978	1979	1980	1981	1982	1983	1984	1985	Pays ou zone
French Guiana	0	0	° 0	0	1	1	1	1	° 1	° 1	Guyane française
Guyana	2	2	2	2	1	1	1	1	1	° 1	Guyana
Paraguay°	59	62	68	77	81	83	84	87	90	90	Paraguay°
Peru*	71	70	69	68	71	77	76	74	71	70	Pérou*
Suriname	1	1	1	1	1	1	1	1	1	° 1	Suriname
Uruguay	* 25	* 24	* 25	* 18	* 17	18	17	18	15	° 16	Uruguay
Venezuela	84	78	81	74	77	79	82	90	102	° 104	Venezuela
Asia	**10 429**	**10 576**	**11 623**	**13 935**	**15 314**	**15 910**	**16 969**	**17 647**	**19 095**	**21 327**	**Asie**
Bhutan°	1	1	1	1	1	1	1	1	1	1	Bhoutan°
Brunei Darussalam°	0	0	1	0	0	0	0	0	0	0	Brunéi Darussalam°
Burma°	68	69	74	78	79	80	81	82	83	83	Birmanie°
China	7 827	7 856	8 609	10 693	11 939	12 479	13 332	13 817	15 179	17 285	Chine
Cyprus	13	14	15	16	15	18	20	21	24	° 24	Chypre
Dem. Kampuchea°	13	12	8	5	9	11	15	18	20	23	Kampuchea démocrat.°
Hong Kong	152	157	157	168	179	187	187	184	° 180	° 179	Hong-kong
India°	55	56	58	64	70	75	80	80	82	85	Inde°
Indonesia	81	84	84	92	° 87	87	° 85	° 85	° 87	° 90	Indonésie
Iran(Islamic Rep.of)	* 2	* 2	* 2	° 1	...	...	...	...	...	...	Iran(Rép.islamique)
Israel	8	10	9	9	9	9	10	9	° 9	° 9	Israël
Japan	1 056	1 169	1 284	1 430	1 475	1 396	1 428	1 429	1 424	1 530	Japon
Korea, D. P. Rp.°	81	90	96	106	115	118	118	130	141	148	Corée, Rp. P. D.°
Korea, Republic of	114	146	172	273	294	262	300	369	429	347	Corée, République de
Lao Peoples Dem.Rep.°	19	23	28	38	41	44	44	47	49	52	Rép. dém. pop. lao°
Lebanon°	1	1	1	1	1	1	1	1	1	1	Liban°
Macau	5	5	6	7	8	8	8	8	8	° 8	Macao
Malaysia°	65	67	65	68	68	78	79	82	82	82	Malaisie°
Mongolia	1	0	1	1	1	1	1	2	2	3	Mongolie
Nepal	5	5	5	° 6	° 6	6	7	7	7	7	Népal
Philippines	* 374	* 337	* 366	* 377	* 408	* 442	* 460	* 500	* 483	° 505	Philippines
Singapore	67	69	66	69	65	60	61	63	68	72	Singapour
Sri Lanka	0	1	1	1	1	1	1	1	° 1	° 1	Sri Lanka
Thailand°	170	140	245	150	150	150	200	200	205	205	Thaïlande°
Turkey°	1	1	1	1	1	1	1	1	1	1	Turquie°
Viet Nam	° 250	° 259	° 270	° 280	292	396	451	511	531	° 587	Viet Nam
Europe	**16 389**	**17 099**	**18 111**	**18 903**	**19 239**	**19 263**	**19 208**	**19 667**	**20 064**	**20 068**	**Europe**
EEC	**8 026**	**8 347**	**8 782**	**9 232**	**9 425**	**9 539**	**9 520**	**9 786**	**9 839**	**9 987**	**CEE**
Denmark	716	744	812	899	972	993	991	1 049	1 041	1 090	Danemark
France	1 614	1 648	1 727	1 803	1 803	1 835	1 807	1 795	1 819	1 810	France
Germany, Fed. Rep.	2 858	2 928	3 086	3 168	3 214	3 182	3 140	3 211	3 222	3 242	Allemagne, Rép. féd.
Greece	111	120	129	135	146	154	155	149	149	* 147	Grèce
Ireland	123	130	135	152	153	150	153	161	139	135	Irlande
Italy	816	904	967	1 033	1 085	1 106	1 108	1 166	1 218	* 1 190	Italie
Netherlands	936	967	1 048	1 107	1 125	1 194	1 211	1 248	1 306	* 1 408	Pays-Bas
United Kingdom	852	905	878	935	926	925	955	1 007	945	965	Royaume-Uni
EFTA	**1 262**	**1 324**	**1 351**	**1 407**	**1 439**	**1 477**	**1 514**	**1 502**	**1 502**	**1 527**	**AELE**
Austria	* 385	* 398	* 398	* 425	* 415	* 439	* 453	* 450	° 463	480	Autriche
Finland	136	140	154	164	169	180	184	185	170	* 168	Finlande
Iceland	1	1	1	1	1	1	1	° 1	° 1	° 1	Islande
Norway	75	79	78	80	86	83	81	81	* 84	* 84	Norvège
Portugal	125	140	155	* 160	* 173	178	179	176	183	* 179	Portugal
Sweden	294	304	307	314	317	321	325	318	324	328	Suède
Switzerland	246	262	258	263	279	275	289	291	276	287	Suisse
East Europe	**5 227**	**5 373**	**5 690**	**5 861**	**5 946**	**5 727**	**5 548**	**5 729**	**5 867**	**5 777**	**Europe de l'est**
Albania	° 8	* 9	° 9	° 9	° 9	° 9	° 9	° 9	° 9	° 9	Albanie
Bulgaria	317	275	276	307	313	326	324	333	334	° 340	Bulgarie
Czechoslovakia	699	751	798	797	819	853	743	796	814	823	Tchécoslovaquie
German Dem. Rep.	1 099	* 1 094	* 1 119	* 1 143	* 1 212	* 1 279	* 1 155	* 1 196	* 1 273	° 1 240	Rép. dém. allemande
Hungary	765	865	853	885	905	906	947	1 049	1 123	* 955	Hongrie
Poland	1 543	1 551	1 785	1 795	1 711	1 346	1 462	1 396	1 304	° 1 500	Pologne
Romania	* 796	* 829	* 852	* 925	* 977	* 1 008	* 908	* 949	° 1 010	° 910	Roumanie
Other Europe	**1 300**	**1 470**	**1 657**	**1 746**	**1 760**	**1 840**	**1 946**	**1 946**	**2 128**	**2 033**	**Autre Europe**
Malta	4	5	4	1	0	0	1	3	° 3	° 3	Malte
Spain	649	735	803	939	986	1 021	1 115	1 119	1 192	° 1 170	Espagne
Yugoslavia	* 647	* 730	* 850	* 805	* 774	* 818	* 830	* 823	* 933	° 860	Yougoslavie

For general note and footnotes, see end of table.

Voir la fin du tableau pour la remarque générale et les notes.

Pork, fresh (Total production) (continued) – Viande de porc, non préparée (Production totale) (suite)

Unit : Thousand metric tons

Unité : Milliers de tonnes métriques

Country or area	1976	1977	1978	1979	1980	1981	1982	1983	1984	1985	Pays ou zone
USSR	**4 228**	**4 950**	**5 302**	**5 266**	**5 183**	**5 219**	**5 300**	**5 760**	**5 927**	**° 5 940**	**URSS**
Oceania	**236**	**254**	**268**	**266**	**286**	**298**	**302**	**313**	**330**	**343**	**Océanie**
Australia	174	185	199	199	220	233	228	239	253	258	Australie
Fiji°	0	0	1	1	1	1	1	1	1	1	Fidji°
French Polynesia	° 1	1	1	1	1	1	1	1	1	° 1	Polynésie française
Guam	0	0	0	1	0	0	° 0	...	...	...	Guam
New Caledonia	° 1	* 1	0	0	1	1	1	1	1	° 1	Nouvelle–Calédonie
New Zealand	33	39	38	36	35	33	40	40	43	48	Nouvelle–Zélande
Pacific Islds(Trust)°	0	1	1	1	1	1	1	1	1	1	I.Pacifique (tutel.)°
Papua New Guinea°	21	21	22	23	23	23	24	24	25	25	Papouasie–Nvl–Guinée°
Samoa	° 2	° 1	° 1	° 1	* 1	* 1	* 1	* 1	* 1	° 2	Samoa
Solomon Islands°	1	1	1	1	1	1	1	1	1	1	Iles Salomon°
Tonga°	1	1	1	1	1	1	1	1	1	1	Tonga°
Vanuatu°	1	2	2	2	2	2	2	2	2	2	Vanuatu°
Total	**39 834**	**41 901**	**44 518**	**48 729**	**51 120**	**51 491**	**51 851**	**53 927**	**55 771**	**58 142**	**Total**

General note.
Fresh, chilled or frozen meat of swine, irrespective of the origin of the animals, expressed in terms of carcass weight, excluding edible offals and lard. Bacon and ham are not included. Includes non–industrial production. (SITC 01130–0).
Source: Food and Agriculture Organization of the United Nations (FAO), Rome.

Remarque générale.
Poids net de viande fraîche, réfrigérée ou congelée, provenant de porcs abattus, quelle que soit la provenance de ces animaux, à l'exclusion des abats comestibles et du saindoux, bacon et jambon non compris. Y compris production non–industrielle. (CTCI 01130–0).
Source: Organisation des Nations Unies pour l'agriculture(FAO), Rome.

Pork, fresh (Industrial production) – Viande de porc, non préparée (Production industrielle)

Unit : Thousand metric tons — Unité : Milliers de tonnes métriques

Country or area	1976	1977	1978	1979	1980	1981	1982	1983	1984	1985	Pays ou zone
Africa	**52**	**57**	**62**	**66**	**69**	**72**	**85**	**93**	**88**	**91**	**Afrique**
South Africa	...	...	...	...	69	72	85	93	88	91	Afrique du Sud
America, North	**8 125**	**7 904**	**7 676**	**7 446**	**7 570**	**6 936**	**6 347**	**6 299**	**6 525**	**6 253**	**Amérique du Nord**
Cuba	...	34	35	34	34	40	42	44	52	58	Cuba
United States	...	...	...	...	7 536	6 896	6 305	6 255	6 473	6 195	Etats-Unis
America, South	**826**	**797**	**768**	**739**	**699**	**709**	**626**	**647**	**567**	**577**	**Amérique du Sud**
Brazil	...	...	...	...	699	709	626	647	567	577	Brésil
Asia	**1 070**	**1 183**	**1 299**	**1 445**	**1 490**	**1 413**	**1 448**	**1 450**	**1 447**	**1 556**	**Asie**
Cyprus	14	14	15	15	15	17	20	21	23	24	Chypre
Japan	1 056	1 169	1 284	1 430	1 475	1 396	1 428	1 429	1 424	1 532	Japon
Europe	**7 878**	**8 238**	**8 793**	**9 168**	**9 162**	**8 835**	**8 801**	**8 978**	**9 083**	**9 064**	**Europe**
EEC	***5 010***	***5 201***	***5 457***	***5 709***	***5 794***	***5 842***	***5 805***	***5 980***	***5 988***	***6 000***	***CEE***
Belgium	568	581	623	650	661	672	672	698	726	717	Belgique
France	1 232	1 268	1 337	1 399	1 411	1 449	1 403	1 424	1 437	1 422	France
Germany, Fed. Rep.[1]	2 589	2 672	2 830	2 929	2 998	2 978	2 959	3 038	3 057	3 068	Allemagne, Rép. féd.[1]
Ireland	...	...	...	...	...	27	37	50	52	56	Irlande
Luxembourg	6	7	7	7	6	6	6	7	7	7	Luxembourg
United Kingdom	597	651	634	694	685	710	728	763	709	730	Royaume-Uni
EFTA	***236***	***251***	***278***	***296***	***306***	***317***	***324***	***335***	***339***	***360***	***AELE***
Finland	161	171	200	215	220	230	241	254	255	...	Finlande
Norway	75	80	78	81	86	87	83	81	* 84	* 84	Norvège
East Europe	***2 392***	***2 461***	***2 728***	***2 817***	***2 738***	***2 338***	***2 347***	***2 348***	***2 360***	***2 377***	***Europe de l'est***
Bulgaria	259	230	227	252	225	227	241	247	252	237	Bulgarie
Czechoslovakia	491	536	576	583	594	622	524	541	559	554	Tchécoslovaquie
Hungary	354	436	422	455	473	471	474	554	619	500	Hongrie
Poland	1 288	1 259	1 503	1 527	1 446	1 018	1 108	1 006	930	1 086	Pologne
Other Europe	***240***	***325***	***330***	***346***	***324***	***338***	***325***	***315***	***396***	***327***	***Autre Europe***
Yugoslavia	240	325	330	346	324	338	325	315	396	327	Yougoslavie
USSR	**2 108**	**2 465**	**2 653**	**2 636**	**2 446**	**2 468**	**2 402**	**2 728**	**2 922**	**2 894**	**URSS**
Byelorussian SSR	*134*	*157*	*173*	*163*	*147*	*134*	*145*	*186*	*206*	*212*	*RSS de Biélorussie*
Ukrainian SSR	*499*	*627*	*635*	*624*	*548*	*557*	*523*	*579*	*614*	*599*	*RSS d'Ukraine*
Total	**20 060**	**20 643**	**21 250**	**21 499**	**21 436**	**20 433**	**19 709**	**20 195**	**20 632**	**20 435**	**Total**

General note.

Fresh, chilled or frozen meat of swine, irrespective of the origin of the animals, expressed in terms of carcass weight, excluding edible offals and lard. Bacon and ham are not included. Data refer to industrial production only.(SITC 01130-0).

[1] Including edible offals.

Remarque générale.

Poids net de viande fraîche, réfrigérée ou congelée, provenant de porcs abattus, quelle que soit la provenance de ces animaux, à l'exclusion des abats comestibles et du saindoux, bacon et jambon non compris. Les données se rapportent à la production industrielle seulement. (CTCI 01130-0).

[1] Y compris les abats comestibles.

Poultry, dressed, fresh (Total production) – Volailles plumées et vidées, non préparées (Production totale)

Unit : Thousand metric tons — Unité : Milliers de tonnes métriques

Country or area	1976	1977	1978	1979	1980	1981	1982	1983	1984	1985	Pays ou zone
Africa	**921**	**981**	**1 059**	**1 115**	**1 219**	**1 275**	**1 404**	**1 493**	**1 519**	**1 604**	**Afrique**
Algeria°	38	40	42	44	46	47	48	49	50	52	Algérie°
Angola°	7	7	7	7	7	7	7	7	7	7	Angola°
Benin°	9	10	11	12	12	13	14	18	21	24	Bénin°
Botswana°	1	1	1	1	1	1	1	1	1	1	Botswana°
Burkina Faso°	10	9	9	10	11	12	14	15	16	16	Burkina Faso°
Burundi°	2	3	3	3	3	3	3	3	3	3	Burundi°
Cameroon°	10	10	10	11	8	7	7	8	8	10	Cameroun°
Central African Rep.°	1	1	1	1	1	2	2	2	2	2	Rép. centrafricaine°
Chad°	3	3	3	3	3	3	3	3	3	3	Tchad°
Congo°	3	3	3	3	3	5	5	5	5	5	Congo°
Côte d'Ivoire°	17	19	22	25	28	29	28	27	25	27	Côte d'Ivoire°
Egypt	100	104	105	103	118	° 135	° 158	° 177	° 185	° 195	Egypte
Ethiopia	56	° 62	° 66	° 67	° 68	° 68	° 69	° 70	° 70	° 71	Ethiopie
Gabon°	1	1	2	2	2	2	2	2	2	2	Gabon°
Gambia°	0	0	0	0	0	0	0	1	1	1	Gambie°
Ghana°	11	15	15	15	15	15	15	15	16	17	Ghana°
Guinea°	7	7	8	9	9	11	11	13	14	15	Guinée°
Kenya°	27	29	30	31	32	33	38	40	39	39	Kenya°
Lesotho°	1	1	1	1	1	1	1	1	1	1	Lesotho°
Liberia°	2	3	3	3	3	3	3	3	4	4	Libéria°
Libyan Arab Jamah.	20	15	20	25	* 27	* 35	° 38	° 40	° 44	° 45	Jamah.arabe libyenne
Madagascar°	36	37	42	42	54	60	64	63	65	69	Madagascar°
Malawi°	7	8	8	9	9	9	9	9	9	9	Malawi°
Mali°	11	10	11	11	11	12	12	13	14	14	Mali°
Mauritania°	2	2	3	3	3	3	3	3	3	3	Mauritanie°
Mauritius°	3	3	3	4	4	5	5	5	5	6	Maurice°
Morocco	° 63	* 75	* 86	* 99	* 99	* 75	* 110	* 128	* 115	* 120	Maroc
Mozambique°	14	14	15	16	16	17	17	18	18	18	Mozambique°
Niger°	7	7	7	8	8	13	13	14	14	16	Niger°
Nigeria°	115	130	150	170	209	231	248	262	258	275	Nigéria°
Réunion	3	4	4	3	4	3	° 4	° 4	° 4	° 4	Réunion
Rwanda°	1	1	1	1	1	1	1	1	1	1	Rwanda°
Senegal°	8	9	10	11	12	13	14	15	16	17	Sénégal°
Sierra Leone°	4	4	5	5	5	6	6	6	7	7	Sierra Leone°
Somalia°	3	3	3	3	3	3	3	3	3	3	Somalie°
South Africa	199	° 199	° 213	215	235	247	266	292	° 304	° 329	Afrique du Sud
Sudan°	17	17	18	20	21	22	23	24	25	26	Soudan°
Swaziland°	1	1	1	1	1	1	1	1	1	1	Swaziland°
Togo°	2	2	3	2	3	3	4	4	4	4	Togo°
Tunisia	° 24	° 30	° 35	° 38	° 40	° 41	50	38	° 40	° 43	Tunisie
Uganda	18	22	20	° 18	° 19	° 19	° 22	° 23	° 24	° 25	Ouganda
United Rep. Tanzania	° 13	° 14	° 15	° 16	17	19	19	° 23	° 24	° 25	Rép.Unie de Tanzanie
Zaire	13	14	13	° 13	° 13	° 13	° 13	° 14	° 14	° 15	Zaïre
Zambia°	25	23	22	22	24	19	20	21	22	22	Zambie°
Zimbabwe°	8	8	9	9	9	9	9	10	10	10	Zimbabwe°
America, North	**6 389**	**6 593**	**7 019**	**7 781**	**7 940**	**8 340**	**8 373**	**8 623**	**8 938**	**9 354**	**Amérique du Nord**
Bahamas	* 5	° 4	° 5	° 5	° 6	° 8	° 7	° 7	° 7	° 8	Bahamas
Barbados	3	4	4	5	5	6	7	6	7	6	Barbade
Belize	2	2	2	° 2	° 2	2	3	3	3	° 3	Belize
Canada	448	458	478	537	527	532	533	533	564	593	Canada
Costa Rica	5	5	6	6	5	4	4	5	° 5	° 5	Costa Rica
Cuba	50	53	61	64	73	82	76	90	107	° 106	Cuba
Dominican Republic	37	39	47	54	66	64	61	74	° 74	° 74	Rép. dominicaine
El Salvador	8	13	15	16	13	* 13	16	16	21	° 20	El Salvador
Guadeloupe°	0	0	0	0	1	1	1	1	1	1	Guadeloupe°
Guatemala°	16	18	30	49	49	49	50	50	50	55	Guatemala°
Haiti°	5	5	5	6	6	7	7	8	9	9	Haïti°
Honduras	6	7	8	8	9	10	12	13	° 13	° 13	Honduras
Jamaica	27	30	31	32	30	30	27	33	34	° 35	Jamaïque
Martinique°	3	3	4	4	4	4	4	4	4	4	Martinique°
Mexico	329	350	378	409	441	469	446	512	489	° 515	Mexique
Neth.Antil and Aruba°	0	0	1	1	1	1	1	1	1	1	Antill.néer.et Aruba°
Nicaragua	° 11	° 10	° 9	* 7	8	7	10	11	° 11	10	Nicaragua
Puerto Rico	17	19	19	25	28	30	28	27	26	31	Porto Rico
Trinidad and Tobago	* 20	* 24	* 24	* 19	* 19	* 21	° 21	° 21	° 21	° 21	Trinité–et–Tobago
United States	5 385	5 536	5 880	6 520	6 631	6 984	7 046	7 194	7 476	7 829	Etats–Unis
America, South	**1 374**	**1 529**	**1 712**	**2 030**	**2 488**	**2 756**	**2 900**	**2 944**	**2 747**	**2 843**	**Amérique du Sud**
Argentina	263	294	300	353	429	476	445	440	° 479	° 482	Argentine

For general note and footnotes, see end of table.

Voir la fin du tableau pour la remarque générale et les notes.

Unit : Thousand metric tons — Unité : Milliers de tonnes métriques

Country or area	1976	1977	1978	1979	1980	1981	1982	1983	1984	1985	Pays ou zone
Bolivia	7	8	8	9	10	° 10	° 11	° 11	° 12	° 12	Bolivie
Brazil	616	710	871	1 110	1 385	1 506	1 619	1 680	1 466	1 536	Brésil
Chile	38	44	59	64	86	109	95	86	70	* 75	Chili
Colombia	70	79	89	103	109	110	125	126	128	133	Colombie
Ecuador°	15	18	20	21	20	25	28	29	30	30	Equateur°
Guyana°	10	11	12	11	12	13	14	14	15	15	Guyana°
Paraguay°	11	12	13	14	15	15	15	16	16	17	Paraguay°
Peru	140	143	119	118	144	183	205	206	182	201	Pérou
Suriname	6	6	8	8	8	8	9	9	9	° 9	Suriname
Uruguay°	17	17	18	18	18	20	20	21	22	22	Uruguay°
Venezuela	182	186	196	201	251	281	315	306	319	° 311	Venezuela
Asia	**3 270**	**3 548**	**3 884**	**4 246**	**4 506**	**4 897**	**5 247**	**5 762**	**6 107**	**6 461**	**Asie**
Afghanistan°	10	11	11	12	12	12	12	13	13	13	Afghanistan°
Bahrain	° 2	* 2	° 3	° 4	° 4	° 4	° 4	3	° 3	° 4	Bahreïn
Bangladesh	54	54	76	° 80	84	88	93	100	107	° 111	Bangladesh
Brunei Darussalam°	2	2	2	2	3	5	5	6	4	4	Brunéi Darussalam°
Burma	52	52	54	61	68	81	91	97	103	° 109	Birmanie
China	828	877	986	1 046	1 113	1 267	1 424	1 603	1 757	1 944	Chine
Cyprus	8	8	9	10	10	10	11	13	13	° 13	Chypre
Dem. Kampuchea°	11	12	11	10	10	11	11	13	15	17	Kampuchea démocrat.°
Democratic Yemen°	1	1	1	1	2	2	2	2	2	2	Yémen démocratique°
Hong Kong	° 24	37	36	42	45	56	57	52	° 48	° 51	Hong–kong
India°	90	90	93	101	113	120	130	137	150	158	Inde°
Indonesia	° 111	° 119	° 119	141	176	187	198	° 191	° 195	° 209	Indonésie
Iran(Islamic Rep.of)°	130	150	170	170	170	200	215	230	235	240	Iran(Rép.islamique)°
Iraq	30	31	42	46	58	65	90	113	125	° 150	Iraq
Israel	139	142	146	150	150	159	170	185	174	170	Israël
Japan	839	944	1 022	1 095	1 120	1 140	1 200	1 270	1 350	1 410	Japon
Jordan	° 22	° 23	° 24	28	° 30	° 33	° 35	° 37	° 38	° 39	Jordanie
Korea, D. P. Rp.°	28	30	31	32	32	33	34	35	36	37	Corée, Rp. P. D.°
Korea, Republic of	63	75	84	123	124	122	101	176	169	129	Corée, République de
Kuwait	7	9	8	16	11	9	* 15	18	* 19	19	Koweït
Lao Peoples Dem.Rep.°	9	9	10	10	10	12	14	16	16	18	Rép. dém. pop. lao°
Lebanon	* 9	* 12	* 19	° 43	° 47	° 47	° 53	° 52	° 51	° 52	Liban
Macau°	3	2	3	3	3	3	3	4	4	4	Macao°
Malaysia°	116	119	124	130	138	138	143	148	152	152	Malaisie°
Nepal	17	17	18	° 18	° 19	° 19	° 20	° 20	° 21	° 21	Népal
Oman°	1	1	1	1	1	1	2	2	2	2	Oman°
Pakistan	26	30	34	40	46	53	61	° 68	° 73	81	Pakistan
Philippines	° 136	132	131	° 149	° 154	° 169	° 174	174	141	° 148	Philippines
Qatar	° 0	1	1	1	1	1	1	1	° 1	° 1	Qatar
Saudi Arabia	° 21	° 23	° 26	° 29	° 42	° 60	° 80	* 136	* 200	° 250	Arabie saoudite
Singapore°	46	49	48	49	50	50	49	49	49	50	Singapour°
Sri Lanka°	10	10	11	11	12	12	13	13	13	14	Sri Lanka°
Syrian Arab Republic	22	25	34	44	49	77	82	86	° 91	° 86	Rép. arabe syrienne
Thailand	° 135	° 145	° 169	° 188	196	° 237	° 249	° 284	° 295	° 302	Thaïlande
Turkey°	175	202	214	229	247	258	247	250	268	271	Turquie°
United Arab Emirates°	1	1	1	2	4	5	5	5	6	6	Emirats arabes unis°
Viet Nam	° 91	° 98	° 109	° 124	145	° 143	° 137	146	150	° 156	Viet Nam
Yemen	1	° 2	° 2	° 3	° 4	° 6	° 9	° 11	° 14	° 15	Yémen
Europe	**5 919**	**6 256**	**6 507**	**6 802**	**7 053**	**7 398**	**7 422**	**7 309**	**7 375**	**7 508**	**Europe**
EEC	**3 334**	**3 453**	**3 589**	**3 749**	**3 893**	**4 059**	**4 286**	**4 168**	**4 151**	**4 263**	**CEE**
Denmark	97	103	98	100	96	104	110	112	109	112	Danemark
France	871	905	963	1 035	1 122	1 236	1 331	1 284	1 249	1 281	France
Germany, Fed. Rep.	297	329	363	376	390	391	395	357	360	366	Allemagne, Rép. féd.
Greece	124	119	121	132	142	143	155	156	155	157	Grèce
Ireland	41	43	44	48	51	50	55	58	56	° 57	Irlande
Italy	897	916	957	985	1 005	1 015	1 047	1 050	1 025	1 057	Italie
Netherlands	313	318	314	321	333	375	386	363	381	395	Pays–Bas
United Kingdom	694	720	729	752	754	746	808	788	° 817	838	Royaume–Uni
EFTA	**251**	**279**	**270**	**274**	**312**	**309**	**297**	**311**	**316**	**319**	**AELE**
Austria	60	63	67	70	71	73	71	76	81	° 81	Autriche
Finland	12	13	12	14	15	17	16	18	20	* 21	Finlande
Iceland	0	1	1	1	1	1	1	° 1	° 1	° 1	Islande
Norway	8	9	10	11	12	12	10	10	11	* 12	Norvège
Portugal	* 110	134	117	113	145	135	128	134	° 130	* 131	Portugal
Sweden	41	38	41	42	44	47	46	47	48	47	Suède
Switzerland	21	22	22	23	23	24	24	25	° 26	° 27	Suisse

For general note and footnotes, see end of table. — Voir la fin du tableau pour la remarque générale et les notes.

Poultry, dressed, fresh (Total production) (continued) – Volailles plumées et vidées, non préparées (Production totale) (suite)

Unit : Thousand metric tons

Unité : Milliers de tonnes métriques

Country or area	1976	1977	1978	1979	1980	1981	1982	1983	1984	1985	Pays ou zone
East Europe	**1 305**	**1 430**	**1 517**	**1 629**	**1 671**	**1 721**	**1 553**	**1 581**	**1 652**	**1 694**	**Europe de l'est**
Albania°	8	8	9	10	10	11	12	12	13	14	Albanie°
Bulgaria	130	148	158	162	145	147	154	160	166	° 165	Bulgarie
Czechoslovakia	155	167	181	189	194	194	195	190	194	200	Tchécoslovaquie
German Dem. Rep.	130	134	135	140	145	149	147	153	° 153	° 155	Rép. dém. allemande
Hungary	302	313	320	319	352	366	418	402	° 403	° 400	Hongrie
Poland	277	320	358	398	419	432	187	189	255	° 285	Pologne
Romania	303	338	356	411	406	422	* 442	* 474	° 468	° 475	Roumanie
Other Europe	**903**	**966**	**1 011**	**1 018**	**1 044**	**1 176**	**1 138**	**1 104**	**1 106**	**1 077**	**Autre Europe**
Malta	4	4	4	5	5	5	4	4	4	4	Malte
Spain	696	735	755	747	762	885	853	813	789	* 757	Espagne
Yugoslavia	* 204	* 227	* 253	* 267	* 277	* 286	* 282	287	313	° 316	Yougoslavie
USSR	**1 414**	**1 691**	**1 902**	**2 034**	**2 139**	**2 255**	**2 425**	**2 596**	**2 686**	**° 2 790**	**URSS**
Oceania	**237**	**251**	**288**	**311**	**352**	**351**	**334**	**359**	**353**	**395**	**Océanie**
Australia	204	218	246	271	313	303	286	313	298	339	Australie
Fiji	1	2	2	3	3	3	3	4	4	4	Fidji
French Polynesia	° 0	0	0	0	1	0	0	0	0	° 1	Polynésie française
New Caledonia°	0	0	0	0	0	0	0	0	1	0	Nouvelle–Calédonie°
New Zealand	° 28	28	° 37	34	32	39	37	34	43	° 44	Nouvelle–Zélande
Papua New Guinea	° 1	° 1	° 1	° 1	° 1	° 3	° 6	6	6	6	Papouasie–Nvl–Guinée
Total	**19 525**	**20 849**	**22 370**	**24 319**	**25 696**	**27 271**	**28 105**	**29 086**	**29 725**	**30 954**	**Total**

General note.
Fresh, chilled or frozen meat of fowls, ducks, geese, turkeys and guinea fowls and edible offals thereof, except liver. Includes non–industrial production. (SITC 01140–1).
Source: Food and Agriculture Organization of the United Nations (FAO), Rome.

Remarque générale.
Viande fraîche, réfrigérée ou congelée, de poulet, de canard, d'oie, de dinde et de pintade, y compris les abats comestibles, à l'exclusion du foie. Y compris production non–industrielle. (CTCI 01140–1).
Source: Organisation des Nations Unies pour l'agriculture(FAO), Rome.

ISIC-BASED CODE
3111-101

Poultry, dressed, fresh (Industrial production) – Volailles plumées et vidées, non préparées (Production industrielle)

CODE BASE CITI
3111-101

Unit : Thousand metric tons

Unité : Milliers de tonnes métriques

Country or area	1976	1977	1978	1979	1980	1981	1982	1983	1984	1985	Pays ou zone
Africa	**12**	**23**	**33**	**44**	**54**	**62**	**67**	**99**	**100**	**98**	**Afrique**
South Africa	...	...	...	...	...	62	67	99	* 100	98	Afrique du Sud
America, North	**460**	**474**	**493**	**561**	**557**	**562**	**598**	**625**	**652**	**674**	**Amérique du Nord**
Canada	442	454	473	532	522	* 516	...	...	...	...	Canada
Cuba	18	20	20	29	35	46	45	54	63	67	Cuba
America, South	**865**	**902**	**938**	**975**	**914**	**1 049**	**1 192**	**1 204**	**1 146**	**1 109**	**Amérique du Sud**
Brazil	...	...	...	...	914	1 049	1 192	1 204	1 146	1 109	Brésil
Asia	**824**	**903**	**1 005**	**1 092**	**1 128**	**1 125**	**1 184**	**1 239**	**1 309**	**1 353**	**Asie**
Japan	824	903	1 005	1 092	1 128	1 125	1 184	1 239	1 309	1 353	Japon
Europe	**2 187**	**2 288**	**2 378**	**2 464**	**2 524**	**2 538**	**2 421**	**2 360**	**2 407**	**2 491**	**Europe**
EEC	***1 512***	***1 528***	***1 542***	***1 562***	***1 581***	***1 555***	***1 652***	***1 568***	***1 542***	***1 592***	***CEE***
Belgium	132	128	119	130	133	133	147	144	144	159	Belgique
France	...	...	...	...	...	1 034	1 118	1 073	1 038	1 064	France
Germany, Fed. Rep.[1]	251	272	296	311	321	329	331	297	304	311	Allemagne, Rép. féd.[1]
Greece	...	...	...	47	55	58	55	53	55	...	Grèce
Luxembourg	1	1	1	1	1	1	1	1	1	1	Luxembourg
EFTA	***19***	***22***	***24***	***26***	***27***	***32***	***32***	***33***	***31***	***35***	***AELE***
Finland	11	13	14	15	15	19	21	22	20	...	Finlande
Norway	8	9	10	11	12	13	11	11	* 11	* 12	Norvège
East Europe	***573***	***648***	***715***	***768***	***807***	***835***	***621***	***624***	***691***	***720***	***Europe de l'est***
Bulgaria	79	92	101	96	95	101	108	110	113	119	Bulgarie
Czechoslovakia	136	146	159	170	175	173	170	168	170	174	Tchécoslovaquie
Hungary	157	165	176	182	193	205	235	235	232	230	Hongrie
Poland	201	245	279	320	344	356	108	111	176	197	Pologne
Other Europe	***83***	***90***	***97***	***108***	***109***	***116***	***116***	***135***	***143***	***144***	***Autre Europe***
Yugoslavia	...	...	...	108	109	116	116	135	143	144	Yougoslavie
USSR	**695**	**898**	**1 033**	**1 139**	**1 224**	**1 350**	**1 460**	**1 573**	**1 667**	**1 743**	**URSS**
Byelorussian SSR	*36*	*43*	*49*	*56*	*68*	*81*	*84*	*88*	*93*	*99*	*RSS de Biélorussie*
Ukrainian SSR	*153*	*184*	*200*	*213*	*228*	*255*	*272*	*279*	*288*	*293*	*RSS d'Ukraine*
Oceania	**2**	**2**	**3**	**3**	**3**	**3**	**3**	**4**	**4**	**4**	**Océanie**
Fiji	2	2	3	3	3	3	3	4	4	4	Fidji
Total	**5 046**	**5 489**	**5 883**	**6 278**	**6 404**	**6 689**	**6 925**	**7 104**	**7 285**	**7 473**	**Total**

General note.
Fresh, chilled or frozen meat of fowls, ducks, geese, turkeys and guinea fowls and edible offals thereof, except liver. Data refer to industrial production only. (SITC 01140–1).

[1] Production of establishments with monthly capacity of 2000 fowls or more.

Remarque générale.
Viande fraîche, réfrigérée ou congelée, de poulet, de canard, d'oie, de dinde et de pintade,y compris les abats comestibles, à l'exclusion du foie. Les données se rapportent à la production industrielle seulement. (SITC 01140–1).

[1] Production des établissements d'un débit mensuel de 2000 volailles ou plus.

Other meat, fresh (Total production) – Autres viandes, non préparées (Production totale)

Unit : Thousand metric tons — Unité : Milliers de tonnes métriques

Country or area	1976	1977	1978	1979	1980	1981	1982	1983	1984	1985	Pays ou zone
Africa	**756**	**783**	**791**	**803**	**825**	**848**	**865**	**889**	**895**	**909**	**Afrique**
Algeria	8	9	9	9	10	10	10	10	11	11	Algérie
Angola	6	6	6	6	6	6	6	6	6	6	Angola
Benin	6	6	6	6	6	6	6	6	6	6	Bénin
Botswana	6	6	6	6	6	6	6	6	6	6	Botswana
Burkina Faso	8	8	7	7	8	8	8	8	8	8	Burkina Faso
Cameroon	4	4	4	4	4	4	4	4	4	4	Cameroun
Central African Rep.	9	9	9	8	7	7	7	7	7	7	Rép. centrafricaine
Chad	4	4	4	4	4	4	4	4	4	4	Tchad
Congo	5	5	5	5	5	5	5	5	5	5	Congo
Côte d'Ivoire	26	26	26	27	28	28	28	28	28	28	Côte d'Ivoire
Egypt	26	27	29	27	25	31	30	34	35	36	Egypte
Ethiopia	93	97	100	102	105	108	110	113	115	118	Ethiopie
Gabon	16	16	16	16	16	16	16	16	16	16	Gabon
Gambia	1	1	1	1	1	1	1	1	1	1	Gambie
Ghana	40	48	54	60	69	75	83	95	92	90	Ghana
Guinea	4	4	4	4	4	4	4	4	4	4	Guinée
Kenya	20	20	21	22	22	23	23	23	24	24	Kenya
Lesotho	4	3	3	3	3	3	3	4	3	4	Lesotho
Liberia	5	5	6	6	6	6	6	6	6	6	Libéria
Libyan Arab Jamah.	6	7	6	7	6	7	7	7	7	7	Jamah.arabe libyenne
Madagascar	2	2	2	2	2	2	2	2	3	3	Madagascar
Mali	22	23	24	24	24	24	26	26	26	27	Mali
Mauritania	10	10	10	10	10	11	11	11	11	11	Mauritanie
Morocco	7	6	6	8	8	8	9	9	9	10	Maroc
Namibia	2	2	2	3	3	3	3	3	3	3	Namibie
Niger	9	9	9	9	10	10	10	10	10	11	Niger
Nigeria	90	95	95	95	100	100	100	100	100	100	Nigéria
Rwanda	6	6	6	6	6	6	6	7	7	7	Rwanda
Senegal	7	7	8	8	7	9	7	7	7	8	Sénégal
Sierra Leone	2	2	2	2	2	2	2	2	2	2	Sierra Leone
Somalia	66	68	68	68	71	73	77	77	77	78	Somalie
South Africa	5	6	7	8	10	11	11	11	11	11	Afrique du Sud
Sudan	67	67	66	60	61	60	60	60	60	64	Soudan
Togo	4	4	4	4	4	4	4	4	4	4	Togo
Tunisia	4	3	3	4	3	4	4	4	4	4	Tunisie
Uganda	13	14	14	15	15	15	15	15	15	16	Ouganda
United Rep. Tanzania	8	8	8	8	9	9	10	10	11	11	Rép.Unie de Tanzanie
Western Sahara	1	1	1	1	1	1	1	1	1	1	Sahara occidental
Zaire	104	103	101	103	103	104	104	106	108	110	Zaïre
Zambia	19	20	20	20	20	20	21	21	21	21	Zambie
Zimbabwe	12	13	13	13	14	14	15	15	15	16	Zimbabwe
America, North	**383**	**392**	**398**	**392**	**390**	**386**	**412**	**393**	**402**	**407**	**Amérique du Nord**
Canada	18	19	21	21	20	18	18	19	18	19	Canada
Cuba	1	1	2	1	2	2	2	2	2	2	Cuba
Guatemala	2	2	2	2	2	2	2	2	2	2	Guatemala
Haiti	8	8	8	8	9	9	9	9	9	9	Haïti
Mexico	49	50	51	51	52	62	63	63	64	66	Mexique
Nicaragua	2	2	3	2	2	2	2	2	2	2	Nicaragua
United States	303	309	311	306	304	290	315	295	303	306	Etats–Unis
America, South	**225**	**215**	**225**	**230**	**207**	**208**	**211**	**211**	**220**	**215**	**Amérique du Sud**
Argentina	86	93	93	97	84	88	97	96	97	97	Argentine
Bolivia	8	8	8	8	7	7	7	7	7	7	Bolivie
Brazil	59	41	48	48	39	36	30	25	30	25	Brésil
Chile	4	5	6	9	10	8	6	11	14	14	Chili
Colombia	2	3	3	3	3	3	3	3	3	3	Colombie
Ecuador	26	27	28	26	26	26	27	27	27	27	Equateur
Paraguay	2	1	1	0	0	0	0	0	0	0	Paraguay
Peru	37	37	37	37	36	37	37	38	38	38	Pérou
Uruguay	2	2	2	2	2	3	3	3	3	3	Uruguay
Asia	**558**	**576**	**585**	**629**	**684**	**710**	**745**	**791**	**821**	**851**	**Asie**
Afghanistan	13	15	15	14	14	13	13	12	12	12	Afghanistan
Bangladesh	1	1	2	2	1	1	3	3	3	4	Bangladesh
China	264	276	296	346	397	424	453	493	514	541	Chine
Cyprus	0	0	0	0	0	0	0	0	1	0	Chypre
Democratic Yemen	2	1	1	1	1	2	1	1	1	1	Yémen démocratique
Hong Kong	4	4	4	5	4	4	5	5	5	5	Hong–kong

For general note, see end of table.

Voir la fin du tableau pour la remarque générale.

Other meat, fresh (Total production) (continued) – Autres viandes, non préparées (Production totale) (suite)

Unit : Thousand metric tons

Unité : Milliers de tonnes métriques

Country or area	1976	1977	1978	1979	1980	1981	1982	1983	1984	1985	Pays ou zone
India	82	84	86	95	103	108	110	110	115	119	Inde
Indonesia	15	15	16	15	15	17	17	17	18	17	Indonésie
Iran(Islamic Rep.of)	16	16	16	16	16	17	17	17	18	18	Iran(Rép.islamique)
Iraq	3	2	2	1	1	1	1	1	1	1	Iraq
Israel	0	0	0	0	0	0	0	0	1	0	Israël
Japan	50	48	29	23	25	22	25	26	27	27	Japon
Jordan	1	0	0	0	1	1	0	0	0	0	Jordanie
Korea, Republic of	7	9	9	9	8	6	5	7	6	6	Corée, République de
Maldives	1	1	1	1	1	1	1	1	1	1	Maldives
Mongolia	40	46	50	43	39	37	35	37	37	38	Mongolie
Oman	1	1	1	1	2	2	3	3	3	3	Oman
Pakistan	11	11	12	12	11	11	12	12	12	12	Pakistan
Philippines	10	10	10	10	11	11	11	11	12	12	Philippines
Saudi Arabia	23	23	22	21	21	19	20	20	20	20	Arabie saoudite
Syrian Arab Republic	1	1	1	1	1	1	1	1	1	1	Rép. arabe syrienne
Turkey	7	5	5	5	4	4	4	5	5	4	Turquie
United Arab Emirates	4	2	2	2	2	2	2	2	2	2	Emirats arabes unis
Viet Nam	3	4	4	4	4	5	5	5	5	6	Viet Nam
Yemen	0	0	1	1	1	1	1	1	1	1	Yémen
Europe	**956**	**996**	**1 014**	**1 051**	**1 062**	**1 058**	**1 003**	**1 020**	**1 036**	**1 042**	**Europe**
EEC	**639**	**653**	**660**	**688**	**684**	**673**	**613**	**646**	**647**	**664**	**CEE**
Denmark	5	5	5	5	5	5	4	4	4	4	Danemark
France	362	351	346	369	355	348	289	322	320	323	France
Germany, Fed. Rep	45	49	50	47	49	45	46	46	45	45	Allemagne, Rép. féd.
Greece	11	11	11	11	11	10	10	10	10	10	Grèce
Ireland	4	4	3	2	3	3	3	2	2	2	Irlande
Italy	196	213	227	239	246	246	244	245	247	261	Italie
Netherlands	6	6	5	5	4	3	2	2	3	3	Pays-Bas
United Kingdom	11	14	14	10	10	12	14	14	15	16	Royaume-Uni
EFTA	**51**	**54**	**58**	**59**	**64**	**69**	**73**	**69**	**72**	**75**	**AELE**
Austria	8	9	9	8	8	8	8	8	8	8	Autriche
Finland	3	3	3	2	2	2	2	2	2	2	Finlande
Iceland	5	5	6	6	8	9	8	6	7	7	Islande
Norway	9	8	8	7	7	8	8	9	9	9	Norvège
Portugal	9	11	11	11	11	11	11	12	12	12	Portugal
Sweden	11	13	16	19	22	25	29	27	29	32	Suède
Switzerland	6	6	5	5	5	5	5	5	5	5	Suisse
East Europe	**131**	**134**	**136**	**139**	**142**	**135**	**132**	**149**	**142**	**142**	**Europe de l'est**
Bulgaria	4	4	6	7	6	4	3	3	3	3	Bulgarie
Czechoslovakia	31	31	30	32	34	37	39	45	48	48	Tchécoslovaquie
German Dem. Rep	31	29	29	27	27	27	21	22	21	22	Rép. dém. allemande
Hungary	21	20	22	23	26	28	28	30	27	27	Hongrie
Poland	36	41	39	40	41	31	33	42	35	35	Pologne
Romania	9	9	9	9	9	7	7	7	8	7	Roumanie
Other Europe	**118**	**138**	**143**	**148**	**154**	**161**	**163**	**134**	**151**	**138**	**Autre Europe**
Spain	114	132	136	142	147	154	157	128	145	131	Espagne
Yugoslavia	4	5	6	6	6	6	6	6	6	6	Yougoslavie
USSR	**323**	**299**	**290**	**274**	**257**	**253**	**240**	**246**	**254**	**247**	**URSS**
Oceania	**37**	**42**	**41**	**42**	**46**	**48**	**52**	**47**	**51**	**49**	**Océanie**
Australia	18	22	22	23	27	29	34	28	31	30	Australie
New Zealand	4	5	4	4	3	3	2	3	3	3	Nouvelle-Zélande
Papua New Guinea	15	15	15	15	16	16	16	16	16	17	Papouasie-Nvl-Guinée
Total	**3 239**	**3 303**	**3 345**	**3 421**	**3 472**	**3 511**	**3 529**	**3 598**	**3 678**	**3 720**	**Total**

General note.
Fresh, chilled or frozen meat of other animals, irrespective of the origin of the animals, in carcass weight, excluding edible offals and tallow. Includes non-industrial production. (SITC 01150-0+).
Source: Food and Agriculture Organization of the United Nations (FAO), Rome.

Remarque générale.
Poids net de viande fraîche, réfrigérée ou congelée, d'autres animaux abattus, quelle que soit leur provenance, à l'exclusion des abats comestibles et du suif. Y compris production non-industrielle. (CTCI 01150-0+).
Source: Organisation des Nations Unies pour l'agriculture(FAO), Rome.

Other meat, fresh (Industrial production) – Autres viandes, non préparées (Production industrielle)

Unit : Thousand metric tons — Unité : Milliers de tonnes métriques

Country or area	1976	1977	1978	1979	1980	1981	1982	1983	1984	1985	Pays ou zone
Europe	**36**	**37**	**37**	**37**	**41**	**42**	**45**	**45**	**45**	**48**	**Europe**
EEC	***27***	***27***	***27***	***28***	***32***	***32***	***35***	***35***	***36***	***39***	***CEE***
Belgium	16	16	16	16	18	18	21	21	21	24	Belgique
Germany, Fed. Rep.	...	...	...	...	6	6	6	7	7	7	Allemagne, Rép. féd.
United Kingdom	6	6	6	6	8	8	8	7	8	8	Royaume-Uni
EFTA	***7***	***7***	***7***	***8***	***8***	***8***	***9***	***9***	***9***	***9***	***AELE***
Finland	...	...	...	...	8	8	9	9	9	...	Finlande
East Europe	***3***	***2***	***2***	***1***	***1***	***2***	***1***	***1***	***0***	***0***	***Europe de l'est***
Hungary	...	...	...	1	1	2	1	1	0	0	Hongrie
USSR	**752**	**763**	**802**	**783**	**732**	**733**	**721**	**779**	**821**	**856**	**URSS**
Byelorussian SSR	...	...	...	*51*	*45*	*40*	*42*	*48*	*52*	*56*	*RSS de Biélorussie*
Ukrainian SSR	*169*	*184*	*191*	*191*	*174*	*173*	*166*	*173*	*181*	*185*	*RSS d'Ukraine*
Total	**788**	**800**	**839**	**820**	**773**	**775**	**766**	**824**	**866**	**904**	**Total**

General note.
Fresh, chilled or frozen meat of other animals, irrespective of the origin of the animals, in carcass weight, excluding edible offals and tallow. Data refer to industrial production only. (SITC 01150-0+).

Remarque générale.
Poids net de viande fraîche, réfrigérée ou congelée, d'autres animaux abattus, quelle que soit leur provenance, à l'exclusion des abats comestibles et du suif. Les données se rapportent à la production industrielle seulement. (CTCI 01150-0+).

Bacon, ham and other dried, salted or smoked pig meat – Bacon, jambon et autres viandes de porc, séchées, salées ou fumées

Unit : Thousand metric tons | Unité : Milliers de tonnes métriques

Country or area	1976	1977	1978	1979	1980	1981	1982	1983	1984	1985	Pays ou zone
Africa	**15**	**16**	**15**	**15**	**15**	**15**	**16**	**18**	**17**	**15**	**Afrique**
Kenya	...	...	2	2	2	1	1	3	2	2	Kenya
South Africa	13	14	13	13	13	14	15	15	* 15	13	Afrique du Sud
America, North	**1 454**	**1 748**	**2 125**	**2 919**	**3 010**	**2 918**	**2 798**	**2 861**	**4 872**	**4 748**	**Amérique du Nord**
Canada[1]	138	139	154	168	174	...	...	...	...	...	Canada[1]
Dominican Republic	1	1	* 2	2	3	3	3	3	3	3	Rép. dominicaine
Jamaica[2]	1	1	1	1	1	1	0	1	0	* 0	Jamaïque[2]
Mexico	21	23	27	27	26	28	29	31	30	32	Mexique
United States	...	1 584	1 941	2 722	2 806	2 702	2 571	2 622	# 4 624	4 488	Etats–Unis
America, South	**118**	**99**	**106**	**142**	**130**	**111**	**115**	**116**	**120**	**121**	**Amérique du Sud**
Brazil	...	49	55	[3] 89	77	...	...	...	...	...	Brésil
Colombia	3	3	4	5	5	4	0	0	...	...	Colombie
Ecuador	0	0	0	...	1	0	0	1	...	...	Equateur
Venezuela	...	...	...	...	...	40	...	...	51	51	Venezuela
Asia	**175**	**203**	**211**	**223**	**224**	**225**	**228**	**232**	**238**	**241**	**Asie**
Japan	174	201	209	221	222	223	226	230	236	239	Japon
Philippines	1	2	...	...	...	...	...	...	...	...	Philippines
Europe	**1 310**	**1 360**	**1 429**	**1 544**	**1 758**	**1 787**	**1 588**	**1 565**	**1 553**	**1 638**	**Europe**
EEC	***825***	***850***	***884***	***849***	***1 004***	***1 030***	***843***	***856***	***838***	***843***	***CEE***
Denmark	215	231	265	221	371	395	212	184	167	167	Danemark
France	284	304	311	328	339	350	358	385	390	...	France
Greece	...	...	...	...	...	2	3	3	4	...	Grèce
Ireland	...	...	...	...	...	80	73	72	69	66	Irlande
United Kingdom	229	221	217	212	210	203	197	212	208	203	Royaume–Uni
EFTA	***139***	***148***	***153***	***176***	***188***	***186***	***184***	***186***	***187***	***191***	***AELE***
Austria[4]	77	79	...	...	...	...	...	...	...	...	Autriche[4]
Finland	3	5	6	9	9	9	8	7	8	...	Finlande
Norway	13	11	11	13	20	19	...	...	...	...	Norvège
Portugal	14	19	23	38	44	43	43	44	45	47	Portugal
Sweden[4]	32	34	35	38	37	37	35	35	32	31	Suède[4]
East Europe	***238***	***242***	***256***	***282***	***310***	***330***	***284***	***287***	***285***	***300***	***Europe de l'est***
Hungary	15	14	15	15	13	14	15	15	15	16	Hongrie
Poland[5]	21	18	20	20	18	8	6	5	4	5	Pologne[5]
Romania[6]	202	210	221	247	279	308	263	267	266	279	Roumanie[6]
Other Europe	***108***	***120***	***136***	***237***	***256***	***241***	***277***	***236***	***244***	***304***	***Autre Europe***
Spain	60	63	77	173	212	197	228	197	198	...	Espagne
Yugoslavia[7]	48	57	59	64	44	44	49	39	46	41	Yougoslavie[7]
Oceania	**59**	**64**	**67**	**77**	**78**	**84**	**85**	**84**	**95**	**93**	**Océanie**
Australia	52	56	58	66	67	71	73	71	79	76	Australie
New Zealand[8]	...	...	...	11	11	13	12	13	16	17	Nouvelle–Zélande[8]
Total	**3 131**	**3 490**	**3 952**	**4 919**	**5 215**	**5 141**	**4 830**	**4 876**	**6 895**	**6 855**	**Total**

General note.
Edible pig meat, salted, in brine, dried or smoked. Including streaky pork with similar meats interlarded with a high proportion of fat, and fat with an adhering layer of meat. Hams enclosed in sausage casings are excluded. (SITC 01210–0).

Remarque générale.
Viandes comestibles de porc, salées, en saumure, séchées ou fumées, y compris le lard maigre et les autres viandes analogues entrelardées de gras en proportion élevée et le lard gras avec couche de viande adhérente, mais à l'exclusion des jambons fermés dans des boyaux, vessies ou enveloppes similaires. (CTCI 01210–0).

[1] Shipments.
[2] Data refer to bacon and ham.
[3] Production by establishments employing 5 or more persons.
[4] Including other meat and edible offals and sausages.
[5] Bacon only.
[6] Including other salted, dried or smoked meats.
[7] Including canned meat.
[8] Twelve months ending 30 September of year stated.

[1] Expéditions.
[2] Données se rapportant à bacon et à jambon.
[3] Production des établissements occupant 5 personnes ou plus.
[4] Y compris les autres viandes et abats comestibles et les saucisses et saucissons.
[5] Lard seulement.
[6] Y compris les autres viandes et abats comestibles séchées, salées, ou fumées.
[7] Y compris les conserves de viande.
[8] Période de douze mois finissant le 30 septembre de l'année indiquée.

Other meat and edible offals, dried, salted or smoked – Autres viandes et abats comestibles, séchés, salés ou fumés

Unit : Thousand metric tons | Unité : Milliers de tonnes métriques

Country or area	1976	1977	1978	1979	1980	1981	1982	1983	1984	1985	Pays ou zone
America, North											**Amérique du Nord**
Canada[1]	20	16	14	15	17	18	...	...	...	...	Canada[1]
Cuba	20	23	22	20	20	24	24	25	24	24	Cuba
Mexico[2]	22	33	37	40	39	46	46	47	51	56	Mexique[2]
United States	...	...	...	265	261	264	269	276	# 683	683	Etats–Unis
Europe											**Europe**
EEC											***CEE***
Belgium[3]	63	63	74	67	69	69	68	70	74	74	Belgique[3]
Denmark	1	1	1	1	1	...	...	...	...	...	Danemark
France	181	197	209	222	232	245	254	270	273	281	France
Greece	15	15	17	18	19	...	...	...	...	...	Grèce
Netherlands[4]	245	257	230	...	...	...	...	...	...	...	Pays–Bas[4]
EFTA											***AELE***
Finland	0	0	0	1	1	1	1	1	1	...	Finlande
Oceania											**Océanie**
New Zealand[5]	* 61	* 58	* 59	* 58	# 15	14	14	14	15	15	Nouvelle–Zélande[5]

General note.
Meat (except pork) and edible meat offals (except poultry liver and poultry fat) salted, in brine, dried or smoked. Meat and offals cooked, prepared or preserved by other processes, and meat flours and meals suitable only for feeding animals are excluded. (SITC 01290–0).

¹ Shipments.
² Edible offals of bovine animals.
³ Edible offals only.
⁴ Industrial sales.
⁵ Twelve months ending 30 September of year stated.

Remarque générale.
Viandes (autres que la viande de porc) et abats comestibles (autres que les foies de volailles et la graisse de volailles), salés, en saumure, séchés ou fumés, à l'exclusion des viandes et des abats cuits, préparés ou mis en conserves par d'autres moyens et des farines et poudres de viande uniquement propres à l'alimentation dex animaux. (CTCI 01290–0).

[1] Expéditions.
[2] Abats comestibles de bovins.
[3] Abats comestibles seulement.
[4] Ventes industrielles.
[5] Période de douze mois finissant le 30 septembre de l'année indiquée.

Unit : Thousand metric tons — Unité : Milliers de tonnes métriques

Country or area	1976	1977	1978	1979	1980	1981	1982	1983	1984	1985	Pays ou zone
Africa	**48**	**47**	**44**	**42**	**46**	**45**	**49**	**51**	**48**	**44**	**Afrique**
Kenya	* 1	* 1	1	1	1	1	1	1	2	2	Kenya
South Africa	43	42	39	37	41	41	44	46	* 42	39	Afrique du Sud
Zambia*	4	4	4	4	4	3	4	...	...	...	Zambie*
America, North	**2 206**	**2 187**	**2 249**	**2 745**	**2 799**	**2 764**	**2 740**	**2 716**	**2 804**	**2 767**	**Amérique du Nord**
Canada[1]	175	173	174	176	183	...	...	...	...	...	Canada[1]
Dominican Republic	1	1	1	9	8	9	9	12	12	11	Rép. dominicaine
Jamaica	1	1	1	1	1	1	1	1	1	1	Jamaïque
Mexico*	23	...	...	...	...	...	...	...	...	...	Mexique*
Panama	3	...	...	...	...	...	...	...	...	...	Panama
United States	2 004	* 1 986	* 2 047	2 533	2 581	2 546	2 521	2 492	2 578	2 540	Etats-Unis
America, South	**94**	**76**	**104**	**93**	**96**	**87**	**102**	**101**	**99**	**105**	**Amérique du Sud**
Bolivia	0	0	1	1	1	1	1	1	1	...	Bolivie
Brazil	72	51	54	[2] 55	53	...	...	...	...	...	Brésil
Chile	...	...	...	14	16	19	25	25	26	26	Chili
Colombia	3	2	3	4	4	9	11	11	...	...	Colombie
Ecuador	* 1	* 1	1	...	6	6	5	7	...	...	Equateur
Venezuela	10	11	32	...	...	6	...	...	15	22	Venezuela
Asia	**181**	**204**	**195**	**210**	**214**	**233**	**262**	**281**	**288**	**312**	**Asie**
Iran(Islamic Rep.of)[3]	8	10	7	9	11	15	36	33	30	...	Iran(Rép.islamique)[3]
Japan	160	178	171	181	181	188	187	204	212	228	Japon
Korea, Republic of	4	6	7	10	12	20	29	33	35	37	Corée, République de
Mongolia	2	3	3	3	3	3	3	4	4	4	Mongolie
Philippines	7	7	...	...	...	...	...	...	...	...	Philippines
Europe	**2 262**	**2 279**	**2 533**	**2 617**	**2 661**	**2 717**	**2 510**	**2 509**	**2 509**	**2 598**	**Europe**
EEC	***844***	***852***	***1 076***	***1 102***	***1 148***	***1 350***	***1 119***	***1 131***	***1 166***	***1 185***	***CEE***
Denmark	78	79	77	82	80	80	70	68	70	74	Danemark
France	184	194	200	209	210	220	220	238	243	242	France
Germany, Fed. Rep.	550	548	769	782	829	1 023	802	798	830	846	Allemagne, Rép. féd.
Greece	4	4	4	5	6	6	7	7	7	7	Grèce
Ireland	...	...	...	...	...	21	20	20	16	16	Irlande
EFTA	***273***	***259***	***270***	***290***	***283***	***282***	***283***	***279***	***281***	***284***	***AELE***
Finland	130	123	132	150	140	142	142	140	142	...	Finlande
Portugal	6	5	6	7	7	6	5	5	5	5	Portugal
Sweden	137	131	132	133	136	134	136	134	134	132	Suède
East Europe	***1 011***	***1 026***	***1 031***	***1 048***	***1 044***	***902***	***919***	***917***	***897***	***963***	***Europe de l'est***
Bulgaria	88	90	93	94	91	93	99	103	113	119	Bulgarie
Hungary	127	133	139	138	142	148	148	148	146	152	Hongrie
Poland[4]	796	803	799	816	811	661	672	666	638	692	Pologne[4]
Other Europe	***134***	***142***	***156***	***177***	***186***	***183***	***189***	***182***	***165***	***166***	***Autre Europe***
Yugoslavia	134	142	156	177	186	183	189	182	165	166	Yougoslavie
Oceania	**7**	**7**	**7**	**7**	**8**	**8**	**8**	**8**	**8**	**9**	**Océanie**
New Zealand[5]	...	...	...	...	...	8	8	8	8	9	Nouvelle-Zélande[5]
Total	**4 799**	**4 799**	**5 131**	**5 714**	**5 823**	**5 854**	**5 671**	**5 666**	**5 756**	**5 836**	**Total**

General note.
Sausages and the like of meat, meat offal or animal blood, whether or not tinned. (SITC 01340-0).

Remarque générale.
Saucissons, saucisses et préparations similaires faites de viande, d'abats ou de sang, contenues ou non dans des récipients fermés hermétiquement. (CTCI 01340-0).

[1] Shipments.
[2] Production by establishments employing 5 or more persons.
[3] Twelve months beginning 21 March of year stated.
[4] Excluding sausages of horse, poultry and rabbit meat and venison.
[5] Twelve months ending 30 September of year stated.

[1] Expéditions.
[2] Production des établissements occupant 5 personnes ou plus.
[3] Période de douze mois commençant le 21 mars de l'année indiquée.
[4] Non compris les saucisses faites de viande de cheval, de volaille et de lapin et de venaison.
[5] Période de douze mois finissant le 30 septembre de l'année indiquée.

Meals, frozen prepared – Repas préparés, congelés

Unit : Metric tons — Unité : Tonnes métriques

Country or area	1976	1977	1978	1979	1980	1981	1982	1983	1984	1985	Pays ou zone
America, North	**672 148**	**659 323**	**723 469**	**710 770**	**690 451**	**709 475**	**753 162**	**730 749**	**749 965**	**759 692**	**Amérique du Nord**
Canada	...	...	13 249	...	...	...	...	...	...	...	Canada
United States	...	646 074	710 220	697 521	677 202	696 226	739 913	717 500	...	...	Etats–Unis
America, South	**34 975**	**44 442**	**42 310**	**99 263**	**59 405**	**87 022**	**97 337**	**107 651**	**117 965**	**128 279**	**Amérique du Sud**
Brazil	34 975	44 442	42 310	[1] 99 263	59 405	...	...	...	...	...	Brésil
Europe	**93 859**	**88 629**	**91 936**	**105 376**	**117 235**	**123 667**	**123 014**	**125 620**	**129 751**	**149 497**	**Europe**
EEC	***26 572***	***26 969***	***27 490***	***32 902***	***33 896***	***44 777***	***42 069***	***48 318***	***53 048***	***67 402***	***CEE***
Denmark	11 768	11 176	7 824	9 279	8 531	15 739	...	...	...	...	Danemark
France	14 804	15 793	19 666	23 623	25 365	29 038	30 013	35 880	40 228	54 200	France
EFTA	***45 472***	***43 185***	***45 936***	***51 834***	***58 907***	***59 435***	***60 345***	***58 229***	***59 387***	***63 621***	***AELE***
Austria	2 799	2 910	2 489	3 154	4 752	5 762	5 669	5 165	5 576	5 804	Autriche
Finland	3 639	3 867	5 039	6 107	6 711	8 841	7 576	7 842	9 060	...	Finlande
Sweden	39 034	36 408	38 408	42 573	47 444	44 832	47 100	45 222	44 751	47 846	Suède
East Europe	***15 435***	***14 702***	***14 810***	***16 684***	***19 351***	***15 185***	***14 011***	***15 706***	***15 102***	***15 067***	***Europe de l'est***
Czechoslovakia	8 468	8 485	9 438	10 445	12 727	14 109	12 217	13 624	13 576	13 616	Tchécoslovaquie
German Dem. Rep.	1 674	1 115	982	1 010	1 131	690	1 492	1 712	1 120	1 130	Rép. dém. allemande
Hungary[2]	5 293	5 102	4 390	5 229	5 493	# 386	302	370	406	321	Hongrie[2]
Other Europe	***6 380***	***3 773***	***3 700***	***3 956***	***5 081***	***4 270***	***6 589***	***3 367***	***2 214***	***3 407***	***Autre Europe***
Yugoslavia[3]	6 380	3 773	3 700	3 956	5 081	4 270	6 589	3 367	2 214	3 407	Yougoslavie[3]
Total	**800 982**	**792 394**	**857 715**	**915 409**	**867 091**	**920 164**	**973 513**	**964 020**	**997 681**	**1 037 468**	**Total**

General note.
More than one food arranged on a shaped container, so as to constitute the main element of a meal, such as mixed frozen dinners and frozen pies of beef, pork and poultry. (SITC 01380–1).

[1] Production by establishments employing 5 or more persons.
[2] Beginning 1981, data are not comparable with those for earlier years.
[3] Untinned and semi–prepared meals. Data on frozen prepared meals are not available separately.

Remarque générale.
Plusieurs plats disposés dans un récipient de forme appropriée, de façon à constituer l'élément principal d'un repas, tels que les repas congelés assortis et les pâtés congelés de viande de boeuf, de porc ou de volaille. (CTCI 01380–1).

[1] Production des établissements occupant 5 personnes ou plus.
[2] A partir de 1981, les données ne sont pas comparables à celles des années antérieures.
[3] Repas non mis en boîte et semi–preparés. Les données relatives aux repas preparés et congelés ne sont pas disponibles séparément.

Meat, tinned – Conserves de Viande

Unit : Metric tons

Unité : Tonnes métriques

Country or area	1976	1977	1978	1979	1980	1981	1982	1983	1984	1985	Pays ou zone
Africa	**22 286**	**18 913**	**22 436**	**17 213**	**19 469**	**20 410**	**17 210**	**17 051**	**17 393**	**15 026**	**Afrique**
Algeria	116	82	66	54	40	33	* 40	* 45	...	...	Algérie
Botswana	...	...	...	...	...	...	2	1	1	...	Botswana
Ethiopia[1]	2 320	# 108	108	64	25	...	...	...	...	...	Ethiopie[1]
Kenya[2 3]	...	...	* 3 969	* 1 728	* 1 018	* 1 314	2 072	1 748	3 897	* 2 700	Kenya[2 3]
Madagascar	* 1 600	* 1 800	1 382	1 281	1 308	1 377	985	418	617	514	Madagascar
South Africa	14 809	14 241	15 475	12 651	15 451	16 250	13 205	13 864	12 006	11 068	Afrique du Sud
Swaziland	290	801	671	430	...	...	...	...	...	...	Swaziland
United Rep. Tanzania	1 650	580	764	1 004	1 078	736	333	...	...	...	Rép.Unie de Tanzanie
America, North	**1 151 890**	**1 069 277**	**1 613 002**	**1 484 362**	**1 377 640**	**1 362 644**	**1 246 348**	**1 210 459**	**1 345 003**	**1 348 796**	**Amérique du Nord**
Cuba[4]	29 015	31 740	31 124	30 484	34 808	41 457	48 809	55 267	61 465	64 240	Cuba[4]
Mexico	2 335	2 449	3 036	3 016	3 038	2 490	2 129	2 814	2 464	1 899	Mexique
United States	1 120 540	1 035 088	1 578 842	1 450 862	1 339 794	1 318 697	1 195 410	1 152 378	...	...	Etats–Unis
America, South	**98 056**	**81 425**	**73 023**	**62 337**	**103 202**	**92 323**	**103 026**	**101 885**	**106 707**	**111 450**	**Amérique du Sud**
Bolivia	1 073	269	793	780	725	323	186	214	* 210	* 250	Bolivie
Brazil	77 990	57 601	49 405	[5] 53 478	91 814	...	92 000	...	...	...	Brésil
Paraguay	8 531	11 959	11 200	307	* 300	257	477	* 500	611	* 600	Paraguay
Venezuela	10 462	11 596	11 625	7 772	...	...	...	...	...	...	Venezuela
Asia	**35 097**	**39 081**	**41 973**	**41 872**	**36 413**	**35 060**	**37 271**	**34 727**	**34 393**	**32 936**	**Asie**
Burma[6]	350	458	692	768	649	# 273	123	122	154	97	Birmanie[6]
India[7]	1 181	* 1 200	1 300	...	...	...	...	...	...	...	Inde[7]
Iran(Islamic Rep.of)[8]	...	...	...	...	...	303	...	...	...	...	Iran(Rép.islamique)[8]
Japan	22 623	26 971	29 134	29 330	23 890	22 913	25 274	22 631	22 165	20 765	Japon
Mongolia[9]	1 100	1 200	1 300	1 000	1 100	1 100	1 100	1 200	1 300	1 300	Mongolie[9]
Philippines[10]	9 540	8 949	...	...	...	...	...	...	...	...	Philippines[10]
Europe	**888 303**	**867 808**	**880 840**	**970 992**	**965 553**	**845 343**	**846 813**	**895 863**	**956 839**	**984 157**	**Europe**
EEC	***333 100***	***320 171***	***321 194***	***310 510***	***306 282***	***286 094***	***283 661***	***289 024***	***294 698***	***287 963***	***CEE***
Belgium[5]	19 091	18 990	21 498	20 836	19 170	20 426	17 793	16 284	15 564	13 814	Belgique[5]
Denmark	66 839	73 055	73 632	66 823	68 132	...	...	...	...	...	Danemark
France	17 500	14 500	13 600	12 100	10 500	11 400	12 907	13 532	14 351	16 880	France
Germany, Fed. Rep.	50 243	48 337	55 947	53 726	48 712	48 139	47 853	47 515	51 114	46 494	Allemagne, Rép. féd.
Greece	...	...	...	...	386	221	207	745	281	* 300	Grèce
Ireland	8 250	10 523	9 768	10 348	9 497	8 636	11 204	10 600	11 600	...	Irlande
Italy	29 874	30 455	30 430	33 350	36 885	34 664	33 952	35 766	33 269	30 539	Italie
United Kingdom	141 000	124 000	116 000	113 000	* 113 000	94 000	91 500	96 700	* 101 000	101 500	Royaume–Uni
EFTA	***39 867***	***43 153***	***38 258***	***40 362***	***40 767***	***44 200***	***45 910***	***44 323***	***35 395***	***55 230***	***AELE***
Austria	12 016	12 738	10 956	12 058	9 346	11 631	18 470	17 385	8 053	26 233	Autriche
Finland	3 326	4 705	3 166	4 346	5 656	6 274	5 122	6 336	6 856	...	Finlande
Portugal	* 9 687	9 365	10 184	10 523	12 499	12 836	9 856	9 094	10 194	10 473	Portugal
Sweden	14 838	16 345	13 952	13 435	13 266	13 459	12 462	11 508	10 292	11 366	Suède
East Europe	***417 129***	***399 082***	***409 080***	***424 911***	***427 716***	***334 934***	***340 109***	***381 406***	***407 847***	***428 910***	***Europe de l'est***
Bulgaria[11]	54 770	30 076	30 142	33 971	37 624	34 224	38 151	52 951	65 204	77 145	Bulgarie[11]
Czechoslovakia	29 988	35 412	36 761	38 206	39 047	39 444	37 670	37 869	38 677	39 627	Tchécoslovaquie
German Dem. Rep.[12]	43 222	43 607	49 785	50 493	52 534	53 488	53 348	53 456	54 214	53 100	Rép. dém. allemande[12]
Hungary[13]	54 438	47 085	51 143	58 599	59 120	52 939	57 016	66 069	74 946	71 336	Hongrie[13]
Poland[14]	179 711	171 902	174 249	166 642	162 391	90 839	78 128	93 181	94 841	105 652	Pologne[14]
Romania	55 000	71 000	67 000	77 000	77 000	64 000	...	...	...	...	Roumanie
Other Europe	***98 207***	***105 402***	***112 308***	***195 209***	***190 788***	***180 115***	***177 133***	***181 110***	***218 899***	***212 054***	***Autre Europe***
Spain[15]	16 550	15 618	18 322	102 361	100 146	76 768	77 963	79 231	...	...	Espagne[15]
Yugoslavia	81 657	89 784	93 986	92 848	90 642	103 347	99 170	101 879	108 550	90 710	Yougoslavie
USSR[16]	**322 012**	**341 016**	**294 453**	**326 358**	**324 613**	**348 366**	**322 233**	**345 298**	**369 917**	**409 740**	**URSS[16]**
Byelorussian SSR[16]	*10 880*	*13 672*	*9 985*	*12 619*	*20 493*	*23 351*	*22 976*	*23 973*	*25 166*	*28 726*	*RSS de Biélorussie[16]*
Ukrainian SSR[16]	*62 187*	*62 818*	*58 724*	*64 686*	*62 868*	*68 058*	*59 035*	*69 676*	*69 162*	*73 587*	*RSS d'Ukraine[16]*
Oceania	**47 839**	**57 106**	**56 550**	**48 125**	**45 611**	**44 756**	**38 831**	**45 023**	**36 467**	**25 846**	**Océanie**
Australia[17]	43 878	52 173	51 778	44 840	41 402	40 603	34 658	40 823	32 331	21 821	Australie[17]

For general note and footnotes, see end of table.

Voir la fin du tableau pour la remarque générale et les notes.

Unit : Metric tons

Unité : Tonnes métriques

Country or area	1976	1977	1978	1979	1980	1981	1982	1983	1984	1985	Pays ou zone
New Zealand[18]	3 807	4 728	4 526	3 025	...	...	...	...	...	...	Nouvelle-Zélande[18]
Vanuatu[3]	154	205	246	260	188	132	152	179	115	4	Vanuatu[3]
Total	**2 565 483**	**2 474 626**	**2 982 277**	**2 951 259**	**2 872 501**	**2 748 902**	**2 611 732**	**2 650 306**	**2 866 719**	**2 927 951**	**Total**

General note.
Meat and meat products (other than meat extracts, soups and broths), packed and heat-processed in hermetically-sealed containers. Tinned meat preparations such as sausages and meat paste are excluded. (SITC 01380-2).

[1] Beginning 1977, data are not comparable with those for earlier years.
[2] Beef only.
[3] Exports.
[4] Including salted and smoked sausages and other preserved meat.
[5] Production by establishments employing 5 or more persons.
[6] Twelve months ending 31 March of year stated.
[7] Production by large and medium scale establishments only.
[8] Production by establishments employing 10 or more persons.
[9] Source: Council for Economic Assistance (COMECON), (Moscow).
[10] Shipments.
[11] Including canned meat and vegetables.
[12] Including canned sausages and meat and sausage preserves.
[13] Including meat pies.
[14] Excluding sausages of horse, poultry and rabbit meat and venison.
[15] Beginning 1979, including sausages.
[16] Including canned sausages, meat pies and vegetable stew.
[17] Twelve months ending 30 June of year stated.
[18] Twelve months ending 30 September of year stated.

Remarque générale.
Viandes et produits de viande (autres que les extraits de viande, les soupes et les bouillons) mis et traités à chaud dans des récipients fermés hermétiquement. Cette rubrique ne comprend pas les produits de viande en boîte, ni les préparations telles que les saucisses, les saucissons et les pâtés de viande. (CTCI 01380-2).

[1] A partir de 1977, les données ne sont pas comparables à celles des années antérieures.
[2] Boeuf seulement.
[3] Exportations.
[4] Y compris les saucisses salées et fumées et autres conserves de viande.
[5] Production des établissements occupant 5 personnes ou plus.
[6] Période de douze mois finissant le 31 mars de l'année indiquée.
[7] Production des grandes et moyennes entreprises seulement.
[8] Production des établissements occupant 10 personnes ou plus.
[9] Source: Conseil d'assistance économique mutuelle (CAEM), (Moscou).
[10] Expéditions.
[11] Y compris les conserves de viande et de légumes.
[12] Y compris les saucisses en boîte et les viandes et saucisses en conserve.
[13] Y compris les pâtés de viande.
[14] Non compris les saucisses faites de viande de cheval, de volaille et de lapin et de venaison.
[15] A partir de 1979, y compris les saucisses.
[16] Y compris les saucisses, les pâtés de viande et les ragoûts de légumes en boîte.
[17] Période de douze mois finissant le 30 juin de l'année indiquée.
[18] Période de douze mois finissant le 30 septembre de l'année indiquée.

Lard (Total production) –
Saindoux (Production totale)

Unit : Thousand metric tons — Unité : Milliers de tonnes métriques

Country or area	1976	1977	1978	1979	1980	1981	1982	1983	1984	1985	Pays ou zone
Africa	**7**	**7**	**7**	**6**	**7**	**8**	**7**	**8**	**8**	**8**	**Afrique**
Angola°	1	1	1	1	1	1	1	1	1	1	Angola°
South Africa°	6	6	5	5	6	7	6	7	7	7	Afrique du Sud°
America, North	**589**	**584**	**571**	**639**	**680**	**661**	**596**	**574**	**567**	**572**	**Amérique du Nord**
Barbados	1	1	1	1	1	°2	2	1	1	°1	Barbade
Canada	51	52	51	63	*74	*74	*71	*72	*73	*73	Canada
Costa Rica°	2	2	2	2	2	2	2	2	2	2	Costa Rica°
Cuba°	3	4	4	4	4	5	5	5	6	6	Cuba°
Dominican Republic	*4	*5	*5	*4	*3	°2	°3	°5	°5	°6	Rép. dominicaine
El Salvador°	3	3	3	3	3	3	3	3	3	3	El Salvador°
Guatemala°	3	3	3	4	4	4	4	4	4	4	Guatemala°
Haiti	2	2	2	3	°2	°1	°1	°0	°0	°0	Haïti
Honduras°	4	3	3	4	4	5	4	3	4	4	Honduras°
Jamaica	2	3	3	3	2	2	3	3	°3	°3	Jamaïque
Mexico°	28	30	31	30	29	32	36	36	36	36	Mexique°
Nicaragua°	4	4	4	4	2	2	3	3	3	3	Nicaragua°
United States	481	471	456	512	547	526	459	435	426	430	Etats-Unis
America, South	**183**	**189**	**189**	**203**	**223**	**218**	**212**	**203**	**201**	**201**	**Amérique du Sud**
Argentina°	35	35	30	36	39	38	35	30	35	35	Argentine°
Brazil*	119	125	128	135	150	146	144	139	132	132	Brésil*
Chile°	1	1	1	2	2	3	2	2	2	2	Chili°
Colombia*	3	3	4	4	4	3	3	3	3	3	Colombie*
Ecuador°	7	7	8	9	10	9	9	9	10	10	Equateur°
Peru	13	°13	°13	12	13	14	°14	°14	°13	°13	Pérou
Uruguay°	2	2	2	1	1	1	1	1	1	1	Uruguay°
Venezuela	4	4	°4	°4	°4	°4	°4	°4	°4	°4	Venezuela
Asia	**598**	**604**	**590**	**672**	**712**	**706**	**719**	**734**	**768**	**821**	**Asie**
China	480	487	470	541	572	565	581	598	637	686	Chine
Hong Kong°	22	23	23	24	27	29	30	31	30	30	Hong-kong°
Japan	95	93	96	105	112	112	107	105	*100	°105	Japon
Europe	**1 935**	**1 919**	**2 025**	**2 121**	**2 130**	**2 148**	**2 129**	**2 204**	**2 263**	**2 212**	**Europe**
EEC	**724**	**748**	**787**	**822**	**844**	**844**	**831**	**856**	**873**	**878**	**CEE**
Denmark	35	36	39	44	47	48	37	39	39	°37	Danemark
France	*86	*89	*93	*97	*98	*100	*100	°103	°100	°100	France
Germany, Fed. Rep.	378	379	399	410	417	409	407	418	422	°425	Allemagne, Rép. féd.
Greece	5	4	5	4	4	5	5	°6	°7	*6	Grèce
Ireland°	6	6	6	7	7	7	7	7	6	6	Irlande°
Italy	154	171	183	195	205	209	209	°217	°232	°237	Italie
Netherlands	*49	*54	51	*54	*52	°52	°52	°53	°53	°53	Pays-Bas
United Kingdom	11	10	11	11	*14	*14	°14	°14	°14	°14	Royaume-Uni
EFTA	**109**	**114**	**111**	**112**	**114**	**117**	**119**	**119**	**123**	**124**	**AELE**
Austria	69	71	71	75	74	°75	°76	°76	80	°80	Autriche
Finland	*2	*2	3	3	3	3	3	3	°3	°3	Finlande
Portugal°	11	13	14	11	14	17	17	16	17	18	Portugal°
Sweden	12	°12	°12	°12	°12	°12	°12	°12	°12	°12	Suède
Switzerland	16	16	12	11	11	11	12	12	11	°11	Suisse
East Europe	**801**	**745**	**758**	**824**	**815**	**817**	**812**	**872**	**888**	**854**	**Europe de l'est**
Bulgaria	51	41	39	42	36	33	33	34	35	°35	Bulgarie
Czechoslovakia	*67	*63	*61	*63	*65	*72	*83	*79	*86	°86	Tchécoslovaquie
German Dem. Rep.	*187	*186	*180	*179	*183	*205	*185	*191	*203	°203	Rép. dém. allemande
Hungary°	186	175	176	219	226	224	237	265	287	256	Hongrie°
Poland	*136	*136	*148	*159	*141	*111	*115	*135	°98	°113	Pologne
Romania°	175	144	154	162	165	171	159	168	179	161	Roumanie°
Other Europe	**206**	**217**	**267**	**257**	**250**	**261**	**260**	**256**	**278**	**257**	**Autre Europe**
Spain	17	20	22	25	26	28	°26	°27	°27	°27	Espagne
Yugoslavia	189	197	245	231	224	233	234	229	251	°230	Yougoslavie
USSR	***575**	***675**	***724**	***719**	***683**	***701**	***676**	***745**	***753**	**°775**	**URSS**

For general note and footnotes, see end of table. — Voir la fin du tableau pour la remarque générale et les notes.

Lard (Total production) (continued) – Saindoux (Production totale) (suite)

Unit : Thousand metric tons

Unité : Milliers de tonnes métriques

Country or area	1976	1977	1978	1979	1980	1981	1982	1983	1984	1985	Pays ou zone
Oceania	**3**	**3**	**4**	**2**	**4**	**3**	**3**	**2**	**1**	**3**	**Océanie**
Australia	2	3	3	2	4	3	3	2	° 1	° 3	Australie
Total	**3 889**	**3 981**	**4 110**	**4 363**	**4 440**	**4 445**	**4 343**	**4 471**	**4 560**	**4 593**	**Total**

General note.
Lard and other rendered pig fat, crude or refined. Includes non–industrial production. (SITC 09130–1).
Source: Food and Agriculture Organization of the United Nations (FAO), Rome.

Remarque générale.
Saindoux et autres graisses de porc, pressées ou fondues, brutes ou raffinées. Y compris production non–industrielle. (CTCI 09130–1).
Source: Organisation des Nations Unies pour l'agriculture(FAO), Rome.

Lard (Industrial production) – Saindoux (Production industrielle)

Unit : Thousand metric tons

Unité : Milliers de tonnes métriques

Country or area	1976	1977	1978	1979	1980	1981	1982	1983	1984	1985	Pays ou zone
America, North	**45**	**45**	**44**	**56**	**63**	**75**	**76**	**82**	**89**	**95**	**Amérique du Nord**
Canada	44	44	* 43	* 55	62	* 74	...	...	...	...	Canada
Cuba	...	1	1	1	1	1	1	1	1	1	Cuba
Asia	**100**	**130**	**142**	**148**	**164**	**153**	**157**	**156**	**192**	**206**	**Asie**
Japan	100	130	142	148	164	153	157	156	192	206	Japon
Europe	**453**	**470**	**489**	**516**	**473**	**414**	**400**	**427**	**454**	**434**	**Europe**
EEC	***75***	***76***	***78***	***80***	***79***	***76***	***76***	***79***	***82***	***84***	***CEE***
Belgium	75	76	78	80	79	76	76	79	82	84	Belgique
EFTA	***3***	***4***	***4***	***4***	***4***	***4***	***6***	***5***	***4***	***5***	***AELE***
Finland[1]	3	4	4	4	4	4	6	5	4	...	Finlande[1]
East Europe	***330***	***346***	***364***	***380***	***355***	***298***	***285***	***318***	***325***	***307***	***Europe de l'est***
Bulgaria	51	41	39	42	36	33	33	34	35	31	Bulgarie
Czechoslovakia	98	110	117	118	116	117	95	101	104	101	Tchécoslovaquie
Hungary	81	93	100	101	101	91	82	107	120	96	Hongrie
Poland	100	102	108	119	102	57	75	76	66	79	Pologne
Other Europe	***45***	***44***	***43***	***52***	***35***	***36***	***33***	***25***	***43***	***38***	***Autre Europe***
Yugoslavia	...	...	...	52	35	36	33	25	43	38	Yougoslavie
Oceania	**3**	**3**	**3**	**3**	**3**	**3**	**3**	**3**	**2**	**3**	**Océanie**
Australia	...	...	...	...	...	3	3	...	2	3	Australie
Total	**601**	**648**	**677**	**723**	**703**	**645**	**636**	**668**	**737**	**738**	**Total**

General note.
Lard and other rendered pig fat, crude or refined. Data refer to industrial production only. (SITC 09130–1).

[1] Including small quantities of rendered poultry fats.

Remarque générale.
Saindoux et autres graisses de porc, pressées ou fondues, brutes ou raffinées. Les données se rapportent à la production industrielle seulement. (CTCI 09130–1).

[1] Y compris de petites quantités de graisse de volaille fondue.

Hides, cattle and horse, undressed (Total production) – Peaux de bovins et d'équidés, non préparées (Production totale)

Unit : Thousand metric tons | Unité : Milliers de tonnes métriques

Country or area	1976	1977	1978	1979	1980	1981	1982	1983	1984	1985	Pays ou zone
Africa	**421**	**447**	**464**	**481**	**475**	**472**	**494**	**495**	**504**	**507**	**Afrique**
Algeria°	8	7	8	8	8	7	9	9	9	9	Algérie°
Angola°	6	6	6	7	7	7	7	7	8	8	Angola°
Benin°	2	2	2	2	2	2	2	2	2	2	Bénin°
Botswana°	5	5	4	6	4	5	6	5	6	6	Botswana°
Burkina Faso°	4	4	4	4	4	4	5	5	5	5	Burkina Faso°
Burundi°	2	2	2	2	2	1	1	1	1	1	Burundi°
Cameroon°	9	9	10	10	10	10	10	9	10	10	Cameroun°
Central African Rep.°	4	3	4	3	4	4	4	4	4	4	Rép. centrafricaine°
Chad°	5	5	5	5	5	5	5	5	5	5	Tchad°
Côte d'Ivoire°	4	4	5	5	6	6	5	6	5	6	Côte d'Ivoire°
Egypt°	34	35	36	37	37	37	39	41	43	43	Egypte°
Ethiopia°	40	40	41	41	41	41	41	41	41	41	Ethiopie°
Gambia°	0	0	0	0	0	0	0	1	0	0	Gambie°
Ghana°	1	1	1	1	1	1	1	1	1	1	Ghana°
Guinea°	3	3	3	3	3	3	3	3	3	3	Guinée°
Guinea–Bissau°	1	1	1	1	1	1	1	1	1	1	Guinée–Bissau°
Kenya°	22	28	30	31	32	27	30	34	35	33	Kenya°
Lesotho°	1	1	1	1	1	1	2	2	2	2	Lesotho°
Liberia°	0	0	1	1	1	1	1	1	1	1	Libéria°
Libyan Arab Jamah.°	2	5	6	6	6	6	6	6	6	6	Jamah.arabe libyenne°
Madagascar°	16	16	16	17	19	19	19	19	19	19	Madagascar°
Malawi°	1	1	1	1	2	2	2	2	2	2	Malawi°
Mali°	7	7	7	6	6	6	6	6	6	6	Mali°
Mauritania°	2	2	2	2	2	2	2	3	3	3	Mauritanie°
Morocco°	17	17	16	17	18	21	20	19	20	20	Maroc°
Mozambique°	6	6	6	6	6	6	6	6	6	6	Mozambique°
Namibia°	4	4	4	4	4	4	5	5	5	5	Namibie°
Niger°	3	5	6	6	6	7	6	6	6	6	Niger°
Nigeria°	31	32	35	38	39	40	40	37	36	35	Nigéria°
Rwanda°	2	2	2	2	2	2	2	2	2	2	Rwanda°
Senegal°	6	7	7	7	6	7	8	8	8	8	Sénégal°
Sierra Leone°	1	1	1	1	1	1	1	1	1	1	Sierra Leone°
Somalia°	8	8	9	8	8	8	8	8	8	8	Somalie°
South Africa°	77	81	90	100	90	81	87	84	89	87	Afrique du Sud°
Sudan°	24	25	24	25	26	32	37	38	38	42	Soudan°
Swaziland°	2	1	2	2	2	2	2	2	1	2	Swaziland°
Togo°	1	1	1	1	1	1	1	1	1	1	Togo°
Tunisia°	6	7	6	4	5	4	4	4	4	4	Tunisie°
Uganda°	11	12	13	13	13	13	13	13	13	13	Ouganda°
United Rep. Tanzania°	25	27	27	28	26	27	29	30	31	32	Rép.Unie de Tanzanie°
Zaire°	3	3	3	3	3	3	3	3	3	3	Zaïre°
Zambia°	4	4	4	4	4	4	4	4	4	5	Zambie°
Zimbabwe°	13	14	14	13	10	9	10	10	10	11	Zimbabwe°
America, North	**1 565**	**1 557**	**1 457**	**1 243**	**1 240**	**1 286**	**1 317**	**1 333**	**1 349**	**1 321**	**Amérique du Nord**
Canada°	137	134	119	99	101	107	111	109	107	105	Canada°
Costa Rica	* 10	* 9	* 10	* 10	* 9	* 9	* 9	* 8	* 9	° 8	Costa Rica
Cuba°	16	17	18	19	20	20	20	20	20	19	Cuba°
Dominican Republic°	5	5	6	6	7	7	7	7	7	8	Rép. dominicaine°
El Salvador	* 4	* 5	* 5	* 5	° 5	° 5	° 5	° 5	° 5	° 5	El Salvador
Guadeloupe°	0	0	1	1	1	1	1	1	1	1	Guadeloupe°
Guatemala	* 9	* 10	* 12	* 13	* 12	15	° 12	° 10	° 10	° 8	Guatemala
Haiti°	3	3	3	3	3	3	4	4	4	4	Haïti°
Honduras	* 7	* 7	* 8	* 11	* 10	* 10	° 8	° 7	° 6	° 6	Honduras
Jamaica°	1	1	1	1	1	1	1	1	2	2	Jamaïque°
Mexico	83	92	° 101	° 92	° 95	° 100	° 101	° 98	° 86	° 95	Mexique
Nicaragua	12	12	* 11	* 11	* 9	* 7	° 8	° 9	° 8	° 8	Nicaragua
Puerto Rico°	3	3	4	5	3	3	2	3	3	3	Porto Rico°
United States°	1 267	1 250	1 151	960	957	992	1 021	1 044	1 073	1 041	Etats–Unis°
America, South	**996**	**1 055**	**1 066**	**983**	**945**	**1 000**	**952**	**936**	**957**	**997**	**Amérique du Sud**
Argentina°	416	442	488	457	415	440	371	336	369	414	Argentine°
Bolivia°	9	10	10	11	11	11	12	12	12	12	Bolivie°
Brazil	° 321	* 375	* 336	* 281	* 280	* 291	* 308	* 322	* 310	° 307	Brésil
Chile°	29	24	23	24	22	25	28	32	31	29	Chili°
Colombia°	76	73	78	83	80	85	81	84	87	87	Colombie°
Ecuador°	11	12	12	13	14	14	13	12	12	16	Equateur°
Guyana°	1	1	1	0	0	0	0	0	0	0	Guyana°
Paraguay°	15	18	17	16	17	17	15	13	13	15	Paraguay°
Peru°	14	13	14	14	13	13	14	15	14	14	Pérou°

For general note and footnotes, see end of table. | Voir la fin du tableau pour la remarque générale et les notes.

Hides, cattle and horse, undressed (Total production) (continued) – Peaux de bovins et d'équidés, non préparées (Production totale) (suite)

Unit : Thousand metric tons — Unité : Milliers de tonnes métriques

Country or area	1976	1977	1978	1979	1980	1981	1982	1983	1984	1985	Pays ou zone
Uruguay°	67	51	49	40	48	59	67	67	67	60	Uruguay°
Venezuela°	36	36	39	43	44	44	43	43	42	43	Venezuela°
Asia	**1 250**	**1 263**	**1 282**	**1 309**	**1 326**	**1 343**	**1 357**	**1 376**	**1 410**	**1 439**	**Asie**
Afghanistan°	10	11	11	12	11	11	11	11	11	11	Afghanistan°
Bangladesh°	34	34	39	34	28	29	24	29	31	31	Bangladesh°
Burma°	23	23	24	24	24	24	25	25	25	25	Birmanie°
China	65	69	69	79	88	81	82	94	107	113	Chine
Dem. Kampuchea°	5	5	4	3	4	4	4	5	5	5	Kampuchea démocrat.°
Hong Kong°	4	4	4	5	5	5	5	4	4	4	Hong-kong°
India°	760	766	771	771	790	800	810	810	817	823	Inde°
Indonesia°	26	27	26	27	25	28	26	26	27	28	Indonésie°
Iran(Islamic Rep.of)°	31	33	33	34	36	35	35	34	34	35	Iran(Rép.islamique)°
Iraq°	7	7	7	8	6	6	5	5	6	5	Iraq°
Israel°	2	3	3	2	3	2	2	2	2	2	Israël°
Japan	21	24	26	25	25	28	28	°29	°30	°31	Japon
Korea, D. P. Rp.°	4	4	4	4	4	4	5	5	5	5	Corée, Rp. P. D.°
Korea, Republic of°	8	7	9	9	11	10	9	8	11	16	Corée, République de°
Kuwait°	0	0	0	1	1	1	2	2	2	3	Koweït°
Lao Peoples Dem.Rep.°	4	4	3	3	4	4	4	4	4	4	Rép. dém. pop. lao°
Lebanon°	0	0	1	1	2	2	2	2	2	2	Liban°
Malaysia°	3	3	3	3	4	3	4	4	4	4	Malaisie°
Mongolia°	11	10	12	13	12	12	11	11	11	11	Mongolie°
Nepal°	16	16	16	17	17	17	17	17	18	18	Népal°
Pakistan°	76	77	78	79	80	81	85	87	89	90	Pakistan°
Philippines°	15	16	18	18	18	17	18	13	13	17	Philippines°
Saudi Arabia°	2	2	4	4	4	4	4	4	4	5	Arabie saoudite°
Sri Lanka°	6	5	5	5	5	5	5	5	6	6	Sri Lanka°
Syrian Arab Republic°	2	2	3	4	4	5	6	5	5	5	Rép. arabe syrienne°
Thailand°	37	38	39	40	41	41	42	42	42	43	Thaïlande°
Turkey°	59	56	50	65	57	64	67	70	72	74	Turquie°
Viet Nam°	12	12	13	14	14	16	17	17	19	20	Viet Nam°
Yemen	2	2	2	2	2	2	°2	°2	°2	°2	Yémen
Europe	**1 185**	**1 156**	**1 134**	**1 165**	**1 186**	**1 157**	**1 149**	**1 154**	**1 217**	**1 227**	**Europe**
EEC	**733**	**714**	**696**	**726**	**752**	**719**	**695**	**713**	**769**	**778**	**CEE**
Denmark°	26	28	27	28	27	27	26	26	28	28	Danemark°
France	174	162	°148	°158	°155	°153	°148	°152	°165	°165	France
Germany, Fed. Rep.	188	180	°186	°198	°208	°201	°193	°195	°211	°214	Allemagne, Rép. féd.
Greece°	13	13	12	10	10	9	9	8	8	8	Grèce°
Ireland	°33	*37	*36	°35	°43	°31	°33	°34	*36	°36	Irlande
Italy°	130	134	131	141	147	142	141	145	149	153	Italie°
Netherlands	43	42	*41	*41	°42	°43	°43	°43	°53	°53	Pays-Bas
United Kingdom°	126	117	115	116	121	113	103	110	120	120	Royaume-Uni°
EFTA	**83**	**78**	**81**	**81**	**81**	**83**	**88**	**83**	**84**	**83**	**AELE**
Austria	23	20	21	°22	°22	°22	°23	°22	°23	°23	Autriche
Finland	13	13	12	12	12	12	13	°13	°13	°13	Finlande
Norway°	5	5	5	5	5	5	6	6	6	6	Norvège°
Portugal°	10	10	12	11	11	13	15	13	12	11	Portugal°
Sweden	*14	*13	°13	°13	°13	°13	°14	°13	°13	°13	Suède
Switzerland	17	17	17	°17	°17	°17	°17	°16	°17	°17	Suisse
East Europe	**241**	**237**	**238**	**249**	**243**	**245**	**255**	**246**	**256**	**258**	**Europe de l'est**
Albania°	3	3	4	4	4	4	4	4	4	4	Albanie°
Bulgaria°	16	18	18	19	19	20	20	21	21	21	Bulgarie°
Czechoslovakia	53	53	54	56	56	54	54	56	58	59	Tchécoslovaquie
German Dem. Rep.°	52	47	48	48	48	49	54	50	50	50	Rép. dém. allemande°
Hungary	16	15	15	17	16	15	15	14	15	°15	Hongrie
Poland	°61	°55	°55	°57	°55	*63	*76	*68	*69	°71	Pologne
Romania°	41	46	44	48	44	40	32	34	38	38	Roumanie°
Other Europe	**100**	**102**	**95**	**83**	**82**	**81**	**86**	**86**	**83**	**83**	**Autre Europe**
Spain	45	45	41	41	44	44	44	44	41	°41	Espagne
Yugoslavia	55	56	53	42	38	37	°42	°42	°42	°42	Yougoslavie
USSR°	**726**	**692**	**715**	**703**	**710**	**718**	**713**	**722**	**760**	**777**	**URSS°**
Oceania	**272**	**291**	**315**	**286**	**221**	**214**	**222**	**230**	**182**	**184**	**Océanie**

For general note and footnotes, see end of table. — Voir la fin du tableau pour la remarque générale et les notes.

Hides, cattle and horse, undressed (Total production) (continued) – Peaux de bovins et d'équidés, non préparées (Production totale) (suite)

Unit : Thousand metric tons — Unité : Milliers de tonnes métriques

Country or area	1976	1977	1978	1979	1980	1981	1982	1983	1984	1985	Pays ou zone
Australia°	212	240	259	238	178	169	173	182	142	144	Australie°
Fiji°	0	0	0	1	1	1	1	1	1	1	Fidji°
New Caledonia°	0	1	1	1	1	0	0	0	0	0	Nouvelle–Calédonie°
New Zealand	* 58	* 50	* 53	* 46	* 41	* 44	* 46	46	38	° 38	Nouvelle–Zélande
Vanuatu°	0	0	0	0	0	0	0	1	1	1	Vanuatu°
Total	**6 415**	**6 461**	**6 432**	**6 170**	**6 104**	**6 191**	**6 204**	**6 246**	**6 379**	**6 452**	**Total**

General note.
Raw hides of bovines and equines, from which the hair has not been removed, in terms of fresh weight. Includes non–industrial production. (SITC 21110–0).
Source: Food and Agriculture Organization of the United Nations (FAO), Rome.

Remarque générale.
Peaux brutes, non épilées, de bovins et d'équidés (poids des cuirs verts). Y compris production non–industrielle. (CTCI 21110–0).
Source: Organisation des Nations Unies pour l'agriculture(FAO), Rome.

Hides, cattle and horse, undressed (Industrial production) – Peaux de bovins et d'équidés, non préparées (Production industrielle)

Unit : Thousand metric tons

Unité : Milliers de tonnes métriques

Country or area	1976	1977	1978	1979	1980	1981	1982	1983	1984	1985	Pays ou zone
Europe	**310**	**293**	**294**	**307**	**305**	**298**	**288**	**288**	**303**	**296**	**Europe**
EEC	***192***	***177***	***178***	***187***	***183***	***185***	***171***	***171***	***178***	***174***	***CEE***
Belgium	...	...	...	...	26	26	22	22	24	23	Belgique
Denmark	22	* 22	* 23	* 28	* 27	* 26	...	...	...	...	Danemark
France	141	127	127	132	129	132	119	118	122	118	France
Luxembourg	1	1	1	1	1	1	1	1	1	1	Luxembourg
EFTA	***13***	***13***	***13***	***13***	***14***	***14***	***15***	***15***	***14***	***14***	***AELE***
Sweden	13	13	13	13	14	14	15	15	14	14	Suède
East Europe	***105***	***103***	***103***	***107***	***108***	***99***	***102***	***102***	***111***	***108***	***Europe de l'est***
Bulgaria[1]	34	33	32	33	33	30	32	33	38	33	Bulgarie[1]
Czechoslovakia	53	53	54	56	56	53	54	55	58	58	Tchécoslovaquie
Hungary	18	17	17	18	19	16	16	14	15	17	Hongrie
Total	**310**	**293**	**294**	**307**	**305**	**298**	**288**	**288**	**303**	**296**	**Total**

General note.
Raw hides of bovines and equines, from which the hair has not been removed, in terms of fresh weight. Data refer to industrial production only. (SITC 21110–0).

[1] Including calf, goat and sheep skins.

Remarque générale.
Peaux brutes, non épilées, de bovins et d'équidés (poids des cuirs verts). Les données se rapportent à la production industrielle seulement. (CTCI 21110–0).

[1] Y compris les peaux de veaux, de caprins et d'ovins.

Skins, calf, goat and sheep, undressed (Total production) – Peaux de veaux, de caprins et d'ovins, non préparées (Production totale)

Unit : Thousand metric tons | Unité : Milliers de tonnes métriques

Country or area	1976	1977	1978	1979	1980	1981	1982	1983	1984	1985	Pays ou zone
Africa	**209**	**215**	**221**	**226**	**229**	**232**	**235**	**247**	**251**	**260**	**Afrique**
Algeria	10	10	11	11	12	12	15	18	19	20	Algérie
Angola	1	1	1	1	1	1	1	1	1	1	Angola
Benin	1	1	1	1	1	1	1	1	1	1	Bénin
Botswana	1	1	1	1	1	0	1	1	1	1	Botswana
Burkina Faso	2	2	2	2	2	2	2	3	3	3	Burkina Faso
Burundi	1	1	1	1	1	1	1	1	1	1	Burundi
Cameroon	3	3	3	3	3	3	3	3	3	3	Cameroun
Central African Rep.	0	1	1	1	1	1	1	1	1	1	Rép. centrafricaine
Chad	3	3	3	3	3	3	3	3	3	3	Tchad
Côte d'Ivoire	2	3	3	3	3	3	3	3	3	3	Côte d'Ivoire
Djibouti	1	1	1	1	1	1	1	1	1	1	Djibouti
Egypt	6	6	6	6	5	5	6	6	7	8	Egypte
Ethiopia	25	25	26	26	27	28	28	29	29	30	Ethiopie
Ghana	2	2	2	2	2	2	2	2	2	2	Ghana
Kenya	8	10	12	12	9	9	9	10	9	11	Kenya
Lesotho	1	1	1	1	1	1	1	1	1	1	Lesotho
Libyan Arab Jamah.	7	9	8	11	12	12	12	13	13	14	Jamah.arabe libyenne
Madagascar	1	1	1	1	1	2	2	1	1	1	Madagascar
Malawi	1	1	1	0	0	0	1	0	0	1	Malawi
Mali	7	8	8	8	9	9	9	9	9	9	Mali
Mauritania	2	2	2	2	2	2	2	2	2	2	Mauritanie
Morocco	9	10	11	11	12	13	10	11	10	11	Maroc
Mozambique	0	0	0	0	0	1	1	1	1	1	Mozambique
Namibia	3	3	3	4	4	4	4	4	4	4	Namibie
Niger	5	6	6	6	7	7	7	7	8	8	Niger
Nigeria	26	26	26	27	27	28	28	29	29	29	Nigéria
Rwanda	1	1	1	1	1	1	1	1	1	1	Rwanda
Senegal	2	2	2	2	2	3	3	3	2	3	Sénégal
Somalia	10	10	11	10	11	11	11	11	10	10	Somalie
South Africa	29	27	28	28	27	27	27	32	32	32	Afrique du Sud
Sudan	17	18	18	20	20	19	19	20	20	22	Soudan
Togo	0	0	0	1	0	0	0	0	0	1	Togo
Tunisia	9	8	8	6	7	6	6	7	7	7	Tunisie
Uganda	3	3	3	3	3	3	3	3	3	4	Ouganda
United Rep. Tanzania	5	6	6	6	6	6	6	6	6	7	Rép.Unie de Tanzanie
Zaire	2	2	2	2	3	3	3	3	3	3	Zaïre
Zimbabwe	1	1	1	1	1	1	1	1	1	1	Zimbabwe
America, North	**34**	**33**	**30**	**30**	**32**	**34**	**36**	**37**	**37**	**36**	**Amérique du Nord**
Canada	1	1	1	1	1	1	1	2	2	2	Canada
Cuba	0	0	0	0	0	0	0	0	0	1	Cuba
Guatemala	0	1	1	1	1	1	1	1	1	1	Guatemala
Haiti	1	1	1	1	1	1	1	1	1	1	Haïti
Mexico	9	9	10	11	11	11	11	12	12	12	Mexique
United States	21	20	17	16	17	19	20	20	21	19	Etats–Unis
America, South	**96**	**96**	**94**	**93**	**88**	**95**	**91**	**89**	**89**	**87**	**Amérique du Sud**
Argentina	45	46	44	44	39	39	38	36	36	34	Argentine
Bolivia	6	6	7	7	7	7	7	7	7	7	Bolivie
Brazil	13	12	10	11	11	11	11	11	11	11	Brésil
Chile	4	4	4	5	4	5	4	4	4	4	Chili
Colombia	2	2	2	2	2	2	2	2	2	2	Colombie
Ecuador	1	1	1	1	1	1	1	1	1	1	Equateur
Paraguay	0	0	0	0	0	0	0	0	0	1	Paraguay
Peru	9	9	10	10	10	9	9	9	8	8	Pérou
Uruguay	13	14	14	12	12	18	16	17	17	17	Uruguay
Venezuela	1	1	1	1	1	1	1	1	1	1	Venezuela
Asia	**456**	**472**	**497**	**496**	**533**	**560**	**564**	**577**	**596**	**612**	**Asie**
Afghanistan	23	22	23	22	23	25	25	25	25	25	Afghanistan
Bahrain	0	0	0	0	0	1	1	1	1	1	Bahreïn
Bangladesh	9	10	14	14	12	11	11	11	13	14	Bangladesh
Burma	1	1	1	1	1	1	1	1	1	1	Birmanie
China	71	74	78	91	109	115	127	133	141	154	Chine
Cyprus	1	1	1	2	2	2	2	2	2	2	Chypre
Democratic Yemen	2	2	2	2	2	2	2	2	2	2	Yémen démocratique
India	104	106	107	108	109	110	110	110	111	113	Inde
Indonesia	10	11	11	12	11	12	11	12	12	12	Indonésie
Iran(Islamic Rep.of)	42	45	46	47	48	47	47	47	48	48	Iran(Rép.islamique)

For general note, see end of table. | Voir la fin du tableau pour la remarque générale.

Skins, calf, goat and sheep, undressed (Total production) (continued) – Peaux de veaux, de caprins et d'ovins, non préparées (Production totale) (suite)

Unit : Thousand metric tons

Unité : Milliers de tonnes métriques

Country or area	1976	1977	1978	1979	1980	1981	1982	1983	1984	1985	Pays ou zone
Iraq	13	12	12	13	13	11	11	11	13	12	Iraq
Israel	1	1	1	1	1	1	1	1	1	1	Israël
Jordan	2	2	2	2	2	2	2	2	3	3	Jordanie
Kuwait	3	4	5	7	9	10	12	12	13	13	Koweït
Lebanon	1	1	1	2	2	2	2	2	2	2	Liban
Mongolia	16	14	17	17	17	18	19	18	18	17	Mongolie
Nepal	5	5	5	3	6	6	6	6	6	6	Népal
Oman	0	0	0	0	0	1	0	1	1	1	Oman
Pakistan	48	52	56	61	66	72	58	60	62	63	Pakistan
Philippines	1	1	1	1	1	2	2	2	2	2	Philippines
Saudi Arabia	5	5	8	11	13	16	17	18	18	19	Arabie saoudite
Syrian Arab Republic	8	10	11	13	15	15	15	15	16	15	Rép. arabe syrienne
Turkey	80	83	84	57	60	72	74	76	77	77	Turquie
United Arab Emirates	0	0	0	0	0	0	0	1	1	1	Emirats arabes unis
Yemen	6	6	6	6	7	7	7	7	7	7	Yémen
Europe	**184**	**180**	**182**	**183**	**185**	**187**	**193**	**195**	**199**	**200**	**Europe**
EEC	***88***	***86***	***88***	***89***	***91***	***92***	***92***	***91***	***93***	***95***	***CEE***
France	14	14	14	14	14	15	16	16	16	16	France
Germany, Fed. Rep.	3	4	4	4	4	4	3	3	4	4	Allemagne, Rép. féd.
Greece	17	17	17	18	18	18	18	18	18	19	Grèce
Ireland	5	5	7	6	6	6	6	6	6	7	Irlande
Italy	15	15	15	16	17	16	16	16	17	17	Italie
Netherlands	2	2	2	2	2	2	2	2	2	2	Pays-Bas
United Kingdom	32	30	30	30	30	30	30	30	30	30	Royaume-Uni
EFTA	***12***	***13***	***14***	***14***	***13***	***14***	***15***	***15***	***14***	***15***	***AELE***
Austria	0	0	0	1	0	0	1	1	1	1	Autriche
Iceland	3	3	3	3	3	3	3	3	3	3	Islande
Norway	2	3	3	3	3	3	4	4	4	4	Norvège
Portugal	5	5	6	6	6	6	6	6	6	7	Portugal
Sweden	0	0	...	0	0	0	1	1	...	...	Suède
Switzerland	1	1	1	1	1	1	1	1	1	1	Suisse
East Europe	***48***	***45***	***45***	***48***	***46***	***47***	***52***	***54***	***57***	***56***	***Europe de l'est***
Albania	3	3	3	3	3	3	3	3	3	3	Albanie
Bulgaria	28	24	24	25	24	26	31	31	33	33	Bulgarie
Czechoslovakia	1	1	1	1	1	1	1	1	2	2	Tchécoslovaquie
German Dem. Rep.	2	2	2	2	2	2	2	1	2	1	Rép. dém. allemande
Hungary	1	1	1	1	1	1	1	1	1	1	Hongrie
Poland	2	3	3	3	3	3	3	3	3	3	Pologne
Romania	11	12	11	13	12	11	11	13	14	13	Roumanie
Other Europe	***35***	***35***	***34***	***31***	***33***	***33***	***34***	***34***	***33***	***33***	***Autre Europe***
Spain	31	31	30	27	29	29	30	30	29	29	Espagne
Yugoslavia	4	4	4	4	4	4	4	4	4	4	Yougoslavie
USSR	**138**	**139**	**134**	**131**	**131**	**133**	**133**	**134**	**135**	**136**	**URSS**
Oceania	**265**	**248**	**251**	**237**	**262**	**276**	**257**	**286**	**255**	**281**	**Océanie**
Australia	164	158	146	134	152	159	141	150	125	131	Australie
New Zealand	100	90	105	103	110	116	116	136	130	150	Nouvelle-Zélande
Total	**1 381**	**1 383**	**1 409**	**1 397**	**1 460**	**1 516**	**1 511**	**1 566**	**1 562**	**1 611**	**Total**

General note.

Raw skins of calves, sheep and goats from which the hair has not been removed, in terms of fresh weight. Calf skins can be distinguished from other bovine hides mainly by their shape, size, weight and appearance. Includes non-industrial production. (SITC 2112, 2114, 2116 and 2117).

Source: Food and Agriculture Organization of the United Nations (FAO), Rome.

Remarque générale.

Peaux brutes, non épilées, de veaux, d'ovins et de caprins (poids des cuirs verts). Les peaux de veaux se distinguent des autres peaux de bovins principalement par leur forme, leurs dimensions, leur poids et leur aspect. Y compris production non-industrielle. (CTCI 2112, 2114, 2116 et 2117).

Source: Organisation des Nations Unies pour l'agriculture(FAO), Rome.

Milk and cream, condensed (Total production) – Lait et crème, concentrés (Production totale)

Unit : Thousand metric tons

Unité : Milliers de tonnes métriques

Country or area	1976	1977	1978	1979	1980	1981	1982	1983	1984	1985	Pays ou zone
Africa	**55.8**	**47.9**	**43.7**	**37.8**	**31.7**	**41.4**	**36.9**	**32.1**	**30.5**	**31.0**	**Afrique**
Kenya	2.1	1.3	0.5	0.2	0.0	...	...	...	...	...	Kenya
South Africa	53.7	46.6	43.2	37.6	31.6	41.4	36.9	32.1	30.5	31.0	Afrique du Sud
America, North	**1 717.9**	**1 814.5**	**1 787.5**	**1 766.6**	**1 737.5**	**1 756.9**	**1 758.7**	**1 725.3**	**1 855.5**	**1 808.5**	**Amérique du Nord**
Barbados	...	0.9	1.0	1.1	1.1	1.1	1.0	1.2	1.3	1.4	Barbade
Canada	112.0	166.9	214.0	220.0	251.4	232.3	250.1	233.6	255.2	232.1	Canada
Cuba	62.1	63.2	62.9	65.2	66.3	65.1	48.8	56.3	61.2	60.0	Cuba
Jamaica	62.2	59.2	62.5	57.5	51.5	53.8	53.4	50.2	50.4	50.4	Jamaïque
Mexico	122.9	157.4	169.4	174.4	169.6	176.1	175.6	130.3	153.1	153.9	Mexique
Nicaragua	0.5	0.5	0.5	0.5	...	0.5	...	...	...	...	Nicaragua
Panama ex.Canal Zone	15.2	15.4	15.6	15.6	15.8	16.4	17.2	18.5	17.1	17.1	Panama ex.zone Canal
United States	1 343.0	1 350.9	1 261.5	1 232.2	1 181.7	1 211.7	1 212.7	1 235.3	1 317.2	1 293.6	Etats–Unis
America, South	**177.2**	**180.0**	**181.4**	**176.2**	**179.7**	**191.7**	**209.2**	**200.9**	**182.3**	**186.5**	**Amérique du Sud**
Argentina	11.9	10.9	7.1	11.2	8.7	5.8	6.2	7.7	8.1	7.0	Argentine
Brazil	32.0	32.0	33.0	34.0	34.0	35.0	35.0	36.0	36.0	36.0	Brésil
Chile	10.4	10.4	11.3	12.5	8.8	4.5	8.5	10.1	9.5	11.5	Chili
Colombia	4.5	4.6	4.6	4.7	4.7	4.8	4.8	4.9	5.0	5.0	Colombie
Peru	118.4	122.1	125.3	113.8	123.4	141.6	154.7	142.3	123.7	127.0	Pérou
Asia	**465.7**	**496.6**	**541.6**	**566.5**	**595.9**	**595.2**	**635.4**	**618.2**	**629.4**	**643.9**	**Asie**
China	20.5	22.4	22.4	23.1	26.1	28.4	32.7	33.0	39.6	42.9	Chine
India	250.0	269.5	284.2	294.0	308.9	323.8	340.0	340.0	350.0	363.4	Inde
Japan	77.3	79.5	92.9	94.9	100.5	95.7	92.6	87.4	84.0	79.4	Japon
Korea, Republic of	2.0	1.6	1.1	1.7	2.0	1.6	1.6	2.0	3.2	2.0	Corée, République de
Lebanon	0.8	0.9	1.2	1.5	1.8	1.8	1.8	1.8	1.7	1.8	Liban
Malaysia	96.7	101.8	110.4	118.9	124.4	117.4	138.3	132.0	133.2	137.0	Malaisie
Singapore	8.2	8.2	13.0	13.2	13.2	10.7	10.7	5.2	4.0	4.0	Singapour
Sri Lanka	7.0	5.9	6.3	6.5	6.5	6.6	6.6	6.6	6.8	6.8	Sri Lanka
Thailand	3.3	6.7	10.0	12.6	12.5	9.2	11.1	10.0	6.9	6.6	Thaïlande
Europe	**1 872.2**	**1 869.0**	**1 904.0**	**1 882.6**	**1 910.6**	**1 944.0**	**1 956.5**	**1 850.6**	**1 871.4**	**1 951.7**	**Europe**
EEC	**1 413.7**	**1 447.7**	**1 430.8**	**1 417.4**	**1 438.6**	**1 502.4**	**1 533.9**	**1 392.8**	**1 415.5**	**1 465.1**	**CEE**
Denmark	20.5	14.2	14.6	16.0	15.1	13.1	11.4	10.2	6.3	8.2	Danemark
France	174.0	165.0	168.0	152.4	169.5	146.6	162.0	166.0	165.0	160.0	France
Germany, Fed. Rep.	480.4	497.0	508.8	492.9	526.5	576.9	583.2	515.1	523.1	566.5	Allemagne, Rép. féd.
Ireland	7.7	8.7	8.0	8.0	5.9	...	...	...	...	...	Irlande
Italy	5.5	4.9	4.5	4.2	4.0	4.0	3.6	3.2	3.0	3.0	Italie
Netherlands	503.1	531.9	497.8	522.8	543.5	577.8	570.6	531.3	560.1	551.4	Pays–Bas
United Kingdom	222.5	226.0	229.0	221.0	174.0	184.0	203.0	167.0	158.0	176.0	Royaume–Uni
EFTA	**52.3**	**48.7**	**53.7**	**51.9**	**49.6**	**53.0**	**53.6**	**49.3**	**46.4**	**47.7**	**AELE**
Austria	17.0	12.9	15.9	15.9	15.1	16.0	15.7	14.6	14.2	14.5	Autriche
Norway	10.0	10.0	10.0	8.0	6.0	6.0	5.0	5.0	5.0	5.0	Norvège
Portugal	3.1	2.7	1.3	1.5	1.7	1.8	1.7	1.8	1.8	1.8	Portugal
Sweden	17.0	16.2	19.7	19.8	21.9	25.0	26.9	23.8	21.5	22.3	Suède
Switzerland	5.2	6.9	6.8	6.7	4.9	4.1	4.3	4.1	3.9	4.1	Suisse
East Europe	**255.9**	**235.8**	**276.4**	**281.6**	**290.0**	**260.6**	**257.9**	**291.8**	**303.0**	**313.8**	**Europe de l'est**
Czechoslovakia	123.1	99.7	138.6	139.2	152.2	127.7	120.4	146.7	154.8	163.0	Tchécoslovaquie
German Dem. Rep.	116.1	117.8	118.0	120.0	115.1	116.0	123.0	125.0	130.0	127.8	Rép. dém. allemande
Hungary	1.4	1.5	1.3	1.6	1.7	2.1	2.2	2.4	2.1	3.0	Hongrie
Poland	15.3	16.7	18.4	20.7	21.0	14.8	12.3	17.7	16.0	20.0	Pologne
Other Europe	**140.9**	**127.5**	**132.9**	**122.3**	**122.7**	**118.1**	**101.4**	**107.4**	**97.3**	**114.0**	**Autre Europe**
Spain	140.9	126.7	132.1	121.4	121.3	116.9	100.7	106.6	96.5	113.2	Espagne
Yugoslavia	...	0.8	0.9	0.9	1.4	1.1	0.8	0.8	0.8	0.8	Yougoslavie
USSR	**564.0**	**559.6**	**543.9**	**538.8**	**548.0**	**530.0**	**535.0**	**550.0**	**560.0**	**575.0**	**URSS**
Oceania	**108.2**	**113.2**	**106.3**	**114.6**	**114.2**	**104.2**	**98.7**	**91.7**	**93.5**	**93.0**	**Océanie**
Australia	95.9	102.1	100.2	109.6	107.9	99.1	93.9	87.4	89.5	88.6	Australie
New Zealand	12.3	11.1	6.0	5.0	6.3	5.1	4.8	4.3	4.0	4.4	Nouvelle–Zélande

For general note, see end of table.

Voir la fin du tableau pour la remarque générale.

Milk and cream, condensed (Total production) (continued) – Lait et crème, concentrés (Production totale) (suite)

Unit : Thousand metric tons

Unité : Milliers de tonnes métriques

Country or area	1976	1977	1978	1979	1980	1981	1982	1983	1984	1985	Pays ou zone
Total	**4 961.0**	**5 080.8**	**5 108.3**	**5 083.1**	**5 117.7**	**5 163.4**	**5 230.5**	**5 068.8**	**5 222.5**	**5 289.6**	**Total**

General note.
Milk and cream (including buttermilk, skim milk and whey), evaporated or condensed (in liquid or semi–solid form). In terms of net weight. (SITC 02210–0).
Source: Food and Agriculture Organization of the United Nations (FAO), Rome.

Remarque générale.
Lait et crème (y compris le babeurre, le lait écrémé et le petit lait), évaporés ou concentrés (à l'état liquide ou pâteux). Poids net. (CTCI 02210–0).
Source: Organisation des Nations Unies pour l'agriculture(FAO), Rome.

Milk and cream, dried (Total production) – Lait et crème, séchés (Production totale)

Unit : Thousand metric tons | Unité : Milliers de tonnes métriques

Country or area	1976	1977	1978	1979	1980	1981	1982	1983	1984	1985	Pays ou zone
Africa	**34.6**	**36.6**	**32.9**	**30.7**	**30.3**	**33.8**	**35.2**	**40.9**	**41.9**	**40.8**	**Afrique**
Kenya	4.5	6.1	5.8	2.7	0.2	1.8	4.1	°4.3	°4.1	°2.6	Kenya
South Africa	28.5	29.0	25.7	26.6	28.7	30.9	30.0	35.3	36.1	°36.5	Afrique du Sud
Zimbabwe°	1.7	1.6	1.3	1.4	1.4	1.1	1.1	1.3	1.7	1.7	Zimbabwe°
America, North	**1 023.0**	**1 100.5**	**1 035.6**	**1 026.2**	**1 120.2**	**1 273.3**	**1 350.1**	**1 416.3**	**1 277.7**	**1 370.3**	**Amérique du Nord**
Canada	202.2	210.4	184.8	170.0	172.4	201.5	227.8	200.8	205.9	157.0	Canada
Costa Rica°	2.9	3.0	3.0	3.1	3.2	3.1	3.1	3.1	2.9	2.9	Costa Rica°
Cuba	2.5	2.5	2.3	2.4	2.5	1.9	2.4	2.4	2.3	°2.3	Cuba
El Salvador°	0.8	0.9	1.1	1.1	1.1	1.1	1.1	1.1	1.1	1.1	El Salvador°
Guatemala°	2.3	2.3	2.4	2.5	2.6	2.6	2.7	2.8	2.8	2.9	Guatemala°
Honduras°	0.3	0.3	0.3	0.3	0.3	0.3	0.3	0.3	0.3	0.3	Honduras°
Mexico	27.0	28.7	36.8	37.5	35.4	44.7	47.1	41.0	50.0	°50.0	Mexique
Nicaragua°	4.2	5.0	4.8	1.5	1.4	1.6	1.9	1.9	1.9	1.9	Nicaragua°
United States	779.4	845.9	798.6	806.4	899.9	1 014.9	1 062.1	1 161.2	1 008.7	1 150.2	Etats-Unis
America, South	**297.8**	**298.5**	**344.1**	**315.6**	**339.9**	**365.8**	**376.3**	**366.8**	**374.0**	**437.1**	**Amérique du Sud**
Argentina	85.0	65.9	62.1	62.7	60.0	63.3	89.5	83.8	72.7	* 100.0	Argentine
Bolivia	1.1	1.4	1.5	1.2	0.9	1.7	°1.8	°1.8	°1.8	°1.8	Bolivie
Brazil	102.7	°120.0	°165.0	* 139.0	* 158.0	* 180.0	* 170.0	* 180.0	* 200.0	°200.0	Brésil
Chile	38.6	38.4	33.9	25.7	31.0	35.0	30.6	23.1	23.3	* 32.0	Chili
Colombia°	11.0	12.1	12.5	13.0	13.2	13.5	13.7	13.8	13.9	14.0	Colombie°
Ecuador°	3.0	3.0	3.0	2.0	2.0	2.2	2.3	2.3	2.3	2.3	Equateur°
Uruguay	...	...	...	°2.0	* 2.8	2.2	3.4	* 3.0	°3.0	°3.0	Uruguay
Venezuela	56.3	57.7	66.0	°70.0	°72.0	°68.0	°65.0	* 59.0	* 57.0	* 84.0	Venezuela
Asia	**206.9**	**229.0**	**255.9**	**282.9**	**290.5**	**275.7**	**279.6**	**306.0**	**316.5**	**342.6**	**Asie**
China	8.8	10.4	12.7	14.9	17.7	19.4	21.4	22.9	24.0	26.0	Chine
Israel	2.9	2.3	1.6	1.9	4.7	2.9	2.3	2.1	°2.3	°2.3	Israël
Japan	174.0	191.1	212.5	230.7	223.5	222.3	222.2	244.2	248.0	272.2	Japon
Korea, Republic of	13.8	18.2	23.0	30.3	40.2	27.2	30.2	33.0	38.1	°38.1	Corée, République de
Sri Lanka	°7.5	°7.0	°6.0	°5.0	°4.5	3.9	3.6	3.8	°4.0	°4.0	Sri Lanka
Europe	**3 826.1**	**3 995.7**	**4 196.5**	**4 173.8**	**4 334.6**	**4 331.1**	**4 412.4**	**4 733.5**	**4 556.4**	**4 331.4**	**Europe**
EEC	**2 827.8**	**2 950.3**	**3 146.5**	**3 135.5**	**3 258.1**	**3 293.9**	**3 384.9**	**3 603.9**	**3 410.1**	**3 248.5**	**CEE**
Denmark	120.6	125.8	145.2	131.6	130.2	129.4	141.4	149.9	131.6	134.5	Danemark
France	1 099.0	1 142.0	1 159.5	1 201.2	1 248.0	1 275.4	1 250.0	1 291.0	1 305.0	1 232.0	France
Germany, Fed. Rep.	778.6	774.1	828.0	870.9	924.2	880.4	900.3	1 013.4	890.0	804.2	Allemagne, Rép. féd.
Ireland	180.0	182.3	204.6	173.6	175.1	177.0	189.3	201.8	222.0	201.6	Irlande
Italy	5.0	4.7	3.1	2.7	2.5	2.3	2.8	2.8	2.7	°2.7	Italie
Netherlands	430.8	427.4	485.1	471.5	480.1	511.4	535.1	573.0	521.8	510.2	Pays-Bas
United Kingdom	213.7	294.0	321.0	284.0	298.0	318.0	366.0	372.0	337.0	363.3	Royaume-Uni
EFTA	**325.4**	**334.0**	**327.1**	**343.6**	**355.7**	**351.3**	**361.1**	**377.3**	**386.5**	**346.2**	**AELE**
Austria	58.8	67.7	58.0	52.8	56.1	61.0	61.9	67.6	68.1	52.0	Autriche
Finland	107.1	112.7	110.4	112.7	116.2	105.6	107.5	113.9	111.5	96.7	Finlande
Iceland	2.9	4.5	5.0	5.6	5.0	4.1	3.6	3.3	°3.7	°3.8	Islande
Norway	10.9	8.8	8.7	9.7	12.8	12.0	14.3	12.4	10.9	9.6	Norvège
Portugal	38.0	44.5	52.5	58.4	65.8	°70.7	67.6	65.0	66.3	71.5	Portugal
Sweden	52.3	46.5	41.6	48.0	47.7	45.1	57.0	61.7	70.3	63.2	Suède
Switzerland	55.5	49.2	50.8	56.3	52.1	52.8	49.1	53.5	55.6	°49.4	Suisse
East Europe	**470.4**	**483.9**	**493.9**	**457.8**	**472.6**	**456.2**	**430.1**	**504.2**	**534.3**	**526.1**	**Europe de l'est**
Bulgaria	5.9	6.1	5.3	°6.0	°5.7	°5.7	°6.6	°6.6	°7.0	°7.0	Bulgarie
Czechoslovakia	83.0	100.1	102.2	70.9	83.8	86.6	80.8	104.6	112.9	115.4	Tchécoslovaquie
German Dem. Rep.	176.3	180.7	183.1	185.5	171.2	163.0	144.3	144.1	°145.0	°145.0	Rép. dém. allemande
Hungary	21.1	29.7	35.9	38.4	42.2	43.7	39.2	41.5	41.8	32.7	Hongrie
Poland	149.0	132.3	131.5	122.0	132.7	122.1	139.1	180.3	197.6	°201.0	Pologne
Romania	°35.0	°35.0	°36.0	°35.0	37.0	°35.0	20.0	27.0	30.0	°25.0	Roumanie
Other Europe	**44.8**	**59.6**	**54.6**	**52.4**	**63.4**	**54.7**	**62.5**	**59.8**	**55.7**	**57.5**	**Autre Europe**
Spain	34.4	42.7	40.0	40.8	48.5	40.2	48.9	45.3	41.0	42.8	Espagne
Yugoslavia	10.4	16.9	14.6	11.6	14.9	14.5	13.6	14.6	14.7	°14.7	Yougoslavie
USSR	**454.2**	**499.9**	**532.5**	**533.0**	**536.0**	**567.0**	**600.0**	**707.0**	**778.0**	**°810.0**	**URSS**

For general note and footnotes, see end of table.
Voir la fin du tableau pour la remarque générale et les notes.

Milk and cream, dried (Total production) (continued) – Lait et crème, séchés (Production totale) (suite)

Unit : Thousand metric tons

Unité : Milliers de tonnes métriques

Country or area	1976	1977	1978	1979	1980	1981	1982	1983	1984	1985	Pays ou zone
Oceania	**476.1**	**467.0**	**434.7**	**441.0**	**427.2**	**449.5**	**484.5**	**475.1**	**564.5**	**597.7**	**Océanie**
Australia	201.7	163.8	168.2	165.9	144.2	140.2	145.5	158.1	178.2	204.2	Australie
New Zealand	274.5	303.2	266.5	275.1	282.9	309.3	339.0	317.0	386.4	393.5	Nouvelle–Zélande
Total	**6 318.7**	**6 627.1**	**6 832.1**	**6 803.2**	**7 078.7**	**7 296.2**	**7 538.1**	**8 045.5**	**7 909.1**	**7 929.9**	**Total**

General note.
Milk and cream (including buttermilk, skim milk and whey), dry (in solid form, such as blocks or powder). (SITC 02220–0).
Source: Food and Agriculture Organization of the United Nations (FAO), Rome.

Remarque générale.
Lait et crème (y compris le babeurre, le lait écrémé et le petit lait), secs (sous forme solide: morceaux ou poudre). (CTCI 02220–0).
Source: Organisation des Nations Unies pour l'agriculture(FAO), Rome.

Butter (Total production) – Beurre (Production totale)

Unit : Thousand metric tons — Unité : Milliers de tonnes métriques

Country or area	1976	1977	1978	1979	1980	1981	1982	1983	1984	1985	Pays ou zone
Africa	**149.4**	**151.6**	**146.2**	**147.2**	**151.4**	**151.3**	**160.6**	**165.2**	**166.5**	**166.9**	**Afrique**
Algeria°	0.6	0.6	0.7	0.7	0.7	0.8	0.8	0.9	0.9	0.9	Algérie°
Angola°	0.7	0.7	0.7	0.7	0.7	0.8	0.8	0.8	0.8	0.8	Angola°
Botswana°	1.0	1.1	1.1	1.2	1.2	1.3	1.3	1.4	1.3	1.3	Botswana°
Burkina Faso°	0.8	0.8	0.9	1.0	1.1	1.1	1.2	1.2	1.3	1.3	Burkina Faso°
Burundi°	0.2	0.2	0.2	0.2	0.2	0.1	0.1	0.1	0.1	0.1	Burundi°
Chad°	2.4	2.9	2.5	2.7	2.7	2.4	2.2	2.1	2.1	2.1	Tchad°
Egypt°	64.5	64.9	65.8	66.7	67.6	68.0	78.0	78.0	78.8	79.6	Egypte°
Ethiopia°	8.6	8.7	8.8	8.8	8.9	8.9	9.0	9.0	8.9	8.9	Ethiopie°
Guinea°	0.1	0.1	0.1	0.1	0.1	0.1	0.1	0.1	0.1	0.1	Guinée°
Kenya	3.1	4.3	3.9	* 3.1	* 2.2	* 2.7	* 3.2	° 3.2	° 3.0	° 2.7	Kenya
Mauritania°	0.5	0.5	0.5	0.6	0.6	0.6	0.6	0.6	0.6	0.6	Mauritanie°
Morocco°	8.4	9.2	10.2	12.0	11.7	12.5	12.7	12.8	13.3	13.6	Maroc°
Namibia°	0.3	0.3	0.3	0.3	0.3	0.3	0.3	0.3	0.3	0.3	Namibie°
Niger°	3.9	4.1	4.4	4.5	4.6	5.0	5.1	5.2	5.2	5.3	Niger°
Nigeria°	7.2	7.2	7.5	7.8	8.2	8.3	8.4	8.2	8.1	8.1	Nigéria°
Rwanda°	0.1	0.2	0.2	0.3	0.3	0.3	0.4	0.3	0.4	0.4	Rwanda°
Senegal°	0.4	0.4	0.4	0.4	0.4	0.3	0.4	0.4	0.3	0.3	Sénégal°
Somalia°	1.5	1.6	1.6	1.5	1.6	1.6	1.6	1.4	1.4	1.4	Somalie°
South Africa	26.9	24.5	17.6	16.4	19.4	17.2	15.2	19.2	18.8	° 18.0	Afrique du Sud
Sudan°	11.2	11.4	11.7	11.9	12.1	12.4	12.6	12.8	13.0	13.0	Soudan°
Swaziland°	0.1	0.2	0.2	0.2	0.2	0.2	0.2	0.2	0.2	0.2	Swaziland°
Tunisia°	1.6	2.2	1.6	0.8	1.3	1.3	1.4	1.4	1.4	1.5	Tunisie°
United Rep. Tanzania°	2.7	2.9	3.0	3.1	3.2	3.2	3.3	3.5	3.6	3.7	Rép.Unie de Tanzanie°
Zambia°	0.2	0.2	0.2	0.2	0.2	0.2	0.2	0.2	0.2	0.2	Zambie°
Zimbabwe°	2.3	2.2	1.9	2.0	2.0	1.5	1.5	1.8	2.4	2.4	Zimbabwe°
America, North	**611.6**	**661.0**	**614.8**	**605.2**	**677.2**	**725.0**	**750.1**	**752.5**	**669.6**	**730.3**	**Amérique du Nord**
Canada	118.5	116.7	105.5	101.4	106.7	116.9	126.4	107.8	111.8	* 102.0	Canada
Costa Rica°	3.0	3.1	3.2	3.4	3.4	3.4	3.5	3.5	3.5	3.5	Costa Rica°
Cuba	5.3	6.2	11.5	10.9	9.5	9.4	9.6	10.3	11.5	° 10.6	Cuba
Dominican Republic	0.8	1.1	1.1	1.2	1.3	1.3	1.3	1.5	° 1.4	° 1.5	Rép. dominicaine
El Salvador°	5.0	5.1	5.2	5.5	5.5	5.5	5.5	5.5	5.5	5.5	El Salvador°
Guatemala°	4.0	4.1	4.2	4.3	4.4	4.5	4.6	4.6	4.4	4.5	Guatemala°
Honduras°	4.0	4.0	4.0	4.0	4.0	4.0	4.0	4.0	4.0	4.0	Honduras°
Mexico	° 23.0	° 24.0	° 25.0	° 24.0	* 21.0	* 21.0	* 23.0	* 24.0	* 25.0	° 25.0	Mexique
Nicaragua°	4.0	4.0	4.0	3.7	1.8	1.8	1.8	1.9	1.9	1.9	Nicaragua°
United States	443.9	492.6	451.0	446.6	519.5	557.1	570.1	589.3	500.5	571.6	Etats–Unis
America, South	**148.6**	**140.7**	**159.4**	**162.3**	**167.1**	**170.1**	**150.3**	**148.7**	**141.8**	**144.9**	**Amérique du Sud**
Argentina	40.2	30.0	29.2	31.9	29.1	31.8	37.0	33.7	28.2	* 30.0	Argentine
Bolivia	0.3	0.4	0.5	0.4	0.3	° 0.4	* 0.5	° 0.5	° 0.5	° 0.5	Bolivie
Brazil	* 66.0	* 69.0	* 90.0	* 92.0	* 94.0	* 95.0	* 70.0	* 70.0	* 70.0	° 70.0	Brésil
Chile	5.5	5.2	4.4	4.0	4.4	3.9	3.3	3.5	3.6	* 4.0	Chili
Colombia°	11.2	11.4	11.6	12.0	12.4	12.5	12.6	12.8	12.8	13.0	Colombie°
Ecuador°	5.5	5.7	5.9	4.2	4.2	4.2	4.4	4.4	4.4	4.4	Equateur°
Peru	5.7	* 5.0	* 4.0	* 5.0	* 5.0	* 4.0	* 4.0	* 3.0	* 2.0	* 2.0	Pérou
Uruguay	° 6.4	° 6.4	° 6.4	5.5	7.8	8.3	8.5	12.8	10.3	° 9.0	Uruguay
Venezuela	7.7	7.5	7.4	7.3	* 10.0	* 10.0	* 10.0	* 8.0	* 10.0	* 12.0	Venezuela
Asia	**1 082.9**	**1 088.2**	**1 151.5**	**1 190.7**	**1 225.9**	**1 275.7**	**1 303.7**	**1 362.7**	**1 387.4**	**1 412.8**	**Asie**
Afghanistan	10.5	10.8	11.1	11.5	11.6	° 12.0	° 12.2	° 12.6	° 12.6	° 12.7	Afghanistan
Bangladesh	° 11.4	° 11.6	° 15.2	° 15.6	14.1	14.4	14.5	14.6	° 14.8	° 15.0	Bangladesh
Bhutan°	0.2	0.2	0.2	0.2	0.2	0.2	0.2	0.2	0.2	0.2	Bhoutan°
Burma°	4.7	5.0	5.2	5.8	6.0	6.9	7.9	9.7	12.3	12.3	Birmanie°
China	25.9	27.1	28.3	29.2	32.5	34.9	39.8	40.5	47.9	48.9	Chine
Democratic Yemen°	0.2	0.2	0.2	0.2	0.2	0.2	0.2	0.2	0.2	0.2	Yémen démocratique°
India	* 570.0	557.9	588.3	608.6	639.7	670.3	° 697.5	° 730.0	° 740.0	° 750.0	Inde
Iran(Islamic Rep.of)°	55.7	57.9	66.4	66.4	66.5	68.0	68.0	69.7	69.7	71.4	Iran(Rép.islamique)°
Iraq°	8.7	8.4	8.0	9.1	8.1	7.5	7.8	8.1	8.3	7.9	Iraq°
Israel	6.3	5.9	4.4	3.8	6.1	4.8	3.9	4.1	° 4.0	° 4.0	Israël
Japan	43.6	54.1	62.2	69.4	64.1	63.6	63.9	74.3	77.6	88.7	Japon
Korea, Republic of°	5.8	7.1	7.7	7.4	8.3	11.6	13.5	16.4	17.8	11.1	Corée, République de°
Mongolia	° 7.0	° 6.8	° 6.5	° 6.0	° 5.4	° 5.0	4.0	4.0	4.4	4.3	Mongolie
Nepal°	8.4	8.8	9.1	9.4	9.8	10.1	10.4	10.7	11.1	11.1	Népal°
Oman°	0.1	0.1	0.1	0.1	0.1	0.1	0.1	0.1	0.1	0.1	Oman°
Pakistan°	202.4	206.0	209.5	213.1	216.8	220.5	229.3	234.1	237.5	241.0	Pakistan°
Saudi Arabia°	1.3	1.3	1.5	1.6	1.7	1.7	2.0	2.0	2.0	2.1	Arabie saoudite°
Sri Lanka	0.3	0.2	0.2	0.1	0.1	0.7	0.3	0.3	° 0.4	° 0.4	Sri Lanka
Syrian Arab Republic	9.7	7.8	9.9	10.6	15.1	14.9	15.1	16.6	13.7	° 17.1	Rép. arabe syrienne

For general note and footnotes, see end of table.

Voir la fin du tableau pour la remarque générale et les notes.

Unit : Thousand metric tons — Unité : Milliers de tonnes métriques

Country or area	1976	1977	1978	1979	1980	1981	1982	1983	1984	1985	Pays ou zone
Turkey	107.7	108.2	114.6	119.3	116.4	124.9	109.9	111.1	109.3	110.8	Turquie
United Arab Emirates°	0.1	0.1	0.1	0.1	0.1	0.1	0.1	0.1	0.2	0.2	Emirats arabes unis°
Yemen°	2.9	2.9	2.9	3.0	3.1	3.1	3.2	3.2	3.3	3.3	Yémen°
Europe	**2 790.0**	**2 840.8**	**3 008.4**	**3 027.4**	**3 031.1**	**2 914.9**	**3 083.4**	**3 383.4**	**3 271.0**	**3 146.3**	**Europe**
EEC	**1 681.3**	**1 701.7**	**1 831.6**	**1 855.4**	**1 843.2**	**1 789.8**	**1 947.3**	**2 134.4**	**1 969.1**	**1 870.3**	**CEE**
Denmark	139.3	131.0	140.3	130.5	113.3	108.5	120.6	131.1	104.4	110.1	Danemark
France	531.0	537.0	538.0	575.0	598.0	580.0	618.5	622.0	597.0	570.0	France
Germany, Fed. Rep.	543.4	535.0	564.3	568.2	576.3	544.1	555.6	627.2	572.1	515.1	Allemagne, Rép. féd.
Greece	5.2	5.2	5.1	4.9	4.6	4.4	4.6	* 5.0	* 4.5	* 5.0	Grèce
Ireland	103.0	107.0	132.0	134.0	124.0	125.0	140.0	158.3	* 164.0	* 158.0	Irlande
Italy	67.2	72.5	76.9	79.1	76.4	72.3	75.6	78.8	81.4	* 83.0	Italie
Netherlands	202.0	179.0	211.0	202.7	180.5	183.4	216.3	270.6	240.6	229.1	Pays–Bas
United Kingdom	90.1	135.0	164.0	161.0	170.0	172.0	216.0	241.5	205.1	200.0	Royaume–Uni
EFTA	**253.4**	**246.5**	**242.2**	**240.7**	**243.0**	**242.7**	**245.1**	**270.0**	**271.0**	**259.1**	**AELE**
Austria	45.1	47.0	42.1	40.0	42.8	43.0	43.0	46.5	45.1	* 42.0	Autriche
Finland	82.6	73.5	72.6	74.3	73.6	72.1	69.9	84.1	79.9	* 76.0	Finlande
Iceland	1.8	1.8	1.7	1.4	1.0	1.0	1.4	° 1.2	° 1.3	° 1.2	Islande
Norway	23.4	23.8	20.4	20.4	21.7	23.1	25.1	26.4	25.0	* 24.0	Norvège
Portugal	° 4.4	° 4.3	4.9	3.3	3.6	3.8	3.8	3.7	3.4	* 4.0	Portugal
Sweden	60.8	61.7	63.0	64.8	65.6	64.4	69.4	73.1	78.0	74.8	Suède
Switzerland	35.3	34.3	37.5	36.6	34.7	35.3	32.5	35.0	38.4	37.0	Suisse
East Europe	**730.1**	**767.4**	**795.2**	**798.9**	**816.6**	**751.3**	**764.2**	**841.5**	**895.3**	**882.8**	**Europe de l'est**
Albania°	2.8	3.4	3.4	3.5	3.6	3.7	3.6	3.7	3.7	3.7	Albanie°
Bulgaria	14.6	17.3	19.7	20.9	19.8	19.9	23.0	24.0	24.6	° 24.0	Bulgarie
Czechoslovakia	113.1	121.3	119.1	120.3	128.1	126.7	138.4	149.2	151.7	152.0	Tchécoslovaquie
German Dem. Rep.	277.8	273.2	281.0	275.5	280.1	272.8	266.2	290.8	309.0	° 315.0	Rép. dém. allemande
Hungary	19.5	26.3	28.8	29.2	31.6	32.3	31.9	32.8	32.6	31.1	Hongrie
Poland	264.0	280.5	298.9	309.4	318.8	259.9	263.3	294.3	* 325.0	* 310.0	Pologne
Romania	38.3	45.3	44.3	40.0	34.6	35.9	37.7	46.7	48.7	47.0	Roumanie
Other Europe	**26.6**	**33.6**	**33.5**	**27.6**	**31.6**	**31.5**	**24.6**	**24.4**	**25.6**	**27.0**	**Autre Europe**
Spain	14.6	18.6	19.5	15.2	20.5	22.0	16.6	13.2	13.6	* 15.0	Espagne
Yugoslavia	12.0	15.0	14.0	12.4	11.1	9.5	8.0	11.2	° 12.0	° 12.0	Yougoslavie
USSR	**1 356.0**	**1 500.0**	**1 472.0**	**1 420.0**	**1 388.0**	**1 318.0**	**1 403.0**	**1 563.0**	**1 588.0**	**° 1 600.0**	**URSS**
Oceania	**424.1**	**406.1**	**361.1**	**375.2**	**352.2**	**349.9**	**326.8**	**350.5**	**410.4**	**409.9**	**Océanie**
Australia	167.3	127.7	125.9	121.4	91.0	83.6	78.1	96.2	118.2	115.9	Australie
Fiji	1.2	1.3	1.5	1.7	1.7	1.4	0.9	0.3	0.3	° 1.0	Fidji
New Zealand	255.6	277.1	233.6	252.1	259.6	264.9	247.8	254.0	291.9	293.0	Nouvelle–Zélande
Total	**6 562.6**	**6 788.4**	**6 913.5**	**6 928.1**	**6 993.0**	**6 904.8**	**7 177.8**	**7 726.0**	**7 634.8**	**7 611.0**	**Total**

General note.
Natural fresh butter, whether salted or not, including melted. Includes non–industrial production. (SITC 02300–0).
Source: Food and Agriculture Organization of the United Nations (FAO), Rome.

Remarque générale.
Beurre, frais, salé ou non, y compris le beurre fondu. Y compris production non–industrielle. (CTCI 02300–0).
Source: Organisation des Nations Unies pour l'agriculture(FAO), Rome.

Butter (Industrial production) – Beurre (Production industrielle)

Unit : Thousand metric tons — Unité : Milliers de tonnes métriques

Country or area	1976	1977	1978	1979	1980	1981	1982	1983	1984	1985	Pays ou zone
America, South	**45.8**	**48.9**	**52.1**	**55.2**	**61.2**	**55.3**	**64.6**	**72.6**	**72.0**	**72.0**	**Amérique du Sud**
Brazil	...	...	...	...	59.1	53.7	...	70.0	70.0	70.0	Brésil
Colombia	...	...	...	...	...	1.6	1.9	2.6	...	...	Colombie
Asia	**8.4**	**8.5**	**9.4**	**9.6**	**8.7**	**9.7**	**10.1**	**10.0**	**10.7**	**10.4**	**Asie**
Indonesia	...	...	...	...	...	0.5	0.5	0.6	0.6	...	Indonésie
Israel	3.1	3.1	3.3	3.3	2.7	2.8	3.0	3.0	3.0	3.1	Israël
Mongolia	3.4	3.3	3.8	3.9	3.8	4.0	4.0	4.1	4.7	4.4	Mongolie
Turkey	...	...	...	...	1.6	2.4	2.4	2.3	2.5	2.4	Turquie
Europe	**1 569.1**	**1 584.2**	**1 636.7**	**1 670.7**	**1 673.9**	**1 605.7**	**1 686.2**	**1 850.9**	**1 789.0**	**1 687.5**	**Europe**
EEC	***1 142.6***	***1 118.0***	***1 162.8***	***1 199.9***	***1 194.4***	***1 157.5***	***1 215.1***	***1 323.2***	***1 232.0***	***1 150.3***	***CEE***
Belgium	70.1	64.3	78.6	78.3	71.3	74.5	76.9	87.4	85.2	83.9	Belgique
France	516.2	505.1	506.7	540.3	532.9	526.0	569.0	595.0	561.0	538.0	France
Germany, Fed. Rep.	541.6	533.3	563.0	566.9	576.3	544.1	555.6	627.2	572.1	515.1	Allemagne, Rép. féd.
Greece	6.5	7.1	6.4	6.2	5.7	5.4	5.7	5.5	5.6	...	Grèce
Luxembourg	8.1	8.1	8.2	8.1	8.2	7.4	7.9	8.1	8.1	8.2	Luxembourg
EFTA	***75.7***	***74.1***	***68.4***	***70.5***	***71.3***	***72.4***	***76.5***	***83.8***	***81.9***	***75.0***	***AELE***
Iceland	1.8	1.8	1.7	1.4	1.0	1.0	0.9	1.0	0.9	0.8	Islande
Norway	25.2	25.4	20.9	21.1	22.0	22.8	23.6	30.2	25.1	25.2	Norvège
Portugal	...	...	...	7.6	...	7.9	7.4	7.5	7.7	6.5	Portugal
Sweden	40.4	38.8	37.8	40.5	40.5	40.7	44.6	45.1	48.1	42.5	Suède
East Europe	***344.7***	***382.6***	***396.8***	***393.5***	***400.7***	***368.5***	***386.2***	***434.3***	***465.8***	***452.1***	***Europe de l'est***
Bulgaria	14.6	17.3	19.6	20.9	19.8	19.9	23.0	24.0	24.7	24.6	Bulgarie
Czechoslovakia	113.1	121.3	119.1	120.3	128.1	126.7	138.4	149.2	151.7	152.0	Tchécoslovaquie
Poland	216.9	244.0	258.0	252.3	252.9	221.8	224.7	261.1	289.4	275.4	Pologne
Other Europe	***6.1***	***9.5***	***8.7***	***6.7***	***7.4***	***7.3***	***8.4***	***9.6***	***9.4***	***10.1***	***Autre Europe***
Yugoslavia	6.1	9.5	8.7	6.7	7.4	7.3	8.4	9.6	9.4	10.1	Yougoslavie
USSR	**1 263.2**	**1 407.6**	**1 381.0**	**1 325.4**	**1 277.6**	**1 209.7**	**1 289.9**	**1 455.0**	**1 497.3**	**1 517.0**	**URSS**
Byelorussian SSR	...	...	...	*99.4*	*100.0*	*88.4*	*99.9*	*108.4*	*120.4*	*125.6*	*RSS de Biélorussie*
Ukrainian SSR	*340.5*	*385.9*	*372.4*	*348.0*	*335.5*	*321.8*	*321.9*	*368.4*	*378.1*	*390.0*	*RSS d'Ukraine*
Oceania	**396.3**	**394.7**	**345.7**	**351.6**	**338.3**	**348.3**	**321.8**	**330.8**	**397.6**	**423.0**	**Océanie**
Australia[1]	140.7	117.6	112.1	99.5	78.7	83.4	74.0	76.8	105.7	129.9	Australie[1]
New Zealand[2]	255.6	277.1	233.6	252.1	259.6	264.9	247.8	254.0	291.9	293.1	Nouvelle–Zélande[2]
Total	**3 282.8**	**3 444.0**	**3 424.8**	**3 412.5**	**3 359.6**	**3 228.6**	**3 372.6**	**3 719.4**	**3 766.7**	**3 710.0**	**Total**

General note.
Natural fresh butter, whether salted or not, including melted. Data refer to industrial production only. (SITC 02300–0).

[1] Twelve months ending 30 June of year stated.
[2] Twelve months ending 31 May of year stated.

Remarque générale.
Beurre, frais, salé ou non, y compris le beurre fondu. Les données se rapportent à la production industrielle seulement. (CTCI 02300–0).

[1] Période de douze mois finissant le 30 juin de l'année indiquée.
[2] Période de douze mois finissant le 31 mai de l'année indiquée.

Cheese (Total production) – Fromage (Production totale)

Unit : Thousand metric tons | Unité : Milliers de tonnes métriques

Country or area	1976	1977	1978	1979	1980	1981	1982	1983	1984	1985	Pays ou zone
Africa	**335.8**	**340.6**	**346.8**	**351.3**	**365.5**	**364.7**	**428.1**	**432.8**	**439.8**	**436.5**	**Afrique**
Algeria°	0.8	0.8	0.9	0.9	0.9	0.9	0.9	0.9	0.9	1.0	Algérie°
Angola°	2.0	2.2	2.2	2.4	2.5	2.5	2.5	2.5	2.5	2.5	Angola°
Botswana°	0.9	0.9	1.0	1.0	1.0	1.1	1.2	1.2	1.1	1.2	Botswana°
Egypt°	224.7	228.5	233.4	237.2	242.5	240.0	298.5	300.0	304.2	306.2	Egypte°
Ethiopia°	3.8	3.9	3.9	3.9	3.9	4.0	4.0	4.0	3.9	3.9	Ethiopie°
Kenya	0.2	0.4	0.3	0.3	0.1	0.2	0.2	° 0.2	° 0.1	° 0.1	Kenya
Mauritania°	1.2	1.5	1.4	1.5	1.5	1.5	1.5	1.6	1.7	1.7	Mauritanie°
Morocco°	4.1	4.3	4.6	4.5	4.4	4.8	4.9	5.0	5.3	5.7	Maroc°
Namibia°	0.1	0.1	0.1	0.1	0.1	0.1	0.1	0.1	0.1	0.1	Namibie°
Niger°	6.8	6.9	7.1	7.3	7.5	8.2	8.4	8.6	8.6	8.8	Niger°
Nigeria°	5.8	5.8	6.0	6.2	6.5	6.7	6.7	6.6	6.4	6.4	Nigéria°
South Africa	29.6	28.8	28.5	27.0	33.6	32.3	34.7	35.9	36.2	° 38.0	Afrique du Sud
Sudan°	49.8	50.5	52.1	53.3	54.7	56.3	57.9	59.5	60.8	52.9	Soudan°
Tunisia	0.9	1.0	0.9	0.9	1.4	2.2	2.5	2.0	° 2.1	° 2.1	Tunisie
United Rep. Tanzania°	0.6	0.7	0.6	0.7	0.8	0.8	0.9	1.0	1.0	1.0	Rép.Unie de Tanzanie°
Zambia°	0.6	0.7	0.7	0.7	0.7	0.7	0.8	0.8	0.8	0.8	Zambie°
Zimbabwe°	3.9	3.7	3.1	3.3	3.3	2.5	2.5	2.9	3.9	4.0	Zimbabwe°
America, North	**2 138.7**	**2 161.3**	**2 250.4**	**2 353.4**	**2 482.9**	**2 612.6**	**2 716.0**	**2 851.6**	**2 790.1**	**2 953.4**	**Amérique du Nord**
Canada	152.3	162.2	175.2	195.7	209.6	211.5	202.7	215.7	224.8	238.9	Canada
Costa Rica	° 5.0	° 5.2	° 5.4	° 5.7	5.8	5.3	° 5.7	° 5.9	° 5.9	° 5.9	Costa Rica
Cuba	7.0	10.1	8.6	10.1	11.1	12.0	9.8	11.1	13.8	° 13.0	Cuba
Dominican Republic	1.0	1.4	1.5	1.6	2.5	2.5	2.5	3.0	° 3.0	° 3.0	Rép. dominicaine
El Salvador°	16.2	16.6	16.8	17.6	17.6	17.6	17.6	17.7	17.7	17.7	El Salvador°
Guatemala°	12.9	13.4	13.8	14.1	14.5	14.8	15.1	15.2	14.6	14.9	Guatemala°
Honduras°	8.0	8.1	8.1	8.1	8.1	8.2	8.2	8.3	8.3	8.3	Honduras°
Mexico	91.1	93.4	95.7	° 95.7	° 96.7	° 98.9	° 100.7	° 99.9	° 99.9	° 99.9	Mexique
Nicaragua°	16.2	16.6	16.3	15.1	7.3	7.5	7.9	8.1	8.1	8.1	Nicaragua°
United States	1 828.6	1 833.9	1 908.7	1 989.3	2 109.5	2 234.0	2 345.4	2 466.5	2 393.7	2 543.5	Etats–Unis
America, South	**458.7**	**461.9**	**457.1**	**453.1**	**463.0**	**450.5**	**450.2**	**457.4**	**413.2**	**430.0**	**Amérique du Sud**
Argentina	240.2	236.1	244.9	241.2	248.5	228.6	232.2	247.7	212.3	* 220.0	Argentine
Bolivia°	6.7	6.8	7.0	7.2	7.2	7.3	7.4	7.5	7.6	7.6	Bolivie°
Brazil°	54.4	55.4	56.4	57.5	58.0	58.0	59.1	59.1	59.1	59.1	Brésil°
Chile	15.4	18.5	17.4	18.2	19.5	23.5	21.5	19.0	18.2	18.7	Chili
Colombia°	39.0	42.0	42.7	43.5	44.2	45.0	46.5	47.2	48.0	49.5	Colombie°
Ecuador°	13.8	14.4	14.5	12.7	12.2	12.4	12.8	12.8	13.1	13.1	Equateur°
Peru	37.4	° 37.9	36.9	33.9	33.9	32.7	32.7	24.9	14.7	14.7	Pérou
Uruguay	° 8.2	° 8.2	° 8.2	* 10.9	11.5	14.9	10.0	* 10.0	11.1	° 15.2	Uruguay
Venezuela	43.6	42.6	29.0	* 28.0	* 28.0	* 28.0	* 28.0	* 29.0	* 29.0	° 32.0	Venezuela
Asia	**525.7**	**538.0**	**572.6**	**600.2**	**609.7**	**631.5**	**648.2**	**667.2**	**672.7**	**694.8**	**Asie**
Afghanistan°	8.7	8.9	9.1	9.3	9.3	9.7	9.9	10.2	10.2	10.2	Afghanistan°
Bangladesh	° 1.0	° 1.0	° 1.4	° 1.4	1.0	1.0	1.0	1.0	° 1.0	° 1.1	Bangladesh
Bhutan°	0.8	0.8	0.8	0.8	0.9	0.9	0.9	0.9	0.9	0.9	Bhoutan°
Burma°	13.4	14.3	14.7	16.6	17.1	19.6	22.6	27.6	35.1	35.1	Birmanie°
China	91.7	94.5	96.1	98.9	102.3	106.1	112.0	115.3	123.5	126.7	Chine
Cyprus	11.4	12.2	12.2	12.5	12.7	13.0	13.3	13.1	13.2	° 13.1	Chypre
Democratic Yemen°	3.2	3.3	3.3	3.3	3.3	3.4	3.4	3.4	3.4	3.4	Yémen démocratique°
Iran(Islamic Rep.of)°	86.8	89.1	98.5	98.4	98.9	101.2	101.8	103.8	104.4	106.4	Iran(Rép.islamique)°
Iraq°	37.0	35.9	35.9	40.5	36.2	32.1	32.6	33.1	33.6	32.9	Iraq°
Israel	46.2	48.7	53.7	55.0	51.6	56.2	60.1	62.8	64.2	° 65.7	Israël
Japan	57.0	60.7	66.4	67.4	65.9	71.2	66.7	67.8	69.3	68.5	Japon
Jordan°	1.7	2.6	2.6	2.8	2.8	2.8	2.9	2.9	2.9	3.0	Jordanie°
Lebanon°	4.3	[illegible]	6.3	8.3	10.7	10.8	10.6	10.9	10.3	10.8	Liban°
Mongolia°	0.8	0.8	0.8	0.9	0.9	0.8	0.8	0.7	0.8	0.7	Mongolie°
Oman°	0.3	0.3	0.3	0.3	0.3	0.3	0.3	0.3	0.3	0.3	Oman°
Syrian Arab Republic	34.6	30.2	33.3	45.4	52.3	57.5	60.6	61.1	° 47.1	° 61.3	Rép. arabe syrienne
Turkey°	113.5	116.7	123.4	124.4	129.1	130.4	134.0	137.0	137.0	139.0	Turquie°
Yemen°	13.4	13.6	13.7	13.9	14.3	14.6	14.9	15.2	15.4	15.5	Yémen°
Europe	**4 883.4**	**5 102.6**	**5 335.0**	**5 530.2**	**5 675.3**	**5 906.4**	**5 903.7**	**5 910.2**	**6 173.0**	**6 263.7**	**Europe**
EEC	**3 141.4**	**3 304.5**	**3 425.6**	**3 580.6**	**3 713.5**	**3 826.3**	**3 894.7**	**3 940.4**	**4 114.1**	**4 190.2**	**CEE**
Denmark	156.9	177.3	182.5	188.8	221.0	242.6	245.2	251.4	295.1	* 256.1	Danemark
France	970.0	1 023.0	1 063.0	1 117.0	1 150.0	1 163.0	1 176.0	1 207.0	1 245.0	1 275.0	France
Germany, Fed. Rep.	650.8	692.2	721.7	743.7	799.2	836.0	857.5	865.3	899.3	939.1	Allemagne, Rép. féd.
Greece	192.2	190.0	192.7	199.0	191.8	198.4	196.4	195.7	196.5	° 196.4	Grèce

For general note and footnotes, see end of table.

Voir la fin du tableau pour la remarque générale et les notes.

Cheese (Total production) (continued) – Fromage (Production totale) (suite)

Unit : Thousand metric tons

Unité : Milliers de tonnes métriques

Country or area	1976	1977	1978	1979	1980	1981	1982	1983	1984	1985	Pays ou zone
Ireland	49.0	53.4	49.7	58.0	49.3	54.2	57.3	53.3	54.0	76.0	Irlande
Italy	536.2	552.3	582.3	610.3	608.0	613.6	637.5	637.9	664.0	669.9	Italie
Netherlands	379.9	410.2	417.6	429.8	456.2	476.6	480.8	484.8	515.1	521.7	Pays–Bas
United Kingdom	206.3	206.0	216.0	234.0	238.0	242.0	244.0	245.0	245.0	256.0	Royaume–Uni
EFTA	**424.5**	**441.7**	**475.8**	**488.0**	**498.5**	**513.5**	**530.2**	**524.8**	**532.2**	**537.0**	**AELE**
Austria	81.5	86.5	90.4	90.7	91.8	97.6	101.9	101.1	100.3	100.4	Autriche
Finland	57.1	60.4	66.5	70.3	73.1	72.3	74.4	72.0	75.9	80.0	Finlande
Iceland	3.3	4.4	5.3	5.3	5.2	4.4	4.4	4.1	º 4.4	º 4.4	Islande
Norway	61.9	59.7	68.3	69.8	71.3	69.7	73.9	67.0	69.6	71.7	Norvège
Portugal	25.1	27.8	31.0	34.8	37.0	37.1	36.7	35.5	36.9	º 38.1	Portugal
Sweden	84.1	87.4	94.1	95.7	100.6	108.1	114.1	* 114.9	* 115.6	* 116.0	Suède
Switzerland	111.4	115.5	120.2	121.4	119.6	124.2	124.9	130.2	129.5	126.4	Suisse
East Europe	**1 031.2**	**1 053.5**	**1 111.8**	**1 137.2**	**1 137.9**	**1 207.3**	**1 151.6**	**1 106.0**	**1 152.5**	**1 164.3**	**Europe de l'est**
Albania	º 9.5	º 9.9	º 10.7	* 12.0	* 9.7	º 12.0	º 12.7	º 14.0	* 16.0	º 12.7	Albanie
Bulgaria	147.0	147.7	150.2	166.9	154.5	163.8	172.8	185.6	186.6	º 182.8	Bulgarie
Czechoslovakia	149.2	157.7	165.8	168.5	172.9	177.9	187.0	188.2	192.9	195.2	Tchécoslovaquie
German Dem. Rep.	195.5	200.2	205.5	206.7	210.0	213.3	222.6	225.2	240.3	º 248.2	Rép. dém. allemande
Hungary	51.3	55.4	60.6	64.2	67.5	72.0	75.4	77.8	82.0	80.9	Hongrie
Poland	352.8	348.3	385.6	380.8	400.0	443.3	358.8	314.2	327.7	346.0	Pologne
Romania	125.8	134.3	133.4	138.0	123.3	125.0	122.4	101.0	106.9	98.5	Roumanie
Other Europe	**244.5**	**256.0**	**276.4**	**280.8**	**278.4**	**308.9**	**274.4**	**293.5**	**324.2**	**320.1**	**Autre Europe**
Maltaº	0.1	0.1	0.1	0.0	0.1	0.1	0.1	0.1	0.1	0.1	Malteº
Spain	110.4	116.9	132.3	133.7	133.3	166.8	137.4	144.5	179.2	º 176.0	Espagne
Yugoslavia	134.0	139.0	144.0	147.0	145.0	142.0	137.0	149.0	º 145.0	º 144.0	Yougoslavie
USSR	**1 363.3**	**1 453.2**	**1 517.1**	**1 585.6**	**1 495.7**	**1 477.3**	**1 555.2**	**1 621.0**	**1 672.5**	**1 710.0**	**URSS**
Oceania	**217.4**	**184.6**	**196.4**	**232.1**	**259.9**	**221.0**	**265.2**	**272.4**	**270.3**	**279.0**	**Océanie**
Australia	112.6	103.5	115.6	141.8	154.2	136.7	153.3	158.0	161.1	159.0	Australie
New Zealand	104.8	81.0	80.7	90.3	105.7	84.3	111.9	114.4	109.3	120.0	Nouvelle–Zélande
Total	**9 923.1**	**10 242.2**	**10 675.4**	**11 105.9**	**11 352.1**	**11 664.0**	**11 966.6**	**12 212.6**	**12 431.7**	**12 767.5**	**Total**

General note.
Cheese made by coagulating animal milk either from a natural process or by addition of rennet or another curdling agent and then removing the whey. Curd and processed cheese are excluded. Includes non–industrial production. (SITC 02400–1).
Source: Food and Agriculture Organization of the United Nations (FAO), Rome.

Remarque générale.
Fromage résultant de la coagulation du lait animal soit par un procédé naturel soit par l'addition la caillebotte et les fromages fondus. Les données se rapportent à la production industrielle seulement.(CTCI02400–1).
Source: Organisation des Nations Unies pour l'agriculture(FAO), Rome.

Cheese (Industrial production) – Fromage (Production Industrielle)

Unit : Thousand metric tons

Unité : Milliers de tonnes métriques

Country or area	1976	1977	1978	1979	1980	1981	1982	1983	1984	1985	Pays ou zone
Africa	**163.4**	**163.0**	**163.3**	**155.4**	**162.4**	**165.2**	**172.5**	**164.1**	**165.4**	**165.7**	**Afrique**
Egypt	...	...	...	155.0	162.0	164.0	171.0	...	...	...	Egypte
Tunisia	...	...	...	0.4	0.4	1.2	1.5	1.1	2.4	2.7	Tunisie
America, North	**1 600.4**	**1 673.7**	**1 746.9**	**1 886.1**	**1 807.3**	**1 940.3**	**2 060.1**	**2 186.1**	**2 120.1**	**2 279.2**	**Amérique du Nord**
United States	...	...	...	1 886.1	1 807.3	1 940.3	2 060.1	2 186.1	2 120.1	2 279.2	Etats–Unis
America, South	**6.1**	**6.1**	**6.1**	**6.1**	**6.1**	**6.2**	**5.8**	**6.3**	**6.1**	**6.1**	**Amérique du Sud**
Colombia	...	...	...	...	...	6.2	5.8	6.3	...	...	Colombie
Asia	**101.6**	**107.2**	**115.4**	**117.9**	**113.8**	**124.2**	**121.1**	**121.7**	**128.1**	**129.1**	**Asie**
Israel	38.9	40.5	42.7	43.9	41.6	44.2	46.7	48.3	49.6	52.0	Israël
Japan	57.0	60.7	66.4	67.4	65.9	71.2	66.7	67.8	69.3	68.4	Japon
Turkey	...	...	...	...	6.3	8.9	7.7	5.6	9.1	8.7	Turquie
Europe	**2 769.2**	**2 871.1**	**2 984.7**	**3 102.5**	**3 194.7**	**3 310.2**	**3 415.4**	**3 463.1**	**3 594.5**	**3 678.5**	**Europe**
EEC	***2 226.8***	***2 319.1***	***2 411.9***	***2 513.4***	***2 599.0***	***2 693.6***	***2 772.8***	***2 805.1***	***2 905.7***	***2 993.6***	***CEE***
Belgium	...	...	...	41.0	43.9	47.4	49.4	41.9	42.2	50.4	Belgique
France	913.0	945.8	990.3	1 040.5	1 062.0	1 098.0	1 125.0	1 153.0	1 191.0	1 219.0	France
Germany, Fed. Rep	649.6	691.1	713.0	732.4	775.2	813.4	839.1	846.7	878.2	913.1	Allemagne, Rép. féd.
Greece	...	...	...	35.3	35.1	33.7	38.0	37.8	37.1	...	Grèce
Luxembourg	2.0	2.3	2.6	2.0	2.1	2.2	2.5	2.9	2.9	2.9	Luxembourg
Netherlands	...	...	...	...	...	457.4	474.7	477.7	507.9	514.4	Pays–Bas
United Kingdom	204.0	206.0	216.0	234.0	238.0	241.6	244.1	245.1	246.4	255.6	Royaume–Uni
EFTA	***89.0***	***87.0***	***95.6***	***91.3***	***95.5***	***104.4***	***106.5***	***95.9***	***99.5***	***93.8***	***AELE***
Norway	61.1	58.9	67.4	65.9	66.9	73.9	75.6	65.7	68.0	68.9	Norvège
Portugal	...	...	...	25.4	...	30.5	30.9	30.2	31.5	24.9	Portugal
East Europe	***409.8***	***421.1***	***432.9***	***453.4***	***453.3***	***465.5***	***492.1***	***520.6***	***541.5***	***541.9***	***Europe de l'est***
Bulgaria	100.2	103.2	105.6	120.2	109.3	117.3	123.6	134.1	135.4	129.5	Bulgarie
Czechoslovakia	95.5	99.0	103.5	105.6	108.7	113.2	120.2	123.1	126.8	128.2	Tchécoslovaquie
German Dem. Rep	92.4	93.2	96.9	99.7	103.6	104.7	108.1	109.6	114.5	121.0	Rép. dém. allemande
Hungary	...	...	...	35.8	38.0	41.7	44.6	47.3	49.5	50.1	Hongrie
Poland	93.2	94.6	93.2	92.0	93.8	88.5	95.7	106.5	115.3	113.0	Pologne
Other Europe	***43.5***	***43.9***	***44.3***	***44.4***	***47.0***	***46.7***	***44.0***	***41.5***	***47.9***	***49.1***	***Autre Europe***
Yugoslavia	...	...	...	44.4	47.0	46.7	44.0	41.5	47.9	49.1	Yougoslavie
USSR[1]	**568.1**	**601.8**	**631.1**	**638.1**	**622.5**	**627.9**	**668.4**	**712.7**	**751.3**	**784.1**	**URSS[1]**
Byelorussian SSR[1]	...	...	...	*36.1*	*36.8*	*36.3*	*39.3*	*42.6*	*46.9*	*49.2*	*RSS de Biélorussie[1]*
Ukrainian SSR	*125.6*	*134.7*	*144.8*	*150.5*	*130.4*	*134.3*	*138.6*	*154.0*	*163.1*	*169.7*	*RSS d'Ukraine*
Oceania	**104.8**	**81.0**	**78.3**	**90.3**	**105.7**	**84.3**	**111.9**	**114.4**	**109.3**	**118.4**	**Océanie**
New Zealand[2]	104.8	81.0	78.3	90.3	105.7	84.3	111.9	114.4	109.3	118.4	Nouvelle–Zélande[2]
Total	**5 313.6**	**5 503.9**	**5 725.9**	**5 996.5**	**6 012.6**	**6 258.3**	**6 555.2**	**6 768.3**	**6 874.7**	**7 161.3**	**Total**

General note.
Cheese made by coagulating animal milk either from a natural process or by addition of rennet or another curdling agent and then removing the whey. Curd and processed cheese are excluded. Data refer to industrial production only. (SITC 02400–1).

Remarque générale.
Fromage résultant de la coagulation du lait animal soit par un procédé naturel soit par l'addition la caillebotte et les fromages fondus. Les données se rapportent à la production industrielle seulement. (CTCI 02400–1).

[1] Including processed cheese containing not less than 20 per cent fat.

[2] Twelve months ending 31 May of year stated.

[1] Y compris les fromages fondus contenant moins de 20 p. 100 de matières grasses.

[2] Période de douze mois finissant le 31 mai de l'année indiquée.

Ice–cream – Crème glacée

Unit : Thousand kiloliters | Unité : Milliers de kiloliters

Country or area	1976	1977	1978	1979	1980	1981	1982	1983	1984	1985	Pays ou zone
Africa											**Afrique**
Egypt[1]	1.9	2.7	2.8	3.4	3.5	3.9	6.0	6.2	...	...	Egypte[1]
Ghana	1.5	2.6	2.9	2.1	2.1	2.1	0.6	0.4	0.7	0.1	Ghana
Kenya	0.7	0.7	0.8	0.7	0.5	0.6	0.4	0.3	0.6	0.6	Kenya
Liberia	...	...	...	0.8	0.2	0.1	0.1	...	...	...	Libéria
South Africa	...	...	...	...	* 47.1	50.7	55.8	* 56.2	57.3	57.2	Afrique du Sud
Tunisia	0.2	0.2	0.3	0.3	0.3	0.3	...	...	...	...	Tunisie
America, North											**Amérique du Nord**
Canada	279.6	291.2	287.6	307.7	311.9	311.4	...	...	...	...	Canada
Cuba	66.2	67.4	71.5	71.9	64.4	69.3	73.5	78.0	79.0	83.5	Cuba
Dominican Republic[1]	2.5	3.1	2.8	4.3	4.9	5.9	5.1	5.9	5.9	6.0	Rép. dominicaine[1]
Jamaica	11.1	11.2	10.0	9.0	5.4	8.8	9.9	...	...	...	Jamaïque
Panama	6.0	6.1	5.7	6.7	* 7.5	9.0	8.2	10.4	...	...	Panama
United States	3 097.4	3 065.6	3 086.5	3 070.3	3 141.1	3 151.2	3 225.3	3 336.9	3 385.8	3 412.3	Etats–Unis
America, South											**Amérique du Sud**
Bolivia[1]	0.5	0.3	0.7	0.7	1.2	0.9	0.5	0.6	1.4	1.5	Bolivie[1]
Brazil[1]	86.3	69.5	79.5	95.3	94.5	...	...	...	...	...	Brésil[1]
Chile	14.9	15.7	15.5	14.5	16.9	15.4	* 15.1	14.2	15.2	17.6	Chili
Colombia[1]	2.9	4.3	3.8	3.6	3.8	13.5	11.4	12.5	...	...	Colombie[1]
Ecuador	1.4	...	2.2	...	1.4	0.5	0.9	1.0	...	...	Equateur
Paraguay	0.9	1.0	1.1	1.3	1.5	1.7	1.9	2.0	2.0	2.1	Paraguay
Asia											**Asie**
India[2]	4.2	4.9	6.5	6.2	...	...	...	...	...	...	Inde[2]
Indonesia[1]	1.5	0.8	0.8	2.1	5.7	2.4	2.1	4.3	2.9	3.0	Indonésie[1]
Iran(Islamic Rep.of)[1]	7.5	8.6	10.0	9.9	7.4	8.6	9.4	8.2	...	...	Iran(Rép.islamique)[1]
Japan[3]	80.5	96.5	99.4	102.0	99.2	104.0	129.4	133.6	130.8	134.9	Japon[3]
Korea, Republic of	26.8	58.1	74.8	90.8	61.0	90.1	81.9	76.7	75.5	72.6	Corée, République de
Philippines	86.1	87.0	...	...	...	...	...	...	...	...	Philippines
Sri Lanka	1.0	1.2	1.9	2.4	2.1	1.7	...	...	...	...	Sri Lanka
Turkey[1]	0.5	0.2	0.3	0.2	0.2	0.3	0.4	0.4	0.5	0.6	Turquie[1]
Europe											**Europe**
EEC											***CEE***
Belgium	34.1	33.2	32.4	49.7	51.2	52.9	51.6	57.2	62.1	73.4	Belgique
Denmark	41.2	43.3	43.4	44.3	39.7	41.2	43.1	42.0	48.1	...	Danemark
France	123.4	111.9	136.1	150.5	154.0	174.2	192.2	197.4	192.2	192.9	France
Germany, Fed. Rep.[1]	175.8	153.8	182.1	180.0	189.6	186.8	182.0	178.9	165.5	172.7	Allemagne, Rép. féd.[1]
Greece[1]	16.4	18.8	20.4	18.2	20.8	20.6	22.6	18.3	17.3	17.0	Grèce[1]
Italy*	289.0	258.0	...	...	...	...	...	...	...	...	Italie*
Netherlands	...	...	28.8	25.0	24.3	23.3	30.6	27.9	32.5	...	Pays–Bas
United Kingdom	206.0	181.0	196.0	175.0	178.0	179.0	200.4	215.1	227.1	* 208.3	Royaume–Uni
EFTA											***AELE***
Finland[1]	12.2	15.2	25.0	29.0	30.1	33.6	35.7	36.0	32.2	...	Finlande[1]
Norway	33.3	34.4	34.8	33.7	35.1	40.8	35.0	34.6	20.4	22.7	Norvège
Portugal[1]	7.6	7.7	4.8	5.6	4.9	6.1	7.4	7.3	7.8	6.1	Portugal[1]
Sweden[1]	51.6	53.9	58.1	59.6	66.9	68.2	56.9	59.7	56.8	54.3	Suède[1]
East Europe											***Europe de l'est***
Czechoslovakia	35.6	35.6	34.8	36.8	35.9	35.4	41.4	40.3	40.8	43.4	Tchécoslovaquie
Hungary	2.5	2.0	3.8	2.9	2.6	3.9	4.4	4.3	4.2	3.2	Hongrie
Poland	29.6	25.8	26.6	25.9	24.9	17.8	16.8	20.0	21.3	18.9	Pologne
Other Europe											***Autre Europe***
Spain	20.6	20.6	25.2	91.5	94.7	95.1	105.0	113.0	...	...	Espagne
Yugoslavia[1]	7.3	8.2	9.3	15.0	13.5	14.6	16.7	17.4	14.7	17.7	Yougoslavie[1]
USSR[1]	470.9	477.6	478.6	491.2	506.1	522.0	535.1	550.4	565.4	587.3	**URSS[1]**
Byelorussian SSR[1]	*16.7*	*16.6*	*16.8*	*17.9*	*18.6*	*19.1*	*19.2*	*19.8*	*20.7*	*22.6*	*RSS de Biélorussie[1]*
Ukrainian SSR	*91.9*	*95.5*	*93.6*	*100.9*	*105.5*	*112.8*	*115.9*	*120.1*	*120.4*	*124.8*	*RSS d'Ukraine*

For general note and footnotes, see end of table.

Voir la fin du tableau pour la remarque générale et les notes.

Unit : Thousand kiloliters

Unité : Milliers de kiloliters

Country or area	1976	1977	1978	1979	1980	1981	1982	1983	1984	1985	Pays ou zone
Oceania											**Océanie**
Australia[4]	213.3	190.7	211.9	211.9	213.3	213.9	214.0	208.7	201.6	205.9	Australie[4]
Fiji	3.5	3.1	3.3	3.3	3.4	3.6	2.5	2.4	2.4	2.2	Fidji
New Zealand[4]	51.9	54.5	57.9	53.5	56.8	53.5	51.3	50.1	57.1	56.7	Nouvelle–Zélande[4]

General note.
Mixture containing 80 per cent cream and milk products, 15 per cent sweeteners and no less than 5 per cent butter fat, with some amounts of colour and flavour. (SITC 09909–1).

[1] In thousand metric tons.
[2] Production by large and medium scale establishments only.
[3] Milk fat content, 8 per cent.
[4] Twelve months ending 30 June of year stated.

Remarque générale.
Mélange contenant 80 p. 100 de crème et de produits laitiers, 15 p. 100 d'édulcorant avec au moins5 p. 100 de butyrine, ainsi qu'une certaine quantité de colorant et de parfum. (CTCI 09909–1).

[1] En milliers de tonnes métriques.
[2] Production des grandes et moyennes entreprises seulement.
[3] Teneur en matières graisses lactiques 8 p. 100.
[4] Période de douze mois finissant le 30 juin de l'année indiquée.

Fruits, dried – Fruits secs

Unit : Metric tons | Unité : Tonnes métriques

Country or area	1976	1977	1978	1979	1980	1981	1982	1983	1984	1985	Pays ou zone
America, North	**266 027**	**374 991**	**284 516**	**400 227**	**432 931**	**365 799**	**368 113**	**467 586**	**415 876**	**429 847**	**Amérique du Nord**
Canada[1 2]	4 077	5 222	...	...	...	...	...	...	...	...	Canada[1 2]
United States	261 950	369 769	279 867	395 578	428 282	361 150	363 464	462 937	411 227	425 198	Etats-Unis
America, South	**3 912**	**4 603**	**4 423**	**4 166**	**3 362**	**3 507**	**3 287**	**3 481**	**3 344**	**3 022**	**Amérique du Sud**
Brazil	3 331	4 022	3 842	[3] 3 585	2 781	...	...	...	...	...	Brésil
Colombia	...	...	...	...	...	454	387	734	750	...	Colombie
Asia	**152 087**	**136 679**	**77 947**	**74 551**	**99 835**	**99 182**	**97 649**	**112 562**	**138 804**	**112 274**	**Asie**
Afghanistan	35 100	40 400	# 7 833	10 204	6 141	5 024	6 100	6 134	5 800	1 920	Afghanistan
Turkey	116 987	96 279	70 114	64 347	93 694	94 158	91 549	106 428	133 004	110 354	Turquie
Europe	**234 250**	**177 291**	**192 420**	**167 148**	**157 191**	**60 896**	**172 535**	**182 901**	**238 419**	**170 065**	**Europe**
EEC	***192 806***	***141 908***	***168 255***	***143 357***	***140 926***	***40 566***	***151 239***	***160 210***	***212 628***	***139 099***	***CEE***
Denmark	113	107	87	87	85	110	115	105	101	75	Danemark
France[4]	26 200	6 100	22 200	24 700	17 800	28 700	35 400	25 200	38 900	25 700	France[4]
Greece[5]	166 493	135 701	145 968	118 570	123 041	11 756	115 724	134 905	173 627	...	Grèce[5]
EFTA	***17 680***	***18 364***	***9 145***	***8 765***	***1 245***	***1 666***	***3 082***	***2 216***	***5 191***	***2 958***	***AELE***
Finland	1	0	0	42	0	0	38	96	136	...	Finlande
Portugal	* 17 679	18 364	9 145	8 723	# 1 245	1 666	3 044	2 120	5 055	2 852	Portugal
East Europe	***3 049***	***3 732***	***2 077***	***3 410***	***3 192***	***3 557***	***3 228***	***2 978***	***2 274***	***4 235***	***Europe de l'est***
Bulgaria	2 239	3 252	1 654	2 873	2 903	3 268	2 257	2 533	1 910	3 629	Bulgarie
Hungary[6]	128	205	82	99	61	17	0	0	0	157	Hongrie[6]
Poland	682	275	341	438	228	272	971	445	364	449	Pologne
Other Europe	***20 715***	***13 287***	***12 943***	***11 616***	***11 828***	***15 107***	***14 986***	***17 497***	***18 326***	***23 773***	***Autre Europe***
Spain[7]	9 997	...	...	8 528	7 713	10 453	7 981	8 130	...	...	Espagne[7]
Yugoslavia	10 718	3 818	3 686	3 088	4 115	4 654	7 005	9 367	10 336	15 994	Yougoslavie
USSR	**33 178**	**51 400**	**45 500**	**52 510**	**39 592**	**36 495**	**38 790**	**56 452**	**56 951**	**61 180**	**URSS**
Byelorussian SSR	*9*	*5*	*59*	*59*	*19*	*84*	*29*	*32*	*8*	*117*	*RSS de Biélorussie*
Ukrainian SSR	*2 723*	*3 454*	*1 806*	*3 064*	*2 265*	*2 587*	*3 831*	*4 801*	*4 788*	*5 595*	*RSS d'Ukraine*
Total	**689 454**	**744 964**	**604 806**	**698 602**	**732 911**	**565 879**	**680 374**	**822 982**	**853 394**	**776 388**	**Total**

General note.
Fruits prepared either by direct drying in the sun or by industrial processes, whether or not containing added sugar. Drained, glace or crystallized fruit as well as dried citrus fruit are excluded. (SITC 05200-0).

1 Shipments.
2 Beginning 1978, data are confidential.
3 Production by establishments employing 5 or more persons.
4 Prunes only.
5 Pasteurized dried figs and raisins.
6 Including crystallised fruit.
7 Including dried vegetables.

Remarque générale.
Fruits séchés, soit par action directe du soleil, soit par des procédés industriels, avec ou sans addition de sucre. Cette rubrique ne comprend ni les fruits confits au sucre (égouttés, glacés ou candis) ni les agrumes séchés. (CTCI 05200-0).

1 Expéditions.
2 A partir de 1978, les données sont confidentielles.
3 Production des établissements occupant 5 personnes ou plus.
4 Pruneaux seulement.
5 Figues et raisins secs pasteurisés.
6 Y compris les fruits candis.
7 Y compris les légumes secs.

Jams, marmalades and fruit jellies
Confitures, marmelades et gelées de fruits

Unit : Thousand metric tons

Unité : Milliers de tonnes métriques

Country or area	1976	1977	1978	1979	1980	1981	1982	1983	1984	1985	Pays ou zone
Africa	**73.5**	**70.1**	**72.9**	**70.3**	**83.2**	**84.4**	**71.2**	**66.5**	**74.7**	**78.9**	**Afrique**
Algeria	...	8.5	12.7	14.1	14.3	14.7	6.9	...	...	...	Algérie
Egypt	9.3	10.7	11.0	12.1	16.9	18.8	24.8	15.7	...	...	Egypte
Kenya	0.9	1.1	1.0	0.9	1.2	0.9	0.8	0.7	0.8	1.0	Kenya
South Africa	...	...	...	39.0	* 45.1	45.3	33.2	32.4	33.4	35.4	Afrique du Sud
Tunisia	3.5	3.7	3.7	4.2	5.8	4.7	...	...	...	...	Tunisie
America, North	**55.8**	**43.5**	**56.1**	**55.4**	**52.9**	**54.4**	**54.9**	**55.4**	**54.8**	**57.1**	**Amérique du Nord**
Canada[1]	40.8	29.4	37.5	38.7	37.0	...	...	...	...	...	Canada[1]
Cuba[2]	14.7	13.7	18.3	16.3	15.3	16.7	16.7	17.0	16.2	18.2	Cuba[2]
Dominican Republic	...	...	0.3	0.4	0.6	0.5	0.9	0.9	0.9	1.0	Rép. dominicaine
El Salvador	0.2	0.2	0.0	0.0	0.0	0.0	0.0	...	...	...	El Salvador
America, South	**14.2**	**15.2**	**16.5**	**164.6**	**157.1**	**133.5**	**154.5**	**176.5**	**198.0**	**219.3**	**Amérique du Sud**
Brazil	[2] 7.9	[2] 7.7	[2] 8.2	# 156.9	148.7	...	...	...	...	...	Brésil
Chile[3]	...	...	...	...	...	4.4	4.3	5.4	5.9	6.2	Chili[3]
Ecuador	0.1	...	...	...	0.0	0.2	0.2	0.2	...	...	Equateur
Paraguay	0.3	0.6	0.1	0.1	0.1	0.0	0.1	0.0	...	...	Paraguay
Venezuela	4.2	4.7	5.4	4.3	...	...	...	...	...	...	Venezuela
Asia	**175.2**	**175.4**	**179.6**	**56.8**	**53.4**	**58.6**	**64.2**	**55.5**	**63.6**	**77.2**	**Asie**
Cyprus	0.3	0.3	0.4	0.4	0.5	0.8	0.9	0.5	0.4	0.5	Chypre
Indonesia	0.2	0.2	0.2	0.2	0.2	0.3	0.2	0.4	0.5	...	Indonésie
Iran(Islamic Rep.of)[4]	124.0	124.0	124.0	# 3.0	5.0	5.5	...	...	...	...	Iran(Rép.islamique)[4]
Japan	43.5	43.3	46.1	45.2	44.2	48.6	47.8	47.1	52.7	62.2	Japon
Mongolia	* 0.3	0.3	* 0.4	* 0.5	0.5	0.6	# 0.0	0.1	0.3	0.9	Mongolie
Philippines	1.0	0.9	...	...	...	...	...	...	...	...	Philippines
Sri Lanka	0.1	0.2	1.2	0.2	1.4	0.3	...	...	...	...	Sri Lanka
Turkey	5.8	6.2	6.4	6.5	0.7	1.5	3.4	2.5	4.6	8.0	Turquie
Europe	**1 051.0**	**1 077.4**	**1 115.5**	**1 096.3**	**1 151.6**	**1 157.4**	**1 201.7**	**1 159.5**	**1 221.0**	**1 303.0**	**Europe**
EEC	***686.8***	***693.9***	***700.0***	***650.0***	***680.2***	***691.5***	***716.8***	***702.3***	***735.0***	***779.7***	***CEE***
Belgium	17.4	16.2	19.6	17.9	19.1	19.5	20.9	19.7	24.1	18.9	Belgique
Denmark	24.0	22.5	23.2	23.5	17.8	22.5	24.5	27.8	25.8	26.4	Danemark
France	189.8	176.6	202.5	169.7	193.6	188.9	195.3	194.2	204.5	212.6	France
Germany, Fed. Rep.	173.4	176.2	174.3	166.2	178.9	178.6	187.2	184.6	195.6	234.0	Allemagne, Rép. féd.
Greece	9.3	10.6	10.6	6.8	11.9	10.7	10.7	9.3	9.0	...	Grèce
Ireland	[5] 11.0	[5] 14.2	12.6	11.9	12.5	13.1	13.5	11.7	12.5	13.2	Irlande
Italy* [5]	51.0	55.0	...	...	...	...	...	...	...	...	Italie* [5]
Netherlands	35.0	37.5	35.2	33.0	34.4	32.1	28.1	24.1	24.6	...	Pays-Bas
United Kingdom	176.0	185.0	169.0	168.0	159.0	173.0	183.6	177.9	186.0	* 188.3	Royaume-Uni
EFTA	***88.4***	***87.8***	***86.0***	***93.7***	***102.1***	***96.0***	***96.3***	***96.2***	***95.5***	***99.7***	***AELE***
Austria	17.3	18.7	18.5	19.0	16.9	18.0	18.8	15.8	16.9	16.5	Autriche
Finland	14.3	10.8	12.3	16.1	22.4	17.9	17.8	18.5	16.6	...	Finlande
Norway[6]	18.4	17.7	18.3	20.9	21.5	15.7	17.1	18.6	17.7	18.3	Norvège[6]
Portugal	3.0	4.8	4.5	4.4	3.9	4.6	5.3	5.4	6.1	4.7	Portugal
Sweden	35.4	35.8	32.4	33.3	37.4	39.8	37.2	37.9	38.3	40.1	Suède
East Europe	***216.2***	***216.3***	***237.2***	***242.8***	***235.1***	***237.8***	***231.8***	***211.8***	***220.3***	***233.1***	***Europe de l'est***
Bulgaria	31.6	28.2	35.8	37.6	27.2	27.2	21.8	21.6	21.9	23.2	Bulgarie
Czechoslovakia	24.4	27.4	29.5	31.6	29.8	30.0	29.3	29.4	27.3	29.9	Tchécoslovaquie
German Dem. Rep.	55.6	51.9	55.8	56.7	54.9	55.5	55.5	53.5	53.6	57.7	Rép. dém. allemande
Hungary	24.9	27.9	25.6	29.7	29.1	30.1	26.9	33.4	36.3	43.4	Hongrie
Poland	79.9	81.0	90.4	87.3	94.2	94.9	98.2	74.0	81.3	78.9	Pologne
Other Europe	***59.5***	***79.4***	***92.4***	***109.9***	***134.2***	***132.2***	***156.8***	***149.1***	***170.2***	***190.5***	***Autre Europe***
Spain	37.8	...	...	89.9	106.3	99.5	123.2	116.4	...	...	Espagne
Yugoslavia	21.7	20.7	22.0	19.9	27.9	32.7	33.6	32.7	30.1	38.7	Yougoslavie
USSR	**266.5**	**330.2**	**307.4**	**295.5**	**301.8**	**321.5**	**375.7**	**425.4**	**338.9**	**304.3**	**URSS**
Byelorussian SSR	*16.6*	*18.3*	*14.5*	*16.4*	*13.2*	*14.1*	*17.4*	*18.5*	*15.3*	*13.9*	*RSS de Biélorussie*
Ukrainian SSR	*54.2*	*68.4*	*63.7*	*59.0*	*57.2*	*67.9*	*79.9*	*89.0*	*73.5*	*73.0*	*RSS d'Ukraine*
Oceania	**36.0**	**33.6**	**33.1**	**34.9**	**27.9**	**34.0**	**37.6**	**36.7**	**35.1**	**36.6**	**Océanie**

For general note and footnotes, see end of table.

Voir la fin du tableau pour la remarque générale et les notes.

Jams, marmalades and fruit jellies (continued) – Confitures, marmelades et gelées de fruits (suite)

Unit : Thousand metric tons

Unité : Milliers de tonnes métriques

Country or area	1976	1977	1978	1979	1980	1981	1982	1983	1984	1985	Pays ou zone
Australia[7]	31.1	27.3	28.6	29.3	22.5	27.5	32.1	30.7	29.1	30.4	Australie[7]
New Zealand[7]	4.9	6.4	4.5	5.7	5.4	6.5	5.5	6.0	6.0	6.2	Nouvelle-Zélande[7]
Total	**1 672.2**	**1 745.4**	**1 781.2**	**1 773.9**	**1 828.0**	**1 843.8**	**1 959.8**	**1 975.5**	**1 986.2**	**2 076.4**	**Total**

General note.
Cooked preparations of fruits, whether or not containing added sugar, including jams made with vegetables or with products such as ginger. In terms of net weight. (SITC 05330-0).

1 Shipments.
2 Fruit jam only.
3 Mamalade only.
4 Including canned or bottled fruits.
5 Source: Industrial Statistics, Statistical Office of the European Communities, (Luxembourg).
6 Including compotes.
7 Twelve months ending 30 June of year stated.

Remarque générale.
Préparations de fruits obtenues par cuisson, avec ou sans addition de sucre, y compris les confitures faites de légumes ou d'autres ingrédients tels que le gingembre. Poids net. (CTCI 05530-0).

1 Expéditions.
2 Confitures de fruits seulement.
3 Marmelades seulement.
4 Y compris les conserves de fruits (en boîtes ou en bocaux).
5 Source: Statistiques industrielles, Office statistique des Communautés européennes, (Luxembourg).
6 Y compris les compotes.
7 Période de douze mois finissant le 30 juin de l'année indiquée.

Fruit and vegetable juices, concentrated, frozen or not – Jus concentrés de fruits et de légumes, congelés ou non

Unit : Thousand metric tons

Unité : Milliers de tonnes métriques

Country or area	1976	1977	1978	1979	1980	1981	1982	1983	1984	1985	Pays ou zone
Africa											**Afrique**
Algeria[1]	17.6	14.7	15.4	16.3	24.4	26.1	1.1	...	...	...	Algérie[1]
Kenya	4.1	3.4	0.5	0.9	0.9	0.2	0.3	0.3	0.3	0.1	Kenya
South Africa[2]	...	...	...	13.6	15.9	15.0	11.8	16.5	19.1	20.0	Afrique du Sud[2]
America, North											**Amérique du Nord**
Canada[3 4]	25.4	43.5	40.0	35.7	...	...	...	...	...	...	Canada[3 4]
Cuba	...	...	...	1.2	1.3	1.4	1.1	2.6	3.4	6.1	Cuba
Dominican Republic[1]	12.7	12.7	12.8	14.8	19.6	17.2	18.0	22.5	21.1	21.3	Rép. dominicaine[1]
El Salvador[2]	...	0.0	0.0	0.4	0.9	0.7	1.1	0.5	1.0	...	El Salvador[2]
United States[5]	925.4	861.3	860.2	917.0	1 164.1	956.0	832.7	888.9	618.5	724.5	Etats-Unis[5]
America, South											**Amérique du Sud**
Brazil[6]	...	199.6	264.1	314.8	350.8	381.3	359.5	...	...	...	Brésil[6]
Paraguay[2]	0.3	0.5	0.6	0.7	0.6	0.7	# 0.0	0.0	0.0	0.0	Paraguay[2]
Asia											**Asie**
Cyprus	0.6	0.7	1.4	1.8	1.1	1.0	1.6	2.1	2.0	3.0	Chypre
Democratic Yemen[1]	...	...	...	...	1.2	0.9	0.8	0.2	0.7	...	Yémen démocratique[1]
Indonesia	0.1	...	...	0.1	0.7	2.9	0.5	1.0	...	...	Indonésie
Iran(Islamic Rep.of)[7]	...	...	...	...	13.9	17.3	...	...	...	...	Iran(Rép.islamique)[7]
Philippines[3]	38.0	56.9	...	...	...	...	...	...	...	...	Philippines[3]
Sri Lanka	0.1	...	1.9	0.5	0.8	0.6	0.7	0.5	...	...	Sri Lanka
Turkey	18.4	10.8	18.1	16.7	2.6	13.2	14.7	16.7	17.2	15.9	Turquie
Europe											**Europe**
EEC											***CEE***
France	10.5	5.9	24.1	17.6	16.4	5.6	25.3	4.8	25.6	15.7	France
Germany, Fed. Rep.[2]	8.4	8.7	8.8	9.9	10.7	10.6	11.0	20.1	19.8	17.6	Allemagne, Rép. féd.[2]
Greece	19.3	18.0	12.5	13.2	33.4	36.2	28.8	31.5	22.8	...	Grèce
EFTA											***AELE***
Austria[2]	15.4	12.6	8.6	9.1	11.8	10.1	21.8	26.0	25.9	24.9	Autriche[2]
Finland[2]	3.0	1.4	7.9	11.1	12.0	11.3	6.8	4.7	4.4	...	Finlande[2]
East Europe											***Europe de l'est***
Czechoslovakia	180.8	168.0	177.7	187.4	172.9	175.1	152.3	195.2	167.6	146.6	Tchécoslovaquie
Hungary	48.1	69.1	47.3	68.6	59.0	51.2	52.8	58.1	50.2	59.6	Hongrie
Other Europe											***Autre Europe***
Yugoslavia	...	96.1	95.3	109.6	171.5	139.7	244.0	202.0	208.0	197.3	Yougoslavie
Oceania											**Océanie**
Australia[2 8 9]	33.7	77.8	84.1	36.7	51.9	49.8	46.9	34.2	37.5	52.8	Australie[2 8 9]

General note.
Unfermented juice of fruit or vegetables, concentrated or in the form of crystals or powder, whether or not containing added sugar (but not containing added alcohol) and whether or not intended for consumption as beverages. Unfermented grape juice is included. In terms of net weight. (SITC 05350-1).

1 Tomato paste only.
2 In thousand kilolitres.
3 Shipments.
4 Beginning 1980, data are confidential.
5 Frozen fruit juice only, concentrated and unconcentrated.
6 Fruit juices only.
7 Production by establishments employing 10 or more persons.
8 Natural fruit juices and tomato paste, puree etc.
9 Twelve months ending 30 June of year stated.

Remarque générale.
Jus non fermentés de fruits ou de légumes, concentrés ou sous forme de cristaux ou de poudre, additionnés ou non de sucre (mais sans addition d'alcool), qu'ils puissent ou non être employés comme boissons. Cette position comprend les moûts de raisins non fermentés. Poids net. (CTCI 05350-1).

1 Purée de tomate seulement.
2 En milliers de kilolitres.
3 Expéditions.
4 A partir de 1980, les données sont confidentielles.
5 Jus de fruits congelé seulement, concentré et non concentré.
6 Jus de fruits seulement.
7 Production des établissements occupant 10 personnes ou plus.
8 Jus de fruits et pâtes, purées, etc. de tomates, naturels.
9 Période de douze mois finissant le 30 juin de l'année indiquée.

Fruit and vegetable juices, unconcentrated, frozen or not – Jus non concentrés de fruits et de légumes, congelés ou non

Unit : Thousand metric tons — Unité : Milliers de tonnes métriques

Country or area	1976	1977	1978	1979	1980	1981	1982	1983	1984	1985	Pays ou zone
Africa											**Afrique**
Algeria[1]	13.3	14.2	17.2	15.8	13.5	16.7	12.3	...	...	...	Algérie[1]
Côte d'Ivoire[2]	14.0	12.4	13.8	16.8	22.8	27.8	2.4	9.1	8.8	* 10.0	Côte d'Ivoire[2]
Kenya	3.1	3.0	6.4	3.7	3.6	3.3	3.5	1.6	1.5	3.6	Kenya
Libyan Arab Jamah.[3]	19.7	5.7	4.4	18.6	19.2	21.7	31.2	40.6	...	...	Jamah.arabe libyenne[3]
Tunisia	0.4	0.5	0.3	0.2	0.2	0.1	...	...	...	...	Tunisie
America, North											**Amérique du Nord**
Canada[4]	395.1	388.7	368.9	382.2	409.8	...	...	...	...	...	Canada[4]
Cuba	...	...	...	...	...	14.3	6.5	18.0	21.0	21.3	Cuba
Dominican Republic[5]	5.5	9.0	10.5	14.5	24.9	28.8	23.9	23.7	25.1	26.3	Rép. dominicaine[5]
Martinique[2]	1.6	1.0	0.6	0.7	0.7	0.5	0.5	1.0	...	...	Martinique[2]
Mexico[5]	60.2	59.5	60.6	67.0	76.3	84.4	111.2	107.4	97.2	111.6	Mexique[5]
Panama[5]	8.5	8.1	10.1	10.4	9.0	7.8	7.7	9.1	5.9	...	Panama[5]
Trinidad and Tobago	15.0	3.4	3.8	6.9	6.7	4.3	...	2.9	3.3	6.1	Trinité-et-Tobago
United States[6]	2 319.9	2 253.6	2 464.5	2 351.1	2 430.7	1 208.0	1 080.5	993.2	879.6	813.5	Etats-Unis[6]
America, South											**Amérique du Sud**
Bolivia	0.0	0.3	0.1	0.2	0.2	0.2	0.1	0.1	0.2	0.2	Bolivie
Brazil[7 8 9]	...	199.6	264.1	313.4	340.0	...	...	...	...	...	Brésil[7 8 9]
Colombia[5 8]	8.9	12.1	11.3	12.4	7.2	5.2	6.2	5.0	...	...	Colombie[5 8]
Asia											**Asie**
Cyprus	3.4	5.9	5.7	6.5	8.5	6.3	6.9	8.2	9.2	11.8	Chypre
Japan[10]	454.0	602.6	572.0	766.2	...	...	...	...	...	...	Japon[10]
Korea, Republic of	0.9	...	...	...	...	...	...	...	...	...	Corée, République de
Malaysia[2 11 12]	1.4	1.9	2.1	1.2	2.8	2.5	2.2	2.0	1.6	1.2	Malaisie[2 11 12]
Sri Lanka	...	0.2	0.2	0.3	0.3	...	...	...	...	...	Sri Lanka
Turkey	46.1	55.7	36.5	32.2	30.0	27.0	20.2	25.4	23.0	17.6	Turquie
Europe											**Europe**
EEC											***CEE***
Denmark[1 8]	85.8	98.4	87.7	89.9	92.2	103.9	62.6	77.3	68.1	...	Danemark[1 8]
France[8]	84.4	77.8	97.1	118.0	120.8	124.2	116.9	126.9	132.7	126.5	France[8]
Germany, Fed. Rep.[8]	819.3	764.5	845.6	1 035.4	1 239.4	1 552.2	1 631.8	1 716.3	1 732.7	1 863.2	Allemagne, Rép. féd.[8]
Greece	8.8	8.4	7.3	5.6	27.8	25.4	28.1	34.4	28.4	...	Grèce
EFTA											***AELE***
Austria[8]	29.3	33.0	54.5	54.9	64.9	77.4	50.5	76.2	88.7	60.1	Autriche[8]
Finland[8]	48.4	51.9	39.6	54.9	81.6	62.7	55.9	44.5	30.4	...	Finlande[8]
Iceland[8]	2.1	2.1	2.0	2.0	2.8	3.6	4.3	5.5	6.6	...	Islande[8]
Norway[5 8]	39.3	45.0	48.0	59.2	63.8	41.6	43.2	54.5	43.0	...	Norvège[5 8]
Portugal[8]	9.1	11.3	13.4	13.1	16.0	20.5	19.7	23.9	20.4	19.3	Portugal[8]
Sweden[5 8]	133.0	125.0	133.0	128.4	124.9	125.1	120.3	110.3	103.4	97.8	Suède[5 8]
Switzerland[13 14]	11.1	12.0	* 11.5	* 10.7	* 10.0	* 9.4	* 9.1	* 10.3	...	...	Suisse[13 14]
East Europe											***Europe de l'est***
Bulgaria[7]	64.6	76.1	85.7	92.2	105.6	104.9	99.6	130.7	104.9	98.9	Bulgarie[7]
Czechoslovakia[8]	30.6	34.3	33.7	39.4	38.2	42.5	47.8	54.0	49.8	29.9	Tchécoslovaquie[8]
German Dem. Rep.[15]	77.0	99.6	106.5	114.6	125.2	139.4	151.4	166.9	159.5	193.1	Rép. dém. allemande[15]
Hungary	4.6	5.2	6.1	9.2	13.3	16.6	23.4	29.6	35.8	35.1	Hongrie
Poland	98.4	98.7	89.1	94.7	100.0	83.7	131.2	153.9	147.6	145.2	Pologne
Other Europe											***Autre Europe***
Spain[5]	106.2	...	...	129.1	167.1	136.7	115.5	154.4	...	...	Espagne[5]
Yugoslavia[5]	73.9	96.1	95.3	109.1	171.5	139.7	244.0	202.0	208.0	197.3	Yougoslavie[5]
USSR[5]	1 123.7	1 240.4	1 037.6	1 258.1	1 117.4	1 353.2	1 438.8	1 554.2	1 397.1	1 471.3	**URSS[5]**
Byelorussian SSR[5]	*56.1*	*55.9*	*55.9*	*45.9*	*44.9*	*55.1*	*34.8*	*33.3*	*34.2*	*39.5*	*RSS de Biélorussie[5]*
Ukrainian SSR[5]	*307.9*	*327.7*	*266.9*	*357.8*	*251.7*	*337.1*	*351.3*	*355.5*	*344.6*	*332.7*	*RSS d'Ukraine[5]*
Oceania											**Océanie**
Australia[8 16 17]	203.4	221.4	263.1	202.0	267.7	227.7	250.1	206.7	228.3	333.5	Australie[8 16 17]

For general note and footnotes, see end of table.

Voir la fin du tableau pour la remarque générale et les notes.

General note.
Unfermented juice of fruit or vegetables presented in liquid form, whether or not containing added sugar (but not containing added alcohol) and whether or not intended for consumption as beverages. Unfermented grape juice is included. In terms of net weight. (SITC 05350–2).

[1] Including concentrated fruit juices.
[2] Pineapple juice only.
[3] Including tomato paste.
[4] Shipments.
[5] Including concentrated fruit and vegetable juices.
[6] Fruit and tomato juices, not frozen, concentrated and unconcentrated.
[7] Fruit juices only.
[8] In thousand kilolitres.
[9] Production by main establishments only.
[10] Pure and mixed tomato juices.
[11] Data refer to Peninsular Malaysia only.
[12] Beginning 1982, scope of series revised.
[13] Sales.
[14] Grape juice only.
[15] Pasteurized fruit juice and drinkable fruit juice.
[16] Single strength natural fruit juice and tomato juice.
[17] Twelve months ending 30 June of year stated.

Remarque générale.
Jus non fermentés de fruits ou de légumes se présentant sous forme liquide, additionnés ou non de sucre (mais sans addition d'alcool), qu'ils puissent ou non être employés comme boissons. Cette position comprend les moûts de raisins non fermentés. Poids net. (CTCI 05350–2).

[1] Y compris les jus concentrés de fruits.
[2] Jus d'ananas seulement.
[3] Y compris la purée de tomate.
[4] Expéditions.
[5] Y compris les jus concentrés de fruits et de légumes.
[6] Jus de fruits et de tomate, non congelés, concentrés et non concentrés.
[7] Jus de fruits seulement.
[8] En milliers de kilolitres.
[9] Production des principaux établissements seulement.
[10] Jus de tomate purs et mélangés.
[11] Données se rapportant à la Malaisie péninsulaire seulement.
[12] A partir de 1982, portée de la série révisée.
[13] Ventes.
[14] Jus de raisin seulement.
[15] Jus de fruits pasteurisés et jus de fruits buvables.
[16] Jus de fruits et jus de tomate naturels de concentration originale.
[17] Période de douze mois finissant le 30 juin de l'année indiquée.

Fruits, frozen – Fruits congelés

Unit : Metric tons

Unité : Tonnes métriques

Country or area	1976	1977	1978	1979	1980	1981	1982	1983	1984	1985	Pays ou zone
America, North	**310 602**	**339 645**	**277 802**	**295 123**	**331 486**	**315 281**	**381 047**	**340 903**	**363 473**	**374 988**	**Amérique du Nord**
Canada	17 388	15 053	18 500	* 21 590	24 630	...	...	...	...	...	Canada
Mexico	6 317	12 793	13 183	12 808	10 433	5 718	2 396	2 617	916	1 132	Mexique
United States	286 897	311 799	246 119	260 725	296 423	283 858	350 854	308 398	330 578	339 786	Etats–Unis
Europe	**191 816**	**182 682**	**212 528**	**198 235**	**196 972**	**188 640**	**214 787**	**257 435**	**257 061**	**281 796**	**Europe**
EEC	***43 077***	***36 318***	***45 842***	***35 541***	***35 113***	***35 604***	***45 978***	***48 430***	***49 811***	***54 174***	***CEE***
Denmark	1 071	859	931	1 152	907	* 850	817	871	1 259	927	Danemark
France[1]	21 682	16 659	21 911	15 789	17 576	17 144	20 576	25 979	27 363	31 825	France[1]
Netherlands	12 624	8 800	11 000	7 600	8 630	5 610	13 020	9 600	...	...	Pays–Bas
United Kingdom[2]	7 700	10 000	12 000	11 000	8 000	12 000	...	...	...	...	Royaume–Uni[2]
EFTA	***6 280***	***7 176***	***7 155***	***5 423***	***5 932***	***5 384***	***6 060***	***8 974***	***11 877***	***10 298***	***AELE***
Austria	820	1 023	859	1 305	...	...	...	...	...	...	Autriche
Finland	1 593	2 158	3 812	879	1 288	1 451	1 634	2 151	1 072	...	Finlande
Portugal	16	60	60	127	609	920	812	1 317	5 972	...	Portugal
Sweden	3 851	3 935	2 424	3 112	3 034	2 012	2 613	4 505	3 832	4 416	Suède
East Europe	***132 684***	***129 927***	***147 314***	***144 037***	***142 954***	***129 038***	***140 542***	***158 729***	***161 527***	***186 713***	***Europe de l'est***
Bulgaria	2 225	1 829	2 615	2 728	2 784	3 796	2 239	2 256	2 947	4 934	Bulgarie
Czechoslovakia	15 379	16 727	16 648	19 330	18 127	14 425	18 985	17 950	17 844	18 353	Tchécoslovaquie
German Dem. Rep.	3 616	1 485	1 539	4 279	2 306	704	3 870	3 130	660	3 273	Rép. dém. allemande
Hungary	18 790	21 541	28 515	25 158	34 082	23 793	24 841	20 096	19 615	15 803	Hongrie
Poland	92 674	88 345	97 997	92 542	85 655	86 320	90 607	115 297	120 461	144 350	Pologne
Other Europe	***9 775***	***9 261***	***12 217***	***13 234***	***12 973***	***18 614***	***22 207***	***41 302***	***33 846***	***30 611***	***Autre Europe***
Spain	2 403	...	...	...	...	...	...	...	...	...	Espagne
Yugoslavia	7 372	6 858	9 814	10 831	10 570	16 211	19 804	38 899	31 443	28 208	Yougoslavie
Oceania	**2**	**56**	**47**	**128**	**58**	**58**	**58**	**58**	**58**	**58**	**Océanie**
New Zealand[3]	2	56	47	128	...	...	...	...	...	...	Nouvelle–Zélande[3]
Total	**502 420**	**522 383**	**490 377**	**493 486**	**528 516**	**503 979**	**595 892**	**598 396**	**620 592**	**656 842**	**Total**

General note.
Fruits, whether or not cooked, frozen by ordinary refrigeration or by the "quick–freezing" process. (SITC 05361 and 05362).

[1] Comprising frozen fruits for immediate consumption and for further transformation.
[2] Data refer to 53–week period.
[3] Twelve months ending 30 June of year stated.

Remarque générale.
Fruits, cuits ou non, congelés ou surgelés. (CTCI 05361 et 05362).

[1] Y compris les fruits surgelés destinés à la consommation immédiate et les fruits surgelés destinés à une transformation ultérieure.
[2] Données se rapportant à une période de 53 semaines.
[3] Période de douze mois finissant le 30 juin de l'année indiquée.

Fruits, tinned or bottled – Fruits en boîtes ou en bocaux

Unit : Thousand metric tons | Unité : Milliers de tonnes métriques

Country or area	1976	1977	1978	1979	1980	1981	1982	1983	1984	1985	Pays ou zone
Africa	**404.5**	**405.5**	**473.6**	**466.3**	**470.3**	**426.0**	**422.2**	**393.3**	**414.5**	**435.6**	**Afrique**
Algeria	6.0	8.1	12.3	...	...	...	...	...	...	...	Algérie
Côte d'Ivoire	59.6	52.1	73.3	65.3	56.3	73.2	72.0	15.0	15.0	15.0	Côte d'Ivoire
Egypt	19.2	20.1	25.9	17.0	5.0	...	3.2	...	...	...	Egypte
Kenya	42.2	54.8	67.4	51.2	49.8	46.6	94.2	132.6	149.3	156.4	Kenya
South Africa	273.9	264.8	290.6	320.0	341.7	287.2	239.8	229.3	236.5	248.1	Afrique du Sud
Tunisia	3.7	5.6	4.1	4.0	8.6	1.3	...	...	...	...	Tunisie
America, North	**1 750.6**	**1 839.5**	**1 672.0**	**1 931.1**	**1 958.5**	**1 265.4**	**1 048.9**	**933.2**	**1 132.6**	**1 172.2**	**Amérique du Nord**
Canada[1]	57.3	53.4	55.5	60.6	61.7	...	...	...	...	...	Canada[1]
Cuba	49.9	57.3	51.7	55.2	69.9	79.6	76.8	100.1	99.4	107.1	Cuba
Martinique[2]	8.6	5.5	8.9	14.5	17.6	19.4	21.0	20.0	...	...	Martinique[2]
Mexico[3]	18.3	18.5	16.1	11.2	10.2	6.2	4.1	5.2	8.8	14.1	Mexique[3]
United States[4]	1 616.6	1 704.8	1 539.8	1 789.7	1 799.0	1 097.7	882.8	742.3	932.4	955.1	Etats–Unis[4]
America, South	**54.0**	**77.4**	**71.7**	**67.9**	**67.2**	**75.1**	**68.6**	**71.7**	**74.7**	**74.6**	**Amérique du Sud**
Bolivia	0.6	0.7	0.7	0.8	0.6	0.3	0.3	0.3	0.1	0.2	Bolivie
Brazil	42.5	62.8	55.3	[5] 51.0	46.2	...	...	...	...	...	Brésil
Chile	...	...	...	9.1	13.9	18.9	13.7	17.0	20.9	21.3	Chili
Colombia	1.1	1.4	1.5	1.1	1.7	0.5	0.4	0.7	...	...	Colombie
Paraguay	0.0	0.6	0.4	0.9	0.5	1.0	0.1	0.0	0.0	0.0	Paraguay
Venezuela	3.7	4.2	4.4	4.9	...	...	...	...	...	...	Venezuela
Asia	**848.7**	**1 312.7**	**863.2**	**679.3**	**676.9**	**850.1**	**836.1**	**853.5**	**812.5**	**794.3**	**Asie**
Afghanistan	...	0.1	1.3	2.2	1.0	0.9	1.2	1.0	0.4	1.0	Afghanistan
Burma[6]	0.5	0.2	0.1	0.1	0.1	0.0	0.0	0.1	0.1	0.0	Birmanie[6]
Cyprus	4.3	5.7	5.3	3.5	2.8	3.4	4.7	5.7	7.3	6.3	Chypre
Iran(Islamic Rep.of)[7]	...	...	...	18.7	19.0	16.8	...	...	...	...	Iran(Rép.islamique)[7]
Japan	362.9	374.1	343.4	359.3	359.6	344.3	323.7	326.5	291.2	263.5	Japon
Malaysia[8 9 10]	46.9	47.5	50.4	48.2	43.0	36.3	38.5	39.1	42.2	43.8	Malaisie[8 9 10]
Philippines[1]	79.8	141.1	...	...	...	...	...	...	...	...	Philippines[1]
Sri Lanka	0.3	0.4	0.2	...	1.4	1.7	...	...	...	...	Sri Lanka
Syrian Arab Republic[11]	10.3	7.3	9.7	9.4	9.8	11.6	13.3	26.1	16.2	24.3	Rép. arabe syrienne[11]
Thailand	...	715.6	...	124.8	128.0	...	...	...	...	...	Thaïlande
Turkey	1.8	2.4	1.5	1.7	...	...	...	...	...	...	Turquie
Europe	**1 628.3**	**1 409.8**	**1 532.2**	**1 569.0**	**1 544.6**	**1 438.6**	**1 584.4**	**1 725.5**	**1 610.1**	**1 596.6**	**Europe**
EEC	***720.1***	***604.6***	***674.2***	***713.5***	***680.1***	***643.2***	***728.9***	***740.8***	***754.6***	***733.9***	***CEE***
Belgium	36.9	33.8	35.1	33.1	33.4	37.7	35.3	36.3	35.8	35.6	Belgique
Denmark	3.5	3.4	1.6	2.4	1.2	3.3	1.7	4.0	6.7	...	Danemark
France[12]	72.5	50.4	73.8	79.2	74.8	* 78.0	111.4	121.2	123.7	118.1	France[12]
Germany, Fed. Rep.	159.2	116.1	133.0	136.8	130.4	116.0	153.6	148.2	129.2	126.1	Allemagne, Rép. féd.
Greece	133.7	133.0	136.1	170.4	174.6	143.9	152.5	153.6	181.7	...	Grèce
Italy* [13]	130.0	...	...	...	...	...	...	...	...	...	Italie* [13]
Netherlands[13]	124.3	86.9	...	...	...	...	...	...	...	...	Pays–Bas[13]
United Kingdom[14]	60.0	51.0	59.0	56.0	30.0	# 28.7	38.7	41.9	42.0	39.1	Royaume–Uni[14]
EFTA	***109.0***	***113.8***	***120.7***	***111.1***	***92.3***	***103.5***	***103.8***	***109.3***	***137.5***	***105.2***	***AELE***
Austria	4.9	4.5	4.8	4.0	3.7	3.4	5.3	4.0	3.9	3.8	Autriche
Portugal	103.1	108.4	115.2	106.4	87.7	99.4	98.0	104.6	133.1	100.6	Portugal
Sweden	1.0	1.0	0.7	0.7	0.9	0.7	0.6	0.7	0.6	0.7	Suède
East Europe	***597.1***	***506.8***	***550.8***	***549.2***	***554.4***	***471.4***	***537.1***	***574.1***	***527.4***	***541.2***	***Europe de l'est***
Bulgaria[15]	70.2	59.0	62.3	63.8	59.9	77.0	58.6	117.8	87.7	90.8	Bulgarie[15]
Czechoslovakia	75.7	51.5	51.0	52.5	73.6	36.2	64.8	67.6	70.8	56.7	Tchécoslovaquie
German Dem. Rep.	63.0	28.7	40.7	70.4	59.2	37.4	68.8	62.5	59.8	75.1	Rép. dém. allemande
Hungary	95.8	96.3	108.5	106.2	107.5	112.4	101.4	108.0	103.5	98.8	Hongrie
Poland	81.4	40.3	51.4	40.3	59.2	32.4	49.6	44.3	51.7	56.8	Pologne
Romania[16]	211.0	231.0	237.0	216.0	195.0	176.0	194.0	174.0	154.0	163.0	Roumanie[16]
Other Europe	***202.0***	***184.6***	***186.5***	***195.2***	***217.8***	***220.5***	***214.5***	***301.3***	***190.5***	***216.3***	***Autre Europe***
Malta	0.0	0.2	0.1	0.1	0.1	0.2	0.2	0.3	0.2	...	Malte
Spain	116.8	...	...	125.0	126.7	113.2	110.8	164.5	* 76.0	...	Espagne
Yugoslavia	85.2	60.6	63.9	70.1	91.0	107.1	103.5	136.5	114.3	102.4	Yougoslavie
USSR	**388.8**	**395.7**	**381.4**	**364.1**	**392.6**	**399.1**	**568.5**	**609.7**	**589.6**	**644.4**	**URSS**

For general note and footnotes, see end of table. | Voir la fin du tableau pour la remarque générale et les notes.

Fruits, tinned or bottled (continued) – Fruits en boîtes ou en bocaux (suite)

Unit : Thousand metric tons

Unité : Milliers de tonnes métriques

Country or area	1976	1977	1978	1979	1980	1981	1982	1983	1984	1985	Pays ou zone
Byelorussian SSR	*12.7*	*10.9*	*10.5*	*6.5*	*7.1*	*14.4*	*33.4*	*37.3*	*32.7*	*40.3*	*RSS de Biélorussie*
Ukrainian SSR	*70.2*	*79.1*	*71.4*	*60.3*	*79.0*	*55.8*	*133.9*	*159.0*	*190.8*	*187.0*	*RSS d'Ukraine*
Oceania	**206.5**	**198.5**	**196.5**	**227.5**	**249.2**	**241.8**	**225.9**	**179.7**	**181.7**	**185.8**	**Océanie**
Australia [17]	186.5	182.8	182.4	210.7	228.5	217.7	204.4	161.2	152.9	166.0	Australie [17]
New Zealand [17 18]	20.0	15.7	14.1	16.8	20.7	24.1	21.5	18.5	28.8	19.8	Nouvelle-Zélande [17 18]
Total	**5 281.5**	**5 639.0**	**5 190.7**	**5 305.2**	**5 359.1**	**4 696.2**	**4 754.6**	**4 766.5**	**4 815.6**	**4 903.4**	**Total**

General note.
Fruits preserved in syrup, in water, in chemicals or in alcohol, and put in hermetically-sealed containers or bottles. In terms of net weight. (SITC 05390-1).

1 Shipments.
2 Pineapple only.
3 Including fruit and vegetable juices.
4 Canned fruits only.
5 Production by establishments employing 5 or more persons.
6 Twelve months ending 31 March of year stated.
7 Production by establishments employing 10 or more persons.
8 Data refer to Peninsular Malaysia only.
9 Canned pineapple only.
10 Beginning 1982, scope of series revised.
11 Including canned vegetables.
12 Fruits preserved in natural state and in syrup.
13 Source: Industrial Statistics, Statistical Office of the European Communities, (Luxembourg).
14 Beginning 1980, scope of series revised.
15 Excluding marinated and cocktail fruits.
16 Including jams, marmalades and fruit jellies.
17 Twelve months ending 30 June of year stated.
18 Including dehydrated fruits.

Remarque générale.
Fruits conservés dans le sirop, l'eau, les produits chimiques ou l'alcool et contenus dans des récipients ou des bocaux fermés hermétiquement. Poids net. (CTCI 05390-1).

1 Expéditions.
2 Ananas seulement.
3 Y compris les jus de fruits et de légumes.
4 Conserves de fruits seulement.
5 Production des établissements occupant 5 personnes ou plus.
6 Période de douze mois finissant le 31 mars de l'année indiquée.
7 Production des établissements occupant 10 personnes ou plus.
8 Données se rapportant à la Malaisie péninsulaire seulement.
9 Conserves d'ananas seulement.
10 A partir de 1982, portée de la série révisée.
11 Y compris les conserves de légumes.
12 Conserves de fruits au sirop et au naturel.
13 Source: Statistiques industrielles, Office statistique des Communautés européennes, (Luxembourg).
14 A partir de 1980, portée de la série révisée.
15 Non compris les fruits marinés et les fruits pour cocktails.
16 Y compris les confitures, marmelades et gelées de fruits.
17 Période de douze mois finissant le 30 juin de l'année indiquée.
18 Y compris les fruits deshydratés.

Unit : Thousand metric tons — Unité : Milliers de tonnes métriques

Country or area	1976	1977	1978	1979	1980	1981	1982	1983	1984	1985	Pays ou zone
America, North	**2 745.4**	**3 170.6**	**3 272.0**	**3 414.6**	**3 139.8**	**3 458.7**	**3 712.2**	**3 541.0**	**3 780.2**	**4 037.8**	**Amérique du Nord**
Canada[1,2]	254.6	337.5	...	...	...	...	...	...	...	...	Canada[1,2]
United States[3]	2 490.7	2 833.1	2 975.9	3 118.6	2 843.7	3 162.6	3 416.2	3 244.9	3 484.1	3 741.7	Etats–Unis[3]
Asia	**60.0**	**83.4**	**77.8**	**80.8**	**76.1**	**83.0**	**85.0**	**86.8**	**99.4**	**94.8**	**Asie**
Japan	60.0	83.4	77.8	80.8	76.1	83.0	85.0	86.8	99.4	94.8	Japon
Europe	**858.7**	**1 037.1**	**1 066.7**	**1 199.6**	**1 213.7**	**1 327.4**	**1 454.7**	**1 474.5**	**1 625.5**	**1 807.0**	**Europe**
EEC	***612.5***	***746.2***	***754.2***	***856.4***	***871.1***	***938.8***	***1 086.2***	***1 090.3***	***1 173.6***	***1 333.7***	***CEE***
Belgium	34.5	49.0	43.2	64.5	74.1	105.0	155.0	165.8	181.4	242.3	Belgique
Denmark	21.1	24.1	24.7	27.7	30.9	33.4	44.5	54.5	43.4	39.4	Danemark
France[4]	90.3	136.0	141.6	141.0	119.0	143.2	171.4	156.7	181.7	231.2	France[4]
Germany, Fed. Rep.[5]	95.5	99.9	84.0	97.5	97.3	99.5	91.5	77.7	95.1	104.0	Allemagne, Rép. féd.[5]
Greece	3.3	3.0	6.7	7.0	8.0	7.1	7.5	8.2	7.2	...	Grèce
Netherlands	59.7	78.2	67.0	60.6	66.8	85.8	86.9	63.3	66.1	...	Pays–Bas
United Kingdom	308.0	356.0	387.0	458.0	475.0	465.0	...	...	...	...	Royaume–Uni
EFTA	***80.0***	***81.9***	***85.3***	***93.3***	***90.4***	***93.0***	***95.0***	***93.1***	***116.5***	***111.6***	***AELE***
Finland	10.2	10.5	13.0	18.0	17.1	17.0	23.8	24.6	22.8	...	Finlande
Norway	10.3	...	18.8	13.8	17.1	15.4	16.9	14.7	19.3	15.6	Norvège
Portugal	5.3	0.9	2.2	9.6	7.0	2.2	2.4	3.5	9.1	6.3	Portugal
Sweden	54.3	56.4	51.4	51.8	49.2	58.5	52.0	50.3	65.4	62.9	Suède
East Europe	***143.9***	***177.0***	***183.7***	***187.6***	***188.4***	***226.7***	***196.6***	***186.4***	***215.3***	***234.9***	***Europe de l'est***
Bulgaria	10.7	11.6	14.6	12.9	12.3	14.4	13.7	12.4	13.3	11.7	Bulgarie
Czechoslovakia	16.8	20.9	22.9	19.6	22.1	25.4	27.1	25.2	28.4	30.8	Tchécoslovaquie
German Dem. Rep.	22.5	29.6	27.5	27.6	29.5	33.2	30.0	30.7	32.4	38.4	Rép. dém. allemande
Hungary	42.6	51.2	48.2	48.4	58.5	56.2	55.7	51.4	66.8	65.2	Hongrie
Poland	51.2	63.7	70.5	79.1	66.0	97.4	70.0	66.8	74.5	88.7	Pologne
Other Europe	***22.4***	***32.0***	***43.5***	***62.3***	***63.8***	***68.8***	***76.8***	***104.6***	***120.0***	***126.8***	***Autre Europe***
Spain[5]	14.7	...	...	50.6	48.2	49.2	54.4	71.4	...	...	Espagne[5]
Yugoslavia	7.7	5.9	10.5	11.8	15.5	19.6	22.4	33.3	45.2	45.0	Yougoslavie
USSR	**3.1**	**3.9**	**2.3**	**2.0**	**2.4**	**2.9**	**3.9**	**3.3**	**2.0**	**3.4**	**URSS**
Ukrainian SSR	*0.4*	*0.4*	*0.1*	*0.6*	*1.2*	*1.4*	*2.2*	*1.4*	*0.8*	*1.8*	*RSS d'Ukraine*
Oceania	**161.1**	**182.5**	**188.0**	**197.3**	**214.2**	**213.1**	**251.7**	**234.2**	**248.0**	**252.7**	**Océanie**
Australia[6]	115.8	129.9	130.3	143.1	160.6	168.7	200.9	183.7	197.6	202.4	Australie[6]
New Zealand[6,7]	45.3	52.6	57.7	54.2	53.6	44.3	...	...	...	...	Nouvelle–Zélande[6,7]
Total	**3 828.3**	**4 477.4**	**4 606.8**	**4 894.3**	**4 646.2**	**5 085.1**	**5 507.4**	**5 339.9**	**5 755.1**	**6 195.7**	**Total**

General note.
Vegetables, whether or not cooked, frozen by ordinary refrigeration or by the "quick–freezing" process. (SITC 05461–0).

[1] Shipments.
[2] Beginning 1978, data are confidential.
[3] Commercial production.
[4] Comprising frozen vegetables for immediate consumption and for further transformation.
[5] Including frozen fruits.
[6] Twelve months ending 30 June of year stated.
[7] Beginning 1982, data are confidential.

Remarque générale.
Légumes, cuits ou non, congelés ou surgelés. (CTCI 05461–0).

[1] Expéditions.
[2] A partir de 1978, les données sont confidentielles.
[3] Production commerciale.
[4] Y compris les légumes surgelés destinés à la consommation immédiate et les légumes surgelés destinés à une transformation ultérieure.
[5] Y compris les fruits congelés.
[6] Période de douze mois finissant le 30 juin de l'année indiquée.
[7] A partir de 1982, les données sont confidentielles.

Vegetables, tinned or bottled – Légumes en boîtes ou en bocaux

Unit : Thousand metric tons — Unité : Milliers de tonnes métriques

Country or area	1976	1977	1978	1979	1980	1981	1982	1983	1984	1985	Pays ou zone
Africa	**141.7**	**139.3**	**132.8**	**129.0**	**142.9**	**206.3**	**159.9**	**142.1**	**141.9**	**144.8**	**Afrique**
Algeria	4.4	5.8	7.8	13.5	7.1	7.7	2.3	...	...	...	Algérie
Egypt[1]	14.9	12.4	* 13.8	7.7	8.6	8.3	9.8	...	...	...	Egypte[1]
Kenya	4.7	2.5	1.1	0.8	0.6	0.7	0.3	0.1	0.4	0.6	Kenya
South Africa	79.5	76.3	70.9	65.8	88.4	141.5	102.4	82.5	82.1	84.8	Afrique du Sud
Sudan* [2]	2.4	2.0	2.0	...	...	...	...	...	...	...	Soudan* [2]
Tunisia	35.9	40.2	37.2	39.0	36.0	46.0	...	...	...	...	Tunisie
America, North	**5 282.1**	**5 846.1**	**5 470.3**	**6 163.0**	**5 640.2**	**3 070.6**	**3 236.5**	**3 042.3**	**3 011.9**	**2 518.4**	**Amérique du Nord**
Canada[3]	275.6	384.9	397.0	463.7	417.8	...	...	...	...	...	Canada[3]
Cuba	32.4	29.4	29.4	...	...	# 5.8	8.1	8.1	9.6	7.4	Cuba
Dominican Republic	6.8	4.8	5.1	6.4	8.5	8.9	9.1	9.9	8.5	...	Rép. dominicaine
Mexico	150.7	140.4	120.7	187.0	198.5	153.2	186.8	159.8	141.7	167.5	Mexique
Panama	5.3	5.4	6.1	5.9	6.0	6.0	6.1	6.0	...	...	Panama
United States	4 811.3	5 281.1	4 912.1	5 478.1	4 990.8	2 400.5	2 494.0	2 290.0	2 241.2	1 686.0	Etats–Unis
America, South	**121.6**	**112.0**	**125.2**	**220.0**	**326.8**	**266.4**	**294.9**	**326.1**	**357.4**	**387.0**	**Amérique du Sud**
Bolivia	0.1	0.6	0.2	0.3	0.4	0.1	0.0	0.2	0.0	...	Bolivie
Brazil	112.1	102.2	115.7	[4] 208.8	315.6	...	...	...	...	...	Brésil
Chile	...	...	...	5.7	4.3	5.0	3.1	4.0	4.1	4.2	Chili
Colombia	2.4	2.5	2.8	4.0	5.3	0.4	1.2	1.0	...	...	Colombie
Paraguay	1.4	1.2	1.3	1.2	1.2	1.2	0.6	0.8	1.3	0.8	Paraguay
Asia	**319.2**	**361.7**	**361.2**	**331.0**	**301.9**	**277.7**	**276.9**	**291.6**	**285.7**	**287.6**	**Asie**
Burma[5]	0.0	0.2	0.2	0.3	0.3	0.2	0.2	0.1	0.2	0.2	Birmanie[5]
Cyprus	4.5	4.1	5.3	4.1	2.7	1.5	2.3	1.2	1.0	1.3	Chypre
Indonesia	0.3	0.4	0.5	0.4	0.1	...	...	...	...	...	Indonésie
Iran(Islamic Rep.of)[6]	...	...	...	...	11.5	14.7	18.8	21.5	...	...	Iran(Rép.islamique)[6]
Japan	227.2	237.8	230.3	217.0	207.4	184.4	186.8	190.0	187.8	188.1	Japon
Korea, Republic of[7]	45.5	72.0	76.2	66.5	56.1	43.1	38.0	51.8	51.6	49.6	Corée, République de[7]
Philippines[3]	8.3	6.8	...	...	...	...	...	...	...	...	Philippines[3]
Turkey	16.6	23.8	24.4	18.5	16.2	26.0	23.0	19.2	20.8	24.0	Turquie
Europe	**4 032.5**	**4 802.0**	**4 629.7**	**4 660.4**	**4 265.3**	**4 560.3**	**4 840.0**	**4 410.3**	**4 776.3**	**4 873.7**	**Europe**
EEC	***2 365.2***	***2 831.1***	***2 650.3***	***2 591.4***	***2 302.8***	***2 564.9***	***2 878.4***	***2 523.9***	***2 666.0***	***2 769.5***	***CEE***
Belgium	145.6	182.6	155.6	152.9	125.6	173.0	232.1	188.8	230.1	258.4	Belgique
Denmark	16.9	14.9	13.3	12.3	15.4	15.3	...	...	...	...	Danemark
France	829.2	1 141.5	1 128.4	1 084.0	890.8	1 062.2	1 262.0	1 005.2	1 114.0	1 170.8	France
Germany, Fed. Rep.	181.5	215.8	177.2	167.8	161.6	169.1	171.5	114.6	123.9	139.3	Allemagne, Rép. féd.
Greece	20.5	23.1	32.7	27.7	25.1	15.2	12.2	16.5	30.5	...	Grèce
Ireland[8]	28.7	30.7	27.7	37.4	33.8	38.7	39.0	37.5	28.9	27.5	Irlande[8]
Netherlands	247.8	326.4	265.4	288.4	272.5	338.7	338.1	337.0	336.0	...	Pays–Bas
United Kingdom[9]	895.0	896.0	850.0	821.0	778.0	# 752.7	809.6	810.6	789.1	786.5	Royaume–Uni[9]
EFTA	***135.0***	***148.5***	***142.7***	***138.9***	***135.5***	***149.4***	***142.3***	***151.0***	***156.8***	***163.3***	***AELE***
Austria	30.4	34.1	30.5	28.0	26.5	33.9	30.7	27.9	33.0	33.5	Autriche
Finland	18.7	22.0	21.5	21.2	21.7	21.0	24.6	27.5	25.2	...	Finlande
Norway	15.8	18.1	19.3	17.3	17.3	20.2	17.5	26.3	...	...	Norvège
Portugal	5.2	6.4	6.7	6.0	4.8	7.9	6.9	7.8	8.2	7.2	Portugal
Sweden	65.0	67.9	64.7	66.4	65.2	66.4	62.7	61.6	67.6	72.3	Suède
East Europe	***1 066.2***	***1 242.8***	***1 275.7***	***1 278.5***	***1 201.5***	***1 284.1***	***1 197.9***	***1 182.6***	***1 343.1***	***1 345.8***	***Europe de l'est***
Bulgaria[10]	198.9	224.4	265.0	265.0	226.2	216.2	215.4	273.2	314.1	256.1	Bulgarie[10]
Czechoslovakia	91.3	124.1	135.6	124.9	119.6	111.7	116.5	120.5	131.0	139.0	Tchécoslovaquie
German Dem. Rep.	125.0	178.9	166.7	162.0	163.5	194.5	185.6	198.1	189.7	215.0	Rép. dém. allemande
Hungary	195.3	235.8	239.1	202.3	239.8	217.5	214.4	194.7	251.5	297.2	Hongrie
Poland	110.7	143.7	139.2	182.3	107.3	179.2	116.1	123.2	120.8	122.5	Pologne
Romania	345.0	336.0	330.0	342.0	345.0	365.0	350.0	273.0	336.0	316.0	Roumanie
Other Europe	***466.1***	***579.6***	***561.1***	***651.5***	***625.6***	***561.9***	***621.3***	***552.7***	***610.4***	***595.0***	***Autre Europe***
Malta	2.3	1.4	1.0	1.8	1.8	1.7	2.4	2.1	2.8	...	Malte
Spain	350.7	...	...	516.0	511.8	416.4	455.4	397.7	...	...	Espagne
Yugoslavia	113.1	153.4	130.1	133.8	112.1	143.8	163.4	152.9	146.3	126.1	Yougoslavie
USSR	**2 099.5**	**2 074.2**	**2 265.1**	**2 408.5**	**2 232.6**	**2 150.8**	**2 195.6**	**2 111.8**	**2 216.7**	**2 243.4**	**URSS**

For general note and footnotes, see end of table.

Voir la fin du tableau pour la remarque générale et les notes.

Vegetables, tinned or bottled (continued) – Légumes en boîtes ou en bocaux (suite)

Unit : Thousand metric tons

Unité : Milliers de tonnes métriques

Country or area	1976	1977	1978	1979	1980	1981	1982	1983	1984	1985	Pays ou zone
Byelorussian SSR	*68.3*	*74.8*	*81.6*	*94.8*	*94.8*	*83.8*	*81.5*	*82.3*	*84.9*	*80.5*	*RSS de Biélorussie*
Ukrainian SSR	*648.9*	*628.6*	*753.1*	*660.7*	*701.6*	*691.2*	*681.9*	*621.6*	*643.9*	*611.0*	*RSS d'Ukraine*
Oceania	**140.6**	**143.3**	**149.6**	**160.7**	**165.1**	**146.5**	**166.0**	**153.8**	**157.6**	**158.4**	**Océanie**
Australia[11]	119.6	122.1	127.8	139.8	141.5	121.3	138.6	129.6	130.1	129.2	Australie[11]
New Zealand[11 12]	21.0	21.1	21.8	20.9	23.6	25.2	27.4	24.2	27.5	29.2	Nouvelle–Zélande[11 12]
Total	**12 137.2**	**13 478.6**	**13 133.9**	**14 072.6**	**13 074.8**	**10 678.6**	**11 169.6**	**10 478.0**	**10 947.4**	**10 613.1**	**Total**

General note.
Vegetables prepared or preserved and put in hermetically–sealed containers or bottles. In terms of net weight. (SITC 05552–1).

[1] Including tomato paste.
[2] Including canned fruits.
[3] Shipments.
[4] Production by establishments employing 5 or more persons.
[5] Twelve months ending 31 March of year stated.
[6] Production by establishments employing 10 or more persons.
[7] Including fruits.
[8] Including frozen vegetables.
[9] Beginning 1980, scope of series revised.
[10] Including vegetable juices.
[11] Twelve months ending 30 June of year stated.
[12] Including dried vegetables.

Remarque générale.
Légumes préparés ou conservés, contenus dans des récipients ou des bocaux fermés hermétiquement. Poids net. (CTCI 05552–1)

[1] Y compris la purée de tomate.
[2] Y compris les conserves de fruits.
[3] Expéditions.
[4] Production des établissements occupant 5 personnes ou plus.
[5] Période de douze mois finissant le 31 mars de l'année indiquée.
[6] Production des établissements occupant 10 personnes ou plus.
[7] Y compris les fruits.
[8] Y compris les légumes congelés.
[9] A partir de 1980, portée de la série révisée.
[10] Y compris les jus de légumes.
[11] Période de douze mois finissant le 30 juin de l'année indiquée.
[12] Y compris les légumes secs.

Fish, frozen – Poisson congelé

Unit : Thousand metric tons

Unité : Milliers de tonnes métriques

Country or area	1976	1977	1978	1979	1980	1981	1982	1983	1984	1985	Pays ou zone
Africa	**118.4**	**132.5**	**148.3**	**162.8**	**152.4**	**225.0**	**269.5**	**261.8**	**273.1**	**263.0**	**Afrique**
Angola* [1]	5.0	8.5	8.9	8.0	8.8	8.7	7.2	7.0	5.0	6.0	Angola* [1]
Cape Verde	0.4	0.3	1.5	1.2	1.9	1.3	1.3	1.8	1.2	1.0	Cap-Vert
Côte d'Ivoire	0.8	0.7	...	...	0.3	...	...	...	...	...	Côte d'Ivoire
Liberia	7.0	16.0	13.0	13.0	7.4	10.0	12.7	10.2	16.1	9.0	Libéria
Mauritania [1] [2]	6.7	5.9	10.1	7.5	2.4	7.9	12.2	6.5	7.9	10.1	Mauritanie [1] [2]
Mauritius [1]	2.3	3.1	2.8	1.9	1.4	1.5	3.8	2.7	2.8	5.0	Maurice [1]
Morocco [1]	8.2	13.4	12.8	11.9	5.4	57.3	85.0	91.8	96.0	84.8	Maroc [1]
Mozambique	...	...	...	0.8	7.4	9.6	9.6	12.8	11.7	...	Mozambique
Réunion	...	...	...	* 0.6	0.7	2.1	2.3	2.0	1.6	1.8	Réunion
Sao Tome – Principe	...	...	...	...	0.0	0.7	1.3	2.4	2.6	* 2.6	Sao Tomé-et-Principe
Senegal [1]	25.9	34.8	37.0	49.0	53.6	60.2	66.2	60.4	57.8	53.4	Sénégal [1]
Seychelles [3] [4]	...	...	...	0.4	0.7	0.3	0.7	0.7	0.7	0.8	Seychelles [3] [4]
South Africa	59.4	42.7	52.9	61.7	56.9	62.8	64.4	60.1	66.2	72.5	Afrique du Sud
Tunisia	[5] 0.2	[5] 0.3	[5] 0.2	2.6	1.7	1.6	...	...	...	...	Tunisie
United Rep. Tanzania [1]	0.5	* 3.7	* 3.7	* 2.8	3.8	0.4	0.1	0.2	0.2	0.5	Rép.Unie de Tanzanie [1]
America, North	**564.1**	**649.2**	**686.2**	**705.4**	**706.2**	**790.5**	**748.6**	**760.1**	**734.6**	**809.9**	**Amérique du Nord**
Canada [5]	172.7	231.3	244.3	252.4	258.6	* [1] 289.5	* [1] 278.1	* [1] 246.4	* [1] 235.2	* [1] 283.5	Canada [5]
Cuba	...	...	...	...	67.7	66.6	76.7	89.1	89.7	...	Cuba
Greenland [3]	...	...	...	10.2	10.1	9.2	11.9	13.2	6.0	8.6	Groënland [3]
Mexico [1]	...	...	...	28.2	46.8	103.8	61.7	52.1	52.7	63.1	Mexique [1]
St.Pierre-Miquelon	2.4	2.1	3.0	3.4	3.3	3.0	2.6	2.4	3.5	5.8	St.Pierre-Miquelon
United States	294.4	312.5	327.1	353.0	319.7	318.4	317.6	357.0	347.5	351.2	Etats-Unis
America, South	**224.2**	**250.4**	**288.5**	**438.5**	**437.5**	**328.3**	**413.2**	**409.3**	**487.6**	**468.5**	**Amérique du Sud**
Argentina [1]	53.6	* 69.3	* 69.3	# 149.5	123.5	122.1	180.0	150.4	109.0	140.7	Argentine [1]
Brazil	50.9	62.2	53.9	[6] 78.8	109.6	68.7	88.1	100.3	101.1	102.4	Brésil
Chile	1.8	11.8	14.0	22.4	13.5	15.4	60.8	52.4	51.2	40.0	Chili
Colombia	0.5	* 0.9	* 0.9	1.1	0.0	0.4	0.3	0.5	...	...	Colombie
Ecuador [1]	* 14.2	* 21.9	* 21.9	25.0	32.2	10.6	13.7	20.1	39.8	34.8	Equateur [1]
Peru	92.5	* 67.9	96.7	116.1	97.0	44.7	22.3	40.8	* 138.3	* 109.0	Pérou
Uruguay [1]	10.6	16.3	31.9	45.6	61.6	66.4	48.0	44.8	47.9	41.4	Uruguay [1]
Asia	**3 689.2**	**3 830.4**	**3 796.3**	**3 817.9**	**3 832.1**	**4 457.7**	**4 804.2**	**4 814.3**	**5 311.0**	**3 977.8**	**Asie**
China* [1]	...	300.0	300.0	286.5	284.6	282.2	291.6	305.8	346.7	351.0	Chine* [1]
Democratic Yemen [1]	...	* 16.4	* 4.9	9.8	10.8	4.0	3.6	* 3.0	4.8	6.0	Yémen démocratique [1]
Hong Kong	...	...	7.3	6.2	4.7	[2] 141.3	[2] 142.6	[2] 158.9	[2] 163.8	[2] 154.0	Hong-kong
India	124.8	...	...	...	...	...	...	...	...	...	Inde
Indonesia [1]	...	11.1	13.9	16.8	31.5	22.7	9.2	28.4	* 32.3	...	Indonésie [1]
Iran(Islamic Rep.of) [7]	...	...	...	...	...	13.9	22.3	7.7	...	...	Iran(Rép.islamique) [7]
Japan	3 111.1	3 200.1	3 153.2	3 171.6	3 134.2	3 622.4	3 902.1	3 933.4	4 338.6	# 2 957.7	Japon
Korea, Republic of	54.4	54.7	69.5	80.9	86.6	121.4	140.2	116.2	117.6	127.7	Corée, République de
Maldives	[1] 8.7	[1] 11.0	* [1] 4.6	* [1] 12.6	* [1] 14.1	* [1] 13.8	* [1] 9.8	* [1] 7.9	* [1] 13.8	# 17.1	Maldives
Philippines	...	...	21.5	34.2	49.1	37.3	51.7	* [1] 21.2	* [1] 16.1	* [1] 14.6	Philippines
Singapore [1]	...	...	...	1.1	0.7	1.2	1.7	1.2	1.3	2.4	Singapour [1]
Sri Lanka [1]	...	...	...	0.1	0.0	0.2	0.0	0.0	0.0	2.9	Sri Lanka [1]
Thailand [1]	...	40.0	69.0	46.0	59.3	56.9	82.5	82.8	116.6	149.5	Thaïlande [1]
Turkey [1]	...	...	...	* 12.6	17.2	15.5	22.3	23.2	20.0	...	Turquie [1]
Europe	**1 275.3**	**1 326.6**	**1 345.0**	**1 487.9**	**1 587.1**	**1 567.6**	**1 602.3**	**1 692.1**	**1 812.0**	**1 862.6**	**Europe**
EEC	***485.6***	***546.4***	***536.7***	***611.2***	***624.0***	***663.7***	***652.4***	***716.4***	***840.4***	***853.1***	***CEE***
Belgium [1]	9.1	10.3	11.1	12.3	12.1	8.7	9.1	9.1	10.5	11.5	Belgique [1]
Denmark	55.3	57.8	56.3	63.4	68.6	80.6	77.0	82.5	95.5	85.7	Danemark
France [8]	100.8	132.6	132.5	117.2	115.2	110.3	100.2	121.7	159.7	176.3	France [8]
Germany, Fed. Rep.	15.6	10.1	11.7	13.2	13.9	13.3	9.3	11.2	13.0	15.4	Allemagne, Rép. féd.
Greece [1]	25.4	27.0	18.1	20.2	22.1	15.0	9.7	8.6	13.0	13.0	Grèce [1]
Ireland [1]	23.9	* 23.9	16.0	17.1	30.1	72.5	91.7	93.6	98.2	94.1	Irlande [1]
Italy [1]	22.2	26.8	28.3	62.3	48.3	42.2	* 40.3	* 42.8	48.3	50.2	Italie [1]
Netherlands [1]	34.4	45.9	66.7	96.5	119.8	132.1	121.0	156.9	207.3	218.2	Pays-Bas [1]
United Kingdom	199.0	212.0	196.0	209.0	194.0	189.0	194.0	190.0	195.0	...	Royaume-Uni
EFTA	***250.2***	***264.1***	***274.8***	***325.5***	***313.6***	***331.8***	***322.2***	***328.5***	***327.9***	***338.0***	***AELE***
Finland	0.9	1.0	1.1	1.2	1.1	1.1	1.2	1.2	3.5	...	Finlande
Iceland	90.7	107.3	117.5	151.4	137.2	125.7	132.6	137.1	131.7	130.8	Islande
Norway [5]	130.9	133.7	137.8	140.8	136.6	179.0	* 169.9	* 169.7	* 171.2	...	Norvège [5]
Portugal	24.9	19.0	14.9	28.0	34.3	19.7	13.7	13.9	15.3	15.8	Portugal

For general note and footnotes, see end of table.

Voir la fin du tableau pour la remarque générale et les notes.

Unit : Thousand metric tons — Unité : Milliers de tonnes métriques

Country or area	1976	1977	1978	1979	1980	1981	1982	1983	1984	1985	Pays ou zone
Sweden[9]	2.7	3.0	3.4	4.0	4.4	6.1	4.8	6.5	6.1	5.9	Suède[9]
Switzerland[1]	0.1	0.1	0.1	0.1	0.1	0.1	0.1	0.1	0.1	0.1	Suisse[1]
East Europe	***369.0***	***332.5***	***352.2***	***345.4***	***435.7***	***337.5***	***376.9***	***404.5***	***383.2***	***368.3***	***Europe de l'est***
Bulgaria[10]	86.7	72.5	98.6	87.4	95.1	81.8	72.9	76.3	75.7	68.0	Bulgarie[10]
German Dem. Rep.	47.7	18.4	25.4	23.2	25.1	28.2	24.3	28.6	30.7	31.6	Rép. dém. allemande
Hungary[1]	...	...	...	4.3	5.0	4.8	2.6	4.8	5.5	6.1	Hongrie[1]
Poland	164.1	164.1	143.8	153.6	219.8	123.7	151.7	164.3	151.8	153.0	Pologne
Romania[1]	...	...	...	76.8	90.8	98.9	125.3	130.4	* 119.5	* 109.5	Roumanie[1]
Other Europe	***170.5***	***183.6***	***181.3***	***205.8***	***213.7***	***234.6***	***250.9***	***242.8***	***260.5***	***303.2***	***Autre Europe***
Faeroe Islands	13.2	18.7	20.8	26.2	26.4	34.3	38.4	48.5	49.5	* 54.5	Iles Féroé
Spain	156.0	162.2	156.8	...	...	197.7	209.8	192.1	209.8	247.9	Espagne
Yugoslavia	[11] 1.3	[11] 2.7	[11] 3.7	# 3.5	2.3	2.6	2.7	2.2	1.2	0.8	Yougoslavie
USSR[1]	**3 508.9**	**3 023.9**	**3 056.3**	**2 885.1**	**3 028.6**	**3 140.5**	**3 174.5**	**2 996.9**	**3 194.1**	**3 290.9**	**URSS[1]**
Oceania	**44.5**	**49.6**	**53.8**	**76.4**	**104.8**	**117.3**	**101.1**	**120.2**	**118.5**	**106.4**	**Océanie**
Australia[1]	1.5	5.6	2.9	3.2	9.0	6.4	13.2	15.0	8.7	2.2	Australie[1]
New Zealand[1]	...	18.2	24.2	44.6	66.0	82.3	68.8	69.9	72.6	73.0	Nouvelle-Zélande[1]
Solomon Islands	...	...	...	[1] 20.8	21.5	23.7	15.3	30.7	33.2	27.2	Iles Salomon
Vanuatu[3]	6.1	10.0	9.2	7.7	8.3	4.8	3.9	4.5	3.9	4.0	Vanuatu[3]
Total	**9 424.6**	**9 262.5**	**9 374.4**	**9 574.0**	**9 848.6**	**10 626.7**	**11 113.5**	**11 054.7**	**11 930.9**	**10 779.2**	**Total**

General note.
Frozen fish and fish products, including production on board fish factory ships. (SITC 03110-3).

[1] Source: Food and Agriculture Organization (FAO), (Rome).
[2] Including chilled fish.
[3] Exports.
[4] Including fresh fish.
[5] Excluding shellfish.
[6] Production by establishments employing 5 or more persons.
[7] Production by establishments employing 10 or more persons.
[8] Comprising frozen fish for immediate consumption and for further transformation.
[9] Frozen fish fillets.
[10] Including salted fish.
[11] Including salted, dried or smoked fish.

Remarque générale.
Poisson et produits de poisson, congelés, y compris la production des navires-usines. (CTCI 03110-3).

[1] Source: Organisation des Nations Unies pour l'alimentation et l'agriculture (FAO), (Rome).
[2] Y compris les poissons réfrigérés.
[3] Exportations.
[4] Y compris le poisson fraîche.
[5] Non compris les coquillages.
[6] Production des établissements occupant 5 personnes ou plus.
[7] Production des établissements occupant 10 personnes ou plus.
[8] Y compris le poisson congelé et surgelé destiné à la consommation immédiate et le poisson congelé destiné à une transformation ultérieure.
[9] Filets de poisson congelés.
[10] Y compris le poisson salé.
[11] Y compris le poisson salé, séché ou fumé.

Fish, salted, dried or smoked – Poisson salé, séché ou fumé

Unit : Thousand metric tons — Unité : Milliers de tonnes métriques

Country or area	1976	1977	1978	1979	1980	1981	1982	1983	1984	1985	Pays ou zone
Africa	**221.1**	**268.1**	**251.0**	**240.8**	**251.9**	**250.9**	**248.9**	**249.2**	**234.6**	**242.5**	**Afrique**
Algeria[1]	1.7	1.9	0.6	0.2	* 0.4	* 0.4	* 0.4	* 0.4	* 0.5	* 0.5	Algérie[1]
Angola* [1]	...	...	...	25.0	27.4	27.4	27.8	27.0	22.0	23.0	Angola* [1]
Benin[1]	2.6	2.6	2.3	* 2.3	* 2.3	* 2.3	* 2.3	* 2.0	* 2.0	* 2.0	Bénin[1]
Cameroon[1]	2.1	2.0	* 2.0	3.6	* 4.0	* 4.0	* 4.0	* 4.0	* 3.8	* 3.8	Cameroun[1]
Cape Verde[1]	0.0	0.1	0.1	* 0.1	...	...	...	...	...	...	Cap-Vert[1]
Chad* [1]	20.0	20.0	20.0	20.0	20.0	20.0	20.0	20.0	19.0	19.0	Tchad* [1]
Côte d'Ivoire[1]	* 15.3	18.0	15.0	15.0	15.0	* 15.0	* 15.0	* 15.0	* 12.0	* 15.0	Côte d'Ivoire[1]
Ethiopia[1]	* 1.1	0.2	* 0.2	* 0.2	* 0.2	* 0.2	0.0	0.0	0.0	0.0	Ethiopie[1]
Gambia[1]	1.7	* 2.0	* 2.0	* 4.3	* 4.6	* 3.1	* 4.0	* 3.0	* 3.1	* 3.0	Gambie[1]
Ghana* [1]	63.6	64.7	64.7	55.1	54.0	58.0	55.0	57.0	55.0	56.0	Ghana* [1]
Kenya[1]	4.5	* 4.2	4.0	5.0	4.6	5.8	11.4	* 12.9	9.4	11.2	Kenya[1]
Madagascar[1]	1.7	2.0	1.6	1.5	1.8	1.2	1.1	2.0	2.0	1.8	Madagascar[1]
Mali[1]	* 5.2	5.8	5.9	7.2	7.8	6.3	6.0	3.6	2.0	2.1	Mali[1]
Mauritania[2]	1.0	* 1.2	* 1.2	0.4	0.4	0.5	0.5	0.4	0.7	0.4	Mauritanie[2]
Mauritius	0.3	0.3	0.3	0.2	0.3	0.2	0.3	0.2	0.1	0.2	Maurice
Morocco[1]	0.1	...	2.6	8.0	6.5	13.7	9.4	4.7	4.8	5.1	Maroc[1]
Mozambique* [1]	...	3.5	3.8	4.5	4.5	4.7	4.8	4.8	4.8	5.0	Mozambique* [1]
Niger	1.2	2.0	2.7	2.7	2.6	2.4	2.0	5.7	2.0	2.0	Niger
Senegal[1]	32.3	19.8	19.2	19.5	22.6	17.7	16.0	16.1	15.8	15.5	Sénégal[1]
Seychelles	...	...	...	* 0.2	* 0.2	* 0.3	* 0.3	* 0.3	* 0.3	0.3	Seychelles
Sierra Leone[1]	14.8	21.0	15.4	19.6	* 16.7	* 17.4	* 18.4	* 18.4	* 18.5	* 18.6	Sierra Leone[1]
Somalia[1]	* 0.9	0.7	1.2	1.0	0.6	0.5	* 0.9	* 0.9	* 0.9	* 1.0	Somalie[1]
South Africa	5.7	7.3	9.7	8.7	* 6.3	4.4	5.2	4.4	3.6	3.1	Afrique du Sud
Sudan* [1]	1.8	1.7	1.6	1.6	2.0	2.2	1.8	1.9	1.9	2.2	Soudan* [1]
Togo* [1]	...	...	...	2.0	2.3	2.5	3.6	3.6	3.4	3.7	Togo* [1]
Tunisia	0.0	0.0	0.1	0.0	0.0	0.2	0.0	...	...	...	Tunisie
United Rep. Tanzania[1]	8.0	50.5	42.7	30.2	44.6	* 38.0	* 35.0	* 37.0	* 42.6	* 41.5	Rép.Unie de Tanzanie[1]
Zambia[1]	...	...	...	...	0.0	2.4	3.8	3.7	4.2	6.4	Zambie[1]
America, North	**104.4**	**90.9**	**85.0**	**92.1**	**107.2**	**103.4**	**113.4**	**88.5**	**92.3**	**102.6**	**Amérique du Nord**
Canada[3]	59.5	52.1	57.0	60.4	74.6	68.2	82.3	55.0	57.6	* 68.0	Canada[3]
Cuba[4]	...	...	...	...	...	0.3	1.2	1.6	1.8	2.0	Cuba[4]
Greenland[2]	...	1.7	2.4	7.1	5.9	7.2	4.8	3.2	3.0	3.8	Groënland[2]
Guatemala[1]	0.3	0.3	0.5	0.6	0.7	0.7	0.8	* 1.0	* 1.0	* 1.0	Guatemala[1]
Jamaica	...	...	...	...	4.0	3.2	2.6	2.2	1.0	0.9	Jamaïque
Mexico[1]	8.7	* 8.7	0.4	0.5	0.6	4.4	* 1.6	* 0.5	* 0.9	...	Mexique[1]
St.Pierre-Miquelon	[1] 0.0	[1] 0.0	[1] 0.0	[1] 0.0	[1] 0.1	0.0	0.2	0.0	0.1	0.2	St.Pierre-Miquelon
United States[5]	24.7	22.1	19.2	18.3	20.6	19.3	* 19.7	* 24.9	* 26.9	* 26.4	Etats-Unis[5]
America, South	**69.2**	**64.2**	**61.9**	**93.9**	**79.2**	**61.7**	**56.4**	**54.1**	**61.7**	**60.2**	**Amérique du Sud**
Argentina[1]	4.4	4.4	2.0	5.7	5.7	5.1	5.2	5.1	5.3	5.8	Argentine[1]
Brazil[1]	35.0	35.3	33.6	36.1	39.5	26.1	19.8	22.4	23.0	20.0	Brésil[1]
Chile	0.2	0.3	0.2	0.2	0.2	0.0	0.1	0.1	0.2	...	Chili
Colombia[1]	11.1	8.9	* 8.9	* 9.4	* 9.3	* 9.6	* 10.1	* 4.9	* 9.6	* 6.3	Colombie[1]
Ecuador	[1] 0.8	[1] 0.8	* [1] 0.8	[1] 0.4	0.2	0.3	0.1	* 0.1	* 0.1	* 0.1	Equateur
Guyana[1]	* 0.1	0.1	0.2	* 0.1	0.1	0.1	0.1	0.0	0.2	0.3	Guyana[1]
Peru	[1] 11.6	* [1] 7.5	[1] 10.1	[1] 37.8	[1] 16.7	13.9	13.7	13.0	* 14.1	* 17.9	Pérou
Suriname[1]	...	...	...	...	0.1	0.2	0.2	0.3	0.3	0.3	Suriname[1]
Uruguay[1]	...	1.0	0.3	0.1	0.1	0.1	0.1	0.1	0.1	0.1	Uruguay[1]
Venezuela[1]	5.4	5.9	5.7	* 4.0	7.3	6.4	7.0	8.1	8.8	9.3	Venezuela[1]
Asia	**2 571.0**	**2 738.2**	**2 760.8**	**2 708.6**	**2 890.2**	**2 923.2**	**2 910.6**	**3 093.0**	**3 268.4**	**3 381.6**	**Asie**
Burma[1 6]	44.1	45.6	47.4	49.7	51.4	54.8	* 54.4	* 54.5	* 57.0	* 57.8	Birmanie[1 6]
China* [1]	...	1 100.0	1 050.0	880.0	900.0	970.0	950.0	1 000.0	1 100.0	1 200.0	Chine* [1]
Democratic Yemen[1]	1.1	10.2	5.4	5.6	9.7	2.9	4.7	3.4	5.0	6.0	Yémen démocratique[1]
Hong Kong	4.1	4.2	4.0	4.9	4.3	4.0	3.5	3.2	2.9	2.6	Hong-kong
India[1]	132.3	139.0	147.4	151.2	158.6	136.8	124.3	136.7	137.8	170.9	Inde[1]
Indonesia[1]	319.4	264.2	313.0	339.0	438.5	434.1	461.9	545.4	616.5	...	Indonésie[1]
Iran(Islamic Rep.of)[1]	1.0	* 1.0	* 1.0	...	...	...	...	...	...	...	Iran(Rép.islamique)[1]
Japan	708.8	733.2	751.4	772.6	796.9	797.7	831.9	863.6	868.9	# 890.9	Japon
Korea, Republic of	52.3	48.8	66.4	71.3	* 84.9	* 95.7	* 54.0	* 46.0	* 45.5	* 50.8	Corée, République de
Macau	[1] 0.4	[1] 0.0	[1] 0.0	[2] 0.7	[2] 0.3	[2] 0.1	[2] 0.2	[2] 0.1	[2] 0.1	[2] 0.1	Macao
Malaysia[1]	6.4	3.7	4.1	# 18.4	17.4	19.3	17.3	22.3	19.2	14.3	Malaisie[1]
Maldives	[1] 1.5	[1] 1.8	[1] 1.8	2.0	* 2.9	2.0	2.2	2.2	1.9	3.5	Maldives
Mongolia	0.2	0.3	0.5	0.5	0.3	0.3	0.2	0.3	0.4	0.4	Mongolie
Pakistan[1]	15.8	19.3	13.3	14.7	7.7	16.1	15.7	* 16.2	20.5	21.6	Pakistan[1]
Philippines[1]	146.9	159.7	160.1	168.0	176.4	188.8	202.7	208.1	210.3	208.1	Philippines[1]
Singapore[1]	3.6	3.2	3.9	4.9	...	...	...	...	...	...	Singapour[1]
Sri Lanka[1]	9.1	9.2	9.4	9.3	12.1	15.5	17.0	14.3	8.8	12.4	Sri Lanka[1]

For general note and footnotes, see end of table.

Voir la fin du tableau pour la remarque générale et les notes.

Fish, salted, dried or smoked (continued) – Poisson salé, séché ou fumé (suite)

Unit : Thousand metric tons

Unité : Milliers de tonnes métriques

Country or area	1976	1977	1978	1979	1980	1981	1982	1983	1984	1985	Pays ou zone
Thailand[1]	124.2	145.7	136.4	174.4	177.5	* 152.9	141.0	149.8	146.7	99.3	Thaïlande[1]
Turkey[1]	...	...	...	* 13.0	21.5	1.3	2.2	2.8	3.0	3.3	Turquie[1]
United Arab Emirates[1]	...	...	...	...	25.0	26.0	22.5	19.0	19.0	18.0	Emirats arabes unis[1]
Europe	**543.7**	**517.3**	**516.7**	**537.0**	**570.9**	**612.9**	**560.5**	**500.0**	**502.6**	**500.4**	**Europe**
EEC	***137.2***	***115.6***	***120.2***	***115.7***	***128.4***	***122.3***	***114.8***	***121.7***	***131.3***	***127.8***	***CEE***
Belgium[7]	11.6	10.7	12.7	11.5	10.8	11.2	12.7	12.2	15.2	17.2	Belgique[7]
Denmark	9.4	10.4	11.2	12.7	13.2	* 5.9	14.1	* 11.7	15.9	...	Danemark
France* [1]	16.9	16.2	15.7	10.8	12.0	11.4	15.2	19.2	23.0	...	France* [1]
Germany, Fed. Rep.	23.0	21.3	20.1	20.1	19.9	18.0	18.5	16.6	16.5	17.2	Allemagne, Rép. féd.
Greece	4.5	4.4	3.9	5.8	4.8	4.6	5.1	4.0	5.4	* 5.0	Grèce
Ireland[1]	7.6	* 7.6	8.5	8.8	10.2	10.1	8.7	10.9	10.0	9.1	Irlande[1]
Italy[1]	10.2	10.1	7.5	7.5	5.5	4.5	3.9	3.2	3.1	5.0	Italie[1]
Netherlands[1]	43.1	30.0	35.6	35.4	44.9	49.6	31.6	36.9	35.1	36.1	Pays–Bas[1]
United Kingdom	11.0	5.0	5.0	3.0	7.0	7.0	5.0	7.0	7.0	...	Royaume–Uni
EFTA	***228.2***	***245.3***	***236.5***	***235.1***	***251.6***	***314.8***	***283.2***	***237.6***	***209.7***	***191.6***	***AELE***
Finland	4.4	4.7	4.9	4.3	3.9	3.5	4.7	4.2	3.6	...	Finlande
Iceland	69.0	71.1	64.6	72.6	102.5	112.2	104.0	79.7	75.5	79.2	Islande
Norway[3]	128.4	139.6	134.2	127.6	120.2	175.0	141.3	118.1	94.4	73.7	Norvège[3]
Portugal	[1] 22.0	25.5	27.9	26.6	21.2	20.7	29.7	31.8	31.9	...	Portugal
Sweden	4.4	4.4	4.9	4.0	3.6	3.4	3.4	3.8	4.3	3.9	Suède
East Europe	***116.3***	***97.5***	***98.8***	***103.9***	***107.6***	***105.3***	***103.5***	***86.1***	***119.3***	***130.5***	***Europe de l'est***
Bulgaria[8]	2.9	3.2	4.0	3.9	4.2	4.7	4.7	4.4	4.0	4.4	Bulgarie[8]
Czechoslovakia[4]	5.6	6.3	6.9	7.4	7.6	7.3	7.3	6.5	6.4	7.1	Tchécoslovaquie[4]
German Dem. Rep.	36.2	28.5	28.0	26.8	27.4	28.8	29.5	22.0	30.6	30.7	Rép. dém. allemande
Poland	60.2	54.2	54.8	53.0	52.6	38.4	38.4	43.6	56.8	57.5	Pologne
Romania[1]	11.4	5.4	5.1	12.9	15.7	26.1	23.6	9.6	21.4	30.8	Roumanie[1]
Other Europe	***62.0***	***58.8***	***61.2***	***82.3***	***83.3***	***70.5***	***59.0***	***54.5***	***42.4***	***50.4***	***Autre Europe***
Faeroe Islands	20.4	19.0	20.5	15.9	18.2	16.9	18.3	18.6	18.6	* 13.4	Iles Féroé
Spain	40.3	37.2	39.0	64.0	62.5	50.5	40.4	35.7	23.6	...	Espagne
Yugoslavia	1.2	2.6	1.7	2.4	2.6	3.1	# 0.3	0.2	0.2	0.1	Yougoslavie
USSR[1]	**710.7**	**669.1**	**629.2**	**672.2**	**683.0**	**710.9**	**773.4**	**792.6**	**793.6**	**850.3**	**URSS[1]**
Oceania	**2.3**	**2.1**	**2.2**	**2.1**	**2.4**	**1.9**	**3.4**	**2.5**	**1.2**	**1.7**	**Océanie**
Fiji[1]	...	0.0	0.0	0.0	0.1	0.1	0.1	0.0	0.0	0.0	Fidji[1]
New Zealand[1]	0.1	0.1	0.3	0.5	0.8	1.0	2.0	0.9	0.3	1.5	Nouvelle–Zélande[1]
Solomon Islands	...	...	...	...	...	0.8	1.3	1.6	0.9	0.2	Iles Salomon
Total	**4 222.4**	**4 349.9**	**4 306.8**	**4 346.7**	**4 584.8**	**4 665.0**	**4 666.6**	**4 779.8**	**4 954.6**	**5 139.3**	**Total**

General note.
Salted, dried or smoked edible fish (whole, in pieces or filleted) including those preserved in brine. Production on fish factory ships is included. (SITC 03120–0).

[1] Source: Food and Agriculture Organization (FAO), (Rome).

[2] Exports.
[3] Excluding shellfish.
[4] Smoked fish only.
[5] Excluding Alaska.
[6] Twelve months ending 30 September of year stated.
[7] Including frozen fish.
[8] Excluding dried fish.

Remarque générale.
Poisson comestible salé, séché ou fumé (poissons entiers ou tronçonnés, et filets de poissons), y compris le poisson conservé dans la saumure. Cette rubrique comprend la production des navires–usines. (CTCI 03120–0).

[1] Source: Organisation des Nations Unies pour l'alimentation et l'agriculture (FAO), (Rome).
[2] Exportations.
[3] Non compris les coquillages.
[4] Poisson fumé seulement.
[5] Non compris l'Alaska.
[6] Période de douze mois finissant le 30 septembre de l'année indiquée.
[7] Y compris le poisson congelé.
[8] Non compris le poisson séché.

Fish, tinned – Conserves de poisson

Unit : Thousand metric tons | Unité : Milliers de tonnes métriques

Country or area	1976	1977	1978	1979	1980	1981	1982	1983	1984	1985	Pays ou zone
Africa	**243.4**	**179.3**	**143.0**	**151.5**	**161.5**	**192.4**	**195.7**	**178.3**	**201.4**	**210.8**	**Afrique**
Algeria[1]	2.7	2.4	1.7	2.4	* 2.9	* 3.4	* 3.9	* 4.0	* 5.0	* 5.5	Algérie[1]
Angola	...	...	...	* 3.0	[1] 3.1	[1] 3.1	[1] 3.5	* [1] 3.5	* [1] 3.0	* [1] 3.2	Angola
Cape Verde	0.2	0.2	0.3	0.2	0.3	0.3	0.3	0.3	* 0.2	0.3	Cap–Vert
Côte d'Ivoire	10.5	12.7	13.2	14.4	17.8	26.2	29.1	25.5	35.2	...	Côte d'Ivoire
Egypt	3.0	3.4	3.9	5.2	5.1	5.0	5.7	...	...	...	Egypte
Ghana	...	...	...	...	1.4	1.9	1.1	1.2	1.0	3.3	Ghana
Libyan Arab Jamah.[1]	0.5	0.4	1.1	1.0	1.0	2.9	2.7	1.5	1.7	1.8	Jamah.arabe libyenne[1]
Mauritius	1.0	1.4	1.3	1.4	2.0	2.4	2.4	2.8	3.5	4.0	Maurice
Morocco[2]	82.3	86.3	* 83.0	84.1	89.8	98.1	82.8	84.6	80.2	...	Maroc[2]
Mozambique	...	...	...	...	0.0	0.2	0.3	0.3	0.5	0.5	Mozambique
Namibia* [1]	126.3	51.3	17.8	18.6	10.4	11.9	12.0	...	...	...	Namibie* [1]
Senegal	11.0	11.9	12.2	11.9	13.1	19.2	23.9	* 20.1	* 28.7	28.2	Sénégal
Somalia[1]	* 0.5	0.5	* 0.5	0.3	0.2	0.1	0.1	* 0.0	* 0.0	0.0	Somalie[1]
South Africa	0.0	2.6	0.9	* 4.2	11.0	13.4	# 23.5	24.8	20.9	20.3	Afrique du Sud
Tunisia	2.0	2.4	3.0	3.6	3.6	4.2	4.3	2.8	4.3	4.9	Tunisie
America, North	**434.0**	**431.9**	**513.2**	**725.3**	**777.3**	**781.1**	**685.8**	**696.3**	**486.9**	**748.9**	**Amérique du Nord**
Canada[3]	38.1	45.1	45.1	43.9	49.0	* 55.0	* 46.2	* 48.8	* 39.1	* 67.8	Canada[3]
Costa Rica[1]	2.4	2.9	3.7	3.8	3.0	1.9	2.2	* 0.9	* 2.3	2.2	Costa Rica[1]
Cuba	2.5	2.3	2.3	1.8	4.5	4.3	5.6	6.5	6.9	7.4	Cuba
Greenland[4]	...	...	...	...	1.1	1.6	2.1	1.2	0.8	0.9	Groënland[4]
Mexico	30.3	20.6	25.3	21.3	32.0	43.8	42.7	26.2	31.3	33.6	Mexique
United States	358.5	358.9	434.9	652.8	687.7	674.5	587.1	* 612.8	* 406.5	...	Etats–Unis
America, South	**235.9**	**176.7**	**203.0**	**319.4**	**407.6**	**350.3**	**277.6**	**229.5**	**289.3**	**237.5**	**Amérique du Sud**
Argentina[1]	23.1	* 23.1	* 23.1	15.7	13.5	14.6	12.7	13.1	12.4	16.6	Argentine[1]
Brazil	39.5	41.1	34.0	[5] 125.6	142.0	* [1] 78.2	* [1] 98.1	* [1] 97.4	* [1] 103.6	* [1] 56.0	Brésil
Chile	9.0	16.5	23.4	27.5	38.0	29.5	23.5	41.7	49.2	40.5	Chili
Colombia	0.3	* 1.3	* 1.3	* 0.8	* 1.6	* 2.4	1.1	0.6	0.3	0.3	Colombie
Ecuador[1]	16.3	28.3	28.3	34.8	44.0	63.0	44.8	22.1	36.8	39.6	Equateur[1]
Peru	98.2	* [1] 49.6	[1] 64.6	[1] 85.1	[1] 140.5	140.1	64.5	26.1	* 45.0	* 37.6	Pérou
Venezuela[1]	49.6	16.8	28.3	* 30.0	* 28.0	* 22.5	* 32.9	* 28.6	* 42.0	* 47.0	Venezuela[1]
Asia	**537.9**	**590.5**	**613.6**	**594.1**	**656.5**	**656.6**	**657.1**	**644.0**	**709.5**	**879.1**	**Asie**
Burma[1,6]	83.8	86.7	90.4	94.5	97.8	104.3	* 82.7	* 82.9	* 86.8	* 87.3	Birmanie[1,6]
China* [1]	...	7.4	7.4	7.4	11.1	9.8	9.6	9.2	9.8	10.0	Chine* [1]
Democratic Yemen[1]	0.0	0.0	0.0	0.3	3.3	5.2	5.8	* 5.8	* 7.5	...	Yémen démocratique[1]
Hong Kong	1.4	0.3	0.5	0.7	...	...	0.0	0.0	0.0	...	Hong–kong
India	7.2	...	...	...	...	...	...	...	...	...	Inde
Indonesia[1]	* 6.7	4.0	2.5	5.1	5.3	5.6	5.6	* 10.7	* 9.5	108.0	Indonésie[1]
Iran(Islamic Rep.of)[7]	1.0	1.0	1.4	2.0	1.1	1.0	1.5	2.5	2.0	2.2	Iran(Rép.islamique)[7]
Israel[1]	4.8	4.1	3.8	* 3.8	3.4	6.3	5.5	6.3	6.7	7.0	Israël[1]
Japan	382.5	405.4	406.3	397.5	448.4	425.8	399.3	361.0	355.7	321.6	Japon
Korea, Republic of	17.2	20.8	18.2	13.5	9.0	13.5	13.9	22.0	25.7	31.9	Corée, République de
Malaysia[1]	3.1	2.4	7.4	8.9	7.1	3.2	3.4	6.8	14.8	12.4	Malaisie[1]
Maldives	...	...	...	...	...	...	0.0	0.0	0.6	0.7	Maldives
Philippines	8.5	20.2	25.0	21.5	32.1	39.4	41.6	46.3	* 44.4	* 45.1	Philippines
Singapore[1]	8.2	8.4	9.9	# 0.4	0.6	1.0	1.1	1.4	1.1	0.8	Singapour[1]
Sri Lanka	* 0.1	0.0	0.0	0.1	0.0	0.0	0.0	0.0	0.0	0.0	Sri Lanka
Thailand[1]	2.9	17.5	26.3	24.2	29.3	33.4	79.6	81.6	137.2	235.5	Thaïlande[1]
Turkey	2.8	4.7	6.9	6.6	0.1	0.0	0.3	0.1	0.5	0.7	Turquie
Europe	**620.7**	**643.3**	**654.9**	**659.5**	**650.4**	**617.3**	**608.5**	**628.5**	**622.9**	**639.7**	**Europe**
EEC	***264.9***	***276.3***	***277.6***	***277.0***	***265.3***	***253.9***	***255.5***	***265.6***	***275.7***	***285.8***	***CEE***
Belgium	5.1	4.3	3.9	4.0	4.5	4.6	4.4	4.2	3.7	3.6	Belgique
Denmark	34.5	32.6	35.6	37.4	33.5	31.0	* 27.0	* 30.0	* 29.2	...	Danemark
France	88.0	98.7	102.0	98.7	84.6	87.0	91.9	98.3	101.7	101.4	France
Germany, Fed. Rep.	57.5	53.2	50.6	46.3	48.9	39.5	40.5	41.4	41.3	41.2	Allemagne, Rép. féd.
Greece	[1] 1.9	[1] 1.9	[1] 1.7	1.8	2.0	2.2	1.6	0.9	0.6	0.7	Grèce
Ireland[1]	3.4	1.5	1.2	0.8	1.0	1.0	1.1	1.0	1.7	1.3	Irlande[1]
Italy[1]	* 55.1	* 57.2	54.2	59.7	64.0	65.5	66.5	70.0	78.3	89.0	Italie[1]
Netherlands[1]	9.6	13.8	* 15.4	15.4	17.8	17.1	15.4	12.8	* 13.1	15.8	Pays–Bas[1]
United Kingdom	10.0	13.0	13.0	13.0	9.0	6.0	7.0	7.0	6.0	...	Royaume–Uni
EFTA	***96.2***	***110.2***	***113.0***	***103.3***	***105.1***	***105.4***	***102.1***	***99.9***	***100.7***	***104.4***	***AELE***
Finland	1.0	1.1	0.2	1.2	1.1	1.2	1.2	1.3	1.9	...	Finlande

For general note and footnotes, see end of table.

Voir la fin du tableau pour la remarque générale et les notes.

Fish, tinned (continued) – Conserves de poisson (suite)

Unit : Thousand metric tons

Unité : Milliers de tonnes métriques

Country or area	1976	1977	1978	1979	1980	1981	1982	1983	1984	1985	Pays ou zone
Iceland	1.4	1.9	1.8	1.9	2.4	2.7	1.2	1.6	1.7	1.9	Islande
Norway	30.4	32.2	33.4	31.2	30.8	28.3	26.8	21.5	...	...	Norvège
Portugal	35.7	47.5	49.8	41.7	43.4	46.8	45.1	46.9	45.0	49.9	Portugal
Sweden	27.3	26.8	27.1	26.6	26.6	25.5	26.7	27.7	27.3	27.4	Suède
Switzerland	...	...	...	...	0.7	0.8	0.9	1.0	1.0	1.1	Suisse
East Europe	***110.6***	***110.1***	***101.6***	***106.0***	***106.3***	***87.2***	***82.5***	***95.1***	***87.7***	***86.3***	***Europe de l'est***
Bulgaria	10.0	10.4	11.5	11.5	12.3	12.3	12.4	12.4	12.3	12.4	Bulgarie
Czechoslovakia	2.8	3.4	3.5	3.6	4.0	4.2	4.2	3.3	3.4	3.6	Tchécoslovaquie
German Dem. Rep	20.8	17.0	16.6	17.1	16.9	18.3	18.4	19.9	20.9	21.6	Rép. dém. allemande
Hungary	4.8	3.6	2.0	2.1	2.0	1.4	2.6	2.1	1.3	0.6	Hongrie
Poland	47.0	49.7	48.0	48.6	46.0	32.1	19.9	30.3	30.8	31.1	Pologne
Romania	25.2	26.0	20.0	23.0	25.0	19.0	25.0	27.0	19.0	17.0	Roumanie
Other Europe	***148.9***	***146.7***	***162.7***	***173.2***	***173.8***	***170.8***	***168.4***	***167.9***	***158.8***	***163.1***	***Autre Europe***
Spain	120.7	117.0	129.8	139.7	139.2	133.6	132.1	128.7	118.8	124.7	Espagne
Yugoslavia	28.2	29.8	32.9	33.6	34.6	37.2	36.3	39.2	40.0	38.4	Yougoslavie
USSR	**831.9**	**863.5**	**934.2**	**1 019.7**	**990.7**	**1 024.4**	**998.7**	**1 021.3**	**1 021.2**	**1 093.1**	**URSS**
Byelorussian SSR	*2.3*	*2.3*	*2.2*	*2.6*	*2.3*	*2.3*	*2.4*	*1.8*	*2.1*	*1.8*	*RSS de Biélorussie*
Ukrainian SSR	*73.2*	*73.1*	*73.1*	*88.5*	*83.6*	*90.8*	*94.5*	*92.2*	*99.3*	*114.6*	*RSS d'Ukraine*
Oceania	**35.7**	**35.0**	**36.4**	**39.1**	**39.8**	**54.2**	**45.7**	**100.2**	**76.9**	**82.7**	**Océanie**
American Samoa	* 26.0	* 26.8	* 26.8	* [1] 30.9	* [1] 30.9	43.8	37.1	* 90.1	...	...	Samoa américaines
Australia[8]	7.8	6.4	7.9	7.3	7.0	8.7	6.5	* 9.0	7.4	6.4	Australie[8]
New Zealand	...	...	...	0.8	1.9	1.7	2.0	0.8	0.9	...	Nouvelle–Zélande
Total	**2 939.6**	**2 920.1**	**3 098.3**	**3 508.7**	**3 683.9**	**3 676.3**	**3 469.1**	**3 498.1**	**3 408.2**	**3 891.9**	**Total**

General note.
Edible fish products packed and heat–processed in hermetically–sealed containers. Prior to packing, the products may have been smoked, dried, seasoned or otherwise prepared. In terms of net weight. (SITC 03201–0).

[1] Source: Food and Agriculture Organization (FAO), (Rome).

[2] Source: Office national des Peches, (Rabat).
[3] Excluding shellfish.
[4] Exports.
[5] Production by establishments employing 5 or more persons.
[6] Twelve months ending 30 September of year stated.
[7] Production by establishments employing 10 or more persons.
[8] Twelve months ending 30 June of year stated.

Remarque générale.
Produits de poisson comestibles, traités par la chaleur et mis dans des récipients fermés hermétiquement. Avant le conditionnement, les produits peuvent avoir été fumés, séchés, assaisonnés ou autrement préparés.Poids net.(CTCI 03201–0).

[1] Source: Organisation des Nations Unies pour l'alimentation et l'agriculture (FAO), (Rome).
[2] Source: Office national des pêches, (Rabat).
[3] Non compris les coquillages.
[4] Exportations.
[5] Production des établissements occupant 5 personnes ou plus.
[6] Période de douze mois finissant le 30 septembre de l'année indiquée.
[7] Production des établissements occupant 10 personnes ou plus.
[8] Période de douze mois finissant le 30 juin de l'année indiquée.

Unit : Thousand metric tons | Unité : Milliers de tonnes métriques

Country or area	1976	1977	1978	1979	1980	1981	1982	1983	1984	1985	Pays ou zone
Africa	**233.3**	**248.0**	**272.9**	**307.7**	**318.6**	**304.8**	**328.4**	**366.7**	**379.1**	**450.3**	**Afrique**
Algeria[1]	8.5	9.0	11.6	12.9	13.4	14.6	14.1	* 13.4	...	...	Algérie[1]
Angola[1]	0.4	...	...	...	...	...	...	...	...	...	Angola[1]
Côte d'Ivoire	1.0	1.6	1.9	1.8	2.2	2.4	2.4	2.9	2.8	...	Côte d'Ivoire
Egypt[1]	128.0	133.2	151.7	160.0	159.0	154.0	166.0	...	...	...	Egypte[1]
Ghana[1]	3.3	1.4	1.3	0.8	0.9	1.3	0.7	0.3	0.5	0.9	Ghana[1]
Kenya	[1] 3.9	[1] 5.4	[1] 6.0	[1] 6.2	[1] 10.6	[1] 6.7	[1] 12.7	# 55.2	50.1	95.2	Kenya
Senegal[1]	0.2	0.1	0.1	0.1	0.2	* 0.1	* 0.3	* 0.3	* 0.3	* 0.3	Sénégal[1]
South Africa	74.1	77.8	78.8	* 108.8	115.8	111.2	110.7	95.9	108.1	126.9	Afrique du Sud
Tunisia[1]	0.4	0.5	0.6	0.6	0.8	0.8	1.5	1.7	1.4	1.7	Tunisie[1]
Zaire[1]	2.1	2.3	3.0	...	...	...	...	...	...	...	Zaïre[1]
Zambia	11.3	16.2	17.5	13.7	12.9	10.9	17.1	20.5	17.7	17.3	Zambie
America, North	**3 320.5**	**3 254.3**	**3 321.8**	**3 434.6**	**3 568.1**	**3 336.0**	**3 103.5**	**3 352.1**	**3 868.5**	**4 143.1**	**Amérique du Nord**
Barbados[1]	1.7	2.0	2.4	2.1	2.2	3.8	2.6	3.5	2.8	2.6	Barbade[1]
Canada[1]	125.3	141.4	127.7	131.2	140.4	...	...	...	...	...	Canada[1]
Dominican Republic	[1] 3.0	[1] 3.3	[1] 4.0	# 3.8	4.3	6.3	6.1	7.7	5.9	8.6	Rép. dominicaine
El Salvador[1]	2.5	2.9	2.9	2.3	2.8	3.2	3.4	4.1	...	...	El Salvador[1]
Jamaica[2]	6.1	8.2	8.6	7.6	5.4	6.7	8.3	8.4	9.0	8.9	Jamaïque[2]
Mexico	200.1	197.7	204.7	214.0	231.9	237.2	247.7	257.2	276.6	285.5	Mexique
Trinidad and Tobago	7.6	6.8	7.6	7.4	5.5	6.8	6.9	8.1	4.0	6.4	Trinité-et-Tobago
United States	2 974.2	2 892.1	2 964.0	3 066.1	3 175.5	2 932.9	2 687.4	2 920.1	3 421.3	3 680.1	Etats-Unis
America, South	**305.8**	**345.9**	**369.9**	**348.0**	**343.7**	**335.0**	**342.0**	**340.7**	**340.9**	**336.1**	**Amérique du Sud**
Brazil[1 3]	154.6	187.6	202.6	...	...	...	...	...	...	...	Brésil[1 3]
Chile[1]	15.5	17.3	17.7	19.9	20.0	18.7	20.1	23.7	26.2	25.5	Chili[1]
Colombia[1]	...	...	...	...	58.2	59.8	63.3	61.8	...	...	Colombie[1]
Ecuador	42.5	...	49.4	...	...	* 31.4	* 35.0	33.0	...	...	Equateur
Guyana	2.1	2.6	2.6	2.7	3.8	3.2	1.1	0.0	...	...	Guyana
Peru[1]	11.5	13.4	14.2	17.6	20.1	18.4	18.7	18.3	* 18.6	* 16.4	Pérou[1]
Suriname[1]	...	...	...	0.8	0.6	0.7	1.0	1.1	1.2	1.4	Suriname[1]
Venezuela[1]	18.5	19.5	22.1	24.4	...	...	...	...	...	...	Venezuela[1]
Asia	**775.8**	**799.6**	**877.9**	**820.2**	**817.1**	**894.1**	**946.6**	**965.9**	**989.1**	**992.1**	**Asie**
Afghanistan[1 4]	11.3	9.9	10.4	9.5	6.5	4.5	2.9	2.1	2.7	3.6	Afghanistan[1 4]
Burma[1 5]	...	0.0	0.0	0.1	0.2	0.3	0.3	0.2	...	...	Birmanie[1 5]
Indonesia	17.9	21.0	14.5	18.4	28.7	25.3	20.6	29.5	19.9	...	Indonésie
Israel[1]	31.2	30.7	33.3	34.2	33.6	32.9	33.9	33.2	34.2	32.7	Israël[1]
Japan	402.0	418.9	439.8	464.6	471.1	491.2	491.0	495.7	499.5	494.3	Japon
Korea, Republic of	30.7	38.6	38.8	39.4	37.7	43.1	...	...	...	...	Corée, République de
Malaysia	...	...	...	...	...	...	12.8	12.9	12.0	12.3	Malaisie
Philippines	34.7	32.8	* 64.9	22.1	24.1	11.3	5.4	9.4	...	...	Philippines
Sri Lanka[1]	4.4	4.1	6.1	6.9	6.4	6.7	...	...	...	...	Sri Lanka[1]
Syrian Arab Republic[1]	6.0	6.2	5.4	5.9	7.3	6.5	7.6	7.1	8.9	8.6	Rép. arabe syrienne[1]
Turkey[1]	225.2	224.9	252.3	206.6	189.1	259.8	320.4	321.9	352.1	350.3	Turquie[1]
Europe	**2 906.2**	**2 914.2**	**2 950.4**	**2 946.2**	**3 055.8**	**3 154.3**	**3 183.2**	**3 128.2**	**3 098.0**	**3 047.6**	**Europe**
EEC	***1 807.2***	***1 827.5***	***1 850.2***	***1 841.3***	***1 915.0***	***1 964.9***	***1 999.0***	***1 956.1***	***1 910.4***	***1 836.7***	***CEE***
Belgium[1]	145.3	141.9	144.8	149.7	158.3	149.9	161.4	158.9	169.6	171.8	Belgique[1]
Denmark	96.6	98.0	94.7	99.8	103.6	108.6	115.7	107.4	115.4	108.4	Danemark
France	164.1	164.8	168.0	158.5	167.2	175.1	175.6	172.6	162.9	154.0	France
Germany, Fed. Rep.	616.0	610.9	612.4	611.1	617.4	611.3	616.4	605.6	590.9	577.6	Allemagne, Rép. féd.
Greece	35.3	35.6	35.7	39.3	43.6	39.9	41.1	42.8	39.2	...	Grèce
Ireland	[1] 13.4	[1] 12.7	[1] 15.0	[1] 17.3	[1] 15.8	28.5	25.4	23.0	24.2	25.0	Irlande
Italy[1]	64.7	65.6	73.5	68.2	68.5	71.6	71.5	68.0	63.9	67.7	Italie[1]
Netherlands[1]	201.8	207.1	207.1	209.4	227.7	229.9	235.9	236.8	247.3	203.0	Pays-Bas[1]
United Kingdom	470.0	491.0	499.0	488.0	513.0	550.0	556.0	541.0	497.0	486.0	Royaume-Uni
EFTA	***380.7***	***395.1***	***393.0***	***393.4***	***400.7***	***412.8***	***404.3***	***398.5***	***401.4***	***400.0***	***AELE***
Austria	60.5	60.3	60.3	61.0	64.9	67.3	67.3	66.5	66.0	65.2	Autriche
Finland[1]	40.1	37.8	39.4	37.7	37.7	52.9	42.7	37.5	38.2	39.8	Finlande[1]
Iceland[1]	2.7	2.9	2.8	2.7	2.8	2.9	2.6	3.1	3.0	...	Islande[1]
Norway	83.0	80.9	79.4	78.6	80.5	73.3	69.1	70.7	69.8	65.5	Norvège
Portugal	38.7	44.6	46.4	48.1	51.4	54.5	56.5	56.2	57.8	57.7	Portugal
Sweden	155.7	168.7	164.8	165.3	163.3	161.8	166.1	164.6	166.5	168.8	Suède
East Europe	***591.0***	***576.2***	***576.3***	***586.2***	***596.5***	***619.1***	***609.4***	***593.7***	***604.6***	***624.6***	***Europe de l'est***

For general note and footnotes, see end of table.

Voir la fin du tableau pour la remarque générale et les notes.

Margarine, imitation lard and other prepared fats (continued) – Margarine, simili–saindoux et autres graisses alimentaires préparées (suite)

Unit : Thousand metric tons

Unité : Milliers de tonnes métriques

Country or area	1976	1977	1978	1979	1980	1981	1982	1983	1984	1985	Pays ou zone
Bulgaria[1]	...	...	...	...	0.0	0.0	0.6	0.7	1.4	1.5	Bulgarie[1]
Czechoslovakia	147.2	148.8	147.5	154.5	155.5	161.6	165.2	161.4	160.1	168.2	Tchécoslovaquie
German Dem. Rep.[1]	179.0	171.7	169.6	169.4	171.9	175.2	180.5	177.3	179.7	180.3	Rép. dém. allemande[1]
Hungary	43.6	46.6	48.4	52.7	53.6	52.6	54.7	53.7	54.5	60.9	Hongrie
Poland	200.7	189.0	188.4	186.9	189.6	203.5	181.2	168.8	176.4	180.6	Pologne
Romania[1]	20.5	20.1	22.3	22.6	25.9	26.1	27.1	31.8	32.5	33.1	Roumanie[1]
Other Europe	***127.2***	***115.3***	***130.9***	***125.3***	***143.6***	***157.5***	***170.6***	***179.8***	***181.7***	***186.3***	***Autre Europe***
Spain	84.1	...	...	73.5	85.3	95.8	112.2	115.5	...	...	Espagne
Yugoslavia	43.2	37.6	47.9	51.8	58.3	61.7	58.3	64.3	67.1	66.5	Yougoslavie
USSR[1]	**1 040.3**	**1 167.9**	**1 225.1**	**1 273.2**	**1 262.6**	**1 360.5**	**1 432.1**	**1 483.5**	**1 427.0**	**1 411.3**	**URSS[1]**
Byelorussian SSR[1]	*84.2*	*90.1*	*96.3*	*101.5*	*105.1*	*110.5*	*114.5*	*117.8*	*115.5*	*119.4*	*RSS de Biélorussie[1]*
Ukrainian SSR[1]	*209.9*	*244.3*	*253.6*	*268.8*	*263.9*	*287.0*	*304.3*	*310.1*	*285.8*	*275.6*	*RSS d'Ukraine[1]*
Oceania	**109.3**	**122.7**	**122.1**	**133.5**	**139.9**	**140.0**	**147.5**	**151.9**	**153.6**	**143.0**	**Océanie**
Australia[1 6]	109.3	122.7	122.1	133.5	139.9	140.0	147.5	151.9	153.6	143.0	Australie[1 6]
Total	**8 691.1**	**8 852.6**	**9 140.0**	**9 263.3**	**9 505.9**	**9 524.8**	**9 483.3**	**9 788.9**	**10 256.3**	**10 523.7**	**Total**

General note.
Solid edible preparations of fats, consisting of mixtures of different animal fats and oils, different vegetable fats and oils, or both. Fats and oils simply refined, or both hydrogenated and refined without further treatment and liquid mixtures of vegetable oils, are excluded. (SITC 09140–0).

[1] Margarine only.
[2] Including lard.
[3] Production by establishments employing 5 or more persons.
[4] Twelve months beginning 21 March of year stated.
[5] Government production only.
[6] Twelve months ending 30 June of year stated.

Remarque générale.
Mélanges solides comestibles de corps gras, composés de mélanges de diverses graisses et huiles animales, de diverses graisses et huiles végétales, soit entre elles, soit les unes avec les autres. Cette position ne comprend pas les graisses et les huiles ayant subi un simple raffinage, ou un raffinage suivi d'une hydrogénation, sans autre traitement, ni les mélanges liquides d'huiles végétales. (CTCI 09140–0).

[1] Margarine seulement.
[2] Y compris le saindoux.
[3] Production des établissements occupant 5 personnes ou plus.
[4] Période de douze mois commençant le 21 mars de l'année indiquée.
[5] Production de l'Etat seulement.
[6] Période de douze mois finissant le 30 juin de l'année indiquée.

Oils and fats of aquatic animal origin – Huiles et graisses d'animaux aquatiques

Unit : Thousand metric tons

Unité : Milliers de tonnes métriques

Country or area	1976	1977	1978	1979	1980	1981	1982	1983	1984	1985	Pays ou zone
Africa	**51**	**36**	**56**	**66**	**52**	**68**	**40**	**67**	**36**	**52**	**Afrique**
Angola* [1]	...	...	...	2	2	2	2	2	1	1	Angola* [1]
Mauritania	...	...	...	...	1	1	1	2	2	3	Mauritanie
Morocco	4	6	6	* 7	4	10	3	* 8	8	* 6	Maroc
South Africa	44	27	47	56	45	55	34	55	25	42	Afrique du Sud
America, North	**122**	**99**	**158**	**144**	**187**	**180**	**192**	**206**	**167**	**228**	**Amérique du Nord**
Canada [1]	12	15	13	12	14	16	8	7	6	8	Canada [1]
Mexico [1]	3	10	6	6	15	11	12	5	6	6	Mexique [1]
Panama	14	13	5	5	17	6	2	5	7	34	Panama
United States	93	61	134	121	141	147	170	* 189	148	180	Etats–Unis
America, South	**168**	**184**	**230**	**257**	**211**	**234**	**361**	**80**	**373**	**179**	**Amérique du Sud**
Argentina [1]	6	* 1	* 1	* 1	* 1	* 1	* 1	* 1	* 1	* 1	Argentine [1]
Brazil [1]	1	* 2	* 1	* 2	* 2	* 1	* 1	* 2	* 1	...	Brésil [1]
Chile [1]	35	60	76	109	111	127	145	57	184	39	Chili [1]
Colombia	...	...	...	...	...	7	9	1	...	...	Colombie
Ecuador	6	6	17	10	13	23	18	3	38	* 11	Equateur
Peru	[1] 114	[1] 109	[1] 129	[1] 129	78	75	187	16	* 143	* 121	Pérou
Asia	**181**	**221**	**256**	**268**	**266**	**281**	**317**	**355**	**427**	**398**	**Asie**
Indonesia [1]	...	1	1	1	0	0	0	1	1	0	Indonésie [1]
Japan [2]	166	208	244	253	263	279	313	350	417	387	Japon [2]
Korea, Republic of [1]	2	1	2	2	* 1	1	2	2	4	5	Corée, République de [1]
Sri Lanka	...	...	...	11	1	0	1	0	0	0	Sri Lanka
Turkey	1	1	1	1	* 1	1	1	[1] 2	[1] 5	[1] 6	Turquie
Europe	**715**	**728**	**708**	**739**	**667**	**665**	**607**	**620**	**685**	**707**	**Europe**
EEC	***307***	***285***	***288***	***312***	***359***	***380***	***389***	***349***	***374***	***405***	***CEE***
Belgium [1]	* 1	0	0	0	0	[3] 28	[3] 33	[3] 30	[3] 41	[3] 50	Belgique [1]
Denmark	97	97	79	84	124	116	101	90	85	87	Danemark
France [1]	7	3	3	3	3	3	3	3	4	4	France [1]
Germany, Fed. Rep.	18	18	13	17	18	15	20	15	18	26	Allemagne, Rép. féd.
Ireland [1]	2	2	3	2	2	1	2	2	2	2	Irlande [1]
United Kingdom	182	165	190	206	212	217	230	209	224	...	Royaume–Uni
EFTA	***393***	***422***	***401***	***408***	***291***	***270***	***204***	***254***	***288***	***279***	***AELE***
Finland	3	3	3	4	4	2	2	3	1	...	Finlande
Iceland	35	76	97	94	89	84	15	27	90	119	Islande
Norway	343	333	291	300	[1] 187	[1] 173	[1] 178	[1] 218	[1] 190	[1] 152	Norvège
Portugal*	7	7	7	7	6	6	5	3	3	3	Portugal*
Sweden	5	3	3	3	5	5	4	* 3	4	4	Suède
East Europe	***3***	***8***	***6***	***7***	***4***	***1***	***1***	***3***	***2***	***2***	***Europe de l'est***
Poland	3	8	6	7	4	1	1	3	2	2	Pologne
Other Europe	***12***	***13***	***13***	***12***	***13***	***14***	***13***	***14***	***21***	***21***	***Autre Europe***
Faeroe Islands [1]	6	7	* 6	* 6	* 7	5	4	8	9	8	Iles Féroé [1]
Spain [1]	6	6	7	6	6	9	9	6	13	12	Espagne [1]
USSR* [1]	**145**	**121**	**131**	**117**	**43**	**50**	**67**	**73**	**93**	**85**	**URSS* [1]**
Oceania	**6**	**4**	**4**	**0**	**0**	**0**	**0**	**0**	**0**	**0**	**Océanie**
Australia [1]	6	4	4	0	0	0	0	0	0	0	Australie [1]
Total	**1 388**	**1 393**	**1 543**	**1 591**	**1 426**	**1 478**	**1 584**	**1 401**	**1 780**	**1 648**	**Total**

General note.
Oils and fats of fish and marine mammals, edible or inedible, crude and refined, but not further prepared, extracted from the body of the aquatic animal or from its liver, viscera or any other part (for example, whale oil, sperm oil, whale liver oil, fish liver oils, fish body oils). Processed products on the basis of these oils are excluded. (SITC 41110–0).

Remarque générale.
Huiles et graisses de poissons et de mammifères marins, comestibles ou non, brutes et raffinées, mais n'ayant subi aucun autre traitement, extraites du corps d'animaux aquatiques ou de leurs foies, viscères ou autres parties du corps (par exemple huile de baleine, huile de cachalot ou huile de spermaceti, huile de foie de baleine, huiles de foie de poisson, huiles de poissons). Cette rubrique ne comprend pas les produits dérivés de ces huiles. (CTCI 41110–0).

For footnotes, see end of table.

Voir la fin du tableau pour les notes.

[1] Source: Food and Agriculture Organization (FAO), (Rome).

[2] Twelve months beginning 1 April of year stated.

[3] Crude oils only.

[1] Source: Organisation des Nations Unies pour l'alimentation et l'agriculture (FAO), (Rome).

[2] Période de douze mois commençant le 1er avril de l'année indiquée.

[3] Huiles brutes seulement.

Oils and fats of animals, unprocessed – Huiles et graisses d'origine animale, non traitées

Unit : Thousand metric tons

Unité : Milliers de tonnes métriques

Country or area	1976	1977	1978	1979	1980	1981	1982	1983	1984	1985	Pays ou zone
Africa	**12**	**13**	**14**	**16**	**14**	**13**	**13**	**13**	**14**	**14**	**Afrique**
South Africa*	12	13	14	16	14	13	13	13	14	14	Afrique du Sud*
America, North	**3 163**	**3 427**	**3 388**	**3 482**	**3 593**	**3 497**	**4 019**	**3 894**	**3 567**	**3 642**	**Amérique du Nord**
Canada* [1,2]	256	295	297	317	366	213	220	215	214	205	Canada* [1,2]
Costa Rica* [1,2]	2	2	2	2	2	2	2	2	2	3	Costa Rica* [1,2]
Cuba	15	16	17	...	...	...	...	...	...	...	Cuba
El Salvador [1,2]	1	1	1	1	1	1	1	* 1	* 1	1	El Salvador [1,2]
Honduras [1,2]	1	1	2	2	2	2	2	* 2	2	2	Honduras [1,2]
Mexico [1,2]	26	27	27	29	31	34	35	* 35	* 35	38	Mexique [1,2]
United States [1]	2 862	3 085	3 042	3 115	3 175	3 229	3 743	3 623	3 297	3 377	Etats-Unis [1]
America, South	**346**	**365**	**372**	**353**	**353**	**350**	**345**	**329**	**328**	**337**	**Amérique du Sud**
Argentina* [1,2]	172	178	193	188	175	172	155	143	156	165	Argentine* [1,2]
Brazil*	117	130	123	115	122	[2] 117	[2] 129	[2] 128	[2] 118	[2] 123	Brésil*
Chile* [1,2]	6	5	5	5	5	5	5	5	5	5	Chili* [1,2]
Colombia*	12	13	12	13	15	15	14	14	14	14	Colombie*
Paraguay [1,2]	0	1	1	0	0	0	0	...	...	...	Paraguay [1,2]
Peru [1]	[2] 5	[2] 5	[2] 5	[2] 5	5	5	7	5	5	5	Pérou [1]
Uruguay [1]	* [2] 26	* [2] 25	* [2] 24	* [2] 17	* [2] 21	* [2] 26	* [2] 25	* [2] 23	...	15	Uruguay [1]
Venezuela* [1,2]	8	8	9	10	10	10	10	10	9	9	Venezuela* [1,2]
Asia	**213**	**260**	**295**	**307**	**334**	**348**	**324**	**343**	**387**	**417**	**Asie**
China* [1,2]	17	18	18	20	21	22	23	26	28	31	Chine* [1,2]
India* [1,2]	26	26	26	27	28	29	30	31	32	33	Inde* [1,2]
Indonesia	1	1	2	9	9	...	3	...	...	...	Indonésie
Iran(Islamic Rep.of)* [1,2]	23	25	25	26	30	48	26	35	35	35	Iran(Rép.islamique)* [1,2]
Japan [3]	132	176	210	210	230	227	233	233	273	299	Japon [3]
Philippines* [1,2]	2	2	2	2	2	2	2	2	2	...	Philippines* [1,2]
Turkey* [1,2]	12	12	12	13	14	14	7	8	8	...	Turquie* [1,2]
Europe	**1 018**	**1 024**	**1 038**	**1 092**	**1 206**	**1 189**	**1 183**	**1 235**	**1 346**	**1 314**	**Europe**
EEC	***727***	***735***	***727***	***797***	***878***	***890***	***875***	***899***	***973***	***958***	***CEE***
Belgium [4]	115	115	121	126	128	139	160	162	183	191	Belgique [4]
Denmark	78	67	75	79	84	...	...	107	96	94	Danemark
France [1,2]	173	186	198	235	* 265	* 260	* 273	* 273	* 273	* 278	France [1,2]
Germany, Fed. Rep. [1,2]	71	69	72	76	78	77	74	75	81	* 79	Allemagne, Rép. féd. [1,2]
Greece* [1,2]	15	14	14	13	13	13	12	12	12	12	Grèce* [1,2]
Ireland* [1,2]	30	29	30	32	25	24	25	25	25	26	Irlande* [1,2]
Italy* [1,2]	21	22	22	23	25	24	24	25	25	26	Italie* [1,2]
Netherlands [1,2]	39	38	42	34	* 33	* 40	* 40	* 40	* 40	* 41	Pays-Bas [1,2]
United Kingdom [1]	185	195	153	179	227	226	* 176	* [2] 180	* [2] 238	* [2] 211	Royaume-Uni [1]
EFTA	***55***	***53***	***47***	***48***	***49***	***51***	***52***	***52***	***55***	***58***	***AELE***
Austria [1]	15	15	8	[2] 8	[2] 8	* [2] 9	* [2] 9	* [2] 9	* [2] 9	* [2] 10	Autriche [1]
Finland	6	5	6	6	6	7	8	9	10	...	Finlande
Iceland [1,2]	* 1	* 1	* 1	* 1	0	* 1	* 1	* 1	...	...	Islande [1,2]
Norway* [1,2]	1	1	1	1	1	1	1	1	1	1	Norvège* [1,2]
Portugal* [1,2]	6	5	5	5	6	6	6	6	6	6	Portugal* [1,2]
Sweden [1,2]	19	19	19	19	* 19	* 19	* 19	* 19	* 19	...	Suède [1,2]
Switzerland [1,2]	7	7	7	8	9	8	8	* 7	* 9	* 11	Suisse [1,2]
East Europe	***199***	***199***	***229***	***214***	***249***	***228***	***236***	***262***	***286***	***266***	***Europe de l'est***
Bulgaria	3	3	* 3	* 3	3	3	3	4	4	4	Bulgarie
Czechoslovakia [1]	19	19	20	19	20	* [2] 17	* [2] 14	* [2] 14	* [2] 12	* [2] 10	Tchécoslovaquie [1]
German Dem. Rep.* [1,2]	14	13	14	13	13	14	14	14	14	14	Rép. dém. allemande* [1,2]
Hungary	124	127	154	137	176	164	171	197	219	193	Hongrie
Poland* [1,2]	31	28	29	32	28	22	27	25	29	37	Pologne* [1,2]
Romania* [1,2]	8	9	9	10	9	8	7	8	8	8	Roumanie* [1,2]
Other Europe	***37***	***37***	***35***	***33***	***30***	***20***	***20***	***22***	***32***	***32***	***Autre Europe***
Spain [1,2]	18	19	18	17	18	* 9	* 9	* 9	* 19	* 19	Espagne [1,2]
Yugoslavia* [1,2]	19	18	17	16	12	11	11	13	13	13	Yougoslavie* [1,2]
USSR* [1,2]	**336**	**322**	**332**	**327**	**330**	**333**	**330**	**334**	**352**	**360**	**URSS* [1,2]**

For general note and footnotes, see end of table.

Voir la fin du tableau pour la remarque générale et les notes.

Oils and fats of animals, unprocessed (continued) – Huiles et graisses d'origine animale, non traitées (suite)

Unit : Thousand metric tons

Unité : Milliers de tonnes métriques

Country or area	1976	1977	1978	1979	1980	1981	1982	1983	1984	1985	Pays ou zone
Oceania	**342**	**511**	**538**	**535**	**471**	**441**	**429**	**471**	**440**	**538**	**Océanie**
Australia[1]	248	379	408	410	346	316	297	339	309	382	Australie[1]
New Zealand[2 5]	94	132	130	125	125	125	132	132	131	156	Nouvelle-Zélande[2 5]
Total	**5 430**	**5 922**	**5 977**	**6 112**	**6 301**	**6 172**	**6 643**	**6 618**	**6 433**	**6 622**	**Total**

General note.
Crude, refined or purified oils, unrendered fats of pigs, poultry, bovine cattle, sheep or goats, tallow, lard stearine, and lard oil, wool grease and degras. Processed products on the basis of these oils are excluded. (SITC 41130-0).

[1] Tallow only.
[2] Source: Food and Agriculture Organization (FAO), (Rome).

[3] Twelve months beginning 1 April of year stated.
[4] Production from imported and indigenous raw material.
[5] Including unprocessed vegetable oils except olive oil.

Remarque générale.
Huiles brutes, raffinées ou épurées, graisses de porc, de volaille, de bovins, d'ovins et de caprins, non pressées ni fondues, suif, stéarine solaire et huile de saindoux, graisses de suint et dégras. Cette rubrique ne comprend pas les produits fabriqués dérivés de ces huiles ou graisses. (CTCI 41130-0).

[1] Suif seulement.
[2] Source: Organisation des Nations Unies pour l'alimentation et l'agriculture (FAO), (Rome).
[3] Période de douze mois commençant le 1er avril de l'année indiquée.
[4] Production à partir de matières premières indigènes et importées.
[5] Y compris les huiles brutes d'origine végétale excepté l'huile d'olive.

Oil, soya bean, crude – Huile de fèves de soya, brute

Unit : Thousand metric tons

Unité : Milliers de tonnes métriques

Country or area	1976	1977	1978	1979	1980	1981	1982	1983	1984	1985	Pays ou zone
America, North	**4 608**	**4 268**	**4 978**	**5 535**	**5 895**	**5 535**	**5 473**	**5 943**	**5 526**	**5 692**	**Amérique du Nord**
Canada	[1] 117	117	125	139	171	149	154	132	168	...	Canada
Cuba	...	...	...	...	...	0	0	0	2	2	Cuba
Mexico	117	* 140	* 170	* 176	* 235	* 260	* 260	* 350	* 360	* 310	Mexique
United States	4 372	4 009	4 681	5 218	5 487	5 126	5 059	5 461	4 996	5 212	Etats-Unis
America, South	**1 350**	**1 723**	**1 719**	**1 726**	**2 156**	**2 948**	**2 765**	**2 645**	**2 872**	**2 643**	**Amérique du Sud**
Argentina	66	77	88	91	141	172	202	292	409	340	Argentine
Brazil	* 1 238	1 583	1 592	[2] 1 600	1 989	2 773	2 560	2 350	2 460	2 300	Brésil
Colombia	1	...	...	5	...	...	...	...	...	...	Colombie
Paraguay	* [1] 45	* [1] 60	...	...	...	0	0	0	0	0	Paraguay
Asia	**999**	**1 038**	**1 049**	**1 142**	**1 134**	**1 116**	**1 065**	**1 147**	**1 142**	**1 148**	**Asie**
China*	...	...	450	520	515	480	430	450	...	...	Chine*
Japan[3]	485	532	598	621	618	635	634	696	698	712	Japon[3]
Turkey	1	1	1	1	* 1	* 1	* 1	* 1	0	...	Turquie
Europe	**1 971**	**2 013**	**2 390**	**2 516**	**2 718**	**2 546**	**2 655**	**2 584**	**2 753**	**2 861**	**Europe**
EEC	***1 593***	***1 612***	***1 917***	***2 029***	***2 082***	***1 911***	***1 991***	***1 948***	***2 018***	***2 075***	***CEE***
Belgium[4]	155	146	184	179	162	91	117	118	120	127	Belgique[4]
Denmark	34	37	40	34	25	14	12	12	8	1	Danemark
France	91	96	138	151	144	97	152	144	111	99	France
Germany, Fed. Rep.* [1]	615	620	650	650	680	...	...	...	...	...	Allemagne, Rép. féd.* [1]
Greece	...	...	...	...	...	34	39	47	36	...	Grèce
Italy*	[1] 200	205	220	275	290	...	...	...	...	...	Italie*
Netherlands	* [1] 270	277	* 430	* 530	547	492	448	445	...	...	Pays-Bas
United Kingdom	189	192	216	171	195	180	179	97	65	63	Royaume-Uni
EFTA	***26***	***41***	***48***	***57***	***38***	***63***	***105***	***125***	***138***	***166***	***AELE***
Finland	17	14	15	17	19	17	21	20	15	...	Finlande
Portugal	9	27	33	40	19	46	84	105	123	147	Portugal
East Europe	***17***	***10***	***25***	***30***	***53***	***32***	***19***	***41***	***18***	***12***	***Europe de l'est***
Hungary	6	7	5	3	6	7	6	9	7	6	Hongrie
Poland	11	3	20	27	47	25	13	32	11	6	Pologne
Other Europe	***335***	***350***	***400***	***400***	***545***	***540***	***540***	***470***	***579***	***609***	***Autre Europe***
Spain	335	* 350	* 400	* 400	* 545	* 540	* 540	* 470	...	...	Espagne
USSR* [1]	...	...	...	...	**280**	**280**	**230**	**220**	**190**	**380**	**URSS* [1]**
Total	**9 151**	**9 270**	**10 371**	**11 160**	**12 182**	**12 425**	**12 188**	**12 539**	**12 483**	**12 724**	**Total**

General note.
Data refer to crude soya bean oil. (SITC 42120-1).

[1] Source: U. S. Department of Agriculture, (Washington, D. C.).
[2] Production by establishments employing 5 or more persons.
[3] Including refined soybean oil.
[4] Production from imported and indigenous raw material.

Remarque générale.
Les données se rapportent à la production d'huile brute de fèves de soya. CTCI 42120-1).

[1] Source: U.S. Department of Agriculture, (Washington, D.C.).
[2] Production des établissements occupant 5 personnes ou plus.
[3] Y compris l'huile de soja raffinée.
[4] Production à partir de matières premières indigènes et importées.

ISIC–BASED CODE
3115–13

Oil, soya bean, refined – Huile de fèves de soya, raffinée

CODE BASE CITI
3115–13

Unit : Thousand metric tons

Unité : Milliers de tonnes métriques

Country or area	1976	1977	1978	1979	1980	1981	1982	1983	1984	1985	Pays ou zone
Africa	**4**	**13**	**14**	**21**	**21**	**21**	**22**	**25**	**24**	**25**	**Afrique**
Egypt	...	2	3	5	7	10	11	14	13	14	Egypte
Zambia	4	...	...	16	14	...	...	...	...	...	Zambie
America, North	**3 472**	**3 724**	**4 121**	**4 341**	**4 290**	**4 508**	**4 634**	**4 840**	**4 671**	**4 770**	**Amérique du Nord**
Canada	121	116	117	122	125	121	...	...	...	...	Canada
Dominican Republic	15	13	13	17	19	28	35	37	30	41	Rép. dominicaine
Mexico	77	61	81	66	70	67	89	89	105	111	Mexique
United States	3 259	3 534	3 910	4 136	4 076	4 292	4 386	4 590	4 411	4 492	Etats–Unis
America, South	**642**	**762**	**843**	**805**	**1 130**	**1 348**	**1 392**	**1 536**	**1 658**	**1 793**	**Amérique du Sud**
Brazil	638	755	827	[1] 794	1 115	1 319	...	...	...	...	Brésil
Colombia	3	6	16	10	13	26	33	50	...	...	Colombie
Paraguay	1	1	0	1	2	3	6	6	5	6	Paraguay
Asia	**65**	**70**	**74**	**74**	**68**	**68**	**74**	**81**	**81**	**71**	**Asie**
Israel	52	57	61	61	55	57	62	69	69	59	Israël
Thailand	...	...	...	...	13	11	...	...	...	...	Thaïlande
Turkey	1	1	1	1	0	0	0	0	0	0	Turquie
Europe	**850**	**880**	**983**	**965**	**989**	**927**	**1 002**	**969**	**960**	**979**	**Europe**
EEC	***531***	***539***	***656***	***622***	***644***	***584***	***665***	***604***	***613***	***614***	***CEE***
Denmark	34	37	40	39	30	26	29	24	19	15	Danemark
France	88	93	134	147	161	91	...	...	...	...	France
Greece	...	...	...	...	...	25	27	25	20	...	Grèce
Netherlands	...	237	272	263	277	263	289	284	...	...	Pays–Bas
United Kingdom	140	148	186	149	152	179	178	122	124	112	Royaume–Uni
EFTA	***92***	***102***	***97***	***96***	***90***	***91***	***97***	***118***	***106***	***121***	***AELE***
Finland	7	6	5	5	4	5	8	4	4	...	Finlande
Norway	...	...	...	...	...	...	...	...	34	33	Norvège
Portugal	* 15	19	17	15	11	9	14	38	29	45	Portugal
Sweden	36	43	41	42	41	43	41	42	39	39	Suède
East Europe	***28***	***26***	***24***	***41***	***49***	***46***	***34***	***41***	***35***	***37***	***Europe de l'est***
Hungary	6	6	6	5	5	7	5	9	7	5	Hongrie
Poland	22	20	18	36	44	39	29	32	28	32	Pologne
Other Europe	***200***	***213***	***207***	***207***	***207***	***207***	***207***	***207***	***207***	***207***	***Autre Europe***
Spain	200	213	...	...	...	...	...	...	...	...	Espagne
Total	**5 033**	**5 449**	**6 036**	**6 206**	**6 498**	**6 872**	**7 124**	**7 452**	**7 395**	**7 638**	**Total**

General note.
Soya bean once–refined (e.g. refined by deacidifying, filtering, washing, decolorizing or deodorizing) and before use in end products. (SITC 42120–2).

[1] Production by establishments employing 5 or more persons.

Remarque générale.
Huile de soya, ayant subi un premier raffinage (notamment par désacidification, filtration, lavage, décoloration, ou désodorisation) et avant emploi dans les produits définitifs. (CTCI 42120–2).

[1] Production des établissements occupant 5 personnes ou plus.

Oil, cotton-seed, crude – Huile de graines de coton, brute

Unit : Thousand metric tons

Unité : Milliers de tonnes métriques

Country or area	1976	1977	1978	1979	1980	1981	1982	1983	1984	1985	Pays ou zone
Africa	**196**	**220**	**221**	**226**	**250**	**263**	**256**	**277**	**292**	**299**	**Afrique**
Burkina Faso	2	2	1	3	4	4	3	4	...	...	Burkina Faso
Côte d'Ivoire	3	6	11	12	12	13	14	21	27	...	Côte d'Ivoire
Egypt	161	167	171	173	196	208	201	...	...	...	Egypte
Sudan* [1]	29	44	...	...	...	...	...	...	...	...	Soudan* [1]
Zaire[2]	1	* 1	* 1	...	...	...	...	...	...	...	Zaïre[2]
America, North	**532**	**676**	**759**	**678**	**781**	**697**	**799**	**624**	**519**	**638**	**Amérique du Nord**
El Salvador[3]	3	...	...	* 6	* 12	* 8	* 12	17	...	...	El Salvador[3]
Mexico[1]	56	...	* 83	* 71	* 88	* 85	* 44	* 60	* 74	* 53	Mexique[1]
Nicaragua[1]	* 27	* 29	...	29	25	36	30	33	30	...	Nicaragua[1]
United States	446	569	642	572	656	568	713	514	399	534	Etats-Unis
America, South	**130**	**203**	**207**	**215**	**226**	**183**	**247**	**205**	**231**	**248**	**Amérique du Sud**
Argentina	33	39	54	49	54	21	35	27	41	38	Argentine
Brazil	* [1] 83	150	139	[4] 152	158	148	* 198	* 164	* 176	...	Brésil
Colombia	...	...	1	1	...	...	...	...	...	...	Colombie
Peru* [1]	13	...	...	...	...	...	...	...	...	...	Pérou* [1]
Asia	**786**	**674**	**650**	**659**	**696**	**734**	**821**	**701**	**791**	**793**	**Asie**
China*	520	...	# [1] 360	[1] 380	[1] 400	...	...	...	...	...	Chine*
India[5]	43	55	44	59	52	53	51	48	61	...	Inde[5]
Indonesia	0	2	3	1	0	0	0	...	...	...	Indonésie
Japan[6]	18	18	19	14	14	12	14	14	16	16	Japon[6]
Pakistan*	117	...	[1] 112	[1] 110	[1] 140	...	[1] 264	[1] 166	[1] 232	...	Pakistan*
Turkey[1]	* 88	* 76	* 112	* 95	* 90	...	* 77	58	67	...	Turquie[1]
Europe	**50**	**43**	**42**	**35**	**39**	**44**	**37**	**37**	**39**	**35**	**Europe**
EEC	***35***	***28***	***27***	***20***	***24***	***29***	***22***	***22***	***24***	***20***	***CEE***
Greece	35	28	27	20	24	29	22	22	24	...	Grèce
Other Europe	***15***	***15***	***15***	***15***	***15***	***15***	***15***	***15***	***15***	***15***	***Autre Europe***
Spain	15	...	...	...	...	...	...	...	...	...	Espagne
USSR*	**640**	**665**	**[1] 650**	**[1] 740**	**[1] 760**	**...**	**[1] 906**	**[1] 898**	**[1] 928**	**...**	**URSS***
Total	**2 334**	**2 481**	**2 528**	**2 553**	**2 752**	**2 739**	**3 065**	**2 743**	**2 800**	**2 995**	**Total**

General note.
Data refer to crude cotton-seed oil. (SITC 42130-1).

[1] Source: U. S. Department of Agriculture, (Washington, D. C.).
[2] Source: Banque du Zaire, (Kinshasa).
[3] Original data in kilolitres.
[4] Production by establishments employing 5 or more persons.
[5] Production by large and medium scale establishments only.
[6] Including refined cotton-seed oil.

Remarque générale.
Les données se rapportent à la production d'huile brute de graines de coton. (CTCI 42130-1).

[1] Source: U.S. Department of Agriculture, (Washington, D.C.).
[2] Source: Banque du Zaire, (Kinshasa).
[3] Données d'origine exprimées en kilolitres.
[4] Production des établissements occupant 5 personnes ou plus.
[5] Production des grandes et moyennes entreprises seulement.
[6] Y compris l'huile de coton raffinée.

Oil, cotton-seed, refined – Huile de graines de coton, raffinée

Unit : Thousand metric tons

Unité : Milliers de tonnes métriques

Country or area	1976	1977	1978	1979	1980	1981	1982	1983	1984	1985	Pays ou zone
Africa	**146**	**158**	**162**	**171**	**161**	**161**	**163**	**161**	**161**	**161**	**Afrique**
Burkina Faso	2	2	2	3	4	4	6	4	4	4	Burkina Faso
Egypt	144	156	160	168	...	...	...	...	...	...	Egypte
America, North	**452**	**592**	**628**	**585**	**659**	**580**	**681**	**528**	**468**	**590**	**Amérique du Nord**
Canada	3	3	...	...	...	...	...	...	...	...	Canada
Haiti	15	12	16	15	23	...	...	...	...	...	Haïti
Mexico	62	63	62	50	47	45	40	44	33	49	Mexique
United States	372	514	547	517	586	510	614	455	404	509	Etats-Unis
America, South	**100**	**115**	**124**	**87**	**94**	**96**	**89**	**82**	**80**	**83**	**Amérique du Sud**
Brazil	84	97	112	[1]78	84	76	...	...	...	...	Brésil
Colombia	11	16	9	7	8	7	5	4	4	4	Colombie
Paraguay	5	2	3	2	2	13	7	4	5	11	Paraguay
Asia	**68**	**92**	**100**	**110**	**83**	**99**	**404**	**441**	**268**	**285**	**Asie**
Iran(Islamic Rep.of)[2]	...	...	...	74	49	63	337	384	...	...	Iran(Rép.islamique)[2]
Israel	5	3	1	11	12	10	15	14	20	13	Israël
Thailand	...	...	...	...	3	2	...	...	...	...	Thaïlande
Turkey	36	38	24	22	19	24	49	41	28	27	Turquie
Europe	**50**	**45**	**45**	**36**	**35**	**39**	**33**	**33**	**35**	**32**	**Europe**
EEC	***26***	***23***	***23***	***16***	***14***	***18***	***12***	***13***	***16***	***12***	***CEE***
Greece	19	15	15	11	10	14	8	12	13	...	Grèce
United Kingdom	7	8	8	5	4	4	4	1	3	3	Royaume-Uni
EFTA	***10***	***8***	***8***	***6***	***7***	***7***	***7***	***6***	***5***	***6***	***AELE***
Sweden	10	8	8	6	7	7	7	6	5	6	Suède
Other Europe	***14***	***14***	***14***	***14***	***14***	***14***	***14***	***14***	***14***	***14***	***Autre Europe***
Spain	14	...	...	...	...	...	...	...	...	...	Espagne
Total	**816**	**1 002**	**1 059**	**989**	**1 032**	**975**	**1 370**	**1 245**	**1 011**	**1 151**	**Total**

General note.
Once-refined cotton-seed oil (for example, refined by deacidifying, filtering, washing, decolourizing or deodorizing) and before use in end products. (SITC 42130-2).

[1] Production by establishments employing 5 or more persons.
[2] Production by establishments employing 10 or more persons.

Remarque générale.
Huile de graines de coton, ayant subi un premier raffinage (notamment par désacidification, filtration, lavage, décoloration ou désodorisation) et avant emploi dans les produits définitifs. (CTCI 42130-2).

[1] Production des établissements occupant 5 personnes ou plus.
[2] Production des établissements occupant 10 personnes ou plus.

Oil, groundnut, crude – Huile d'arachides, brute

Unit : Thousand metric tons

Unité : Milliers de tonnes métriques

Country or area	1976	1977	1978	1979	1980	1981	1982	1983	1984	1985	Pays ou zone
Africa	**564**	**533**	**265**	**368**	**315**	**236**	**401**	**332**	**239**	**194**	**Afrique**
Burkina Faso	0	0	1	1	0	0	0	0	0	0	Burkina Faso
Congo	1	0	0	0	1	1	1	* 1	0	...	Congo
Mali[1]	11	15	10	11	8	6	2	1	...	...	Mali[1]
Niger	10	5	5	6	1	1	0	2	...	...	Niger
Nigeria* [1]	1	3	...	...	...	...	...	...	...	...	Nigéria* [1]
Senegal[2 3 4]	222	231	67	147	90	31	219	192	126	88	Sénégal[2 3 4]
South Africa	49	39	40	33	37	43	32	23	17	27	Afrique du Sud
Sudan*	270	240	[1] 140	[1] 168	[1] 176	[1] 152	[1] 145	...	...	...	Soudan*
America, North	**218**	**115**	**67**	**67**	**84**	**64**	**54**	**46**	**49**	**67**	**Amérique du Nord**
United States	218	115	67	67	84	64	54	46	49	67	Etats-Unis
America, South	**192**	**170**	**191**	**256**	**176**	**130**	**155**	**193**	**166**	**131**	**Amérique du Sud**
Argentina	60	119	124	130	75	32	63	87	64	28	Argentine
Brazil	* [1] 132	51	67	[5] 126	101	...	* 92	* 106	* 102	...	Brésil
Asia	**2 228**	**1 954**	**1 818**	**1 814**	**1 803**	**1 862**	**2 213**	**2 547**	**2 534**	**2 411**	**Asie**
Burma* [6]	94	...	...	...	...	...	...	...	...	...	Birmanie* [6]
China* [1]	450	390	280	352	405	...	...	...	...	...	Chine* [1]
Hong Kong	15	11	10	15	13	15	19	18	20	...	Hong-kong
India*	1 640	1 440	[1] 1 420	[1] 1 340	[1] 1 276	[1] 1 400	[1] 1 776	[1] 2 112	[1] 2 112	...	Inde*
Indonesia	29	...	14	13	15	16	0	...	...	...	Indonésie
Europe	**145**	**94**	**104**	**78**	**53**	**52**	**60**	**62**	**51**	**68**	**Europe**
EEC	***134***	***83***	***93***	***67***	***42***	***41***	***49***	***51***	***40***	***57***	***CEE***
Belgium[7]	1	1	1	1	1	# 10	17	19	17	17	Belgique[7]
France	114	63	70	41	30	12	13	...	...	21	France
Italy* [8]	...	...	22	25	11	...	...	...	...	...	Italie* [8]
Other Europe	***11***	***11***	***11***	***11***	***11***	***11***	***11***	***11***	***11***	***11***	***Autre Europe***
Spain	11	...	...	...	...	...	...	...	...	...	Espagne
Total	**3 347**	**2 867**	**2 445**	**2 583**	**2 431**	**2 345**	**2 884**	**3 180**	**3 039**	**2 871**	**Total**

General note.
Data refer to crude groundnut oil. (SITC 42140-1).

Remarque générale.
Les données se rapportent à la production d'huile brute d'arachide. (CTCI 42140-1).

1 Source: U. S. Department of Agriculture , (Washington, D. C.).
2 Crop year production.
3 Sales.
4 Source: Syndicat des fabricants d'huile et de tourteaux du Sénégal, (Dakar).
5 Production by establishments employing 5 or more persons.
6 Twelve months ending 30 September of year stated.
7 Production from imported and indigenous raw material.
8 Twelve months ending 30 June of year stated.

1 Source: U.S. Department of Agriculture, (Washington, D.C.).
2 Production par campagne.
3 Ventes.
4 Source: Syndicat des fabricants d'huile et de tourteaux du Sénégal, (Dakar).
5 Production des établissements occupant 5 personnes ou plus.
6 Période de douze mois finissant le 30 septembre de l'année indiquée.
7 Production à partir de matières premières indigènes et importées.
8 Période de douze mois finissant le 30 juin de l'année indiquée.

Oil, groundnut, refined – Huile d'arachides, raffinée

Unit : Thousand metric tons

Unité : Milliers de tonnes métriques

Country or area	1976	1977	1978	1979	1980	1981	1982	1983	1984	1985	Pays ou zone
Africa	**100**	**65**	**33**	**67**	**40**	**24**	**40**	**53**	**35**	**29**	**Afrique**
Congo	1	0	0	0	0	1	1	...	...	...	Congo
Madagascar	6	6	4	4	4	3	2	1	2	1	Madagascar
Mali	8	4	1	0	1	1	...	...	...	...	Mali
Senegal[1 2 3]	85	55	28	63	35	19	36	51	32	26	Sénégal[1 2 3]
America, North	**148**	**149**	**210**	**101**	**99**	**97**	**91**	**91**	**98**	**81**	**Amérique du Nord**
Canada	* 6	7	6	...	...	...	...	...	...	...	Canada
Dominican Republic	24	29	32	39	46	35	33	33	30	21	Rép. dominicaine
United States	118	113	172	56	47	56	52	52	62	54	Etats-Unis
America, South	**15**	**10**	**10**	**30**	**14**	**20**	**21**	**25**	**25**	**26**	**Amérique du Sud**
Brazil	13	8	8	[4] 28	11	...	...	...	...	...	Brésil
Paraguay	2	2	2	2	3	2	1	3	2	1	Paraguay
Asia	**13**	**13**	**13**	**13**	**14**	**12**	**13**	**13**	**13**	**13**	**Asie**
Thailand	...	...	...	...	14	12	...	...	...	...	Thaïlande
Europe	**171**	**131**	**106**	**77**	**56**	**102**	**109**	**118**	**104**	**132**	**Europe**
EEC	***128***	***74***	***78***	***50***	***42***	***90***	***94***	***98***	***90***	***121***	***CEE***
France	108	59	66	39	28	...	...	...	...	# 116	France
United Kingdom	20	15	12	11	14	15	16	18	7	5	Royaume-Uni
EFTA	***32***	***46***	***17***	***16***	***3***	***1***	***4***	***9***	***3***	***0***	***AELE***
Portugal	31	45	16	15	2	1	4	9	3	0	Portugal
Sweden	1	1	1	1	1	0	0	0	0	...	Suède
Other Europe	***11***	***11***	***11***	***11***	***11***	***11***	***11***	***11***	***11***	***11***	***Autre Europe***
Spain	11	...	...	...	...	...	...	...	...	...	Espagne
Total	**447**	**368**	**372**	**289**	**224**	**255**	**274**	**300**	**276**	**282**	**Total**

General note.
Groundnut or peanut oil once-refined (for example, refined by deacidifying, filtering, washing, decolourizing or deodorizing) and before use in end products. (SITC 42140-2).

[1] Crop year production.
[2] Sales.
[3] Source: Syndicat des fabricants d'huile et de tourteaux du Sénégal, (Dakar).
[4] Production by establishments employing 5 or more persons.

Remarque générale.
Huile d'arachides, ayant subi un premier raffinage (notamment par désacidification, filtration, lavage, décoloration, ou désodorisation) et avant emploi dans les produits définitifs. (CTCI 42140-2).

[1] Production par campagne.
[2] Ventes.
[3] Source: Syndicat des fabricants d'huile et de tourteaux du Sénégal, (Dakar).
[4] Production des établissements occupant 5 personnes ou plus.

Oil, olive, crude – Huile d'olives, brute

Unit : Thousand metric tons

Unité : Milliers de tonnes métriques

Country or area	1976	1977	1978	1979	1980	1981	1982	1983	1984	1985	Pays ou zone
Africa	**176**	**176**	**169**	**163**	**213**	**145**	**160**	**234**	**162**	**196**	**Afrique**
Algeria	11	11	22	12	25	20	20	° 24	° 14	° 24	Algérie
Libyan Arab Jamah.	33	9	31	18	° 34	° 26	27	24	16	26	Jamah.arabe libyenne
Morocco	* 41	* 17	* 24	* 39	* 25	* 20	54	° 24	31	31	Maroc
Tunisia	91	139	92	94	130	78	58	162	100	115	Tunisie
America, North	**2**	**2**	**3**	**2**	**2**	**2**	**2**	**2**	**2**	**2**	**Amérique du Nord**
El Salvador°	0	0	0	0	0	0	0	0	0	1	El Salvador°
Mexico	* 1	* 1	* 1	* 1	* 1	* 1	* 1	* 1	° 1	° 1	Mexique
United States	* 1	* 0	* 1	* 0	* 0	° 0	° 0	° 0	° 0	° 0	Etats–Unis
America, South	**14**	**13**	**16**	**23**	**13**	**16**	**14**	**17**	**10**	**9**	**Amérique du Sud**
Argentina	13	12	15	22	12	15	13	* 16	* 9	* 9	Argentine
Chile°	1	1	1	1	1	1	1	1	1	1	Chili°
Asia	**277**	**140**	**296**	**133**	**358**	**126**	**357**	**94**	**174**	**128**	**Asie**
Cyprus°	3	3	2	5	7	3	6	3	4	3	Chypre°
Iran(Islamic Rep.of)°	1	1	1	1	1	1	1	1	1	2	Iran(Rép.islamique)°
Israel	1	1	0	0	0	0	0	0	0	* 1	Israël
Jordan	° 5	2	7	° 1	8	4	8	7	6	8	Jordanie
Lebanon	10	5	9	2	14	3	14	° 4	° 10	° 4	Liban
Syrian Arab Republic	58	42	73	43	88	47	101	29	54	38	Rép. arabe syrienne
Turkey	199	86	203	80	239	68	226	49	98	73	Turquie
Europe	**1 070**	**1 434**	**1 327**	**1 342**	**1 649**	**1 292**	**1 730**	**1 513**	**1 371**	**1 257**	**Europe**
EEC	**577**	**1 002**	**725**	**783**	**1 102**	**931**	**906**	**1 203**	**602**	**828**	**CEE**
France	1	1	2	2	2	2	2	2	2	1	France
Greece	251	262	269	270	360	275	443	317	233	290	Grèce
Italy	325	739	454	510	741	655	461	885	367	537	Italie
EFTA	**43**	**36**	**47**	**67**	**44**	**29**	**95**	**13**	**46**	**33**	**AELE**
Portugal	43	36	47	67	44	29	95	13	46	° 33	Portugal
East Europe	**6**	**8**	**4**	**7**	**4**	**3**	**2**	**7**	**3**	**7**	**Europe de l'est**
Albania°	6	8	4	7	4	3	2	7	3	7	Albanie°
Other Europe	**444**	**388**	**550**	**486**	**500**	**329**	**726**	**290**	**721**	**389**	**Autre Europe**
Spain	442	386	548	483	498	323	726	288	718	387	Espagne
Yugoslavia	2	2	2	2	1	6	° 1	2	2	° 2	Yougoslavie
Total	**1 540**	**1 765**	**1 810**	**1 663**	**2 236**	**1 582**	**2 263**	**1 860**	**1 718**	**1 592**	**Total**

General note.
Data refer to crude olive oil. Processed products based on olive oil such as mayonnaise, salad dressings etc. are excluded. (SITC 42150–1).
Source: Food and Agriculture Organization of the United Nations (FAO), Rome.

Remarque générale.
Les données se rapportent à la production d'huile brute d'olives. (CTCI 42150–1).
Source: Organisation des Nations Unies pour l'agriculture(FAO), Rome.

° Unofficial figure

° ...

Oil, olive, refined – Huile d'olives, raffinée

Unit : Thousand metric tons

Unité : Milliers de tonnes métriques

Country or area	1976	1977	1978	1979	1980	1981	1982	1983	1984	1985	Pays ou zone
America, South	**5**	**8**	**13**	**8**	**8**	**10**	**11**	**11**	**12**	**13**	**Amérique du Sud**
Brazil	5	8	13	[1] 8	8	...	...	...	...	...	Brésil
Asia	**22**	**27**	**25**	**31**	**19**	**39**	**40**	**79**	**54**	**62**	**Asie**
Israel	1	1	2	1	1	1	1	1	1	1	Israël
Turkey	21	26	23	30	18	38	39	78	53	61	Turquie
Europe	**147**	**124**	**155**	**176**	**173**	**184**	**135**	**181**	**176**	**181**	**Europe**
EEC	***21***	***20***	***19***	***18***	***18***	***14***	***14***	***16***	***11***	***12***	***CEE***
France	1	1	2	2	2	2	2	2	...	...	France
Greece	...	...	...	...	16	12	12	14	9	...	Grèce
EFTA	***3***	***8***	***8***	***5***	***7***	***8***	***4***	***6***	***5***	***4***	***AELE***
Portugal	3	8	8	5	7	8	4	6	5	4	Portugal
Other Europe	***123***	***96***	***128***	***153***	***148***	***162***	***117***	***159***	***160***	***166***	***Autre Europe***
Spain	123	96	...	153	148	162	117	159	...	...	Espagne
Total	**174**	**159**	**193**	**215**	**200**	**233**	**186**	**271**	**242**	**256**	**Total**

General note.
Hundred per cent olive oil presented as end product. (SITC 42150–2).

Remarque générale.
Produit définitif à 100 p. 100 d'huile d'olives pure. (CTCI 42150–2).

[1] Production by establishments employing 5 or more persons.

[1] Production des établissements occupant 5 personnes ou plus.

Unit : Thousand metric tons

Unité : Milliers de tonnes métriques

Country or area	1976	1977	1978	1979	1980	1981	1982	1983	1984	1985	Pays ou zone
Africa	**1 518**	**1 471**	**1 600**	**1 520**	**1 674**	**1 723**	**1 721**	**1 611**	**1 817**	**1 746**	**Afrique**
Angola* [1,2]	40	42	40	40	40	40	40	40	40	40	Angola* [1,2]
Benin[2,3]	44	36	16	23	26	27	* 36	* 33	* 34	* 37	Bénin[2,3]
Burkina Faso	2	1	2	1	* 1	1	1	2	4	...	Burkina Faso
Burundi* [1,2]	1	1	1	1	2	2	2	2	2	2	Burundi* [1,2]
Cameroon	[1] 40	[1] 37	[1] 37	[1] 45	[1] 69	[1] 70	* [1] 71	[1] 39	77	66	Cameroun
Central African Rep.* [1,2]	2	2	2	2	2	2	2	2	2	2	Rép. centrafricaine* [1,2]
Congo* [1,2]	7	...	...	...	9	14	15	15	15	15	Congo* [1,2]
Côte d'Ivoire[3]	144	118	151	132	182	155	177	200	244	...	Côte d'Ivoire[3]
Equatorial Guinea* [1,2]	4	5	5	5	5	5	5	5	5	5	Guinée équatoriale* [1,2]
Gabon[1,2]	2	1	1	* 2	* 2	* 2	* 2	3	* 3	* 4	Gabon[1,2]
Gambia* [1]	[2] 1	[2] 1	[2] 2	[2] 3	[2] 2	[2] 3	[2] 3	[2] 3	3	3	Gambie* [1]
Ghana* [1,2]	21	20	21	21	21	21	23	20	30	42	Ghana* [1,2]
Guinea* [1,2]	35	40	41	40	42	42	45	45	45	45	Guinée* [1,2]
Guinea–Bissau* [1,2]	5	5	5	5	5	7	4	3	3	3	Guinée–Bissau* [1,2]
Kenya	2	3	...	...	...	...	...	...	...	...	Kenya
Liberia* [1,2]	24	25	25	26	27	25	30	30	34	34	Libéria* [1,2]
Madagascar* [1,2]	1	2	2	2	2	2	3	3	3	3	Madagascar* [1,2]
Mali	10	15	10	11	8	...	...	...	...	...	Mali
Nigeria* [1,2]	655	660	670	650	675	675	700	730	740	730	Nigéria* [1,2]
Sao Tome – Principe[1,2]	1	1	1	1	0	0	0	0	0	0	Sao Tomé–et–Principe[1,2]
Senegal[1]	3	4	3	* 6	* 6	* 6	* 6	* 6	* 6	* 6	Sénégal[1]
Seychelles[4]	* 1	* 1	* 1	1	1	0	0	1	1	1	Seychelles[4]
Sierra Leone[1,2]	* 44	* 53	* 45	* 45	* 47	* 48	* 48	46	* 37	* 44	Sierra Leone[1,2]
South Africa	77	111	185	168	# 221	231	234	153	154	154	Afrique du Sud
Togo* [1,2]	18	18	18	19	20	20	20	14	14	14	Togo* [1,2]
Tunisia	180	85	130	85	85	145	85	58	155	95	Tunisie
Un. Rp. Tanzania* [1,2]	2	3	3	3	3	4	4	4	4	4	Rp.Unie Tanzanie* [1,2]
Zaire[3]	152	173	171	* 170	* 168	* 165	* 155	* 145	* 153	* 160	Zaïre[3]
America, North	**336**	**367**	**366**	**388**	**417**	**442**	**467**	**502**	**489**	**541**	**Amérique du Nord**
Costa Rica* [1,2]	23	23	23	32	31	31	35	40	40	40	Costa Rica* [1,2]
Cuba	1	2	2	2	1	1	1	2	3	4	Cuba
Dominican Republic	2	2	2	2	2	1	2	3	3	2	Rép. dominicaine
Honduras[1]	9	10	* 10	* 11	* 4	* 6	10	14	12	25	Honduras[1]
Jamaica	15	14	13	13	10	13	11	13	12	15	Jamaïque
Mexico	221	...	...	...	...	...	...	...	...	...	Mexique
Nicaragua* [1]	2	2	3	3	3	3	3	3	3	3	Nicaragua* [1]
Saint Lucia[4,5]	3	4	4	4	4	2	3	3	3	...	Sainte–Lucie[4,5]
Trinidad and Tobago[4]	6	7	6	6	3	...	...	...	...	...	Trinité–et–Tobago[4]
United States	...	82	82	94	139	161	178	201	190	...	Etats–Unis
America, South	**552**	**691**	**770**	**832**	**960**	**694**	**847**	**1 134**	**1 117**	**1 465**	**Amérique du Sud**
Argentina[6]	442	582	656	692	808	523	656	923	874	1 211	Argentine[6]
Brazil* [2]	7	7	15	16	13	17	17	18	21	29	Brésil* [2]
Colombia* [1]	61	43	49	62	70	80	90	90	110	...	Colombie* [1]
Ecuador[1,2]	15	* 22	* 22	* 31	* 37	* 41	* 43	* 62	* 75	* 80	Equateur[1,2]
Paraguay	26	32	21	23	22	22	29	26	20	18	Paraguay
Peru[1,2]	0	* 3	* 4	* 4	* 6	* 6	* 6	* 8	* 10	* 10	Pérou[1,2]
Suriname[1]	[2] 1	* [2] 2	* [2] 3	4	4	5	6	7	7	8	Suriname[1]
Asia	**4 160**	**4 625**	**4 461**	**5 083**	**5 479**	**5 654**	**6 286**	**5 935**	**6 871**	**7 349**	**Asie**
Afghanistan[7]	...	...	...	10	6	5	4	2	1	3	Afghanistan[7]
Bangladesh[8]	5	7	6	4	5	4	4	3	2	...	Bangladesh[8]
China* [1,2]	160	160	161	172	160	164	180	181	184	192	Chine* [1,2]
Indonesia	584	634	645	744	691	752	807	922	1 087	1 118	Indonésie
Japan[9]	602	622	622	728	724	800	808	810	845	920	Japon[9]
Malaysia[10]	[11] 1 467	[11] 1 682	[11] 1 843	[11] 2 256	[11] 2 641	[11] 2 890	[1,2] 3 511	[1,2] 3 016	[1,2] 3 715	[1,2] 4 132	Malaisie[10]
Pakistan[8,12]	277	326	360	422	452	505	531	513	595	...	Pakistan[8,12]
Philippines[13]	...	782	456	386	407	233	186	...	...	...	Philippines[13]
Singapore[14]	69	75	67	89	117	...	...	...	...	...	Singapour[14]
Sri Lanka[15]	116	48	79	23	[16] 6	[16] 1	[16] 15	[16] 7	[16] 2	[16] 4	Sri Lanka[15]
Syrian Arab Republic	25	24	24	26	21	20	20	24	24	22	Rép. arabe syrienne
Thailand* [1,2]	2	3	4	6	12	19	30	21	34	22	Thaïlande* [1,2]
Turkey	...	...	185	217	237	...	# [17] 63	[17] 92	[17] 78	...	Turquie
Europe	**2 492**	**2 472**	**2 806**	**2 940**	**2 904**	**3 714**	**3 390**	**4 111**	**3 955**	**3 971**	**Europe**
EEC	***1 474***	***1 210***	***1 324***	***1 377***	***1 413***	***1 447***	***1 528***	***1 675***	***1 425***	***1 260***	***CEE***

For general note and footnotes, see end of table.

Voir la fin du tableau pour la remarque générale et les notes.

Oils, other, of vegetable origin, crude (continued) – Autres huiles brutes d'origine végétale (suite)

Unit : Thousand metric tons

Unité : Milliers de tonnes métriques

Country or area	1976	1977	1978	1979	1980	1981	1982	1983	1984	1985	Pays ou zone
Belgium[18 19]	22	20	36	22	48	# 145	149	176	109	130	Belgique[18 19]
Denmark	15	11	8	9	5	...	13	17	* 23	29	Danemark
France[14 20 21]	799	853	972	979	974	886	953	945	...	666	France[14 20 21]
Greece	...	...	...	...	...	4	7	21	24	...	Grèce
Netherlands	[13 22] 453	# 113	102	92	88	128	154	215	...	...	Pays–Bas
United Kingdom	171	199	192	261	284	269	252	301	318	344	Royaume–Uni
EFTA	***153***	***173***	***181***	***173***	***172***	***196***	***183***	***215***	***207***	***209***	***AELE***
Austria[14]	47	53	51	52	55	57	58	65	71	63	Autriche[14]
Finland	20	19	22	17	27	45	31	60	45	...	Finlande
Norway	...	52	...	...	...	...	...	...	...	...	Norvège
Portugal	9	25	30	36	...	...	...	...	...	...	Portugal
Sweden	25	24	26	16	13	17	17	13	14	15	Suède
East Europe	***560***	***640***	***620***	***556***	***553***	***723***	***664***	***679***	***760***	***780***	***Europe de l'est***
Czechoslovakia[14]	115	115	121	126	138	143	140	145	161	151	Tchécoslovaquie[14]
German Dem. Rep.	143	141	145	124	122	122	122	147	151	152	Rép. dém. allemande
Hungary	82	102	107	115	156	222	247	237	240	238	Hongrie
Poland	220	282	247	191	137	236	155	150	208	239	Pologne
Other Europe	***305***	***449***	***681***	***834***	***766***	***1 348***	***1 015***	***1 542***	***1 563***	***1 721***	***Autre Europe***
Spain[23]	185	...	...	539	534	1 145	844	1 379	...	...	Espagne[23]
Yugoslavia	120	183	256	295	232	203	171	163	180	179	Yougoslavie
USSR	**907**	**856**	**946**	**912**	**941**	**864**	**937**	**1 001**	**880**	**938**	**URSS**
Ukrainian SSR[13]	*907*	*856*	*946*	...	*941*	*864*	*937*	*1 001*	*880*	...	*RSS d'Ukraine[13]*
Oceania	**132**	**126**	**145**	**170**	**181**	**165**	**235**	**227**	**261**	**269**	**Océanie**
Australia[13]	66	61	79	97	107	79	112	103	108	107	Australie[13]
Fiji[4]	17	18	17	15	15	14	15	16	16	12	Fidji[4]
French Polynesia[4]	13	9	8	9	12	10	12	8	6	8	Polynésie française[4]
Papua New Guinea[1 2]	32	32	30	36	33	44	77	80	111	123	Papouasie–Nvl–Guinée[1 2]
Solomon Islands[1]	* [2] 4	* [2] 6	[2] 11	* [2] 13	* [2] 14	* [2] 18	* [2] 19	20	20	19	Iles Salomon[1]
Total	**10 097**	**10 608**	**11 094**	**11 844**	**12 556**	**13 257**	**13 883**	**14 521**	**15 390**	**16 279**	**Total**

General note.
Data refer to crude oils of other vegetable origin and include linseed oil, palm oil, coconut (copra) oil, palm kernel oil and those oils covered under SITC 4229. (SITC 42200–1).

1 Palm oil only.
2 Source: Food and Agriculture Organization (FAO), (Rome).
3 Data refer to palm and palm kernel oil.
4 Coconut oil only.
5 Original data in gallons.
6 Edible and inedible vegetable oils.
7 Twelve months beginning 21 March of year stated.
8 All vegetable oils.
9 Including refined oils.
10 Data refer to Peninsular Malaysia and Sabah.
11 Data refer to coconut and palm oil.
12 Twelve months ending 30 June of year stated.
13 All crude vegetable oils.
14 All crude and refined vegetable oils.
15 Crude and refined coconut oil only.
16 Government production only.
17 Sunflower seed oil.
18 Including small quantities of animal oils and fats.
19 Production from imported and indigenous raw material.
20 Deliveries.
21 Including animal oils and fats and unprocessed olive oil.
22 Source: Industrial Statistics, Statistical Office of the European Communities, (Luxembourg).
23 Including cotton–seed, groundnut and soya bean oil.

Remarque générale.
Les autres huiles brutes d'origine végétale comprises dans cette position sont suivantes: huile de lin, huile de palme, huile de coprah, huile de palmiste, huile de ricin et les huiles énumérées dans la rubrique 4229 de la CTCI. (CTCI 42200–1).

1 Huile de palme seulement.
2 Source: Organisation des Nations Unies pour l'alimentation et l'agriculture (FAO), (Rome).
3 Données se rapportant à l'huile de palme et de palmiste.
4 Huile de coco seulement.
5 Données d'origine exprimées en gallons.
6 Huiles végétales comestibles ou non.
7 Période de douze mois commençant le 21 mars de l'année indiquée.
8 Huiles végétales de toutes catégories.
9 Y compris les huiles raffinées.
10 Données se rapportant à la Malaisie péninsulaire et au Sabah.
11 Données se rapportant à l'huile de coco et à l'huile de palme.
12 Période de douze mois finissant le 30 juin de l'année indiquée.
13 Huiles végétales brutes de toutes catégories.
14 Huiles végétales brutes et raffinées de toutes catégories.
15 Huile de coco brute et raffinée seulement.
16 Production de l'Etat seulement.
17 Huile de tournesol.
18 Y compris de petites quantités d'huiles et de graisses d'origine animale.
19 Production à partir de matières premières indigènes et importées.
20 Livraisons.
21 Y compris les huiles et graisses d'origine animale et l'huile d'olive non traitée.
22 Source: Statistiques industrielles, Office statistique des Communautés européennes, (Luxembourg).
23 Y compris huile de graines de coton, huile d'arachides et huile de fèves de soya.

Oils, other, of vegetable origin, refined – Autres huiles d'origine végétale, raffinées

Unit : Thousand metric tons — Unité : Milliers de tonnes métriques

Country or area	1976	1977	1978	1979	1980	1981	1982	1983	1984	1985	Pays ou zone
Africa	**193**	**236**	**263**	**275**	**281**	**298**	**312**	**329**	**336**	**350**	**Afrique**
Algeria[1]	153	190	198	203	224	232	249	...	...	...	Algérie[1]
Côte d'Ivoire[2]	29	36	58	66	49	58	58	61	50	50	Côte d'Ivoire[2]
Egypt	5	5	2	2	...	...	...	...	...	...	Egypte
Kenya	5	4	4	3	3	3	0	0	3	3	Kenya
Tunisia[3]	1	1	1	1	1	1	1	...	...	...	Tunisie[3]
America, North	**1 130**	**1 227**	**1 189**	**1 336**	**990**	**1 194**	**1 243**	**1 176**	**1 124**	**1 176**	**Amérique du Nord**
Canada	124	207	211	258	46	...	...	...	...	...	Canada
Cuba[4]	46	60	53	63	60	65	65	72	73	86	Cuba[4]
Dominican Republic	3	3	2	3	3	3	3	2	2	2	Rép. dominicaine
Mexico	246	250	225	244	268	314	321	306	334	355	Mexique
Saint Lucia[5 6]	2	2	2	2	2	1	2	3	2	2	Sainte–Lucie[5 6]
S.Vincent–Grenadines	[5 7] 1	* [5] 1	* [5] 1	* [5] 1	* [5] 1	* [5] 1	# 0	0	0	0	S.Vincent–Grenadines
Trinidad and Tobago	[5] 9	[5] 9	[5] 8	[5] 8	[4] 8	[4] 24	[4] 10	[4] 9	[4] 6	[4] 5	Trinité–et–Tobago
United States	699	695	687	757	602	648	715	667	600	...	Etats–Unis
America, South	**177**	**170**	**161**	**221**	**221**	**270**	**287**	**247**	**260**	**270**	**Amérique du Sud**
Brazil	92	75	61	105	79	...	...	...	...	...	Brésil
Chile	54	60	66	67	71	89	95	90	78	82	Chili
Colombia	...	...	...	...	...	22	19	23	...	...	Colombie
Ecuador	...	13	12	...	...	55	63	29	...	...	Equateur
Paraguay[8]	2	1	1	1	# 17	20	26	21	17	17	Paraguay[8]
Asia	**870**	**958**	**884**	**916**	**966**	**1 058**	**1 098**	**1 086**	**1 051**	**1 115**	**Asie**
Burma* [9]	36	...	...	...	...	...	...	...	...	...	Birmanie* [9]
Indonesia	172	144	154	189	224	170	228	...	...	...	Indonésie
Iran(Islamic Rep.of)[10]	269	308	303	317	255	294	320	...	...	...	Iran(Rép.islamique)[10]
Israel	1	1	1	1	1	1	1	1	1	1	Israël
Malaysia[5 11 12]	13	13	7	10	9	8	51	51	44	...	Malaisie[5 11 12]
Philippines[4]	...	230	# [13] 162	[13] 139	[13] 164	[13] 184	[13] 162	[13] 186	...	...	Philippines[4]
Singapore	48	59	48	75	96	98	125	77	78	94	Singapour
Sri Lanka[5]	4	12	20	21	11	...	[14] 1	[14] 1	[14] 1	[14] 1	Sri Lanka[5]
Thailand	...	...	...	...	76	75	...	...	...	...	Thaïlande
Turkey[15]	64	79	77	52	94	185	99	128	110	...	Turquie[15]
Europe	**2 479**	**2 425**	**2 489**	**2 537**	**2 688**	**2 761**	**2 935**	**3 167**	**2 994**	**3 118**	**Europe**
EEC	***1 236***	***1 066***	***1 048***	***1 129***	***1 183***	***1 233***	***1 342***	***1 498***	***1 422***	***1 535***	***CEE***
Denmark	24	21	18	17	20	23	19	29	...	...	Danemark
France	243	347	340	391	408	426	...	...	...	554	France
Greece	...	...	...	...	...	3	6	18	19	* 20	Grèce
Netherlands[16]	551	283	295	322	364	370	406	457	...	...	Pays–Bas[16]
United Kingdom	415	412	393	395	384	411	445	497	458	541	Royaume–Uni
EFTA	***98***	***99***	***191***	***190***	***209***	***189***	***180***	***170***	***140***	***139***	***AELE***
Finland	8	8	9	9	10	12	12	14	14	...	Finlande
Norway	0	0	45	44	45	33	...	...	9	...	Norvège
Portugal	44	43	90	90	106	100	101	97	91	65	Portugal
Sweden	46	48	47	47	48	44	38	29	26	26	Suède
East Europe	***793***	***840***	***857***	***858***	***879***	***861***	***906***	***918***	***890***	***880***	***Europe de l'est***
Bulgaria[16]	158	145	155	148	175	163	183	202	182	177	Bulgarie[16]
German Dem. Rep.	223	229	244	241	244	248	248	239	232	240	Rép. dém. allemande
Hungary	60	66	62	70	72	69	73	69	67	74	Hongrie
Poland	30	33	55	24	19	46	50	37	61	61	Pologne
Romania[16]	322	367	341	375	369	335	352	371	348	328	Roumanie[16]
Other Europe	***352***	***420***	***393***	***360***	***417***	***478***	***507***	***580***	***542***	***564***	***Autre Europe***
Spain[17]	177	233	...	142	188	235	283	343	...	...	Espagne[17]
Yugoslavia	175	187	196	218	229	243	224	237	233	236	Yougoslavie
Oceania	**63**	**97**	**112**	**97**	**112**	**113**	**122**	**77**	**88**	**116**	**Océanie**
Australia[4]	63	97	112	97	112	113	122	77	88	116	Australie[4]
Total	**4 912**	**5 113**	**5 097**	**5 382**	**5 258**	**5 693**	**5 998**	**6 082**	**5 852**	**6 145**	**Total**

For general note and footnotes, see end of table.

Voir la fin du tableau pour la remarque générale et les notes.

Oils, other, of vegetable origin, refined (continued) – Autres huiles d'origine végétale, raffinées (suite)

General note.
Linseed oil, palm oil, coconut (copra) oil, palm kernel oil, castor oil and those oils covered under SITC 4229, refined (for description of refining see 3115–19) and before use in end products. (SITC 42200–2).

[1] Including refined olive oil.
[2] Including groundnut oil.
[3] Linseed oil.
[4] All refined vegetable oils.
[5] Coconut oil only.
[6] Original data in gallons.
[7] Source: United Nations Economic Commission for Latin America (ECLA), (Santiago).
[8] Beginning 1980, scope of series revised.
[9] Twelve months ending 30 September of year stated.
[10] Production by establishments employing 50 or more persons.
[11] Data refer to Peninsular Malaysia only.
[12] Beginning 1982, scope of series revised.
[13] Shipments.
[14] Government production only.
[15] Sunflower seed oil.
[16] All crude and refined vegetable oils.
[17] Including cotton–seed and groundnut oil.

Remarque générale.
Huile de lin, huile de palme, huile de coprah, huile de palmiste, huile de ricin et huiles énumérées dans la rubrique 4229 de la CTCI, raffinées (notamment par désacidification, filtration, lavage, décoloration, ou désodorisation) et avant emploi dans les produits définitifs. (CTCI 42200–2).

[1] Y compris l'huile d'olive raffinée.
[2] Y compris l'huile d'arachide.
[3] Huile de lin.
[4] Huiles végétales raffinées de toutes catégories.
[5] Huile de coco seulement.
[6] Données d'origine exprimées en gallons.
[7] Source: Commission économique des Nations Unies pour l'Amérique Latine (CEPAL), (Santiago).
[8] A partir de 1980, portée de la série révisée.
[9] Période de douze mois finissant le 30 septembre de l'année indiquée.
[10] Production des établissements occupant 50 personnes ou plus.
[11] Données se rapportant à la Malaisie péninsulaire seulement.
[12] A partir de 1982, portée de la série révisée.
[13] Expéditions.
[14] Production de l'Etat seulement.
[15] Huile de tournesol.
[16] Huiles végétales brutes et raffinées de toutes catégories.
[17] Y compris huile de graines de coton et huile d'arachides.

Flour, wheat – Farines de froment

Unit : Thousand metric tons — Unité : Milliers de tonnes métriques

Country or area	1976	1977	1978	1979	1980	1981	1982	1983	1984	1985	Pays ou zone
Africa	**7 608**	**8 120**	**8 394**	**8 588**	**8 975**	**10 048**	**10 251**	**9 799**	**9 903**	**10 405**	**Afrique**
Algeria[1]	715	541	547	568	643	694	769	* 650	...	...	Algérie[1]
Angola* [2]	88	96	50	50	35	50	75	50	40	50	Angola* [2]
Burkina Faso	14	20	16	13	5	19	18	21	18	...	Burkina Faso
Burundi	...	...	...	...	...	...	3	5	4	7	Burundi
Cameroon	31	33	18	32	50	45	53	59	73	52	Cameroun
Central African Rep.	[2] 1	[2] 1	[2] 1	[2] 1	[2] 1	[2] 1	4	1	0	0	Rép. centrafricaine
Chad	2	3	3	4	4	* 1	* 1	* 1	* 1	...	Tchad
Congo	15	5	0	3	4	8	9	8	3	0	Congo
Côte d'Ivoire	76	119	105	135	115	140	145	129	163	...	Côte d'Ivoire
Egypt	2 878	3 240	3 480	3 507	3 138	3 487	3 487	3 648	3 707	3 598	Egypte
Ethiopia[3]	80	107	81	115	175	160	164	* 160	134	...	Ethiopie[3]
Gabon[4]	15	16	15	15	17	16	* 19	21	23	26	Gabon[4]
Ghana	68	74	82	93	90	73	25	18	40	45	Ghana
Kenya	138	149	170	141	199	217	267	272	222	293	Kenya
Libyan Arab Jamah.	118	124	121	114	102	132	176	135	...	...	Jamah.arabe libyenne
Morocco[1 2]	930	935	1 100	1 379	1 503	1 759	1 688	1 747	...	...	Maroc[1 2]
Mozambique	[2] 65	[2] 85	[2] 85	92	98	110	95	82	71	...	Mozambique
Nigeria[2]	441	550	707	569	1 092	1 197	1 335	813	526	844	Nigéria[2]
Senegal	88	79	111	93	76	86	70	89	87	65	Sénégal
Sierra Leone[2]	20	22	20	21	20	8	* 5	* 2	...	...	Sierra Leone[2]
South Africa[5]	951	917	674	643	638	718	727	692	727	745	Afrique du Sud[5]
Sudan	237	267	280	270	244	315	265	* 270	...	...	Soudan
Togo	7	18	15	16	20	29	32	37	31	32	Togo
Tunisia	258	324	309	333	340	390	420	463	462	498	Tunisie
Uganda	2	9	10	8	8	8	* 4	* 5	...	...	Ouganda
United Rep. Tanzania	72	81	88	54	32	26	27	* 69	* 53	...	Rép.Unie de Tanzanie
Zaire	...	...	...	...	...	...	123	117	...	...	Zaïre
Zambia	88	90	76	74	81	84	95	75	63	43	Zambie
Zimbabwe[2]	85	90	105	120	120	150	150	160	187	...	Zimbabwe[2]
America, North	**16 886**	**16 911**	**17 195**	**17 559**	**17 811**	**18 295**	**18 608**	**19 738**	**19 282**	**19 516**	**Amérique du Nord**
Barbados	...	...	...	...	...	12	8	10	10	11	Barbade
Canada	1 933	1 866	1 982	1 916	1 868	1 900	1 718	* 1 710	* 1 877	...	Canada
Costa Rica[2]	70	75	80	82	80	80	75	90	66	...	Costa Rica[2]
Cuba	165	176	175	170	271	354	386	428	422	442	Cuba
Dominican Republic	92	92	92	107	115	108	117	127	122	139	Rép. dominicaine
El Salvador	65	76	82	81	82	80	92	100	...	...	El Salvador
Guadeloupe	35	34	34	35	36	37	33	33	34	...	Guadeloupe
Guatemala	87	73	83	85	90	110	95	97	...	...	Guatemala
Haiti	68	71	63	75	117	110	104	139	111	132	Haïti
Honduras	35	43	40	42	40	65	# 142	158	* 41	...	Honduras
Jamaica	50	54	49	38	49	45	55	62	86	132	Jamaïque
Mexico	1 714	1 753	1 814	1 951	2 147	2 422	2 484	2 544	2 630	2 523	Mexique
Nicaragua	45	40	42	40	40	45	55	47	43	...	Nicaragua
Panama[6]	39	39	43	43	45	47	49	60	52	...	Panama[6]
United States	12 477	12 509	12 606	12 884	12 821	12 880	13 195	14 133	13 584	13 831	Etats–Unis
America, South	**7 238**	**9 211**	**9 433**	**10 311**	**10 815**	**10 350**	**10 515**	**10 647**	**11 045**	**10 883**	**Amérique du Sud**
Argentina	2 529	2 530	2 523	2 482	2 438	2 456	2 550	2 678	2 754	2 801	Argentine
Bolivia[2]	82	245	161	190	225	207	* 180	234	209	...	Bolivie[2]
Brazil	2 288	4 006	4 345	4 698	5 154	4 666	4 647	4 540	4 812	4 722	Brésil
Chile	501	493	455	866	874	914	894	913	911	* 919	Chili
Colombia	252	329	300	317	329	353	* 350	376	...	...	Colombie
Ecuador[1 7]	180	189	206	199	164	191	181	185	[2] 278	...	Equateur[1 7]
Guyana	* 37	35	36	40	36	34	8	0	...	...	Guyana
Paraguay	50	59	85	82	82	101	97	100	90	99	Paraguay
Peru	609	595	572	657	733	760	766	761	* 788	* 703	Pérou
Uruguay	210	210	200	230	240	118	* 242	* 260	* 200	153	Uruguay
Venezuela[2]	500	520	550	550	540	550	600	600	...	...	Venezuela[2]
Asia	**55 709**	**54 854**	**62 160**	**70 678**	**69 973**	**73 614**	**78 349**	**81 735**	**87 304**	**91 329**	**Asie**
Afghanistan	...	81	97	123	113	123	124	136	154	173	Afghanistan
Bangladesh	...	...	...	...	...	11	16	11	14	20	Bangladesh
Burma[8]	53	64	67	56	50	50	* 55	* 55	...	...	Birmanie[8]
China[2]	37 000	35 000	42 000	50 000	50 000	52 000	56 000	58 500	...	...	Chine[2]
Cyprus	...	...	60	46	50	47	48	47	49	51	Chypre
Democratic Yemen	...	...	...	...	32	34	19	15	28	...	Yémen démocratique
Hong Kong	90	90	123	99	93	94	110	96	88	...	Hong–kong
India[9]	1 666	2 337	2 660	1 636	2 409	2 327	2 405	2 475	3 237	3 430	Inde[9]

For general note and footnotes, see end of table. — Voir la fin du tableau pour la remarque générale et les notes.

Unit : Thousand metric tons

Unité : Milliers de tonnes métriques

Country or area	1976	1977	1978	1979	1980	1981	1982	1983	1984	1985	Pays ou zone
Indonesia	696	774	837	866	998	1 012	1 040	1 234	1 142	...	Indonésie
Iran(Islamic Rep.of)[2]	4 705	4 710	4 730	4 750	4 674	5 404	5 500	5 800	...	...	Iran(Rép.islamique)[2]
Iraq[2]	1 307	1 543	1 541	2 445	1 716	1 622	1 790	1 850	...	...	Iraq[2]
Israel	444	460	489	476	455	464	498	506	516	507	Israël
Japan[10]	3 954	3 970	4 013	4 150	4 184	4 184	4 369	4 356	4 445	4 425	Japon[10]
Jordan	142	144	112	163	183	299	196	390	375	330	Jordanie
Korea, Republic of	1 316	1 384	1 184	1 242	1 472	1 439	1 444	1 476	1 547	1 616	Corée, République de
Kuwait	109	113	127	154	156	200	210	176	186	143	Koweït
Lebanon[2]	145	165	165	185	180	290	270	190	...	...	Liban[2]
Malaysia[11 12]	266	289	311	301	308	314	332	344	357	...	Malaisie[11 12]
Mongolia	131	116	112	141	83	125	120	150	185	176	Mongolie
Philippines	465	483	443	582	570	630	692	650	...	...	Philippines
Qatar	19	21	17	25	28	27	31	...	...	...	Qatar
Sri Lanka	94	73	62	69	58	[2] 320	[2] 386	[2] 400	...	...	Sri Lanka
Syrian Arab Republic	538	488	473	424	447	865	887	997	1 116	1 161	Rép. arabe syrienne
Thailand	68	73	91	112	111	109	117	* 90	...	...	Thaïlande
Turkey	2 217	2 266	2 276	2 437	1 437	1 424	1 480	1 582	1 481	1 491	Turquie
Europe	**35 465**	**34 369**	**34 602**	**35 204**	**35 480**	**36 556**	**36 377**	**33 772**	**35 123**	**35 759**	**Europe**
EEC	***17 307***	***17 362***	***17 921***	***18 224***	***18 168***	***19 200***	***18 935***	***17 566***	***19 090***	***19 734***	***CEE***
Belgium[13]	749	776	744	766	859	947	891	776	881	897	Belgique[13]
Denmark	205	211	218	219	223	244	246	246	259	268	Danemark
France[14]	3 366	3 302	3 385	3 467	3 489	4 871	4 796	4 266	4 975	5 042	France[14]
Germany, Fed. Rep.	2 466	2 388	2 447	2 528	2 713	2 601	2 480	2 280	2 433	2 519	Allemagne, Rép. féd.
Greece	[15] 665	[15] 736	# 1 168	1 123	1 016	885	861	* 927	...	...	Grèce
Ireland	203	223	217	224	221	226	213	188	187	174	Irlande
Italy[2]	4 650	4 780	4 846	5 074	4 921	4 770	4 890	4 462	...	...	Italie[2]
Luxembourg	25	26	25	28	34	39	44	45	45	40	Luxembourg
Netherlands[1 2]	1 027	1 024	1 023	1 010	990	1 021	1 010	* 950	965	1 066	Pays-Bas[1 2]
United Kingdom	3 951	3 896	3 848	3 785	3 702	3 596	3 504	3 426	3 604	3 983	Royaume-Uni
EFTA	***2 052***	***2 042***	***2 009***	***2 020***	***2 028***	***2 204***	***2 126***	***2 161***	***2 180***	***2 178***	***AELE***
Austria	212	204	201	202	209	243	225	234	224	222	Autriche
Finland	217	227	222	228	189	226	197	212	218	236	Finlande
Norway	219	225	223	224	237	300	* 264	* 250	...	...	Norvège
Portugal[1]	576	540	544	552	522	585	580	583	618	570	Portugal[1]
Sweden[15 16]	440	451	423	423	459	438	454	458	448	455	Suède[15 16]
Switzerland	388	395	396	391	412	412	406	424	394	409	Suisse
East Europe	***10 675***	***9 541***	***9 745***	***9 539***	***9 841***	***9 756***	***10 320***	***9 373***	***8 989***	***9 050***	***Europe de l'est***
Bulgaria[1]	1 577	1 500	1 551	1 428	1 356	1 317	1 308	1 277	1 246	1 258	Bulgarie[1]
Czechoslovakia	1 245	1 198	1 260	1 237	1 236	1 315	1 339	1 296	1 305	1 336	Tchécoslovaquie
German Dem. Rep.	[1] 1 332	# 887	905	909	910	919	941	889	920	924	Rép. dém. allemande
Hungary	1 239	1 224	1 230	1 232	1 197	1 190	1 205	1 172	1 155	1 153	Hongrie
Poland	2 462	2 262	2 324	2 533	2 642	2 815	2 827	2 539	2 116	2 177	Pologne
Romania[1 2]	2 820	2 470	2 475	2 200	2 500	2 200	2 700	2 200	...	...	Roumanie[1 2]
Other Europe	***5 431***	***5 424***	***4 927***	***5 421***	***5 443***	***5 396***	***4 996***	***4 672***	***4 865***	***4 797***	***Autre Europe***
Malta	41	36	36	23	23	21	22	23	22	...	Malte
Spain	2 963	3 006	2 504	3 002	3 127	3 044	2 542	2 249	...	...	Espagne
Yugoslavia	2 427	2 382	2 387	2 396	2 293	2 331	2 432	2 400	2 337	2 342	Yougoslavie
USSR[1]	**42 183**	**42 863**	**42 414**	**42 592**	**[2] 43 000**	**[2] 43 000**	**[2] 43 000**	**[2] 43 000**	**[2] 43 000**	...	**URSS[1]**
Byelorussian SSR[1]	*2 693*	*3 078*	*2 967*	*2 733*	...	...	...	...	...	...	*RSS de Biélorussie[1]*
Ukrainian SSR[1]	*7 277*	*7 352*	*7 465*	*7 503*	...	...	...	...	...	...	*RSS d'Ukraine[1]*
Oceania	**1 460**	**1 264**	**1 297**	**1 272**	**1 287**	**1 313**	**1 328**	**1 298**	**1 367**	**1 421**	**Océanie**
Australia[7]	1 240	1 033	1 062	1 039	1 045	1 069	1 086	1 055	1 136	1 186	Australie[7]
Fiji	9	11	16	19	19	20	21	23	22	24	Fidji
New Zealand	211	220	219	214	223	224	221	220	209	211	Nouvelle-Zélande
Total	**166 549**	**167 591**	**175 494**	**186 203**	**187 341**	**193 176**	**198 428**	**199 988**	**207 025**	**212 534**	**Total**

General note.
Sifted (bolted) flour made from wheat or meslin. (SITC 04601-0).

Remarque générale.
Farines tamisées (blutées) de froment ou de méteil. (CTCI 04601-0).

[1] Including flour produced from other grains.

[1] Y compris les farines d'autres grains.

[2] Source: World Wheat Statistics, International Wheat Council, (London).
[3] Twelve months ending 10 September of year stated.
[4] Sales.
[5] Twelve months ending 31 October of year stated.
[6] Including groats.
[7] Twelve months ending 30 June of year stated.
[8] Twelve months ending 30 September of year stated.
[9] Production by large and medium scale establishments only.
[10] Twelve months beginning 1 April of year stated.
[11] Data refer to Peninsular Malaysia only.
[12] Beginning 1982, scope of series revised.
[13] Industrial production only.
[14] Deliveries.
[15] Production for sale only.
[16] Including wheat flour mixed with rye.

[2] Source: World Wheat Statistics, International Wheat Council, (Londres).
[3] Période de douze mois finissant le 10 septembre de l'année indiquée.
[4] Ventes.
[5] Période de douze mois finissant le 31 octobre de l'année indiquée.
[6] Y compris le gruau.
[7] Période de douze mois finissant le 30 juin de l'année indiquée.
[8] Période de douze mois finissant le 30 septembre de l'année indiquée.
[9] Production des grandes et moyennes entreprises seulement.
[10] Période de douze mois commençant le 1er avril de l'année indiquée.
[11] Données se rapportant à la Malaisie péninsulaire seulement.
[12] A partir de 1982, portée de la série révisée.
[13] Production industrielle seulement.
[14] Livraisons.
[15] Production destinée à la vente seulement.
[16] Y compris la farine de froment mélangée avec du seigle.

Meal and groats of all cereals – Semoules et gruaux de toutes céréales

Unit : Thousand metric tons | Unité : Milliers de tonnes métriques

Country or area	1976	1977	1978	1979	1980	1981	1982	1983	1984	1985	Pays ou zone
Africa	**1 890**	**2 122**	**2 442**	**2 507**	**2 573**	**2 653**	**2 781**	**2 714**	**2 799**	**2 878**	**Afrique**
Algeria	* 775	956	938	866	928	927	1 010	1 000	...	...	Algérie
Burkina Faso	5	...	...	...	...	...	...	...	...	...	Burkina Faso
Kenya[1]	219	196	227	256	257	290	337	227	302	320	Kenya[1]
South Africa	405	405	633	741	799	846	831	878	879	906	Afrique du Sud
Tunisia	226	261	330	333	337	373	350	373	368	369	Tunisie
Zambia	260	299	309	306	247	212	248	231	220	230	Zambie
America, North	**1 542**	**1 627**	**1 466**	**1 417**	**1 511**	**1 407**	**1 383**	**1 341**	**1 315**	**1 310**	**Amérique du Nord**
Canada	...	6	6	5	6	...	...	...	...	...	Canada
Cuba	54	56	...	...	...	...	...	...	...	...	Cuba
Dominican Republic	10	10	10	12	12	13	16	18	18	19	Rép. dominicaine
United States	1 472	1 555	1 395	1 345	1 438	1 333	1 306	1 262	1 236	1 230	Etats–Unis
America, South	**229**	**214**	**191**	**190**	**190**	**171**	**199**	**191**	**190**	**187**	**Amérique du Sud**
Argentina[2]	93	86	71	73	80	83	94	93	98	98	Argentine[2]
Bolivia	19	14	...	...	...	0	1	1	1	...	Bolivie
Chile[2]	...	...	...	86	81	71	76	72	...	...	Chili[2]
Colombia	...	...	...	...	...	17	28	24	...	...	Colombie
Ecuador	...	...	* 0	...	...	0	0	1	...	...	Equateur
Asia	**38**	**44**	**46**	**58**	**64**	**72**	**80**	**80**	**84**	**94**	**Asie**
Kuwait	19	22	23	29	32	36	40	40	42	...	Koweït
Europe	**1 120**	**1 278**	**1 382**	**1 579**	**1 698**	**1 642**	**1 472**	**1 413**	**1 527**	**1 482**	**Europe**
EEC	***282***	***483***	***408***	***461***	***472***	***516***	***458***	***522***	***476***	***470***	***CEE***
Denmark[3]	24	22	22	23	21	20	18	16	15	16	Danemark[3]
France[4 5]	240	437	365	416	430	420	392	456	411	408	France[4 5]
United Kingdom[6]	18	24	21	22	21	76	48	50	50	46	Royaume–Uni[6]
EFTA	***118***	***134***	***156***	***166***	***165***	***173***	***190***	***175***	***172***	***175***	***AELE***
Finland[7]	16	16	15	20	23	23	37	25	20	...	Finlande[7]
Portugal	81	96	119	126	119	123	127	121	120	114	Portugal
Sweden	21	22	22	20	23	27	26	29	32	32	Suède
East Europe	***667***	***621***	***687***	***737***	***723***	***709***	***644***	***638***	***654***	***595***	***Europe de l'est***
Hungary[8]	436	400	423	454	412	397	420	421	425	419	Hongrie[8]
Poland	231	221	264	283	311	312	224	217	229	176	Pologne
Other Europe	***53***	***40***	***131***	***215***	***338***	***244***	***180***	***78***	***225***	***242***	***Autre Europe***
Spain	39	37	...	201	320	228	170	73	...	...	Espagne
Yugoslavia	14	3	6	14	18	16	10	5	5	6	Yougoslavie
USSR	**3 767**	**3 977**	**4 049**	**3 956**	...	...	...	...	...	...	**URSS**
Byelorussian SSR	*163*	*176*	*178*	*179*	*189*	...	...	...	...	...	*RSS de Biélorussie*
Ukrainian SSR[9]	*792*	*834*	*839*	*765*	...	...	...	...	...	...	*RSS d'Ukraine[9]*
Oceania	**118**	**117**	**117**	**116**	**114**	**120**	**106**	**117**	**114**	**112**	**Océanie**
Australia	...	...	...	110	108	114	100	109	...	...	Australie
New Zealand[10]	...	...	6	6	6	6	6	8	9	8	Nouvelle–Zélande[10]
Total	**8 704**	**9 379**	**9 693**	**9 823**	**10 087**	**10 002**	**9 959**	**9 793**	**9 967**	**10 000**	**Total**

General note.
Small fragments of floury kernels obtained by the rough grinding of grains of all cereals (groats) and granules obtained either from the first sifting after the initial milling operation, or by regrinding and resifting the groats resulting from that initial milling (meal). (SITC 04602 and 04702).

1 Corn meal only.
2 Wheat meal and groats only.
3 Oat meal and barley groats only.
4 Crop year production.

Remarque générale.
Petits fragments de grains farineux obtenus par mouture grossière de toutes céréales (gruaux) et granules résultant soit d'un blutage après la première mouture, soit d'un nouveau blutage après remouture des gruaux issus de la première opération (semoule). (CTCI 04602 et 04702).

1 Farine de maïs seulement.
2 Farine et gruau de blé seulement.
3 Farine d'avoine et gruau d'orge seulement.
4 Production par campagne.

[5] Deliveries.
[6] Other cuts and groats of oatmeal only.
[7] Including meslin flour.
[8] Low–grade flour and bran.
[9] Data refer to meal only.
[10] Wheat meal only.

[5] Livraisons.
[6] Autres variétés d'avoine et gruaux d'avoine seulement.
[7] Y compris les farines de méteil.
[8] Farines et sons de qualité inférieure.
[9] Données se rapportant à aux semoules seulement.
[10] Semoules de forment.

Flour, cereal, other than wheat – Farines de céréales autres que le froment

Unit : Thousand metric tons — Unité : Milliers de tonnes métriques

Country or area	1976	1977	1978	1979	1980	1981	1982	1983	1984	1985	Pays ou zone
Africa	**454**	**423**	**465**	**487**	**553**	**601**	**598**	**475**	**500**	**374**	**Afrique**
Algeria	0	0	1	1	1	2	2	1	...	...	Algérie
Burkina Faso	6	7	7	4	2	6	* 6	* 6	* 5	...	Burkina Faso
Kenya	277	249	286	296	369	414	456	347	356	236	Kenya
Zaire	171	167	171	* 186	181	179	134	121	...	...	Zaïre
America, North	**538**	**551**	**586**	**532**	**591**	**569**	**591**	**688**	**737**	**697**	**Amérique du Nord**
Canada[1]	10	15	12	12	14	...	...	...	...	...	Canada[1]
Cuba[2]	53	56	57	32	33	22	1	4	5	4	Cuba[2]
Dominican Republic	4	5	9	9	10	7	8	9	8	10	Rép. dominicaine
Jamaica	18	18	19	20	25	22	21	24	...	...	Jamaïque
Mexico	364	380	412	386	434	431	475	567	617	579	Mexique
Panama	2	2	2	2	2	2	2	1	...	...	Panama
United States[3]	87	75	75	71	73	71	69	68	65	61	Etats–Unis[3]
America, South	**1 630**	**561**	**670**	**881**	**1 201**	**818**	**767**	**713**	**662**	**608**	**Amérique du Sud**
Brazil[4]	1 616	548	656	[5] 867	1 188	...	...	...	...	...	Brésil[4]
Colombia	...	...	...	...	...	3	6	5	...	...	Colombie
Ecuador	...	...	9	9	9	0	0	0	...	...	Equateur
Asia	**149**	**167**	**175**	**188**	**195**	**221**	**206**	**217**	**231**	**242**	**Asie**
Indonesia	37	62	68	65	69	101	...	...	...	...	Indonésie
Japan	78	77	80	93	98	94	88	87	93	...	Japon
Sri Lanka[6]	34	28	27	30	28	26	17	...	...	...	Sri Lanka[6]
Europe	**2 517**	**2 483**	**2 517**	**2 699**	**2 480**	**2 555**	**2 571**	**2 702**	**3 389**	**3 365**	**Europe**
EEC	***501***	***473***	***494***	***498***	***493***	***482***	***487***	***482***	***515***	***587***	***CEE***
Denmark	108	112	116	121	114	105	108	103	101	99	Danemark
Germany, Fed. Rep.	391	360	377	376	378	376	378	378	413	487	Allemagne, Rép. féd.
Luxembourg	1	0	0	0	0	0	0	0	0	0	Luxembourg
United Kingdom[7]	1	1	1	1	1	1	1	1	1	1	Royaume–Uni[7]
EFTA	***493***	***471***	***459***	***441***	***448***	***476***	***471***	***466***	***610***	***505***	***AELE***
Austria	100	96	102	104	102	108	98	96	93	89	Autriche
Finland	10	16	12	18	15	19	20	21	20	...	Finlande
Norway[4]	263	246	227	203	214	218	220	227	379	...	Norvège[4]
Portugal	42	41	39	36	42	43	44	40	39	41	Portugal
Sweden	78	72	79	80	75	88	89	82	79	74	Suède
East Europe	***1 190***	***1 171***	***1 181***	***1 252***	***1 220***	***1 285***	***1 104***	***1 261***	***1 783***	***1 777***	***Europe de l'est***
Bulgaria	19	19	24	23	23	27	27	22	18	116	Bulgarie
Czechoslovakia	288	292	293	284	293	302	296	305	311	309	Tchécoslovaquie
Hungary	15	17	17	16	28	18	21	25	27	28	Hongrie
Poland	868	843	847	929	876	938	760	909	1 427	1 324	Pologne
Other Europe	***333***	***368***	***383***	***508***	***319***	***312***	***509***	***493***	***481***	***496***	***Autre Europe***
Spain	...	...	...	463	298	293	486	474	...	...	Espagne
Yugoslavia	34	49	43	45	21	19	23	19	16	10	Yougoslavie
Oceania	**123**	**139**	**147**	**151**	**160**	**164**	**221**	**123**	**128**	**128**	**Océanie**
Australia	123	139	147	151	160	164	221	123	[4] 128	[4] 128	Australie
Total	**5 411**	**4 325**	**4 560**	**4 937**	**5 181**	**4 928**	**4 954**	**4 918**	**5 647**	**5 414**	**Total**

General note.
Sifted (bolted) flour of cereals other than wheat or meslin. (SITC 04701–0).

Remarque générale.
Farines tamisées (blutées) de céréales autres que le froment ou le méteil. (CTCI 04701–0).

[1] Shipments.
[2] Including corn flour.
[3] Rye flour.
[4] Including meal and groats of all cereals.
[5] Production by establishments employing 5 or more persons.
[6] State sector only.
[7] Oat flour only.

[1] Expéditions.
[2] Y compris la farine de maïs.
[3] Farine de seigle.
[4] Y compris les farines et gruaux de toutes céréales.
[5] Production des établissements occupant 5 personnes ou plus.
[6] Secteur public seulement.
[7] Farine d'avoine seulement.

Cereal breakfast food – Aliments à base de céréales, pour le petit déjeûner

Unit : Thousand metric tons

Unité : Milliers de tonnes métriques

Country or area	1976	1977	1978	1979	1980	1981	1982	1983	1984	1985	Pays ou zone
Africa	**18.8**	**19.2**	**19.5**	**19.4**	**20.4**	**20.8**	**21.4**	**22.5**	**21.8**	**22.0**	**Afrique**
Algeria	0.5	...	...	...	...	...	...	...	...	...	Algérie
Kenya	0.2	0.2	0.1	0.2	0.2	0.2	0.1	0.2	0.5	0.5	Kenya
South Africa	...	...	...	18.8	19.7	20.1	20.8	21.8	20.8	21.1	Afrique du Sud
America, North	**1 720.0**	**1 411.7**	**2 011.9**	**2 301.9**	**2 656.9**	**2 482.3**	**2 497.7**	**2 566.5**	**2 702.6**	**2 783.0**	**Amérique du Nord**
Canada	117.2	116.6	124.1	117.2	127.8	...	...	...	...	...	Canada
Cuba	...	...	...	...	3.2	2.4	0.7	1.1	1.2	...	Cuba
United States	...	1 291.9	1 884.8	2 182.0	2 526.0	2 352.8	2 367.7	2 433.9	2 567.8	2 646.0	Etats-Unis
America, South	**0.5**	**0.5**	**0.5**	**0.5**	**0.5**	**0.5**	**0.5**	**0.5**	**0.5**	**0.5**	**Amérique du Sud**
Colombia	...	...	...	...	...	0.5	0.5	0.5	...	...	Colombie
Asia	**0.8**	**0.9**	**0.9**	**0.6**	**0.8**	**0.8**	**0.8**	**0.8**	**0.8**	**0.8**	**Asie**
India[1]	0.8	* 0.9	0.9	0.6	...	...	...	...	...	...	Inde[1]
Europe	**260.6**	**259.0**	**263.6**	**235.2**	**264.9**	**254.5**	**266.0**	**276.5**	**292.0**	**296.3**	**Europe**
EEC	***249.5***	***247.8***	***251.8***	***224.6***	***252.5***	***241.5***	***253.9***	***264.2***	***279.2***	***284.1***	***CEE***
Denmark	16.7	17.0	18.5	13.4	20.5	19.5	21.3	26.2	27.7	28.7	Danemark
France	3.8	4.8	4.3	3.2	3.0	3.0	3.6	4.0	4.6	6.4	France
United Kingdom[2]	229.0	226.0	229.0	208.0	229.0	219.0	229.0	234.0	247.0	249.0	Royaume-Uni[2]
EFTA	***11.1***	***11.2***	***11.8***	***10.5***	***12.4***	***13.0***	***12.1***	***12.3***	***12.7***	***12.2***	***AELE***
Finland	2.0	2.5	2.4	2.6	3.4	2.4	# 0.6	0.6	0.5	...	Finlande
Norway	2.7	2.8	3.4	3.4	3.9	3.8	3.2	3.1	3.1	3.1	Norvège
Sweden	6.3	5.9	5.9	4.6	5.2	6.8	8.4	8.6	9.1	8.6	Suède
Oceania	**84.5**	**91.5**	**96.7**	**97.8**	**95.2**	**101.6**	**106.2**	**101.1**	**131.8**	**61.0**	**Océanie**
Australia	67.3	73.8	77.8	78.9	75.0	81.5	86.0	80.3	109.6	37.9	Australie
New Zealand	17.1	17.7	18.8	19.0	20.2	20.1	20.2	20.8	22.2	23.1	Nouvelle-Zélande
Total	**2 085.2**	**1 782.7**	**2 393.1**	**2 655.4**	**3 038.7**	**2 860.5**	**2 892.5**	**2 967.9**	**3 149.5**	**3 163.6**	**Total**

General note.
Prepared foods (ready to serve or to be cooked before serving) obtained by swelling or roasting of cereals or cereal products such as puffed rice, corn flakes and similar products. (SITC 04812-0).

[1] Production by large and medium scale establishments only.
[2] Data refer to 53-week period.

Remarque générale.
Produits alimentaires (pour consommation immédiate, ou après cuisson) obtenus par gonflage, le soufflage ou le grillage de céréales ou de produits à base de céréales (riz soufflé, flocons de maïs et produits similaires). (CTCI 04812-0).

[1] Production des grandes et moyennes entreprises seulement.
[2] Données se rapportant à une période de 53 semaines.

Macaroni and noodle products, uncooked – Pâtes alimentaires

Unit : Thousand metric tons | Unité : Milliers de tonnes métriques

Country or area	1976	1977	1978	1979	1980	1981	1982	1983	1984	1985	Pays ou zone
Africa	**241**	**261**	**277**	**290**	**347**	**333**	**371**	**446**	**436**	**455**	**Afrique**
Algeria	62	65	69	68	80	84	83	...	...	...	Algérie
Cameroon	1	1	1	2	2	...	...	2	3	3	Cameroun
Côte d'Ivoire	2	2	2	2	2	2	2	2	2	...	Côte d'Ivoire
Egypt	79	88	97	100	102	108	138	202	...	...	Egypte
Ethiopia[1]	9	6	7	14	54	24	11	10	17	14	Ethiopie[1]
Libyan Arab Jamah.	48	49	50	57	54	59	62	61	...	...	Jamah.arabe libyenne
Madagascar	1	* 1	* 1	* 1	* 1	* 1	* 1	* 1	* 1	* 1	Madagascar
Tunisia	39	49	50	46	52	53	72	79	80	82	Tunisie
America, North	**1 112**	**1 245**	**1 202**	**1 208**	**1 208**	**1 180**	**1 291**	**1 243**	**1 287**	**1 321**	**Amérique du Nord**
Barbados	1	1	1	1	2	2	2	2	2	2	Barbade
Canada[2]	83	92	99	105	107	...	...	...	...	...	Canada[2]
Cuba	52	52	52	53	59	60	57	59	56	56	Cuba
Dominican Republic	20	22	22	25	24	24	26	28	29	36	Rép. dominicaine
El Salvador	3	5	2	2	2	2	0	1	...	...	El Salvador
Mexico	119	126	129	134	136	138	146	150	146	144	Mexique
Panama	5	6	6	6	5	6	6	6	...	...	Panama
United States	829	941	891	882	873	833	933	870	914	937	Etats–Unis
America, South	**874**	**876**	**929**	**1 019**	**1 078**	**1 039**	**1 100**	**1 141**	**1 191**	**1 238**	**Amérique du Sud**
Bolivia	24	25	27	30	36	30	30	35	38	...	Bolivie
Brazil	550	542	582	[3] 646	690	656	...	...	...	...	Brésil
Chile	77	73	82	96	83	75	74	71	76	83	Chili
Colombia	47	55	61	56	66	73	70	73	...	...	Colombie
Ecuador	...	...	24	...	...	...	...	...	...	...	Equateur
Peru	152	157	153	167	179	...	...	...	...	...	Pérou
Asia	**1 440**	**1 462**	**1 501**	**1 582**	**1 572**	**1 557**	**1 647**	**1 653**	**1 754**	**1 760**	**Asie**
Burma[4]	* 14	...	...	* 11	* 12	16	17	18	18	19	Birmanie[4]
Hong Kong	36	44	42	43	62	32	92	35	85	80	Hong–kong
Indonesia	23	25	27	33	38	33	41	50	75	...	Indonésie
Iran(Islamic Rep.of)	4	...	...	...	...	...	...	...	...	...	Iran(Rép.islamique)
Japan[5]	1 264	1 262	1 287	1 359	1 321	1 338	1 348	1 373	1 392	1 397	Japon[5]
Kuwait	2	2	2	2	2	3	3	3	3	4	Koweït
Singapore	9	9	11	16	...	...	...	...	...	...	Singapour
Syrian Arab Republic	7	7	8	8	9	12	14	15	15	11	Rép. arabe syrienne
Turkey	79	95	105	104	111	105	113	141	147	166	Turquie
Europe	**3 078**	**3 074**	**3 103**	**3 185**	**3 191**	**3 220**	**3 181**	**3 187**	**3 206**	**3 210**	**Europe**
EEC	***2 587***	***2 578***	***2 579***	***2 591***	***2 605***	***2 619***	***2 595***	***2 605***	***2 622***	***2 607***	***CEE***
Belgium	21	20	21	22	22	19	19	21	24	23	Belgique
Denmark	2	1	1	1	1	1	1	0	0	0	Danemark
France	301	285	289	294	301	303	291	302	298	285	France
Germany, Fed. Rep.	213	182	188	190	196	211	201	199	218	213	Allemagne, Rép. féd.
Greece	71	64	72	72	79	80	77	77	76	...	Grèce
Italy[6]	1 916	1 969	...	...	...	...	...	...	...	...	Italie[6]
Luxembourg[7]	2	2	2	2	2	1	2	...	...	...	Luxembourg[7]
Netherlands* [6]	34	31	41	43	...	...	...	...	...	...	Pays–Bas* [6]
United Kingdom	27	24	22	...	...	...	...	...	...	...	Royaume–Uni
EFTA	***111***	***119***	***116***	***125***	***125***	***120***	***122***	***131***	***118***	***121***	***AELE***
Austria	21	19	19	20	20	20	19	36	19	24	Autriche
Finland	8	8	7	8	9	10	13	8	9	...	Finlande
Portugal	68	77	74	82	79	73	72	69	71	69	Portugal
Sweden	14	15	16	15	17	17	18	18	19	18	Suède
East Europe	***221***	***210***	***235***	***243***	***249***	***266***	***266***	***252***	***261***	***269***	***Europe de l'est***
Bulgaria	13	14	15	17	17	19	18	18	18	19	Bulgarie
Czechoslovakia	38	39	39	40	42	44	46	47	46	49	Tchécoslovaquie
German Dem. Rep.	53	55	58	61	61	63	65	69	69	68	Rép. dém. allemande
Hungary	36	29	36	35	34	39	42	40	42	50	Hongrie
Poland	81	73	87	90	95	101	95	78	86	83	Pologne
Other Europe	***159***	***167***	***173***	***226***	***212***	***215***	***198***	***199***	***205***	***213***	***Autre Europe***

For general note and footnotes, see end of table.

Voir la fin du tableau pour la remarque générale et les notes.

Unit : Thousand metric tons

Unité : Milliers de tonnes métriques

Country or area	1976	1977	1978	1979	1980	1981	1982	1983	1984	1985	Pays ou zone
Malta	7	4	4	5	5	5	7	8	9	...	Malte
Spain	89	109	...	164	137	123	101	102	...	...	Espagne
Yugoslavia	63	54	52	57	70	87	90	89	76	84	Yougoslavie
USSR	**1 476**	**1 491**	**1 454**	**1 499**	**1 554**	**1 619**	**1 634**	**1 598**	**1 607**	**1 654**	**URSS**
Byelorussian SSR	*47*	*49*	*48*	*48*	*48*	*50*	*51*	*51*	*52*	*52*	*RSS de Biélorussie*
Ukrainian SSR	*299*	*293*	*283*	*291*	*309*	*332*	*330*	*325*	*330*	*330*	*RSS d'Ukraine*
Oceania	**33**	**36**	**36**	**34**	**36**	**36**	**34**	**35**	**37**	**40**	**Océanie**
Australia	28	31	30	28	33	33	31	31	32	34	Australie
New Zealand	...	...	6	6	3	3	3	4	5	6	Nouvelle–Zélande
Total	**8 254**	**8 445**	**8 502**	**8 817**	**8 985**	**8 985**	**9 258**	**9 303**	**9 517**	**9 677**	**Total**

General note.
Uncooked products made generally from semolina or wheat flour doughs by extrusion, moulding or rolling. "Couscous" made of hard wheat semolina, steamed and dried, is included. Stuffed dough products (for example, ravioli, tortellini etc.) and cooked macaroni, spaghetti etc. are excluded. (SITC 04830–0).

1 Twelve months ending 10 September of year stated.
2 Shipments.
3 Production by establishments employing 5 or more persons.
4 Twelve months ending 31 March of year stated.
5 Twelve months beginning 1 April of year stated.
6 Source: Industrial Statistics, Statistical Office of the European Communities, (Luxembourg).
7 Beginning 1983, data are confidential.

Remarque générale.
Produits non cuits généralement préparés par extrusion, pressage ou laminage à partir de pâte de semoule ou de farine de blé. Cette rubrique comprend le couscous, préparé à partir de semoule de blé dur traitée à la vapeur et séchée, mais non les produits farcis (raviolis, tortellinis etc.) ni les pâtes cuites. (CTCI 04830–0).

1 Période de douze mois finissant le 10 septembre de l'année indiquée.
2 Expéditions.
3 Production des établissements occupant 5 personnes ou plus.
4 Période de douze mois finissant le 31 mars de l'année indiquée.
5 Période de douze mois commençant le 1er avril de l'année indiquée.
6 Source: Statistiques industrielles, Office statistique des Communautés européennes, (Luxembourg).
7 A partir de 1983, les données sont confidentielles.

Bread, ships' biscuits and other ordinary bakers' wares – Pain, biscuits de mer et autres produits de boulangerie ordinaire

Unit : Thousand metric tons — Unité : Milliers de tonnes métriques

Country or area	1976	1977	1978	1979	1980	1981	1982	1983	1984	1985	Pays ou zone
Africa	**1 402**	**1 448**	**1 449**	**1 515**	**1 799**	**1 856**	**1 876**	**1 958**	**1 974**	**2 054**	**Afrique**
Cape Verde	1	1	2	2	2	2	2	2	2	2	Cap-Vert
Côte d'Ivoire	78	117	...	146	124	108	84	86	85	84	Côte d'Ivoire
Gabon	3	6	5	5	5	6	6	6	7	7	Gabon
Kenya[1]	89	96	103	79	153	104	148	181	116	115	Kenya[1]
Sierra Leone[1]	...	...	...	0	1	0	0	0	0	...	Sierra Leone[1]
South Africa[1]	1 104	1 130	1 125	1 165	* 1 400	1 496	1 506	1 550	* 1 627	1 705	Afrique du Sud[1]
Tunisia	127	98	104	118	114	140	...	...	...	...	Tunisie
America, North	**7 694**	**8 007**	**7 733**	**7 714**	**7 720**	**9 026**	**9 101**	**9 076**	**9 215**	**9 206**	**Amérique du Nord**
Bermuda*	2	2	2	2	2	...	...	...	...	...	Bermudes*
Canada[1 2 3]	776	750	750	710	732	...	...	...	...	...	Canada[1 2 3]
Cuba[1]	422	429	444	441	447	510	518	524	530	531	Cuba[1]
Dominican Republic	58	61	56	63	71	66	80	81	82	89	Rép. dominicaine
Jamaica	44	46	36	36	32	26	32	32	...	...	Jamaïque
Panama	15	19	20	20	20	22	22	21	...	...	Panama
United States	6 377	6 700	6 425	6 442	6 416	7 694	7 754	7 736	7 885	7 882	Etats-Unis
America, South	**1 746**	**1 749**	**1 826**	**1 831**	**1 987**	**1 984**	**2 050**	**2 111**	**2 171**	**2 230**	**Amérique du Sud**
Bolivia[1]	11	12	5	5	7	5	4	6	9	8	Bolivie[1]
Brazil[1]	1 642	1 647	1 709	1 734	1 886	...	...	...	...	...	Brésil[1]
Colombia	...	44	58	44	40	45	43	44	* 43	* 45	Colombie
Ecuador	24	...	32	...	30	14	...	...	...	...	Equateur
Paraguay[1 4]	21	21	22	23	24	25	...	...	...	...	Paraguay[1 4]
Asia	**1 280**	**1 337**	**1 427**	**1 486**	**1 489**	**1 505**	**1 513**	**1 544**	**1 600**	**1 661**	**Asie**
Afghanistan	...	20	20	22	20	20	25	30	32	33	Afghanistan
Indonesia	16	15	16	15	23	16	17	...	...	...	Indonésie
Japan[5]	1 098	1 147	1 168	1 168	1 189	1 211	1 192	1 194	1 203	1 178	Japon[5]
Korea, Republic of	64	63	123	178	146	143	158	172	210	290	Corée, République de
Kuwait	5	4	* 5	6	7	7	7	7	7	* 7	Koweït
Mongolia	49	55	55	56	60	63	69	76	80	83	Mongolie
Philippines[2]	# 12	15	19	20	22	23	* 23	* 24	...	...	Philippines[2]
Singapore	14	12	14	13	...	...	...	...	...	...	Singapour
Yemen	...	...	...	...	...	2	2	2	2	2	Yémen
Europe	**12 524**	**12 748**	**13 412**	**13 497**	**13 572**	**14 140**	**13 826**	**13 661**	**13 805**	**13 962**	**Europe**
EEC	***2 068***	***2 482***	***2 847***	***2 868***	***2 838***	***2 969***	***2 711***	***2 771***	***2 900***	***3 018***	***CEE***
Belgium[1 6]	135	127	119	119	128	133	140	144	...	...	Belgique[1 6]
Denmark	169	167	168	171	159	189	188	179	181	198	Danemark
France	149	148	166	175	130	132	123	120	...	...	France
Germany, Fed. Rep.	1 112	1 110	1 485	1 518	1 521	1 529	[1] 1 273	[1] 1 319	[1] 1 355	[1] 1 411	Allemagne, Rép. féd.
Ireland[1]	189	...	...	...	...	...	...	...	...	...	Irlande[1]
Netherlands[7]	314	# 741	720	696	711	797	798	820	...	...	Pays-Bas[7]
EFTA	***1 189***	***1 072***	***1 045***	***1 048***	***1 021***	***985***	***964***	***938***	***967***	***913***	***AELE***
Finland	270	190	188	190	194	195	196	195	201	...	Finlande
Iceland	8	9	9	9	9	9	10	10	11	...	Islande
Portugal	624	592	559	557	528	491	464	440	455	...	Portugal
Sweden	287	281	289	292	290	290	294	293	300	312	Suède
East Europe	***8 160***	***8 046***	***8 243***	***8 250***	***8 315***	***8 710***	***8 648***	***8 416***	***8 356***	***8 408***	***Europe de l'est***
Bulgaria	1 642	1 619	1 639	1 622	1 574	1 634	1 498	1 438	1 392	1 544	Bulgarie
Czechoslovakia	1 346	1 343	1 365	1 354	1 378	1 393	1 445	1 428	1 435	1 443	Tchécoslovaquie
German Dem. Rep.	789	766	801	836	845	867	877	893	910	928	Rép. dém. allemande
Hungary	989	991	996	1 013	995	984	966	928	884	875	Hongrie
Poland	3 394	3 327	3 442	3 425	3 523	3 832	3 862	3 729	3 735	3 618	Pologne
Other Europe	***1 107***	***1 148***	***1 277***	***1 331***	***1 398***	***1 476***	***1 503***	***1 536***	***1 582***	***1 623***	***Autre Europe***
Malta	29	22	23	21	20	27	26	23	25	...	Malte
Spain	...	...	...	174	206	214	196	247	...	...	Espagne
Yugoslavia	938	973	1 087	1 136	1 172	1 235	1 281	1 266	1 309	1 338	Yougoslavie
USSR	**34 635**	**33 665**	**34 331**	**34 229**	**35 201**	**35 631**	**35 863**	**35 953**	**35 676**	**34 733**	**URSS**
Byelorussian SSR	*1 610*	*1 556*	*1 622*	*1 559*	*1 632*	*1 712*	*1 706*	*1 733*	*1 704*	*1 648*	*RSS de Biélorussie*

For general note and footnotes, see end of table. — Voir la fin du tableau pour la remarque générale et les notes.

Unit : Thousand metric tons | Unité : Milliers de tonnes métriques

Country or area	1976	1977	1978	1979	1980	1981	1982	1983	1984	1985	Pays ou zone
Ukrainian SSR	*7 476*	*7 078*	*7 305*	*7 145*	*7 375*	*7 591*	*7 654*	*7 702*	*7 702*	*7 348*	*RSS d'Ukraine*
Oceania	**746**	**737**	**784**	**732**	**745**	**735**	**770**	**752**	**772**	**784**	**Océanie**
Australia[1]	746	737	784	732	745	735	770	752	772	784	Australie[1]
Total	**60 028**	**59 691**	**60 962**	**61 004**	**62 512**	**64 878**	**64 999**	**65 055**	**65 214**	**64 630**	**Total**

General note.
Ordinary bakers' wares (including wholemeal bread and ships' biscuits), that is, containing only normal bread ingredients (cereal flours, leavens, salt) in terms of baked weight. Bakers' wares containing added sugar, honey, eggs, fats, cheeses, fruit or cocoa are excluded. (SITC 04841-0).

[1] Bread only.
[2] Shipments.
[3] Including bread produced by merchandising establishments.
[4] Industrial production only.
[5] Quantity of wheat flour used for making bread.
[6] Production by establishments employing 5 or more persons.
[7] Production by main establishments only.

Remarque générale.
Produits de boulangerie ordinaire (y compris le pain entier et les biscuits de mer), c'est-à-dire contenant seulement les ingrédients normaux du pain (farines de céréales, levures, sel). Cette position ne comprend pas les produits de boulangerie additionnés de sucre, de miel, d'oeufs, de matières grasses, de fromage, de fruits ou de cacao. Poids en tonnes métriques de produits cuits. (CTCI 04841-0).

[1] Pain seulement.
[2] Expéditions.
[3] Y compris le pain fabriqué par les établissements de marchandisage.
[4] Production industrielle seulement.
[5] Quantité de farine de froment destinée à la panification.
[6] Production des établissements occupant 5 personnes ou plus.
[7] Production des principaux établissements seulement.

Unit : Thousand metric tons

Unité : Milliers de tonnes métriques

Country or area	1976	1977	1978	1979	1980	1981	1982	1983	1984	1985	Pays ou zone
Africa	**142.3**	**148.3**	**160.9**	**176.3**	**177.5**	**192.3**	**187.6**	**180.9**	**174.8**	**194.7**	**Afrique**
Algeria	19.2	18.2	21.2	30.5	26.7	27.0	15.3	...	...	...	Algérie
Cameroon	* 0.4	* 0.5	...	...	1.1	1.1	* 1.0	* 1.0	1.2	1.4	Cameroun
Cape Verde	0.1	0.2	0.2	0.3	0.3	0.4	0.4	0.4	0.4	0.4	Cap–Vert
Côte d'Ivoire	1.6	1.8	2.3	2.5	2.9	4.5	4.6	4.0	4.5	...	Côte d'Ivoire
Egypt	16.3	18.3	21.0	26.4	22.4	23.1	26.1	28.3	...	...	Egypte
Ethiopia[1]	0.7	0.2	0.3	0.1	0.2	0.1	0.1	0.4	0.2	...	Ethiopie[1]
Ghana	3.4	1.4	2.6	1.2	1.9	1.4	1.0	0.5	...	...	Ghana
Kenya	1.7	1.7	3.3	2.9	3.0	2.5	1.9	1.4	4.5	3.3	Kenya
Libyan Arab Jamah	...	...	...	10.4	12.5	7.5	9.2	12.7	...	...	Jamah.arabe libyenne
Mali	0.5	0.5	0.6	0.8	1.3	1.0	1.0	1.0	0.9	0.9	Mali
Nigeria	29.0	32.8	35.9	...	...	48.8	48.9	31.0	20.1	37.9	Nigéria
Senegal	11.7	10.4	9.5	10.7	10.4	9.6	9.4	8.9	8.2	7.9	Sénégal
Sierra Leone	...	...	...	0.7	0.9	0.9	0.5	0.7	0.9	...	Sierra Leone
South Africa	...	...	...	40.2	42.9	48.1	50.6	47.5	* 47.6	47.1	Afrique du Sud
Tunisia	2.8	4.9	5.9	8.0	10.2	10.4	...	...	...	...	Tunisie
Uganda	0.6	...	...	...	...	...	...	...	...	...	Ouganda
United Rep. Tanzania	0.4	0.6	0.8	0.9	0.7	0.4	0.3	...	...	...	Rép.Unie de Tanzanie
Zaire	3.6	4.6	3.2	...	4.0	4.8	4.0	3.6	...	...	Zaïre
America, North	**2 269.9**	**2 344.5**	**2 418.0**	**2 455.4**	**2 435.5**	**1 478.8**	**1 535.0**	**1 612.4**	**1 716.3**	**1 755.5**	**Amérique du Nord**
Antigua and Barbuda	...	0.0	0.0	0.0	0.0	0.0	0.1	0.3	...	...	Antigua–et–Barbuda
Barbados	4.0	3.8	3.7	3.7	3.9	3.5	3.5	3.2	2.9	3.0	Barbade
Canada	[2] 167.4	[2] 160.4	[2] 169.6	[2] 168.9	[2] 175.9	...	...	...	...	184.1	Canada
Cuba	65.2	63.2	65.6	63.6	71.8	# 29.6	28.0	27.8	27.6	25.3	Cuba
Dominican Republic	4.8	6.7	7.5	9.4	13.1	9.4	11.4	12.3	12.5	12.6	Rép. dominicaine
Mexico	244.7	232.4	253.5	261.3	285.6	292.6	301.3	298.0	295.6	296.7	Mexique
Nicaragua	...	...	...	2.4	3.5	4.3	3.6	3.5	3.5	...	Nicaragua
Panama	4.2	4.7	4.4	4.3	4.0	3.5	4.0	4.3	...	...	Panama
United States	1 776.9	1 870.4	1 910.7	1 941.7	1 877.6	960.6	1 005.7	1 083.1	1 187.9	1 225.8	Etats–Unis
America, South	**566.3**	**581.0**	**628.5**	**709.2**	**731.7**	**808.4**	**828.6**	**876.2**	**928.6**	**972.9**	**Amérique du Sud**
Bolivia	2.1	2.8	3.1	3.2	3.2	3.5	2.1	3.1	9.6	8.0	Bolivie
Brazil	444.4	444.4	477.1	[3] 542.6	561.1	636.8	...	...	...	...	Brésil
Chile	12.7	12.5	13.3	19.7	19.1	19.0	16.2	11.7	11.0	11.3	Chili
Colombia	26.4	32.5	41.5	47.1	48.5	49.1	50.6	50.5	...	...	Colombie
Ecuador	6.7	12.5	13.0	...	...	17.2	19.9	30.7	...	...	Equateur
Guyana	2.3	3.0	2.8	1.9	2.1	1.6	1.4	1.0	...	...	Guyana
Paraguay	44.3	45.6	46.9	49.3	50.8	52.3	53.9	55.5	57.1	57.6	Paraguay
Venezuela	27.4	27.7	30.8	30.0	...	...	...	...	...	...	Venezuela
Asia	**692.0**	**730.0**	**740.9**	**731.4**	**742.9**	**803.3**	**867.8**	**894.2**	**836.0**	**827.6**	**Asie**
Burma[4]	7.1	7.5	7.7	7.9	8.1	8.5	8.5	8.6	8.8	9.0	Birmanie[4]
Hong Kong	13.3	12.7	11.3	12.5	10.5	14.4	14.9	19.1	13.3	...	Hong–kong
India[5]	70.3	83.1	84.8	99.7	100.5	142.3	155.6	158.8	127.9	130.7	Inde[5]
Indonesia	15.6	15.3	15.6	16.1	15.8	20.3	20.7	29.0	28.9	...	Indonésie
Iran(Islamic Rep.of)[6]	60.0	64.4	73.6	43.6	51.5	54.5	67.4	71.9	...	...	Iran(Rép.islamique)[6]
Japan	292.0	281.0	267.0	253.0	266.0	266.0	267.0	267.0	257.0	247.0	Japon
Korea, Republic of	58.8	68.1	68.1	78.7	106.9	99.7	126.0	116.3	101.4	108.4	Corée, République de
Kuwait	1.9	1.8	1.6	2.6	3.0	3.1	2.8	2.4	2.0	2.2	Koweït
Malaysia[7 8]	35.5	40.0	42.4	43.0	43.9	43.1	# 44.8	48.1	53.1	...	Malaisie[7 8]
Mongolia	2.2	2.3	2.3	2.6	2.7	2.7	2.1	2.8	3.9	6.7	Mongolie
Nepal[9]	0.7	1.2	2.0	1.9	1.7	2.3	2.3	3.6	4.3	...	Népal[9]
Philippines[2]	17.4	23.8	21.4	21.3	21.1	21.0	* 20.0	18.6	...	...	Philippines[2]
Singapore	9.0	7.7	8.0	8.4	8.2	10.3	7.4	7.3	6.6	5.8	Singapour
Sri Lanka	7.2	12.2	7.8	17.5	12.4	18.3	...	...	...	...	Sri Lanka
Syrian Arab Republic	5.7	6.2	6.0	6.3	7.2	8.0	10.0	11.0	8.0	10.0	Rép. arabe syrienne
Turkey	75.0	84.9	104.6	95.0	80.4	85.8	96.3	106.0	112.3	96.0	Turquie
Yemen	...	...	15.1	18.9	0.0	0.0	0.0	0.0	0.0	0.0	Yémen
Europe	**2 410.0**	**2 557.4**	**2 667.6**	**2 672.7**	**2 921.2**	**2 958.6**	**3 011.5**	**3 130.1**	**3 258.0**	**3 356.2**	**Europe**
EEC	***1 842.8***	***1 950.5***	***2 045.9***	***2 043.9***	***2 216.9***	***2 268.8***	***2 290.5***	***2 430.5***	***2 523.3***	***2 637.9***	***CEE***
Belgium	102.2	115.6	114.5	113.3	119.3	124.9	130.1	139.4	144.9	141.3	Belgique
Denmark[10]	11.8	11.6	9.6	8.6	8.9	7.6	6.8	7.9	7.8	9.0	Danemark[10]
France	355.0	373.0	375.0	359.0	377.0	379.0	380.0	397.0	400.1	402.0	France
Germany, Fed. Rep.	[11] 205.8	[11] 217.3	...	...	...	...	...	...	393.1	403.0	Allemagne, Rép. féd.
Greece	22.6	22.3	29.9	32.2	40.6	40.4	41.1	40.1	37.9	...	Grèce
Italy[11]	* 333.0	...	...	...	459.7	483.9	526.8	558.0	596.6	613.8	Italie[11]

For general note and footnotes, see end of table.

Voir la fin du tableau pour la remarque générale et les notes.

Unit : Thousand metric tons

Unité : Milliers de tonnes métriques

Country or area	1976	1977	1978	1979	1980	1981	1982	1983	1984	1985	Pays ou zone
Netherlands[11]	182.5	195.0	* 171.4	* 172.4	278.0	286.9	279.1	285.7	299.8	318.3	Pays–Bas[11]
United Kingdom	630.0	652.0	644.9	625.8	628.7	641.3	621.8	697.6	643.0	704.3	Royaume–Uni
EFTA	***141.4***	***145.5***	***146.7***	***150.5***	***152.1***	***156.4***	***165.3***	***159.9***	***169.8***	***164.4***	***AELE***
Austria	38.7	40.1	40.5	42.5	45.0	45.1	48.2	44.8	50.1	48.2	Autriche
Finland	12.2	13.7	13.3	14.5	15.4	14.2	15.1	15.6	15.0	14.7	Finlande
Iceland	0.7	0.9	1.1	1.0	0.6	0.8	0.8	0.9	0.8	...	Islande
Norway	7.6	8.1	7.9	8.6	8.6	9.4	...	...	...	...	Norvège
Portugal	29.4	30.1	31.5	32.4	29.2	33.9	38.5	35.3	37.0	31.8	Portugal
Sweden	25.1	23.5	23.5	23.2	23.2	22.2	23.9	24.1	24.8	25.9	Suède
Switzerland[12]	27.8	29.1	28.9	28.3	29.9	30.8	29.3	29.4	31.9	32.6	Suisse[12]
East Europe	***178.9***	***177.2***	***180.8***	***189.1***	***198.0***	***202.4***	***205.9***	***207.0***	***209.6***	***210.8***	***Europe de l'est***
Bulgaria	22.8	22.8	21.5	22.6	23.7	24.7	25.4	23.5	23.9	24.3	Bulgarie
Czechoslovakia	72.9	74.9	76.4	79.8	83.8	83.9	85.9	86.6	88.1	88.3	Tchécoslovaquie
German Dem. Rep.	82.4	78.9	82.4	86.3	90.1	93.4	94.1	96.5	97.1	97.8	Rép. dém. allemande
Hungary	0.8	0.6	0.6	0.3	0.4	0.5	0.5	0.4	0.4	0.4	Hongrie
Other Europe	***247.0***	***284.1***	***294.3***	***289.2***	***354.2***	***330.9***	***349.9***	***332.7***	***355.3***	***343.1***	***Autre Europe***
Spain	166.3	197.4	...	185.3	238.5	208.2	224.4	201.3	...	...	Espagne
Yugoslavia	80.7	86.7	101.0	103.9	115.7	122.8	125.5	131.4	127.9	110.0	Yougoslavie
USSR	**614.3**	**653.7**	**669.8**	**684.1**	**705.6**	**726.7**	**740.0**	**762.2**	**784.0**	**815.6**	**URSS**
Byelorussian SSR	*26.9*	*29.0*	*29.1*	*29.2*	*29.0*	*29.3*	*29.8*	*30.9*	*32.6*	*34.5*	*RSS de Biélorussie*
Ukrainian SSR	*119.7*	*125.3*	*126.0*	*127.7*	*127.7*	*132.3*	*134.8*	*139.2*	*145.0*	*153.8*	*RSS d'Ukraine*
Oceania	**146.9**	**149.9**	**146.6**	**149.1**	**149.1**	**155.5**	**159.1**	**159.6**	**166.5**	**166.6**	**Océanie**
Australia[13]	117.8	124.7	121.3	125.2	124.1	129.7	131.6	129.1	132.3	134.4	Australie[13]
New Zealand	29.1	25.2	25.3	23.9	25.1	25.7	27.5	30.5	34.2	32.3	Nouvelle–Zélande
Total	**6 841.8**	**7 164.7**	**7 432.3**	**7 578.2**	**7 863.5**	**7 123.4**	**7 329.7**	**7 615.5**	**7 864.2**	**8 089.3**	**Total**

General note.
Fine bakers' wares without leavening made from flour, sugar and shortening, usually crisp, dry and hard and in the form of small flat thin cakes, in terms of baked weight. Ships' biscuits, crisp bread, matzos and rusks are excluded. (SITC 04842–1).

[1] Twelve months ending 10 September of year stated.
[2] Shipments.
[3] Production by establishments employing 5 or more persons.
[4] Twelve months ending 31 March of year stated.
[5] Production by large and medium scale establishments only.
[6] Production by establishments employing 10 or more persons.
[7] Data refer to Peninsular Malaysia only.
[8] Beginning 1982, scope of series revised.
[9] Twelve months beginning 16 July of year stated.
[10] Including crackers.
[11] Source: Industrial Statistics, Statistical Office of the European Communities, (Luxembourg).
[12] Sales.
[13] Twelve months ending 30 June of year stated.

Remarque générale.
Produits de boulangerie fine préparés sans levain à partir de farine, sucre et corps gras, généralement croustillants, secs et durs et se présentant sous forme de petits gâteaux plats. Cette rubrique ne comprend pas les biscuits de mer, le pain dur, le pain azyme et les biscottes. Poids en tonnes métriques de produits cuits. (CTCI 04842–1).

[1] Période de douze mois finissant le 10 septembre de l'année indiquée.
[2] Expéditions.
[3] Production des établissements occupant 5 personnes ou plus.
[4] Période de douze mois finissant le 31 mars de l'année indiquée.
[5] Production des grandes et moyennes entreprises seulement.
[6] Production des établissements occupant 10 personnes ou plus.
[7] Données se rapportant à la Malaisie péninsulaire seulement.
[8] A partir de 1982, portée de la série révisée.
[9] Période de douze mois commençant le 16 juillet de l'année indiquée.
[10] Y compris les biscuits durs.
[11] Source: Statistiques industrielles, Office statistique des Communautés européennes, (Luxembourg).
[12] Ventes.
[13] Période de douze mois finissant le 30 juin de l'année indiquée.

Pastry, cakes, and other fine bakers' wares – Pâtisseries, gâteaux et autres produits de boulangerie

Unit : Thousand metric tons

Unité : Milliers de tonnes métriques

Country or area	1976	1977	1978	1979	1980	1981	1982	1983	1984	1985	Pays ou zone
Africa											**Afrique**
Kenya	1.0	2.9	1.7	2.5	3.6	2.0	1.9	1.9	1.0	1.1	Kenya
America, North											**Amérique du Nord**
United States	1 283.7	1 348.7	1 293.4	1 296.9	1 291.6	1 361.7	1 363.1	1 333.2	1 388.3	1 366.9	Etats-Unis
America, South											**Amérique du Sud**
Brazil	115.3	117.6	110.8	[1] 116.8	128.2	...	...	...	...	...	Brésil
Colombia	...	...	...	...	...	17.8	19.2	16.5	...	...	Colombie
Asia											**Asie**
Indonesia	1.0	4.6	4.7	9.5	7.8	8.1	9.5	11.5	8.2	...	Indonésie
Korea, Republic of	...	...	...	...	47.9	56.8	52.6	61.2	73.5	76.1	Corée, République de
Philippines[2]	3.0	1.6	...	...	...	...	...	...	...	...	Philippines[2]
Turkey	...	12.7	...	...	...	...	...	...	...	...	Turquie
Europe											**Europe**
EEC											***CEE***
Denmark	46.5	50.9	57.2	64.2	74.2	81.3	...	...	...	...	Danemark
France	...	...	85.4	75.2	80.0	...	...	...	...	...	France
Germany, Fed. Rep.[3]	101.4	105.3	173.9	182.2	189.9	190.9	...	...	...	...	Allemagne, Rép. féd.[3]
EFTA											***AELE***
Austria	10.8	14.6	16.4	18.2	18.4	19.1	20.1	20.5	26.0	25.5	Autriche
Finland	85.7	61.3	57.9	58.4	79.6	60.5	61.1	58.7	62.6	...	Finlande
Iceland	1.4	1.6	1.8	2.1	2.2	2.1	2.0	2.3	2.3	...	Islande
Other Europe											***Autre Europe***
Spain	...	...	...	212.8	142.2	156.5	197.5	223.6	...	...	Espagne
East Europe											***Europe de l'est***
Bulgaria	23.8	24.9	27.1	27.7	27.1	24.4	26.2	26.3	28.0	42.7	Bulgarie
Czechoslovakia	50.8	53.4	54.0	55.5	58.1	59.2	59.2	59.8	59.8	60.3	Tchécoslovaquie
Hungary	117.3	122.5	124.1	135.5	138.6	134.5	138.7	111.8	101.2	101.3	Hongrie

General note.
Bakery products containing sugar, honey, eggs, fats, cheese, fruit, or cocoa, in terms of baked weight. Products containing meat and fish are excluded.

[1] Production by establishments employing 5 or more persons.
[2] Shipments.
[3] Beginning 1982, series discontinued.

Remarque générale.
Produits de boulangerie contenant un ou plusieurs des ingrédients suivants: sucre, miel, oeufs, matières grasses, fromage, fruits, cacao, à l'exclusion des produits contenant de la viande ou du poisson. Poids en tonnesmétriques de produits cuits. (CTCI 04842-2).

[1] Production des établissements occupant 5 personnes ou plus.
[2] Expéditions.
[3] A partir de 1982, la série a été abandonnée.

Raw sugar – Sucre brut

Unit : Thousand metric tons

Unité : Milliers de tonnes métriques

Country or area	1976	1977	1978	1979	1980	1981	1982	1983	1984	1985	Pays ou zone
Africa	**5 747**	**6 108**	**5 983**	**6 171**	**5 263**	**5 584**	**6 196**	**5 562**	**5 962**	**6 358**	**Afrique**
Algeria[1]	* 20	3	4	3	5	* 4	* 4	* 5	* 7	0	Algérie[1]
Angola* [1]	50	50	50	50	50	50	35	60	50	50	Angola* [1]
Burkina Faso[1]	0	30	31	31	27	30	28	28	* 27	* 10	Burkina Faso[1]
Cameroon	* [1] 32	* [1] 35	* [1] 37	56	60	66	* 70	58	54	* 70	Cameroun
Chad[2]	0	* 15	* 20	* 24	* 30	* 25	* 25	* 22	* 22	* 15	Tchad[2]
Congo	34	16	6	12	12	12	28	21	* 31	46	Congo
Côte d'Ivoire	22	37	32	63	114	147	170	150	130	* 112	Côte d'Ivoire
Egypt[1]	576	657	589	668	662	658	745	723	780	900	Egypte[1]
Ethiopia[1 3]	136	137	161	167	163	154	177	207	200	191	Ethiopie[1 3]
Gabon[2]	0	* 3	* 8	* 10	* 12	* 20	* 15	17	* 15	* 15	Gabon[2]
Ghana[1]	12	* 25	* 20	15	4	2	0	0	0	0	Ghana[1]
Guinea[1]	* 13	* 13	* 15	* 20	20	22	22	14	10	5	Guinée[1]
Kenya	182	185	236	296	383	368	308	325	405	395	Kenya
Liberia[1]	0	0	0	0	0	0	* 1	* 2	* 3	* 3	Libéria[1]
Madagascar	114	117	123	117	116	105	82	96	73	93	Madagascar
Malawi	87	95	97	108	147	114	115	122	86	69	Malawi
Mali[1]	* 5	* 15	* 25	* 18	* 19	9	5	* 12	10	21	Mali[1]
Mauritius	637	618	623	646	444	538	647	567	536	597	Maurice
Morocco	319	239	257	216	243	233	234	239	210	167	Maroc
Mozambique[1]	* 220	320	190	212	170	177	126	74	39	60	Mozambique[1]
Nigeria[2 4]	38	53	51	* 35	* 35	* 25	* 20	* 55	* 58	* 33	Nigéria[2 4]
Réunion[5]	250	249	272	261	227	251	258	230	246	228	Réunion[5]
Rwanda[2]	1	1	1	3	3	3	2	2	2	3	Rwanda[2]
Senegal	[1] 17	[1] 20	[1] 40	[1] 33	[1] 41	37	40	50	47	51	Sénégal
Sierra Leone	0	0	0	0	0	1	* 3	* 3	* 6	* 5	Sierra Leone
Somalia[1]	33	* 30	* 24	* 20	* 35	* 50	* 55	* 60	* 45	* 54	Somalie[1]
South Africa	2 030	2 201	2 100	* 2 143	# 1 098	1 234	1 656	949	1 334	1 558	Afrique du Sud
Sudan[1]	* 140	151	152	116	* 195	* 230	* 270	* 400	* 360	* 450	Soudan[1]
Swaziland	[1] 208	[1] 224	[1] 248	[1] 241	310	349	380	380	402	375	Swaziland
Tunisia	8	10	8	6	7	6	10	5	15	16	Tunisie
Uganda	20	12	8	5	4	4	3	* 2	* 3	* 6	Ouganda
United Rep. Tanzania[1]	110	108	136	123	122	122	* 105	* 116	129	105	Rép.Unie de Tanzanie[1]
Zaire[1]	* 65	* 65	36	* 52	* 55	* 60	* 58	* 51	* 59	* 65	Zaïre[1]
Zambia[1]	84	71	73	102	111	107	102	108	109	152	Zambie[1]
Zimbabwe	284	303	310	299	339	371	397	409	459	438	Zimbabwe
America, North	**18 917**	**17 925**	**18 117**	**18 414**	**16 883**	**18 323**	**18 558**	**18 029**	**18 569**	**18 654**	**Amérique du Nord**
Barbados	104	120	101	119	137	94	86	83	98	97	Barbade
Belize	63	92	115	100	103	98	106	114	104	* 110	Belize
Canada	156	* 144	123	112	85	* 99	* 129	* 132	* 110	* 60	Canada
Costa Rica	173	195	191	194	190	190	* 194	193	241	* 234	Costa Rica
Cuba[1]	6 151	6 953	7 662	7 800	6 805	7 926	8 040	7 460	7 783	7 889	Cuba[1]
Dominican Republic	1 168	1 130	1 069	1 070	911	1 018	1 232	1 122	1 130	900	Rép. dominicaine
El Salvador[1]	261	318	279	274	217	182	199	259	242	279	El Salvador[1]
Grenada	0	1	1	1	1	1	0	0	0	0	Grenade
Guadeloupe[5]	96	91	81	105	92	59	72	57	41	53	Guadeloupe[5]
Guatemala[1]	517	487	446	415	452	474	580	614	555	500	Guatemala[1]
Haiti	* 65	56	57	* 60	61	41	48	35	39	* 18	Haïti
Honduras[1]	81	* 115	131	164	191	196	217	221	207	235	Honduras[1]
Jamaica[1 6]	368	295	292	283	232	200	196	198	188	225	Jamaïque[1 6]
Martinique[5]	14	14	13	9	6	3	2	4	5	9	Martinique[5]
Mexico	2 548	1 459	1 637	1 611	1 448	1 387	1 322	1 685	1 811	2 011	Mexique
Nicaragua	* 242	226	222	202	190	214	247	249	242	195	Nicaragua
Panama[1]	161	181	187	226	200	186	239	215	176	160	Panama[1]
Puerto Rico[7]	308	264	201	191	175	151	112	99	96	96	Porto Rico[7]
St.Kitts–Nevis	35	42	40	40	35	32	36	28	31	27	St–Kitts–Nevis
Trinidad and Tobago	204	176	147	143	113	93	80	78	96	114	Trinité–et–Tobago
United States	6 167	5 524	5 082	5 255	5 204	5 647	5 385	5 155	5 343	5 415	Etats–Unis
America, South	**11 638**	**12 873**	**12 404**	**11 752**	**12 849**	**13 196**	**13 499**	**14 057**	**14 022**	**13 164**	**Amérique du Sud**
Argentina[1]	1 559	1 666	1 397	1 411	1 716	1 624	1 623	1 624	1 545	1 188	Argentine[1]
Bolivia	[1] 282	[1] 282	[1] 285	[1] 288	[1] 262	239	211	396	396	...	Bolivie
Brazil	6 851	8 306	7 475	6 980	7 844	8 266	8 496	9 027	8 777	7 995	Brésil
Chile[1]	* 319	* 315	131	97	60	235	132	229	360	351	Chili[1]
Colombia[1]	935	853	1 014	1 107	1 247	1 212	1 318	1 340	* 1 177	1 367	Colombie[1]
Ecuador[1]	309	266	347	355	368	330	246	164	329	* 300	Equateur[1]
Guyana	[1] 343	246	330	303	274	303	293	256	246	* 258	Guyana
Paraguay	56	53	69	76	69	71	75	92	92	* 80	Paraguay
Peru	[1] 319	[1] 315	[1] 856	694	542	508	613	442	* 603	* 727	Pérou
Suriname	9	8	6	10	7	8	7	6	7	7	Suriname

For general note and footnotes, see end of table.

Voir la fin du tableau pour la remarque générale et les notes.

Unit : Thousand metric tons | Unité : Milliers de tonnes métriques

Country or area	1976	1977	1978	1979	1980	1981	1982	1983	1984	1985	Pays ou zone
Uruguay[1]	* 120	120	91	84	102	97	103	104	100	90	Uruguay[1]
Venezuela	536	443	403	347	358	303	382	377	390	[1] 457	Venezuela
Asia	**15 659**	**15 321**	**17 676**	**16 028**	**14 582**	**18 115**	**22 670**	**21 948**	**20 937**	**21 252**	**Asie**
Afghanistan[8]	[1] 11	[1] 11	[1] 11	[1] 10	8	2	1	0	1	0	Afghanistan[8]
Bangladesh	110	115	120	125	135	175	190	186	242	300	Bangladesh
Burma* [1]	80	85	65	60	65	65	65	75	88	101	Birmanie* [1]
China[1]	1 650	# 1 816	2 267	2 500	2 571	3 170	3 380	3 770	3 800	4 500	Chine[1]
India[1]	5 033	5 019	7 103	6 080	4 528	5 991	9 126	8 452	6 635	7 016	Inde[1]
Indonesia	1 056	1 105	1 126	1 200	1 183	1 081	1 565	1 572	1 500	1 739	Indonésie
Iran(Islamic Rep.of)[1 8]	* 650	752	* 620	* 450	* 350	* 400	* 400	* 500	* 600	* 700	Iran(Rép.islamique)[1 8]
Iraq[1]	11	* 25	19	* 19	* 20	* 25	0	0	0	0	Iraq[1]
Israel[1]	40	34	* 10	* 16	* 10	* 20	0	0	0	0	Israël[1]
Japan	506	566	645	733	# 234	253	261	276	320	309	Japon
Lebanon[1]	* 10	* 10	* 10	* 10	* 10	6	5	0	0	0	Liban[1]
Malaysia[1]	* 50	* 60	* 70	* 40	* 50	* 55	* 60	* 70	* 75	70	Malaisie[1]
Nepal[1 9]	16	27	27	14	12	21	22	17	11	23	Népal[1 9]
Pakistan[1]	677	764	* 700	670	686	970	* 1 530	* 1 200	* 1 355	* 1 410	Pakistan[1]
Philippines[1]	2 984	2 624	2 273	2 390	2 332	2 376	2 709	2 112	2 577	1 665	Philippines[1]
Sri Lanka	24	23	26	20	26	25	24	22	18	20	Sri Lanka
Syrian Arab Republic[1]	26	21	19	25	47	35	81	* 110	* 110	50	Rép. arabe syrienne[1]
Thailand	1 594	1 026	1 280	526	1 000	1 988	1 387	1 436	1 568	* 1 517	Thaïlande
Turkey[1]	1 090	1 158	1 185	1 060	1 140	1 211	1 642	1 844	1 654	1 398	Turquie[1]
Viet Nam[1]	41	* 80	* 100	* 80	175	246	222	306	383	434	Viet Nam[1]
Europe	**16 486**	**18 857**	**18 775**	**19 148**	**18 363**	**22 037**	**21 436**	**18 437**	**19 950**	**19 859**	**Europe**
EEC	***10 729***	***12 045***	***12 248***	***12 858***	***12 804***	***15 472***	***14 444***	***11 345***	***12 899***	***13 106***	***CEE***
Belgium	721	757	842	966	874	1 038	1 246	847	910	961	Belgique
Denmark	432	472	544	469	499	* 522	* 584	* 376	595	...	Danemark
France[10]	2 736	3 927	3 738	3 979	3 921	5 130	4 446	3 560	3 956	3 978	France[10]
Germany, Fed. Rep.[2]	2 844	3 169	2 997	3 087	2 935	3 702	3 586	* 2 720	* 3 150	* 3 427	Allemagne, Rép. féd.[2]
Greece	[1] 386	[1] 294	[1] 354	[1] 309	[1] 198	# [2] 351	* [2] 322	* [2] 326	* [2] 236	* [2] 345	Grèce
Ireland	249	* 182	* 204	* 190	* 187	* 196	* 242	* 203	* 239	* 189	Irlande
Italy[2]	1 758	1 362	* 1 620	1 707	* 1 892	* 2 207	* 1 282	* 1 352	* 1 385	* 1 350	Italie[2]
Netherlands	946	* 904	880	915	951	* 1 139	1 195	* 807	* 1 000	* 1 000	Pays-Bas
United Kingdom[11]	657	978	1 069	1 236	1 347	1 187	1 541	1 154	1 428	1 315	Royaume-Uni[11]
EFTA	***898***	***1 023***	***922***	***1 009***	***1 045***	***1 125***	***1 277***	***1 000***	***1 132***	***1 087***	***AELE***
Austria	426	515	373	421	479	520	641	405	* 464	* 468	Autriche
Finland[1]	77	75	104	100	125	99	116	155	129	103	Finlande[1]
Portugal	[1] 11	9	10	12	3	1	1	8	8	* 9	Portugal
Sweden[1]	301	339	328	358	333	370	399	308	400	369	Suède[1]
Switzerland[1]	83	85	107	118	105	135	120	124	131	138	Suisse[1]
East Europe	***3 998***	***4 492***	***4 420***	***4 281***	***3 546***	***4 359***	***4 592***	***4 771***	***4 698***	***4 576***	***Europe de l'est***
Albania[1]	21	25	20	20	* 25	* 25	* 20	* 38	* 40	* 33	Albanie[1]
Bulgaria	394	391	425	418	371	440	433	477	487	497	Bulgarie
Czechoslovakia	149	262	257	250	183	187	216	175	201	229	Tchécoslovaquie
German Dem. Rep.	609	700	777	674	662	681	822	750	750	798	Rép. dém. allemande
Hungary	403	486	551	552	519	544	509	529	452	536	Hongrie
Poland	1 812	1 853	1 783	1 762	1 186	1 872	1 992	2 202	1 963	1 898	Pologne
Romania[1]	610	775	607	605	* 600	610	* 600	* 600	* 805	* 585	Roumanie[1]
Other Europe	***861***	***1 297***	***1 185***	***1 000***	***968***	***1 081***	***1 123***	***1 321***	***1 221***	***1 090***	***Autre Europe***
Spain[1]	861	1 297	1 185	* 1 000	968	1 081	1 123	1 321	1 221	1 090	Espagne[1]
USSR[1]	*** 8 500**	**8 885**	**9 353**	**7 927**	**7 174**	**6 413**	*** 7 391**	*** 8 695**	*** 8 587**	*** 8 600**	**URSS[1]**
Oceania	**3 152**	**3 650**	**3 690**	**3 462**	**3 393**	**3 793**	**3 933**	**3 808**	**3 628**	**3 915**	**Océanie**
Australia[7]	2 856	3 288	3 343	2 989	2 997	3 323	3 435	* 3 500	3 113	3 545	Australie[7]
Fiji	296	362	347	473	396	470	486	275	480	340	Fidji
Papua New Guinea	0	0	0	0	0	0	12	33	* 35	30	Papouasie-Nvl-Guinée
Total	**80 099**	**83 619**	**85 998**	**82 902**	**78 507**	**87 461**	**93 683**	**90 537**	**91 655**	**91 801**	**Total**

General note.
Crude beet and cane sugars in crystalline form. Aqueous solutions of raw sugar are excluded. (SITC 06110-0).

Remarque générale.
Sucre brut de betterave ou de canne sous forme cristallisée. Cette rubrique ne comprend pas les solutions aqueuses de sucre brut. (CTCI 06110-0).

For footnotes, see end of table.

Voir la fin du tableau pour les notes.

1 Source: International Sugar Organization, (London).
2 Source: Food and Agriculture Organization (FAO), (Rome).

3 Twelve months ending 10 September of year stated.
4 Including refined sugar.
5 Crop year production.
6 Telle quelle
7 Twelve months ending 30 June of year stated.
8 Twelve months beginning 21 March of year stated.
9 Twelve months beginning 16 July of year stated.
10 Crop year ending 30 September.
11 Sugar produced from home–grown sugar beet.

1 Source: Organisation Internationale du Sucre, (Londres).
2 Source: Organisation des Nations Unies pour l'alimentation et l'agriculture (FAO), (Rome).
3 Période de douze mois finissant le 10 septembre de l'année indiquée.
4 Y compris le sucre raffiné.
5 Production par campagne.
6 Production telle quelle.
7 Période de douze mois finissant le 30 juin de l'année indiquée.
8 Période de douze mois commençant le 21 mars de l'année indiquée.
9 Période de douze mois commençant le 16 juillet de l'année indiquée.
10 Production par campagne se terminant au 30 septembre de l'année indiquée.
11 Sucre provenant de betteraves récoltées localement.

Refined sugar – Sucre raffiné

Unit : Thousand metric tons

Unité : Milliers de tonnes métriques

Country or area	1976	1977	1978	1979	1980	1981	1982	1983	1984	1985	Pays ou zone
Africa	**2 506**	**2 658**	**2 875**	**3 040**	**3 119**	**3 262**	**3 369**	**3 529**	**3 672**	**3 811**	**Afrique**
Algeria	2	0	0	0	0	0	0	...	...	...	Algérie
Burkina Faso	21	37	57	30	28	26	28	28	26	28	Burkina Faso
Chad	12	16	17	17	17	...	...	...	...	...	Tchad
Côte d'Ivoire	23	38	32	41	41	69	80	56	75	...	Côte d'Ivoire
Egypt	# 574	603	630	617	616	619	599	746	...	...	Egypte
Gabon	4	3	7	9	* 13	14	14	16	10	15	Gabon
Kenya*	150	160	200	270	344	331	318	292	364	356	Kenya*
Mali	8	16	20	18	12	9	* 6	* 8	...	...	Mali
Mauritius	53	48	42	42	31	37	41	38	40	49	Maurice
Morocco	445	471	547	558	577	588	591	687	632	623	Maroc
Nigeria	38	34	44	...	...	...	...	...	...	...	Nigéria
Senegal	33	44	40	47	39	37	44	46	52	56	Sénégal
Sierra Leone	...	...	...	...	0	0	0	2	0	...	Sierra Leone
South Africa	...	...	...	1 042	1 077	1 112	1 154	* 1 108	1 250	1 302	Afrique du Sud
Sudan	114	139	138	...	135	214	307	...	...	...	Soudan
Tunisia	45	30	48	51	54	52	36	67	65	62	Tunisie
Zambia	75	70	64	85	96	96	92	97	98	137	Zambie
America, North	**12 435**	**12 577**	**12 367**	**12 258**	**12 094**	**13 538**	**11 294**	**11 460**	**11 792**	**11 251**	**Amérique du Nord**
Canada	1 033	1 154	1 131	1 089	921	1 054	1 025	1 017	1 084	1 076	Canada
Cuba	698	742	861	899	872	944	945	967	845	910	Cuba
Dominican Republic	82	94	106	97	102	114	109	112	108	86	Rép. dominicaine
El Salvador	...	25	26	0	0	0	0	...	...	...	El Salvador
Mexico	...	1 171	1 213	1 270	1 094	1 126	1 013	1 195	1 096	1 026	Mexique
Panama	46	51	46	52	50	51	55	52	...	...	Panama
United States	9 330	9 340	8 984	8 851	9 055	10 249	8 147	8 106	8 594	8 088	Etats–Unis
America, South	**4 376**	**5 031**	**4 475**	**4 572**	**5 075**	**5 242**	**4 940**	**5 089**	**4 977**	**4 499**	**Amérique du Sud**
Argentina	1 288	1 662	1 292	1 280	1 572	1 516	1 485	1 459	1 412	1 099	Argentine
Brazil	1 832	2 109	2 056	[1] 2 261	2 440	2 790	2 539	2 835	2 651	2 418	Brésil
Chile	351	403	313	258	237	175	146	193	308	285	Chili
Colombia	138	151	149	156	152	191	160	176	...	...	Colombie
Paraguay	56	77	69	68	89	77	81	98	85	78	Paraguay
Peru	...	...	...	...	251	229	306	146	197	* 330	Pérou
Venezuela	494	408	371	320	* 334	...	...	...	...	...	Venezuela
Asia	**11 806**	**12 367**	**13 994**	**13 429**	**11 836**	**13 284**	**17 943**	**17 681**	**15 803**	**15 890**	**Asie**
Bangladesh[2]	87	141	177	133	94	145	202	178	151	88	Bangladesh[2]
Burma[3]	19	31	38	37	41	47	43	47	62	60	Birmanie[3]
India	4 640	4 637	6 557	5 614	4 191	5 540	8 439	7 871	6 123	6 504	Inde
Indonesia	1 056	1 145	936	1 091	1 149	1 117	1 361	1 590	1 573	...	Indonésie
Iran(Islamic Rep.of)[4]	808	718	628	636	588	565	933	986	...	...	Iran(Rép.islamique)[4]
Israel	36	34	12	14	...	9	0	0	0	...	Israël
Japan	2 615	2 920	2 620	3 102	2 760	2 540	2 683	2 546	2 587	2 579	Japon
Korea, Republic of	298	386	511	625	757	690	646	772	748	823	Corée, République de
Malaysia	...	389	422	437	...	462	478	584	603	591	Malaisie
Pakistan[2]	630	736	861	607	586	851	1 301	1 127	1 145	...	Pakistan[2]
Syrian Arab Republic	126	104	105	118	90	148	183	206	199	54	Rép. arabe syrienne
Turkey	1 105	1 080	1 090	972	1 048	1 117	1 617	1 714	1 703	1 430	Turquie
Viet Nam	32	46	37	43	52	...	...	...	...	...	Viet Nam
Europe	**13 359**	**15 215**	**15 115**	**16 026**	**15 266**	**16 537**	**16 733**	**16 037**	**16 865**	**16 648**	**Europe**
EEC	***7 346***	***8 089***	***7 979***	***8 191***	***8 367***	***8 587***	***8 358***	***7 655***	***7 976***	***7 789***	***CEE***
Belgium	215	227	231	244	248	261	253	227	220	220	Belgique
Denmark[5]	397	435	501	432	460	474	454	472	405	533	Danemark[5]
France	719	727	664	646	610	672	655	593	594	497	France
Germany, Fed. Rep.	2 401	3 250	2 705	...	...	...	...	...	...	...	Allemagne, Rép. féd.
Greece	355	270	325	285	182	323	299	298	218	...	Grèce
Ireland	...	...	...	...	...	189	205	220	213	213	Irlande
Italy	1 613	1 229	1 510	1 564	1 816	1 946	1 249	1 258	1 287	1 190	Italie
Netherlands	872	876	879	912	835	845	1 040	740	940	897	Pays–Bas
United Kingdom	605	900	984	1 137	1 239	1 092	1 418	1 062	1 314	1 210	Royaume–Uni
EFTA	***1 228***	***1 409***	***1 273***	***1 407***	***1 483***	***1 486***	***1 623***	***1 372***	***1 386***	***1 288***	***AELE***
Austria	375	446	328	375	418	447	558	350	418	423	Autriche
Finland	166	199	212	213	278	243	292	286	228	* 150	Finlande

For general note and footnotes, see end of table.

Voir la fin du tableau pour la remarque générale et les notes.

Unit : Thousand metric tons

Unité : Milliers de tonnes métriques

Country or area	1976	1977	1978	1979	1980	1981	1982	1983	1984	1985	Pays ou zone
Portugal	276	314	299	354	338	304	288	351	286	279	Portugal
Sweden	334	371	335	357	353	371	372	265	345	294	Suède
Switzerland	77	79	99	108	96	121	113	120	109	142	Suisse
East Europe	***4 203***	***4 726***	***4 694***	***4 691***	***3 887***	***4 780***	***5 036***	***5 133***	***5 232***	***5 108***	***Europe de l'est***
Bulgaria	362	360	391	385	341	405	399	438	448	457	Bulgarie
Czechoslovakia	629	863	907	919	779	778	894	836	936	969	Tchécoslovaquie
German Dem. Rep.	667	697	754	792	733	818	896	846	869	911	Rép. dém. allemande
Hungary	353	425	482	484	458	485	458	475	406	481	Hongrie
Poland	1 631	1 668	1 605	1 586	1 067	1 685	1 793	1 982	1 767	1 708	Pologne
Romania	561	713	555	525	509	609	596	556	806	582	Roumanie
Other Europe	***582***	***991***	***1 169***	***1 737***	***1 529***	***1 684***	***1 716***	***1 877***	***2 270***	***2 463***	***Autre Europe***
Spain	6	...	...	954	771	893	1 033	1 155	...	...	Espagne
Yugoslavia	576	666	693	783	758	791	683	722	891	933	Yougoslavie
USSR	**9 249**	**12 036**	**12 207**	**10 647**	**10 127**	**9 491**	**12 070**	**12 394**	**12 464**	**11 799**	**URSS**
Byelorussian SSR	*244*	*298*	*319*	*314*	*298*	*278*	*306*	*302*	*317*	*335*	*RSS de Biélorussie*
Ukrainian SSR	*5 032*	*6 778*	*6 903*	*5 935*	*5 302*	*5 181*	*6 608*	*6 942*	*6 873*	*6 247*	*RSS d'Ukraine*
Oceania	**877**	**951**	**691**	**690**	**690**	**682**	**822**	**695**	**712**	**706**	**Océanie**
Australia[2]	723	791	...	...	...	...	701	...	...	...	Australie[2]
New Zealand	154	160	134	133	133	125	121	138	155	149	Nouvelle–Zélande
Total	**54 609**	**60 835**	**61 724**	**60 663**	**58 206**	**62 036**	**67 171**	**66 886**	**66 284**	**64 604**	**Total**

General note.
Beet sugar and cane sugar, refined, in solid form or powder, including white sugar derived directly from the processing of sugar beet. Aqueous solutions of sugar with added flavouring or colouring matter are excluded. (SITC 06120–0).

1 Production by establishments employing 5 or more persons.
2 Twelve months ending 30 June of year stated.
3 Government production only.
4 Production by establishments employing 10 or more persons.
5 Solid beet and cane sugar.

Remarque générale.
Sucre de betterave et sucre de canne, raffiné, à l'état solide (même en poudre), y compris le sucre blanc obtenu directement par traitement des betteraves sucrières. Cette rubrique ne comprend pas les solutions aqueuses de sucre aromatisées ou additionnées de colorants. (CTCI 06120–0).

1 Production des établissements occupant 5 personnes ou plus.
2 Période de douze mois finissant le 30 juin de l'année indiquée.
3 Production de l'Etat seulement.
4 Production des établissements occupant 10 personnes ou plus.
5 Sucres de betterave et de canne, à l'état solide.

Fruit, glace or crystallized – Fruits glacés ou candis

Unit : Metric tons

Unité : Tonnes métriques

Country or area	1976	1977	1978	1979	1980	1981	1982	1983	1984	1985	Pays ou zone
America, North	**13**	**13**	**13**	**13**	**13**	**41**	**2**	**1**	**8**	**13**	**Amérique du Nord**
Cuba	...	...	...	...	...	41	2	1	8	...	Cuba
America, South	**3 059**	**1 921**	**2 439**	**3 151**	**2 796**	**2 883**	**2 953**	**3 023**	**3 093**	**3 163**	**Amérique du Sud**
Brazil	3 059	1 921	2 439	[1]3 151	2 796	...	...	...	...	...	Brésil
Europe	**4 069**	**3 991**	**3 645**	**4 152**	**3 662**	**3 343**	**3 274**	**3 434**	**3 126**	**3 147**	**Europe**
EEC	***1 959***	***1 874***	***1 870***	***1 665***	***1 619***	***1 383***	***1 104***	***1 147***	***963***	***994***	***CEE***
Denmark	484	449	495	415	399	358	489	487	468	329	Danemark
France[2]	1 475	1 425	1 375	1 250	1 220	1 025	615	660	495	665	France[2]
EFTA	***2 057***	***2 055***	***1 775***	***2 487***	***2 043***	***1 960***	***2 170***	***2 287***	***2 163***	***2 153***	***AELE***
Austria	374	380	491	538	394	259	393	364	320	266	Autriche
Finland	36	32	46	38	36	37	38	166	158	...	Finlande
Norway	...	...	...	...	...	...	...	...	...	338	Norvège
Portugal	774	966	587	1 280	1 011	1 054	1 147	1 106	1 052	...	Portugal
Sweden	535	339	313	293	264	272	254	313	295	213	Suède
East Europe	***53***	***62***	***0***	***0***	***0***	***0***	***0***	***0***	***0***	***0***	***Europe de l'est***
Hungary	53	62	0	0	0	0	0	0	0	0	Hongrie
Oceania	**1 479**	**2 060**	**2 351**	**1 580**	**1 718**	**4 750**	**1 493**	**1 627**	**4 906**	**2 206**	**Océanie**
Australia	1 479	2 060	2 351	1 580	1 718	4 750	1 493	1 627	4 906	2 206	Australie
Total	**8 620**	**7 985**	**8 448**	**8 896**	**8 189**	**11 017**	**7 722**	**8 085**	**11 133**	**8 529**	**Total**

General note.
Fruit, fruit–peel and parts of plants, preserved by sugar either drained, glace or crystallized. (SITC 05320–0).

[1] Production by establishments employing 5 or more persons.
[2] Chestnuts glacé only.

Remarque générale.
Fruits, peaux de fruits et parties de plantes conservés au sucre, égouttés, glacés ou cristallisées.(CTCI 05320–0).

[1] Production des établissements occupant 5 personnes ou plus.
[2] Marrons glacés uniquement.

Sugar confectionery – Sucreries

Unit : Thousand metric tons

Unité : Milliers de tonnes métriques

Country or area	1976	1977	1978	1979	1980	1981	1982	1983	1984	1985	Pays ou zone
Africa	**219.9**	**233.3**	**239.8**	**233.2**	**261.3**	**273.7**	**275.8**	**248.1**	**254.1**	**245.8**	**Afrique**
Algeria	16.6	16.2	13.0	12.9	11.3	12.3	* 0.3	...	...	...	Algérie
Cameroon	...	...	...	5.6	5.2	5.0	4.5	4.0	4.7	4.4	Cameroun
Côte d'Ivoire	* 3.0	* 3.7	6.0	4.8	5.6	8.4	9.0	6.9	8.8	...	Côte d'Ivoire
Egypt	63.0	65.0	64.0	62.0	65.0	77.0	89.0	...	...	...	Egypte
Ethiopia[1 2]	2.1	1.7	2.4	4.1	3.4	3.3	3.5	3.7	4.2	4.0	Ethiopie[1 2]
Mali	1.1	1.4	1.3	1.7	1.5	1.1	2.3	2.3	...	...	Mali
Nigeria	22.8	31.4	...	...	65.9	56.5	47.9	33.8	28.8	26.0	Nigéria
Sierra Leone	1.5	1.7	1.7	1.7	2.1	2.2	1.4	1.0	1.3	...	Sierra Leone
South Africa	98.0	100.2	101.0	95.6	95.2	* [3] 101.7	[3] 111.5	[3] 102.8	* [3] 108.9	[3] 99.6	Afrique du Sud
Tunisia	5.1	5.3	5.2	5.1	5.9	5.9	...	...	...	...	Tunisie
Uganda	0.3	...	...	...	...	...	...	...	...	...	Ouganda
Zaire[1]	0.4	0.6	0.2	...	0.0	0.1	0.1	0.2	...	...	Zaïre[1]
America, North	**829.5**	**897.1**	**854.4**	**880.6**	**888.1**	**903.8**	**892.3**	**896.7**	**979.3**	**1 059.8**	**Amérique du Nord**
Canada[4]	59.4	58.1	62.0	68.6	72.1	...	...	...	...	...	Canada[4]
Cuba	21.9	22.3	25.1	21.6	25.1	25.5	23.8	24.7	24.9	24.8	Cuba
Dominican Republic	5.7	6.0	6.1	6.6	8.6	7.2	5.5	6.3	4.8	4.2	Rép. dominicaine
Panama	1.8	2.0	1.7	2.1	2.1	2.2	2.3	2.3	...	...	Panama
United States	...	808.7	759.5	781.7	780.2	794.2	782.4	781.6	861.8	939.4	Etats–Unis
America, South	**18.0**	**23.2**	**20.9**	**20.6**	**20.8**	**20.8**	**20.6**	**20.8**	**20.9**	**20.9**	**Amérique du Sud**
Bolivia	0.0	0.3	0.0	0.0	0.0	0.1	0.0	0.0	0.1	0.1	Bolivie
Chile	11.6	16.8	...	...	...	...	...	...	...	...	Chili
Ecuador	...	4.9	5.5	...	...	...	...	...	...	...	Equateur
Guyana	0.6	0.7	0.6	0.6	0.7	0.7	0.5	...	...	...	Guyana
Paraguay	0.6	0.6	0.6	0.6	0.7	0.7	0.7	0.7	0.8	0.8	Paraguay
Asia	**508.4**	**503.2**	**516.7**	**539.7**	**549.4**	**549.3**	**549.4**	**574.8**	**581.1**	**588.0**	**Asie**
Burma[5]	1.6	1.6	2.3	2.5	2.5	2.8	3.0	3.1	3.3	3.4	Birmanie[5]
Hong Kong[6]	4.6	4.0	3.1	4.1	3.2	6.3	9.3	8.0	...	...	Hong–kong[6]
India[7]	13.1	15.1	18.7	21.1	15.7	17.2	19.6	20.9	19.0	...	Inde[7]
Indonesia	9.7	* 7.2	8.1	10.4	19.2	18.9	11.7	15.5	14.3	...	Indonésie
Japan	415.0	409.9	...	...	...	...	...	...	...	...	Japon
Korea, Republic of[1]	27.4	28.4	34.5	47.2	53.9	49.5	53.0	74.9	81.1	81.2	Corée, République de[1]
Malaysia	8.3	9.6	9.9	10.7	13.2	12.5	10.3	9.6	...	...	Malaisie
Singapore[8]	4.5	4.2	4.6	5.3	...	...	...	...	...	...	Singapour[8]
Sri Lanka	0.5	0.6	1.3	2.0	1.5	2.0	...	...	...	...	Sri Lanka
Turkey[9]	23.7	22.5	21.8	24.0	...	...	...	...	...	...	Turquie[9]
Europe	**2 034.6**	**2 516.2**	**2 603.8**	**2 597.1**	**2 529.6**	**2 521.5**	**2 616.3**	**2 303.2**	**2 655.6**	**2 717.5**	**Europe**
EEC	***1 211.3***	***1 619.7***	***1 670.8***	***1 632.6***	***1 587.4***	***1 588.4***	***1 627.1***	***1 294.4***	***1 685.6***	***1 714.0***	***CEE***
Belgium[10]	39.2	33.4	35.3	34.9	37.4	39.6	45.6	46.9	50.1	54.1	Belgique[10]
Denmark	26.7	28.1	29.4	30.4	30.5	32.4	33.9	35.5	38.4	34.8	Danemark
France	178.9	187.8	191.2	182.2	177.6	175.4	177.3	175.0	178.0	172.0	France
Germany, Fed. Rep.	320.8	339.2	357.1	350.3	362.8	373.5	375.7	36.1	381.6	392.9	Allemagne, Rép. féd.
Ireland	23.0	24.8	24.5	26.5	24.3	21.0	20.5	25.8	21.8	24.5	Irlande
Italy[11]	...	...	...	...	123.5	116.5	110.1	113.9	109.7	109.0	Italie[11]
Netherlands	97.5	96.8	* 97.8	* 97.6	98.4	104.4	101.7	99.5	104.0	* 110.0	Pays–Bas
United Kingdom[12]	394.9	781.8	810.3	788.0	732.9	725.6	762.3	761.7	802.1	816.7	Royaume–Uni[12]
EFTA	***116.1***	***116.2***	***116.9***	***118.9***	***122.9***	***121.7***	***118.5***	***126.1***	***125.7***	***127.3***	***AELE***
Austria[1]	15.6	15.2	14.7	14.1	13.8	14.0	13.4	14.5	13.5	16.0	Autriche[1]
Finland	20.0	18.5	19.4	21.6	22.7	22.0	22.6	21.9	22.1	18.4	Finlande
Iceland	0.9	0.9	1.0	1.0	0.8	0.9	0.7	0.7	0.6	...	Islande
Norway	8.7	8.1	7.8	8.1	8.4	9.0	7.0	7.4	7.0	7.2	Norvège
Portugal	16.7	17.9	18.7	18.9	20.1	19.1	19.2	21.2	19.9	...	Portugal
Sweden	37.1	37.9	37.4	37.6	38.3	37.4	* 36.8	41.2	43.4	42.5	Suède
Switzerland[13]	17.1	17.7	17.9	17.5	18.9	19.3	18.8	19.2	19.2	21.5	Suisse[13]
East Europe	***592.7***	***624.1***	***656.5***	***673.4***	***643.4***	***649.1***	***689.9***	***712.6***	***748.5***	***785.5***	***Europe de l'est***
Bulgaria[1 14]	120.4	117.0	113.6	111.5	110.2	112.9	114.1	111.5	113.3	114.1	Bulgarie[1 14]
Czechoslovakia	41.7	42.8	49.9	51.3	50.4	50.4	52.5	53.9	52.7	54.1	Tchécoslovaquie
German Dem. Rep.	83.9	79.9	82.4	84.1	88.5	92.5	90.4	92.8	92.5	93.0	Rép. dém. allemande
Hungary	26.3	28.8	23.2	25.6	30.1	30.2	26.0	25.9	25.4	26.2	Hongrie
Poland[15]	144.4	156.7	165.4	155.8	119.2	98.1	128.9	145.6	161.5	169.1	Pologne[15]

For general note and footnotes, see end of table.

Voir la fin du tableau pour la remarque générale et les notes.

Unit : Thousand metric tons

Unité : Milliers de tonnes métriques

Country or area	1976	1977	1978	1979	1980	1981	1982	1983	1984	1985	Pays ou zone
Romania[1]	176.0	199.0	222.0	245.0	245.0	265.0	278.0	283.0	303.0	329.0	Roumanie[1]
Other Europe	***114.5***	***156.2***	***159.6***	***172.2***	***175.9***	***162.4***	***180.8***	***170.1***	***95.7***	***90.7***	***Autre Europe***
Spain	72.4	...	...	111.0	110.6	107.5	120.4	114.9	35.0	33.2	Espagne
Yugoslavia	42.0	47.9	55.9	61.2	65.3	54.9	60.4	55.2	60.7	57.5	Yougoslavie
USSR[16]	**1 443.6**	**1 692.1**	**1 780.6**	**1 756.6**	**1 786.6**	**1 805.8**	**1 840.0**	**1 768.4**	**1 722.0**	**1 736.4**	**URSS[16]**
Byelorussian SSR	*61.3*	*72.0*	*75.0*	*74.3*	*73.1*	*73.6*	*75.8*	*69.7*	*68.7*	*67.2*	*RSS de Biélorussie*
Ukrainian SSR[1]	*336.5*	*405.0*	*425.1*	*424.2*	*426.4*	*430.5*	*434.6*	*410.5*	*405.9*	*411.3*	*RSS d'Ukraine[1]*
Oceania	**74.0**	**70.8**	**70.4**	**67.1**	**65.1**	**66.6**	**70.0**	**68.6**	**75.6**	**73.7**	**Océanie**
Australia[17]	63.3	59.0	59.3	56.0	53.6	56.3	60.1	57.5	63.3	61.6	Australie[17]
New Zealand	10.8	11.9	11.1	11.1	11.5	10.3	9.9	11.1	12.3	12.1	Nouvelle-Zélande
Total	**5 128.0**	**5 935.8**	**6 086.5**	**6 095.0**	**6 100.9**	**6 141.7**	**6 264.4**	**5 880.6**	**6 288.7**	**6 442.3**	**Total**

General note.
Sugar preparations marketed in a solid or semi-solid form and collectively referred to as sweetmeats or confectionery. Sugar preparations containing cocoa are excluded. (SITC 06201-0).

1 Including chocolate and chocolate products.
2 Twelve months ending 10 September of year stated.
3 Including drinking chocolate, cocoa powder, cocoa butter and grindings from cocoa beans.
4 Shipments.
5 Twelve months ending 31 March of year stated.
6 Beginning 1984, data are confidential.
7 Production by large and medium scale establishments only.
8 Including chocolate.
9 Including jams, marmalades and fruit jellies.
10 Production by establishments employing 5 or more persons.
11 Source: Industrial Statistics, Statistical Office of the European Communities, (Luxembourg).
12 Including chocolate confectionery.
13 Sales.
14 Including biscuits, waffles, halva and Turkish delight.
15 Excluding chocolate confectionery.
16 Including soybean chocolate only.
17 Twelve months ending 30 June of year stated.

Remarque générale.
Préparations au sucre, solides ou semi-solides, et généralement désignées sous le nom de sucreries ou de confiseries. Cette rubrique ne comprend pas les préparations sucrées contenant du cacao. (CTCI 06201-0).

1 Y compris le chocolat et les produits à base de chocolat.
2 Période de douze mois finissant le 10 septembre de l'année indiquée.
3 Y compris le chocolat à boire, le cacao en poudre, le beurre de cacao et les brisures de fèves de cacao.
4 Expéditions.
5 Période de douze mois finissant le 31 mars de l'année indiquée.
6 A partir de 1984, les données sont confidentielles.
7 Production des grandes et moyennes entreprises seulement.
8 Y compris le chocolat.
9 Y compris les confitures, marmelades et gelées de fruits.
10 Production des établissements occupant 5 personnes ou plus.
11 Source: Statistiques industrielles, Office statistique des Communautés européennes, (Luxembourg).
12 Y compris les confiseries au chocolat.
13 Ventes.
14 Y compris les biscuits, les gaufres, le halva et le rahat loukoum.
15 Non compris les confiseries au chocolat.
16 Y compris le chocolat de soja seulement.
17 Période de douze mois finissant le 30 juin de l'année indiquée.

Cocoa powder – Cacao en poudre

Unit : Metric tons

Unité : Tonnes métriques

Country or area	1976	1977	1978	1979	1980	1981	1982	1983	1984	1985	Pays ou zone
Africa	**37 245**	**32 717**	**48 662**	**40 778**	**46 053**	**39 749**	**35 760**	**45 832**	**39 165**	**50 110**	**Afrique**
Cameroon[1]	10 477	11 173	15 259	13 094	12 674	12 583	6 046	5 340	4 914	7 872	Cameroun[1]
Côte d'Ivoire[1]	20 056	12 715	25 415	21 372	21 000	16 800	16 800	22 400	20 400	* 26 609	Côte d'Ivoire[1]
Egypt	...	...	...	2 865	3 256	3 757	4 374	5 010	...	...	Egypte
Ghana	914	307	318	97	560	735	646	656	435	475	Ghana
Nigeria* [1]	...	6 603	5 214	3 160	8 325	5 660	7 680	12 212	7 740	8 941	Nigéria* [1]
Tunisia	...	...	...	190	238	...	...	...	...	...	Tunisie
America, North	**163 472**	**168 334**	**175 101**	**184 157**	**193 897**	**194 685**	**202 518**	**210 195**	**212 861**	**222 285**	**Amérique du Nord**
Canada[2 3]	4 035	4 622	4 680	4 435	...	...	...	...	...	...	Canada[2 3]
Costa Rica[1]	469	425	321	394	901	468	361	569	400	* 691	Costa Rica[1]
Dominican Republic	295	446	497	822	1 248	1 769	2 050	2 045	2 997	3 296	Rép. dominicaine
Guatemala	...	...	...	...	5	5	10	15	21	20	Guatemala
United States	...	162 840	169 600	178 500	187 300	188 000	195 654	203 123	205 000	...	Etats-Unis
America, South	**5 545**	**8 046**	**12 081**	**22 379**	**22 843**	**16 716**	**28 304**	**28 870**	**46 151**	**42 068**	**Amérique du Sud**
Brazil	4 790	4 516	7 013	13 905	16 506	4 698	[1] 23 368	[1] 27 108	[1] 41 367	[1] 36 526	Brésil
Colombia	76	...	122	...	...	4 318	2 655	715	...	...	Colombie
Ecuador	564	2 898	4 763	6 917	4 464	7 470	1 911	377	[1] 1 447	[1] 2 015	Equateur
Peru	...	0	0	0	181	199	* 370	* 670	* 440	* 300	Pérou
Venezuela[1]	77	46	183	310	115	31	0	0	0	0	Venezuela[1]
Asia	**10 231**	**11 512**	**7 491**	**8 314**	**7 178**	**6 986**	**7 486**	**8 910**	**7 594**	**6 841**	**Asie**
India[4]	105	29	33	40	...	...	...	...	...	...	Inde[4]
Indonesia	1 572	* 2 350	2 539	2 442	1 791	1 011	775	...	1 153	...	Indonésie
Japan[5]	7 584	6 784	3 441	4 471	4 261	4 754	5 530	5 243	4 579	4 872	Japon[5]
Philippines[2]	667	2 170	1 268	1 081	894	888	823	1 539	...	...	Philippines[2]
Sri Lanka	...	40	42	43	39	10	36	50	40	0	Sri Lanka
Turkey	257	139	168	237	142	272	271	903	710	* 100	Turquie
Europe	**163 470**	**168 469**	**164 943**	**166 368**	**180 668**	**183 504**	**182 100**	**189 919**	**195 118**	**200 012**	**Europe**
EEC	***132 169***	***140 313***	***136 965***	***136 550***	***151 865***	***148 473***	***152 490***	***159 972***	***167 324***	***171 817***	***CEE***
Denmark	300	300	269	403	637	596	589	506	378	322	Danemark
France[6]	15 200	18 200	17 000	15 700	13 200	14 700	13 600	13 500	11 700	13 430	France[6]
Germany, Fed. Rep.	44 027	46 084	44 037	44 138	47 452	47 344	48 183	52 507	55 585	52 789	Allemagne, Rép. féd.
Greece	1 295	1 267	1 496	1 404	1 265	1 242	1 183	1 281	1 314	...	Grèce
Italy	* [7] 5 000	...	...	...	[7] 11 451	[1] 2 119	[1] 1 640	[1] 2 453	[1] 2 327	[1] 2 587	Italie
Netherlands	45 478	47 200	49 400	53 660	61 685	62 772	67 700	71 300	75 800	...	Pays-Bas
United Kingdom[8]	20 869	20 912	18 940	15 950	16 175	19 700	19 595	18 425	20 220	22 055	Royaume-Uni[8]
EFTA	***6 581***	***6 012***	***5 582***	***5 896***	***5 789***	***6 846***	***7 004***	***7 619***	***6 861***	***6 856***	***AELE***
Austria	4 420	4 073	3 841	4 418	4 238	5 333	5 347	5 755	5 181	5 325	Autriche
Finland	...	2	0	5	21	15	0	15	25	...	Finlande
Portugal	1 199	988	994	867	817	822	965	1 190	1 039	754	Portugal
Sweden	960	949	747	606	713	676	692	659	616	760	Suède
East Europe	***17 229***	***14 659***	***15 523***	***16 076***	***14 158***	***18 591***	***12 247***	***12 933***	***12 707***	***11 224***	***Europe de l'est***
Czechoslovakia	6 579	6 292	6 037	6 472	5 296	6 662	4 751	5 352	4 668	4 527	Tchécoslovaquie
Hungary	3 553	3 721	4 189	4 206	4 252	4 634	4 271	4 516	4 846	4 122	Hongrie
Poland	7 097	4 646	5 297	5 398	4 610	7 295	3 225	3 065	3 193	2 575	Pologne
Other Europe	***7 491***	***7 485***	***6 873***	***7 846***	***8 856***	***9 594***	***10 359***	***9 395***	***8 226***	***10 115***	***Autre Europe***
Spain	5 505	...	...	...	...	...	...	...	...	...	Espagne
Yugoslavia	1 986	1 980	1 368	2 341	3 351	4 089	4 854	3 890	2 721	4 610	Yougoslavie
Oceania	**6 173**	**6 744**	**6 085**	**4 710**	**4 399**	**3 653**	**3 987**	**3 046**	**2 531**	**2 016**	**Océanie**
Australia[9]	6 173	6 744	6 085	4 710	4 399	3 653	3 987	...	...	...	Australie[9]
Total	**386 136**	**395 822**	**414 363**	**426 706**	**455 038**	**445 293**	**460 155**	**486 772**	**503 420**	**523 332**	**Total**

General note.
Unsweetened powder obtained by pulverising the partly defatted cocoa paste. Sweetened cocoa powder and cocoa powder to which milk powder or peptones have been added are excluded. (SITC 07220-0).

Remarque générale.
Poudre non sucrée provenant de la pulvérisation de la pâte de cacao partiellement dégraissée. Cette rubrique ne comprend pas le cacao en poudre sucré et le cacao additionné de poudre de lait ou de peptones. (CTCI 07220-0).

For footnotes, see end of table.

Voir la fin du tableau pour les notes.

[1] Exports.
[2] Shipments.
[3] Beginning 1980, data are confidential.
[4] Production by large and medium scale establishments only.
[5] Including sweetened cocoa powder.
[6] Cocoa powder for sale.
[7] Source: Industrial Statistics, Statistical Office of the European Communities, (Luxembourg).
[8] Including sweetened cocoa and drinking chocolate.
[9] Twelve months ending 30 June of year stated.

[1] Exportations.
[2] Expéditions.
[3] A partir de 1980, les données sont confidentielles.
[4] Production des grandes et moyennes entreprises seulement.
[5] Y compris le cacao en poudre sucré.
[6] Cacao en poudre pour vente en l'état.
[7] Source: Statistiques industrielles, Office statistique des Communautés européennes, (Luxembourg).
[8] Y compris le cacao sucré et les chocolats à boire.
[9] Période de douze mois finissant le 30 juin de l'année indiquée.

Cocoa butter – Beurre de cacao

Unit : Metric tons

Unité : Tonnes métriques

Country or area	1976	1977	1978	1979	1980	1981	1982	1983	1984	1985	Pays ou zone
Africa	**44 808**	**42 312**	**42 513**	**37 096**	**36 200**	**33 828**	**34 127**	**39 925**	**33 838**	**42 339**	**Afrique**
Cameroon[1]	6 619	6 910	7 696	5 700	4 730	2 200	2 986	5 510	3 312	3 482	Cameroun[1]
Côte d'Ivoire[1]	12 113	11 211	14 323	12 632	12 400	13 600	15 480	16 340	18 580	21 689	Côte d'Ivoire[1]
Ghana	19 568	17 027	13 994	10 560	10 985	9 928	8 764	8 818	3 866	7 674	Ghana
Nigeria* [1]	6 508	7 164	6 500	8 204	8 085	8 100	6 897	9 257	8 080	9 494	Nigéria* [1]
America, North	**10 850**	**9 010**	**11 896**	**13 809**	**13 957**	**11 878**	**11 639**	**12 338**	**14 063**	**16 171**	**Amérique du Nord**
Costa Rica[1]	695	864	1 378	1 676	1 723	1 208	1 042	414	* 682	* 985	Costa Rica[1]
Cuba	...	...	...	...	* 350	450	392	489	546	531	Cuba
Dominican Republic	190	307	299	362	437	793	1 114	525	781	851	Rép. dominicaine
Haiti	731	207	694	...	...	...	...	...	...	...	Haïti
Jamaica[1]	55	10	25	* 97	59	* 40	30	76	* 315	* 202	Jamaïque[1]
Mexico[1]	3 819	1 967	3 607	* 4 900	* 4 544	* 2 393	* 1 746	* 3 239	* 4 070	* 5 550	Mexique[1]
United States	...	5 398	5 600	5 900	6 300	6 450	6 771	7 051	7 125	...	Etats–Unis
America, South	**34 130**	**29 084**	**31 281**	**36 831**	**37 719**	**33 289**	**32 211**	**30 510**	**39 655**	**45 362**	**Amérique du Sud**
Bolivia	1	72	101	69	213	135	102	157	61	...	Bolivie
Brazil	31 481	25 393	25 506	29 883	34 274	26 310	29 020	27 898	36 067	41 922	Brésil
Colombia	309	565	679	966	785	1 283	870	879	* 1 560	* 1 338	Colombie
Ecuador	2 339	3 054	4 995	5 913	2 447	5 561	2 219	1 576	1 967	1 954	Equateur
Asia	**5 692**	**5 592**	**4 374**	**6 223**	**7 453**	**11 860**	**12 440**	**8 165**	**7 889**	**6 617**	**Asie**
Indonesia	690	...	728	1 292	1 441	...	1 156	817	467	...	Indonésie
Japan	4 051	3 191	2 395	2 448	3 371	3 460	5 284	5 848	5 606	4 071	Japon
Philippines[1]	951	1 409	1 251	...	...	* 7 470	* 6 000	* 1 500	* 1 816	* 1 677	Philippines[1]
Europe	**122 670**	**118 063**	**124 315**	**125 951**	**126 318**	**126 591**	**126 212**	**144 626**	**151 658**	**142 413**	**Europe**
EEC	***113 923***	***109 531***	***115 359***	***117 262***	***118 369***	***118 730***	***118 461***	***136 906***	***143 541***	***134 533***	***CEE***
Denmark	0	5	0	0	0	0	...	...	9	4	Danemark
France	115	0	1 200	2 100	1 100	1 100	600	10 140	3 425	3 415	France
Germany, Fed. Rep.	31 171	33 450	38 564	41 364	43 493	46 494	44 585	45 945	50 335	49 096	Allemagne, Rép. féd.
Greece	1 094	842	1 085	1 163	978	961	1 005	1 076	862	...	Grèce
Italy	...	...	...	...	8 634	...	...	...	...	...	Italie
Netherlands	60 730	54 900	55 800	54 976	56 190	54 630	59 200	66 800	75 700	* 69 126	Pays–Bas
United Kingdom	...	[2] 11 700	...	...	...	[1] 6 911	[1] 4 434	[1] 4 308	[1] 4 576	[1] 3 300	Royaume–Uni
EFTA	***1 761***	***1 517***	***1 511***	***1 429***	***951***	***763***	***551***	***434***	***502***	***366***	***AELE***
Austria	306	235	310	294	467	482	270	167	133	90	Autriche
Portugal	663	592	692	507	244	281	281	267	369	276	Portugal
Sweden	792	690	509	628	240	0	0	0	0	0	Suède
East Europe	***72***	***101***	***531***	***346***	***84***	***184***	***286***	***372***	***701***	***600***	***Europe de l'est***
Hungary	72	101	531	346	84	184	286	372	701	600	Hongrie
Other Europe	***6 914***	***6 914***	***6 914***	***6 914***	***6 914***	***6 914***	***6 914***	***6 914***	***6 914***	***6 914***	***Autre Europe***
Spain	6 914	...	...	...	...	...	...	...	...	...	Espagne
Total	**218 150**	**204 061**	**214 379**	**219 910**	**221 647**	**217 446**	**216 629**	**235 564**	**247 103**	**252 902**	**Total**

General note.
Fat and oil contained in cocoa beans. (SITC 07232–0).

[1] Exports.
[2] Source: Industrial Statistics, Statistical Office of the European Communities, (Luxembourg).

Remarque générale.
Graisse et huile contenues dans les fèves de cacao. (CTCI 07232–0).

[1] Exportations.
[2] Source: Statistiques industrielles, Office statistique des Communautés européennes, (Luxembourg).

Chocolate and chocolate products
Chocolat et produits à base de chocolat

Unit : Thousand metric tons — Unité : Milliers de tonnes métriques

Country or area	1976	1977	1978	1979	1980	1981	1982	1983	1984	1985	Pays ou zone
Africa	**31.5**	**33.4**	**37.6**	**35.3**	**41.8**	**54.2**	**53.6**	**56.0**	**58.0**	**62.6**	**Afrique**
Algeria	3.1	3.6	3.6	3.7	4.1	3.2	0.3	...	...	...	Algérie
Cameroon	...	...	...	1.2	1.2	...	...	2.2	2.2	3.3	Cameroun
Côte d'Ivoire	0.0	1.3	5.6	1.4	3.7	9.0	9.5	8.4	8.6	...	Côte d'Ivoire
Egypt	2.2	3.9	4.2	4.0	4.7	4.5	4.4	5.0	...	...	Egypte
Kenya	0.3	0.2	0.2	0.3	0.3	0.4	0.3	0.3	0.3	0.4	Kenya
South Africa	25.0	23.1	22.1	22.3	* 25.4	33.3	34.1	34.9	36.3	36.9	Afrique du Sud
Tunisia	0.8	0.8	1.3	2.4	2.4	2.2	...	...	...	...	Tunisie
America, North	**857.3**	**890.0**	**893.5**	**959.5**	**981.2**	**986.0**	**1 032.3**	**1 089.9**	**1 123.2**	**1 123.3**	**Amérique du Nord**
Canada[1]	99.3	85.4	88.4	94.7	92.5	...	...	...	...	...	Canada[1]
Cuba	...	...	...	...	...	5.2	5.1	4.7	5.5	5.6	Cuba
Dominican Republic	3.6	2.9	3.1	4.4	5.8	5.8	6.9	6.9	4.2	4.6	Rép. dominicaine
El Salvador	0.2	0.4	0.0	0.0	0.1	0.2	0.1	0.2	...	...	El Salvador
United States	...	796.8	797.3	855.7	877.9	884.0	929.8	988.0	1 023.8	1 023.9	Etats–Unis
America, South	**96.1**	**130.4**	**153.8**	**193.5**	**193.5**	**129.1**	**195.0**	**199.8**	**212.7**	**223.2**	**Amérique du Sud**
Bolivia	0.6	0.5	0.6	0.4	0.2	0.1	0.1	0.4	1.0	...	Bolivie
Brazil	38.0	75.3	94.5	[2] 136.5	118.6	* 54.5	...	...	...	...	Brésil
Chile	3.1	3.1	3.3	5.1	7.6	10.1	8.5	9.4	9.6	10.0	Chili
Colombia	54.0	48.9	52.0	44.5	53.9	57.2	57.5	57.2	...	...	Colombie
Ecuador	...	...	3.3	...	13.2	7.2	17.1	13.9	...	...	Equateur
Asia	**141.3**	**127.0**	**115.7**	**117.7**	**135.6**	**161.2**	**165.6**	**180.0**	**165.1**	**174.5**	**Asie**
India[3]	2.0	2.0	1.8	1.1	...	...	...	...	...	...	Inde[3]
Indonesia	1.8	* 1.1	1.4	1.9	4.5	8.3	9.6	12.3	4.1	...	Indonésie
Japan	128.9	116.2	105.2	108.1	122.6	141.6	146.4	146.1	144.5	147.2	Japon
Sri Lanka	0.2	0.2	0.3	0.1	0.1	0.1	...	...	...	...	Sri Lanka
Syrian Arab Republic	1.7	1.9	2.0	2.7	3.2	3.5	3.6	5.7	4.1	4.1	Rép. arabe syrienne
Turkey	6.6	5.5	5.0	3.8	3.5	6.0	4.2	14.2	10.7	* 11.0	Turquie
Europe	**1 958.7**	**1 948.2**	**1 988.5**	**2 056.4**	**2 122.3**	**2 150.6**	**2 139.6**	**2 127.5**	**2 244.9**	**2 217.8**	**Europe**
EEC	***1 393.6***	***1 409.5***	***1 452.4***	***1 502.3***	***1 559.8***	***1 532.5***	***1 574.5***	***1 585.3***	***1 679.1***	***1 668.5***	***CEE***
Belgium[2]	103.5	99.9	93.7	105.3	122.0	127.0	132.4	137.2	145.7	154.3	Belgique[2]
Denmark	34.2	32.1	31.7	33.5	32.2	* 24.0	23.4	25.4	19.8	20.1	Danemark
France	209.0	218.5	236.3	250.2	264.1	282.6	289.3	314.3	321.3	324.4	France
Germany, Fed. Rep.	403.9	406.0	408.2	425.4	466.3	415.4	401.7	404.4	434.1	414.8	Allemagne, Rép. féd.
Greece	14.7	13.6	14.5	16.9	19.0	18.6	19.7	18.3	16.3	...	Grèce
Ireland	20.7	20.1	21.7	20.9	21.4	23.7	24.1	20.7	24.5	23.3	Irlande
Italy	68.0	65.0	...	...	77.4	81.0	88.2	91.1	98.2	69.9	Italie
Netherlands	149.5	156.9	* 149.4	149.8	150.3	153.6	161.2	167.3	149.6	170.0	Pays–Bas
United Kingdom[4]	390.1	397.2	424.0	425.0	407.0	406.6	434.6	406.6	* 469.6	472.2	Royaume–Uni[4]
EFTA	***187.1***	***192.3***	***190.3***	***200.1***	***214.4***	***233.0***	***247.6***	***256.6***	***268.4***	***250.0***	***AELE***
Austria	32.3	31.4	32.3	34.6	37.0	40.4	40.6	42.6	43.9	27.4	Autriche
Finland	14.9	14.7	14.5	16.8	18.6	22.5	21.9	22.1	24.4	21.2	Finlande
Iceland	0.5	0.5	0.6	0.6	0.8	0.9	1.0	1.1	1.2	...	Islande
Norway[5]	21.4	23.0	23.5	24.9	25.0	31.1	26.0	27.2	32.5	...	Norvège[5]
Portugal	10.6	9.0	9.7	9.3	7.2	8.1	7.1	8.9	7.3	6.9	Portugal
Sweden	46.4	47.6	47.7	51.0	54.4	52.2	74.3	77.5	77.1	79.0	Suède
Switzerland[6]	61.0	66.1	62.0	62.9	71.4	77.8	76.6	77.2	82.1	82.6	Suisse[6]
East Europe	***266.6***	***247.8***	***246.4***	***260.7***	***246.9***	***275.7***	***217.1***	***191.0***	***200.0***	***205.2***	***Europe de l'est***
Czechoslovakia	46.8	44.9	36.0	40.5	42.7	46.5	48.0	49.8	53.4	54.6	Tchécoslovaquie
German Dem. Rep.	52.1	53.2	54.4	57.8	58.5	61.6	58.7	65.0	70.9	73.7	Rép. dém. allemande
Hungary	30.8	32.6	30.8	28.4	31.1	36.3	32.9	30.7	30.8	32.2	Hongrie
Poland	137.0	117.1	125.2	134.0	114.6	131.3	77.5	45.6	44.9	44.6	Pologne
Other Europe	***111.4***	***98.7***	***99.4***	***93.2***	***101.1***	***109.4***	***100.3***	***94.6***	***97.3***	***94.1***	***Autre Europe***
Spain	64.1	...	...	43.8	50.5	57.8	55.3	52.8	51.8	51.4	Espagne
Yugoslavia	47.3	42.2	43.6	49.4	50.6	51.6	45.1	41.9	45.5	42.7	Yougoslavie
USSR[7 8]	**545.4**	**341.1**	**362.6**	**426.2**	**433.2**	**456.5**	**446.3**	**558.8**	**641.4**	**684.9**	**URSS[7 8]**
Byelorussian SSR[7]	*25.9*	*13.8*	*14.4*	*17.3*	*18.4*	*18.1*	*15.9*	*22.5*	*24.3*	*27.4*	*RSS de Biélorussie[7]*
Ukrainian SSR	*129.0*	*65.8*	*72.2*	*84.7*	*84.5*	*89.9*	*92.7*	*131.0*	*148.9*	*165.6*	*RSS d'Ukraine*

For general note and footnotes, see end of table.

Voir la fin du tableau pour la remarque générale et les notes.

Chocolate and chocolate products (continued) – Chocolat et produits à base de chocolat (suite)

Unit : Thousand metric tons

Unité : Milliers de tonnes métriques

Country or area	1976	1977	1978	1979	1980	1981	1982	1983	1984	1985	Pays ou zone
Oceania	**80.0**	**64.5**	**63.2**	**61.1**	**63.2**	**68.9**	**77.4**	**95.9**	**80.9**	**104.2**	**Océanie**
Australia[9]	70.1	55.7	54.4	51.6	53.2	58.0	65.3	83.2	68.5	91.9	Australie[9]
New Zealand	9.9	8.8	8.8	9.6	10.0	10.9	12.1	12.7	12.4	12.3	Nouvelle–Zélande
Total	**3 710.3**	**3 534.6**	**3 614.8**	**3 849.7**	**3 970.7**	**4 006.4**	**4 109.7**	**4 307.9**	**4 526.2**	**4 590.5**	**Total**

General note.
Chocolate and food preparations containing cocoa or chocolate, including all sugar confectionery containing cocoa in any proportion, sweetened cocoa powder, chocolate powder and chocolate spreads. The product known as "white chocolate" (composed of cocoa butter, sugar and powdered milk) is excluded. (SITC 07300–0).

1 Shipments.
2 Production by establishments employing 5 or more persons.
3 Production by large and medium scale establishments only.
4 Source: Industrial Statistics, Statistical Office of the European Communities, (Luxembourg).
5 Including pudding powder without cocoa.
6 Sales.
7 Excluding soft candies glazed with chocolate as well as soybean chocolate included in sugar confectionery.
8 Excluding soybean chocolate only.
9 Twelve months ending 30 June of year stated.

Remarque générale.
Chocolat et préparations alimentaires contenant du cacao ou du chocolat, y compris toutes les sucreries contenant du cacao, en proportion quelconque, les cacaos en poudre sucrés, les chocolats en poudre et les produits pâteux à base de chocolat. La préparation dite "chocolat blanc" (composé de beurre de cacao, de sucre et de lait en poudre) n'est pas comprise dans cette position. (CTCI 07300–0).

1 Expéditions.
2 Production des établissements occupant 5 personnes ou plus.
3 Production des grandes et moyennes entreprises seulement.
4 Source: Statistiques industrielles, Office statistique des Communautés européennes, (Luxembourg).
5 Y compris les flans en poudre sans cacao.
6 Ventes.
7 Non compris les bonbons mous glacés au chocolat ainsi que le chocolat de soya entrant dans la composition de confiseries au sucre.
8 Non compris le chocolat de soja seulement.
9 Période de douze mois finissant le 30 juin de l'année indiquée.

Coffee extracts, including instant coffee – Les extraits et essences de café, y compris le café soluble

Unit : Metric tones | Unité : Tonnes métriques

Country or area	1976	1977	1978	1979	1980	1981	1982	1983	1984	1985	Pays ou zone
Africa	**93 701**	**99 157**	**103 423**	**92 464**	**112 755**	**123 752**	**131 603**	**113 564**	**131 824**	**120 032**	**Afrique**
Côte d'Ivoire	2 424	1 875	4 079	6 027	4 742	7 630	7 570	8 475	8 200	...	Côte d'Ivoire
Kenya	77 505	84 541	85 366	70 052	80 249	88 695	94 663	74 181	90 621	80 116	Kenya
South Africa	13 732	12 681	13 958	16 365	* 27 764	27 427	29 353	30 895	32 993	29 951	Afrique du Sud
Zimbabwe[1 2]	* 40	* 60	* 20	* 20	0	0	...	...	...	...	Zimbabwe[1 2]
America, North	**80 978**	**69 299**	**81 700**	**81 458**	**79 483**	**78 586**	**84 426**	**85 783**	**87 879**	**87 690**	**Amérique du Nord**
Canada[3]	* 11 000	9 180	* 19 640	10 240	...	10 660	...	...	...	...	Canada[3]
Dominican Republic	5 762	5 763	6 044	6 018	6 158	6 568	8 076	7 565	7 521	...	Rép. dominicaine
El Salvador[2 4]	480	500	800	1 000	940	820	1 131	1 144	...	...	El Salvador[2 4]
Guatemala[4]	[2] 340	[2] 40	[2] 60	[2] 160	[2] 100	[2] 260	255	364	...	...	Guatemala[4]
Jamaica	...	...	...	...	2 216	1 379	1 516	1 632	1 745	1 274	Jamaïque
Mexico[2 4]	380	100	540	1 460	1 300	720	...	...	...	...	Mexique[2 4]
Nicaragua[1]	20	0	200	244	500	800	1 864	1 216	1 781	...	Nicaragua[1]
Trinidad and Tobago[2 4]	240	280	100	140	200	300	...	...	...	...	Trinité–et–Tobago[2 4]
United States	60 480	51 260	52 240	60 220	56 060	57 079	58 134	60 305	61 609	60 993	Etats–Unis
America, South	**49 307**	**38 741**	**51 081**	**67 103**	**93 164**	**93 229**	**106 121**	**115 611**	**128 160**	**139 099**	**Amérique du Sud**
Brazil	[1 2] 43 580	[1 2] 31 740	[1 2] 43 920	[5] 58 269	82 840	...	...	...	...	...	Brésil
Chile	1 779	1 459	1 801	3 226	1 759	1 513	2 094	2 216	2 519	2 200	Chili
Colombia	2 100	3 614	3 632	2 933	3 878	3 984	4 823	5 364	...	...	Colombie
Ecuador[1]	[2] 360	[2] 480	[2] 320	[2] 1 120	3 675	3 061	3 814	2 596	...	...	Equateur[1]
Paraguay[1 2]	...	...	...	...	339	356	374	393	413	442	Paraguay[1 2]
Peru	...	...	...	1 240	673	893	1 144	720	* 774	* 671	Pérou
Asia	**23 301**	**30 225**	**29 754**	**38 968**	**39 239**	**42 333**	**47 066**	**44 218**	**51 812**	**54 207**	**Asie**
India[2 4]	320	440	360	820	* 2 520	...	...	...	...	...	Inde[2 4]
Indonesia	491	1 639	1 700	540	553	870	849	1 505	1 891	...	Indonésie
Japan	* 13 200	19 707	19 169	26 917	25 089	26 472	29 345	30 069	32 224	33 005	Japon
Korea, Republic of	1 325	1 231	2 007	2 759	4 021	4 766	5 651	6 874	8 723	10 699	Corée, République de
Philippines	...	7 208	6 518	7 932	7 056	8 359	9 031	3 257	...	...	Philippines
Europe	**62 298**	**48 470**	**52 915**	**55 657**	**53 015**	**50 660**	**48 395**	**47 802**	**46 649**	**44 661**	**Europe**
EEC	***48 962***	***35 198***	***38 121***	***40 800***	***40 037***	***37 280***	***33 979***	***33 013***	***32 510***	***30 718***	***CEE***
Belgium*	500	480	460	...	...	...	...	...	...	...	Belgique*
Denmark	0	0	269	220	193	...	...	...	...	...	Danemark
Germany, Fed. Rep.	21 802	16 938	18 672	22 460	20 284	21 171	19 361	19 887	20 876	20 576	Allemagne, Rép. féd.
United Kingdom*[6]	26 660	17 780	18 720	17 640	19 080	...	...	...	...	...	Royaume–Uni*[6]
EFTA	***4 337***	***4 810***	***5 288***	***5 698***	***4 759***	***5 141***	***5 738***	***6 238***	***5 973***	***6 097***	***AELE***
Finland	215	188	182	94	0	0	0	0	0	...	Finlande
Portugal	...	...	2 326	2 744	2 039	2 741	2 915	3 331	2 982	3 016	Portugal
Switzerland*[2 7]	2 020	2 400	2 780	2 860	2 720	2 400	...	...	...	...	Suisse*[2 7]
East Europe	***7 577***	***7 045***	***7 429***	***6 468***	***6 674***	***6 327***	***6 705***	***6 732***	***6 540***	***5 974***	***Europe de l'est***
German Dem. Rep.	218	131	46	24	26	29	29	26	30	27	Rép. dém. allemande
Hungary	...	...	...	...	...	0	0	0	4	112	Hongrie
Poland	7 355	6 910	7 379	6 443	6 640	6 298	6 676	6 706	6 506	5 835	Pologne
Other Europe	***1 422***	***1 417***	***2 077***	***2 691***	***1 545***	***1 912***	***1 973***	***1 819***	***1 626***	***1 872***	***Autre Europe***
Yugoslavia	1 422	1 417	2 077	2 691	1 545	1 912	1 973	1 819	1 626	1 872	Yougoslavie
Oceania	**10 387**	**11 298**	**10 158**	**11 190**	**13 268**	**13 635**	**13 547**	**11 582**	**13 912**	**15 042**	**Océanie**
Australia[8]	10 387	11 298	10 158	11 190	13 268	13 635	13 547	11 582	13 912	15 042	Australie[8]
Total	**319 972**	**297 190**	**329 031**	**346 840**	**390 924**	**402 195**	**431 158**	**418 560**	**460 236**	**460 731**	**Total**

General note.
Data under this heading relate to coffee extracts, essences and concentrates. These may be made from real coffee (whether or not caffeine has been removed) or from a mixture of real coffee and coffee substitutes in any proportion. They may be in liquid or powder form, usually highly concentrated. The heading includes instant or pulverized coffee. (SITC 07130–0).

Remarque générale.
Les données se rapportent aux extraits et essences de café. Ils peuvent être préparés à partir de véritable café, décaféine ou non, ou à partir d'un mélange, en toutes proportions, de véritable café et de succédanés de café. Ces extraits ou essences se présentent à l'état liquide ou en poudre et sont généralement très concentrés. Cette rubrique comprend le café soluble. (CTCI 07130–0).

For footnotes, see end of table.

Voir la fin du tableau pour les notes.

[1] Exports of soluble coffee.
[2] Source: International Coffee Organization , (London).
[3] 1980, data are confidential.
[4] Exports of soluble coffee. Data refer to crop years ending September.
[5] Production by establishments employing 5 or more persons.
[6] Source: International Coffee Organization, (London). Estimated data, figures relate to roastings for soluble coffee.
[7] Estimated data. Figures relate to roastings for soluble coffee.
[8] Excluding coffee essence.

[1] Exportations de café soluble.
[2] Source: Organisation internationale du café , (Londres).
[3] Pour 1980, les données sont confidentielles.
[4] Exportations de café soluble. Données se rapportant à la production par compagne se terminant au 30 septembre de l'année indiguée.
[5] Production des établissements occupant 5 personnes ou plus.
[6] Source: Organisation internationale du café , (London). Données estimatives, les chiffres se rapportent à la torréfaction pour le café soluble.
[7] Données estimatives. Les chiffres se rapportent à la torréfaction pour le café soluble.
[8] Non compris les essences de cafe.

Vinegar – Vinaigres

Unit : Thousand hectolitres | Unité : Milliers de hectolitres

Country or area	1976	1977	1978	1979	1980	1981	1982	1983	1984	1985	Pays ou zone
Africa	**180**	**183**	**167**	**212**	**224**	**281**	**284**	**285**	**289**	**295**	**Afrique**
Algeria	80	74	58	89	106	153	* 155	* 155	* 155	* 150	Algérie
Egypt	90	100	100	110	110	120	120	* 120	* 125	136	Egypte
Mali	3	4	3	8	3	3	4	4	...	...	Mali
Mauritius	1	1	1	1	1	1	1	1	1	1	Maurice
Tunisia	6	4	5	4	4	4	* 4	* 5	...	...	Tunisie
America, North	**4 557**	**5 418**	**6 807**	**5 861**	**6 066**	**6 074**	**8 692**	**9 272**	**9 539**	**9 701**	**Amérique du Nord**
Canada[1]	...	850	775	647	672	...	...	...	...	...	Canada[1]
Cuba	106	110	117	107	112	125	122	115	125	115	Cuba
Dominican Republic	17	21	22	26	29	34	32	32	37	36	Rép. dominicaine
Panama	3	4	3	5	5	4	0	2	...	...	Panama
United States	...	4 433	5 890	5 076	5 248	5 175	7 802	8 387	8 639	8 812	Etats–Unis
America, South	**798**	**935**	**1 066**	**1 141**	**1 251**	**1 359**	**1 478**	**1 593**	**1 701**	**1 810**	**Amérique du Sud**
Brazil	769	905	1 035	[2] 1 106	1 206	...	...	...	...	...	Brésil
Colombia	25	25	26	30	40	29	27	34	...	...	Colombie
Ecuador	...	1	1	...	...	1	1	1	...	...	Equateur
Paraguay	3	4	4	4	4	4	18	19	20	21	Paraguay
Asia	**4 749**	**4 899**	**5 389**	**5 701**	**5 383**	**5 500**	**5 670**	**5 724**	**5 860**	**5 939**	**Asie**
Cyprus	2	2	2	3	2	2	2	3	3	3	Chypre
Japan	2 591	2 720	2 786	2 944	2 959	3 066	3 229	3 325	3 435	3 514	Japon
Philippines	...	...	...	...	...	56	63	* 20	...	...	Philippines
Turkey	2 110	2 131	2 555	2 708	...	...	...	...	...	...	Turquie
Europe	**5 684**	**5 816**	**5 959**	**6 250**	**6 345**	**6 581**	**6 978**	**6 339**	**6 360**	**6 643**	**Europe**
EEC	***3 746***	***3 789***	***3 792***	***3 920***	***3 835***	***3 961***	***4 155***	***3 689***	***3 606***	***3 716***	***CEE***
Belgium[3]	146	136	124	126	140	152	205	234	168	190	Belgique[3]
Denmark	184	202	182	179	197	199	219	189	195	199	Danemark
France	1 040	977	983	1 052	1 005	1 009	1 071	622	651	613	France
Germany, Fed. Rep.	1 076	1 070	1 144	1 194	1 095	1 199	1 258	1 240	1 182	1 289	Allemagne, Rép. féd.
Greece[4]	* 36	* 39	* 44	* 54	* 83	* 87	* 87	89	95	...	Grèce[4]
Ireland	1 264	1 365	...	...	...	...	...	...	...	...	Irlande
EFTA	***128***	***118***	***127***	***140***	***150***	***151***	***147***	***155***	***158***	***159***	***AELE***
Austria	42	40	41	48	51	52	56	59	59	56	Autriche
Finland[4 5]	* 22	22	26	32	35	32	27	29	34	...	Finlande[4 5]
Norway[4]	* 21	* 20	21	...	...	...	...	...	...	...	Norvège[4]
Sweden	43	36	39	39	43	46	43	46	44	48	Suède
East Europe	***1 575***	***1 601***	***1 568***	***1 682***	***1 721***	***1 718***	***1 767***	***1 612***	***1 562***	***1 689***	***Europe de l'est***
Bulgaria	413	417	371	470	458	469	478	436	457	492	Bulgarie
Czechoslovakia	397	407	404	449	482	462	489	497	415	415	Tchécoslovaquie
Hungary	279	299	289	301	313	314	323	273	302	367	Hongrie
Poland	486	478	504	462	468	473	477	406	388	415	Pologne
Other Europe	***235***	***308***	***472***	***509***	***640***	***752***	***910***	***884***	***1 035***	***1 079***	***Autre Europe***
Spain[6]	...	...	...	224	341	446	532	482	...	...	Espagne[6]
Yugoslavia* [4]	181	184	278	285	299	306	378	402	419	393	Yougoslavie* [4]
Oceania	**160**	**160**	**160**	**175**	**171**	**175**	**187**	**150**	**249**	**174**	**Océanie**
Australia[7]	160	160	160	175	171	175	187	150	249	174	Australie[7]
Total	**16 128**	**17 411**	**19 548**	**19 340**	**19 440**	**19 970**	**23 289**	**23 363**	**23 998**	**24 562**	**Total**

General note.
Wine vinegar, beer and malt vinegar, fermented fruit vinegar, spirit vinegar and substitutes for vinegar (obtained by diluting acetic acid with water), in terms of 10 per cent of vinegar. Toilet vinegar is excluded. (SITC 09907–0).

Remarque générale.
Vinaigres de vin, de bière ou de malt, vinaigres de fruits fermentés, vinaigres d'alcools et succédanés du vinaigre (obtenus par dilution d'acide acétique dans l'eau) exprimés en vinaigre à 10 p. 100. Cette rubrique ne comprend pas le vinaigre de toilette. (CTCI 09907–0).

[1] Shipments.

[1] Expéditions.

Vinegar (continued) – Vinaigres (suite)

[2] Production by establishments employing 5 or more persons.
[3] Including data for Luxembourg.
[4] Original data in metric tons.
[5] Including grape must.
[6] Wine vinegar only.
[7] Bulk and bottled vinegar, including imitation vinegar.

[2] Production des établissements occupant 5 personnes ou plus.
[3] Y compris les données relatives au Luxembourg.
[4] Données d'origine exprimées en tonnes.
[5] Y compris les moûts de raisin.
[6] Vinegar de vin seulement.
[7] Vinaigres en vrac et en bouteilles y compris les succédanés de vinaigre.

Prepared animal feeds – Aliments préparés pour animaux

Unit : Thousand metric tons | Unité : Milliers de tonnes métriques

Country or area	1976	1977	1978	1979	1980	1981	1982	1983	1984	1985	Pays ou zone
Africa	**2 758**	**3 065**	**3 006**	**3 188**	**2 733**	**2 837**	**3 243**	**3 426**	**3 146**	**3 253**	**Afrique**
Algeria	3	7	50	39	53	47	47	...	...	...	Algérie
Côte d'Ivoire	13	17	20	28	35	24	23	45	41	...	Côte d'Ivoire
Gabon*	3	3	3	4	4	...	...	...	...	...	Gabon*
Kenya	97	139	124	119	113	135	118	154	139	138	Kenya
Malawi	12	...	...	...	...	...	...	...	...	...	Malawi
Mauritius	4	7	20	27	28	27	27	30	31	30	Maurice
Mozambique	...	...	...	52	50	66	50	28	35	...	Mozambique
Nigeria	19	23	36	...	58	53	110	20	17	67	Nigéria
Sierra Leone	9	4	3	...	...	...	...	...	...	...	Sierra Leone
South Africa	2 304	2 417	2 344	2 404	* 1 898	2 081	2 348	* 2 522	* 2 213	2 227	Afrique du Sud
Tunisia	68	161	200	297	323	262	...	...	...	...	Tunisie
Uganda	12	8	* 7	* 6	5	3	2	* 1	...	...	Ouganda
Zaire	14	73	9	...	26	27	23	26	...	...	Zaïre
Zambia	127	126	114	126	123	90	...	...	...	...	Zambie
America, North	**39 562**	**43 986**	**44 721**	**47 196**	**47 299**	**49 837**	**57 007**	**56 717**	**57 961**	**57 565**	**Amérique du Nord**
Barbados	35	38	35	40	40	45	50	43	43	45	Barbade
Canada[1]	4 685	5 142	6 262	6 317	6 754	...	...	...	...	...	Canada[1]
Cuba	1 096	1 124	1 256	1 264	1 387	1 510	1 364	1 489	1 609	1 630	Cuba
Dominican Republic	96	101	115	97	131	157	141	180	162	164	Rép. dominicaine
El Salvador	70	122	100	77	81	79	73	82	...	...	El Salvador
Guadeloupe	12	15	* 16	17	19	21	16	17	18	...	Guadeloupe
Jamaica	199	198	211	203	204	208	184	217	216	165	Jamaïque
Mexico	2 337	2 315	2 346	2 597	2 929	2 999	3 123	2 584	2 334	2 344	Mexique
Panama	56	51	60	84	90	103	101	107	...	...	Panama
Trinidad and Tobago	...	3 079	1 364	1 688	# 283	227	262	297	290	256	Trinité–et–Tobago
United States[2]	28 672	31 801	32 956	34 812	35 381	37 070	43 748	43 226	44 091	43 209	Etats–Unis[2]
America, South	**7 318**	**7 281**	**8 687**	**9 780**	**10 500**	**10 174**	**11 808**	**12 385**	**12 970**	**13 825**	**Amérique du Sud**
Bolivia	22	30	36	45	23	37	25	23	27	...	Bolivie
Brazil	4 504	4 396	5 583	[3] 7 147	7 544	7 064	...	...	...	...	Brésil
Colombia	761	843	887	980	927	954	1 131	1 116	...	...	Colombie
Ecuador	...	...	53	...	76	114	130	147	...	...	Equateur
Guyana	* 34	37	50	58	54	53	32	25	* 25	...	Guyana
Paraguay	69	61	64	74	91	104	109	115	121	108	Paraguay
Peru	741	643	670	491	611	666	775	673	* 492	...	Pérou
Suriname	29	35	43	48	43	50	55	55	59	67	Suriname
Venezuela	1 149	1 207	1 301	869	...	...	...	...	...	...	Venezuela
Asia	**24 166**	**26 092**	**28 417**	**31 585**	**30 890**	**31 126**	**32 589**	**35 538**	**36 307**	**37 634**	**Asie**
Hong Kong	...	...	...	...	65	145	326	232	241	...	Hong–kong
Indonesia	229	222	293	587	585	935	708	943	1 072	...	Indonésie
Iran(Islamic Rep.of)[4]	...	...	...	391	375	452	549	528	...	...	Iran(Rép.islamique)[4]
Israel[5]	1 684	1 642	1 614	1 702	1 579	1 580	1 652	1 697	1 668	1 564	Israël[5]
Japan	18 618	19 878	21 067	22 438	22 252	22 159	22 877	24 280	24 494	25 233	Japon
Jordan	51	42	52	52	48	55	64	61	61	45	Jordanie
Korea, Republic of	1 305	1 810	2 625	3 924	3 567	3 500	4 126	5 491	5 676	6 262	Corée, République de
Malaysia[6 7 8]	390	406	445	457	549	565	591	653	726	736	Malaisie[6 7 8]
Mongolia	178	171	140	131	77	61	72	130	153	156	Mongolie
Philippines	591	590	647	647	669	660	...	522	...	...	Philippines
Singapore	253	305	304	320	342	269	248	223	238	186	Singapour
Sri Lanka	47	42	42	63	104	67	...	...	...	...	Sri Lanka
Turkey	539	636	774	762	...	...	...	...	...	...	Turquie
Europe	**87 604**	**89 414**	**96 220**	**101 342**	**104 566**	**103 107**	**100 855**	**103 111**	**103 254**	**103 562**	**Europe**
EEC	***58 402***	***57 656***	***60 738***	***63 748***	***65 293***	***65 311***	***66 082***	***68 266***	***66 014***	***65 194***	***CEE***
Belgium	5 122	4 949	4 996	4 952	4 883	4 763	4 989	5 047	4 990	5 003	Belgique
Denmark	399	388	428	480	382	...	...	...	...	...	Danemark
France	12 305	12 492	13 296	13 924	14 611	15 070	15 299	15 193	14 942	14 693	France
Germany, Fed. Rep.	9 894	10 522	11 686	12 289	13 419	13 260	12 545	13 140	12 394	11 849	Allemagne, Rép. féd.
Greece	528	552	622	745	722	742	721	635	581	...	Grèce
Italy	7 413	...	...	...	...	...	...	...	...	...	Italie
Netherlands	11 390	10 550	11 324	12 302	12 755	12 687	12 822	14 160	14 501	...	Pays–Bas
United Kingdom	11 351	10 790	10 973	11 643	11 108	10 943	11 855	12 234	10 743	10 356	Royaume–Uni
EFTA	***6 982***	***7 906***	***8 188***	***8 717***	***10 194***	***10 260***	***9 940***	***9 560***	***9 035***	***9 389***	***AELE***

For general note and footnotes, see end of table. | Voir la fin du tableau pour la remarque générale et les notes.

Prepared animal feeds (continued) – Aliments préparés pour animaux (suite)

Unit : Thousand metric tons

Unité : Milliers de tonnes métriques

Country or area	1976	1977	1978	1979	1980	1981	1982	1983	1984	1985	Pays ou zone
Austria	709	681	741	776	821	806	815	766	780	718	Autriche
Finland	656	934	1 235	1 515	1 897	1 884	1 993	1 763	1 686	...	Finlande
Norway	1 343	1 369	1 402	1 540	1 659	...	...	...	...	1 633	Norvège
Portugal	2 242	2 801	2 592	2 662	3 509	3 683	3 174	3 139	2 571	2 462	Portugal
Sweden	2 032	2 121	2 218	2 224	2 308	2 331	2 367	2 265	2 336	2 361	Suède
East Europe	***13 668***	***14 265***	***15 577***	***16 256***	***15 751***	***14 480***	***11 612***	***12 271***	***13 772***	***14 617***	***Europe de l'est***
Bulgaria	3 005	2 996	2 993	3 387	3 276	3 453	3 275	3 672	4 072	4 513	Bulgarie
Hungary	2 222	2 589	2 630	2 743	2 741	2 479	2 584	2 665	2 822	2 542	Hongrie
Poland	8 441	8 680	9 954	10 126	9 734	8 548	5 753	5 934	6 878	7 562	Pologne
Other Europe	***8 552***	***9 587***	***11 717***	***12 621***	***13 328***	***13 056***	***13 220***	***13 014***	***14 433***	***14 362***	***Autre Europe***
Malta	112	112	98	94	78	87	99	117	133	...	Malte
Spain	6 685	7 427	8 885	9 592	10 140	9 595	9 893	9 312	...	...	Espagne
Yugoslavia	1 755	2 048	2 734	2 935	3 110	3 374	3 228	3 585	3 570	3 123	Yougoslavie
Oceania	**2 062**	**2 180**	**2 300**	**2 351**	**2 638**	**1 904**	**1 842**	**2 482**	**2 976**	**2 834**	**Océanie**
Australia[9]	2 048	2 163	2 281	2 331	2 615	1 884	1 824	2 460	2 958	2 816	Australie[9]
Fiji	14	17	19	20	23	20	18	22	18	18	Fidji
Total	**163 469**	**172 018**	**183 351**	**195 443**	**198 626**	**198 984**	**207 344**	**213 659**	**216 613**	**218 672**	**Total**

General note.

Preparations of vegetable or animal origin with or without added mineral or chemical materials. They may be ready for direct consumption or may be in concentrated form requiring dilution before use. Inorganic esters and their salts, medicaments and simple mixtures of cereal grain, of cereal flours or of flours of leguminous vegetables are excluded. Biscuits for dogs and other animals, bird foods, fish foods and chemical preparations, such as egg–laying mixtures, are included. (SITC 08199–0).

1 Shipments.
2 Source: U. S. Department of Agriculture , (Washington, D. C.).
3 Production by establishments employing 5 or more persons.
4 Production by establishments employing 10 or more persons.
5 Twelve months ending 30 September of year stated.
6 Data refer to Peninsular Malaysia only.
7 Mixed poultry feeds and pig feeds.
8 Beginning 1982, scope of series revised.
9 Twelve months ending 30 June of year stated.

Remarque générale.

Produits d'origine végétale ou animale additionnés ou non de produits chimiques ou de sels minéraux, soit tout préparés et prêts à la consommation, soit présentés sous forme concentrée et devant être dilués avant consommation. Cette position ne comprend pas les esters et les sels d'acides minéraux, les médicaments, et les simples mélanges de céréales en grain ou en farine et de farines de légumineuses. Toutefois, elle inclut les biscuits pour chiens ou autres animaux, les nourritures pour oiseaux et poissons et les produits minéraux ou chimiques comme par exemple les pâtées servant à favoriser la ponte. (CTCI 08199–0).

1 Expéditions.
2 Source: U.S. Department of Agriculture, (Washington, D.C.).
3 Production des établissements occupant 5 personnes ou plus.
4 Production des établissements occupant 10 personnes ou plus.
5 Période de douze mois finissant le 30 septembre de l'année indiquée.
6 Données se rapportant à la Malaisie péninsulaire seulement.
7 Aliments mélangés pour volaille et porcins.
8 A partir de 1982, portée de la série révisée.
9 Période de douze mois finissant le 30 juin de l'année indiquée.

Distilled alcoholic beverages, excluding ethyl alcohol – Boissons alcooliques distillées, à l'exclusion de l'alcool éthylique

Unit : Thousand hectolitres | Unité : Milliers de hectolitres

Country or area	1976	1977	1978	1979	1980	1981	1982	1983	1984	1985	Pays ou zone
Africa	**451**	**475**	**524**	**518**	**563**	**625**	**601**	**612**	**686**	**742**	**Afrique**
Cape Verde	0	2	2	1	2	2	2	2	2	2	Cap-Vert
Egypt	...	...	...	6	6	6	6	...	...	...	Egypte
Ethiopia[1]	26	27	60	30	33	36	46	45	59	...	Ethiopie[1]
Kenya	4	3	4	4	5	6	5	5	5	5	Kenya
Liberia	7	8	4	6	11	9	9	8	2	2	Liberia
Mauritius[2]	53	55	56	58	54	51	52	51	49	46	Maurice[2]
Réunion[2]	68	64	62	59	69	80	68	84	90	102	Réunion[2]
Sierra Leone	...	...	...	...	2	3	3	1	0	...	Sierra Leone
South Africa	...	...	...	...	* 368	419	396	397	460	511	Afrique du Sud
Tunisia	6	5	4	6	6	7	...	...	...	...	Tunisie
Uganda	5	5	4	1	4	2	4	...	...	...	Ouganda
Zambia	3	3	* 2	3	* 3	4	...	...	...	...	Zambie
America, North	**16 595**	**16 669**	**17 835**	**19 754**	**20 687**	**20 876**	**21 177**	**20 808**	**20 655**	**20 190**	**Amérique du Nord**
Antigua and Barbuda[2]	5	3	5	3	3	5	5	5	7	...	Antigua-et-Barbuda[2]
Barbados[2]	50	61	61	43	58	33	27	28	27	39	Barbade[2]
Canada	1 530	1 617	1 229	1 720	1 814	...	...	...	...	...	Canada
Cuba	320	284	319	359	402	385	570	586	656	618	Cuba
Dominica[2 3]	6	5	* 5	* 6	* 6	...	...	...	...	...	Dominique[2 3]
Dominican Republic	195	209	200	200	201	196	219	222	269	...	Rép. dominicaine
El Salvador	215	152	152	141	163	158	50	50	...	...	El Salvador
Grenada[2]	4	4	3	4	3	4	4	4	3	4	Grenade[2]
Guadeloupe[2]	103	94	88	98	93	92	92	69	65	73	Guadeloupe[2]
Guatemala	140	179	...	...	370	* 354	242	260	...	...	Guatemala
Jamaica[4]	174	177	168	180	205	222	173	147	173	148	Jamaïque[4]
Martinique[2]	110	110	110	112	115	108	101	105	99	93	Martinique[2]
Mexico	1 389	1 538	1 358	1 399	1 465	1 702	...	...	...	...	Mexique
Nicaragua	...	...	...	73	93	120	120	147	119	...	Nicaragua
Panama	73	76	83	65	76	85	83	82	86	79	Panama
Puerto Rico[2 5]	611	492	...	...	...	...	...	...	...	...	Porto Rico[2 5]
Saint Lucia[2 6]	9	9	9	5	5	4	3	4	4	...	Sainte-Lucie[2 6]
S.Vincent-Grenadines[2]	5	4	3	3	4	5	5	5	4	7	S.Vincent-Grenadines[2]
Trinidad and Tobago[2]	106	110	121	111	128	120	108	73	74	104	Trinité-et-Tobago[2]
United States	11 500	11 483	...	14 440	14 931	14 944	15 355	14 894	14 447	13 893	Etats-Unis
America, South	**9 531**	**9 769**	**8 482**	**9 124**	**10 809**	**9 534**	**9 660**	**9 537**	**9 616**	**9 633**	**Amérique du Sud**
Brazil	...	9 225	7 911	[7] 8 523	10 183	...	...	...	...	...	Brésil
Colombia	...	...	...	...	...	...	...	192	...	...	Colombie
Ecuador	131	...	* 129	...	...	133	228	141	...	...	Equateur
French Guiana[2]	* 2	2	2	3	3	3	3	3	3	2	Guyane française[2]
Guyana[2 8]	* 157	100	103	107	118	108	130	139	154	...	Guyana[2 8]
Paraguay	88	118	145	153	160	137	146	101	127	155	Paraguay
Asia	**11 565**	**12 421**	**12 800**	**13 573**	**14 248**	**14 833**	**16 059**	**17 938**	**19 475**	**19 386**	**Asie**
Burma	82	149	165	...	...	...	...	...	...	...	Birmanie
Cyprus	10	11	11	11	11	13	13	13	14	14	Chypre
Hong Kong	65	40	55	36	31	* 41	* 38	* 43	* 36	...	Hong-kong
Indonesia	30	16	19	35	17	15	31	12	9	...	Indonésie
Iran(Islamic Rep.of)[9]	197	217	...	...	...	...	...	...	...	...	Iran(Rép.islamique)[9]
Israel[10]	93	...	80	57	57	56	49	55	60	52	Israël[10]
Japan[11]	4 949	5 381	5 509	6 262	6 310	6 433	7 272	8 508	9 546	9 702	Japon[11]
Jordan	6	6	6	7	7	10	9	9	9	5	Jordanie
Korea, Republic of	4 396	4 603	4 654	4 551	5 051	5 354	5 493	5 850	6 301	5 889	Corée, République de
Mongolia	43	52	53	59	60	64	64	65	69	61	Mongolie
Nepal	5	6	5	7	8	5	3	4	10	...	Népal
Philippines[12]	1 248	1 389	1 469	1 572	1 675	1 848	...	* 2 430	...	...	Philippines[12]
Sri Lanka	70	61	69	66	* 59	* 59	[13] 72	[13] 49	[13] 64	[13] 62	Sri Lanka
Syrian Arab Republic	130	110	110	130	140	170	* 180	150	170	180	Rép. arabe syrienne
Turkey[14]	241	303	388	441	483	426	389	411	428	456	Turquie[14]
Europe	**23 133**	**23 747**	**25 651**	**26 792**	**25 025**	**25 573**	**25 307**	**25 222**	**25 932**	**26 460**	**Europe**
EEC	***12 527***	***12 007***	***13 748***	***13 742***	***13 228***	***13 491***	***13 402***	***13 536***	***13 750***	***13 973***	*CEE*
Denmark	192	193	174	189	193	194	204	218	213	234	Danemark
France	2 709	2 689	2 900	2 854	2 830	2 715	2 771	...	...	...	France
Germany, Fed. Rep.	4 349	3 412	3 981	3 930	3 882	3 647	3 279	3 114	3 037	2 946	Allemagne, Rép. féd.
Greece[15]	* 270	* 270	* 320	* 330	* 394	* 401	* 363	* 385	400	...	Grèce[15]
Luxembourg	4	3	2	3	2	2	2	3	1	2	Luxembourg

For general note and footnotes, see end of table. | Voir la fin du tableau pour la remarque générale et les notes.

Distilled alcoholic beverages, excluding ethyl alcohol (continued) – Boissons alcooliques distillées, à l'exclusion de l'alcool éthylique (suite)

Unit : Thousand hectolitres — Unité : Milliers de hectolitres

Country or area	1976	1977	1978	1979	1980	1981	1982	1983	1984	1985	Pays ou zone
Netherlands[16]	1 023	1 147	1 176	1 356	1 077	1 098	1 098	* 1 074	* 1 100	...	Pays-Bas[16]
United Kingdom	3 980	4 293	5 195	* 5 080	* 4 850	...	...	...	...	...	Royaume-Uni
EFTA	***1 333***	***1 385***	***1 407***	***1 509***	***1 539***	***1 452***	***1 465***	***1 350***	***1 396***	***1 370***	*AELE*
Austria	289	293	285	305	315	308	300	301	300	303	Autriche
Finland	581	631	561	568	566	588	596	546	568	...	Finlande
Norway[16]	23	23	18	19	19	34	...	...	...	...	Norvège[16]
Portugal	62	78	75	87	82	84	89	86	85	71	Portugal
Sweden[17]	378	360	468	530	557	438	453	389	413	405	Suède[17]
East Europe	***6 186***	***6 793***	***6 931***	***6 896***	***7 093***	***6 899***	***6 961***	***7 010***	***7 202***	***7 529***	*Europe de l'est*
Bulgaria	586	618	625	691	538	586	...	...	...	...	Bulgarie
Czechoslovakia	1 162	1 244	1 344	1 220	1 250	1 327	1 405	1 196	1 264	1 205	Tchécoslovaquie
German Dem. Rep.	1 564	1 684	1 813	1 972	2 095	2 221	2 234	2 496	2 521	2 601	Rép. dém. allemande
Hungary	971	1 087	1 070	984	1 089	1 150	1 156	1 125	1 184	1 353	Hongrie
Poland[16]	1 903	2 160	2 079	2 029	2 121	1 615	1 576	1 608	1 653	1 795	Pologne[16]
Other Europe	***3 087***	***3 562***	***3 565***	***4 645***	***3 165***	***3 731***	***3 479***	***3 326***	***3 585***	***3 588***	*Autre Europe*
Spain	3 087	...	...	4 645	3 165	3 731	3 479	3 326	...	...	Espagne
Oceania	**1 980**	**2 060**	**2 010**	**1 764**	**1 309**	**1 627**	**1 672**	**1 288**	**1 273**	**1 376**	**Océanie**
Australia	1 980	2 060	2 010	1 764	1 309	1 627	* 1 672	1 288	1 273	1 376	Australie
Total	**63 255**	**65 140**	**67 303**	**71 526**	**72 641**	**73 068**	**74 477**	**75 405**	**77 638**	**77 788**	**Total**

General note.
Spirits produced by distilling wine, cides etc., or fermented grain or other vegetable products, without adding flavouring; spirits, liqueurs and cordials containing added flavouring and other spirituous beverages. The average alcoholic content should be indicated. (SITC 11240–1).

1 Twelve months ending 10 September of year stated.
2 Rum only.
3 Source: United Nations Economic Commission for Latin America (ECLA), (Santiago).
4 Rum and gin.
5 Twelve months ending 30 June of year stated.
6 Original data in proof gallons.
7 Production by establishments employing 5 or more persons.
8 Original data in British proof gallons.
9 Including wine.
10 Marketed quantities.
11 Twelve months beginning 1 April of year stated.
12 Shipments.
13 Coconut spirit.
14 Government production only.
15 Original data in metric tons.
16 In terms of 100 per cent alcohol.
17 Vermouths, blended from imported wines.

Remarque générale.
Eaux de vie obtenues par distillation du vin, du cidre etc., ou de grains fermentés ou d'autres produitsvégétaux, non additionnés d'aromates; alcools et liqueurs additionnés d'aromates et toutes autres boissons spiritueuses. In diquer le dégre moyen d'alcool. (CTCI 11241–1).

1 Période de douze mois finissant le 10 septembre de l'année indiquée.
2 Rhum seulement.
3 Source: Commission économique des Nations Unies pour l'Amérique Latine (CEPAL), (Santiago).
4 Rhum et gin.
5 Période de douze mois finissant le 30 juin de l'année indiquée.
6 Données d'origine exprimées en gallons d'alcool du titre normal.
7 Production des établissements occupant 5 personnes ou plus.
8 Données d'origine exprimées en gallons impériaux d'alcool de titre normal.
9 Y compris le vin.
10 Quantités commercialisées.
11 Période de douze mois commençant le 1er avril de l'année indiquée.
12 Expéditions.
13 Liqueur de coco.
14 Production de l'Etat seulement.
15 Données d'origine exprimées en tonnes.
16 Sur la base de 100 p. 100 d'alcool.
17 Vermouths constitués à partir de vins importés.

Ethyl alcohol for all purposes – Alcool éthylique pour tous usages

Unit : Thousand hectolitres

Unité : Milliers de hectolitres

Country or area	1976	1977	1978	1979	1980	1981	1982	1983	1984	1985	Pays ou zone
Africa	**811**	**821**	**802**	**747**	**754**	**754**	**780**	**749**	**742**	**733**	**Afrique**
Algeria	32	23	19	...	...	...	...	...	...	...	Algérie
Egypt	301	316	294	240	260	260	290	...	...	...	Egypte
Ethiopia[1]	8	9	11	6	7	8	5	7	9	...	Ethiopie[1]
Ghana	439	...	...	...	...	...	...	...	...	...	Ghana
Mauritius	31	34	39	37	23	22	21	24	21	21	Maurice
America, North	**20 761**	**20 980**	**19 337**	**16 922**	**16 602**	**16 823**	**16 758**	**14 829**	**14 903**	**13 428**	**Amérique du Nord**
Canada	227	240	...	...	...	...	...	...	...	...	Canada
Cuba	769	914	1 265	1 186	1 091	1 154	1 439	1 395	1 504	1 393	Cuba
Dominican Republic	109	131	102	109	117	102	113	121	135	130	Rép. dominicaine
El Salvador	...	0	83	91	101	96	77	84	...	...	El Salvador
Jamaica	31	29	35	...	...	...	...	...	...	...	Jamaïque
Mexico	636	763	785	924	905	1 145	...	...	...	...	Mexique
Panama	38	43	46	50	40	61	61	52	62	57	Panama
United States[2]	18 910	18 860	...	14 297	14 083	14 000	13 632	11 653	11 478	...	Etats–Unis[2]
America, South	**6 644**	**13 815**	**23 536**	**34 734**	**37 013**	**42 373**	**56 559**	**79 970**	**92 505**	**118 304**	**Amérique du Sud**
Brazil	6 419	13 656	23 361	34 503	36 762	42 024	56 211	79 501	92 071	117 834	Brésil
Colombia	123	54	65	128	155	260	216	375	...	...	Colombie
Ecuador	40	...	47	...	32	47	42	39	...	...	Equateur
Paraguay	43	49	46	47	52	34	82	42	39	19	Paraguay
Suriname	19	14	17	15	12	8	8	13	12	30	Suriname
Asia	**7 357**	**8 109**	**7 496**	**7 549**	**8 696**	**9 448**	**10 148**	**10 503**	**11 381**	**11 408**	**Asie**
India[3]	2 908	3 474	2 879	3 060	4 230	4 810	5 144	5 219	...	...	Inde[3]
Japan[4]	2 216	2 219	2 278	2 179	2 107	2 105	2 345	2 554	2 849	2 666	Japon[4]
Jordan	3	2	2	2	1	1	4	6	10	3	Jordanie
Korea, Republic of	1 216	1 321	1 290	1 256	1 306	1 476	1 602	1 670	1 812	1 661	Corée, République de
Philippines[5]	580	663	...	...	...	...	...	...	...	...	Philippines[5]
Syrian Arab Republic	20	25	24	18	22	26	23	24	28	21	Rép. arabe syrienne
Turkey	414	405	401	412	...	...	...	...	...	...	Turquie
Europe	**23 603**	**24 296**	**23 948**	**24 272**	**24 691**	**25 580**	**25 655**	**26 612**	**27 270**	**27 996**	**Europe**
EEC	***14 683***	***15 101***	***14 692***	***15 127***	***15 892***	***15 716***	***16 094***	***16 698***	***17 657***	***17 901***	***CEE***
Belgium	488	537	512	432	* 164	* 143	* 142	* 158	* 163	176	Belgique
Denmark	195	171	139	130	135	127	136	145	142	155	Danemark
France[6 7 8]	7 695	8 556	8 300	8 983	10 737	10 401	...	...	...	...	France[6 7 8]
Germany, Fed. Rep.	2 146	2 116	1 823	1 821	2 179	2 290	1 678	1 351	1 072	1 425	Allemagne, Rép. féd.
Greece[6]	* 260	* 280	...	* 214	* 257	* 250	259	258	239	...	Grèce[6]
Netherlands	1 410	# [9] 724	[9] 689	[9] 738	[9] 609	[9] 665	[9] 621	[9] 608	[9] 626	[9] 601	Pays–Bas
United Kingdom[10]	2 489	2 717	2 973	2 809	1 811	1 840	2 071	2 399	3 043	...	Royaume–Uni[10]
EFTA	***1 130***	***1 131***	***1 068***	***1 094***	***1 093***	***1 152***	***1 275***	***1 259***	***1 333***	***1 267***	***AELE***
Finland[6]	247	349	322	323	371	467	459	477	483	...	Finlande[6]
Norway	217	200	161	202	195	205	...	202	334	...	Norvège
Portugal	123	126	101	89	91	117	126	132	105	76	Portugal
Sweden	543	456	484	480	436	363	452	448	411	387	Suède
East Europe	***5 800***	***6 210***	***6 235***	***6 401***	***5 849***	***6 062***	***5 909***	***6 191***	***5 740***	***6 190***	***Europe de l'est***
Czechoslovakia	1 528	1 189	1 130	1 138	1 141	1 277	1 461	1 427	1 356	1 322	Tchécoslovaquie
German Dem. Rep.	336	315	411	435	445	462	458	486	490	494	Rép. dém. allemande
Hungary	530	589	636	676	683	670	829	854	878	865	Hongrie
Poland	2 622	3 297	3 235	3 266	2 703	2 747	2 346	2 658	2 202	2 680	Pologne
Romania	784	820	823	886	877	906	815	766	814	829	Roumanie
Other Europe	***1 990***	***1 854***	***1 952***	***1 650***	***1 857***	***2 650***	***2 377***	***2 464***	***2 540***	***2 638***	***Autre Europe***
Spain	* 1 990	...	...	1 650	1 857	[11] 2 650	[11] 2 377	[11] 2 464	...	...	Espagne
USSR	**31 683**	**32 551**	**32 251**	**31 177**	**30 556**	**31 576**	**32 807**	**32 002**	...	...	**URSS**
Byelorussian SSR	*1 453*	*1 473*	*1 400*	*1 547*	*1 431*	*1 612*	*1 667*	*1 511*	...	...	*RSS de Biélorussie*
Ukrainian SSR	*6 306*	*6 975*	*7 308*	*6 613*	*6 852*	*6 467*	*7 243*	*7 084*	*6 952*	...	*RSS d'Ukraine*
Total	**90 859**	**100 572**	**107 369**	**115 401**	**118 311**	**126 553**	**142 705**	**164 665**	**178 673**	**203 751**	**Total**

For general note and footnotes, see end of table.

Voir la fin du tableau pour la remarque générale et les notes.

General note.
Ethyl alcohol of any strength, denatured or undenatured, irrespective of its use, in terms of 100 per cent spirit. SITC 51224 and part of 1124).

[1] Twelve months ending 10 September of year stated.
[2] Twelve months ending 30 June of year stated.
[3] Production by large and medium scale establishments only.
[4] Twelve months beginning 1 April of year stated.
[5] Shipments.
[6] Original data in metric tons.
[7] Source: The Chemical Industry, Organisation for Economic Co–operation and Development (OECD), (Paris).
[8] Including the production by the state and by large distillers as well as home distillers.
[9] In terms of 100 per cent alcohol.
[10] Ethyl alcohol for industrial purposes including industrial alcohol made from processes and derived from other processes.
[11] Including household production.

Remarque générale.
Alcool éthylique quel que soit son degré alcoolique, dénaturé ou non, et quel que soit son usage, exprimé en alcool à 100 p. 100. (CTCI 51224, plus partie de 1124).

[1] Période de douze mois finissant le 10 septembre de l'année indiquée.
[2] Période de douze mois finissant le 30 juin de l'année indiquée.
[3] Production des grandes et moyennes entreprises seulement.
[4] Période de douze mois commençant le 1er avril de l'année indiquée.
[5] Expéditions.
[6] Données d'origine exprimées en tonnes.
[7] Source: l'Industrie chimique, Organisation de coopération et de développement économiques (OCDE), (Paris).
[8] Y compris la production par la régie d'Etat et la production des grands distillateurs ainsi que des bouilleurs de cru.
[9] Sur la base de 100 p. 100 d'alcool.
[10] Alcool éthylique à usage industriel y compris l'alcool industriel provenant de procédés ou obtenu par d'autres procédés.
[11] Y compris la production ménagère.

Unit : Thousand hectolitres | Unité : Milliers de hectolitres

Country or area	1976	1977	1978	1979	1980	1981	1982	1983	1984	1985	Pays ou zone
Africa	**11 371**	**9 095**	**7 072**	**8 115**	**8 482**	**8 015**	**10 619**	**11 705**	**11 915**	**11 280**	**Afrique**
Algeria[1]	3 783	2 549	1 840	2 710	2 837	2 669	* 1 510	* 1 880	* 2 150	* 2 200	Algérie[1]
Egypt[1]	11	13	* 15	* 10	* 20	* 20	* 20	* 20	* 20	* 20	Egypte[1]
Ethiopia[2]	56	67	66	71	77	74	86	86	89	...	Ethiopie[2]
Kenya	0	4	4	4	...	...	...	...	...	...	Kenya
Madagascar[1]	84	96	97	98	* 70	* 70	* 70	* 70	* 80	* 80	Madagascar[1]
Mauritius	23	26	27	32	33	32	41	43	51	43	Maurice
Morocco	770	810	1 137	1 105	910	514	350	436	395	309	Maroc
Nigeria	...	...	...	...	...	27	23	43	32	14	Nigéria
South Africa	5 975	4 823	3 387	3 396	3 831	4 006	7 963	8 505	* 8 372	7 907	Afrique du Sud
Sudan	46	41	39	...	50	44	40	...	...	...	Soudan
Tunisia	583	628	424	611	618	556	513	576	680	567	Tunisie
America, North	**17 612**	**17 766**	**19 622**	**19 988**	**19 465**	**16 803**	**20 075**	**14 966**	**16 840**	**18 120**	**Amérique du Nord**
Antigua and Barbuda[3]	...	...	...	...	...	1	1	1	0	...	Antigua-et-Barbuda[3]
Canada	650	662	920	973	1 028	* [1] 460	* [1] 460	* [1] 530	* [1] 550	* [1] 550	Canada
Cuba	125	135	137	137	135	131	138	151	160	147	Cuba
Dominican Republic	14	19	21	20	25	28	32	27	27	28	Rép. dominicaine
El Salvador	5	7	6	7	7	6	4	5	...	...	El Salvador
Mexico	723	880	630	675	708	1 078	* [1] 630	* [1] 500	* [1] 630	* [1] 640	Mexique
Panama	3	3	3	2	2	3	3	2	2	2	Panama
United States[4]	* 16 091	* 16 059	* 17 904	* 18 173	17 559	15 096	18 807	13 750	15 466	16 747	Etats-Unis[4]
America, South	**37 294**	**33 444**	**30 544**	**37 007**	**34 361**	**31 362**	**34 925**	**34 620**	**27 276**	**25 239**	**Amérique du Sud**
Argentina	28 197	23 319	20 267	25 975	23 302	21 633	24 984	24 719	18 808	16 800	Argentine
Bolivia	12	10	7	6	12	13	14	15	15	20	Bolivie
Brazil* [1]	2 700	4 340	4 283	4 530	4 532	2 700	2 750	2 275	2 730	2 800	Brésil* [1]
Chile	* 5 143	* 5 000	* 5 200	5 611	* 5 700	* 5 720	* 6 000	* 6 500	* 4 500	* 4 500	Chili
Colombia	71	76	74	95	106	94	82	86	...	...	Colombie
Ecuador	15	18	29	...	...	15	13	12	...	...	Equateur
Paraguay	67	66	68	76	91	76	110	121	132	136	Paraguay
Peru* [1]	87	93	94	95	90	80	80	90	90	90	Pérou* [1]
Uruguay	* [1] 950	* [1] 470	* [1] 470	* [1] 550	* [1] 460	* [1] 970	* [1] 840	* [1] 750	* [1] 850	731	Uruguay
Venezuela	...	...	...	...	...	61	...	...	42	...	Venezuela
Asia	**2 508**	**2 523**	**2 370**	**2 382**	**1 962**	**1 759**	**1 993**	**2 070**	**2 039**	**1 993**	**Asie**
Afghanistan	...	...	...	370	142	179	204	256	262	264	Afghanistan
Cyprus	* 473	* 460	565	594	* 600	416	483	450	442	387	Chypre
India[5]	530	565	480	...	...	...	...	...	...	...	Inde[5]
Indonesia	18	27	23	25	19	17	2	65	82	...	Indonésie
Israel[6]	376	* 360	209	185	189	166	160	165	176	183	Israël[6]
Japan[7 8]	179	166	179	241	281	232	377	402	314	341	Japon[7 8]
Jordan	2	3	3	1	4	5	7	6	4	2	Jordanie
Lebanon* [1]	43	43	43	43	43	50	50	50	40	50	Liban* [1]
Macau	...	...	...	...	...	...	5	5	6	7	Macao
Syrian Arab Republic	7	4	3	2	1	1	* 4	* 3	* 3	4	Rép. arabe syrienne
Turkey	* [1] 634	* [1] 650	* [1] 620	* [1] 390	# 152	162	176	143	185	172	Turquie
Europe	**219 531**	**189 549**	**207 674**	**266 744**	**248 606**	**218 166**	**260 608**	**246 401**	**224 640**	**212 846**	**Europe**
EEC	***153 377***	***130 845***	***142 304***	***181 988***	***166 567***	***141 036***	***169 297***	***170 996***	***149 731***	***147 492***	***CEE***
Belgium[1]	132	159	* 164	* 167	* 160	* 100	* 260	* 190	* 190	* 170	Belgique[1]
Denmark	...	...	...	...	...	...	120	129	119	...	Danemark
France[9]	74 145	52 708	58 429	84 105	69 598	57 435	79 801	68 810	64 148	70 291	France[9]
Germany, Fed. Rep.[1]	8 928	9 558	6 714	7 139	* 4 870	* 7 480	* 10 610	* 13 390	* 8 880	* 6 000	Allemagne, Rép. féd.[1]
Greece[1]	4 070	4 000	4 360	5 240	5 220	5 240	* 5 600	* 5 190	* 5 340	* 5 300	Grèce[1]
Italy[1]	65 850	64 140	72 440	* 85 150	86 545	70 560	72 648	83 100	70 900	65 500	Italie[1]
Luxembourg	128	155	72	63	50	97	256	185	152	107	Luxembourg
United Kingdom	1	2	2	...	...	...	...	...	...	...	Royaume-Uni
EFTA	***13 916***	***11 143***	***11 040***	***15 725***	***14 602***	***12 202***	***17 201***	***14 102***	***12 632***	***12 396***	***AELE***
Austria	2 901	2 594	3 366	2 773	3 086	2 085	4 906	3 699	2 519	1 126	Autriche
Finland	192	201	183	194	212	271	246	357	348	322	Finlande
Norway	105	102	81	114	135	134	...	...	...	...	Norvège
Portugal	9 486	6 908	6 594	11 498	10 289	8 819	10 031	8 249	8 393	9 567	Portugal
Sweden[10]	38	38	...	...	...	...	...	...	...	...	Suède[10]
Switzerland	1 194	1 300	778	1 108	842	855	1 840	1 612	1 179	1 180	Suisse
East Europe	***21 519***	***19 427***	***18 955***	***20 618***	***18 888***	***21 262***	***24 445***	***20 663***	***22 420***	***16 173***	***Europe de l'est***

For general note and footnotes, see end of table.

Voir la fin du tableau pour la remarque générale et les notes.

Unit : Thousand hectolitres

Unité : Milliers de hectolitres

Country or area	1976	1977	1978	1979	1980	1981	1982	1983	1984	1985	Pays ou zone
Albania* [1]	187	199	205	214	210	210	210	220	230	230	Albanie* [1]
Bulgaria	5 116	3 588	4 366	4 492	4 182	5 059	5 803	4 549	5 155	3 859	Bulgarie
Czechoslovakia	1 325	1 386	1 417	1 317	1 421	1 427	1 303	1 378	1 563	1 763	Tchécoslovaquie
German Dem. Rep.	32	37	31	36	22	14	14	23	26	21	Rép. dém. allemande
Hungary	2 356	2 095	2 280	2 471	2 410	2 330	2 245	2 492	2 652	2 276	Hongrie
Poland	2 835	3 014	3 023	3 219	3 044	2 271	1 801	2 514	2 756	2 675	Pologne
Romania	9 668	9 108	7 633	8 869	7 599	9 951	13 069	9 487	10 038	5 349	Roumanie
Other Europe	***30 719***	***28 134***	***35 375***	***48 413***	***48 549***	***43 666***	***49 666***	***40 640***	***39 857***	***36 784***	***Autre Europe***
Malta [1]	* 12	* 14	* 14	* 14	20	10	20	20	20	20	Malte [1]
Spain	24 327	21 820	29 481	41 656	40 359	36 766	44 261	36 299	35 540	33 270	Espagne
Yugoslavia	6 380	6 300	5 880	6 743	* 8 170	6 890	5 385	4 321	4 297	3 494	Yougoslavie
USSR	**31 486**	**30 726**	**24 707**	**29 415**	**32 273**	**34 420**	**34 850**	**35 101**	**34 025**	**26 527**	**URSS**
Byelorussian SSR	*1 310*	*1 258*	*957*	*1 072*	*1 307*	*1 351*	*1 360*	*1 363*	*1 339*	*1 157*	*RSS de Biélorussie*
Ukrainian SSR	*5 888*	*5 724*	*4 185*	...	*5 465*	*5 927*	*6 007*	*6 326*	*5 777*	*4 876*	*RSS d'Ukraine*
Oceania	**3 862**	**4 163**	**3 805**	**3 773**	**4 606**	**4 184**	**4 472**	**3 980**	**4 262**	**4 413**	**Océanie**
Australia	[1] 3 562	[1] 3 831	* [1] 3 400	* [1] 3 350	* [1] 4 140	* [1] 3 740	* [1] 4 000	* [1] 3 400	3 840	3 810	Australie
New Zealand [4]	300	332	405	423	466	444	472	580	422	603	Nouvelle-Zélande [4]
Total	**323 662**	**287 265**	**295 794**	**367 424**	**349 755**	**314 709**	**367 542**	**348 843**	**320 997**	**300 417**	**Total**

General note.
Ordinary wine of fresh grapes produced in wineries (red, white, rose), sparkling wines, dessert wines (malaga, port, sherry, mistelles), vermouth and other wines flavoured with aromatic extracts. Unfermented grape juice and grape must are excluded. (SITC 11212 and 11213).

1 Source: Food and Agriculture Organization (FAO), (Rome).

2 Twelve months ending 10 September of year stated.
3 Including vodka.
4 Twelve months ending 30 June of year stated.
5 Production by large and medium scale establishments only.
6 Marketed quantities.
7 Including liqueurs of apples and other fruits.
8 Twelve months beginning 1 April of year stated.
9 Including grape must.
10 Wines blended from imported wines.

Remarque générale.
Vins ordinaires (vins rouges, rosés ou blancs), vins mousseux, vins de dessert (malaga, porto, sherry, mistelle), vermouths et autres vins de raisins frais aromatisés. Cette rubrique ne comprend pas les moûts de raisins ni les jus de raisin non fermentés. (CTCI 11212 et 11213).

1 Source: Organisation des Nations Unies pour l'alimentation et l'agriculture (FAO), (Rome).
2 Période de douze mois finissant le 10 septembre de l'année indiquée.
3 Y compris la vodka.
4 Période de douze mois finissant le 30 juin de l'année indiquée.
5 Production des grandes et moyennes entreprises seulement.
6 Quantités commercialisées.
7 Y compris les liqueurs de pomme et d'autres fruits.
8 Période de douze mois commençant le 1er avril de l'année indiquée.
9 Y compris les moûts de raisin.
10 Vins constitués à partir de vins importés.

Unit : Thousand metric tons — Unité : Milliers de tonnes métriques

Country or area	1976	1977	1978	1979	1980	1981	1982	1983	1984	1985	Pays ou zone
Africa	**207**	**228**	**227**	**504**	**548**	**550**	**627**	**688**	**734**	**825**	**Afrique**
Egypt	3	2	2	# 283	297	294	295	...	...	...	Egypte
Kenya	19	33	23	25	30	27	72	25	18	22	Kenya
South Africa	...	...	...	196	221	229	260	244	235	259	Afrique du Sud
America, North	**2 627**	**2 373**	**2 659**	**2 664**	**2 778**	**2 721**	**2 583**	**2 536**	**2 497**	**2 468**	**Amérique du Nord**
Barbados* [1]	3	3	4	2	3	3	3	3	3	3	Barbade* [1]
Cuba[1]	* 37	* 28	* 18	* 22	23	21	20	19	19	...	Cuba[1]
Grenada	2	2	4	5	5	6	6	5	3	4	Grenade
Mexico	216	228	229	248	273	294	331	292	299	262	Mexique
United States	...	2 112	2 404	2 387	2 474	2 397	2 223	2 217	2 173	2 184	Etats–Unis
America, South	**553**	**448**	**793**	**736**	**830**	**527**	**627**	**587**	**653**	**671**	**Amérique du Sud**
Argentina	14	11	9	8	5	11	12	15	15	31	Argentine
Brazil	30	28	46	[2] 85	121	...	...	...	...	...	Brésil
Colombia	501	399	730	635	694	412	496	441	...	...	Colombie
Ecuador	8	10	8	...	10	5	8	6	...	...	Equateur
Asia	**241**	**248**	**258**	**268**	**255**	**254**	**259**	**254**	**248**	**255**	**Asie**
Israel	76	70	57	54	60	99	105	103	114	162	Israël
Japan[3 4]	136	144	162	173	161	129	136	124	105	69	Japon[3 4]
Korea, Republic of	20	* 24	* 29	31	26	18	15	18	20	...	Corée, République de
Turkey	9	10	10	10	...	...	[5] 3	[5] 9	[5] 9	...	Turquie
Europe	**4 726**	**4 638**	**5 290**	**4 930**	**4 923**	**5 042**	**5 086**	**5 098**	**4 936**	**4 963**	**Europe**
EEC	***3 146***	***2 994***	***3 175***	***3 162***	***3 115***	***3 139***	***3 241***	***3 220***	***3 164***	***3 121***	***CEE***
Belgium	545	520	558	484	422	457	461	466	468	476	Belgique
Denmark[6]	61	56	68	51	61	62	69	78	48	72	Danemark[6]
France[7]	861	863	948	980	1 035	1 046	1 094	1 107	1 106	1 091	France[7]
Germany, Fed. Rep.	1 475	1 355	1 391	1 433	1 393	1 372	1 406	1 349	1 329	1 266	Allemagne, Rép. féd.
Greece	18	29	29	29	30	33	40	42	40	...	Grèce
Ireland[8]	116	101	111	115	104	99	101	108	103	...	Irlande[8]
Italy[9]	...	...	70	...	...	...	...	...	...	...	Italie[9]
EFTA	***274***	***290***	***284***	***287***	***300***	***334***	***338***	***333***	***252***	***319***	***AELE***
Austria	117	126	119	121	114	123	121	139	55	133	Autriche
Finland	64	75	76	82	92	97	98	95	92	...	Finlande
Portugal	44	43	41	40	41	57	54	41	51	37	Portugal
Sweden	49	46	48	44	53	57	65	58	54	44	Suède
East Europe	***1 095***	***1 131***	***1 184***	***1 170***	***1 155***	***1 192***	***1 148***	***1 199***	***1 148***	***1 178***	***Europe de l'est***
Bulgaria	69	74	77	78	49	67	73	85	84	87	Bulgarie
Czechoslovakia	508	535	543	542	540	546	543	552	544	541	Tchécoslovaquie
German Dem. Rep.	264	262	270	283	282	295	297	297	300	290	Rép. dém. allemande
Hungary	59	63	62	65	65	74	76	95	76	76	Hongrie
Poland	195	197	232	202	219	210	159	170	144	184	Pologne
Other Europe	***211***	***223***	***647***	***311***	***353***	***377***	***359***	***346***	***372***	***345***	***Autre Europe***
Spain	135	121	...	185	208	222	192	186	...	...	Espagne
Yugoslavia	76	102	487	126	145	155	167	160	147	109	Yougoslavie
Oceania	**389**	**388**	**423**	**460**	**530**	**565**	**558**	**536**	**481**	**438**	**Océanie**
Australia	389	388	423	460	530	565	558	536	481	438	Australie
Total	**8 743**	**8 323**	**9 649**	**9 562**	**9 864**	**9 659**	**9 740**	**9 698**	**9 549**	**9 620**	**Total**

General note.
Roasted malt (most frequently roasted barley) as whole malt, ground malt or malt flour. Malt extracts are excluded. (SITC 04820–0).

[1] Original data in thousand kilolitres.
[2] Production by establishments employing 5 or more persons.
[3] Twelve months beginning 1 April of year stated.

Remarque générale.
Malt grillé (en général obtenu à partir de l'orge), en grains, en semoule ou en farine, à l'exclusion des extraits de malt. (CTCI 04820–0).

[1] Données d'origine exprimées en milliers de kilolitres.
[2] Production des établissements occupant 5 personnes ou plus.
[3] Période de douze mois commençant le 1er avril de l'année indiquée.

[4] For use in alcoholic liquors only.
[5] Government production only.
[6] Sales of manufacturing industry's own products.
[7] Malt of barley and other cereals.
[8] 1985, data are confidential.
[9] Source: Industrial Statistics, Statistical Office of the European Communities, (Luxembourg).

[4] Pour l'emploi dans les boissons alcooliques seulement.
[5] Production de l'Etat seulement.
[6] Ventes des produits directement fabriqués par les industries manufacturières.
[7] Malt d'orge et d'autres céréales.
[8] Pour 1985, les données sont confidentielles.
[9] Source: Statistiques industrielles, Office statistique des Communautés européennes, (Luxembourg).

Beer – Bières

Unit : Thousand hectolitres

Unité : Milliers de hectolitres

Country or area	1976	1977	1978	1979	1980	1981	1982	1983	1984	1985	Pays ou zone
Africa	**29 871**	**31 501**	**34 903**	**35 312**	**40 837**	**61 684**	**64 882**	**64 391**	**46 991**	**46 261**	**Afrique**
Algeria	590	616	601	588	544	497	470	...	...	...	Algérie
Angola	1 250	* 1 300	* 1 300	* 1 350	...	...	...	...	...	...	Angola
Benin	145	200	* 210	* 220	* 225	...	...	...	...	...	Bénin
Botswana	81	48	37	98	# 368	471	591	648	667	...	Botswana
Burkina Faso	195	326	421	503	652	748	693	701	623	...	Burkina Faso
Burundi	480	525	525	526	662	687	684	644	798	817	Burundi
Cameroon	1 146	1 526	2 037	2 229	1 884	...	2 859	3 354	3 976	4 904	Cameroun
Central African Rep.	144	163	241	216	240	203	187	211	218	276	Rép. centrafricaine
Chad	154	152	159	161	163	...	...	...	...	...	Tchad
Congo	395	416	518	500	517	646	691	788	906	882	Congo
Côte d'Ivoire	809	972	655	772	1 598	1 348	1 285	1 400	1 245	...	Côte d'Ivoire
Egypt	302	388	423	360	420	460	* 500	* 500	...	...	Egypte
Ethiopia[1]	376	411	415	496	552	604	616	655	613	...	Ethiopie[1]
Gabon	374	462	519	543	594	628	696	733	770	850	Gabon
Ghana	775	718	496	451	445	527	339	310	452	429	Ghana
Kenya	1 658	1 952	2 214	2 127	2 324	2 283	2 337	2 175	2 303	2 633	Kenya
Liberia	108	125	152	180	161	* 156	123	117	111	97	Libéria
Madagascar	257	274	257	284	318	210	190	236	229	241	Madagascar
Malawi	458	479	553	591	651	729	657	889	622	658	Malawi
Mali	12	18	19	20	17	10	9	9	...	...	Mali
Mauritius	133	155	148	137	137	132	137	150	166	172	Maurice
Morocco[2]	316	* 469	* 411	* 420	453	402	376	383	393	411	Maroc[2]
Mozambique	* 655	* 650	* 665	573	538	511	450	445	373	...	Mozambique
Namibia*	130	130	130	130	130	...	...	...	...	...	Namibie*
Niger	45	54	65	79	83	86	90	100	...	...	Niger
Nigeria	3 160	3 150	4 694	5 004	3 994	8 185	8 376	7 516	7 355	8 052	Nigéria
Rwanda	355	425	498	386	505	599	629	555	576	631	Rwanda
Senegal	224	283	248	270	211	178	176	189	164	168	Sénégal
Seychelles	33	37	48	49	53	46	44	38	38	41	Seychelles
Sierra Leone	107	103	123	65	125	104	62	65	102	57	Sierra Leone
South Africa	5 389	5 608	5 951	6 023	7 508	9 203	11 440	11 586	* 12 400	12 284	Afrique du Sud
Sudan	96	88	100	68	42	11	...	...	...	...	Soudan
Togo	171	233	290	307	384	494	482	392	359	423	Togo
Tunisia	278	314	337	353	323	323	357	423	396	373	Tunisie
Uganda	233	221	228	10	12	7	10	* 10	...	* 54	Ouganda
United Rep. Tanzania	664	741	815	752	638	643	642	...	...	...	Rép.Unie de Tanzanie
Zaire	4 548	4 289	4 984	* 5 010	2 628	2 874	2 954	3 069	...	...	Zaïre
Zambia	* 2 725	* 2 750	* 2 750	* 2 775	...	22 006	22 760	21 861	* 4 169	* [3] 717	Zambie
Zimbabwe	* 900	730	666	686	812	963	1 074	1 235	920	1 100	Zimbabwe
America, North	**226 873**	**217 806**	**247 149**	**273 288**	**285 484**	**287 134**	**286 748**	**284 607**	**286 322**	**287 891**	**Amérique du Nord**
Barbados	50	61	75	61	71	77	73	74	58	55	Barbade
Canada	21 712	21 898	22 032	24 106	22 655	23 085	22 658	23 332	23 558	23 237	Canada
Costa Rica[4]	139	168	170	...	...	...	...	...	...	...	Costa Rica[4]
Cuba	2 169	2 199	2 338	2 307	2 365	2 243	2 421	2 582	2 607	2 736	Cuba
Dominican Republic	475	648	804	991	1 173	1 101	1 119	1 261	1 189	1 181	Rép. dominicaine
El Salvador	484	578	581	414	351	427	420	344	...	...	El Salvador
Grenada	6	12	14	14	14	12	13	12	12	14	Grenade
Guatemala	572	* 598	* 700	* 700	* 700	* 789	718	645	...	...	Guatemala
Honduras	233	309	374	* 380	433	471	397	469	511	...	Honduras
Jamaica	606	558	612	515	636	563	581	604	517	568	Jamaïque
Mexico	19 358	21 642	22 568	25 461	26 876	28 635	28 028	24 139	25 616	27 215	Mexique
Neth.Antil and Aruba	103	110	121	120	134	...	...	...	...	...	Antill.néer.et Aruba
Nicaragua	* 160	* 160	* 165	357	477	480	470	503	522	...	Nicaragua
Panama	433	355	433	559	670	694	713	708	734	796	Panama
Puerto Rico[5]	601	463	509	736	721	692	546	377	347	266	Porto Rico[5]
St.Kitts–Nevis	9	10	10	11	13	12	10	9	9	10	St–Kitts–Nevis
Trinidad and Tobago	231	238	198	230	251	239	258	282	279	274	Trinité–et–Tobago
United States	[5] 179 523	[4] 167 789	[4] 195 434	[4] 216 155	[4] 227 772	[4] 227 303	[4] 228 007	[4] 228 945	[4] 228 955	[4] 228 960	Etats–Unis
America, South	**66 772**	**49 584**	**59 900**	**59 161**	**58 021**	**59 645**	**56 818**	**57 016**	**57 379**	**56 891**	**Amérique du Sud**
Argentina	2 839	2 710	2 048	2 148	2 280	2 102	2 225	3 157	4 079	3 827	Argentine
Bolivia	957	1 058	1 113	814	1 162	1 141	901	717	701	...	Bolivie
Brazil	40 285	21 519	31 897	[6] 30 089	27 824	28 928	...	...	...	...	Brésil
Chile	1 083	1 361	1 404	1 591	1 808	1 904	1 797	1 760	1 781	1 892	Chili
Colombia	9 577	10 578	11 317	11 467	12 871	13 536	13 383	14 494	...	...	Colombie
Ecuador	1 370	* 1 677	1 957	* 2 010	632	728	769	626	...	...	Equateur
Guyana	139	178	162	157	117	157	130	79	* 71	...	Guyana
Paraguay	332	451	514	591	621	632	696	717	753	768	Paraguay
Peru	5 096	4 691	3 964	4 600	5 325	5 141	5 430	5 128	* 5 201	* 5 450	Pérou

For general note and footnotes, see end of table.

Voir la fin du tableau pour la remarque générale et les notes.

Beer (continued) – Bières (suite)

Unit : Thousand hectolitres | Unité : Milliers de hectolitres

Country or area	1976	1977	1978	1979	1980	1981	1982	1983	1984	1985	Pays ou zone
Suriname	94	111	114	124	128	142	147	151	150	142	Suriname
Uruguay	* 600	* 650	* 660	* 670	...	...	...	...	...	468	Uruguay
Venezuela*	4 400	4 600	4 750	4 900	...	...	...	...	...	...	Venezuela*
Asia	**56 252**	**64 281**	**68 788**	**75 843**	**73 582**	**76 763**	**82 342**	**88 001**	**91 093**	**100 299**	**Asie**
Burma	29	33	37	* 40	32	36	33	34	40	48	Birmanie
China[7]	* 3 000	3 500	4 000	5 000	6 880	9 100	11 730	16 300	22 400	31 000	Chine[7]
Cyprus	113	135	152	174	181	198	210	228	232	247	Chypre
Democratic Yemen	...	...	...	...	0	3	55	61	66	...	Yémen démocratique
Hong Kong* [8]	450	500	550	570	...	...	...	...	...	...	Hong–kong* [8]
India[9]	817	1 071	948	869	945	1 575	1 924	1 610	1 950	1 779	Inde[9]
Indonesia	470	513	522	608	708	778	901	942	847	* 474	Indonésie
Iran(Islamic Rep.of)	546	520	...	...	...	...	...	...	...	...	Iran(Rép.islamique)
Iraq*	190	200	200	200	...	...	...	...	...	...	Iraq*
Israel	351	353	389	407	394	439	402	408	415	511	Israël
Japan[10]	37 236	42 972	44 210	46 814	45 589	45 416	48 389	50 534	45 978	48 522	Japon[10]
Jordan	50	47	47	61	57	74	77	63	50	46	Jordanie
Korea, Republic of	1 897	2 430	4 443	6 406	5 790	5 992	6 268	7 096	7 626	7 919	Corée, République de
Lebanon*	130	115	130	130	...	...	...	...	...	...	Liban*
Malaysia	...	767	883	1 072	1 200	1 176	1 181	954	998	1 026	Malaisie
Mongolia	77	78	81	89	98	101	94	91	97	89	Mongolie
Nepal[11]	6	8	12	13	15	13	20	31	23	...	Népal[11]
Pakistan[5]	35	* 39	* 57	* 72	...	...	...	...	...	...	Pakistan[5]
Philippines	* 6 000	* 6 500	* 7 000	* 7 500	5 246	5 219	...	* 2 357	...	...	Philippines
Singapore*	480	500	500	525	...	...	...	...	...	...	Singapour*
Sri Lanka	30	71	44	71	74	52	...	...	...	...	Sri Lanka
Syrian Arab Republic	68	59	67	78	73	89	83	81	89	94	Rép. arabe syrienne
Thailand	750	1 031	1 084	1 563	1 241	1 054	1 217	1 456	1 639	1 052	Thaïlande
Turkey	1 709	1 931	2 002	2 094	2 533	2 932	3 036	3 226	2 622	1 965	Turquie
Viet Nam	880	905	893	942	600	590	558	527	915	866	Viet Nam
Europe	**357 813**	**356 333**	**356 772**	**368 911**	**368 964**	**370 553**	**373 845**	**377 125**	**363 677**	**364 923**	**Europe**
EEC	***232 191***	***229 363***	***227 634***	***231 956***	***231 048***	***232 517***	***232 264***	***234 630***	***224 955***	***224 781***	***CEE***
Belgium	14 544	13 819	13 395	13 681	14 291	13 811	14 629	14 224	14 311	13 931	Belgique
Denmark	8 328	8 450	8 056	8 307	9 168	9 747	10 122	11 038	8 671	8 286	Danemark
France	24 585	23 540	22 781	22 793	21 289	21 852	22 409	22 086	20 280	19 300	France
Germany, Fed. Rep.	91 391	90 017	87 298	87 659	89 321	90 857	90 916	91 382	87 309	87 895	Allemagne, Rép. féd.
Greece[7]	1 380	1 800	1 990	2 460	2 560	3 100	2 930	2 850	2 970	...	Grèce[7]
Ireland[4]	4 300	4 400	...	...	...	* 5 000	* 4 000	...	...	...	Irlande[4]
Italy	7 377	7 402	7 939	9 115	8 718	9 016	10 543	10 320	9 201	10 381	Italie
Luxembourg	789	703	682	713	757	779	751	651	634	738	Luxembourg
Netherlands[12]	13 862	13 993	14 650	15 387	15 683	16 639	16 180	17 330	17 050	17 530	Pays–Bas[12]
United Kingdom	65 635	65 239	66 418	67 416	64 836	61 716	59 784	* 60 324	60 104	...	Royaume–Uni
EFTA	***24 476***	***23 940***	***24 107***	***24 289***	***24 312***	***25 083***	***24 677***	***25 325***	***24 764***	***25 545***	***AELE***
Austria	7 783	7 778	7 720	7 771	7 698	8 181	8 313	8 403	8 440	8 836	Autriche
Finland	2 963	2 732	2 668	2 650	2 879	2 818	2 810	2 840	2 968	...	Finlande
Iceland	29	32	32	33	32	33	34	30	36	34	Islande
Norway	1 857	1 867	1 926	1 923	1 974	2 131	2 013	1 911	1 944	1 991	Norvège
Portugal	2 812	2 795	3 610	3 786	3 780	4 035	3 608	4 265	3 682	3 943	Portugal
Sweden	4 793	4 703	4 153	4 104	3 867	3 684	3 694	3 705	3 616	3 784	Suède
Switzerland[13]	4 239	4 033	3 998	4 022	4 082	4 201	4 205	4 171	4 078	4 076	Suisse[13]
East Europe	***75 234***	***76 059***	***77 111***	***80 512***	***81 173***	***81 384***	***84 203***	***83 839***	***81 706***	***82 145***	***Europe de l'est***
Bulgaria	4 695	4 927	5 165	5 303	5 254	5 128	5 477	5 505	5 764	5 838	Bulgarie
Czechoslovakia	22 629	22 442	22 058	23 601	23 393	23 934	24 912	24 957	23 768	22 354	Tchécoslovaquie
German Dem. Rep.	21 202	21 705	22 297	23 061	23 633	24 091	25 404	25 313	24 500	24 288	Rép. dém. allemande
Hungary	6 765	6 998	7 233	7 412	7 841	7 987	7 882	7 830	7 962	8 740	Hongrie
Poland	12 318	12 069	11 378	11 293	11 155	10 514	10 617	10 306	9 867	11 078	Pologne
Romania	7 625	7 918	8 980	9 842	9 897	9 730	9 911	9 928	9 845	9 847	Roumanie
Other Europe	***25 912***	***26 971***	***27 920***	***32 154***	***32 431***	***31 569***	***32 701***	***33 331***	***32 252***	***32 452***	***Autre Europe***
Malta*	100	110	115	115	...	...	...	...	...	...	Malte*
Spain	17 127	17 273	* 17 800	20 785	20 609	19 296	19 122	20 823	...	...	Espagne
Yugoslavia	8 685	9 588	10 005	11 254	11 712	12 163	13 469	12 398	10 925	10 656	Yougoslavie
USSR	**59 152**	**61 861**	**64 138**	**63 315**	**61 330**	**62 976**	**64 673**	**66 081**	**65 385**	**65 721**	**URSS**
Byelorussian SSR	*2 372*	*2 803*	*2 979*	*3 083*	*3 073*	*3 095*	*3 206*	*3 241*	*3 296*	*3 360*	*RSS de Biélorussie*
Ukrainian SSR	*13 274*	*13 609*	*14 090*	*13 878*	*13 314*	*13 804*	*14 256*	*14 627*	*14 460*	*14 756*	*RSS d'Ukraine*

For general note and footnotes, see end of table.

Voir la fin du tableau pour la remarque générale et les notes.

Unit : Thousand hectolitres

Unité : Milliers de hectolitres

Country or area	1976	1977	1978	1979	1980	1981	1982	1983	1984	1985	Pays ou zone
Oceania	**23 643**	**24 188**	**24 867**	**24 410**	**24 848**	**24 469**	**24 287**	**24 204**	**23 380**	**23 360**	**Océanie**
Australia[5]	19 158	19 554	20 045	19 860	20 232	19 868	19 677	19 724	18 729	18 610	Australie[5]
Fiji	161	159	162	178	180	182	195	191	185	178	Fidji
French Polynesia	* 95	* 100	* 95	* 100	* 100	82	91	96	94	95	Polynésie française
New Caledonia	13	16	21	26	35	42	47	...	...	...	Nouvelle–Calédonie
New Zealand[13]	3 804	3 903	4 059	3 753	3 783	3 826	3 755	3 679	3 839	3 863	Nouvelle–Zélande[13]
Papua New Guinea	412	456	485	493	518	469	522	461	* 474	* 550	Papouasie–Nvl–Guinée
Total	**820 376**	**805 554**	**856 517**	**900 240**	**913 067**	**943 225**	**953 595**	**961 426**	**934 226**	**945 346**	**Total**

General note.
Beer made from malt (including ale, stout, porter). (SITC 11230–0).

1 Twelve months ending 10 September of year stated.
2 Including some carbonated drinks.
3 Incomplete coverage.
4 Twelve months ending 30 September of year stated.
5 Twelve months ending 30 June of year stated.
6 Production by establishments employing 5 or more persons.
7 Original data in metric tons.
8 Beginning 1980, data are confidential.
9 Production by large and medium scale establishments only.
10 Twelve months beginning 1 April of year stated.
11 Twelve months beginning 16 July of year stated.
12 Industrial sales.
13 Sales by breweries.

Remarque générale.
Bières obtenues à partir du malt (y compris l'ale, le stout et le porter). (CTCI 11230–0).

1 Période de douze mois finissant le 10 septembre de l'année indiquée.
2 Y compris certaines boissons gazeuses.
3 Couverture incomplète.
4 Période de douze mois finissant le 30 septembre de l'année indiquée.
5 Période de douze mois finissant le 30 juin de l'année indiquée.
6 Production des établissements occupant 5 personnes ou plus.
7 Données d'origine exprimées en tonnes.
8 A partir de 1980, les données sont confidentielles.
9 Production des grandes et moyennes entreprises seulement.
10 Période de douze mois commençant le 1er avril de l'année indiquée.
11 Période de douze mois commençant le 16 juillet de l'année indiquée.
12 Ventes industrielles.
13 Ventes des brasseries.

Mineral waters – Eaux minérales

Unit : Thousand hectolitres — Unité : Milliers de hectolitres

Country or area	1976	1977	1978	1979	1980	1981	1982	1983	1984	1985	Pays ou zone
Africa	**1 941**	**2 173**	**2 348**	**2 613**	**2 890**	**3 155**	**3 110**	**2 967**	**3 275**	**3 330**	**Afrique**
Algeria	696	771	827	864	950	1 026	1 065	...	...	...	Algérie
Central African Rep.	3	3	3	4	4	4	4	4	5	7	Rép. centrafricaine
Ethiopia[1]	172	144	145	139	160	173	177	203	201	...	Ethiopie[1]
Kenya	797	994	1 080	1 280	1 430	1 508	1 378	1 188	1 420	1 334	Kenya
Libyan Arab Jamah.	106	78	94	100	103	148	155	106	...	...	Jamah.arabe libyenne
Tunisia	167	183	199	226	243	296	331	332	312	383	Tunisie
America, North	**1 955**	**2 099**	**2 475**	**2 812**	**2 978**	**3 447**	**3 523**	**3 518**	**3 262**	**3 455**	**Amérique du Nord**
Canada[2]	106	112	...	...	196	...	...	...	...	...	Canada[2]
Cuba	399	394	510	469	461	798	802	890	886	1 050	Cuba
Dominican Republic	24	23	23	21	27	18	22	21	18	13	Rép. dominicaine
Mexico	1 426	1 570	1 804	2 184	2 294	2 493	2 561	2 469	2 220	2 254	Mexique
America, South	**3 743**	**5 031**	**4 645**	**5 392**	**6 193**	**6 414**	**6 581**	**6 893**	**6 959**	**7 698**	**Amérique du Sud**
Bolivia	2	2	1	2	11	14	9	5	1	2	Bolivie
Brazil	3 191	4 176	3 891	[3] 4 515	5 196	5 416	5 287	5 694	5 625	...	Brésil
Colombia	123	237	123	133	178	170	165	168	...	...	Colombie
Ecuador	351	523	538	...	...	716	1 013	931	...	...	Equateur
Paraguay	76	93	92	106	87	98	107	95	103	104	Paraguay
Asia	**855**	**1 014**	**1 110**	**1 277**	**1 463**	**1 281**	**1 479**	**1 458**	**1 542**	**1 473**	**Asie**
Democratic Yemen[4]	...	...	...	...	40	125	135	150	135	140	Yémen démocratique[4]
Indonesia	...	...	...	...	...	...	...	64	143	* 150	Indonésie
Japan	432	460	596	680	780	850	870	890	910	830	Japon
Philippines[2]	5	5	...	...	...	...	...	...	...	...	Philippines[2]
Sri Lanka[5]	203	320	266	334	445	* 108	...	...	...	...	Sri Lanka[5]
Turkey	76	75	73	73	...	...	...	...	...	...	Turquie
Europe	**104 925**	**107 824**	**108 900**	**109 656**	**116 241**	**111 630**	**122 630**	**130 741**	**127 003**	**134 212**	**Europe**
EEC	***57 645***	***57 115***	***59 371***	***63 041***	***63 198***	***65 782***	***74 664***	***79 021***	***78 976***	***82 626***	***CEE***
Belgium	3 211	3 029	3 163	3 383	3 418	4 894	6 888	7 098	6 975	7 050	Belgique
Denmark	282	299	325	326	350	347	366	372	315	334	Danemark
France[6]	29 500	28 280	29 460	30 760	29 800	29 445	32 585	33 791	34 220	35 807	France[6]
Germany, Fed. Rep.	24 082	24 757	25 613	28 052	29 210	30 696	34 355	37 334	36 976	39 070	Allemagne, Rép. féd.
Greece* [7]	570	750	810	520	420	400	470	426	490	...	Grèce* [7]
EFTA	***6 301***	***7 160***	***8 891***	***9 961***	***10 265***	***10 719***	***11 704***	***12 555***	***10 914***	***13 018***	***AELE***
Austria	224	558	* 2 098	2 896	2 848	3 044	3 571	4 122	2 375	3 945	Autriche
Finland	147	472	506	436	420	372	380	367	404	...	Finlande
Norway[5]	2 072	2 305	2 344	2 415	2 507	2 303	2 444	2 526	2 665	2 986	Norvège[5]
Portugal	1 263	1 333	1 435	1 571	1 713	2 078	2 172	2 202	2 160	2 129	Portugal
Sweden	538	528	549	571	618	610	625	629	616	651	Suède
Switzerland[6]	2 057	1 964	1 959	2 072	2 159	2 312	2 512	2 709	2 694	2 885	Suisse[6]
East Europe	***32 592***	***34 383***	***31 059***	***26 716***	***31 513***	***24 004***	***24 472***	***26 577***	***24 197***	***25 447***	***Europe de l'est***
Czechoslovakia	1 856	2 019	2 073	2 093	2 107	2 338	2 783	2 986	3 068	2 890	Tchécoslovaquie
German Dem. Rep.	1 181	1 237	1 320	1 363	1 430	1 696	2 628	2 419	2 131	2 266	Rép. dém. allemande
Hungary	1 160	1 100	960	975	877	861	788	724	668	626	Hongrie
Poland	28 395	30 027	26 706	22 285	27 099	19 109	18 273	20 448	18 330	19 665	Pologne
Other Europe	***8 387***	***9 166***	***9 579***	***9 938***	***11 265***	***11 125***	***11 790***	***12 588***	***12 916***	***13 121***	***Autre Europe***
Malta	7	58	60	19	16	14	5	0	0	...	Malte
Spain	4 324	...	...	4 876	5 724	5 648	5 886	6 084	...	...	Espagne
Yugoslavia	4 056	4 514	4 663	5 043	5 525	5 463	5 899	6 504	6 488	6 426	Yougoslavie
Total	**113 419**	**118 141**	**119 478**	**121 751**	**129 765**	**125 927**	**137 323**	**145 578**	**142 040**	**150 169**	**Total**

General note.
Natural and artificial spa waters, aerated waters. Ordinary natural waters, sweetened and flavoured waters are excluded. (SITC 11101–1).

[1] Twelve months ending 10 September of year stated.
[2] Shipments.

Remarque générale.
Eaux minérales naturelles et artificielles, eaux gazeuses, à l'exclusion des eaux naturelles ordinaires et des eaux sucrées ou aromatisées. (CTCI 11101–1).

[1] Période de douze mois finissant le 10 septembre de l'année indiquée.
[2] Expéditions.

[3] Production by establishments employing 5 or more persons.
[4] Aerated water only.
[5] Including soft drinks.
[6] Sales.
[7] Original data in metric tons.

[3] Production des établissements occupant 5 personnes ou plus.
[4] Eaux gazeuses seulement.
[5] Y compris les boissons non alcooliques.
[6] Ventes.
[7] Données d'origine exprimées en tonnes.

Soft drinks – Boissons non alcooliques

Unit : Thousand hectolitres

Unité : Milliers de hectolitres

Country or area	1976	1977	1978	1979	1980	1981	1982	1983	1984	1985	Pays ou zone
Africa	**16 505**	**18 454**	**18 871**	**19 616**	**23 136**	**26 978**	**31 044**	**31 845**	**33 257**	**35 398**	**Afrique**
Algeria	499	1 271	1 294	1 508	1 519	815	751	938	* 1 310	* 1 300	Algérie
Benin	75	100	* 120	* 130	* 150	...	...	...	...	...	Bénin
Botswana	...	0	0	0	57	73	93	99	98	...	Botswana
Burkina Faso	83	98	98	123	136	146	143	253	* 118	...	Burkina Faso
Burundi	35	48	78	96	109	115	122	140	144	127	Burundi
Cameroon	430	626	708	750	525	...	...	1 033	1 244	1 397	Cameroun
Cape Verde	1	1	1	* 1	1	* 1	1	1	2	2	Cap–Vert
Central African Rep.	31	40	33	33	40	50	63	57	46	50	Rép. centrafricaine
Chad	24	* 25	* 25	...	...	...	...	...	...	...	Tchad
Congo	154	156	163	172	188	223	247	278	279	* 299	Congo
Côte d'Ivoire	421	590	655	772	943	748	426	564	400	...	Côte d'Ivoire
Ethiopia[1]	326	325	328	264	711	720	625	650	719	...	Ethiopie[1]
Gabon	126	168	183	189	170	199	237	298	369	435	Gabon
Ghana[2]	233	294	158	131	93	129	71	30	...	...	Ghana[2]
Kenya	1 054	1 046	1 228	1 379	1 850	2 825	2 746	2 720	3 256	...	Kenya
Liberia	80	111	104	122	169	86	102	101	121	119	Libéria
Libyan Arab Jamah.	718	1 185	729	825	714	738	694	736	...	...	Jamah.arabe libyenne
Mali	27	29	34	46	20	15	* 23	22	...	...	Mali
Mauritius	465	567	605	534	474	404	308	313	273	266	Maurice
Mozambique[2]	...	...	...	246	288	226	184	128	77	...	Mozambique[2]
Niger	30	39	48	61	71	70	80	108	* 110	...	Niger
Nigeria[2]	1 822	1 910	2 091	1 586	3 233	5 151	8 376	7 516	7 355	8 052	Nigéria[2]
Senegal	290	362	412	472	353	329	287	258	238	266	Sénégal
Seychelles	14	19	23	28	30	30	32	34	32	35	Seychelles
Sierra Leone	...	...	...	...	0	115	101	172	271	...	Sierra Leone
South Africa[2]	6 924	6 682	6 767	7 280	8 432	9 507	10 824	11 677	* 12 395	12 809	Afrique du Sud[2]
Togo	39	52	59	73	87	90	90	76	68	...	Togo
Tunisia	571	784	860	1 183	1 218	1 354	1 604	...	...	...	Tunisie
Uganda	59	46	53	28	25	16	6	...	...	...	Ouganda
United Rep. Tanzania	353	...	...	...	...	...	...	...	...	...	Rép.Unie de Tanzanie
Zaire	567	573	716	...	593	783	807	820	...	...	Zaïre
Zambia	565	515	531	433	559	563	430	495	267	317	Zambie
America, North	**52 494**	**56 196**	**64 476**	**73 999**	**75 799**	**76 276**	**79 879**	**77 206**	**75 680**	**82 733**	**Amérique du Nord**
Antigua and Barbuda	...	...	...	...	...	20	24	36	36	...	Antigua–et–Barbuda
Barbados	169	177	166	158	158	176	168	162	155	146	Barbade
Canada[3]	14 694	14 467	16 014	17 014	16 172	16 907	...	...	...	...	Canada[3]
Cuba	1 501	1 062	1 250	1 339	1 867	1 308	2 056	2 203	2 128	2 108	Cuba
Dominican Republic	742	792	796	716	850	614	740	858	653	693	Rép. dominicaine
El Salvador[2]	823	1 131	1 360	2 328	1 881	1 816	1 227	1 065	...	...	El Salvador[2]
Honduras	...	...	1 692	1 827	1 695	# 662	782	694	748	614	Honduras
Jamaica	483	550	501	444	470	385	373	393	371	372	Jamaïque
Mexico	30 030	34 125	40 721	48 227	50 493	52 248	54 720	51 859	49 324	55 942	Mexique
Nicaragua	...	...	...	857	1 123	1 000	1 150	815	932	...	Nicaragua
Panama	812	853	882	1 006	1 000	1 079	987	975	...	...	Panama
St.Kitts–Nevis	21	21	23	27	31	31	29	30	30	30	St–Kitts–Nevis
America, South	**56 385**	**52 377**	**60 545**	**90 356**	**59 282**	**56 605**	**64 430**	**66 248**	**67 254**	**68 602**	**Amérique du Sud**
Bolivia	790	755	796	989	1 100	970	542	753	784	...	Bolivie
Brazil	36 959	31 543	39 421	[4] 66 603	34 505	30 781	...	...	...	...	Brésil
Chile	...	...	...	3 877	4 050	4 606	* 3 649	3 345	3 248	3 524	Chili
Colombia	11 249	12 358	12 424	15 097	15 752	15 665	16 019	17 120	...	...	Colombie
Ecuador	2 134	2 422	2 323	...	...	2 837	1 820	2 871	...	...	Equateur
Paraguay	354	542	965	1 111	1 161	1 457	1 602	1 221	1 373	1 387	Paraguay
Suriname	...	...	...	300	291	289	312	304	267	302	Suriname
Asia	**51 976**	**59 984**	**68 519**	**69 936**	**66 383**	**64 226**	**65 058**	**71 760**	**73 883**	**75 570**	**Asie**
Afghanistan[5]	...	...	...	3 700	4 700	4 100	5 300	7 000	7 300	7 600	Afghanistan[5]
Cyprus	179	259	294	286	261	264	289	307	316	355	Chypre
Hong Kong	915	1 122	1 276	1 245	1 934	2 324	2 347	3 336	2 169	* 2 200	Hong–kong
India[6 7]	1 340	1 036	1 250	1 191	...	...	...	...	...	...	Inde[6 7]
Indonesia	801	688	758	736	[8] 1 214	[8] 1 301	[8] 1 669	[8] 2 022	[8] 2 305	...	Indonésie
Iran(Islamic Rep.of)[9]	1 092	5 895	6 836	6 715	6 680	6 573	5 936	...	...	...	Iran(Rép.islamique)[9]
Japan[2]	27 945	31 740	34 078	33 620	28 550	26 680	26 410	27 820	28 940	29 440	Japon[2]
Korea, Republic of	1 893	3 267	4 857	5 755	5 229	5 368	6 254	6 556	7 499	7 915	Corée, République de
Malaysia[2 10]	1 230	1 634	1 986	2 406	2 537	2 238	1 784	1 802	1 596	1 775	Malaisie[2 10]
Philippines[3]	11 013	7 540	...	...	...	...	...	...	...	...	Philippines[3]
Singapore	1 259	1 385	1 713	1 695	1 751	1 896	1 820	1 934	1 597	1 623	Singapour
Thailand	906	...	...	...	...	...	...	...	...	...	Thaïlande

For general note and footnotes, see end of table.

Voir la fin du tableau pour la remarque générale et les notes.

Unit : Thousand hectolitres

Unité : Milliers de hectolitres

Country or area	1976	1977	1978	1979	1980	1981	1982	1983	1984	1985	Pays ou zone
Turkey	1 788	2 113	2 115	2 006	...	...	1 568	1 379	1 996	...	Turquie
Viet Nam	186	263	330	398	...	...	...	...	...	...	Viet Nam
Europe	**177 717**	**175 037**	**181 781**	**198 420**	**192 933**	**194 634**	**197 715**	**197 844**	**196 419**	**198 846**	**Europe**
EEC	***125 058***	***117 645***	***122 540***	***131 116***	***128 874***	***129 964***	***133 437***	***130 775***	***128 908***	***130 055***	***CEE***
Belgium	5 927	5 385	5 374	5 463	5 533	6 528	8 346	8 335	8 079	8 272	Belgique
Denmark	2 305	2 538	2 702	2 551	2 449	2 340	2 508	2 517	2 217	2 499	Danemark
France[11]	13 790	12 070	12 700	12 790	12 540	12 500	13 175	13 755	...	...	France[11]
Germany, Fed. Rep.	43 966	41 426	43 478	45 862	46 434	47 463	49 464	46 458	44 143	46 442	Allemagne, Rép. féd.
Greece[12]	2 560	3 120	3 410	3 370	3 370	3 073	3 014	3 020	3 297	...	Grèce[12]
Netherlands[2]	9 690	9 214	9 165	9 607	9 350	9 760	9 630	9 690	9 820	9 570	Pays–Bas[2]
United Kingdom[13]	46 820	43 892	45 711	51 473	49 198	48 300	47 300	47 000	48 200	* 46 800	Royaume–Uni[13]
EFTA	***11 913***	***11 870***	***11 847***	***12 415***	***12 852***	***13 390***	***13 737***	***14 242***	***13 844***	***14 810***	***AELE***
Austria	2 684	2 766	2 816	3 145	3 157	3 219	3 646	3 928	3 630	4 314	Autriche
Finland	1 769	1 658	1 371	1 446	1 574	1 896	1 623	1 627	1 693	...	Finlande
Iceland	137	154	176	175	179	180	183	167	166	187	Islande
Portugal	1 905	2 085	2 028	1 925	2 214	2 207	2 175	2 172	2 105	1 828	Portugal
Sweden	2 422	2 257	2 414	2 516	2 451	2 371	2 469	2 595	2 453	2 799	Suède
Switzerland[14]	2 996	2 950	3 042	3 208	3 277	3 517	3 641	3 753	3 797	4 007	Suisse[14]
East Europe	***23 660***	***24 181***	***24 897***	***25 117***	***25 223***	***26 468***	***26 841***	***28 280***	***27 355***	***27 035***	***Europe de l'est***
Bulgaria	3 254	3 602	3 592	3 601	3 736	3 816	4 051	5 337	5 504	5 695	Bulgarie
Czechoslovakia	7 995	7 853	7 755	7 656	7 511	7 759	7 886	7 857	7 324	6 474	Tchécoslovaquie
German Dem. Rep.	10 870	10 932	11 594	11 661	11 651	12 272	12 170	12 392	11 922	12 143	Rép. dém. allemande
Hungary	1 541	1 794	1 956	2 199	2 325	2 621	2 734	2 694	2 605	2 723	Hongrie
Other Europe	***17 086***	***21 341***	***22 497***	***29 772***	***25 984***	***24 812***	***23 700***	***24 547***	***26 312***	***26 946***	***Autre Europe***
Malta	181	138	128	133	182	259	625	331	229	...	Malte
Spain	14 055	...	...	25 574	21 623	20 636	18 798	20 046	...	...	Espagne
Yugoslavia[2]	2 850	2 771	3 403	4 065	4 179	3 917	4 277	4 170	3 915	3 842	Yougoslavie[2]
USSR	**30 282**	**32 561**	**32 767**	**35 655**	**35 093**	**37 534**	**34 850**	**35 734**	**35 715**	**38 334**	**URSS**
Byelorussian SSR	*1 161*	*1 209*	*1 293*	*1 450*	*1 420*	*1 487*	*1 505*	*1 556*	*1 516*	*1 732*	*RSS de Biélorussie*
Ukrainian SSR	*7 557*	*8 053*	*8 474*	*9 484*	*9 059*	*9 848*	*9 008*	*9 372*	*9 293*	*9 717*	*RSS d'Ukraine*
Oceania	**11 096**	**10 509**	**11 074**	**10 913**	**10 387**	**11 416**	**11 211**	**11 205**	**14 522**	**14 929**	**Océanie**
Australia[2 15]	* 10 103	9 482	9 987	9 858	9 389	10 313	10 073	10 094	13 329	13 729	Australie[2 15]
Fiji	36	46	52	55	43	42	36	37	35	38	Fidji
New Caledonia	28	30	* 29	* 32	* 32	...	...	...	...	...	Nouvelle–Calédonie
New Zealand[2]	929	951	1 006	968	923	1 028	1 068	1 039	1 122	1 125	Nouvelle–Zélande[2]
Total	**396 454**	**405 119**	**438 033**	**498 895**	**463 013**	**467 670**	**484 187**	**491 842**	**496 730**	**514 413**	**Total**

General note.
Sweetened and flavoured spa waters (natural or artificial), lemonade, orangeade etc. (SITC 11102–0).

1 Twelve months ending 10 September of year stated.
2 Including mineral waters.
3 Shipments.
4 Production by establishments employing 5 or more persons.
5 Twelve months beginning 21 March of year stated.
6 Production by large and medium scale establishments only.
7 Original data in million bottles converted on the basis of 200 ml per bottle.
8 Including fruit juice.
9 Production by establishments employing 10 or more persons.
10 Data refer to Peninsular Malaysia only.
11 Including syrups.
12 Original data in metric tons.
13 Including fruit juices and mineral waters. Excluding spa water.
14 Sales.
15 Twelve months ending 30 June of year stated.

Remarque générale.
Eaux minérales sucrées ou aromatisées, naturelles et artificielles, limonades, orangeades etc. (CTCI 11102–0).

1 Période de douze mois finissant le 10 septembre de l'année indiquée.
2 Y compris les eaux minérales.
3 Expéditions.
4 Production des établissements occupant 5 personnes ou plus.
5 Période de douze mois commençant le 21 mars de l'année indiquée.
6 Production des grandes et moyennes entreprises seulement.
7 Données d'origine exprimées en millions de bouteilles converties sur la base de 200 ml par boutei
8 Y compris les jus de fruits.
9 Production des établissements occupant 10 personnes ou plus.
10 Données se rapportant à la Malaisie péninsulaire seulement.
11 Y compris les sirops.
12 Données d'origine exprimées en tonnes.
13 Y compris les jus de fruits et les eaux minérales. Non compris les eaux minérales naturelles.
14 Ventes.
15 Période de douze mois finissant le 30 juin de l'année indiquée.

ISIC–BASED CODE
3140–01

Tobacco, prepared leaf – Feuilles de tabac, traitées

CODE BASE CITI
3140–01

Unit : Thousand metric tons

Unité : Milliers de tonnes métriques

Country or area	1976	1977	1978	1979	1980	1981	1982	1983	1984	1985	Pays ou zone
Africa	**5**	**5**	**4**	**3**	**4**	**3**	**2**	**1**	**1**	**1**	**Afrique**
Uganda	...	...	...	3	4	[1] 3	[1] 2	[1] 1	* [1] 1	* [1] 1	Ouganda
America, North	**97**	**124**	**140**	**107**	**122**	**140**	**125**	**156**	**131**	**123**	**Amérique du Nord**
Canada	81	104	116	79	108	101	62	110	91	79	Canada
Cuba	...	...	...	...	14	39	63	46	40	44	Cuba
America, South	**570**	**633**	**663**	**701**	**676**	**532**	**686**	**827**	**738**	**714**	**Amérique du Sud**
Brazil	177	240	270	[2] 308	283	223	* [1] 321	* [1] 322	* [1] 345	* [1] 321	Brésil
Colombia	...	...	...	...	...	309	365	505	...	...	Colombie
Asia	**506**	**554**	**547**	**578**	**516**	**485**	**431**	**436**	**493**	**439**	**Asie**
Burma[3]	46	61	58	51	53	55	* 43	* 48	* 52	* 60	Birmanie[3]
Indonesia	18	22	15	24	26	16	15	16	17	...	Indonésie
Japan	163	174	171	155	148	143	133	133	* 135	* 105	Japon
Malaysia	...	7	9	39	10	7	10	10	7	9	Malaisie
Philippines	59	50	57	51	42	39	46	* 48	* 55	* 50	Philippines
Thailand	43	43	44	47	37	52	47	40	39	...	Thaïlande
Turkey	160	197	193	211	200	173	137	141	188	156	Turquie
Europe	**242**	**248**	**227**	**241**	**243**	**205**	**255**	**267**	**256**	**272**	**Europe**
EEC	***138***	***144***	***134***	***144***	***150***	***117***	***152***	***154***	***133***	***141***	***CEE***
Belgium	39	40	38	39	39	40	42	42	40	40	Belgique
Greece	99	104	96	105	111	77	110	112	93	...	Grèce
East Europe	***21***	***23***	***25***	***25***	***23***	***21***	***26***	***26***	***22***	***23***	***Europe de l'est***
Czechoslovakia	5	5	5	5	5	5	5	6	5	5	Tchécoslovaquie
Hungary	16	18	20	20	18	16	21	20	17	18	Hongrie
Other Europe	***83***	***81***	***68***	***72***	***70***	***67***	***77***	***87***	***101***	***108***	***Autre Europe***
Spain	...	...	...	6	8	7	7	12	36	35	Espagne
Yugoslavia	77	75	65	66	62	60	70	75	65	73	Yougoslavie
Total	**1 420**	**1 563**	**1 581**	**1 630**	**1 561**	**1 365**	**1 499**	**1 687**	**1 619**	**1 548**	**Total**

General note.
Tobacco leaves cured, stripped and cut to shape in industrial establishments. (SITC 12100–3).

[1] Source: U. S. Department of Agriculture , (Washington, D. C.).
[2] Production by establishments employing 5 or more persons.
[3] Twelve months ending 30 September of year stated.

Remarque générale.
Feuilles de tabac séchées ou fermentées, écotées et découpées à la forme voulue dans des établissements industriels. (CTCI 12100–3).

[1] Source: U.S. Department of Agriculture, (Washington, D.C.).
[2] Production des établissements occupant 5 personnes ou plus.
[3] Période de douze mois finissant le 30 septembre de l'année indiquée.

Unit : Million units

Unité : En million

Country or area	1976	1977	1978	1979	1980	1981	1982	1983	1984	1985	Pays ou zone
Africa	**152**	**156**	**168**	**161**	**193**	**192**	**177**	**145**	**126**	**139**	**Afrique**
Algeria[1]	4	4	5	7	6	9	3	...	...	...	Algérie[1]
Central African Rep.	...	10	20	30	41	48	38	33	34	33	Rép. centrafricaine
Côte d'Ivoire	* 80	94	94	77	97	96	99	69	56	...	Côte d'Ivoire
Egypt	1	1	1	1	1	1	* 1	* 1	* 1	* 1	Egypte
South Africa[1]	46	45	47	45	47	37	35	34	27	24	Afrique du Sud[1]
Tunisia	1	2	1	1	1	1	1	1	1	1	Tunisie
America, North	**7 771**	**6 817**	**6 617**	**6 057**	**5 661**	**4 903**	**4 722**	**4 499**	**4 368**	**4 098**	**Amérique du Nord**
Canada	560	460	448	431	449	434	404	342	379	302	Canada
Cuba	361	353	354	295	167	230	358	333	302	366	Cuba
Dominican Republic	8	10	9	11	13	21	21	24	25	26	Rép. dominicaine
Guatemala	125	* 130	* 135	* 140	* 125	# 230	* 223	* 217	...	...	Guatemala
Jamaica	16	16	17	31	25	26	21	19	22	21	Jamaïque
United States[2]	6 701	5 848	5 654	5 149	4 882	3 962	3 695	3 564	3 401	3 127	Etats–Unis[2]
America, South	**402**	**312**	**292**	**386**	**377**	**363**	**353**	**349**	**389**	**384**	**Amérique du Sud**
Argentina[1]	40	48	44	57	53	54	41	50	47	34	Argentine[1]
Bolivia	6	7	* 7	6	6	6	* 4	* 4	...	...	Bolivie
Brazil	128	90	73	[3] 138	147	...	...	...	...	...	Brésil
Chile	1	1	1	1	0	0	0	0	0	0	Chili
Colombia	128	...	...	...	...	63	59	37	...	...	Colombie
Paraguay	10	10	6	6	7	7	8	8	8	8	Paraguay
Peru*	1	1	1	1	...	...	...	...	...	...	Pérou*
Venezuela	88	83	88	105	...	...	...	...	...	...	Venezuela
Asia	**256**	**368**	**278**	**237**	**213**	**202**	**192**	**179**	**189**	**179**	**Asie**
Burma[4]	3	3	3	3	3	3	3	3	3	3	Birmanie[4]
Indonesia	26	30	# 4	4	4	4	3	3	3	...	Indonésie
Iran(Islamic Rep.of)	* 6	6	...	...	...	...	...	...	...	...	Iran(Rép.islamique)
Israel[1]	1	1	1	1	1	2	1	1	1	1	Israël[1]
Japan[5]	34	148	101	49	22	17	17	12	...	...	Japon[5]
Malaysia[1 6]	116	110	109	111	93	79	68	63	* 80	...	Malaisie[1 6]
Philippines[2]	22	* 25	* 30	* 35	* 70	* 70	* 70	* 70	* 70	* 70	Philippines[2]
Singapore	10	9	* 10	* 10	* 10	17	21	...	...	...	Singapour
Sri Lanka	34	32	11	* 15	2	1	0	* 1	* 1	1	Sri Lanka
Turkey	4	4	3	3	2	3	3	1	...	1	Turquie
Europe	**11 490**	**11 313**	**10 814**	**9 584**	**9 713**	**9 079**	**8 396**	**7 799**	**7 903**	**7 643**	**Europe**
EEC	***8 430***	***8 373***	***8 134***	***7 170***	***7 342***	***6 935***	***6 306***	***5 841***	***5 805***	***5 785***	***CEE***
Belgium[7]	714	676	693	214	649	601	579	483	469	444	Belgique[7]
Denmark	889	890	840	811	778	716	653	625	610	604	Danemark
France	1 237	1 164	1 081	989	977	948	906	765	779	788	France
Germany, Fed. Rep.	2 417	2 521	2 370	2 100	2 051	1 997	1 701	1 656	1 635	1 551	Allemagne, Rép. féd.
Greece[1]	* 6	1	1	1	1	1	0	...	...	...	Grèce[1]
Italy[1]	131	173	179	184	132	136	120	129	112	113	Italie[1]
Netherlands	2 430	2 325	2 287	2 149	2 028	1 918	1 788	1 631	1 631	1 731	Pays–Bas
United Kingdom[1 8]	606	623	683	722	726	618	559	552	569	553	Royaume–Uni[1 8]
EFTA	***934***	***852***	***758***	***686***	***697***	***678***	***634***	***538***	***548***	***530***	***AELE***
Austria	52	58	61	47	55	53	48	41	34	44	Autriche
Finland	123	91	74	73	64	65	56	56	57	...	Finlande
Portugal[1]	1	1	1	1	1	1	2	2	4	4	Portugal[1]
Sweden	265	219	181	176	170	165	155	139	162	152	Suède
Switzerland	493	483	441	389	407	394	373	300	291	291	Suisse
East Europe	***1 083***	***1 024***	***902***	***858***	***805***	***644***	***619***	***603***	***580***	***530***	***Europe de l'est***
Albania[1]	4	...	...	...	...	...	...	...	...	...	Albanie[1]
Czechoslovakia	70	62	58	59	57	54	48	34	32	31	Tchécoslovaquie
German Dem. Rep.	973	917	799	760	706	554	532	530	521	477	Rép. dém. allemande
Hungary	27	29	29	23	26	21	22	18	16	16	Hongrie
Poland	9	12	12	12	12	11	13	17	7	2	Pologne
Other Europe	***1 043***	***1 064***	***1 020***	***870***	***869***	***822***	***837***	***817***	***970***	***799***	***Autre Europe***
Spain	976	990	970	775	809	757	772	752	950	...	Espagne

For general note and footnotes, see end of table.

Voir la fin du tableau pour la remarque générale et les notes.

Unit : Million units

Unité : En million

Country or area	1976	1977	1978	1979	1980	1981	1982	1983	1984	1985	Pays ou zone
Yugoslavia....................	67	74	50	95	* 60	65	* 65	* 65	20	40	Yougoslavie
Total.............................	**20 071**	**18 965**	**18 169**	**16 425**	**16 157**	**14 739**	**13 840**	**12 971**	**12 976**	**12 444**	**Total**

General note.
Cigars of all sizes, cigarillos and cheroots. (SITC 12210-0).

[1] Original data in units of weight. Computed on the basis of 250000 cigars per ton.
[2] Twelve months ending 30 June of year stated.
[3] Production by establishments employing 5 or more persons.
[4] Twelve months ending 31 March of year stated.
[5] Twelve months beginning 1 April of year stated.
[6] Data refer to Peninsular Malaysia only.
[7] Excluding cigarillos.
[8] Sales by manufacturers employing 25 or more persons.

Remarque générale.
Cigares de toutes dimensions, cigarillos et cigares à bouts coupés (cheroots). (CTCI 12210-0).

[1] Données d'origine exprimées en poids. Calcul sur la base de 250 000 cigares par tonne.
[2] Période de douze mois finissant le 30 juin de l'année indiquée.
[3] Production des établissements occupant 5 personnes ou plus.
[4] Période de douze mois finissant le 31 mars de l'année indiquée.
[5] Période de douze mois commençant le 1er avril de l'année indiquée.
[6] Données se rapportant à la Malaisie péninsulaire seulement.
[7] Non compris les cigarillos.
[8] Ventes des fabricants employant 25 personnes ou plus.

Unit : Million units

Unité : En million

Country or area	1976	1977	1978	1979	1980	1981	1982	1983	1984	1985	Pays ou zone
Africa	**126 757**	**129 596**	**135 312**	**141 089**	**149 500**	**147 651**	**156 020**	**156 391**	**172 703**	**174 776**	**Afrique**
Algeria[1]	10 217	* 11 016	* 13 578	* 14 678	* 15 444	* 16 178	17 542	17 500	18 000	18 500	Algérie[1]
Angola* [2]	2 400	2 300	2 300	2 400	2 400	2 400	2 400	2 400	2 400	2 400	Angola* [2]
Burkina Faso	460	561	570	692	957	565	708	700	670	...	Burkina Faso
Burundi	0	0	0	130	123	260	235	294	334	293	Burundi
Cameroon	1 538	1 755	1 350	992	1 340	* 1 500	* 1 550	1 954	2 319	2 128	Cameroun
Central African Rep.	298	281	285	362	409	435	431	403	413	539	Rép. centrafricaine
Chad	350	325	338	344	349	...	...	...	...	...	Tchad
Congo[1]	586	641	857	676	706	830	801	895	903	1 027	Congo[1]
Côte d'Ivoire	* 2 700	3 240	3 500	3 489	3 480	3 700	3 500	3 640	3 210	4 000	Côte d'Ivoire
Egypt	23 248	25 132	27 558	30 000	35 570	33 249	36 008	35 571	48 008	47 000	Egypte
Ethiopia[3]	1 572	1 084	1 005	1 406	1 458	1 575	1 741	1 946	2 036	1 250	Ethiopie[3]
Gabon	357	303	301	301	* 315	262	288	328	317	355	Gabon
Ghana	3 121	3 219	2 095	1 666	2 028	1 611	1 209	1 074	2 008	1 942	Ghana
Kenya	3 703	4 315	4 547	4 554	4 556	4 972	4 904	5 584	5 391	5 661	Kenya
Liberia	[2] 24	[2] 100	[2] 200	[2] 104	# 20	18	20	59	123	82	Libéria
Libyan Arab Jamah.	2 526	2 063	1 980	1 937	2 134	2 306	* [2] 2 924	* [2] 3 400	* [2] 3 500	* [2] 3 500	Jamah.arabe libyenne
Madagascar[1]	1 439	1 804	1 983	2 014	1 983	1 867	2 065	1 780	2 137	2 368	Madagascar[1]
Malawi	541	487	582	663	630	646	743	778	824	1 450	Malawi
Mauritius[1]	978	984	1 031	1 030	959	1 117	1 010	982	1 253	1 418	Maurice[1]
Morocco	9 043	10 620	11 266	11 820	11 491	12 441	11 493	12 677	13 986	13 813	Maroc
Mozambique	[2] 2 300	[2] 1 600	[2] 1 500	1 000	1 100	1 300	1 100	900	700	...	Mozambique
Nigeria	12 606	11 590	12 178	* 11 372	* 11 063	* [2] 8 640	* [2] 9 000	* [2] 9 800	* [2] 9 000	* [2] 9 100	Nigéria
Senegal[1]	2 217	1 572	2 511	2 518	2 703	2 400	2 176	2 516	2 501	2 979	Sénégal[1]
Seychelles	20	23	23	24	31	45	52	52	65	56	Seychelles
Sierra Leone	1 544	1 503	1 599	1 539	1 711	1 774	1 156	966	1 341	* 1 500	Sierra Leone
Somalia[1]	296	294	239	...	...	...	...	...	...	...	Somalie[1]
South Africa	23 405	22 620	22 517	26 658	28 151	30 025	32 463	31 101	32 501	31 704	Afrique du Sud
Sudan[2]	690	700	710	720	730	730	740	700	* 700	* 740	Soudan[2]
Tunisia	5 035	5 399	4 975	4 835	4 419	3 965	6 016	5 900	5 527	6 334	Tunisie
Uganda	1 813	1 867	1 303	537	636	233	746	...	...	1 416	Ouganda
United Rep. Tanzania	3 678	4 013	4 292	4 153	4 735	3 865	4 693	3 800	4 000	4 050	Rép.Unie de Tanzanie
Zaire[4]	2 860	3 068	2 892	* 3 500	2 739	3 130	3 282	3 472	3 500	3 525	Zaïre[4]
Zambia	1 192	1 217	* 1 247	1 099	* 1 283	1 239	* 1 350	* 1 400	* 1 400	* 1 400	Zambie
Zimbabwe[2]	4 000	3 900	4 000	3 600	3 571	3 750	3 050	2 400	2 300	2 318	Zimbabwe[2]
America, North	**830 103**	**823 492**	**837 409**	**863 349**	**854 106**	**894 339**	**853 940**	**815 891**	**820 882**	**810 464**	**Amérique du Nord**
Barbados[1]	189	190	229	229	224	260	271	241	238	200	Barbade[1]
Belize	81	80	69	61	63	68	56	57	65	* 100	Belize
Canada	61 559	65 530	62 106	65 443	67 180	68 611	68 232	63 900	61 600	63 486	Canada
Costa Rica[2]	2 270	2 381	2 322	2 403	2 252	2 320	1 976	2 200	2 200	2 200	Costa Rica[2]
Cuba	14 760	15 881	16 908	17 377	15 109	15 409	17 044	16 802	18 697	17 961	Cuba
Dominican Republic	3 227	3 128	3 230	3 364	3 375	3 439	3 612	3 604	3 696	3 828	Rép. dominicaine
El Salvador	1 912	2 157	2 035	2 481	2 570	2 328	2 291	2 128	* 2 500	* 2 300	El Salvador
Grenada	[5] 36	[5] 29	# [1] 134	* [1] 113	[1] 101	[1] 98	[1] 104	* [1] 128	* [1] 126	* [1] 118	Grenade
Guatemala	[2] 3 187	[2] 3 307	[2] 3 462	[2] 3 615	2 699	2 162	2 273	2 156	* 2 700	* 2 400	Guatemala
Haiti	746	782	919	988	1 094	1 061	921	909	886	806	Haïti
Honduras	1 965	2 151	2 170	2 311	2 475	2 160	2 279	2 022	2 145	2 311	Honduras
Jamaica	1 544	1 480	1 328	1 349	1 284	1 246	1 414	1 359	1 270	1 314	Jamaïque
Mexico	46 653	49 933	50 580	52 791	54 520	54 660	54 979	49 337	51 666	54 332	Mexique
Nicaragua	[2] 1 695	[2] 1 838	[2] 1 831	[2] 1 904	[2] 2 228	[2] 2 117	[2] 2 200	1 919	2 318	2 400	Nicaragua
Panama	1 077	983	1 081	1 057	1 083	1 050	1 001	981	911	873	Panama
Trinidad and Tobago[1]	1 031	1 003	1 017	889	849	850	1 087	1 148	1 064	* 535	Trinité–et–Tobago[1]
United States[6]	688 171	672 639	687 988	706 974	697 000	736 500	694 200	667 000	668 800	655 300	Etats–Unis[6]
America, South	**209 747**	**226 734**	**233 503**	**237 219**	**253 573**	**230 655**	**218 577**	**218 755**	**224 893**	**242 231**	**Amérique du Sud**
Argentina[1]	37 526	35 926	33 558	33 368	34 680	29 085	26 930	28 241	30 843	31 092	Argentine[1]
Bolivia[2]	1 650	1 336	1 400	1 260	1 265	1 122	624	628	368	...	Bolivie[2]
Brazil	112 101	128 613	136 565	136 710	151 415	137 997	[2] 132 300	[2] 129 200	[2] 127 800	[2] 146 300	Brésil
Chile	8 850	9 502	9 860	9 988	10 510	9 201	7 669	7 680	8 107	8 053	Chili
Colombia[2]	18 344	18 520	18 500	20 600	21 200	19 255	17 907	19 141	23 400	* 24 050	Colombie[2]
Ecuador	[2] 3 736	[2] 4 224	[2] 3 931	[2] 4 090	3 858	4 227	5 149	4 980	5 000	4 800	Equateur
Guyana	559	558	519	549	578	602	430	408	* 344	* 600	Guyana
Paraguay	681	787	818	808	648	757	758	931	878	834	Paraguay
Peru	[2] 3 750	[2] 3 657	[2] 3 378	3 622	3 826	3 965	3 179	3 180	* 3 189	* 2 803	Pérou
Suriname	342	354	353	361	379	402	444	460	521	514	Suriname
Uruguay[2]	* 3 453	* 3 377	* 3 548	* 3 863	* 3 914	* 4 242	* 3 700	* 3 750	* 3 800	3 098	Uruguay[2]
Venezuela[2]	18 755	19 880	21 073	22 000	21 300	19 800	19 487	20 156	20 643	* 19 760	Venezuela[2]
Asia	**1 521 541**	**1 546 265**	**1 552 453**	**1 591 261**	**1 605 198**	**1 722 994**	**1 818 566**	**1 839 959**	**1 947 707**	**2 050 602**	**Asie**

For general note and footnotes, see end of table.

Voir la fin du tableau pour la remarque générale et les notes.

Unit : Million units

Unité : En million

Country or area	1976	1977	1978	1979	1980	1981	1982	1983	1984	1985	Pays ou zone
Bangladesh[6]	11 907	11 631	11 974	13 531	13 830	14 906	15 778	14 031	14 843	14 393	Bangladesh[6]
Burma[7]	2 181	2 185	2 451	2 429	2 724	2 792	3 117	2 949	2 515	3 375	Birmanie[7]
China[2]	...	...	...	...	...	866 000	942 000	968 800	1 066 000	1 180 000	Chine[2]
Cyprus	2 044	2 408	2 896	2 855	2 901	3 320	3 353	2 878	2 586	2 366	Chypre
Democratic Kampuchea* [2]	4 100	4 100	4 100	4 100	4 100	4 100	4 100	4 100	4 100	4 150	Kampuchea démocrat.* [2]
Democratic Yemen	...	...	...	...	1 248	1 150	1 142	1 204	1 202	...	Yémen démocratique
Hong Kong[8]	4 006	4 181	3 983	4 527	4 234	5 250	5 116	6 577	8 681	...	Hong–kong[8]
India[9]	67 201	67 996	70 913	78 578	77 376	88 283	97 391	86 850	86 760	80 428	Inde[9]
Indonesia	[2] 67 218	# 67 996	73 156	73 397	80 194	85 274	85 068	91 463	95 634	102 300	Indonésie
Iran(Islamic Rep.of)[10]	15 591	13 456	10 565	14 359	12 884	12 549	13 546	15 104	12 000	13 000	Iran(Rép.islamique)[10]
Iraq[2]	7 100	7 200	7 250	7 300	7 500	7 725	7 000	7 900	7 000	7 000	Iraq[2]
Israel[1]	5 488	4 751	4 939	4 855	5 337	5 985	6 043	6 373	6 714	6 709	Israël[1]
Japan[11]	288 812	303 461	302 574	308 260	303 177	306 624	309 063	306 320	306 867	303 000	Japon[11]
Jordan	2 224	2 464	2 628	3 414	4 188	4 711	4 614	4 535	5 027	3 905	Jordanie
Korea, Republic of	54 773	58 974	62 662	64 391	70 351	72 139	71 528	75 275	77 984	75 552	Corée, République de
Lao Peoples Dem.Rep.* [2]	1 000	1 100	1 100	1 100	1 100	1 100	1 100	1 100	1 100	1 125	Rép. dém. pop. lao* [2]
Lebanon[2]	1 000	100	100	131	150	280	200	* 200	* 200	* 200	Liban[2]
Malaysia[1 12 13]	11 289	12 257	12 464	13 479	13 529	13 744	14 054	13 502	14 671	13 839	Malaisie[1 12 13]
Nepal	[2] 1 250	# 1 633	2 068	1 642	1 811	2 835	3 209	3 741	4 252	...	Népal
Pakistan[6]	27 454	28 379	31 304	32 536	34 647	35 891	38 132	38 199	40 096	38 921	Pakistan[6]
Philippines[6]	50 950	51 373	50 920	55 273	58 810	55 050	* 70 565	* 57 812	* 58 600	* 62 300	Philippines[6]
Singapore[1]	3 060	3 248	3 311	3 278	3 147	3 203	3 792	3 165	* 2 283	* 2 400	Singapour[1]
Sri Lanka	4 461	4 841	5 098	* 4 637	5 225	* 5 200	5 802	5 858	5 200	6 168	Sri Lanka
Syrian Arab Republic[1]	5 888	5 268	6 335	6 748	6 943	9 939	10 880	13 211	11 274	12 127	Rép. arabe syrienne[1]
Thailand[1]	24 637	23 472	23 900	27 157	30 783	32 807	26 919	29 089	29 211	29 215	Thaïlande[1]
Turkey	47 555	54 523	46 606	55 043	51 977	71 697	62 254	61 497	62 085	62 000	Turquie
Viet Nam	[2] 9 140	[2] 8 060	[2] 7 952	[2] 7 040	[2] 7 032	[2] 10 440	[2] 12 800	[2] 18 226	[2] 20 822	20 640	Viet Nam
Europe	**963 050**	**971 980**	**993 410**	**1 021 702**	**1 058 044**	**1 040 355**	**1 018 305**	**1 048 560**	**1 050 262**	**1 060 753**	**Europe**
EEC	***529 783***	***519 320***	***540 839***	***539 641***	***555 268***	***539 708***	***521 876***	***540 818***	***543 441***	***547 891***	***CEE***
Belgium[8]	26 459	27 070	26 327	20 089	28 167	28 714	30 461	29 738	29 422	30 184	Belgique[8]
Denmark	9 430	9 436	9 477	9 629	9 390	9 660	10 353	9 846	10 583	10 966	Danemark
France	86 546	80 055	80 856	77 491	72 478	62 454	62 510	62 147	60 729	67 376	France
Germany, Fed. Rep.	148 966	141 178	151 765	156 273	160 993	163 979	146 713	155 883	160 680	163 267	Allemagne, Rép. féd.
Greece	[1] 22 933	[1] 23 965	[1] 25 194	[1] 25 268	[1] 25 017	[1] 22 861	17 660	24 286	25 699	28 000	Grèce
Ireland	8 942	8 701	9 265	9 080	9 660	8 823	8 136	7 531	7 289	6 562	Irlande
Italy[1]	73 636	75 175	71 551	68 823	73 090	72 168	80 551	83 700	80 452	78 774	Italie[1]
Netherlands	30 502	34 815	35 212	41 889	40 705	39 189	43 772	46 337	47 287	54 038	Pays–Bas
United Kingdom[1 14]	122 369	118 925	131 192	131 099	135 768	131 860	121 720	121 350	121 300	108 724	Royaume–Uni[1 14]
EFTA	***73 948***	***76 771***	***76 666***	***76 640***	***80 720***	***79 564***	***77 374***	***76 427***	***74 709***	***73 265***	***AELE***
Austria	14 041	14 318	15 008	15 400	15 260	14 671	15 538	15 625	14 907	16 051	Autriche
Finland	7 722	7 483	7 560	6 941	9 162	12 710	8 491	8 375	8 345	* 8 225	Finlande
Norway[2]	710	720	730	750	820	740	* 740	* 792	* 790	* 1 082	Norvège[2]
Portugal	12 409	13 352	13 583	13 507	13 281	13 605	15 016	15 531	14 798	14 667	Portugal
Sweden	11 278	10 361	10 050	10 760	10 933	10 269	11 092	10 423	10 420	10 090	Suède
Switzerland	27 788	30 537	29 735	29 282	31 264	27 569	26 497	25 681	25 449	23 150	Suisse
East Europe	***262 697***	***272 605***	***279 519***	***287 261***	***293 469***	***289 643***	***293 538***	***294 298***	***299 918***	***303 375***	***Europe de l'est***
Albania* [2]	5 800	5 900	6 000	6 000	6 100	6 200	6 200	6 100	6 200	6 000	Albanie* [2]
Bulgaria[15]	73 110	76 575	78 002	81 907	85 214	88 593	88 132	91 296	92 055	93 975	Bulgarie[15]
Czechoslovakia	23 232	24 011	24 075	23 099	22 543	23 734	24 006	25 016	24 603	23 840	Tchécoslovaquie
German Dem. Rep.	19 828	21 661	23 504	24 841	26 008	26 004	25 605	27 387	28 018	26 909	Rép. dém. allemande
Hungary	24 896	24 865	25 152	24 972	27 158	27 102	26 135	25 676	26 679	26 430	Hongrie
Poland	88 831	89 593	90 786	91 442	93 446	83 010	87 460	82 823	86 363	90 021	Pologne
Romania[2 15]	27 000	30 000	32 000	35 000	33 000	* 35 000	* 36 000	* 36 000	* 36 000	* 36 200	Roumanie[2 15]
Other Europe	***96 622***	***103 284***	***96 386***	***118 160***	***128 587***	***131 440***	***125 517***	***137 017***	***132 194***	***136 222***	***Autre Europe***
Malta	988	1 315	1 148	1 127	1 115	1 209	1 307	1 128	1 129	1 300	Malte
Spain[2]	53 394	53 873	41 500	58 241	68 369	67 135	65 269	77 396	* 75 100	* 77 270	Espagne[2]
Yugoslavia	42 240	48 096	53 738	58 792	59 103	63 096	58 941	58 493	55 965	57 652	Yougoslavie
USSR	**375 201**	**378 451**	**376 868**	**360 302**	**363 971**	**365 218**	**359 440**	**369 193**	**373 794**	**381 274**	**URSS**
Byelorussian SSR	*18 537*	*18 926*	*18 872*	*18 912*	*19 229*	*19 218*	*19 254*	*19 285*	*19 525*	*19 843*	*RSS de Biélorussie*
Ukrainian SSR	*74 834*	*75 769*	*77 112*	*77 708*	*78 084*	*78 602*	*77 858*	*79 716*	*81 084*	*82 020*	*RSS d'Ukraine*
Oceania	**38 788**	**36 904**	**37 376**	**36 636**	**39 971**	**40 972**	**42 888**	**42 114**	**39 454**	**38 733**	**Océanie**

For general note and footnotes, see end of table.

Voir la fin du tableau pour la remarque générale et les notes.

Unit : Million units

Unité : En million

Country or area	1976	1977	1978	1979	1980	1981	1982	1983	1984	1985	Pays ou zone
Australia[15]	31 725	29 856	30 389	29 670	33 146	34 215	36 018	35 385	32 667	32 453	Australie[15]
Fiji	528	536	544	560	549	566	536	533	513	513	Fidji
New Zealand	6 535	6 512	6 443	6 406	6 276	6 191	6 334	6 196	6 274	5 767	Nouvelle–Zélande
Total	**4 065 187**	**4 113 422**	**4 166 331**	**4 251 558**	**4 324 364**	**4 442 184**	**4 467 736**	**4 490 863**	**4 629 695**	**4 758 833**	**Total**

General note.
Cigarettes only. (SITC 12220–0).

1 Original data in units of weight. Computed on the basis of one million cigarettes per ton.
2 Source: U. S. Department of Agriculture , (Washington, D. C.).
3 Twelve months ending 10 September of year stated.
4 Including cut tobacco.
5 Original data in cartons.
6 Twelve months ending 30 June of year stated.
7 Government production only.
8 Including cigarillos.
9 Production by large and medium scale establishments only.
10 Production by establishments employing 10 or more persons.
11 Twelve months beginning 1 April of year stated.
12 Data refer to Peninsular Malaysia only.
13 Beginning 1982, scope of series revised.
14 Sales by manufacturers employing 25 or more persons.
15 Including cigars.

Remarque générale.
Cigarettes seulement. (CTCI 12220–0).

1 Données d'origine exprimées en poids. Calcul sur la base d'un million cigarettes par tonne.
2 Source: U.S. Department of Agriculture, (Washington, D.C.).
3 Période de douze mois finissant le 10 septembre de l'année indiquée.
4 Y compris le tabac haché.
5 Données d'origine exprimées en cartons.
6 Période de douze mois finissant le 30 juin de l'année indiquée.
7 Production de l'Etat seulement.
8 Y compris les cigarillos.
9 Production des grandes et moyennes entreprises seulement.
10 Production des établissements occupant 10 personnes ou plus.
11 Période de douze mois commençant le 1er avril de l'année indiquée.
12 Données se rapportant à la Malaisie péninsulaire seulement.
13 A partir de 1982, portée de la série révisée.
14 Ventes des fabricants employant 25 personnes ou plus.
15 Y compris les cigares.

Tobacco, manufactured – Tabacs manufacturés

Unit : Metric tons

Unité : Tonnes métriques

Country or area	1976	1977	1978	1979	1980	1981	1982	1983	1984	1985	Pays ou zone
Africa	**24 325**	**28 749**	**30 436**	**30 990**	**31 756**	**31 452**	**30 865**	**30 094**	**24 793**	**30 219**	**Afrique**
Algeria	5 025	5 417	6 604	6 803	7 130	6 883	7 962	* 5 115	* 4 900	...	Algérie
Cape Verde	8	8	21	14	19	14	32	39	70	74	Cap–Vert
Egypt	# 3 022	7 734	8 173	9 091	10 274	11 732	10 696	12 000	7 520	...	Egypte
Ghana	763	500	672	...	...	...	...	...	...	...	Ghana
Kenya	6	6	4	5	4	5	6	7	6	3	Kenya
Liberia	...	...	194	106	128	118	153	188	184	196	Libéria
Libyan Arab Jamah.	131	143	186	147	146	133	126	136	125	...	Jamah.arabe libyenne
Madagascar	2 164	1 994	2 276	2 247	2 204	1 678	1 641	1 496	1 345	1 034	Madagascar
South Africa[1]	12 256	11 957	11 481	11 203	* 10 550	9 501	8 878	9 764	9 376	8 876	Afrique du Sud[1]
Tunisia	717	766	758	719	643	742	692	700	612	813	Tunisie
Uganda[1]	115	98	66	9	12	0	33	...	...	...	Ouganda[1]
Zaire*	1	1	1	1	1	1	1	1	1	1	Zaïre*
America, North	**77 220**	**77 812**	**77 362**	**76 005**	**79 319**	**78 452**	**79 723**	**79 765**	**80 378**	**78 133**	**Amérique du Nord**
Canada	7 763	7 353	6 576	5 988	5 583	5 395	6 003	6 493	6 568	6 545	Canada
Cuba[1]	22	10	3	5	17	11	10	16	10	...	Cuba[1]
United States	69 435	70 449	70 783	70 012	73 719	73 046	73 710	73 256	73 800	71 578	Etats–Unis
America, South	**4 264**	**7 654**	**8 833**	**10 843**	**14 933**	**14 500**	**13 600**	**17 489**	**19 196**	**20 903**	**Amérique du Sud**
Brazil	4 264	7 654	8 833	[2] 10 843	14 933	* 14 500	* 13 600	...	...	...	Brésil
Asia	**25 849**	**24 615**	**22 327**	**24 740**	**21 172**	**21 296**	**21 016**	**20 283**	**21 635**	**20 131**	**Asie**
Indonesia	...	2 680	2 121	3 884	2 749	2 300	2 958	3 441	5 083	...	Indonésie
Iran(Islamic Rep.of)[3]	5 987	5 706	4 596	5 957	4 779	4 972	4 442	4 995	5 000	...	Iran(Rép.islamique)[3]
Iraq	...	...	...	...	* 7 800	* 7 500	6 872	* 6 800	...	...	Iraq
Israel	99	101	102	93	77	62	60	52	50	49	Israël
Japan[4]	464	404	287	48	58	44	49	46	...	...	Japon[4]
Jordan	11	8	12	19	25	43	48	54	77	81	Jordanie
Korea, Republic of	1 860	1 708	1 402	782	692	494	...	...	...	...	Corée, République de
Malaysia[5]	667	659	643	652	636	602	580	535	...	...	Malaisie[5]
Philippines[6]	1 933	1 223	1 153	1 161	1 160	1 130	* 1 130	* 1 130	...	...	Philippines[6]
Sri Lanka	2	2	2	2	2	3	* 3	3	3	4	Sri Lanka
Syrian Arab Republic	2 597	2 509	2 503	* 2 042	2 042	2 802	2 700	1 482	1 379	...	Rép. arabe syrienne
Turkey[7]	2 916	2 372	2 263	2 857	1 152	1 344	1 584	1 332	1 056	840	Turquie[7]
Europe	**84 591**	**88 337**	**83 343**	**79 895**	**80 008**	**81 864**	**90 556**	**90 709**	**87 998**	**89 375**	**Europe**
EEC	***66 097***	***72 197***	***67 403***	***63 224***	***63 382***	***65 181***	***74 001***	***73 811***	***72 255***	***73 003***	***CEE***
Belgium	4 619	5 203	4 741	4 647	4 460	4 443	4 814	5 808	6 307	5 989	Belgique
Denmark	3 120	3 463	3 804	3 754	4 189	4 357	4 762	4 838	4 658	4 706	Danemark
France	8 299	7 599	7 125	6 697	6 436	5 961	5 891	6 184	5 271	5 970	France
Germany, Fed. Rep.[8]	6 058	9 148	7 747	7 150	7 202	7 224	10 896	8 559	7 954	8 696	Allemagne, Rép. féd.[8]
Greece	26	22	21	18	16	12	11	11	10	...	Grèce
Ireland[9]	3 794	3 645	...	...	...	...	...	...	...	...	Irlande[9]
Italy	1 714	1 655	1 352	782	962	953	668	620	504	512	Italie
Netherlands	23 762	25 263	24 091	24 631	25 281	27 249	31 519	31 872	32 326	32 545	Pays–Bas
United Kingdom[10]	14 705	16 199	14 803	11 826	11 117	11 263	11 721	12 200	11 506	10 860	Royaume–Uni[10]
EFTA	***14 113***	***13 558***	***13 330***	***13 243***	***13 156***	***13 237***	***13 505***	***13 560***	***13 702***	***13 704***	***AELE***
Austria	280	244	229	218	181	211	236	384	240	223	Autriche
Finland	1 162	1 277	1 123	1 128	865	886	894	859	864	...	Finlande
Iceland[11]	17	15	14	15	15	14	15	14	15	13	Islande[11]
Norway	5 076	4 801	4 823	4 894	4 885	4 906	5 049	5 084	4 897	4 867	Norvège
Portugal	192	214	220	260	205	181	190	185	191	169	Portugal
Sweden	6 565	6 200	6 182	6 049	6 298	6 392	6 500	6 461	6 963	7 191	Suède
Switzerland[12]	821	807	739	679	707	647	621	573	532	497	Suisse[12]
East Europe	***1 857***	***1 581***	***1 390***	***1 400***	***1 323***	***1 289***	***1 165***	***975***	***831***	***808***	***Europe de l'est***
Czechoslovakia	720	623	570	516	459	486	423	305	324	321	Tchécoslovaquie
German Dem. Rep.[12]	682	601	498	515	466	405	438	408	356	326	Rép. dém. allemande[12]
Hungary[12]	265	205	166	191	195	159	137	89	104	78	Hongrie[12]
Poland	190	152	156	178	203	239	167	173	47	83	Pologne
Other Europe	***2 524***	***1 001***	***1 220***	***2 028***	***2 147***	***2 157***	***1 885***	***2 363***	***1 210***	***1 860***	***Autre Europe***
Spain[13]	2 352	826	1 050	1 853	1 967	1 987	1 715	2 193	1 050	...	Espagne[13]

For general note and footnotes, see end of table.

Voir la fin du tableau pour la remarque générale et les notes.

Unit : Metric tons

Unité : Tonnes métriques

Country or area	1976	1977	1978	1979	1980	1981	1982	1983	1984	1985	Pays ou zone
Yugoslavia	172	175	170	* 175	* 180	* 170	* 170	* 170	* 160	...	Yougoslavie
USSR[14]	**955**	**1 135**	**1 142**	**1 136**	**1 142**	**1 170**	**1 193**	**1 200**	**1 362**	**1 426**	**URSS[14]**
Ukrainian SSR[14]	*9*	*3*	*3*	*1*	*3*	*1*	*1*	*2*	*2*	*0*	*RSS d'Ukraine[14]*
Oceania	**2 931**	**2 675**	**2 627**	**2 992**	**2 965**	**2 969**	**3 964**	**2 955**	**2 930**	**2 857**	**Océanie**
Australia[6 13]	2 101	1 935	1 947	...	...	...	3 365	...	...	...	Australie[6 13]
Fiji	16	12	12	10	12	10	12	9	10	7	Fidji
New Zealand	814	728	668	645	616	622	587	609	583	513	Nouvelle–Zélande
Total	**220 135**	**230 977**	**226 070**	**226 601**	**231 295**	**231 703**	**240 917**	**242 495**	**238 292**	**243 044**	**Total**

General note.
Smoking tobacco, chewing tobacco, snuff. (SITC 12230–0).

1 Pipe tobacco only.
2 Production by establishments employing 5 or more persons.
3 Production by establishments employing 10 or more persons.
4 Twelve months beginning 1 April of year stated.
5 Data refer to Peninsular Malaysia only.
6 Twelve months ending 30 June of year stated.
7 Twelve months ending 21 March of year stated.
8 Excluding chewing tobacco.
9 Including cigars.
10 Sales by manufacturers employing 25 or more persons.
11 Snuff tobacco only.
12 Smoking tobacco only.
13 Excluding snuff.
14 Excluding chewing tobacco and snuff.

Remarque générale.
Tabac à fumer, tabac à chiquer, tabac à priser. (CTCI 12230–0).

1 Tabacs à pipe seulement.
2 Production des établissements occupant 5 personnes ou plus.
3 Production des établissements occupant 10 personnes ou plus.
4 Période de douze mois commençant le 1er avril de l'année indiquée.
5 Données se rapportant à la Malaisie péninsulaire seulement.
6 Période de douze mois finissant le 30 juin de l'année indiquée.
7 Période de douze mois finissant le 21 mars de l'année indiquée.
8 Non compris le tabac à chiquer.
9 Y compris les cigares.
10 Ventes des fabricants employant 25 personnes ou plus.
11 Tabac à priser seulement.
12 Tabac à fumer seulement.
13 Non compris le tabac à priser.
14 Non compris le tabac à chiquer et à priser.

Wool yarn, pure and mixed (total) – Filés de laine pure et mélangée (production totale)

Unit : Thousand metric tons | Unité : Milliers de tonnes métriques

Country or area	1976	1977	1978	1979	1980	1981	1982	1983	1984	1985	Pays ou zone
Africa	**30.8**	**33.7**	**26.3**	**28.2**	**28.4**	**29.3**	**28.7**	**27.4**	**27.6**	**27.6**	**Afrique**
Algeria	0.2	0.3	0.5	0.8	0.8	* 0.8	* 0.8	* 0.9	...	...	Algérie
Egypt	12.9	13.4	10.2	11.4	12.2	14.2	14.6	14.9	14.3	...	Egypte
South Africa	15.6	17.6	13.6	13.9	* 13.6	13.0	11.3	9.5	* 10.5	9.8	Afrique du Sud
Tunisia	2.0	2.4	2.1	2.1	1.8	1.4	* 2.0	* 2.0	* 1.8	...	Tunisie
America, North	**94.9**	**99.6**	**95.6**	**93.4**	**88.6**	**97.1**	**87.2**	**88.8**	**82.4**	**81.9**	**Amérique du Nord**
Canada[1]	3.2	3.8	4.0	# [2] 4.2	[2] 3.5	...	...	...	...	...	Canada[1]
Cuba[3]	...	...	...	0.1	0.1	0.1	0.1	0.1	0.1	0.1	Cuba[3]
Mexico	...	31.8	28.0	25.6	28.0	31.1	28.4	25.5	20.8	* 26.9	Mexique
United States	60.8	63.9	63.5	* 63.6	57.0	61.9	54.5	59.0	57.2	50.5	Etats–Unis
America, South	**7.3**	**5.0**	**11.0**	**4.8**	**10.5**	**7.7**	**9.6**	**9.9**	**10.2**	**10.8**	**Amérique du Sud**
Bolivia[3]	0.5	0.2	0.1	0.0	0.0	0.0	* 0.0	* 0.0	0.0	0.0	Bolivie[3]
Brazil[4]	5.4	3.5	9.7	3.7	9.1	7.0	...	...	...	...	Brésil[4]
Colombia	1.0	0.9	0.8	0.7	0.8	0.6	0.8	0.6	* 0.5	* 0.5	Colombie
Ecuador	...	...	...	...	0.4	0.0	0.4	0.5	...	...	Equateur
Paraguay[3]	0.0	0.0	0.0	0.0	0.0	0.1	0.0	0.0	0.0	0.0	Paraguay[3]
Asia	**318.2**	**311.4**	**308.5**	**301.2**	**308.5**	**335.7**	**357.6**	**372.7**	**397.5**	**415.6**	**Asie**
Afghanistan[5]	...	...	...	0.2	0.2	0.0	0.0	0.0	0.0	0.0	Afghanistan[5]
China	27.8	31.1	37.8	44.4	57.3	76.5	92.5	* 102.1	110.0	125.9	Chine
Hong Kong	9.2	6.9	6.1	6.3	6.1	5.5	# [3] 3.6	[3] 3.1	[3] 3.7	[3] 4.0	Hong–kong
India	41.5	50.5	52.9	55.2	61.0	68.6	* 65.0	...	...	...	Inde
Indonesia[4]	0.1	0.0	0.1	0.1	0.0	* 0.1	* 0.1	* 0.2	* 0.2	...	Indonésie[4]
Iran(Islamic Rep.of)[6]	38.0	39.9	42.2	11.3	18.5	15.7	...	...	...	...	Iran(Rép.islamique)[6]
Israel[7]	8.9	8.8	9.1	8.4	7.6	7.1	6.5	6.2	5.6	5.9	Israël[7]
Japan	159.4	130.2	109.4	124.2	119.2	114.4	120.4	110.0	120.9	123.4	Japon
Korea, Republic of	16.7	22.2	27.7	29.8	28.7	33.0	36.3	41.7	45.2	41.4	Corée, République de
Syrian Arab Republic	0.5	0.8	2.2	1.7	1.6	1.6	1.7	1.1	1.8	2.1	Rép. arabe syrienne
Turkey	15.9	20.9	20.8	19.6	8.2	13.3	16.8	24.7	26.3	28.7	Turquie
Europe	**1 253.3**	**1 256.7**	**1 258.2**	**1 287.4**	**1 283.2**	**1 217.4**	**1 132.8**	**1 160.4**	**1 126.2**	**1 151.0**	**Europe**
EEC	***805.8***	***797.9***	***780.8***	***815.2***	***789.3***	***738.0***	***672.9***	***691.1***	***656.6***	***678.8***	***CEE***
Belgium	81.1	76.9	74.0	76.3	80.8	78.6	73.7	86.7	92.4	90.6	Belgique
Denmark	3.9	3.6	3.6	4.4	5.1	8.2	* 9.1	9.0	* 9.0	...	Danemark
France	145.2	154.8	136.8	138.3	147.0	124.8	114.0	107.9	34.6	34.3	France
Germany, Fed. Rep.	59.7	53.9	52.8	55.9	60.2	52.1	46.7	46.4	48.5	55.7	Allemagne, Rép. féd.
Greece	16.5	15.5	20.0	19.2	17.3	16.3	15.0	14.5	13.3	...	Grèce
Ireland	13.5	12.3	12.3	12.6	9.8	10.1	8.0	8.0	8.1	8.6	Irlande
Italy	286.1	283.7	289.2	325.3	319.5	309.9	284.9	290.8	317.7	326.2	Italie
Netherlands[8]	11.0	10.3	8.9	9.0	8.5	7.1	6.6	6.5	6.4	...	Pays–Bas[8]
United Kingdom[9]	188.8	186.9	183.2	174.3	141.0	130.9	114.9	121.2	126.6	133.6	Royaume–Uni[9]
EFTA	***45.3***	***46.8***	***41.0***	***43.3***	***46.8***	***46.4***	***43.1***	***41.4***	***43.9***	***48.3***	***AELE***
Austria	5.4	5.4	4.9	4.0	5.1	5.0	5.1	5.3	6.0	6.3	Autriche
Finland	2.8	3.1	2.2	2.6	2.5	2.6	2.3	1.7	1.8	...	Finlande
Iceland	1.6	1.9	1.6	1.8	2.1	2.5	2.2	2.1	2.0	...	Islande
Norway	4.0	4.3	3.9	4.3	4.2	4.1	3.9	3.2	3.0	3.0	Norvège
Portugal	12.2	13.6	11.9	14.3	15.5	14.0	12.4	12.0	12.5	15.9	Portugal
Sweden	2.4	2.0	1.9	1.9	1.8	1.6	1.7	1.6	1.5	1.2	Suède
Switzerland	16.9	16.5	14.6	14.3	15.6	16.6	15.5	15.6	17.0	17.8	Suisse
East Europe	***341.8***	***345.8***	***360.1***	***356.5***	***361.7***	***345.2***	***335.6***	***343.4***	***337.1***	***334.8***	***Europe de l'est***
Bulgaria[10]	34.0	34.9	43.0	35.6	35.9	36.9	37.9	37.8	36.5	35.1	Bulgarie[10]
Czechoslovakia	52.7	54.0	53.6	55.1	56.6	57.3	58.0	58.4	57.5	58.0	Tchécoslovaquie
German Dem. Rep.[11]	83.6	79.1	77.4	76.2	76.5	74.8	75.8	76.4	75.5	75.0	Rép. dém. allemande[11]
Hungary	9.8	10.6	11.0	11.5	12.3	12.9	11.5	10.8	10.9	10.5	Hongrie
Poland	106.0	106.5	107.5	107.2	106.7	88.2	74.8	81.3	83.3	84.2	Pologne
Romania	55.8	60.8	67.6	70.9	73.7	75.0	77.6	78.8	73.4	72.0	Roumanie
Other Europe	***60.4***	***66.1***	***76.3***	***72.4***	***85.5***	***87.9***	***81.3***	***84.4***	***88.7***	***89.1***	***Autre Europe***
Spain	16.2	20.0	31.8	29.0	31.8	31.8	28.3	[12] 33.3	...	...	Espagne
Yugoslavia	44.2	46.1	44.5	43.4	53.7	56.2	53.0	51.1	52.2	50.6	Yougoslavie
USSR	**428.5**	**436.7**	**446.8**	**449.5**	**456.5**	**452.7**	**448.9**	**447.1**	**432.7**	**420.9**	**URSS**

For general note and footnotes, see end of table. | Voir la fin du tableau pour la remarque générale et les notes.

Wool yarn, pure and mixed (total) (continued) – Filés de laine pure et mélangée (production totale) (suite)

Unit : Thousand metric tons

Unité : Milliers de tonnes métriques

Country or area	1976	1977	1978	1979	1980	1981	1982	1983	1984	1985	Pays ou zone
Byelorussian SSR	*29.5*	*31.2*	*34.3*	*36.0*	*37.3*	*37.4*	*37.3*	*38.1*	*38.1*	*39.1*	*RSS de Biélorussie*
Ukrainian SSR	*39.6*	*43.9*	*44.8*	*45.9*	*48.0*	*45.5*	*45.0*	*44.8*	*43.1*	*42.5*	*RSS d'Ukraine*
Oceania	**44.0**	**38.2**	**37.0**	**38.5**	**36.6**	**38.8**	**40.1**	**38.7**	**42.3**	**49.3**	**Océanie**
Australia[13]	22.4	19.4	19.3	20.4	17.9	19.2	19.9	19.4	17.5	23.0	Australie[13]
New Zealand	21.6	18.8	17.7	18.1	18.7	19.6	20.2	19.3	24.8	26.3	Nouvelle-Zélande
Total	**2 177.0**	**2 181.2**	**2 183.3**	**2 203.0**	**2 212.3**	**2 178.8**	**2 105.0**	**2 145.0**	**2 119.0**	**2 157.1**	**Total**

General note.
Data refer to total production of pure yarn of carded and combed (worsted) wool, and mixed yarn in which wool is predominant material by weight, containing less than 10 per cent by weight of silk, noil or other waste silk or any combination thereof. (SITC 65121-0 and 65125-0).

1 Including yarn produced in carpet mills.
2 Shipments.
3 Pure wool yarn only.
4 Mixed wool yarn only.
5 Twelve months beginning 21 March of year stated.
6 Production by establishments employing 10 or more persons.
7 Including vicuna.
8 Including hand-knit wool yarn.
9 Estimated production in the woollen system and deliveries in the worsted system. Including man-made fibres and yarn of wholly wool and hair.
10 Including yarn of man-made staple.
11 Including thread.
12 Including household production.
13 Twelve months ending 30 June of year stated.

Remarque générale.
Les données se rapportent à la production totale de filés de laine pure (cardée ou peignée) et de filés mélangées dans lesquels le poids de laine prédomine, qui contiennent moins de 10 p. 100 en poids de soie, de bourre de soie ou d'autres déchets de soie, ou de mélange de ces fibres. (CTCI 65121-0 et 65125-0).

1 Y compris les filés produits dans les fabriques de tapis.
2 Expéditions.
3 Filés de laine pure seulement.
4 Filés de laine mélangée seulement.
5 Période de douze mois commençant le 21 mars de l'année indiquée.
6 Production des établissements occupant 10 personnes ou plus.
7 Y compris la vigogne.
8 Y compris filés de laine tricotés à main.
9 Production estimative du cardage et quantités obtenues par peignage. Y compris les fibres artificielles et les filés entièrement constitués de laine et de poils.
10 Y compris les filés de fibres synthétiques discontinues.
11 Y compris les fils.
12 Y compris la production ménagère.
13 Période de douze mois finissant le 30 juin de l'année indiquée.

Wool yarn, mixed – Filés de laine mélangée

Unit : Thousand metric tons | Unité : Milliers de tonnes métriques

Country or area	1976	1977	1978	1979	1980	1981	1982	1983	1984	1985	Pays ou zone
Africa	**12.2**	**14.5**	**12.0**	**11.4**	**10.9**	**10.2**	**9.8**	**8.5**	**8.8**	**9.1**	**Afrique**
South Africa	12.2	14.5	12.0	11.4	* 10.9	10.2	9.0	7.7	* 8.0	8.2	Afrique du Sud
Tunisia	0.0	0.0	0.0	0.0	0.0	0.0	* 0.8	* 0.8	...	...	Tunisie
America, North	**17.6**	**18.0**	**19.0**	**19.7**	**19.2**	**20.7**	**21.8**	**20.3**	**16.8**	**22.6**	**Amérique du Nord**
Canada[1]	1.9	2.3	1.9	# [2] 2.3	[2] 1.0	...	...	...	...	...	Canada[1]
Mexico	15.7	15.8	17.1	17.4	18.1	19.4	20.6	19.3	15.9	21.9	Mexique
America, South	**5.8**	**4.0**	**10.2**	**4.1**	**9.7**	**7.5**	**8.8**	**9.2**	**9.8**	**10.3**	**Amérique du Sud**
Brazil	5.4	3.5	9.7	3.7	9.1	7.0	...	...	...	...	Brésil
Colombia	0.4	0.4	0.4	0.4	0.6	0.5	0.5	0.4	0.4	0.4	Colombie
Ecuador	0.1	0.0	0.0	...	...	...	...	...	...	...	Equateur
Asia	**54.5**	**66.6**	**77.6**	**94.3**	**100.3**	**118.5**	**142.9**	**157.4**	**170.4**	**179.3**	**Asie**
China	...	...	...	...	43.5	57.9	74.8	81.7	86.0	98.1	Chine
Hong Kong[3]	2.1	2.0	1.5	2.0	1.4	0.7	...	...	...	...	Hong–kong[3]
Indonesia	0.1	0.0	0.1	0.1	0.0	* 0.1	* 0.1	* 0.2	...	...	Indonésie
Japan	33.1	28.3	26.2	29.1	30.3	31.0	34.9	34.7	39.0	39.5	Japon
Korea, Republic of	11.1	17.1	19.6	22.7	22.0	24.2	27.1	34.6	38.0	33.9	Corée, République de
Turkey	1.9	2.7	3.3	3.2	3.1	4.5	5.2	5.7	6.9	7.6	Turquie
Europe	**429.5**	**437.0**	**456.9**	**468.7**	**467.8**	**435.4**	**395.1**	**401.8**	**430.3**	**441.4**	**Europe**
EEC	***292.5***	***290.9***	***303.6***	***325.2***	***316.5***	***302.9***	***277.3***	***280.5***	***303.0***	***310.9***	***CEE***
Denmark	1.8	1.9	2.0	2.5	3.0	5.1	5.9	7.0	7.0	...	Danemark
France[4]	59.7	56.2	59.6	55.5	56.0	49.0	40.4	34.1	34.6	34.3	France[4]
Greece	...	...	* 3.8	4.0	3.8	3.0	3.6	3.4	3.7	...	Grèce
Italy	227.1	229.0	238.2	263.2	253.7	245.8	227.3	236.0	257.7	265.3	Italie
EFTA	***11.2***	***13.1***	***10.5***	***12.0***	***13.5***	***12.0***	***11.2***	***10.3***	***14.0***	***17.0***	***AELE***
Austria	...	2.2	2.0	1.5	2.1	2.1	2.2	2.0	4.0	4.4	Autriche
Portugal	8.5	9.8	7.4	9.4	10.5	9.3	8.3	7.8	9.5	12.2	Portugal
Sweden	1.5	1.1	1.1	1.1	0.9	0.5	0.7	0.5	0.5	0.4	Suède
East Europe	***104.7***	***106.9***	***108.1***	***105.3***	***107.7***	***91.1***	***77.9***	***84.0***	***85.4***	***86.0***	***Europe de l'est***
Hungary	7.7	8.0	8.9	9.1	9.7	10.1	9.0	8.4	8.4	7.9	Hongrie
Poland	97.1	98.8	99.2	96.1	97.9	81.0	68.9	75.6	77.1	78.1	Pologne
Other Europe	***21.1***	***26.1***	***34.7***	***26.2***	***30.1***	***29.4***	***28.7***	***27.0***	***27.9***	***27.6***	***Autre Europe***
Spain	12.6	15.9	23.6	...	...	...	...	...	...	...	Espagne
Yugoslavia	8.6	10.2	11.1	8.9	12.8	12.0	11.3	9.6	10.6	10.2	Yougoslavie
Oceania	**9.2**	**8.4**	**8.3**	**7.4**	**7.0**	**8.3**	**8.6**	**8.6**	**7.0**	**10.1**	**Océanie**
Australia[5]	9.2	8.4	8.3	7.4	7.0	8.3	8.6	8.6	7.0	10.1	Australie[5]
Total	**528.9**	**548.6**	**584.0**	**605.7**	**615.0**	**600.6**	**587.0**	**605.8**	**643.0**	**672.8**	**Total**

General note.
Mixed yarn in which wool is the predominant material by weight, containing less than 10 per cent by weight of silk, noil or other waste silk or any combination thereof. (Parts of SITC 65121, 65122 and 65125).

[1] Including yarn produced in carpet mills.
[2] Shipments.
[3] Beginning 1982, data are confidential.
[4] More than 50 per cent wool.
[5] Twelve months ending 30 June of year stated.

Remarque générale.
Filés de laine mélangée dans lesquels la laine prédomine en poids et contenant moins de 10 p. 100 en poids de soie, de bourre de soie (schappe) ou de bourette de soie, ou de mélange de ces fibres. (Parties de CTCI 65121, 65122 et 65125).

[1] Y compris les filés produits dans les fabriques de tapis.
[2] Expéditions.
[3] A partir de 1982, les données sont confidentielles.
[4] Plus de 50 p. 100 de laine.
[5] Période de douze mois finissant le 30 juin de l'année indiquée.

Wool yarn, pure – Filés de laine pure

Unit : Thousand metric tons

Unité : Milliers de tonnes métriques

Country or area	1976	1977	1978	1979	1980	1981	1982	1983	1984	1985	Pays ou zone
Africa	**5.4**	**5.5**	**3.7**	**4.6**	**4.6**	**4.1**	**3.4**	**3.1**	**3.5**	**2.4**	**Afrique**
South Africa	3.3	3.1	1.6	2.5	2.7	2.8	2.2	1.9	2.4	1.6	Afrique du Sud
Tunisia	2.0	2.4	2.1	2.1	1.8	1.4	* 1.2	* 1.2	...	...	Tunisie
America, North	**16.5**	**17.6**	**13.0**	**12.2**	**12.4**	**14.5**	**10.8**	**9.5**	**8.5**	**8.8**	**Amérique du Nord**
Canada[1]	1.3	1.6	2.1	[2] 1.9	[2] 2.5	...	...	...	...	...	Canada[1]
Cuba	...	...	...	0.1	0.1	0.1	0.1	0.1	0.1	0.1	Cuba
Mexico	...	16.0	10.9	10.2	9.8	11.8	7.8	6.2	4.9	* 5.0	Mexique
America, South	**1.2**	**0.7**	**0.4**	**0.4**	**0.3**	**0.2**	**0.4**	**0.3**	**0.2**	**0.1**	**Amérique du Sud**
Bolivia	0.5	0.2	0.1	0.0	0.0	0.0	* 0.0	* 0.0	0.0	0.0	Bolivie
Colombia	0.6	0.5	0.4	0.3	0.2	0.0	0.3	0.2	* 0.1	* 0.1	Colombie
Paraguay	0.0	0.0	0.0	0.0	0.0	0.1	0.0	0.0	0.0	0.0	Paraguay
Asia	**156.9**	**136.4**	**122.3**	**134.5**	**119.2**	**124.2**	**127.6**	**124.8**	**136.1**	**144.3**	**Asie**
China	...	...	...	...	13.8	18.6	17.7	20.4	24.0	27.8	Chine
Hong Kong	7.1	4.8	4.5	4.3	4.7	4.7	3.6	3.1	3.7	4.0	Hong–kong
Japan	126.3	101.9	83.2	95.1	88.9	83.3	85.5	75.3	81.9	84.0	Japon
Korea, Republic of	5.6	5.1	8.1	7.1	6.7	8.7	9.2	7.1	7.1	7.5	Corée, République de
Turkey	14.0	18.2	17.5	16.4	5.1	8.8	11.6	19.0	19.4	21.1	Turquie
Europe	**135.9**	**130.1**	**129.1**	**140.7**	**147.8**	**148.5**	**135.5**	**131.2**	**133.3**	**133.4**	**Europe**
EEC	***77.7***	***71.8***	***68.9***	***79.2***	***81.4***	***80.5***	***72.2***	***67.9***	***71.6***	***72.7***	***CEE***
Denmark	2.1	1.7	1.7	1.9	2.1	3.1	3.2	* 2.0	* 2.0	...	Danemark
Greece	16.5	15.5	16.2	15.2	13.6	13.3	11.4	11.1	9.6	...	Grèce
Italy	59.0	54.7	51.0	62.1	65.7	64.1	57.6	54.8	60.0	60.9	Italie
EFTA	***7.9***	***8.0***	***8.1***	***8.3***	***8.9***	***8.6***	***8.0***	***8.5***	***6.0***	***6.4***	***AELE***
Austria	...	3.3	2.9	2.6	3.0	2.8	2.8	3.3	2.0	1.9	Autriche
Portugal	3.7	3.8	4.5	4.9	5.0	4.7	4.1	4.2	3.1	3.7	Portugal
Sweden	0.9	0.9	0.8	0.8	0.9	1.1	1.0	1.0	1.0	0.8	Suède
East Europe	***11.0***	***10.3***	***10.5***	***13.4***	***11.3***	***10.0***	***8.4***	***8.1***	***8.8***	***8.7***	***Europe de l'est***
Hungary	2.1	2.6	2.1	2.3	2.5	2.8	2.5	2.4	2.6	2.6	Hongrie
Poland	8.9	7.7	8.3	11.1	8.8	7.2	5.9	5.7	6.3	6.1	Pologne
Other Europe	***39.3***	***40.0***	***41.6***	***39.8***	***46.2***	***49.4***	***47.0***	***46.7***	***46.9***	***45.7***	***Autre Europe***
Spain[3]	3.6	4.1	8.2	...	...	...	...	...	...	...	Espagne[3]
Yugoslavia	35.7	35.9	33.4	34.5	40.9	44.1	41.7	41.4	41.6	40.4	Yougoslavie
Oceania	**13.2**	**11.0**	**10.9**	**13.0**	**10.9**	**11.2**	**11.4**	**10.8**	**10.5**	**12.9**	**Océanie**
Australia[4]	13.2	11.0	10.9	13.0	10.9	11.2	11.4	10.8	10.5	12.9	Australie[4]
Total	**329.1**	**301.3**	**279.5**	**305.3**	**295.1**	**302.7**	**289.2**	**279.7**	**292.0**	**302.0**	**Total**

General note.
Pure yarn of carded and combed (worsted) wool. (Parts of SITC 65121, 65122 and 65125).

[1] Including yarn produced in carpet mills.
[2] Shipments.
[3] Incomplete coverage (about 95 per cent of total production).
[4] Twelve months ending 30 June of year stated.

Remarque générale.
Filés de pure laine cardée ou peignée. (Parties de CTCI 65121, 65122 et 65125).

[1] Y compris les filés produits dans les fabriques de tapis.
[2] Expéditions.
[3] Couverture incomplète (environ 95 p. 100 de la production totale).
[4] Période de douze mois finissant le 30 juin de l'année indiquée.

Cotton yarn, pure and mixed (total) – Filés de coton pur et mélangé (production totale)

Unit : Thousand metric tons — Unité : Milliers de tonnes métriques

Country or area	1976	1977	1978	1979	1980	1981	1982	1983	1984	1985	Pays ou zone
Africa	**351.2**	**356.4**	**359.9**	**378.1**	**414.0**	**430.2**	**409.4**	**404.6**	**415.3**	**430.7**	**Afrique**
Algeria	13.9	14.0	16.0	11.8	15.5	21.4	19.9	...	...	...	Algérie
Burkina Faso[1]	0.8	0.4	0.6	0.6	0.3	1.0	1.2	* 1.3	1.5	* 1.4	Burkina Faso[1]
Côte d'Ivoire[1]	...	7.0	9.4	10.7	10.9	22.1	13.1	15.9	15.6	18.5	Côte d'Ivoire[1]
Egypt[1]	193.0	210.4	212.2	219.0	236.0	239.0	245.0	229.1	243.6	250.8	Egypte[1]
Ethiopia[1 2 3]	9.8	8.9	7.9	7.9	9.3	7.0	9.2	9.3	9.3	9.4	Ethiopie[1 2 3]
Kenya	3.6	3.4	3.1	4.8	5.5	5.5	2.8	1.4	1.7	2.6	Kenya
Mali[1]	...	...	45.7	48.6	51.1	46.3	40.8	54.3	...	...	Mali[1]
Mozambique[1 4]	3.4	...	...	...	...	...	...	...	...	...	Mozambique[1 4]
Nigeria[1]	6.4	4.4	5.0	...	...	...	...	...	...	...	Nigéria[1]
Senegal[5]	0.6	0.6	0.5	0.6	0.6	0.6	0.7	0.7	0.6	0.6	Sénégal[5]
South Africa	59.0	48.4	47.8	54.9	63.9	67.3	* 55.9	* 51.1	49.8	51.8	Afrique du Sud
Tunisia[1]	7.5	9.1	8.3	10.5	12.2	11.1	* 12.0	* 12.0	...	...	Tunisie[1]
America, North	**1 311.4**	**1 233.3**	**1 161.2**	**1 173.2**	**1 189.7**	**1 058.2**	**1 004.9**	**1 132.3**	**1 031.6**	**1 054.7**	**Amérique du Nord**
Canada[6 7]	62.6	61.2	[8] 33.5	[8] 34.9	...	41.4	45.5	45.2	44.6	43.5	Canada[6 7]
Cuba[9]	22.2	24.0	24.3	21.7	25.0	26.2	23.9	26.4	26.7	30.8	Cuba[9]
Dominican Republic[9]	0.5	0.8	1.1	0.8	0.7	0.4	0.5	0.9	0.9	0.8	Rép. dominicaine[9]
El Salvador[1]	4.5	5.9	6.1	3.6	3.9	2.9	3.0	4.7	...	...	El Salvador[1]
United States	1 221.5	1 141.3	1 096.2	* 1 112.1	1 113.7	987.4	932.0	1 055.1	956.4	976.8	Etats-Unis
America, South	**252.3**	**609.8**	**677.0**	**710.6**	**735.8**	**709.9**	**705.2**	**690.0**	**734.6**	**891.5**	**Amérique du Sud**
Argentina[1]	91.7	95.0	83.6	92.4	74.9	61.3	68.4	83.0	92.9	112.6	Argentine[1]
Bolivia[1]	0.6	2.0	1.0	1.0	0.8	0.7	* 4.5	3.5	6.8	8.6	Bolivie[1]
Brazil	[1 10] 69.7	383.1	450.0	483.2	526.6	483.3	492.9	473.2	472.2	544.0	Brésil
Chile[1]	...	...	...	3.8	4.8	4.0	4.6	3.6	7.5	8.3	Chili[1]
Colombia	53.7	54.0	47.8	55.5	51.6	54.0	42.6	48.0	49.0	56.8	Colombie
Ecuador	1.7	1.1	...	...	2.2	0.8	1.5	1.5	1.0	...	Equateur
Paraguay[1]	33.8	72.8	90.7	73.3	74.9	105.9	90.8	77.2	105.3	160.0	Paraguay[1]
Asia	**4 862.2**	**5 023.9**	**5 350.5**	**5 875.8**	**6 274.0**	**6 508.4**	**6 722.3**	**6 777.0**	**6 913.8**	**7 308.7**	**Asie**
Afghanistan[1 11]	1.1	1.2	0.9	0.6	0.3	0.1	0.1	0.1	0.3	0.3	Afghanistan[1 11]
Bangladesh[1 12]	39.9	37.4	40.7	43.8	43.2	46.2	43.2	44.4	46.2	48.2	Bangladesh[1 12]
Burma	[13] 13.8	[13] 14.4	[13] 14.4	[13] 13.2	[13] 15.6	16.4	16.0	12.0	10.6	10.2	Birmanie
China	1 960.0	2 230.0	2 382.0	2 634.6	2 925.5	3 170.1	3 354.0	3 270.0	3 219.0	3 535.0	Chine
Hong Kong	221.9	200.4	209.5	224.3	200.6	161.3	148.3	162.1	153.3	154.0	Hong-kong
India	1 062.1	1 009.4	1 107.0	1 100.6	1 158.7	1 129.2	1 058.1	1 179.5	1 225.5	[1] 1 260.0	Inde
Indonesia	40.7	56.9	77.5	100.6	133.2	154.6	156.5	147.8	220.8	...	Indonésie
Iran(Islamic Rep.of)[14]	65.0	72.0	78.3	58.6	84.9	88.3	...	...	...	...	Iran(Rép.islamique)[14]
Israel	24.4	25.5	24.3	22.4	20.0	17.3	16.5	17.0	16.5	15.2	Israël
Japan[15]	498.3	440.9	447.9	507.7	503.8	455.5	470.2	437.7	436.8	437.0	Japon[15]
Korea, Republic of	251.1	277.5	293.7	385.2	425.1	426.5	439.5	476.8	492.0	466.4	Corée, République de
Malaysia	...	...	...	...	[1] 15.6	[1] 14.4	23.4	23.6	24.9	25.2	Malaisie
Pakistan[2 12]	349.7	282.6	297.9	350.0	396.1	413.7	463.0	448.4	464.0	493.6	Pakistan[2 12]
Philippines[1 4]	32.6	30.8	32.0	35.9	38.4	36.3	35.6	19.8	25.2	22.5	Philippines[1 4]
Sri Lanka[1]	7.4	5.1	5.7	6.2	4.3	6.4	7.6	7.6	6.9	9.4	Sri Lanka[1]
Syrian Arab Republic[1]	14.4	15.0	12.5	24.8	20.5	31.4	28.2	37.0	33.6	34.9	Rép. arabe syrienne[1]
Thailand[1 4]	85.9	93.8	102.0	96.4	96.2	97.3	101.2	109.7	115.6	131.5	Thaïlande[1 4]
Turkey	[2] 153.8	[2] 184.3	[2] 173.4	[2] 221.6	162.8	212.1	237.2	247.0	274.1	292.6	Turquie
Viet Nam	33.8	38.1	39.8	35.9	29.3	31.1	35.5	44.7	52.5	51.6	Viet Nam
Europe	**2 131.3**	**2 047.5**	**2 056.7**	**2 110.3**	**2 133.1**	**1 996.8**	**2 026.4**	**2 036.1**	**2 082.6**	**2 096.2**	**Europe**
EEC	***982.1***	***877.4***	***862.4***	***891.4***	***879.4***	***776.6***	***813.0***	***820.9***	***838.2***	***833.4***	***CEE***
Belgium	53.5	40.7	40.7	47.7	47.4	40.6	45.9	45.7	46.7	47.8	Belgique
Denmark	2.3	1.9	1.5	1.7	1.9	2.0	2.0	1.9	* 1.6	1.5	Danemark
France[1]	201.8	185.4	172.3	170.6	171.4	148.7	149.3	148.5	146.9	133.6	France[1]
Germany, Fed. Rep.[6]	208.0	177.6	163.3	160.6	169.9	146.0	168.3	181.4	194.0	202.6	Allemagne, Rép. féd.[6]
Greece[16]	109.7	101.3	115.7	128.1	135.5	127.6	127.9	137.2	133.9	132.2	Grèce[16]
Ireland[17]	4.7	[1] 3.1	[1] 2.6	[1] 3.4	[1] 15.6	[1] 17.6	[1] 15.3	[1] 13.5	[1] 12.8	...	Irlande[17]
Italy	233.8	211.8	225.9	242.0	231.2	215.5	224.8	216.6	230.5	...	Italie
Netherlands	34.7	30.1	22.2	19.0	15.9	12.2	12.9	9.1	7.5	9.1	Pays-Bas
United Kingdom	133.5	125.5	118.1	118.2	90.5	66.5	66.6	67.0	64.5	64.7	Royaume-Uni
EFTA	***179.8***	***183.3***	***170.9***	***194.0***	***207.3***	***198.8***	***208.7***	***224.7***	***229.1***	***228.9***	***AELE***
Austria	20.7	20.1	17.7	18.6	18.4	17.4	15.8	16.9	17.2	15.3	Autriche
Finland	17.8	14.9	12.0	14.0	14.5	10.8	10.1	11.1	6.9	3.5	Finlande
Norway	1.7	1.3	1.1	1.7	2.1	1.7	1.8	2.4	2.4	...	Norvège

For general note and footnotes, see end of table.

Voir la fin du tableau pour la remarque générale et les notes.

Cotton yarn, pure and mixed (total) (continued) – Filés de coton pur et mélangé (production totale) (suite)

Unit : Thousand metric tons

Unité : Milliers de tonnes métriques

Country or area	1976	1977	1978	1979	1980	1981	1982	1983	1984	1985	Pays ou zone
Portugal[6]	89.1	96.7	92.9	108.6	118.7	116.7	125.9	136.1	140.3	144.8	Portugal[6]
Sweden	6.9	5.6	5.3	5.1	4.9	4.5	4.8	5.2	5.7	5.4	Suède
Switzerland	43.6	44.7	41.9	46.1	48.8	47.8	50.3	52.9	56.5	57.5	Suisse
East Europe	***781.6***	***796.7***	***811.8***	***804.1***	***819.3***	***801.7***	***775.7***	***764.3***	***766.1***	***774.8***	***Europe de l'est***
Bulgaria	78.8	86.2	84.4	85.5	87.4	87.3	85.8	85.2	83.5	82.7	Bulgarie
Czechoslovakia	122.7	125.1	128.9	134.1	135.7	137.1	138.8	140.1	140.0	142.2	Tchécoslovaquie
German Dem. Rep.[4 6 18]	138.1	135.4	135.8	134.8	136.0	134.5	135.3	134.7	138.2	138.1	Rép. dém. allemande[4 6 18]
Hungary[4]	58.5	60.1	62.8	60.6	59.9	58.2	55.7	56.5	56.7	57.9	Hongrie[4]
Poland	218.5	219.0	224.9	214.1	217.3	195.5	173.2	176.7	178.6	183.9	Pologne
Romania[6]	165.0	171.0	175.0	175.0	183.0	189.0	187.0	171.0	169.0	170.0	Roumanie[6]
Other Europe	***187.8***	***190.2***	***211.6***	***220.7***	***227.1***	***219.7***	***229.0***	***226.1***	***249.2***	***259.0***	***Autre Europe***
Spain	70.4	69.3	93.7	100.9	109.9	102.2	108.2	[19] 105.6	...	...	Espagne
Yugoslavia	117.4	120.9	117.8	119.9	117.2	117.5	120.8	120.5	128.7	132.9	Yougoslavie
USSR	**1 583.0**	**1 597.3**	**1 627.4**	**1 623.3**	**1 636.3**	**1 645.3**	**1 634.0**	**1 658.5**	**1 688.5**	**1 742.2**	**URSS**
Byelorussian SSR	*46.1*	*46.2*	*47.1*	*47.4*	*47.9*	*47.2*	*45.9*	*45.8*	*46.3*	*48.5*	*RSS de Biélorussie*
Ukrainian SSR	*120.5*	*123.6*	*128.1*	*131.0*	*135.7*	*139.9*	*142.5*	*146.3*	*149.2*	*153.1*	*RSS d'Ukraine*
Oceania	**25.8**	**22.2**	**22.5**	**21.1**	**21.8**	**21.7**	**22.0**	**18.9**	**18.5**	**20.3**	**Océanie**
Australia[6 12]	25.8	22.2	22.5	21.1	21.8	21.7	22.0	18.9	18.5	20.3	Australie[6 12]
Total	**10 517.2**	**10 890.4**	**11 255.0**	**11 892.5**	**12 404.7**	**12 370.4**	**12 524.2**	**12 717.4**	**12 884.9**	**13 544.3**	**Total**

General note.
Data refer to pure cotton yarn including yarn from cotton waste and mixed yarn in which cotton or cotton waste is predominant material by weight, containing less than 10 per cent by weight of silk, noil or other waste silk or any combination thereof. (SITC 65130-0).

1 Pure cotton yarn only.
2 Factory production only.
3 Twelve months ending 10 September of year stated.
4 Excluding yarn made from waste.
5 Production for sale only.
6 Including tire-cord yarn.
7 Beginning 1980, data are confidential.
8 Shipments.
9 Mixed cotton yarn only.
10 Data refer to Sao Paulo only.
11 Twelve months beginning 21 March of year stated.
12 Twelve months ending 30 June of year stated.
13 Production by government-owned enterprises only.
14 Production by establishments employing 10 or more persons.
15 Including condenser cotton yarn.
16 Including all mixed yarns, irrespective of predominant raw material.
17 1985, data are confidential.
18 Including thread.
19 Including household production.

Remarque générale.
Les données se rapportent à la production totale de filés de coton pur ou mélangé à d'autres matières textiles dans lesquelles le poids de coton et les déchets de coton prédominent, et où le poids de la soie, de la bourrette et autres déchets de soie ou mélangé de ces textiles représente moins de 10 p. 100 du poids total. (CTCI 65130-0).

1 Filés de coton pur seulement.
2 Production des fabriques seulement.
3 Période de douze mois finissant le 10 septembre de l'année indiquée.
4 Non compris les filés à base de déchets de coton.
5 Production destinée à la vente seulement.
6 Y compris les filés de coton pour pneumatiques à cordes.
7 A partir de 1980, les données sont confidentielles.
8 Expéditions.
9 Filés de coton mélangé seulement.
10 Données se rapportant à Sao Paulo seulement.
11 Période de douze mois commençant le 21 mars de l'année indiquée.
12 Période de douze mois finissant le 30 juin de l'année indiquée.
13 Production des établissements d'Etat seulement.
14 Production des établissements occupant 10 personnes ou plus.
15 Y compris les filés de coton obtenus sur carde fileuse.
16 Y compris les filés mélangés, quelle que soit la matière première principale.
17 Pour 1985, les données sont confidentielles.
18 Y compris les fils.
19 Y compris la production ménagère.

Cotton yarn, mixed – Filés de coton mélangé

Unit : Thousand metric tons — Unité : Milliers de tonnes métriques

Country or area	1976	1977	1978	1979	1980	1981	1982	1983	1984	1985	Pays ou zone
Africa	**11.0**	**10.8**	**12.0**	**9.6**	**12.6**	**13.7**	**14.3**	**14.0**	**12.0**	**12.6**	**Afrique**
Senegal	* 0.3	* 0.3	* 0.2	0.0	0.2	0.3	0.3	0.2	0.2	0.2	Sénégal
South Africa	10.7	10.5	11.8	9.6	12.4	13.4	* 14.0	13.8	11.8	12.4	Afrique du Sud
America, North	**174.6**	**181.0**	**169.6**	**170.4**	**175.7**	**176.6**	**174.4**	**177.1**	**171.5**	**187.5**	**Amérique du Nord**
Canada[1 2]	21.0	25.2	13.4	17.0	...	...	...	...	...	...	Canada[1 2]
Cuba	22.2	24.0	24.3	21.7	25.0	26.2	23.9	26.4	26.7	30.8	Cuba
Dominican Republic	0.5	0.8	1.1	0.8	0.7	0.4	0.5	0.7	0.7	0.8	Rép. dominicaine
United States	...	...	...	...	...	...	...	...	125.0	136.8	Etats–Unis
America, South	**339.7**	**361.0**	**448.6**	**474.3**	**530.3**	**538.6**	**600.1**	**644.0**	**687.3**	**730.7**	**Amérique du Sud**
Brazil	...	358.2	444.3	469.7	526.6	535.2	...	...	...	...	Brésil
Colombia	2.2	2.1	2.2	3.4	2.5	2.2	2.1	2.5	2.5	...	Colombie
Ecuador	0.9	0.7	2.0	...	...	...	...	...	...	...	Equateur
Asia	**612.9**	**843.6**	**929.2**	**1 136.8**	**1 197.3**	**1 410.1**	**1 218.0**	**1 401.8**	**1 567.6**	**1 641.1**	**Asie**
Burma	...	...	...	...	...	2.9	2.5	1.2	0.4	0.2	Birmanie
China	...	...	484.6	685.8	793.1	966.9	836.0	977.8	1 121.3	1 226.9	Chine
Hong Kong	25.8	31.0	39.9	39.0	36.6	31.9	21.9	21.6	16.8	11.6	Hong–kong
India	56.1	163.3	195.4	148.4	100.9	114.4	84.9	85.7	83.5	* 81.0	Inde
Indonesia	7.9	16.9	27.1	49.2	...	...	...	...	...	...	Indonésie
Israel	3.2	3.2	3.7	3.3	4.3	3.5	3.8	3.9	3.7	3.4	Israël
Japan[3]	33.4	32.1	35.3	32.3	31.0	32.1	36.0	37.9	46.1	44.5	Japon[3]
Korea, Republic of	75.2	88.4	104.5	140.7	160.1	181.4	167.6	205.5	217.4	198.8	Corée, République de
Pakistan	...	...	...	22.2	33.2	38.8	32.8	33.3	44.0	40.0	Pakistan
Turkey	11.6	13.9	10.7	13.3	10.4	13.0	7.2	9.8	9.2	9.5	Turquie
Europe	**285.4**	**270.8**	**297.9**	**295.5**	**271.6**	**245.1**	**250.5**	**267.3**	**270.2**	**278.8**	**Europe**
EEC	***101.6***	***96.0***	***95.8***	***106.5***	***87.8***	***79.9***	***89.7***	***92.3***	***91.7***	***88.3***	***CEE***
Greece[4]	...	...	3.0	8.7	8.5	9.4	8.5	8.7	8.6	8.6	Grèce[4]
Italy	69.6	62.6	66.0	70.4	61.0	55.0	65.6	66.6	65.9	...	Italie
United Kingdom	26.5	27.4	26.8	27.4	18.4	15.5	15.6	17.1	17.1	16.5	Royaume–Uni
EFTA	***8.3***	***13.3***	***12.8***	***13.0***	***13.1***	***14.8***	***22.0***	***25.8***	***26.2***	***34.7***	***AELE***
Austria	2.6	2.8	1.8	1.8	1.7	1.3	1.4	1.2	1.8	1.7	Autriche
Portugal	5.7	10.4	11.1	11.3	11.4	13.5	20.6	24.7	24.4	33.0	Portugal
East Europe	***121.2***	***118.5***	***124.7***	***118.9***	***120.4***	***99.4***	***85.4***	***97.4***	***100.1***	***102.2***	***Europe de l'est***
Hungary	13.4	13.1	13.1	12.6	13.2	13.8	13.3	14.3	13.9	14.6	Hongrie
Poland	107.8	105.4	111.5	106.4	107.2	85.6	72.2	83.1	86.1	87.7	Pologne
Other Europe	***54.4***	***43.1***	***64.5***	***57.0***	***50.3***	***51.0***	***53.4***	***51.7***	***52.2***	***53.6***	***Autre Europe***
Spain	23.6	24.2	42.1	...	...	...	...	...	...	...	Espagne
Yugoslavia	30.8	18.9	22.4	27.0	20.3	21.1	23.4	21.7	22.3	23.6	Yougoslavie
Oceania	**0.3**	**1.6**	**4.0**	**4.1**	**4.4**	**3.6**	**4.4**	**5.6**	**6.2**	**6.9**	**Océanie**
Australia[5 6]	0.3	1.6	4.0	4.1	4.4	3.6	4.4	...	...	...	Australie[5 6]
Total	**1 424.0**	**1 668.8**	**1 861.2**	**2 090.6**	**2 191.9**	**2 387.8**	**2 261.7**	**2 509.8**	**2 714.8**	**2 857.6**	**Total**

General note.
Mixed yarn in which cotton or cotton waste is the predominant material by weight, containing less than 10 per cent by weight of silk, noil or other waste silk or any combination thereof. (SITC 65130–1).

[1] Shipments.
[2] Beginning 1980, data are confidential.
[3] Including condenser cotton yarn.
[4] Including all mixed yarns, irrespective of predominant raw material.
[5] Twelve months ending 30 June of year stated.
[6] Beginning 1983, series discontinued.

Remarque générale.
Filés de coton mélangé dans lesquels le coton ou les déchets de coton prédominent en poids et contenant moins de 10 p. 100 en poids de soie, de bourre de soie ou d'autres déchets de soie, ou de mélange de ces fibres. (CTCI 65130–1).

[1] Expéditions.
[2] A partir de 1980, les données sont confidentielles.
[3] Y compris les filés de coton obtenus sur carde fileuse.
[4] Y compris les filés mélangés, quelle que soit la matière première principale.
[5] Période de douze mois finissant le 30 juin de l'année indiquée.
[6] A partir 1983, la série a été interrompue.

Cotton yarn, pure – Filés de coton pur

Unit : Thousand metric tons

Unité : Milliers de tonnes métriques

Country or area	1976	1977	1978	1979	1980	1981	1982	1983	1984	1985	Pays ou zone
Africa	**320.9**	**327.8**	**329.8**	**354.2**	**387.3**	**394.5**	**375.1**	**375.2**	**388.4**	**405.8**	**Afrique**
Burkina Faso	0.8	0.4	0.6	0.6	0.3	1.0	1.2	* 1.3	1.5	* 1.4	Burkina Faso
Central African Rep.	...	...	...	...	10.3	8.4	6.2	10.3	12.1	17.0	Rép. centrafricaine
Côte d'Ivoire	...	7.0	9.4	10.7	10.9	22.1	13.1	15.9	15.6	18.5	Côte d'Ivoire
Egypt	193.0	210.4	212.2	219.0	236.0	239.0	245.0	229.1	243.6	250.8	Egypte
Ethiopia[1,2]	9.8	8.9	7.9	7.9	9.3	7.0	9.2	9.3	9.3	9.4	Ethiopie[1,2]
Mali	...	...	45.7	48.6	51.1	46.3	40.8	54.3	...	...	Mali
Nigeria	6.4	4.4	5.0	...	...	...	...	...	...	...	Nigéria
Senegal[3]	0.3	0.3	0.3	0.6	0.4	0.3	0.4	0.5	0.4	0.1	Sénégal[3]
South Africa	48.3	37.9	36.1	45.3	51.5	54.0	* 41.9	37.3	38.0	39.5	Afrique du Sud
Tunisia	7.4	9.1	8.3	10.5	12.2	11.1	* 12.0	* 12.0	...	...	Tunisie
America, North	**881.9**	**877.5**	**861.7**	**857.3**	**875.9**	**879.9**	**884.2**	**885.6**	**879.0**	**886.3**	**Amérique du Nord**
Canada[4,5]	41.7	36.0	[6] 19.9	[6] 17.9	...	41.4	45.5	45.2	44.6	43.5	Canada[4,5]
El Salvador	4.5	5.9	6.1	3.6	3.9	2.9	3.0	4.7	...	...	El Salvador
United States	...	...	...	...	...	...	...	...	831.4	840.0	Etats–Unis
America, South	**249.2**	**248.8**	**229.4**	**236.6**	**233.5**	**211.3**	**206.3**	**204.7**	**247.1**	**326.9**	**Amérique du Sud**
Argentina	91.7	95.0	83.6	92.4	74.9	61.3	68.4	83.0	92.9	112.6	Argentine
Bolivia	0.6	2.0	1.0	1.0	0.8	0.7	* 4.5	3.5	6.8	8.6	Bolivie
Brazil	69.7	24.9	5.7	13.5	...	...	...	...	...	...	Brésil
Chile	...	...	...	3.8	4.8	4.0	4.6	3.6	7.5	8.3	Chili
Colombia	51.5	51.8	45.5	52.1	49.1	10.5	9.1	8.5	...	...	Colombie
Ecuador	0.8	0.4	0.4	...	...	...	...	...	...	...	Equateur
Paraguay	33.8	72.8	90.7	73.3	74.9	105.9	90.8	77.2	105.3	160.0	Paraguay
Asia	**4 405.4**	**4 262.6**	**4 362.4**	**4 650.4**	**4 926.4**	**4 935.5**	**5 325.8**	**5 203.9**	**5 099.7**	**5 499.9**	**Asie**
Afghanistan[7]	1.1	1.2	0.9	0.6	0.3	0.1	0.1	0.1	0.3	0.3	Afghanistan[7]
Bangladesh[8]	39.9	37.4	40.7	43.8	43.2	46.2	43.2	44.4	46.2	48.2	Bangladesh[8]
Burma[9]	13.8	14.4	14.4	13.2	15.6	13.5	13.5	10.8	10.3	10.0	Birmanie[9]
China	...	1 897.8	1 898.4	1 948.8	2 132.4	2 203.2	2 518.0	2 292.2	2 097.7	2 308.1	Chine
Hong Kong	196.1	169.4	169.6	185.3	164.0	129.4	126.4	140.6	136.5	142.5	Hong–kong
India[1]	1 005.9	846.1	911.6	952.2	1 057.8	1 014.9	973.2	1 093.8	1 142.0	1 260.0	Inde[1]
Indonesia	32.8	40.0	50.4	51.4	...	86.0	85.3	100.6	116.4	111.9	Indonésie
Israel	21.2	22.4	20.6	19.2	15.7	13.8	12.7	13.1	12.8	11.9	Israël
Japan[10]	464.9	408.8	412.6	475.4	472.7	423.5	434.2	399.8	390.7	392.5	Japon[10]
Korea, Republic of	176.0	189.1	189.2	244.5	265.0	245.1	271.9	271.3	274.7	267.6	Corée, République de
Malaysia	...	...	...	...	15.6	14.4	14.3	10.9	10.0	12.0	Malaisie
Pakistan	...	...	...	* 327.8	362.9	374.9	430.2	415.2	420.0	453.6	Pakistan
Philippines[11]	32.6	30.8	32.0	35.9	38.4	36.3	35.6	19.8	21.2	22.5	Philippines[11]
Sri Lanka	7.4	5.1	5.7	6.2	4.3	6.4	7.6	7.6	6.9	9.4	Sri Lanka
Syrian Arab Republic	14.4	15.0	12.5	24.8	20.5	31.4	28.2	37.0	33.6	34.9	Rép. arabe syrienne
Thailand[11]	85.9	93.8	102.0	96.4	96.2	97.3	101.2	109.7	115.6	131.5	Thaïlande[11]
Turkey	[1] 142.2	170.4	162.7	208.3	152.3	199.1	230.0	237.1	264.9	283.1	Turquie
Europe	**989.6**	**950.8**	**948.1**	**986.0**	**1 009.0**	**959.0**	**949.8**	**951.2**	**975.1**	**961.0**	**Europe**
EEC	***587.3***	***539.7***	***540.3***	***557.6***	***558.4***	***498.0***	***496.2***	***492.4***	***498.5***	***486.9***	***CEE***
Denmark	2.3	1.9	1.5	1.7	1.9	* 2.0	2.0	1.9	* 1.6	...	Danemark
France	201.8	185.4	172.3	170.6	171.4	148.7	[12] 149.3	[12] 148.5	[12] 146.9	...	France
Greece	109.7	101.3	112.7	119.4	127.0	118.2	119.4	128.5	125.3	123.6	Grèce
Ireland[13]	...	3.8	2.6	3.4	15.6	17.6	15.3	13.5	12.8	...	Irlande[13]
Italy	164.2	149.1	159.9	171.6	170.2	160.5	159.2	150.0	164.6	161.6	Italie
United Kingdom	106.9	98.1	91.3	90.8	72.2	51.0	51.0	49.9	47.3	48.1	Royaume–Uni
EFTA	***101.5***	***103.5***	***97.8***	***114.2***	***123.9***	***119.3***	***119.7***	***127.2***	***131.3***	***125.4***	***AELE***
Austria	18.1	17.2	16.0	16.8	16.6	16.1	14.4	15.7	15.3	13.6	Autriche
Portugal[12]	83.4	86.3	81.8	97.3	107.3	103.2	105.3	111.5	116.0	111.8	Portugal[12]
East Europe	***155.8***	***160.6***	***163.0***	***155.8***	***156.8***	***154.3***	***143.4***	***135.8***	***135.3***	***139.6***	***Europe de l'est***
Hungary[11]	45.1	47.0	49.6	48.0	46.7	44.3	42.4	42.2	42.8	43.3	Hongrie[11]
Poland	110.7	113.6	113.4	107.7	110.1	110.0	101.0	93.6	92.4	96.3	Pologne
Other Europe	***145.0***	***147.1***	***147.0***	***158.5***	***169.9***	***187.4***	***190.5***	***195.8***	***210.0***	***209.1***	***Autre Europe***
Spain	46.8	45.0	51.6	...	...	90.9	93.1	97.0	103.6	99.8	Espagne
Yugoslavia	98.1	102.0	95.4	92.8	96.9	96.5	97.4	98.8	106.4	109.3	Yougoslavie

For general note and footnotes, see end of table.

Voir la fin du tableau pour la remarque générale et les notes.

Unit : Thousand metric tons — Unité : Milliers de tonnes métriques

Country or area	1976	1977	1978	1979	1980	1981	1982	1983	1984	1985	Pays ou zone
Oceania	**25.5**	**20.6**	**18.5**	**17.0**	**17.4**	**18.0**	**17.6**	**15.0**	**13.9**	**12.8**	**Océanie**
Australia[8] [14]	25.5	20.6	18.5	17.0	17.4	18.0	17.6	...	...	...	Australie[8] [14]
Total	**6 872.6**	**6 688.1**	**6 749.9**	**7 101.5**	**7 449.4**	**7 398.2**	**7 758.8**	**7 635.7**	**7 603.2**	**8 092.7**	**Total**

General note.
Pure cotton yarn, including yarn from cotton waste. (SITC 65130–2).

1 Factory production only.
2 Twelve months ending 10 September of year stated.
3 Production for sale only.
4 Including mixed cotton yarn.
5 Beginning 1980, data are confidential.
6 Shipments.
7 Twelve months beginning 21 March of year stated.
8 Twelve months ending 30 June of year stated.
9 Production by government–owned enterprises only.
10 Including condenser cotton yarn.
11 Excluding yarn made from waste.
12 Including tire–cord yarn.
13 1985, data are confidential.
14 Beginning 1983, series discontinued.

Remarque générale.
Filés de coton pur, y compris les filés obtenus à partir de déchets de coton. (CTCI 65130–2).

1 Production des fabriques seulement.
2 Période de douze mois finissant le 10 septembre de l'année indiquée.
3 Production destinée à la vente seulement.
4 Y compris les filés de coton mélangé.
5 A partir de 1980, les données sont confidentielles.
6 Expéditions.
7 Période de douze mois commençant le 21 mars de l'année indiquée.
8 Période de douze mois finissant le 30 juin de l'année indiquée.
9 Production des établissements d'Etat seulement.
10 Y compris les filés de coton obtenus sur carde fileuse.
11 Non compris les filés à base de déchets de coton.
12 Y compris les filés de coton pour pneumatiques à cordes.
13 Pour 1985, les données sont confidentielles.
14 A partir 1983, la série a été interrompue.

Flax, ramie and true hemp yarn
Filés de lin, de ramie et de chanvre

Unit : Thousand metric tons

Unité : Milliers de tonnes métriques

Country or area	1976	1977	1978	1979	1980	1981	1982	1983	1984	1985	Pays ou zone
Africa	**1.1**	**1.0**	**0.8**	**0.7**	**0.7**	**0.7**	**0.6**	**0.7**	**0.6**	**0.7**	**Afrique**
Egypt[1,2]	1.0	0.9	0.7	0.7	0.6	0.6	0.5	0.5	* 0.4	* 0.5	Egypte[1,2]
Tunisia	0.1	0.1	0.1	0.1	0.1	0.1	* 0.1	* 0.2	* 0.2	...	Tunisie
America, South	**4.0**	**3.7**	**3.9**	**2.3**	**5.8**	**4.6**	**4.8**	**5.0**	**5.2**	**5.4**	**Amérique du Sud**
Brazil	4.0	* 3.7	3.9	[3] 2.3	5.8	...	...	...	...	...	Brésil
Asia	**2.8**	**2.8**	**2.7**	**2.6**	**2.8**	**3.0**	**4.1**	**5.9**	**7.0**	**6.9**	**Asie**
Japan	2.1	2.2	2.1	2.0	2.1	2.4	3.5	5.2	6.4	6.3	Japon
Korea, Republic of[1]	0.6	...	...	...	...	...	...	...	...	...	Corée, République de[1]
Europe	**190.6**	**183.5**	**174.9**	**171.3**	**174.1**	**161.3**	**151.4**	**145.7**	**145.0**	**141.8**	**Europe**
EEC	***45.9***	***40.3***	***36.6***	***38.1***	***39.5***	***33.7***	***33.0***	***31.4***	***28.7***	***27.9***	***CEE***
Belgium[1]	10.6	9.0	9.0	9.6	9.4	8.1	8.5	9.3	10.6	9.0	Belgique[1]
France	13.3	11.5	10.9	12.7	11.2	* 9.8	* 9.2	* 8.5	8.9	7.7	France
Germany, Fed. Rep.[4]	6.3	4.6	4.4	4.1	3.4	...	...	...	...	...	Allemagne, Rép. féd.[4]
Greece	4.4	4.9	4.2	4.3	[5] 9.8	[5] 9.2	[5] 9.2	[5] 8.5	[5] 5.8	...	Grèce
Italy	[6] 11.4	# 10.3	[1] 8.0	[1] 7.4	[1] 5.6	[1] 3.9	[1] 4.0	...	...	...	Italie
EFTA	***5.8***	***5.4***	***4.6***	***4.9***	***4.0***	***3.7***	***3.1***	***3.3***	***3.3***	***3.5***	***AELE***
Austria[6]	2.3	2.4	2.1	2.4	2.1	2.2	2.2	2.4	2.5	2.7	Autriche[6]
Finland[1]	1.7	1.4	1.3	1.2	0.9	0.9	0.4	0.5	0.5	...	Finlande[1]
Portugal[7,8]	0.3	0.2	0.2	0.3	0.3	0.4	0.3	0.3	0.3	0.6	Portugal[7,8]
Sweden	1.6	1.4	0.9	0.9	0.7	0.2	0.1	0.1	0.1	0.1	Suède
East Europe	***131.1***	***129.8***	***126.1***	***120.6***	***123.1***	***116.7***	***108.1***	***103.4***	***103.4***	***102.4***	***Europe de l'est***
Bulgaria[6]	8.9	9.1	9.6	10.1	10.5	9.1	9.9	9.8	9.8	9.5	Bulgarie[6]
Czechoslovakia[6]	19.5	17.9	17.7	17.5	17.7	17.8	17.7	17.4	17.1	16.4	Tchécoslovaquie[6]
German Dem. Rep.	1.3	1.6	0.4	0.2	0.0	0.0	0.0	0.2	0.2	0.0	Rép. dém. allemande
Hungary	13.1	12.2	11.4	10.2	10.6	10.0	8.9	8.4	8.9	8.7	Hongrie
Poland	52.3	50.6	46.3	40.8	38.9	33.5	30.1	29.1	29.5	30.1	Pologne
Romania[6,9]	36.1	38.4	40.7	41.8	45.5	46.3	41.6	38.6	38.0	37.7	Roumanie[6,9]
Other Europe	***7.7***	***8.1***	***7.6***	***7.7***	***7.6***	***7.2***	***7.2***	***7.6***	***9.5***	***8.0***	***Autre Europe***
Spain[10]	1.1	1.0	1.1	...	...	...	...	...	...	...	Espagne[10]
Yugoslavia	6.7	7.1	6.5	6.6	6.5	6.2	6.2	6.5	8.5	7.0	Yougoslavie
USSR[1]	**267.7**	**268.7**	**267.8**	**245.1**	**213.8**	**201.7**	**196.1**	**208.0**	**212.0**	**213.6**	**URSS[1]**
Byelorussian SSR[1]	*30.0*	*30.6*	*31.1*	*31.2*	*27.8*	*26.1*	*25.3*	*25.8*	*26.2*	*27.0*	*RSS de Biélorussie[1]*
Ukrainian SSR[1]	*24.6*	*24.9*	*25.9*	*26.4*	*24.1*	*23.4*	*20.9*	*22.6*	*23.5*	*24.8*	*RSS d'Ukraine[1]*
Total	**466.1**	**459.6**	**450.2**	**422.1**	**397.2**	**371.3**	**357.1**	**365.3**	**369.8**	**368.5**	**Total**

General note.
Flax, ramie and true hemp yarn, including yarns put up for sale. (SITC 65150–1).

Remarque générale.
Filés de lin, de ramie et de chanvre, y compris les fils conditionnés pour la vente au détail. (CTCI 65150–1).

[1] Flax yarn only.
[2] Including waste.
[3] Production by establishments employing 5 or more persons.
[4] Beginning 1981, data are confidential.
[5] Including yarn of jute.
[6] Yarn of flax and true hemp.
[7] Including yarn made from tow.
[8] Linen only.
[9] Including mixed yarn and jute.
[10] Including mixed yarn.

[1] Filés de lin seulement.
[2] Y compris les déchets.
[3] Production des établissements occupant 5 personnes ou plus.
[4] A partir de 1981, les données sont confidentielles.
[5] Y compris les filés de jute.
[6] Filés de lin et de chanvre.
[7] Y compris les filés d'étoupe.
[8] Toile de lin seulement.
[9] Y compris les filés mélangés et le jute.
[10] Y compris les filés mélangés.

Yarn of man–made staple – Filés de fibres synthétiques et artificielles

Unit : Thousand metric tons

Unité : Milliers de tonnes métriques

Country or area	1976	1977	1978	1979	1980	1981	1982	1983	1984	1985	Pays ou zone
Africa	**13.8**	**19.2**	**14.3**	**18.0**	**22.1**	**24.7**	**24.6**	**20.8**	**21.7**	**25.2**	**Afrique**
South Africa	13.4	18.2	13.3	16.2	20.3	21.7	21.6	17.8	* 18.0	...	Afrique du Sud
Tunisia	0.4	1.0	1.1	1.8	1.9	3.0	* 3.0	* 3.0	...	...	Tunisie
America, North	**1 321.1**	**1 355.8**	**1 387.4**	**1 416.4**	**1 455.2**	**1 517.2**	**1 424.6**	**1 658.0**	**1 647.5**	**1 588.3**	**Amérique du Nord**
Canada[1 2]	35.6	32.3	25.8	[3] 16.8	[3] 18.3	...	...	...	...	...	Canada[1 2]
Cuba	...	...	...	...	2.1	3.2	3.1	3.4	4.7	6.3	Cuba
United States	...	...	...	...	...	1 494.1	1 403.9	1 639.1	1 629.5	1 571.0	Etats–Unis
America, South	**13.0**	**16.5**	**14.7**	**16.7**	**16.9**	**18.1**	**12.6**	**14.5**	**16.0**	**16.8**	**Amérique du Sud**
Chile	...	...	...	8.7	7.1	6.8	4.1	5.3	7.0	6.2	Chili
Colombia	1.4	2.2	1.4	2.0	3.0	2.1	* 2.5	2.3	2.0	...	Colombie
Ecuador	3.2	6.2	5.5	...	6.9	9.2	6.0	6.9	* 7.0	...	Equateur
Asia	**1 015.7**	**1 025.3**	**1 052.7**	**1 143.9**	**1 208.0**	**1 164.2**	**1 208.8**	**1 258.1**	**1 350.4**	**1 411.1**	**Asie**
India	84.7	112.6	133.1	137.2	126.7	153.0	135.7	130.8	130.3	...	Inde
Japan	648.2	589.1	603.2	660.7	649.3	593.5	613.3	617.1	655.2	648.9	Japon
Korea, Republic of	245.8	276.7	286.1	308.9	336.1	363.0	407.8	434.6	466.0	502.4	Corée, République de
Philippines	...	...	18.2	22.5	72.4	25.5	23.5	...	...	...	Philippines
Turkey	10.0	18.6	12.2	14.5	# 23.5	29.2	28.5	39.2	61.1	72.0	Turquie
Europe	**968.9**	**925.8**	**933.3**	**1 084.3**	**1 037.5**	**1 039.3**	**1 003.9**	**1 016.2**	**1 143.5**	**1 197.4**	**Europe**
EEC	***719.4***	***671.0***	***663.4***	***637.2***	***599.3***	***612.8***	***581.4***	***582.4***	***594.7***	***650.2***	***CEE***
Belgium	15.3	12.3	11.2	9.5	9.2	8.7	9.5	10.2	11.8	13.4	Belgique
Denmark[4]	6.0	5.4	5.6	5.1	5.1	...	3.4	3.3	3.5	5.4	Danemark[4]
France	140.7	141.0	141.3	140.0	133.2	130.8	133.1	130.4	132.4	137.0	France
Germany, Fed. Rep.	450.8	394.3	386.6	377.6	358.2	377.6	350.9	356.9	363.9	411.2	Allemagne, Rép. féd.
Greece	46.9	57.6	61.1	50.1	51.1	55.0	48.6	45.5	46.6	...	Grèce
Netherlands	14.4	15.3	13.9	13.2	11.4	10.4	9.6	8.1	7.5	...	Pays–Bas
United Kingdom[5]	45.3	45.2	43.7	41.7	31.1	25.6	26.4	28.1	29.0	30.1	Royaume–Uni[5]
EFTA	***43.1***	***43.8***	***43.5***	***45.8***	***51.4***	***51.8***	***49.7***	***48.4***	***50.6***	***50.4***	***AELE***
Austria	8.8	7.3	4.4	4.4	4.8	5.0	4.9	4.5	4.6	5.0	Autriche
Finland	4.7	4.3	5.3	5.2	4.7	4.6	4.1	3.2	3.1	...	Finlande
Norway	3.1	2.8	3.1	3.2	3.7	3.5	...	...	...	...	Norvège
Portugal	20.4	24.7	26.9	29.4	34.5	36.2	34.2	33.7	35.6	* 35.0	Portugal
Sweden	6.1	4.5	3.8	3.6	3.8	2.5	2.8	3.2	3.2	2.9	Suède
East Europe	***199.5***	***205.0***	***219.3***	***217.8***	***227.3***	***227.1***	***243.9***	***257.6***	***302.8***	***279.3***	***Europe de l'est***
Hungary	20.7	21.1	21.9	21.6	21.5	21.8	21.5	22.1	21.5	22.1	Hongrie
Romania	178.8	183.8	197.5	196.2	205.8	205.3	222.4	235.5	281.3	257.2	Roumanie
Other Europe	***6.8***	***6.0***	***7.1***	***183.5***	***159.5***	***147.6***	***128.9***	***127.8***	***195.5***	***217.6***	***Autre Europe***
Spain	6.8	6.0	7.1	[6] 183.5	[6] 159.5	[6] 147.6	[6] 128.9	[6] 127.8	...	...	Espagne
USSR	**152.1**	**152.7**	**159.2**	**153.6**	**158.0**	**162.9**	**155.7**	**161.0**	**167.1**	**168.6**	**URSS**
Total	**3 484.6**	**3 495.3**	**3 561.6**	**3 832.9**	**3 897.8**	**3 926.3**	**3 830.2**	**4 128.5**	**4 346.2**	**4 407.6**	**Total**

General note.

Yarns obtained by converting discontinuous man–made fibres other than textile glass fibres into slivers, rovings and yarns by processes generally similar to those used for cotton and wool. Monofils, yarns obtained by grouping together a number of filaments as they emerge from the spinnerets, either reeled parallel without twist or twisted, and continuous filament tow are excluded. (Parts of SITC 65164, 65165, 65174 and 65175).

Remarque générale.

Filés obtenus à partir de fibres artificielles ou synthétiques discontinues autres que les fibres de verre par transformation en rubans, mèches et filés par des procédés en général analogues à ceux que l'on emploie pour le coton et la laine. Cette rubrique ne comprend pas les monofils, les fils constitués par la juxtaposition d'un certain nombre de filaments simples à la sortie des filières, moulinés ou non moulinés, et les câbles de fibres continues. (Parties de CTCI 65164, 65165, 65174 et 65175).

[1] Including yarn produced in carpet mills.
[2] Including tire–cord yarn.
[3] Shipments.
[4] Yarns containing at least 50 per cent discontinuous man–made fibres.
[5] Production in cotton spinning sector only.
[6] Including household production.

[1] Y compris les filés produits dans les fabriques de tapis.
[2] Y compris les filés de coton pour pneumatiques à cordes.
[3] Expéditions.
[4] Filés contenant au moins 50 p. 100 de fibres synthétiques discontinues.
[5] Production du secteur des filatures de coton seulement.
[6] Y compris la production ménagère.

Jute yarn – Filés de jute

Unit : Thousand metric tons

Unité : Milliers de tonnes métriques

Country or area	1976	1977	1978	1979	1980	1981	1982	1983	1984	1985	Pays ou zone
Africa	**36.8**	**38.2**	**35.2**	**39.6**	**41.7**	**40.5**	**39.9**	**35.7**	**36.3**	**33.6**	**Afrique**
Algeria	0.0	0.0	1.4	3.7	5.5	5.0	5.6	* 6.0	...	...	Algérie
Egypt	36.7	38.1	33.7	35.8	36.2	35.4	34.2	29.6	28.4	24.7	Egypte
Tunisia	0.1	0.1	0.1	0.1	0.1	0.1	* 0.1	* 0.1	...	...	Tunisie
America, South	**57.3**	**55.2**	**64.7**	**61.4**	**71.7**	**57.2**	**65.8**	**67.1**	**68.4**	**69.7**	**Amérique du Sud**
Brazil	57.3	55.2	64.7	[1] 61.4	71.7	57.2	...	...	...	...	Brésil
Asia	**31.4**	**29.5**	**25.1**	**22.5**	**22.0**	**14.8**	**10.7**	**9.5**	**8.8**	**6.6**	**Asie**
Japan	31.3	29.4	25.1	22.5	21.9	14.8	10.7	9.5	8.8	6.6	Japon
Europe	**213.9**	**188.2**	**164.8**	**147.1**	**126.7**	**108.6**	**97.7**	**85.0**	**75.0**	**70.1**	**Europe**
EEC	***147.8***	***123.9***	***106.0***	***93.7***	***74.8***	***61.4***	***54.8***	***46.0***	***39.7***	***35.3***	***CEE***
Belgium	37.2	29.7	23.1	16.9	14.4	14.0	12.9	15.2	14.1	13.6	Belgique
France[2]	30.9	24.7	18.9	16.8	15.0	11.2	8.2	3.3	0.7	0.5	France[2]
Germany, Fed. Rep.	11.7	11.1	9.7	8.6	7.5	5.7	5.1	3.4	3.1	[3] 0.8	Allemagne, Rép. féd.
Greece	...	...	...	...	...	...	...	...	1.2	...	Grèce
Italy	14.1	10.4	8.0	7.4	5.6	4.0	5.7	...	...	...	Italie
United Kingdom	52.7	46.8	45.1	42.8	31.1	25.3	21.8	19.0	17.8	17.5	Royaume–Uni
EFTA	***10.9***	***11.1***	***10.8***	***10.0***	***9.0***	***6.9***	***6.2***	***5.2***	***5.1***	***3.7***	***AELE***
Austria	0.2	0.1	0.4	0.1	0.0	0.0	0.0	0.0	0.0	0.0	Autriche
Finland	0.6	0.6	0.5	0.4	0.4	0.4	0.5	0.5	0.5	...	Finlande
Portugal	9.1	9.4	8.7	8.6	8.0	6.1	5.5	4.5	4.5	3.3	Portugal
Sweden	1.1	1.0	1.1	0.9	0.6	0.3	0.3	0.2	0.1	0.0	Suède
East Europe	***44.0***	***40.9***	***34.4***	***30.7***	***30.0***	***26.9***	***24.1***	***22.3***	***20.6***	***21.3***	***Europe de l'est***
Czechoslovakia[4]	12.9	11.8	8.7	7.7	7.2	7.2	6.7	5.8	5.5	5.6	Tchécoslovaquie[4]
German Dem. Rep.	1.3	0.9	0.9	0.9	0.8	0.7	0.8	0.7	0.4	0.6	Rép. dém. allemande
Hungary	4.3	4.0	2.6	1.6	1.5	1.1	0.7	0.7	0.6	0.6	Hongrie
Poland	25.5	24.2	22.2	20.5	20.4	17.9	16.0	15.1	14.1	14.4	Pologne
Other Europe	***11.2***	***12.4***	***13.4***	***12.7***	***12.9***	***13.4***	***12.6***	***11.6***	***9.6***	***9.8***	***Autre Europe***
Spain[5]	0.5	1.7	1.6	...	...	...	...	...	...	...	Espagne[5]
Yugoslavia	10.7	10.7	11.9	11.5	11.6	12.1	11.3	10.3	8.3	8.6	Yougoslavie
Total	**339.3**	**311.1**	**289.7**	**270.6**	**262.1**	**221.1**	**214.1**	**197.3**	**188.5**	**180.0**	**Total**

General note.
Jute yarns obtained by spinning slivers of jute. (SITC 65192–1).

Remarque générale.
Filé de jute résultant du filage de rubans de jute. (CTCI 65192–1).

[1] Production by establishments employing 5 or more persons.
[2] Yarn of pure jute or mixed with sisal.
[3] Marketable production.
[4] Including yarn made from tow.
[5] Including mixed yarn.

[1] Production des établissements occupant 5 personnes ou plus.
[2] Filés de jute pur ou mélangé de sisal.
[3] Production commercialisable.
[4] Y compris les filés d'étoupe.
[5] Y compris les filés mélangés.

Yarn of other vegetable textile fibres –
Filés d'autres fibres textile végétales

Unit : Thousand metric tons

Unité : Milliers de tonnes métriques

Country or area	1976	1977	1978	1979	1980	1981	1982	1983	1984	1985	Pays ou zone
Africa	**8.8**	**8.1**	**6.8**	**5.8**	**4.4**	**4.4**	**4.3**	**2.2**	**1.3**	**1.0**	**Afrique**
Mauritius[1]	0.7	0.7	0.3	0.1	0.0	0.0	0.0	0.0	0.0	0.0	Maurice[1]
South Africa	...	...	...	...	4.4	4.4	4.3	2.2	1.3	1.0	Afrique du Sud
America, North	**59.2**	**65.5**	**56.7**	**61.9**	**58.5**	**60.8**	**60.8**	**54.8**	**59.0**	**64.5**	**Amérique du Nord**
Cuba	...	...	...	...	...	...	2.9	4.2	3.7	3.5	Cuba
Mexico	55.6	61.9	53.2	58.3	55.0	57.2	57.9	50.6	55.4	61.0	Mexique
America, South	**53.9**	**80.3**	**58.3**	**76.8**	**82.3**	**85.0**	**92.0**	**97.0**	**102.1**	**107.4**	**Amérique du Sud**
Brazil	51.2	77.6	55.3	[2] 74.1	79.6	...	...	...	...	...	Brésil
Ecuador[3]	...	...	3.0	...	...	1.6	3.2	2.9	...	...	Equateur[3]
Europe	**102.0**	**80.1**	**69.2**	**87.2**	**82.3**	**70.9**	**65.6**	**59.2**	**66.3**	**64.5**	**Europe**
EEC	***88.9***	***68.3***	***58.3***	***59.3***	***53.9***	***51.8***	***47.3***	***42.8***	***41.4***	***39.1***	***CEE***
Belgium	33.7	22.5	22.0	22.7	19.1	18.9	17.5	16.0	17.6	18.3	Belgique
Denmark	0.0	0.0	0.0	0.0	0.0	0.1	0.1	0.1	0.1	0.1	Danemark
France[4]	40.6	33.7	30.5	33.1	25.8	...	...	...	...	...	France[4]
Germany, Fed. Rep.[5]	14.0	11.4	5.1	2.9	...	...	...	...	...	...	Allemagne, Rép. féd.[5]
Greece	...	...	...	...	...	...	0.6	0.6	0.6	...	Grèce
EFTA	***1.6***	***1.5***	***1.3***	***1.3***	***1.1***	***0.8***	***0.7***	***0.6***	***0.6***	***0.5***	***AELE***
Austria	1.6	1.5	1.3	1.3	1.1	0.8	0.7	0.6	0.6	0.5	Autriche
East Europe	***3.6***	***4.3***	***3.5***	***3.2***	***3.0***	***2.7***	***2.6***	***2.3***	***2.2***	***2.0***	***Europe de l'est***
Czechoslovakia[6]	1.2	1.2	1.2	1.2	1.1	1.1	1.0	1.0	0.9	0.9	Tchécoslovaquie[6]
German Dem. Rep.	2.4	3.1	2.3	2.1	1.9	1.6	1.6	1.4	1.3	1.1	Rép. dém. allemande
Other Europe	***7.9***	***6.0***	***6.2***	***23.3***	***24.3***	***15.6***	***15.1***	***13.4***	***22.1***	***22.8***	***Autre Europe***
Spain[7 8]	0.7	0.6	0.6	19.5	18.4	9.1	10.4	10.6	...	...	Espagne[7 8]
Yugoslavia	7.2	5.4	5.6	3.8	6.0	6.5	4.7	2.8	5.7	4.7	Yougoslavie
Total	**223.9**	**233.9**	**191.1**	**231.7**	**227.5**	**221.1**	**222.7**	**213.3**	**228.7**	**237.3**	**Total**

General note.
Yarns obtained by spinning vegetable textile fibres other than cotton, flax, ramie, true hemp and jute. (SITC 65193–0).

[1] Production of aloe fibre.
[2] Production by establishments employing 5 or more persons.
[3] Yarn of agave and abaca.
[4] Essentially yarn for ropes and cordage,
[5] Beginning 1980, data are confidential.
[6] Yarn of sisal.
[7] Including continuous fibres.
[8] Including flax, ramie and ture hemp yarn.

Remarque générale.
Filés obtenus par filage de fibres textiles végétales autres que le coton, le lin, la ramie, le chanvre et le jute. (CTCI 65193–0).

[1] Production de fibre d'aloès.
[2] Production des établissements occupant 5 personnes ou plus.
[3] Filés d'agave et d'abaca.
[4] Essentiellement filés pour la ficellerie et la corderie.
[5] A partir de 1980, les données sont confidentielles.
[6] Filés de sisal.
[7] Y compris de fibres continues.
[8] Y compris filés de lin, de ramie et de chanvre.

Cotton woven fabrics – Tissus de coton

Unit : Million square metres

Unité : Millions de mètres carrés

Country or area	1976	1977	1978	1979	1980	1981	1982	1983	1984	1985	Pays ou zone
Africa	**1 938**	**1 956**	**1 931**	**1 967**	**2 159**	**2 337**	**2 554**	**2 221**	**2 041**	**1 904**	**Afrique**
Algeria	53	56	66	* 67	* 88	109	102	* 105	* 105	* 103	Algérie
Central African Rep.	6	4	3	* 4	* 4	* 4	* 4	* 4	* 4	...	Rép. centrafricaine
Chad	22	17	18	18	19	...	...	...	...	...	Tchad
Côte d'Ivoire[1]	...	81	82	89	94	146	103	129	118	...	Côte d'Ivoire[1]
Egypt[2]	673	711	722	729	756	754	996	* 922	* 899	* 740	Egypte[2]
Ethiopia[3]	81	76	65	88	86	87	92	92	85	...	Ethiopie[3]
Ghana[4]	123	113	105	79	44	36	8	8	8	...	Ghana[4]
Kenya	26	38	39	40	38	47	38	46	51	54	Kenya
Madagascar	93	95	93	100	95	75	87	91	82	78	Madagascar
Mali[2]	20	26	28	23	28	21	22	* 12	...	...	Mali[2]
Niger*	11	7	8	17	16	8	8	7	7	6	Niger*
Nigeria[5]	367	300	290	276	423	543	656	401	267	285	Nigéria[5]
Senegal	3	4	3	4	6	7	8	10	* 8	* 3	Sénégal
South Africa	126	156	147	181	195	226	194	* 147	147	139	Afrique du Sud
Togo	18	18	20	* 20	* 20	* 18	* 18	* 17	...	...	Togo
Tunisia	26	30	30	39	...	...	...	...	...	...	Tunisie
Uganda[4 6]	39	36	28	15	21	19	20	...	...	...	Ouganda[4 6]
United Rep. Tanzania	83	79	73	85	93	96	86	...	...	...	Rép.Unie de Tanzanie
Zaire[5]	80	95	97	* 83	* 89	* 76	50	61	* 58	* 50	Zaïre[5]
Zambia	14	14	14	10	13	17	15	16	16	21	Zambie
America, North	**5 651**	**5 257**	**4 953**	**4 761**	**4 416**	**3 984**	**3 840**	**4 186**	**4 032**	**4 022**	**Amérique du Nord**
Cuba[7]	133	145	147	143	148	149	138	156	156	177	Cuba[7]
Dominican Republic[6]	10	9	12	17	17	9	9	12	13	13	Rép. dominicaine[6]
El Salvador[5]	16	20	26	22	19	18	* 17	* [2] 4	...	...	El Salvador[5]
Haiti	2	1	2	1	1	1	1	1	1	1	Haïti
Honduras[5]	16	17	17	9	9	* 9	* 8	9	11	10	Honduras[5]
Jamaica[2]	7	10	11	7	5	4	4	4	...	...	Jamaïque[2]
Mexico[5 8]	523	498	479	487	482	512	473	476	460	510	Mexique[5 8]
Nicaragua[2]	...	...	...	6	9	10	17	19	31	...	Nicaragua[2]
United States	[2] 4 942	[2] 4 553	[2] 4 252	[2] 4 069	[2] 3 726	3 272	3 173	3 505	3 346	3 278	Etats–Unis
America, South	**1 722**	**1 873**	**2 028**	**2 108**	**2 128**	**1 811**	**2 040**	**2 087**	**2 150**	**2 207**	**Amérique du Sud**
Argentina[8]	525	...	...	...	...	...	...	...	...	...	Argentine[8]
Bolivia	8	5	12	12	13	7	* 5	* 8	* 7	...	Bolivie
Brazil[2]	1 076	1 208	1 342	[9] 1 444	1 497	1 216	...	...	...	...	Brésil[2]
Chile[2]	60	70	82	80	63	44	32	34	48	54	Chili[2]
Ecuador[4]	35	41	42	...	[2] 10	[2] 4	[2] 3	...	...	...	Equateur[4]
Paraguay	18	24	25	24	20	15	11	7	7	* 11	Paraguay
Asia	**16 290**	**24 094**	**25 764**	**27 180**	**29 226**	**29 737**	**34 000**	**34 720**	**33 824**	**33 123**	**Asie**
Afghanistan[10]	88	92	92	75	51	32	27	38	45	45	Afghanistan[10]
Bangladesh[11]	81	74	90	93	97	94	79	* 71	* 70	* 75	Bangladesh[11]
Burma[12]	[2] 87	[2] 93	[2] 89	[2] 99	[2] 107	95	74	80	84	33	Birmanie[12]
China	...	9 228	10 286	11 426	12 795	13 637	[2] 18 343	[2] 17 782	[2] 16 372	15 202	Chine
Democratic Yemen	...	...	...	...	2	2	3	4	4	...	Yémen démocratique
Hong Kong	822	676	654	717	661	616	566	642	659	639	Hong–kong
India	9 495	8 248	8 753	9 000	9 935	9 703	9 357	10 315	10 547	* 11 152	Inde
Indonesia[2 13]	703	...	...	* 751	858	* 950	* 936	* 1 001	* 1 135	...	Indonésie[2 13]
Iran(Islamic Rep.of)[2 14]	203	170	140	180	160	140	128	...	...	...	Iran(Rép.islamique)[2 14]
Japan	2 237	2 266	2 315	2 339	2 202	2 067	2 030	2 079	2 090	2 061	Japon
Jordan[6]	1	1	1	2	2	2	1	1	2	* 2	Jordanie[6]
Korea, Republic of[4]	295	288	273	317	366	354	447	442	395	470	Corée, République de[4]
Malaysia	209	226	248	253	262	267	257	241	...	...	Malaisie
Nepal[2 15]	6	5	3	4	6	8	10	12	...	...	Népal[2 15]
Pakistan[5 16]	520	408	391	339	342	308	325	336	297	274	Pakistan[5 16]
Philippines[2 4]	244	242	218	213	199	244	190	* 216	...	...	Philippines[2 4]
Sri Lanka[5]	71	82	89	56	43	[2] 25	[2] 21	[2] 17	[2] 21	[2] 31	Sri Lanka[5]
Syrian Arab Republic[8]	264	253	262	278	* 122	* 122	* 129	* 180	* 273	* 158	Rép. arabe syrienne[8]
Thailand[4]	585	598	634	...	...	...	...	...	...	...	Thaïlande[4]
Turkey[2 17]	188	196	202	201	195	272	197	185	189	211	Turquie[2 17]
Viet Nam	187	233	257	224	209	189	266	343	435	439	Viet Nam
Yemen[2]	...	...	2	5	6	4	8	7	7	7	Yémen[2]
Europe	**9 937**	**9 635**	**9 467**	**9 422**	**9 659**	**9 128**	**9 258**	**9 199**	**9 440**	**9 540**	**Europe**
EEC	***4 726***	***4 355***	***4 198***	***4 392***	***4 499***	***4 136***	***4 525***	***4 398***	***4 629***	***4 714***	***CEE***
Belgium[18]	435	336	315	361	352	331	374	361	361	373	Belgique[18]

For general note and footnotes, see end of table.

Voir la fin du tableau pour la remarque générale et les notes.

Cotton woven fabrics (continued) – Tissus de coton (suite)

Unit : Million square metres — Unité : Millions de mètres carrés

Country or area	1976	1977	1978	1979	1980	1981	1982	1983	1984	1985	Pays ou zone
Denmark	11	12	12	14	15	...	...	...	...	...	Danemark
France[8]	1 127	1 068	1 002	999	986	923	965	920	907	861	France[8]
Germany, Fed. Rep.[4]	906	809	746	748	791	518	822	884	943	990	Allemagne, Rép. féd.[4]
Greece[8]	212	205	200	211	280	278	276	300	281	...	Grèce[8]
Ireland[4 19]	19	18	14	17	36	43	40	36	34	...	Irlande[4 19]
Italy[8]	1 304	1 230	1 259	1 422	1 469	1 552	1 592	1 482	1 665	...	Italie[8]
Netherlands[4 8]	278	253	205	186	200	155	136	107	114	105	Pays-Bas[4 8]
United Kingdom	434	424	445	434	370	320	303	290	305	315	Royaume-Uni
EFTA	***775***	***785***	***742***	***749***	***847***	***807***	***811***	***840***	***864***	***891***	***AELE***
Austria	90	83	76	82	84	80	75	77	64	85	Autriche
Finland	80	87	57	60	66	61	71	72	73	...	Finlande
Norway[4]	23	24	17	15	24	17	15	12	19	16	Norvège[4]
Portugal[8]	* 373	* 382	* 388	* 392	* 466	* 460	462	499	523	542	Portugal[8]
Sweden* [8]	56	50	44	45	50	50	50	50	58	...	Suède* [8]
Switzerland[2]	153	159	160	155	157	139	138	130	127	130	Suisse[2]
East Europe	***3 103***	***3 165***	***3 167***	***3 107***	***3 165***	***3 079***	***2 981***	***3 025***	***3 135***	***3 159***	***Europe de l'est***
Bulgaria[4]	337	351	343	343	339	355	364	371	374	356	Bulgarie[4]
Czechoslovakia[4]	517	520	530	537	546	559	568	570	624	631	Tchécoslovaquie[4]
German Dem. Rep.	274	272	270	262	277	286	288	298	294	298	Rép. dém. allemande
Hungary[4]	319	332	328	306	295	287	282	280	278	287	Hongrie[4]
Poland[4 20]	979	987	979	952	960	860	741	797	868	887	Pologne[4 20]
Romania[4]	677	703	717	707	748	732	738	709	697	700	Roumanie[4]
Other Europe	***1 333***	***1 330***	***1 360***	***1 174***	***1 148***	***1 106***	***941***	***936***	***812***	***776***	***Autre Europe***
Spain[8]	948	946	950	756	762	729	569	...	...	...	Espagne[8]
Yugoslavia[21]	385	384	410	418	386	377	372	379	318	344	Yougoslavie[21]
USSR[4]	**7 408**	**7 461**	**7 619**	**7 662**	**7 798**	**7 878**	**7 877**	**8 029**	**8 313**	**8 580**	**URSS[4]**
Byelorussian SSR	*116*	...	...	...	...	...	...	...	...	...	*RSS de Biélorussie*
Oceania	**47**	**40**	**38**	**40**	**43**	**43**	**39**	**32**	**33**	**35**	**Océanie**
Australia[5 11]	47	40	38	40	43	43	39	32	33	35	Australie[5 11]
Total	**42 993**	**50 317**	**51 799**	**53 140**	**55 429**	**54 918**	**59 607**	**60 474**	**59 832**	**59 412**	**Total**

General note.
Woven cotton fabrics (at loom stage) before undergoing finishing processes such as bleaching, dyeing, printing, mercerizing, lazing etc. (SITC 65210–0).

1 Finished fabrics.
2 Original data in metres.
3 Twelve months ending 10 September of year stated.
4 After undergoing finishing processes.
5 Including finished fabrics.
6 Including cellulosic fabrics.
7 Including mixed cotton fabrics.
8 Original data in metric tons.
9 Production by establishments employing 5 or more persons.
10 Twelve months beginning 21 March of year stated.
11 Twelve months ending 30 June of year stated.
12 Production by government-owned enterprises only.
13 Including synthetic fabrics.
14 Including linen fabrics.
15 Twelve months beginning 16 July of year stated.
16 Factory production only.
17 Government production only.
18 Including cotton blankets and carpets.
19 1985, data are confidential.
20 Including fabrics of cotton substitutes.
21 Including woven cellulosic fabrics.

Remarque générale.
Tissus de coton sortant du métier à tisser, avant les opérations de finition, c'est-à-dire avant d'être blanchis, teints, imprimés, mercerisés, glacés etc. (CTCI 65210–0).

1 Tissus finis.
2 Données d'origine exprimées en mètres.
3 Période de douze mois finissant le 10 septembre de l'année indiquée.
4 Après opérations de finition.
5 Y compris les tissus finis.
6 Y compris les tissus en fibres cellulosiques.
7 Y compris les tissus de cotton mélangé.
8 Données d'origine exprimées en tonnes.
9 Production des établissements occupant 5 personnes ou plus.
10 Période de douze mois commençant le 21 mars de l'année indiquée.
11 Période de douze mois finissant le 30 juin de l'année indiquée.
12 Production des établissements d'Etat seulement.
13 Y compris les tissus synthétiques.
14 Y compris les tissus de lin.
15 Période de douze mois commençant le 16 juillet de l'année indiquée.
16 Production des fabriques seulement.
17 Production de l'Etat seulement.
18 Y compris les couvertures et les tapis en coton.
19 Pour 1985, les données sont confidentielles.
20 Y compris les tissus de succédanés de coton.
21 Y compris les tissus en fibres cellulosiques.

Cotton woven fabrics – Tissus de coton

Unit : Million metres | Unité : Million de mètres

Country or area	1976	1977	1978	1979	1980	1981	1982	1983	1984	1985	Pays ou zone
Africa	**1 018.5**	**1 061.0**	**1 069.4**	**1 067.3**	**1 091.7**	**1 117.8**	**1 253.1**	**1 216.4**	**1 222.4**	**1 085.2**	**Afrique**
Algeria	...	46.9	55.3	56.1	73.7	91.2	85.1	...	...	...	Algérie
Cameroon	...	...	...	55.1	62.8	...	...	27.0	50.8	24.5	Cameroun
Central African Rep.	5.3	3.7	2.6	...	...	...	...	...	...	...	Rép. centrafricaine
Chad	18.4	14.6	15.1	15.4	15.6	...	...	...	...	...	Tchad
Côte d'Ivoire[1]	...	68.0	69.0	74.5	78.0	121.7	85.9	107.4	100.8	...	Côte d'Ivoire[1]
Egypt	563.0	595.0	604.0	610.1	632.5	631.2	834.0	771.6	752.4	619.0	Egypte
Ghana	102.9	94.4	88.1	66.0	36.5	30.5	7.1	7.1	10.3	12.6	Ghana
Madagascar	78.1	79.5	78.2	85.3	79.3	74.4	72.9	76.0	68.6	64.9	Madagascar
Mali	12.0	16.0	17.0	14.0	17.0	12.6	13.1	* 10.0	...	...	Mali
Niger	* 9.0	* 5.8	7.0	14.0	13.1	7.1	6.8	...	...	...	Niger
Senegal	2.4	3.2	2.7	3.5	4.9	5.6	6.9	8.6	7.1	2.2	Sénégal
Somalia	6.7	11.8	12.6	...	...	...	...	...	...	...	Somalie
Togo	14.7	15.3	16.3	* 16.4	* 16.5	...	...	...	...	...	Togo
Tunisia	21.9	25.3	24.8	32.7	33.3	33.7	...	...	...	...	Tunisie
Zambia	11.5	11.7	* 11.8	9.9	14.2	13.9	12.6	13.5	13.6	17.2	Zambie
America, North	**4 499.2**	**3 636.2**	**3 264.2**	**3 039.4**	**3 506.5**	**3 036.6**	**2 823.8**	**3 131.4**	**3 539.0**	**3 476.2**	**Amérique du Nord**
Cuba[2]	...	...	149.0	144.0	146.0	129.2	119.1	150.9	143.0	155.9	Cuba[2]
Dominican Republic[3]	9.5	8.8	12.2	16.8	14.5	7.9	7.6	9.7	10.5	12.7	Rép. dominicaine[3]
El Salvador	13.3	16.4	21.7	18.6	16.2	14.9	# 3.3	3.2	...	...	El Salvador
Haiti	1.8	1.0	1.3	0.7	0.7	0.7	0.5	1.2	0.7	* 0.6	Haïti
Honduras	13.7	13.9	14.2	7.5	7.6	...	...	...	...	...	Honduras
Jamaica	5.9	8.0	9.3	5.9	4.6	3.2	3.7	3.7	...	...	Jamaïque
Nicaragua	...	...	...	4.8	7.4	8.8	14.0	15.7	25.7	...	Nicaragua
United States	4 314.3	# 3 445.0	3 051.0	2 841.0	3 309.6	2 863.2	2 667.6	2 940.0	3 345.6	3 278.4	Etats–Unis
America, South	**1 181.1**	**1 133.1**	**1 261.7**	**1 328.3**	**1 346.5**	**1 083.6**	**1 216.6**	**1 220.6**	**1 251.6**	**1 275.6**	**Amérique du Sud**
Bolivia	6.4	4.2	9.9	9.9	10.5	6.0	* 4.4	2.7	0.9	...	Bolivie
Brazil	1 075.4	1 010.8	1 122.7	[4] 1 207.3	1 252.5	1 018.0	...	...	...	...	Brésil
Chile	50.1	58.6	68.5	67.1	53.1	36.4	27.1	28.2	40.6	44.9	Chili
Colombia	...	...	...	...	...	7.2	6.8	1.0	...	...	Colombie
Ecuador	28.9	34.2	34.8	...	8.8	3.5	2.4	...	...	...	Equateur
Paraguay	15.3	20.3	20.9	20.3	16.6	12.5	9.2	5.8	6.1	9.2	Paraguay
Asia	**19 178.0**	**19 440.6**	**20 830.2**	**22 001.8**	**24 025.4**	**24 718.4**	**25 430.1**	**25 878.2**	**25 037.5**	**26 476.2**	**Asie**
Afghanistan[5]	73.7	76.8	76.6	63.0	43.0	26.5	23.0	37.8	45.3	45.3	Afghanistan[5]
Bangladesh	68.1	62.3	75.5	77.7	81.0	78.6	66.3	59.7	58.8	62.7	Bangladesh
Burma[6]	72.8	77.7	74.8	82.9	89.8	97.7	86.0	89.7	91.4	57.2	Birmanie[6]
China	8 840.0	10 151.0	11 029.0	12 150.0	13 470.0	14 268.0	15 350.0	14 880.0	13 700.0	14 670.0	Chine
Democratic Yemen	...	...	...	...	1.8	1.8	2.7	3.1	3.2	...	Yémen démocratique
India	7 945.4	6 901.8	7 324.9	7 531.6	8 314.1	8 119.9	7 830.3	8 632.2	8 826.2	9 332.4	Inde
Indonesia[7]	588.1	...	662.0	* 628.4	717.7	794.6	783.3	837.5	949.9	...	Indonésie[7]
Iran(Islamic Rep.of)	127.0	139.0	114.0	150.0	133.0	113.0	107.0	...	...	...	Iran(Rép.islamique)
Jordan	0.8	0.8	1.0	1.3	...	...	...	...	...	...	Jordanie
Malaysia	174.6	189.3	207.6	211.9	218.7	223.2	214.9	201.7	...	...	Malaisie
Nepal[8]	5.2	3.9	2.4	3.5	5.3	6.9	8.0	10.2	10.5	* 10.0	Népal[8]
Pakistan[9 10]	621.4	* 487.6	* 467.2	* 405.0	* 408.7	* 368.1	* 388.4	* 370.0	...	...	Pakistan[9 10]
Philippines	204.0	202.5	182.8	178.5	166.2	204.0	156.3	* 180.0	...	...	Philippines
Sri Lanka	59.1	68.3	73.9	47.0	36.1	30.0	25.2	20.4	25.2	37.2	Sri Lanka
Turkey[11]	157.5	178.9	208.9	182.7	163.7	227.3	164.9	154.7	158.4	176.9	Turquie[11]
Viet Nam	240.0	299.3	328.7	287.0	175.3	158.0	223.0	287.3	364.3	367.0	Viet Nam
Europe	**2 464.8**	**2 474.3**	**2 452.1**	**2 409.6**	**2 378.6**	**2 245.7**	**2 123.8**	**2 168.5**	**2 240.6**	**2 282.8**	**Europe**
EEC	***374.5***	***368.3***	***380.0***	***364.7***	***313.8***	***277.9***	***260.8***	***254.6***	***264.8***	***273.8***	***CEE***
United Kingdom[12]	374.5	368.3	380.0	364.7	313.8	277.9	260.8	254.6	264.8	273.8	Royaume–Uni[12]
EFTA	***252.2***	***250.5***	***240.7***	***240.1***	***255.3***	***234.7***	***221.4***	***217.5***	***198.3***	***220.3***	***AELE***
Austria	...	76.8	73.3	78.1	82.4	82.4	72.9	78.4	54.4	73.7	Autriche
Norway	19.4	19.9	13.9	12.5	20.1	14.3	12.4	10.4	15.7	13.7	Norvège
Sweden	23.4	21.0	19.6	19.8	21.7	21.0	21.0	19.9	22.1	24.0	Suède
Switzerland	128.3	132.8	134.0	129.7	131.1	117.0	115.1	108.8	106.1	108.9	Suisse
East Europe	***1 838.1***	***1 855.5***	***1 831.5***	***1 804.9***	***1 809.5***	***1 733.1***	***1 641.6***	***1 696.5***	***1 777.5***	***1 788.7***	***Europe de l'est***
Bulgaria	359.4	371.0	352.8	348.8	346.1	353.8	366.6	367.4	367.8	351.3	Bulgarie
Czechoslovakia	530.7	533.4	543.7	551.1	560.4	574.2	582.9	585.3	597.9	606.4	Tchécoslovaquie

For general note and footnotes, see end of table. | Voir la fin du tableau pour la remarque générale et les notes.

Unit : Million metres

Unité : Million de mètres

Country or area	1976	1977	1978	1979	1980	1981	1982	1983	1984	1985	Pays ou zone
Poland[13 14]	948.0	951.1	935.0	904.9	902.9	805.2	692.0	743.8	811.8	831.0	Pologne[13 14]
USSR	**7 888.2**	**7 910.6**	**8 034.7**	**8 035.3**	**8 097.8**	**8 143.4**	**8 094.7**	**8 224.1**	**8 499.9**	**8 755.5**	**URSS**
Total	**36 229.7**	**35 655.8**	**36 912.4**	**37 881.8**	**40 446.5**	**40 345.6**	**40 942.0**	**41 839.3**	**41 790.9**	**43 351.6**	**Total**

General note.
Woven cotton fabrics (at loom stage) before undergoing finishing processes such as bleaching, dyeing, printing, mercerizing, lazing etc. (SITC 65210–A).

1 Finished fabrics.
2 Including mixed cotton fabrics.
3 Including cellulosic fabrics.
4 Production by establishments employing 5 or more persons.
5 Twelve months beginning 21 March of year stated.
6 Production by government–owned enterprises only.
7 Including synthetic fabrics.
8 Twelve months beginning 16 July of year stated.
9 Twelve months ending 30 June of year stated.
10 Factory production only. Including finished fabrics.
11 Government production only.
12 Data refer to 53–week period.
13 After undergoing finishing processes.
14 Including fabrics of cotton substitutes.

Remarque générale.
Tissus de coton sortant du métier à tisser, avant les opérations de finition, c'est–à–dire avant d'être blanchis, teints, imprimés, mercerisés, glacés etc. (CTCI 65210–A).

1 Tissus finis.
2 Y compris les tissus de cotton mélangé.
3 Y compris les tissus en fibres cellulosiques.
4 Production des établissements occupant 5 personnes ou plus.
5 Période de douze mois commençant le 21 mars de l'année indiquée.
6 Production des établissements d'Etat seulement.
7 Y compris les tissus synthétiques.
8 Période de douze mois commençant le 16 juillet de l'année indiquée.
9 Période de douze mois finissant le 30 juin de l'année indiquée.
10 Production des fabriques seulement. Y compris les tissus finis.
11 Production de l'Etat seulement.
12 Données se rapportant à une période de 53 semaines.
13 Après opérations de finition.
14 Y compris les tissus de succédanés de coton.

Unit : Thousand metric tons

Unité : Milliers de tonnes métriques

Country or area	1976	1977	1978	1979	1980	1981	1982	1983	1984	1985	Pays ou zone
Africa	**596**	**596**	**596**	**596**	**596**	**596**	**614**	**586**	**599**	**586**	**Afrique**
Egypt	...	...	...	...	...	...	613	585	599	585	Egypte
Niger	...	...	...	1	1	1	1	* 1	* 1	* 1	Niger
America, North	**778**	**723**	**679**	**653**	**605**	**542**	**524**	**571**	**760**	**578**	**Amérique du Nord**
Cuba[1]	19	21	21	20	20	23	15	19	19	21	Cuba[1]
Mexico	73	69	67	68	67	71	66	66	64	71	Mexique
United States	687	633	591	566	518	448	443	* 486	* 677	...	Etats–Unis
America, South	**165**	**173**	**204**	**251**	**243**	**218**	**261**	**276**	**291**	**306**	**Amérique du Sud**
Argentina	73	...	...	...	...	...	...	...	...	...	Argentine
Brazil	92	100	131	[2] 178	170	145	...	...	...	...	Brésil
Asia	**2 105**	**1 931**	**2 042**	**2 089**	**2 232**	**2 218**	**2 145**	**2 331**	**2 392**	**2 388**	**Asie**
India	1 320	1 146	1 217	1 251	1 381	1 349	1 301	1 434	1 466	...	Inde
Philippines	34	34	30	30	28	* 34	* 26	* 30	...	...	Philippines
Syrian Arab Republic[3]	37	35	36	39	17	17	18	25	38	22	Rép. arabe syrienne[3]
Thailand	...	716	758	770	806	818	* 800	...	...	...	Thaïlande
Europe	**1 059**	**995**	**957**	**957**	**984**	**938**	**914**	**934**	**967**	**986**	**Europe**
EEC	***668***	***602***	***577***	***604***	***622***	***598***	***616***	***611***	***641***	***653***	***CEE***
Belgium[4]	63	49	* 46	52	51	47	53	51	51	53	Belgique[4]
France	157	148	139	139	137	128	134	128	126	120	France
Germany, Fed. Rep.	199	170	160	160	163	146	159	169	177	189	Allemagne, Rép. féd.
Greece	30	29	28	29	39	39	38	42	39	...	Grèce
Italy	181	171	175	198	204	216	212	206	231	...	Italie
Netherlands	39	35	28	26	28	22	19	15	16	15	Pays–Bas
EFTA	***100***	***101***	***88***	***96***	***104***	***102***	***105***	***110***	***108***	***111***	***AELE***
Austria	17	16	15	16	16	16	15	15	12	16	Autriche
Finland	20	22	11	14	16	13	17	17	13	9	Finlande
Norway	3	3	2	2	3	2	2	2	3	2	Norvège
Portugal	52	53	54	58	61	64	64	69	73	75	Portugal
Sweden	8	7	6	6	7	7	7	7	8	8	Suède
East Europe	***159***	***161***	***161***	***152***	***152***	***137***	***115***	***125***	***136***	***139***	***Europe de l'est***
Poland[5 6]	159	161	161	152	152	137	115	125	136	139	Pologne[5 6]
Other Europe	***132***	***132***	***132***	***105***	***106***	***101***	***79***	***88***	***82***	***84***	***Autre Europe***
Spain	132	132	132	105	106	101	79	[7] 88	* 82	* 84	Espagne
Total	**4 703**	**4 419**	**4 478**	**4 547**	**4 660**	**4 512**	**4 458**	**4 698**	**5 009**	**4 844**	**Total**

General note.
Woven cotton fabrics (at loom stage) before undergoing finishing processes such as bleaching, dyeing, printing, mercerizing, lazing etc. (SITC 65210–B).

Remarque générale.
Tissus de coton sortant du métier à tisser, avant les opérations de finition, c'est–à–dire avant d'être blanchis, teints, imprimés, mercerisés, glacés etc. (CTCI 65210–B).

[1] Including mixed cotton fabrics.
[2] Production by establishments employing 5 or more persons.
[3] Including silk fabrics.
[4] Including cotton blankets and carpets.
[5] After undergoing finishing processes.
[6] Including fabrics of cotton substitutes.
[7] Including household production.

[1] Y compris les tissus de cotton mélangé.
[2] Production des établissements occupant 5 personnes ou plus.
[3] Y compris les tissus de soie.
[4] Y compris les couvertures et les tapis en coton.
[5] Après opérations de finition.
[6] Y compris les tissus de succédanés de coton.
[7] Y compris la production ménagère.

Silk fabrics – Tissus de soie

Unit : Thousand square metres — Unité : Millions de mètres carrés

Country or area	1976	1977	1978	1979	1980	1981	1982	1983	1984	1985	Pays ou zone
Africa	**24 006**	**28 052**	**25 813**	**21 319**	**21 397**	**24 171**	**22 771**	**26 566**	**23 547**	**23 389**	**Afrique**
Algeria	276	# 5 252	6 333	6 339	8 437	9 301	7 901	...	...	...	Algérie
Egypt	23 730	22 800	19 480	14 980	12 960	14 870	* [1] 14 870	* [1] 15 578	...	...	Egypte
America, North	**5 763**	**3 302**	**2 175**	**8 187**	**11 587**	**23 390**	**15 391**	**14 634**	**17 013**	**28 288**	**Amérique du Nord**
Cuba[2]	5 117	2 656	1 529	7 541	10 941	# 22 744	14 745	13 988	16 347	27 663	Cuba[2]
United States[1]	...	...	...	...	...	...	...	...	# 666	625	Etats–Unis[1]
America, South	**1 682**	**2 717**	**3 694**	**4 835**	**5 870**	**6 000**	**7 350**	**8 270**	**9 189**	**10 108**	**Amérique du Sud**
Brazil[1]	1 682	2 717	3 694	4 835	5 870	* 6 000	...	...	...	...	Brésil[1]
Asia	**516 395**	**926 630**	**777 718**	**829 844**	**932 719**	**1 018 597**	**1 285 842**	**1 545 812**	**1 782 417**	**1 783 937**	**Asie**
China	...	724 730	565 560	621 040	733 590	826 130	1 091 848	1 368 630	1 613 860	1 615 640	Chine
Hong Kong	15	# 510	1 469	2 575	2 456	2 972	2 168	1 606	1 208	1 126	Hong–kong
Indonesia[1]	32 847	...	...	...	...	...	...	...	...	...	Indonésie[1]
Japan	163 120	155 609	159 234	157 975	151 889	137 111	136 459	121 794	115 116	114 538	Japon
Korea, Republic of	14 458	11 289	17 050	13 846	11 317	18 649	21 379	19 619	18 404	18 602	Corée, République de
Turkey[1]	1 561	1 645	1 558	1 561	# 620	888	1 141	1 316	982	1 184	Turquie[1]
Europe	**284 675**	**296 966**	**298 918**	**302 060**	**302 195**	**311 017**	**308 507**	**306 127**	**307 050**	**314 336**	**Europe**
EEC	***152 852***	***153 583***	***153 114***	***152 497***	***153 122***	***152 725***	***153 196***	***153 384***	***153 708***	***153 539***	***CEE***
France	4 427	5 374	5 185	4 959	5 158	4 905	5 500	5 464	5 582	5 520	France
Germany, Fed. Rep.[3]	2 272	2 029	1 930	1 629	...	...	...	...	...	...	Allemagne, Rép. féd.[3]
Greece[4]	117	144	153	153	153	144	135	99	135	...	Grèce[4]
Italy[4]	145 176	...	...	...	...	...	...	...	...	...	Italie[4]
United Kingdom[5]	860	860	670	580	670	535	420	680	850	750	Royaume–Uni[5]
EFTA	***24 173***	***21 650***	***18 032***	***17 526***	***17 227***	***16 998***	***18 102***	***22 476***	***24 012***	***24 628***	***AELE***
Austria	51	56	51	53	76	131	129	165	191	149	Autriche
Portugal[4]	* 0	* 0	* 0	* 0	* 271	* 9	0	9	27	81	Portugal[4]
Switzerland[1 2]	24 122	21 594	17 981	17 473	16 880	16 858	17 973	22 302	23 794	24 398	Suisse[1 2]
East Europe	***107 329***	***121 452***	***127 478***	***131 758***	***131 489***	***140 563***	***136 951***	***130 047***	***129 158***	***135 935***	***Europe de l'est***
Czechoslovakia	157	147	155	139	138	134	102	151	118	103	Tchécoslovaquie
Hungary[6]	71	64	101	78	122	184	157	9	0	0	Hongrie[6]
Poland[6]	1 101	1 241	1 222	1 541	1 229	1 245	692	887	1 040	832	Pologne[6]
Romania	106 000	120 000	126 000	130 000	130 000	139 000	136 000	129 000	128 000	135 000	Roumanie
Other Europe	***321***	***281***	***294***	***279***	***357***	***731***	***258***	***220***	***172***	***234***	***Autre Europe***
Spain[4]	243	252	234	198	180	180	...	...	...	...	Espagne[4]
Yugoslavia	78	29	60	81	177	551	100	78	47	125	Yougoslavie
USSR[6]	**43 567**	**43 665**	**49 351**	**51 183**	**53 241**	**52 620**	**54 182**	**56 637**	**57 178**	**57 319**	**URSS[6]**
Total	**876 087**	**1 301 332**	**1 157 669**	**1 217 428**	**1 327 009**	**1 435 795**	**1 694 043**	**1 958 045**	**2 196 395**	**2 217 377**	**Total**

General note.
Woven fabrics of silk with more than 10 per cent by weight of silk or of waste silk (noil silk and other) at loom stage. (SITC 65310–0).

1 Original data in metres.
2 Including artificial silk fabrics.
3 Beginning 1980, data are confidential.
4 Original data in metric tons.
5 Deliveries.
6 After undergoing finishing processes.

Remarque générale.
Tissus contenant plus de 10 p. 100 en poids de soie, de bourre de soie ou d'autres déchets de soie, au sortir du métier à tisser. (CTCI 65310–0).

1 Données d'origine exprimées en mètres.
2 Y compris les tissus de soie artificielle.
3 A partir de 1980, les données sont confidentielles.
4 Données d'origine exprimées en tonnes.
5 Livraisons.
6 Après opérations de finition.

Silk fabrics – Tissus de soie

Unit : Thousand metres — Unité : Milliers de mètres

Country or area	1976	1977	1978	1979	1980	1981	1982	1983	1984	1985	Pays ou zone
Africa	**17 321**	**16 644**	**14 216**	**10 935**	**9 460**	**9 945**	**10 857**	**11 371**	**8 047**	**7 036**	**Afrique**
Egypt	17 321	16 644	14 216	10 935	9 460	9 945	10 857	11 371	...	...	Egypte
America, North	**1 243**	**3 355**	**1 400**	**7 408**	**10 862**	**19 900**	**14 467**	**12 716**	**14 368**	**21 755**	**Amérique du Nord**
Cuba	...	...	1 400	7 408	10 862	19 900	14 467	12 716	14 368	21 755	Cuba
America, South	**1 228**	**1 983**	**2 696**	**3 529**	**4 285**	**4 280**	**5 299**	**5 956**	**6 612**	**7 269**	**Amérique du Sud**
Brazil	1 228	1 983	2 696	[1] 3 529	4 285	* 4 280	...	...	...	...	Brésil
Asia	**365 719**	**530 251**	**611 657**	**664 589**	**759 912**	**835 378**	**914 513**	**999 961**	**1 178 717**	**1 449 754**	**Asie**
China	...	529 050	610 520	663 450	759 460	834 730	913 680	999 000	1 178 000	1 449 000	Chine
Turkey	1 139	1 201	1 137	1 139	# 452	648	833	961	717	754	Turquie
Europe	**19 952**	**18 258**	**15 395**	**15 280**	**14 632**	**14 462**	**14 520**	**18 203**	**19 598**	**19 670**	**Europe**
EEC	***900***	***900***	***700***	***600***	***700***	***500***	***400***	***600***	***700***	***700***	***CEE***
United Kingdom	900	900	700	600	700	500	400	600	700	700	Royaume-Uni
EFTA	***17 633***	***15 822***	***13 184***	***12 818***	***12 403***	***12 439***	***13 251***	***16 463***	***17 590***	***17 959***	***AELE***
Austria	...	60	59	64	82	134	132	184	222	150	Autriche
Switzerland[2]	17 607	15 762	13 125	12 754	12 321	12 305	13 119	16 279	17 368	17 809	Suisse[2]
East Europe	***1 419***	***1 536***	***1 511***	***1 862***	***1 529***	***1 523***	***869***	***1 140***	***1 308***	***1 011***	***Europe de l'est***
Czechoslovakia	146	136	144	129	128	124	95	140	115	100	Tchécoslovaquie
Poland[3]	1 273	1 400	1 367	1 733	1 401	1 399	774	1 000	1 193	911	Pologne[3]
USSR	**47 427**	**47 732**	**54 278**	**56 393**	**58 615**	**58 116**	**60 090**	**62 079**	**62 597**	**63 045**	**URSS**
Total	**452 890**	**618 223**	**699 642**	**758 134**	**857 766**	**942 081**	**1 019 746**	**1 110 286**	**1 289 939**	**1 568 530**	**Total**

General note.
Woven fabrics of silk with more than 10 per cent by weight of silk or of waste silk (noil silk and other) at loom stage. (SITC 65310-A).

[1] Production by establishments employing 5 or more persons.
[2] Including artificial silk fabrics.
[3] After undergoing finishing processes.

Remarque générale.
Tissus contenant plus de 10 p. 100 en poids de soie, de bourre de soie ou d'autres déchets de soie, au sortir du métier à tisser. (CTCI 65310-A).

[1] Production des établissements occupant 5 personnes ou plus.
[2] Y compris les tissus de soie artificielle.
[3] Après opérations de finition.

ISIC-BASED CODE 3211–31B

Silk fabrics – Tissus de soie

CODE BASE CITI 3211–31B

Unit : Metric tons — Unité : Tonnes métriques

Country or area	1976	1977	1978	1979	1980	1981	1982	1983	1984	1985	Pays ou zone
Africa	**6 400**	**6 500**	**9 800**	**9 753**	**7 000**	**7 250**	**7 500**	**7 500**	**7 835**	**7 863**	**Afrique**
Egypt	6 400	6 500	9 800	9 753	7 000	7 250	7 500	7 500	...	...	Egypte
America, North	**947**	**1 224**	**1 500**	**1 332**	**1 953**	**3 578**	**2 601**	**2 262**	**2 612**	**3 913**	**Amérique du Nord**
Cuba	...	...	...	1 332	1 953	3 578	2 601	2 262	2 612	3 913	Cuba
America, South	**92**	**125**	**147**	**318**	**100**	**218**	**239**	**260**	**281**	**301**	**Amérique du Sud**
Brazil	92	125	147	[1] 318	100	...	...	...	...	...	Brésil
Asia	**238**	**238**	**188**	**289**	**238**	**238**	**238**	**238**	**238**	**238**	**Asie**
Indonesia	...	...	15	116	...	...	...	...	...	...	Indonésie
Turkey	173	...	...	...	...	...	...	...	...	...	Turquie
Europe	**16 637**	**16 745**	**16 723**	**16 694**	**16 746**	**16 693**	**16 754**	**16 749**	**16 770**	**16 761**	**Europe**
EEC	***16 604***	***16 712***	***16 692***	***16 667***	***16 689***	***16 660***	***16 725***	***16 717***	***16 734***	***16 726***	***CEE***
France	491	596	575	550	572	544	610	606	619	612	France
Greece	13	16	17	17	17	16	15	11	15	...	Grèce
Italy	16 100	...	...	...	...	...	...	...	...	...	Italie
EFTA	***6***	***5***	***5***	***5***	***37***	***13***	***12***	***17***	***22***	***23***	***AELE***
Austria	6	5	5	5	7	12	12	16	19	14	Autriche
Portugal	0	0	0	0	30	1	0	1	3	9	Portugal
Other Europe	***27***	***28***	***26***	***22***	***20***	***20***	***17***	***15***	***14***	***12***	***Autre Europe***
Spain	27	28	26	22	20	20	...	...	...	...	Espagne
Total	**24 314**	**24 832**	**28 358**	**28 386**	**26 037**	**27 977**	**27 332**	**27 009**	**27 736**	**29 076**	**Total**

General note.
Woven fabrics of silk with more than 10 per cent by weight of silk or of waste silk (noil silk and other) at loom stage. (SITC 65310–B).

[1] Production by establishments employing 5 or more persons.

Remarque générale.
Tissus contenant plus de 10 p. 100 en poids de soie, de bourre de soie ou d'autres déchets de soie, au sortir du métier à tisser. (CTCI 65310–B).

[1] Production des établissements occupant 5 personnes ou plus.

Woolen woven fabrics – Tissus de laine

Unit : Million square metres

Unité : Millions de mètres carrés

Country or area	1976	1977	1978	1979	1980	1981	1982	1983	1984	1985	Pays ou zone
Africa	**27.0**	**26.7**	**27.3**	**27.4**	**31.2**	**32.5**	**32.6**	**31.3**	**34.0**	**32.4**	**Afrique**
Algeria	0.1	0.5	1.3	1.2	2.2	2.2	2.1	* 2.0	...	...	Algérie
Egypt[1]	19.0	16.5	15.8	16.1	17.6	17.8	18.3	18.5	...	...	Egypte[1]
Kenya	0.8	2.0	2.3	2.0	2.3	3.1	3.3	4.3	3.3	3.8	Kenya
South Africa[2]	3.8	4.2	5.2	5.3	6.1	6.4	5.6	4.3	7.1	4.6	Afrique du Sud[2]
Tunisia	0.7	0.9	0.1	0.4	0.4	0.4	...	...	...	...	Tunisie
Zaire	...	...	...	...	...	...	3.1	2.0	...	...	Zaïre
America, North	**176.6**	**182.7**	**206.0**	**205.1**	**205.0**	**179.7**	**142.2**	**160.5**	**174.5**	**157.0**	**Amérique du Nord**
Canada[3 4]	28.9	28.0	28.1	...	...	...	...	...	...	...	Canada[3 4]
Cuba[5]	0.3	0.3	0.3	0.3	0.3	0.3	0.3	0.3	0.2	0.3	Cuba[5]
Mexico	9.4	9.9	11.8	12.2	13.2	13.1	12.2	11.8	12.6	12.7	Mexique
United States	138.0	144.4	165.7	164.3	163.1	138.0	101.3	120.0	133.2	115.6	Etats–Unis
America, South	**10.1**	**8.8**	**8.3**	**8.5**	**8.9**	**11.2**	**8.9**	**6.9**	**8.0**	**7.9**	**Amérique du Sud**
Bolivia[2]	0.5	0.3	0.2	0.4	0.6	0.4	0.4	0.1	0.0	* 0.0	Bolivie[2]
Brazil[1]	9.0	6.8	5.9	[6] 5.4	* 5.2	* 5.0	...	...	...	...	Brésil[1]
Ecuador[1]	0.5	...	...	...	* 3.1	* 5.7	* 4.8	* 3.8	...	...	Equateur[1]
Paraguay[2]	0.1	0.1	0.1	0.0	0.1	0.2	0.0	0.0	0.0	* 0.0	Paraguay[2]
Asia	**578.3**	**657.4**	**679.7**	**685.9**	**676.0**	**721.3**	**763.2**	**820.8**	**937.7**	**1 004.6**	**Asie**
Afghanistan[7]	0.7	0.5	0.9	0.7	0.7	0.4	0.5	* 0.5	* 0.5	* 0.4	Afghanistan[7]
China	...	129.4	146.6	148.8	166.6	186.6	209.0	235.8	297.8	[1] 360.0	Chine
Hong Kong	0.2	0.2	0.2	0.1	0.0	0.0	0.0	0.0	0.0	0.0	Hong–kong
India[1 8]	38.3	83.6	90.7	95.7	116.4	142.9	...	...	...	...	Inde[1 8]
Iran(Islamic Rep.of)[1 2]	21.4	21.5	18.2	19.8	21.5	23.1	26.4	...	...	...	Iran(Rép.islamique)[1 2]
Japan[9]	373.7	347.3	336.0	325.7	294.2	290.7	294.5	301.8	327.1	325.6	Japon[9]
Korea, Republic of[3]	41.2	49.9	63.4	72.7	59.6	57.9	57.9	65.0	76.8	64.4	Corée, République de[3]
Mongolia	1.3	1.4	1.4	1.4	1.4	1.3	1.6	1.7	1.9	2.1	Mongolie
Pakistan[10]	...	...	0.8	1.7	1.4	1.7	1.6	1.2	1.4	...	Pakistan[10]
Syrian Arab Republic	11.3	12.6	11.0	9.2	5.9	6.9	6.2	[11] 4.4	[11] 4.4	[11] 4.7	Rép. arabe syrienne
Turkey[1 12]	12.6	9.7	10.4	10.1	8.3	9.7	8.3	10.5	9.3	8.7	Turquie[1 12]
Europe	**1 617.3**	**1 618.3**	**1 594.9**	**1 628.8**	**1 542.0**	**1 462.3**	**1 369.7**	**1 396.8**	**1 393.1**	**1 439.7**	**Europe**
EEC	***899.7***	***876.9***	***863.0***	***928.8***	***802.4***	***754.1***	***686.7***	***695.2***	***726.0***	***764.9***	***CEE***
Belgium[13]	19.9	12.7	12.6	12.7	14.1	13.0	11.7	12.2	11.4	9.8	Belgique[13]
Denmark[9]	2.2	2.3	2.1	3.0	3.0	2.0	0.7	...	...	...	Danemark[9]
France	73.3	64.8	64.5	70.0	62.4	53.8	44.7	40.8	41.4	44.6	France
Germany, Fed. Rep.[3]	104.4	96.0	97.2	97.1	109.2	95.8	81.7	79.2	87.1	104.1	Allemagne, Rép. féd.[3]
Greece[3 11]	9.1	10.3	10.9	8.2	10.9	9.3	10.3	9.1	7.9	...	Grèce[3 11]
Ireland[3]	3.1	3.7	4.0	3.3	2.7	2.7	2.9	2.7	3.2	3.3	Irlande[3]
Italy[11]	523.3	519.9	521.3	591.4	476.4	476.9	431.5	452.9	479.8	497.5	Italie[11]
Netherlands[3 14]	21.3	17.2	# 6.3	5.3	5.5	3.8	2.9	2.7	3.1	4.4	Pays–Bas[3 14]
United Kingdom[15]	143.1	150.1	144.1	137.7	118.2	96.7	100.3	94.0	90.7	90.9	Royaume–Uni[15]
EFTA	***77.1***	***69.3***	***63.7***	***68.3***	***74.9***	***68.0***	***62.4***	***62.6***	***64.2***	***67.5***	***AELE***
Austria	18.9	18.6	17.0	16.4	19.9	18.3	17.8	15.8	15.5	15.6	Autriche
Finland[3]	9.9	5.0	2.8	2.2	2.2	2.9	2.8	2.1	2.5	...	Finlande[3]
Iceland	0.2	0.2	0.2	0.2	0.2	0.1	0.3	0.3	0.4	...	Islande
Norway[2 3]	3.4	3.0	2.5	2.7	3.6	3.7	2.7	2.2	2.6	2.9	Norvège[2 3]
Portugal[11]	* 22.7	* 20.6	* 23.0	* 29.1	* 28.6	26.6	* 24.7	26.7	27.4	32.1	Portugal[11]
Sweden[11]	1.2	1.1	1.0	* 1.1	* 1.5	* 1.4	* 1.6	* 1.7	* 1.7	...	Suède[11]
Switzerland[2]	20.7	20.6	17.3	16.6	18.9	15.1	12.4	13.8	14.1	14.3	Suisse[2]
East Europe	***496.0***	***513.3***	***510.8***	***513.5***	***523.4***	***503.8***	***497.6***	***517.8***	***489.8***	***501.2***	***Europe de l'est***
Bulgaria[3]	52.1	53.1	51.6	53.7	59.6	57.3	59.6	70.1	61.0	61.4	Bulgarie[3]
Czechoslovakia[3]	92.5	92.3	87.6	87.4	87.9	90.6	91.9	92.9	85.3	87.0	Tchécoslovaquie[3]
German Dem. Rep.	38.6	38.7	37.5	38.2	38.9	38.9	39.6	39.0	40.7	41.3	Rép. dém. allemande
Hungary[3]	22.0	24.4	25.1	24.2	27.2	28.9	26.4	23.3	24.4	22.6	Hongrie[3]
Poland[3 16]	185.8	185.8	186.0	185.0	181.9	160.1	138.1	148.5	155.5	157.9	Pologne[3 16]
Romania[3]	105.0	119.0	123.0	125.0	128.0	128.0	142.0	144.0	123.0	131.0	Roumanie[3]
Other Europe	***144.5***	***158.8***	***157.4***	***118.1***	***141.3***	***136.5***	***123.1***	***121.2***	***113.0***	***106.1***	***Autre Europe***
Spain[11]	77.5	80.1	84.0	47.3	49.4	40.7	28.9	25.0	...	...	Espagne[11]
Yugoslavia[17]	67.0	78.7	73.4	70.8	91.9	95.8	94.2	96.2	99.2	101.2	Yougoslavie[17]

For general note and footnotes, see end of table.

Voir la fin du tableau pour la remarque générale et les notes.

Unit : Million square metres

Unité : Millions de mètres carrés

Country or area	1976	1977	1978	1979	1980	1981	1982	1983	1984	1985	Pays ou zone
USSR	**986.0**	**989.1**	**992.9**	**979.3**	**971.5**	**972.9**	**950.7**	**911.3**	**872.3**	**840.7**	**URSS**
Byelorussian SSR	*42.7*	...	...	...	...	...	...	...	...	...	*RSS de Biélorussie*
Oceania	**17.2**	**14.1**	**13.5**	**13.9**	**14.9**	**15.5**	**14.1**	**15.1**	**13.1**	**13.4**	**Océanie**
Australia[10]	14.4	11.5	11.0	11.2	12.0	12.7	10.9	12.3	10.0	10.5	Australie[10]
New Zealand	2.8	2.7	2.4	2.7	2.8	2.7	3.2	2.8	3.1	2.9	Nouvelle–Zélande
Total	**3 412.6**	**3 497.1**	**3 522.5**	**3 548.9**	**3 449.4**	**3 395.3**	**3 281.3**	**3 342.6**	**3 432.6**	**3 495.6**	**Total**

General note.
Woollen and worsted fabrics in the piece (at loom stage) before undergoing finishing processes such as bleaching, dyeing, making up etc. Fabrics of fine hair are excluded. (SITC 65320–0).

[1] Original data in metres.
[2] Pure woollen fabrics only.
[3] After undergoing finishing processes.
[4] Shipments.
[5] Including mixed wool fabrics.
[6] Production by establishments employing 5 or more persons.
[7] Twelve months beginning 21 March of year stated.
[8] Mill production relating to wearable woollen fabrics only.
[9] Including finished fabrics.
[10] Twelve months ending 30 June of year stated.
[11] Original data in metric tons.
[12] Government production only.
[13] Including woollen blankets and carpets.
[14] Beginning 1978, data are not comparable with those for earlier years.
[15] Deliveries of woollen and worsted fabrics, except blankets, containing, by weight, more than 15 per cent wool or animal fibres. Including finished fabrics.
[16] Including fabrics of wool substitutes.
[17] Including woven cellulosic fabrics.

Remarque générale.
Tissus de laine cardée ou peignée, en pièces, sortant du métier à tisser, avant les opérations de finition, c'est–à–dire avant d'être blanchis, teints, confectionnés etc., à l'exclusion des tissus de poils fins. (CTCI 65320–0).

[1] Données d'origine exprimées en mètres.
[2] Tissus de laine pure seulement.
[3] Après opérations de finition.
[4] Expéditions.
[5] Y compris les tissues de laine mélangée.
[6] Production des établissements occupant 5 personnes ou plus.
[7] Période de douze mois commençant le 21 mars de l'année indiquée.
[8] Production des usines correspondant aux tissus d'habillement en laine seulement.
[9] Y compris les tissus finis.
[10] Période de douze mois finissant le 30 juin de l'année indiquée.
[11] Données d'origine exprimées en tonnes.
[12] Production de l'Etat seulement.
[13] Y compris les couvertures et tapis en laine.
[14] A partir de 1978, les données ne sont pas comparables à celles des années antérieures.
[15] Quantités livrées de tissus de laine cardée et peignée, à l'exception des couvertures, contenant, en poids, plus de l5 p. 100 de laine ou de fibres animales. Y compris les tissus finis.
[16] Y compris les tissus de succédanés de laine.
[17] Y compris les tissus en fibres cellulosiques.

Woolen woven fabrics – Tissus de laine

Unit : Million metres

Unité : Million de mètres

Country or area	1976	1977	1978	1979	1980	1981	1982	1983	1984	1985	Pays ou zone
Africa	**14.3**	**12.8**	**12.8**	**13.1**	**14.3**	**15.9**	**16.0**	**15.9**	**15.1**	**16.3**	**Afrique**
Egypt	11.5	9.6	9.6	9.6	10.7	10.8	11.1	11.2	...	...	Egypte
South Africa	2.3	2.6	3.2	3.2	3.3	4.9	4.8	4.6	4.0	...	Afrique du Sud
Tunisia	0.4	0.6	0.1	0.3	0.2	0.3	...	...	...	...	Tunisie
America, North	**89.2**	**93.1**	**106.8**	**106.3**	**105.2**	**95.8**	**59.2**	**60.9**	**85.9**	**71.2**	**Amérique du Nord**
Cuba[1]	...	...	0.2	0.2	0.2	0.2	0.2	0.2	0.2	0.2	Cuba[1]
United States	89.0	92.9	106.6	106.1	105.0	95.6	59.0	* 60.7	85.7	...	Etats–Unis
America, South	**6.1**	**5.0**	**4.1**	**5.0**	**5.5**	**6.8**	**5.4**	**4.3**	**4.9**	**5.0**	**Amérique du Sud**
Bolivia	0.3	0.2	0.1	0.2	0.3	0.2	0.2	0.2	0.0	...	Bolivie
Brazil	5.4	4.1	3.6	[2] 3.3	3.2	* 3.0	...	...	...	...	Brésil
Ecuador	0.3	...	0.3	...	1.9	3.4	2.9	2.3	...	...	Equateur
Paraguay	0.1	0.1	0.0	0.0	0.0	0.1	0.0	0.0	0.0	0.0	Paraguay
Asia	**91.4**	**149.2**	**162.7**	**167.7**	**190.9**	**220.8**	**244.2**	**271.6**	**319.8**	**368.8**	**Asie**
Afghanistan[3]	0.4	0.3	0.5	0.4	0.4	0.2	0.3	0.3	0.3	0.2	Afghanistan[3]
China	...	78.4	88.8	90.2	100.9	113.1	126.7	142.9	180.5	218.2	Chine
India	23.2	50.7	55.0	58.0	70.5	86.6	...	...	...	...	Inde
Iran(Islamic Rep.of)	13.0	13.0	11.0	12.0	13.0	14.0	16.0	...	...	...	Iran(Rép.islamique)
Mongolia	0.9	0.9	1.0	1.0	1.0	1.0	1.0	1.0	1.0	1.4	Mongolie
Turkey[4]	7.6	5.9	6.3	6.1	5.0	5.9	5.0	6.3	5.6	5.3	Turquie[4]
Europe	**349.0**	**358.2**	**357.9**	**360.6**	**373.1**	**348.2**	**329.7**	**341.6**	**348.3**	**353.7**	**Europe**
EEC	***99.3***	***109.1***	***116.7***	***120.9***	***127.2***	***118.7***	***113.1***	***111.4***	***120.3***	***122.0***	***CEE***
Belgium[5]	...	7.7	7.7	7.7	8.5	7.9	7.1	* 7.4	* 6.9	...	Belgique[5]
France	91.2	101.4	109.1	113.2	118.7	110.8	* 106.0	* 104.0	...	...	France
EFTA	***27.5***	***27.1***	***23.8***	***22.1***	***26.8***	***23.6***	***21.7***	***21.3***	***21.6***	***21.9***	***AELE***
Austria	...	...	...	9.6	12.1	11.3	11.3	10.3	10.5	10.6	Autriche
Iceland	0.2	0.2	0.1	0.1	0.2	0.1	0.2	0.2	0.3	...	Islande
Norway	2.1	1.8	1.5	1.7	2.2	2.2	1.6	1.3	1.3	...	Norvège
Sweden	0.8	0.8	0.7	0.7	1.0	0.9	1.0	1.1	1.0	1.0	Suède
Switzerland	13.3	13.2	10.5	10.1	11.5	9.2	7.5	8.3	8.6	8.7	Suisse
East Europe	***222.2***	***222.0***	***217.3***	***217.5***	***219.0***	***205.9***	***194.9***	***209.0***	***206.4***	***209.9***	***Europe de l'est***
Bulgaria[6]	35.6	36.2	35.1	36.5	39.5	39.6	42.0	48.7	41.5	41.9	Bulgarie[6]
Czechoslovakia	61.5	61.3	58.2	58.0	58.4	60.2	61.0	61.7	61.8	63.0	Tchécoslovaquie
Poland[6 7]	125.1	124.5	124.1	123.0	121.1	106.1	91.8	98.5	103.2	105.0	Pologne[6 7]
USSR	**599.2**	**605.6**	**609.0**	**601.2**	**598.4**	**600.0**	**584.0**	**558.2**	**536.3**	**522.0**	**URSS**
Total	**1 149.1**	**1 223.8**	**1 253.3**	**1 253.8**	**1 287.2**	**1 287.5**	**1 238.5**	**1 252.7**	**1 310.2**	**1 337.1**	**Total**

General note.
Woollen and worsted fabrics in the piece (at loom stage) before undergoing finishing processes such as bleaching, dyeing, making up etc. Fabrics of fine hair are excluded. (SITC 65320–A).

[1] Including mixed wool fabrics.
[2] Production by establishments employing 5 or more persons.
[3] Twelve months beginning 21 March of year stated.
[4] Government production only.
[5] Including woollen blankets and carpets.
[6] After undergoing finishing processes.
[7] Including fabrics of wool substitutes.

Remarque générale.
Tissus de laine cardée ou peignée, en pièces, sortant du métier à tisser, avant les opérations de finition, c'est–à–dire avant d'être blanchis, teints, confectionnés etc., à l'exclusion des tissus de poils fins. (CTCI 65320–A).

[1] Y compris les tissues de laine mélangée.
[2] Production des établissements occupant 5 personnes ou plus.
[3] Période de douze mois commençant le 21 mars de l'année indiquée.
[4] Production de l'Etat seulement.
[5] Y compris les couvertures et tapis en laine.
[6] Après opérations de finition.
[7] Y compris les tissus de succédanés de laine.

Woolen woven fabrics – Tissus de laine

CODE BASE CITI
3211–34B

Unit : Thousand metric tons — Unité : Milliers de tonnes métriques

Country or area	1976	1977	1978	1979	1980	1981	1982	1983	1984	1985	Pays ou zone
America, North	**61.31**	**63.43**	**71.83**	**71.53**	**71.52**	**66.43**	**47.73**	**55.50**	**49.14**	**51.23**	**Amérique du Nord**
Canada[1]	8.61	8.25	8.51	...	...	...	...	...	...	...	Canada[1]
Cuba[2]	...	...	...	...	0.05	0.05	0.06	0.06	0.05	0.05	Cuba[2]
Mexico	3.48	3.66	4.21	4.49	4.89	4.85	4.52	4.21	4.49	4.53	Mexique
United States	49.17	51.46	59.05	58.53	58.11	53.07	34.69	* 42.76	36.13	...	Etats–Unis
America, South	**1.93**	**1.47**	**1.28**	**1.12**	**0.97**	**0.81**	**0.87**	**0.75**	**0.63**	**0.51**	**Amérique du Sud**
Brazil	1.93	1.47	1.28	[3] 1.12	0.97	0.81	...	...	...	...	Brésil
Asia	**15.11**	**31.41**	**33.73**	**35.28**	**42.59**	**52.82**	**57.05**	**63.95**	**70.33**	**76.79**	**Asie**
India	13.66	29.80	32.32	34.10	41.46	50.92	...	...	...	...	Inde
Syrian Arab Republic	1.44	1.61	1.40	1.18	1.13	1.90	1.05	1.58	1.58	1.67	Rép. arabe syrienne
Europe	**409.56**	**419.18**	**424.25**	**439.63**	**407.93**	**389.27**	**346.94**	**355.69**	**370.68**	**385.43**	**Europe**
EEC	***304.20***	***314.92***	***319.03***	***346.05***	***313.06***	***305.96***	***276.25***	***282.65***	***299.87***	***315.83***	***CEE***
Belgium[4]	12.06	27.36	27.61	30.69	35.72	35.58	33.37	35.95	38.11	35.73	Belgique[4]
France	62.00	62.00	66.00	63.54	64.26	63.23	57.27	55.20	59.19	65.97	France
Germany, Fed. Rep.	40.47	36.67	35.80	36.47	39.43	33.90	28.16	26.88	28.79	33.66	Allemagne, Rép. féd.
Greece[5]	3.21	3.66	3.88	4.62	3.90	3.32	3.68	3.26	2.82	...	Grèce[5]
Italy	186.47	185.23	185.74	210.73	169.75	169.91	153.76	161.36	170.96	177.24	Italie
EFTA	***18.48***	***15.91***	***15.22***	***17.09***	***18.53***	***17.54***	***16.36***	***16.11***	***16.32***	***17.53***	***AELE***
Austria	5.38	5.28	4.82	4.65	5.65	5.19	5.07	4.47	4.41	4.42	Autriche
Finland	3.34	1.78	0.97	0.72	0.89	1.06	0.95	0.71	0.79	...	Finlande
Norway	1.23	1.09	0.88	0.97	1.27	1.30	0.97	0.79	0.77	1.05	Norvège
Portugal	8.09	7.36	8.19	10.36	10.19	9.49	8.78	9.53	9.75	11.42	Portugal
Sweden	0.44	0.41	0.36	0.38	0.53	0.50	0.59	0.61	0.60	0.49	Suède
East Europe	***59.25***	***59.81***	***60.08***	***59.62***	***58.74***	***51.28***	***44.05***	***48.01***	***49.56***	***50.31***	***Europe de l'est***
Poland[5 6]	59.25	59.81	60.08	59.62	58.74	51.28	44.05	48.01	49.56	50.31	Pologne[5 6]
Other Europe	***27.62***	***28.54***	***29.92***	***16.87***	***17.60***	***14.48***	***10.29***	***8.92***	***4.94***	***1.75***	***Autre Europe***
Spain	27.62	28.54	29.92	16.87	17.60	14.48	10.29	[7] 8.92	...	...	Espagne
Total	**487.91**	**515.49**	**531.08**	**547.56**	**523.01**	**509.32**	**452.60**	**475.89**	**490.78**	**513.95**	**Total**

General note.
Woollen and worsted fabrics in the piece (at loom stage) before undergoing finishing processes such as bleaching, dyeing, making up etc. Fabrics of fine hair are excluded. (SITC 65320–B).

1 Shipments.
2 Including mixed wool fabrics.
3 Production by establishments employing 5 or more persons.
4 Including woollen blankets and carpets.
5 After undergoing finishing processes.
6 Including fabrics of wool substitutes.
7 Including household production.

Remarque générale.
Tissus de laine cardée ou peignée, en pièces, sortant du métier à tisser, avant les opérations de finition, c'est–à–dire avant d'être blanchis, teints, confectionnés etc., à l'exclusion des tissus de poils fins. (CTCI 65320–B).

1 Expéditions.
2 Y compris les tissues de laine mélangée.
3 Production des établissements occupant 5 personnes ou plus.
4 Y compris les couvertures et tapis en laine.
5 Après opérations de finition.
6 Y compris les tissus de succédanés de laine.
7 Y compris la production ménagère.

Unit : Million square metres

Unité : Millions de mètres carrés

Country or area	1976	1977	1978	1979	1980	1981	1982	1983	1984	1985	Pays ou zone
Africa	**6.3**	**6.5**	**6.3**	**7.1**	**6.4**	**6.1**	**6.1**	**8.1**	**8.0**	**7.6**	**Afrique**
Egypt[1]	6.3	6.5	6.3	7.1	* 6.4	* 6.1	* 6.1	* 8.1	* 8.0	...	Egypte[1]
Asia	**38.9**	**33.7**	**34.7**	**36.1**	**34.7**	**37.4**	**43.4**	**41.6**	**46.2**	**46.9**	**Asie**
Iran(Islamic Rep.of)[2]	24.1	18.1	17.6	17.6	18.6	22.3	23.2	...	...	...	Iran(Rép.islamique)[2]
Japan	14.7	15.6	17.1	18.5	16.1	15.1	20.2	20.5	24.8	25.3	Japon
Europe	**495.9**	**494.6**	**508.3**	**469.2**	**479.5**	**450.4**	**424.7**	**420.8**	**427.1**	**435.1**	**Europe**
EEC	***90.8***	***87.2***	***87.3***	***83.8***	***74.7***	***67.1***	***65.8***	***67.7***	***68.4***	***58.0***	***CEE***
Belgium	13.7	11.8	15.1	13.3	13.1	12.6	12.9	13.7	16.1	14.8	Belgique
Denmark	0.2	0.1	0.1	0.1	0.1	0.1	0.1	0.1	0.0	0.0	Danemark
France	26.6	25.0	28.2	25.0	22.4	19.3	18.3	22.8	20.0	12.9	France
Germany, Fed. Rep.	14.9	12.1	10.5	10.1	10.0	9.1	7.6	6.9	6.4	5.3	Allemagne, Rép. féd.
Greece[1,3,4]	5.9	7.9	7.6	10.0	8.7	7.9	8.2	...	...	...	Grèce[1,3,4]
Netherlands[1,5]	0.5	0.4	0.7	...	...	...	...	...	...	...	Pays-Bas[1,5]
United Kingdom[6]	29.0	29.8	25.1	24.8	19.9	17.6	18.2	14.5	15.8	14.8	Royaume-Uni[6]
EFTA	***10.0***	***8.8***	***5.7***	***6.1***	***5.9***	***6.1***	***5.1***	***4.0***	***4.4***	***2.6***	***AELE***
Austria	1.8	1.7	1.8	1.6	2.1	1.9	1.4	1.2	1.7	1.2	Autriche
Finland	0.7	0.5	0.1	0.5	0.4	0.4	0.3	0.2	0.2	...	Finlande
Portugal	0.1	0.1	0.2	0.4	0.4	0.3	0.4	0.3	0.3	*[1] 0.3	Portugal
Sweden[1,7]	7.4	6.5	3.6	3.6	3.0	3.5	3.0	2.3	2.2	...	Suède[1,7]
East Europe	***384.2***	***390.6***	***406.5***	***371.1***	***391.7***	***370.4***	***347.1***	***342.1***	***347.3***	***367.8***	***Europe de l'est***
Bulgaria[4,5]	16.6	18.6	19.5	19.5	19.6	19.9	19.5	19.4	20.0	20.9	Bulgarie[4,5]
Czechoslovakia[5]	74.4	76.0	91.7	94.2	99.1	97.1	98.2	99.8	101.9	98.1	Tchécoslovaquie[5]
German Dem. Rep.	9.4	8.4	8.8	8.3	9.1	8.8	7.2	6.9	7.5	6.9	Rép. dém. allemande
Hungary[5]	15.9	14.2	14.3	13.6	13.1	11.7	9.4	8.9	9.8	8.7	Hongrie[5]
Poland[3,5]	146.1	146.8	137.6	110.5	102.8	82.0	75.7	81.2	85.2	84.1	Pologne[3,5]
Romania[5,8]	121.9	126.6	134.7	125.0	148.0	151.0	137.0	126.0	123.0	149.0	Roumanie[5,8]
Other Europe	***10.9***	***7.9***	***8.8***	***8.2***	***7.1***	***6.8***	***6.7***	***6.9***	***7.0***	***6.7***	***Autre Europe***
Spain	6.0	6.1	6.4	...	...	...	...	...	...	...	Espagne
Yugoslavia	4.9	1.9	2.4	2.0	0.9	0.7	0.6	0.8	0.9	0.6	Yougoslavie
USSR	**830.5**	**842.9**	**854.7**	**790.3**	**706.8**	**682.7**	**695.0**	**752.7**	**812.2**	**832.9**	**URSS**
Total	**1 371.6**	**1 377.7**	**1 404.0**	**1 302.6**	**1 227.4**	**1 176.6**	**1 169.2**	**1 223.3**	**1 293.5**	**1 322.5**	**Total**

General note.
Woven fabrics of flax or ramie yarn (at loom stage) before undergoing finishing processes. (SITC 65331-0).

1 Original data in metric tons.
2 Original data in metres.
3 Including fabrics of hemp.
4 Including jute fabrics.
5 After undergoing finishing processes.
6 Deliveries by weavers in Great Britain plus production in Northern Ireland. Including union cloths.
7 Woven fabrics of linen and ramie.
8 Including fabrics of flax, hemp, jute and mixed yarns.

Remarque générale.
Tissus de fil de lin ou de ramie sortant du métier à tisser, avant les opérations de finition. (CTCI 65331-0).

1 Données d'origine exprimées en tonnes.
2 Données d'origine exprimées en mètres.
3 Y compris les tissus de chanvre.
4 Y compris les tissus de jute.
5 Après opérations de finition.
6 Quantités produites par les tissages de Grande Bretagne majorées de la production de l'Irlande du Nord. Y compris les tissus mi-laine.
7 Tissus de lin et de ramie.
8 Y compris les tissus de lin, de chanvre, de jute et de filés mélangés.

Linen fabrics – Tissus de lin

Unit : Thousand metres

Unité : Milliers de mètres

Country or area	1976	1977	1978	1979	1980	1981	1982	1983	1984	1985	Pays ou zone
Africa	**552**	**387**	**207**	**214**	**194**	**275**	**269**	**145**	**106**	**67**	**Afrique**
Egypt	552	387	207	214	194	* 275	* 269	...	...	...	Egypte
America, South	**3 923**	**5 545**	**3 522**	**3 243**	**4 563**	**4 586**	**4 372**	**4 390**	**4 425**	**4 460**	**Amérique du Sud**
Brazil	2 954	4 716	2 949	[1] 2 527	3 791	* 3 814	* 3 600	...	...	...	Brésil
Colombia	969	829	573	716	...	...	...	...	...	...	Colombie
Asia	**76 000**	**21 000**	**19 000**	**19 000**	**20 000**	**24 000**	**25 000**	**16 490**	**13 006**	**9 522**	**Asie**
Iran(Islamic Rep.of)*	76 000	21 000	19 000	19 000	20 000	24 000	25 000	...	...	...	Iran(Rép.islamique)*
Europe	**248 528**	**251 429**	**254 538**	**235 268**	**233 864**	**213 154**	**201 274**	**208 301**	**205 391**	**218 169**	**Europe**
EFTA	***8 055***	***7 506***	***7 271***	***6 724***	***6 593***	***6 926***	***5 711***	***5 286***	***4 958***	***4 868***	***AELE***
Austria	1 602	1 377	1 466	1 243	1 787	1 506	1 243	1 141	1 478	1 103	Autriche
Sweden	...	...	...	...	4 806	5 420	4 468	4 145	3 480	3 765	Suède
East Europe	***240 473***	***243 923***	***247 267***	***228 544***	***227 271***	***206 228***	***195 563***	***203 015***	***200 433***	***213 301***	***Europe de l'est***
Bulgaria[2 3]	16 340	18 036	18 271	18 187	18 114	18 275	17 944	17 620	18 148	20 057	Bulgarie[2 3]
Czechoslovakia	78 305	80 008	96 466	99 147	104 289	102 169	103 332	104 983	99 682	...	Tchécoslovaquie
Poland[2 4]	145 828	145 879	132 530	111 210	104 868	85 784	74 287	80 412	82 603	81 992	Pologne[2 4]
USSR	**763 524**	**771 270**	**779 561**	**715 419**	**641 818**	**614 391**	**625 831**	**672 641**	**720 836**	**735 710**	**URSS**
Total	**1 092 527**	**1 049 631**	**1 056 828**	**973 144**	**900 439**	**856 406**	**856 746**	**901 967**	**943 763**	**967 928**	**Total**

General note.
Woven fabrics of flax or ramie yarn (at loom stage) before undergoing finishing processes. (SITC 65331-A).

[1] Production by establishments employing 5 or more persons.
[2] After undergoing finishing processes.
[3] Including jute fabrics.
[4] Including fabrics of hemp.

Remarque générale.
Tissus de fil de lin ou de ramie sortant du métier à tisser, avant les opérations de finition. (CTCI 65331-A).

[1] Production des établissements occupant 5 personnes ou plus.
[2] Après opérations de finition.
[3] Y compris les tissus de jute.
[4] Y compris les tissus de chanvre.

Linen fabrics – Tissus de lin

Unit : Metric tons — Unité : Tonnes métriques

Country or area	1976	1977	1978	1979	1980	1981	1982	1983	1984	1985	Pays ou zone
Africa	**2 326**	**2 407**	**2 328**	**2 000**	**2 343**	**2 250**	**2 250**	**3 000**	**2 579**	**2 627**	**Afrique**
Egypt	2 326	2 407	2 328	2 000	2 343	2 250	2 250	3 000	...	...	Egypte
Europe	**67 878**	**65 441**	**63 334**	**54 523**	**49 403**	**42 246**	**38 072**	**41 739**	**41 958**	**38 806**	**Europe**
EEC	***17 179***	***16 602***	***18 980***	***17 967***	***15 815***	***14 081***	***13 834***	***16 168***	***15 835***	***13 030***	***CEE***
Belgium	5 032	4 346	5 588	4 876	4 153	3 888	3 910	4 213	4 809	4 514	Belgique
France[1]	9 774	9 190	10 356	9 198	8 250	7 080	6 721	8 386	7 354	4 740	France[1]
Greece	2 183	2 906	2 776	3 690	3 209	2 910	3 000	...	...	...	Grèce
Netherlands	190	160	260	...	...	...	...	...	...	...	Pays-Bas
EFTA	***3 909***	***3 223***	***2 030***	***2 194***	***2 138***	***2 151***	***1 754***	***1 436***	***1 512***	***1 273***	***AELE***
Austria	576	561	580	512	699	640	447	395	558	422	Autriche
Finland	574	226	48	206	181	115	91	67	50	...	Finlande
Portugal	45	39	76	151	148	113	100	112	99	103	Portugal
Sweden[2]	2 714	2 397	1 326	1 325	1 110	1 283	1 116	862	805	700	Suède[2]
East Europe	***44 590***	***43 388***	***39 984***	***32 106***	***29 194***	***23 758***	***20 228***	***21 879***	***22 355***	***22 247***	***Europe de l'est***
Poland[3 4]	44 590	43 388	39 984	32 106	29 194	23 758	20 228	21 879	22 355	22 247	Pologne[3 4]
Other Europe	***2 200***	***2 228***	***2 340***	***2 256***	***2 256***	***2 256***	***2 256***	***2 256***	***2 256***	***2 256***	***Autre Europe***
Spain	2 200	2 228	2 340	...	...	...	...	...	...	...	Espagne
Total	**70 204**	**67 848**	**65 662**	**56 523**	**51 746**	**44 496**	**40 322**	**44 739**	**44 537**	**41 433**	**Total**

General note.
Woven fabrics of flax or ramie yarn (at loom stage) before undergoing finishing processes. (SITC 65331-B).

[1] Woven fabrics of flax or ramie yarn, or mixed yarn (50 percent cotton and 50 per cent flax).
[2] Woven fabrics of linen and ramie.
[3] After undergoing finishing processes.
[4] Including fabrics of hemp.

Remarque générale.
Tissus de fil de lin ou de ramie sortant du métier à tisser, avant les opérations de finition. (CTCI 65331-B).

[1] Tissus de filés de lin ou de ramie ou filés mélangés (50 p. 100 de lin).
[2] Tissus de lin et de ramie.
[3] Après opérations de finition.
[4] Y compris les tissus de chanvre.

Jute fabrics – Tissus de jute

Unit : Million square metres

Unité : Millions de mètres carrés

Country or area	1976	1977	1978	1979	1980	1981	1982	1983	1984	1985	Pays ou zone
Africa											**Afrique**
Algeria	0.5	0.7	3.3	7.1	7.1	8.5	9.7	...	...	...	Algérie
Egypt[1]	70.3	71.0	61.9	65.0	64.7	67.1	64.4	59.9	...	...	Egypte[1]
Zambia	0.7	0.2	8.6	9.0	9.4	10.9	* 11.0	* 10.0	...	...	Zambie
Asia											**Asie**
Bangladesh[1 2]	1 022.5	1 048.5	1 168.9	1 072.0	1 120.3	1 243.6	1 236.9	1 201.6	1 147.3	1 096.3	Bangladesh[1 2]
India[1]	2 507.9	2 496.7	2 545.4	2 420.9	2 919.4	2 877.8	2 726.7	2 815.7	2 431.4	* 2 714.8	Inde[1]
Iran(Islamic Rep.of)* [3]	...	...	...	2.1	6.3	10.5	...	...	...	...	Iran(Rép.islamique)* [3]
Japan	17.3	13.7	12.9	12.9	11.0	5.0	4.3	3.1	0.6	0.5	Japon
Pakistan[1 4]	88.5	71.3	70.3	77.9	88.1	106.9	118.0	140.0	168.1	...	Pakistan[1 4]
Europe											**Europe**
EEC											***CEE***
Belgium	9.0	5.9	5.2	8.1	5.8	5.4	5.4	5.5	5.8	4.6	Belgique
France	36.2	28.7	23.0	19.7	17.0	15.2	11.4	5.8	* 6.0	...	France
Germany, Fed. Rep.[1]	25.4	25.9	24.0	* 27.4	* 23.1	* 19.2	* 17.5	* 16.2	* 15.9	* 13.0	Allemagne, Rép. féd.[1]
Greece[1]	...	...	...	...	...	...	...	...	0.4	...	Grèce[1]
Italy[1]	12.7	11.0	14.9	15.2	14.9	12.5	11.1	...	...	...	Italie[1]
United Kingdom	33.8	29.0	27.5	26.5	21.6	15.4	15.4	15.2	14.0	13.9	Royaume–Uni
EFTA											***AELE***
Austria	0.5	2.0	2.5	2.6	4.3	3.1	2.2	0.8	0.6	* 0.2	Autriche
Finland	...	...	0.5	0.2	0.1	0.2	0.0	0.0	0.1	...	Finlande
Portugal* [1]	15.5	16.3	13.4	13.1	11.7	7.8	6.3	6.8	7.2	5.0	Portugal* [1]
Sweden[1]	1.2	1.5	4.8	* 3.9	* 2.5	* 1.6	* 0.8	* 0.8	* 0.4	...	Suède[1]
East Europe											***Europe de l'est***
Czechoslovakia	36.2	38.4	40.8	43.6	48.9	51.8	54.9	57.8	76.6	77.8	Tchécoslovaquie
Hungary[5]	3.2	3.0	5.8	9.0	2.9	3.0	2.2	1.9	1.7	1.6	Hongrie[5]
Poland[6]	71.9	75.3	73.2	70.7	70.3	60.2	51.7	44.0	35.5	37.3	Pologne[6]
Other Europe											***Autre Europe***
Spain[1 7]	0.8	3.4	3.2	...	6.1	4.8	4.2	4.4	...	...	Espagne[1 7]
Yugoslavia	30.7	33.6	32.1	37.6	36.9	34.1	31.5	31.2	30.1	22.1	Yougoslavie
USSR	152.5	152.8	151.9	146.7	132.5	125.4	124.3	123.9	119.5	116.3	**URSS**

General note.
Woven fabrics manufactured with yarns of jute at loom stage. (SITC 65340–0).

Remarque générale.
Tissus sortant du métier à tisser, fabriqués à partir de fils de jute. (CTCI 65340–0).

[1] Original data in metric tons.
[2] Twelve months ending 30 June of year stated. Production of jute mills.
[3] Production by establishments employing 10 or more persons.
[4] Twelve months ending 30 June of year stated.
[5] Finished fabrics.
[6] After undergoing finishing processes.
[7] Including fabrics of flax, hemp, jute and mixed yarns.

[1] Données d'origine exprimées en tonnes.
[2] Période de douze mois finissant le 30 juin de l'année indiquée. Production d'usines de jute.
[3] Production des établissements occupant 10 personnes ou plus.
[4] Période de douze mois finissant le 30 juin de l'année indiquée.
[5] Tissus finis.
[6] Après opérations de finition.
[7] Y compris les tissus de lin, de chanvre, de jute et de filés mélangés.

Jute fabrics – Tissus de jute

Unit : Thousand metres

Unité : Milliers de mètres

Country or area	1976	1977	1978	1979	1980	1981	1982	1983	1984	1985	Pays ou zone
America, South	**122 164**	**40 313**	**89 785**	**112 514**	**128 700**	**128 700**	**128 000**	**128 000**	**142 569**	**149 858**	**Amérique du Sud**
Brazil	122 164	* 40 313	* 89 785	112 514	128 700	* 128 700	* 128 000	* 128 000	...	...	Brésil
Europe	**92 419**	**96 111**	**96 609**	**96 381**	**99 640**	**93 359**	**88 694**	**83 503**	**78 951**	**81 525**	**Europe**
EFTA	***5 103***	***6 183***	***6 292***	***6 088***	***6 102***	***4 287***	***2 359***	***1 733***	***905***	***1 345***	***AELE***
Austria	518	1 971	2 453	2 622	2 020	1 457	1 031	379	301	116	Autriche
Sweden	...	...	...	...	4 082	2 830	1 328	1 354	604	...	Suède
East Europe	***87 316***	***89 928***	***90 317***	***90 293***	***93 538***	***89 072***	***86 335***	***81 770***	***78 046***	***80 180***	***Europe de l'est***
Czechoslovakia	31 073	32 953	35 029	37 395	41 992	44 472	47 126	49 546	51 302	52 595	Tchécoslovaquie
Poland[1]	56 243	56 975	55 288	52 898	51 546	44 600	39 209	32 224	26 744	27 585	Pologne[1]
USSR	**129 850**	**129 947**	**129 713**	**125 265**	**114 541**	**108 505**	**107 524**	**106 936**	**102 959**	**99 979**	**URSS**
Total	**344 433**	**266 371**	**316 107**	**334 160**	**342 881**	**330 564**	**324 218**	**318 439**	**324 479**	**331 362**	**Total**

General note.
Woven fabrics manufactured with yarns of jute at loom stage. (SITC 65340–A).

Remarque générale.
Tissus sortant du métier à tisser, fabriqués à partir de fils de jute. (CTCI 65340–A).

[1] After undergoing finishing processes.

[1] Après opérations de finition.

Jute fabrics – Tissus de jute

Unit : Metric tons — Unité : Tonnes métriques

Country or area	1976	1977	1978	1979	1980	1981	1982	1983	1984	1985	Pays ou zone
Africa	**34 257**	**34 667**	**31 587**	**35 133**	**34 579**	**36 511**	**35 949**	**34 824**	**35 965**	**36 248**	**Afrique**
Algeria	237	320	1 563	3 387	3 389	4 043	4 629	...	...	...	Algérie
Egypt	33 381	33 708	29 385	31 107	30 690	31 868	30 563	28 408	...	...	Egypte
Uganda	...	...	...	...	500	* 600	757	* 700	...	...	Ouganda
America, South	**38 015**	**26 122**	**26 336**	**24 208**	**6 148**	**13 082**	**9 274**	**5 465**	**1 657**	**6 148**	**Amérique du Sud**
Brazil	* 38 015	26 122	26 336	[1] 24 208	6 148	...	...	...	...	...	Brésil
Asia	**1 885 488**	**1 845 669**	**1 964 858**	**1 888 553**	**2 163 534**	**2 208 999**	**2 131 065**	**2 149 646**	**1 973 469**	**2 042 858**	**Asie**
Bangladesh[2]	485 590	497 944	555 127	509 109	531 439	589 927	586 723	569 998	544 235	520 072	Bangladesh[2]
India	1 191 000	1 184 700	1 208 800	1 150 600	1 384 900	1 365 200	1 293 500	1 335 700	1 153 400	1 287 800	Inde
Iran(Islamic Rep.of)* [3]	...	...	...	1 000	3 000	5 000	4 000	...	...	...	Iran(Rép.islamique)* [3]
Pakistan	42 011	33 859	33 383	36 976	41 808	50 173	55 996	66 422	79 733	...	Pakistan
Thailand	...	125 916	164 298	190 868	202 387	198 699	190 846	174 276	* 192 851	157 224	Thaïlande
Europe	**78 628**	**75 708**	**71 857**	**73 287**	**67 696**	**57 944**	**51 132**	**48 108**	**45 923**	**41 487**	**Europe**
EEC	***49 627***	***44 634***	***42 060***	***43 592***	***39 920***	***35 055***	***31 785***	***29 791***	***28 849***	***25 248***	***CEE***
Belgium[4]	5 826	5 171	4 485	5 986	5 922	5 023	5 509	5 461	5 950	5 491	Belgique[4]
France	17 197	13 629	10 912	9 340	8 094	7 211	5 391	2 767	...	...	France
Germany, Fed. Rep.	12 077	12 288	11 379	13 034	10 970	9 104	8 296	7 703	7 556	6 161	Allemagne, Rép. féd.
Greece	...	...	...	...	...	...	...	...	494	...	Grèce
Italy	6 030	5 205	7 098	7 202	7 060	5 922	5 295	...	...	...	Italie
United Kingdom	...	...	...	...	...	7 301	6 800	7 223	6 655	6 587	Royaume–Uni
EFTA	***8 316***	***9 292***	***9 332***	***8 745***	***7 254***	***5 151***	***3 604***	***4 242***	***3 603***	***2 500***	***AELE***
Austria	150	612	553	579	436	331	235	95	81	32	Autriche
Finland	232	211	120	55	52	35	13	13	17	...	Finlande
Portugal	7 353	7 749	6 359	6 240	5 563	4 048	2 968	3 752	3 314	2 372	Portugal
Sweden	581	720	2 300	1 871	1 203	737	388	382	191	83	Suède
East Europe	***20 294***	***20 151***	***18 920***	***17 551***	***17 612***	***15 480***	***13 752***	***11 994***	***10 627***	***10 713***	***Europe de l'est***
Poland[5]	20 294	20 151	18 920	17 551	17 612	15 480	13 752	11 994	10 627	10 713	Pologne[5]
Other Europe	***391***	***1 631***	***1 545***	***3 399***	***2 910***	***2 258***	***1 991***	***2 081***	***2 844***	***3 026***	***Autre Europe***
Spain[6]	391	1 631	1 545	3 399	2 910	2 258	1 991	2 081	...	...	Espagne[6]
Total	**2 036 388**	**1 982 166**	**2 094 638**	**2 021 181**	**2 271 957**	**2 316 536**	**2 227 420**	**2 238 043**	**2 057 014**	**2 126 741**	**Total**

General note.
Woven fabrics manufactured with yarns of jute at loom stage. (SITC 65340–B).

Remarque générale.
Tissus sortant du métier à tisser, fabriqués à partir de fils de jute. (CTCI 65340–B).

[1] Production by establishments employing 5 or more persons.
[2] Twelve months ending 30 June of year stated. Production of jute mills.
[3] Production by establishments employing 10 or more persons.
[4] Including carpets of jute.
[5] After undergoing finishing processes.
[6] Including fabrics of flax, hemp, jute and mixed yarns.

[1] Production des établissements occupant 5 personnes ou plus.
[2] Période de douze mois finissant le 30 juin de l'année indiquée. Production d'usines de jute.
[3] Production des établissements occupant 10 personnes ou plus.
[4] Y compris les carpettes et tapis en jute.
[5] Après opérations de finition.
[6] Y compris les tissus de lin, de chanvre, de jute et de filés mélangés.

Woven fabrics of cellulosic fibres – Tissus de fibres cellulosiques

Unit : Million square metres — Unité : Millions de mètres carrés

Country or area	1976	1977	1978	1979	1980	1981	1982	1983	1984	1985	Pays ou zone
Africa	**35.3**	**31.3**	**30.8**	**28.6**	**33.7**	**33.9**	**33.9**	**35.2**	**35.9**	**36.5**	**Afrique**
Egypt[1]	23.7	22.8	19.5	15.0	...	...	...	...	...	...	Egypte[1]
Tunisia	11.5	8.5	11.4	13.7	13.5	13.6	* 13.7	...	...	...	Tunisie
America, North	**1 170.3**	**1 324.3**	**1 468.7**	**1 454.6**	**1 453.6**	**1 590.9**	**1 651.0**	**1 669.4**	**1 719.6**	**1 834.6**	**Amérique du Nord**
Canada[2]	56.4	...	70.3	...	...	...	...	...	...	...	Canada[2]
Cuba	...	...	...	...	10.9	22.7	14.8	14.0	16.3	27.7	Cuba
El Salvador	24.2	38.2	30.2	18.7	17.4	23.8	36.7	* 34.0	...	...	El Salvador
Mexico	451.8	464.5	480.2	526.0	526.3	548.0	554.1	527.0	530.0	584.1	Mexique
United States	632.0	750.6	878.6	835.2	835.5	...	...	...	...	...	Etats–Unis
America, South	**316.0**	**311.5**	**311.5**	**311.5**	**311.5**	**310.9**	**309.1**	**310.2**	**311.5**	**311.5**	**Amérique du Sud**
Brazil[3 4]	307.6	...	...	...	...	...	...	...	...	...	Brésil[3 4]
Ecuador[5]	8.4	...	...	...	...	* 3.2	* 1.5	* 2.6	...	...	Equateur[5]
Asia	**2 622.0**	**2 826.1**	**2 944.7**	**3 200.3**	**3 082.3**	**3 286.3**	**3 149.6**	**3 085.9**	**3 112.1**	**3 352.7**	**Asie**
Afghanistan[6]	38.2	40.7	31.6	29.2	20.3	14.8	21.4	...	...	...	Afghanistan[6]
Hong Kong[7]	0.4	0.4	0.2	0.1	0.3	* 0.2	...	...	...	...	Hong–kong[7]
India	1 043.3	1 198.8	1 252.9	1 388.3	1 254.0	1 424.0	1 238.0	1 097.7	1 072.7	...	Inde
Iran(Islamic Rep.of)	232.9	215.1	182.2	204.1	215.1	243.9	249.3	...	...	...	Iran(Rép.islamique)
Japan	926.4	882.4	850.9	901.9	881.9	775.0	740.4	708.4	696.9	719.3	Japon
Korea, Republic of[8]	47.4	49.3	47.3	44.1	40.0	43.0	32.3	* 75.0	...	...	Corée, République de[8]
Pakistan[9 10]	13.6	24.0	21.3	19.2	...	...	...	...	...	...	Pakistan[9 10]
Sri Lanka	7.5	5.5	5.5	4.7	3.9	4.5	[3 5 11] 2.0	[3 5 11] 1.5	[3 5 11] 1.0	[3 5 11] 1.1	Sri Lanka
Thailand[12]	290.6	386.8	525.5	579.1	622.0	...	...	...	...	...	Thaïlande[12]
Turkey[5]	21.7	23.0	27.2	29.5	...	...	...	...	...	...	Turquie[5]
Europe	**1 852.4**	**1 809.7**	**1 795.9**	**1 823.2**	**1 677.5**	**1 531.5**	**1 423.5**	**1 406.6**	**1 383.7**	**1 429.0**	**Europe**
EEC	***1 245.2***	***1 242.3***	***1 226.7***	***1 267.3***	***1 136.3***	***1 020.1***	***923.9***	***895.6***	***859.4***	***912.6***	***CEE***
Belgium[13]	273.6	288.8	299.5	306.3	303.6	321.1	300.3	295.3	253.7	258.0	Belgique[13]
Denmark[14]	3.6	3.1	3.0	1.6	0.2	...	...	...	...	...	Danemark[14]
France	184.9	178.3	180.0	179.2	164.8	126.3	117.6	110.3	113.6	144.7	France
Germany, Fed. Rep.[8]	448.4	408.2	430.7	458.3	422.0	381.9	333.2	320.9	323.6	375.2	Allemagne, Rép. féd.[8]
Greece[14]	14.8	14.9	13.9	14.7	14.2	13.5	13.0	11.4	* 9.2	...	Grèce[14]
Ireland[3 8]	16.7	48.2	58.8	64.3	53.3	50.9	45.7	48.3	55.6	27.4	Irlande[3 8]
Italy	35.2	34.3	35.2	36.5	...	...	...	...	...	...	Italie
Netherlands[8]	28.2	19.1	11.8	9.0	5.1	9.7	11.1	9.8	9.2	...	Pays–Bas[8]
United Kingdom	239.8	247.4	193.7	197.3	137.8	80.4	67.3	64.4	59.0	57.6	Royaume–Uni
EFTA	***131.6***	***116.3***	***110.8***	***115.2***	***117.1***	***106.3***	***104.6***	***113.3***	***116.3***	***102.1***	***AELE***
Austria	13.9	12.6	15.3	12.8	10.7	6.0	6.9	6.4	6.3	6.2	Autriche
Finland[8]	12.5	11.2	7.6	8.3	10.7	9.0	1.8	1.5	2.5	...	Finlande[8]
Norway[8]	5.3	13.6	12.9	12.7	14.8	15.4	17.8	9.4	...	...	Norvège[8]
Portugal	16.4	13.7	13.7	23.3	22.4	* [1] 18.9	* [1] 19.0	* [1] 28.9	* [1] 26.1	* [1] 20.8	Portugal
Sweden[12]	83.5	65.1	61.3	58.1	58.6	57.1	59.2	67.1	65.5	...	Suède[12]
East Europe	***316.7***	***296.8***	***299.1***	***277.4***	***278.1***	***263.8***	***253.4***	***255.5***	***264.1***	***265.4***	***Europe de l'est***
Bulgaria[3 8 9]	33.3	31.7	35.8	34.7	39.1	42.0	42.9	44.6	45.4	44.7	Bulgarie[3 8 9]
Czechoslovakia	64.0	65.2	62.6	55.4	53.5	53.5	54.4	54.7	59.2	59.8	Tchécoslovaquie
German Dem. Rep.	58.3	53.5	50.9	48.6	48.5	49.9	50.4	48.6	47.4	48.7	Rép. dém. allemande
Hungary[8]	54.0	50.3	61.6	54.1	54.7	55.1	48.2	43.1	44.9	45.2	Hongrie[8]
Poland[8]	107.1	96.0	88.2	84.6	82.3	63.3	57.5	64.5	67.2	67.0	Pologne[8]
Other Europe	***158.9***	***154.4***	***159.3***	***163.3***	***145.9***	***141.3***	***141.6***	***142.1***	***143.9***	***148.8***	***Autre Europe***
Spain	121.8	115.7	117.1	...	...	...	...	...	...	...	Espagne
Yugoslavia[3]	37.1	38.7	42.2	45.1	27.8	23.1	23.4	23.9	25.7	30.6	Yougoslavie[3]
USSR	**1 155.7**	**1 144.1**	**1 128.1**	**1 136.5**	**1 145.3**	**1 179.4**	**1 157.2**	**1 178.6**	**1 114.4**	**1 071.9**	**URSS**
Oceania	**16.7**	**16.6**	**15.2**	**17.9**	**19.0**	**18.7**	**14.5**	**15.0**	**10.9**	**9.6**	**Océanie**
Australia[10 14]	16.7	16.6	15.2	17.9	19.0	18.7	14.5	* 15.0	10.9	9.6	Australie[10 14]
Total	**7 168.3**	**7 463.7**	**7 695.1**	**7 972.6**	**7 722.9**	**7 951.5**	**7 738.8**	**7 700.8**	**7 688.2**	**8 045.9**	**Total**

For general note and footnotes, see end of table.

Voir la fin du tableau pour la remarque générale et les notes.

Woven fabrics of cellulosic fibres (continued) – Tissus de fibres cellulosiques (suite)

General note.
Fabrics of continuous and discontinuous rayon and acetate fibres, including pile and chenille fabrics at loom stage. (Parts of SITC 6535 and 6536).

[1] Original data in metric tons.
[2] Shipments.
[3] Including fabrics of non–cellulosic fibres.
[4] Production by main establishments only.
[5] Original data in metres.
[6] Twelve months beginning 21 March of year stated.
[7] Beginning 1982, data are confidential.
[8] After undergoing finishing processes.
[9] Including silk fabrics.
[10] Twelve months ending 30 June of year stated.
[11] Government production only.
[12] Including woven non–cellulosic fabrics.
[13] Including blankets and carpets of cellulosic fibres.
[14] Including finished fabrics.

Remarque générale.
Tissus de fibres de rayonne et d'acétate, continues ou discontinues, sortant du métier à tisser, y compris les velours, peluches, tissus bouclés et tissus chenille. (Parties de CTCI 6535 et 6536).

[1] Données d'origine exprimées en tonnes.
[2] Expéditions.
[3] Y compris les tissus en fibres non cellulosiques.
[4] Production des principaux établissements seulement.
[5] Données d'origine exprimées en mètres.
[6] Période de douze mois commençant le 21 mars de l'année indiquée.
[7] A partir de 1982, les données sont confidentielles.
[8] Après opérations de finition.
[9] Y compris les tissus de soie.
[10] Période de douze mois finissant le 30 juin de l'année indiquée.
[11] Production de l'Etat seulement.
[12] Y compris les tissus en fibres non cellulosiques.
[13] Y compris les couvertures et les tapis en fibres cellulosiques.
[14] Y compris les tissus finis.

Woven fabrics of cellulosic fibres – Tissus de fibres cellulosiques

Unit : Thousand metres

Unité : Milliers de mètres

Country or area	1976	1977	1978	1979	1980	1981	1982	1983	1984	1985	Pays ou zone
Africa	**25 744**	**22 861**	**22 503**	**20 361**	**19 278**	**19 446**	**19 500**	**19 200**	**17 208**	**16 341**	**Afrique**
Egypt	17 321	16 644	14 216	10 387	9 460	* 9 500	* 9 500	* 9 200	...	...	Egypte
Tunisia	8 423	6 217	8 287	9 974	9 818	9 946	* 10 000	* 10 000	...	...	Tunisie
America, North	**529 696**	**623 461**	**707 724**	**675 511**	**675 786**	**732 562**	**441 544**	**618 338**	**610 385**	**609 503**	**Amérique du Nord**
El Salvador	...	...	...	...	...	17 362	27 544	26 076	* 21 000	...	El Salvador
United States	506 700	600 465	684 728	652 515	652 790	715 200	414 000	...	...	...	Etats-Unis
America, South	**230 657**	**229 763**	**229 113**	**228 464**	**227 814**	**226 908**	**225 642**	**226 426**	**225 539**	**224 566**	**Amérique du Sud**
Brazil[1 2]	224 539	...	...	...	...	...	...	...	...	...	Brésil[1 2]
Ecuador	6 118	...	...	...	...	2 369	1 103	1 887	* 1 000	...	Equateur
Asia	**991 463**	**1 100 712**	**1 110 670**	**1 223 230**	**1 123 124**	**1 264 294**	**1 135 473**	**1 021 874**	**1 001 577**	**1 102 253**	**Asie**
Afghanistan[3]	27 900	29 700	23 100	21 300	14 800	10 800	15 600	6 800	3 700	4 600	Afghanistan[3]
India	761 515	875 041	914 548	1 013 391	915 295	1 039 426	903 659	801 210	782 990	...	Inde
Iran(Islamic Rep.of)*	170 000	157 000	133 000	149 000	157 000	178 000	182 000	180 000	...	...	Iran(Rép.islamique)*
Pakistan	9 922	17 548	15 585	13 996	...	...	...	...	...	...	Pakistan
Sri Lanka	6 314	4 638	4 580	3 976	3 261	* 3 300	[1 4] 1 446	[1 4] 1 096	[1 4] 762	[1 4] 774	Sri Lanka
Turkey	15 812	16 785	19 857	21 567	...	...	...	...	...	...	Turquie
Europe	**429 197**	**426 199**	**409 716**	**389 407**	**330 663**	**260 788**	**253 268**	**241 944**	**247 007**	**245 465**	**Europe**
EEC	***170 100***	***173 000***	***154 800***	***152 600***	***107 400***	***63 600***	***53 700***	***43 800***	***39 100***	***37 800***	***CEE***
United Kingdom	170 100	173 000	154 800	152 600	107 400	63 600	53 700	43 800	39 100	37 800	Royaume-Uni
EFTA	***67 114***	***75 249***	***83 320***	***76 439***	***65 281***	***54 880***	***61 238***	***51 998***	***60 877***	***61 812***	***AELE***
Austria	37 119	39 638	48 681	42 417	30 514	20 371	23 042	23 076	27 646	27 371	Autriche
Norway	3 877	9 958	9 451	9 300	10 781	11 215	12 973	6 852	...	...	Norvège
Sweden	...	...	...	...	23 986	23 294	25 223	22 070	21 644	22 346	Suède
East Europe	***191 983***	***177 950***	***171 596***	***160 368***	***157 982***	***142 308***	***138 330***	***146 146***	***147 030***	***145 853***	***Europe de l'est***
Bulgaria[1 5 6]	32 049	29 031	31 818	30 592	33 564	35 412	35 923	37 114	37 157	36 393	Bulgarie[1 5 6]
Czechoslovakia	59 365	60 445	58 053	51 377	49 637	49 586	50 426	50 717	49 329	49 692	Tchécoslovaquie
Poland[5]	100 569	88 474	81 725	78 399	74 781	57 310	51 981	58 315	60 544	59 768	Pologne[5]
USSR	**1 130 724**	**1 143 717**	**1 103 207**	**1 088 015**	**1 075 411**	**1 091 596**	**1 069 791**	**1 093 549**	**1 069 638**	**1 032 539**	**URSS**
Total	**3 337 481**	**3 546 713**	**3 582 933**	**3 624 988**	**3 452 076**	**3 595 594**	**3 145 218**	**3 221 331**	**3 171 354**	**3 230 666**	**Total**

General note.
Fabrics of continuous and discontinuous rayon and acetate fibres, including pile and chenille fabrics at loom stage. (Parts of SITC 6535 and 6536).

Remarque générale.
Tissus de fibres de rayonne et d'acétate, continues ou discontinues, sortant du métier à tisser, y compris les velours, peluches, tissus bouclés et tissus chenille. (Parties de CTCI 6535 et 6536).

[1] Including fabrics of non-cellulosic fibres.
[2] Production by main establishments only.
[3] Twelve months beginning 21 March of year stated.
[4] Government production only.
[5] After undergoing finishing processes.
[6] Including silk fabrics.

[1] Y compris les tissus en fibres non cellulosiques.
[2] Production des principaux établissements seulement.
[3] Période de douze mois commençant le 21 mars de l'année indiquée.
[4] Production de l'Etat seulement.
[5] Après opérations de finition.
[6] Y compris les tissus de soie.

Woven fabrics of cellulosic fibres – Tissus de fibres cellulosiques

Unit : Metric tons — Unité : Tonnes métriques

Country or area	1976	1977	1978	1979	1980	1981	1982	1983	1984	1985	Pays ou zone
Africa	**6 400**	**6 500**	**9 800**	**9 753**	**10 000**	**11 000**	**12 252**	**13 207**	**14 163**	**15 118**	**Afrique**
Egypt	6 400	6 500	9 800	9 753	* 10 000	* 11 000	...	...	...	...	Egypte
America, North	**57 900**	**59 313**	**60 977**	**66 166**	**62 777**	**65 038**	**65 672**	**62 847**	**63 157**	**68 815**	**Amérique du Nord**
Canada[1]	...	...	7 795	...	...	...	...	...	...	...	Canada[1]
Mexico	50 105	51 518	53 182	58 371	54 982	57 243	57 877	55 052	55 362	61 020	Mexique
Asia	**135 007**	**152 256**	**155 267**	**173 883**	**159 063**	**178 923**	**156 604**	**141 038**	**132 270**	**150 149**	**Asie**
India	115 699	132 948	138 950	153 967	139 063	157 923	137 296	121 730	112 962	...	Inde
Indonesia	...	...	16 317	19 916	* 20 000	* 21 000	...	...	...	...	Indonésie
Europe	**163 438**	**155 313**	**156 101**	**157 288**	**151 552**	**138 902**	**125 613**	**122 933**	**120 172**	**132 762**	**Europe**
EEC	***131 130***	***125 649***	***125 569***	***125 726***	***119 534***	***109 928***	***97 639***	***94 321***	***91 176***	***103 533***	***CEE***
Belgium[2]	30 343	32 029	33 217	33 971	33 668	35 606	33 299	32 746	28 134	28 617	Belgique[2]
France	20 504	19 769	19 963	19 875	18 280	14 012	13 041	12 231	12 600	16 051	France
Germany, Fed. Rep.	71 641	66 295	65 610	65 345	61 387	53 537	44 446	42 752	44 088	51 817	Allemagne, Rép. féd.
Greece	1 640	1 653	1 546	1 634	1 577	1 493	1 440	1 259	1 025	...	Grèce
Italy	3 902	3 803	...	3 901	4 052	* 4 200	...	...	...	...	Italie
Netherlands	3 100	2 100	1 300	1 000	570	1 080	1 228	1 085	1 018	1 533	Pays-Bas
EFTA	***18 291***	***16 163***	***16 252***	***17 630***	***18 086***	***15 042***	***14 042***	***14 680***	***15 064***	***15 297***	***AELE***
Austria	5 071	4 595	5 563	4 673	3 880	2 171	2 530	2 326	2 305	2 242	Autriche
Finland	1 554	1 317	944	2 520	3 254	2 733	875	659	837	...	Finlande
Norway	589	1 513	1 436	1 413	1 638	1 704	1 971	1 041	...	...	Norvège
Portugal	1 819	1 518	1 514	2 579	2 488	2 102	2 106	3 204	2 896	2 307	Portugal
Sweden[3]	9 258	7 220	6 795	6 445	6 826	6 332	6 560	7 450	7 266	7 676	Suède[3]
Other Europe	***14 017***	***13 501***	***14 280***	***13 932***	***13 932***	***13 932***	***13 932***	***13 932***	***13 932***	***13 932***	***Autre Europe***
Spain	14 017	13 501	14 280	...	...	...	...	...	...	...	Espagne
Total	**362 745**	**373 382**	**382 145**	**407 090**	**383 392**	**393 863**	**360 141**	**340 025**	**329 762**	**366 844**	**Total**

General note.
Fabrics of continuous and discontinuous rayon and acetate fibres, including pile and chenille fabrics at loom stage. (Parts of SITC 6535 and 6536).

[1] Shipments.
[2] Including blankets and carpets of cellulosic fibres.
[3] Including woven non-cellulosic fabrics.

Remarque générale.
Tissus de fibres de rayonne et d'acétate, continues ou discontinues, sortant du métier à tisser, y compris les velours, peluches, tissus bouclés et tissus chenille. (Parties de CTCI 6535 et 6536).

[1] Expéditions.
[2] Y compris les couvertures et les tapis en fibres cellulosiques.
[3] Y compris les tissus en fibres non cellulosiques.

Woven fabrics of non–cellulosic fibres – Tissus de fibres non cellulosiques

Unit : Million square metres

Unité : Millions de mètres carrés

Country or area	1976	1977	1978	1979	1980	1981	1982	1983	1984	1985	Pays ou zone
Africa	**38.4**	**41.6**	**36.7**	**34.2**	**38.6**	**37.9**	**37.7**	**36.6**	**35.1**	**36.0**	**Afrique**
Algeria[1]	...	25.6	22.7	18.6	23.0	22.0	* 22.0	* 21.0	* 20.0	* 20.0	Algérie[1]
Côte d'Ivoire[2]	...	* 2.6	2.2	2.3	3.0	3.0	3.0	3.1	2.4	...	Côte d'Ivoire[2]
Ethiopia[3]	4.8	6.2	5.1	5.6	5.9	5.9	5.9	5.9	6.1	...	Ethiopie[3]
Tunisia	3.8	3.7	3.2	3.8	2.7	2.9	* 2.7	* 2.6	* 2.4	* 2.4	Tunisie
Zaire	3.5	3.4	3.5	* 4.0	* 4.0	* 4.0	* 4.0	* 4.0	...	...	Zaïre
America, North	**300.5**	**482.7**	**327.1**	**370.1**	**370.1**	**370.1**	**370.1**	**370.1**	**370.1**	**370.1**	**Amérique du Nord**
Canada[4 5]	300.5	482.7	327.1	...	...	...	...	...	...	...	Canada[4 5]
America, South	**20.2**	**20.2**	**20.2**	**20.2**	**23.5**	**20.6**	**21.2**	**15.6**	**20.2**	**20.2**	**Amérique du Sud**
Ecuador* [2]	...	...	...	...	23.5	20.6	21.2	15.6	...	...	Equateur* [2]
Asia	**4 319.0**	**4 509.6**	**4 836.2**	**5 021.2**	**5 432.1**	**5 791.8**	**5 769.5**	**6 390.3**	**6 910.0**	**6 411.4**	**Asie**
India	309.4	390.7	589.9	538.0	566.1	583.1	695.3	1 076.4	1 378.0	...	Inde
Iran(Islamic Rep.of)	257.6	269.9	224.7	265.8	263.0	282.2	291.8	...	...	...	Iran(Rép.islamique)
Japan[6 7]	2 808.2	2 883.5	2 915.9	2 980.6	3 138.6	3 121.0	3 024.3	3 218.7	3 296.8	3 067.6	Japon[6 7]
Korea, Republic of	942.2	963.1	1 103.2	1 233.8	1 461.3	1 801.9	1 754.0	1 801.6	1 936.1	1 808.4	Corée, République de
Nepal[2 8]	1.5	2.4	2.4	3.0	3.2	3.7	4.1	4.9	4.5	...	Népal[2 8]
Europe	**4 098.7**	**4 158.0**	**4 191.8**	**4 727.7**	**4 823.5**	**4 860.5**	**4 661.0**	**4 962.9**	**5 303.4**	**5 443.7**	**Europe**
EEC	***3 531.7***	***3 599.7***	***3 632.0***	***4 010.1***	***3 939.3***	***3 985.3***	***3 799.6***	***4 030.7***	***4 273.9***	***4 344.4***	***CEE***
Belgium[9]	1 440.2	1 527.6	1 487.3	1 717.6	1 854.2	2 058.4	1 894.9	2 251.9	2 387.7	2 371.8	Belgique[9]
Denmark	18.8	19.9	19.9	22.2	19.9	...	...	...	...	...	Danemark
France	722.4	715.9	722.5	756.7	726.9	678.9	665.1	600.6	601.9	598.5	France
Germany, Fed. Rep.	544.7	539.3	541.0	564.5	573.8	544.3	560.8	528.5	577.3	629.3	Allemagne, Rép. féd.
Greece	171.9	168.4	190.4	271.0	234.3	208.7	* 210.0	* 210.0	...	...	Grèce
Netherlands[10]	178.5	164.1	200.6	192.5	156.2	135.5	128.3	113.8	120.6	123.5	Pays–Bas[10]
United Kingdom	455.0	464.5	470.4	485.5	374.0	338.0	318.6	303.4	329.0	357.7	Royaume–Uni
EFTA	***140.4***	***125.0***	***117.2***	***124.8***	***132.6***	***124.0***	***125.8***	***126.5***	***135.0***	***141.9***	***AELE***
Austria	71.7	73.3	63.0	68.9	78.9	67.3	83.4	83.6	77.8	96.2	Autriche
Finland	43.9	31.8	38.7	44.1	41.9	45.0	29.8	32.7	32.3	...	Finlande
Norway	24.8	19.9	15.5	11.7	11.7	11.7	12.5	10.1	24.9	...	Norvège
East Europe	***179.9***	***187.5***	***181.5***	***193.0***	***196.3***	***189.0***	***180.0***	***184.3***	***183.3***	***183.9***	***Europe de l'est***
Czechoslovakia	36.3	38.0	37.6	40.5	45.8	46.5	46.2	47.7	50.8	51.8	Tchécoslovaquie
Hungary[10]	49.2	54.6	50.8	57.9	50.7	47.5	47.4	47.5	45.6	45.6	Hongrie[10]
Poland[10]	94.4	95.0	93.2	94.7	99.8	95.0	86.5	89.1	86.9	86.5	Pologne[10]
Other Europe	***246.7***	***245.8***	***261.1***	***399.9***	***555.3***	***562.2***	***555.6***	***621.4***	***711.2***	***773.5***	***Autre Europe***
Spain[4]	246.7	245.8	261.1	...	[11] 555.3	[11] 562.2	[11] 555.6	[11] 621.4	...	...	Espagne[4]
USSR	**399.5**	**460.4**	**517.1**	**536.4**	**570.4**	**574.1**	**609.9**	**649.2**	**742.8**	**805.5**	**URSS**
Oceania	**97.8**	**96.9**	**104.1**	**115.3**	**119.3**	**122.3**	**120.5**	**120.5**	**129.7**	**145.3**	**Océanie**
Australia[12]	97.8	96.9	104.1	115.3	119.3	122.3	120.5	120.5	129.7	145.3	Australie[12]
Total	**9 274.1**	**9 769.5**	**10 033.1**	**10 825.2**	**11 377.6**	**11 777.3**	**11 589.8**	**12 545.2**	**13 511.3**	**13 232.1**	**Total**

General note.
Fabrics of continuous and discontinuous non–cellulosic fibres other than textile glass fibres, including pile and chenille fabrics at loom stage. (Parts of SITC 6535 and 6536).

1 Including cellulosic fabrics.
2 Original data in metres.
3 Twelve months ending 10 September of year stated.
4 Including woven cellulosic fabrics.
5 Shipments.
6 Including finished fabrics.
7 Including blanketing made of synthetic fibres.
8 Twelve months beginning 16 July of year stated.
9 Including blankets and carpets of non–cellulosic fibres.
10 After undergoing finishing processes.
11 Original data in metric tons.
12 Twelve months ending 30 June of year stated.

Remarque générale.
Tissus sortant du métier à tisser, composés de fibres non cellulosiques, continues ou discontinues, autres que les fibres de verre. Cette rubrique comprend les velours, peluches, tissus bouclés et tissus chenille. (Parties de CTCI 6535 et 6536).

1 Y compris les tissus en fibres cellulosiques.
2 Données d'origine exprimées en mètres.
3 Période de douze mois finissant le 10 septembre de l'année indiquée.
4 Y compris les tissus en fibres cellulosiques.
5 Expéditions.
6 Y compris les tissus finis.
7 Y compris les couvertures en fibres synthétiques.
8 Période de douze mois commençant le 16 juillet de l'année indiquée.
9 Y compris les couvertures et les tapis en fibres non cellulosiques.
10 Après opérations de finition.
11 Données d'origine exprimées en tonnes.
12 Période de douze mois finissant le 30 juin de l'année indiquée.

Woven fabrics of non–cellulosic fibres – Tissus de fibres non cellulosiques

Unit : Thousand metres

Unité : Milliers de mètres

Country or area	1976	1977	1978	1979	1980	1981	1982	1983	1984	1985	Pays ou zone
Africa	**4 470**	**4 624**	**3 966**	**4 422**	**3 663**	**3 818**	**3 700**	**4 350**	**3 535**	**3 408**	**Afrique**
Côte d'Ivoire	...	* 1 900	1 600	1 646	* 1 700	* 1 700	* 1 700	2 250	1 710	* 1 700	Côte d'Ivoire
Tunisia	2 764	2 724	2 366	2 776	1 963	2 118	* 2 000	* 2 100	...	...	Tunisie
America, South	**14 752**	**14 752**	**14 752**	**14 752**	**17 153**	**15 000**	**15 444**	**11 410**	**14 752**	**14 752**	**Amérique du Sud**
Ecuador	...	...	...	...	17 153	* 15 000	15 444	11 410	...	...	Equateur
Asia	**414 996**	**483 896**	**596 346**	**588 927**	**607 514**	**634 265**	**723 512**	**1 000 010**	**1 224 163**	**1 120 237**	**Asie**
India	225 868	285 179	430 571	392 737	413 185	425 588	507 489	785 705	1 005 828	...	Inde
Iran(Islamic Rep.of)	188 000	197 000	164 000	194 000	192 000	206 000	213 000	...	...	...	Iran(Rép.islamique)
Nepal[1]	1 128	1 717	1 775	2 190	2 329	2 677	3 023	3 591	3 300	3 300	Népal[1]
Europe	**514 002**	**514 035**	**479 205**	**492 842**	**437 046**	**392 341**	**380 787**	**371 196**	**390 842**	**412 055**	**Europe**
EEC	***322 700***	***324 800***	***305 500***	***314 500***	***243 400***	***209 300***	***196 600***	***184 600***	***199 700***	***217 100***	***CEE***
United Kingdom	322 700	324 800	305 500	314 500	243 400	209 300	196 600	184 600	199 700	217 100	Royaume–Uni
EFTA	***71 266***	***67 179***	***54 476***	***57 506***	***64 400***	***57 135***	***66 790***	***65 897***	***71 073***	***74 110***	***AELE***
Austria	53 166	52 627	43 182	48 976	55 863	48 612	57 635	58 499	52 907	64 650	Autriche
Norway	18 100	14 552	11 294	8 530	8 537	8 523	9 155	7 398	18 166	...	Norvège
East Europe	***120 036***	***122 056***	***119 229***	***120 836***	***129 246***	***125 906***	***117 397***	***120 699***	***120 069***	***120 845***	***Europe de l'est***
Czechoslovakia	33 687	35 212	34 845	37 516	42 512	43 151	42 821	44 228	45 163	45 774	Tchécoslovaquie
Poland[2]	86 349	86 844	84 384	83 320	86 734	82 755	74 576	76 471	74 906	75 071	Pologne[2]
USSR	**409 992**	**417 468**	**461 411**	**471 024**	**497 976**	**501 758**	**524 106**	**548 463**	**577 631**	**622 019**	**URSS**
Total	**1 358 212**	**1 434 775**	**1 555 680**	**1 571 967**	**1 563 352**	**1 547 182**	**1 647 549**	**1 935 429**	**2 210 923**	**2 172 471**	**Total**

General note.
Fabrics of continuous and discontinuous non–cellulosic fibres other than textile glass fibres, including pile and chenille fabrics at loom stage. (Parts of SITC 6535 and 6536).

1 Twelve months beginning 16 July of year stated.
2 After undergoing finishing processes.

Remarque générale.
Tissus sortant du métier à tisser, composés de fibres non cellulosiques, continues ou discontinues, autres que les fibres de verre. Cette rubrique comprend les velours, peluches, tissus bouclés et tissus chenille. (Parties en CTCI 6535 et 6536).

1 Période de douze mois commençant le 16 juillet de l'année indiquée.
2 Après opérations de finition.

Woven fabrics of non–cellulosic fibres – Tissus de fibres non cellulosiques

Unit : Metric tons

Unité : Tonnes métriques

Country or area	1976	1977	1978	1979	1980	1981	1982	1983	1984	1985	Pays ou zone
Asia	**34 317**	**43 328**	**65 418**	**59 670**	**62 776**	**64 661**	**77 104**	**119 374**	**152 818**	**136 371**	**Asie**
India	34 317	43 328	65 418	59 670	62 776	64 661	77 104	119 374	152 818	...	Inde
Europe	**330 272**	**332 729**	**335 214**	**430 609**	**395 565**	**410 666**	**387 694**	**424 167**	**456 104**	**450 940**	**Europe**
EEC	***278 707***	***285 679***	***288 420***	***313 748***	***315 517***	***329 298***	***309 421***	***338 545***	***353 576***	***343 903***	***CEE***
Belgium[1]	159 722	169 411	164 938	190 481	205 634	228 272	210 145	249 732	264 800	263 035	Belgique[1]
France	80 118	79 397	80 120	83 917	80 609	75 294	73 756	66 613	66 751	60 828	France
Greece	19 067	18 671	21 112	* 18 000	11 949	10 707	11 297	9 583	8 648	...	Grèce
Netherlands	19 800	18 200	22 250	21 350	17 325	15 025	14 223	12 617	13 377	13 692	Pays–Bas
EFTA	***24 203***	***19 792***	***17 837***	***18 928***	***18 463***	***19 021***	***16 660***	***16 710***	***19 830***	***18 072***	***AELE***
Austria	11 918	12 067	10 403	11 387	11 777	10 014	10 502	10 796	11 676	12 115	Autriche
Finland	9 535	5 514	5 718	6 245	5 389	7 712	4 767	4 790	5 394	...	Finlande
Norway	2 750	2 211	1 716	1 296	1 297	1 295	1 391	1 124	2 760	...	Norvège
Other Europe	***27 362***	***27 258***	***28 957***	***97 933***	***61 585***	***62 347***	***61 613***	***68 912***	***82 698***	***88 965***	***Autre Europe***
Spain[2 3]	27 362	27 258	28 957	97 933	61 585	62 347	61 613	68 912	...	...	Espagne[2 3]
Total	**364 589**	**376 057**	**400 632**	**490 279**	**458 341**	**475 327**	**464 798**	**543 541**	**608 922**	**587 311**	**Total**

General note.
Fabrics of continuous and discontinuous non–cellulosic fibres other than textile glass fibres, including pile and chenille fabrics at loom stage. (Parts of SITC 6535 and 6536).

[1] Including blankets and carpets of non–cellulosic fibres.
[2] Including woven cellulosic fabrics.
[3] Including household production.

Remarque générale.
Tissus sortant du métier à tisser, composés de fibres non cellulosiques, continues ou discontinues, autres que les fibres de verre. Cette rubrique comprend les velours, peluches, tissus bouclés et tissus chenille. (Parties de CTCI 6535 et 6536).

[1] Y compris les couvertures et les tapis en fibres non cellulosiques.
[2] Y compris les tissus en fibres cellulosiques.
[3] Y compris la production ménagère.

Blankets – Couvertures

Unit : Thousand units

Unité : En milliers

Country or area	1976	1977	1978	1979	1980	1981	1982	1983	1984	1985	Pays ou zone
Africa											**Afrique**
Algeria	5 131	887	964	1 144	1 105	1 486	1 242	...	...	...	Algérie
Burundi	416	429	435	400	373	381	345	359	340	364	Burundi
Cameroon	...	...	...	400	400	* 400	* 400	537	482	523	Cameroun
Central African Rep.	77	...	41	...	...	...	...	...	...	...	Rép. centrafricaine
Ethiopia[1]	845	955	871	687	1 158	847	* 1 170	1 207	1 233	...	Ethiopie[1]
Kenya	2 788	3 127	3 295	4 257	4 982	3 256	3 435	2 303	2 253	2 642	Kenya
Malawi	420	510	573	711	815	769	740	688	676	681	Malawi
Senegal	703	585	347	695	624	439	473	662	111	112	Sénégal
South Africa	11 592	12 763	9 444	12 056	12 679	13 059	12 729	9 198	8 098	9 722	Afrique du Sud
Tunisia	626	851	534	725	814	1 310	...	...	...	...	Tunisie
Uganda	236	253	174	76	93	133	124	* 130	* 120	* 130	Ouganda
United Rep. Tanzania[2]	3 676	3 514	2 706	2 549	...	...	...	...	...	...	Rép.Unie de Tanzanie[2]
Zaire	2 239	1 751	1 229	* 1 000	978	1 189	803	1 041	...	...	Zaïre
Zambia	* 1 523	* 1 133	* 1 181	* 1 118	1 552	1 442	1 065	893	629	636	Zambie
America, North											**Amérique du Nord**
Canada[3 4]	5 189	5 025	6 378	6 486	5 953	...	...	...	...	...	Canada[3 4]
Cuba[5]	1 452	1 591	1 400	1 280	1 280	1 218	879	934	499	551	Cuba[5]
El Salvador	...	1 381	414	431	508	344	58	141	...	...	El Salvador
Mexico[6]	1 071	691	384	384	282	367	372	* 400	668	670	Mexique[6]
America, South											**Amérique du Sud**
Brazil	14 861	15 937	15 397	[7] 16 629	14 404	11 273	* 12 000	* 12 000	...	...	Brésil
Ecuador	4	3	50	...	530	613	709	...	...	...	Equateur
Paraguay	72	89	88	51	93	89	86	79	83	80	Paraguay
Asia											**Asie**
Afghanistan	...	...	77	69	27	47	50	67	62	23	Afghanistan
Burma[8]	1 287	1 356	1 879	1 043	2 311	1 395	1 351	1 365	1 224	1 119	Birmanie[8]
China	...	5 390	6 250	6 900	8 840	10 670	13 790	16 220	17 450	20 150	Chine
Indonesia	3 678	1 753	2 140	2 023	3 497	5 028	7 083	5 365	6 585	...	Indonésie
Iran(Islamic Rep.of)[9]	2 446	2 948	2 586	3 356	3 823	4 244	6 676	7 775	...	...	Iran(Rép.islamique)[9]
Japan[2 10]	7 864	7 856	6 686	5 967	5 570	5 588	5 533	5 050	4 587	4 398	Japon[2 10]
Korea, Republic of[2]	4 433	6 253	8 022	8 556	10 229	10 240	14 057	10 247	10 438	9 207	Corée, République de[2]
Pakistan	285	297	342	181	179	227	326	301	355	...	Pakistan
Philippines[3 11]	847	868	...	...	...	...	...	...	...	...	Philippines[3 11]
Turkey	647	774	884	692	730	1 980	1 123	1 793	2 265	1 967	Turquie
Europe											**Europe**
EEC											***CEE***
Belgium[6]	4 020	3 233	2 652	3 222	3 036	2 921	2 422	1 781	1 762	1 982	Belgique[6]
Denmark	67	59	59	45	37	* 32	30	47	* 32	34	Danemark
France	[2] 19 457	[2] 18 440	[2] 17 427	[2] 18 644	[2] 18 690	[2] 15 975	[2] 17 100	[2] 14 578	12 170	6 998	France
Germany, Fed. Rep.[12]	5 371	6 262	6 856	7 698	7 311	6 756	6 923	...	...	...	Allemagne, Rép. féd.[12]
Greece[6]	9 269	9 323	9 655	12 641	10 759	10 989	9 808	8 109	8 354	...	Grèce[6]
Ireland	43	48	40	51	52	61	61	65	70	85	Irlande
Netherlands[13]	900	...	...	...	...	...	...	...	...	...	Pays–Bas[13]
United Kingdom[14]	5 412	5 255	5 374	4 471	3 611	2 354	2 236	1 927	2 080	2 017	Royaume–Uni[14]
EFTA											***AELE***
Austria	526	635	563	683	622	562	448	370	338	238	Autriche
Finland	118	32	168	144	205	155	175	172	191	...	Finlande
Iceland	124	135	154	139	178	102	130	110	62	...	Islande
Norway[6]	135	148	191	202	176	178	...	136	154	...	Norvège[6]
Portugal[6]	5 182	3 137	2 910	3 678	3 000	2 905	2 723	3 246	2 817	1 758	Portugal[6]
Sweden[15]	118	34	38	22	28	37	43	39	41	29	Suède[15]
Switzerland[16]	806	770	728	803	878	832	725	736	747	...	Suisse[16]
East Europe											***Europe de l'est***
Bulgaria	2 427	2 923	2 549	2 545	2 446	2 599	2 546	2 580	2 699	2 722	Bulgarie
Hungary	850	750	1 231	786	710	750	653	573	508	529	Hongrie
Other Europe											***Autre Europe***
Spain[17]	...	...	...	12 887	13 928	15 210	14 996	16 584	...	...	Espagne[17]

For general note and footnotes, see end of table.

Voir la fin du tableau pour la remarque générale et les notes.

Unit : Thousand units

Unité : En milliers

Country or area	1976	1977	1978	1979	1980	1981	1982	1983	1984	1985	Pays ou zone
Yugoslavia	3 935	4 059	4 130	5 201	5 459	5 445	5 144	5 685	5 638	5 937	Yougoslavie
Oceania											**Océanie**
Australia	2 031	1 580	1 427	1 167	972	856	961	1 096	732	483	Australie
New Zealand	430	400	306	276	184	...	...	...	...	...	Nouvelle-Zélande

General note.
Blankets, travelling rugs and coverlets. Specially-shaped rugs and blankets for animals, bedspreads and counterpanes, and quilted or stuffed bed coverings are excluded. (SITC 65660-0).

Remarque générale.
Couvertures de lits, couvertures de voyage, couvertures de berceaux, de voitures d'enfants. Cette rubrique ne comprend pas les couvertures de forme spéciale pour animaux, les couvre-lits, les couvre-pieds et les articles de literie rembourrés ou garnis intérieurement de toutes matières. (CTCI 65660-0).

1 Twelve months ending 10 September of year stated.
2 In thousand square metres.
3 Shipments.
4 Excluding electric blankets.
5 Including bedspreads.
6 In metric tons.
7 Production by establishments employing 5 or more persons.
8 Government production only.
9 Production by establishments employing 50 or more persons.
10 Blanketing made of wool and remanufactured fibres only.
11 Including bedspreads, bedsheets and pillow slips.
12 Beginning 1983, data are confidential.
13 Excluding cotton blankets.
14 Deliveries by the woolen textile industry. Including cotton blankets.
15 Including woollen blankets.
16 In thousand metres.
17 Including household production.

1 Période de douze mois finissant le 10 septembre de l'année indiquée.
2 En milliers de mètres carrés.
3 Expéditions.
4 Non compris les couvertures électriques.
5 Y compris les couvre-lits.
6 En tonnes métriques.
7 Production des établissements occupant 5 personnes ou plus.
8 Production de l'Etat seulement.
9 Production des établissements occupant 50 personnes ou plus.
10 Tissus pour couvertures en laine et fibres recyclées seulement.
11 Y compris les couvre-lits, draps de lit et taies d'oreiller.
12 A partir de 1983, les données sont confidentielles.
13 Non compris les couvertures de coton.
14 Quantités produites par l'industrie lainière. Y compris les couvertures en coton.
15 Y compris les couvertures en laine.
16 En milliers de mètres.
17 Y compris la production ménagère.

Bed linen, articles – Linge de literie

Unit : Thousand units — Unité : En milliers

Country or area	1976	1977	1978	1979	1980	1981	1982	1983	1984	1985	Pays ou zone
Africa											**Afrique**
South Africa	1 231	1 565	6 043	6 905	* 9 699	10 035	10 878	9 353	* 9 392	9 415	Afrique du Sud
America, North											**Amérique du Nord**
Cuba	9 525	10 057	10 231	9 896	9 858	11 603	8 892	9 361	10 460	10 203	Cuba
United States	336 420	370 392	392 424	369 888	383 148	382 236	334 428	392 940	387 276	343 980	Etats-Unis
America, South											**Amérique du Sud**
Brazil	33 931	27 100	39 975	[1] 51 916	62 315	48 242	...	...	...	...	Brésil
Colombia	1 040	1 472	1 645	1 670	1 768	1 847	1 945	1 592	* 1 600	...	Colombie
Ecuador	4	...	...	...	# 274	120	137	161	* 170	...	Equateur
Asia											**Asie**
Indonesia	559	503	422	430	340	757	176	252	212	...	Indonésie
Syrian Arab Republic	148	131	138	145	152	456	...	...	# 79	74	Rép. arabe syrienne
Europe											**Europe**
EEC											***CEE***
Denmark	816	694	1 223	1 599	2 600	...	...	...	...	...	Danemark
Germany, Fed. Rep.	78 952	68 201	68 855	74 125	74 872	63 833	58 638	56 755	52 372	48 602	Allemagne, Rép. féd.
EFTA											***AELE***
Austria	2 694	2 913	3 334	3 320	3 772	3 614	3 602	3 334	3 364	4 201	Autriche
Finland	2 032	1 393	997	1 178	1 585	1 534	1 826	1 976	1 712	...	Finlande
Norway	3 470	4 066	3 118	3 183	3 848	4 011	3 575	2 461	2 800	1 471	Norvège
Sweden	...	...	...	...	3 325	2 819	2 587	2 867	2 981	2 906	Suède
East Europe											***Europe de l'est***
Hungary	15 529	13 773	16 057	15 866	16 059	15 239	14 124	15 251	14 012	13 837	Hongrie
Other Europe											***Autre Europe***
Spain	...	...	...	3 133	4 685	3 751	5 004	6 124	...	...	Espagne
Yugoslavia[2]	26 557	29 165	35 579	37 063	40 532	44 471	49 181	49 763	51 563	52 684	Yougoslavie[2]

General note.
Articles made of cotton, flax, hemp, ramie or man-made fibres, such as bed sheets, pillow cases, mattress covers etc. Table linens and other furnishing articles are excluded. (SITC 65691-1).

[1] Production by establishments employing 5 or more persons.
[2] In thousand square metres.

Remarque générale.
Articles fabriqués en coton, lin, chanvre, ramie ou fibres artificielles, tels que draps de lit, taies d'oreiller, couvre-matelas etc. Cette rubrique ne comprend pas le linge de table et autres articles d'ameublement. (CTCI 65691-1).

[1] Production des établissements occupant 5 personnes ou plus.
[2] En milliers de mètres carrés.

Towelling – Serviettes

Unit : Thousand units

Unité : En milliers

Country or area	1976	1977	1978	1979	1980	1981	1982	1983	1984	1985	Pays ou zone
Africa											**Afrique**
South Africa	...	...	20 113	19 454	20 916	20 659	18 826	* 12 123	* 11 815	14 235	Afrique du Sud
America, North											**Amérique du Nord**
Cuba	3 207	3 526	3 394	2 946	4 191	5 408	7 833	8 550	6 639	9 045	Cuba
Dominican Republic	436	232	300	206	134	130	215	304	268	222	Rép. dominicaine
El Salvador	2 687	6 022	5 365	6 315	6 146	6 549	* 2 416	4 278	...	...	El Salvador
United States	546 672	543 828	539 712	565 416	541 992	539 172	493 404	596 904	563 448	539 688	Etats–Unis
America, South											**Amérique du Sud**
Bolivia	10	15	13	30	32	33	140	187	51	* 60	Bolivie
Brazil[1]	20 435	15 279	21 297	[2] 25 825	47 381	...	...	...	...	...	Brésil[1]
Colombia	6 543	6 050	8 108	3 912	5 847	7 138	6 971	7 384	...	...	Colombie
Ecuador	529	295	663	...	592	364	357	...	...	...	Equateur
Asia											**Asie**
Burma[3]	1 910	1 789	1 554	1 647	1 780	1 886	2 024	1 963	1 647	1 747	Birmanie[3]
China	...	...	...	...	1 261 790	1 250 700	1 284 000	1 297 000	1 363 000	1 314 000	Chine
Hong Kong[4]	15 444	8 844	8 367	9 357	5 993	4 565	3 245	1 500	...	...	Hong–kong[4]
Indonesia	6 513	4 934	5 063	6 685	6 645	9 537	11 052	9 047	9 181	...	Indonésie
Iran(Islamic Rep.of)[5]	...	...	...	...	...	1 325	842	751	...	...	Iran(Rép.islamique)[5]
Japan[5]	59 428	54 614	56 689	61 985	65 487	57 631	55 348	52 053	58 909	62 476	Japon[5]
Korea, Republic of[5]	4 218	4 184	4 405	4 561	4 701	5 116	4 822	5 252	4 676	5 356	Corée, République de[5]
Philippines[6]	8 674	8 303	...	...	...	...	...	...	...	...	Philippines[6]
Syrian Arab Republic	4 845	4 015	4 216	4 427	4 648	4 752	4 819	5 753	3 121	1 534	Rép. arabe syrienne
Viet Nam	29 859	31 576	35 946	37 193	...	...	...	...	...	...	Viet Nam
Europe											**Europe**
EEC											***CEE***
Denmark[7]	...	...	...	...	...	1 027	1 006	751	847	...	Danemark[7]
Germany, Fed. Rep.	80 751	69 039	63 635	72 783	74 814	69 953	70 303	72 364	59 922	62 001	Allemagne, Rép. féd.
EFTA											***AELE***
Finland	2 943	4 283	3 228	4 270	4 182	3 409	3 158	3 303	2 764	...	Finlande
Sweden[5]	47	75	64	35	44	28	18	...	...	...	Suède[5]
East Europe											***Europe de l'est***
Hungary	5 428	5 702	6 303	5 040	5 312	5 446	5 953	5 681	6 351	6 423	Hongrie
Other Europe											***Autre Europe***
Spain	...	...	...	18 356	12 042	12 735	9 920	11 275	...	...	Espagne
Oceania											**Océanie**
Australia[7]	9 400	9 732	10 056	11 196	11 184	11 304	11 338	7 532	8 146	8 205	Australie[7]

General note.
Toilet linen, that is, hand and face towels (including roller towels), bath towels, face cloths and toilet gloves. (SITC 65691–2).

[1] In thousand metres.
[2] Production by establishments employing 5 or more persons.
[3] Government production only.
[4] Beginning 1984, data are confidential.
[5] In metric tons.
[6] Shipments.
[7] In thousand square metres.

Remarque générale.
Linge de toilette, c'est–à–dire serviettes de toilette, essuie–mains (y compris les touailles), serviettes de bain, débarbouillettes et gants de toilette. (CTCI 65691–2).

[1] En milliers de mètres.
[2] Production des établissements occupant 5 personnes ou plus.
[3] Production de l'Etat seulement.
[4] A partir de 1984, les données sont confidentielles.
[5] En tonnes métriques.
[6] Expéditions.
[7] En milliers de mètres carrés.

Knitted fabrics – Etoffes de bonneterie

Unit : Thousand metric tons | Unité : Milliers de tonnes métriques

Country or area	1976	1977	1978	1979	1980	1981	1982	1983	1984	1985	Pays ou zone
Africa	**25.0**	**25.3**	**37.1**	**36.1**	**42.3**	**39.5**	**32.9**	**30.8**	**32.7**	**28.9**	**Afrique**
Algeria	* 5.0	6.3	9.6	7.7	7.3	6.5	* 6.0	* 6.0	* 7.0	* 7.5	Algérie
Egypt	...	0.8	0.4	0.6	0.7	0.6	0.7	...	...	...	Egypte
Nigeria	5.2	6.2	6.2	4.4	3.0	3.7	3.9	3.2	3.1	2.7	Nigéria
South Africa	14.3	12.0	20.9	23.5	31.3	28.6	22.3	20.9	21.9	18.0	Afrique du Sud
America, North	**854.4**	**808.9**	**784.7**	**819.0**	**763.2**	**678.7**	**632.5**	**723.7**	**725.4**	**717.2**	**Amérique du Nord**
Canada[1]	41.9	35.1	...	...	...	...	...	...	...	...	Canada[1]
Dominican Republic	0.2	0.2	0.3	0.3	0.3	0.2	0.3	0.2	0.3	0.3	Rép. dominicaine
United States	812.3	773.5	745.9	780.2	724.4	640.0	593.8	684.9	686.6	678.4	Etats–Unis
America, South	**3.7**	**1.6**	**1.4**	**1.2**	**0.3**	**0.2**	**0.7**	**0.3**	**0.8**	**0.2**	**Amérique du Sud**
Ecuador	3.7	...	...	...	0.3	0.2	0.7	0.3	0.8	...	Equateur
Asia	**315.7**	**312.4**	**298.2**	**284.2**	**279.7**	**281.4**	**280.7**	**282.9**	**312.1**	**291.4**	**Asie**
Indonesia	...	...	1.0	0.9	0.2	* 0.1	0.1	...	35.4	...	Indonésie
Iran(Islamic Rep.of)	57.0	...	...	...	...	...	...	...	...	...	Iran(Rép.islamique)
Japan	204.0	193.9	198.2	178.5	170.0	175.2	174.9	167.3	172.4	173.2	Japon
Philippines	18.5	21.1	12.8	14.5	17.8	14.3	13.9	13.7	...	...	Philippines
Turkey	36.1	40.3	29.3	33.4	...	...	...	...	...	...	Turquie
Europe	**776.6**	**742.4**	**748.1**	**772.0**	**775.6**	**749.2**	**743.2**	**748.6**	**755.7**	**782.1**	**Europe**
EEC	***631.2***	***600.1***	***597.1***	***609.7***	***596.3***	***570.4***	***561.1***	***573.1***	***570.8***	***590.2***	***CEE***
Belgium	12.4	9.3	8.4	9.2	9.4	8.7	9.0	9.3	8.2	8.0	Belgique
Denmark	6.1	5.2	4.6	5.4	6.1	* 6.2	...	...	...	...	Danemark
France	39.2	36.2	35.5	41.0	37.8	37.2	40.7	41.3	41.3	40.4	France
Germany, Fed. Rep.	89.2	65.4	69.2	77.2	75.8	65.7	63.0	64.6	62.6	74.6	Allemagne, Rép. féd.
Greece	...	...	...	17.1	17.3	19.5	19.9	22.0	21.7	...	Grèce
Italy	...	364.6	...	...	...	...	...	...	...	...	Italie
Netherlands[2]	10.1	8.2	8.9	8.6	7.1	6.5	5.6	6.2	5.6	6.6	Pays–Bas[2]
United Kingdom[3]	96.0	96.4	90.0	86.4	78.1	61.9	52.2	59.0	60.5	66.4	Royaume–Uni[3]
EFTA	***56.6***	***53.3***	***55.5***	***63.6***	***75.8***	***71.6***	***73.3***	***69.3***	***75.5***	***78.4***	***AELE***
Austria	10.2	10.0	10.0	11.4	11.8	10.1	13.5	12.7	14.3	16.3	Autriche
Finland	11.0	9.6	6.9	6.6	12.1	12.2	10.5	9.3	10.1	...	Finlande
Iceland	0.1	0.2	0.1	0.2	0.3	0.2	0.2	0.3	0.3	...	Islande
Norway	2.5	2.9	3.0	4.1	3.4	2.1	1.5	1.7	...	...	Norvège
Portugal	26.9	26.7	31.1	35.2	42.5	42.0	42.8	40.2	43.5	44.0	Portugal
Sweden[2]	5.9	3.9	4.4	6.1	5.8	5.0	4.7	5.2	5.5	5.7	Suède[2]
East Europe	***49.2***	***50.2***	***52.3***	***53.4***	***55.5***	***58.2***	***57.6***	***54.8***	***53.4***	***53.9***	***Europe de l'est***
Czechoslovakia	30.4	30.6	32.0	33.2	34.4	37.2	37.5	35.4	33.4	34.3	Tchécoslovaquie
Hungary	18.8	19.5	20.3	20.2	21.1	21.0	20.1	19.5	20.0	19.6	Hongrie
Other Europe	***39.7***	***38.9***	***43.2***	***45.4***	***48.0***	***49.0***	***51.2***	***51.3***	***56.0***	***59.7***	***Autre Europe***
Spain[4]	13.9	14.1	16.9	16.4	17.8	18.3	20.6	20.7	...	...	Espagne[4]
Yugoslavia	25.8	24.7	26.3	29.1	30.2	30.7	30.6	30.6	34.1	36.7	Yougoslavie
Oceania	**19.3**	**20.0**	**20.7**	**21.2**	**20.0**	**23.1**	**23.4**	**22.8**	**26.8**	**24.9**	**Océanie**
Australia	13.9	15.0	16.1	16.6	14.7	16.4	16.8	16.5	19.4	17.6	Australie
New Zealand	5.4	5.0	4.6	4.6	5.3	6.6	6.6	6.4	7.4	7.3	Nouvelle–Zélande
Total	**1 994.7**	**1 910.6**	**1 890.2**	**1 933.8**	**1 881.2**	**1 772.2**	**1 713.4**	**1 809.1**	**1 853.4**	**1 844.8**	**Total**

General note.
Knitted or crocheted fabrics (of all textile fibres), neither elastic nor rubberized. Knitted garments are excluded. (SITC 65370–0).

[1] Shipments.
[2] Knitted fabrics for sale only.
[3] Manufacturers' sales.
[4] Including household production.

Remarque générale.
Etoffes de bonneterie (en tous textiles), ni élastiques ni caoutchoutées. Cette rubrique ne comprend pas les vêtements tricotés. (CTCI 65370–0).

[1] Expéditions.
[2] Etoffes de bonneterie destinées à la vente seulement.
[3] Ventes des fabricants.
[4] Y compris la production ménagère.

Socks and other stockings, except women's stockings – Bas, chaussettes et socquettes

Unit : Million pairs

Unité : Million de paires

Country or area	1976	1977	1978	1979	1980	1981	1982	1983	1984	1985	Pays ou zone
Africa	**34.5**	**47.3**	**44.5**	**40.9**	**50.8**	**48.8**	**39.2**	**36.3**	**38.3**	**34.6**	**Afrique**
Algeria[1]	10.1	11.4	13.9	10.7	10.9	10.8	2.2	2.7	3.1	* 4.0	Algérie[1]
Ethiopia[1 2]	4.1	5.5	2.4	4.8	6.3	* 5.0	* 4.0	* 3.0	* 4.0	...	Ethiopie[1 2]
Kenya	1.3	...	0.4	0.3	0.9	0.3	0.3	0.2	0.7	0.3	Kenya
South Africa	15.4	23.0	21.0	19.7	22.8	25.0	24.4	22.0	20.8	16.3	Afrique du Sud
Tunisia	3.2	6.3	6.6	5.0	9.5	7.4	* 8.0	* 8.0	...	...	Tunisie
Uganda	0.4	0.2	0.3	* 0.3	* 0.3	* 0.2	* 0.2	* 0.2	* 0.3	0.0	Ouganda
Zambia	0.1	...	...	...	...	...	...	...	...	...	Zambie
America, North	**1 894.8**	**1 969.0**	**1 922.7**	**1 920.3**	**1 777.7**	**1 974.6**	**1 687.4**	**1 832.3**	**1 795.8**	**1 827.3**	**Amérique du Nord**
Canada[3]	178.1	180.4	# [4] 51.3	[5] 56.2	[5] 57.4	[5] 40.8	...	...	...	...	Canada[3]
Cuba	19.6	19.8	21.7	23.3	23.0	25.1	22.8	19.1	25.4	23.9	Cuba
Dominican Republic[1]	5.6	6.2	6.0	5.2	6.6	5.5	5.9	8.1	7.9	...	Rép. dominicaine[1]
El Salvador	10.3	0.9	8.9	2.0	2.3	2.4	4.9	4.2	* 4.0	* 4.0	El Salvador
United States[6 7]	1 681.2	1 761.6	1 834.8	1 833.6	1 688.4	1 900.8	1 609.2	1 772.4	1 746.0	...	Etats-Unis[6 7]
America, South	**132.2**	**143.9**	**147.2**	**144.3**	**147.4**	**145.7**	**145.8**	**138.6**	**148.5**	**150.6**	**Amérique du Sud**
Bolivia	1.2	1.4	1.1	1.2	1.7	0.7	0.6	0.9	0.8	* 0.9	Bolivie
Brazil	86.0	95.0	91.0	[8] 88.3	95.7	94.2	...	...	...	...	Brésil
Chile	11.7	11.5	11.1	11.7	9.4	9.8	* 8.0	8.5	10.3	11.0	Chili
Colombia	29.9	33.0	36.6	39.4	38.9	37.0	39.1	30.1	...	...	Colombie
Ecuador	3.4	2.9	7.4	...	1.7	4.1	2.3	2.2	...	...	Equateur
Asia	**1 645.7**	**1 473.5**	**1 433.1**	**1 547.7**	**1 524.9**	**1 584.3**	**1 564.8**	**1 478.0**	**1 563.0**	**1 632.2**	**Asie**
Burma[9 10]	0.1	0.1	0.2	...	...	0.4	0.3	0.2	0.1	0.5	Birmanie[9 10]
China[1]	...	...	...	...	851.5	875.1	834.0	726.9	749.2	817.2	Chine[1]
Hong Kong	24.1	26.5	22.7	20.4	19.4	17.9	19.5	21.9	50.3	...	Hong-kong
Indonesia	10.3	13.6	12.5	14.1	14.4	13.9	16.4	20.5	11.6	...	Indonésie
Iran(Islamic Rep.of)[11]	[1] 190.0	# 1.9	2.1	2.2	2.4	45.5	48.8	62.3	...	...	Iran(Rép.islamique)[11]
Japan	289.4	333.3	308.4	[12] 421.2	[12] 456.4	[12] 462.6	[12] 468.2	[12] 420.1	[12] 443.9	[12] 428.2	Japon
Korea, Republic of[1]	152.6	140.9	145.0	162.5	129.3	117.2	121.0	170.0	235.0	257.5	Corée, République de[1]
Malaysia[1 13 14]	9.2	12.0	15.9	15.6	16.6	16.5	18.9	18.0	17.7	21.9	Malaisie[1 13 14]
Philippines[3]	7.6	3.5	...	...	...	...	...	...	...	...	Philippines[3]
Sri Lanka[1]	1.0	1.0	1.0	0.8	1.4	1.7	...	...	...	...	Sri Lanka[1]
Syrian Arab Republic[1]	16.3	14.9	15.9	16.7	17.7	18.0	19.3	19.5	21.4	18.9	Rép. arabe syrienne[1]
Turkey[15]	9.1	# 4.6	3.3	4.9	2.2	2.3	3.6	3.8	2.7	14.6	Turquie[15]
Viet Nam	5.0	9.2	7.4	8.9	...	...	...	...	...	...	Viet Nam
Europe	**1 966.5**	**2 048.0**	**2 167.4**	**2 159.5**	**2 190.6**	**2 199.8**	**2 229.2**	**2 253.9**	**2 313.0**	**2 349.7**	**Europe**
EEC	***930.8***	***968.0***	***965.2***	***970.6***	***936.5***	***910.8***	***952.3***	***940.0***	***945.9***	***944.4***	***CEE***
Belgium	23.6	20.0	21.0	21.6	20.3	19.6	18.7	18.0	15.9	16.5	Belgique
Denmark	6.1	6.3	4.5	3.6	3.5	* 3.0	* 3.0	5.0	* 5.0	6.0	Danemark
France[16]	170.6	177.3	177.0	185.6	180.2	177.8	204.5	207.2	205.8	228.4	France[16]
Germany, Fed. Rep.	111.6	107.9	111.6	111.6	106.3	94.6	96.3	90.1	97.4	71.2	Allemagne, Rép. féd.
Greece	26.6	25.5	26.5	25.0	24.8	28.4	27.2	26.5	27.0	...	Grèce
Italy[17]	322.7	357.2	...	...	...	...	...	...	...	...	Italie[17]
Netherlands	27.3	23.6	23.3	22.1	22.4	20.7	20.4	17.4	14.1	11.9	Pays-Bas
United Kingdom[18]	242.4	250.3	261.2	261.2	239.2	226.8	242.2	236.0	240.8	243.2	Royaume-Uni[18]
EFTA	***59.7***	***62.1***	***65.8***	***67.2***	***66.3***	***72.1***	***66.3***	***65.7***	***81.0***	***58.6***	***AELE***
Finland	11.1	10.0	9.6	9.7	10.8	13.2	11.7	9.6	10.3	...	Finlande
Iceland	0.5	0.4	0.5	0.4	0.4	0.5	0.5	0.5	0.4	...	Islande
Norway	7.3	7.4	7.2	8.7	7.8	6.4	5.0	3.5	3.1	...	Norvège
Portugal	23.6	22.8	29.5	29.4	28.9	# 35.8	31.4	34.8	48.9	28.6	Portugal
Sweden	17.2	21.5	19.0	19.0	18.4	16.3	17.7	17.3	18.2	15.3	Suède
East Europe	***762.8***	***798.8***	***861.2***	***882.4***	***914.7***	***907.9***	***902.4***	***930.2***	***967.5***	***1 020.9***	***Europe de l'est***
Bulgaria[1]	55.9	57.1	58.8	59.3	63.2	64.6	68.2	71.3	74.0	76.0	Bulgarie[1]
German Dem. Rep.[1]	291.3	302.1	306.6	316.8	322.0	338.2	343.9	356.9	372.0	388.0	Rép. dém. allemande[1]
Hungary[19]	30.9	32.7	35.5	33.7	35.8	38.2	32.3	34.2	37.8	38.0	Hongrie[19]
Poland	197.7	225.8	251.3	250.5	258.7	226.8	218.0	230.8	246.7	274.9	Pologne
Romania[1]	187.0	181.0	209.0	222.0	235.0	240.0	240.0	237.0	237.0	244.0	Roumanie[1]
Other Europe	***213.1***	***219.0***	***275.2***	***239.3***	***273.2***	***309.0***	***308.2***	***317.9***	***318.6***	***325.8***	***Autre Europe***
Spain[1 20]	141.8	147.6	174.8	171.1	192.2	207.6	208.3	209.1	...	...	Espagne[1 20]

For general note and footnotes, see end of table.

Voir la fin du tableau pour la remarque générale et les notes.

Socks and other stockings, except women's stockings (continued) – Bas, chaussettes et socquettes (suite)

Unit : Million pairs — Unité : Million de paires

Country or area	1976	1977	1978	1979	1980	1981	1982	1983	1984	1985	Pays ou zone
Yugoslavia	71.3	71.4	100.4	68.2	81.0	101.4	99.9	108.8	89.1	85.6	Yougoslavie
USSR	**815.0**	**837.3**	**860.0**	**899.5**	**951.0**	**975.8**	**1 015.4**	**1 038.2**	**1 072.8**	**1 124.3**	**URSS**
Byelorussian SSR	*76.4*	*78.7*	*81.4*	*82.5*	*83.5*	*82.7*	*83.4*	*85.5*	*87.8*	*91.7*	*RSS de Biélorussie*
Ukrainian SSR	*192.3*	*197.6*	*196.6*	*202.7*	*212.6*	*214.2*	*221.9*	*233.1*	*239.7*	*240.6*	*RSS d'Ukraine*
Oceania	**51.1**	**44.0**	**42.9**	**44.5**	**50.5**	**54.6**	**55.3**	**54.1**	**45.2**	**60.9**	**Océanie**
Australia[21]	43.2	36.0	35.7	37.1	42.9	47.0	47.1	46.9	35.7	51.4	Australie[21]
New Zealand	7.9	8.0	7.2	7.3	7.6	7.6	8.2	7.3	9.5	9.5	Nouvelle–Zélande
Total	**6 539.9**	**6 563.0**	**6 617.9**	**6 756.6**	**6 692.9**	**6 983.7**	**6 737.1**	**6 831.4**	**6 976.5**	**7 179.5**	**Total**

General note.
Knitted or crocheted socks for men, women and children, extending from the ankle to below the knee, and knitted or crocheted stockings for men and children extending above the knee, of man–made fibres, cotton, wool or other textile fibres, made in knitting mills. Elastic and rubberized socks of all kinds and stockings for men and children are excluded, but those having rubber threads or elastic forming merely a supporting band are included. (SITC 84142–1).

1 Including women's stockings.
2 Twelve months ending 10 September of year stated.
3 Shipments.
4 Data for men's and boy's only.
5 Men's and children's socks and stockings only.

6 Including socks and other stockings.
7 Source: Hosiery Statistics, National Association of Hosiery Manufacturers, (Charlotte, N.C.).
8 Production by establishments employing 5 or more persons.
9 Twelve months ending 30 September of year stated.
10 Socks only.
11 Production by establishments employing 10 or more persons.
12 Including seamless stockings.
13 Data refer to Peninsular Malaysia only.
14 Beginning 1982, scope of series revised.
15 Beginning 1977, data are not comparable with those for earlier years.

16 Put up for sale. Excluding own consumption.
17 Source: Industrial Statistics, Statistical Office of the European Communities, (Luxembourg).
18 Manufacturers' sales.
19 Including elastic socks and stockings.
20 Including household production.
21 Twelve months ending 30 June of year stated.

Remarque générale.
Bas, chaussettes et socquettes en bonneterie, faits en usine, pour hommes, femmes et enfants, montant jusqu'à la cheville, à mi–jambe ou jusqu'au–dessous du genou, et bas en bonneterie, pour hommes et enfants montant plus haut que le genou, en fibres artificielles, en coton, en laine ou en d'autres fibres textiles. Cette rubrique ne comprend pas les chaussettes élastiques et caoutchoutées de tous types et les bas élastiques et caoutchoutés pour hommes et enfants, mais comprend les chaussettes et les bas possédant des fils de caoutchouc ou des élastiques qui ne constituent qu'une bande de serrage. (CTCI 84142–1).

1 Y compris les bas de dames.
2 Période de douze mois finissant le 10 septembre de l'année indiquée.
3 Expéditions.
4 Données pour hommes et garçonnets seulement.
5 Bas, chaussettes et socquettes en bonneterie pour hommes et garçonnets seulement.
6 Y compris les bas, chaussettes et socquettes.
7 Source: Hosiery Statistics, National Association of Hosiery Manufacturers, (Charlotte, N.C.).
8 Production des établissements occupant 5 personnes ou plus.
9 Période de douze mois finissant le 30 septembre de l'année indiquée.
10 Chaussettes seulement.
11 Production des établissements occupant 10 personnes ou plus.
12 Y compris les bas sans couture.
13 Données se rapportant à la Malaisie péninsulaire seulement.
14 A partir de 1982, portée de la série révisée.
15 A partir de 1977, les données ne sont pas comparables à celles des années antérieures.
16 Pour la vente au mètre, auto–consommation exclue.
17 Source: Statistiques industrielles, Office statistique des Communautés européennes, (Luxembourg).
18 Ventes des fabricants.
19 Y compris les bas et chaussettes élastiques.
20 Y compris la production ménagère.
21 Période de douze mois finissant le 30 juin de l'année indiquée.

Women's stockings – Bas de dames

Unit : Million pairs — Unité : Million de paires

Country or area	1976	1977	1978	1979	1980	1981	1982	1983	1984	1985	Pays ou zone
Africa	**107.7**	**108.2**	**110.3**	**82.7**	**107.7**	**110.0**	**105.0**	**107.5**	**122.8**	**126.5**	**Afrique**
Mali	0.2	0.3	0.3	0.2	0.2	0.1	...	0.1	...	...	Mali
South Africa	105.6	105.3	108.7	69.5	82.1	81.5	79.7	78.3	89.6	89.4	Afrique du Sud
Tunisia	1.8	2.6	1.2	12.9	25.5	28.4	...	...	...	...	Tunisie
America, North	**1 414.0**	**1 384.3**	**1 470.1**	**1 843.3**	**1 839.0**	**1 963.5**	**1 929.9**	**2 111.1**	**2 130.7**	**2 282.6**	**Amérique du Nord**
Canada	43.8	47.7	[1] 130.6	[1] 134.8	[1] 157.6	...	...	...	...	...	Canada
Cuba	4.2	5.1	5.2	4.8	4.0	2.8	3.1	2.4	3.9	4.3	Cuba
El Salvador	0.4	4.3	3.5	3.3	2.1	1.0	1.5	1.8	...	...	El Salvador
United States[2]	1 365.6	1 327.2	1 330.8	1 700.4	1 675.2	1 820.4	1 772.4	1 940.4	1 945.2	...	Etats–Unis[2]
America, South	**45.2**	**42.8**	**46.1**	**48.0**	**54.3**	**54.3**	**56.7**	**62.6**	**67.4**	**71.8**	**Amérique du Sud**
Bolivia	1.1	0.7	1.5	1.2	1.7	0.5	0.1	0.2	0.7	...	Bolivie
Brazil	20.3	26.1	26.8	[3] 32.3	34.4	35.5	...	...	...	...	Brésil
Chile	8.8	8.7	8.9	8.9	9.8	12.5	* 12.8	15.8	18.3	20.7	Chili
Colombia[4]	11.6	3.5	5.1	2.3	2.3	2.8	3.5	3.2	...	...	Colombie[4]
Ecuador	3.4	3.8	...	...	6.1	3.0	* 0.4	0.5	* 1.0	* 1.0	Equateur
Asia	**720.4**	**776.9**	**875.5**	**839.4**	**894.6**	**1 023.0**	**1 043.4**	**1 106.4**	**1 155.5**	**1 096.2**	**Asie**
Afghanistan	...	1.4	1.4	0.4	0.7	0.8	1.0	0.7	0.6	0.5	Afghanistan
Hong Kong[1 5]	3.6	6.0	4.2	5.2	6.9	7.8	12.8	...	13.2	...	Hong–kong[1 5]
Indonesia	...	...	11.1	...	...	...	...	...	...	...	Indonésie
Japan[6]	692.7	748.0	848.5	[7] 813.5	[7] 868.3	[7] 986.3	[7] 1 002.6	[7] 1 064.8	[7] 1 099.3	[7] 1 016.3	Japon[6]
Philippines[8]	0.7	0.9	...	...	...	...	...	...	...	...	Philippines[8]
Turkey[1]	11.1	* 9.6	9.6	8.6	6.8	16.1	15.2	17.4	30.6	53.4	Turquie[1]
Europe	**2 122.7**	**2 095.2**	**2 111.9**	**2 185.3**	**2 175.3**	**2 143.8**	**2 155.8**	**2 185.6**	**2 218.1**	**2 304.8**	**Europe**
EEC	***1 735.6***	***1 725.2***	***1 756.3***	***1 786.7***	***1 773.7***	***1 745.3***	***1 734.4***	***1 777.4***	***1 792.5***	***1 851.9***	***CEE***
Belgium	17.8	16.6	14.0	13.2	13.3	10.3	11.3	11.8	14.8	17.5	Belgique
Denmark	3.5	3.2	3.7	3.3	3.5	* 2.3	...	...	...	...	Danemark
France	259.4	277.5	297.7	339.8	312.7	301.1	290.5	295.8	329.2	325.8	France
Germany, Fed. Rep.	66.6	62.6	60.5	59.0	66.7	66.3	68.5	76.8	88.4	86.4	Allemagne, Rép. féd.
Greece	58.2	54.5	64.4	67.0	75.7	71.6	65.9	63.9	55.9	...	Grèce
Ireland	91.5	80.1	90.8	82.7	80.7	75.7	73.6	74.8	76.9	81.4	Irlande
Italy[9]	746.8	770.2	...	...	...	...	...	...	...	...	Italie[9]
Netherlands	* 7.1	7.9	7.9	7.5	5.6	...	...	...	...	...	Pays–Bas
United Kingdom[10]	484.8	452.6	458.9	455.7	457.1	453.2	457.7	487.8	461.3	508.8	Royaume–Uni[10]
EFTA	***70.9***	***63.3***	***58.1***	***67.1***	***72.0***	***69.5***	***80.5***	***84.0***	***81.9***	***117.1***	***AELE***
Austria[11]	27.3	22.5	21.6	17.9	21.0	21.1	18.2	21.2	18.9	24.0	Autriche[11]
Finland	11.2	6.9	8.0	10.2	9.0	9.6	10.8	12.3	10.8	...	Finlande
Norway	0.1	0.0	0.0	0.0	...	...	...	...	...	...	Norvège
Portugal	* 22.8	27.8	22.9	33.0	35.3	34.4	46.9	45.1	48.1	77.1	Portugal
Sweden	9.4	6.0	5.6	6.0	6.6	4.4	4.6	5.4	4.1	4.4	Suède
East Europe	***149.0***	***139.9***	***148.3***	***137.8***	***138.4***	***138.2***	***147.2***	***149.6***	***152.6***	***145.4***	***Europe de l'est***
Czechoslovakia[11]	99.0	102.0	97.6	95.2	96.6	101.8	104.3	106.6	109.6	111.6	Tchécoslovaquie[11]
Hungary[12]	5.6	5.9	5.6	4.5	6.3	6.2	6.1	9.0	9.1	6.3	Hongrie[12]
Poland	44.5	31.9	45.1	38.1	35.5	30.2	36.8	33.9	34.0	27.4	Pologne
Other Europe	***167.2***	***166.8***	***149.2***	***193.6***	***191.2***	***190.8***	***193.7***	***174.6***	***191.2***	***190.5***	***Autre Europe***
Spain[13]	...	...	...	85.6	80.0	78.2	84.8	81.4	...	...	Espagne[13]
Yugoslavia	83.4	83.3	66.1	108.0	111.2	112.6	108.9	93.2	110.2	109.9	Yougoslavie
USSR	**451.1**	**405.7**	**368.0**	**327.0**	**297.3**	**290.1**	**293.3**	**295.1**	**274.1**	**253.8**	**URSS**
Byelorussian SSR	*39.0*	*36.1*	*30.0*	*27.6*	*26.3*	*27.6*	*25.4*	*25.4*	*24.8*	*23.4*	*RSS de Biélorussie*
Ukrainian SSR	*87.9*	*80.4*	*78.5*	*72.1*	*68.7*	*65.9*	*68.7*	*67.1*	*60.6*	*53.6*	*RSS d'Ukraine*
Oceania	**87.7**	**87.3**	**77.1**	**85.6**	**87.4**	**101.0**	**89.6**	**106.2**	**112.0**	**109.8**	**Océanie**
Australia[14]	75.8	74.9	66.2	74.9	76.9	88.1	77.0	90.7	96.7	96.6	Australie[14]
New Zealand[15]	11.9	12.4	10.9	10.7	10.5	13.0	12.7	15.5	15.4	13.2	Nouvelle–Zélande[15]
Total	**4 948.8**	**4 900.4**	**5 059.0**	**5 411.3**	**5 455.7**	**5 685.8**	**5 673.7**	**5 974.4**	**6 080.7**	**6 245.5**	**Total**

For general note and footnotes, see end of table.

Voir la fin du tableau pour la remarque générale et les notes.

General note.
Knitted or crocheted women's stockings extending above the knee, of man–made fibres, silk, cotton, wool or other textile fibres, made in knitting mills. Elastic and rubberized stockings are excluded, but those having rubber threads or elastic forming merely a supporting band are included. (SITC 84142–2).

1 Including pantyhose.
2 Source: Hosiery Statistics, National Association of Hosiery Manufacturers, (Charlotte, N.C.).
3 Production by establishments employing 5 or more persons.
4 Nylon stockings for women only.
5 Including socks for women and girls.
6 Seamless stockings and pantyhose only.
7 Including seamless stockings.
8 Shipments.
9 Source: Industrial Statistics, Statistical Office of the European Communities, (Luxembourg).
10 Manufacturers' sales.
11 Including socks and other stockings.
12 Excluding pantyhose.
13 Including household production.
14 Twelve months ending 30 June of year stated.
15 Data refer to pantyhose only.

Remarque générale.
Bas en bonneterie, pour dames, faits en usine, montant plus haut que le genou, en fibres artificielles, en soie, en coton, en laine ou en d'autres fibres textiles. Cette rubrique ne comprend pas les bas élastiques ou caoutchoutés, mais comprend les bas possédant des fils de caoutchouc ou des élastiques qui ne constituent qu'une bande de serrage. (CTCI 84142–2).

1 Y compris les bas–culottes.
2 Source: Hosiery Statistics, National Association of Hosiery Manufacturers, (Charlotte, N.C.).
3 Production des établissements occupant 5 personnes ou plus.
4 Bas de nylon pour dames seulement.
5 Y compris les bas de dames et de filletes.
6 Collants de ville et bas sans couture seulement.
7 Y compris les bas sans couture.
8 Expéditions.
9 Source: Statistiques industrielles, Office statistique des Communautés européennes, (Luxembourg).
10 Ventes des fabricants.
11 Y compris les bas, chaussettes et socquettes.
12 Non compris les bas–culottes.
13 Y compris la production ménagère.
14 Période de douze mois finissant le 30 juin de l'année indiquée.
15 Les données se rapportant aux bas–culottes seulement.

Knitted undergarments – Sous-vêtements en bonneterie

Unit : Thousand units — Unité : En milliers

Country or area	1976	1977	1978	1979	1980	1981	1982	1983	1984	1985	Pays ou zone
Africa	**7 075**	**8 177**	**7 537**	**9 463**	**9 580**	**10 090**	**8 427**	**8 496**	**9 621**	**9 847**	**Afrique**
Algeria[1]	5 717	6 744	5 930	7 552	7 705	8 117	6 265	* 6 200	...	...	Algérie[1]
South Africa	...	1 433	1 607	1 911	1 875	1 973	...	...	...	...	Afrique du Sud
America, North	**75 740**	**92 307**	**117 116**	**119 143**	**109 679**	**129 259**	**145 074**	**152 040**	**163 520**	**173 305**	**Amérique du Nord**
Canada	41 560	67 760	81 443	89 016	82 165	...	...	...	...	...	Canada
Cuba	22 323	16 308	23 772	21 938	20 217	23 483	25 452	24 269	27 102	27 755	Cuba
El Salvador	11 857	8 239	11 901	8 189	7 297	2 806	6 459	4 414	...	...	El Salvador
America, South	**92 997**	**78 569**	**83 285**	**69 625**	**94 644**	**76 990**	**79 364**	**78 409**	**81 899**	**79 328**	**Amérique du Sud**
Brazil	64 130	60 070	66 283	[2] 54 119	73 674	...	...	...	...	...	Brésil
Colombia	27 685	...	...	...	...	6 874	8 354	5 095	* 6 000	...	Colombie
Ecuador	1 182	...	...	...	10 885	2 540	2 127	3 124	...	...	Equateur
Asia	**432 194**	**431 539**	**439 748**	**513 858**	**501 594**	**490 447**	**491 045**	**474 184**	**1 039 485**	**695 681**	**Asie**
Indonesia	...	...	7 747	15 952	14 545	18 162	27 282	* 27 000	586 000	...	Indonésie
Japan	420 700	420 670	430 020	[3] 495 618	[3] 485 055	[3] 470 430	[3] 462 155	[3] 445 817	[3] 452 355	[3] 460 661	Japon
Malaysia	3 290	2 138	1 260	1 567	1 273	1 134	887	646	...	...	Malaisie
Philippines[4]	457	984	...	...	...	...	...	...	...	...	Philippines[4]
Europe	**2 005 017**	**2 019 292**	**1 945 344**	**1 928 597**	**1 935 282**	**1 873 474**	**1 828 489**	**1 819 533**	**1 783 049**	**1 744 093**	**Europe**
EEC	***1 263 900***	***1 254 346***	***1 204 252***	***1 203 434***	***1 180 913***	***1 116 006***	***1 109 828***	***1 108 834***	***1 064 585***	***1 011 242***	***CEE***
Belgium	27 749	25 977	24 503	22 984	25 339	20 790	21 134	19 803	16 138	16 912	Belgique
Denmark	55 717	45 437	43 010	44 242	40 310	45 554	49 038	51 605	53 638	45 296	Danemark
France	242 181	248 229	228 945	237 169	231 214	210 950	216 972	220 017	203 210	198 596	France
Germany, Fed. Rep.[5]	301 661	281 194	263 146	267 770	257 870	225 032	215 584	...	...	...	Allemagne, Rép. féd.[5]
Greece	56 134	57 193	63 984	70 189	68 262	70 014	67 450	69 241	63 533	...	Grèce
Italy[6]	353 600	364 600	...	...	...	...	...	...	...	...	Italie[6]
Netherlands	52 030	56 060	49 280	45 440	43 730	40 650	42 370	45 730	43 730	45 080	Pays-Bas
United Kingdom[7]	174 828	175 656	172 284	156 540	155 088	143 916	138 180	138 132	133 452	96 744	Royaume-Uni[7]
EFTA	***94 471***	***92 591***	***78 660***	***80 059***	***81 355***	***76 286***	***72 087***	***62 880***	***59 099***	***59 543***	***AELE***
Austria	26 760	29 981	27 589	28 218	28 901	26 961	25 123	23 408	23 298	22 518	Autriche
Finland	10 971	12 169	10 206	11 051	12 012	12 489	11 748	8 615	6 114	...	Finlande
Iceland	81	72	69	39	38	7	7	2	2	...	Islande
Norway	9 044	9 819	8 761	9 069	9 028	7 230	5 744	5 183	...	4 102	Norvège
Sweden	47 615	40 550	32 035	31 682	31 376	29 599	29 465	25 672	24 672	24 455	Suède
East Europe	***553 054***	***575 219***	***561 751***	***545 621***	***565 601***	***563 632***	***524 432***	***537 844***	***537 419***	***547 817***	***Europe de l'est***
Bulgaria	70 035	71 210	71 295	73 618	75 790	75 310	78 477	77 376	65 393	69 485	Bulgarie
Czechoslovakia	67 441	64 777	70 152	71 704	75 505	73 057	68 169	68 069	69 729	70 474	Tchécoslovaquie
German Dem. Rep.	163 005	170 417	172 614	174 869	177 151	181 789	185 507	180 750	178 441	174 851	Rép. dém. allemande
Hungary	53 673	49 753	49 187	41 883	41 409	45 492	38 260	36 565	32 727	31 386	Hongrie
Poland	198 900	219 062	198 503	183 547	195 746	187 984	154 019	175 084	191 129	201 621	Pologne
Other Europe	***93 592***	***97 136***	***100 681***	***99 483***	***107 413***	***117 550***	***122 142***	***109 976***	***121 946***	***125 491***	***Autre Europe***
Spain[8]	...	...	...	99 483	107 413	117 550	122 142	109 976	...	...	Espagne[8]
Oceania	**94 715**	**94 715**	**94 715**	**94 715**	**94 715**	**94 715**	**94 715**	**94 715**	**94 715**	**94 715**	**Océanie**
Australia	...	...	...	...	...	...	...	...	...	94 715	Australie
Total	**2 707 738**	**2 724 600**	**2 687 745**	**2 735 400**	**2 745 493**	**2 674 975**	**2 647 113**	**2 627 376**	**3 172 290**	**2 796 967**	**Total**

General note.
Knitted or crocheted undergarments made in knitting mills, such as undershirts, pyjamas, night-gowns, drawers, slips, petticoats, camisoles, theatrical flesh tights. Elastic and rubberized undergarments (corsets, brassieres, braces etc.) are excluded. (SITC 84143-1).

Remarque générale.
Sous-vêtements en bonneterie, faits en usine, tels que gilets, pyjamas, chemises de nuit, caleçons, combinaisons, jupons, chemises américaines, collants. Cette rubrique ne comprend pas les sous-vêtements élastiques ou caoutchoutés (corsets, soutien-gorge, bretelles etc.). (CTCI 84143-1).

[1] Including knitted sports shirts.
[2] Production by establishments employing 5 or more persons.
[3] Excluding night gowns.
[4] Shipments.

[1] Y compris les chemisettes en bonneterie.
[2] Production des établissements occupant 5 personnes ou plus.
[3] Non compris les chemises de nuit.
[4] Expéditions.

[5] Beginning 1983, data are confidential.
[6] Source: Industrial Statistics, Statistical Office of the European Communities, (Luxembourg).
[7] Including knitted sports shirts and underwear for children.
[8] Including household production.

[5] A partir de 1983, les données sont confidentielles.
[6] Source: Statistiques industrielles, Office statistique des Communautés européennes, (Luxembourg).
[7] Y compris les chemisettes en bonneterie et les sous-vêtements pour enfants.
[8] Y compris la production ménagère.

Knitted sports shirts – Chemisettes en bonneterie

Unit : Thousand units | Unité : En milliers

Country or area	1976	1977	1978	1979	1980	1981	1982	1983	1984	1985	Pays ou zone
Africa	**3 755**	**4 219**	**3 888**	**4 581**	**18 104**	**14 179**	**34 964**	**30 970**	**34 531**	**31 768**	**Afrique**
South Africa	3 755	4 219	3 888	4 581	* 18 104	14 179	34 964	30 970	34 531	31 768	Afrique du Sud
America, North	**670 844**	**732 431**	**757 189**	**784 503**	**854 366**	**883 175**	**900 410**	**896 368**	**811 111**	**809 650**	**Amérique du Nord**
Canada[1 2]	10 928	12 695	33 577	33 927	38 642	...	...	...	...	...	Canada[1 2]
United States	659 916	719 736	723 612	750 576	815 724	848 700	862 716	855 456	766 980	762 300	Etats–Unis
America, South	**564**	**564**	**564**	**542**	**585**	**564**	**564**	**564**	**564**	**564**	**Amérique du Sud**
Brazil	...	...	...	# 185	228	...	...	...	...	...	Brésil
Ecuador	357	...	...	...	...	...	...	...	...	...	Equateur
Asia	**43 760**	**47 795**	**44 395**	**53 447**	**58 930**	**51 969**	**63 105**	**62 767**	**64 047**	**62 547**	**Asie**
Indonesia	8 491	13 444	11 582	12 292	18 917	12 784	14 442	15 093	17 283	...	Indonésie
Japan[3]	25 889	26 304	24 580	33 022	31 921	30 733	40 613	39 175	38 838	37 126	Japon[3]
Malaysia[4 5]	4 692	2 456	2 579	2 117	2 605	2 965	# 2 563	3 012	2 439	2 259	Malaisie[4 5]
Philippines[1]	3 151	3 919	...	...	...	...	...	...	...	...	Philippines[1]
Turkey	1 537	1 672	2 119	2 481	...	...	...	...	...	...	Turquie
Europe	**40 600**	**39 716**	**39 271**	**36 194**	**35 237**	**34 466**	**55 364**	**44 658**	**45 075**	**42 237**	**Europe**
EEC	***39 896***	***39 155***	***38 969***	***35 908***	***34 983***	***33 924***	***54 804***	***43 998***	***44 608***	***41 821***	***CEE***
Belgium	...	1 506	1 484	2 192	2 334	2 197	2 228	2 658	2 379	2 047	Belgique
Denmark	117	100	# [6] 2 487	[6] 3 289	[6] 3 709	[6] 4 399	[6] 5 853	[6] 7 175	[6] 7 790	[6] 5 412	Danemark
Germany, Fed. Rep.[7]	19 310	15 757	15 138	15 139	14 540	13 384	31 879	...	...	...	Allemagne, Rép. féd.[7]
United Kingdom	18 828	21 792	19 860	15 288	14 400	13 944	14 844	11 664	...	...	Royaume–Uni
EFTA	***704***	***561***	***302***	***286***	***254***	***542***	***560***	***660***	***467***	***416***	***AELE***
Austria	129	138	59	66	111	64	143	184	123	39	Autriche
Norway	575	423	243	* 220	143	478	417	476	344	377	Norvège
Oceania	**26 143**	**21 874**	**24 525**	**19 661**	**22 046**	**24 234**	**24 233**	**25 263**	**24 752**	**13 388**	**Océanie**
Australia	26 143	21 874	24 525	19 661	22 046	24 234	24 233	25 263	24 752	13 388	Australie
Total	**785 665**	**846 599**	**869 832**	**898 928**	**989 268**	**1 008 587**	**1 078 639**	**1 060 590**	**980 079**	**960 153**	**Total**

General note.
Knitted and crocheted sports shirts for men, women and children, made in knitting mills. (SITC 84144–1).

[1] Shipments.
[2] Excluding tailored sports shirts and knitted dress shirts.
[3] Including knitted sweaters and other knitted outer garments.
[4] Data refer to Peninsular Malaysia only.
[5] Beginning 1982, scope of series revised.
[6] Including t–shirts and pully shirts.
[7] Beginning 1983, data are confidential.

Remarque générale.
Chemisettes de bonneterie, pour hommes, femmes et enfants, faites en usine. (CTCI 84144–1).

[1] Expéditions.
[2] Non compris les chemises de coupe sport et les chemises habillées en tricot.
[3] Y compris les chandails tricotés et autres vêtements de dessus en bonneterie.
[4] Données se rapportant à la Malaisie péninsulaire seulement.
[5] A partir de 1982, portée de la série révisée.
[6] Y compris les 'tee–shirts' et les chemises de sport en bonneterie.
[7] A partir de 1983, les données sont confidentielles.

Knitted sweaters – Tricots

Unit : Thousand units

Unité : En milliers

Country or area	1976	1977	1978	1979	1980	1981	1982	1983	1984	1985	Pays ou zone
Africa	**12 063**	**11 013**	**11 987**	**17 255**	**16 282**	**17 876**	**19 424**	**20 856**	**22 288**	**23 720**	**Afrique**
Algeria[1]	3 212	3 065	2 904	2 927	2 188	2 449	...	...	...	...	Algérie[1]
South Africa	8 851	7 948	9 083	14 328	14 094	15 427	...	...	...	...	Afrique du Sud
America, North	**152 289**	**162 779**	**147 220**	**127 154**	**123 239**	**141 488**	**141 867**	**141 981**	**142 750**	**148 130**	**Amérique du Nord**
Canada[2]	23 906	18 982	17 576	17 182	18 743	...	...	...	...	...	Canada[2]
Cuba	...	...	500	100	300	261	191	251	198	100	Cuba
United States	127 980	143 424	129 144	109 872	104 196	125 568	127 224	128 484	130 512	137 196	Etats-Unis
America, South	**1 683**	**1 427**	**1 479**	**1 466**	**2 121**	**1 315**	**1 605**	**1 611**	**1 618**	**1 624**	**Amérique du Sud**
Brazil[3]	1 683	1 427	1 479	[4] 1 466	2 121	* 1 315	...	...	...	...	Brésil[3]
Asia	**215 896**	**185 287**	**170 864**	**249 777**	**268 441**	**322 815**	**277 795**	**325 688**	**336 024**	**344 463**	**Asie**
Hong Kong	91 516	78 993	76 904	80 865	96 835	119 738	97 757	147 537	150 965	...	Hong-kong
Indonesia	88	49	112	56	1 181	1 056	86	57	37	...	Indonésie
Japan	17 607	17 271	15 523	104 088	93 614	99 917	89 699	80 541	80 130	74 688	Japon
Korea, Republic of	105 160	86 425	76 363	62 751	74 809	98 760	88 043	95 320	102 635	118 894	Corée, République de
Philippines[2]	458	1 434	...	...	...	...	...	...	...	...	Philippines[2]
Sri Lanka	60	...	2	8	39	[5] 1 381	...	...	...	...	Sri Lanka
Turkey	1 007	984	1 014	1 063	...	...	...	...	...	...	Turquie
Europe	**600 714**	**567 171**	**563 317**	**572 032**	**590 597**	**598 735**	**648 332**	**649 140**	**654 203**	**586 854**	**Europe**
EEC	***291 633***	***266 978***	***243 024***	***223 555***	***216 753***	***202 850***	***235 281***	***232 942***	***232 100***	***226 343***	***CEE***
Belgium[1]	18 510	14 731	13 281	12 332	12 739	11 829	11 900	11 143	10 921	10 951	Belgique[1]
Denmark	17 307	15 552	[6] 12 811	[6] 13 436	[6] 14 438	* [6] 15 000	[6] 15 110	[6] 18 898	[6] 20 098	[6] 21 497	Danemark
France	66 060	58 370	53 769	49 802	51 108	43 235	40 974	41 643	41 467	37 920	France
Germany, Fed. Rep.	72 984	65 203	57 913	54 207	55 426	50 232	55 653	54 702	54 680	56 017	Allemagne, Rép. féd.
Netherlands	3 480	3 790	3 070	3 490	4 250	4 950	5 420	5 300	5 490	5 830	Pays-Bas
United Kingdom	113 292	109 332	102 180	90 288	78 792	77 604	106 224	101 256	99 444	94 128	Royaume-Uni
EFTA	***9 891***	***8 969***	***8 457***	***6 302***	***5 921***	***5 761***	***4 837***	***4 955***	***4 991***	***4 997***	***AELE***
Austria	9	16	5	10	1	1	1	8	4	4	Autriche
Finland	1 261	1 356	1 471	1 532	1 612	1 717	1 631	1 772	1 857	...	Finlande
Iceland	394	410	285	218	306	231	221	252	217	...	Islande
Sweden	8 227	7 187	6 696	4 542	4 002	3 812	2 984	2 923	2 913	2 896	Suède
East Europe	***299 190***	***291 224***	***311 836***	***342 175***	***367 923***	***390 124***	***408 214***	***411 243***	***417 112***	***355 514***	***Europe de l'est***
Bulgaria[7]	42 282	46 350	46 354	48 337	51 753	55 263	53 310	56 923	59 762	61 423	Bulgarie[7]
Hungary	16 714	17 874	18 482	18 838	20 170	20 861	18 904	15 320	17 350	15 091	Hongrie
Romania[1]	...	227 000	247 000	275 000	296 000	314 000	336 000	339 000	340 000	279 000	Roumanie[1]
Oceania	**25 652**	**29 176**	**28 557**	**27 695**	**27 635**	**27 271**	**25 177**	**22 953**	**25 154**	**22 461**	**Océanie**
Australia[8]	21 336	24 739	24 561	23 892	24 355	22 910	21 180	19 332	21 845	19 183	Australie[8]
New Zealand	4 316	4 437	3 996	3 803	3 280	4 361	3 997	3 621	3 309	3 278	Nouvelle-Zélande
Total	**1 008 298**	**956 853**	**923 424**	**995 379**	**1 028 315**	**1 109 500**	**1 114 201**	**1 162 230**	**1 182 036**	**1 127 252**	**Total**

General note.
Knitted and crocheted sweaters, cardigans, pull-overs and jackets for men, women and children, made in knitting mills. (SITC 84144-2).

1 Including other knitted outer garments.
2 Shipments.
3 Including knitted coats.
4 Production by establishments employing 5 or more persons.
5 Data are not comparable with those for earlier years.
6 Including t-shirts and pully shirts.
7 Including knitted sports shirts and other knitted outer garments.
8 Including knitted sweaters for infants.

Remarque générale.
Sweaters, cardigans, pull-overs et gilets en bonneterie, faits en usine. (CTCI 84144-2).

1 Y compris autres vêtements de dessus en bonneterie.
2 Expéditions.
3 Y compris les manteaux en bonneterie.
4 Production des établissements occupant 5 personnes ou plus.
5 Données établies selon des critères différents de ceux des années antérieures.
6 Y compris les 'tee-shirts' et les chemises de sport en bonneterie.
7 Y compris les chemisettes et autres vêtements de dessus en bonneterie.
8 Y compris les chandails tricotés pour enfants.

Other knitted outer garments – Autres vêtements de dessus, en bonneterie

Unit : Thousand units | Unité : En milliers

Country or area	1976	1977	1978	1979	1980	1981	1982	1983	1984	1985	Pays ou zone
Africa	**14 182**	**13 654**	**13 126**	**12 598**	**11 173**	**12 477**	**12 077**	**9 178**	**10 148**	**9 451**	**Afrique**
South Africa	...	...	...	...	11 173	12 477	12 077	9 178	10 148	9 451	Afrique du Sud
America, North	**20 041**	**14 473**	**14 908**	**14 717**	**15 516**	**16 764**	**17 635**	**18 017**	**16 082**	**14 997**	**Amérique du Nord**
Canada	9 141	...	...	...	...	...	...	...	...	...	Canada
Cuba	5 702	2 720	4 880	5 230	5 320	6 943	7 952	8 446	6 429	5 510	Cuba
El Salvador	5 198	2 612	887	346	1 055	680	542	430	512	...	El Salvador
America, South	**82 313**	**58 486**	**41 178**	**48 368**	**68 053**	**49 162**	**44 624**	**39 520**	**37 113**	**33 368**	**Amérique du Sud**
Brazil	79 199	55 871	38 563	[1] 45 753	65 438	...	...	...	...	...	Brésil
Colombia	3 114	...	...	...	...	3 431	2 637	1 278	...	...	Colombie
Asia	**3 864**	**4 914**	**4 389**	**4 389**	**4 389**	**4 389**	**4 389**	**4 389**	**4 389**	**4 389**	**Asie**
Philippines[2]	# 3 864	4 914	...	...	...	...	...	...	...	...	Philippines[2]
Europe	**543 233**	**541 991**	**540 927**	**541 163**	**533 375**	**492 197**	**498 020**	**496 940**	**496 091**	**475 463**	**Europe**
EEC	***143 904***	***143 990***	***139 092***	***145 973***	***143 989***	***135 173***	***141 021***	***139 888***	***138 596***	***123 204***	***CEE***
Denmark	8 224	7 369	7 258	7 062	5 897	...	...	...	...	...	Danemark
France	44 730	44 130	38 994	40 960	43 999	42 004	41 872	39 946	38 081	28 620	France
Germany, Fed. Rep.	9 318	7 972	6 833	6 450	6 566	5 970	8 469	8 529	7 163	6 363	Allemagne, Rép. féd.
Greece[3]	43 852	42 873	41 235	46 435	48 539	44 532	45 816	46 955	49 781	...	Grèce[3]
Netherlands	3 400	3 510	2 820	2 610	[4] 1 560	[4] 1 010	[4] 1 220	5 480	4 810	5 090	Pays–Bas
United Kingdom[5]	34 380	38 136	41 952	42 456	37 428	35 976	38 456	34 284	34 560	30 264	Royaume–Uni[5]
EFTA	***15 709***	***15 285***	***12 579***	***13 809***	***14 165***	***14 835***	***13 070***	***13 032***	***12 744***	***12 837***	***AELE***
Austria	516	481	434	465	576	603	535	176	214	255	Autriche
Finland	2 371	2 444	2 191	3 212	3 375	4 151	3 220	3 268	3 445	...	Finlande
Iceland[6]	178	1 068	336	862	556	463	505	898	2 014	...	Islande[6]
Norway	3 528	3 629	3 108	3 455	3 158	3 038	2 878	3 157	1 369	1 620	Norvège
Sweden[7]	9 116	7 663	6 510	5 815	6 500	6 580	5 932	5 533	5 702	5 744	Suède[7]
East Europe	***297 117***	***300 126***	***310 454***	***305 589***	***305 627***	***276 470***	***275 870***	***286 997***	***288 804***	***287 492***	***Europe de l'est***
Czechoslovakia	69 042	69 719	73 582	78 246	79 379	73 180	68 958	69 469	73 435	74 133	Tchécoslovaquie
German Dem. Rep.	54 292	54 255	55 289	57 727	59 063	60 311	57 963	58 349	59 504	59 372	Rép. dém. allemande
Hungary	21 172	21 330	20 829	20 783	22 298	22 392	20 966	20 754	21 440	20 865	Hongrie
Poland	152 611	154 822	160 754	148 833	144 887	120 587	127 983	138 425	134 425	133 122	Pologne
Other Europe	***86 503***	***82 590***	***78 802***	***75 792***	***69 594***	***65 719***	***68 059***	***57 023***	***55 947***	***51 931***	***Autre Europe***
Malta	1 170	1 026	1 008	1 102	951	349	647	711	772	...	Malte
Spain[8]	...	...	...	74 690	68 643	65 370	67 412	56 312	...	...	Espagne[8]
Total	**663 633**	**633 518**	**614 528**	**621 235**	**632 506**	**574 989**	**576 744**	**568 044**	**563 823**	**537 669**	**Total**

General note.
Other knitted and crocheted outer garments made in knitting mills, such as dresses, coats, minor articles of apparel, curtains etc. (SITC 84144–3).

1 Production by establishments employing 5 or more persons.
2 Shipments.
3 Data refer to all knitted outer garments.
4 Incomplete coverage.
5 Including dresses, skirts and two– and three–piece suits for women.
6 Including children's garments.
7 Excluding knitted outer garments for infants.
8 Including household production.

Remarque générale.
Autres vêtements de dessus, en bonneterie, faits en usine, tels que robes, manteaux, divers articles d'habillement, rideaux etc. (CTCI 84144–3).

1 Production des établissements occupant 5 personnes ou plus.
2 Expéditions.
3 Données se rapportant aux vêtements de dessus tricotés de toutes catégories.
4 Couverture incomplète.
5 Y compris les robes, jupes et costumes deux–pièces et trois–pièces pour dames.
6 Y compris les vêtements pour enfants.
7 Non compris les vêtements de dessus en tricot pour enfants.
8 Y compris la production ménagère.

Carpets and rugs of wool, knotted – Tapis de laine à points noués

Unit : Thousand square metres — Unité : Milliers de mètres carrés

Country or area	1976	1977	1978	1979	1980	1981	1982	1983	1984	1985	Pays ou zone
Africa											**Afrique**
Algeria	133	168	113	146	211	61	* 70	* 70	...	...	Algérie
Egypt[1 2]	288	287	318	...	...	...	...	...	...	...	Egypte[1 2]
Ethiopia[3]	11	9	6	16	21	17	17	17	...	...	Ethiopie[3]
Libyan Arab Jamah.*	1	1	1	1	1	1	1	2	...	...	Jamah.arabe libyenne*
Morocco	...	...	1 724	1 918	1 582	1 635	1 668	1 807	1 623	1 444	Maroc
America, North											**Amérique du Nord**
Canada[4 5]	1 288	...	...	...	...	...	...	...	...	...	Canada[4 5]
America, South											**Amérique du Sud**
Chile	84	100	94	...	...	...	...	...	...	...	Chili
Colombia[6]	125	...	...	...	...	21	23	7	...	...	Colombie[6]
Ecuador	132	145	238	...	...	...	...	...	...	...	Equateur
Asia											**Asie**
Hong Kong	0	0	233	242	976	328	225	235	228	210	Hong–kong
India*	...	...	...	...	...	...	858	1 453	...	...	Inde*
Indonesia	# 78	416	630	607	712	463	195	186	498	...	Indonésie
Japan	8 569	8 109	9 145	13 188	13 041	10 995	11 518	10 734	10 645	9 353	Japon
Mongolia	322	340	376	422	464	547	915	1 039	1 380	1 586	Mongolie
Pakistan	...	485	545	587	669	615	403	371	501	...	Pakistan
Philippines[5]	582	381	...	...	...	...	...	...	...	...	Philippines[5]
Syrian Arab Republic	284	298	342	365	376	483	412	588	517	564	Rép. arabe syrienne
Turkey[7]	123	184	173	188	98	157	109	96	140	108	Turquie[7]
Europe											**Europe**
EEC											***CEE***
Belgium[1]	26 894	22 841	23 108	26 150	30 694	30 940	29 219	31 606	34 054	32 225	Belgique[1]
France[6]	2 107	1 796	1 535	1 410	1 325	1 206	1 119	928	836	828	France[6]
Germany, Fed. Rep.[8]	3 800	4 000	...	...	...	...	...	...	...	...	Allemagne, Rép. féd.[8]
Greece	...	...	...	1 814	1 768	1 179	1 232	1 038	873	...	Grèce
Ireland	3 494	3 104	2 651	2 790	2 157	2 372	1 874	1 504	...	...	Irlande
EFTA											***AELE***
Austria	344	630	688	664	759	837	793	834	743	677	Autriche
Iceland	52	47	47	37	38	36	32	32	29	16	Islande
Switzerland[1]	11 770	12 695	13 029	12 072	14 503	13 708	12 132	13 393	13 960	15 219	Suisse[1]
East Europe											***Europe de l'est***
Bulgaria[6]	5 860	6 522	6 011	5 956	5 384	5 536	5 516	5 854	4 122	3 599	Bulgarie[6]
Czechoslovakia	1 728	1 931	2 127	2 325	2 020	2 200	2 364	2 411	2 325	1 459	Tchécoslovaquie
Hungary	762	696	764	1 248	739	637	569	504	476	400	Hongrie
Poland[6]	15 264	15 265	15 164	15 144	15 659	13 259	12 104	13 143	13 890	15 042	Pologne[6]
Other Europe											***Autre Europe***
Yugoslavia[6]	11 603	14 677	15 824	18 447	20 173	21 189	20 861	22 052	22 532	19 137	Yougoslavie[6]
USSR[9]	52 304	62 897	67 802	77 453	93 415	100 423	104 147	106 249	107 875	108 548	**URSS[9]**
Byelorussian SSR	*7 071*	*7 195*	*7 227*	*7 198*	*6 977*	*6 915*	*6 753*	*6 827*	*7 389*	*8 037*	*RSS de Biélorussie*
Ukrainian SSR[6]	*1 536*	*1 943*	*2 389*	*2 449*	*2 565*	*2 723*	*2 886*	*2 987*	*2 787*	*2 653*	*RSS d'Ukraine[6]*
Oceania											**Océanie**
Australia[6 10]	31 939	29 901	27 422	28 528	30 582	31 956	34 531	...	...	...	Australie[6 10]
New Zealand[6]	11 315	10 042	8 546	9 203	9 263	9 304	10 274	9 050	11 783	12 733	Nouvelle–Zélande[6]

General note.
Knotted wool carpets and rugs made up or not, composed of a taut warp around which the pile threads are knotted (giordes or Turkish knot, Senna or Persian knot, and single warp knots) in a complete turn. (SITC 65750–0).

Remarque générale.
Tapis de laine à points noués, même confectionnés, constitués par une chaîne de fond tendue sur laquelle les fils de poil sont noués ou enroulés (noeud "ghiordès" ou point de Smyrne, noeud "senneh" ou point de Perse, noeud sur un seul fil de chaîne). (CTCI 65750–0).

1 In metric tons.
2 Including blankets.

1 En tonnes métriques.
2 Y compris les couvertures.

[3] Twelve months ending 10 September of year stated.
[4] Excluding automobile rugs and scatter–type mats.
[5] Shipments.
[6] Including other carpets.
[7] Government production only.
[8] Source: Industrial Statistics, Statistical Office of the European Communities, (Luxembourg).
[9] Including other carpets and rugs.
[10] Twelve months ending 30 June of year stated.

[3] Période de douze mois finissant le 10 septembre de l'année indiquée.
[4] Non compris les tapis et carpettes de voitures.
[5] Expéditions.
[6] Y compris les autres tapis.
[7] Production de l'Etat seulement.
[8] Source: Statistiques industrielles, Office statistique des Communautés européennes, (Luxembourg).
[9] Y compris les autres tapis et carpettes.
[10] Période de douze mois finissant le 30 juin de l'année indiquée.

Carpets and rugs, other – Autres tapis

Unit : Thousand square metres — Unité : Milliers de mètres carrés

Country or area	1976	1977	1978	1979	1980	1981	1982	1983	1984	1985	Pays ou zone
Africa											**Afrique**
Algeria	48	52	62	94	80	75	...	...	...	...	Algérie
Morocco	...	...	103	118	139	161	...	...	...	...	Maroc
Nigeria	...	...	...	...	...	767	614	727	689	1 340	Nigéria
South Africa	15 441	14 678	16 338	18 829	23 122	27 135	23 057	17 969	20 359	19 021	Afrique du Sud
America, North											**Amérique du Nord**
Canada[1,2]	63 715	[3] 78 205	[3] 71 279	[3] 80 572	[3] 76 462	...	...	...	...	...	Canada[1,2]
Mexico[4]	1 267	668	459	194	782	780	632	815	858	702	Mexique[4]
United States[2,3]	770 069	857 721	928 122	976 499	904 859	828 286	740 653	911 441	932 073	969 764	Etats–Unis[2,3]
America, South											**Amérique du Sud**
Brazil	13 707	10 876	8 556	[5] 11 627	21 817	...	...	...	...	...	Brésil
Colombia	885	...	...	...	...	122	61	72	...	...	Colombie
Asia											**Asie**
Afghanistan	...	...	12	11	11	9	12	17	18	20	Afghanistan
Indonesia	3	3	1	3	4	1	11	6	3	...	Indonésie
Japan[6]	67 834	66 867	66 653	79 295	80 505	76 621	79 970	78 367	88 440	83 946	Japon[6]
Philippines[2,3]	168	123	...	...	...	...	...	...	...	...	Philippines[2,3]
Sri Lanka	12	...	...	23	5	8	...	...	...	...	Sri Lanka
Syrian Arab Republic	661	670	640	632	651	682	707	1 586	480	266	Rép. arabe syrienne
Turkey	2 157	3 376	4 811	4 935	...	...	6 254	9 816	7 703	9 927	Turquie
Europe											**Europe**
EEC											***CEE***
Belgium[4]	137 873	147 669	142 253	166 971	182 054	202 652	184 209	220 762	228 021	222 647	Belgique[4]
Denmark	24 356	23 790	21 423	21 832	19 100	17 590	...	...	...	19 894	Danemark
France	37 916	38 983	46 819	50 509	49 730	47 214	45 372	47 652	46 867	49 620	France
Germany, Fed. Rep.	161 210	168 839	163 211	158 764	152 952	148 733	135 501	141 334	140 642	144 074	Allemagne, Rép. féd.
Greece[7]	3 887	4 321	5 250	3 769	4 304	1 461	1 608	1 455	1 506	...	Grèce[7]
Ireland	4 237	5 062	5 754	4 786	3 091	2 999	2 383	2 258	[3] 3 579	[3] 3 468	Irlande
Netherlands[3]	48 020	49 270	51 773	56 555	59 656	59 370	59 350	62 890	67 690	67 650	Pays–Bas[3]
United Kingdom[8]	176 726	169 562	169 704	164 343	138 204	130 500	125 951	138 511	122 346	139 081	Royaume–Uni[8]
EFTA											***AELE***
Austria	10 057	10 171	8 999	10 316	10 678	10 581	8 779	9 652	9 581	10 388	Autriche
Finland	...	...	...	...	...	...	1 615	2 367	3 405	...	Finlande
Portugal	828	819	913	1 275	1 654	1 194	1 406	1 364	1 659	...	Portugal
Sweden[4,9,10]	11 013	11 095	9 478	12 613	13 731	10 857	10 729	10 644	13 869	11 738	Suède[4,9,10]
East Europe											***Europe de l'est***
Czechoslovakia	17 945	21 353	22 694	23 404	26 067	27 083	26 851	27 503	28 001	30 098	Tchécoslovaquie
German Dem. Rep.[3]	26 652	28 858	30 336	29 569	30 678	32 709	33 833	36 562	39 955	41 775	Rép. dém. allemande[3]
Hungary	5 029	5 302	5 538	5 043	5 663	6 353	6 145	6 129	6 360	6 263	Hongrie
Other Europe											***Autre Europe***
Spain[3]	...	...	...	14 915	16 123	16 656	16 669	17 472	...	...	Espagne[3]

General note.
Other carpets, carpeting and rugs, mats and matting, kelem, "schumacks" and "karamanic" rugs and the like, made up or not. (SITC 65760–0).

Remarque générale.
Autres tapis et moquettes, tissus et matières pour tapis, paillassons, dessous de tapis, tissus kilim, soumack, karamanic ou similaires, même confectionnés. (CTCI 65760–0).

1 Excluding automobile rugs and scatter–type mats.
2 Shipments.
3 Including carpets and rugs of wool.
4 In metric tons.
5 Production by establishments employing 5 or more persons.
6 Excluding tufted carpets.
7 Machine–woven carpets and rugs only.
8 Manufacturers' sales, including carpets and rugs of wool.
9 Excluding those made up from strips of artificial plastics materials.
10 Excluding those woven and wall–to–wall with a surface of synthetic or regenerated textile fibre.

1 Non compris les tapis et carpettes de voitures.
2 Expéditions.
3 Y compris les carpettes et les tapis de laine.
4 En tonnes métriques.
5 Production des établissements occupant 5 personnes ou plus.
6 Non compris les tapis tuftés.
7 Tapis et carpettes tissés à la machine seulement.
8 Ventes des fabricants, y compris les tapis et carpettes en laine.
9 Non compris les tapis et carpettes qui sont faits de bandes de matière plastique artificielle.
10 Non compris les tapis et moquettes tissés dont une surface est composée de fibres textiles synthétiques ou régénérées.

Cordage, rope and twine – Cordes, câbles, cordages et ficelles

Unit : Metric tons — Unité : Tonnes métriques

Country or area	1976	1977	1978	1979	1980	1981	1982	1983	1984	1985	Pays ou zone
Africa	**62 830**	**56 957**	**50 869**	**59 361**	**54 351**	**34 325**	**41 235**	**33 353**	**30 874**	**25 175**	**Afrique**
Algeria	1 645	1 736	1 033	1 232	1 905	699	1 609	* 1 600	...	...	Algérie
Egypt[1]	5 842	4 918	4 997	...	...	...	...	...	...	...	Egypte[1]
Kenya	2 125	3 733	1 536	1 446	1 797	1 662	1 920	2 139	2 136	2 874	Kenya
Madagascar	807	623	705	705	710	707	732	897	1 060	1 241	Madagascar
South Africa[2]	8 429	7 813	9 542	10 985	11 962	11 505	9 805	* 7 643	* 9 529	7 400	Afrique du Sud[2]
Tunisia	941	804	918	1 067	306	313	...	...	...	...	Tunisie
Uganda	175	313	...	...	26	...	...	...	...	...	Ouganda
United Rep. Tanzania	42 377	36 535	31 423	37 911	31 616	13 246	20 595	...	...	...	Rép.Unie de Tanzanie
Zaire	53	48	119	...	51	114	92	119	* 100	...	Zaïre
Zambia	436	* 434	* 425	* 513	* 726	* 656	* 650	* 650	...	57	Zambie
America, North	**20 195**	**19 717**	**18 217**	**20 559**	**18 857**	**16 948**	**19 211**	**19 572**	**19 037**	**19 215**	**Amérique du Nord**
Canada[3 4]	9 070	8 926	8 243	10 875	...	...	...	...	...	...	Canada[3 4]
Cuba	7 037	6 105	6 144	5 518	5 647	3 574	5 824	6 192	5 861	5 970	Cuba
Dominican Republic	633	601	359	489	364	486	520	516	327	398	Rép. dominicaine
Haiti	3 243	3 959	3 347	3 588	...	...	...	...	...	...	Haïti
Jamaica	212	126	124	89	34	...	55	52	37	35	Jamaïque
America, South	**29 676**	**28 668**	**26 109**	**21 467**	**57 207**	**46 841**	**51 860**	**57 987**	**64 247**	**69 640**	**Amérique du Sud**
Brazil	21 072	23 871	21 791	[5] 17 171	52 789	...	...	...	...	...	Brésil
Colombia	6 267	...	...	...	...	1 372	1 300	1 908	...	...	Colombie
Ecuador	...	...	1 607	...	1 707	1 198	645	520	...	...	Equateur
Asia	**88 589**	**93 692**	**98 602**	**100 901**	**103 279**	**101 985**	**97 477**	**106 574**	**109 398**	**106 005**	**Asie**
Hong Kong	1 682	1 331	4 054	2 919	3 110	3 078	1 327	1 537	3 518	...	Hong–kong
Indonesia	2 860	2 004	2 114	1 939	1 840	1 507	1 650	1 562	2 537	...	Indonésie
Japan	48 884	48 952	46 852	51 183	48 737	39 046	39 775	39 196	41 654	40 089	Japon
Korea, Republic of	17 531	24 573	28 585	28 011	33 360	38 608	34 397	41 074	39 880	38 969	Corée, République de
Philippines[4]	16 616	15 754	16 123	15 647	15 032	...	...	22 100	...	...	Philippines[4]
Sri Lanka	...	...	13	...	360	423	...	...	...	...	Sri Lanka
Turkey	751	813	861	937	...	...	...	...	...	...	Turquie
Europe	**182 790**	**182 851**	**178 456**	**191 280**	**203 855**	**186 820**	**185 985**	**186 694**	**207 444**	**222 321**	**Europe**
EEC	***53 891***	***46 882***	***47 670***	***52 049***	***59 652***	***54 092***	***55 364***	***45 798***	***52 286***	***62 230***	***CEE***
Belgium	4 864	4 680	5 680	6 764	8 662	8 494	7 879	4 464	5 751	5 908	Belgique
Denmark	10 721	7 205	5 919	7 120	8 844	8 949	8 882	7 890	...	...	Danemark
France	26 027	23 976	26 014	27 991	32 376	28 425	31 150	26 452	31 005	42 152	France
Germany, Fed. Rep.[6]	7 357	5 534	4 950	4 589	4 307	3 516	3 703	3 128	3 244	...	Allemagne, Rép. féd.[6]
Greece	4 922	5 487	5 107	5 585	5 463	4 708	3 750	3 864	4 128	...	Grèce
EFTA	***36 117***	***44 200***	***41 952***	***58 988***	***67 764***	***60 498***	***57 123***	***61 201***	***77 767***	***80 504***	***AELE***
Austria	795	823	679	2 366	4 398	4 241	3 594	3 743	3 642	1 741	Autriche
Finland	972	702	747	1 008	936	612	451	367	371	...	Finlande
Iceland	1 009	1 197	1 434	1 676	1 830	1 991	2 176	1 747	1 580	1 758	Islande
Norway	3 810	6 079	5 735	5 231	5 561	4 889	3 389	2 834	3 096	...	Norvège
Portugal	26 834	32 743	30 779	46 231	52 820	46 405	45 439	50 649	67 297	72 019	Portugal
Sweden	2 697	2 656	2 578	2 476	2 219	2 360	2 074	1 861	1 781	1 623	Suède
East Europe	***69 431***	***62 968***	***61 998***	***61 391***	***60 742***	***56 134***	***58 182***	***61 655***	***64 303***	***68 623***	***Europe de l'est***
Czechoslovakia	14 758	14 910	14 231	13 681	13 727	11 933	13 243	13 248	13 167	13 400	Tchécoslovaquie
Hungary	8 897	9 320	10 402	8 471	9 031	9 669	11 211	12 453	9 365	10 610	Hongrie
Poland	45 776	38 738	37 365	39 239	37 984	34 532	33 728	35 954	41 771	44 613	Pologne
Other Europe	***23 351***	***28 801***	***26 836***	***18 852***	***15 697***	***16 096***	***15 316***	***18 040***	***13 088***	***10 964***	***Autre Europe***
Spain	17 544	22 664	18 534	12 744	8 808	9 529	9 011	11 502	...	...	Espagne
Yugoslavia	5 807	6 137	8 302	6 108	6 889	6 567	6 305	6 538	6 877	6 438	Yougoslavie
USSR	**149 722**	**151 078**	**148 931**	**141 197**	**134 709**	**133 417**	**134 290**	**139 262**	**141 484**	**140 700**	**URSS**
Byelorussian SSR	*6 598*	*7 621*	*7 771*	*7 712*	*6 592*	*6 512*	*6 529*	*7 025*	*7 467*	*7 353*	*RSS de Biélorussie*
Ukrainian SSR	*37 072*	*36 494*	*36 796*	*34 423*	*31 157*	*30 353*	*30 526*	*32 996*	*33 410*	*33 795*	*RSS d'Ukraine*
Oceania	**12 344**	**10 359**	**8 430**	**8 824**	**6 950**	**7 243**	**6 487**	**6 187**	**6 370**	**6 874**	**Océanie**
Australia	12 344	10 359	8 430	8 824	6 950	7 243	6 487	6 187	6 370	6 874	Australie

For general note and footnotes, see end of table.

Voir la fin du tableau pour la remarque générale et les notes.

Cordage, rope and twine (continued) – Cordes, câbles, cordages et ficelles (suite)

Unit : Metric tons

Unité : Tonnes métriques

Country or area	1976	1977	1978	1979	1980	1981	1982	1983	1984	1985	Pays ou zone
Total	**546 146**	**543 322**	**529 614**	**543 589**	**579 208**	**527 579**	**536 545**	**549 629**	**578 854**	**589 930**	**Total**

General note.
Twine, cordage, ropes and cables of all fibres produced by twisting or by plaiting. Textile yarns reinforced with metal are included. Twine, cordage, ropes and cables of paper yarn are included only if plaited or reinforced with metal. Fancy cords, cords of a kind commonly used in machinery or plant as packing or lubricating materials, abrasives, coated twine, cord etc. Gymnasium apparatus and articles of twine, cordage, ropes and cables are excluded. (SITC 65561–0).

[1] Products of flax only.
[2] Excluding paper rope and cord.
[3] All types of related textile products (including binder and baler twines).
[4] Shipments.
[5] Production by establishments employing 5 or more persons.
[6] Beginning 1984, data are confidential.

Remarque générale.
Ficelles, cordages, cordes et câbles en toutes fibres fabriqués par commettage ou tressage, y compris les fils textiles armés de métal. Cette rubrique comprend aussi les ficelles en papier et les cordages, cordes et câbles en ficelle de papier, à condition qu'ils soient armés de métal ou obtenus par tressage. Elle ne comprend pas les cordonnets employés comme ficelles de fantaisie, les cordons du type généralement utilisé dans la mécanique ou l'industrie pour le bourrage ou le graissage, les cordes et ficelles revêtues de poudres abrasives, les agrès de gymnastique et les articles fabriqués en ficelles, cordes ou cordages. (CTCI 65561–0).

[1] Produits en lin seulement.
[2] Non compris les ficelles et cordes de papier.
[3] Produits textiles analogues de toutes catégories (y compris ficelles et cordes).
[4] Expéditions.
[5] Production des établissements occupant 5 personnes ou plus.
[6] A partir de 1984, les données sont confidentielles.

Unit : Thousand square metres — Unité : Milliers de mètres carrés

Country or area	1976	1977	1978	1979	1980	1981	1982	1983	1984	1985	Pays ou zone
America, South											**Amérique du Sud**
Brazil	11 910	7 210	15 228	[1] 18 212	12 063	9 349	...	...	...	...	Brésil
Asia											**Asie**
Cyprus	31	57	49	46	* 49	30	25	13	13	11	Chypre
India[2 3]	1 314	933	...	...	...	...	...	...	...	...	Inde[2 3]
Thailand[4]	708	836	1 166	1 391	1 788	1 700	1 695	1 700	...	...	Thaïlande[4]
Europe											**Europe**
EEC											***CEE***
Greece	...	...	...	...	...	4 223	4 173	3 937	5 312	...	Grèce
EFTA											***AELE***
Sweden[5]	404	592	406	170	1 339	1 229	1 517	1 447	1 686	2 209	Suède[5]
East Europe											***Europe de l'est***
Bulgaria	11 064	14 048	14 584	14 283	16 694	17 561	18 551	22 717	28 363	30 072	Bulgarie
Czechoslovakia	6 740	6 675	6 711	6 711	6 758	5 784	4 295	4 350	3 198	2 039	Tchécoslovaquie
Hungary[6]	1 936	1 747	1 677	1 477	986	836	916	964	856	913	Hongrie[6]
USSR[7]	78 666	82 999	85 164	87 810	93 130	95 072	96 195	99 902	106 181	112 657	**URSS[7]**
Byelorussian SSR[7]	*4 313*	*4 393*	*4 155*	*3 555*	*3 576*	*3 028*	*2 851*	*3 185*	*3 591*	*3 728*	*RSS de Biélorussie[7]*
Ukrainian SSR[7]	*16 738*	*16 284*	*16 898*	*18 000*	*19 238*	*20 330*	*21 014*	*21 570*	*23 726*	*24 366*	*RSS d'Ukraine[7]*
Oceania											**Océanie**

General note.
Floor covering (other than carpets and blankets) on base of paper, paperboard or felt paper (whether or not coated with linoleum); and linoleum; and linoleum textile base, cut in sheets or tiles. (SITC 65740-0).

1 Production by establishments employing 5 or more persons.
2 In thousand metres.
3 Production by large and medium scale establishments only.
4 Data refer to vinyl floor tiles.
5 In metric tons.
6 Data refer to wooden floor covering.
7 Including linoleum without base.

Remarque générale.
Couvre-parquets (autres que les tapis et les couvertures) à support de papier, de carton ou de feutre cellulosique, revêtu ou non de linoléum; linoléum à support de matières textiles; découpés en feuilles ou en carreaux. (CTCI 65740-0).

1 Production des établissements occupant 5 personnes ou plus.
2 En milliers de mètres.
3 Production des grandes et moyennes entreprises seulement.
4 Données se rapportant aux revêtements de sol en vinyl.
5 En tonnes métriques.
6 Données se rapportant aux revêtements de sol en bois.
7 Y compris les linoléums sans semelle.

ISIC–BASED CODE
3220–01

Jackets, men's and boys' – Vestes pour hommes et garçonnets

CODE BASE CITI
3220–01

Unit : Thousand units — Unité : En milliers

Country or area	1976	1977	1978	1979	1980	1981	1982	1983	1984	1985	Pays ou zone
Africa	**3 631**	**2 975**	**2 240**	**2 578**	**2 609**	**2 776**	**2 715**	**2 440**	**2 591**	**2 526**	**Afrique**
South Africa	3 594	2 774	2 099	2 123	* 1 964	2 141	2 075	1 800	* 1 733	1 572	Afrique du Sud
Tunisia	37	201	141	455	645	635	* 640	* 640	...	...	Tunisie
America, North	**27 764**	**24 636**	**20 943**	**21 290**	**20 656**	**20 425**	**24 085**	**23 445**	**22 490**	**21 490**	**Amérique du Nord**
Canada[1]	1 055	1 410	1 457	1 420	1 415	...	...	...	...	...	Canada[1]
United States	26 709	23 226	19 486	19 870	19 241	18 856	22 443	21 730	20 703	19 630	Etats–Unis
America, South	**933**	**1 102**	**1 040**	**883**	**988**	**1 087**	**947**	**878**	**921**	**907**	**Amérique du Sud**
Chile	428	531	* 540	...	...	...	...	...	...	...	Chili
Colombia	502	567	493	373	474	585	417	354	...	...	Colombie
Ecuador	3	4	...	...	* 14	2	30	24	...	...	Equateur
Asia	**26 279**	**30 871**	**26 849**	**27 795**	**23 375**	**27 721**	**26 704**	**32 067**	**39 765**	**34 818**	**Asie**
Hong Kong	15 549	19 024	14 837	14 773	10 771	14 905	13 744	19 547	24 938	...	Hong–kong
Indonesia	...	...	298	283	144	418	361	* 365	1 089	...	Indonésie
Japan	...	...	...	10 156	10 201	10 060	10 285	9 666	11 229	12 301	Japon
Mongolia	117	140	158	133	179	189	...	...	...	...	Mongolie
Philippines[1 2]	1 608	2 135	...	...	...	...	...	...	...	...	Philippines[1 2]
Turkey[3]	90	# 309	284	578	208	277	245	407	414	236	Turquie[3]
Europe	**44 747**	**42 724**	**43 654**	**42 973**	**38 760**	**37 749**	**37 020**	**37 145**	**36 764**	**37 346**	**Europe**
EEC	***33 638***	***32 730***	***33 760***	***32 567***	***30 061***	***28 089***	***27 168***	***26 374***	***25 894***	***26 950***	***CEE***
Belgium	833	863	818	672	753	815	923	765	717	937	Belgique
Denmark	273	162	154	110	77	98	116	152	209	230	Danemark
France	12 205	12 454	13 286	13 043	...	...	...	...	...	...	France
Germany, Fed. Rep.	9 083	8 145	8 080	7 163	6 744	5 722	5 151	4 904	4 577	4 935	Allemagne, Rép. féd.
Ireland	354	375	369	492	400	458	339	296	250	173	Irlande
Italy[4]	4 500	4 600	...	...	...	...	...	...	...	...	Italie[4]
Netherlands[5]	1 340	970	980	920	860	640	591	439	315	285	Pays–Bas[5]
United Kingdom[6]	5 050	5 161	5 523	5 617	3 930	3 059	2 751	2 521	2 529	3 093	Royaume–Uni[6]
EFTA	***4 072***	***3 700***	***3 787***	***4 554***	***4 014***	***4 374***	***4 615***	***4 679***	***4 580***	***4 279***	***AELE***
Austria	748	673	623	546	549	511	437	439	441	402	Autriche
Finland	342	602	584	1 001	638	557	522	447	358	...	Finlande
Iceland	14	14	13	20	29	21	19	25	37	...	Islande
Norway	418	387	328	294	452	362	374	...	395	...	Norvège
Portugal	1 198	949	1 386	1 950	1 703	2 163	2 654	2 828	2 894	2 673	Portugal
Sweden	1 352	1 075	853	743	643	760	609	561	455	311	Suède
East Europe	***1 074***	***963***	***883***	***1 040***	***887***	***949***	***1 061***	***1 088***	***1 358***	***1 221***	***Europe de l'est***
Hungary[7]	1 074	963	883	1 040	887	949	1 061	1 088	1 358	1 221	Hongrie[7]
Other Europe	***5 963***	***5 331***	***5 224***	***4 812***	***3 798***	***4 337***	***4 176***	***5 004***	***4 932***	***4 896***	***Autre Europe***
Malta	101	97	135	207	272	274	290	208	227	...	Malte
Spain[8 9]	4 205	...	...	3 730	2 872	3 143	3 026	4 032	...	...	Espagne[8 9]
Yugoslavia	1 657	1 449	1 394	875	654	920	860	764	1 547	1 525	Yougoslavie
Oceania	**2 626**	**2 409**	**2 070**	**1 976**	**2 031**	**1 817**	**1 854**	**1 911**	**2 230**	**1 647**	**Océanie**
Australia[10]	2 341	2 086	1 709	1 577	1 593	1 403	1 351	1 263	1 553	1 127	Australie[10]
New Zealand	...	...	...	...	...	414	503	648	677	520	Nouvelle–Zélande
Total	**105 979**	**104 717**	**96 796**	**97 495**	**88 418**	**91 574**	**93 325**	**97 885**	**104 761**	**98 734**	**Total**

General note.
Jackets produced for sale as individual garments rather than as a part of a combined costume. Waistcoats, blazers, sports jackets and jackets of battledress type are included. Smoking–jackets designed primarily for indoor wear are excluded. (SITC 84111–1).

[1] Shipments.
[2] Including sweaters, coats and loafers.
[3] Beginning 1977, data are not comparable with those for earlier years.

Remarque générale.
Ces vêtements sont fabriqués pour être vendus séparément et non comme partie d'un costume complet. Cette rubrique comprend les gilets, les blazers, les sahariennes, les blousons, les vestes de sport, mais non les vestons d'intérieur. (CTCI 84111–1).

[1] Expéditions.
[2] Y compris les chandails, manteaux et blousons.
[3] A partir de 1977, les données ne sont pas comparables à celles des années antérieures.

[4] Source: Industrial Statistics, Statistical Office of the European Communities, (Luxembourg).
[5] Jackets and sports jackets only.
[6] Manufacturers' sales.
[7] Excluding work jackets.
[8] Excluding children's wear.
[9] Including household production.
[10] Twelve months ending 30 June of year stated.

[4] Source: Statistiques industrielles, Office statistique des Communautés européennes, (Luxembourg).
[5] Vestons et vestes de sport seulement.
[6] Ventes des fabricants.
[7] Non compris les vestes de travail.
[8] Non compris les vêtements d'enfants.
[9] Y compris la production ménagère.
[10] Période de douze mois finissant le 30 juin de l'année indiquée.

ISIC–BASED CODE
3220–04

Overcoats, men's and boys' – Vêtements de dessus pour hommes et garçonnets

CODE BASE CITI
3220–04

Unit : Thousand units — Unité : En milliers

Country or area	1976	1977	1978	1979	1980	1981	1982	1983	1984	1985	Pays ou zone
Africa	**1 032**	**1 139**	**888**	**829**	**912**	**577**	**532**	**253**	**273**	**211**	**Afrique**
Cameroon	842	* 955	823	765	830	...	...	# 136	157	93	Cameroun
South Africa	190	184	65	64	82	80	139	117	116	118	Afrique du Sud
America, North	**7 275**	**7 922**	**11 954**	**10 472**	**10 446**	**9 971**	**9 788**	**10 362**	**10 576**	**10 880**	**Amérique du Nord**
Canada[1]	991	* 660	5 638	5 840	5 442	...	...	...	...	...	Canada[1]
Dominican Republic[2]	886	865	872	520	1 228	1 140	1 006	1 682	2 090	...	Rép. dominicaine[2]
United States	5 398	6 397	5 444	4 112	3 776	3 660	3 050	2 387	1 632	1 642	Etats–Unis
America, South	**5 402**	**1 478**	**1 529**	**1 273**	**2 509**	**2 470**	**2 447**	**2 434**	**2 473**	**2 479**	**Amérique du Sud**
Bolivia	1	1	1	1	1	1	1	2	2	2	Bolivie
Brazil[3 4]	5 322	1 410	1 476	1 183	...	...	...	...	...	...	Brésil[3 4]
Chile	78	64	50	62	...	...	...	...	...	...	Chili
Ecuador	1	3	2	...	# 97	58	35	21	...	...	Equateur
Asia	**11 478**	**14 938**	**5 067**	**3 509**	**2 695**	**2 417**	**2 645**	**1 447**	**2 060**	**2 046**	**Asie**
Hong Kong	5 970	9 599	560	358	177	164	247	50	244	...	Hong–kong
Indonesia	11	...	10	...	...	...	...	...	...	...	Indonésie
Japan[5]	5 406	5 204	4 357	2 998	2 383	2 118	2 263	1 262	1 681	1 861	Japon[5]
Turkey	91	124	140	142	...	...	...	...	...	...	Turquie
Europe	**20 239**	**19 446**	**19 530**	**19 585**	**26 841**	**26 315**	**25 654**	**21 622**	**20 353**	**20 276**	**Europe**
EEC	***13 802***	***12 513***	***12 385***	***11 748***	***11 358***	***10 815***	***10 077***	***9 446***	***9 114***	***8 834***	***CEE***
Belgium	1 371	1 055	1 308	1 237	925	706	786	508	467	629	Belgique
Denmark	549	459	462	485	449	* 541	16	11	9	8	Danemark
France	1 277	1 040	990	935	...	...	...	...	...	...	France
Germany, Fed. Rep.[6]	2 973	2 489	2 361	1 925	1 857	1 533	1 319	...	...	...	Allemagne, Rép. féd.[6]
Greece	...	...	...	...	111	105	78	102	64	...	Grèce
Ireland	267	219	220	202	247	290	330	332	360	376	Irlande
Italy[7 8]	5 800	5 700	...	...	...	...	...	...	...	...	Italie[7 8]
Netherlands	340	410	320	300	260	...	...	...	...	...	Pays–Bas
United Kingdom[9]	1 075	1 001	844	793	698	584	519	479	491	325	Royaume–Uni[9]
EFTA	***1 505***	***1 407***	***1 255***	***1 371***	***1 250***	***1 313***	***1 133***	***981***	***1 065***	***1 117***	***AELE***
Austria	485	402	360	400	425	472	404	367	358	308	Autriche
Finland	457	558	532	673	497	569	570	481	457	...	Finlande
Iceland	5	5	5	3	3	2	1	1	1	...	Islande
Norway	68	56	60	57	121	71	57	40	142	172	Norvège
Portugal	203	112	91	99	53	52	13	17	33	41	Portugal
Sweden[10]	287	274	207	139	151	147	88	75	74	85	Suède[10]
East Europe	***2 547***	***2 579***	***2 646***	***2 521***	***2 721***	***2 726***	***2 559***	***2 387***	***2 194***	***1 923***	***Europe de l'est***
German Dem. Rep.	1 288	1 374	1 526	1 469	1 592	1 706	1 619	1 648	1 397	1 216	Rép. dém. allemande
Hungary[11]	1 259	1 205	1 120	1 052	1 129	1 020	940	739	797	707	Hongrie[11]
Other Europe	***2 385***	***2 947***	***3 243***	***3 945***	***11 512***	***11 461***	***11 885***	***8 808***	***7 980***	***8 401***	***Autre Europe***
Malta	...	4	6	3	4	2	5	11	19	...	Malte
Spain[5 12]	901	...	...	1 971	1 682	1 441	1 262	1 185	...	...	Espagne[5 12]
Yugoslavia	1 483	1 591	1 868	1 971	# 9 826	10 018	10 618	7 612	6 487	6 899	Yougoslavie
Oceania	**439**	**406**	**332**	**359**	**243**	**352**	**406**	**327**	**296**	**483**	**Océanie**
Australia[10 13]	422	388	313	339	222	324	388	302	279	449	Australie[10 13]
New Zealand	...	...	...	...	...	28	18	25	17	34	Nouvelle–Zélande
Total	**45 865**	**45 328**	**39 300**	**36 027**	**43 646**	**42 102**	**41 472**	**36 445**	**36 031**	**36 375**	**Total**

General note.
Men's and boys' overcoats of all types other than raincoats, such as overcoats, topcoats, greatcoats, duffel coats (with or without hoods), capes and cloaks. Dressing–gowns, bath–robes and similar indoor wear are excluded. (SITC 84111–2).

[1] Shipments.

Remarque générale.
Vêtements de tous types autres que les imperméables, tels que pardessus, manteaux, capotes, trois–quarts, paletots, redingotes, jaquettes, capes, pèlerines et duffel–coats. Cette rubrique ne comprend pas les robes de chambre, les peignoirs de bain et autres vêtements d'intérieur analogues. (CTCI 84111–2).

[1] Expéditions.

[2] Including coats for women and girls.
[3] Production by establishments employing 5 or more persons.
[4] Including overcoats for girls.
[5] Excluding children's wear.
[6] Beginning 1983, data are confidential.
[7] Including raincoats for women and girls.
[8] Source: Industrial Statistics, Statistical Office of the European Communities, (Luxembourg).
[9] Manufacturers' sales.
[10] Including raincoats for men and boys.
[11] Excluding overcoats for work and for uniforms.
[12] Including household production.
[13] Twelve months ending 30 June of year stated.

[2] Y compris les manteaux de dames et de fillettes.
[3] Production des établissements occupant 5 personnes ou plus.
[4] Y compris les pardessus pour fillettes.
[5] Non compris les vêtements d'enfants.
[6] A partir de 1983, les données sont confidentielles.
[7] Y compris les imperméables pour dames et fillettes.
[8] Source: Statistiques industrielles, Office statistique des Communautés européennes, (Luxembourg).
[9] Ventes des fabricants.
[10] Y compris les imperméables pour hommes et garçonnets.
[11] Non compris les pardessus de travail et d'uniformes.
[12] Y compris la production ménagère.
[13] Période de douze mois finissant le 30 juin de l'année indiquée.

Raincoats, men's and boys' – Imperméables pour hommes et garçonnets

Unit : Thousand units | Unité : En milliers

Country or area	1976	1977	1978	1979	1980	1981	1982	1983	1984	1985	Pays ou zone
Africa	**996**	**825**	**835**	**852**	**905**	**1 108**	**1 093**	**795**	**955**	**856**	**Afrique**
Algeria	27	49	73	141	162	106	114	126	115	...	Algérie
South Africa	969	776	762	711	743	1 002	979	669	* 840	702	Afrique du Sud
America, North	**5 144**	**5 916**	**5 189**	**4 134**	**4 319**	**3 639**	**3 272**	**3 342**	**3 850**	**3 821**	**Amérique du Nord**
Canada[1,2]	860	* 576	315	412	613	...	...	...	...	...	Canada[1,2]
United States	4 284	5 340	4 874	3 722	3 706	3 280	2 979	3 114	3 688	3 724	Etats-Unis
America, South	**2 251**	**729**	**684**	**715**	**1 025**	**854**	**720**	**596**	**513**	**411**	**Amérique du Sud**
Brazil[3,4]	2 105	554	554	547	904	...	...	...	...	...	Brésil[3,4]
Colombia	145	174	129	167	* 120	181	146	122	...	...	Colombie
Ecuador	...	1	1	...	...	...	...	...	...	...	Equateur
Asia	**914**	**1 779**	**3 992**	**10 372**	**3 196**	**1 767**	**2 039**	**4 012**	**713**	**2 639**	**Asie**
Burma[5,6]	144	122	89	...	...	181	140	131	109	132	Birmanie[5,6]
Hong Kong	746	1 613	3 858	10 173	...	1 542	1 855	3 836	547	...	Hong-kong
Indonesia	...	...	...	5	1	* 1	1	* 2	14	...	Indonésie
Sri Lanka[3]	23	...	...	64	43	...	...	...	...	...	Sri Lanka[3]
Europe	**16 533**	**16 264**	**14 884**	**13 531**	**15 746**	**15 185**	**14 030**	**12 327**	**12 832**	**12 979**	**Europe**
EEC	***13 088***	***12 417***	***11 167***	***9 504***	***10 538***	***10 886***	***10 002***	***9 023***	***8 784***	***8 840***	***CEE***
Belgium[3]	3 771	3 270	3 713	3 617	3 109	2 785	2 610	2 381	2 339	2 270	Belgique[3]
Denmark	167	166	218	201	174	346	...	...	114	134	Danemark
France	6 144	6 375	5 018	3 510	...	...	...	...	...	...	France
Germany, Fed. Rep.[3]	509	261	265	232	337	403	318	219	231	268	Allemagne, Rép. féd.[3]
Netherlands	570	480	360	340	155	# [7] 1 046	[7] 744	[7] 335	[7] 175	[7] 240	Pays-Bas
United Kingdom[8]	1 927	1 865	1 593	1 604	1 501	1 044	887	650	* [1] 663	666	Royaume-Uni[8]
EFTA	***1 316***	***1 356***	***1 482***	***1 529***	***1 749***	***1 471***	***1 397***	***1 303***	***1 354***	***1 569***	***AELE***
Austria[3]	306	262	260	233	215	278	267	181	188	132	Autriche[3]
Finland	499	522	517	720	631	670	653	642	657	...	Finlande
Iceland[3]	35	28	40	26	14	24	28	46	38	...	Islande[3]
Norway	314	374	317	194	515	272	233	* 200	169	382	Norvège
Portugal	162	170	348	356	374	227	216	234	302	307	Portugal
East Europe	***374***	***459***	***384***	***232***	***211***	***198***	***179***	***204***	***144***	***130***	***Europe de l'est***
Hungary[9]	374	459	384	232	211	198	179	204	144	130	Hongrie[9]
Other Europe	***1 755***	***2 032***	***1 851***	***2 266***	***3 248***	***2 630***	***2 452***	***1 797***	***2 550***	***2 441***	***Autre Europe***
Spain[3,10]	1 549	...	...	1 956	1 375	1 039	862	598	...	...	Espagne[3,10]
Yugoslavia	206	307	282	310	1 873	1 591	1 590	1 199	1 920	1 967	Yougoslavie
Oceania	**111**	**105**	**100**	**94**	**89**	**101**	**57**	**60**	**84**	**60**	**Océanie**
New Zealand	...	...	...	...	...	101	57	60	84	60	Nouvelle-Zélande
Total	**25 949**	**25 618**	**25 683**	**29 698**	**25 279**	**22 654**	**21 211**	**21 133**	**18 947**	**20 766**	**Total**

General note.
Men's and boys' raincoats of all types and materials, except rubber. (Parts of SITC 84111 and 8930).

[1] Excluding rubber and rubberized raincoats.
[2] Shipments.
[3] Including raincoats for women and girls.
[4] Production by establishments employing 5 or more persons.
[5] Government production only.
[6] Twelve months ending 30 September of year stated.
[7] Including overcoats and suits for men and boys.
[8] Manufacturers' sales.
[9] Excluding raincoats for work and for uniforms.
[10] Including household production.

Remarque générale.
Imperméables de tous types et en toutes matières pour hommes et garçonnets, sauf ceux en caoutchouc. (Parties de CTCI 84111 et 8930).

[1] Non compris les imperméables en caoutchouc ou enduits de caoutchouc.
[2] Expéditions.
[3] Y compris les imperméables pour dames et fillettes.
[4] Production des établissements occupant 5 personnes ou plus.
[5] Production de l'Etat seulement.
[6] Période de douze mois finissant le 30 septembre de l'année indiquée.
[7] Y compris les vêtements de dessus et costumes pour hommes et garçonnets.
[8] Ventes des fabricants.
[9] Non compris les imperméables de travail et d'uniformes.
[10] Y compris la production ménagère.

Suits, men's and boys' – Costumes pour hommes et garçonnets

Unit : Thousand units

Unité : En milliers

Country or area	1976	1977	1978	1979	1980	1981	1982	1983	1984	1985	Pays ou zone
Africa	**4 114**	**3 679**	**3 674**	**3 979**	**4 009**	**4 188**	**3 962**	**3 293**	**3 436**	**3 375**	**Afrique**
Algeria[1]	1 821	1 889	2 030	...	...	...	...	...	...	...	Algérie[1]
Kenya	...	68	70	238	498	466	427	257	321	337	Kenya
South Africa[2]	1 905	1 418	1 425	1 635	1 413	1 659	1 494	1 017	* 1 118	1 063	Afrique du Sud[2]
Tunisia	240	304	149	193	185	150	...	...	...	...	Tunisie
America, North	**28 949**	**25 369**	**26 255**	**25 894**	**22 618**	**23 099**	**20 574**	**20 214**	**23 502**	**23 415**	**Amérique du Nord**
Canada[3]	2 608	2 218	3 182	4 318	4 201	...	...	...	...	...	Canada[3]
Cuba	76	77	48	43	71	28	58	36	29	18	Cuba
Dominican Republic	7	7	7	18	10	13	10	10	11	11	Rép. dominicaine
El Salvador	1	2	4	4	2	3	0	0	...	...	El Salvador
Panama	5	2	2	1	...	2	2	7	7	8	Panama
United States	26 252	23 063	23 012	21 510	18 330	18 170	15 095	14 226	16 994	16 391	Etats–Unis
America, South	**1 437**	**1 337**	**2 010**	**2 063**	**1 760**	**2 870**	**2 056**	**2 157**	**2 551**	**2 682**	**Amérique du Sud**
Bolivia	7	3	2	2	1	1	1	1	1	...	Bolivie
Brazil[4 5]	1 142	1 057	1 612	1 639	1 381	...	...	...	...	...	Brésil[4 5]
Colombia	...	...	...	...	...	275	251	240	...	...	Colombie
Ecuador	33	22	...	...	# 123	911	16	23	...	...	Equateur
Asia	**35 124**	**31 569**	**32 500**	**27 750**	**24 889**	**33 745**	**24 926**	**23 373**	**23 290**	**23 880**	**Asie**
Hong Kong	6 613	4 939	4 092	2 821	1 798	10 350	2 053	844	630	...	Hong–kong
Indonesia	...	...	65	33	87	87	27	...	...	...	Indonésie
Iran(Islamic Rep.of)	10 835	...	...	...	...	...	...	...	...	...	Iran(Rép.islamique)
Japan[6]	17 607	15 729	17 508	14 061	12 169	12 473	12 011	11 641	11 774	11 933	Japon[6]
Europe	**41 905**	**42 540**	**39 566**	**37 702**	**36 544**	**35 019**	**33 211**	**32 025**	**31 397**	**30 946**	**Europe**
EEC	***28 645***	***27 978***	***25 867***	***24 714***	***23 544***	***22 249***	***20 885***	***20 612***	***20 135***	***19 367***	***CEE***
Belgium	903	827	596	597	380	344	216	203	209	239	Belgique
Denmark	244	187	155	150	114	61	109	87	91	89	Danemark
France	5 844	5 324	5 131	5 265	...	...	...	...	...	...	France
Germany, Fed. Rep.[7]	6 861	6 769	6 527	5 706	5 519	5 224	4 442	...	...	...	Allemagne, Rép. féd.[7]
Greece	...	...	...	...	549	433	314	224	292	...	Grèce
Ireland	230	190	109	211	203	162	163	148	167	167	Irlande
Italy[8]	7 900	7 500	...	...	...	...	...	...	...	...	Italie[8]
Netherlands	1 460	1 230	1 190	1 170	1 050	...	...	495	325	240	Pays–Bas
United Kingdom[9]	4 411	5 230	3 810	3 338	2 638	2 142	1 895	2 122	2 124	1 963	Royaume–Uni[9]
EFTA	***2 554***	***3 393***	***3 032***	***3 447***	***2 874***	***3 321***	***3 281***	***2 992***	***2 928***	***3 088***	***AELE***
Austria	591	592	539	586	624	644	624	604	585	522	Autriche
Finland	735	1 892	1 578	1 782	1 349	1 567	1 455	1 207	1 280	...	Finlande
Iceland	17	16	18	16	14	11	12	9	6	...	Islande
Norway	166	154	147	148	124	102	125	92	86	86	Norvège
Portugal	265	172	368	572	459	660	790	803	703	811	Portugal
Sweden	780	567	382	343	304	337	275	277	268	263	Suède
East Europe	***6 267***	***6 290***	***5 349***	***5 600***	***5 711***	***5 415***	***4 971***	***4 511***	***4 219***	***4 136***	***Europe de l'est***
German Dem. Rep.	3 872	3 837	2 901	3 300	3 413	3 327	3 131	2 964	2 847	2 666	Rép. dém. allemande
Hungary[10]	2 395	2 453	2 448	2 300	2 298	2 088	1 840	1 547	1 372	1 470	Hongrie[10]
Other Europe	***4 439***	***4 879***	***5 318***	***3 941***	***4 415***	***4 034***	***4 074***	***3 910***	***4 114***	***4 355***	***Autre Europe***
Malta	55	76	92	102	95	70	100	75	93	...	Malte
Spain[6 11]	1 896	...	...	1 184	1 176	740	804	792	...	...	Espagne[6 11]
Yugoslavia	2 488	3 176	3 766	2 655	3 144	3 224	3 170	3 043	3 562	3 967	Yougoslavie
Oceania	**206**	**218**	**167**	**133**	**124**	**101**	**120**	**79**	**96**	**81**	**Océanie**
New Zealand	206	218	167	133	124	101	120	79	96	81	Nouvelle–Zélande
Total	**111 736**	**104 712**	**104 172**	**97 522**	**89 944**	**99 022**	**84 849**	**81 141**	**84 272**	**84 379**	**Total**

For general note and footnotes, see end of table.

Voir la fin du tableau pour la remarque générale et les notes.

General note.
Men's and boys' suits of all types, such as lounge suits, dress suits, dinner–jacket suits, morning suits, clerical suits, plus–fours, siren suits, skiing, hunting and other sports suits and uniforms of all kinds (including liveries). They consist of a jacket and a pair of trousers (usually matching) and may include a vest and an extra pair of trousers. Suits for small boys consisting of a jacket and a pair of short pants are included. (SITC 84111–4).

[1] Including overcoats, jackets and slacks.
[2] Lounge suits only.
[3] Shipments.
[4] Production by establishments employing 5 or more persons.
[5] Including suits for boys.
[6] Excluding children's wear.
[7] Beginning 1983, data are confidential.
[8] Source: Industrial Statistics, Statistical Office of the European Communities, (Luxembourg).
[9] Manufacturers' sales.
[10] Excluding work suits and uniforms.
[11] Including household production.

Remarque générale.
Costumes de tous types pour hommes et garçonnets, tels que complets de ville et costumes de sport (pour le ski, la chasse etc.), costumes de soirée ou de cérémonie (tels que smokings, spencers ou fracs), vêtements ecclésiastiques, uniformes militaires, administratifs et autres (y compris les livrées). Ils se composent d'une veste et d'un pantalon (habituellement du même tissu) et peuvent comprendre un gilet et un second pantalon. Cette rubrique comprend les costumes pour garçonnets composés d'une veste et d'une culotte courte. (CTCI 84111–4).

[1] Y compris les pardessus, vestes et pantalons.
[2] Complets vestons seulement.
[3] Expéditions.
[4] Production des établissements occupant 5 personnes ou plus.
[5] Y compris les costumes pour garçonnets.
[6] Non compris les vêtements d'enfants.
[7] A partir de 1983, les données sont confidentielles.
[8] Source: Statistiques industrielles, Office statistique des Communautés européennes, (Luxembourg).
[9] Ventes des fabricants.
[10] Non compris les vêtements de travail et les uniformes.
[11] Y compris la production ménagère.

Trousers, men's and boys' – Pantalons pour hommes et garçonnets

Unit : Thousand units | Unité : En milliers

Country or area	1976	1977	1978	1979	1980	1981	1982	1983	1984	1985	Pays ou zone
Africa	**23 686**	**24 373**	**20 561**	**21 790**	**24 400**	**29 705**	**28 657**	**27 676**	**27 376**	**26 970**	**Afrique**
Kenya	588	569	886	948	816	960	1 212	1 428	1 370	1 085	Kenya
Malawi	280	280	176	181	121	147	253	285	199	284	Malawi
Senegal	115	110	76	105	77	62	52	* 60	...	...	Sénégal
South Africa	20 013	17 980	13 026	14 926	16 856	19 747	17 928	15 749	* 14 668	13 528	Afrique du Sud
Tunisia	2 690	5 434	6 397	5 630	6 530	8 789	...	...	...	...	Tunisie
America, North	**226 460**	**211 619**	**215 397**	**207 855**	**204 527**	**204 806**	**199 683**	**196 921**	**195 740**	**191 105**	**Amérique du Nord**
Canada[1]	31 963	26 623	31 735	32 827	36 520	...	...	...	...	...	Canada[1]
Cuba	13 397	13 532	13 971	14 617	11 836	13 722	14 644	15 340	14 303	15 629	Cuba
Dominican Republic	492	425	583	682	506	381	451	683	1 542	...	Rép. dominicaine
El Salvador	533	610	1 198	976	917	1 001	182	87	...	...	El Salvador
Panama	1 923	2 224	2 179	2 242	...	2 530	2 844	2 127	...	...	Panama
United States	178 152	168 205	165 731	156 511	152 414	150 667	143 533	139 131	135 843	128 897	Etats–Unis
America, South	**68 444**	**79 708**	**94 305**	**93 227**	**83 784**	**79 841**	**80 206**	**80 312**	**82 860**	**82 945**	**Amérique du Sud**
Brazil[2]	57 964	76 077	90 597	[3] 88 343	...	...	...	...	...	...	Brésil[2]
Chile	440	479	512	1 402	...	...	...	...	...	...	Chili
Colombia	9 728	...	...	...	...	307	637	469	...	...	Colombie
Ecuador	312	367	411	...	2 045	580	615	889	...	...	Equateur
Asia	**128 450**	**118 394**	**116 004**	**130 442**	**134 055**	**141 310**	**134 423**	**145 910**	**119 806**	**133 989**	**Asie**
Burma	473	406	328	...	...	786	1 147	569	466	541	Birmanie
Hong Kong	119 682	109 932	106 794	120 085	120 057	123 912	116 423	115 649	96 041	...	Hong–kong
Indonesia	...	...	80	570	3 403	4 685	5 503	* 17 286	8 769	...	Indonésie
Malaysia[4 5]	4 603	4 967	4 684	4 278	5 330	7 624	# 7 233	8 289	10 413	9 174	Malaisie[4 5]
Philippines[1]	2 986	840	...	...	...	...	...	...	...	...	Philippines[1]
Sri Lanka	72	...	...	2 369	2 180	1 788	...	...	...	...	Sri Lanka
Turkey	554	567	603	683	...	. .	...	...	...	...	Turquie
Europe	**309 734**	**324 173**	**310 496**	**322 253**	**319 140**	**302 671**	**306 798**	**305 298**	**310 607**	**314 306**	**Europe**
EEC	***240 597***	***241 906***	***228 345***	***224 920***	***221 122***	***213 773***	***214 881***	***211 529***	***203 759***	***205 000***	***CEE***
Belgium	26 973	25 902	26 519	25 633	26 074	23 818	24 735	22 923	16 315	16 547	Belgique
Denmark	3 744	4 081	3 493	2 808	2 146	2 047	1 853	1 804	2 203	2 152	Danemark
France	66 767	71 262	59 013	59 538	...	...	...	...	...	...	France
Germany, Fed. Rep.	50 815	46 601	44 797	45 535	42 435	40 258	39 262	37 643	36 499	36 128	Allemagne, Rép. féd.
Greece	...	...	...	...	12 751	11 178	10 703	9 174	9 523	...	Grèce
Ireland[6]	891	1 082	1 076	838	654	914	1 572	2 096	2 063	2 200	Irlande[6]
Italy[7]	48 000	49 400	...	...	...	...	...	...	...	...	Italie[7]
Netherlands	5 770	5 810	7 510	6 170	4 760	4 670	4 610	4 600	3 685	3 525	Pays–Bas
United Kingdom[8 9]	21 939	22 909	23 216	22 516	19 457	18 043	19 301	20 444	20 626	23 454	Royaume–Uni[8 9]
EFTA	***27 274***	***29 269***	***25 952***	***27 000***	***28 750***	***28 326***	***28 701***	***28 527***	***29 215***	***30 725***	***AELE***
Austria	4 335	4 068	3 963	4 402	4 930	4 757	4 344	5 646	5 802	5 865	Autriche
Finland	2 876	5 885	5 955	5 690	6 792	6 844	6 909	5 612	5 052	...	Finlande
Iceland	87	84	145	101	123	115	108	77	67	...	Islande
Norway	1 644	1 718	1 404	1 509	1 738	2 369	2 547	...	...	...	Norvège
Portugal	10 682	11 536	10 050	11 075	11 317	10 896	11 721	12 301	13 247	13 114	Portugal
Sweden	7 650	5 978	4 435	4 223	3 850	3 345	3 072	2 423	2 424	2 233	Suède
East Europe	***16 449***	***16 859***	***17 287***	***18 350***	***18 188***	***17 841***	***18 049***	***19 428***	***20 887***	***20 066***	***Europe de l'est***
German Dem. Rep.	11 535	11 932	12 390	12 616	12 332	11 764	12 182	13 773	14 337	14 371	Rép. dém. allemande
Hungary[10]	4 914	4 927	4 897	5 734	5 856	6 077	5 867	5 655	6 550	5 695	Hongrie[10]
Other Europe	***25 414***	***36 139***	***38 912***	***51 983***	***51 080***	***42 731***	***45 167***	***45 814***	***56 746***	***58 515***	***Autre Europe***
Malta[11]	774	853	946	733	994	637	877	620	960	...	Malte[11]
Spain[12 13]	19 165	...	...	44 177	42 969	35 299	37 090	37 505	...	...	Espagne[12 13]
Yugoslavia	5 475	5 940	6 508	7 073	7 117	6 795	* 7 200	7 689	11 656	11 467	Yougoslavie
Oceania	**22 634**	**21 677**	**20 065**	**21 353**	**22 222**	**23 897**	**23 948**	**21 728**	**22 839**	**20 745**	**Océanie**
Australia	17 786	16 845	15 825	16 770	18 505	18 305	17 934	15 604	16 826	14 701	Australie
New Zealand	4 848	4 832	4 240	4 583	3 717	# 5 592	6 014	6 124	6 013	6 044	Nouvelle–Zélande
Total	**779 408**	**779 945**	**776 828**	**796 920**	**788 128**	**782 230**	**773 714**	**777 845**	**759 230**	**770 061**	**Total**

For general note and footnotes, see end of table. | Voir la fin du tableau pour la remarque générale et les notes.

Trousers, men's and boys' (continued) – Pantalons pour hommes et garçonnets (suite)

General note.
Trousers for men and boys produced for sale as individual garments rather than as part of a combined costume. Knickerbockers, breeches and shorts are included. (SITC 84111–5).

1 Shipments.
2 Including trousers for girls.
3 Production by establishments employing 5 or more persons.
4 Data refer to Peninsular Malaysia only.
5 Beginning 1982, scope of series revised.
6 Excluding cotton jeans.
7 Source: Industrial Statistics, Statistical Office of the European Communities, (Luxembourg).
8 Excluding jeans and trousers made on 2– or 3–needle machines.
9 Manufacturers' sales.
10 Excluding work trousers.
11 Including women's and girls' dresses.
12 Excluding children's wear.
13 Including household production.

Remarque générale.
Ces vêtements sont fabriqués pour être vendus séparément et non comme partie d'un costume complet. Cette rubrique comprend les pantalons de golf, les culottes et les shorts. (CTCI 84111–5).

1 Expéditions.
2 Y compris les pantalous pour fillettes.
3 Production des établissements occupant 5 personnes ou plus.
4 Données se rapportant à la Malaisie péninsulaire seulement.
5 A partir de 1982, portée de la série révisée.
6 Non compris les 'jeans' en coton.
7 Source: Statistiques industrielles, Office statistique des Communautés européennes, (Luxembourg).
8 Non compris les 'jeans' et pantalons cousus sur machines à 2 ou 3 aiguilles.
9 Ventes des fabricants.
10 Non compris les pantalons de travail.
11 Y compris les robes de dames et de fillettes.
12 Non compris les vêtements d'enfants.
13 Y compris la production ménagère.

Blouses, women's and girls' – Blouses de dames et de fillettes

Unit : Thousand units

Unité : En milliers

Country or area	1976	1977	1978	1979	1980	1981	1982	1983	1984	1985	Pays ou zone
Africa	**14 902**	**10 457**	**10 259**	**11 455**	**7 380**	**7 644**	**6 774**	**7 231**	**5 569**	**7 595**	**Afrique**
Kenya	...	...	...	5 460	1 344	1 008	780	612	* 131	24	Kenya
South Africa	9 026	5 326	5 873	5 995	6 036	6 636	5 994	6 619	* 5 438	7 571	Afrique du Sud
America, North	**297 453**	**358 938**	**371 507**	**395 487**	**385 591**	**361 786**	**395 537**	**422 237**	**316 354**	**307 225**	**Amérique du Nord**
Canada[1]	20 143	16 989	13 241	17 432	18 386	...	...	...	...	...	Canada[1]
Cuba	2 303	2 329	2 636	2 183	1 599	2 699	1 827	2 679	3 257	3 297	Cuba
Panama	315	248	334	344	...	465	450	311	...	...	Panama
United States	274 692	339 372	355 296	375 528	365 244	342 300	377 244	403 536	# 297 264	288 384	Etats–Unis
America, South	**145 043**	**187 148**	**214 223**	**328 391**	**217 726**	**217 200**	**216 589**	**216 723**	**215 899**	**215 459**	**Amérique du Sud**
Brazil	139 573	182 809	210 704	324 934	...	...	...	...	...	...	Brésil
Chile	107	103	161	164	...	...	...	...	...	...	Chili
Colombia	5 300	4 156	3 282	3 184	2 817	2 512	1 873	1 888	...	...	Colombie
Ecuador	63	80	76	...	# 270	49	77	196	...	...	Equateur
Asia	**173 296**	**193 734**	**190 026**	**186 390**	**233 526**	**203 239**	**189 229**	**232 475**	**249 395**	**251 165**	**Asie**
Hong Kong	137 872	155 368	149 255	153 633	202 540	170 882	159 057	196 350	212 080	...	Hong–kong
Indonesia	...	...	64	64	662	1 925	1 750	4 278	3 315	...	Indonésie
Japan[2]	[3] 30 238	[3] 34 656	[3] 35 359	[3] 25 890	# 23 636	22 293	20 320	23 448	21 084	23 399	Japon[2]
Malaysia[4 5]	3 944	2 775	4 451	5 570	5 357	7 096	# 6 898	7 380	11 038	13 975	Malaisie[4 5]
Turkey[6]	1 178	# 871	897	1 233	1 331	1 043	1 204	1 019	1 878	1 780	Turquie[6]
Europe	**145 445**	**154 454**	**160 099**	**161 047**	**164 775**	**164 621**	**161 087**	**168 926**	**175 707**	**169 227**	**Europe**
EEC	***122 595***	***126 209***	***130 586***	***127 230***	***130 079***	***128 761***	***129 003***	***134 643***	***136 484***	***132 373***	***CEE***
Belgium	6 133	5 458	6 175	6 081	5 128	5 062	5 573	5 217	4 935	5 293	Belgique
Denmark	1 804	1 712	1 915	1 812	1 716	1 783	1 659	1 899	2 163	2 775	Danemark
France	21 063	21 773	21 390	16 220	22 194	23 080	23 626	25 297	23 139	21 638	France
Germany, Fed. Rep.	35 958	35 630	37 377	37 716	40 398	40 233	40 092	40 170	39 878	38 000	Allemagne, Rép. féd.
Greece	...	...	...	...	...	...	11 203	13 857	14 598	...	Grèce
Ireland	519	508	777	1 261	1 075	975	1 049	1 370	2 289	1 933	Irlande
Italy[7]	18 000	19 200	...	...	...	...	...	...	...	...	Italie[7]
Netherlands	3 150	2 640	2 220	2 100	1 600	1 510	1 695	1 750	1 710	2 160	Pays–Bas
United Kingdom[8]	22 749	26 069	28 913	30 221	26 149	24 299	25 506	26 483	29 172	28 755	Royaume–Uni[8]
EFTA	***5 373***	***5 533***	***5 187***	***5 909***	***6 150***	***6 139***	***5 972***	***5 693***	***5 809***	***5 265***	***AELE***
Austria	2 622	2 699	2 812	3 353	3 739	3 976	3 425	3 155	3 072	2 814	Autriche
Finland	1 428	1 783	1 404	1 460	1 373	1 350	1 688	1 573	1 783	...	Finlande
Iceland	13	9	6	9	7	8	2	2	3	...	Islande
Norway	206	216	189	198	173	219	229	181	...	...	Norvège
Sweden	1 104	826	776	889	858	586	628	782	752	610	Suède
East Europe	***8 780***	***9 872***	***9 709***	***10 240***	***10 201***	***10 446***	***9 593***	***9 127***	***8 907***	***8 408***	***Europe de l'est***
German Dem. Rep.	6 000	6 473	6 044	6 162	5 901	5 121	4 592	4 623	4 615	4 405	Rép. dém. allemande
Hungary[9]	2 780	3 399	3 665	4 078	4 300	5 325	5 001	4 504	4 292	4 003	Hongrie[9]
Other Europe	***8 697***	***12 839***	***14 617***	***17 668***	***18 345***	***19 275***	***16 519***	***19 463***	***24 507***	***23 180***	***Autre Europe***
Malta	1 867	5 442	5 776	5 895	5 495	5 401	4 030	5 610	8 045	...	Malte
Spain[2 10]	3 958	...	...	5 149	5 716	6 369	4 669	5 086	...	...	Espagne[2 10]
Yugoslavia	2 872	2 735	4 022	6 624	7 134	7 505	7 820	8 767	10 704	10 212	Yougoslavie
Oceania	**9 001**	**9 124**	**9 561**	**11 228**	**10 667**	**12 177**	**11 557**	**6 467**	**11 775**	**7 166**	**Océanie**
Australia	7 218	7 160	7 955	9 278	9 062	10 144	9 499	4 568	9 521	4 267	Australie
New Zealand	1 783	1 964	1 606	1 950	1 605	# 2 033	2 058	1 899	2 254	2 899	Nouvelle–Zélande
Total	**785 140**	**913 855**	**955 675**	**1 093 998**	**1 019 665**	**966 667**	**980 773**	**1 054 058**	**974 699**	**957 837**	**Total**

General note.
Women's and girls' blouses of all types, with or without sleeves, extending from the shoulders to the waist. They may button down the front or back or may be pulled on over the head and shoulders. (SITC 84112–1).

Remarque générale.
Blouses de tous types, pour dames et fillettes, avec ou sans manches, allant des épaules à la taille. Elles peuvent se boutonner devant ou derrière ou être enfilées par la tête. (CTCI 84112–1).

For footnotes, see end of table.

Voir la fin du tableau pour les notes.

[1] Shipments.
[2] Excluding children's wear.
[3] Excluding dress shirts.
[4] Data refer to Peninsular Malaysia only.
[5] Beginning 1982, scope of series revised.
[6] Beginning 1977, data are not comparable with those for earlier years.
[7] Source: Industrial Statistics, Statistical Office of the European Communities, (Luxembourg).
[8] Manufacturers' sales.
[9] Excluding blouses for work and for uniforms.
[10] Including household production.

[1] Expéditions.
[2] Non compris les vêtements d'enfants.
[3] Non compris les chemises habillées.
[4] Données se rapportant à la Malaisie péninsulaire seulement.
[5] A partir de 1982, portée de la série révisée.
[6] A partir de 1977, les données ne sont pas comparables à celles des années antérieures.
[7] Source: Statistiques industrielles, Office statistique des Communautés européennes, (Luxembourg).
[8] Ventes des fabricants.
[9] Non compris les blouses de travail et d'uniformes.
[10] Y compris la production ménagère.

Coats, women's and girls' – Manteaux de dames et de fillettes

Unit : Thousand units

Unité : En milliers

Country or area	1976	1977	1978	1979	1980	1981	1982	1983	1984	1985	Pays ou zone
Africa	**735**	**579**	**885**	**785**	**569**	**785**	**841**	**608**	**430**	**403**	**Afrique**
Cameroon	583	499	469	377	236	...	...	...	...	...	Cameroun
South Africa	152	80	416	408	333	476	575	385	251	267	Afrique du Sud
America, North	**34 529**	**39 653**	**34 676**	**28 385**	**26 722**	**20 986**	**16 730**	**17 222**	**23 469**	**20 728**	**Amérique du Nord**
Canada[1]	2 656	2 726	2 432	3 020	2 717	...	...	...	...	...	Canada[1]
United States	31 873	36 927	32 244	25 365	24 005	18 152	13 854	14 305	20 510	17 728	Etats–Unis
America, South	**1 649**	**905**	**663**	**531**	**938**	**933**	**918**	**918**	**923**	**928**	**Amérique du Sud**
Brazil[2]	1 565	796	564	436	...	...	...	...	...	...	Brésil[2]
Chile	51	78	70	68	...	...	...	...	...	...	Chili
Colombia	...	...	...	...	...	8	6	4	...	...	Colombie
Ecuador	...	...	...	...	25	18	5	7	* 10	* 15	Equateur
Asia	**9 324**	**10 883**	**8 901**	**9 784**	**6 870**	**7 332**	**6 149**	**6 027**	**6 138**	**5 690**	**Asie**
Hong Kong	...	...	1 335	3 874	1 429	1 096	1 180	2 069	1 461	...	Hong–kong
Japan[3]	6 679	7 678	6 487	5 559	5 189	6 005	4 803	3 806	4 549	4 285	Japon[3]
Philippines[1 4]	29	135	...	...	...	...	...	...	...	...	Philippines[1 4]
Turkey	217	795	997	269	170	149	84	70	46	43	Turquie
Europe	**54 057**	**51 102**	**50 505**	**49 943**	**49 907**	**46 576**	**43 173**	**40 422**	**39 807**	**42 205**	**Europe**
EEC	***40 014***	***36 989***	***36 919***	***36 453***	***34 462***	***31 117***	***29 477***	***28 288***	***27 152***	***27 780***	***CEE***
Belgium	1 319	1 150	1 266	1 344	1 231	949	961	1 009	960	1 465	Belgique
Denmark	1 436	1 364	1 342	1 197	1 094	...	986	1 131	874	926	Danemark
France[5]	4 280	3 380	3 416	3 342	...	...	...	...	...	...	France[5]
Germany, Fed. Rep.	15 948	13 880	14 065	14 092	12 721	10 938	10 053	9 950	9 769	10 013	Allemagne, Rép. féd.
Ireland	1 511	1 478	1 464	1 200	1 172	957	721	588	464	254	Irlande
Italy[3 6]	9 000	9 700	...	...	...	...	...	...	...	...	Italie[3 6]
Netherlands	1 620	900	820	720	630	440	580	540	300	390	Pays–Bas
United Kingdom[7]	4 900	5 137	5 196	5 208	4 659	3 761	3 221	2 115	1 830	1 777	Royaume–Uni[7]
EFTA	***3 920***	***3 750***	***3 536***	***3 556***	***3 680***	***3 392***	***3 359***	***2 513***	***2 800***	***2 404***	***AELE***
Austria	1 515	1 345	1 346	1 545	1 436	1 379	1 380	1 372	1 009	936	Autriche
Finland	1 354	1 407	1 436	1 295	1 486	1 356	1 478	685	1 453	...	Finlande
Iceland	23	23	26	21	26	20	15	11	14	...	Islande
Norway	243	222	177	148	142	151	90	...	...	...	Norvège
Portugal	148	134	112	169	177	141	120	127	79	115	Portugal
Sweden[3]	637	619	439	378	413	345	276	241	191	117	Suède[3]
East Europe	***5 678***	***5 289***	***4 846***	***4 813***	***4 900***	***4 358***	***4 298***	***3 928***	***3 874***	***3 664***	***Europe de l'est***
German Dem. Rep.	3 384	2 901	2 677	2 531	2 524	2 342	2 115	2 109	2 024	1 774	Rép. dém. allemande
Hungary[8]	2 294	2 388	2 169	2 282	2 376	2 016	2 183	1 819	1 850	1 890	Hongrie[8]
Other Europe	***4 445***	***5 074***	***5 204***	***5 121***	***6 865***	***7 709***	***6 039***	***5 694***	***5 981***	***8 358***	***Autre Europe***
Spain[9 10]	2 027	...	...	2 568	2 866	3 459	2 550	2 375	...	...	Espagne[9 10]
Yugoslavia[3]	2 418	2 676	2 730	2 553	3 999	4 250	3 489	3 319	3 046	5 346	Yougoslavie[3]
Oceania	**1 142**	**1 307**	**854**	**848**	**1 032**	**1 091**	**952**	**714**	**313**	**588**	**Océanie**
Australia	1 090	1 252	797	789	971	1 016	896	666	228	517	Australie
New Zealand	...	...	...	...	...	75	56	48	85	71	Nouvelle–Zélande
Total	**101 436**	**104 428**	**96 484**	**90 275**	**86 037**	**77 704**	**68 762**	**65 911**	**71 080**	**70 542**	**Total**

General note.
Women's and girls' coats of all types other than raincoats, such as overcoats, spring coats, duffel coats (with or without hoods), capes and cloaks. Jackets, boleros and beach wraps are excluded as well as dressing–gowns, bathrobes, negligees, bed jackets, house coats and similar indoor wear. (SITC 84112–2).

[1] Shipments.
[2] Excluding coats for girls.
[3] Including raincoats for women and girls.

Remarque générale.
Manteaux de tous types pour dames et fillettes, autres que les imperméables, tels que manteaux d'hiver, manteaux d'été, capes, pèlerines et duffel–coats. Cette rubrique ne comprend pas les jaquettes, les boléros, les pyjamas de plage, les robes de chambre, les déshabillés, les négligés, les saut–de–lit, les liseuses, les peignoirs de bain et les autres vêtements d'intérieur de même genre. (CTCI 84112–2).

[1] Expéditions.
[2] Non compris les manteaux de fillettes.
[3] Y compris les imperméables pour dames et fillettes.

4 Including sweaters and jackets.
5 Ready–to–wear articles made from fabrics.
6 Source: Industrial Statistics, Statistical Office of the European Communities, (Luxembourg).
7 Manufacturers' sales.
8 Excluding work coats and uniforms.
9 Excluding children's wear.
10 Including household production.

4 Y compris les chandails et vestes.
5 Articles de confection en tissus.
6 Source: Statistiques industrielles, Office statistique des Communautés européennes, (Luxembourg).
7 Ventes des fabricants.
8 Non compris les blouses de travail et les uniformes.
9 Non compris les vêtements d'enfants.
10 Y compris la production ménagère.

Dresses, women's and girls' – Robes de dames et de fillettes

Unit : Thousand units

Unité : En milliers

Country or area	1976	1977	1978	1979	1980	1981	1982	1983	1984	1985	Pays ou zone
Africa	**10 229**	**13 370**	**17 974**	**24 160**	**26 496**	**26 961**	**27 721**	**28 267**	**28 488**	**24 365**	**Afrique**
Algeria[1]	492	730	581	...	...	...	...	...	...	...	Algérie[1]
Kenya	316	720	1 227	1 500	1 680	2 508	2 484	2 336	2 306	1 943	Kenya
South Africa	8 808	10 891	15 429	19 888	22 653	22 464	23 236	23 930	* 23 827	19 963	Afrique du Sud
Tunisia	613	1 029	737	2 171	1 562	1 388	* 1 400	* 1 400	...	...	Tunisie
America, North	**250 830**	**287 693**	**275 181**	**270 050**	**266 493**	**200 107**	**200 262**	**204 308**	**253 411**	**241 673**	**Amérique du Nord**
Canada[2]	15 789	21 832	14 876	16 055	16 051	...	...	...	...	...	Canada[2]
Cuba	350	469	521	400	361	492	454	526	558	438	Cuba
United States	234 691	265 392	259 784	253 595	250 081	184 262	184 978	189 474	239 068	227 972	Etats–Unis
America, South	**24 910**	**25 899**	**30 821**	**31 779**	**34 039**	**23 768**	**29 692**	**30 954**	**31 250**	**31 753**	**Amérique du Sud**
Bolivia	13	3	6	6	4	11	* 10	* 11	* 12	...	Bolivie
Brazil[3]	22 730	23 896	28 608	28 978	31 593	20 800	...	...	...	...	Brésil[3]
Chile	68	89	107	...	...	...	...	...	...	...	Chili
Colombia	2 085	1 886	2 072	2 676	2 290	2 847	2 077	2 937	...	...	Colombie
Ecuador	14	...	...	...	64	22	36	42	...	...	Equateur
Asia	**53 997**	**55 488**	**63 838**	**62 799**	**64 201**	**59 344**	**55 155**	**52 713**	**48 510**	**52 125**	**Asie**
Hong Kong	13 095	11 840	18 937	22 623	24 229	13 597	16 827	16 174	15 344	...	Hong–kong
Indonesia	...	...	2 601	2 389	3 784	4 815	3 549	* 3 600	3 147	...	Indonésie
Japan[3 4]	21 698	21 568	23 914	21 276	19 013	16 897	15 521	13 275	10 774	11 205	Japon[3 4]
Malaysia[5 6]	985	1 320	1 694	2 013	2 820	2 812	# 2 566	2 972	2 553	2 577	Malaisie[5 6]
Philippines[2 7 8]	9 988	12 392	...	...	...	...	...	...	...	...	Philippines[2 7 8]
Sri Lanka	...	...	...	3 308	3 165	10 033	...	...	...	...	Sri Lanka
Europe	**197 118**	**195 872**	**181 363**	**186 252**	**176 219**	**161 162**	**154 163**	**149 359**	**150 420**	**136 529**	**Europe**
EEC	***168 943***	***165 196***	***152 687***	***153 647***	***144 643***	***129 692***	***124 899***	***120 889***	***119 051***	***109 647***	***CEE***
Belgium	7 243	7 354	6 792	7 424	7 361	6 962	7 016	5 724	5 738	5 231	Belgique
Denmark	1 123	1 121	1 037	1 170	1 214	1 080	871	865	840	699	Danemark
France[9]	27 867	27 624	25 905	26 662	23 884	20 585	...	21 790	20 003	20 626	France[9]
Germany, Fed. Rep.	53 093	46 612	41 780	41 409	37 678	32 515	31 317	31 155	31 090	25 884	Allemagne, Rép. féd.
Greece	...	...	...	...	7 668	6 013	4 310	4 275	4 209	...	Grèce
Ireland	1 509	949	561	423	514	412	383	417	224	557	Irlande
Italy[10]	19 000	21 700	...	...	...	...	...	...	...	...	Italie[10]
Netherlands	7 090	6 690	6 040	5 790	3 810	3 510	3 490	2 470	2 090	1 100	Pays–Bas
United Kingdom[11]	41 574	43 560	41 494	42 550	42 164	38 265	34 849	33 843	34 507	32 480	Royaume–Uni[11]
EFTA	***5 727***	***6 485***	***5 338***	***7 380***	***6 019***	***7 270***	***6 100***	***5 854***	***5 421***	***4 357***	***AELE***
Austria	1 823	2 039	1 718	1 994	2 159	2 355	2 273	1 934	1 890	1 416	Autriche
Finland	1 652	2 629	1 853	3 244	1 893	2 788	1 694	1 835	1 953	...	Finlande
Iceland	9	4	4	3	3	3	4	3	2	...	Islande
Norway	572	461	372	318	147	200	181	128	...	...	Norvège
Portugal	523	503	809	1 187	1 201	1 368	1 492	1 529	1 178	603	Portugal
Sweden	1 148	849	582	634	616	556	456	425	324	307	Suède
East Europe	***16 455***	***15 950***	***14 857***	***13 731***	***13 035***	***12 374***	***13 370***	***12 522***	***12 233***	***12 490***	***Europe de l'est***
German Dem. Rep.	8 194	7 189	6 461	5 917	5 595	5 593	5 107	5 298	5 656	5 301	Rép. dém. allemande
Hungary[12]	8 261	8 761	8 396	7 814	7 440	6 781	8 263	7 224	6 577	7 189	Hongrie[12]
Other Europe	***5 993***	***8 242***	***8 482***	***11 494***	***12 522***	***11 826***	***9 794***	***10 094***	***13 716***	***10 034***	***Autre Europe***
Spain[4 13]	3 841	...	...	7 209	7 846	7 153	5 038	5 835	...	...	Espagne[4 13]
Yugoslavia	2 152	2 705	2 750	4 285	4 676	4 673	4 756	4 259	6 815	2 939	Yougoslavie
Oceania	**16 249**	**15 990**	**16 073**	**18 883**	**18 682**	**18 862**	**17 799**	**17 543**	**13 312**	**14 073**	**Océanie**
Australia	15 137	14 839	14 847	17 269	17 206	16 772	15 823	15 542	11 153	12 010	Australie
New Zealand	1 112	1 151	1 226	1 614	1 476	# 2 090	1 976	2 001	2 159	2 063	Nouvelle–Zélande
Total	**553 333**	**594 312**	**585 250**	**593 923**	**586 130**	**490 204**	**484 792**	**483 143**	**525 392**	**500 517**	**Total**

General note.
Women's and girls' dresses of all types, such as street dresses, cocktail dresses, evening dresses, house dresses and schoolgirls' tunics. They may include a matching jacket or bolero. Two–piece dresses consisting of a matching blouse and skirt are included. Knitted dresses made in knitting mills are excluded. (SITC 84112–3).

Remarque générale.
Robes de tous types pour dames et fillettes, telles que robes de ville, robes de cocktail, robes du soir, robes de maison et uniformes d'écolière. Elles peuvent comprendre une jaquette ou un boléro du même tissu. Cette rubrique comprend les costumes deux–pièces, qui consistent en une blouse et une jupe du même tissu, mais ne comprend pas les robes en bonneterie faites en usine. (CTCI 84112–3).

For footnotes, see end of table.

Voir la fin du tableau pour les notes.

Dresses, women's and girls' (continued) – Robes de dames et de fillettes (suite)

[1] Including coats, skirts, slacks and suits.
[2] Shipments.
[3] Including suits for women and girls.
[4] Excluding children's wear.
[5] Data refer to Peninsular Malaysia only.
[6] Beginning 1982, scope of series revised.
[7] Including skirts and blouses.
[8] Establishments with ten or more workers.
[9] Dresses for beach and street, and ensemble dresses.
[10] Source: Industrial Statistics, Statistical Office of the European Communities, (Luxembourg).
[11] Manufacturers' sales.
[12] Excluding work dresses and uniforms.
[13] Including household production.

[1] Y compris manteaux, jupes, pantalons et costumes.
[2] Expéditions.
[3] Y compris les costumes pour dames et fillettes.
[4] Non compris les vêtements d'enfants.
[5] Données se rapportant à la Malaisie péninsulaire seulement.
[6] A partir de 1982, portée de la série révisée.
[7] Y compris les jupes et les blouses.
[8] Etablissements employant 10 ouvriers ou plus.
[9] Robes de ville, de plage et ensembles.
[10] Source: Statistiques industrielles, Office statistique des Communautés européennes, (Luxembourg).
[11] Ventes des fabricants.
[12] Non compris les habits de travail et les uniformes.
[13] Y compris la production ménagère.

Raincoats, women's and girls' – Imperméables pour dames et fillettes

Unit : Thousand units

Unité : En milliers

Country or area	1976	1977	1978	1979	1980	1981	1982	1983	1984	1985	Pays ou zone
Africa	**316**	**704**	**161**	**261**	**120**	**274**	**357**	**221**	**375**	**138**	**Afrique**
South Africa	316	704	161	261	120	274	357	221	* 375	138	Afrique du Sud
America, North	**8 687**	**7 494**	**6 898**	**7 302**	**7 276**	**6 862**	**5 894**	**5 995**	**5 995**	**5 074**	**Amérique du Nord**
Canada[1 2]	803	747	692	809	986	...	...	...	...	...	Canada[1 2]
United States	7 884	6 747	6 206	6 493	6 290	5 927	4 916	4 975	4 932	3 969	Etats–Unis
Asia	**2 242**	**4 147**	**6 369**	**10 235**	**12 429**	**3 353**	**3 599**	**4 826**	**2 033**	**4 493**	**Asie**
Hong Kong	1 924	2 838	5 555	9 421	11 615	2 539	2 785	4 012	1 219	...	Hong–kong
Philippines[2 3]	318	1 309	...	...	...	...	...	...	...	...	Philippines[2 3]
Europe	**9 424**	**8 577**	**9 527**	**7 469**	**7 963**	**7 839**	**7 562**	**7 138**	**7 047**	**7 474**	**Europe**
EEC	***7 013***	***6 232***	***7 073***	***5 076***	***5 618***	***5 589***	***5 380***	***4 957***	***4 876***	***5 352***	***CEE***
Denmark	58	57	64	47	39	50	101	58	39	27	Danemark
France	3 157	3 001	4 081	2 297	...	...	...	...	...	...	France
Netherlands	730	450	490	390	200	150	...	...	...	...	Pays–Bas
United Kingdom[4]	3 068	2 724	2 438	2 342	2 245	2 255	1 953	1 639	1 642	2 041	Royaume–Uni[4]
EFTA	***388***	***354***	***367***	***424***	***378***	***261***	***202***	***192***	***210***	***160***	***AELE***
Finland	384	349	357	410	361	240	178	166	171	...	Finlande
Norway	4	5	...	...	...	...	...	26	39	30	Norvège
East Europe	***186***	***154***	***250***	***132***	***130***	***152***	***143***	***152***	***124***	***125***	***Europe de l'est***
Hungary[5]	186	154	250	132	130	152	143	152	124	125	Hongrie[5]
Other Europe	***1 837***	***1 837***	***1 837***	***1 837***	***1 837***	***1 837***	***1 837***	***1 837***	***1 837***	***1 837***	***Autre Europe***
Spain	1 837	...	...	...	...	...	...	...	...	...	Espagne
Oceania	**260**	**239**	**218**	**198**	**177**	**220**	**88**	**97**	**93**	**73**	**Océanie**
New Zealand	...	...	...	...	...	220	88	97	93	73	Nouvelle–Zélande
Total	**20 929**	**21 161**	**23 173**	**25 464**	**27 965**	**18 547**	**17 499**	**18 277**	**15 542**	**17 253**	**Total**

General note.
Women's and girls' raincoats of all types and materials, except rubber. (SITC 84112–4).

1 Excluding rubber and rubberized raincoats.
2 Shipments.
3 Including raincoats for men and boys.
4 Manufacturers' sales.
5 Excluding raincoats for work and for uniforms.

Remarque générale.
Imperméables de tous types et en toutes matières pour dames et fillettes, sauf en caoutchouc. (CTCI 84112–4).

1 Non compris les imperméables en caoutchouc ou enduits de caoutchouc.
2 Expéditions.
3 Y compris les imperméables pour hommes et garçonnets.
4 Ventes des fabricants.
5 Non compris les imperméables de travail et d'uniformes.

Skirts, slacks and shorts, women's and girls' – Jupes, pantalons et shorts pour dames et fillettes

Unit : Thousand units

Unité : En milliers

Country or area	1976	1977	1978	1979	1980	1981	1982	1983	1984	1985	Pays ou zone
Africa	**7 656**	**7 428**	**7 930**	**11 508**	**12 553**	**14 653**	**16 970**	**18 300**	**20 017**	**16 237**	**Afrique**
Kenya	90	107	107	138	...	168	511	80	124	28	Kenya
South Africa	6 703	6 638	6 677	10 452	11 161	13 115	* 15 023	* 16 670	* 18 229	14 431	Afrique du Sud
Tunisia	863	683	1 146	918	1 244	1 370	...	...	...	...	Tunisie
America, North	**381 589**	**384 578**	**351 606**	**452 858**	**474 714**	**428 907**	**442 297**	**470 567**	**517 151**	**514 108**	**Amérique du Nord**
Canada[1]	30 765	30 775	29 885	27 471	28 469	...	...	...	...	...	Canada[1]
Cuba	...	...	4 349	2 251	1 325	2 069	1 491	1 833	2 024	1 893	Cuba
El Salvador	8	6	15	14	11	8	67	74	...	...	El Salvador
Panama	724	504	729	564	...	556	555	457	...	...	Panama
United States	346 800	350 208	316 628	422 558	444 339	399 158	413 853	442 658	489 834	487 723	Etats-Unis
America, South	**15 057**	**4 964**	**5 478**	**5 041**	**7 619**	**7 852**	**7 657**	**7 352**	**7 614**	**7 611**	**Amérique du Sud**
Brazil[2]	13 596	# 3 500	4 023	[3] 3 589	...	...	...	...	...	...	Brésil[2]
Colombia	...	...	...	...	...	1 665	1 469	1 156	...	...	Colombie
Ecuador	...	34	...	...	* 12	10	11	19	...	...	Equateur
Asia	**110 020**	**103 834**	**105 578**	**127 726**	**154 228**	**130 626**	**147 638**	**146 612**	**152 028**	**155 387**	**Asie**
Hong Kong	75 566	69 629	71 836	86 735	111 113	84 358	99 288	96 857	105 732	...	Hong-kong
Indonesia	...	...	48	259	188	483	519	675	1 219	...	Indonésie
Japan[4]	34 406	34 168	33 694	40 732	42 927	45 785	47 831	49 080	45 077	44 298	Japon[4]
Europe	**252 843**	**235 264**	**241 902**	**346 294**	**279 490**	**272 757**	**271 476**	**267 192**	**267 721**	**274 879**	**Europe**
EEC	***229 535***	***212 944***	***218 836***	***323 177***	***253 454***	***246 862***	***245 090***	***240 792***	***240 097***	***248 087***	***CEE***
Belgium	7 179	7 261	6 849	7 197	7 218	6 929	6 487	6 595	7 112	8 296	Belgique
Denmark	5 303	5 119	5 188	6 352	7 510	...	...	...	...	...	Danemark
France[5]	33 055	27 838	26 120	126 191	...	...	...	...	...	...	France[5]
Germany, Fed. Rep.	68 059	60 129	64 510	68 931	72 192	69 141	65 271	64 808	64 739	68 047	Allemagne, Rép. féd.
Greece	...	...	...	...	8 665	9 524	10 878	11 232	9 931	...	Grèce
Ireland	1 025	1 685	1 883	2 320	2 294	2 410	1 945	1 711	2 318	2 407	Irlande
Italy[6]	58 300	54 500	...	...	...	...	...	...	...	...	Italie[6]
Netherlands[7]	9 690	7 200	7 010	6 820	7 260	6 660	6 500	3 220	2 710	2 440	Pays-Bas[7]
United Kingdom[8]	39 400	41 268	42 511	40 181	38 614	34 917	36 166	34 822	34 321	36 062	Royaume-Uni[8]
EFTA	***11 156***	***10 226***	***10 030***	***10 697***	***11 302***	***11 330***	***11 778***	***11 247***	***11 727***	***10 808***	***AELE***
Austria	2 037	2 176	2 489	2 464	2 700	2 693	2 595	2 541	2 444	2 642	Autriche
Finland	2 026	2 085	1 888	1 954	1 961	1 971	3 172	3 314	3 889	...	Finlande
Iceland	43	30	63	84	56	57	65	62	82	...	Islande
Norway	1 618	1 496	1 398	1 386	1 349	1 123	1 052	534	644	...	Norvège
Portugal[2]	1 576	1 446	1 856	2 299	2 757	3 097	2 794	2 654	2 722	2 316	Portugal[2]
Sweden	3 856	2 993	2 336	2 510	2 479	2 389	2 100	2 142	1 946	1 621	Suède
East Europe	***3 638***	***3 464***	***4 105***	***4 180***	***4 452***	***4 552***	***4 442***	***4 981***	***5 200***	***5 001***	***Europe de l'est***
Hungary[9]	3 638	3 464	4 105	4 180	4 452	4 552	4 442	4 981	5 200	5 001	Hongrie[9]
Other Europe	***8 514***	***8 630***	***8 932***	***8 240***	***10 282***	***10 013***	***10 166***	***10 172***	***10 697***	***10 983***	***Autre Europe***
Malta	29	21	44	67	33	43	178	90	138	...	Malte
Spain[4,10]	8 485	...	...	8 173	10 249	9 970	9 988	10 082	...	...	Espagne[4,10]
Oceania	**11 455**	**10 569**	**10 802**	**12 362**	**12 882**	**18 405**	**19 417**	**17 900**	**19 088**	**17 725**	**Océanie**
Australia	10 760	9 869	10 078	11 199	11 458	14 784	14 806	13 296	13 894	12 460	Australie
New Zealand[11]	695	700	724	1 163	1 424	# 3 621	4 611	4 604	5 194	5 265	Nouvelle-Zélande[11]
Total	**778 621**	**746 638**	**723 296**	**955 789**	**941 487**	**873 200**	**905 455**	**927 924**	**983 619**	**985 946**	**Total**

General note.
Women's and girls' skirts, slacks or shorts of all types, produced for sale as individual garments rather than as part of a combined costume, other than those made in knitting mills. (SITC 84112-5).

[1] Shipments.
[2] Skirts only.
[3] Production by establishments employing 5 or more persons.

Remarque générale.
Jupes, pantalons et shorts de tous types pour dames et fillettes, fabriqués pour être vendus séparément en non comme partie d'un costume deux-pièces. Cette rubrique ne comprend pas les jupes en bonneterie faites en usine. (CTCI 84112-5).

[1] Expéditions.
[2] Jupes seulement.
[3] Production des établissements occupant 5 personnes ou plus.

[4] Excluding children's wear.
[5] Beginning 1979, data are not comparable with those of previous years.
[6] Source: Industrial Statistics, Statistical Office of the European Communities, (Luxembourg).
[7] Excluding shorts and slacks.
[8] Manufacturers' sales.
[9] Excluding skirts, slacks and shorts for work and for uniforms.
[10] Including household production.
[11] Beginning 1981, data are not comparable with those for earlier years.

[4] Non compris les vêtements d'enfants.
[5] A partir de 1979, les données ne sont pas comparables à celles des années antérieures.
[6] Source: Statistiques industrielles, Office statistique des Communautés européennes, (Luxembourg).
[7] Non compris les shorts et pantalons tout–aller.
[8] Ventes des fabricants.
[9] Non compris les jupes, shorts et pantalons de travail ou d'uniformes.
[10] Y compris la production ménagère.
[11] A partir de 1981, les données ne sont pas comparables à celles des années antérieures.

Suits, women's and girls' – Costumes pour dames et fillettes

Unit : Thousand units

Unité : En milliers

Country or area	1976	1977	1978	1979	1980	1981	1982	1983	1984	1985	Pays ou zone
Africa	**1 411**	**1 784**	**2 065**	**4 513**	**5 726**	**4 536**	**3 858**	**3 158**	**2 447**	**1 983**	**Afrique**
South Africa	1 411	1 784	2 065	4 513	5 726	4 536	3 858	3 158	* 2 447	1 983	Afrique du Sud
America, North	**46 745**	**47 966**	**42 128**	**33 577**	**26 342**	**27 440**	**19 465**	**17 836**	**15 609**	**15 153**	**Amérique du Nord**
Canada[1]	3 599	3 551	3 404	2 838	2 609	...	...	...	...	...	Canada[1]
El Salvador	...	...	433	233	254	667	243	158	...	...	El Salvador
Panama	239	400	442	530	...	685	1 133	861	...	...	Panama
United States[2]	42 456	43 591	37 849	29 976	22 806	...	15 960	14 956	12 681	12 414	Etats–Unis[2]
America, South	**38**	**20**	**19**	**19**	**21**	**18**	**11**	**4**	**17**	**17**	**Amérique du Sud**
Bolivia	4	3	2	2	1	1	1	* 1	...	...	Bolivie
Ecuador	34	...	...	...	* 20	...	* 10	3	...	...	Equateur
Asia	**9 641**	**6 350**	**3 841**	**5 557**	**4 953**	**4 114**	**5 222**	**6 797**	**6 286**	**4 885**	**Asie**
Hong Kong	9 616	6 326	3 813	5 524	4 919	4 077	4 979	6 529	5 590	...	Hong–kong
Turkey	25	24	28	33	* 34	* 37	# 243	268	696	394	Turquie
Europe	**17 064**	**14 465**	**15 892**	**16 831**	**15 644**	**16 169**	**15 326**	**14 324**	**15 040**	**16 002**	**Europe**
EEC	***14 394***	***11 908***	***13 351***	***14 225***	***12 612***	***12 355***	***11 748***	***11 043***	***11 095***	***11 924***	***CEE***
Belgium	206	185	186	184	218	126	160	232	409	326	Belgique
Denmark	380	212	194	219	301	306	272	230	236	243	Danemark
France[3]	1 981	1 937	2 668	3 320	...	...	...	...	...	...	France[3]
Germany, Fed. Rep.	3 389	3 721	3 619	3 357	3 361	3 391	2 697	2 448	2 414	2 409	Allemagne, Rép. féd.
Greece	...	...	...	...	296	376	543	453	430	...	Grèce
Ireland	192	118	130	230	122	112	87	81	63	118	Irlande
Italy[4]	5 100	3 500	...	...	...	...	...	...	...	...	Italie[4]
Netherlands	1 200	870	1 040	1 060	770	530	590	300	210	220	Pays–Bas
United Kingdom[5]	1 732	1 116	931	1 238	767	737	622	522	556	1 309	Royaume–Uni[5]
EFTA	***989***	***911***	***819***	***922***	***901***	***915***	***828***	***752***	***732***	***729***	***AELE***
Austria	268	293	286	370	373	359	327	338	314	324	Autriche
Finland	302	319	279	332	311	331	223	174	141	...	Finlande
Iceland	3	3	1	1	1	0	0	1	0	...	Islande
Norway	352	244	207	183	192	205	249	224	254	...	Norvège
Sweden	64	52	46	36	24	20	29	15	23	31	Suède
East Europe	***238***	***257***	***290***	***234***	***358***	***538***	***879***	***707***	***618***	***524***	***Europe de l'est***
Hungary[6]	238	257	290	234	358	538	879	707	618	524	Hongrie[6]
Other Europe	***1 443***	***1 390***	***1 432***	***1 450***	***1 773***	***2 361***	***1 871***	***1 822***	***2 596***	***2 825***	***Autre Europe***
Spain[7 8]	946	...	...	673	1 040	1 331	885	1 008	...	...	Espagne[7 8]
Yugoslavia	497	480	500	777	733	1 030	986	814	1 530	1 737	Yougoslavie
Oceania	**3 629**	**3 360**	**2 660**	**2 610**	**1 955**	**2 219**	**1 703**	**1 328**	**762**	**549**	**Océanie**
Australia	3 238	2 997	2 325	2 303	1 676	1 893	1 464	1 143	615	...	Australie
New Zealand	...	...	...	...	...	326	239	185	147	103	Nouvelle–Zélande
Total	**78 529**	**73 946**	**66 605**	**63 107**	**54 641**	**54 495**	**45 584**	**43 446**	**40 161**	**38 589**	**Total**

General note.
Women's and girls' suits of all types, consisting essentially of a jacket and skirt or a jacket and a pair of trousers (usually matching), including skiing, riding, hunting and other sports suits. Knitted suits made in knitting mills are excluded. (SITC 84112–6).

Remarque générale.
Costumes de tous types pour dames et fillettes, comprenant essentiellement une jaquette et une jupe ou une jaquette et un pantalon (habituellement du même tissu), y compris les costumes de ski, d'équitation, de chasse et autres costumes pour le sport. Cette rubrique ne comprend pas les costumes en bonneterie faits en usine. (CTCI 84112–6).

[1] Shipments.
[2] Including pants suits.
[3] Dresses for beach and street, and ensemble dresses.
[4] Source: Industrial Statistics, Statistical Office of the European Communities, (Luxembourg).
[5] Manufacturers' sales.
[6] Excluding work suits and uniforms.
[7] Excluding children's wear.
[8] Including household production.

[1] Expéditions.
[2] Y compris les ensembles pantalon.
[3] Robes de ville, de plage et ensembles.
[4] Source: Statistiques industrielles, Office statistique des Communautés européennes, (Luxembourg).
[5] Ventes des fabricants.
[6] Non compris les vêtements de travail et les uniformes.
[7] Non compris les vêtements d'enfants.
[8] Y compris la production ménagère.

Shirts, men's and boys' – Chemises d'hommes et de garçonnets

Unit : Thousand units — Unité : En milliers

Country or area	1976	1977	1978	1979	1980	1981	1982	1983	1984	1985	Pays ou zone
Africa	**41 212**	**37 406**	**37 532**	**37 901**	**46 194**	**42 783**	**38 877**	**35 608**	**37 454**	**34 025**	**Afrique**
Algeria	3 094	3 202	3 146	2 949	3 221	3 540	2 140	* 2 100	...	...	Algérie
Kenya	2 475	3 515	3 632	3 000	2 628	2 964	3 000	3 074	2 963	1 177	Kenya
Malawi	421	583	567	552	834	866	1 001	1 068	620	632	Malawi
Senegal	63	65	56	58	60	* 30	12	* 15	...	...	Sénégal
South Africa	32 189	27 636	27 677	29 085	* 35 516	33 387	30 102	26 743	* 28 923	27 419	Afrique du Sud
Tunisia	2 970	2 405	2 454	2 257	3 935	1 996	...	...	...	...	Tunisie
America, North	**345 758**	**349 482**	**301 593**	**303 952**	**281 199**	**257 476**	**236 863**	**219 082**	**177 857**	**177 256**	**Amérique du Nord**
Canada[1 2]	24 062	21 085	20 386	18 572	18 654	...	...	...	...	...	Canada[1 2]
Cuba[3]	16 036	16 026	16 604	16 880	15 622	16 545	16 377	15 725	14 744	15 250	Cuba[3]
Dominican Republic	1 111	743	751	773	829	675	732	890	1 162	...	Rép. dominicaine
El Salvador	1 445	1 456	1 631	896	916	1 055	523	540	...	...	El Salvador
Panama	2 024	1 772	2 037	1 847	...	1 911	1 795	1 645	...	...	Panama
United States	301 080	308 400	260 184	264 984	243 336	220 716	202 188	186 360	147 276	147 948	Etats–Unis
America, South	**98 477**	**44 177**	**76 001**	**34 122**	**72 150**	**42 923**	**37 981**	**31 014**	**24 038**	**17 279**	**Amérique du Sud**
Bolivia	341	387	363	274	291	259	187	133	88	...	Bolivie
Brazil	86 338	32 422	65 241	[4] 22 835	60 604	...	...	...	...	...	Brésil
Chile	1 509	1 804	1 792	3 510	...	...	...	...	...	...	Chili
Colombia	9 997	9 111	8 018	6 896	7 319	5 209	5 557	5 320	...	...	Colombie
Ecuador	292	453	...	...	1 783	36	892	289	...	...	Equateur
Asia	**315 502**	**309 843**	**307 069**	**263 664**	**283 367**	**261 399**	**232 596**	**226 754**	**279 750**	**254 217**	**Asie**
Burma[5 6]	680	748	629	...	...	987	983	782	598	303	Birmanie[5 6]
Hong Kong	159 363	168 900	157 874	189 315	201 216	174 366	150 190	148 562	189 790	...	Hong–kong
Indonesia	...	...	2 265	2 544	5 717	8 154	8 988	8 958	13 620	...	Indonésie
Japan[7]	94 694	86 948	90 073	# 8 197	9 518	8 324	7 330	6 956	5 563	6 025	Japon[7]
Malaysia[8 9]	16 819	14 574	17 880	20 117	23 962	25 388	# 22 354	19 018	24 235	21 381	Malaisie[8 9]
Philippines[1]	21 387	10 092	...	...	...	...	...	...	...	...	Philippines[1]
Singapore	16 140	20 916	20 364	21 048	20 316	19 560	20 232	20 880	21 204	16 788	Singapour
Sri Lanka	...	...	2 149	3 993	5 299	7 921	...	...	...	...	Sri Lanka
Turkey	354	519	95	1 968	874	959	1 939	1 018	4 160	4 592	Turquie
Europe	**240 081**	**242 479**	**242 002**	**235 153**	**241 528**	**213 519**	**206 825**	**208 994**	**209 926**	**219 044**	**Europe**
EEC	***153 922***	***151 227***	***149 715***	***144 489***	***132 474***	***116 162***	***113 677***	***116 688***	***116 231***	***123 263***	*CEE*
Belgium	9 704	8 512	7 163	5 590	4 128	3 481	3 593	3 864	4 174	4 656	Belgique
Denmark	916	903	891	1 023	830	697	800	853	882	1 115	Danemark
France	36 060	36 793	37 139	35 518	* 32 375	27 994	28 969	30 717	27 708	32 351	France
Germany, Fed. Rep.	30 249	27 773	26 959	26 104	22 459	17 095	13 541	13 691	13 052	12 512	Allemagne, Rép. féd.
Ireland	2 344	2 536	3 047	3 158	3 009	2 814	3 732	3 855	4 401	4 481	Irlande
Italy[10]	35 000	35 000	...	...	...	...	...	...	...	...	Italie[10]
Netherlands	4 580	3 740	2 950	2 220	2 500	1 290	1 220	1 190	1 330	...	Pays–Bas
United Kingdom[11 12]	35 069	35 970	36 566	35 876	32 173	27 791	26 822	27 518	29 684	32 899	Royaume–Uni[11 12]
EFTA	***22 914***	***23 581***	***24 394***	***23 827***	***26 153***	***22 245***	***22 957***	***24 532***	***24 246***	***22 767***	*AELE*
Austria	4 509	4 569	4 377	4 104	4 477	4 208	4 294	4 621	4 750	4 493	Autriche
Finland	2 100	2 599	2 414	2 328	2 231	2 125	1 293	762	1 546	...	Finlande
Iceland	21	16	18	10	9	6	3	3	1	...	Islande
Norway[13]	737	739	852	816	975	937	940	734	764	810	Norvège[13]
Portugal	11 852	13 131	14 776	14 886	16 558	13 583	15 088	17 085	16 022	15 199	Portugal
Sweden[14]	3 695	2 527	1 957	1 683	1 903	1 386	1 339	1 327	1 163	1 179	Suède[14]
East Europe	***26 025***	***24 478***	***22 570***	***21 170***	***20 714***	***17 227***	***15 413***	***14 680***	***14 385***	***13 994***	*Europe de l'est*
German Dem. Rep.	14 993	14 236	13 507	13 153	12 326	10 856	10 574	9 954	9 968	9 863	Rép. dém. allemande
Hungary	11 032	10 242	9 063	8 017	8 388	6 371	4 839	4 726	4 417	4 131	Hongrie
Other Europe	***37 220***	***43 193***	***45 323***	***45 667***	***62 187***	***57 885***	***54 778***	***53 094***	***55 064***	***59 020***	*Autre Europe*
Malta	535	649	561	753	310	290	307	206	379	...	Malte
Spain	20 799	...	...	23 420	28 394	24 301	20 002	21 125	...	...	Espagne
Yugoslavia	15 886	19 338	21 619	21 494	33 483	33 294	34 469	31 763	31 920	36 118	Yougoslavie
Oceania	**40 550**	**35 562**	**38 683**	**39 086**	**43 816**	**48 471**	**48 889**	**48 091**	**23 101**	**24 413**	**Océanie**
Australia[15]	34 176	30 593	33 932	34 068	38 992	42 434	42 000	41 860	16 402	17 418	Australie[15]

For general note and footnotes, see end of table.

Voir la fin du tableau pour la remarque générale et les notes.

Shirts, men's and boys' (continued) – Chemises d'hommes et de garçonnets (suite)

Unit : Thousand units

Unité : En milliers

Country or area	1976	1977	1978	1979	1980	1981	1982	1983	1984	1985	Pays ou zone
New Zealand...............	6 374	4 969	4 751	5 018	4 824	6 037	6 889	6 231	6 699	6 995	Nouvelle–Zélande
Total............................	**1 081 580**	**1 018 949**	**1 002 880**	**913 878**	**968 254**	**866 570**	**802 031**	**769 543**	**752 126**	**726 235**	**Total**

General note.
Men's and boys' shirts of all types, with full length or short sleeves, designed to be worn with or without a tie, such as shirts for street wear, dress shirts, work shirts and sports shirts. Knitted sports shirts made in knitting mills are excluded. (SITC 84113–1).

1 Shipments.
2 Excluding tailored sports shirts and knitted dress shirts.
3 Excluding pyjamas.
4 Production by establishments employing 5 or more persons.
5 Government production only.
6 Twelve months ending 30 September of year stated.
7 Beginning 1979, data are not comparable with those of previous years.
8 Data refer to Peninsular Malaysia only.
9 Beginning 1982, scope of series revised.
10 Source: Industrial Statistics, Statistical Office of the European Communities, (Luxembourg).
11 Excluding those manufactured in hosiery industry.
12 Manufacturers' sales.
13 Excluding knitted sports shirts.
14 Including knitted or crocheted shirts.
15 Twelve months ending 30 June of year stated.

Remarque générale.
Chemises de tous types, pour hommes et garçonnets, à manches longues ou courtes, conçues pour être portées avec ou sans cravate, telles que les chemises de ville, les chemises habillées, les chemises de travail et les chemises de sport, à l'exclusion des chemisettes en bonneterie faites en usine. (CTCI 84113–1).

1 Expéditions.
2 Non compris les chemises de coupe sport et les chemises habillées en tricot.
3 Non compris les pyjamas.
4 Production des établissements occupant 5 personnes ou plus.
5 Production de l'Etat seulement.
6 Période de douze mois finissant le 30 septembre de l'année indiquée.
7 A partir de 1979, les données ne sont pas comparables à celles des années antérieures.
8 Données se rapportant à la Malaisie péninsulaire seulement.
9 A partir de 1982, portée de la série révisée.
10 Source: Statistiques industrielles, Office statistique des Communautés européennes, (Luxembourg).
11 Non compris les articles fabriqués par l'industrie de la bonneterie.
12 Ventes des fabricants.
13 Non compris les chemisettes en bonneterie.
14 Y compris les chemises en bonneterie.
15 Période de douze mois finissant le 30 juin de l'année indiquée.

Underwear, men's and boys' – Sous–vétements pour hommes et garçonnets

Unit : Thousand units — Unité : En milliers

Country or area	1976	1977	1978	1979	1980	1981	1982	1983	1984	1985	Pays ou zone
Africa	**17 901**	**17 009**	**18 037**	**15 618**	**17 654**	**21 627**	**19 383**	**16 246**	**18 013**	**18 216**	**Afrique**
Cameroon	...	...	...	179	* 175	* 170	* 165	...	...	...	Cameroun
Kenya[1]	2 832	2 408	4 381	3 672	3 732	3 708	3 720	3 720	3 059	...	Kenya[1]
South Africa	14 897	14 429	13 484	11 767	13 747	17 749	15 498	12 354	* 14 782	14 277	Afrique du Sud
America, North	**906 770**	**861 490**	**868 548**	**877 320**	**780 744**	**767 358**	**777 027**	**790 894**	**854 023**	**836 473**	**Amérique du Nord**
Canada	11 427	9 401	# [2] 588	[2] 540	[2] 645	...	...	...	...	...	Canada
Cuba	11 508	7 358	10 454	11 551	9 629	13 666	13 684	13 795	13 360	14 264	Cuba
Dominican Republic	2 571	2 649	3 514	5 621	4 688	4 523	4 474	5 738	...	...	Rép. dominicaine
Panama	2 660	2 334	2 328	3 192	...	3 292	4 802	4 621	...	...	Panama
United States[3]	878 604	839 748	851 664	856 416	762 264	744 180	753 492	766 200	829 200	810 000	Etats–Unis[3]
America, South	**27 809**	**31 232**	**47 329**	**45 069**	**55 920**	**62 588**	**70 439**	**76 327**	**83 868**	**90 858**	**Amérique du Sud**
Bolivia	33	58	298	60	19	11	14	23	93	...	Bolivie
Brazil	25 055	27 188	43 771	[4] 41 733	53 161	...	...	...	...	...	Brésil
Colombia	...	...	...	...	...	1 546	2 736	1 584	...	...	Colombie
Ecuador	766	2 031	...	...	785	1 732	1 351	1 343	...	...	Equateur
Asia	**264 789**	**269 502**	**253 751**	**206 671**	**185 663**	**270 236**	**205 439**	**167 415**	**199 475**	**233 066**	**Asie**
Burma	370	230	159	...	...	223	95	327	266	449	Birmanie
Hong Kong	105 553	107 939	75 944	140 179	111 903	192 532	123 305	102 801	118 527	...	Hong–kong
Indonesia	2 546	...	[1] 15 158	7 008	[1] 17 669	[1] 18 918	[1] 29 583	[1] 15 792	[1] 27 397	...	Indonésie
Japan[1]	131 963	131 400	137 415	[5] 29 994	[5] 28 096	[5] 27 126	[5] 20 970	[5] 21 190	[5] 23 208	[5] 20 959	Japon[1]
Malaysia	5 282	5 373	5 425	6 335	6 119	7 055	6 198	5 029	...	...	Malaisie
Philippines[6]	5 437	4 207	...	...	...	...	...	...	...	...	Philippines[6]
Sri Lanka	...	...	212	202	79	300	...	...	...	...	Sri Lanka
Syrian Arab Republic	13 440	12 684	14 616	17 880	16 716	19 260	20 268	17 256	18 828	35 688	Rép. arabe syrienne
Europe	**51 125**	**51 743**	**51 003**	**49 815**	**50 467**	**53 285**	**54 914**	**51 300**	**56 561**	**73 487**	**Europe**
EEC	***37 560***	***36 905***	***33 798***	***30 071***	***28 807***	***29 353***	***28 606***	***23 615***	***26 168***	***40 943***	***CEE***
Belgium[7]	7 542	7 035	6 720	4 103	4 617	4 512	3 717	3 773	3 429	2 000	Belgique[7]
Denmark*	1 176	981	975	1 120	897	...	...	...	...	...	Danemark*
France	12 005	10 878	6 598	7 688	7 814	7 397	7 289	5 530	7 291	7 799	France
Germany, Fed. Rep.	7 686	...	7 780	7 675	5 424	6 712	6 544	5 176	5 335	4 362	Allemagne, Rép. féd.
Netherlands	370	210	...	...	...	...	...	...	...	...	Pays–Bas
United Kingdom	8 781	10 040	11 435	9 195	9 765	9 537	9 903	8 025	9 043	25 754	Royaume–Uni
EFTA	***238***	***302***	***218***	***283***	***273***	***239***	***201***	***239***	***172***	***182***	***AELE***
Austria	26	38	22	14	45	24	20	10	10	4	Autriche
Finland	142	141	114	75	96	101	73	60	30	...	Finlande
Iceland[1]	35	32	29	31	26	24	43	52	42	...	Islande[1]
Sweden	35	91	53	163	106	90	65	117	90	104	Suède
East Europe	***3 994***	***2 778***	***2 868***	***2 489***	***2 989***	***2 778***	***2 162***	***1 601***	***1 936***	***1 715***	***Europe de l'est***
Hungary	3 994	2 778	2 868	2 489	2 989	2 778	2 162	1 601	1 936	1 715	Hongrie
Other Europe	***9 333***	***11 758***	***14 119***	***16 972***	***18 398***	***20 915***	***23 945***	***25 845***	***28 286***	***30 647***	***Autre Europe***
Spain[8 9]	9 333	...	...	16 972	18 398	20 915	23 945	25 845	...	...	Espagne[8 9]
Oceania	**31 447**	**35 076**	**32 946**	**30 252**	**33 588**	**35 784**	**35 445**	**34 480**	**38 448**	**39 432**	**Océanie**
Australia[7]	25 596	29 089	28 207	24 936	29 205	31 328	30 576	29 966	32 656	34 245	Australie[7]
New Zealand	5 851	5 987	4 739	5 316	4 383	4 456	4 869	4 514	5 792	5 187	Nouvelle–Zélande
Total	**1 299 842**	**1 266 052**	**1 271 614**	**1 224 745**	**1 124 036**	**1 210 878**	**1 162 647**	**1 136 663**	**1 250 388**	**1 291 532**	**Total**

General note.
Underwear made from woven or knitted fabrics other than knitted garments made in knitting mills. Elastic or rubberized garments are excluded. (Parts of SITC 84113 and 84143).

[1] Including underwear for women and girls.
[2] Excluding knitted underwear.
[3] Including knitted undergarments except body supporting garments.

Remarque générale.
Sous–vêtements faits d'étoffe tissée ou tricotée, autres que les articles de bonneterie faits en usine. Cette rubrique ne comprend pas les articles élastiques ou caoutchoutés. (Parties de CTCI 84113 et 84143).

[1] Y compris les sous–vêtements pour dames et fillettes.
[2] Non compris les sous–vêtements en bonneterie.
[3] Y compris les sous–vêtements en bonneterie autres que les sous–vêtements élastiques ou caoutchoutés.

[4] Production by establishments employing 5 or more persons.
[5] Excluding underwear for boys.
[6] Shipments.
[7] Including knitted undergarments.
[8] Underwear for men only.
[9] Including household production.

[4] Production des établissements occupant 5 personnes ou plus.
[5] Non compris les sous–vêtements pour garçonnets.
[6] Expéditions.
[7] Y compris les sous–vêtements en bonneterie.
[8] Sous–vêtements pour hommes seulement.
[9] Y compris la production ménagère.

Underwear, women's and girls' – Sous-vêtements de dames et de fillettes

Unit : Thousand units | Unité : En milliers

Country or area	1976	1977	1978	1979	1980	1981	1982	1983	1984	1985	Pays ou zone
Africa	**38 614**	**33 339**	**31 363**	**33 737**	**35 796**	**41 473**	**39 116**	**37 923**	**40 115**	**40 108**	**Afrique**
Kenya	...	4 163	1 004	...	1 815	2 149	2 169	714	1 247	514	Kenya
South Africa	35 423	29 176	30 359	31 386	33 981	* 39 324	36 947	37 209	* 38 868	39 594	Afrique du Sud
America, North	**896 348**	**887 893**	**836 764**	**840 010**	**865 643**	**812 071**	**817 164**	**835 292**	**797 006**	**775 611**	**Amérique du Nord**
Canada	43 062	43 726	31 328	25 564	25 333	...	...	...	...	...	Canada
Cuba	...	...	27 317	28 769	28 660	26 374	27 576	26 851	29 676	30 279	Cuba
Dominican Republic	6 119	4 949	5 471	6 158	8 975	6 851	7 082	8 780	10 740	...	Rép. dominicaine
Panama	5 161	4 234	5 164	4 979	...	7 041	4 937	4 699	...	...	Panama
United States[1]	815 196	807 924	767 484	774 540	797 460	743 748	751 704	771 288	729 600	710 400	Etats-Unis[1]
America, South	**482 263**	**141 981**	**159 167**	**137 301**	**210 585**	**166 482**	**144 672**	**126 095**	**100 105**	**77 679**	**Amérique du Sud**
Bolivia	78	5	13	3	10	7	* 8	* 7	...	...	Bolivie
Brazil	468 248	129 020	152 190	129 254	202 256	...	...	...	...	...	Brésil
Colombia	13 764	12 806	6 837	7 375	8 062	8 345	7 269	10 328	...	...	Colombie
Ecuador	173	* 150	127	...	257	599	2 067	2 636	...	...	Equateur
Asia	**247 938**	**246 518**	**237 594**	**292 367**	**316 517**	**215 810**	**287 616**	**294 366**	**372 549**	**331 911**	**Asie**
Hong Kong	155 728	155 885	152 389	206 187	236 070	139 573	217 294	227 401	298 208	...	Hong-kong
Indonesia	...	...	7 023	9 363	...	...	...	...	...	...	Indonésie
Japan	...	...	...	63 896	59 119	53 323	51 263	45 383	48 597	42 951	Japon
Philippines[2]	2 929	4 601	...	...	...	...	...	...	...	...	Philippines[2]
Sri Lanka	...	...	422	353	567	2 153	* 600	...	...	...	Sri Lanka
Turkey	...	...	...	...	...	...	6 501	8 882	13 014	6 813	Turquie
Europe	**208 525**	**202 379**	**202 046**	**198 159**	**207 269**	**196 401**	**209 765**	**186 692**	**199 831**	**234 056**	**Europe**
EEC	***160 865***	***151 291***	***151 208***	***147 065***	***138 358***	***129 995***	***131 813***	***123 008***	***125 553***	***151 097***	***CEE***
Belgium[3]	12 522	11 568	7 827	6 953	4 714	3 913	3 857	3 153	2 618	3 065	Belgique[3]
Denmark*	554	353	408	500	513	...	...	...	...	...	Danemark*
France[4]	45 365	45 326	47 765	47 450	...	44 129	42 897	38 502	36 575	32 203	France[4]
Germany, Fed. Rep.	41 326	32 912	29 168	30 445	27 505	22 987	27 895	22 978	22 713	24 123	Allemagne, Rép. féd.
Netherlands[5]	16 570	15 460	13 330	11 970	11 330	10 140	8 660	7 850	5 850	6 410	Pays-Bas[5]
United Kingdom	44 528	45 672	52 710	49 747	51 247	48 341	48 013	50 027	57 293	84 785	Royaume-Uni
EFTA	***7 140***	***8 005***	***7 031***	***12 148***	***14 891***	***18 960***	***24 087***	***24 749***	***25 308***	***32 078***	***AELE***
Austria	4 385	4 287	3 563	6 696	8 564	12 403	15 538	17 199	16 753	20 515	Autriche
Finland	782	808	349	381	436	503	719	729	317	...	Finlande
Norway	...	...	180	269	206	192	257	211	...	...	Norvège
Portugal[5]	1 226	2 329	2 662	4 356	5 250	5 471	7 158	6 197	7 642	10 447	Portugal[5]
Sweden	541	372	277	446	435	391	415	413	366	428	Suède
East Europe	***6 091***	***5 507***	***4 912***	***4 399***	***3 643***	***3 190***	***3 577***	***2 320***	***2 163***	***2 755***	***Europe de l'est***
Hungary	6 091	5 507	4 912	4 399	3 643	3 190	3 577	2 320	2 163	2 755	Hongrie
Other Europe	***34 429***	***37 576***	***38 895***	***34 547***	***50 377***	***44 256***	***50 288***	***36 615***	***46 807***	***48 126***	***Autre Europe***
Spain[6 7]	34 429	...	...	34 547	50 377	44 256	50 288	36 615	...	...	Espagne[6 7]
Oceania	**51 735**	**61 592**	**54 591**	**54 837**	**63 174**	**64 851**	**65 591**	**57 851**	**60 599**	**64 021**	**Océanie**
Australia[3]	43 764	54 329	47 962	48 180	55 993	57 568	57 528	50 300	52 406	54 633	Australie[3]
New Zealand	7 971	7 263	6 629	6 657	7 181	7 283	8 063	7 551	8 193	9 388	Nouvelle-Zélande
Total	**1 925 422**	**1 573 702**	**1 521 524**	**1 556 411**	**1 698 984**	**1 497 088**	**1 563 924**	**1 538 219**	**1 570 205**	**1 523 385**	**Total**

General note.
Underwear made from woven or knitted fabrics, other than knitted garments made in knitting mills. Elastic or rubberized garments are excluded. (Parts of SITC 84114 and 84143).

[1] Including knitted undergarments except body supporting garments.
[2] Shipments.
[3] Including knitted undergarments.
[4] Ready-to-wear articles made from fabrics.
[5] Including underwear for men and boys.
[6] Underwear for women only.
[7] Including household production.

Remarque générale.
Sous-vêtements faits d'étoffe tissée ou tricotée, autres que la bonneterie. Cette rubrique ne comprend pas les sous-vêtements élastiques ou caoutchoutés. (Parties de CTCI 84114 et 84143).

[1] Y compris les sous-vêtements en bonneterie autres que les sous-vêtements élastiques ou caoutchoutés.
[2] Expéditions.
[3] Y compris les sous-vêtements en bonneterie.
[4] Articles de confection en tissus.
[5] Y compris les sous-vêtements pour hommes et garçonnets.
[6] Sous-vêtements pour dames seulement.
[7] Y compris la production ménagère.

Heavy leather – Cuirs forts

Unit : Metric tons

Unité : Tonnes métriques

Country or area	1976	1977	1978	1979	1980	1981	1982	1983	1984	1985	Pays ou zone
Africa											**Afrique**
Algeria	854	775	678	580	763	855	849	* 850	...	...	Algérie
Ethiopia[1]	251	216	201	289	880	322	318	* 300	...	...	Ethiopie[1]
South Africa[2]	1 574	1 333	1 438	1 387	1 178	* 1 264	3 165	2 967	2 602	2 720	Afrique du Sud[2]
Sudan	36	105	112	...	...	...	...	...	...	...	Soudan
Tunisia	226	269	216	199	212	347	* 340	* 340	...	...	Tunisie
America, North											**Amérique du Nord**
Canada[3 4]	2 760	2 845	3 371	3 731	...	...	...	...	...	...	Canada[3 4]
Cuba	2 138	1 482	1 908	1 927	1 712	1 764	1 336	1 007	1 196	1 376	Cuba
Dominican Republic	387	307	355	382	455	527	441	458	429	...	Rép. dominicaine
El Salvador	...	64	256	52	55	76	86	99	* 100	* 98	El Salvador
Mexico[5]	5 364	6 025	...	...	...	...	...	...	...	...	Mexique[5]
Panama	143	128	85	92	...	69	122	49	...	...	Panama
United States	52 800	50 394	48 271	39 950	36 795	...	...	24 200	23 310	...	Etats–Unis
America, South											**Amérique du Sud**
Brazil	177 355	196 339	233 228	223 323	223 760	...	...	...	...	...	Brésil
Paraguay	13 283	14 667	13 787	9 444	8 972	9 519	9 527	11 036	8 260	7 785	Paraguay
Asia											**Asie**
Indonesia	16 705	9 724	9 946	15 569	10 616	16 558	12 419	* 13 000	13 217	...	Indonésie
Iran(Islamic Rep.of)[6]	1 180	922	672	884	571	931	727	1 120	...	...	Iran(Rép.islamique)[6]
Japan[6]	4 776	4 853	4 656	4 269	3 818	3 600	3 480	2 876	2 207	1 810	Japon[6]
Jordan[2]	92	75	147	47	66	106	33	40	27	18	Jordanie[2]
Mongolia	1 138	1 165	836	161	1 400	1 202	1 036	898	884	848	Mongolie
Philippines[4]	488	80	...	...	...	...	...	...	...	...	Philippines[4]
Sri Lanka	...	92	121	101	91	* 100	* 103	71	48	88	Sri Lanka
Turkey	[7] 3 125	[7] 3 235	[7] 3 194	[7] 3 586	# 666	295	846	788	1 405	* 1 000	Turquie
Europe											**Europe**
EEC											***CEE***
Belgium	2 014	1 956	1 570	1 563	1 643	1 640	1 492	1 374	1 585	1 548	Belgique
Denmark	62	74	83	40	25	28	26	21	18	17	Danemark
France	30 598	30 196	27 940	25 310	# 23 237	22 690	22 329	20 620	16 724	15 228	France
Germany, Fed. Rep.	4 307	4 427	5 460	5 745	4 859	3 777	4 138	4 210	3 729	3 854	Allemagne, Rép. féd.
Greece	1 933	2 151	2 463	2 762	2 270	2 302	2 346	2 229	2 358	...	Grèce
Italy* [7]	53 000	41 810	42 900	48 700	45 000	43 000	...	...	...	...	Italie* [7]
Netherlands[8]	800	650	440	371	378	263	16	0	2	6	Pays–Bas[8]
United Kingdom	8 260	7 671	7 275	5 865	5 744	5 407	4 685	5 436	4 359	3 442	Royaume–Uni
EFTA											***AELE***
Austria	347	340	312	324	296	251	208	232	227	15	Autriche
Finland	111	132	121	132	126	127	131	135	137	...	Finlande
Norway* [7]	425	510	375	...	...	...	...	...	...	...	Norvège* [7]
Portugal	* 1 490	* 2 010	* 2 281	1 873	2 054	1 940	2 623	3 213	2 536	1 577	Portugal
East Europe											***Europe de l'est***
Bulgaria	1 968	1 911	1 956	1 804	1 608	1 441	1 430	1 513	1 612	1 413	Bulgarie
Czechoslovakia	6 943	6 913	6 913	6 873	6 215	5 699	5 784	4 899	3 869	3 723	Tchécoslovaquie
German Dem. Rep.	2 853	2 684	2 497	2 447	2 281	2 168	1 913	1 941	1 868	1 945	Rép. dém. allemande
Hungary	2 726	2 837	2 734	1 793	1 607	1 361	1 502	1 432	1 247	973	Hongrie
Poland	9 952	9 612	9 593	9 337	9 168	7 133	6 229	7 150	6 938	5 804	Pologne
Other Europe											***Autre Europe***
Spain[7]	25 845	* 25 200	* 24 533	* 23 886	* 29 200	...	...	...	...	...	Espagne[7]
Yugoslavia	3 828	3 935	4 338	4 667	3 369	3 410	2 961	3 306	3 465	3 879	Yougoslavie
USSR											***URSS***
Byelorussian SSR	*7 084*	*7 156*	*6 759*	*6 788*	*6 702*	*5 769*	*5 543*	*5 557*	*5 701*	*5 704*	*RSS de Biélorussie*
Ukrainian SSR	*29 707*	*29 401*	*29 302*	*27 577*	*26 968*	*25 915*	*25 041*	*25 182*	*24 832*	*25 066*	*RSS d'Ukraine*
Oceania											**Océanie**

For general note and footnotes, see end of table.

Voir la fin du tableau pour la remarque générale et les notes.

General note.
Hides and skins, tanned (including chamois–dressed), parchment dressed or otherwise prepared as leather, undressed or dressed, but excluding those tanned or dressed with the hair on. Reconstituted and artificial leather are excluded. The heavy and light leather together correspond to SITC 6113, 6114 and 6119. The headings include, inter alia, sole leather (in heavy leather), upper and lining leather, leather for hand–bags (in light leather). (SITC 61130–1A+).

[1] Twelve months ending 10 September of year stated.
[2] Sole leather only.
[3] Including belting and harness leather.
[4] Shipments.
[5] Hides and skins of all types.
[6] Production by establishments employing 10 or more persons.
[7] Source: Organisation for Economic Co–operation and Development (OECD), (Paris).
[8] Industrial sales.

Remarque générale.
Peaux tannées, chamoisées, corroyées ou autrement préparées (parcheminées, vernies etc.), à l'exception de celles revêtues de leurs poils. Les cuirs artificiels ou reconstitués ne sont pas compris dans cette rubrique. L'ensemble des deux rubriques représente les positions 6113, 6114 et 6119 de la CTCI. Elles comprennent notamment le cuir pour semelles (cuir fort), les cuirs pour empeignes et doublures, le cuir pour sacs à main (cuir léger). (CTCI 61130–1A+).

[1] Période de douze mois finissant le 10 septembre de l'année indiquée.
[2] Cuir pour semelles seulement.
[3] Y compris les cuirs pour courroies et harnais.
[4] Expéditions.
[5] Cuirs et peaux de toutes catégories.
[6] Production des établissements occupant 10 personnes ou plus.
[7] Source: Organisation de coopération et de développement économiques (OCDE), (Paris).
[8] Ventes industrielles.

Unit : Thousand square metres

Unité : Milliers de mètres carrés

Country or area	1976	1977	1978	1979	1980	1981	1982	1983	1984	1985	Pays ou zone
Africa	**11 198**	**10 751**	**12 087**	**11 678**	**12 029**	**11 995**	**11 919**	**12 639**	**13 453**	**12 914**	**Afrique**
Algeria	1 789	1 893	2 155	2 689	2 901	2 385	2 648	* 2 700	* 2 700	* 2 800	Algérie
Ethiopia[1]	539	445	569	754	797	908	* 850	* 850	...	...	Ethiopie[1]
Nigeria	3 540	...	...	...	...	...	...	...	...	...	Nigéria
South Africa	4 586	4 126	5 051	3 934	4 076	* 4 368	4 081	4 769	5 424	4 716	Afrique du Sud
Tunisia	744	747	772	761	715	794	* 800	* 780	...	...	Tunisie
America, North	**87 501**	**80 794**	**79 566**	**85 409**	**79 856**	**83 343**	**81 919**	**86 013**	**79 233**	**81 304**	**Amérique du Nord**
Canada[2]	11 058	10 701	11 154	...	...	...	...	...	...	...	Canada[2]
Cuba	2 704	2 637	3 217	2 925	2 726	2 904	2 899	3 045	2 988	2 953	Cuba
Dominican Republic	949	976	952	813	710	784	834	881	823	...	Rép. dominicaine
Panama	604	637	594	809	...	684	478	716	...	...	Panama
United States	72 186	65 843	63 649	69 891	64 802	* 68 000	...	70 400	63 800	...	Etats–Unis
America, South	**54 936**	**61 592**	**69 141**	**70 756**	**66 862**	**74 511**	**77 796**	**81 080**	**84 364**	**87 649**	**Amérique du Sud**
Brazil	54 936	61 592	69 141	70 756	66 862	...	...	...	...	...	Brésil
Asia	**66 063**	**73 749**	**73 154**	**73 170**	**63 615**	**78 150**	**75 328**	**79 735**	**85 560**	**86 969**	**Asie**
Iran(Islamic Rep.of)[3]	2 759	2 976	3 056	3 640	3 186	4 213	5 701	6 473	...	...	Iran(Rép.islamique)[3]
Japan	40 496	41 735	36 732	35 974	33 995	37 453	34 813	34 548	40 533	37 506	Japon
Jordan[4]	181	235	244	317	389	438	253	245	140	...	Jordanie[4]
Korea, Republic of[5]	15 712	20 859	24 808	21 001	17 319	25 717	25 561	29 084	29 183	33 005	Corée, République de[5]
Mongolia	2 248	2 655	2 845	2 844	2 346	2 815	2 569	2 928	2 937	2 885	Mongolie
Sri Lanka	...	115	119	165	332	1 466	...	...	...	...	Sri Lanka
Turkey[6]	4 439	5 174	5 350	9 229	...	...	...	...	...	...	Turquie[6]
Europe	**410 799**	**386 994**	**406 678**	**419 207**	**377 196**	**382 968**	**388 406**	**394 286**	**395 599**	**395 361**	**Europe**
EEC	***243 807***	***215 876***	***229 966***	***246 356***	***204 642***	***209 222***	***216 483***	***218 845***	***216 211***	***212 990***	***CEE***
Belgium	3 876	3 315	2 650	2 104	1 615	2 066	2 322	2 352	2 390	2 242	Belgique
Denmark	2 337	1 951	1 876	1 568	1 345	...	...	...	...	...	Danemark
France[6]	* 39 760	* 37 500	* 35 150	* 34 670	* 33 380	33 790	...	...	...	...	France[6]
Germany, Fed. Rep.	26 283	26 001	26 559	26 006	24 025	25 139	27 157	29 473	27 768	26 579	Allemagne, Rép. féd.
Greece[6]	4 245	4 243	3 983	3 810	4 948	5 347	4 869	4 813	4 092	...	Grèce[6]
Ireland[7]	4 073	2 840	2 628	2 157	1 799	1 747	1 469	1 280	...	...	Irlande[7]
Italy* [6]	121 300	100 900	120 300	142 050	111 200	113 060	...	...	...	...	Italie* [6]
Netherlands[8]	5 500	5 400	4 680	4 805	4 893	5 131	5 610	6 230	6 995	7 335	Pays–Bas[8]
United Kingdom	36 433	33 726	32 140	29 186	21 437	21 833	23 462	24 230	24 953	23 448	Royaume–Uni
EFTA	***18 680***	***17 511***	***18 145***	***18 782***	***18 714***	***19 222***	***20 361***	***22 110***	***23 392***	***22 801***	***AELE***
Austria	3 846	3 552	3 276	3 747	3 865	3 913	4 320	5 029	5 300	5 155	Autriche
Finland	3 626	3 133	3 502	3 616	3 951	4 130	4 201	4 474	4 869	...	Finlande
Norway	1 001	972	916	977	885	569	...	...	...	...	Norvège
Portugal* [6]	4 640	4 720	5 475	6 092	6 165	...	...	...	...	...	Portugal* [6]
Sweden	5 567	5 134	4 976	4 350	3 848	* 3 872	* 4 011	4 406	4 649	...	Suède
East Europe	***91 277***	***91 880***	***93 551***	***93 600***	***93 173***	***89 745***	***88 060***	***90 289***	***91 544***	***93 431***	***Europe de l'est***
Bulgaria	6 680	6 900	6 790	6 660	7 095	7 419	7 520	7 649	7 748	7 904	Bulgarie
Czechoslovakia	23 837	23 774	24 331	24 539	24 548	24 617	23 998	23 127	23 774	24 311	Tchécoslovaquie
German Dem. Rep.	16 509	16 668	17 134	17 174	17 120	17 357	16 880	17 029	17 666	18 094	Rép. dém. allemande
Hungary	12 246	12 586	13 362	13 465	12 647	12 784	12 469	12 403	12 483	12 394	Hongrie
Poland	32 005	31 952	31 934	31 762	31 763	27 568	27 193	30 081	29 873	30 728	Pologne
Other Europe	***57 035***	***61 727***	***65 016***	***60 469***	***60 667***	***64 779***	***63 502***	***63 042***	***64 452***	***66 139***	***Autre Europe***
Spain* [6]	41 100	44 680	48 700	43 250	42 730	...	...	...	...	...	Espagne* [6]
Yugoslavia	15 935	17 047	16 316	17 219	17 937	20 141	18 682	18 040	19 268	20 773	Yougoslavie
USSR	**114 885**	**117 942**	**116 323**	**113 781**	**115 196**	**113 116**	**111 695**	**114 022**	**113 986**	**113 791**	**URSS**
Byelorussian SSR	*6 860*	*7 251*	*7 470*	*7 598*	*7 721*	*7 001*	*7 380*	*7 249*	*7 579*	*7 703*	*RSS de Biélorussie*
Ukrainian SSR	*23 639*	*23 662*	*23 569*	*24 326*	*25 601*	*25 313*	*24 155*	*25 020*	*24 967*	*24 516*	*RSS d'Ukraine*
Oceania	**5 015**	**5 090**	**6 250**	**8 330**	**6 171**	**6 171**	**6 171**	**6 171**	**6 171**	**6 171**	**Océanie**
Australia* [6]	5 015	5 090	6 250	8 330	...	...	...	...	...	...	Australie* [6]
Total	**750 397**	**736 912**	**763 199**	**782 331**	**720 925**	**750 255**	**753 234**	**773 947**	**778 367**	**784 159**	**Total**

For general note and footnotes, see end of table.

Voir la fin du tableau pour la remarque générale et les notes.

General note.
Hides and skins, tanned (including chamois–dressed), parchment dressed or otherwise prepared as leather, undressed or dressed, but excluding those tanned or dressed with the hair on. Reconstituted and artificial leather are excluded. The heavy and light leather together correspond to SITC 6113, 6114 and 6119. The headings include, inter alia, sole leather (in heavy leather), upper and lining leather, leather for hand–bags (in light leather). (SITC 61130–2B+).

1 Twelve months ending 10 September of year stated.
2 Shipments.
3 Production by establishments employing 10 or more persons.
4 Upper leather only.
5 Including heavy leather.
6 Source: Organisation for Economic Co–operation and Development (OECD), (Paris).
7 Beginning 1984, data are confidential.
8 Industrial sales.

Remarque générale.
Peaux tannées, chamoisées, corroyées ou autrement préparées (parcheminées, vernies etc.), à l'exception de celles revêtues de leurs poils. Les cuirs artificiels ou reconstitués ne sont pas compris dans cette rubrique. L'ensemble des deux rubriques représente les positions 6113, 6114 et 6119 de la CTCI. Elles comprennent notamment le cuir pour semelles (cuir fort), les cuirs pour empeignes et doublures, le cuir pour sacs à main (cuir léger). (CTCI 61130–2B+).

1 Période de douze mois finissant le 10 septembre de l'année indiquée.
2 Expéditions.
3 Production des établissements occupant 10 personnes ou plus.
4 Cuirs pour empeignes seulement.
5 Y compris les cuirs forts.
6 Source: Organisation de coopération et de développement économiques (OCDE), (Paris).
7 A partir de 1984, les données sont confidentielles.
8 Ventes industrielles.

Footwear, total production, excluding rubber footwear – Chaussures, production totale, non compris les chaussures de caoutchouc

Unit : Thousand pairs — Unité : Milliers de paires

Country or area	1976	1977	1978	1979	1980	1981	1982	1983	1984	1985	Pays ou zone
Africa	**163 245**	**168 751**	**175 515**	**176 151**	**184 356**	**192 916**	**180 501**	**190 786**	**193 570**	**193 894**	**Afrique**
Algeria	15 314	14 152	14 806	16 417	19 078	22 183	* 16 112	* 16 780	...	...	Algérie
Burkina Faso	713	651	580	578	536	377	461	280	811	...	Burkina Faso
Cameroon[1]	4 215	5 126	2 945	3 456	8 333	...	...	6 108	3 572	3 964	Cameroun[1]
Central African Rep.	631	743	749	409	473	380	367	266	582	611	Rép. centrafricaine
Congo[2]	712	714	725	696	836	857	876	928	995	1 127	Congo[2]
Côte d'Ivoire	...	7 400	6 389	6 267	6 440	7 010	5 930	6 380	5 900	...	Côte d'Ivoire
Egypt	37 389	39 809	47 777	53 472	56 144	56 457	57 330	59 414	...	...	Egypte
Ethiopia[3 4]	5 388	5 139	2 517	5 514	6 625	6 936	7 511	7 985	8 794	...	Ethiopie[3 4]
Madagascar[5]	2 305	2 201	2 584	3 186	3 027	2 770	1 988	2 302	2 133	2 172	Madagascar[5]
Mali	19	22	0	0	0	0	* 0	* 0	...	...	Mali
Nigeria	6 284	...	...	...	12 554	14 387	6 308	10 618	10 118	8 256	Nigéria
Senegal	6 151	6 043	7 779	14 071	3 360	3 693	4 794	3 250	3 234	2 851	Sénégal
South Africa[1]	45 478	43 545	48 676	36 478	42 531	* 48 508	44 089	45 542	* 46 316	45 117	Afrique du Sud[1]
Sudan	14 400	12 400	13 600	* 10 000	9 000	9 400	10 300	...	...	...	Soudan
Togo	902	1 025	740	932	1 155	1 011	796	559	485	* 520	Togo
Tunisia[2]	5 616	7 109	6 835	6 801	7 405	6 268	* 6 200	* 6 200	...	...	Tunisie[2]
United Rep. Tanzania	3 689	6 331	6 363	5 760	4 135	...	...	...	...	...	Rép.Unie de Tanzanie
Zaire	6 986	7 215	3 179	2 698	2 724	2 599	7 310	10 730	...	...	Zaïre
America, North	**495 093**	**484 769**	**492 613**	**475 375**	**457 615**	**449 404**	**427 872**	**409 383**	**379 090**	**341 803**	**Amérique du Nord**
Canada	43 840	38 114	43 483	45 167	39 834	43 355	36 670	39 119	45 458	44 286	Canada
Cuba	14 967	12 466	14 685	13 759	12 927	15 518	13 508	13 172	12 473	12 394	Cuba
Dominican Republic	4 513	5 508	5 472	7 306	9 193	8 975	9 074	9 275	9 636	...	Rép. dominicaine
El Salvador	3 983	4 975	4 257	4 957	3 722	3 373	3 154	2 732	...	...	El Salvador
Haiti	219	335	288	390	768	577	514	* 519	528	...	Haïti
Jamaica	1 690	1 856	1 542	1 260	927	1 029	593	* 600	...	...	Jamaïque
Nicaragua	...	...	...	2 050	2 127	3 330	3 062	2 812	2 549	...	Nicaragua
Panama	1 247	1 151	1 578	1 880	...	1 603	2 092	1 807	...	...	Panama
St.Kitts–Nevis	...	...	...	...	63	39	49	80	59	23	St–Kitts–Nevis
United States	422 507	418 120	418 948	398 480	386 311	371 566	359 107	339 187	303 174	265 474	Etats–Unis
America, South	**125 585**	**125 682**	**126 535**	**125 226**	**128 097**	**131 235**	**131 671**	**131 289**	**132 531**	**132 970**	**Amérique du Sud**
Bolivia	2 565	2 572	3 144	1 769	1 800	1 710	923	1 739	...	...	Bolivie
Brazil[6]	101 704	...	...	...	...	...	...	...	...	...	Brésil[6]
Chile	9 191	9 306	...	...	...	...	...	...	...	...	Chili
Colombia	9 017	8 968	9 137	8 626	10 731	13 016	* 14 000	12 286	...	...	Colombie
Ecuador	284	270	353	...	...	952	1 052	1 424	...	...	Equateur
Paraguay	2 824	2 862	2 948	3 238	3 809	4 604	4 744	4 887	5 034	4 790	Paraguay
Asia	**287 256**	**291 901**	**306 032**	**335 355**	**368 930**	**819 790**	**800 339**	**857 787**	**925 693**	**1 036 492**	**Asie**
Afghanistan	...	299	305	309	265	238	229	297	344	380	Afghanistan
Burma[7]	4 846	...	...	...	...	...	...	...	...	...	Birmanie[7]
China	...	91 190	100 530	116 080	157 450	557 050	533 880	565 070	638 920	730 610	Chine
Cyprus	3 027	4 094	4 730	5 153	5 725	7 239	6 525	6 741	7 296	7 281	Chypre
Democratic Yemen	...	...	...	...	94	105	157	168	219	...	Yémen démocratique
Hong Kong	23 398	17 392	24 953	27 231	32 760	69 262	75 458	96 371	# 77 821	...	Hong–kong
India[8]	15 152	14 277	11 437	13 416	12 277	14 343	12 939	14 292	14 221	14 402	Inde[8]
Indonesia[5]	6 459	# 32 915	* 28 000	27 928	31 525	31 783	36 507	38 308	48 315	...	Indonésie[5]
Iran(Islamic Rep.of)[9]	36 800	20 227	19 382	19 478	14 395	24 556	[5]31 375	[5]34 208	...	...	Iran(Rép.islamique)[9]
Japan[9]	49 446	49 511	51 442	53 426	50 195	51 227	50 012	48 387	55 707	53 387	Japon[9]
Mongolia	1 998	1 900	1 717	1 962	2 104	1 916	1 727	2 226	2 677	2 883	Mongolie
Nepal[10]	55	59	56	70	82	61	88	73	83	...	Népal[10]
Singapore[11]	4 219	4 212	5 304	9 058	6 849	6 464	3 690	3 914	4 755	3 789	Singapour[11]
Sri Lanka	[1]7 630	[1]8 195	[1]10 535	[1]13 591	[1]7 663	* [1]8 000	206	186	163	197	Sri Lanka
Turkey	42 700	...	...	...	...	...	...	...	...	...	Turquie
Europe	**1 696 561**	**1 671 720**	**1 702 060**	**1 754 512**	**1 690 192**	**1 749 983**	**1 756 333**	**1 804 693**	**1 833 048**	**1 854 198**	**Europe**
EEC	***905 967***	***861 259***	***899 240***	***977 824***	***909 552***	***945 505***	***970 594***	***1 000 616***	***1 022 980***	***1 047 425***	***CEE***
Belgium	8 549	7 223	6 202	6 067	6 328	5 916	6 311	6 018	5 837	5 343	Belgique
Denmark	7 940	7 430	6 161	6 362	6 663	...	...	...	...	...	Danemark
France[12]	213 000	216 100	198 360	205 020	206 387	196 356	202 372	206 074	201 809	196 992	France[12]
Germany, Fed. Rep.	141 218	113 690	106 343	104 964	105 942	97 786	96 313	94 518	92 472	86 678	Allemagne, Rép. féd.
Greece	14 553	13 943	14 293	16 308	14 628	16 141	13 134	12 599	11 108	...	Grèce
Ireland	4 511	4 499	4 359	4 148	3 483	3 047	2 786	2 609	2 716	1 914	Irlande
Italy[13]	350 400	* 331 420	* 402 284	* 479 826	* 421 751	...	...	...	...	...	Italie[13]
Netherlands[1 14]	13 650	12 900	12 560	11 923	12 113	11 043	10 857	10 599	9 585	9 452	Pays–Bas[1 14]
United Kingdom[15]	152 146	154 054	148 678	143 206	132 257	125 367	120 373	121 152	123 807	130 414	Royaume–Uni[15]

For general note and footnotes, see end of table.

Voir la fin du tableau pour la remarque générale et les notes.

Footwear, total production, excluding rubber footwear (continued) – Chaussures, production totale, non compris les chaussures de caoutchouc (suite)

Unit : Thousand pairs

Unité : Milliers de paires

Country or area	1976	1977	1978	1979	1980	1981	1982	1983	1984	1985	Pays ou zone
EFTA	***66 604***	***67 534***	***67 098***	***70 000***	***76 628***	***77 103***	***71 558***	***70 089***	***73 765***	***76 439***	***AELE***
Austria	24 366	25 085	23 543	25 133	28 069	28 108	28 016	26 986	25 453	26 107	Autriche
Finland	10 144	8 950	8 580	9 664	11 086	11 497	7 842	6 666	7 867	...	Finlande
Norway	...	...	...	...	...	1 276	1 632	1 244	...	...	Norvège
Portugal	12 249	13 684	17 969	19 337	21 605	23 010	21 880	24 157	28 790	31 465	Portugal
Sweden	12 434	12 174	9 746	8 650	8 505	7 342	6 502	5 618	4 490	3 826	Suède
Switzerland	6 027	6 257	5 876	5 832	5 979	5 870	5 686	5 418	5 781	5 813	Suisse
East Europe	***470 987***	***471 842***	***478 249***	***484 120***	***482 020***	***516 063***	***517 424***	***538 137***	***552 004***	***559 087***	***Europe de l'est***
Bulgaria	23 597	24 236	23 706	22 860	24 404	25 821	25 537	26 057	27 997	29 623	Bulgarie
Czechoslovakia	127 950	127 665	128 926	129 800	127 484	128 022	128 474	127 638	130 584	131 402	Tchécoslovaquie
German Dem. Rep.	80 067	79 813	78 254	78 100	78 817	80 395	82 112	81 683	82 425	83 551	Rép. dém. allemande
Hungary	48 802	49 477	50 362	48 720	47 043	48 345	48 233	47 761	49 035	49 756	Hongrie
Poland	135 672	133 054	135 864	140 013	140 634	126 238	126 199	141 497	147 076	147 603	Pologne
Romania	[16] 54 899	[16] 57 597	[16] 61 137	[16] 64 627	[16] 63 638	[1] 107 242	[1] 106 869	[1] 113 501	[1] 114 887	[1] 117 152	Roumanie
Other Europe	***253 003***	***271 085***	***257 473***	***222 568***	***221 992***	***211 312***	***196 757***	***195 851***	***184 300***	***171 247***	***Autre Europe***
Malta	325	667	1 113	1 188	1 484	1 522	1 519	1 524	1 691	...	Malte
Spain	203 204	* 217 000	* 198 800	158 801	150 577	134 948	119 199	114 190	...	...	Espagne
Yugoslavia	49 474	53 418	57 560	62 579	69 931	74 842	76 039	80 137	90 798	93 063	Yougoslavie
USSR[17]	**724 394**	**735 918**	**740 076**	**740 296**	**742 930**	**737 974**	**734 417**	**745 303**	**763 514**	**787 610**	**URSS[17]**
Byelorussian SSR	*42 277*	*41 979*	*41 795*	*41 246*	*41 537*	*41 466*	*41 984*	*42 151*	*43 080*	*44 222*	*RSS de Biélorussie*
Ukrainian SSR	*170 163*	*172 882*	*174 031*	*175 793*	*177 169*	*175 234*	*173 618*	*177 861*	*182 216*	*185 726*	*RSS d'Ukraine*
Oceania	**37 145**	**33 633**	**34 599**	**37 728**	**39 340**	**42 440**	**40 028**	**38 557**	**42 139**	**44 105**	**Océanie**
Australia[18 19]	30 017	26 943	28 453	30 656	32 030	35 288	32 476	31 124	33 675	36 404	Australie[18 19]
New Zealand	7 128	6 690	6 146	7 072	7 310	7 152	7 552	7 433	8 464	7 701	Nouvelle–Zélande
Total	**3 529 280**	**3 512 373**	**3 577 430**	**3 644 643**	**3 611 461**	**4 123 741**	**4 071 161**	**4 177 798**	**4 269 586**	**4 391 071**	**Total**

General note.
Data refer to total production of leather footwear for children, men and women and all other footwear such as footwear with outer soles of wood or cork, sports footwear and orthopedic leather footwear. House slippers and sandals of various types are included. Rubber footwear, however, are excluded. (SITC 85102 and 85104 and parts of 85103 and 85105).

[1] Including rubber footwear.
[2] Including rubber and plastic footwear.
[3] Twelve months ending 10 September of year stated.
[4] Including canvas, plastic and rubber footwear.
[5] Including plastic footwear.
[6] Production by main establishments only.
[7] Twelve months ending 30 September of year stated.
[8] Production by large and medium scale establishments only.
[9] Production by establishments employing 10 or more persons.
[10] Twelve months beginning 16 July of year stated.
[11] Data refer to leather, rubber and plastic footwear.
[12] Including other footwear, house footwear, sandals and other light footwear. Also including rubber footwear.
[13] Source: Organisation for Economic Co–operation and Development (OECD), (Paris).
[14] Industrial sales.
[15] Manufacturers' sales.
[16] Excluding production of private workshops and small–scale private industry.
[17] Including sporting footwear of all types and orthopedic shoes.
[18] Twelve months ending 30 June of year stated.
[19] Including footwear of materials other than leather.

Remarque générale.
Les données se rapportent à la production totale de chaussures de cuir pour enfants, hommes et dames et toutes les autres chaussures telles que chaussures à semelles en bois ou en liège, chaussures pour sports et chaussures orthopediques en cuir. Chaussures en caoutchouc ne sont pas compris. (CTCI 85102 et 85104 et parties de 85103 et 85105).

[1] Y compris les chaussures en caoutchouc.
[2] Y compris chaussures en caoutchouc et en matière plastique.
[3] Période de douze mois finissant le 10 septembre de l'année indiquée.
[4] Y compris les chaussures en toile, en matière plastique et en caoutchouc.
[5] Y compris les chaussures en matière plastique.
[6] Production des principaux établissements seulement.
[7] Période de douze mois finissant le 30 septembre de l'année indiquée.
[8] Production des grandes et moyennes entreprises seulement.
[9] Production des établissements occupant 10 personnes ou plus.
[10] Période de douze mois commençant le 16 juillet de l'année indiquée.
[11] Données se rapportant aux chaussures en cuir, en caoutchouc et en plastique.
[12] Y compris les autres chaussures, chaussures de maison, sandales et autres chaussures légères. Y compris également les chaussures en caoutchouc.
[13] Source: Organisation de coopération et de développement économiques (OCDE), (Paris).
[14] Ventes industrielles.
[15] Ventes des fabricants.
[16] Non compris la production des ateliers privés et de la petite industrie privée.
[17] Y compris les chaussures de sport de tous genres et les chaussures orthopédiques.
[18] Période de douze mois finissant le 30 juin de l'année indiquée.
[19] Y compris les chaussures en matières autres que le cuir.

Footwear, leather, children's – Chaussures de cuir pour enfants

Unit : Thousand pairs

Unité : Milliers de paires

Country or area	1976	1977	1978	1979	1980	1981	1982	1983	1984	1985	Pays ou zone
Africa	**7 252**	**6 633**	**7 702**	**6 434**	**5 604**	**7 521**	**6 269**	**6 964**	**7 135**	**6 527**	**Afrique**
Kenya	454	394	576	277	357	1 641	307	331	365	323	Kenya
South Africa	6 798	6 239	7 126	6 157	5 247	5 880	5 962	6 633	6 770	6 204	Afrique du Sud
America, North	**90 895**	**80 348**	**79 318**	**77 127**	**74 759**	**68 964**	**65 741**	**56 886**	**50 028**	**46 730**	**Amérique du Nord**
Canada	5 167	4 607	3 904	5 656	4 426	4 832	3 818	3 849	4 268	3 613	Canada
Cuba	4 429	4 412	5 252	5 144	5 114	4 906	3 968	3 283	3 534	3 846	Cuba
Dominican Republic	279	344	404	477	472	338	425	494	483	...	Rép. dominicaine
El Salvador	592	1 146	1 152	1 298	911	749	524	270	...	...	El Salvador
Panama	388	385	466	646	...	433	445	362	...	...	Panama
United States[1]	80 040	69 454	68 140	63 906	63 391	57 706	56 561	48 628	40 849	37 952	Etats–Unis[1]
America, South	**26 121**	**24 173**	**25 996**	**30 080**	**29 743**	**31 478**	**31 681**	**33 544**	**34 745**	**35 813**	**Amérique du Sud**
Bolivia	923	922	987	666	656	606	377	756	...	...	Bolivie
Brazil[2]	17 638	17 488	19 318	22 787	22 324	...	...	...	...	...	Brésil[2]
Chile	2 262	1 870	1 838	3 104	2 955	2 906	2 068	2 237	2 328	2 064	Chili
Colombia	3 160	2 595	3 125	2 601	2 825	2 565	2 432	2 283	...	...	Colombie
Ecuador	...	13	16	...	...	...	...	...	...	...	Equateur
Peru	2 123	1 285	712	907	968	...	...	1 045	* 1 021	* 1 053	Pérou
Asia	**6 086**	**4 535**	**6 181**	**3 706**	**6 047**	**9 245**	**12 553**	**4 115**	**3 606**	**6 573**	**Asie**
Cyprus	719	811	900	980	934	1 161	977	1 029	1 048	1 103	Chypre
Hong Kong	4 404	2 748	4 220	1 469	3 804	6 656	10 534	1 966	# 1 707	...	Hong–kong
Indonesia	147	127	219	400	406	547	182	33	34	...	Indonésie
Japan[3]	572	564	459	474	520	498	477	468	434	352	Japon[3]
Philippines[4]	# 244	285	...	...	...	...	...	619	...	...	Philippines[4]
Europe	**166 770**	**159 444**	**151 216**	**143 699**	**139 457**	**113 436**	**108 647**	**108 199**	**104 146**	**101 244**	**Europe**
EEC	***113 384***	***113 172***	***107 158***	***106 428***	***105 761***	***78 957***	***76 911***	***77 805***	***75 873***	***75 631***	***CEE***
Belgium	707	589	590	546	550	488	712	586	487	442	Belgique
Denmark[2]	1 587	1 519	1 158	941	1 278	...	...	...	...	...	Danemark[2]
France[5]	46 000	46 800	42 615	44 054	44 089	19 824	21 702	22 354	20 599	21 624	France[5]
Germany, Fed. Rep.	8 492	7 850	7 333	6 694	6 864	5 674	5 054	5 055	4 846	4 114	Allemagne, Rép. féd.
Greece	1 798	2 057	1 698	1 780	1 633	1 865	1 389	1 107	997	...	Grèce
Ireland	734	472	337	324	224	265	280	280	120	83	Irlande
Italy	29 487	...	...	...	...	...	...	...	...	...	Italie
Netherlands[6]	2 570	2 200	1 920	1 794	1 654	1 459	1 281	1 296	1 104	1 047	Pays–Bas[6]
United Kingdom[7]	22 009	22 198	22 020	20 808	19 982	18 955	16 185	16 938	17 650	17 328	Royaume–Uni[7]
EFTA	***5 189***	***4 978***	***4 618***	***4 320***	***3 789***	***3 307***	***3 510***	***3 769***	***4 257***	***4 373***	***AELE***
Austria	1 442	1 398	1 353	1 556	1 502	1 547	1 784	1 676	1 831	1 852	Autriche
Finland	448	276	234	236	335	267	191	163	89	...	Finlande
Iceland	20	22	17	14	7	14	2	2	3	...	Islande
Norway	...	...	...	...	...	24	22	6	26	...	Norvège
Portugal	2 860	2 856	2 654	2 169	1 578	1 143	1 193	1 562	1 935	2 078	Portugal
Sweden	399	406	340	325	347	312	318	360	373	326	Suède
East Europe	***9 014***	***10 288***	***10 153***	***9 903***	***10 106***	***10 376***	***10 022***	***9 764***	***10 961***	***11 219***	***Europe de l'est***
Hungary	9 014	10 288	10 153	9 903	10 106	10 376	10 022	9 764	10 961	11 219	Hongrie
Other Europe	***39 183***	***31 006***	***29 288***	***23 048***	***19 801***	***20 796***	***18 204***	***16 862***	***13 055***	***10 020***	***Autre Europe***
Malta	18	24	30	37	29	33	31	21	33	...	Malte
Spain	32 787	25 022	...	16 719	12 597	13 722	11 073	8 580	...	...	Espagne
Yugoslavia	6 378	5 960	6 526	6 292	7 175	7 041	7 100	8 261	9 601	9 785	Yougoslavie
USSR[8]	**269 452**	**274 632**	**281 639**	**288 640**	**293 832**	**294 402**	**296 717**	**297 152**	**307 448**	**331 557**	**URSS[8]**
Byelorussian SSR[8]	*15 405*	*15 320*	*15 617*	*15 800*	*16 503*	*15 906*	*16 236*	*16 342*	*16 816*	*17 902*	*RSS de Biélorussie[8]*
Ukrainian SSR[8]	*58 193*	*59 287*	*61 780*	*62 464*	*63 994*	*63 615*	*64 824*	*63 475*	*65 561*	*67 777*	*RSS d'Ukraine[8]*
Oceania	**7 272**	**6 564**	**6 961**	**7 480**	**7 243**	**7 850**	**6 949**	**6 155**	**6 492**	**6 916**	**Océanie**
Australia[9 10]	6 331	5 608	6 063	6 581	6 315	6 798	6 152	5 282	5 599	6 187	Australie[9 10]
New Zealand[10]	941	956	898	899	928	1 052	797	873	893	729	Nouvelle–Zélande[10]
Total	**573 847**	**556 329**	**559 013**	**557 165**	**556 684**	**532 895**	**528 557**	**513 015**	**513 600**	**535 360**	**Total**

For general note and footnotes, see end of table.

Voir la fin du tableau pour la remarque générale et les notes.

General note.
Boots and shoes with leather, rubber, composition leather or plastic soles, and with leather or mainly leather uppers. Rubber footwear is excluded. (SITC 85102–1).

[1] Including non–leather footwear.
[2] Including sandals and light footwear.
[3] Production by establishments employing 10 or more persons.
[4] Shipments.
[5] Including other footwear, house footwear, sandals and other light footwear. Also including rubber footwear.
[6] Industrial sales.
[7] Manufacturers' sales.
[8] Including sporting footwear of all types and orthopedic shoes.

[9] Twelve months ending 30 June of year stated.
[10] Including footwear of materials other than leather.

Remarque générale.
Bottes et chaussures à semelle en cuir naturel, en caoutchouc, en cuir artificiel ou reconstitué ou en matière plastique, et à dessus en cuir ou principalement en cuir. Les chaussures en caoutchouc ne sont pas comprises. (CTCI 85102–1).

[1] Y compris les chaussures en toutes matières autres que le cuir.
[2] Y compris les sandales et chaussures légères.
[3] Production des établissements occupant 10 personnes ou plus.
[4] Expéditions.
[5] Y compris les autres chaussures, chaussures de maison, sandales et autres chaussures légères. Y compris également les chaussures en caoutchouc.
[6] Ventes industrielles.
[7] Ventes des fabricants.
[8] Y compris les chaussures de sport de tous genres et les chaussures orthopédiques.
[9] Période de douze mois finissant le 30 juin de l'année indiquée.
[10] Y compris les chaussures en matières autres que le cuir.

Footwear, leather, men's – Chaussures en cuir pour hommes

Unit : Thousand pairs

Unité : Milliers de paires

Country or area	1976	1977	1978	1979	1980	1981	1982	1983	1984	1985	Pays ou zone
Africa	**15 012**	**13 533**	**14 163**	**12 217**	**12 369**	**14 262**	**15 094**	**15 024**	**15 563**	**15 623**	**Afrique**
Kenya	733	832	856	1 048	803	879	886	703	627	725	Kenya
South Africa	14 279	12 701	13 307	11 169	11 566	13 383	14 208	14 321	14 936	14 898	Afrique du Sud
America, North	**125 425**	**124 556**	**121 489**	**108 636**	**102 763**	**103 875**	**93 609**	**90 987**	**87 185**	**78 129**	**Amérique du Nord**
Canada	7 346	9 848	10 299	8 176	6 837	7 418	5 720	6 547	6 443	5 677	Canada
Cuba	4 572	5 466	5 433	4 989	4 304	5 230	4 918	5 592	5 529	5 705	Cuba
Dominican Republic	949	1 236	1 006	1 157	1 167	1 131	1 047	1 008	975	...	Rép. dominicaine
El Salvador	2 653	2 484	1 828	2 144	1 772	1 738	1 690	1 683	...	...	El Salvador
Panama	411	288	425	475	...	522	507	540	...	...	Panama
United States[1]	109 494	105 234	102 498	91 695	88 215	87 836	79 727	75 617	72 273	63 859	Etats–Unis[1]
America, South	**54 119**	**53 299**	**56 373**	**62 181**	**64 748**	**70 365**	**71 504**	**73 821**	**77 454**	**80 287**	**Amérique du Sud**
Bolivia	769	793	1 023	539	591	454	361	476	...	...	Bolivie
Brazil[2]	43 896	42 113	45 395	50 500	51 715	...	...	...	...	...	Brésil[2]
Chile	2 348	2 220	2 606	2 948	2 302	2 433	1 914	2 258	2 007	2 246	Chili
Colombia	3 757	4 744	3 834	4 394	5 775	8 434	7 659	6 936	...	...	Colombie
Ecuador	5	9	11	...	...	...	...	...	...	...	Equateur
Paraguay[3]	2 724	2 800	2 884	3 172	3 737	4 522	4 658	4 798	4 942	4 695	Paraguay[3]
Peru	...	...	...	...	...	...	...	671	* 643	* 545	Pérou
Asia	**60 867**	**60 063**	**61 690**	**67 029**	**57 741**	**72 022**	**60 295**	**65 597**	**68 571**	**68 649**	**Asie**
Burma[3 4 5]	4 236	...	...	...	...	...	...	...	...	...	Birmanie[3 4 5]
Cyprus	1 345	2 338	2 890	3 069	3 539	4 691	4 313	4 446	4 979	5 093	Chypre
Hong Kong	3 811	2 278	3 149	3 096	1 803	3 152	1 216	7 108	6 864	...	Hong–kong
India[6]	8 252	8 253	5 773	7 724	6 986	7 906	7 051	7 538	7 106	6 923	Inde[6]
Indonesia[7]	1 968	1 850	1 886	5 099	3 918	7 084	4 294	3 342	3 638	...	Indonésie[7]
Iran(Islamic Rep.of)[8]	8 353	8 343	10 626	10 681	8 249	14 973	9 589	10 689	...	...	Iran(Rép.islamique)[8]
Japan[8]	24 237	23 323	23 112	23 816	22 498	23 021	22 536	21 286	23 059	22 846	Japon[8]
Korea, Republic of	4 019	4 792	5 518	4 862	2 932	2 883	2 921	2 333	2 561	2 637	Corée, République de
Philippines[9]	1 407	961	...	...	...	...	...	1 665	...	...	Philippines[9]
Turkey	3 239	3 689	3 156	3 102	2 236	2 732	2 795	2 954	2 818	2 520	Turquie
Europe	**309 931**	**318 921**	**304 045**	**306 844**	**295 053**	**287 722**	**280 652**	**273 011**	**271 042**	**274 891**	**Europe**
EEC	***191 058***	***193 429***	***188 743***	***188 617***	***180 074***	***175 604***	***173 671***	***169 980***	***169 456***	***170 509***	***CEE***
Belgium	1 426	1 270	998	1 071	1 467	972	946	942	752	845	Belgique
Denmark[2]	2 756	2 293	2 057	2 187	2 454	...	...	...	...	...	Danemark[2]
France[10]	79 300	80 700	76 250	78 640	74 212	72 315	76 267	74 389	75 220	74 771	France[10]
Germany, Fed. Rep.	17 630	17 594	18 104	17 598	16 915	16 578	15 457	14 313	14 183	14 265	Allemagne, Rép. féd.
Greece	2 649	2 756	2 896	2 895	2 972	3 834	3 650	3 625	3 383	...	Grèce
Ireland	1 943	2 280	2 270	2 035	1 537	1 506	1 422	1 315	1 100	1 022	Irlande
Italy[11]	56 515	...	...	...	...	...	...	...	...	...	Italie[11]
Netherlands[12]	2 420	2 300	2 480	2 195	2 120	1 729	1 732	1 505	1 311	1 356	Pays–Bas[12]
United Kingdom[13 14]	26 419	27 721	27 173	25 481	21 882	20 018	15 615	15 380	15 066	16 030	Royaume–Uni[13 14]
EFTA	***13 048***	***14 290***	***13 155***	***15 374***	***16 244***	***15 535***	***14 174***	***14 375***	***15 891***	***17 801***	***AELE***
Austria	3 183	4 214	2 935	3 564	3 678	3 473	3 841	3 650	2 621	3 777	Autriche
Finland	2 606	2 291	2 767	3 003	3 321	3 851	1 782	1 568	1 435	...	Finlande
Iceland	8	11	8	7	8	7	15	14	17	...	Islande
Norway	1 929	# [3] 2 011	[3] 1 766	[3] 1 610	[3] 1 641	368	308	227	...	...	Norvège
Portugal	3 852	4 478	4 526	6 535	6 936	7 274	7 687	8 462	11 373	11 588	Portugal
Sweden	1 470	1 285	1 153	655	660	562	541	454	350	344	Suède
East Europe	***53 914***	***52 420***	***51 254***	***50 436***	***48 712***	***48 537***	***49 102***	***45 087***	***44 928***	***47 185***	***Europe de l'est***
Bulgaria	...	...	...	...	...	39 481	39 818	35 571	35 868	37 840	Bulgarie
Hungary	11 185	10 407	9 957	9 856	8 848	9 056	9 284	9 516	9 060	9 345	Hongrie
Other Europe	***51 911***	***58 782***	***50 893***	***52 417***	***50 023***	***48 046***	***43 705***	***43 569***	***40 767***	***39 396***	***Autre Europe***
Malta	56	265	663	825	1 007	1 018	1 030	1 075	1 166	...	Malte
Spain	38 758	44 281	...	36 406	29 750	26 124	21 990	21 019	...	...	Espagne
Yugoslavia	13 097	14 236	13 443	15 186	19 266	20 904	20 685	21 475	22 405	24 026	Yougoslavie
USSR[15]	**211 992**	**219 354**	**221 074**	**219 165**	**215 472**	**212 961**	**212 022**	**220 999**	**227 840**	**228 551**	**URSS[15]**
Byelorussian SSR[15]	*12 798*	*12 728*	*12 990*	*12 970*	*12 514*	*12 388*	*12 782*	*13 180*	*13 123*	*13 120*	*RSS de Biélorussie[15]*
Ukrainian SSR[15]	*47 799*	*49 729*	*51 169*	*52 479*	*52 274*	*51 976*	*50 503*	*52 981*	*53 548*	*53 080*	*RSS d'Ukraine[15]*

For general note and footnotes, see end of table.

Voir la fin du tableau pour la remarque générale et les notes.

Footwear, leather, men's (continued) – Chaussures en cuir pour hommes (suite)

Unit : Thousand pairs

Unité : Milliers de paires

Country or area	1976	1977	1978	1979	1980	1981	1982	1983	1984	1985	Pays ou zone
Oceania	**12 083**	**11 242**	**11 681**	**12 663**	**13 189**	**14 117**	**12 586**	**10 911**	**11 676**	**12 503**	**Océanie**
Australia[16 17]	10 321	9 672	10 179	10 965	11 764	12 966	11 428	9 901	10 583	11 350	Australie[16 17]
New Zealand[17]	1 762	1 570	1 502	1 698	1 425	1 151	1 158	1 010	1 093	1 153	Nouvelle–Zélande[17]
Total	**789 429**	**800 968**	**790 515**	**788 736**	**761 336**	**775 325**	**745 762**	**750 351**	**759 331**	**758 633**	**Total**

General note.
Boots and shoes with leather, rubber, composition leather or plastic soles, and with leather or mainly leather uppers. Rubber footwear is excluded. (SITC 85102–2).

1 Including non–leather footwear.
2 Including sandals and light footwear.
3 Including footwear for women and children.
4 Twelve months ending 30 September of year stated.
5 Including slippers.
6 Production by large and medium scale establishments only.
7 Including footwear for women.
8 Production by establishments employing 10 or more persons.
9 Shipments.
10 Including other footwear, house footwear, sandals and other light footwear. Also including rubber footwear.
11 Source: Organisation for Economic Co–operation and Development (OECD), (Paris).
12 Industrial sales.
13 Including sports shoes with leather uppers and excluding safety footwear with leather uppers.
14 Manufacturers' sales.
15 Including sporting footwear of all types and orthopedic shoes.
16 Twelve months ending 30 June of year stated.
17 Including footwear of materials other than leather.

Remarque générale.
Bottes et chaussures à semelle en cuir naturel, en caoutchouc, en cuir artificiel ou reconstitué ou en matière plastique, et à dessus en cuir ou principalement en cuir. Les chaussures en caoutchouc ne sont pas comprises. (CTCI 85102–2).

1 Y compris les chaussures en toutes matières autres que le cuir.
2 Y compris les sandales et chaussures légères.
3 Y compris les chaussures pour dames et enfants.
4 Période de douze mois finissant le 30 septembre de l'année indiquée.
5 Y compris les pantoufles.
6 Production des grandes et moyennes entreprises seulement.
7 Y compris les chaussures pour dames.
8 Production des établissements occupant 10 personnes ou plus.
9 Expéditions.
10 Y compris les autres chaussures, chaussures de maison, sandales et autres chaussures légères. Y compris également les chaussures en caoutchouc.
11 Source: Organisation de coopération et de développement économiques (OCDE), (Paris).
12 Ventes industrielles.
13 Y compris les chaussures de sport à empeigne en cuir et, à l'exclusion des chaussures de sécurité à empeigne en cuir.
14 Ventes des fabricants.
15 Y compris les chaussures de sport de tous genres et les chaussures orthopédiques.
16 Période de douze mois finissant le 30 juin de l'année indiquée.
17 Y compris les chaussures en matières autres que le cuir.

Footwear, leather, women's – Chaussures en cuir pour dames

Unit : Thousand pairs

Unité : Milliers de paires

Country or area	1976	1977	1978	1979	1980	1981	1982	1983	1984	1985	Pays ou zone
Africa	**24 491**	**22 938**	**24 694**	**18 471**	**20 857**	**23 755**	**23 130**	**25 270**	**26 962**	**26 708**	**Afrique**
Algeria[1]	6 754	6 465	6 582	* 6 600	* 6 800	...	...	...	...	...	Algérie[1]
Kenya	1 026	727	757	552	442	410	387	269	190	313	Kenya
South Africa	16 711	15 746	17 355	11 319	13 615	16 637	16 012	18 248	19 996	19 597	Afrique du Sud
America, North	**175 286**	**164 296**	**166 429**	**167 027**	**162 391**	**157 141**	**162 343**	**153 356**	**134 141**	**116 621**	**Amérique du Nord**
Canada	15 100	12 589	15 855	15 829	14 613	15 591	14 046	14 709	16 349	16 547	Canada
Cuba	3 196	2 827	3 069	2 813	2 615	4 524	3 589	3 146	2 457	2 119	Cuba
Dominican Republic	119	185	353	447	742	671	683	625	633	...	Rép. dominicaine
El Salvador	710	1 345	1 277	1 515	1 039	886	940	780	...	...	El Salvador
Panama	271	303	439	503	...	400	569	412	...	...	Panama
United States[2]	155 890	147 047	145 436	145 920	142 954	135 069	142 516	133 684	113 282	95 697	Etats–Unis[2]
America, South	**71 403**	**71 257**	**87 255**	**93 373**	**90 739**	**100 265**	**105 899**	**112 617**	**118 451**	**123 970**	**Amérique du Sud**
Bolivia	826	841	1 058	541	719	833	171	486	...	...	Bolivie
Brazil	66 977	[3] 66 735	[3] 83 012	[3] 87 489	[3] 86 736	...	...	...	...	...	Brésil
Chile	2 285	2 350	2 058	4 003	1 841	1 959	2 036	2 596	2 512	2 047	Chili
Colombia	840	857	650	865	968	820	1 043	889	...	...	Colombie
Ecuador	...	4	7	...	...	...	...	...	...	...	Equateur
Peru	...	...	...	...	...	...	...	471	* 449	* 489	Pérou
Asia	**26 302**	**24 036**	**31 419**	**34 045**	**32 362**	**34 627**	**30 478**	**31 725**	**36 260**	**36 202**	**Asie**
Cyprus	963	945	940	1 104	1 252	1 387	1 235	1 266	1 269	1 085	Chypre
Hong Kong	4 452	2 620	6 326	8 295	9 194	10 798	7 387	8 598	11 039	...	Hong–kong
Japan[4]	17 084	16 038	18 943	19 749	18 081	18 364	17 872	17 444	19 693	19 216	Japon[4]
Korea, Republic of	1 270	1 900	2 677	2 364	1 302	1 545	1 451	1 884	1 726	1 658	Corée, République de
Philippines	...	...	...	...	...	...	...	2 533	...	...	Philippines
Europe	**600 571**	**591 283**	**575 222**	**578 851**	**585 005**	**586 574**	**580 592**	**591 185**	**593 117**	**579 889**	**Europe**
EEC	***332 014***	***330 547***	***320 143***	***328 594***	***331 685***	***343 672***	***339 931***	***345 298***	***342 925***	***334 856***	***CEE***
Belgium	1 794	1 223	1 037	1 246	1 181	1 033	1 179	1 354	1 178	788	Belgique
Denmark[3]	2 757	2 743	2 350	2 592	2 329	...	...	...	...	...	Danemark[3]
France[5]	87 700	88 600	79 493	82 326	88 086	104 217	104 403	109 331	105 990	101 723	France[5]
Germany, Fed. Rep.	35 251	32 948	31 991	32 745	32 958	31 328	30 390	29 887	30 720	28 949	Allemagne, Rép. féd.
Greece	5 909	5 741	5 546	5 489	5 444	5 482	4 271	4 176	3 950	...	Grèce
Ireland	1 277	1 747	1 719	1 789	1 722	1 276	1 084	1 014	1 494	809	Irlande
Italy[6]	172 128	...	...	...	...	...	...	...	...	...	Italie[6]
Netherlands[7]	4 270	4 100	4 060	4 153	4 309	3 772	3 836	3 544	3 307	3 116	Pays–Bas[7]
United Kingdom[8]	20 928	21 317	21 819	26 126	23 528	22 182	20 487	21 811	22 205	21 635	Royaume–Uni[8]
EFTA	***18 495***	***18 109***	***18 380***	***21 183***	***24 978***	***25 290***	***24 827***	***24 889***	***28 350***	***31 791***	***AELE***
Austria	8 188	7 795	8 264	8 835	10 351	10 171	10 250	10 456	10 643	12 053	Autriche
Finland	3 374	2 934	2 938	3 482	4 535	5 119	4 346	3 619	4 469	...	Finlande
Iceland	2	1	2	2	2	5	8	13	14	...	Islande
Norway	...	...	...	...	...	221	169	110	...	...	Norvège
Portugal	3 488	4 091	4 308	5 770	6 759	6 937	7 579	8 312	10 530	12 325	Portugal
Sweden	1 141	1 005	713	822	892	...	...	...	460	429	Suède
Switzerland	...	...	1 988	2 105	2 272	2 138	1 848	1 823	2 067	2 028	Suisse
East Europe	***183 086***	***177 404***	***176 460***	***174 036***	***171 700***	***165 256***	***165 113***	***169 308***	***173 994***	***169 492***	***Europe de l'est***
Bulgaria[9]	18 454	18 354	18 670	17 692	18 274	19 125	19 171	19 599	21 642	...	Bulgarie[9]
Czechoslovakia[10]	62 555	61 164	61 271	61 402	59 485	58 865	57 617	57 374	58 312	57 887	Tchécoslovaquie[10]
Hungary[11]	22 030	21 927	23 025	22 150	21 554	21 099	21 042	20 121	20 854	20 698	Hongrie[11]
Poland[10]	80 047	75 959	73 494	72 792	72 387	66 167	67 283	72 214	73 186	70 332	Pologne[10]
Other Europe	***66 976***	***65 223***	***60 240***	***55 038***	***56 642***	***52 357***	***50 720***	***51 690***	***47 848***	***43 750***	***Autre Europe***
Malta	251	378	420	326	448	471	458	428	491	...	Malte
Spain	47 642	43 944	...	32 065	28 689	22 981	20 962	21 418	...	...	Espagne
Yugoslavia	19 083	20 901	21 628	22 647	27 505	28 905	29 300	29 844	33 986	33 997	Yougoslavie
USSR[12]	**242 950**	**241 932**	**237 363**	**232 491**	**233 626**	**230 611**	**225 678**	**227 152**	**228 226**	**227 451**	**URSS[12]**
Byelorussian SSR[12]	*14 074*	*13 931*	*13 188*	*12 476*	*12 520*	*13 172*	*12 966*	*12 629*	*13 141*	*13 200*	*RSS de Biélorussie[12]*
Ukrainian SSR[12]	*64 171*	*63 866*	*61 082*	*60 850*	*60 901*	*59 643*	*58 291*	*59 552*	*60 738*	*61 507*	*RSS d'Ukraine[12]*
Oceania	**15 535**	**13 700**	**14 398**	**15 807**	**16 767**	**18 227**	**17 876**	**18 931**	**20 861**	**22 026**	**Océanie**

For general note and footnotes, see end of table.

Voir la fin du tableau pour la remarque générale et les notes.

Footwear, leather, women's (continued) – Chaussures en cuir pour dames (suite)

Unit : Thousand pairs

Unité : Milliers de paires

Country or area	1976	1977	1978	1979	1980	1981	1982	1983	1984	1985	Pays ou zone
Australia[13 14]	13 365	11 663	12 211	13 110	13 952	15 524	14 896	15 941	17 493	18 867	Australie[13 14]
New Zealand[14]	2 170	2 037	2 187	2 697	2 815	2 703	2 980	2 990	3 368	3 159	Nouvelle–Zélande[14]
Total	**1 156 538**	**1 129 442**	**1 136 780**	**1 140 065**	**1 141 747**	**1 151 201**	**1 145 995**	**1 160 237**	**1 158 018**	**1 132 867**	**Total**

General note.
Boots and shoes with leather, rubber, composition leather or plastic soles, and with leather or mainly leather uppers. Rubber footwear is excluded. (SITC 85102–3).

1 Including footwear for men.
2 Including non–leather footwear.
3 Including sandals and light footwear.
4 Production by establishments employing 10 or more persons.
5 Including other footwear, house footwear, sandals and other light footwear. Also including rubber footwear.
6 Source: Organisation for Economic Co–operation and Development (OECD), (Paris).
7 Industrial sales.
8 Manufacturers' sales.
9 Including footwear for men and children, and other footwear.
10 Including footwear for men and children.
11 Including sandals.
12 Including sporting footwear of all types and orthopedic shoes.
13 Twelve months ending 30 June of year stated.
14 Including footwear of materials other than leather.

Remarque générale.
Bottes et chaussures à semelle en cuir naturel, en caoutchouc, en cuir artificiel ou reconstitué ou en matière plastique, et à dessus en cuir ou principalement en cuir. Les chaussures en caoutchouc ne sont pas comprises. (CTCI 85102–3).

1 Y compris les chaussures pour hommes.
2 Y compris les chaussures en toutes matières autres que le cuir.
3 Y compris les sandales et chaussures légères.
4 Production des établissements occupant 10 personnes ou plus.
5 Y compris les autres chaussures, chaussures de maison, sandales et autres chaussures légères. Y compris également les chaussures en caoutchouc.
6 Source: Organisation de coopération et de développement économiques (OCDE), (Paris).
7 Ventes industrielles.
8 Ventes des fabricants.
9 Y compris les chaussures pour hommes et enfants, et autres chaussures.
10 Y compris les chaussures pour hommes et enfants.
11 Y compris les sandales.
12 Y compris les chaussures de sport de tous genres et les chaussures orthopédiques.
13 Période de douze mois finissant le 30 juin de l'année indiquée.
14 Y compris les chaussures en matières autres que le cuir.

Footwear, other (sports, orthopedic etc.) – Autres chaussures (pour sports, orthopédiques etc.)

Unit : Thousand pairs — Unité : Milliers de paires

Country or area	1976	1977	1978	1979	1980	1981	1982	1983	1984	1985	Pays ou zone
Africa	**24 329**	**26 411**	**25 323**	**25 495**	**30 876**	**31 692**	**26 055**	**23 488**	**23 006**	**23 000**	**Afrique**
Algeria[1]	7 258	7 287	8 224	...	...	...	...	...	...	...	Algérie[1]
Egypt	...	...	...	...	...	292	...	...	...	...	Egypte
Ethiopia[2]	5 388	5 139	2 517	5 514	6 625	6 936	* 6 000	* 5 000	...	...	Ethiopie[2]
South Africa[3]	7 690	8 862	10 024	7 833	12 103	12 608	7 907	6 340	* 4 614	4 418	Afrique du Sud[3]
Tunisia[4]	3 701	4 831	...	...	...	...	...	...	...	...	Tunisie[4]
America, North	**21 573**	**28 717**	**33 371**	**39 547**	**46 026**	**40 632**	**47 514**	**47 085**	**41 312**	**40 470**	**Amérique du Nord**
Canada	5 342	5 506	4 934	9 623	10 825	11 706	...	...	...	...	Canada
Cuba	843	655	898	813	894	858	1 033	1 151	953	724	Cuba
Dominican Republic	3 166	3 743	3 960	4 860	6 512	6 835	6 919	7 148	6 463	...	Rép. dominicaine
Panama	28	30	58	71	...	47	87	493	...	...	Panama
United States[5]	12 194	18 783	23 521	24 180	27 654	21 186	26 242	23 561	17 355	13 545	Etats–Unis[5]
America, South	**2 125**	**2 495**	**810**	**2 424**	**3 607**	**2 902**	**3 470**	**4 013**	**4 103**	**4 405**	**Amérique du Sud**
Bolivia	47	16	76	23	...	...	14	20	18	...	Bolivie
Brazil	2 057	2 248	542	[6] 2 127	3 219	...	...	...	...	...	Brésil
Colombia	...	231	192	274	358	180	541	859	...	...	Colombie
Asia	**471 267**	**476 234**	**469 941**	**467 217**	**450 871**	**476 320**	**476 458**	**474 656**	**474 215**	**473 541**	**Asie**
Burma[7]	228	...	...	...	...	...	...	...	...	...	Birmanie[7]
China[4 8]	...	...	...	...	408 740	430 530	430 000	...	...	...	Chine[4 8]
India[9 10]	6 900	6 024	5 664	5 692	5 291	6 437	5 888	6 754	7 115	7 479	Inde[9 10]
Indonesia	...	1 284	717	715	1 237	861	2 657	3 174	2 208	...	Indonésie
Iran(Islamic Rep.of)[11]	...	11 884	8 756	8 997	6 146	9 583	[12] 11 617	[12] 16 234	...	...	Iran(Rép.islamique)[11]
Japan[11]	7 552	9 586	8 928	9 387	9 096	9 343	9 127	9 188	12 521	10 974	Japon[11]
Malaysia[13 14]	17 334	18 278	17 508	15 394	15 766	15 189	12 292	11 128	...	...	Malaisie[13 14]
Sri Lanka	2 875	...	...	78	6	2	...	...	...	...	Sri Lanka
Syrian Arab Republic[4]	2 821	2 657	1 847	1 173	1 898	1 684	1 446	1 657	1 547	1 621	Rép. arabe syrienne[4]
Turkey[15]	...	...	...	...	...	...	...	...	...	2 463	Turquie[15]
Europe	**304 567**	**312 341**	**304 177**	**301 856**	**299 009**	**289 125**	**287 141**	**297 435**	**299 929**	**297 600**	**Europe**
EEC	***101 105***	***102 904***	***92 438***	***83 386***	***83 050***	***76 944***	***75 208***	***73 001***	***67 960***	***62 545***	***CEE***
Belgium[16]	1 136	1 047	985	753	427	562	528	537	708	640	Belgique[16]
Denmark[17]	362	482	262	305	123	...	...	...	...	...	Danemark[17]
Germany, Fed. Rep.	52 250	53 014	46 453	45 223	47 027	40 863	39 928	40 871	38 623	35 073	Allemagne, Rép. féd.
Greece[15]	...	...	...	484	1 048	967	746	1 264	724	...	Grèce[15]
Netherlands[3 18 19]	4 400	4 300	1 420	1 380	1 409	1 500	1 349	1 387	1 151	1 231	Pays–Bas[3 18 19]
United Kingdom[20 21]	42 340	43 398	42 608	35 241	33 016	32 858	32 502	...	...	...	Royaume–Uni[20 21]
EFTA	***17 830***	***19 582***	***16 458***	***17 102***	***14 829***	***14 619***	***11 399***	***9 915***	***8 550***	***6 487***	***AELE***
Austria	3 873	3 879	3 392	3 490	3 745	3 651	3 530	2 964	2 632	2 555	Autriche
Finland	2 674	2 471	1 955	2 259	1 815	1 513	927	555	1 071	...	Finlande
Iceland	6	6	4	6	19	10	24	22	20	...	Islande
Norway	196	125	153	200	211	289	125	...	...	...	Norvège
Portugal	2 865	4 854	4 466	5 886	...	5 070	3 199	3 318	2 777	1 991	Portugal
Sweden	8 216	8 247	6 488	5 261	5 096	4 086	3 594	2 846	1 834	1 247	Suède
East Europe	***160 136***	***163 501***	***168 396***	***174 421***	***175 682***	***171 306***	***173 499***	***184 676***	***191 546***	***196 885***	***Europe de l'est***
Czechoslovakia	55 125	57 726	59 465	60 793	60 591	62 295	64 071	63 803	66 132	67 316	Tchécoslovaquie
German Dem. Rep.	42 813	41 825	39 990	39 597	40 308	41 126	42 627	43 230	43 364	43 803	Rép. dém. allemande
Hungary[22]	6 573	6 855	6 571	6 810	6 536	7 814	7 885	8 360	8 160	8 495	Hongrie[22]
Poland	55 625	57 095	62 370	67 221	68 247	60 071	58 916	69 283	73 890	77 271	Pologne
Other Europe	***25 496***	***26 354***	***26 885***	***26 947***	***25 448***	***26 256***	***27 035***	***29 842***	***31 872***	***31 682***	***Autre Europe***
Spain	13 489	...	...	8 493	9 463	8 264	8 081	9 285	...	...	Espagne
Yugoslavia	12 007	14 820	15 990	18 454	15 985	17 992	18 954	20 557	24 806	25 255	Yougoslavie
Oceania	**1 825**	**1 825**	**1 825**	**1 825**	**1 825**	**1 825**	**1 562**	**1 682**	**2 159**	**1 896**	**Océanie**
New Zealand[23]	...	...	...	...	...	...	1 562	1 682	2 159	1 896	Nouvelle–Zélande[23]
Total	**825 686**	**848 023**	**835 447**	**838 363**	**832 213**	**842 496**	**842 201**	**848 359**	**844 724**	**840 912**	**Total**

For general note and footnotes, see end of table.

Voir la fin du tableau pour la remarque générale et les notes.

General note.
All other footwear such as sports footwear equipped with spikes, studs, bars etc., and orthopedic leather footwear. Rubber footwear is excluded. (Parts of SITC 85102, 85103 and 85105).

[1] Excluding leather footwear.
[2] Excluding canvas shoes.
[3] Including rubber footwear.
[4] Including rubber and plastic footwear.
[5] Including non–leather footwear.
[6] Production by establishments employing 5 or more persons.
[7] Twelve months ending 30 September of year stated.
[8] Including footwear for men, women and children.
[9] Indigenous–type footwear.
[10] Production by large and medium scale establishments only.
[11] Production by establishments employing 10 or more persons.
[12] Including canvas, plastic and rubber footwear.
[13] Canvas shoes with rubber soles.
[14] Data refer to Peninsular Malaysia only.
[15] Sporting footwear of all types.
[16] Including sandals and similar light footwear.
[17] Including sandals and light footwear.
[18] Including slippers and sandals with leather uppers.
[19] Industrial sales.
[20] Including safety footwear with uppers of all materials.
[21] Manufacturers' sales.
[22] Including leather top–boots, brogues, sports shoes and slippers.
[23] Including sporting footwear of all types.

Remarque générale.
Toutes autres chaussures, telles que chaussures pour sports, équipées de pointes, de crampons, de barrettes etc., et chaussures orthopédiques en cuir. Cette rubrique ne comprend pas les chaussures en caoutchouc. (Parties de CTCI 85102, 85103 et 85105).

[1] Non compris les chaussures en cuir.
[2] Non compris les chaussures en toile.
[3] Y compris les chaussures en caoutchouc.
[4] Y compris chaussures en caoutchouc et en matière plastique.
[5] Y compris les chaussures en toutes matières autres que le cuir.
[6] Production des établissements occupant 5 personnes ou plus.
[7] Période de douze mois finissant le 30 septembre de l'année indiquée.
[8] Y compris les chaussures pour hommes, dames et enfants.
[9] Chaussures de type indigène.
[10] Production des grandes et moyennes entreprises seulement.
[11] Production des établissements occupant 10 personnes ou plus.
[12] Y compris les chaussures en toile, en matière plastique et en caoutchouc.
[13] Chaussures en toile à semelles de caoutchouc.
[14] Données se rapportant à la Malaisie péninsulaire seulement.
[15] Les chaussures de sport de tous genres.
[16] Y compris les sandales et chaussures légères analogues.
[17] Y compris les sandales et chaussures légères.
[18] Y compris les pantoufles et sandales à empeigne en cuir.
[19] Ventes industrielles.
[20] Y compris les chaussures de sécurité à empeigne en matières de toutes sortes.
[21] Ventes des fabricants.
[22] Y compris les bottes à revers, les brogues, les chaussures de sport et les pantoufles en cuir.
[23] Y compris les chaussures de sport de tous genres.

Unit : Thousand pairs — Unité : Milliers de paires

Country or area	1976	1977	1978	1979	1980	1981	1982	1983	1984	1985	Pays ou zone
Africa	**428**	**1 000**	**822**	**821**	**815**	**599**	**577**	**600**	**623**	**604**	**Afrique**
Algeria	234	843	716	690	599	420	* 400	* 420	...	...	Algérie
Tunisia	194	157	106	131	216	179	...	...	...	...	Tunisie
America, North	**72 151**	**83 144**	**85 519**	**78 662**	**78 966**	**75 542**	**59 065**	**62 970**	**66 462**	**61 520**	**Amérique du Nord**
Canada[1 2]	7 271	5 542	6 166	5 883	5 629	5 773	5 024	5 278	7 047	7 099	Canada[1 2]
United States	64 880	77 602	79 353	72 779	73 337	69 769	54 041	57 692	59 415	54 421	Etats-Unis
America, South	**426**	**472**	**611**	**477**	**856**	**874**	**1 046**	**910**	**1 116**	**1 206**	**Amérique du Sud**
Colombia	...	410	547	411	784	792	960	821	...	...	Colombie
Paraguay[3]	100	62	64	66	72	82	86	89	92	95	Paraguay[3]
Asia	**45 804**	**46 674**	**41 818**	**40 297**	**38 491**	**43 469**	**34 300**	**71 780**	**47 868**	**53 457**	**Asie**
Hong Kong	10 731	9 746	11 258	14 371	17 959	19 816	12 217	54 277	33 808	...	Hong-kong
Korea, Republic of	...	...	...	...	18 974	22 120	20 670	16 088	12 622	12 135	Corée, République de
Philippines	...	...	...	...	...	...	...	543	...	...	Philippines
Sri Lanka	4 430	8 195	...	237	205	180	61	62	86	66	Sri Lanka
Turkey	519	529	865	1 325	...	...	...	...	...	...	Turquie
Europe	**220 406**	**206 771**	**196 371**	**186 658**	**186 401**	**183 639**	**174 820**	**168 865**	**158 862**	**154 503**	**Europe**
EEC	***138 492***	***132 696***	***125 961***	***125 713***	***128 132***	***122 373***	***116 299***	***113 334***	***111 552***	***110 559***	***CEE***
Belgium	3 485	3 094	2 591	2 451	2 703	2 861	2 946	2 599	2 712	2 629	Belgique
Denmark	478	393	334	337	479	* 350	313	242	...	...	Danemark
France[4]	52 600	51 300	48 325	48 268	51 512	48 690	44 689	44 846	43 356	42 600	France[4]
Germany, Fed. Rep.	19 402	18 303	18 742	18 492	18 743	18 329	17 650	16 231	15 334	13 918	Allemagne, Rép. féd.
Greece	588	548	526	518	530	510	405	334	343	...	Grèce
Italy[5]	18 971	16 419	...	...	...	...	...	...	...	...	Italie[5]
Netherlands	2 518	3 219	2 690	2 402	2 621	2 584	2 658	2 905	2 657	2 980	Pays-Bas
United Kingdom[6]	40 450	39 420	35 058	35 550	33 849	31 354	29 943	28 482	29 189	30 171	Royaume-Uni[6]
EFTA	***7 156***	***6 597***	***6 199***	***5 072***	***5 499***	***5 788***	***5 608***	***5 018***	***5 318***	***5 278***	***AELE***
Austria	3 343	2 725	2 195	2 268	2 311	2 822	3 211	2 714	3 067	3 110	Autriche
Finland	545	673	429	400	723	472	376	530	566	...	Finlande
Iceland[7]	14	17	19	26	20	16	21	16	11	...	Islande[7]
Norway	463	364	330	329	330	311	128	68	...	...	Norvège
Portugal	460	* 605	1 402	286	357	340	257	210	243	220	Portugal
Sweden	1 208	1 214	1 045	934	887	914	891	883	890	860	Suède
Switzerland	[8] 1 123	...	779	829	871	913	724	597	465	551	Suisse
East Europe	***37 190***	***38 164***	***38 524***	***38 272***	***39 216***	***41 304***	***40 529***	***38 986***	***38 139***	***38 448***	***Europe de l'est***
Bulgaria	5 143	5 882	5 033	5 168	6 130	6 696	6 366	6 458	6 355	5 735	Bulgarie
German Dem. Rep.	27 961	28 385	29 280	29 267	29 268	29 784	29 644	28 394	27 318	28 127	Rép. dém. allemande
Hungary	4 086	3 897	4 211	3 837	3 818	4 824	4 519	4 134	4 466	4 586	Hongrie
Other Europe	***37 568***	***29 315***	***25 687***	***17 601***	***13 554***	***14 174***	***12 384***	***11 527***	***3 853***	***219***	***Autre Europe***
Malta	2	3	12	12	12	15	2	1	1	...	Malte
Spain	37 566	...	...	17 589	13 542	14 159	12 382	11 526	...	...	Espagne
Oceania	**1 180**	**1 098**	**964**	**1 078**	**1 047**	**1 111**	**1 124**	**878**	**951**	**763**	**Océanie**
New Zealand	1 180	1 098	964	1 078	1 047	1 111	1 124	878	951	763	Nouvelle-Zélande
Total	**340 396**	**339 160**	**326 104**	**307 993**	**306 576**	**305 234**	**270 932**	**306 003**	**275 881**	**272 052**	**Total**

General note.
House slippers, underwedge slippers such as slip-on type, without laces, buckles, zippers or other closures, of underwedge heel construction, or with leather upper and split leather tread sole and heel held together by a blown sponge rubber midsole created and simultaneously attached thereto. Slipper socks are excluded. (SITC 85104-1).

[1] Excluding felt.
[2] Including Indian type slippers.
[3] Slippers only.

Remarque générale.
Pantoufles, babouches, mules et autres chaussons, sans lacets, boucles, fermetures à glissière ni autres fermetures, du type à semelle compensée ou avec empeigne de cuir et semelle et talon en cuir refendu, réunis par un cambrion intégral en caoutchouc mousse. Cette rubrique ne comprend pas les chaussettes à semelle renforcée. (CTCI 85104-1).

[1] Non compris les feutres.
[2] Y compris les pantoufles de type indien.
[3] Pantoufles seulement.

[4] Also included with data for leather footwear for men, women and children.

[5] Source: Industrial Statistics, Statistical Office of the European Communities, (Luxembourg).

[6] Manufacturers' sales.

[7] Including sandals and light footwear.

[8] Source: Organisation for Economic Co–operation and Development (OECD), (Paris).

[4] Aussi comptées dans les données concernant les chaussures en cuir pour hommes, pour dames et pour enfants.

[5] Source: Statistiques industrielles, Office statistique des Communautés européennes, (Luxembourg).

[6] Ventes des fabricants.

[7] Y compris les sandales et chaussures légères.

[8] Source: Organisation de coopération et de développement économiques (OCDE), (Paris).

Sandals and similar light footwear –
Sandales et autres chaussures légères

Unit : Thousand pairs

Unité : Milliers de paires

Country or area	1976	1977	1978	1979	1980	1981	1982	1983	1984	1985	Pays ou zone
Africa	**6 439**	**7 063**	**7 285**	**5 793**	**6 857**	**7 016**	**7 145**	**6 787**	**7 063**	**7 122**	**Afrique**
Algeria[1]	1 068	1 021	2 113	731	1 857	2 472	* 2 500	* 2 300	...	...	Algérie[1]
Niger	1 864	1 348	1 097	1 335	...	...	...	...	...	...	Niger
Tunisia	3 507	4 694	4 075	3 727	3 589	3 133	...	...	...	...	Tunisie
America, North	**1 580**	**1 472**	**1 720**	**1 696**	**1 336**	**778**	**777**	**1 433**	**1 422**	**1 411**	**Amérique du Nord**
Canada	151	100	...	...	...	...	...	...	...	...	Canada
Cuba[2]	...	...	1 404	1 385	935	451	167	...	...	...	Cuba[2]
Panama	149	145	190	185	...	201	484	...	...	...	Panama
America, South	**596**	**596**	**628**	**606**	**606**	**596**	**698**	**526**	**606**	**606**	**Amérique du Sud**
Colombia	...	...	...	...	...	581	683	511	...	...	Colombie
Ecuador	4	4	36	...	...	...	...	...	...	...	Equateur
Asia	**5 932**	**28 971**	**26 318**	**23 693**	**27 542**	**24 918**	**30 962**	**34 789**	**43 984**	**42 471**	**Asie**
Burma[3]	382	...	...	...	...	...	...	...	...	...	Birmanie[3]
Indonesia	4 344	# 27 383	24 730	22 105	25 954	23 330	29 374	33 201	42 396	...	Indonésie
Turkey[4]	...	...	...	...	...	...	...	...	...	1 206	Turquie[4]
Europe	**67 092**	**73 038**	**71 916**	**75 703**	**82 629**	**73 740**	**72 034**	**66 756**	**72 260**	**68 242**	**Europe**
EEC	***12 569***	***12 085***	***10 791***	***12 987***	***10 612***	***11 860***	***12 630***	***11 429***	***12 189***	***11 032***	***CEE***
Germany, Fed. Rep.	8 193	8 639	6 532	7 215	6 964	7 801	9 269	8 886	9 977	8 530	Allemagne, Rép. féd.
Greece	3 609	2 841	3 627	5 142	3 001	3 483	2 673	2 093	1 711	...	Grèce
Ireland[5 6]	767	605	632	630	647	576	688	450	501	...	Irlande[5 6]
EFTA	***5 899***	***6 262***	***6 683***	***7 185***	***8 752***	***8 980***	***7 610***	***7 771***	***6 844***	***6 070***	***AELE***
Austria	4 337	5 074	5 404	5 420	6 484	6 444	5 400	5 326	4 659	2 760	Autriche
Finland	497	305	257	284	357	275	220	231	237	...	Finlande
Norway	125	139	81	90	60	63	39	27	33	...	Norvège
Portugal[7]	940	744	941	1 391	1 851	2 198	1 951	2 187	1 915	3 121	Portugal[7]
East Europe	***10 174***	***11 689***	***12 217***	***11 431***	***11 708***	***12 556***	***12 249***	***12 924***	***13 622***	***12 330***	***Europe de l'est***
Hungary	10 174	11 689	12 217	11 431	11 708	12 556	12 249	12 924	13 622	12 330	Hongrie
Other Europe	***38 450***	***43 002***	***42 225***	***44 100***	***51 557***	***40 344***	***39 545***	***34 632***	***39 605***	***38 810***	***Autre Europe***
Malta	78	118	90	107	102	102	100	132	98	...	Malte
Spain	32 962	...	...	37 677	43 994	34 220	32 559	29 220	...	...	Espagne
Yugoslavia	5 410	5 968	5 791	6 316	7 461	6 022	6 886	5 280	6 594	6 354	Yougoslavie
Oceania	**1 076**	**1 028**	**596**	**701**	**1 096**	**1 211**	**1 029**	**1 066**	**1 092**	**1 118**	**Océanie**
New Zealand	1 076	1 028	596	701	1 096	1 211	1 029	...	...	...	Nouvelle–Zélande
Total	**82 715**	**112 167**	**108 463**	**108 192**	**120 067**	**108 258**	**112 645**	**111 357**	**126 428**	**120 971**	**Total**

General note.
Sandals of various types, "espadrilles", "alpargatas" (shoes with canvas uppers and soles of plaited vegetable material) and similar light footwear. Rubber footwear is excluded. (SITC 85104–2).

1 Footwear made of textile fabrics.
2 Begining 1983, series discontinued.
3 Twelve months ending 30 September of year stated.
4 Slippers only.
5 Including house footwear.
6 1985, data are confidential.
7 Tennis shoes only.

Remarque générale.
Sandales de types divers, "espadrilles", "alpargates" (chaussures avec dessus de toile et semelle de sparte tressée) et autres chaussures légères, à l'exclusion des chaussures en caoutchouc. (CTCI 85104–2).

1 Chaussures en tissus.
2 A partir de 1983, la série a été interrompue.
3 Période de douze mois finissant le 30 septembre de l'année indiquée.
4 Pantoufles seulement.
5 Y compris les chaussures d'intérieur.
6 Pour 1985, les données sont confidentielles.
7 Chaussures de tennis seulement.

Unit : Thousand cubic metres | Unité : Milliers de mètres cubes

Country or area	1976	1977	1978	1979	1980	1981	1982	1983	1984	1985	Pays ou zone
Africa	**344**	**366**	**312**	**305**	**288**	**349**	**340**	**330**	**330**	**330**	**Afrique**
Algeria	3	3	3	3	3	3	3	3	3	3	Algérie
Angola	10	0	0	0	0	0	0	0	0	0	Angola
Cameroon	98	43	55	55	30	85	85	85	85	85	Cameroun
Côte d'Ivoire	2	1	0	0	0	0	0	0	0	0	Côte d'Ivoire
Equatorial Guinea	9	6	1	1	3	9	9	9	9	9	Guinée équatoriale
Gabon	20	20	20	20	20	20	20	20	20	20	Gabon
Ghana	65	65	65	65	65	65	65	65	65	65	Ghana
Liberia	12	95	100	100	100	100	100	100	100	100	Libéria
Madagascar	3	3	3	3	3	3	3	3	3	3	Madagascar
Morocco	2	0	0	0	0	0	0	0	0	0	Maroc
Mozambique	80	80	11	11	11	14	6	4	4	4	Mozambique
Nigeria	12	12	12	12	12	12	12	12	12	12	Nigéria
South Africa	9	14	19	10	12	13	17	17	17	17	Afrique du Sud
Sudan	4	4	4	4	4	4	4	4	4	4	Soudan
Tunisia	1	1	1	1	1	1	1	1	1	1	Tunisie
United Rep. Tanzania	1	0	0	0	0	0	0	0	0	0	Rép.Unie de Tanzanie
Zimbabwe	14	20	18	20	24	20	15	7	7	7	Zimbabwe
America, North	**388**	**306**	**530**	**564**	**721**	**663**	**566**	**474**	**474**	**474**	**Amérique du Nord**
Costa Rica	8	11	11	0	0	0	0	0	0	0	Costa Rica
Cuba	55	55	55	26	31	23	23	23	23	23	Cuba
El Salvador	5	6	6	7	7	7	5	6	6	6	El Salvador
Guatemala	6	6	3	0	0	2	1	0	0	0	Guatemala
Haiti	2	2	2	2	2	2	2	2	2	2	Haïti
Honduras	17	17	17	17	15	15	15	15	15	15	Honduras
Mexico	219	161	373	296	361	402	308	215	215	215	Mexique
Nicaragua	2	2	2	2	2	2	2	2	2	2	Nicaragua
United States	74	46	61	214	303	210	210	210	210	210	Etats–Unis
America, South	**125**	**131**	**90**	**123**	**109**	**139**	**132**	**132**	**130**	**130**	**Amérique du Sud**
Argentina	78	86	27	68	37	67	67	67	67	67	Argentine
Bolivia	8	22	27	14	4	4	4	4	4	4	Bolivie
Chile	0	0	3	3	3	3	3	3	3	3	Chili
Colombia	4	4	4	6	40	40	40	40	40	40	Colombie
Ecuador	2	2	2	2	2	2	2	2	2	2	Equateur
Paraguay	5	4	5	7	6	6	6	6	6	6	Paraguay
Peru	3	2	4	5	4	5	5	5	5	5	Pérou
Suriname	1	2	9	9	5	2	2	2	0	0	Suriname
Uruguay	24	9	9	9	9	10	3	3	3	3	Uruguay
Asia	**559**	**572**	**580**	**727**	**752**	**765**	**796**	**790**	**790**	**790**	**Asie**
Bangladesh	6	6	6	6	6	6	6	6	6	6	Bangladesh
Burma	11	11	11	11	11	11	11	11	11	11	Birmanie
China	62	64	66	66	66	66	66	66	66	66	Chine
India	161	124	124	252	252	252	252	252	252	252	Inde
Indonesia	12	10	0	7	7	7	7	7	7	7	Indonésie
Iran(Islamic Rep.of)	54	73	73	73	73	73	73	73	73	73	Iran(Rép.islamique)
Japan	56	27	27	45	35	42	69	69	69	69	Japon
Korea, Republic of	0	50	66	66	66	66	66	66	66	66	Corée, République de
Malaysia	100	100	100	100	100	100	100	100	100	100	Malaisie
Pakistan	15	15	15	15	15	15	15	15	15	15	Pakistan
Singapore	18	37	33	27	54	54	54	54	54	54	Singapour
Sri Lanka	10	4	4	4	4	4	4	4	4	4	Sri Lanka
Thailand	11	7	7	8	16	22	26	20	20	20	Thaïlande
Turkey	43	44	48	48	48	48	48	48	48	48	Turquie
Europe	**1 747**	**1 751**	**1 606**	**1 624**	**1 699**	**1 460**	**1 336**	**1 324**	**1 266**	**1 229**	**Europe**
EEC	**570**	**502**	**540**	**544**	**574**	**562**	**475**	**409**	**361**	**351**	**CEE**
Denmark	10	10	6	0	0	29	29	29	29	29	Danemark
France	326	261	271	295	319	304	261	209	185	185	France
Germany, Fed. Rep.	181	171	198	178	168	146	119	107	93	90	Allemagne, Rép. féd.
Greece	1	0	0	0	0	0	0	0	0	0	Grèce
Italy	49	57	62	69	85	81	64	62	52	45	Italie
United Kingdom	3	3	3	2	2	2	2	2	2	2	Royaume–Uni
EFTA	**195**	**249**	**180**	**168**	**171**	**158**	**160**	**186**	**198**	**193**	**AELE**

For general note, see end of table. | Voir la fin du tableau pour la remarque générale.

Wooden railway sleepers (continued) – Traverses en bois pour voies ferrées (suite)

Unit : Thousand cubic metres

Unité : Milliers de mètres cubes

Country or area	1976	1977	1978	1979	1980	1981	1982	1983	1984	1985	Pays ou zone
Austria	0	43	0	0	0	0	0	35	43	37	Autriche
Finland	50	45	39	30	28	20	22	28	33	33	Finlande
Norway	3	11	2	2	2	2	2	2	2	2	Norvège
Portugal	80	80	70	70	70	70	70	60	60	60	Portugal
Sweden	27	30	29	26	26	26	26	26	26	26	Suède
Switzerland	35	40	40	40	45	40	40	35	35	35	Suisse
East Europe	**870**	**879**	**750**	**786**	**844**	**623**	**576**	**615**	**601**	**576**	**Europe de l'est**
Bulgaria	26	22	22	22	22	22	22	24	24	19	Bulgarie
Czechoslovakia	113	125	133	133	126	135	134	128	127	121	Tchécoslovaquie
German Dem. Rep.	155	171	137	126	201	124	96	96	96	96	Rép. dém. allemande
Hungary	9	17	13	8	5	10	15	18	15	15	Hongrie
Poland	470	447	348	414	406	277	251	291	281	267	Pologne
Romania	97	97	97	83	84	55	58	58	58	58	Roumanie
Other Europe	**70**	**73**	**91**	**78**	**58**	**65**	**73**	**62**	**53**	**57**	**Autre Europe**
Spain	64	58	78	61	42	48	56	45	43	43	Espagne
Yugoslavia	6	15	13	17	16	17	17	17	10	14	Yougoslavie
Oceania	**226**	**212**	**235**	**268**	**281**	**241**	**225**	**210**	**210**	**210**	**Océanie**
Australia	205	192	216	249	229	220	207	196	196	196	Australie
New Zealand	21	20	19	19	52	21	18	14	14	14	Nouvelle–Zélande
Total	**3 388**	**3 337**	**3 352**	**3 610**	**3 851**	**3 616**	**3 395**	**3 260**	**3 200**	**3 163**	**Total**

General note.
Pieces of wood of more or less rectangular section, suitable for laying transversely on the railway road–bed to support the rails. (SITC 24310–0).
Source: Food and Agriculture Organization of the United Nations (FAO), Rome.

Remarque générale.
Pièces de bois scié de section plus ou moins rectangulaire pouvant être posées transversalement sur le ballast pour supporter les rails. (CTCI 24310–0).
Source: Organisation des Nations Unies pour l'agriculture(FAO), Rome.

Sawnwood, coniferous – Sciages de résineux

Unit : Thousand cubic metres

Unité : Milliers de mètres cubes

Country or area	1976	1977	1978	1979	1980	1981	1982	1983	1984	1985	Pays ou zone
Africa	**2 000**	**1 920**	**1 855**	**1 877**	**1 919**	**2 151**	**1 903**	**1 898**	**1 921**	**1 829**	**Afrique**
Algeria	8	8	8	8	8	8	8	8	8	8	Algérie
Burundi	1	1	1	1	1	1	1	1	4	3	Burundi
Ethiopia	64	66	49	49	49	49	34	34	34	34	Ethiopie
Kenya	147	140	116	125	113	113	113	113	113	113	Kenya
Malawi	19	19	19	19	17	17	17	17	17	17	Malawi
Mauritius	5	2	4	2	3	2	2	3	3	3	Maurice
Morocco	50	45	38	40	30	63	94	94	94	94	Maroc
Mozambique	0	0	0	0	3	4	4	5	12	8	Mozambique
South Africa	1 494	1 395	1 398	1 385	1 411	1 581	1 317	1 363	1 363	1 276	Afrique du Sud
Swaziland	100	100	100	120	121	136	136	136	136	136	Swaziland
Tunisia	2	2	2	2	2	2	2	2	2	2	Tunisie
Uganda	8	8	8	8	8	7	7	7	7	7	Ouganda
United Rep. Tanzania	20	2	2	2	1	0	0	0	0	0	Rép.Unie de Tanzanie
Zambia	3	4	4	4	4	4	4	5	5	5	Zambie
Zimbabwe	80	128	106	112	148	164	164	110	123	123	Zimbabwe
America, North	**109 135**	**120 131**	**125 338**	**124 799**	**111 754**	**100 140**	**97 499**	**119 757**	**124 377**	**127 422**	**Amérique du Nord**
Bahamas	1	1	1	1	1	1	1	1	1	1	Bahamas
Belize	1	1	2	2	2	4	6	9	10	10	Belize
Canada	35 463	40 651	43 447	43 645	42 895	38 715	36 689	47 161	48 587	52 519	Canada
Costa Rica	2	2	2	2	12	12	12	12	12	12	Costa Rica
Cuba	5	5	5	9	13	13	24	26	32	35	Cuba
El Salvador	12	13	13	10	10	30	30	25	30	31	El Salvador
Guatemala	241	205	246	126	60	81	74	72	77	98	Guatemala
Haiti	7	7	7	7	7	7	7	7	7	7	Haïti
Honduras	564	599	605	599	* 538	* 538	472	450	409	409	Honduras
Mexico	1 798	1 977	1 840	1 729	1 546	1 468	1 314	1 529	1 611	1 840	Mexique
Nicaragua	170	170	170	170	170	170	170	93	93	93	Nicaragua
United States	70 871	76 500	79 000	78 500	66 500	59 100	58 700	70 372	73 508	72 367	Etats–Unis
America, South	**6 894**	**7 561**	**8 398**	**9 495**	**9 192**	**9 175**	**8 776**	**9 209**	**9 497**	**9 658**	**Amérique du Sud**
Argentina	20	20	20	223	146	180	269	304	304	304	Argentine
Brazil	5 846	6 590	6 952	7 334	7 143	7 475	7 475	7 475	7 475	7 475	Brésil
Chile	956	872	1 353	1 870	1 833	1 454	1 013	1 423	1 710	* 1 871	Chili
Colombia	30	30	30	30	30	30	1	1	1	1	Colombie
Peru	...	5	3	3	5	1	1	1	2	2	Pérou
Uruguay	42	44	40	35	35	35	17	5	5	5	Uruguay
Asia	**46 251**	**49 860**	**50 560**	**51 565**	**51 067**	**47 281**	**48 873**	**48 174**	**49 937**	**50 199**	**Asie**
Afghanistan	380	380	380	380	380	380	380	380	380	380	Afghanistan
China	10 973	11 449	12 012	12 591	13 169	13 799	14 455	14 993	17 432	17 432	Chine
Cyprus	70	89	67	75	69	58	61	51	56	56	Chypre
India	1 014	1 114	1 225	1 347	1 480	1 627	1 788	1 965	2 160	2 374	Inde
Indonesia	10	...	1	1	11	12	13	14	14	14	Indonésie
Japan	29 685	31 930	30 705	30 679	29 905	25 944	26 445	24 110	23 788	23 869	Japon
Korea,Dem.Ppl's.Rep	185	185	185	185	185	185	185	185	185	185	Corée,Rép.pop.dém.de
Korea, Republic of	846	1 668	1 740	2 048	1 570	2 126	2 120	2 510	1 952	1 919	Corée, République de
Lebanon	22	22	22	22	36	27	18	22	22	22	Liban
Malaysia	2	6	6	8	37	39	41	43	45	45	Malaisie
Mongolia	470	470	470	470	470	470	470	470	470	470	Mongolie
Nepal	10	10	10	10	10	10	10	10	10	10	Népal
Pakistan	71	12	24	40	40	40	40	40	40	40	Pakistan
Syrian Arab Republic	...	...	...	2	7	7	7	7	7	7	Rép. arabe syrienne
Turkey	2 444	2 441	3 635	3 635	3 635	2 500	2 788	3 328	3 330	3 330	Turquie
Viet Nam	69	84	78	72	63	57	52	47	47	47	Viet Nam
Europe	**63 070**	**64 788**	**64 846**	**69 246**	**70 374**	**65 564**	**64 838**	**67 713**	**69 048**	**67 629**	**Europe**
EEC	**15 783**	**16 300**	**15 881**	**16 565**	**17 088**	**16 021**	**15 595**	**16 430**	**17 198**	**17 615**	**CEE**
Denmark	400	400	400	400	400	400	400	400	400	400	Danemark
France	5 189	5 365	5 353	5 579	5 678	5 412	5 388	5 483	5 667	5 667	France
Germany, Fed. Rep	8 338	8 279	7 908	8 204	8 359	7 530	7 038	7 818	8 321	8 321	Allemagne, Rép. féd.
Greece	203	250	250	205	205	222	178	191	191	191	Grèce
Ireland	30	104	114	108	134	202	224	245	285	285	Irlande
Italy	780	920	852	983	1 144	1 145	1 070	920	1 003	1 166	Italie
Netherlands	75	102	96	88	103	100	72	146	153	166	Pays–Bas
United Kingdom	768	880	908	998	1 065	1 010	1 225	1 227	1 178	1 419	Royaume–Uni

For general note and footnotes, see end of table.

Voir la fin du tableau pour la remarque générale et les notes.

Sawnwood, coniferous (continued) – Sciages de résineux (suite)

Unit : Thousand cubic metres — Unité : Milliers de mètres cubes

Country or area	1976	1977	1978	1979	1980	1981	1982	1983	1984	1985	Pays ou zone
EFTA	**27 204**	**28 776**	**28 847**	**32 419**	**33 510**	**30 140**	**29 450**	**31 339**	**31 957**	**30 092**	**AELE**
Austria	5 709	5 841	5 526	6 108	6 301	6 024	5 518	6 048	6 041	5 749	Autriche
Finland	5 708	6 925	7 558	9 574	10 152	8 185	7 230	7 925	8 146	7 240	Finlande
Norway	2 007	2 000	2 086	2 350	2 450	2 450	2 250	2 300	2 350	2 350	Norvège
Portugal	1 600	1 700	1 750	2 000	2 000	1 650	1 855	1 980	2 000	2 000	Portugal
Sweden	11 005	10 850	10 577	10 987	11 077	10 266	10 977	11 546	12 120	11 275	Suède
Switzerland	1 175	1 460	1 350	1 400	1 530	1 565	1 620	1 540	1 300	1 478	Suisse
East Europe	**15 740**	**15 566**	**15 812**	**15 629**	**15 494**	**15 009**	**14 853**	**15 364**	**15 325**	**15 338**	**Europe de l'est**
Albania	105	105	105	105	105	105	105	105	105	105	Albanie
Bulgaria	1 203	1 032	1 099	1 205	1 007	988	1 063	1 047	964	979	Bulgarie
Czechoslovakia	3 599	3 631	3 790	3 855	3 996	4 024	4 140	4 206	4 300	4 303	Tchécoslovaquie
German Dem. Rep.	1 747	1 737	1 760	1 762	1 825	1 831	1 879	1 900	1 983	1 983	Rép. dém. allemande
Hungary	481	565	568	477	512	508	383	438	514	513	Hongrie
Poland	6 757	6 665	6 508	6 128	5 920	5 568	5 414	5 818	5 689	5 685	Pologne
Romania	1 848	1 831	1 982	2 097	2 129	1 985	1 869	1 850	1 770	1 770	Roumanie
Other Europe	**4 023**	**3 824**	**3 976**	**4 302**	**3 943**	**4 073**	**4 567**	**4 153**	**4 128**	**4 144**	**Autre Europe**
Spain	1 840	1 540	1 693	1 912	1 602	1 789	2 103	1 695	1 636	1 636	Espagne
Yugoslavia	2 183	2 284	2 283	2 390	2 341	2 284	2 464	2 458	2 492	2 508	Yougoslavie
USSR	**98 900**	**95 400**	**92 800**	**87 200**	**86 000**	**85 800**	**85 737**	**84 900**	**84 900**	**84 900**	**URSS**
Oceania	**3 111**	**2 957**	**2 598**	**2 785**	**3 173**	**3 432**	**3 474**	**3 201**	**3 216**	**3 336**	**Océanie**
Australia	905	991	946	967	1 133	1 226	1 181	1 042	1 096	1 218	Australie
Fiji	14	14	14	17	18	16	12	13	13	14	Fidji
New Caledonia	1	1	...	...	...	...	...	...	...	...	Nouvelle–Calédonie
New Zealand	2 162	1 926	1 613	1 776	1 968	2 144	2 233	2 099	2 060	2 060	Nouvelle–Zélande
Papua New Guinea	29	25	25	25	54	46	46	46	46	* 43	Papouasie–Nvl–Guinée
Tonga	...	...	...	...	...	...	2	1	1	1	Tonga
Total	**329 361**	**342 617**	**346 395**	**346 967**	**333 479**	**313 543**	**311 100**	**334 852**	**342 897**	**344 974**	**Total**

General note.
Sawnwood includes wood simply sawn lengthwise (for example, planks, beams, joists, boards, rafters, scantlings, laths etc.) and wood which has been sliced, peeled or rotary cut, and which is more than 5 mm thick. Rough sawnwood is often further processed in the same establishment into planed, tongued, grooved, chamfered, rabbeted, v–jointed and beaded wood etc. Where this occurs, production may be counted at the sawn stage or at a later stage, but steps should be taken to ensure that the sawn wood is not counted more than once. Boxes, whether assembled or not (part of SITC 6321) and sawn railway sleepers (part of SITC 2431) are excluded, as is wood sawn into sheets of a thickness of 5 mm or less (part of SITC 6311). (SITC 24320–0).
Source: Food and Agriculture Organization of the United Nations (FAO), Rome.

Remarque générale.
Les sciages comprennent les bois simplement sciés longitudinalement (par exemple: madriers, poutres, solives, planches, chevrons, voliges, lattes etc.) et les bois tranchés ou déroulés, de plus de 5 mm d'épaisseur. Dans le même établissement, on fait souvent subir aux sciages bruts un traitement ultérieur pour en faire des bois rabotés, bouvetés, rainés, languetés, chamfreinés, feuillurés, chevronnés et moulurés etc. Dans ce cas, la production peut être comptée au stade du sciage ou à un stade ultérieur, mais on doit veiller à ne pas compter deux fois le même bois. N'entrent dans cette rubrique ni les caisses ni les planches de caisserie (ex CTCI 6321), ni les traverses de chemin de fer sciées (ex CTCI 2431), ni le bois scié en feuilles d'une épaisseur de 5 mm ou moins (ex CTCI 6311). (CTCI 24320–0).
Source: Organisation des Nations Unies pour l'agriculture(FAO), Rome.

Sawnwood, broadleaved – Sciages de feuillus

Unit : Thousand cubic metres — Unité : Milliers de mètres cubes

Country or area	1976	1977	1978	1979	1980	1981	1982	1983	1984	1985	Pays ou zone
Africa	**3 405**	**3 758**	**4 536**	**4 612**	**5 397**	**5 519**	**5 350**	**5 110**	**5 397**	**5 673**	**Afrique**
Algeria	2	2	2	2	2	2	2	2	2	2	Algérie
Angola	90	60	40	20	10	10	10	10	10	10	Angola
Benin	9	9	9	9	9	9	9	9	5	9	Bénin
Burkina Faso	1	1	1	1	2	2	2	2	2	1	Burkina Faso
Cameroon	235	258	465	361	380	383	383	* 341	552	565	Cameroun
Central African Rep.	75	90	104	68	71	70	63	61	58	56	Rép. centrafricaine
Chad	1	1	1	1	1	1	1	1	1	1	Tchad
Congo	60	49	43	53	64	73	66	66	60	50	Congo
Côte d'Ivoire	583	681	665	670	664	611	748	718	646	646	Côte d'Ivoire
Equatorial Guinea	7	5	1	1	3	4	9	14	15	30	Guinée équatoriale
Ethiopia	21	22	16	16	16	16	11	11	11	11	Ethiopie
Gabon	55	88	88	88	88	88	88	88	97	106	Gabon
Gambia	1	1	1	1	1	1	1	1	1	1	Gambie
Ghana	316	520	320	280	160	160	150	210	220	302	Ghana
Guinea	90	90	90	90	90	90	90	90	90	90	Guinée
Guinea–Bissau	16	16	16	16	16	16	16	16	16	16	Guinée–Bissau
Kenya	26	33	15	26	68	68	68	68	68	68	Kenya
Liberia	128	138	40	66	43	99	72	61	53	53	Libéria
Libyan Arab Jamah.	9	21	31	31	31	31	31	31	31	31	Jamah.arabe libyenne
Madagascar	99	231	231	231	231	231	231	231	231	231	Madagascar
Malawi	15	15	15	15	31	26	26	26	26	26	Malawi
Mali	5	6	6	6	6	6	6	6	6	4	Mali
Mauritius	3	2	3	3	1	1	2	1	1	1	Maurice
Morocco	10	36	30	33	98	51	55	55	55	55	Maroc
Mozambique	112	65	55	55	51	47	33	29	24	20	Mozambique
Nigeria	937	937	1 803	2 000	2 782	2 950	2 655	2 390	2 500	2 700	Nigéria
Réunion	1	1	1	1	1	1	1	1	1	1	Réunion
Rwanda	2	2	2	2	2	2	2	2	2	2	Rwanda
Sao Tome – Principe	2	2	2	2	4	3	1	3	3	3	Sao Tomé–et–Principe
Senegal	5	6	8	11	11	11	11	11	11	11	Sénégal
Sierra Leone	41	11	23	23	24	22	20	19	19	19	Sierra Leone
Somalia	14	14	14	14	14	14	14	14	14	14	Somalie
South Africa	206	140	143	153	170	178	229	240	255	217	Afrique du Sud
Sudan	6	12	12	6	2	2	2	9	9	9	Soudan
Togo	5	5	5	5	5	5	5	5	5	5	Togo
Uganda	37	16	16	16	16	16	16	16	16	16	Ouganda
United Rep. Tanzania	46	29	36	48	52	60	70	80	90	100	Rép.Unie de Tanzanie
Zaire	78	90	* 123	* 136	121	* 105	* 95	* 114	* 121	121	Zaïre
Zambia	38	38	38	38	38	38	38	45	45	45	Zambie
Zimbabwe	19	15	22	15	19	16	19	14	27	27	Zimbabwe
America, North	**17 562**	**17 972**	**18 531**	**19 306**	**19 761**	**18 190**	**13 242**	**14 947**	**16 947**	**16 478**	**Amérique du Nord**
Belize	19	15	15	16	39	34	36	24	28	28	Belize
Canada	1 170	1 045	1 333	1 164	1 429	956	1 057	908	1 384	1 348	Canada
Costa Rica	503	676	676	362	512	522	366	294	400	400	Costa Rica
Cuba	45	45	45	67	69	72	60	55	53	46	Cuba
El Salvador	14	15	14	20	20	10	10	8	10	10	El Salvador
Guadeloupe	1	2	2	1	1	1	1	1	1	1	Guadeloupe
Guatemala	79	142	97	12	33	53	55	32	26	33	Guatemala
Haiti	5	5	5	5	5	5	5	5	5	5	Haïti
Honduras	17	12	11	8	* 7	* 7	2	3	3	3	Honduras
Jamaica	30	29	24	25	25	25	25	23	31	31	Jamaïque
Martinique	3	1	0	0	0	0	0	0	0	0	Martinique
Mexico	130	121	86	84	84	58	47	83	149	150	Mexique
Nicaragua	230	230	230	230	230	230	230	127	127	127	Nicaragua
Panama ex.Canal Zone	81	33	12	12	53	53	53	53	53	53	Panama ex.zone Canal
Trinidad and Tobago	32	32	32	32	33	33	28	22	21	21	Trinité–et–Tobago
United States	15 203	15 569	15 949	17 268	17 221	16 131	11 267	13 309	14 657	14 223	Etats–Unis
America, South	**9 655**	**10 367**	**10 282**	**11 293**	**12 625**	**13 393**	**12 779**	**12 923**	**13 164**	**13 195**	**Amérique du Sud**
Argentina	533	753	593	617	700	800	856	866	866	866	Argentine
Bolivia	135	87	140	219	216	168	113	93	93	93	Bolivie
Brazil	5 397	6 053	6 385	6 736	7 738	8 377	8 377	8 377	8 377	8 377	Brésil
Chile	267	395	122	326	350	278	160	184	288	* 320	Chili
Colombia	900	900	900	947	900	936	680	680	680	680	Colombie
Ecuador	750	850	760	828	903	984	978	1 140	1 210	1 213	Equateur
French Guiana	10	10	14	19	19	19	19	19	19	19	Guyane française
Guyana	82	75	51	61	70	70	70	70	60	65	Guyana
Paraguay	340	310	375	517	649	649	649	649	828	745	Paraguay
Peru	783	469	479	538	602	647	571	571	472	528	Pérou

For general note and footnotes, see end of table. — Voir la fin du tableau pour la remarque générale et les notes.

Unit : Thousand cubic metres — Unité : Milliers de mètres cubes

Country or area	1976	1977	1978	1979	1980	1981	1982	1983	1984	1985	Pays ou zone
Suriname	58	62	59	81	74	61	59	56	53	71	Suriname
Uruguay	51	54	55	55	55	55	27	8	8	8	Uruguay
Venezuela	349	349	349	349	349	349	220	210	210	210	Venezuela
Asia	**37 845**	**36 663**	**40 550**	**41 504**	**42 290**	**42 148**	**44 694**	**45 829**	**48 019**	**49 614**	**Asie**
Afghanistan	20	20	20	20	20	20	20	20	20	20	Afghanistan
Bangladesh	142	159	170	170	170	170	197	156	148	143	Bangladesh
Bhutan	...	...	5	5	5	5	5	5	5	5	Bhoutan
Brunei Darussalam	65	72	63	67	60	95	99	90	90	90	Brunéi Darussalam
Burma	324	404	404	404	404	404	404	404	404	404	Birmanie
China	6 450	6 759	7 078	7 419	7 775	8 142	8 543	8 846	10 297	10 297	Chine
Cyprus	0	1	5	8	7	6	12	4	3	3	Chypre
Dem. Kampuchea	43	43	43	43	43	43	43	43	43	43	Kampuchea démocrat.
Hong Kong	166	228	262	257	235	273	319	271	248	248	Hong–kong
India	6 332	6 961	7 650	8 410	9 244	10 161	11 169	12 278	13 495	14 834	Inde
Indonesia	3 000	3 500	3 500	3 400	* 4 797	* 5 250	6 798	6 296	6 600	7 065	Indonésie
Iran(Islamic Rep.of)	90	90	90	90	90	90	90	90	90	90	Iran(Rép.islamique)
Iraq	8	8	8	8	8	8	8	8	8	8	Iraq
Japan	9 630	6 241	8 162	8 907	7 015	6 533	6 023	5 491	4 810	4 534	Japon
Korea, D. P. Rp.	95	95	95	95	95	95	95	95	95	95	Corée, Rp. P. D.
Korea, Republic of	1 396	1 277	1 557	1 025	1 407	786	824	942	956	1 033	Corée, République de
Lao Peoples Dem.Rep.	44	46	56	41	41	16	22	25	26	26	Rép. dém. pop. lao
Lebanon	11	11	11	11	11	11	11	11	11	11	Liban
Malaysia	5 128	5 654	5 913	5 913	5 913	6 173	6 444	7 138	7 138	7 138	Malaisie
Nepal	210	210	210	210	210	210	210	210	210	210	Népal
Philippines	1 609	1 567	1 781	1 626	1 529	1 219	1 200	1 222	1 080	* 1 200	Philippines
Singapore	443	302	364	371	282	188	175	178	157	137	Singapour
Sri Lanka	27	21	57	13	22	27	17	25	19	21	Sri Lanka
Syrian Arab Republic	2	2	2	6	2	2	2	2	2	2	Rép. arabe syrienne
Thailand	1 659	1 737	1 565	1 550	1 527	899	885	930	1 016	909	Thaïlande
Turkey	500	707	967	967	967	950	741	741	741	741	Turquie
Viet Nam	451	548	512	468	410	372	338	307	307	307	Viet Nam
Europe	**17 561**	**18 336**	**18 703**	**18 962**	**18 497**	**17 441**	**17 155**	**16 792**	**17 692**	**17 929**	**Europe**
EEC	**8 227**	**8 615**	**8 444**	**8 640**	**8 675**	**7 686**	**7 344**	**6 947**	**7 323**	**7 543**	**CEE**
Denmark	400	400	400	400	400	400	400	400	400	400	Danemark
France	3 598	3 713	3 672	3 790	3 722	3 300	3 400	3 313	3 485	3 485	France
Germany, Fed. Rep.	1 965	2 069	2 103	2 041	1 989	1 740	1 557	1 488	1 602	1 602	Allemagne, Rép. féd.
Greece	162	170	175	185	175	128	185	132	130	130	Grèce
Ireland	20	14	6	7	9	13	14	13	5	5	Irlande
Italy	1 177	1 289	1 131	1 293	1 492	1 374	1 196	1 043	1 179	1 388	Italie
Netherlands	215	196	202	158	234	200	132	168	182	240	Pays–Bas
United Kingdom	690	764	755	766	654	531	460	390	340	293	Royaume–Uni
EFTA	**905**	**1 110**	**1 104**	**1 062**	**1 093**	**1 028**	**1 110**	**1 000**	**1 245**	**1 236**	**AELE**
Austria	278	405	449	441	438	403	326	225	231	252	Autriche
Finland	49	75	50	76	78	75	70	70	86	60	Finlande
Norway	10	10	5	5	11	10	10	10	12	12	Norvège
Portugal	140	150	150	170	200	150	304	320	546	546	Portugal
Sweden	293	300	300	210	196	210	210	190	190	190	Suède
Switzerland	135	170	150	160	170	180	190	185	180	176	Suisse
East Europe	**5 931**	**5 951**	**6 165**	**6 238**	**6 060**	**5 969**	**5 860**	**6 155**	**6 257**	**6 197**	**Europe de l'est**
Albania	95	95	95	95	95	95	95	95	95	95	Albanie
Bulgaria	482	430	416	488	404	463	426	433	365	367	Bulgarie
Czechoslovakia	743	768	772	774	801	797	819	809	800	794	Tchécoslovaquie
German Dem. Rep.	400	432	437	443	430	439	447	447	497	497	Rép. dém. allemande
Hungary	523	648	711	768	806	809	729	748	751	756	Hongrie
Poland	1 227	1 147	1 251	1 113	1 060	906	703	653	709	648	Pologne
Romania	2 461	2 431	2 483	2 557	2 464	2 460	2 641	2 970	3 040	3 040	Roumanie
Other Europe	**2 168**	**2 340**	**2 486**	**2 730**	**2 374**	**2 478**	**2 590**	**2 416**	**2 617**	**2 703**	**Autre Europe**
Spain	714	647	712	865	492	550	639	478	461	461	Espagne
Yugoslavia	1 454	1 693	1 774	1 865	1 882	1 928	1 951	1 938	2 156	2 242	Yougoslavie
USSR	**14 100**	**13 600**	**13 200**	**12 400**	**12 200**	**12 300**	**11 763**	**12 100**	**12 100**	**12 100**	**URSS**
Oceania	**2 649**	**2 553**	**2 279**	**2 223**	**2 332**	**2 345**	**2 197**	**1 981**	**1 941**	**2 035**	**Océanie**

For general note and footnotes, see end of table. — Voir la fin du tableau pour la remarque générale et les notes.

Sawnwood, broadleaved (continued) – Sciages de feuillus (suite)

Unit : Thousand cubic metres | Unité : Milliers de mètres cubes

Country or area	1976	1977	1978	1979	1980	1981	1982	1983	1984	1985	Pays ou zone
Australia	2 380	2 305	2 029	1 952	2 027	2 107	1 976	1 753	1 711	1 805	Australie
Fiji	67	67	67	79	85	77	60	67	70	74	Fidji
New Caledonia	4	5	3	4	4	4	4	4	4	4	Nouvelle–Calédonie
New Zealand	50	35	34	34	42	38	37	37	36	36	Nouvelle–Zélande
Papua New Guinea	123	113	113	113	133	78	78	78	78	* 74	Papouasie–Nvl–Guinée
Samoa	14	18	20	21	21	21	21	21	21	21	Samoa
Solomon Islands	9	8	11	18	18	18	18	18	18	18	Iles Salomon
Tonga	...	...	...	...	...	...	1	0	0	0	Tonga
Vanuatu	2	2	2	2	2	2	2	3	3	3	Vanuatu
Total	**102 777**	**103 248**	**108 081**	**110 300**	**113 101**	**111 335**	**107 180**	**109 682**	**115 261**	**117 026**	**Total**

General note.
Sawnwood includes wood simply sawn lengthwise (for example, planks, beams, joists, boards, rafters, scantlings, laths etc.) and wood which has been sliced, peeled or rotary cut, and which is more than 5 mm thick. Rough sawnwood is often further processed in the same establishment into planed, tongued, grooved, chamfered, rabbeted, v–jointed and beaded wood etc. Where this occurs, production may be counted at the sawn stage or at a later stage, but steps should be taken to ensure that the sawn wood is not counted more than once. Boxes, whether assembled or not (part of SITC 6321) and sawn railway sleepers (part of SITC 2431) are excluded, as is wood sawn into sheets of a thickness of 5 mm or less (part of SITC 6311). (SITC 24330–0).
Source: Food and Agriculture Organization of the United Nations (FAO), Rome.

Remarque générale.
Les sciages comprennent les bois simplement sciés longitudinalement (par exemple: madriers, poutres, solives, planches, chevrons, voliges, lattes etc.) et les bois tranchés ou déroulés, de plus de 5 mm d'épaisseur. Dans le même établissement, on fait souvent subir aux sciages bruts un traitement ultérieur pour en faire des bois rabotés, bouvetés, rainés, languetés, chamfreinés, feuillurés, chevronnés et moulurés etc. Dans ce cas, la production peut être comptée au stade du sciage ou à un stade ultérieur, mais on doit veiller à ne pas compter deux fois le même bois. N'entrent dans cette rubrique ni les caisses ni les planches de caisserie (ex CTCI 6321), ni les traverses de chemin de fer sciées (ex CTCI 2431), ni le bois scié en feuilles d'une épaisseur de 5 mm ou moins (ex CTCI 6311). (CTCI 24330–0).
Source: Organisation des Nations Unies pour l'agriculture(FAO), Rome.

ISIC–BASED CODE
3311–10

Veneer sheets – Feuilles de placage

CODE BASE CITI
3311–10

Unit : Thousand cubic metres — Unité : Milliers de mètres cubes

Country or area	1976	1977	1978	1979	1980	1981	1982	1983	1984	1985	Pays ou zone
Africa	**292**	**358**	**391**	**435**	**525**	**514**	**488**	**517**	**522**	**543**	**Afrique**
Algeria	2	2	2	2	2	2	2	2	2	2	Algérie
Angola	3	3	3	3	3	3	3	3	3	3	Angola
Cameroon	63	63	63	63	63	63	63	63	63	63	Cameroun
Central African Rep.	3	1	1	2	3	3	4	3	1	2	Rép. centrafricaine
Congo	55	72	78	70	75	68	63	74	63	67	Congo
Côte d'Ivoire	38	43	38	49	122	108	100	127	122	122	Côte d'Ivoire
Egypt	2	2	2	2	2	2	1	1	1	1	Egypte
Equatorial Guinea	1	1	0	0	0	1	1	2	3	10	Guinée équatoriale
Gabon	41	45	60	101	97	97	97	97	97	97	Gabon
Ghana	14	18	19	17	22	23	21	15	24	34	Ghana
Liberia	...	...	...	2	2	2	2	2	2	2	Libéria
Malawi	3	3	3	3	5	6	6	6	6	6	Malawi
Morocco	25	52	51	26	25	25	25	25	25	25	Maroc
Mozambique	1	1	1	1	1	1	1	1	1	1	Mozambique
Nigeria	2	2	3	3	* 3	3	3	3	3	3	Nigéria
South Africa	22	41	53	75	72	73	70	70	70	70	Afrique du Sud
Zaire	18	9	* 13	* 13	* 27	* 31	* 21	* 20	* 33	33	Zaïre
Zimbabwe	...	...	1	3	1	3	4	4	3	3	Zimbabwe
America, North	**488**	**486**	**507**	**497**	**489**	**497**	**493**	**487**	**483**	**483**	**Amérique du Nord**
Canada	474	474	474	474	474	474	474	474	474	474	Canada
Costa Rica	5	5	3	5	5	8	8	5	6	6	Costa Rica
Guatemala	2	1	2	2	2	1	1	1	1	1	Guatemala
Mexico	7	6	28	16	8	14	10	8	2	2	Mexique
America, South	**206**	**260**	**266**	**304**	**357**	**379**	**362**	**364**	**364**	**364**	**Amérique du Sud**
Argentina	9	2	2	7	3	4	5	6	6	6	Argentine
Bolivia	3	18	16	19	22	22	22	22	22	22	Bolivie
Brazil	169	* 190	190	200	216	234	234	234	234	234	Brésil
Chile	3	5	6	7	7	8	8	9	9	9	Chili
Colombia	4	4	4	4	9	7	7	7	7	7	Colombie
Ecuador	3	3	2	2	2	2	3	3	3	3	Equateur
Paraguay	9	14	22	37	63	63	63	63	63	63	Paraguay
Peru	6	24	24	28	35	38	20	20	20	20	Pérou
Asia	**899**	**955**	**981**	**1 023**	**1 054**	**1 096**	**1 086**	**1 160**	**1 187**	**1 190**	**Asie**
Bangladesh	30	30	30	1	1	1	1	1	1	1	Bangladesh
China	2	2	4	4	7	7	7	7	7	7	Chine
India	11	19	4	4	4	4	4	4	4	4	Inde
Iran(Islamic Rep.of)	8	4	3	2	2	2	2	2	2	2	Iran(Rép.islamique)
Japan	300	300	300	300	300	300	300	300	300	300	Japon
Korea, Republic of	1	1	...	...	...	...	...	...	...	...	Corée, République de
Malaysia	348	377	408	442	475	511	549	598	642	642	Malaisie
Philippines	89	110	121	140	133	138	98	123	71	71	Philippines
Singapore	90	90	90	90	90	90	90	90	90	90	Singapour
Syrian Arab Republic	...	...	...	7	10	10	10	10	10	10	Rép. arabe syrienne
Thailand	11	13	11	23	23	23	15	15	50	53	Thaïlande
Turkey	8	9	10	10	10	10	10	10	10	10	Turquie
Europe	**1 553**	**1 515**	**1 463**	**1 470**	**1 501**	**1 532**	**1 481**	**1 566**	**1 631**	**1 606**	**Europe**
EEC	**828**	**805**	**822**	**854**	**854**	**824**	**667**	**774**	**812**	**789**	**CEE**
Denmark	14	11	9	12	8	6	6	6	6	6	Danemark
France	52	52	58	58	58	58	58	58	58	58	France
Germany, Fed. Rep.	285	292	300	289	300	255	235	381	405	398	Allemagne, Rép. féd.
Greece	10	12	11	13	14	11	10	12	12	12	Grèce
Ireland	2	2	2	2	2	2	...	...	...	...	Irlande
Italy	427	400	405	441	450	470	336	295	309	293	Italie
Netherlands	9	12	12	12	...	...	...	...	...	...	Pays–Bas
United Kingdom	29	24	25	27	22	22	22	22	22	22	Royaume–Uni
EFTA	**63**	**78**	**73**	**75**	**84**	**90**	**79**	**79**	**78**	**83**	**AELE**
Austria	15	15	17	19	20	18	18	* 18	19	19	Autriche
Finland	16	21	17	18	18	18	18	18	18	18	Finlande
Portugal	2	9	6	5	13	21	10	10	8	9	Portugal
Sweden	13	* 13	13	13	13	13	13	13	13	13	Suède
Switzerland	17	20	20	20	20	20	20	20	20	24	Suisse

For general note and footnotes, see end of table. — Voir la fin du tableau pour la remarque générale et les notes.

Unit : Thousand cubic metres

Unité : Milliers de mètres cubes

Country or area	1976	1977	1978	1979	1980	1981	1982	1983	1984	1985	Pays ou zone
East Europe	**251**	**263**	**236**	**240**	**248**	**320**	**329**	**322**	**324**	**314**	**Europe de l'est**
Albania	5	5	5	5	5	5	5	5	5	5	Albanie
Bulgaria	50	52	48	48	53	55	55	51	49	46	Bulgarie
Czechoslovakia	66	75	52	57	58	59	57	59	60	56	Tchécoslovaquie
German Dem. Rep.	...	...	...	...	...	74	81	81	81	81	Rép. dém. allemande
Hungary	14	17	17	17	16	16	14	14	15	15	Hongrie
Poland	59	51	47	46	46	39	38	33	35	32	Pologne
Romania	57	63	67	67	70	72	79	79	79	79	Roumanie
Other Europe	**381**	**339**	**302**	**266**	**276**	**262**	**373**	**358**	**382**	**385**	**Autre Europe**
Spain	146	120	68	36	26	25	140	125	137	137	Espagne
Yugoslavia	235	219	234	230	250	237	233	* 233	245	248	Yougoslavie
USSR	**476**	**476**	**476**	**476**	**476**	**476**	**476**	**476**	**476**	**476**	**URSS**
Oceania	**53**	**49**	**52**	**58**	**49**	**52**	**58**	**52**	**48**	**48**	**Océanie**
Australia	31	26	23	25	28	29	29	29	29	29	Australie
Fiji	7	7	7	8	7	7	7	7	4	4	Fidji
New Zealand	10	8	11	14	3	5	11	4	4	4	Nouvelle–Zélande
Papua New Guinea	5	8	10	10	10	10	10	10	10	10	Papouasie–Nvl–Guinée
Solomon Islands	0	0	1	1	1	1	1	1	1	1	Iles Salomon
Total	**3 967**	**4 099**	**4 136**	**4 263**	**4 452**	**4 545**	**4 443**	**4 621**	**4 712**	**4 711**	**Total**

General note.
Thin sheets of wood of a uniform thickness not exceeding 5 mm (excluding any reinforcing material), produced by a sawing, slicing or peeling (rotary cutting) process for use in making plywood and other types of laminated boards, furniture, veneer containers etc. (SITC 63110–0).
Source: Food and Agriculture Organization of the United Nations (FAO), Rome.

Remarque générale.
Minces feuilles de bois d'épaisseur uniforme ne dépassant pas 5 mm (à l'exclusion de tout matériau de renforcement), sciées, tranchées ou déroulées pour être utilisées dans la fabrication du contreplaqué, des bois laminés, des muebles, des emballages etc. (CTCI 63110–0).
Source: Organisation des Nations Unies pour l'agriculture(FAO), Rome.

Plywood – Contreplaqués

Unit : Thousand cubic metres — Unité : Milliers de mètres cubes

Country or area	1976	1977	1978	1979	1980	1981	1982	1983	1984	1985	Pays ou zone
Africa	**404**	**424**	**462**	**478**	**514**	**525**	**569**	**569**	**573**	**593**	**Afrique**
Algeria	23	23	23	23	23	23	23	23	23	23	Algérie
Angola	27	27	27	27	27	27	27	27	27	27	Angola
Cameroon	10	10	10	10	10	10	10	10	10	10	Cameroun
Central African Rep.	1	4	6	3	4	5	9	8	5	5	Rép. centrafricaine
Congo	...	1	2	2	4	3	4	5	6	7	Congo
Côte d'Ivoire	55	72	65	54	63	25	24	33	26	26	Côte d'Ivoire
Egypt	8	10	10	6	7	5	5	8	9	9	Egypte
Ethiopia	3	3	3	3	3	3	2	2	2	2	Ethiopie
Gabon	50	43	69	73	95	70	* 104	104	110	131	Gabon
Ghana	59	47	40	38	49	43	39	27	26	24	Ghana
Guinea	2	2	2	2	2	2	2	2	2	2	Guinée
Kenya	12	14	17	19	23	15	16	18	21	21	Kenya
Liberia	3	3	7	15	7	2	2	3	3	3	Libéria
Malawi	2	2	2	2	3	4	4	4	4	4	Malawi
Morocco	19	31	29	32	45	45	50	50	50	50	Maroc
Mozambique	6	2	1	1	1	3	2	1	0	0	Mozambique
Nigeria	66	66	78	86	68	151	151	151	151	151	Nigéria
Rwanda	...	...	...	1	1	2	2	2	2	2	Rwanda
South Africa	23	18	21	29	28	29	27	27	27	27	Afrique du Sud
Swaziland	4	4	4	1	5	5	5	5	5	5	Swaziland
Tunisia	10	11	12	13	14	18	24	24	24	24	Tunisie
Uganda	1	1	1	1	1	1	4	5	6	6	Ouganda
United Rep. Tanzania	2	3	4	4	3	3	2	2	2	2	Rép.Unie de Tanzanie
Zaire	9	9	* 12	* 12	* 12	* 16	* 16	* 14	* 19	19	Zaïre
Zambia	3	4	4	4	4	4	4	6	6	6	Zambie
Zimbabwe	5	15	15	16	12	12	13	10	9	9	Zimbabwe
America, North	**19 382**	**20 897**	**20 123**	**19 923**	**17 523**	**18 758**	**15 369**	**19 497**	**20 177**	**21 157**	**Amérique du Nord**
Canada	2 442	2 660	2 807	2 510	2 338	2 086	1 682	2 064	1 846	1 958	Canada
Costa Rica	40	44	30	31	31	26	33	23	25	25	Costa Rica
Cuba	2	2	2	2	2	2	2	2	2	2	Cuba
Guatemala	4	4	4	4	4	3	1	1	...	...	Guatemala
Honduras	11	13	* 14	* 14	* 11	* 11	5	6	8	8	Honduras
Mexico	139	171	188	206	254	304	313	286	286	270	Mexique
Nicaragua	10	10	10	16	14	14	22	14	14	14	Nicaragua
Panama ex.Canal Zone	8	12	12	12	12	12	12	12	12	12	Panama ex.zone Canal
United States	16 726	17 981	17 056	17 128	14 857	16 300	13 300	17 090	17 984	18 868	Etats–Unis
America, South	**1 014**	**966**	**981**	**1 059**	**1 148**	**1 219**	**1 174**	**1 186**	**1 196**	**1 184**	**Amérique du Sud**
Argentina	58	50	47	53	53	50	47	48	48	48	Argentine
Bolivia	2	3	1	4	6	6	1	1	1	1	Bolivie
Brazil	695	698	722	762	826	902	902	902	902	902	Brésil
Chile	7	9	13	16	20	18	10	15	20	20	Chili
Colombia	75	75	75	52	52	40	48	48	48	48	Colombie
Ecuador	38	40	50	55	59	65	65	65	65	65	Equateur
Paraguay	2	3	3	4	4	4	4	4	17	15	Paraguay
Peru	76	39	24	38	49	40	37	37	30	20	Pérou
Suriname	18	15	17	18	17	19	20	15	14	14	Suriname
Uruguay	4	5	6	7	7	7	3	4	4	4	Uruguay
Venezuela	40	* 29	* 22	50	55	69	37	47	47	47	Venezuela
Asia	**12 114**	**13 249**	**14 678**	**15 356**	**14 449**	**14 095**	**14 705**	**13 718**	**14 054**	**15 229**	**Asie**
Bangladesh	4	2	2	2	1	1	1	1	1	1	Bangladesh
Burma	12	12	12	12	12	15	15	15	15	15	Birmanie
China	* 1 133	* 1 155	1 535	1 575	1 613	1 634	1 677	1 738	1 773	1 773	Chine
Dem. Kampuchea	2	2	2	2	2	2	2	2	2	2	Kampuchea démocrat.
Hong Kong	12	12	12	12	12	12	12	12	12	12	Hong–kong
India	141	149	176	180	* 200	* 280	* 300	* 300	* 360	360	Inde
Indonesia	* 214	* 279	* 424	624	* 1 011	* 1 552	2 487	3 138	3 600	4 615	Indonésie
Iran(Islamic Rep.of)	26	22	16	16	16	16	16	16	16	16	Iran(Rép.islamique)
Israel	71	71	71	71	71	71	71	71	71	71	Israël
Japan	7 136	7 476	8 016	8 532	8 000	7 096	6 740	4 884	4 880	5 032	Japon
Korea, Republic of	1 671	2 289	2 560	2 338	1 575	1 599	1 423	1 491	1 326	1 229	Corée, République de
Lao Peoples Dem.Rep.	2	1	1	1	2	3	5	5	5	5	Rép. dém. pop. lao
Lebanon	34	34	34	34	34	34	34	34	34	34	Liban
Malaysia	525	565	465	490	601	603	787	787	787	787	Malaisie
Mongolia	3	3	3	3	3	3	3	3	3	3	Mongolie
Pakistan	2	1	1	3	3	3	3	3	3	3	Pakistan
Philippines	416	489	490	515	553	463	434	469	414	515	Philippines

For general note and footnotes, see end of table.

Voir la fin du tableau pour la remarque générale et les notes.

Unit : Thousand cubic metres

Unité : Milliers de mètres cubes

Country or area	1976	1977	1978	1979	1980	1981	1982	1983	1984	1985	Pays ou zone
Singapore	558	515	675	778	579	527	460	460	460	460	Singapour
Sri Lanka	21	17	15	3	12	12	10	13	14	13	Sri Lanka
Syrian Arab Republic	7	9	10	9	8	8	8	8	8	8	Rép. arabe syrienne
Thailand	63	68	75	93	89	106	160	165	165	170	Thaïlande
Turkey	45	50	53	45	34	34	34	54	65	65	Turquie
Viet Nam	16	28	30	18	18	* 21	* 23	* 49	* 40	40	Viet Nam
Europe	**3 779**	**3 629**	**3 537**	**3 676**	**3 585**	**3 445**	**3 271**	**3 071**	**3 167**	**3 162**	**Europe**
EEC	**1 613**	**1 548**	**1 461**	**1 566**	**1 514**	**1 531**	**1 346**	**1 259**	**1 323**	**1 333**	**CEE**
Denmark	28	28	30	30	30	30	30	30	30	30	Danemark
France	573	567	509	539	527	516	477	483	476	476	France
Germany, Fed. Rep.	449	443	445	444	429	354	331	334	340	336	Allemagne, Rép. féd.
Greece	64	65	63	77	68	69	47	52	97	97	Grèce
Italy	420	380	350	410	400	500	425	325	346	360	Italie
Netherlands	54	42	40	44	45	45	20	18	17	17	Pays-Bas
United Kingdom	25	23	24	22	15	17	16	17	17	17	Royaume-Uni
EFTA	**666**	**620**	**698**	**791**	**785**	**730**	**718**	**706**	**717**	**720**	**AELE**
Austria	7	7	8	8	7	5	4	4	4	4	Autriche
Finland	491	464	549	639	639	603	596	580	592	592	Finlande
Norway	9	8	8	8	9	9	10	10	11	11	Norvège
Portugal	28	25	23	20	19	21	22	19	20	21	Portugal
Sweden	111	95	87	92	87	72	65	71	66	68	Suède
Switzerland	20	21	23	24	24	20	21	22	24	24	Suisse
East Europe	**974**	**973**	**958**	**941**	**907**	**861**	**847**	**781**	**799**	**777**	**Europe de l'est**
Albania	7	7	7	7	7	7	7	7	7	7	Albanie
Bulgaria	63	64	62	58	56	53	57	55	53	51	Bulgarie
Czechoslovakia	282	283	286	300	283	276	272	258	260	247	Tchécoslovaquie
German Dem. Rep.	45	42	42	42	40	41	41	41	40	40	Rép. dém. allemande
Hungary	13	13	13	14	16	15	15	15	16	15	Hongrie
Poland	269	260	240	225	214	192	172	172	175	169	Pologne
Romania	295	304	308	295	291	277	283	233	248	248	Roumanie
Other Europe	**466**	**438**	**373**	**328**	**324**	**263**	**292**	**255**	**270**	**274**	**Autre Europe**
Spain	290	236	178	134	162	110	150	120	129	129	Espagne
Yugoslavia	176	202	195	194	162	153	142	135	141	145	Yougoslavie
USSR	**2 174**	**2 178**	**2 122**	**1 988**	**2 022**	**2 035**	**2 015**	**2 103**	**2 385**	**2 385**	**URSS**
Oceania	**116**	**128**	**149**	**147**	**155**	**162**	**161**	**139**	**150**	**158**	**Océanie**
Australia	73	78	85	87	87	89	89	71	82	89	Australie
Fiji	1	2	3	3	3	4	4	4	4	5	Fidji
New Zealand	26	33	46	42	54	60	59	55	55	55	Nouvelle-Zélande
Papua New Guinea	15	15	15	15	10	9	9	9	9	9	Papouasie-Nvl-Guinée
Total	**38 983**	**41 470**	**42 052**	**42 627**	**39 396**	**40 240**	**37 265**	**40 284**	**41 703**	**43 868**	**Total**

General note.
A wooden sheet material consisting of three or more layers of veneers glued or cemented together, the grains of adjoining plies usually being at right angles to one another. This item includes veneered panels, that is, sheets or panels consisting of a thin veneer of wood affixed to a base, usually of inferior wood, by gluing under pressure. (SITC 63121-2).
Source: Food and Agriculture Organization of the United Nations (FAO), Rome.

Remarque générale.
Panneaux de bois faits de trois couches au moins de feuilles de placage assemblées à la colle ou à l'adhesif et généralement superposées de façon que le fil de chaque feuille soit perpendiculaire à celui de la feuille contiguë. Cette rubrique comprend les panneaux de bois plaqué, c'est-à-dire des feuilles ou des panneaux constitués par des feuilles de placage appliquées par collage et pressage sur un support normalement en bois de qualité inférieure. (CTCI 63121-2).
Source: Organisation des Nations Unies pour l'agriculture(FAO), Rome.

Particle board – Panneaux de particules

Unit : Thousand cubic metres | Unité : Milliers de mètres cubes

Country or area	1976	1977	1978	1979	1980	1981	1982	1983	1984	1985	Pays ou zone
Africa	**290**	**366**	**364**	**382**	**391**	**403**	**426**	**463**	**465**	**465**	**Afrique**
Algeria	24	24	24	24	24	24	24	24	24	24	Algérie
Côte d'Ivoire	* 5	* 4	4	5	6	6	6	6	6	6	Côte d'Ivoire
Egypt	29	30	30	42	32	32	26	29	36	36	Egypte
Ethiopia	3	3	3	3	3	3	5	5	5	5	Ethiopie
Ghana	...	8	8	8	8	8	8	8	8	8	Ghana
Mauritius	2	...	...	...	...	...	...	...	...	...	Maurice
Morocco	1	10	18	17	15	25	30	30	30	30	Maroc
Nigeria	* 35	* 35	35	38	45	55	55	55	55	55	Nigéria
Somalia	2	2	2	2	2	2	2	2	2	2	Somalie
South Africa	164	* 213	* 202	202	202	202	202	202	202	202	Afrique du Sud
Sudan	5	4	4	2	2	2	2	2	2	2	Soudan
Tunisia	14	14	17	21	21	24	35	70	70	70	Tunisie
United Rep. Tanzania	5	4	3	3	3	4	4	2	2	2	Rép.Unie de Tanzanie
Zaire	...	1	1	1	1	1	1	1	1	1	Zaïre
Zambia	...	...	...	...	...	...	...	5	7	7	Zambie
Zimbabwe	2	16	14	16	29	17	29	25	17	17	Zimbabwe
America, North	**6 243**	**8 215**	**9 088**	**8 722**	**7 897**	**7 885**	**6 731**	**8 505**	**9 445**	**10 130**	**Amérique du Nord**
Canada	808	880	1 089	1 279	1 267	1 411	1 054	1 581	2 034	2 380	Canada
Costa Rica	6	24	28	31	32	23	11	11	15	15	Costa Rica
Cuba	4	4	4	4	4	4	44	48	85	73	Cuba
Guatemala	4	6	3	4	3	3	4	4	4	5	Guatemala
Jamaica	11	4	4	4	4	4	4	4	4	4	Jamaïque
Mexico	99	155	162	194	316	339	412	335	379	425	Mexique
Panama ex.Canal Zone	2	2	2	2	2	2	2	2	2	2	Panama ex.zone Canal
United States	5 310	7 140	7 797	7 204	6 269	6 100	5 200	6 520	6 923	7 226	Etats-Unis
America, South	**793**	**829**	**852**	**943**	**1 108**	**1 099**	**1 083**	**1 143**	**1 185**	**1 242**	**Amérique du Sud**
Argentina	225	176	185	248	268	217	215	241	241	241	Argentine
Brazil	461	541	541	550	660	660	660	660	660	660	Brésil
Chile	29	32	42	46	43	72	37	72	114	114	Chili
Colombia	* 17	* 20	20	* 30	31	42	50	50	50	50	Colombie
Ecuador	...	8	14	19	26	28	49	30	32	89	Equateur
Paraguay	2	2	2	2	2	2	2	2	2	2	Paraguay
Peru	5	1	...	...	...	...	...	...	...	...	Pérou
Suriname	13	8	7	6	6	6	6	5	3	3	Suriname
Uruguay	7	6	6	7	7	6	4	5	5	5	Uruguay
Venezuela	35	35	35	35	65	66	60	78	78	78	Venezuela
Asia	**1 484**	**1 663**	**1 741**	**2 126**	**2 169**	**2 028**	**2 123**	**2 154**	**2 355**	**2 458**	**Asie**
Afghanistan	1	1	1	1	1	1	1	1	1	1	Afghanistan
Bangladesh	1	5	5	5	5	5	5	5	5	5	Bangladesh
China	* 70	* 72	87	96	121	120	146	170	208	208	Chine
India	13	14	16	21	* 28	* 31	* 28	* 30	* 32	32	Inde
Iran(Islamic Rep.of)	43	135	101	126	126	126	126	126	126	126	Iran(Rép.islamique)
Iraq	2	2	2	2	2	2	2	2	2	2	Iraq
Israel	57	57	57	57	57	57	57	57	57	57	Israël
Japan	901	941	941	1 260	1 312	1 141	1 232	1 221	1 170	1 170	Japon
Korea, Republic of	56	57	45	53	45	70	36	44	45	57	Corée, République de
Lebanon	15	12	12	12	12	12	12	12	12	12	Liban
Malaysia	1	1	2	2	2	2	2	2	2	2	Malaisie
Mongolia	1	1	1	1	1	1	1	1	1	1	Mongolie
Pakistan	18	16	40	40	100	100	100	100	100	100	Pakistan
Philippines	...	...	3	4	5	5	5	8	3	3	Philippines
Sri Lanka	2	3	3	3	3	3	3	3	3	3	Sri Lanka
Syrian Arab Republic	5	3	7	9	9	9	9	9	9	9	Rép. arabe syrienne
Thailand	6	5	5	10	9	11	28	33	33	34	Thaïlande
Turkey	292	339	415	425	332	332	330	330	546	636	Turquie
Europe	**21 181**	**21 939**	**22 780**	**23 783**	**23 888**	**22 475**	**21 810**	**22 244**	**22 541**	**22 542**	**Europe**
EEC	**11 190**	**11 087**	**11 257**	**11 510**	**11 397**	**10 630**	**10 045**	**10 192**	**10 146**	**10 062**	**CEE**
Denmark	358	316	365	400	317	306	237	240	240	240	Danemark
France	2 090	2 012	2 061	2 191	2 289	2 169	1 988	1 904	1 760	1 760	France
Germany, Fed. Rep.	6 125	6 149	6 322	6 373	6 243	5 741	5 486	5 768	5 974	5 830	Allemagne, Rép. féd.
Greece	178	190	190	289	288	298	288	289	270	270	Grèce
Ireland	100	100	100	53	69	34	42	30	30	30	Irlande
Italy	1 600	1 700	1 600	1 500	1 500	1 480	1 430	1 380	1 300	1 350	Italie

For general note and footnotes, see end of table.

Voir la fin du tableau pour la remarque générale et les notes.

Unit : Thousand cubic metres

Unité : Milliers de mètres cubes

Country or area	1976	1977	1978	1979	1980	1981	1982	1983	1984	1985	Pays ou zone
Netherlands	56	58	90	100	75	66	59	63	30	40	Pays–Bas
United Kingdom	683	562	529	604	616	536	515	518	542	542	Royaume–Uni
EFTA	**3 915**	**4 040**	**4 277**	**4 517**	**4 720**	**4 293**	**3 862**	**3 992**	**3 998**	**4 070**	**AELE**
Austria	1 069	1 092	1 097	1 161	1 309	1 156	1 045	1 126	1 152	1 200	Autriche
Finland	657	572	673	800	809	707	636	605	541	571	Finlande
Norway	335	316	360	348	400	358	363	361	411	423	Norvège
Portugal	237	294	322	321	364	378	371	420	395	456	Portugal
Sweden	1 090	1 180	1 255	1 235	1 193	1 094	952	980	978	902	Suède
Switzerland	527	586	570	652	645	600	495	500	521	518	Suisse
East Europe	**2 996**	**3 437**	**3 829**	**3 950**	**3 964**	**3 853**	**4 163**	**4 390**	**4 678**	**4 769**	**Europe de l'est**
Bulgaria	265	280	291	313	327	324	383	376	377	389	Bulgarie
Czechoslovakia	348	446	531	563	592	657	700	813	900	898	Tchécoslovaquie
German Dem. Rep.	662	677	713	766	735	701	812	859	897	897	Rép. dém. allemande
Hungary	194	229	248	267	285	235	278	285	259	286	Hongrie
Poland	743	908	1 086	1 010	1 087	1 040	1 073	1 193	1 244	1 298	Pologne
Romania	784	897	960	1 031	938	896	917	864	1 001	1 001	Roumanie
Other Europe	**1 380**	**1 825**	**1 842**	**2 106**	**2 142**	**2 089**	**2 090**	**1 945**	**1 969**	**1 891**	**Autre Europe**
Spain	896	1 199	1 210	1 380	1 330	1 300	1 300	1 200	1 210	1 210	Espagne
Yugoslavia	484	626	632	726	812	789	790	745	759	681	Yougoslavie
USSR	**4 222**	**4 590**	**4 777**	**4 695**	**5 118**	**5 390**	**5 583**	**5 749**	**6 860**	**6 860**	**URSS**
Oceania	**641**	**608**	**638**	**652**	**769**	**791**	**792**	**675**	**785**	**815**	**Océanie**
Australia	481	501	517	531	622	635	637	535	645	675	Australie
New Zealand	160	107	121	121	147	156	155	140	140	140	Nouvelle–Zélande
Total	**34 855**	**38 210**	**40 240**	**41 303**	**41 339**	**40 070**	**38 547**	**40 932**	**43 635**	**44 511**	**Total**

General note.
Sheet material manufactured from small pieces of wood or other ligno–cellulosic materials (for example, chips, flakes, splinters, strands, shreds, shives etc.) agglomerated by use of an organic binder together with one or more of the following agents – heat, pressure, humidity, a catalyst etc. Wood wool or other particle boards agglomerated by means of an inorganic binder such as cement or plaster are excluded. (SITC 63142–0).
Source: Food and Agriculture Organization of the United Nations (FAO), Rome.

Remarque générale.
Matériaux en feuilles, fabriqués à partir de petits fragments de bois ou d'autres substances ligno–cellulosiques (copeaux, flocons, éclats, fils, brins etc.) agglomérés sous l'action d'unliant organique, ainsi que d'un ou plusieurs des agents suivants: chaleur, pression, humidité, catalyseur etc. Cette rubrique ne comprend pas les panneaux faits de fibres de bois ou autres particules agglomérées au moyen de liants inorganiques tels que le ciment ou le plâtre. (CTCI 62142–0).
Source: Organisation des Nations Unies pour l'agriculture(FAO), Rome.

For footnotes, see end of table.

Voir la fin du tableau pour les notes.

Mattresses – Matelas

Unit : Thousand units

Unité : En milliers

Country or area	1976	1977	1978	1979	1980	1981	1982	1983	1984	1985	Pays ou zone
Africa	**802**	**805**	**774**	**735**	**890**	**872**	**935**	**1 109**	**1 134**	**1 292**	**Afrique**
Algeria	126	149	152	164	165	237	165	* 170	...	...	Algérie
Kenya	134	203	...	...	...	25	24	...	107	240	Kenya
South Africa	493	413	446	393	543	539	682	* 756	* 755	769	Afrique du Sud
Tunisia	39	35	48	49	54	65	* 60	* 60	...	...	Tunisie
Zaire	10	5	4	...	5	6	4	3	...	...	Zaïre
America, North	**14 266**	**16 632**	**16 602**	**19 692**	**17 745**	**19 985**	**20 812**	**21 859**	**22 546**	**23 627**	**Amérique du Nord**
Antigua and Barbuda[1]	...	...	3	9	12	11	10	15	13	...	Antigua–et–Barbuda[1]
Canada	1 656	...	...	...	...	...	...	...	...	...	Canada
Cuba	774	859	793	1 043	1 106	1 220	1 152	1 285	1 106	1 263	Cuba
Dominican Republic	117	137	173	243	273	264	285	289	307	...	Rép. dominicaine
El Salvador	41	29	42	39	38	43	15	30	...	...	El Salvador
Panama	75	66	57	46	...	63	97	117	...	...	Panama
United States	11 600	13 880	13 878	16 656	14 582	...	...	...	...	...	Etats–Unis
America, South	**113**	**190**	**144**	**240**	**294**	**489**	**326**	**419**	**488**	**534**	**Amérique du Sud**
Bolivia	7	12	2	3	16	22	3	1	1	...	Bolivie
Colombia	66	61	69	99	98	147	146	204	...	...	Colombie
Ecuador	13	90	44	...	143	276	128	144	...	...	Equateur
Paraguay	27	27	29	31	37	44	49	70	72	73	Paraguay
Asia	**234**	**168**	**217**	**209**	**217**	**217**	**230**	**214**	**220**	**223**	**Asie**
Cyprus	28	26	36	42	43	43	56	40	46	49	Chypre
Indonesia	...	...	15	1	...	...	...	...	...	...	Indonésie
Philippines[2]	198	134	...	...	...	...	...	...	...	...	Philippines[2]
Europe	**10 459**	**10 477**	**11 496**	**11 518**	**10 332**	**10 697**	**10 741**	**10 688**	**9 986**	**10 310**	**Europe**
EEC	***8 348***	***8 234***	***9 351***	***9 320***	***8 701***	***9 212***	***9 256***	***9 368***	***8 799***	***9 071***	***CEE***
Denmark	241	251	333	316	224	* 380	634	517	366	625	Danemark
Germany, Fed. Rep.	3 944	3 925	4 455	4 296	4 317	4 333	4 031	4 208	3 725	3 676	Allemagne, Rép. féd.
Greece[3]	146	150	164	175	135	131	160	148	149	...	Grèce[3]
United Kingdom[4]	4 017	3 908	4 399	4 533	4 025	...	...	...	...	...	Royaume–Uni[4]
EFTA	***1 298***	***1 304***	***1 272***	***1 281***	***1 339***	***1 204***	***1 196***	***1 069***	***970***	***1 069***	***AELE***
Austria	425	410	312	320	285	225	232	225	195	189	Autriche
Finland	444	425	563	597	677	623	649	489	492	...	Finlande
Portugal	429	469	397	364	377	356	315	355	283	...	Portugal
East Europe	***98***	***58***	***43***	***31***	***24***	***19***	***25***	***20***	***21***	***18***	***Europe de l'est***
Hungary	98	58	43	31	24	19	25	20	21	18	Hongrie
Other Europe	***715***	***881***	***830***	***886***	***268***	***262***	***264***	***231***	***196***	***152***	***Autre Europe***
Malta	26	24	17	25	29	23	33	22	22	...	Malte
Yugoslavia	689	857	813	861	239	239	231	209	174	127	Yougoslavie
Oceania	**1 239**	**1 311**	**1 275**	**1 197**	**1 271**	**1 236**	**1 241**	**1 172**	**1 516**	**1 072**	**Océanie**
Australia[5]	1 239	1 311	1 275	1 197	1 271	1 236	1 241	1 172	1 516	1 072	Australie[5]
Total	**27 113**	**29 583**	**30 508**	**33 591**	**30 749**	**33 495**	**34 286**	**35 461**	**35 890**	**37 057**	**Total**

General note.
Mattresses fitted with inner springs or filled with any material (cotton, wool, horsehair, down etc.) or of expanded foam or sponge rubber or artificial materials (whether or not covered with woven fabrics, plastic materials etc.). (SITC 82103–1).

Remarque générale.
Matelas qui sont, soit pourvus de ressorts ou rembourrés ou garnis intérieurement de toutes matières (coton, laine, crin, duvet etc.), soit consistant en caoutchouc ou en matières artificielles à l'état spongieux ou cellulaire, recouverts ou non de tissu, de matière plastique etc. Cette rubrique ne comprend pas les sommiers. (CTCI 82103–1).

1 Including mattress supports.
2 Shipments.
3 Mattresses filled with springs only.
4 Inner spring only.
5 Twelve months ending 30 June of year stated.

1 Y compris les sommiers.
2 Expéditions.
3 Matelas garnis de ressorts seulement.
4 Ressorts intérieurs seulement.
5 Période de douze mois finissant le 30 juin de l'année indiquée.

Wood pulp, mechanical – Pâte de bois mécanique

Unit : Thousand metric tons

Unité : Milliers de tonnes métriques

Country or area	1976	1977	1978	1979	1980	1981	1982	1983	1984	1985	Pays ou zone
Africa	**209**	**201**	**188**	**171**	**220**	**272**	**335**	**297**	**170**	**276**	**Afrique**
Madagascar	3	4	4	4	4	4	4	5	5	4	Madagascar
South Africa	194	185	170	152	200	250	313	273	148	255	Afrique du Sud
Zimbabwe	12	12	14	15	16	18	18	19	17	17	Zimbabwe
America, North	**11 276**	**11 355**	**11 869**	**11 509**	**11 730**	**12 510**	**11 513**	**12 448**	**13 865**	**13 678**	**Amérique du Nord**
Canada	7 049	6 856	7 545	7 414	7 510	7 631	6 832	7 793	8 800	8 800	Canada
Costa Rica	...	...	...	5	5	3	3	2	2	3	Costa Rica
Mexico	54	54	60	60	46	50	53	56	65	103	Mexique
United States	4 173	4 445	4 264	4 030	4 169	4 826	4 625	4 597	4 998	4 772	Etats–Unis
America, South	**271**	**305**	**283**	**312**	**432**	**390**	**396**	**450**	**431**	**513**	**Amérique du Sud**
Argentina	31	34	27	33	22	19	25	30	* 30	22	Argentine
Brazil	117	140	120	141	* 270	* 240	* 250	* 275	* 237	324	Brésil
Chile	121	125	129	130	131	125	115	140	157	158	Chili
Uruguay	2	2	1	2	2	2	2	1	3	3	Uruguay
Venezuela	...	* 3	* 6	* 6	* 7	* 4	* 4	* 4	* 4	6	Venezuela
Asia	**1 977**	**2 062**	**2 239**	**2 430**	**2 467**	**2 351**	**2 299**	**2 379**	**2 399**	**2 497**	**Asie**
Bangladesh	9	3	6	14	14	14	14	18	14	14	Bangladesh
China	238	253	295	328	345	345	345	354	378	417	Chine
India	23	25	25	25	25	40	60	75	77	77	Inde
Japan	1 464	1 513	1 671	1 757	1 770	1 638	1 540	1 595	1 580	1 646	Japon
Korea,Dem.Ppl's.Rep	9	10	11	12	13	13	13	13	13	13	Corée,Rép.pop.dém.de
Korea, Republic of	87	110	93	139	137	137	127	126	139	138	Corée, République de
Philippines	45	40	43	42	39	40	37	40	* 38	* 32	Philippines
Turkey	94	100	87	105	116	116	155	150	152	152	Turquie
Viet Nam	8	8	8	8	8	8	8	8	8	8	Viet Nam
Europe	**7 702**	**7 850**	**8 435**	**9 102**	**9 234**	**9 190**	**8 695**	**9 124**	**10 322**	**10 437**	**Europe**
EEC	**2 267**	**2 303**	**2 425**	**2 525**	**2 512**	**2 401**	**2 285**	**2 322**	**2 576**	**2 535**	**CEE**
Denmark	6	5	6	6	...	...	...	...	...	...	Danemark
France	413	433	458	453	419	398	407	397	454	* 436	France
Germany, Fed. Rep	963	1 018	1 063	1 136	1 148	1 210	1 213	1 281	1 399	* 1 392	Allemagne, Rép. féd.
Greece	...	...	...	29	28	22	21	15	15	15	Grèce
Ireland	14	19	20	26	19	...	...	...	...	...	Irlande
Italy	545	534	566	557	533	493	448	409	474	434	Italie
Netherlands	138	145	149	146	201	200	135	146	153	138	Pays–Bas
United Kingdom	188	149	163	172	164	78	61	74	81	120	Royaume–Uni
EFTA	**4 397**	**4 427**	**4 896**	**5 533**	**5 630**	**5 716**	**5 359**	**5 740**	**6 603**	**6 801**	**AELE**
Austria	195	208	196	221	221	223	210	192	180	197	Autriche
Finland	1 689	1 774	1 984	2 238	2 349	2 485	2 326	2 483	2 958	2 931	Finlande
Norway	836	763	802	919	918	911	881	925	1 083	1 182	Norvège
Sweden	1 532	1 527	1 748	1 981	1 960	1 901	1 762	1 965	2 197	2 298	Suède
Switzerland	145	155	166	174	182	196	180	175	185	193	Suisse
East Europe	**604**	**640**	**625**	**628**	**629**	**607**	**601**	**588**	**657**	**648**	**Europe de l'est**
Bulgaria	10	18	18	19	18	19	19	18	17	16	Bulgarie
Czechoslovakia	166	172	169	166	172	173	169	164	159	157	Tchécoslovaquie
German Dem. Rep	190	187	185	180	176	176	175	175	* 250	250	Rép. dém. allemande
Hungary	22	22	23	21	20	16	19	13	13	14	Hongrie
Poland	155	158	148	143	145	123	126	125	125	118	Pologne
Romania	61	83	82	99	98	100	93	93	93	93	Roumanie
Other Europe	**284**	**336**	**356**	**291**	**323**	**338**	**333**	**357**	**366**	**333**	**Autre Europe**
Spain	184	215	240	186	208	217	205	229	237	204	Espagne
Yugoslavia	100	121	116	105	115	121	128	128	129	129	Yougoslavie
USSR	**1 815**	**1 825**	**1 840**	**1 710**	**1 729**	**1 777**	**1 807**	**1 921**	**1 921**	**1 921**	**URSS**
Oceania	**689**	**709**	**667**	**662**	**778**	**800**	**855**	**792**	**834**	**839**	**Océanie**
Australia	167	182	177	198	212	235	324	321	363	357	Australie
New Zealand	522	527	490	464	566	565	531	471	471	482	Nouvelle–Zélande

For general note and footnotes, see end of table.

Voir la fin du tableau pour la remarque générale et les notes.

Wood pulp, mechanical (continued) – Pâte de bois mécanique (suite)

Unit : Thousand metric tons

Unité : Milliers de tonnes métriques

Country or area	1976	1977	1978	1979	1980	1981	1982	1983	1984	1985	Pays ou zone
Total	**23 939**	**24 306**	**25 520**	**25 896**	**26 589**	**27 289**	**25 899**	**27 411**	**29 942**	**30 161**	**Total**

General note.
Fibrous material prepared from wood by mechanical disintegration. It includes exploded and defibrated pulp and mechanical screenings. In terms of air–dry weight (10 per cent moisture content). (SITC 25120–0).
Source: Food and Agriculture Organization of the United Nations (FAO), Rome.

Remarque générale.
Matériaux fibreux préparés en soumettant le bois à la désintégration mécanique. Cette rubrique comprend le bois éclaté et défibré ainsi que les refus du traitement mécanique. Poids après séchage à l'air (pâte à 10 p. 100 d'humidité). (CTCI 25120–0).
Source: Organisation des Nations Unies pour l'agriculture(FAO), Rome.

Pulp of fibres other than wood – Pâtes de fibres autres que le bois

Unit : Thousand metric tons

Unité : Milliers de tonnes métriques

Country or area	1976	1977	1978	1979	1980	1981	1982	1983	1984	1985	Pays ou zone
Africa	**113**	**129**	**157**	**224**	**230**	**225**	**203**	**198**	**279**	**321**	**Afrique**
Algeria	12	12	12	24	24	31	10	7	7	21	Algérie
Angola	2	2	2	2	2	2	2	2	2	...	Angola
Botswana	...	...	...	...	...	...	...	...	86	99	Botswana
Egypt	37	37	46	85	91	80	80	80	80	80	Egypte
Madagascar	2	2	2	2	2	2	2	2	2	2	Madagascar
Morocco	6	6	5	5	5	5	5	5	5	5	Maroc
South Africa	32	49	68	84	84	84	84	84	86	99	Afrique du Sud
Tunisia	22	21	22	22	22	21	20	18	11	15	Tunisie
America, North	**974**	**887**	**892**	**936**	**1 050**	**1 027**	**1 095**	**674**	**659**	**647**	**Amérique du Nord**
Canada	40	40	40	40	40	40	40	40	40	40	Canada
Costa Rica	...	...	...	...	...	...	...	8	8	7	Costa Rica
Cuba	44	38	14	30	30	32	33	34	38	49	Cuba
Mexico	208	239	236	262	230	285	272	289	270	248	Mexique
United States	682	570	602	604	* 750	670	750	303	303	303	Etats–Unis
America, South	**334**	**386**	**405**	**493**	**486**	**489**	**477**	**454**	**450**	**470**	**Amérique du Sud**
Argentina	51	74	54	54	45	44	45	74	74	108	Argentine
Bolivia	1	1	1	1	1	1	1	1	1	1	Bolivie
Brazil	80	88	108	150	150	150	150	168	164	142	Brésil
Colombia	64	68	87	82	84	88	79	75	75	* 80	Colombie
Ecuador	6	7	8	5	5	5	5	5	5	5	Equateur
Peru	* 91	* 98	97	155	155	155	155	75	75	* 72	Pérou
Uruguay	4	4	4	...	...	...	...	...	...	...	Uruguay
Venezuela	* 37	* 46	46	46	46	46	42	56	56	62	Venezuela
Asia	**3 385**	**3 653**	**4 156**	**4 560**	**4 744**	**4 763**	**4 796**	**6 171**	**6 748**	**7 948**	**Asie**
Bangladesh	35	35	49	51	51	51	51	77	77	77	Bangladesh
Burma	13	13	13	13	13	13	13	13	13	13	Birmanie
China	2 340	2 583	3 008	3 300	3 466	3 466	3 466	3 918	4 386	5 467	Chine
India	676	695	760	760	760	760	760	1 640	1 710	1 830	Inde
Indonesia	45	45	45	45	45	45	45	45	45	45	Indonésie
Iran(Islamic Rep.of)	28	28	28	50	50	50	50	50	50	50	Iran(Rép.islamique)
Iraq	10	9	9	9	9	9	9	9	9	9	Iraq
Japan	15	14	15	18	15	11	10	13	17	17	Japon
Jordan	8	8	8	8	8	8	8	8	8	8	Jordanie
Korea,Dem.Ppl's.Rep	50	50	50	50	50	50	50	50	50	50	Corée,Rép.pop.dém.de
Korea, Republic of	3	12	3	67	67	67	67	67	67	67	Corée, République de
Malaysia	1	1	1	1	1	1	1	1	1	1	Malaisie
Mongolia	2	2	2	2	2	2	2	2	2	2	Mongolie
Nepal	15	15	15	15	15	15	15	15	15	15	Népal
Pakistan	50	50	56	56	56	56	56	80	108	108	Pakistan
Philippines	25	23	23	29	19	31	51	51	51	51	Philippines
Sri Lanka	5	6	10	9	10	10	10	10	14	12	Sri Lanka
Thailand	52	52	38	36	37	37	51	41	43	44	Thaïlande
Turkey	6	6	17	35	64	75	75	75	75	75	Turquie
Viet Nam	7	7	7	7	7	7	7	7	7	7	Viet Nam
Europe	**1 059**	**947**	**900**	**805**	**694**	**621**	**581**	**574**	**495**	**493**	**Europe**
EEC	**588**	**560**	**580**	**481**	**404**	**310**	**303**	**314**	**244**	**235**	**CEE**
Denmark	43	40	43	45	45	45	45	62	63	63	Danemark
France	10	9	12	15	15	16	16	16	23	23	France
Greece	18	18	25	38	38	13	6	6	6	6	Grèce
Italy	410	415	435	355	285	215	215	216	140	130	Italie
Netherlands	53	24	11	6	6	6	6	2	...	1	Pays–Bas
United Kingdom	54	54	54	22	15	15	15	12	12	12	Royaume–Uni
EFTA	**30**	**33**	**5**	**35**	**33**	**33**	**26**	**22**	**22**	**22**	**AELE**
Portugal	30	33	5	35	33	33	26	22	22	22	Portugal
East Europe	**194**	**198**	**192**	**163**	**134**	**153**	**135**	**135**	**139**	**137**	**Europe de l'est**
Bulgaria	25	20	20	20	20	20	20	20	20	20	Bulgarie
Czechoslovakia	...	5	5	2	2	2	2	2	2	2	Tchécoslovaquie
German Dem. Rep.	45	45	45	45	45	45	45	45	45	45	Rép. dém. allemande
Hungary	22	21	21	20	15	22	14	16	21	19	Hongrie

For general note and footnotes, see end of table.

Voir la fin du tableau pour la remarque générale et les notes.

Pulp of fibres other than wood (continued) – Pâtes de fibres autres que le bois (suite)

Unit : Thousand metric tons

Unité : Milliers de tonnes métriques

Country or area	1976	1977	1978	1979	1980	1981	1982	1983	1984	1985	Pays ou zone
Poland	18	23	17	7	6	6	4	2	1	1	Pologne
Romania	84	84	84	69	46	58	50	50	50	50	Roumanie
Other Europe	**247**	**156**	**123**	**126**	**123**	**125**	**117**	**103**	**89**	**99**	**Autre Europe**
Spain	244	153	120	123	120	122	114	100	86	86	Espagne
Yugoslavia	3	3	3	3	3	3	3	3	3	13	Yougoslavie
USSR	**335**	**360**	**380**	**355**	**355**	**355**	**355**	**355**	**355**	**355**	**URSS**
Oceania	...	**2**	**4**	**6**	**5**	**5**	**9**	**1**	**10**	**11**	**Océanie**
Australia	...	2	4	6	5	5	9	1	10	11	Australie
Total	**6 200**	**6 364**	**6 894**	**7 378**	**7 564**	**7 484**	**7 516**	**8 427**	**8 995**	**10 245**	**Total**

General note.
Pulp other than wood pulp, derived from fibrous materials such as straw, bagasse, cotton, flax, bamboo, esparto and other grasses, used for the manufacture of paper, paperboard and fibreboard. In terms of air–dry weight (10 per cent moisture content). (SITC 25150–0).
Source: Food and Agriculture Organization of the United Nations (FAO), Rome.

Remarque générale.
Pâtes autres que la pâte de bois, dérivées de matières fibreuses telles que paille, bagasse, coton, lin, bambou, alfa, spart et autres herbes servant à la fabrication de papiers, de cartons et de panneaux de fibres. Poids après séchage à l'air (pâte à 10 p. 100 d'humidité). (CTCI 25150–0).
Source: Organisation des Nations Unies pour l'agriculture(FAO), Rome.

Wood pulp, dissolving grades – Pâte de bois chimiques, solubles

Unit : Thousand metric tons

Unité : Milliers de tonnes métriques

Country or area	1976	1977	1978	1979	1980	1981	1982	1983	1984	1985	Pays ou zone
Africa	**328**	**348**	**405**	**420**	**420**	**420**	**386**	**369**	**406**	**581**	**Afrique**
South Africa	328	348	405	420	420	420	386	369	406	581	Afrique du Sud
America, North	**1 535**	**1 543**	**1 639**	**1 732**	**1 685**	**1 517**	**1 215**	**1 365**	**1 319**	**1 294**	**Amérique du Nord**
Canada	222	268	351	368	313	274	220	217	221	222	Canada
Mexico	4	4	4	4	4	4	4	4	4	4	Mexique
United States	1 309	1 271	1 284	1 360	1 368	1 239	991	1 144	1 094	1 068	Etats–Unis
America, South	**69**	**48**	**47**	**43**	**43**	**41**	**41**	**43**	**63**	**60**	**Amérique du Sud**
Argentina	6	6	5	5	5	3	3	3	3	...	Argentine
Brazil	63	42	42	38	38	38	38	40	* 60	60	Brésil
Asia	**460**	**469**	**463**	**468**	**453**	**410**	**418**	**444**	**436**	**458**	**Asie**
India	126	127	139	143	143	143	143	175	175	200	Inde
Japan	324	330	321	316	300	256	266	260	252	249	Japon
Turkey	10	12	3	9	10	11	9	9	9	9	Turquie
Europe	**1 482**	**1 495**	**1 506**	**1 434**	**1 353**	**1 339**	**1 208**	**1 204**	**1 209**	**1 152**	**Europe**
EEC	**310**	**331**	**314**	**299**	**284**	**298**	**207**	**201**	**201**	**201**	**CEE**
France	75	91	96	99	94	94	10	10	8	8	France
Germany, Fed. Rep.	173	175	170	166	156	169	150	146	163	163	Allemagne, Rép. féd.
Italy	62	65	48	34	34	35	47	45	30	30	Italie
EFTA	**670**	**624**	**645**	**632**	**572**	**560**	**527**	**545**	**556**	**492**	**AELE**
Austria	121	120	116	119	120	127	126	126	126	125	Autriche
Finland	163	164	190	199	209	202	192	184	204	140	Finlande
Norway	142	106	108	118	121	134	112	135	126	127	Norvège
Sweden	244	234	231	196	122	97	97	100	100	100	Suède
East Europe	**382**	**399**	**388**	**345**	**394**	**345**	**348**	**331**	**316**	**325**	**Europe de l'est**
Czechoslovakia	58	61	61	46	52	48	45	33	26	31	Tchécoslovaquie
German Dem. Rep.	170	170	170	170	170	170	170	170	170	170	Rép. dém. allemande
Poland	91	108	92	64	97	59	59	54	46	50	Pologne
Romania	63	60	65	65	75	68	74	74	74	74	Roumanie
Other Europe	**120**	**141**	**159**	**158**	**103**	**136**	**126**	**127**	**136**	**134**	**Autre Europe**
Spain	39	41	53	53	53	48	36	37	53	53	Espagne
Yugoslavia	81	100	106	105	50	88	90	* 90	83	81	Yougoslavie
USSR	**794**	**800**	**810**	**753**	**761**	**782**	**796**	**846**	**846**	**846**	**URSS**
Total	**4 668**	**4 703**	**4 870**	**4 850**	**4 715**	**4 509**	**4 064**	**4 271**	**4 279**	**4 391**	**Total**

General note.
Bleached hardwood or softwood chemical pulp (sulphite or sulphate), of high alpha–cellulose content readily adaptable for uses other than paper–making (rayon, cellophane, lacquers etc.). In terms of air–dry weight (10 per cent moisture content). (SITC 25160–0).
Source: Food and Agriculture Organization of the United Nations (FAO), Rome.

Remarque générale.
Pâtes chimiques blanchies de bois feuillus ou résineux (au bisulfite ou au sulfate), à haute teneur en cellulose alfa, qui peuvent être facilement adaptées à des emplois autres que la fabrication du papier (rayonne, cellophane, laques etc.). Poids après séchage à l'air (pâte à 10 p. 100 d'humidité). (CTCI 25160–0).
Source: Organisation des Nations Unies pour l'agriculture(FAO), Rome.

Wood pulp, sulphate and soda – Pâte de bois chimiques, au sulfate

Unit : Thousand metric tons — Unité : Milliers de tonnes métriques

Country or area	1976	1977	1978	1979	1980	1981	1982	1983	1984	1985	Pays ou zone
Africa	**484**	**497**	**545**	**628**	**649**	**677**	**615**	**615**	**587**	**546**	**Afrique**
Angola	35	35	35	35	35	35	...	...	...	...	Angola
Cameroon	...	...	...	...	25	60	...	...	...	...	Cameroun
Morocco	42	55	66	82	83	75	80	86	83	81	Maroc
Nigeria	...	...	...	...	...	...	...	...	1	1	Nigéria
South Africa	227	255	289	350	350	350	378	354	325	290	Afrique du Sud
Swaziland	180	152	155	161	156	157	157	175	178	174	Swaziland
America, North	**37 963**	**39 370**	**41 500**	**43 656**	**45 250**	**45 368**	**42 767**	**46 590**	**48 876**	**47 999**	**Amérique du Nord**
Canada	7 885	8 155	8 686	9 171	9 549	9 102	7 978	9 248	9 411	9 511	Canada
Mexico	342	365	393	376	384	400	414	383	428	458	Mexique
United States	29 736	30 850	32 421	34 109	35 317	35 866	34 375	36 959	39 037	38 030	Etats–Unis
America, South	**1 639**	**1 934**	**2 420**	**2 493**	**3 326**	**3 197**	**3 505**	**3 848**	**3 933**	**4 107**	**Amérique du Sud**
Argentina	145	138	175	238	133	86	151	282	346	371	Argentine
Brazil	1 027	1 242	1 631	1 603	2 468	2 403	2 707	2 823	2 818	2 950	Brésil
Chile	375	459	516	551	614	602	536	634	659	656	Chili
Colombia	77	81	78	79	86	85	93	89	89	111	Colombie
Peru	5	5	5	5	7	4	1	1	1	1	Pérou
Uruguay	10	10	15	17	19	17	17	19	20	18	Uruguay
Asia	**6 389**	**6 438**	**6 505**	**7 165**	**7 050**	**6 335**	**6 655**	**7 070**	**7 481**	**7 702**	**Asie**
Bangladesh	10	10	12	17	17	17	17	17	17	17	Bangladesh
India	250	240	290	290	290	290	290	393	420	460	Inde
Indonesia	1	1	1	1	1	1	1	1	1	1	Indonésie
Japan	5 937	5 973	6 018	6 604	6 519	5 767	6 079	6 339	6 675	6 848	Japon
Korea, Republic of	4	8	...	...	30	69	108	116	121	129	Corée, République de
Philippines	104	106	130	131	105	93	89	106	122	122	Philippines
Turkey	83	100	54	123	88	98	71	98	125	125	Turquie
Europe	**11 686**	**11 459**	**12 736**	**13 737**	**13 636**	**13 993**	**13 585**	**15 101**	**16 154**	**16 164**	**Europe**
EEC	**987**	**1 087**	**1 099**	**995**	**870**	**954**	**1 004**	**1 117**	**1 219**	**1 170**	**CEE**
France	916	1 041	1 024	976	870	954	1 004	1 117	1 219	1 170	France
Italy	71	46	75	19	...	...	...	...	...	...	Italie
EFTA	**8 456**	**8 051**	**9 297**	**10 343**	**10 165**	**10 431**	**9 764**	**10 813**	**11 650**	**11 735**	**AELE**
Austria	216	229	253	287	299	302	301	290	327	458	Autriche
Finland	2 470	2 445	3 109	3 739	3 796	3 792	3 487	3 792	4 180	4 241	Finlande
Norway	341	269	205	168	158	325	314	353	403	406	Norvège
Portugal	397	428	512	609	544	577	795	856	889	1 027	Portugal
Sweden	5 032	4 680	5 218	5 540	5 368	5 435	4 867	5 522	5 851	5 603	Suède
East Europe	**1 165**	**1 098**	**1 171**	**1 184**	**1 235**	**1 226**	**1 410**	**1 720**	**1 696**	**1 683**	**Europe de l'est**
Bulgaria	181	179	209	221	216	223	212	203	195	174	Bulgarie
Czechoslovakia	231	246	253	257	276	301	499	612	655	658	Tchécoslovaquie
Poland	383	347	323	311	334	316	316	522	463	468	Pologne
Romania	370	326	386	395	409	386	383	383	383	383	Roumanie
Other Europe	**908**	**1 024**	**993**	**1 020**	**1 167**	**1 191**	**1 220**	**1 264**	**1 396**	**1 383**	**Autre Europe**
Spain	716	816	835	816	940	968	993	1 037	1 070	1 101	Espagne
Yugoslavia	192	208	158	204	227	223	227	227	326	282	Yougoslavie
USSR	**3 645**	**3 770**	**3 835**	**3 567**	**3 604**	**3 703**	**3 766**	**4 003**	**4 003**	**4 003**	**URSS**
Oceania	**685**	**747**	**746**	**721**	**711**	**796**	**743**	**727**	**762**	**815**	**Océanie**
Australia	125	153	156	158	171	177	165	176	211	274	Australie
New Zealand	560	594	590	563	540	619	578	551	551	541	Nouvelle–Zélande
Total	**62 491**	**64 215**	**68 287**	**71 967**	**74 226**	**74 068**	**71 636**	**77 954**	**81 796**	**81 336**	**Total**

For general note, see end of table.

Voir la fin du tableau pour la remarque générale.

General note.
Wood pulp prepared by an alkaline process in which the liquor used for digestion contains a mixture of sodium hydroxide and sodium sulphide (sulphate method), and sodium hydroxide alone (soda method). Includes chemical sulphate screenings. In terms of air–dry weight (10 per cent moisture content). (SITC 25170–0).
Source: Food and Agriculture Organization of the United Nations (FAO), Rome.

Remarque générale.
Pâtes de bois préparées par un procédé alcalin dans lequel la liqueur utilisée pour la délignification contient soit un mélange de soude caustique et de sulfure de sodium (procédé au sulfate) soit uniquement de la soude (procédé à la soude). Cette rubrique comprend les produits obtenus par tamisage après traitement chimique. Poids après séchage à l'air (pâte à 10 p. 100 d'humidité). (CTCI 25170–0).
Source: Organisation des Nations Unies pour l'agriculture(FAO), Rome.

Wood pulp, sulphite –
Pâte de bois chimiques, au bisulfite

Unit : Thousand metric tons

Unité : Milliers de tonnes métriques

Country or area	1976	1977	1978	1979	1980	1981	1982	1983	1984	1985	Pays ou zone
Africa	...	...	**5**	**0**	**50**	**52**	**53**	**53**	**53**	**53**	**Afrique**
Kenya	...	...	...	...	50	52	53	53	53	53	Kenya
South Africa	...	...	5	0	0	0	0	0	0	...	Afrique du Sud
America, North	**4 123**	**4 035**	**3 880**	**3 854**	**3 924**	**3 956**	**3 175**	**3 136**	**3 249**	**3 210**	**Amérique du Nord**
Canada	2 263	2 207	2 267	2 240	2 240	2 249	1 725	1 658	1 688	1 688	Canada
Mexico	15	14	19	21	12	10	11	12	12	13	Mexique
United States	1 845	1 814	1 594	1 593	1 672	1 697	1 439	1 466	1 549	1 509	Etats–Unis
America, South	**160**	**153**	**134**	**184**	**221**	**201**	**236**	**246**	**246**	**254**	**Amérique du Sud**
Argentina	36	33	41	55	31	18	32	28	27	26	Argentine
Brazil	105	105	73	110	172	167	188	196	196	205	Brésil
Chile	19	15	20	19	18	16	16	22	23	23	Chili
Asia	**309**	**303**	**237**	**254**	**250**	**201**	**152**	**159**	**166**	**126**	**Asie**
Japan	275	271	216	208	182	143	110	101	80	40	Japon
Turkey	34	32	21	46	68	58	42	58	86	86	Turquie
Europe	**4 641**	**4 088**	**4 085**	**4 213**	**4 237**	**3 902**	**3 599**	**3 767**	**3 996**	**3 791**	**Europe**
EEC	**837**	**870**	**818**	**868**	**939**	**846**	**864**	**915**	**941**	**863**	**CEE**
France	174	196	206	182	258	198	210	234	228	218	France
Germany, Fed. Rep.	587	608	541	593	619	573	573	576	583	580	Allemagne, Rép. féd.
Italy	15	8	10	35	28	75	81	105	130	65	Italie
United Kingdom	61	58	61	58	34	...	...	...	...	...	Royaume–Uni
EFTA	**3 053**	**2 450**	**2 434**	**2 577**	**2 538**	**2 325**	**2 027**	**2 171**	**2 276**	**2 119**	**AELE**
Austria	464	468	490	553	589	558	552	561	596	506	Autriche
Finland	815	618	530	571	601	557	400	403	388	338	Finlande
Norway	393	315	242	248	223	170	149	157	179	180	Norvège
Portugal	65	66	88	89	101	108	75	94	99	114	Portugal
Sweden	1 239	908	1 009	1 018	921	832	747	847	897	859	Suède
Switzerland	77	75	75	98	103	100	104	109	117	122	Suisse
East Europe	**573**	**558**	**565**	**543**	**503**	**479**	**459**	**430**	**509**	**549**	**Europe de l'est**
Czechoslovakia	293	288	292	299	275	268	263	230	318	359	Tchécoslovaquie
Hungary	24	32	20	19	15	10	13	13	12	10	Hongrie
Poland	116	114	108	91	89	84	84	88	80	81	Pologne
Romania	140	124	145	134	124	117	99	99	99	99	Roumanie
Other Europe	**144**	**181**	**242**	**207**	**238**	**234**	**231**	**233**	**238**	**228**	**Autre Europe**
Spain	22	26	10	13	25	23	17	19	20	20	Espagne
Yugoslavia	122	155	232	194	213	211	214	214	218	208	Yougoslavie
USSR	**2 430**	**2 513**	**2 556**	**2 376**	**2 401**	**2 467**	**2 509**	**2 667**	**2 667**	**2 667**	**URSS**
Oceania	**38**	**39**	**34**	**39**	**45**	**38**	**40**	**40**	**42**	**37**	**Océanie**
Australia	38	39	34	39	45	38	40	40	42	37	Australie
Total	**11 701**	**11 131**	**10 931**	**10 921**	**11 128**	**10 817**	**9 764**	**10 068**	**10 419**	**10 138**	**Total**

General note.
Wood pulp prepared by an acid pulping process. The liquor used is an aqueous solution of sulphurous acid in which lime or some other base has been dissolved. It may be bleached or not. Includes chemical sulphite screenings. In terms of air–dry weight (10 per cent moisture content). (SITC 25180–0).
Source: Food and Agriculture Organization of the United Nations (FAO), Rome.

Remarque générale.
Pâtes de bois préparées par un procédé acide de délignification. La liqueur utilisée est une solution aqueuse de gaz sulfureux dans laquelle on a dissous de la chaux ou une autre base. Pâte blanchie ou écrue. Cette rubrique comprend les produits obtenus par tamisage après traitement chimique. Poids après séchage à l'air (pâte à 10 p. 100 d'humidité). (CTCI 25180–0).
Source: Organisation des Nations Unies pour l'agriculture(FAO), Rome.

Wood pulp, semi–chemical – Pâte de bois mi–chimiques

Unit : Thousand metric tons

Unité : Milliers de tonnes métriques

Country or area	1976	1977	1978	1979	1980	1981	1982	1983	1984	1985	Pays ou zone
Africa	**77**	**128**	**117**	**93**	**94**	**92**	**114**	**93**	**129**	**137**	**Afrique**
Madagascar	2	2	2	2	2	2	2	2	2	1	Madagascar
Nigeria	...	...	...	...	...	...	...	...	1	1	Nigéria
South Africa	71	122	108	82	82	82	105	84	117	126	Afrique du Sud
Zimbabwe	4	4	7	9	10	8	7	7	9	9	Zimbabwe
America, North	**3 513**	**3 525**	**3 949**	**4 549**	**3 994**	**3 894**	**3 608**	**3 799**	**4 051**	**3 940**	**Amérique du Nord**
Canada	269	287	367	323	333	322	252	305	331	* 258	Canada
United States	3 244	3 238	3 582	4 226	3 661	3 572	3 356	3 494	3 720	3 682	Etats–Unis
America, South	**188**	**205**	**178**	**199**	**257**	**274**	**243**	**275**	**294**	**302**	**Amérique du Sud**
Argentina	57	54	39	56	118	126	122	153	* 160	155	Argentine
Brazil	103	120	110	100	* 99	* 104	* 96	* 94	104	114	Brésil
Colombia	26	29	27	40	37	41	22	25	25	* 28	Colombie
Uruguay	2	2	2	3	3	3	3	3	5	5	Uruguay
Asia	**1 530**	**1 366**	**1 178**	**1 117**	**1 028**	**844**	**689**	**631**	**620**	**576**	**Asie**
India	10	10	25	25	25	40	60	75	77	77	Inde
Japan	1 503	1 336	1 150	1 090	1 002	797	622	553	540	496	Japon
Turkey	17	20	3	2	1	7	7	3	3	3	Turquie
Europe	**1 666**	**1 591**	**1 602**	**1 631**	**1 631**	**1 524**	**1 456**	**1 483**	**1 528**	**1 619**	**Europe**
EEC	**637**	**559**	**505**	**500**	**493**	**445**	**421**	**446**	**446**	**488**	**CEE**
Denmark	63	53	52	59	64	65	58	51	68	63	Danemark
France	235	256	220	203	174	127	118	119	120	* 115	France
Germany, Fed. Rep.	52	61	68	71	73	69	69	78	77	* 76	Allemagne, Rép. féd.
Italy	166	83	63	73	94	94	96	99	72	73	Italie
Netherlands	24	7	...	...	...	...	...	...	...	...	Pays–Bas
United Kingdom	97	99	102	94	88	90	80	99	109	161	Royaume–Uni
EFTA	**699**	**672**	**730**	**770**	**745**	**686**	**648**	**645**	**661**	**711**	**AELE**
Austria	51	54	48	43	52	45	39	39	39	39	Autriche
Finland	258	255	275	303	291	308	309	301	301	326	Finlande
Norway	59	56	56	75	74	68	67	71	73	83	Norvège
Portugal	...	...	...	1	...	...	...	...	...	...	Portugal
Sweden	331	307	351	348	328	265	233	234	248	263	Suède
East Europe	**198**	**245**	**276**	**257**	**284**	**276**	**266**	**275**	**277**	**264**	**Europe de l'est**
Bulgaria	41	31	29	25	28	27	28	30	28	25	Bulgarie
Czechoslovakia	74	80	82	82	86	91	90	92	89	90	Tchécoslovaquie
German Dem. Rep.	5	5	5	5	5	5	5	5	5	5	Rép. dém. allemande
Hungary	28	49	62	62	61	64	60	61	62	50	Hongrie
Poland	16	34	53	53	69	59	59	63	69	70	Pologne
Romania	34	46	45	30	35	30	24	24	24	24	Roumanie
Other Europe	**132**	**115**	**91**	**104**	**109**	**117**	**121**	**117**	**144**	**156**	**Autre Europe**
Spain	64	50	30	33	36	35	31	27	22	22	Espagne
Yugoslavia	68	65	61	71	73	82	90	90	122	134	Yougoslavie
USSR	**300**	**320**	**350**	**326**	**329**	**338**	**344**	**366**	**366**	**366**	**URSS**
Oceania	**248**	**221**	**248**	**271**	**285**	**274**	**249**	**234**	**229**	**241**	**Océanie**
Australia	227	205	231	255	269	253	224	214	207	219	Australie
New Zealand	21	16	17	16	16	21	25	20	* 22	22	Nouvelle–Zélande
Total	**7 522**	**7 356**	**7 622**	**8 185**	**7 617**	**7 239**	**6 702**	**6 881**	**7 217**	**7 181**	**Total**

General note.
Wood pulp in which the fibres are partly separated without material damage by a sequence of chemical and mechanical actions and where the conditions of the separation treatment are not sufficiently severe in themselves to bring about a complete separation of the fibres. In terms of air–dry weight (10 per cent moisture content). (SITC 25190–0).
Source: Food and Agriculture Organization of the United Nations (FAO), Rome.

Remarque générale.
Pâtes de bois dans lesquelles les fibres sont partiellement séparées, sans dommage important, par une suite de traitements chimiques et mécaniques qui ne sont pas suffisamment vigoureux pour entraîner une séparation complète des fibres. Poids après séchage à l'air (pâte à 10 p. 100 d'humidité). (CTCI 25190–0).
Source: Organisation des Nations Unies pour l'agriculture(FAO), Rome.

Newsprint – Papier journal

Unit : Thousand metric tons

Unité : Milliers de tonnes métriques

Country or area	1976	1977	1978	1979	1980	1981	1982	1983	1984	1985	Pays ou zone
Africa	**229**	**271**	**230**	**245**	**247**	**249**	**322**	**260**	**320**	**345**	**Afrique**
Angola* [1]	1	1	1	1	1	1	1	1	1	1	Angola* [1]
Madagascar	[1] 4	* [1] 4	* [1] 4	* [1] 4	* [1] 4	* [1] 4	* [1] 4	1	1	1	Madagascar
South Africa[2]	212	254	212	226	* 226	* 226	* 300	* 240	* 301	* 325	Afrique du Sud[2]
Zimbabwe[1]	* 12	* 12	13	14	16	18	17	18	* 17	* 18	Zimbabwe[1]
America, North	**11 229**	**11 411**	**12 064**	**12 248**	**12 923**	**13 780**	**12 767**	**13 286**	**14 132**	**14 020**	**Amérique du Nord**
Canada	8 088	8 154	8 841	8 756	8 625	8 946	8 117	8 495	9 013	* 8 988	Canada
Mexico	57	59	59	65	71	69	77	72	94	108	Mexique
United States	3 084	3 198	3 164	3 427	4 227	4 765	4 573	4 719	5 025	4 924	Etats–Unis
America, South	**274**	**265**	**296**	**360**	**335**	**372**	**693**	**451**	**594**	**709**	**Amérique du Sud**
Argentina	3	15	36	102	98	109	95	125	202	197	Argentine
Brazil	137	117	127	109	105	105	107	106	109	208	Brésil
Chile	133	132	132	148	131	129	124	154	173	180	Chili
Colombia	...	0	0	0	0	28	366	65	...	...	Colombie
Uruguay*	1	1	1	1	1	1	1	1	...	...	Uruguay*
Asia	**3 851**	**3 099**	**3 233**	**3 354**	**3 523**	**3 467**	**3 539**	**3 575**	**3 633**	**3 815**	**Asie**
Bangladesh[3]	20	15	28	34	39	31	39	27	29	46	Bangladesh[3]
China	* [1] 1 154	# 327	339	357	376	355	* 400	* 400	* 400	425	Chine
India	57	56	49	48	48	58	101	160	199	269	Inde
Indonesia*	1	2	2	2	2	1	1	0	0	30	Indonésie*
Israel	13	16	12	5	5	6	3	2	1	1	Israël
Japan	2 341	2 370	2 482	2 566	2 674	2 575	2 580	2 562	2 553	2 592	Japon
Korea, Republic of	111	147	163	174	213	236	213	207	216	244	Corée, République de
Philippines[1]	74	78	80	81	80	79	63	70	83	59	Philippines[1]
Turkey	80	88	78	87	86	126	139	147	152	149	Turquie
Europe	**4 916**	**5 094**	**5 574**	**6 092**	**6 267**	**6 392**	**5 680**	**5 884**	**6 784**	**6 839**	**Europe**
EEC	***1 558***	***1 552***	***1 605***	***1 749***	***1 785***	***1 576***	***1 455***	***1 463***	***1 713***	***1 795***	***CEE***
Belgium	88	83	84	99	102	102	98	112	102	100	Belgique
France	255	265	287	280	261	267	248	218	265	262	France
Germany, Fed. Rep.	501	544	524	600	593	670	666	659	696	694	Allemagne, Rép. féd.
Greece	[1] 0	[1] 0	[1] 0	13	9	5	6	4	7	8	Grèce
Ireland	...	...	1	2	...	...	...	...	...	...	Irlande
Italy	263	234	262	272	277	234	198	194	207	178	Italie
Netherlands	123	123	128	119	177	183	151	* 194	* 198	* 199	Pays–Bas
United Kingdom	326	301	319	364	364	113	86	80	236	352	Royaume–Uni
EFTA	***2 818***	***2 978***	***3 394***	***3 780***	***3 946***	***4 277***	***3 731***	***3 930***	***4 553***	***4 526***	***AELE***
Austria	154	171	161	171	176	178	182	176	199	141	Autriche
Finland	879	1 068	1 279	1 330	1 430	1 593	1 355	1 398	1 697	* 1 490	Finlande
Norway	466	435	482	566	588	696	662	704	841	919	Norvège
Portugal	1	0	0	0	0	0	0	0	0	3	Portugal
Sweden	1 164	1 131	1 282	1 517	1 542	1 592	1 322	1 434	1 585	1 741	Suède
Switzerland[1]	154	173	190	196	210	218	210	218	* 231	* 232	Suisse[1]
East Europe	***343***	***362***	***369***	***371***	***381***	***379***	***358***	***348***	***365***	***357***	***Europe de l'est***
Czechoslovakia	79	80	74	74	71	76	79	68	72	72	Tchécoslovaquie
German Dem. Rep.	104	100	103	104	116	118	113	106	108	113	Rép. dém. allemande
Poland	83	84	89	91	91	82	75	83	86	82	Pologne
Romania	77	98	103	102	103	103	91	91	99	* 90	Roumanie
Other Europe	***197***	***202***	***206***	***192***	***155***	***160***	***136***	***143***	***153***	***161***	***Autre Europe***
Spain[1]	107	106	110	108	110	108	107	115	* 124	* 134	Espagne[1]
Yugoslavia	90	96	96	84	45	52	29	28	29	27	Yougoslavie
USSR	**1 390**	**1 388**	**1 432**	**1 420**	**1 535**	**1 532**	**1 508**	**1 528**	**1 532**	**1 565**	**URSS**
Oceania	**481**	**482**	**485**	**468**	**540**	**537**	**686**	**645**	**607**	**663**	**Océanie**
Australia[3]	206	207	208	208	221	214	364	376	365	365	Australie[3]
New Zealand[4]	275	275	277	260	319	323	322	269	242	298	Nouvelle–Zélande[4]
Total	**22 370**	**22 010**	**23 314**	**24 187**	**25 370**	**26 329**	**25 195**	**25 629**	**27 601**	**27 956**	**Total**

For general note and footnotes, see end of table.

Voir la fin du tableau pour la remarque générale et les notes.

General note.
Bleached, unsized or slack–sized printing paper, without coating, of the type usually used for newspapers, weight from 45 to 60 grammes per square metre, usually with at least 70 per cent of the weight of the fibrous material derived from mechanical pulp. (SITC 64110–0).

[1] Source: Food and Agriculture Organization (FAO), (Rome).

[2] Twelve months beginning 1 April of year stated.
[3] Twelve months ending 30 June of year stated.
[4] Twelve months ending 31 March of year stated.

Remarque générale.
Papier d'impression, blanchi, non encollé ou peu collé, non couché, du type utilisé d'ordinaire pour les journaux, poids de 45 à 60 g au m^2, contenant généralement au moins 70 p. 100 en poids de matière fibreuse tirée de la pâte mécanique. (CTCI 64110–0).

[1] Source: Organisation des Nations Unies pour l'alimentation et l'agriculture (FAO), (Rome).
[2] Période de douze mois commençant le 1er avril de l'année indiquée.
[3] Période de douze mois finissant le 30 juin de l'année indiquée.
[4] Période de douze mois finissant le 31 mars de l'année indiquée.

Other printing and writing paper – Autres papiers d'imprimerie et d'écriture

Unit : Thousand metric tons — Unité : Milliers de tonnes métriques

Country or area	1976	1977	1978	1979	1980	1981	1982	1983	1984	1985	Pays ou zone
Africa	**201**	**234**	**287**	**342**	**341**	**349**	**321**	**407**	**429**	**427**	**Afrique**
Algeria	18	18	18	30	26	32	32	29	32	30	Algérie
Angola	3	3	3	3	3	3	...	...	...	...	Angola
Egypt	38	38	45	66	66	66	39	39	* 52	* 52	Egypte
Ethiopia	4	4	4	4	4	4	4	6	7	8	Ethiopie
Kenya	12	18	19	20	19	18	18	17	23	23	Kenya
Madagascar	...	...	...	...	...	...	...	7	6	7	Madagascar
Morocco	2	12	13	17	25	24	24	23	24	23	Maroc
Nigeria	2	2	3	4	4	4	4	4	2	2	Nigéria
South Africa	105	118	161	178	177	182	182	260	260	256	Afrique du Sud
Tunisia	17	21	21	21	18	17	19	22	23	26	Tunisie
America, North	**12 884**	**13 758**	**14 646**	**15 526**	**15 915**	**15 867**	**15 817**	**17 584**	**19 059**	**19 465**	**Amérique du Nord**
Canada	842	1 109	1 316	1 525	1 511	1 431	1 480	1 726	1 943	2 141	Canada
Cuba	30	31	31	31	31	31	37	34	44	59	Cuba
Guatemala	7	12	13	15	15	15	7	10	11	9	Guatemala
Mexico	297	304	350	360	526	427	390	404	708	783	Mexique
Panama ex.Canal Zone	3	3	3	3	3	5	5	5	5	5	Panama ex.zone Canal
United States	* 11 705	* 12 299	* 12 933	* 13 592	* 13 829	* 13 958	* 13 898	15 405	16 348	16 468	Etats-Unis
America, South	**808**	**948**	**1 040**	**1 256**	**1 299**	**1 336**	**1 354**	**1 390**	**1 585**	**1 671**	**Amérique du Sud**
Argentina	129	142	142	236	152	139	156	174	185	161	Argentine
Brazil	454	577	638	764	870	876	913	952	1 075	1 164	Brésil
Chile	48	44	56	34	48	* 52	* 37	53	61	63	Chili
Colombia	58	61	65	66	71	84	70	67	85	* 106	Colombie
Ecuador	3	3	4	4	4	5	5	5	5	5	Equateur
Paraguay	...	...	1	2	2	2	2	2	2	2	Paraguay
Peru	* 46	* 41	36	41	42	68	68	37	* 41	* 49	Pérou
Uruguay	11	11	18	25	25	23	19	18	18	* 18	Uruguay
Venezuela	* 59	* 69	* 81	* 84	* 84	* 87	84	82	* 113	103	Venezuela
Asia	**5 449**	**5 673**	**6 312**	**6 802**	**7 216**	**7 105**	**7 453**	**8 304**	**9 009**	**9 663**	**Asie**
Bangladesh	19	24	19	27	27	32	32	71	71	71	Bangladesh
Burma	7	7	7	7	7	7	7	7	7	7	Birmanie
China	1 343	1 419	1 655	1 631	1 751	1 767	1 908	2 166	2 491	2 868	Chine
India	523	552	550	591	514	710	680	815	805	866	Inde
Indonesia	45	61	* 94	119	* 121	* 135	161	173	186	201	Indonésie
Iran(Islamic Rep.of)	30	38	38	45	45	45	45	45	45	45	Iran(Rép.islamique)
Iraq	12	9	9	9	9	9	9	9	9	9	Iraq
Israel	39	41	41	41	41	41	41	67	68	53	Israël
Japan	3 050	3 103	3 416	3 771	4 137	3 814	4 017	4 319	4 551	4 746	Japon
Korea, Republic of	* 158	187	247	298	293	303	333	416	475	483	Corée, République de
Malaysia	1	1	1	1	1	1	1	1	3	3	Malaisie
Pakistan	19	21	25	25	* 28	* 33	* 33	33	49	49	Pakistan
Philippines	43	40	43	73	70	30	34	28	35	58	Philippines
Sri Lanka	8	10	15	14	13	13	13	16	16	16	Sri Lanka
Thailand	57	62	65	70	73	73	36	36	87	88	Thaïlande
Turkey	77	72	62	61	69	75	86	85	92	75	Turquie
Viet Nam	18	26	25	19	17	17	17	17	* 19	* 25	Viet Nam
Europe	**12 115**	**12 833**	**14 279**	**14 888**	**15 050**	**15 056**	**15 033**	**15 987**	**18 039**	**18 116**	**Europe**
EEC	**6 905**	**7 101**	**8 175**	**8 437**	**8 413**	**8 425**	**8 315**	**8 796**	**9 854**	**9 650**	**CEE**
Denmark	73	79	95	117	113	133	157	155	165	135	Danemark
France	1 630	1 684	2 180	2 027	2 011	2 001	2 011	2 120	2 248	* 2 158	France
Germany, Fed. Rep.	2 202	2 326	2 525	2 709	2 879	3 000	3 071	3 368	3 779	* 3 782	Allemagne, Rép. féd.
Greece	37	37	62	80	80	74	72	53	53	53	Grèce
Ireland	24	26	20	23	23	17	...	...	...	...	Irlande
Italy	1 470	1 481	1 718	1 887	1 799	1 807	1 679	1 671	2 005	1 940	Italie
Netherlands	518	501	541	564	571	500	492	526	580	560	Pays-Bas
United Kingdom	951	967	1 034	1 030	937	893	833	903	1 024	1 022	Royaume-Uni
EFTA	**3 204**	**3 661**	**4 058**	**4 225**	**4 351**	**4 368**	**4 428**	**4 841**	**5 767**	**6 077**	**AELE**
Austria	601	594	596	624	618	646	661	721	762	850	Autriche
Finland	1 527	1 686	1 906	1 877	2 027	2 093	2 171	2 382	2 970	3 166	Finlande
Norway	300	287	304	350	337	267	250	243	298	304	Norvège
Portugal	59	79	82	91	87	92	97	99	116	93	Portugal
Sweden	506	766	907	999	998	996	992	1 121	1 334	1 364	Suède

For general note and footnotes, see end of table.

Voir la fin du tableau pour la remarque générale et les notes.

Other printing and writing paper (continued) – Autres papiers d'imprimerie et d'écriture (suite)

Unit : Thousand metric tons — Unité : Milliers de tonnes métriques

Country or area	1976	1977	1978	1979	1980	1981	1982	1983	1984	1985	Pays ou zone
Switzerland	211	249	263	284	284	274	257	275	287	300	Suisse
East Europe	**831**	**874**	**832**	**839**	**841**	**827**	**836**	**907**	**904**	**910**	**Europe de l'est**
Bulgaria	42	49	33	35	36	39	40	79	76	80	Bulgarie
Czechoslovakia	162	168	174	163	168	164	161	173	155	153	Tchécoslovaquie
German Dem. Rep.	179	170	176	179	182	184	184	182	189	* 188	Rép. dém. allemande
Hungary	108	110	109	118	115	120	120	126	140	136	Hongrie
Poland	219	233	213	195	199	173	192	208	205	214	Pologne
Romania	121	144	127	149	141	147	139	139	139	139	Roumanie
Other Europe	**772**	**803**	**800**	**958**	**1 009**	**1 013**	**1 037**	**1 026**	**1 076**	**1 041**	**Autre Europe**
Spain	591	602	585	730	717	716	703	692	737	712	Espagne
Yugoslavia	181	201	215	228	292	297	334	334	339	329	Yougoslavie
USSR	**1 163**	**1 187**	**1 205**	**1 140**	**1 141**	**1 170**	**1 173**	**1 249**	**1 284**	**1 306**	**URSS**
Oceania	**155**	**192**	**175**	**223**	**243**	**276**	**230**	**214**	**260**	**276**	**Océanie**
Australia	116	169	153	190	210	235	193	179	222	228	Australie
New Zealand	39	23	22	33	33	41	37	35	38	* 48	Nouvelle-Zélande
Total	**32 775**	**34 825**	**37 944**	**40 177**	**41 205**	**41 158**	**41 381**	**45 134**	**49 665**	**50 924**	**Total**

General note.
Machine-made papers in rolls or rectangular sheets (other than newsprint) of a quality rendering them suitable for use as printing and writing papers. The rolls should exceed 15 cm in width and the sheets should have at least one side exceeding 36 cm. To avoid double counting in this item, these papers should be counted only at the end of the paper manufacturing stage resulting in the formation of the dried web. (SITC 64120-0).
Source: Food and Agriculture Organization of the United Nations (FAO), Rome.

Remarque générale.
Papiers, autres que le papier journal, fabriqués à la machine, en rouleaux ou en feuilles rectangulaires et dont la qualité permet l'emploi pour l'impression ou l'écriture. Rouleaux d'une largeur supérieure à 15 cm et feuilles dont une dimension au moins est supérieure à 36 cm. Pour eviter de compter deux fois cette rubrique, ces papiers ne devraient être comptés qu'à la fin de l'étape de fabrication qui aboutit à la formation de la feuille sèche. (CTCI 64120-0).
Source: Organisation des Nations Unies pour l'agriculture(FAO), Rome.

Kraft paper and kraft paperboard – Papier kraft et carton kraft

Unit : Thousand metric tons

Unité : Milliers de tonnes métriques

Country or area	1976	1977	1978	1979	1980	1981	1982	1983	1984	1985	Pays ou zone
Africa	**131**	**690**	**703**	**763**	**869**	**956**	**942**	**1 024**	**1 058**	**1 089**	**Afrique**
Algeria	12	12	12	47	59	70	68	76	82	78	Algérie
Cameroon	5	5	5	5	5	5	5	5	5	5	Cameroun
Egypt	59	59	58	41	41	65	56	56	73	73	Egypte
Ethiopia	4	4	4	4	4	4	4	3	3	2	Ethiopie
Kenya	...	...	...	...	...	42	39	39	34	34	Kenya
Libyan Arab Jamah	5	5	5	5	5	5	5	5	5	5	Jamah.arabe libyenne
Morocco	40	62	60	48	53	54	54	54	58	56	Maroc
Mozambique	1	1	1	1	3	2	2	2	1	1	Mozambique
Nigeria	...	...	...	...	...	...	...	...	13	13	Nigéria
South Africa	...	537	553	607	687	697	697	772	774	810	Afrique du Sud
Sudan	5	5	5	5	5	5	5	5	5	5	Soudan
Tunisia	...	...	...	...	7	7	7	8	5	7	Tunisie
America, North	**32 059**	**32 823**	**34 283**	**35 455**	**35 133**	**34 575**	**33 126**	**36 019**	**38 059**	**36 812**	**Amérique du Nord**
Canada	2 390	2 407	2 560	2 708	2 680	2 848	2 436	2 756	2 865	2 910	Canada
Cuba	...	...	...	...	...	...	27	33	34	32	Cuba
Dominican Republic	9	9	9	9	9	9	9	9	10	10	Rép. dominicaine
El Salvador	2	2	2	10	10	10	10	10	10	10	El Salvador
Guatemala	9	9	12	3	5	4	3	3	3	4	Guatemala
Jamaica	...	...	...	...	...	...	12	12	12	12	Jamaïque
Mexico	821	881	970	1 013	1 109	106	1 106	1 153	1 198	1 290	Mexique
Panama ex.Canal Zone	13	13	13	13	13	25	25	25	25	25	Panama ex.zone Canal
United States	* 28 815	* 29 502	* 30 718	* 31 699	* 31 308	* 31 573	* 29 498	32 018	33 902	32 519	Etats–Unis
America, South	**1 932**	**2 051**	**2 274**	**2 547**	**2 791**	**2 671**	**2 838**	**2 896**	**3 174**	**2 984**	**Amérique du Sud**
Argentina	275	270	327	379	377	352	407	455	469	382	Argentine
Brazil	967	1 053	1 193	1 415	1 616	1 479	1 624	1 733	1 911	1 824	Brésil
Chile	83	95	81	79	137	95	102	85	111	100	Chili
Colombia	191	193	206	215	221	253	227	229	245	* 252	Colombie
Ecuador	26	26	28	8	8	9	10	10	10	10	Equateur
Paraguay	1	1	1	1	1	10	10	10	10	3	Paraguay
Peru	* 88	* 88	100	100	111	157	157	78	* 65	68	Pérou
Uruguay	16	16	14	20	20	20	14	20	23	* 22	Uruguay
Venezuela	* 285	* 309	* 324	* 330	* 300	* 296	* 287	* 276	* 330	323	Venezuela
Asia	**8 268**	**8 941**	**9 310**	**10 200**	**9 787**	**9 111**	**8 990**	**11 619**	**11 422**	**12 216**	**Asie**
Bangladesh	5	5	4	5	7	9	12	16	17	17	Bangladesh
Burma	3	3	3	3	3	3	3	3	3	3	Birmanie
Hong Kong	8	11	13	15	15	15	15	31	35	35	Hong–kong
India	199	234	240	240	240	281	281	281	317	341	Inde
Iraq	13	19	19	19	19	19	19	19	19	19	Iraq
Israel	23	52	52	52	52	52	52	59	53	51	Israël
Japan	7 229	7 397	7 603	8 243	7 805	7 048	7 069	9 563	8 984	9 757	Japon
Korea, Republic of	323	682	806	960	973	1 037	996	1 129	1 262	1 295	Corée, République de
Lebanon	43	43	43	43	43	43	43	43	43	43	Liban
Malaysia	...	16	14	15	15	25	25	25	29	29	Malaisie
Pakistan	4	2	10	10	* 12	* 12	* 15	42	60	60	Pakistan
Philippines	152	167	198	177	169	122	111	100	111	84	Philippines
Sri Lanka	10	10	9	7	5	8	6	7	7	7	Sri Lanka
Thailand	128	154	174	217	216	232	142	197	322	337	Thaïlande
Turkey	128	146	122	194	213	205	201	104	160	138	Turquie
Europe	**19 365**	**19 894**	**20 171**	**20 810**	**20 367**	**20 070**	**19 956**	**21 276**	**22 204**	**22 082**	**Europe**
EEC	**10 097**	**10 350**	**10 211**	**10 679**	**10 019**	**9 854**	**9 622**	**10 322**	**10 952**	**10 813**	**CEE**
Denmark	125	132	146	140	92	76	12	117	117	132	Danemark
France	2 244	2 326	2 172	2 067	2 000	2 000	1 950	2 556	2 669	2 562	France
Germany, Fed. Rep.	2 290	2 763	2 855	3 091	3 050	3 089	3 029	3 168	3 447	3 451	Allemagne, Rép. féd.
Greece	...	...	...	...	...	...	...	83	83	83	Grèce
Ireland	83	105	67	72	32	35	20	20	20	20	Irlande
Italy	2 445	2 172	2 142	2 463	2 367	2 303	2 149	* 1 927	2 004	1 917	Italie
Netherlands	861	880	880	885	800	750	905	902	973	1 000	Pays–Bas
United Kingdom	2 049	1 972	1 949	1 961	1 678	1 601	1 557	1 549	1 639	1 648	Royaume–Uni
EFTA	**5 753**	**5 714**	**6 104**	**6 942**	**6 629**	**6 580**	**6 547**	**7 103**	**7 421**	**7 452**	**AELE**
Austria	507	533	560	647	691	711	725	760	819	883	Autriche
Finland	1 659	1 568	1 725	1 873	1 891	1 907	1 800	1 918	2 009	1 973	Finlande

For general note and footnotes, see end of table.

Voir la fin du tableau pour la remarque générale et les notes.

Kraft paper and kraft paperboard (continued) – Papier kraft et carton kraft (suite)

Unit : Thousand metric tons

Unité : Milliers de tonnes métriques

Country or area	1976	1977	1978	1979	1980	1981	1982	1983	1984	1985	Pays ou zone
Norway	425	398	387	398	371	343	325	347	355	354	Norvège
Portugal	219	320	284	307	285	301	329	391	379	356	Portugal
Sweden	2 716	2 652	2 903	3 382	3 042	2 971	3 033	3 348	3 477	3 490	Suède
Switzerland	227	243	245	335	349	347	335	339	382	396	Suisse
East Europe	**2 106**	**2 164**	**2 208**	**1 523**	**2 014**	**1 886**	**1 879**	**1 915**	**1 923**	**1 928**	**Europe de l'est**
Czechoslovakia	632	640	652	66	662	668	678	692	682	674	Tchécoslovaquie
Hungary	232	283	283	267	277	283	240	249	254	252	Hongrie
Poland	796	795	782	700	576	444	467	480	493	508	Pologne
Romania	446	446	491	490	499	491	494	494	494	494	Roumanie
Other Europe	**1 225**	**1 507**	**1 480**	**1 468**	**1 513**	**1 542**	**1 724**	**1 752**	**1 887**	**1 868**	**Autre Europe**
Spain	1 089	1 338	1 360	1 347	1 377	1 370	1 450	1 464	1 565	1 533	Espagne
Yugoslavia	136	169	120	121	136	172	274	288	322	335	Yougoslavie
Oceania	**894**	**983**	**971**	**1 091**	**1 144**	**1 127**	**704**	**630**	**663**	**652**	**Océanie**
Australia	686	783	771	813	889	841	396	328	355	336	Australie
New Zealand	208	200	200	278	255	286	308	302	308	316	Nouvelle–Zélande
Total	**62 649**	**65 383**	**67 712**	**70 866**	**70 091**	**68 510**	**66 555**	**73 464**	**76 580**	**75 835**	**Total**

General note.
Machine–made paper and paperboard of high mechanical strength, consisting mainly of soda or sulphate pulp. It may be coloured in the mass and may contain a certain amount of bleached pulp. This heading applies only to kraft paper when in strips or rolls exceeding 15 cm in width or in rectangular sheets of which one side exceeds 36 cm. (SITC 64130–0).
Source: Food and Agriculture Organization of the United Nations (FAO), Rome.

Remarque générale.
Papier et carton fabriqués à la machine, ayant une résistance mécanique élevée, fabriqués principalement à partir de pâte à la soude ou au sulfate, éventuellement teintés dans la masse et contenant une certaine quantité de pâte blanchie. Cette rubrique ne comprend que le papier kraft en rouleaux dont la largeur est supérieure à 15 cm ou en feuilles dont une dimension au moins est supérieure à 36 cm. (CTCI 64130–0).
Source: Organisation des Nations Unies pour l'agriculture(FAO), Rome.

Cigarette paper – Papier à cigarettes

Unit : Metric tons | Unité : Tonnes métriques

Country or area	1976	1977	1978	1979	1980	1981	1982	1983	1984	1985	Pays ou zone
America, North	**2 691**	**2 579**	**2 656**	**2 674**	**2 943**	**2 658**	**2 997**	**2 601**	**2 784**	**3 065**	**Amérique du Nord**
Mexico	2 691	2 579	2 656	2 674	2 943	2 658	2 997	2 601	2 784	3 065	Mexique
America, South	**9 544**	**11 657**	**10 743**	**11 742**	**9 756**	**9 807**	**10 079**	**11 388**	**9 314**	**10 709**	**Amérique du Sud**
Brazil	7 662	9 922	9 059	10 269	8 271	8 575	8 167	8 109	6 980	8 264	Brésil
Colombia	1 882	1 735	1 684	1 473	1 485	1 232	1 912	3 279	...	...	Colombie
Asia	**25 240**	**24 511**	**22 331**	**25 987**	**26 733**	**26 878**	**30 379**	**29 236**	**29 145**	**32 343**	**Asie**
Indonesia	2 956	...	2 204	2 385	3 315	2 969	4 867	3 080	3 361	...	Indonésie
Japan	17 100	15 695	15 201	16 808	16 095	15 275	16 644	16 926	15 466	16 162	Japon
Korea, Republic of	3 062	3 975	2 563	4 887	5 246	6 112	...	...	...	...	Corée, République de
Turkey	2 122	2 196	2 363	1 907	2 077	2 522	2 423	2 175	2 652	4 081	Turquie
Europe	**23 931**	**27 786**	**27 959**	**29 621**	**30 746**	**29 159**	**28 150**	**31 426**	**31 501**	**33 501**	**Europe**
EEC	***2 670***	***2 581***	***2 588***	***2 368***	***1 979***	***2 265***	***2 111***	***1 993***	***2 542***	***2 428***	***CEE***
France[1]	2 670	2 581	2 588	2 368	1 979	2 265	2 111	1 993	2 542	2 428	France[1]
EFTA	***2 171***	***1 244***	***2 271***	***3 342***	***3 916***	***2 561***	***1 831***	***2 549***	***3 551***	***3 251***	***AELE***
Finland	2 171	1 244	2 271	3 342	3 916	2 561	1 831	2 549	3 551	...	Finlande
East Europe	***7 204***	***7 857***	***7 751***	***7 940***	***8 120***	***7 446***	***7 926***	***7 635***	***7 309***	***7 953***	***Europe de l'est***
Czechoslovakia	3 395	3 461	3 374	3 678	3 759	3 670	3 776	3 663	3 461	3 548	Tchécoslovaquie
Poland	3 809	4 396	4 377	4 262	4 361	3 776	4 150	3 972	3 848	4 405	Pologne
Other Europe	***11 886***	***16 104***	***15 349***	***15 971***	***16 731***	***16 887***	***16 282***	***19 249***	***18 099***	***19 869***	***Autre Europe***
Spain	7 389	10 793	...	...	...	10 648	11 130	12 386	...	...	Espagne
Yugoslavia	4 497	5 311	5 743	5 886	6 166	6 239	5 152	6 863	5 617	6 908	Yougoslavie
Total	**61 406**	**66 533**	**63 689**	**70 024**	**70 178**	**68 502**	**71 605**	**74 651**	**72 744**	**79 618**	**Total**

General note.
Cigarette paper in rolls exceeding 15 cm in width or in rectangular sheets of which at least one side exceeds 36 cm. It is a specially made tissue, strong, opaque, generally white but occasionally coloured, containing fillers such as calcium or magnesium carbonate. Its rate of combustion varies. The pulp from which this paper is made is very carefully refined and is drawn on narrow gauge machines. (SITC 64140-0).

[1] Consumption.

Remarque générale.
Papier à cigarettes en rouleaux d'une largeur supérieure à 15 cm ou en feuilles rectangulaires dont une dimension au moins est supérieure à 36 cm. C'est un papier de soie spécial, solide, opaque, généralement blanc mais parfois coloré, contenant une charge d'un produit tel que le carbonate de calcium ou de magnésium. Sa vitesse de combustion est variable. Le papier est fabriqué sur des machines étroites, à partir d'une pâte raffinée avec soin. (CTCI 64140-0).

[1] Consommation.

Other machine–made paper and paperboard, simply finished – Autres papiers et cartons fabriqués à la machine simplement finis

Unit : Thousand metric tons | Unité : Milliers de tonnes métriques

Country or area	1976	1977	1978	1979	1980	1981	1982	1983	1984	1985	Pays ou zone
Africa	**824**	**870**	**918**	**1 014**	**1 125**	**1 175**	**1 166**	**1 239**	**1 255**	**1 287**	**Afrique**
Algeria	12	12	12	47	59	70	68	76	82	78	Algérie
Angola	10	10	10	10	10	10	...	...	...	...	Angola
Cameroon	5	5	5	5	5	5	5	5	5	5	Cameroun
Egypt	80	80	79	56	56	80	71	71	* 93	* 93	Egypte
Ethiopia	4	4	4	4	4	4	4	3	3	2	Ethiopie
Kenya	29	37	39	41	43	45	42	43	38	38	Kenya
Libyan Arab Jamah.	5	5	5	5	5	5	5	5	5	5	Jamah.arabe libyenne
Madagascar	1	1	1	1	1	1	1	2	3	3	Madagascar
Morocco	44	62	60	65	71	72	73	73	77	75	Maroc
Mozambique	2	2	2	2	3	2	2	2	1	1	Mozambique
Nigeria	11	11	13	14	14	14	14	14	13	13	Nigéria
South Africa	587	607	644	718	796	806	806	875	869	908	Afrique du Sud
Sudan	6	7	7	7	9	9	9	9	9	9	Soudan
Tunisia	...	...	...	...	7	7	7	8	5	7	Tunisie
Uganda	1	1	...	...	...	...	0	0	0	0	Ouganda
Zaire	2	2	2	2	2	2	2	2	2	2	Zaïre
Zambia	...	...	...	...	...	...	8	5	3	1	Zambie
Zimbabwe	26	26	37	39	41	44	50	47	47	47	Zimbabwe
America, North	**40 684**	**41 585**	**43 226**	**44 733**	**43 485**	**43 894**	**40 826**	**43 486**	**45 965**	**44 717**	**Amérique du Nord**
Canada	2 887	2 888	3 158	3 252	3 254	3 458	2 811	3 141	3 265	3 316	Canada
Costa Rica	7	8	8	11	12	15	18	13	13	13	Costa Rica
Cuba	93	39	41	41	41	41	75	75	78	73	Cuba
Dominican Republic	9	9	9	9	9	9	9	9	10	10	Rép. dominicaine
El Salvador	5	5	5	16	16	16	16	16	16	16	El Salvador
Guatemala	11	11	14	15	17	14	5	6	7	5	Guatemala
Jamaica	...	4	9	10	10	10	18	18	18	18	Jamaïque
Mexico	993	* 1 069	1 162	1 229	1 337	1 337	1 409	1 458	1 531	1 660	Mexique
Panama ex.Canal Zone	17	17	17	17	17	38	38	38	38	38	Panama ex.zone Canal
United States	* 36 663	* 37 536	* 38 803	* 40 133	* 38 772	* 38 956	* 36 427	38 712	40 989	39 568	Etats–Unis
America, South	**2 707**	**2 832**	**3 191**	**3 536**	**3 918**	**3 657**	**3 868**	**3 891**	**4 213**	**4 224**	**Amérique du Sud**
Argentina	397	381	465	459	464	420	480	537	554	457	Argentine
Bolivia	1	1	1	1	1	1	1	1	1	1	Bolivie
Brazil	1 464	1 552	1 780	2 106	2 386	2 121	2 309	2 368	2 584	2 682	Brésil
Chile	95	120	106	108	177	135	145	117	144	136	Chili
Colombia	225	220	242	259	280	323	296	299	320	* 340	Colombie
Ecuador	31	31	33	17	22	27	29	29	29	29	Equateur
Paraguay	1	1	7	10	11	11	11	11	11	5	Paraguay
Peru	* 106	* 108	123	121	133	179	179	99	97	* 100	Pérou
Uruguay	24	24	24	27	27	25	20	25	29	* 27	Uruguay
Venezuela	* 364	* 395	411	428	417	416	398	405	* 444	448	Venezuela
Asia	**14 034**	**14 979**	**16 092**	**18 238**	**18 359**	**17 660**	**18 186**	**20 154**	**22 135**	**24 266**	**Asie**
Bangladesh	6	6	7	7	10	13	18	23	24	24	Bangladesh
Burma	3	3	3	3	3	3	3	3	3	3	Birmanie
China	2 466	2 680	3 104	3 951	4 223	4 260	4 578	5 696	6 510	7 673	Chine
Hong Kong	8	11	14	17	17	17	17	32	36	36	Hong–kong
India	356	384	408	408	408	301	301	291	327	351	Inde
Indonesia	13	17	* 60	93	* 110	* 123	168	201	217	236	Indonésie
Iran(Islamic Rep.of)	39	39	39	33	33	33	33	33	33	33	Iran(Rép.islamique)
Iraq	13	19	19	19	19	19	19	19	19	19	Iraq
Israel	54	64	64	64	64	64	64	88	78	77	Israël
Japan	10 003	10 229	10 601	11 524	11 277	10 591	10 856	11 561	12 241	13 131	Japon
Jordan	6	6	6	6	6	6	6	5	7	13	Jordanie
Korea,Dem.Ppl's.Rep.	80	80	80	80	80	80	80	80	80	80	Corée,Rép.pop.dém.de
Korea, Republic of	375	739	935	1 102	1 138	1 210	1 160	1 334	1 512	1 591	Corée, République de
Lebanon	45	45	45	45	45	45	45	45	45	45	Liban
Malaysia	17	19	37	45	45	50	50	50	77	77	Malaisie
Mongolia	2	2	2	2	2	2	2	2	2	2	Mongolie
Nepal	2	2	2	2	2	2	2	2	2	2	Népal
Pakistan	14	13	35	35	35	35	35	43	61	61	Pakistan
Philippines	169	187	218	196	187	138	125	114	133	102	Philippines
Singapore	6	8	20	6	30	40	* 56	56	56	56	Singapour
Sri Lanka	10	10	9	7	5	8	6	7	7	7	Sri Lanka
Syrian Arab Republic	3	3	3	3	3	3	3	3	3	3	Rép. arabe syrienne
Thailand	160	190	212	262	265	276	222	278	387	404	Thaïlande
Turkey	153	179	126	294	323	312	307	159	244	210	Turquie
Viet Nam	32	45	44	35	30	30	30	30	* 31	* 30	Viet Nam

For general note and footnotes, see end of table.

Voir la fin du tableau pour la remarque générale et les notes.

Unit : Thousand metric tons — Unité : Milliers de tonnes métriques

Country or area	1976	1977	1978	1979	1980	1981	1982	1983	1984	1985	Pays ou zone
Europe	**26 681**	**26 784**	**27 082**	**29 291**	**28 664**	**28 441**	**28 277**	**28 997**	**30 560**	**30 564**	**Europe**
EEC	**13 405**	**13 328**	**13 136**	**14 333**	**13 642**	**13 452**	**13 176**	**13 231**	**14 069**	**13 942**	**CEE**
Denmark	158	164	174	167	112	94	144	167	167	187	Danemark
France	2 664	2 697	2 496	2 953	2 880	2 880	2 808	2 924	3 054	* 2 932	France
Germany, Fed. Rep.	3 717	3 734	3 804	4 124	4 095	4 148	4 053	4 251	4 659	* 4 664	Allemagne, Rép. féd.
Greece	177	176	134	219	218	208	188	209	209	209	Grèce
Ireland	83	105	67	72	32	35	20	20	20	20	Irlande
Italy	2 765	2 573	2 635	2 941	2 858	2 814	2 626	2 394	2 510	2 469	Italie
Netherlands	963	1 001	1 014	1 028	959	900	1 029	1 041	1 123	1 154	Pays-Bas
United Kingdom	2 878	2 878	2 812	2 829	2 488	2 373	2 308	2 225	2 327	2 307	Royaume-Uni
EFTA	**7 109**	**6 986**	**7 493**	**8 207**	**8 038**	**7 952**	**7 929**	**8 501**	**8 830**	**8 901**	**AELE**
Austria	640	659	676	770	822	847	865	892	961	1 036	Autriche
Finland	2 032	1 955	2 108	2 348	2 323	2 339	2 223	2 393	2 470	2 467	Finlande
Norway	491	464	454	482	447	415	387	414	424	423	Norvège
Portugal	273	370	356	402	376	393	430	493	478	449	Portugal
Sweden	3 335	3 183	3 537	3 798	3 650	3 530	3 604	3 879	4 029	4 044	Suède
Switzerland	338	355	362	407	420	428	420	430	468	482	Suisse
East Europe	**4 023**	**4 129**	**4 083**	**4 050**	**4 157**	**4 115**	**4 189**	**4 183**	**4 286**	**4 333**	**Europe de l'est**
Albania	8	8	8	8	8	8	8	8	8	8	Albanie
Bulgaria	455	464	330	347	359	388	395	363	369	373	Bulgarie
Czechoslovakia	875	893	897	910	946	961	988	990	1 010	1 034	Tchécoslovaquie
German Dem. Rep.	917	895	924	938	954	967	970	957	995	* 992	Rép. dém. allemande
Hungary	262	314	336	318	325	337	342	353	366	358	Hongrie
Poland	1 022	1 044	1 024	961	987	870	914	940	966	996	Pologne
Romania	484	511	564	568	578	584	572	572	572	572	Roumanie
Other Europe	**1 853**	**2 075**	**2 074**	**2 365**	**2 501**	**2 567**	**2 671**	**2 770**	**3 011**	**3 024**	**Autre Europe**
Spain	1 365	1 452	1 480	1 695	1 741	1 765	1 889	1 947	2 091	2 067	Espagne
Yugoslavia	488	623	594	670	760	802	782	823	920	957	Yougoslavie
USSR	**6 363**	**6 489**	**6 599**	**6 236**	**6 238**	**6 396**	**6 413**	**6 825**	**7 017**	**7 141**	**URSS**
Oceania	**1 125**	**1 215**	**1 207**	**1 251**	**1 321**	**1 306**	**1 329**	**1 242**	**1 334**	**1 351**	**Océanie**
Australia	804	873	865	913	999	946	965	875	920	927	Australie
New Zealand	321	342	342	338	322	360	364	367	414	* 424	Nouvelle-Zélande
Total	**92 418**	**94 754**	**98 315**	**104 299**	**103 110**	**102 530**	**100 064**	**105 834**	**112 478**	**113 550**	**Total**

General note.
All kinds of simply finished paper and paperboard in the form of rolls (exceeding 15 cm in width) or rectangular sheets (of which one side exceeds 36 cm) other than newsprint, printing and writing paper, kraft paper and kraft paperboard and cigarette paper. Examples of paper falling under this heading are blotting paper, filter paper, carbon tissue, wrapping paper other than kraft, felt, duplex, triplex and multiplex paperboards, straw paper and strawboard, cable paper etc. Excludes tranformed paper and paperboards such as parchment paper, composite paper or paperboard, impregnated, coated, surface coloured paper and paperboard etc. (SITC 64150-0).
Source: Food and Agriculture Organization of the United Nations (FAO), Rome.

Remarque générale.
Papiers et cartons de toute nature simplement finis, en rouleaux d'une largeur supérieure à 15 cm ou en feuilles rectangulaires dont une dimension au moins est supérieure à 36 cm, autres que le papier journal, les papiers d'imprimerie et d'écriture, le papier kraft, le carton kraft et le papier à cigarettes. Sont notamment compris dans cette rubrique le papier buvard, le papier filtre, le papier carbone, les papiers d'emballage autres que le papier kraft, le carton de feutre, les cartons duplex, triplex et multiplex, le papier et le carton de paille, le papier de cordages etc. Cette rubrique ne comprend pas les papiers et les cartons ayant subi une transformation, tels que le papier parchemin, les sandwiches de papier ou de carton et d'autres matières, les papiers et cartons imprégnés, à revêtement, enduits de couleur etc. (CTCI 64150-0).
Source: Organisation des Nations Unies pour l'agriculture(FAO), Rome.

Fibreboard, compressed – Panneaux de fibres, comprimés

Unit : Thousand cubic metres — Unité : Milliers de mètres cubes

Country or area	1976	1977	1978	1979	1980	1981	1982	1983	1984	1985	Pays ou zone
Africa	**126**	**77**	**53**	**54**	**100**	**99**	**131**	**124**	**131**	**131**	**Afrique**
Kenya	...	...	...	...	38	37	49	41	48	48	Kenya
Madagascar	1	1	1	1	1	1	1	1	1	1	Madagascar
South Africa	115	* 68	* 44	44	* 53	53	* 74	* 74	74	74	Afrique du Sud
Tunisia	* 5	* 5	* 5	* 5	* 5	* 5	* 5	* 5	5	5	Tunisie
United Rep. Tanzania	4	3	3	3	3	3	2	3	3	3	Rép.Unie de Tanzanie
America, North	**2 248**	**2 351**	**2 265**	**2 259**	**1 939**	**1 993**	**1 788**	**2 315**	**2 269**	**2 264**	**Amérique du Nord**
Canada	208	185	211	206	205	167	118	170	161	156	Canada
Cuba	...	...	...	...	...	...	44	48	48	48	Cuba
Mexico	25	30	26	26	26	26	26	67	65	65	Mexique
United States	2 015	2 136	2 028	2 027	1 708	1 800	1 600	2 030	1 995	1 995	Etats–Unis
America, South	**514**	**595**	**661**	**603**	**709**	**706**	**568**	**659**	**657**	**657**	**Amérique du Sud**
Argentina	51	52	68	59	67	65	65	72	72	72	Argentine
Brazil	426	500	545	* 484	* 580	580	* 442	* 527	527	527	Brésil
Chile	22	28	33	44	45	44	44	42	40	40	Chili
Colombia	12	12	12	13	15	13	14	* 15	15	15	Colombie
Uruguay	3	3	3	3	2	4	3	3	3	3	Uruguay
Asia	**709**	**772**	**891**	**1 008**	**1 079**	**1 123**	**1 225**	**1 309**	**1 307**	**1 329**	**Asie**
Bangladesh	5	5	5	4	* 5	* 5	* 5	* 5	5	5	Bangladesh
China	* 202	* 253	361	461	538	600	707	772	773	773	Chine
India	18	19	30	30	19	39	42	47	43	43	Inde
Indonesia	1	1	1	1	1	1	1	1	1	1	Indonésie
Iran(Islamic Rep.of)	31	33	25	22	* 26	* 26	* 26	* 26	26	26	Iran(Rép.islamique)
Japan	280	277	277	290	304	262	259	253	255	270	Japon
Korea, Republic of	19	18	18	18	14	7	10	11	9	13	Corée, République de
Pakistan	7	7	6	9	* 5	5	* 11	* 11	11	11	Pakistan
Philippines	51	54	64	73	68	66	* 63	* 63	63	63	Philippines
Thailand	42	42	42	31	30	42	31	35	51	54	Thaïlande
Turkey	53	63	63	70	70	70	70	85	70	70	Turquie
Europe	**3 085**	**3 050**	**3 247**	**3 129**	**3 117**	**2 957**	**2 742**	**2 865**	**2 881**	**2 794**	**Europe**
EEC	**809**	**794**	**831**	**686**	**666**	**641**	**602**	**651**	**706**	**677**	**CEE**
France	221	171	207	210	201	188	148	156	143	143	France
Germany, Fed. Rep.	256	290	290	252	224	189	193	212	222	219	Allemagne, Rép. féd.
Greece	14	16	18	17	17	20	18	18	18	18	Grèce
Ireland	19	19	18	...	...	...	...	...	...	...	Irlande
Italy	250	250	250	180	200	220	201	208	250	250	Italie
Netherlands	24	24	24	3	...	...	...	...	...	...	Pays–Bas
United Kingdom	25	24	24	24	24	24	42	57	73	47	Royaume–Uni
EFTA	**854**	**780**	**758**	**800**	**809**	**714**	**639**	**655**	**629**	**605**	**AELE**
Austria	71	69	69	76	81	64	64	66	70	68	Autriche
Finland	110	98	109	127	141	130	106	107	103	97	Finlande
Norway	104	97	86	78	93	91	70	75	66	68	Norvège
Portugal	48	59	47	69	74	72	67	73	72	60	Portugal
Sweden	493	424	411	412	374	317	291	290	273	269	Suède
Switzerland	28	33	36	38	46	40	41	44	45	43	Suisse
East Europe	**1 161**	**1 174**	**1 278**	**1 190**	**1 217**	**1 155**	**1 149**	**1 122**	**1 108**	**1 098**	**Europe de l'est**
Bulgaria	101	127	126	137	141	126	123	108	107	109	Bulgarie
Czechoslovakia	134	147	150	154	160	153	151	138	140	132	Tchécoslovaquie
German Dem. Rep.	217	222	265	274	281	280	264	283	264	264	Rép. dém. allemande
Hungary	74	66	94	94	99	97	82	89	84	80	Hongrie
Poland	329	340	347	332	328	297	331	318	328	328	Pologne
Romania	306	272	296	199	208	202	198	* 186	185	185	Roumanie
Other Europe	**208**	**258**	**336**	**409**	**417**	**439**	**352**	**437**	**438**	**414**	**Autre Europe**
Spain	116	165	246	310	310	325	240	280	250	250	Espagne
Yugoslavia	92	93	90	99	107	114	112	157	188	164	Yougoslavie
USSR	**1 476**	**1 561**	**1 571**	**1 598**	**1 595**	**1 639**	**1 595**	**1 707**	**1 707**	**1 707**	**URSS**

For general note and footnotes, see end of table.

Voir la fin du tableau pour la remarque générale et les notes.

Fibreboard, compressed (continued) – Panneaux de fibres, comprimés (suite)

Unit : Thousand cubic metres

Unité : Milliers de mètres cubes

Country or area	1976	1977	1978	1979	1980	1981	1982	1983	1984	1985	Pays ou zone
Oceania	**157**	**160**	**129**	**125**	**180**	**199**	**203**	**180**	**200**	**204**	**Océanie**
Australia	123	135	105	101	95	97	102	86	90	94	Australie
New Zealand	34	25	* 24	24	85	102	101	94	110	110	Nouvelle–Zélande
Total	**8 314**	**8 566**	**8 818**	**8 776**	**8 719**	**8 716**	**8 252**	**9 159**	**9 152**	**9 086**	**Total**

General note.
Sheet material manufactured from fibres of wood or other ligno–cellulosic materials, with the primary bond deriving from the arrangement of the fibres and their inherent adhesive properties, with a density over 0.40 gr./cubic centimetre (25 lb./cubic foot). It includes semi–hardboard, hardboard and super hardboard as variously defined. (SITC 64160–1).
Source: Food and Agriculture Organization of the United Nations (FAO), Rome.

Remarque générale.
Panneaux d'une densité supérieure à 0.4 (25 livres par pied cube), fabriqués à partir de fibres de bois ou d'autres matières ligneuses ou cellulosiques, dont la cohésion est due principalement à l'arrangement des fibres et à leur adhérence propre. Cette rubrique comprend les panneaux semi–durs, durs et extra–durs définis ailleurs. (CTCI 64160–1).
Source: Organisation des Nations Unies pour l'agriculture(FAO), Rome.

Fibreboard, non–compressed – Panneaux de fibres, non comprimés

Unit : Thousand cubic metres | Unité : Milliers de mètres cubes

Country or area	1976	1977	1978	1979	1980	1981	1982	1983	1984	1985	Pays ou zone
Africa	**48**	**31**	**33**	**33**	**33**	**33**	**33**	**33**	**33**	**33**	**Afrique**
Ethiopia	8	8	8	8	8	8	8	8	8	8	Ethiopie
South Africa	40	* 23	* 25	25	25	25	25	25	25	25	Afrique du Sud
America, North	**5 877**	**5 818**	**5 826**	**5 821**	**3 908**	**3 673**	**3 362**	**3 313**	**3 238**	**3 345**	**Amérique du Nord**
Canada	673	611	684	661	518	573	462	553	529	636	Canada
United States	5 204	5 207	5 142	5 160	3 390	3 100	2 900	2 760	2 709	2 709	Etats–Unis
America, South	**214**	**221**	**233**	**260**	**243**	**241**	**183**	**231**	**231**	**231**	**Amérique du Sud**
Argentina	...	...	...	...	23	21	15	23	23	23	Argentine
Brazil	205	210	220	* 240	* 200	200	* 160	* 200	200	200	Brésil
Colombia	* 1	1	1	4	4	4	4	4	4	4	Colombie
Venezuela	8	10	12	* 16	* 16	16	* 4	* 4	4	4	Venezuela
Asia	**298**	**327**	**302**	**369**	**375**	**296**	**322**	**327**	**333**	**365**	**Asie**
India	4	6	2	2	1	3	3	3	3	3	Inde
Israel	10	10	10	10	10	10	10	10	10	10	Israël
Japan	284	311	290	357	364	283	305	298	304	336	Japon
Thailand	...	...	...	...	...	...	4	16	16	16	Thaïlande
Europe	**1 415**	**1 334**	**1 268**	**1 378**	**1 332**	**1 135**	**1 217**	**1 195**	**1 151**	**1 089**	**Europe**
EEC	**216**	**200**	**203**	**201**	**178**	**181**	**161**	**160**	**170**	**150**	**CEE**
France	91	72	89	77	65	69	54	57	52	52	France
Germany, Fed. Rep.	55	57	50	58	55	50	50	50	50	50	Allemagne, Rép. féd.
Netherlands	42	37	30	36	33	34	25	21	39	20	Pays–Bas
United Kingdom	28	34	34	30	25	28	32	32	29	28	Royaume–Uni
EFTA	**679**	**621**	**584**	**624**	**578**	**451**	**513**	**512**	**458**	**412**	**AELE**
Austria	45	47	49	47	46	43	34	20	18	18	Autriche
Finland	143	123	121	145	157	93	133	131	111	71	Finlande
Norway	168	123	108	137	118	116	171	183	163	166	Norvège
Sweden	308	312	293	279	236	176	148	147	136	128	Suède
Switzerland	15	16	13	16	21	23	27	31	30	29	Suisse
East Europe	**492**	**489**	**462**	**517**	**510**	**423**	**459**	**440**	**437**	**441**	**Europe de l'est**
Czechoslovakia	61	64	65	61	65	70	70	70	59	63	Tchécoslovaquie
Poland	420	415	387	352	342	246	276	265	273	273	Pologne
Romania	11	10	10	104	103	107	113	* 105	* 105	* 105	Roumanie
Other Europe	**...**	**...**	**19**	**36**	**66**	**80**	**80**	**80**	**80**	**80**	**Autre Europe**
Spain	...	...	19	36	66	80	80	80	80	80	Espagne
USSR	**1 302**	**1 377**	**1 386**	**1 410**	**1 407**	**1 446**	**1 407**	**1 506**	**1 506**	**1 506**	**URSS**
Oceania	**116**	**130**	**127**	**128**	**45**	**42**	**45**	**39**	**44**	**44**	**Océanie**
Australia	20	18	15	16	15	15	14	12	12	12	Australie
New Zealand	96	112	112	112	30	27	31	27	32	32	Nouvelle–Zélande
Total	**9 270**	**9 238**	**9 175**	**9 399**	**7 343**	**6 866**	**6 569**	**6 644**	**6 536**	**6 613**	**Total**

General note.
Sheet material manufactured from fibres of wood or other ligno–cellulosic materials, with the primary bond deriving from the arrangement of the fibres and their inherent adhesive properties, with a density of 0.40 gr./cubic centimetre (25 lb./cubic foot) or less. (SITC 64160–2).
Source: Food and Agriculture Organization of the United Nations (FAO), Rome.

Remarque générale.
Panneaux d'une densité inférieure à 0.4 (25 livres par pied cube), fabriqués à partir de fibres de bois ou autres matières ligneuses ou cellulosiques, dont la cohésion est due principalement à l'arrangement des fibres et à leur adhérence propre. (CTCI 64160–2).
Source: Organisation des Nations Unies pour l'agriculture(FAO), Rome.

Voir la fin du tableau pour les notes.

Packing containers of paper or paperboard – Récipients d'emballage en papier ou en carton

Unit : Thousand metric tons | Unité : Milliers de tonnes métriques

Country or area	1976	1977	1978	1979	1980	1981	1982	1983	1984	1985	Pays ou zone
Africa	**441**	**414**	**465**	**552**	**704**	**704**	**664**	**692**	**751**	**731**	**Afrique**
Algeria	...	38	41	81	84	69	55	...	...	...	Algérie
Côte d'Ivoire	...	31	53	52	51	55	45	46	57	...	Côte d'Ivoire
Madagascar	...	...	...	3	3	* 3	...	...	...	...	Madagascar
Senegal	7	7	7	8	8	9	8	9	9	9	Sénégal
South Africa	322	311	331	376	* 522	* 529	521	525	565	536	Afrique du Sud
Tunisia	23	24	30	32	36	39	32	30	34	39	Tunisie
America, North	**551**	**664**	**711**	**886**	**929**	**812**	**867**	**964**	**985**	**1 064**	**Amérique du Nord**
Dominican Republic	129	236	251	376	382	301	357	470	503	...	Rép. dominicaine
Mexico	373	377	397	448	486	442	438	441	414	466	Mexique
Panama	49	51	63	62	...	69	72	53	...	...	Panama
America, South	**492**	**492**	**492**	**492**	**492**	**328**	**322**	**827**	**492**	**492**	**Amérique du Sud**
Chile	12	12	12	...	...	...	...	...	...	...	Chili
Colombia	...	...	...	...	...	316	310	815	...	...	Colombie
Asia	**5 367**	**5 469**	**5 571**	**6 167**	**5 838**	**5 229**	**5 189**	**5 535**	**5 884**	**6 595**	**Asie**
India	* 141	* 157	* 168	* 172	177	205	210	194	231	...	Inde
Iran(Islamic Rep.of)[1]	85	91	97	83	77	99	...	...	...	...	Iran(Rép.islamique)[1]
Japan[2]	4 619	4 694	4 812	5 350	5 063	4 487	4 415	4 787	5 110	5 829	Japon[2]
Korea, Republic of	522	527	494	562	521	438	...	...	...	...	Corée, République de
Europe	**9 437**	**9 569**	**9 942**	**10 330**	**10 744**	**10 515**	**10 272**	**10 602**	**11 063**	**11 319**	**Europe**
EEC	***5 485***	***5 471***	***5 620***	***5 915***	***6 052***	***6 051***	***6 037***	***6 275***	***6 551***	***6 709***	***CEE***
Belgium	401	379	393	408	416	416	439	467	502	519	Belgique
Denmark	273	295	288	315	301	...	...	...	...	...	Danemark
France[3]	1 769	1 768	1 810	1 891	1 872	1 870	...	...	...	...	France[3]
Germany, Fed. Rep.	3 004	2 987	3 087	3 266	3 359	3 342	3 249	3 426	3 598	3 701	Allemagne, Rép. féd.
Greece[4]	38	42	42	35	# 104	106	105	104	140	...	Grèce[4]
EFTA	***1 088***	***1 098***	***1 199***	***1 126***	***1 253***	***1 178***	***1 113***	***1 119***	***1 167***	***1 203***	***AELE***
Austria	256	244	236	260	281	311	300	296	322	353	Autriche
Finland	346	373	489	361	446	383	302	339	345	...	Finlande
Iceland	7	7	8	10	9	8	8	9	9	...	Islande
Portugal[5]	33	41	40	40	44	43	41	41	37	33	Portugal[5]
Sweden	446	433	426	455	473	433	462	434	454	470	Suède
East Europe	***1 683***	***1 708***	***1 720***	***1 695***	***1 783***	***1 666***	***1 654***	***1 629***	***1 686***	***1 723***	***Europe de l'est***
Bulgaria[6]	44	39	...	...	...	...	...	...	...	...	Bulgarie[6]
Czechoslovakia	376	382	393	412	420	429	430	434	441	427	Tchécoslovaquie
German Dem. Rep.[6]	401	402	391	394	400	398	404	384	422	435	Rép. dém. allemande[6]
Hungary	266	301	308	311	323	333	340	324	342	341	Hongrie
Poland	596	584	586	536	598	464	438	445	439	478	Pologne
Other Europe	***1 181***	***1 292***	***1 404***	***1 594***	***1 656***	***1 620***	***1 468***	***1 580***	***1 660***	***1 683***	***Autre Europe***
Spain	854	900	...	1 121	1 144	1 066	947	1 032	...	...	Espagne
Yugoslavia	327	392	431	473	512	554	521	548	560	562	Yougoslavie
Total	**16 288**	**16 608**	**17 182**	**18 427**	**18 707**	**17 588**	**17 314**	**18 619**	**19 177**	**20 201**	**Total**

General note.
Bags, boxes, cartons and other containers made of paper or paperboard used for the packing, transport, storage or sale of merchandise. (SITC 64211-0).

Remarque générale.
Sacs, boîtes, cartons et autres récipients fabriqués en papier ou en carton, utilisés pour l'emballage, le transport, le magasinage ou la vente de marchandises. (CTCI 64211-0).

[1] Production by establishments employing 10 or more persons.
[2] Packing containers of paperboard only.
[3] Primary materials consumed for the production of paper and paperboard containers.
[4] Paper bags and paper sacks only.
[5] Paper bags only, including envelopes.
[6] Paper bags only.

[1] Production des établissements occupant 10 personnes ou plus.
[2] Emballages en carton seulement.
[3] Matières primaires consommées pour la fabrication des récipients en papier ou en carton.
[4] Sacs et sachets en papier seulement.
[5] Sacs en papier seulement, y compris les enveloppes.
[6] Sacs en papier seulement.

Sulphur, recovered as by-product – Soufre en tant que sous-produit

Unit : Thousand metric tons — Unité : Milliers de tonnes métriques

Country or area	1976	1977	1978	1979	1980	1981	1982	1983	1984	1985	Pays ou zone
Africa	**279**	**286**	**306**	**267**	**285**	**275**	**298**	**308**	**279**	**277**	**Afrique**
Algeria[1]	10	10	15	15	14	15	* 10	* 15	* 20	* 20	Algérie[1]
Egypt[1]	2	3	3	3	3	2	* 2	* 1	* 2	* 2	Egypte[1]
Libyan Arab Jamah.* [1]	16	17	19	20	22	11	12	14	14	14	Jamah.arabe libyenne* [1]
South Africa[1]	118	133	* 125	* 125	* 125	* 127	* 160	* 157	121	120	Afrique du Sud[1]
Zaire* [1]	37	31	30	25	25	25	25	36	37	36	Zaïre* [1]
Zambia[1]	91	87	109	74	91	90	84	* 80	* 80	* 80	Zambie[1]
Zimbabwe* [1]	5	5	5	5	5	5	5	5	5	5	Zimbabwe* [1]
America, North	**8 194**	**9 789**	**10 812**	**11 815**	**11 888**	**11 624**	**11 217**	**12 011**	**12 354**	**12 520**	**Amérique du Nord**
Bahamas* [1]	5	5	5	5	5	5	5	5	3	1	Bahamas* [1]
Canada	4 735	5 943	6 428	7 323	[1]7 260	[1]6 799	[1]6 280	* [1]6 577	* [1]6 606	* [1]6 748	Canada
Cuba	* 1	* 0	* 0	* 0	* 0	1	0	0	0	0	Cuba
Mexico	96	146	168	249	402	426	425	377	461	475	Mexique
Neth.Antil and Aruba[1]	95	94	95	91	91	* 90	* 90	87	63	* 25	Antill.néer.et Aruba[1]
Trinidad and Tobago	[1]74	[1]34	[1]54	[1]77	[1]57	[1]44	* [1]13	* [1]10	* [1]7	* 5	Trinité-et-Tobago
United States	3 188	3 567	4 062	4 070	4 073	4 259	4 404	4 955	5 214	5 266	Etats-Unis
America, South	**178**	**203**	**206**	**238**	**276**	**293**	**352**	**491**	**500**	**531**	**Amérique du Sud**
Brazil[1]	30	47	57	92	131	119	130	260	* 260	* 285	Brésil[1]
Chile[1]	30	29	21	27	27	28	32	32	* 32	30	Chili[1]
Colombia	[1]2	[1]2	[1]3	[1]2	[1]1	29	36	37	...	...	Colombie
Ecuador[1]	8	8	10	10	* 10	* 10	* 10	* 10	* 10	* 10	Equateur[1]
Peru[1]	16	20	18	* 20	* 20	* 20	* 58	* 65	* 70	* 70	Pérou[1]
Uruguay[1]	2	2	2	2	2	2	2	2	* 2	* 2	Uruguay[1]
Venezuela	[1]90	[1]95	[1]95	[1]85	# 85	* 85	* 84	* 85	* 86	* 88	Venezuela
Asia	**3 461**	**3 788**	**3 635**	**3 901**	**4 527**	**4 576**	**5 298**	**5 121**	**5 318**	**5 943**	**Asie**
Bahrain	[1]10	[1]7	[1]26	[1]25	[1]33	[1]36	[1]34	[1]49	[1]50	* 50	Bahreïn
China[1]	300	* 300	* 200	* 300	* 300	* 300	* 300	* 350	* 350	* 350	Chine[1]
India* [1]	122	122	123	119	120	96	105	114	120	120	Inde* [1]
Iran(Islamic Rep.of)[1]	399	* 400	* 300	* 200	* 150	* 6	* 10	* 25	* 30	* 180	Iran(Rép.islamique)[1]
Iraq* [1]	40	40	40	70	40	40	40	40	70	70	Iraq* [1]
Israel[1]	* 10	* 10	* 10	* 10	* 10	* 10	* 10	10	* 10	* 10	Israël[1]
Japan[1]	2 178	2 436	2 401	2 591	2 473	2 316	2 319	2 341	2 333	* 2 257	Japon[1]
Korea, D. P. Rp.* [1]	20	12	10	30	30	30	30	30	30	30	Corée, Rp. P. D.* [1]
Korea, Republic of* [1]	47	64	81	90	90	90	90	90	90	90	Corée, République de* [1]
Kuwait	61	79	100	114	82	109	141	147	147	202	Koweït
Pakistan* [1]	12	12	14	14	14	14	19	26	26	26	Pakistan* [1]
Philippines	...	...	...	...	...	...	...	57	130	100	Philippines
Saudi Arabia[1]	* 12	12	14	17	460	600	900	793	* 833	* 1 068	Arabie saoudite[1]
Singapore[1]	7	23	20	* 20	12	0	15	4	6	* 5	Singapour[1]
Syrian Arab Republic[1]	* 5	* 4	* 6	4	5	6	22	* 30	* 35	* 35	Rép. arabe syrienne[1]
Turkey* [1]	69	80	80	70	70	118	126	75	78	80	Turquie* [1]
Europe	**4 446**	**4 753**	**4 747**	**4 840**	**5 014**	**4 884**	**4 974**	**4 662**	**4 784**	**4 542**	**Europe**
EEC	***3 160***	***3 553***	***3 611***	***3 702***	***3 859***	***3 714***	***3 770***	***3 472***	***3 625***	***3 385***	***CEE***
Belgium[1]	218	257	267	270	* 270	* 270	* 270	* 250	* 240	* 240	Belgique[1]
Denmark	10	11	14	8	8	[1]6	[1]7	* [1]9	[1]11	* [1]7	Danemark
France[2]	1 868	2 062	2 063	2 128	2 064	1 922	1 925	1 810	1 752	1 569	France[2]
Germany, Fed. Rep.	606	839	883	934	1 095	1 109	1 163	941	1 142	1 107	Allemagne, Rép. féd.
Greece	[1]41	[1]47	[1]51	37	26	15	33	25	43	...	Grèce
Italy* [1]	211	259	250	250	250	230	210	210	200	200	Italie* [1]
Netherlands	150	30	24	18	12	28	39	* [1]100	* [1]90	* [1]85	Pays-Bas
United Kingdom	56	48	59	57	* [1]134	[1]134	[1]123	[1]127	* [1]147	* [1]151	Royaume-Uni
EFTA	***349***	***335***	***292***	***306***	***305***	***286***	***334***	***338***	***303***	***293***	***AELE***
Austria[1]	49	60	58	61	52	62	75	* 66	* 65	* 61	Autriche[1]
Finland[3]	86	58	38	29	37	39	30	...	...	...	Finlande[3]
Norway[1]	40	45	44	46	46	* 45	* 91	* 103	* 66	* 68	Norvège[1]
Portugal	4	5	1	1	0	1	2	* [1]5	* [1]4	* [1]5	Portugal
Sweden[1]	* 168	* 165	* 148	* 166	* 167	136	133	145	157	* 155	Suède[1]
Switzerland[1]	2	2	3	3	3	* 3	* 3	* 3	* 3	* 3	Suisse[1]
East Europe	***574***	***502***	***509***	***494***	***505***	***530***	***523***	***538***	***556***	***565***	***Europe de l'est***
Bulgaria* [1]	60	65	70	75	70	70	70	70	70	70	Bulgarie* [1]

For general note and footnotes, see end of table.

Voir la fin du tableau pour la remarque générale et les notes.

Sulphur, recovered as by-product (continued) – Soufre en tant que sous-produit (suite)

Unit : Thousand metric tons

Unité : Milliers de tonnes métriques

Country or area	1976	1977	1978	1979	1980	1981	1982	1983	1984	1985	Pays ou zone
Czechoslovakia* [1]	10	9	10	10	10	10	10	10	10	12	Tchécoslovaquie* [1]
German Dem. Rep.	79	75	75	70	71	80	92	97	108	109	Rép. dém. allemande
Hungary	8	8	9	9	9	10	11	11	18	24	Hongrie
Poland* [1]	319	235	225	200	205	210	190	200	200	200	Pologne* [1]
Romania [1 4]	98	110	120	130	* 140	* 150	* 150	* 150	* 150	* 150	Roumanie [1 4]
Other Europe	***363***	***363***	***335***	***338***	***345***	***354***	***347***	***314***	***300***	***299***	***Autre Europe***
Spain [1]	158	158	130	133	140	150	143	* 131	* 137	* 126	Espagne [1]
Yugoslavia [1]	205	* 205	* 205	* 205	* 205	* 204	* 204	* 183	* 163	* 173	Yougoslavie [1]
USSR* [1]	**3 100**	**3 340**	**3 040**	**3 040**	**3 240**	**3 300**	**3 550**	**3 650**	**3 700**	**3 825**	**URSS* [1]**
Oceania	**129**	**127**	**151**	**157**	**180**	**185**	**174**	**174**	**174**	**176**	**Océanie**
Australia* [1]	128	126	150	156	180	185	174	173	173	175	Australie* [1]
New Zealand [1]	* 1	* 1	* 1	* 1	0	0	0	1	* 1	* 1	Nouvelle-Zélande [1]
Total	**19 787**	**22 286**	**22 897**	**24 258**	**25 410**	**25 137**	**25 863**	**26 417**	**27 110**	**27 814**	**Total**

General note.
Sulphur recovered as by-product in the purification of coal-gas, in petroleum refineries and gas plants and from copper, lead and zinc sulphide ores. (SITC 27410-2).

[1] Source: U. S. Bureau of Mines, (Washington, D. C.).
[2] Crude sulfur and sulfur recovered in petroleum refineries.
[3] Beginning 1983, data are confidential.
[4] Beginning 1974, data are not comparable with those of earlier years.

Remarque générale.
Soufre récupéré comme sous-produit lors de la purification du gaz de houille, dans les raffineries de pétrole et les usines à gaz et lors du traitement des minerais sulfurés de cuivre, de plomb et de zinc. (CTCI 27410-2).

[1] Source: U.S. Bureau of Mines, (Washington, D.C.).
[2] Soufre sorti des raffineries françaises et des vapocraqueurs intégrés.
[3] A partir de 1983, les données sont confidentielles.
[4] A partir de 1974, les données ne sont pas comparables à celles des années antérieures.

Sulphur, recovered from pyrites etc. – Soufre de récupération

Unit : Thousand metric tons

Unité : Milliers de tonnes métriques

Country or area	1976	1977	1978	1979	1980	1981	1982	1983	1984	1985	Pays ou zone
Africa	**371**	**411**	**308**	**339**	**563**	**557**	**549**	**605**	**612**	**634**	**Afrique**
Morocco[1]	24	45	61	63	* 36	* 22	* 0	* 0	0	...	Maroc[1]
Namibia[1]	4	4	3	4	4	8	58	81	105	* 100	Namibie[1]
South Africa[1]	294	332	219	243	493	502	465	474	464	474	Afrique du Sud[1]
Zambia[1]	9	8	1	1	1	0	1	25	18	* 25	Zambie[1]
Zimbabwe* [1]	40	22	24	28	29	25	25	25	25	25	Zimbabwe* [1]
America, North	**322**	**212**	**326**	**424**	**356**	**331**	**293**	**339**	**343**	**353**	**Amérique du Nord**
Canada[2]	11	9	4	12	* 12	* 10	* 8	* 9	* 10	* 10	Canada[2]
Cuba* [1]	20	34	21	12	22	14	20	5	0	...	Cuba* [1]
United States	291	169	301	400	322	307	265	...	...	...	Etats–Unis
America, South	**31**	**34**	**37**	**41**	**44**	**44**	**54**	**55**	**55**	**60**	**Amérique du Sud**
Brazil[1]	...	...	...	...	...	44	54	55	* 55	* 60	Brésil[1]
Asia	**1 863**	**2 042**	**2 229**	**2 158**	**2 400**	**2 433**	**2 387**	**2 882**	**2 864**	**2 941**	**Asie**
China[1]	* 900	* 1 252	* 1 500	* 1 500	* 1 700	* 1 800	* 1 800	* 2 300	2 300	2 300	Chine[1]
Cyprus	113	69	55	21	25	7	26	21	10	31	Chypre
India[1]	19	14	26	27	34	23	22	26	* 18	* 7	Inde[1]
Japan[1]	471	389	327	300	311	293	276	272	259	253	Japon[1]
Korea,Dem.Ppl's.Rep.* [1]	245	250	255	255	250	225	200	200	200	200	Corée,Rép.pop.dém.de* [1]
Philippines[1 3]	77	50	52	41	54	46	30	29	35	107	Philippines[1 3]
Turkey	[1] 38	[1] 18	* [1] 14	* [1] 14	26	39	33	34	42	43	Turquie
Europe	**3 545**	**3 393**	**3 260**	**3 438**	**3 461**	**3 364**	**3 233**	**3 222**	**3 270**	**3 381**	**Europe**
EEC	***704***	***681***	***631***	***581***	***625***	***561***	***564***	***552***	***482***	***571***	***CEE***
Germany, Fed. Rep.[1]	233	235	221	203	222	213	229	...	...	...	Allemagne, Rép. féd.[1]
Greece[1]	74	54	61	63	61	* 76	* 55	* 67	* 78	* 78	Grèce[1]
Ireland[1]	* 31	21	19	13	11	* 11	* 11	0	0	...	Irlande[1]
Italy[1]	366	371	330	302	331	261	269	271	192	280	Italie[1]
EFTA	***883***	***729***	***688***	***788***	***765***	***726***	***714***	***726***	***815***	***780***	***AELE***
Finland	309	209	150	204	196	181	182	218	230	210	Finlande
Norway	[1] 188	158	152	150	150	* 218	* 213	178	215	200	Norvège
Portugal	181	158	137	152	170	125	115	* [1] 124	* [1] 140	* [1] 145	Portugal
Sweden	205	204	249	282	249	202	204	206	* 230	* 225	Suède
East Europe	***673***	***718***	***724***	***788***	***723***	***673***	***573***	***573***	***572***	***574***	***Europe de l'est***
Bulgaria* [1]	280	305	310	315	300	300	300	300	300	300	Bulgarie* [1]
Czechoslovakia	5	5	1	* [1] 60	* [1] 60	* [1] 60	* [1] 60	* [1] 60	* [1] 60	* [1] 62	Tchécoslovaquie
German Dem. Rep.* [1]	10	10	10	10	10	10	...	...	...	...	Rép. dém. allemande* [1]
Hungary* [1]	3	3	3	3	3	3	3	3	2	2	Hongrie* [1]
Romania* [1]	375	395	400	400	350	300	200	200	200	200	Roumanie* [1]
Other Europe	***1 285***	***1 265***	***1 217***	***1 281***	***1 348***	***1 404***	***1 382***	***1 371***	***1 401***	***1 456***	***Autre Europe***
Spain[4]	1 100	1 099	1 046	1 091	1 096	1 118	1 029	1 073	* 1 100	* 1 133	Espagne[4]
Yugoslavia[1]	* 185	166	171	190	252	* 286	* 353	* 298	* 301	* 323	Yougoslavie[1]
USSR* [1]	**3 300**	**3 500**	**3 500**	**3 500**	**3 550**	**3 600**	**3 500**	**3 400**	**3 400**	**3 350**	**URSS* [1]**
Oceania	**108**	**108**	**93**	**29**	**0**	**0**	**0**	**0**	**29**	**29**	**Océanie**
Australia[5]	108	108	93	29	0	0	0	0	...	...	Australie[5]
Total	**9 540**	**9 700**	**9 753**	**9 929**	**10 374**	**10 329**	**10 016**	**10 503**	**10 573**	**10 748**	**Total**

General note.
Sulphur content of iron and copper pyrites, including pyrite concentrates obtained from copper, lead and zinc ores. (SITC 27410–3).

[1] Source: U. S. Bureau of Mines, (Washington, D. C.).
[2] Shipments.
[3] Twelve months ending 30 June of year stated.
[4] Sulphur from iron pyrites only.
[5] Sales.

Remarque générale.
Soufre contenu dans les pyrites de fer et de cuivre, y compris celui des concentrés de pyrites obtenus à partir des minerais de cuivre, de plomb et de zinc. (CTCI 27410–3).

[1] Source: U.S. Bureau of Mines, (Washington, D.C.).
[2] Expéditions.
[3] Période de douze mois finissant le 30 juin de l'année indiquée.
[4] Soufre provenant de pyrites de fer seulement.
[5] Ventes.

Styrene – Styrène

Unit : Thousand metric tons

Unité : Milliers de tonnes métriques

Country or area	1976	1977	1978	1979	1980	1981	1982	1983	1984	1985	Pays ou zone
America, North	**2 178.9**	**3 151.4**	**3 157.8**	**3 425.6**	**3 031.6**	**3 062.7**	**2 724.3**	**2 982.9**	**3 525.4**	**3 413.9**	**Amérique du Nord**
Mexico	34.9	36.4	37.8	31.0	31.3	33.0	29.0	24.0	30.0	33.0	Mexique
United States	2 144.0	3 115.0	3 120.0	3 394.6	...	3 029.7	2 695.3	2 958.9	3 495.4	3 380.9	Etats-Unis
America, South	**61.8**	**64.1**	**145.4**	**197.8**	**193.5**	**187.1**	**203.7**	**210.2**	**229.1**	**243.0**	**Amérique du Sud**
Brazil	61.8	64.1	145.4	197.8	193.5	187.1	203.7	210.2	229.1	243.0	Brésil
Asia	**1 124.9**	**1 063.6**	**1 169.8**	**1 291.3**	**1 173.8**	**1 160.4**	**1 149.6**	**1 245.4**	**1 505.8**	**1 503.5**	**Asie**
Japan	1 088.7	1 021.7	1 122.4	1 238.3	1 114.2	1 095.1	1 085.5	1 167.2	1 423.3	1 418.1	Japon
Korea, Republic of	...	...	...	...	59.5	65.2	64.1	78.2	82.5	85.4	Corée, République de
Europe	**882.5**	**927.8**	**917.7**	**912.2**	**872.5**	**827.2**	**747.8**	**911.9**	**874.3**	**840.5**	**Europe**
EEC	***750.3***	***792.2***	***785.1***	***761.4***	***721.7***	***679.9***	***585.5***	***732.0***	***692.4***	***648.4***	***CEE***
France	...	...	...	...	...	...	321.7	484.9	462.1	434.9	France
Italy	324.4	366.3	359.1	335.5	295.8	254.0	...	...	...	...	Italie
East Europe	***64.5***	***64.8***	***66.0***	***66.7***	***67.7***	***70.1***	***70.3***	***82.0***	***85.2***	***93.7***	***Europe de l'est***
Czechoslovakia	64.5	64.8	66.0	66.7	67.7	70.1	70.3	82.0	85.2	93.7	Tchécoslovaquie
Other Europe	***67.8***	***70.8***	***66.6***	***84.1***	***83.1***	***77.1***	***92.0***	***97.9***	***96.7***	***98.4***	***Autre Europe***
Spain	...	...	56.7	80.4	74.2	70.0	88.2	89.5	88.1	91.3	Espagne
Yugoslavia	10.6	9.4	10.0	3.7	8.8	7.1	3.8	8.4	8.6	7.1	Yougoslavie
Oceania	**1.0**	**1.0**	**0.7**	**0.7**	**0.6**	**0.9**	**0.6**	**0.5**	**0.5**	**0.4**	**Océanie**
Australia	1.0	1.0	0.7	0.7	0.6	0.9	0.6	...	...	...	Australie
Total	**4 249.2**	**5 207.8**	**5 391.5**	**5 827.6**	**5 272.1**	**5 238.3**	**4 826.0**	**5 350.9**	**6 135.2**	**6 001.3**	**Total**

General note.
Pure C6H5.CH=CH2. (SITC 51211-0).

Remarque générale.
C6H5.CH=CH2 pur. (CTCI 51211-0).

Unit : Thousand metric tons | Unité : Milliers de tonnes métriques

Country or area	1976	1977	1978	1979	1980	1981	1982	1983	1984	1985	Pays ou zone
Africa	**9.3**	**9.4**	**9.6**	**9.3**	**10.1**	**9.8**	**9.7**	**9.6**	**9.5**	**9.6**	**Afrique**
Algeria	0.9	1.0	1.1	...	...	...	...	...	...	...	Algérie
Cameroon[1]	0.2	0.1	0.1	0.1	0.2	...	...	0.2	0.2	0.1	Cameroun[1]
Congo	0.1	0.1	0.1	0.1	0.1	0.1	0.1	0.1	0.1	0.1	Congo
Côte d'Ivoire	0.2	0.3	0.3	0.3	0.3	0.3	0.2	0.2	0.2	...	Côte d'Ivoire
Egypt	1.0	1.2	1.2	1.2	1.4	1.2	1.2	1.3	...	...	Egypte
Gabon	...	...	0.1	0.1	0.1	...	...	...	...	...	Gabon
Madagascar[1]	0.1	0.1	0.1	0.1	0.1	0.2	0.2	0.1	0.2	0.2	Madagascar[1]
Mozambique[1]	...	...	0.2	...	...	...	...	...	...	...	Mozambique[1]
Senegal	0.1	0.1	0.1	0.1	0.1	0.1	0.1	0.1	0.1	0.1	Sénégal
South Africa	...	...	...	5.2	* 5.8	* 5.7	5.6	5.4	5.3	5.4	Afrique du Sud
Tunisia	0.4	0.3	0.4	0.4	0.5	0.5	0.5	0.5	0.5	0.5	Tunisie
Zaire	0.1	0.1	0.1	...	0.1	0.1	0.1	0.1	...	...	Zaïre
Zambia	0.3	0.3	0.3	0.3	0.3	0.3	0.3	0.3	0.3	0.3	Zambie
America, North	**232.8**	**197.9**	**175.9**	**190.3**	**182.5**	**172.4**	**130.5**	**128.0**	**163.5**	**152.2**	**Amérique du Nord**
Canada	8.3	8.0	7.5	...	...	...	...	...	...	...	Canada
Cuba	1.8	1.8	2.1	2.5	2.5	2.7	2.7	2.9	3.4	3.8	Cuba
Jamaica	0.2	0.2	0.2	0.2	0.2	0.2	0.2	0.2	0.2	0.2	Jamaïque
United States	222.5	187.8	166.0	179.6	171.9	161.5	119.6	116.9	151.9	140.2	Etats–Unis
America, South	**43.4**	**37.1**	**34.1**	**41.3**	**38.0**	**31.9**	**37.3**	**38.6**	**38.8**	**31.3**	**Amérique du Sud**
Argentina	15.1	19.3	15.2	20.5	17.2	16.5	21.9	25.8	27.0	21.1	Argentine
Brazil	27.1	16.3	17.6	[2] 19.3	19.5	13.8	...	...	...	...	Brésil
Chile	0.2	0.3	0.3	0.4	0.4	0.4	0.3	0.3	0.4	0.4	Chili
Colombia	0.8	0.8	0.9	0.9	0.9	0.9	0.7	0.6	...	...	Colombie
Ecuador	0.2	0.4	0.2	...	0.1	0.3	1.0	0.1	...	...	Equateur
Asia	**109.3**	**103.6**	**99.1**	**85.5**	**71.1**	**66.4**	**63.7**	**68.1**	**70.7**	**70.3**	**Asie**
Burma[3]	0.2	0.2	0.2	...	...	0.2	0.2	* 0.1	...	...	Birmanie[3]
India[1]	9.0	9.8	10.0	10.4	10.9	11.4	11.9	11.6	11.7	11.9	Inde[1]
Japan[4]	58.1	53.7	50.8	33.2	17.6	12.4	6.4	...	...	...	Japon[4]
Korea, Republic of	12.2	12.6	11.3	7.8	5.6	5.2	5.9	9.9	9.7	7.1	Corée, République de
Philippines	28.4	26.3	25.8	32.4	35.3	...	...	...	...	...	Philippines
Sri Lanka	0.2	...	0.2	0.3	0.3	0.3	...	0.3	0.3	0.3	Sri Lanka
Thailand	0.2	0.2	0.2	0.2	0.2	0.4	0.3	0.3	0.3	...	Thaïlande
Turkey	0.6	0.1	0.2	0.5	0.4	0.5	0.6	0.0	0.0	0.0	Turquie
United Arab Emirates	...	...	0.2	...	...	...	...	...	...	...	Emirats arabes unis
Viet Nam[1]	# 0.3	0.3	0.3	0.3	...	...	...	...	...	...	Viet Nam[1]
Europe	**570.2**	**496.6**	**458.0**	**452.9**	**434.7**	**386.3**	**342.7**	**342.8**	**363.5**	**362.6**	**Europe**
EEC	***461.1***	***390.0***	***352.3***	***352.8***	***332.1***	***296.4***	***257.7***	***258.9***	***279.8***	***277.0***	***CEE***
Belgium[2]	2.6	2.7	2.8	2.4	2.3	2.3	2.1	2.2	2.1	2.1	Belgique[2]
Denmark	2.8	2.8	2.5	2.5	2.5	2.3	2.4	2.3	2.3	...	Danemark
France[1]	14.7	14.7	14.0	13.9	14.5	13.8	# 12.9	12.0	12.2	11.0	France[1]
Germany, Fed. Rep.	251.5	203.8	209.1	224.8	219.4	209.0	187.0	189.8	204.0	208.8	Allemagne, Rép. féd.
Greece[1]	1.3	1.6	1.5	1.3	1.4	1.5	1.4	1.2	1.1	...	Grèce[1]
Italy	188.2	164.5	122.4	107.9	92.0	67.4	51.9	51.4	58.2	51.8	Italie
EFTA	***8.8***	***8.1***	***7.5***	***7.4***	***7.6***	***7.4***	***7.0***	***6.7***	***6.7***	***6.4***	***AELE***
Finland[5]	2.6	2.4	2.2	2.3	2.5	2.4	2.4	...	...	...	Finlande[5]
Portugal	1.3	1.5	1.5	1.5	1.5	1.5	1.4	1.3	1.4	...	Portugal
Sweden	4.9	4.2	3.7	3.6	3.6	3.4	3.3	3.0	2.9	2.6	Suède
East Europe	***69.6***	***69.6***	***66.8***	***61.4***	***62.8***	***49.7***	***45.4***	***44.2***	***44.1***	***46.2***	***Europe de l'est***
Bulgaria	12.7	12.2	13.1	11.9	12.8	11.2	6.8	8.3	6.9	6.6	Bulgarie
Czechoslovakia	15.8	16.2	16.5	16.2	16.4	16.7	16.6	16.6	16.4	16.5	Tchécoslovaquie
Hungary	24.5	24.4	21.7	17.7	17.1	7.5	5.7	5.5	5.4	5.4	Hongrie
Poland	16.6	16.8	15.5	15.6	16.6	14.4	16.2	13.8	15.4	17.6	Pologne
Other Europe	***30.7***	***28.9***	***31.4***	***31.3***	***32.2***	***32.8***	***32.6***	***33.0***	***32.9***	***33.0***	***Autre Europe***
Spain	24.9	23.9	...	...	...	...	...	...	...	...	Espagne
Yugoslavia	5.8	5.1	7.0	6.9	7.8	8.5	8.2	8.6	8.6	8.6	Yougoslavie
USSR[6]	...	...	...	...	**311.0**	**301.0**	**294.0**	**277.0**	**291.0**	...	**URSS[6]**

For general note and footnotes, see end of table.

Voir la fin du tableau pour la remarque générale et les notes.

Unit : Thousand metric tons | Unité : Milliers de tonnes métriques

Country or area	1976	1977	1978	1979	1980	1981	1982	1983	1984	1985	Pays ou zone
Total	**1 297.9**	**1 171.1**	**1 097.0**	**1 093.3**	**1 047.5**	**967.8**	**878.0**	**864.1**	**937.0**	**901.8**	**Total**

General note.
Pure C2H2. (SITC 51212-1).

Remarque générale.
C2H2 pur. (CTCI 51212-1).

[1] Original data in units of volume.
[2] Production by establishments employing 5 or more persons.
[3] Twelve months ending 30 September of year stated.
[4] Production from petroleum and gas only.
[5] Beginning 1983, data are confidential.
[6] Source: United Nations Economic Commission for Europe (ECE), (Geneva).

[1] Données d'origine exprimées en unités de volume.
[2] Production des établissements occupant 5 personnes ou plus.
[3] Période de douze mois finissant le 30 septembre de l'année indiquée.
[4] Production à partir de pétrol et de gaz naturel seulement.
[5] A partir de 1983, les données sont confidentielles.
[6] Source: Commission économique des Nations Unies pour l'Europe (CEE), (Genève).

Benzene (Benzol) – Benzène (Benzol)

Unit : Thousand metric tons | Unité : Milliers de tonnes métriques

Country or area	1976	1977	1978	1979	1980	1981	1982	1983	1984	1985	Pays ou zone
Africa	**4.4**	**4.8**	**4.9**	**4.8**	**5.4**	**5.5**	**5.7**	**5.9**	**6.1**	**6.3**	**Afrique**
Egypt	4.4	4.8	4.9	4.8	5.4	...	...	...	...	...	Egypte
America, North	**5 305.5**	**5 296.3**	**5 674.8**	**6 291.9**	**7 136.3**	**4 986.7**	**4 107.6**	**4 812.4**	**4 871.3**	**4 884.8**	**Amérique du Nord**
Canada[1]	411.3	435.2	558.6	492.9	560.0	566.5	519.0	580.0	548.7	691.3	Canada[1]
Mexico	99.2	74.5	78.8	70.5	79.3	77.0	96.0	139.0	156.0	178.0	Mexique
United States	4 795.0	4 786.7	5 037.4	5 728.5	6 497.0	4 343.3	3 492.5	4 093.5	...	...	Etats–Unis
America, South	**121.3**	**144.9**	**171.7**	**259.3**	**308.5**	**316.6**	**357.8**	**435.8**	**490.0**	**520.9**	**Amérique du Sud**
Brazil[2]	121.3	144.9	171.7	259.3	308.5	316.6	357.8	435.8	490.0	...	Brésil[2]
Asia	**1 960.8**	**2 043.6**	**2 148.6**	**2 324.3**	**2 229.6**	**2 087.4**	**2 026.5**	**2 198.5**	**2 546.2**	**2 627.2**	**Asie**
India	52.5	64.2	68.2	74.8	63.6	65.0	79.9	92.4	143.2	...	Inde
Japan	1 878.6	1 951.3	2 014.6	2 179.0	2 059.7	1 898.8	1 814.7	1 938.0	2 217.6	2 279.4	Japon
Korea, Republic of	25.9	21.4	54.4	57.1	92.9	109.3	120.0	158.9	171.0	215.9	Corée, République de
Turkey[3]	3.8	6.7	11.4	13.5	13.4	14.3	12.0	9.2	...	...	Turquie[3]
Europe	**4 279.5**	**4 370.7**	**4 596.5**	**5 207.8**	**4 555.0**	**4 501.2**	**4 388.6**	**5 459.6**	**5 742.3**	**5 626.5**	**Europe**
EEC	***3 393.6***	***3 409.3***	***3 673.5***	***4 208.5***	***3 512.5***	***3 388.1***	***3 295.4***	***4 288.6***	***4 454.8***	***4 318.6***	***CEE***
Belgium[4,5]	42.2	43.1	38.6	45.9	39.1	46.7	41.0	40.8	33.9	...	Belgique[4,5]
France	456.6	493.8	518.6	595.2	547.3	500.2	# 513.9	626.7	601.0	632.8	France
Germany, Fed. Rep.	918.4	824.4	893.5	1 006.5	919.1	921.6	1 026.5	1 335.8	1 437.9	...	Allemagne, Rép. féd.
Italy	592.8	593.5	522.0	529.5	449.5	423.8	382.4	527.5	535.9	488.5	Italie
Netherlands	456.0	610.0	910.0	975.0	732.0	744.0	772.0	1 032.0	1 091.4	975.0	Pays–Bas
United Kingdom	927.7	844.6	790.7	1 056.3	825.5	751.9	559.6	725.9	754.7	836.2	Royaume–Uni
EFTA	***28.1***	***28.1***	***28.1***	***108.3***	***102.9***	***95.3***	***64.0***	***114.6***	***129.1***	***143.9***	***AELE***
Finland[6]	0.0	0.0	0.0	80.2	74.9	67.2	43.4	...	...	...	Finlande[6]
Portugal	...	...	...	...	...	...	20.6	28.1	30.5	33.1	Portugal
East Europe	***654.3***	***687.3***	***683.4***	***639.7***	***709.3***	***772.8***	***833.4***	***836.9***	***903.9***	***887.1***	***Europe de l'est***
Bulgaria	57.4	61.4	...	...	...	...	...	...	...	...	Bulgarie
Czechoslovakia	167.9	195.4	203.1	178.0	184.2	240.0	279.4	267.8	277.7	291.1	Tchécoslovaquie
Hungary	35.0	33.8	29.5	43.2	103.5	87.5	101.5	104.4	103.9	119.5	Hongrie
Poland[7]	...	...	...	...	240.2	235.8	232.1	201.3	255.9	...	Pologne[7]
Romania	159.0	162.0	157.0	125.0	122.0	150.0	161.0	204.0	207.0	185.0	Roumanie
Other Europe	***203.5***	***246.0***	***211.6***	***251.4***	***230.2***	***244.9***	***195.8***	***219.5***	***254.5***	***277.0***	***Autre Europe***
Spain	147.9	191.0	174.0	212.0	212.0	204.7	174.6	194.1	229.4	258.0	Espagne
Yugoslavia	55.6	55.0	37.6	39.4	18.2	40.3	21.2	25.4	25.1	19.0	Yougoslavie
USSR	...	...	...	...	**1 644.0**	**1 698.2**	**1 689.6**	**1 853.3**	**1 956.3**	**1 971.4**	**URSS**
Total	**12 995.9**	**13 258.2**	**14 067.9**	**15 633.1**	**15 878.8**	**13 595.6**	**12 575.7**	**14 765.5**	**15 612.1**	**15 637.0**	**Total**

General note.
Pure C6H6. Includes benzene obtained by dealkylation. (SITC 51212–3).

Remarque générale.
C6H6 pur. Comprend le benzène obtenu par desalkylation. (CTCI 51212–3).

[1] Shipments.
[2] Production by main establishments only.
[3] Source: The Chemical Industry, Organisation for Economic Co–operation and Development (OECD), (Paris).
[4] Production by establishments employing 5 or more persons.
[5] 1985, data are confidential.
[6] Beginning 1983, data are confidential.
[7] Source: United Nations Economic Commission for Europe (ECE), (Geneva).

[1] Expéditions.
[2] Production des principaux établissements seulement.
[3] Source: l'Industrie chimique, Organisation de coopération et de développement économiques (OCDE), (Paris).
[4] Production des établissements occupant 5 personnes ou plus.
[5] Pour 1985, les données sont confidentielles.
[6] A partir de 1983, les données sont confidentielles.
[7] Source: Commission économique des Nations Unies pour l'Europe (CEE), (Genève).

Butylenes, butadiene – Butylènes, butadiène

Unit : Thousand metric tons

Unité : Milliers de tonnes métriques

Country or area	1976	1977	1978	1979	1980	1981	1982	1983	1984	1985	Pays ou zone
America, North	**4 552.4**	**5 927.7**	**4 771.0**	**5 779.4**	**789.1**	**1 095.3**	**1 052.9**	**1 338.5**	**1 424.6**	**1 447.1**	**Amérique du Nord**
Canada[1]	145.0	...	...	...	...	250.2	214.9	270.6	256.4	...	Canada[1]
Mexico	18.4	23.3	18.3	17.0	17.0	12.0	15.0	19.0	20.0	18.0	Mexique
United States	4 389.0	5 739.0	4 572.5	5 567.5	# 562.4	833.1	823.0	1 048.9	1 148.2	1 145.5	Etats-Unis
America, South	**81.3**	**80.5**	**81.1**	**131.8**	**134.1**	**140.9**	**150.1**	**161.7**	**197.0**	**199.8**	**Amérique du Sud**
Brazil	81.3	80.5	81.1	131.8	134.1	140.9	150.1	161.7	197.0	...	Brésil
Asia	**2 261.0**	**2 266.1**	**2 456.2**	**2 443.4**	**2 160.0**	**2 059.8**	**2 055.7**	**2 073.8**	**2 243.8**	**2 291.8**	**Asie**
India	5.0	5.7	6.7	...	...	...	...	...	...	...	Inde
Japan	2 240.2	2 247.4	2 427.3	2 414.8	2 086.2	1 993.7	1 988.0	1 990.2	2 152.4	2 191.4	Japon
Korea, Republic of	15.8	13.0	22.2	22.8	68.0	60.2	61.8	77.8	85.6	94.5	Corée, République de
Europe	**2 195.6**	**2 193.1**	**2 516.8**	**2 840.8**	**2 738.5**	**2 732.8**	**2 709.0**	**3 023.3**	**3 405.0**	**3 385.3**	**Europe**
EEC	***2 004.1***	***2 011.1***	***2 306.3***	***2 578.3***	***2 494.9***	***2 485.9***	***2 414.9***	***2 704.5***	***3 062.2***	***3 022.6***	***CEE***
France	236.0	255.0	287.0	299.6	260.1	266.2	# 262.6	284.6	303.1	289.4	France
Germany, Fed. Rep.	940.5	974.8	1 214.2	1 443.7	1 311.7	1 241.4	1 145.2	1 351.6	1 618.0	1 553.4	Allemagne, Rép. féd.
Italy	181.3	185.6	174.7	165.9	183.2	166.4	156.9	172.6	181.4	139.3	Italie
Netherlands	416.0	374.0	421.0	442.0	548.0	604.0	...	...	...	...	Pays-Bas
United Kingdom	230.2	221.7	209.4	227.0	191.9	207.9	234.4	237.7	259.2	297.6	Royaume-Uni
EFTA	***116.9***	***92.7***	***107.3***	***114.7***	***91.1***	***84.4***	***90.9***	***99.1***	***105.9***	***90.4***	***AELE***
Finland[2]	14.0	15.0	18.0	17.0	18.0	14.1	14.4	...	...	...	Finlande[2]
Portugal	...	...	...	...	...	...	15.1	8.8	17.9	15.2	Portugal
Sweden	88.7	63.5	75.1	83.5	58.8	56.0	61.5	74.5	72.3	59.5	Suède
East Europe	***33.6***	***30.6***	***30.7***	***41.8***	***49.0***	***61.7***	***67.2***	***68.0***	***72.8***	***75.4***	***Europe de l'est***
Czechoslovakia	33.6	30.6	30.7	41.8	49.0	61.7	67.2	68.0	72.8	75.4	Tchécoslovaquie
Other Europe	***41.0***	***58.8***	***72.4***	***106.0***	***103.5***	***100.9***	***136.1***	***151.7***	***164.1***	***196.9***	***Autre Europe***
Spain	28.8	41.0	49.0	77.0	77.2	70.8	95.1	105.3	100.7	123.9	Espagne
Yugoslavia	...	...	...	...	26.3	30.1	41.0	46.4	63.4	73.1	Yougoslavie
Total	**9 090.3**	**10 467.5**	**9 825.1**	**11 195.5**	**5 821.8**	**6 028.8**	**5 967.7**	**6 597.4**	**7 270.4**	**7 324.0**	**Total**

General note.
Pure C4H8. Including butene-1, cisbutene-2, transbutene-2 and isobutene. (SITC 51212-4).

[1] Source: The Chemical Industry, Organisation for Economic Co-operation and Development (OECD), (Paris).
[2] Beginning 1983, data are confidential.

Remarque générale.
C4H8 pur. Comprend le butène-1, le cisbutène-2, le transbutène-2 et l'isobutène. (CTCI 51212-4).

[1] Source: l'Industrie chimique, Organisation de coopération et de développement économiques (OCDE), (Paris).
[2] A partir de 1983, les données sont confidentielles.

Unit : Thousand metric tons — Unité : Milliers de tonnes métriques

Country or area	1976	1977	1978	1979	1980	1981	1982	1983	1984	1985	Pays ou zone
Africa	**37.0**	**40.0**	**42.9**	**41.3**	**26.0**	**52.7**	**76.8**	**28.0**	**50.3**	**51.9**	**Afrique**
Algeria	* 37.0	* 40.0	42.9	41.3	26.0	52.7	76.8	28.0	...	...	Algérie
America, North	**10 727.7**	**12 330.2**	**13 844.7**	**14 595.9**	**14 565.3**	**15 052.0**	**12 522.7**	**14 808.3**	**16 249.8**	**16 272.5**	**Amérique du Nord**
Canada	508.9	567.3	825.8	1 013.8	1 196.7	1 330.2	1 013.0	1 196.0	1 464.4	1 745.4	Canada
Mexico	227.9	229.9	258.0	343.0	365.5	378.0	396.0	645.0	643.0	670.0	Mexique
United States	9 991.0	11 533.0	12 761.0	13 239.1	13 003.0	13 343.8	11 113.6	12 967.3	14 142.4	13 857.1	Etats–Unis
America, South	**364.0**	**367.7**	**413.3**	**640.7**	**745.6**	**732.9**	**867.1**	**1 177.9**	**1 276.5**	**1 319.2**	**Amérique du Sud**
Brazil	349.4	362.2	398.8	631.2	715.5	719.6	852.5	1 163.3	1 262.0	...	Brésil
Colombia	...	5.5	...	9.4	30.1	13.3	...	...	...	...	Colombie
Asia	**4 302.9**	**4 644.9**	**5 201.5**	**5 719.4**	**5 304.4**	**4 788.3**	**4 781.1**	**5 113.9**	**5 877.2**	**5 710.0**	**Asie**
China	133.5	302.7	380.3	434.9	489.9	504.8	565.0	654.0	648.0	652.1	Chine
India	48.5	56.6	74.3	102.4	...	...	...	...	...	...	Inde
Israel	22.3	18.3	18.7	15.0	4.3	1.2	...	...	...	...	Israël
Japan	3 802.9	3 978.6	4 387.4	4 783.7	4 175.3	3 654.6	3 589.7	3 687.7	4 385.7	4 226.9	Japon
Korea, Republic of	97.4	86.3	140.8	190.4	368.2	373.7	373.6	491.4	525.7	561.6	Corée, République de
Qatar	...	...	...	...	...	133.0	127.0	* 155.0	* 204.0	...	Qatar
Turkey	43.4	47.7	45.3	38.4	41.6	50.5	51.5	54.4	42.1	43.0	Turquie
Europe	**10 558.0**	**10 771.9**	**11 242.5**	**12 506.1**	**11 602.3**	**11 137.9**	**11 129.0**	**12 389.1**	**12 938.1**	**12 846.7**	**Europe**
EEC	***9 101.0***	***9 212.7***	***9 433.9***	***10 424.0***	***9 227.6***	***8 656.8***	***8 373.5***	***9 352.6***	***9 681.8***	***9 521.1***	***CEE***
France[1]	1 689.0	1 879.0	1 922.0	2 248.0	2 073.0	1 856.8	1 860.0	2 045.8	2 080.9	2 160.2	France[1]
Germany, Fed. Rep.	2 786.7	2 988.9	3 219.4	3 548.7	3 065.4	2 889.5	2 640.2	3 172.8	3 224.0	3 027.7	Allemagne, Rép. féd.
Greece	12.5	13.4	14.1	13.9	13.9	13.9	13.7	12.9	12.4	...	Grèce
Italy	1 442.8	1 414.0	1 224.7	1 180.9	1 074.4	914.2	874.0	1 062.5	1 138.2	973.4	Italie
Netherlands	1 884.0	1 780.0	1 958.0	2 199.0	1 906.0	1 747.0	...	...	...	...	Pays–Bas
United Kingdom[2]	1 286.1	1 137.5	1 095.7	1 233.6	1 094.9	1 235.5	1 079.9	1 154.6	1 324.3	1 446.5	Royaume–Uni[2]
EFTA	***445.0***	***366.0***	***414.1***	***501.5***	***451.4***	***366.2***	***445.7***	***540.4***	***648.7***	***582.6***	***AELE***
Finland[3]	123.0	129.0	155.0	165.0	180.0	156.7	140.4	...	...	...	Finlande[3]
Portugal	...	...	...	...	...	4.1	70.2	58.0	139.8	142.5	Portugal
Sweden[1]	317.9	232.9	255.0	321.2	238.4	205.3	235.1	313.6	335.3	261.8	Suède[1]
East Europe	***707.3***	***870.3***	***942.1***	***954.9***	***1 200.7***	***1 402.3***	***1 454.0***	***1 531.6***	***1 634.1***	***1 673.4***	***Europe de l'est***
Bulgaria	75.4	78.4	81.2	95.3	150.0	192.9	202.1	213.1	239.6	242.2	Bulgarie
Czechoslovakia	92.8	201.4	229.3	252.0	323.4	479.3	533.1	543.3	556.5	592.0	Tchécoslovaquie
Hungary	202.5	231.0	253.2	266.2	275.5	262.0	255.8	261.3	264.9	270.9	Hongrie
Poland	94.6	96.5	98.3	98.4	184.7	182.1	175.0	198.0	256.0	261.2	Pologne
Romania	242.0	263.0	280.0	243.0	267.0	286.0	288.0	316.0	317.0	307.0	Roumanie
Other Europe	***304.6***	***322.8***	***452.5***	***625.6***	***722.5***	***712.7***	***855.7***	***964.4***	***973.6***	***1 069.6***	***Autre Europe***
Spain	282.5	301.4	432.0	610.3	609.0	569.2	688.3	798.4	765.9	855.7	Espagne
Yugoslavia	22.1	21.5	20.5	15.3	113.5	143.4	167.5	166.1	207.7	213.9	Yougoslavie
USSR[4]	**...**	**...**	**...**	**...**	**1 773.0**	**2 093.0**	**2 132.0**	**2 267.0**	**2 543.0**	**...**	**URSS[4]**
Total	**27 131.6**	**29 466.8**	**32 226.9**	**35 155.2**	**34 016.5**	**33 856.9**	**31 508.6**	**35 784.1**	**38 935.0**	**38 871.7**	**Total**

General note.
Pure C2H4. (SITC 51212–5).

Remarque générale.
C2H4 pur. (CTCI 51212–5).

[1] Including acetylene used partly for welding.
[2] Produced from oil base, other than for use as fuel.
[3] Beginning 1983, data are confidential.
[4] Source: United Nations Economic Commission for Europe (ECE), (Geneva).

[1] Y compris l'acétylène utilisé en partie pour la soudure.
[2] Obtenu à partir de pétrole autre que celui servant de combustible.
[3] A partir de 1983, les données sont confidentielles.
[4] Source: Commission économique des Nations Unies pour l'Europe (CEE), (Genève).

Naphthalene – Naphtalène

Unit : Thousand metric tons

Unité : Milliers de tonnes métriques

Country or area	1976	1977	1978	1979	1980	1981	1982	1983	1984	1985	Pays ou zone
Africa	**1.1**	**1.1**	**1.1**	**1.1**	**1.1**	**1.0**	**1.0**	**1.0**	**1.0**	**0.9**	**Afrique**
Egypt	...	...	...	1.1	1.1	1.0	1.0	1.0	...	...	Egypte
America, North	**255.2**	**68.4**	**72.4**	**74.4**	**46.9**	**64.5**	**57.4**	**36.5**	**21.5**	**6.4**	**Amérique du Nord**
United States[1]	255.2	68.4	72.4	74.4	* 46.9	64.5	57.4	...	...	...	Etats–Unis[1]
America, South	**8.9**	**9.0**	**9.3**	**8.7**	**11.3**	**10.3**	**10.1**	**11.1**	**11.4**	**11.7**	**Amérique du Sud**
Brazil	8.5	8.6	9.1	7.0	11.1	9.3	10.1	11.0	11.0	...	Brésil
Colombia	0.4	0.3	0.2	1.7	0.2	1.1	0.1	0.1	...	...	Colombie
Asia	**104.5**	**119.4**	**118.9**	**143.1**	**135.6**	**129.8**	**139.4**	**141.2**	**163.1**	**183.4**	**Asie**
India	1.6	1.5	1.7	1.7	1.5	1.1	0.9	0.9	1.3	...	Inde
Japan	98.0	112.9	111.7	135.2	128.6	122.3	133.0	133.7	154.9	175.5	Japon
Korea, Republic of	...	...	...	...	3.8	3.9	3.1	4.1	4.4	4.4	Corée, République de
Turkey	1.8	1.9	2.3	2.7	* 1.6	* 2.5	...	...	...	...	Turquie
Europe	**180.2**	**182.7**	**184.0**	**182.1**	**163.3**	**169.6**	**193.6**	**180.6**	**187.6**	**183.7**	**Europe**
EEC	***113.6***	***114.8***	***114.3***	***119.0***	***102.2***	***115.9***	***133.3***	***117.8***	***123.0***	***124.4***	***CEE***
Belgium[2]	0.3	4.3	0.4	...	...	...	...	...	...	...	Belgique[2]
France* [3]	33.0	29.0	...	...	...	...	...	...	...	...	France* [3]
Germany, Fed. Rep.[4]	37.7	44.5	49.1	46.3	37.5	50.0	68.7	54.5	...	...	Allemagne, Rép. féd.[4]
Greece	1.3	1.2	1.2	1.3	0.9	...	...	...	...	...	Grèce
Italy	19.3	* 17.0	* 14.0	* 17.0	...	...	...	...	...	...	Italie
United Kingdom[5]	22.0	18.8	18.6	21.8	14.4	...	...	...	...	...	Royaume–Uni[5]
East Europe	***57.9***	***58.5***	***58.5***	***53.6***	***49.9***	***46.3***	***50.1***	***50.9***	***52.8***	***48.3***	***Europe de l'est***
Bulgaria	2.4	2.4	2.5	1.2	0.7	1.2	1.7	1.5	1.3	1.3	Bulgarie
Czechoslovakia	37.6	38.3	39.9	37.6	36.4	35.4	37.8	38.6	38.7	37.6	Tchécoslovaquie
Hungary	2.6	2.4	2.3	2.4	2.7	2.3	2.6	2.2	1.6	1.2	Hongrie
Poland	15.3	15.4	13.7	12.4	10.0	7.4	7.9	8.5	11.2	8.1	Pologne
Other Europe	***8.6***	***9.4***	***11.2***	***9.5***	***11.2***	***7.4***	***10.3***	***12.0***	***11.8***	***11.0***	***Autre Europe***
Spain	6.2	6.9	8.3	6.3	8.4	4.5	7.2	8.3	...	...	Espagne
Yugoslavia	2.5	2.5	2.9	3.2	2.9	2.9	3.0	3.6	4.4	3.5	Yougoslavie
Total	**549.9**	**380.6**	**385.6**	**409.4**	**358.2**	**375.2**	**401.6**	**370.5**	**384.6**	**386.1**	**Total**

General note.
Pure C10H8 hydrocarbon with two condensed rings. Crude naphthalene is excluded. (SITC 51212–6).

[1] Petroleum naphthalene only.
[2] Production by establishments employing 5 or more persons.
[3] Source: Industrial Statistics, Statistical Office of the European Communities, (Luxembourg).
[4] Beginning 1984, data are confidential.
[5] Sales by manufacturers employing 25 or more persons.

Remarque générale.
C10H8. Hydrocarbure résultant de la condensation de deux noyaux. A l'état pur, à l'exclusion du naphtalène brut. (CTCI 51212–6).

[1] Naphtalène de pétrole seulement.
[2] Production des établissements occupant 5 personnes ou plus.
[3] Source: Statistiques industrielles, Office statistique des Communautés européennes, (Luxembourg).
[4] A partir de 1984, les données sont confidentielles.
[5] Ventes des fabricants employant 25 personnes ou plus.

Propylene – Propylène

Unit : Thousand metric tons

Unité : Milliers de tonnes métriques

Country or area	1976	1977	1978	1979	1980	1981	1982	1983	1984	1985	Pays ou zone
America, North	**4 682.6**	**6 348.5**	**6 968.4**	**7 039.2**	**6 879.8**	**6 948.6**	**6 433.9**	**7 248.7**	**7 881.3**	**7 647.4**	**Amérique du Nord**
Canada	* 143.0	* 165.0	* 310.0	...	539.9	677.3	693.3	714.7	656.4	646.9	Canada
Mexico	113.6	137.5	138.4	159.9	136.9	156.0	158.0	191.0	208.0	207.0	Mexique
United States	4 426.0	6 046.0	6 520.0	6 485.5	6 203.0	6 115.3	5 582.6	6 343.0	7 016.9	6 793.5	Etats-Unis
America, South	**105.4**	**140.2**	**226.6**	**376.5**	**418.1**	**437.0**	**461.2**	**590.7**	**673.6**	**727.2**	**Amérique du Sud**
Brazil[1]	105.4	140.2	226.6	376.5	418.1	437.0	461.2	590.7	673.6	...	Brésil[1]
Asia	**2 760.9**	**2 848.8**	**3 138.0**	**3 310.2**	**2 921.3**	**2 835.7**	**2 870.2**	**3 013.1**	**3 352.8**	**3 452.6**	**Asie**
India	33.1	37.1	49.7	57.7	...	...	...	...	...	...	Inde
Japan	2 635.5	2 716.4	2 963.7	3 112.5	2 636.9	2 537.7	2 564.6	2 657.5	2 980.5	3 057.2	Japon
Korea, Republic of	61.6	55.1	89.1	110.9	208.0	215.9	224.4	272.5	297.6	318.0	Corée, République de
Turkey	30.6	40.2	35.5	29.1	31.9	37.7	36.9	38.6	30.3	33.0	Turquie
Europe	**5 650.2**	**5 687.6**	**6 201.8**	**6 644.9**	**5 898.8**	**6 058.6**	**6 288.2**	**6 814.9**	**7 315.4**	**7 264.7**	**Europe**
EEC	***4 901.6***	***4 871.6***	***5 208.4***	***5 592.3***	***4 784.5***	***4 791.8***	***4 902.6***	***5 285.5***	***5 668.6***	***5 479.0***	***CEE***
France[2]	874.0	941.0	1 063.0	1 156.0	988.0	1 005.6	# 1 135.3	1 189.0	1 297.1	1 345.2	France[2]
Germany, Fed. Rep.	1 431.6	1 535.9	1 703.6	1 844.0	1 591.5	1 613.4	1 481.3	1 724.0	1 803.9	1 666.0	Allemagne, Rép. féd.
Italy	868.6	830.2	747.9	677.5	648.3	492.2	446.0	519.5	565.6	463.2	Italie
Netherlands	980.0	905.0	1 023.0	1 149.0	984.0	944.0	...	...	...	...	Pays-Bas
United Kingdom	747.5	659.6	670.8	765.8	572.7	736.6	824.2	831.9	975.8	973.2	Royaume-Uni
EFTA	***165.4***	***110.9***	***185.6***	***212.2***	***144.1***	***162.6***	***182.9***	***244.7***	***310.2***	***281.3***	***AELE***
Finland[3]	5.0	5.0	61.0	68.0	54.0	69.0	51.4	...	...	...	Finlande[3]
Portugal	...	...	...	...	...	1.6	29.4	25.0	64.7	59.7	Portugal
Sweden	158.8	104.3	123.0	137.7	75.9	92.0	102.1	137.7	154.2	121.1	Suède
East Europe	***426.4***	***531.3***	***579.6***	***536.6***	***652.0***	***786.6***	***813.4***	***871.7***	***899.6***	***984.9***	***Europe de l'est***
Bulgaria	60.5	62.2	62.1	63.0	79.4	110.5	121.5	136.1	145.7	141.1	Bulgarie
Czechoslovakia	46.5	98.8	108.9	116.0	150.7	220.8	246.0	256.9	266.6	276.5	Tchécoslovaquie
Hungary	105.5	116.6	130.2	130.6	133.2	137.8	132.7	131.2	156.5	176.8	Hongrie
Poland	50.9	83.7	96.3	85.0	128.6	121.5	117.2	125.7	104.8	166.6	Pologne
Romania	163.0	170.0	182.0	142.0	160.0	196.0	196.0	222.0	226.0	224.0	Roumanie
Other Europe	***156.8***	***173.8***	***228.2***	***303.7***	***318.1***	***317.6***	***389.3***	***413.0***	***436.9***	***519.4***	***Autre Europe***
Spain	148.9	156.7	202.0	268.4	278.6	263.4	318.2	345.7	348.5	435.5	Espagne
Yugoslavia	...	...	...	...	39.6	54.2	71.1	67.2	88.5	83.9	Yougoslavie
USSR[4]	**...**	**...**	**...**	**...**	**824.0**	**919.0**	**981.0**	**1 035.0**	**1 094.0**	**...**	**URSS[4]**
Total	**13 779.6**	**15 670.6**	**17 245.3**	**18 146.3**	**16 942.0**	**17 198.9**	**17 034.5**	**18 702.3**	**20 317.1**	**20 257.5**	**Total**

General note.
Pure C3H6 should be shown at 100 per cent. However, the tonnage of the C3 cuts should be counted as pure propylene when the propylene content is at least 90 per cent. (SITC 51212-7).

[1] Production by establishments employing 5 or more persons.
[2] Source: The Chemical Industry, Organisation for Economic Co-operation and Development (OECD), (Paris).
[3] Beginning 1983, data are confidential.
[4] Source: United Nations Economic Commission for Europe (ECE), (Geneva).

Remarque générale.
Exprimé en C3H6 pur à 100 p. 100. Néanmoins, les fractions à 3 atomes de carbone seront à compter comme du propylène pur si la concentration de propylène est au moins égale à 90 p. 100. (CTCI 51212-7).

[1] Production des établissements occupant 5 personnes ou plus.
[2] Source: l'Industrie chimique, Organisation de coopération et de développement économiques (OCDE), (Paris).
[3] A partir de 1983, les données sont confidentielles.
[4] Source: Commission économique des Nations Unies pour l'Europe (CEE), (Genève).

Toluene – Toluène

Unit : Thousand metric tons

Unité : Milliers de tonnes métriques

Country or area	1976	1977	1978	1979	1980	1981	1982	1983	1984	1985	Pays ou zone
Africa	**0.5**	**0.5**	**0.5**	**0.5**	**0.5**	**0.5**	**0.5**	**0.5**	**0.5**	**0.5**	**Afrique**
Egypt	...	...	...	0.5	0.5	0.5	...	...	...	...	Egypte
America, North	**4 022.7**	**3 748.0**	**4 596.4**	**5 795.2**	**3 896.7**	**3 398.3**	**2 943.7**	**3 184.1**	**2 496.6**	**2 635.0**	**Amérique du Nord**
Canada[1]	182.4	...	283.0	341.0	469.8	480.3	470.4	410.6	395.5	471.9	Canada[1]
Mexico	132.3	116.3	123.8	107.9	124.9	132.0	138.0	223.0	216.0	220.0	Mexique
United States	3 708.0	3 346.3	4 189.6	5 346.3	3 302.0	2 786.0	2 335.3	2 550.5	1 885.1	...	Etats–Unis
America, South	**55.9**	**71.0**	**78.0**	**85.7**	**111.7**	**146.7**	**132.6**	**146.8**	**141.4**	**169.4**	**Amérique du Sud**
Brazil	55.9	71.0	78.0	85.7	111.7	146.7	132.6	146.8	141.4	...	Brésil
Asia	**941.3**	**973.3**	**975.7**	**1 065.5**	**1 063.0**	**970.6**	**977.6**	**1 022.7**	**1 002.7**	**1 034.5**	**Asie**
India[2]	6.3	14.0	16.3	19.8	...	...	...	...	...	...	Inde[2]
Japan	878.2	891.6	884.1	961.9	907.6	843.2	833.6	856.0	811.2	829.3	Japon
Korea, Republic of	55.7	66.8	74.3	82.5	139.8	112.0	128.3	151.5	176.0	190.2	Corée, République de
Turkey	1.0	1.0	0.9	1.3	1.5	1.3	1.5	1.1	1.3	1.0	Turquie
Europe	**1 706.6**	**1 666.2**	**1 535.6**	**1 732.6**	**1 486.0**	**1 528.0**	**1 501.6**	**1 646.5**	**1 713.2**	**1 781.7**	**Europe**
EEC	***1 185.0***	***1 087.6***	***972.1***	***1 188.6***	***920.6***	***915.8***	***881.3***	***965.1***	***1 022.0***	***1 082.0***	***CEE***
Belgium[3]	...	55.0	54.0	65.0	...	...	...	...	...	...	Belgique[3]
Denmark[4]	...	...	...	...	...	0.2	0.1	0.0	0.0	0.0	Danemark[4]
France	73.9	70.5	53.6	83.5	63.7	56.1	# 41.4	41.9	39.7	40.3	France
Germany, Fed. Rep.	232.8	243.1	226.2	298.5	260.6	262.7	268.3	314.3	370.8	390.8	Allemagne, Rép. féd.
Italy	466.0	424.9	357.7	366.8	287.0	278.8	263.5	299.0	312.9	348.1	Italie
Netherlands[5]	81.0	...	...	...	...	...	...	...	...	...	Pays–Bas[5]
United Kingdom	273.1	212.9	199.5	293.7	170.1	179.0	169.0	...	...	163.8	Royaume–Uni
EFTA	***84.2***	***84.2***	***84.2***	***84.2***	***84.2***	***84.2***	***73.7***	***88.0***	***85.9***	***89.1***	***AELE***
Portugal	...	...	...	...	...	...	73.7	88.0	85.9	89.1	Portugal
East Europe	***372.7***	***414.4***	***408.3***	***375.7***	***405.7***	***438.4***	***448.3***	***490.5***	***506.9***	***508.8***	***Europe de l'est***
Bulgaria	55.1	48.0	56.0	52.4	54.4	59.2	62.7	...	...	...	Bulgarie
Czechoslovakia	46.0	48.5	48.6	44.4	48.6	46.0	43.4	50.9	50.8	49.6	Tchécoslovaquie
Hungary	48.1	61.8	59.2	58.1	72.1	76.1	91.7	90.6	98.7	109.3	Hongrie
Poland	75.6	99.0	95.5	92.7	92.6	89.2	91.5	102.4	92.1	99.1	Pologne
Romania	148.0	157.0	149.0	128.0	138.0	168.0	159.0	185.0	202.0	186.0	Roumanie
Other Europe	***64.7***	***80.1***	***70.9***	***84.1***	***75.5***	***89.6***	***98.2***	***102.9***	***98.4***	***101.9***	***Autre Europe***
Spain	51.2	66.6	63.0	74.0	69.7	82.6	91.9	81.1	73.3	85.3	Espagne
Yugoslavia	13.5	13.5	7.9	10.1	5.8	7.1	6.3	21.8	25.2	16.6	Yougoslavie
Total	**6 727.0**	**6 459.0**	**7 186.1**	**8 679.5**	**6 557.8**	**6 044.1**	**5 555.9**	**6 000.5**	**5 354.3**	**5 621.1**	**Total**

General note.
Pure methylbenzene C6H5CH3 excluding toluene intended for dealkylation. (SITC 51212–8).

1 Shipments.
2 Excluding toluene recovered as a by–product from coke–oven plants.
3 Source: The Chemical Industry, Organisation for Economic Co–operation and Development (OECD), (Paris).
4 Exports.
5 Source: Industrial Statistics, Statistical Office of the European Communities, (Luxembourg).

Remarque générale.
Méthylbenzène pur C6H5CH3, à l'exclusion du toluène destiné à la desalkylation. (CTCI 51212–8).

1 Expéditions.
2 Non compris le toluène récupéré comme sous–produit des fours de cokéfaction.
3 Source: l'Industrie chimique, Organisation de coopération et de développement économiques (OCDE), (Paris).
4 Exportations.
5 Source: Statistiques industrielles, Office statistique des Communautés européennes, (Luxembourg).

Xylenes – Xylènes

Unit : Thousand metric tons

Unité : Milliers de tonnes métriques

Country or area	1976	1977	1978	1979	1980	1981	1982	1983	1984	1985	Pays ou zone
Africa	**0.1**	**0.1**	**0.1**	**0.1**	**0.1**	**0.1**	**0.1**	**0.1**	**0.1**	**0.1**	**Afrique**
Egypt	0.1	...	...	...	...	...	...	...	...	...	Egypte
America, North	**2 660.2**	**3 059.2**	**3 390.8**	**3 790.7**	**3 662.2**	**3 023.9**	**2 848.9**	**3 287.4**	**3 561.0**	**3 341.0**	**Amérique du Nord**
Canada[1]	161.8	* 280.0	352.0	...	402.7	409.8	430.5	432.4	405.7	405.7	Canada[1]
Mexico	124.0	112.0	130.0	118.0	132.5	142.0	151.0	352.0	405.0	501.0	Mexique
United States	2 374.4	2 667.2	2 908.8	3 346.6	3 127.0	2 472.1	2 267.3	2 503.0	2 750.2	2 434.3	Etats-Unis
America, South	**21.4**	**28.7**	**33.2**	**180.1**	**203.9**	**244.6**	**256.1**	**300.8**	**362.3**	**405.4**	**Amérique du Sud**
Brazil[2]	21.4	28.7	33.2	180.1	203.9	244.6	256.1	300.8	362.3	...	Brésil[2]
Asia	**1 253.0**	**1 299.9**	**1 336.2**	**1 419.4**	**1 416.4**	**1 446.0**	**1 479.1**	**1 570.3**	**1 711.6**	**1 661.4**	**Asie**
Japan	1 169.2	1 212.6	1 248.9	1 318.2	1 195.1	1 201.8	1 229.3	1 270.4	1 407.0	...	Japon
Korea, Republic of	83.5	86.9	87.0	100.9	221.0	243.9	249.4	299.7	304.4	330.1	Corée, République de
Turkey	0.4	0.4	0.3	0.3	0.3	0.4	0.3	0.2	0.2	0.2	Turquie
Europe	**1 532.5**	**1 544.2**	**1 492.1**	**1 568.1**	**1 386.0**	**1 512.8**	**1 518.6**	**1 795.5**	**1 741.1**	**1 792.6**	**Europe**
EEC	***955.6***	***898.8***	***868.8***	***960.4***	***752.2***	***829.1***	***816.1***	***1 007.4***	***970.8***	***1 037.4***	***CEE***
Belgium[3]	...	28.0	33.0	40.0	...	...	...	...	...	...	Belgique[3]
Denmark[4]	...	...	...	...	...	0.1	0.0	0.0	0.0	0.0	Danemark[4]
France	75.9	72.5	111.1	102.8	78.2	52.2	# 52.2	96.0	* 85.3	...	France
Germany, Fed. Rep.	474.2	455.8	412.3	493.2	356.0	486.6	460.0	512.4	455.9	495.2	Allemagne, Rép. féd.
Italy	371.7	342.4	312.3	324.3	284.2	256.5	270.2	365.3	396.0	432.9	Italie
EFTA	***100.9***	***100.9***	***100.9***	***100.9***	***100.9***	***100.9***	***83.6***	***109.7***	***104.3***	***105.9***	***AELE***
Portugal	...	...	...	...	...	...	83.6	109.7	104.3	105.9	Portugal
East Europe	***453.6***	***466.9***	***488.3***	***462.9***	***489.5***	***542.5***	***569.4***	***620.6***	***612.5***	***596.5***	***Europe de l'est***
Bulgaria	34.5	30.9	32.4	33.2	30.1	32.2	32.2	28.9	31.6	31.2	Bulgarie
Czechoslovakia	106.0	96.8	114.7	110.9	114.1	138.3	148.0	160.2	160.8	159.2	Tchécoslovaquie
Hungary	13.6	43.1	54.5	55.6	58.6	76.1	79.0	93.3	93.9	94.7	Hongrie
Poland	78.5	75.1	91.8	93.2	83.6	71.8	56.2	69.3	72.2	86.4	Pologne
Romania	221.0	221.0	195.0	170.0	203.0	224.0	254.0	269.0	254.0	225.0	Roumanie
Other Europe	***22.4***	***77.6***	***34.0***	***44.0***	***43.4***	***40.3***	***49.5***	***57.7***	***53.5***	***52.7***	***Autre Europe***
Spain	22.4	77.6	34.0	44.0	43.4	40.3	49.5	57.7	53.5	52.7	Espagne
USSR	**433.6**	**405.1**	**432.8**	**435.0**	**458.6**	**468.4**	**409.1**	**555.7**	**849.3**	**937.1**	**URSS**
Ukrainian SSR	...	...	*8.3*	*6.8*	*6.1*	*5.6*	*4.8*	*5.3*	*5.0*	*4.0*	*RSS d'Ukraine*
Total	**5 900.7**	**6 337.2**	**6 685.2**	**7 393.4**	**7 127.1**	**6 695.9**	**6 511.8**	**7 509.8**	**8 225.4**	**8 137.7**	**Total**

General note.
Pure dimethylbenzene (C6H4(CH3)2) total of three isomers : orthoxylene, metaxylene and paraxylene. (SITC 51212–9).

[1] Shipments.
[2] Excluding metaxylene.
[3] Source: The Chemical Industry, Organisation for Economic Co-operation and Development (OECD), (Paris).
[4] Exports.

Remarque générale.
Diméthyl benzène pur (C6H4(CH3)2). Poids total des trois isomères: l'orthoxylène, le métaxylène et le paraxylène. (CTCI 51212–9).

[1] Expéditions.
[2] Non compris le métaxylène.
[3] Source: l'Industrie chimique, Organisation de coopération et de développement économiques (OCDE), (Paris).
[4] Exportations.

Trichloroethylene – Trichloro-éthylène

Unit : Thousand metric tons

Unité : Milliers de tonnes métriques

Country or area	1976	1977	1978	1979	1980	1981	1982	1983	1984	1985	Pays ou zone
America, North	**530.1**	**521.9**	**522.6**	**531.9**	**574.1**	**495.1**	**666.0**	**653.0**	**690.0**	**655.5**	**Amérique du Nord**
Mexico	...	...	...	...	...	378.0	396.0	...	...	...	Mexique
United States	143.1	134.9	135.6	144.9	...	117.1	270.0	266.0	303.0	268.5	Etats-Unis
America, South	**0.0**	**0.1**	**0.1**	**0.0**	**0.1**	**0.1**	**0.1**	**0.1**	**0.1**	**0.1**	**Amérique du Sud**
Brazil	0.0	0.1	0.1	0.0	0.1	...	...	...	...	...	Brésil
Asia	**79.9**	**80.6**	**74.9**	**80.8**	**82.5**	**74.5**	**67.5**	**66.7**	**74.1**	**72.5**	**Asie**
Japan	79.9	80.6	74.9	80.8	82.5	74.5	67.5	66.7	74.1	72.5	Japon
Europe	**133.5**	**121.5**	**122.9**	**113.9**	**99.0**	**97.7**	**85.9**	**83.0**	**76.4**	**66.8**	**Europe**
EEC	***63.3***	***61.0***	***57.0***	***45.5***	***40.8***	***35.5***	***29.5***	***23.5***	***17.5***	***11.4***	***CEE***
Italy	63.3	61.0	57.0	45.5	40.8	...	...	...	...	...	Italie
EFTA	***13.6***	***15.1***	***13.1***	***13.8***	***9.9***	***11.9***	***8.4***	***9.9***	***10.5***	***10.7***	***AELE***
Finland	0.9	0.9	0.8	0.8	0.9	0.6	...	...	...	...	Finlande
Portugal	0.5	...	...	...	...	...	...	...	...	...	Portugal
Sweden	12.1	13.7	11.8	12.5	8.5	10.8	7.3	8.7	9.4	9.7	Suède
East Europe	***29.8***	***31.8***	***20.8***	***17.5***	***17.6***	***18.5***	***17.9***	***18.2***	***17.9***	***16.3***	***Europe de l'est***
Czechoslovakia	28.4	30.2	19.4	16.2	16.5	17.4	16.9	17.4	17.6	16.3	Tchécoslovaquie
Hungary	1.5	1.6	1.4	1.3	1.1	1.1	1.0	0.7	0.3	0.0	Hongrie
Other Europe	***26.7***	***13.6***	***31.9***	***37.1***	***30.6***	***31.8***	***30.1***	***31.5***	***30.7***	***28.3***	***Autre Europe***
Spain	20.1	9.9	24.4	29.5	24.4	24.0	24.4	27.7	26.6	23.3	Espagne
Yugoslavia	6.6	3.7	7.6	7.6	6.2	7.8	5.6	3.7	4.1	5.0	Yougoslavie
Total	**743.5**	**724.1**	**720.5**	**726.7**	**755.6**	**667.4**	**819.4**	**802.7**	**840.6**	**794.9**	**Total**

General note.
ClHC=CCl2 halogenated derivative of unsaturated acyclic hydrocarbons. (SITC 51213-3).

Remarque générale.
CHCl=CCl2, dérivé halogéné d'hydrocarbures acycliques non saturés. (CTCI 51213-3).

Methanol (methyl alcohol) – Alcool méthylique (méthanol)

Unit : Thousand metric tons

Unité : Milliers de tonnes métriques

Country or area	1976	1977	1978	1979	1980	1981	1982	1983	1984	1985	Pays ou zone
Africa	**39.0**	**44.0**	**47.7**	**47.0**	**42.9**	**38.9**	**34.9**	**61.0**	**48.6**	**49.5**	**Afrique**
Algeria	39.0	44.0	47.7	47.0	42.9	38.9	34.9	* 61.0	...	...	Algérie
America, North	**4 633.7**	**4 731.7**	**4 759.2**	**5 307.3**	**5 190.1**	**5 841.8**	**5 389.3**	**4 880.2**	**5 825.2**	**4 675.7**	**Amérique du Nord**
Canada	...	...	...	...	...	...	...	1 670.7	1 872.4	...	Canada
Mexico	32.1	33.1	102.7	174.1	173.6	180.0	191.0	205.0	197.0	192.0	Mexique
United States	2 830.0	2 927.0	2 884.8	3 361.6	3 245.0	3 890.3	3 426.7	3 004.5	3 755.8	2 712.1	Etats-Unis
America, South	**85.0**	**85.2**	**97.2**	**109.2**	**146.5**	**126.5**	**134.7**	**142.8**	**147.8**	**162.5**	**Amérique du Sud**
Brazil	...	81.3	95.2	107.2	126.6	120.4	127.8	136.1	137.9	...	Brésil
Colombia	...	4.0	2.1	2.0	19.9	6.1	6.9	6.7	...	...	Colombie
Asia	**1 063.9**	**983.1**	**1 216.8**	**1 310.6**	**1 092.0**	**947.4**	**782.0**	**486.1**	**326.7**	**300.6**	**Asie**
India	32.9	45.1	42.1	52.1	...	...	...	...	...	...	Inde
Israel	0.9	...	1.7	...	...	...	...	...	...	...	Israël
Japan	951.2	762.0	907.3	940.2	835.7	734.3	625.3	373.2	280.1	254.3	Japon
Korea, Republic of	78.9	174.7	265.6	317.0	211.9	168.7	112.4	68.6	2.3	1.9	Corée, République de
Europe	**2 480.0**	**2 442.9**	**2 359.3**	**2 494.1**	**2 469.1**	**2 321.5**	**2 350.3**	**2 274.6**	**2 317.4**	**2 374.3**	**Europe**
EEC	***1 692.6***	***1 496.5***	***1 304.7***	***1 397.4***	***1 382.2***	***1 255.4***	***1 268.5***	***1 223.5***	***1 225.5***	***1 138.5***	***CEE***
Denmark[1]	...	...	...	...	...	0.7	0.1	0.0	...	...	Danemark[1]
France	345.2	375.7	347.2	353.1	344.9	347.6	# 344.9	341.2	327.2	...	France
Germany, Fed. Rep.	1 052.3	887.2	800.3	871.0	822.6	692.6	708.8	668.0	683.5	591.7	Allemagne, Rép. féd.
Greece	...	...	...	...	...	...	0.9	0.5	0.7	...	Grèce
Italy	294.1	232.7	156.3	172.4	...	...	...	...	...	...	Italie
EFTA	***51.8***	***39.4***	***50.3***	***53.0***	***48.6***	***48.6***	***48.6***	***48.6***	***48.6***	***48.6***	***AELE***
Norway	51.8	39.3	50.2	53.0	...	...	...	...	...	...	Norvège
Sweden	0.1	0.1	0.1	0.0	0.0	0.0	0.0	0.0	0.0	0.0	Suède
East Europe	***691.8***	***787.9***	***844.2***	***824.4***	***864.4***	***858.0***	***834.2***	***847.8***	***835.3***	***983.9***	***Europe de l'est***
Bulgaria	27.1	27.3	24.3	25.7	27.2	28.1	28.2	28.0	26.3	38.3	Bulgarie
Czechoslovakia	99.4	99.2	102.5	103.3	105.2	114.8	115.2	116.5	98.6	109.3	Tchécoslovaquie
German Dem. Rep.	243.5	240.1	248.6	227.1	249.3	242.8	230.6	242.6	238.7	309.9	Rép. dém. allemande
Poland	197.5	193.5	195.8	193.4	187.7	185.2	168.8	173.5	182.8	177.5	Pologne
Romania	124.3	227.9	273.0	274.9	295.0	287.0	291.3	287.2	289.0	349.0	Roumanie
Other Europe	***43.8***	***119.0***	***160.1***	***219.3***	***173.8***	***159.5***	***199.0***	***154.6***	***208.1***	***203.3***	***Autre Europe***
Spain	5.8	69.5	99.0	167.7	72.2	61.5	90.5	24.4	...	...	Espagne
Yugoslavia	...	...	...	51.5	101.6	98.0	108.6	130.2	132.8	127.7	Yougoslavie
USSR	**1 591.0**	**1 758.0**	**1 809.0**	**1 774.0**	**1 900.0**	[2] **2 030.0**	[2] **1 989.0**	[2] **2 174.0**	[2] **2 467.0**	**...**	**URSS**
Total	**9 892.6**	**10 044.9**	**10 289.2**	**11 042.2**	**10 840.6**	**11 306.1**	**10 680.2**	**10 018.7**	**11 132.8**	**9 953.5**	**Total**

General note.
Pure CH3OH, Crude methyl alcohol (wood naphtha) is excluded. (SITC 51221–0).

[1] Exports.
[2] Source: United Nations Economic Commission for Europe (ECE), (Geneva).

Remarque générale.
CH3OH pur, à l'exclusion de l'alcool méthylique brut (esprit de bois). (CTCI 51221–0).

[1] Exportations.
[2] Source: Commission économique des Nations Unies pour l'Europe (CEE), (Genève).

Butyl alcohol (butanol) – Alcools butyliques (butanols)

Unit : Thousand metric tons

Unité : Milliers de tonnes métriques

Country or area	1976	1977	1978	1979	1980	1981	1982	1983	1984	1985	Pays ou zone
America, North	**362.9**	**381.2**	**342.8**	**347.7**	**413.0**	**366.9**	**331.3**	**363.2**	**416.5**	**330.4**	**Amérique du Nord**
United States	362.9	381.2	342.8	347.7	413.0	366.9	331.3	363.2	416.5	330.4	Etats–Unis
America, South	**4.3**	**3.7**	**4.3**	**8.2**	**11.2**	**12.2**	**15.3**	**25.8**	**34.1**	**30.8**	**Amérique du Sud**
Brazil	4.3	3.7	4.3	8.2	11.2	12.2	15.3	25.8	34.1	...	Brésil
Asia	**197.7**	**202.4**	**230.2**	**259.7**	**230.7**	**245.5**	**236.1**	**286.5**	**251.1**	**265.8**	**Asie**
India	7.3	8.8	8.6	8.2	...	...	...	...	...	...	Inde
Japan	190.4	193.7	221.6	251.6	222.5	237.3	227.9	228.3	242.9	257.5	Japon
Europe	**652.0**	**636.6**	**670.5**	**721.6**	**679.1**	**641.1**	**657.1**	**714.1**	**709.8**	**710.3**	**Europe**
EEC	***472.3***	***464.9***	***504.1***	***563.0***	***523.7***	***478.0***	***494.1***	***532.1***	***522.8***	***539.7***	***CEE***
Denmark	0.0	0.0	0.0	0.0	0.0	0.0	0.9	0.9	0.4	0.1	Danemark
France	7.7	13.2	19.5	24.9	28.9	30.5	...	...	...	...	France
Germany, Fed. Rep.	433.1	426.2	456.1	509.6	466.2	419.0	427.3	460.5	446.9	459.4	Allemagne, Rép. féd.
Italy	31.5	25.5	...	...	...	...	...	...	...	...	Italie
EFTA	***16.0***	***8.2***	***2.0***	***3.4***	***4.7***	***14.7***	***15.5***	***20.7***	***25.4***	***24.3***	***AELE***
Sweden	16.0	8.2	2.0	3.4	4.7	14.7	15.5	20.7	25.4	24.3	Suède
East Europe	***149.1***	***144.1***	***145.7***	***135.7***	***135.3***	***135.3***	***137.4***	***145.6***	***148.3***	***133.3***	***Europe de l'est***
Czechoslovakia	19.7	20.5	20.5	18.9	17.5	18.5	19.8	20.1	21.7	22.0	Tchécoslovaquie
German Dem. Rep.	59.3	53.6	55.9	55.3	51.4	52.7	55.3	55.7	56.0	54.3	Rép. dém. allemande
Poland	25.9	23.7	23.6	20.5	21.7	19.6	20.0	20.5	22.2	16.3	Pologne
Romania	44.1	46.4	45.6	41.1	44.7	44.4	42.3	49.4	48.4	40.6	Roumanie
Other Europe	***14.7***	***19.3***	***18.8***	***19.5***	***15.4***	***13.1***	***10.1***	***15.8***	***13.3***	***13.0***	***Autre Europe***
Spain	14.7	19.3	18.8	19.5	15.4	13.1	10.1	15.8	13.3	13.0	Espagne
USSR[1]	**181.0**	**187.0**	**186.0**	**184.0**	**205.0**	**274.0**	**276.0**	**278.0**	**297.0**	...	**URSS[1]**
Total	**1 397.9**	**1 411.0**	**1 434.0**	**1 521.2**	**1 539.0**	**1 539.6**	**1 515.8**	**1 617.6**	**1 708.4**	**1 651.1**	**Total**

General note.
Including n–Butyl, isobutyl, sec–butyl and tert–butyl alcohols. Methyl, ethyl alcohols and glycerol are excluded. (SITC 51222–1).

[1] Source: United Nations Economic Commission for Europe (ECE), (Geneva).

Remarque générale.
Y compris les alcools n–butylique, isobutylique et les alcools butyliques secondaires et tertiaires, mais à l'exclusion du méthanol, de l'éthanol et du glycérol. (CTCI 51222–1).

[1] Source: Commission économique des Nations Unies pour l'Europe (CEE), (Genève).

Ethanediol (ethylene glycol)
Ethane–diol (glycol)

Unit : Thousand metric tons

Unité : Milliers de tonnes métriques

Country or area	1976	1977	1978	1979	1980	1981	1982	1983	1984	1985	Pays ou zone
America, North	**1 512.5**	**1 667.2**	**1 770.8**	**2 144.8**	**2 145.4**	**1 972.4**	**1 954.6**	**2 019.0**	**2 196.2**	**2 122.2**	**Amérique du Nord**
United States	1 512.5	1 667.2	1 770.8	2 144.8	2 145.4	1 972.4	1 954.6	2 019.0	2 196.2	2 122.2	Etats–Unis
America, South	**16.9**	**20.0**	**19.8**	**73.9**	**96.0**	**89.0**	**104.9**	**121.6**	**125.7**	**151.3**	**Amérique du Sud**
Brazil	16.9	20.0	19.8	73.9	96.0	89.0	104.9	121.6	125.7	...	Brésil
Asia	**655.7**	**633.3**	**749.0**	**698.9**	**616.3**	**550.6**	**521.5**	**507.5**	**570.5**	**596.3**	**Asie**
India	6.4	5.3	8.6	11.9	...	...	...	...	...	...	Inde
Japan	549.3	522.9	630.2	571.6	492.2	410.6	384.9	357.5	428.8	439.8	Japon
Korea, Republic of	...	...	...	...	63.4	79.3	75.9	89.4	81.0	95.7	Corée, République de
Turkey	...	...	...	...	...	52.7	...	...	...	...	Turquie
Europe	**377.3**	**391.5**	**426.5**	**485.8**	**500.2**	**510.3**	**462.7**	**484.4**	**522.5**	**525.9**	**Europe**
EEC	***323.2***	***312.3***	***339.8***	***405.8***	***369.2***	***377.2***	***339.9***	***361.4***	***388.4***	***386.5***	***CEE***
France[1]	108.1	107.9	...	...	...	...	...	...	...	...	France[1]
Germany, Fed. Rep.	166.2	157.3	191.2	254.1	208.5	221.3	183.6	204.7	231.3	229.0	Allemagne, Rép. féd.
Italy[1]	48.8	47.1	40.5	43.7	52.7	...	...	...	...	...	Italie[1]
EFTA	***12.5***	***6.5***	***9.9***	***8.8***	***6.0***	***9.6***	***9.2***	***9.7***	***6.7***	***3.6***	***AELE***
Finland	...	...	...	...	0.0	1.5	...	...	...	...	Finlande
Sweden	11.8	5.8	9.2	8.0	6.0	8.2	8.5	9.0	5.9	2.8	Suède
East Europe	***35.3***	***61.7***	***61.1***	***69.7***	***82.4***	***81.5***	***82.0***	***82.7***	***83.8***	***87.6***	***Europe de l'est***
Czechoslovakia	35.1	61.6	61.0	69.6	82.4	81.4	81.9	82.6	83.7	87.5	Tchécoslovaquie
Hungary	0.1	0.1	0.1	0.1	0.0	0.1	0.1	0.1	0.1	0.1	Hongrie
Other Europe	***6.4***	***11.0***	***15.7***	***1.5***	***42.6***	***42.0***	***31.6***	***30.6***	***43.6***	***48.3***	***Autre Europe***
Spain	...	...	...	1.5	42.6	42.0	31.6	30.6	...	...	Espagne
Total	**2 562.5**	**2 712.0**	**2 966.1**	**3 403.4**	**3 357.9**	**3 122.3**	**3 043.8**	**3 132.5**	**3 415.0**	**3 395.7**	**Total**

General note.
Ethylene glycol, glycol CH2OHCH2OH. (SITC 51222–2).

[1] Source: Industrial Statistics, Statistical Office of the European Communities, (Luxembourg).

Remarque générale.
Ethylène–glycol, glycol CH2OHCH2OH. (CTCI 51222–2).

[1] Source: Statistiques industrielles, Office statistique des Communautés européennes, (Luxembourg).

Glycerine (Glycerol) – Glycérine (glycérol)

Unit : Thousand metric tons

Unité : Milliers de tonnes métriques

Country or area	1976	1977	1978	1979	1980	1981	1982	1983	1984	1985	Pays ou zone
Africa	**6.0**	**7.1**	**6.6**	**6.7**	**6.3**	**7.6**	**8.2**	**8.0**	**8.5**	**8.9**	**Afrique**
Algeria	0.8	1.0	0.9	0.5	0.2	0.2	0.1	...	...	...	Algérie
Côte d'Ivoire	0.7	1.0	...	...	...	...	...	...	...	...	Côte d'Ivoire
Egypt	3.8	4.3	4.0	4.7	4.7	6.0	6.7	6.5	...	...	Egypte
Zaire	0.7	0.8	0.8	...	0.5	0.5	0.6	0.6	...	...	Zaïre
America, North	**162.1**	**156.4**	**151.9**	**171.9**	**151.8**	**146.1**	**118.5**	**134.9**	**151.4**	**161.0**	**Amérique du Nord**
Canada[1]	6.2	...	...	...	...	...	...	...	...	...	Canada[1]
Cuba	2.3	2.0	1.8	1.8	1.9	1.8	1.3	1.3	1.5	1.5	Cuba
Mexico	6.3	7.2	6.6	7.0	7.0	6.4	6.9	6.9	6.3	7.7	Mexique
United States	147.3	141.0	137.3	156.9	136.6	131.7	104.0	120.4	137.3	145.6	Etats-Unis
America, South	**11.1**	**11.4**	**10.2**	**13.4**	**19.9**	**18.9**	**17.2**	**19.3**	**18.4**	**21.5**	**Amérique du Sud**
Brazil[2]	11.1	11.4	10.2	13.4	19.9	18.9	17.2	19.3	18.4	...	Brésil[2]
Asia	**62.4**	**64.1**	**65.3**	**63.6**	**65.3**	**63.8**	**69.3**	**71.0**	**69.3**	**80.6**	**Asie**
Burma[3]	0.8	0.7	0.7	0.7	1.0	1.0	0.2	0.3	...	...	Birmanie[3]
India[4]	8.8	8.9	9.8	6.0	8.5	11.1	11.1	11.9	10.8	...	Inde[4]
Indonesia	2.6	2.6	2.5	2.9	7.3	4.1	6.7	2.6	2.5	...	Indonésie
Japan	40.3	40.4	41.5	44.2	38.3	34.5	36.1	40.1	40.4	45.2	Japon
Korea, Republic of	5.1	6.1	6.4	7.5	7.3	8.5	10.4	9.5	10.1	13.5	Corée, République de
Philippines	4.2	4.8	4.0	1.7	2.5	...	...	6.2	...	...	Philippines
Sri Lanka	0.1	0.1	0.0	0.1	0.1	0.0	0.0	0.0	0.0	0.0	Sri Lanka
Turkey	0.4	0.5	0.4	0.5	...	...	...	...	...	...	Turquie
Europe	**143.1**	**164.9**	**168.5**	**176.1**	**175.5**	**165.8**	**173.5**	**178.6**	**178.2**	**171.1**	**Europe**
EEC	***125.9***	***144.9***	***148.6***	***155.5***	***152.0***	***143.9***	***154.9***	***161.5***	***160.1***	***153.7***	***CEE***
Denmark	2.3	2.6	3.1	2.7	2.4	1.9	2.0	2.0	1.8	1.1	Danemark
France[5]	...	...	16.2	15.2	15.8	14.6	30.2	30.9	33.7	30.8	France[5]
Germany, Fed. Rep.	60.2	75.5	74.8	80.3	85.1	93.3	92.7	98.5	97.2	92.8	Allemagne, Rép. féd.
Greece	...	...	...	0.5	0.4	0.4	0.4	0.3	0.3	...	Grèce
Italy	12.3	9.9	5.7	...	...	...	...	...	...	...	Italie
United Kingdom[6]	43.8	46.6	48.3	47.6	39.0	# 24.3	20.3	20.5	17.9	19.5	Royaume-Uni[6]
EFTA	***4.1***	***4.9***	***4.2***	***4.7***	***4.5***	***5.1***	***4.3***	***3.6***	***3.6***	***2.6***	***AELE***
Finland	0.1	0.1	0.1	0.1	0.1	0.1	0.2	0.3	0.2	...	Finlande
Portugal	3.6	4.4	3.7	4.2	3.9	4.5	3.6	2.9	3.0	2.1	Portugal
Sweden	0.4	0.4	0.4	0.4	0.5	0.5	0.5	0.5	0.4	0.3	Suède
East Europe	***9.2***	***9.7***	***9.9***	***10.0***	***10.8***	***10.3***	***10.1***	***9.1***	***9.2***	***9.5***	***Europe de l'est***
Bulgaria	0.2	0.3	0.4	0.3	0.5	0.4	0.3	0.3	0.4	0.3	Bulgarie
Czechoslovakia	7.3	7.7	7.8	8.0	8.6	8.5	8.5	7.3	7.3	7.7	Tchécoslovaquie
Hungary	1.7	1.7	1.7	1.7	1.7	1.5	1.2	1.5	1.5	1.5	Hongrie
Other Europe	***3.9***	***5.4***	***5.8***	***5.9***	***8.2***	***6.5***	***4.3***	***4.4***	***5.3***	***5.3***	***Autre Europe***
Spain	3.1	...	...	4.4	7.0	5.7	3.4	3.8	...	...	Espagne
Yugoslavia	0.8	1.1	1.4	1.5	1.2	0.8	0.9	0.6	0.4	0.4	Yougoslavie
Oceania	**5.0**	**9.6**	**8.6**	**8.4**	**8.2**	**8.3**	**9.3**	**8.0**	**8.0**	**8.9**	**Océanie**
Australia	5.0	9.6	8.6	8.4	...	...	9.3	8.0	8.0	...	Australie
Total	**389.8**	**413.7**	**411.1**	**440.1**	**426.9**	**410.5**	**396.0**	**419.8**	**433.7**	**452.1**	**Total**

General note.
Glycerol and glycerol lyes, including both synthetic and chemically pure glycerol. Glycerol put up as a medicament, perfumed glycerol and glycerol with added pharmaceutical substances or cosmetics are excluded. (SITC 51226-1).

Remarque générale.
Glycérol, y compris les eaux et lessives glycérinées ainsi que le glycérol synthétique chimiquement pur. Cette rubrique ne comprend pas le glycérol présenté sous conditionnement pharmaceutique, le glycérol parfumé et le glycérol additionné de substances médicamenteuses ou de cosmétiques. (CTCI 51226-1).

1 Shipments.
2 Production by main establishments only.
3 Twelve months ending 30 September of year stated.
4 Production by large and medium scale establishments only.
5 Crude glycerine (100 per cent glycerol).
6 Crude natural glycerine plus glycerine processed into distilled glycerine. Including crude glycerol.

1 Expéditions.
2 Production des principaux établissements seulement.
3 Période de douze mois finissant le 30 septembre de l'année indiquée.
4 Production des grandes et moyennes entreprises seulement.
5 Glycérine brute (100 pour cent glycérol).
6 Glycérine naturelle brute et glycérine épurée. Y compris le glycérol brut.

Phenol – Phénol

Unit : Thousand metric tons

Unité : Milliers de tonnes métriques

Country or area	1976	1977	1978	1979	1980	1981	1982	1983	1984	1985	Pays ou zone
Africa	**0.1**	**0.0**	**0.1**	**0.1**	**0.1**	**0.1**	**0.2**	**0.2**	**0.2**	**0.2**	**Afrique**
Egypt	0.1	0.0	0.1	0.1	0.1	0.1	...	...	...	...	Egypte
America, North	**1 013.5**	**1 074.0**	**1 234.6**	**1 372.6**	**1 186.0**	**1 192.2**	**938.5**	**1 206.7**	**1 315.1**	**1 286.9**	**Amérique du Nord**
Mexico	10.5	13.6	18.2	20.3	21.0	23.0	20.7	22.0	24.5	27.1	Mexique
United States	1 003.0	1 060.4	1 216.4	1 352.3	1 165.0	1 169.2	917.7	1 184.7	1 290.7	1 259.8	Etats–Unis
America, South	**63.5**	**71.2**	**70.1**	**68.8**	**87.1**	**72.9**	**91.5**	**95.8**	**99.6**	**102.1**	**Amérique du Sud**
Brazil[1]	63.5	71.2	70.1	68.8	87.1	72.9	91.5	95.8	99.6	...	Brésil[1]
Asia	**239.7**	**235.3**	**269.5**	**264.2**	**231.7**	**232.7**	**239.3**	**290.8**	**291.2**	**282.0**	**Asie**
India	11.5	12.4	14.3	14.2	...	...	...	...	...	...	Inde
Japan	221.7	221.3	248.8	243.5	215.0	214.4	210.9	271.3	271.7	262.4	Japon
Korea, Republic of	...	1.5	...	...	3.4	5.0	15.1	...	...	...	Corée, République de
Turkey	0.1	0.2	0.2	0.3	...	...	...	...	...	...	Turquie
Europe	**1 121.9**	**1 098.0**	**1 073.3**	**1 142.1**	**1 104.1**	**1 058.8**	**1 118.5**	**1 120.1**	**1 191.4**	**1 115.8**	**Europe**
EEC	***899.1***	***887.4***	***852.4***	***892.8***	***840.5***	***800.1***	***826.2***	***825.2***	***862.3***	***791.2***	***CEE***
France* [2]	148.0	...	...	...	...	...	...	...	...	...	France* [2]
Germany, Fed. Rep.[3]	276.5	273.3	245.3	291.2	246.6	...	...	...	...	...	Allemagne, Rép. féd.[3]
Italy* [4]	290.0	298.0	290.0	275.0	...	...	...	...	...	...	Italie* [4]
United Kingdom[5]	184.6	168.1	169.1	178.6	...	109.7	140.0	143.2	184.4	117.5	Royaume–Uni[5]
EFTA	***0.8***	***0.0***	***0.0***	***0.0***	***0.0***	***2.9***	***29.9***	***8.9***	***10.0***	***11.2***	***AELE***
Finland[6]	...	0.0	0.0	0.0	0.0	2.9	29.9	...	...	...	Finlande[6]
East Europe	***212.0***	***206.5***	***210.6***	***202.1***	***212.1***	***211.0***	***221.9***	***242.7***	***251.3***	***236.1***	***Europe de l'est***
Bulgaria	35.1	36.2	37.0	34.9	34.9	38.3	38.7	39.2	37.8	39.8	Bulgarie
Czechoslovakia	43.9	36.8	45.8	45.9	43.9	42.1	45.1	45.3	43.6	42.6	Tchécoslovaquie
Poland	70.6	64.9	67.3	68.5	67.7	64.5	66.4	69.9	70.3	65.8	Pologne
Romania	62.4	68.6	60.5	52.7	65.7	66.0	71.7	88.4	99.6	87.9	Roumanie
Other Europe	***10.0***	***4.2***	***10.2***	***47.3***	***51.4***	***44.8***	***40.5***	***43.3***	***67.8***	***77.4***	***Autre Europe***
Spain	0.0	0.0	# 10.2	47.3	47.9	41.3	37.0	39.7	64.3	73.8	Espagne
Yugoslavia	10.0	4.2	0.0	0.0	...	...	...	...	...	...	Yougoslavie
USSR[4]	*** 424.0**	*** 431.0**	*** 469.0**	*** 487.0**	*** 496.0**	**497.0**	**459.0**	**484.0**	**511.0**	**...**	**URSS[4]**
Total	**2 862.7**	**2 909.5**	**3 116.5**	**3 334.9**	**3 105.0**	**3 053.8**	**2 846.9**	**3 197.6**	**3 408.6**	**3 301.6**	**Total**

General note.
Pure C6H5.OH obtained by fractional distillation of coal tars or by synthesis. Crude phenol is excluded. (SITC 51227–1).

[1] Production by main establishments only.
[2] Beginning 1977, data are confidential.
[3] Beginning 1981, data are confidential.
[4] Source: United Nations Economic Commission for Europe (ECE), (Geneva).
[5] Synthetic phenol only.
[6] Beginning 1983, data are confidential.

Remarque générale.
C6H5.OH pur, obtenu par distillation fractionnée des goudrons de houille, ou par synthèse, à l'exclusion du phénol brut. (CTCI 51227–1).

[1] Production des principaux établissements seulement.
[2] A partir de 1977 ,les données sont confidentielles.
[3] A partir de 1981, les données sont confidentielles.
[4] Source: Commission économique des Nations Unies pour l'Europe (CEE), (Genève).
[5] Phénol synthétique seulement.
[6] A partir de 1983, les données sont confidentielles.

Ethylene oxide – Oxide d'éthylène

Unit : Thousand metric tons

Unité : Milliers de tonnes métriques

Country or area	1976	1977	1978	1979	1980	1981	1982	1983	1984	1985	Pays ou zone
America, North	**1 877.4**	**2 006.4**	**2 299.9**	**2 593.5**	**2 397.7**	**2 365.4**	**2 341.2**	**2 631.0**	**2 799.3**	**2 716.9**	**Amérique du Nord**
Mexico	25.4	26.8	26.3	23.8	29.7	48.0	79.0	112.0	97.0	71.0	Mexique
United States	1 852.0	1 979.5	2 273.6	2 569.8	2 368.0	2 317.4	2 262.2	2 519.0	2 702.3	2 645.9	Etats-Unis
America, South	**78.8**	**85.4**	**91.9**	**98.5**	**112.2**	**103.9**	**124.0**	**107.3**	**143.6**	**137.9**	**Amérique du Sud**
Brazil	...	...	...	...	112.2	103.9	124.0	107.3	143.6	...	Brésil
Asia	**556.3**	**549.5**	**644.4**	**605.2**	**540.5**	**489.6**	**483.0**	**479.8**	**544.6**	**566.8**	**Asie**
India	9.6	11.9	13.8	12.1	...	...	...	...	...	...	Inde
Japan	546.8	537.6	630.6	593.1	528.6	477.8	471.2	467.9	532.8	555.0	Japon
Europe	**875.8**	**863.0**	**965.3**	**1 089.1**	**1 073.3**	**1 116.2**	**1 078.0**	**1 170.8**	**1 216.7**	**1 244.9**	**Europe**
EEC	***781.4***	***751.7***	***849.6***	***929.1***	***931.7***	***970.3***	***951.3***	***1 025.4***	***1 064.9***	***1 094.4***	***CEE***
France*	178.0	...	...	...	...	...	...	...	...	...	France*
Germany, Fed. Rep.	300.5	295.1	361.1	434.4	385.1	434.0	393.5	451.3	474.5	487.6	Allemagne, Rép. féd.
Italy	82.9	78.6	75.6	77.7	...	...	...	...	...	...	Italie
Netherlands*	220.0	200.0	235.0	239.0	290.0	279.6	...	...	...	...	Pays-Bas*
EFTA	***27.3***	***28.8***	***30.9***	***32.6***	***25.9***	***28.5***	***10.7***	***28.4***	***32.1***	***28.1***	***AELE***
Sweden	27.3	28.8	30.9	32.6	25.9	28.5	10.7	28.4	32.1	28.1	Suède
East Europe	***43.4***	***57.5***	***57.4***	***51.5***	***58.2***	***62.5***	***67.3***	***68.4***	***70.0***	***72.9***	***Europe de l'est***
Bulgaria	9.8	10.4	10.4	9.9	10.9	12.5	16.8	...	...	...	Bulgarie
Czechoslovakia	8.5	11.1	11.3	11.3	12.5	13.4	12.5	13.8	13.1	13.6	Tchécoslovaquie
Romania	* 25.0	* 36.0	35.7	30.4	34.9	...	...	...	...	...	Roumanie
Other Europe	***23.8***	***25.0***	***27.3***	***75.9***	***57.4***	***54.9***	***48.7***	***48.7***	***49.7***	***49.6***	***Autre Europe***
Spain	23.8	* 25.0	27.3	75.9	57.4	54.9	48.7	48.7	49.7	49.6	Espagne
Total	**3 388.4**	**3 504.2**	**4 001.5**	**4 386.4**	**4 123.6**	**4 075.1**	**4 026.2**	**4 388.9**	**4 704.2**	**4 666.5**	**Total**

General note.
Pure CH2CH2O. (SITC 51232-1).

Remarque générale.
CH2CH2O pur. (CTCI 51232-1).

Acetaldehyde (ethanal) – Aldéhyde acétique (éthanal)

Unit : Thousand metric tons

Unité : Milliers de tonnes métriques

Country or area	1976	1977	1978	1979	1980	1981	1982	1983	1984	1985	Pays ou zone
America, North	**46.6**	**44.0**	**45.3**	**48.8**	**47.6**	**122.0**	**149.0**	**153.0**	**147.0**	**145.0**	**Amérique du Nord**
Mexico	46.6	44.0	45.3	48.8	47.6	122.0	149.0	153.0	147.0	145.0	Mexique
America, South	**25.0**	**31.2**	**37.4**	**43.5**	**56.3**	**48.8**	**63.8**	**58.7**	**82.4**	**80.5**	**Amérique du Sud**
Brazil	...	...	...	...	56.3	48.8	63.8	58.7	82.4	...	Brésil
Asia	**615.3**	**624.5**	**586.7**	**583.3**	**431.7**	**323.7**	**278.7**	**254.7**	**297.3**	**271.4**	**Asie**
Japan	615.3	624.5	586.7	583.3	431.7	323.7	278.7	254.7	297.3	271.4	Japon
Europe	**940.9**	**1 470.0**	**1 553.8**	**1 643.3**	**1 576.6**	**1 667.8**	**1 836.2**	**1 995.7**	**2 177.0**	**2 296.6**	**Europe**
EEC	***801.5***	***1 329.7***	***1 402.1***	***1 507.1***	***1 455.8***	***1 520.5***	***1 703.1***	***1 865.6***	***2 037.1***	***2 162.4***	***CEE***
France	*[1] 58.0	# 617.0	676.0	735.0	794.0	853.0	...	...	...	...	France
Germany, Fed. Rep.	352.6	346.2	367.0	405.3	330.2	304.5	261.7	293.9	335.0	330.0	Allemagne, Rép. féd.
Italy	169.5	145.1	124.1	127.8	...	...	...	...	...	...	Italie
Netherlands	...	...	235.0	239.0	190.0	...	...	...	...	...	Pays-Bas
EFTA	***7.6***	***7.7***	***5.9***	***7.2***	***4.1***	***0.2***	***0.9***	***4.4***	***6.4***	***6.8***	***AELE***
Sweden	7.6	7.7	5.9	7.2	4.1	0.2	0.9	...	6.4	6.8	Suède
East Europe	***76.8***	***77.8***	***66.4***	***59.3***	***69.0***	***100.4***	***97.3***	***91.2***	***93.9***	***96.1***	***Europe de l'est***
Bulgaria	0.0	0.0	0.0	0.0	8.1	41.3	47.1	44.0	49.7	55.1	Bulgarie
Czechoslovakia	19.8	18.8	18.4	14.3	15.8	19.7	14.5	15.3	16.1	16.6	Tchécoslovaquie
Romania[1]	57.0	59.0	48.0	45.0	45.0	...	...	...	...	...	Roumanie[1]
Other Europe	***55.0***	***54.8***	***79.5***	***69.7***	***47.7***	***46.7***	***34.8***	***34.5***	***39.5***	***31.2***	***Autre Europe***
Spain	55.0	54.8	79.5	69.7	47.7	46.7	34.8	34.5	39.5	31.2	Espagne
Total	**1 627.8**	**2 169.7**	**2 223.2**	**2 319.0**	**2 112.2**	**2 162.3**	**2 327.6**	**2 462.2**	**2 703.7**	**2 793.5**	**Total**

General note.
Pure CH3.CHO (ethanal), saturated acyclic aldehyde. (SITC 51241-1).

[1] Source: United Nations Economic Commission for Europe (ECE), (Geneva).

Remarque générale.
Aldéhyde acyclique saturé pur CH3.CHO (éthanal). (CTCI 51241-1).

[1] Source: Commission économique des Nations Unies pour l'Europe (CEE), (Genève).

Methanal (formaldehyde) – Méthanal (formaldéhyde)

Unit : Thousand metric tons

Unité : Milliers de tonnes métriques

Country or area	1976	1977	1978	1979	1980	1981	1982	1983	1984	1985	Pays ou zone
America, North	**2 524.4**	**2 795.0**	**2 978.1**	**2 848.8**	**2 728.6**	**2 755.6**	**2 337.8**	**2 617.4**	**2 775.2**	**2 806.0**	**Amérique du Nord**
Canada[1]	13.0	10.0	...	84.0	...	85.5	70.0	89.9	96.8	...	Canada[1]
Mexico	39.6	42.4	43.9	56.3	74.3	75.2	83.1	79.0	87.3	106.0	Mexique
United States[2]	2 471.8	2 742.6	2 894.4	2 708.4	...	2 594.9	2 184.7	2 448.5	2 591.1	2 585.8	Etats–Unis[2]
America, South	**125.3**	**114.8**	**118.4**	**138.1**	**185.9**	**113.6**	**152.4**	**159.2**	**185.3**	**178.4**	**Amérique du Sud**
Brazil	125.3	114.8	118.4	138.1	185.9	113.6	152.4	159.2	185.3	...	Brésil
Asia	**509.5**	**499.6**	**510.7**	**564.1**	**603.7**	**576.9**	**554.3**	**577.2**	**598.7**	**605.9**	**Asie**
India	32.9	47.1	38.8	36.2	40.1	43.0	46.3	46.8	46.9	...	Inde
Japan	386.4	384.9	415.1	447.5	412.8	384.4	381.1	403.0	427.0	437.1	Japon
Korea, Republic of	80.8	58.2	47.4	71.0	141.3	140.2	117.6	118.0	115.4	110.9	Corée, République de
Turkey[1]	...	...	...	...	...	9.4	...	...	...	...	Turquie[1]
Europe	**1 961.2**	**1 919.7**	**1 969.6**	**2 008.8**	**1 943.7**	**1 999.9**	**1 967.2**	**2 053.6**	**2 129.6**	**2 158.4**	**Europe**
EEC	***920.9***	***892.2***	***876.6***	***923.1***	***876.2***	***878.0***	***823.6***	***871.9***	***934.4***	***928.9***	***CEE***
Denmark	2.9	3.2	3.6	3.7	3.9	2.9	3.6	3.5	4.0	2.7	Danemark
France	150.2	148.7	146.8	158.5	136.1	120.6	# 99.8	94.7	96.1	92.6	France
Germany, Fed. Rep.	485.9	460.8	466.1	488.7	481.3	507.5	488.1	534.0	582.9	573.4	Allemagne, Rép. féd.
Italy	149.2	133.3	128.5	134.3	131.0	134.0	125.0	141.9	147.9	136.6	Italie
United Kingdom	132.7	146.1	131.6	137.8	123.9	113.0	107.2	97.8	103.6	123.7	Royaume–Uni
EFTA	***313.5***	***249.3***	***273.2***	***291.2***	***253.6***	***245.3***	***240.7***	***266.3***	***290.2***	***282.1***	***AELE***
Finland	87.5	33.0	38.2	55.1	48.8	43.7	39.7	39.4	41.5	...	Finlande
Portugal* [1]	6.0	11.0	13.0	...	...	...	...	...	...	...	Portugal* [1]
Sweden	220.1	205.3	222.1	226.1	194.8	191.6	191.1	216.9	238.7	239.1	Suède
East Europe	***504.4***	***552.4***	***583.9***	***607.5***	***627.1***	***676.6***	***707.6***	***749.6***	***710.2***	***771.3***	***Europe de l'est***
Czechoslovakia	189.9	193.8	201.3	217.3	226.3	243.7	253.7	259.3	265.0	265.8	Tchécoslovaquie
Hungary	29.8	30.9	31.9	33.4	34.1	31.6	33.4	32.8	29.5	33.7	Hongrie
Poland[1]	...	...	...	...	...	219.1	219.1	236.9	175.9	...	Pologne[1]
Romania* [1]	72.0	115.0	138.0	144.0	154.0	...	...	...	...	...	Roumanie* [1]
Other Europe	***222.4***	***225.8***	***235.9***	***187.0***	***186.8***	***200.0***	***195.2***	***165.8***	***194.7***	***176.1***	***Autre Europe***
Spain	140.5	128.3	142.0	79.5	85.2	77.4	73.5	74.8	79.9	79.8	Espagne
Yugoslavia	81.9	97.5	93.9	107.5	101.6	122.6	121.7	91.0	114.8	96.2	Yougoslavie
Total	**5 120.4**	**5 329.1**	**5 576.9**	**5 559.8**	**5 461.8**	**5 446.0**	**5 011.8**	**5 407.5**	**5 688.8**	**5 748.7**	**Total**

General note.
Formaldehyde H.CHO saturated acyclic aldehyde also known as formalin or formol. (SITC 51241–2).

[1] Source: United Nations Economic Commission for Europe (ECE), (Geneva).

[2] 37% by weight.

Remarque générale.
Aldéhyde formique H.CHO, aldéhyde acyclique saturé, appelé aussi formal ou formol. (CTCI 51241–2).

[1] Source: Commission économique des Nations Unies pour l'Europe (CEE), (Genève).

[2] 37 p.100 en poids.

Acetone – Acétone

Unit : Thousand metric tons

Unité : Milliers de tonnes métriques

Country or area	1976	1977	1978	1979	1980	1981	1982	1983	1984	1985	Pays ou zone
America, North	**887.9**	**1 047.2**	**1 005.3**	**1 183.8**	**972.7**	**1 026.3**	**829.1**	**924.5**	**930.4**	**894.3**	**Amérique du Nord**
Canada	...	...	...	...	...	24.8	22.6	25.1	25.0	22.8	Canada
Mexico	14.9	15.8	21.2	24.2	25.8	28.9	38.1	49.7	49.5	53.7	Mexique
United States	847.7	1 006.3	959.3	1 134.9	...	972.5	768.5	849.7	855.9	817.8	Etats–Unis
America, South	**39.5**	**44.2**	**43.6**	**42.4**	**53.2**	**44.1**	**56.2**	**58.9**	**62.0**	**62.8**	**Amérique du Sud**
Brazil[1]	39.5	44.2	43.6	42.4	53.2	44.1	56.2	58.9	62.0	...	Brésil[1]
Asia	**257.2**	**263.4**	**289.0**	**281.5**	**256.6**	**251.8**	**254.2**	**282.9**	**279.9**	**270.1**	**Asie**
India	18.1	19.5	22.4	21.2	17.9	18.9	19.4	29.6	28.4	...	Inde
Japan	233.3	238.1	260.8	254.5	234.6	225.4	228.9	247.4	245.6	237.3	Japon
Korea, Republic of	...	...	...	...	4.1	7.5	...	...	...	...	Corée, République de
Europe	**358.2**	**358.8**	**372.0**	**387.9**	**342.1**	**344.7**	**369.1**	**360.9**	**406.6**	**398.0**	**Europe**
EEC	***260.2***	***266.6***	***267.0***	***270.0***	***221.9***	***217.5***	***243.1***	***229.7***	***265.8***	***249.2***	***CEE***
France	111.2	122.9	121.4	123.1	99.3	106.3	# 109.9	107.9	...	...	France
United Kingdom	149.0	143.7	145.6	146.9	122.6	111.2	133.2	121.8	161.5	146.8	Royaume–Uni
EFTA	***0.0***	***0.0***	***0.0***	***0.0***	***0.0***	***1.9***	***1.4***	***1.7***	***1.9***	***2.2***	***AELE***
Finland	0.0	0.0	0.0	0.0	0.0	1.9	...	...	...	...	Finlande
East Europe	***83.0***	***81.7***	***89.4***	***90.8***	***91.1***	***90.1***	***91.1***	***94.5***	***92.4***	***94.7***	***Europe de l'est***
Bulgaria	21.6	22.4	23.4	22.2	22.0	23.6	23.3	24.1	23.5	25.1	Bulgarie
Czechoslovakia	19.8	15.2	20.8	22.8	20.7	19.8	22.4	21.9	21.6	19.5	Tchécoslovaquie
German Dem. Rep.	22.2	22.9	23.2	22.8	24.5	24.7	25.1	25.2	25.4	28.7	Rép. dém. allemande
Poland	19.4	21.2	21.9	22.9	23.9	22.0	20.3	23.3	22.1	21.4	Pologne
Other Europe	***15.0***	***10.5***	***15.6***	***27.1***	***29.1***	***35.1***	***33.5***	***35.1***	***46.4***	***51.8***	***Autre Europe***
Spain	9.0	8.0	15.6	27.1	27.0	33.0	31.4	33.0	44.3	49.7	Espagne
Yugoslavia	6.0	2.5	0.0	0.0	...	...	...	...	...	...	Yougoslavie
Total	**1 542.8**	**1 713.7**	**1 710.0**	**1 895.7**	**1 624.5**	**1 666.9**	**1 508.5**	**1 627.2**	**1 678.9**	**1 625.1**	**Total**

General note.
Propanone CH3.CO.CH3. (SITC 51243–1).

[1] Production by main establishments only.

Remarque générale.
Propanone CH3.CO.CH3. (CTCI 51243–1).

[1] Production des principaux établissements seulement.

Acetates (methyl, ethyl, butyl) –
Acétates de méthyle, d'éthyle et de butyle

Unit : Thousand metric tons

Unité : Milliers de tonnes métriques

Country or area	1976	1977	1978	1979	1980	1981	1982	1983	1984	1985	Pays ou zone
America, North	**98.0**	**99.0**	**98.7**	**98.0**	**97.3**	**106.8**	**90.8**	**96.6**	**87.7**	**97.3**	**Amérique du Nord**
United States[1]	98.0	99.0	...	...	...	106.8	90.8	96.6	87.7	97.3	Etats-Unis[1]
America, South	**13.8**	**17.5**	**25.0**	**31.4**	**36.8**	**29.9**	**32.8**	**38.8**	**45.6**	**47.3**	**Amérique du Sud**
Brazil	13.8	17.5	25.0	31.4	36.8	29.9	32.8	38.8	45.6	...	Brésil
Asia	**120.9**	**131.9**	**125.6**	**147.6**	**135.4**	**135.0**	**122.5**	**136.7**	**154.8**	**152.7**	**Asie**
India[2]	4.9	4.4	3.0	4.8	6.3	6.1	6.1	4.7	4.2	...	Inde[2]
Japan	115.9	127.5	122.6	142.8	129.1	128.9	116.4	132.0	150.6	147.3	Japon
Europe	**264.8**	**259.5**	**265.8**	**273.0**	**269.2**	**242.9**	**235.7**	**248.1**	**279.3**	**288.1**	**Europe**
EEC	***220.8***	***214.4***	***225.3***	***228.0***	***225.0***	***206.4***	***202.3***	***213.7***	***248.2***	***256.7***	***CEE***
France	4.2	3.3	2.0	2.4	2.0	...	...	...	...	...	France
Germany, Fed. Rep.	128.1	127.7	165.3	161.1	157.9	142.3	127.3	133.9	154.5	157.1	Allemagne, Rép. féd.
Italy	88.6	83.3	58.1	64.6	65.1	61.9	73.0	78.1	92.1	98.2	Italie
EFTA	***13.2***	***12.2***	***8.4***	***11.4***	***9.2***	***5.6***	***7.6***	***4.2***	***1.5***	***1.6***	***AELE***
Sweden[2]	13.2	12.2	8.4	11.4	9.2	5.6	7.6	...	1.5	...	Suède[2]
East Europe	***9.4***	***9.2***	***8.7***	***7.9***	***8.3***	***8.2***	***8.6***	***8.5***	***8.6***	***9.1***	***Europe de l'est***
Czechoslovakia	8.0	7.9	8.1	7.4	8.2	8.2	8.6	8.5	8.6	9.1	Tchécoslovaquie
Hungary	1.4	1.2	0.6	0.5	0.1	0.0	0.0	0.0	0.0	0.0	Hongrie
Other Europe	***21.4***	***23.7***	***23.3***	***25.6***	***26.6***	***22.7***	***17.3***	***21.6***	***21.1***	***20.7***	***Autre Europe***
Spain	21.4	...	...	25.6	26.6	22.7	17.3	21.6	...	...	Espagne
Total	**497.4**	**507.8**	**515.1**	**550.0**	**538.8**	**514.6**	**481.8**	**520.1**	**567.5**	**585.4**	**Total**

General note.
Esters of acetic acid responding to the formula in which the hydrogen atom of the carboxyl group (COOH) is replaced by an alkyl or aryl radical. (SITC 51251-1).

[1] Ethyl acetate only.
[2] Ethyl and butyl acetates only.

Remarque générale.
Esters de l'acide acétique dans la formule desquels l'atome d'hydrogène du groupement carboxyde (COOH) est remplacé par un radical alkyle ou aryle. (CTCI 51251-1).

[1] Acétate d'éthyle seulement.
[2] Acétates d'éthyle et de butyle seulement.

Acetic acid – Acide acétique

Unit : Thousand metric tons

Unité : Milliers de tonnes métriques

Country or area	1976	1977	1978	1979	1980	1981	1982	1983	1984	1985	Pays ou zone
America, North	**1 136.5**	**1 202.1**	**1 320.8**	**1 574.4**	**1 424.2**	**1 479.2**	**1 359.0**	**1 395.8**	**1 351.0**	**1 464.7**	**Amérique du Nord**
Mexico	34.5	36.1	57.1	64.3	74.0	84.8	112.5	128.4	152.7	160.7	Mexique
United States	1 102.0	1 166.0	1 263.7	1 510.0	* 1 350.2	1 394.4	1 246.5	1 267.3	1 198.3	1 304.0	Etats–Unis
America, South	**28.5**	**39.7**	**49.3**	**53.7**	**61.3**	**53.6**	**60.7**	**69.2**	**79.9**	**81.5**	**Amérique du Sud**
Brazil	27.9	38.9	47.5	52.9	59.0	53.1	60.1	68.8	79.2	...	Brésil
Colombia	0.6	0.8	1.8	0.8	2.2	0.5	0.6	0.4	...	...	Colombie
Asia	**571.5**	**563.3**	**541.1**	**523.8**	**439.2**	**397.2**	**389.7**	**369.1**	**389.9**	**386.6**	**Asie**
India	25.0	23.4	26.7	25.1	24.1	34.7	38.8	42.6	41.7	...	Inde
Japan	544.9	538.3	512.8	497.1	413.4	361.1	349.4	324.9	346.6	340.5	Japon
Turkey[1]	...	...	...	...	1.6	1.5	...	...	...	...	Turquie[1]
Europe	**740.6**	**730.0**	**732.4**	**789.6**	**734.2**	**729.1**	**649.0**	**609.9**	**596.9**	**569.9**	**Europe**
EEC	***482.7***	***459.9***	***457.8***	***525.5***	***482.3***	***476.0***	***411.5***	***376.1***	***367.4***	***356.4***	***CEE***
Germany, Fed. Rep.	266.2	249.6	266.2	344.3	286.7	293.5	255.7	268.3	303.6	297.7	Allemagne, Rép. féd.
Italy	216.5	210.3	191.6	181.2	195.6	182.4	155.9	107.8	63.8	58.7	Italie
EFTA	***11.3***	***11.0***	***8.6***	***10.8***	***9.5***	***4.6***	***4.9***	***6.3***	***5.3***	***6.0***	***AELE***
Finland	0.8	0.4	0.5	0.6	2.0	2.5	2.4	3.2	3.3	...	Finlande
Sweden	10.5	10.5	8.2	10.2	7.5	2.0	2.5	3.1	2.0	2.3	Suède
East Europe	***212.4***	***209.6***	***206.4***	***200.1***	***204.3***	***206.3***	***202.8***	***207.0***	***199.4***	***196.3***	***Europe de l'est***
Bulgaria	0.4	0.4	0.5	0.5	0.6	0.7	0.7	0.6	0.4	0.6	Bulgarie
Czechoslovakia	22.6	21.7	21.0	17.7	20.1	22.9	17.9	18.7	19.0	19.5	Tchécoslovaquie
German Dem. Rep.	128.2	130.1	138.1	134.9	134.7	131.6	131.9	130.5	123.6	121.9	Rép. dém. allemande
Hungary	0.0	0.0	0.0	0.0	0.0	0.0	0.6	0.5	0.8	0.1	Hongrie
Poland	30.9	29.3	25.1	24.6	25.9	21.1	19.0	19.0	20.1	18.4	Pologne
Romania	30.2	28.1	21.6	22.4	23.0	30.0	32.7	37.8	35.5	35.8	Roumanie
Other Europe	***34.3***	***49.6***	***59.7***	***53.2***	***38.1***	***42.3***	***29.7***	***20.5***	***24.8***	***11.3***	***Autre Europe***
Spain	32.5	47.8	56.7	49.4	33.8	36.7	24.1	18.1	* 21.9	8.4	Espagne
Yugoslavia	1.8	1.8	3.0	3.8	4.3	5.5	* 5.6	2.4	2.9	2.9	Yougoslavie
USSR[1]	...	...	...	...	**239.0**	**297.0**	**308.0**	**339.0**	**343.0**	...	**URSS[1]**
Total	**2 633.5**	**2 716.3**	**2 849.7**	**3 172.3**	**2 898.0**	**2 956.2**	**2 766.4**	**2 783.0**	**2 760.8**	**2 882.3**	**Total**

General note.
CH3.COOH in terms of 100 per cent obtained by the dry distillation of wood or by synthesis. (SITC 51251–2).

[1] Source: United Nations Economic Commission for Europe (ECE), (Geneva).

Remarque générale.
Acide obtenu par synthèse ou par distillation sèche du bois. Poids exprimé sur la base de CH3.COOH pur. (CTCI 51251–2).

[1] Source: Commission économique des Nations Unies pour l'Europe (CEE), (Genève).

Formic acid – Acide formique

Unit : Thousand metric tons

Unité : Milliers de tonnes métriques

Country or area	1976	1977	1978	1979	1980	1981	1982	1983	1984	1985	Pays ou zone
America, South	**2.1**	**1.7**	**2.1**	**2.1**	**2.1**	**1.4**	**2.5**	**2.3**	**2.5**	**2.4**	**Amérique du Sud**
Brazil	2.1	1.7	2.1	2.1	2.1	1.4	2.5	2.3	2.5	...	Brésil
Asia	**8.7**	**9.9**	**10.7**	**11.6**	**12.2**	**11.4**	**10.9**	**11.4**	**12.3**	**11.6**	**Asie**
India	0.8	1.2	1.3	0.9	...	...	...	...	...	...	Inde
Japan	7.9	8.7	9.4	10.6	11.2	10.4	9.9	10.4	11.3	10.6	Japon
Europe	**77.0**	**72.8**	**81.3**	**92.7**	**96.0**	**87.0**	**92.2**	**118.0**	**132.8**	**134.3**	**Europe**
EEC	***54.2***	***50.8***	***59.1***	***68.6***	***73.4***	***69.6***	***74.1***	***91.0***	***99.8***	***108.5***	***CEE***
Germany, Fed. Rep.	48.5	48.0	57.1	65.8	70.0	66.3	70.8	87.7	96.5	105.1	Allemagne, Rép. féd.
Italy[1]	5.7	2.8	2.0	2.8	...	...	...	...	...	...	Italie[1]
EFTA	***12.7***	***12.0***	***12.0***	***13.6***	***12.4***	***7.0***	***7.8***	***16.7***	***22.7***	***15.7***	***AELE***
Finland	...	...	...	...	...	1.0	3.0	11.6	16.3	...	Finlande
Sweden	4.7	4.0	4.0	5.6	4.5	6.1	4.8	5.1	6.5	7.7	Suède
East Europe	***10.1***	***10.1***	***10.2***	***10.5***	***10.2***	***10.4***	***10.3***	***10.2***	***10.3***	***10.2***	***Europe de l'est***
Czechoslovakia	10.1	10.1	10.2	10.5	10.2	10.4	10.3	10.2	10.3	10.2	Tchécoslovaquie
Total	**87.8**	**84.5**	**94.1**	**106.4**	**110.3**	**99.8**	**105.6**	**131.7**	**147.6**	**148.3**	**Total**

General note.
H.COOH in terms of 100 per cent either native or obtained by synthesis. (SITC 51251-3).

[1] Source: Industrial Statistics, Statistical Office of the European Communities, (Luxembourg).

Remarque générale.
Sur la base de H.COOH pur, naturel ou synthétique. (CTCI 51251-3).

[1] Source: Statistiques industrielles, Office statistique des Communautés européennes, (Luxembourg).

Phthalic anhydride – Anhydride phtalique

Unit : Thousand metric tons

Unité : Milliers de tonnes métriques

Country or area	1976	1977	1978	1979	1980	1981	1982	1983	1984	1985	Pays ou zone
America, North	**430.5**	**441.1**	**468.8**	**486.6**	**398.2**	**422.7**	**337.9**	**414.4**	**425.5**	**418.9**	**Amérique du Nord**
Mexico	21.2	21.1	23.8	26.6	27.2	28.3	27.5	28.9	32.5	39.9	Mexique
United States	409.3	420.0	* 445.0	460.0	* 371.0	394.4	310.4	385.6	393.0	379.1	Etats–Unis
America, South	**56.2**	**53.3**	**60.8**	**76.3**	**80.3**	**80.8**	**86.6**	**78.5**	**82.8**	**92.7**	**Amérique du Sud**
Brazil	35.9	36.1	44.2	59.5	62.6	58.8	65.3	59.9	62.6	...	Brésil
Colombia	5.9	2.3	3.2	4.5	4.3	3.9	5.6	2.6	...	...	Colombie
Venezuela	14.3	14.9	13.4	12.3	13.5	18.0	...	...	...	...	Venezuela
Asia	**272.0**	**290.6**	**330.2**	**328.0**	**284.9**	**314.9**	**321.6**	**321.6**	**338.7**	**371.8**	**Asie**
India	11.6	19.1	20.5	21.8	29.1	24.2	27.7	35.6	27.3	...	Inde
Japan	249.1	259.8	288.1	283.7	235.2	253.8	253.6	242.0	259.3	278.9	Japon
Korea, Republic of	11.3	11.7	21.7	22.5	20.6	36.8	40.3	43.9	52.0	58.0	Corée, République de
Europe	**732.6**	**744.6**	**781.2**	**773.9**	**668.8**	**704.7**	**695.1**	**677.9**	**652.0**	**594.7**	**Europe**
EEC	***587.3***	***575.3***	***594.5***	***604.1***	***488.8***	***493.2***	***480.3***	***453.7***	***415.1***	***376.1***	***CEE***
France	83.7	86.7	88.7	87.5	77.0	[1] 76.1	[1] 72.4	...	...	...	France
Germany, Fed. Rep.	253.1	246.3	267.1	267.3	224.4	215.6	199.4	195.0	205.7	171.7	Allemagne, Rép. féd.
Italy	146.5	144.0	147.9	153.8	141.1	140.4	135.5	135.5	96.2	101.0	Italie
United Kingdom	...	98.2	90.9	95.5	46.3	61.1	73.0	...	...	...	Royaume–Uni
EFTA	***12.8***	***13.3***	***30.3***	***7.2***	***9.7***	***13.6***	***14.8***	***18.0***	***17.8***	***18.2***	***AELE***
Portugal*	...	...	...	...	...	...	...	...	1.5	...	Portugal*
Sweden	11.3	11.8	28.7	5.7	8.2	12.0	13.3	16.5	16.3	16.6	Suède
East Europe	***100.8***	***99.0***	***99.3***	***98.6***	***114.5***	***123.4***	***122.7***	***123.9***	***134.3***	***136.3***	***Europe de l'est***
Bulgaria	0.1	0.0	0.0	3.0	7.2	8.3	12.0	15.9	16.9	14.1	Bulgarie
Czechoslovakia	24.2	23.5	24.8	24.8	24.6	23.9	23.6	21.2	27.1	30.3	Tchécoslovaquie
Hungary	6.3	6.4	6.2	6.7	17.1	23.3	20.9	22.3	24.0	23.2	Hongrie
Poland	36.2	33.6	32.9	33.7	33.0	32.4	31.6	30.7	32.4	35.2	Pologne
Romania	34.0	35.5	35.6	30.4	32.6	35.5	34.6	33.7	33.9	33.5	Roumanie
Other Europe	***31.7***	***57.1***	***57.1***	***64.0***	***55.8***	***74.5***	***77.2***	***82.4***	***84.9***	***64.2***	***Autre Europe***
Spain	30.2	55.7	47.5	47.8	39.0	52.9	54.9	52.1	49.9	31.0	Espagne
Yugoslavia	1.6	1.4	9.6	16.2	16.8	21.6	22.3	30.3	34.9	33.2	Yougoslavie
USSR[1]	**...**	**...**	**...**	**...**	**175.0**	**189.0**	**185.0**	**202.0**	**216.0**	**...**	**URSS[1]**
Total	**1 628.2**	**1 675.9**	**1 796.9**	**1 829.9**	**1 607.2**	**1 712.1**	**1 626.2**	**1 694.5**	**1 715.0**	**1 699.9**	**Total**

General note.
Pure C6H4(CO)2O. (SITC 51252–1).

Remarque générale.
C6H4(CO)2O, pur. (CTCI 51252–1).

[1] Source: United Nations Economic Commission for Europe (ECE), (Geneva).

[1] Source: Commission économique des Nations Unies pour l'Europe (CEE), (Genève).

Acetylsalicylic acid (aspirin) – Acide acétyl-salicylique (aspirin)

Unit : Metric tons

Unité : Tonnes métriques

Country or area	1976	1977	1978	1979	1980	1981	1982	1983	1984	1985	Pays ou zone
America, North	**12 800**	**14 200**	**14 598**	**14 616**	**13 287**	**13 452**	**10 261**	**13 949**	**13 996**	**10 573**	**Amérique du Nord**
United States	12 800	14 200	14 598	14 616	...	13 452	10 261	13 949	13 996	10 573	Etats-Unis
America, South	**587**	**582**	**620**	**604**	**602**	**609**	**542**	**327**	**624**	**502**	**Amérique du Sud**
Brazil	415	410	448	432	430	437	370	155	452	...	Brésil
Colombia	172	...	...	...	...	...	...	...	...	...	Colombie
Asia	**1 042**	**1 065**	**1 295**	**1 092**	**834**	**1 065**	**1 065**	**1 065**	**1 065**	**1 065**	**Asie**
India	1 042	...	1 295	1 092	834	...	...	...	...	...	Inde
Europe	**592**	**930**	**930**	**930**	**930**	**1 050**	**1 205**	**874**	**930**	**930**	**Europe**
Other Europe	***592***	***930***	***930***	***930***	***930***	***1 050***	***1 205***	***874***	***930***	***930***	***Autre Europe***
Spain	592	...	...	...	...	1 050	1 205	874	...	...	Espagne
Total	**15 021**	**16 777**	**17 443**	**17 242**	**15 653**	**16 176**	**13 073**	**16 215**	**16 615**	**13 070**	**Total**

General note.
C2H3O2C6H4CO2H, also known as ortho-acetoxy-benzoic acid (aspirin). (SITC 51253-1).

Remarque générale.
C2H3O2C6H4CO2H, connu aussi sous les noms d'acide ortho-acétoxybenzoïque ou d'aspirine. (CTCI 51253-1).

Tartaric acid – Acides tartriques

Unit : Metric tons

Unité : Tonnes métriques

Country or area	1976	1977	1978	1979	1980	1981	1982	1983	1984	1985	Pays ou zone
America, South	**5 320**	**4 146**	**4 729**	**4 568**	**4 401**	**3 802**	**4 273**	**4 421**	**3 292**	**2 989**	**Amérique du Sud**
Argentina	5 159	3 952	4 568	4 407	4 273	3 641	4 112	4 260	3 131	2 828	Argentine
Brazil	...	[1] 194	...	...	128	...	...	...	...	...	Brésil
Asia	**858**	**821**	**859**	**983**	**1 142**	**999**	**926**	**870**	**858**	**948**	**Asie**
Japan	853	816	854	978	1 137	993	920	865	853	...	Japon
Korea, Republic of	...	...	...	...	5	6	6	...	...	...	Corée, République de
Europe	**13 397**	**12 678**	**8 828**	**3 928**	**6 813**	**7 179**	**6 547**	**7 122**	**4 932**	**4 274**	**Europe**
EEC	***5 709***	***3 598***	***2 701***	***1 253***	***3 233***	***3 234***	***3 290***	***3 284***	***3 279***	***3 269***	***CEE***
Denmark	...	...	...	...	...	4	3	4	6	3	Danemark
Greece	156	99	74	0	0	0	...	...	...	...	Grèce
Italy	5 550	3 496	2 624	1 250	...	...	...	...	...	...	Italie
East Europe	***245***	***233***	***237***	***218***	***260***	***199***	***242***	***209***	***151***	***234***	***Europe de l'est***
Czechoslovakia	189	199	187	155	232	199	242	209	151	234	Tchécoslovaquie
Hungary	56	34	50	63	28	0	0	0	0	0	Hongrie
Other Europe	***7 443***	***8 847***	***5 890***	***2 457***	***3 320***	***3 746***	***3 015***	***3 629***	***1 502***	***771***	***Autre Europe***
Spain	7 443	8 847	...	2 457	3 320	3 746	3 015	3 629	...	...	Espagne
Total	**19 575**	**17 645**	**14 416**	**9 479**	**12 356**	**11 980**	**11 746**	**12 413**	**9 082**	**8 211**	**Total**

General note.
HOOC.CH(OH).CH(OH).COOH (SITC 51253-2).

Remarque générale.
COOH.CH(OH).CH(OH).COOH pur. (CTCI 51253-2).

[1] Production by establishments employing 5 or more persons.

[1] Production des établissements occupant 5 personnes ou plus.

Aniline

Unit : Metric tons

Unité : Tonnes métriques

Country or area	1976	1977	1978	1979	1980	1981	1982	1983	1984	1985	Pays ou zone
America, North	**267 911**	**286 752**	**277 150**	**315 126**	**296 131**	**289 839**	**254 782**	**303 354**	**358 242**	**346 047**	**Amérique du Nord**
Mexico	1 660	1 819	2 377	2 246	2 073	2 130	1 937	1 909	1 700	2 144	Mexique
United States	...	284 933	274 773	312 880	...	287 709	252 845	301 445	356 542	343 903	Etats–Unis
America, South	**25 195**	**22 679**	**20 496**	**22 898**	**22 817**	**22 817**	**22 817**	**22 817**	**22 817**	**22 817**	**Amérique du Sud**
Brazil	25 195	22 679	20 496	[1] 22 898	...	...	...	...	...	...	Brésil
Asia	**58 969**	**63 931**	**81 731**	**86 289**	**83 675**	**76 630**	**83 691**	**104 891**	**108 405**	**102 051**	**Asie**
India	5 535	7 659	9 062	...	...	...	...	...	...	...	Inde
Japan	53 434	56 272	72 669	78 871	76 257	69 212	76 273	97 473	100 987	94 633	Japon
Europe	**162 567**	**177 084**	**170 913**	**190 162**	**160 035**	**154 489**	**168 491**	**184 776**	**213 161**	**219 352**	**Europe**
EEC	***148 808***	***158 994***	***149 205***	***166 131***	***133 574***	***132 125***	***140 753***	***150 487***	***169 636***	***167 669***	***CEE***
Germany, Fed. Rep.	148 808	158 994	149 205	166 131	133 574	132 125	140 753	150 487	169 636	167 669	Allemagne, Rép. féd.
EFTA	***5 336***	***8 142***	***10 948***	***13 754***	***15 139***	***11 985***	***18 205***	***24 729***	***33 208***	***33 305***	***AELE***
Portugal	...	...	...	...	15 139	11 985	18 205	24 729	33 208	33 305	Portugal
East Europe	***8 423***	***9 948***	***10 760***	***10 277***	***11 322***	***10 379***	***9 533***	***9 560***	***10 317***	***18 378***	***Europe de l'est***
Czechoslovakia	7 053	7 479	7 794	7 730	8 323	8 262	9 533	9 560	10 317	18 378	Tchécoslovaquie
Hungary	1 370	2 469	2 966	2 547	2 999	2 117	0	0	0	0	Hongrie
Total	**514 642**	**550 446**	**550 290**	**614 475**	**562 658**	**543 775**	**529 781**	**615 838**	**702 625**	**690 267**	**Total**

General note.
$C6H5NH2$, phenylamine, aromatic monoamine. (SITC 51271–1).

[1] Production by establishments employing 5 or more persons.

Remarque générale.
$C6H5NH2$, phénylamine, monoamine aromatique. (CTCI 51271–1).

[1] Production des établissements occupant 5 personnes ou plus.

Acrylonitrile

Unit : Thousand metric tons

Unité : Milliers de tonnes métriques

Country or area	1976	1977	1978	1979	1980	1981	1982	1983	1984	1985	Pays ou zone
America, North	**753.4**	**766.0**	**813.6**	**938.6**	**884.3**	**959.6**	**976.2**	**1 028.6**	**1 047.5**	**1 113.1**	**Amérique du Nord**
Mexico	22.0	19.3	19.1	23.3	54.3	54.0	53.0	55.0	49.0	49.0	Mexique
United States	...	746.6	794.5	915.3	830.1	905.5	923.2	973.6	998.5	1 064.1	Etats-Unis
America, South	**0.0**	**0.0**	**0.0**	**3.0**	**49.7**	**56.5**	**57.1**	**57.6**	**69.6**	**84.2**	**Amérique du Sud**
Brazil	0.0	0.0	0.0	3.0	49.7	56.5	57.1	57.6	69.6	...	Brésil
Asia	**668.0**	**629.1**	**656.4**	**658.8**	**525.2**	**527.4**	**531.2**	**503.8**	**570.1**	**591.6**	**Asie**
Japan	633.4	595.7	609.3	578.7	468.6	477.2	488.6	459.1	522.5	540.9	Japon
Korea, Republic of	34.7	33.4	47.1	80.1	56.5	50.1	42.7	44.7	47.6	50.8	Corée, République de
Europe	**766.0**	**689.8**	**811.2**	**765.5**	**721.0**	**706.5**	**692.6**	**689.6**	**703.0**	**699.0**	**Europe**
EEC	***627.5***	***550.4***	***633.4***	***588.2***	***570.3***	***551.3***	***540.2***	***526.9***	***513.6***	***500.3***	***CEE***
Germany, Fed. Rep.[1]	442.4	383.7	452.1	452.9	...	...	...	...	...	...	Allemagne, Rép. féd.[1]
Italy	185.1	166.7	181.3	135.4	137.5	118.5	...	...	...	...	Italie
EFTA	***0.2***	***0.1***	***0.1***	***0.1***	***0.0***	***0.0***	***0.0***	***0.0***	***0.0***	***0.0***	***AELE***
Sweden	0.2	0.1	0.1	0.1	0.0	0.0	0.0	0.0	0.0	...	Suède
East Europe	***82.4***	***91.7***	***105.1***	***97.9***	***85.5***	***96.6***	***93.8***	***99.4***	***105.9***	***111.8***	***Europe de l'est***
Bulgaria	...	26.3	28.1	27.5	* 26.9	26.3	27.0	25.0	26.3	25.2	Bulgarie
Poland	13.1	12.7	13.2	12.2	12.4	9.5	9.7	12.8	13.1	12.6	Pologne
Romania	41.6	52.6	63.7	58.3	46.2	60.8	57.1	61.6	...	74.0	Roumanie
Other Europe	***55.8***	***47.6***	***72.7***	***79.2***	***65.2***	***58.6***	***58.6***	***63.2***	***83.5***	***86.9***	***Autre Europe***
Spain	...	47.6	72.7	* 79.2	* 65.2	58.6	58.6	63.2	83.5	86.9	Espagne
Total	**2 187.5**	**2 084.9**	**2 281.3**	**2 366.0**	**2 180.2**	**2 250.0**	**2 257.1**	**2 279.5**	**2 390.2**	**2 488.0**	**Total**

General note.
Pure CH2=CHCN. Acrylonitrile polymers and co-polymers are excluded. (SITC 51276-1).

[1] Beginning 1980, data are confidential.

Remarque générale.
H2C=CHCN pur, à l'exclusion des polymères et copolymères de l'acrylonitrile. (CTCI 51276-1).

[1] A partir de 1980, les données sont confidentielles.

Chlorine – Chlore

Unit : Thousand metric tons — Unité : Milliers de tonnes métriques

Country or area	1976	1977	1978	1979	1980	1981	1982	1983	1984	1985	Pays ou zone
Africa	**11**	**12**	**11**	**13**	**23**	**21**	**24**	**28**	**30**	**32**	**Afrique**
Algeria	6	7	7	7	17	15	18	...	...	...	Algérie
Egypt	5	5	4	6	6	6	6	8	...	...	Egypte
America, North	**10 168**	**10 652**	**11 142**	**12 352**	**11 833**	**11 301**	**9 862**	**10 636**	**11 404**	**11 164**	**Amérique du Nord**
Canada	898	888	941	1 031	1 303	1 292	1 233	1 385	1 424	1 424	Canada
Cuba	2	2	2	2	1	3	3	4	4	3	Cuba
Mexico	142	172	175	171	170	241	303	300	299	302	Mexique
United States	9 126	9 590	10 024	11 148	10 359	9 765	8 323	8 947	9 677	9 435	Etats–Unis
America, South	**258**	**345**	**569**	**633**	**660**	**716**	**754**	**745**	**852**	**952**	**Amérique du Sud**
Brazil	226	313	536	587	628	684	725	713	819	...	Brésil
Chile	25	23	27	38	25	25	22	24	26	26	Chili
Colombia	7	9	6	8	7	7	7	8	...	...	Colombie
Asia	**931**	**996**	**1 002**	**1 099**	**1 171**	**1 220**	**1 256**	**1 319**	**1 445**	**1 515**	**Asie**
Bangladesh[1]	4	3	4	4	3	4	4	4	4	5	Bangladesh[1]
India	180	201	219	212	227	244	254	272	305	315	Inde
Israel	23	26	22	26	35	34	30	29	31	33	Israël
Japan[2]	666	689	651	729	763	764	794	818	897	926	Japon[2]
Korea, Republic of	...	...	...	...	89	121	122	145	166	183	Corée, République de
Kuwait	4	4	7	8	8	8	8	9	8	10	Koweït
Pakistan[1]	6	4	6	8	9	8	8	8	8	...	Pakistan[1]
Sri Lanka	1	1	1	1	1	1	1	1	1	0	Sri Lanka
Turkey	22	25	28	28	28	28	27	24	17	...	Turquie
Europe	**8 692**	**8 746**	**8 933**	**9 292**	**8 915**	**8 689**	**8 568**	**9 315**	**9 350**	**9 543**	**Europe**
EEC	***6 611***	***6 624***	***6 678***	***6 977***	***6 602***	***6 384***	***6 343***	***6 905***	***6 815***	***6 886***	***CEE***
Denmark	11	11	14	16	14	16	17	18	19	...	Danemark
France	1 687	1 742	1 779	1 834	1 822	1 748	1 840	1 928	# 1 410	1 392	France
Germany, Fed. Rep.	2 809	2 808	3 011	3 202	2 997	3 013	2 842	3 136	3 426	3 493	Allemagne, Rép. féd.
Greece	28	31	31	30	30	29	29	26	28	...	Grèce
Italy[3]	1 022	998	883	867	828	707	735	897	952	923	Italie[3]
United Kingdom	1 054	1 034	960	1 028	911	871	880	900	980	1 031	Royaume–Uni
EFTA	***643***	***596***	***693***	***758***	***761***	***747***	***690***	***782***	***846***	***914***	***AELE***
Finland	154	159	193	221	241	257	188	186	202	...	Finlande
Norway[4]	66	64	89	150	161	153	...	199	214	...	Norvège[4]
Portugal	35	38	35	39	44	45	49	60	67	70	Portugal
Sweden	388	335	376	348	315	292	272	337	363	378	Suède
East Europe	***971***	***1 057***	***1 086***	***1 049***	***1 051***	***1 049***	***1 011***	***1 073***	***1 087***	***1 098***	***Europe de l'est***
Czechoslovakia[2]	264	282	283	282	295	300	293	299	298	302	Tchécoslovaquie[2]
Hungary	13	14	21	23	17	17	21	25	24	23	Hongrie
Poland	265	322	350	329	309	303	268	320	336	344	Pologne
Romania[4]	...	439	432	415	430	...	...	...	...	...	Roumanie[4]
Other Europe	***467***	***469***	***476***	***508***	***501***	***509***	***524***	***555***	***602***	***645***	***Autre Europe***
Spain	428	424	431	454	428	396	416	441	471	506	Espagne
Yugoslavia	39	45	45	54	73	113	108	114	131	139	Yougoslavie
Oceania	**115**	**111**	**106**	**112**	**111**	**111**	**111**	**111**	**111**	**111**	**Océanie**
Australia[1]	115	111	106	112	...	...	...	...	...	...	Australie[1]
Total	**20 175**	**20 862**	**21 763**	**23 501**	**22 713**	**22 058**	**20 576**	**22 154**	**23 192**	**23 317**	**Total**

General note.
Gas usually obtained by electrolysis of alkali chlorides, especially sodium chloride. (SITC 51321–0).

[1] Twelve months ending 30 June of year stated.
[2] Liquid chlorine only.
[3] Excluding chlorine used in production of calcium hypochlorite and sodium hypochlorite.
[4] Source: United Nations Economic Commission for Europe (ECE), (Geneva).

Remarque générale.
Gaz généralement obtenu par électrolyse des chlorures alcalins, particulièrement du chlorure de sodium. (CTCI 51321–0).

[1] Période de douze mois finissant le 30 juin de l'année indiquée.
[2] Chlore liquide seulement.
[3] Non compris le chlore utilisé pour fabriquer de l'hypochlorite de calcium et de l'hypochlorite de sodium.
[4] Source: Commission économique des Nations Unies pour l'Europe (CEE), (Genève).

Hydrochloric acid – Acide chlorhydrique

Unit : Thousand metric tons

Unité : Milliers de tonnes métriques

Country or area	1976	1977	1978	1979	1980	1981	1982	1983	1984	1985	Pays ou zone
Africa	**126.8**	**127.6**	**125.5**	**126.7**	**144.7**	**113.1**	**116.7**	**116.9**	**128.3**	**132.3**	**Afrique**
Algeria	1.5	# 5.2	5.5	6.1	11.2	11.8	* 12.3	* 11.5	...	...	Algérie
Egypt	3.4	3.1	3.3	4.2	5.6	6.0	6.7	7.4	...	...	Egypte
South Africa	...	...	...	116.4	127.9	95.3	97.6	98.0	105.3	107.1	Afrique du Sud
America, North	**2 391.5**	**2 643.4**	**2 792.6**	**3 083.3**	**2 930.1**	**2 656.5**	**2 509.6**	**2 553.2**	**2 751.5**	**2 869.2**	**Amérique du Nord**
Canada	109.5	136.2	154.6	154.4	176.8	185.7	143.1	169.9	161.3	157.6	Canada
Cuba	7.0	7.2	7.4	7.1	7.0	8.0	9.6	11.6	12.4	11.4	Cuba
Mexico	72.1	79.6	97.4	119.1	127.0	127.9	134.5	133.3	135.6	154.2	Mexique
United States	2 202.9	2 420.3	2 533.2	2 802.7	2 619.4	2 334.9	2 222.5	2 238.3	2 442.2	2 546.0	Etats-Unis
America, South	**104.0**	**171.1**	**194.4**	**170.2**	**123.9**	**221.8**	**145.3**	**105.0**	**137.9**	**143.1**	**Amérique du Sud**
Bolivia	0.1	0.1	0.2	0.2	...	0.7	0.4	0.6	0.8	...	Bolivie
Brazil	91.7	159.9	178.5	153.5	108.2	207.2	129.8	90.1	121.9	...	Brésil
Chile	6.0	4.8	7.9	8.6	...	...	...	...	...	...	Chili
Colombia[1]	6.3	6.3	7.7	7.9	8.5	7.1	8.2	7.5	...	...	Colombie[1]
Asia	**1 730.5**	**1 847.4**	**1 983.0**	**1 990.6**	**2 118.4**	**2 183.0**	**2 433.1**	**2 541.4**	**2 775.3**	**2 900.3**	**Asie**
Bangladesh[2]	1.7	1.5	1.7	1.9	2.2	2.5	1.1	1.4	1.5	1.4	Bangladesh[2]
China	...	962.0	1 115.0	1 078.0	1 177.0	1 292.0	1 483.0	1 583.0	1 704.0	1 856.0	Chine
India	228.3	179.1	200.9	201.6	193.8	116.8	155.4	149.4	215.6	...	Inde
Indonesia	3.8	1.3	1.7	4.0	12.0	12.0	8.4	7.9	14.4	...	Indonésie
Iran(Islamic Rep.of)	30.2	...	...	...	...	...	...	...	...	...	Iran(Rép.islamique)
Japan	486.7	487.4	455.5	489.7	528.6	528.2	548.5	560.1	593.4	624.7	Japon
Korea, Republic of	43.9	45.2	43.4	39.1	31.0	42.3	42.7	50.9	58.3	...	Corée, République de
Philippines	...	...	...	...	...	58.4	...	...	...	...	Philippines
Sri Lanka	0.6	0.5	0.7	1.0	1.5	1.3	# 0.6	0.6	0.6	0.0	Sri Lanka
Thailand[1]	59.5	71.8	66.6	76.2	72.6	87.4	90.5	85.9	84.9	...	Thaïlande[1]
Turkey[1]	3.4	3.1	2.8	3.7	4.1	5.0	7.4	...	...	...	Turquie[1]
Viet Nam	7.9	6.9	6.1	6.7	...	...	...	...	...	...	Viet Nam
Europe	**2 412.9**	**2 486.0**	**2 547.5**	**2 676.7**	**2 620.7**	**2 656.7**	**2 590.7**	**2 690.4**	**2 869.9**	**2 880.3**	**Europe**
EEC	***1 794.0***	***1 824.4***	***1 868.4***	***1 960.1***	***1 892.0***	***1 902.1***	***1 827.8***	***1 913.1***	***2 029.1***	***1 981.1***	***CEE***
Denmark	1.7	4.2	3.8	3.0	3.0	7.3	7.0	...	...	...	Danemark
France	210.9	229.1	233.1	243.6	229.8	238.4	# 212.5	242.5	261.1	230.3	France
Germany, Fed. Rep.	869.6	857.4	891.6	945.3	890.7	887.9	847.5	899.9	956.4	945.2	Allemagne, Rép. féd.
Greece	34.6	39.9	46.3	51.4	52.6	49.7	40.1	40.5	48.8	...	Grèce
Italy	512.4	523.8	530.2	...	...	...	...	...	...	...	Italie
Netherlands	26.9	29.7	31.8	36.9	56.4	79.8	80.0	70.5	76.0	74.5	Pays-Bas
United Kingdom[3]	137.9	140.4	131.7	157.7	137.3	116.8	118.4	130.2	156.6	151.6	Royaume-Uni[3]
EFTA	***120.1***	***128.4***	***129.6***	***133.6***	***131.0***	***138.7***	***136.6***	***144.5***	***137.0***	***149.6***	***AELE***
Finland[4]	4.7	2.4	5.8	6.6	6.9	7.2	7.9	7.2	11.7	...	Finlande[4]
Portugal	46.3	55.9	54.4	54.4	53.6	58.4	56.7	61.9	47.2	53.6	Portugal
Sweden	69.1	70.1	69.4	72.7	70.5	73.0	72.0	75.4	78.1	85.3	Suède
East Europe	***319.5***	***331.6***	***351.2***	***365.1***	***379.9***	***388.3***	***397.0***	***408.7***	***449.8***	***472.0***	***Europe de l'est***
Bulgaria	7.9	10.2	12.3	12.9	15.4	16.5	17.2	18.0	22.2	22.8	Bulgarie
Czechoslovakia	50.8	54.7	61.9	65.6	72.2	70.4	71.5	71.9	73.0	75.6	Tchécoslovaquie
German Dem. Rep.	107.4	107.7	103.4	105.2	106.0	104.1	106.0	115.5	135.3	136.8	Rép. dém. allemande
Hungary	22.0	21.8	25.0	24.7	23.4	28.4	32.0	32.1	35.2	36.2	Hongrie
Poland	51.1	55.0	64.2	69.3	70.5	64.8	55.0	56.7	50.4	57.6	Pologne
Romania	80.3	82.2	84.5	87.4	92.5	104.0	115.2	114.6	133.8	143.0	Roumanie
Other Europe	***179.3***	***201.5***	***198.3***	***217.9***	***217.9***	***227.7***	***229.4***	***224.1***	***253.9***	***277.6***	***Autre Europe***
Spain	132.9	143.7	128.5	145.0	138.7	141.0	140.0	135.3	160.0	165.0	Espagne
Yugoslavia	46.4	57.8	69.8	72.9	79.2	86.7	89.4	88.8	93.9	112.6	Yougoslavie
Oceania	**47.0**	**47.7**	**50.2**	**55.0**	**62.7**	**59.0**	**54.6**	**61.0**	**58.9**	**57.9**	**Océanie**
Australia[2]	47.0	47.7	50.2	55.0	62.7	59.0	54.6	61.0	58.9	57.9	Australie[2]
Total	**6 812.7**	**7 323.1**	**7 693.2**	**8 102.3**	**8 000.5**	**7 890.2**	**7 849.9**	**8 067.8**	**8 721.8**	**8 983.1**	**Total**

For general note and footnotes, see end of table.

Voir la fin du tableau pour la remarque générale et les notes.

General note.
HCl in all forms, in terms of 100 per cent HCl. Chloro–sulphuric acids are excluded. (SITC 51331–1).

[1] Strength of acid not known.
[2] Twelve months ending 30 June of year stated.
[3] Sales by manufacturers employing 25 or more persons.
[4] Original data in 33 per cent HCl.

Remarque générale.
HCl sous toutes ses formes sur la base de 100 p. 100 de HCl, à l'exclusion de l'acide chlorosulfonique. (CTCI 51331–1).

[1] Titre de l'acide inconnu.
[2] Période de douze mois finissant le 30 juin de l'année indiquée.
[3] Ventes des fabricants employant 25 personnes ou plus.
[4] Données d'origine en HCl de 33 p. 100.

Sulphuric acid – Acide sulfurique

Unit : Thousand metric tons | Unité : Milliers de tonnes métriques

Country or area	1976	1977	1978	1979	1980	1981	1982	1983	1984	1985	Pays ou zone
Africa	**1 980**	**2 283**	**2 376**	**2 787**	**3 007**	**3 524**	**3 772**	**4 214**	**4 138**	**3 883**	**Afrique**
Algeria	23	52	44	191	97	56	192	* 200	...	...	Algérie
Côte d'Ivoire	...	...	1	0	1	1	1	1	1	...	Côte d'Ivoire
Egypt	27	30	33	33	35	44	46	45	47	...	Egypte
Morocco[1]	358	526	694	695	806	768	665	727	758	660	Maroc[1]
Mozambique	...	...	9	9	6	14	11	1	0	...	Mozambique
Tunisia	1 081	1 208	1 238	1 476	1 634	2 221	2 456	2 808	2 716	2 559	Tunisie
Uganda	1	1	1	1	0	0	0	...	...	...	Ouganda
Zaire	173	172	138	* 135	150	144	146	* 160	* 153	* 150	Zaïre
Zambia	303	281	218	247	278	276	255	271	255	229	Zambie
America, North	**35 903**	**40 624**	**43 555**	**45 205**	**47 121**	**44 113**	**36 304**	**41 027**	**45 505**	**43 565**	**Amérique du Nord**
Canada	2 842	3 140	3 261	3 666	4 295	4 117	3 085	3 679	4 043	3 890	Canada
Cuba	392	375	347	296	401	413	332	356	336	373	Cuba
El Salvador	12	28	88	1	1	0	0	4	...	...	El Salvador
Jamaica	19	...	...	...	...	11	12	17	...	...	Jamaïque
Mexico	2 178	2 295	2 372	2 041	2 359	2 619	2 732	2 996	3 196	3 322	Mexique
United States[2]	30 460	34 771	37 472	39 186	40 050	36 953	30 143	33 975	37 914	35 964	Etats-Unis[2]
America, South	**2 014**	**2 107**	**2 189**	**2 553**	**3 030**	**3 197**	**3 452**	**3 784**	**4 288**	**4 349**	**Amérique du Sud**
Argentina	234	251	244	279	250	232	250	262	254	235	Argentine
Bolivia	1	0	6	0	0	1	1	1	1	...	Bolivie
Brazil	1 439	1 556	1 596	1 910	2 408	2 516	2 681	2 983	3 484	...	Brésil
Chile[1]	130	132	127	100	...	...	...	...	...	...	Chili[1]
Colombia	49	42	45	54	59	49	40	53	...	...	Colombie
Peru	65	70	65	68	62	184	231	210	* 205	* 213	Pérou
Uruguay[3]	...	...	...	...	14	...	...	...	...	...	Uruguay[3]
Venezuela	82	42	92	128	114	79	113	139	157	157	Venezuela
Asia	**14 268**	**16 070**	**17 746**	**18 863**	**19 235**	**18 921**	**20 002**	**20 551**	**20 652**	**19 586**	**Asie**
Bangladesh[4]	4	3	5	13	4	4	2	3	4	4	Bangladesh[4]
China	4 508	5 375	6 610	6 998	7 643	7 807	8 175	8 696	8 172	6 764	Chine
India	1 635	2 017	2 086	2 228	2 217	2 278	2 391	2 388	2 732	...	Inde
Indonesia	8	17	16	11	19	15	34	35	44	...	Indonésie
Iran(Islamic Rep.of)[5]	351	* 260	* 200	* 100	* 100	* 70	* 100	* 150	* 200	* 200	Iran(Rép.islamique)[5]
Israel	208	198	183	226	209	182	154	171	189	178	Israël
Japan	6 095	6 392	6 437	6 582	6 777	6 572	6 531	6 662	6 458	6 580	Japon
Korea, Republic of	696	1 034	1 461	1 645	1 702	1 304	1 596	1 610	1 975	2 028	Corée, République de
Kuwait	5	1	0	18	2	5	9	7	4	5	Koweït
Pakistan[4]	46	45	52	65	67	71	72	71	81	82	Pakistan[4]
Philippines	280	267	168	210	...	...	...	...	...	...	Philippines
Saudi Arabia	0	10	13	14	27	39	50	63	71	...	Arabie saoudite
Thailand[1]	46	56	60	60	54	34	49	56	63	66	Thaïlande[1]
Turkey	381	384	442	661	# [6] 154	[6] 265	[6] 549	[6] 338	[6] 353	[6] 514	Turquie
Europe	**33 880**	**35 710**	**35 739**	**37 162**	**36 470**	**34 843**	**32 863**	**33 926**	**35 856**	**34 263**	**Europe**
EEC	***19 024***	***20 240***	***20 683***	***21 739***	***20 938***	***19 377***	***17 733***	***18 203***	***19 168***	***17 746***	***CEE***
Belgium[7]	1 891	2 011	2 112	2 299	2 151	1 974	1 718	1 898	2 247	2 107	Belgique[7]
Denmark[8]	17	16	57	68	36	20	21	20	27	36	Danemark[8]
France	3 959	4 501	4 584	4 957	4 952	4 412	# 4 166	4 309	4 531	4 321	France
Germany, Fed. Rep.	4 668	4 678	4 671	5 067	4 777	4 832	4 411	4 340	4 309	3 456	Allemagne, Rép. féd.
Greece	920	1 111	1 181	1 151	1 088	980	1 000	1 016	1 155	1 069	Grèce
Italy	2 896	2 946	2 945	2 955	2 827	2 544	2 221	2 540	2 636	2 724	Italie
Netherlands	1 402	1 572	1 680	1 744	1 726	1 726	1 609	1 451	1 609	1 508	Pays-Bas
United Kingdom	3 271	3 405	3 453	3 498	3 381	2 889	2 587	2 629	2 654	2 525	Royaume-Uni
EFTA	***2 616***	***2 780***	***2 532***	***2 950***	***2 808***	***2 968***	***2 821***	***3 025***	***3 224***	***3 392***	***AELE***
Finland	1 016	982	849	1 048	1 039	1 058	1 032	1 145	1 165	1 439	Finlande
Norway	405	384	381	386	354	407	412	440	460	448	Norvège
Portugal	309	476	380	633	636	546	472	431	553	428	Portugal
Sweden	767	816	807	764	660	838	786	890	927	958	Suède
Switzerland[9]	...	122	115	...	...	...	...	...	...	...	Suisse[9]
East Europe	***8 440***	***8 532***	***8 657***	***8 548***	***8 486***	***8 375***	***8 187***	***8 403***	***8 310***	***8 245***	***Europe de l'est***
Bulgaria	857	860	974	998	852	920	916	861	908	810	Bulgarie
Czechoslovakia	1 240	1 276	1 195	1 253	1 285	1 315	1 252	1 244	1 246	1 298	Tchécoslovaquie

For general note and footnotes, see end of table.

Voir la fin du tableau pour la remarque générale et les notes.

Sulphuric acid (continued) – Acide sulfurique (suite)

Unit : Thousand metric tons

Unité : Milliers de tonnes métriques

Country or area	1976	1977	1978	1979	1980	1981	1982	1983	1984	1985	Pays ou zone
German Dem. Rep.	957	927	971	952	958	948	920	926	885	883	Rép. dém. allemande
Hungary[10]	652	678	690	612	616	602	603	645	587	556	Hongrie[10]
Poland	3 179	3 268	3 172	2 983	3 019	2 776	2 676	2 786	2 769	2 863	Pologne
Romania	1 555	1 523	1 655	1 750	1 756	1 814	...	1 941	1 915	1 835	Roumanie
Other Europe	***3 800***	***4 158***	***3 867***	***3 925***	***4 238***	***4 123***	***4 123***	***4 295***	***5 154***	***4 880***	***Autre Europe***
Spain	2 958	3 284	2 965	2 950	3 052	2 875	2 940	2 995	3 683	3 391	Espagne
Yugoslavia	842	874	902	975	1 186	1 248	1 183	1 300	1 471	1 489	Yougoslavie
USSR	**20 015**	**21 104**	**22 411**	**22 364**	**23 033**	**24 095**	**23 801**	**24 714**	**25 338**	**26 037**	**URSS**
Byelorussian SSR	*689*	*700*	*698*	*707*	*860*	*1 143*	*1 158*	*1 228*	*1 258*	*1 194*	*RSS de Biélorussie*
Ukrainian SSR	*4 247*	*4 413*	*4 893*	*4 742*	*4 507*	*4 753*	*4 431*	*4 505*	*4 426*	*4 125*	*RSS d'Ukraine*
Oceania	**1 295**	**1 752**	**1 837**	**1 940**	**2 175**	**1 963**	**2 027**	**1 734**	**1 706**	**1 783**	**Océanie**
Australia[4]	1 295	1 752	1 837	1 940	2 175	1 963	2 027	1 734	1 706	1 783	Australie[4]
Total	**109 355**	**119 650**	**125 852**	**130 874**	**134 070**	**130 656**	**122 222**	**129 950**	**137 483**	**133 465**	**Total**

General note.
H_2SO_4 in terms of pure monohydrate sulphuric acid, including the sulphuric acid equivalent of oleum or fuming sulphuric acid (H_2SO_4 + N SO_3). (SITC 51333–0).

1 Strength of acid not known.
2 Including data for government–owned, but privately–operated plants.
3 Source: United Nations Economic Commission for Latin America (ECLA), (Santiago).
4 Twelve months ending 30 June of year stated.
5 Source: U. S. Bureau of Mines, (Washington, D. C.).
6 Output of steel industry only.
7 Production by establishments employing 5 or more persons.
8 Excluding quantities consumed by superphosphate industry.
9 Source: Organisation for Economic Co–operation and Development (OECD), (Paris).
10 Including regenerated sulphuric acid.

Remarque générale.
H_2SO_4 sur la base de l'acide sulfurique monohydraté, y compris l'équivalent en acide sulfurique de l'oléum ou acide sulfurique fumant (H_2SO_4 + N SO_3). (CTCI 51333–0).

1 Titre de l'acide inconnu.
2 Y compris les données relatives à des usines appartenant à l'Etat mais exploitées par des entreprises privées.
3 Source: Commission économique des Nations Unies pour l'Amérique Latine (CEPAL), (Santiago).
4 Période de douze mois finissant le 30 juin de l'année indiquée.
5 Source: U.S. Bureau of Mines, (Washington, D.C.).
6 Production de l'industrie sidérurgique seulement.
7 Production des établissements occupant 5 personnes ou plus.
8 Non compris les quantités utilisées par l'industrie des superphosphates.
9 Source: Organisation de coopération et de développement économiques (OCDE), (Paris).
10 Y compris l'acide sulfurique régénéré.

Nitric acid – Acide nitrique

Unit : Thousand metric tons

Unité : Milliers de tonnes métriques

Country or area	1976	1977	1978	1979	1980	1981	1982	1983	1984	1985	Pays ou zone
Africa	**74**	**86**	**13**	**41**	**63**	**24**	**109**	**100**	**83**	**87**	**Afrique**
Algeria	72	83	12	39	61	22	108	* 98	...	...	Algérie
Egypt	2	3	1	2	2	2	1	2	...	...	Egypte
America, North	**7 556**	**8 045**	**8 148**	**9 237**	**9 525**	**9 569**	**8 024**	**7 487**	**8 632**	**8 508**	**Amérique du Nord**
Canada	...	...	...	...	713	861	977	855	1 101	1 128	Canada
Cuba	117	99	...	304	269	300	177	145	287	283	Cuba
Mexico	183	182	174	174	170	161	167	167	171	173	Mexique
United States[1]	6 813	7 244	7 196	8 087	8 373	8 247	6 703	6 320	7 073	6 924	Etats-Unis[1]
America, South	**399**	**375**	**377**	**381**	**419**	**383**	**417**	**351**	**420**	**397**	**Amérique du Sud**
Brazil	374	341	353	346	381	349	308	321	356	...	Brésil
Colombia	20	28	24	31	31	30	100	27	...	...	Colombie
Venezuela	5	6	0	4	7	4	9	3	5	3	Venezuela
Asia	**1 288**	**1 260**	**1 272**	**1 410**	**1 172**	**1 227**	**1 167**	**1 253**	**1 261**	**1 267**	**Asie**
India	539	474	467	583	454	561	487	551	529	...	Inde
Israel	...	...	129	...	...	...	...	...	...	...	Israël
Japan	611	646	642	664	565	508	521	540	569	567	Japon
Korea, Republic of	3	6	28	27	20	25	25	28	30	33	Corée, République de
Turkey	6	5	6	7	[2] 4	[2] 4	[2] 5	[2] 5	...	...	Turquie
Europe	**16 456**	**16 998**	**17 847**	**18 561**	**18 618**	**18 484**	**18 101**	**18 897**	**19 804**	**19 759**	**Europe**
EEC	***10 213***	***10 617***	***10 950***	***11 572***	***11 574***	***11 535***	***11 179***	***11 786***	***12 249***	***12 529***	***CEE***
Belgium[3]	711	985	1 048	1 055	1 167	1 315	1 297	1 445	1 496	1 533	Belgique[3]
Denmark	3	9	9	10	15	11	22	23	12	24	Danemark
France[4]	3 069	...	...	...	...	...	...	...	...	...	France[4]
Germany, Fed. Rep.	2 792	2 849	2 896	3 146	3 174	2 888	2 291	2 626	2 858	2 891	Allemagne, Rép. féd.
Greece	167	153	177	313	313	274	395	440	478	...	Grèce
Italy	918	929	1 038	1 070	1 011	1 005	1 021	1 038	1 100	1 181	Italie
United Kingdom[5]	2 553	2 623	2 713	2 909	2 825	2 973	3 084	3 145	...	...	Royaume-Uni[5]
EFTA	***842***	***886***	***1 124***	***1 197***	***1 236***	***1 010***	***1 040***	***1 166***	***1 252***	***1 161***	***AELE***
Finland	304	291	357	408	445	420	409	541	545	* 484	Finlande
Norway	12	12	14	18	...	...	...	...	...	...	Norvège
Portugal	227	271	405	422	431	222	260	204	259	222	Portugal
Sweden	299	312	348	349	346	354	357	407	434	441	Suède
East Europe	***3 870***	***3 941***	***3 983***	***3 939***	***3 851***	***3 988***	***3 954***	***4 149***	***4 191***	***3 988***	***Europe de l'est***
Bulgaria	783	892	862	878	931	956	977	...	...	...	Bulgarie
Hungary	902	936	1 010	1 059	1 038	1 100	1 054	1 076	1 063	1 041	Hongrie
Poland	2 185	2 113	2 111	2 002	1 882	1 932	1 923	2 065	2 092	1 883	Pologne
Other Europe	***1 531***	***1 554***	***1 790***	***1 853***	***1 957***	***1 951***	***1 928***	***1 796***	***2 112***	***2 082***	***Autre Europe***
Spain	898	892	1 134	1 187	1 266	1 226	1 199	1 055	1 285	1 246	Espagne
Yugoslavia	633	662	656	666	691	725	729	741	827	836	Yougoslavie
Oceania	**148**	**153**	**174**	**177**	**180**	**182**	**193**	**190**	**190**	**202**	**Océanie**
Australia[6]	148	153	174	177	180	182	193	190	190	202	Australie[6]
Total	**25 921**	**26 917**	**27 831**	**29 807**	**29 977**	**29 869**	**28 011**	**28 278**	**30 390**	**30 220**	**Total**

General note.
HNO3 in terms of 100 per cent HNO3. Sulpho-nitric acids are excluded. (SITC 51334-0).

[1] Including data for government-owned, but privately-operated plants.
[2] State sector only.
[3] Production by establishments employing 5 or more persons.
[4] Beginning 1977, data are confidential.
[5] Sales by manufacturers employing 25 or more persons.
[6] Twelve months ending 30 June of year stated.

Remarque générale.
HNO3 sur la base de HNO3 à 100 p. 100, à l'exclusion des acides sulfonitriques. (CTCI 51334-0).

[1] Y compris les données relatives à des usines appartenant à l'Etat mais exploitées par des entreprises privées.
[2] Secteur public seulement.
[3] Production des établissements occupant 5 personnes ou plus.
[4] A partir de 1977 ,les données sont confidentielles.
[5] Ventes des fabricants employant 25 personnes ou plus.
[6] Période de douze mois finissant le 30 juin de l'année indiquée.

Unit : Thousand metric tons

Unité : Milliers de tonnes métriques

Country or area	1976	1977	1978	1979	1980	1981	1982	1983	1984	1985	Pays ou zone
Africa	**236.8**	**221.7**	**227.0**	**273.3**	**823.8**	**970.9**	**1 264.3**	**1 585.7**	**1 675.0**	**1 508.0**	**Afrique**
Morocco	...	...	0.2	0.3	349.4	517.9	758.1	965.6	1 125.1	1 032.8	Maroc
Tunisia	236.6	221.4	226.7	273.1	474.4	453.0	506.2	620.1	549.9	475.2	Tunisie
America, North	**7 731.9**	**8 879.8**	**9 641.1**	**10 423.2**	**10 930.6**	**10 170.8**	**8 440.0**	**9 912.0**	**11 432.3**	**10 574.4**	**Amérique du Nord**
Canada	522.6	555.7	553.8	747.7	807.9	743.8	552.6	655.5	690.8	628.6	Canada
Mexico	362.8	392.0	346.2	317.0	283.4	395.4	402.2	398.1	407.2	406.0	Mexique
United States	6 846.5	7 932.1	8 741.0	9 358.5	9 839.3	9 031.7	7 485.2	8 858.3	10 334.3	9 539.8	Etats-Unis
America, South	**183.0**	**181.0**	**179.6**	**200.6**	**328.4**	**429.6**	**501.4**	**594.1**	**677.5**	**704.7**	**Amérique du Sud**
Brazil	183.0	180.9	179.6	200.6	328.4	429.6	501.4	594.1	677.5	...	Brésil
Asia	**442.0**	**428.8**	**361.3**	**391.6**	**384.5**	**397.9**	**265.6**	**255.0**	**253.1**	**247.3**	**Asie**
India	15.4	22.2	22.9	12.2	13.7	5.5	9.3	12.3	4.6	...	Inde
Japan	191.9	194.2	198.4	211.4	194.8	174.4	183.3	203.7	203.5	202.4	Japon
Turkey	...	...	[1] 140.0	...	176.0	218.0	# 73.0	39.0	45.0	40.6	Turquie
Europe	**3 152.7**	**3 373.9**	**3 660.6**	**3 582.2**	**3 705.3**	**3 532.6**	**3 902.2**	**4 160.5**	**4 209.6**	**3 923.7**	**Europe**
EEC	***1 962.6***	***2 084.6***	***2 166.9***	***2 038.0***	***2 098.1***	***1 936.1***	***2 287.4***	***2 393.8***	***2 290.0***	***2 037.8***	*CEE*
Belgium	* [1] 308.0	358.0	373.0	295.1	298.6	268.3	273.4	...	...	...	Belgique
France[2]	118.3	110.9	169.5	189.7	202.2	181.7	# 583.0	617.6	488.8	398.8	France[2]
Germany, Fed. Rep.	318.9	330.9	332.6	330.8	339.2	329.7	310.8	317.6	336.1	323.4	Allemagne, Rép. féd.
Greece	* 308.0	307.0	327.6	263.2	289.6	259.5	271.5	298.9	358.1	...	Grèce
Italy	427.4	476.0	464.8	493.0	474.4	445.0	440.9	454.0	452.9	402.9	Italie
United Kingdom	482.0	501.8	499.5	466.2	494.1	452.0	407.9	446.1	407.3	375.6	Royaume-Uni
EFTA	***244.8***	***251.4***	***306.1***	***357.2***	***367.1***	***380.0***	***399.8***	***465.9***	***454.9***	***461.6***	*AELE*
Finland	103.8	98.2	126.0	163.9	183.6	182.8	206.6	235.6	224.0	* 242.3	Finlande
Portugal	24.6	30.8	48.6	47.8	45.4	38.9	35.0	30.4	42.0	...	Portugal
Sweden[3]	116.5	122.5	131.5	145.5	138.1	158.3	158.2	199.9	188.8	178.5	Suède[3]
East Europe	***475.0***	***475.4***	***493.8***	***517.5***	***541.1***	***494.2***	***545.5***	***563.9***	***568.0***	***547.9***	*Europe de l'est*
Czechoslovakia	16.5	16.9	35.4	55.9	61.1	52.5	61.4	62.2	64.4	63.5	Tchécoslovaquie
Hungary	0.0	0.0	0.0	3.1	21.5	22.1	23.2	26.2	25.8	25.9	Hongrie
Poland[4]	...	...	...	...	...	419.6	460.9	475.5	477.8	...	Pologne[4]
Other Europe	***470.3***	***562.5***	***693.7***	***669.5***	***699.1***	***722.3***	***669.6***	***736.8***	***896.8***	***876.3***	*Autre Europe*
Spain	* 308.0	406.2	* 517.0	* 466.0	419.8	426.4	397.6	431.7	548.3	531.8	Espagne
Yugoslavia	162.3	156.2	176.7	203.5	279.3	295.9	271.9	305.2	348.5	344.5	Yougoslavie
USSR[4]	**...**	**...**	**...**	**...**	**...**	**611.0**	**562.0**	**546.0**	**622.0**	**...**	**URSS[4]**
Oceania	**76.6**	**95.0**	**103.6**	**106.3**	**110.1**	**111.6**	**83.2**	**76.0**	**66.0**	**72.0**	**Océanie**
Australia[5]	76.6	95.0	103.6	106.3	110.1	111.6	83.2	76.0	66.0	72.0	Australie[5]
Total	**12 408.2**	**13 765.4**	**14 758.4**	**15 562.4**	**16 868.1**	**16 224.3**	**15 018.8**	**17 129.2**	**18 935.5**	**17 615.4**	**Total**

General note.
In terms of phosphorus pentoxide (P2O5), orthophosphoric acid (H3PO4), pyrophosphoric acid (H4P2O7) and metaphosphoric acid (HPO3) produced by the thermal process, by sulphuric acid reaction or by other processes. (SITC 51335-1).

[1] Source: The Chemical Industry, Organisation for Economic Co-operation and Development (OECD), (Paris).
[2] In terms of P2O5, coloured or not, for industrial use.
[3] Orthophosphoric acid.
[4] Source: United Nations Economic Commission for Europe (ECE), (Geneva).
[5] Twelve months ending 30 June of year stated.

Remarque générale.
Acide orthophosphorique (H3PO4), acide pyrophosphorique (H4P2O7) et acide métaphosphorique (HPO3) obtenus par l'action de la chaleur, par réaction avec l'acide sulfurique ou par d'autres procédés. Exprimé sur la base d'anhydride phosphorique (P2O5). (CTCI 51335-1).

[1] Source: l'Industrie chimique, Organisation de coopération et de développement économiques (OCDE), (Paris).
[2] En poids de P2O5, coloré ou non, pour usages industriels.
[3] Acide orthophosphorique.
[4] Source: Commission économique des Nations Unies pour l'Europe (CEE), (Genève).
[5] Période de douze mois finissant le 30 juin de l'année indiquée.

Carbon bisulphide – Sulfure de carbone

Unit : Thousand metric tons

Unité : Milliers de tonnes métriques

Country or area	1976	1977	1978	1979	1980	1981	1982	1983	1984	1985	Pays ou zone
America, North	**232.2**	**230.5**	**217.9**	**214.3**	**214.6**	**177.7**	**214.2**	**214.2**	**214.2**	**214.3**	**Amérique du Nord**
Cuba	...	1.7	1.9	1.6	1.8	1.8	1.4	1.4	1.5	1.5	Cuba
United States	* 230.4	* 228.8	216.0	...	...	175.9	...	...	...	...	Etats–Unis
America, South	**27.8**	**23.4**	**28.9**	**35.2**	**38.6**	**30.6**	**29.3**	**30.1**	**30.4**	**32.8**	**Amérique du Sud**
Brazil	23.5	18.2	23.0	29.5	32.2	24.5	23.0	24.1	23.7	...	Brésil
Colombia	4.3	...	5.9	...	6.4	6.2	...	6.0	...	...	Colombie
Asia	**96.7**	**103.7**	**101.0**	**102.4**	**103.3**	**94.2**	**90.3**	**91.9**	**92.3**	**88.3**	**Asie**
Japan	95.5	102.2	100.6	102.1	102.9	93.7	88.9	91.3	91.6	87.7	Japon
Korea, Republic of	1.2	1.6	0.4	0.3	0.5	0.5	1.5	...	...	...	Corée, République de
Europe	**180.7**	**163.3**	**147.4**	**160.6**	**176.2**	**176.5**	**203.2**	**238.2**	**240.0**	**249.3**	**Europe**
EEC	***55.8***	***55.1***	***55.4***	***55.4***	***55.4***	***55.4***	***55.4***	***55.4***	***55.4***	***55.4***	***CEE***
Italy	55.8	55.1	...	...	...	...	...	...	...	...	Italie
EFTA	***12.5***	***12.1***	***12.6***	***12.4***	***9.8***	***8.1***	***6.2***	***42.4***	***37.9***	***40.4***	***AELE***
Austria	10.7	10.2	10.5	10.2	8.1	7.0	5.2	# 42.3	37.5	40.2	Autriche
Portugal	1.8	2.0	2.1	2.2	1.7	1.1	1.0	0.1	...	...	Portugal
East Europe	***101.1***	***83.5***	***67.8***	***81.3***	***106.5***	***105.6***	***133.0***	***133.3***	***138.2***	***145.8***	***Europe de l'est***
Czechoslovakia	12.9	10.9	0.7	...	...	...	...	...	...	...	Tchécoslovaquie
German Dem. Rep.	49.4	40.9	34.5	23.4	0.0	0.0	0.0	0.0	0.0	0.0	Rép. dém. allemande
Poland	38.7	31.7	32.5	49.7	98.3	97.4	124.8	125.1	130.0	137.6	Pologne
Other Europe	***11.4***	***12.6***	***11.5***	***11.4***	***4.5***	***7.4***	***8.5***	***7.1***	***8.5***	***7.7***	***Autre Europe***
Yugoslavia	11.4	12.6	11.5	11.4	4.5	7.4	8.5	7.1	8.5	7.7	Yougoslavie
Total	**537.5**	**520.9**	**495.2**	**512.5**	**532.8**	**479.1**	**537.0**	**574.5**	**576.9**	**584.7**	**Total**

General note.
CS2. (SITC 51342–1).

Remarque générale.
CS2. (CTCI 51342–1).

Zinc oxide – Oxyde de zinc

Unit : Thousand metric tons

Unité : Milliers de tonnes métriques

Country or area	1976	1977	1978	1979	1980	1981	1982	1983	1984	1985	Pays ou zone
Africa	**0.2**	**0.2**	**0.5**	**0.1**	**0.4**	**0.2**	**0.2**	**0.3**	**0.4**	**0.3**	**Afrique**
Kenya	0.2	0.2	0.5	0.1	0.4	0.2	0.2	0.3	0.4	0.3	Kenya
America, North	**176.4**	**188.4**	**186.8**	**172.7**	**145.5**	**145.3**	**123.5**	**129.6**	**115.4**	**105.9**	**Amérique du Nord**
United States	176.4	188.4	186.8	172.7	145.5	145.3	123.5	129.6	...	...	Etats-Unis
America, South	**12.2**	**15.4**	**16.7**	**18.1**	**24.5**	**20.5**	**23.2**	**17.5**	**21.4**	**23.7**	**Amérique du Sud**
Brazil	12.1	12.8	15.3	16.3	22.5	18.6	20.7	15.8	19.0	...	Brésil
Colombia	0.2	2.6	1.3	1.8	2.0	1.8	2.5	1.7	...	...	Colombie
Asia	**64.2**	**66.2**	**65.8**	**74.1**	**78.7**	**69.8**	**65.3**	**71.0**	**79.7**	**79.6**	**Asie**
India[1]	4.6	5.0	6.2	5.1	4.6	4.7	4.1	4.4	4.5	...	Inde[1]
Japan	59.2	58.3	56.8	61.5	63.5	64.7	60.9	64.8	72.8	72.8	Japon
Korea, Republic of	0.5	2.9	2.8	7.5	10.5	0.4	0.2	1.8	2.4	...	Corée, République de
Europe	**133.1**	**145.6**	**149.3**	**149.4**	**149.8**	**167.3**	**127.0**	**127.7**	**140.1**	**138.9**	**Europe**
EEC	***116.6***	***128.5***	***131.9***	***130.3***	***123.9***	***136.2***	***98.4***	***105.2***	***112.4***	***108.3***	***CEE***
France	42.8	44.9	46.8	45.6	51.1	69.7	# 34.0	36.5	...	...	France
Germany, Fed. Rep.	29.9	34.8	36.9	42.4	43.3	40.4	39.8	40.7	40.5	44.3	Allemagne, Rép. féd.
Greece	0.3	0.4	0.3	0.4	0.4	0.3	0.3	0.3	0.3	...	Grèce
Italy	10.3	10.6	...	...	...	...	...	...	...	...	Italie
United Kingdom[2 3]	33.3	37.7	37.4	31.5	18.6	15.4	13.8	17.1	16.1	...	Royaume-Uni[2 3]
EFTA	***7.7***	***6.5***	***6.3***	***7.5***	***13.9***	***14.3***	***14.0***	***13.6***	***13.8***	***16.3***	***AELE***
Finland	2.1	1.6	1.7	1.9	1.9	1.8	1.7	1.8	1.6	...	Finlande
Portugal	2.8	2.3	1.9	2.4	9.0	9.9	9.4	8.9	9.1	...	Portugal
Sweden	2.8	2.5	2.6	3.2	3.0	2.6	2.9	2.9	3.1	2.8	Suède
Other Europe	***8.7***	***10.7***	***11.1***	***11.6***	***12.0***	***16.8***	***14.6***	***8.9***	***13.9***	***14.3***	***Autre Europe***
Spain	8.7	...	...	...	12.0	16.8	14.6	8.9	...	...	Espagne
Oceania	**7.5**	**7.8**	**5.8**	**8.1**	**8.1**	**7.9**	**7.5**	**6.8**	**4.2**	**4.8**	**Océanie**
Australia	7.5	7.8	5.8	8.1	8.1	7.9	7.5	6.8	4.2	4.8	Australie
Total	**393.6**	**423.6**	**424.7**	**422.5**	**407.0**	**411.1**	**346.6**	**352.9**	**361.2**	**353.3**	**Total**

General note.
ZnO zinc white including zinc peroxide (ZnO2). Natural zinc oxide or zincite is excluded. (SITC 51351-1).

[1] Production by large and medium scale establishments only.
[2] Sales by manufacturers employing 25 or more persons.
[3] Data refer to zinc oxide and peroxide.

Remarque générale.
Blanc de zinc ZnO, y compris le peroxyde de zinc (ZnO2), mais non compris l'oxyde de zinc naturel ou zincite. (CTCI 51351-1).

[1] Production des grandes et moyennes entreprises seulement.
[2] Ventes des fabricants employant 25 personnes ou plus.
[3] Données se rapportant aux oxydes et peroxydes de zinc.

Titanium oxides – Oxydes de titane

Unit : Thousand metric tons — Unité : Milliers de tonnes métriques

Country or area	1976	1977	1978	1979	1980	1981	1982	1983	1984	1985	Pays ou zone
America, North	**669.2**	**650.7**	**664.1**	**708.0**	**698.9**	**730.4**	**635.9**	**730.2**	**802.0**	**828.0**	**Amérique du Nord**
Mexico	22.4	27.5	28.5	35.0	39.1	40.0	37.5	40.5	44.7	...	Mexique
United States	646.8	623.2	635.6	673.0	659.7	690.4	598.4	689.7	757.2	780.4	Etats–Unis
America, South	**11.4**	**15.6**	**19.8**	**24.1**	**29.9**	**32.8**	**30.9**	**45.3**	**45.0**	**49.5**	**Amérique du Sud**
Brazil	...	...	...	...	29.9	32.8	30.9	45.3	45.0	...	Brésil
Asia	**168.7**	**167.8**	**190.5**	**200.3**	**190.7**	**195.8**	**205.0**	**220.1**	**228.5**	**242.8**	**Asie**
India[1]	9.7	9.9	9.9	...	...	...	...	...	...	...	Inde[1]
Japan	156.0	150.3	171.4	185.4	172.8	176.2	184.0	195.9	204.7	217.7	Japon
Korea, Republic of	2.9	7.6	9.2	5.1	8.0	9.8	11.1	14.4	...	...	Corée, République de
Europe	**320.3**	**344.5**	**364.9**	**364.7**	**343.7**	**339.3**	**346.7**	**366.9**	**381.7**	**399.5**	**Europe**
EEC	***254.8***	***263.8***	***269.8***	***257.4***	***251.0***	***234.1***	***236.9***	***259.4***	***270.5***	***283.6***	***CEE***
Italy	63.4	65.7	...	...	...	...	...	...	...	...	Italie
United Kingdom	191.4	198.1	205.3	192.9	186.5	169.6	172.3	194.9	206.0	219.1	Royaume–Uni
East Europe	***19.6***	***19.6***	***19.6***	***19.6***	***19.6***	***16.7***	***21.0***	***21.0***	***19.6***	***19.6***	***Europe de l'est***
Czechoslovakia[2]	...	...	...	...	...	16.7	21.0	21.0	...	...	Tchécoslovaquie[2]
Other Europe	***46.0***	***61.1***	***75.5***	***87.7***	***73.1***	***88.5***	***88.8***	***86.5***	***91.7***	***96.3***	***Autre Europe***
Spain[3]	24.3	39.5	* 53.9	* 66.1	51.4	66.6	67.4	64.9	70.0	74.7	Espagne[3]
Yugoslavia[2]	...	...	...	...	...	21.9	21.4	...	...	...	Yougoslavie[2]
USSR[2]	...	...	...	...	...	**4.7**	**5.0**	**5.0**	**6.4**	...	**URSS[2]**
Total	**1 174.8**	**1 183.9**	**1 244.6**	**1 302.4**	**1 268.4**	**1 303.0**	**1 223.5**	**1 367.5**	**1 463.6**	**1 525.1**	**Total**

General note.
TiO2 and TiO3. Natural titanium dioxide is excluded. (SITC 51355–0).

[1] Production by large and medium scale establishments only.
[2] Source: United Nations Economic Commission for Europe (ECE), (Geneva).
[3] Data refer to titanium dioxide.

Remarque générale.
TiO2 et TiO3, à l'exclusion du bioxyde de titane naturel. (CTCI 51355–0).

[1] Production des grandes et moyennes entreprises seulement.
[2] Source: Commission économique des Nations Unies pour l'Europe (CEE), (Genève).
[3] Données se rapportant au bioxyde de titane.

Lead oxides – Oxydes de plomb

Unit : Thousand metric tons

Unité : Milliers de tonnes métriques

Country or area	1976	1977	1978	1979	1980	1981	1982	1983	1984	1985	Pays ou zone
Africa	**1.3**	**1.4**	**1.5**	**1.8**	**1.5**	**1.6**	**1.7**	**2.1**	**2.0**	**2.1**	**Afrique**
Egypt	...	...	...	1.8	1.5	1.6	1.7	2.1	...	...	Egypte
America, South	**16.5**	**16.5**	**16.5**	**15.0**	**18.0**	**16.5**	**16.5**	**16.5**	**16.5**	**16.5**	**Amérique du Sud**
Brazil	...	...	...	[1] 15.0	18.0	...	...	...	...	...	Brésil
Asia	**62.8**	**65.4**	**62.5**	**67.6**	**71.0**	**75.3**	**71.7**	**76.1**	**82.3**	**81.7**	**Asie**
India[2]	7.4	7.4	7.0	5.7	7.4	8.3	9.2	10.3	10.1	...	Inde[2]
Japan	55.3	56.1	55.1	59.3	63.1	64.5	62.2	64.3	70.7	69.9	Japon
Korea, Republic of	0.2	2.0	0.4	2.6	0.4	2.5	0.3	...	...	...	Corée, République de
Europe	**188.7**	**184.2**	**184.5**	**182.6**	**181.3**	**182.0**	**179.8**	**180.8**	**167.7**	**172.4**	**Europe**
EEC	***164.0***	***163.9***	***163.7***	***161.2***	***159.7***	***161.1***	***158.6***	***162.5***	***145.2***	***152.5***	***CEE***
France[3]	29.8	32.9	28.0	33.9	35.2	...	...	...	...	...	France[3]
Germany, Fed. Rep.	54.1	54.0	55.9	52.3	54.8	56.2	54.7	59.5	43.3	...	Allemagne, Rép. féd.
Greece	0.7	0.8	0.8	0.6	0.6	0.6	0.7	0.7	0.8	...	Grèce
Italy	55.4	54.8	55.7	...	...	...	...	...	...	...	Italie
United Kingdom[4]	24.0	21.4	23.3	19.2	13.8	...	...	...	...	...	Royaume–Uni[4]
EFTA	***6.6***	***6.3***	***6.7***	***7.3***	***7.5***	***6.8***	***7.1***	***8.3***	***8.5***	***5.8***	***AELE***
Portugal	...	2.2	2.5	3.0	3.1	2.7	2.0	2.8	3.0	1.4	Portugal
Sweden	3.9	4.1	4.3	4.3	4.4	4.1	5.1	5.5	5.5	4.4	Suède
Other Europe	***18.1***	***14.0***	***14.0***	***14.0***	***14.0***	***14.0***	***14.0***	***10.0***	***14.0***	***14.0***	***Autre Europe***
Spain	18.1	...	...	...	...	...	...	10.0	...	...	Espagne
Total	**269.4**	**267.5**	**265.0**	**267.0**	**271.7**	**275.4**	**269.7**	**275.5**	**268.5**	**272.7**	**Total**

General note.
Such as oxide, dioxide, litharge, massicot, minium, orange lead, puce oxide etc. (SITC 51356–0).

[1] Production by establishments employing 5 or more persons.
[2] Production by large and medium scale establishments only.
[3] Beginning 1981, data are confidential.
[4] Sales by manufacturers employing 25 or more persons.

Remarque générale.
Notamment le protoxyde de plomb (litharge, massicot), le minium, la mine orange, le bioxyde de plomb (oxyde puce de plomb) etc. (CTCI 51356–0).

[1] Production des établissements occupant 5 personnes ou plus.
[2] Production des grandes et moyennes entreprises seulement.
[3] A partir de 1981, les données sont confidentielles.
[4] Ventes des fabricants employant 25 personnes ou plus.

Ammonia – Ammoniac

Unit : Thousand metric tons

Unité : Milliers de tonnes métriques

Country or area	1976	1977	1978	1979	1980	1981	1982	1983	1984	1985	Pays ou zone
Africa	**25**	**0**	**0**	**82**	**107**	**74**	**197**	**183**	**208**	**233**	**Afrique**
Algeria	25	0	0	...	...	74	197	...	...	...	Algérie
America, North	**14 438**	**16 522**	**16 822**	**18 201**	**19 311**	**16 761**	**15 296**	**17 766**	**17 913**	**20 307**	**Amérique du Nord**
Canada	907	2 162	2 343	2 405	2 556	2 654	2 509	2 888	3 494	3 620	Canada
Cuba	97	70	47	155	136	166	98	86	169	163	Cuba
Mexico	865	944	1 579	1 653	1 883	2 183	2 469	2 354	2 156	2 261	Mexique
United States	12 569	13 346	12 853	13 988	14 736	11 758	10 220	12 438	12 094	14 263	Etats–Unis
America, South	**571**	**584**	**620**	**730**	**879**	**960**	**1 142**	**1 270**	**1 672**	**1 546**	**Amérique du Sud**
Brazil	176	184	259	339	444	463	580	904	1 070	...	Brésil
Colombia	...	70	90	75	85	92	27	25	...	...	Colombie
Venezuela	294	330	271	316	350	405	535	341	571	490	Venezuela
Asia	**13 122**	**14 616**	**15 281**	**16 936**	**18 165**	**17 266**	**17 108**	**18 325**	**20 028**	**18 824**	**Asie**
China	...	...	11 835	13 482	14 974	14 833	15 463	16 771	18 374	17 188	Chine
Indonesia	...	8	9	7	16	24	23	36	27	...	Indonésie
Israel	79	83	90	83	67	52	95	97	101	106	Israël
Japan	165	167	126	119	125	...	...	...	...	...	Japon
Korea, Republic of	733	882	1 091	1 169	1 032	908	661	523	565	538	Corée, République de
Qatar	...	128	201	371	506	447	528	482	* 547	* 640	Qatar
Turkey	1 078	1 623	1 929	1 705	1 445	...	249	339	350	265	Turquie
Europe	**18 458**	**18 986**	**19 711**	**19 867**	**19 496**	**19 412**	**18 133**	**18 575**	**20 412**	**20 471**	**Europe**
EEC	***7 921***	***8 072***	***8 305***	***8 636***	***8 451***	***8 379***	***7 193***	***7 273***	***8 473***	***8 488***	***CEE***
Belgium[1]	539	584	540	531	542	589	513	449	452	388	Belgique[1]
Denmark	* 14	* 16	* 11	* 10	* 7	...	8	5	5	5	Danemark
France[2]	1 781	2 034	2 016	...	...	[3] 2 250	[3] 1 900	[3] 1 960	1 959	...	France[2]
Germany, Fed. Rep.	1 863	1 989	1 955	2 161	2 044	1 962	1 570	1 703	1 963	1 908	Allemagne, Rép. féd.
Greece	290	287	285	269	286	284	272	276	305	...	Grèce
Italy	1 483	1 378	1 756	1 773	1 714	1 472	1 275	1 134	1 469	1 477	Italie
Netherlands	1 951	1 784	1 742	1 916	1 874	1 814	1 655	1 746	2 320	2 396	Pays–Bas
EFTA	***1 033***	***1 044***	***1 042***	***976***	***847***	***837***	***822***	***746***	***791***	***781***	***AELE***
Finland	205	160	182	139	85	84	79	82	84	* 79	Finlande
Norway	468	484	512	476	437	505	502	488	...	...	Norvège
Portugal	251	298	251	270	237	165	164	126	165	188	Portugal
Sweden	109	102	97	91	88	83	77	50	49	19	Suède
East Europe	***7 982***	***8 265***	***8 788***	***8 740***	***8 804***	***8 761***	***8 949***	***9 441***	***9 721***	***9 703***	***Europe de l'est***
Bulgaria	920	995	960	951	1 009	1 023	1 033	1 124	1 138	1 138	Bulgarie
Czechoslovakia	881	962	987	977	1 029	865	881	984	1 006	994	Tchécoslovaquie
German Dem. Rep.	1 361	1 374	1 383	1 312	1 436	1 463	1 419	1 471	1 467	1 471	Rép. dém. allemande
Hungary	703	730	747	803	795	819	792	812	814	791	Hongrie
Poland[4]	2 099	2 024	1 965	1 860	1 803	1 694	1 683	1 739	1 822	1 812	Pologne[4]
Romania	2 018	2 180	2 746	2 837	2 732	2 897	3 141	3 311	3 474	3 497	Roumanie
Other Europe	***1 522***	***1 605***	***1 576***	***1 515***	***1 394***	***1 435***	***1 169***	***1 115***	***1 427***	***1 499***	***Autre Europe***
Spain	1 051	1 098	1 070	1 006	902	923	654	615	818	733	Espagne
Yugoslavia	471	507	506	509	492	512	515	500	609	766	Yougoslavie
USSR[3]	...	...	...	...	...	**17 894**	**17 757**	**20 552**	**21 492**	...	**URSS[3]**
Total	**66 038**	**70 131**	**71 858**	**75 239**	**77 382**	**72 368**	**69 633**	**76 670**	**81 726**	**80 805**	**Total**

General note.
Ammonia obtained from impure ammoniacal gas liquors in coal gas purification and coke works or by synthesis from hydrogen and nitrogen, expressed in terms of 100 per cent N. (SITC 51361–0).

[1] Production by establishments employing 5 or more persons.
[2] 1979 and 1980, data are confidential.
[3] Source: United Nations Economic Commission for Europe (ECE), (Geneva).
[4] Synthetic ammonia.

Remarque générale.
Ammoniac obtenu à partir d'eaux ammoniacales impures provenant de l'épuration du gaz d'éclairage et des cokeries, ou par synthèse de l'hydrogène et de l'azote. Exprimé sur la base d'azote pur. (CTCI 51361–0).

[1] Production des établissements occupant 5 personnes ou plus.
[2] 1979 et 1980, les données sont confidentielles.
[3] Source: Commission économique des Nations Unies pour l'Europe (CEE), (Genève).
[4] Ammoniac synthétique.

Caustic soda – Soude caustique

Unit : Thousand metric tons

Unité : Milliers de tonnes métriques

Country or area	1976	1977	1978	1979	1980	1981	1982	1983	1984	1985	Pays ou zone
Africa	**29**	**34**	**39**	**45**	**53**	**52**	**53**	**57**	**48**	**52**	**Afrique**
Algeria	2	6	8	8	9	9	8	* 8	* 1	* 1	Algérie
Egypt	27	28	31	37	44	43	45	49	47	51	Egypte
America, North	**10 432**	**11 259**	**11 546**	**12 946**	**12 230**	**11 395**	**10 255**	**11 013**	**11 842**	**11 771**	**Amérique du Nord**
Canada	1 000	1 014	1 036	1 138	1 459	1 458	1 367	1 528	1 575	1 589	Canada
Cuba	2	5	5	5	3	8	11	16	18	14	Cuba
Mexico	228	263	247	231	224	296	365	363	350	363	Mexique
United States	9 202	9 977	10 258	11 572	10 544	9 633	8 512	9 106	9 899	9 805	Etats-Unis
America, South	**455**	**514**	**751**	**830**	**881**	**961**	**973**	**988**	**1 079**	**1 174**	**Amérique du Sud**
Argentina	110	121	101	110	104	105	115	128	125	121	Argentine
Brazil	259	317	577	645	691	759	760	746	857	950	Brésil
Chile	29	30	33	43	44	34	35	42	43	47	Chili
Colombia	56	36	32	24	20	38	33	38	28	...	Colombie
Venezuela	1	10	8	8	22	25	30	34	26	30	Venezuela
Asia	**4 839**	**4 981**	**5 179**	**5 630**	**5 922**	**5 775**	**5 805**	**5 975**	**6 377**	**6 524**	**Asie**
Bangladesh[1]	4	5	6	6	6	6	6	6	6	7	Bangladesh[1]
China	1 215	1 386	1 640	1 826	1 923	1 923	2 073	2 123	2 222	2 353	Chine
India	504	517	548	565	549	613	595	609	698	707	Inde
Iran(Islamic Rep.of)	[2] 28	[2] 20	[2] 15	[2] 17	[3] 8	[3] 10	[3] 12	[3] 13	[3] 12	[3] 12	Iran(Rép.islamique)
Israel	24	27	22	26	35	35	29	31	29	31	Israël
Japan	2 819	2 785	2 693	2 930	3 063	2 786	2 709	2 778	2 993	2 982	Japon
Korea, Republic of	67	74	76	76	148	190	166	202	215	229	Corée, République de
Kuwait	9	8	8	9	9	9	9	10	9	11	Koweït
Pakistan[1]	38	25	35	36	40	38	41	41	40	45	Pakistan[1]
Philippines	17	19	21	26	24	41	...	27	...	...	Philippines
Sri Lanka	2	2	2	2	2	2	1	1	1	0	Sri Lanka
Thailand	60	65	62	67	68	68	77	82	81	84	Thaïlande
Turkey	39	35	38	31	34	42	42	38	22	11	Turquie
Viet Nam	4	5	5	4	4	3	4	4	4	3	Viet Nam
Europe	**9 496**	**9 579**	**9 816**	**10 381**	**10 123**	**10 065**	**9 853**	**10 522**	**11 168**	**11 257**	**Europe**
EEC	***6 262***	***6 265***	***6 347***	***6 614***	***6 233***	***6 165***	***6 030***	***6 551***	***6 969***	***7 008***	***CEE***
Belgium* [4]	720	...	...	...	...	...	...	...	...	...	Belgique* [4]
Denmark	12	13	17	19	16	44	54	49	50	...	Danemark
France	1 274	1 313	1 339	1 450	1 333	1 315	1 335	1 393	1 485	1 467	France
Germany, Fed. Rep.	3 090	3 081	3 260	3 415	3 177	3 209	3 027	3 350	3 611	3 697	Allemagne, Rép. féd.
Greece	32	23	24	24	34	33	33	30	31	...	Grèce
Italy	1 134	1 115	987	986	953	844	861	1 009	1 072	1 031	Italie
EFTA	***741***	***714***	***811***	***886***	***876***	***861***	***759***	***858***	***931***	***984***	***AELE***
Finland	178	187	216	247	274	291	204	213	231	...	Finlande
Norway	75	74	102	171	184	184	182	205	223	210	Norvège
Portugal	39	69	66	72	57	55	62	76	85	132	Portugal
Sweden	449	384	427	396	361	331	311	364	392	389	Suède
East Europe	***1 963***	***2 088***	***2 135***	***2 281***	***2 429***	***2 451***	***2 465***	***2 484***	***2 588***	***2 559***	***Europe de l'est***
Bulgaria	87	96	102	107	162	151	155	147	163	151	Bulgarie
Czechoslovakia	293	312	311	312	325	331	325	332	329	332	Tchécoslovaquie
German Dem. Rep.	441	423	415	548	626	631	695	687	694	667	Rép. dém. allemande
Hungary	81	82	128	174	177	170	167	181	181	181	Hongrie
Poland	388	440	454	436	416	401	363	392	416	414	Pologne
Romania	673	735	725	704	723	767	760	745	805	814	Roumanie
Other Europe	***530***	***512***	***523***	***600***	***585***	***588***	***599***	***629***	***680***	***706***	***Autre Europe***
Spain	440	416	437	498	448	410	430	458	489	518	Espagne
Yugoslavia	90	96	86	102	137	178	169	171	191	188	Yougoslavie
USSR	**2 604**	**2 658**	**2 763**	**2 680**	**2 755**	**2 757**	**2 783**	**2 853**	**2 972**	**3 056**	**URSS**
Ukrainian SSR	*437*	*458*	*438*	*398*	*396*	*392*	*395*	*401*	*489*	*500*	*RSS d'Ukraine*
Oceania	**137**	**135**	**131**	**132**	**139**	**135**	**135**	**135**	**135**	**135**	**Océanie**

For general note and footnotes, see end of table.

Voir la fin du tableau pour la remarque générale et les notes.

Unit : Thousand metric tons

Unité : Milliers de tonnes métriques

Country or area	1976	1977	1978	1979	1980	1981	1982	1983	1984	1985	Pays ou zone
Australia[1]	137	135	131	132	139	...	...	...	...	...	Australie[1]
Total	**27 992**	**29 160**	**30 225**	**32 644**	**32 103**	**31 140**	**29 857**	**31 544**	**33 622**	**33 970**	**Total**

General note.
NaOH. This item excludes soda lyes obtained as residual products from the manufacture of wood pulp by the alkali or sulphate processes, and mixtures of sodium hydroxide and lime known as soda lime. (SITC 51362–0).

[1] Twelve months ending 30 June of year stated.
[2] Production in urban areas only.
[3] Source: U. S. Bureau of Mines, (Washington, D. C.).
[4] Source: Industrial Statistics, Statistical Office of the European Communities, (Luxembourg).

Remarque générale.
NaOH. Cette rubrique ne comprend pas les lessives sodiques résiduaires du traitement à la soude ou au sulfate des pâtes de bois ni les mélanges de soude caustique et de chaux appelés chaux sodées. (CTCI 51362–0).

[1] Période de douze mois finissant le 30 juin de l'année indiquée.
[2] Production des zones urbaines seulement.
[3] Source: U.S. Bureau of Mines, (Washington, D.C.).
[4] Source: Statistiques industrielles, Office statistique des Communautés européennes, (Luxembourg).

Aluminium oxide – Oxyde d"aluminium

Unit : Thousand metric tons

Unité : Milliers de tonnes métriques

Country or area	1976	1977	1978	1979	1980	1981	1982	1983	1984	1985	Pays ou zone
America, North	**5 366.3**	**5 580.0**	**5 550.0**	**5 784.8**	**5 923.1**	**5 141.8**	**3 254.1**	**2 939.1**	**3 586.5**	**3 175.4**	**Amérique du Nord**
United States	5 366.3	5 580.0	5 550.0	5 784.8	5 923.1	5 141.8	3 254.1	2 939.1	3 586.5	3 175.4	Etats-Unis
America, South	**323.8**	**365.6**	**387.3**	**457.4**	**510.5**	**571.9**	**587.6**	**659.1**	**941.6**	**856.1**	**Amérique du Sud**
Brazil	323.8	365.6	387.3	457.4	510.5	571.9	587.6	659.1	941.6	...	Brésil
Europe	**3 197.6**	**3 402.4**	**3 356.9**	**3 334.7**	**3 506.7**	**3 509.8**	**3 216.5**	**3 214.3**	**3 352.7**	**3 128.3**	**Europe**
EEC	***2 496.6***	***2 678.1***	***2 609.4***	***2 564.7***	***2 737.8***	***2 665.1***	***2 392.1***	***2 342.3***	***2 458.5***	***2 245.2***	***CEE***
France	1 020.0	1 080.9	1 056.4	1 069.2	1 172.8	1 095.3	# 962.6	853.1	898.0	734.5	France
Germany, Fed. Rep.	1 333.4	1 453.9	1 409.8	1 352.4	1 421.8	1 426.6	1 286.3	1 346.0	1 417.3	1 367.5	Allemagne, Rép. féd.
Italy[1]	143.2	...	...	...	...	...	...	...	...	...	Italie[1]
EFTA	***0.7***	***0.3***	***0.5***	***0.5***	***0.3***	***0.2***	***0.3***	***0.2***	***0.1***	***0.1***	***AELE***
Sweden	0.7	0.3	0.5	0.5	0.3	0.1	0.3	...	...	...	Suède
East Europe	***138.0***	***141.2***	***143.4***	***145.2***	***147.5***	***149.3***	***151.2***	***152.5***	***152.5***	***154.2***	***Europe de l'est***
Czechoslovakia	138.0	141.2	143.4	145.2	147.5	149.3	151.2	152.5	152.5	154.2	Tchécoslovaquie
Other Europe	***562.2***	***582.9***	***603.5***	***624.2***	***621.1***	***695.2***	***673.0***	***719.3***	***741.6***	***728.8***	***Autre Europe***
Spain	...	...	...	...	* 621.1	# 695.2	673.0	* 719.3	741.6	728.8	Espagne
Total	**8 887.8**	**9 348.0**	**9 294.2**	**9 576.9**	**9 940.3**	**9 223.5**	**7 058.3**	**6 812.5**	**7 880.8**	**7 159.7**	**Total**

General note.
Al2O3 anhydrous or calcined alumina. Natural alumina is excluded. (SITC 51365-1).

[1] Source: Industrial Statistics, Statistical Office of the European Communities, (Luxembourg).

Remarque générale.
Alumine anhydre ou calcinée Al2O3, à l'exclusion de l'alumine naturelle. (CTCI 51365-1).

[1] Source: Statistiques industrielles, Office statistique des Communautés européennes, (Luxembourg).

Hydrated alumina – Alumine hydratrée

Unit : Thousand metric tons

Unité : Milliers de tonnes métriques

Country or area	1976	1977	1978	1979	1980	1981	1982	1983	1984	1985	Pays ou zone
America, North	**352.5**	**367.4**	**316.5**	**371.3**	**376.3**	**372.2**	**377.3**	**382.5**	**387.6**	**392.7**	**Amérique du Nord**
United States	352.5	367.4	316.5	371.3	376.3	...	...	...	...	...	Etats-Unis
America, South	**0.5**	**0.5**	**0.5**	**0.5**	**0.5**	**0.5**	**0.5**	**0.5**	**0.5**	**0.5**	**Amérique du Sud**
Colombia	...	...	...	...	...	...	...	0.5	...	...	Colombie
Europe	**2 862.3**	**3 052.3**	**2 969.4**	**2 971.6**	**3 140.9**	**3 076.5**	**2 790.7**	**2 786.2**	**2 943.2**	**2 737.0**	**Europe**
EEC	***2 853.8***	***3 047.6***	***2 963.4***	***2 964.3***	***3 134.2***	***3 073.5***	***2 783.5***	***2 776.3***	***2 921.5***	***2 719.6***	***CEE***
France	1 184.1	1 241.6	1 220.9	1 238.4	1 339.4	1 235.9	1 086.7	1 009.1	1 034.0	876.1	France
Germany, Fed. Rep.	1 483.4	1 618.4	1 555.5	1 538.9	1 607.9	1 650.6	1 509.9	1 580.2	1 700.6	1 656.6	Allemagne, Rép. féd.
Italy	186.3	187.5	...	...	...	...	...	...	...	...	Italie
Other Europe	***8.5***	***4.7***	***6.0***	***7.3***	***6.7***	***3.1***	***7.2***	***10.0***	***21.7***	***17.3***	***Autre Europe***
Spain	8.5	...	...	7.3	6.7	3.1	7.2	10.0	21.7	17.3	Espagne
Total	**3 215.2**	**3 420.2**	**3 286.4**	**3 343.4**	**3 517.7**	**3 449.2**	**3 168.5**	**3 169.2**	**3 331.3**	**3 130.2**	**Total**

General note.
Aluminium hydroxide (Al2O3.3H2O or Al(OH)3) in terms of Al2O3. (SITC 51365-2).

Remarque générale.
Hydroxyde d'aluminium (Al2O3.3H2O ou Al(OH)3), exprimé en poids de Al2O3. (CTCI 51365-2).

Aluminium sulphate – Sulfate d'aluminium

Unit : Thousand metric tons

Unité : Milliers de tonnes métriques

Country or area	1976	1977	1978	1979	1980	1981	1982	1983	1984	1985	Pays ou zone
Africa	**3.5**	**5.8**	**9.7**	**14.5**	**21.1**	**25.4**	**19.6**	**10.6**	**9.4**	**10.2**	**Afrique**
Tunisia	3.5	5.8	9.7	14.5	21.1	25.4	19.6	10.6	9.4	10.2	Tunisie
America, North	**1 124.2**	**1 146.6**	**1 195.9**	**1 201.1**	**1 178.1**	**1 184.0**	**1 057.6**	**1 026.4**	**1 135.4**	**1 092.2**	**Amérique du Nord**
Cuba	...	8.6	8.9	8.7	11.2	10.5	11.2	10.8	11.6	12.3	Cuba
United States	1 116.0	1 138.0	1 187.0	1 192.5	1 166.8	1 173.5	1 046.4	1 015.6	1 123.8	1 079.9	Etats-Unis
America, South	**182.8**	**205.4**	**210.6**	**245.7**	**251.9**	**265.2**	**297.0**	**313.2**	**368.6**	**365.0**	**Amérique du Sud**
Brazil	122.3	134.0	141.9	163.2	176.4	197.9	216.1	228.7	283.7	...	Brésil
Chile	10.2	...	...	...	...	...	...	...	...	...	Chili
Colombia	39.6	38.6	34.1	50.0	41.8	28.9	40.0	40.9	...	...	Colombie
Venezuela	10.7	22.6	24.5	22.3	23.5	...	...	...	...	...	Venezuela
Asia	**1 457.4**	**1 357.5**	**1 295.5**	**1 305.2**	**1 288.0**	**1 264.7**	**1 211.8**	**1 165.3**	**1 164.5**	**1 318.1**	**Asie**
Indonesia	13.6	11.3	13.2	6.4	15.7	17.2	19.2	19.6	32.2	...	Indonésie
Japan	768.9	724.3	712.1	731.9	756.7	727.1	770.1	794.9	824.3	811.6	Japon
Korea, Republic of	26.4	23.4	21.8	68.6	67.3	42.8	108.5	121.5	131.9	185.8	Corée, République de
Turkey	...	...	...	...	...	477.7	314.0	229.3	176.0	294.0	Turquie
Europe	**639.1**	**675.3**	**679.5**	**625.8**	**644.4**	**732.6**	**702.6**	**736.0**	**734.9**	**750.9**	**Europe**
EEC	***349.3***	***361.9***	***390.2***	***383.8***	***378.4***	***394.1***	***396.8***	***402.1***	***410.7***	***415.5***	***CEE***
France	133.5	130.3	136.3	135.3	120.9	...	...	...	...	...	France
Germany, Fed. Rep.[1]	...	...	...	...	...	* 150.0	159.6	161.4	174.8	179.3	Allemagne, Rép. féd.[1]
Greece	10.0	10.7	14.0	11.7	13.3	17.8	12.9	18.3	15.6	...	Grèce
Italy	92.0	99.7	111.5	...	...	...	...	...	...	...	Italie
EFTA	***61.5***	***64.4***	***72.4***	***76.0***	***81.0***	***81.2***	***69.3***	***68.8***	***67.7***	***73.0***	***AELE***
Finland	54.2	55.5	60.1	64.0	66.7	66.5	56.1	55.0	56.6	...	Finlande
Portugal	7.3	8.9	12.3	12.0	14.3	14.7	13.2	13.8	11.1	13.4	Portugal
East Europe	***43.6***	***51.5***	***52.5***	***58.3***	***58.2***	***55.9***	***63.0***	***60.5***	***66.3***	***65.4***	***Europe de l'est***
Bulgaria	12.1	16.8	13.7	12.8	13.0	11.7	12.2	12.7	14.1	15.8	Bulgarie
Czechoslovakia	31.5	34.7	38.8	45.5	45.3	44.2	50.9	47.8	52.2	49.6	Tchécoslovaquie
Other Europe	***184.6***	***197.5***	***164.5***	***107.7***	***126.8***	***201.3***	***173.5***	***204.6***	***190.3***	***197.0***	***Autre Europe***
Spain	129.2	145.1	...	59.7	71.7	144.7	116.4	141.5	...	...	Espagne
Yugoslavia	55.4	52.4	49.9	48.0	55.1	56.6	57.1	63.1	72.5	78.6	Yougoslavie
Total	**3 406.9**	**3 390.6**	**3 391.2**	**3 392.4**	**3 383.3**	**3 472.0**	**3 288.6**	**3 251.5**	**3 412.8**	**3 536.4**	**Total**

General note.
Al2(SO4)3 ordinary or pure, in terms of Al2O3. (SITC 51424-1).

Remarque générale.
Al2(SO4)3 ordinaire ou pur, exprimé en poids de Al2O3. (CTCI 51424-1).

[1] Prior to 1981, data are confidential.

[1] Avant 1981, les données sont confidentielles.

Copper sulphate – Sulfate de cuivre

Unit : Metric tons

Unité : Tonnes métriques

Country or area	1976	1977	1978	1979	1980	1981	1982	1983	1984	1985	Pays ou zone
Africa	**4 552**	**5 618**	**6 684**	**7 750**	**7 053**	**7 340**	**10 964**	**13 453**	**12 940**	**15 329**	**Afrique**
South Africa	...	...	...	...	7 053	7 340	10 964	13 453	12 940	15 329	Afrique du Sud
America, North	**29 141**	**27 306**	**31 881**	**35 005**	**31 010**	**35 636**	**32 227**	**37 500**	**33 000**	**36 467**	**Amérique du Nord**
United States	29 141	27 306	31 881	35 005	31 010	35 636	32 227	37 500	33 000	...	Etats–Unis
America, South	**2 935**	**3 206**	**3 482**	**659**	**7 499**	**5 166**	**5 016**	**3 326**	**5 177**	**5 457**	**Amérique du Sud**
Brazil	...	...	...	637	7 410	5 078	4 921	3 254	...	...	Brésil
Colombia	37	36	40	22	89	88	95	72	...	...	Colombie
Asia	**16 333**	**17 671**	**21 044**	**21 241**	**22 752**	**20 348**	**20 466**	**24 561**	**23 011**	**24 078**	**Asie**
India	2 620	2 110	2 580	...	...	...	...	...	...	...	Inde
Japan	12 517	14 353	16 424	16 685	17 708	16 599	15 580	...	...	...	Japon
Korea, Republic of	1 196	1 208	2 040	2 120	2 608	1 313	2 450	4 293	2 208	2 741	Corée, République de
Europe	**81 632**	**96 822**	**95 328**	**95 173**	**94 535**	**78 902**	**69 629**	**55 692**	**61 081**	**65 197**	**Europe**
EEC	***33 217***	***43 373***	***41 765***	***39 805***	***37 535***	***32 035***	***29 795***	***27 205***	***30 385***	***30 073***	***CEE***
France	19 370	20 450	23 380	21 420	19 150	# 13 650	11 410	8 820	12 000	11 688	France
Germany, Fed. Rep.	559	...	...	...	...	...	...	...	...	...	Allemagne, Rép. féd.
Italy	13 288	22 364	...	...	...	...	...	...	...	...	Italie
EFTA	***1 285***	***1 476***	***1 634***	***1 797***	***1 404***	***1 119***	***1 278***	***974***	***1 238***	***1 099***	***AELE***
Finland	1 285	1 476	1 634	1 797	1 404	1 119	1 278	974	1 238	...	Finlande
East Europe	***24 282***	***25 098***	***25 669***	***26 154***	***25 430***	***23 875***	***18 163***	***10 427***	***12 867***	***13 625***	***Europe de l'est***
Bulgaria	15 040	15 284	15 193	15 110	14 495	14 602	6 647	852	73	80	Bulgarie
Czechoslovakia	3 906	4 658	5 427	5 548	5 475	4 469	5 545	5 502	6 048	5 769	Tchécoslovaquie
Poland	5 336	5 156	5 049	5 496	5 460	4 804	5 971	4 073	6 746	7 776	Pologne
Other Europe	***22 848***	***26 875***	***26 260***	***27 417***	***30 166***	***21 873***	***20 393***	***17 086***	***16 591***	***20 400***	***Autre Europe***
Spain	4 614	6 960	...	4 016	...	3 968	6 500	5 611	...	...	Espagne
Yugoslavia	18 234	19 915	21 025	23 401	24 880	17 905	13 893	11 475	11 203	14 986	Yougoslavie
Total	**134 593**	**150 623**	**158 419**	**159 828**	**162 849**	**147 392**	**138 302**	**134 532**	**135 209**	**146 528**	**Total**

General note.
$CuSO_4.5H_2O$ (cupric sulphate). Cuprous sulphate Cu_2SO_4 is excluded. (SITC 51424–2).

Remarque générale.
$CuSO_4.5H_2O$ (sulfate cuivrique). Cette rubrique ne comprend pas le sulfate cuivreux Cu_2SO_4. (CTCI 51424–2).

Soda ash – Cendres sodiques

Unit : Thousand metric tons

Unité : Milliers de tonnes métriques

Country or area	1976	1977	1978	1979	1980	1981	1982	1983	1984	1985	Pays ou zone
Africa	**107**	**122**	**186**	**207**	**217**	**158**	**139**	**194**	**226**	**228**	**Afrique**
Kenya	107	122	186	207	217	158	139	194	226	228	Kenya
America, North	**7 248**	**7 707**	**7 956**	**7 899**	**7 913**	**7 913**	**7 483**	**8 076**	**8 144**	**8 177**	**Amérique du Nord**
Mexico	390	413	435	412	406	401	390	395	424	457	Mexique
United States[1]	6 858	7 294	7 521	7 487	7 507	7 512	7 093	7 681	7 720	7 720	Etats–Unis[1]
America, South	**286**	**276**	**288**	**252**	**301**	**294**	**310**	**328**	**345**	**317**	**Amérique du Sud**
Brazil	136	140	121	119	176	188	199	210	215	190	Brésil
Colombia[2]	150	136	167	133	125	106	111	118	130	127	Colombie[2]
Asia	**3 062**	**3 108**	**3 375**	**3 721**	**3 827**	**3 823**	**3 842**	**4 020**	**4 153**	**4 317**	**Asie**
China	1 117	1 077	1 329	1 486	1 613	1 652	1 735	1 793	1 880	2 011	Chine
India	565	568	581	544	504	641	597	744	827	825	Inde
Japan	1 080	1 173	1 156	1 348	1 349	1 172	1 157	1 098	1 031	1 052	Japon
Korea, Republic of	155	170	176	204	222	202	186	231	248	251	Corée, République de
Pakistan[3]	79	55	69	71	79	96	107	94	107	118	Pakistan[3]
Turkey* [2]	...	...	64	68	60	60	60	60	60	60	Turquie* [2]
Europe	**8 284**	**7 834**	**8 008**	**8 679**	**8 836**	**8 598**	**7 927**	**7 771**	**8 211**	**8 077**	**Europe**
EEC	***3 992***	***3 535***	***3 400***	***3 748***	***3 694***	***3 576***	***2 939***	***2 979***	***3 162***	***3 251***	***CEE***
Belgium	* 362	# [2] 442	[2] 427	[2] 400	[2] 327	[2] 273	[2] 328	[2] 260	[2] 409	* [2] 450	Belgique
Denmark	1	1	2	3	0	0	0	0	0	0	Danemark
France[4]	1 317	1 365	1 353	1 550	1 560	* 1 601	* 998	* 998	* 898	* 898	France[4]
Germany, Fed. Rep.	1 364	1 351	1 230	1 401	1 411	1 189	1 105	1 218	1 364	1 412	Allemagne, Rép. féd.
Greece	5	5	5	* [2] 1	* [2] 1	* [2] 1	* [2] 1	* [2] 1	* [2] 1	* [2] 1	Grèce
Italy* [2]	672	95	95	95	95	95	90	85	90	90	Italie* [2]
Netherlands	271	276	288	298	300	* [2] 417	* [2] 417	* [2] 417	* [2] 400	* [2] 400	Pays–Bas
EFTA	***130***	***138***	***138***	***195***	***205***	***173***	***169***	***164***	***178***	***183***	***AELE***
Finland	...	...	...	...	...	...	2	0	0	...	Finlande
Norway	14	16	5	10	# [2] 27	[2] 0	[2] 0	* [2] 0	* [2] 0	...	Norvège
Portugal	114	120	131	183	176	172	167	164	178	180	Portugal
Sweden[2]	* 1	* 1	* 1	1	* 1	* 0	* 0	* 0	* 0	...	Suède[2]
East Europe	***3 513***	***3 684***	***3 804***	***4 024***	***4 122***	***4 047***	***4 019***	***3 823***	***3 991***	***3 767***	***Europe de l'est***
Bulgaria	1 025	1 194	1 268	1 468	1 449	1 439	1 430	1 245	1 188	1 016	Bulgarie
Czechoslovakia	119	118	121	119	123	118	106	95	101	110	Tchécoslovaquie
German Dem. Rep.	829	840	852	860	866	878	882	887	890	884	Rép. dém. allemande
Poland	726	671	664	684	747	686	731	808	900	921	Pologne
Romania	814	861	899	893	937	926	870	788	912	836	Roumanie
Other Europe	***649***	***477***	***666***	***712***	***815***	***802***	***800***	***805***	***880***	***876***	***Autre Europe***
Spain	512	320	500	548	686	655	618	622	692	676	Espagne
Yugoslavia	137	157	166	164	129	147	182	183	188	200	Yougoslavie
USSR	**4 842**	**4 876**	**4 858**	**4 782**	**4 780**	**4 860**	**4 763**	**5 099**	**5 116**	**5 027**	**URSS**
Ukrainian SSR	*964*	*1 024*	*1 023*	*1 073*	*1 077*	*1 166*	*1 202*	*1 301*	*1 296*	*1 161*	*RSS d'Ukraine*
Total	**23 829**	**23 923**	**24 671**	**25 540**	**25 874**	**25 646**	**24 464**	**25 488**	**26 195**	**26 143**	**Total**

General note.
Na_2CO_3. Sodium bicarbonate ($NaHCO_3$) and natural sodium carbonate are excluded. (SITC 51428–0).

[1] Including natural sodium carbonate (Na_2CO_3).
[2] Source: U. S. Bureau of Mines, (Washington, D. C.).
[3] Twelve months ending 30 June of year stated.
[4] Beginning 1981, data are confidential.

Remarque générale.
Na_2CO_3. Cette rubrique ne comprend pas le bicarbonate de sodium ($NaHCO_3$)ni le carbonate de sodium naturel. (CTCI 51428–0).

[1] Y compris le carbonate de sodium naturel (Na_2CO_3).
[2] Source: U.S. Bureau of Mines, (Washington, D.C.).
[3] Période de douze mois finissant le 30 juin de l'année indiquée.
[4] A partir de 1981, les données sont confidentielles.

Sodium silicates – Silicate de sodium

Unit : Thousand metric tons

Unité : Milliers de tonnes métriques

Country or area	1976	1977	1978	1979	1980	1981	1982	1983	1984	1985	Pays ou zone
Africa	**2.2**	**2.2**	**1.3**	**1.9**	**1.9**	**1.9**	**1.9**	**1.9**	**1.9**	**1.9**	**Afrique**
Tunisia	2.2	2.2	1.3	...	...	...	...	...	...	...	Tunisie
America, North	**685.1**	**937.7**	**998.7**	**1 017.9**	**722.4**	**707.4**	**610.0**	**653.7**	**629.4**	**661.6**	**Amérique du Nord**
Cuba	...	6.5	8.4	7.5	9.3	8.2	7.7	9.7	8.1	7.3	Cuba
United States	677.5	931.2	990.3	1 010.4	713.0	699.3	602.3	644.0	621.3	654.2	Etats–Unis
America, South	**51.0**	**106.6**	**122.7**	**130.8**	**78.0**	**104.3**	**100.2**	**79.2**	**116.3**	**107.7**	**Amérique du Sud**
Brazil	37.8	97.6	110.0	109.3	62.1	...	...	66.9	100.2	...	Brésil
Colombia	13.2	8.9	12.7	21.5	15.9	18.8	13.2	12.3	...	...	Colombie
Asia	**673.1**	**699.6**	**701.5**	**782.9**	**770.5**	**781.0**	**781.5**	**660.1**	**733.5**	**735.3**	**Asie**
Japan	623.6	632.1	653.8	714.3	712.2	692.5	649.8	587.7	595.9	594.1	Japon
Korea, Republic of	38.2	54.8	34.3	52.1	39.0	68.4	111.2	49.6	112.9	114.7	Corée, République de
Thailand	11.2	12.8	13.4	16.5	19.2	20.2	20.5	22.8	24.8	...	Thaïlande
Europe	**577.8**	**667.7**	**576.8**	**572.4**	**537.3**	**545.7**	**539.3**	**531.1**	**555.7**	**543.3**	**Europe**
EEC	***404.1***	***402.0***	***387.6***	***396.8***	***396.6***	***396.6***	***395.1***	***394.2***	***395.5***	***395.7***	***CEE***
Denmark	* 5.1	* 4.8	* 3.5	* 3.3	3.1	3.1	1.6	0.8	2.0	2.3	Danemark
France[1]	399.0	397.1	384.1	...	...	...	...	...	...	...	France[1]
EFTA	***38.2***	***44.1***	***41.5***	***38.3***	***42.1***	***46.6***	***41.8***	***44.7***	***66.0***	***49.1***	***AELE***
Finland	18.1	22.6	20.9	16.9	15.4	16.4	14.8	16.0	35.1	...	Finlande
Portugal	20.1	21.5	20.6	21.4	26.7	30.2	27.1	28.7	31.0	26.6	Portugal
East Europe	***15.2***	***16.1***	***16.0***	***15.6***	***16.1***	***15.8***	***16.2***	***15.8***	***16.7***	***18.3***	***Europe de l'est***
Hungary	15.2	16.1	16.0	15.6	16.1	15.8	16.2	15.8	16.7	18.3	Hongrie
Other Europe	***120.3***	***205.5***	***131.6***	***121.7***	***82.4***	***86.7***	***86.2***	***76.4***	***77.5***	***80.2***	***Autre Europe***
Spain	120.3	205.5	...	...	82.4	86.7	86.2	76.4	77.5	80.2	Espagne
Total	**1 989.3**	**2 413.7**	**2 401.0**	**2 505.8**	**2 110.0**	**2 140.4**	**2 033.0**	**1 926.0**	**2 036.8**	**2 049.8**	**Total**

General note.
In terms of SiO_2. (SITC 51433–1).

Remarque générale.
En poids de SiO_2 combiné. (CTCI 51433–1).

[1] Beginning 1979, data are confidential.

[1] A partir de 1979, les données sont confidentielles.

Sodium dichromate – Bichromate de sodium

Unit : Thousand metric tons

Unité : Milliers de tonnes métriques

Country or area	1976	1977	1978	1979	1980	1981	1982	1983	1984	1985	Pays ou zone
America, North	**141.3**	**142.2**	**159.0**	**152.0**	**141.8**	**150.5**	**151.6**	**152.6**	**153.7**	**154.8**	**Amérique du Nord**
United States	141.3	142.2	159.0	152.0	141.8	...	...	...	...	...	Etats–Unis
America, South	**26.5**	**26.5**	**26.5**	**26.6**	**25.6**	**23.0**	**33.0**	**28.5**	**22.9**	**26.6**	**Amérique du Sud**
Brazil	...	...	...	...	25.6	23.0	33.0	28.5	22.9	...	Brésil
Asia	**58.5**	**60.4**	**53.2**	**66.4**	**60.7**	**65.7**	**67.2**	**69.0**	**70.8**	**72.6**	**Asie**
India	29.0	31.3	30.3	39.3	33.6	38.6	...	...	...	...	Inde
Japan	29.5	29.1	22.9	...	...	...	...	...	...	...	Japon
Europe	**25.4**	**24.7**	**24.5**	**44.9**	**41.5**	**38.3**	**42.1**	**44.7**	**48.0**	**50.6**	**Europe**
EEC	***1.5***	***0.0***	***0.0***	***19.0***	***16.5***	***14.7***	***17.3***	***19.8***	***22.4***	***25.0***	***CEE***
France[1]	1.5	0.0	0.0	19.0	16.5	...	...	...	...	...	France[1]
East Europe	***19.2***	***19.1***	***18.8***	***18.8***	***18.6***	***17.5***	***18.5***	***18.5***	***18.7***	***18.6***	***Europe de l'est***
Poland	19.2	19.1	18.8	18.8	18.6	17.5	18.5	18.5	18.7	18.6	Pologne
Other Europe	***4.7***	***5.6***	***5.8***	***7.1***	***6.4***	***6.1***	***6.3***	***6.3***	***6.9***	***7.0***	***Autre Europe***
Spain	4.7	...	...	7.1	6.4	6.1	6.3	6.3	...	...	Espagne
Total	**251.7**	**253.8**	**263.3**	**289.8**	**269.6**	**277.5**	**293.8**	**294.9**	**295.4**	**304.7**	**Total**

General note.
Na2Cr2O7.2H2O, in terms of Cr2O3. (SITC 51435–1).

[1] Beginning 1981, data are confidential.

Remarque générale.
Na2Cr2O7.2H2O, en poids de Cr2O3 combiné. (CTCI 51435–1).

[1] A partir de 1981, les données sont confidentielles.

Hydrogen peroxide – Péroxyde d'hydrogène

Unit : Thousand metric tons — Unité : Milliers de tonnes métriques

Country or area	1976	1977	1978	1979	1980	1981	1982	1983	1984	1985	Pays ou zone
America, North	**85.0**	**85.0**	**95.1**	**103.2**	**105.6**	**100.4**	**98.3**	**106.6**	**126.0**	**131.0**	**Amérique du Nord**
United States	85.0	85.0	95.1	103.2	105.6	100.4	98.3	106.6	126.0	131.0	Etats-Unis
America, South	**7.5**	**7.1**	**7.7**	**8.7**	**9.6**	**10.2**	**12.8**	**15.5**	**15.5**	**16.3**	**Amérique du Sud**
Brazil	4.8	4.6	5.7	6.2	6.9	7.4	10.1	12.8	12.6	...	Brésil
Chile	0.4	0.4	0.1	...	...	...	...	...	...	...	Chili
Colombia	2.3	2.2	2.0	2.3	2.4	2.5	2.5	2.5	...	...	Colombie
Asia	**61.5**	**67.0**	**77.1**	**79.5**	**82.6**	**87.6**	**89.0**	**88.7**	**99.5**	**100.0**	**Asie**
India	1.8	5.0	4.6	5.1	4.7	5.2	4.1	3.6	...	...	Inde
Japan	59.7	62.0	72.5	74.4	77.9	82.4	84.9	85.1	94.7	95.1	Japon
Europe	**485.2**	**458.7**	**482.2**	**517.0**	**473.2**	**485.4**	**438.5**	**435.8**	**492.2**	**581.2**	**Europe**
EEC	***461.0***	***430.6***	***450.4***	***477.9***	***434.4***	***443.4***	***391.0***	***385.7***	***430.2***	***508.9***	***CEE***
France	184.1	177.6	178.1	203.6	...	...	...	...	...	...	France
Germany, Fed. Rep.	168.3	160.9	172.0	174.0	148.2	157.2	104.8	99.4	144.0	222.6	Allemagne, Rép. féd.
Italy	108.6	92.1	...	...	...	...	...	...	...	...	Italie
EFTA	***9.8***	***11.9***	***14.1***	***18.8***	***19.0***	***19.3***	***22.4***	***26.0***	***34.9***	***44.4***	***AELE***
Portugal	2.3	2.4	2.2	3.4	3.5	3.1	3.4	4.5	4.2	4.7	Portugal
Sweden	7.5	9.5	11.9	15.4	15.5	16.2	19.0	21.5	30.6	39.6	Suède
East Europe	***1.6***	***2.0***	***2.3***	***2.3***	***2.3***	***2.4***	***1.9***	***1.8***	***2.4***	***2.1***	***Europe de l'est***
Hungary	1.6	2.0	2.3	2.3	2.3	2.4	1.9	1.8	2.4	2.1	Hongrie
Other Europe	***12.8***	***14.2***	***15.4***	***18.0***	***17.4***	***20.2***	***23.1***	***22.4***	***24.8***	***25.8***	***Autre Europe***
Spain	...	...	15.4	18.0	17.4	20.2	23.1	22.4	24.8	25.8	Espagne
Total	**639.2**	**617.8**	**662.2**	**708.5**	**671.0**	**683.6**	**638.7**	**646.6**	**733.3**	**828.4**	**Total**

General note.
H2O2 including solid hydrogen peroxide combined with urea, whether or not stabilized. Hydrogen peroxide put up as a pharmaceutical preparation is excluded. (SITC 51492-0).

Remarque générale.
H2O2, y compris le péroxyde d'hydrogène sous forme solide en combinaison avec l'urée, stabilisé ou non, à l'exclusion de l'eau oxygénée pharmaceutique. (CTCI 51492-0).

Calcium carbide – Carbure de calcium

Unit : Thousand metric tons — Unité : Milliers de tonnes métriques

Country or area	1976	1977	1978	1979	1980	1981	1982	1983	1984	1985	Pays ou zone
America, North	**227**	**233**	**245**	**254**	**246**	**262**	**186**	**195**	**215**	**220**	**Amérique du Nord**
Cuba	6	5	9	11	10	9	11	9	11	11	Cuba
United States	221	228	236	243	236	253	175	186	204	209	Etats-Unis
America, South	**113**	**106**	**120**	**112**	**125**	**118**	**112**	**111**	**116**	**116**	**Amérique du Sud**
Brazil	97	92	105	95	106	100	...	...	...	...	Brésil
Colombia	16	14	15	17	19	18	8	6	...	...	Colombie
Asia	**1 678**	**1 694**	**1 954**	**2 110**	**2 211**	**2 154**	**2 302**	**2 446**	**2 518**	**2 549**	**Asie**
China	963	989	1 238	1 407	1 520	1 513	1 675	1 808	1 846	1 953	Chine
India	84	83	93	95	75	81	70	85	99	67	Inde
Japan	552	541	555	570	550	495	483	476	478	445	Japon
Korea, Republic of	67	68	50	21	41	46	57	61	63	58	Corée, République de
Turkey	12	13	18	17	25	19	17	16	32	...	Turquie
Europe	**3 443**	**3 355**	**3 202**	**3 053**	**3 016**	**2 895**	**2 811**	**2 824**	**2 825**	**2 733**	**Europe**
EEC	***665***	***679***	***619***	***577***	***588***	***562***	***542***	***521***	***501***	***480***	***CEE***
France[1]	94	98	101	97	91	87	...	...	...	...	France[1]
Germany, Fed. Rep.[1]	517	530	476	452	457	432	...	...	...	...	Allemagne, Rép. féd.[1]
Italy	51	48	35	27	...	...	...	...	...	...	Italie
Netherlands[2]	...	...	7	1	0	...	...	...	...	...	Pays-Bas[2]
EFTA	***168***	***168***	***151***	***164***	***157***	***129***	***151***	***153***	***175***	***190***	***AELE***
Finland	...	...	...	...	...	...	4	0	0	...	Finlande
Norway	110	105	85	94	90	79	81	86	101	121	Norvège
Portugal	22	31	35	39	34	26	32	30	35	32	Portugal
Sweden	35	31	30	30	32	23	34	37	39	36	Suède
East Europe	***2 398***	***2 320***	***2 311***	***2 176***	***2 118***	***2 069***	***1 992***	***2 024***	***2 019***	***1 938***	***Europe de l'est***
Bulgaria[3]	73	76	78	77	78	68	42	54	48	48	Bulgarie[3]
Czechoslovakia	140	130	121	107	107	106	89	82	61	65	Tchécoslovaquie
German Dem. Rep.	1 248	1 211	1 223	1 200	1 199	1 187	1 179	1 176	1 177	1 135	Rép. dém. allemande
Hungary	13	13	10	1	0	0	0	0	0	0	Hongrie
Poland[4]	603	579	560	473	455	421	403	441	469	434	Pologne[4]
Romania[5]	321	311	319	318	279	...	...	...	...	...	Roumanie[5]
Other Europe	***212***	***188***	***121***	***136***	***152***	***135***	***126***	***125***	***131***	***125***	***Autre Europe***
Spain	167	160	92	100	114	95	87	89	90	87	Espagne
Yugoslavia	45	28	29	36	38	40	39	36	41	38	Yougoslavie
USSR[6]	**851**	**802**	**791**	**790**	**766**	**699**	**678**	**658**	**646**	**...**	**URSS[6]**
Ukrainian SSR	...	...	*8*	*9*	*9*	*9*	*9*	*9*	*10*	...	*RSS d'Ukraine*
Total	**6 312**	**6 190**	**6 312**	**6 319**	**6 364**	**6 128**	**6 089**	**6 234**	**6 320**	**6 230**	**Total**

General note.
CaC2 in terms of 75 per cent of C. (SITC 51494–0).

Remarque générale.
CaC2 rapporté à une teneur de 75 p. 100 de C. (CTCI 51494–0).

[1] Beginning 1982, data are confidential.
[2] Source: Industrial Statistics, Statistical Office of the European Communities, (Luxembourg).
[3] 220 litres of C2H2 per kilogramme.
[4] In terms of 75 percent calcium carbide.
[5] 260 litres of C2H2 per kilogramme.
[6] Source: United Nations Economic Commission for Europe (ECE), (Geneva).

[1] A partir de 1982, les données sont confidentielles.
[2] Source: Statistiques industrielles, Office statistique des Communautés européennes, (Luxembourg).
[3] 220 litres de C2H2 par kilogramme.
[4] Sur la base de 75 p. 100 de carbure de calcium.
[5] 260 litres de C2H2 par kilogramme.
[6] Source: Commission économique des Nations Unies pour l'Europe (CEE), (Genève).

Dyestuffs, synthetic – Colorant synthétiques

Unit : Metric tons

Unité : Tonnes métriques

Country or area	1976	1977	1978	1979	1980	1981	1982	1983	1984	1985	Pays ou zone
Africa	**172**	**66**	**51**	**20**	**62**	**39**	**26**	**13**	**10**	**20**	**Afrique**
Algeria	172	66	51	20	62	...	...	...	...	...	Algérie
America, North	**120 191**	**124 211**	**118 265**	**125 096**	**122 361**	**122 478**	**122 883**	**122 312**	**122 340**	**122 793**	**Amérique du Nord**
Mexico	3 961	4 295	4 513	4 495	4 737	4 854	5 259	4 688	4 716	5 169	Mexique
United States	116 230	119 916	113 752	120 601	...	...	...	...	...	...	Etats–Unis
America, South	**23 574**	**25 505**	**21 628**	**20 536**	**39 198**	**19 604**	**27 014**	**27 587**	**28 161**	**28 734**	**Amérique du Sud**
Colombia	...	25 505	21 628	20 536	39 198	19 604	...	...	...	...	Colombie
Asia	**163 965**	**163 360**	**165 927**	**170 174**	**161 190**	**138 664**	**184 104**	**169 729**	**170 600**	**168 421**	**Asie**
India[1]	17 804	18 024	19 800	...	...	...	...	...	...	...	Inde[1]
Japan[2]	55 259	54 109	54 513	59 993	51 415	50 174	54 321	54 608	56 738	54 928	Japon[2]
Korea, Republic of	4 207	4 532	4 919	4 944	4 538	4 906	5 049	7 727	8 625	8 256	Corée, République de
Turkey[3]	...	...	...	...	...	65 042	106 192	88 852	...	...	Turquie[3]
Europe	**341 739**	**330 991**	**319 544**	**343 225**	**308 815**	**307 661**	**313 754**	**319 073**	**326 143**	**325 626**	**Europe**
EEC	***260 786***	***249 121***	***236 505***	***256 922***	***223 597***	***227 624***	***227 589***	***233 473***	***241 520***	***241 527***	***CEE***
Belgium	2 296	...	...	...	...	...	...	...	...	...	Belgique
Denmark	...	...	...	...	...	...	4 254	4 457	4 598	4 388	Danemark
France	34 300	35 000	28 210	31 730	29 220	28 030	42 470	42 580	46 754	40 076	France
Germany, Fed. Rep.[4]	150 257	134 821	135 836	145 187	124 297	133 638	119 726	129 381	133 823	134 264	Allemagne, Rép. féd.[4]
Greece[5]	842	1 028	1 210	1 353	1 752	1 631	700	697	735	...	Grèce[5]
Italy	14 287	15 963	14 546	16 791	15 333	13 165	13 987	10 178	8 288	14 971	Italie
Netherlands[6]	* 1 880	1 870	1 800	1 900	1 800	...	...	...	...	...	Pays–Bas[6]
United Kingdom[7]	52 500	53 719	48 183	53 241	44 475	42 629	42 358	42 099	43 254	42 848	Royaume–Uni[7]
EFTA	***46***	***46***	***56***	***57***	***419***	***599***	***822***	***772***	***888***	***1 008***	***AELE***
Finland	2	0	1	0	0	1	9	1	0	...	Finlande
Sweden	44	46	55	57	...	# [3] 598	[3] 813	...	...	...	Suède
East Europe	***62 823***	***64 031***	***64 821***	***66 448***	***67 449***	***64 153***	***62 866***	***64 047***	***63 358***	***62 344***	***Europe de l'est***
Bulgaria[8]	2 080	2 023	1 602	1 691	1 430	1 646	1 660	1 639	1 181	638	Bulgarie[8]
Czechoslovakia	11 385	12 689	12 492	12 649	13 878	14 166	14 902	14 811	14 749	15 127	Tchécoslovaquie
German Dem. Rep.	10 179	9 934	10 183	10 479	10 396	10 853	10 949	10 790	10 958	12 371	Rép. dém. allemande
Hungary	101	85	95	118	92	96	77	100	118	175	Hongrie
Poland[9]	25 781	25 679	26 632	25 766	25 113	21 297	20 192	22 383	22 297	18 152	Pologne[9]
Romania[10]	13 297	13 621	13 817	15 745	16 540	16 095	...	14 324	14 055	15 881	Roumanie[10]
Other Europe	***18 084***	***17 793***	***18 162***	***19 798***	***17 350***	***15 285***	***22 477***	***20 781***	***20 377***	***20 747***	***Autre Europe***
Spain	16 123	...	...	17 837	15 389	13 422	20 417	18 820	...	...	Espagne
Yugoslavia[3]	...	...	...	...	...	1 863	2 060	...	...	...	Yougoslavie[3]
USSR	**89 286**	**92 158**	**91 904**	**83 629**	**81 033**	**82 411**	**82 794**	**80 914**	**74 891**	**73 355**	**URSS**
Ukrainian SSR	*34 792*	*36 336*	*34 519*	*31 693*	*27 936*	*27 035*	*28 529*	*28 246*	*20 995*	*20 754*	*RSS d'Ukraine*
Total	**738 927**	**736 291**	**717 319**	**742 680**	**712 659**	**670 857**	**730 575**	**719 628**	**722 145**	**718 949**	**Total**

General note.
Synthetic organic dyestuffs (including pigment dyestuffs), synthetic organic products of a kind used as luminophores, products of the kind known as optical bleaching agents, substantive to the fibre, natural indigo, colour lakes, in terms of 60 per cent concentration basis. (SITC 53100–0).

[1] Production by large and medium scale establishments only.
[2] Excluding pigment resin colours and lakes.
[3] Source: United Nations Economic Commission for Europe (ECE), (Geneva).
[4] Excluding luminophores, optical bleaching agents, natural indigo and colour lakes.
[5] Including organic colours.
[6] Source: Industrial Statistics, Statistical Office of the European Communities, (Luxembourg).
[7] Sales by manufacturers employing 25 or more persons.
[8] In terms of 100 per cent synthetic dyestuffs.
[9] Data relate to gross weight of organic dyestuffs.
[10] Organic dyestuffs only.

Remarque générale.
Colorants organiques synthétiques (y compris les pigments), produits organiques synthétiques du genre de ceux utilisés comme "luminophores", produits des types dits "agents de blanchiment optique" fixables sur la fibre, indigo naturel, laques colorantes, dont le poids est ramené à une concentration de 60 p. 100. (CTCI 53100–0).

[1] Production des grandes et moyennes entreprises seulement.
[2] Non compris les couleurs et laques à base de pigments et de résines.
[3] Source: Commission économique des Nations Unies pour l'Europe (CEE), (Genève).
[4] Non compris les luminophores, les agents de blanchiment optique, l'indigo naturel et les laques colorantes.
[5] Y compris les colorants organiques.
[6] Source: Statistiques industrielles, Office statistique des Communautés européennes, (Luxembourg).
[7] Ventes des fabricants employant 25 personnes ou plus.
[8] Sur la base de 100 p. 100 de matières colorantes synthétiques.
[9] Données se rapportant au poids brut des colorants organiques.
[10] Colorants organiques seulement.

Vegetable tanning extracts – Extraits tannants d'origine végétale

Unit : Metric tons

Unité : Tonnes métriques

Country or area	1976	1977	1978	1979	1980	1981	1982	1983	1984	1985	Pays ou zone
America, South	**109 833**	**117 869**	**114 550**	**110 973**	**111 127**	**105 455**	**121 233**	**98 174**	**76 869**	**72 712**	**Amérique du Sud**
Argentina	91 929	104 752	97 198	104 314	95 433	92 248	110 571	85 296	65 660	61 774	Argentine
Paraguay	17 904	13 117	17 352	6 659	15 694	13 207	10 662	12 878	11 209	10 938	Paraguay
Asia	**2 130**	**2 499**	**2 114**	**2 753**	**2 374**	**2 374**	**2 374**	**2 374**	**2 374**	**2 374**	**Asie**
Turkey[1]	2 130	2 499	2 114	2 753	...	...	...	...	...	...	Turquie[1]
Europe	**36 447**	**36 210**	**38 109**	**42 334**	**37 789**	**37 746**	**36 186**	**37 009**	**35 886**	**35 868**	**Europe**
EEC	***31 285***	***30 963***	***33 401***	***36 916***	***33 141***	***33 141***	***33 141***	***33 141***	***33 141***	***33 141***	***CEE***
Italy	31 285	30 963	33 401	36 916	...	...	...	...	...	...	Italie
East Europe	***4 815***	***4 900***	***4 361***	***5 071***	***4 301***	***4 258***	***2 698***	***3 521***	***2 398***	***2 380***	***Europe de l'est***
Bulgaria	104	24	...	...	...	...	...	...	...	...	Bulgarie
Poland	2 735	2 961	2 456	3 139	2 431	2 429	907	1 769	684	705	Pologne
Romania	1 976	1 915	1 841	1 868	1 806	...	...	...	...	...	Roumanie
Other Europe	***347***	***347***	***347***	***347***	***347***	***347***	***347***	***347***	***347***	***347***	***Autre Europe***
Spain	347	...	...	...	...	...	...	...	...	...	Espagne
Total	**148 410**	**156 578**	**154 773**	**156 060**	**151 290**	**145 575**	**159 793**	**137 557**	**115 129**	**110 954**	**Total**

General note.
Tannin content (Shake method) of various tanning extracts of vegetable origin from oak, chestnut, quebracho, pines, wattle, sumach, myrobolans, vallonia, gambier, mangrove and divi–divi. Tanning, tanning extracts mixed with synthetic tanning substances and concentrated sulphite lye are excluded. (SITC 53240–0).

[1] Source: The Chemical Industry, Organisation for Economic Co–operation and Development (OECD), (Paris).

Remarque générale.
Teneur en tanin (déterminée par la méthode Shake) des divers extraits d'origine végétale provenant du chêne, du marronnier, du quebracho, de certains pins et acacias, du sumac, du myrobalan, de la vallonée, du gambier, du palétuvier, du dividivi. Cette rubrique ne comprend ni les tanins et extraits tannants mélangés à des produits tannants synthétiques ni les lignosulfites. (CTCI 53240–0).

[1] Source: l'Industrie chimique, Organisation de coopération et de développement économiques (OCDE), (Paris).

Lithopone

Unit : Thousand metric tons

Unité : Milliers de tonnes métriques

Country or area	1976	1977	1978	1979	1980	1981	1982	1983	1984	1985	Pays ou zone
Europe	**83.2**	**80.8**	**86.9**	**84.0**	**82.6**	**82.0**	**80.1**	**82.0**	**84.1**	**84.1**	**Europe**
EEC	***12.5***	***14.2***	***15.6***	***14.9***	***14.3***	***14.3***	***14.3***	***14.3***	***14.3***	***14.3***	***CEE***
France[1]	9.8	12.4	13.4	12.7	...	...	...	...	...	...	France[1]
Italy	2.7	1.8	...	...	...	...	...	...	...	...	Italie
East Europe	***57.5***	***56.9***	***58.6***	***57.6***	***56.9***	***55.3***	***54.3***	***56.1***	***57.2***	***56.8***	***Europe de l'est***
Czechoslovakia	19.4	19.6	19.8	19.0	19.5	19.9	20.3	20.4	20.3	19.9	Tchécoslovaquie
German Dem. Rep.	19.6	19.3	20.8	20.8	21.0	21.0	...	...	...	...	Rép. dém. allemande
Poland	18.6	18.0	18.0	17.9	16.4	14.4	12.4	13.7	14.6	14.1	Pologne
Other Europe	***13.3***	***9.7***	***12.7***	***11.4***	***11.4***	***12.4***	***11.4***	***11.6***	***12.6***	***13.0***	***Autre Europe***
Spain	9.7	6.3	...	...	...	...	...	...	...	...	Espagne
Yugoslavia	3.5	3.4	4.7	3.4	3.4	4.4	3.4	3.5	4.6	5.0	Yougoslavie
USSR	**404.0**	**402.6**	**379.3**	**352.6**	**363.7**	**364.5**	**363.2**	**360.6**	**371.9**	**371.4**	**URSS**
Byelorussian SSR	*0.2*	*0.2*	*0.2*	*0.2*	*0.1*	*0.0*	*0.0*	*0.1*	*0.1*	*0.1*	*RSS de Biélorussie*
Ukrainian SSR	*147.6*	*151.3*	*160.9*	*150.7*	*159.7*	*164.9*	*159.1*	*158.5*	*170.0*	*170.0*	*RSS d'Ukraine*
Total	**487.3**	**483.4**	**466.2**	**436.6**	**446.4**	**446.5**	**443.2**	**442.6**	**456.1**	**455.5**	**Total**

General note.
Lithopone and other pigments with a basis of zinc sulphide, such as white pigments consisting of mixtures in varying proportions of zinc sulphide and barium sulphate. (SITC 53310–2).

[1] Beginning 1980, data are confidential.

Remarque générale.
Lithopone et produits similaires à base de sulfure de zinc, tels que les pigments blancs constitués par un mélange en proportions variables de sulfure de zinc et de sulfate de baryum. (CTCI 53310–2).

[1] A partir de 1980, les données sont confidentielles.

Activated carbon – Charbons activés

Unit : Thousand metric tons

Unité : Milliers de tonnes métriques

Country or area	1976	1977	1978	1979	1980	1981	1982	1983	1984	1985	Pays ou zone
America, North	**71.5**	**79.5**	**104.0**	**89.2**	**88.2**	**85.2**	**97.8**	**92.9**	**107.9**	**90.6**	**Amérique du Nord**
United States	71.5	79.5	104.0	89.2	88.2	85.2	97.8	92.9	107.9	90.6	Etats-Unis
Asia	**47.1**	**50.5**	**56.2**	**57.2**	**54.5**	**54.5**	**56.6**	**56.7**	**60.0**	**64.0**	**Asie**
India	1.5	1.6	1.7	...	...	...	...	...	...	...	Inde
Japan	40.1	41.5	48.0	49.1	46.4	46.5	48.6	48.7	51.9	56.0	Japon
Korea, Republic of	2.5	...	...	...	...	...	...	...	...	...	Corée, République de
Philippines [1]	3.0	4.9	...	...	...	...	...	...	...	...	Philippines [1]
Europe	**634.1**	**633.6**	**596.6**	**575.8**	**644.2**	**521.7**	**499.3**	**528.4**	**488.4**	**504.1**	**Europe**
EEC	***404.6***	***425.3***	***409.2***	***431.2***	***433.7***	***432.9***	***429.1***	***418.8***	***426.1***	***462.9***	***CEE***
Germany, Fed. Rep.	400.7	421.9	405.6	427.6	430.1	429.3	425.5	415.2	422.5	459.3	Allemagne, Rép. féd.
Italy	3.8	3.4	...	...	...	...	...	...	...	...	Italie
East Europe	***0.9***	***0.6***	***0.6***	***0.6***	***0.5***	***0.7***	***0.5***	***0.6***	***0.7***	***0.5***	***Europe de l'est***
Hungary	0.9	0.6	0.6	0.6	0.5	0.7	0.5	0.6	0.7	0.5	Hongrie
Other Europe	***228.6***	***207.7***	***186.8***	***144.1***	***210.1***	***88.1***	***69.8***	***109.0***	***61.6***	***40.7***	***Autre Europe***
Spain	...	...	...	144.1	210.1	88.1	69.8	109.0	...	...	Espagne
Total	**752.7**	**763.5**	**756.7**	**722.3**	**786.9**	**661.4**	**653.8**	**678.1**	**656.3**	**658.7**	**Total**

General note.
Activated carbon and activated natural mineral products (that is, activated diatomite, certain volcanic minerals, activated clays and earths, activated bauxite). Activated carbons having the character of medicament, catalysts consisting of chemical products are excluded. (SITC 59992-0).

[1] Shipments.

Remarque générale.
Charbons activés et produits minéraux naturels activés (silices fossiles activées, certaines roches volcaniques, argiles et terres activées, bauxite activée). Cette rubrique ne comprend pas les charbons activés à caractère médicamenteux et les catalyseurs constitués par un produit chimique fixé sur une matière activée. (CTCI 59992-0).

[1] Expéditions.

Nitrogenous fertilizers, N content – Engrais azotés, N contenu

Unit : Thousand metric tons | Unité : Milliers de tonnes métriques

Country or area	1976	1977	1978	1979	1980	1981	1982	1983	1984	1985	Pays ou zone
Africa	**623**	**742**	**805**	**810**	**1 172**	**1 387**	**1 588**	**1 567**	**1 531**	**1 731**	**Afrique**
Algeria* [1]	31	33	42	42	21	24	51	47	65	...	Algérie* [1]
Cameroon	1	1	* 1	* 1	...	...	* 9	...	...	...	Cameroun
Côte d'Ivoire	* [1] 4	* [1] 5	* [1] 5	* [1] 5	4	6	2	5	5	...	Côte d'Ivoire
Egypt [1,2]	151	170	195	216	264	400	* 482	* 626	646	680	Egypte [1,2]
Mauritius	6	9	8	8	9	9	8	8	11	10	Maurice
Morocco [1]	* 13	* 21	* 26	* 20	* 36	* 26	39	55	34	...	Maroc [1]
Mozambique [1,2]	* 2	* 5	* 6	* 6	* 5	* 7	* 3	* 2	1	...	Mozambique [1,2]
Senegal [1,2]	9	9	10	9	* 5	* 6	* 5	* 3	* 4	10	Sénégal [1,2]
South Africa	* [1] 332	* [1] 414	* [1] 451	* [1] 433	# 742	710	759	576	* 463	577	Afrique du Sud
Tunisia [1]	0	* 5	* 5	* 5	* 9	* 47	69	73	83	* 124	Tunisie [1]
United Rep. Tanzania [1]	3	4	3	* 5	* 4	* # 69	* 73	83	124	...	Rép.Unie de Tanzanie [1]
Zambia [1]	* 6	* 6	* 8	* 10	* 9	* 7	* 4	* 9	16	15	Zambie [1]
Zimbabwe [1]	65	60	45	50	59	70	84	71	* 69	...	Zimbabwe [1]
America, North	**11 088**	**11 676**	**11 734**	**12 426**	**13 707**	**14 510**	**13 409**	**11 640**	**13 252**	**13 914**	**Amérique du Nord**
Canada* [1,2]	775	1 204	1 578	1 674	1 709	1 755	1 825	1 897	2 371	2 543	Canada* [1,2]
Costa Rica [1]	* 30	31	32	* 33	* 36	* 42	* 46	* 36	41	...	Costa Rica [1]
Cuba	81	40	27	113	* 162	* 142	* 96	74	144	149	Cuba
El Salvador [1]	* 5	* 4	* 12	24	* 15	...	...	3	...	...	El Salvador [1]
Guatemala [1,2]	* 6	* 6	* 7	* 2	* 11	* 9	* 9	12	* 8	9	Guatemala [1,2]
Jamaica [1]	4	2	...	5	8	9	...	...	...	...	Jamaïque [1]
Mexico	[1,2] 546	[1,2] 553	[1,2] 535	[1,2] 450	# 542	676	874	861	959	1 133	Mexique
Neth.Antil and Aruba [1,2]	6	2	0	0	0	0	...	...	...	...	Antill.néer.et Aruba [1,2]
Trinidad and Tobago [1]	44	46	43	49	44	41	24	30	23	67	Trinité–et–Tobago [1]
United States [2]	9 591	9 788	9 495	10 076	11 180	11 825	10 513	8 715	9 682	9 943	Etats–Unis [2]
America, South	**495**	**553**	**581**	**592**	**765**	**763**	**808**	**941**	**1 107**	**1 108**	**Amérique du Sud**
Argentina [1]	* 18	* 21	27	28	* 25	* 25	* 29	32	34	...	Argentine [1]
Brazil	200	232	273	237	383	349	397	518	670	...	Brésil
Chile [1,3]	100	96	89	94	101	94	92	* 98	114	...	Chili [1,3]
Colombia [1]	66	72	59	57	* 42	* 42	* 48	54	60	...	Colombie [1]
Ecuador [1]	2	2	2	* 2	2	* 2	* 3	* 3	...	...	Equateur [1]
Peru [1]	34	55	69	71	67	86	74	28	* 19	...	Pérou [1]
Venezuela [1]	* 75	75	62	103	* 145	* 165	* 165	* 208	* 207	255	Venezuela [1]
Asia	**9 718**	**11 756**	**14 829**	**17 134**	**19 083**	**19 457**	**20 006**	**21 605**	**24 176**	**24 209**	**Asie**
Afghanistan [1,2]	26	38	48	48	49	48	48	48	50	48	Afghanistan [1,2]
Bangladesh [1,2]	131	126	106	200	371	161	193	237	337	343	Bangladesh [1,2]
Burma [1,4]	47	55	53	58	62	60	* 51	60	* 87	...	Birmanie [1,4]
China	3 815	5 509	7 639	8 821	9 993	9 857	10 219	11 094	12 210	11 440	Chine
India [2]	[1] 1 332	[1] 1 648	[1] 1 723	[1] 2 173	[1] 2 224	# 2 987	3 359	3 358	3 835	4 232	Inde [2]
Indonesia [1]	208	184	396	* 694	958	971	940	1 077	* 1 402	...	Indonésie [1]
Iran(Islamic Rep.of)* [1,2]	126	136	124	72	93	71	21	22	24	14	Iran(Rép.islamique)* [1,2]
Iraq [1]	* 24	25	125	166	387	* 355	...	14	11	...	Iraq [1]
Israel [2]	43	45	45	54	51	41	41	44	48	...	Israël [2]
Japan [2]	1 567	1 653	1 807	1 784	1 626	1 423	1 241	1 152	1 225	1 131	Japon [2]
Korea,Dem.Ppl's.Rep. [1]	370	440	540	550	553	600	* 588	* 608	620	...	Corée,Rép.pop.dém.de [1]
Korea, Republic of [1,5]	579	535	636	751	* 786	* 688	* 666	* 616	* 580	...	Corée, République de [1,5]
Kuwait [1]	259	228	291	* 310	307	* 183	* 234	* 224	281	...	Koweït [1]
Lebanon* [1]	1	1	1	1	0	0	...	...	...	...	Liban* [1]
Malaysia [1,2,6]	34	42	43	37	37	35	20	20	44	47	Malaisie [1,2,6]
Pakistan [1,2]	316	312	311	336	367	541	715	999	1 015	1 028	Pakistan [1,2]
Philippines [1]	50	38	* 46	* 35	* 34	21	4	7	8	...	Philippines [1]
Qatar [1]	* 87	95	76	118	229	286	265	305	318	341	Qatar [1]
Saudi Arabia [1]	* 100	84	93	121	138	* 152	159	161	266	* 397	Arabie saoudite [1]
Syrian Arab Republic [1,2]	26	22	24	25	21	13	37	80	74	117	Rép. arabe syrienne [1,2]
Thailand [1]	4	7	9	4	...	...	...	...	...	...	Thaïlande [1]
Turkey	* [1] 189	* [1] 187	* [1] 269	* [1] 305	306	608	646	1 072	1 172	1 050	Turquie
Viet Nam* [1]	25	34	40	40	40	15	15	15	15	15	Viet Nam* [1]
Europe	**13 368**	**14 104**	**14 898**	**14 970**	**15 636**	**15 237**	**15 056**	**15 485**	**16 068**	**16 563**	**Europe**
EEC	***5 997***	***6 606***	***6 936***	***7 247***	***7 819***	***7 321***	***7 095***	***7 388***	***7 743***	***8 018***	***CEE***
Belgium [1,2,7]	466	468	442	570	562	544	739	755	706	715	Belgique [1,2,7]
Denmark [2]	28	28	29	27	28	* 35	112	130	110	101	Danemark [2]
France [2]	[1] 1 361	* [1] 1 462	* [1] 1 470	* [1] 1 781	* [1] 1 780	1 640	1 553	1 530	1 687	1 715	France [2]
Germany, Fed. Rep.	925	922	903	975	1 113	996	666	744	838	830	Allemagne, Rép. féd.
Greece [1]	288	273	* 278	311	320	* 317	* 364	* 402	* 430	...	Grèce [1]

For general note and footnotes, see end of table.

Voir la fin du tableau pour la remarque générale et les notes.

Nitrogenous fertilizers, N content (continued) – Engrais azotés, N contenu (suite)

Unit : Thousand metric tons

Unité : Milliers de tonnes métriques

Country or area	1976	1977	1978	1979	1980	1981	1982	1983	1984	1985	Pays ou zone
Ireland* [1,2]	100	100	120	66	102	190	205	235	265	260	Irlande* [1,2]
Italy [1,2]	1 000	985	1 042	1 127	1 187	1 071	899	858	835	1 060	Italie [1,2]
Netherlands [1,2]	1 155	1 297	1 453	1 243	1 411	1 361	1 287	1 335	1 500	1 551	Pays-Bas [1,2]
United Kingdom	674	1 071	1 199	1 147	1 316	1 167	1 270	1 399	1 372	1 360	Royaume-Uni
EFTA	***1 117***	***1 044***	***1 107***	***869***	***849***	***843***	***763***	***756***	***789***	***762***	***AELE***
Austria [1,2]	256	* 239	* 285	* 295	* 275	* 300	* 238	* 255	* 220	* 233	Autriche [1,2]
Finland [2]	202	190	185	82	71	80	61	49	57	...	Finlande [2]
Iceland [1,5]	9	11	10	3	3	2	2	[8] 8	[8] 10	...	Islande [1,5]
Norway [1,2]	356	337	336	* 180	195	177	183	174	196	184	Norvège [1,2]
Portugal	190	177	194	204	198	178	165	139	161	186	Portugal
Sweden [1,5]	78	62	69	73	72	73	81	101	111	116	Suède [1,5]
Switzerland [1,2]	26	28	28	32	35	33	* 33	* 30	* 34	* 34	Suisse [1,2]
East Europe	***5 307***	***5 493***	***5 879***	***5 762***	***5 813***	***5 913***	***6 118***	***6 385***	***6 502***	***6 636***	***Europe de l'est***
Albania* [1]	45	50	72	73	73	73	71	73	75	...	Albanie* [1]
Bulgaria [9]	663	705	685	677	730	753	758	831	836	838	Bulgarie [9]
Czechoslovakia	568	605	625	591	618	539	568	591	576	582	Tchécoslovaquie
German Dem. Rep.	776	839	892	875	943	967	948	968	959	1 078	Rép. dém. allemande
Hungary	492	514	534	550	559	589	571	594	583	604	Hongrie
Poland	1 432	1 399	1 348	1 258	1 183	1 170	1 194	1 237	1 261	1 254	Pologne
Romania [1]	1 331	1 381	1 723	1 738	1 707	1 822	2 008	2 091	2 212	2 197	Roumanie [1]
Other Europe	***947***	***961***	***976***	***1 092***	***1 155***	***1 160***	***1 080***	***956***	***1 034***	***1 148***	***Autre Europe***
Spain [1,2]	659	682	* 688	778	859	856	785	654	677	776	Espagne [1,2]
Yugoslavia	288	279	288	314	296	304	295	302	357	372	Yougoslavie
USSR	**8 609**	**9 114**	**9 299**	**9 151**	**10 241**	**10 705**	**11 593**	**13 014**	**13 328**	**14 223**	**URSS**
Ukrainian SSR	*2 308*	*2 405*	*2 386*	*2 284*	*2 403*	*2 565*	*2 892*	*3 109*	*3 044*	*3 220*	*RSS d'Ukraine*
Oceania	**216**	**256**	**251**	**242**	**246**	**250**	**242**	**205**	**221**	**286**	**Océanie**
Australia [1,2,8]	180	220	215	206	210	214	206	200	173	231	Australie [1,2,8]
New Zealand* [1,2]	...	...	...	...	...	...	...	5	48	55	Nouvelle-Zélande* [1,2]
Total	**44 117**	**48 201**	**52 397**	**55 325**	**60 850**	**62 309**	**62 702**	**64 457**	**69 683**	**72 034**	**Total**

General note.
N content of nitrogenous fertilizer materials (other than natural). Intermediary products such as ammonia for further processing into fertilizers and part of separate chemically defined compounds and compounds of a high degree of purity are excluded. (SITC 5611 and part of SITC 5619).

[1] Source: Food and Agriculture Organization (FAO), (Rome).

[2] Fertilizer year ending 30 June of year stated.
[3] Including complex fertilizers.
[4] Twelve months ending 30 September of year stated.
[5] Fertilizer year ending 30 April of year stated.
[6] Data refer to Peninsular Malaysia only.
[7] Including data for Luxembourg.
[8] Including multinutrient fertilizers.
[9] Including urea.

Remarque générale.
Poids de l'azote contenu dans les produits fertilisants azotés (autres que naturels). Les produits intermédiaires, tels que l'ammoniac devant servir à la fabrication d'engrais, les composés chimiques définis séparément et les corps composés d'une grande pureté ne sont pas compris dans cette rubrique. (CTCI 5611 et partie de CTCI 5619).

[1] Source: Organisation des Nations Unies pour l'alimentation et l'agriculture (FAO), (Rome).
[2] Campagne d'engrais se terminant le 30 juin de l'année indiquée.
[3] Y compris les engrais complexes.
[4] Période de douze mois finissant le 30 septembre de l'année indiquée.
[5] Campagne d'engrais se terminant le 30 avril de l'année indiquée.
[6] Données se rapportant à la Malaisie péninsulaire seulement.
[7] Y compris les données relatives au Luxembourg.
[8] Y compris les engrais composés.
[9] Y compris l'urée.

Superphosphates, P2O5 content – Superphosphates, P2O5 contenu

Unit : Thousand metric tons — Unité : Milliers de tonnes métriques

Country or area	1976	1977	1978	1979	1980	1981	1982	1983	1984	1985	Pays ou zone
Africa	**855**	**966**	**977**	**995**	**1 298**	**1 498**	**1 472**	**1 619**	**1 291**	**1 454**	**Afrique**
Algeria* [1]	64	70	46	38	31	23	48	53	77	...	Algérie* [1]
Cameroon [1]	2	* 1	* 1	* 2	...	...	...	...	...	...	Cameroun [1]
Côte d'Ivoire	* [1] 1	* [1] 2	* [1] 2	* [1] 2	3	3	3	2	3	...	Côte d'Ivoire
Egypt [1,2]	74	74	88	* 86	84	84	* 93	146	123	112	Egypte [1,2]
Morocco [1]	102	115	121	86	* 177	* 199	* 296	493	336	...	Maroc [1]
Mozambique [1,2]	* 1	* 2	* 1	* 1	* 1	* 0	* 2	1	0	...	Mozambique [1,2]
Nigeria* [1]	1	3	4	4	6	10	7	4	5	...	Nigéria* [1]
Senegal	7	# [1,3] 21	* [1,3] 20	* [1,3] 28	* [1,3] 28	* [1,3] 25	* [1,3] 16	* [1,3] 30	* [1,3] 30	...	Sénégal
South Africa [4]	* [1] 394	* [1] 403	* [1] 425	* [1] 444	# 644	825	687	552	385	415	Afrique du Sud [4]
Tunisia	163	228	238	269	285	287	280	291	290	368	Tunisie
Uganda	* [1] 1	[1] 4	* [1] 1	0	0	0	0	...	...	...	Ouganda
Zimbabwe* [1]	45	43	30	35	37	40	38	45	40	...	Zimbabwe* [1]
America, North	**1 960**	**2 127**	**2 093**	**2 157**	**2 014**	**1 652**	**1 190**	**1 381**	**1 226**	**1 256**	**Amérique du Nord**
Cuba	1	3	8	3	4	7	5	2	2	4	Cuba
El Salvador* [1]	2	4	5	4	2	...	...	...	...	...	El Salvador* [1]
Guatemala [1,2]	* 6	* 5	* 5	* 2	* 6	8	8	* 11	* 9	* 10	Guatemala [1,2]
Mexico	157	182	160	158	# 53	68	55	125	114	118	Mexique
United States	1 794	1 933	1 915	1 990	1 949	1 566	* 1 119	1 240	1 098	1 121	Etats-Unis
America, South	**600**	**773**	**746**	**683**	**903**	**682**	**591**	**549**	**863**	**718**	**Amérique du Sud**
Argentina* [1]	7	8	4	1	1	1	0	0	0	0	Argentine* [1]
Brazil	525	680	659	613	820	594	483	452	745	...	Brésil
Chile [1]	7	6	...	...	...	...	...	...	...	...	Chili [1]
Colombia* [1]	33	50	50	45	35	...	...	...	...	...	Colombie* [1]
Peru [1]	2	2	* 2	* 1	* 2	* 4	3	2	1	...	Pérou [1]
Uruguay* [1]	10	10	11	14	14	20	17	6	...	...	Uruguay* [1]
Venezuela [1,4]	* 16	* 17	* 13	* 2	* 24	14	* 39	* 40	* 54	...	Venezuela [1,4]
Asia	**2 295**	**2 639**	**1 970**	**2 810**	**3 382**	**3 539**	**3 475**	**3 693**	**3 566**	**3 099**	**Asie**
Bangladesh [1,2]	22	20	18	58	68	33	30	32	37	26	Bangladesh [1,2]
China	1 418	1 708	1 033	1 817	2 308	2 508	2 537	2 666	2 360	1 760	Chine
India [1,2]	112	127	161	187	178	197	215	222	248	308	Inde [1,2]
Indonesia [1,2]	0	0	0	0	214	257	257	271	368	461	Indonésie [1,2]
Israel	44	21	24	17	34	39	36	57	96	...	Israël
Japan	119	142	135	142	137	113	116	115	120	119	Japon
Korea,Dem.Ppl's.Rep. [1,4]	127	127	127	127	127	127	130	130	* 130	...	Corée,Rép.pop.dém.de [1,4]
Korea, Republic of [1,2]	23	20	20	21	* 24	...	...	...	...	...	Corée, République de [1,2]
Lebanon* [1]	30	66	62	98	103	51	10	5	14	...	Liban* [1]
Malaysia [1,2,5]	22	25	29	33	27	20	20	26	48	10	Malaisie [1,2,5]
Pakistan [1,2,6]	11	12	14	18	18	18	18	19	19	19	Pakistan [1,2,6]
Syrian Arab Republic [1,2]	0	0	0	0	0	0	26	54	58	88	Rép. arabe syrienne [1,2]
Turkey	[1] 267	* [1] 276	* [1] 221	* [1] 162	114	131	29	...	...	...	Turquie
Viet Nam [1]	* 100	* 95	* 126	* 130	* 30	23	28	* 30	* 35	* 38	Viet Nam [1]
Europe	**4 015**	**4 100**	**4 158**	**4 392**	**4 325**	**4 280**	**3 881**	**3 822**	**3 848**	**3 864**	**Europe**
EEC	***1 529***	***1 593***	***1 566***	***1 713***	***1 750***	***1 632***	***1 460***	***1 344***	***1 406***	***1 494***	***CEE***
Belgium* [1,2]	...	...	...	32	61	...	...	...	...	...	Belgique* [1,2]
Denmark [7]	65	55	11	20	25	104	93	40	85	76	Danemark [7]
France [2,8]	814	875	835	890	907	795	758	664	661	776	France [2,8]
Germany, Fed. Rep.	40	43	42	37	41	39	35	29	11	9	Allemagne, Rép. féd.
Greece [1,2]	[4] 114	[4] 134	[4] 180	[4] 208	[4] 189	[4] 170	[4] 143	* 167	* 194	* 197	Grèce [1,2]
Ireland [1,2,4]	89	79	95	50	42	44	37	13	15	8	Irlande [1,2,4]
Italy [1,2]	125	113	166	167	196	170	142	167	157	146	Italie [1,2]
Netherlands [1,2]	102	121	76	202	178	153	131	137	* 164	...	Pays-Bas [1,2]
United Kingdom [9]	...	...	114	* [1] 107	* [1] 111	* [1] 110	* [1] 74	...	...	...	Royaume-Uni [9]
EFTA	***277***	***202***	***215***	***202***	***208***	***208***	***179***	***185***	***214***	***223***	***AELE***
Austria [1,2]	90	105	108	104	* 108	* 105	* 96	* 95	* 110	* 112	Autriche [1,2]
Finland [2]	5	4	3	3	3	2	3	2	2	...	Finlande [2]
Portugal	101	74	88	87	84	79	65	59	80	84	Portugal
Sweden [1,2]	80	17	15	7	12	21	14	28	21	25	Suède [1,2]
Switzerland [1,2]	1	2	1	1	1	1	1	1	1	1	Suisse [1,2]
East Europe	***1 902***	***2 001***	***2 179***	***2 109***	***1 940***	***2 043***	***2 004***	***2 042***	***2 007***	***1 943***	***Europe de l'est***

For general note and footnotes, see end of table. — Voir la fin du tableau pour la remarque générale et les notes.

Unit : Thousand metric tons — Unité : Milliers de tonnes métriques

Country or area	1976	1977	1978	1979	1980	1981	1982	1983	1984	1985	Pays ou zone
Albania* [1 4]	22	21	24	23	17	6	23	25	18	...	Albanie* [1 4]
Bulgaria	242	279	283	282	217	258	239	204	211	172	Bulgarie
Czechoslovakia	180	189	162	148	147	143	131	127	129	129	Tchécoslovaquie
German Dem. Rep.	224	228	237	227	222	225	199	196	192	187	Rép. dém. allemande
Hungary	188	165	185	165	149	158	156	167	160	130	Hongrie
Poland	553	571	628	555	501	536	532	590	532	519	Pologne
Romania	493	548	660	709	687	717	...	733	765	788	Roumanie
Other Europe	***307***	***304***	***198***	***368***	***427***	***397***	***238***	***251***	***221***	***204***	***Autre Europe***
Spain [1 2]	211	204	114	252	331	253	100	111	105	110	Espagne [1 2]
Yugoslavia	96	100	84	116	96	144	138	140	116	94	Yougoslavie
USSR	**5 664**	**6 024**	**6 153**	**6 344**	**6 455**	**6 836**	**7 057**	**7 417**	**7 695**	**8 596**	**URSS**
Byelorussian SSR	*232*	*236*	*241*	*260*	*254*	*228*	*219*	*209*	*209*	*225*	*RSS de Biélorussie*
Ukrainian SSR	*1 332*	*1 363*	*1 340*	*1 415*	*1 344*	*1 467*	*1 536*	*1 590*	*1 460*	*1 563*	*RSS d'Ukraine*
Oceania	**915**	**1 149**	**1 202**	**871**	**1 369**	**1 181**	**1 149**	**948**	**1 058**	**959**	**Océanie**
Australia [1 2]	481	722	755	420	* 919	* 800	785	* 591	* 678	* 590	Australie [1 2]
Christmas Isl.(Aust) [1 2]	52	48	49	51	40	35	28	27	22	...	Ile Christmas (Aust) [1 2]
New Zealand [1 2]	* 382	* 379	* 398	* 400	* 410	* 346	* 336	* 330	358	350	Nouvelle-Zélande [1 2]
Total	**16 304**	**17 778**	**17 298**	**18 252**	**19 745**	**19 668**	**18 814**	**19 429**	**19 547**	**19 946**	**Total**

General note.
P2O5 content of single, double and concentrated superphosphates. (Parts of SITC 56129 and 5619).

[1] Source: Food and Agriculture Organization (FAO), (Rome).
[2] Fertilizer year ending 30 June of year stated.
[3] Including other phosphatic fertilizers and complex fertilizers.
[4] Including other phosphatic fertilizers.
[5] Peninsular Malaysia only.
[6] Twelve months ending 30 June of year stated.
[7] Fertilizer year ending 31 July of year stated.
[8] Crude weight. Nutrient content not known.
[9] Fertilizer year ending 31 May of year stated.

Remarque générale.
Poids de P2O5 contenu dans les superphosphates simples, doubles et composés. (Parties de CTCI 56129 et 5619).

[1] Source: Organisation des Nations Unies pour l'alimentation et l'agriculture (FAO), (Rome).
[2] Campagne d'engrais se terminant le 30 juin de l'année indiquée.
[3] Y compris les autres engrais phosphatés et les engrais composés.
[4] Y compris les autres engrais phosphatés.
[5] Malaisie péninsulaire seulement.
[6] Période de douze mois finissant le 30 juin de l'année indiquée.
[7] Campagne d'engrais se terminant le 31 juillet de l'année indiquée.
[8] Poids brut. Teneur en éléments nutritifs inconnue.
[9] Campagne d'engrais se terminant le 31 mai de l'année indiquée.

Phosphatic fertilizers, other, P2O5 content – Autres engrais phosphatés, P2O5 contenu

Unit : Thousand metric tons — Unité : Milliers de tonnes métriques

Country or area	1976	1977	1978	1979	1980	1981	1982	1983	1984	1985	Pays ou zone
Africa	**9**	**16**	**12**	**11**	**12**	**12**	**11**	**4**	**9**	**11**	**Afrique**
Tunisia	9	16	12	11	12	12	11	4	9	11	Tunisie
America, North	**3 729**	**4 884**	**4 961**	**5 692**	**6 472**	**5 505**	**6 757**	**7 267**	**6 853**	**6 884**	**Amérique du Nord**
Canada[1 2 3]	610	632	651	660	703	724	658	581	655	645	Canada[1 2 3]
Cuba[1 3]	10	9	7	12	...	...	6	4	2	2	Cuba[1 3]
Mexico	94	100	68	61	147	95	186	148	180	192	Mexique
United States[1]	3 015	4 143	4 235	4 959	5 615	4 680	5 907	6 534	6 016	6 045	Etats-Unis[1]
America, South	**376**	**310**	**549**	**663**	**823**	**620**	**699**	**693**	**854**	**898**	**Amérique du Sud**
Brazil	351	293	474	637	760	556	612	598	739	...	Brésil
Colombia	...	7	59	5	...	50	48	...	...	...	Colombie
Venezuela[3]	12	* 10	...	...	...	[1] 14	39	40	54	...	Venezuela[3]
Asia	**401**	**551**	**710**	**818**	**961**	**891**	**889**	**1 103**	**1 299**	**1 425**	**Asie**
India[1 3]	57	69	126	138	268	260	294	373	529	633	Inde[1 3]
Indonesia[1 3]	0	0	0	0	0	0	0	6	...	...	Indonésie[1 3]
Iran(Islamic Rep.of)[1 3]	83	109	91	68	* 46	* 30	* 3	7	4	...	Iran(Rép.islamique)[1 3]
Japan[1]	134	164	170	170	169	124	119	129	132	132	Japon[1]
Korea, Republic of[1 2 3]	43	124	222	330	356	...	324	447	458	488	Corée, République de[1 2 3]
Philippines[3]	...	...	...	...	...	19	5	7	7	...	Philippines[3]
Turkey[1 3]	74	75	...	...	...	...	144	134	165	155	Turquie[1 3]
Europe	**1 653**	**1 917**	**1 938**	**2 027**	**1 984**	**1 869**	**1 742**	**1 863**	**1 920**	**1 789**	**Europe**
EEC	***1 122***	***1 415***	***1 404***	***1 506***	***1 497***	***1 420***	***1 328***	***1 429***	***1 470***	***1 325***	***CEE***
Belgium[1 3]	56	...	...	* 61	* 48	...	...	...	...	...	Belgique[1 3]
Denmark	0	0	49	49	46	46	46	48	47	...	Danemark
France[1 4]	858	1 081	1 062	1 139	1 177	1 117	1 040	1 148	1 169	1 039	France[1 4]
Germany, Fed. Rep.[1]	144	194	167	174	177	163	126	116	135	117	Allemagne, Rép. féd.[1]
Netherlands[1 3]	63	85	71	82	46	34	48	57	59	...	Pays-Bas[1 3]
United Kingdom[5]	...	0	0	1	3	* 5	* 13	...	...	...	Royaume-Uni[5]
EFTA	***69***	***58***	***83***	***80***	***80***	***76***	***81***	***73***	***83***	***90***	***AELE***
Finland[1]	[3] 22	[3] 11	[3] 12	# 10	11	12	12	10	7	...	Finlande[1]
Portugal	0	0	27	34	32	31	33	29	36	...	Portugal
Sweden[1 3]	45	45	42	34	35	31	34	32	38	36	Suède[1 3]
Switzerland[1 3]	2	2	2	2	2	2	2	* 2	* 2	* 3	Suisse[1 3]
East Europe	***462***	***444***	***451***	***441***	***407***	***373***	***333***	***361***	***367***	***374***	***Europe de l'est***
Czechoslovakia	196	200	205	209	214	197	204	199	215	224	Tchécoslovaquie
German Dem. Rep.	200	175	176	169	136	125	75	110	106	101	Rép. dém. allemande
Poland	66	69	70	63	57	51	54	52	46	49	Pologne
Total	**6 168**	**7 678**	**8 170**	**9 210**	**10 252**	**8 897**	**10 098**	**10 930**	**10 936**	**11 007**	**Total**

General note.
P2O5 content of phosphatic fertilizers and fertilizing materials other than natural, superphosphates and Thomas basic slag. Intermediary products such as liquid phosphoric and superphosphoric acids are excluded. (Parts of SITC 56129 and 5619).

[1] Fertilizer year ending 30 June of year stated.
[2] Including superphosphates.
[3] Source: Food and Agriculture Organization (FAO), (Rome).
[4] Crude weight. Nutrient content not known.
[5] Fertilizer year ending 31 May of year stated.

Remarque générale.
Poids de P2O5 contenu dans les engrais phosphatés et les produits fertilisants autres que les engrais phosphatés naturels, les superphosphates et les scories de déphosphoration Thomas. Cette rubrique ne comprend pas les produits intermédiaires tels que les solutions d'acide phosphorique et l'acide superphosphorique. (Parties de CTCI 56129 et 5619).

[1] Campagne d'engrais se terminant le 30 juin de l'année indiquée.
[2] Y compris les superphosphates.
[3] Source: Organisation des Nations Unies pour l'alimentation et l'agriculture (FAO), (Rome).
[4] Poids brut. Teneur en éléments nutritifs inconnue.
[5] Campagne d'engrais se terminant le 31 mai de l'année indiquée.

Potassic fertilizers, K2O content – Engrais potassiques, K2O contenu

Unit : Thousand metric tons

Unité : Milliers de tonnes métriques

Country or area	1976	1977	1978	1979	1980	1981	1982	1983	1984	1985	Pays ou zone
Africa	**277**	**267**	**81**	**121**	**0**	**0**	**0**	**0**	**0**	**0**	**Afrique**
Congo[1 2]	277	267	81	...	0	0	0	0	0	0	Congo[1 2]
America, North	**6 941**	**7 999**	**8 182**	**8 673**	**8 230**	**9 504**	**7 972**	**7 015**	**8 646**	**8 609**	**Amérique du Nord**
Canada[1 2]	* 4 842	* 5 655	* 6 207	* 6 387	* 7 063	* 7 337	* 6 043	5 378	7 154	7 154	Canada[1 2]
United States[1]	2 099	2 344	1 975	2 286	1 167	2 167	1 929	1 637	1 492	1 455	Etats-Unis[1]
America, South	**9**	**9**	**9**	**11**	**11**	**7**	**5**	**9**	**9**	**9**	**Amérique du Sud**
Chile* [2]	...	...	...	11	11	7	5	...	...	...	Chili* [2]
Asia	**723**	**666**	**704**	**692**	**812**	**837**	**910**	**969**	**988**	**1 013**	**Asie**
China	11	21	21	16	20	25	* 25	29	32	24	Chine
Israel[1]	712	645	683	676	792	812	* 885	940	956	...	Israël[1]
Europe	**7 613**	**7 868**	**8 313**	**8 816**	**9 164**	**9 109**	**8 372**	**8 481**	**9 080**	**15 050**	**Europe**
EEC	***3 754***	***3 886***	***4 246***	***4 559***	***4 870***	***4 752***	***4 006***	***4 224***	***4 745***	***10 707***	***CEE***
Denmark	0	0	...	...	...	...	7	11	15	15	Danemark
France[1]	*[2] 1 734	*[2] 1 567	*[2] 1 704	*[2] 1 831	*[2] 1 915	1 933	1 726	1 601	1 833	7 863	France[1]
Germany, Fed. Rep.	1 905	2 206	2 336	2 472	2 601	2 453	1 925	2 275	2 488	2 414	Allemagne, Rép. féd.
Italy[1 2]	78	64	83	80	72	51	65	74	92	83	Italie[1 2]
Netherlands[1 2]	3	0	0	0	0	0	...	...	...	...	Pays-Bas[1 2]
United Kingdom[3]	34	49	121	172	276	307	281	261	315	329	Royaume-Uni[3]
EFTA	***2***	***4***	***1***	***0***	***0***	***0***	***0***	***0***	***0***	***1***	***AELE***
Portugal	2	4	1	0	0	0	0	0	0	...	Portugal
East Europe	***3 345***	***3 412***	***3 514***	***3 594***	***3 625***	***3 666***	***3 645***	***3 637***	***3 681***	***3 680***	***Europe de l'est***
Czechoslovakia	184	183	191	199	203	206	211	206	216	215	Tchécoslovaquie
German Dem. Rep.	3 161	3 229	3 323	3 395	3 422	3 460	3 434	3 431	3 465	3 465	Rép. dém. allemande
Other Europe	***512***	***566***	***552***	***663***	***669***	***691***	***721***	***620***	***654***	***662***	***Autre Europe***
Spain[1 2]	512	566	552	663	669	691	721	620	654	662	Espagne[1 2]
USSR	**8 310**	**8 347**	**8 193**	**6 635**	**8 064**	**8 449**	**8 079**	**9 294**	**9 776**	**10 367**	**URSS**
Byelorussian SSR	*3 555*	*3 633*	*3 746*	*3 705*	*4 187*	*4 369*	*4 333*	*4 670*	*4 829*	*5 144*	*RSS de Biélorussie*
Ukrainian SSR	*430*	*397*	*395*	*339*	*337*	*317*	*272*	*292*	*284*	*290*	*RSS d'Ukraine*
Total	**23 873**	**25 156**	**25 482**	**24 948**	**26 281**	**27 906**	**25 338**	**25 768**	**28 499**	**35 047**	**Total**

General note.
K2O content of potassic fertilizers and potassic fertilizer materials, except crude potash salts. (SITC 5613 and part of SITC 5619).

[1] Fertilizer year ending 30 June of year stated.
[2] Source: Food and Agriculture Organization (FAO), (Rome).

[3] Fertilizer year ending 31 May of year stated.

Remarque générale.
Poids de K2O contenu dans les engrais potassiques et les produits potassiques fertilisants à l'exception des sels bruts de potassium. (CTCI 5613 et partie de CTCI 5619).

[1] Campagne d'engrais se terminant le 30 juin de l'année indiquée.
[2] Source: Organisation des Nations Unies pour l'alimentation et l'agriculture (FAO), (Rome).
[3] Campagne d'engrais se terminant le 31 mai de l'année indiquée.

Multinutrient fertilizers, N content – Engrais composés, N contenu

Unit : Thousand metric tons — Unité : Milliers de tonnes métriques

Country or area	1976	1977	1978	1979	1980	1981	1982	1983	1984	1985	Pays ou zone
Africa	**91**	**91**	**93**	**94**	**94**	**95**	**95**	**96**	**97**	**97**	**Afrique**
Senegal	0	0	2	1	2	...	...	...	...	...	Sénégal
Sudan	...	...	...	...	...	...	90	...	...	...	Soudan
United Rep. Tanzania[1]	1	1	1	* 3	* 2	* 3	...	...	...	...	Rép.Unie de Tanzanie[1]
America, North	**76**	**74**	**60**	**54**	**61**	**60**	**54**	**52**	**55**	**53**	**Amérique du Nord**
Cuba	17	16	15	17	18	17	13	9	17	19	Cuba
Mexico[1 2]	59	58	45	37	43	43	41	43	38	...	Mexique[1 2]
America, South	**59**	**58**	**98**	**124**	**108**	**91**	**100**	**97**	**110**	**114**	**Amérique du Sud**
Brazil[1]	16	9	32	47	42	27	36	28	...	...	Brésil[1]
Chile[1]	17	* 15	12	26	25	23	22	...	...	...	Chili[1]
Colombia[1]	24	* 32	52	49	...	...	...	...	...	...	Colombie[1]
Ecuador* [1 2]	2	2	2	2	2	2	3	3	...	...	Equateur* [1 2]
Asia	**831**	**927**	**999**	**1 081**	**993**	**920**	**950**	**950**	**901**	**963**	**Asie**
India[1 2]	170	214	277	334	201	241	258	240	191	246	Inde[1 2]
Indonesia[1 2]	0	0	0	0	1	0	0	0	...	...	Indonésie[1 2]
Israel[1 2]	2	* 12	* 23	* 25	27	22	22	31	33	...	Israël[1 2]
Japan[2]	499	554	545	568	580	461	477	477	477	466	Japon[2]
Korea, Republic of[1]	148	137	142	133	* 140	...	...	...	...	...	Corée, République de[1]
Pakistan[1 2]	0	0	0	9	32	39	48	55	...	...	Pakistan[1 2]
Philippines[1]	12	10	...	...	...	...	...	17	7	...	Philippines[1]
Syrian Arab Republic[1 2]	0	0	0	0	0	11	1	0	1	4	Rép. arabe syrienne[1 2]
Europe	**2 501**	**2 726**	**2 924**	**3 121**	**3 156**	**2 988**	**2 829**	**3 110**	**3 290**	**3 279**	**Europe**
EEC	***1 462***	***1 626***	***1 758***	***1 865***	***1 878***	***1 701***	***1 634***	***1 723***	***1 848***	***1 822***	***CEE***
Belgium[1 2]	144	177	167	181	194	200	...	...	...	...	Belgique[1 2]
Denmark[1 3]	52	82	88	94	102	116	101	133	174	...	Danemark[1 3]
France	...	...	...	...	672	601	605	611	633	626	France
Germany, Fed. Rep.[2]	304	371	389	363	373	346	288	313	349	326	Allemagne, Rép. féd.[2]
Italy[1 2]	191	219	260	315	336	247	251	275	261	278	Italie[1 2]
Netherlands[1 2]	123	132	213	275	201	191	177	169	200	189	Pays–Bas[1 2]
EFTA	***445***	***458***	***476***	***552***	***572***	***565***	***533***	***636***	***665***	***666***	***AELE***
Finland[1 2]	127	127	127	164	188	186	175	213	236	...	Finlande[1 2]
Iceland[1 2]	6	8	7	7	7	7	7	...	...	...	Islande[1 2]
Norway[1 2]	211	216	214	264	258	250	242	284	298	296	Norvège[1 2]
Portugal[1 2]	...	15	18	14	17	12	16	42	38	...	Portugal[1 2]
Sweden[1]	92	89	107	100	99	107	90	87	83	84	Suède[1]
Switzerland[1 2]	3	3	3	3	3	3	...	...	...	...	Suisse[1 2]
East Europe	***263***	***271***	***291***	***299***	***289***	***296***	***294***	***301***	***303***	***306***	***Europe de l'est***
Czechoslovakia* [1]	90	90	...	...	...	...	...	...	...	...	Tchécoslovaquie* [1]
Hungary	57	59	79	91	92	102	100	106	105	97	Hongrie
Poland	116	122	122	118	107	104	104	105	108	119	Pologne
Other Europe	***330***	***371***	***399***	***405***	***417***	***426***	***368***	***450***	***473***	***485***	***Autre Europe***
Spain[1 2]	* 166	* 201	218	214	208	208	157	197	181	202	Espagne[1 2]
Yugoslavia	164	170	181	191	209	218	211	253	292	283	Yougoslavie
Total	**3 558**	**3 876**	**4 174**	**4 474**	**4 412**	**4 153**	**4 028**	**4 304**	**4 452**	**4 507**	**Total**

General note.
N content of multinutrient fertilizers (physical mixtures and chemical combinations), containing two or three different minerals or chemical fertilizing substances (nitrogen, phosphorus or potassium). (SITC 56190–1A).

[1] Source: Food and Agriculture Organization (FAO), (Rome).

[2] Fertilizer year ending 30 June of year stated.
[3] Fertilizer year ending 31 July of year stated.

Remarque générale.
Poids de l'azote contenu dans les engrais composés (mélanges physiques et combinaisons chimiques) contenant deux ou trois minéraux ou éléments chimiques fertilisants différents (azote, phosphore ou potassium). (CTCI 56190–1A).

[1] Source: Organisation des Nations Unies pour l'alimentation et l'agriculture (FAO), (Rome).
[2] Campagne d'engrais se terminant le 30 juin de l'année indiquée.
[3] Campagne d'engrais se terminant le 31 juillet de l'année indiquée.

Multinutrient fertilizers, P205 content – Engrais composés, P2O5 contenu

Unit : Thousand metric tons

Unité : Milliers de tonnes métriques

Country or area	1976	1977	1978	1979	1980	1981	1982	1983	1984	1985	Pays ou zone
Africa	**36**	**28**	**31**	**43**	**18**	**34**	**29**	**25**	**26**	**26**	**Afrique**
Algeria* [1]	...	...	...	34	15	...	...	...	...	...	Algérie* [1]
United Rep. Tanzania[1]	* 11	3	6	* 9	* 3	* 9	* 4	* 0	...	...	Rép.Unie de Tanzanie[1]
America, North	**102**	**107**	**113**	**48**	**43**	**42**	**42**	**42**	**46**	**20**	**Amérique du Nord**
Cuba	13	13	13	13	14	14	11	9	16	15	Cuba
Mexico[1 2]	89	94	100	35	29	28	31	33	30	...	Mexique[1 2]
America, South	**54**	**52**	**116**	**244**	**239**	**154**	**191**	**191**	**239**	**260**	**Amérique du Sud**
Brazil[1 2]	49	47	112	237	* 232	144	181	179	...	...	Brésil[1 2]
Ecuador[1 2]	5	5	4	* 7	* 7	* 7	* 8	* 10	0	0	Equateur[1 2]
Peru[1 2]	0	0	0	0	0	3	2	2	2	...	Pérou[1 2]
Asia	**930**	**1 115**	**1 234**	**1 346**	**1 243**	**1 175**	**1 243**	**1 209**	**1 101**	**1 179**	**Asie**
India[1 2]	151	283	386	453	318	385	441	389	286	377	Inde[1 2]
Indonesia[1 2]	0	0	0	0	1	0	0	0	...	...	Indonésie[1 2]
Israel[2]	3	* 3	* 3	* 2	2	2	3	3	3	...	Israël[2]
Japan[2]	618	679	685	731	762	612	627	642	643	621	Japon[2]
Korea, Republic of[1]	148	137	147	138	* 114	...	...	...	...	...	Corée, République de[1]
Pakistan[1 2]	0	0	0	9	32	39	48	55	...	...	Pakistan[1 2]
Philippines[1]	10	...	...	...	...	20	14	17	8	...	Philippines[1]
Europe	**2 680**	**3 214**	**3 529**	**3 673**	**3 843**	**3 406**	**3 801**	**4 071**	**4 133**	**4 125**	**Europe**
EEC	***1 515***	***1 848***	***2 107***	***2 226***	***2 376***	***1 916***	***2 459***	***2 489***	***2 542***	***2 483***	***CEE***
Belgium[1 2]	161	...	...	* 249	* 241	...	...	...	...	...	Belgique[1 2]
Denmark[1 3]	22	32	38	37	44	59	52	58	75	...	Danemark[1 3]
France	...	...	...	...	851	739	1 282	1 262	1 282	1 232	France
Germany, Fed. Rep.[2]	299	357	366	342	353	328	273	286	316	302	Allemagne, Rép. féd.[2]
Italy[1 2]	226	323	373	455	434	254	253	309	296	295	Italie[1 2]
Netherlands[1 2]	41	68	185	130	139	141	146	150	164	...	Pays-Bas[1 2]
United Kingdom[1 4]	...	...	271	* 256	* 314	* 178	* 236	...	...	...	Royaume-Uni[1 4]
EFTA	***338***	***331***	***366***	***380***	***409***	***377***	***382***	***501***	***482***	***477***	***AELE***
Finland	139	122	144	149	172	145	150	204	182	...	Finlande
Norway[1 2]	114	125	126	141	146	143	148	163	163	164	Norvège[1 2]
Portugal	...	9	9	7	9	8	12	63	57	...	Portugal
Sweden[1]	78	75	87	83	82	81	72	71	80	79	Suède[1]
East Europe	***388***	***419***	***451***	***444***	***419***	***427***	***426***	***429***	***442***	***464***	***Europe de l'est***
Hungary	78	93	123	131	134	148	144	147	151	143	Hongrie
Poland	310	326	328	313	285	279	282	282	291	321	Pologne
Other Europe	***439***	***616***	***605***	***623***	***639***	***686***	***534***	***652***	***667***	***700***	***Autre Europe***
Spain[1 2]	* 245	* 388	365	361	370	375	272	338	304	353	Espagne[1 2]
Yugoslavia	194	228	240	262	269	311	262	314	363	347	Yougoslavie
Total	**3 801**	**4 516**	**5 022**	**5 354**	**5 386**	**4 810**	**5 306**	**5 538**	**5 546**	**5 609**	**Total**

General note.
P2O5 content of multinutrient fertilizers (physical mixtures and chemical combinations), containing two or three different minerals or fertilizing substances (nitrogen, phosphorus or potassium). (SITC 56190–1B).

[1] Source: Food and Agriculture Organization (FAO), (Rome).

[2] Fertilizer year ending 30 June of year stated.
[3] Fertilizer year ending 31 July of year stated.
[4] Fertilizer year ending 31 May of year stated.

Remarque générale.
Poids de P2O5 contenu dans les engrais composés (mélanges physiques et combinaisons chimiques) contenant deux ou trois minéraux ou éléments chimiques fertilisants (azote, phosphore ou potassium). CTCI 56190–1B).

[1] Source: Organisation des Nations Unies pour l'alimentation et l'agriculture (FAO), (Rome).
[2] Campagne d'engrais se terminant le 30 juin de l'année indiquée.
[3] Campagne d'engrais se terminant le 31 juillet de l'année indiquée.
[4] Campagne d'engrais se terminant le 31 mai de l'année indiquée.

Multinutrient fertilizers, K2O content – Engrais composés, K2O contenu

Unit : Thousand metric tons

Unité : Milliers de tonnes métriques

Country or area	1976	1977	1978	1979	1980	1981	1982	1983	1984	1985	Pays ou zone
America, South											**Amérique du Sud**
Chile[1]	16	11	11	24	* 11	* 7	...	...	...	...	Chili[1]
Asia											**Asie**
Israel[2 3]	48	# 2	2	2	2	...	...	...	...	...	Israël[2 3]
Japan[2]	457	519	506	508	496	414	422	419	422	401	Japon[2]
Europe											**Europe**
EEC											***CEE***
France	...	...	...	...	765	697	1 270	1 274	1 328	1 351	France
Germany, Fed. Rep.	734	770	771	781	779	708	578	602	593	569	Allemagne, Rép. féd.
Italy[1 2]	64	77	51	54	46	44	55	61	34	58	Italie[1 2]
EFTA											***AELE***
Finland	...	...	...	130	135	130	131	140	140	...	Finlande
East Europe											***Europe de l'est***
Hungary	87	109	136	143	139	152	142	140	139	130	Hongrie
Poland	120	123	124	111	105	101	118	111	118	127	Pologne
Other Europe											***Autre Europe***
Yugoslavia	178	208	225	232	234	262	235	252	305	279	Yougoslavie

General note.
K2O content of multinutrient fertilizers (physical mixtures and chemical combinations), containing two or three different minerals or fertilizing substances (nitrogen, phosphorus or potassium). (SITC 56190–1C).

[1] Source: Food and Agriculture Organization (FAO), (Rome).

[2] Fertilizer year ending 30 June of year stated.

[3] Beginning 1977, data are not comparable with those for earlier years.

Remarque générale.
Poids de K2O contenu dans les engrais composés (mélanges physiques et combinaisons chimiques) contenant deux ou trois minéraux ou éléments chimiques fertilisants (azote, phosphore ou potassium). (CTCI 56190–1C).

[1] Source: Organisation des Nations Unies pour l'alimentation et l'agriculture (FAO), (Rome).

[2] Campagne d'engrais se terminant le 30 juin de l'année indiquée.

[3] A partir de 1977, les données ne sont pas comparables à celles des années antérieures.

Insecticides, fungicides, disinfectants etc. – Insecticides, fongicides, désinfectants etc.

Unit : Thousand metric tons

Unité : Milliers de tonnes métriques

Country or area	1976	1977	1978	1979	1980	1981	1982	1983	1984	1985	Pays ou zone
Africa	**43.1**	**49.6**	**45.2**	**42.9**	**58.1**	**69.7**	**52.1**	**40.9**	**46.5**	**41.0**	**Afrique**
Algeria	0.9	0.6	0.7	0.7	0.7	0.8	0.7	...	...	...	Algérie
Burundi	1.6	1.7	2.1	1.3	1.5	1.9	2.1	3.0	1.4	2.2	Burundi
Côte d'Ivoire	8.0	11.0	5.7	4.8	6.0	6.3	2.5	3.4	3.9	...	Côte d'Ivoire
Egypt	15.0	15.5	...	...	10.0	13.8	...	...	...	...	Egypte
Kenya	1.3	# 4.1	5.7	4.4	5.0	4.1	5.0	4.6	3.9	1.0	Kenya
South Africa[1]	13.8	14.1	16.3	17.1	33.3	40.3	26.6	14.2	21.6	20.1	Afrique du Sud[1]
Tunisia	2.6	2.6	1.1	1.1	1.5	2.6	...	...	...	...	Tunisie
America, North	**625.5**	**634.4**	**648.8**	**657.1**	**672.5**	**680.2**	**690.7**	**703.7**	**714.6**	**726.9**	**Amérique du Nord**
Cuba	6.7	5.2	6.4	8.8	6.7	5.5	4.8	6.5	6.2	7.2	Cuba
United States	618.8	629.3	642.4	648.3	665.9	...	...	...	...	...	Etats–Unis
America, South	**36.2**	**51.3**	**58.4**	**72.4**	**95.6**	**83.3**	**72.9**	**80.5**	**91.5**	**100.4**	**Amérique du Sud**
Brazil	16.8	28.2	40.1	53.5	70.4	60.5	52.2	55.7	67.4	...	Brésil
Colombia	...	22.3	17.2	18.2	24.8	22.3	20.5	24.0	...	...	Colombie
Ecuador	0.3	0.8	1.2	...	0.3	0.5	0.3	0.8	...	...	Equateur
Asia	**907.2**	**713.2**	**780.7**	**859.6**	**818.4**	**743.6**	**728.1**	**669.0**	**679.1**	**521.0**	**Asie**
China	...	457.3	533.2	536.7	536.5	484.3	457.0	331.3	298.5	210.8	Chine
India[2]	34.7	40.8	49.9	...	...	...	...	...	...	...	Inde[2]
Indonesia	...	...	...	2.9	9.7	25.8	42.0	34.6	34.4	...	Indonésie
Korea, Republic of	180.0	153.1	132.1	192.8	166.5	129.3	125.9	196.4	240.3	163.0	Corée, République de
Sri Lanka	...	...	0.8	0.8	...	...	...	...	...	...	Sri Lanka
Turkey	63.5	38.2	37.1	66.2	...	...	...	...	...	...	Turquie
Viet Nam[3]	16.4	19.0	19.7	18.4	11.7	10.3	9.4	12.7	12.0	17.4	Viet Nam[3]
Europe	**664.6**	**745.5**	**779.3**	**883.9**	**895.7**	**945.6**	**1 068.1**	**1 106.0**	**1 165.4**	**1 132.8**	**Europe**
EEC	***285.2***	***315.2***	***327.3***	***411.3***	***437.2***	***466.9***	***565.7***	***562.9***	***609.0***	***583.5***	***CEE***
Denmark	16.0	15.9	16.9	15.2	14.5	...	...	...	...	...	Danemark
France	29.4	38.3	31.9	...	...	...	268.7	274.6	280.1	264.0	France
Germany, Fed. Rep.[4]	236.4	257.9	275.2	281.1	273.0	270.1	279.4	271.4	312.7	303.3	Allemagne, Rép. féd.[4]
Greece[5]	3.4	3.2	3.3	2.8	4.0	3.0	3.3	3.0	2.7	...	Grèce[5]
EFTA	***50.7***	***67.3***	***68.7***	***68.0***	***66.1***	***61.4***	***62.7***	***55.5***	***57.4***	***57.9***	***AELE***
Austria	12.1	13.3	12.7	14.8	13.0	13.4	14.2	15.6	18.0	20.1	Autriche
Finland	2.5	8.9	9.4	11.7	11.3	12.7	14.6	# 5.6	7.2	...	Finlande
Portugal	28.8	37.3	39.2	34.6	34.4	27.9	26.6	27.0	24.9	19.4	Portugal
Sweden	...	7.8	7.4	6.9	...	...	...	...	...	...	Suède
East Europe	***229.5***	***239.5***	***241.9***	***241.6***	***221.0***	***230.9***	***241.2***	***265.8***	***268.0***	***258.7***	***Europe de l'est***
Bulgaria	15.9	17.9	17.3	16.9	18.9	20.2	20.0	20.7	20.3	18.3	Bulgarie
Czechoslovakia	14.4	15.3	15.9	16.1	15.7	15.8	16.4	15.8	17.4	19.4	Tchécoslovaquie
German Dem. Rep.	43.2	47.1	46.3	51.2	50.5	53.2	53.4	54.0	57.7	59.9	Rép. dém. allemande
Hungary	48.3	48.9	56.8	56.5	61.7	62.5	57.9	73.5	73.0	71.1	Hongrie
Poland	67.2	67.9	59.6	53.9	34.5	36.2	48.0	53.7	46.4	37.4	Pologne
Romania	40.4	42.4	46.0	47.0	39.7	42.9	45.4	48.1	53.1	52.6	Roumanie
Other Europe	***99.2***	***123.5***	***141.5***	***163.1***	***171.4***	***186.4***	***198.5***	***221.7***	***231.0***	***232.8***	***Autre Europe***
Spain	...	...	...	87.7	91.3	106.6	126.4	135.7	...	...	Espagne
Yugoslavia	54.7	66.0	71.0	75.3	80.1	79.8	72.1	86.0	82.5	71.3	Yougoslavie
USSR	**275.6**	**290.3**	**295.7**	**284.4**	**285.4**	**298.8**	**315.8**	**332.4**	**343.0**	**347.7**	**URSS**
Ukrainian SSR	*60.8*	*63.4*	*63.1*	*56.5*	*63.1*	*66.5*	*66.7*	*78.5*	*82.0*	*88.1*	*RSS d'Ukraine*
Total	**2 552.2**	**2 484.3**	**2 608.3**	**2 800.3**	**2 825.7**	**2 821.3**	**2 927.8**	**2 932.4**	**3 040.1**	**2 869.8**	**Total**

General note.
Preparations, other than solutions, dilutions and suspensions of single chemical compounds in a liquid (unless the liquid plays an active part in the preparations) of products intended to destroy or combat pathogenic germs, insects, mosses and moulds, weeds, rodents, wild birds etc., to disinfect seeds or to prevent vegetables from sprouting. Excluded are separately–defined chemical compounds, medicaments, fumigants, deodorizers and disinfectant soaps. (SITC 59920–0).

Remarque générale.
Préparations autres que les solutions, dilutions et suspensions de composés chimiques uniques dans un liquide (à moins que le liquide ne joue un rôle actif dans les préparations) de produits conçus pour détruire ou pour repousser les germes pathogènes, les insectes, les mousses et moisissures, les mauvaises herbes, les rongeurs, les oiseaux etc., pour désinfecter les semences ou prévenir la germination des végétaux. Cette rubrique ne comprend pas les composés chimiques définis sous d'autres rubriques, les médicaments, les produits pour fumigation, les désodorisants et les savons désinfectants. (CTCI 59920–0).

For footnotes, see end of table.

Voir la fin du tableau pour les notes.

[1] Excluding products usually measured in units of volume.
[2] Excluding quantities consumed by fertilizer industry.
[3] Insecticides only.
[4] Excluding disinfectants.
[5] Insecticides for household use.

[1] Non compris les produits normalement mesurés en unités de volume.
[2] Non compris les quantités utilisées par l'industrie des engrais.
[3] Insecticides seulement.
[4] Non compris les désinfectants.
[5] Insecticides pour usage domestique.

Rubber, synthetic – Caoutchoucs synthétiques

Unit : Thousand metric tons

Unité : Milliers de tonnes métriques

Country or area	1976	1977	1978	1979	1980	1981	1982	1983	1984	1985	Pays ou zone
Africa	**34.6**	**27.2**	**31.8**	**31.2**	**38.7**	**36.5**	**32.4**	**27.5**	**42.4**	**42.8**	**Afrique**
South Africa [1]	34.6	27.2	31.8	31.2	38.7	36.5	32.4	27.5	42.4	* 42.8	Afrique du Sud [1]
America, North	**2 708.8**	**2 967.9**	**2 994.1**	**3 087.2**	**2 584.6**	**2 592.7**	**2 105.6**	**2 302.7**	**2 627.6**	**2 375.4**	**Amérique du Nord**
Canada	214.5	241.4	252.1	282.5	252.8	263.3	181.7	183.4	217.4	209.2	Canada
Mexico	68.8	66.6	80.3	84.4	90.8	104.3	106.7	131.9	125.0	* 140.0	Mexique
United States	2 425.5	2 660.0	2 661.7	2 720.3	2 241.0	2 225.1	1 817.2	1 987.4	2 285.1	2 026.2	Etats–Unis
America, South	**204.1**	**238.1**	**240.0**	**260.8**	**282.1**	**250.8**	**273.8**	**268.4**	**306.2**	**316.7**	**Amérique du Sud**
Argentina	39.7	50.0	33.9	37.0	33.0	28.0	45.7	47.5	47.8	50.8	Argentine
Brazil	164.4	188.1	206.1	223.8	249.1	222.9	228.1	220.9	258.4	265.9	Brésil
Asia	**1 078.7**	**1 142.6**	**1 235.9**	**1 344.2**	**1 335.1**	**1 275.0**	**1 190.1**	**1 315.6**	**1 499.5**	**1 503.4**	**Asie**
China	60.0	78.0	101.9	120.6	123.0	124.9	136.0	168.9	174.1	181.1	Chine
India	23.5	28.4	25.6	32.8	22.6	28.7	29.0	29.0	37.8	36.7	Inde
Japan	941.3	971.0	1 028.9	1 107.3	1 094.1	1 010.3	930.7	1 002.5	1 160.5	1 158.0	Japon
Korea, Republic of	35.3	43.9	63.6	60.6	75.4	82.1	64.0	91.2	99.8	99.6	Corée, République de
Turkey	[1] 18.7	[1] 21.4	[1] 15.9	* [1] 23.0	20.0	29.0	30.3	24.0	27.3	28.0	Turquie
Europe	**2 259.4**	**2 428.9**	**2 440.9**	**2 532.3**	**2 342.6**	**2 279.1**	**2 117.7**	**2 350.7**	**2 447.0**	**2 549.7**	**Europe**
EEC	***1 738.2***	***1 837.3***	***1 825.2***	***1 921.1***	***1 727.0***	***1 687.9***	***1 554.1***	***1 732.7***	***1 833.3***	***1 896.7***	***CEE***
Belgium* [1]	115.0	119.0	124.0	125.0	125.0	108.0	100.0	108.0	110.0	110.0	Belgique* [1]
France	438.2	480.6	491.5	541.4	510.8	486.3	389.6	# 513.5	554.8	597.9	France
Germany, Fed. Rep.	379.5	431.4	424.2	445.9	408.8	415.4	403.8	432.4	448.9	457.8	Allemagne, Rép. féd.
Italy	238.0	237.1	268.8	291.1	258.5	243.2	215.9	229.8	234.0	* 234.7	Italie
Netherlands	247.0	240.0	223.0	240.0	212.0	211.0	201.0	196.0	207.0	235.0	Pays–Bas
United Kingdom	320.4	329.2	293.7	277.7	211.8	224.0	243.9	253.0	278.6	261.2	Royaume–Uni
EFTA	***12.3***	***18.2***	***27.4***	***22.5***	***26.6***	***31.1***	***32.8***	***43.5***	***50.1***	***59.7***	***AELE***
Austria [1]	0.0	* 3.0	* 4.0	* 4.0	* 5.0	* 5.0	* 5.0	* 5.0	* 5.0	* 5.0	Autriche [1]
Finland* [1]	6.0	7.0	8.0	9.0	9.0	9.0	9.0	9.0	9.0	8.5	Finlande* [1]
Sweden [1]	6.3	8.2	15.4	9.5	12.6	* 17.1	* 18.8	* 29.5	36.1	46.2	Suède [1]
East Europe	***435.6***	***486.3***	***501.9***	***518.0***	***521.4***	***505.0***	***475.5***	***520.0***	***512.6***	***538.6***	***Europe de l'est***
Bulgaria* [1]	21.0	25.0	25.0	25.0	30.0	30.0	25.0	25.0	26.0	26.0	Bulgarie* [1]
Czechoslovakia	57.0	58.8	58.9	59.3	60.1	63.2	65.2	67.2	70.9	69.6	Tchécoslovaquie
German Dem. Rep. [1]	145.5	* 147.0	* 145.0	* 155.0	* 163.0	* 155.0	* 148.0	* 161.0	* 137.0	* 161.0	Rép. dém. allemande [1]
Poland	116.9	119.4	125.6	129.9	117.9	111.1	99.9	119.7	119.4	126.1	Pologne
Romania	95.2	136.2	147.5	148.8	150.4	145.7	137.5	147.2	159.3	155.9	Roumanie
Other Europe	***73.3***	***87.1***	***86.3***	***70.7***	***67.7***	***55.1***	***55.3***	***54.5***	***50.9***	***54.7***	***Autre Europe***
Spain	73.3	87.1	86.3	70.7	67.7	55.1	55.3	54.5	* 50.9	* 54.7	Espagne
USSR* [1]	**1 700.0**	**1 800.0**	**1 950.0**	**2 025.0**	**2 040.0**	**2 000.0**	**1 950.0**	**1 970.0**	**2 085.0**	**2 125.0**	**URSS* [1]**
Oceania	**42.2**	**43.5**	**43.5**	**42.8**	**46.0**	**43.0**	**43.0**	**32.0**	**45.2**	**31.2**	**Océanie**
Australia	[1] 42.2	[1] 43.5	[1] 43.5	[1] 42.8	46.0	43.0	43.0	32.0	45.2	* 31.2	Australie
Total	**8 027.9**	**8 648.3**	**8 936.2**	**9 323.6**	**8 669.2**	**8 477.2**	**7 712.6**	**8 266.9**	**9 052.8**	**8 944.3**	**Total**

General note.
Copolymers of butadiene with styrene and acrylonitrile, and neoprene and butyl–type rubber. Latices should be included (dry weight). (SITC 23120–0).

[1] Source: International Rubber Study Group, (London).

Remarque générale.
Copolymères du butadiène associé au styrène ou à l'acrylonitrile, néoprène et caoutchouc butyle, y compris les latex (poids du produit sec). (CTCI 23120–0).

[1] Source: International Rubber Study Group , (Londres).

Non–cellulosic staple and tow – Fibres discontinues et câbles non cellulosiques

Unit : Thousand metric tons

Unité : Milliers de tonnes métriques

Country or area	1976	1977	1978	1979	1980	1981	1982	1983	1984	1985	Pays ou zone
Africa	**13.6**	**13.9**	**19.9**	**23.9**	**27.5**	**29.0**	**38.7**	**46.1**	**58.3**	**62.4**	**Afrique**
Egypt[1]	0.6	0.4	0.4	0.4	5.0	5.0	17.6	20.6	25.6	27.6	Egypte[1]
Nigeria[1]	0.0	0.0	3.0	4.0	2.5	4.0	1.1	2.5	3.0	3.0	Nigéria[1]
South Africa[1]	13.0	13.5	16.5	19.5	20.0	20.0	20.0	23.0	29.7	31.8	Afrique du Sud[1]
America, North	**1 601.2**	**1 763.3**	**1 919.0**	**2 071.8**	**1 970.2**	**1 995.7**	**1 643.3**	**1 912.7**	**1 887.5**	**1 790.0**	**Amérique du Nord**
Canada[2]	34.5	43.5	50.9	48.5	48.0	* 43.9	* 45.0	* 53.0	* 59.0	* 54.0	Canada[2]
Mexico	59.8	61.8	73.9	80.1	91.7	115.1	116.6	144.7	151.4	* 158.1	Mexique
United States	1 506.9	1 658.0	1 794.2	1 943.2	1 830.5	1 836.7	1 481.7	1 715.0	1 677.1	1 577.9	Etats–Unis
America, South	**111.9**	**114.4**	**126.6**	**153.3**	**152.4**	**138.0**	**138.9**	**144.2**	**173.4**	**174.8**	**Amérique du Sud**
Argentina[1]	16.9	17.0	16.8	22.0	12.9	8.3	11.9	16.0	21.0	17.0	Argentine[1]
Brazil[1]	60.7	64.2	74.5	91.4	95.0	86.8	82.1	79.6	97.6	100.8	Brésil[1]
Chile[1]	3.0	2.2	1.5	2.4	2.5	2.5	0.8	1.0	1.1	2.0	Chili[1]
Colombia[1]	6.2	6.1	7.8	8.0	10.9	11.2	8.8	8.9	10.7	12.0	Colombie[1]
Peru[1]	19.8	19.2	20.5	21.0	22.5	21.1	29.4	31.0	34.1	33.0	Pérou[1]
Uruguay[1]	0.0	0.0	0.0	2.4	2.6	2.1	2.3	3.7	3.4	4.0	Uruguay[1]
Venezuela	5.3	5.7	5.5	6.1	6.0	6.0	3.6	4.0	5.5	[1] 6.0	Venezuela
Asia	**1 026.6**	**1 143.3**	**1 313.4**	**1 386.8**	**1 504.8**	**1 659.7**	**1 660.8**	**1 739.5**	**2 112.8**	**2 249.4**	**Asie**
Bangladesh[1]	0.0	0.0	0.0	0.0	0.0	0.0	0.0	5.0	10.0	0.0	Bangladesh[1]
China[1]	* 37.0	* 42.0	* 106.6	* 128.0	* 205.0	* 292.0	* 302.0	* 325.0	586.0	632.0	Chine[1]
India[1]	21.8	21.8	25.8	* 27.8	30.8	39.8	44.2	40.8	56.0	65.4	Inde[1]
Indonesia[1]	25.0	37.2	45.4	50.3	53.9	55.1	55.2	54.5	73.3	70.3	Indonésie[1]
Iran(Islamic Rep.of)[1]	0.0	0.0	0.0	0.0	0.0	10.0	20.0	27.1	24.0	31.0	Iran(Rép.islamique)[1]
Israel[1]	6.2	5.6	6.2	6.4	6.6	6.8	7.0	7.0	7.0	7.3	Israël[1]
Japan	678.6	715.4	774.2	760.7	757.8	747.9	736.2	750.0	767.0	792.3	Japon
Korea, Republic of[1]	161.7	179.9	209.4	240.1	281.2	326.4	311.0	327.6	376.9	402.9	Corée, République de[1]
Malaysia[1]	15.0	30.0	33.0	35.0	36.0	35.0	32.0	35.0	35.5	38.8	Malaisie[1]
Philippines[1]	7.8	7.8	8.6	11.6	14.0	14.0	15.0	16.0	16.0	16.5	Philippines[1]
Thailand[1]	29.4	38.1	43.6	49.9	49.5	56.3	48.0	50.0	52.4	55.0	Thaïlande[1]
Turkey[1]	44.2	65.5	60.6	77.0	70.0	76.4	90.2	101.5	108.7	137.9	Turquie[1]
Europe	**1 618.5**	**1 577.5**	**1 785.1**	**1 832.3**	**1 796.6**	**1 891.6**	**1 781.0**	**1 941.1**	**2 078.5**	**2 357.8**	**Europe**
EEC	***1 090.8***	***1 005.7***	***1 146.2***	***1 145.5***	***1 103.5***	***1 174.5***	***1 066.3***	***1 176.5***	***1 259.8***	***1 501.5***	***CEE***
Belgium	20.0	13.4	18.4	19.4	[1,3] 32.4	[1,3] 25.3	[1,3] 19.2	[1,3] 21.3	[1,3] 23.0	[1,3] 29.0	Belgique
Denmark	4.2	5.1	5.5	5.0	5.0	...	...	...	...	...	Danemark
France	145.5	143.4	156.9	147.4	129.5	137.8	135.8	139.0	146.6	137.0	France
Germany, Fed. Rep.	396.4	375.2	408.3	431.8	418.4	447.5	377.9	425.6	421.3	439.5	Allemagne, Rép. féd.
Greece[1]	5.0	7.5	7.9	9.5	10.0	8.9	9.3	10.0	10.0	10.0	Grèce[1]
Ireland[1]	9.0	12.5	26.0	32.0	31.7	31.3	28.0	32.0	...	...	Irlande[1]
Italy	284.8	253.9	284.7	281.2	282.4	344.6	333.5	373.9	437.1	[4] 660.0	Italie
Netherlands[1]	...	12.6	* 13.0	9.5	# [5] 32.4	[5] 25.3	[5] 19.2	[5] 21.3	[5] 23.0	[5] 29.0	Pays–Bas[1]
United Kingdom	214.1	182.1	225.5	209.6	161.7	* 148.4	* 137.8	* 147.7	* 154.0	* 149.0	Royaume–Uni
EFTA	***84.0***	***91.1***	***111.6***	***119.7***	***106.4***	***110.7***	***112.1***	***113.6***	***124.8***	***132.5***	***AELE***
Austria[1]	27.4	25.9	30.4	29.3	25.4	18.7	16.2	18.0	18.1	18.1	Autriche[1]
Finland	...	0.0	0.3	0.3	0.2	0.2	0.2	0.1	0.2	...	Finlande
Portugal	29.1	36.5	47.5	60.1	57.1	63.9	68.7	67.5	78.2	86.8	Portugal
Switzerland[1]	27.3	28.7	33.4	30.0	23.7	27.9	27.0	28.0	28.3	27.5	Suisse[1]
East Europe	***334.2***	***355.6***	***368.4***	***379.1***	***394.7***	***386.5***	***383.8***	***403.8***	***417.1***	***435.7***	***Europe de l'est***
Bulgaria[1]	28.9	31.5	33.0	35.0	37.0	39.0	35.0	42.0	43.8	46.8	Bulgarie[1]
Czechoslovakia	24.7	26.0	21.2	21.9	32.9	33.6	35.7	36.3	38.1	39.4	Tchécoslovaquie
German Dem. Rep.	117.6	124.0	131.1	135.8	138.7	146.2	148.6	150.5	153.8	157.7	Rép. dém. allemande
Hungary	8.6	13.7	16.1	15.4	14.5	14.2	12.5	13.4	13.6	14.8	Hongrie
Poland	68.4	65.4	67.0	65.9	68.5	39.0	40.0	49.1	51.3	51.5	Pologne
Romania[1]	86.0	95.0	100.0	105.0	103.0	114.5	112.0	112.5	116.5	125.5	Roumanie[1]
Other Europe	***109.5***	***125.1***	***158.8***	***188.0***	***192.0***	***219.9***	***218.9***	***247.2***	***276.8***	***288.0***	***Autre Europe***
Spain[1]	94.0	104.6	129.1	141.4	142.1	168.9	157.7	173.1	176.8	189.0	Espagne[1]
Yugoslavia	15.5	20.5	29.7	46.6	49.9	51.0	61.2	74.1	100.0	99.0	Yougoslavie
USSR	**145.4**	**167.5**	**187.2**	**212.6**	**246.0**	**269.3**	**287.9**	**303.7**	**318.0**	**336.4**	**URSS**
Ukrainian SSR	*9.8*	*11.7*	*14.0*	*14.4*	*14.3*	*15.9*	*16.3*	*17.4*	*16.3*	*14.3*	*RSS d'Ukraine*

For general note and footnotes, see end of table.

Voir la fin du tableau pour la remarque générale et les notes.

Non–cellulosic staple and tow (continued) – Fibres discontinues et câbles non cellulosiques (suite)

Unit : Thousand metric tons

Unité : Milliers de tonnes métriques

Country or area	1976	1977	1978	1979	1980	1981	1982	1983	1984	1985	Pays ou zone
Oceania	**1.0**	**1.2**	**1.1**	**0.5**	**0.0**	**0.0**	**0.5**	**1.0**	**1.0**	**1.0**	**Océanie**
Australia[1] [6]	1.0	1.2	1.1	0.5	0.0	0.0	* 0.5	* 1.0	* 1.0	* 1.0	Australie[1] [6]
Total	**4 518.3**	**4 781.0**	**5 352.3**	**5 681.2**	**5 697.5**	**5 983.3**	**5 551.1**	**6 088.3**	**6 629.6**	**6 971.8**	**Total**

General note.
Non–cellulosic (synthetic) discontinuous fibres ranging from around 3/4 inch to 18 inches and tow (a collection of many parallel, continuous filaments without twist grouped together in rope–like form) made of natural polymers based on materials such as casein, or of synthetic polymers mainly from coal and oil distillation products. Waste, spun yarns and other manufactures are excluded. (SITC 26620–1).

[1] Source: Textile Economics Bureau, Inc. (New York).
[2] Excluding olefin.
[3] Including production in Netherlands and Luxembourg.
[4] Including continuous fibres.
[5] Including production in Belgium and Luxembourg.
[6] Including production in New Zealand.

Remarque générale.
Fibres discontinues longues d'environ 2 à 45 centimètres et câbles (ensemble filaments continus, parallèles, sans torsion) de matières non cellulosiques artificielles ou synthétiques. Polymères naturels obtenus à partir de produits tels que la caséine ou polymères synthétiques obtenus principalement à partir de produits de la distillation du charbon ou du pétrole. Cette rubrique ne comprend pas les déchets, les filés de fibres discontinues et les autres produits non cellulosiques. (CTCI 26620–1).

[1] Source: Textile Economics Bureau, Inc. (New York).
[2] Non compris l'oléfine.
[3] Y compris la production en Pays–Bas et Luxembourg.
[4] Y compris de fibres continues.
[5] Y compris la production en Belgique et Luxembourg.
[6] Y compris la production de la Nouvelle–Zélande.

Cellulosic staple and tow – Fibres et câbles cellulosiques

Unit : Thousand metric tons

Unité : Milliers de tonnes métriques

Country or area	1976	1977	1978	1979	1980	1981	1982	1983	1984	1985	Pays ou zone
Africa	**3.2**	**2.3**	**3.7**	**4.2**	**4.0**	**4.0**	**4.5**	**4.6**	**4.6**	**4.7**	**Afrique**
Egypt[1]	3.2	2.3	3.7	4.2	4.0	4.0	* 4.5	* 4.6	* 4.6	* 4.7	Egypte[1]
America, North	**259.8**	**286.7**	**291.6**	**304.0**	**256.0**	**258.1**	**201.8**	**207.3**	**213.8**	**191.5**	**Amérique du Nord**
Canada[1]	21.2	26.2	26.8	31.3	30.0	28.2	* 28.0	* 30.0	* 31.0	* 23.9	Canada[1]
Mexico	18.0	17.8	19.1	20.3	21.7	19.2	12.8	6.7	6.1	7.5	Mexique
United States[1]	220.6	242.7	245.7	252.4	204.3	210.7	161.0	170.6	176.7	160.1	Etats–Unis[1]
America, South	**27.7**	**30.3**	**29.5**	**33.2**	**29.8**	**28.3**	**27.4**	**25.2**	**34.2**	**31.8**	**Amérique du Sud**
Argentina[1 2]	5.0	5.7	3.8	4.7	1.5	0.0	0.0	0.0	1.5	1.5	Argentine[1 2]
Brazil[1]	19.7	21.7	22.4	25.5	25.3	25.3	24.2	22.0	29.0	26.5	Brésil[1]
Chile[1 2]	3.0	2.9	3.3	3.0	3.0	3.0	3.2	3.2	3.7	3.8	Chili[1 2]
Asia	**458.1**	**503.0**	**522.6**	**540.1**	**524.7**	**550.4**	**502.3**	**551.8**	**593.1**	**560.8**	**Asie**
Bangladesh[1]	0.0	0.0	0.0	0.0	0.0	0.0	0.0	1.0	1.0	1.0	Bangladesh[1]
China[1 2]	* 70.0	* 77.0	* 80.0	* 85.0	* 95.0	* 105.0	* 105.0	* 112.0	* 115.0	112.0	Chine[1 2]
India[1]	82.4	84.7	89.9	92.2	74.7	94.5	52.8	69.9	100.1	95.0	Inde[1]
Indonesia[1]	0.0	0.0	0.0	0.0	0.0	0.0	18.1	34.1	41.3	40.0	Indonésie[1]
Iraq[1]	5.5	5.3	5.5	5.4	5.5	5.5	5.5	5.5	5.5	5.5	Iraq[1]
Japan[3]	282.7	306.8	314.2	326.0	313.1	310.1	294.6	307.8	307.7	283.3	Japon[3]
Korea, Republic of[1]	11.6	14.6	15.4	10.4	15.0	13.9	* 5.8	0.0	0.0	0.0	Corée, République de[1]
Thailand[1]	2.0	10.7	13.5	15.1	16.4	16.4	15.5	17.5	18.0	19.0	Thaïlande[1]
Turkey[1 2]	3.9	4.0	4.0	6.0	5.0	5.0	5.0	4.0	4.5	5.0	Turquie[1 2]
Europe	**961.2**	**975.0**	**984.5**	**1 004.4**	**963.0**	**1 010.4**	**953.1**	**918.1**	**948.5**	**900.2**	**Europe**
EEC	***350.3***	***349.2***	***345.4***	***363.2***	***321.9***	***384.5***	***332.8***	***331.4***	***321.3***	***274.5***	***CEE***
Belgium[2]	21.4	23.0	24.6	26.8	22.0	14.6	8.4	0.0	0.0	0.0	Belgique[2]
Denmark	* 0.8	0.2	0.1	0.1	0.0	0.0	...	...	...	...	Danemark
France[3]	60.3	60.7	55.2	60.3	50.7	43.9	37.8	29.9	21.0	* 15.0	France[3]
Germany, Fed. Rep.[3]	72.1	68.0	73.1	76.1	73.1	148.7	[4] 142.1	[4] 150.5	[4] 163.2	[4] 169.1	Allemagne, Rép. féd.[3]
Italy[5]	62.1	64.2	48.3	40.2	28.6	60.3	46.3	29.7	30.9	30.3	Italie[5]
Netherlands	0.0	2.7	* 3.0	3.7	[1 6] 22.0	[1 6] 14.6	[1 6] 8.9	[1 6] 6.1	[1 6] 0.0	[1 6] 0.0	Pays–Bas
United Kingdom	133.6	130.3	141.1	156.1	* 125.5	* 102.4	* 89.2	* 115.2	* 106.2	* 60.2	Royaume–Uni
EFTA	***179.5***	***191.2***	***207.8***	***217.6***	***218.3***	***219.1***	***214.5***	***208.9***	***216.4***	***214.0***	***AELE***
Austria[1 2]	88.9	90.2	96.0	98.8	100.6	107.9	100.8	109.7	110.0	110.0	Autriche[1 2]
Finland[2]	31.2	40.3	43.0	48.3	50.7	46.3	53.1	57.6	65.5	...	Finlande[2]
Norway[2]	26.1	24.7	28.4	29.3	28.3	28.2	20.0	0.0	0.0	...	Norvège[2]
Portugal[2]	2.7	2.7	3.5	4.3	3.7	3.0	2.6	1.5	0.8	0.7	Portugal[2]
Sweden	30.6	33.4	36.9	36.9	34.9	33.7	38.0	40.1	40.1	33.4	Suède
East Europe	***340.5***	***335.6***	***333.5***	***308.7***	***314.4***	***304.0***	***301.8***	***312.5***	***319.0***	***316.0***	***Europe de l'est***
Bulgaria[1]	23.6	25.7	27.8	30.0	33.0	34.7	34.0	35.0	37.1	37.6	Bulgarie[1]
Czechoslovakia[2]	50.3	50.7	49.2	33.5	35.1	36.3	37.0	38.0	37.2	37.3	Tchécoslovaquie[2]
German Dem. Rep.[2]	136.9	132.6	129.2	125.0	122.9	126.1	127.8	130.6	133.8	131.4	Rép. dém. allemande[2]
Hungary	9.0	9.1	9.0	8.6	8.4	7.5	7.6	6.1	6.1	6.1	Hongrie
Poland	66.9	67.1	65.4	56.6	61.0	44.3	45.5	51.9	53.8	50.6	Pologne
Romania[1 2]	53.9	50.4	53.0	55.0	54.0	55.0	50.0	51.0	51.0	53.0	Roumanie[1 2]
Other Europe	***91.0***	***98.9***	***97.8***	***114.8***	***108.4***	***102.8***	***104.1***	***65.3***	***91.8***	***95.7***	***Autre Europe***
Spain[1 7]	41.0	43.1	46.6	45.3	40.1	* 37.8	* 38.0	* 21.5	* 26.1	* 30.0	Espagne[1 7]
Yugoslavia[2]	50.0	55.8	51.2	69.5	68.3	65.0	66.1	43.8	65.7	65.7	Yougoslavie[2]
USSR	**325.8**	**339.6**	**343.6**	**290.8**	**318.8**	**323.3**	**309.9**	**366.4**	**391.2**	**358.5**	**URSS**
Ukrainian SSR	*39.5*	*44.0*	*42.2*	*28.1*	*33.5*	*34.4*	*33.9*	*46.1*	*45.6*	*32.7*	*RSS d'Ukraine*
Total	**2 036.0**	**2 136.9**	**2 175.6**	**2 176.8**	**2 096.4**	**2 174.4**	**1 999.1**	**2 073.5**	**2 185.5**	**2 047.5**	**Total**

General note.
Rayon and acetate (artificial) discontinuous fibres ranging from around 3/4 inch to 18 inches and tow (a collection of many parallel, continuous filaments without twist grouped together in rope–like form) produced by chemical transformation of natural organic polymers from cellulose. Waste of these fibres, spun yarn and other manufactures of rayon and acetate are excluded. (SITC 26630–1).

Remarque générale.
Fibres discontinues de rayonne et d'acétate longues d'environ 2 à 45 centimètres, et câbles (ensemble de filaments continus parallèles, sans torsion) artificiels obtenus par transformation chimique de polymères organiques naturels cellulosiques. Cette rubrique ne comprend pas les déchets de ces fibres, les fils de fibres discontinues et les autres produits fabriqués à partir de rayonne ou d'acétate. (CTCI 26630–1).

For footnotes, see end of table.

Voir la fin du tableau pour les notes.

Cellulosic staple and tow (continued) – Fibres et câbles cellulosiques (suite)

1 Source: Textile Economics Bureau, Inc. (New York).
2 Production of acetate fibres is nil or negligible.
3 Including cigarette filtration tow.
4 Including cellulosic continuous filaments.
5 Including continuous fibres.
6 Including production in Belgium.
7 Including waste.

1 Source: Textile Economics Bureau, Inc. (New York).
2 Production de fibres d'acétate nulle ou négligeable.
3 Y compris l'étoupe pour filtres de cigarettes.
4 Y compris les filaments cellulosiques continus.
5 Y compris de fibres continues.
6 Y compris la production de la Belgique.
7 Y compris les déchets.

Alkyd resins – Résines alkyliques

Unit : Thousand metric tons

Unité : Milliers de tonnes métriques

Country or area	1976	1977	1978	1979	1980	1981	1982	1983	1984	1985	Pays ou zone
America, North	**335.6**	**358.0**	**358.9**	**361.4**	**340.4**	**329.6**	**259.0**	**345.8**	**304.7**	**298.1**	**Amérique du Nord**
Mexico	16.0	16.4	17.1	19.0	21.6	23.7	21.8	19.6	20.6	21.2	Mexique
United States	319.6	341.7	341.9	342.4	318.8	...	237.2	326.2	...	...	Etats-Unis
America, South	**15.6**	**16.1**	**15.0**	**15.6**	**15.2**	**13.3**	**11.0**	**13.4**	**13.7**	**11.6**	**Amérique du Sud**
Argentina	6.6	6.8	5.7	6.6	4.9	3.0	3.0	3.6	3.3	2.0	Argentine
Chile	2.7	...	...	2.7	4.0	4.2	2.0	3.0	4.1	3.3	Chili
Colombia	...	...	...	...	...	6.1	6.0	6.8	...	...	Colombie
Asia	**266.5**	**276.4**	**311.5**	**346.5**	**317.8**	**313.8**	**328.1**	**327.5**	**339.8**	**347.4**	**Asie**
Indonesia	...	...	...	...	...	1.1	1.2	1.1	1.8	...	Indonésie
Japan	265.2	275.1	310.2	345.2	316.5	312.7	326.8	326.4	338.0	346.0	Japon
Europe	**450.4**	**453.7**	**468.4**	**481.0**	**464.7**	**483.4**	**499.1**	**461.6**	**469.9**	**427.8**	**Europe**
EEC	***363.7***	***366.9***	***374.4***	***385.2***	***370.4***	***380.7***	***403.2***	***362.3***	***367.7***	***321.4***	***CEE***
Denmark	...	...	...	...	...	...	0.7	...	...	...	Danemark
France	43.8	46.4	47.4	41.9	41.7	44.8	# 63.1	47.1	43.2	47.2	France
Germany, Fed. Rep.	101.6	99.0	113.5	115.4	121.4	127.2	126.2	123.9	132.9	123.0	Allemagne, Rép. féd.
Italy	30.5	28.5	31.1	31.8	29.1	32.8	29.5	22.8	23.2	22.1	Italie
Netherlands	61.2	60.3	58.6	65.6	65.6	72.7	84.6	69.6	69.8	49.2	Pays-Bas
United Kingdom	125.9	132.0	123.1	129.8	111.8	102.5	99.1	98.2	97.8	79.2	Royaume-Uni
EFTA	***40.8***	***41.1***	***43.3***	***41.1***	***39.6***	***49.9***	***44.1***	***45.7***	***47.1***	***44.4***	***AELE***
Finland	3.3	3.9	3.5	3.8	3.8	3.5	4.8	4.8	4.9	...	Finlande
Portugal	4.9	5.0	5.5	6.1	5.9	6.1	6.4	6.4	6.5	6.4	Portugal
Sweden	32.6	32.3	34.2	31.2	29.8	40.4	32.9	34.5	35.7	32.9	Suède
East Europe	***35.2***	***38.1***	***39.6***	***40.9***	***41.6***	***38.4***	***38.2***	***40.7***	***41.8***	***43.1***	***Europe de l'est***
Czechoslovakia	25.1	26.7	28.0	29.9	31.2	27.0	26.4	28.4	29.8	31.1	Tchécoslovaquie
Hungary	10.1	11.4	11.7	11.1	10.4	11.4	11.8	12.3	12.0	12.0	Hongrie
Other Europe	***10.7***	***7.6***	***11.1***	***13.9***	***13.1***	***14.4***	***13.6***	***12.9***	***13.3***	***19.0***	***Autre Europe***
Spain	10.5	7.3	...	13.5	12.6	13.9	13.2	12.4	12.7	18.4	Espagne
Yugoslavia	0.2	0.2	0.3	0.3	0.4	0.5	0.4	0.5	0.6	0.6	Yougoslavie
Oceania	**25.7**	**26.4**	**26.9**	**31.0**	**36.4**	**36.2**	**24.4**	**18.2**	**20.6**	**20.3**	**Océanie**
Australia	25.7	26.4	26.9	31.0	36.4	36.2	24.4	18.2	20.6	20.3	Australie
Total	**1 093.8**	**1 130.7**	**1 180.7**	**1 235.6**	**1 174.5**	**1 176.3**	**1 121.6**	**1 166.4**	**1 148.8**	**1 105.1**	**Total**

General note.
Polycondensation products of polyhydric alcohols (glycerol) with polybasic organic acids (glycerophthalic resins) and maleic acids (glyceromaleic resins). Dry weight of resins. (SITC 58110-1).

Remarque générale.
Produits de la polycondensation des polyalcools (glycérol) avec des acides organiques polybasiques (résines glycéro-phtaliques) ou l'acide maléique (résines glycéro-maléiques). Poids sec des résines. (CTCI 58110-1).

Amino plastics – Aminoplastes

Unit : Thousand metric tons — Unité : Milliers de tonnes métriques

Country or area	1976	1977	1978	1979	1980	1981	1982	1983	1984	1985	Pays ou zone
America, North	**580.5**	**637.3**	**750.6**	**756.3**	**718.8**	**664.2**	**546.6**	**652.6**	**650.2**	**647.3**	**Amérique du Nord**
Mexico	22.7	20.1	23.1	31.0	39.8	46.3	53.0	40.6	...	...	Mexique
United States	557.7	617.2	727.5	725.2	679.0	...	493.6	612.0	...	...	Etats–Unis
America, South	**15.1**	**11.4**	**8.0**	**12.0**	**11.8**	**10.3**	**9.6**	**9.7**	**10.8**	**9.8**	**Amérique du Sud**
Argentina	15.1	11.4	8.0	12.0	11.8	10.3	9.6	9.7	10.8	9.8	Argentine
Asia	**686.8**	**708.1**	**763.0**	**790.2**	**749.1**	**659.3**	**616.9**	**656.2**	**627.1**	**596.7**	**Asie**
Japan	665.3	665.8	706.5	733.8	716.1	629.2	606.0	631.8	605.5	578.0	Japon
Turkey	21.5	42.3	56.5	56.4	...	...	10.9	...	...	...	Turquie
Europe	**1 747.5**	**1 767.7**	**1 697.8**	**1 816.3**	**1 718.8**	**1 607.8**	**1 584.4**	**1 575.5**	**1 537.0**	**1 547.2**	**Europe**
EEC	***1 395.1***	***1 374.9***	***1 329.1***	***1 412.3***	***1 311.9***	***1 192.3***	***1 154.9***	***1 109.1***	***1 115.4***	***1 112.5***	***CEE***
Denmark	56.3	46.9	45.9	52.7	42.8	...	...	...	...	...	Danemark
France	207.4	194.8	173.6	191.0	168.5	150.1	# 167.6	150.8	129.9	128.5	France
Germany, Fed. Rep.[1]	833.2	814.8	792.4	859.0	804.9	730.5	679.4	665.8	684.0	682.7	Allemagne, Rép. féd.[1]
Netherlands	126.0	140.0	150.0	145.0	131.0	114.0	128.0	119.0	104.2	...	Pays–Bas
United Kingdom[2]	172.1	178.4	167.2	164.5	164.8	155.1	139.4	135.1	161.0	157.2	Royaume–Uni[2]
EFTA	***183.1***	***206.3***	***234.0***	***249.8***	***247.9***	***231.3***	***222.4***	***251.3***	***243.3***	***260.3***	***AELE***
Finland	34.6	45.3	66.7	83.0	85.8	75.8	61.7	61.9	54.3	...	Finlande
Portugal	27.3	35.4	39.4	42.3	47.9	44.7	48.3	63.5	63.9	63.5	Portugal
Sweden	121.2	125.7	127.9	124.5	114.1	110.8	112.4	125.9	125.1	124.3	Suède
East Europe	***59.9***	***65.4***	***68.0***	***69.1***	***68.4***	***68.4***	***71.6***	***78.1***	***71.6***	***72.6***	***Europe de l'est***
Bulgaria	31.5	35.5	34.8	37.7	36.6	39.8	42.1	44.5	42.0	41.4	Bulgarie
Czechoslovakia	2.3	2.2	2.2	2.1	2.2	2.5	2.4	2.5	1.4	2.2	Tchécoslovaquie
Hungary	17.6	17.5	18.1	16.9	17.3	16.6	17.5	19.0	15.8	17.2	Hongrie
Poland	8.5	10.2	12.9	12.4	12.2	9.5	9.5	12.1	12.4	11.7	Pologne
Other Europe	***109.3***	***121.1***	***66.7***	***85.2***	***90.6***	***115.8***	***135.5***	***136.9***	***106.8***	***101.9***	***Autre Europe***
Spain	109.3	121.1	66.7	85.2	90.6	# 115.8	135.5	136.9	* 106.8	* 101.9	Espagne
Total	**3 029.8**	**3 124.6**	**3 219.4**	**3 374.7**	**3 198.5**	**2 941.6**	**2 757.5**	**2 894.0**	**2 825.1**	**2 801.0**	**Total**

General note.
Materials derived by condensation of amines or amides with formaldehyde, furfuraldehyde etc., such as urea–formal–dehyde, thiourea–formaldehyde, melamine–formaldehyde, aniline–formaldehyde etc. Dry resin content of moulding powders. (SITC 58110–2).

[1] Including phenolic and cresylic plastics.
[2] Including actual weight of aminoplastics, phenolic and cresylic resins.

Remarque générale.
Matières dérivées par condensation des amines ou des amides avec des aldéhydes (formaldéhyde, furfural etc.) telles que les résines urée–formol, thiourée–formol, mélamine–formol, aniline–formol etc. Teneur des poudres de moulage en résine sèche. (CTCI 58110–2).

[1] Y compris les résines phénoliques et crésyliques.
[2] Y compris le poids effectif des aminoplastes et des résines phénoliques et crésyliques.

Phenolic and cresylic plastics – Phénoplastes

Unit : Thousand metric tons

Unité : Milliers de tonnes métriques

Country or area	1976	1977	1978	1979	1980	1981	1982	1983	1984	1985	Pays ou zone
America, North	**599.6**	**823.2**	**883.9**	**818.4**	**660.3**	**779.7**	**645.6**	**686.1**	**681.5**	**658.5**	**Amérique du Nord**
Mexico	7.5	8.0	10.3	11.7	13.3	14.1	11.6	11.4	14.5	...	Mexique
United States	592.1	815.2	873.6	806.7	647.0	765.6	634.0	674.7	667.0	643.5	Etats–Unis
America, South	**5.2**	**6.0**	**4.7**	**6.5**	**6.0**	**4.7**	**5.0**	**4.5**	**4.9**	**3.4**	**Amérique du Sud**
Argentina	5.2	6.0	4.7	6.5	6.0	4.7	5.0	4.5	4.9	3.4	Argentine
Asia	**253.8**	**246.2**	**267.5**	**300.4**	**303.7**	**294.4**	**281.1**	**303.2**	**334.1**	**326.6**	**Asie**
Japan	253.8	246.2	267.5	300.4	303.7	294.4	281.1	303.2	334.1	326.6	Japon
Europe	**334.1**	**329.0**	**324.3**	**357.5**	**328.3**	**325.7**	**350.4**	**313.3**	**327.3**	**365.2**	**Europe**
EEC	***169.1***	***164.6***	***154.2***	***164.8***	***146.3***	***157.6***	***172.6***	***137.9***	***140.3***	***180.8***	***CEE***
Denmark	0.6	0.5	0.5	0.5	0.5	...	...	...	...	...	Danemark
France	73.9	65.4	57.2	63.7	57.8	62.1	# 77.9	35.5	35.9	72.0	France
Italy	38.4	37.4	39.9	40.9	42.7	49.6	47.4	51.6	55.1	57.1	Italie
Netherlands	2.9	3.4	3.5	5.1	4.2	6.0	5.5	6.8	10.2	12.2	Pays–Bas
United Kingdom[1]	53.3	57.9	53.0	54.7	41.1	39.4	41.3	43.6	38.7	39.0	Royaume–Uni[1]
EFTA	***109.1***	***104.8***	***116.1***	***131.4***	***125.5***	***107.5***	***120.8***	***115.1***	***121.1***	***120.6***	***AELE***
Finland	52.8	51.4	60.6	70.5	69.0	64.4	75.1	68.6	76.0	...	Finlande
Portugal	1.6	3.2	3.6	4.2	4.8	4.7	4.8	5.0	4.8	5.0	Portugal
Sweden	54.7	50.2	51.8	56.6	51.8	38.4	40.9	41.4	40.3	36.4	Suède
East Europe	***41.9***	***38.9***	***32.7***	***33.6***	***34.4***	***29.9***	***27.4***	***29.4***	***31.2***	***26.9***	***Europe de l'est***
Czechoslovakia	18.5	18.0	18.5	18.8	19.2	17.9	17.5	17.0	16.9	14.7	Tchécoslovaquie
Hungary	4.3	4.3	5.0	4.7	5.2	4.5	4.1	6.1	8.0	6.6	Hongrie
Poland	19.1	16.6	9.3	10.1	10.0	7.5	5.8	6.3	6.4	5.7	Pologne
Other Europe	***14.0***	***20.7***	***21.3***	***27.7***	***22.1***	***30.8***	***29.7***	***30.9***	***34.6***	***36.8***	***Autre Europe***
Spain	14.0	20.7	...	27.7	22.1	30.8	29.7	30.9	...	...	Espagne
Oceania	**6.3**	**8.2**	**7.6**	**7.6**	**8.6**	**8.7**	**8.0**	**8.5**	**8.5**	**8.7**	**Océanie**
Australia	6.3	8.2	7.6	7.6	8.6	8.7	8.0	...	8.5	8.7	Australie
Total	**1 199.0**	**1 412.6**	**1 488.1**	**1 490.4**	**1 307.0**	**1 413.2**	**1 290.1**	**1 315.7**	**1 356.3**	**1 362.4**	**Total**

General note.
Material derived from condensation of phenol, cresol, xylenol etc. or substituted phenols with aldehydes, such as, resins (novolaks), thermosetting phenol–formaldehyde resins, oil–soluble resins prepared from butylphenol, amyphenol, parahydroxydiphenyl or other substituted phenol, and modified phenolic resins. Dry resin content of moulding powders. (SITC 58110–3).

[1] Including actual weight of aminoplastics, phenolic and cresylic resins.

Remarque générale.
Matières dérivées de la condensation, avec des aldéhydes, du phénol, du crésol, du xylénol etc., ou de phénols de substitution, telles que: résines "novolaques", résines formophénoliques thermodurcissables, résines oléosolubles préparées à partir du butylphénol, de l'amylphénol, du paraphénylphénol ou d'autres phénols de substitution, résines phénoliques modifiées. Teneur en résine sèche des poudres de moulage. (CTCI 58110–3).

[1] Y compris le poids effectif des aminoplastes et des résines phénoliques et crésyliques.

Polyethylene – Polyéthylène

Unit : Thousand metric tons

Unité : Milliers de tonnes métriques

Country or area	1976	1977	1978	1979	1980	1981	1982	1983	1984	1985	Pays ou zone
America, North	**4 374.7**	**5 021.4**	**5 728.8**	**6 409.6**	**5 911.7**	**6 481.5**	**6 355.5**	**7 082.2**	**7 521.4**	**8 100.9**	**Amérique du Nord**
Canada	300.9	345.0	477.5	628.2	641.7	673.3	570.5	623.0	755.4	962.1	Canada
Mexico	93.7	95.0	99.7	154.1	91.4	91.2	93.3	88.3	133.5	160.0	Mexique
United States	3 980.1	4 581.3	5 151.7	5 627.4	5 178.6	5 716.9	5 691.7	6 370.8	6 632.5	6 978.8	Etats–Unis
America, South	**295.4**	**362.2**	**384.3**	**521.5**	**564.3**	**589.2**	**754.5**	**832.1**	**927.8**	**948.3**	**Amérique du Sud**
Argentina	29.1	33.6	31.9	34.1	34.3	34.2	146.6	183.1	188.6	160.8	Argentine
Brazil	229.9	253.3	272.2	409.2	435.9	440.0	478.8	...	...	...	Brésil
Chile	30.7	34.2	30.3	36.1	38.5	33.1	22.5	32.4	32.3	30.5	Chili
Colombia	0.2	0.7	7.0	8.7	14.8	34.0	41.7	# 0.2	...	...	Colombie
Venezuela	5.5	40.4	43.0	33.5	40.7	47.9	...	...	88.6	...	Venezuela
Asia	**1 786.7**	**1 843.2**	**2 253.2**	**2 731.7**	**2 592.9**	**2 375.4**	**2 453.2**	**2 629.0**	**3 191.1**	**3 023.9**	**Asie**
China	...	197.8	244.1	263.4	302.2	305.8	313.2	341.3	337.2	335.0	Chine
Hong Kong	2.5	11.0	13.0	10.4	27.7	5.6	19.6	6.9	38.7	...	Hong–kong
India	49.4	47.0	71.7	99.8	97.9	128.3	134.9	136.0	147.0	144.0	Inde
Israel	33.6	32.7	35.6	40.1	61.0	48.0	66.6	62.5	74.0	73.9	Israël
Japan	1 392.5	1 466.7	1 766.6	2 165.3	1 860.2	1 670.7	1 674.1	1 773.0	2 251.1	2 027.3	Japon
Korea, Republic of	75.3	61.9	96.9	122.4	227.9	200.0	218.0	279.0	317.3	352.9	Corée, République de
Turkey	23.0	26.2	25.4	30.3	16.0	17.0	26.8	30.3	25.8	* 64.0	Turquie
Europe	**4 777.7**	**4 879.4**	**4 965.0**	**5 535.9**	**5 415.5**	**4 730.0**	**4 690.6**	**5 467.1**	**5 518.1**	**5 610.1**	**Europe**
EEC	***3 695.7***	***3 663.5***	***3 633.7***	***3 972.7***	***3 663.2***	***3 099.6***	***3 008.0***	***3 451.4***	***3 457.1***	***3 496.9***	***CEE***
Denmark	...	...	...	...	...	...	6.5	6.2	...	...	Danemark
France[1]	913.7	954.5	980.9	1 173.3	1 074.5	883.5	# 921.5	965.0	1 006.2	1 089.6	France[1]
Germany, Fed. Rep.	1 469.8	1 433.6	1 521.6	1 578.0	1 399.9	1 199.6	1 124.0	1 362.0	1 310.2	1 238.6	Allemagne, Rép. féd.
Italy	831.4	779.7	696.6	731.4	747.6	555.8	530.3	711.0	728.2	640.0	Italie
United Kingdom	474.4	489.4	428.4	483.6	434.8	454.4	425.8	407.2	406.1	# 522.3	Royaume–Uni
EFTA	***397.0***	***298.6***	***342.1***	***481.1***	***506.4***	***396.0***	***379.1***	***469.0***	***501.4***	***506.0***	***AELE***
Finland[2]	124.8	115.4	129.5	141.8	148.6	134.4	131.4	...	...	...	Finlande[2]
Norway	...	5.0	17.0	100.0	135.0	...	...	...	...	...	Norvège
Portugal	3.6	4.8	4.9	5.0	4.6	3.4	4.1	4.2	4.9	5.1	Portugal
Sweden	204.4	173.4	190.6	234.4	218.3	194.0	179.3	257.3	286.2	287.9	Suède
East Europe	***396.9***	***486.8***	***509.8***	***516.0***	***657.0***	***688.8***	***727.1***	***779.3***	***804.5***	***805.6***	***Europe de l'est***
Bulgaria	51.6	54.3	56.4	65.9	93.1	94.2	88.6	94.1	104.4	100.3	Bulgarie
Czechoslovakia	60.5	112.2	139.9	152.8	164.2	141.2	151.3	167.9	154.2	166.7	Tchécoslovaquie
German Dem. Rep.	...	87.4	84.5	92.7	112.4	159.7	173.0	175.1	179.0	178.0	Rép. dém. allemande
Hungary	46.2	49.8	51.2	52.2	52.6	52.9	53.1	54.2	54.3	56.1	Hongrie
Poland	48.5	47.8	46.3	43.1	110.8	111.3	118.1	129.4	140.6	141.9	Pologne
Romania	124.8	135.4	131.4	109.3	123.9	129.5	143.0	158.6	172.1	162.6	Roumanie
Other Europe	***288.1***	***430.5***	***479.4***	***566.1***	***588.9***	***545.6***	***576.4***	***767.4***	***755.1***	***801.7***	***Autre Europe***
Spain	258.5	398.7	450.0	531.0	489.4	429.6	489.4	611.3	586.8	619.7	Espagne
Yugoslavia	29.6	31.8	29.4	35.1	99.5	115.9	87.0	156.1	168.3	182.0	Yougoslavie
Oceania	**119.8**	**149.5**	**159.2**	**160.9**	**178.3**	**191.8**	**182.3**	**201.9**	**226.4**	**236.6**	**Océanie**
Australia	119.8	149.5	159.2	160.9	178.3	191.8	182.3	201.9	226.4	236.6	Australie
Total	**11 354.2**	**12 255.8**	**13 490.6**	**15 359.7**	**14 662.6**	**14 367.9**	**14 436.1**	**16 212.4**	**17 384.7**	**17 919.8**	**Total**

General note.
Dry resin content of polymerized ethylene. (SITC 58120–1).

Remarque générale.
Teneur en résine sèche de l'éthylène polymérisé. (CTCI 58120–1).

[1] Polystyrene and its copolymers.
[2] Beginning 1983, data are confidential.

[1] Polystyréne et ses copolyméres.
[2] A partir de 1983, les données sont confidentielles.

Polypropylene – Polypropylène

Unit : Thousand metric tons

Unité : Milliers de tonnes métriques

Country or area	1976	1977	1978	1979	1980	1981	1982	1983	1984	1985	Pays ou zone
America, North	**1 160.0**	**1 227.3**	**1 385.6**	**1 734.2**	**1 516.6**	**1 817.9**	**1 594.4**	**2 021.6**	**2 250.2**	**2 349.7**	**Amérique du Nord**
United States	1 160.0	1 227.3	1 385.6	1 734.2	1 516.6	1 817.9	1 594.4	2 021.6	2 250.2	2 349.7	Etats–Unis
America, South	**24.3**	**44.0**	**24.7**	**95.9**	**119.9**	**129.9**	**155.6**	**200.0**	**232.1**	**201.6**	**Amérique du Sud**
Brazil	...	...	24.5	95.3	119.6	129.9	155.4	199.6	231.8	...	Brésil
Colombia	0.1	0.1	...	0.5	0.3	0.0	0.2	0.4	...	...	Colombie
Asia	**829.7**	**805.5**	**924.6**	**1 241.6**	**1 212.3**	**1 253.4**	**1 258.5**	**1 418.3**	**1 672.0**	**1 748.0**	**Asie**
China	...	57.1	72.0	75.0	95.0	101.0	116.0	120.8	119.9	132.0	Chine
Hong Kong	0.0	0.0	1.8	0.0	...	0.0	4.1	1.4	20.3	...	Hong–kong
India	...	...	...	...	...	0.3	0.2	0.3	0.8	...	Inde
Japan	669.0	607.8	744.7	1 022.7	927.2	958.6	940.9	1 062.1	1 271.5	1 303.8	Japon
Korea, Republic of	79.9	109.2	74.0	110.2	151.5	155.8	160.4	195.1	218.9	258.8	Corée, République de
Turkey	* 28.0	* 31.0	...	...	...	[1] 37.7	[1] 36.9	[1] 38.6	...	...	Turquie
Europe	**937.5**	**1 099.2**	**1 226.1**	**1 370.1**	**1 221.5**	**1 364.5**	**1 455.2**	**1 614.4**	**1 936.1**	**2 053.5**	**Europe**
EEC	***804.2***	***939.8***	***1 048.8***	***1 108.3***	***966.6***	***1 084.4***	***1 140.7***	***1 269.6***	***1 483.1***	***1 565.2***	***CEE***
France	65.3	90.6	145.3	206.6	211.0	298.0	# 315.2	381.5	401.5	430.8	France
Germany, Fed. Rep.[2]	...	290.0	298.0	311.0	287.0	323.0	316.0	361.0	418.0	...	Allemagne, Rép. féd.[2]
Italy	[2] 190.4	[2] 256.0	# 265.6	279.7	230.6	218.5	240.5	249.6	357.9	424.7	Italie
Netherlands	40.0	55.0	...	...	...	...	...	...	...	...	Pays–Bas
United Kingdom	250.7	248.2	292.3	263.4	190.4	197.5	221.4	229.9	258.2	269.0	Royaume–Uni
EFTA	***14.0***	***20.5***	***19.6***	***54.3***	***49.6***	***53.9***	***62.9***	***66.6***	***78.2***	***88.0***	***AELE***
Finland	0.0	0.0	0.3	0.3	0.3	0.3	0.5	0.2	0.1	...	Finlande
Norway	...	...	[2] 7.0	[2] 37.0	[2] 34.0	[1] 36.3	[1] 48.5	[1] 51.3	...	...	Norvège
Portugal	11.5	10.6	12.3	17.0	15.3	17.3	13.8	15.2	16.5	18.8	Portugal
East Europe	***89.1***	***100.1***	***113.7***	***144.4***	***144.3***	***156.9***	***174.3***	***188.9***	***252.5***	***272.9***	***Europe de l'est***
Czechoslovakia	89.1	100.1	105.6	111.6	101.5	109.4	124.2	131.8	159.4	174.2	Tchécoslovaquie
Hungary	0.0	0.0	8.2	32.9	42.8	47.5	50.1	57.0	93.0	98.6	Hongrie
Other Europe	***30.2***	***38.9***	***44.0***	***63.0***	***61.2***	***69.2***	***77.4***	***89.4***	***122.3***	***127.4***	***Autre Europe***
Spain	30.2	38.9	44.0	63.0	61.2	69.2	77.4	89.4	122.3	127.4	Espagne
Oceania	**120.3**	**120.3**	**120.3**	**120.3**	**120.3**	**120.3**	**103.6**	**113.5**	**124.1**	**140.2**	**Océanie**
Australia	...	...	...	...	...	...	103.6	113.5	124.1	140.2	Australie
Total	**3 071.8**	**3 296.4**	**3 681.5**	**4 562.1**	**4 190.7**	**4 686.0**	**4 567.2**	**5 367.8**	**6 214.4**	**6 493.0**	**Total**

General note.
Dry resin content of polymerized propylene. (SITC 58120–2).

Remarque générale.
Teneur en résine sèche du propylène polymérisé. (CTCI 58120–2).

[1] Source: United Nations Economic Commission for Europe (ECE), (Geneva).

[2] Source: The Chemical Industry, Organisation for Economic Co–operation and Development (OECD), (Paris).

[1] Source: Commission économique des Nations Unies pour l'Europe (CEE), (Genève).

[2] Source: l'Industrie chimique, Organisation de coopération et de développement économiques (OCDE), (Paris).

Polystyrene – Polystyrène

Unit : Thousand metric tons | Unité : Milliers de tonnes métriques

Country or area	1976	1977	1978	1979	1980	1981	1982	1983	1984	1985	Pays ou zone
America, North	**1 274.6**	**2 499.3**	**2 866.1**	**3 073.3**	**2 243.0**	**2 895.3**	**2 762.3**	**2 757.9**	**2 918.1**	**2 808.3**	**Amérique du Nord**
Canada[1]	75.9	90.5	98.7	123.8	109.8	122.6	126.0	...	170.9	178.1	Canada[1]
Mexico	41.6	48.7	51.4	80.1	81.8	89.7	92.3	87.9	88.5	96.4	Mexique
United States	1 157.1	2 360.0	2 715.9	2 869.4	2 051.4	2 683.1	2 544.0	2 518.4	2 658.7	2 533.9	Etats–Unis
America, South	**100.0**	**110.2**	**146.8**	**185.2**	**203.7**	**161.5**	**182.2**	**171.6**	**202.9**	**208.5**	**Amérique du Sud**
Argentina	21.6	26.0	25.1	32.2	21.6	21.2	29.4	30.8	34.0	24.1	Argentine
Brazil	55.7	52.2	86.0	[2] 114.3	132.2	99.3	105.9	96.6	116.1	...	Brésil
Chile	2.0	...	...	0.7	0.9	0.7	0.9	0.6	0.7	0.5	Chili
Colombia	7.0	8.0	12.8	13.0	16.7	9.8	10.1	4.2	...	...	Colombie
Venezuela	13.7	22.6	21.5	25.2	32.3	30.5	...	...	...	...	Venezuela
Asia	**1 011.4**	**1 013.6**	**1 219.3**	**1 392.0**	**1 296.8**	**1 386.3**	**1 403.1**	**1 501.1**	**1 736.6**	**1 839.0**	**Asie**
China	...	9.6	11.8	13.7	16.8	20.2	21.2	21.2	25.8	31.5	Chine
Hong Kong	...	44.6	98.8	82.0	75.3	82.3	76.2	15.2	41.8	...	Hong–kong
India	12.3	14.7	12.7	13.5	10.5	8.1	11.4	15.0	18.9	18.1	Inde
Japan	875.1	900.3	1 031.8	1 226.9	1 128.8	1 183.4	1 190.3	1 310.5	1 503.2	1 599.2	Japon
Korea, Republic of	22.9	37.3	51.2	43.8	54.4	80.3	93.7	123.3	131.6	133.8	Corée, République de
Turkey	5.8	7.1	13.1	12.1	11.0	12.0	10.2	15.9	15.2	* 16.0	Turquie
Europe	**1 165.1**	**1 175.4**	**1 263.9**	**1 327.6**	**1 361.9**	**1 343.2**	**1 394.8**	**1 444.7**	**1 447.6**	**1 477.2**	**Europe**
EEC	***943.6***	***921.0***	***1 002.3***	***1 048.2***	***1 060.7***	***1 043.5***	***1 103.4***	***1 146.2***	***1 120.6***	***1 122.0***	***CEE***
Denmark	2.0	1.5	1.7	5.5	5.4	...	5.9	5.2	4.8	11.2	Danemark
France	238.7	233.3	319.3	366.4	366.3	386.5	# 444.8	480.7	484.4	489.6	France
Italy	267.3	262.3	277.2	264.7	324.7	290.2	306.5	329.6	316.1	321.4	Italie
Netherlands[3]	195.0	...	...	...	...	...	...	...	...	...	Pays–Bas[3]
United Kingdom	240.6	228.9	209.2	216.5	169.3	...	...	...	...	...	Royaume–Uni
EFTA	***37.7***	***43.9***	***36.8***	***52.5***	***58.8***	***61.4***	***61.3***	***67.0***	***69.6***	***71.1***	***AELE***
Finland[4]	24.0	28.7	23.5	36.5	33.8	33.1	29.8	...	...	...	Finlande[4]
Norway[3]	...	5.0	...	...	...	...	...	...	...	...	Norvège[3]
Sweden	8.7	10.2	8.3	11.0	20.1	23.4	26.4	26.9	28.2	28.4	Suède
East Europe	***94.8***	***99.7***	***104.1***	***105.1***	***111.4***	***104.8***	***105.0***	***111.3***	***120.4***	***134.4***	***Europe de l'est***
Bulgaria	19.2	19.0	20.0	17.5	16.3	19.3	19.4	22.2	24.4	25.1	Bulgarie
Czechoslovakia	43.1	47.0	50.2	54.6	61.2	63.0	63.8	68.9	72.3	86.2	Tchécoslovaquie
Poland	32.5	33.8	33.9	32.9	33.9	22.6	21.8	20.2	23.6	23.2	Pologne
Other Europe	***89.0***	***110.8***	***120.7***	***121.8***	***130.9***	***133.4***	***125.2***	***120.1***	***137.1***	***149.6***	***Autre Europe***
Spain	69.9	96.7	98.0	83.0	85.0	91.2	95.1	86.4	101.4	108.7	Espagne
Yugoslavia	19.1	14.1	22.7	38.8	45.9	42.2	30.1	33.6	35.7	40.8	Yougoslavie
Oceania	**6.6**	**6.6**	**6.6**	**6.6**	**7.6**	**7.1**	**5.1**	**6.6**	**6.6**	**6.6**	**Océanie**
Australia	...	...	...	...	7.6	7.1	5.1	...	...	...	Australie
Total	**3 557.7**	**4 805.1**	**5 502.6**	**5 984.7**	**5 113.0**	**5 793.4**	**5 747.4**	**5 881.9**	**6 311.9**	**6 339.6**	**Total**

General note.
Dry resin content of polymerized styrene. (SITC 58120–3).

Remarque générale.
Teneur en résine sèche du styrène polymérisé. (CTCI 58120–3).

1 1983, data are confidential.
2 Production by establishments employing 5 or more persons.
3 Source: The Chemical Industry, Organisation for Economic Co–operation and Development (OECD), (Paris).
4 Beginning 1983, data are confidential.

1 1983, les données sont confidentielles.
2 Production des établissements occupant 5 personnes ou plus.
3 Source: l'Industrie chimique, Organisation de coopération et de développement économiques (OCDE), (Paris).
4 A partir de 1983, les données sont confidentielles.

Polyvinylchloride – Chlorure de polyvinyle

Unit : Thousand metric tons

Unité : Milliers de tonnes métriques

Country or area	1976	1977	1978	1979	1980	1981	1982	1983	1984	1985	Pays ou zone
America, North	**2 250.3**	**2 573.8**	**2 872.6**	**3 043.8**	**2 771.5**	**2 923.7**	**2 791.5**	**2 994.5**	**3 670.8**	**3 673.7**	**Amérique du Nord**
Canada[1]	96.7	99.7	124.8	149.4	190.4	222.1	192.6	243.3	251.7	...	Canada[1]
Mexico	60.2	55.7	55.8	55.7	62.5	131.5	142.5	190.0	251.3	262.9	Mexique
Nicaragua	...	...	...	22.3	22.5	21.6	8.3	10.8	11.8	...	Nicaragua
United States	2 061.4	2 389.2	2 665.8	2 816.5	2 496.1	2 548.4	2 448.1	2 550.4	3 155.9	3 125.2	Etats-Unis
America, South	**233.2**	**251.8**	**271.6**	**305.3**	**293.5**	**252.3**	**295.4**	**327.0**	**323.9**	**309.9**	**Amérique du Sud**
Argentina	39.2	52.2	44.0	58.4	54.5	49.5	64.5	78.2	75.7	56.2	Argentine
Brazil	151.3	160.1	179.3	196.2	202.2	142.0	165.9	...	...	...	Brésil
Chile	8.9	10.1	9.8	9.2	...	...	...	...	...	...	Chili
Colombia	26.4	20.7	28.8	31.9	17.3	40.3	43.9	51.7	...	...	Colombie
Peru	7.4	8.7	9.7	9.7	10.0	...	...	...	...	...	Pérou
Asia	**1 445.9**	**1 482.3**	**1 758.3**	**2 284.3**	**2 196.8**	**1 946.3**	**2 118.1**	**2 393.3**	**2 516.5**	**2 638.1**	**Asie**
China	...	185.2	256.2	331.6	377.8	371.8	424.4	481.9	503.9	507.8	Chine
Hong Kong	0.0	0.0	7.2	4.6	...	...	10.8	18.1	...	...	Hong-kong
India	45.9	57.0	59.1	59.0	...	...	...	...	...	...	Inde
Indonesia	...	...	...	...	...	...	...	4.1	...	...	Indonésie
Japan	1 044.0	1 030.8	1 204.3	1 592.1	1 429.3	1 129.5	1 218.1	1 420.4	1 503.8	1 549.5	Japon
Korea, Republic of	95.1	116.0	131.0	191.8	231.4	287.3	312.2	322.8	344.3	410.7	Corée, République de
Thailand	...	...	...	...	...	45.0	52.0	...	...	...	Thaïlande
Turkey	24.4	40.8	48.0	52.6	...	41.5	41.3	42.2	37.8	41.0	Turquie
Europe	**3 945.4**	**3 973.1**	**4 283.0**	**4 638.9**	**4 405.3**	**4 223.7**	**4 316.4**	**4 676.2**	**4 903.2**	**4 854.6**	**Europe**
EEC	***2 969.1***	***2 946.5***	***3 055.4***	***3 307.3***	***3 007.9***	***2 833.8***	***2 874.2***	***3 158.2***	***3 216.3***	***3 225.1***	***CEE***
Denmark	2.3	2.2	2.2	2.4	2.1	...	3.2	3.2	3.3	...	Danemark
France	616.4	645.2	664.6	782.8	725.4	710.4	791.6	816.7	* 796.6	808.8	France
Germany, Fed. Rep.	965.1	897.4	1 006.3	1 084.8	953.2	918.6	864.4	1 089.9	1 131.9	1 208.3	Allemagne, Rép. féd.
Greece	34.4	39.9	44.1	47.6	50.1	49.4	41.0	50.7	57.2	...	Grèce
Italy	713.8	685.4	673.1	694.5	672.3	582.7	591.7	632.4	678.8	617.1	Italie
Netherlands[2]	220.0	290.0	...	...	...	...	...	...	...	...	Pays-Bas[2]
United Kingdom	417.1	386.4	410.1	440.2	349.7	314.8	...	...	...	...	Royaume-Uni
EFTA	***255.1***	***247.4***	***266.5***	***298.9***	***276.4***	***313.8***	***372.1***	***371.3***	***478.5***	***450.4***	***AELE***
Finland[3]	38.6	38.7	50.5	60.3	57.1	...	...	...	...	...	Finlande[3]
Norway[2]	55.0	59.0	54.0	63.0	* 62.1	* 97.7	* 122.7	* 97.7	* 199.7	...	Norvège[2]
Portugal	24.3	30.7	32.5	38.2	39.3	44.2	52.3	55.9	47.9	52.1	Portugal
Sweden[4]	137.3	119.0	129.4	137.3	117.9	105.4	124.7	139.6	146.9	146.1	Suède[4]
East Europe	***482.6***	***556.3***	***632.9***	***655.1***	***765.6***	***735.7***	***741.0***	***806.3***	***834.7***	***807.9***	***Europe de l'est***
Bulgaria	27.5	29.4	29.4	38.7	63.5	78.8	93.3	108.9	117.1	98.5	Bulgarie
Czechoslovakia	140.3	174.3	188.7	193.4	204.2	200.5	198.7	201.4	206.0	209.4	Tchécoslovaquie
Hungary	42.7	42.8	95.1	150.6	173.2	157.8	166.5	170.1	172.4	169.8	Hongrie
Poland	124.9	122.2	125.5	101.9	118.6	92.9	79.5	106.2	128.2	126.3	Pologne
Romania	147.0	187.6	194.3	170.6	206.1	205.8	...	219.8	211.0	203.9	Roumanie
Other Europe	***238.6***	***222.8***	***328.2***	***377.5***	***355.5***	***340.4***	***329.1***	***340.4***	***373.7***	***371.2***	***Autre Europe***
Spain	186.2	139.0	210.0	240.0	216.0	185.0	201.7	226.8	230.2	218.2	Espagne
Yugoslavia	52.4	83.8	118.2	137.5	139.5	155.4	127.4	113.6	143.6	152.9	Yougoslavie
Oceania	**18.3**	**18.3**	**18.3**	**18.3**	**17.5**	**17.9**	**19.7**	**18.3**	**18.3**	**18.3**	**Océanie**
Australia	...	...	...	...	17.5	17.9	19.7	...	...	...	Australie
Total	**7 893.1**	**8 299.4**	**9 203.8**	**10 290.8**	**9 684.6**	**9 363.9**	**9 541.2**	**10 409.4**	**11 432.7**	**11 494.6**	**Total**

General note.

Dry resin content of polyvinylchloride (PVC) derived from polymerisation of vinylchloride monomer and peroxide catalysts. (SITC 58120-4).

[1] Shipments.
[2] Source: The Chemical Industry, Organisation for Economic Co-operation and Development (OECD), (Paris).
[3] Beginning 1981, data are confidential.
[4] Including other polyvinyl resins.

Remarque générale.

Teneur en résine sèche du chlorure de polyvinyle obtenu par polymérisation du chlorure de vinyle en présence de catalyseurs (péroxydes). (CTCI 58120-4).

[1] Expéditions.
[2] Source: l'Industrie chimique, Organisation de coopération et de développement économiques (OCDE), (Paris).
[3] A partir de 1981, les données sont confidentielles.
[4] Y compris les autres résines de polyvinyle.

Regenerated cellulose – Cellulose régénérée

Unit : Thousand metric tons

Unité : Milliers de tonnes métriques

Country or area	1976	1977	1978	1979	1980	1981	1982	1983	1984	1985	Pays ou zone
America, North											**Amérique du Nord**
Mexico	19.6	20.0	20.2	21.9	21.2	18.4	16.0	17.1	14.5	12.8	Mexique
Europe											**Europe**
EEC											***CEE***
Denmark	...	...	...	...	...	...	0.4	...	...	...	Danemark
Germany, Fed. Rep.[1]	...	...	...	...	...	183.0	161.0	171.0	...	...	Allemagne, Rép. féd.[1]
Netherlands[1]	...	...	...	...	...	53.5	50.3	57.1	...	...	Pays-Bas[1]
United Kingdom	81.4	77.7	79.8	73.8	78.8	76.7	62.7	57.0	54.6	55.0	Royaume-Uni
EFTA											***AELE***
Finland	0.1	0.2	...	0.1	0.1	0.1	...	...	...	...	Finlande
Sweden	1.6	1.7	1.5	1.9	2.0	2.4	2.5	3.0	3.8	4.1	Suède
East Europe											***Europe de l'est***
Czechoslovakia	17.9	18.5	18.4	18.2	18.2	17.4	16.2	15.6	14.6	15.5	Tchécoslovaquie
Hungary[1]	...	...	...	...	...	4.6	4.4	7.0	...	...	Hongrie[1]
Poland[1]	...	...	...	...	...	11.5	10.2	10.3	11.2	...	Pologne[1]
Other Europe											***Autre Europe***
Spain	0.9	...	10.6	12.5	13.7	15.2	16.7	16.3	17.4	14.2	Espagne
Yugoslavia[1]	...	...	...	...	...	24.8	21.6	...	...	...	Yougoslavie[1]
USSR[1]	...	...	...	...	...	58.9	73.0	79.3	79.2	...	**URSS[1]**

General note.
Net dry content of regenerated cellulose, cellulose nitrate, cellulose acetate and other cellulose derivatives. Collodions and vulcanized fibres are excluded. (SITC 58132-0).

[1] Source: United Nations Economic Commission for Europe (ECE), (Geneva).

Remarque générale.
Teneur en cellulose sèche de la cellulose régénérée, du nitrate de cellulose, de l'acétate de cellulose et d'autres dérivés de la cellulose. Cette rubrique ne comprend pas les collodions et les fibres vulcanisées. (CTCI 58132-0).

[1] Source: Commission économique des Nations Unies pour l'Europe (CEE), (Genève).

Non-cellulosic continuous fibres – Fibres continues non cellulosiques

Unit : Thousand metric tons

Unité : Milliers de tonnes métriques

Country or area	1976	1977	1978	1979	1980	1981	1982	1983	1984	1985	Pays ou zone
Africa	**28.0**	**26.5**	**30.2**	**33.7**	**35.3**	**34.6**	**38.3**	**41.5**	**49.5**	**54.8**	**Afrique**
Egypt[1]	0.6	0.8	0.8	1.5	1.8	* 2.0	* 3.3	* 3.5	* 3.0	...	Egypte[1]
South Africa[1]	27.4	25.7	29.4	32.2	33.5	32.6	35.0	38.0	46.5	51.0	Afrique du Sud[1]
America, North	**1 637.0**	**1 834.0**	**1 908.7**	**2 062.9**	**1 591.0**	**1 624.3**	**1 286.6**	**1 474.0**	**1 448.0**	**1 493.7**	**Amérique du Nord**
Canada[1 2]	63.8	71.3	72.2	73.1	74.0	* 65.9	* 52.0	* 59.3	* 69.6	* 75.1	Canada[1 2]
Costa Rica[1]	0.0	0.0	2.0	2.0	3.0	3.2	3.5	3.5	* 3.5	* 3.5	Costa Rica[1]
Mexico	73.3	96.5	96.7	103.3	102.4	116.4	109.7	117.7	115.1	128.8	Mexique
United States	1 499.9	1 666.2	1 737.8	1 884.5	1 411.6	1 438.8	1 121.4	1 293.5	1 259.8	1 286.3	Etats-Unis
America, South	**170.6**	**179.5**	**186.7**	**209.1**	**217.9**	**191.2**	**195.5**	**201.6**	**219.0**	**213.7**	**Amérique du Sud**
Argentina	24.1	26.5	22.7	29.7	21.8	16.6	19.3	26.9	30.2	20.1	Argentine
Brazil[1]	96.6	95.6	105.7	122.5	136.4	115.0	116.0	105.7	118.2	121.7	Brésil[1]
Chile[1]	4.0	4.0	4.4	5.0	5.0	5.0	4.6	2.6	2.8	3.3	Chili[1]
Colombia[1]	27.7	32.7	33.2	28.7	28.2	32.7	31.3	38.6	38.3	...	Colombie[1]
Ecuador[1]	1.8	2.3	2.5	3.4	3.5	3.5	4.0	4.0	4.8	4.9	Equateur[1]
Peru[1]	3.8	5.6	5.6	7.0	10.5	10.0	11.2	12.5	13.0	13.3	Pérou[1]
Uruguay[1]	1.1	1.1	1.1	1.1	1.0	0.9	0.9	1.6	1.6	2.1	Uruguay[1]
Venezuela[1]	11.5	11.7	11.5	11.7	11.5	7.5	8.2	9.7	10.2	10.9	Venezuela[1]
Asia	**834.5**	**907.7**	**1 030.9**	**1 092.6**	**1 133.8**	**1 184.0**	**1 230.1**	**1 305.8**	**1 447.9**	**1 546.5**	**Asie**
Bangladesh[1]	0.4	0.3	0.5	0.2	0.3	0.2	0.2	0.2	0.3	0.4	Bangladesh[1]
China[1]	* 15.0	* 18.0	* 30.0	* 36.0	* 43.0	* 55.0	61.0	66.0	103.1	125.0	Chine[1]
India[1]	24.2	25.6	32.8	35.8	39.7	50.9	62.0	87.2	106.3	127.5	Inde[1]
Indonesia[1]	11.0	17.3	21.3	22.7	41.5	46.4	60.9	60.5	75.5	...	Indonésie[1]
Iran(Islamic Rep.of)[1]	8.7	8.5	9.0	5.0	6.0	10.0	11.5	15.0	13.5	13.5	Iran(Rép.islamique)[1]
Israel[1]	5.7	5.8	8.9	9.9	10.5	10.5	9.0	8.7	9.5	10.5	Israël[1]
Japan	566.9	604.9	644.5	649.1	641.6	620.8	607.8	611.3	648.1	653.6	Japon
Korea, Republic of[1]	142.0	163.5	209.2	237.2	255.2	283.8	* 301.4	336.3	369.6	408.7	Corée, République de[1]
Pakistan[1]	2.4	2.2	1.9	2.0	1.5	1.5	5.1	8.1	12.0	15.6	Pakistan[1]
Philippines[1]	14.0	14.9	16.0	25.0	30.0	32.0	29.0	24.5	20.5	22.0	Philippines[1]
Thailand[1]	25.8	31.7	34.7	39.7	36.5	40.5	37.1	40.0	37.0	37.1	Thaïlande[1]
Turkey[1]	18.5	15.0	22.1	30.0	28.0	32.4	45.1	48.0	52.5	52.0	Turquie[1]
Europe	**1 167.3**	**1 106.6**	**1 138.9**	**1 177.5**	**1 162.7**	**1 194.7**	**1 160.0**	**1 189.6**	**1 255.9**	**1 317.6**	**Europe**
EEC	***841.1***	***764.8***	***771.1***	***786.2***	***751.9***	***772.5***	***729.6***	***735.4***	***764.6***	***794.8***	***CEE***
Belgium	3.8	5.5	11.3	14.0	[1 3] 71.9	[1 3] 80.4	[1 3] 70.6	[1 3] 61.9	[1 3] 62.5	[1 3] 71.0	Belgique
Denmark	0.0	0.0	0.0	0.0	0.0	10.8	10.9	12.6	14.0	13.4	Danemark
France	105.1	101.3	91.8	86.3	65.2	66.4	64.8	63.2	63.5	62.0	France
Germany, Fed. Rep.	374.7	337.7	337.9	354.0	317.8	320.7	324.0	332.1	349.7	357.5	Allemagne, Rép. féd.
Greece[1]	8.3	7.7	8.5	9.2	9.0	9.0	8.5	9.0	9.0	9.0	Grèce[1]
Ireland[1]	6.3	2.4	8.3	10.8	10.0	15.0	12.3	11.0	11.5	11.5	Irlande[1]
Italy[4]	142.7	133.4	132.5	140.5	152.2	170.8	172.0	165.5	170.9	...	Italie[4]
United Kingdom	200.1	176.7	180.8	171.4	125.9	99.4	* 66.5	* 80.0	* 83.5	* 90.5	Royaume-Uni
EFTA	***56.4***	***54.6***	***56.2***	***58.0***	***67.0***	***63.0***	***59.3***	***62.6***	***74.9***	***77.0***	***AELE***
Finland	4.2	3.8	4.3	4.9	4.2	4.1	4.0	3.7	4.2	...	Finlande
Portugal	1.8	1.7	2.0	3.9	2.0	1.7	1.8	0.9	1.0	0.9	Portugal
Sweden	1.0	0.1	0.1	0.1	0.1	0.1	...	...	...	...	Suède
Switzerland[1]	49.4	49.0	49.8	49.1	60.7	57.1	53.4	58.0	69.7	72.0	Suisse[1]
East Europe	***210.1***	***226.9***	***244.6***	***256.3***	***273.3***	***279.7***	***289.1***	***312.7***	***329.9***	***345.9***	***Europe de l'est***
Bulgaria[1]	13.0	12.5	13.0	13.0	17.3	17.5	17.5	18.0	20.0	23.0	Bulgarie[1]
Czechoslovakia	50.2	53.3	64.9	69.0	70.5	79.3	89.1	91.7	95.6	97.1	Tchécoslovaquie
German Dem. Rep.[1]	51.0	53.0	53.5	54.6	57.0	56.0	55.0	62.0	61.0	69.0	Rép. dém. allemande[1]
Hungary	3.2	3.2	3.3	3.2	6.1	7.2	7.8	7.7	8.6	9.0	Hongrie
Poland	64.6	76.0	79.9	81.5	89.4	78.7	74.8	80.3	84.7	87.9	Pologne
Romania[1]	28.0	29.0	30.0	35.0	33.0	41.0	45.0	53.0	60.0	60.0	Roumanie[1]
Other Europe	***59.8***	***60.3***	***66.9***	***77.0***	***70.4***	***79.4***	***82.0***	***78.9***	***86.4***	***99.9***	***Autre Europe***
Spain	54.5	55.1	60.8	71.7	64.0	72.3	73.6	64.6	69.4	* 85.0	Espagne
Yugoslavia	5.3	5.2	6.1	5.3	6.4	7.1	8.4	14.3	17.0	14.9	Yougoslavie
USSR	**263.0**	**291.8**	**310.1**	**317.1**	**323.9**	**340.0**	**367.0**	**403.9**	**426.4**	**452.6**	**URSS**
Byelorussian SSR	*29.9*	*30.1*	*38.0*	*43.1*	*41.7*	*40.6*	*48.4*	*50.6*	*53.2*	*56.5*	*RSS de Biélorussie*

For general note and footnotes, see end of table.

Voir la fin du tableau pour la remarque générale et les notes.

Non-cellulosic continuous fibres (continued) – Fibres continues non cellulosiques (suite)

Unit : Thousand metric tons

Unité : Milliers de tonnes métriques

Country or area	1976	1977	1978	1979	1980	1981	1982	1983	1984	1985	Pays ou zone
Ukrainian SSR	*79.2*	*84.0*	*84.4*	*86.2*	*86.0*	*87.2*	*90.0*	*91.3*	*119.9*	*118.9*	*RSS d'Ukraine*
Oceania	**20.0**	**17.5**	**18.1**	**16.4**	**13.0**	**10.0**	**14.5**	**14.5**	**12.9**	**5.7**	**Océanie**
Australia	20.0	17.5	18.1	16.4	13.0	10.0	14.5	14.5	12.9	5.7	Australie
Total	**4 120.5**	**4 363.6**	**4 623.5**	**4 909.3**	**4 477.6**	**4 578.7**	**4 292.0**	**4 630.7**	**4 859.6**	**5 084.6**	**Total**

General note.
Non-cellulosic (synthetic) continuous fibres made of natural polymers based on materials such as casein, or of synthetic polymers mainly from coal and oil distillation products. Textile glass fibres are excluded. They comprise filament yarn composed of two or more grouped, continuous, fine filaments, usually slightly twisted together, monofilaments other than those for use as bristle, and slit film mainly an olefin product made by slitting attenuated film to desired widths and often fibrillated by twisting. Waste, spun yarns and other manufactures are excluded. (SITC 65160-1).

[1] Source: Textile Economics Bureau, Inc. (New York).
[2] Excluding olefin.
[3] Including production in Netherlands and Luxembourg.
[4] Beginning 1985, series discontinued.

Remarque générale.
Fibres continues non cellulosiques artificielles ou synthétiques de polymères naturels obtenus à partir de matériaux comme la caséine, ou de polymères synthétiques obtenus principalement à partir de produits de la distillation du charbon ou du pétrole. Cette rubrique comprend les filés constitués d'un ensemble d'au moins deux filaments fins et continus soumis en général à une légère torsion. Les monofils autres que ceux servant à la fabrication des soies de brosserie, les lames obtenues en refendant à la largeur désirée un film fin de matière à base d'oléfines et en leur donnant souvent par torsion le crochet désiré. Cette rubrique ne comprend pas les fibres textiles de verre, les déchets, les filés de fibres discontinues et les autres produits non cellulosiques. (CTCI 65160-1).

[1] Source: Textile Economics Bureau, Inc. (New York).
[2] Non compris l'oléfine.
[3] Y compris la production en Pays-Bas et Luxembourg.
[4] A partir de 1985, la série a été abandonnée.

Cellulosic continuous filaments – Filaments cellulosiques continus

Unit : Thousand metric tons

Unité : Milliers de tonnes métriques

Country or area	1976	1977	1978	1979	1980	1981	1982	1983	1984	1985	Pays ou zone
Africa	**6.3**	**6.1**	**5.3**	**5.0**	**6.0**	**6.0**	**7.0**	**7.0**	**7.0**	**7.0**	**Afrique**
Egypt	6.3	6.1	5.3	5.0	* 6.0	* 6.0	* 7.0	* 7.0	* 7.0	* 7.0	Egypte
America, North	**185.4**	**189.4**	**194.0**	**200.2**	**192.8**	**171.6**	**128.2**	**143.7**	**131.3**	**116.6**	**Amérique du Nord**
Canada	5.7	11.0	12.3	14.1	14.0	13.5	9.5	10.0	10.0	10.0	Canada
Cuba	[1,2] 2.5	[1,2] 2.4	[1,2] 2.3	[1,2] 2.4	[1,2] 2.2	4.9	3.2	3.6	3.8	3.5	Cuba
Mexico	16.4	16.0	14.8	14.3	15.3	14.6	11.9	10.4	9.2	10.1	Mexique
United States[2]	160.8	160.0	164.6	169.4	161.3	138.6	103.6	119.7	108.4	93.0	Etats–Unis[2]
America, South	**49.9**	**44.0**	**38.1**	**39.6**	**37.1**	**30.0**	**28.0**	**26.4**	**27.0**	**29.4**	**Amérique du Sud**
Argentina	5.3	5.5	4.4	5.1	2.1	1.1	1.6	1.7	2.1	1.4	Argentine
Brazil[2]	34.2	28.8	24.1	24.4	26.0	21.0	20.8	18.4	17.7	20.1	Brésil[2]
Chile[1,2]	1.0	0.9	0.8	1.0	1.0	1.0	1.0	1.0	1.2	1.3	Chili[1,2]
Colombia[2]	3.4	3.3	3.4	3.4	2.4	1.8	1.8	1.8	1.8	1.8	Colombie[2]
Peru[2]	2.1	1.3	1.1	1.3	1.5	1.3	1.0	1.0	1.7	1.7	Pérou[2]
Uruguay[2,3]	1.1	1.2	1.3	1.4	1.3	1.0	0.6	1.0	1.0	1.0	Uruguay[2,3]
Venezuela[3,4]	2.8	3.0	3.0	3.0	2.8	2.8	1.2	1.5	1.5	2.1	Venezuela[3,4]
Asia	**245.9**	**247.2**	**258.5**	**265.3**	**273.9**	**276.1**	**266.6**	**269.4**	**261.2**	**261.5**	**Asie**
Bangladesh[2]	0.9	1.4	3.0	4.1	3.5	3.0	2.5	2.5	2.5	2.7	Bangladesh[2]
China[1,2]	* 55.0	* 61.0	* 65.0	* 68.0	* 75.0	* 80.0	* 80.0	* 85.0	87.0	87.0	Chine[1,2]
India[2]	60.6	58.9	62.4	60.5	57.7	55.9	48.6	46.2	41.7	46.9	Inde[2]
Iraq[2]	3.0	2.8	3.0	2.9	3.0	3.0	3.0	3.0	3.0	3.0	Iraq[2]
Japan	109.3	107.4	109.8	114.3	119.3	118.7	120.5	116.8	110.8	104.6	Japon
Korea, Republic of[2]	14.2	12.8	12.7	13.2	* 12.4	* 12.8	* 9.9	* 12.9	12.8	13.8	Corée, République de[2]
Pakistan[2]	2.6	2.6	2.3	2.0	2.7	2.4	1.8	2.7	3.1	3.2	Pakistan[2]
Turkey[2]	0.3	0.3	0.3	0.3	0.3	0.3	0.3	0.3	0.3	0.3	Turquie[2]
Europe	**366.5**	**340.5**	**322.7**	**319.3**	**315.7**	**288.3**	**268.9**	**267.8**	**273.9**	**269.8**	**Europe**
EEC	***212.5***	***190.8***	***179.8***	***176.8***	***172.2***	***152.7***	***143.2***	***143.9***	***151.0***	***144.2***	***CEE***
Belgium[5]	4.0	3.2	3.9	4.1	4.5	4.2	4.3	4.1	4.5	5.2	Belgique[5]
France	24.4	20.8	18.9	18.1	16.8	11.0	8.6	8.4	7.5	* 7.0	France
Germany, Fed. Rep.	71.3	66.0	62.2	62.0	69.6	# [2] 65.0	* [2] 61.0	* [2] 59.0	* [2] 66.0	* [2] 64.0	Allemagne, Rép. féd.
Greece[1]	6.7	7.0	6.8	7.2	7.2	7.2	7.2	6.3	6.0	7.0	Grèce[1]
Netherlands	35.3	31.2	28.2	26.3	# [2,6] 37.4	[2,6] 38.3	[2,6] 38.1	[2,6] 41.1	[2,6] 41.1	[2,6] 42.0	Pays–Bas
United Kingdom	70.7	62.6	59.8	59.2	* 36.7	* 27.0	* 24.0	* 25.0	25.9	19.0	Royaume–Uni
EFTA	***22.8***	***21.0***	***18.7***	***18.9***	***20.4***	***18.2***	***16.1***	***12.2***	***15.5***	***15.4***	***AELE***
Austria[1,2]	15.0	12.6	11.3	12.0	15.3	15.6	13.8	11.4	14.8	14.8	Autriche[1,2]
Finland[1]	0.9	1.2	1.2	1.2	0.6	0.0	0.0	0.0	0.0	0.0	Finlande[1]
Portugal[1]	2.5	2.6	2.1	2.4	2.7	2.6	2.3	0.8	0.7	0.6	Portugal[1]
Switzerland[1,2]	4.4	4.7	4.1	3.3	1.8	0.0	0.0	0.0	0.0	0.0	Suisse[1,2]
East Europe	***100.8***	***98.5***	***96.0***	***95.6***	***94.5***	***89.2***	***82.8***	***86.0***	***85.6***	***87.4***	***Europe de l'est***
Bulgaria[2]	3.0	3.0	3.2	3.2	3.3	4.3	4.0	4.1	4.1	4.1	Bulgarie[2]
Czechoslovakia[1]	22.0	21.9	21.3	20.5	19.9	18.7	17.6	18.9	17.3	18.8	Tchécoslovaquie[1]
German Dem. Rep.[1,2]	36.2	36.0	34.0	35.0	36.5	37.0	34.0	35.0	35.2	35.4	Rép. dém. allemande[1,2]
Poland	28.7	28.6	28.0	27.2	25.4	19.5	19.0	19.5	20.5	20.3	Pologne
Romania[1,2]	11.0	9.0	9.5	9.7	9.5	9.6	8.2	8.5	8.5	8.8	Roumanie[1,2]
Other Europe	***30.4***	***30.1***	***28.2***	***27.9***	***28.5***	***28.2***	***26.7***	***25.7***	***21.8***	***22.8***	***Autre Europe***
Spain[2]	15.6	15.0	13.8	12.6	12.8	12.6	11.3	10.5	7.2	7.5	Espagne[2]
Yugoslavia[1]	14.8	15.1	14.4	15.3	15.7	15.6	15.4	15.2	14.6	15.3	Yougoslavie[1]
USSR	**286.1**	**288.9**	**289.7**	**280.0**	**287.6**	**280.4**	**270.6**	**279.0**	**265.7**	**246.4**	**URSS**
Byelorussian SSR	*52.9*	*56.0*	*55.9*	*53.4*	*54.5*	*54.2*	*54.1*	*53.6*	*54.0*	*52.8*	*RSS de Biélorussie*
Ukrainian SSR	*26.6*	*27.9*	*28.4*	*27.5*	*27.3*	*26.8*	*26.8*	*27.0*	*27.2*	*27.0*	*RSS d'Ukraine*
Total	**1 140.1**	**1 116.2**	**1 108.2**	**1 109.3**	**1 113.1**	**1 052.4**	**969.3**	**993.3**	**966.2**	**930.7**	**Total**

For general note and footnotes, see end of table.

Voir la fin du tableau pour la remarque générale et les notes.

General note.
Rayon and acetate (artificial) continuous filaments produced by chemical transformation of natural organic polymers from cellulose. They comprise filament yarn composed of two or more grouped, continuous, fine filaments, usually slightly twisted together, and monofilaments other than those for use as bristle. Waste of these fibres, spun yarn and other manufactures of rayon and acetate are excluded. (SITC 65170–1).

1 Production of acetate fibres is nil or negligible.
2 Source: Textile Economics Bureau, Inc. (New York).
3 Production of rayon is nil or negligible.
4 Including spun yarn.
5 Excluding acetate fibres.
6 Including production in Netherlands and Luxembourg.

Remarque générale.
Filaments artificiels continus de rayonne ou d'acétate obtenus par une transformation chimique de polymères organiques naturels cellulosiques. Cette rubrique comprend les filés constitués d'un ensemble d'au moins deux filaments fins continus, soumis en général à une légère torsion, ainsi que les monofils autres que ceux servant à la fabrication des soies de brosserie, mais non les déchets de ces fibres, les filés de fibres discontinues et les autres produits fabriqués à partir de rayonne ou d'acétate. (CTCI 65170–1).

1 Production de fibres d'acétate nulle ou négligeable.
2 Source: Textile Economics Bureau, Inc. (New York).
3 Production de rayonne nulle ou négligeable.
4 Y compris les filés.
5 Non compris les fibres d'acétate.
6 Y compris la production en Pays–Bas et Luxembourg.

Paints, cellulose – Peintures cellulosiques

Unit : Thousand metric tons

Unité : Milliers de tonnes métriques

Country or area	1976	1977	1978	1979	1980	1981	1982	1983	1984	1985	Pays ou zone
Africa											**Afrique**
Burundi[1]	0.4	0.3	0.4	0.4	0.5	0.6	0.7	0.7	0.6	0.6	Burundi[1]
Kenya[2]	4.0	2.8	3.5	4.3	5.6	2.5	4.5	3.8	4.6	5.7	Kenya[2]
Madagascar[3]	3.1	3.1	3.7	3.8	4.2	3.1	1.8	1.8	1.8	2.0	Madagascar[3]
Nigeria[2 4]	20.8	25.8	34.6	30.4	47.0	58.4	58.7	25.6	30.1	21.9	Nigéria[2 4]
Rwanda[5]	0.2	0.4	0.5	0.6	0.6	0.5	0.8	0.9	0.9	0.8	Rwanda[5]
South Africa[2]	21.9	23.9	23.9	24.6	25.1	28.0	...	...	...	...	Afrique du Sud[2]
Asia											**Asie**
Afghanistan	...	0.0	0.1	0.0	0.1	0.0	0.0	0.0	0.0	...	Afghanistan
Democratic Yemen[2]	...	...	...	...	1.5	1.9	1.6	2.0	2.3	...	Yémen démocratique[2]
India[6]	73.7	74.4	86.5	77.0	88.1	95.6	108.2	113.0	119.9	139.9	Inde[6]
Indonesia	6.2	11.3	11.3	9.2	6.6	4.5	5.2	...	...	...	Indonésie
Japan	64.1	59.6	60.2	67.7	57.6	55.3	49.6	48.1	46.2	48.1	Japon
Korea, Republic of[2 7]	9.0	11.8	18.5	19.7	16.5	17.7	18.7	21.8	22.4	24.6	Corée, République de[2 7]
Pakistan[2]	7.1	7.2	7.9	8.3	8.0	9.0	9.7	9.9	12.4	...	Pakistan[2]
Singapore	10.2	12.6	14.7	15.3	17.5	21.6	20.7	19.6	23.1	24.3	Singapour
Sri Lanka	0.2	...	0.6	0.4	1.0	1.6	...	...	...	...	Sri Lanka
Turkey	4.4	5.9	6.2	7.3	9.0	4.6	4.2	5.6	6.2	* 7.0	Turquie
Europe											**Europe**
EEC											***CEE***
Belgium[8]	5.5	...	...	...	...	...	...	...	...	...	Belgique[8]
Denmark	2.0	2.0	2.0	2.2	1.9	...	2.6	2.3	3.1	2.9	Danemark
France	44.6	26.9	25.9	23.2	20.3	...	...	...	...	...	France
Germany, Fed. Rep.	89.3	78.4	78.3	76.4	70.7	65.1	59.4	61.0	61.7	61.1	Allemagne, Rép. féd.
Greece[9]	19.9	20.8	20.4	22.8	22.2	23.1	20.6	19.8	19.1	...	Grèce[9]
Netherlands	27.0	19.3	17.9	21.3	19.0	19.9	17.2	11.6	11.8	12.2	Pays-Bas
United Kingdom[10]	58.9	64.7	69.5	76.9	57.4	52.0	44.1	48.1	50.1	46.2	Royaume-Uni[10]
EFTA											***AELE***
Austria	19.9	20.1	...	...	22.5	...	...	* 17.5	* 18.9	...	Autriche
Portugal	2.5	2.7	5.0	4.6	5.2	4.6	4.6	4.6	4.2	3.9	Portugal
Sweden	3.8	2.7	2.3	2.3	1.5	1.4	1.2	1.0	1.1	1.0	Suède
East Europe											***Europe de l'est***
Bulgaria[4]	65.7	77.9	89.5	94.6	94.5	95.0	98.2	104.2	110.9	120.5	Bulgarie[4]
Hungary	13.2	14.1	14.7	14.0	14.2	13.3	13.5	12.7	13.9	13.1	Hongrie
Romania[4]	145.0	160.0	173.0	179.0	182.0	184.0	167.0	160.0	175.0	184.0	Roumanie[4]
Other Europe											***Autre Europe***
Spain	16.7	...	...	...	...	9.7	9.7	9.1	...	...	Espagne
USSR	153.4	169.7	175.1	157.9	162.9	181.6	182.5	194.3	197.3	207.5	**URSS**
Byelorussian SSR[4]	*153.4*	*169.7*	*175.1*	*157.9*	*162.9*	*181.6*	*182.5*	*194.3*	*197.3*	*207.5*	*RSS de Biélorussie[4]*
Oceania											**Océanie**
Australia[2 11]	4.9	4.0	4.2	5.1	5.3	5.3	5.7	4.8	4.9	4.9	Australie[2 11]

General note.
Paints, enamels and varnishes with cellulose derivative bases. (SITC 53332-1A).

1 Including cellulose paints and other paints.
2 In thousand kilolitres.
3 Including water paints and other paints.
4 Including other paints.
5 Including water paints.
6 Production by large and medium scale establishments only.
7 Varnishes and lacquers with cellulose derivative base.
8 Source: Industrial Statistics, Statistical Office of the European Communities, (Luxembourg).
9 Varnishes only.
10 Sales by manufacturers employing 25 or more persons.
11 Twelve months ending 30 June of year stated.

Remarque générale.
Peintures, laques et vernis à base de dérivés de la cellulose. (CTCI 53332-1A).

1 Y compris les peintures cellulosiques et les autres peintures.
2 En milliers de kilolitres.
3 Y compris les peintures à l'eau et les autres peintures.
4 Y compris les autres peintures.
5 Y compris les peintures à l'eau.
6 Production des grandes et moyennes entreprises seulement.
7 Vernis et lacques à base de dérivés de la cellulose.
8 Source: Statistiques industrielles, Office statistique des Communautés européennes, (Luxembourg).
9 Vernis seulement.
10 Ventes des fabricants employant 25 personnes ou plus.
11 Période de douze mois finissant le 30 juin de l'année indiquée.

Unit : Thousand metric tons — Unité : Milliers de tonnes métriques

Country or area	1976	1977	1978	1979	1980	1981	1982	1983	1984	1985	Pays ou zone
Africa											**Afrique**
Kenya[1]	0.5	# 2.4	2.3	3.1	2.9	2.6	2.2	...	0.3	3.3	Kenya[1]
Liberia	0.6	0.6	0.5	1.1	0.8	0.8	0.9	0.7	0.7	0.3	Libéria
Niger	0.3	0.4	0.3	0.6	0.1	0.3	0.4	...	...	...	Niger
Sierra Leone[1]	0.4	0.3	0.3	0.5	0.6	0.3	0.5	0.1	0.1	...	Sierra Leone[1]
South Africa[1]	26.9	24.0	32.3	35.8	* 42.6	44.7	44.7	44.7	55.7	48.3	Afrique du Sud[1]
United Rep. Tanzania[1]	3.0	3.0	4.7	2.5	1.4	1.5	1.1	...	...	...	Rép.Unie de Tanzanie[1]
America, North											**Amérique du Nord**
Antigua and Barbuda	...	...	...	...	0.3	0.3	0.4	0.3	...	...	Antigua–et–Barbuda
Canada[1 2]	...	...	60.8	56.9	62.4	...	...	...	...	...	Canada[1 2]
Cuba[1]	7.1	7.3	8.6	...	...	...	...	...	...	...	Cuba[1]
Jamaica[3]	5.6	4.7	5.5	5.8	3.6	4.8	6.2	7.4	5.8	5.4	Jamaïque[3]
Mexico	41.1	43.4	47.2	53.2	57.2	65.5	72.0	52.7	52.5	63.5	Mexique
America, South											**Amérique du Sud**
Argentina	26.9	37.1	46.4	50.6	58.1	54.5	43.5	39.1	44.6	42.7	Argentine
Brazil	343.1	301.3	330.7	[4] 347.7	361.2	297.9	...	...	...	...	Brésil
Chile	6.0	7.8	8.5	8.7	10.9	15.2	13.0	13.0	...	...	Chili
Ecuador[1]	...	...	...	...	...	10.9	3.0	1.6	...	...	Equateur[1]
Asia											**Asie**
Indonesia	...	0.0	0.0	0.0	0.1	0.0	0.1	...	...	...	Indonésie
Japan	171.7	179.6	209.8	255.6	244.7	230.6	251.8	268.6	294.9	315.2	Japon
Korea, Republic of[1]	13.1	16.5	26.8	32.1	31.1	38.4	32.1	35.0	40.9	44.2	Corée, République de[1]
Malaysia[1 5]	2.7	3.5	3.4	4.1	4.7	4.8	# 14.8	17.3	19.8	23.9	Malaisie[1 5]
Singapore	8.2	11.2	11.8	11.2	12.3	12.8	14.7	20.7	27.6	25.0	Singapour
Sri Lanka	0.6	...	1.0	0.7	1.9	2.0	...	...	...	...	Sri Lanka
Europe											**Europe**
EEC											***CEE***
Belgium[6]	38.9	39.2	...	...	...	...	...	...	...	...	Belgique[6]
Denmark	22.0	21.9	22.7	23.5	21.2	22.4	23.2	29.3	33.6	36.4	Danemark
France	15.4	11.5	10.1	8.3	7.2	...	...	...	...	...	France
Germany, Fed. Rep.	605.1	586.0	593.2	632.0	645.8	640.9	564.2	580.9	591.2	574.5	Allemagne, Rép. féd.
Greece	...	...	...	...	...	0.1	0.1	0.1	0.1	...	Grèce
Netherlands	40.0	43.4	50.9	47.2	48.3	51.3	51.8	57.0	60.4	62.4	Pays–Bas
United Kingdom[7]	254.0	263.7	268.7	273.4	239.1	252.8	272.7	283.2	296.7	322.7	Royaume–Uni[7]
EFTA											***AELE***
Austria	...	1.1	0.8	0.8	0.8	...	...	...	...	...	Autriche
Finland	19.5	19.4	17.6	19.6	21.1	17.8	20.7	21.3	22.4	...	Finlande
Portugal	31.6	37.2	40.3	46.2	44.2	50.6	54.9	57.2	52.3	50.7	Portugal
Sweden	44.8	43.0	42.0	43.6	46.5	46.8	48.7	49.5	53.3	50.8	Suède
East Europe											***Europe de l'est***
Hungary	0.1	0.1	0.1	0.1	0.1	0.1	0.2	0.1	0.2	0.2	Hongrie
Other Europe											***Autre Europe***
Spain	95.4	101.8	...	95.4	83.4	76.8	67.4	81.8	...	...	Espagne
Oceania											**Océanie**
Australia[1 8]	32.1	36.2	36.2	39.7	44.8	48.9	49.8	50.1	53.9	58.4	Australie[1 8]
Fiji[1 3]	1.4	1.5	1.7	1.7	1.8	1.8	1.8	2.3	1.8	2.3	Fidji[1 3]
New Zealand	7.9	7.8	8.5	9.0	9.6	11.4	11.6	11.4	12.4	13.1	Nouvelle–Zélande

General note.
Water paints including aqueous emulsions and distempers in paste form or ready for use. (SITC 53332–2A).

[1] In thousand kilolitres.
[2] Shipments.
[3] Including cellulose paints and other paints.
[4] Production by establishments employing 5 or more persons.

Remarque générale.
Peintures à l'eau, y compris les émulsions aqueuses et les détrempes à l'état pâteux ou prêtes à l'emploi. (CTCI 53332–2A).

[1] En milliers de kilolitres.
[2] Expéditions.
[3] Y compris les peintures cellulosiques et les autres peintures.
[4] Production des établissements occupant 5 personnes ou plus.

[5] Data refer to Peninsular Malaysia only.
[6] Source: Industrial Statistics, Statistical Office of the European Communities, (Luxembourg).
[7] Sales by manufacturers employing 25 or more persons.
[8] Twelve months ending 30 June of year stated.

[5] Données se rapportant à la Malaisie péninsulaire seulement.
[6] Source: Statistiques industrielles, Office statistique des Communautés européennes, (Luxembourg).
[7] Ventes des fabricants employant 25 personnes ou plus.
[8] Période de douze mois finissant le 30 juin de l'année indiquée.

Paints, other – Autres peintures

Unit : Thousand metric tons

Unité : Milliers de tonnes métriques

Country or area	1976	1977	1978	1979	1980	1981	1982	1983	1984	1985	Pays ou zone
Africa											**Afrique**
Algeria[1]	45.8	51.6	61.8	69.0	81.7	91.4	100.3	...	...	...	Algérie[1]
Cameroon	2.5	4.2	3.1	7.2	4.0	...	...	7.5	8.8	9.9	Cameroun
Central African Rep.	0.5	0.5	0.5	0.4	0.4	0.5	0.5	0.5	0.6	0.6	Rép. centrafricaine
Côte d'Ivoire	8.0	9.0	10.1	13.3	11.5	12.2	9.5	11.2	13.5	...	Côte d'Ivoire
Gabon	3.0	3.3	2.9	2.6	* 3.0	5.5	6.3	6.2	6.4	6.8	Gabon
Libyan Arab Jamah.[1]	16.4	13.2	13.1	17.9	19.5	25.2	25.9	30.3	...	...	Jamah.arabe libyenne[1]
Senegal	3.8	3.4	3.4	3.5	2.7	2.7	2.8	3.0	2.8	2.9	Sénégal
South Africa[2]	71.6	75.5	82.1	71.5	* 80.6	84.3	80.5	77.5	123.6	108.9	Afrique du Sud[2]
Tunisia[1 3]	12.9	11.5	12.2	16.7	14.1	19.4	...	...	...	...	Tunisie[1 3]
Uganda[1 2]	0.4	0.6	0.8	0.2	0.3	0.0	0.1	...	...	...	Ouganda[1 2]
Zaire	6.1	4.3	2.3	...	3.2	3.3	3.3	3.5	...	...	Zaïre
America, North											**Amérique du Nord**
Barbados[1]	1.0	1.0	1.1	1.3	1.6	1.4	1.5	1.4	1.2	1.3	Barbade[1]
Canada[2 4]	...	...	54.7	46.6	48.0	...	...	...	...	...	Canada[2 4]
Cuba[2]	7.1	7.3	7.1	7.2	6.7	6.2	3.7	7.9	13.8	13.4	Cuba[2]
Dominican Republic	6.8	6.0	7.5	9.2	10.1	7.6	8.4	9.7	7.9	9.3	Rép. dominicaine
Mexico	92.1	92.4	101.8	111.9	139.7	154.9	144.7	126.1	148.8	158.2	Mexique
America, South											**Amérique du Sud**
Argentina[5]	84.0	112.0	103.4	102.3	88.1	76.4	74.3	79.7	79.9	61.0	Argentine[5]
Brazil[6]	# 192.4	242.3	191.1	260.1	218.6	...	...	...	...	...	Brésil[6]
Chile	11.8	14.0	15.9	18.1	16.4	22.2	17.9	18.7	...	...	Chili
Ecuador[2 3]	4.7	...	...	...	2.0	0.3	7.6	3.5	...	...	Equateur[2 3]
Asia											**Asie**
Cyprus	1.5	1.7	2.2	2.2	2.1	2.5	2.7	2.7	2.7	3.1	Chypre
Indonesia	1.6	2.7	5.8	8.1	7.0	9.7	17.0	[3] 22.9	[3] 23.8	...	Indonésie
Iran(Islamic Rep.of)[7]	45.8	56.6	50.9	40.8	43.2	46.6	51.6	70.2	...	...	Iran(Rép.islamique)[7]
Israel[1 8]	27.3	26.7	30.7	31.6	27.0	31.4	31.5	35.2	31.9	33.9	Israël[1 8]
Japan	1 062.4	1 102.3	1 178.4	1 274.9	1 239.6	1 269.2	1 272.7	1 301.2	1 461.9	1 485.3	Japon
Korea, Republic of[2 9]	38.6	46.4	63.9	59.4	57.4	60.8	66.0	87.5	98.0	99.1	Corée, République de[2 9]
Malaysia[2 10]	20.5	23.2	27.6	31.2	34.0	38.7	# 10.9	10.1	11.3	10.4	Malaisie[2 10]
Pakistan[1 11]	4.0	4.4	5.9	5.6	6.6	9.7	12.0	...	...	...	Pakistan[1 11]
Philippines[12]	50.1	41.3	...	...	...	...	...	...	...	...	Philippines[12]
Sri Lanka[2]	0.4	...	...	0.6	1.1	0.5	...	...	...	...	Sri Lanka[2]
Syrian Arab Republic	4.3	5.3	4.9	6.0	6.8	7.0	9.0	14.0	12.0	13.0	Rép. arabe syrienne
Turkey	35.6	51.1	39.7	44.1	39.2	48.4	55.4	64.2	59.2	* 66.0	Turquie
Viet Nam	5.3	7.7	5.5	6.1	...	...	...	...	...	...	Viet Nam
Yemen[13]	0.3	...	# [2] 1.4	[2] 1.8	[2] 2.2	[2] 2.7	[2] 3.1	[2] 5.1	[2] 5.1	[2] 6.9	Yémen[13]
Europe											**Europe**
EEC											***CEE***
Belgium[1 14]	[15] 89.1	[15] 87.0	# 116.9	115.8	106.3	114.1	112.8	113.4	123.4	120.4	Belgique[1 14]
Denmark	61.5	61.5	61.0	63.6	59.7	62.6	59.2	...	...	...	Danemark
France	604.1	672.1	681.7	656.5	659.5	...	...	...	...	...	France
Germany, Fed. Rep.	479.0	466.8	485.7	484.9	470.3	467.2	508.5	515.9	515.2	525.8	Allemagne, Rép. féd.
Greece	26.2	30.3	35.3	36.3	38.9	38.4	35.3	31.9	34.2	...	Grèce
Netherlands	139.0	134.8	138.0	145.3	144.6	141.6	139.8	144.3	153.2	158.0	Pays-Bas
United Kingdom[16]	454.0	483.7	499.8	524.7	455.2	437.8	417.7	...	412.7	407.2	Royaume-Uni[16]
EFTA											***AELE***
Austria[17]	19.2	41.0	41.2	* 40.9	* 41.0	...	...	...	...	...	Autriche[17]
Finland	33.9	32.7	31.1	20.0	53.7	76.1	54.1	53.5	55.8	...	Finlande
Norway[1]	58.9	60.8	62.9	52.9	58.9	62.2	61.2	61.8	63.0	...	Norvège[1]
Portugal	13.5	24.3	22.1	23.7	22.5	23.5	22.1	20.2	19.6	19.3	Portugal
Sweden	94.8	88.3	83.7	85.2	85.9	83.2	83.7	83.4	85.1	81.9	Suède
East Europe											***Europe de l'est***
Czechoslovakia[5]	146.3	151.4	156.4	162.5	163.1	162.9	161.8	165.8	165.7	171.4	Tchécoslovaquie[5]
German Dem. Rep.[1]	310.0	361.0	382.2	388.2	379.8	382.5	333.3	380.4	397.7	396.7	Rép. dém. allemande[1]
Hungary	117.3	120.0	122.9	115.9	116.1	125.3	126.8	127.3	125.1	127.4	Hongrie
Other Europe											***Autre Europe***

For general note and footnotes, see end of table.

Voir la fin du tableau pour la remarque générale et les notes.

Unit : Thousand metric tons — Unité : Milliers de tonnes métriques

Country or area	1976	1977	1978	1979	1980	1981	1982	1983	1984	1985	Pays ou zone
Spain	123.6	...	...	...	...	...	...	...	...	...	Espagne
Yugoslavia[1]	109.1	105.2	111.5	185.1	191.6	209.2	191.1	199.9	294.0	302.9	Yougoslavie[1]
USSR[5]	2 981.1	3 015.5	3 098.8	2 942.8	2 879.1	3 027.7	2 984.2	3 131.0	3 234.4	3 301.1	**URSS[5]**
Ukrainian SSR[5]	*596.0*	*580.4*	*609.2*	*573.6*	*560.0*	*554.3*	*537.9*	*565.0*	*592.1*	*600.2*	*RSS d'Ukraine[5]*
Oceania											**Océanie**
Australia[2 11]	113.7	105.2	102.7	103.7	105.6	106.9	104.3	94.0	93.5	91.8	Australie[2 11]
New Zealand[5]	15.9	15.2	15.3	15.6	18.2	19.1	18.9	18.1	21.0	20.0	Nouvelle–Zélande[5]

General note.
Other paints, enamels, pigments and extenders, varnishes, lacquers and stains other than cellulose, siccatives and other ancillary products ready for use, responding to products based on glycerophthalic resins, epoxy, acrylic or vinyl resin polyesters, polyurethanes, rubber derivatives, bituminous protective products, and products based on other resins and oils. Artists' colours, printing inks and printers' colours, theatrical grease paint and other make–up and coloured crayons and pastels are excluded. (SITC 53332–3A).

[1] Including water paints and cellulose paints.
[2] In thousand kilolitres.
[3] Including cellulose and water paints.
[4] Shipments.
[5] Including cellulose paints.
[6] Production by establishments employing 5 or more persons.
[7] Production by establishments employing 10 or more persons.
[8] Production of establishments employing 15 or more persons.
[9] Data relate to oil paints and enamels.
[10] Data refer to Peninsular Malaysia only.
[11] Twelve months ending 30 June of year stated.
[12] Incomplete coverage.
[13] Beginning 1978, data are not comparable with those for earlier years.
[14] Excluding enamels.
[15] Source: Industrial Statistics, Statistical Office of the European Communities, (Luxembourg).
[16] Sales by manufacturers employing 25 or more persons.
[17] Source: The Chemical Industry, Organisation for Economic Co–operation and Development (OECD), (Paris).

Remarque générale.
Autres peintures, peintures–émaux, pigments et diluants, vernis, laques et teintures autres que celles à base de cellulose, siccatifs et autres produits connexes prêts à l'emploi, correspondant aux produits à base de résines glycérophtaliques, polyesters des résines époxiques, acryliques ou vinyliques, polyuréthanes, dérivés du caoutchouc, enduits protecteurs bitumineux, produits à base d'autres résines et huiles. Cette rubrique ne comprend pas les couleurs pour la peinture artistique, les encres et les couleurs d'imprimerie, les fards et autres produits de maquillage et les pastels. (CTCI 53332–3A).

[1] Y compris les peintures à l'eau et les peintures cellulosiques.
[2] En milliers de kilolitres.
[3] Y compris les peintures cellulosiques et les peintures à l'eau.
[4] Expéditions.
[5] Y compris les peintures cellulosiques.
[6] Production des établissements occupant 5 personnes ou plus.
[7] Production des établissements occupant 10 personnes ou plus.
[8] Production des établissements occupant 15 personnes ou plus.
[9] Données se rapportant aux peintures à l'huile et peintures–émaux.
[10] Données se rapportant à la Malaisie péninsulaire seulement.
[11] Période de douze mois finissant le 30 juin de l'année indiquée.
[12] Couverture incomplète.
[13] A partir de 1978, les données ne sont pas comparables à celles des années antérieures.
[14] Non compris les émaux.
[15] Source: Statistiques industrielles, Office statistique des Communautés européennes, (Luxembourg).
[16] Ventes des fabricants employant 25 personnes ou plus.
[17] Source: l'Industrie chimique, Organisation de coopération et de développement économiques (OCDE), (Paris).

Mastics

Unit : Thousand metric tons — Unité : Milliers de tonnes métriques

Country or area	1976	1977	1978	1979	1980	1981	1982	1983	1984	1985	Pays ou zone
Africa	**0.6**	**0.5**	**0.6**	**0.7**	**0.3**	**0.4**	**0.4**	**0.4**	**0.4**	**0.3**	**Afrique**
Algeria	0.1	0.0	0.0	0.0	0.1	0.2	...	...	...	...	Algérie
Cameroon	...	...	...	0.0	0.1	...	...	0.1	0.2	0.2	Cameroun
Tunisia	0.4	0.5	0.5	0.7	0.2	0.1	...	...	...	...	Tunisie
America, South	**1.1**	**0.9**	**0.8**	**1.8**	**0.7**	**0.8**	**0.9**	**0.9**	**0.8**	**0.8**	**Amérique du Sud**
Colombia	...	0.9	0.8	1.8	0.7	0.8	...	...	...	...	Colombie
Asia	**32.6**	**33.7**	**31.4**	**32.0**	**32.7**	**31.8**	**31.5**	**31.5**	**31.3**	**31.1**	**Asie**
Hong Kong[1]	...	3.3	0.2	1.2	1.9	1.0	0.7	0.7	...	...	Hong-kong[1]
Japan[2]	...	30.4	31.2	...	...	...	...	...	...	...	Japon[2]
Europe	**547.8**	**467.8**	**462.6**	**497.8**	**525.7**	**550.2**	**553.0**	**478.2**	**507.2**	**506.9**	**Europe**
EEC	***405.8***	***321.9***	***317.0***	***332.0***	***343.1***	***346.8***	***348.1***	***290.6***	***306.7***	***306.2***	***CEE***
Belgium[2 3]	# 6.3	8.3	5.7	10.0	6.6	5.4	5.1	5.0	5.0	4.5	Belgique[2 3]
Denmark	17.7	12.2	13.7	14.9	19.1	...	...	...	...	...	Danemark
France	130.8	49.3	43.4	38.4	25.6	...	...	...	...	...	France
Germany, Fed. Rep.	186.0	192.6	188.4	204.5	227.5	224.9	225.0	172.4	187.9	181.1	Allemagne, Rép. féd.
United Kingdom[4]	65.0	59.6	65.9	64.3	64.3	64.0	73.5	76.8	85.5	100.2	Royaume-Uni[4]
EFTA	***85.8***	***87.2***	***84.3***	***104.3***	***119.5***	***132.0***	***137.2***	***129.2***	***136.3***	***134.3***	***AELE***
Austria	...	5.5	5.1	4.5	2.2	1.9	1.7	0.8	0.7	0.7	Autriche
Finland	0.6	0.6	0.6	0.6	0.5	0.4	0.5	0.7	0.3	...	Finlande
Norway	...	...	...	...	...	13.0	12.9	8.1	8.4	10.4	Norvège
Portugal	1.8	2.5	2.6	2.9	3.8	3.5	3.8	3.5	3.6	3.0	Portugal
Sweden	60.2	62.3	60.7	81.8	99.5	113.2	118.3	116.0	123.3	119.7	Suède
East Europe	***27.4***	***29.6***	***32.6***	***33.1***	***32.8***	***34.4***	***33.9***	***35.7***	***35.6***	***37.8***	***Europe de l'est***
Czechoslovakia	27.4	29.6	32.6	33.1	32.8	34.4	33.9	35.7	35.6	37.8	Tchécoslovaquie
Other Europe	***28.8***	***29.1***	***28.7***	***28.4***	***30.3***	***37.0***	***33.8***	***22.6***	***28.6***	***28.6***	***Autre Europe***
Spain[2]	...	...	...	...	...	32.4	29.7	17.2	...	...	Espagne[2]
Yugoslavia	2.4	2.6	2.3	2.0	3.9	4.6	4.1	5.5	2.1	2.2	Yougoslavie
Total	**582.1**	**502.8**	**495.5**	**532.4**	**559.5**	**583.1**	**585.7**	**510.9**	**539.7**	**539.1**	**Total**

General note.
Glazier's putty, grafting putty, painters' fillings and stopping, sealing and similar mastics, including resin mastics and cements. This heading covers mastics based on: oil, sodium silicate, zinc oxychloride, magnesium oxychloride, sulphur, plaster, artificial plastic materials, zinc oxide, glycerol, rubber and luting wax. Plasters, lime and cement are excluded, as well as bituminous mastic, dental cements, brewers' pitch, factory cements and mortars. (SITC 53335-0).

1 Beginning 1984, data are confidential.
2 Source: The Chemical Industry, Organisation for Economic Co-operation and Development (OECD), (Paris).
3 Production by establishments employing 5 or more persons.
4 Sales.

Remarque générale.
Mastic de vitrier, mastic de jardinier, mastic de peintre en bâtiment et autres mastics pour l'obturation, le colmatage et autres fonctions, y compris les résines et les ciments. Cette rubrique comprend les mastics à base des produits suivants: huile, silicate de sodium, oxychlorure de zinc, oxychlorure de magnésium, soufre, plâtre, matières plastiques artificielles, oxyde de zinc, glycérine, caoutchouc, cire à luter. Elle ne comprend pas le plâtre, la chaux et le ciment, ni les mastics bitumineux, les ciments dentaires, le brai des brasseurs, les ciments et mortiers produits en usines. (CTCI 53335-0).

1 A partir de 1984, les données sont confidentielles.
2 Source: l'Industrie chimique, Organisation de coopération et de développement économiques (OCDE), (Paris).
3 Production des établissements occupant 5 personnes ou plus.
4 Ventes.

Unit : Thousand metric tons

Unité : Milliers de tonnes métriques

Country or area	1976	1977	1978	1979	1980	1981	1982	1983	1984	1985	Pays ou zone
Africa	**804.9**	**859.7**	**887.9**	**928.1**	**909.4**	**985.7**	**977.2**	**1 092.7**	**1 029.0**	**1 070.0**	**Afrique**
Algeria	53.4	58.1	64.7	74.0	73.9	77.2	79.9	76.8	...	...	Algérie
Burkina Faso	4.1	5.0	5.7	7.4	8.7	10.0	11.2	30.2	12.0	...	Burkina Faso
Burundi	...	...	...	1.5	1.8	2.4	2.8	2.8	2.6	2.8	Burundi
Cameroon	14.0	15.2	16.0	18.7	13.0	...	...	25.1	30.7	26.1	Cameroun
Congo	5.0	5.1	3.4	2.5	4.6	4.4	5.8	5.1	...	* 1.9	Congo
Côte d'Ivoire	22.0	25.0	33.8	41.4	38.5	39.9	32.1	45.0	55.6	...	Côte d'Ivoire
Egypt	227.0	218.0	230.0	242.5	289.7	303.7	312.5	338.9	...	...	Egypte
Ethiopia[1]	12.8	8.9	9.0	8.8	10.3	10.6	12.2	14.8	14.2	...	Ethiopie[1]
Gabon	...	...	...	0.6	0.1	* 0.1	...	...	...	...	Gabon
Ghana	2.6	6.5	4.2	5.8	7.7	9.4	4.7	3.1	5.9	12.4	Ghana
Kenya	43.1	22.4	20.9	21.1	35.2	35.4	29.7	23.8	46.6	53.5	Kenya
Liberia	2.9	...	...	...	2.7	3.2	3.8	4.5	5.2	4.3	Libéria
Madagascar	14.4	16.4	16.6	19.3	18.0	10.1	9.0	11.0	13.4	12.3	Madagascar
Mali	2.1	2.2	3.0	2.1	1.6	...	1.7	2.0	...	...	Mali
Morocco	24.3	25.8	21.5	24.6	30.6	30.3	29.7	31.2	28.4	20.2	Maroc
Mozambique	...	...	...	0.5	1.3	1.9	1.2	1.0	0.4	...	Mozambique
Niger	4.9	4.7	4.2	4.2	4.2	6.2	6.6	...	...	...	Niger
Nigeria[2]	134.0	137.6	155.3	139.5	162.5	201.6	200.2	249.6	143.2	157.7	Nigéria[2]
Rwanda	3.4	2.5	4.4	3.9	5.3	6.8	7.2	8.1	12.4	15.1	Rwanda
Senegal	24.3	27.9	30.1	35.1	34.2	36.1	35.9	37.7	35.1	30.4	Sénégal
Sierra Leone	...	...	...	* 1.0	* 1.0	* 5.0	4.0	3.0	4.0	...	Sierra Leone
South Africa	93.4	146.3	137.2	152.9	* 43.1	* 46.7	* 47.5	51.1	44.7	48.1	Afrique du Sud
Sudan*	43.1	50.7	48.7	...	...	...	...	...	...	...	Soudan*
Tunisia[3]	19.3	21.0	20.5	20.9	22.3	24.0	...	...	...	...	Tunisie[3]
Uganda[2]	2.5	1.1	0.8	0.1	0.0	0.2	0.2	...	...	...	Ouganda[2]
Zaire	43.1	45.3	44.8	...	47.5	46.9	41.0	45.9	...	...	Zaïre
Zambia	...	7.2	5.7	4.3	4.0	2.9	3.5	3.2	5.4	4.9	Zambie
America, North	**704.0**	**673.1**	**673.6**	**677.9**	**753.5**	**752.9**	**745.3**	**774.1**	**782.6**	**770.2**	**Amérique du Nord**
Canada[2 4]	383.0	349.1	322.0	331.7	386.5	...	...	...	...	...	Canada[2 4]
Cuba	61.9	52.5	57.2	52.8	54.1	59.5	49.8	62.0	64.4	56.4	Cuba
Dominica[5]	0.8	2.1	3.4	2.4	5.7	6.9	7.3	6.6	6.6	...	Dominique[5]
Dominican Republic	20.6	22.3	25.2	23.1	24.6	24.3	23.4	25.5	25.3	25.5	Rép. dominicaine
El Salvador	12.3	12.1	10.3	6.9	9.7	10.7	16.3	15.7	...	...	El Salvador
Grenada	0.0	0.0	0.0	0.0	0.0	0.1	0.1	0.0	0.0	0.0	Grenade
Haiti	8.7	9.5	11.0	11.3	13.1	11.4	14.5	14.7	14.0	...	Haïti
Jamaica	6.4	5.5	6.1	6.0	5.3	6.0	5.1	6.1	5.9	5.5	Jamaïque
Mexico	197.5	206.3	220.3	220.8	226.0	247.0	244.1	255.9	257.8	245.4	Mexique
Nicaragua	...	...	...	16.0	21.4	28.4	29.0	32.3	40.1	...	Nicaragua
Panama	2.6	2.4	2.7	3.0	...	4.1	3.2	3.6	...	...	Panama
Saint Lucia	0.4	0.5	0.4	0.3	0.4	0.4	0.5	0.6	0.2	...	Sainte–Lucie
Trinidad and Tobago	6.1	3.0	2.5	3.5	3.3	2.6	1.6	1.7	1.7	2.9	Trinité–et–Tobago
America, South	**828.7**	**836.3**	**858.1**	**885.5**	**853.4**	**874.0**	**909.8**	**931.7**	**935.9**	**957.7**	**Amérique du Sud**
Argentina[6]	183.9	158.0	140.7	138.5	124.0	123.5	134.4	141.9	123.1	124.4	Argentine[6]
Bolivia	4.0	4.8	3.5	5.5	6.6	4.2	5.1	7.0	3.5	...	Bolivie
Brazil	471.6	500.7	532.8	[7] 567.1	502.1	525.4	...	...	...	...	Brésil
Chile	8.4	7.2	7.0	3.7	3.5	3.7	4.1	4.3	4.3	4.2	Chili
Colombia	103.6	97.1	107.9	97.6	134.2	133.4	128.9	126.6	...	...	Colombie
Ecuador	19.7	...	30.3	...	34.9	34.1	38.0	42.7	...	...	Equateur
Guyana	2.1	1.9	1.7	1.6	2.0	2.3	2.3	1.2	...	...	Guyana
Paraguay	8.4	8.6	2.9	9.2	9.6	10.1	10.6	11.1	11.6	11.7	Paraguay
Peru	27.1	33.3	31.3	32.0	36.5	...	...	...	...	...	Pérou
Asia	**4 677.5**	**4 711.6**	**5 067.8**	**5 885.4**	**2 147.9**	**2 297.5**	**2 166.9**	**2 233.5**	**2 306.8**	**2 392.7**	**Asie**
Afghanistan	...	0.2	0.1	0.1	0.1	0.2	0.1	0.1	0.0	0.0	Afghanistan
Burma[8]	48.0	44.5	36.5	39.5	46.1	49.3	53.0	39.4	28.2	49.5	Birmanie[8]
China	...	551.3	596.3	752.6	851.9	933.3	851.5	864.7	942.6	995.6	Chine
Cyprus	2.1	2.2	1.8	2.0	2.7	2.8	4.1	3.8	4.2	4.6	Chypre
India[9]	269.5	294.5	337.4	289.7	308.8	331.7	333.0	355.5	377.6	371.0	Inde[9]
Indonesia	45.0	47.9	50.2	55.7	69.0	67.8	23.0	53.0	51.5	...	Indonésie
Iran(Islamic Rep.of)[10]	37.5	38.4	39.7	14.1	24.6	32.7	35.8	44.0	...	...	Iran(Rép.islamique)[10]
Israel	8.1	8.5	8.0	7.4	6.3	5.7	6.1	6.5	6.4	5.7	Israël
Japan	147.2	150.6	156.1	174.4	198.5	189.7	181.2	188.0	197.2	184.4	Japon
Jordan[11]	7.5	13.7	4.2	7.6	12.1	11.9	* 7.4	* 5.9	12.1	8.1	Jordanie[11]
Korea, Republic of	108.6	132.2	133.4	152.1	147.6	185.1	201.3	195.5	200.9	226.3	Corée, République de
Malaysia[12 13]	37.2	47.1	42.8	49.1	49.0	49.7	# 48.3	52.9	47.4	58.5	Malaisie[12 13]
Mongolia	2 991.8	2 956.7	3 265.0	3 935.0	3.9	3.4	4.1	4.7	4.7	4.1	Mongolie
Nepal[14]	1.9	1.3	1.1	1.2	2.6	3.0	5.1	5.6	7.7	...	Népal[14]

For general note and footnotes, see end of table.

Voir la fin du tableau pour la remarque générale et les notes.

Unit : Thousand metric tons — Unité : Milliers de tonnes métriques

Country or area	1976	1977	1978	1979	1980	1981	1982	1983	1984	1985	Pays ou zone
Pakistan[15]	...	16.5	20.4	21.1	23.3	24.3	27.0	28.9	26.2	...	Pakistan[15]
Philippines	71.6	83.6	52.0	37.6	65.9	44.0	...	...	...	...	Philippines
Singapore[2]	26.0	26.4	24.9	27.6	28.6	29.9	25.2	26.7	25.4	23.6	Singapour[2]
Sri Lanka	...	[2] 18.2	[2] 18.4	[2] 30.9	[2] 19.6	[2] 27.8	[8] 3.5	[8] 4.1	[8] 3.0	[8] 4.5	Sri Lanka
Syrian Arab Republic	31.2	34.6	35.8	34.6	37.4	46.0	48.0	52.0	37.0	25.0	Rép. arabe syrienne
Thailand	11.0	12.7	17.1	22.4	...	...	...	...	...	...	Thaïlande
Turkey	46.4	51.5	48.2	55.2	52.2	52.8	66.3	68.7	68.7	* 59.0	Turquie
United Arab Emirates	...	...	153.6	...	...	...	...	...	...	...	Emirats arabes unis
Viet Nam	24.7	25.5	24.8	21.8	27.4	35.1	31.4	27.2	[16] 29.4	51.0	Viet Nam
Yemen	...	0.0	0.0	0.0	0.9	2.0	* 3.7	4.2	5.9	7.7	Yémen
Europe	**1 160.0**	**1 178.1**	**1 163.1**	**1 151.4**	**1 181.9**	**1 168.7**	**1 133.1**	**1 108.3**	**1 068.4**	**1 053.5**	**Europe**
EEC	***581.8***	***580.3***	***573.0***	***559.6***	***574.7***	***555.5***	***549.7***	***524.3***	***523.5***	***512.9***	***CEE***
Belgium	30.3	31.1	29.9	28.6	29.9	30.5	31.3	32.3	31.0	30.7	Belgique
Denmark	10.9	9.3	9.5	8.8	8.5	8.4	8.3	9.6	7.7	7.1	Danemark
France	101.5	99.5	96.8	90.5	99.7	91.2	# 116.0	114.5	113.0	109.9	France
Germany, Fed. Rep.	113.6	110.7	112.1	116.6	125.8	124.1	112.2	110.0	109.2	111.4	Allemagne, Rép. féd.
Greece	16.0	18.4	16.2	15.6	14.4	14.7	13.0	14.5	11.8	...	Grèce
Netherlands[17]	24.5	...	...	...	...	...	...	...	...	...	Pays–Bas[17]
United Kingdom[18]	285.0	286.8	283.9	* 275.0	* 272.0	* 262.1	* 244.4	* 218.9	...	...	Royaume–Uni[18]
EFTA	***233.7***	***247.1***	***236.6***	***245.4***	***255.2***	***263.8***	***247.1***	***256.5***	***243.5***	***235.1***	***AELE***
Austria	5.9	6.1	5.9	6.0	6.1	6.3	6.5	5.5	6.7	7.5	Autriche
Finland	4.5	5.3	5.2	8.2	13.4	17.2	11.2	14.7	# 6.2	...	Finlande
Norway	15.0	15.1	14.6	18.3	18.0	9.2	11.3	9.5	8.9	...	Norvège
Portugal	68.3	77.8	65.7	63.9	69.8	78.7	66.4	71.7	66.8	50.8	Portugal
Sweden	13.1	...	...	11.5	9.3	9.9	9.2	10.8	9.3	9.0	Suède
Switzerland[19 20]	126.9	131.0	133.7	137.5	138.6	142.4	142.4	144.3	145.4	145.0	Suisse[19 20]
East Europe	***237.6***	***247.4***	***247.6***	***248.7***	***259.7***	***240.2***	***241.1***	***238.1***	***218.6***	***229.2***	***Europe de l'est***
Bulgaria	25.3	24.2	25.0	25.1	28.7	26.6	25.8	29.9	27.2	25.8	Bulgarie
Czechoslovakia	30.7	32.9	33.7	34.9	37.3	37.7	34.7	32.5	32.8	36.1	Tchécoslovaquie
German Dem. Rep.	38.0	39.3	39.8	37.7	36.5	37.4	37.2	38.6	38.7	40.3	Rép. dém. allemande
Hungary	17.5	17.6	16.5	17.8	19.0	20.0	16.0	18.3	16.6	16.1	Hongrie
Poland	73.1	71.5	71.6	72.2	72.2	69.4	75.3	73.8	54.5	63.8	Pologne
Romania	53.0	62.0	61.0	61.0	66.0	49.0	...	45.0	...	...	Roumanie
Other Europe	***106.8***	***103.3***	***106.0***	***97.7***	***92.3***	***109.2***	***95.2***	***89.4***	***82.8***	***76.3***	***Autre Europe***
Spain	88.1	...	...	70.5	63.9	76.9	63.3	52.2	...	...	Espagne
Yugoslavia	18.7	20.6	27.6	27.2	28.4	32.3	32.0	37.2	30.1	27.9	Yougoslavie
USSR	**1 541.7**	**1 409.8**	**1 420.2**	**1 406.4**	**1 566.8**	**1 593.8**	**1 636.6**	**1 646.6**	**1 535.9**	**1 464.4**	**URSS**
Byelorussian SSR	*49.6*	*46.4*	*47.1*	*47.2*	*49.8*	*49.9*	*51.4*	*52.1*	*48.4*	*46.0*	*RSS de Biélorussie*
Ukrainian SSR[21]	*266.8*	*225.2*	*219.2*	*245.0*	*269.2*	*271.7*	*278.2*	*283.2*	*252.9*	*234.6*	*RSS d'Ukraine[21]*
Oceania	**72.0**	**81.1**	**70.5**	**72.2**	**69.6**	**69.2**	**73.0**	**75.3**	**77.7**	**65.9**	**Océanie**
Australia[22]	58.1	67.6	57.8	59.3	57.0	55.7	58.8	60.8	62.2	50.6	Australie[22]
Fiji	5.0	4.6	5.2	6.0	6.0	5.6	6.2	6.8	7.3	6.1	Fidji
New Caledonia	0.3	0.3	0.3	0.3	0.3	0.3	0.3	...	...	...	Nouvelle–Calédonie
New Zealand	8.6	8.6	7.2	6.7	6.3	7.6	7.6	7.4	8.0	8.8	Nouvelle–Zélande
Total	**9 788.9**	**9 749.8**	**10 141.2**	**11 006.9**	**7 482.5**	**7 741.8**	**7 641.9**	**7 862.1**	**7 736.4**	**7 774.5**	**Total**

General note.
Normal soaps of commerce, including both hard and soft soaps. Included are, in particular, household soaps, toilet soaps, transparent soaps, shaving soaps, medicated soaps, disinfectant soaps, abrasive soaps, resin and naphthenate soaps, and industrial soaps. (SITC 55410–0).

Remarque générale.
Produits commercialement désignés sous le nom de savon, y compris les savons durs et les savons mous. Cette rubrique comprend notamment: les savons de ménage, les savons de toilette, les savons translucides, les savons à barbe, les savons médicinaux, les savons désinfectants, les savons abrasifs, les savons de résines ou de naphténates et les savons industriels. (CTCI 55410–0).

1 Twelve months ending 10 September of year stated.
2 Including washing powder and detergents.
3 Excluding toilet soap.
4 Shipments.
5 Source: United Nations Economic Commission for Latin America (ECLA), (Santiago).
6 Excluding liquid toilet soap.
7 Production by establishments employing 5 or more persons.

1 Période de douze mois finissant le 10 septembre de l'année indiquée.
2 Y compris les poudres pour lessives et les détersifs.
3 Non compris les savons de toilette.
4 Expéditions.
5 Source: Commission économique des Nations Unies pour l'Amérique Latine (CEPAL), (Santiago).
6 Non compris le savon liquide de toilette.
7 Production des établissements occupant 5 personnes ou plus.

[8] Government production only.
[9] Production by large and medium scale establishments only.
[10] Production by establishments employing 10 or more persons.
[11] Including washing powder.
[12] Data refer to Peninsular Malaysia only.
[13] Beginning 1982, scope of series revised.
[14] Twelve months beginning 16 July of year stated.
[15] Toilet soap only.
[16] Excluding perfumed soaps.
[17] Source: Industrial Statistics, Statistical Office of the European Communities, (Luxembourg).
[18] Deliveries.
[19] Sales.
[20] Including other cleaning products.
[21] In terms of 40 per cent fat content.
[22] Twelve months ending 30 June of year stated.

[8] Production de l'Etat seulement.
[9] Production des grandes et moyennes entreprises seulement.
[10] Production des établissements occupant 10 personnes ou plus.
[11] Y compris les poudres pour lessives.
[12] Données se rapportant à la Malaisie péninsulaire seulement.
[13] A partir de 1982, portée de la série révisée.
[14] Période de douze mois commençant le 16 juillet de l'année indiquée.
[15] Savons de toilette seulement.
[16] Non compris savons parfumés.
[17] Source: Statistiques industrielles, Office statistique des Communautés européennes, (Luxembourg).
[18] Livraisons.
[19] Ventes.
[20] Y compris les autres produits de nettoyage.
[21] Sur la base de 40 p. 100 de matières grasses.
[22] Période de douze mois finissant le 30 juin de l'année indiquée.

Washing powders and detergents – Poudres pour lessives et détersifs

Unit : Thousand metric tons — Unité : Milliers de tonnes métriques

Country or area	1976	1977	1978	1979	1980	1981	1982	1983	1984	1985	Pays ou zone
Africa	**122.8**	**132.9**	**143.0**	**150.1**	**275.5**	**291.9**	**295.6**	**306.9**	**300.9**	**322.2**	**Afrique**
Algeria	25.0	27.7	31.7	37.5	37.0	35.2	29.0	...	...	...	Algérie
Côte d'Ivoire	3.5	8.0	7.2	7.0	7.7	7.6	6.5	9.6	9.2	...	Côte d'Ivoire
Egypt	21.0	21.9	22.9	27.9	32.8	40.3	46.7	48.1	...	...	Egypte
Libyan Arab Jamah.[1]	12.8	17.2	17.9	17.3	16.6	17.0	16.4	19.2	...	...	Jamah.arabe libyenne[1]
Mozambique	...	...	...	15.5	16.3	23.7	21.2	19.3	14.2	...	Mozambique
South Africa[2]	12.8	11.5	13.7	12.0	* 131.1	* 133.8	139.7	134.3	* 128.7	137.8	Afrique du Sud[2]
Tunisia	22.7	21.5	24.6	25.9	30.7	28.6	...	...	...	...	Tunisie
Zambia	...	6.9	6.6	7.1	3.3	5.8	4.5	6.8	4.9	5.0	Zambie
America, North	**449.6**	**509.5**	**498.4**	**529.8**	**599.5**	**644.8**	**716.2**	**702.2**	**691.8**	**666.8**	**Amérique du Nord**
Cuba[3]	29.7	25.2	29.6	23.0	30.3	35.6	30.0	33.6	32.8	35.5	Cuba[3]
Dominican Republic	5.0	5.9	5.9	8.5	9.2	9.9	11.8	12.4	13.7	13.4	Rép. dominicaine
El Salvador	8.0	9.0	14.5	14.8	14.1	* 10.9	13.9	16.7	...	...	El Salvador
Haiti	0.2	0.3	0.4	0.5	0.6	0.5	0.6	0.8	...	...	Haïti
Jamaica	6.1	8.3	7.5	6.2	3.8	4.2	5.8	7.2	6.7	7.1	Jamaïque
Mexico	393.7	454.3	433.2	469.9	533.3	574.1	646.1	621.4	611.0	581.8	Mexique
Panama	6.9	6.5	7.4	7.0	...	9.6	8.1	10.0	...	...	Panama
America, South	**410.0**	**496.5**	**593.8**	**765.4**	**692.1**	**732.3**	**851.9**	**925.1**	**986.3**	**1 045.8**	**Amérique du Sud**
Argentina	44.0	32.1	26.8	26.8	25.1	26.1	26.5	24.1	21.3	16.5	Argentine
Brazil	257.2	353.2	445.3	[4] 570.5	527.8	556.8	...	...	...	...	Brésil
Chile	35.2	36.3	37.4	43.3	44.5	47.8	48.2	44.4	45.2	41.2	Chili
Colombia	37.3	37.4	43.0	84.8	49.6	54.1	60.5	77.8	...	...	Colombie
Ecuador	3.0	...	11.7	...	* 12.0	17.8	21.0	22.3	...	...	Equateur
Guyana	1.0	0.3	0.6	1.0	0.7	0.4	0.3	0.1	...	...	Guyana
Peru	32.3	30.6	29.0	27.1	32.4	...	...	...	...	...	Pérou
Asia	**1 213.5**	**1 494.4**	**1 718.9**	**1 950.0**	**1 885.8**	**2 058.4**	**2 300.2**	**2 499.0**	**2 732.5**	**3 035.1**	**Asie**
Afghanistan	...	2.5	2.7	2.1	0.8	0.6	0.8	0.5	0.3	0.3	Afghanistan
China	...	257.0	324.0	397.0	393.0	478.0	569.0	677.0	809.6	1 004.6	Chine
Cyprus	3.6	3.5	3.7	3.3	3.7	4.6	3.7	4.6	4.8	5.2	Chypre
Hong Kong	5.3	11.6	10.8	10.2	12.4	15.7	13.9	19.4	28.9	...	Hong-kong
India[5]	79.7	104.3	120.9	151.1	147.8	172.9	158.2	149.7	156.8	190.4	Inde[5]
Indonesia	33.4	38.5	44.2	46.5	54.4	69.5	117.1	82.7	79.2	...	Indonésie
Iran(Islamic Rep.of)[6]	95.5	118.5	110.2	98.1	102.1	107.2	126.4	161.9	...	...	Iran(Rép.islamique)[6]
Israel	...	43.6	46.8	45.4	42.7	...	...	...	...	...	Israël
Japan[7]	607.2	660.1	724.9	810.9	684.8	761.4	802.6	834.0	870.3	894.0	Japon[7]
Jordan	5.0	6.0	7.0	10.6	15.3	18.8	15.2	12.7	25.5	15.0	Jordanie
Korea, Republic of	35.5	47.9	64.4	69.6	63.6	56.9	52.3	57.5	61.9	68.0	Corée, République de
Kuwait	0.4	0.8	1.0	1.1	1.6	1.9	1.7	1.6	1.5	1.4	Koweït
Pakistan	...	6.7	9.3	7.3	8.5	16.3	10.7	10.6	12.5	...	Pakistan
Philippines	58.7	66.3	91.4	127.4	158.1	126.2	...	...	...	...	Philippines
Syrian Arab Republic	7.1	7.5	6.5	6.8	7.5	10.4	16.3	25.8	23.2	24.4	Rép. arabe syrienne
Thailand	55.0	59.3	61.2	73.2	84.6	82.7	83.6	86.9	91.5	...	Thaïlande
Turkey	59.1	59.6	88.9	88.1	103.2	88.6	112.9	139.8	172.1	* 172.0	Turquie
Europe	**5 248.1**	**5 259.4**	**5 484.4**	**6 113.9**	**6 492.7**	**6 546.0**	**6 824.2**	**7 025.7**	**7 180.9**	**7 499.7**	**Europe**
EEC	***4 083.0***	***4 062.7***	***4 286.1***	***4 504.9***	***4 545.7***	***4 615.4***	***4 768.8***	***4 816.2***	***4 843.7***	***4 988.7***	***CEE***
Belgium	223.9	236.4	257.2	246.5	271.5	286.3	308.6	307.2	305.8	306.7	Belgique
Denmark	146.8	153.2	154.6	157.8	164.2	177.0	189.3	191.6	204.4	208.6	Danemark
France	490.8	490.5	490.0	524.1	543.1	549.7	# 597.5	638.4	639.1	649.6	France
Germany, Fed. Rep.[8]	1 463.6	1 441.5	1 556.6	1 651.0	1 680.2	1 665.6	1 693.4	1 638.5	1 615.1	1 624.9	Allemagne, Rép. féd.[8]
Greece	112.4	108.6	115.9	131.0	142.6	146.3	145.1	156.1	153.5	...	Grèce
Italy[9]	...	606.3	653.8	...	...	...	...	...	...	...	Italie[9]
Netherlands	258.0	247.0	238.0	243.0	240.0	257.5	253.8	261.5	265.8	273.5	Pays-Bas
United Kingdom[10]	757.5	779.1	820.0	921.4	874.0	902.9	951.1	992.8	1 029.9	1 129.0	Royaume-Uni[10]
EFTA	***407.1***	***426.6***	***416.4***	***452.4***	***485.0***	***502.2***	***488.5***	***519.2***	***501.8***	***520.9***	***AELE***
Austria	97.6	92.4	101.5	110.3	117.4	118.4	113.6	111.0	107.7	107.1	Autriche
Finland	33.3	42.6	44.2	49.9	67.7	76.5	58.4	57.5	58.5	...	Finlande
Norway	67.6	64.7	40.6	46.7	48.7	43.2	49.1	58.4	47.8	51.1	Norvège
Portugal	69.5	85.2	87.8	98.7	99.3	107.1	110.2	118.0	123.0	122.4	Portugal
Sweden	139.2	141.6	142.3	146.7	152.0	157.0	157.1	174.2	164.7	169.3	Suède
East Europe	***315.7***	***340.1***	***347.7***	***348.2***	***376.1***	***370.6***	***401.2***	***374.3***	***388.0***	***414.4***	***Europe de l'est***

For general note and footnotes, see end of table. — Voir la fin du tableau pour la remarque générale et les notes.

Washing powders and detergents (continued) – Poudres pour lessives et détersifs (suite)

Unit : Thousand metric tons

Unité : Milliers de tonnes métriques

Country or area	1976	1977	1978	1979	1980	1981	1982	1983	1984	1985	Pays ou zone
Bulgaria	1.5	1.2	1.6	2.2	1.5	1.3	1.4	1.5	1.3	1.6	Bulgarie
Czechoslovakia	67.6	68.1	69.9	69.5	74.8	78.7	87.4	77.2	79.1	82.2	Tchécoslovaquie
Hungary	77.2	81.1	86.9	77.7	92.2	93.8	91.6	100.5	99.4	98.1	Hongrie
Poland[11]	154.3	172.8	171.3	179.8	187.9	178.1	200.2	173.8	186.0	209.6	Pologne[11]
Romania[12]	15.1	16.9	18.0	19.0	19.7	18.7	...	...	...	...	Roumanie[12]
Other Europe	***442.2***	***430.0***	***434.2***	***808.4***	***1 086.0***	***1 057.8***	***1 165.7***	***1 316.0***	***1 447.4***	***1 575.8***	***Autre Europe***
Spain	288.5	268.0	258.6	616.0	848.2	805.1	925.9	1 042.9	...	...	Espagne
Yugoslavia	153.6	162.0	175.6	192.4	237.8	252.7	239.8	273.1	256.4	260.5	Yougoslavie
USSR	**828.4**	**824.4**	**876.7**	**858.9**	**1 012.0**	**1 076.3**	**1 076.2**	**1 106.6**	**1 096.4**	**1 150.3**	**URSS**
Byelorussian SSR	*26.2*	*24.3*	*23.1*	*22.2*	*27.6*	*29.7*	*30.6*	*30.7*	*30.7*	*31.3*	*RSS de Biélorussie*
Ukrainian SSR	*135.7*	*147.5*	*153.3*	*165.3*	*204.2*	*211.7*	*219.2*	*243.3*	*250.9*	*253.8*	*RSS d'Ukraine*
Oceania	**217.3**	**230.2**	**224.9**	**231.5**	**236.5**	**267.0**	**289.5**	**329.0**	**309.0**	**319.3**	**Océanie**
Australia[13]	208.7	221.3	218.1	225.4	231.6	250.8	265.3	304.2	283.6	295.7	Australie[13]
New Zealand[14 15]	8.6	8.9	6.8	6.1	4.8	...	24.2	24.8	25.3	23.6	Nouvelle-Zélande[14 15]
Total	**8 489.6**	**8 947.3**	**9 540.1**	**10 599.7**	**11 194.2**	**11 616.6**	**12 353.7**	**12 894.6**	**13 297.7**	**14 039.2**	**Total**

General note.
Organic surface-active agents, surface-active preparations and washing preparations, whether or not containing soap. (SITC 55420-0).

1 Including soap.
2 Synthetic detergents in powder form only.
3 Detergents only.
4 Production by establishments employing 5 or more persons.
5 Production by large and medium scale establishments only.
6 Production by establishments employing 10 or more persons.
7 Surface-active agents only.
8 Excluding surface-active organic agents.
9 Source: Industrial Statistics, Statistical Office of the European Communities, (Luxembourg).
10 Estimates of manufacturers' sales of finished detergents for washing purposes, in terms of actual weight sold.
11 Washing powder only.
12 On the basis of 100 per cent active substances.
13 Twelve months ending 30 June of year stated.
14 Data refer to soap flakes and powder only.
15 1981, data are confidential.

Remarque générale.
Produits organiques tensio-actifs, préparations tensio-actives et préparations pour lessives contenant ou non du savon. (CTCI 55420-0).

1 Y compris le savon.
2 Détersifs synthétiques en poudre seulement.
3 Détersifs seulement.
4 Production des établissements occupant 5 personnes ou plus.
5 Production des grandes et moyennes entreprises seulement.
6 Production des établissements occupant 10 personnes ou plus.
7 Produits tensio-actifs seulement.
8 Non compris les produits organiques tensio-actifs.
9 Source: Statistiques industrielles, Office statistique des Communautés européennes, (Luxembourg).
10 Estimations des ventes de détersifs pour lessives par les fabricants, sur la base du poids de produits effectivement ecoulé.
11 Poudres pour lessive seulement.
12 Sur la base de 100 p. 100 de substances actives.
13 Période de douze mois finissant le 30 juin de l'année indiquée.
14 Données se rapportant aux savons en paillettes et en poudre seulement.
15 Pour 1981, les données sont confidentielles.

Carbon black – Noirs de carbone

Unit : Thousand metric tons

Unité : Milliers de tonnes métriques

Country or area	1976	1977	1978	1979	1980	1981	1982	1983	1984	1985	Pays ou zone
Africa	**43.0**	**45.0**	**45.0**	**45.0**	**45.0**	**57.0**	**53.7**	**55.7**	**57.7**	**59.7**	**Afrique**
South Africa* [1]	43.0	45.0	45.0	45.0	45.0	57.0	...	...	...	...	Afrique du Sud* [1]
America, North	**1 541.1**	**1 777.7**	**1 851.3**	**1 713.6**	**1 367.1**	**1 458.2**	**1 276.1**	**1 375.7**	**1 524.3**	**1 343.6**	**Amérique du Nord**
Canada[2]	134.5	141.9	143.3	159.5	137.3	143.0	126.6	...	176.5	173.0	Canada[2]
Mexico	43.8	51.7	108.1	127.5	# 73.6	77.1	84.5	85.7	95.7	112.4	Mexique
United States	1 362.7	1 584.1	1 600.0	1 426.5	1 156.2	1 238.2	1 065.0	1 132.0	1 252.0	...	Etats–Unis
America, South	**213.4**	**239.6**	**212.7**	**200.9**	**227.3**	**197.8**	**194.9**	**191.4**	**245.3**	**264.5**	**Amérique du Sud**
Argentina* [1]	30.0	30.0	...	...	...	...	...	...	...	...	Argentine* [1]
Brazil[1]	103.0	121.7	125.5	132.4	148.8	125.8	122.5	123.2	141.0	156.5	Brésil[1]
Colombia* [1]	26.3	4.2	20.6	19.3	20.0	18.8	18.4	18.0	18.0	18.0	Colombie* [1]
Peru[1]	2.1	5.7	5.7	3.2	5.5	4.2	6.0	2.2	* 5.3	* 5.0	Pérou[1]
Venezuela* [1]	52.0	78.0	31.0	16.0	23.0	19.0	18.0	18.0	51.0	55.0	Venezuela* [1]
Asia	**511.3**	**557.2**	**625.9**	**683.7**	**726.1**	**692.6**	**649.7**	**747.6**	**805.8**	**828.5**	**Asie**
India	56.3	63.3	71.6	71.9	66.9	55.7	67.1	78.2	91.8	...	Inde
Indonesia[1]	* 1.7	* 1.0	0.9	0.8	1.0	1.1	...	...	...	...	Indonésie[1]
Japan	408.8	438.9	489.0	538.2	575.2	556.7	503.8	568.0	605.9	632.3	Japon
Korea, Republic of	31.6	38.2	52.0	58.3	67.1	60.9	58.0	75.4	82.4	91.0	Corée, République de
Turkey	12.9	15.8	12.5	14.5	16.0	18.1	19.9	25.3	25.2	* 22.0	Turquie
Europe	**1 214.7**	**1 227.2**	**1 210.6**	**1 290.9**	**1 268.8**	**1 322.1**	**1 273.1**	**1 311.8**	**1 368.3**	**1 383.1**	**Europe**
EEC	***927.8***	***928.2***	***897.0***	***994.9***	***965.0***	***979.8***	***940.5***	***978.2***	***1 018.1***	***1 017.0***	***CEE***
Belgium* [1]	2.0	2.0	2.0	2.0	2.0	2.0	2.0	2.0	1.8	1.7	Belgique* [1]
France	* 170.0	* 170.0	* 170.0	* 180.0	* 170.0	220.0	# 205.7	218.6	227.0	220.8	France
Germany, Fed. Rep.	292.3	301.7	279.5	340.6	353.6	354.2	348.0	362.1	382.4	387.1	Allemagne, Rép. féd.
Italy	155.2	158.6	155.8	171.7	171.8	153.3	152.0	154.3	172.9	183.2	Italie
Netherlands	90.0	90.7	86.8	93.0	95.3	97.8	82.7	91.2	102.0	103.4	Pays–Bas
United Kingdom[3]	218.2	205.2	202.9	207.6	172.3	152.5	150.0	150.0	...	...	Royaume–Uni[3]
EFTA	***23.0***	***23.5***	***25.5***	***26.0***	***26.7***	***25.8***	***22.6***	***24.4***	***26.3***	***30.8***	***AELE***
Sweden	23.0	23.5	25.5	26.0	26.7	25.8	22.6	24.4	26.3	30.8	Suède
East Europe	***191.8***	***198.9***	***209.3***	***193.7***	***196.9***	***200.6***	***208.5***	***209.7***	***219.3***	***219.5***	***Europe de l'est***
Bulgaria[4]	11.7	9.2	8.0	6.9	5.9	6.3	6.8	...	...	...	Bulgarie[4]
Czechoslovakia	30.6	30.7	32.0	33.2	33.7	34.3	45.4	50.4	53.6	54.3	Tchécoslovaquie
Hungary* [1]	4.0	5.0	5.0	5.0	5.0	5.0	5.0	5.0	5.0	5.0	Hongrie* [1]
Poland	54.3	53.5	55.2	53.5	50.5	50.6	47.3	48.6	50.0	48.5	Pologne
Romania	91.3	100.4	109.0	95.1	101.8	104.4	...	101.2	106.9	108.6	Roumanie
Other Europe	***72.1***	***76.6***	***78.8***	***76.3***	***80.2***	***116.0***	***101.5***	***99.5***	***104.6***	***115.9***	***Autre Europe***
Spain	[1] 50.3	[1] 52.7	[1] 53.0	[1] 53.0	[1] 54.0	# [5] 92.1	[5] 76.8	[5] 74.8	[5] 76.5	...	Espagne
Yugoslavia	21.8	23.9	25.8	23.3	26.2	23.9	24.7	24.7	28.1	29.6	Yougoslavie
USSR[5]	...	...	...	...	...	**140.0**	**129.0**	**129.0**	**132.0**	...	**URSS[5]**
Oceania	**77.0**	**77.0**	**77.0**	**77.0**	**77.0**	**77.0**	**77.0**	**77.0**	**77.0**	**77.0**	**Océanie**
Australia* [1]	77.0	...	...	...	...	...	...	...	...	...	Australie* [1]
Total	**3 733.1**	**4 056.3**	**4 155.0**	**4 143.6**	**3 843.9**	**3 944.7**	**3 653.4**	**3 888.2**	**4 210.4**	**4 088.9**	**Total**

General note.
All forms of carbon, other than natural and artificial graphite, natural carbons in the form of solid fuels, black mineral colouring matter, animal black, activated carbon, wood charcoal and crystalline carbon in the form of diamonds. (SITC 51327–0).

[1] Source: U. S. Bureau of Mines, (Washington, D. C.).
[2] 1983, data are confidential.
[3] Excluding acetylene and base black.
[4] Vegetable black only.
[5] Source: United Nations Economic Commission for Europe (ECE), (Geneva).

Remarque générale.
Toutes les formes de carbone autres que le graphite naturel et artificiel, les charbons naturels constituant des combustibles solides, les pigments noirs minéraux, les noirs d'origine animale, les charbons activés, le charbon de bois et le carbone cristallisé sous forme de diamant. (CTCI 51327–0).

[1] Source: U.S. Bureau of Mines, (Washington, D.C.).
[2] 1983, les données sont confidentielles.
[3] Non compris l'acétylène et les pigments noirs de base.
[4] Noir végétal seulement.
[5] Source: Commission économique des Nations Unies pour l'Europe (CEE), (Genève).

Unit : Thousand metric tons

Unité : Milliers de tonnes métriques

Country or area	1976	1977	1978	1979	1980	1981	1982	1983	1984	1985	Pays ou zone
Africa	**0.2**	**0.2**	**0.2**	**0.2**	**0.3**	**0.3**	**0.3**	**0.3**	**0.3**	**0.3**	**Afrique**
Tunisia	0.1	0.1	0.1	0.1	0.1	0.1	...	...	...	...	Tunisie
Zambia	0.1	0.1	0.1	0.1	0.1	...	...	...	...	...	Zambie
America, North	**27.2**	**27.4**	**27.6**	**41.3**	**47.4**	**49.9**	**55.4**	**61.0**	**66.3**	**72.0**	**Amérique du Nord**
Canada[1]	26.3	26.7	26.8	40.3	46.3	...	...	...	...	...	Canada[1]
Cuba	0.9	0.7	0.8	1.0	1.1	0.7	0.8	1.0	1.0	1.4	Cuba
America, South	**17.6**	**37.0**	**34.4**	**34.7**	**42.9**	**26.6**	**38.0**	**39.9**	**41.9**	**43.6**	**Amérique du Sud**
Brazil	16.0	35.2	32.6	[2] 32.7	40.6	24.4	...	...	...	...	Brésil
Chile	0.9	1.2	1.2	1.3	1.5	1.5	1.3	1.5	1.8	1.8	Chili
Colombia	0.7	0.6	0.6	0.7	0.8	0.6	0.7	0.7	...	...	Colombie
Asia	**201.7**	**217.3**	**231.6**	**253.7**	**250.6**	**261.3**	**278.0**	**300.9**	**319.3**	**330.5**	**Asie**
Hong Kong	...	0.8	0.9	1.9	1.0	1.5	1.2	1.0	1.5	...	Hong-kong
Indonesia	0.8	1.3	1.9	2.7	3.0	3.3	3.5	4.3	5.5	...	Indonésie
Iran(Islamic Rep.of)[3]	...	...	...	...	...	0.9	...	...	...	...	Iran(Rép.islamique)[3]
Japan	187.5	202.2	213.2	233.5	229.9	239.7	253.8	274.2	287.6	295.7	Japon
Korea, Republic of	4.0	4.6	6.4	6.2	7.3	7.4	8.0	9.2	11.8	14.7	Corée, République de
Malaysia[4 5]	1.2	1.2	1.4	1.6	1.7	1.8	# 4.0	4.7	5.5	5.6	Malaisie[4 5]
Philippines	...	...	2.6	...	...	...	...	...	...	...	Philippines
Sri Lanka	...	...	...	0.1	0.3	0.3	...	...	...	...	Sri Lanka
Turkey	3.4	3.5	4.2	4.3	...	...	...	...	...	...	Turquie
Europe	**348.1**	**361.3**	**374.8**	**407.1**	**411.4**	**407.3**	**407.9**	**411.8**	**442.2**	**462.5**	**Europe**
EEC	***301.0***	***303.2***	***316.1***	***339.2***	***342.1***	***339.9***	***342.8***	***349.2***	***371.4***	***388.2***	***CEE***
Belgium[2]	14.2	13.7	14.5	17.5	19.2	17.5	20.3	21.2	22.2	22.4	Belgique[2]
Denmark	6.4	6.3	6.7	7.1	7.6	* 7.6	7.7	8.4	8.8	8.8	Danemark
France	47.5	50.1	50.6	49.2	51.6	# 51.1	45.0	46.0	49.0	56.4	France
Germany, Fed. Rep.	121.3	122.6	126.4	137.1	139.2	138.7	139.5	151.7	164.7	169.6	Allemagne, Rép. féd.
Greece	1.2	1.0	0.9	1.1	0.9	0.7	0.8	0.6	0.3	...	Grèce
Italy	* 32.0	31.7	36.3	40.8	46.9	46.7	49.3	49.5	50.6	50.3	Italie
Netherlands	13.3	14.1	15.0	15.9	14.4	14.0	14.7	14.8	16.1	17.6	Pays-Bas
United Kingdom	65.2	63.6	65.6	70.5	62.3	63.5	65.6	57.1	59.6	62.8	Royaume-Uni
EFTA	***23.3***	***29.4***	***28.4***	***33.2***	***33.5***	***33.3***	***33.1***	***34.0***	***36.7***	***38.2***	***AELE***
Austria	5.5	5.8	4.3	6.9	6.6	7.7	6.7	7.0	8.7	9.1	Autriche
Finland	5.7	5.9	6.5	7.1	7.3	7.2	7.7	7.6	8.3	...	Finlande
Norway[6]	0.0	5.6	5.0	* 5.2	* 5.4	5.7	5.8	5.4	5.8	5.8	Norvège[6]
Portugal	1.6	1.8	2.0	2.4	2.7	2.7	2.6	2.7	2.0	2.2	Portugal
Sweden	10.6	10.4	10.5	11.7	11.5	10.0	10.4	11.3	11.8	12.5	Suède
East Europe	***3.8***	***4.0***	***4.0***	***3.5***	***4.2***	***4.0***	***4.2***	***4.6***	***4.5***	***6.3***	***Europe de l'est***
Bulgaria	0.8	0.8	0.9	0.9	1.0	1.0	1.0	1.0	1.0	1.1	Bulgarie
Hungary	3.0	3.2	3.1	2.6	3.2	3.0	3.2	3.5	3.4	5.2	Hongrie
Other Europe	***20.0***	***24.7***	***26.3***	***31.2***	***31.7***	***30.2***	***27.7***	***23.9***	***29.7***	***29.8***	***Autre Europe***
Spain	12.0	16.3	...	21.6	22.7	21.1	20.3	16.1	...	...	Espagne
Yugoslavia	8.0	8.4	9.0	9.6	9.0	9.0	7.4	7.8	7.9	7.4	Yougoslavie
Oceania	**16.1**	**21.7**	**23.3**	**25.2**	**23.0**	**22.9**	**24.3**	**23.3**	**21.8**	**25.5**	**Océanie**
Australia[7]	16.1	21.7	23.3	25.2	23.0	22.9	24.3	23.3	21.8	25.5	Australie[7]
Total	**610.9**	**664.8**	**692.0**	**762.2**	**775.4**	**768.4**	**803.8**	**837.2**	**891.8**	**934.4**	**Total**

General note.
Printing ink, including printing colours. (SITC 53320-0).

Remarque générale.
Encres d'imprimerie, y compris les couleurs d'imprimerie. (CTCI 53320-0).

[1] Shipments.
[2] Production by establishments employing 5 or more persons.
[3] Production by establishments employing 10 or more persons.
[4] Data refer to Peninsular Malaysia only.
[5] Beginning 1982, scope of series revised.
[6] Source: The Chemical Industry, Organisation for Economic Co-operation and Development (OECD), (Paris).
[7] Twelve months ending 30 June of year stated.

[1] Expéditions.
[2] Production des établissements occupant 5 personnes ou plus.
[3] Production des établissements occupant 10 personnes ou plus.
[4] Données se rapportant à la Malaisie péninsulaire seulement.
[5] A partir de 1982, portée de la série révisée.
[6] Source: l'Industrie chimique, Organisation de coopération et de développement économiques (OCDE), (Paris).
[7] Période de douze mois finissant le 30 juin de l'année indiquée.

Explosives – Explosifs

Unit : Thousand metric tons — Unité : Milliers de tonnes métriques

Country or area	1976	1977	1978	1979	1980	1981	1982	1983	1984	1985	Pays ou zone
Africa	**42.2**	**42.8**	**35.1**	**39.3**	**32.5**	**31.7**	**29.8**	**29.8**	**25.3**	**22.6**	**Afrique**
Algeria	8.5	11.4	9.8	9.5	...	...	...	...	...	...	Algérie
Tunisia	2.7	3.3	3.1	4.2	4.5	4.4	4.3	3.8	3.7	3.2	Tunisie
Zaire	5.9	3.9	2.9	...	4.9	4.5	5.8	8.8	...	...	Zaïre
Zambia	25.2	24.1	19.3	20.6	13.3	12.9	...	...	...	...	Zambie
America, North	**1 870.9**	**2 043.8**	**2 143.3**	**2 216.5**	**2 299.9**	**2 330.1**	**2 134.8**	**2 053.1**	**2 337.3**	**2 324.7**	**Amérique du Nord**
Canada	...	...	...	...	361.1	...	...	...	...	...	Canada
United States[1]	1 509.8	1 682.7	1 782.2	1 855.4	1 938.9	1 969.1	1 773.8	1 692.0	1 976.2	...	Etats–Unis[1]
America, South	**73.7**	**74.4**	**75.8**	**88.1**	**77.5**	**82.6**	**82.9**	**83.8**	**87.5**	**89.3**	**Amérique du Sud**
Brazil	43.9	44.2	45.0	[2] 53.8	48.5	...	...	...	...	...	Brésil
Chile	29.8	30.2	30.8	34.2	29.0	29.9	28.4	27.4	29.3	29.1	Chili
Asia	**124.3**	**123.9**	**143.4**	**141.3**	**150.5**	**158.7**	**165.1**	**170.1**	**179.2**	**188.4**	**Asie**
India	46.6	45.8	55.9	52.6	58.4	67.1	75.8	82.0	89.2	93.8	Inde
Japan[3]	61.3	60.3	67.8	69.2	72.1	69.4	64.4	63.3	63.2	...	Japon[3]
Korea, Republic of	8.8	10.3	12.0	12.0	12.4	14.7	17.9	17.4	...	...	Corée, République de
Turkey	...	...	...	...	...	...	6.9	7.4	8.0	* 8.0	Turquie
Europe	**255.7**	**284.0**	**280.6**	**306.0**	**299.0**	**280.4**	**275.7**	**283.7**	**271.0**	**274.7**	**Europe**
EEC	***134.4***	***152.9***	***153.6***	***154.4***	***165.4***	***168.4***	***154.1***	***153.4***	***149.3***	***150.3***	***CEE***
France	46.9	55.9	54.3	51.5	53.8	52.8	48.5	44.1	42.0	38.8	France
Germany, Fed. Rep.	53.9	59.1	62.5	66.0	64.6	64.1	61.0	63.2	65.6	66.4	Allemagne, Rép. féd.
Greece	18.5	22.2	21.6	22.6	22.6	25.4	18.7	22.6	19.9	...	Grèce
Italy	15.0	15.8	15.2	14.2	24.4	26.1	25.8	23.6	21.8	23.2	Italie
EFTA	***40.0***	***50.8***	***49.9***	***51.4***	***57.3***	***51.9***	***54.9***	***53.8***	***48.0***	***50.5***	***AELE***
Finland	7.5	9.4	9.0	8.0	11.8	10.4	11.1	11.0	13.7	...	Finlande
Portugal	6.3	5.7	7.1	7.6	9.4	7.9	8.4	7.7	7.0	6.4	Portugal
Sweden	26.2	35.7	33.7	35.8	36.1	33.7	35.4	35.1	27.3	30.8	Suède
East Europe	***14.7***	***13.6***	***10.6***	***10.3***	***9.7***	***9.4***	***9.0***	***8.3***	***7.0***	***7.4***	***Europe de l'est***
Hungary	14.7	13.6	10.6	10.3	9.7	9.4	9.0	8.3	7.0	7.4	Hongrie
Other Europe	***66.6***	***66.6***	***66.6***	***89.8***	***66.6***	***50.8***	***57.7***	***68.2***	***66.6***	***66.6***	***Autre Europe***
Spain	...	...	...	89.8	...	50.8	57.7	68.2	...	...	Espagne
Total	**2 366.8**	**2 568.9**	**2 678.2**	**2 791.2**	**2 859.4**	**2 883.6**	**2 688.4**	**2 620.5**	**2 900.4**	**2 899.8**	**Total**

General note.
Mixtures based on nitric esters of polyhydric alcohols, other organic nitrated derivatives, ammonium nitrate, chlorate or perchlorates. Initiatory explosives are included. (SITC 57112–0).

[1] Industrial explosives and blasting agents sold for consumption.
[2] Production by establishments employing 5 or more persons.
[3] Gunpowder for industrial use only.

Remarque générale.
Mélanges à base des produits suivants: esters nitriques de polyalcools, autres dérivés nitrés organiques, nitrate d'ammonium, chlorates et perchlorates. Cette rubrique comprend les explosifs d'amorçage. (CTCI 57112–0).

[1] Expolsifs industriels et matières de démolition vendus pour la consommation.
[2] Production des établissements occupant 5 personnes ou plus.
[3] Poudre à canon pour usages industriels seulement.

Photographic film, sensitized, in rolls – Pellicules photographiques sensibilisées, en rouleaux

Unit : Thousand square metres | Unité : Milliers de mètres carrés

Country or area	1976	1977	1978	1979	1980	1981	1982	1983	1984	1985	Pays ou zone
Asia	**70 386**	**85 431**	**91 045**	**101 894**	**108 920**	**114 171**	**123 670**	**138 435**	**147 348**	**158 441**	**Asie**
Japan	70 386	85 431	91 045	101 894	108 920	114 171	123 670	138 435	147 348	158 441	Japon
Europe	**3 878**	**4 003**	**3 972**	**4 381**	**4 130**	**4 411**	**4 393**	**3 863**	**4 207**	**4 388**	**Europe**
East Europe	***2 394***	***2 270***	***2 537***	***2 705***	***2 619***	***2 591***	***2 540***	***2 425***	***2 298***	***2 392***	***Europe de l'est***
Czechoslovakia	1 828	1 668	1 844	1 996	1 970	1 973	1 928	1 836	1 808	1 872	Tchécoslovaquie
Hungary	566	602	693	709	649	618	612	589	490	520	Hongrie
Other Europe	***1 484***	***1 733***	***1 435***	***1 676***	***1 511***	***1 820***	***1 853***	***1 438***	***1 909***	***1 996***	***Autre Europe***
Spain	...	...	...	...	406	280	244	178	...	...	Espagne
Yugoslavia	1 207	1 456	1 158	1 399	1 105	1 540	1 609	1 260	1 632	1 719	Yougoslavie
Total	**74 264**	**89 434**	**95 017**	**106 275**	**113 050**	**118 582**	**128 063**	**142 298**	**151 555**	**162 829**	**Total**

General note.
Unexposed, sensitized films in rolls (as opposed to plates in the flat), usually of celluloid, cellulose acetate or similar flexible materials, which normally provide for a number of exposures. Cinematographic film (raw stock) is included. (SITC 86242–0).

Remarque générale.
Pellicules sensibilisées non impressionnées, en rouleaux (par opposition aux films plans), habituellement en celluloïd, en acétate de cellulose ou en d'autres matières flexibles analogues, qui servent normalement à prendre un certain nombre d'images. Cette rubrique comprend les films cinématographiques vierges. (CTCI 86242–0).

Photographic paper – Papiers photographiques

Unit : Thousand sqaure metres

Unité : Milliers de mètres carrés

Country or area	1976	1977	1978	1979	1980	1981	1982	1983	1984	1985	Pays ou zone
America, North											**Amérique du Nord**
United States[1]	...	38 615	...	...	...	...	...	...	...	...	Etats–Unis[1]
Asia											**Asie**
India	5 219	4 333	4 673	5 036	5 796	5 715	6 389	6 437	5 936	...	Inde
Japan[2]	86 253	95 271	112 083	133 556	167 665	188 512	215 235	247 642	244 535	280 135	Japon[2]
Europe											**Europe**
EEC											***CEE***
Denmark	4 100	...	...	...	...	...	...	...	...	...	Danemark
Germany, Fed. Rep.	114 845	127 780	117 986	117 098	99 542	105 767	128 586	130 015	153 679	171 821	Allemagne, Rép. féd.
Greece[3]	7 815	7 896	8 615	7 132	12 442	10 036	10 959	14 417	...	...	Grèce[3]
EFTA											***AELE***
Finland[4]	825	1 144	1 111	1 253	994	1 105	1 057	1 299	1 582	...	Finlande[4]
Sweden[4]	3 547	...	...	...	...	...	...	...	...	...	Suède[4]
East Europe											***Europe de l'est***
Bulgaria	4 878	5 161	5 872	8 616	9 703	10 342	9 473	12 121	12 716	12 177	Bulgarie
Czechoslovakia	6 684	6 562	7 200	7 278	6 886	7 069	7 489	7 701	6 898	6 513	Tchécoslovaquie
Hungary	8 856	9 446	9 834	7 055	5 427	6 285	5 407	6 090	6 226	6 201	Hongrie
Poland	7 100	6 750	6 070	5 688	6 140	5 682	4 390	5 166	6 033	6 539	Pologne
Other Europe											***Autre Europe***
Spain	36 715	...	...	...	...	...	...	...	...	...	Espagne
Yugoslavia	3 179	3 746	4 233	2 774	2 108	1 934	1 460	1 372	1 680	2 082	Yougoslavie

General note.
Sensitized paper, unexposed, not developed, for the production of positive photographic prints (amateur, professional, recording, x–ray, photo–copying etc. work) for the production of negatives by exposure in a camera, and papers used to produce blue–prints, tracings etc. Sensitized paperboard and cloth are excluded. (SITC 86243–0).

[1] Shipments.
[2] Excluding sensitized paper for blue–prints and office use.
[3] Including heliogravure and photo–copy paper.
[4] In metric tons.

Remarque générale.
Papiers sensibilisés, non impressionnés, non développés, pour la production de positifs (papiers pour photographie d'amateurs, photographie d'art, photocopie, radiographie, appareils enregistreurs etc.), et la production de négatifs par exposition dans un appareil photographique, et papiers utilisés pour la production de calques photographiques, la reproduction de plans et de dessins etc. Cette rubrique ne comprend pas les cartons et les tissus sensibilisés. (CTCI 86243–0).

[1] Expéditions.
[2] Non compris les papiers sensibilisés pour bleus et usages de bureau.
[3] Y compris les papiers pour héliogravure et photocopie.
[4] En tonnes métriques.

Aviation gasolene – Essence d'aviation

Unit : Thousand metric tons

Unité : Milliers de tonnes métriques

Country or area	1976	1977	1978	1979	1980	1981	1982	1983	1984	1985	Pays ou zone
Africa	**10**	**8**	**4**	**4**	**15**	**18**	**21**	**22**	**24**	**24**	**Afrique**
Cameroon	...	...	...	...	10	13	15	16	18	17	Cameroun
Somalia	...	...	1	2	3	3	4	4	4	5	Somalie
Sudan	10	8	3	2	2	2	2	2	2	2	Soudan
America, North	**2 016**	**2 112**	**2 095**	**2 106**	**1 947**	**1 770**	**1 393**	**1 436**	**1 425**	**1 349**	**Amérique du Nord**
Canada	171	172	170	182	171	172	124	125	150	131	Canada
Mexico	64	61	68	74	72	64	76	46	48	45	Mexique
Neth.Antil and Aruba	169	152	178	212	170	170	127	179	150	70	Antill.néer.et Aruba
Puerto Rico	27	33	26	12	0	0	0	0	0	0	Porto Rico
Trinidad and Tobago	38	44	42	32	45	25	36	18	20	20	Trinité–et–Tobago
United States	1 547	1 650	1 611	1 594	1 489	1 339	1 030	1 068	1 057	1 083	Etats–Unis
America, South	**148**	**156**	**103**	**131**	**123**	**120**	**132**	**136**	**138**	**195**	**Amérique du Sud**
Argentina	18	19	22	26	21	15	16	15	15	16	Argentine
Bolivia	0	0	0	8	14	14	11	11	11	10	Bolivie
Brazil	...	...	...	...	...	...	0	0	0	66	Brésil
Chile	9	11	14	15	4	6	11	10	6	3	Chili
Colombia	42	43	43	51	50	44	47	49	43	39	Colombie
Uruguay	1	1	1	1	1	1	2	1	3	1	Uruguay
Venezuela	78	82	23	30	33	40	45	50	60	60	Venezuela
Asia	**444**	**378**	**534**	**434**	**332**	**195**	**171**	**174**	**181**	**200**	**Asie**
Burma	1	1	2	1	1	1	0	0	0	0	Birmanie
China	...	...	90	101	103	74	57	70	61	70	Chine
Indonesia	15	13	16	15	15	14	12	12	8	7	Indonésie
Iran(Islamic Rep.of)	367	304	340	250	150	60	70	60	80	90	Iran(Rép.islamique)
Japan	23	19	21	16	14	13	13	10	10	9	Japon
Jordan	16	18	17	16	20	14	0	3	19	21	Jordanie
Philippines	0	2	5	4	0	0	0	0	0	0	Philippines
Turkey	1	2	0	1	3	0	0	1	0	0	Turquie
Europe	**267**	**258**	**259**	**291**	**386**	**331**	**269**	**237**	**254**	**243**	**Europe**
EEC	***250***	***240***	***243***	***275***	***375***	***320***	***258***	***215***	***241***	***232***	***CEE***
Belgium	0	0	0	0	0	0	0	10	21	17	Belgique
France incl. Monaco	38	29	42	41	30	25	63	47	46	62	France y comp.Monaco
Italy and San Marino	48	47	34	65	192	147	99	96	89	84	Italie y comp. S.Mrn
Netherlands	138	123	130	102	87	91	52	62	84	65	Pays–Bas
United Kingdom	26	41	37	67	66	57	44	0	1	4	Royaume–Uni
EFTA	***0***	***2***	***0***	***0***	***0***	***0***	***0***	***0***	***0***	***0***	***AELE***
Norway,Svlbd,J.Myn I.	0	2	0	0	0	0	0	0	0	0	Norvège,Svalbd,J.May
East Europe	***15***	***15***	***15***	***15***	***10***	***10***	***10***	***10***	***10***	***10***	***Europe de l'est***
Romania	15	15	15	15	10	10	10	10	10	10	Roumanie
Other Europe	***2***	***1***	***1***	***1***	***1***	***1***	***1***	***12***	***3***	***1***	***Autre Europe***
Spain	0	0	0	0	0	0	0	11	2	0	Espagne
Yugoslavia	2	1	1	1	1	1	1	1	1	1	Yougoslavie
Oceania	**25**	**40**	**34**	**37**	**67**	**78**	**123**	**111**	**144**	**116**	**Océanie**
Australia	25	40	34	37	67	78	123	111	144	116	Australie
Total	**2 910**	**2 952**	**3 029**	**3 003**	**2 870**	**2 512**	**2 109**	**2 116**	**2 166**	**2 127**	**Total**

General note.
Any of the specially–blended grades of gasolene with high anti–knock value, high stability, high volatility and low freezing point, intended for use in aviation piston–engined power units only. Natural gasolene and motor gasolene are excluded. Jet fuels are also excluded. (SITC 33210–2A).

Remarque générale.
Tout mélange spécial d'essences de diverses qualités présentant un caractère anti–détonant prononcé, une stabilité et une volatilité élevées et une basse température de congélation, destiné uniquement à l'emploi dans les moteurs d'avion à pistons. Cette rubrique ne comprend ni la gazoline naturelle ni le carburant pour moteurs. (CTCI 33210–2A).

Unit : Thousand metric tons | Unité : Milliers de tonnes métriques

Country or area	1976	1977	1978	1979	1980	1981	1982	1983	1984	1985	Pays ou zone
Africa	**1 927**	**2 141**	**2 442**	**2 457**	**2 735**	**2 796**	**2 772**	**2 776**	**2 728**	**2 788**	**Afrique**
Algeria	180	200	330	350	370	514	530	520	487	500	Algérie
Angola	57	57	62	58	60	62	60	70	65	70	Angola
Cameroon	...	...	...	...	110	130	135	137	150	155	Cameroun
Côte d'Ivoire	80	90	90	90	95	95	95	97	96	98	Côte d'Ivoire
Egypt	117	123	136	183	0	0	0	0	0	0	Egypte
Ethiopia	25	26	29	26	39	44	52	53	51	52	Ethiopie
Gabon	81	80	74	75	75	85	90	87	90	90	Gabon
Ghana	50	41	32	39	38	31	28	31	28	30	Ghana
Kenya	347	302	289	137	310	380	302	249	250	246	Kenya
Liberia	36	0	6	50	55	54	56	55	57	60	Libéria
Libyan Arab Jamah.	238	489	611	484	603	465	510	530	540	540	Jamah.arabe libyenne
Madagascar	12	12	12	12	1	1	1	1	1	1	Madagascar
Morocco	171	154	150	263	247	198	180	203	198	208	Maroc
Mozambique	7	16	16	10	12	15	15	18	16	17	Mozambique
Nigeria	0	10	20	30	40	45	50	50	42	50	Nigéria
Senegal	95	121	122	119	118	100	79	48	53	54	Sénégal
Sierra Leone	14	14	13	12	19	17	15	14	16	15	Sierra Leone
Somalia	...	...	13	55	58	65	62	65	63	65	Somalie
South Africa	283	302	305	310	350	360	400	420	400	410	Afrique du Sud
Sudan	50	35	34	38	25	27	32	30	30	33	Soudan
United Rep. Tanzania	44	31	22	31	30	28	28	25	27	27	Rép.Unie de Tanzanie
Zaire	...	...	30	35	40	40	22	43	40	42	Zaïre
Zambia	40	38	46	50	40	40	30	30	28	25	Zambie
America, North	**51 760**	**53 839**	**54 341**	**56 904**	**56 940**	**54 512**	**54 879**	**56 432**	**61 750**	**63 328**	**Amérique du Nord**
Bahamas	993	954	1 045	1 000	1 084	1 128	1 100	1 000	600	400	Bahamas
Canada	3 240	3 298	3 620	3 977	3 934	3 832	3 389	3 403	3 403	3 568	Canada
Costa Rica	...	...	...	25	19	15	14	11	13	13	Costa Rica
Cuba	...	...	21	40	39	57	76	66	89	81	Cuba
Dominican Republic	32	32	36	40	42	45	17	19	20	20	Rép. dominicaine
El Salvador	18	18	21	21	17	17	17	20	18	18	El Salvador
Guatemala	30	34	41	46	32	27	25	28	29	30	Guatemala
Honduras	12	13	14	19	20	18	10	10	12	12	Honduras
Jamaica	82	40	55	65	53	35	37	45	40	42	Jamaïque
Mexico	797	998	952	1 179	1 299	1 360	1 439	1 272	1 573	1 547	Mexique
Neth.Antil and Aruba	2 112	1 302	1 474	1 645	1 697	1 500	1 300	1 400	1 100	500	Antill.néer.et Aruba
Nicaragua	28	29	20	14	18	16	21	15	16	15	Nicaragua
Panama ex.Canal Zone	220	238	148	135	...	...	...	...	...	...	Panama ex.zone Canal
Panama	...	...	...	...	125	100	100	100	75	60	Panama
Puerto Rico	115	118	101	141	142	103	142	129	270	200	Porto Rico
Trinidad and Tobago	551	296	286	299	413	172	323	259	246	291	Trinité–et–Tobago
United States	43 250	45 722	45 580	47 548	47 081	45 487	45 974	48 055	53 356	55 876	Etats–Unis
U.S. Virgin Islands	500	985	1 075	845	925	600	895	600	890	655	Iles Vierges amér.
America, South	**3 884**	**4 167**	**4 753**	**5 171**	**5 717**	**6 147**	**6 387**	**6 610**	**6 590**	**7 026**	**Amérique du Sud**
Argentina	469	517	580	627	782	786	661	608	662	690	Argentine
Bolivia	52	62	78	70	92	91	68	73	76	82	Bolivie
Brazil	1 436	1 449	1 683	1 905	2 170	2 503	2 573	2 260	2 884	2 749	Brésil
Chile	120	135	164	165	158	195	147	145	164	156	Chili
Colombia	351	371	406	453	453	502	539	541	450	475	Colombie
Ecuador	60	48	127	146	139	148	137	117	135	145	Equateur
Paraguay	7	9	10	12	9	14	13	11	2	15	Paraguay
Peru	210	171	233	342	388	425	371	350	342	340	Pérou
Uruguay	34	29	29	38	28	26	28	19	9	22	Uruguay
Venezuela	1 145	1 376	1 443	1 413	1 498	1 457	1 850	2 486	1 866	2 352	Venezuela
Asia	**15 882**	**16 751**	**17 299**	**17 945**	**16 710**	**15 298**	**16 116**	**17 109**	**19 237**	**19 801**	**Asie**
Bahrain	1 009	1 512	1 514	1 520	1 783	1 734	1 076	1 269	1 565	1 479	Bahreïn
Bangladesh	17	12	5	13	4	3	4	1	4	7	Bangladesh
Brunei Darussalam	0	0	0	0	0	0	0	0	25	29	Brunéi Darussalam
Burma	27	31	28	39	39	39	40	35	37	40	Birmanie
Cyprus	22	33	26	29	46	48	41	46	46	21	Chypre
Democratic Yemen	261	160	160	160	160	200	200	200	210	220	Yémen démocratique
India	972	1 020	1 166	1 176	1 010	981	1 092	1 163	1 332	1 462	Inde
Indonesia	108	94	130	185	241	223	275	355	325	340	Indonésie
Iran(Islamic Rep.of)	1 140	1 712	1 547	870	617	380	400	350	300	350	Iran(Rép.islamique)
Iraq	173	606	249	260	507	360	400	360	370	380	Iraq
Israel	582	474	479	510	530	510	538	520	473	470	Israël
Japan	2 918	3 256	3 322	3 541	3 719	3 642	3 478	3 030	3 030	3 505	Japon

For general note, see end of table.

Voir la fin du tableau pour la remarque générale.

Unit : Thousand metric tons — Unité : Milliers de tonnes métriques

Country or area	1976	1977	1978	1979	1980	1981	1982	1983	1984	1985	Pays ou zone
Jordan	88	109	127	172	200	256	300	247	220	220	Jordanie
Korea, Republic of	639	521	694	708	633	696	839	1 168	1 347	1 381	Corée, République de
Kuwait,part Ntl.Zone	538	558	393	877	538	689	800	1 016	887	1 218	Koweït et prt.Zne.N.
Lebanon	166	124	131	130	140	130	110	80	10	20	Liban
Malaysia	200	203	150	175	208	212	249	251	250	195	Malaisie
Oman	...	...	...	...	...	...	0	110	180	190	Oman
Pakistan	378	392	439	520	544	540	512	468	474	464	Pakistan
Philippines	303	343	346	266	292	281	359	387	425	520	Philippines
Qatar	52	58	59	61	63	62	63	61	103	105	Qatar
S.Arabia,pt.Ntrl.Zn	559	265	28	31	44	38	202	484	500	510	Arab.saoud,p.Zn.neut
Singapore	4 165	3 756	4 708	5 033	3 709	2 291	2 341	2 544	2 992	2 394	Singapour
Sri Lanka	77	71	35	31	62	84	115	65	116	73	Sri Lanka
Syrian Arab Republic	80	50	130	136	146	221	230	183	176	140	Rép. arabe syrienne
Thailand	680	609	612	634	629	749	769	858	828	834	Thaïlande
Turkey	178	182	171	188	146	209	328	283	309	359	Turquie
United Arab Emirates	...	...	...	...	...	0	620	665	1 063	1 070	Emirats arabes unis
Europe	**19 515**	**20 173**	**21 597**	**24 117**	**23 807**	**22 494**	**22 985**	**24 005**	**24 818**	**24 829**	**Europe**
EEC	***15 883***	***16 338***	***17 588***	***19 661***	***19 853***	***18 738***	***19 072***	***19 514***	***19 632***	***19 461***	***CEE***
Belgium	1 107	1 753	1 496	1 515	1 707	1 783	1 649	1 369	1 192	1 196	Belgique
Denmark	0	9	10	8	10	6	22	33	83	125	Danemark
France incl. Monaco	3 511	3 586	4 002	4 318	4 603	4 366	4 051	4 462	4 449	4 280	France y comp.Monaco
Germany, Fed. Rep.	1 350	1 358	1 329	1 293	1 229	1 460	1 387	1 410	1 665	1 728	Allemagne, Rép. féd.
Greece	591	502	701	1 278	1 372	1 650	1 900	1 640	1 465	1 341	Grèce
Ireland	20	78	12	15	19	7	0	0	0	0	Irlande
Italy and San Marino	1 942	1 916	2 463	2 408	2 414	1 990	2 305	2 403	1 890	2 124	Italie y comp. S.Mrn
Netherlands	2 986	3 040	2 716	3 503	3 301	2 917	3 301	3 474	3 536	3 410	Pays–Bas
United Kingdom	4 376	4 096	4 859	5 323	5 198	4 559	4 457	4 723	5 352	5 257	Royaume–Uni
EFTA	***1 128***	***1 328***	***1 332***	***1 493***	***1 445***	***1 612***	***1 393***	***1 906***	***2 498***	***2 523***	***AELE***
Austria	109	102	102	113	132	148	130	137	183	180	Autriche
Finland	194	198	221	226	242	248	215	327	362	350	Finlande
Norway,Svlbd,J.Myn I.	210	306	280	309	120	257	205	437	672	722	Norvège,Svalbd,J.May
Portugal	361	396	354	456	532	552	424	468	551	517	Portugal
Sweden	82	139	173	181	197	175	193	282	473	514	Suède
Switzrld,Liechtenst	172	187	202	208	222	232	226	255	257	240	Suisse,Liechtenstein
Other Europe	***2 504***	***2 507***	***2 677***	***2 963***	***2 509***	***2 144***	***2 520***	***2 585***	***2 688***	***2 845***	***Autre Europe***
Spain	2 189	2 172	2 405	2 655	2 194	1 862	2 216	2 310	2 412	2 460	Espagne
Yugoslavia	315	335	272	308	315	282	304	275	276	385	Yougoslavie
Oceania	**2 486**	**2 413**	**2 577**	**2 546**	**2 526**	**2 485**	**2 565**	**2 452**	**2 517**	**2 629**	**Océanie**
Australia	1 655	1 676	1 804	1 756	1 736	1 815	1 978	1 891	1 967	2 054	Australie
Guam	831	737	773	790	790	670	587	561	550	575	Guam
Total	**95 454**	**99 484**	**103 009**	**109 140**	**108 435**	**103 732**	**105 704**	**109 384**	**117 640**	**120 401**	**Total**

General note.
Fuel meeting the required properties for use in jet engines and aircraft–turbine engines, mainly refined from kerosene. Gasolene–type jet fuel (light hydrocarbons, also naphtha type, intended for use in aviation gas–turbine units) is included. (Part of SITC 33210 and mainly part of 33220).

Remarque générale.
Carburants ayant les propriétés requises pour l'emploi dans les moteurs à réaction et les moteurs d'avion à turbine, obtenus principalement par raffinage du kérosène, y compris les carburéacteurs analogues à l'essence (hydrocarbures légers, y compris ceux analogues au naphta, devant servir dans les moteurs d'avion à turbine à gaz). (Partie de CTCI 33210 et principalement partie de 33220).

Motor gasolene – Carburants pour moteurs

Unit : Thousand metric tons

Unité : Milliers de tonnes métriques

Country or area	1976	1977	1978	1979	1980	1981	1982	1983	1984	1985	Pays ou zone
Africa	**9 143**	**9 752**	**10 422**	**11 118**	**11 540**	**12 899**	**13 397**	**13 776**	**14 918**	**15 245**	**Afrique**
Algeria	816	1 164	1 215	1 078	1 150	1 469	1 417	1 400	1 774	1 800	Algérie
Angola	51	62	60	59	60	60	65	70	70	75	Angola
Cameroon	...	...	...	...	150	370	420	430	650	655	Cameroun
Congo	...	...	0	0	0	0	0	0	0	3	Congo
Côte d'Ivoire	258	254	266	286	200	233	240	250	245	250	Côte d'Ivoire
Egypt	1 476	1 530	1 704	1 768	1 949	2 054	2 213	2 312	2 506	2 712	Egypte
Ethiopia	75	75	83	84	81	94	99	103	99	101	Ethiopie
Gabon	134	146	120	97	100	90	120	110	113	110	Gabon
Ghana	222	227	262	259	246	262	243	253	172	175	Ghana
Kenya	351	366	378	371	429	369	322	301	304	319	Kenya
Liberia	65	0	13	69	70	70	75	73	75	75	Libéria
Libyan Arab Jamah	279	341	490	417	525	429	500	550	560	580	Jamah.arabe libyenne
Madagascar	93	97	69	56	88	64	56	28	30	32	Madagascar
Morocco	356	380	391	452	362	331	360	344	342	360	Maroc
Mozambique	65	73	60	89	90	85	85	90	90	85	Mozambique
Nigeria	632	726	906	1 500	1 500	2 173	2 200	2 175	2 663	2 700	Nigéria
Senegal	114	131	132	134	124	135	87	56	66	65	Sénégal
Sierra Leone	41	41	46	44	20	23	24	25	28	27	Sierra Leone
Somalia	...	...	20	75	80	80	85	80	85	83	Somalie
South Africa	3 504	3 539	3 540	3 600	3 700	3 900	4 200	4 500	4 400	4 400	Afrique du Sud
Sudan	116	134	139	140	145	145	150	147	148	150	Soudan
Togo	...	...	58	40	68	0	0	0	0	0	Togo
Tunisia	130	141	149	152	150	163	176	182	211	228	Tunisie
United Rep. Tanzania	117	105	93	91	25	85	75	80	82	85	Rép.Unie de Tanzanie
Zaire	68	32	33	57	48	50	25	57	55	35	Zaïre
Zambia	180	188	195	200	180	165	160	160	150	140	Zambie
America, North	**342 712**	**353 067**	**359 216**	**347 769**	**335 505**	**329 335**	**322 351**	**320 743**	**326 124**	**322 182**	**Amérique du Nord**
Antigua and Barbuda	0	0	0	0	0	0	11	0	0	0	Antigua–et–Barbuda
Bahamas	...	...	...	43	43	43	45	45	20	20	Bahamas
Barbados	37	39	39	41	41	44	42	43	42	44	Barbade
Canada	26 255	26 598	27 192	28 340	28 486	27 268	24 976	24 070	23 965	23 976	Canada
Costa Rica	48	65	74	70	88	83	85	69	73	69	Costa Rica
Cuba	909	833	887	872	807	989	847	890	984	953	Cuba
Dominican Republic	315	315	321	301	289	267	240	260	295	290	Rép. dominicaine
El Salvador	133	142	155	153	128	115	107	120	127	130	El Salvador
Guatemala	136	131	144	132	109	109	100	104	122	120	Guatemala
Honduras	106	104	90	86	81	42	26	50	55	60	Honduras
Jamaica	247	242	238	224	185	155	191	160	150	155	Jamaïque
Martinique	135	140	130	135	135	136	137	136	135	110	Martinique
Mexico	8 971	9 816	10 429	12 105	13 983	15 360	14 736	14 708	15 057	14 891	Mexique
Neth.Antil and Aruba	1 779	2 580	2 138	2 400	2 700	2 491	1 950	2 400	2 050	1 050	Antill.néer.et Aruba
Nicaragua	166	172	140	127	137	133	107	90	61	72	Nicaragua
Panama ex.Canal Zone	281	289	305	277	...	...	...	...	...	...	Panama ex.zone Canal
Panama	...	...	...	...	240	220	210	200	190	170	Panama
Puerto Rico	3 218	3 769	3 531	3 294	2 901	2 676	1 808	1 755	1 959	1 900	Porto Rico
Trinidad and Tobago	2 351	2 253	1 976	1 745	1 772	1 532	1 305	986	702	768	Trinité–et–Tobago
United States	294 556	302 009	307 850	294 223	280 194	275 053	272 153	272 257	277 887	275 654	Etats–Unis
U.S. Virgin Islands	3 350	3 859	3 882	3 478	3 186	2 619	3 275	2 400	2 250	1 750	Iles Vierges amér.
America, South	**25 978**	**26 056**	**27 276**	**27 466**	**26 549**	**27 416**	**28 445**	**27 914**	**29 334**	**29 085**	**Amérique du Sud**
Argentina	4 013	4 347	4 506	4 652	5 157	5 121	5 146	5 137	4 971	4 615	Argentine
Bolivia	399	502	352	477	406	324	385	332	342	324	Bolivie
Brazil	10 937	10 033	10 880	10 279	8 336	8 691	8 803	7 651	8 623	8 483	Brésil
Chile	932	926	1 003	1 010	990	1 052	856	947	956	960	Chili
Colombia	2 215	2 426	1 963	1 897	2 138	2 438	2 434	2 456	2 765	3 000	Colombie
Ecuador	715	581	858	958	968	918	890	720	922	913	Equateur
Paraguay	56	76	94	85	64	59	55	51	38	53	Paraguay
Peru	1 383	1 389	1 287	1 518	1 511	1 619	1 577	1 256	1 348	1 375	Pérou
Uruguay	229	216	238	225	207	185	204	164	173	162	Uruguay
Venezuela	5 099	5 560	6 095	6 365	6 772	7 009	8 095	9 200	9 196	9 200	Venezuela
Asia	**51 545**	**55 821**	**61 644**	**64 884**	**64 586**	**66 733**	**67 793**	**72 075**	**75 163**	**79 125**	**Asie**
Bahrain	1 117	1 156	1 306	1 088	1 043	1 314	1 185	653	663	911	Bahreïn
Bangladesh	55	51	53	55	58	45	49	29	38	39	Bangladesh
Brunei Darussalam	18	17	19	19	21	48	82	65	73	81	Brunéi Darussalam
Burma	194	205	219	222	246	240	242	237	259	258	Birmanie
China	8 000	8 670	9 567	10 295	10 380	10 938	10 944	12 277	13 502	14 382	Chine
Cyprus	76	90	93	100	101	96	95	105	101	93	Chypre

For general note, see end of table.

Voir la fin du tableau pour la remarque générale.

Unit : Thousand metric tons — Unité : Milliers de tonnes métriques

Country or area	1976	1977	1978	1979	1980	1981	1982	1983	1984	1985	Pays ou zone
Democratic Yemen	84	209	210	600	386	392	194	230	230	240	Yémen démocratique
India	1 314	1 370	1 526	1 569	1 459	1 629	1 750	1 880	2 062	2 252	Inde
Indonesia	1 531	1 847	2 082	2 294	2 812	2 929	1 971	1 597	2 271	3 234	Indonésie
Iran(Islamic Rep.of)	3 468	3 715	3 951	4 298	3 627	3 065	3 368	3 704	4 368	4 547	Iran(Rép.islamique)
Iraq	652	953	1 442	1 530	1 318	1 340	1 350	1 500	1 600	1 650	Iraq
Israel	889	902	957	866	898	970	1 037	1 107	1 117	1 175	Israël
Japan	22 314	23 535	25 130	25 461	25 251	25 840	26 245	26 371	26 866	26 907	Japon
Jordan	203	211	248	274	266	296	326	315	352	335	Jordanie
Korea,Dem.Ppl's.Rep	...	48	500	600	600	650	700	750	800	850	Corée,Rép.pop.dém.de
Korea, Republic of	627	824	940	1 025	834	730	604	577	646	1 145	Corée, République de
Kuwait,part Ntl.Zone	687	732	877	1 004	935	963	1 199	1 174	1 253	1 317	Koweït et prt.Zne.N.
Lebanon	459	330	473	490	500	450	150	120	110	150	Liban
Malaysia	731	767	934	985	888	872	904	982	1 148	1 130	Malaisie
Oman	...	...	...	...	...	...	0	300	450	450	Oman
Pakistan	282	298	333	401	468	511	574	570	642	675	Pakistan
Philippines	1 832	1 698	1 692	1 699	1 386	1 271	1 231	1 100	1 021	1 025	Philippines
Qatar	78	90	94	107	131	135	121	128	237	240	Qatar
S.Arabia,pt.Ntrl.Zn	1 054	1 480	2 319	2 520	3 516	3 213	4 314	5 752	5 500	5 800	Arab.saoud,p.Zn.neut
Singapore	1 084	1 124	1 420	2 078	2 252	3 114	2 807	3 306	2 175	2 200	Singapour
Sri Lanka	100	103	121	102	109	100	114	95	116	124	Sri Lanka
Syrian Arab Republic	294	150	185	185	168	442	380	734	848	963	Rép. arabe syrienne
Thailand	1 408	1 567	1 523	1 567	1 353	1 348	1 467	1 526	1 485	1 511	Thaïlande
Turkey	1 950	2 421	2 004	1 847	1 904	1 936	2 030	1 994	2 224	2 251	Turquie
United Arab Emirates	65	126	130	155	162	344	713	864	947	980	Emirats arabes unis
Europe	**109 152**	**111 983**	**116 919**	**124 652**	**123 712**	**118 259**	**120 061**	**122 674**	**127 260**	**129 886**	**Europe**
EEC	***79 129***	***80 908***	***83 760***	***90 410***	***89 962***	***85 234***	***87 568***	***88 688***	***90 364***	***92 376***	***CEE***
Belgium	3 934	5 077	4 815	5 088	5 460	4 773	3 676	3 943	3 709	3 853	Belgique
Denmark	1 397	1 405	1 416	1 416	1 106	1 160	996	1 241	1 227	1 203	Danemark
France incl. Monaco	18 565	17 754	17 801	19 646	19 263	18 744	18 110	16 348	16 141	17 191	France y comp.Monaco
Germany, Fed. Rep	17 369	18 358	19 065	21 539	22 472	20 024	19 986	19 913	19 813	20 141	Allemagne, Rép. féd.
Greece	991	995	1 250	1 272	1 139	1 559	1 550	1 634	1 663	1 954	Grèce
Ireland	415	474	530	519	489	186	114	314	307	317	Irlande
Italy and San Marino	14 271	15 633	15 593	16 660	14 284	14 376	15 325	15 030	15 370	15 283	Italie y comp. S.Mrn
Netherlands	6 955	6 407	7 331	8 159	9 140	7 272	8 676	9 212	9 897	10 180	Pays-Bas
United Kingdom	15 232	14 805	15 959	16 111	16 609	17 140	19 135	21 053	22 237	22 254	Royaume-Uni
EFTA	***8 571***	***8 696***	***8 876***	***9 632***	***9 731***	***9 630***	***9 135***	***9 910***	***10 810***	***10 648***	***AELE***
Austria	1 579	1 463	1 620	1 758	1 778	1 885	1 776	1 895	1 987	2 071	Autriche
Finland	1 692	1 839	1 970	2 161	1 941	2 052	1 988	2 383	2 475	2 420	Finlande
Norway,Svlbd,J.Myn I.	1 087	1 206	1 187	1 230	1 196	1 095	1 135	1 178	1 290	1 319	Norvège,Svalbd,J.May
Portugal	764	753	776	1 033	975	1 116	895	846	783	844	Portugal
Sweden	2 459	2 480	2 437	2 464	2 745	2 379	2 276	2 509	3 286	2 996	Suède
Switzrld,Liechtenst	990	955	886	986	1 096	1 103	1 065	1 099	989	998	Suisse,Liechtenstein
East Europe	***14 363***	***15 269***	***16 689***	***16 548***	***16 095***	***15 975***	***15 616***	***15 840***	***16 312***	***16 645***	***Europe de l'est***
Albania	125	130	150	155	160	155	250	260	270	280	Albanie
Bulgaria	1 680	1 700	1 720	1 800	1 850	1 800	1 800	1 800	1 800	1 800	Bulgarie
Czechoslovakia	1 585	1 639	1 675	1 740	1 518	1 523	1 365	1 499	1 500	1 500	Tchécoslovaquie
German Dem. Rep	2 982	3 083	3 237	3 274	3 333	3 442	3 891	3 955	4 140	4 302	Rép. dém. allemande
Hungary	1 157	1 144	1 325	1 405	1 136	1 044	948	803	1 019	1 147	Hongrie
Poland	2 317	3 107	3 589	3 290	3 333	3 025	2 362	2 421	2 262	2 311	Pologne
Romania	4 517	4 466	4 993	4 884	4 765	4 986	5 000	5 102	5 321	5 305	Roumanie
Other Europe	***7 089***	***7 110***	***7 594***	***8 062***	***7 924***	***7 420***	***7 742***	***8 236***	***9 774***	***10 217***	***Autre Europe***
Spain	5 166	4 879	5 214	5 453	5 344	5 053	5 153	5 739	5 871	6 709	Espagne
Yugoslavia	1 923	2 231	2 380	2 609	2 580	2 367	2 589	2 497	3 903	3 508	Yougoslavie
USSR	**67 300**	**68 500**	**69 720**	**71 500**	**73 500**	**75 000**	**76 500**	**77 000**	**76 000**	**75 000**	**URSS**
Oceania	**10 599**	**10 906**	**11 628**	**11 615**	**12 152**	**11 922**	**12 237**	**12 261**	**12 545**	**12 040**	**Océanie**
Australia	9 223	9 630	10 382	10 342	10 872	10 660	11 083	11 006	11 255	11 334	Australie
New Zealand	1 376	1 276	1 246	1 273	1 280	1 262	1 154	1 255	1 290	706	Nouvelle-Zélande
Total	**616 429**	**636 085**	**656 825**	**659 004**	**647 544**	**641 564**	**640 784**	**646 443**	**661 344**	**662 563**	**Total**

For general note, see end of table.

Voir la fin du tableau pour la remarque générale.

General note.
Mixture of relatively volatile hydrocarbons with or without small quantities of additives, which have been blended to form a fuel suitable for use in spark–ignition internal combustion engines. Natural gasolene and aviation gasolene are excluded. Napthas are also excluded. (SITC 33210–4A).

Africa
  Egypt: Including naphthas.

America, South
  Brazil: Including alcohol.

Remarque générale.
Mélange d'hydrocarbures relativement volatils, comportant ou non de petites quantités d'additif incorporées pour donner un carburant pouvant convenir aux moteurs à combustion interne, à allumage par étincelles. Cette rubrique ne comprend ni la gazoline naturelle ni l'essence d'aviation ni les naphtas. (CTCI 33210–4A).

Afrique
  Egypte: Y compris les naphthas.

Amérique, du Sud
  Brésil: Y compris l'alcool.

Unit : Thousand metric tons

Unité : Milliers de tonnes métriques

Country or area	1976	1977	1978	1979	1980	1981	1982	1983	1984	1985	Pays ou zone
Africa	**2 428**	**2 865**	**2 882**	**2 709**	**3 606**	**4 355**	**5 806**	**5 741**	**5 915**	**6 005**	**Afrique**
Algeria	452	562	723	489	1 848	2 557	3 961	3 677	4 022	4 060	Algérie
Gabon	67	110	...	...	...	...	...	...	...	...	Gabon
Libyan Arab Jamah	1 835	2 075	2 041	1 935	1 422	1 444	1 440	1 640	1 450	1 550	Jamah.arabe libyenne
Morocco	15	40	40	140	175	207	197	233	235	240	Maroc
Sierra Leone	7	6	2	3	5	7	5	3	4	5	Sierra Leone
Sudan	11	15	18	12	15	15	17	17	16	18	Soudan
Tunisia	41	57	58	130	141	125	186	171	188	132	Tunisie
America, North	**6 278**	**7 244**	**6 912**	**7 024**	**7 162**	**6 018**	**5 183**	**5 016**	**4 458**	**4 429**	**Amérique du Nord**
Bahamas	1 235	2 110	1 265	1 200	1 300	1 500	1 300	900	700	600	Bahamas
Canada	426	424	400	483	550	538	500	473	340	368	Canada
Cuba	154	310	333	383	438	233	367	350	311	361	Cuba
Mexico	57	54	61	68	75	141	212	235	200	200	Mexique
Panama ex.Canal Zone	47	50	55	58	...	...	...	...	...	...	Panama ex.zone Canal
Panama	...	...	...	...	50	48	50	45	40	30	Panama
Puerto Rico	538	641	549	584	492	343	458	561	561	550	Porto Rico
Trinidad and Tobago	132	107	97	115	139	127	86	45	50	50	Trinité–et–Tobago
United States	3 736	3 598	4 207	4 191	4 118	3 088	2 210	2 407	2 256	2 270	Etats–Unis
America, South	**4 857**	**4 636**	**4 724**	**5 085**	**4 799**	**4 473**	**4 812**	**7 261**	**7 221**	**7 961**	**Amérique du Sud**
Argentina	528	420	353	361	300	226	250	605	707	716	Argentine
Brazil	1 634	1 711	2 264	2 674	2 955	3 189	3 432	4 268	4 239	4 999	Brésil
Chile	61	56	46	50	39	46	26	46	62	31	Chili
Colombia	0	136	70	50	29	25	43	45	45	40	Colombie
Uruguay	...	4	9	13	10	10	10	9	11	9	Uruguay
Venezuela	2 634	2 309	1 982	1 937	1 466	977	1 051	2 288	2 157	2 166	Venezuela
Asia	**36 130**	**38 062**	**35 964**	**36 101**	**31 122**	**28 419**	**26 564**	**29 094**	**29 932**	**30 692**	**Asie**
Bahrain	907	1 037	1 052	1 285	1 238	1 166	903	1 182	1 282	1 334	Bahreïn
Bangladesh	62	92	84	65	77	99	108	87	85	82	Bangladesh
Brunei Darussalam	4	4	4	5	7	4	3	7	4	5	Brunéi Darussalam
India	2 012	2 093	2 162	2 533	2 017	2 865	2 871	3 474	3 479	4 586	Inde
Indonesia	371	914	900	870	850	830	845	2 183	1 687	1 769	Indonésie
Iran(Islamic Rep.of)	605	1 350	1 097	1 171	805	91	124	141	136	142	Iran(Rép.islamique)
Iraq	460	500	510	650	500	460	200	300	400	500	Iraq
Israel	145	145	206	306	326	298	287	274	274	265	Israël
Japan	20 975	20 163	18 351	17 991	15 080	12 351	9 241	8 357	7 994	7 451	Japon
Korea, Republic of	2 002	2 265	2 373	2 570	2 378	2 454	2 402	2 488	3 100	3 137	Corée, République de
Kuwait,part Ntl.Zone	2 182	2 107	2 073	2 569	1 850	1 456	2 444	3 026	2 809	3 502	Koweït et prt.Zne.N.
Malaysia	232	196	108	108	79	116	106	176	329	350	Malaisie
Pakistan	96	145	189	119	213	165	210	185	103	145	Pakistan
Philippines	8	7	0	18	89	75	173	261	174	200	Philippines
S.Arabia,pt.Ntrl.Zn	3 010	2 920	2 181	1 526	1 065	935	1 072	1 260	1 100	970	Arab.saoud,p.Zn.neut
Singapore	1 884	2 613	2 748	2 557	2 750	3 275	3 675	3 550	3 675	3 085	Singapour
Sri Lanka	103	102	82	84	151	138	158	120	149	127	Sri Lanka
Syrian Arab Republic	110	393	430	639	851	677	600	535	612	620	Rép. arabe syrienne
Thailand	207	265	224	220	175	146	149	145	150	155	Thaïlande
Turkey	364	366	395	333	505	549	770	895	1 089	897	Turquie
United Arab Emirates	...	...	...	...	...	234	155	235	528	540	Emirats arabes unis
Europe	**36 195**	**33 132**	**33 862**	**35 178**	**32 398**	**32 519**	**31 237**	**35 203**	**32 976**	**30 364**	**Europe**
EEC	***30 016***	***26 498***	***27 028***	***28 563***	***25 762***	***25 666***	***24 573***	***27 944***	***25 438***	***22 613***	***CEE***
Belgium	1 827	1 709	1 937	1 759	1 486	1 457	931	1 785	1 290	1 304	Belgique
Denmark	70	76	85	93	107	76	104	118	145	154	Danemark
France incl. Monaco	5 822	5 572	5 716	5 774	4 349	2 152	2 299	3 128	3 030	2 806	France y comp.Monaco
Germany, Fed. Rep.	4 370	3 791	3 930	4 336	7 435	7 603	6 216	6 825	6 371	5 937	Allemagne, Rép. féd.
Greece	714	651	513	990	889	782	789	927	678	386	Grèce
Ireland	20	24	6	1	0	0	1	5	11	0	Irlande
Italy and San Marino	7 209	5 589	5 958	5 862	4 184	3 929	3 999	3 591	3 166	3 219	Italie y comp. S.Mrn
Netherlands	5 401	4 598	4 074	4 344	3 646	6 179	6 659	7 969	7 504	5 898	Pays–Bas
United Kingdom	4 583	4 488	4 809	5 404	3 666	3 488	3 575	3 596	3 243	2 909	Royaume–Uni
EFTA	***1 699***	***1 466***	***1 502***	***1 712***	***1 583***	***1 463***	***1 300***	***1 489***	***1 195***	***1 505***	***AELE***
Austria	26	10	4	17	18	17	19	26	64	62	Autriche
Finland	716	640	613	633	738	513	384	382	347	328	Finlande
Norway,Svlbd,J.Myn I.	445	428	502	461	485	549	436	587	381	426	Norvège,Svalbd,J.May

For general note, see end of table.

Voir la fin du tableau pour la remarque générale.

Naphthas (continued) – Naphtas (suite)

Unit : Thousand metric tons

Unité : Milliers de tonnes métriques

Country or area	1976	1977	1978	1979	1980	1981	1982	1983	1984	1985	Pays ou zone
Portugal	269	290	296	304	203	155	293	282	194	551	Portugal
Sweden	200	76	65	272	119	212	158	193	200	129	Suède
Switzrld,Liechtenst	43	22	22	25	20	17	10	19	9	9	Suisse,Liechtenstein
East Europe	***1 424***	***1 210***	***1 570***	***1 526***	***2 050***	***2 109***	***2 162***	***2 224***	***2 408***	***2 403***	***Europe de l'est***
Hungary	757	544	562	519	759	834	902	931	950	927	Hongrie
Poland	...	...	265	273	576	529	520	558	728	736	Pologne
Romania	667	666	743	734	715	746	740	735	730	740	Roumanie
Other Europe	***3 056***	***3 958***	***3 762***	***3 377***	***3 003***	***3 281***	***3 202***	***3 546***	***3 935***	***3 843***	***Autre Europe***
Spain	2 411	2 995	2 812	2 552	2 603	2 921	2 531	2 846	3 079	2 943	Espagne
Yugoslavia	645	963	950	825	400	360	671	700	856	900	Yougoslavie
Oceania	**...**	**...**	**436**	**426**	**457**	**89**	**29**	**50**	**144**	**136**	**Océanie**
Australia	...	...	436	426	457	89	29	50	144	136	Australie
Total	**85 888**	**85 939**	**84 780**	**86 523**	**79 544**	**75 873**	**73 631**	**82 365**	**80 646**	**79 587**	**Total**

General note.
Refined or partly refined light distillates derived from crude petroleum, with a boiling range roughly between 27 degrees centigrade and 221 centigrade (80 degrees fahrenheit and 430 degrees fahrenheit), which are to be further blended or mixed with other materials to make high grade motor gasolene or jet fuel, or to be used as raw materials for town gas or feedstocks to make various kinds of chemical products, or to be also used as various solvents, depending on the character of the naphthas derived and the demands of various industries. Chemical feedstocks originated from other than crude petroleum but used as chemical feedstocks are excluded. (Parts of SITC 33210 and 33220).

Remarque générale.
Dérivés légers de la distillation du pétrole brut, totalement ou partiellement raffinés, dont l'ébullition se produit approximativement entre 27° C et 221° C (80° F et 430° F), qui sont destinés à être mélangés entre eux ou à d'autres produits pour donner du carburant pour moteurs ou du carburéacteur de haute qualité, ou à servir de matières premières dans la fabrication du gaz de ville ou de produits de départ dans l'élaboration de divers produits chimiques, ou à être utilisés comme solvants selon leurs caractéristiques et les exigences des diverses industries. Cette rubrique ne comprend pas les charges de départ des industries chimiques dont l'origine est autre que le pétrole brut ni le gaz de pétrole liquéfié dérivé du pétrole brut mais utilisé comme produit de départ dans l'industrie chimique. (Parties de CTCI 33210 et 33220).

Kerosene – Kérosène

Unit : Thousand metric tons

Unité : Milliers de tonnes métriques

Country or area	1976	1977	1978	1979	1980	1981	1982	1983	1984	1985	Pays ou zone
Africa	**3 175**	**3 104**	**3 470**	**3 617**	**4 134**	**4 500**	**5 058**	**5 277**	**5 711**	**5 867**	**Afrique**
Algeria	227	195	322	270	59	50	100	110	120	130	Algérie
Angola	18	21	21	21	21	21	20	25	23	25	Angola
Cameroon	...	...	...	...	120	398	450	470	520	525	Cameroun
Côte d'Ivoire	60	67	65	115	143	112	134	261	318	320	Côte d'Ivoire
Egypt	1 320	1 379	1 508	1 452	1 678	1 659	1 974	2 128	2 245	2 257	Egypte
Ethiopia	0	0	2	0	0	0	0	12	10	5	Ethiopie
Gabon	24	25	24	20	20	25	26	25	26	26	Gabon
Ghana	98	113	135	129	108	143	128	77	86	120	Ghana
Kenya	89	75	47	60	67	95	76	78	107	105	Kenya
Liberia	8	0	3	7	8	7	8	8	8	8	Libéria
Libyan Arab Jamah.	96	99	103	136	108	61	70	110	170	190	Jamah.arabe libyenne
Madagascar	50	56	35	35	49	43	38	23	25	25	Madagascar
Morocco	94	54	69	72	71	49	56	68	60	54	Maroc
Mozambique	25	23	22	50	55	50	50	60	55	55	Mozambique
Nigeria	386	310	387	500	820	1 040	1 175	1 080	1 203	1 300	Nigéria
Senegal	22	22	20	19	21	18	11	7	11	12	Sénégal
Sierra Leone	24	15	15	13	5	7	10	12	12	12	Sierra Leone
Somalia	...	...	...	13	14	16	15	10	12	12	Somalie
South Africa	403	429	430	430	450	460	480	480	450	440	Afrique du Sud
Sudan	37	34	25	25	26	28	18	16	15	17	Soudan
Togo	...	...	30	45	72	0	0	0	0	0	Togo
Tunisia	108	101	110	109	115	123	118	110	126	133	Tunisie
United Rep. Tanzania	26	45	42	38	39	35	36	35	36	36	Rép.Unie de Tanzanie
Zaire	40	19	29	30	40	40	45	47	50	40	Zaïre
Zambia	20	22	26	28	25	20	20	25	23	20	Zambie
America, North	**14 639**	**15 642**	**14 320**	**15 729**	**13 539**	**11 506**	**11 214**	**10 172**	**10 401**	**9 264**	**Amérique du Nord**
Barbados	9	8	8	8	6	6	5	5	5	5	Barbade
Canada	3 485	3 359	3 036	3 219	3 116	2 394	2 095	1 777	1 780	1 748	Canada
Costa Rica	19	22	24	27	18	12	11	10	12	15	Costa Rica
Cuba	454	415	427	415	438	429	456	494	506	528	Cuba
Dominican Republic	16	44	53	64	69	71	72	81	93	90	Rép. dominicaine
El Salvador	27	29	30	29	27	23	27	27	26	28	El Salvador
Guatemala	30	30	31	35	37	35	29	32	33	30	Guatemala
Honduras	34	33	39	40	40	8	0	5	8	8	Honduras
Jamaica	42	65	81	93	80	50	50	75	70	72	Jamaïque
Martinique	120	125	115	120	120	125	127	125	125	127	Martinique
Mexico	1 736	1 599	1 782	1 893	1 953	1 938	2 130	1 813	1 477	1 456	Mexique
Neth.Antil and Aruba	42	77	56	94	94	80	50	50	45	20	Antill.néer.et Aruba
Nicaragua	15	15	16	15	15	17	19	20	27	21	Nicaragua
Panama ex.Canal Zone	19	25	11	10	...	...	...	...	...	...	Panama ex.zone Canal
Panama	...	...	...	...	10	12	15	16	15	10	Panama
Puerto Rico	134	147	207	141	189	135	120	125	100	100	Porto Rico
Trinidad and Tobago	881	750	580	418	409	276	192	139	154	115	Trinité–et–Tobago
United States	7 178	8 064	7 254	8 601	6 447	5 613	5 406	5 153	5 385	4 441	Etats–Unis
U.S. Virgin Islands	417	860	581	517	471	282	410	225	540	450	Iles Vierges amér.
America, South	**4 033**	**4 131**	**3 885**	**3 773**	**3 691**	**3 550**	**3 310**	**3 353**	**3 136**	**2 873**	**Amérique du Sud**
Argentina	796	756	656	525	591	425	437	527	457	420	Argentine
Bolivia	139	135	137	136	129	92	90	83	87	89	Bolivie
Brazil	554	587	648	700	530	510	518	576	495	411	Brésil
Chile	367	344	311	260	227	215	164	172	111	97	Chili
Colombia	424	403	395	413	352	336	291	293	263	285	Colombie
Ecuador	245	245	350	322	292	284	325	265	293	274	Equateur
Paraguay	16	17	19	17	18	12	8	10	11	7	Paraguay
Peru	643	646	713	793	868	902	916	775	801	805	Pérou
Uruguay	168	153	145	131	124	96	88	80	66	49	Uruguay
Venezuela	681	845	511	476	560	678	473	572	552	436	Venezuela
Asia	**41 803**	**43 291**	**44 729**	**48 580**	**45 078**	**43 180**	**44 218**	**47 482**	**48 649**	**47 589**	**Asie**
Bahrain	691	420	118	112	71	338	343	155	306	348	Bahreïn
Bangladesh	202	247	263	306	311	321	296	234	285	281	Bangladesh
Burma	144	131	113	86	89	17	22	19	18	11	Birmanie
China	3 000	3 170	3 560	4 090	3 980	3 670	3 840	4 102	4 080	4 075	Chine
Cyprus	9	8	7	8	10	8	8	8	8	7	Chypre
Democratic Yemen	100	100	140	140	200	135	150	140	150	175	Yémen démocratique
India	2 607	2 488	2 414	2 651	2 343	2 844	3 253	3 467	3 304	3 842	Inde
Indonesia	2 925	3 902	3 863	4 507	4 396	4 611	4 288	4 078	4 874	5 329	Indonésie
Iran(Islamic Rep.of)	4 223	4 350	3 886	5 197	4 434	3 536	4 112	3 000	3 100	3 100	Iran(Rép.islamique)

For general note, see end of table.

Voir la fin du tableau pour la remarque générale.

Unit : Thousand metric tons — Unité : Milliers de tonnes métriques

Country or area	1976	1977	1978	1979	1980	1981	1982	1983	1984	1985	Pays ou zone
Iraq	449	610	665	670	700	550	620	570	700	750	Iraq
Israel	244	250	250	250	230	210	210	180	190	210	Israël
Japan	20 510	19 936	21 160	21 498	19 175	18 487	17 789	20 363	21 741	19 641	Japon
Jordan	160	107	148	153	169	157	186	224	147	191	Jordanie
Korea,Dem.Ppl's.Rep	...	7	71	100	120	140	160	170	180	190	Corée,Rép.pop.dém.de
Korea, Republic of	547	578	868	1 159	1 127	1 049	1 061	1 184	1 172	1 377	Corée, République de
Kuwait,part Ntl.Zone	758	837	1 343	1 516	1 426	945	973	1 081	1 148	1 698	Koweït et prt.Zne.N.
Lebanon	24	27	19	25	25	30	10	30	10	30	Liban
Malaysia	178	256	226	230	225	266	277	525	788	691	Malaisie
Mongolia	2	2	3	3	...	...	...	...	...	...	Mongolie
Oman	...	...	...	...	...	...	0	10	50	40	Oman
Pakistan	243	221	274	154	171	169	211	240	258	307	Pakistan
Philippines	389	403	461	538	466	578	528	443	307	351	Philippines
Qatar	5	5	5	5	4	4	4	4	10	10	Qatar
S.Arabia,pt.Ntrl.Zn	1 098	1 104	1 269	1 277	1 506	1 546	1 321	1 469	1 226	1 330	Arab.saoud,p.Zn.neut
Singapore	1 950	2 730	2 270	2 617	2 654	2 358	3 521	4 746	3 675	2 622	Singapour
Sri Lanka	188	185	212	189	179	149	155	132	148	154	Sri Lanka
Syrian Arab Republic	285	335	288	361	320	273	270	240	203	164	Rép. arabe syrienne
Thailand	230	228	213	258	237	286	292	351	198	133	Thaïlande
Turkey	521	589	577	442	475	306	305	306	335	463	Turquie
United Arab Emirates	3	24	43	28	35	197	0	0	30	40	Emirats arabes unis
Europe	**9 587**	**9 062**	**8 834**	**10 232**	**7 874**	**7 366**	**7 322**	**7 013**	**7 499**	**7 713**	**Europe**
EEC	***7 338***	***6 882***	***6 491***	***7 557***	***5 232***	***5 075***	***5 018***	***4 650***	***5 238***	***5 079***	***CEE***
Belgium	38	130	90	144	23	33	38	38	9	22	Belgique
Denmark	102	100	84	69	26	7	9	10	55	16	Danemark
France incl. Monaco	120	99	91	113	136	173	121	185	50	60	France y comp.Monaco
Germany, Fed. Rep.	49	59	43	71	77	46	83	80	81	74	Allemagne, Rép. féd.
Greece	51	13	41	46	41	25	29	34	26	39	Grèce
Ireland	0	1	0	0	0	0	0	0	0	0	Irlande
Italy and San Marino	3 850	3 439	3 030	3 854	2 423	2 491	2 447	1 954	2 372	2 103	Italie y comp. S.Mrn
Netherlands	670	579	498	551	472	396	440	579	579	458	Pays–Bas
United Kingdom	2 458	2 462	2 614	2 709	2 034	1 904	1 851	1 770	2 066	2 307	Royaume–Uni
EFTA	***311***	***313***	***316***	***606***	***623***	***323***	***421***	***311***	***130***	***144***	***AELE***
Austria	40	40	26	11	4	12	7	3	6	7	Autriche
Finland	4	4	4	5	6	16	21	19	13	8	Finlande
Norway,Svlbd,J.Myn I.	178	175	197	446	531	218	321	226	60	70	Norvège,Svalbd,J.May
Portugal	76	82	83	128	73	55	51	38	33	29	Portugal
Sweden	8	8	1	11	4	16	16	20	15	26	Suède
Switzrld,Liechtenst	5	4	5	5	5	6	5	5	3	4	Suisse,Liechtenstein
East Europe	***1 811***	***1 796***	***1 904***	***1 912***	***1 937***	***1 869***	***1 717***	***1 898***	***2 000***	***2 099***	***Europe de l'est***
Albania	50	60	60	65	70	65	80	85	90	95	Albanie
Bulgaria	170	190	200	220	230	220	220	220	220	220	Bulgarie
Czechoslovakia	298	337	460	485	527	470	309	390	404	425	Tchécoslovaquie
German Dem. Rep.	19	18	18	17	17	17	16	16	15	16	Rép. dém. allemande
Hungary	0	1	1	2	0	9	17	112	196	260	Hongrie
Poland	146	154	160	160	225	177	175	175	175	183	Pologne
Romania	1 128	1 036	1 005	963	868	911	900	900	900	900	Roumanie
Other Europe	***127***	***71***	***123***	***157***	***82***	***99***	***166***	***154***	***131***	***391***	***Autre Europe***
Spain	117	61	80	95	42	57	152	130	106	356	Espagne
Yugoslavia	10	10	43	62	40	42	14	24	25	35	Yougoslavie
USSR	**31 400**	**32 200**	**33 018**	**35 000**	**36 000**	**37 000**	**37 000**	**37 000**	**37 000**	**36 000**	**URSS**
Oceania	**786**	**938**	**940**	**738**	**548**	**357**	**398**	**362**	**281**	**265**	**Océanie**
Australia	786	938	940	738	548	357	398	362	281	265	Australie
Total	**105 423**	**108 368**	**109 196**	**117 669**	**110 864**	**107 459**	**108 520**	**110 659**	**112 677**	**109 571**	**Total**

General note.
Mixtures of hydrocarbons with a flash point above 21 degrees centigrade, distilling less than 90 per cent in volume at 210 degrees centigrade, including losses. This is a refined crude petroleum fuel, in volatility between motor gasolene and gas oil, free of gasolenes and heavy hydrocarbons such as gas oil and lubricating oil. It is used as a fuel in certain types of spark–ignition engines such as those used for

Remarque générale.
Mélange d'hydrocarbures dont le point d'éclair est supérieur à 21° C, donnant moins de 90 p. 100 en volume de distillat à 210° C, y compris les pertes. C'est un carburant qui provient du raffinage du pétrole brut et dont la volatilité se situe entre celle du carburant pour moteurs et celle du gas–oil. Il est exempt d'essences et d'hydrocarbures lourds tels que le gas–oil et les huiles de graissage. Il sert de

agricultural tractors and stationary engines. Jet fuel is excluded. Kerosene–type jet fuel, white spirit, naphthas and special boiling–point products are excluded. (SITC 33220–1A).

carburant dans certains types de moteurs à allumage par étincelles, tels que ceux utilisés dans les tracteurs agricoles et les installations stationnaires. Cette rubrique ne comprend pas les carburéacteurs, qu'ils soient ou non analogues au kérosène, ni le "white spirit", les naphtas ou les produits à point d'ébullition défini. (CTCI 33220–1A).

White spirit – White spirit

Jnit : Thousand metric tons — Unité : Milliers de tonnes métriques

Country or area	1976	1977	1978	1979	1980	1981	1982	1983	1984	1985	Pays ou zone
Africa	**0**	**0**	**0**	**0**	**11**	**7**	**8**	**11**	**19**	**21**	**Afrique**
Cameroon*	...	...	...	0	5	7	8	10	15	17	Cameroun*
Togo*	...	...	0	0	6	0	0	0	0	0	Togo*
Tunisia	0	0	0	0	0	0	0	1	4	4	Tunisie
America, North	**68**	**65**	**74**	**69**	**71**	**82**	**99**	**95**	**93**	**93**	**Amérique du Nord**
Mexico	66	64	71	67	69	80	97	94	* 90	* 90	Mexique
Trinidad and Tobago	2	1	3	2	2	2	2	1	* 3	* 3	Trinité–et–Tobago
America, South	**325**	**362**	**359**	**459**	**455**	**514**	**381**	**436**	**402**	**478**	**Amérique du Sud**
Brazil	114	109	* 110	* 200	* 200	* 224	* 100	* 175	126	198	Brésil
Chile	19	30	22	25	23	27	15	14	15	18	Chili
Colombia	177	194	198	204	202	236	245	231	239	* 240	Colombie
Ecuador	3	3	5	5	7	6	7	6	7	* 9	Equateur
Uruguay	...	13	12	14	13	12	4	2	4	3	Uruguay
Venezuela*	12	13	12	11	10	9	10	8	11	10	Venezuela*
Asia	**695**	**634**	**513**	**602**	**588**	**649**	**615**	**662**	**610**	**627**	**Asie**
India	130	132	146	156	155	145	139	117	133	137	Inde
Indonesia	21	25	* 20	* 20	* 23	* 21	* 19	* 35	* 50	* 100	Indonésie
Iran(Islamic Rep.of)*	94	100	100	90	90	70	70	70	80	80	Iran(Rép.islamique)*
Japan	199	74	65	72	71	135	100	* 85	52	49	Japon
Korea, Republic of	55	115	15	74	47	53	83	128	105	52	Corée, République de
Philippines	33	28	34	33	29	* 31	* 36	44	* 24	* 29	Philippines
Singapore	* 105	93	* 80	* 95	* 120	* 135	* 120	* 125	* 130	* 125	Singapour
Sri Lanka	...	...	...	...	...	0	0	0	0	2	Sri Lanka
Turkey	16	29	19	23	16	30	24	31	8	28	Turquie
Europe	**1 515**	**1 555**	**1 692**	**1 668**	**1 507**	**1 398**	**1 329**	**1 390**	**1 474**	**1 227**	**Europe**
EEC	***1 332***	***1 336***	***1 319***	***1 377***	***1 176***	***1 071***	***998***	***1 011***	***1 034***	***971***	***CEE***
Belgium	169	255	242	270	231	218	253	234	270	258	Belgique
Denmark	29	25	25	26	12	0	0	0	0	0	Danemark
France incl. Monaco	391	331	307	322	290	266	226	252	156	84	France y comp.Monaco
Germany, Fed. Rep.	228	234	218	228	236	244	240	201	237	262	Allemagne, Rép. féd.
Italy and San Marino	69	69	78	97	117	68	9	40	33	35	Italie y comp. S.Mrn
Netherlands	337	326	368	345	217	160	155	150	196	192	Pays–Bas
United Kingdom	109	96	81	89	73	115	115	134	142	140	Royaume–Uni
EFTA	***91***	***83***	***230***	***179***	***161***	***96***	***174***	***221***	***291***	***101***	***AELE***
Austria	18	19	18	23	16	10	14	8	8	6	Autriche
Finland	17	25	23	21	39	38	27	47	40	41	Finlande
Norway,Svlbd,J.Myn I..	5	4	3	33	29	31	35	36	30	41	Norvège,Svalbd,J.May
Portugal	4	5	5	7	9	3	93	103	202	4	Portugal
Sweden	47	30	181	95	68	14	5	27	11	9	Suède
East Europe	***60***	***61***	***66***	***43***	***48***	***47***	***42***	***47***	***50***	***54***	***Europe de l'est***
Hungary	60	61	54	39	37	38	34	40	39	36	Hongrie
Poland	...	...	12	4	11	9	8	7	11	18	Pologne
Other Europe	***32***	***75***	***77***	***69***	***122***	***184***	***115***	***111***	***99***	***101***	***Autre Europe***
Spain	* 3	43	44	* 40	96	155	85	77	65	71	Espagne
Yugoslavia	29	32	33	29	26	29	30	34	34	* 30	Yougoslavie
Oceania	**161**	**188**	**173**	**157**	**177**	**101**	**85**	**85**	**76**	**63**	**Océanie**
Australia	161	188	173	157	177	101	85	85	76	63	Australie
Total	**2 764**	**2 804**	**2 811**	**2 955**	**2 809**	**2 751**	**2 517**	**2 679**	**2 674**	**2 509**	**Total**

General note.
A highly–refined distillate with a boiling–point range about 150 to 200 degrees centigrade used as a paint solvent and for dry–cleaning purposes. (SITC 33220–2A).

Remarque générale.
Produit de distillation hautement raffiné dont le point d'ébullition se situe entre 150° C et 200° C, utilisé comme diluant de peinture et comme solvant de dégraissage. (CTCI 33220–2A).

Distillate fuel oils –
Gas-oil, fuel-oil domestique et fuel-oil léger

Unit : Thousand metric tons

Unité : Milliers de tonnes métriques

Country or area	1976	1977	1978	1979	1980	1981	1982	1983	1984	1985	Pays ou zone
Africa	**13 492**	**14 192**	**16 552**	**16 707**	**19 292**	**21 288**	**23 992**	**24 228**	**25 002**	**26 286**	**Afrique**
Algeria	1 459	1 348	2 757	2 130	3 726	4 670	7 088	6 456	7 260	7 300	Algérie
Angola	190	203	217	207	210	215	210	250	225	250	Angola
Cameroon	...	...	...	...	165	570	635	610	650	655	Cameroun
Congo	...	...	0	0	0	0	0	0	0	34	Congo
Côte d'Ivoire	489	517	497	240	170	416	190	512	450	475	Côte d'Ivoire
Egypt	1 717	1 961	2 180	2 312	2 521	2 610	2 691	2 815	3 107	3 326	Egypte
Ethiopia	191	176	219	138	154	146	193	209	191	180	Ethiopie
Gabon	344	392	453	316	320	290	320	345	355	350	Gabon
Ghana	337	406	340	332	308	325	292	164	170	165	Ghana
Kenya	499	553	550	548	508	535	464	448	469	498	Kenya
Liberia	140	0	23	120	130	125	135	137	136	137	Libéria
Libyan Arab Jamah	617	1 191	1 414	1 149	1 281	1 015	1 090	1 270	1 280	2 100	Jamah.arabe libyenne
Madagascar	153	126	88	69	128	102	101	56	60	65	Madagascar
Morocco	734	659	733	1 240	1 202	1 173	1 229	1 203	1 143	1 250	Maroc
Mozambique	85	120	88	139	120	120	130	150	140	145	Mozambique
Nigeria	703	677	845	1 200	1 723	2 292	2 330	2 340	2 325	2 350	Nigéria
Senegal	151	190	195	180	185	150	210	10	50	50	Sénégal
Sierra Leone	36	23	32	88	72	93	82	90	95	93	Sierra Leone
Somalia	...	...	59	155	160	188	192	175	180	170	Somalie
South Africa	4 326	4 414	4 420	4 500	4 600	4 750	5 000	5 500	5 200	5 250	Afrique du Sud
Sudan	326	337	505	511	498	510	530	490	510	495	Soudan
Togo	...	...	73	87	62	0	0	0	0	0	Togo
Tunisia	324	340	317	426	439	423	405	401	423	418	Tunisie
United Rep. Tanzania	193	162	135	135	150	130	140	140	138	140	Rép.Unie de Tanzanie
Zaire	97	44	40	94	110	115	15	137	135	90	Zaïre
Zambia	361	353	372	391	350	325	320	320	310	300	Zambie
America, North	**195 276**	**217 088**	**211 437**	**213 019**	**190 630**	**183 623**	**175 598**	**166 565**	**178 746**	**176 133**	**Amérique du Nord**
Antigua and Barbuda	0	0	0	0	0	0	14	0	0	0	Antigua-et-Barbuda
Bahamas	1 235	2 967	1 600	1 464	1 620	1 666	1 600	1 615	1 100	600	Bahamas
Barbados	52	32	37	37	44	45	43	42	40	34	Barbade
Canada	22 129	23 572	23 218	25 547	25 253	22 647	19 404	19 036	20 115	19 410	Canada
Costa Rica	63	75	96	83	147	143	116	75	104	88	Costa Rica
Cuba	962	996	1 083	1 094	1 098	1 118	1 117	1 060	1 020	979	Cuba
Dominican Republic	338	357	357	347	393	374	351	476	407	400	Rép. dominicaine
El Salvador	198	219	232	240	194	182	171	185	181	180	El Salvador
Guatemala	216	204	261	259	242	222	204	200	232	230	Guatemala
Honduras	199	235	171	190	202	58	12	89	90	90	Honduras
Jamaica	255	249	259	170	203	136	217	201	200	210	Jamaïque
Martinique	55	60	40	45	40	38	40	40	38	40	Martinique
Mexico	8 727	9 209	10 023	10 869	12 364	13 629	11 652	11 309	11 792	12 376	Mexique
Neth.Antil and Aruba	3 170	3 100	3 475	3 736	3 797	3 433	2 600	2 900	2 650	1 200	Antill.néer.et Aruba
Nicaragua	170	192	181	131	174	198	168	160	127	129	Nicaragua
Panama ex.Canal Zone	657	607	632	576	...	...	...	...	...	...	Panama ex.zone Canal
Panama	...	...	...	...	462	400	400	400	350	300	Panama
Puerto Rico	3 125	2 615	2 524	2 204	2 221	1 636	1 471	1 346	1 091	1 000	Porto Rico
Trinidad and Tobago	1 682	1 486	1 402	1 624	1 915	1 424	1 314	625	587	585	Trinité-et-Tobago
United States	148 030	165 470	159 910	159 173	134 743	131 932	131 579	124 006	135 722	135 682	Etats-Unis
U.S. Virgin Islands	4 670	6 050	6 568	5 806	5 518	4 342	3 125	2 800	2 900	2 600	Iles Vierges amér.
America, South	**28 605**	**30 839**	**33 484**	**35 734**	**39 122**	**38 103**	**38 725**	**39 107**	**41 466**	**44 248**	**Amérique du Sud**
Argentina	6 035	6 468	6 496	7 011	7 621	7 778	7 752	7 793	7 921	7 645	Argentine
Bolivia	189	232	268	262	261	272	235	214	230	210	Bolivie
Brazil	12 221	13 455	14 867	15 473	16 986	16 013	16 889	16 817	17 734	17 757	Brésil
Chile	885	929	1 053	1 207	1 211	1 089	850	1 048	1 107	1 193	Chili
Colombia	1 036	1 039	1 101	1 074	1 187	1 337	1 335	1 430	1 436	1 526	Colombie
Ecuador	399	285	625	711	785	694	723	605	749	748	Equateur
Paraguay	80	70	110	105	119	112	99	97	71	86	Paraguay
Peru	1 044	987	1 320	1 618	1 670	1 778	1 671	1 333	1 647	1 850	Pérou
Uruguay	453	451	513	460	473	468	492	432	444	388	Uruguay
Venezuela	6 263	6 923	7 131	7 813	8 809	8 562	8 679	9 338	10 127	12 845	Venezuela
Asia	**100 325**	**109 767**	**118 483**	**123 570**	**121 939**	**124 727**	**131 302**	**145 709**	**151 886**	**160 711**	**Asie**
Bahrain	2 709	3 260	3 303	3 297	3 312	3 534	2 726	2 378	3 048	2 607	Bahreïn
Bangladesh	137	181	150	123	155	147	165	162	238	211	Bangladesh
Brunei Darussalam	29	30	51	55	60	37	43	48	109	120	Brunéi Darussalam
Burma	282	327	326	360	369	368	392	371	410	438	Birmanie
China	15 000	16 160	18 260	18 730	18 280	17 780	17 460	19 035	19 465	19 892	Chine
Cyprus	98	111	120	132	153	139	137	154	156	133	Chypre

For general note, see end of table.

Voir la fin du tableau pour la remarque générale.

Distillate fuel oils (continued) – Gas–oil, fuel–oil domestique et fuel–oil léger (suite)

Unit : Thousand metric tons

Unité : Milliers de tonnes métriques

Country or area	1976	1977	1978	1979	1980	1981	1982	1983	1984	1985	Pays ou zone
Democratic Yemen.........	277	374	404	40	940	945	830	800	850	1 010	Yémen démocratique
India..............................	7 308	8 176	8 525	9 519	8 132	9 865	10 468	11 666	12 154	14 882	Inde
Indonesia......................	2 697	3 793	4 163	4 689	4 731	4 440	4 855	5 188	5 685	6 927	Indonésie
Iran(Islamic Rep.of).......	6 845	7 514	7 756	7 893	7 840	6 412	6 977	9 428	10 667	11 359	Iran(Rép.islamique)
Iraq..............................	1 166	1 181	1 784	1 700	2 379	2 398	2 400	3 000	3 400	3 900	Iraq
Israel............................	1 141	1 345	1 405	1 405	1 351	1 410	1 566	1 462	1 499	1 595	Israël
Japan............................	32 300	34 177	36 129	38 267	36 818	35 308	34 706	36 741	38 265	38 651	Japon
Jordan..........................	336	349	417	469	470	648	686	689	686	738	Jordanie
Korea,Dem.Ppl's.Rep.....	...	39	405	500	600	700	750	800	850	900	Corée,Rép.pop.dém.de
Korea, Republic of........	3 545	4 183	4 764	5 264	5 278	5 619	5 632	6 716	7 492	7 568	Corée, République de
Kuwait,part Ntl.Zone.....	4 244	4 032	4 037	4 132	3 703	3 298	5 282	6 127	5 324	6 056	Koweït et prt.Zne.N.
Lebanon........................	429	336	326	330	345	330	100	100	190	210	Liban
Malaysia.......................	1 231	1 323	1 542	1 668	1 714	1 730	1 883	2 337	2 489	2 340	Malaisie
Oman............................	...	...	...	...	...	...	0	310	450	450	Oman
Pakistan........................	837	923	1 074	1 068	1 152	1 115	1 283	1 342	1 341	1 538	Pakistan
Philippines....................	1 996	2 064	2 070	2 278	2 382	2 427	2 325	2 426	2 466	2 507	Philippines
Qatar............................	116	128	126	136	152	154	151	192	350	350	Qatar
S.Arabia,pt.Ntrl.Zn.......	3 723	4 442	5 185	5 312	6 156	7 469	9 264	11 563	11 600	11 650	Arab.saoud,p.Zn.neut
Singapore.....................	5 046	5 569	6 780	6 566	4 619	6 991	7 644	7 806	6 707	7 729	Singapour
Sri Lanka......................	365	368	359	340	480	416	471	391	466	376	Sri Lanka
Syrian Arab Republic.....	708	1 118	1 070	1 407	1 514	1 969	1 980	2 433	2 865	3 700	Rép. arabe syrienne
Thailand........................	2 216	2 435	2 241	2 412	2 431	2 394	2 475	2 656	2 408	2 923	Thaïlande
Turkey..........................	3 314	3 393	2 686	2 421	3 106	3 538	4 600	4 582	5 152	5 089	Turquie
United Arab Emirates.....	129	187	185	202	216	273	1 313	1 777	2 065	2 080	Emirats arabes unis
Europe........................	**222 026**	**227 639**	**232 293**	**254 553**	**232 497**	**201 952**	**195 764**	**195 112**	**201 707**	**200 707**	**Europe**
EEC..............................	***164 982***	***167 337***	***170 379***	***188 930***	***167 925***	***142 891***	***137 707***	***135 170***	***141 031***	***138 651***	***CEE***
Belgium.........................	9 034	11 560	10 730	11 803	10 932	8 776	7 947	7 543	8 028	7 336	Belgique
Denmark........................	3 362	3 430	3 304	3 543	2 789	2 671	2 599	2 997	3 130	3 017	Danemark
France incl. Monaco......	41 020	40 349	40 002	45 537	41 532	31 305	28 408	27 475	29 265	29 691	France y comp.Monaco
Germany, Fed. Rep.......	40 523	40 704	40 431	47 363	41 986	36 324	35 489	33 790	34 886	34 429	Allemagne, Rép. féd.
Greece..........................	2 670	2 736	2 801	3 634	3 649	3 945	3 939	3 856	3 798	3 231	Grèce
Ireland..........................	512	617	641	614	539	189	156	375	416	434	Irlande
Italy and San Marino.....	25 634	26 506	29 599	31 097	26 815	25 291	24 950	23 698	23 868	23 891	Italie y comp. S.Mrn
Netherlands...................	18 029	17 959	18 807	19 857	17 511	13 961	13 621	14 405	16 091	14 920	Pays–Bas
United Kingdom............	24 198	23 476	24 064	25 482	22 172	20 429	20 598	21 031	21 549	21 702	Royaume–Uni
EFTA...........................	***16 918***	***18 225***	***18 202***	***20 022***	***20 155***	***17 651***	***16 776***	***18 152***	***17 613***	***18 233***	***AELE***
Austria..........................	2 459	2 346	2 640	2 812	2 543	2 113	2 076	2 047	2 083	2 209	Autriche
Finland..........................	3 329	3 896	3 618	4 293	4 281	3 915	3 496	3 960	4 004	4 054	Finlande
Norway,Svlbd,J.Myn l..	3 069	3 974	3 742	3 763	3 442	3 251	3 255	3 454	3 321	3 594	Norvège,Svalbd,J.May
Portugal........................	1 289	1 246	1 308	1 901	1 866	2 057	1 851	2 188	1 856	1 945	Portugal
Sweden.........................	4 633	4 840	5 079	5 283	6 005	4 629	4 440	4 729	4 582	4 622	Suède
Switzrld,Liechtenst.........	2 139	1 923	1 815	1 970	2 018	1 686	1 658	1 774	1 767	1 809	Suisse,Liechtenstein
East Europe.................	***27 009***	***28 164***	***29 664***	***30 520***	***30 304***	***28 033***	***28 024***	***27 837***	***28 625***	***28 931***	***Europe de l'est***
Albania.........................	200	210	220	250	300	250	350	365	380	390	Albanie
Bulgaria........................	3 150	3 300	3 400	3 450	3 500	3 400	3 400	3 400	3 400	3 400	Bulgarie
Czechoslovakia..............	3 962	4 160	4 369	4 444	4 145	4 071	3 798	3 753	3 688	3 595	Tchécoslovaquie
German Dem. Rep.........	5 089	5 383	5 585	5 961	6 119	5 614	6 142	6 054	6 132	6 350	Rép. dém. allemande
Hungary........................	3 446	3 528	3 721	3 943	3 672	3 712	3 481	3 257	3 522	3 512	Hongrie
Poland...........................	4 875	5 101	5 355	5 193	5 093	4 248	4 353	4 568	4 694	4 842	Pologne
Romania........................	6 287	6 482	7 014	7 279	7 475	6 738	6 500	6 440	6 809	6 842	Roumanie
Other Europe..............	***13 117***	***13 913***	***14 048***	***15 081***	***14 113***	***13 377***	***13 257***	***13 953***	***14 438***	***14 892***	***Autre Europe***
Spain.............................	10 148	10 463	10 577	11 165	10 790	10 304	9 964	10 487	10 782	11 495	Espagne
Yugoslavia....................	2 969	3 450	3 471	3 916	3 323	3 073	3 293	3 466	3 656	3 397	Yougoslavie
USSR...........................	**101 000**	**103 800**	**107 000**	**112 000**	**115 000**	**118 000**	**120 000**	**120 000**	**120 000**	**118 000**	**URSS**
Oceania.......................	**7 255**	**7 323**	**7 739**	**7 827**	**8 160**	**8 155**	**8 048**	**7 806**	**7 997**	**7 734**	**Océanie**
Australia.......................	6 219	6 491	6 904	6 965	7 281	7 122	7 173	6 925	7 081	7 106	Australie
Guam............................	326	176	206	210	225	355	321	270	300	300	Guam
New Zealand.................	710	656	629	652	654	678	554	611	616	328	Nouvelle–Zélande
Total...........................	**667 979**	**710 648**	**726 988**	**763 410**	**726 640**	**695 848**	**693 429**	**698 527**	**726 804**	**733 819**	**Total**

For general note, see end of table.

Voir la fin du tableau pour la remarque générale.

General note.
Gas oils (with a flash point in a closed vessel of at least 55 degrees centigrade and distilling 90 per cent or more in volume at 360 degrees centigrade); fuel oils (with a flash point in a closed vessel of between 55 degrees centigrade and 190 degrees centigrade and a needle penetration at 25 degrees centigrade of 400 or more); domestic fuel oil (with a viscosity of less than 12 centistokes at 20 degrees centigrade and an asphalt content of not less than 0.5 per cent), used as a fuel for internal combustion in diesel engines, as a burner fuel in heating installations such as furnaces and for enriching water gas to increase its luminosity.

Remarque générale.
Gas–oil (point d'éclair en vase clos au moins égal à 55 ° C et donnant en volume 90 p. 100 ou plus de distillat à 360° C); fuel–oil (point d'éclair en vase clos compris entre 55° C et 190° C et pénétration à l'aiguille à 25° C égale ou supérieure à 400° C); fuel–oil domestique (viscosité à 20° C inférieure à 12 centistokes et teneur en asphaltène supérieure ou égale à 0,5 p. 100); produits servant de carburants dans les moteurs diesel, de combustibles dans les installations de chauffage telles que les chaudières ou d'additifs pour augmenter la luminosité de la flamme du gaz à l'eau. (CTCI 33230–0A).

Residual fuel oils – Fuel-oil lourd

Unit : Thousand metric tons

Unité : Milliers de tonnes métriques

Country or area	1976	1977	1978	1979	1980	1981	1982	1983	1984	1985	Pays ou zone
Africa	**18 819**	**19 311**	**20 958**	**21 988**	**25 447**	**26 775**	**29 149**	**29 560**	**30 020**	**30 290**	**Afrique**
Algeria	1 389	1 141	2 012	1 792	2 703	3 765	5 392	5 177	5 108	5 200	Algérie
Angola	423	539	549	535	550	560	525	600	575	600	Angola
Cameroon	...	...	...	...	200	850	910	975	995	997	Cameroun
Congo	...	...	0	0	0	0	0	0	0	9	Congo
Côte d'Ivoire	728	690	644	717	684	590	580	518	510	520	Côte d'Ivoire
Egypt	5 056	5 262	5 462	5 540	6 700	7 657	8 336	8 912	9 475	9 482	Egypte
Ethiopia	256	273	253	303	243	193	300	303	308	310	Ethiopie
Gabon	439	551	856	627	652	575	620	491	535	510	Gabon
Ghana	287	368	314	271	280	314	271	395	318	320	Ghana
Kenya	1 133	1 117	1 197	1 144	1 332	648	735	605	613	653	Kenya
Liberia	270	0	48	335	350	345	350	348	350	351	Libéria
Libyan Arab Jamah	1 047	1 912	2 289	2 077	2 416	2 034	2 160	2 400	2 440	2 540	Jamah.arabe libyenne
Madagascar	213	215	160	174	240	144	155	85	90	87	Madagascar
Morocco	1 153	1 180	1 266	1 864	1 757	1 804	1 821	1 948	2 063	1 980	Maroc
Mozambique	173	217	171	268	200	180	180	200	190	195	Mozambique
Nigeria	986	657	695	900	1 746	1 699	1 650	1 650	1 612	1 700	Nigéria
Senegal	281	310	257	300	270	265	350	155	152	153	Sénégal
Sierra Leone	160	40	48	35	33	56	57	60	65	63	Sierra Leone
Somalia	...	...	1	4	4	6	5	5	6	6	Somalie
South Africa	3 187	3 328	3 330	3 380	3 500	3 600	3 500	3 300	3 200	3 250	Afrique du Sud
Sudan	460	484	270	275	267	280	310	295	298	297	Soudan
Togo	...	...	136	180	110	0	0	0	0	0	Togo
Tunisia	487	509	502	645	675	658	532	591	591	587	Tunisie
United Rep. Tanzania	358	279	238	258	250	230	235	230	232	225	Rép.Unie de Tanzanie
Zaire	132	53	79	189	105	145	25	157	139	105	Zaïre
Zambia	201	186	181	175	180	177	150	160	155	150	Zambie
America, North	**166 641**	**188 285**	**178 041**	**176 421**	**172 865**	**150 740**	**130 501**	**111 674**	**112 674**	**104 166**	**Amérique du Nord**
Antigua and Barbuda	0	0	0	0	0	0	50	0	0	0	Antigua-et-Barbuda
Bahamas	5 560	8 200	5 300	4 500	5 500	4 024	5 000	4 100	3 100	1 900	Bahamas
Barbados	42	78	75	87	92	94	101	91	105	122	Barbade
Canada	17 558	18 972	18 191	18 932	17 105	14 959	10 843	8 885	8 261	6 682	Canada
Costa Rica	112	162	172	175	216	212	176	144	183	202	Costa Rica
Cuba	3 033	3 209	3 101	3 213	3 026	3 130	3 198	3 414	3 340	3 318	Cuba
Dominican Republic	406	610	554	646	563	659	457	815	537	540	Rép. dominicaine
El Salvador	246	235	227	213	191	193	182	190	196	190	El Salvador
Guatemala	298	303	326	307	313	334	246	209	251	250	Guatemala
Honduras	148	130	99	118	141	56	32	87	90	90	Honduras
Jamaica	674	359	346	504	383	315	294	504	400	410	Jamaïque
Martinique	140	145	130	130	120	125	130	130	132	134	Martinique
Mexico	11 663	12 857	13 438	13 093	17 053	19 131	19 279	19 306	20 724	21 810	Mexique
Neth.Antil and Aruba	17 500	17 403	18 000	16 000	17 500	16 000	14 750	14 000	12 500	6 800	Antill.néer.et Aruba
Nicaragua	233	270	188	125	156	217	228	221	180	222	Nicaragua
Panama ex.Canal Zone	1 554	1 590	1 191	1 021	...	...	...	...	...	...	Panama ex.zone Canal
Panama	...	...	...	...	1 001	900	940	875	775	640	Panama
Puerto Rico	4 533	4 580	4 533	4 165	3 383	2 525	1 498	1 555	1 824	1 800	Porto Rico
Trinidad and Tobago	10 241	8 515	6 869	6 573	6 450	4 467	4 135	2 196	2 209	2 622	Trinité-et-Tobago
United States	76 116	96 685	91 927	92 976	87 364	72 814	58 962	46 952	49 267	48 634	Etats-Unis
U.S. Virgin Islands	18 138	15 572	14 565	14 664	12 308	10 585	10 000	8 000	8 600	7 800	Iles Vierges amér.
America, South	**63 620**	**63 179**	**66 640**	**66 078**	**60 289**	**55 418**	**51 655**	**46 261**	**46 993**	**43 219**	**Amérique du Sud**
Argentina	7 911	8 750	8 437	8 583	8 134	8 129	7 231	6 539	6 113	5 550	Argentine
Bolivia	204	226	187	169	151	124	128	140	101	76	Bolivie
Brazil	15 278	15 698	17 318	17 404	16 515	15 517	13 644	12 238	12 499	11 807	Brésil
Chile	1 503	1 575	1 649	1 645	1 629	1 430	1 008	1 065	1 005	958	Chili
Colombia	2 786	2 783	2 862	2 304	2 566	2 462	2 691	2 943	2 912	3 015	Colombie
Ecuador	570	748	1 966	2 096	2 260	2 163	2 189	1 886	2 131	1 865	Equateur
Paraguay	43	45	56	58	47	59	35	30	22	28	Paraguay
Peru	1 985	2 308	2 170	2 310	2 489	2 526	2 875	3 498	4 076	3 300	Pérou
Uruguay	776	804	763	788	845	788	701	437	392	310	Uruguay
Venezuela	32 564	30 242	31 232	30 721	25 653	22 220	21 153	17 485	17 742	16 310	Venezuela
Asia	**236 478**	**244 444**	**244 781**	**249 994**	**235 701**	**215 077**	**205 552**	**210 044**	**211 914**	**195 990**	**Asie**
Bahrain	3 998	5 088	4 437	4 655	4 097	4 322	3 005	2 569	2 582	1 972	Bahreïn
Bangladesh	336	455	420	431	535	545	477	299	305	267	Bangladesh
Brunei Darussalam	0	0	0	1	1	0	1	1	0	0	Brunéi Darussalam
Burma	152	192	203	211	220	241	223	210	213	212	Birmanie
China	27 000	28 000	28 143	28 161	31 420	28 175	26 096	28 967	28 570	29 505	Chine
Cyprus	140	141	147	218	231	168	179	187	190	147	Chypre

For general note, see end of table.

Voir la fin du tableau pour la remarque générale.

Unit : Thousand metric tons | Unité : Milliers de tonnes métriques

Country or area	1976	1977	1978	1979	1980	1981	1982	1983	1984	1985	Pays ou zone
Democratic Yemen	819	956	923	950	1 030	810	1 700	1 600	1 600	1 800	Yémen démocratique
India	4 779	5 242	5 496	6 285	6 113	6 643	7 811	7 821	7 915	8 096	Inde
Indonesia	7 662	9 440	9 787	11 101	11 267	11 434	10 059	9 314	10 144	6 165	Indonésie
Iran(Islamic Rep.of)	14 471	16 341	15 103	17 643	14 915	8 856	8 923	10 195	11 265	11 683	Iran(Rép.islamique)
Iraq	1 700	1 750	2 143	2 300	2 920	2 100	2 500	4 600	4 900	5 100	Iraq
Israel	3 151	3 236	3 532	2 960	2 436	2 530	3 574	3 427	2 993	2 024	Israël
Japan	102 694	100 753	98 683	95 158	82 557	69 388	59 502	57 230	54 378	43 850	Japon
Jordan	240	234	291	388	497	578	722	775	886	709	Jordanie
Korea,Dem.Ppl's.Rep.	...	21	214	250	300	350	400	450	500	550	Corée,Rép.pop.dém.de
Korea, Republic of	10 583	11 665	12 565	13 238	13 657	12 920	12 293	13 005	12 820	11 110	Corée, République de
Kuwait,part Ntl.Zone	9 662	9 258	8 975	10 174	8 021	6 050	9 448	10 680	11 907	13 837	Koweït et prt.Zne.N.
Lebanon	832	843	820	820	820	770	92	150	400	185	Liban
Malaysia	1 948	2 326	2 480	2 465	2 257	1 979	1 554	1 986	2 044	1 952	Malaisie
Mongolia	2	3	3	3	...	...	...	...	...	...	Mongolie
Oman	...	...	...	...	...	...	0	180	250	240	Oman
Pakistan	916	878	1 316	1 292	1 483	1 493	1 669	1 459	1 534	1 539	Pakistan
Philippines	3 798	4 115	4 456	4 422	4 128	4 140	3 850	3 723	2 985	3 240	Philippines
Qatar	0	0	0	0	0	226	215	220	1 900	2 100	Qatar
S.Arabia,pt.Ntrl.Zn.	15 837	14 844	14 411	14 377	13 443	12 916	14 160	14 888	12 800	13 100	Arab.saoud,p.Zn.neut
Singapore	9 127	10 209	10 154	12 945	12 281	14 994	12 219	12 371	13 500	12 171	Singapour
Sri Lanka	514	545	547	543	746	699	721	490	658	606	Sri Lanka
Syrian Arab Republic	1 092	1 321	1 808	2 282	2 875	4 680	4 900	4 405	4 675	4 700	Rép. arabe syrienne
Thailand	2 559	2 687	2 968	3 314	2 389	2 495	2 251	2 053	2 340	1 931	Thaïlande
Turkey	5 856	6 408	5 797	4 565	5 264	5 527	6 990	6 418	6 833	6 800	Turquie
United Arab Emirates	105	157	159	154	133	943	1 389	1 608	2 305	2 400	Emirats arabes unis
Europe	**282 859**	**276 418**	**275 460**	**284 188**	**256 882**	**230 341**	**196 395**	**181 629**	**171 394**	**158 342**	**Europe**
EEC	***192 786***	***189 989***	***187 609***	***190 764***	***162 814***	***145 720***	***119 596***	***106 875***	***100 460***	***89 752***	***CEE***
Belgium	10 648	13 153	12 053	10 950	10 898	9 546	8 300	6 000	6 535	4 274	Belgique
Denmark	2 450	2 346	2 476	2 952	2 116	1 801	1 851	2 063	2 179	1 994	Danemark
France incl. Monaco	40 588	39 965	38 224	40 826	33 997	29 934	20 913	18 147	15 691	14 690	France y comp.Monaco
Germany, Fed. Rep.	27 938	26 307	24 412	26 025	24 675	21 477	19 146	15 725	14 245	12 377	Allemagne, Rép. féd.
Greece	5 583	5 190	5 710	7 460	6 490	7 188	6 165	5 180	4 283	4 435	Grèce
Ireland	867	1 003	966	1 074	898	327	197	444	458	487	Irlande
Italy and San Marino	45 401	46 716	49 317	49 296	39 468	38 827	30 816	27 740	26 154	23 513	Italie y comp. S.Mrn
Netherlands	23 550	21 855	20 659	20 125	17 046	14 561	13 427	15 577	15 427	12 898	Pays-Bas
United Kingdom	35 761	33 454	33 792	32 056	27 226	22 059	18 781	15 999	15 488	15 084	Royaume-Uni
EFTA	***20 738***	***19 653***	***20 637***	***21 600***	***22 389***	***17 796***	***15 604***	***15 219***	***13 211***	***12 739***	***AELE***
Austria	3 856	3 556	4 429	4 437	4 277	3 407	2 664	1 809	1 748	2 408	Autriche
Finland	4 200	4 104	3 710	3 753	4 249	3 255	2 405	2 280	2 094	2 047	Finlande
Norway,Svlbd,J.Myn I.	2 879	2 226	1 956	1 809	1 830	1 408	1 246	1 187	1 070	815	Norvège,Svalbd,J.May
Portugal	2 553	2 568	2 844	3 716	3 473	3 460	3 543	3 470	3 087	2 672	Portugal
Sweden	6 149	6 151	6 777	6 927	7 758	5 679	5 062	5 730	4 449	4 085	Suède
Switzrld,Liechtenst.	1 101	1 048	921	958	802	587	684	743	763	712	Suisse,Liechtenstein
East Europe	***38 892***	***38 378***	***40 821***	***42 849***	***42 105***	***39 142***	***35 677***	***35 268***	***35 717***	***36 043***	***Europe de l'est***
Albania	360	375	400	450	500	450	550	575	600	610	Albanie
Bulgaria	5 090	5 300	5 500	5 800	6 000	5 900	5 900	5 900	5 900	5 900	Bulgarie
Czechoslovakia	8 469	8 602	8 948	9 245	9 396	9 065	7 543	7 452	7 357	7 363	Tchécoslovaquie
German Dem. Rep.	8 836	8 536	8 820	8 850	8 900	9 000	8 500	8 500	9 000	9 000	Rép. dém. allemande
Hungary	3 509	3 535	3 686	3 922	3 147	3 082	2 472	2 353	2 374	2 339	Hongrie
Poland	4 996	4 374	4 321	4 463	3 931	3 200	2 712	2 505	2 366	2 399	Pologne
Romania	7 632	7 656	9 146	10 119	10 231	8 445	8 000	7 983	8 120	8 432	Roumanie
Other Europe	***30 443***	***28 398***	***26 393***	***28 975***	***29 574***	***27 683***	***25 518***	***24 267***	***22 006***	***19 808***	***Autre Europe***
Spain	25 643	22 580	20 274	22 486	22 924	22 066	20 114	18 831	17 117	15 280	Espagne
Yugoslavia	4 800	5 818	6 119	6 489	6 650	5 617	5 404	5 436	4 889	4 528	Yougoslavie
USSR	**134 700**	**137 400**	**140 200**	**145 000**	**149 000**	**152 000**	**153 000**	**153 000**	**153 000**	**151 000**	**URSS**
Oceania	**5 826**	**6 085**	**5 442**	**5 702**	**5 095**	**4 791**	**4 473**	**3 739**	**3 792**	**3 731**	**Océanie**
Australia	4 340	4 604	4 138	4 354	3 830	3 719	3 601	2 894	2 947	2 930	Australie
Guam	328	416	453	470	480	510	476	500	500	500	Guam
New Zealand	1 158	1 065	851	878	785	562	396	345	345	301	Nouvelle-Zélande
Total	**908 943**	**935 122**	**931 522**	**949 371**	**905 279**	**835 142**	**770 725**	**735 907**	**729 787**	**686 738**	**Total**

For general note, see end of table. | Voir la fin du tableau pour la remarque générale.

General note.
Mixtures of hydrocarbons with a viscosity of at least 49 centistokes at 20 degrees centigrade and an asphalt content of at least one per cent. These oils are crude petroleum residues, such as viscous residuum, obtained by the refinery operations of crude petroleum after gasolene, kerosene and sometimes heavier distillates (such as gas oil or diesel oil) have been removed. They are commonly used by ships and industrial large–scale heating installations as a fuel in furnaces or boilers to produce heat and power. (SITC 33240–0A).

Remarque générale.
Mélanges d'hydrocarbures ayant une viscosité à 20° C égale ou supérieure à 49 centistokes et une teneur en asphaltène égale ou supérieure à 1 p. 100. Ce sont des résidus du raffinage du pétrole brut, qui comprennent notamment les produits visqueux restant après élimination de l'essence, du kérosène et parfois des distillats plus lourds, tels que le gas–oil et le combustible pour moteurs diesel. On les utilise généralement comme combustibles pour produire la chaleur et l'énergie dans les chaudières des navires ou les grandes installations de chauffage utilisées dans l'industrie. (CTCI 33240–0A).

Lubricating oils – Huiles lubrifiantes

Unit : Thousand metric tons

Unité : Milliers de tonnes métriques

Country or area	1976	1977	1978	1979	1980	1981	1982	1983	1984	1985	Pays ou zone
Africa	**516**	**551**	**566**	**570**	**575**	**708**	**767**	**849**	**881**	**893**	**Afrique**
Algeria	18	32	52	52	47	52	42	47	83	90	Algérie
Cameroon	...	...	...	...	50	175	210	220	210	215	Cameroun
Egypt	54	73	72	42	73	68	78	127	154	167	Egypte
Ghana	38	22	22	19	19	22	23	25	23	23	Ghana
Madagascar	5	2	3	4	0	0	0	0	0	0	Madagascar
Nigeria	57	60	60	70	...	...	...	...	...	...	Nigéria
Senegal	...	22	22	20	15	8	9	7	11	12	Sénégal
Sierra Leone	18	15	10	12	10	10	11	10	11	11	Sierra Leone
Somalia	...	...	...	4	4	4	3	3	4	4	Somalie
South Africa	319	320	320	340	350	360	380	400	375	360	Afrique du Sud
Sudan	7	5	5	7	7	9	11	10	10	11	Soudan
America, North	**10 918**	**11 410**	**12 023**	**12 523**	**11 786**	**11 078**	**9 480**	**9 618**	**10 352**	**9 294**	**Amérique du Nord**
Canada	596	643	688	804	870	845	696	707	831	823	Canada
Cuba	104	120	122	127	130	115	137	138	130	128	Cuba
Jamaica	30	30	32	31	5	28	25	25	28	30	Jamaïque
Mexico	437	391	408	395	404	494	408	344	358	348	Mexique
Neth.Antil and Aruba	604	595	500	625	628	574	470	400	350	100	Antill.néer.et Aruba
Puerto Rico	186	272	229	286	286	243	286	286	300	250	Porto Rico
Trinidad and Tobago	118	132	104	98	145	113	69	19	20	20	Trinité–et–Tobago
United States	8 843	9 227	9 940	10 157	9 318	8 666	7 389	7 699	8 335	7 595	Etats–Unis
America, South	**970**	**1 008**	**1 020**	**1 339**	**1 394**	**1 357**	**1 447**	**1 436**	**1 445**	**1 414**	**Amérique du Sud**
Argentina	237	265	243	307	277	268	282	282	258	275	Argentine
Bolivia	15	16	14	22	22	19	21	15	16	15	Bolivie
Brazil	315	331	288	485	556	546	659	675	700	659	Brésil
Chile	...	...	...	...	...	62	51	47	59	55	Chili
Colombia	8	5	7	10	10	6	5	10	15	10	Colombie
Ecuador	24	28	33	37	42	43	46	32	39	40	Equateur
Peru	15	16	18	18	11	15	21	26	17	19	Pérou
Uruguay	3	5	6	7	7	6	7	6	6	6	Uruguay
Venezuela	353	342	411	453	469	392	355	343	335	335	Venezuela
Asia	**3 501**	**4 017**	**6 306**	**6 672**	**6 302**	**5 747**	**5 656**	**6 580**	**6 847**	**6 847**	**Asie**
Afghanistan	...	...	...	...	6	...	21	34	21	3	Afghanistan
Bahrain	10	47	54	21	0	0	52	214	168	170	Bahreïn
Bangladesh	29	28	36	33	31	35	30	30	19	24	Bangladesh
Burma	20	19	22	20	22	20	20	18	16	18	Birmanie
China	...	...	1 806	1 915	1 970	1 599	1 550	1 482	1 637	1 700	Chine
India	340	404	488	481	439	416	404	462	455	459	Inde
Indonesia	2	3	76	78	71	0	75	53	77	79	Indonésie
Iran(Islamic Rep.of)	118	266	192	232	177	130	130	460	460	394	Iran(Rép.islamique)
Iraq	52	58	60	80	60	60	60	100	100	100	Iraq
Israel	37	40	40	40	40	40	40	40	40	40	Israël
Japan	1 908	1 976	2 024	2 098	2 073	1 896	1 802	1 958	2 025	2 024	Japon
Jordan	...	1	3	5	5	8	18	8	8	9	Jordanie
Korea, Republic of	136	170	198	216	201	216	238	268	282	343	Corée, République de
Malaysia	0	53	68	77	77	66	77	79	80	85	Malaisie
Oman	0	0	0	0	0	0	0	0	60	80	Oman
Pakistan	92	88	77	73	96	103	93	103	106	125	Pakistan
Philippines	89	109	126	128	119	118	118	142	120	120	Philippines
S.Arabia,pt.Ntrl.Zn.	...	...	155	225	0	224	209	216	230	250	Arab.saoud,p.Zn.neut
Singapore	429	469	540	618	611	535	451	551	575	516	Singapour
Sri Lanka	16	14	17	19	23	18	20	20	20	18	Sri Lanka
Turkey	129	163	193	178	158	148	148	223	212	168	Turquie
Europe	**8 401**	**8 979**	**9 354**	**9 831**	**9 565**	**8 980**	**8 876**	**9 049**	**9 584**	**9 737**	**Europe**
EEC	***5 592***	***5 791***	***5 896***	***6 191***	***6 168***	***5 743***	***5 607***	***5 714***	***6 193***	***6 128***	***CEE***
Belgium	102	102	88	98	66	40	26	36	37	66	Belgique
France incl. Monaco	1 228	1 241	1 544	1 503	1 631	1 539	1 471	1 616	1 523	1 628	France y comp.Monaco
Germany, Fed. Rep.	1 524	1 586	1 510	1 568	1 524	1 604	1 671	1 541	1 504	1 359	Allemagne, Rép. féd.
Greece	55	101	105	84	103	63	92	94	156	121	Grèce
Italy and San Marino	807	786	843	1 039	1 028	908	882	1 003	1 056	974	Italie y comp. S.Mrn
Netherlands	543	556	600	565	566	522	471	495	807	792	Pays–Bas
United Kingdom	1 333	1 419	1 206	1 334	1 250	1 067	994	929	1 110	1 188	Royaume–Uni
EFTA	***342***	***301***	***295***	***316***	***257***	***293***	***276***	***267***	***261***	***264***	***AELE***

For general note, see end of table.

Voir la fin du tableau pour la remarque générale.

Lubricating oils (continued) – Huiles lubrifiantes (suite)

Unit : Thousand metric tons

Unité : Milliers de tonnes métriques

Country or area	1976	1977	1978	1979	1980	1981	1982	1983	1984	1985	Pays ou zone
Austria	184	171	167	173	119	136	88	99	92	101	Autriche
Norway,Svlbd,J.Myn I.	41	28	40	41	24	20	18	17	17	3	Norvège,Svalbd,J.May
Portugal	74	91	67	64	73	90	81	81	81	103	Portugal
Sweden	43	11	21	38	41	47	89	70	71	57	Suède
East Europe	***2 047***	***2 044***	***2 228***	***2 364***	***2 361***	***2 183***	***2 205***	***2 213***	***2 244***	***2 314***	***Europe de l'est***
Albania	12	12	15	15	20	20	25	25	25	25	Albanie
Bulgaria	85	100	110	120	150	130	130	130	130	130	Bulgarie
Czechoslovakia	256	280	275	300	368	350	336	346	348	356	Tchécoslovaquie
German Dem. Rep.	381	391	402	416	414	430	437	463	462	478	Rép. dém. allemande
Hungary	209	195	178	180	172	192	207	223	200	216	Hongrie
Poland	436	460	581	604	573	460	470	465	502	537	Pologne
Romania	668	606	667	729	664	601	600	561	577	572	Roumanie
Other Europe	***420***	***843***	***935***	***960***	***779***	***761***	***788***	***855***	***886***	***1 031***	***Autre Europe***
Spain	240	605	555	529	319	325	382	394	433	427	Espagne
Yugoslavia	180	238	380	431	460	436	406	461	453	604	Yougoslavie
USSR	**9 000**	**9 300**	**9 600**	**10 500**	**11 000**	**11 000**	**11 000**	**11 000**	**11 000**	**10 000**	**URSS**
Oceania	**387**	**486**	**532**	**518**	**553**	**521**	**508**	**478**	**507**	**541**	**Océanie**
Australia	387	486	532	518	553	521	508	478	507	541	Australie
Total	**33 693**	**35 751**	**39 401**	**41 953**	**41 175**	**39 391**	**37 734**	**39 010**	**40 616**	**38 726**	**Total**

General note.
Mixtures of hydrocarbons distilling less than 30 per cent in volume at 300 degrees centigrade and with a flow point lower than 30 degrees centigrade. These are heavy liquid distillates obtained by refining crude petroleum. Lubricating preparations consisting of mixtures of oils of any kind (animal, vegetable, mineral, silicon etc.) are also included. Solid lubricants (for example, grease) are excluded. (SITC 33250–1A).

Remarque générale.
Mélanges d'hydrocarbures donnant moins de 30 p. 100 en volume de distillat à 300° C et présentant un point d'écoulement inférieur à 30° C. Ce sont des distillats liquides lourds résultant du raffinage du pétrole brut. Cette rubrique comprend aussi les préparations lubrifiantes consistant en mélanges d'huiles de toutes espèces (huiles animales, végétales, minérales, huiles de silicones etc.) Les lubrifiants solides tels que les graisses ne sont pas compris dans cette rubrique. (CTCI 33250–1A).

Paraffin wax – Paraffine

Unit : Thousand metric tons

Unité : Milliers de tonnes métriques

Country or area	1976	1977	1978	1979	1980	1981	1982	1983	1984	1985	Pays ou zone
Africa	...	...	**9**	**14**	**5**	**5**	**3**	**4**	**5**	**5**	**Afrique**
Morocco	...	...	* 9	* 14	5	5	3	* 4	* 5	* 5	Maroc
America, North	**968**	**932**	**976**	**961**	**905**	**970**	**740**	**825**	**773**	**761**	**Amérique du Nord**
Mexico	78	86	94	84	101	87	87	121	88	61	Mexique
United States	890	846	882	877	804	883	653	704	685	700	Etats–Unis
America, South	**95**	**102**	**115**	**122**	**128**	**119**	**137**	**131**	**134**	**158**	**Amérique du Sud**
Argentina	* 5	* 4	* 9	* 4	* 6	* 4	* 6	* 5	* 6	10	Argentine
Bolivia	* 0	* 0	* 0	0	0	1	1	1	* 1	* 1	Bolivie
Brazil	64	74	81	94	99	89	105	* 100	* 100	* 110	Brésil
Venezuela	26	24	25	24	23	25	* 25	* 25	* 27	* 37	Venezuela
Asia	**568**	**614**	**681**	**750**	**743**	**738**	**722**	**770**	**822**	**848**	**Asie**
Burma	9	10	11	* 13	* 12	* 13	* 12	* 13	* 12	* 13	Birmanie
China	* 350	* 350	394	426	476	459	466	470	505	* 520	Chine
India	48	49	55	69	32	52	57	63	66	77	Inde
Indonesia	34	42	38	43	32	18	13	* 18	* 20	* 27	Indonésie
Iraq	* 10	* 12	* 15	* 20	* 20	20	* 20	* 60	* 60	* 60	Iraq
Israel	5	5	* 5	* 5	* 5	* 5	* 5	* 1	* 1	* 0	Israël
Japan	112	146	163	174	166	163	145	138	151	141	Japon
Turkey	...	...	...	...	...	8	4	7	7	10	Turquie
Europe	**518**	**631**	**622**	**634**	**738**	**681**	**536**	**576**	**704**	**646**	**Europe**
EEC	***386***	***489***	***471***	***486***	***473***	***443***	***375***	***416***	***528***	***467***	***CEE***
France incl. Monaco	68	73	77	81	80	75	69	80	103	109	France y comp.Monaco
Germany, Fed. Rep.	157	176	179	179	163	149	146	166	183	176	Allemagne, Rép. féd.
Greece	0	0	0	10	17	10	6	0	0	0	Grèce
Italy and San Marino	26	30	34	31	32	31	7	37	39	41	Italie y comp. S.Mrn
Netherlands	54	124	90	87	95	96	76	77	123	* 70	Pays–Bas
United Kingdom	81	86	91	98	86	82	71	56	80	71	Royaume–Uni
EFTA	***3***	***5***	***5***	***5***	***4***	***8***	***7***	***7***	***6***	***9***	***AELE***
Portugal	3	5	5	5	4	8	7	7	6	9	Portugal
East Europe	***104***	***103***	***109***	***108***	***111***	***104***	***105***	***107***	***111***	***115***	***Europe de l'est***
Czechoslovakia	14	14	16	18	16	15	15	15	* 15	* 15	Tchécoslovaquie
Hungary	26	25	26	25	31	30	33	33	34	32	Hongrie
Poland	22	24	27	25	24	24	22	24	27	33	Pologne
Romania*	42	40	40	40	40	35	35	35	35	35	Roumanie*
Other Europe	***25***	***34***	***37***	***35***	***150***	***126***	***49***	***46***	***59***	***55***	***Autre Europe***
Spain	* 15	24	27	* 25	140	116	39	36	49	45	Espagne
Yugoslavia	10	10	* 10	* 10	* 10	* 10	* 10	* 10	* 10	* 10	Yougoslavie
Oceania	...	...	...	...	...	**2**	**14**	**10**	**15**	**10**	**Océanie**
Australia	...	...	...	...	...	2	14	10	15	10	Australie
Total	**2 149**	**2 279**	**2 403**	**2 481**	**2 519**	**2 515**	**2 152**	**2 316**	**2 453**	**2 428**	**Total**

General note.
Includes paraffin wax which is a translucent, white or yellowish crystalline hydrocarbon material of low oil content normally obtained during the refining of lubricating oil distillate, paraffin scale, slack wax, micricystalline wax and wax–emulsions, used for candle manufacture, polishes and water–proofing in food containers, wrappings etc. (SITC 33262–1).

Remarque générale.
Y compris la paraffine déshuilée qui est une substance hydrocarbure translucide blanche ou jaunâtre, de structure cristalline, à faible teneur en huile, normalement obtenue pendant le raffinage de la fraction donnant les huiles de graissage, le gatsch et autres résidus paraffineux, la cire de pétrole et les émulsions de paraffine servant à la fabrication des bougies et des encaustiques, à l'imperméabilisation des récipients et emballages contenant des produits alimentaires etc. (CTCI 33262–1).

Petroleum coke – Coke de pétrole

Unit : Thousand metric tons

Unité : Milliers de tonnes métriques

Country or area	1976	1977	1978	1979	1980	1981	1982	1983	1984	1985	Pays ou zone
America, North	**24 334**	**25 366**	**25 409**	**25 895**	**25 607**	**26 834**	**28 158**	**28 737**	**29 968**	**30 886**	**Amérique du Nord**
Canada	651	884	972	933	977	928	915	833	797	748	Canada
Cuba	15	18	19	15	20	18	18	20	24	25	Cuba
Mexico	54	17	0	40	30	46	93	68	29	23	Mexique
United States	23 614	24 447	24 418	24 907	24 580	25 842	27 132	27 816	29 118	30 090	Etats–Unis
America, South	**1 077**	**1 218**	**1 306**	**1 369**	**1 182**	**1 382**	**1 381**	**1 452**	**1 534**	**1 632**	**Amérique du Sud**
Argentina	681	746	896	810	710	869	970	983	944	941	Argentine
Brazil	118	156	176	250	182	212	210	225	278	291	Brésil
Colombia	149	151	155	200	150	140	90	100	175	150	Colombie
Uruguay	9	13	14	13	15	12	12	12	11	11	Uruguay
Venezuela	120	152	65	96	125	149	99	132	126	239	Venezuela
Asia	**1 332**	**1 378**	**1 312**	**1 341**	**1 331**	**1 357**	**1 380**	**1 316**	**1 569**	**1 639**	**Asie**
Burma	15	14	13	16	17	18	20	23	25	28	Birmanie
China	800	800	848	826	813	842	819	872	959	966	Chine
India	151	162	128	129	94	126	159	127	174	180	Inde
Indonesia	28	34	35	30	34	32	33	35	25	30	Indonésie
Japan	208	224	158	201	254	213	219	166	216	284	Japon
Syrian Arab Republic	130	144	130	139	119	126	130	93	170	151	Rép. arabe syrienne
Europe	**1 321**	**1 644**	**2 980**	**3 054**	**3 339**	**3 420**	**3 730**	**4 723**	**4 653**	**4 911**	**Europe**
EEC	***1 035***	***1 232***	***2 518***	***2 559***	***2 938***	***2 968***	***3 214***	***4 176***	***4 097***	***4 352***	***CEE***
Belgium	0	0	161	167	181	167	157	196	180	186	Belgique
France incl. Monaco	0	0	0	0	0	0	0	564	667	723	France y comp.Monaco
Germany, Fed. Rep.	882	908	948	1 020	1 056	969	1 013	1 093	1 188	1 299	Allemagne, Rép. féd.
Italy and San Marino	153	324	296	176	542	587	526	684	674	741	Italie y comp. S.Mrn
Netherlands	...	...	250	241	211	254	412	372	0	0	Pays–Bas
United Kingdom	...	...	863	955	948	991	1 106	1 267	1 388	1 403	Royaume–Uni
EFTA	***0***	***124***	***139***	***181***	***100***	***152***	***176***	***146***	***179***	***161***	***AELE***
Norway,Svlbd,J.Myn I..	0	124	139	181	100	152	176	146	179	161	Norvège,Svalbd,J.May
East Europe	***230***	***240***	***245***	***250***	***250***	***220***	***220***	***220***	***220***	***220***	***Europe de l'est***
Romania	230	240	245	250	250	220	220	220	220	220	Roumanie
Other Europe	***56***	***48***	***78***	***64***	***51***	***80***	***120***	***181***	***157***	***178***	***Autre Europe***
Spain	...	...	...	...	...	...	50	121	107	128	Espagne
Yugoslavia	56	48	78	64	51	80	70	60	50	50	Yougoslavie
Oceania	**501**	**505**	**510**	**515**	**510**	**314**	**415**	**396**	**421**	**443**	**Océanie**
Australia	501	505	510	515	510	314	415	396	421	443	Australie
Total	**28 565**	**30 111**	**31 517**	**32 174**	**31 969**	**33 307**	**35 064**	**36 624**	**38 145**	**39 511**	**Total**

General note.
The solid residue obtained by the distillation of heavier petroleum oils, used mainly in metallurgical processes. (SITC 33294–0).

Remarque générale.
Résidu solide de la distillation des fractions les plus lourdes des huiles de pétrole, utilisé principalement en métallurgie. (CTCI 33294–0).

Bitumen (asphalt) – Bitume (bral)

Unit : Thousand metric tons

Unité : Milliers de tonnes métriques

Country or area	1976	1977	1978	1979	1980	1981	1982	1983	1984	1985	Pays ou zone
Africa	**660**	**687**	**724**	**829**	**838**	**925**	**1 059**	**1 323**	**1 415**	**1 441**	**Afrique**
Algeria	56	56	57	91	54	84	115	184	209	210	Algérie
Angola	5	10	8	10	10	10	8	10	12	12	Angola
Cameroon	...	...	...	...	10	11	13	15	14	15	Cameroun
Egypt	135	147	192	220	272	280	378	509	564	599	Egypte
Ethiopia	9	11	11	15	12	18	15	14	15	12	Ethiopie
Gabon	5	13	7	15	13	13	14	12	14	13	Gabon
Kenya	44	34	22	37	31	33	29	26	31	27	Kenya
Liberia	5	4	5	3	4	3	4	4	5	5	Libéria
Libyan Arab Jamah	0	0	0	0	0	0	0	78	91	100	Jamah.arabe libyenne
Madagascar	7	3	4	4	1	1	1	0	0	0	Madagascar
Morocco	83	85	90	95	46	62	75	62	70	70	Maroc
Mozambique	16	18	18	7	25	20	20	22	22	20	Mozambique
Somalia	...	...	3	4	3	3	2	2	3	3	Somalie
South Africa	290	300	300	320	350	380	380	380	360	350	Afrique du Sud
Zambia	5	6	7	8	7	7	5	5	5	5	Zambie
America, North	**27 953**	**30 465**	**33 761**	**33 571**	**29 093**	**25 977**	**24 799**	**27 239**	**28 297**	**29 139**	**Amérique du Nord**
Barbados	5	5	5	5	6	4	4	5	4	5	Barbade
Canada	2 877	3 046	3 080	3 513	3 457	3 167	2 658	2 754	2 662	3 015	Canada
Costa Rica	6	12	17	15	14	11	9	12	12	12	Costa Rica
Cuba	179	176	202	173	196	210	198	223	234	238	Cuba
El Salvador	20	18	22	18	16	20	20	22	21	21	El Salvador
Jamaica	35	23	15	15	15	15	17	13	15	15	Jamaïque
Mexico	712	728	797	891	1 017	1 100	1 205	1 023	1 371	1 382	Mexique
Neth.Antil and Aruba	1 020	983	990	975	950	950	850	700	550	200	Antill.néer.et Aruba
Nicaragua	35	32	16	12	20	13	6	4	3	6	Nicaragua
Panama ex.Canal Zone	15	15	20	20	...	...	...	...	...	...	Panama ex.zone Canal
Panama	...	...	...	...	18	20	25	20	20	15	Panama
Trinidad and Tobago	21	32	29	46	45	55	64	32	35	35	Trinité-et-Tobago
United States	23 043	25 410	28 588	27 908	23 339	20 412	19 743	22 431	23 370	24 195	Etats-Unis
America, South	**2 154**	**2 417**	**2 983**	**3 614**	**3 110**	**3 387**	**3 365**	**2 891**	**2 891**	**3 382**	**Amérique du Sud**
Argentina	431	545	572	677	640	623	487	393	367	381	Argentine
Bolivia	0	0	0	0	0	0	3	0	1	1	Bolivie
Brazil	913	977	1 230	1 265	1 028	888	973	800	740	1 020	Brésil
Chile	9	12	15	15	6	31	23	8	7	4	Chili
Colombia	94	76	99	117	156	187	184	148	159	150	Colombie
Ecuador	0	22	65	80	52	48	49	42	66	75	Equateur
Paraguay	4	2	2	2	2	0	0	0	0	0	Paraguay
Peru	49	41	35	30	39	42	52	28	35	35	Pérou
Uruguay	37	33	48	59	51	37	54	40	37	27	Uruguay
Venezuela	617	709	917	1 369	1 136	1 531	1 540	1 432	1 479	1 689	Venezuela
Asia	**8 638**	**10 320**	**12 531**	**12 703**	**13 214**	**13 727**	**14 430**	**15 585**	**16 232**	**17 703**	**Asie**
Afghanistan	...	...	...	...	33	37	45	176	190	187	Afghanistan
Bahrain	139	179	216	228	332	356	284	217	175	167	Bahreïn
Bangladesh	0	0	0	0	0	0	0	0	13	31	Bangladesh
China	...	...	1 383	1 457	1 612	1 737	1 749	1 769	2 089	2 100	Chine
Cyprus	13	15	17	18	16	24	22	27	28	24	Chypre
India	884	959	1 025	1 027	1 102	1 285	1 300	1 216	919	1 069	Inde
Indonesia	47	83	80	85	95	83	87	19	135	150	Indonésie
Iran(Islamic Rep.of)	750	981	1 015	877	1 068	1 038	1 136	1 474	1 444	1 624	Iran(Rép.islamique)
Iraq	270	280	285	350	280	280	280	280	340	400	Iraq
Israel	...	...	...	...	40	50	109	122	90	69	Israël
Japan	4 121	4 593	5 229	5 065	4 721	4 600	4 564	4 965	5 137	4 999	Japon
Jordan	64	82	106	95	96	118	158	130	123	136	Jordanie
Korea, Republic of	184	327	326	379	317	322	333	328	415	478	Corée, République de
Kuwait,part Ntl.Zone	65	83	115	159	193	249	206	119	145	158	Koweït et prt.Zne.N.
Malaysia	0	85	104	124	135	139	144	130	168	179	Malaisie
Oman	0	0	0	0	0	0	0	25	100	120	Oman
Pakistan	89	88	100	103	121	124	122	124	127	155	Pakistan
Philippines	72	62	67	66	58	59	71	101	75	78	Philippines
S.Arabia,pt.Ntrl.Zn.	840	1 104	1 020	1 312	1 596	1 707	2 095	2 497	2 400	2 400	Arab.saoud,p.Zn.neut
Singapore	280	280	335	400	425	385	540	545	660	1 468	Singapour
Sri Lanka	27	25	25	24	26	16	25	23	35	32	Sri Lanka
Syrian Arab Republic	111	171	95	199	248	319	320	350	402	472	Rép. arabe syrienne
Thailand	141	163	158	127	119	141	129	133	153	150	Thaïlande
Turkey	264	379	431	325	292	359	336	418	488	562	Turquie
Europe	**22 735**	**22 810**	**22 891**	**23 105**	**22 047**	**20 468**	**20 280**	**20 664**	**20 451**	**20 525**	**Europe**

For general note, see end of table.

Voir la fin du tableau pour la remarque générale.

Unit : Thousand metric tons

Unité : Milliers de tonnes métriques

Country or area	1976	1977	1978	1979	1980	1981	1982	1983	1984	1985	Pays ou zone
EEC	***13 401***	***12 817***	***13 019***	***13 312***	***12 484***	***11 409***	***10 982***	***11 228***	***10 628***	***10 506***	***CEE***
Belgium	763	664	671	680	757	672	554	708	532	516	Belgique
Denmark	318	264	265	229	140	164	76	72	86	84	Danemark
France incl. Monaco	3 588	3 345	3 411	3 325	3 210	3 053	2 738	2 516	2 302	2 396	France y comp.Monaco
Germany, Fed. Rep.	3 809	3 935	3 880	3 920	3 430	3 078	2 918	3 212	3 059	2 818	Allemagne, Rép. féd.
Greece	112	62	100	121	75	108	107	172	152	163	Grèce
Italy and San Marino	1 867	1 713	1 884	2 043	2 065	2 066	1 972	1 970	1 897	2 064	Italie y comp. S.Mrn
Netherlands	1 033	934	907	918	879	533	755	780	805	701	Pays–Bas
United Kingdom	1 911	1 900	1 901	2 076	1 928	1 735	1 862	1 798	1 795	1 764	Royaume–Uni
EFTA	***1 448***	***1 553***	***1 346***	***1 695***	***1 533***	***1 389***	***1 436***	***1 393***	***1 640***	***1 605***	***AELE***
Austria	351	394	365	377	359	273	265	201	274	225	Autriche
Finland	221	255	270	314	246	271	284	353	379	334	Finlande
Norway,Svlbd,J.Myn I.	88	93	93	88	89	77	91	93	101	64	Norvège,Svalbd,J.May
Portugal	34	54	58	97	147	124	127	117	82	116	Portugal
Sweden	585	591	422	662	561	518	546	515	665	752	Suède
Switzrld,Liechtenst.	169	166	138	157	131	126	123	114	139	114	Suisse,Liechtenstein
East Europe	***6 306***	***6 720***	***6 895***	***6 456***	***6 373***	***5 712***	***5 705***	***6 026***	***6 092***	***6 173***	***Europe de l'est***
Albania	1 125	1 150	1 200	1 200	1 300	1 200	1 400	1 450	1 500	1 550	Albanie
Bulgaria	394	491	541	529	550	550	550	550	550	550	Bulgarie
Czechoslovakia	1 309	1 293	1 310	1 337	1 299	1 246	1 023	1 042	1 074	1 086	Tchécoslovaquie
German Dem. Rep.	1 088	1 199	1 119	827	650	497	520	594	670	681	Rép. dém. allemande
Hungary	594	661	684	652	648	649	616	586	530	527	Hongrie
Poland	1 144	1 207	1 315	1 215	1 255	970	996	1 154	1 118	1 129	Pologne
Romania	652	719	726	696	671	600	600	650	650	650	Roumanie
Other Europe	***1 580***	***1 720***	***1 631***	***1 642***	***1 657***	***1 958***	***2 157***	***2 017***	***2 091***	***2 241***	***Autre Europe***
Spain	1 189	1 183	997	900	1 014	1 376	1 620	1 397	1 365	1 491	Espagne
Yugoslavia	391	537	634	742	643	582	537	620	726	750	Yougoslavie
USSR	**24 300**	**25 600**	**27 000**	**30 000**	**31 000**	**31 000**	**31 000**	**31 000**	**31 000**	**30 000**	**URSS**
Oceania	**586**	**604**	**628**	**631**	**626**	**608**	**590**	**617**	**602**	**675**	**Océanie**
Australia	476	492	523	517	521	513	514	502	464	540	Australie
Guam	...	2	3	4	5	5	7	2	5	5	Guam
New Zealand	110	110	102	110	100	90	69	113	133	130	Nouvelle–Zélande
Total	**87 026**	**92 903**	**100 518**	**104 453**	**99 928**	**96 092**	**95 523**	**99 319**	**100 888**	**102 865**	**Total**

General note.
Brown to black solid or semi–solid material obtained as a residue in petroleum distillation used mainly in road surfacing. Natural asphalt is excluded. (SITC 33295–0A).

Remarque générale.
Résidu solide ou semi–solide, noir ou brun, de la distillation du pétrole, utilisé principalement pour le revêtement des routes. Cette rubrique ne comprend pas l'asphalte naturel. (CTCI 33295–0A).

Liquefied petroleum gas from natural gas plants – Gaz de pétrole liquéfiés provenant du gaz naturel

Unit : Thousand metric tons

Unité : Milliers de tonnes métriques

Country or area	1976	1977	1978	1979	1980	1981	1982	1983	1984	1985	Pays ou zone
Africa	**716**	**811**	**778**	**994**	**829**	**892**	**1 423**	**1 443**	**2 769**	**2 904**	**Afrique**
Algeria	508	535	542	652	408	470	995	944	2 206	* 2 300	Algérie
Egypt	...	...	...	...	66	72	78	99	163	204	Egypte
Libyan Arab Jamah	208	276	236	342	355	* 350	* 350	* 400	* 400	* 400	Jamah.arabe libyenne
America, North	**43 763**	**44 387**	**43 168**	**47 079**	**47 923**	**48 596**	**48 654**	**51 103**	**52 565**	**51 998**	**Amérique du Nord**
Canada	4 859	4 944	4 599	6 843	7 110	7 180	6 936	6 943	7 542	7 280	Canada
Mexico	1 356	1 414	1 520	2 126	2 959	2 047	2 312	2 987	3 106	* 3 567	Mexique
United States	37 548	38 029	37 049	38 110	37 854	39 369	39 406	41 173	41 917	41 151	Etats–Unis
America, South	**2 610**	**2 588**	**2 315**	**2 478**	**2 340**	**2 455**	**2 609**	**2 663**	**2 825**	**3 076**	**Amérique du Sud**
Argentina	285	251	* 262	* 280	* 350	533	* 625	730	774	775	Argentine
Bolivia	24	30	45	33	50	96	130	131	* 123	* 125	Bolivie
Brazil	131	141	143	147	150	167	192	219	323	430	Brésil
Chile	246	255	264	* 255	248	244	* 190	242	252	248	Chili
Colombia	152	134	134	* 126	121	123	104	* 120	* 110	* 90	Colombie
Ecuador	3	3	* 2	* 2	* 2	* 6	* 12	22	41	* 42	Equateur
Peru	7	6	6	4	7	8	6	1	5	* 5	Pérou
Venezuela	1 762	1 768	1 459	1 631	1 412	1 278	1 350	1 198	1 197	1 361	Venezuela
Asia	**6 258**	**7 587**	**8 563**	**11 531**	**12 309**	**14 404**	**19 320**	**17 245**	**17 886**	**18 414**	**Asie**
Bahrain	...	...	...	* 30	129	163	160	163	160	47	Bahreïn
Brunei Darussalam	13	14	14	18	20	9	10	20	29	* 32	Brunéi Darussalam
Indonesia	1	* 2	1	1	1	1	1	* 1	* 1	* 1	Indonésie
Iran(Islamic Rep.of)*	550	1 000	1 200	1 000	550	500	500	500	400	600	Iran(Rép.islamique)*
Iraq*	150	215	260	260	260	260	260	160	160	200	Iraq*
Japan	25	24	21	22	16	14	14	14	13	13	Japon
Kuwait,part Ntl.Zone	1 248	1 283	1 189	3 095	2 400	1 409	890	1 591	1 279	1 611	Koweït et prt.Zne.N.
Malaysia	...	...	...	...	...	...	...	...	...	162	Malaisie
Oman	...	...	...	...	...	* 400	4 387	* 4 400	* 4 500	* 4 600	Oman
Qatar	* 230	* 25	* 0	* 0	106	392	401	517	690	* 710	Qatar
S.Arabia,pt.Ntrl.Zn.	* 3 987	* 4 943	* 5 518	* 6 600	8 061	10 347	10 698	7 867	8 684	8 115	Arab.saoud,p.Zn.neut
Thailand	...	...	...	...	...	...	...	...	...	343	Thaïlande
United Arab Emirates	0	81	360	505	766	909	* 1 999	2 012	1 970	* 1 980	Emirats arabes unis
Europe	**842**	**1 157**	**1 554**	**2 251**	**1 833**	**2 000**	**3 490**	**3 948**	**4 519**	**3 540**	**Europe**
EEC	***427***	***707***	***1 066***	***1 759***	***1 409***	***1 490***	***2 236***	***2 683***	***3 143***	***2 271***	***CEE***
France incl. Monaco	293	322	306	298	300	287	271	262	256	239	France y comp.Monaco
Netherlands	...	...	135	633	700	729	933	1 009	1 410	* 945	Pays–Bas
United Kingdom	134	385	625	828	409	474	1 032	1 412	1 477	1 087	Royaume–Uni
EFTA	...	...	...	...	...	...	***710***	***737***	***852***	***776***	***AELE***
Norway,Svlbd,J.Myn I..	...	...	...	...	...	...	710	737	852	776	Norvège,Svalbd,J.May
East Europe	***155***	***209***	***256***	***239***	***224***	***227***	***235***	***232***	***238***	***213***	***Europe de l'est***
Hungary	150	204	251	234	219	221	231	232	238	213	Hongrie
Poland	5	5	5	5	5	6	4	0	0	0	Pologne
Other Europe	***260***	***241***	***232***	***253***	***200***	***283***	***309***	***296***	***286***	***280***	***Autre Europe***
Spain	260	241	232	253	153	219	226	208	196	200	Espagne
Yugoslavia	...	...	...	...	47	64	83	88	90	* 80	Yougoslavie
USSR	**1 041**	**972**	**937**	**975**	**987**	*** 995**	*** 1 015**	*** 1 035**	*** 1 060**	*** 1 080**	**URSS**
Oceania	**1 208**	**1 372**	**1 585**	**1 722**	**1 691**	**1 634**	**1 663**	**1 599**	**1 738**	**2 130**	**Océanie**
Australia	1 204	1 366	1 577	1 714	1 682	1 612	1 637	1 569	1 691	2 080	Australie
New Zealand	4	6	8	* 8	* 9	22	26	* 30	47	* 50	Nouvelle–Zélande
Total	**56 438**	**58 874**	**58 900**	**67 030**	**67 912**	**70 976**	**78 174**	**79 036**	**83 362**	**83 142**	**Total**

For general note and footnotes, see end of table.

Voir la fin du tableau pour la remarque générale et les notes.

General note.
A hydrocarbon fraction of the paraffin series lighter than gasolene produced in natural gas procesing plants. It is presented in the liquid state by compression or absorption process to facilitate storage, transport and handling. It mainly consists of butanes and propane or a mixture of them, and used in domestic heating, as fuel and as solvent. Measured at 15 degrees centigrade and standard sea–level atmospheric pressure. The data for liquefied petroleum gas from petroleum refineries are given in a separate table. (SITC 34110–2A).

Remarque générale.
Les fractions d'hydrocarbures de la série paraffinique, plus légère que la gazoline et obtenues dans les usines de traitement du gaz naturel. Ces gaz sont mis à l'etat liquide parcompression ou absorption afin d'en faciliter l'emmagasinage, la manutention et le transport. Ils se composent principalement de butanes (butane normal et isobutane), de propane ou d'un mélange de ces deux hydrocarbures. Ils sont utilisés comme combustible pour le chaffage domestique et comme solvant. Mesurés à 15 ° C et à la pression atmosphérique normale au niveau de la me. (CTCI 34110–2A).

Liquefied petroleum gas from petroleum refineries – Gaz de pétrole liquéfiés, des raffineries de pétrole

Unit : Thousand metric tons

Unité : Milliers de tonnes métriques

Country or area	1976	1977	1978	1979	1980	1981	1982	1983	1984	1985	Pays ou zone
Africa	**481**	**613**	**602**	**672**	**940**	**1 106**	**1 233**	**1 330**	**1 446**	**1 475**	**Afrique**
Algeria	144	270	235	154	295	451	558	537	600	* 610	Algérie
Angola*	7	9	10	10	12	13	10	15	13	15	Angola*
Cameroon*	...	...	...	...	10	14	16	17	19	18	Cameroun*
Congo	* 0	* 0	0	0	* 0	* 0	* 0	* 0	* 0	* 3	Congo
Côte d'Ivoire	9	11	10	* 10	* 10	10	10	* 10	* 8	* 8	Côte d'Ivoire
Egypt	59	64	70	100	138	166	169	223	254	258	Egypte
Ethiopia	3	3	3	4	4	5	5	5	5	* 5	Ethiopie
Gabon	5	6	* 6	* 6	* 5	* 5	* 6	* 5	* 6	* 6	Gabon
Ghana	* 5	13	* 7	7	7	7	7	* 7	* 7	* 7	Ghana
Kenya	18	19	19	* 21	* 24	* 22	20	* 20	23	22	Kenya
Liberia	1	0	* 1	* 0	* 1	* 1	* 1	* 1	* 1	* 1	Libéria
Libyan Arab Jamah.	18	17	27	23	47	25	* 25	* 80	* 80	* 80	Jamah.arabe libyenne
Madagascar	7	5	4	4	5	3	2	1	1	* 1	Madagascar
Morocco	71	57	70	180	196	167	195	199	207	* 210	Maroc
Mozambique	* 7	* 7	* 7	13	* 7	* 7	* 8	* 10	* 10	* 10	Mozambique
Nigeria	14	15	* 20	* 17	* 61	* 76	* 70	* 80	94	* 100	Nigéria
Senegal	6	8	8	9	8	6	3	* 2	2	* 2	Sénégal
South Africa*	59	60	60	70	70	75	80	70	65	70	Afrique du Sud*
Sudan	6	* 6	* 5	* 4	* 5	* 5	* 7	* 6	* 7	* 7	Soudan
Tunisia	26	26	27	31	28	29	30	31	31	29	Tunisie
United Rep. Tanzania	6	* 6	* 6	* 6	* 4	* 8	* 5	* 5	* 7	* 7	Rép.Unie de Tanzanie
Zaire	1	1	1	* 1	* 1	* 1	* 1	* 1	* 1	* 1	Zaïre
Zambia*	9	10	6	2	2	10	5	5	5	5	Zambie*
America, North	**13 023**	**13 667**	**14 046**	**13 624**	**13 519**	**14 457**	**13 112**	**14 636**	**15 723**	**16 330**	**Amérique du Nord**
Bahamas*	10	15	20	25	25	30	30	30	20	10	Bahamas*
Canada	1 053	1 096	1 214	1 339	1 422	1 519	1 489	1 754	1 804	1 753	Canada
Costa Rica	5	7	9	7	8	7	7	3	4	5	Costa Rica
Cuba	91	97	102	92	107	104	112	106	116	125	Cuba
Dominican Republic	49	53	62	* 65	51	42	45	45	43	* 40	Rép. dominicaine
El Salvador	22	23	26	* 28	26	24	22	* 25	* 27	* 28	El Salvador
Guatemala	5	4	4	3	2	2	2	3	5	* 5	Guatemala
Honduras	8	7	4	3	3	* 4	* 3	* 4	* 4	* 4	Honduras
Jamaica	25	22	20	23	19	12	16	18	* 19	* 20	Jamaïque
Martinique*	16	17	12	13	11	15	17	16	15	17	Martinique*
Mexico	394	649	800	712	803	* 2 211	2 414	1 867	1 797	* 1 669	Mexique
Neth.Antil and Aruba*	115	117	120	110	130	125	100	85	75	30	Antill.néer.et Aruba*
Nicaragua	16	* 17	16	15	17	* 17	16	16	14	18	Nicaragua
Panama ex.Canal Zone	31	31	27	23	...	...	...	...	...	...	Panama ex.zone Canal
Panama	...	...	...	...	22	* 20	* 25	* 20	* 20	* 20	Panama
Puerto Rico*	455	429	429	429	378	352	249	275	275	250	Porto Rico*
Trinidad and Tobago	35	40	52	65	75	77	66	* 60	57	* 50	Trinité–et–Tobago
United States	10 694	11 044	11 120	10 655	10 375	9 856	8 459	10 269	11 393	12 246	Etats–Unis
U.S. Virgin Islands*	30	30	36	40	45	40	40	40	35	40	Iles Vierges amér.*
America, South	**2 634**	**2 790**	**3 070**	**3 341**	**3 470**	**3 435**	**3 327**	**3 570**	**4 005**	**4 106**	**Amérique du Sud**
Argentina	345	384	312	* 366	* 400	350	* 400	443	429	363	Argentine
Bolivia	15	17	25	43	55	52	53	41	39	34	Bolivie
Brazil	1 570	1 567	1 918	2 007	2 192	2 265	2 099	2 369	2 516	2 853	Brésil
Chile	224	216	245	* 226	* 231	* 239	213	201	196	177	Chili
Colombia	180	175	156	148	139	158	159	234	244	* 150	Colombie
Ecuador	0	11	* 61	* 71	* 73	* 59	* 66	33	53	* 53	Equateur
Paraguay	* 4	* 4	2	3	5	3	6	7	3	4	Paraguay
Peru	95	106	105	107	100	122	132	101	124	* 125	Pérou
Uruguay	35	35	38	37	40	36	44	41	47	47	Uruguay
Venezuela	166	275	208	333	235	151	* 155	* 100	354	* 300	Venezuela
Asia	**6 963**	**7 735**	**7 908**	**8 557**	**8 104**	**8 393**	**8 643**	**9 482**	**10 202**	**14 610**	**Asie**
Bahrain	22	32	38	41	50	25	25	38	44	* 40	Bahreïn
Bangladesh	0	0	0	1	3	5	5	4	6	8	Bangladesh
Brunei Darussalam	0	0	15	* 17	* 20	9	* 5	5	3	* 5	Brunéi Darussalam
Burma*	2	2	4	2	3	3	4	3	3	4	Birmanie*
Cyprus	13	17	18	22	21	19	17	20	19	15	Chypre
Democratic Yemen	5	8	* 8	* 8	* 10	* 15	* 18	* 18	* 20	* 20	Yémen démocratique
India	354	377	401	416	367	456	522	692	844	1 130	Inde
Indonesia	25	26	32	* 375	567	560	469	* 513	* 520	580	Indonésie
Iran(Islamic Rep.of)	* 359	984	697	755	560	549	573	* 580	* 600	* 600	Iran(Rép.islamique)
Iraq*	130	140	150	150	0	100	100	100	120	200	Iraq*
Israel	136	142	* 138	* 154	* 179	* 170	* 211	* 222	* 194	* 218	Israël

For general note and footnotes, see end of table.

Voir la fin du tableau pour la remarque générale et les notes.

Unit : Thousand metric tons

Unité : Milliers de tonnes métriques

Country or area	1976	1977	1978	1979	1980	1981	1982	1983	1984	1985	Pays ou zone
Japan	4 353	4 292	4 458	4 652	4 115	4 167	4 138	4 272	4 225	8 353	Japon
Jordan	37	36	43	45	41	59	85	75	77	80	Jordanie
Korea, Republic of	223	264	282	276	328	348	425	524	556	636	Corée, République de
Lebanon*	60	50	60	60	60	50	10	10	15	20	Liban*
Malaysia	* 50	68	105	75	76	69	97	102	130	127	Malaisie
Oman	...	...	...	...	...	...	0	0	* 350	* 350	Oman
Pakistan	21	23	30	34	37	39	46	46	67	70	Pakistan
Philippines	170	148	160	168	158	124	114	141	* 148	* 155	Philippines
Qatar	4	5	6	6	8	7	6	6	37	* 50	Qatar
S.Arabia,pt.Ntrl.Zn	* 50	* 64	* 90	* 100	288	373	441	* 516	* 590	* 560	Arab.saoud,p.Zn.neut
Singapore	* 138	* 141	* 174	* 193	161	188	227	241	266	* 72	Singapour
Sri Lanka	2	3	5	6	7	6	8	7	9	12	Sri Lanka
Syrian Arab Republic	21	32	31	45	53	122	* 130	197	141	107	Rép. arabe syrienne
Thailand	121	130	118	135	125	132	105	123	132	133	Thaïlande
Turkey	344	393	366	383	394	354	371	419	496	481	Turquie
United Arab Emirates	1	3	6	9	15	9	91	143	154	* 158	Emirats arabes unis
Europe	**14 455**	**14 898**	**14 800**	**15 775**	**13 977**	**13 059**	**13 010**	**13 344**	**13 617**	**13 745**	**Europe**
EEC	***11 471***	***11 747***	***11 830***	***12 698***	***10 948***	***10 077***	***10 133***	***10 075***	***10 180***	***10 061***	***CEE***
Belgium	328	534	503	552	516	465	391	373	371	421	Belgique
Denmark	95	119	129	132	107	108	117	130	144	131	Danemark
France incl. Monaco	2 915	2 999	2 943	3 343	3 133	2 831	2 555	2 438	2 408	2 655	France y comp.Monaco
Germany, Fed. Rep.	2 821	2 760	2 835	3 165	2 468	2 278	2 265	2 065	2 148	2 230	Allemagne, Rép. féd.
Greece	137	128	146	186	182	265	258	280	246	217	Grèce
Ireland	52	60	40	36	30	7	14	23	16	16	Irlande
Italy and San Marino	2 480	2 581	2 525	2 467	2 084	1 968	2 076	2 081	2 039	1 876	Italie y comp. S.Mrn
Netherlands	1 068	1 027	1 096	1 213	931	753	1 039	1 136	1 134	* 1 000	Pays-Bas
United Kingdom	1 575	1 539	1 613	1 604	1 497	1 402	1 418	1 549	1 674	1 515	Royaume-Uni
EFTA	***579***	***675***	***606***	***780***	***861***	***908***	***876***	***978***	***940***	***998***	***AELE***
Austria	115	126	122	159	151	139	124	100	76	90	Autriche
Finland	87	100	85	112	116	143	123	146	147	158	Finlande
Norway,Svlbd,J.Myn I.	31	46	53	84	170	185	192	204	159	176	Norvège,Svalbd,J.May
Portugal	128	143	134	182	220	270	244	275	253	246	Portugal
Sweden	152	158	117	141	110	82	80	112	163	180	Suède
Switzrld,Liechtenst.	66	102	95	102	94	89	113	141	142	148	Suisse,Liechtenstein
East Europe	***984***	***1 033***	***1 048***	***983***	***965***	***959***	***987***	***1 009***	***970***	***998***	***Europe de l'est***
Bulgaria	47	56	65	70	79	67	64	85	86	85	Bulgarie
Czechoslovakia	130	133	147	164	146	143	145	141	138	138	Tchécoslovaquie
German Dem. Rep.	265	284	274	244	240	248	276	275	239	252	Rép. dém. allemande
Hungary	92	95	105	108	79	74	69	79	95	103	Hongrie
Poland	183	194	215	200	199	185	183	179	162	170	Pologne
Romania	267	271	242	197	222	242	* 250	* 250	* 250	* 250	Roumanie
Other Europe	***1 421***	***1 443***	***1 316***	***1 314***	***1 203***	***1 115***	***1 014***	***1 282***	***1 527***	***1 688***	***Autre Europe***
Spain	1 111	1 132	1 035	1 031	962	872	784	1 091	1 284	1 457	Espagne
Yugoslavia	310	311	281	283	241	243	230	191	243	* 231	Yougoslavie
USSR	**6 282**	**6 718**	**7 036**	**7 400**	**7 534**	*** 7 500**	*** 7 670**	*** 7 930**	*** 8 090**	*** 8 200**	**URSS**
Oceania	**352**	**351**	**377**	**321**	**338**	**345**	**374**	**519**	**517**	**522**	**Océanie**
Australia	349	348	374	318	334	341	371	514	512	517	Australie
Guam	* 3	3	* 3	* 3	* 4	4	3	5	* 5	* 5	Guam
Total	**44 190**	**46 772**	**47 839**	**49 690**	**47 882**	**48 295**	**47 369**	**50 811**	**53 600**	**58 988**	**Total**

General note.
A hydrocarbon fraction of the paraffin series lighter than gasolene derived from the distillation of crude petroleum only. It is presented in the liquid state by compression or absorption process to facilitate storage, transport and handling. It mainly consists of butanes and propane or a mixture of them, and used in domestic heating, as fuel and as solvent. Measured at 15 degrees centigrade and standard sea-level atmospheric pressure. The data for liquefied petroleum gas from natural gas plants are given in a separate table. (SITC 34110-3A)

Remarque générale.
Les fractions d'hydrocarbures de la série paraffinique, plus légère que la gazoline et obtunues exclusivement par distillation du pétrole brut. Ces gaz sont mis à l'etat liquide par compression ou absorption afin d'en faciliter l'emmagasinage, la manutention et le transport. Ils se composent principalement de butanes (butane normal et isobutane), de propane d'un mélange de ces deux hydrocarbures. Ils sont utilisés comme combustible pour le chauffage domestique et comme solvant. Mesurés à 15° C et à la pression atmosphérique normale au niveau de la mer. (CTCI 34110-3A).

Hard-coal briquettes – Agglomérés (briquettes de houille)

Unit : Thousand metric tons — Unité : Milliers de tonnes métriques

Country or area	1976	1977	1978	1979	1980	1981	1982	1983	1984	1985	Pays ou zone
Africa	**17**	**11**	**7**	**5**	**0**	**0**	**0**	**0**	**0**	**0**	**Afrique**
Morocco	17	11	7	5	0	0	* 0	* 0	* 0	* 0	Maroc
Asia	**14 501**	**16 573**	**15 281**	**15 329**	**18 497**	**18 955**	**18 248**	**19 288**	**21 587**	**23 440**	**Asie**
Afghanistan	44	35	49	30	38	* 42	* 40	* 42	* 40	* 40	Afghanistan
Japan	495	511	412	517	422	370	321	286	231	300	Japon
Korea, Republic of	13 962	16 027	14 820	14 782	18 037	18 543	17 887	18 960	21 316	23 100	Corée, République de
Europe	**7 558**	**7 090**	**7 230**	**7 359**	**6 580**	**6 265**	**6 094**	**5 500**	**4 436**	**5 281**	**Europe**
EEC	***5 247***	***4 754***	***4 818***	***4 961***	***4 230***	***3 968***	***3 743***	***3 599***	***3 101***	***3 662***	***CEE***
Belgium	166	126	125	152	82	54	50	45	45	28	Belgique
France incl. Monaco	2 516	2 222	2 175	2 134	1 757	1 596	1 491	1 509	1 448	1 408	France y comp.Monaco
Germany, Fed. Rep.	1 357	1 305	1 453	1 673	1 455	1 332	1 283	1 244	1 437	1 564	Allemagne, Rép. féd.
Italy and San Marino	25	28	12	22	10	10	0	0	0	0	Italie y comp. S.Mrn
United Kingdom	1 183	1 073	1 053	980	926	976	919	801	171	662	Royaume-Uni
EFTA	***1***	***1***	***0***	***0***	***0***	***0***	***0***	***0***	***0***	***0***	***AELE***
Portugal	1	1	0	0	0	0	0	* 0	* 0	* 0	Portugal
East Europe	***2 217***	***2 259***	***2 362***	***2 356***	***2 317***	***2 261***	***2 325***	***1 878***	***1 319***	***1 608***	***Europe de l'est***
Poland	1 517	1 539	1 612	1 606	1 567	1 511	1 575	1 128	569	858	Pologne
Romania*	700	720	750	750	750	750	750	750	750	750	Roumanie*
Other Europe	***93***	***76***	***50***	***42***	***33***	***36***	***26***	***23***	***16***	***11***	***Autre Europe***
Spain	93	76	50	42	33	36	26	23	16	11	Espagne
USSR*	**1 355**	**755**	**700**	**427**	**285**	**271**	**234**	**200**	**200**	**200**	**URSS***
Oceania	**11**	**10**	**10**	**10**	**17**	**7**	**6**	**6**	**6**	**6**	**Océanie**
New Zealand	11	10	10	* 10	* 17	7	6	* 6	6	* 6	Nouvelle-Zélande
Total	**23 442**	**24 439**	**23 228**	**23 130**	**25 379**	**25 498**	**24 582**	**24 994**	**26 229**	**28 927**	**Total**

General note.
Briquettes, ovoids and similar solid fuels manufactured from hard coal by agglomerating the particles of coal with pitch. Solid smokeless patent fuels are included. (SITC 32150-0).

Remarque générale.
Briquettes, boulets et combustibles solides analogues fabriqués à partir de la houille par agglomération du poussier de houille avec du brai. Cette rubrique comprend les agglomérés solides brûlant sans fumée. (CTCI 32150-0).

Brown–coal briquettes – Briquettes de lignite

Unit : Thousand metric tons

Unité : Milliers de tonnes métriques

Country or area	1976	1977	1978	1979	1980	1981	1982	1983	1984	1985	Pays ou zone
Asia	**65**	**62**	**69**	**42**	**75**	**136**	**156**	**161**	**166**	**242**	**Asie**
India	48	43	49	24	55	115	133	* 130	144	* 205	Inde
Turkey	17	19	20	18	20	21	23	31	22	37	Turquie
Europe	**57 429**	**57 196**	**56 652**	**58 028**	**60 686**	**61 716**	**61 719**	**61 667**	**61 139**	**62 071**	**Europe**
EEC	***4 710***	***4 338***	***4 173***	***5 044***	***6 628***	***6 617***	***6 132***	***6 021***	***6 438***	***6 646***	***CEE***
Germany, Fed. Rep.	4 390	4 104	3 889	4 752	6 381	6 419	6 022	5 868	6 254	6 517	Allemagne, Rép. féd.
Greece	320	234	284	292	247	198	110	153	184	129	Grèce
East Europe	***52 573***	***52 749***	***52 303***	***52 821***	***54 058***	***54 169***	***54 613***	***54 646***	***54 701***	***55 425***	***Europe de l'est***
Bulgaria	1 209	1 263	1 146	1 336	1 493	1 428	1 443	1 360	1 213	1 316	Bulgarie
Czechoslovakia	1 311	1 255	1 130	1 117	1 159	1 069	1 111	1 104	1 069	1 118	Tchécoslovaquie
German Dem. Rep.	48 679	48 749	48 468	48 698	49 693	49 803	50 005	50 047	50 270	50 666	Rép. dém. allemande
Hungary	1 018	1 105	1 169	1 251	1 250	1 327	1 492	1 533	1 549	1 722	Hongrie
Poland	156	157	140	144	163	142	162	152	150	153	Pologne
Romania*	200	220	250	275	300	400	400	450	450	450	Roumanie*
Other Europe	***146***	***109***	***176***	***163***	...	***930***	***974***	***1 000***	***0***	***0***	***Autre Europe***
Yugoslavia	146	109	176	163	...	930	974	* 1 000	* 0	* 0	Yougoslavie
USSR	*** 7 200**	*** 7 800**	*** 7 300**	*** 7 000**	**6 785**	**6 800**	**6 434**	**5 376**	**5 519**	**4 884**	**URSS**
Oceania	**947**	**1 037**	**1 064**	**1 131**	**1 253**	**1 081**	**993**	**745**	**818**	**802**	**Océanie**
Australia	947	1 037	1 064	1 131	1 253	1 081	993	745	818	802	Australie
Total	**65 641**	**66 095**	**65 085**	**66 201**	**68 799**	**69 733**	**69 302**	**67 949**	**67 642**	**67 999**	**Total**

General note.
A solid fuel manufactured from brown coal by a process in which the brown coal is partly dried, warmed to expel additional water, and then compressed in moulds into briquettes, usually without the use of a binding substance. (SITC 32160–2).

Remarque générale.
Combustible solide fabriqué à partir du lignite par un procédé qui consiste à sécher partiellement le lignite, à le chauffer pour en éliminer l'eau en excédent, et à le presser ensuite dans des moules pour en faire des briquettes, habituellement sans addition de liants. (CTCI 32160–2).

Unit : Thosusand metric tons

Unité : Milliers de tonnes métriques

Country or area	1976	1977	1978	1979	1980	1981	1982	1983	1984	1985	Pays ou zone
Africa	**2 469**	**2 927**	**2 601**	**2 607**	**2 591**	**2 799**	**2 906**	**2 870**	**2 895**	**2 951**	**Afrique**
Egypt	628	693	691	* 755	* 730	* 950	974	915	* 930	* 980	Egypte
South Africa	1 576	1 964	* 1 660	1 592	* 1 584	* 1 590	* 1 620	* 1 700	* 1 750	* 1 750	Afrique du Sud
United Rep. Tanzania*	...	1	0	0	0	0	0	0	0	1	Rép.Unie de Tanzanie*
Zambia	* 50	* 75	* 73	60	50	* 50	55	* 35	* 35	* 30	Zambie
Zimbabwe	215	194	177	200	227	209	* 257	* 220	* 180	* 190	Zimbabwe
America, North	**64 422**	**60 527**	**56 069**	**60 238**	**50 006**	**46 417**	**32 491**	**30 529**	**35 556**	**33 278**	**Amérique du Nord**
Canada	5 289	4 845	4 968	5 685	5 250	4 659	3 999	4 120	4 901	4 684	Canada
Mexico	2 275	3 007	3 021	3 174	2 906	2 943	2 986	2 996	2 931	2 613	Mexique
United States	56 858	52 675	48 080	51 379	41 850	38 815	25 506	23 413	27 724	25 981	Etats-Unis
America, South	**4 314**	**4 740**	**4 911**	**5 287**	**5 487**	**5 211**	**5 033**	**5 619**	**7 319**	**8 528**	**Amérique du Sud**
Argentina	738	610	620	539	* 520	467	* 425	* 318	* 336	663	Argentine
Brazil	2 877	3 428	3 575	4 048	4 265	4 068	4 020	4 715	6 357	7 216	Brésil
Chile	235	256	240	270	286	310	240	252	290	301	Chili
Colombia*	420	400	439	396	377	327	313	300	300	310	Colombie*
Peru	44	45	35	31	33	33	34	31	35	* 37	Pérou
Uruguay	0	1	2	3	6	6	1	3	1	1	Uruguay
Asia	**86 002**	**88 162**	**90 883**	**97 123**	**101 360**	**100 553**	**100 187**	**101 640**	**106 726**	**110 493**	**Asie**
China	* 25 000	26 830	32 690	33 540	34 047	31 718	33 106	34 508	36 150	38 360	Chine
India	9 620	* 12 000	11 661	11 422	11 342	11 773	11 721	11 610	10 969	11 637	Inde
Iran(Islamic Rep.of)*	400	400	450	400	400	300	300	300	350	400	Iran(Rép.islamique)*
Japan	46 084	43 838	40 720	44 345	47 464	47 242	44 777	44 833	48 145	48 622	Japon
Korea,Dem.Ppl's.Rep.*	2 500	2 600	2 700	2 800	3 000	3 000	3 300	3 400	3 400	3 500	Corée,Rép.pop.dém.de*
Korea, Republic of	960	1 165	1 319	2 331	2 965	4 401	4 539	4 682	5 199	5 253	Corée, République de
Turkey	1 210	1 100	1 106	2 045	1 915	1 900	2 285	2 157	2 372	2 589	Turquie
Europe	**119 741**	**113 366**	**109 720**	**113 961**	**114 883**	**109 805**	**106 276**	**99 681**	**98 837**	**102 323**	**Europe**
EEC	***76 244***	***68 464***	***64 318***	***67 542***	***67 538***	***64 427***	***60 702***	***53 721***	***53 043***	***57 546***	***CEE***
Belgium	6 216	5 569	5 747	6 450	6 048	6 004	5 217	5 106	5 926	5 964	Belgique
Denmark	...	...	...	...	...	...	67	23	0	0	Danemark
France incl. Monaco	11 313	10 770	10 682	11 615	11 118	10 723	9 934	8 458	8 999	8 691	France y comp.Monaco
Germany, Fed. Rep.	31 951	27 499	25 593	26 697	29 347	28 300	26 665	22 984	21 467	23 232	Allemagne, Rép. féd.
Greece	337	255	186	228	246	45	0	0	* 0	0	Grèce
Italy and San Marino	7 970	7 676	7 315	7 501	8 264	8 054	7 672	6 492	6 943	7 410	Italie y comp. S.Mrn
Netherlands	2 693	2 501	2 401	2 530	2 455	2 242	2 428	2 126	2 726	2 973	Pays-Bas
United Kingdom	15 764	14 194	12 394	12 521	10 060	9 059	8 719	8 532	6 982	9 276	Royaume-Uni
EFTA	***3 219***	***2 951***	***2 981***	***3 405***	***3 482***	***3 290***	***3 400***	***3 452***	***3 643***	***3 541***	***AELE***
Austria	1 615	1 458	1 484	1 689	1 729	1 652	1 662	1 725	1 854	1 751	Autriche
Norway,Svlbd,J.Myn I.	286	317	320	341	349	346	341	314	321	312	Norvège,Svalbd,J.May
Portugal	246	258	244	223	216	198	214	249	237	* 275	Portugal
Sweden	1 072	918	933	1 152	1 188	1 094	1 183	1 164	1 231	1 203	Suède
East Europe	***34 136***	***35 909***	***36 465***	***36 684***	***37 084***	***35 327***	***35 269***	***35 544***	***35 352***	***34 251***	***Europe de l'est***
Albania*	15	15	15	15	15	15	15	16	17	18	Albanie*
Bulgaria	1 408	1 446	1 411	1 351	1 348	1 381	1 274	1 270	1 186	1 087	Bulgarie
Czechoslovakia	10 893	10 861	10 785	10 458	10 323	10 324	10 566	10 340	10 303	* 10 300	Tchécoslovaquie
German Dem. Rep.	660	625	603	596	1 322	1 238	1 226	1 193	1 179	1 257	Rép. dém. allemande
Hungary	773	759	764	788	975	958	947	877	703	607	Hongrie
Poland	17 915	19 055	19 429	20 410	20 068	18 478	17 728	17 580	17 115	16 239	Pologne
Romania	2 472	3 148	3 458	3 066	3 033	2 933	3 513	4 268	4 849	4 743	Roumanie
Other Europe	***6 142***	***6 042***	***5 956***	***6 330***	***6 779***	***6 761***	***6 905***	***6 964***	***6 799***	***6 985***	***Autre Europe***
Spain	4 356	4 277	3 886	3 843	4 151	4 068	4 126	3 524	3 283	3 440	Espagne
Yugoslavia	1 786	1 765	2 070	2 487	2 628	2 693	2 779	3 440	3 516	3 545	Yougoslavie
USSR*	**84 400**	**86 000**	**86 400**	**86 000**	**86 000**	**82 000**	**83 000**	**84 000**	**84 000**	**86 000**	**URSS***
Oceania	**5 310**	**5 163**	**4 944**	**5 336**	**4 987**	**5 425**	**4 747**	**3 685**	**3 571**	**3 611**	**Océanie**
Australia	5 310	5 132	4 916	5 306	4 987	5 421	4 745	3 678	3 563	3 603	Australie
New Zealand	0	31	28	* 30	0	4	2	7	8	* 8	Nouvelle-Zélande

For general note and footnotes, see end of table.

Voir la fin du tableau pour la remarque générale et les notes.

Unit : Thousand metric tons

Unité : Milliers de tonnes métriques

Country or area	1976	1977	1978	1979	1980	1981	1982	1983	1984	1985	Pays ou zone
Total	**366 658**	**360 885**	**355 528**	**370 552**	**365 314**	**352 210**	**334 640**	**328 024**	**338 904**	**347 184**	**Total**

General note.
Coke is the solid residue obtained in the dry distillation of hard coal or lignite in the total or partial absence of air (carbonization). The data include: gas coke – a by–product of coal used for the production of manufactured or town gas in gasworks; and coke–oven coke – all other coke produced from hard coal. (SITC 32180–0).

Remarque générale.
Résidu solide obtenu lors de la distillation à sec de houille ou de lignite en l'absence totale ou partielle d'air (carbonisation). Les données comprennent le coke de gaz, sous–produit de l'utilisation du charbon pour la production de gas manufacturé ou de gaz de ville dans les usines à gas, et le coke de four, regroupant tous les cokes produits à partir de houille. (CTCI 32180–0)

Gas produced by cokeries – Gaz de cokerie

Unit : Terajoules | Unité : Terajoules

Country or area	1976	1977	1978	1979	1980	1981	1982	1983	1984	1985	Pays ou zone
Africa	**34 146**	**38 925**	**37 925**	**40 600**	**44 410**	**45 000**	**45 500**	**47 500**	**45 600**	**46 100**	**Afrique**
South Africa	32 221	37 000	36 000	39 500	42 410	* 43 000	* 44 000	* 46 000	* 44 500	* 45 000	Afrique du Sud
Zimbabwe*	1 925	1 925	1 925	1 100	2 000	2 000	1 500	1 500	1 100	1 100	Zimbabwe*
America, North	**597 863**	**560 989**	**528 596**	**564 842**	**506 918**	**440 649**	**313 213**	**282 493**	**331 324**	**316 101**	**Amérique du Nord**
Canada	50 136	45 770	47 268	53 548	49 540	43 778	37 786	38 943	45 453	43 101	Canada
Mexico*	18 268	24 777	27 450	27 164	27 128	27 000	27 000	28 000	25 500	26 000	Mexique*
United States	529 459	490 442	453 878	484 130	430 250	369 871	248 427	215 550	260 371	* 247 000	Etats–Unis
America, South	**31 891**	**38 834**	**41 430**	**42 909**	**44 299**	**40 174**	**43 224**	**49 729**	**61 435**	**70 116**	**Amérique du Sud**
Argentina	* 5 012	* 4 674	* 5 286	* 4 495	* 3 957	* 3 693	* 3 371	3 605	3 836	6 040	Argentine
Brazil	* 22 432	27 215	28 343	31 429	32 653	29 844	32 312	38 266	50 494	57 088	Brésil
Chile	4 199	3 869	4 530	* 3 868	* 5 000	* 3 931	* 4 962	* 5 000	4 111	3 843	Chili
Colombia*	...	2 849	3 065	2 880	2 421	2 448	2 311	2 600	2 700	2 850	Colombie*
Peru*	248	227	206	237	268	258	268	258	294	295	Pérou*
Asia	**426 666**	**406 208**	**379 058**	**389 432**	**419 613**	**438 564**	**418 966**	**412 397**	**367 459**	**372 157**	**Asie**
India*	31 401	31 401	31 401	31 500	31 650	31 775	32 000	29 000	27 500	30 300	Inde*
Indonesia*	46	46	50	56	60	65	75	80	90	95	Indonésie*
Japan	385 173	365 761	342 043	352 267	* 373 403	391 068	371 771	366 221	321 747	322 208	Japon
Turkey	10 046	9 000	5 564	5 609	14 500	15 656	15 120	17 096	18 122	19 554	Turquie
Europe	**904 811**	**854 808**	**826 634**	**833 999**	**832 623**	**799 948**	**771 925**	**750 257**	**711 266**	**745 915**	**Europe**
EEC	***606 898***	***545 111***	***512 249***	***532 188***	***525 084***	***508 794***	***477 505***	***461 133***	***424 033***	***454 431***	***CEE***
Belgium	47 490	42 768	43 132	48 039	44 973	45 199	39 202	39 563	45 850	44 945	Belgique
France incl. Monaco	101 452	97 193	93 999	94 845	95 638	89 964	85 456	75 639	79 491	76 325	France y comp.Monaco
Germany, Fed. Rep.	258 025	222 331	207 852	215 709	233 261	229 671	215 973	218 737	173 634	188 177	Allemagne, Rép. féd.
Greece	3 164	2 395	1 746	2 139	2 311	418	0	* 0	* 0	0	Grèce
Italy and San Marino	67 331	64 205	61 798	60 341	60 739	61 446	56 913	50 064	53 409	56 574	Italie y comp. S.Mrn
Netherlands	23 422	20 971	21 427	23 440	22 854	21 114	23 304	20 262	25 439	24 683	Pays–Bas
United Kingdom	106 014	95 248	82 295	87 675	65 308	60 982	56 657	56 868	46 210	63 727	Royaume–Uni
EFTA	***27 430***	***25 133***	***24 536***	***26 695***	***27 261***	***26 021***	***27 624***	***26 444***	***28 987***	***27 115***	***AELE***
Austria	15 308	13 826	13 434	13 631	13 964	13 499	13 318	13 511	15 412	13 025	Autriche
Norway,Svlbd,J.Myn I.	2 323	3 072	2 882	3 053	3 053	2 961	3 177	2 653	2 522	2 628	Norvège,Svalbd,J.May
Portugal	1 796	1 789	1 522	1 688	1 837	1 623	1 734	1 854	1 959	2 252	Portugal
Sweden	8 003	6 446	6 698	8 323	8 407	7 938	9 395	8 426	9 094	9 210	Suède
East Europe	***229 603***	***243 428***	***250 743***	***236 791***	***238 611***	***223 013***	***212 238***	***210 069***	***209 232***	***211 966***	***Europe de l'est***
Bulgaria	5 027	4 943	4 780	4 500	4 065	3 830	3 646	3 454	3 206	3 323	Bulgarie
Czechoslovakia	71 990	81 487	84 329	79 081	77 321	75 264	68 946	67 355	67 718	66 662	Tchécoslovaquie
Hungary	5 081	6 445	6 284	6 472	6 398	6 212	6 005	5 356	4 079	3 477	Hongrie
Poland	125 320	128 577	132 746	123 738	126 827	113 707	109 641	108 904	108 229	112 504	Pologne
Romania*	22 185	21 976	22 604	23 000	24 000	24 000	24 000	25 000	26 000	26 000	Roumanie*
Other Europe	***40 880***	***41 136***	***39 106***	***38 325***	***41 667***	***42 120***	***54 558***	***52 611***	***49 014***	***52 403***	***Autre Europe***
Spain	32 290	32 336	31 179	29 048	31 140	30 995	34 920	27 369	26 681	29 789	Espagne
Yugoslavia	8 590	8 800	7 927	9 277	10 527	11 125	19 638	25 242	22 333	22 614	Yougoslavie
USSR	**593 038**	**607 355**	**605 999**	**593 424**	**595 969**	*** 575 000**	**562 582**	**562 361**	**564 477**	**552 652**	**URSS**
Oceania	**56 418**	**55 219**	**39 022**	**41 647**	**39 457**	**41 062**	**37 660**	**28 879**	**28 280**	**26 833**	**Océanie**
Australia	56 418	55 219	39 022	41 647	39 457	41 062	37 660	28 879	28 280	26 833	Australie
Total	**2 644 833**	**2 562 338**	**2 458 664**	**2 506 853**	**2 483 289**	**2 380 397**	**2 193 070**	**2 133 616**	**2 109 841**	**2 129 874**	**Total**

General note.
Gas made in coke ovens or plants for the gasification of coal owned by industrial groups not dependent on gas undertakings proper, measured at 15 degrees centigrade and standard sea–level atmospheric pressure (760 mm Hg). Production should include gas consumed for heating furnaces and other internal uses by the producing establishment. (SITC 34120–1B).

Remarque générale.
Gaz produits dans les fours à coke ou les installations de gazéfication de la houille, appartenant à des groupements industriels dont la production de gaz n'est pas l'activité principale, mesurés à 15° C à la pression atmosphérique normale au niveau de la mer (760 mm de mercure). La production indiquée devrait comprendre le gaz consommé pour le chauffage des fours et pour d'autres utilisations internes de l'établissement producteur. (CTCI 34120–1B).

Tars – Goudrons

Unit : Thousand metric tons

Unité : Milliers de tonnes métriques

Country or area	1976	1977	1978	1979	1980	1981	1982	1983	1984	1985	Pays ou zone
America, North	**2 907**	**2 729**	**2 825**	**2 827**	**2 827**	**2 826**	**2 827**	**2 819**	**2 820**	**2 825**	**Amérique du Nord**
Mexico	20	40	37	39	39	38	39	31	32	...	Mexique
United States	2 887	2 689	...	...	...	...	...	...	...	...	Etats–Unis
America, South	**176**	**127**	**170**	**207**	**199**	**176**	**176**	**176**	**176**	**176**	**Amérique du Sud**
Brazil	...	127	170	207	199	...	...	...	...	...	Brésil
Asia	**2 484**	**2 520**	**2 330**	**2 429**	**2 613**	**2 576**	**2 583**	**2 604**	**2 629**	**2 653**	**Asie**
Japan	2 484	2 520	2 330	2 429	2 613	2 576	2 583	...	...	...	Japon
Europe	**3 484**	**3 313**	**3 090**	**3 174**	**3 303**	**3 124**	**3 046**	**2 893**	**2 843**	**2 852**	**Europe**
EEC	***2 302***	***2 096***	***1 856***	***1 987***	***2 092***	***2 016***	***1 964***	***1 811***	***1 810***	***1 820***	***CEE***
Belgium	230	209	164	203	188	198	174	170	195	203	Belgique
Denmark	0	0	0	...	...	18	33	31	42	34	Danemark
France	437	421	419	423	431	384	390	344	344	317	France
Germany, Fed. Rep.	1 247	1 090	1 011	1 067	1 130	1 089	1 040	939	902	939	Allemagne, Rép. féd.
Italy	285	282	258	275	...	...	...	...	...	...	Italie
Netherlands	103	94	4	8	...	...	...	...	...	...	Pays–Bas
EFTA	***160***	***158***	***155***	***152***	***146***	***149***	***130***	***145***	***116***	***151***	***AELE***
Austria	133	123	123	110	103	108	86	98	69	105	Autriche
Finland	2	0	0	0	...	...	...	...	...	...	Finlande
Sweden	25	35	32	42	42	40	43	46	46	45	Suède
East Europe	***838***	***878***	***911***	***879***	***860***	***792***	***783***	***793***	***761***	***729***	***Europe de l'est***
Hungary	43	39	40	41	41	41	39	34	27	23	Hongrie
Poland	795	839	871	838	819	751	744	759	734	706	Pologne
Other Europe	***184***	***181***	***168***	***156***	***205***	***167***	***169***	***144***	***156***	***153***	***Autre Europe***
Spain	184	181	168	156	205	167	169	144	...	...	Espagne
Total	**9 051**	**8 689**	**8 415**	**8 637**	**8 942**	**8 702**	**8 632**	**8 491**	**8 467**	**8 506**	**Total**

General note.
Tars obtained from coal, lignite, peat and water gas. Tars extracted from non–mineral sources are excluded. (SITC 52110–0).

Remarque générale.
Goudrons obtenus à partir de la houille, du lignite, de la tourbe et du gaz à l'eau. Cette rubrique ne comprend pas les goudrons de provenance non minérale. (CTCI 52110–0).

Inner tubes, rubber, for motor vehicles – Chambres à air en caoutchouc pour véhicules à moteur

Unit : Thousand units — Unité : En milliers

Country or area	1976	1977	1978	1979	1980	1981	1982	1983	1984	1985	Pays ou zone
Africa	**4 551**	**4 696**	**4 990**	**4 843**	**5 509**	**5 954**	**5 787**	**5 513**	**5 682**	**5 758**	**Afrique**
Egypt	...	...	...	484	599	649	670	770	...	...	Egypte
Nigeria	725	...	...	...	...	...	...	...	...	...	Nigéria
South Africa	3 417	3 432	3 566	3 364	3 917	4 275	4 047	3 652	3 735	3 629	Afrique du Sud
Tunisia	94	160	256	270	268	305	345	366	396	514	Tunisie
America, North	**35 930**	**50 384**	**46 300**	**47 497**	**43 085**	**39 087**	**42 505**	**41 857**	**42 049**	**41 438**	**Amérique du Nord**
Canada[1,2]	2 264	...	...	3 401	3 010	...	...	...	...	...	Canada[1,2]
Cuba[2]	190	151	221	193	354	359	185	268	313	322	Cuba[2]
Jamaica	154	123	142	111	92	110	101	87	70	67	Jamaïque
Mexico[3]	6 122	5 318	6 045	6 192	7 629	6 726	7 220	7 077	7 815	7 772	Mexique[3]
United States	27 200	41 900	37 000	37 600	32 000	29 000	...	...	...	...	Etats–Unis
America, South	**18 777**	**19 760**	**20 832**	**23 913**	**22 809**	**17 288**	**20 673**	**20 887**	**19 109**	**19 003**	**Amérique du Sud**
Argentina[4]	3 537	3 515	3 269	4 165	3 711	2 373	3 549	4 560	3 407	2 269	Argentine[4]
Brazil	13 110	14 050	15 611	17 569	16 798	12 948	15 655	14 830	14 189	...	Brésil
Chile	319	439	402	743	864	726	382	336	427	424	Chili
Ecuador	231	270	235	...	362	331	457	699	...	...	Equateur
Peru[5]	...	...	...	350	379	348	302	220	220	277	Pérou[5]
Venezuela	1 138	1 068	921	747	* 695	562	328	242	258	221	Venezuela
Asia	**57 324**	**57 642**	**61 038**	**66 948**	**72 529**	**67 583**	**61 928**	**71 843**	**81 326**	**79 773**	**Asie**
India	3 392	3 570	4 035	3 887	4 366	4 741	4 822	4 902	5 649	...	Inde
Indonesia	* 626	1 374	1 883	1 663	2 550	2 930	2 411	2 910	3 695	...	Indonésie
Iran(Islamic Rep.of)[6]	3 490	3 328	1 541	1 734	985	1 175	1 440	...	...	...	Iran(Rép.islamique)[6]
Israel	593	572	618	555	455	401	439	362	333	237	Israël
Japan	37 028	35 643	34 949	35 645	35 639	31 514	27 100	30 886	28 328	27 774	Japon
Korea, Republic of	3 628	5 025	8 797	13 658	17 535	16 201	16 073	21 833	32 298	27 189	Corée, République de
Malaysia[7,8]	5 130	5 246	5 793	6 099	6 169	6 493	# 5 199	4 939	4 487	5 948	Malaisie[7,8]
Pakistan[9]	143	137	159	197	201	189	136	134	122	...	Pakistan[9]
Philippines[1]	566	94	...	...	...	...	...	...	...	...	Philippines[1]
Sri Lanka	[10] 147	[10] 183	[10] 241	[10] 266	# 178	143	* 165	* 173	219	178	Sri Lanka
Thailand	918	# [2] 1 049	[2] 1 088	[2] 1 297	[2] 1 219	[2] 1 369	...	...	...	...	Thaïlande
Turkey	1 663	1 421	1 604	1 617	2 902	2 097	2 359	2 936	3 626	6 443	Turquie
Europe	**85 708**	**96 972**	**94 288**	**95 235**	**90 143**	**84 083**	**74 609**	**65 253**	**66 939**	**66 002**	**Europe**
EEC	***65 164***	***69 056***	***67 959***	***65 840***	***63 946***	***56 095***	***49 302***	***43 383***	***42 622***	***41 585***	***CEE***
France	23 430	23 520	22 600	22 020	22 400	20 008	18 739	17 816	19 093	17 964	France
Germany, Fed. Rep.	5 612	5 652	5 764	5 450	4 722	3 885	2 715	2 080	1 329	1 159	Allemagne, Rép. féd.
Italy	26 749	30 915	30 855	29 975	28 929	25 497	23 159	18 438	17 845	18 801	Italie
United Kingdom	9 373	8 969	8 740	8 395	7 895	6 705	4 689	...	...	...	Royaume–Uni
EFTA	***2 373***	***2 469***	***2 524***	***2 611***	***2 518***	***2 311***	***1 933***	***2 087***	***1 967***	***1 581***	***AELE***
Finland	730	513	587	564	457	476	376	422	297	...	Finlande
Portugal	935	1 070	1 060	1 131	1 227	1 289	1 155	1 139	1 071	761	Portugal
Sweden	708	886	877	916	834	546	402	526	599	538	Suède
East Europe	***6 911***	***6 796***	***6 529***	***6 707***	***6 807***	***7 165***	***6 880***	***6 993***	***7 218***	***7 572***	***Europe de l'est***
Bulgaria[11]	1 470	1 435	1 219	1 170	1 223	1 601	1 658	1 812	1 871	2 110	Bulgarie[11]
Czechoslovakia	4 798	4 777	4 758	4 962	5 000	5 070	4 626	4 661	4 706	4 683	Tchécoslovaquie
Hungary	643	584	552	575	584	494	596	520	641	779	Hongrie
Other Europe	***11 260***	***18 651***	***17 276***	***20 077***	***16 872***	***18 512***	***16 494***	***12 790***	***15 132***	***15 264***	***Autre Europe***
Spain	8 187	15 301	...	14 726	10 916	13 234	12 412	9 139	...	...	Espagne
Yugoslavia	3 073	3 350	5 117	5 351	5 956	5 278	4 082	3 651	3 571	3 802	Yougoslavie
Oceania	**5 626**	**5 263**	**5 484**	**5 191**	**4 956**	**4 469**	**3 805**	**3 734**	**3 401**	**3 101**	**Océanie**
Australia[9,11]	4 727	4 259	4 435	4 147	3 936	3 488	2 840	...	...	...	Australie[9,11]
New Zealand[3]	899	1 004	1 049	1 044	1 020	981	965	858	800	775	Nouvelle–Zélande[3]
Total	**207 916**	**234 717**	**232 932**	**243 627**	**239 031**	**218 464**	**209 307**	**209 087**	**218 506**	**215 074**	**Total**

General note. — **Remarque générale.**

Inner tubes, rubber, for motor vehicles (continued) – Chambres à air en caoutchouc pour véhicules à moteur (suite)

Rubber inner tubes for motor vehicles other than bicycles and motorcycles. (Part of SITC 62910–1).

[1] Shipments.
[2] Inner tubes of all types.
[3] Including inner tubes for bicycles and motorcycles.
[4] Including inner tubes for agricultural vehicles and aircraft.
[5] Including inner tubes for agricultural vehicles.
[6] Production by establishments employing 50 or more persons.
[7] Data refer to Peninsular Malaysia only.
[8] Beginning 1982, scope of series revised.
[9] Twelve months ending 30 June of year stated.
[10] Including flaps.
[11] Including inner tubes for motorcycles.

Chambres à air en caoutchouc pour véhicules à moteur, à l'exclusion des chambres à air pour bicyclettes et motocyclettes. (Partie de CTCI 62910–1).

[1] Expéditions.
[2] Chambres à air de tous genres.
[3] Y compris les chambres à air pour bicyclettes et motocyclettes.
[4] Y compris les chambres à air pour véhicules agricoles et pour aéronefs.
[5] Y compris les chambres à air pour véhicules agricoles.
[6] Production des établissements occupant 50 personnes ou plus.
[7] Données se rapportant à la Malaisie péninsulaire seulement.
[8] A partir de 1982, portée de la série révisée.
[9] Période de douze mois finissant le 30 juin de l'année indiquée.
[10] Y compris les 'flaps'.
[11] Y compris les chambres à air pour motocyclettes.

Inner tubes, rubber, for bicycles and motorcycles – Chambres à air en caoutchouc pour bicyclettes et motocyclettes

Unit : Thousand units | Unité : En milliers

Country or area	1976	1977	1978	1979	1980	1981	1982	1983	1984	1985	Pays ou zone
Africa	**4 322**	**5 466**	**5 329**	**4 863**	**4 990**	**5 016**	**5 109**	**5 714**	**5 348**	**5 281**	**Afrique**
Egypt[1]	497	1 075	901	512	632	693	688	796	...	...	Egypte[1]
Mozambique	...	...	...	...	81	135	96	78	43	...	Mozambique
Nigeria	3 382	3 859	3 970	...	...	...	...	...	...	...	Nigéria
Tunisia	277	379	319	488	540	451	588	1 103	862	795	Tunisie
America, South	**9 270**	**11 169**	**9 127**	**10 361**	**10 573**	**9 045**	**8 019**	**8 422**	**9 638**	**8 754**	**Amérique du Sud**
Argentina[2]	2 643	3 234	2 491	2 557	1 559	1 368	1 865	2 311	1 951	1 654	Argentine[2]
Brazil[3]	6 627	7 935	6 636	7 804	9 014	7 677	6 154	6 111	7 687	...	Brésil[3]
Asia	**91 284**	**101 800**	**101 280**	**103 613**	**114 714**	**109 061**	**103 881**	**112 325**	**107 483**	**106 329**	**Asie**
India[4]	17 512	15 811	15 344	16 419	12 992	13 372	16 689	17 117	19 413	...	Inde[4]
Indonesia	4 152	4 041	3 008	5 037	5 512	8 807	8 070	5 564	6 398	...	Indonésie
Japan	32 942	34 541	33 050	30 605	39 076	38 074	38 454	39 795	38 107	38 198	Japon
Korea, Republic of[5]	24 341	33 365	35 702	39 141	43 414	34 920	26 016	33 582	26 826	27 266	Corée, République de[5]
Pakistan[5]	4 219	4 131	5 202	4 154	5 147	5 425	5 449	5 226	6 056	...	Pakistan[5]
Philippines[5 6]	128	1 515	...	...	...	...	...	149	...	...	Philippines[5 6]
Sri Lanka	1 004	1 917	...	...	1 196	1 232	...	...	...	...	Sri Lanka
Turkey	1 895	1 909	1 987	2 001	...	...	...	...	...	...	Turquie
Viet Nam	5 091	4 570	5 052	4 321	4 832	4 686	5 320	7 607	6 800	6 035	Viet Nam
Europe	**38 877**	**42 314**	**43 610**	**46 542**	**47 113**	**48 044**	**44 442**	**43 450**	**47 650**	**48 219**	**Europe**
EEC	***21 652***	***23 851***	***24 527***	***23 451***	***25 087***	***24 075***	***21 343***	***21 582***	***22 731***	***23 821***	***CEE***
France	11 535	14 555	14 871	14 046	15 431	14 258	11 728	11 939	13 091	14 183	France
Germany, Fed. Rep.[7]	9 581	8 770	...	...	...	...	...	...	...	...	Allemagne, Rép. féd.[7]
United Kingdom[8]	536	526	480	229	480	641	439	...	...	...	Royaume-Uni[8]
EFTA	***2 473***	***1 916***	***2 044***	***2 349***	***2 855***	***3 278***	***2 332***	***2 053***	***2 568***	***2 461***	***AELE***
Finland	564	829	836	1 288	1 595	1 640	1 059	926	1 302	...	Finlande
Portugal	816	908	983	993	1 197	1 566	1 198	1 060	1 235	990	Portugal
Sweden	1 093	179	225	68	63	72	75	67	31	19	Suède
East Europe	***8 295***	***8 498***	***8 532***	***8 525***	***8 364***	***8 601***	***8 774***	***8 928***	***9 293***	***8 411***	***Europe de l'est***
Bulgaria	726	628	568	593	708	709	711	902	823	1 283	Bulgarie
German Dem. Rep.	5 292	5 207	5 345	5 651	5 775	6 118	6 326	6 721	7 533	6 435	Rép. dém. allemande
Hungary	2 277	2 663	2 619	2 281	1 881	1 774	1 737	1 305	937	693	Hongrie
Other Europe	***6 457***	***8 049***	***8 507***	***12 217***	***10 807***	***12 090***	***11 993***	***10 887***	***13 058***	***13 525***	***Autre Europe***
Spain	2 374	...	...	7 080	5 453	6 308	6 024	5 128	...	...	Espagne
Yugoslavia	4 083	3 863	3 940	5 137	5 354	5 782	5 969	5 759	6 200	6 286	Yougoslavie
Total	**143 753**	**160 748**	**159 346**	**165 378**	**177 390**	**171 166**	**161 450**	**169 911**	**170 118**	**168 583**	**Total**

General note.
Rubber inner tubes for bicycles and motorcycles. (Part of SITC 62910-1).

[1] Including inner tubes for motor vehicles.
[2] Including inner tubes for baby carriages and tricycles used for transporting goods.
[3] For bicycles only.
[4] Production by large and medium scale establishments only.
[5] Inner tubes for bicycles only.
[6] Shipments.
[7] Beginning 1978, data are confidential.
[8] Inner tubes for motor cycles only.

Remarque générale.
Les données se rapportent à la production de chambres à air en caoutchouc pour bicyclettes et motocyclettes. (Partie de CTCI 62910-1).

[1] Y compris les chambres à air pour véhicules à moteur.
[2] Y compris les chambres à air pour voitures d'enfant et pour triporteurs.
[3] Pour bicyclettes seulement.
[4] Production des grandes et moyennes entreprises seulement.
[5] Chambres à air pour bicyclettes seulement.
[6] Expéditions.
[7] A partir de 1978, les données sont confidentielles.
[8] Chambres à air pour motocyclettes seulement.

Tires for agricultural and other off-the-road vehicles – Pneumatiques et bandages pour véhicules agricoles et autres véhicules tous terrains

Unit : Thousand units

Unité : En milliers

Country or area	1976	1977	1978	1979	1980	1981	1982	1983	1984	1985	Pays ou zone
Africa	**240**	**235**	**238**	**192**	**293**	**315**	**257**	**208**	**254**	**256**	**Afrique**
South Africa	230	222	223	178	272	293	231	177	216	206	Afrique du Sud
Tunisia	10	13	15	14	21	22	26	31	38	50	Tunisie
America, North	**5 875**	**6 175**	**5 325**	**6 482**	**5 145**	**4 989**	**4 940**	**4 801**	**4 649**	**4 511**	**Amérique du Nord**
Canada[1 2 3]	754	599	...	714	...	...	...	...	...	...	Canada[1 2 3]
Cuba[4]	68	65	101	108	136	75	35	99	123	127	Cuba[4]
Jamaica[4]	2	2	2	3	1	2	1	2	2	2	Jamaïque[4]
Mexico[4]	103	98	120	117	124	110	114	101	117	166	Mexique[4]
United States[5]	4 948	5 411	4 413	5 540	4 195	4 113	...	...	...	...	Etats-Unis[5]
America, South	**1 566**	**1 354**	**1 302**	**1 504**	**1 665**	**1 288**	**1 490**	**1 525**	**1 817**	**1 599**	**Amérique du Sud**
Argentina	418	446	218	365	212	152	235	338	379	210	Argentine
Brazil	1 091	850	1 036	1 086	1 401	1 089	1 209	1 143	1 395	...	Brésil
Colombia	...	58	48	53	52	47	...	...	...	...	Colombie
Asia	**745**	**781**	**1 033**	**1 061**	**1 220**	**1 240**	**1 221**	**1 510**	**1 671**	**1 681**	**Asie**
India	440	484	592	613	661	705	705	788	934	969	Inde
Indonesia	2	3	1	3	2	5	4	55	5	...	Indonésie
Philippines[1]	38	11	...	...	...	...	...	...	...	...	Philippines[1]
Sri Lanka	10	8	19	25	27	20	26	26	* 8	* 9	Sri Lanka
Turkey	255	275	396	395	505	485	462	617	700	655	Turquie
Europe	**7 739**	**7 676**	**7 472**	**7 591**	**7 117**	**6 870**	**6 383**	**6 569**	**6 800**	**6 748**	**Europe**
EEC	***3 967***	***3 824***	***3 638***	***3 109***	***2 855***	***2 602***	***2 489***	***2 151***	***1 860***	***1 673***	***CEE***
Germany, Fed. Rep.	1 967	1 980	1 841	1 761	1 543	1 369	1 383	1 242	1 031	917	Allemagne, Rép. féd.
Italy	868	685	855	617	775	710	684	507	527	554	Italie
United Kingdom[6]	1 132	1 159	942	731	537	523	422	...	...	...	Royaume-Uni[6]
EFTA	***66***	***77***	***83***	***69***	***75***	***81***	***71***	***40***	***46***	***56***	***AELE***
Finland	29	27	31	31	42	52	44	14	18	...	Finlande
Portugal	37	50	52	38	33	29	27	26	28	27	Portugal
East Europe	***2 957***	***2 654***	***2 513***	***2 579***	***2 792***	***2 684***	***2 599***	***2 919***	***3 173***	***3 213***	***Europe de l'est***
Czechoslovakia	634	666	644	673	687	667	649	675	688	674	Tchécoslovaquie
German Dem. Rep.	368	348	345	327	367	371	376	381	374	381	Rép. dém. allemande
Hungary	463	143	115	125	251	316	295	252	308	325	Hongrie
Poland	1 492	1 497	1 409	1 454	1 487	1 330	1 279	1 611	1 803	1 833	Pologne
Other Europe	***749***	***1 121***	***1 238***	***1 834***	***1 395***	***1 503***	***1 224***	***1 459***	***1 721***	***1 806***	***Autre Europe***
Spain	429	...	...	1 354	792	825	521	602	...	...	Espagne
Yugoslavia	320	352	474	480	603	678	703	857	986	1 076	Yougoslavie
USSR	**10 294**	**10 967**	**...**	**...**	**...**	**...**	**...**	**...**	**...**	**...**	**URSS**
Oceania	**276**	**214**	**182**	**196**	**204**	**212**	**179**	**170**	**160**	**151**	**Océanie**
Australia[7]	276	214	182	196	204	212	179	...	...	...	Australie[7]
Total	**26 735**	**27 402**	**26 182**	**27 656**	**26 274**	**25 544**	**25 101**	**25 414**	**25 982**	**25 576**	**Total**

General note.
Solid rubber tires, cushion tires, reinforced tires, tires not requiring inner tubes and tire cases (outer covers) for all types of agricultural and other off-the-road tractors, construction machinery and aircraft. Excluding inner tubes, tires for bicycles and motorcycles, tires for road vehicles other than bicycles and motorcycles, tires for wheeled toys, articles of furniture etc. (SITC 62910-2).

¹ Shipments.
² Including tires for trucks and buses.
³ Excluding tires for industrial, pneumatic and semi-pneumatic and boat trailers.
⁴ Tires for agricultural vehicles only.
⁵ Source: International Rubber Study Group, (London).
⁶ Excluding solid tires.
⁷ Twelve months ending 30 June of year stated.

Remarque générale.
Bandages pleins ou creux ("mi-pleins"), chambres à air renforcées, pneumatiques ne nécessitant pas de chambre à air et enveloppes pour machines de tous types tels que les tracteurs agricoles et autres tracteurs tous terrains, le matériel de travaux publics et les aérodynes. Cette rubrique ne comprend pas les chambres à air, les pneumatiques pour bicyclettes, motocyclettes et autres véhicules routiers, les pneumatiques pour jouets ou meubles etc. (CTCI 62910-2).

¹ Expéditions.
² Y compris les pneumatiques pour camions et autobus.
³ Non compris les bandages pneumatiques et semi-pneumatiques pour véhicules industriels et les pneumatiques pour remorques à embarcation.
⁴ Pneumatiques pour véhicules agricoles seulement.
⁵ Source: International Rubber Study Group, (Londres).
⁶ Non compris les bandages pleins.
⁷ Période de douze mois finissant le 30 juin de l'année indiquée.

Tires for bicycles and motorcycles – Pneumatiques pour bicyclettes et motocyclettes

Unit : Thousand units

Unité : En milliers

Country or area	1976	1977	1978	1979	1980	1981	1982	1983	1984	1985	Pays ou zone
Africa	**5 061**	**6 459**	**7 353**	**6 862**	**6 452**	**5 098**	**5 299**	**5 087**	**5 508**	**5 236**	**Afrique**
Burkina Faso[1]	1 400	2 003	2 718	2 576	2 096	773	1 077	745	1 017	...	Burkina Faso[1]
Egypt	374	437	375	443	522	505	552	586	...	...	Egypte
Nigeria	2 982	3 557	3 864	...	...	...	...	...	...	...	Nigéria
Tunisia	125	249	226	267	346	322	178	259	394	374	Tunisie
Zaire	180	213	170	...	* 20	30	24	29	...	...	Zaïre
America, North	**3 425**	**2 405**	**2 308**	**2 053**	**2 758**	**2 971**	**3 113**	**2 734**	**2 928**	**3 233**	**Amérique du Nord**
Cuba	61	73	69	52	33	62	66	56	26	3	Cuba
Mexico	3 364	2 332	2 239	2 001	2 725	2 909	3 047	2 678	2 902	3 230	Mexique
America, South	**12 036**	**12 853**	**13 084**	**14 472**	**16 339**	**12 784**	**10 393**	**18 310**	**15 409**	**15 965**	**Amérique du Sud**
Argentina	3 881	3 606	3 698	3 346	2 125	1 849	1 891	2 346	2 519	1 713	Argentine
Brazil	7 439	8 541	8 918	10 034	13 456	10 225	7 816	15 676	12 357	...	Brésil
Colombia	716	706	468	1 092	758	710	686	288	...	...	Colombie
Asia	**89 395**	**100 998**	**107 183**	**110 436**	**121 207**	**114 683**	**115 759**	**128 666**	**121 086**	**124 057**	**Asie**
Bangladesh[1 2]	329	374	383	182	176	194	171	151	520	340	Bangladesh[1 2]
Burma[3 4]	103	...	...	...	...	...	...	...	...	...	Birmanie[3 4]
India[5]	24 622	27 954	32 563	30 898	27 893	27 979	29 216	31 065	35 470	37 491	Inde[5]
Indonesia	* 5 808	* 5 471	5 193	4 310	5 412	6 794	6 220	9 513	5 190	* 2 500	Indonésie
Japan	31 189	33 201	32 743	33 585	41 831	40 050	39 304	40 335	38 841	39 931	Japon
Korea, Republic of[3]	14 898	22 022	23 819	28 792	32 639	25 640	21 556	29 175	23 267	24 055	Corée, République de[3]
Pakistan[1 2 3]	3 180	3 461	3 675	3 731	3 937	4 072	4 304	3 984	3 734	...	Pakistan[1 2 3]
Philippines[6]	672	400	...	...	...	...	...	...	...	...	Philippines[6]
Sri Lanka	922	864	...	...	1 256	1 082	...	...	8	15	Sri Lanka
Syrian Arab Republic	228	176	126	58	83	17	46	...	...	...	Rép. arabe syrienne
Thailand	855	784	947	1 269	1 146	...	...	...	...	...	Thaïlande
Turkey	939	908	914	986	1 278	...	...	...	...	...	Turquie
Viet Nam	5 650	5 280	5 216	5 131	4 917	5 667	11 045	10 460	10 307	11 559	Viet Nam
Europe	**71 941**	**72 702**	**69 669**	**68 375**	**73 756**	**72 560**	**65 019**	**58 813**	**61 651**	**63 537**	**Europe**
EEC	***42 946***	***44 037***	***41 357***	***40 120***	***44 078***	***41 403***	***33 766***	***27 252***	***29 618***	***33 366***	***CEE***
Denmark	108	107	10	0	0	0	0	0	0	0	Danemark
France	16 840	18 410	19 950	21 021	23 424	21 139	15 996	12 322	14 316	17 842	France
Germany, Fed. Rep.[7]	7 384	8 763	...	...	...	...	...	...	...	...	Allemagne, Rép. féd.[7]
Italy[1 8]	17 851	16 072	12 669	10 669	12 109	11 664	9 398	6 591	7 031	7 321	Italie[1 8]
United Kingdom[9]	763	685	654	356	471	526	298	...	...	...	Royaume-Uni[9]
EFTA	***3 306***	***2 965***	***2 539***	***2 927***	***3 547***	***3 440***	***3 747***	***2 974***	***2 376***	***2 411***	***AELE***
Finland	585	715	752	1 012	1 281	1 024	1 404	973	1 077	...	Finlande
Portugal	717	705	613	704	866	932	766	856	883	790	Portugal
Sweden	2 004	1 545	1 174	1 211	1 400	1 484	1 577	1 145	416	303	Suède
East Europe	***19 931***	***20 215***	***19 952***	***18 745***	***18 960***	***19 663***	***19 406***	***20 506***	***20 449***	***18 008***	***Europe de l'est***
Bulgaria	442	393	373	314	358	368	376	396	492	507	Bulgarie
Czechoslovakia[10]	4 623	4 795	4 666	4 857	4 979	5 072	5 092	5 047	5 046	4 992	Tchécoslovaquie[10]
German Dem. Rep.	4 653	4 305	4 264	4 144	4 531	4 822	5 266	5 838	5 327	4 558	Rép. dém. allemande
Hungary	1 855	2 200	2 158	1 754	1 700	1 562	1 563	1 211	815	193	Hongrie
Poland	7 390	7 484	7 706	7 213	7 141	7 316	6 333	6 656	6 615	6 190	Pologne
Romania	968	1 038	785	463	251	523	776	1 358	2 154	1 568	Roumanie
Other Europe	***5 758***	***5 485***	***5 822***	***6 583***	***7 171***	***8 054***	***8 100***	***8 081***	***9 208***	***9 751***	***Autre Europe***
Spain	2 650	...	...	3 196	3 274	4 130	3 987	3 732	...	...	Espagne
Yugoslavia[3]	3 108	2 607	2 749	3 387	3 897	3 924	4 113	4 349	4 966	5 314	Yougoslavie[3]
USSR[3]	**16 107**	**16 748**	**17 934**	**19 005**	**19 210**	**18 914**	**19 081**	**19 458**	**19 195**	**19 161**	**URSS[3]**
Total	**197 965**	**212 164**	**217 530**	**221 203**	**239 721**	**227 009**	**218 663**	**233 067**	**225 778**	**231 189**	**Total**

General note.
Data refer to bicycle and motorcycle tires, excluding inner tubes. (SITC 62910-3).

Remarque générale.
Les données se rapportent à la production de pneumatiques pour bicyclettes et motocyclettes, à l'exclusion des chambres à air. (CTCI 62910-3).

[1] Including inner tubes.
[2] Twelve months ending 30 June of year stated.
[3] Tires for bicycles only.
[4] Twelve months ending 30 September of year stated.
[5] Production by large and medium scale establishments only.
[6] Shipments.
[7] Beginning 1978, data are confidential.
[8] Excluding tires for motorcycles and scooters.
[9] Excluding tires for bicycles.
[10] Tires for motorcycles only.

[1] Y compris les chambres à air.
[2] Période de douze mois finissant le 30 juin de l'année indiquée.
[3] Pneumatiques pour bicyclettes seulement.
[4] Période de douze mois finissant le 30 septembre de l'année indiquée.
[5] Production des grandes et moyennes entreprises seulement.
[6] Expéditions.
[7] A partir de 1978, les données sont confidentielles.
[8] Non compris les pneumatiques pour motocyclettes et scooters.
[9] Non compris les pneumatiques pour bicyclettes.
[10] Pneumatiques pour motocyclettes seulement.

Tires for road motor vehicles – Pneumatiques pour véhicules à moteur

Unit : Thousand units

Unité : En milliers

Country or area	1976	1977	1978	1979	1980	1981	1982	1983	1984	1985	Pays ou zone
Africa	**6 432**	**7 008**	**7 725**	**7 491**	**9 093**	**10 163**	**10 191**	**10 172**	**9 491**	**9 655**	**Afrique**
Algeria	...	11	11	7	7	6	* 5	* 6	...	...	Algérie
Côte d'Ivoire	...	...	32	33	37	25	16	12	...	...	Côte d'Ivoire
Egypt[1]	485	921	858	938	1 113	1 106	1 212	1 116	* 816	...	Egypte[1]
Ghana	302	312	200	...	...	...	112	...	...	...	Ghana
Morocco	379	395	403	367	782	681	745	763	796	776	Maroc
Nigeria	754	...	...	...	...	# 2 246	2 046	2 205	1 604	2 154	Nigéria
South Africa	4 308	4 017	4 735	4 359	* 5 250	5 761	5 923	5 666	* 5 825	5 041	Afrique du Sud
Tunisia	146	135	174	107	88	106	132	172	205	261	Tunisie
America, North	**213 086**	**257 725**	**250 572**	**239 522**	**190 155**	**212 213**	**211 466**	**219 713**	**245 290**	**233 736**	**Amérique du Nord**
Canada	* 18 412	* 19 509	* 18 700	24 627	22 335	[2] 21 574	[2] 22 965	[2] 23 533	[2] 25 519	[2] 26 655	Canada
Cuba	266	172	295	302	387	252	184	255	328	345	Cuba
Jamaica	242	233	257	220	177	232	216	196	209	210	Jamaïque
Mexico	6 152	6 093	7 842	7 617	8 749	8 328	9 522	8 722	9 779	10 472	Mexique
Panama	58	81	72	69	72	65	79	83	...	...	Panama
United States	187 956	231 637	223 406	206 687	158 435	181 762	178 500	186 924	209 375	195 972	Etats-Unis
America, South	**28 369**	**28 510**	**30 433**	**33 112**	**36 997**	**28 291**	**28 512**	**29 678**	**33 473**	**34 891**	**Amérique du Sud**
Argentina	4 437	4 482	4 203	5 255	5 297	3 883	3 799	4 463	5 024	3 741	Argentine
Brazil	17 896	17 625	19 223	20 627	24 000	16 585	17 438	18 230	21 020	22 152	Brésil
Chile	605	852	766	893	931	870	482	595	913	858	Chili
Colombia	1 512	1 396	2 027	1 670	1 899	1 703	1 750	1 625	1 950	2 000	Colombie
Ecuador	219	345	385	507	510	601	643	...	...	...	Equateur
Peru	963	876	740	716	877	968	810	676	782	* 780	Pérou
Venezuela	2 737	2 934	3 089	3 444	3 483	3 681	3 590	3 358	2 985	4 492	Venezuela
Asia	**110 840**	**121 772**	**133 475**	**149 925**	**163 670**	**151 794**	**150 499**	**173 032**	**187 646**	**196 415**	**Asie**
China[3]	6 760	7 720	9 360	11 690	11 460	7 290	8 640	12 710	15 690	19 260	Chine[3]
India	3 637	4 066	4 455	4 541	4 720	4 744	5 323	5 491	5 951	6 193	Inde
Indonesia	1 987	2 416	2 789	3 064	4 031	4 131	3 098	3 332	3 406	3 420	Indonésie
Iran(Islamic Rep.of)[4]	...	4 132	3 244	3 253	2 099	2 943	3 897	...	...	...	Iran(Rép.islamique)[4]
Israel	1 680	1 720	1 538	1 317	1 242	1 106	1 227	1 045	1 009	930	Israël
Japan	80 456	86 397	94 065	104 651	116 384	110 924	109 968	123 094	131 199	135 745	Japon
Korea, Republic of	3 491	4 767	6 905	10 024	12 327	9 101	7 855	12 033	15 126	15 163	Corée, République de
Malaysia[3 5 6]	4 261	4 885	4 638	4 657	4 634	5 375	4 010	4 262	3 700	3 622	Malaisie[3 5 6]
Pakistan[7]	166	148	182	183	204	227	193	216	238	...	Pakistan[7]
Philippines	1 222	1 548	1 681	1 853	1 637	1 387	1 632	1 737	1 450	1 300	Philippines
Sri Lanka	181	149	238	244	241	193	189	197	164	120	Sri Lanka
Thailand	1 225	1 652	1 707	1 898	1 762	1 940	1 562	2 199	2 177	* 2 744	Thaïlande
Turkey	2 190	2 172	2 673	2 550	2 929	2 433	2 905	3 777	4 690	4 922	Turquie
Europe	**185 452**	**196 709**	**195 283**	**210 351**	**203 185**	**190 483**	**184 629**	**191 570**	**202 201**	**183 925**	**Europe**
EEC	***142 656***	***145 201***	***141 746***	***147 523***	***146 565***	***133 394***	***131 423***	***136 077***	***140 610***	***120 209***	***CEE***
France	43 995	46 590	46 405	49 630	50 601	43 196	41 478	45 606	47 817	47 316	France
Germany, Fed. Rep.	37 699	37 936	37 519	38 878	37 799	36 843	36 335	37 878	39 254	40 475	Allemagne, Rép. féd.
Italy	28 692	29 330	28 897	29 734	29 681	27 513	27 146	26 598	27 460	27 955	Italie
Luxembourg[8]	2 400	2 434	2 260	2 386	2 138	2 118	2 088	...	...	...	Luxembourg[8]
United Kingdom	29 870	28 911	26 665	26 895	26 346	23 724	24 376	23 976	24 120	* 2 565	Royaume-Uni
EFTA	***5 123***	***5 713***	***5 654***	***6 138***	***5 651***	***4 820***	***5 221***	***5 979***	***6 322***	***6 774***	***AELE***
Finland	726	776	970	1 039	1 127	912	1 341	1 352	1 427	...	Finlande
Portugal	1 427	1 690	1 679	1 682	1 833	1 878	1 852	2 011	2 154	2 275	Portugal
Sweden	2 970	3 247	3 005	3 417	2 691	2 030	2 028	2 616	2 741	2 996	Suède
East Europe	***21 574***	***23 039***	***23 860***	***24 842***	***25 759***	***24 287***	***23 118***	***24 424***	***26 407***	***27 042***	***Europe de l'est***
Bulgaria	1 236	1 320	1 250	1 261	1 532	1 567	1 577	1 613	1 666	1 659	Bulgarie
Czechoslovakia	4 339	4 673	4 768	4 841	4 969	5 097	4 506	4 465	4 621	4 547	Tchécoslovaquie
German Dem. Rep.	6 432	6 652	6 728	6 890	7 067	7 026	7 051	7 379	7 784	8 362	Rép. dém. allemande
Hungary	688	706	663	650	655	615	549	537	552	578	Hongrie
Poland	4 764	5 425	5 854	6 559	6 533	4 804	4 043	5 084	5 902	6 254	Pologne
Romania[9]	4 115	4 263	4 597	4 641	5 003	5 178	5 392	5 346	5 882	5 642	Roumanie[9]
Other Europe	***16 099***	***22 756***	***24 023***	***31 848***	***25 210***	***27 982***	***24 867***	***25 090***	***28 862***	***29 899***	***Autre Europe***
Spain	10 455	...	...	22 687	15 626	17 470	15 479	15 670	* 19 004	* 18 705	Espagne

For general note and footnotes, see end of table.

Voir la fin du tableau pour la remarque générale et les notes.

Tires for road motor vehicles (continued) – Pneumatiques pour véhicules à moteur (suite)

Unit : Thousand units

Unité : En milliers

Country or area	1976	1977	1978	1979	1980	1981	1982	1983	1984	1985	Pays ou zone
Yugoslavia[10]	5 644	8 126	8 862	9 161	9 584	10 512	9 388	9 420	9 858	11 194	Yougoslavie[10]
USSR[10]	**37 394**	**39 446**	**[9] 59 018**	**[9] 59 981**	**[9] 60 066**	**[9] 60 476**	**[9] 61 675**	**[9] 62 025**	**[9] 63 737**	**[9] 65 171**	**URSS[10]**
Oceania	**9 781**	**10 288**	**8 966**	**9 709**	**9 337**	**8 828**	**8 680**	**7 057**	**7 447**	**7 068**	**Océanie**
Australia[7 10]	8 108	8 483	7 441	8 060	7 674	7 245	6 943	5 821	6 165	5 846	Australie[7 10]
New Zealand[9]	1 673	1 805	1 525	1 649	1 663	1 583	1 737	1 236	1 282	1 222	Nouvelle–Zélande[9]
Total	**591 355**	**661 458**	**685 471**	**710 091**	**672 503**	**662 248**	**655 652**	**693 247**	**749 285**	**730 860**	**Total**

General note.
Solid rubber tires, cushion tires, reinforced tires, tires not requiring inner rubes, tire cases (outer covers) for motor cars, lorries and all types of road vehicles other than bicycles and motorcycles. Inner tubes are excluded. (SITC 62910–4).

1 Including inner tubes for bicycles and motorcycles.
2 Source: International Rubber Study Group, (London).
3 Tires of all types.
4 Including tires for bicycles, agricultural and other off–the road vehicles.

5 Data refer to Peninsular Malaysia only.
6 Beginning 1982, scope of series revised.
7 Twelve months ending 30 June of year stated.
8 Beginning 1983, data are confidential.
9 Including tires for vehicles operating off–the–road.
10 Including motorcycle tires.

Remarque générale.
Bandages pleins ou creux ("mi–pleins"), chambres à air renforcées, pneumatiques ne nécessitant pas de chambre à air, enveloppes pour voitures automobiles, camions et autres types de véhicules routiers à l'exception des bicyclettes et des motocyclettes. (CTCI 62910–4).

1 Y compris les chambres à air pour bicyclettes et motocyclettes.
2 Source: International Rubber Study Group , (Londres).
3 Pneumatiques de tous genres.
4 Y compris les pneumatiques pour bicyclettes, pour véhicules agricoles et autres véhicules tous terrains.
5 Données se rapportant à la Malaisie péninsulaire seulement.
6 A partir de 1982, portée de la série révisée.
7 Période de douze mois finissant le 30 juin de l'année indiquée.
8 A partir de 1983, les données sont confidentielles.
9 Y compris les pneumatiques pour véhicules tous terrains.
10 Y compris les pneumatiques pour motocyclettes.

Rubber, reclaimed – Caoutchouc régénéré

Unit : Metric tons

Unité : Tonnes métriques

Country or area	1976	1977	1978	1979	1980	1981	1982	1983	1984	1985	Pays ou zone
America, North	**115 324**	**124 563**	**127 355**	**128 916**	**89 907**	**91 800**	**77 825**	**78 798**	**76 026**	**65 647**	**Amérique du Nord**
Canada	4 623	3 431	3 799	5 174	3 015	3 020	4 177	...	...	...	Canada
United States	110 701	121 132	123 556	123 742	86 892	88 780	73 648	75 328	72 661	62 387	Etats-Unis
America, South	**32 048**	**32 077**	**32 998**	**32 921**	**38 194**	**26 376**	**23 974**	**23 467**	**25 636**	**23 403**	**Amérique du Sud**
Brazil	[1] 31 577	[1] 31 632	[1] 32 568	32 459	37 744	25 959	23 544	23 037	25 217	...	Brésil
Colombia	471	445	430	462	450	417	430	430	...	...	Colombie
Asia	**81 003**	**82 713**	**87 650**	**91 947**	**97 525**	**90 288**	**84 996**	**90 846**	**95 529**	**98 108**	**Asie**
India	18 876	18 070	19 175	19 673	20 353	22 956	22 031	24 443	26 359	...	Inde
Japan	58 087	56 676	59 645	63 285	67 175	56 581	54 536	57 974	60 741	63 516	Japon
Sri Lanka	33	...	...	...	5 491	6 245	...	...	...	...	Sri Lanka
Turkey	4 007	4 044	4 907	5 066	...	...	...	...	...	...	Turquie
Europe	**108 104**	**97 720**	**96 551**	**90 537**	**85 439**	**76 019**	**70 012**	**68 786**	**59 744**	**55 436**	**Europe**
EEC	***56 610***	***52 680***	***48 293***	***45 774***	***40 419***	***36 124***	***32 883***	***28 792***	***24 783***	***22 641***	***CEE***
France	21 490	20 980	20 010	17 540	17 630	15 470	15 060	...	...	...	France
Germany, Fed. Rep.	10 817	8 586	7 546	8 499	7 392	6 322	5 599	5 035	4 301	5 435	Allemagne, Rép. féd.
United Kingdom	24 303	23 114	20 737	19 735	15 397	...	...	...	...	...	Royaume-Uni
EFTA	***4 109***	***930***	***1 000***	***300***	***596***	***0***	***0***	***0***	***0***	***77***	***AELE***
Finland	250	428	534	0	0	0	0	0	0	...	Finlande
Sweden	3 859	502	466	300	596	0	0	0	0	0	Suède
East Europe	***16 908***	***16 035***	***19 812***	***19 804***	***19 329***	***20 259***	***20 116***	***20 137***	***19 153***	***18 520***	***Europe de l'est***
Czechoslovakia	15 446	15 950	19 812	19 804	19 329	20 259	20 086	20 058	19 050	18 401	Tchécoslovaquie
Hungary	1 462	85	0	0	0	0	30	79	103	119	Hongrie
Other Europe	***30 477***	***28 075***	***27 446***	***24 659***	***25 095***	***19 636***	***17 013***	***19 857***	***15 808***	***14 198***	***Autre Europe***
Spain	...	...	...	18 163	17 723	11 862	9 927	11 901	...	...	Espagne
Yugoslavia	6 480	6 095	7 482	6 496	7 372	7 774	7 086	7 956	7 943	8 350	Yougoslavie
Oceania	**4 237**	**1 096**	**921**	**618**	**159**	**202**	**120**	**120**	**120**	**120**	**Océanie**
Australia	4 237	1 096	921	618	159	202	120	...	...	...	Australie
Total	**340 716**	**338 169**	**345 475**	**344 939**	**311 224**	**284 685**	**256 927**	**262 017**	**257 055**	**242 714**	**Total**

General note.
Rubber otained from old rubber articles, or from waste or scrap of vulcanized rubber. (SITC 23130-0).

[1] Source: International Rubber Study Group, (London).

Remarque générale.
Caoutchouc provenant du traitement de vieux ouvrages en caoutchouc ou de déchets et rognures de caoutchouc vulcanisé. (CTCI 23130-0).

[1] Source: International Rubber Study Group, (Londres).

Rubber, unhardened vulcanized plated, sheets etc. – Plaques, feuilles etc. en caoutchouc vulcanisé non durci

Unit : Metric tons

Unité : Tonnes métriques

Country or area	1976	1977	1978	1979	1980	1981	1982	1983	1984	1985	Pays ou zone
America, South	**25 271**	**10 549**	**11 015**	**18 083**	**14 769**	**13 466**	**14 009**	**13 641**	**13 273**	**12 905**	**Amérique du Sud**
Brazil	21 247	5 179	[1] 7 831	14 524	...	...	...	...	...	...	Brésil
Colombia	...	5 370	3 184	3 559	2 574	1 271	...	...	...	...	Colombie
Asia	**2 362**	**3 109**	**3 171**	**3 345**	**3 295**	**3 129**	**2 814**	**3 973**	**4 861**	**3 728**	**Asie**
Malaysia[2 3]	2 362	3 109	3 171	3 345	3 295	3 129	# 2 814	3 973	4 861	3 728	Malaisie[2 3]
Europe	**251 999**	**274 925**	**269 488**	**290 863**	**294 147**	**290 928**	**243 216**	**247 228**	**278 911**	**301 531**	**Europe**
EEC	***112 886***	***116 680***	***118 067***	***114 541***	***114 736***	***108 015***	***65 929***	***72 959***	***80 103***	***96 063***	***CEE***
Denmark	982	1 024	1 155	1 079	1 073	...	...	...	...	...	Danemark
Germany, Fed. Rep.	111 904	115 656	116 912	113 462	113 663	106 882	64 773	71 779	78 899	94 836	Allemagne, Rép. féd.
EFTA	***127 577***	***140 340***	***130 730***	***148 947***	***153 349***	***149 426***	***144 242***	***145 422***	***161 407***	***165 282***	***AELE***
Austria[4]	110 254	123 801	113 468	130 312	135 425	132 419	127 289	127 906	145 175	149 781	Autriche[4]
Finland	2 229	1 652	1 594	1 782	1 717	1 822	1 770	1 635	1 003	...	Finlande
Portugal	663	738	659	1 070	1 024	960	1 023	1 074	1 211	1 103	Portugal
Sweden	14 431	14 149	15 009	15 783	15 183	14 225	14 160	14 807	14 018	13 089	Suède
Other Europe	***11 536***	***17 905***	***20 691***	***27 375***	***26 062***	***33 487***	***33 045***	***28 847***	***37 401***	***40 186***	***Autre Europe***
Spain	11 536	...	...	27 375	26 062	33 487	33 045	28 847	...	...	Espagne
Total	**279 632**	**288 583**	**283 674**	**312 291**	**312 211**	**307 523**	**260 039**	**264 842**	**297 045**	**318 164**	**Total**

General note.
Unhardened vulcanized plates, sheets, strips, rods and profile shapes of rubber including covered rubber material without further working. (SITC 62104–0).

[1] Production by establishments employing 5 or more persons.
[2] Data refer to Peninsular Malaysia only.
[3] Beginning 1982, scope of series revised.
[4] All hardened and unhardened rubber products.

Remarque générale.
Plaques, feuilles, bandes, fils et profilés en caoutchouc vulcanisé non durci, découpés en rectangles ou se présentant sous la forme de fils ou de profilés, y compris les matières en caoutchouc recouvert mais n'ayant pas subi d'autre façon. (CTCI 62104–0).

[1] Production des établissements occupant 5 personnes ou plus.
[2] Données se rapportant à la Malaisie péninsulaire seulement.
[3] A partir de 1982, portée de la série révisée.
[4] Produits de caoutchouc durci et non durci de toutes catégories.

Rubber, unhardened vulcanized piping and tubing – Tubes et tuyaux en caoutchouc vulcanisé non durci

Unit : Metric tons

Unité : Tonnes métriques

Country or area	1976	1977	1978	1979	1980	1981	1982	1983	1984	1985	Pays ou zone
Asia	**17 105**	**18 661**	**20 453**	**23 054**	**23 658**	**24 565**	**21 673**	**21 335**	**24 567**	**27 279**	**Asie**
Japan	16 515	17 923	19 561	21 907	22 611	23 909	21 407	21 101	24 174	26 954	Japon
Malaysia	590	738	892	1 147	1 047	656	266	234	...	...	Malaisie
Europe	**138 690**	**140 012**	**146 300**	**152 490**	**147 976**	**141 349**	**101 799**	**92 576**	**96 553**	**100 893**	**Europe**
EEC	***107 551***	***112 673***	***120 032***	***129 286***	***127 282***	***116 728***	***76 974***	***68 607***	***75 169***	***80 076***	***CEE***
Belgium	5 270	5 811	5 124	4 851	5 155	3 707	4 590	4 478	4 711	5 387	Belgique
Denmark	2 895	3 557	3 866	4 550	3 821	...	...	...	...	...	Danemark
France	28 080	29 160	27 650	29 320	28 330	24 530	22 670	15 680	20 000	20 853	France
Germany, Fed. Rep.	66 554	69 093	77 813	87 109	87 154	80 593	42 324	41 225	43 405	46 961	Allemagne, Rép. féd.
Greece	...	...	...	...	...	682	632	644	...	...	Grèce
Netherlands	4 100	4 400	4 927	2 804	2 170	2 630	...	...	...	...	Pays–Bas
EFTA	***12 050***	***12 409***	***12 290***	***12 940***	***12 709***	***12 533***	***12 675***	***12 553***	***12 494***	***12 732***	***AELE***
Finland	773	1 073	1 410	1 519	1 481	1 305	1 447	1 325	1 266	...	Finlande
Sweden	11 277	11 336	10 880	11 421	...	...	...	...	...	...	Suède
East Europe	***1 047***	***914***	***794***	***909***	***964***	***833***	***280***	***656***	***693***	***720***	***Europe de l'est***
Hungary	1 047	914	794	909	964	833	280	656	693	720	Hongrie
Other Europe	***18 042***	***14 016***	***13 184***	***9 355***	***7 021***	***11 255***	***11 870***	***10 760***	***8 197***	***7 365***	***Autre Europe***
Spain	18 042	...	...	9 355	7 021	11 255	11 870	10 760	...	...	Espagne
Total	**155 795**	**158 673**	**166 753**	**175 544**	**171 634**	**165 914**	**123 472**	**113 911**	**121 120**	**128 172**	**Total**

General note.
Piping and tubing consisting wholly of vulcanized rubber and vulcanized piping and tubing reinforced by stratification of textile fabric. Inner rubber tubes for tires are excluded. (SITC 62105–0).

Remarque générale.
Tubes et tuyaux entièrement constitués de caoutchouc vulcanisé, et tubes et tuyaux vulcanisés renforcés par une stratification d'un ou plusieurs plis textiles. Cette rubrique ne comprend pas les chambres à air pour pneumatiques. (CTCI 62105–0).

Rubber, hardened (ebonite and vulcanite in blocks, plates, sheets etc.) – Caoutchouc durci

Unit : Metric tons | Unité : Tonnes métriques

Country or area	1976	1977	1978	1979	1980	1981	1982	1983	1984	1985	Pays ou zone
Europe	**45 227**	**47 956**	**46 452**	**50 840**	**46 295**	**44 813**	**42 242**	**40 973**	**36 144**	**36 813**	**Europe**
EEC	***38 170***	***40 343***	***38 764***	***44 255***	***42 092***	***40 462***	***34 965***	***35 518***	***31 362***	***33 506***	***CEE***
France	2 070	1 970	1 890	1 640	820	700	450	...	...	...	France
Germany, Fed. Rep.	[1] 30 600	[1] 31 573	[1] 31 704	[1] 36 965	# 35 872	34 461	29 349	30 019	26 233	28 293	Allemagne, Rép. féd.
Netherlands[1]	5 500	6 800	5 170	5 650	5 400	...	...	...	...	...	Pays-Bas[1]
EFTA	***588***	***614***	***34***	***71***	***70***	***64***	***54***	***142***	***103***	***358***	***AELE***
Finland	542	538	0	0	0	0	0	0	0	...	Finlande
Portugal	46	76	34	71	70	64	54	142	103	...	Portugal
East Europe	***6 437***	***6 967***	***7 622***	***6 482***	***4 101***	***4 257***	***7 201***	***5 269***	***4 647***	***2 917***	***Europe de l'est***
Hungary	6 437	6 967	7 622	6 482	4 101	4 257	7 201	5 269	4 647	2 917	Hongrie
Other Europe	***32***	***32***	***32***	***32***	***32***	***30***	***22***	***44***	***32***	***32***	***Autre Europe***
Spain	...	...	...	...	...	30	22	44	...	...	Espagne
Total	**45 227**	**47 956**	**46 452**	**50 840**	**46 295**	**44 813**	**42 242**	**40 973**	**36 144**	**36 813**	**Total**

General note.
Ebonite and vulcanite in blocks, plates, sheets, strips, rods, profile shapes, powder and manufacturing waste. Articles of hardened rubber are excluded. (SITC 62106-1).

[1] Source: Industrial Statistics, Statistical Office of the European Communities, (Luxembourg).

Remarque générale.
Ebonite ou autre caoutchouc durci, en blocs, plaques, feuilles, bandes, bâtons, profilés et poudres, y compris les déchets de fabrication. Cette rubrique ne comprend pas les articles en caoutchouc durci. (CTCI 62106-1).

[1] Source: Statistiques industrielles, Office statistique des Communautés européennes, (Luxembourg).

Rubber, transmission, conveyor, elevator belts etc. – Courroies transporteuses, de transmission etc., en caoutchouc

Unit : Metric tons

Unité : Tonnes métriques

Country or area	1976	1977	1978	1979	1980	1981	1982	1983	1984	1985	Pays ou zone
America, North											**Amérique du Nord**
Canada[1]	449	401	...	...	...	...	...	...	...	...	Canada[1]
America, South											**Amérique du Sud**
Colombia	...	654	128	256	230	449	491	280	...	...	Colombie
Asia											**Asie**
India[2]	7 145	5 804	6 940	7 027	8 159	8 085	8 518	8 946	9 138	...	Inde[2]
Japan	27 184	25 149	26 882	29 091	32 415	30 319	28 456	29 284	33 071	33 354	Japon
Turkey	24 006	24 683	33 922	34 385	...	...	...	...	...	...	Turquie
Europe											**Europe**
EEC											***CEE***
Belgium	3 585	3 716	3 777	3 413	3 557	2 753	2 605	2 545	3 165	3 418	Belgique
Denmark	5 032	5 604	5 810	5 735	6 551	4 130	* 4 300	4 507	4 852	4 865	Danemark
France	17 950	16 110	16 070	16 020	16 230	16 190	15 530	# 12 280	9 451	16 017	France
Germany, Fed. Rep.	42 895	43 905	46 401	43 834	45 363	47 062	52 737	52 950	42 519	52 747	Allemagne, Rép. féd.
Greece	...	...	...	...	...	3 650	3 543	3 701	...	...	Grèce
Italy[3]	9 600	9 900	...	...	...	...	...	...	...	...	Italie[3]
Netherlands	5 400	6 500	5 273	[4] 10 038	[4] 10 517	[4] 9 788	[4] 9 631	[4] 10 338	[4] 11 322	...	Pays–Bas
United Kingdom	17 000	19 693	15 050	19 043	14 710	9 492	11 021	9 473	7 223	6 470	Royaume–Uni
EFTA											***AELE***
Finland	1 529	1 261	1 566	2 054	1 824	1 540	1 606	1 493	1 554	...	Finlande
Portugal	461	761	934	762	816	499	486	473	414	315	Portugal
Sweden	3 113	3 120	2 818	3 175	...	3 263	3 259	4 435	3 692	3 809	Suède
East Europe											***Europe de l'est***
Hungary	5 780	6 855	6 971	6 008	5 838	4 549	5 720	6 144	6 226	6 000	Hongrie
Other Europe											***Autre Europe***
Spain	8 631	...	...	9 337	9 504	10 407	9 457	8 287	...	...	Espagne

General note.
Transmission, conveyor or elevator belts or belting of vulcanized rubber. Data represent belting and belts of wholly vulcanized rubber or of fabric impregnated, coated, covered or laminated with rubber or made from textile yarns or cord impregnated or coated with rubber. (SITC 62940–0).

[1] In thousand metres.
[2] Production by large and medium scale establishments only.
[3] Source: Industrial Statistics, Statistical Office of the European Communities, (Luxembourg).
[4] Including production in Belgium and Luxembourg.

Remarque générale.
Courroies et matières pour courroies transporteuses, élévatrices, de transmission, entièrement en caoutchouc vulcanisé ou en tissu imprégné, enduit ou recouvert de caoutchouc ou laminé avec du caoutchouc, ou faites en fils ou ficelles textiles imprégnés ou enduits de caoutchouc. (CTCI 62940–0).

[1] En milliers de mètres.
[2] Production des grandes et moyennes entreprises seulement.
[3] Source: Statistiques industrielles, Office statistique des Communautés européennes, (Luxembourg).
[4] Y compris la production en Belgique et Luxembourg.

Rubber footwear – Chaussures en caoutchouc

Unit : Thousand pairs

Unité : Milliers de paires

Country or area	1976	1977	1978	1979	1980	1981	1982	1983	1984	1985	Pays ou zone
Africa	**14 893**	**41 029**	**36 577**	**24 513**	**45 471**	**41 200**	**43 251**	**43 589**	**45 949**	**49 753**	**Afrique**
Algeria	3 463	4 733	2 373	2 333	1 140	...	...	...	...	...	Algérie
Burkina Faso	990	1 099	1 227	1 833	1 698	1 478	1 628	1 313	811	1 191	Burkina Faso
Burundi[1]	174	275	386	471	440	460	390	301	237	373	Burundi[1]
Kenya	6 663	6 204	7 828	5 730	4 756	6 973	6 546	4 546	4 997	5 928	Kenya
Morocco	189	2 684	2 461	2 811	2 664	1 580	1 558	1 610	1 247	888	Maroc
Nigeria	1 359	24 200	20 504	9 260	32 554	...	...	...	...	...	Nigéria
Sierra Leone[2]	454	233	132	475	536	875	477	497	...	...	Sierra Leone[2]
Zaire	...	...	1 666	...	1 683	1 453	...	...	...	...	Zaïre
America, North	**166 732**	**159 339**	**153 986**	**144 937**	**130 030**	**127 118**	**124 850**	**117 914**	**102 000**	**94 227**	**Amérique du Nord**
Canada[3]	3 207	3 974	6 426	5 968	3 213	...	...	...	...	...	Canada[3]
Cuba[1]	11 745	8 189	8 826	8 060	8 489	9 694	9 011	10 015	8 281	8 956	Cuba[1]
Dominican Republic	3 530	3 239	3 622	2 421	2 158	3 216	3 550	4 453	4 166	...	Rép. dominicaine
El Salvador	143	4 001	3 347	4 894	4 181	3 001	2 856	2 212	...	...	El Salvador
United States	...	...	...	...	111 989	106 051	104 077	95 679	80 343	71 836	Etats-Unis
America, South	**158 115**	**158 506**	**156 172**	**157 666**	**158 582**	**157 590**	**158 619**	**154 759**	**156 550**	**156 339**	**Amérique du Sud**
Bolivia	629	973	...	...	929	270	870	921	...	...	Bolivie
Brazil	...	...	...	...	146 200	...	...	...	...	...	Brésil
Colombia	...	10 493	8 298	9 058	7 862	9 300	9 481	5 141	...	...	Colombie
Ecuador	...	840	914	...	# 3 591	1 820	2 068	2 497	...	...	Equateur
Asia	**325 625**	**336 023**	**272 503**	**272 164**	**301 025**	**236 575**	**253 123**	**227 946**	**230 497**	**219 921**	**Asie**
Afghanistan	...	3 800	4 570	3 712	2 886	2 537	2 450	2 600	2 400	2 400	Afghanistan
Burma[4]	3 123	...	...	...	...	...	...	...	...	...	Birmanie[4]
Democratic Yemen[5]	...	...	...	...	634	831	1 110	1 186	1 146	...	Yémen démocratique[5]
Hong Kong	61 820	74 568	26 066	30 967	63 390	16 906	33 957	11 975	10 954	...	Hong-kong
India[6]	40 500	42 820	38 100	43 225	44 545	37 281	38 118	36 320	37 047	36 320	Inde[6]
Indonesia	4 195	7 784	6 136	3 339	4 031	7 037	5 515	9 958	10 946	...	Indonésie
Iran(Islamic Rep.of)[7 8]	6 055	8 194	7 483	4 720	4 645	5 495	5 432	5 728	...	...	Iran(Rép.islamique)[7 8]
Japan	88 503	83 463	73 070	73 136	73 830	71 339	71 768	72 093	71 774	70 703	Japon
Korea, Republic of	50 909	55 821	55 801	58 683	38 882	26 913	26 668	20 680	22 589	20 340	Corée, République de
Malaysia[9]	13 672	13 073	13 906	13 692	16 163	15 998	16 049	14 975	...	...	Malaisie[9]
Philippines	22 075	11 488	...	...	...	...	...	...	...	...	Philippines
Sri Lanka	4 446	...	6 045	1 619	5 818	6 792	...	...	...	...	Sri Lanka
Syrian Arab Republic	663	669	866	767	960	685	738	806	752	695	Rép. arabe syrienne
Turkey	24 410	25 296	19 761	15 608	...	...	...	...	...	...	Turquie
Yemen	...	...	360	2 220	4 068	3 588	4 128	4 100	3 800	4 700	Yémen
Europe	**110 740**	**155 715**	**164 266**	**220 957**	**207 734**	**197 525**	**196 708**	**180 653**	**217 415**	**228 021**	**Europe**
EEC	***5 845***	***5 620***	***5 683***	***6 317***	***5 876***	***5 235***	***5 375***	***5 129***	***3 702***	***4 439***	***CEE***
Denmark	0	0	0	17	34	...	...	...	...	...	Danemark
France	2 600	2 120	2 110	2 347	2 199	1 753	2 040	2 120	1 489	...	France
Greece	1 190	1 445	1 518	1 898	1 588	1 402	1 250	919	118	...	Grèce
United Kingdom[10 11]	2 055	...	...	...	...	...	...	...	...	...	Royaume-Uni[10 11]
EFTA	***5 505***	***5 373***	***5 306***	***3 469***	***4 366***	***4 795***	***4 451***	***4 178***	***4 532***	***3 992***	***AELE***
Finland	1 852	1 633	1 632	1 739	1 878	1 934	1 808	1 550	1 460	...	Finlande
Portugal	2 628	2 879	2 822	1 024	1 797	2 231	2 044	2 158	2 747	...	Portugal
Sweden	1 025	861	852	706	691	630	599	470	325	288	Suède
East Europe	***76 043***	***71 084***	***68 010***	***66 054***	***68 312***	***65 275***	***65 256***	***62 437***	***57 989***	***56 529***	***Europe de l'est***
Bulgaria	11 495	11 703	11 658	11 067	12 464	13 660	14 281	9 514	7 871	8 217	Bulgarie
Czechoslovakia	10 270	8 775	8 190	7 605	7 408	6 862	6 786	6 461	6 140	6 199	Tchécoslovaquie
German Dem. Rep.	4 300	4 000	4 600	5 000	4 963	5 400	5 300	5 785	4 911	5 263	Rép. dém. allemande
Hungary	2 886	2 764	2 882	2 916	2 659	2 745	2 771	3 087	2 955	2 617	Hongrie
Poland	27 786	25 604	23 393	21 547	21 677	18 423	17 998	19 535	18 121	16 307	Pologne
Romania[12]	19 306	18 238	17 287	17 919	19 141	...	...	...	...	...	Roumanie[12]
Other Europe	***23 347***	***73 638***	***85 267***	***145 117***	***129 180***	***122 221***	***121 626***	***108 909***	***151 192***	***163 061***	***Autre Europe***
Spain	7 493	...	...	129 225	113 714	105 103	104 831	92 878	...	...	Espagne
Yugoslavia[7]	15 854	16 554	17 092	15 892	15 466	17 118	16 795	16 031	16 467	17 244	Yougoslavie[7]
USSR	**202 543**	**197 150**	**195 326**	**193 918**	**193 477**	**191 678**	**192 335**	**199 463**	**208 484**	**218 437**	**URSS**

For general note and footnotes, see end of table.

Voir la fin du tableau pour la remarque générale et les notes.

Unit : Thousand pairs

Unité : Milliers de paires

Country or area	1976	1977	1978	1979	1980	1981	1982	1983	1984	1985	Pays ou zone
Byelorussian SSR	*6 613*	*7 603*	*7 965*	*7 990*	*7 942*	*8 062*	*8 304*	*8 553*	*8 867*	*9 291*	*RSS de Biélorussie*
Ukrainian SSR	*20 600*	*20 996*	*21 119*	*21 813*	*22 380*	*22 471*	*23 408*	*25 495*	*27 666*	*29 323*	*RSS d'Ukraine*
Oceania	**1 139**	**1 091**	**983**	**1 265**	**1 189**	**1 108**	**875**	**1 014**	**994**	**975**	**Océanie**
New Zealand	1 139	1 091	983	1 265	1 189	1 108	875	...	...	...	Nouvelle–Zélande
Total	**979 786**	**1 048 853**	**979 814**	**1 015 420**	**1 037 508**	**952 795**	**969 761**	**925 339**	**961 889**	**967 672**	**Total**

General note.
Footwear, including overshoes, with both outer soles and uppers of rubber. (SITC 85101–1).

[1] Including plastic footwear.
[2] Plastic shoes only.
[3] Shipments.
[4] Twelve months ending 30 September of year stated.
[5] Rubber sandals only.
[6] Production by large and medium scale establishments only.
[7] Excluding rubber overshoes.
[8] Production by establishments employing 10 or more persons.
[9] Data refer to Peninsular Malaysia only.
[10] Excluding safety footwear with rubber uppers.
[11] Manufacturers' sales.
[12] Excluding production of private workshops and small–scale private industry.

Remarque générale.
Chaussures, y compris les couvre–chaussures, dont la semelle extérieure et le dessus sont en caoutchouc. (CTCI 85101–1).

[1] Y compris les chaussures en matière plastique.
[2] Chaussures en matière plastique seulement.
[3] Expéditions.
[4] Période de douze mois finissant le 30 septembre de l'année indiquée.
[5] Sandales en caoutchouc seulement.
[6] Production des grandes et moyennes entreprises seulement.
[7] Non compris les couvre–chaussures en caoutchouc.
[8] Production des établissements occupant 10 personnes ou plus.
[9] Données se rapportant à la Malaisie péninsulaire seulement.
[10] Non compris les chaussures de sécurité à empeignes en caoutchouc.
[11] Ventes des fabricants.
[12] Non compris la production des ateliers privés et de la petite industrie privée.

Household ware of porcelain or china – Articles de ménage en porcelaine

Unit : Thousand units

Unité : En milliers

Country or area	1976	1977	1978	1979	1980	1981	1982	1983	1984	1985	Pays ou zone
Asia											**Asie**
Indonesia[1]	6 702	12 477	13 539	21 874	26 837	31 722	47 783	38 027	45 290	...	Indonésie[1]
Korea, Republic of	32 088	56 395	63 958	87 811	125 342	149 656	148 921	161 822	155 019	152 897	Corée, République de
Philippines[2]	26 979	7 454	...	...	...	...	...	...	...	...	Philippines[2]
Syrian Arab Republic	10 354	15 810	17 801	13 855	16 350	16 182	12 920	22 577	31 816	37 084	Rép. arabe syrienne
Europe											**Europe**
EEC											***CEE***
Greece	25 181	28 764	30 210	25 577	25 204	24 030	20 992	20 384	18 949	...	Grèce
EFTA											***AELE***
Finland	1 915	3 339	2 365	1 877	1 358	477	254	# 13	...	...	Finlande
East Europe											***Europe de l'est***
Bulgaria	36 539	38 605	35 195	38 429	39 440	39 198	42 206	41 026	37 585	39 027	Bulgarie
USSR	1 046 883	1 063 601	1 081 947	1 080 505	1 105 088	1 110 446	1 137 659	1 155 074	1 158 347	1 166 036	**URSS**
Ukrainian SSR	*351 066*	*345 693*	*349 875*	*346 626*	*344 710*	*340 536*	*336 967*	*340 697*	*341 955*	*334 177*	*RSS d'Ukraine*

General note.
Tableware and other articles of a kind commonly used for domestic purposes, of porcelain or china, including biscuit porcelain, parain and bone china. (SITC 66640-0A).

[1] Including household ware of other ceramic materials.
[2] Shipments.

Remarque générale.
Vaisselle et autres articles du type communément utilisé à des fins ménagères, faits en porcelaine, y compris le biscuit, le parian et la porcelaine phosphatique. (CTCI 66640-0A).

[1] Y compris les articles de ménage faits d'autres matières céramiques.
[2] Expéditions.

Household ware of porcelain or china – Articles de ménage en porcelaine

Unit : Metric tones

Unité : Tonnes métriques

Country or area	1976	1977	1978	1979	1980	1981	1982	1983	1984	1985	Pays ou zone
Africa	**3 183**	**3 510**	**4 270**	**3 902**	**4 277**	**5 472**	**7 148**	**6 793**	**8 244**	**9 214**	**Afrique**
Algeria	1 556	1 955	2 573	2 097	2 430	3 664	5 286	...	...	...	Algérie
Egypt	1 312	* 1 105	...	...	...	...	...	...	...	...	Egypte
Tunisia	315	450	489	597	639	600	654	725	1 659	2 113	Tunisie
America, South	**3 799**	**3 849**	**4 795**	**3 274**	**3 929**	**3 929**	**3 929**	**3 929**	**3 929**	**3 929**	**Amérique du Sud**
Chile	3 799	3 849	4 795	3 274	...	...	...	...	...	...	Chili
Asia	**761 005**	**794 267**	**733 758**	**718 581**	**740 597**	**644 216**	**620 287**	**635 582**	**633 014**	**595 258**	**Asie**
Japan[1 2]	761 005	794 267	733 758	718 581	740 597	644 216	620 287	635 582	633 014	595 258	Japon[1 2]
Europe	**266 483**	**277 945**	**274 145**	**269 711**	**274 181**	**277 414**	**264 590**	**255 342**	**259 323**	**257 949**	**Europe**
EEC	***138 101***	***139 605***	***136 780***	***131 548***	***133 290***	***125 391***	***125 510***	***116 143***	***112 184***	***111 600***	***CEE***
Belgium	9 412	10 058	9 831	8 941	8 761	8 377	8 067	7 982	6 958	6 220	Belgique
France	38 400	38 800	38 800	35 000	37 000	28 800	28 500	22 200	19 600	18 840	France
Germany, Fed. Rep.	90 289	90 747	88 149	87 607	87 529	88 214	88 943	85 961	85 626	86 540	Allemagne, Rép. féd.
EFTA	***12 057***	***11 949***	***11 024***	***11 582***	***11 945***	***13 556***	***13 648***	***15 923***	***18 114***	***19 761***	***AELE***
Austria	3 495	3 219	3 112	3 409	3 491	3 404	3 153	3 024	3 565	...	Autriche
Finland	451	797	581	...	...	...	...	...	...	...	Finlande
Portugal	5 350	5 133	5 080	4 986	5 547	6 993	6 901	8 107	10 524	12 299	Portugal
Sweden	2 761	2 800	2 251	2 578	2 298	2 550	2 985	4 183	...	...	Suède
East Europe	***99 669***	***100 259***	***100 209***	***100 449***	***102 814***	***99 592***	***98 726***	***100 983***	***102 893***	***100 456***	***Europe de l'est***
Czechoslovakia	19 266	20 105	20 199	20 053	20 483	20 574	21 066	21 482	22 444	22 675	Tchécoslovaquie
German Dem. Rep.[3]	39 514	38 866	38 693	38 013	39 217	39 336	39 876	39 989	40 499	39 738	Rép. dém. allemande[3]
Hungary	5 548	6 221	6 305	6 298	6 910	6 261	6 491	6 499	6 763	6 342	Hongrie
Poland	35 341	35 067	35 012	36 085	36 204	33 421	31 293	33 013	33 187	31 701	Pologne
Other Europe	***16 656***	***26 132***	***26 132***	***26 132***	***26 132***	***38 875***	***26 706***	***22 293***	***26 132***	***26 132***	***Autre Europe***
Spain	16 656	...	...	...	...	38 875	26 706	22 293	...	...	Espagne
Total	**1 034 470**	**1 079 571**	**1 016 968**	**995 468**	**1 022 984**	**931 031**	**895 954**	**901 646**	**904 510**	**866 350**	**Total**

General note.

Tableware and other articles of a kind commonly used for domestic purposes, of porcelain or china, including biscuit porcelain, parian and bone china. (SITC 66640–0B).

[1] Production of establishments employing 5 or more persons.

[2] Including household ware of other ceramic materials.

[3] Porcelain for household and hotel use.

Remarque générale.

Vaisselle et autres articles du type communément utilisé à des fins ménagères, faits en porcelaine, y compris le biscuit, le parian et la porcelaine phosphatique. (CTCI 66640–0B).

[1] Production des établissements occupant 5 personnes ou plus.

[2] Y compris les articles de ménage faits d'autres matières céramiques.

[3] Porcelaines à usages ménagers et hôteliers.

Household ware of other ceramic materials – Articles de ménage en autres matières céramiques

Unit : Metric tons — Unité : Tonnes métriques

Country or area	1976	1977	1978	1979	1980	1981	1982	1983	1984	1985	Pays ou zone
Africa	**2 242**	**3 625**	**3 525**	**4 900**	**4 066**	**4 435**	**5 893**	**5 971**	**6 439**	**6 908**	**Afrique**
Egypt	2 242	3 625	3 525	4 900	4 066	4 435	5 893	...	...	...	Egypte
Asia	**10 897**	**9 582**	**9 953**	**9 984**	**9 694**	**9 379**	**7 588**	**10 181**	**9 891**	**9 624**	**Asie**
Sri Lanka[1]	2 422	2 947	3 541	3 572	3 282	2 967	3 461	3 769	3 479	3 212	Sri Lanka[1]
Turkey	8 475	6 635	...	...	...	...	4 127	...	...	...	Turquie
Europe	**272 139**	**281 539**	**285 314**	**283 423**	**278 804**	**271 499**	**273 181**	**276 578**	**284 314**	**262 642**	**Europe**
EEC	***192 014***	***197 687***	***202 626***	***194 122***	***184 800***	***173 332***	***176 269***	***168 997***	***156 200***	***135 196***	***CEE***
Belgium	30 593	30 378	28 163	24 120	26 481	20 062	20 660	20 048	20 842	18 160	Belgique
France	130 100	134 200	135 900	137 200	126 000	122 000	124 900	117 400	105 000	92 000	France
Germany, Fed. Rep.	31 321	33 109	38 563	32 802	32 319	31 270	30 709	31 549	30 358	25 036	Allemagne, Rép. féd.
EFTA	***28 558***	***31 186***	***28 986***	***34 224***	***39 419***	***35 582***	***47 050***	***56 068***	***72 259***	***71 199***	***AELE***
Austria	4 237	3 439	3 484	4 194	3 860	2 419	3 430	3 526	5 127	5 828	Autriche
Finland	2 873	2 211	1 063	...	...	...	...	...	...	...	Finlande
Portugal	16 339	21 178	20 665	24 577	30 262	28 221	38 730	47 124	62 668	61 175	Portugal
Sweden	5 109	4 358	3 774	3 404	3 248	2 893	2 841	3 369	...	...	Suède
East Europe	***17 222***	***18 321***	***19 357***	***20 732***	***20 240***	***21 027***	***19 265***	***20 632***	***21 510***	***21 902***	***Europe de l'est***
Hungary	5 787	5 965	5 246	5 198	4 309	4 020	2 205	2 590	2 696	2 791	Hongrie
Poland	11 435	12 356	14 111	15 534	15 931	17 007	17 060	18 042	18 814	19 111	Pologne
Other Europe	***34 345***	***34 345***	***34 345***	***34 345***	***34 345***	***41 558***	***30 597***	***30 881***	***34 345***	***34 345***	***Autre Europe***
Spain	...	...	...	...	...	41 558	30 597	30 881	...	...	Espagne
Total	**285 278**	**294 746**	**298 792**	**298 307**	**292 564**	**285 313**	**286 662**	**292 730**	**300 644**	**279 174**	**Total**

General note.
Tableware and other utensils and articles of a kind commonly used for domestic purposes of other ceramic materials, such as common pottery, stoneware, earthenware and imitation porcelain. (SITC 66650–0B).

[1] State sector only.

Remarque générale.
Vaisselle et autres ustensiles et articles du type communément utilisé à des fins ménagères, faits en autres matières céramiques telles que la terre cuite, le grés, la faïence et la porcelaine imitation. (CTCI 66650–0B).

[1] Secteur public seulement.

Sanitary ceramic fittings – Appareils sanitaires en céramique

Unit : Thousand units — Unité : En milliers

Country or area	1976	1977	1978	1979	1980	1981	1982	1983	1984	1985	Pays ou zone
Africa	**196**	**163**	**196**	**223**	**275**	**241**	**234**	**325**	**326**	**267**	**Afrique**
Tunisia	196	163	196	223	275	241	234	325	326	267	Tunisie
America, North	**171**	**214**	**245**	**231**	**298**	**318**	**358**	**350**	**336**	**338**	**Amérique du Nord**
Cuba	171	214	245	231	298	318	358	350	336	338	Cuba
America, South	**685**	**695**	**1 110**	**1 357**	**1 493**	**1 379**	**1 729**	**1 903**	**2 077**	**2 251**	**Amérique du Sud**
Colombia	...	695	1 110	1 357	1 493	1 379	...	...	...	...	Colombie
Asia	**1 046**	**1 109**	**1 322**	**1 514**	**2 349**	**2 372**	**1 743**	**2 103**	**2 251**	**2 361**	**Asie**
Indonesia	105	122	107	159	751	495	211	302	401	...	Indonésie
Israel	329	...	240	293	294	300	258	230	237	246	Israël
Korea, Republic of	612	686	975	1 062	1 304	1 577	1 274	1 571	1 613	1 631	Corée, République de
Europe	**4 375**	**3 901**	**3 952**	**3 559**	**4 850**	**5 497**	**4 438**	**3 908**	**4 339**	**3 672**	**Europe**
EEC	***3 364***	***2 842***	***2 873***	***2 492***	***2 723***	***2 442***	***1 980***	***2 020***	***1 883***	***1 661***	***CEE***
Greece	3 364	2 842	2 873	2 492	2 723	2 442	1 980	2 020	1 883	...	Grèce
EFTA	***563***	***563***	***563***	***563***	***563***	***641***	***514***	***562***	***535***	***563***	***AELE***
Finland	...	...	...	...	...	641	514	562	535	...	Finlande
East Europe	***448***	***496***	***516***	***504***	***1 564***	***2 414***	***1 944***	***1 326***	***1 921***	***1 448***	***Europe de l'est***
Bulgaria	448	496	516	504	1 564	2 414	1 944	1 326	1 921	1 448	Bulgarie
Oceania	**536**	**546**	**555**	**557**	**534**	**390**	**404**	**293**	**779**	**896**	**Océanie**
Australia[1]	536	546	555	557	534	390	404	293	779	896	Australie[1]
Total	**7 009**	**6 628**	**7 380**	**7 441**	**9 799**	**10 197**	**8 906**	**8 882**	**10 108**	**9 785**	**Total**

General note.
China or earthenware fittings designed to be permanently fixed in place, normally by connection to the water or sewage system (for example, sinks, wash basins, bidets, water closet pans, urinals and the like). Small accessory bathroom or sanitary fittings are excluded. (SITC 81220-0A).

[1] Twelve months ending 30 June of year stated.

Remarque générale.
Appareils en porcelaine ou en faïence destinés à être fixés à demeure, généralement par branchement sur une conduite d'eau ou d'égout (par exemple, les éviers, les lavabos, les bidets, les cuvettes de cabinets d'aisances, les urinoirs etc.). Cette rubrique ne comprend pas les petits accessoires de salle de bains ou autres petits articles sanitaires. (CTCI 81220-0A).

[1] Période de douze mois finissant le 30 juin de l'année indiquée.

Unit : Metric tons — Unité : Tonnes métriques

Country or area	1976	1977	1978	1979	1980	1981	1982	1983	1984	1985	Pays ou zone
Africa	**6 724**	**6 256**	**7 364**	**7 796**	**8 688**	**8 218**	**8 035**	**9 653**	**9 824**	**9 214**	**Afrique**
Egypt	3 946	3 991	4 475	4 876	5 206	5 074	4 785	...	...	...	Egypte
Tunisia	2 778	2 265	2 889	2 920	3 482	3 144	3 250	4 258	4 236	3 433	Tunisie
America, South	**4 017**	**4 536**	**5 085**	**5 174**	**6 048**	**5 508**	**673**	**8 203**	**10 745**	**6 929**	**Amérique du Sud**
Chile	4 017	4 536	5 085	5 174	6 048	5 508	673	8 203	10 745	6 929	Chili
Asia	**134 647**	**132 699**	**137 446**	**154 098**	**167 580**	**150 404**	**153 030**	**157 284**	**164 540**	**172 470**	**Asie**
India[1]	20 008	20 423	21 385	23 157	24 773	25 653	28 858	33 569	34 167	...	Inde[1]
Japan[2]	111 646	109 217	112 303	127 192	138 765	120 760	119 090	119 621	126 658	133 468	Japon[2]
Sri Lanka[3]	550	648	790	781	1 074	1 023	1 030	1 126	747	798	Sri Lanka[3]
Turkey	2 443	2 411	...	...	...	...	4 052	...	...	...	Turquie
Europe	**754 256**	**773 968**	**786 511**	**792 981**	**792 622**	**785 778**	**757 162**	**725 117**	**753 635**	**740 167**	**Europe**
EEC	***557 340***	***561 470***	***569 505***	***556 046***	***561 288***	***553 855***	***528 155***	***514 581***	***516 769***	***505 856***	***CEE***
France	146 500	144 130	132 123	135 300	143 900	145 700	129 300	119 900	126 000	122 000	France
Germany, Fed. Rep.	86 762	89 849	93 184	88 824	85 466	76 233	66 933	62 759	58 847	51 934	Allemagne, Rép. féd.
Italy[4]	215 000	...	...	...	...	...	...	...	...	...	Italie[4]
Netherlands[4]	30 700	...	...	...	...	...	...	...	...	...	Pays-Bas[4]
United Kingdom	78 378	81 791	98 498	...	...	...	...	...	...	...	Royaume-Uni
EFTA	***39 959***	***37 712***	***37 065***	***37 640***	***33 871***	***35 075***	***38 640***	***39 680***	***42 428***	***42 465***	***AELE***
Finland	7 565	7 155	7 142	...	...	...	...	...	...	...	Finlande
Portugal	11 089	12 245	12 722	12 575	12 360	14 993	18 165	19 694	21 842	20 966	Portugal
Sweden	21 305	18 312	17 201	17 778	14 224	12 795	13 188	12 699	13 299	14 212	Suède
East Europe	***68 424***	***69 765***	***73 332***	***75 887***	***77 250***	***75 817***	***74 369***	***78 744***	***80 266***	***75 825***	***Europe de l'est***
Czechoslovakia	19 980	21 141	21 229	21 038	20 899	19 625	21 058	24 013	24 174	24 014	Tchécoslovaquie
German Dem. Rep.	13 698	14 001	14 365	19 012	21 161	21 670	22 156	22 795	23 132	20 222	Rép. dém. allemande
Hungary	10 902	10 437	10 282	10 064	10 720	12 511	11 844	12 929	12 325	11 940	Hongrie
Poland	23 844	24 186	27 456	25 773	24 470	22 011	19 311	19 007	20 635	19 649	Pologne
Other Europe	***88 533***	***105 021***	***106 609***	***123 408***	***120 213***	***121 031***	***115 998***	***92 112***	***114 172***	***116 021***	***Autre Europe***
Spain	77 522	...	...	111 638	107 865	108 248	102 105	78 485	...	...	Espagne
Yugoslavia	11 011	10 309	10 971	11 770	12 348	12 783	13 893	13 627	12 980	13 903	Yougoslavie
Total	**899 644**	**917 459**	**936 406**	**960 049**	**974 938**	**949 908**	**918 900**	**900 257**	**938 744**	**928 780**	**Total**

General note.
China or earthenware fittings designed to be permanently fixed in place, normally by connection to the water or sewage system (for example, sinks, wash basins, bidets, water closet pans, urinals and the like). Small accessory bathroom or sanitary fittings are excluded. (SITC 81220-0B).

[1] Production by large and medium scale establishments only.
[2] Production of establishments employing 5 or more persons.
[3] State sector only.
[4] Source: Industrial Statistics, Statistical Office of the European Communities, (Luxembourg).

Remarque générale.
Appareils en porcelaine ou en faïence destinés à être fixés à demeure, généralement par branchement sur une conduite d'eau ou d'égout (par exemple, les éviers, les lavabos, les bidets, les cuvettes de cabinets d'aisances, les urinoirs etc.). Cette rubrique ne comprend pas les petits accessoires de salle de bains ou autres petits articles sanitaires. (CTCI 81220-0B).

[1] Production des grandes et moyennes entreprises seulement.
[2] Production des établissements occupant 5 personnes ou plus.
[3] Secteur public seulement.
[4] Source: Statistiques industrielles, Office statistique des Communautés européennes, (Luxembourg).

Glass, drawn or blown, in rectangles, unworked – Verres étirés ou soufflés, de forme rectangulaire, non travaillés

Unit : Thousand metric tons — Unité : Milliers de tonnes métriques

Country or area	1976	1977	1978	1979	1980	1981	1982	1983	1984	1985	Pays ou zone
America, North	**3 187**	**3 170**	**3 346**	**3 249**	**2 832**	**2 986**	**2 546**	**2 917**	**3 299**	**2 857**	**Amérique du Nord**
Mexico	126	134	141	135	159	171	153	110	110	110	Mexique
United States	...	3 036	3 205	3 114	2 673	2 815	2 393	2 807	3 189	...	Etats-Unis
Asia	**307**	**318**	**296**	**349**	**342**	**417**	**450**	**438**	**473**	**478**	**Asie**
Iran(Islamic Rep.of)[1]	108	102	91	135	170	148	160	...	...	...	Iran(Rép.islamique)[1]
Syrian Arab Republic	25	25	23	35	46	58	51	47	63	50	Rép. arabe syrienne
Thailand	43	46	33	39	...	...	...	...	...	...	Thaïlande
Turkey	131	145	149	140	86	171	199	...	...	...	Turquie
Europe	**1 597**	**1 576**	**1 537**	**1 603**	**1 724**	**1 633**	**1 583**	**1 578**	**1 654**	**1 598**	**Europe**
EEC	***922***	***873***	***859***	***916***	***1 019***	***982***	***949***	***915***	***954***	***935***	***CEE***
Belgium* [2]	389	...	...	...	...	...	...	...	...	...	Belgique* [2]
Denmark	52	38	55	53	55	...	...	...	...	...	Danemark
France	199	199	* 180	* 240	* 279	* 270	...	...	...	...	France
Germany, Fed. Rep.	144	113	108	76	22	9	14	9	46	18	Allemagne, Rép. féd.
Italy	104	100	93	124	240	223	160	110	91	79	Italie
Netherlands* [2]	34	...	...	...	...	...	...	...	...	...	Pays-Bas* [2]
EFTA	***144***	***112***	***100***	***112***	***122***	***134***	***130***	***122***	***121***	***119***	***AELE***
Austria	66	49	44	50	64	68	64	61	65	69	Autriche
Portugal	44	34	41	52	53	63	66	61	56	50	Portugal
Sweden	34	29	15	10	5	3	0	0	0	0	Suède
East Europe	***411***	***450***	***447***	***444***	***452***	***387***	***373***	***410***	***449***	***414***	***Europe de l'est***
Hungary	81	88	94	89	104	86	94	94	101	96	Hongrie
Poland[3 4]	330	362	353	355	348	301	279	316	348	318	Pologne[3 4]
Other Europe	***120***	***141***	***131***	***131***	***131***	***131***	***131***	***131***	***131***	***131***	***Autre Europe***
Spain	120	141	...	...	...	...	...	...	...	...	Espagne
Total	**5 091**	**5 064**	**5 179**	**5 201**	**4 898**	**5 037**	**4 579**	**4 933**	**5 426**	**4 933**	**Total**

General note.
Unworked drawn or blown glass (including flashed glass) in rectangles, used mainly for windows, doors, display cases, greenhouses, clocks and pictures, and sometimes as parts of articles of furniture, for photographic plates, plain spectacle glasses etc. Glass cut otherwise than into rectangles is excluded. (SITC 66430-0A).

Remarque générale.
Verres étirés ou soufflés, non travaillés (y compris les verres plaqués) de forme rectangulaire, utilisés principalement dans le garnissage des fenêtres, des portes, des vitrines, des serres, des horloges et des tableaux, et servant parfois pour recouvrir des meubles, pour fabriquer des plaques photographiques, des lunettes ordinaires etc. Cette rubrique ne comprend pas les verres qui ne sont pas de forme rectangulaire. (CTCI 66430-0A).

[1] Production by establishments employing 50 or more persons.
[2] Source: Industrial Statistics, Statistical Office of the European Communities, (Luxembourg).
[3] Drawn window glass.
[4] In terms of 2 mm thickness.

[1] Production des établissements occupant 50 personnes ou plus.
[2] Source: Statistiques industrielles, Office statistique des Communautés européennes, (Luxembourg).
[3] Verre à vitres étirés.
[4] Sur la base de 2 mm d'épaisseur.

Glass, drawn or blown, in rectangles, unworked – Verres étirés ou soufflés, de forme rectangulaire, non travaillés

Unit : Thousand square metres — Unité : Milliers de mètres carrés

Country or area	1976	1977	1978	1979	1980	1981	1982	1983	1984	1985	Pays ou zone
America, North	**328 601**	**369 418**	**398 676**	**378 283**	**337 442**	**356 058**	**317 603**	**351 602**	**396 513**	**359 931**	**Amérique du Nord**
Cuba	351	408	335	293	189	88	284	345	284	579	Cuba
Mexico	24 713	26 815	27 610	26 349	31 294	33 687	30 068	21 575	21 553	23 132	Mexique
United States[1]	303 537	342 195	370 731	351 641	305 959	322 283	287 251	329 682	374 676	...	Etats–Unis[1]
America, South	**33 535**	**36 023**	**39 444**	**37 626**	**31 088**	**34 463**	**32 994**	**35 401**	**34 476**	**35 276**	**Amérique du Sud**
Brazil	30 649	32 455	36 445	[2] 35 702	29 122	32 283	...	...	...	...	Brésil
Chile	2 886	3 568	2 999	1 924	1 966	2 180	475	2 956	2 104	2 977	Chili
Asia	**51 557**	**53 216**	**55 551**	**71 483**	**53 241**	**66 953**	**62 215**	**73 150**	**67 921**	**73 289**	**Asie**
India[3]	20 660	21 196	19 972	24 963	23 146	22 749	22 468	26 779	18 213	...	Inde[3]
Indonesia	...	...	11 879	14 429	14 303	18 502	17 420	25 357	27 803	...	Indonésie
Israel	3 496	3 609	3 750	3 818	3 778	3 726	3 185	2 325	3 668	3 535	Israël
Philippines[4]	966	951	...	...	...	...	...	...	...	...	Philippines[4]
Turkey	...	19 324	18 991	27 314	11 055	21 017	...	...	...	...	Turquie
Europe	**290 901**	**298 490**	**300 119**	**307 170**	**289 249**	**268 127**	**260 542**	**261 652**	**259 565**	**253 756**	**Europe**
EEC	***20 559***	***18 282***	***17 549***	***15 758***	***5 120***	***1 793***	***2 843***	***1 793***	***2 473***	***2 325***	***CEE***
Denmark	...	...	...	...	...	...	...	...	5	5	Danemark
Germany, Fed. Rep.	20 554	18 277	17 544	15 753	5 115	1 788	2 838	1 788	2 468	2 320	Allemagne, Rép. féd.
EFTA	***17 789***	***12 588***	***12 140***	***14 474***	***14 889***	***14 725***	***13 447***	***14 289***	***11 603***	***14 306***	***AELE***
Austria	7 661	4 194	3 909	3 569	4 118	4 237	2 759	3 679	4 246	4 571	Autriche
Finland	10 128	8 394	8 231	10 905	10 771	10 488	10 688	10 610	7 357	...	Finlande
East Europe	***238 639***	***250 399***	***253 730***	***260 201***	***254 814***	***235 922***	***226 779***	***230 065***	***231 786***	***222 587***	***Europe de l'est***
Bulgaria	27 615	24 959	26 514	27 659	24 538	22 352	24 860	23 012	20 642	23 459	Bulgarie
Czechoslovakia	37 366	38 992	38 102	40 783	39 132	34 312	35 476	35 942	32 151	31 577	Tchécoslovaquie
German Dem. Rep.	20 498	23 868	23 488	23 956	23 296	24 741	24 399	23 645	23 923	22 798	Rép. dém. allemande
Hungary	16 238	17 484	18 513	17 659	20 797	17 121	18 872	18 834	20 114	19 166	Hongrie
Poland[5, 6]	65 919	72 428	70 546	71 070	69 547	60 106	55 707	63 000	69 706	63 593	Pologne[5, 6]
Romania[6]	71 003	72 668	76 567	79 074	77 504	77 290	67 465	65 632	65 250	61 994	Roumanie[6]
Other Europe	***13 914***	***17 221***	***16 700***	***16 737***	***14 426***	***15 687***	***17 473***	***15 505***	***13 703***	***14 538***	***Autre Europe***
Yugoslavia	13 914	17 221	16 700	16 737	14 426	15 687	17 473	15 505	13 703	14 538	Yougoslavie
USSR	**267 007**	**268 746**	**265 575**	**255 131**	**244 802**	**245 156**	**243 229**	**247 247**	**247 238**	**242 874**	**URSS**
Byelorussian SSR	*15 040*	*15 342*	*16 578*	*15 138*	*15 898*	*14 869*	*14 333*	*15 415*	*14 290*	*14 986*	*RSS de Biélorussie*
Ukrainian SSR	*61 462*	*62 098*	*55 252*	*48 469*	*39 912*	*45 458*	*45 964*	*49 041*	*47 237*	*50 512*	*RSS d'Ukraine*
Total	**971 601**	**1 025 893**	**1 059 365**	**1 049 693**	**955 822**	**970 757**	**916 583**	**969 053**	**1 005 713**	**965 126**	**Total**

General note.
Unworked drawn or blown glass (including flashed glass) in rectangles, used mainly for windows, doors, display cases, greenhouses, clocks and pictures, and sometimes as parts of articles of furniture, for photographic plates, plain spectacle glasses etc. Glass cut otherwise than into rectangles is excluded. (SITC 66430–0B).

[1] Flat glass only.
[2] Production by establishments employing 5 or more persons.
[3] Production by large and medium scale establishments only.
[4] Shipments.
[5] Drawn window glass.
[6] In terms of 2 mm thickness.

Remarque générale.
Verres étirés ou soufflés, non travaillés (y compris les verres plauqés) de forme rectangulaire, utilisés principalement dans le garnissage des fenêtres, des portes, des vitrines, des serres, des horloges et des tableaux, et servant parfois pour recouvrir des meubles, pour fabriquer des plaques photographiques, des lunettes ordinaires etc. Cette rubrique ne comprend pas les verres qui ne sont pas de forme rectangulaire. (CTCI 66430–0B).

[1] Verre plat seulement.
[2] Production des établissements occupant 5 personnes ou plus.
[3] Production des grandes et moyennes entreprises seulement.
[4] Expéditions.
[5] Verre à vitres étirés.
[6] Sur la base de 2 mm d'épaisseur.

Glass, cast, rolled, drawn or blown – Verres coulés, laminés, étirés ou soufflés

Unit : Thousand metric tons

Unité : Milliers de tonnes métriques

Country or area	1976	1977	1978	1979	1980	1981	1982	1983	1984	1985	Pays ou zone
Africa											**Afrique**
Egypt	23	21	19	28	27	25	23	26	...	...	Egypte
America, North											**Amérique du Nord**
Mexico	7	6	8	9	10	12	10	7	10	13	Mexique
America, South											**Amérique du Sud**
Brazil	145	182	122	[1,2] 229	[1,2] 289	...	...	...	...	...	Brésil
Asia											**Asie**
United Arab Emirates[1]	...	...	844	...	...	...	...	...	...	...	Emirats arabes unis[1]
Europe											**Europe**
EEC											***CEE***
Belgium* [3]	303	...	...	...	...	...	...	...	...	...	Belgique* [3]
Denmark	1	1	1	1	1	...	...	...	...	...	Danemark
France	334	303	* 270	* 360	* 415	* 405	...	...	...	...	France
Germany, Fed. Rep.	760	966	932	998	1 149	1 041	1 033	1 104	1 064	1 080	Allemagne, Rép. féd.
Greece	58	46	66	52	65	60	66	39	18	...	Grèce
Italy	391	383	392	398	335	377	444	549	670	700	Italie
EFTA											***AELE***
Finland	...	...	...	...	...	750	842	1 087	904	...	Finlande
Sweden	50	140	146	169	167	144	171	181	160	176	Suède
East Europe											***Europe de l'est***
Bulgaria[1]	37	12	9	24	...	...	...	...	...	...	Bulgarie[1]
Czechoslovakia[1]	10 459	11 106	18 666	23 975	23 891	22 365	21 806	15 904	24 095	24 511	Tchécoslovaquie[1]
Hungary	42	56	56	50	60	54	60	55	50	51	Hongrie
Other Europe											***Autre Europe***
Spain	188	80	...	...	...	...	...	...	...	...	Espagne
USSR[1]	24 889	27 180	31 749	35 015	35 855	34 826	35 847	38 238	38 932	...	**URSS[1]**
Ukrainian SSR[1]	*3 161*	*4 156*	*4 963*	*5 036*	*4 578*	*5 249*	*5 226*	*4 914*	*6 116*	*6 404*	*RSS d'Ukraine[1]*

General note.

Cast, rolled, drawn or blown glass (including flashed or wired glass) in rectangles, surface ground or polished, but not further worked, used mainly in furniture, for the manufacture of mirrors etc., in bay windows and display windows, show cases, ships etc. Glass cut to shape other than rectangular, bent and curved glass are excluded. (SITC 66440–0A).

[1] In thousand square metres.
[2] Production by establishments employing 5 or more persons.
[3] Source: Industrial Statistics, Statistical Office of the European Communities, (Luxembourg).

Remarque générale.

Verres coulés, laminés, étirés ou soufflés (y compris les verres plaqués ou armés) de forme rectangulaire, simplement doucis ou polis, utilisés principalement dans l'ameublement, dans la fabrication d'articles de miroiterie etc., dans la garniture de baies de maisons, de vitrines de magasins, dans l'équipement des navires etc. Cette rubrique ne comprend pas les verres qui ne sont pas de forme rectangulaire ou sont incurvés et bombés. (CTCI 66440–0A).

[1] En milliers de mètres carrés.
[2] Production des établissements occupant 5 personnes ou plus.
[3] Source: Statistiques industrielles, Office statistique des Communautés européennes, (Luxembourg).

Glass, safety, of toughened or laminated glass – Glaces ou verres de sécurité consistant en verre trempé ou feuilleté

Unit : Thousand metric tons — Unité : Milliers de tonnes métriques

Country or area	1976	1977	1978	1979	1980	1981	1982	1983	1984	1985	Pays ou zone
Africa											**Afrique**
Egypt	1	1	...	1	1	1	1	...	...	...	Egypte
Tunisia	...	3	...	...	...	...	...	...	...	...	Tunisie
America, North											**Amérique du Nord**
Mexico	5	6	8	15	15	16	13	10	13	19	Mexique
Asia											**Asie**
Turkey	...	...	...	5	3	4	5	7	12	13	Turquie
Europe											**Europe**
EEC											***CEE***
Belgium* [1]	76	...	...	...	...	...	...	...	...	...	Belgique* [1]
Denmark	7	7	2	2	2	2	* 1	1	...	...	Danemark
Germany, Fed. Rep.[2]	171	171	166	176	165	149	...	...	...	...	Allemagne, Rép. féd.[2]
Greece	1	1	1	1	2	2	2	2	2	...	Grèce
Italy	111	112	121	129	127	108	106	103	150	157	Italie
EFTA											***AELE***
Austria	1	1	1	1	1	3	3	4	4	6	Autriche
Finland	...	...	...	...	...	...	1 466	1 737	...	...	Finlande
Portugal	4	4	3	3	5	5	5	5	4	3	Portugal
Sweden	18	17	19	20	20	19	21	25	31	28	Suède
East Europe											***Europe de l'est***
Czechoslovakia[3]	1 258	1 375	1 480	1 434	1 460	1 455	1 576	1 608	1 693	1 819	Tchécoslovaquie[3]
Hungary	6	6	7	7	7	8	9	10	10	10	Hongrie

General note.
Toughened or laminated glass, shaped or not, used for motor–car windscreens and windows, in doors, in ships' portholes, in protective goggles for industrial workers and drivers, and for eye–pieces for gas masks and divers' helmets. Ordinary wired glass and selective absorption glasses are excluded. (SITC 66470–0A).

[1] Source: Industrial Statistics, Statistical Office of the European Communities, (Luxembourg).
[2] Beginning 1982, data are confidential.
[3] In thousand square metres.

Remarque générale.
Glaces ou verres trempés ou feuilletés, façonnés ou non, utilisés pour la fabrication de pare–brise et de fenêtres d'automobiles, de portes, de hublots de navires, de lunettes de protection pour ouvriers et conducteurs, ainsi que des verres de masques à gaz et de casques de scaphandriers. Cette rubrique ne comprend pas les verres armés ordinaires et les verres à absorption sélective. (CTCI 66470–0A).

[1] Source: Statistiques industrielles, Office statistique des Communautés européennes, (Luxembourg).
[2] A partir de 1982, les données sont confidentielles.
[3] En milliers de mètres carrés.

Glass bottles and other containers of common glass – Bouteilles et autres récipients en verre ordinaire

Unit : Million units | Unité : En millions

Country or area	1976	1977	1978	1979	1980	1981	1982	1983	1984	1985	Pays ou zone
Africa	**42**	**42**	**50**	**48**	**49**	**58**	**63**	**73**	**71**	**76**	**Afrique**
Tunisia	21	25	32	34	34	...	...	...	...	...	Tunisie
Zaire	21	...	...	14	15	18	20	26	...	...	Zaïre
America, North	**46 795**	**47 234**	**51 099**	**51 130**	**52 021**	**51 276**	**48 682**	**46 351**	**46 250**	**44 608**	**Amérique du Nord**
Cuba	182	166	229	184	176	157	233	187	265	263	Cuba
Dominican Republic	46	54	51	68	70	73	56	75	75	77	Rép. dominicaine
Mexico	3 007	3 360	3 643	3 938	4 547	4 168	3 727	3 882	4 157	4 982	Mexique
United States	43 560	43 654	47 176	46 940	47 228	46 878	44 666	42 207	41 753	39 286	Etats-Unis
America, South	**10 710**	**3 228**	**3 873**	**3 827**	**4 367**	**3 794**	**3 407**	**2 932**	**2 439**	**1 949**	**Amérique du Sud**
Bolivia	14	15	36	39	31	21	1	16	16	...	Bolivie
Brazil	10 085	2 729	3 177	3 089	3 795	3 291	...	...	...	...	Brésil
Colombia	...	483	657	696	536	476	...	...	...	...	Colombie
Paraguay	1	1	3	3	5	6	6	11	12	18	Paraguay
Asia	**565**	**592**	**1 002**	**1 126**	**1 497**	**981**	**1 577**	**1 420**	**1 510**	**1 897**	**Asie**
Burma[1]	18	16	17	9	42	44	41	43	38	21	Birmanie[1]
Indonesia	92	54	450	430	499	159	676	248	167	...	Indonésie
Iran(Islamic Rep.of)[2]	180	195	148	231	198	194	295	...	...	...	Iran(Rép.islamique)[2]
Korea, Republic of	275	327	387	456	758	584	565	867	1 029	1 189	Corée, République de
Europe	**19 968**	**20 579**	**20 113**	**20 429**	**20 340**	**19 936**	**19 459**	**18 770**	**19 950**	**20 507**	**Europe**
EEC	***17 421***	***17 945***	***17 681***	***17 599***	***17 394***	***16 861***	***16 586***	***15 768***	***16 840***	***17 439***	***CEE***
Denmark	494	510	427	411	420	456	429	449	485	467	Danemark
Germany, Fed. Rep.	10 101	10 572	10 183	10 349	10 535	10 416	10 168	9 883	10 908	11 459	Allemagne, Rép. féd.
United Kingdom	6 826	6 863	7 071	6 839	6 439	5 989	5 989	5 436	5 447	5 513	Royaume-Uni
EFTA	***740***	***818***	***964***	***915***	***995***	***1 000***	***848***	***881***	***1 011***	***923***	***AELE***
Finland	236	198	222	129	247	214	110	155	150	...	Finlande
Portugal	504	620	742	786	748	786	738	726	861	789	Portugal
East Europe	***1 807***	***1 816***	***1 468***	***1 915***	***1 951***	***2 075***	***2 025***	***2 121***	***2 099***	***2 145***	***Europe de l'est***
Czechoslovakia	1 189	1 209	1 218	1 263	1 273	1 363	1 329	1 455	1 387	1 376	Tchécoslovaquie
Hungary	618	607	250	652	678	712	696	666	712	769	Hongrie
Total	**78 080**	**71 675**	**76 137**	**76 560**	**78 274**	**76 045**	**73 188**	**69 546**	**70 220**	**69 036**	**Total**

General note.
Bottles of all shapes and sizes, jars, pots and similar containers, and stoppers and closures of common glass, blown, pressed or moulded, but not otherwise worked. Inners for vacuum vessels are excluded. (SITC 66511-0A).

Remarque générale.
Bouteilles de toutes formes et de toutes dimensions, bocaux, pots et récipients similaires et bouchons, couvercles et autres dispositifs de fermeture en verre ordinaire fabriqués par soufflage, pressage ou moulage, mais n'ayant subi aucune autre ouvraison. Cette rubrique ne comprend pas les ampoules en verre pour récipients isolants. (CTCI 66511-0A).

[1] Government production only.
[2] Production by establishments employing 50 or more persons.

[1] Production de l'Etat seulement.
[2] Production des établissements occupant 50 personnes ou plus.

Glass bottles and other containers of common glass – Bouteilles et autres récipients en verre ordinaire

Unit : Thousand metric tons — Unité : Milliers de tonnes métriques

Country or area	1976	1977	1978	1979	1980	1981	1982	1983	1984	1985	Pays ou zone
Africa	**35**	**40**	**62**	**53**	**60**	**61**	**60**	**74**	**76**	**74**	**Afrique**
Algeria	19	22	35	27	27	27	28	...	...	...	Algérie
Tunisia	8	9	15	15	17	18	14	24	23	18	Tunisie
United Rep. Tanzania	8	9	* 12	11	* 16	* 16	...	...	...	...	Rép.Unie de Tanzanie
America, North	**11 866**	**11 782**	**12 687**	**12 268**	**12 152**	**12 132**	**11 543**	**11 149**	**10 714**	**10 066**	**Amérique du Nord**
United States	11 866	11 782	12 687	12 268	12 152	12 132	11 543	11 149	10 714	10 066	Etats–Unis
America, South	**559**	**556**	**552**	**553**	**551**	**554**	**529**	**536**	**540**	**542**	**Amérique du Sud**
Chile	...	...	...	56	55	48	* 30	31	35	36	Chili
Colombia	...	...	...	...	...	475	468	486	...	...	Colombie
Ecuador	...	...	17	...	19	31	31	19	...	...	Equateur
Asia	**2 563**	**2 435**	**2 640**	**2 810**	**2 675**	**2 490**	**2 742**	**2 969**	**2 965**	**2 894**	**Asie**
India[1]	229	246	292	315	324	350	386	432	324	...	Inde[1]
Japan[2]	2 008	2 000	2 085	2 220	2 157	1 942	2 073	2 305	2 413	2 251	Japon[2]
Philippines[3]	206	56	...	...	...	...	...	...	...	...	Philippines[3]
Syrian Arab Republic	6	7	8	7	5	8	6	7	...	...	Rép. arabe syrienne
Turkey[4]	114	126	124	137	58	59	146	...	...	...	Turquie[4]
Europe	**11 344**	**11 624**	**11 673**	**12 074**	**12 857**	**12 417**	**12 378**	**12 993**	**13 466**	**13 006**	**Europe**
EEC	***7 810***	***8 145***	***8 062***	***8 410***	***8 913***	***8 531***	***8 486***	***9 146***	***9 442***	***8 915***	***CEE***
Belgium[5]	400	...	...	...	...	...	...	...	...	...	Belgique[5]
France	2 637	2 861	2 875	2 883	3 093	2 977	3 020	# 3 233	3 248	2 785	France
Germany, Fed. Rep.	2 930	2 929	2 805	2 861	2 884	2 848	2 771	2 693	2 933	2 991	Allemagne, Rép. féd.
Greece	62	71	72	70	40	65	66	78	73	...	Grèce
Italy	1 382	1 485	1 511	1 797	2 097	1 842	1 830	2 343	2 389	2 270	Italie
Netherlands[5]	399	...	...	...	...	...	...	...	...	...	Pays–Bas[5]
EFTA	***435***	***427***	***395***	***428***	***449***	***463***	***467***	***450***	***433***	***448***	***AELE***
Austria	174	186	171	208	223	245	251	231	229	254	Autriche
Finland	88	77	82	...	...	...	...	...	...	...	Finlande
Sweden	173	164	142	138	144	136	134	137	122	112	Suède
East Europe	***1 806***	***1 779***	***1 846***	***1 883***	***1 929***	***1 920***	***1 891***	***1 970***	***2 064***	***2 084***	***Europe de l'est***
Bulgaria	533	535	549	568	595	595	609	620	642	657	Bulgarie
Hungary	274	266	294	301	305	321	305	308	337	344	Hongrie
Poland	629	614	619	620	638	609	593	624	673	696	Pologne
Romania	370	364	384	394	391	395	384	418	412	387	Roumanie
Other Europe	***1 293***	***1 273***	***1 370***	***1 353***	***1 566***	***1 503***	***1 534***	***1 427***	***1 526***	***1 558***	***Autre Europe***
Spain	1 044	985	...	1 004	1 230	1 119	1 123	1 061	...	...	Espagne
Yugoslavia	249	288	314	349	336	384	411	366	383	400	Yougoslavie
Total	**26 367**	**26 437**	**27 613**	**27 758**	**28 295**	**27 654**	**27 253**	**27 722**	**27 761**	**26 582**	**Total**

General note.
Bottles of all shapes and sizes, jars, pots and similar containers, and stoppers and closures of common glass, blown, pressed or moulded, but not otherwise worked. Inners for vacuum vessels are excluded. (SITC 66511–0B).

Remarque générale.
Bouteilles de toutes formes et de toutes dimensions, bocaux, pots et récipients similaires et bouchons, couvercles et autres dispositifs de fermeture en verre ordinaire fabriqués par soufflage, pressage ou moulage, mais n'ayant subi aucune autre ouvraison. Cette rubrique ne comprend pas les ampoules en verre pour récipients isolants. (CTCI 665110–0B).

[1] Production by large and medium scale establishments only.
[2] Production by establishments employing 10 or more persons.
[3] Shipments.
[4] Bottles only.
[5] Source: Industrial Statistics, Statistical Office of the European Communities, (Luxembourg).

[1] Production des grandes et moyennes entreprises seulement.
[2] Production des établissements occupant 10 personnes ou plus.
[3] Expéditions.
[4] Bouteilles seulement.
[5] Source: Statistiques industrielles, Office statistique des Communautés européennes, (Luxembourg).

Building bricks, made of clay – Briques de construction en argile

Unit : Million units

Unité : En millions

Country or area	1976	1977	1978	1979	1980	1981	1982	1983	1984	1985	Pays ou zone
Africa	**3 049**	**2 430**	**2 500**	**3 066**	**3 232**	**3 707**	**3 631**	**3 754**	**3 824**	**3 212**	**Afrique**
Egypt	500	400	300	408	220	# 38	66	24	...	...	Egypte
Ethiopia[1]	17	12	14	20	23	23	20	25	22	...	Ethiopie[1]
South Africa	2 215	1 752	1 931	2 349	* 2 685	* 3 082	2 913	3 025	* 3 031	2 369	Afrique du Sud
Togo	1	1	1	* 1	* 1	...	...	...	...	521	Togo
Tunisia	164	...	...	...	...	...	...	...	...	...	Tunisie
Zimbabwe	152	101	90	124	139	130	123	98	90	108	Zimbabwe
America, North	**8 051**	**9 023**	**9 454**	**9 165**	**7 181**	**6 140**	**5 518**	**6 719**	**7 823**	**7 868**	**Amérique du Nord**
Canada	595	599	613	644	* 556	...	...	...	...	...	Canada
Cuba	100	113	115	115	109	118	111	125	128	147	Cuba
El Salvador[2]	15	12	29	2	2	1	4	4	...	...	El Salvador[2]
United States	7 341	8 299	8 697	8 404	6 514	5 429	4 815	6 005	7 112	7 142	Etats–Unis
America, South	**3 783**	**4 746**	**4 977**	**5 066**	**9 682**	**9 673**	**8 625**	**9 625**	**9 637**	**9 634**	**Amérique du Sud**
Brazil	3 275	4 223	4 446	[3] 4 540	9 035	...	...	...	...	...	Brésil
Chile	...	...	...	56	52	63	* 15	21	35	38	Chili
Colombia	...	272	270	244	261	267	287	307	...	...	Colombie
Ecuador	...	4	8	...	# 65	20	19	12	...	...	Equateur
Paraguay	176	184	194	207	269	323	304	285	279	265	Paraguay
Asia	**14 481**	**2 023**	**2 061**	**9 340**	**9 425**	**10 137**	**11 404**	**12 619**	**1 973**	**1 935**	**Asie**
Burma[4]	34	44	41	35	40	46	41	42	45	36	Birmanie[4]
Cyprus	14	30	38	50	53	49	47	49	48	47	Chypre
Indonesia	56	59	57	80	63	42	54	89	68	...	Indonésie
Iran(Islamic Rep.of)[5]	12 510	...	...	7 285	7 465	8 277	9 761	10 682	...	...	Iran(Rép.islamique)[5]
Korea, Republic of	153	148	190	176	193	161	210	247	255	263	Corée, République de
Malaysia	...	...	...	...	...	...	493	573	661	561	Malaisie
Mongolia	89	81	103	105	110	109	113	123	127	143	Mongolie
Philippines[6]	7	9	...	...	...	...	...	...	...	...	Philippines[6]
Singapore	128	128	109	126	127	127	127	176	176	129	Singapour
Turkey	917	950	942	901	...	...	549	624	580	671	Turquie
Yemen	...	...	...	...	5	2	* 1	6	5	6	Yémen
Europe	**35 415**	**35 330**	**35 019**	**36 039**	**35 227**	**32 195**	**30 457**	**30 314**	**29 603**	**28 316**	**Europe**
EEC	***19 963***	***19 980***	***20 009***	***20 563***	***20 077***	***17 798***	***16 297***	***16 302***	***16 415***	***15 803***	***CEE***
Belgium[7]	559	544	450	403	380	253	196	170	164	178	Belgique[7]
Denmark	675	627	657	634	452	344	296	342	409	417	Danemark
France	2 853	2 843	* 2 705	* 2 783	* 2 836	* 2 329	* 2 073	* 1 857	...	...	France
Germany, Fed. Rep.	3 609	3 841	4 187	4 683	4 593	4 214	3 599	3 779	3 627	2 966	Allemagne, Rép. féd.
Greece	...	...	...	...	...	1 405	1 490	1 341	1 160	...	Grèce
Italy[8]	4 033	3 950	...	...	...	...	...	...	...	...	Italie[8]
Netherlands	2 145	2 331	2 417	2 419	2 369	1 905	1 507	1 413	1 556	1 467	Pays–Bas
United Kingdom	4 740	4 495	4 253	4 301	4 107	3 357	3 145	3 409	3 610	3 679	Royaume–Uni
EFTA	***646***	***622***	***563***	***550***	***561***	***540***	***508***	***491***	***492***	***440***	***AELE***
Austria	288	275	250	251	248	231	215	203	212	198	Autriche
Finland	125	124	113	124	135	131	134	143	160	* 141	Finlande
Norway	31	35	38	36	38	40	39	40	28	30	Norvège
Sweden	202	188	162	139	* 140	138	120	105	92	71	Suède
East Europe	***11 464***	***10 985***	***10 477***	***10 036***	***9 907***	***9 922***	***9 802***	***9 781***	***9 320***	***8 737***	***Europe de l'est***
Bulgaria	1 446	1 451	1 413	1 433	1 425	1 435	1 404	1 464	1 376	1 122	Bulgarie
Czechoslovakia	2 479	2 212	2 096	2 028	2 145	2 246	2 340	2 214	1 824	1 823	Tchécoslovaquie
German Dem. Rep.	1 347	1 346	1 307	1 229	1 230	1 242	1 104	1 118	1 131	1 116	Rép. dém. allemande
Hungary	1 898	1 953	1 943	1 916	1 946	1 967	1 956	2 010	2 086	1 921	Hongrie
Poland	2 608	2 399	2 245	1 917	1 738	1 560	1 629	1 653	1 628	1 526	Pologne
Romania	1 686	1 624	1 473	1 513	1 423	1 472	...	...	...	...	Roumanie
Other Europe	***3 342***	***3 743***	***3 970***	***4 890***	***4 682***	***3 935***	***3 850***	***3 740***	***3 376***	***3 336***	***Autre Europe***
Yugoslavia	3 342	3 743	3 970	4 890	4 682	3 935	3 850	3 740	3 376	3 336	Yougoslavie
USSR[9]	**32 478**	**31 263**	**30 079**	**28 255**	**27 462**	**27 424**	**27 099**	**27 619**	**27 057**	**26 616**	**URSS[9]**
Byelorussian SSR	*1 257*	*1 156*	*1 098*	*1 054*	*1 053*	*1 063*	*1 015*	*1 077*	*1 055*	*1 042*	*RSS de Biélorussie*
Ukrainian SSR	*8 034*	*7 639*	*7 256*	*6 860*	*6 400*	*6 245*	*6 239*	*6 435*	*6 327*	*6 093*	*RSS d'Ukraine*

For general note and footnotes, see end of table.

Voir la fin du tableau pour la remarque générale et les notes.

Building bricks, made of clay (continued) – Briques de construction en argile (suite)

Unit : Million units

Unité : En millions

Country or area	1976	1977	1978	1979	1980	1981	1982	1983	1984	1985	Pays ou zone
Oceania	**1 845**	**1 938**	**1 956**	**1 937**	**2 197**	**2 311**	**2 258**	**1 718**	**1 795**	**2 006**	**Océanie**
Australia	1 818	1 910	1 936	1 914	2 173	2 287	2 234	1 694	1 771	1 982	Australie
New Zealand	27	28	20	23	...	...	...	...	...	...	Nouvelle–Zélande
Total	**99 102**	**86 753**	**86 046**	**92 869**	**94 407**	**91 588**	**88 993**	**92 369**	**81 713**	**79 588**	**Total**

General note.
Clay bricks for building purposes, including common and facing bricks (solid, hollow, shaped or perforated). Glazed, refractory, paving, concrete, shale and sand–lime bricks are excluded. (SITC 66241–0A).

[1] Twelve months ending 30 September of year stated.
[2] Including concrete bricks.
[3] Production by establishments employing 5 or more persons.
[4] Government production only.
[5] Production by establishments employing 10 or more persons.
[6] Shipments.
[7] Excluding hollow bricks.
[8] Source: Industrial Statistics, Statistical Office of the European Communities, (Luxembourg).
[9] Standard size.

Remarque générale.
Briques en argile pour la construction, y compris les briques ordinaires et les briques de parement (pleines, creuses, faconnées ou perforées). Cette rubrique ne comprend pas les briques vernissées, les briques réfractaires, les briques de pavement, les briques en béton et en schiste et les briques silico–calcaires. (CTCI 66241–0A).

[1] Période de douze mois finissant le 30 septembre de l'année indiquée.
[2] Y compris les briques en béton.
[3] Production des établissements occupant 5 personnes ou plus.
[4] Production de l'Etat seulement.
[5] Production des établissements occupant 10 personnes ou plus.
[6] Expéditions.
[7] Non compris les briques creuses.
[8] Source: Statistiques industrielles, Office statistique des Communautés européennes, (Luxembourg).
[9] De taille courante.

Building bricks, made of clay – Briques de construction en argile

Unit : Thousand cubic metres

Unité : Milliers de mètres cubes

Country or area	1976	1977	1978	1979	1980	1981	1982	1983	1984	1985	Pays ou zone
Africa											**Afrique**
Algeria	...	...	1 252	...	...	...	...	...	...	...	Algérie
Burkina Faso	5	5	5	4	4	5	5	4	5	[1] 3	Burkina Faso
Côte d'Ivoire[1]	14	17	0	0	197	164	111	82	80	...	Côte d'Ivoire[1]
Kenya	20	25	13	23	20	6	5	10	10	...	Kenya
Niger[1]	13	14	24	27	12	11	10	...	...	...	Niger[1]
South Africa[1]	420	308	258	349	431	493	...	...	...	...	Afrique du Sud[1]
Tunisia	586	760	878	968	1 117	...	...	...	...	...	Tunisie
America, North											**Amérique du Nord**
Canada[2]	654	659	674	708	...	...	...	...	...	...	Canada[2]
Asia											**Asie**
Cyprus	94	194	239	315	321	294	282	293	290	282	Chypre
Europe											**Europe**
EEC											***CEE***
Belgium[1 3]	2 558	2 808	2 714	2 636	2 479	1 599	1 318	1 284	1 377	1 436	Belgique[1 3]
Denmark[4]	1 153	1 072	1 123	1 084	773	588	505	584	...	...	Danemark[4]
France[1]	4 867	4 819	4 592	4 723	4 807	3 947	3 515	3 149	2 900	2 964	France[1]
Germany, Fed. Rep.	11 497	9 368	10 213	11 422	11 202	10 278	8 779	9 217	8 847	7 233	Allemagne, Rép. féd.
Italy[1]	10 164	9 973	10 137	10 251	11 435	11 621	10 169	...	...	...	Italie[1]
Netherlands	...	2 800	2 900	2 900	2 840	2 290	1 810	...	...	...	Pays–Bas
EFTA											***AELE***
Austria[5]	1 604	1 531	1 392	1 398	1 381	1 286	1 197	1 130	1 181	1 103	Autriche[5]
Finland[1]	463	471	413	451	500	...	...	...	...	...	Finlande[1]
Norway	51	57	60	58	62	64	...	...	...	...	Norvège
Portugal[1]	3 199	3 499	3 304	2 955	3 260	3 813	4 065	3 664	2 977	2 875	Portugal[1]
Sweden	383	357	307	263	266	262	228	200	174	135	Suède
East Europe											***Europe de l'est***
Czechoslovakia	4 834	4 313	4 087	3 955	4 183	4 380	4 563	4 317	3 557	3 554	Tchécoslovaquie
German Dem. Rep.[6]	2 101	2 100	2 039	1 917	1 919	1 938	1 722	1 744	1 764	1 741	Rép. dém. allemande[6]
Hungary	3 465	3 572	3 549	3 502	3 529	3 568	3 550	3 655	3 534	3 256	Hongrie
Poland[6]	4 069	3 743	3 502	2 991	2 712	2 434	2 541	2 578	2 540	2 380	Pologne[6]
Romania[7]	2 932	2 824	2 562	2 631	2 475	2 560	...	...	...	...	Roumanie[7]
USSR	64 955	62 526	60 157	56 509	54 923	54 849	54 199	55 238	54 115	53 232	**URSS**
Byelorussian SSR	*2 514*	*2 312*	*2 196*	*2 108*	*2 106*	*2 126*	*2 030*	*2 154*	*2 110*	*2 084*	*RSS de Biélorussie*
Ukrainian SSR	*16 068*	*15 278*	*14 511*	*13 720*	*12 799*	*12 491*	*12 478*	*12 869*	*12 653*	*12 186*	*RSS d'Ukraine*
Oceania											**Océanie**

General note.
Clay bricks for building purposes, including common and facing bricks (solid, hollow, shaped or perforated). Glazed, refractory, paving, concrete, shale and sand–lime bricks are excluded. (SITC 66241–0B).

[1] In thousand metric tons.
[2] Shipments.
[3] Excluding hollow bricks for partitions and ceilings.
[4] Original data in pieces, 585 pieces = 1 cubic metre.
[5] Original data in thousand standard bricks of dimensions 0.25 x 0.12 x 0.065 m.
[6] Original data in pieces, 641 pieces = 1 cubic metre.
[7] Original data in pieces, 575 pieces = 1 cubic metre.

Remarque générale.
Briques en argile pour la construction, y compris les briques ordinaires et les briques de parement (pleines, creuses, façonnées ou perforées). Cette rubrique ne comprend pas les briques vernissées, les briques réfractaires, les briques de pavement, les briques en béton et en schiste et les briques silico–calcaires. (CTCI 66241–0B).

[1] En milliers de tonnes métriques.
[2] Expéditions.
[3] Non compris les briques creuses pour hourdis.
[4] Données d'origine exprimées en unités (585 unités = 1 mètre cube).
[5] Données d'origine exprimées en milliers de briques type des dimensions suivantes: 0,25 x 0,12 x 0,065
[6] Données d'origine exprimées en unités (641 unités = 1 mètre cube).
[7] Données d'origine exprimées en unités (575 unités = 1 mètre cube).

Tiles, roofing, made of clay – Tuiles de couverture en argile

Unit : Million units

Unité : En millions

Country or area	1976	1977	1978	1979	1980	1981	1982	1983	1984	1985	Pays ou zone
Africa	**1**	**1**	**2**	**1**	**1**	**1**	**1**	**1**	**1**	**1**	**Afrique**
Tunisia	1	* 1	* 2	...	...	...	...	...	...	...	Tunisie
America, North	**3**	**2**	**6**	**6**	**7**	**7**	**8**	**8**	**8**	**8**	**Amérique du Nord**
Cuba	3	2	6	6	7	7	8	8	8	8	Cuba
America, South	**818**	**863**	**927**	**996**	**1 722**	**1 653**	**1 845**	**2 034**	**2 225**	**2 416**	**Amérique du Sud**
Brazil	796	839	904	[1] 975	1 693	...	...	...	...	...	Brésil
Colombia	4	5	4	0	2	3	5	4	...	...	Colombie
Paraguay	18	19	19	21	27	33	31	29	28	27	Paraguay
Asia	**321**	**302**	**311**	**304**	**364**	**353**	**315**	**350**	**319**	**339**	**Asie**
Democratic Yemen	...	...	...	...	1	1	1	1	1	...	Yémen démocratique
Indonesia[2]	56	49	53	65	71	82	89	97	121	...	Indonésie[2]
Malaysia[3 4]	21	23	36	44	57	52	# 61	64	52	27	Malaisie[3 4]
Philippines[5]	1	1	...	...	...	...	...	...	...	...	Philippines[5]
Sri Lanka	25	18	18	23	55	43	12	17	16	18	Sri Lanka
Turkey	216	210	201	168	...	...	144	164	120	167	Turquie
Yemen	...	...	...	...	1	4	* 7	6	8	8	Yémen
Europe	**1 397**	**1 487**	**1 509**	**1 406**	**1 376**	**1 442**	**1 437**	**1 487**	**1 528**	**1 545**	**Europe**
EEC	***296***	***405***	***430***	***461***	***488***	***482***	***512***	***543***	***554***	***522***	***CEE***
Denmark	10	10	11	10	12	14	...	...	21	22	Danemark
Germany, Fed. Rep.	203	307	328	356	372	374	405	420	426	393	Allemagne, Rép. féd.
Greece	...	...	...	...	57	52	57	69	69	...	Grèce
Netherlands	46	47	46	46	47	42	33	36	38	...	Pays–Bas
EFTA	***23***	***22***	***22***	***22***	***20***	***19***	***18***	***23***	***28***	***29***	***AELE***
Austria	3	2	3	3	2	2	3	4	6	11	Autriche
Finland	...	...	...	...	...	12	10	13	15	...	Finlande
Sweden	8	8	7	7	6	5	5	6	7	6	Suède
East Europe	***491***	***461***	***443***	***410***	***400***	***384***	***360***	***368***	***367***	***391***	***Europe de l'est***
Bulgaria	57	60	68	75	79	76	49	55	45	49	Bulgarie
Czechoslovakia	64	64	53	50	48	45	49	52	55	55	Tchécoslovaquie
German Dem. Rep.	78	60	50	44	33	22	19	13	15	39	Rép. dém. allemande
Hungary	160	130	133	124	130	111	111	109	114	114	Hongrie
Poland	31	29	28	24	25	23	19	20	21	19	Pologne
Romania	...	118	111	93	85	107	113	119	117	115	Roumanie
Other Europe	***586***	***598***	***614***	***512***	***467***	***557***	***547***	***553***	***579***	***602***	***Autre Europe***
Spain	264	...	...	201	196	230	178	185	...	...	Espagne
Yugoslavia	322	356	382	311	271	327	369	368	410	444	Yougoslavie
Oceania	**210**	**227**	**206**	**202**	**233**	**239**	**219**	**169**	**203**	**227**	**Océanie**
Australia[6]	210	227	206	202	233	239	219	169	203	227	Australie[6]
Total	**2 750**	**2 882**	**2 962**	**2 915**	**3 703**	**3 696**	**3 825**	**4 049**	**4 283**	**4 536**	**Total**

General note.
Clay tiles for roofs, for topping walls etc. They may be flat, half cyclinders, or of special shapes for eaves, ridges, hips or valleys. (SITC 66242–0A).

Remarque générale.
Tuiles d'argile pour toitures, couronnement des murs etc. Elles peuvent être plates, demi–rondes ou de forme spéciale (tuiles pour pignons, tuiles faîtières, tuiles de rives, tuiles d'arêtiers). (CTCI 66242–0A).

[1] Production by establishments employing 5 or more persons.
[2] Including tiles of cement.
[3] Data refer to Peninsular Malaysia only.
[4] Beginning 1982, scope of series revised.
[5] Shipments.
[6] Including concrete tiles.

[1] Production des établissements occupant 5 personnes ou plus.
[2] Y compris les tuiles de ciment.
[3] Données se rapportant à la Malaisie péninsulaire seulement.
[4] A partir de 1982, portée de la série révisée.
[5] Expéditions.
[6] Y compris les tuiles en béton.

Tiles, roofing, made of clay – Tuiles de couverture en argile

Unit : Million square metres

Unité : Millions de mètres carrés

Country or area	1976	1977	1978	1979	1980	1981	1982	1983	1984	1985	Pays ou zone
Africa											**Afrique**
Egypt	3	4	4	8	6	6	7	8	...	...	Egypte
Nigeria	...	...	...	...	3	...	...	...	...	...	Nigéria
Europe											**Europe**
EEC											***CEE***
Belgium[1]	2	2	2	...	...	...	...	...	...	...	Belgique[1]
France	39	41	46	50	52	* 44	* 45	* 45	* 45	...	France
Germany, Fed. Rep.	12	18	20	21	22	22	24	25	24	22	Allemagne, Rép. féd.
Italy	17	18	20	21	26	26	26	...	...	...	Italie
Netherlands	3	3	3	3	* 3	* 3	2	2	2	...	Pays–Bas
United Kingdom[2]	1	1	1	2	2	2	2	2	2	2	Royaume–Uni[2]
East Europe											***Europe de l'est***
Czechoslovakia	3	3	3	2	2	2	3	3	3	3	Tchécoslovaquie
Hungary	10	8	8	8	8	8	8	8	7	8	Hongrie
USSR[3]	1	1	1	1	1	1	1	1	1	1	**URSS[3]**
Ukrainian SSR[3]	*1*	...	*0*	*0*	*0*	*0*	*0*	*0*	*0*	*0*	*RSS d'Ukraine[3]*
Oceania											**Océanie**
Australia[4]	18	20	17	18	18	24	20	15	19	21	Australie[4]

General note.
Clay tiles for roofs, for topping walls etc. They may be flat, half cyclinders, or of special shapes for eaves, ridges, hips or valleys. (SITC 66242–0B).

Remarque générale.
Tuiles d'argile pour toitures, couronnement des murs etc. Elles peuvent être plates, demi–rondes ou de forme spéciale (tuiles pour pignons, tuiles faîtières, tuiles de rives, tuiles d'arêtiers). (CTCI 66242–0B).

1 Source: Industrial Statistics, Statistical Office of the European Communities, (Luxembourg).
2 Sales by manufacturers employing 25 or more persons.
3 Including tiles of cement and sand and lime.
4 Twelve months ending 30 June of year stated.

1 Source: Statistiques industrielles, Office statistique des Communautés européennes, (Luxembourg).
2 Ventes des fabricants employant 25 personnes ou plus.
3 Y compris les tuiles de ciment, sable et chaux.
4 Période de douze mois finissant le 30 juin de l'année indiquée.

Tiles, floor and wall – Carreaux pour planchers et murs

Unit : Thousand units

Unité : En milliers

Country or area	1976	1977	1978	1979	1980	1981	1982	1983	1984	1985	Pays ou zone
America, North											**Amérique du Nord**
Cuba	36	30	...	...	...	...	...	...	...	...	Cuba
Dominican Republic	5 800	5 658	8 215	9 771	11 255	19 558	21 633	22 722	22 163	23 252	Rép. dominicaine
America, South											**Amérique du Sud**
Colombia	...	...	...	...	...	54 012	21 140	23 611	...	...	Colombie
Paraguay	361	397	437	503	654	760	714	671	655	648	Paraguay
Asia											**Asie**
India[1]	39 375	40 844	41 778	44 173	...	...	...	...	...	...	Inde[1]
Indonesia	103 244	110 208	96 488	93 055	120 495	...	...	...	...	...	Indonésie
Israel	51 131	38 815	39 092	43 726	44 094	50 677	49 239	56 100	63 573	63 099	Israël
Malaysia	5 800	8 719	14 139	13 555	12 152	9 284	11 082	11 355	...	...	Malaisie
Philippines[2]	206 735	218 556	...	...	...	...	...	...	...	...	Philippines[2]
Sri Lanka	2	2	2	2	2	2	1	0	...	...	Sri Lanka
Europe											**Europe**
EEC											***CEE***
Denmark[3]	33 200	* 32 200	* 29 662	* 10 405	* 8 613	...	...	...	...	...	Danemark[3]
EFTA											***AELE***
Portugal[4]	29	35	36	47	94	120	139	103	129	...	Portugal[4]
Sweden[4]	15	16	16	21	17	16	17	14	11	12	Suède[4]
East Europe											***Europe de l'est***
Poland	22 803	20 853	19 778	17 358	16 224	17 346	15 903	19 005	20 369	19 405	Pologne
Other Europe											***Autre Europe***
Spain	728 752	...	...	...	...	...	...	...	...	...	Espagne
Yugoslavia[4]	108	218	237	267	283	355	344	333	365	315	Yougoslavie[4]

General note.
Setts, flags and other tiles commonly used for paving or for facing walls, hearths etc., whether or not glazed. Vitrified brick and roofing tiles are excluded. This item corresponds to SITC 66244 and 66245.

[1] Production by large and medium scale establishments only.
[2] Shipments.
[3] Glazed wall and fireplace tiles only.
[4] In thousand metric tons.

Remarque générale.
Carreaux, pavés et dalles de pavement ou de revêtement, émaillés ou non, communément utilisés pour le pavement des sols et le revêtement des murs, foyers de cheminée etc. Cette rubrique ne comprend pas les briques vitrifiées et les tuiles de toiture. Elle correspond aux postes 66244 et 66245 de la CTCI.

[1] Production des grandes et moyennes entreprises seulement.
[2] Expéditions.
[3] Carreaux vitrifiés pour murs et cheminées seulement.
[4] En milliers de tonnes métriques.

Tiles, floor and wall – Carreaux pour planchers et murs

Unit : Thousand square metres

Unité : Milliers de mètres carrés

Country or area	1976	1977	1978	1979	1980	1981	1982	1983	1984	1985	Pays ou zone
Africa	**5 512**	**8 612**	**8 801**	**10 496**	**15 981**	**16 658**	**17 370**	**18 328**	**16 891**	**19 863**	**Afrique**
Algeria	1 220	2 231	2 347	2 492	2 355	2 086	1 918	...	...	...	Algérie
Côte d'Ivoire	...	268	104	185	235	342	113	143	157	...	Côte d'Ivoire
Nigeria	357	...	...	...	2 566	3 009	2 755	2 182	357	3 352	Nigéria
South Africa	[1] 792	[1] 852	* [1] 675	[1] 1 086	# 4 731	5 204	* 5 565	5 980	5 638	4 894	Afrique du Sud
Tunisia	2 775	3 809	4 155	5 042	5 935	5 897	...	...	...	...	Tunisie
Zaire	138	128	30	* 35	159	120	130	130	...	...	Zaïre
America, North	**42 109**	**42 924**	**40 691**	**43 053**	**42 744**	**40 088**	**40 079**	**43 454**	**49 028**	**47 914**	**Amérique du Nord**
Canada	10 528	8 423	8 169	8 038	8 193	...	...	...	...	...	Canada
Cuba	4 874	4 640	4 775	4 724	4 393	4 503	4 569	4 525	4 981	5 780	Cuba
Panama	382	340	418	336	...	577	548	219	...	...	Panama
United States[2 3]	26 325	29 521	27 329	29 955	29 752	27 846	28 303	32 554	37 967	36 552	Etats–Unis[2 3]
America, South	**88 877**	**100 272**	**103 940**	**133 299**	**182 791**	**132 703**	**173 230**	**186 607**	**201 066**	**215 178**	**Amérique du Sud**
Brazil	87 465	98 799	102 187	[4] 130 833	180 387	129 363	...	...	...	...	Brésil
Chile	171	268	270	331	802	416	405	337	373	336	Chili
Colombia	...	482	492	569	58	137	...	...	...	...	Colombie
Ecuador	784	723	991	...	1 544	2 787	2 905	2 612	...	...	Equateur
Asia	**22 288**	**33 032**	**35 097**	**39 735**	**41 495**	**40 736**	**40 055**	**50 036**	**50 879**	**53 768**	**Asie**
Cyprus	498	895	1 155	1 393	1 504	1 484	1 513	1 515	1 634	1 540	Chypre
Indonesia	1 971	3 292	3 164	3 934	4 533	5 175	5 817	8 665	5 682	...	Indonésie
Iran(Islamic Rep.of)[5]	8 906	12 455	11 157	12 665	12 933	15 094	17 022	...	...	...	Iran(Rép.islamique)[5]
Korea, Republic of	10 205	15 553	18 456	20 352	21 500	17 958	14 678	21 455	24 040	23 765	Corée, République de
Thailand[6]	708	837	1 165	1 391	...	...	...	...	...	...	Thaïlande[6]
Europe	**291 738**	**296 383**	**291 217**	**301 891**	**307 875**	**304 185**	**269 662**	**279 948**	**276 777**	**265 924**	**Europe**
EEC	***218 723***	***226 402***	***224 436***	***237 358***	***245 316***	***240 691***	***213 914***	***226 628***	***227 476***	***219 493***	***CEE***
Belgium	1 432	1 703	1 753	568	665	499	211	135	73	60	Belgique
France	24 333	25 542	21 530	22 772	23 774	23 388	23 387	22 862	22 780	18 068	France
Germany, Fed. Rep.	68 779	72 867	71 049	72 393	76 606	75 951	69 418	66 151	65 903	61 249	Allemagne, Rép. féd.
Greece	5 467	5 859	6 100	6 640	6 591	6 327	5 260	5 518	5 413	...	Grèce
Italy	91 847	93 493	95 680	106 437	107 816	107 553	90 611	...	...	...	Italie
Netherlands[7]	9 500	9 500	10 300	11 900	13 500	11 600	11 600	11 700	11 700	* 12 000	Pays–Bas[7]
United Kingdom[8]	17 365	17 438	18 024	...	...	15 373	13 427	15 979	16 018	15 583	Royaume–Uni[8]
EFTA	***5 712***	***5 885***	***5 363***	***5 291***	***4 987***	***5 417***	***4 443***	***4 493***	***3 603***	***4 395***	***AELE***
Austria	4 970	4 850	4 221	4 040	3 776	4 187	3 213	3 253	2 352	3 013	Autriche
Finland	742	1 035	1 142	1 251	1 211	1 230	1 230	1 240	1 251	...	Finlande
East Europe	***27 270***	***28 025***	***29 310***	***31 283***	***33 761***	***36 226***	***36 138***	***36 512***	***37 367***	***37 668***	***Europe de l'est***
Czechoslovakia	14 326	14 808	15 758	16 720	18 228	20 046	20 419	20 989	21 605	21 455	Tchécoslovaquie
German Dem. Rep.	...	...	...	...	6 190	...	...	...	6 800	7 085	Rép. dém. allemande
Hungary	6 252	6 525	6 860	7 871	9 343	9 488	9 027	8 831	8 962	9 128	Hongrie
Other Europe	***40 034***	***36 071***	***32 108***	***27 959***	***23 811***	***21 851***	***15 167***	***12 315***	***8 332***	***4 369***	***Autre Europe***
Spain	...	...	...	27 959	23 811	21 851	15 167	12 315	...	...	Espagne
USSR	**48 811**	**51 425**	**53 948**	**52 426**	**55 809**	**61 346**	**65 056**	**68 802**	**70 702**	**72 686**	**URSS**
Ukrainian SSR	*16 936*	*17 750*	*18 367*	*16 922*	*16 228*	*18 340*	*19 688*	*20 694*	*21 231*	*22 162*	*RSS d'Ukraine*
Oceania	**3 855**	**4 519**	**4 546**	**5 165**	**6 000**	**4 718**	**6 256**	**4 643**	**5 675**	**1 991**	**Océanie**
Australia[9]	3 855	4 519	4 546	5 165	6 000	...	6 256	...	5 675	1 991	Australie[9]
Total	**503 191**	**537 166**	**538 240**	**586 064**	**652 695**	**600 434**	**611 707**	**651 818**	**671 018**	**677 325**	**Total**

General note.
Setts, flags and other tiles commonly used for paving or for facing walls, hearths etc., whether or not glazed. Vitrified brick and roofing tiles are excluded. The item corresponds to SITC 66244 and 66245.

Remarque générale.
Carreaux, pavés et dalles de pavement ou de revêtement, émaillés ou non, communément utilisés pour le pavement des sols et le revêtement des murs, foyers de cheminée etc. Cette rubrique ne comprend pas les briques vitrifiées et les tuiles de toiture. Elle correspond aux postes 66244 et 66245 de la CTCI.

For footnotes, see end of table.

Voir la fin du tableau pour les notes.

[1] Tiles for cement and terazzo flooring.
[2] Shipments.
[3] Data refer to clay tiles, including quarry tiles.
[4] Production by establishments employing 5 or more persons.
[5] Production by establishments employing 50 or more persons.
[6] Vinyl floor tiles only.
[7] Industrial sales.
[8] Sales by manufacturers employing 25 or more persons.
[9] Twelve months ending 30 June of year stated.

[1] Carreaux de revêtement de sol en ciment et terazzo.
[2] Expéditions.
[3] Données se rapportant aux carreaux d'argile, y compris les carreaux machine non vernissés.
[4] Production des établissements occupant 5 personnes ou plus.
[5] Production des établissements occupant 50 personnes ou plus.
[6] Carreaux pour planchers en vinyle seulement.
[7] Ventes industrielles.
[8] Ventes des fabricants employant 25 personnes ou plus.
[9] Période de douze mois finissant le 30 juin de l'année indiquée.

Unit : Thousand metric tons

Unité : Milliers de tonnes métriques

Country or area	1976	1977	1978	1979	1980	1981	1982	1983	1984	1985	Pays ou zone
Africa	**2 480**	**2 678**	**3 025**	**2 852**	**3 392**	**3 527**	**3 346**	**3 619**	**3 958**	**3 879**	**Afrique**
Algeria	32	38	42	36	22	47	24	*[1] 41	*[1] 41	*[1] 41	Algérie
Egypt[1]	* 82	100	100	88	87	91	* 95	* 94	* 97	* 97	Egypte[1]
Ethiopia[2]	35	5	3	7	9	5	4	5	6	...	Ethiopie[2]
Kenya	30	78	50	27	21	13	13	25	18	* 36	Kenya
Libyan Arab Jamah.[1]	325	300	220	225	230	235	225	260	* 260	* 272	Jamah.arabe libyenne[1]
Mauritius	7	7	8	8	7	5	6	5	5	6	Maurice
South Africa[1 3]	1 387	1 504	1 875	1 721	2 184	2 251	2 150	1 892	2 110	2 014	Afrique du Sud[1 3]
Tunisia	[1] 318	[1] 338	[1] 427	[1] 430	529	466	471	580	594	595	Tunisie
Uganda[1]	20	20	25	28	15	84	74	413	* 499	* 499	Ouganda[1]
United Rep. Tanzania* [1]	2	2	5	6	6	6	6	3	3	3	Rép.Unie de Tanzanie* [1]
Zaire	98	101	* 109	* 115	111	124	104	107	109	* 110	Zaïre
Zambia	144	185	161	161	171	200	174	194	216	203	Zambie
America, North	**20 759**	**21 867**	**22 970**	**23 395**	**23 900**	**24 553**	**19 328**	**19 608**	**20 987**	**20 765**	**Amérique du Nord**
Canada	1 569	1 646	1 858	1 662	1 853	* 2 555	* 2 197	* 2 232	2 266	2 269	Canada
Costa Rica* [1]	5	6	7	9	7	7	9	10	10	10	Costa Rica* [1]
Cuba	[4] 119	[4] 163	[4] 184	[4] 181	[4] 146	[4] 140	[4] 146	# 26	36	30	Cuba
Dominican Republic	* 22	21	* 27	31	33	21	31	32	33	33	Rép. dominicaine
Guatemala[1]	45	45	44	41	36	25	* 25	27	* 51	* 51	Guatemala[1]
Jamaica[1]	122	144	157	204	159	132	114	122	* 115	* 115	Jamaïque[1]
Martinique[1]	...	...	...	...	...	6	* 6	* 6	* 6	* 6	Martinique[1]
Mexico[1]	3 492	4 150	4 445	4 579	* 4 350	4 500	* 3 992	* 3 629	* 3 992	* 3 992	Mexique[1]
Nicaragua* [1]	26	36	37	36	40	30	6	5	3	4	Nicaragua* [1]
United States	15 353	15 650	16 205	16 646	17 270	17 137	12 802	13 519	14 475	14 255	Etats–Unis
America, South	**6 006**	**4 637**	**4 934**	**5 002**	**5 533**	**4 995**	**7 004**	**7 098**	**7 151**	**7 134**	**Amérique du Sud**
Brazil	* 4 300	2 593	2 890	[5] 2 944	3 381	2 939	* 4 990	* 4 990	* 4 990	...	Brésil
Chile[1]	600	617	617	635	778	648	645	723	* 778	* 798	Chili[1]
Colombia* [1]	1 000	1 300	1 300	1 300	1 300	1 297	1 297	1 297	1 297	1 297	Colombie* [1]
Ecuador	4	3	3	...	5	...	...	...	...	...	Equateur
Paraguay	32	54	39	38	49	57	54	74	72	71	Paraguay
Uruguay	[1] 70	[1] 70	[1] 85	[1] 81	[1] 20	50	14	10	10	* 5	Uruguay
Asia	**11 763**	**11 524**	**11 410**	**11 859**	**12 686**	**11 263**	**11 060**	**11 015**	**11 496**	**11 155**	**Asie**
Cyprus	32	28	15	18	16	13	11	9	7	8	Chypre
India* [1]	180	182	220	408	400	400	400	400	500	500	Inde* [1]
Indonesia	...	...	...	...	...	328	375	309	401	...	Indonésie
Iran(Islamic Rep.of)* [1]	1 000	1 000	900	500	500	500	544	635	635	635	Iran(Rép.islamique)* [1]
Israel[1]	200	102	124	* 124	* 124	80	50	41	* 50	* 50	Israël[1]
Japan	9 116	9 022	9 063	9 628	9 350	8 026	7 777	7 436	7 754	7 441	Japon
Jordan[1]	3	3	3	4	* 4	20	60	276	* 224	* 224	Jordanie[1]
Korea,Dem.Ppl's.Rep.* [1]	340	350	350	380	400	...	...	...	...	...	Corée,Rép.pop.dém.de* [1]
Korea, Republic of[1]	* 109	60	* 60	60	210	200	200	200	200	* 200	Corée, République de[1]
Kuwait	12	20	4	6	18	22	10	* 14	6	* 15	Koweït
Lebanon* [1]	181	162	100	118	20	61	50	20	20	10	Liban* [1]
Mongolia	36	37	36	46	64	79	90	90	106	103	Mongolie
Philippines[1]	27	28	33	54	87	85	66	51	50	* 45	Philippines[1]
Qatar	...	...	...	14	19	21	20	...	...	...	Qatar
Saudi Arabia	10	7	15	25	29	28	...	* 9	* 10	* 12	Arabie saoudite
Turkey	83	83	55	48	*[1] 1 000	*[1] 900	*[1] 900	*[1] 1 000	*[1] 1 000	*[1] 1 000	Turquie
United Arab Emirates* [1]	...	...	...	...	45	41	41	45	45	45	Emirats arabes unis* [1]
Europe	**40 366**	**38 822**	**39 501**	**40 755**	**39 549**	**35 549**	**33 038**	**33 301**	**34 216**	**33 639**	**Europe**
EEC	***22 107***	***20 671***	***20 869***	***21 675***	***20 331***	***16 315***	***14 157***	***14 278***	***14 603***	***14 434***	***CEE***
Belgium	2 304	2 311	2 301	2 481	2 326	2 000	1 371	1 595	1 974	1 816	Belgique
Denmark	203	150	137	157	123	* 125	84	94	113	106	Danemark
France	3 750	3 590	3 728	3 870	3 610	3 366	2 994	[1] 2 946	*[1] 2 994	[1] 3 100	France
Germany, Fed. Rep.	9 645	8 770	8 990	9 238	8 575	7 916	6 898	6 871	6 941	6 845	Allemagne, Rép. féd.
Greece	...	...	...	...	...	412	348	302	267	...	Grèce
Ireland[1]	69	80	92	73	32	51	51	* 65	* 75	* 80	Irlande[1]
Italy	2 188	2 196	2 141	2 214	2 353	# 1 390	1 427	1 407	1 384	1 310	Italie
United Kingdom	[1] 3 616	[1] 3 242	[1] 3 148	[1] 3 310	[1] 2 980	1 055	984	998	855	845	Royaume–Uni
EFTA	***1 882***	***1 787***	***1 836***	***1 900***	***1 823***	***1 663***	***1 474***	***1 663***	***1 767***	***1 664***	***AELE***
Austria	436	408	376	351	348	343	303	292	291	288	Autriche

For general note and footnotes, see end of table.

Voir la fin du tableau pour la remarque générale et les notes.

Unit : Thousand metric tons | Unité : Milliers de tonnes métriques

Country or area	1976	1977	1978	1979	1980	1981	1982	1983	1984	1985	Pays ou zone
Finland	236	234	260	326	295	271	118	300	403	354	Finlande
Norway	67	75	123	107	102	79	* [1] 130	* [1] 130	* [1] 130	* [1] 100	Norvège
Portugal	215	235	261	270	270	272	296	289	254	236	Portugal
Sweden	857	769	748	776	744	641	581	610	648	649	Suède
Switzerland[1]	71	66	68	70	64	57	46	42	41	37	Suisse[1]
East Europe	***14 824***	***14 671***	***15 117***	***15 224***	***15 025***	***14 987***	***14 915***	***14 651***	***14 836***	***14 488***	***Europe de l'est***
Bulgaria	1 599	1 725	1 782	1 868	1 848	1 758	1 776	1 634	1 526	1 331	Bulgarie
Czechoslovakia	2 986	3 021	3 077	2 968	3 018	3 234	3 088	3 100	3 117	3 227	Tchécoslovaquie
German Dem. Rep.	3 404	3 367	3 443	3 470	3 401	3 441	3 510	3 458	3 597	3 567	Rép. dém. allemande
Hungary	732	743	740	714	698	757	845	822	823	801	Hongrie
Poland	2 783	2 369	2 418	2 375	2 247	2 055	1 904	2 014	1 925	1 845	Pologne
Romania	3 320	3 446	3 657	3 829	3 813	3 742	3 792	3 623	3 848	3 717	Roumanie
Other Europe	***1 553***	***1 693***	***1 679***	***1 956***	***2 370***	***2 584***	***2 492***	***2 709***	***3 010***	***3 053***	***Autre Europe***
Malta[1]	27	32	28	30	# 6	* 6	* 7	* 5	* 5	* 5	Malte[1]
Spain	359	* 400	* 354	* 400	860	965	935	1 008	* 1 008	* 1 100	Espagne
Yugoslavia	1 167	1 261	1 297	1 526	1 504	1 613	1 550	1 696	1 997	1 948	Yougoslavie
USSR	**27 199**	**28 243**	**29 056**	**28 341**	**28 427**	**28 426**	**28 731**	**29 542**	**29 452**	**29 233**	**URSS**
Byelorussian SSR	*852*	*865*	*804*	*799*	*790*	*808*	*851*	*910*	*923*	*928*	*RSS de Biélorussie*
Ukrainian SSR	*8 701*	*9 578*	*9 473*	*9 245*	*8 856*	*8 637*	*8 727*	*9 303*	*9 093*	*8 633*	*RSS d'Ukraine*
Oceania	**730**	**706**	**723**	**595**	**603**	**583**	**640**	**683**	**684**	**821**	**Océanie**
Australia	564	532	563	422	429	390	446	500	516	643	Australie
Fiji[1]	3	2	1	1	2	3	4	* 3	* 3	* 3	Fidji[1]
New Zealand* [1]	163	172	159	172	172	190	190	180	165	175	Nouvelle–Zélande* [1]
Total	**109 304**	**108 477**	**111 620**	**112 799**	**114 091**	**108 896**	**103 146**	**104 866**	**107 944**	**106 626**	**Total**

General note.
Impure calcium oxide obtained by calcining limestone containing very little or no clay. Hydraulic lime and slaked lime are excluded. (SITC 66110–1).

Remarque générale.
Oxyde de calcium impur obtenu par calcination de pierres calcaires contenant très peu d'argile ou pas d'argile. Cette rubrique ne comprend pas la chaux hydraulique et la chaux éteinte. (CTCI 66110–1).

[1] Source: U. S. Bureau of Mines, (Washington, D. C.).
[2] Twelve months ending 10 September of year stated.
[3] Domestic sales plus exports.
[4] Including other types of lime.
[5] Production by establishments employing 5 or more persons.

[1] Source: U.S. Bureau of Mines, (Washington, D.C.).
[2] Période de douze mois finissant le 10 septembre de l'année indiquée.
[3] Ventes nationales plus exportations.
[4] Y compris les autres types de chaux.
[5] Production des établissements occupant 5 personnes ou plus.

Unit : Thousand metric tons

Unité : Milliers de tonnes métriques

Country or area	1976	1977	1978	1979	1980	1981	1982	19	1984	1985	Pays ou zone
Africa	**22 938**	**23 653**	**25 276**	**27 900**	**30 968**	**34 669**	**34 387**	**35 855**	**37 196**	**38 913**	**Afrique**
Algeria	1 336	1 782	2 700	3 775	4 156	4 457	3 743	*[1] 4 808	*[1] 5 534	*[1] 5 534	Algérie
Angola*[1]	300	300	400	400	240	250	250	220	350	350	Angola*[1]
Benin	* 164	* 179	136	255	[1] 285	[1] 297	[1] 315	[1] 300	[1] 300	[1] 300	Bénin
Burundi	...	...	0	0	0	1	0	0	0	0	Burundi
Cameroon	210	278	403	*[1] 489	*[1] 508	*[1] 516	530	598	694	785	Cameroun
Congo	52	45	65	55	34	52	39	28	...	62	Congo
Côte d'Ivoire	804	875	964	1 030	1 157	1 317	988	636	552	535	Côte d'Ivoire
Egypt	3 362	3 232	2 722	2 987	3 638	3 446	3 627	4 080	4 596	5 364	Egypte
Ethiopia[2]	100	199	103	95	123	142	146	[1] 150	[1] 160	[1] 160	Ethiopie[2]
Gabon	107	164	134	96	137	150	178	194	207	244	Gabon
Ghana	678	565	489	248	294	396	252	278	285	336	Ghana
Kenya	971	1 137	1 133	1 148	1 280	1 280	1 238	1 280	1 134	1 115	Kenya
Liberia	105	104	132	185	108	100	66	88	86	94	Libéria
Libyan Arab Jamah.	675	659	1 079	1 594	1 787	2 722	3 139	3 093	...	...	Jamah.arabe libyenne
Madagascar	70	52	66	63	60	36	36	36	37	28	Madagascar
Malawi	85	94	108	113	92	78	53	70	70	62	Malawi
Mali	38	35	34	27	20	35	* 27	* 20	* 26	* 26	Mali
Morocco	2 140	2 604	2 819	3 317	3 561	3 606	3 739	3 848	3 573	3 694	Maroc
Mozambique	218	323	327	274	236	261	270	188	110	...	Mozambique
Niger	35	36	41	34	41	41	36	30	* 38	* 38	Niger
Nigeria[3]	1 294	1 262	1 289	1 655	1 714	* 2 566	* 3 009	* 2 755	* 2 182	* 3 352	Nigéria[3]
Réunion[4]	155	158	132	160	145	162	...	...	...	...	Réunion[4]
Senegal	396	329	357	380	371	396	375	388	414	408	Sénégal
Sierra Leone	...	...	...	...	...	...	...	42	...	17	Sierra Leone
South Africa	7 048	6 573	6 823	6 199	7 125	8 095	8 080	7 897	8 084	6 880	Afrique du Sud
Sudan*[1]	130	151	188	184	185	150	170	232	200	162	Soudan*[1]
Togo	158	239	327	298	307	279	272	232	243	284	Togo
Tunisia	478	572	882	1 383	1 780	2 023	1 834	2 532	2 777	3 033	Tunisie
Uganda	87	73	4	2	10	* 6	* 19	* 31	* 25	* 4	Ouganda
United Rep. Tanzania	244	247	231	280	312	396	336	240	272	372	Rép.Unie de Tanzanie
Zaire	540	542	475	454	453	494	541	513	400	480	Zaïre
Zambia	387	328	279	299	310	302	319	392	278	160	Zambie
Zimbabwe	541	486	404	391	469	588	576	501	650	614	Zimbabwe
America, North	**98 065**	**104 040**	**110 696**	**112 162**	**104 071**	**102 054**	**93 227**	**97 110**	**107 007**	**108 495**	**Amérique du Nord**
Bahamas[1]	271	...	364	496	472	# 29	64	26	...	...	Bahamas[1]
Canada	9 898	9 933	10 473	11 459	10 340	10 152	8 136	7 089	8 609	9 559	Canada
Costa Rica[1]	362	406	490	528	554	460	424	386	350	350	Costa Rica[1]
Cuba	2 501	2 656	2 712	2 613	2 831	3 292	3 163	3 231	3 347	3 182	Cuba
Dominican Republic	654	862	839	876	928	902	955	1 057	1 109	970	Rép. dominicaine
El Salvador	322	334	520	571	* 519	459	276	296	* 407	* 400	El Salvador
Guadeloupe	...	...	...	...	...	160	* 160	200	203	186	Guadeloupe
Guatemala	[1] 445	[1] 491	[1] 515	574	569	514	613	491	* 786	* 790	Guatemala
Haiti	246	268	247	195	243	229	213	219	248	263	Haïti
Honduras	234	184	206	205	311	307	278	485	368	* 216	Honduras
Jamaica	365	324	288	216	144	159	237	278	259	241	Jamaïque
Martinique[1]	...	...	...	144	180	180	* 207	* 189	* 200	191	Martinique[1]
Mexico	12 691	13 328	14 150	15 352	16 398	18 173	19 343	17 363	18 702	20 255	Mexique
Nicaragua[1]	226	226	199	86	* 154	* 100	* 100	298	280	100	Nicaragua[1]
Panama[1]	282	271	300	510	565	520	350	327	330	300	Panama[1]
Puerto Rico[5]	1 485	1 296	1 331	1 327	1 282	1 225	1 044	855	896	865	Porto Rico[5]
Trinidad and Tobago	242	218	224	218	186	139	189	393	406	329	Trinité–et–Tobago
United States	67 581	72 629	77 546	76 648	68 241	65 054	57 475	63 927	70 452	70 284	Etats–Unis
America, South	**36 176**	**38 540**	**41 487**	**45 840**	**50 633**	**49 510**	**48 033**	**41 366**	**40 644**	**41 201**	**Amérique du Sud**
Argentina	5 707	6 030	6 322	6 698	7 289	6 913	5 818	5 882	5 220	4 795	Argentine
Bolivia	220	[1] 267	[1] 257	[1] 253	[1] 318	374	326	310	220	* 145	Bolivie
Brazil	18 675	20 545	22 348	24 871	27 194	26 051	25 644	20 870	19 497	20 635	Brésil
Chile	968	1 140	1 203	1 357	1 583	1 863	1 131	1 255	1 390	1 430	Chili
Colombia	3 612	3 298	4 153	4 257	4 356	4 610	4 707	4 787	5 280	5 412	Colombie
Ecuador	608	[1] 623	[1] 834	[1] 1 099	1 389	1 380	1 800	1 530	1 730	* 1 400	Equateur
Paraguay	155	200	166	155	177	156	111	153	109	46	Paraguay
Peru	1 966	1 968	2 047	2 428	2 758	2 584	2 477	1 949	1 925	1 648	Pérou
Suriname	51	45	57	69	43	71	74	70	50	79	Suriname
Uruguay	676	682	674	680	684	604	550	401	* 347	317	Uruguay
Venezuela	[1] 3 538	3 742	3 426	3 973	4 842	4 904	5 395	4 159	4 876	5 294	Venezuela
Asia	**203 822**	**224 377**	**254 716**	**275 543**	**280 435**	**293 650**	**310 627**	**337 079**	**363 455**	**405 004**	**Asie**
Afghanistan[6]	125	150	127	99	87	77	87	130	112	127	Afghanistan[6]

For general note and footnotes, see end of table.

Voir la fin du tableau pour la remarque générale et les notes.

Unit : Thousand metric tons

Unité : Milliers de tonnes métriques

Country or area	1976	1977	1978	1979	1980	1981	1982	1983	1984	1985	Pays ou zone
Bangladesh[5]	157	308	339	322	336	345	326	307	273	240	Bangladesh[5]
Burma	233	269	254	391	386	317	344	334	301	429	Birmanie
China	46 700	55 647	65 236	73 896	79 857	82 897	95 200	108 250	123 020	145 950	Chine
Cyprus	1 025	1 071	1 107	1 154	1 233	1 036	1 068	943	853	659	Chypre
Democratic Kampuchea[1]	* 50	* 50	* 10	0	0	0	0	...	...	...	Kampuchea démocrat.[1]
Hong Kong	765	1 029	1 236	1 279	1 489	1 517	1 436	1 717	1 847	1 835	Hong-kong
India	18 516	19 173	19 626	18 270	17 803	20 908	22 650	25 422	29 635	31 903	Inde
Indonesia	1 810	2 549	3 649	4 432	5 259	5 719	5 832	6 150	6 612	* 10 104	Indonésie
Iran(Islamic Rep.of)[7]	5 955	6 323	6 241	8 103	8 114	9 319	10 103	10 665	10 500	10 977	Iran(Rép.islamique)[7]
Iraq[1]	2 728	3 170	4 599	5 098	* 5 500	* 5 600	* 5 600	* 5 600	* 8 000	* 8 000	Iraq[1]
Israel	2 055	1 964	1 996	1 919	2 092	2 361	2 189	2 058	1 889	1 596	Israël
Japan	68 712	73 138	84 882	87 804	87 957	84 828	80 686	80 891	78 860	72 847	Japon
Jordan	582	538	553	623	913	965	788	1 269	2 026	2 023	Jordanie
Korea,Dem.Ppl's.Rep.* [1]	7 000	7 000	7 000	8 000	8 000	8 000	8 000	8 000	8 000	8 000	Corée,Rép.pop.dém.de* [1]
Korea, Republic of	11 873	14 198	15 133	16 413	15 612	15 617	17 887	21 282	20 413	20 424	Corée, République de
Kuwait	351	329	621	1 040	1 308	1 549	1 553	1 124	1 184	10 665	Koweït
Lebanon[1]	1 704	1 360	1 381	2 031	* 1 484	2 391	1 700	1 500	1 250	* 1 000	Liban[1]
Malaysia[8 9]	1 739	1 777	2 196	2 265	2 349	2 833	# 3 123	3 231	3 469	3 128	Malaisie[8 9]
Mongolia	163	100	166	185	178	106	179	165	141	151	Mongolie
Nepal	27	43	38	21	29	30	37	39	31	32	Népal
Pakistan[5]	3 196	3 071	3 224	3 023	3 343	3 538	3 657	3 840	4 502	4 800	Pakistan[5]
Philippines	4 229	4 112	4 201	6 857	4 516	4 008	4 393	4 560	3 660	3 072	Philippines
Qatar	179	170	208	180	150	188	172	* [1] 375	* [1] 478	* [1] 319	Qatar
Saudi Arabia	1 104	1 267	1 638	2 674	2 888	4 237	5 263	8 126	* 9 000	* 8 981	Arabie saoudite
Singapore	1 532	1 550	1 628	1 808	1 952	2 253	2 695	3 153	2 511	1 897	Singapour
Sri Lanka	336	361	575	661	633	706	538	480	401	380	Sri Lanka
Syrian Arab Republic	1 110	1 395	1 497	1 847	1 995	2 310	2 850	3 719	4 279	4 357	Rép. arabe syrienne
Thailand	4 438	5 083	5 055	5 233	5 359	6 323	6 656	7 301	8 271	* 7 916	Thaïlande
Turkey	12 154	13 390	15 572	13 573	12 975	15 043	15 778	13 595	15 738	17 412	Turquie
United Arab Emirates	...	...	...	...	1 720	2 220	2 068	* 2 068	* 4 000	* 3 990	Emirats arabes unis
Viet Nam	* [1] 738	* [1] 845	* [1] 843	* [1] 729	[1] 641	[1] 538	[1] 710	[1] 910	[1] 1 296	1 436	Viet Nam
Yemen	60	60	66	68	81	85	243	623	709	698	Yémen
Europe	**257 050**	**265 332**	**271 962**	**274 609**	**274 897**	**263 839**	**259 152**	**258 751**	**246 757**	**231 248**	**Europe**
EEC	***140 821***	***142 062***	***145 181***	***148 081***	***147 943***	***141 811***	***135 880***	***134 644***	***129 211***	***123 403***	***CEE***
Belgium	7 504	7 764	7 576	7 703	7 482	6 691	6 320	5 719	5 708	5 537	Belgique
Denmark	2 355	2 309	2 627	2 409	1 917	1 602	1 770	1 654	1 668	1 983	Danemark
France	30 614	29 835	29 074	28 825	29 104	28 229	26 141	24 503	22 724	22 224	France
Germany, Fed. Rep.	34 152	32 163	34 258	35 659	34 551	31 498	30 079	30 466	28 909	25 758	Allemagne, Rép. féd.
Greece	8 740	10 564	11 463	11 973	12 340	13 366	13 297	14 196	13 521	12 744	Grèce
Ireland	1 569	1 580	1 806	2 064	1 812	1 944	1 619	1 486	1 377	1 457	Irlande
Italy	36 327	38 204	38 232	39 289	41 862	42 094	40 245	39 763	38 307	37 155	Italie
Luxembourg	299	291	311	318	325	342	344	353	340	295	Luxembourg
Netherlands	3 481	3 895	3 918	3 701	3 745	3 316	3 103	3 108	3 176	2 911	Pays-Bas
United Kingdom	15 780	15 457	15 916	16 140	14 805	12 729	12 962	13 396	13 481	13 339	Royaume-Uni
EFTA	***20 705***	***20 959***	***19 798***	***21 538***	***22 190***	***21 802***	***21 123***	***21 110***	***20 304***	***19 067***	***AELE***
Austria	5 880	5 993	5 732	5 611	5 455	5 288	5 012	4 907	4 899	4 560	Autriche
Finland	1 934	1 813	1 796	1 876	1 787	1 863	1 906	1 979	1 656	* 1 623	Finlande
Iceland	144	139	134	127	131	115	128	120	114	117	Islande
Norway	2 680	2 314	2 232	2 251	2 206	1 837	1 704	1 666	1 547	1 343	Norvège
Portugal	3 794	4 436	3 856	5 352	5 914	6 033	5 969	6 060	5 514	5 069	Portugal
Sweden	2 727	2 615	2 351	2 387	2 445	2 318	2 304	2 240	2 393	2 101	Suède
Switzerland	3 546	3 649	3 697	3 934	4 252	4 348	4 100	4 138	4 181	4 254	Suisse
East Europe	***62 607***	***66 309***	***68 981***	***67 465***	***67 040***	***61 694***	***62 825***	***62 197***	***62 427***	***57 874***	***Europe de l'est***
Albania* [1]	700	750	800	840	1 000	790	830	840	840	848	Albanie* [1]
Bulgaria	4 362	4 665	5 149	5 401	5 359	5 433	5 614	5 644	5 717	5 296	Bulgarie
Czechoslovakia	9 552	9 749	10 204	10 258	10 546	10 646	10 325	10 498	10 530	10 265	Tchécoslovaquie
German Dem. Rep.	11 344	12 102	12 521	12 273	12 440	12 204	11 721	11 782	11 555	11 608	Rép. dém. allemande
Hungary	4 298	4 620	4 764	4 857	4 660	4 635	4 369	4 243	4 145	3 678	Hongrie
Poland	19 803	21 301	21 651	19 180	18 428	14 224	16 035	16 163	16 649	14 990	Pologne
Romania	12 548	13 122	13 892	14 656	14 607	13 762	13 931	13 027	12 991	11 189	Roumanie
Other Europe	***32 917***	***36 002***	***38 002***	***37 525***	***37 724***	***38 532***	***39 324***	***40 800***	***34 815***	***30 904***	***Autre Europe***
Spain	25 296	27 996	29 304	28 056	28 008	28 752	29 604	31 212	25 500	21 876	Espagne
Yugoslavia	7 621	8 006	8 698	9 469	9 716	9 780	9 720	9 588	9 315	9 028	Yougoslavie
USSR	**124 246**	**127 056**	**126 956**	**123 019**	**125 049**	**127 169**	**123 681**	**128 156**	**129 866**	**130 772**	**URSS**

For general note and footnotes, see end of table.

Voir la fin du tableau pour la remarque générale et les notes.

Unit : Thousand metric tons

Unité : Milliers de tonnes métriques

Country or area	1976	1977	1978	1979	1980	1981	1982	1983	1984	1985	Pays ou zone
Byelorussian SSR	*2 180*	...	...	...	...	...	...	...	...	...	*RSS de Biélorussie*
Oceania	**6 162**	**6 119**	**5 952**	**5 981**	**6 057**	**6 553**	**7 054**	**6 262**	**5 636**	**6 667**	**Océanie**
Australia	5 040	5 083	5 016	5 085	5 201	5 656	6 136	5 351	4 655	5 680	Australie
Fiji	69	78	87	87	83	92	88	110	98	93	Fidji
New Caledonia	54	48	51	57	53	46	49	41	* 60	31	Nouvelle–Calédonie
New Zealand	999	910	798	752	720	759	781	760	823	863	Nouvelle–Zélande
Total	**748 458**	**789 116**	**837 045**	**865 054**	**872 109**	**877 444**	**876 161**	**904 579**	**930 562**	**962 301**	**Total**

General note.
All hydraulic cements used for construction (portland, metallurgic, aluminous, natural etc.). (SITC 66120–0).

[1] Source: U. S. Bureau of Mines, (Washington, D. C.).
[2] Twelve months ending 10 September of year stated.
[3] Incomplete coverage.
[4] Beginning 1982, data are confidential.
[5] Twelve months ending 30 June of year stated.
[6] Twelve months beginning 21 March of year stated.
[7] Production by establishments employing 10 or more persons.
[8] Data refer to Peninsular Malaysia only.
[9] Beginning 1982, scope of series revised.

Remarque générale.
Tous les ciments hydrauliques utilisés dans la construction (ciments portland, métallurgique, alumineux, naturel etc.). (CTCI 66120–0).

[1] Source: U.S. Bureau of Mines, (Washington, D.C.).
[2] Période de douze mois finissant le 10 septembre de l'année indiquée.
[3] Couverture incomplète.
[4] A partir de 1982, les données sont confidentielles.
[5] Période de douze mois finissant le 30 juin de l'année indiquée.
[6] Période de douze mois commençant le 21 mars de l'année indiquée.
[7] Production des établissements occupant 10 personnes ou plus.
[8] Données se rapportant à la Malaisie péninsulaire seulement.
[9] A partir de 1982, portée de la série révisée.

Asbestos-cement articles – Ouvrages en amiante-ciment, cellulose-ciment et similaires

Unit : Thousand metric tons

Unité : Milliers de tonnes métriques

Country or area	1976	1977	1978	1979	1980	1981	1982	1983	1984	1985	Pays ou zone
Africa	**158**	**205**	**215**	**220**	**221**	**262**	**262**	**282**	**274**	**285**	**Afrique**
Algeria	47	90	104	107	94	116	128	...	...	...	Algérie
Egypt	69	78	...	...	...	...	...	...	...	...	Egypte
Senegal	2	2	1	1	1	1	1	2	2	2	Sénégal
Tunisia	13	12	16	20	28	47	35	43	33	41	Tunisie
Uganda	2	* 2	* 2	0	2	1	1	...	...	...	Ouganda
Zambia	25	21	18	18	22	23	23	24	16	9	Zambie
America, North	**369**	**298**	**347**	**431**	**423**	**477**	**470**	**352**	**524**	**301**	**Amérique du Nord**
Mexico	369	298	347	431	423	477	470	352	524	301	Mexique
America, South	**1 123**	**1 202**	**1 476**	**1 644**	**1 798**	**1 668**	**1 945**	**2 077**	**2 208**	**2 340**	**Amérique du Sud**
Brazil	863	944	1 178	[1] 1 341	1 458	1 408	...	...	...	...	Brésil
Chile	57	70	77	79	...	...	...	...	...	...	Chili
Colombia	...	188	221	224	269	189	...	...	...	...	Colombie
Asia	**553**	**580**	**580**	**783**	**689**	**824**	**811**	**742**	**791**	**867**	**Asie**
India	488	507	551	620	644	733	716	642	686	...	Inde
Indonesia	13	18	12	22	34	36	...	...	...	...	Indonésie
Sri Lanka	52	...	17	141	11	...	...	...	...	...	Sri Lanka
Europe	**4 661**	**4 527**	**4 372**	**4 333**	**4 302**	**3 718**	**3 415**	**3 467**	**3 233**	**2 999**	**Europe**
EEC	***2 648***	***2 561***	***2 375***	***2 428***	***2 363***	***1 887***	***1 725***	***1 676***	***1 474***	***1 270***	***CEE***
Denmark	234	234	244	255	134	135	126	135	...	...	Danemark
France	1 020	959	881	906	984	831	785	670	606	528	France
Germany, Fed. Rep.	939	907	810	851	881	644	541	619	503	400	Allemagne, Rép. féd.
Greece	...	...	...	11	12	11	11	12	...	...	Grèce
United Kingdom[2]	444	450	429	405	352	266	262	240	256	253	Royaume-Uni[2]
EFTA	***134***	***97***	***60***	***61***	***62***	***58***	***59***	***73***	***62***	***63***	***AELE***
Finland	65	65	60	61	62	58	59	54	46	...	Finlande
Sweden	69	32	0	0	0	0	0	...	...	...	Suède
East Europe	***1 013***	***947***	***1 019***	***916***	***947***	***787***	***782***	***867***	***805***	***790***	***Europe de l'est***
Bulgaria	140	89	168	100	123	96	99	107	89	100	Bulgarie
Hungary	217	224	249	245	256	232	237	258	248	244	Hongrie
Poland	656	634	602	571	568	459	446	502	468	446	Pologne
Other Europe	***866***	***922***	***918***	***928***	***930***	***986***	***849***	***851***	***892***	***876***	***Autre Europe***
Spain	...	...	...	...	...	605	459	480	...	...	Espagne
Yugoslavia	351	407	403	413	415	381	390	371	377	361	Yougoslavie
Total	**6 864**	**6 812**	**6 989**	**7 410**	**7 432**	**6 949**	**6 903**	**6 920**	**7 030**	**6 792**	**Total**

General note.
Articles consisting essentially of an intimate mixture of fibres (asbestos, cellulose or other vegetable fibres) and cement or other hydraulic binders. Control panels of asbestos-cement are excluded. (SITC 66183-0A).

Remarque générale.
Ouvrages consistant essentiellement en un mélange intime de fibres (amiante, cellulose ou autres fibres végétales) et de ciment ou autres liants hydrauliques. Cette rubrique ne comprend pas les tableaux de commande en amiante-ciment. (CTCI 66183-0A).

[1] Production by establishments employing 5 or more persons.
[2] Including fibre-cement articles.

[1] Production des établissements occupant 5 personnes ou plus.
[2] Y compris ouvrages en fibres-ciment.

Abrasives, agglomerated or not (millstones, grindstones, grinding wheels etc.) – Abrasifs, agglomerés ou non (meules et pierres à moudre, à aiguiser etc.)

Unit : Metric tons

Unité : Tonnes métriques

Country or area	1976	1977	1978	1979	1980	1981	1982	1983	1984	1985	Pays ou zone
America, South	**535**	**535**	**535**	**535**	**535**	**438**	**686**	**481**	**535**	**535**	**Amérique du Sud**
Colombia	...	...	...	...	...	438	686	481	...	...	Colombie
Asia	**58 248**	**58 443**	**59 618**	**68 030**	**70 003**	**64 854**	**64 517**	**62 282**	**66 148**	**66 310**	**Asie**
Japan	58 248	58 443	59 618	68 030	70 003	64 854	64 517	62 282	66 148	66 310	Japon
Europe	**109 121**	**101 376**	**98 041**	**98 696**	**94 188**	**92 083**	**88 437**	**84 327**	**83 047**	**81 704**	**Europe**
EEC	***65 654***	***68 034***	***66 782***	***66 444***	***65 935***	***67 300***	***67 287***	***67 102***	***67 292***	***67 395***	***CEE***
Belgium[1]	1 391	1 248	546	520	751	...	...	...	...	...	Belgique[1]
Denmark	1 127	...	...	304	1 885	2 134	2 234	2 162	...	...	Danemark
France	17 636	19 627	19 212	19 770	17 449	...	...	...	...	...	France
Germany, Fed. Rep.[2]	19 300	20 000	...	...	...	...	...	...	...	...	Allemagne, Rép. féd.[2]
Italy[2]	26 200	...	...	...	...	...	...	...	...	...	Italie[2]
EFTA	***6 896***	***7 072***	***6 257***	***6 955***	***6 684***	***6 125***	***5 460***	***5 555***	***4 524***	***5 047***	***AELE***
Finland	1 247	1 644	292	354	361	382	391	385	395	...	Finlande
Portugal	629	780	1 049	1 078	1 148	1 091	1 172	1 074	1 019	700	Portugal
Sweden	5 020	4 648	4 916	5 523	5 175	4 652	3 897	4 096	3 110	4 322	Suède
East Europe	***6 689***	***6 488***	***7 206***	***7 253***	***6 362***	***5 849***	***6 027***	***5 326***	***5 351***	***5 368***	***Europe de l'est***
Hungary	6 689	6 488	7 206	7 253	6 362	5 849	6 027	5 326	5 351	5 368	Hongrie
Other Europe	***29 882***	***19 782***	***17 796***	***18 044***	***15 207***	***12 809***	***9 663***	***6 344***	***5 880***	***3 894***	***Autre Europe***
Spain	29 882	...	...	18 044	15 207	12 809	9 663	6 344	...	...	Espagne
Total	**167 904**	**160 354**	**158 194**	**167 261**	**164 726**	**157 375**	**153 640**	**147 090**	**149 730**	**148 549**	**Total**

General note.
Millstones, grindstones, grinding wheels and the like made essentially of natural stone (agglomerated or not), of agglomerated natural or artificial abrasives or of pottery. This item does not include the natural or artificial abrasive powder or grain coated onto fabric, paper and dental burrs. (SITC 66310-0).

[1] Beginning 1981, data are confidential.
[2] Source: Industrial Statistics, Statistical Office of the European Communities, (Luxembourg).

Remarque générale.
Meules et pierres à moudre, à aiguiser, à polir et articles analogues, essentiellement fabriqués en pierre naturelle (aggloméré ou non), en abrasifs agglomérés naturels ou artificiels ou en poterie. Cette rubrique ne comprend ni les abrasifs naturels ou artificiels en poudre ou en grains appliqués sur tissu ou sur papier, ni les fraises dentaires. (CTCI 66310-0).

[1] A partir de 1981, les données sont confidentielles.
[2] Source: Statistiques industrielles, Office statistique des Communautés européennes, (Luxembourg).

Concrete blocks and bricks – Blocs et briques en béton

Unit : Thousand metric tons

Unité : Milliers de tonnes métriques

Country or area	1976	1977	1978	1979	1980	1981	1982	1983	1984	1985	Pays ou zone
Africa	**263**	**218**	**1 076**	**834**	**1 046**	**424**	**407**	**430**	**392**	**466**	**Afrique**
Côte d'Ivoire	100	118	96	266	408	317	328	338	372	...	Côte d'Ivoire
Kenya	95	46	# 945	535	611	81	52	70	2	4	Kenya
Tunisia	68	54	35	33	27	26	...	...	...	...	Tunisie
America, North	**13**	**17**	**17**	**16**	**16**	**16**	**16**	**16**	**16**	**16**	**Amérique du Nord**
Cuba	13	17	17	...	...	...	...	...	...	...	Cuba
America, South	**23 621**	**24 737**	**21 362**	**24 765**	**23 621**	**23 621**	**23 621**	**23 621**	**23 621**	**23 621**	**Amérique du Sud**
Brazil	...	24 737	21 362	[1] 24 765	...	...	...	...	...	...	Brésil
Asia	**355**	**355**	**355**	**355**	**355**	**355**	**355**	**355**	**355**	**355**	**Asie**
Korea, Republic of	153	...	...	...	...	...	...	...	...	...	Corée, République de
Sri Lanka	...	...	...	202	...	...	...	...	...	...	Sri Lanka
Europe	**52 045**	**55 934**	**56 856**	**60 406**	**60 431**	**56 330**	**54 626**	**53 447**	**60 708**	**59 787**	**Europe**
EEC	***21 929***	***23 279***	***24 083***	***25 302***	***25 252***	***23 357***	***21 922***	***23 469***	***23 499***	***23 106***	***CEE***
Belgium	2 040	2 089	1 954	1 822	1 585	1 260	1 070	993	978	...	Belgique
France	17 308	18 323	19 040	20 245	20 449	19 034	17 429	...	...	...	France
Ireland	2 581	2 867	3 089	3 235	3 218	3 063	3 423	3 187	3 118	2 879	Irlande
EFTA	***3 505***	***3 491***	***3 085***	***3 014***	***3 168***	***2 873***	***3 006***	***3 100***	***3 220***	***2 962***	***AELE***
Austria	1 733	1 856	1 685	1 620	1 704	1 560	1 607	1 686	1 707	1 436	Autriche
Finland	465	353	292	354	433	393	458	488	673	...	Finlande
Portugal	...	541	553	554	637	684	745	741	627	...	Portugal
Sweden	788	741	555	486	394	236	196	185	213	207	Suède
East Europe	***23 874***	***24 331***	***24 436***	***24 743***	***24 957***	***22 937***	***21 944***	***21 985***	***26 228***	***25 539***	***Europe de l'est***
German Dem. Rep.[2]	23 576	24 033	24 040	24 326	24 618	22 627	21 676	21 704	25 936	25 309	Rép. dém. allemande[2]
Hungary	298	298	396	417	339	310	268	281	292	230	Hongrie
Other Europe	***2 737***	***4 833***	***5 252***	***7 347***	***7 054***	***7 163***	***7 754***	***4 893***	***7 761***	***8 180***	***Autre Europe***
Spain	2 737	...	...	7 347	7 054	7 163	7 754	4 893	...	...	Espagne
Total	**76 298**	**81 261**	**79 666**	**86 376**	**85 469**	**80 746**	**79 025**	**77 869**	**85 092**	**84 246**	**Total**

General note.
Structural blocks and bricks made of light or heavy weight aggregates. Decorative blocks are included. (SITC 66362–1A).

[1] Production by establishments employing 5 or more persons.
[2] Including concrete pipes and other concrete products.

Remarque générale.
Blocs et briques de construction faits en agrégats légers ou lourds, y compris les blocs décoratifs. (CTCI 66362–1A).

[1] Production des établissements occupant 5 personnes ou plus.
[2] Y compris les conduites en béton et autres produits en béton.

Concrete blocks and bricks – Blocs et briques en béton

Unit : Thousand cubic metres

Unité : Milliers de mètres cubes

Country or area	1976	1977	1978	1979	1980	1981	1982	1983	1984	1985	Pays ou zone
Africa											**Afrique**
Mozambique	...	...	...	8	11	9	9	7	3	...	Mozambique
South Africa[1]	25	18	...	...	...	...	...	...	...	...	Afrique du Sud[1]
America, North											**Amérique du Nord**
Canada	3 669	3 305	3 107	...	...	...	...	...	...	...	Canada
Cuba[1]	38	45	48	46	48	51	53	56	56	65	Cuba[1]
Dominican Republic[1]	25	28	38	40	46	38	37	44	80	75	Rép. dominicaine[1]
Panama[1]	15	17	19	16	...	13	8	13	...	...	Panama[1]
Trinidad and Tobago[1]	21	26	25	27	29	27	22	...	...	...	Trinité–et–Tobago[1]
America, South											**Amérique du Sud**
Brazil	539	788	1 061	4 557	...	...	...	...	...	...	Brésil
Ecuador[1]	19	26	28	...	43	20	22	17	...	...	Equateur[1]
Asia											**Asie**
Democratic Yemen[1]	0	1	1	1	1	1	1	1	1	...	Yémen démocratique[1]
Israel	...	...	...	...	...	266	267	258	239	230	Israël
Korea, Republic of[1]	153	148	190	176	193	161	210	246	255	263	Corée, République de[1]
Philippines[1]	32	14	...	...	...	...	...	...	...	...	Philippines[1]
Singapore[1]	32	30	24	25	40	44	62	88	64	28	Singapour[1]
Sri Lanka[1]	...	...	...	...	...	...	5	3	2	4	Sri Lanka[1]
Yemen	...	...	...	12	22	31	* 32	81	89	90	Yémen
Europe											**Europe**
EEC											***CEE***
Belgium	1 638	1 694	1 534	1 469	1 298	1 009	853	813	793	...	Belgique
Germany, Fed. Rep.	21 216	17 663	18 560	19 357	18 304	15 950	13 637	14 629	13 415	10 288	Allemagne, Rép. féd.
Greece[1]	40	41	38	40	42	33	36	34	28	...	Grèce[1]
Netherlands	1 660	1 815	1 917	1 939	2 092	1 852	1 750	1 642	1 608	...	Pays–Bas
United Kingdom[2 3]	69 761	66 865	71 061	73 088	66 820	55 565	63 685	75 641	81 642	74 445	Royaume–Uni[2 3]
East Europe											***Europe de l'est***
Czechoslovakia	6 518	6 745	6 998	7 192	7 296	7 093	6 396	6 300	6 401	6 433	Tchécoslovaquie
Hungary	184	176	201	196	177	182	149	157	151	125	Hongrie
Poland[1 4]	6	6	7	7	6	6	8	8	6	6	Pologne[1 4]
Other Europe											***Autre Europe***
Malta[1]	1	1	2	2	2	2	3	2	2	...	Malte[1]
Yugoslavia[1]	411	356	404	633	645	650	704	868	698	604	Yougoslavie[1]
USSR[5]	118 703	121 296	123 168	120 842	122 223	124 478	123 511	128 284	132 425	136 631	**URSS[5]**
Byelorussian SSR[6]	*4 621*	*4 764*	*4 918*	*4 923*	*5 144*	*5 279*	*5 223*	*5 421*	*5 755*	*6 010*	*RSS de Biélorussie[6]*
Ukrainian SSR[6]	*20 088*	*20 659*	*20 734*	*20 354*	*20 117*	*20 168*	*19 834*	*20 427*	*21 197*	*21 513*	*RSS d'Ukraine[6]*

General note.
Structural blocks and bricks made of light or heavy weight aggregates. Decorative blocks are included. (SITC 66362–1B).

[1] In million pieces.
[2] Concrete blocks only.
[3] In thousand square metres.
[4] Ferro–concrete and concrete wall materials in terms of full brick.
[5] Data refer to metal reinforced concrete blocks, bricks, pipes and other concrete products.
[6] Including concrete pipes and other concrete products.

Remarque générale.
Blocs et briques de construction faits en agrégats légers ou lourds, y compris les blocs décoratifs. (CTCI 66362–1B).

[1] En millions d'unités.
[2] Blocs en béton seulement.
[3] En milliers de mètres carrés.
[4] Béton armé et autres produits en béton pour murs exprimés en briques pleines.
[5] Données se rapportant aux dalles, briques et conduites en béton armé et autres articles en béton.
[6] Y compris les conduites en béton et autres produits en béton.

Concrete pipes – Conduites en béton

Unit : Thousand metric tons

Unité : Milliers de tonnes métriques

Country or area	1976	1977	1978	1979	1980	1981	1982	1983	1984	1985	Pays ou zone
Africa	**595**	**573**	**861**	**853**	**905**	**952**	**877**	**839**	**906**	**761**	**Afrique**
Egypt[1]	37	41	38	32	35	46	46	...	...	...	Egypte[1]
Kenya	13	28	24	39	32	12	20	14	12	8	Kenya
South Africa[2]	412	394	683	639	673	* 749	647	619	746	601	Afrique du Sud[2]
Tunisia	133	110	116	143	165	145	164	162	103	105	Tunisie
America, North	**1 405**	**1 423**	**1 313**	**1 424**	**1 409**	**1 417**	**1 388**	**1 363**	**1 427**	**1 411**	**Amérique du Nord**
Canada	1 316	1 351	1 197	...	...	...	...	...	...	...	Canada
Mexico	89	72	116	136	121	129	100	75	139	...	Mexique
America, South	**1 411**	**1 411**	**1 411**	**1 411**	**1 374**	**1 448**	**1 411**	**1 411**	**1 411**	**1 411**	**Amérique du Sud**
Brazil	...	...	...	...	1 374	1 448	...	...	...	...	Brésil
Asia	**4 608**	**4 940**	**5 645**	**5 307**	**5 054**	**4 806**	**4 625**	**4 462**	**4 453**	**4 564**	**Asie**
Indonesia	117	...	...	...	2	25	32	10	15	...	Indonésie
Iran(Islamic Rep.of)	1 125	1 406	1 437	...	...	...	...	...	...	...	Iran(Rép.islamique)
Japan	2 980	3 040	3 631	3 527	3 372	3 161	2 872	2 725	2 681	2 561	Japon
Korea, Republic of	...	443	533	420	357	297	398	404	434	678	Corée, République de
Europe	**14 598**	**13 645**	**14 113**	**14 152**	**14 088**	**13 340**	**11 988**	**11 697**	**11 631**	**11 329**	**Europe**
EEC	***10 196***	***8 892***	***9 411***	***9 709***	***9 408***	***8 280***	***7 524***	***7 480***	***7 220***	***6 908***	***CEE***
Belgium[3]	981	803	813	901	906	774	705	611	523	...	Belgique[3]
France	2 872	2 623	2 468	2 592	2 762	2 596	2 398	...	...	...	France
Germany, Fed. Rep.	4 881	4 246	4 841	5 023	4 883	4 121	3 581	3 544	3 472	3 325	Allemagne, Rép. féd.
Ireland	[4] 88	# 109	131	130	143	136	146	134	119	101	Irlande
United Kingdom[5]	1 374	1 111	1 158	1 063	714	653	694	744	701	569	Royaume-Uni[5]
EFTA	***2 444***	***2 547***	***2 414***	***2 085***	***1 978***	***2 428***	***1 956***	***1 849***	***1 802***	***1 788***	***AELE***
Austria	502	521	509	470	501	524	569	549	567	576	Autriche
Finland	485	744	685	484	434	944	524	467	481	...	Finlande
Portugal	...	...	...	...	...	284	290	274	278	...	Portugal
Sweden	1 175	1 000	938	849	761	676	573	559	476	406	Suède
East Europe	***223***	***210***	***213***	***220***	***208***	***201***	***181***	***164***	***158***	***136***	***Europe de l'est***
Hungary	223	210	213	220	208	201	181	164	158	136	Hongrie
Other Europe	***1 735***	***1 997***	***2 076***	***2 138***	***2 494***	***2 431***	***2 327***	***2 204***	***2 451***	***2 497***	***Autre Europe***
Spain	1 411	...	...	1 658	2 028	1 968	1 887	1 807	...	...	Espagne
Yugoslavia	324	416	428	480	466	463	440	397	401	380	Yougoslavie
Oceania	**707**	**666**	**691**	**626**	**673**	**652**	**442**	**383**	**324**	**132**	**Océanie**
Australia	707	666	691	626	673	652	...	...	...	132	Australie
Total	**23 324**	**22 659**	**24 035**	**23 773**	**23 502**	**22 615**	**20 730**	**20 155**	**20 152**	**19 607**	**Total**

General note.
Culvert, sewer, pressure, irrigation etc., reinforced or nonreinforced, concrete pipes. (SITC 66362-2A).

[1] Including other concrete products.
[2] Cement pipes and fittings.
[3] Production by establishments employing 5 or more persons.
[4] Source: Industrial Statistics, Statistical Office of the European Communities, (Luxembourg).
[5] Including fittings.

Remarque générale.
Tuyaux d'écoulement, conduites d'égouts, conduites forcées, conduites d'irrigation, en béton armé ou non. (CTCI 66362-2A).

[1] Y compris les autres produits en béton.
[2] Conduits et accessoires en ciment.
[3] Production des établissements occupant 5 personnes ou plus.
[4] Source: Statistiques industrielles, Office statistique des Communautés européennes, (Luxembourg).
[5] Y compris les joints et accessoires.

Concrete pipes – Conduites en béton

Unit : Thousand cubic metres | Unité : Milliers de mètres cubes

Country or area	1976	1977	1978	1979	1980	1981	1982	1983	1984	1985	Pays ou zone
America, North											**Amérique du Nord**
Cuba[1]	373	423	482	432	391	460	434	441	449	422	Cuba[1]
Panama[2]	104	183	177	169	...	123	...	92	...	...	Panama[2]
Asia											**Asie**
Burma[2 3]	15	18	...	...	...	24	20	15	...	...	Birmanie[2 3]
Europe											**Europe**
EEC											***CEE***
Denmark[1]	4 602	4 075	3 761	3 159	2 563	1 989	1 561	1 494	1 557	1 653	Danemark[1]
Greece[1]	982	1 014	974	969	961	1 097	912	785	788	...	Grèce[1]
Ireland	...	...	...	132	145	136	...	...	...	...	Irlande
Netherlands	326	306	280	267	267	252	233	187	303	...	Pays-Bas
East Europe											***Europe de l'est***
Bulgaria	[1] 1 201	[1] 1 445	[1] 1 503	[1] 1 543	[1] 1 610	[1] 1 591	[1] 1 650	[1] 1 604	[1] 1 441	901	Bulgarie
Czechoslovakia	[1] 1 202	[1] 940	[1] 758	[1] 626	[1] 538	[1] 421	[1] 380	[1] 318	[1] 294	343	Tchécoslovaquie
Hungary	96	90	91	93	89	85	78	70	67	57	Hongrie

General note.
Culvert, sewer, pressure, irrigation etc., reinforced or nonreinforced, concrete pipes. (SITC 66362-2B).

[1] In thousand metres.
[2] In thousand pieces.
[3] Twelve months ending 30 September of year stated.

Remarque générale.
Tuyaux d'écoulement, conduites d'égouts, conduites forcées, conduites d'irrigation, en béton armé ou non. (CTCI 66362-2B).

[1] En milliers de mètres.
[2] En milliers d'unités.
[3] Période de douze mois finissant le 30 septembre de l'année indiquée.

Concrete, other products – Autres produits en béton

Unit : Thousand metric tons

Unité : Milliers de tonnes métriques

Country or area	1976	1977	1978	1979	1980	1981	1982	1983	1984	1985	Pays ou zone
Africa	**1 475**	**1 245**	**1 016**	**985**	**1 230**	**1 424**	**968**	**691**	**687**	**446**	**Afrique**
Algeria[1]	1 149	1 017	834	720	659	707	310	...	...	...	Algérie[1]
South Africa[2]	323	226	179	262	569	714	655	391	505	382	Afrique du Sud[2]
Tunisia	3	2	3	3	2	3	...	...	...	...	Tunisie
America, North	**280**	**226**	**231**	**295**	**302**	**348**	**370**	**277**	**384**	**376**	**Amérique du Nord**
Mexico	280	226	231	295	302	348	370	277	384	...	Mexique
America, South	**2 868**	**2 895**	**3 406**	**1 772**	**1 456**	**1 844**	**1 624**	**1 404**	**1 184**	**964**	**Amérique du Sud**
Brazil	2 867	2 894	3 405	[3] 1 772	1 455	...	...	...	...	...	Brésil
Ecuador	...	...	...	0	1	0	0	...	...	...	Equateur
Asia	**9 479**	**10 384**	**12 321**	**12 817**	**11 644**	**11 199**	**9 990**	**12 027**	**12 551**	**11 982**	**Asie**
Iran(Islamic Rep.of)	1 623	...	...	...	...	...	...	...	...	...	Iran(Rép.islamique)
Japan	7 856	8 761	10 698	11 194	10 021	9 576	8 367	10 404	10 928	10 359	Japon
Europe	**64 110**	**67 905**	**66 753**	**73 467**	**65 993**	**54 414**	**55 371**	**56 534**	**53 269**	**50 773**	**Europe**
EEC	***12 351***	***12 120***	***11 874***	***12 079***	***11 687***	***10 205***	***9 640***	***9 281***	***9 158***	***8 630***	***CEE***
Belgium[1 3]	7 024	6 958	6 816	6 808	6 421	5 278	5 072	4 561	4 529	...	Belgique[1 3]
France	5 327	5 162	5 058	5 271	5 266	4 927	4 568	...	...	...	France
EFTA	***6 617***	***6 658***	***6 975***	***6 711***	***6 526***	***5 778***	***6 296***	***6 283***	***6 073***	***6 213***	***AELE***
Austria	767	840	699	732	767	747	666	706	738	750	Autriche
Finland	562	1 823	2 007	1 935	1 741	1 549	2 085	2 036	1 882	...	Finlande
Portugal[1]	2 536	1 370	1 652	1 358	1 387	1 363	1 345	1 351	1 187	...	Portugal[1]
Sweden	2 752	2 625	2 617	2 686	2 631	2 119	2 200	2 190	2 266	2 253	Suède
East Europe	***39 981***	***43 554***	***42 116***	***42 601***	***35 846***	***27 072***	***28 731***	***31 194***	***29 727***	***27 659***	***Europe de l'est***
Hungary	1 904	1 896	1 892	1 908	1 927	1 665	1 519	1 669	1 801	1 372	Hongrie
Poland[1]	38 077	41 658	40 224	40 693	33 919	25 407	27 212	29 525	27 926	26 287	Pologne[1]
Other Europe	***5 161***	***5 573***	***5 788***	***12 076***	***11 934***	***11 359***	***10 704***	***9 776***	***8 311***	***8 271***	***Autre Europe***
Spain	...	...	...	...	...	4 391	4 330	4 079	...	...	Espagne
Yugoslavia	894	1 306	1 521	7 809	7 667	6 968	6 374	5 697	4 044	4 004	Yougoslavie
Total	**78 211**	**82 654**	**83 726**	**89 336**	**80 625**	**69 229**	**68 323**	**70 933**	**68 075**	**64 541**	**Total**

General note.
Other moulded, pressed or centrifuged articles of cement except blocks, bricks and pipes. (SITC 66362–3A).

[1] Including concrete blocks, bricks and pipes.
[2] Railway sleepers of concrete.
[3] Production by establishments employing 5 or more persons.

Remarque générale.
Autres ouvrages en béton obtenus par moulage, pressage ou centrifugation, à l'exception des blocs, des briques et des conduites. (CTCI 66362–3A).

[1] Y compris les blocs, briques et conduits en béton.
[2] Traverses en béton pour voies ferrées.
[3] Production des établissements occupant 5 personnes ou plus.

Concrete, other products – Autres produits en béton

Unit : Thousand cubic metres — Unité : Milliers de mètres cubes

Country or area	1976	1977	1978	1979	1980	1981	1982	1983	1984	1985	Pays ou zone
Africa											**Afrique**
Algeria[1]	...	56	90	101	115	114	117	...	...	...	Algérie[1]
America, North											**Amérique du Nord**
Cuba	919	915	894	883	737	762	780	833	905	961	Cuba
America, South											**Amérique du Sud**
Brazil	9 436	4 857	5 621	[2] 6 561	14 018	6 672	...	...	...	...	Brésil
Europe											**Europe**
EEC											***CEE***
Netherlands	3 527	3 777	3 864	3 775	3 752	3 489	3 256	3 295	3 214	...	Pays-Bas
United Kingdom[3 4]	29 839	24 151	27 899	28 263	28 813	23 345	25 551	33 243	34 685	27 870	Royaume-Uni[3 4]
East Europe											***Europe de l'est***
Bulgaria[1]	957	1 023	1 055	1 027	994	1 006	1 145	1 131	1 152	1 134	Bulgarie[1]
Hungary	802	785	784	784	836	685	645	692	744	650	Hongrie
Poland	20 335	21 107	21 294	21 307	18 546	14 170	14 535	15 926	16 804	15 406	Pologne
Romania[1]	4 658	5 187	6 179	7 147	7 454	6 582	...	...	...	...	Roumanie[1]
Other Europe											***Autre Europe***
Malta	31	38	62	67	67	106	230	395	416	...	Malte

General note.
Other moulded, pressed or centrifuged articles of cement except blocks, bricks and pipes. (SITC 66362–3B).

[1] Including concrete blocks, bricks and pipes.
[2] Production by establishments employing 5 or more persons.
[3] In thousand square metres.
[4] Concrete roofing tiles only.

Remarque générale.
Autres ouvrages en béton obtenus par moulage, pressage ou centrifugation, à l'exception des blocs, des briques et des conduites. (CTCI 66362–3B).

[1] Y compris les blocs, briques et conduits en béton.
[2] Production des établissements occupant 5 personnes ou plus.
[3] En milliers de mètres carrés.
[4] Tuiles de couverture en béton seulement.

Thomas (basic) slag – Scories Thomas

Unit : Thousand metric tons | Unité : Milliers de tonnes métriques

Country or area	1976	1977	1978	1979	1980	1981	1982	1983	1984	1985	Pays ou zone
Africa	**34**	**32**	**29**	**18**	**19**	**18**	**71**	**2**	**2**	**14**	**Afrique**
Egypt	...	...	...	18	19	18	71	# [1]2	[1]2	...	Egypte
America, South	**7**	**8**	**4**	**1**	**1**	**1**	**0**	**0**	**0**	**1**	**Amérique du Sud**
Argentina[2]	* 7	* 8	* 4	1	* 1	1	0	0	0	...	Argentine[2]
Europe	**1 479**	**2 100**	**1 493**	**1 440**	**1 469**	**1 316**	**1 155**	**1 145**	**1 234**	**1 194**	**Europe**
EEC	***1 456***	***2 077***	***1 395***	***1 365***	***1 364***	***1 175***	***1 027***	***1 002***	***1 076***	***1 020***	***CEE***
Belgium[3]	139	841	* 115	* 139	* 144	* 129	* [1]71	* [1]45	* [1]63	...	Belgique[3]
France[4]	374	356	341	323	339	296	258	242	220	209	France[4]
Germany, Fed. Rep.[2 3]	175	141	142	143	163	154	125	128	64	64	Allemagne, Rép. féd.[2 3]
Luxembourg	733	713	771	730	688	595	572	586	728	701	Luxembourg
United Kingdom[5]	35	26	26	30	30	1	1	1	1	...	Royaume–Uni[5]
EFTA	***6***	***5***	***83***	***58***	***88***	***124***	***111***	***126***	***142***	***157***	***AELE***
Sweden[4 6]	6	5	83	58	88	124	...	...	...	...	Suède[4 6]
East Europe	***13***	***13***	***13***	***13***	***13***	***13***	***13***	***13***	***13***	***13***	***Europe de l'est***
German Dem. Rep.	13	13	...	...	...	...	...	...	...	...	Rép. dém. allemande
Other Europe	***4***	***5***	***2***	***4***	***4***	***4***	***4***	***4***	***4***	***4***	***Autre Europe***
Spain[2]	...	5	2	...	...	...	...	...	...	...	Espagne[2]
Total	**1 519**	**2 140**	**1 526**	**1 459**	**1 489**	**1 335**	**1 226**	**1 147**	**1 236**	**1 208**	**Total**

General note.
P2O5 content of phosphatic slag produced as a by–product of the manufacture of steel from phosphatic iron (Thomas slag), including slag not for use as fertilizer. (SITC 56121–0).

[1] Source: U. S. Bureau of Mines, (Washington, D. C.).
[2] Source: Food and Agriculture Organization (FAO), (Rome).

[3] Fertilizer year ending 30 June of year stated.
[4] Fertilizer year ending 31 May of year stated.
[5] Production for use as fertilizer only.
[6] P2O5 content 15 to 20 per cent.

Remarque générale.
Poids du P2O5 contenu dans les scories phosphatées obtenues comme sous–produit de la fabrication de l'acier à partir de fontes phosphoreuses (scories Thomas), y compris les scories non utilisées comme engrais. (CTCI 56121–0).

[1] Source: U.S. Bureau of Mines, (Washington, D.C.).
[2] Source: Organisation des Nations Unies pour l'alimentation et l'agriculture (FAO), (Rome).
[3] Campagne d'engrais se terminant le 30 juin de l'année indiquée.
[4] Campagne d'engrais se terminant le 31 mai de l'année indiquée.
[5] Production à utiliser comme engrais seulement.
[6] Teneur en P2O5 entre 15 et 20 p. 100.

Spiegeleisen and ferro–manganese – Fonte Spiegel et ferro–manganèse

Unit : Thousand metric tons

Unité : Milliers de tonnes métriques

Country or area	1976	1977	1978	1979	1980	1981	1982	1983	1984	1985	Pays ou zone
Africa	**2**	**2**	**2**	**2**	**2**	**2**	**2**	**2**	**2**	**2**	**Afrique**
Zimbabwe[1,2]	2	2	2	2	* 2	2	2	2	2	2	Zimbabwe[1,2]
America, North	**663**	**496**	**487**	**460**	**464**	**457**	**326**	**249**	**356**	**366**	**Amérique du Nord**
Canada[3,4]	225	193	240	172	292	282	* 218	178	201	* 227	Canada[3,4]
United States[5]	438	303	247	288	172	175	108	71	155	139	Etats–Unis[5]
America, South	**130**	**162**	**148**	**174**	**171**	**137**	**150**	**135**	**137**	**164**	**Amérique du Sud**
Argentina	24	28	25	34	[2] 24	[2] 22	[2] 24	[2] 25	[2] 24	[2] 21	Argentine
Brazil	99	129	118	134	140	108	121	103	106	135	Brésil
Chile*	[2] 7	[2] 5	[2] 5	[2] 5	[2] 5	[2] 5	[2] 3	[2] 5	[2] 5	6	Chili*
Venezuela[1,2]	0	0	0	1	* 2	* 2	* 2	* 2	* 2	* 2	Venezuela[1,2]
Asia	**894**	**818**	**772**	**888**	**827**	**871**	**790**	**631**	**699**	**701**	**Asie**
India[2]	176	194	220	187	158	206	158	154	122	163	Inde[2]
Japan	678	564	487	636	599	595	562	407	507	468	Japon
Korea, D. P. Rp.*	40	60	65	65	70	70	70	70	70	70	Corée, Rp. P. D.*
Europe	**1 538**	**1 382**	**1 376**	**1 650**	**1 458**	**1 137**	**1 434**	**1 086**	**1 432**	**1 363**	**Europe**
EEC	***796***	***719***	***678***	***822***	***737***	***612***	***949***	***527***	***870***	***802***	***CEE***
Belgium[3]	84	68	0	0	0	0	0	0	0	0	Belgique[3]
France	367	373	397	449	480	313	332	270	329	336	France
Germany, Fed. Rep.	220	175	209	233	200	214	[6] 555	[6] 174	[6] 465	[6] 388	Allemagne, Rép. féd.
Italy	3	6	3	3	5	1	1	1	1	1	Italie
United Kingdom	122	97	69	137	52	84	61	82	75	77	Royaume–Uni
EFTA	***430***	***338***	***388***	***455***	***371***	***298***	***251***	***317***	***315***	***297***	***AELE***
Norway	375	283	310	380	297	233	224	283	285	* 268	Norvège
Portugal*[1,2]	55	55	78	75	74	65	27	34	30	29	Portugal*[1,2]
East Europe	***179***	***184***	***176***	***188***	***186***	***167***	***149***	***133***	***133***	***144***	***Europe de l'est***
Bulgaria[3]	54	50	46	50	54	55	55	47	39	43	Bulgarie[3]
Czechoslovakia	1	0	0	0	0	0	0	0	0	0	Tchécoslovaquie
German Dem. Rep.[7]	0	0	4	0	0	2	2	0	2	0	Rép. dém. allemande[7]
Poland	124	134	126	138	132	110	92	86	92	101	Pologne
Other Europe	***133***	***141***	***134***	***185***	***164***	***60***	***85***	***109***	***114***	***120***	***Autre Europe***
Spain[1]	133	141	134	185	164	60	85	109	114	120	Espagne[1]
Oceania	**50**	**71**	**95**	**86**	**94**	**68**	**55**	**53**	**75**	**60**	**Océanie**
Australia[1,2,8]	50	71	95	86	94	68	55	53	75	60	Australie[1,2,8]
Total	**3 277**	**2 931**	**2 880**	**3 260**	**3 016**	**2 672**	**2 757**	**2 156**	**2 701**	**2 656**	**Total**

General note.
Spiegeleisen is a ferrous product containing, by weight, at least 6 per cent but not more than 25 per cent manganese and otherwise conforming to the definition of pig iron. Ferro–manganese is a ferro–alloy containing, by weight, more than 25 per cent manganese. (The sum of SITC 6711 and 6714).

1 Ferro–manganese only.
2 Source: U. S. Bureau of Mines, (Washington, D. C.).
3 Including other ferro–alloys.
4 Shipments.
5 Gross weight, including fused salt electrolytic low carbon ferro–manganese.
6 Including other raw iron, ferrosilicon and iron sponge.
7 Source: Annual Bulletin of Steel Statistics for Europe, United Nations Economic Commission of Europe (Geneva).
8 Twelve months ending 30 November of the year stated.

Remarque générale.
La fonte Spiegel est un produit ferreux contenant en poids de 6 à 25 p. 100 de manganèse et répondant, en ce qui concerne les autres caractéristiques, à la définition de la fonte. Le ferro–manganèse est un ferro–alliage contenant en poids plus de 25 p. 100 de manganèse. (CTCI 6711 et 6714).

1 Ferro–manganèse seulement.
2 Source: U.S. Bureau of Mines, (Washington, D.C.).
3 Y compris les autres ferro–alliages.
4 Expéditions.
5 Poids brut. Y compris le ferro–manganèse à faible teneur en carbone obtenu par électrolyse en présence de sels fondus.
6 Y compris les fontes brutes, le ferro–silicium et le fer spongieux.
7 Source: Bulletin annuel de statistiques de l'acier pour l'Europe, Commission économique des Nations Unies pour l'Europe (Genève).
8 Période de douze mois finissant le 30 novembre de l'année indiquée.

Pig iron, foundry – Fonte de moulage

Unit : Thousand metric tons

Unité : Milliers de tonnes métriques

Country or area	1976	1977	1978	1979	1980	1981	1982	1983	1984	1985	Pays ou zone
Africa	**1 285**	**1 229**	**1 152**	**1 090**	**1 068**	**1 064**	**723**	**446**	**505**	**540**	**Afrique**
Egypt*[1,2]	300	300	300	300	250	220	113	196	225	225	Egypte*[1,2]
South Africa	...	...	...	...	666	686	513	103	133	174	Afrique du Sud
Tunisia	112	136	138	155	152	158	97	147	147	141	Tunisie
America, North	**3 125**	**3 087**	**3 380**	**3 179**	**2 408**	**2 790**	**1 152**	**1 216**	**1 220**	**1 216**	**Amérique du Nord**
Canada	634	562	825	505	877	736	537	...	...	...	Canada
Mexico	29	27	36	43	36	44	26	36	62	68	Mexique
United States	2 462	2 498	2 519	2 631	1 495	2 010	# 589	496	471	457	Etats–Unis
America, South	**147**	**98**	**87**	**109**	**127**	**57**	**111**	**65**	**63**	**47**	**Amérique du Sud**
Argentina	113	56	44	63	79	29	72	* 26	24	9	Argentine
Chile[3]	34	42	43	46	48	28	...	...	...	...	Chili[3]
Asia	**2 623**	**2 299**	**2 144**	**2 121**	**2 308**	**1 708**	**1 698**	**1 923**	**2 102**	**1 968**	**Asie**
Iran(Islamic Rep.of)[1,2,4]	625	700	900	800	800	500	600	700	700	700	Iran(Rép.islamique)[1,2,4]
Japan	1 525	1 232	986	994	1 278	981	821	915	1 179	991	Japon
Turkey	473	367	258	327	230	227	277	308	223	277	Turquie
Europe	**7 245**	**6 939**	**6 663**	**6 608**	**6 505**	**5 713**	**5 210**	**5 023**	**5 037**	**5 090**	**Europe**
EEC	***4 116***	***3 823***	***3 549***	***3 696***	***3 416***	***2 756***	***2 448***	***2 146***	***2 049***	***2 279***	***CEE***
Belgium	12	0	0	0	0	0	0	0	0	0	Belgique
France	1 297	1 184	1 177	1 252	1 251	1 146	1 180	869	742	900	France
Germany, Fed. Rep.	1 377	1 226	1 223	1 371	1 272	1 090	816	693	800	914	Allemagne, Rép. féd.
Greece	421	323	282	328	303	*[2] 91	*[2] 110	*[2] 138	*[2] 138	*[2] 140	Grèce
Italy	230	320	277	284	328	293	242	298	314	325	Italie
United Kingdom[5]	779	770	590	461	262	136	100	148	55	0	Royaume–Uni[5]
EFTA	***185***	***161***	***153***	***128***	***98***	***85***	***35***	***29***	***67***	***75***	***AELE***
Austria[6]	25	8	3	23	5	4	0	0	0	0	Autriche[6]
Finland	96	66	0	0	0	0	0	0	0	0	Finlande
Portugal	14	7	9	28	22	10	8	10	9	9	Portugal
Sweden	27	53	106	47	38	38	17	9	4	0	Suède
Switzerland[1,6]	23	27	35	* 30	33	33	10	10	54	66	Suisse[1,6]
East Europe	***2 425***	***2 451***	***2 530***	***2 334***	***2 563***	***2 545***	***2 435***	***2 537***	***2 638***	***2 459***	***Europe de l'est***
Bulgaria	5	4	4	1	2	4	4	3	5	10	Bulgarie
Czechoslovakia	479	485	475	450	480	510	456	468	474	386	Tchécoslovaquie
German Dem. Rep.	400	394	398	407	414	377	401	397	422	415	Rép. dém. allemande
Hungary	110	112	78	107	120	128	116	81	67	88	Hongrie
Poland	978	953	1 006	895	1 021	849	802	891	886	886	Pologne
Romania[6]	# 453	503	569	474	526	677	656	697	784	674	Roumanie[6]
Other Europe	***519***	***504***	***431***	***450***	***428***	***327***	***292***	***311***	***283***	***277***	***Autre Europe***
Spain	284	283	216	219	184	81	44	50	34	31	Espagne
Yugoslavia	235	221	215	231	244	246	248	261	249	246	Yougoslavie
Total	**14 425**	**13 652**	**13 426**	**13 107**	**12 416**	**11 332**	**8 894**	**8 673**	**8 927**	**8 862**	**Total**

General note.
Pig iron is iron in liquid or solid form, containing at least 3 per cent of carbon and possibly one or more of the following elements within the weight limits specified : less than 6 per cent of silicon, less than 6 per cent of manganese, and less than 3 per cent of phosphorus. It may also contain small proportions of other elements, for example, chromium and nickel. Foundry pig iron is pig iron for use in making cast iron, including forge pig iron and pig iron for direct casting. (SITC 67120–1).

[1] Including pig–iron for steel making.
[2] Source: U. S. Bureau of Mines, (Washington, D. C.).
[3] Source: Instituto Latino Americano del Fierro y el Acero, (Santiago).
[4] Twelve months beginning 21 March of year stated.
[5] Including refined pig iron.
[6] Source: Annual Bulletin of Steel Statistics for Europe, United Nations Economic Commission of Europe (Geneva).

Remarque générale.
La fonte est du fer à l'état liquide ou solide contenant au moins 3 p. 100 de carbone et pouvant contenir un ou plusieurs des éléments suivants dans les limites de poids indiquées: moins de 6 p. 100 de silicium, moins de 6 p. 100 de manganèse et moins de 3 p. 100 de phosphore. Elle peut aussi contenir de faibles proportions d'autres éléments, tels que le chrome et le nickel. La fonte de moulage est de la fonte servant à la fabrication de pièces moulées en fonte et comprend notamment la fonte pour forge et la fonte pour moulages de première coulé. (CTCI 67120–1).

[1] Y compris la fonte d'affinage.
[2] Source: U.S. Bureau of Mines, (Washington, D.C.).
[3] Source: Instituto Latino Americano del Fierro y el Acero, (Santiago).
[4] Période de douze mois commençant le 21 mars de l'année indiquée.
[5] Y compris la fonte affinée.
[6] Source: Bulletin annuel de statistiques de l'acier pour l'Europe, Commission économique des Nations Unies pour l'Europe (Genève).

Pig iron, steel-making – Fonte d'affinage

Unit : Thousand metric tons

Unité : Milliers de tonnes métriques

Country or area	1976	1977	1978	1979	1980	1981	1982	1983	1984	1985	Pays ou zone
Africa	**6 528**	**6 825**	**6 809**	**8 139**	**8 129**	**8 088**	**7 590**	**7 164**	**7 364**	**9 120**	**Afrique**
Algeria	413	389	287	496	669	897	1 059	1 113	1 100	* 1 100	Algérie
Morocco* [1]	10	12	12	12	11	12	12	15	15	15	Maroc* [1]
South Africa	5 795	6 114	5 910	7 031	* 6 849	* 6 779	* 6 249	* 5 110	* 5 322	7 005	Afrique du Sud
Zimbabwe [1]	* 310	* 310	* 600	* 600	* 600	* 400	* 270	926	927	* 1 000	Zimbabwe [1]
America, North	**88 950**	**84 418**	**91 401**	**91 493**	**75 960**	**79 058**	**51 145**	**57 177**	**61 539**	**56 750**	**Amérique du Nord**
Canada	9 167	9 099	9 513	10 401	10 016	9 007	7 463	[2] 8 567	[2] 9 643	[2] 6 423	Canada
Mexico	3 437	4 037	4 865	4 795	5 095	5 320	4 981	4 920	5 277	5 021	Mexique
United States	76 346	71 282	77 023	76 297	60 849	64 731	38 701	43 690	46 619	45 306	Etats-Unis
America, South	**10 679**	**11 815**	**12 915**	**14 272**	**15 340**	**13 097**	**12 833**	**14 899**	**19 241**	**21 687**	**Amérique du Sud**
Argentina	1 167	1 044	1 391	1 072	969	886	944	891	820	1 301	Argentine
Brazil	8 170	9 380	10 043	11 594	12 685	10 791	10 827	12 945	17 230	18 961	Brésil
Chile	403	427	539	611	648	582	453	540	594	575	Chili
Colombia [1 2]	286	223	297	240	279	233	246	241	271	246	Colombie [1 2]
Peru [1 2]	231	244	244	257	262	187	161	113	0	163	Pérou [1 2]
Venezuela [2]	422	497	401	498	497	418	202	169	326	* 441	Venezuela [2]
Asia	**124 985**	**127 894**	**130 955**	**140 236**	**145 067**	**137 367**	**137 813**	**134 658**	**145 871**	**150 846**	**Asie**
China [2]	22 330	25 050	34 790	36 730	38 020	34 170	35 510	37 380	40 010	43 840	Chine [2]
India [2]	9 731	9 785	9 431	8 687	8 480	9 465	9 613	9 087	9 382	9 701	Inde [2]
Japan	85 051	84 654	77 603	82 831	85 763	79 067	76 837	72 022	79 224	79 578	Japon
Korea, D. P. Rp.* [1 2]	4 400	4 600	4 800	5 000	5 400	5 000	5 300	5 500	5 700	5 800	Corée, Rp. P. D.* [1 2]
Korea, Republic of	1 937	2 425	2 741	5 063	5 577	7 928	8 445	8 024	8 763	8 833	Corée, République de
Thailand [2]	18	20	21	24	17	10	6	0	0	0	Thaïlande [2]
Turkey	1 518	1 360	1 569	1 901	1 810	1 727	2 102	2 645	2 792	3 094	Turquie
Europe	**135 519**	**130 546**	**135 574**	**145 866**	**136 991**	**133 946**	**119 683**	**118 942**	**129 914**	**132 805**	**Europe**
EEC	***89 930***	***83 194***	***86 099***	***94 063***	***85 427***	***84 979***	***73 395***	***71 797***	***80 371***	***82 811***	***CEE***
Belgium	9 865	8 910	10 128	10 776	9 845	9 791	7 832	8 033	8 968	8 719	Belgique
France	17 359	16 700	16 923	17 714	17 428	15 815	13 535	12 631	13 968	14 172	France
Germany, Fed. Rep.	30 161	27 471	28 708	33 483	32 337	30 522	26 250	25 659	28 937	30 229	Allemagne, Rép. féd.
Italy	11 401	11 090	11 064	11 043	11 822	11 967	11 295	10 015	11 317	11 737	Italie
Luxembourg	3 756	3 568	3 721	3 801	3 568	2 889	2 587	2 316	2 768	2 754	Luxembourg
Netherlands	4 265	3 922	4 613	4 814	4 328	4 600	3 617	3 747	4 926	4 819	Pays-Bas
United Kingdom	13 123	11 533	10 942	12 432	6 099	9 395	8 279	9 396	9 487	10 381	Royaume-Uni
EFTA	***9 030***	***8 213***	***8 533***	***10 190***	***9 365***	***8 995***	***8 178***	***8 909***	***9 615***	***9 674***	***AELE***
Austria	3 294	2 957	3 074	3 679	3 480	3 473	3 115	3 319	3 745	3 704	Autriche
Finland	1 233	1 698	1 858	2 038	2 019	1 965	1 944	1 898	2 034	1 890	Finlande
Norway [3]	1 209	959	1 000	1 272	1 131	1 487	1 146	1 337	1 264	1 250	Norvège [3]
Portugal	* 330	348	344	352	349	305	214	355	373	415	Portugal
Sweden	2 964	2 251	2 257	2 849	2 386	1 765	1 759	2 000	2 199	2 415	Suède
East Europe	***28 534***	***31 084***	***33 049***	***33 239***	***33 838***	***31 223***	***29 702***	***30 276***	***32 037***	***32 022***	***Europe de l'est***
Bulgaria	1 553	1 610	1 489	1 450	1 527	1 512	1 558	1 623	1 578	1 702	Bulgarie
Czechoslovakia	8 994	9 229	9 469	9 080	9 339	9 393	9 069	8 999	9 088	9 176	Tchécoslovaquie
German Dem. Rep.	2 119	2 225	2 150	1 971	2 034	2 052	1 735	1 799	1 921	2 150	Rép. dém. allemande
Hungary	2 111	2 175	2 252	2 262	2 094	2 065	2 065	1 966	2 029	2 007	Hongrie
Poland	6 795	8 564	10 103	10 071	10 357	8 021	7 294	8 395	8 647	8 449	Pologne
Romania [4]	6 962	7 281	7 586	8 405	8 487	8 180	7 981	7 494	8 774	8 538	Roumanie [4]
Other Europe	***8 025***	***8 055***	***7 893***	***8 374***	***8 361***	***8 749***	***8 408***	***7 960***	***7 891***	***8 298***	***Autre Europe***
Spain	6 342	6 338	6 027	6 245	6 180	6 178	5 953	5 376	5 285	5 424	Espagne
Yugoslavia	1 683	1 717	1 866	2 129	2 181	2 571	2 455	2 584	2 606	2 874	Yougoslavie
USSR [5]	**105 374**	**107 368**	**110 702**	**108 998**	**107 283**	**107 766**	**106 723**	**110 453**	**110 893**	**109 977**	**URSS [5]**
Ukrainian SSR	*47 287*	...	...	...	...	...	...	...	...	...	*RSS d'Ukraine*
Oceania	**7 519**	**7 055**	**6 989**	**7 349**	**7 276**	**7 403**	**6 606**	**4 990**	**5 258**	**5 341**	**Océanie**
Australia [2 6]	7 519	7 055	6 989	7 349	7 276	7 403	6 606	4 990	5 258	5 341	Australie [2 6]
Total	**479 554**	**475 921**	**495 345**	**516 353**	**496 046**	**486 725**	**442 393**	**448 283**	**480 080**	**486 526**	**Total**

For general note and footnotes, see end of table.

Voir la fin du tableau pour la remarque générale et les notes.

General note.
Pig iron is iron in liquid or solid form, containing at least 3 per cent of carbon and possibly one or more of the following elements within the weight limits specified : less than 6 per cent of silicon, less than 6 per cent of manganese, and less than 3 per cent of phosphorus. It may also contain small proportions of other elements, for example, chromium and nickel. Steel–making pig iron is distinguished from foundry pig iron on the basis of the uses to which it is put. Steel–making pig iron is pig iron for use in making crude steel. (SITC 67120–2).

[1] Source: U. S. Bureau of Mines, (Washington, D. C.).
[2] Including foundry pig iron.
[3] Including foundry pig iron and other ferro–alloys.
[4] Source: Annual Bulletin of Steel Statistics for Europe, United Nations Economic Commission of Europe (Geneva).
[5] Including foundry pig iron, spiegeleisen, ferromanganese and other ferro–alloys.
[6] Twelve months ending 30 June of year stated.

Remarque générale.
La fonte est du fer à l'état liquide ou solide contenant au moins 3 p. 100 de carbone et pouvant contenir un ou plusieurs des éléments suivants dans les limites de poids indiquées: moins de 6 p. 100 de silicium, moins de 6 p. 100 de manganèse et moins de 3 p. 100 de phosphore. Elle peut aussi contenir de faibles proportions d'autres éléments, tels que le chrome et le nickel. La fonte d'affinage ne se distingue de la fonte de moulage que par sa destination. La fonte d'affinage est de la fonte servant à la fabrication d'acier brut. (CTCI 67120–2).

[1] Source: U.S. Bureau of Mines, (Washington, D.C.).
[2] Y compris la fonte de moulage.
[3] Y compris la fonte de moulage et les autres ferro–alliages.
[4] Source: Bulletin annuel de statistiques de l'acier pour l'Europe, Commission économique des Nations Unies pour l'Europe (Genève).
[5] Y compris fonte de moulage, spiegel, ferro–manganèse et autres ferro–alliages.
[6] Période de douze mois finissant le 30 juin de l'année indiquée.

Other ferro-alloys – Autres ferro-alliages

Unit : Thousand metric tons — Unité : Milliers de tonnes métriques

Country or area	1976	1977	1978	1979	1980	1981	1982	1983	1984	1985	Pays ou zone
Africa	**1 023**	**990**	**1 320**	**1 001**	**1 602**	**1 460**	**1 302**	**1 160**	**1 396**	**1 604**	**Afrique**
South Africa[1]	823	780	1 110	791	1 332	1 241	1 099	* 965	1 166	1 384	Afrique du Sud[1]
Zambia	10	* 10	* 10	...	...	...	...	...	...	...	Zambie
Zimbabwe* [2]	190	200	200	200	260	209	193	185	220	210	Zimbabwe* [2]
America, North	**1 377**	**1 430**	**1 421**	**1 601**	**1 431**	**1 396**	**851**	**846**	**1 081**	**989**	**Amérique du Nord**
Mexico	82	142	157	188	199	191	216	205	249	242	Mexique
United States	1 295	1 288	1 264	1 413	1 232	1 205	635	641	832	747	Etats-Unis
America, South	**237**	**268**	**329**	**403**	**372**	**321**	**292**	**437**	**374**	**395**	**Amérique du Sud**
Argentina[3]	17	15	10	14	12	11	10	15	20	19	Argentine[3]
Brazil	208	237	286	345	291	252	227	359	292	324	Brésil
Chile*	8	3	2	7	7	3	3	7	8	2	Chili*
Colombia* [2]	1	1	1	1	1	1	1	1	1	1	Colombie* [2]
Peru[2]	0	* 1	2	1	* 1	0	0	0	0	0	Pérou[2]
Venezuela[2]	3	* # 11	* 28	35	60	54	51	55	53	49	Venezuela[2]
Asia	**2 443**	**2 380**	**2 336**	**2 905**	**2 700**	**2 315**	**2 320**	**2 352**	**2 694**	**2 929**	**Asie**
China	659	732	939	1 173	994	799	889	1 088	1 275	1 494	Chine
India[2]	76	78	81	82	75	106	97	111	142	132	Inde[2]
Japan[4]	1 618	1 468	1 194	1 508	1 490	1 241	1 164	990	1 078	1 097	Japon[4]
Korea, Republic of	65	64	79	112	109	128	126	129	144	151	Corée, République de
Turkey[2]	* 25	* 38	* 43	* 30	* 32	41	* 44	* 34	* 55	* 55	Turquie[2]
Europe	**2 032**	**2 006**	**1 986**	**2 444**	**2 210**	**1 941**	**1 729**	**1 685**	**1 975**	**1 986**	**Europe**
EEC	***1 047***	***1 036***	***906***	***1 078***	***938***	***753***	***707***	***658***	***791***	***704***	***CEE***
France	463	490	440	523	436	345	331	346	382	320	France
Germany, Fed. Rep.	330	297	217	274	246	204	132	107	151	102	Allemagne, Rép. féd.
Italy	254	249	249	281	256	204	244	205	258	282	Italie
EFTA	***280***	***257***	***262***	***419***	***372***	***290***	***312***	***312***	***349***	***434***	***AELE***
Austria[5]	8	[2] 7	[2] 7	[2] 9	* [2] 10	* [2] 12	* [2] 14	* [2] 14	* [2] 13	* [2] 14	Autriche[5]
Finland	50	34	45	49	53	52	54	58	59	* 133	Finlande
Portugal	[3] 12	[3] 12	[3] 12	137	132	52	87	78	84	93	Portugal
Sweden	205	196	194	220	172	169	152	158	188	189	Suède
Switzerland* [2]	5	8	4	4	5	5	5	4	5	5	Suisse* [2]
East Europe	***335***	***371***	***372***	***387***	***368***	***356***	***357***	***360***	***350***	***365***	***Europe de l'est***
Czechoslovakia	136	175	177	175	173	173	164	162	151	161	Tchécoslovaquie
German Dem. Rep.	...	7	8	8	10	9	11	11	12	13	Rép. dém. allemande
Hungary	12	13	13	12	13	14	13	12	13	14	Hongrie
Poland	181	176	174	192	172	160	169	175	174	177	Pologne
Other Europe	***370***	***342***	***446***	***560***	***532***	***542***	***353***	***355***	***485***	***483***	***Autre Europe***
Spain	170	153	226	310	289	278	132	104	181	184	Espagne
Yugoslavia	200	189	220	250	243	264	221	251	304	299	Yougoslavie
Oceania	**22**	**43**	**19**	**39**	**36**	**48**	**49**	**38**	**56**	**40**	**Océanie**
Australia[2] [6]	22	43	19	39	36	48	49	38	* 56	40	Australie[2] [6]
Total	**7 135**	**7 117**	**7 411**	**8 394**	**8 351**	**7 481**	**6 543**	**6 518**	**7 576**	**7 943**	**Total**

General note.
All ferro-alloys, other than ferro-manganese, which are produced in blast furnaces, low-shaft furnaces, electric furnaces and other types of iron-making installations. (SITC 67150-0).

[1] Including ferro-manganese.
[2] Source: U. S. Bureau of Mines, (Washington, D. C.).
[3] Ferro-silicon only.
[4] Including silico-chromium.
[5] Ferro-alloys produced in electric furnaces.
[6] Twelve months ending 30 November of the year stated.

Remarque générale.
Tous les ferro-alliages autres que le ferro-manganèse, produits au haut fourneau, au bas fourneau, au four électrique ou dans d'autres types d'installations pour la fabrication de la fonte. (CTCI 67150-0).

[1] Y compris le ferromanganèse.
[2] Source: U.S. Bureau of Mines, (Washington, D.C.).
[3] Ferro-silicium seulement.
[4] Y compris le silico-chrome.
[5] Ferro-alliages produits dans les fourneaux électriques.
[6] Période de douze mois finissant le 30 novembre de l'année indiquée.

Ferro–chromium (including ferro–silico–chromium and charge chrome) – Ferro–chrome (y compris le ferro–silicochrome et chrome de charge)

Unit : Thousand metric tons | Unité : Milliers tonnes métriques

Country or area	1976	1977	1978	1979	1980	1981	1982	1983	1984	1985	Pays ou zone
Africa	**558**	**573**	**883**	**1 008**	**978**	**789**	**651**	**923**	**1 133**	**1 017**	**Afrique**
South Africa[1]	*[2] 372	*[2] 373	*[2] 683	*[2] 808	*[2] 718	*[2] 580	*[2] 458	*[2] 738	*[2] 913	# 807	Afrique du Sud[1]
Zimbabwe[2]	186	* 200	* 200	* 200	* 260	* 209	* 193	* 185	* 220	* 210	Zimbabwe[2]
America, North	**248**	**248**	**203**	**301**	**216**	**208**	**114**	**36**	**93**	**105**	**Amérique du Nord**
Mexico[2]	4	3	4	4	0	3	6	3	7	6	Mexique[2]
United States[1]	244	245	199	297	216	205	108	33	86	99	Etats–Unis[1]
America, South	**66**	**71**	**67**	**92**	**102**	**119**	**97**	**74**	**125**	**127**	**Amérique du Sud**
Brazil	[1,2] 66	[1,2] 71	[1,2] 67	[1,2] 92	[1,2] 102	119	97	74	125	127	Brésil
Asia	**673**	**590**	**961**	**558**	**604**	**551**	**578**	**568**	**619**	**660**	**Asie**
China* [1,2]	60	70	90	90	100	120	120	120	120	120	Chine* [1,2]
India[1,2]	22	22	25	26	21	36	46	61	59	79	Inde[1,2]
Japan	565	459	796	402	441	344	360	335	359	373	Japon
Philippines* [2]	...	...	10	10	10	10	12	22	33	40	Philippines* [2]
Turkey[2]	* 25	* 35	* 40	* 30	* 32	41	40	30	48	48	Turquie[2]
Europe	**582**	**568**	**596**	**672**	**555**	**508**	**504**	**478**	**550**	**674**	**Europe**
EEC	***199***	***203***	***180***	***198***	***146***	***87***	***116***	***68***	***101***	***149***	***CEE***
France	102	102	93	95	45	27	# 38	18	19	19	France
Germany, Fed. Rep.* [2]	...	61	50	60	60	50	42	38	70	72	Allemagne, Rép. féd.* [2]
Italy[1,2]	45	40	37	43	41	10	36	12	12	58	Italie[1,2]
EFTA	***205***	***199***	***232***	***281***	***216***	***213***	***202***	***205***	***227***	***297***	***AELE***
Finland	50	34	45	49	53	52	54	58	59	* 133	Finlande
Norway[1]	33	23	16	13	11	13	12	9	* 4	0	Norvège[1]
Sweden[1]	122	142	171	219	152	148	136	138	164	164	Suède[1]
East Europe	***108***	***108***	***111***	***101***	***98***	***117***	***115***	***129***	***135***	***136***	***Europe de l'est***
Albania* [2]	...	...	...	...	4	28	30	35	40	43	Albanie* [2]
Czechoslovakia	...	30	30	27	28	28	30	29	28	25	Tchécoslovaquie
German Dem. Rep.* [2]	...	24	25	21	19	20	20	17	19	19	Rép. dém. allemande* [2]
Poland* [2]	50	50	50	49	47	41	35	48	48	49	Pologne* [2]
Other Europe	***69***	***58***	***73***	***92***	***95***	***91***	***71***	***76***	***87***	***92***	***Autre Europe***
Spain[2]	19	16	14	20	16	17	15	* 14	* 14	* 17	Espagne[2]
Yugoslavia[2]	50	42	59	72	79	74	56	* 62	...	...	Yougoslavie[2]
USSR* [1,2]	**480**	**540**	**550**	**550**	**390**	**400**	**415**	**415**	**420**	**420**	**URSS* [1,2]**
Total	**2 606**	**2 590**	**3 260**	**3 181**	**2 845**	**2 575**	**2 359**	**2 494**	**2 940**	**3 003**	**Total**

General note.
Data refer to ferro–chromium and include ferro–silico–chromium and charge chrome. (SITC 67150–1).

[1] Including ferrochromium–silicon.
[2] Source: U. S. Bureau of Mines, (Washington, D. C.).

Remarque générale.
Les données se rapportent au ferro–chrome et comprennent le ferro–silico–chrome. (CTCI 67150–1).

[1] Y compris ferro–silico–chrome.
[2] Source: U.S. Bureau of Mines, (Washington, D.C.).

Ferro-nickel

Unit : Thousand metric tons

Unité : Milliers de tonnes métriques

Country or area	1976	1977	1978	1979	1980	1981	1982	1983	1984	1985	Pays ou zone
America, North	**77**	**79**	**49**	**75**	**53**	**59**	**17**	**52**	**73**	**70**	**Amérique du Nord**
Dominican Republic	64	67	38	66	43	50	14	52	64	67	Rép. dominicaine
United States	...	...	...	...	10	9	3	0	9	...	Etats-Unis
America, South	**10**	**11**	**11**	**11**	**11**	**11**	**11**	**9**	**9**	**9**	**Amérique du Sud**
Brazil	10	11	11	11	11	11	11	9	9	9	Brésil
Asia	**216**	**246**	**219**	**322**	**295**	**264**	**237**	**202**	**240**	**251**	**Asie**
Indonesia[1]	17	22	20	18	18	20	22	21	23	24	Indonésie[1]
Japan	199	224	199	304	277	244	215	181	217	227	Japon
Europe	**61**	**35**	**61**	**63**	**52**	**51**	**51**	**50**	**53**	**55**	**Europe**
EEC	***61***	***35***	***61***	***63***	***52***	***51***	***51***	***50***	***53***	***55***	***CEE***
Greece[1]	61	35	61	63	52	* 51	* 51	* 50	* 53	* 55	Grèce[1]
Total	**364**	**371**	**340**	**472**	**411**	**385**	**316**	**313**	**375**	**385**	**Total**

General note.
Data refer to ferro-nickel. (SITC 67150-2).

Remarque générale.
Les données se rapportent au ferro-nickel. (CTCI 67150-2).

[1] Source: U. S. Bureau of Mines, (Washington, D. C.).

[1] Source: U.S. Bureau of Mines, (Washington, D.C.).

Ferro-silicon – Ferro-silicium

Unit : Thousand metric tons — Unité : Milliers de tonnes métriques

Country or area	1976	1977	1978	1979	1980	1981	1982	1983	1984	1985	Pays ou zone
Africa	**84**	**105**	**80**	**153**	**166**	**115**	**105**	**103**	**117**	**82**	**Afrique**
Egypt	5	5	5	4	4	* 5	* 5	* 3	* 7	* 7	Egypte
South Africa* [1]	79	100	75	149	162	110	100	100	110	75	Afrique du Sud* [1]
America, North	**884**	**948**	**885**	**897**	**789**	**783**	**475**	**505**	**509**	**513**	**Amérique du Nord**
Canada[1]	85	114	* 118	95	139	116	* 105	85	* 80	84	Canada[1]
Mexico[1]	18	23	24	24	27	23	29	24	23	28	Mexique[1]
United States	781	811	743	778	623	644	341	396	406	401	Etats-Unis
America, South	**72**	**90**	**118**	**123**	**175**	**179**	**169**	**222**	**229**	**249**	**Amérique du Sud**
Argentina	17	15	10	14	12	11	10	15	20	19	Argentine
Brazil	45	60	73	67	109	121	115	155	158	187	Brésil
Chile* [1]	6	3	2	5	5	2	1	5	6	0	Chili* [1]
Colombia* [1]	1	1	1	1	1	1	1	1	1	1	Colombie* [1]
Peru[1]	0	0	* 1	* 1	* 1	0	0	* 0	0	0	Pérou[1]
Venezuela[1]	3	* 11	* 31	35	47	44	42	46	44	42	Venezuela[1]
Asia	**546**	**525**	**563**	**632**	**651**	**587**	**532**	**495**	**497**	**484**	**Asie**
China* [1]	100	110	150	160	200	200	200	200	200	200	Chine* [1]
India[1]	54	45	52	53	54	60	40	47	51	39	Inde[1]
Japan	320	298	278	330	317	239	197	161	156	153	Japon
Korea, D. P. Rp.* [1]	20	20	30	30	30	30	30	30	30	30	Corée, Rp. P. D.* [1]
Korea, Republic of[1]	34	...	...	38	30	32	32	33	35	35	Corée, République de[1]
Philippines* [1]	...	15	14	18	20	26	29	20	18	20	Philippines* [1]
Thailand[1]	1	0	2	3	0	0	0	0	0	0	Thaïlande[1]
Turkey[1]	...	* 3	* 3	0	0	0	* 4	* 4	* 7	* 7	Turquie[1]
Europe	**1 045**	**1 057**	**1 023**	**1 275**	**1 245**	**1 093**	**1 067**	**1 152**	**1 192**	**1 124**	**Europe**
EEC	***407***	***464***	***360***	***447***	***397***	***310***	***339***	***344***	***351***	***331***	***CEE***
France	237	284	199	272	246	189	226	247	206	197	France
Germany, Fed. Rep.	91	87	78	79	64	50	* [1] 34	* [1] 31	* [1] 60	* [1] 60	Allemagne, Rép. féd.
Italy[1]	79	93	83	96	87	71	79	66	85	* 74	Italie[1]
EFTA	***343***	***290***	***310***	***465***	***482***	***447***	***433***	***516***	***554***	***509***	***AELE***
Iceland	0	0	0	17	28	33	* 42	51	61	60	Islande
Norway	278	223	266	406	406	369	349	421	437	398	Norvège
Portugal* [1]	23	24	30	25	25	24	21	22	20	19	Portugal* [1]
Sweden	37	35	10	13	18	16	16	18	31	27	Suède
Switzerland[1]	5	* 8	* 4	* 4	* 5	* 5	* 5	* 4	* 5	* 5	Suisse[1]
East Europe	***139***	***136***	***144***	***129***	***127***	***125***	***113***	***116***	***118***	***118***	***Europe de l'est***
Bulgaria	...	7	7	9	10	13	13	8	11	8	Bulgarie
Czechoslovakia[1]	...	* 40	* 41	22	29	31	26	20	19	21	Tchécoslovaquie[1]
German Dem. Rep.* [1]	...	25	34	34	26	25	24	24	24	23	Rép. dém. allemande* [1]
Hungary	7	9	9	10	12	13	13	12	13	14	Hongrie
Poland* [1]	52	55	53	54	50	43	37	52	51	52	Pologne* [1]
Other Europe	***156***	***167***	***209***	***234***	***239***	***211***	***182***	***176***	***169***	***166***	***Autre Europe***
Spain	[1] 57	* [1] 84	* [1] 118	* [1] 134	* [1] 143	* [1] 103	* [1] 81	# 61	75	74	Espagne
Yugoslavia	99	83	91	100	96	108	101	* 115	94	92	Yougoslavie
USSR* [1]	**600**	**600**	**620**	**630**	**630**	**650**	**680**	**720**	**750**	**750**	**URSS* [1]**
Oceania	**7**	**19**	**19**	**19**	**18**	**18**	**20**	**19**	**25**	**20**	**Océanie**
Australia[1] [2]	7	19	19	19	18	18	20	19	* 25	20	Australie[1] [2]
Total	**3 238**	**3 344**	**3 308**	**3 729**	**3 674**	**3 425**	**3 048**	**3 216**	**3 319**	**3 222**	**Total**

General note.
Data refer to ferro-silicon. (SITC 67150-4).

Remarque générale.
Les données se rapportent au ferrosilicium. (CTCI 67150-4).

[1] Source: U. S. Bureau of Mines, (Washington, D. C.).
[2] Twelve months ending 30 November of the year stated.

[1] Source: U.S. Bureau of Mines, (Washington, D.C.).
[2] Période de douze mois finissant le 30 novembre de l'année indiquée.

Crude steel for castings – Acier brut pour moulages

Unit : Thousand metric tons

Unité : Milliers de tonnes métriques

Country or area	1976	1977	1978	1979	1980	1981	1982	1983	1984	1985	Pays ou zone
Africa	**315**	**365**	**336**	**285**	**276**	**280**	**223**	**264**	**285**	**268**	**Afrique**
Egypt	0	3	2	0	0	0	0	...	...	...	Egypte
Morocco* [1]	1	5	6	6	6	6	6	6	6	6	Maroc* [1]
South Africa	211	201	168	103	92	101	112	94	112	101	Afrique du Sud
Tunisia	103	156	160	176	178	173	105	163	166	160	Tunisie
America, North	**186**	**165**	**188**	**243**	**239**	**196**	**125**	**115**	**145**	**111**	**Amérique du Nord**
Canada	167	149	170	223	217	174	109	104	131	99	Canada
Mexico	19	16	18	20	22	22	16	11	14	12	Mexique
America, South	**178**	**173**	**172**	**159**	**174**	**141**	**101**	**88**	**115**	**135**	**Amérique du Sud**
Argentina	46	46	51	51	40	20	21	26	25	27	Argentine
Brazil	...	...	...	108	134	121	80	62	90	108	Brésil
Asia	**2 573**	**2 663**	**2 716**	**2 964**	**2 904**	**2 988**	**2 882**	**3 232**	**3 281**	**3 659**	**Asie**
India	63	67	76	73	72	80	86	89	87	93	Inde
Indonesia [1 2]	139	145	150	305	360	500	500	800	* 1 000	* 1 400	Indonésie [1 2]
Iran(Islamic Rep.of)* [1 3]	1 300	1 400	1 400	1 400	1 200	1 200	1 200	1 400	1 200	1 200	Iran(Rép.islamique)* [1 3]
Japan	1 044	1 024	1 048	1 130	1 224	1 139	1 030	876	910	886	Japon
Korea, Republic of	27	27	42	56	48	69	66	67	84	80	Corée, République de
Europe	**5 631**	**6 445**	**6 992**	**7 956**	**5 742**	**6 014**	**6 294**	**6 702**	**7 223**	**7 230**	**Europe**
EEC	***1 789***	***1 646***	***1 562***	***1 617***	***1 573***	***1 437***	***1 438***	***1 158***	***1 167***	***1 162***	***CEE***
Belgium	46	33	23	22	23	16	* 110	112	113	98	Belgique
Denmark [4]	26	14	15	14	13	13	11	9	3	0	Danemark [4]
France	399	356	347	354	365	367	319	254	241	239	France
Germany, Fed. Rep.	567	512	491	545	538	514	466	382	398	412	Allemagne, Rép. féd.
Italy	239	242	234	277	248	211	179	146	155	174	Italie
Luxembourg	5	4	4	4	5	0	0	0	0	0	Luxembourg
Netherlands	18	10	7	6	8	8	8	8	8	0	Pays–Bas
United Kingdom	489	475	441	395	373	308	345	247	249	239	Royaume–Uni
EFTA	***1 401***	***1 662***	***1 843***	***2 471***	***2 496***	***3 032***	***3 380***	***3 950***	***4 414***	***4 426***	***AELE***
Austria	1 276	1 566	1 759	2 380	2 408	2 946	3 317	3 883	4 350	4 370	Autriche
Finland	30	25	29	34	37	35	[4] 23	[4] 21	[4] 21	[4] 23	Finlande
Norway	29	20	11	12	13	15	9	8	7	7	Norvège
Sweden	45	30	28	30	* 29	* 27	22	29	31	26	Suède
Switzerland [4]	21	21	16	...	9	9	9	9	5	0	Suisse [4]
East Europe	***2 198***	***2 927***	***3 273***	***3 655***	***1 440***	***1 335***	***1 267***	***1 387***	***1 423***	***1 457***	***Europe de l'est***
Hungary	117	113	104	100	103	104	93	90	81	81	Hongrie
Poland	592	613	623	607	609	536	501	588	550	581	Pologne
Romania [4]	1 489	2 201	2 546	2 948	728	695	673	709	792	795	Roumanie [4]
Other Europe	***243***	***210***	***314***	***213***	***233***	***210***	***209***	***207***	***219***	***185***	***Autre Europe***
Spain	188	168	200	152	166	139	138	143	131	127	Espagne
Yugoslavia	55	42	114	61	67	71	71	64	88	58	Yougoslavie
Total	**8 883**	**9 811**	**10 404**	**11 607**	**9 335**	**9 619**	**9 625**	**10 401**	**11 049**	**11 403**	**Total**

General note.
Crude steel is steel (including alloy steel) in the form in which it emerges from the Bessemer, Thomas, open–hearth or electric process or from one of the various oxygen–blowing processes. Puddled iron is excluded. Steel for castings is crude steel which is used directly in liquid form for producing steel castings. Steel for castings produced by independent foundries is included. Continuously–cast blooms, billets and slabs are included as ingots. (SITC 67230–1).

[1] Source: U. S. Bureau of Mines, (Washington, D. C.).
[2] Including ingots.
[3] Twelve months beginning 21 March of year stated.
[4] Source: Annual Bulletin of Steel Statistics for Europe, United Nations Economic Commission of Europe (Geneva).

Remarque générale.
On entend par acier brut l'acier (y compris l'acier allié), produit par les procédés Bessemer, Thomas, Martin ou électrique ou par les procédés à l'oxygène. Cette rubrique ne comprend pas le fer puddlé. L'acier pour moulage est de l'acier brut utilisé directement à l'état liquide pour la fabrication de pièces moulées en acier. Cette rubrique comprend l'acier pour moulages produit par les fonderies indépendantes. (CTCI 67230–1).

[1] Source: U.S. Bureau of Mines, (Washington, D.C.).
[2] Y compris les lingots.
[3] Période de douze mois commençant le 21 mars de l'année indiquée.
[4] Source: Bulletin annuel de statistiques de l'acier pour l'Europe, Commission économique des Nations Unies pour l'Europe (Genève).

Crude steel, ingots – Acier brut (lingots)

Unit : Thousand metric tons — Unité : Milliers de tonnes métriques

Country or area	1976	1977	1978	1979	1980	1981	1982	1983	1984	1985	Pays ou zone
Africa	**8 349**	**8 486**	**9 356**	**10 697**	**10 975**	**11 078**	**10 147**	**8 935**	**9 196**	**10 427**	**Afrique**
Algeria[1]	206	285	211	450	370	557	868	892	* 700	* 750	Algérie[1]
Angola*[2]	5	5	10	10	10	10	10	10	10	10	Angola*[2]
Egypt[2]	457	263	* 600	800	800	900	480	125	200	533	Egypte[2]
Nigeria*[2]	15	15	15	15	15	15	100	140	180	254	Nigéria*[2]
South Africa[3]	6 926	7 178	7 735	8 678	* 8 972	* 8 903	* 8 159	* 7 096	* 7 715	* 8 481	Afrique du Sud[3]
Uganda[1]	6	6	7	4	4	2	2	0	0	...	Ouganda[1]
Zimbabwe[2]	* 734	* 734	* 778	* 740	804	691	528	672	391	399	Zimbabwe[2]
America, North	**134 718**	**132 976**	**146 060**	**146 859**	**124 413**	**131 994**	**86 618**	**96 578**	**106 112**	**100 983**	**Amérique du Nord**
Canada	13 123	13 432	14 728	15 855	15 684	14 637	11 762	12 728	14 568	13 353	Canada
Cuba	250	330	324	313	292	317	290	352	325	401	Cuba
Mexico	5 224	5 513	6 694	7 003	6 981	7 426	6 910	6 736	7 279	7 162	Mexique
United States[1 4]	116 121	113 701	124 314	123 688	101 456	109 614	67 656	76 762	83 940	80 067	Etats–Unis[1 4]
America, South	**12 262**	**13 816**	**13 728**	**15 778**	**15 838**	**13 770**	**13 499**	**14 484**	**17 310**	**16 228**	**Amérique du Sud**
Argentina	2 198	2 625	2 600	3 039	2 516	2 369	2 731	2 802	2 483	2 748	Argentine
Brazil	8 050	9 206	9 032	9 930	10 098	8 289	7 580	8 104	10 707	8 949	Brésil
Chile	448	509	574	642	695	625	429	* 618	* 692	* 681	Chili
Colombia[1]	252	209	265	234	263	262	215	272	257	274	Colombie[1]
Ecuador[2]	...	...	...	8	17	28	28	23	18	18	Equateur[2]
Peru[1 2]	349	379	374	436	447	364	273	299	342	411	Pérou[1 2]
Uruguay[1]	[5] 14	[5] 18	[5] 7	[5] 16	[5] 18	[5] 15	[5] 28	[5] 46	[5] 41	# 86	Uruguay[1]
Venezuela[1]	937	855	860	1 473	1 784	1 818	2 215	2 320	2 770	3 061	Venezuela[1]
Asia	**146 260**	**145 220**	**153 668**	**168 478**	**170 920**	**160 637**	**160 672**	**161 266**	**175 018**	**179 497**	**Asie**
Bangladesh[6]	90	108	117	126	137	139	109	58	79	112	Bangladesh[6]
China[1]	20 460	23 740	31 780	34 480	37 120	35 600	37 160	40 020	43 470	46 790	Chine[1]
India[1]	9 250	9 828	9 948	9 931	9 355	10 617	10 834	10 050	10 261	10 963	Inde[1]
Iraq[2]	...	...	* 50	* 352	* 260	* 45	* 45	0	0	0	Iraq[2]
Israel*[1 2]	70	70	90	110	115	120	120	150	200	150	Israël*[1 2]
Japan	106 355	101 381	101 057	110 618	110 171	100 537	98 518	96 303	104 676	104 392	Japon
Korea, D. P. Rp.*[1 2]	5 300	5 400	5 500	5 700	5 800	5 500	5 800	6 100	6 500	6 500	Corée, Rp. P. D.*[1 2]
Korea, Republic of	2 698	2 737	3 138	5 200	5 712	5 891	5 636	5 062	5 014	4 851	Corée, République de
Saudi Arabia	* 5	* 5	* 5	* 45	* 50	# [2] 72	* [2] 70	* [2] 400	* [2] 842	* [2] 1 106	Arabie saoudite
Thailand[1 2]	275	300	350	440	450	300	312	244	381	447	Thaïlande[1 2]
Turkey[1]	1 469	1 397	1 628	1 431	1 700	1 744	1 998	2 479	2 753	3 080	Turquie[1]
Europe	**209 521**	**202 738**	**213 161**	**223 759**	**211 855**	**204 222**	**187 285**	**187 036**	**199 255**	**199 742**	**Europe**
EEC	***132 993***	***124 996***	***131 766***	***139 460***	***126 949***	***123 640***	***108 620***	***106 769***	***116 855***	***116 544***	***CEE***
Belgium	12 099	11 223	12 601	13 442	12 321	12 283	9 992	10 154	11 301	10 684	Belgique
Denmark[7]	697	672	849	791	721	600	549	483	545	528	Danemark[7]
France	22 822	21 738	22 494	23 006	22 811	20 891	18 083	17 328	18 759	18 840	France
Germany, Fed. Rep.	41 848	38 473	40 762	45 495	43 300	41 096	35 414	35 346	38 991	38 794	Allemagne, Rép. féd.
Greece[1]	715	573	700	813	1 067	812	831	755	772	* 985	Grèce[1]
Ireland[1 2]	88	47	69	72	2	32	* 55	* 136	* 154	* 200	Irlande[1 2]
Italy	23 207	23 092	24 049	24 023	26 253	24 567	23 830	21 664	23 955	23 724	Italie
Luxembourg	4 561	4 325	4 787	4 950	4 619	3 790	3 510	3 294	3 987	3 945	Luxembourg
Netherlands	5 172	4 917	5 584	5 799	4 951	4 305	2 996	2 869	3 518	3 361	Pays–Bas
United Kingdom	21 784	19 936	19 871	21 069	10 904	15 264	13 360	14 740	14 873	15 483	Royaume–Uni
EFTA	***11 630***	***10 287***	***11 097***	***11 786***	***11 032***	***9 973***	***9 106***	***9 171***	***10 079***	***9 543***	***AELE***
Austria	3 100	2 526	2 576	2 537	2 216	1 711	940	527	520	291	Autriche
Finland	1 614	2 171	2 304	2 429	2 472	2 384	2 391	2 395	2 611	2 496	Finlande
Norway	880	691	797	910	840	847	759	895	920	572	Norvège
Portugal	* 389	341	366	411	382	338	266	353	412	372	Portugal
Sweden	5 123	3 923	4 286	4 613	4 202	3 768	3 924	4 175	4 643	4 825	Suède
Switzerland[7]	524	635	768	886	920	925	826	826	973	987	Suisse[7]
East Europe	***51 305***	***54 018***	***55 689***	***56 935***	***59 248***	***55 542***	***54 296***	***56 039***	***57 119***	***57 077***	***Europe de l'est***
Bulgaria[1]	2 460	2 589	2 470	2 482	2 565	2 484	2 584	2 831	2 878	2 944	Bulgarie[1]
Czechoslovakia[8]	14 693	15 064	15 294	14 817	15 225	15 270	14 992	15 024	14 831	15 036	Tchécoslovaquie[8]
German Dem. Rep.[1]	6 732	6 850	6 976	7 023	7 308	7 467	7 168	7 219	7 573	7 853	Rép. dém. allemande[1]
Hungary	3 535	3 610	3 773	3 807	3 663	3 433	3 529	3 433	3 562	3 464	Hongrie
Poland	14 640	16 649	17 943	18 845	18 039	14 558	13 641	15 648	14 630	14 780	Pologne
Romania[7]	9 245	9 256	9 233	9 961	12 448	12 330	12 382	11 884	13 645	13 000	Roumanie[7]

For general note and footnotes, see end of table.

Voir la fin du tableau pour la remarque générale et les notes.

Unit : Thousand metric tons

Unité : Milliers de tonnes métriques

Country or area	1976	1977	1978	1979	1980	1981	1982	1983	1984	1985	Pays ou zone
Other Europe	***13 593***	***13 437***	***14 609***	***15 578***	***14 626***	***15 067***	***15 263***	***15 057***	***15 202***	***16 578***	***Autre Europe***
Spain	10 897	11 102	11 269	12 102	12 387	12 881	13 311	13 119	13 248	14 552	Espagne
Yugoslavia	2 696	2 335	3 340	3 476	2 239	2 186	1 952	1 938	1 954	2 026	Yougoslavie
USSR[1]	**144 805**	**146 678**	**151 453**	**127 248**	**147 941**	**148 445**	**147 165**	**152 514**	**154 238**	**154 668**	**URSS[1]**
Ukrainian SSR[1]	*53 125*	*53 671*	*54 440*	*53 863*	*51 473*	...	...	...	...	...	*RSS d'Ukraine[1]*
Oceania	**8 148**	**7 695**	**7 747**	**7 762**	**8 112**	**8 185**	**7 512**	**5 625**	**4 913**	**6 529**	**Océanie**
Australia[1 6]	7 937	7 473	7 532	7 541	7 895	7 954	7 260	5 392	4 639	6 301	Australie[1 6]
New Zealand	211	222	215	221	217	231	252	233	274	228	Nouvelle-Zélande
Total	**664 063**	**657 609**	**695 173**	**700 581**	**690 054**	**678 331**	**612 898**	**626 438**	**666 042**	**668 074**	**Total**

General note.
Crude steel is steel (including alloy steel) in the form in which it emerges from the Bessemer, Thomas, open-hearth or electric process or from one of the various oxygen-blowing processes. Puddled iron is excluded. Steel ingots are primary products for rolling or forging obtained by casting the molten steel into moulds which are usually square, rectangular or octagonal in cross-section with one end thicker than the other, to facilitate removal from the mould. Continuously-cast blooms, billets and slabs are included as ingots. (SITC 67230-2).

1 Including crude steel for casting.
2 Source: U. S. Bureau of Mines, (Washington, D. C.).
3 Including concast steel billets.
4 Excluding steel for castings made in foundries operated by companies not producing ingots.
5 Source: Instituto Latino Americano del Fierro y el Acero, (Santiago).
6 Twelve months ending 30 June of year stated.
7 Source: Annual Bulletin of Steel Statistics for Europe, United Nations Economic Commission of Europe (Geneva).
8 Including crude steel for casting and for tubes.

Remarque générale.
On entend par acier brut l'acier (y compris l'acier allié), produit par les procédés Bessemer, Thomas, Martin ou électrique ou par les procédés à l'oxygène. Cette rubrique ne comprend pas le fer puddlé. Les lingots d'acier sont des produits de base destinés à être transformés par laminage ou forgeage et obtenus en coulant l'acier liquide dans des lingotières qui sont ordinairement de section carrée, rectangulaire ou octogonale et dont l'une des extrémités est plus épaisse que l'autre pour faciliter le démoulage. Les blooms, les billettes et les brames obtenus par coulée continue sont classés parmi les lingots. (CTCI 67230-2).

1 Y compris l'acier brut pour moulages.
2 Source: U.S. Bureau of Mines, (Washington, D.C.).
3 Y compris les billettes d'acier coulées en continu.
4 Non compris l'acier pour les moulages fabriqués dans des fonderies exploitées par des entreprises ne produisant pas de lingots.
5 Source: Instituto Latino Americano del Fierro y el Acero , (Santiago).
6 Période de douze mois finissant le 30 juin de l'année indiquée.
7 Source: Bulletin annuel de statistiques de l'acier pour l'Europe, Commission économique des Nations Unies pour l'Europe (Genève).
8 Y compris l'acier brut pour moulages et tubes.

Ingots for tubes – Lingots pour tubes

Unit : Thousand metric tons

Unité : Milliers de tonnes métriques

Country or area	1976	1977	1978	1979	1980	1981	1982	1983	1984	1985	Pays ou zone
America, North	**516**	**509**	**609**	**521**	**547**	**566**	**456**	**361**	**547**	**530**	**Amérique du Nord**
Canada[1 2]	199	229	272	266	306	315	191	128	223	228	Canada[1 2]
Mexico	317	280	337	255	241	251	265	233	324	302	Mexique
America, South	**214**	**206**	**180**	**164**	**171**	**158**	**181**	**163**	**169**	**197**	**Amérique du Sud**
Argentina	214	206	180	164	171	158	181	163	169	197	Argentine
Asia	**170**	**151**	**92**	**18**	**33**	**30**	**33**	**27**	**26**	**27**	**Asie**
Japan	170	151	92	18	33	30	33	27	26	27	Japon
Europe	**3 052**	**3 150**	**3 251**	**3 140**	**3 105**	**3 551**	**3 102**	**3 092**	**4 168**	**4 196**	**Europe**
EEC	***2 379***	***2 471***	***2 689***	***2 572***	***2 444***	***2 862***	***2 579***	***2 584***	***3 494***	***3 614***	***CEE***
France[2]	130	132	119	115	179	123	102	0	146	105	France[2]
Germany, Fed. Rep.	1 183	1 373	1 675	1 678	1 656	1 995	1 902	2 031	2 825	3 059	Allemagne, Rép. féd.
Italy	745	648	536	481	390	409	298	196	218	146	Italie
United Kingdom[3]	321	318	359	298	219	335	277	* 357	...	...	Royaume-Uni[3]
East Europe	***475***	***504***	***387***	***379***	***434***	***389***	***343***	***362***	***382***	***313***	***Europe de l'est***
Hungary	110	143	129	116	104	106	80	94	107	101	Hongrie
Poland	365	361	258	263	330	283	263	268	275	212	Pologne
Other Europe	***198***	***175***	***175***	***189***	***227***	***300***	***180***	***146***	***292***	***269***	***Autre Europe***
Spain	74	61	52	65	108	168	35	17	157	128	Espagne
Yugoslavia	124	114	123	124	119	132	145	129	135	141	Yougoslavie
USSR	**1 688**	**1 811**	**1 862**	**1 880**	**1 976**	**1 917**	**1 848**	**1 862**	**1 931**	**1 930**	**URSS**
Ukrainian SSR	*904*	*896*	*847*	*866*	*879*	*850*	*811*	*847*	*847*	*842*	*RSS d'Ukraine*
Total	**5 640**	**5 827**	**5 994**	**5 723**	**5 832**	**6 222**	**5 620**	**5 505**	**6 841**	**6 880**	**Total**

General note.

Ingots which are used directly for making seamless tubes, and which do not, therefore, pass through the stage of being rolled into a semi-manufactured product. (SITC 67230-3).

[1] Including semis for tubes.

[2] Source: Annual Bulletin of Steel Statistics for Europe, United Nations Economic Commission of Europe (Geneva).

[3] Deliveries.

Remarque générale.

Lingots qui sont utilisés directement pour la fabrication de tubes sans soudure et qui ne sont donc pas laminés en un produit semi-fini. (CTCI 67230-3).

[1] Y compris les demi-produits pour tubes.

[2] Source: Bulletin annuel de statistiques de l'acier pour l'Europe, Commission économique des Nations Unies pour l'Europe (Genève).

[3] Livraisons.

Semis for tubes – Demi-produits pour tubes

Unit : Thousand metric tons

Unité : Milliers de tonnes métriques

Country or area	1976	1977	1978	1979	1980	1981	1982	1983	1984	1985	Pays ou zone
America, North	**2 594**	**3 171**	**3 522**	**3 435**	**3 833**	**4 344**	**1 736**	**847**	**1 502**	**1 153**	**Amérique du Nord**
United States[1 2]	2 594	3 171	3 522	3 435	3 833	4 344	1 736	847	1 502	1 153	Etats-Unis[1 2]
Asia	**5 898**	**7 380**	**9 127**	**11 812**	**11 963**	**14 880**	**15 275**	**14 661**	**17 605**	**18 246**	**Asie**
Japan	2 356	2 735	3 825	4 082	4 567	4 969	4 348	3 426	4 709	4 655	Japon
Korea, Republic of	3 455	4 528	5 184	7 632	7 385	9 841	10 863	11 227	12 735	13 591	Corée, République de
Turkey	87	117	118	98	11	...	...	8	161	0	Turquie
Europe	**4 337**	**4 333**	**4 630**	**4 828**	**5 061**	**5 585**	**5 121**	**4 682**	**5 223**	**5 096**	**Europe**
EEC	***2 286***	***2 180***	***2 470***	***2 579***	***2 520***	***3 077***	***2 453***	***1 842***	***2 451***	***2 128***	***CEE***
Belgium	0	0	0	63	78	122	168	197	255	246	Belgique
France[3]	551	522	578	601	639	828	725	480	783	573	France[3]
Germany, Fed. Rep.	1 022	911	929	971	890	984	480	188	179	170	Allemagne, Rép. féd.
Italy	315	364	553	577	699	836	844	752	980	880	Italie
Netherlands	8	14	42	18	0	0	0	0	0	0	Pays-Bas
United Kingdom	390	369	368	349	214	307	236	225	254	259	Royaume-Uni
EFTA	***228***	***207***	***202***	***211***	***225***	***247***	***223***	***178***	***165***	***197***	***AELE***
Finland	...	...	...	...	0	0	0	1	0	0	Finlande
Sweden[3]	227	206	201	210	225	* 247	* 223	* 177	165	197	Suède[3]
East Europe	***1 610***	***1 757***	***1 758***	***1 816***	***2 020***	***1 985***	***1 992***	***2 211***	***2 130***	***2 186***	***Europe de l'est***
Czechoslovakia	664	714	720	718	764	747	766	814	834	862	Tchécoslovaquie
Hungary	90	93	94	95	86	58	81	82	73	86	Hongrie
Poland	381	409	323	346	342	373	346	373	355	362	Pologne
Romania[3]	475	541	621	657	828	807	799	942	868	876	Roumanie[3]
Other Europe	***213***	***189***	***200***	***222***	***296***	***276***	***453***	***451***	***477***	***585***	***Autre Europe***
Spain	171	* 157	164	184	257	237	408	415	445	546	Espagne
Yugoslavia	42	32	36	38	39	39	45	36	32	39	Yougoslavie
USSR	**5 871**	**5 844**	**6 071**	**6 040**	**6 021**	**6 122**	**6 245**	**6 435**	**6 409**	**6 587**	**URSS**
Ukrainian SSR	*1 956*	*1 974*	*2 032*	*2 029*	*2 037*	*2 049*	*2 173*	*2 277*	*2 247*	*2 272*	*RSS d'Ukraine*
Total	**18 700**	**20 728**	**23 350**	**26 115**	**26 878**	**30 931**	**28 377**	**26 625**	**30 739**	**31 082**	**Total**

General note.
All semi-manufactured products for use in making seamless tubes. Output of these products should be measured at the stage at which they are still solids, that is, before piercing. (SITC 67250-1).

[1] Including ingots for tubes.
[2] Shipments.
[3] Source: Annual Bulletin of Steel Statistics for Europe, United Nations Economic Commission of Europe (Geneva).

Remarque générale.
Tous les produits semi-finis servant à la fabrication de tubes sans soudure. La quantité de ces produits doit être mesurée au stade où ils sont encore pleins, c'est-à-dire avant le perçage. (CTCI 67250-1).

[1] Y compris les lingots pour tubes.
[2] Expéditions.
[3] Source: Bulletin annuel de statistiques de l'acier pour l'Europe, Commission économique des Nations Unies pour l'Europe (Genève).

Wire rods – Fil machine

Unit : Thousand metric tons

Unité : Milliers de tonnes métriques

Country or area	1976	1977	1978	1979	1980	1981	1982	1983	1984	1985	Pays ou zone
Africa	**447**	**356**	**441**	**532**	**796**	**762**	**816**	**916**	**994**	**1 078**	**Afrique**
Egypt	207	231	261	298	289	297	* 293	...	...	...	Egypte
Mozambique	...	...	...	3	9	10	8	8	5	...	Mozambique
South Africa[1]	234	118	173	231	498	455	...	...	...	...	Afrique du Sud[1]
America, North	**5 472**	**5 489**	**6 651**	**7 162**	**6 719**	**6 760**	**5 644**	**6 138**	**6 377**	**6 043**	**Amérique du Nord**
Canada[2]	729	784	998	1 141	1 237	987	898	1 025	1 088	1 048	Canada[2]
Mexico	787	891	1 059	1 204	1 439	1 517	1 372	1 288	1 376	1 261	Mexique
United States[3]	3 956	3 814	4 594	4 817	4 043	4 256	3 374	3 825	3 913	3 734	Etats–Unis[3]
America, South	**1 064**	**1 125**	**1 241**	**1 357**	**1 600**	**1 342**	**1 423**	**1 358**	**1 569**	**1 888**	**Amérique du Sud**
Brazil	995	1 070	1 174	1 282	1 523	1 283	1 394	1 297	1 505	1 835	Brésil
Chile	...	40	52	60	62	44	22	48	...	...	Chili
Ecuador*	...	...	...	...	...	...	7	13	25	...	Equateur*
Asia	**10 686**	**10 919**	**11 077**	**11 556**	**12 187**	**11 194**	**10 436**	**11 796**	**13 323**	**15 129**	**Asie**
Burma[4]	22	22	16	...	...	15	25	19	...	...	Birmanie[4]
China	...	...	...	...	4 432	4 629	4 141	4 454	5 098	5 983	Chine
Indonesia	...	...	...	...	...	81	106	154	46	...	Indonésie
Japan	6 984	6 889	6 663	6 743	6 682	5 458	5 115	6 032	6 742	7 538	Japon
Korea, Republic of	191	241	299	425	553	590	636	668	713	1 004	Corée, République de
Malaysia	181	190	240	244	236	233	266	306	543	323	Malaisie
Philippines	...	...	...	...	...	...	...	19	...	...	Philippines
Sri Lanka	6	6	* 9	11	12	10	4	3	2	0	Sri Lanka
Syrian Arab Republic	98	98	109	93	80	102	67	84	84	89	Rép. arabe syrienne
Turkey[2]	57	55	53	61	...	...	...	...	...	...	Turquie[2]
Europe	**16 115**	**16 082**	**17 217**	**18 742**	**17 596**	**16 866**	**16 141**	**16 623**	**18 025**	**18 379**	**Europe**
EEC	***10 521***	***10 371***	***11 271***	***12 559***	***11 549***	***11 026***	***10 166***	***10 246***	***11 060***	***11 387***	***CEE***
Belgium	656	581	698	799	787	781	733	685	713	475	Belgique
Denmark	[2] 2	[2] 1	[2] 5	[2] 12	[2] 6	[2] 1	[2] 0	[2] 1	1	2	Danemark
France	2 259	2 218	2 418	2 630	2 538	2 402	2 196	2 074	2 219	2 256	France
Germany, Fed. Rep.	3 521	3 247	3 379	4 016	3 626	3 384	2 846	3 158	3 319	3 438	Allemagne, Rép. féd.
Greece[5 6]	540	557	605	917	1 021	846	826	803	818	...	Grèce[5 6]
Italy	1 309	1 484	1 775	1 758	1 933	1 936	2 098	2 027	2 256	2 310	Italie
Luxembourg	354	331	334	330	317	271	224	240	349	510	Luxembourg
Netherlands	342	302	313	337	349	302	269	238	234	228	Pays–Bas
United Kingdom[7]	1 538	1 650	1 744	1 760	972	1 103	974	1 020	1 151	1 213	Royaume–Uni[7]
EFTA	***879***	***784***	***831***	***879***	***924***	***874***	***894***	***983***	***1 084***	***1 155***	***AELE***
Austria	433	374	416	465	497	513	455	467	503	464	Autriche
Finland	106	108	133	140	139	93	142	179	193	199	Finlande
Norway[2]	29	24	23	6	2	17	26	36	41	44	Norvège[2]
Portugal	71	75	87	102	108	101	103	149	185	209	Portugal
Sweden	240	203	172	166	178	150	168	152	162	* 239	Suède
East Europe	***3 594***	***3 661***	***3 863***	***4 067***	***3 936***	***3 581***	***3 455***	***3 615***	***3 922***	***3 743***	***Europe de l'est***
Bulgaria	429	463	457	498	438	420	413	421	446	442	Bulgarie
Czechoslovakia	933	867	979	960	941	892	901	992	1 048	1 022	Tchécoslovaquie
Hungary	328	373	391	465	402	334	314	361	365	346	Hongrie
Poland	1 326	1 379	1 409	1 399	1 390	1 116	1 004	1 104	1 147	1 133	Pologne
Romania[2]	578	579	627	745	765	819	823	737	916	800	Roumanie[2]
Other Europe	***1 121***	***1 266***	***1 252***	***1 237***	***1 187***	***1 385***	***1 626***	***1 779***	***1 959***	***2 094***	***Autre Europe***
Spain	833	881	828	763	704	888	1 115	1 092	1 193	1 280	Espagne
Yugoslavia	288	385	424	474	483	497	511	687	766	814	Yougoslavie
USSR	**8 352**	**8 360**	**8 233**	**7 991**	**8 055**	**7 878**	**7 884**	**8 318**	**8 421**	**8 386**	**URSS**
Ukrainian SSR	*4 011*	*4 000*	*3 859*	*3 793*	*3 695*	*3 490*	*3 642*	*3 815*	*3 841*	*3 652*	*RSS d'Ukraine*
Oceania	**587**	**657**	**735**	**739**	**777**	**698**	**697**	**679**	**678**	**592**	**Océanie**
Australia	587	657	735	739	777	698	697	...	...	592	Australie
Total	**42 724**	**42 987**	**45 595**	**48 079**	**47 730**	**45 500**	**43 041**	**45 828**	**49 387**	**51 494**	**Total**

For general note and footnotes, see end of table.

Voir la fin du tableau pour la remarque générale et les notes.

General note.
Round, oval, hexagonal etc., hot–rolled products with a diameter of 13 mm and less, delivered in coils. Straightened rods are excluded. (SITC 67310–0).

[1] Including barbed wire and stranded wire.
[2] Source: Annual Bulletin of Steel Statistics for Europe, United Nations Economic Commission of Europe (Geneva).
[3] Shipments.
[4] Twelve months ending 30 September of year stated.
[5] Including concrete reinforcement bars.
[6] Including cold–drawn rods.
[7] Excluding other bars and rods in coil.

Remarque générale.
Produits ronds, ovales, hexagonaux etc., laminés à chaud, d'un diamètre maximal de 13 mm, livrés en couronnes ou en torches. Cette rubrique ne comprend pas le fil machine redressé. (CTCI 67310–0).

[1] Y compris les fils barbelés et câbles métalliques.
[2] Source: Bulletin annuel de statistiques de l'acier pour l'Europe, Commission économique des Nations Unies pour l'Europe (Genève).
[3] Expéditions.
[4] Période de douze mois finissant le 30 septembre de l'année indiquée.
[5] Y compris les barres d'armature pour béton.
[6] Y compris les ronds étirés à froid.
[7] Non compris les barres et tiges en rouleaux.

Angles, shapes and sections (total production) – Cornières, profilés et poutrelles (production totale)

Unit : Thousand metric tons | Unité : Milliers de tonnes métriques

Country or area	1976	1977	1978	1979	1980	1981	1982	1983	1984	1985	Pays ou zone
Africa	**1 003**	**1 165**	**1 319**	**1 541**	**1 812**	**1 864**	**2 051**	**2 240**	**2 427**	**2 591**	**Afrique**
Algeria	...	12	36	42	46	49	49	...	...	...	Algérie
Egypt	...	213	211	264	387	372	417	...	...	...	Egypte
South Africa	715	788	925	1 074	1 210	1 280	...	...	...	...	Afrique du Sud
Tunisia	124	152	147	161	169	163	163	162	174	164	Tunisie
America, North	**17 914**	**19 216**	**21 555**	**22 913**	**18 007**	**18 184**	**14 181**	**16 644**	**18 982**	**18 575**	**Amérique du Nord**
Canada[1]	619	749	1 004	1 150	577	521	* 632	2 314	2 673	2 849	Canada[1]
Mexico	583	503	646	718	679	670	507	430	534	517	Mexique
United States[2]	16 712	17 964	19 905	21 045	16 751	16 993	13 042	13 900	15 775	15 209	Etats–Unis[2]
America, South	**870**	**890**	**864**	**956**	**924**	**818**	**807**	**682**	**769**	**783**	**Amérique du Sud**
Argentina[3]	427	407	337	...	...	...	...	...	...	...	Argentine[3]
Brazil[4]	440	480	524	563	531	425	414	289	376	390	Brésil[4]
Ecuador	...	...	3	...	...	...	...	...	...	...	Equateur
Asia	**26 317**	**24 939**	**27 247**	**32 650**	**32 615**	**30 193**	**31 239**	**31 612**	**32 830**	**33 850**	**Asie**
Japan	25 136	23 401	25 446	30 673	30 770	27 997	28 617	28 845	29 803	30 666	Japon
Korea, Republic of	215	290	424	417	361	465	631	671	767	851	Corée, République de
Malaysia	10	11	14	12	13	13	14	13	...	...	Malaisie
Philippines[5]	747	945	1 097	1 272	1 371	...	...	...	...	...	Philippines[5]
Turkey	209	292	266	276	100	162	264	213	219	135	Turquie
Europe	**48 659**	**47 344**	**50 131**	**52 775**	**51 298**	**47 862**	**43 857**	**44 743**	**44 767**	**46 392**	**Europe**
EEC	***28 404***	***26 759***	***27 599***	***28 631***	***26 659***	***23 809***	***20 653***	***20 640***	***20 695***	***21 029***	***CEE***
Belgium	2 643	2 220	2 166	2 263	1 880	1 082	1 006	993	870	714	Belgique
Denmark[1]	222	211	223	230	193	165	129	139	151	169	Danemark[1]
France	4 305	3 756	3 844	4 041	3 821	3 412	2 911	2 849	2 810	2 784	France
Germany, Fed. Rep.	6 941	6 253	6 508	6 856	6 641	5 730	4 661	4 668	4 570	4 714	Allemagne, Rép. féd.
Greece	5	5	6	4	4	4	4	3	5	...	Grèce
Italy	7 185	7 590	7 964	8 331	8 782	7 812	6 908	6 874	7 135	6 935	Italie
Luxembourg	1 637	1 554	1 637	1 653	1 677	1 471	1 433	1 383	1 504	1 766	Luxembourg
Netherlands	228	292	302	316	247	234	181	214	226	262	Pays–Bas
United Kingdom	5 238	4 878	4 949	4 937	3 414	3 899	3 420	3 517	3 424	3 681	Royaume–Uni
EFTA	***2 635***	***2 553***	***2 767***	***3 003***	***3 020***	***2 866***	***2 730***	***2 610***	***2 390***	***2 833***	***AELE***
Austria	580	581	584	577	550	482	462	620	311	441	Autriche
Finland	297	296	310	357	351	356	[1]265	[1]276	[1]285	[1]291	Finlande
Norway[1]	386	317	379	466	474	434	387	432	511	581	Norvège[1]
Portugal[6]	259	349	438	414	457	464	511	406	390	364	Portugal[6]
Sweden[7]	1 113	1 010	1 056	1 189	1 188	* 1 130	* 1 105	876	893	1 156	Suède[7]
East Europe	***12 921***	***13 200***	***14 278***	***15 243***	***15 683***	***14 769***	***14 182***	***15 103***	***15 631***	***16 015***	***Europe de l'est***
Bulgaria	891	895	890	872	923	1 012	905	843	943	935	Bulgarie
Czechoslovakia	3 455	3 564	3 485	3 610	3 586	3 638	3 537	3 604	3 570	3 560	Tchécoslovaquie
German Dem. Rep.	1 646	1 848	2 022	2 076	2 083	2 084	2 057	2 091	2 142	2 274	Rép. dém. allemande
Hungary	1 217	1 278	1 371	1 357	1 329	1 195	1 233	1 213	1 229	1 212	Hongrie
Poland	3 502	3 241	3 980	4 706	4 890	3 922	3 761	4 455	4 536	4 636	Pologne
Romania[1 8]	2 210	2 374	2 530	2 622	2 872	2 918	2 689	2 897	3 211	3 398	Roumanie[1 8]
Other Europe	***4 699***	***4 832***	***5 487***	***5 898***	***5 936***	***6 418***	***6 292***	***6 390***	***6 051***	***6 515***	***Autre Europe***
Spain	3 677	3 583	4 011	4 332	4 501	4 774	4 726	5 003	5 427	5 661	Espagne
Yugoslavia	1 022	1 249	1 476	1 566	1 435	1 644	1 566	1 387	624	854	Yougoslavie
USSR	**38 064**	**38 682**	**39 812**	**38 670**	**38 459**	**38 598**	**37 698**	**39 613**	**39 997**	**39 926**	**URSS**
Oceania	**535**	**470**	**491**	**555**	**674**	**698**	**664**	**580**	**584**	**438**	**Océanie**
Australia	535	470	491	555	674	698	664	...	...	438	Australie
Total	**133 362**	**132 706**	**141 419**	**150 060**	**143 789**	**138 218**	**130 498**	**136 114**	**140 356**	**142 554**	**Total**

General note.
Angles, shapes and sections of iron and steel commonly known as H, I, T, capital omega, Z and U, obtuse and right (L) angles. Sheet piling is included but rails are excluded. (The sum of SITC 6734 and 6735).

Remarque générale.
Profilés en fer et en acier, communément désignés d'après leurs sections: profilés en H, I, T, Z et U, profilés zorès (à section en forme d'oméga), cornières et équerres à angle obtus, aigu ou droit (en forme d'L). Cette rubrique comprend les palplanches mais non les rails. (CTCI 6734 et 6735).

For footnotes, see end of table.

Voir la fin du tableau pour les notes.

Angles, shapes and sections (total production) (continued) – Cornières, profilés et poutrelles (production totale) (suite)

[1] Source: Annual Bulletin of Steel Statistics for Europe, United Nations Economic Commission of Europe (Geneva).
[2] Shipments.
[3] Source: Instituto Latino Americano del Fierro y el Acero, (Santiago).
[4] Structural shapes only.
[5] Including wire rods.
[6] Heavy and light profiles.
[7] Including bars and rods, except wire rod and hollow mining drills of iron and steel. Hot-rolled products only.
[8] Including rail accessories.

[1] Source: Bulletin annuel de statistiques de l'acier pour l'Europe, Commission économique des Nations Unies pour l'Europe (Genève).
[2] Expéditions.
[3] Source: Instituto Latino Americano del Fierro y el Acero , (Santiago).
[4] Profilés de construction seulement.
[5] Y compris les fils machine.
[6] Profilés lourds et légers.
[7] Y compris les barres et tiges, à l'exclusion des fils machine et des tiges de forage creuses en fer et en acier. Produits laminés à chaud seulement.
[8] Y compris le matériel de voie ferrée.

Angles, shapes and sections of 80 mm or more (heavy sections) – Cornières, profilés et poutrelles de 80 mm ou plus (profilés lourds)

Unit : Thousand metric tons

Unité : Milliers de tonnes métriques

Country or area	1976	1977	1978	1979	1980	1981	1982	1983	1984	1985	Pays ou zone
Africa	**56**	**57**	**57**	**57**	**57**	**57**	**57**	**57**	**57**	**57**	**Afrique**
Egypt	56	57	...	...	...	...	...	...	...	...	Egypte
America, North	**4 310**	**4 582**	**5 369**	**5 911**	**5 140**	**4 803**	**3 533**	**4 006**	**4 585**	**5 093**	**Amérique du Nord**
Canada[1]	511	607	809	834	416	355	* 300	720	814	852	Canada[1]
United States[2]	3 799	3 975	4 560	5 077	4 724	4 448	3 233	3 286	3 771	4 241	Etats-Unis[2]
America, South	**235**	**249**	**230**	**194**	**223**	**224**	**171**	**114**	**124**	**178**	**Amérique du Sud**
Brazil[3]	235	249	230	194	223	224	171	114	124	178	Brésil[3]
Asia	**6 744**	**6 424**	**6 192**	**7 448**	**7 430**	**7 537**	**7 734**	**7 211**	**7 559**	**7 050**	**Asie**
Japan[4]	6 634	6 246	6 041	7 301	7 330	7 375	7 470	6 998	7 340	6 915	Japon[4]
Turkey	110	178	151	147	[5] 100	[5] 162	[5] 264	[5] 213	[5] 219	[5] 135	Turquie
Europe	**14 525**	**14 522**	**15 900**	**15 635**	**15 325**	**15 289**	**13 519**	**13 795**	**13 252**	**13 812**	**Europe**
EEC	***7 934***	***7 950***	***8 407***	***7 713***	***7 205***	***7 351***	***5 914***	***6 051***	***5 428***	***5 862***	***CEE***
Belgium[1]	1 152	1 200	1 254	1 130	943	796	439	528	405	317	Belgique[1]
Denmark[1]	8	11	14	10	7	0	0	0	0	0	Danemark[1]
France[1]	1 194	1 051	1 131	1 014	985	877	715	769	695	696	France[1]
Germany, Fed. Rep.	2 141	2 096	2 304	2 022	2 209	1 975	1 508	1 549	1 404	1 553	Allemagne, Rép. féd.
Italy	669	732	839	679	747	914	832	809	632	581	Italie
Luxembourg	852	922	809	789	877	861	739	678	690	935	Luxembourg
United Kingdom[1]	1 918	1 938	2 056	2 069	1 437	1 928	1 681	1 718	1 602	1 780	Royaume-Uni[1]
EFTA	***311***	***294***	***351***	***423***	***472***	***496***	***392***	***454***	***548***	***532***	***AELE***
Austria[1]	57	58	74	59	50	58	38	44	40	43	Autriche[1]
Finland	12	13	19	12	10	11	[1] 8	[1] 13	[1] 135	[1] 135	Finlande
Norway[1]	110	112	148	162	205	193	153	190	210	227	Norvège[1]
Portugal	18	17	24	19	24	37	3	2	2	28	Portugal
Sweden	114	94	86	171	183	* 197	* 190	* 205	* 161	* 99	Suède
East Europe	***4 530***	***4 677***	***5 301***	***5 714***	***5 754***	***5 335***	***5 329***	***5 530***	***5 684***	***5 696***	***Europe de l'est***
Bulgaria[1]	401	430	427	454	365	371	353	363	379	312	Bulgarie[1]
Czechoslovakia[1 6]	1 730	1 779	1 727	1 773	1 751	1 767	1 665	1 809	1 819	1 803	Tchécoslovaquie[1 6]
German Dem. Rep.	635	671	678	714	663	650	639	641	646	716	Rép. dém. allemande
Hungary	329	338	342	320	326	263	276	243	249	237	Hongrie
Poland[1 7]	1 154	1 186	1 810	2 116	2 278	1 825	...	2 176	2 266	2 239	Pologne[1 7]
Romania[1 8]	281	273	317	337	371	459	314	298	325	389	Roumanie[1 8]
Other Europe	***1 750***	***1 601***	***1 841***	***1 785***	***1 894***	***2 107***	***1 884***	***1 760***	***1 592***	***1 722***	***Autre Europe***
Spain	1 618	1 440	1 651	1 583	1 709	1 895	1 682	1 581	1 511	1 612	Espagne
Yugoslavia	132	161	190	202	185	212	202	179	81	110	Yougoslavie
Ukrainian SSR[9]	*14 937*	*14 935*	*14 964*	*14 709*	*13 971*	*13 540*	*13 428*	*15 046*	...	...	*RSS d'Ukraine*[9]
Total	**25 870**	**25 834**	**27 748**	**29 245**	**28 175**	**27 910**	**25 014**	**25 183**	**25 577**	**26 190**	**Total**

General note.
Angles, shapes and sections of iron and steel commonly known as H, I, T, capital omega, Z and U, obtuse, acute and right (L) angles. Sheet piling is included but rails are excluded. This item relates to heavy sections of 80 mm or more. (SITC 67340-0).

[1] Source: Annual Bulletin of Steel Statistics for Europe, United Nations Economic Commission of Europe (Geneva).
[2] Deliveries.
[3] Structural shapes only.
[4] 100 mm and over.
[5] Including those less than 80 mm.
[6] Cross-section, over 840 square millimetres.
[7] 60 mm and over.
[8] Including rail accessories.
[9] All sizes from 10 mm and over.

Remarque générale.
Profilés en fer et en acier, communément désignés d'après leurs sections: profilés en H, I, T, Z et U, profilés zorès (à section en forme d'oméga), cornières et équerres à angle obtus, aigu ou droit (en forme d'L). Cette rubrique comprend les palplanches mais non les rails. Les données se rapportent aux profilés lourds de 80 mm ou plus. (CTCI 67340-0).

[1] Source: Bulletin annuel de statistiques de l'acier pour l'Europe, Commission économique des Nations Unies pour l'Europe (Genève).
[2] Livraisons.
[3] Profilés de construction seulement.
[4] 100 mm et plus.
[5] Y compris ceux de moins de 80mm.
[6] Section transversale supérieure à 840 millimètres carrés.
[7] 60 mm et plus.
[8] Y compris le matériel de voie ferrée.
[9] Toutes dimensions à partir de 10 mm.

Angles, shapes and sections, less than 80 mm (light sections) – Cornières, profilés et poutrelles de moins de 80 mm (profilés légers)

Unit : Thousand metric tons

Unité : Milliers de tonnes métriques

Country or area	1976	1977	1978	1979	1980	1981	1982	1983	1984	1985	Pays ou zone
Africa	**26**	**45**	**36**	**36**	**36**	**36**	**36**	**36**	**36**	**36**	**Afrique**
Egypt	26	45	...	...	...	...	...	...	...	...	Egypte
America, North	**13 021**	**14 131**	**15 540**	**16 177**	**12 188**	**12 711**	**10 141**	**12 208**	**13 863**	**12 965**	**Amérique du Nord**
Canada[1]	108	142	195	209	161	166	332	1 594	1 859	1 997	Canada[1]
United States	12 913	13 989	15 345	15 968	12 027	12 545	9 809	10 614	12 004	10 968	Etats–Unis
America, South	**205**	**231**	**294**	**369**	**308**	**201**	**243**	**175**	**252**	**212**	**Amérique du Sud**
Brazil[2]	205	231	294	369	308	201	243	175	252	212	Brésil[2]
Asia	**17 904**	**16 699**	**18 690**	**22 471**	**22 403**	**19 653**	**20 207**	**20 975**	**21 510**	**22 888**	**Asie**
Japan[3]	17 805	16 585	18 575	22 342	22 289	19 539	20 093	20 861	21 396	22 774	Japon[3]
Turkey	99	114	115	129	...	...	...	...	...	...	Turquie
Europe	**34 397**	**32 828**	**34 347**	**36 832**	**35 500**	**32 092**	**30 648**	**30 663**	**31 237**	**32 049**	**Europe**
EEC	***20 461***	***18 806***	***19 186***	***20 913***	***19 451***	***16 453***	***14 737***	***14 586***	***15 259***	***15 166***	***CEE***
Belgium[1 4]	1 491	1 020	912	1 133	937	286	567	465	465	397	Belgique[1 4]
Denmark[1 5]	214	200	209	220	186	165	129	139	151	169	Danemark[1 5]
France[1]	3 111	2 706	2 713	3 026	2 837	2 535	2 196	2 080	2 115	2 088	France[1]
Germany, Fed. Rep.	4 795	4 157	4 203	4 834	4 432	3 755	3 155	3 119	3 164	3 161	Allemagne, Rép. féd.
Italy[1]	6 517	6 859	7 126	7 652	8 035	6 898	6 076	6 065	6 502	6 357	Italie[1]
Luxembourg	[1] 785	[1] 632	[1] 828	[1] 864	# 800	609	694	705	814	831	Luxembourg
Netherlands	228	292	302	316	247	234	181	214	226	262	Pays–Bas
United Kingdom[6]	3 320	2 940	2 893	2 868	1 977	1 971	1 739	1 799	1 822	1 901	Royaume–Uni[6]
EFTA	***2 434***	***2 259***	***2 416***	***2 580***	***2 548***	***2 370***	***2 338***	***2 156***	***1 842***	***2 302***	***AELE***
Austria	523	523	510	518	500	424	424	576	271	398	Autriche
Finland	285	283	291	345	341	345	[1] 257	[1] 263	[1] 150	[1] 156	Finlande
Norway[1]	276	205	231	304	269	241	234	242	301	354	Norvège[1]
Portugal	241	332	414	395	433	427	508	404	388	337	Portugal
Sweden	1 109	916	970	1 018	1 005	* 933	* 915	* 671	* 732	* 1 057	Suède
East Europe	***8 086***	***8 532***	***9 099***	***9 226***	***9 459***	***8 958***	***9 165***	***9 289***	***9 677***	***9 889***	***Europe de l'est***
Bulgaria	180	178	214	225	218	218	204	193	204	215	Bulgarie
Czechoslovakia[1 7]	1 695	1 759	1 732	1 813	1 807	1 847	1 843	1 771	1 732	1 736	Tchécoslovaquie[1 7]
German Dem. Rep.	1 011	1 177	1 344	1 362	1 420	1 434	1 418	1 450	1 496	1 558	Rép. dém. allemande
Hungary	888	940	1 029	1 037	1 003	932	958	970	981	974	Hongrie
Poland[1 8]	2 383	2 377	2 567	2 504	2 510	2 068	...	2 306	2 378	2 397	Pologne[1 8]
Romania[1 9]	1 929	2 101	2 213	2 285	2 501	2 459	2 375	2 599	2 886	3 009	Roumanie[1 9]
Other Europe	***3 416***	***3 231***	***3 646***	***4 113***	***4 042***	***4 311***	***4 408***	***4 632***	***4 459***	***4 692***	***Autre Europe***
Spain	2 526	2 143	2 360	2 749	2 792	2 879	3 044	3 422	3 916	3 949	Espagne
Yugoslavia	890	1 088	1 286	1 364	1 250	1 432	1 364	1 210	543	743	Yougoslavie
Total	**65 553**	**63 934**	**68 907**	**75 885**	**70 435**	**64 693**	**61 275**	**64 057**	**66 898**	**68 150**	**Total**

General note.
Angles, shapes and sections of iron and steel commonly known as H, I, T, capital omega, Z and U, obtuse and right (L) angles. Sheet piling is included but rails are excluded. This item relates to light sections of less than 80 mm. (SITC 67350–0).

Remarque générale.
Profilés en fer et en acier, communément désignés d'après leurs sections: profilés en H, I, T, Z et U, profilés zorès (à section en forme d'oméga), cornières et équerres à angle obtus, aigu ou droit (en forme d'L). Cette rubrique comprend les palplanches mais non les rails. Les données se rapportent aux profilés légers de moins de 80 mm. (CTCI 67350–0).

[1] Source: Annual Bulletin of Steel Statistics for Europe, United Nations Economic Commission of Europe (Geneva).
[2] Structural shapes only.
[3] Under 100 mm.
[4] Including rolled wrought–iron products.
[5] Including merchant bars.
[6] 13 mm and over.
[7] Cross–section up to and including 840 square millimetres.
[8] Under 60 mm.
[9] Including rail accessories.

[1] Source: Bulletin annuel de statistiques de l'acier pour l'Europe, Commission économique des Nations Unies pour l'Europe (Genève).
[2] Profilés de construction seulement.
[3] Moins de 100 mm.
[4] Y compris les articles en fer laminé et forgé.
[5] Y compris les barres marchandes.
[6] 13 mm et plus.
[7] Surface de section: jusqu' à 840 millimètres carrés.
[8] Moins de 60 mm.
[9] Y compris le matériel de voie ferrée.

Plates (heavy), over 4.75 mm – Tôles fortes de plus de 4,75 mm

Unit : Thousand metric tons — Unité : Milliers de tonnes métriques

Country or area	1976	1977	1978	1979	1980	1981	1982	1983	1984	1985	Pays ou zone
Africa	**1 220**	**1 510**	**1 499**	**1 710**	**1 705**	**1 837**	**2 021**	**2 109**	**2 225**	**2 342**	**Afrique**
Algeria	...	# 213	178	247	227	332	399	...	...	...	Algérie
Egypt	...	34	41	50	61	61	57	...	...	...	Egypte
South Africa[1]	1 059	1 263	1 280	1 413	1 417	1 444	...	...	...	...	Afrique du Sud[1]
America, North	**9 311**	**9 866**	**11 637**	**12 070**	**11 058**	**10 732**	**6 988**	**6 348**	**7 731**	**7 681**	**Amérique du Nord**
Canada[1 2]	1 072	1 137	1 484	1 465	1 536	1 622	1 123	1 015	1 479	1 476	Canada[1 2]
Mexico	1 744	1 899	2 350	2 408	2 192	2 399	2 104	1 871	2 316	2 289	Mexique
United States[1 3]	6 495	6 830	7 803	8 197	7 330	6 711	3 761	3 462	3 936	3 916	Etats–Unis[1 3]
America, South	**1 046**	**1 585**	**1 719**	**2 215**	**2 559**	**2 149**	**1 828**	**1 754**	**2 380**	**2 808**	**Amérique du Sud**
Argentina	91	154	89	112	79	66	87	100	102	70	Argentine
Brazil[1]	875	1 350	1 554	2 024	2 401	2 004	1 662	1 575	2 199	2 659	Brésil[1]
Venezuela	80	81	76	...	...	...	...	...	...	...	Venezuela
Asia	**18 273**	**15 919**	**18 762**	**17 304**	**17 933**	**18 416**	**18 574**	**16 945**	**18 665**	**19 194**	**Asie**
China[4]	2 558	2 190	3 410	3 140	2 865	3 080	3 620	3 911	4 312	...	Chine[4]
Japan[5 6]	14 414	12 785	13 881	12 074	12 897	12 888	12 449	10 488	11 660	12 180	Japon[5 6]
Korea, Republic of[1]	437	502	821	1 439	1 497	1 765	1 814	1 847	1 977	2 022	Corée, République de[1]
Philippines[3]	776	376	...	...	...	...	...	...	...	...	Philippines[3]
Turkey[2]	88	66	74	75	...	...	...	...	140	...	Turquie[2]
Europe	**22 973**	**23 186**	**24 481**	**25 301**	**24 425**	**25 599**	**23 234**	**20 802**	**22 941**	**23 493**	**Europe**
EEC	***11 516***	***11 484***	***12 314***	***13 008***	***12 186***	***13 338***	***11 056***	***9 470***	***10 488***	***11 074***	***CEE***
Belgium	1 070	1 238	1 595	1 731	1 788	1 960	1 519	1 233	1 493	1 652	Belgique
Denmark[2]	315	341	410	434	450	390	332	266	310	342	Danemark[2]
France	1 697	1 878	2 136	1 930	2 239	2 272	1 515	1 204	1 504	1 536	France
Germany, Fed. Rep.	3 764	3 612	4 004	4 183	4 137	4 408	3 664	3 382	3 536	4 139	Allemagne, Rép. féd.
Italy	2 389	2 206	2 053	2 320	2 068	2 215	2 156	1 776	1 926	1 894	Italie
Luxembourg	117	128	128	145	141	124	135	137	106	* 3	Luxembourg
Netherlands	285	282	283	283	251	259	216	171	228	207	Pays–Bas
United Kingdom[7 8]	1 879	1 799	1 705	1 982	1 112	1 710	1 519	1 301	1 385	1 301	Royaume–Uni[7 8]
EFTA	***1 580***	***1 393***	***1 403***	***1 648***	***1 690***	***1 896***	***1 851***	***1 478***	***1 446***	***1 592***	***AELE***
Austria	296	316	349	421	476	517	501	436	470	513	Autriche
Finland	319	490	495	572	626	670	[2] 646	[2] 415	[2] 367	[2] 465	Finlande
Sweden	965	587	559	655	588	* 709	* 704	627	609	614	Suède
East Europe	***8 282***	***8 730***	***9 153***	***9 224***	***9 056***	***8 785***	***8 986***	***8 764***	***9 811***	***9 413***	***Europe de l'est***
Bulgaria[1]	844	941	1 051	1 144	1 152	1 168	1 278	1 338	1 291	1 254	Bulgarie[1]
Czechoslovakia[4]	1 835	1 841	1 862	1 862	1 811	1 873	2 073	2 000	2 051	2 091	Tchécoslovaquie[4]
German Dem. Rep.[9]	883	893	918	941	944	885	912	998	1 135	1 032	Rép. dém. allemande[9]
Hungary[1]	673	723	736	756	646	664	676	634	714	676	Hongrie[1]
Poland	2 037	2 142	2 265	2 201	2 074	1 592	1 490	1 671	1 777	1 666	Pologne
Romania[2 9]	2 010	2 190	2 321	2 320	2 429	2 603	2 557	2 123	2 843	2 694	Roumanie[2 9]
Other Europe	***1 595***	***1 579***	***1 611***	***1 421***	***1 493***	***1 580***	***1 341***	***1 090***	***1 196***	***1 414***	***Autre Europe***
Spain	1 225	1 165	1 137	979	1 074	1 087	945	694	753	931	Espagne
Yugoslavia	370	414	474	442	419	493	396	396	443	483	Yougoslavie
USSR	**13 625**	**13 826**	**14 076**	**13 592**	*** 13 916**	...	...	...	...	...	**URSS**
Ukrainian SSR[10]	*4 555*	*4 639*	*5 241*	*4 496*	*4 695*	...	...	...	...	...	*RSS d'Ukraine[10]*
Total	**66 448**	**65 892**	**72 174**	**72 192**	**71 596**	**72 644**	**66 590**	**61 938**	**67 957**	**69 567**	**Total**

General note.
Universals and plates which are more than 4.75 mm thick. (SITC 67410–0).

Remarque générale.
Larges plats et tôles de plus de 4.75 mm d'épaisseur. (CTCI 67410–0).

1 Including medium plates 3 to 4.75 mm thick.
2 Source: Annual Bulletin of Steel Statistics for Europe, United Nations Economic Commission of Europe (Geneva).
3 Shipments.
4 Heavy plates of 4 mm and over.

1 Y compris les tôles moyennes de 3 à 4,75 mm d'épaisseur.
2 Source: Bulletin annuel de statistiques de l'acier pour l'Europe, Commission économique des Nations Unies pour l'Europe (Genève).
3 Expéditions.
4 Tôles fortes de 4 mm et plus.

[5] Heavy plates over 6 mm thick.
[6] Including medium plates of high tensile steel.
[7] Deliveries.
[8] 13 mm and over.
[9] 4 mm and over.
[10] Over 5 mm.

[5] Tôles fortes de plus de 6 mm d'épaisseur.
[6] Y compris les tôles moyennes d'acier à haute résistance à la traction.
[7] Livraisons.
[8] 13 mm et plus.
[9] 4 mm et plus.
[10] Plus de 5 mm.

Plates (medium) 3 to 4.75 mm – Tôles moyennes de 3 à 4,75 mm

Unit : Thousand metric tons

Unité : Milliers de tonnes métriques

Country or area	1976	1977	1978	1979	1980	1981	1982	1983	1984	1985	Pays ou zone
Africa	**200**	**216**	**178**	**267**	**220**	**216**	**216**	**216**	**216**	**216**	**Afrique**
Algeria	200	...	178	267	220	...	...	...	...	...	Algérie
America, North	**530**	**505**	**673**	**756**	**736**	**817**	**633**	**448**	**556**	**585**	**Amérique du Nord**
Mexico	530	505	673	756	736	817	633	448	556	585	Mexique
America, South	**2**	**2**	**2**	**2**	**2**	**2**	**2**	**2**	**2**	**2**	**Amérique du Sud**
Ecuador	...	...	2	...	...	...	...	...	...	...	Equateur
Asia	**1 671**	**1 676**	**1 699**	**1 600**	**1 288**	**1 007**	**1 016**	**1 351**	**1 226**	**1 135**	**Asie**
Japan[1]	1 565	1 568	1 600	1 500	1 141	893	900	1 209	1 139	1 016	Japon[1]
Turkey	[2] 106	[2] 108	[2] 99	[2] 100	[2] 147	...	...	142	87	...	Turquie
Europe	**5 443**	**6 091**	**6 639**	**6 856**	**6 419**	**6 458**	**5 960**	**6 457**	**6 807**	**6 739**	**Europe**
EEC	***2 196***	***2 559***	***2 971***	***3 152***	***2 858***	***3 112***	***2 506***	***2 671***	***2 867***	***2 944***	***CEE***
Belgium	478	584	901	1 004	771	767	632	600	777	834	Belgique
France	695	944	1 022	1 047	1 128	1 094	887	884	891	920	France
Germany, Fed. Rep.	472	477	520	534	499	476	372	415	474	433	Allemagne, Rép. féd.
Italy	76	104	85	80	62	50	45	40	35	33	Italie
Luxembourg	47	50	39	45	39	40	36	40	32	* 2	Luxembourg
Netherlands	46	57	36	51	58	44	33	43	52	49	Pays-Bas
United Kingdom[3]	382	343	368	391	301	641	501	649	606	673	Royaume-Uni[3]
EFTA	***246***	***213***	***365***	***410***	***344***	***440***	***506***	***730***	***779***	***766***	***AELE***
Austria	108	110	112	126	128	126	97	93	98	113	Autriche
Finland	57	39	180	209	145	259	[2] 339	[2] 561	[2] 600	[2] 589	Finlande
Sweden	81	64	73	75	71	55	70	76	81	64	Suède
East Europe	***1 792***	***2 043***	***2 240***	***2 255***	***2 221***	***2 049***	***2 103***	***2 038***	***2 084***	***1 957***	***Europe de l'est***
Poland	904	872	885	913	972	830	837	782	912	896	Pologne
Romania[2,4]	888	1 171	1 355	1 342	1 249	1 219	1 266	1 256	1 172	1 061	Roumanie[2,4]
Other Europe	***1 209***	***1 276***	***1 063***	***1 039***	***996***	***857***	***845***	***1 018***	***1 077***	***1 072***	***Autre Europe***
Spain	1 148	1 191	975	957	908	780	761	957	1 010	986	Espagne
Yugoslavia	61	85	88	82	88	77	84	61	67	86	Yougoslavie
USSR	**6 714**	**6 750**	**7 700**	**7 506**	*** 7 802**	...	...	...	...	...	**URSS**
Ukrainian SSR[5]	*2 235*	*2 318*	*1 780*	*2 146*	*2 147*	...	...	...	...	...	*RSS d'Ukraine[5]*
Total	**14 560**	**15 240**	**16 891**	**16 987**	**16 467**	**16 670**	**16 288**	**17 227**	**17 852**	**18 014**	**Total**

General note.
Plates which are at least 3 mm but not more than 4.75 mm thick, including strip which is more than 500 mm wide and 3 mm or more thick used as such. (SITC 67420-0).

[1] Medium plates 3 to 6 mm thick.
[2] Source: Annual Bulletin of Steel Statistics for Europe, United Nations Economic Commission of Europe (Geneva).
[3] 3 mm to 13 mm.
[4] Under 4 mm.
[5] From 3 mm to 5 mm.

Remarque générale.
Tôles de 3 mm au moins et de 4.75 mm au plus d'épaisseur, y compris les bandes de plus de 500 mm de largeur et de 3 mm d'épaisseur ou plus, utilisées en l'état. (CTCI 67420-0).

[1] Tôles moyennes de 3 à 6 mm d'épaisseur.
[2] Source: Bulletin annuel de statistiques de l'acier pour l'Europe, Commission économique des Nations Unies pour l'Europe (Genève).
[3] De 3 à 13 mm.
[4] Moins de 4 mm.
[5] De 3 à 5 mm.

Sheets, electrical – Tôles magnétiques

Unit : Thousand metric tons

Unité : Milliers de tonnes métriques

Country or area	1976	1977	1978	1979	1980	1981	1982	1983	1984	1985	Pays ou zone
America, North	**537**	**555**	**593**	**646**	**557**	**554**	**413**	**425**	**455**	**386**	**Amérique du Nord**
Cuba	...	...	13	14	12	10	9	9	10	12	Cuba
United States[1]	523	542	580	632	545	544	404	416	445	374	Etats–Unis[1]
America, South	**26**	**27**	**22**	**15**	**32**	**31**	**46**	**49**	**51**	**59**	**Amérique du Sud**
Brazil	26	27	22	15	32	31	46	49	51	59	Brésil
Asia	**2 015**	**2 183**	**2 608**	**2 518**	**1 091**	**1 023**	**1 096**	**1 271**	**1 407**	**1 355**	**Asie**
India	20	35	36	45	44	51	27	26	32	...	Inde
Japan	1 076	1 023	1 142	1 102	1 028	935	1 035	1 186	1 305	1 254	Japon
Korea, Republic of	[2] 919	[2] 1 125	[2] 1 430	[2] 1 371	# 19	37	34	59	70	65	Corée, République de
Europe	**1 497**	**1 469**	**1 557**	**1 565**	**1 439**	**1 369**	**1 354**	**1 490**	**1 534**	**1 539**	**Europe**
EEC	***1 106***	***1 018***	***1 067***	***1 021***	***907***	***856***	***871***	***997***	***1 076***	***1 081***	***CEE***
Belgium	91	89	86	86	87	70	63	93	93	100	Belgique
France	199	178	181	195	178	167	160	184	171	168	France
Germany, Fed. Rep.	374	333	378	361	372	363	352	406	480	483	Allemagne, Rép. féd.
Italy	201	184	208	209	197	155	177	192	188	198	Italie
United Kingdom	241	234	214	170	73	101	119	122	144	132	Royaume–Uni
EFTA	***62***	***65***	***62***	***75***	***65***	***59***	***59***	***74***	***55***	***60***	***AELE***
Austria[3]	36	41	38	47	38	32	27	36	37	48	Autriche[3]
Norway[3]	26	24	24	28	27	27	32	38	18	12	Norvège[3]
East Europe	***282***	***329***	***372***	***403***	***385***	***390***	***369***	***371***	***359***	***356***	***Europe de l'est***
Czechoslovakia	143	148	145	142	145	162	148	152	160	159	Tchécoslovaquie
German Dem. Rep.	...	84	85	87	85	88	85	86	67	66	Rép. dém. allemande
Hungary	15	15	15	16	10	6	4	4	3	2	Hongrie
Poland	27	61	85	94	86	81	81	78	74	73	Pologne
Romania[3]	5	21	42	64	59	53	51	51	55	56	Roumanie[3]
Other Europe	***47***	***57***	***56***	***66***	***82***	***64***	***55***	***48***	***44***	***42***	***Autre Europe***
Spain	39	42	32	41	50	25	24	20	15	4	Espagne
Yugoslavia	8	15	24	25	# [3] 32	[3] 39	[3] 31	[3] 28	[3] 29	...	Yougoslavie
USSR	**1 150**	**1 153**	**1 172**	**1 150**	**1 172**	**1 136**	**1 113**	**1 139**	**1 138**	**1 133**	**URSS**
Ukrainian SSR	*64*	*63*	*54*	*55*	*60*	*55*	*50*	*45*	*45*	*44*	*RSS d'Ukraine*
Total	**5 225**	**5 387**	**5 952**	**5 894**	**4 291**	**4 113**	**4 022**	**4 374**	**4 585**	**4 472**	**Total**

General note.

Uncoated hot–rolled or cold–rolled sheets and strip of silicon steel for use in making electric equipment, notably motors, transformers and dynamos. (Part of SITC 6743 and part of SITC 675).

[1] Shipments.
[2] Including hot and cold rolled sheets under 3 mm.
[3] Source: Annual Bulletin of Steel Statistics for Europe, United Nations Economic Commission of Europe (Geneva).

Remarque générale.

Tôles sans revêtement laminées à chaud ou à froid et bandes d'acier au silicium, utilisées pour la fabrication d'outillage électrique, notamment de moteurs, de transformateurs et de dynamos. (Parties de CTCI 6743 et CTCI 675).

[1] Expéditions.
[2] Y compris tôles laminées à froid et á chaud, de moins de 3 mm d'épaisseur.
[3] Source: Bulletin annuel de statistiques de l'acier pour l'Europe, Commission économique des Nations Unies pour l'Europe (Genève).

Sheets under 3 mm, cold–rolled, uncoated – Tôles de moins de 3 mm, laminées à froid, sans revêtement

Unit : Thousand metric tons

Unité : Milliers de tonnes métriques

Country or area	1976	1977	1978	1979	1980	1981	1982	1983	1984	1985	Pays ou zone
America, North	**18 335**	**17 816**	**18 079**	**17 480**	**13 652**	**14 643**	**11 313**	**13 768**	**13 777**	**13 709**	**Amérique du Nord**
Canada[1 2]	1 765	1 774	1 912	1 800	1 575	1 583	1 214	1 266	1 381	1 415	Canada[1 2]
United States[3]	16 570	16 042	16 167	15 680	12 077	13 060	10 099	12 502	12 396	12 294	Etats–Unis[3]
America, South	**1 069**	**510**	**545**	**578**	**568**	**424**	**407**	**378**	**421**	**422**	**Amérique du Sud**
Brazil	1 069	# 510	545	578	568	424	407	378	421	422	Brésil
Asia	**22 121**	**22 400**	**22 136**	**24 261**	**25 303**	**24 117**	**23 958**	**26 149**	**27 950**	**28 520**	**Asie**
Burma[4]	4	4	3	...	...	1	3	1	...	...	Birmanie[4]
China[5]	...	968	1 327	1 689	2 422	3 033	3 080	3 167	3 517	3 751	Chine[5]
Japan	20 930	20 839	20 102	21 782	21 938	20 087	20 083	21 767	23 097	23 447	Japon
Korea, Republic of	...	...	...	...	780	841	643	1 071	1 218	1 190	Corée, République de
Turkey[2]	125	198	210	190	...	...	...	...	117	...	Turquie[2]
Europe	**31 735**	**32 941**	**33 639**	**34 413**	**33 891**	**33 142**	**31 750**	**32 622**	**34 656**	**34 817**	**Europe**
EEC	***25 526***	***26 005***	***26 621***	***27 807***	***26 188***	***25 876***	***24 419***	***24 925***	***26 538***	***26 547***	***CEE***
Belgium	3 033	3 209	3 366	3 640	3 411	2 928	2 584	2 585	3 017	3 084	Belgique
France	6 023	6 120	6 482	6 577	6 375	5 831	5 454	5 346	5 715	5 844	France
Germany, Fed. Rep.	7 570	7 889	7 960	8 562	8 565	8 216	7 804	8 023	8 465	8 473	Allemagne, Rép. féd.
Greece	...	...	...	...	...	126	121	238	304	...	Grèce
Italy	2 893	2 829	2 785	2 851	3 923	3 845	3 854	3 892	3 989	4 067	Italie
Luxembourg	247	271	287	291	274	246	152	143	145	177	Luxembourg
Netherlands	1 710	1 650	1 826	1 761	1 570	1 603	1 486	1 490	1 546	1 464	Pays–Bas
United Kingdom	3 853	3 840	3 718	3 928	1 873	3 081	2 964	3 208	3 357	3 241	Royaume–Uni
EFTA	***1 676***	***1 828***	***1 982***	***2 009***	***1 992***	***1 886***	***1 981***	***2 216***	***2 372***	***2 323***	***AELE***
Austria	1 023	1 040	1 118	1 145	1 068	980	978	1 075	1 129	1 101	Autriche
Finland	170	299	369	343	436	438	[2] 445	[2] 515	[2] 543	[2] 522	Finlande
Norway[2]	7	9	18	8	7	6	11	3	5	3	Norvège[2]
Sweden	476	480	477	513	481	* 462	* 547	623	695	697	Suède
East Europe	***2 751***	***2 913***	***2 905***	***3 026***	***3 384***	***3 069***	***2 987***	***2 951***	***3 080***	***3 194***	***Europe de l'est***
German Dem. Rep.	716	708	700	764	803	792	755	700	691	810	Rép. dém. allemande
Hungary	430	468	468	452	456	426	414	425	456	451	Hongrie
Poland	1 189	1 231	1 219	1 258	1 542	1 335	1 288	1 336	1 403	1 414	Pologne
Romania[2]	416	506	518	552	583	516	530	490	530	519	Roumanie[2]
Other Europe	***1 782***	***2 195***	***2 131***	***1 571***	***2 327***	***2 311***	***2 363***	***2 530***	***2 666***	***2 753***	***Autre Europe***
Spain	1 515	1 864	1 754	1 187	1 912	1 889	2 004	2 024	2 077	2 158	Espagne
Yugoslavia	267	331	377	384	415	422	359	506	589	595	Yougoslavie
USSR	**6 965**	**7 074**	**7 037**	**7 046**	**6 905**	**7 548**	**7 818**	**8 774**	**9 396**	**9 602**	**URSS**
Ukrainian SSR	*2 275*	*2 368*	*2 321*	*2 292*	*2 172*	*2 099*	*2 020*	*2 142*	*2 152*	*2 083*	*RSS d'Ukraine*
Total	**80 225**	**80 741**	**81 436**	**83 778**	**80 320**	**79 874**	**75 246**	**81 691**	**86 200**	**87 070**	**Total**

General note.
Uncoated sheets less than 3 mm thick, produced from hot–rolled products by a cold–rolling process to improve their technical properties. (SITC 67430–2).

Remarque générale.
Tôles sans revêtement de moins de 3 mm d'épaisseur, fabriquées à partir de produits laminés à chaud et dont on a amélioré les propriétés techniques par laminage à froid. (CTCI 67430–2).

[1] Including hoop and strip, tinplate, electrical sheets and cold–reduced hoop and strip.
[2] Source: Annual Bulletin of Steel Statistics for Europe, United Nations Economic Commission of Europe (Geneva).
[3] Shipments.
[4] Twelve months ending 30 September of year stated.
[5] Including hot–rolled sheets under 3 mm.

[1] Y compris les feuillards, le fer blanc, les tôles magnétiques et les feuillards laminés à froid.
[2] Source: Bulletin annuel de statistiques de l'acier pour l'Europe, Commission économique des Nations Unies pour l'Europe (Genève).
[3] Expéditions.
[4] Période de douze mois finissant le 30 septembre de l'année indiquée.
[5] Y compris les tôles laminées à chaud de moins de 3 mm d'épaisseur.

Sheets under 3 mm, hot–rolled – Tôles de moins de 3 mm, laminées à chaud

Unit : Thousand metric tons — Unité : Milliers de tonnes métriques

Country or area	1976	1977	1978	1979	1980	1981	1982	1983	1984	1985	Pays ou zone
Africa	**547**	**608**	**818**	**1 128**	**1 187**	**1 204**	**1 153**	**1 172**	**1 206**	**1 291**	**Afrique**
South Africa	547	608	818	1 128	1 187	1 204	1 153	1 172	1 206	1 291	Afrique du Sud
America, North	**45 542**	**45 093**	**17 903**	**18 298**	**14 452**	**15 940**	**11 661**	**14 125**	**16 412**	**16 334**	**Amérique du Nord**
Canada[1]	[2] 2 451	[2] 2 441	[2] 2 476	[2] 2 376	[2] 1 893	[2] 2 094	[2] 1 999	[2] 2 113	[2] 2 769	[3] 2 740	Canada[1]
Mexico	1 005	1 101	1 414	1 411	1 568	1 644	1 450	1 472	1 729	1 800	Mexique
United States[4]	[2] 42 086	[2] 41 551	14 013	14 511	10 991	12 202	8 212	10 540	11 914	11 794	Etats–Unis[4]
America, South	**1 202**	**475**	**540**	**503**	**524**	**465**	**456**	**520**	**564**	**629**	**Amérique du Sud**
Brazil	881	# 202	220	198	219	160	151	215	259	324	Brésil
Venezuela	321	* 273	* 320	...	...	...	...	...	...	...	Venezuela
Asia	**40 716**	**40 541**	**40 249**	**44 495**	**43 907**	**39 695**	**39 381**	**39 890**	**43 788**	**41 751**	**Asie**
Japan	40 181	40 022	39 730	43 968	43 166	38 884	38 491	38 959	42 688	...	Japon
Korea, Republic of	...	...	...	...	266	272	287	263	307	338	Corée, République de
Turkey[2]	328	299	287	282	...	...	...	...	793	...	Turquie[2]
Europe	**15 090**	**16 374**	**17 098**	**17 201**	**14 359**	**14 914**	**13 846**	**14 693**	**16 009**	**15 199**	**Europe**
EEC	***9 746***	***10 553***	***11 317***	***11 573***	***8 421***	***9 100***	***8 290***	***8 690***	***9 810***	***9 624***	***CEE***
Belgium	3 450	3 892	4 233	4 450	4 169	3 721	3 239	3 321	3 982	4 082	Belgique
France	1 023	1 450	1 571	1 580	1 500	1 571	1 530	1 569	1 790	1 644	France
Germany, Fed. Rep.	60	85	100	42	54	50	76	62	56	76	Allemagne, Rép. féd.
Greece[5]	[6] 487	[6] 398	[6] 605	[6] 473	[6] 304	102	114	29	40	...	Grèce[5]
Italy	31	34	15	6	0	1	12	10	9	10	Italie
Netherlands	12	15	8	12	5	6	8	13	18	17	Pays–Bas
United Kingdom	4 683	4 679	4 785	5 010	2 389	3 649	3 311	3 686	3 915	3 766	Royaume–Uni
EFTA	***103***	***64***	***123***	***103***	***110***	***105***	***113***	***120***	***123***	***106***	***AELE***
Austria	45	36	44	...	...	...	...	...	...	...	Autriche
Finland	...	24	72	...	60	56	...	...	...	...	Finlande
Sweden	5	4	7	8	8	7	18	25	28	11	Suède
East Europe	***3 723***	***3 961***	***4 090***	***4 066***	***4 137***	***4 006***	***4 008***	***3 951***	***4 166***	***3 929***	***Europe de l'est***
Bulgaria	592	632	651	615	615	701	658	633	674	695	Bulgarie
Czechoslovakia[7]	1 218	1 186	1 260	1 283	1 230	1 284	1 297	1 311	1 300	1 256	Tchécoslovaquie[7]
Hungary	553	616	599	580	582	527	536	527	570	550	Hongrie
Poland	922	941	921	938	1 046	821	767	873	898	861	Pologne
Romania	438	586	659	650	664	673	750	607	724	567	Roumanie
Other Europe	***1 518***	***1 796***	***1 568***	***1 459***	***1 691***	***1 703***	***1 435***	***1 932***	***1 910***	***1 540***	***Autre Europe***
Spain[8]	1 505	1 785	1 562	1 455	1 688	1 701	1 430	1 925	1 902	1 536	Espagne[8]
Yugoslavia	13	11	6	4	3	2	5	7	8	4	Yougoslavie
USSR[9]	**12 277**	**12 205**	**12 440**	**12 176**	*** 12 782**	**...**	**...**	**...**	**...**	**...**	**URSS[9]**
Ukrainian SSR[9]	*3 196*	*3 264*	*3 265*	*3 176*	*3 260*	...	...	...	...	...	*RSS d'Ukraine[9]*
Total	**115 374**	**115 296**	**89 048**	**93 800**	**87 210**	**84 886**	**79 263**	**83 263**	**90 940**	**88 262**	**Total**

General note.
Hot–rolled sheets which are less than 3 mm thick, including strip which is more than 500 mm wide and less than 3 mm thick, and which is used as such in the country concerned. Coils for re–rolling which are exported, are considered as semi–manufactured products for sale, and are therefore excluded from this item. (SITC 67430–3).

1 Including hot–rolled sheets over 3 mm thick.
2 Source: Annual Bulletin of Steel Statistics for Europe, United Nations Economic Commission of Europe (Geneva).
3 Including rail passenger carriages.
4 Shipments.
5 Data refer to sheets and strips of various thicknesses.
6 Including cold–rolled sheets.
7 Plates and sheets under 4 mm.
8 Black sheets.
9 Including cold–rolled sheets by weight of rolled products.

Remarque générale.
Tôles laminées à chaud, de moins de 3 mm d'épaisseur, y compris les bandes qui ont plus de 500 mm de largeur et moins de 3 mm d'épaisseur et sont utilisées en l'état dans le pays déclarant. Les ébauches en rouleaux pour relaminage destinées à l'exportation sont considérées comme des demi–produits pour la vente et ne sont donc pas comprises dans cette rubrique. (CTCI 67430–3).

1 Y compris les tôles laminées à chaud de plus de 3 mm d'épaisseur.
2 Source: Bulletin annuel de statistiques de l'acier pour l'Europe, Commission économique des Nations Unies pour l'Europe (Genève).
3 Y compris les wagons pour passagers.
4 Expéditions.
5 Données se rapportant aux tôles et feuillards de différentes épaisseurs.
6 Y compris les tôles laminées à froid.
7 Tôles de moins de 4 mm.
8 Tôles noires.
9 Y compris les tôles laminées à froid en fonction du poids de produits laminés.

Tinplate – Tôles étamées

Unit : Thousand metric tons

Unité : Milliers de tonnes métriques

Country or area	1976	1977	1978	1979	1980	1981	1982	1983	1984	1985	Pays ou zone
Africa	**217**	**216**	**209**	**238**	**207**	**245**	**211**	**257**	**219**	**255**	**Afrique**
South Africa	217	216	209	238	207	245	211	257	219	255	Afrique du Sud
America, North	**5 924**	**5 939**	**5 612**	**5 778**	**5 361**	**4 552**	**4 143**	**4 127**	**4 075**	**3 542**	**Amérique du Nord**
Canada[1 2]	477	533	461	445	492	365	385	394	475	388	Canada[1 2]
Mexico	165	193	183	179	147	99	127	144	174	148	Mexique
United States[3]	5 282	5 213	4 968	5 154	4 722	4 088	3 631	3 589	3 426	3 006	Etats–Unis[3]
America, South	**530**	**689**	**735**	**783**	**813**	**607**	**629**	**631**	**596**	**579**	**Amérique du Sud**
Argentina	67	[2] 79	[2] 53	[2] 67	[2] 40	[2] 52	[2] 84	[2] 100	[2] 84	* [2] 82	Argentine
Brazil	320	462	501	537	595	407	433	369	349	336	Brésil
Chile	34	42	43	47	48	28	21	40	39	33	Chili
Colombia[2]	* 40	* 40	56	59	65	50	55	52	54	* 58	Colombie[2]
Venezuela	69	66	82	73	65	# [2] 70	* [2] 36	* [2] 70	* [2] 70	* [2] 70	Venezuela
Asia	**2 079**	**2 233**	**2 203**	**2 308**	**2 344**	**2 134**	**2 106**	**2 150**	**2 232**	**2 089**	**Asie**
India* [2]	120	100	120	160	200	200	160	160	160	160	Inde* [2]
Japan	1 797	1 865	1 810	1 887	1 869	1 666	1 638	1 588	1 653	1 564	Japon
Korea, Republic of	42	57	83	67	71	85	105	127	150	148	Corée, République de
Philippines	[3] 18	[3] 95	# [2] 64	[2] 57	[2] 59	[2] 41	[2] 43	[2] 103	[2] 85	[2] 56	Philippines
Thailand	26	36	44	65	70	79	63	73	92	* 68	Thaïlande
Turkey[2]	76	* 80	82	72	75	63	97	99	92	93	Turquie[2]
Europe	**4 696**	**5 018**	**4 912**	**5 099**	**4 869**	**4 782**	**4 896**	**4 939**	**5 077**	**4 846**	**Europe**
EEC	***4 044***	***4 276***	***4 101***	***4 276***	***3 954***	***3 909***	***3 998***	***4 050***	***4 010***	***3 816***	***CEE***
Belgium	331	363	298	332	334	326	276	303	336	302	Belgique
Denmark	0	0	0	0	0	4	3	3	...	3	Danemark
France	863	931	978	952	1 043	894	988	921	914	900	France
Germany, Fed. Rep.	903	893	859	925	989	871	878	890	914	891	Allemagne, Rép. féd.
Greece	39	52	50	40	50	50	40	40	47	42	Grèce
Italy	338	400	387	421	436	375	413	485	485	455	Italie
Netherlands	452	461	462	498	505	513	517	524	565	532	Pays–Bas
United Kingdom	1 118	1 176	1 067	1 108	597	876	883	884	746	691	Royaume–Uni
EFTA	***209***	***206***	***241***	***269***	***276***	***273***	***267***	***280***	***310***	***326***	***AELE***
Austria	75	85	105	131	126	143	137	147	151	190	Autriche
Norway[1]	76	72	73	79	80	75	64	70	91	91	Norvège[1]
Portugal	* 58	49	63	59	70	55	66	63	68	45	Portugal
East Europe	***228***	***225***	***245***	***253***	***247***	***188***	***179***	***203***	***204***	***203***	***Europe de l'est***
Czechoslovakia	82	87	96	108	103	95	98	101	105	107	Tchécoslovaquie
Hungary	8	9	10	8	10	10	8	8	7	6	Hongrie
Poland	136	127	137	135	132	81	71	92	90	88	Pologne
Romania[1]	2	2	2	2	2	2	2	2	2	2	Roumanie[1]
Other Europe	***215***	***311***	***325***	***301***	***392***	***412***	***452***	***406***	***553***	***501***	***Autre Europe***
Spain	215	311	325	301	392	412	452	399	519	468	Espagne
Yugoslavia	0	0	0	0	0	0	0	7	34	33	Yougoslavie
Oceania	**257**	**341**	**333**	**337**	**379**	**333**	**368**	**301**	**376**	**394**	**Océanie**
Australia[4]	257	341	333	337	379	333	368	301	376	394	Australie[4]
Total	**13 703**	**14 436**	**14 004**	**14 543**	**13 973**	**12 653**	**12 353**	**12 405**	**12 575**	**11 705**	**Total**

General note.
A product made by coating hot–rolled or cold–rolled sheets and strip on both sides with commercially–pure tin. (SITC 6747 and part of SITC 675).

[1] Source: Annual Bulletin of Steel Statistics for Europe, United Nations Economic Commission of Europe (Geneva).
[2] Source: International Tin Council, (London).
[3] Shipments.
[4] Twelve months ending 30 June of year stated.

Remarque générale.
Produit que l'on obtient en revêtant d'étain commercialement pur les deux faces des tôles et des bandes laminées à chaud ou à froid. (CTCI 6747 et partie de CTCI 675).

[1] Source: Bulletin annuel de statistiques de l'acier pour l'Europe, Commission économique des Nations Unies pour l'Europe (Genève).
[2] Source: Conseil international de l'étain, (Londres).
[3] Expéditions.
[4] Période de douze mois finissant le 30 juin de l'année indiquée.

Sheets, galvanized – Tôles galvanisées

Unit : Thousand metric tons

Unité : Milliers de tonnes métriques

Country or area	1976	1977	1978	1979	1980	1981	1982	1983	1984	1985	Pays ou zone
Africa	**348**	**444**	**501**	**548**	**509**	**519**	**584**	**613**	**646**	**676**	**Afrique**
Madagascar	3	6	9	15	12	2	2	2	4	3	Madagascar
South Africa	319	410	462	503	480	507	...	...	...	...	Afrique du Sud
United Rep. Tanzania	26	28	30	30	17	10	16	...	...	...	Rép.Unie de Tanzanie
America, North	**5 526**	**6 024**	**6 899**	**6 819**	**5 754**	**6 324**	**5 799**	**6 787**	**7 205**	**8 056**	**Amérique du Nord**
Canada[1]	827	892	1 065	1 066	997	951	928	950	1 073	1 212	Canada[1]
United States[2]	4 699	5 132	5 834	5 753	4 757	5 373	4 871	5 837	6 132	6 844	Etats–Unis[2]
America, South	**141**	**162**	**219**	**223**	**221**	**231**	**248**	**232**	**264**	**399**	**Amérique du Sud**
Brazil	113	129	175	181	182	169	188	167	194	323	Brésil
Colombia	...	33	44	42	39	62	...	...	...	...	Colombie
Asia	**6 100**	**6 259**	**6 282**	**7 305**	**7 342**	**6 778**	**7 174**	**7 822**	**8 799**	**9 385**	**Asie**
Japan	5 824	5 904	5 915	6 897	6 899	6 200	6 600	7 169	8 085	8 632	Japon
Korea, Republic of	67	131	167	185	191	301	339	419	471	511	Corée, République de
Malaysia	56	58	54	62	65	70	49	52	51	51	Malaisie
Sri Lanka	1	* 2	* 3	...	3	...	...	...	...	...	Sri Lanka
Thailand	89	102	85	102	124	145	124	120	130	* 129	Thaïlande
Turkey[1]	63	62	58	57	...	...	...	...	...	...	Turquie[1]
Europe	**5 290**	**5 403**	**6 027**	**6 841**	**6 606**	**6 846**	**6 935**	**6 989**	**7 696**	**7 679**	**Europe**
EEC	***3 920***	***3 828***	***4 396***	***5 034***	***4 810***	***5 032***	***5 028***	***5 128***	***5 675***	***5 630***	***CEE***
Belgium	739	703	831	911	931	897	810	866	953	942	Belgique
France	704	742	873	955	1 014	1 039	1 042	1 015	1 136	1 164	France
Germany, Fed. Rep.[3]	1 442	1 391	1 417	1 685	1 717	1 654	1 635	1 726	1 929	1 894	Allemagne, Rép. féd.[3]
Greece	13	11	15	17	15	13	16	15	35	...	Grèce
Italy	488	489	543	553	600	669	668	642	705	652	Italie
Luxembourg	49	50	52	57	65	64	68	61	70	62	Luxembourg
United Kingdom	485	442	665	856	468	696	789	...	...	...	Royaume–Uni
EFTA	***358***	***334***	***351***	***518***	***554***	***521***	***609***	***626***	***684***	***738***	***AELE***
Finland	121	127	146	154	180	167	215	209	196	201	Finlande
Portugal	26	35	38	41	38	36	38	32	65	88	Portugal
Sweden	211	172	167	323	336	318	356	385	423	449	Suède
East Europe	***742***	***917***	***942***	***919***	***908***	***864***	***839***	***800***	***829***	***833***	***Europe de l'est***
Bulgaria	93	100	98	98	93	108	114	138	142	140	Bulgarie
Czechoslovakia[4]	280	288	290	283	282	272	254	232	260	261	Tchécoslovaquie[4]
Hungary	9	7	9	9	8	9	9	8	7	5	Hongrie
Poland	225	339	352	343	360	310	309	338	344	347	Pologne
Romania	135	183	193	186	165	165	153	84	76	80	Roumanie
Other Europe	***270***	***324***	***338***	***370***	***334***	***429***	***459***	***435***	***508***	***478***	***Autre Europe***
Spain	263	289	298	303	276	320	369	354	396	407	Espagne
Yugoslavia	7	35	40	67	58	109	90	81	112	71	Yougoslavie
Oceania	**49**	**68**	**72**	**120**	**100**	**121**	**67**	**81**	**28**	**45**	**Océanie**
Australia	49	68	72	120	100	121	67	81	28	45	Australie
Total	**17 454**	**18 360**	**20 000**	**21 856**	**20 532**	**20 819**	**20 807**	**22 525**	**24 639**	**26 240**	**Total**

General note.

A product made by coating hot–rolled or cold–rolled sheets and strip on both sides with zinc containing small proportions of certain other metals. (Parts of SITC 6748 and 675).

1 Source: Annual Bulletin of Steel Statistics for Europe, United Nations Economic Commission of Europe (Geneva).
2 Shipments.
3 Including galvanized strip.
4 Including sheets coated with lead.

Remarque générale.

Produits que l'on obtient en revêtant de zinc contenant de faibles proportions de certains autres métaux les deux faces des tôles et des bandes laminées à chaud ou à froid. (Parties de CTCI 6748 et 675).

1 Source: Bulletin annuel de statistiques de l'acier pour l'Europe, Commission économique des Nations Unies pour l'Europe (Genève).
2 Expéditions.
3 Y compris les feuillards galvanisés.
4 Y compris les tôles à revêtement de plomb.

Hoop and strip, cold-reduced – Feuillards laminés à froid

Unit : Thousand metric tons | Unité : Milliers de tonnes métriques

Country or area	1976	1977	1978	1979	1980	1981	1982	1983	1984	1985	Pays ou zone
America, North	**1 046**	**1 076**	**1 133**	**1 116**	**844**	**961**	**657**	**835**	**909**	**797**	**Amérique du Nord**
United States[1,2]	1 046	1 076	1 133	1 116	844	961	657	835	909	797	Etats-Unis[1,2]
America, South	**19**	**27**	**23**	**38**	**15**	**11**	**23**	**18**	**17**	**16**	**Amérique du Sud**
Argentina	[3] 19	[3] 27	[3] 23	[3] 38	# 15	11	23	...	...	...	Argentine
Asia	**523**	**533**	**523**	**555**	**596**	**540**	**545**	**574**	**648**	**574**	**Asie**
Japan	512	522	512	544	585	529	534	563	637	563	Japon
Turkey[4]	11	...	...	...	...	...	...	...	...	...	Turquie[4]
Europe	**4 739**	**4 836**	**4 726**	**5 029**	**4 735**	**4 434**	**4 270**	**4 414**	**4 940**	**4 589**	**Europe**
EEC	***3 461***	***3 320***	***3 266***	***3 448***	***3 131***	***2 793***	***2 613***	***2 735***	***3 246***	***2 922***	***CEE***
Denmark	0	0	0	0	0	5	8	9	0	10	Danemark
France[5]	175	173	166	167	165	139	143	122	115	106	France[5]
Germany, Fed. Rep.	2 068	1 957	1 869	2 112	1 971	1 715	1 573	1 679	1 784	1 732	Allemagne, Rép. féd.
Greece	...	...	...	...	...	124	131	175	160	...	Grèce
Italy	549	534	570	548	508	481	442	440	843	...	Italie
Luxembourg	37	50	61	47	33	29	26	22	23	28	Luxembourg
United Kingdom[5]	484	458	452	426	306	300	290	288	321	305	Royaume-Uni[5]
EFTA	***174***	***181***	***162***	***220***	***241***	***211***	***208***	***223***	***224***	***229***	***AELE***
Austria	46	50	47	46	42	35	25	25	32	29	Autriche
Finland	23	32	0	38	30	27	...	...	...	...	Finlande
Sweden	105	99	115	136	169	149	153	166	159	165	Suède
East Europe	***811***	***902***	***914***	***909***	***948***	***1 023***	***1 033***	***1 033***	***1 093***	***1 090***	***Europe de l'est***
Czechoslovakia	354	354	357	361	370	379	362	376	368	371	Tchécoslovaquie
Hungary	71	74	77	69	80	79	81	86	87	80	Hongrie
Poland	244	252	250	262	311	305	287	292	315	323	Pologne
Romania[4]	142	222	230	217	187	260	303	279	323	316	Roumanie[4]
Other Europe	***293***	***433***	***384***	***452***	***415***	***407***	***416***	***423***	***377***	***348***	***Autre Europe***
Spain	245	352	296	311	240	214	228	218	155	155	Espagne
Yugoslavia	48	81	88	141	175	193	188	205	222	193	Yougoslavie
USSR	**435**	**431**	**469**	**477**	*** 520**	...	...	...	...	...	**URSS**
Ukrainian SSR	*49*	*48*	*48*	*47*	*45*	*40*	...	...	...	...	*RSS d'Ukraine*
Total	**6 762**	**6 903**	**6 874**	**7 215**	**6 710**	**6 477**	**6 048**	**6 415**	**7 110**	**6 593**	**Total**

General note.
A flat, cold-rolled product which is not more than 500 mm wide and is normally delivered in coils. (SITC 67500-1).

[1] Cold-reduced strip only.
[2] Shipments.
[3] Source: Instituto Latino Americano del Fierro y el Acero, (Santiago).
[4] Source: Annual Bulletin of Steel Statistics for Europe, United Nations Economic Commission of Europe (Geneva).
[5] Deliveries.

Remarque générale.
Produits plats laminé à froid, de moins de 500 mm de largeur et normalement livrés en rouleaux. (CTCI 67500-1).

[1] Feuillards laminé à froid seulement.
[2] Expéditions.
[3] Source: Instituto Latino Americano del Fierro y el Acero , (Santiago).
[4] Source: Bulletin annuel de statistiques de l'acier pour l'Europe, Commission économique des Nations Unies pour l'Europe (Genève).
[5] Livraisons.

Hoop and strip, hot-rolled – Feuillards laminés à chaud

Unit : Thousand metric tons

Unité : Milliers de tonnes métriques

Country or area	1976	1977	1978	1979	1980	1981	1982	1983	1984	1985	Pays ou zone
Africa	**76**	**56**	**67**	**76**	**69**	**69**	**69**	**69**	**69**	**69**	**Afrique**
South Africa	76	56	67	76	...	...	...	...	...	...	Afrique du Sud
America, North	**5 245**	**5 710**	**6 190**	**6 083**	**5 892**	**6 563**	**3 934**	**3 504**	**3 885**	**3 549**	**Amérique du Nord**
United States[1,2]	5 245	5 710	6 190	6 083	5 892	6 563	3 934	3 504	3 885	3 549	Etats-Unis[1,2]
America, South	**52**	**54**	**32**	**61**	**71**	**85**	**88**	**101**	**78**	**111**	**Amérique du Sud**
Argentina	52	54	32	61	71	85	88	101	78	111	Argentine
Asia	**1 987**	**1 902**	**1 814**	**2 000**	**2 027**	**1 556**	**1 447**	**1 418**	**1 499**	**1 357**	**Asie**
Japan	1 916	1 834	1 738	1 912	1 931	1 474	1 381	1 350	1 422	...	Japon
Sri Lanka	28	25	33	45	53	39	23	25	...	...	Sri Lanka
Turkey[3]	43	...	...	...	...	...	...	...	...	...	Turquie[3]
Europe	**10 591**	**10 017**	**10 298**	**10 741**	**9 663**	**8 838**	**7 974**	**7 913**	**8 637**	**8 161**	**Europe**
EEC	***7 046***	***6 373***	***6 553***	***7 074***	***5 938***	***5 091***	***4 377***	***4 197***	***4 302***	***3 732***	***CEE***
Belgium	160	99	69	37	26	66	62	57	90	90	Belgique
France	1 338	1 213	1 306	1 300	1 125	892	807	683	614	288	France
Germany, Fed. Rep.	2 595	2 329	2 330	2 654	2 516	2 384	2 115	2 100	2 150	2 085	Allemagne, Rép. féd.
Italy	859	823	822	870	871	782	593	461	526	338	Italie
Luxembourg	649	604	660	791	755	481	331	366	373	371	Luxembourg
Netherlands	181	171	222	288	232	237	202	230	229	254	Pays-Bas
United Kingdom	1 264	1 134	1 144	1 134	413	249	267	300	320	306	Royaume-Uni
EFTA	***341***	***283***	***339***	***320***	***274***	***226***	***87***	***96***	***92***	***99***	***AELE***
Austria	207	178	177	179	166	131	7	0	0	0	Autriche
Finland[3]	11	20	67	64	66	55	50	51	46	48	Finlande[3]
Portugal	3	0	0	0	0	0	0	0	0	0	Portugal
Sweden[4]	120	85	95	77	42	* 40	* 30	45	46	51	Suède[4]
East Europe	***2 535***	***2 477***	***2 488***	***2 445***	***2 447***	***2 377***	***2 325***	***2 306***	***2 382***	***2 464***	***Europe de l'est***
Czechoslovakia	985	856	882	825	826	801	819	797	811	823	Tchécoslovaquie
German Dem. Rep.	383	406	414	419	437	457	467	439	453	468	Rép. dém. allemande
Hungary	13	14	14	11	13	14	15	11	10	8	Hongrie
Poland	1 091	1 130	1 111	1 145	1 122	1 069	993	1 028	1 034	1 032	Pologne
Romania[3]	63	71	67	45	49	36	31	31	74	133	Roumanie[3]
Other Europe	***669***	***884***	***918***	***902***	***1 004***	***1 144***	***1 185***	***1 314***	***1 861***	***1 866***	***Autre Europe***
Spain	307	242	247	310	325	230	243	235	285	254	Espagne
Yugoslavia	362	642	671	592	679	914	942	1 079	1 576	1 612	Yougoslavie
USSR	**10 599**	**10 716**	**11 112**	**11 472**	**10 892**	**[5] 10 705**	**[5] 10 225**	**[5] 11 015**	**[5] 10 489**	**[5] 11 333**	**URSS**
Ukrainian SSR	*4 098*	*3 982*	*4 023*	*4 092*	*3 551*	...	...	...	...	...	*RSS d'Ukraine*
Oceania	**2 310**	**2 518**	**2 790**	**2 832**	**3 552**	**3 318**	**3 485**	**2 649**	**2 812**	**2 739**	**Océanie**
Australia[5]	2 310	2 518	2 790	2 832	3 552	3 318	3 485	2 649	2 812	2 739	Australie[5]
Total	**30 860**	**30 973**	**32 303**	**33 265**	**32 166**	**31 134**	**27 222**	**26 669**	**27 468**	**27 319**	**Total**

General note.
A flat, hot-rolled product which is not more than 500 mm wide and is normally delivered in coils, including strip for use in making welded tubes. (SITC 67500-2).

[1] Shipments.
[2] Including welded pipes and tubing.
[3] Source: Annual Bulletin of Steel Statistics for Europe, United Nations Economic Commission of Europe (Geneva).
[4] Hot-rolled products only.
[5] Including cold-reduced hoop and strip.

Remarque générale.
Produits plats laminés à chaud, de moins de 500 mm de largeur et normalement livrés en rouleaux. Cette rubrique comprend les bandes pour la fabrication des tubes soudés. (CTCI 67500-2).

[1] Expéditions.
[2] Y compris les conduits et tubes soudés.
[3] Source: Bulletin annuel de statistiques de l'acier pour l'Europe, Commission économique des Nations Unies pour l'Europe (Genève).
[4] Produits laminés à chaud seulement.
[5] Y compris les feuillards laminés à froid.

Railway track material – Matériel de voie

Unit : Thousand metric tons | Unité : Milliers de tonnes métriques

Country or area	1976	1977	1978	1979	1980	1981	1982	1983	1984	1985	Pays ou zone
Africa	**289**	**269**	**254**	**199**	**268**	**250**	**257**	**215**	**201**	**168**	**Afrique**
South Africa[1]	289	269	254	199	268	250	257	215	201	168	Afrique du Sud[1]
America, North	**1 981**	**1 774**	**1 553**	**1 894**	**1 756**	**1 601**	**780**	**786**	**1 110**	**767**	**Amérique du Nord**
Canada[2]	426	386	328	417	445	469	* 169	50	69	49	Canada[2]
United States[3]	1 555	1 388	1 225	1 477	1 311	1 132	611	736	1 041	718	Etats-Unis[3]
America, South	**82**	**71**	**29**	**109**	**123**	**67**	**108**	**83**	**79**	**114**	**Amérique du Sud**
Brazil	82	71	29	109	123	67	108	83	79	114	Brésil
Asia	**941**	**1 219**	**1 333**	**1 311**	**1 335**	**1 351**	**1 427**	**1 532**	**1 783**	**1 733**	**Asie**
China	...	...	...	...	816	893	901	1 059	1 141	1 121	Chine
Japan	377	590	640	548	504	439	500	442	613	592	Japon
Philippines[3]	7	15	...	...	...	...	...	...	...	...	Philippines[3]
Turkey	[2] 19	# 6	5	6	4	8	15	20	18	9	Turquie
Europe	**2 817**	**2 534**	**2 481**	**2 650**	**2 439**	**2 364**	**2 242**	**2 050**	**2 170**	**2 236**	**Europe**
EEC	***1 555***	***1 322***	***1 301***	***1 530***	***1 368***	***1 349***	***1 250***	***1 112***	***1 209***	***1 285***	***CEE***
France	468	343	314	383	396	321	319	244	267	252	France
Germany, Fed. Rep.	519	414	440	531	456	477	380	310	336	397	Allemagne, Rép. féd.
Italy	234	199	197	222	217	216	240	234	280	278	Italie
Luxembourg	108	104	117	137	123	116	102	64	99	132	Luxembourg
United Kingdom[4]	226	262	233	257	176	219	209	260	227	226	Royaume-Uni[4]
EFTA	***222***	***195***	***212***	***225***	***193***	***195***	***221***	***180***	***225***	***198***	***AELE***
Austria	141	127	137	161	124	122	138	116	159	142	Autriche
Finland	11	12	9	11	12	13	10	8	18	18	Finlande
Norway[2]	0	0	0	1	0	0	0	0	0	0	Norvège[2]
Portugal	3	0	7	0	0	2	7	2	0	0	Portugal
Sweden	67	56	59	52	57	58	* 66	* 54	48	38	Suède
East Europe	***875***	***818***	***790***	***690***	***709***	***629***	***614***	***597***	***615***	***607***	***Europe de l'est***
Czechoslovakia[5]	156	194	200	197	198	218	209	212	217	213	Tchécoslovaquie[5]
German Dem. Rep.	91	90	93	82	90	79	85	62	78	72	Rép. dém. allemande
Hungary	74	73	77	69	72	71	73	69	65	71	Hongrie
Poland	470	386	348	262	262	194	176	180	188	200	Pologne
Romania[1 2]	84	75	72	80	87	67	71	74	67	51	Roumanie[1 2]
Other Europe	***165***	***199***	***178***	***205***	***169***	***191***	***157***	***161***	***121***	***146***	***Autre Europe***
Spain	71	100	82	80	94	122	99	109	56	56	Espagne
Yugoslavia	94	99	96	125	75	69	58	52	65	90	Yougoslavie
USSR	**3 940**	**3 944**	**4 134**	**3 969**	**4 132**	**3 904**	**4 131**	**4 056**	**4 285**	**4 367**	**URSS**
Ukrainian SSR	*1 885*	*1 895*	*1 901*	*1 805*	*1 751*	*1 580*	*1 674*	*1 463*	*1 605*	*1 643*	*RSS d'Ukraine*
Oceania	**150**	**141**	**131**	**174**	**184**	**175**	**131**	**134**	**113**	**110**	**Océanie**
Australia[6]	150	141	131	174	184	175	131	...	113	110	Australie[6]
Total	**10 200**	**9 952**	**9 915**	**10 306**	**10 237**	**9 712**	**9 076**	**8 856**	**9 741**	**9 495**	**Total**

General note.
Hot-rolled steel products for the construction of railway and tramway track, that is, rails (including check-rails and rack rails), sleepers and products used as accessories for track construction, such as fishplates, soleplates, bedplates etc. This item does not include fabricated steel products for railway and tramway track construction, such as fishplates, soleplates, bedplates etc. This item does not include fabricated steel products for railway and tramway track construction, such as the following: (a) assembled track, turntables, platform buffers and loading gauges, (b) switch blades, crossings (or frogs), crossing pieces and point rods, and (c) screws, bolts, nuts, rivets and spikes used for fixing track construction materials. (SITC 6761 and part of SITC 6762).

[1] Rails only.

Remarque générale.
Produits sidérurgiques laminés à chaud utilisés pour la construction de voies ferrées, rails (y compris les contre-rails et les crémaillères), traverses et produits utilisés accessoirement pour la construction de voies ferrées (éclisses, plaques de serrage, plaques d'écartement etc.). Cette rubrique ne comprend pas les articles manufacturés en acier pour la construction de voies ferrées tels que:(a) voies assemblées, plaques tournantes, butoirs et gabarits, (b) aiguilles, pointes de coeur, croisements et changements de voies et tringles d'aiguillages, (c) tire-fonds, boulons, écrous, rivets, clous etc., utilisés pour fixer les éléments servant à la construction des voies ferrées. (CTCI 6761 et partie de CTCI 6762).

[1] Rails seulement.

[2] Source: Annual Bulletin of Steel Statistics for Europe, United Nations Economic Commission of Europe (Geneva).
[3] Shipments.
[4] Deliveries.
[5] Heavy rails and tram rails only.
[6] Twelve months ending 30 June of year stated.

[2] Source: Bulletin annuel de statistiques de l'acier pour l'Europe, Commission économique des Nations Unies pour l'Europe (Genève).
[3] Expéditions.
[4] Livraisons.
[5] Rails lourds et rails à ornière seulement.
[6] Période de douze mois finissant le 30 juin de l'année indiquée.

Wire, plain – Fil ordinaire

Unit : Thousand metric tons

Unité : Milliers de tonnes métriques

Country or area	1976	1977	1978	1979	1980	1981	1982	1983	1984	1985	Pays ou zone
Africa	**152**	**206**	**220**	**248**	**301**	**275**	**254**	**274**	**302**	**288**	**Afrique**
Egypt	23	26	29	31	36	36	42	...	...	...	Egypte
Mozambique	...	...	...	2	1	2	2	1	1	...	Mozambique
South Africa	127	...	...	215	* 264	237	210	229	254	237	Afrique du Sud
America, North	**3 108**	**3 094**	**3 326**	**3 361**	**2 681**	**2 435**	**2 053**	**2 194**	**2 101**	**2 009**	**Amérique du Nord**
Canada[1]	454	484	508	540	490	...	258	240	267	...	Canada[1]
El Salvador	6	2	1	4	6	2	0	1	...	...	El Salvador
Mexico	417	430	540	596	581	531	608	720	724	679	Mexique
United States[2]	2 231	2 178	2 277	2 221	1 604	1 537	1 187	1 233	1 109	1 109	Etats–Unis[2]
America, South	**1 208**	**597**	**695**	**738**	**1 049**	**885**	**811**	**890**	**911**	**870**	**Amérique du Sud**
Brazil	1 153	556	652	[3] 644	870	726	...	...	...	...	Brésil
Chile	3	10	6	...	...	...	...	...	...	...	Chili
Venezuela[4]	52	31	37	88	173	153	158	271	326	...	Venezuela[4]
Asia	**7 444**	**7 245**	**7 088**	**6 989**	**6 900**	**6 821**	**6 839**	**6 800**	**7 013**	**7 002**	**Asie**
China	...	...	...	...	4 432	4 629	...	...	...	...	Chine
Hong Kong	0	0	0	0	0	...	7	45	...	...	Hong–kong
Indonesia	58	63	63	48	160	76	102	50	78	...	Indonésie
Japan	2 724	2 484	2 290	2 231	2 128	1 905	2 022	1 995	2 169	2 142	Japon
Korea, Republic of	62	89	130	103	105	117	103	105	124	122	Corée, République de
Philippines[2]	14	25	...	...	...	...	...	...	...	...	Philippines[2]
Turkey[1]	55	53	55	57	...	...	...	...	...	...	Turquie[1]
Europe	**5 553**	**5 444**	**5 588**	**6 091**	**6 026**	**5 584**	**5 469**	**5 471**	**5 382**	**5 374**	**Europe**
EEC	***2 721***	***2 617***	***2 749***	***2 929***	***2 814***	***2 653***	***2 521***	***2 552***	***2 502***	***2 615***	***CEE***
France[5]	486	478	494	507	486	460	444	468	480	438	France[5]
Germany, Fed. Rep.	1 902	1 786	1 881	2 042	1 997	1 852	1 741	1 725	1 674	1 810	Allemagne, Rép. féd.
Greece[6]	65	75	77	91	117	117	127	128	116	...	Grèce[6]
Netherlands[7]	268	278	297	289	214	224	209	231	232	225	Pays–Bas[7]
EFTA	***509***	***486***	***510***	***529***	***536***	***455***	***454***	***471***	***489***	***474***	***AELE***
Austria	185	174	193	200	195	125	129	127	141	140	Autriche
Finland	8	13	27	25	23	24	22	28	30	27	Finlande
Norway	...	46	43	...	...	...	...	...	...	...	Norvège
Portugal	62	66	72	76	79	84	85	73	67	62	Portugal
Sweden[8]	209	187	175	183	194	177	173	198	206	200	Suède[8]
East Europe	***1 929***	***1 936***	***1 920***	***2 058***	***2 041***	***1 933***	***1 885***	***1 874***	***1 917***	***1 816***	***Europe de l'est***
Czechoslovakia	515	518	544	568	535	541	564	566	577	576	Tchécoslovaquie
Hungary	181	186	189	203	209	199	203	197	200	199	Hongrie
Poland[1,9]	623	614	582	591	578	487	428	446	444	437	Pologne[1,9]
Romania[1]	610	618	605	696	719	706	690	665	696	604	Roumanie[1]
Other Europe	***394***	***405***	***409***	***575***	***635***	***543***	***609***	***574***	***474***	***469***	***Autre Europe***
Spain	162	167	133	257	283	236	255	229	* 154	* 137	Espagne
Yugoslavia	232	238	276	318	352	307	354	345	320	332	Yougoslavie
Oceania	**257**	**429**	**419**	**450**	**510**	**483**	**480**	**373**	**426**	**480**	**Océanie**
Australia[10]	257	429	419	450	510	483	480	373	426	...	Australie[10]
Total	**17 721**	**17 015**	**17 336**	**17 877**	**17 466**	**16 483**	**15 906**	**16 001**	**16 134**	**16 024**	**Total**

General note.
A cold–drawn steel product of solid section of any cross–sectional shape, of which no cross–sectional dimension exceeds 13 mm, produced from wire rod by drawing it through a die. Fabricated wire products are excluded. (SITC 67700–0).

Remarque générale.
Produit sidérurgique de section pleine, étiré ou tréfilé à froid, dont la coupe transversale, de forme quelconque, n'excède pas 13 mm dans sa plus grande dimension, obtenu par étirage du fil machine à travers une filière. Cette rubrique ne comprend pas les ouvrages en fil. (CTCI 67700–0).

[1] Source: Annual Bulletin of Steel Statistics for Europe, United Nations Economic Commission of Europe (Geneva).
[2] Shipments.

[1] Source: Bulletin annuel de statistiques de l'acier pour l'Europe, Commission économique des Nations Unies pour l'Europe (Genève).
[2] Expéditions.

[3] Production by establishments employing 5 or more persons.
[4] Source: Instituto Latino Americano del Fierro y el Acero, (Santiago).
[5] Deliveries.
[6] Black wire and wire coated with zinc.
[7] Production by wire industry only.
[8] Excluding wire of iron or steel covered metal.
[9] Production for sale only.
[10] Twelve months ending 30 June of year stated.

[3] Production des établissements occupant 5 personnes ou plus.
[4] Source: Instituto Latino Americano del Fierro y el Acero, (Santiago).
[5] Livraisons.
[6] Fils noirs et fils galvanisés.
[7] Production de l'industrie du fil métallique seulement.
[8] Non compris les fils métalliques recouverts de fer ou d'acier.
[9] Production destinée à la vente seulement.
[10] Période de douze mois finissant le 30 juin de l'année indiquée.

Tubes, seamless – Tubes sans soudure

Unit : Thousand metric tons — Unité : Milliers de tonnes métriques

Country or area	1976	1977	1978	1979	1980	1981	1982	1983	1984	1985	Pays ou zone
America, North	**2 825**	**3 396**	**3 778**	**3 695**	**4 078**	**4 595**	**2 001**	**1 080**	**1 826**	**1 819**	**Amérique du Nord**
Cuba	...	...	...	5	4	0	0	0	0	0	Cuba
Mexico	225	220	252	255	241	251	265	233	324	302	Mexique
United States[1]	2 594	3 171	3 522	3 435	3 833	4 344	1 736	847	1 502	1 517	Etats–Unis[1]
America, South	**445**	**485**	**559**	**592**	**664**	**757**	**710**	**622**	**749**	**871**	**Amérique du Sud**
Argentina	152	214	267	261	283	309	303	315	311	367	Argentine
Brazil	203	197	220	260	309	357	300	209	340	385	Brésil
Venezuela[2]	90	74	72	71	72	91	107	98	98	119	Venezuela[2]
Asia	**3 181**	**3 642**	**4 927**	**5 385**	**5 977**	**6 739**	**6 279**	**5 838**	**7 267**	**7 460**	**Asie**
China	...	...	...	...	919	919	1 012	1 151	1 277	1 392	Chine
India	33	17	31	30	28	36	45	51	46	46	Inde
Japan	2 145	2 381	3 258	3 468	3 894	4 324	3 893	2 959	4 031	4 082	Japon
Korea, Republic of	514	668	946	1 090	1 092	1 415	1 282	1 633	1 864	1 889	Corée, République de
Malaysia	10	14	18	21	22	23	25	22	...	...	Malaisie
Philippines[1]	31	12	...	...	...	...	...	...	...	...	Philippines[1]
Europe	**6 307**	**6 331**	**6 890**	**6 822**	**6 783**	**7 659**	**6 912**	**6 827**	**7 089**	**7 175**	**Europe**
EEC	***3 566***	***3 402***	***3 888***	***3 740***	***3 727***	***4 524***	***3 912***	***3 756***	***4 209***	***4 332***	***CEE***
Belgium	49	37	86	53	60	109	124	156	254	240	Belgique
France[3]	582	526	588	603	646	740	662	912	...	...	France[3]
Germany, Fed. Rep.	1 616	1 564	1 832	1 759	1 786	2 155	1 655	1 559	1 821	1 946	Allemagne, Rép. féd.
Italy	806	773	836	824	880	1 093	1 010	753	871	851	Italie
United Kingdom[4]	513	502	546	501	355	427	461	376	419	409	Royaume–Uni[4]
EFTA	***206***	***188***	***184***	***221***	***190***	***205***	***186***	***148***	***163***	***163***	***AELE***
Finland	...	...	...	...	...	3	3	3	3	3	Finlande
Sweden[5]	203	185	181	218	187	202	* 183	* 145	* 160	* 160	Suède[5]
East Europe	***2 362***	***2 434***	***2 460***	***2 476***	***2 447***	***2 443***	***2 358***	***2 400***	***2 496***	***2 440***	***Europe de l'est***
Bulgaria	71	78	80	78	76	79	70	72	69	71	Bulgarie
Czechoslovakia	944	958	938	958	963	953	945	940	941	959	Tchécoslovaquie
Hungary	184	186	188	184	167	167	155	169	172	174	Hongrie
Poland	492	521	518	509	498	461	423	449	455	410	Pologne
Romania[6]	671	691	736	747	743	783	765	770	859	826	Roumanie[6]
Other Europe	***173***	***307***	***358***	***385***	***419***	***487***	***456***	***523***	***221***	***240***	***Autre Europe***
Spain	51	# 204	241	259	288	342	308	401	* 79	* 100	Espagne
Yugoslavia	122	103	117	126	131	145	148	122	142	140	Yougoslavie
USSR	**6 741**	**6 902**	**7 051**	**7 197**	**7 234**	**7 382**	**7 347**	**7 547**	**7 679**	**7 794**	**URSS**
Ukrainian SSR	*2 840*	*2 803*	*2 847*	*2 937*	*2 937*	*3 012*	...	...	...	...	*RSS d'Ukraine*
Total	**19 499**	**20 756**	**23 205**	**23 691**	**24 736**	**27 132**	**23 249**	**21 914**	**24 610**	**25 119**	**Total**

General note.
Steel tubes produced from an ingot or a semi–manufactured product by a number of different methods involving piercing followed by a series of finishing operations. (SITC 67820–0).

[1] Shipments.
[2] Source: Instituto Latino Americano del Fierro y el Acero, (Santiago).
[3] Deliveries.
[4] Deliveries from home production. Including all types of alloy tubes.
[5] Primary production of hot–rolled seamless tubes.
[6] Source: Annual Bulletin of Steel Statistics for Europe, United Nations Economic Commission of Europe (Geneva).

Remarque générale.
Tubes d'acier fabriqués à partir d'un lingot ou demi–produit par divers procédés comprenant un perçage suivi d'une série d'opérations de finition. (CTCI 67820–0).

[1] Expéditions.
[2] Source: Instituto Latino Americano del Fierro y el Acero , (Santiago).
[3] Livraisons.
[4] Production nationale. Y compris les tubes en alliage de toutes catégories.
[5] Production primaire de tubes sans soudure laminés à chaud.
[6] Source: Bulletin annuel de statistiques de l'acier pour l'Europe, Commission économique des Nations Unies pour l'Europe (Genève).

Tubes, welded – Tubes soudés

Unit : Thousand metric tons — Unité : Milliers de tonnes métriques

Country or area	1976	1977	1978	1979	1980	1981	1982	1983	1984	1985	Pays ou zone
Africa	**486**	**515**	**653**	**727**	**737**	**699**	**671**	**612**	**620**	**694**	**Afrique**
Algeria	118	126	209	212	146	147	148	...	...	...	Algérie
Egypt	32	37	...	...	...	...	...	...	...	...	Egypte
South Africa	336	352	409	480	556	517	488	410	415	487	Afrique du Sud
America, North	**4 532**	**5 043**	**5 852**	**6 015**	**6 483**	**7 398**	**4 559**	**3 482**	**3 227**	**4 015**	**Amérique du Nord**
Canada[1 2 3]	1 186	1 104	1 290	1 412	1 459	1 852	1 226	995	394	1 460	Canada[1 2 3]
Cuba	...	...	0	1	1	1	0	0	0	0	Cuba
Mexico	255	314	465	559	604	558	509	392	456	355	Mexique
United States[2]	3 090	3 624	4 097	4 043	4 419	4 987	2 824	2 095	2 377	2 200	Etats-Unis[2]
America, South	**798**	**581**	**736**	**834**	**943**	**974**	**979**	**1 026**	**1 075**	**1 119**	**Amérique du Sud**
Argentina	238	199	174	224	243	221	187	176	170	158	Argentine
Brazil	560	380	557	[4] 603	690	744	...	...	...	...	Brésil
Ecuador	...	...	5	...	10	9	13	17	...	...	Equateur
Asia	**7 590**	**7 668**	**8 327**	**9 294**	**9 154**	**9 590**	**9 165**	**7 733**	**8 495**	**9 123**	**Asie**
Cyprus	0	0	0	2	3	1	4	6	7	5	Chypre
India[5]	450	540	551	567	546	...	...	...	...	...	Inde[5]
Japan	7 050	7 004	7 648	8 578	8 386	8 773	8 296	6 778	7 488	8 142	Japon
Korea, Republic of	32	48	43	63	76	75	77	99	124	108	Corée, République de
Malaysia	58	76	85	84	143	145	170	210	214	185	Malaisie
Europe	**10 274**	**10 139**	**11 275**	**11 533**	**11 203**	**11 822**	**11 083**	**10 943**	**11 658**	**11 677**	**Europe**
EEC	***7 343***	***6 632***	***7 398***	***7 510***	***7 182***	***7 837***	***7 202***	***7 040***	***8 133***	***8 017***	***CEE***
Belgium	202	163	199	192	166	117	69	52	60	65	Belgique
France[6]	1 367	1 291	1 515	1 527	1 455	1 409	1 229	863	[1] 1 739	[1] 1 750	France[6]
Germany, Fed. Rep.[7]	1 975	1 761	2 109	2 261	2 077	2 434	2 168	2 357	2 373	2 618	Allemagne, Rép. féd.[7]
Greece[8]	213	224	294	275	263	320	281	241	308	...	Grèce[8]
Italy	2 599	2 271	2 336	2 260	2 525	2 709	2 537	2 549	2 575	2 232	Italie
Luxembourg	93	111	118	122	113	124	120	147	147	143	Luxembourg
United Kingdom	894	811	827	873	583	724	798	831	931	903	Royaume-Uni
EFTA	***463***	***515***	***564***	***570***	***651***	***662***	***637***	***620***	***623***	***679***	***AELE***
Austria[1]	91	87	104	106	101	95	92	80	85	68	Autriche[1]
Finland	26	89	125	120	197	191	169	177	181	200	Finlande
Portugal	...	...	71	71	76	76	85	66	48	62	Portugal
Sweden[9]	107	99	117	118	127	...	...	...	...	...	Suède[9]
Switzerland[1 3]	157	160	147	155	150	169	154	154	160	194	Suisse[1 3]
East Europe	***1 926***	***2 046***	***2 163***	***2 252***	***2 218***	***2 107***	***2 073***	***2 076***	***2 109***	***2 187***	***Europe de l'est***
Bulgaria	109	113	145	164	175	190	205	211	224	215	Bulgarie
Czechoslovakia	517	525	572	578	580	576	583	581	580	595	Tchécoslovaquie
Hungary	115	116	117	115	107	114	111	97	103	108	Hongrie
Poland	643	663	646	642	635	581	517	546	554	582	Pologne
Romania[3]	542	629	683	753	721	646	657	641	648	687	Roumanie[3]
Other Europe	***542***	***946***	***1 150***	***1 201***	***1 152***	***1 216***	***1 171***	***1 207***	***793***	***794***	***Autre Europe***
Spain	245	# 717	743	756	724	758	698	788	* 280	* 271	Espagne
Yugoslavia	297	229	407	445	428	458	473	419	513	523	Yougoslavie
USSR	**10 066**	**10 121**	**10 502**	**10 988**	**10 935**	**10 886**	**10 597**	**11 185**	**11 204**	**11 560**	**URSS**
Ukrainian SSR	*3 543*	*3 496*	*3 178*	*3 591*	*3 409*	*3 580*	...	...	...	...	*RSS d'Ukraine*
Oceania	**407**	**383**	**413**	**456**	**527**	**553**	**471**	**595**	**462**	**563**	**Océanie**
Australia[10 11]	407	383	413	456	527	553	471	595	462	...	Australie[10 11]
Total	**34 153**	**34 450**	**37 758**	**39 846**	**39 981**	**41 922**	**37 524**	**35 576**	**36 740**	**38 752**	**Total**

General note.
Steel tubes generally produced from strip or sheets by a number of different processes involving welding, which may be followed by a cold-drawing finishing operation. (SITC 67830-0).

Remarque générale.
Tubes d'acier fabriqués généralement à partir de bandes ou de tôles par divers procédés comprenant la soudure et, éventuellement, une opération ultérieure de finition par étirage à froid. (CTCI 67830-0).

For footnotes, see end of table.

Voir la fin du tableau pour les notes.

1 Including seamless tubes.
2 Shipments.
3 Source: Annual Bulletin of Steel Statistics for Europe, United Nations Economic Commission of Europe (Geneva).
4 Production by establishments employing 5 or more persons.
5 Production by large and medium scale establishments only.
6 Deliveries.
7 Excluding welded precision tubes.
8 Including seamless tubes and iron pipes of all kinds.
9 Including welded tubes of stainless steel.
10 Twelve months ending 30 June of year stated.
11 Excluding seamless tubes.

1 Y compris les tubes sans soudure.
2 Expéditions.
3 Source: Bulletin annuel de statistiques de l'acier pour l'Europe, Commission économique des Nations Unies pour l'Europe (Genève).
4 Production des établissements occupant 5 personnes ou plus.
5 Production des grandes et moyennes entreprises seulement.
6 Livraisons.
7 Non compris les tuyaux de précision soudés.
8 Y compris les tubes sans soudure et tuyaux en fonte de toutes sortes.
9 Y compris les tubes soudés en acier inoxydable.
10 Période de douze mois finissant le 30 juin de l'année indiquée.
11 Non compris les tubes sans soudure.

Steel castings in the rough state – Moulages d'acier non usinés

Unit : Thousand metric tons | Unité : Milliers de tonnes métriques

Country or area	1976	1977	1978	1979	1980	1981	1982	1983	1984	1985	Pays ou zone
Africa	**177**	**218**	**196**	**138**	**146**	**130**	**137**	**119**	**139**	**128**	**Afrique**
South Africa	140	* 184	* 161	* 103	* 112	101	112	94	112	101	Afrique du Sud
Zambia	...	# 34	35	35	34	29	25	25	27	27	Zambie
America, North	**1 833**	**1 775**	**1 924**	**2 098**	**1 958**	**1 899**	**1 213**	**1 013**	**1 178**	**1 254**	**Amérique du Nord**
Cuba	...	...	...	...	...	317	290	352	325	401	Cuba
United States[1]	1 637	1 559	1 688	1 841	1 681	1 582	923	661	853	853	Etats–Unis[1]
Asia	**795**	**791**	**840**	**902**	**1 023**	**1 039**	**946**	**908**	**985**	**983**	**Asie**
India[2]	65	68	76	72	...	...	...	...	...	...	Inde[2]
Japan	621	612	623	682	733	683	613	519	546	538	Japon
Korea, Republic of	106	107	137	144	216	282	259	315	365	371	Corée, République de
Philippines[1]	3	4	...	...	...	...	...	...	...	...	Philippines[1]
Europe	**2 634**	**2 592**	**2 536**	**2 574**	**2 618**	**2 472**	**2 353**	**2 207**	**2 224**	**2 237**	**Europe**
EEC	***970***	***887***	***824***	***851***	***849***	***766***	***701***	***570***	***569***	***580***	***CEE***
Belgium	26	19	15	8	13	10	0	0	0	0	Belgique
Denmark[3]	10	7	7	7	6	9	9	5	0	0	Danemark[3]
France	232	201	194	206	218	202	180	142	136	135	France
Germany, Fed. Rep.	306	275	268	301	294	281	252	207	218	228	Allemagne, Rép. féd.
Italy	128	131	130	134	140	115	103	100	87	94	Italie
Luxembourg	3	2	2	0	0	0	0	0	0	0	Luxembourg
Netherlands	10	6	4	3	4	4	4	4	4	...	Pays–Bas
United Kingdom	255	246	204	192	174	145	153	112	124	121	Royaume–Uni
EFTA	***120***	***117***	***99***	***107***	***118***	***121***	***107***	***100***	***111***	***114***	***AELE***
Austria	26	* 23	21	24	27	31	[3] 23	[3] 17	[3] 21	[3] 25	Autriche
Finland	51	56	49	51	59	58	57	55	59	...	Finlande
Norway[3]	6	* 10	4	6	8	8	5	4	5	4	Norvège[3]
Sweden	26	16	15	15	15	13	* 11	* 13	15	15	Suède
Switzerland*	11	12	10	...	9	...	...	...	...	...	Suisse*
East Europe	***1 365***	***1 406***	***1 424***	***1 421***	***1 437***	***1 372***	***1 340***	***1 333***	***1 335***	***1 335***	***Europe de l'est***
Bulgaria	52	60	67	68	69	69	73	78	85	88	Bulgarie
Czechoslovakia	356	359	361	363	367	364	358	342	328	320	Tchécoslovaquie
German Dem. Rep.	238	242	240	234	235	238	236	235	230	230	Rép. dém. allemande
Hungary	60	59	55	54	54	53	50	49	45	44	Hongrie
Poland	361	369	374	365	355	291	266	267	258	275	Pologne
Romania[3]	298	317	327	337	357	357	357	362	389	378	Roumanie[3]
Other Europe	***179***	***182***	***189***	***195***	***214***	***213***	***205***	***204***	***209***	***208***	***Autre Europe***
Spain	120	117	122	125	141	136	133	119	109	106	Espagne
Yugoslavia	59	65	67	70	73	77	72	85	100	102	Yougoslavie
Total	**5 439**	**5 376**	**5 496**	**5 711**	**5 744**	**5 539**	**4 648**	**4 246**	**4 525**	**4 602**	**Total**

General note.
Steel castings at the black stage, after fettling. (SITC 67920–0).

Remarque générale.
Moulages d'acier noirs après ébarbage. (CTCI 67920–0).

[1] Shipments.
[2] Production by large and medium scale establishments only.
[3] Source: Annual Bulletin of Steel Statistics for Europe, United Nations Economic Commission of Europe (Geneva).

[1] Expéditions.
[2] Production des grandes et moyennes entreprises seulement.
[3] Source: Bulletin annuel de statistiques de l'acier pour l'Europe, Commission économique des Nations Unies pour l'Europe (Genève).

Steel forgings – Pièces de forge

Unit : Thousand metric tons | Unité : Milliers de tonnes métriques

Country or area	1976	1977	1978	1979	1980	1981	1982	1983	1984	1985	Pays ou zone
America, North	**1 730**	**1 977**	**2 116**	**2 269**	**1 804**	**2 111**	**2 155**	**2 199**	**2 244**	**2 288**	**Amérique du Nord**
Cuba	1	1	1	1	1	1	2	2	3	3	Cuba
United States[1]	1 729	1 976	2 115	2 268	1 803	...	...	...	...	...	Etats-Unis[1]
Asia	**725**	**705**	**704**	**862**	**914**	**914**	**824**	**783**	**837**	**825**	**Asie**
India[2]	96	95	98	119	141	158	156	169	152	156	Inde[2]
Japan	590	568	565	701	732	715	627	573	644	628	Japon
Korea, Republic of	36	...	...	...	...	...	...	...	...	...	Corée, République de
Philippines[1]	0	2	...	...	...	...	...	...	...	...	Philippines[1]
Turkey[3]	3	4	4	5	...	...	...	...	...	...	Turquie[3]
Europe	**3 957**	**4 090**	**3 998**	**4 247**	**4 407**	**4 220**	**4 081**	**3 902**	**3 795**	**3 903**	**Europe**
EEC	***995***	***1 104***	***932***	***1 034***	***1 116***	***1 066***	***989***	***831***	***649***	***721***	***CEE***
Belgium	6	11	14	14	15	8	4	1	0	0	Belgique
Denmark[3]	3	0	0	0	0	3	4	0	0	0	Danemark[3]
France[4]	122	150	# 22	...	...	...	...	...	...	...	France[4]
Germany, Fed. Rep.	289	292	299	303	320	324	305	244	259	282	Allemagne, Rép. féd.
Italy	442	538	501	538	616	568	511	435	239	304	Italie
Luxembourg	12	10	* 3	0	0	0	0	0	0	0	Luxembourg
United Kingdom[5]	121	103	93	81	67	65	67	53	53	...	Royaume-Uni[5]
EFTA	***204***	***195***	***186***	***216***	***206***	***188***	***200***	***197***	***204***	***254***	***AELE***
Austria	82	89	88	92	83	71	72	56	56	68	Autriche
Finland	4	4	5	5	7	4	5	4	3	1	Finlande
Sweden[6]	93	83	78	101	96	103	* 110	124	133	144	Suède[6]
Switzerland[3]	25	19	15	18	20	10	13	13	12	41	Suisse[3]
East Europe	***2 597***	***2 633***	***2 722***	***2 801***	***2 835***	***2 787***	***2 709***	***2 711***	***2 775***	***2 762***	***Europe de l'est***
Czechoslovakia	629	630	638	647	659	690	668	638	627	616	Tchécoslovaquie
German Dem. Rep.	504	495	503	513	519	524	515	517	531	529	Rép. dém. allemande
Hungary	143	141	142	141	139	134	132	124	127	130	Hongrie
Poland	626	656	669	661	648	564	524	531	526	528	Pologne
Romania[3]	695	711	770	839	870	875	870	901	964	959	Roumanie[3]
Other Europe	***161***	***158***	***158***	***196***	***250***	***179***	***183***	***163***	***167***	***166***	***Autre Europe***
Spain	84	76	71	92	146	72	76	57	* 49	* 44	Espagne
Yugoslavia	77	82	87	104	104	107	107	106	...	...	Yougoslavie
USSR	**1 286**	**1 332**	**1 311**	**1 340**	**1 361**	**1 362**	**1 353**	**1 395**	**1 432**	**1 446**	**URSS**
Ukrainian SSR	*280*	*281*	*299*	*313*	*330*	*321*	*319*	*348*	*352*	*358*	*RSS d'Ukraine*
Oceania	**25**	**27**	**25**	**27**	**33**	**82**	**90**	**75**	**79**	**97**	**Océanie**
Australia	25	27	25	27	33	82	90	75	79	...	Australie
Total	**7 723**	**8 131**	**8 154**	**8 745**	**8 519**	**8 689**	**8 503**	**8 354**	**8 386**	**8 559**	**Total**

General note.
Finished steel products produced by forging (including drop forging), hammering and pressing operations. (SITC 67930-0).

1 Shipments.
2 Production by large and medium scale establishments only.
3 Source: Annual Bulletin of Steel Statistics for Europe, United Nations Economic Commission of Europe (Geneva).
4 Deliveries.
5 Deliveries from home production. Excluding drop forgings.
6 Including forged bars.

Remarque générale.
Produits en acier obtenus par forgeage (y compris l'estampage), travail au marteau ou formage. (CTCI 67930-0).

1 Expéditions.
2 Production des grandes et moyennes entreprises seulement.
3 Source: Bulletin annuel de statistiques de l'acier pour l'Europe, Commission économique des Nations Unies pour l'Europe (Genève).
4 Livraisons.
5 Production nationale. Estampages non compris.
6 Y compris les barres forgées.

Wheels, wheel centres, tires and axles – Roues, centres de roues, bandages et essieux

Unit : Thousand metric tons

Unité : Milliers de tonnes métriques

Country or area	1976	1977	1978	1979	1980	1981	1982	1983	1984	1985	Pays ou zone
America, North	**275**	**302**	**320**	**361**	**320**	**191**	**98**	**66**	**83**	**66**	**Amérique du Nord**
United States[1]	275	302	320	361	320	191	98	66	83	66	Etats–Unis[1]
Asia	**116**	**98**	**85**	**96**	**104**	**74**	**65**	**86**	**69**	**52**	**Asie**
Japan	116	98	85	96	104	74	65	86	69	52	Japon
Europe	**454**	**402**	**390**	**365**	**412**	**400**	**371**	**323**	**304**	**294**	**Europe**
EEC	***209***	***175***	***160***	***174***	***204***	***199***	***169***	***155***	***142***	***136***	***CEE***
Belgium	8	7	2	3	3	1	1	1	3	1	Belgique
France	13	10	10	11	11	11	7	4	7	5	France
Germany, Fed. Rep.	74	65	56	64	91	84	71	64	76	66	Allemagne, Rép. féd.
Italy[2]	41	36	35	39	47	44	42	47	39	37	Italie[2]
United Kingdom[3]	73	57	57	57	52	59	48	39	17	...	Royaume–Uni[3]
EFTA	***25***	***27***	***28***	***0***	***0***	***0***	***0***	***0***	***0***	***0***	***AELE***
Finland	25	27	28	0	0	0	0	0	0	0	Finlande
East Europe	***189***	***177***	***170***	***162***	***169***	***158***	***166***	***136***	***140***	***135***	***Europe de l'est***
Hungary	20	18	16	19	22	24	22	21	18	17	Hongrie
Poland	132	119	115	110	118	102	111	88	94	90	Pologne
Romania[2 4]	37	40	39	33	29	32	33	27	28	28	Roumanie[2 4]
Other Europe	***31***	***23***	***32***	***29***	***39***	***43***	***36***	***32***	***22***	***23***	***Autre Europe***
Spain	18	19	22	19	27	31	25	19	8	10	Espagne
Yugoslavia	13	4	10	10	12	12	11	13	14	13	Yougoslavie
USSR	**1 188**	**1 117**	**1 124**	**1 067**	**1 116**	**1 085**	**1 016**	**1 104**	**1 073**	**1 078**	**URSS**
Ukrainian SSR	*310*	*326*	*324*	*305*	*333*	*323*	*322*	*361*	*353*	*327*	*RSS d'Ukraine*
Total	**2 033**	**1 919**	**1 919**	**1 889**	**1 952**	**1 750**	**1 550**	**1 579**	**1 529**	**1 490**	**Total**

General note.
Wheels, parts of wheels and axles of steel for use in constructing vehicles running on rails. Although this item is classified under transport equipment in the SITC, the products concerned are generally made in steel works. (SITC 73170–1).

[1] Shipments.
[2] Excluding axles.
[3] Deliveries.
[4] Source: Annual Bulletin of Steel Statistics for Europe, United Nations Economic Commission of Europe (Geneva).

Remarque générale.
Roues, parties de roues et essieux en acier servant à la construction de véhicules se déplaçant sur rails. Bien que ces articles soient classés dans la CTCI parmi le matériel de transport, il convient de noter qu'ils sont généralement fabriqués dans les établissements sidérurgiques. (CTCI 73170–1).

[1] Expéditions.
[2] Non compris les essieux.
[3] Livraisons.
[4] Source: Bulletin annuel de statistiques de l'acier pour l'Europe, Commission économique des Nations Unies pour l'Europe (Genève).

Copper, blister and other unrefined – Cuivre blister et autre cuivre non affiné

Unit : Thousand metric tons

Unité : Milliers de tonnes métriques

Country or area	1976	1977	1978	1979	1980	1981	1982	1983	1984	1985	Pays ou zone
Africa	**1 358.5**	**1 374.9**	**1 317.1**	**1 211.7**	**1 309.4**	**1 295.7**	**1 330.2**	**1 338.0**	**1 254.9**	**1 189.7**	**Afrique**
Namibia[1]	36.1	53.4	45.9	42.7	40.0	39.7	49.8	54.2	46.4	43.3	Namibie[1]
South Africa[2 3]	168.0	188.4	189.4	182.3	185.8	185.4	191.8	192.3	178.7	159.7	Afrique du Sud[2 3]
Uganda	5.0	2.3	1.3	0.4	0.0	0.0	0.0	0.0	0.0	0.0	Ouganda
Zaire[1 2]	413.0	443.0	390.7	370.1	447.8	480.4	473.5	479.1	480.6	480.0	Zaïre[1 2]
Zambia[2]	712.9	659.8	655.6	584.8	609.5	560.1	* 584.7	* 581.2	* 525.0	* 482.3	Zambie[2]
Zimbabwe[3]	23.5	28.0	34.2	31.4	26.3	30.1	30.5	31.2	24.2	24.4	Zimbabwe[3]
America, North	**1 946.1**	**1 882.7**	**1 788.8**	**1 818.1**	**1 589.0**	**1 865.0**	**1 465.6**	**1 426.1**	**1 534.3**	**1 504.1**	**Amérique du Nord**
Canada	468.7	493.3	413.4	398.6	[3] 492.7	[3] 479.0	[3] 412.4	[3] 406.4	[3] 440.0	[3] 480.0	Canada
Mexico[2]	85.2	[1] 87.5	[1] 87.0	[1] 83.9	[1] 87.9	[1] 69.2	[1] 77.5	[1] 92.0	[1] 80.3	[1] 80.6	Mexique[2]
United States[2]	1 392.2	1 302.0	1 288.4	1 335.6	1 008.4	1 316.8	975.7	927.7	1 014.0	943.5	Etats-Unis[2]
America, South	**1 054.6**	**1 209.5**	**1 246.4**	**1 321.0**	**1 301.7**	**1 256.1**	**1 229.3**	**1 250.1**	**1 330.4**	**1 351.5**	**Amérique du Sud**
Brazil[3]	0.0	0.0	0.0	0.0	0.0	0.0	9.6	60.9	61.3	93.9	Brésil[3]
Chile[2]	856.3	888.4	927.4	949.6	953.1	953.8	896.5	893.3	938.0	* 903.6	Chili[2]
Peru[2]	198.3	[3] 321.1	[3] 319.0	[3] 371.4	[3] 348.6	[3] 302.3	[3] 323.2	[3] 295.9	[3] 331.1	[3] 354.0	Pérou[2]
Asia	**1 496.9**	**1 674.3**	**1 688.4**	**1 765.1**	**1 767.2**	**1 882.7**	**1 954.9**	**2 012.4**	**1 882.9**	**1 863.9**	**Asie**
China* [1]	150.0	150.0	170.0	170.0	175.0	190.0	205.0	195.0	210.0	225.0	Chine* [1]
India	24.7	23.5	19.5	19.7	24.6	23.1	33.2	34.2	40.5	33.6	Inde
Iran(Islamic Rep.of)* [1 4]	4.0	7.0	6.0	0.7	0.8	0.8	18.0	18.0	50.0	40.0	Iran(Rép.islamique)* [1 4]
Japan	1 002.1	1 127.0	1 131.2	1 173.7	1 155.5	1 224.2	1 285.4	1 336.4	1 180.5	1 163.3	Japon
Korea, D. P. Rp.* [1]	20.0	20.0	20.0	18.0	18.0	18.0	18.0	18.0	18.0	18.0	Corée, Rp. P. D.* [1]
Korea, Republic of[5]	30.9	42.9	52.4	63.1	72.9	108.0	110.8	123.3	129.1	140.1	Corée, République de[5]
Philippines	237.2	272.5	263.1	297.7	304.1	291.3	259.2	269.0	222.7	210.0	Philippines
Turkey[2]	27.9	31.5	26.2	22.2	16.3	27.3	25.4	18.5	32.0	34.0	Turquie[2]
Europe	**1 041.3**	**1 113.2**	**1 114.2**	**1 104.2**	**1 110.3**	**1 117.0**	**1 193.5**	**1 192.6**	**1 259.7**	**1 241.7**	**Europe**
EEC	***182.1***	***178.3***	***161.6***	***156.5***	***153.9***	***163.1***	***161.8***	***158.9***	***148.8***	***152.4***	***CEE***
Germany, Fed. Rep.	182.1	178.3	161.6	156.5	153.9	163.1	161.8	158.9	[6] 148.8	[6] 152.4	Allemagne, Rép. féd.
EFTA	***140.0***	***152.8***	***144.1***	***150.2***	***147.4***	***172.7***	***194.3***	***210.2***	***232.4***	***218.9***	***AELE***
Austria[5]	1.8	0.0	0.0	0.0	6.5	8.2	9.0	7.9	10.6	8.7	Autriche[5]
Finland	50.3	60.8	53.1	54.6	47.2	54.0	66.2	70.1	77.6	68.9	Finlande
Norway	23.4	26.6	20.1	27.3	33.7	32.0	24.4	25.7	36.8	37.8	Norvège
Portugal	2.5	3.8	3.9	3.7	3.7	4.7	4.8	4.7	4.7	3.3	Portugal
Sweden[3]	62.0	61.7	67.0	64.5	56.4	73.8	89.9	101.8	102.7	100.1	Suède[3]
East Europe	***434.7***	***470.9***	***500.9***	***509.3***	***533.5***	***494.6***	***531.5***	***537.8***	***575.0***	***560.7***	***Europe de l'est***
Albania[6]	8.5	9.7	9.5	9.7	11.5	10.0	12.0	12.0	12.6	13.0	Albanie[6]
Bulgaria[6]	57.0	57.0	57.0	58.0	59.0	62.0	62.0	60.0	70.0	70.0	Bulgarie[6]
Czechoslovakia	26.4	30.0	31.0	31.3	31.0	30.2	30.3	33.0	32.9	33.5	Tchécoslovaquie
German Dem. Rep.* [6]	16.0	18.0	16.0	18.0	16.0	16.0	17.0	17.0	14.0	14.0	Rép. dém. allemande* [6]
Hungary	5.2	3.8	1.0	2.3	2.1	2.4	2.6	2.8	3.0	3.3	Hongrie
Poland	281.2	311.0	347.6	348.8	373.3	334.6	367.5	372.8	404.4	390.9	Pologne
Romania	40.5	41.4	38.9	41.1	40.7	39.4	[6] 40.0	[6] 40.2	[6] 38.0	[6] 36.0	Roumanie
Other Europe	***284.4***	***311.3***	***307.7***	***288.3***	***275.5***	***286.6***	***305.9***	***285.7***	***303.5***	***309.7***	***Autre Europe***
Spain	120.3	145.4	# [3] 112.5	[3] 108.3	[3] 103.1	[3] 107.9	[3] 135.0	[3] 118.0	[3] 127.2	[3] 120.5	Espagne
Yugoslavia	164.1	165.8	195.2	180.0	172.4	178.7	170.9	167.7	176.3	189.2	Yougoslavie
USSR* [6]	**1 130.0**	**1 100.0**	**1 130.0**	**1 130.0**	**1 130.0**	**1 150.0**	**1 130.0**	**1 120.0**	**1 120.0**	**1 140.0**	**URSS* [6]**
Oceania	**174.2**	**171.4**	**167.8**	**173.4**	**163.6**	**167.8**	**177.3**	**172.2**	**182.1**	**167.7**	**Océanie**
Australia[7]	174.2	171.4	167.8	173.4	163.6	167.8	177.3	172.2	182.1	167.7	Australie[7]
Total	**8 201.6**	**8 526.1**	**8 452.8**	**8 523.6**	**8 371.2**	**8 734.2**	**8 480.9**	**8 511.3**	**8 564.4**	**8 458.6**	**Total**

General note.
Unwrought product obtained by smelting (black or blister copper), by precipitation or concentration (cement copper or copper precipitate) of ores and concentrates. (SITC 68211-0).

Remarque générale.
Produit non travaillé obtenu à partir des minerais ou concentrés par convertissage (cuivre noir ou cuivre blister), ou par précipitation ("cémentation") (cuivre de cément ou précipités de cuivre). (CTCI 68211-0).

For footnotes, see end of table.

Voir la fin du tableau pour les notes.

Copper, blister and other unrefined (continued) – Cuivre blister et autre cuivre non affiné (suite)

[1] Source: U. S. Bureau of Mines, (Washington, D. C.).
[2] Including some production at the refined stage.
[3] Source: World Metal Statistics, (London).
[4] Twelve months beginning 21 March of year stated.
[5] Production at the refined stage.
[6] Source: Metallgesellschaft Aktiengesellschaft, (Frankfurt).
[7] Twelve months ending 30 June of year stated.

[1] Source: U.S. Bureau of Mines, (Washington, D.C.).
[2] Y compris certaines productions au stade affiné.
[3] Source: World Metal Statistics, (Londres).
[4] Période de douze mois commençant le 21 mars de l'année indiquée.
[5] Données se rapportant au cuivre affiné.
[6] Source: Metallgesellschaft Aktiengesellschaft, (Francfort).
[7] Période de douze mois finissant le 30 juin de l'année indiquée.

Copper, refined, unwrought (total production) – Cuivre affiné, non travaillé (production totale)

Unit : Thousand metric tons | Unité : Milliers de tonnes métriques

Country or area	1976	1977	1978	1979	1980	1981	1982	1983	1984	1985	Pays ou zone
Africa	**897.5**	**928.4**	**918.1**	**849.5**	**926.1**	**881.3**	**926.7**	**982.5**	**919.2**	**867.9**	**Afrique**
South Africa[1]	95.6	145.9	152.5	152.3	147.9	144.8	142.5	157.7	148.4	143.3	Afrique du Sud[1]
Zaire[2]	66.0	98.7	102.8	103.2	144.0	151.3	175.0	227.2	224.8	226.8	Zaïre[2]
Zambia	694.6	649.0	629.0	564.4	607.2	560.6	584.4	576.0	523.5	477.4	Zambie
Zimbabwe	41.3	34.8	33.8	29.6	27.0	24.6	24.8	21.6	22.6	20.4	Zimbabwe
America, North	**2 322.7**	**2 288.9**	**2 390.4**	**2 494.2**	**2 321.1**	**2 575.5**	**2 093.5**	**2 128.9**	**2 074.7**	**2 001.6**	**Amérique du Nord**
Canada	510.5	508.9	446.3	397.3	505.2	476.7	337.8	464.3	504.3	499.6	Canada
Mexico	75.4	73.1	75.0	81.8	85.6	61.3	61.3	80.9	60.7	65.7	Mexique
United States	1 736.8	1 707.0	1 869.2	2 015.1	1 730.3	2 037.6	1 694.3	1 583.7	1 509.7	1 436.3	Etats-Unis
America, South	**802.9**	**909.9**	**979.5**	**1 065.2**	**1 104.3**	**1 020.9**	**1 010.4**	**990.4**	**1 069.3**	**1 028.8**	**Amérique du Sud**
Brazil	39.3	45.8	45.0	53.1	63.0	45.0	56.8	103.0	97.3	142.0	Brésil
Chile	632.0	676.0	749.1	781.8	810.7	775.5	729.1	692.7	753.0	* 660.0	Chili
Peru	131.7	[1] 188.1	[1] 185.4	[1] 230.3	[1] 230.6	[1] 200.4	[1] 224.5	[1] 194.7	[1] 219.0	[1] 226.8	Pérou
Asia	**1 220.0**	**1 323.8**	**1 368.0**	**1 403.4**	**1 449.4**	**1 528.7**	**1 567.8**	**1 618.4**	**1 478.8**	**1 569.1**	**Asie**
China* [2]	240.0	260.0	290.0	290.0	295.0	300.0	300.0	310.0	310.0	400.0	Chine* [2]
India	24.7	23.5	19.5	[2] 19.3	[2] 25.6	[2] 25.2	[2] 26.8	[2] 29.4	[2] 33.6	[2] 29.0	Inde
Iran(Islamic Rep.of)* [2 3]	7.0	7.0	6.0	3.0	0.8	1.0	1.0	10.0	10.0	12.0	Iran(Rép.islamique)* [2 3]
Japan[4]	864.4	933.7	959.1	983.7	1 014.3	1 050.1	1 075.0	1 091.9	935.2	936.0	Japon[4]
Korea, D. P. Rp.* [2]	25.0	25.0	25.0	22.0	22.0	22.0	22.0	22.0	22.0	22.0	Corée, Rp. P. D.* [2]
Korea, Republic of	30.9	42.9	52.4	63.1	72.9	108.0	110.8	123.3	129.1	140.1	Corée, République de
Turkey[1]	28.0	31.7	16.0	22.3	18.8	22.4	32.2	31.8	39.0	30.0	Turquie[1]
Europe	**2 006.6**	**2 131.4**	**2 017.2**	**2 034.4**	**2 101.1**	**1 974.7**	**2 073.2**	**2 086.4**	**2 070.7**	**2 159.1**	**Europe**
EEC	***1 131.8***	***1 190.8***	***1 062.8***	***1 092.5***	***1 120.8***	***1 030.2***	***1 094.6***	***1 072.2***	***1 034.3***	***1 103.3***	***CEE***
Belgium[5]	481.8	563.3	504.9	519.9	526.3	436.6	501.6	431.3	427.7	455.5	Belgique[5]
Denmark	0.0	0.1	0.0	0.0	0.0	0.0	0.0	0.0	0.0	0.0	Danemark
France	39.4	45.0	41.9	45.9	47.1	46.4	# 45.6	45.1	40.7	43.7	France
Germany, Fed. Rep.	446.6	440.2	372.9	389.3	373.8	387.4	393.6	420.3	378.8	414.4	Allemagne, Rép. féd.
Italy[6]	26.8	20.0	17.5	15.6	12.2	23.7	19.6	31.2	50.3	64.3	Italie[6]
United Kingdom	137.2	122.2	125.6	121.7	161.3	136.2	134.1	144.4	136.8	125.4	Royaume-Uni
EFTA	***156.8***	***162.2***	***159.7***	***162.7***	***170.8***	***164.2***	***168.3***	***186.0***	***193.1***	***196.2***	***AELE***
Austria	29.0	31.8	28.5	26.3	36.8	30.9	32.5	34.0	34.2	35.2	Autriche
Finland	38.1	42.8	42.7	43.0	40.5	33.8	48.0	55.4	57.3	58.8	Finlande
Norway	24.0	22.5	21.3	28.3	33.2	32.8	20.9	28.6	32.3	33.1	Norvège
Portugal	* 2.8	3.4	2.8	3.4	4.5	4.9	4.6	4.6	5.3	4.5	Portugal
Sweden	62.9	61.7	64.4	61.7	55.7	61.9	62.3	63.4	63.9	64.7	Suède
East Europe	***419.8***	***465.2***	***496.9***	***501.1***	***524.6***	***495.5***	***511.6***	***545.9***	***559.3***	***572.5***	***Europe de l'est***
Bulgaria[7]	55.0	58.0	62.0	62.0	63.0	60.0	55.2	68.0	70.0	73.0	Bulgarie[7]
Czechoslovakia	22.1	23.1	23.8	24.6	25.6	25.5	25.6	25.7	26.1	26.4	Tchécoslovaquie
German Dem. Rep.* [7]	50.0	51.0	49.0	51.0	51.0	54.0	60.0	68.0	65.0	63.0	Rép. dém. allemande* [7]
Hungary	22.6	26.6	29.8	27.7	27.8	28.8	22.8	24.0	25.9	23.0	Hongrie
Poland	270.1	306.6	332.2	335.8	357.3	327.2	348.0	360.1	372.4	387.0	Pologne
Other Europe	***298.2***	***313.1***	***297.8***	***278.1***	***285.0***	***284.7***	***298.8***	***282.3***	***284.0***	***287.1***	***Autre Europe***
Spain	161.7	169.6	# [1] 147.0	[1] 140.6	[1] 153.7	[1] 152.1	[1] 171.9	[1] 158.6	[1] 156.4	[1] 151.7	Espagne
Yugoslavia	136.5	143.5	150.8	137.5	131.3	132.6	126.9	123.7	127.6	135.4	Yougoslavie
USSR* [7]	**1 250.0**	**1 250.0**	**1 280.0**	**1 300.0**	**1 300.0**	**1 320.0**	**1 350.0**	**1 400.0**	**1 380.0**	**1 400.0**	**URSS* [7]**
Oceania	**177.1**	**183.2**	**173.0**	**155.6**	**158.4**	**185.2**	**191.6**	**200.1**	**208.9**	**196.7**	**Océanie**
Australia[8]	177.1	183.2	173.0	155.6	158.4	185.2	191.6	200.1	208.9	196.7	Australie[8]
Total	**8 676.8**	**9 015.5**	**9 126.3**	**9 302.2**	**9 360.4**	**9 486.4**	**9 213.1**	**9 406.7**	**9 201.7**	**9 223.4**	**Total**

General note.
Refined copper obtained by fire-refining or electrolysis of primary crude metal (blister, black or cement copper). It can also be recovered from secondary materials (scrap). Electrolytic copper obtained directly from ores by leaching is included. (SITC 68212-0).

Remarque générale.
Cuivre affiné par affinage thermique ou électrolytique de la matière première (métal brut), (cuivre blister, cuivre noir ou cuivre de cément) ou par récupération à partir de produits secondaires (déchets de cuivre). Cette rubrique comprend le cuivre électrolytique obtenu directement à partir des minerais après lixiviation. (CTCI 68212-0).

For footnotes, see end of table.

Voir la fin du tableau pour les notes.

[1] Source: World Metal Statistics, (London).
[2] Source: U. S. Bureau of Mines, (Washington, D. C.).
[3] Twelve months beginning 21 March of year stated.
[4] Electrolytic cathode copper.
[5] Including alloys and processing of refined copper imported from Zaire.
[6] Secondary metal production only.
[7] Source: Metallgesellschaft Aktiengesellschaft, (Frankfurt).
[8] Twelve months ending 30 June of year stated.

[1] Source: World Metal Statistics, (Londres).
[2] Source: U.S. Bureau of Mines, (Washington, D.C.).
[3] Période de douze mois commençant le 21 mars de l'année indiquée.
[4] Cuivre électrolytique à cathode.
[5] Y compris les alliages et le traitement ultérieur du cuivre raffiné importé du Zaïre.
[6] Production du métal de deuxième fusion seulement.
[7] Source: Metallgesellschaft Aktiengesellschaft, (Francfort).
[8] Période de douze mois finissant le 30 juin de l'année indiquée.

Copper, primary, refined – Cuivre, neuf, affiné

Unit : Thousand metric tons

Unité : Milliers de tonnes métriques

Country or area	1976	1977	1978	1979	1980	1981	1982	1983	1984	1985	Pays ou zone
Africa	**897.5**	**928.4**	**918.1**	**849.5**	**926.1**	**881.3**	**926.7**	**982.5**	**919.2**	**867.9**	**Afrique**
South Africa[1]	95.6	145.9	152.5	152.3	147.9	144.8	142.5	157.7	148.4	143.3	Afrique du Sud[1]
Zaire[2]	66.0	98.7	102.8	103.2	144.0	151.3	175.0	227.2	224.8	226.8	Zaïre[2]
Zambia	694.6	649.0	629.0	564.4	607.2	560.6	584.4	576.0	523.5	477.4	Zambie
Zimbabwe	41.3	34.8	33.8	29.6	27.0	24.6	24.8	21.6	22.6	20.4	Zimbabwe
America, North	**1 957.1**	**1 906.8**	**1 941.9**	**1 963.6**	**1 776.0**	**2 082.0**	**1 625.9**	**1 727.3**	**1 765.2**	**1 622.4**	**Amérique du Nord**
Canada	485.3	476.4	417.8	365.2	475.2	[3] 476.7	[3] 337.8	[3] 464.3	[3] 504.3	[3] 499.6	Canada
Mexico	75.4	73.1	75.0	81.8	85.6	61.3	61.3	80.9	60.7	65.7	Mexique
United States	1 396.4	1 357.3	1 449.1	1 516.7	1 215.2	1 544.0	1 226.8	1 182.1	1 200.2	1 057.2	Etats–Unis
America, South	**763.7**	**864.1**	**934.5**	**1 012.1**	**1 041.3**	**975.9**	**958.4**	**950.5**	**1 033.3**	**976.8**	**Amérique du Sud**
Brazil	0.0	0.0	0.0	0.0	0.0	0.0	4.8	63.1	61.3	90.0	Brésil
Chile	632.0	676.0	749.1	781.8	810.7	775.5	729.1	692.7	753.0	* 660.0	Chili
Peru	131.7	[1] 188.1	[1] 185.4	[1] 230.3	[1] 230.6	[1] 200.4	[1] 224.5	[1] 194.7	[1] 219.0	[1] 226.8	Pérou
Asia	**921.8**	**1 014.9**	**1 020.5**	**1 022.8**	**1 077.5**	**1 162.3**	**1 200.1**	**1 226.9**	**1 098.9**	**1 081.0**	**Asie**
India	[3] 24.7	[3] 23.5	[2] 11.8	[2] 14.7	[2] 24.6	[2] 24.0	[2] 25.6	[2] 28.4	[2] 32.6	[2] 28.0	Inde
Iran(Islamic Rep.of)* [2]	7.0	7.0	6.0	3.0	0.8	1.0	1.0	10.0	10.0	12.0	Iran(Rép.islamique)* [2]
Japan	806.2	884.9	909.3	897.7	938.4	984.9	1 008.5	1 011.4	866.2	848.9	Japon
Korea, D. P. Rp.* [2 3]	25.0	25.0	25.0	22.0	22.0	22.0	22.0	22.0	22.0	22.0	Corée, Rp. P. D.* [2 3]
Korea, Republic of	30.9	42.9	52.4	63.1	72.9	108.0	110.8	123.3	129.1	140.1	Corée, République de
Turkey[1 3]	28.0	31.7	16.0	22.3	18.8	22.4	32.2	31.8	39.0	30.0	Turquie[1 3]
Europe	**1 646.6**	**1 755.4**	**1 640.2**	**1 637.3**	**1 705.2**	**1 584.7**	**1 675.2**	**1 636.3**	**1 628.9**	**1 683.9**	**Europe**
EEC	***861.0***	***935.3***	***820.3***	***800.5***	***828.4***	***749.8***	***820.3***	***746.8***	***737.2***	***768.3***	***CEE***
Belgium[4]	481.8	563.3	504.9	519.9	526.3	436.6	501.6	431.3	427.7	455.5	Belgique[4]
France	38.6	44.4	41.3	45.3	46.5	46.0	[3] 45.6	[3] 45.1	[3] 40.7	[3] 43.7	France
Germany, Fed. Rep.	289.1	283.2	228.0	186.7	187.4	207.4	209.9	202.9	199.3	205.3	Allemagne, Rép. féd.
United Kingdom	51.6	44.4	46.2	48.5	68.3	59.8	63.2	67.5	69.5	63.9	Royaume–Uni
EFTA	***115.1***	***128.2***	***126.4***	***126.0***	***123.8***	***124.4***	***123.5***	***133.7***	***146.1***	***150.0***	***AELE***
Austria	0.9	13.1	12.6	11.1	8.9	8.8	8.8	8.8	9.6	7.8	Autriche
Finland	38.1	42.8	42.7	43.0	40.5	33.8	48.0	55.4	57.3	58.8	Finlande
Norway	17.8	21.2	15.7	22.0	26.7	26.8	18.6	22.7	30.3	31.1	Norvège
Portugal	* 2.8	3.4	2.8	3.4	4.5	4.9	4.6	4.6	5.3	4.5	Portugal
Sweden	55.6	47.7	52.5	46.4	43.2	50.1	43.6	42.3	43.5	47.9	Suède
East Europe	***409.2***	***453.3***	***483.8***	***489.1***	***512.5***	***482.7***	***501.6***	***535.3***	***548.0***	***562.3***	***Europe de l'est***
Bulgaria[5]	55.0	58.0	62.0	62.0	63.0	60.0	55.2	68.0	70.0	73.0	Bulgarie[5]
Czechoslovakia	22.1	23.1	23.8	24.6	25.6	25.5	25.6	25.7	26.1	26.4	Tchécoslovaquie
German Dem. Rep.[3 5]	50.0	51.0	49.0	51.0	51.0	54.0	60.0	68.0	65.0	63.0	Rép. dém. allemande[3 5]
Hungary	12.0	14.7	16.8	15.7	15.7	16.0	12.7	13.5	14.6	12.8	Hongrie
Poland	270.1	306.6	332.2	335.8	357.3	327.2	348.0	360.1	372.4	387.0	Pologne
Other Europe	***261.3***	***238.6***	***209.7***	***221.8***	***240.5***	***227.8***	***229.9***	***220.5***	***197.7***	***203.4***	***Autre Europe***
Spain	139.7	145.6	[1] 122.0	[1] 122.6	[1] 148.7	[1] 137.1	[1] 145.9	[1] 137.6	[1] 117.4	[1] 101.7	Espagne
Yugoslavia	121.6	93.0	87.7	99.2	91.8	90.7	84.0	82.9	80.3	101.7	Yougoslavie
USSR* [3 5]	**1 250.0**	**1 250.0**	**1 280.0**	**1 300.0**	**1 300.0**	**1 320.0**	**1 350.0**	**1 400.0**	**1 380.0**	**1 400.0**	**URSS* [3 5]**
Oceania	**164.3**	**157.5**	**155.4**	**137.9**	**137.0**	**159.0**	**163.0**	**172.5**	**166.0**	**165.0**	**Océanie**
Australia[6]	164.3	157.5	155.4	137.9	137.0	159.0	163.0	172.5	166.0	165.0	Australie[6]
Total	**7 601.1**	**7 877.0**	**7 890.5**	**7 923.2**	**7 963.2**	**8 165.2**	**7 899.4**	**8 095.9**	**7 991.5**	**7 797.2**	**Total**

General note.
Refined copper obtained by fire–refining or electrolysis of primary crude metal (blister, black or cement copper). Electrolytic copper obtained directly from ores by leaching is included. (SITC 68212–1).

[1] Source: World Metal Statistics, (London).
[2] Source: U. S. Bureau of Mines, (Washington, D. C.).

Remarque générale.
Cuivre affiné par affinage thermique ou électrolytique de la matière première (métal brut), (cuivre blister, cuivre noir ou cuivre de cément). Le cuivre électrolytique obtenu directement à partir des minerais après lixiviation est compris. (CTCI 68212–1).

[1] Source: World Metal Statistics, (Londres).
[2] Source: U.S. Bureau of Mines, (Washington, D.C.).

[3] Including secondary metal production.
[4] Including alloys and processing of refined copper imported from Zaire.
[5] Source: Metallgesellschaft Aktiengesellschaft, (Frankfurt).
[6] Twelve months ending 30 June of year stated.

[3] Y compris la production de métal de deuxième fusion.
[4] Y compris les alliages et le traitement ultérieur du cuivre raffiné importé du Zaïre.
[5] Source: Metallgesellschaft Aktiengesellschaft, (Francfort).
[6] Période de douze mois finissant le 30 juin de l'année indiquée.

Copper, secondary, refined – Cuivre, récupéré, affiné

Unit : Thousand metric tons — Unité : Milliers de tonnes métriques

Country or area	1976	1977	1978	1979	1980	1981	1982	1983	1984	1985	Pays ou zone
America, North	**365.5**	**382.0**	**448.6**	**530.5**	**545.1**	**522.6**	**498.6**	**433.1**	**341.4**	**411.6**	**Amérique du Nord**
Canada	25.2	32.4	28.5	32.1	30.0	...	...	...	...	...	Canada
United States	340.3	349.6	420.1	498.5	515.1	493.6	467.5	401.6	309.5	379.2	Etats-Unis
America, South	**39.3**	**45.8**	**45.0**	**53.1**	**63.0**	**45.0**	**52.0**	**39.9**	**36.0**	**40.0**	**Amérique du Sud**
Brazil	39.3	45.8	45.0	53.1	63.0	45.0	52.0	39.9	36.0	40.0	Brésil
Asia	**64.7**	**54.6**	**57.5**	**90.6**	**76.8**	**66.4**	**67.6**	**81.5**	**69.9**	**88.1**	**Asie**
India	...	...	* 7.7	[1] 4.6	[1] 1.0	[1] 1.2	[1] 1.2	* [1] 1.0	* [1] 1.0	* [1] 1.0	Inde
Japan	58.1	48.8	49.8	86.0	75.8	65.2	66.5	80.5	68.9	87.1	Japon
Europe	**360.0**	**379.9**	**417.8**	**397.0**	**395.9**	**390.0**	**398.4**	**446.6**	**441.4**	**475.3**	**Europe**
EEC	***270.8***	***255.5***	***242.5***	***292.0***	***292.3***	***280.4***	***274.7***	***325.7***	***297.4***	***335.2***	***CEE***
Denmark	0.0	0.1	0.0	0.0	0.0	0.0	0.0	0.0	0.0	0.0	Danemark
France	0.8	0.6	0.6	0.6	0.6	0.4	...	...	...	...	France
Germany, Fed. Rep.	157.5	157.0	144.9	202.6	186.4	180.0	183.7	217.4	179.5	209.1	Allemagne, Rép. féd.
Italy	26.8	20.0	17.5	15.6	12.2	23.7	19.6	31.2	50.3	64.3	Italie
United Kingdom	85.7	77.8	79.4	73.2	93.0	76.3	71.0	76.8	67.4	61.6	Royaume-Uni
EFTA	***41.7***	***38.0***	***33.3***	***36.8***	***47.0***	***39.9***	***44.8***	***48.3***	***46.0***	***46.2***	***AELE***
Austria	28.1	18.7	15.9	15.2	27.9	22.1	23.7	25.3	23.6	27.4	Autriche
Norway	6.2	5.2	5.6	6.4	6.5	* [1] 6.0	* [1] 2.3	* [1] 2.0	* [1] 2.0	* [1] 2.0	Norvège
Sweden	7.3	14.0	11.9	15.2	12.5	11.7	18.7	21.1	20.4	16.7	Suède
East Europe	***10.6***	***11.9***	***13.1***	***12.0***	***12.1***	***12.8***	***10.1***	***10.8***	***11.7***	***10.2***	***Europe de l'est***
Hungary	10.6	11.9	13.1	12.0	12.1	12.8	10.1	10.8	11.7	10.2	Hongrie
Other Europe	***36.9***	***74.5***	***128.9***	***56.3***	***44.5***	***56.9***	***68.9***	***61.8***	***86.4***	***83.8***	***Autre Europe***
Spain	22.0	24.0	[2] 25.0	[2] 18.0	[2] 5.0	[2] 15.0	[2] 26.0	[2] 21.0	[2] 39.0	[2] 50.0	Espagne
Yugoslavia	14.9	50.5	103.9	38.3	39.5	41.9	42.9	40.8	47.4	33.8	Yougoslavie
Oceania	**12.8**	**25.7**	**17.7**	**17.7**	**21.3**	**26.2**	**28.6**	**27.7**	**42.9**	**31.7**	**Océanie**
Australia[3]	12.8	25.7	17.7	17.7	21.3	26.2	28.6	27.7	42.9	31.7	Australie[3]
Total	**842.3**	**888.2**	**986.5**	**1 089.0**	**1 102.2**	**1 050.2**	**1 045.2**	**1 028.8**	**931.7**	**1 046.8**	**Total**

General note.
Secondary refined copper recovered from scrap and other similar materials. (SITC 68212-2).

[1] Source: U. S. Bureau of Mines, (Washington, D. C.).
[2] Source: World Metal Statistics, (London).
[3] Twelve months ending 30 June of year stated.

Remarque générale.
Cuivre de deuxième fusion récupéré à partir de produits secondaires (déchets de cuivre). (CTCI 68212-2).

[1] Source: U.S. Bureau of Mines, (Washington, D.C.).
[2] Source: World Metal Statistics, (Londres).
[3] Période de douze mois finissant le 30 juin de l'année indiquée.

Copper–base alloys – Cupro–alliages

Unit : Thousand metric tons | Unité : Milliers de tonnes métriques

Country or area	1976	1977	1978	1979	1980	1981	1982	1983	1984	1985	Pays ou zone
Africa	**7.4**	**5.6**	**4.9**	**6.0**	**6.0**	**6.0**	**6.0**	**6.0**	**6.0**	**6.0**	**Afrique**
South Africa*	7.4	5.6	4.9	...	...	...	...	...	...	...	Afrique du Sud*
America, North	**653.1**	**688.5**	**720.1**	**809.9**	**790.8**	**856.1**	**565.6**	**660.9**	**601.6**	**603.7**	**Amérique du Nord**
United States	653.1	688.5	720.1	809.9	790.8	856.1	565.6	* 660.9	* 601.6	* 603.7	Etats–Unis
America, South	**0.8**	**0.8**	**0.9**	**0.7**	**0.9**	**0.9**	**0.8**	**0.7**	**0.8**	**0.8**	**Amérique du Sud**
Colombia	...	0.8	0.9	0.7	0.9	0.9	...	0.7	...	...	Colombie
Asia	**99.9**	**87.8**	**87.2**	**102.1**	**101.8**	**103.0**	**98.9**	**94.0**	**100.6**	**102.1**	**Asie**
India[1 2]	26.5	22.5	20.2	...	...	...	...	...	...	...	Inde[1 2]
Japan	...	62.4	61.2	73.3	73.0	74.1	70.0	65.1	71.7	73.2	Japon
Philippines[3]	8.7	2.9	...	...	...	...	...	...	...	...	Philippines[3]
Europe	**200.6**	**209.4**	**201.0**	**203.3**	**216.3**	**188.2**	**188.3**	**174.8**	**207.7**	**155.7**	**Europe**
EEC	***167.4***	***176.8***	***169.1***	***172.3***	***182.1***	***155.6***	***153.9***	***147.4***	***176.5***	***125.5***	***CEE***
Denmark	2.9	2.2	1.7	2.3	2.1	1.8	1.7	1.5	2.0	0.7	Danemark
France	17.7	20.2	17.1	18.2	17.7	14.9	# 29.9	25.1	51.6	12.9	France
Italy	56.0	65.0	68.0	76.9	88.9	77.2	68.9	69.5	69.7	69.6	Italie
Netherlands[4]	9.2	8.5	5.8	...	...	...	...	...	...	...	Pays–Bas[4]
United Kingdom	81.6	80.8	76.5	67.1	65.6	53.9	45.5	43.5	45.3	...	Royaume–Uni
EFTA	***19.9***	***18.2***	***17.1***	***18.0***	***19.0***	***18.1***	***18.7***	***15.7***	***17.3***	***17.3***	***AELE***
Austria	15.9	14.3	13.8	14.7	15.1	14.6	15.3	12.3	14.0	14.1	Autriche
Norway[4]	4.0	3.9	3.3	3.3	3.9	...	...	...	...	...	Norvège[4]
Portugal	* 0.1	0.0	0.0	0.0	0.0	0.0	0.0	0.0	0.0	0.0	Portugal
East Europe	***5.7***	***6.9***	***7.4***	***7.5***	***6.4***	***6.8***	***7.5***	***6.6***	***7.3***	***6.4***	***Europe de l'est***
Hungary	5.7	6.9	7.4	7.5	6.4	6.8	7.5	6.6	7.3	6.4	Hongrie
Other Europe	***7.7***	***7.5***	***7.4***	***5.4***	***8.8***	***7.6***	***8.2***	***5.0***	***6.6***	***6.5***	***Autre Europe***
Spain[4]	...	...	...	5.4	8.8	7.6	8.2	5.0	...	...	Espagne[4]
Total	**961.8**	**992.0**	**1 014.1**	**1 121.9**	**1 115.9**	**1 154.2**	**859.6**	**936.4**	**916.7**	**868.4**	**Total**

General note.
Copper–base alloys in which copper predominates by weight over each of the other metals. (SITC 68213–0).

[1] Production by large and medium scale establishments only.
[2] Including other non–ferrous alloys.
[3] Shipments.
[4] Including other copper alloys.

Remarque générale.
Alliages à base de cuivre dans lesquels le cuivre prédomine en poids sur tous les autres métaux. (CTCI 68213–0).

[1] Production des grandes et moyennes entreprises seulement.
[2] Y compris les autres alliages non ferreux.
[3] Expéditions.
[4] Y compris les autres alliages de cuivre.

Copper bars, rods, angles, shapes, sections – Barres, cornières et profilés de cuivre

Unit : Thousand metric tons

Unité : Milliers de tonnes métriques

Country or area	1976	1977	1978	1979	1980	1981	1982	1983	1984	1985	Pays ou zone
America, North	**399.4**	**431.1**	**434.4**	**454.0**	**66.3**	**65.0**	**55.7**	**54.7**	**75.9**	**52.6**	**Amérique du Nord**
Canada	6.3	6.8	8.9	11.4	...	...	...	...	...	...	Canada
Mexico	0.8	0.6	0.5	0.8	0.8	0.8	1.5	1.8	1.3	1.1	Mexique
United States[1]	392.4	423.7	425.0	441.8	# 57.2	55.8	45.8	44.5	66.2	43.1	Etats-Unis[1]
America, South	**102.0**	**18.3**	**18.3**	**16.4**	**10.6**	**13.2**	**12.3**	**8.9**	**9.1**	**9.0**	**Amérique du Sud**
Brazil[2]	101.0	17.0	16.3	15.0	9.1	[3] 11.4	[3] 10.8	[3] 7.4	[3] 7.6	...	Brésil[2]
Chile	0.6	1.3	1.9	...	...	...	...	...	...	...	Chili
Colombia	0.3	0.1	0.1	0.2	0.2	0.5	0.2	0.2	...	...	Colombie
Asia	**80.6**	**80.8**	**82.8**	**85.1**	**60.7**	**90.9**	**115.9**	**78.3**	**100.7**	**91.4**	**Asie**
Hong Kong	5.9	4.8	4.6	5.2	4.3	4.1	2.7	5.1	4.3	...	Hong-kong
Indonesia	...	...	...	...	...	12.9	18.1	1.6	18.8	...	Indonésie
Japan	17.5	18.9	21.1	22.8	24.2	27.0	28.6	27.4	33.3	30.6	Japon
Korea, Republic of	...	...	...	...	19.4	46.9	66.6	...	...	...	Corée, République de
Europe	**360.9**	**344.0**	**337.3**	**373.9**	**387.6**	**307.5**	**289.0**	**300.4**	**320.6**	**343.7**	**Europe**
EEC	***317.4***	***304.9***	***295.9***	***328.7***	***340.9***	***267.9***	***250.1***	***260.6***	***281.3***	***307.8***	***CEE***
Denmark	15.1	15.0	12.3	12.6	11.3	* 6.8	6.9	9.6	12.9	12.2	Danemark
France[4]	115.7	121.0	117.9	131.8	141.5	120.5	# 106.9	105.8	105.0	108.0	France[4]
Germany, Fed. Rep.[5]	155.0	136.3	132.9	151.2	162.0	123.2	110.9	121.2	135.9	158.9	Allemagne, Rép. féd.[5]
Greece[6]	3.7	4.7	4.9	6.4	3.0	2.6	# 12.6	11.1	11.3	...	Grèce[6]
Italy	16.0	16.1	16.7	16.0	16.5	10.7	8.3	9.4	8.2	9.0	Italie
United Kingdom	11.9	11.9	11.2	10.6	6.7	4.1	4.5	3.5	8.0	7.8	Royaume-Uni
EFTA	***29.2***	***26.4***	***28.9***	***32.1***	***33.1***	***27.3***	***27.4***	***29.3***	***29.4***	***26.0***	***AELE***
Finland	10.5	6.2	5.7	5.9	5.5	4.7	4.1	4.5	4.6	...	Finlande
Sweden	18.6	20.2	23.1	26.2	27.6	22.7	23.4	24.8	24.9	23.1	Suède
East Europe	***7.2***	***6.8***	***7.8***	***7.8***	***7.8***	***7.4***	***6.9***	***6.1***	***5.9***	***6.1***	***Europe de l'est***
Czechoslovakia	4.3	4.1	4.5	4.6	4.8	4.3	4.0	4.1	3.9	3.9	Tchécoslovaquie
Hungary	2.9	2.7	3.3	3.2	3.0	3.1	2.9	2.0	2.0	2.3	Hongrie
Other Europe	***7.1***	***5.9***	***4.8***	***5.3***	***5.8***	***4.8***	***4.6***	***4.4***	***3.9***	***3.7***	***Autre Europe***
Spain	7.1	# [3] 5.9	[3] 4.8	[3] 5.3	[3] 5.8	[3] 4.8	[3] 4.6	[3] 4.4	[3] 3.9	[3] 3.7	Espagne
Oceania	**2.3**	**2.1**	**2.6**	**2.9**	**3.4**	**4.6**	**4.1**	**108.3**	**102.3**	**114.1**	**Océanie**
Australia[7]	2.3	2.1	2.6	2.9	3.4	4.6	4.1	# 108.3	102.3	114.1	Australie[7]
Total	**945.2**	**876.3**	**875.4**	**932.2**	**528.7**	**481.2**	**477.0**	**550.6**	**608.6**	**610.9**	**Total**

General note.
Rolled, extruded, drawn or forged copper products of solid section, of which the maximum cross-sectional dimension exceeds 6 mm and which, if they are flat, have a thickness exceeding one-tenth of the width. (SITC 68221-1).

1 Beginning 1980, data are not comparable with those for earlier years.

2 Copper bars and sections only.
3 Source: World Metal Statistics, (London).
4 Products of copper and copper alloys (brass or bronze).
5 Including products of copper alloys, except alloys with aluminium.

6 Beginning 1982, data are not comparable with those of previous years.

7 Twelve months ending 30 June of year stated.

Remarque générale.
Produits en cuivre de section pleine, laminés, filés, étirés ou forgés, dont la plus grande dimension transversale est supérieure à 6 mm et, en ce qui concerne les produits plats, dont l'épaisseur dépasse le dixième de la largeur. (CTCI 68221-1).

1 A partir de 1980, les données ne sont pas comparables à celles des années antérieures.
2 Barres et profilés de cuivre seulement.
3 Source: World Metal Statistics, (Londres).
4 Produits en cuivre et en alliages à base de cuivre (laiton ou bronze).
5 Y compris les produits en alliages de cuivre, autres que les alliages contenant de l'aluminum.
6 A partir de 1982, les données ne sont pas comparables à celles des années antérieures.
7 Période de douze mois finissant le 30 juin de l'année indiquée.

Copper wire – Fil de cuivre

Unit : Thousand metric tons

Unité : Milliers de tonnes métriques

Country or area	1976	1977	1978	1979	1980	1981	1982	1983	1984	1985	Pays ou zone
America, North	**1 123.0**	**1 248.7**	**1 359.8**	**1 436.4**	**1 334.2**	**1 370.8**	**1 136.3**	**1 225.4**	**1 362.3**	**1 337.4**	**Amérique du Nord**
Mexico	42.1	39.0	39.4	53.9	57.4	79.4	50.9	46.9	59.6	51.5	Mexique
United States	1 080.9	1 209.7	1 320.4	1 382.5	1 276.7	1 291.4	1 085.5	* 1 178.4	* 1 302.7	* 1 285.9	Etats–Unis
America, South	**31.0**	**28.4**	**27.3**	**27.8**	**25.4**	**24.3**	**19.9**	**16.1**	**17.5**	**13.4**	**Amérique du Sud**
Brazil	7.7	5.3	5.9	[1] 5.7	4.3	* [2] 3.2	* [2] 3.0	* [2] 2.1	* [2] 2.1	...	Brésil
Chile[3]	21.3	21.1	19.7	19.5	19.0	20.1	15.8	13.3	14.6	11.7	Chili[3]
Colombia	1.9	2.0	1.7	2.5	2.1	0.9	1.2	0.7	...	...	Colombie
Asia	**166.9**	**189.0**	**227.4**	**223.8**	**194.8**	**217.6**	**256.8**	**264.3**	**299.9**	**282.4**	**Asie**
Hong Kong	0.0	0.0	0.4	0.2	0.0	...	...	16.6	...	...	Hong–kong
Indonesia	...	...	...	...	...	...	...	...	1.9	...	Indonésie
Japan	129.2	144.3	153.5	155.4	144.3	142.0	158.8	153.3	180.6	155.9	Japon
Korea, Republic of	35.7	42.7	71.5	66.1	48.6	64.5	84.4	92.5	100.8	105.3	Corée, République de
Europe	**1 217.9**	**1 289.9**	**1 298.6**	**1 307.4**	**1 332.2**	**1 277.2**	**1 299.1**	**1 324.2**	**1 270.7**	**1 263.8**	**Europe**
EEC	***915.2***	***983.9***	***967.5***	***970.2***	***1 000.1***	***950.9***	***973.6***	***1 000.5***	***960.9***	***938.7***	***CEE***
Denmark	16.4	14.7	14.0	14.2	0.2	...	...	...	...	...	Danemark
France[4]	299.7	324.5	329.5	332.0	374.3	384.9	# 416.7	459.0	410.0	387.0	France[4]
Germany, Fed. Rep.[5]	30.2	36.6	33.9	36.8	40.5	33.5	35.7	38.1	42.3	42.2	Allemagne, Rép. féd.[5]
Italy	231.5	238.0	231.1	236.0	265.0	247.0	227.0	210.0	216.0	218.0	Italie
Netherlands[6]	71.2	72.3	66.3	...	...	...	...	...	...	...	Pays–Bas[6]
United Kingdom	266.2	297.8	292.7	281.2	250.1	210.6	221.6	223.1	222.4	221.3	Royaume–Uni
EFTA	***109.7***	***96.6***	***114.3***	***124.7***	***138.5***	***137.2***	***132.0***	***128.8***	***120.8***	***123.8***	***AELE***
Austria[7]	33.0	33.7	34.2	39.7	46.9	46.2	40.7	37.2	38.4	36.7	Autriche[7]
Finland	23.2	15.8	20.8	21.7	27.6	28.5	27.7	29.7	30.0	...	Finlande
Sweden	53.5	47.1	59.3	63.3	64.0	62.6	63.7	61.9	52.4	54.7	Suède
East Europe	***58.3***	***70.1***	***69.6***	***70.5***	***59.7***	***68.0***	***61.2***	***61.1***	***63.6***	***68.3***	***Europe de l'est***
Czechoslovakia	39.4	42.7	41.1	42.1	33.6	35.3	31.7	35.8	38.2	40.1	Tchécoslovaquie
Hungary	18.8	27.4	28.5	28.4	26.1	32.7	29.5	25.4	25.4	28.2	Hongrie
Other Europe	***134.7***	***139.3***	***147.2***	***141.9***	***134.0***	***121.2***	***132.2***	***133.7***	***125.4***	***133.0***	***Autre Europe***
Spain	93.8	* [2] 94.0	* [2] 93.0	[2] 87.1	[2] 82.9	[2] 69.9	[2] 78.0	[2] 79.0	[2] 69.6	[2] 74.1	Espagne
Yugoslavia	40.9	45.3	54.2	54.9	51.1	51.3	54.2	54.7	55.9	58.9	Yougoslavie
Oceania	**46.1**	**38.4**	**42.5**	**42.4**	**46.1**	**50.5**	**58.0**	**54.3**	**47.9**	**49.2**	**Océanie**
Australia[8]	46.1	38.4	42.5	42.4	46.1	50.5	58.0	54.3	47.9	49.2	Australie[8]
Total	**2 584.9**	**2 794.3**	**2 955.4**	**3 037.7**	**2 932.7**	**2 940.5**	**2 770.2**	**2 884.4**	**2 998.3**	**2 946.2**	**Total**

General note.
Rolled, extruded or drawn copper products of solid section of any cross–sectional shape, of which no cross–sectional dimension exceeds 6 mm. (SITC 68221–2).

1 Production by establishments employing 5 or more persons.
2 Source: World Metal Statistics, (London).
3 Including bare wire.
4 Products of copper and copper alloys (brass or bronze).
5 Including products of copper alloys, except alloys with aluminium.
6 Semi–finished products of copper and copper alloys.
7 Including all other copper products.
8 Twelve months ending 30 June of year stated.

Remarque générale.
Produits de cuivre de section pleine, laminés, filés, étirés ou tréfilés, dont la coupe transversale, de forme quelconque, n'excède pas 6 mm dans sa plus grande dimension. (CTCI 68221–2).

1 Production des établissements occupant 5 personnes ou plus.
2 Source: World Metal Statistics, (Londres).
3 Y compris les fils nus.
4 Produits en cuivre et en alliages à base de cuivre (laiton ou bronze).
5 Y compris les produits en alliages de cuivre, autres que les alliages contenant de l'aluminum.
6 Produits semi–finis de cuivre et d'alliages de cuivre.
7 Y compris tous les autres produits en cuivre.
8 Période de douze mois finissant le 30 juin de l'année indiquée.

ISIC-BASED CODE
3720-16

Copper plates, sheets, strip, foil – Tôles, bandes et feuilles et papier de cuivre

CODE BASE CITI
3720-16

Unit : Thousand metric tons

Unité : Milliers de tonnes métriques

Country or area	1976	1977	1978	1979	1980	1981	1982	1983	1984	1985	Pays ou zone
America, North	**456.6**	**464.4**	**459.7**	**499.2**	**109.0**	**112.1**	**87.3**	**86.4**	**120.2**	**102.9**	**Amérique du Nord**
Canada	14.8	16.1	16.6	15.8	...	...	...	...	...	...	Canada
Mexico	2.3	2.0	2.3	2.1	1.6	2.9	4.5	4.8	7.3	5.4	Mexique
United States[1]	439.5	446.3	440.9	481.3	# 91.6	93.4	67.0	65.8	97.1	81.6	Etats-Unis[1]
America, South	**119.0**	**24.0**	**27.0**	**25.6**	**19.3**	**15.2**	**17.7**	**16.3**	**15.8**	**15.5**	**Amérique du Sud**
Brazil	114.8	16.3	17.6	[2] 18.5	12.1	8.4	* [3] 10.6	* [3] 9.1	* [3] 8.7	...	Brésil
Chile	4.0	7.4	9.0	...	...	...	...	...	...	...	Chili
Colombia	0.2	0.3	0.4	0.3	0.4	0.0	0.3	0.4	...	...	Colombie
Asia	**90.4**	**98.4**	**121.2**	**144.8**	**142.3**	**157.8**	**169.0**	**189.3**	**228.8**	**217.0**	**Asie**
India	2.1	1.9	1.9	1.4	1.6	1.2	1.2	1.6	1.6	1.4	Inde
Japan[4]	82.1	89.2	106.5	126.5	127.5	121.8	120.0	129.6	162.3	150.1	Japon[4]
Korea, Republic of[5]	3.6	4.4	8.7	12.7	9.8	31.3	44.4	54.7	61.5	62.0	Corée, République de[5]
Turkey	2.6	2.9	4.1	4.2	...	...	...	...	...	...	Turquie
Europe	**380.0**	**394.9**	**427.4**	**453.2**	**439.2**	**463.3**	**498.6**	**495.4**	**566.2**	**501.5**	**Europe**
EEC	***299.0***	***308.6***	***332.7***	***351.2***	***347.0***	***364.4***	***397.0***	***405.0***	***466.1***	***411.8***	***CEE***
Denmark	2.1	2.9	1.9	6.0	5.8	...	...	...	...	...	Danemark
France[6]	64.7	65.0	66.3	73.6	74.4	75.5	# 99.2	86.7	96.0	66.6	France[6]
Germany, Fed. Rep.[7]	158.2	163.8	179.0	194.7	199.5	214.1	219.7	246.6	291.8	265.0	Allemagne, Rép. féd.[7]
Italy	22.0	24.9	28.4	27.0	33.2	41.9	43.1	41.5	44.6	50.9	Italie
United Kingdom	51.9	52.0	57.2	50.0	34.0	27.8	29.3	24.0	26.9	22.1	Royaume-Uni
EFTA	***69.3***	***73.7***	***81.7***	***88.9***	***79.5***	***86.0***	***89.0***	***78.3***	***87.5***	***78.9***	***AELE***
Finland	7.9	8.3	9.5	11.2	11.2	10.5	11.2	14.2	19.3	...	Finlande
Sweden	61.4	65.4	72.2	77.7	68.3	75.5	77.8	64.1	68.3	62.0	Suède
East Europe	***7.4***	***7.9***	***8.1***	***8.1***	***8.3***	***8.9***	***8.8***	***7.9***	***8.2***	***7.7***	***Europe de l'est***
Czechoslovakia	5.3	5.6	5.7	5.7	6.1	6.5	6.3	5.9	6.2	6.2	Tchécoslovaquie
Hungary	2.1	2.2	2.4	2.4	2.2	2.4	2.5	1.9	2.0	1.5	Hongrie
Other Europe	***4.3***	***4.8***	***4.8***	***5.0***	***4.4***	***3.9***	***3.7***	***4.2***	***4.4***	***3.0***	***Autre Europe***
Spain[3]	4.3	4.8	4.8	5.0	4.4	3.9	3.7	4.2	4.4	3.0	Espagne[3]
Oceania	**11.3**	**12.0**	**11.6**	**11.6**	**11.6**	**11.6**	**11.6**	**11.6**	**11.6**	**11.6**	**Océanie**
Australia* [8]	11.3	12.0	...	...	...	...	...	...	...	...	Australie* [8]
Total	**1 057.3**	**993.7**	**1 046.9**	**1 134.5**	**721.5**	**760.0**	**784.3**	**798.9**	**942.6**	**848.5**	**Total**

General note.
Flat-surfaced, wrought copper products (coiled or not), of which the maximum cross-sectional dimension exceeds 6 mm, and of which the thickness exceeds 0.15 mm but does not exceed one-tenth of the width (plates, sheets, strip), thin sheets, not exceeding 0.15 mm in thickness, whether or not embossed, cut to shape, perforated, coated, printed or backed with paper or other reinforcing material (copper foil). (SITC 68222 and 68223).

[1] Beginning 1980, data are not comparable with those for earlier years.

[2] Production by establishments employing 5 or more persons.
[3] Source: World Metal Statistics, (London).
[4] Excluding copper foil.
[5] Including copper bars and sections.
[6] Products of copper and copper alloys (brass or bronze).
[7] Including products of copper alloys, except alloys with aluminium.

[8] Twelve months ending 30 June of year stated.

Remarque générale.
Produits plats en cuivre (enroulés ou non), dont la plus grande dimension transversale est supérieure à 6 mm et dont l'épaisseur, supérieure à 0.15 mm, ne dépasse pas le dixième de la largeur (tôles, feuilles et bandes), feuilles et bandes minces d'une épaisseur de 0.15 mm au maximum, même gaufrées, découpées, perforées, revêtues, imprimées ou fixées sur papier ou support similaire (feuilles minces ou papier de cuivre). (CTCI 68222 et 68223).

[1] A partir de 1980, les données ne sont pas comparables à celles des années antérieures.
[2] Production des établissements occupant 5 personnes ou plus.
[3] Source: World Metal Statistics, (Londres).
[4] Non compris les feuilles de cuivre.
[5] Y compris les barres et profilés de cuivre.
[6] Produits en cuivre et en alliages à base de cuivre (laiton ou bronze).
[7] Y compris les produits en alliages de cuivre, autres que les alliages contenant de l'aluminum.
[8] Période de douze mois finissant le 30 juin de l'année indiquée.

Copper tubes and pipes – Tuyaux et tubes de cuivre

Unit : Thousand metric tons — Unité : Milliers de tonnes métriques

Country or area	1976	1977	1978	1979	1980	1981	1982	1983	1984	1985	Pays ou zone
America, North	**355.8**	**387.6**	**416.5**	**470.0**	**342.2**	**324.9**	**309.9**	**342.0**	**371.6**	**383.4**	**Amérique du Nord**
Canada	34.1	35.6	38.4	39.5	[1] 37.4	[1] 35.8	[1] 26.1	[1] 32.9	[1] 33.0	[1] 35.9	Canada
Mexico	12.4	11.9	13.8	14.5	18.6	17.9	17.8	24.3	22.8	20.1	Mexique
United States	309.3	340.2	364.2	415.9	286.2	271.2	266.0	284.9	315.7	327.5	Etats-Unis
America, South	**15.6**	**15.9**	**17.4**	**17.1**	**15.8**	**19.8**	**19.1**	**19.9**	**22.4**	**21.8**	**Amérique du Sud**
Brazil	9.2	9.5	10.2	[2] 10.5	9.2	* [1] 13.1	* [1] 12.5	* [1] 13.3	* [1] 15.8	...	Brésil
Chile	6.3	6.3	7.2	...	...	...	...	...	...	...	Chili
Colombia	0.1	0.0	0.0	0.0	0.0	0.1	0.0	0.0	...	...	Colombie
Asia	**102.9**	**107.3**	**123.0**	**147.1**	**125.4**	**130.6**	**138.6**	**156.6**	**181.8**	**187.6**	**Asie**
India	0.5	0.4	0.5	0.7	...	...	...	...	...	...	Inde
Japan	99.5	103.9	120.8	141.8	121.9	122.3	131.2	139.1	160.1	160.2	Japon
Korea, Republic of	...	...	...	...	3.0	7.8	6.9	17.0	21.2	26.9	Corée, République de
Europe	**357.8**	**358.7**	**384.0**	**405.9**	**395.9**	**365.0**	**372.1**	**387.6**	**412.8**	**405.4**	**Europe**
EEC	***311.4***	***308.1***	***322.0***	***336.8***	***329.1***	***304.7***	***307.3***	***320.5***	***343.8***	***334.5***	***CEE***
France[3]	58.6	59.1	63.3	66.5	61.3	62.3	# 62.6	51.9	59.0	55.2	France[3]
Germany, Fed. Rep.[4]	151.8	148.4	149.1	162.6	164.6	143.7	145.3	165.9	174.4	171.8	Allemagne, Rép. féd.[4]
Italy	27.5	27.2	29.8	29.0	33.8	30.4	27.8	28.5	36.0	34.5	Italie
United Kingdom[5]	73.4	73.4	79.8	78.7	69.4	68.4	71.6	74.2	74.4	73.0	Royaume-Uni[5]
EFTA	***30.1***	***31.7***	***40.3***	***42.8***	***42.4***	***41.3***	***41.7***	***44.4***	***44.7***	***45.6***	***AELE***
Finland	14.0	15.3	20.7	21.1	21.2	22.0	23.1	22.6	24.8	...	Finlande
Sweden	16.1	16.4	19.6	21.6	21.2	19.3	18.6	21.8	19.9	19.1	Suède
East Europe	***8.8***	***8.6***	***9.2***	***9.2***	***9.3***	***8.1***	***8.1***	***7.2***	***7.7***	***6.7***	***Europe de l'est***
Czechoslovakia	5.3	4.8	5.1	# 5.3	5.5	5.5	5.2	4.7	4.7	4.6	Tchécoslovaquie
Hungary	3.5	3.8	4.1	3.9	3.8	2.7	2.9	2.5	3.0	2.1	Hongrie
Other Europe	***7.5***	***10.3***	***12.5***	***17.1***	***15.2***	***10.8***	***15.0***	***15.5***	***16.6***	***18.5***	***Autre Europe***
Spain	7.5	# [1] 10.3	[1] 12.5	[1] 17.1	[1] 15.2	[1] 10.8	[1] 15.0	[1] 15.5	[1] 16.6	[1] 18.5	Espagne
Oceania	**19.7**	**22.9**	**22.0**	**21.5**	**21.5**	**21.5**	**21.5**	**21.5**	**21.5**	**21.5**	**Océanie**
Australia[6]	19.7	22.9	22.0	...	...	...	...	...	...	...	Australie[6]
Total	**851.8**	**892.4**	**962.8**	**1 061.7**	**900.9**	**861.9**	**861.3**	**927.7**	**1 010.2**	**1 019.8**	**Total**

General note.
Seamless and welded tubes and pipes, including blanks therefore, but excluding tube and pipe fittings. (SITC 68225-1).

1 Source: World Metal Statistics, (London).
2 Production by establishments employing 5 or more persons.
3 Products of copper and copper alloys (brass or bronze).
4 Including products of copper alloys, except alloys with aluminium.
5 Copper tubes only.
6 Twelve months ending 30 June of year stated.

Remarque générale.
Tuyaux et tubes sans soudure et soudés, y compris leurs ébauches mais non les accessoires de tuyauterie en cuivre. (CTCI 68225-1).

1 Source: World Metal Statistics, (Londres).
2 Production des établissements occupant 5 personnes ou plus.
3 Produits en cuivre et en alliages à base de cuivre (laiton ou bronze).
4 Y compris les produits en alliages de cuivre, autres que les alliages contenant de l'aluminum.
5 Tubes et tuyaux de cuivre seulement.
6 Période de douze mois finissant le 30 juin de l'année indiquée.

Nickel unwrought – Nickel brut

Unit : Metric tons — Unité : Tonnes métriques

Country or area	1976	1977	1978	1979	1980	1981	1982	1983	1984	1985	Pays ou zone
Africa	**26 944**	**35 925**	**35 470**	**21 280**	**33 172**	**30 978**	**27 734**	**27 147**	**30 751**	**29 881**	**Afrique**
South Africa[1]	16 964	22 955	22 500	8 040	18 098	17 960	14 425	* 17 000	20 500	20 000	Afrique du Sud[1]
Zimbabwe	9 980	12 970	12 970	13 240	15 074	13 018	13 309	10 147	10 251	9 881	Zimbabwe
America, North	**241 911**	**218 208**	**144 774**	**157 052**	**216 696**	**181 087**	**114 088**	**147 086**	**177 520**	**176 973**	**Amérique du Nord**
Canada[1 2]	168 250	151 967	89 200	83 750	152 300	109 303	58 636	87 200	104 000	110 100	Canada[1 2]
Cuba[1 3]	* 18 416	6 928	7 414	8 100	7 926	8 487	9 001	9 342	8 447	8 500	Cuba[1 3]
Dominican Republic[4]	24 400	24 899	14 302	25 112	16 350	19 022	5 668	20 244	24 311	25 366	Rép. dominicaine[4]
Mexico[1]	56	34	22	1	0	0	0	0	0	...	Mexique[1]
United States	30 789	34 380	33 836	40 089	40 120	44 275	40 783	* 30 300	40 762	33 006	Etats–Unis
America, South	**3 469**	**3 850**	**3 608**	**2 463**	**2 504**	**2 334**	**6 133**	**23 801**	**29 764**	**25 000**	**Amérique du Sud**
Brazil[4]	2 149	2 530	2 288	2 463	2 504	2 334	4 813	10 741	12 700	13 200	Brésil[4]
Colombia[1 4]	...	...	...	0	0	0	1 320	13 060	17 064	11 800	Colombie[1 4]
Asia	**122 966**	**127 830**	**113 646**	**136 478**	**139 662**	**123 987**	**111 591**	**93 503**	**96 552**	**113 949**	**Asie**
China* [1]	9 070	9 980	9 980	10 000	11 000	11 000	12 000	13 000	14 000	15 000	Chine* [1]
Indonesia[1 4]	3 857	2 077	5 729	4 000	4 421	4 703	5 010	4 855	4 826	4 802	Indonésie[1 4]
Japan[1]	94 800	93 900	79 200	101 000	98 360	86 799	83 358	69 551	74 198	77 491	Japon[1]
Philippines[1]	15 239	21 873	18 737	21 478	25 881	21 485	11 223	6 097	3 528	16 656	Philippines[1]
Europe	**108 935**	**97 406**	**82 835**	**86 784**	**101 592**	**105 515**	**64 839**	**96 071**	**104 845**	**105 154**	**Europe**
EEC	***62 016***	***43 126***	***44 905***	***38 038***	***45 262***	***49 351***	***20 002***	***45 138***	***44 513***	***41 485***	***CEE***
France[2]	12 313	10 279	7 750	3 320	10 847	10 051	# 7 360	4 878	5 384	7 019	France[2]
Germany, Fed. Rep.[5]	130	91	901	1 223	1 235	* 1 200	* 1 200	* 1 200	* 1 000	* 700	Allemagne, Rép. féd.[5]
Greece[1]	16 448	9 600	14 887	14 632	13 880	12 700	* 4 540	15 860	15 829	15 966	Grèce[1]
United Kingdom[6]	33 125	23 156	21 367	18 863	19 300	25 400	6 902	23 200	22 300	17 800	Royaume–Uni[6]
EFTA	***40 309***	***47 670***	***31 240***	***42 146***	***49 930***	***50 264***	***38 137***	***43 133***	***50 832***	***53 169***	***AELE***
Finland	7 624	9 447	7 501	11 460	12 807	13 310	12 304	14 514	15 284	15 656	Finlande
Norway	32 685	38 223	23 739	30 686	37 123	36 954	25 833	28 619	35 548	37 513	Norvège
East Europe	***6 610***	***6 610***	***6 690***	***6 600***	***6 400***	***5 900***	***5 200***	***6 300***	***7 500***	***7 500***	***Europe de l'est***
Czechoslovakia* [1]	1 600	1 600	1 600	1 600	1 600	1 600	1 500	3 000	4 500	4 500	Tchécoslovaquie* [1]
German Dem. Rep.* [1]	2 810	2 810	2 990	3 000	3 000	2 800	3 000	3 000	3 000	3 000	Rép. dém. allemande* [1]
Poland[7]	* 2 200	* 2 200	* 2 100	* 2 000	* 1 800	* 1 500	* 700	* 300	0	0	Pologne[7]
Other Europe	***0***	***0***	***0***	***0***	***0***	***0***	***1 500***	***1 500***	***2 000***	***3 000***	***Autre Europe***
Yugoslavia[1]	...	...	0	0	0	0	* 1 500	* 1 500	* 2 000	* 3 000	Yougoslavie[1]
USSR* [1]	**160 570**	**166 920**	**167 010**	**165 000**	**172 000**	**178 000**	**180 000**	**185 000**	**191 000**	**198 000**	**URSS* [1]**
Oceania	**78 020**	**62 423**	**57 216**	**69 714**	**67 909**	**70 493**	**74 054**	**63 517**	**67 818**	**76 910**	**Océanie**
Australia[1 8]	39 868	34 140	37 327	39 341	35 309	42 505	45 931	41 800	38 660	40 807	Australie[1 8]
New Caledonia[4]	38 152	28 283	19 889	30 373	32 600	27 988	28 123	* 21 717	29 158	36 103	Nouvelle–Calédonie[4]
Total	**742 815**	**712 562**	**604 559**	**638 771**	**733 535**	**692 394**	**578 439**	**636 125**	**698 250**	**725 867**	**Total**

General note.
Production of refined nickel plus nickel content of ferro–nickel and nickel oxide. (SITC 68310–0).

[1] Source: U. S. Bureau of Mines, (Washington, D. C.).
[2] Including nickel content of refined nickel, nickel oxide and nickel matte.
[3] Including nickel content of nickel alloys.
[4] Nickel content of ferronickel only.
[5] Beginning 1982, official data are confidential. Data shown are U. S. Bureau of Mines (Washington, D.C.) estimates.
[6] Calcined alumina plus calcined alumina equivalent of alumina hydrate.
[7] Source: Metallgesellschaft Aktiengesellschaft, (Frankfurt).
[8] Refined nickel plus the nickel content of oxide.

Remarque générale.
Production de nickel raffiné et nickel contenu dans les oxydes de nickel et dans le ferro–nickel. (CTCI 68310–0).

[1] Source: U.S. Bureau of Mines, (Washington, D.C.).
[2] Y compris la teneur en nickel de nickel affiné, de l'oxyde de nickel et de mattes de nickel.
[3] Y compris la teneur en nickel des alliages de nickel.
[4] La teneur en nickel de ferro–nickel seulement.
[5] A partir de 1982, les chiffres sont confidentiels. Les données officielles publiées se rapportent aux estimations du 'U. S. Bureau of Mines' (Washington D.C.).
[6] Alumine calcinée et l'equivalent en alumine calcinée de l'alumine hydratée.
[7] Source: Metallgesellschaft Aktiengesellschaft, (Francfort).
[8] Nickel affiné et la teneur en nickel de l'oxyde de nickel.

Alumina, calcined equivalent – Alumine calcinée

Unit : Thousand metric tons

Unité : Milliers de tonnes métriques

Country or area	1976	1977	1978	1979	1980	1981	1982	1983	1984	1985	Pays ou zone
Africa	**560**	**562**	**610**	**660**	**708**	**608**	**549**	**583**	**508**	**580**	**Afrique**
Guinea[1]	560	562	610	660	708	608	549	583	508	580	Guinée[1]
America, North	**7 934**	**9 142**	**9 131**	**9 497**	**10 468**	**9 724**	**7 018**	**6 970**	**7 422**	**5 996**	**Amérique du Nord**
Canada[1]	490	1 061	1 054	953	1 202	1 208	1 127	1 116	1 126	1 019	Canada[1]
Jamaica	1 644	2 051	2 117	2 094	2 456	2 556	1 761	1 854	1 751	1 512	Jamaïque
United States	* 5 800	* 6 030	* 5 960	6 450	6 810	5 960	4 130	4 000	4 545	3 465	Etats–Unis
America, South	**1 931**	**2 067**	**2 323**	**1 962**	**2 176**	**1 924**	**1 677**	**2 343**	**3 267**	**3 218**	**Amérique du Sud**
Brazil	306	368	434	449	517	519	552	629	891	891	Brésil
Guyana[1 2]	281	271	250	200	214	157	73	0	0	0	Guyana[1 2]
Suriname	1 162	1 172	1 310	1 313	1 445	1 248	1 052	1 154	1 237	1 242	Suriname
Venezuela[1]	...	...	...	0	0	0	0	560	* 1 139	* 1 085	Venezuela[1]
Asia	**2 742**	**3 092**	**2 806**	**2 858**	**3 324**	**2 725**	**2 343**	**2 372**	**2 607**	**2 476**	**Asie**
China* [1]	750	750	750	750	750	750	800	800	800	825	Chine* [1]
India[1]	442	387	480	493	* 500	* 500	* 500	* 450	* 560	* 560	Inde[1]
Japan	1 411	1 785	1 502	1 545	1 936	1 344	959	1 065	1 172	978	Japon
Turkey[1]	139	170	74	70	138	131	84	57	75	113	Turquie[1]
Europe	**5 455**	**5 754**	**5 712**	**6 116**	**6 679**	**7 109**	**6 512**	**6 463**	**6 792**	**6 510**	**Europe**
EEC	***3 709***	***3 896***	***3 857***	***3 859***	***4 091***	***3 892***	***3 439***	***3 171***	***3 512***	***3 256***	***CEE***
France	1 020	1 081	1 056	1 069	1 173	1 095	# 963	853	898	734	France
Germany, Fed. Rep.	1 333	1 454	1 410	1 352	1 422	1 427	1 286	1 346	1 417	1 367	Allemagne, Rép. féd.
Greece[1]	462	474	478	496	494	494	404	413	485	500	Grèce[1]
Italy[1]	798	788	819	854	900	786	698	466	607	555	Italie[1]
United Kingdom[1]	96	99	94	88	102	90	88	93	105	100	Royaume–Uni[1]
EFTA	***0***	***0***	***0***	***0***	***0***	***0***	***0***	***70***	***47***	***55***	***AELE***
Iceland	0	0	0	0	0	0	0	70	...	...	Islande
East Europe	***1 291***	***1 359***	***1 359***	***1 421***	***1 472***	***1 485***	***1 383***	***1 470***	***1 491***	***1 474***	***Europe de l'est***
Czechoslovakia* [1]	90	95	90	90	90	90	80	80	85	85	Tchécoslovaquie* [1]
German Dem. Rep.[1]	44	39	38	41	43	45	46	42	43	43	Rép. dém. allemande[1]
Hungary	732	783	782	788	805	792	743	836	811	798	Hongrie
Romania	425	442	449	502	534	558	514	512	552	548	Roumanie
Other Europe	***455***	***499***	***496***	***836***	***1 116***	***1 732***	***1 690***	***1 752***	***1 742***	***1 725***	***Autre Europe***
Spain[1]	0	0	0	0	58	695	673	737	742	725	Espagne[1]
Yugoslavia[1]	455	499	496	836	1 058	1 037	1 017	* 1 015	* 1 000	* 1 000	Yougoslavie[1]
USSR* [1]	**2 500**	**2 600**	**2 600**	**2 600**	**2 700**	**2 800**	**3 000**	**3 200**	**3 300**	**3 500**	**URSS* [1]**
Oceania	**6 206**	**6 659**	**6 776**	**7 415**	**7 246**	**7 079**	**6 631**	**7 230**	**8 781**	**8 792**	**Océanie**
Australia[1]	6 206	6 659	6 776	7 415	7 246	7 079	6 631	7 230	8 781	8 792	Australie[1]
Total	**27 328**	**29 876**	**29 958**	**31 108**	**33 301**	**31 969**	**27 730**	**29 161**	**32 677**	**31 072**	**Total**

General note.
Alumina (aluminium oxide – Al2O3) (anyhdrous or calcined alumina) is obtained by calcining the aluminium hydroxide or from aluminium alum. Aluminium hydroxide (hydrated alumina) is recovered from bauxite during aluminium metallurgy. Most of the calcined oxide is used to make the metal. (SITC 51365–0).

[1] Source: U. S. Bureau of Mines, (Washington, D. C.).
[2] Calcined alumina plus calcined alumina equivalent of alumina hydrate.

Remarque générale.
L'alumine (oxyde d'aluminium – Al2O3) (alumine anhydre ou calcinée) est obtenu par calcination de l'hydrate d'aluminium ou à partir de l'alun ammoniacal. L'hydroxide d'aluminium (alumine hydratée) est obtenu au cours de la métallurgie de l'aluminium par le traitement de la bauxite. La plus grande partie de l'oxyde calciné sert à la fabrication du métal. (CTCI 51365–0).

[1] Source: U.S. Bureau of Mines, (Washington, D.C.).
[2] Alumine calcinée et l'equivalent en alumine calcinée de l'alumine hydratée.

Aluminium, unwrought (total production) – Aluminium non travaillé (production totale)

Unit : Thousand metric tons

Unité : Milliers de tonnes métriques

Country or area	1976	1977	1978	1979	1980	1981	1982	1983	1984	1985	Pays ou zone
Africa	**341.2**	**377.1**	**334.1**	**404.2**	**432.4**	**456.5**	**499.2**	**397.6**	**458.8**	**502.5**	**Afrique**
Cameroon[1]	57.7	56.6	41.0	48.4	* 43.0	* 65.4	64.1	53.6	125.4	81.8	Cameroun[1]
Egypt[1]	# 54.0	89.0	101.0	102.0	116.0	134.0	141.0	140.2	166.0	208.6	Egypte[1]
Ghana[1]	[2] 151.5	[2] 153.5	[2] 111.4	168.7	187.7	173.3	188.5	42.5	0.0	47.5	Ghana[1]
South Africa[1 2]	78.0	78.0	80.7	85.0	85.7	83.7	105.5	161.3	167.4	164.6	Afrique du Sud[1 2]
America, North	**5 816.4**	**6 537.3**	**6 934.0**	**7 045.3**	**7 298.3**	**7 374.3**	**5 991.3**	**6 195.6**	**7 039.9**	**6 651.8**	**Amérique du Nord**
Canada[2]	673.5	1 021.8	1 123.2	944.7	1 133.3	1 175.0	1 126.8	1 154.2	1 291.0	1 347.0	Canada[2]
Mexico[1]	42.4	42.7	43.1	43.2	42.6	43.2	42.3	39.8	43.6	42.8	Mexique[1]
United States[3]	5 100.6	5 472.8	5 767.7	6 057.4	6 122.3	6 156.1	4 822.3	5 001.6	5 705.3	5 262.0	Etats-Unis[3]
America, South	**299.2**	**343.9**	**391.8**	**655.8**	**857.0**	**780.4**	**802.0**	**949.0**	**1 049.8**	**1 166.1**	**Amérique du Sud**
Argentina[1]	[4] 43.1	[4] 49.9	[4] 49.5	[4] 118.4	[4] 133.1	[4] 133.9	140.5	136.4	137.8	139.9	Argentine[1]
Brazil	164.9	200.6	218.2	290.7	340.8	292.5	345.3	443.8	503.9	594.7	Brésil
Suriname	45.9	50.0	58.0	53.9	54.9	40.5	42.5	33.6	23.0	28.8	Suriname
Venezuela	45.3	43.4	66.1	192.8	328.2	313.5	273.6	335.3	385.1	402.8	Venezuela
Asia	**2 221.4**	**2 556.5**	**2 485.0**	**2 569.4**	**2 623.9**	**2 378.9**	**2 017.2**	**2 092.8**	**2 282.6**	**2 273.9**	**Asie**
Bahrain	122.1	121.4	[4] 122.8	[4] 126.1	[4] 126.0	[4] 130.0	[4] 171.0	[4] 171.7	[4] 177.3	[4] 174.8	Bahreïn
China* [2]	320.0	350.0	350.0	350.0	350.0	350.0	380.0	400.0	400.0	410.0	Chine* [2]
India	211.4	183.9	205.4	211.9	184.5	212.0	216.5	203.9	268.5	260.0	Inde
Indonesia	...	...	...	...	0.0	0.0	0.0	138.6	206.9	* 216.8	Indonésie
Iran(Islamic Rep.of)[1 2]	* 30.8	* 20.9	* 25.5	* 14.0	16.0	12.5	45.0	39.4	42.4	42.0	Iran(Rép.islamique)[1 2]
Japan[3]	1 450.7	1 779.8	1 721.8	1 782.5	1 896.2	1 616.4	1 153.2	1 096.2	1 131.4	1 098.5	Japon[3]
Korea, Republic of	17.9	18.3	20.2	21.8	17.6	17.5	15.2	12.6	18.3	17.7	Corée, République de
Turkey[1 4]	37.5	51.3	32.3	31.8	33.6	40.4	36.3	30.4	37.9	54.1	Turquie[1 4]
Europe	**4 719.1**	**5 003.3**	**5 016.4**	**5 196.7**	**5 388.5**	**5 314.9**	**5 021.0**	**5 270.1**	**5 448.8**	**5 177.9**	**Europe**
EEC	***2 631.1***	***2 782.3***	***2 820.7***	***2 863.3***	***2 933.2***	***2 866.6***	***2 624.6***	***2 611.5***	***2 764.3***	***2 612.6***	***CEE***
Belgium[4 5]	2.6	3.6	1.1	2.0	0.0	0.0	0.0	1.0	2.0	2.0	Belgique[4 5]
France[3]	518.3	545.7	552.2	560.8	601.9	591.3	554.8	522.9	504.0	457.3	France[3]
Germany, Fed. Rep.	737.0	785.1	784.0	784.4	767.8	766.5	761.4	781.5	815.1	786.2	Allemagne, Rép. féd.
Greece[1]	134.3	131.4	145.6	168.0	184.0	185.6	177.4	157.9	189.0	145.0	Grèce[1]
Italy	404.5	485.1	492.8	514.1	537.2	523.8	474.9	473.7	513.2	506.1	Italie
Netherlands	294.0	280.9	305.2	297.8	305.8	312.2	300.7	293.5	309.1	312.9	Pays-Bas
United Kingdom[6]	540.4	550.6	539.9	536.2	536.5	487.2	355.4	380.8	431.8	403.0	Royaume-Uni[6]
EFTA	***1 181.3***	***1 269.6***	***1 244.3***	***1 305.1***	***1 283.1***	***1 282.8***	***1 271.9***	***1 479.3***	***1 438.6***	***1 311.7***	***AELE***
Austria	291.0	368.5	328.8	362.1	339.4	358.9	357.9	482.6	380.7	285.0	Autriche
Finland[5]	5.7	9.3	8.9	7.7	11.5	11.0	11.6	14.9	18.7	* 21.0	Finlande[5]
Iceland	65.2	70.7	73.5	71.0	73.0	73.6	75.2	76.1	80.4	73.4	Islande
Norway	632.5	632.2	645.2	671.6	665.7	648.1	645.6	717.6	770.7	748.7	Norvège
Portugal[5]	2.1	2.3	3.1	3.8	2.7	1.9	1.9	2.4	2.4	2.1	Portugal[5]
Sweden	106.5	106.7	105.2	106.0	104.4	107.1	* 104.5	109.7	106.5	108.7	Suède
Switzerland	78.2	79.8	79.5	83.0	86.3	82.2	75.3	76.0	79.2	72.7	Suisse
East Europe	***495.0***	***502.4***	***504.4***	***537.3***	***562.5***	***537.6***	***475.9***	***500.9***	***523.0***	***524.9***	***Europe de l'est***
Czechoslovakia	[1] 36.0	[1] 36.5	[1] 36.8	64.2	65.6	66.8	62.6	66.3	66.0	66.0	Tchécoslovaquie
German Dem. Rep.* [1 4]	60.0	65.0	65.0	60.0	60.0	60.0	58.0	59.0	58.0	60.0	Rép. dém. allemande* [1 4]
Hungary	70.5	71.3	71.4	80.5	82.8	83.8	84.6	87.2	89.0	86.9	Hongrie
Poland	103.5	103.5	100.2	96.6	95.1	66.0	42.7	44.4	45.9	47.0	Pologne
Romania[6]	225.0	226.0	231.0	236.0	259.0	261.0	228.0	244.0	264.0	265.0	Roumanie[6]
Other Europe	***411.7***	***449.0***	***447.0***	***491.0***	***609.8***	***627.9***	***648.6***	***678.5***	***723.0***	***728.7***	***Autre Europe***
Spain	214.0	251.5	# [7] 251.3	[7] 301.5	[7] 425.0	[7] 431.1	[7] 402.2	[7] 394.9	[7] 421.4	[7] 412.6	Espagne
Yugoslavia	197.7	197.5	195.7	189.5	184.8	196.8	246.4	283.6	301.6	316.1	Yougoslavie
USSR* [2]	**1 750.0**	**1 790.0**	**1 820.0**	**1 910.0**	**1 930.0**	**1 980.0**	**2 040.0**	**2 200.0**	**2 310.0**	**2 415.0**	**URSS* [2]**
Oceania	**388.6**	**405.3**	**433.8**	**448.9**	**475.7**	**542.7**	**585.4**	**660.2**	**924.6**	**1 167.3**	**Océanie**
Australia[8]	250.5	261.5	284.0	295.3	321.0	388.8	422.0	441.6	681.8	926.4	Australie[8]
New Zealand	138.1	143.7	149.8	153.6	154.7	154.0	163.4	218.6	242.9	240.8	Nouvelle-Zélande
Total	**15 535.9**	**17 013.4**	**17 415.1**	**18 230.2**	**19 005.8**	**18 827.6**	**16 956.0**	**17 765.4**	**19 514.6**	**19 354.5**	**Total**

For general note and footnotes, see end of table.

Voir la fin du tableau pour la remarque générale et les notes.

General note.
Aluminium obtained by electrolytic reduction of alumina (primary) and remelting metal waste or scrap (secondary). (SITC 68410–0).

[1] Primary metal production only.
[2] Source: U. S. Bureau of Mines, (Washington, D. C.).
[3] Including alloys.
[4] Source: Metallgesellschaft Aktiengesellschaft, (Frankfurt).
[5] Secondary metal production only.
[6] Including pure content of virgin alloys.
[7] Source: World Metal Statistics, (London).
[8] Twelve months ending 30 June of year stated.

Remarque générale.
Aluminium obtenu par réduction électrolytique de l'alumine (formes primaires) ou refonte des déchets et débris de métal (formes secondaires). (CTCI 68410–0).

[1] Production du métal de première fusion seulement.
[2] Source: U.S. Bureau of Mines, (Washington, D.C.).
[3] Y compris les alliages.
[4] Source: Metallgesellschaft Aktiengesellschaft, (Francfort).
[5] Production du métal de deuxième fusion seulement.
[6] Y compris la teneur pure des alliages de première fusion.
[7] Source: World Metal Statistics, (Londres).
[8] Période de douze mois finissant le 30 juin de l'année indiquée.

Aluminium, unwrought, primary – Aluminium non travaillé, neuf

Unit : Thousand metric tons — Unité : Milliers de tonnes métriques

Country or area	1976	1977	1978	1979	1980	1981	1982	1983	1984	1985	Pays ou zone
Africa	**341.2**	**377.1**	**334.1**	**404.2**	**432.4**	**456.3**	**499.1**	**397.6**	**458.8**	**502.4**	**Afrique**
Cameroon	57.7	56.6	41.0	48.4	* 43.0	* 65.4	64.1	53.6	125.4	81.8	Cameroun
Egypt	54.0	89.0	101.0	102.0	116.0	133.8	141.0	140.2	166.0	208.6	Egypte
Ghana	[1] 151.5	[1] 153.5	[1] 111.4	168.7	187.7	173.3	188.5	42.5	0.0	47.5	Ghana
South Africa[1]	78.0	78.0	80.7	85.0	85.7	83.7	105.5	161.3	167.4	164.6	Afrique du Sud[1]
America, North	**4 530.2**	**5 133.7**	**5 449.5**	**5 460.3**	**5 764.4**	**5 647.6**	**4 380.7**	**4 484.3**	**5 369.6**	**4 824.8**	**Amérique du Nord**
Canada[1]	631.0	973.5	1 048.5	860.3	1 068.2	1 115.7	1 064.8	1 091.2	1 227.0	1 282.0	Canada[1]
Mexico	42.4	42.7	43.1	43.2	42.6	43.2	42.3	39.8	43.6	42.8	Mexique
United States	3 856.8	4 117.4	4 357.9	4 556.9	4 653.6	4 488.7	3 273.7	3 353.2	4 099.0	3 500.0	Etats-Unis
America, South	**273.5**	**310.4**	**360.0**	**603.4**	**806.9**	**744.4**	**755.7**	**906.0**	**1 000.9**	**1 121.3**	**Amérique du Sud**
Argentina[2]	43.1	49.9	49.5	118.4	133.1	133.9	140.5	136.4	137.8	139.9	Argentine[2]
Brazil	139.2	167.1	186.4	238.3	290.7	256.4	299.1	400.7	455.0	549.8	Brésil
Suriname	45.9	50.0	58.0	53.9	54.9	40.5	42.5	33.6	23.0	28.8	Suriname
Venezuela	45.3	43.4	66.1	192.8	328.2	313.5	273.6	335.3	385.1	402.8	Venezuela
Asia	**1 694.0**	**1 969.6**	**1 825.0**	**1 801.1**	**1 823.5**	**1 539.2**	**1 219.1**	**1 255.2**	**1 442.4**	**1 406.8**	**Asie**
Bahrain	122.1	121.4	[2] 122.8	[2] 126.1	[2] 126.0	[2] 130.0	[2] 171.0	[2] 171.7	[2] 177.3	[2] 174.8	Bahreïn
China* [1]	320.0	350.0	350.0	350.0	350.0	350.0	380.0	400.0	400.0	410.0	Chine* [1]
India	211.4	183.9	205.4	211.9	184.5	212.0	216.5	203.9	268.5	260.0	Inde
Indonesia	...	...	...	...	0.0	0.0	0.0	138.6	206.9	* 216.8	Indonésie
Iran(Islamic Rep.of)[1]	* 30.8	* 20.9	* 25.5	* 14.0	16.0	12.5	45.0	39.4	42.4	42.0	Iran(Rép.islamique)[1]
Japan	923.3	1 192.9	1 061.7	1 014.3	1 095.7	776.8	355.1	258.6	291.1	231.3	Japon
Korea, Republic of	17.9	18.3	20.2	21.8	17.6	17.5	15.2	12.6	18.3	17.7	Corée, République de
Turkey[2]	37.5	51.3	32.3	31.8	33.6	40.4	36.3	30.4	37.9	54.1	Turquie[2]
Europe	**3 829.8**	**3 895.1**	**3 945.3**	**4 093.5**	**4 293.5**	**4 235.2**	**3 991.7**	**4 039.2**	**4 360.7**	**4 194.9**	**Europe**
EEC	***2 012.9***	***2 123.9***	***2 154.6***	***2 191.3***	***2 250.9***	***2 225.0***	***2 025.7***	***1 945.7***	***2 074.5***	***1 933.6***	***CEE***
France	385.1	399.7	391.4	395.1	431.9	435.6	400.0	360.8	341.0	293.1	France
Germany, Fed. Rep.	697.1	741.8	739.5	741.9	730.7	728.9	723.7	743.4	777.2	745.5	Allemagne, Rép. féd.
Greece	134.3	131.4	145.6	168.0	184.0	185.6	177.4	157.9	189.0	145.0	Grèce
Italy	206.5	260.1	270.8	269.1	271.2	273.8	232.9	195.7	230.2	224.1	Italie
Netherlands	255.5	241.3	261.2	257.7	258.6	262.0	250.9	235.3	249.2	250.6	Pays-Bas
United Kingdom[3]	334.5	349.7	346.2	359.5	374.4	339.2	240.8	252.5	287.9	275.4	Royaume-Uni[3]
EFTA	***932.2***	***947.3***	***963.5***	***992.6***	***988.3***	***965.9***	***962.7***	***1 041.3***	***1 159.3***	***1 125.2***	***AELE***
Austria	88.7	91.8	91.3	92.7	94.4	94.2	93.9	94.2	151.9	152.7	Autriche
Iceland	65.2	70.7	73.5	71.0	73.0	73.6	75.2	76.1	80.4	73.4	Islande
Norway	617.6	622.7	638.6	663.9	653.4	633.6	636.9	713.0	765.1	742.7	Norvège
Sweden	82.5	82.2	80.6	82.0	81.2	82.3	81.3	82.0	82.8	83.7	Suède
Switzerland	78.2	79.8	79.5	83.0	86.3	82.2	75.3	76.0	79.2	72.7	Suisse
East Europe	***477.0***	***485.4***	***486.4***	***482.4***	***507.9***	***475.0***	***416.7***	***436.6***	***453.8***	***459.6***	***Europe de l'est***
Czechoslovakia	36.0	36.5	36.8	36.9	38.3	32.7	33.8	36.2	31.6	31.7	Tchécoslovaquie
German Dem. Rep.* [2]	60.0	65.0	65.0	60.0	60.0	60.0	58.0	59.0	58.0	60.0	Rép. dém. allemande* [2]
Hungary	70.5	71.3	71.4	71.9	73.5	74.3	74.2	74.0	74.2	73.9	Hongrie
Poland	103.5	103.5	100.2	96.6	95.1	66.0	42.7	44.4	45.9	47.0	Pologne
Romania[3]	207.0	209.0	213.0	217.0	241.0	242.0	208.0	223.0	244.0	247.0	Roumanie[3]
Other Europe	***407.7***	***338.5***	***340.8***	***427.2***	***546.4***	***569.3***	***586.6***	***615.7***	***673.1***	***676.4***	***Autre Europe***
Spain	210.0	211.2	[4] 212.2	[4] 259.5	[4] 385.0	[4] 396.6	[4] 366.5	[4] 357.5	[4] 380.8	[4] 370.1	Espagne
Yugoslavia	[5] 197.7	127.3	128.6	167.7	161.4	172.7	220.1	258.2	292.3	306.3	Yougoslavie
USSR* [1]	**1 600.0**	**1 640.0**	**1 670.0**	**1 750.0**	**1 760.0**	**1 800.0**	**1 850.0**	**2 000.0**	**2 100.0**	**2 200.0**	**URSS* [1]**
Oceania	**358.1**	**380.7**	**409.4**	**418.4**	**437.7**	**498.7**	**541.0**	**622.5**	**860.8**	**1 063.1**	**Océanie**
Australia[6]	220.0	236.9	259.6	264.8	283.0	344.8	377.6	403.9	617.9	822.3	Australie[6]
New Zealand	138.1	143.7	149.8	153.6	154.7	154.0	163.4	218.6	242.9	240.8	Nouvelle-Zélande
Total	**12 626.8**	**13 706.6**	**13 993.2**	**14 530.8**	**15 318.4**	**14 921.4**	**13 237.3**	**13 704.8**	**15 593.1**	**15 313.4**	**Total**

General note.

For footnotes, see end of table.

Remarque générale.

Voir la fin du tableau pour les notes.

Primary aluminium recovered by the electrolytic reduction of alumina from domestic and imported ores. (SITC 68410–1).

[1] Source: U. S. Bureau of Mines, (Washington, D. C.).
[2] Source: Metallgesellschaft Aktiengesellschaft, (Frankfurt).
[3] Including pure content of virgin alloys.
[4] Source: World Metal Statistics, (London).
[5] Including secondary metal production.
[6] Twelve months ending 30 June of year stated.

Aluminium de première fusion obtenu par réduction électrolytique de l'alumine contenue dans les minerais nationaux ou importés. (CTCI 68410–1).

[1] Source: U.S. Bureau of Mines, (Washington, D.C.).
[2] Source: Metallgesellschaft Aktiengesellschaft, (Francfort).
[3] Y compris la teneur pure des alliages de première fusion.
[4] Source: World Metal Statistics, (Londres).
[5] Y compris la production de métal de deuxième fusion.
[6] Période de douze mois finissant le 30 juin de l'année indiquée.

Aluminium, unwrought, secondary – Aluminium non travaillé, récupéré

Unit : Thousand metric tons

Unité : Milliers de tonnes métriques

Country or area	1976	1977	1978	1979	1980	1981	1982	1983	1984	1985	Pays ou zone
America, North	**1 295.1**	**1 414.6**	**1 497.5**	**1 599.9**	**1 551.0**	**1 747.0**	**1 636.3**	**1 727.1**	**1 692.8**	**1 859.0**	**Amérique du Nord**
Canada[1]	42.5	48.3	74.8	84.5	65.1	59.3	62.0	63.0	64.0	65.0	Canada[1]
Mexico[1]	...	...	...	14.9	17.1	20.3	25.8	15.7	22.5	32.0	Mexique[1]
United States[2]	1 243.8	1 355.3	1 409.8	1 500.5	1 468.7	1 667.4	1 548.6	1 648.4	1 606.3	1 762.0	Etats-Unis[2]
America, South	**25.7**	**33.5**	**31.8**	**52.4**	**50.1**	**36.0**	**46.3**	**43.0**	**48.9**	**44.8**	**Amérique du Sud**
Brazil	25.7	33.5	31.8	52.4	50.1	36.0	46.3	43.0	48.9	44.8	Brésil
Asia	**527.4**	**586.9**	**660.0**	**768.3**	**800.4**	**839.6**	**798.1**	**837.7**	**840.3**	**867.2**	**Asie**
Japan[2]	527.4	586.9	660.0	768.3	800.4	839.6	798.1	837.7	840.3	867.2	Japon[2]
Europe	**971.9**	**1 093.2**	**1 053.1**	**1 048.2**	**1 039.0**	**1 017.0**	**970.2**	**1 166.6**	**1 019.0**	**913.3**	**Europe**
EEC	***618.2***	***660.4***	***666.1***	***671.9***	***682.3***	***641.6***	***598.9***	***665.8***	***689.8***	***674.6***	***CEE***
Belgium[3]	* 2.6	* 3.6	* 1.1	* 2.0	0.0	0.0	0.0	1.0	2.0	2.0	Belgique[3]
France[2]	133.3	146.0	160.8	165.7	170.0	155.7	154.8	162.1	163.0	164.3	France[2]
Germany, Fed. Rep.[4]	39.9	43.3	44.5	42.4	37.1	37.7	37.7	38.2	...	...	Allemagne, Rép. féd.[4]
Italy	198.0	225.0	222.0	245.0	266.0	250.0	242.0	278.0	283.0	282.0	Italie
Netherlands	38.5	41.6	44.0	40.1	47.1	50.2	49.8	58.2	59.9	62.3	Pays-Bas
United Kingdom	205.8	200.8	193.7	176.7	162.1	148.0	114.6	128.3	143.9	127.6	Royaume-Uni
EFTA	***249.1***	***322.4***	***280.8***	***312.5***	***294.8***	***316.9***	***309.3***	***438.0***	***279.3***	***186.4***	***AELE***
Austria[5]	202.3	276.7	237.5	269.4	245.0	264.7	264.0	388.4	228.8	132.3	Autriche[5]
Finland	5.7	9.3	8.9	7.7	11.5	11.0	11.6	14.9	18.7	* 21.0	Finlande
Norway	14.9	9.5	6.6	7.6	12.3	14.5	8.7	4.6	5.6	6.0	Norvège
Portugal	2.1	2.3	3.1	3.8	2.7	1.9	1.9	2.4	2.4	2.1	Portugal
Sweden[3]	24.0	24.5	24.6	24.0	23.2	24.7	* 23.2	27.7	23.8	25.0	Suède[3]
Other Europe	***104.6***	***110.4***	***106.2***	***63.8***	***61.9***	***58.6***	***62.0***	***62.8***	***49.9***	***52.2***	***Autre Europe***
Spain	40.0	40.3	# [6] 39.1	[6] 42.0	[6] 38.5	[6] 34.5	[6] 35.7	[6] 37.4	[6] 40.6	[6] 42.5	Espagne
Yugoslavia	...	70.1	67.1	21.8	23.4	24.1	26.3	25.4	9.3	9.7	Yougoslavie
USSR* [1]	**150.0**	**150.0**	**150.0**	**160.0**	**170.0**	**180.0**	**190.0**	**200.0**	**210.0**	**215.0**	**URSS* [1]**
Oceania	**30.5**	**24.6**	**24.4**	**30.5**	**38.0**	**44.0**	**44.4**	**37.7**	**63.9**	**104.1**	**Océanie**
Australia[7]	30.5	24.6	24.4	30.5	38.0	44.0	44.4	37.7	63.9	104.1	Australie[7]
Total	**3 000.6**	**3 302.7**	**3 416.8**	**3 659.3**	**3 648.5**	**3 863.8**	**3 685.3**	**4 012.1**	**3 874.8**	**4 003.4**	**Total**

General note.
Secondary aluminium obtained by remelting metal waste or scrap. (SITC 68410-2).

[1] Source: U. S. Bureau of Mines, (Washington, D. C.).
[2] Including alloys.
[3] Source: Metallgesellschaft Aktiengesellschaft, (Frankfurt).
[4] Beginning 1984, data are confidential.
[5] Secondary aluminium produced from old scrap only.
[6] Source: World Metal Statistics, (London).
[7] Twelve months ending 30 June of year stated.

Remarque générale.
Aluminium de deuxième fusion récupéré à partir de déchets et de débris d'ouvrages. (CTCI 68410-2).

[1] Source: U.S. Bureau of Mines, (Washington, D.C.).
[2] Y compris les alliages.
[3] Source: Metallgesellschaft Aktiengesellschaft, (Francfort).
[4] A partir de 1984, les données sont confidentielles.
[5] Aluminium de deuxième fusion obtenu à partir de vieux déchets seulement.
[6] Source: World Metal Statistics, (Londres).
[7] Période de douze mois finissant le 30 juin de l'année indiquée.

Aluminium–base alloys – Alliages à base d'aluminium

Unit : Thousand metric tons

Unité : Milliers de tonnes métriques

Country or area	1976	1977	1978	1979	1980	1981	1982	1983	1984	1985	Pays ou zone
America, South	**7.4**	**9.2**	**13.2**	**97.1**	**4.3**	**65.7**	**77.6**	**89.7**	**101.4**	**113.3**	**Amérique du Sud**
Brazil	7.3	9.1	13.2	97.1	4.3	...	...	...	...	...	Brésil
Colombia	0.0	0.1	0.0	0.0	0.0	0.0	0.0	0.3	...	...	Colombie
Asia	**120.6**	**114.8**	**128.6**	**136.7**	**138.2**	**115.9**	**114.0**	**133.4**	**128.6**	**146.8**	**Asie**
Japan	...	110.2	123.2	130.6	131.0	108.0	106.5	125.1	119.9	135.5	Japon
Korea, Republic of	...	...	...	...	6.6	7.3	6.9	7.7	8.0	10.7	Corée, République de
Philippines[1]	0.7	0.5	...	...	...	...	...	...	...	...	Philippines[1]
Europe	**811.0**	**904.9**	**939.1**	**988.2**	**984.4**	**867.0**	**905.6**	**970.0**	**1 067.2**	**1 078.8**	**Europe**
EEC	***315.3***	***358.6***	***378.8***	***390.7***	***379.0***	***364.6***	***378.0***	***397.7***	***413.6***	***431.6***	***CEE***
Denmark	10.8	11.9	10.7	10.1	11.2	10.9	11.5	12.6	14.2	16.4	Danemark
Germany, Fed. Rep.	304.5	346.8	368.1	380.6	367.8	353.8	366.6	385.0	399.5	415.2	Allemagne, Rép. féd.
EFTA	***242.2***	***248.2***	***262.9***	***274.2***	***277.2***	***218.4***	***248.1***	***339.9***	***370.1***	***367.0***	***AELE***
Finland	18.7	18.7	27.9	22.6	37.2	31.7	27.8	29.5	27.3	...	Finlande
Norway	221.9	228.5	235.0	251.6	239.9	186.7	220.3	310.4	342.7	333.9	Norvège
Portugal	* 1.5	1.0	0.0	0.0	0.0	0.0	0.0	0.0	0.0	0.0	Portugal
East Europe	***76.8***	***83.2***	***82.4***	***75.4***	***74.4***	***59.4***	***63.7***	***60.8***	***68.3***	***65.0***	***Europe de l'est***
Poland	76.8	83.2	82.4	75.4	74.4	59.4	63.7	60.8	68.3	65.0	Pologne
Other Europe	***176.7***	***215.0***	***215.0***	***247.9***	***253.8***	***224.6***	***215.7***	***171.6***	***215.2***	***215.2***	***Autre Europe***
Spain[2]	176.7	...	...	247.9	253.8	224.6	215.7	171.6	...	...	Espagne[2]
Total	**939.0**	**1 029.0**	**1 080.9**	**1 222.1**	**1 126.9**	**1 048.6**	**1 097.2**	**1 193.2**	**1 297.2**	**1 338.9**	**Total**

General note.
Aluminium–base alloys in which aluminium predominates by weight over each of the other metals. (SITC 68410–3).

[1] Shipments.
[2] Including other aluminium alloys.

Remarque générale.
Alliages à base d'aluminium dans lesquels l'aluminium prédomine en poids sur tous les autres métaux. (CTCI 68410–3).

[1] Expéditions.
[2] Y compris autres alliages d'aluminium.

Aluminium bars, rods, angles, shapes, sections – Barres, cornières et profilés d'aluminium

Unit : Thousand metric tons — Unité : Milliers de tonnes métriques

Country or area	1976	1977	1978	1979	1980	1981	1982	1983	1984	1985	Pays ou zone
America, North	**1 016.6**	**1 079.2**	**1 251.1**	**1 235.9**	**1 209.3**	**1 104.2**	**1 034.8**	**1 212.8**	**1 368.3**	**1 346.4**	**Amérique du Nord**
Cuba	1.8	1.2	1.3	1.5	2.0	4.2	2.9	2.4	3.0	3.6	Cuba
Dominican Republic	35.2	50.6	57.7	39.4	61.3	50.8	57.2	79.5	78.7	71.9	Rép. dominicaine
Mexico	17.8	15.0	19.8	24.8	29.5	30.5	26.8	15.6	16.8	24.6	Mexique
United States[1]	961.8	1 012.4	1 172.4	1 170.2	1 116.4	1 018.8	947.9	1 115.4	1 269.8	1 246.4	Etats-Unis[1]
America, South	**52.6**	**46.1**	**73.5**	**49.9**	**93.5**	**87.5**	**96.0**	**105.2**	**113.1**	**121.5**	**Amérique du Sud**
Brazil	49.7	42.3	69.5	[2] 44.5	88.0	...	...	...	...	...	Brésil
Colombia	2.9	3.8	4.0	5.4	5.5	5.2	5.8	7.2	...	...	Colombie
Asia	**811.5**	**770.9**	**853.7**	**981.1**	**925.5**	**803.2**	**871.3**	**940.0**	**911.4**	**942.1**	**Asie**
India	11.8	15.4	18.0	21.9	21.7	24.4	28.8	29.8	39.5	39.9	Inde
Japan[3]	761.1	715.1	794.4	912.1	859.4	723.4	774.5	831.9	796.1	825.7	Japon[3]
Korea, Republic of	...	...	...	...	32.1	40.4	49.0	57.5	53.8	54.4	Corée, République de
Philippines[4]	6.6	1.7	...	...	...	...	...	...	...	...	Philippines[4]
Turkey	14.0	16.0	9.9	11.1	8.2	10.9	15.0	16.6	17.9	18.0	Turquie
Europe	**1 056.1**	**1 067.1**	**1 127.7**	**1 238.9**	**1 252.8**	**1 140.6**	**1 221.0**	**1 322.7**	**970.8**	**1 006.3**	**Europe**
EEC	***909.1***	***942.8***	***1 002.4***	***1 142.3***	***1 130.8***	***1 023.2***	***1 110.5***	***1 191.6***	***856.0***	***895.2***	***CEE***
France[5]	260.2	282.3	304.9	345.0	326.6	345.9	412.5	422.7	# [6] 112.0	112.5	France[5]
Germany, Fed. Rep.[3]	261.2	255.2	263.9	300.8	293.4	237.7	227.6	263.2	251.9	258.1	Allemagne, Rép. féd.[3]
Greece	39.4	45.3	54.8	58.3	66.2	58.1	67.4	59.5	63.4	...	Grèce
Italy	122.3	132.5	144.5	178.0	204.6	172.6	184.8	201.2	180.8	202.3	Italie
Netherlands[7]	107.7	106.2	103.5	111.9	107.0	93.9	95.2	109.3	113.0	122.8	Pays-Bas[7]
United Kingdom[4]	118.2	121.4	130.7	148.3	132.9	115.0	123.0	135.7	134.9	128.9	Royaume-Uni[4]
EFTA	***17.5***	***16.1***	***16.4***	***18.3***	***18.2***	***16.6***	***17.6***	***20.7***	***21.5***	***20.2***	***AELE***
Sweden	17.5	16.1	16.4	18.3	18.2	16.6	17.6	20.7	21.5	20.2	Suède
East Europe	***60.0***	***64.4***	***69.6***	***76.9***	***77.5***	***76.1***	***71.2***	***75.9***	***80.7***	***82.9***	***Europe de l'est***
Czechoslovakia	21.2	22.6	22.8	26.9	27.7	28.1	26.8	24.8	25.7	26.1	Tchécoslovaquie
Hungary	17.0	18.8	22.8	24.8	25.6	27.8	25.6	30.8	33.2	34.2	Hongrie
Poland	21.7	23.0	23.9	25.2	24.2	20.3	18.8	20.4	21.8	22.6	Pologne
Other Europe	***69.5***	***43.8***	***39.3***	***1.4***	***26.3***	***24.7***	***21.6***	***34.4***	***12.5***	***8.1***	***Autre Europe***
Spain	69.5	...	...	1.4	26.3	24.7	21.6	34.4	...	...	Espagne
Oceania	**45.7**	**50.4**	**50.4**	**55.3**	**63.6**	**62.5**	**67.3**	**56.7**	**83.6**	**92.6**	**Océanie**
Australia[8]	45.7	50.4	50.4	55.3	63.6	62.5	67.3	56.7	83.6	92.6	Australie[8]
Total	**2 982.7**	**3 013.7**	**3 356.5**	**3 561.1**	**3 544.5**	**3 198.1**	**3 290.4**	**3 637.3**	**3 447.3**	**3 509.0**	**Total**

General note.
Rolled, extruded, drawn or forged aluminium products of solid section, of which the maximum cross-sectional dimension exceeds 6 mm and which, if they are flat, have a thickness exceeding one-tenth of the width. (SITC 68421-1).

1 Including bare wire.
2 Production by establishments employing 5 or more persons.
3 Including products of alloys containing aluminium.
4 Shipments.
5 Aluminium and light alloys.
6 Aluminium bars, rods and sections and other light metals.
7 Semi-finished products.
8 Twelve months ending 30 June of year stated.

Remarque générale.
Produits en aluminium de section pleine, laminés, filés, étirés ou forgés, dont la plus grande dimension transversale est supérieure à 6 mm et, en ce qui concerne les produits plats, dont l'épaisseur dépasse le dixième de la largeur. (CTCI 68421-1).

1 Y compris les fils nus.
2 Production des établissements occupant 5 personnes ou plus.
3 Y compris les produits en alliages contenant de l'aluminum.
4 Expéditions.
5 Aluminium et alliages légers.
6 Barres et profilés en aluminium et autres métaux légers.
7 Produits semi-finis.
8 Période de douze mois finissant le 30 juin de l'année indiquée.

Aluminium wire – Fil d'aluminium

Unit : Thousand metric tons | Unité : Milliers de tonnes métriques

Country or area	1976	1977	1978	1979	1980	1981	1982	1983	1984	1985	Pays ou zone
America, North	**304.3**	**328.8**	**389.2**	**402.5**	**369.6**	**349.6**	**296.9**	**320.6**	**349.7**	**416.5**	**Amérique du Nord**
Mexico	20.6	13.0	21.9	19.3	23.5	32.0	15.2	7.4	14.2	25.3	Mexique
United States[1]	283.7	315.8	367.4	383.2	346.1	317.7	281.7	313.2	335.5	391.1	Etats–Unis[1]
America, South	**2.5**	**2.0**	**3.5**	**2.8**	**1.9**	**2.4**	**2.4**	**2.3**	**2.3**	**2.2**	**Amérique du Sud**
Brazil	2.2	1.5	1.6	* 1.6	1.6	...	...	...	...	...	Brésil
Colombia	0.3	0.5	1.9	1.2	0.3	...	...	...	...	...	Colombie
Asia	**185.4**	**192.2**	**199.2**	**196.3**	**216.5**	**174.5**	**146.3**	**146.5**	**149.3**	**133.1**	**Asie**
India	42.0	25.7	19.9	23.7	25.6	25.7	14.4	14.1	17.3	18.9	Inde
Japan[2]	134.1	157.7	170.6	164.7	182.2	140.1	123.2	123.6	123.3	105.5	Japon[2]
Turkey	9.3	8.9	8.7	7.9	...	...	...	...	...	...	Turquie
Europe	**376.4**	**366.6**	**372.9**	**377.0**	**430.4**	**418.1**	**410.6**	**453.2**	**451.0**	**459.3**	**Europe**
EEC	***153.4***	***143.9***	***157.6***	***175.9***	***199.8***	***196.7***	***197.0***	***206.4***	***200.4***	***205.4***	***CEE***
Denmark	0.7	1.0	3.2	3.4	...	...	...	...	...	...	Danemark
France	90.6	89.9	98.4	112.6	131.9	134.4	# 146.1	146.2	130.0	134.3	France
Germany, Fed. Rep.[2]	7.3	7.7	6.4	7.7	7.5	6.9	6.4	9.0	9.1	10.1	Allemagne, Rép. féd.[2]
Italy	13.0	10.5	14.5	14.0	25.0	21.8	10.5	20.0	30.3	29.1	Italie
United Kingdom[3]	41.8	34.8	35.0	38.2	33.3	31.6	31.9	29.2	28.9	29.9	Royaume–Uni[3]
EFTA	***116.5***	***118.8***	***115.1***	***120.3***	***115.6***	***115.7***	***117.5***	***149.9***	***148.9***	***152.0***	***AELE***
Austria[4]	85.8	86.6	88.3	95.5	91.9	89.1	90.4	118.9	124.8	126.9	Autriche[4]
Finland	8.6	12.3	8.2	3.0	4.1	4.9	3.4	3.7	3.4	...	Finlande
Sweden[5]	22.1	19.8	18.5	21.7	19.5	21.6	23.7	27.2	20.8	23.9	Suède[5]
East Europe	***58.5***	***57.3***	***55.3***	***53.6***	***54.9***	***61.1***	***56.5***	***62.4***	***65.3***	***66.1***	***Europe de l'est***
Czechoslovakia	24.4	23.0	23.1	21.4	21.3	18.8	17.7	19.5	20.1	20.6	Tchécoslovaquie
Hungary	34.1	34.2	32.2	32.2	33.6	42.3	38.9	42.9	45.2	45.5	Hongrie
Other Europe	***47.9***	***46.7***	***44.9***	***27.3***	***60.2***	***44.6***	***39.6***	***34.4***	***36.4***	***35.7***	***Autre Europe***
Spain	30.6	...	...	2.3	32.3	32.9	24.8	24.0	...	...	Espagne
Yugoslavia	17.3	22.7	20.8	25.0	27.9	11.8	14.8	10.4	11.3	10.4	Yougoslavie
Oceania	**16.9**	**15.7**	**17.3**	**17.0**	**17.9**	**21.3**	**23.4**	**21.4**	**19.0**	**23.0**	**Océanie**
Australia[6]	16.9	15.7	17.3	17.0	17.9	21.3	23.4	21.4	19.0	23.0	Australie[6]
Total	**885.5**	**905.4**	**982.2**	**995.5**	**1 036.4**	**965.9**	**879.7**	**943.9**	**971.4**	**1 034.1**	**Total**

General note.
Rolled, extruded or drawn aluminium products of solid section of any cross–sectional shape, of which no cross–sectional dimension exceeds 6 mm. (SITC 68421–2).

1 Excluding bare wire.
2 Including products of alloys containing aluminium.
3 Shipments.
4 Including all other aluminium products.
5 Aluminium wire, rolled only.
6 Twelve months ending 30 June of year stated.

Remarque générale.
Produits en aluminium de section pleine, laminés, filés, étirés ou tréfilés), dont la coupe transversale, de forme quelconque, n'excède pas 6 mm dans sa plus grande dimension (fil). (CTCI 68421–2).

1 Non compris les fils nus.
2 Y compris les produits en alliages contenant de l'aluminum.
3 Expéditions.
4 Y compris tous les autres produits en aluminium.
5 Fils d'aluminium, laminés seulement.
6 Période de douze mois finissant le 30 juin de l'année indiquée.

Aluminium plates, sheets, strip, foil – Tôles, bandes et feuilles d'aluminium:

Unit : Thousand metric tons

Unité : Milliers de tonnes métriques

Country or area	1976	1977	1978	1979	1980	1981	1982	1983	1984	1985	Pays ou zone
Africa	**11.9**	**13.6**	**16.2**	**16.4**	**14.6**	**15.1**	**13.8**	**14.5**	**14.5**	**14.5**	**Afrique**
Egypt	8.4	9.6	12.1	12.4	...	...	...	...	...	...	Egypte
United Rep. Tanzania	3.4	4.0	4.0	4.0	4.0	4.5	3.1	...	...	...	Rép.Unie de Tanzanie
America, North	**2 893.6**	**3 120.7**	**3 322.9**	**3 279.5**	**3 057.5**	**3 117.0**	**2 929.3**	**3 483.2**	**3 428.1**	**3 483.5**	**Amérique du Nord**
Mexico	15.0	15.4	18.4	21.2	21.8	19.6	15.3	12.2	12.0	20.4	Mexique
United States	2 878.6	3 105.3	3 304.6	3 258.3	3 035.7	3 097.4	2 914.0	3 471.0	3 416.1	3 463.1	Etats–Unis
America, South	**114.9**	**155.0**	**152.9**	**174.5**	**240.4**	**243.0**	**269.2**	**294.7**	**321.4**	**347.2**	**Amérique du Sud**
Brazil	99.8	136.7	134.5	* [1] 156.8	221.3	...	...	...	...	...	Brésil
Colombia	4.1	7.2	7.4	6.7	8.0	3.6	3.6	2.9	...	...	Colombie
Venezuela	11.0	...	...	...	...	...	...	...	...	...	Venezuela
Asia	**632.0**	**613.6**	**731.6**	**765.4**	**685.0**	**753.3**	**851.2**	**955.0**	**1 042.0**	**1 083.9**	**Asie**
Burma[2]	0.6	...	...	...	...	...	...	...	...	...	Birmanie[2]
India	44.0	49.8	52.9	52.4	47.5	55.0	57.3	59.5	71.0	81.8	Inde
Japan[3]	563.1	534.9	650.4	671.2	596.3	643.4	735.1	819.4	890.0	914.4	Japon[3]
Korea, Republic of	9.0	11.4	16.8	19.8	13.8	23.5	24.6	33.5	37.2	40.2	Corée, République de
Turkey	15.2	16.9	10.9	21.4	26.8	...	33.5	42.0	43.1	...	Turquie
Europe	**1 280.3**	**1 273.9**	**1 299.9**	**1 414.6**	**1 360.3**	**1 348.7**	**1 369.8**	**1 470.8**	**1 524.0**	**1 524.6**	**Europe**
EEC	***925.6***	***926.6***	***962.4***	***1 048.5***	***1 020.5***	***1 014.5***	***1 040.2***	***1 122.9***	***1 192.2***	***1 189.3***	***CEE***
France[4]	39.4	42.0	44.5	48.4	46.7	47.3	# 45.1	43.0	39.0	34.5	France[4]
Germany, Fed. Rep.[3]	487.2	487.7	521.2	588.3	568.1	600.5	611.2	703.1	742.9	745.1	Allemagne, Rép. féd.[3]
Greece	...	...	...	...	...	...	...	25.0	27.5	...	Grèce
Italy	155.8	167.0	181.0	176.0	180.0	174.6	184.0	177.0	191.6	188.9	Italie
United Kingdom[5]	217.0	203.8	189.5	209.5	199.4	165.8	173.7	174.9	191.2	194.5	Royaume–Uni[5]
EFTA	***137.8***	***137.5***	***118.4***	***165.0***	***130.9***	***123.0***	***124.5***	***118.2***	***110.5***	***113.5***	***AELE***
Norway	...	...	49.9	97.9	...	...	...	...	...	...	Norvège
Sweden[6]	63.9	63.6	68.4	67.1	57.0	49.1	50.6	44.3	36.6	39.6	Suède[6]
East Europe	***141.6***	***149.3***	***160.7***	***161.4***	***162.8***	***156.1***	***159.0***	***168.2***	***175.1***	***177.7***	***Europe de l'est***
Czechoslovakia	61.9	65.7	70.2	72.5	74.1	64.2	62.2	61.7	63.0	59.6	Tchécoslovaquie
Hungary	75.1	78.6	85.4	83.9	83.5	87.3	91.9	101.3	106.7	112.7	Hongrie
Poland	4.7	5.0	5.1	5.1	5.2	4.7	4.9	5.2	5.3	5.4	Pologne
Other Europe	***75.3***	***60.4***	***58.4***	***39.7***	***46.1***	***55.1***	***46.2***	***61.6***	***46.2***	***44.2***	***Autre Europe***
Spain	75.3	...	...	39.7	46.1	55.1	46.2	61.6	...	...	Espagne
Oceania	**83.3**	**94.3**	**98.7**	**109.2**	**135.9**	**145.5**	**146.3**	**144.7**	**159.4**	**172.8**	**Océanie**
Australia[7]	83.3	94.3	98.7	109.2	135.9	145.5	146.3	144.7	159.4	172.8	Australie[7]
Total	**5 016.0**	**5 271.0**	**5 622.2**	**5 759.6**	**5 493.7**	**5 622.6**	**5 579.5**	**6 362.9**	**6 489.5**	**6 626.5**	**Total**

General note.
Flat–surfaced, wrought aluminium products (coiled or not), of which the maximum cross–sectional dimension exceeds 6 mm and of which the thickness exceeds 0.15 mm but does not exceed one–tenth of the width (plates, sheets, strip), thin sheets, not exceeding 0.15 mm in thickness, whether or not embossed, cut to shape, perforated, coated, printed or backed with paper or other reinforcing material (aluminium foil). (SITC 68422 and 68423).

1 Production by establishments employing 5 or more persons.
2 Twelve months ending 30 September of year stated.
3 Including products of alloys containing aluminium.
4 Aluminium and light alloys.
5 Shipments.
6 Excluding aluminium foil of a thickness less than 0.05 mm.
7 Twelve months ending 30 June of year stated.

Remarque générale.
Produits plats en aluminium (enroulés ou non), dont la plus grande dimension transversale est supérieure à 6 mm et dont l'épaisseur, supérieure à 0.15 mm, ne dépasse pas le dixième de la largeur (tôles, feuilles et bandes), feuilles et bandes minces d'une épaisseur de 0.15 mm au maximum, même gaufrées, découpées, perforées, revêtues, imprimées ou fixées sur papier ou support similaire (feuilles minces ou papier d'aluminium). (CTCI 68422 et 68423).

1 Production des établissements occupant 5 personnes ou plus.
2 Période de douze mois finissant le 30 septembre de l'année indiquée.
3 Y compris les produits en alliages contenant de l'aluminum.
4 Aluminium et alliages légers.
5 Expéditions.
6 Non compris les feuilles d'aluminium d'une épaisseur inférieure à 0,05 mm.
7 Période de douze mois finissant le 30 juin de l'année indiquée.

Aluminium tubes and pipes – Tubes et tuyaux d'aluminium

Unit : Thousand metric tons

Unité : Milliers de tonnes métriques

Country or area	1976	1977	1978	1979	1980	1981	1982	1983	1984	1985	Pays ou zone
Africa	**3.8**	**3.7**	**3.5**	**3.4**	**2.9**	**3.4**	**3.0**	**2.6**	**2.5**	**2.4**	**Afrique**
South Africa	...	...	...	...	2.9	3.4	3.0	2.6	* 2.5	2.4	Afrique du Sud
America, North	**179.0**	**188.3**	**184.0**	**156.8**	**152.0**	**150.6**	**122.1**	**139.4**	**140.5**	**117.9**	**Amérique du Nord**
Mexico	6.2	5.6	5.4	6.6	7.7	7.2	5.9	4.2	5.2	4.8	Mexique
United States	172.8	182.6	178.7	150.2	144.3	143.4	116.2	135.3	135.3	113.0	Etats–Unis
America, South	**88.2**	**6.7**	**4.9**	**4.4**	**29.7**	**12.0**	**6.9**	**0.7**	**3.7**	**3.6**	**Amérique du Sud**
Brazil	87.5	5.5	3.4	[1] 4.3	29.6	...	...	...	...	...	Brésil
Colombia	0.7	1.2	1.5	0.1	0.1	0.7	1.0	0.2	...	...	Colombie
Asia	**29.6**	**26.1**	**31.1**	**39.4**	**40.3**	**41.3**	**41.9**	**50.5**	**54.1**	**53.2**	**Asie**
Japan[2]	29.6	26.1	31.1	39.4	40.3	41.3	41.9	50.5	54.1	53.2	Japon[2]
Europe	**110.7**	**111.3**	**102.6**	**105.1**	**111.6**	**100.7**	**103.0**	**99.7**	**101.1**	**99.8**	**Europe**
EEC	***89.4***	***88.5***	***79.0***	***82.6***	***82.8***	***74.4***	***74.5***	***75.6***	***72.4***	***72.0***	***CEE***
Denmark	...	...	3.9	4.5	5.1	...	...	...	...	...	Danemark
France[3]	17.1	18.2	14.6	15.0	14.4	12.9	# 9.6	[4] 9.6	[4] 9.0	[4] 8.5	France[3]
Germany, Fed. Rep.[2]	30.3	29.9	26.4	27.4	27.1	25.2	24.9	26.5	27.4	26.6	Allemagne, Rép. féd.[2]
Greece	1.4	2.1	1.6	0.6	0.2	0.8	2.0	2.9	3.0	...	Grèce
Italy	15.2	13.5	15.0	17.0	20.0	18.0	19.0	19.8	18.0	20.0	Italie
United Kingdom[5]	20.9	20.2	17.4	18.1	16.0	13.1	14.4	12.4	10.4	9.9	Royaume–Uni[5]
EFTA	***7.9***	***8.6***	***8.9***	***10.7***	***11.2***	***9.6***	***10.3***	***12.0***	***12.9***	***11.0***	***AELE***
Finland	0.1	0.1	0.1	0.1	0.1	0.1	0.1	0.1	0.1	...	Finlande
Sweden	7.8	8.4	8.8	10.6	11.1	9.5	10.1	11.8	12.7	10.8	Suède
East Europe	***11.7***	***12.1***	***12.0***	***10.9***	***12.2***	***11.5***	***10.7***	***9.7***	***10.0***	***10.4***	***Europe de l'est***
Czechoslovakia	7.9	8.3	8.1	6.6	7.8	7.3	6.6	5.2	5.5	5.8	Tchécoslovaquie
Hungary	3.8	3.8	3.8	4.3	4.4	4.2	4.1	4.5	4.5	4.6	Hongrie
Other Europe	***1.6***	***2.2***	***2.7***	***0.9***	***5.4***	***5.2***	***7.5***	***2.4***	***5.9***	***6.4***	***Autre Europe***
Spain	1.6	...	...	0.9	5.4	5.2	7.5	2.4	...	...	Espagne
Oceania	**2.6**	**2.5**	**3.3**	**3.2**	**3.0**	**4.0**	**3.6**	**3.7**	**2.7**	**3.6**	**Océanie**
Australia[6]	* 2.6	* 2.5	* 3.3	3.2	3.0	4.0	3.6	3.7	2.7	...	Australie[6]
Total	**413.8**	**338.6**	**329.4**	**312.3**	**339.5**	**312.0**	**280.4**	**296.7**	**304.6**	**280.5**	**Total**

General note.
Seamless and welded tubes and pipes, including blanks therefore, but excluding tube and pipe fittings. (SITC 68425–0).

[1] Production by establishments employing 5 or more persons.
[2] Including products of alloys containing aluminium.
[3] Aluminium and light alloys.
[4] Pipes, tubes and hollow rods of aluminium.
[5] Shipments of aluminium tubes only.
[6] Twelve months ending 30 June of year stated.

Remarque générale.
Tuyaux et tubes sans soudure et soudés, y compris leurs ébauches mais non les accessoires de tuyauterie en aluminium. (CTCI 68425–0).

[1] Production des établissements occupant 5 personnes ou plus.
[2] Y compris les produits en alliages contenant de l'aluminum.
[3] Aluminium et alliages légers.
[4] Tubes, tuyaux et barres creuses en aluminium.
[5] Expéditions de tubes d'aluminium seulement.
[6] Période de douze mois finissant le 30 juin de l'année indiquée.

ISIC-BASED CODE
3720-37

Lead, refined, unwrought (total production) – Plomb non travaillé, affiné (production totale)

CODE BASE CITI
3720-37

Unit : Thousand metric tons

Unité : Milliers de tonnes métriques

Country or area	1976	1977	1978	1979	1980	1981	1982	1983	1984	1985	Pays ou zone
Africa	**105.1**	**112.7**	**101.0**	**112.7**	**118.4**	**125.9**	**133.3**	**122.3**	**98.6**	**118.2**	**Afrique**
Egypt	1.8	2.6	...	...	...	...	...	...	...	...	Egypte
Morocco[1]	26.3	34.6	30.0	36.8	42.4	52.3	58.6	57.6	48.3	63.5	Maroc[1]
Namibia[2]	39.6	42.7	39.5	41.7	42.7	41.7	40.6	35.4	28.9	38.5	Namibie[2]
Nigeria[2 3]	0.0	0.0	0.0	1.5	2.0	2.0	2.0	2.0	2.0	3.0	Nigéria[2 3]
Tunisia	23.9	19.5	16.6	17.7	19.2	17.8	15.3	10.5	8.4	2.0	Tunisie
Zambia	13.5	13.3	12.7	12.8	10.0	9.9	14.6	14.6	8.8	9.0	Zambie
America, North	**1 468.2**	**1 551.3**	**1 588.0**	**1 581.0**	**1 518.3**	**1 461.3**	**1 412.4**	**1 370.4**	**1 392.7**	**1 463.9**	**Amérique du Nord**
Canada[4]	231.0	240.6	245.9	252.4	234.6	238.1	241.9	242.0	252.0	240.0	Canada[4]
Guatemala[2]	0.1	0.1	0.1	0.1	0.1	0.0	0.0	0.1	0.1	0.1	Guatemala[2]
Mexico	128.0	137.5	150.3	158.3	131.1	138.3	128.8	152.6	153.8	185.2	Mexique
United States	1 109.1	1 173.1	1 191.7	1 170.3	1 152.6	1 084.9	1 041.6	975.8	986.8	1 038.7	Etats-Unis
America, South	**200.5**	**214.7**	**198.8**	**250.3**	**230.0**	**201.9**	**181.2**	**174.2**	**183.4**	**218.1**	**Amérique du Sud**
Argentina	50.0	45.0	29.7	50.0	41.7	34.6	30.6	30.7	31.3	35.0	Argentine
Bolivia[5]	0.2	0.2	0.1	0.5	0.8	0.3	[2] 0.2	[2] 0.3	[2] 0.2	[2] 0.2	Bolivie[5]
Brazil	69.2	77.2	80.5	99.1	90.4	70.8	53.4	63.1	63.7	81.6	Brésil
Peru	74.1	# [6] 84.3	[6] 79.6	[6] 90.7	[6] 87.0	[6] 84.2	[6] 82.0	[6] 65.1	[6] 71.2	[6] 83.3	Pérou
Venezuela* [2 3]	7.0	8.0	9.0	10.0	10.0	12.0	15.0	15.0	17.0	18.0	Venezuela* [2 3]
Asia	**449.3**	**464.0**	**488.8**	**490.9**	**495.4**	**504.0**	**503.9**	**548.2**	**628.3**	**640.9**	**Asie**
Burma[2]	3.5	5.0	5.1	6.4	6.2	5.3	8.1	7.9	7.2	9.9	Birmanie[2]
China* [2]	140.0	150.0	160.0	170.0	175.0	175.0	175.0	195.0	195.0	195.0	Chine* [2]
India	5.4	7.6	10.0	9.7	14.8	14.3	14.4	13.7	15.7	15.8	Inde
Iran(Islamic Rep.of)* [6]	0.3	0.3	0.0	0.0	0.0	0.0	0.0	5.0	7.5	7.5	Iran(Rép.islamique)* [6]
Japan	219.1	221.4	228.4	221.2	220.9	226.2	223.9	241.3	278.5	285.4	Japon
Korea, D. P. Rp.* [2]	70.0	70.0	75.0	70.0	65.0	65.0	60.0	60.0	95.0	95.0	Corée, Rp. P. D.* [2]
Korea, Republic of	7.8	6.7	7.2	7.6	10.4	14.7	16.1	17.8	20.3	22.4	Corée, République de
Turkey[6]	3.2	3.0	3.0	5.9	3.0	3.5	6.5	7.5	9.0	* 10.0	Turquie[6]
Europe	**1 651.2**	**1 777.4**	**1 795.0**	**1 830.4**	**1 766.6**	**1 708.7**	**1 646.4**	**1 699.0**	**1 712.9**	**1 754.7**	**Europe**
EEC	***1 095.9***	***1 149.4***	***1 162.6***	***1 214.9***	***1 167.0***	***1 161.2***	***1 064.7***	***1 088.2***	***1 127.7***	***1 098.7***	***CEE***
Belgium[7]	121.5	122.8	125.0	113.4	127.9	109.9	99.7	134.2	127.7	114.3	Belgique[7]
Denmark[3]	8.0	10.5	7.6	12.0	11.9	12.9	15.9	10.1	13.1	4.5	Danemark[3]
France	172.2	184.1	208.5	219.7	218.8	228.0	# 220.9	204.2	203.0	205.8	France
Germany, Fed. Rep.[8]	278.3	309.6	305.1	316.8	301.4	304.2	[9] 260.6	[9] 261.5	[9] 262.3	[9] 260.9	Allemagne, Rép. féd.[8]
Greece	19.1	20.4	22.6	28.3	20.9	20.2	4.2	0.0	9.1	* 13.7	Grèce
Italy	118.2	117.7	116.2	126.2	133.7	133.0	133.7	130.0	140.5	135.0	Italie
Netherlands	36.7	33.2	31.9	30.1	27.7	19.7	23.5	26.0	* 33.6	* 37.3	Pays-Bas
United Kingdom[10]	341.9	351.1	345.8	368.3	324.8	333.4	306.2	322.2	338.4	327.2	Royaume-Uni[10]
EFTA	***73.2***	***77.5***	***83.3***	***74.7***	***71.4***	***45.1***	***59.5***	***58.1***	***43.0***	***72.7***	***AELE***
Austria	17.1	17.8	16.4	17.7	18.3	16.7	18.4	17.8	19.6	18.8	Autriche
Finland	4.0	4.8	5.3	5.4	3.7	3.5	2.9	4.0	1.5	* 4.6	Finlande
Norway[11]	0.6	0.9	0.9	0.4	0.3	0.1	0.0	0.0	0.0	0.0	Norvège[11]
Portugal* [6]	2.0	2.0	2.0	2.0	2.0	3.0	4.0	6.0	6.0	6.0	Portugal* [6]
Sweden[12]	49.5	51.9	58.7	49.3	47.1	21.8	34.1	30.3	15.9	43.2	Suède[12]
East Europe	***289.5***	***302.0***	***310.1***	***302.8***	***302.5***	***298.9***	***309.4***	***311.4***	***311.4***	***328.4***	***Europe de l'est***
Bulgaria* [6]	112.0	120.0	125.0	120.0	118.0	123.0	118.0	116.0	114.0	116.0	Bulgarie* [6]
Czechoslovakia	19.1	19.0	19.0	19.0	20.0	20.7	21.1	21.0	21.1	21.4	Tchécoslovaquie
German Dem. Rep.* [6]	32.1	34.1	36.5	38.5	41.2	45.0	45.0	44.0	47.0	55.0	Rép. dém. allemande* [6]
Hungary	3.2	1.8	0.0	0.1	0.3	0.6	0.8	0.0	0.0	0.0	Hongrie
Poland	80.6	85.4	86.7	84.2	82.0	69.0	78.8	81.0	83.4	87.3	Pologne
Romania	42.5	41.7	42.8	40.9	41.0	40.7	45.7	49.3	45.9	48.6	Roumanie
Other Europe	***192.6***	***248.5***	***238.9***	***238.0***	***225.8***	***203.5***	***212.8***	***241.3***	***230.8***	***255.0***	***Autre Europe***
Spain	81.4	[2] 118.6	[2] 122.2	[2] 127.0	[2] 124.0	[2] 117.1	[2] 131.6	[2] 143.8	[2] 148.0	[2] 155.0	Espagne
Yugoslavia	111.2	129.9	116.7	111.0	101.8	86.4	81.2	97.5	82.8	100.0	Yougoslavie
USSR* [2]	**600.0**	**610.0**	**620.0**	**690.0**	**700.0**	**715.0**	**730.0**	**745.0**	**755.0**	**765.0**	**URSS* [2]**
Oceania	**211.5**	**216.3**	**239.3**	**254.7**	**232.6**	**239.2**	**252.2**	**238.9**	**220.6**	**215.0**	**Océanie**

For general note and footnotes, see end of table.

Voir la fin du tableau pour la remarque générale et les notes.

Unit : Thousand metric tons | Unité : Milliers de tonnes métriques

Country or area	1976	1977	1978	1979	1980	1981	1982	1983	1984	1985	Pays ou zone
Australia[13]	211.5	216.3	239.3	254.7	232.6	239.2	252.2	238.9	220.6	215.0	Australie[13]
Total	**4 685.8**	**4 946.4**	**5 030.8**	**5 210.1**	**5 061.3**	**4 955.9**	**4 859.4**	**4 898.0**	**4 991.5**	**5 175.8**	**Total**

General note.
Soft lead and the lead content of antimonial lead recovered directly from lead ores and concentrates (primary) or from scrap (secondary). Unless otherwise stated, remelted lead (soft and hard lead produced by simple remelting without further processing), lead bullions produced for export and the amount of lead recovered in the form of alloys are excluded. (SITC 68510-0).

[1] Source: World Metal Statistics, (London).
[2] Source: U. S. Bureau of Mines, (Washington, D. C.).
[3] Secondary metal production only.
[4] Including secondary lead.
[5] Exports.
[6] Source: Metallgesellschaft Aktiengesellschaft, (Frankfurt).
[7] Including lead remelted and recovered in alloys.
[8] Production from imported bullion is included with secondary lead.
[9] Excluding antimonial lead.
[10] Excluding hard lead.
[11] Secondary lead, including remelted lead.
[12] Primary metal production only.
[13] Twelve months ending 30 June of year stated.

Remarque générale.
Plomb antimonieux obtenu directement à partir de minerais et des concentrés de plomb (formes primaires) ou des déchets de plomb (formes secondaires). Sauf avis contraire, le plomb refondu (plomb doux et antimonieux obtenu par simple refonte sans processus ultérieur), le plomb d'oeuvre pour l'exportation et les quantités de plomb obtenues sous forme d'alliages sont exclus. (CTCI 68510-0).

[1] Source: World Metal Statistics, (Londres).
[2] Source: U.S. Bureau of Mines, (Washington, D.C.).
[3] Production du métal de deuxième fusion seulement.
[4] Y compris plombde deuxiéme fusion.
[5] Exportations.
[6] Source: Metallgesellschaft Aktiengesellschaft, (Francfort).
[7] Y compris le plomb refondu et le plomb récupéré à partir des alliages.
[8] La production obtenue à partir de gueuses importées est incluse dans les données relatives au plombde deuxième fusion.
[9] Non compris les plomb antimonieux.
[10] Non compris le plomb antimonié.
[11] Plomb de deuxième fusion, y compris le plomb refondu.
[12] Production du métal de première fusion seulement.
[13] Période de douze mois finissant le 30 juin de l'année indiquée.

Lead, primary, refined soft – Plomb, neuf, doux affiné

Unit : Thousand metric tons

Unité : Milliers de tonnes métriques

Country or area	1976	1977	1978	1979	1980	1981	1982	1983	1984	1985	Pays ou zone
Africa	**102.6**	**109.6**	**98.3**	**108.7**	**114.2**	**121.4**	**129.0**	**118.0**	**94.5**	**113.1**	**Afrique**
Morocco[1,2]	26.3	34.6	30.0	36.8	42.4	52.3	58.6	57.6	48.3	63.5	Maroc[1,2]
Namibia[3,4]	39.6	42.7	39.5	41.7	42.7	41.7	40.6	35.4	28.9	38.5	Namibie[3,4]
Tunisia	23.2	19.0	16.1	17.4	19.2	17.5	15.1	10.4	8.4	2.0	Tunisie
Zambia	13.5	13.3	12.7	12.8	10.0	9.9	14.6	14.6	8.8	9.0	Zambie
America, North	**896.1**	**873.9**	**910.9**	**920.6**	**843.3**	**802.1**	**815.4**	**845.3**	**724.4**	**845.9**	**Amérique du Nord**
Canada	175.7	187.5	194.1	183.8	162.5	168.4	174.3	178.0	175.0	173.2	Canada
Guatemala[3,4]	0.1	0.1	0.1	0.1	0.1	0.0	0.0	0.1	0.1	0.1	Guatemala[3,4]
Mexico	128.0	137.5	150.3	158.3	131.1	138.3	128.8	152.6	153.8	185.2	Mexique
United States	592.3	548.8	566.4	578.5	549.7	495.3	512.2	514.6	395.6	487.4	Etats–Unis
America, South	**157.7**	**170.6**	**146.5**	**177.8**	**154.7**	**137.9**	**119.9**	**100.9**	**113.5**	**127.3**	**Amérique du Sud**
Argentina	40.0	38.0	19.7	32.0	23.2	19.0	15.9	15.2	16.3	17.0	Argentine
Brazil	43.7	48.3	47.2	55.1	44.5	34.7	21.9	20.6	26.0	* 27.0	Brésil
Peru	74.1	[5] 84.3	[5] 79.6	[5] 90.7	[5] 87.0	[5] 84.2	[5] 82.0	[5] 65.1	[5] 71.2	[5] 83.3	Pérou
Asia	**413.0**	**426.6**	**450.0**	**449.1**	**445.9**	**463.7**	**476.3**	**513.7**	**593.4**	**604.6**	**Asie**
Burma[6]	[4] 3.3	[4] 4.8	[4] 5.0	[4] 6.2	[4] 6.0	# 5.1	7.8	7.6	7.0	9.6	Birmanie[6]
China* [4,7]	125.0	135.0	140.0	150.0	145.0	150.0	155.0	165.0	165.0	165.0	Chine* [4,7]
India	5.4	7.6	10.0	9.7	14.8	14.3	14.4	13.7	15.7	15.8	Inde
Iran(Islamic Rep.of)* [5]	0.3	0.3	0.0	0.0	0.0	0.0	0.0	5.0	7.5	7.5	Iran(Rép.islamique)* [5]
Japan	202.9	204.1	214.8	204.7	206.6	211.1	216.5	237.1	273.9	279.4	Japon
Korea, D. P. Rp.* [4]	65.0	65.0	70.0	65.0	60.0	65.0	60.0	60.0	95.0	95.0	Corée, Rp. P. D.* [4]
Korea, Republic of	7.8	6.7	7.2	7.6	10.4	14.7	16.1	17.8	20.3	22.4	Corée, République de
Turkey[2,5]	3.2	3.0	3.0	5.9	3.0	3.5	6.5	7.5	9.0	* 10.0	Turquie[2,5]
Europe	**1 081.4**	**1 144.6**	**1 120.7**	**1 090.0**	**1 092.7**	**1 029.6**	**1 063.8**	**1 114.2**	**1 080.5**	**1 150.8**	**Europe**
EEC	***554.2***	***565.3***	***545.3***	***533.7***	***551.6***	***536.1***	***536.1***	***557.1***	***549.7***	***559.0***	***CEE***
Belgium[8]	121.5	122.8	125.0	113.4	127.9	109.9	99.7	134.2	127.7	114.3	Belgique[8]
France	118.4	126.1	125.9	129.0	126.8	128.6	# 144.2	114.9	118.0	133.0	France
Germany, Fed. Rep	101.0	105.1	105.2	103.4	111.9	107.5	110.7	116.2	102.3	109.7	Allemagne, Rép. féd.
Greece	13.2	16.2	17.1	22.1	15.6	12.1	3.3	0.0	8.8	9.1	Grèce
Italy[7]	46.0	34.2	31.1	25.2	42.1	35.6	36.4	40.0	37.6	38.3	Italie[7]
Netherlands[6]	21.9	21.1	18.2	16.4	13.9	7.0	10.8	* 14.9	...	...	Pays–Bas[6]
United Kingdom	132.2	139.7	122.8	124.1	113.4	135.4	131.0	136.9	147.1	148.1	Royaume–Uni
EFTA	***56.2***	***59.8***	***65.2***	***55.3***	***52.5***	***25.2***	***37.6***	***40.4***	***26.5***	***53.4***	***AELE***
Austria	6.3	7.5	6.3	6.0	5.4	3.3	3.4	10.1	10.6	10.2	Autriche
Portugal	0.4	0.4	0.2	0.1	0.0	0.1	0.1	0.0	0.0	0.0	Portugal
Sweden	49.5	51.9	58.7	49.3	47.1	21.8	34.1	30.3	15.9	* 43.2	Suède
East Europe	***286.5***	***300.4***	***310.1***	***302.8***	***302.5***	***298.9***	***309.4***	***311.4***	***311.4***	***328.4***	***Europe de l'est***
Bulgaria* [5,9]	112.0	120.0	125.0	120.0	118.0	123.0	118.0	116.0	114.0	116.0	Bulgarie* [5,9]
Czechoslovakia	19.1	19.0	19.0	19.0	20.0	20.7	21.1	21.0	21.1	21.4	Tchécoslovaquie
German Dem. Rep.* [5,10]	32.1	34.1	36.5	38.5	41.2	45.0	45.0	44.0	47.0	55.0	Rép. dém. allemande* [5,10]
Hungary	0.3	0.2	0.0	0.1	0.3	0.6	0.8	0.0	0.0	0.0	Hongrie
Poland[10]	80.6	85.4	86.7	84.2	82.0	69.0	78.8	81.0	83.4	87.3	Pologne[10]
Romania[6]	42.5	41.7	42.8	40.9	41.0	40.7	45.7	49.3	45.9	48.6	Roumanie[6]
Other Europe	***184.5***	***219.1***	***200.1***	***198.2***	***186.1***	***169.4***	***180.7***	***205.3***	***192.9***	***210.0***	***Autre Europe***
Spain	73.2	[4] 89.2	[4] 83.4	[4] 87.2	[4] 84.3	[4] 83.0	[4] 99.5	[4] 107.8	[4] 110.1	[4] 110.0	Espagne
Yugoslavia	111.2	129.9	116.7	111.0	101.8	86.4	81.2	97.5	82.8	100.0	Yougoslavie
USSR* [4]	**400.0**	**405.0**	**410.0**	**475.0**	**475.0**	**480.0**	**485.0**	**490.0**	**495.0**	**500.0**	**URSS* [4]**
Oceania	**168.2**	**165.6**	**207.9**	**218.0**	**204.3**	**207.7**	**218.8**	**212.2**	**190.1**	**189.0**	**Océanie**
Australia[11]	168.2	165.6	207.9	218.0	204.3	207.7	218.8	212.2	190.1	189.0	Australie[11]
Total	**3 218.9**	**3 295.8**	**3 344.4**	**3 439.2**	**3 330.1**	**3 242.4**	**3 308.1**	**3 394.2**	**3 291.4**	**3 530.7**	**Total**

General note.
Soft lead recovered directly from lead ores and concentrates. (SITC 68510–1).

Remarque générale.
Plomb doux obtenu directement à partir des minerais et des concentrés de plomb. (CTCI 68510–1).

For footnotes, see end of table.

Voir la fin du tableau pour les notes.

[1] Source: World Metal Statistics, (London).
[2] Including primary and secondary antimonial lead and secondary refined soft lead.
[3] Including recovery from secondary materials.
[4] Source: U. S. Bureau of Mines, (Washington, D. C.).
[5] Source: Metallgesellschaft Aktiengesellschaft, (Frankfurt).
[6] Including secondary refined soft lead.
[7] Including antimonial lead.
[8] Including lead remelted and recovered in alloys.
[9] Including secondary antimonial lead.
[10] Including secondary metal production.
[11] Twelve months ending 30 June of year stated.

[1] Source: World Metal Statistics, (Londres).
[2] Y compris le plomb antimonieux de première et deuxième fusion et le plomb doux de è deuxième.
[3] Y compris le plomb récupéré dans les déchets.
[4] Source: U.S. Bureau of Mines, (Washington, D.C.).
[5] Source: Metallgesellschaft Aktiengesellschaft, (Francfort).
[6] Y compris le plomb raffiné de deuxième fusion doux.
[7] Y compris le plomb antimonié.
[8] Y compris le plomb refondu et le plomb récupéré à partir des alliages.
[9] Y compris le plomb antimonié de deuxième fusion.
[10] Y compris la production de métal de deuxième fusion.
[11] Période de douze mois finissant le 30 juin de l'année indiquée.

Lead, primary, refined hard, antimonial – Plomb, neuf, antimonieux affiné

Unit : Thousand metric tons — Unité : Milliers de tonnes métriques

Country or area	1976	1977	1978	1979	1980	1981	1982	1983	1984	1985	Pays ou zone
Africa	**0.7**	**0.5**	**0.5**	**0.3**	**0.0**	**0.3**	**0.2**	**0.1**	**0.0**	**0.0**	**Afrique**
Tunisia	0.7	0.5	0.5	0.3	0.0	0.3	0.2	0.1	0.0	0.0	Tunisie
America, North	**6.1**	**6.9**	**5.0**	**2.6**	**0.9**	**3.0**	**4.6**	**1.8**	**1.2**	**0.6**	**Amérique du Nord**
United States[1]	6.1	6.9	5.0	2.6	0.9	3.0	4.6	...	...	...	Etats-Unis[1]
Asia	**0.2**	**0.1**	**0.1**	**0.2**	**0.2**	**0.3**	**0.3**	**0.3**	**0.3**	**0.3**	**Asie**
Burma[2]	0.2	0.1	0.1	0.2	0.2	0.3	0.3	0.3	0.3	* 0.3	Birmanie[2]
Europe	**23.3**	**17.2**	**20.6**	**21.9**	**22.0**	**22.7**	**18.0**	**9.9**	**11.2**	**15.0**	**Europe**
EEC	***19.8***	***16.1***	***19.2***	***19.9***	***19.1***	***20.8***	***13.6***	***9.1***	***11.2***	***15.0***	***CEE***
Greece	5.6	4.0	5.5	6.2	5.3	8.1	0.9	0.0	0.4	* 4.6	Grèce
Netherlands[3]	...	12.1	13.7	13.7	13.8	12.7	12.7	9.1	...	...	Pays-Bas[3]
EFTA	***3.5***	***1.2***	***1.4***	***2.0***	***2.9***	***1.9***	***4.4***	***0.8***	***0.0***	***0.0***	***AELE***
Austria	3.5	1.2	1.4	2.0	2.9	1.9	4.4	0.8	0.0	0.0	Autriche
Total	**30.3**	**24.7**	**26.2**	**25.0**	**23.0**	**26.2**	**23.1**	**12.2**	**12.7**	**16.0**	**Total**

General note.
Lead content of antimonial lead recovered from lead ores and concentrates. (SITC 68510-2).

[1] Beginning 1983, data are confidential.
[2] Source: U. S. Bureau of Mines, (Washington, D. C.).
[3] Including secondary refined hard (antimonial) lead.

Remarque générale.
Plomb contenu dans le plomb antimonieux obtenu à partir des minerais et des concentrés de plomb. (CTCI 68510-2).

[1] A partir de 1983, les données sont confidentielles.
[2] Source: U.S. Bureau of Mines, (Washington, D.C.).
[3] Y compris le plomb raffiné dur de deuxième fusion antimonié.

Lead, secondary, refined, soft – Plomb, récupéré, doux affiné

Unit : Thousand metric tons

Unité : Milliers de tonnes métriques

Country or area	1976	1977	1978	1979	1980	1981	1982	1983	1984	1985	Pays ou zone
Africa	**0.0**	**0.0**	**0.0**	**1.5**	**2.0**	**2.0**	**2.0**	**2.0**	**2.0**	**3.0**	**Afrique**
Nigeria[1]	0.0	0.0	0.0	1.5	2.0	2.0	2.0	2.0	2.0	3.0	Nigéria[1]
America, North	**255.7**	**287.1**	**262.2**	**278.9**	**367.5**	**351.8**	**308.0**	**253.5**	**342.4**	**330.1**	**Amérique du Nord**
Canada[1]	55.3	53.1	51.8	68.5	72.1	69.7	67.6	63.9	79.0	66.8	Canada[1]
United States	200.4	234.0	210.4	210.4	295.3	282.2	240.5	189.6	263.4	263.3	Etats-Unis
America, South	**42.5**	**44.0**	**52.2**	**72.0**	**68.9**	**56.6**	**55.9**	**59.4**	**69.7**	**76.0**	**Amérique du Sud**
Argentina	10.0	7.0	10.0	18.0	18.5	15.6	14.6	15.5	15.0	18.0	Argentine
Brazil	25.5	29.0	33.2	44.0	40.4	29.0	26.3	28.9	37.7	* 40.0	Brésil
Venezuela* [1]	7.0	8.0	9.0	10.0	10.0	12.0	15.0	15.0	17.0	18.0	Venezuela* [1]
Asia	**36.1**	**37.3**	**38.6**	**41.6**	**49.3**	**40.1**	**27.4**	**34.2**	**34.6**	**36.0**	**Asie**
China* [1 2]	15.0	15.0	20.0	20.0	30.0	25.0	20.0	30.0	30.0	30.0	Chine* [1 2]
Japan	16.1	17.3	13.6	16.6	14.3	15.1	7.4	4.2	4.6	6.0	Japon
Korea,Dem.Ppl's.Rep.* [1]	5.0	5.0	5.0	5.0	5.0	0.0	0.0	0.0	0.0	0.0	Corée,Rép.pop.dém.de* [1]
Europe	**531.4**	**600.0**	**640.1**	**703.4**	**638.7**	**641.8**	**656.6**	**673.2**	**724.0**	**670.7**	**Europe**
EEC	***521.0***	***567.9***	***598.1***	***661.3***	***596.3***	***604.4***	***620.4***	***627.1***	***664.1***	***615.9***	***CEE***
Denmark	8.0	10.5	7.6	12.0	11.9	12.9	15.9	10.1	13.1	4.5	Danemark
France	53.8	58.0	82.6	90.6	92.0	99.4	76.7	89.3	85.0	72.8	France
Germany, Fed. Rep.[3]	177.3	204.5	199.8	213.4	189.5	196.7	255.2	252.5	271.8	262.8	Allemagne, Rép. féd.[3]
Italy[2]	72.2	83.5	85.1	101.0	91.6	97.4	97.3	90.0	102.9	96.7	Italie[2]
United Kingdom[2]	209.7	211.4	222.9	244.2	211.4	198.0	175.2	185.3	191.3	179.1	Royaume-Uni[2]
EFTA	***2.2***	***2.7***	***3.3***	***2.3***	***2.7***	***3.3***	***4.2***	***10.1***	***10.0***	***9.8***	***AELE***
Austria	0.0	0.2	0.5	0.0	0.4	0.3	0.2	4.1	4.0	3.8	Autriche
Norway[4]	0.6	0.9	0.9	0.4	0.3	0.1	0.0	0.0	0.0	0.0	Norvège[4]
Portugal*	1.6	1.6	1.8	1.9	2.0	2.9	3.9	6.0	6.0	6.0	Portugal*
Other Europe	***8.2***	***29.4***	***38.8***	***39.8***	***39.7***	***34.1***	***32.1***	***36.0***	***49.9***	***45.0***	***Autre Europe***
Spain	8.2	[1] 29.4	[1] 38.8	[1] 39.8	[1] 39.7	[1] 34.1	[1] 32.1	[1] 36.0	[1] 49.9	[1] 45.0	Espagne
USSR* [1]	**200.0**	**205.0**	**210.0**	**215.0**	**225.0**	**235.0**	**245.0**	**255.0**	**260.0**	**265.0**	**URSS* [1]**
Total	**1 065.8**	**1 173.4**	**1 203.2**	**1 312.3**	**1 351.4**	**1 327.3**	**1 295.0**	**1 277.4**	**1 432.8**	**1 380.7**	**Total**

General note.
Secondary soft lead recovered from scrap or other similar materials. (SITC 68510-4).

[1] Source: U. S. Bureau of Mines, (Washington, D. C.).
[2] Including antimonial lead.
[3] Production from imported bullion is included with secondary lead.
[4] Including remelted lead.

Remarque générale.
Plomb doux de deuxième fusion récupéré à partir des déchets de plomb. (CTCI 68510-4).

[1] Source: U.S. Bureau of Mines, (Washington, D.C.).
[2] Y compris le plomb antimonié.
[3] La production obtenue à partir de gueuses importées est incluse dans les données relatives au plombde deuxième fusion.
[4] Y compris le plomb refondu.

Lead, secondary, refined hard, antimonial – Plomb, récupéré, antimonieux affiné

Unit : Thousand metric tons

Unité : Milliers de tonnes métriques

Country or area	1976	1977	1978	1979	1980	1981	1982	1983	1984	1985	Pays ou zone
America, North	**310.2**	**383.4**	**409.9**	**378.8**	**306.7**	**304.4**	**284.4**	**271.6**	**327.8**	**288.0**	**Amérique du Nord**
United States	310.2	383.4	409.9	378.8	306.7	304.4	284.4	271.6	327.8	288.0	Etats-Unis
Europe	**7.3**	**8.9**	**8.2**	**9.7**	**9.6**	**11.1**	**10.6**	**6.9**	**9.0**	**8.6**	**Europe**
EFTA	***7.3***	***8.9***	***8.2***	***9.7***	***9.6***	***11.1***	***10.6***	***6.9***	***9.0***	***8.6***	***AELE***
Austria	7.3	8.9	8.2	9.7	9.6	11.1	10.6	6.9	9.0	8.6	Autriche
Oceania	**31.6**	**36.5**	**35.1**	**38.5**	**32.2**	**31.5**	**33.4**	**26.8**	**19.6**	**26.0**	**Océanie**
Australia[1 2]	31.6	36.5	35.1	38.5	32.2	31.5	33.4	26.8	19.6	26.0	Australie[1 2]
Total	**349.1**	**428.8**	**453.2**	**427.0**	**348.4**	**347.0**	**328.3**	**305.3**	**356.4**	**322.5**	**Total**

General note.
Secondary antimonial lead recovered from scrap or other similar materials. (SITC 68510-5).

[1] Twelve months ending 30 June of year stated.
[2] Including secondary refined soft lead.

Remarque générale.
Plomb antimonieux de deuxième fusion obtenu à partir des déchets de plomb. (CTCI 68510-5).

[1] Période de douze mois finissant le 30 juin de l'année indiquée.
[2] Y compris le plomb raffiné de deuxième fusion doux.

Lead-base alloys – Alliages à base de plomb

Unit : Thousand metric tons

Unité : Milliers de tonnes métriques

Country or area	1976	1977	1978	1979	1980	1981	1982	1983	1984	1985	Pays ou zone
Africa	**19.9**	**21.5**	**25.6**	**32.1**	**34.9**	**32.7**	**31.7**	**27.8**	**30.8**	**32.8**	**Afrique**
South Africa	19.9	21.5	25.6	32.1	34.9	* 32.7	31.7	27.8	* 30.8	32.8	Afrique du Sud
America, North	**54.0**	**55.7**	**58.7**	**51.3**	**41.5**	**40.1**	**30.7**	**27.2**	**24.6**	**20.1**	**Amérique du Nord**
United States	54.0	55.7	58.7	51.3	41.5	40.1	30.7	27.2	...	...	Etats-Unis
America, South	**1.9**	**2.1**	**2.3**	**2.9**	**2.2**	**3.3**	**3.1**	**2.2**	**3.0**	**3.1**	**Amérique du Sud**
Colombia	1.9	2.1	2.3	2.9	2.2	3.3	3.1	2.2	...	...	Colombie
Europe	**50.8**	**45.0**	**37.9**	**32.2**	**28.6**	**31.4**	**22.3**	**26.3**	**24.2**	**24.9**	**Europe**
EEC	***32.8***	***34.5***	***31.6***	***28.9***	***22.5***	***25.2***	***18.4***	***22.0***	***20.5***	***21.5***	***CEE***
Denmark	10.7	12.7	13.0	13.2	11.7	11.2	...	...	...	...	Danemark
Germany, Fed. Rep.	7.9	8.3	6.6	6.0	5.6	5.0	4.0	3.4	2.9	2.4	Allemagne, Rép. féd.
Greece	...	...	...	...	...	7.6	0.7	...	3.0	...	Grèce
Italy	10.5	9.7	8.2	6.0	1.5	1.4	1.7	2.8	2.6	3.4	Italie
EFTA	***0.8***	***0.6***	***1.2***	***0.8***	***3.3***	***1.6***	***1.0***	***1.8***	***1.8***	***2.1***	***AELE***
Finland	0.5	0.5	1.1	0.7	3.2	1.5	0.9	1.8	1.7	...	Finlande
Norway	0.2	0.0	0.0	0.0	0.0	0.0	0.0	0.0	0.0	0.0	Norvège
Portugal	0.1	0.1	0.1	0.1	0.1	0.0	0.0	0.0	0.0	0.0	Portugal
East Europe	***7.0***	***4.3***	***0.0***	***0.0***	***0.0***	***0.0***	***0.0***	***0.0***	***0.0***	***0.0***	***Europe de l'est***
Hungary	7.0	4.3	0.0	0.0	0.0	0.0	0.0	0.0	0.0	0.0	Hongrie
Other Europe	***10.2***	***5.7***	***5.1***	***2.5***	***2.8***	***4.7***	***2.9***	***2.5***	***1.8***	***1.2***	***Autre Europe***
Spain[1]	10.2	...	...	2.5	2.8	4.7	2.9	2.5	...	...	Espagne[1]
Total	**126.6**	**124.4**	**124.4**	**118.5**	**107.3**	**107.5**	**87.9**	**83.5**	**82.6**	**81.0**	**Total**

General note.
Lead-base alloys in which lead predominates by weight over each of the other metals. (SITC 68510-8).

[1] Including other lead alloys.

Remarque générale.
Alliages à base de plomb dans lesquels le plomb prédomine en poids sur tous les autres métaux. (CTCI 68510-8).

[1] Y compris autres alliages de plomb.

Lead tubes and pipes – Tuyaux et tubes de plomb

Unit : Thousand metric tons | Unité : Milliers de tonnes métriques

Country or area	1976	1977	1978	1979	1980	1981	1982	1983	1984	1985	Pays ou zone
Africa	**4.5**	**4.0**	**4.7**	**4.3**	**4.2**	**4.1**	**3.4**	**3.3**	**2.9**	**2.9**	**Afrique**
Algeria	...	2.1	3.1	...	...	...	...	...	...	...	Algérie
Tunisia	2.0	2.0	1.6	1.7	1.6	1.6	0.8	0.7	0.3	0.3	Tunisie
America, South	**1.4**	**0.3**	**0.3**	**1.4**	**1.5**	**1.2**	**1.3**	**1.2**	**1.4**	**1.5**	**Amérique du Sud**
Brazil	1.4	0.2	0.1	[1] 1.3	1.2	...	...	...	...	...	Brésil
Colombia	0.0	0.1	0.2	0.1	0.3	0.1	0.2	0.0	...	...	Colombie
Asia	**23.1**	**21.7**	**23.2**	**20.9**	**18.8**	**17.0**	**14.6**	**13.7**	**12.0**	**10.9**	**Asie**
India	0.0	0.0	0.6	0.4	0.5	0.4	0.4	...	...	...	Inde
Japan	21.2	19.9	20.5	18.3	16.3	14.7	12.2	11.1	9.4	8.2	Japon
Turkey	1.8	1.8	2.0	2.1	...	...	...	...	...	...	Turquie
Europe	**106.0**	**103.4**	**106.5**	**103.4**	**109.6**	**97.5**	**78.4**	**79.1**	**88.6**	**56.4**	**Europe**
EEC	***73.8***	***67.9***	***67.7***	***62.4***	***64.3***	***59.2***	***54.9***	***52.5***	***70.1***	***44.9***	***CEE***
Belgium	15.8	18.1	...	...	...	...	...	...	...	...	Belgique
France	6.0	5.0	4.3	4.0	3.9	3.0	[2] 4.2	[2] 4.1	# [2] 25.0	[2] 3.2	France
Germany, Fed. Rep.	3.3	2.3	2.8	1.5	3.0	2.2	2.2	4.1	1.9	1.7	Allemagne, Rép. féd.
Greece	2.6	2.3	2.1	1.9	1.9	1.2	1.6	1.3	1.6	...	Grèce
Italy	30.5	24.5	24.5	24.0	23.0	20.2	14.3	10.5	9.1	6.3	Italie
Netherlands[3]	...	15.7	17.1	14.0	...	...	...	...	...	...	Pays–Bas[3]
EFTA	***0.4***	***0.3***	***0.5***	***0.4***	***0.3***	***0.5***	***0.5***	***0.2***	***0.2***	***0.2***	***AELE***
Sweden	0.4	0.3	0.5	0.4	0.3	0.5	0.5	0.2	0.2	0.2	Suède
East Europe	***1.5***	***1.2***	***1.3***	***0.7***	***0.7***	***0.7***	***0.9***	***0.6***	***0.3***	***0.5***	***Europe de l'est***
Hungary	1.5	1.2	1.3	0.7	0.7	0.7	0.9	0.6	0.3	0.5	Hongrie
Other Europe	***30.3***	***34.1***	***37.0***	***39.8***	***44.3***	***37.1***	***22.2***	***25.8***	***18.0***	***10.8***	***Autre Europe***
Spain	18.8	...	...	18.9	21.3	14.2	8.7	6.8	...	...	Espagne
Yugoslavia[4]	11.5	13.5	18.2	21.0	23.0	22.9	13.5	19.0	10.3	5.0	Yougoslavie[4]
Total	**135.1**	**129.4**	**134.7**	**130.0**	**134.1**	**119.8**	**97.7**	**97.3**	**104.9**	**71.6**	**Total**

General note.
Seamless and welded tubes and pipes, including blanks therefore, but excluding tube and pipe fittings. (SITC 68524–1).

[1] Production by establishments employing 5 or more persons.
[2] Pipes, tubes and hollow rods of lead.
[3] Industrial sales.
[4] Rolled lead products.

Remarque générale.
Tuyaux et tubes sans soudure ou soudés, y compris leurs ébauches mais non les accessoires de tuyauterie. (CTCI 68524–1).

[1] Production des établissements occupant 5 personnes ou plus.
[2] Tubes, tuyaux et barres creuses en plomb.
[3] Ventes industrielles.
[4] Produits en plomb laminé.

Zinc, unwrought (total production) – Zinc non travaillé, affiné (production totale)

Unit : Thousand metric tons

Unité : Milliers de tonnes métriques

Country or area	1976	1977	1978	1979	1980	1981	1982	1983	1984	1985	Pays ou zone
Africa	**103.7**	**104.0**	**115.0**	**103.2**	**104.5**	**123.2**	**132.4**	**131.9**	**130.3**	**122.1**	**Afrique**
Algeria	[1] 6.0	# 13.0	29.0	21.5	28.0	32.3	28.8	31.2	* 35.0	* 31.2	Algérie
Zaire	60.6	51.0	43.5	43.5	* 43.8	* 57.6	* 64.4	* 62.8	* 66.1	* 67.9	Zaïre
Zambia	37.1	40.0	42.5	38.2	32.7	33.3	39.2	37.9	29.2	23.0	Zambie
America, North	**1 162.4**	**1 123.6**	**1 110.0**	**1 267.9**	**1 105.3**	**1 141.9**	**941.3**	**1 096.2**	**1 180.8**	**1 178.9**	**Amérique du Nord**
Canada[2]	472.3	494.9	495.4	580.4	591.6	618.6	511.9	617.0	683.1	692.4	Canada[2]
Mexico	175.3	174.4	173.1	161.7	143.9	126.5	127.0	174.1	166.5	175.0	Mexique
United States	514.7	454.3	441.5	525.7	369.9	396.8	302.5	305.1	331.2	311.6	Etats–Unis
America, South	**150.9**	**151.8**	**154.7**	**182.5**	**187.8**	**266.3**	**302.6**	**297.0**	**292.2**	**316.4**	**Amérique du Sud**
Argentina	31.3	29.3	23.6	35.5	27.9	29.3	31.4	32.0	29.9	32.9	Argentine
Brazil	52.7	55.6	68.3	78.8	96.0	110.8	110.4	111.0	113.7	120.7	Brésil
Peru	66.8	[3] 66.9	[3] 62.9	[3] 68.2	[3] 63.8	[3] 126.2	[3] 160.7	[3] 154.0	[3] 148.6	[3] 162.8	Pérou
Asia	**1 081.4**	**1 137.2**	**1 175.6**	**1 215.6**	**1 138.5**	**1 091.5**	**1 094.2**	**1 157.4**	**1 223.3**	**1 252.1**	**Asie**
China* [3]	150.0	155.0	160.0	160.0	160.0	160.0	160.0	175.0	185.0	190.0	Chine* [3]
India	26.8	36.0	58.7	63.3	44.1	57.4	52.6	53.3	55.4	70.8	Inde
Japan	742.1	778.4	767.9	789.4	735.2	670.2	662.4	701.3	754.4	739.6	Japon
Korea,Dem.Ppl's.Rep.* [2 3]	135.0	135.0	130.0	120.0	120.0	120.0	120.0	120.0	120.0	140.0	Corée,Rép.pop.dém.de* [2 3]
Korea, Republic of	27.5	32.8	59.0	83.0	79.1	83.9	99.2	107.9	108.5	111.7	Corée, République de
Europe	**2 031.1**	**2 109.6**	**2 088.2**	**2 235.0**	**2 229.1**	**2 189.3**	**2 134.2**	**2 188.9**	**2 296.2**	**2 335.0**	**Europe**
EEC	***1 183.4***	***1 242.3***	***1 208.9***	***1 342.8***	***1 372.3***	***1 350.1***	***1 302.1***	***1 348.3***	***1 409.1***	***1 439.0***	***CEE***
Belgium[4]	241.2	258.2	240.5	261.7	249.2	250.4	240.9	275.8	285.3	289.6	Belgique[4]
Denmark[5]	0.5	0.8	0.9	0.1	0.0	0.0	0.0	0.0	0.0	0.4	Danemark[5]
France	251.5	252.3	245.7	262.4	264.3	270.6	283.2	273.2	290.0	278.0	France
Germany, Fed. Rep.	304.8	341.6	306.8	355.5	374.4	366.6	335.1	349.7	356.4	367.8	Allemagne, Rép. féd.
Greece	0.0	0.0	0.0	0.1	0.1	0.4	0.4	0.4	0.4	...	Grèce
Italy	191.2	169.4	177.6	202.8	206.7	180.9	158.2	155.6	166.8	210.1	Italie
Netherlands[2]	125.5	109.4	135.4	154.0	165.9	177.4	186.0	187.5	209.7	201.7	Pays–Bas[2]
United Kingdom	68.7	110.6	102.0	106.2	111.6	103.8	98.3	106.1	100.6	90.9	Royaume–Uni
EFTA	***191.5***	***224.5***	***226.2***	***247.6***	***248.2***	***243.0***	***242.8***	***238.9***	***257.0***	***273.6***	***AELE***
Austria	16.5	16.8	21.7	23.2	22.1	22.7	20.1	19.7	21.0	20.5	Autriche
Finland	110.6	138.0	132.9	146.6	146.7	140.0	144.0	128.5	141.7	160.4	Finlande
Norway[2]	64.4	69.8	71.6	77.8	79.4	80.3	78.7	90.7	94.2	92.8	Norvège[2]
East Europe	***399.5***	***387.3***	***380.9***	***363.0***	***372.3***	***320.3***	***320.8***	***323.8***	***335.8***	***333.7***	***Europe de l'est***
Bulgaria[1 6]	92.5	* 90.0	91.0	89.0	91.0	90.0	92.0	93.0	93.0	90.0	Bulgarie[1 6]
Czechoslovakia	1.7	1.7	2.1	1.3	1.9	2.0	2.4	2.1	1.2	1.2	Tchécoslovaquie
German Dem. Rep.* [1]	15.0	15.5	16.0	17.0	16.0	16.0	17.0	16.5	17.0	17.0	Rép. dém. allemande* [1]
Hungary[5]	0.3	0.0	0.0	0.0	0.0	0.0	0.0	0.0	0.7	0.4	Hongrie[5]
Poland	236.7	228.2	222.0	209.2	217.5	167.1	165.4	170.3	176.1	180.1	Pologne
Romania	53.4	51.9	49.8	46.5	45.9	45.2	[1] 44.0	[1] 42.0	[1] 47.8	* [1] 45.0	Roumanie
Other Europe	***256.6***	***255.4***	***272.2***	***281.6***	***236.3***	***275.9***	***268.6***	***277.9***	***294.3***	***288.7***	***Autre Europe***
Spain	161.1	[3] 156.6	[3] 177.0	[3] 182.7	[3] 151.8	[3] 179.5	[3] 181.8	[3] 189.9	[3] 207.4	[3] 205.3	Espagne
Yugoslavia[6]	95.5	98.8	95.2	98.9	84.5	96.4	86.8	88.0	86.9	83.4	Yougoslavie[6]
USSR* [3]	**800.0**	**815.0**	**850.0**	**880.0**	**895.0**	**905.0**	**920.0**	**955.0**	**985.0**	**1 000.0**	**URSS* [3]**
Oceania	**211.1**	**268.6**	**266.8**	**312.8**	**304.6**	**279.0**	**305.5**	**292.7**	**302.6**	**302.3**	**Océanie**
Australia[7]	* 211.1	268.6	266.8	312.8	304.6	279.0	305.5	292.7	302.6	302.3	Australie[7]
Total	**5 540.6**	**5 709.8**	**5 760.4**	**6 197.1**	**5 964.7**	**5 996.2**	**5 830.1**	**6 119.2**	**6 410.4**	**6 506.9**	**Total**

General note.
Zinc recovered from zinc ores and concentrates and distilled zinc and zinc produced directly from ores by electrolysis (primary), zinc recovered from scrap (secondary). Unless otherwise stated, remelted zinc (metal produced by simple remelting without further processing) and the amount of zinc recovered in the form of alloys are excluded. (SITC 68610–0).

Remarque générale.
Zinc obtenu à partir des minerais et des concentrés de zinc, zinc distilé et zinc obtenu directement à partir de minerais par électrolyse (formes primaires), zinc obtenu à partir de déchets (formes secondaires). Sauf avis contraire, le zinc refondu (zinc obtenu par simple refonte sans processus ultérieur) et les quantités de zinc obtenues sous forme d'alliages sont exclus. (CTCI 68610–0).

For footnotes, see end of table.

Voir la fin du tableau pour les notes.

Zinc, unwrought (total production) (continued) –
Zinc non travaillé, affiné (production totale) (suite)

[1] Source: Metallgesellschaft Aktiengesellschaft, (Frankfurt).
[2] Primary metal production only.
[3] Source: U. S. Bureau of Mines, (Washington, D. C.).
[4] Including zinc remelted and recovered in alloys.
[5] Secondary metal production only.
[6] Including zinc dust.
[7] Twelve months ending 30 June of year stated.

[1] Source: Metallgesellschaft Aktiengesellschaft, (Francfort).
[2] Production du métal de première fusion seulement.
[3] Source: U.S. Bureau of Mines, (Washington, D.C.).
[4] Y compris le zinc refondu et récupéré à partir des alliages.
[5] Production du métal de deuxième fusion seulement.
[6] Y compris la poudre de zinc.
[7] Période de douze mois finissant le 30 juin de l'année indiquée.

Zinc, unwrought, primary – Zinc, neuf, affiné

Unit : Thousand metric tons — Unité : Milliers de tonnes métriques

Country or area	1976	1977	1978	1979	1980	1981	1982	1983	1984	1985	Pays ou zone
Africa	**103.7**	**104.0**	**115.0**	**103.2**	**104.5**	**123.2**	**132.4**	**131.9**	**130.3**	**122.1**	**Afrique**
Algeria	[1] 6.0	# 13.0	29.0	21.5	28.0	32.3	28.8	31.2	* 35.0	* 31.2	Algérie
Zaire	60.6	51.0	43.5	43.5	* 43.8	* 57.6	* 64.4	* 62.8	* 66.1	* 67.9	Zaïre
Zambia	37.1	40.0	42.5	38.2	32.7	33.3	39.2	37.9	29.2	23.0	Zambie
America, North	**1 100.2**	**1 077.7**	**1 075.2**	**1 214.7**	**1 075.9**	**1 091.7**	**867.0**	**1 026.9**	**1 102.7**	**1 103.4**	**Amérique du Nord**
Canada	472.3	494.9	495.4	580.4	591.6	618.6	511.9	617.0	683.1	692.4	Canada
Mexico	175.3	174.4	173.1	161.7	143.9	126.5	127.0	174.1	166.5	175.0	Mexique
United States	452.6	408.4	406.7	472.5	340.5	346.6	228.2	235.7	253.1	236.0	Etats-Unis
America, South	**141.3**	**143.3**	**142.5**	**167.2**	**170.1**	**247.3**	**288.2**	**285.9**	**284.7**	**311.8**	**Amérique du Sud**
Argentina	31.3	29.3	23.6	35.5	27.9	29.3	31.4	32.0	29.9	32.9	Argentine
Brazil	43.2	47.0	56.1	63.5	78.4	91.8	96.0	99.9	106.2	116.1	Brésil
Peru	66.8	# [2] 66.9	[2] 62.9	[2] 68.2	[2] 63.8	[2] 126.2	[2] 160.7	[2] 154.0	[2] 148.6	[2] 162.8	Pérou
Asia	**1 052.7**	**1 097.6**	**1 144.2**	**1 188.0**	**1 104.9**	**1 047.4**	**1 038.0**	**1 093.2**	**1 154.2**	**1 187.9**	**Asie**
China* [2 3]	150.0	155.0	160.0	160.0	160.0	160.0	160.0	175.0	185.0	190.0	Chine* [2 3]
India	26.8	36.0	58.7	63.3	44.1	57.4	52.6	53.3	55.4	70.8	Inde
Japan	713.3	738.8	736.5	761.7	701.6	626.1	606.2	637.1	685.4	675.5	Japon
Korea,Dem.Ppl's.Rep.* [2]	135.0	135.0	130.0	120.0	120.0	120.0	120.0	120.0	120.0	140.0	Corée,Rép.pop.dém.de* [2]
Korea, Republic of	27.5	32.8	59.0	83.0	79.1	83.9	99.2	107.9	108.5	111.7	Corée, République de
Europe	**1 828.7**	**1 881.8**	**1 900.9**	**1 997.1**	**1 991.8**	**1 944.8**	**1 922.4**	**1 982.3**	**2 070.0**	**2 112.5**	**Europe**
EEC	***1 035.1***	***1 066.7***	***1 072.0***	***1 155.1***	***1 186.7***	***1 174.4***	***1 143.4***	***1 191.0***	***1 265.7***	***1 292.2***	***CEE***
Belgium[4]	241.2	258.2	240.5	261.7	249.2	250.4	240.9	275.8	285.3	289.6	Belgique[4]
France	233.5	238.3	231.2	248.6	252.8	257.1	# 243.7	237.6	257.6	247.2	France
Germany, Fed. Rep.	202.0	209.9	213.8	211.4	225.4	227.0	235.3	246.8	260.8	269.3	Allemagne, Rép. féd.
Italy	191.2	169.4	177.6	202.7	206.7	180.9	158.2	155.6	166.8	210.1	Italie
Netherlands	125.5	109.4	135.4	154.0	165.9	177.4	186.0	187.5	209.7	201.7	Pays-Bas
United Kingdom	41.6	81.5	73.6	76.7	86.7	81.7	79.3	87.7	85.6	74.3	Royaume-Uni
EFTA	***191.2***	***224.2***	***225.6***	***246.8***	***247.5***	***242.2***	***242.0***	***237.9***	***255.4***	***272.1***	***AELE***
Austria	16.2	16.4	21.0	22.5	21.3	21.9	19.3	18.8	19.4	19.0	Autriche
Finland	110.6	138.0	132.9	146.6	146.7	140.0	144.0	128.5	141.7	160.4	Finlande
Norway	64.4	69.8	71.6	77.8	79.4	80.3	78.7	90.7	94.2	92.8	Norvège
East Europe	***345.8***	***335.4***	***331.1***	***316.5***	***326.4***	***275.1***	***276.8***	***281.8***	***287.3***	***288.3***	***Europe de l'est***
Bulgaria[1 5]	92.5	* 90.0	91.0	89.0	91.0	90.0	92.0	93.0	93.0	90.0	Bulgarie[1 5]
Czechoslovakia	1.7	1.7	2.1	1.3	1.9	2.0	2.4	2.1	1.2	1.2	Tchécoslovaquie
German Dem. Rep.* [1 3]	15.0	15.5	16.0	17.0	16.0	16.0	17.0	16.5	17.0	17.0	Rép. dém. allemande* [1 3]
Poland[3]	236.7	228.2	222.0	209.2	217.5	167.1	165.4	170.3	176.1	180.1	Pologne[3]
Other Europe	***256.6***	***255.5***	***272.2***	***278.8***	***231.3***	***253.1***	***260.2***	***271.5***	***261.7***	***259.9***	***Autre Europe***
Spain	161.1	156.6	177.0	179.9	146.7	156.8	173.4	183.5	...	...	Espagne
Yugoslavia[5]	95.5	98.8	95.2	98.9	84.5	96.4	86.8	88.0	86.9	83.4	Yougoslavie[5]
USSR* [2]	**720.0**	**735.0**	**770.0**	**800.0**	**815.0**	**870.0**	**830.0**	**860.0**	**890.0**	**900.0**	**URSS* [2]**
Oceania	**204.5**	**261.9**	**262.6**	**308.6**	**299.6**	**274.0**	**301.0**	**288.2**	**299.7**	**299.0**	**Océanie**
Australia	204.5	261.9	262.6	308.6	299.6	274.0	301.0	288.2	299.7	299.0	Australie
Total	**5 151.2**	**5 301.4**	**5 410.5**	**5 778.8**	**5 561.8**	**5 598.5**	**5 378.9**	**5 668.4**	**5 931.8**	**6 036.7**	**Total**

General note.
Zinc recovered from zinc ores and concentrates and distilled zinc and zinc produced directly from ores by electrolysis. (SITC 68610-1).

[1] Source: Metallgesellschaft Aktiengesellschaft, (Frankfurt).
[2] Source: U. S. Bureau of Mines, (Washington, D. C.).
[3] Including secondary metal production.
[4] Including zinc remelted and recovered in alloys.
[5] Including zinc dust.

Remarque générale.
Zinc de première fusion obtenu à partir des minerais et concentrés de zinc, zinc distilé et zinc obtenu directement à partir des minerais par électrolyse. (CTCI 68610-1).

[1] Source: Metallgesellschaft Aktiengesellschaft, (Francfort).
[2] Source: U.S. Bureau of Mines, (Washington, D.C.).
[3] Y compris la production de métal de deuxième fusion.
[4] Y compris le zinc refondu et récupéré à partir des alliages.
[5] Y compris la poudre de zinc.

Zinc, unwrought, secondary – Zinc, récupéré, affiné

Unit : Thousand metric tons

Unité : Milliers de tonnes métriques

Country or area	1976	1977	1978	1979	1980	1981	1982	1983	1984	1985	Pays ou zone
America, North	**62.2**	**45.9**	**34.8**	**53.2**	**29.4**	**50.2**	**74.3**	**69.4**	**78.1**	**75.6**	**Amérique du Nord**
United States	62.2	45.9	34.8	53.2	29.4	50.2	74.3	69.4	78.1	75.6	Etats–Unis
America, South	**9.6**	**8.5**	**12.2**	**15.3**	**17.7**	**19.0**	**14.4**	**11.0**	**7.5**	**4.6**	**Amérique du Sud**
Brazil	9.6	8.5	12.2	15.3	17.7	19.0	14.4	11.0	7.5	* 4.6	Brésil
Asia	**28.7**	**39.6**	**31.4**	**27.7**	**33.5**	**44.1**	**56.1**	**64.2**	**69.0**	**64.2**	**Asie**
Japan	28.7	39.6	31.4	27.7	33.5	44.1	56.1	64.2	69.0	64.2	Japon
Europe	**296.6**	**323.8**	**308.5**	**322.2**	**329.6**	**355.7**	**375.5**	**375.3**	**387.0**	**388.7**	**Europe**
EEC	***295.9***	***320.9***	***303.7***	***318.6***	***323.9***	***332.2***	***366.3***	***368.1***	***371.6***	***372.0***	***CEE***
Denmark	0.5	0.8	0.9	0.1	0.0	0.0	0.0	0.0	0.0	0.4	Danemark
France	18.0	14.0	14.5	13.8	11.5	13.5	# 39.5	35.6	32.4	30.8	France
Germany, Fed. Rep.	250.3	276.9	259.9	275.1	287.4	296.5	307.8	314.1	324.1	324.1	Allemagne, Rép. féd.
Italy	0.0	0.0	0.0	0.1	0.0	0.0	0.0	0.0	0.0	...	Italie
United Kingdom	27.1	29.1	28.4	29.5	25.0	22.2	19.0	18.4	15.0	16.6	Royaume–Uni
EFTA	***0.3***	***0.3***	***0.6***	***0.8***	***0.8***	***0.8***	***0.8***	***0.8***	***1.1***	***1.2***	***AELE***
Austria	0.3	0.3	0.6	0.8	0.8	0.8	0.8	0.8	1.1	1.2	Autriche
East Europe	***0.3***	***0.0***	***0.0***	***0.0***	***0.0***	***0.0***	***0.0***	***0.0***	***0.7***	***0.4***	***Europe de l'est***
Hungary	0.3	0.0	0.0	0.0	0.0	0.0	0.0	0.0	0.7	0.4	Hongrie
Other Europe	***0.0***	***2.6***	***4.2***	***2.8***	***5.0***	***22.7***	***8.4***	***6.4***	***13.6***	***15.1***	***Autre Europe***
Spain	0.0	...	...	2.8	5.0	22.7	8.4	6.4	...	...	Espagne
USSR* [1]	**80.0**	**80.0**	**80.0**	**80.0**	**80.0**	**85.0**	**90.0**	**95.0**	**95.0**	**100.0**	**URSS* [1]**
Oceania	**6.6**	**6.7**	**4.2**	**4.2**	**5.0**	**5.0**	**4.5**	**4.5**	**2.8**	**3.3**	**Océanie**
Australia	* 6.6	* 6.7	* 4.2	* 4.2	* 5.0	* 5.0	* 4.5	* 4.5	* 2.8	3.3	Australie
Total	**483.7**	**504.5**	**471.2**	**502.6**	**495.2**	**558.9**	**614.8**	**619.5**	**639.5**	**636.3**	**Total**

General note.
Secondary zinc recovered from waste and scrap. Remelted zinc (metal produced by simple remelting without further processing) and the amount of zinc recovered in the form of alloys are excluded. (SITC 68610–2).

[1] Source: U. S. Bureau of Mines, (Washington, D. C.).

Remarque générale.
Zinc de deuxième fusion obtenu à partir de déchets et de débris d'ouvrages. Zinc refondu (le zinc obtenu par simple refonte sans processus ultérieur) et les quantités de zinc obtenues sous forme d'alliages sont exclus. (CTCI 68610–2).

[1] Source: U.S. Bureau of Mines, (Washington, D.C.).

Zinc-base alloys – Alliages à base de zinc

Unit : Thousand metric tons — Unité : Milliers de tonnes métriques

Country or area	1976	1977	1978	1979	1980	1981	1982	1983	1984	1985	Pays ou zone
America, North	**231.3**	**190.4**	**209.3**	**220.7**	**180.8**	**185.7**	**121.0**	**174.3**	**143.3**	**133.1**	**Amérique du Nord**
United States	231.3	190.4	209.3	220.7	180.8	185.7	121.0	174.3	...	...	Etats-Unis
America, South	**28.6**	**28.8**	**23.7**	**39.6**	**77.8**	**39.7**	**39.7**	**39.9**	**39.8**	**39.8**	**Amérique du Sud**
Brazil	6.3	6.4	1.3	...	55.4	...	...	...	...	...	Brésil
Colombia	0.1	0.2	0.1	0.0	0.1	0.1	0.1	0.3	...	...	Colombie
Peru	...	...	...	...	...	...	...	...	22.2	...	Pérou
Asia	**0.9**	**0.9**	**0.9**	**0.9**	**0.9**	**0.9**	**0.9**	**0.9**	**0.9**	**0.9**	**Asie**
Turkey	...	...	...	...	...	...	0.9	...	...	...	Turquie
Europe	**131.4**	**115.4**	**123.1**	**118.8**	**115.8**	**119.5**	**123.2**	**120.2**	**111.7**	**114.2**	**Europe**
EEC	***85.5***	***83.8***	***88.5***	***99.0***	***96.4***	***82.2***	***85.8***	***81.6***	***80.5***	***83.0***	***CEE***
Denmark	1.8	2.0	0.1	0.0	0.0	0.0	0.0	0.0	0.0	...	Danemark
Italy	48.0	45.6	49.4	61.0	65.0	55.0	53.9	52.1	48.0	48.3	Italie
United Kingdom	35.7	36.2	38.9	38.0	31.4	27.2	31.9	29.5	32.5	34.6	Royaume-Uni
EFTA	***15.0***	***11.1***	***13.4***	***10.7***	***10.1***	***12.5***	***13.5***	***13.2***	***11.7***	***12.9***	***AELE***
Austria	3.0	3.0	3.2	3.2	3.4	3.1	3.5	4.6	4.5	5.1	Autriche
Finland	0.2	0.6	0.5	1.0	0.8	0.7	0.2	0.0	0.0	...	Finlande
Norway[1]	11.9	7.4	9.6	6.4	5.9	8.7	9.8	8.6	7.1	7.7	Norvège[1]
East Europe	***3.1***	***2.9***	***3.9***	***3.8***	***3.9***	***4.5***	***4.3***	***4.1***	***4.1***	***3.3***	***Europe de l'est***
Hungary	3.1	2.9	3.9	3.8	3.9	4.5	4.3	4.1	4.1	3.3	Hongrie
Other Europe	***27.8***	***17.6***	***17.3***	***5.3***	***5.4***	***20.3***	***19.6***	***21.3***	***15.4***	***15.1***	***Autre Europe***
Spain	27.8	...	...	5.3	5.4	20.3	19.6	21.3	...	...	Espagne
Total	**392.3**	**335.5**	**357.0**	**380.1**	**375.3**	**345.8**	**284.9**	**335.3**	**295.7**	**288.0**	**Total**

General note.
Zinc-base alloys in which zinc predominates by weight over each of the other metals. (SITC 68610-4).

[1] Including other zinc alloys.

Remarque générale.
Alliages à base de zinc dans lesquels le zinc prédomine en poids sur tous les autres métaux. (CTCI 68610-4).

[1] Y compris les autres alliages de zinc.

Zinc plates, sheets, strip, foil – Tôles, plaques, bandes et feuilles de zinc

Unit : Thousand metric tons

Unité : Milliers de tonnes métriques

Country or area	1976	1977	1978	1979	1980	1981	1982	1983	1984	1985	Pays ou zone
America, South	**27.4**	**27.0**	**38.9**	**42.7**	**45.0**	**58.6**	**33.7**	**52.3**	**55.6**	**59.0**	**Amérique du Sud**
Brazil	8.2	4.7	4.8	* 5.2	...	...	...	...	...	...	Brésil
Chile	19.2	22.3	34.1	37.5	39.3	52.9	28.0	...	...	...	Chili
Asia	**46.2**	**42.4**	**45.4**	**44.7**	**45.4**	**38.9**	**43.7**	**45.2**	**43.1**	**43.3**	**Asie**
India	7.2	6.7	9.3	9.7	10.1	8.1	10.0	10.1	9.5	...	Inde
Japan[1 2]	36.9	33.5	33.6	32.5	33.0	28.5	31.4	32.9	31.3	30.4	Japon[1 2]
Turkey	2.1	2.1	2.5	2.5	...	...	...	...	...	...	Turquie
Europe	**159.6**	**162.8**	**174.5**	**185.4**	**188.3**	**174.1**	**178.0**	**170.5**	**168.2**	**158.2**	**Europe**
EEC	***143.5***	***148.6***	***160.6***	***168.9***	***171.2***	***159.6***	***163.4***	***155.3***	***152.3***	***139.3***	***CEE***
France	87.5	87.3	96.8	106.0	106.2	99.1	# 104.5	94.0	93.0	86.1	France
Germany, Fed. Rep.	35.4	37.9	40.6	42.3	45.8	44.7	44.8	52.7	53.7	47.4	Allemagne, Rép. féd.
United Kingdom[3]	20.6	23.4	23.2	20.6	19.1	15.9	14.1	8.6	5.6	5.8	Royaume-Uni[3]
EFTA	***0.1***	***0.0***	***0.1***	***0.1***	***0.1***	***0.1***	***0.1***	***0.1***	***0.1***	***0.1***	***AELE***
Finland	0.1	0.0	...	...	...	...	...	...	...	...	Finlande
East Europe	***1.1***	***1.5***	***1.9***	***2.3***	***2.3***	***2.6***	***2.6***	***2.4***	***2.3***	***2.4***	***Europe de l'est***
Hungary	1.1	1.5	1.9	2.3	2.3	2.6	2.6	2.4	2.3	2.4	Hongrie
Other Europe	***14.9***	***12.6***	***12.0***	***14.1***	***14.8***	***11.8***	***11.9***	***12.7***	***13.5***	***16.5***	***Autre Europe***
Spain	8.0	...	...	...	...	2.6	2.5	4.2	...	...	Espagne
Yugoslavia[4]	6.8	8.3	7.6	9.8	10.4	9.2	9.4	8.5	9.1	12.1	Yougoslavie[4]
Total	**233.1**	**232.1**	**258.8**	**272.7**	**278.7**	**271.6**	**255.5**	**268.1**	**267.0**	**260.4**	**Total**

General note.

Flat-surfaced, wrought zinc products (coiled or not), of which the maximum cross-sectional dimension exceeds 6 mm, and of which the thickness exceeds 0.15 mm but does not exceed one-tenth of the width (plates, sheets, strip), thin sheets, not exceeding 0.15 mm in thickness, whether or not embossed, cut to shape, perforated, coated, printed or backed with paper or other reinforcing material (zinc foil). (SITC 68622-0).

[1] Including zinc plates for dry battery.
[2] Excluding strip and foil.
[3] Including zinc wire.
[4] Rolled zinc products.

Remarque générale.

Produits plats en zinc (enroulés ou non), dont la plus grande dimension transversale est supérieure à 6 mm et dont l'épaisseur, supérieure à 0.15 mm, ne dépasse pas le dixième de la largeur (tôles, feuilles et bandes), feuilles et bandes minces d'une épaisseur de 0.15 mm au maximum, même gaufrées, découpées, perforées, revêtues, imprimées ou fixées sur papier ou support similaire (feuilles minces ou papier de zinc). (CTCI 68622-0).

[1] Y compris les tôles de zinc pour piles sèches.
[2] Non compris les feuilles et feuillards.
[3] Y compris le fil de zinc.
[4] Produits en zinc laminé.

Tin, unwrought (total production) – Etain, non travaillé (production totale)

Unit : Metric tons — Unité : Tonnes métriques

Country or area	1976	1977	1978	1979	1980	1981	1982	1983	1984	1985	Pays ou zone
Africa	**6 562**	**6 358**	**5 926**	**5 883**	**6 439**	**6 264**	**5 423**	**4 813**	**4 841**	**4 375**	**Afrique**
Nigeria	3 809	3 315	2 985	2 858	2 978	2 483	1 677	* 1 244	* 1 334	* 1 027	Nigéria
South Africa[1,2]	* 1 400	* 1 500	* 1 500	* 1 600	2 207	2 174	2 197	* 2 200	* 2 200	* 2 056	Afrique du Sud[1,2]
Zaire[2]	478	663	496	458	320	450	352	134	98	85	Zaïre[2]
Zimbabwe	[2] 875	[2] 880	# 945	967	934	1 157	1 197	1 235	1 209	1 207	Zimbabwe
America, North	**8 180**	**9 572**	**8 645**	**7 838**	**6 265**	**4 633**	**5 718**	**4 660**	**6 087**	**4 822**	**Amérique du Nord**
Canada* [2,3]	180	180	180	180	180	180	180	180	180	180	Canada* [2,3]
Mexico[1]	* [2] 800	* [2] 1 000	* [2] 1 000	* [2] 1 291	* [2] 1 382	* [2] 866	* [2] 971	* [2] 800	* [2] 800	340	Mexique[1]
United States	7 200	8 392	7 465	6 367	4 703	3 587	4 567	3 680	5 107	* 4 302	Etats–Unis
America, South	**16 335**	**20 652**	**25 633**	**25 948**	**26 644**	**28 350**	**26 770**	**26 565**	**34 247**	**39 273**	**Amérique du Sud**
Argentina	* [2] 120	* [2] 120	* [2] 120	* [2] 120	* [2] 200	457	323	282	290	365	Argentine
Bolivia	9 792	12 846	16 184	15 696	17 648	20 104	17 149	13 542	15 842	* 14 205	Bolivie
Brazil[1]	[2] 6 423	[2] 7 686	# 9 329	10 132	8 796	7 789	9 298	12 741	18 115	* 24 703	Brésil[1]
Asia	**142 352**	**132 930**	**146 073**	**152 391**	**153 997**	**153 010**	**135 593**	**118 748**	**107 708**	**104 038**	**Asie**
China* [1,4]	20 000	18 000	18 000	17 000	16 000	16 000	16 000	17 000	17 500	18 000	Chine* [1,4]
India* [2,3]	100	100	100	100	120	120	120	120	120	120	Inde* [2,3]
Indonesia[2]	23 322	24 005	25 830	27 790	30 465	32 519	29 755	28 390	22 467	20 909	Indonésie[2]
Japan	1 234	1 323	1 150	1 251	1 319	1 314	1 296	1 260	1 354	1 391	Japon
Malaysia	[5] 77 297	[5] 66 304	71 953	73 068	71 318	70 326	62 836	53 338	46 300	45 500	Malaisie
Thailand	[2] 20 399	[2] 23 198	[2] 29 040	[2] 33 182	34 775	32 731	25 586	18 640	19 967	18 118	Thaïlande
Europe	**42 673**	**42 666**	**37 855**	**38 937**	**36 734**	**36 982**	**35 517**	**36 509**	**38 053**	**36 223**	**Europe**
EEC	***35 383***	***34 680***	***32 162***	***31 896***	***29 189***	***29 699***	***28 662***	***29 270***	***29 756***	***27 600***	***CEE***
Belgium	6 060	5 004	5 196	4 740	5 052	2 508	2 208	2 214	2 408	2 298	Belgique
Denmark[3]	61	70	76	183	48	911	1 122	1 728	1 220	283	Danemark[3]
France[3]	11 095	9 500	9 000	9 410	8 900	7 436	# 8 004	5 792	5 137	2 904	France[3]
Germany, Fed. Rep.	2 247	3 932	4 767	4 096	2 257	2 006	599	399	289	865	Allemagne, Rép. féd.
Greece[3]	34	38	162	175	240	224	209	198	133	200	Grèce[3]
Netherlands* [2]	2 180	2 280	1 805	1 900	1 328	3 680	2 937	5 602	6 721	6 237	Pays–Bas* [2]
United Kingdom	13 706	13 856	11 156	11 392	11 364	12 934	13 583	13 337	13 848	14 813	Royaume–Uni
EFTA	***691***	***751***	***818***	***675***	***705***	***599***	***660***	***570***	***496***	***575***	***AELE***
Austria[3]	7	0	6	0	1	0	0	0	0	0	Autriche[3]
Finland	125	106	96	35	37	52	58	59	14	...	Finlande
Norway[3]	60	54	44	54	59	46	44	42	38	46	Norvège[3]
Portugal	385	533	603	512	537	424	503	421	409	457	Portugal
Sweden[3]	114	58	69	74	71	77	55	48	35	61	Suède[3]
East Europe	***2 142***	***1 792***	***1 520***	***1 720***	***2 015***	***2 289***	***2 495***	***2 907***	***3 425***	***3 807***	***Europe de l'est***
Czechoslovakia[3]	120	120	120	120	215	289	295	307	425	507	Tchécoslovaquie[3]
German Dem. Rep.* [1,4]	1 400	1 400	1 400	1 600	1 800	2 000	2 200	2 600	3 000	3 300	Rép. dém. allemande* [1,4]
Hungary	622	272	0	0	0	0	0	0	0	0	Hongrie
Other Europe	***4 457***	***5 443***	***3 355***	***4 646***	***4 825***	***4 395***	***3 700***	***3 762***	***4 376***	***4 241***	***Autre Europe***
Spain	4 457	* [2] 5 443	* [2] 3 355	* [2] 4 646	* [2] 4 825	* [2] 4 395	* [2] 3 700	* [2] 3 762	* [2] 4 376	* [2] 4 241	Espagne
USSR* [1,4]	**17 000**	**17 500**	**18 000**	**18 000**	**17 000**	**16 000**	**17 000**	**18 500**	**18 500**	**18 200**	**URSS* [1,4]**
Oceania	**5 641**	**5 578**	**6 314**	**5 297**	**5 733**	**5 100**	**4 072**	**3 378**	**3 490**	**3 483**	**Océanie**
Australia	5 641	5 578	6 314	5 297	5 733	5 100	4 072	3 378	3 490	3 483	Australie
Total	**238 743**	**235 256**	**248 446**	**254 294**	**252 812**	**250 339**	**230 093**	**213 173**	**212 926**	**210 414**	**Total**

General note.
Production of virgin metal (primary) and tin derived from scrap (secondary). (SITC 68710–0).

1 Primary metal production only.
2 Source: International Tin Council, (London).
3 Secondary metal production only.
4 Source: Metallgesellschaft Aktiengesellschaft, (Frankfurt).
5 Including data for Singapore.

Remarque générale.
Production de métal vierge (formes primaires) et d'étain de récupération (formes secondaires), y compris les alliages d'étain. (CTCI 68710–0).

1 Production du métal de première fusion seulement.
2 Source: Conseil international de l'étain, (Londres).
3 Production du métal de deuxième fusion seulement.
4 Source: Metallgesellschaft Aktiengesellschaft, (Francfort).
5 Y compris les données relatives à Singapour.

Tin, unwrought, primary – Etain, non travaillé, neuf

Unit : Metric tons

Unité : Tonnes métriques

Country or area	1976	1977	1978	1979	1980	1981	1982	1983	1984	1985	Pays ou zone
Africa	**6 562**	**6 358**	**5 926**	**5 883**	**6 439**	**6 264**	**5 423**	**4 813**	**4 841**	**4 375**	**Afrique**
Nigeria	3 809	3 315	2 985	2 858	2 978	2 483	1 677	* 1 244	* 1 334	* 1 027	Nigéria
South Africa[1]	1 400	1 500	1 500	1 600	2 207	2 174	2 197	* 2 200	* 2 200	* 2 056	Afrique du Sud[1]
Zaire[1]	478	663	496	458	320	450	352	134	98	85	Zaïre[1]
Zimbabwe	[1] 875	[1] 880	# 945	967	934	1 157	1 197	1 235	1 209	1 207	Zimbabwe
America, North	**6 533**	**7 724**	**6 900**	**5 891**	**4 382**	**2 866**	**4 471**	**3 300**	**4 800**	**3 340**	**Amérique du Nord**
Mexico	* [1] 800	* [1] 1 000	* [1] 1 000	* [1] 1 291	* [1] 1 382	* [1] 866	* [1] 971	* [1] 800	* [1] 800	340	Mexique
United States	5 733	6 724	5 900	4 600	3 000	2 000	3 500	2 500	4 000	* 3 000	Etats–Unis
America, South	**16 335**	**20 652**	**25 633**	**25 948**	**26 644**	**28 350**	**26 770**	**26 565**	**34 247**	**39 273**	**Amérique du Sud**
Argentina	* [1] 120	* [1] 120	* [1] 120	* [1] 120	* [1] 200	457	323	282	290	365	Argentine
Bolivia	9 792	12 846	16 184	15 696	17 648	20 104	17 149	13 542	15 842	* 14 205	Bolivie
Brazil	[1] 6 423	[1] 7 686	# 9 329	10 132	8 796	7 789	9 298	12 741	18 115	* 24 703	Brésil
Asia	**142 100**	**132 691**	**145 870**	**152 167**	**153 791**	**152 795**	**135 366**	**118 455**	**107 350**	**103 796**	**Asie**
China* [2]	20 000	18 000	18 000	17 000	16 000	16 000	16 000	17 000	17 500	18 000	Chine* [2]
Indonesia[1]	23 322	24 005	25 830	27 790	30 465	32 519	29 755	28 390	22 467	20 909	Indonésie[1]
Japan	1 144	1 280	1 142	1 251	1 319	1 314	1 296	1 260	1 354	1 391	Japon
Malaysia	77 297	66 304	71 953	73 068	71 318	70 326	62 836	53 338	46 300	45 500	Malaisie
Thailand	[1] 20 337	[1] 23 102	[1] 28 945	[1] 33 058	34 689	32 636	25 479	18 467	19 729	17 996	Thaïlande
Europe	**27 021**	**27 860**	**23 919**	**23 666**	**18 881**	**19 119**	**19 739**	**20 816**	**23 581**	**23 461**	**Europe**
EEC	***20 671***	***20 459***	***18 507***	***16 973***	***12 667***	***13 433***	***14 058***	***14 732***	***16 407***	***15 980***	***CEE***
Belgium[3]	6 060	5 004	5 196	4 740	5 052	2 508	2 208	2 214	2 408	2 298	Belgique[3]
Germany, Fed. Rep.	1 450	[1] 2 897	[1] 3 241	[1] 2 488	[1] 638	* [1] 562	...	...	...	...	Allemagne, Rép. féd.
Netherlands	* [1] 2 000	* [1] 2 100	* [1] 1 625	* [1] 1 720	* [1] 1 148	3 500	2 757	5 398	6 517	6 033	Pays–Bas
United Kingdom	[1] 11 161	10 458	8 445	8 025	5 829	6 863	8 164	6 467	7 105	7 548	Royaume–Uni
EFTA	***501***	***639***	***699***	***547***	***574***	***476***	***561***	***480***	***423***	***470***	***AELE***
Finland	116	106	96	35	37	52	58	59	14	...	Finlande
Portugal	385	533	603	512	537	424	503	421	409	457	Portugal
East Europe	***1 490***	***1 419***	***1 458***	***1 600***	***1 890***	***2 140***	***2 370***	***2 792***	***3 325***	***3 720***	***Europe de l'est***
Czechoslovakia	...	...	...	0	90	140	170	192	325	420	Tchécoslovaquie
German Dem. Rep.* [2]	1 400	1 400	1 400	1 600	1 800	2 000	2 200	2 600	3 000	3 300	Rép. dém. allemande* [2]
Other Europe	***4 359***	***5 343***	***3 255***	***4 546***	***3 750***	***3 070***	***2 750***	***2 812***	***3 426***	***3 291***	***Autre Europe***
Spain	4 359	[1] 5 343	[1] 3 255	[1] 4 546	* [1] 3 750	* [1] 3 070	* [1] 2 750	[1] 2 812	[1] 3 426	[1] 3 291	Espagne
USSR* [2]	**17 000**	**17 500**	**18 000**	**18 000**	**17 000**	**16 000**	**17 000**	**18 500**	**18 500**	**18 200**	**URSS* [2]**
Oceania	**5 386**	**5 373**	**5 994**	**4 857**	**5 249**	**4 669**	**3 617**	**2 898**	**2 937**	**2 824**	**Océanie**
Australia	5 386	5 373	5 994	4 857	5 249	4 669	3 617	2 898	2 937	2 824	Australie
Total	**220 937**	**218 158**	**232 242**	**236 412**	**232 386**	**230 063**	**212 386**	**195 347**	**196 256**	**195 269**	**Total**

General note.
Primary (virgin) metal recovered from tin ores and concentrates. (SITC 68710–1).

[1] Source: International Tin Council, (London).
[2] Source: Metallgesellschaft Aktiengesellschaft, (Frankfurt).
[3] Including secondary metal production.

Remarque générale.
Production de métal neuf (vierge) obtenu par l'affinage de concentrés d'étain. (CTCI 68710–1).

[1] Source: Conseil international de l'étain, (Londres).
[2] Source: Metallgesellschaft Aktiengesellschaft, (Francfort).
[3] Y compris la production de métal de deuxième fusion.

Tin, unwrought, secondary – Etain, non travaillé, récupéré

Unit : Metric tons

Unité : Tonnes métriques

Country or area	1976	1977	1978	1979	1980	1981	1982	1983	1984	1985	Pays ou zone
America, North	**1 647**	**1 848**	**1 745**	**1 947**	**1 883**	**1 767**	**1 247**	**1 360**	**1 287**	**1 482**	**Amérique du Nord**
Canada* [1]	180	180	180	180	180	180	180	180	180	180	Canada* [1]
United States	1 467	1 668	1 565	1 767	1 703	1 587	1 067	1 180	1 107	1 302	Etats-Unis
America, South	**240**	**240**	**240**	**240**	**240**	**240**	**240**	**240**	**240**	**240**	**Amérique du Sud**
Brazil* [1]	240	240	240	240	240	240	240	240	240	240	Brésil* [1]
Asia	**252**	**239**	**203**	**224**	**206**	**215**	**227**	**293**	**358**	**242**	**Asie**
India* [1]	100	100	100	100	120	120	120	120	120	120	Inde* [1]
Japan	90	43	8	0	0	0	0	0	0	0	Japon
Thailand	[1] 62	[1] 96	[1] 95	[1] 124	86	95	107	173	238	122	Thaïlande
Europe	**15 401**	**14 844**	**14 268**	**15 545**	**18 127**	**17 944**	**18 097**	**18 052**	**16 778**	**14 347**	**Europe**
EEC	***14 712***	***14 229***	***13 655***	***14 923***	***16 522***	***16 073***	***16 649***	***16 623***	***15 385***	***12 920***	***CEE***
Denmark	61	70	76	183	48	911	1 122	1 728	1 220	283	Danemark
France	11 095	9 500	9 000	9 410	8 900	7 436	# 8 004	5 792	5 137	2 904	France
Germany, Fed. Rep.	797	1 043	[1] 1 526	[1] 1 608	[1] 1 619	* [1] 1 251	...	...	...	...	Allemagne, Rép. féd.
Greece	34	38	162	175	240	224	209	198	133	200	Grèce
Netherlands* [1]	180	180	180	180	180	180	180	204	204	204	Pays-Bas* [1]
United Kingdom	[1] 2 545	3 398	2 711	3 367	5 535	6 071	5 419	6 870	6 743	7 265	Royaume-Uni
EFTA	***190***	***112***	***119***	***128***	***131***	***123***	***99***	***90***	***73***	***111***	***AELE***
Austria	7	0	6	0	1	0	0	0	0	0	Autriche
Finland	9	0	0	0	0	0	0	0	0	...	Finlande
Norway	60	54	44	54	59	46	44	42	38	46	Norvège
Sweden	114	58	69	74	71	77	55	48	35	61	Suède
East Europe	***127***	***129***	***120***	***120***	***125***	***149***	***125***	***115***	***100***	***87***	***Europe de l'est***
Czechoslovakia	120	120	120	120	125	149	125	115	100	87	Tchécoslovaquie
Hungary	7	9	0	0	0	0	0	0	0	0	Hongrie
Other Europe	***372***	***374***	***374***	***374***	***1 349***	***1 599***	***1 224***	***1 224***	***1 220***	***1 229***	***Autre Europe***
Spain	98	# [1] 100	* [1] 100	* [1] 100	* [1] 1 075	* [1] 1 325	* [1] 950	* [1] 950	* [1] 950	* [1] 950	Espagne
Yugoslavia	...	...	...	...	...	...	...	...	270	279	Yougoslavie
Oceania	**255**	**205**	**320**	**440**	**484**	**431**	**455**	**480**	**553**	**660**	**Océanie**
Australia	255	205	320	440	484	* 431	* 455	* 480	553	660	Australie
Total	**17 795**	**17 376**	**16 776**	**18 396**	**20 940**	**20 597**	**20 266**	**20 425**	**19 216**	**16 971**	**Total**

General note.
Secondary metal recovered from scrap waste or detinning. (SITC 68710-2).

[1] Source: International Tin Council, (London).

Remarque générale.
Production de métal de deuxième fusion provenant du vieux métal ou du désétamage. (CTCI 68710-2).

[1] Source: Conseil international de l'étain, (Londres).

Cadmium unwrought – Cadmium brut

Unit : Metric tons

Unité : Tonnes métriques

Country or area	1976	1977	1978	1979	1980	1981	1982	1983	1984	1985	Pays ou zone
Africa	**385**	**471**	**299**	**357**	**298**	**295**	**456**	**409**	**400**	**373**	**Afrique**
Algeria[1]	29	133	34	64	60	* 65	* 65	* 50	* 50	* 50	Algérie[1]
Namibia[1]	83	88	79	81	69	0	110	51	* 40	30	Namibie[1]
Zaire	266	246	186	212	168	230	281	308	* 310	...	Zaïre
Zambia[1]	7	4	0	0	1	0	0	0	0	...	Zambie[1]
America, North	**4 071**	**4 092**	**3 815**	**4 108**	**3 659**	**3 491**	**2 468**	**3 408**	**3 859**	**3 737**	**Amérique du Nord**
Canada[1 2]	1 314	1 185	1 265	1 455	1 303	1 298	854	1 456	1 602	1 400	Canada[1 2]
Mexico[1 2]	710	908	897	830	778	590	607	900	571	734	Mexique[1 2]
United States[3]	2 047	1 999	1 653	1 823	1 578	1 603	1 007	1 052	1 686	1 603	Etats–Unis[3]
America, South	**231**	**237**	**219**	**247**	**230**	**335**	**515**	**661**	**660**	**690**	**Amérique du Sud**
Argentina	* 35	40	22	36	18	0	* 21	21	46	46	Argentine
Brazil	22	15	28	21	40	28	73	* [1] 189	* [1] 224	224	Brésil
Peru[1]	174	182	169	190	172	307	421	* 451	* 390	* 420	Pérou[1]
Asia	**2 884**	**3 258**	**3 054**	**3 213**	**3 017**	**2 800**	**2 885**	**3 065**	**3 243**	**3 429**	**Asie**
China* [1]	200	200	220	250	250	270	300	300	300	300	Chine* [1]
India	34	* 44	113	166	89	113	131	131	120	194	Inde
Japan	2 500	2 844	2 531	2 597	2 173	1 977	2 034	2 214	2 423	2 535	Japon
Korea,Dem.Ppl's.Rep.* [1]	150	150	150	150	140	140	100	100	100	100	Corée,Rép.pop.dém.de* [1]
Korea, Republic of[1]	0	20	40	50	365	300	320	* 320	* 300	* 300	Corée, République de[1]
Europe	**6 086**	**6 815**	**6 394**	**7 100**	**7 171**	**6 511**	**5 986**	**6 070**	**6 861**	**6 619**	**Europe**
EEC	***4 033***	***4 609***	***4 109***	***4 762***	***4 905***	***4 316***	***3 937***	***4 109***	***4 629***	***4 367***	***CEE***
Belgium[1]	1 200	1 440	1 164	1 440	1 524	1 176	1 001	1 264	1 472	1 252	Belgique[1]
France	532	790	694	689	789	663	# 580	513	568	482	France
Germany, Fed. Rep.[4]	1 275	1 336	1 182	1 266	1 194	# 1 192	* 1 030	* 1 094	* 1 111	* 1 075	Allemagne, Rép. féd.[4]
Italy[1]	436	448	378	527	568	489	475	385	452	* 588	Italie[1]
Netherlands[1]	* 400	* 300	* 400	* 416	* 455	* 518	497	513	636	600	Pays–Bas[1]
United Kingdom[1]	190	295	291	424	375	278	354	* 340	390	370	Royaume–Uni[1]
EFTA	***537***	***650***	***764***	***739***	***747***	***793***	***723***	***770***	***812***	***812***	***AELE***
Austria	29	26	33	34	36	55	49	46	48	52	Autriche
Finland	428	527	611	590	581	621	570	620	614	610	Finlande
Norway	80	97	120	115	130	117	104	104	150	150	Norvège
East Europe	***1 090***	***1 064***	***1 081***	***1 088***	***1 009***	***891***	***866***	***865***	***860***	***890***	***Europe de l'est***
Bulgaria* [1]	220	200	210	210	210	210	200	200	200	200	Bulgarie* [1]
German Dem. Rep.* [1]	20	20	20	15	16	16	16	15	15	15	Rép. dém. allemande* [1]
Poland[1]	* 750	754	761	773	698	580	570	* 570	* 570	* 600	Pologne[1]
Romania* [1]	100	90	90	90	85	85	80	80	75	75	Roumanie* [1]
Other Europe	***426***	***492***	***440***	***511***	***510***	***511***	***460***	***326***	***560***	***550***	***Autre Europe***
Spain[1]	246	303	253	222	309	303	286	278	290	300	Espagne[1]
Yugoslavia[1]	* 180	189	187	289	201	208	174	48	270	250	Yougoslavie[1]
USSR* [1]	**2 700**	**2 750**	**2 800**	**2 850**	**2 850**	**2 900**	**2 900**	**3 000**	**3 000**	**3 000**	**URSS* [1]**
Oceania	**649**	**670**	**747**	**804**	**1 012**	**1 031**	**1 010**	**1 121**	**1 049**	**1 000**	**Océanie**
Australia[1 2]	649	670	747	804	1 012	1 031	1 010	1 121	* 1 049	* 1 000	Australie[1 2]
Total	**17 006**	**18 293**	**17 328**	**18 679**	**18 237**	**17 363**	**16 220**	**17 734**	**19 072**	**18 848**	**Total**

General note.
Production of refined cadmium recovered from ores and other materials, but not from cadmium cast directly from remelted secondary cadmium. (SITC 68950–1).

[1] Source: U. S. Bureau of Mines, (Washington, D. C.).
[2] Refined cadmium.
[3] Including secondary metal production.
[4] Beginning 1981, official data are confidential. Data shown are U. S. Bureau of Mines (Washington, D.C.) estimates.

Remarque générale.
Production de cadmium raffiné provenant de minerais ou autres matières, à l'exclusion du cadmium coulé directement à partir de cadmium refondu de deuxième fusion. (CTCI 68950–1).

[1] Source: U.S. Bureau of Mines, (Washington, D.C.).
[2] Cadmium affiné.
[3] Y compris la production de métal de deuxième fusion.
[4] A partir de 1981, les chiffres sont confidentiels. Les données officielles publiées se rapportent aux estimations du 'U. S. Bureau of Mines' (Washington D.C.).

Magnesium, unwrought (total production) – Magnésium, non travaillé (production totale)

Unit : Metric tons

Unité : Tonnes métriques

Country or area	1976	1977	1978	1979	1980	1981	1982	1983	1984	1985	Pays ou zone
America, North	**142 632**	**151 560**	**176 765**	**190 167**	**199 705**	**190 247**	**139 831**	**152 746**	**196 299**	**184 026**	**Amérique du Nord**
Canada[1]	6 092	7 633	8 309	9 015	9 252	8 775	7 900	6 000	8 000	7 000	Canada[1]
United States	136 540	143 927	168 456	181 152	190 453	181 472	131 931	146 746	188 299	177 026	Etats-Unis
Asia	**23 584**	**22 000**	**28 101**	**33 750**	**40 122**	**41 104**	**34 225**	**26 038**	**29 758**	**34 996**	**Asie**
China* [2]	5 000	5 000	6 000	6 000	7 000	7 000	7 000	7 000	7 000	7 000	Chine* [2]
Japan	18 584	17 000	22 101	27 750	33 122	34 104	27 225	19 038	22 758	27 996	Japon
Europe	**59 151**	**58 944**	**60 645**	**65 732**	**67 194**	**68 511**	**57 404**	**53 033**	**72 554**	**78 405**	**Europe**
EEC	***20 343***	***20 779***	***21 485***	***21 055***	***22 342***	***20 556***	***21 904***	***23 189***	***23 253***	***23 701***	***CEE***
Denmark	0	0	0	0	0	0	2	0	0	0	Danemark
France	8 006	8 683	8 500	9 040	9 300	7 263	9 610	11 075	12 953	13 873	France
Germany, Fed. Rep.[3]	545	638	...	...	...	...	...	...	...	...	Allemagne, Rép. féd.[3]
Italy	8 836	8 766	9 678	8 757	9 676	10 800	9 943	9 799	8 148	7 862	Italie
United Kingdom	2 956	2 692	2 716	2 667	2 775	1 902	1 758	* 1 724	...	...	Royaume-Uni
EFTA	***38 808***	***38 165***	***39 160***	***44 177***	***44 352***	***47 455***	***35 000***	***29 844***	***49 301***	***54 704***	***AELE***
Norway[4]	38 808	38 165	39 160	44 177	44 352	47 455	35 000	* 29 844	49 301	54 704	Norvège[4]
East Europe	***0***	***0***	***0***	***500***	***500***	***500***	***500***	***0***	***0***	***0***	***Europe de l'est***
Poland[5]	0	0	0	500	500	500	500	0	0	0	Pologne[5]
USSR* [2]	**[6] 62 600**	**[6] 65 300**	**[6] 69 850**	**78 930**	**82 560**	**86 180**	**88 900**	**90 710**	**93 440**	**95 250**	**URSS* [2]**
Total	**287 967**	**297 804**	**335 361**	**368 579**	**389 581**	**386 042**	**320 360**	**322 527**	**392 051**	**392 677**	**Total**

General note.
Magnesium recovered from both domestic and imported ores (primary) and metal derived from scrap and waste (secondary). (SITC 68931-0).

[1] Factory shipments.
[2] Source: U. S. Bureau of Mines, (Washington, D. C.).
[3] Beginning 1978, data are confidential.
[4] Including magnesium-based alloys.
[5] Source: Metallgesellschaft Aktiengesellschaft, (Frankfurt).
[6] Primary metal production only.

Remarque générale.
Magnésium obtenu à partir des minerais et de concentrés nationaux ou importés (formes primaires) et le métal récupéré à partir de déchets et de débris d'ouvrages (formes secondaires). (CTCI 68931-0).

[1] Livraisons des fabriques.
[2] Source: U.S. Bureau of Mines, (Washington, D.C.).
[3] A partir de 1978, les données sont confidentielles.
[4] Y compris les alliages à base de magnésium.
[5] Source: Metallgesellschaft Aktiengesellschaft, (Francfort).
[6] Production du métal de première fusion seulement.

Razor blades – Lames de rasoir

Unit : Million units

Unité : En million

Country or area	1976	1977	1978	1979	1980	1981	1982	1983	1984	1985	Pays ou zone
Africa											**Afrique**
Algeria	...	53	73	76	80	81	100	...	...	...	Algérie
Tunisia	27	38	25	24	27	29	35	34	17	14	Tunisie
America, South											**Amérique du Sud**
Brazil	...	...	541	* 477	1 121	...	...	...	...	...	Brésil
Colombia	185	193	224	183	213	159	217	195	...	...	Colombie
Asia											**Asie**
India	912	985	1 213	1 491	1 264	1 353	1 670	1 906	1 916	2 028	Inde
Indonesia	...	30	...	15	49	49	77	49	79	...	Indonésie
Philippines	...	...	...	...	...	...	...	58	...	...	Philippines
Sri Lanka	34	22	39	39	30	...	...	...	...	...	Sri Lanka
Turkey	...	...	...	...	...	...	127	...	...	...	Turquie
Europe											**Europe**
EEC											***CEE***
Denmark	2	2	1	2	0	21	3	3	8	8	Danemark
Germany, Fed. Rep.	738	777	878	798	1 084	977	1 113	1 163	1 348	1 299	Allemagne, Rép. féd.
Greece	375	539	576	868	919	992	908	1 075	1 154	...	Grèce
United Kingdom[1]	2 775	...	...	...	...	...	...	...	...	...	Royaume–Uni[1]
East Europe											***Europe de l'est***
Hungary	41	39	54	47	33	39	32	31	32	37	Hongrie
Other Europe											***Autre Europe***
Spain	172	...	...	398	131	# 20	20	55	...	...	Espagne
Yugoslavia[2]	81	82	84	99	102	119	119	49	255	281	Yougoslavie[2]
USSR	1 907	1 566	1 610	1 461	1 497	1 411	1 487	1 459	1 541	1 644	**URSS**

General note.
Blades for safety razors. (SITC 69603–1).

Remarque générale.
Lames pour rasoirs mécaniques dits de sûreté. (CTCI 69603–1).

[1] Deliveries of U.K. manufactured goods.
[2] Estimated data.

[1] Quantités livrées de marchandises fabriquées au Royaume–Uni.
[2] Données estimatives.

Locksmiths' wares – locks, padlocks, keys etc. – Articles de serrurerie – serrures, cadenas, clefs etc.

Unit : Metric tons

Unité : Tonnes métriques

Country or area	1976	1977	1978	1979	1980	1981	1982	1983	1984	1985	Pays ou zone
Africa	**2 312**	**1 657**	**3 364**	**3 374**	**2 094**	**3 578**	**1 743**	**2 712**	**2 743**	**2 774**	**Afrique**
Algeria	2 312	1 657	3 364	3 374	2 094	3 578	1 743	...	...	...	Algérie
Europe	**328 424**	**335 099**	**337 255**	**354 377**	**319 182**	**326 825**	**330 053**	**319 022**	**304 949**	**302 679**	**Europe**
EEC	***188 051***	***198 597***	***204 951***	***212 317***	***205 313***	***213 212***	***214 780***	***204 339***	***190 107***	***200 349***	***CEE***
Belgium[1]	2 004	1 893	1 665	# [2] 1 457	[2] 1 628	[2] 1 308	[2] 1 322	[2] 1 380	[2] 1 465	[2] 1 474	Belgique[1]
France[3]	20 200	24 000	24 900	25 600	26 000	26 300	29 400	30 600	30 640	34 188	France[3]
Germany, Fed. Rep.	165 847	172 704	178 386	185 260	177 685	185 604	184 058	172 359	158 002	164 687	Allemagne, Rép. féd.
EFTA	***4 012***	***4 195***	***4 085***	***4 032***	***4 630***	***4 297***	***3 690***	***4 057***	***4 633***	***4 176***	***AELE***
Austria	1 607	1 729	1 759	1 793	2 071	2 367	1 813	1 767	2 323	2 086	Autriche
Sweden[4]	2 405	2 466	2 326	2 239	2 559	1 930	1 877	2 290	2 310	...	Suède[4]
East Europe	***112 156***	***109 536***	***106 882***	***114 841***	***92 580***	***96 956***	***94 224***	***95 015***	***97 477***	***86 856***	***Europe de l'est***
Hungary	6 645	6 670	6 661	6 791	7 498	7 872	7 495	7 057	7 091	6 655	Hongrie
Poland	...	...	...	108 050	85 082	89 084	86 729	87 958	90 386	80 201	Pologne
Other Europe	***24 205***	***22 771***	***21 337***	***23 187***	***16 659***	***12 360***	***17 359***	***15 611***	***12 732***	***11 298***	***Autre Europe***
Spain	...	...	...	23 187	16 659	12 360	17 359	15 611	...	...	Espagne
Total	**330 736**	**336 756**	**340 619**	**357 751**	**321 276**	**330 403**	**331 796**	**321 734**	**307 692**	**305 453**	**Total**

General note.
Locks, padlocks and keys therefore of base metal. (SITC 69811-0A).

[1] Production by establishments employing 5 or more persons.
[2] Shipments.
[3] Deliveries.
[4] Excluding keys and key-blanks.

Remarque générale.
Serrures, cadenas et clefs pour ces articles, en métaux communs. (CTCI 69811-0A).

[1] Production des établissements occupant 5 personnes ou plus.
[2] Expéditions.
[3] Livraisons.
[4] Non compris les clefs et leurs ébauches.

Locksmiths' wares – locks, padlocks, keys etc. – Articles de serrurerie – serrures, cadenas, clefs etc.

Unit : Thousand units

Unité : En milliers

Country or area	1976	1977	1978	1979	1980	1981	1982	1983	1984	1985	Pays ou zone
Africa	**90**	**407**	**206**	**353**	**242**	**385**	**404**	**432**	**465**	**498**	**Afrique**
Tunisia	90	407	206	353	242	385	404	...	...	...	Tunisie
America, South	**252 263**	**286 411**	**174 237**	**297 145**	**261 534**	**256 867**	**256 678**	**251 261**	**256 300**	**256 707**	**Amérique du Sud**
Brazil	...	282 493	169 035	287 537	251 338	...	...	...	...	...	Brésil
Chile	...	...	...	842	729	673	* 661	494	549	519	Chili
Colombia	3 701	3 011	4 348	8 766	9 467	8 593	8 416	3 166	...	...	Colombie
Asia	**11 231**	**12 014**	**12 948**	**6 835**	**5 985**	**6 402**	**17 356**	**19 940**	**20 255**	**14 965**	**Asie**
Indonesia	2 879	3 727	4 334	1 210	1 440	1 526	1 405	1 991	2 671	...	Indonésie
Sri Lanka	121	...	...	35	40	9	...	...	...	...	Sri Lanka
Turkey	8 231	8 236	8 563	5 590	4 505	4 867	15 900	17 898	17 533	13 525	Turquie
Europe	**173 761**	**173 985**	**167 283**	**154 079**	**179 553**	**131 420**	**167 279**	**149 967**	**146 513**	**144 571**	**Europe**
EEC	***4 334***	***5 338***	***4 979***	***4 982***	***4 910***	***5 663***	***5 298***	***4 486***	***4 342***	***4 825***	***CEE***
Denmark	2 216	2 459	2 413	2 403	2 608	2 777	3 100	...	...	...	Danemark
Greece	2 118	2 879	2 566	2 579	2 302	2 886	2 198	1 420	1 152	...	Grèce
EFTA	***5 674***	***6 787***	***5 508***	***6 550***	***5 850***	***5 921***	***5 954***	***6 135***	***5 172***	***5 642***	***AELE***
Finland	5 674	6 787	5 508	6 550	5 850	5 921	5 954	6 135	5 172	...	Finlande
East Europe	***55 265***	***55 720***	***53 003***	***40 565***	***54 969***	***52 636***	***48 670***	***45 959***	***47 293***	***46 745***	***Europe de l'est***
Hungary	55 265	55 720	53 003	40 565	54 969	52 636	48 670	45 959	47 293	46 745	Hongrie
Other Europe	***108 488***	***106 140***	***103 793***	***101 982***	***113 824***	***67 200***	***107 357***	***93 387***	***89 707***	***87 359***	***Autre Europe***
Spain	...	...	...	101 982	113 824	67 200	107 357	93 387	...	...	Espagne
Total	**437 345**	**472 818**	**354 673**	**458 412**	**447 314**	**395 074**	**441 717**	**421 599**	**423 534**	**416 741**	**Total**

General note.
Locks, padlocks and keys therefore of base metal. (SITC 69811-0B).

Remarque générale.
Serrures, cadenas et clefs pour ces articles, en métaux communs. (CTCI 68911-0B).

Hardware, general – Articles de quincaillerie, en général

Unit : Metric tons

Unité : Tonnes métriques

Country or area	1976	1977	1978	1979	1980	1981	1982	1983	1984	1985	Pays ou zone
Africa											**Afrique**
Algeria	...	174	129	101	0	0	0	...	...	...	Algérie
Europe											**Europe**
EEC											***CEE***
Belgium[1]	22 569	23 321	21 810	[2] 20 220	[2] 19 225	[2] 19 041	[2] 17 325	[2] 19 166	[2] 19 587	[2] 21 942	Belgique[1]
France[3]	119 870	152 800	160 700	170 700	196 400	181 800	215 800	194 200	194 297	191 856	France[3]
Germany, Fed. Rep.	203 055	201 702	200 977	108 638	271 685	250 258	248 032	276 279	297 400	303 647	Allemagne, Rép. féd.
EFTA											***AELE***
Austria	912	467	466	434	383	314	317	407	328	291	Autriche
East Europe											***Europe de l'est***
Czechoslovakia	8 435	8 931	8 862	9 495	10 601	12 524	12 228	13 796	12 916	14 210	Tchécoslovaquie
Hungary	16 183	16 770	16 787	18 725	16 347	15 709	16 026	15 866	16 057	14 635	Hongrie

General note.
Base–metal fittings and mountings of a kind suitable for furniture, doors, windows, staircases, blinds, coachwork, saddlery, trunks, caskets and the like. Base–metal hat–racks, hat–pegs, baskets etc. (SITC 69812–0A).

[1] Production by establishments employing 5 or more persons.
[2] Shipments.
[3] Deliveries.

Remarque générale.
Garnitures et ferrures en métaux communs utilisées pour les meubles, les portes, les fenêtres, les escaliers, les volets, la carrosserie, la sellerie, les coffres et autres boîtes. Porte–chapeaux (râteliers ou patères) et paniers etc., en métaux communs. (CTCI 69812–0A).

[1] Production des établissements occupant 5 personnes ou plus.
[2] Expéditions.
[3] Livraisons.

Hardware, general – Articles de quincaillerie, en général

Unit : Thousand units

Unité : En milliers

Country or area	1976	1977	1978	1979	1980	1981	1982	1983	1984	1985	Pays ou zone
Africa											**Afrique**
South Africa	...	...	...	...	13 534	12 368	10 802	7 575	7 611	8 570	Afrique du Sud
Tunisia	712	2 013	3 603	4 998	4 788	4 973	3 271	...	...	...	Tunisie
America, North											**Amérique du Nord**
El Salvador[1]	1 457	1 440	1 708	1 684	1 729	1 835	1 623	1 414	1 594	1 372	El Salvador[1]
Asia											**Asie**
Turkey	4 413	6 475	6 920	...	4 505	...	...	...	...	...	Turquie
Europe											**Europe**
EFTA											***AELE***
Finland	12 182	14 177	14 365	14 958	19 721	20 236	20 762	21 234	22 301	...	Finlande
East Europe											***Europe de l'est***
Hungary	300 412	286 172	262 092	289 989	203 119	242 516	239 846	189 485	156 519	237 794	Hongrie

General note.
Base metal fittings and mountings of a kind suitable for furniture, doors, windows, staircases, blinds, coachwork, saddlery, trunks, caskets and the like. Base–metal hat–racks, hat–pegs, baskets etc. (SITC 69812–0B).

[1] Including machetes.

Remarque générale.
Garnitures et ferrures en métaux communs utilisées pour les meubles, les portes, les fenêtres, les escaliers, les volets, la carrosserie, la sellerie, les coffres et autres boîtes. Porte–chapeaux (râteliers ou patères) et paniers etc., en métaux communs. (CTCI 69812–0B).

[1] Y compris les machettes.

Tanks and vats – Citernes et cuves

Unit : Thousand metric tons

Unité : Milliers de tonnes métriques

Country or area	1976	1977	1978	1979	1980	1981	1982	1983	1984	1985	Pays ou zone
Africa											**Afrique**
Algeria	3	1	2	2	2	2	2	...	...	...	Algérie
Asia											**Asie**
Iran(Islamic Rep.of)	23	...	...	...	...	...	...	...	...	...	Iran(Rép.islamique)
Japan	164	209	280	242	275	79	47	195	195	123	Japon
Korea, Republic of	...	...	...	...	112	120	371	190	547	192	Corée, République de
Europe											**Europe**
EEC											***CEE***
Denmark[1]	38	* 33	...	...	...	...	...	...	...	...	Danemark[1]
France[2 3]	[4] 183	[4] 142	[4] 134	[4] 141	[4] 124	[4] 106	[4] 108	# 87	63	...	France[2 3]
Germany, Fed. Rep.	200	192	185	162	211	183	182	143	103	121	Allemagne, Rép. féd.
Netherlands[5]	71	54	54	44	49	40	33	...	...	...	Pays–Bas[5]
EFTA											***AELE***
Austria	16	16	16	16	5	7	7	8	8	16	Autriche
Finland	3	...	...	...	...	...	...	...	...	...	Finlande
East Europe											***Europe de l'est***
Bulgaria[1]	3 500	3 902	...	...	...	...	...	...	...	...	Bulgarie[1]
Hungary	38	32	24	23	22	21	24	20	20	15	Hongrie
Poland	...	...	...	98	61	88	66	69	80	67	Pologne
Other Europe											***Autre Europe***
Spain	...	...	...	80	88	83	57	58	...	...	Espagne
Yugoslavia	16	17	23	29	26	29	* 50	24	24	26	Yougoslavie

General note.
Reservoirs, tanks, vats and similar containers, for any material, of iron and steel, copper or aluminium of a capacity exceeding 300 litres, whether or not lined or heat–insulated, but not fitted with mechanical or thermal equipment, normally installed as permanent fixtures for storage or manufacturing use, in chemical works, dye works, gasworks etc. (SITC 69210–0A).

[1] In number of units.
[2] Deliveries.
[3] Including containers of one cubic metre and over.
[4] Storage tanks for petroleum and petro–chemicals.
[5] Industrial sales.

Remarque générale.
Réservoirs, citernes, cuves et autres récipients analogues, pour toutes matières, en fonte ou acier, en cuivre ou en aluminium, d'une contenance supérieure à 300 litres, sans dispositifs mécaniques ou thermiques, même avec revêtement intérieur ou calorifuge, normalement installé en permanence pour le magasinage ou la fabrication, dans les usines de produits chimiques, de matières colorantes, les usines à gaz etc. (CTCI 69210–0A).

[1] En nombre d'unités.
[2] Livraisons.
[3] Y compris les récipients d'un mètre cube et plus.
[4] Réservoirs de stockage pour pétrole et produits pétrochimiques.
[5] Ventes industrielles.

Unit : Number units

Unité : Nombre

Country or area	1976	1977	1978	1979	1980	1981	1982	1983	1984	1985	Pays ou zone
Africa											**Afrique**
Algeria[1]	5	7	8	11	10	9	12	...	...	...	Algérie[1]
America, North											**Amérique du Nord**
United States[2]	3 619	3 790	3 970	3 915	3 770	...	...	...	...	...	Etats–Unis[2]
America, South											**Amérique du Sud**
Brazil	3 836	2 204	2 928	[3] 2 356	4 533	...	...	...	...	...	Brésil
Asia											**Asie**
Japan[4 5]	5 354	7 038	9 278	9 427	12 938	13 031	12 241	13 269	14 250	13 843	Japon[4 5]
Korea, Republic of	964	975	1 526	1 627	1 444	1 457	...	...	...	...	Corée, République de
Turkey	2 966	12 601	12 466	13 718	...	...	...	...	...	...	Turquie
Europe											**Europe**
EEC											***CEE***
Belgium[1]	...	...	...	...	...	...	...	11	...	...	Belgique[1]
France[1 6]	29	24	9	23	13	...	...	26	...	...	France[1 6]
Germany, Fed. Rep.[1]	160	137	128	129	109	107	119	106	104	79	Allemagne, Rép. féd.[1]
Greece	...	...	...	...	...	...	727	884	907	...	Grèce
Netherlands[7]	214	209	250	158	126	136	150	119	175	...	Pays–Bas[7]
EFTA											***AELE***
Austria[1]	...	...	...	...	...	...	...	29	...	...	Autriche[1]
East Europe											***Europe de l'est***
Bulgaria	434	381	240	307	162	86	152	195	189	212	Bulgarie
Czechoslovakia	177	350	362	285	225	210	222	150	209	192	Tchécoslovaquie
Hungary	710	790	813	604	514	381	457	501	235	246	Hongrie
Poland	276	316	275	201	159	104	105	128	120	115	Pologne
Romania	528	541	435	528	515	469	491	387	...	262	Roumanie
Other Europe											***Autre Europe***
Spain	...	...	...	477	499	555	598	469	...	...	Espagne
Yugoslavia	17	203	315	385	289	* 239	262	286	368	405	Yougoslavie
USSR[4 8]	706	693	615	585	687	735	714	707	732	864	**URSS[4 8]**
Oceania											**Océanie**
Australia	833	901	999	970	901	1 071	1 223	505	253	...	Australie

General note.
Steam and other vapour generating boilers (excluding central heating hot water boilers capable of producing low pressure steam), tank boilers, firetube boilers, water–tube boilers. (SITC 71110–0A).

[1] In thousand metric tons.
[2] Excluding power boilers. Figures reported relate to new orders.
[3] Production by establishments employing 5 or more persons.
[4] Excluding steam–generating boilers for ships.
[5] Including central–heating boilers.
[6] Source: Industrial Statistics, Statistical Office of the European Communities, (Luxembourg).
[7] Industrial sales.
[8] Boilers with a capacity over 10 tons of steam per hour.

Remarque générale.
Générateurs de vapeur d'eau ou d'autres vapeurs (à l'exclusion des chaudières pour le chauffage central conçues pour produire à la fois de l'eau chaude et de la vapeur à basse pression). Chaudières à bouilleurs et chaudières à tubes de fumée et chaudières à tubes d'eau. (CTCI 71110–0A).

[1] En milliers de tonnes métriques.
[2] Non compris les chaudières de production d'énergie. Les chiffres indiqués correspondent à de nouvelles commandes.
[3] Production des établissements occupant 5 personnes ou plus.
[4] Non compris les chaudières de navire.
[5] Y compris les chaudières de chauffage central.
[6] Source: Statistiques industrielles, Office statistique des Communautés européennes, (Luxembourg).
[7] Ventes industrielles.
[8] Chaudières d'une capacité de plus de 10 tonnes de vapeur par heure.

Boilers, steam–generating – Chaudières à vapeur

Unit : Tons of steam per hour

Unité : Tonnes de vapeurs par heure

Country or area	1976	1977	1978	1979	1980	1981	1982	1983	1984	1985	Pays ou zone
America, North	**143 500**	**143 500**	**143 500**	**143 500**	**143 500**	**143 500**	**143 500**	**143 500**	**143 500**	**143 500**	**Amérique du Nord**
United States	143 500	...	...	...	...	...	...	...	...	...	Etats–Unis
Asia	**35 501**	**47 832**	**31 050**	**41 851**	**40 048**	**54 589**	**49 365**	**39 839**	**34 645**	**46 077**	**Asie**
Japan[1 2]	33 638	45 214	27 678	37 725	35 830	49 045	45 538	33 620	27 885	33 706	Japon[1 2]
Korea, Republic of	...	...	...	...	4 218	5 544	3 827	6 219	6 760	12 371	Corée, République de
Europe	**50 360**	**63 746**	**61 248**	**38 194**	**43 381**	**36 549**	**34 285**	**39 227**	**54 128**	**51 452**	**Europe**
EEC	***13 342***	***18 428***	***18 989***	***6 856***	***7 390***	***7 801***	***4 064***	***5 206***	***10 883***	***4 202***	***CEE***
France[3]	7 125	3 686	5 407	3 565	3 876	3 474	350	3 149	9 319	...	France[3]
Netherlands[4]	6 217	14 742	13 582	3 291	3 514	4 327	3 714	2 057	1 564	...	Pays–Bas[4]
East Europe	***22 774***	***26 714***	***20 076***	***14 067***	***16 861***	***11 891***	***13 997***	***13 383***	***14 387***	***18 235***	***Europe de l'est***
Bulgaria	2 458	1 752	1 202	1 595	833	444	832	1 002	944	930	Bulgarie
Czechoslovakia	4 822	6 862	8 731	4 071	5 431	3 699	3 196	1 496	4 987	4 744	Tchécoslovaquie
Hungary	942	1 231	1 140	2 100	1 686	1 581	1 405	1 094	817	2 692	Hongrie
Poland	7 731	8 890	3 227	1 949	4 799	1 699	4 460	4 820	4 480	7 475	Pologne
Romania	6 821	7 979	5 776	4 352	4 112	4 468	...	4 971	...	2 394	Roumanie
Other Europe	***14 244***	***18 604***	***22 183***	***17 271***	***19 130***	***16 857***	***16 224***	***20 638***	***28 858***	***29 015***	***Autre Europe***
Spain	...	...	...	12 292	13 979	13 266	...	...	...	...	Espagne
Yugoslavia	1 065	5 425	9 004	4 979	5 151	* 3 591	3 045	7 459	15 679	15 836	Yougoslavie
USSR[1 5]	**53 151**	**52 206**	**55 808**	**54 928**	**51 044**	**53 098**	**43 105**	**50 777**	**46 462**	**43 653**	**URSS[1 5]**
Total	**282 512**	**307 284**	**291 606**	**278 473**	**277 973**	**287 736**	**270 255**	**273 343**	**278 735**	**284 682**	**Total**

General note.
Steam and other vapour generating boilers (excluding central heating hot water boilers capable of producing low pressure steam), tank boilers, firetube boilers, water–tube boilers. (SITC 71110–0B).

[1] Excluding steam–generating boilers for ships.
[2] Including central–heating boilers.
[3] Boilers with a capacity of 50 tons of steam per hour and over.
[4] Industrial sales.
[5] Boilers with a capacity over 10 tons of steam per hour.

Remarque générale.
Générateurs de vapeur d'eau ou d'autres vapeurs (à l'exclusion des chaudières pour le chauffage central conçues pour produire à la fois de l'eau chaude et de la vapeur à basse pression). Chaudières à bouilleurs et chaudières à tubes de fumée et chaudières à tubes d'eau. (CTCI 71110–0B).

[1] Non compris les chaudières de navire.
[2] Y compris les chaudières de chauffage central.
[3] Chaudières d'une capacité de 50 tonnes de vapeur par heure et plus.
[4] Ventes industrielles.
[5] Chaudières d'une capacité de plus de 10 tonnes de vapeur par heure.

Cans, metal – Récipients métalliques

Unit : Thousand metric tons — Unité : Milliers de tonnes métriques

Country or area	1976	1977	1978	1979	1980	1981	1982	1983	1984	1985	Pays ou zone
Africa											**Afrique**
Algeria	17	20	28	31	32	36	34	...	...	...	Algérie
Senegal	141	175	163	180	...	...	525	663	607	517	Sénégal
Tunisia	12	14	16	15	14	19	19	15	17	...	Tunisie
America, North											**Amérique du Nord**
United States[1]	5 372	5 310	5 722	5 620	5 035	5 574	5 854	...	...	...	Etats–Unis[1]
Asia											**Asie**
Hong Kong[2 3]	...	...	51	76	45	39	61	111	...	...	Hong–kong[2 3]
Indonesia[2]	93	68	72	85	130	175	206	391	...	...	Indonésie[2]
Japan[4]	979	1 106	1 191	1 235	1 175	1 189	1 186	1 241	1 346	1 371	Japon[4]
Korea, Republic of[2]	223	307	347	357	341	429	490	569	636	659	Corée, République de[2]
Malaysia[2]	236	314	368	450	433	392	352	377	404	433	Malaisie[2]
Philippines[1 2]	133	358	...	...	...	...	...	...	...	...	Philippines[1 2]
Turkey	77	162	110	86	87	...	134	...	...	...	Turquie
Europe											**Europe**
EEC											***CEE***
Belgium	...	...	...	...	...	...	...	367	...	...	Belgique
Denmark[2]	668	675	634	646	759	...	554	505	512	446	Danemark[2]
France[5 6 7]	462	625	655	689	689	...	...	...	...	...	France[5 6 7]
Germany, Fed. Rep.	543	518	504	528	566	605	615	623	567	576	Allemagne, Rép. féd.
Greece	...	...	...	...	...	...	...	...	4	...	Grèce
EFTA											***AELE***
Austria	29	32	28	22	33	32	31	33	36	28	Autriche
Finland[2]	397	435	632	1 515	1 561	1 532	1 543	1 554	1 663	...	Finlande[2]
Norway	5	5	6	6	5	5	5	5	7	...	Norvège
Portugal	24	30	31	33	36	57	54	53	54	52	Portugal
East Europe											***Europe de l'est***
Czechoslovakia	...	...	...	...	...	...	...	123	...	...	Tchécoslovaquie
Hungary	3	3	4	4	4	4	4	4	4	4	Hongrie
Poland	...	...	...	...	...	...	...	65	...	...	Pologne
Other Europe											***Autre Europe***
Spain[8]	164	...	...	210	297	271	222	289	...	...	Espagne[8]
Yugoslavia	48	56	61	* 65	57	55	43	37	44	36	Yougoslavie

General note.
All types of metal cans made of tinplate, terneplate, blackplate or enamelled sheet metal used for packing food and non–food products, of a capacity not exceeding 300 litres. (SITC 69220–1).

1 Shipments.
2 In million units.
3 Beginning 1984, data are confidential.
4 Total drum cans, food cans and 18–litre cans.
5 Consumption of metal.
6 Deliveries.
7 Boxes, drums and barrels of metal.
8 Made of aluminium and tin.

Remarque générale.
Boîtes métalliques de tous types, d'une capacité ne dépassant pas 300 litres, fabriquées en fer blanc, en tôle plombée, en fer noir ou en tôle émaillée, utilisées pour l'emballage de produits alimentaires ou autres. (CTCI 69220–1).

1 Expéditions.
2 En millions d'unités.
3 A partir de 1984, les données sont confidentielles.
4 Nombre total de boîtes cylindriques, de boîtes pour aliments et de boîtes de 18 litres.
5 Consommation de métal.
6 Livraisons.
7 Futs, tonnelets, boîtes et bidons métalliques.
8 En aluminium et en étain.

Casks, drums etc., made of metal – Foudres, fûts etc., en metal.

Unit : Thousand units

Unité : En milliers

Country or area	1976	1977	1978	1979	1980	1981	1982	1983	1984	1985	Pays ou zone
Asia											**Asie**
Korea, Republic of	461	764	953	897	900	1 027	925	1 091	1 081	1 035	Corée, République de
Malaysia	1 420	2 030	2 090	2 227	2 726	2 161	2 108	1 883	2 246	2 449	Malaisie
Philippines	908	# [1] 479	...	...	...	...	...	...	...	...	Philippines
Sri Lanka	4	...	0	0	205	64	...	...	...	...	Sri Lanka
Europe											**Europe**
EFTA											***AELE***
Austria[2]	15 877	15 592	16 087	15 649	4 774	8 659	8 679	10 084	9 427	17 853	Autriche[2]
East Europe											***Europe de l'est***
Hungary	1 062	817	968	843	1 060	935	726	728	681	613	Hongrie

General note.
Iron, steel or aluminium containers with capacity of over 300 litres, commonly used for the conveyance or packing of goods, such as casks, drums, cans, boxes etc. Reservoirs, gas cylinders and road–rail containers are excluded. (SITC 69220–2A).

[1] Shipments.
[2] In metric tons.

Remarque générale.
Récipients en fer, en acier ou en aluminium, d'une contenance supérieure à 300 litres, couramment utilisés pour le transport de marchandises, tels que foudres, fûts, bidons, boîtes etc. Cette rubrique ne comprend pas les réservoirs, les bouteilles à gaz et les conteneurs rail–route. (CTCI 69220–2A).

[1] Expéditions.
[2] En tonnes métriques.

Compressed gas cylinders, made of metal – Bouteilles cylindriques à gaz comprimé, en métal

Unit : Thousand units

Unité : En milliers

Country or area	1976	1977	1978	1979	1980	1981	1982	1983	1984	1985	Pays ou zone
Africa											**Afrique**
Tunisia	74	63	65	126	105	129	148	115	126	110	Tunisie
America, South											**Amérique du Sud**
Chile	76	58	32	# 108	107	182	163	84	122	134	Chili
Ecuador	29	61	67	...	164	161	71	64	...	...	Equateur
Europe											**Europe**
EEC											***CEE***
Denmark	152	107	109	122	325	518	...	...	...	...	Danemark
France[1] [2]	17	22	19	27	29	20	14	# 26	17	23	France[1] [2]
Greece	...	139	131	109	137	26	21	21	12	...	Grèce
EFTA											***AELE***
Sweden[2]	9	7	...	...	...	...	...	...	...	...	Suède[2]
East Europe											***Europe de l'est***
Hungary	294	284	304	373	369	288	285	214	263	391	Hongrie
Other Europe											***Autre Europe***
Spain	1 664	...	...	3 404	2 208	2 459	1 447	1 027	...	...	Espagne
Yugoslavia	675	642	985	942	1 060	1 194	740	293	265	292	Yougoslavie

General note.
Cylinders made of iron, steel or aluminium which are used for the transport and storage of compressed gases (oxygen, hydrogen, carbon dioxide or butane). (SITC 69230-0A).

[1] Deliveries.
[2] In metric tons.

Remarque générale.
Bouteilles cylindriques en fer, en acier ou en aluminium, utilisées pour le transport et le magasinage de gaz comprimés (oxygène, hydrogène, gaz carbonique ou butane). (CTCI 69230-0A).

[1] Livraisons.
[2] En tonnes métriques.

Cables – Câbles

Unit : Thousand metric tons

Unité : Milliers de tonnes métriques

Country or area	1976	1977	1978	1979	1980	1981	1982	1983	1984	1985	Pays ou zone
Africa	**7.4**	**7.4**	**7.4**	**6.6**	**7.4**	**8.1**	**7.4**	**7.4**	**7.4**	**7.4**	**Afrique**
Egypt	...	...	...	6.6	...	8.1	...	...	...	...	Egypte
America, North	**56.3**	**60.7**	**64.0**	**68.8**	**62.8**	**63.5**	**62.5**	**63.1**	**63.1**	**63.8**	**Amérique du Nord**
Canada[1]	55.1	59.4	62.5	67.2	...	...	...	...	...	...	Canada[1]
Cuba	...	...	...	...	...	2.4	1.4	2.0	2.1	2.8	Cuba
America, South	**26.2**	**22.9**	**28.6**	**42.4**	**43.4**	**46.3**	**49.1**	**55.6**	**60.2**	**64.9**	**Amérique du Sud**
Brazil	20.7	19.6	23.2	[2] 31.4	36.9	...	...	...	...	...	Brésil
Colombia	...	3.3	5.4	11.0	6.5	...	5.2	...	...	...	Colombie
Asia	**94.9**	**76.2**	**78.7**	**89.2**	**111.9**	**116.9**	**183.2**	**95.5**	**89.0**	**129.9**	**Asie**
India[3]	84.0	65.6	62.5	71.0	75.6	79.1	51.4	50.0	46.6	59.9	Inde[3]
Indonesia	7.6	7.5	11.7	14.0	27.0	27.2	119.0	31.6	31.0	...	Indonésie
Syrian Arab Republic	3.1	2.9	4.3	4.0	9.1	10.5	12.7	13.8	11.2	6.4	Rép. arabe syrienne
Viet Nam	0.2	0.2	0.2	0.2	...	...	...	...	...	...	Viet Nam
Europe	**900.3**	**927.6**	**979.9**	**971.8**	**1 005.2**	**957.7**	**1 162.3**	**958.4**	**1 006.6**	**1 034.5**	**Europe**
EEC	***329.6***	***328.2***	***344.3***	***345.5***	***384.7***	***374.9***	***373.2***	***374.7***	***385.0***	***418.8***	***CEE***
Belgium[2]	96.3	95.2	100.2	# [1] 103.3	[1] 92.4	[1] 91.8	[1] 90.9	[1] 95.8	[1] 105.6	[1] 113.5	Belgique[2]
Denmark	4.3	4.4	4.5	4.2	4.9	...	...	...	...	...	Danemark
France[4 5]	77.0	72.3	76.0	80.4	86.7	83.5	84.5	87.8	84.0	78.0	France[4 5]
Germany, Fed. Rep.	136.0	141.2	150.5	144.7	137.7	135.8	136.4	132.1	135.6	150.2	Allemagne, Rép. féd.
Greece	16.0	15.2	13.1	12.8	63.0	59.1	56.5	54.1	54.7	...	Grèce
EFTA	***62.5***	***70.9***	***70.6***	***76.3***	***74.5***	***63.1***	***75.3***	***74.3***	***74.6***	***74.5***	***AELE***
Finland	15.2	15.6	15.2	16.4	14.9	16.0	21.2	18.4	19.0	...	Finlande
Norway	26.1	27.5	30.4	32.8	31.8	22.9	...	...	20.4	...	Norvège
Portugal	4.5	6.8	6.3	4.1	7.0	7.1	8.4	6.6	6.7	6.3	Portugal
Sweden	16.7	21.0	18.6	23.0	20.9	17.2	20.8	25.2	28.5	26.1	Suède
East Europe	***320.5***	***316.6***	***326.4***	***344.4***	***325.5***	***280.0***	***250.8***	***251.4***	***261.2***	***265.9***	***Europe de l'est***
Bulgaria	...	...	...	...	...	...	...	20.1	...	...	Bulgarie
Czechoslovakia	43.0	42.9	45.0	52.0	49.7	45.4	40.5	39.5	38.1	39.3	Tchécoslovaquie
Hungary	40.0	39.1	40.1	41.0	40.9	44.7	41.9	38.3	44.4	44.1	Hongrie
Poland	106.2	113.5	128.1	129.3	115.8	75.7	64.2	83.5	92.5	96.3	Pologne
Romania[6]	...	101.0	93.0	102.0	99.0	94.0	84.0	70.0	66.0	66.0	Roumanie[6]
Other Europe	***187.6***	***211.9***	***238.6***	***205.7***	***220.4***	***239.7***	***463.0***	***257.9***	***285.8***	***275.4***	***Autre Europe***
Spain	101.2	...	...	124.9	133.0	148.9	123.3	119.2	...	...	Espagne
Yugoslavia	86.4	96.9	120.4	80.8	87.4	90.7	339.8	138.7	148.5	134.9	Yougoslavie
Oceania	**20.6**	**18.4**	**21.1**	**21.4**	**21.9**	**26.6**	**27.9**	**26.7**	**23.1**	**27.6**	**Océanie**
Australia	20.6	18.4	21.1	21.4	21.9	26.6	27.9	26.7	23.1	...	Australie
Total	**1 105.6**	**1 113.2**	**1 179.7**	**1 200.3**	**1 252.4**	**1 219.0**	**1 492.4**	**1 206.6**	**1 249.4**	**1 328.1**	**Total**

General note.
Stranded wire, cables, cordage, ropes, plaited bands, strings and the like of iron and steel, copper or aluminium, but excluding insulated electric cables. Uninsulated stranded copper wire for electrical purposes is included. (SITC 69310–0).

1 Shipments.
2 Production by establishments employing 5 or more persons.
3 Production by large and medium scale establishments only.
4 Deliveries.
5 Steel cables only.
6 Electric cables and conductors.

Remarque générale.
Câbles, cordages, tresses, élingues et similaires, en fil de fer, d'acier, de cuivre ou d'aluminium, à l'exclusion des articles isolés pour l'électricité mais y compris les câbles de cuivre non isolés pour l'électricité. (CTCI 69310–0).

1 Expéditions.
2 Production des établissements occupant 5 personnes ou plus.
3 Production des grandes et moyennes entreprises seulement.
4 Livraisons.
5 Câbles en acier seulement.
6 Conductuers et cables electriques.

Nails, screws, nuts, bolts, rivets etc. – Clous, vis, écrous, boulons, rivets et articles similaires

Unit : Thousand metric tons

Unité : Milliers de tonnes métriques

Country or area	1976	1977	1978	1979	1980	1981	1982	1983	1984	1985	Pays ou zone
Africa	**83.4**	**83.1**	**106.3**	**131.6**	**145.0**	**164.0**	**169.5**	**138.4**	**149.7**	**155.8**	**Afrique**
Algeria	4.6	6.0	9.6	13.8	12.2	12.9	10.6	...	...	...	Algérie
Côte d'Ivoire	...	5.3	3.5	3.9	...	...	...	...	...	...	Côte d'Ivoire
Egypt	8.6	8.6	8.6	9.3	10.1	10.2	11.4	32.3	...	...	Egypte
Ethiopia[1 2]	2.5	2.5	2.8	3.7	4.9	4.2	5.1	3.2	3.6	4.0	Ethiopie[1 2]
Madagascar	0.3	0.6	0.8	0.8	0.9	0.5	1.1	0.9	1.5	...	Madagascar
Sierra Leone[3]	0.5	0.5	0.7	0.6	0.6	0.4	0.4	0.4	0.1	0.2	Sierra Leone[3]
South Africa[4]	59.6	57.6	78.3	97.7	* 109.5	129.1	134.3	80.0	* 99.4	101.7	Afrique du Sud[4]
Tunisia	1.6	0.8	0.9	0.8	1.9	2.0	...	...	...	...	Tunisie
Zaire	1.4	1.3	...	...	0.6	0.4	0.5	...	...	...	Zaïre
America, North	**146.6**	**164.2**	**164.5**	**163.7**	**157.3**	**163.1**	**164.5**	**167.4**	**169.9**	**169.5**	**Amérique du Nord**
Barbados	0.1	0.1	0.1	0.2	0.1	0.2	0.1	0.2	0.1	0.1	Barbade
Canada[5]	134.4	150.6	151.4	148.9	143.6	...	...	...	...	...	Canada[5]
Cuba	5.5	6.8	7.6	7.4	8.6	8.3	8.3	9.0	9.7	8.9	Cuba
Dominican Republic	4.8	5.5	3.4	3.7	2.8	2.6	2.5	3.0	3.1	...	Rép. dominicaine
El Salvador[6]	1.2	0.3	...	2.7	1.3	0.6	0.3	0.4	...	...	El Salvador[6]
Haiti[3]	0.7	0.8	0.7	0.7	0.8	0.7	0.8	0.7	0.7	0.5	Haïti[3]
America, South	**314.7**	**339.0**	**322.2**	**354.2**	**367.8**	**344.0**	**340.7**	**339.0**	**343.3**	**345.8**	**Amérique du Sud**
Bolivia[3]	1.1	1.4	1.7	1.4	1.8	2.1	1.2	1.0	0.8	...	Bolivie[3]
Brazil	293.6	...	296.4	[7] 329.0	339.4	...	...	...	...	...	Brésil
Chile[3]	...	...	...	9.6	11.4	11.8	* 8.1	9.8	11.6	13.3	Chili[3]
Colombia	...	...	...	...	...	8.6	8.6	8.0	...	...	Colombie
Ecuador[3]	2.9	5.5	6.3	...	6.8	6.9	8.2	5.6	...	...	Equateur[3]
Asia	**781.3**	**825.3**	**889.5**	**954.7**	**1 015.0**	**998.9**	**974.4**	**1 005.2**	**1 134.5**	**1 112.4**	**Asie**
Burma[8]	5.0	...	...	...	...	...	...	...	...	...	Birmanie[8]
Cyprus[3]	0.2	0.2	0.6	0.7	0.4	0.2	0.8	1.0	0.5	0.5	Chypre[3]
Democratic Yemen[3]	...	...	...	...	0.3	0.2	0.3	0.4	0.5	...	Yémen démocratique[3]
India[9]	26.5	27.6	28.3	28.8	29.6	29.2	22.4	18.6	16.5	19.2	Inde[9]
Indonesia	14.4	33.8	26.9	33.3	39.0	39.9	47.9	46.4	63.0	...	Indonésie
Iran(Islamic Rep.of)[10]	17.6	22.0	14.8	16.6	18.7	28.2	25.0	...	...	...	Iran(Rép.islamique)[10]
Israel	4.3	...	...	...	...	...	...	...	...	...	Israël
Japan	665.1	673.9	736.2	791.9	851.6	804.7	775.4	792.8	889.3	878.2	Japon
Korea, Republic of[11]	21.6	31.2	45.9	48.6	43.7	60.8	64.8	81.8	91.6	91.8	Corée, République de[11]
Philippines[12]	...	...	12.1	13.0	8.2	...	...	...	...	...	Philippines[12]
Sri Lanka	1.2	...	3.3	4.9	3.7	1.1	...	...	...	...	Sri Lanka
Turkey	14.1	13.5	12.0	7.4	10.4	14.2	14.1	14.5	21.9	8.0	Turquie
Europe	**2 008.3**	**1 974.2**	**2 006.1**	**2 057.4**	**2 101.0**	**1 985.6**	**1 909.4**	**1 972.3**	**1 983.7**	**2 012.9**	**Europe**
EEC	***989.1***	***978.5***	***950.5***	***1 012.2***	***1 023.4***	***847.6***	***817.2***	***797.4***	***841.9***	***855.9***	***CEE***
Belgium[7]	74.8	77.7	65.5	# [13] 77.3	[13] 68.2	[13] 58.7	[13] 48.5	[13] 41.6	[13] 41.6	[13] 42.2	Belgique[7]
Denmark	31.9	31.9	39.6	35.9	21.5	...	14.0	15.8	20.7	...	Danemark
France[14 15]	65.6	67.1	62.6	59.6	55.9	54.9	47.8	51.8	47.3	40.8	France[14 15]
Germany, Fed. Rep.	792.0	775.0	756.4	812.0	849.8	685.4	685.8	668.5	714.3	740.8	Allemagne, Rép. féd.
Greece	24.9	26.9	26.4	27.3	27.9	25.1	21.0	19.7	18.1	...	Grèce
EFTA	***175.6***	***158.0***	***162.3***	***166.5***	***173.2***	***169.4***	***171.9***	***164.8***	***168.8***	***168.8***	***AELE***
Austria	41.8	38.9	34.7	33.9	37.3	33.9	32.3	26.4	36.9	35.0	Autriche
Finland	28.6	22.0	23.9	29.5	28.8	27.3	27.4	28.3	27.1	...	Finlande
Portugal	23.3	22.8	25.5	25.0	29.0	30.1	34.1	31.9	26.7	27.2	Portugal
Sweden	81.9	74.4	...	...	...	...	...	...	...	...	Suède
East Europe	***588.1***	***578.6***	***585.5***	***591.9***	***603.6***	***683.0***	***675.0***	***664.4***	***665.5***	***674.2***	***Europe de l'est***
Bulgaria[16]	49.3	51.4	53.3	54.0	58.4	60.0	57.6	58.2	60.0	61.1	Bulgarie[16]
Czechoslovakia	124.1	119.9	121.2	126.4	133.6	134.2	135.9	135.2	136.6	125.9	Tchécoslovaquie
German Dem. Rep.	102.5	91.1	93.9	94.4	96.8	200.6	200.3	191.2	191.7	223.0	Rép. dém. allemande
Hungary	60.3	61.9	63.9	64.7	63.6	65.5	68.5	62.5	64.5	59.5	Hongrie
Poland	252.0	254.2	253.2	252.3	251.2	222.7	212.7	217.3	212.6	204.7	Pologne
Other Europe	***255.4***	***259.1***	***307.8***	***286.8***	***300.9***	***285.6***	***245.4***	***345.8***	***307.5***	***314.0***	***Autre Europe***
Spain	148.0	...	...	169.3	156.4	154.7	163.6	182.7	...	...	Espagne
Yugoslavia	107.3	107.6	152.8	117.6	144.5	130.9	81.8	163.1	131.8	134.9	Yougoslavie
Oceania	**22.6**	**22.3**	**20.2**	**19.2**	**25.0**	**23.0**	**20.9**	**16.5**	**18.1**	**18.3**	**Océanie**

For general note and footnotes, see end of table.

Voir la fin du tableau pour la remarque générale et les notes.

Unit : Thousand metric tons — Unité : Milliers de tonnes métriques

Country or area	1976	1977	1978	1979	1980	1981	1982	1983	1984	1985	Pays ou zone
Australia[3 17]	22.6	22.3	20.2	19.2	25.0	23.0	20.9	16.5	18.1	...	Australie[3 17]
Total	**3 356.9**	**3 408.1**	**3 508.8**	**3 680.7**	**3 811.1**	**3 678.7**	**3 579.4**	**3 638.7**	**3 799.1**	**3 814.9**	**Total**

General note.
Nails, tacks, staples, hook–nails, corrugated nails, spiked cramps, studs, spikes and drawing pins, bolts, nuts (including bolt ends and screw studs), whether or not threaded or tapped, screws (including screw hooks and screw rings), rivets, cotters, cotter pins, washers, and spring washers, or iron, steel or copper. (SITC 69400–0).

1 Eritrea only.
2 Twelve months ending 10 September of year stated.
3 Nails only.
4 Excluding rivets.
5 Shipments of nails and spikes of iron and steel wire.
6 Nails and clasps only.
7 Production by establishments employing 5 or more persons.
8 Twelve months ending 30 September of year stated.
9 Production by large and medium scale establishments only.
10 Production by establishments employing 50 or more persons.
11 Nuts and bolts only.
12 Steel and copper nails only.
13 Shipments.
14 Deliveries.
15 Steel products only.
16 Excluding pins, drawing pins, clasps etc.
17 Twelve months ending 30 June of year stated.

Remarque générale.
Clous, semences, agrafes, crochets, clous cannelés, crampons appointés, clous d'ornementation, pointes et punaises, boulons, écrous (y compris ceux des boulons et des goujons), filetés ou non, taraudés ou non, vis (y compris les crochets à vis et les pitons à vis), rivets, clavettes, goupilles, rondelles, élastiques ou non, en fer, en acier ou en cuivre. (CTCI 69400–0).

1 Erythrée seulement.
2 Période de douze mois finissant le 10 septembre de l'année indiquée.
3 Clous seulement.
4 Non compris les rivets.
5 Expéditions de clous et pointes de fer et de fil d'acier.
6 Clous et àgràfès seulement.
7 Production des établissements occupant 5 personnes ou plus.
8 Période de douze mois finissant le 30 septembre de l'année indiquée.
9 Production des grandes et moyennes entreprises seulement.
10 Production des établissements occupant 50 personnes ou plus.
11 Ecrous et boulons seulement.
12 Clous en acier et en cuivre seulement.
13 Expéditions.
14 Livraisons.
15 Produits en acier seulement.
16 Non compris les épingles, punaises, agrafes etc.
17 Période de douze mois finissant le 30 juin de l'année indiquée.

Containers, one cubic metre and over – Cadres et autres conteneurs d'un mètre cube et plus

Unit : Thousand units

Unité : En milliers

Country or area	1976	1977	1978	1979	1980	1981	1982	1983	1984	1985	Pays ou zone
Asia											**Asie**
Japan[1]	194	321	443	304	380	290	224	179	290	237	Japon[1]
Europe											**Europe**
EEC											***CEE***
Denmark	11	9	* 5	* 3	3	...	...	3	...	...	Danemark
France	...	...	...	...	...	...	...	13	...	...	France
Germany, Fed. Rep.	33	37	41	66	68	48	58	32	38	42	Allemagne, Rép. féd.
EFTA											***AELE***
Finland	1	0	0	6	5	7	6	4	6	...	Finlande
East Europe											***Europe de l'est***
Bulgaria	...	...	...	...	...	...	...	5	...	...	Bulgarie
Hungary	44	21	22	46	49	51	35	11	12	14	Hongrie
Poland	...	...	...	19	22	17	8	8	10	12	Pologne
Other Europe											***Autre Europe***
Spain	302	...	...	92	197	183	196	93	...	...	Espagne

General note.
An article of transport equipment (lift–van, movable tank or other similar structure) with an internal volume of one cubic metre or more, which is (a) of a permanent character and accordingly strong enough to be suitable for repeated use, (b) specially designed to facilitate the carriage of goods, by one or more modes of transport, without intermediate reloading, (c) fitted with devices permitting its ready handling, particularly its transfer from one mode of transport to another, and (d) so designed as to be easy to fill and empty. This item does not include vehicles of any kind or conventional packing. (SITC 73163–1A).

[1] In thousand metric tons.

Remarque générale.
Engin de transport (cadre, citerne amovible ou autre engin analogue) ayant un volume intérieur d'un mètre cube ou plus: (a) ayant un caractère permanent et étant de ce fait suffisamment résistant pour permettre son usage répété, (b) spécialement conçu pour faciliter le transport de marchandises sans rupture de charge par un ou plusieurs moyens de transport, (c) muni de dispositifs le rendant facile à manipuler, notamment lors de son transbordement d'un moyen de transport à un autre, et (d) conçu de façon à être facile à remplir et à vider. Cette rubrique ne comprend ni les véhicules de toute espèce ni les emballages conventionnels. (CTCI 73163–1A).

[1] En milliers de tonnes métriques.

Central-heating apparatus, non-electric – Appareils de chauffage central, non électriques

Unit : Thousand units

Unité : En milliers

Country or area	1976	1977	1978	1979	1980	1981	1982	1983	1984	1985	Pays ou zone
Asia											**Asie**
Iran(Islamic Rep.of)[1]	136	151	150	180	200	130	134	...	...	...	Iran(Rép.islamique)[1]
Japan	247	328	486	493	344	434	458	427	...	...	Japon
Europe											**Europe**
EEC											***CEE***
Belgium[2 3]	19	18	16	18	15	12	12	13	15	13	Belgique[2 3]
Denmark	48	50	49	67	50	...	...	...	...	...	Danemark
France[4]	97	92	97	105	78	53	45	38	46	60	France[4]
Germany, Fed. Rep	554	490	509	606	591	440	462	442	443	481	Allemagne, Rép. féd.
Greece	10	13	16	15	14	13	14	15	15	...	Grèce
Netherlands[5 6]	188	193	192	202	219	166	173	128	126	...	Pays-Bas[5 6]
EFTA											***AELE***
Austria	44	46	44	58	66	55	62	53	46	49	Autriche
Finland	27	25	27	31	32	68	21	16	25	...	Finlande
Sweden[2]	44	[7] 22	...	...	...	...	...	...	...	...	Suède[2]
East Europe											***Europe de l'est***
Hungary	923	921	1 021	1 105	1 068	1 098	1 033	1 203	1 322	1 390	Hongrie
Other Europe											***Autre Europe***
Yugoslavia	28	34	54	58	60	66	68	61	66	73	Yougoslavie

General note.
Boilers (excluding steam-generating boilers) and radiators for central heating, air heaters and hot-air distributors, not electric. (SITC 81210-1).

Remarque générale.
Chaudières (à l'exclusion des générateurs de vapeur d'eau) et radiateurs de chauffage central. Générateurs et distributeurs d'air chaud. Cette rubrique ne comprend pas les appareils électriques. (CTCI 81210-1).

1 Production by establishments employing 50 or more persons.
2 In thousand metric tons.
3 Shipments.
4 Deliveries.
5 Industrial sales.
6 Including central heating radiators.
7 Excluding boilers for central heating and parts thereof other than those made of cast iron.

1 Production des établissements occupant 50 personnes ou plus.
2 En milliers de tonnes métriques.
3 Expéditions.
4 Livraisons.
5 Ventes industrielles.
6 Y compris les radiateurs pour le chauffage central.
7 Non compris les chaudières de chauffage central ou leurs éléments autres que ceux qui sont en fonte.

Steam turbines – Turbines à vapeur

Unit : Number units — Unité : Nombre

Country or area	1976	1977	1978	1979	1980	1981	1982	1983	1984	1985	Pays ou zone
America, North											**Amérique du Nord**
United States[1 2]	98	71	49	62	54	47	38	34	36	41	Etats–Unis[1 2]
America, South											**Amérique du Sud**
Brazil	[3] 834	[3] 357	[3] 257	[3] 266	1 228	...	...	...	...	...	Brésil
Asia											**Asie**
Japan[4 5]	155	400	462	323	426	597	586	487	406	374	Japon[4 5]
Europe											**Europe**
EEC											***CEE***
Belgium[6]	...	...	...	...	...	...	...	350	...	...	Belgique[6]
France[6 7]	3 000	2 540	2 410	3 200	5 670	2 720	1 080	910	[4] 2 210	1 050	France[6 7]
Germany, Fed. Rep.	1 035	858	646	592	651	647	646	666	520	794	Allemagne, Rép. féd.
United Kingdom[8]	355	150	117	116	105	...	87	87	...	...	Royaume–Uni[8]
EFTA											***AELE***
Sweden	96	80	...	...	...	...	...	...	...	...	Suède
East Europe											***Europe de l'est***
Czechoslovakia	92	55	65	51	45	46	30	50	63	64	Tchécoslovaquie
Hungary	9	10	20	44	67	29	7	6	10	8	Hongrie
Poland	20	19	26	16	12	7	7	3	9	11	Pologne
Romania[9]	9	10	17	12	13	23	23	13	...	9	Roumanie[9]
Other Europe											***Autre Europe***
Yugoslavia	15	17	16	16	7	18	16	23	6	20	Yougoslavie
USSR[10]	456	478	513	525	481	484	504	465	532	523	**URSS[10]**

General note.
Impulse turbines, reaction turbines and compound turbines. Mercury–vapour turbines are excluded. Steam piston–valve engines and parts of steam turbines are also excluded. (SITC 71132–1A).

1 Shipments.
2 Conventional and nuclear steam turbine–generator sets, 4000 kW and larger.
3 Production by establishments employing 5 or more persons.
4 Including gas turbines.
5 Excluding steam turbines for ships.
6 In metric tons.
7 Deliveries.
8 Excluding turbines for electricity generation, marine engines and steam locomotives.
9 Steam turbines of over 500 kW.
10 Including gas and hydraulic turbines.

Remarque générale.
Turbines à action, turbines à réaction et turbines compound. Cette rubrique ne comprend pas les turbines à vapeur de mercure, les machines à vapeur à piston et les pièces détachées de turbines à vapeur. (CTCI 71132–1A).

1 Expéditions.
2 Turbogénérateurs à vapeur, de type classique ou nucléaire, de 4000 kW et plus.
3 Production des établissements occupant 5 personnes ou plus.
4 Y compris les turbines à gaz.
5 Non compris les turbines à vapeur de marine.
6 En tonnes métriques.
7 Livraisons.
8 Non compris les turbo–générateurs, les moteurs marins et les locomotives à vapeur.
9 Turbines à vapeur de plus de 500 kW.
10 Y compris les turbines à gaz et les turbines hydrauliques.

Steam turbines Turbines à vapeur

Unit : Thousand kilowatts

Unité : Milliers de kilowatts

Country or area	1976	1977	1978	1979	1980	1981	1982	1983	1984	1985	Pays ou zone
America, North	**34 518**	**28 682**	**26 503**	**28 983**	**19 213**	**13 466**	**9 116**	**11 905**	**10 802**	**7 255**	**Amérique du Nord**
United States[1]	34 518	28 682	26 503	28 983	19 213	13 466	9 116	11 905	10 802	7 255	Etats–Unis[1]
Asia	**9 764**	**5 903**	**8 796**	**12 002**	**8 607**	**14 845**	**15 188**	**11 014**	**9 296**	**9 669**	**Asie**
Japan[2]	9 764	5 903	8 796	12 002	8 607	14 845	15 188	11 014	9 296	9 669	Japon[2]
Europe	**15 262**	**15 163**	**13 629**	**10 772**	**8 066**	**8 847**	**8 122**	**9 793**	**8 492**	**7 124**	**Europe**
EEC	***10 954***	***11 024***	***10 024***	***7 399***	***5 825***	***6 340***	***4 908***	***7 785***	***6 144***	***4 599***	***CEE***
Germany, Fed. Rep.	10 954	11 024	10 024	7 399	5 825	6 340	4 908	7 785	6 144	4 599	Allemagne, Rép. féd.
East Europe	***4 290***	***4 066***	***3 551***	***3 319***	***2 159***	***2 398***	***3 178***	***1 947***	***2 231***	***2 396***	***Europe de l'est***
Czechoslovakia	1 447	1 279	1 273	856	312	1 082	1 681	951	1 060	1 227	Tchécoslovaquie
Hungary	334	521	96	76	32	11	7	152	11	51	Hongrie
Poland	1 831	1 532	1 579	1 872	1 318	968	893	587	834	786	Pologne
Romania[3]	678	734	603	515	497	337	597	257	...	332	Roumanie[3]
Other Europe	***18***	***73***	***54***	***54***	***82***	***109***	***36***	***61***	***117***	***129***	***Autre Europe***
Yugoslavia	18	73	54	54	82	109	36	61	117	129	Yougoslavie
USSR[2 4]	**19 594**	**19 010**	**18 340**	**20 003**	**19 613**	**14 628**	**17 258**	**15 458**	**21 329**	**21 608**	**URSS[2 4]**
Total	**79 138**	**68 758**	**67 268**	**71 760**	**55 499**	**51 786**	**49 684**	**48 170**	**49 919**	**45 656**	**Total**

General note.
Impulse turbines, reaction turbines and compound turbines. Mercury–vapour turbines are excluded. Steam piston–valve engines and parts of steam turbines are also excluded. (SITC 71132–1B).

[1] Conventional and nuclear steam turbine–generator sets, 4000 kW and larger.
[2] Including gas turbines.
[3] Steam turbines of over 500 kW.
[4] Including hydraulic turbines.

Remarque générale.
Turbines à action, turbines à réaction et turbines compound. Cette rubrique ne comprend pas les turbines à vapeur de mercure, les machines à vapeur à piston et les pièces détachées de turbines à vapeur. (CTCI 71132–1B).

[1] Turbogénérateurs à vapeur, de type classique ou nucléaire, de 4000 kW et plus.
[2] Y compris les turbines à gaz.
[3] Turbines à vapeur de plus de 500 kW.
[4] Y compris les turbines hydrauliques.

Engines, diesel – Moteurs diesel

Unit : Number units

Unité : Nombre

Country or area	1976	1977	1978	1979	1980	1981	1982	1983	1984	1985	Pays ou zone
Africa	**2 626**	**3 455**	**4 896**	**6 225**	**7 431**	**7 051**	**7 401**	**11 375**	**10 976**	**12 075**	**Afrique**
Algeria	...	3 455	4 896	6 225	7 431	7 051	7 401	11 375	10 976	...	Algérie
America, North	**315 274**	**368 367**	**388 438**	**403 769**	**344 119**	**349 262**	**209 496**	**169 552**	**211 019**	**174 764**	**Amérique du Nord**
United States	315 274	368 367	388 438	403 769	344 119	349 262	209 496	169 552	211 019	174 764	Etats–Unis
America, South	**105 450**	**92 675**	**80 941**	**80 998**	**92 401**	**56 097**	**60 019**	**52 951**	**45 882**	**38 814**	**Amérique du Sud**
Brazil	105 450	92 675	80 941	80 998	92 401	56 097	...	...	...	...	Brésil
Asia	**952 487**	**1 035 406**	**956 665**	**1 062 127**	**1 171 495**	**1 265 914**	**1 104 299**	**1 184 399**	**1 252 049**	**1 177 691**	**Asie**
India	110 068	136 031	136 934	143 290	138 934	171 800	156 901	149 292	166 210	168 433	Inde
Indonesia	33 000	27 126	24 567	21 036	58 705	72 000	70 254	53 000	52 000	...	Indonésie
Japan	775 334	844 631	765 907	864 688	949 523	1 000 201	860 196	965 032	1 019 184	926 616	Japon
Turkey	34 085	27 618	29 257	33 113	...	...	16 948	...	...	...	Turquie
Europe	**664 424**	**667 897**	**687 998**	**609 977**	**623 607**	**657 385**	**620 422**	**591 697**	**596 882**	**574 933**	**Europe**
EEC	***464 509***	***505 514***	***527 979***	***516 966***	***506 299***	***488 765***	***477 474***	***444 122***	***456 004***	***449 201***	***CEE***
Denmark	7 995	...	...	...	...	...	...	...	...	...	Danemark
Germany, Fed. Rep.	220 111	240 698	252 766	281 359	263 628	255 177	244 134	215 465	230 407	228 998	Allemagne, Rép. féd.
Netherlands[1]	302	287	441	350	304	357	323	218	1 737	...	Pays–Bas[1]
United Kingdom	236 101	256 534	266 777	227 262	234 372	225 236	...	...	...	...	Royaume–Uni
EFTA	***28 612***	***28 186***	***31 020***	***32 224***	***41 377***	***48 788***	***43 003***	***47 759***	***52 156***	***39 416***	***AELE***
Austria	806	951	911	692	1 075	2 548	1 752	947	808	748	Autriche
Finland	...	2 483	2 464	2 431	2 835	1 926	1 924	2 338	2 209	...	Finlande
Portugal	* 1 000	* 2 000	2 989	3 210	3 122	3 309	...	...	...	...	Portugal
Sweden	24 214	22 752	24 656	25 891	34 345	41 005	35 210	39 925	44 158	31 196	Suède
East Europe	***12 675***	***17 405***	***19 212***	***18 884***	***19 237***	***23 392***	***26 650***	***33 127***	***39 439***	***42 487***	***Europe de l'est***
Bulgaria	6 590	10 699	12 709	11 570	12 338	16 929	19 746	25 873	32 038	34 647	Bulgarie
Czechoslovakia	3 359	4 133	3 590	4 308	4 474	4 170	4 597	4 911	5 306	5 661	Tchécoslovaquie
German Dem. Rep.	1 951	...	...	...	...	...	...	...	...	...	Rép. dém. allemande
Hungary	775	622	962	1 055	474	342	356	392	144	228	Hongrie
Other Europe	***158 628***	***116 792***	***109 787***	***41 903***	***56 694***	***96 440***	***73 295***	***66 689***	***49 283***	***43 829***	***Autre Europe***
Spain	121 182	...	...	20 470	33 207	77 067	58 580	51 191	...	...	Espagne
Yugoslavia	37 446	34 153	34 208	21 433	23 487	19 373	14 715	15 498	16 064	17 670	Yougoslavie
Total	**2 040 261**	**2 167 800**	**2 118 938**	**2 163 096**	**2 239 053**	**2 335 709**	**2 001 637**	**2 009 974**	**2 116 808**	**1 978 277**	**Total**

General note.
Compression–ignition engines (Diesel, semi–Diesel and other heavy oil engines). Diesel engines for motor vehicles are excluded. (SITC 71150–1A).

[1] Industrial sales.

Remarque générale.
Moteurs à allumage par compression (diesels, semi–diesels et autres moteurs à huile lourde), non compris les diesels pour véhicules automobiles. (CTCI 71150–1A).

[1] Ventes industrielles.

Engines, internal combustion – Moteurs à explosion, à essence

Unit : Thousand units

Unité : En milliers

Country or area	1976	1977	1978	1979	1980	1981	1982	1983	1984	1985	Pays ou zone
Africa	**3**	**3**	**4**	**3**	**2**	**4**	**4**	**4**	**4**	**4**	**Afrique**
Tunisia	3	3	4	3	2	4	4	4	4	4	Tunisie
America, North	**10 804**	**12 076**	**13 741**	**15 929**	**14 431**	**10 331**	**9 685**	**8 739**	**11 756**	**10 544**	**Amérique du Nord**
United States	10 804	12 076	13 741	15 929	14 431	10 331	9 685	8 739	11 756	10 544	Etats–Unis
America, South	**62**	**56**	**47**	**47**	**61**	**51**	**50**	**49**	**48**	**47**	**Amérique du Sud**
Brazil	62	56	47	[1] 47	61	...	...	...	...	...	Brésil
Asia	**3 424**	**4 076**	**4 285**	**4 834**	**4 862**	**4 669**	**4 744**	**5 346**	**6 532**	**6 455**	**Asie**
Japan[2]	3 423	4 074	4 283	4 832	4 860	4 667	4 742	5 344	6 530	6 453	Japon[2]
Philippines[3]	1	2	...	...	...	...	...	...	...	...	Philippines[3]
Europe	**2 258**	**1 539**	**1 670**	**2 203**	**2 093**	**2 017**	**2 000**	**2 019**	**1 952**	**1 944**	**Europe**
EEC	***1 292***	***728***	***778***	***752***	***719***	***703***	***696***	***664***	***683***	***682***	***CEE***
Denmark	8	...	...	...	...	...	...	...	...	...	Danemark
Germany, Fed. Rep.	1 035	454	459	470	438	423	415	383	404	403	Allemagne, Rép. féd.
Greece	10	9	10	9	8	7	8	7	6	...	Grèce
Netherlands[4]	3	1	1	1	1	1	1	2	...	...	Pays–Bas[4]
United Kingdom[5]	236	256	300	...	...	...	...	...	...	...	Royaume–Uni[5]
EFTA	***534***	***461***	***487***	***508***	***433***	***448***	***458***	***532***	***554***	***524***	***AELE***
Austria	93	75	88	103	68	57	30	45	57	54	Autriche
Finland	5	4	5	5	5	5	5	5	5	...	Finlande
Portugal	* 13	21	33	24	17	13	...	...	...	...	Portugal
Sweden	423	361	361	376	343	373	405	465	475	...	Suède
East Europe	***250***	***274***	***284***	***861***	***842***	***732***	***708***	***678***	***674***	***690***	***Europe de l'est***
Bulgaria	7	11	13	12	14	21	24	28	36	38	Bulgarie
Hungary	1	0	0	0	0	0	0	0	0	0	Hongrie
Poland	32	31	32	# 617	595	496	462	422	402	399	Pologne
Romania	210	232	239	232	233	215	222	228	236	253	Roumanie
Other Europe	***182***	***76***	***121***	***82***	***100***	***134***	***138***	***145***	***41***	***48***	***Autre Europe***
Spain	161	...	...	# 17	15	15	7	7	...	...	Espagne
Yugoslavia	21	6	63	65	85	119	131	138	34	41	Yougoslavie
Oceania	**341**	**311**	**245**	**230**	**248**	**215**	**262**	**204**	**189**	**173**	**Océanie**
Australia	341	311	245	230	248	215	* 262	...	...	...	Australie
Total	**16 892**	**18 061**	**19 991**	**23 245**	**21 697**	**17 287**	**16 745**	**16 361**	**20 480**	**19 166**	**Total**

General note.
Spark–ignition, internal combustion, piston engines, equipped with fuel injection pumps, ignition parts, fuel and oil reservoirs, water radiators, oil coolers, water, oil and fuel pumps, blowers, air and oil filters, starting devices etc. Automobile, bus, truck and aircraft engines are excluded. (SITC 71150–2A)).

1 Production by establishments employing 5 or more persons.
2 Excluding internal–combustion engines for ships and gas engines.
3 Shipments.
4 Industrial sales.
5 Excluding engines for road vehicles, wheeled agricultural tractors, heavy slow–speed diesel engines for marine propulsion, other marine engines, petrol and spark ignition engines.

Remarque générale.
Moteurs à explosion à pistons, à allumage par étincelle, muni des appareils suivants: dispositif d'alimentation en carburant, accessoires d'allumage, réservoirs à essence et à huile, radiateur à eau, refroidisseur à huile, pompes à eau, à huile et à essence, compresseur d'air, filtres à air et huile, dispositif de démarrage etc. Cette rubrique ne comprend pas les moteurs d'automobile, d'autocar et d'avion. (CTCI 71150–2A).

1 Production des établissements occupant 5 personnes ou plus.
2 Non compris les moteurs à combustion interne pour bateaux et les moteurs à essence.
3 Expéditions.
4 Ventes industrielles.
5 Non compris les moteurs pour véhicules routiers, les tracteurs agricoles à roues, les moteurs Diesel lourds et lents pour propulsion marine, les autres moteurs marins, les moteurs à essence et les moteurs à allumage commandé.

Engines, internal combustion – Moteurs à explosion, à essence

Unit : Thousand horsepower

Unité : Milliers de cheval–vapeur

Country or area	1976	1977	1978	1979	1980	1981	1982	1983	1984	1985	Pays ou zone
Asia	**48 159**	**60 362**	**65 553**	**72 450**	**68 836**	**62 992**	**65 182**	**73 295**	**90 682**	**106 370**	**Asie**
China	...	27 410	28 180	29 080	25 390	20 040	22 960	28 990	40 720	55 470	Chine
Japan[1]	29 403	32 709	37 053	43 101	42 690	42 119	41 087	42 898	48 799	49 817	Japon[1]
Korea, Republic of	111	243	320	269	756	833	1 135	1 407	1 163	1 083	Corée, République de
Europe	**30 011**	**31 902**	**32 845**	**32 950**	**33 633**	**32 973**	**34 128**	**34 757**	**35 832**	**35 979**	**Europe**
EEC	***1 324***	***1 377***	***1 503***	***1 753***	***1 662***	***1 704***	***2 173***	***1 979***	***1 963***	***1 914***	***CEE***
Germany, Fed. Rep.	1 290	1 343	1 469	1 720	1 629	1 685	2 145	1 925	1 929	1 881	Allemagne, Rép. féd.
Netherlands	...	...	...	...	...	19	28	54	...	...	Pays–Bas
EFTA	***30***	***50***	***75***	***50***	***37***	***27***	***37***	***35***	***32***	***30***	***AELE***
Portugal	* 30	50	75	50	37	27	...	...	...	...	Portugal
East Europe	***22 287***	***24 597***	***24 918***	***24 797***	***25 697***	***25 005***	***25 681***	***26 507***	***27 600***	***27 798***	***Europe de l'est***
Bulgaria	350	527	604	525	814	1 360	1 600	1 874	2 655	2 705	Bulgarie
Hungary	15	5	1	1	0	0	0	0	0	0	Hongrie
Poland	4 036	4 485	4 538	4 677	4 714	3 476	3 670	3 956	4 003	4 170	Pologne
Romania	17 886	19 580	19 775	19 594	20 169	20 169	...	...	...	20 923	Roumanie
Other Europe	***6 370***	***5 878***	***6 349***	***6 350***	***6 237***	***6 237***	***6 237***	***6 237***	***6 237***	***6 237***	***Autre Europe***
Spain	5 860	...	...	...	...	...	...	...	...	...	Espagne
Yugoslavia	510	18	489	490	...	...	...	...	...	...	Yougoslavie
USSR[2]	**19 014**	**18 926**	**19 163**	**18 620**	**19 003**	**18 724**	**18 560**	**16 291**	**16 103**	**16 579**	**URSS[2]**
Ukrainian SSR	...	...	*3 934*	*3 952*	*3 947*	*4 112*	*4 219*	*3 748*	*3 845*	*3 893*	*RSS d'Ukraine*
Total	**97 184**	**111 190**	**117 561**	**124 020**	**121 472**	**114 689**	**117 870**	**124 343**	**142 617**	**158 928**	**Total**

General note.
Spark–ignition, internal combustion, piston engines, equipped with fuel injection pumps, ignition parts, fuel and oil reservoirs, water radiators, oil coolers, water, oil and fuel pumps, blowers, air and oil filters, starting devices etc. Automobile, bus, truck and aircraft engines are excluded. (SITC 71150–2B).

[1] Excluding internal–combustion engines for ships and gas engines.

[2] Diesel engines only.

Remarque générale.
Moteurs à explosion à pistons, à allumage par étincelle, muni des appareils suivants: dispositif d'alimentation en carburant, accessoires d'allumage, réservoirs à essence et à huile, radiateur à eau, refroidisseur à huile, pompes à eau, à huile et à essence, compresseur d'air, filtres à air et huile, dispositif de démarrage etc. Cette rubrique ne comprend pas les moteurs d'automobile, d'autocar et d'avion. (CTCI 71150–2B).

[1] Non compris les moteurs à combustion interne pour bateaux et les moteurs à essence.

[2] Moteurs Diesel seulement.

Gas turbines – Turbines à gaz

Unit : Number units

Unité : Nombre

Country or area	1976	1977	1978	1979	1980	1981	1982	1983	1984	1985	Pays ou zone
America, North											**Amérique du Nord**
United States[1]	35	43	36	35	29	12	21	14	30	28	Etats–Unis[1]
Europe											**Europe**
EEC											***CEE***
France[2] [3]	3 360	750	225	274	299	719	1 170	500	...	...	France[2] [3]
United Kingdom[4]	86	109	90	59	101	134	115	...	...	...	Royaume–Uni[4]
EFTA											***AELE***
Sweden	2	4	2	12	10	12	12	...	...	...	Suède
East Europe											***Europe de l'est***
Czechoslovakia	8	8	22	34	24	8	0	8	6	11	Tchécoslovaquie

General note.
Turbines composed of a rotary compressor which compresses a considerable volume of air in a combustion chamber where it is heated to a high temperature by burners fed by gas or liquid fuel. The kinetic energy of the heated air and combustion gases acts on the blades of a rotor which drives the power shaft and also the compressor. Gas turbines for aircraft are excluded. (SITC 71160–0A).

[1] Generators for gas turbines of 4000 kW and larger.
[2] Deliveries.
[3] In metric tons.
[4] Excluding turbines for marine use, road vehicles or for electricity generation.

Remarque générale.
Turbines composées d'un compresseur rotatif qui comprime une masse d'air considérable dans une chambre de combustion où elle est portée à haute température par des brûleurs alimentés par un gaz ou un liquide combustibles. L'énergie cinétique de la masse d'air et des gaz de combustion agit sur les ailettes du rotor de la turbine, entraînant lui–même l'arbre de transmission ainsi que le compresseur. Cette rubrique ne comprend pas les turbines à gaz pour avions. (CTCI 71160–0A).

[1] Génératrices pour entraînement par turbines à gaz de 4000 kW et plus.
[2] Livraisons.
[3] En tonnes métriques.
[4] Non compris les turbines pour usages marins, pour les véhicules routiers ou pour la production d'électricité.

Hydraulic turbines – Turbines hydrauliques

Unit : Number units | Unité : Nombre

Country or area	1976	1977	1978	1979	1980	1981	1982	1983	1984	1985	Pays ou zone
America, North											**Amérique du Nord**
United States[1 2]	6	13	12	2	7	14	1	8	10	8	Etats-Unis[1 2]
America, South											**Amérique du Sud**
Brazil	[3] 1 844	[3] 8 698	[3] 6 204	[3] 4 110	* 15 067	...	...	...	...	...	Brésil
Asia											**Asie**
Japan	33	29	35	49	44	41	71	63	58	43	Japon
Europe											**Europe**
EEC											***CEE***
France[4 5]	6 483	5 862	2 609	2 607	6 459	5 317	5 077	7 230	9 740	6 190	France[4 5]
EFTA											***AELE***
Finland	687	1 772	1 739	2 949	2 497	1 755	1 657	1 966	1 521	...	Finlande
East Europe											***Europe de l'est***
Czechoslovakia	3	6	4	4	7	4	5	9	19	33	Tchécoslovaquie
Hungary	3	2	4	0	0	0	0	0	3	0	Hongrie
Romania	14	12	6	9	10	15	31	54	85	132	Roumanie
Other Europe											***Autre Europe***
Spain	47	...	...	8	35	35	52	46	...	...	Espagne
Yugoslavia	13	1	4	11	3	5	9	3	...	...	Yougoslavie

General note.
Turbines consisting of a rotor encased in a stator which directs jets of water on to the blades of the rotor. There are three types of hydraulic turbines – the Pelton type, the Francis type and the Kaplan type. Regulators for water engines are also included. (SITC 71181-1A).

[1] Shipments.
[2] Hydraulic turbines of 5000 HP and larger.
[3] Production by establishments employing 5 or more persons.
[4] Deliveries.
[5] In metric tons.

Remarque générale.
Turbines se composant d'un rotor enveloppé d'un stator destiné à orienter les filets d'eau sur les aubages du rotor. Il existe trois types de turbines hydrauliques: les turbines du type Pelton, les turbines du type Francis et les turbines du type Kaplan. Cette rubrique comprend les organes régulateurs chargés de régler le débit d'eau des tuyères. (CTCI 71181-1A).

[1] Expéditions.
[2] Turbines hydrauliques de 5000 ch et plus.
[3] Production des établissements occupant 5 personnes ou plus.
[4] Livraisons.
[5] En tonnes métriques.

Hydraulic turbines – Turbines hydrauliques

Unit : Thousand kilowatts

Unité : Milliers de kilowatts

Country or area	1976	1977	1978	1979	1980	1981	1982	1983	1984	1985	Pays ou zone
America, North											**Amérique du Nord**
United States[1 2]	545	1 723	1 089	224	744	710	18	1 496	1 700	711	Etats-Unis[1 2]
Asia											**Asie**
Japan	3 950	2 081	4 054	8 038	4 092	5 749	8 610	3 728	3 184	2 424	Japon
Europe											**Europe**
East Europe											***Europe de l'est***
Czechoslovakia	169	466	592	705	808	589	423	552	836	1 349	Tchécoslovaquie
Hungary	48	47	15	0	0	0	0	0	4	0	Hongrie
Romania	334	356	66	323	213	300	230	178	371	400	Roumanie
Other Europe											***Autre Europe***
Spain	103	...	...	...	...	...	...	...	...	...	Espagne
Yugoslavia	773	37	34	301	1	65	110	27	9	10	Yougoslavie

General note.
Turbines consisting of a rotor encased in a stator which directs jets of water on to the blades of the rotor. There are three types of hydraulic turbines – the Pelton type, the Francis type and the Kaplan type. Regulatorss for water engines are also included. (SITC 71181-1B).

1 Hydraulic turbines of 5000 HP and larger.
2 In thousand horsepower.

Remarque générale.
Turbines se composant d'un rotor enveloppé d'un stator destiné à orienter les filets d'eau sur les aubages du rotor. Il existe trois types de turbines hydrauliques: les turbines du type Pelton, les turbines du type Francis et les turbines du type Kaplan. Cette rubrique comprend les organes régulateurs chargés de régler le débit d'eau des tuyères. (CTCI 71181-1B).

1 Turbines hydrauliques de 5000 ch et plus.
2 En milliers de chevaux-vapeur.

Cultivators, scarifiers, weeders, hoes etc. – Cultivateurs, scarificateurs, extirpateurs, houes etc.

Unit : Number units | Unité : Nombre

Country or area	1976	1977	1978	1979	1980	1981	1982	1983	1984	1985	Pays ou zone
Africa	**456**	**800**	**920**	**131**	**753**	**987**	**1 379**	**1 200**	**1 306**	**1 412**	**Afrique**
Algeria	...	800	920	131	753	...	1 379	...	...	...	Algérie
America, North	**208 541**	**183 280**	**169 271**	**229 826**	**138 328**	**104 655**	**71 950**	**47 832**	**49 495**	**35 358**	**Amérique du Nord**
Canada[1,2]	30 029	19 146	15 055	20 319	16 508	...	...	...	...	...	Canada[1,2]
Cuba[3]	4 900	0	879	15	95	3 215	1 115	979	1 720	1 088	Cuba[3]
United States[2]	173 612	164 134	153 337	209 492	121 725	88 950	60 918	39 510	43 005	32 074	Etats–Unis[2]
America, South	**14 939**	**28 121**	**7 603**	**16 202**	**22 660**	**19 022**	**19 406**	**19 802**	**20 159**	**20 579**	**Amérique du Sud**
Brazil	14 769	27 835	7 311	16 149	22 631	...	...	...	...	...	Brésil
Colombia	170	286	292	53	29	78	61	55	...	...	Colombie
Asia	**1 937**	**2 950**	**3 014**	**4 396**	**3 074**	**3 074**	**3 074**	**3 074**	**3 074**	**3 074**	**Asie**
Turkey	1 937	2 950	3 014	4 396	...	...	...	...	...	...	Turquie
Europe	**480 088**	**498 326**	**497 505**	**481 114**	**403 104**	**387 531**	**414 309**	**450 260**	**439 523**	**377 876**	**Europe**
EEC	***365 056***	***383 448***	***385 591***	***356 293***	***288 738***	***263 455***	***246 430***	***247 920***	***222 670***	***216 017***	***CEE***
Belgium[3]	...	...	...	...	1 397	...	...	...	1 704	...	Belgique[3]
Denmark	27 459	20 009	20 522	20 257	18 051	...	7 644	9 036	6 610	5 430	Danemark
France[4]	154 000	160 800	172 500	156 600	148 700	122 500	130 600	123 600	114 000	107 000	France[4]
Germany, Fed. Rep.	129 461	130 467	129 431	125 996	81 721	95 461	81 344	87 138	77 334	77 920	Allemagne, Rép. féd.
Greece	5 386	6 372	7 551	11 675	11 153	6 276	8 150	8 433	9 408	...	Grèce
Netherlands[5]	16 350	17 440	9 545	9 030	9 260	10 610	9 950	9 320	9 600	...	Pays–Bas[5]
United Kingdom	30 850	46 810	44 492	31 185	18 456	13 375	7 192	...	...	...	Royaume–Uni
EFTA	***15 602***	***14 919***	***16 287***	***20 179***	***24 390***	***18 822***	***21 225***	***24 160***	***15 875***	***15 381***	***AELE***
Austria	6 320	6 012	6 624	7 292	10 239	7 091	6 851	9 951	7 766	7 290	Autriche
Portugal	1 643	456	2 224	3 189	3 540	3 787	3 927	4 518	2 957	2 733	Portugal
Sweden[6]	7 639	8 451	7 439	9 698	10 611	7 944	10 447	9 691	5 152	5 358	Suède[6]
East Europe	***68 595***	***61 247***	***54 519***	***53 932***	***45 398***	***45 757***	***60 674***	***101 231***	***124 130***	***62 767***	***Europe de l'est***
Bulgaria	17 527	13 208	11 677	1 419	120	380	532	1 321	2 620	762	Bulgarie
Hungary	26 422	27 312	24 649	20 558	18 886	14 624	16 528	10 790	4 662	5 027	Hongrie
Poland	21 137	16 694	15 586	28 227	23 319	25 108	38 957	84 208	111 682	51 557	Pologne
Romania[7]	3 509	4 033	2 607	3 728	3 073	5 645	...	...	...	...	Roumanie[7]
Other Europe	***30 835***	***38 712***	***41 108***	***50 710***	***44 578***	***59 497***	***85 980***	***76 949***	***76 848***	***83 711***	***Autre Europe***
Spain	...	...	...	9 856	9 615	4 351	7 121	11 256	...	...	Espagne
Yugoslavia	22 548	30 394	32 760	40 854	34 963	55 146	78 859	65 693	68 318	75 150	Yougoslavie
USSR[7]	**190 026**	**186 787**	**192 608**	**201 616**	**203 548**	**218 209**	**217 897**	**223 265**	**250 956**	**267 119**	**URSS[7]**
Oceania	**8 932**	**8 881**	**5 738**	**4 624**	**4 277**	**5 944**	**5 744**	**2 736**	**3 474**	**2 191**	**Océanie**
Australia	8 932	8 881	5 738	4 624	4 277	5 944	5 744	2 736	3 474	2 191	Australie
Total	**904 919**	**909 145**	**876 659**	**937 909**	**775 744**	**739 422**	**733 759**	**748 169**	**767 987**	**707 609**	**Total**

General note.
Animal– or tractor–operated. Cultivators, scarifiers, weeders, hoes and like machines usually consisting of a horizontal frame fitted with several rows of various types of tools (shares, discs, teeth etc.) which may be rigid or springy, fixed or movable, and are sometimes interchangeable, used for working, weeding or smoothing the soil after ploughing or during the growth of the crops. Corn and cotton–type cultivators are excluded. (SITC 71210–1).

[1] Cultivators and weeders only.
[2] Shipments.
[3] Cultivators only.
[4] Excluding rollers.
[5] Industrial sales.
[6] Including harrows.
[7] Tractor–drawn machines only.

Remarque générale.
Cultivateurs, scarificateurs, extirpateurs, houes etc., consistant habituellement en un bâti horizontal garni de plusieurs rangées d'outils (dents, socs, disques) rigides ou flexibles, fixes ou mobiles, parfois interchangeables, utilisées pour ameublir, désherber ou niveler le sol après labour ou pour entretenir les cultures. Cette rubrique ne comprend pas les cultivateurs des types utilisés pour le maïs et le coton. (CTCI 71210–1).

[1] Cultivateurs et extirpateurs seulement.
[2] Expéditions.
[3] Cultivateurs seulement.
[4] Non compris les rouleaux.
[5] Ventes industrielles.
[6] Y compris les herses.
[7] Machines tractées seulement.

Harrows, rotary, animal– or tractor–operated – Herses rotatives, à traction animale ou tractées

Unit : Number units — Unité : Nombre

Country or area	1976	1977	1978	1979	1980	1981	1982	1983	1984	1985	Pays ou zone
America, North	**583 674**	**504 101**	**492 182**	**685 449**	**425 843**	**406 808**	**290 259**	**272 840**	**291 626**	**253 559**	**Amérique du Nord**
Canada	163 242	114 452	104 670	161 830	144 009	...	...	...	...	...	Canada
Cuba	4 889	81	2 570	1 635	1 550	1 315	184	1 304	5 719	3 454	Cuba
United States	415 543	389 568	384 942	521 984	280 284	265 193	148 889	129 463	142 947	106 259	Etats–Unis
America, South	**74 303**	**62 022**	**49 003**	**58 414**	**65 810**	**34 796**	**39 724**	**34 676**	**29 628**	**24 581**	**Amérique du Sud**
Brazil	74 303	62 022	49 003	[1] 58 414	65 810	34 796	...	...	...	...	Brésil
Asia	**5 293**	**11 574**	**36 428**	**37 500**	**25 537**	**28 376**	**31 719**	**29 527**	**23 884**	**29 615**	**Asie**
Korea, Republic of	670	...	870	810	...	6 592	9 935	7 743	2 100	...	Corée, République de
Turkey	4 623	10 268	35 558	36 690	...	...	...	...	...	...	Turquie
Europe	**239 697**	**234 897**	**230 154**	**229 821**	**185 726**	**197 761**	**189 469**	**195 566**	**168 403**	**163 204**	**Europe**
EEC	***199 672***	***198 353***	***196 313***	***193 333***	***148 591***	***162 773***	***155 910***	***155 550***	***138 971***	***135 585***	***CEE***
Belgium	...	...	...	...	56 664	...	...	...	55 514	...	Belgique
France	34 600	29 600	26 300	27 100	22 200	21 200	28 100	22 300	20 000	16 000	France
Germany, Fed. Rep.	99 549	102 705	102 578	96 961	56 957	73 449	60 779	67 163	57 232	54 066	Allemagne, Rép. féd.
Greece	5 298	6 286	7 500	10 287	9 860	9 859	8 393	8 871	5 008	...	Grèce
United Kingdom	4 136	3 673	3 846	2 896	2 910	2 176	2 549	1 127	...	...	Royaume–Uni
EFTA	***30 819***	***25 642***	***22 888***	***24 088***	***21 170***	***26 579***	***24 799***	***26 489***	***19 860***	***22 121***	***AELE***
Austria	3 946	3 341	3 428	3 892	2 987	3 486	2 932	2 930	1 130	1 888	Autriche
Finland	18 413	12 289	10 544	11 524	10 122	15 249	13 676	14 361	11 229	...	Finlande
Portugal	1 802	2 618	2 549	3 280	3 383	3 888	4 021	4 925	3 742	3 885	Portugal
Sweden	6 658	7 394	6 367	5 392	4 678	3 956	4 170	4 273	3 759	4 347	Suède
East Europe	***2 684***	***2 893***	***3 608***	***4 508***	***5 406***	***3 695***	***6 197***	***10 334***	***6 210***	***2 800***	***Europe de l'est***
Poland	2 684	2 893	3 608	4 508	5 406	3 695	6 197	10 334	6 210	2 800	Pologne
Other Europe	***6 522***	***8 009***	***7 345***	***7 892***	***10 559***	***4 714***	***2 563***	***3 193***	***3 362***	***2 698***	***Autre Europe***
Spain	6 522	...	...	7 892	10 559	4 714	2 563	3 193	...	...	Espagne
USSR	**32 060**	**33 332**	**25 190**	**31 579**	**31 877**	**35 559**	**36 469**	**41 135**	**44 018**	**45 189**	**URSS**
Oceania	**33 839**	**46 535**	**25 691**	**45 964**	**54 603**	**32 066**	**29 081**	**17 041**	**20 686**	**14 412**	**Océanie**
Australia	33 839	46 535	25 691	45 964	54 603	32 066	29 081	17 041	20 686	14 412	Australie
Total	**968 866**	**892 461**	**858 648**	**1 088 727**	**789 396**	**735 366**	**616 721**	**590 785**	**578 245**	**530 560**	**Total**

General note.
Animal– or tractor–operated rotary harrows which are used for breaking up the soil after ploughing. (SITC 71210–2).

[1] Production by establishments employing 5 or more persons.

Remarque générale.
Herses servant à émietter le sol après le labourage. (CTCI 71210–2).

[1] Production des établissements occupant 5 personnes ou plus.

Ploughs, animal– or tractor–operated – Charrues à traction animale ou tractées

Unit : Number units — Unité : Nombre

Country or area	1976	1977	1978	1979	1980	1981	1982	1983	1984	1985	Pays ou zone
Africa	**1 599**	**1 999**	**2 438**	**3 324**	**3 978**	**4 773**	**4 161**	**5 291**	**5 817**	**6 345**	**Afrique**
Algeria	...	1 987	2 428	3 313	3 966	4 763	4 151	...	...	...	Algérie
Mali	11	12	10	11	12	10	10	10	...	...	Mali
America, North	**203 012**	**177 571**	**165 513**	**227 633**	**99 915**	**88 866**	**54 820**	**45 980**	**47 797**	**40 721**	**Amérique du Nord**
Cuba	813	800	410	707	1 200	2 759	836	3 013	1 677	2 110	Cuba
Mexico	5 979	3 874	6 058	7 308	8 088	9 709	5 923	3 993	2 244	4 186	Mexique
United States[1]	196 220	172 897	159 045	219 618	90 627	76 398	48 061	38 974	43 876	34 425	Etats–Unis[1]
America, South	**144 063**	**139 115**	**50 877**	**78 145**	**201 911**	**138 570**	**143 201**	**148 332**	**153 915**	**159 114**	**Amérique du Sud**
Brazil	143 817	138 525	49 282	[2] 76 780	201 160	...	...	...	...	...	Brésil
Colombia	246	590	1 595	1 365	751	857	222	86	...	...	Colombie
Asia	**59 945**	**45 289**	**44 909**	**66 033**	**109 779**	**176 561**	**264 161**	**295 587**	**148 172**	**80 241**	**Asie**
Korea, Republic of	38 323	21 992	23 583	44 114	98 091	168 048	263 248	295 145	145 353	79 799	Corée, République de
Turkey	21 622	23 297	21 326	21 919	...	...	913	442	2 819	...	Turquie
Europe	**473 731**	**480 062**	**481 387**	**491 635**	**476 725**	**455 825**	**413 427**	**461 690**	**402 039**	**373 105**	**Europe**
EEC	***255 976***	***276 967***	***300 031***	***274 356***	***257 184***	***219 660***	***207 752***	***196 493***	***153 889***	***157 230***	***CEE***
Belgium	...	...	...	...	69 079	...	59 535	...	56 982	...	Belgique
Denmark	6 090	5 452	4 708	5 547	3 889	...	4 850	6 061	3 904	4 065	Danemark
France	143 200	161 100	187 100	167 800	150 100	114 400	105 700	87 339	60 000	56 000	France
Germany, Fed. Rep	25 186	26 467	23 997	20 997	16 982	18 222	19 905	21 664	16 300	18 197	Allemagne, Rép. féd.
Greece	8 821	9 504	9 395	9 261	8 708	7 900	8 457	8 150	7 934	...	Grèce
Netherlands[3]	1 940	1 860	1 613	1 250	1 370	1 090	970	2 060	800	...	Pays–Bas[3]
United Kingdom	8 874	10 719	11 353	7 636	7 056	11 311	8 335	9 354	7 969	...	Royaume–Uni
EFTA	***36 124***	***30 171***	***21 725***	***56 117***	***52 139***	***76 901***	***24 805***	***29 022***	***23 147***	***23 419***	***AELE***
Austria	3 795	3 462	3 191	5 359	4 303	3 975	3 973	4 334	4 641	4 879	Autriche
Finland	13 242	8 249	3 584	4 433	4 527	5 295	5 898	8 716	2 977	...	Finlande
Portugal	9 716	10 905	8 647	40 593	37 724	61 978	9 734	11 472	9 189	9 194	Portugal
Sweden	9 371	7 555	6 303	5 732	5 585	5 653	5 200	4 500	6 340	5 869	Suède
East Europe	***120 220***	***85 952***	***64 127***	***68 442***	***65 981***	***78 699***	***102 603***	***134 659***	***150 255***	***113 468***	***Europe de l'est***
Bulgaria	3 624	771	1 166	1 650	2 145	1 475	1 111	1 475	1 342	2 136	Bulgarie
Czechoslovakia	1 876	1 365	1 001	1 100	1 212	1 510	1 661	1 700	4 735	3 613	Tchécoslovaquie
German Dem. Rep.[4]	2 343	2 567	3 432	...	2 676	4 525	7 185	9 753	13 035	6 323	Rép. dém. allemande[4]
Hungary	4 616	2 583	1 590	707	1 327	851	1 052	545	393	521	Hongrie
Poland	84 511	62 989	42 182	51 158	45 803	51 957	73 352	108 438	117 563	88 243	Pologne
Romania[4]	23 250	15 677	14 756	9 597	12 818	18 381	18 242	12 748	...	...	Roumanie[4]
Other Europe	***61 411***	***86 972***	***95 504***	***92 720***	***101 421***	***80 565***	***78 267***	***101 516***	***74 748***	***78 988***	***Autre Europe***
Spain	21 377	...	...	29 535	29 005	14 660	11 382	10 934	...	...	Espagne
Yugoslavia	40 034	60 887	71 504	63 185	72 416	65 905	66 885	90 582	63 260	69 586	Yougoslavie
USSR[4]	**202 321**	**184 940**	**216 117**	**210 851**	**202 246**	**202 546**	**208 025**	**201 844**	**207 464**	**206 704**	**URSS[4]**
Ukrainian SSR[4]	*127 504*	*113 133*	*123 205*	*115 399*	*105 704*	*101 503*	*106 834*	*104 199*	*106 598*	*103 313*	*RSS d'Ukraine[4]*
Oceania	**6 766**	**4 971**	**4 552**	**2 783**	**2 015**	**1 742**	**1 628**	**810**	**1 408**	**1 243**	**Océanie**
Australia	6 766	4 971	4 552	2 783	2 015	1 742	1 628	810	1 408	1 243	Australie
Total	**1 091 437**	**1 033 947**	**965 793**	**1 080 404**	**1 096 569**	**1 068 883**	**1 089 423**	**1 159 534**	**966 612**	**867 473**	**Total**

General note.
Implements which cut a furrow slice by means of sharp–edged steel discs, of saucer–like shape, set obliquely to the ground surface (disc ploughs, animal– and tractor–operated) and machines which by means of a coulter and a share detach a slice of soil vertically from the undersoil (mouldboard ploughs, animal– and tractor–operated). (SITC 71210–3 and 71210–4).

Remarque générale.
Charrues qui découpent la bande de terre au moyen de disques d'acier à bord tranchant, en forme de soucoupes, inclinés par rapport à la surface du sol (charrues à disques, à traction animale et tractées), et machines qui detachent du sol une tranche verticale de terre au moyen d'un coutre et d'un soc (charrues à soc, à traction animale et tractées). (CTCI 71210–3 et 71210–4).

[1] Shipments.
[2] Production by establishments employing 5 or more persons.
[3] Industrial sales.
[4] Tractor–drawn ploughs only.

[1] Expéditions.
[2] Production des établissements occupant 5 personnes ou plus.
[3] Ventes industrielles.
[4] Charrues tractées seulement.

Unit : Number units

Unité : Nombre

Country or area	1976	1977	1978	1979	1980	1981	1982	1983	1984	1985	Pays ou zone
America, North	**252 270**	**254 788**	**218 025**	**296 332**	**244 459**	**252 053**	**596 848**	**433 318**	**491 292**	**267 032**	**Amérique du Nord**
Cuba[1]	...	...	...	...	...	...	...	21	29	...	Cuba[1]
United States[2]	252 245	254 763	* 218 000	...	244 434	252 028	596 823	433 297	491 263	267 007	Etats–Unis[2]
America, South	**59 455**	**408 055**	**375 354**	**511 438**	**142 014**	**388 204**	**412 127**	**440 117**	**468 182**	**496 201**	**Amérique du Sud**
Brazil	[3] 59 410	[3] 407 991	[3] 374 876	[3] 511 335	141 958	388 063	...	...	...	...	Brésil
Colombia	45	64	478	103	56	141	76	34	...	...	Colombie
Asia	**246 412**	**287 009**	**204 170**	**176 209**	**222 766**	**151 976**	**137 353**	**136 856**	**137 246**	**139 898**	**Asie**
Japan[4]	238 887	279 635	196 836	169 779	210 206	141 618	130 092	128 514	131 966	132 039	Japon[4]
Korea, Republic of	...	2 193	2 318	1 408	9 192	7 563	6 341	7 743	2 847	...	Corée, République de
Turkey	4 979	5 181	5 016	5 022	...	...	920	599	2 433	...	Turquie
Europe	**355 315**	**349 600**	**315 030**	**308 713**	**276 781**	**250 197**	**242 206**	**253 267**	**277 152**	**252 231**	**Europe**
EEC	***233 874***	***219 620***	***204 255***	***195 144***	***167 497***	***160 359***	***148 521***	***144 785***	***144 448***	***136 527***	***CEE***
Belgium	...	...	...	...	23 347	...	...	...	41 708	...	Belgique
Denmark	21 078	19 622	12 110	11 624	6 881	...	6 610	...	...	6 455	Danemark
France	63 500	60 000	56 300	61 400	58 700	51 000	48 600	52 400	54 000	59 000	France
Germany, Fed. Rep.[5]	100 781	87 614	86 785	80 329	68 145	61 892	...	...	...	...	Allemagne, Rép. féd.[5]
Greece	2 446	4 020	2 591	2 020	2 303	2 491	3 613	3 642	3 416	...	Grèce
Netherlands[6]	520	490	210	480	790	460	170	420	400	...	Pays–Bas[6]
United Kingdom	13 022	15 347	13 732	6 764	7 331	2 345	1 995	...	...	...	Royaume–Uni
EFTA	***13 778***	***20 443***	***12 157***	***11 548***	***11 450***	***11 165***	***11 427***	***14 166***	***15 410***	***11 446***	***AELE***
Austria	1 436	3 025	1 617	1 128	2 413	* 1 438	1 978	2 591	1 874	1 404	Autriche
Finland	10 347	14 804	8 093	7 933	6 300	7 078	7 228	9 139	10 913	...	Finlande
Portugal	623	826	867	907	1 157	1 069	641	856	1 043	813	Portugal
Sweden	1 372	1 788	...	...	...	...	...	...	...	...	Suède
East Europe	***92 612***	***87 981***	***76 273***	***67 448***	***66 156***	***43 842***	***58 941***	***63 142***	***77 474***	***62 120***	***Europe de l'est***
Bulgaria	26 361	28 442	26 712	25 792	20 404	3 825	3 758	4 700	4 863	5 532	Bulgarie
Czechoslovakia	5 090	5 325	3 547	2 492	4 178	2 810	2 995	4 028	6 811	6 371	Tchécoslovaquie
Hungary	4 486	6 263	6 086	3 328	1 789	2 477	2 126	1 393	1 493	1 210	Hongrie
Poland	38 055	20 897	16 721	13 400	20 434	24 041	35 603	38 993	45 733	31 081	Pologne
Romania[7]	18 620	27 054	23 207	22 436	19 351	10 689	14 459	14 028	18 574	17 926	Roumanie[7]
Other Europe	***15 051***	***21 556***	***22 345***	***34 573***	***31 678***	***34 831***	***23 317***	***31 174***	***39 820***	***42 138***	***Autre Europe***
Spain	8 804	...	...	21 982	16 891	11 640	9 168	6 259	...	...	Espagne
Yugoslavia	6 247	6 952	8 419	12 591	14 787	23 191	14 149	24 915	29 962	32 958	Yougoslavie
USSR[7]	**191 051**	**196 891**	**194 789**	**202 008**	**201 181**	**213 227**	**204 847**	**208 658**	**214 613**	**229 666**	**URSS[7]**
Ukrainian SSR[7]	*96 011*	*98 094*	*89 516*	*86 626*	*78 024*	*79 613*	*70 314*	*68 720*	*72 343*	*75 180*	*RSS d'Ukraine[7]*
Oceania	**4 386**	**4 837**	**3 779**	**3 359**	**3 293**	**4 645**	**4 017**	**2 248**	**3 351**	**2 644**	**Océanie**
Australia	4 386	4 837	3 779	3 359	3 293	4 645	4 017	2 248	3 351	2 644	Australie
Total	**1 108 889**	**1 501 180**	**1 311 147**	**1 498 059**	**1 090 494**	**1 260 302**	**1 597 398**	**1 474 464**	**1 591 836**	**1 387 672**	**Total**

General note.
Boxes or hoppers mounted on wheels and fitted with devices for setting seeds. They may include devices for opening or recovering the furrow. This item includes animal– or tractor–operated seeders, planters and transplanters. (SITC 71210–5).

Remarque générale.
Bacs ou trémies sur roues, munis de mécanismes distributeurs. Ils peuvent être dotés d'outils traceurs ou de dispositifs de recouvrement. Cette rubrique comprend les semoirs, planteuses et repiqueuses, à traction animale ou tractés. (CTCI 71210–5).

1 Seeders and transplanters only.
2 Shipments.
3 Production by establishments employing 5 or more persons.
4 Including rice transplanters.
5 Beginning 1982, series discontinued.
6 Industrial sales.
7 Tractor–drawn seeders only.

1 Semoirs et repiqueuses seulement.
2 Expéditions.
3 Production des établissements occupant 5 personnes ou plus.
4 Y compris les appareils à repiquer le riz.
5 A partir de 1982, la série a été abandonnée.
6 Ventes industrielles.
7 Semoirs tractés seulement.

Combine harvester-threshers – Moissonneuses-batteuses

Unit : Number units

Unité : Nombre

Country or area	1976	1977	1978	1979	1980	1981	1982	1983	1984	1985	Pays ou zone
America, North	**31 712**	**31 973**	**32 185**	**32 717**	**29 003**	**32 667**	**23 328**	**14 323**	**11 927**	**7 633**	**Amérique du Nord**
Cuba	0	30	165	360	501	605	602	650	631	606	Cuba
United States[1]	31 712	31 943	32 020	32 357	28 502	32 062	22 726	13 673	11 296	7 027	Etats-Unis[1]
Asia	**180 231**	**174 911**	**122 709**	**102 706**	**114 657**	**90 437**	**102 282**	**102 665**	**117 924**	**129 072**	**Asie**
China	...	...	...	...	6 025	6 005	4 630	19 530	19 990	22 230	Chine
Iran(Islamic Rep.of)[2]	...	...	...	62	68	...	315	619	...	...	Iran(Rép.islamique)[2]
Japan	172 351	172 908	117 098	94 374	105 817	82 777	84 730	80 973	94 598	102 593	Japon
Korea, Republic of	2 984	552	1 860	2 486	2 747	1 389	12 607	1 543	3 070	3 983	Corée, République de
Europe	**48 895**	**46 438**	**41 027**	**39 220**	**40 850**	**41 740**	**40 551**	**37 729**	**87 251**	**96 134**	**Europe**
EEC	***32 856***	***30 178***	***27 649***	***27 322***	***26 890***	***25 882***	***24 386***	***23 725***	***23 647***	***24 889***	***CEE***
Belgium	...	...	...	7 700	...	8 086	7 940	7 287	7 381	7 702	Belgique
Denmark	1 625	1 355	1 068	788	851	244	* 400	615	772	1 298	Danemark
France	4 200	3 700	3 400	3 000	2 400	2 000	2 100	1 411	1 000	...	France
Germany, Fed. Rep.	15 206	13 506	12 460	12 448	12 431	12 166	10 560	11 026	11 108	11 863	Allemagne, Rép. féd.
United Kingdom	3 764	3 616	2 780	...	...	...	...	...	...	...	Royaume-Uni
EFTA	***3 605***	***2 642***	***1 546***	***1 749***	***2 156***	***2 267***	***1 842***	***1 648***	***1 851***	***1 982***	***AELE***
Austria	230	154	74	19	17	0	0	0	0	0	Autriche
Finland	1 342	1 078	854	1 009	1 311	1 418	1 417	1 311	1 361	...	Finlande
Portugal	...	...	...	0	1	61	36	6	19	11	Portugal
Sweden	2 017	1 394	601	721	827	788	389	331	471	546	Suède
East Europe	***9 154***	***9 368***	***8 188***	***7 284***	***9 483***	***10 272***	***9 806***	***9 644***	***9 580***	***11 937***	***Europe de l'est***
Poland	3 956	4 003	4 301	4 268	4 593	4 255	4 533	4 550	4 678	5 131	Pologne
Romania	5 198	5 365	3 887	3 016	4 890	6 017	...	5 094	4 902	6 806	Roumanie
Other Europe	***3 280***	***4 250***	***3 644***	***2 865***	***2 321***	***3 319***	***4 517***	***2 712***	***52 173***	***57 326***	***Autre Europe***
Spain	643	...	...	...	...	...	...	...	...	...	Espagne
Yugoslavia	2 637	3 607	3 001	2 222	1 678	2 676	3 874	2 069	# 51 530	56 683	Yougoslavie
USSR	**101 700**	**105 510**	**112 620**	**114 759**	**117 365**	**106 469**	**111 551**	**118 058**	**117 891**	**111 992**	**URSS**
Oceania	**2 553**	**1 948**	**1 715**	**1 113**	**1 327**	**1 194**	**824**	**825**	**365**	**1 006**	**Océanie**
Australia	2 553	1 948	1 715	1 113	1 327	...	824	...	365	1 006	Australie
Total	**365 091**	**360 780**	**310 256**	**290 515**	**303 202**	**272 507**	**278 536**	**273 600**	**335 358**	**345 837**	**Total**

General note.
Tractor-operated or self-propelled. Machines which successively reap, thresh, clean and bag the grain. (SITC 71220-1).

[1] Shipments.
[2] Production by establishments employing 10 or more persons.

Remarque générale.
Tractées ou automotrices. Machines qui réalisent successivement la coupe, l'égrenage, le nettoyage et la mise en sacs du grain. (CTCI 71220-1).

[1] Expéditions.
[2] Production des établissements occupant 10 personnes ou plus.

Mowers, animal– or tractor–operated and self–propelled – Faucheuses, à traction animale ou tractèes et automotrices

Unit : Number units

Unité : Nombre

Country or area	1976	1977	1978	1979	1980	1981	1982	1983	1984	1985	Pays ou zone
America, North	**14 695**	**14 712**	**12 636**	**15 659**	**47 082**	**39 207**	**32 866**	**19 954**	**26 049**	**18 066**	**Amérique du Nord**
Cuba	500	750	502	450	325	461	252	391	1 392	1 735	Cuba
United States[1]	14 195	13 962	12 134	15 209	46 757	38 746	32 614	19 563	24 657	16 331	Etats–Unis[1]
America, South	**2 826**	**6 855**	**6 059**	**28 396**	**52 722**	**39 882**	**46 928**	**53 973**	**61 019**	**68 065**	**Amérique du Sud**
Brazil	2 826	6 855	6 059	[2] 28 396	52 722	...	...	...	...	...	Brésil
Asia	**2 764**	**2 764**	**3 761**	**9 031**	**2 764**	**6 286**	**33 182**	**43 359**	**56 973**	**19 032**	**Asie**
Korea, Republic of	...	...	...	...	2 764	6 286	33 182	43 359	56 973	19 032	Corée, République de
Europe	**286 910**	**241 073**	**269 853**	**261 964**	**294 711**	**269 804**	**304 591**	**325 504**	**331 582**	**351 321**	**Europe**
EEC	***129 258***	***122 914***	***122 340***	***116 539***	***111 691***	***99 167***	***94 547***	***92 834***	***87 931***	***77 033***	***CEE***
Belgium	...	...	...	...	...	...	24 221	...	...	...	Belgique
Denmark	...	...	...	...	...	...	9 070	10 118	9 685	...	Danemark
France	26 400	25 400	29 000	25 600	29 400	22 100	19 500	17 200	16 000	15 000	France
Germany, Fed. Rep.	59 990	54 689	51 474	49 904	42 922	41 371	39 760	39 058	36 320	26 643	Allemagne, Rép. féd.
Greece	...	...	...	...	...	118	145	173	358	...	Grèce
United Kingdom	8 825	8 782	7 823	6 992	5 326	1 733	1 851	2 064	1 347	...	Royaume–Uni
EFTA	***95 881***	***74 077***	***116 611***	***115 324***	***151 639***	***138 670***	***163 313***	***179 751***	***190 606***	***226 296***	***AELE***
Austria	82 432	62 647	106 316	106 550	144 216	128 230	153 459	164 814	179 246	214 921	Autriche
Finland	7 512	6 859	5 311	4 785	4 751	6 067	8 438	13 862	...	...	Finlande
Sweden	5 937	4 571	4 984	3 989	2 672	4 373	1 416	1 075	1 239	604	Suède
East Europe	***59 936***	***41 482***	***28 145***	***27 215***	***28 264***	***26 374***	***43 828***	***50 657***	***49 342***	***44 131***	***Europe de l'est***
Bulgaria	34	0	27	252	1 151	945	414	143	131	230	Bulgarie
Poland	59 902	41 482	28 118	26 963	27 113	25 429	43 414	50 514	49 211	43 901	Pologne
Other Europe	***1 835***	***2 600***	***2 757***	***2 886***	***3 117***	***5 593***	***2 903***	***2 262***	***3 703***	***3 861***	***Autre Europe***
Spain	1 835	...	...	2 886	3 117	5 593	2 903	2 262	...	...	Espagne
USSR	**89 403**	**97 235**	**109 222**	**101 765**	**86 225**	**84 245**	**87 715**	**90 406**	**99 705**	**79 081**	**URSS**
Oceania	**70 395**	**73 071**	**76 511**	**82 779**	**89 723**	**101 914**	**108 526**	**71 075**	**112 007**	**119 464**	**Océanie**
Australia	10 496	8 259	6 786	8 141	10 172	10 339	9 844	7 102	9 012	5 242	Australie
New Zealand	...	...	...	...	...	91 575	98 682	63 973	102 995	114 222	Nouvelle–Zélande
Total	**466 993**	**435 710**	**478 042**	**499 594**	**573 227**	**541 338**	**613 808**	**604 271**	**687 335**	**655 029**	**Total**

General note.
Animal– or tractor–operated and self–propelled mowers for cutting hay etc., consisting of a wheeled frame, supporting a horizontal cutter bar and a toothed knife. (SITC 71220–2).

[1] Shipments.
[2] Production by establishments employing 5 or more persons.

Remarque générale.
Faucheuses (à traction animale, tractées ou automotrices) servant à couper les foins etc., consistant en un cadre sur roues portant une barre de coupe horizontale et une lame à dents tranchantes. (CTCI 71220–2).

[1] Expéditions.
[2] Production des établissements occupant 5 personnes ou plus.

Rakes, animal- or tractor-operated and self-propelled - Râteaux, à traction animale ou tractés et automotrices

Unit : Number units | Unité : Nombre

Country or area	1976	1977	1978	1979	1980	1981	1982	1983	1984	1985	Pays ou zone
America, North	**27 435**	**22 867**	**25 345**	**24 801**	**25 961**	**20 691**	**14 881**	**10 234**	**11 348**	**11 265**	**Amérique du Nord**
Mexico	5 539	2 539	4 725	5 675	6 254	7 076	4 792	2 968	2 279	3 193	Mexique
United States[1]	21 896	20 328	20 620	19 126	19 707	13 615	10 089	7 266	9 069	8 072	Etats-Unis[1]
Europe	**84 848**	**80 907**	**89 522**	**93 362**	**92 349**	**72 961**	**71 351**	**75 541**	**89 065**	**72 066**	**Europe**
EEC	***68 212***	***67 735***	***74 476***	***79 368***	***77 844***	***57 460***	***57 411***	***61 099***	***74 272***	***57 540***	***CEE***
Denmark	134	0	0	0	0	0	0	0	0	...	Danemark
France	25 000	27 800	29 400	30 200	29 700	20 200	22 700	23 300	25 000	21 000	France
Germany, Fed. Rep.	* 38 110	* 35 181	40 211	44 306	43 282	32 398	29 849	32 937	44 410	31 609	Allemagne, Rép. féd.
United Kingdom	4 968	4 754	4 865	...	...	...	...	...	...	...	Royaume-Uni
EFTA	***16 636***	***13 172***	***15 046***	***13 994***	***14 505***	***15 501***	***13 940***	***14 442***	***14 793***	***14 526***	***AELE***
Austria	9 768	8 438	10 212	8 711	8 631	7 553	6 001	5 437	4 882	4 528	Autriche
Finland	5 868	3 834	3 934	4 983	5 574	7 648	7 639	8 705	9 661	...	Finlande
Sweden	1 000	900	900	300	300	300	300	300	250	250	Suède
USSR	**42 502**	**46 670**	**48 324**	**50 911**	**53 058**	**48 881**	**56 106**	**59 253**	**65 136**	**69 924**	**URSS**
Ukrainian SSR	*5 800*	*8 500*	*9 000*	*9 000*	*9 500*	*9 600*	*9 000*	*9 000*	*9 000*	*9 003*	*RSS d'Ukraine*
Oceania	**1 308**	**1 070**	**1 127**	**1 174**	**1 786**	**963**	**437**	**50**	**158**	**126**	**Océanie**
Australia	1 308	1 070	1 127	1 174	1 786	963	437	50	158	...	Australie
Total	**156 093**	**151 514**	**164 318**	**170 248**	**173 154**	**143 496**	**142 775**	**145 078**	**165 707**	**153 381**	**Total**

General note.
Animal-operated, self-propelled or tractor-operated tedder-rakes, windrower-rakes and bundling rakes. (SITC 71220-3).

[1] Shipments.

Remarque générale.
Râteaux-faneurs, râteaux-daineurs et râteaux (à traction animale, ou tractés et automotrices). (CTCI 71220-3).

[1] Expéditions.

Threshing machines – Batteuses

Unit : Number units | Unité : Nombre

Country or area	1976	1977	1978	1979	1980	1981	1982	1983	1984	1985	Pays ou zone
America, North	**6**	**6**	**6**	**6**	**6**	**6**	**6**	**12**	**0**	**6**	**Amérique du Nord**
Cuba	...	...	...	...	...	...	...	12	0	...	Cuba
America, South	**4 980**	**3 122**	**2 514**	**13 925**	**17 248**	**13 898**	**15 881**	**17 719**	**19 694**	**21 626**	**Amérique du Sud**
Brazil	[1] 4 887	[1] 3 029	[1] 2 421	[1] 13 832	17 160	...	...	...	...	...	Brésil
Colombia	...	...	...	...	88	92	144	50	...	...	Colombie
Asia	**107 405**	**96 598**	**98 771**	**107 496**	**106 348**	**76 428**	**78 332**	**70 146**	**72 614**	**61 432**	**Asie**
Japan	83 341	72 106	66 509	76 183	75 718	52 861	50 190	45 720	46 879	42 901	Japon
Korea, Republic of	17 376	16 064	23 866	23 251	24 417	17 945	22 280	21 910	21 603	15 274	Corée, République de
Philippines	...	...	...	...	...	...	...	1 547	...	...	Philippines
Turkey	5 141	6 881	6 849	6 515	...	...	4 315	969	2 585	...	Turquie
Europe	**11 965**	**17 143**	**17 634**	**22 192**	**22 499**	**25 890**	**15 931**	**18 009**	**22 656**	**24 775**	**Europe**
EEC	***91***	***63***	***95***	***78***	***63***	***79***	***50***	***63***	***43***	***53***	***CEE***
France	61	35	70	68	57	69	44	60	39	...	France
Greece	30	28	25	10	6	...	6	3	4	...	Grèce
EFTA	***85***	***98***	***46***	***48***	***33***	***53***	***170***	***57***	***80***	***68***	***AELE***
Portugal	85	98	46	48	33	53	170	57	80	68	Portugal
East Europe	***11 613***	***11 637***	***11 544***	***11 970***	***12 125***	***11 383***	***12 141***	***12 831***	***12 959***	***14 475***	***Europe de l'est***
Poland	11 613	11 637	11 544	11 970	12 125	11 383	12 141	12 831	12 959	14 475	Pologne
Other Europe	***176***	***5 345***	***5 949***	***10 096***	***10 278***	***14 375***	***3 570***	***5 058***	***9 574***	***10 179***	***Autre Europe***
Spain	176	...	...	10 096	10 278	14 375	3 570	5 058	...	...	Espagne
USSR	**1 513**	**1 759**	**4 533**	**2 437**	**2 643**	**3 051**	**1 220**	**1 549**	**1 026**	**1 621**	**URSS**
Total	**125 869**	**118 628**	**123 458**	**146 056**	**148 744**	**119 273**	**111 370**	**107 435**	**115 990**	**109 460**	**Total**

General note.
Machines used in place of hand tools for threshing grain. They may be driven by a steam engine, tractor etc. (SITC 71220–4).

[1] Production by establishments employing 5 or more persons.

Remarque générale.
Machines utilisées au lieu d'outils à main pour le battage du grain. Elles peuvent être actionnées par une locomobile, un tracteur etc. (CTCI 71220–4).

[1] Production des établissements occupant 5 personnes ou plus.

Milking machines – Trayeuses

Unit : Number units | Unité : Nombre

Country or area	1976	1977	1978	1979	1980	1981	1982	1983	1984	1985	Pays ou zone
America, North	**11 623**	**12 920**	**12 967**	**14 274**	**10 041**	**9 124**	**9 843**	**9 277**	**8 711**	**8 144**	**Amérique du Nord**
United States[1]	11 623	12 920	12 967	14 274	10 041	9 124	...	...	...	...	Etats–Unis[1]
America, South	**2 823**	**2 982**	**2 823**	**2 823**	**2 665**	**2 806**	**2 839**	**2 826**	**2 823**	**2 823**	**Amérique du Sud**
Brazil	...	[2] 2 933	...	...	2 616	...	...	...	...	...	Brésil
Colombia	...	...	...	...	...	32	65	52	...	...	Colombie
Asia	**8 763**	**8 749**	**8 758**	**12 246**	**10 832**	**12 187**	**18 070**	**10 563**	**32 121**	**13 152**	**Asie**
Japan	2 222	2 208	2 221	2 244	2 022	1 415	2 426	1 696	1 589	1 575	Japon
Korea, Republic of	234	234	230	# 3 695	2 503	4 465	4 317	1 271	30 532	5 270	Corée, République de
Turkey	...	...	...	...	...	...	11 327	7 596	0	...	Turquie
Europe	**133 899**	**122 044**	**125 329**	**132 800**	**122 438**	**123 277**	**114 643**	**110 329**	**105 772**	**112 595**	**Europe**
EEC	***75 374***	***72 002***	***74 306***	***79 939***	***72 703***	***72 820***	***62 847***	***61 215***	***55 146***	***53 321***	***CEE***
Belgium	...	...	...	44 956	43 930	44 465	40 548	43 047	40 834	41 009	Belgique
France	24 540	21 700	25 300	29 400	23 900	27 200	21 500	17 500	14 000	12 000	France
United Kingdom	3 983	4 145	3 544	5 583	4 873	1 155	799	668	312	...	Royaume–Uni
EFTA	***17 171***	***16 309***	***6 925***	***6 057***	***7 309***	***10 915***	***7 429***	***5 590***	***2 378***	***4 911***	***AELE***
Austria	7 711	7 550	6 925	6 057	7 309	10 915	7 429	5 590	2 378	992	Autriche
Sweden	9 460	8 759	0	0	0	0	0	0	0	...	Suède
East Europe	***19 625***	***13 399***	***19 415***	***22 387***	***19 524***	***16 140***	***21 729***	***21 761***	***23 563***	***27 909***	***Europe de l'est***
Czechoslovakia	1 322	1 439	1 587	1 734	1 942	1 922	1 793	1 632	1 720	5 024	Tchécoslovaquie
Hungary	959	762	1 691	1 711	1 466	1 155	784	0	1 000	1 470	Hongrie
Poland	17 344	11 198	16 137	18 942	16 116	13 063	19 152	20 129	20 843	21 415	Pologne
Other Europe	***21 729***	***20 334***	***24 683***	***24 417***	***22 902***	***23 402***	***22 638***	***21 763***	***24 685***	***26 454***	***Autre Europe***
Spain	...	...	...	4 515	3 000	3 500	2 736	1 861	...	...	Espagne
Yugoslavia	15 842	* 15 000	...	...	...	...	...	...	23 222	25 544	Yougoslavie
USSR	**53 090**	**54 905**	**53 420**	**57 706**	**56 666**	**62 573**	**68 577**	**67 906**	**67 600**	**68 447**	**URSS**
Total	**210 198**	**201 600**	**203 297**	**219 849**	**202 642**	**209 967**	**213 972**	**200 901**	**217 027**	**205 161**	**Total**

General note.
Machines comprising a rust–proof milking pail with a special cover to which is fitted a pulsator for causing intermittent suction in the attached teat cup assembly. In the cases where the air pump for causing a comparative vacuum in the milk pails forms an integral part of the pail, the whole unit (machine plus pump) is included under this heading. (SITC 71239–1).

[1] Shipments.
[2] Production by establishments employing 5 or more persons.

Remarque générale.
Machines comprenant un pot collecteur en métal inoxydable, et des gobelets trayeurs, reliés à un organe pulsateur disposé sur le couvercle. Lorsque la motopompe destinée à créer un vide relatif dans les gobelets trayeurs fait corps avec le récipient collecteur, l'ensemble (machine et pompe) est compris dans cette rubrique. (CTCI 71239–1).

[1] Expéditions.
[2] Production des établissements occupant 5 personnes ou plus.

Garden tractors – Tracteurs horticoles

Unit : Number units

Unité : Nombre

Country or area	1976	1977	1978	1979	1980	1981	1982	1983	1984	1985	Pays ou zone
America, North	**440 186**	**453 685**	**362 281**	**213 355**	**178 742**	**150 702**	**106 855**	**96 545**	**106 947**	**112 146**	**Amérique du Nord**
United States[1]	440 186	453 685	362 281	213 355	178 742	150 702	106 855	96 545	106 947	112 146	Etats–Unis[1]
America, South	**8 003**	**6 405**	**6 487**	**6 535**	**7 793**	**6 958**	**6 929**	**6 900**	**6 871**	**6 842**	**Amérique du Sud**
Brazil	8 003	6 405	6 487	6 535	7 793	...	...	...	...	...	Brésil
Asia	**594 926**	**691 321**	**666 165**	**648 803**	**540 930**	**583 966**	**744 879**	**918 966**	**1 050 580**	**1 101 412**	**Asie**
China	240 000	320 500	324 200	317 500	217 900	198 900	298 300	497 700	688 600	822 500	Chine
Japan	354 713	370 473	341 593	330 912	322 699	384 735	446 248	420 935	361 649	278 581	Japon
Korea, Republic of	213	348	372	391	...	...	...	...	...	...	Corée, République de
Europe	**36 195**	**35 362**	**33 132**	**31 755**	**25 909**	**24 393**	**20 490**	**24 971**	**16 395**	**15 393**	**Europe**
EEC	***13 707***	***15 073***	***14 783***	***15 170***	***11 781***	***11 616***	***11 653***	***15 952***	***10 207***	***11 232***	***CEE***
Belgium	...	...	...	8 715	5 337	5 828	5 708	9 041	5 520	5 678	Belgique
Germany, Fed. Rep.[2]	2 499	4 063	3 971	2 979	2 968	2 233	...	...	...	...	Allemagne, Rép. féd.[2]
Greece	...	...	...	...	...	3 555	3 387	4 513	2 449	...	Grèce
Other Europe	***22 488***	***20 289***	***18 349***	***16 585***	***14 128***	***12 777***	***8 837***	***9 019***	***6 188***	***4 161***	***Autre Europe***
Spain	...	...	...	16 469	14 012	12 661	8 721	8 903	...	...	Espagne
Yugoslavia	202	30	...	...	...	...	...	...	...	...	Yougoslavie
Total	**1 079 310**	**1 186 773**	**1 068 065**	**900 448**	**753 374**	**766 019**	**879 153**	**1 047 382**	**1 180 793**	**1 235 793**	**Total**

General note.
Small tractors and mechanical cultivators developing less than 10 horsepower, used mainly for horticultural purposes. Motor tillers are included. (SITC 71250–1A).

[1] Shipments.
[2] Beginning 1982, data are confidential.

Remarque générale.
Petits tracteurs et cultivateurs mécaniques de moins de 10 CV utilisés surtout en horticulture, y compris les motobineuses. (CTCI 71250–1A).

[1] Expéditions.
[2] A partir de 1982, les données sont confidentielles.

ISIC-BASED CODE
3822-61A

Tractors of 10 HP and over, other than industrial and road tractors – Tracteurs (autres que les tracteurs industriels et ceux pour train routier) de 10 CV et plus

CODE BASE CITI
3822-61A

Unit : Number units

Unité : Nombre

Country or area	1976	1977	1978	1979	1980	1981	1982	1983	1984	1985	Pays ou zone
Africa	**4 774**	**5 600**	**6 649**	**7 651**	**6 668**	**7 038**	**7 779**	**8 294**	**8 720**	**9 145**	**Afrique**
Algeria	2 110	2 839	3 724	4 868	4 206	4 379	4 500	...	...	...	Algérie
Egypt	...	2 761	2 925	2 783	2 462	2 659	3 279	...	...	...	Egypte
America, North	**224 728**	**179 377**	**149 843**	**175 568**	**196 635**	**169 600**	**122 569**	**107 332**	**117 776**	**99 021**	**Amérique du Nord**
Mexico	11 574	10 489	13 005	15 595	17 893	18 898	15 714	10 787	10 829	11 763	Mexique
United States[1]	213 154	168 888	136 838	159 973	178 742	150 702	106 855	96 545	106 947	...	Etats-Unis[1]
America, South	**83 732**	**75 452**	**50 339**	**60 720**	**54 063**	**35 658**	**29 727**	**34 656**	**62 260**	**55 450**	**Amérique du Sud**
Argentina[2]	24 098	25 631	5 997	10 901	3 618	1 100	3 974	7 884	12 241	6 332	Argentine[2]
Brazil[2]	59 178	49 452	44 084	49 488	50 238	34 309	25 531	26 576	49 850	48 976	Brésil[2]
Peru[3]	456	369	258	331	207	...	...	...	...	...	Pérou[3]
Asia	**473 293**	**466 378**	**410 080**	**479 316**	**414 083**	**371 255**	**356 620**	**356 416**	**402 151**	**404 855**	**Asie**
Burma	882	844	700	945	831	674	391	820	419	587	Birmanie
China	73 700	99 300	113 500	125 600	97 700	52 800	40 300	37 000	39 700	45 000	Chine
India	36 675	34 675	52 368	60 094	67 517	84 317	68 153	72 608	82 462	80 657	Inde
Iran(Islamic Rep.of)[4]	13 442	10 032	7 011	13 125	7 083	12 044	13 570	13 570	...	...	Iran(Rép.islamique)[4]
Japan[5]	309 909	288 073	227 196	266 141	227 932	199 027	197 974	189 293	217 309	224 052	Japon[5]
Korea, Republic of	1 796	1 796	1 121	551	594	411	2 096	2 818	3 600	4 559	Corée, République de
Turkey	36 889	31 658	8 184	12 860	12 426	21 982	34 136	40 307	45 946	36 956	Turquie
Europe	**878 730**	**911 533**	**832 295**	**819 715**	**778 607**	**707 377**	**714 755**	**703 331**	**693 505**	**646 825**	**Europe**
EEC	***659 208***	***681 818***	***604 441***	***605 430***	***556 666***	***501 338***	***492 394***	***473 557***	***469 066***	***430 354***	***CEE***
Belgium	100 950	101 165	101 110	104 948	107 024	104 895	106 937	101 866	108 925	108 583	Belgique
France[6]	166 700	162 300	165 000	157 200	123 500	113 000	113 400	93 000	84 000	61 848	France[6]
Germany, Fed. Rep.	125 152	128 727	108 480	110 646	94 587	88 869	93 382	98 265	80 638	88 210	Allemagne, Rép. féd.
Greece	1 689	1 879	1 571	861	1 232	447	571	309	1 247	...	Grèce
Italy	128 217	140 547	116 380	115 775	127 023	109 027	92 869	88 411	94 093	95 803	Italie
United Kingdom[7]	136 500	147 200	111 900	116 000	103 300	85 100	85 235	91 706	100 163	...	Royaume-Uni[7]
EFTA	***25 866***	***25 638***	***25 218***	***25 818***	***30 524***	***26 843***	***28 429***	***28 715***	***29 921***	***30 093***	***AELE***
Austria	9 000	9 251	9 241	8 281	10 049	10 202	9 936	8 022	8 191	8 740	Autriche
Finland	2 629	3 727	3 433	3 399	4 241	3 092	3 713	5 659	6 443	...	Finlande
Sweden	14 237	12 660	12 544	14 138	16 234	13 549	...	...	...	...	Suède
East Europe	***154 624***	***164 358***	***170 634***	***162 199***	***172 674***	***161 596***	***169 112***	***177 573***	***179 350***	***174 024***	***Europe de l'est***
Bulgaria	5 919	6 258	7 675	5 944	6 767	6 614	6 216	5 880	5 784	5 350	Bulgarie
Czechoslovakia	31 458	35 040	33 317	35 370	33 359	32 110	33 523	34 176	34 160	35 184	Tchécoslovaquie
German Dem. Rep.	4 018	...	...	...	...	...	...	...	...	...	Rép. dém. allemande
Hungary	513	658	400	142	108	224	300	400	108	254	Hongrie
Poland	58 805	59 078	59 509	54 231	57 549	50 537	53 240	55 957	58 824	59 019	Pologne
Romania[8]	53 911	59 306	65 715	62 494	70 873	68 093	71 815	77 142	76 456	70 199	Roumanie[8]
Other Europe	***39 032***	***39 719***	***32 002***	***26 268***	***18 743***	***17 600***	***24 820***	***23 486***	***15 168***	***12 354***	***Autre Europe***
Spain	38 830	39 594	31 709	25 954	18 614	17 418	24 620	23 276	...	...	Espagne
Yugoslavia	202	125	293	314	129	182	200	210	200	171	Yougoslavie
USSR	**562 175**	**569 145**	**576 113**	**557 415**	**554 916**	**558 538**	**555 159**	**563 995**	**571 403**	**585 472**	**URSS**
Byelorussian SSR	*86 526*	*87 126*	*87 835*	*89 145*	*89 550*	*89 975*	*90 850*	*92 300*	*94 710*	*95 953*	*RSS de Biélorussie*
Ukrainian SSR	*140 794*	*141 331*	*141 752*	*142 039*	*135 630*	*133 091*	*131 845*	*134 716*	*128 775*	*135 912*	*RSS d'Ukraine*
Oceania	**6 876**	**6 676**	**5 831**	**4 547**	**4 971**	**5 014**	**6 996**	**3 512**	**3 429**	**3 811**	**Océanie**
Australia[9]	6 876	6 676	5 831	4 547	4 971	5 014	6 996	3 512	3 429	3 811	Australie[9]
Total	**2 234 308**	**2 214 161**	**2 031 150**	**2 104 932**	**2 009 943**	**1 854 480**	**1 793 605**	**1 777 536**	**1 859 244**	**1 804 579**	**Total**

General note.
Vehicles constructed essentially for hauling or pushing another vehicle, appliance or load, whether or not they contain subsidiary provision for the transport, in connection with the main use of the tractor, of tools, seeds, fertilizers or other goods etc., irrespective of their mode of propulsion (internal combustion engine, steam engine etc.). This heading includes agricultural as well as other tractors, for

For footnotes, see end of table.

Remarque générale.
Véhicules essentiellement conçus, soit pour remorquer ou pousser d'autres engins, véhicules ou charges. Ils peuvent cependant comporter un plateau accessoire ou un dispositif analogue permettant le transport, en corrélation avec leur usage principal, d'outils, de semences, d'engrais etc., quelle que soit la source d'énergie qui les actionne (moteur à explosion, moteur à vapeur etc.). Cette rubrique comprend les

Voir la fin du tableau pour les notes.

Tractors of 10 HP and over, other than industrial and road tractors (continued) – Tracteurs (autres que les tracteurs industriels et ceux pour train routier) de 10 CV et plus (suite)

example, for use in forestry or in construction. Road tractors for tractor–trailer combinations and industrial tractors are, however, excluded. Walking tractors, equipped with a single driving axle carried on one or two wheels, the steering of which is effected by means of two handles, used like normal tractors and possibly with interchangeable implements, are also included. Tractors of less than 10 horsepower (garden tractors) are excluded. (SITC 71250–2A).

1 Shipments.
2 Agricultural tractors only.
3 Data refer to assembly.
4 Production by establishments employing 10 or more persons.
5 Including bulldozers.
6 Agricultural tractors of all sizes.
7 Deliveries of wheeled and half–track tractors. Production of wheeled tractors.
8 Including road tractors.
9 Including tractors of less than 10 HP.

tracteurs agricoles et autres (tracteurs forestiers et tracteurs de travaux publics, par example). Elle ne comprend pas les tracteurs pour trains routiers ni les tracteurs industriels. Elle comprend aussi les moto–culteurs comportant un seul essieu moteur, à une ou deux roues, et guidés à la main au moyen de deux mancherons, qui sont utilisés comme les tracteurs proprement dits et sont munis éventuellement d'outils interchangeables. Elle ne comprend pas les tracteurs de moins de 10 CV (tracteurs horticoles). (CTCI 71250–2A).

1 Expéditions.
2 Tracteurs agricoles seulement.
3 Données se rapportant à l'assemblage.
4 Production des établissements occupant 10 personnes ou plus.
5 Y compris les bouteurs.
6 Tracteurs agricoles de toutes dimensions.
7 Nombre réceptionné de tracteurs à roues et semi–chenillés. Production de tracteurs à roues.
8 Y compris les tracteurs routiers.
9 Y compris les tracteurs de moins de 10 ch.

Fertilizer distributors, animal–, hand– or tractor–operated – Distributeurs d'engrais, à traction animale, à bras ou tractés

Unit : Number units — Unité : Nombre

Country or area	1976	1977	1978	1979	1980	1981	1982	1983	1984	1985	Pays ou zone
America, North	**27 403**	**24 627**	**24 480**	**26 482**	**26 326**	**24 118**	**16 213**	**14 961**	**17 825**	**12 421**	**Amérique du Nord**
United States	27 403	24 627	24 480	26 482	26 326	24 118	16 213	14 961	17 825	12 421	Etats–Unis
America, South	**7 272**	**5 162**	**4 119**	**13 534**	**12 205**	**11 574**	**12 642**	**13 711**	**14 779**	**15 847**	**Amérique du Sud**
Brazil	7 272	5 162	4 119	[1] 13 534	12 205	...	...	...	...	...	Brésil
Asia	**10 973**	**15 345**	**14 824**	**17 089**	**14 557**	**14 557**	**14 557**	**14 557**	**14 557**	**14 557**	**Asie**
Philippines[2]	4 504	2 735	...	...	...	...	...	...	...	...	Philippines[2]
Turkey	6 469	12 610	11 205	13 470	...	...	...	...	...	...	Turquie
Europe	**250 302**	**239 781**	**239 282**	**230 100**	**202 789**	**214 146**	**227 529**	**190 241**	**187 486**	**170 053**	**Europe**
EEC	***228 382***	***214 897***	***212 190***	***201 985***	***174 032***	***176 681***	***174 427***	***159 542***	***154 967***	***152 829***	***CEE***
Belgium	...	...	...	...	...	53 138	...	50 990	...	52 694	Belgique
Denmark	24 119	23 891	23 601	16 817	10 701	...	13 269	...	...	...	Danemark
France	33 900	32 300	32 000	32 400	25 200	24 600	22 500	21 300	17 300	17 000	France
Germany, Fed. Rep.	67 567	58 086	57 997	50 692	41 584	36 952	34 654	34 535	32 228	32 907	Allemagne, Rép. féd.
Greece	942	827	683	1 586	4 263	3 189	3 700	5 547	5 104	...	Grèce
Netherlands[3]	41 640	39 220	38 789	42 210	34 210	* 42 464	44 490	36 530	40 700	...	Pays–Bas[3]
United Kingdom	7 940	8 299	6 846	6 006	5 800	3 182	3 540	2 264	1 374	...	Royaume–Uni
EFTA	***10 406***	***13 837***	***16 138***	***16 983***	***17 646***	***26 666***	***38 845***	***17 856***	***16 226***	***17 024***	***AELE***
Austria	4 100	7 912	8 101	7 065	6 688	16 510	29 244	7 103	5 789	5 556	Autriche
Finland	2 241	1 745	3 499	5 279	7 010	6 290	5 584	6 382	6 013	...	Finlande
Portugal	151	102	146	273	480	476	585	657	588	369	Portugal
Sweden	3 914	4 078	4 392	4 366	3 468	3 390	3 432	3 714	3 836	3 358	Suède
East Europe	***11 514***	***11 047***	***10 954***	***11 132***	***11 111***	***10 799***	***14 257***	***12 843***	***16 293***	***200***	***Europe de l'est***
Bulgaria	1 000	533	440	618	597	285	659	477	200	200	Bulgarie
Poland	...	...	...	...	...	...	13 598	12 366	16 093	0	Pologne
Oceania	**2 487**	**1 513**	**1 207**	**1 325**	**1 567**	**1 188**	**1 939**	**1 313**	**648**	**380**	**Océanie**
Australia	2 487	1 513	1 207	1 325	1 567	1 188	1 939	1 313	648	380	Australie
Total	**298 437**	**286 428**	**283 912**	**288 530**	**257 444**	**265 583**	**272 880**	**234 783**	**235 295**	**213 258**	**Total**

General note.
Distributors for spreading manure or solid fertilizers, usually consisting of long box hoppers mounted on wheels and fitted with a distributing mechanism (animal–, hand– or tractor–operated). (SITC 71964–1).

[1] Production by establishments employing 5 or more persons.
[2] Shipments.
[3] Industrial sales.

Remarque générale.
Distributeurs destinés à répandre le fumier ou les engrais solides, consistant en général en longues trémies–réservoirs montées sur roues et munies d'un mécanisme distributeur (à traction animale, à bras ou tractés). (CTCI 71964–1).

[1] Production des établissements occupant 5 personnes ou plus.
[2] Expéditions.
[3] Ventes industrielles.

Drilling and boring machines – Perceuses

Unit : Number units | Unité : Nombre

Country or area	1976	1977	1978	1979	1980	1981	1982	1983	1984	1985	Pays ou zone
America, North	**41 326**	**45 000**	**53 169**	**46 368**	**36 691**	**28 894**	**18 040**	**13 915**	**12 526**	**9 809**	**Amérique du Nord**
United States[1]	41 326	45 000	53 169	46 368	36 691	28 894	18 040	13 915	12 526	9 809	Etats–Unis[1]
America, South	**38 348**	**35 570**	**20 149**	**89 042**	**76 642**	**74 647**	**82 397**	**90 146**	**97 896**	**105 646**	**Amérique du Sud**
Brazil	38 348	35 570	20 149	[2] 89 042	76 642	...	...	...	...	...	Brésil
Asia	**41 866**	**43 787**	**38 217**	**45 633**	**44 597**	**38 880**	**36 934**	**33 255**	**42 862**	**38 445**	**Asie**
Japan	40 981	42 022	36 431	43 516	42 959	37 242	35 296	31 617	41 224	36 807	Japon
Turkey	885	1 765	1 786	2 117	...	...	...	...	...	...	Turquie
Europe	**113 234**	**110 535**	**109 394**	**111 460**	**109 291**	**104 846**	**95 256**	**96 203**	**100 871**	**103 519**	**Europe**
EEC	***78 168***	***79 564***	***77 260***	***74 689***	***73 771***	***68 579***	***59 683***	***60 318***	***57 530***	***56 475***	***CEE***
Belgium	...	...	...	...	39 142	...	...	...	37 528	...	Belgique
Denmark	879	848	403	230	184	...	...	43	...	185	Danemark
France	4 195	3 752	3 316	[3] 3 304	[3] 4 790	* [3] 5 840	* [3] 1 700	[3] 3 396	[3] 3 081	[3] 3 769	France
Germany, Fed. Rep.[4]	24 125	24 839	22 262	19 934	20 742	18 558	...	...	...	...	Allemagne, Rép. féd.[4]
United Kingdom	10 634	11 790	12 944	12 886	8 913	5 557	1 942	2 257	...	...	Royaume–Uni
EFTA	***14 718***	***11 579***	***11 109***	***13 324***	***13 307***	***13 113***	***10 247***	***11 210***	***14 150***	***14 582***	***AELE***
Austria	769	698	778	814	782	859	1 075	1 746	1 881	1 593	Autriche
Finland	14	0	0	0	90	131	40	50	...	...	Finlande
Portugal	1 439	1 743	3 794	3 189	3 458	3 757	3 592	...	...	...	Portugal
Sweden	12 496	9 138	6 537	9 321	8 977	8 366	5 540	4 968	7 371	7 717	Suède
East Europe	***15 635***	***14 496***	***14 818***	***14 807***	***16 361***	***15 812***	***16 533***	***16 978***	***21 500***	***24 258***	***Europe de l'est***
Bulgaria	3 446	3 645	4 212	4 571	5 132	5 211	4 641	4 122	4 731	6 563	Bulgarie
Czechoslovakia	1 388	1 222	1 164	1 278	1 490	1 504	1 543	1 631	1 492	1 512	Tchécoslovaquie
Hungary	4 862	3 756	3 340	3 507	3 468	3 389	3 173	2 925	4 147	5 744	Hongrie
Poland	5 939	5 873	6 102	5 451	6 271	5 708	7 176	8 300	11 130	10 439	Pologne
Other Europe	***4 713***	***4 896***	***6 207***	***8 640***	***5 852***	***7 342***	***8 793***	***7 697***	***7 691***	***8 204***	***Autre Europe***
Spain	3 636	...	...	5 239	1 730	3 662	5 711	5 937	...	...	Espagne
Yugoslavia	1 077	1 480	2 506	3 401	4 122	3 680	3 082	1 760	2 279	2 507	Yougoslavie
Total	**234 774**	**234 892**	**220 929**	**292 503**	**267 221**	**247 267**	**232 627**	**233 519**	**254 155**	**257 419**	**Total**

General note.
Metal–working machines fitted with a baseplate, stand or other device for mounting on the floor, or on a bench, wall or another machine. (SITC 71510–1).

[1] Shipments.
[2] Production by establishments employing 5 or more persons.
[3] Limited coverage.
[4] Beginning 1982, data are confidential.

Remarque générale.
Machines–outils pour le travail des métaux, munies d'un socle, d'un pied ou d'un autre dispositif permettant de les fixer au sol, à un établi, à une paroi ou à une autre machine. (CTCI 71510–1).

[1] Expéditions.
[2] Production des établissements occupant 5 personnes ou plus.
[3] Couverture limitée.
[4] A partir de 1982, les données sont confidentielles.

Forging, stamping and die–stamping machines – Marteaux, martinets et moutons

Unit : Number units — Unité : Nombre

Country or area	1976	1977	1978	1979	1980	1981	1982	1983	1984	1985	Pays ou zone
America, North	**543**	**494**	**533**	**609**	**631**	**479**	**383**	**206**	**198**	**213**	**Amérique du Nord**
United States[1 2]	543	494	533	609	631	479	383	206	198	213	Etats–Unis[1 2]
Asia	**492**	**413**	**507**	**482**	**561**	**466**	**346**	**302**	**844**	**838**	**Asie**
Japan	492	413	507	482	561	466	346	302	844	838	Japon
Europe	**15 083**	**10 975**	**11 010**	**7 169**	**7 881**	**7 841**	**7 894**	**7 952**	**8 963**	**8 550**	**Europe**
EEC	***589***	***314***	***540***	***873***	***1 424***	***1 382***	***1 538***	***1 713***	***2 066***	***2 210***	***CEE***
Germany, Fed. Rep.	311	96	318	625	673	502	266	53	...	...	Allemagne, Rép. féd.
United Kingdom[2]	278	218	222	248	751	880	1 272	1 660	1 730	...	Royaume–Uni[2]
EFTA	***185***	***135***	***145***	***137***	***195***	***132***	***112***	***76***	***82***	***69***	***AELE***
Austria	117	131	106	105	157	86	75	51	67	...	Autriche
Finland	...	2	0	1	0	0	0	0	0	...	Finlande
Portugal	67	2	39	31	38	46	37	25	15	12	Portugal
East Europe	***5 344***	***5 472***	***5 764***	***6 030***	***6 244***	***6 307***	***6 226***	***6 124***	***5 212***	***5 161***	***Europe de l'est***
Bulgaria	0	0	75	0	176	240	273	325	318	318	Bulgarie
Czechoslovakia	52	53	26	43	55	35	37	33	24	10	Tchécoslovaquie
German Dem. Rep.[3]	5 279	5 406	5 649	5 979	6 008	6 026	5 912	5 764	4 867	4 827	Rép. dém. allemande[3]
Hungary	13	13	14	8	5	6	4	2	3	6	Hongrie
Other Europe	***8 965***	***5 054***	***4 561***	***129***	***18***	***20***	***18***	***39***	***1 603***	***1 110***	***Autre Europe***
Spain	8 965	...	...	129	18	20	17	38	...	...	Espagne
Yugoslavia	0	0	0	0	0	0	...	...	2	3	Yougoslavie
Total	**16 118**	**11 882**	**12 050**	**8 260**	**9 073**	**8 786**	**8 623**	**8 460**	**10 005**	**9 601**	**Total**

General note.
Mechanical, hydraulic, pneumatic and steam forge hammers and die–stamping hammers. Metal–working presses are excluded. (SITC 71510–3).

[1] Shipments.
[2] Including swaging machines.
[3] Data refer to forging and pressing equipment.

Remarque générale.
Marteaux à forger, à estamper et à matricer, à commande mécanique, hydraulique, pneumatique ou à vapeur. Cette rubrique ne comprend pas les presses à former les métaux. (CTCI 71510–3).

[1] Expéditions.
[2] Y compris les machines à étamper.
[3] Données se rapportant aux machines de forgeage et d'emboutissage.

Grinding and sharpening machines – Meuleuses et affûteuses

Unit : Number units

Unité : Nombre

Country or area	1976	1977	1978	1979	1980	1981	1982	1983	1984	1985	Pays ou zone
America, North	**86 315**	**95 234**	**110 202**	**107 288**	**97 004**	**91 548**	**58 284**	**57 196**	**60 189**	**51 807**	**Amérique du Nord**
United States[1]	86 315	95 234	110 202	107 288	97 004	91 548	58 284	57 196	60 189	51 807	Etats–Unis[1]
America, South	**53 740**	**54 316**	**53 314**	**78 559**	**28 772**	**53 740**	**53 740**	**53 740**	**53 740**	**53 740**	**Amérique du Sud**
Brazil	...	54 316	53 314	[2] 78 559	28 772	...	...	...	...	...	Brésil
Asia	**29 403**	**27 334**	**29 556**	**29 782**	**30 671**	**25 441**	**22 209**	**23 732**	**28 323**	**25 489**	**Asie**
China	...	19 736	21 363	20 488	19 608	13 659	10 969	13 949	14 866	...	Chine
Japan	6 913	7 598	8 193	9 294	11 063	11 782	11 240	9 783	13 457	14 320	Japon
Europe	**136 656**	**132 645**	**185 122**	**125 831**	**104 238**	**120 412**	**83 989**	**91 538**	**96 884**	**108 638**	**Europe**
EEC	***96 402***	***97 502***	***146 818***	***83 353***	***63 002***	***75 646***	***34 620***	***45 873***	***43 781***	***58 382***	***CEE***
Denmark	42 447	35 037	84 223	33 694	925	...	2 438	...	...	22 481	Danemark
Germany, Fed. Rep.	44 088	54 051	52 777	41 116	55 277	46 158	30 089	28 071	30 665	35 854	Allemagne, Rép. féd.
United Kingdom	9 867	8 414	9 818	8 543	6 800	4 440	2 093	1 935	1 839	...	Royaume–Uni
EFTA	***5 690***	***4 264***	***2 934***	***4 986***	***4 654***	***4 342***	***4 668***	***5 907***	***7 193***	***6 825***	***AELE***
Austria	687	180	104	247	299	235	1 075	2 561	3 929	3 495	Autriche
Finland	773	630	694	1 962	1 174	1 073	1 042	910	987	...	Finlande
Portugal	54	69	103	89	13	58	80	136	148	220	Portugal
Sweden	4 176	3 385	2 033	2 688	3 168	2 976	...	...	...	...	Suède
East Europe	***22 011***	***20 712***	***26 286***	***29 653***	***30 488***	***33 205***	***34 596***	***35 157***	***42 700***	***41 162***	***Europe de l'est***
Czechoslovakia	13 626	13 606	13 387	14 166	15 100	14 989	16 454	15 957	17 161	17 056	Tchécoslovaquie
German Dem. Rep.	4 515	3 490	3 325	3 425	3 439	3 321	3 847	3 235	3 384	2 819	Rép. dém. allemande
Hungary	106	103	48	42	11	19	6	0	2	1	Hongrie
Poland	3 764	3 513	9 526	12 020	11 938	14 876	14 289	15 965	22 153	21 286	Pologne
Other Europe	***12 553***	***10 167***	***9 084***	***7 839***	***6 094***	***7 219***	***10 105***	***4 601***	***3 210***	***2 269***	***Autre Europe***
Spain	11 646	...	...	6 023	4 144	5 079	6 057	2 618	...	...	Espagne
Yugoslavia	907	800	804	1 816	1 950	2 140	4 048	1 983	1 446	1 591	Yougoslavie
Total	**306 114**	**309 529**	**378 194**	**341 460**	**260 685**	**291 141**	**218 222**	**226 206**	**239 136**	**239 674**	**Total**

General note.
Metal–working grinding, filing and sharpening machines. Including machines for grinding metallic carbide or hard metal tool tips and machines with metal brushes and abrasives. (SITC 71510–4).

[1] Shipments.
[2] Production by establishments employing 5 or more persons.

Remarque générale.
Machines–outils pour le travail des métaux, destinées au meulage, au limage et à l'affûtage, y compris celles servant à meuler le tranchant en carbure métallique ou en métal dur des outils et les machines équipées de brosses et d'abrasifs. (CTCI 71510–4).

[1] Expéditions.
[2] Production des établissements occupant 5 personnes ou plus.

Unit : Number units | Unité : Nombre

Country or area	1976	1977	1978	1979	1980	1981	1982	1983	1984	1985	Pays ou zone
America, North	**14 085**	**11 249**	**13 557**	**20 107**	**17 937**	**16 904**	**4 508**	**9 692**	**4 300**	**3 836**	**Amérique du Nord**
United States[1]	14 085	11 249	13 557	20 107	17 937	16 904	4 508	9 692	4 300	3 836	Etats-Unis[1]
America, South	**16 305**	**31 487**	**28 317**	**61 184**	**57 845**	**53 279**	**58 158**	**63 353**	**68 667**	**73 840**	**Amérique du Sud**
Brazil	16 016	31 110	27 878	[2] 60 585	57 383	...	...	...	...	...	Brésil
Colombia	289	377	439	599	462	403	68	49	...	...	Colombie
Asia	**106 783**	**112 778**	**110 884**	**94 800**	**98 321**	**83 394**	**73 055**	**77 428**	**93 330**	**75 989**	**Asie**
China	...	84 240	80 278	57 522	58 388	44 493	43 148	49 694	55 675	...	Chine
Japan	21 450	22 713	22 870	28 429	34 710	33 025	24 783	21 816	31 455	33 527	Japon
Korea, Republic of	2 748	4 262	5 793	6 260	4 493	4 583	4 299	5 141	6 020	5 170	Corée, République de
Turkey	1 447	1 563	1 943	2 589	730	1 293	825	777	180	71	Turquie
Europe	**72 810**	**75 360**	**77 619**	**77 272**	**72 334**	**62 836**	**58 653**	**51 093**	**49 981**	**47 503**	**Europe**
EEC	***31 942***	***31 254***	***33 733***	***32 019***	***29 186***	***19 817***	***15 567***	***15 361***	***13 211***	***11 746***	***CEE***
France[3]	4 716	3 918	3 927	3 708	3 175	* 2 350	* 1 800	1 488	1 077	1 284	France[3]
Germany, Fed. Rep.	10 383	10 805	11 607	10 729	10 906	9 400	7 025	6 516	6 772	6 864	Allemagne, Rép. féd.
Greece	29	29	32	19	28	23	2	...	...	...	Grèce
United Kingdom	16 814	16 502	18 167	17 563	15 077	8 044	6 740	7 348	...	...	Royaume-Uni
EFTA	***2 157***	***4 164***	***3 913***	***4 853***	***3 366***	***3 902***	***4 588***	***2 001***	***2 256***	***2 522***	***AELE***
Austria[4]	780	# 2 841	2 787	3 626	2 307	3 019	3 728	1 251	1 613	1 939	Autriche[4]
Finland	0	0	0	4	1	0	3	2	...	...	Finlande
Portugal	197	252	264	314	318	178	257	177	141	150	Portugal
Sweden[5]	1 180	1 071	862	909	740	705	600	571	500	431	Suède[5]
East Europe	***32 541***	***32 532***	***33 148***	***32 947***	***34 643***	***33 375***	***33 297***	***29 995***	***30 329***	***29 315***	***Europe de l'est***
Bulgaria	5 902	5 928	6 484	7 634	8 880	8 829	8 540	6 310	5 564	5 477	Bulgarie
Czechoslovakia	7 335	7 368	7 408	7 120	7 617	7 251	7 686	6 896	7 254	7 157	Tchécoslovaquie
German Dem. Rep.[6]	3 163	3 059	3 007	2 900	2 819	2 459	2 351	2 629	3 225	2 598	Rép. dém. allemande[6]
Hungary	2 980	3 117	2 653	1 985	1 808	1 912	1 990	1 526	1 113	952	Hongrie
Poland	6 285	5 633	6 308	5 915	5 740	4 980	4 630	4 348	4 701	4 474	Pologne
Romania	6 876	7 427	7 288	7 393	7 779	7 944	...	...	...	...	Roumanie
Other Europe	***6 170***	***7 410***	***6 825***	***7 453***	***5 139***	***5 742***	***5 201***	***3 736***	***4 185***	***3 920***	***Autre Europe***
Spain	5 211	...	...	5 184	2 764	3 569	2 658	1 158	...	...	Espagne
Yugoslavia	959	2 231	2 200	2 269	2 375	2 173	2 543	2 578	2 887	3 176	Yougoslavie
Total	**209 983**	**230 874**	**230 377**	**253 363**	**246 437**	**216 413**	**194 374**	**201 566**	**216 278**	**201 168**	**Total**

General note.
Metal-working lathes of all kinds, whether or not automatic, including slide leathes, vertical lathes, capstan and turret lathes, production (or copying) lathes. (SITC 71510-5).

[1] Shipments.
[2] Production by establishments employing 5 or more persons.
[3] Deliveries.
[4] Beginning 1977, data are not comparable with those for earlier years.
[5] Excluding automatic lathes not numerically controlled.
[6] Excluding turning lathes for clock-makers.

Remarque générale.
Tours à métaux, de tous types, automatiques ou non, y compris les tours parallèles, les tours verticaux, les tours à revolver, les tours à reproduire. (CTCI 71510-5).

[1] Expéditions.
[2] Production des établissements occupant 5 personnes ou plus.
[3] Livraisons.
[4] A partir de 1977, les données ne sont pas comparables à celles des années antérieures.
[5] Non compris les tours automatiques sans contrôle numérique.
[6] Non compris les tours d'horloger.

Milling machines – Fraiseuses

Unit : Number units

Unité : Nombre

Country or area	1976	1977	1978	1979	1980	1981	1982	1983	1984	1985	Pays ou zone
America, North	**10 122**	**12 479**	**14 602**	**15 553**	**17 098**	**17 193**	**7 737**	**7 349**	**7 981**	**8 308**	**Amérique du Nord**
United States[1]	10 122	12 479	14 602	15 553	17 098	17 193	7 737	7 349	7 981	8 308	Etats–Unis[1]
America, South	**1 455**	**1 142**	**1 351**	**1 478**	**1 752**	**1 961**	**1 818**	**1 977**	**2 105**	**2 214**	**Amérique du Sud**
Brazil	1 182	1 071	1 208	[2] 1 358	1 647	...	...	...	...	...	Brésil
Colombia	273	71	143	120	105	305	41	79	...	...	Colombie
Asia	**21 245**	**22 797**	**21 947**	**22 593**	**24 402**	**22 739**	**21 326**	**22 190**	**24 176**	**22 653**	**Asie**
China	...	15 054	13 486	12 383	13 192	9 756	9 441	10 781	11 134	...	Chine
Japan	6 077	7 141	7 670	9 231	10 364	11 761	10 631	9 713	10 723	11 399	Japon
Korea, Republic of	...	...	...	...	788	1 164	1 196	1 638	2 261	2 145	Corée, République de
Turkey	58	...	...	...	...	...	...	...	...	...	Turquie
Europe	**32 735**	**33 148**	**35 319**	**34 779**	**33 090**	**35 657**	**32 608**	**30 954**	**32 908**	**33 004**	**Europe**
EEC	***18 422***	***18 089***	***19 423***	***17 510***	***17 397***	***14 422***	***12 903***	***12 400***	***12 259***	***11 057***	***CEE***
Denmark	350	675	644	547	509	...	523	413	...	...	Danemark
France[3]	3 357	2 621	2 870	2 913	2 741	2 043	1 670	1 959	1 665	1 434	France[3]
Germany, Fed. Rep.[4]	10 488	9 097	9 498	8 908	9 615	9 106	...	...	...	...	Allemagne, Rép. féd.[4]
United Kingdom	4 227	5 696	6 411	5 142	4 532	2 766	1 853	1 341	1 596	...	Royaume–Uni
EFTA	***943***	***842***	***747***	***763***	***1 378***	***1 523***	***1 228***	***1 075***	***1 201***	***1 101***	***AELE***
Austria	21	16	16	8	# 629	886	578	552	682	713	Autriche
Portugal	...	...	...	32	22	11	137	135	107	95	Portugal
Sweden	911	822	712	723	727	626	513	388	412	293	Suède
East Europe	***8 674***	***8 411***	***8 595***	***8 110***	***8 246***	***8 662***	***8 598***	***8 678***	***8 803***	***9 457***	***Europe de l'est***
Bulgaria	1 115	991	812	516	745	832	1 000	1 082	1 209	1 981	Bulgarie
Czechoslovakia	2 590	2 642	2 772	2 643	2 655	2 843	2 729	2 617	2 548	2 260	Tchécoslovaquie
Hungary	298	255	244	304	248	273	164	118	78	94	Hongrie
Poland	1 908	1 635	1 775	1 670	1 565	1 365	1 370	1 431	1 442	1 500	Pologne
Romania	2 763	2 888	2 992	2 977	3 033	3 349	...	...	...	...	Roumanie
Other Europe	***4 696***	***5 806***	***6 554***	***8 396***	***6 069***	***11 050***	***9 879***	***8 801***	***10 645***	***11 389***	***Autre Europe***
Spain	3 936	...	...	7 472	5 043	9 928	8 698	7 459	...	...	Espagne
Yugoslavia	760	709	828	924	1 026	1 122	1 181	1 342	1 145	1 260	Yougoslavie
Total	**65 557**	**69 566**	**73 219**	**74 403**	**76 342**	**77 550**	**63 489**	**62 470**	**67 170**	**66 179**	**Total**

General note.
Metal–working machines designed to work a plane or profile surface by means of rotating tools, known as milling cutters. (SITC 71510–6).

[1] Shipments.
[2] Production by establishments employing 5 or more persons.
[3] Deliveries.
[4] Beginning 1982, data are confidential.

Remarque générale.
Machines–outils pour le travail des métaux conçues pour usiner une surface plane ou un profil au moyen d'outils tournants appelés fraises. (CTCI 71510–6).

[1] Expéditions.
[2] Production des établissements occupant 5 personnes ou plus.
[3] Livraisons.
[4] A partir de 1982, les données sont confidentielles.

Other metal–cutting machine–tools – Autres machines–outils pour le travail des métaux

Unit : Number units

Unité : Nombre

Country or area	1976	1977	1978	1979	1980	1981	1982	1983	1984	1985	Pays ou zone
America, North	**59 764**	**56 855**	**65 239**	**69 924**	**75 458**	**76 041**	**39 154**	**16 913**	**18 709**	**19 273**	**Amérique du Nord**
United States[1 2]	59 764	56 855	65 239	69 924	75 458	76 041	39 154	16 913	18 709	19 273	Etats–Unis[1 2]
America, South	**153**	**153**	**153**	**153**	**153**	**226**	**117**	**117**	**153**	**153**	**Amérique du Sud**
Colombia	...	...	...	...	...	226	117	117	...	...	Colombie
Asia	**195 488**	**243 808**	**236 992**	**202 726**	**199 146**	**157 407**	**148 232**	**171 372**	**188 676**	**220 867**	**Asie**
China	157 000	198 700	183 200	139 600	133 600	102 600	99 800	121 300	133 500	167 200	Chine
Japan	38 488	45 108	53 792	63 126	65 546	54 807	48 432	50 072	55 176	53 667	Japon
Europe	**120 956**	**108 327**	**122 056**	**115 724**	**91 781**	**110 282**	**102 566**	**106 222**	**85 087**	**72 903**	**Europe**
EEC	***100 900***	***88 592***	***84 556***	***82 524***	***64 700***	***71 391***	***75 168***	***68 032***	***41 985***	***49 023***	***CEE***
Denmark	...	1 050	1 129	1 219	2 587	...	...	...	...	...	Danemark
France[3 4]	5 567	3 876	3 866	3 751	3 443	3 230	2 820	2 702	2 197	3 009	France[3 4]
Germany, Fed. Rep.[5]	41 590	36 996	34 857	33 997	35 819	32 645	...	...	...	...	Allemagne, Rép. féd.[5]
Greece	...	...	...	...	15 161	32 935	37 937	27 606	530	...	Grèce
United Kingdom	8 838	6 690	8 154	10 436	7 690	1 085	1 841	6 556	9 493	...	Royaume–Uni
EFTA	***1 448***	***2 269***	***19 794***	***16 861***	***16 196***	***19 902***	***15 583***	***30 721***	***33 524***	***15 872***	***AELE***
Austria[6]	1 062	1 825	# 19 193	16 291	15 813	19 515	15 282	30 404	33 297	15 586	Autriche[6]
Finland	237	215	306	253	212	230	184	182	116	...	Finlande
Portugal	149	229	295	317	171	157	117	135	111	142	Portugal
East Europe	***4 119***	***3 377***	***4 133***	***4 205***	***4 502***	***4 212***	***4 100***	***4 097***	***4 307***	***3 883***	***Europe de l'est***
Bulgaria	3 776	3 179	3 789	3 664	3 982	3 635	3 554	3 493	3 582	3 000	Bulgarie
Hungary	343	198	344	541	520	577	546	604	725	883	Hongrie
Other Europe	***14 489***	***14 089***	***13 573***	***12 134***	***6 383***	***14 777***	***7 715***	***3 372***	***5 271***	***4 125***	***Autre Europe***
Spain	13 434	...	...	11 470	5 340	13 869	6 851	2 466	...	...	Espagne
Yugoslavia	1 055	1 165	1 918	664	1 043	908	864	906	1 233	1 356	Yougoslavie
Total	**376 361**	**409 143**	**424 440**	**388 527**	**366 538**	**343 956**	**290 069**	**294 624**	**292 625**	**313 196**	**Total**

General note.
Broaching, centering and dividing, sawing, gear cutting, engraving, polishing, lapping and honing machine–tools. (SITC 71510–7).

[1] Shipments.
[2] Including planing, shaping and slotting machines.
[3] Deliveries.
[4] Sawing, cutting and straightening machines.
[5] Beginning 1982, data are confidential.
[6] Beginning 1978, data are not comparable with those for earlier years.

Remarque générale.
Machines à brocher, machines à pointer et à diviser, scies mécaniques, machines à tailler les engrenages, machines à graver, machines à polir, à roder et à affiler. (CTCI 71510–7).

[1] Expéditions.
[2] Y compris les raboteuses, étaux–limeurs et mortaiseuses.
[3] Livraisons.
[4] Machines à scier, à tronconner et à rectifier.
[5] A partir de 1982, les données sont confidentielles.
[6] A partir de 1978, les données ne sont pas comparables à celles des années antérieures.

Planing, shaping and slotting machines – Raboteuses, étaux–limeurs, mortaiseuses

Unit : Number units

Unité : Nombre

Country or area	1976	1977	1978	1979	1980	1981	1982	1983	1984	1985	Pays ou zone
America, South	**2 211**	**1 758**	**2 181**	**378**	**409**	**436**	**519**	**347**	**479**	**487**	**Amérique du Sud**
Brazil	2 179	1 732	1 847	# [1] 334	358	340	...	...	...	...	Brésil
Colombia	32	26	334	44	51	96	111	172	...	...	Colombie
Asia	**19 628**	**29 384**	**24 669**	**14 932**	**10 531**	**19 743**	**19 562**	**19 428**	**19 531**	**19 505**	**Asie**
China	...	28 000	23 000	13 000	9 000	...	...	...	...	...	Chine
Japan	818	808	876	936	800	762	581	447	550	524	Japon
Turkey	560	576	793	996	...	...	...	...	...	...	Turquie
Europe	**8 496**	**8 281**	**8 111**	**8 057**	**5 913**	**6 002**	**5 880**	**5 653**	**5 446**	**5 410**	**Europe**
EEC	***3 222***	***2 964***	***3 076***	***3 042***	***1 501***	***1 514***	***1 274***	***1 135***	***992***	***1 015***	***CEE***
Denmark	4	7	3	3	0	0	0	0	0	0	Danemark
France	225	182	...	...	...	...	...	...	...	...	France
Germany, Fed. Rep.	2 657	2 388	2 346	2 421	883	896	656	517	374	397	Allemagne, Rép. féd.
United Kingdom	336	387	524	...	...	...	...	...	...	...	Royaume–Uni
EFTA	***183***	***177***	***109***	***112***	***135***	***86***	***60***	***29***	***28***	***56***	***AELE***
Austria	43	46	30	45	44	36	25	12	12	13	Autriche
Portugal	* 33	37	36	24	48	48	33	17	16	41	Portugal
Sweden	107	94	43	43	43	2	2	0	0	...	Suède
East Europe	***4 045***	***4 009***	***3 739***	***3 832***	***3 471***	***3 584***	***3 591***	***3 677***	***3 644***	***3 579***	***Europe de l'est***
Bulgaria	204	...	18	81	103	127	125	116	135	170	Bulgarie
Czechoslovakia	119	64	78	80	69	20	6	5	16	7	Tchécoslovaquie
German Dem. Rep.	3 162	3 321	3 163	3 066	3 051	3 167	3 148	3 447	3 429	3 335	Rép. dém. allemande
Hungary	426	412	372	422	151	101	81	5	0	0	Hongrie
Poland	134	105	108	183	97	169	231	104	64	67	Pologne
Other Europe	***1 046***	***1 131***	***1 187***	***1 071***	***806***	***818***	***955***	***812***	***782***	***760***	***Autre Europe***
Spain	...	...	...	932	619	727	885	623	...	...	Espagne
Yugoslavia	115	235	326	139	187	91	70	189	130	143	Yougoslavie
Total	**30 335**	**39 423**	**34 961**	**23 367**	**16 853**	**26 181**	**25 961**	**25 428**	**25 456**	**25 402**	**Total**

General note.
Machines whose function is to remove metal. These machines are fitted with a baseplate, stand or other device for mounting on the floor or on a bench, wall or another machine. (SITC 71510–8).

[1] Production by establishments employing 5 or more persons.

Remarque générale.
Machines–outils dont la fonction est d'enlever du métal. Ces machines sont équipées d'un socle, d'un pied ou d'un autre dispositif permettant de les fixer au sol, à un établi, à une paroi ou à une autre machine. (CTCI 71510–8).

[1] Production des établissements occupant 5 personnes ou plus.

Metal–working presses – Presses pour le travail des métaux

Unit : Number units | Unité : Nombre

Country or area	1976	1977	1978	1979	1980	1981	1982	1983	1984	1985	Pays ou zone
America, North	**14 623**	**16 575**	**17 052**	**24 895**	**20 938**	**18 588**	**12 370**	**10 104**	**11 514**	**9 884**	**Amérique du Nord**
Canada	321	381	397	477	510	...	...	...	...	...	Canada
United States[1]	14 302	16 194	16 655	24 418	20 428	18 030	11 765	9 452	10 814	9 137	Etats–Unis[1]
America, South	**23 067**	**47 188**	**11 405**	**19 235**	**14 405**	**15 427**	**12 960**	**10 353**	**7 881**	**5 317**	**Amérique du Sud**
Brazil	22 602	46 811	10 966	[2] 18 636	13 943	...	...	...	...	...	Brésil
Colombia	...	377	439	599	462	61	106	12	...	...	Colombie
Asia	**13 258**	**13 529**	**15 525**	**18 876**	**21 524**	**22 658**	**15 934**	**16 978**	**22 731**	**20 162**	**Asie**
Japan	10 552	10 170	11 802	16 350	20 007	20 261	14 073	15 358	21 351	19 023	Japon
Korea, Republic of	2 382	3 011	3 364	2 150	1 166	2 046	...	...	...	...	Corée, République de
Turkey	324	348	359	376	...	...	...	...	...	...	Turquie
Europe	**40 035**	**48 441**	**36 961**	**34 012**	**29 597**	**27 491**	**27 689**	**29 757**	**29 661**	**28 681**	**Europe**
EEC	***29 758***	***38 789***	***27 506***	***23 832***	***20 174***	***17 157***	***17 546***	***18 230***	***19 800***	***18 676***	***CEE***
Denmark	4 120	4 418	3 529	3 240	* 4 037	...	...	...	...	...	Danemark
France[3]	2 686	2 376	2 441	2 295	1 983	1 388	1 120	1 171	1 166	1 082	France[3]
Germany, Fed. Rep.	19 031	24 729	14 537	12 783	11 483	10 296	11 550	12 538	14 153	13 289	Allemagne, Rép. féd.
Greece	...	...	...	...	...	...	...	...	475	...	Grèce
Netherlands[4]	...	619	638	550	657	634	511	284	...	...	Pays–Bas[4]
United Kingdom	2 723	6 172	5 886	4 489	1 539	897	557	562	552	...	Royaume–Uni
EFTA	***443***	***495***	***798***	***993***	***1 330***	***1 419***	***2 700***	***2 855***	***3 004***	***3 309***	***AELE***
Austria	117	131	106	105	157	86	75	51	69	79	Autriche
Finland	130	197	427	610	897	1 072	2 386	2 682	2 803	...	Finlande
Portugal	* 196	167	265	278	276	261	239	122	132	108	Portugal
East Europe	***3 576***	***3 220***	***3 027***	***3 084***	***3 407***	***3 738***	***3 596***	***3 733***	***3 635***	***3 765***	***Europe de l'est***
Bulgaria	1 290	1 318	1 198	937	...	...	...	...	...	...	Bulgarie
Czechoslovakia	1 994	1 681	1 704	1 819	1 817	1 749	1 729	1 753	1 540	1 581	Tchécoslovaquie
Poland	24	5	7	56	10	33	22	44	67	64	Pologne
Romania	268	216	118	272	395	771	...	...	...	...	Roumanie
Other Europe	***6 258***	***5 937***	***5 630***	***6 103***	***4 686***	***5 177***	***3 847***	***4 939***	***3 222***	***2 931***	***Autre Europe***
Spain	...	...	...	4 271	2 631	3 339	1 550	2 447	...	...	Espagne
Yugoslavia	1 065	1 213	1 375	1 832	2 055	1 838	2 297	2 492	1 783	1 961	Yougoslavie
Total	**90 983**	**125 733**	**80 943**	**97 018**	**86 464**	**84 164**	**68 953**	**67 192**	**71 787**	**64 044**	**Total**

General note.
Mechanical, hydraulic and pneumatic presses used for forging, stamping, cutting out etc. Forge hammers are excluded. (SITC 71511–1).

[1] Shipments.
[2] Production by establishments employing 5 or more persons.
[3] Deliveries.
[4] Industrial sales.

Remarque générale.
Presses à commande mécanique, hydraulique et pneumatique servant à forger, à estamper, à matricer etc. Cette rubrique ne comprend pas les outils agissant par chocs. (CTCI 71511–1).

[1] Expéditions.
[2] Production des établissements occupant 5 personnes ou plus.
[3] Livraisons.
[4] Ventes industrielles.

Other metal–forming machine–tools – Autres machines–outils à former les métaux

Unit : Number units

Unité : Nombre

Country or area	1976	1977	1978	1979	1980	1981	1982	1983	1984	1985	Pays ou zone
America, North	**43 271**	**47 389**	**52 625**	**57 172**	**54 908**	**48 636**	**36 439**	**38 315**	**45 884**	**44 327**	**Amérique du Nord**
United States[1]	43 271	47 389	52 625	57 172	54 908	48 636	36 439	38 315	45 884	44 327	Etats–Unis[1]
America, South	**2 051**	**530**	**2 051**	**1 766**	**1 363**	**4 547**	**2 051**	**2 051**	**2 051**	**2 051**	**Amérique du Sud**
Colombia	...	530	...	1 766	1 363	4 547	...	...	...	...	Colombie
Asia	**27 762**	**27 562**	**27 662**	**27 662**	**27 662**	**27 662**	**27 662**	**27 662**	**27 662**	**27 662**	**Asie**
Japan	27 762	27 562	...	...	...	...	...	...	...	...	Japon
Europe	**116 338**	**119 303**	**113 191**	**135 975**	**113 495**	**112 708**	**110 023**	**76 023**	**73 728**	**100 297**	**Europe**
EEC	***107 966***	***110 678***	***105 388***	***122 675***	***104 923***	***104 820***	***102 804***	***71 137***	***67 484***	***93 480***	***CEE***
Denmark	7 831	...	...	...	...	...	...	...	...	...	Danemark
France[2 3]	5 025	3 461	4 141	3 320	3 145	2 875	...	...	3 893	4 235	France[2 3]
Germany, Fed. Rep.	78 116	84 445	76 388	87 720	82 496	84 036	83 233	52 584	50 480	77 187	Allemagne, Rép. féd.
Netherlands[4]	6 350	4 919	5 235	5 543	4 600	3 732	3 099	4 108	...	...	Pays–Bas[4]
United Kingdom	10 644	10 022	11 793	18 261	6 851	6 346	4 948	2 955	2 203	...	Royaume–Uni
EFTA	***611***	***898***	***757***	***626***	***856***	***635***	***814***	***615***	***625***	***866***	***AELE***
Austria	483	462	276	433	496	356	443	384	433	611	Autriche
Portugal	128	436	481	193	360	279	371	231	192	...	Portugal
East Europe	***1 084***	***1 301***	***832***	***834***	***855***	***870***	***788***	***1 054***	***941***	***1 522***	***Europe de l'est***
Hungary	1 084	1 301	832	834	855	870	788	1 054	941	1 522	Hongrie
Other Europe	***6 677***	***6 426***	***6 214***	***11 840***	***6 861***	***6 383***	***5 617***	***3 217***	***4 678***	***4 429***	***Autre Europe***
Spain	...	...	...	11 362	6 763	6 294	5 523	3 180	...	...	Espagne
Yugoslavia	15	18	60	478	98	89	94	37	50	55	Yougoslavie
Total	**189 422**	**194 784**	**195 529**	**222 575**	**197 428**	**193 553**	**176 175**	**144 051**	**149 325**	**174 337**	**Total**

General note.
Other machine–tools for changing the shape or form of the metal without removing any of it, such as: riveting machines, bending and straightening machines, drawing machines, plate–working machines, shearing and notching machines, wire–drawing machines, thread–rolling machines. (SITC 71511–2).

[1] Shipments.
[2] Deliveries.
[3] 1982 and 1983, data are confidential.
[4] Industrial sales.

Remarque générale.
Autres machines–outils travaillant par déformation sans enlèvement de métal, notamment: machines à river, à cintrer, à dresser, à étirer, machines à travailler les tôles, à cisailler et à grignoter, machines à tréfiler, machines à fileter par roulage. (CTCI 71511–2).

[1] Expéditions.
[2] Livraisons.
[3] 1982 et 1983, les données sont confidentielles.
[4] Ventes industrielles.

Rolling mills for rolling metals – Laminoirs à métaux

Unit : Number units

Unité : Nombre

Country or area	1976	1977	1978	1979	1980	1981	1982	1983	1984	1985	Pays ou zone
Asia											**Asie**
Japan[1]	393	292	457	336	519	285	230	173	385	425	Japon[1]
Europe											**Europe**
EEC											***CEE***
Belgium[2]	...	...	...	...	...	...	...	13 867	...	...	Belgique[2]
Denmark	...	86	55	42	53	...	...	50	...	46	Danemark
Germany, Fed. Rep.[2]	183 413	125 802	119 763	136 059	139 490	172 481	172 288	134 285	152 931	105 958	Allemagne, Rép. féd.[2]
EFTA											***AELE***
Austria	11 669	10 161	10 978	9 555	...	...	...	...	...	...	Autriche
East Europe											***Europe de l'est***
Hungary	211	178	206	196	128	81	145	123	150	140	Hongrie
Poland	5	7	13	5	20	1	5	27	25	78	Pologne

General note.
Hot and cold rolling-mill machinery designed for rolling out to reduce the thickness with the corresponding increase in length, rolling of blooms, billets etc., to form a particular cross-section, rolling tubes, and rolling of wheel blanks or wheel-rim blanks. (SITC 71522-0).

[1] Including auxiliary equipment.
[2] In metric tons.

Remarque générale.
Machines pour laminage à chaud ou à froid destinées à réduire l'épaisseur du métal avec une augmentation correspondante de la longueur, laminoirs à blooms, à billettes etc., donnant des barres ou profilés de la section désirée, laminoirs à tubes, laminoirs à roues et à bandages. (CTCI 71522-0).

[1] Y compris l'équipement auxiliaire.
[2] En tonnes métriques.

Machine–tools for working wood –
Machines–outils pour le travail du bois

Unit : Number units

Unité : Nombre

Country or area	1976	1977	1978	1979	1980	1981	1982	1983	1984	1985	Pays ou zone
America, South											**Amérique du Sud**
Colombia	...	437	293	358	594	735	1 006	946	...	...	Colombie
Ecuador	...	185	194	...	1 650	1 911	313	7 376	...	...	Equateur
Asia											**Asie**
Japan	50 469	48 068	49 031	66 845	62 042	90 541	86 173	103 320	105 413	124 136	Japon
Turkey	4 373	4 430	5 684	5 836	...	...	...	...	...	...	Turquie
Europe											**Europe**
EEC											***CEE***
Belgium[1 2]	2 618	2 364	2 258	2 915	1 583	975	277	706	1 052	2 340	Belgique[1 2]
Denmark[3]	300	...	...	...	...	...	...	...	...	...	Danemark[3]
France[4 5]	15 437	17 028	17 437	16 135	17 311	17 836	...	16 330	66 393	49 476	France[4 5]
Germany, Fed. Rep.	824 565	920 393	1 066 227	1 111 362	1 331 101	1 274 472	...	...	...	...	Allemagne, Rép. féd.
Greece	1 989	2 058	1 851	1 847	2 800	2 496	2 283	2 921	2 437	...	Grèce
United Kingdom	16 787	19 681	21 192	18 873	15 113	16 122	11 328	6 881	6 350	...	Royaume–Uni
EFTA											***AELE***
Austria	39 844	31 695	25 454	30 433	32 089	29 193	31 816	32 260	34 764	32 611	Autriche
Finland[6]	1 855	2 135	3 136	1 743	2 286	3 819	3 405	3 651	4 662	...	Finlande[6]
Portugal	1 562	1 541	1 446	3 284	3 352	3 692	3 922	3 455	1 690	2 274	Portugal
East Europe											***Europe de l'est***
Bulgaria	2 434	2 240	2 130	771	1 155	1 231	5 941	8 435	12 406	12 173	Bulgarie
Czechoslovakia	39 329	40 031	42 206	47 386	51 690	57 204	45 685	62 033	59 429	56 092	Tchécoslovaquie
Hungary	2 112	2 021	3 045	1 521	1 223	1 766	1 703	857	1 367	2 097	Hongrie
Poland	28 264	31 705	25 908	33 020	39 946	32 653	32 757	31 341	41 847	44 193	Pologne
Romania[1]	29 928	32 338	31 592	31 545	31 396	...	...	...	...	...	Roumanie[1]
Other Europe											***Autre Europe***
Spain	6 190	...	...	13 397	8 958	7 737	4 573	4 335	...	...	Espagne
Yugoslavia	3 303	6 047	8 546	10 373	14 880	20 575	11 992	12 502	13 848	15 233	Yougoslavie
USSR											***URSS***
Ukrainian SSR	*8 908*	*8 948*	*9 502*	*8 305*	*9 099*	*8 867*	*8 654*	*8 691*	*8 968*	*9 327*	*RSS d'Ukraine*

General note.
Machines for shaping or surface–working wood (and also cork, bone, ebonite, plastic materials etc.), generally power–driven and designed to be mounted on the floor, a bench or a wall, such as wood de–barking machinery, sawing machines, slicing and paring machines, planing, profiling, grooving, mortising and tenoning, drilling, sandpapering machines, lathes, machinery for the cooperage industry etc. Tools for working in the hand, pneumatic or with self–contained electric or non–electric motor, are excluded. (SITC 71952–0).

[1] In metric tons.
[2] Shipments.
[3] Source: Industrial Statistics, Statistical Office of the European Communities, (Luxembourg).
[4] Deliveries.
[5] Machines over 150 kilogrammes.
[6] Main types of wood–working machines only.

Remarque générale.
Machines servant à façonner ou à travailler en surface le bois (et aussi le liège, l'os, l'ébonite, les matières plastiques etc.), généralement actionnées mécaniquement et conçues pour être fixées au sol, à un établi ou à une paroi, telles que machines à écorcer le bois, scies, machines à trancher et à dérouler, machines à raboter, à profiler, à rainurer, à mortaiser, à faire les tenons, à percer, à poncer, à meuler ou à polir, tours de tous types, machines pour tonnellerie etc. Cette rubrique ne comprend pas les outils à main pneumatiques ou à moteur électrique ou non électrique incorporé. (CTCI 71952–0).

[1] En tonnes métriques.
[2] Expéditions.
[3] Source: Statistiques industrielles, Office statistique des Communautés européennes, (Luxembourg).
[4] Livraisons.
[5] Machines de plus de 150 kilogrammes.
[6] Principaux types de machines à travailler le bois seulement.

Electro-mechanical hand tools – Outils et machines-outils électromécaniques, pour emploi à la main

Unit : Thousand units

Unité : En milliers

Country or area	1976	1977	1978	1979	1980	1981	1982	1983	1984	1985	Pays ou zone
America, North	**23 973**	**20 840**	**23 130**	**24 290**	**25 500**	**21 468**	**18 087**	**20 466**	**19 965**	**19 464**	**Amérique du Nord**
United States	...	20 840	23 130	24 290	25 500	...	18 087	...	...	...	Etats-Unis
Asia	**4 321**	**5 339**	**5 645**	**6 948**	**7 848**	**7 813**	**8 171**	**9 234**	**11 021**	**10 815**	**Asie**
Japan	4 321	5 339	5 645	6 948	7 848	7 813	8 171	9 234	11 021	10 815	Japon
Europe	**5 948**	**6 418**	**6 592**	**8 217**	**9 279**	**9 501**	**10 651**	**10 690**	**11 423**	**11 436**	**Europe**
EEC	***5 218***	***5 450***	***5 556***	***6 118***	***6 447***	***6 577***	***7 672***	***8 226***	***8 516***	***8 245***	***CEE***
Denmark	1	1	1	1	1	0	0	0	...	...	Danemark
Germany, Fed. Rep.	5 217	5 449	5 555	6 117	6 446	6 577	7 672	8 226	8 515	8 244	Allemagne, Rép. féd.
EFTA	***163***	***362***	***360***	***1 446***	***1 972***	***1 521***	***1 765***	***2 007***	***2 248***	***2 489***	***AELE***
Finland	122	311	315	1 397	1 865	1 434	...	...	...	...	Finlande
Sweden	41	51	45	49	107	...	...	...	...	...	Suède
East Europe	***45***	***50***	***50***	***54***	***42***	***60***	***77***	***77***	***50***	***51***	***Europe de l'est***
Hungary	45	50	50	54	42	60	77	77	50	51	Hongrie
Other Europe	***522***	***556***	***626***	***599***	***818***	***1 343***	***1 137***	***380***	***609***	***651***	***Autre Europe***
Spain	214	...	...	274	339	577	519	240	...	...	Espagne
Yugoslavia	308	282	325	325	479	766	618	140	144	158	Yougoslavie
Oceania	**353**	**346**	**337**	**307**	**307**	**307**	**193**	**307**	**307**	**307**	**Océanie**
Australia	353	346	337	...	...	...	193	...	...	...	Australie
Total	**34 595**	**32 943**	**35 704**	**39 762**	**42 934**	**39 089**	**37 102**	**40 696**	**42 716**	**42 022**	**Total**

General note.
Tools for working in the hand, with self-contained electric motor or vibrator. This heading excludes portable mechanical tools permanently fitted with a baseplate, stand or other device for mounting on the wall, bench or floor, electrical lawn mowers, electro-mechanical domestic appliances, and electric shavers and hair clippers. (SITC 72960-0).

Remarque générale.
Outils et machines-outils pour emploi à la main, avec moteur électrique ou vibreur incorporé. Cette rubrique ne comprend pas les outils ou machines-outils portatifs munis en permanence d'un socle, d'un pied ou d'un autre dispositif permettant de les fixer sur une paroi, sur un établi ou sur le sol, les tondeuses à gazon électriques, les appareils ménagers électromécaniques, les rasoirs et tondeuses électriques. (CTCI 72960-0).

Spinning machines – Machines à filer les textiles

Unit : Number of spindles

Unité : Nombre de broches

Country or area	1976	1977	1978	1979	1980	1981	1982	1983	1984	1985	Pays ou zone
America, North											**Amérique du Nord**
United States[1]	...	169 700	150 000	150 000	...	...	...	...	...	...	Etats–Unis[1]
America, South											**Amérique du Sud**
Asia											**Asie**
Japan[2]	5 207	5 145	4 689	4 813	5 598	4 114	3 222	3 543	4 686	5 177	Japon[2]
Pakistan	...	...	...	...	3 731	3 983	4 180	4 265	4 224	...	Pakistan
Europe											**Europe**
EEC											***CEE***
Belgium[3 4]	5 242	5 317	6 144	[1] 5 499	[1] 5 466	[1] 5 893	[1] 6 547	[1] 6 811	[1] 9 029	[1] 9 204	Belgique[3 4]
France[5]	240 262	237 877	261 840	138 904	97 034	97 055	57 745	# 12 372	23 690	24 930	France[5]
Germany, Fed. Rep.[3 6]	67 500	...	...	...	...	...	...	47 871	...	...	Allemagne, Rép. féd.[3 6]
East Europe											***Europe de l'est***
Czechoslovakia	289 463	244 314	212 096	210 725	237 352	193 592	197 112	194 990	200 496	207 536	Tchécoslovaquie
German Dem. Rep.[2]	594	379	391	463	378	483	207	224	242	142	Rép. dém. allemande[2]
Hungary	25 000	27 000	20 000	5 000	0	1 000	6 000	6 000	1 000	2 000	Hongrie
Poland	184 689	189 998	209 106	183 538	84 444	47 950	47 570	43 380	36 778	44 052	Pologne
Other Europe											***Autre Europe***
Yugoslavia	61 612	19 352	55 118	56 347	52 452	55 492	41 276	44 664	60 100	66 110	Yougoslavie
USSR[2]	5 025	5 188	4 997	4 892	4 372	4 826	4 334	3 328	3 862	3 911	**URSS[2]**

General note.
Machines for working up the various textile fibres, after preparation or special preliminary treatment, into yarns; spinning frames, the essential feature of which is the spinning mechanism associated with a revolving vertical or oblique spindle; flax, hemp, jute etc., spinning machines, intermittent spinning frames and continuous spinning frames for cotton, wool; throwing machines for twisting together continuous filaments of silk or of man–made textiles and "tow–to–yarn" machines (for breaking the filaments of the tow of synthetic or artificial continuous fibres, drawing out into a roving, and spinning into yarn). Machines for extruding man–made textiles in the form of monofilaments or of several filaments from a chemical composition forced through nozzles, and twisting and doubling machines for giving a supplementary torsion to yarns, are excluded. (SITC 71711–2).

[1] Shipments.
[2] In number of machines.
[3] In metric tons.
[4] Production of establishments employing 5 or more persons.
[5] Deliveries.
[6] Source: Industrial Statistics, Statistical Office of the European Communities, (Luxembourg).

Remarque générale.
Machines pour la transformation en filés des diverses matières textiles après préparation ou traitement préliminaire spécial; métiers à filer dont l'organe essentiel est le dispositif de torsion associé à un axe tournant vertical ou oblique (broche); métiers à filer le lin, le chanvre, le jute etc.; métiers à filer intermittents et métiers à filer continus pour le coton, la laine etc., machines à mouliner la soie ou à tordre les filaments continus de fibres synthétiques, machines dites "tow–to–yarn" ("câble–à–filé") (qui assurent la rupture des câbles de fibres snythétiques ou artificielles continues, l'étirage de la mèche de fibres discontinues ainsi formée et la filature). Cette rubrique ne comprend pas les machines à filer les matières textiles artificielles ou synthétiques sous la forme de fibres continues composées soit d'un monofilament ou de plusieurs filaments juxtaposés et obtenus par extrusion dans des presses à filer à partir d'une composition chimique, les métiers à retordre, les machines à doubler et à câbler et les assembleuses–retordeuses, qui ont pour fonction de donner aux fils une torsion supplémentaire. (CTCI 71711–2).

[1] Expéditions.
[2] En nombre de machines.
[3] En tonnes métriques.
[4] Production des établissements occupant 5 personnes ou plus.
[5] Livraisons.
[6] Source: Statistiques industrielles, Office statistique des Communautés européennes, (Luxembourg).

Knitting machines – Métiers à bonneterie

Unit : Number units | Unité : Nombre

Country or area	1976	1977	1978	1979	1980	1981	1982	1983	1984	1985	Pays ou zone
America, North											**Amérique du Nord**
United States*	...	1 500	1 500	1 500	...	...	...	...	...	...	Etats-Unis*
America, South											**Amérique du Sud**
Colombia	...	...	425	123	...	22	0	0	...	...	Colombie
Asia											**Asie**
Iran(Islamic Rep.of) [1]	6 250	...	...	...	...	232	444	337	...	...	Iran(Rép.islamique) [1]
Japan	6 390	6 606	7 406	8 103	8 856	11 658	10 950	14 834	15 209	14 623	Japon
Korea, Republic of	2 372	2 002	1 845	1 164	1 576	1 411	1 109	1 129	885	802	Corée, République de
Thailand	...	...	...	...	...	30 245	31 442	33 503	37 067	...	Thaïlande
Europe											**Europe**
EEC											***CEE***
Belgium [2] [3]	19 192	19 186	16 038	[4] 14 248	[4] 17 376	[4] 15 790	[4] 17 021	[4] 12 101	[4] 15 391	[4] 16 373	Belgique [2] [3]
Denmark	69	213	39	4	0	0	0	0	0	0	Danemark
France [5]	25	58	94	37	4	...	...	...	...	...	France [5]
Germany, Fed. Rep.	3 300	3 616	3 719	3 672	3 480	3 365	2 793	2 758	3 188	2 865	Allemagne, Rép. féd.
EFTA											***AELE***
Austria [2]	0	0	0	0	5	8	0	0	0	0	Autriche [2]
East Europe											***Europe de l'est***
Czechoslovakia	3 289	2 892	3 274	3 428	3 290	3 607	3 973	4 073	4 345	3 979	Tchécoslovaquie
Hungary	6	0	0	0	0	0	0	0	0	0	Hongrie
Poland [2]	546	37	132	113	69	94	71	103	273	312	Pologne [2]
Other Europe											***Autre Europe***
Spain	3 212	...	...	3 095	4 652	5 222	3 521	2 684	...	...	Espagne
Yugoslavia	1 661	737	696	397	581	342	188	190	...	...	Yougoslavie

General note.
Flat and circular knitting machines. Small domestic knitting machines are excluded. (SITC 71712-1).

[1] Production by establishments employing 10 or more persons.
[2] In metric tons.
[3] Including looms.
[4] Shipments.
[5] Deliveries.

Remarque générale.
Métiers à bonneterie rectilignes ou circulaires. Cette rubrique ne comprend pas les petites machines de ménage. (CTCI 71712-1).

[1] Production des établissements occupant 10 personnes ou plus.
[2] En tonnes métriques.
[3] Y compris les métiers à tisser.
[4] Expéditions.
[5] Livraisons.

Looms – Métiers à tisser

Unit : Number units

Unité : Nombre

Country or area	1976	1977	1978	1979	1980	1981	1982	1983	1984	1985	Pays ou zone
America, North											**Amérique du Nord**
United States	...	2 700	2 500	2 500	...	...	...	...	...	...	Etats–Unis
America, South											**Amérique du Sud**
Brazil	1 094	1 936	250	[1] 539	474	...	...	...	...	...	Brésil
Asia											**Asie**
Japan	17 817	15 158	16 765	21 402	25 733	22 412	15 547	17 867	23 158	16 998	Japon
Korea, Republic of	18 670	9 773	7 873	10 498	4 111	4 368	4 056	8 804	7 814	5 359	Corée, République de
Pakistan	...	...	...	...	26	25	25	24	24	...	Pakistan
Turkey	190	198	214	267	182	274	203	125	345	141	Turquie
Europe											**Europe**
EEC											***CEE***
Austria	580	247	649	599	570	1 007	829	395	470	685	Autriche
Denmark	...	...	2 819	2 756	3 052	2 950	2 767	2 662	2 325	2 151	Danemark
France	3 025	2 997	2 223	2 456	1 939	2 038	1 347	1 476	1 664	1 430	France
Germany, Fed. Rep.	2 032	1 852	2 061	2 080	1 932	1 905	1 766	1 873	1 889	2 061	Allemagne, Rép. féd.
EFTA											***AELE***
Austria	580	247	649	599	570	1 007	829	395	470	685	Autriche
Finland	396	395	592	351	362	373	381	382	391	...	Finlande
Portugal	51	132	152	249	423	448	542	315	252	339	Portugal
East Europe											***Europe de l'est***
Bulgaria	0	15	20	0	0	0	0	0	...	...	Bulgarie
Czechoslovakia	7 864	6 991	7 531	7 963	8 737	9 014	8 818	6 945	6 803	6 831	Tchécoslovaquie
German Dem. Rep.	2 788	2 800	2 719	2 905	3 059	2 757	2 572	1 639	2 044	2 148	Rép. dém. allemande
Hungary	14	5	7	9	6	10	15	0	0	0	Hongrie
Poland	2 292	1 654	964	678	622	539	478	436	308	329	Pologne
Other Europe											***Autre Europe***
Spain	1 348	...	...	742	772	609	575	660	...	...	Espagne
Yugoslavia	309	209	190	163	89	289	258	192	190	209	Yougoslavie
USSR	30 897	25 356	21 187	22 169	21 812	22 579	22 189	21 388	21 672	21 279	**URSS**

General note.
Machines for interlacing warp and weft yarns at right angles to form a fabric. They usually produce a flat fabric, but there are circular looms which produce a tubular fabric. Knitting machines and machines for making knotted net, tulle, braid etc. are excluded. (SITC 71712–2).

[1] Production by establishments employing 5 or more persons.

Remarque générale.
Machines servant à entrelacer à angle droit les fils de chaîne et les fils de trame de manière à former le tissu. Le plus souvent, elles produisent un tissu plat mais il existe des métiers circulaires qui produisent un tissu cylindrique. Cette rubrique ne comprend pas les machines à tricoter, les machines pour la fabrication des filets, des tulles, des tresses etc. (CTCI 71712–2).

[1] Production des établissements occupant 5 personnes ou plus.

Machinery for making or finishing cellulosic pulp etc. – Machines pour la fabrication ou le finissage de pâte cellulosique etc.

Unit : Number units

Unité : Nombre

Country or area	1976	1977	1978	1979	1980	1981	1982	1983	1984	1985	Pays ou zone
America, North											**Amérique du Nord**
United States	...	1 582	...	...	...	...	...	...	...	...	Etats-Unis
Asia											**Asie**
Japan	711	969	776	978	1 723	1 037	1 151	755	796	820	Japon
Europe											**Europe**
EEC											***CEE***
France[1 2]	13 890	13 310	13 010	12 350	16 260	15 060	12 770	14 640	14 200	11 000	France[1 2]
Germany, Fed. Rep.[2]	36 761	38 260	38 613	35 963	50 201	46 336	38 319	33 806	32 885	48 693	Allemagne, Rép. féd.[2]
EFTA											***AELE***
Austria[2 3]	3 885	7 554	12 681	7 370	5 692	4 657	7 650	6 405	4 118	9 442	Autriche[2 3]
Finland	521	983	1 426	2 621	3 531	6 550	7 488	5 502	# 17 542	...	Finlande
East Europe											***Europe de l'est***
Poland	98	14	4	6	...	...	...	...	...	...	Pologne
Other Europe											***Autre Europe***
Spain	9 985	...	...	1 085	2 493	1 587	1 306	2 048	...	...	Espagne

General note.
Machines for making pulp from various cellulosic materials (wood, esparto, grass, straw, rags, waste paper etc.). Including machinery for making paper or paper board, and machinery for finishing paper or paperboard ready for its various uses (that is, pulpmill machinery, papermill machinery, paper and paperboard converting equipment). (SITC 71811-1).

[1] Deliveries.
[2] In metric tons.
[3] Including papercutting, trimming etc. machines.

Remarque générale.
Machines pour transformer en pâte diverses matières riches en cellulose (bois, alfa, paille, chiffons, déchets de papier etc.). Y compris les machines à fabriquer ou à finir le papier ou le carton en vue de leurs diverses utilisations (c'est-à-dire machines pour usines de pâte à papier, machines de papeteries, matériel pour la transformation du papier et du carton). (CTCI 71811-1).

[1] Livraisons.
[2] En tonnes métriques.
[3] Y compris les coupeuses, rogneuses et autres machines à façonner le papier.

Paper cutting machines etc. – Coupeuses à papier etc.

Unit : Number units — Unité : Nombre

Country or area	1976	1977	1978	1979	1980	1981	1982	1983	1984	1985	Pays ou zone
Europe											**Europe**
EEC											***CEE***
France[1 2]	8 430	7 100	7 480	5 830	5 880	5 100	4 350	4 570	4 870	7 200	France[1 2]
Germany, Fed. Rep.[2]	61 011	56 405	58 479	65 372	65 073	68 585	59 971	57 793	63 536	74 818	Allemagne, Rép. féd.[2]
EFTA											***AELE***
Austria[2]	73	85	52	80	52	26	18	8	10	1	Autriche[2]
Finland	142	181	190	185	194	205	231	220	236	...	Finlande
East Europe											***Europe de l'est***
Hungary	2	13	21	72	175	119	198	264	280	322	Hongrie
Other Europe											***Autre Europe***
Spain	...	...	...	998	795	545	446	935	...	...	Espagne
Yugoslavia	60	48	54	* 55	90	92	95	246	846	931	Yougoslavie

General note.
This heading includes paper cutting and paper trimming machines, slitter–reelers, stacking machines, machines for making envelopes, for die–cutting, for cutting or grooving paper, for folding, for making paper bags, for folding and gluing cartons and boxes, for stapling, for forming waxed paper cups etc., and for moulding articles in paper pulp, paper or paperboard. (SITC 71812–0).

[1] Deliveries.
[2] In metric tons.

Remarque générale.
Cette rubrique comprend les machines à découper et à rogner le papier, les coupeuses–bobineuses, les machines à taquer et égaliser les feuilles, les machines à fabriquer les enveloppes, à découper à l'emporte–pièce, à couper ou à rainer le papier, les plieuses, les machines à fabriquer les sacs en papier, celles à plier et à coller les cartons et les boîtes, les machines à agrafer, les machines à former les gobelets en papier paraffiné etc., et les machines à mouler les articles en pâte à papier, papier ou carton. (CTCI 71812–0).

[1] Livraisons.
[2] En tonnes métriques.

Unit : Number units — Unité : Nombre

Country or area	1976	1977	1978	1979	1980	1981	1982	1983	1984	1985	Pays ou zone
Asia											**Asie**
Japan	4 473	4 422	4 990	5 089	5 627	5 915	5 893	6 199	8 323	8 053	Japon
Europe											**Europe**
EEC											***CEE***
France[1 2]	6 500	7 060	7 630	5 730	6 240	7 560	7 080	6 540	8 220	7 960	France[1 2]
Germany, Fed. Rep.[2]	78 656	93 108	114 549	113 286	118 160	113 476	109 316	113 801	123 928	144 429	Allemagne, Rép. féd.[2]
EFTA											***AELE***
Austria[2]	635	412	494	766	912	861	558	1 515	853	1 067	Autriche[2]
Finland	1	...	1	8	15	14	16	16	17	...	Finlande
East Europe											***Europe de l'est***
Hungary	283	113	42	35	26	22	21	4	5	403	Hongrie
Other Europe											***Autre Europe***
Spain	306	...	...	168	88	104	458	256	...	...	Espagne
USSR	1 861	1 951	1 178	1 121	1 074	1 047	812	745	705	1 173	**URSS**

General note.
Sheet– and roll–fed ordinary and platen presses, cylinder printing presses, and rotary presses, used industrially for typography, offset printing, photogravure or rotogravure. (SITC 71829–1).

1 Deliveries.
2 In metric tons.

Remarque générale.
Presses ordinaires et presses à platine, travaillant à plat ou sur rouleaux, presses à cylindre, presses rotatives, utilisées industriellement en typographie, en impression offset, en héliogravure et en rotogravure. (CTCI 71829–1).

1 Livraisons.
2 En tonnes métriques.

Unit : Number units — Unité : Nombre

Country or area	1976	1977	1978	1979	1980	1981	1982	1983	1984	1985	Pays ou zone
America, North	**19 430**	**19 877**	**22 058**	**16 735**	**13 179**	**12 318**	**8 476**	**4 657**	**8 160**	**7 321**	**Amérique du Nord**
United States[1 2]	19 430	19 877	22 058	16 735	13 179	12 318	8 476	4 657	8 160	7 321	Etats-Unis[1 2]
America, South	**11 631**	**10 069**	**12 181**	**10 574**	**2 581**	**1 569**	**3 095**	**1 596**	**98**	**1 569**	**Amérique du Sud**
Brazil	11 631	10 069	12 181	[3] 10 574	2 581	1 569	...	...	...	...	Brésil
Asia	**14 691**	**15 260**	**17 867**	**20 151**	**19 624**	**17 625**	**17 551**	**17 982**	**15 037**	**13 717**	**Asie**
India	796	863	941	...	...	...	...	...	...	...	Inde
Iran(Islamic Rep.of)[4 5]	...	...	...	54	163	367	461	421	...	...	Iran(Rép.islamique)[4 5]
Japan	13 785	14 244	16 731	19 155	18 514	16 269	16 148	16 592	13 789	12 264	Japon
Korea, Republic of	...	...	...	...	81	123	76	103	67	241	Corée, République de
Europe	**8 297**	**8 012**	**9 048**	**10 788**	**12 541**	**11 050**	**12 260**	**12 367**	**13 922**	**14 545**	**Europe**
EEC	***7 281***	***7 626***	***7 434***	***9 132***	***10 848***	***9 248***	***10 713***	***11 319***	***11 924***	***12 529***	***CEE***
Germany, Fed. Rep.[6]	7 281	7 626	7 434	9 132	10 848	9 248	...	...	...	...	Allemagne, Rép. féd.[6]
East Europe	***256***	***67***	***765***	***716***	***809***	***710***	***511***	***528***	***792***	***689***	***Europe de l'est***
Bulgaria	221	12	710	626	651	606	394	387	648	520	Bulgarie
Czechoslovakia	35	55	55	90	85	...	...	...	...	...	Tchécoslovaquie
Poland	0	0	0	0	73	0	0	10	0	...	Pologne
Other Europe	***760***	***319***	***849***	***940***	***884***	***1 092***	***1 036***	***520***	***1 206***	***1 327***	***Autre Europe***
Yugoslavia	760	319	849	940	884	1 092	1 036	520	1 206	1 327	Yougoslavie
USSR	**49 122**	**52 329**	**45 269**	**44 851**	**45 497**	**46 113**	**42 983**	**42 594**	**41 618**	**41 310**	**URSS**
Byelorussian SSR	*763*	*362*	*300*	*618*	*468*	*523*	*428*	*445*	*463*	*431*	*RSS de Biélorussie*
Ukrainian SSR	*23 431*	*27 040*	*25 250*	*24 515*	*23 975*	*23 994*	*18 100*	*15 438*	*15 009*	*12 986*	*RSS d'Ukraine*
Oceania	**658**	**610**	**562**	**572**	**463**	**521**	**123**	**321**	**272**	**316**	**Océanie**
Australia	...	...	...	572	463	521	123	...	272	316	Australie
Total	**103 829**	**106 157**	**106 985**	**103 671**	**93 885**	**89 196**	**84 488**	**79 517**	**79 107**	**78 778**	**Total**

General note.
Machines with large blades mounted squarely in front of a tractor unit used to level or clear away excess soil, debris etc. Angle dozers (or bullgraders) with blades mounted at an angle, and bulldozers designed for pushing down trees or for cutting through brush are included. (SITC 71842-1A).

Remarque générale.
Grandes lames conçues pour être montées sur tracteurs perpendiculairement au sens de la marche et destinées aux travaux de nivellement ou de déblaiement. Cette rubrique comprend les angledozers, ou lames montées obliquement et les bulldozers concus pour l'abattage des arbres par simple poussée sur le tronc ou pour le débroussaillage. (CTCI 71842-1A).

[1] Shipments.
[2] Bulldozers to be mounted on tracklaying tractors.
[3] Production by establishments employing 5 or more persons.
[4] Including excavating machines, and graders and levellers.
[5] Production by establishments employing 10 or more persons.
[6] Beginning 1982, series discontinued.

[1] Expéditions.
[2] Bouteurs à monter sur tracteurs chenillés.
[3] Production des établissements occupant 5 personnes ou plus.
[4] Y compris les machines d'excavation et les niveleuses-régleuses.
[5] Production des établissements occupant 10 personnes ou plus.
[6] A partir de 1982, la série a été abandonnée.

Excavating machines – Machines d'excavation

Unit : Number units — Unité : Nombre

Country or area	1976	1977	1978	1979	1980	1981	1982	1983	1984	1985	Pays ou zone
America, North	**4 420**	**5 239**	**6 199**	**6 519**	**4 044**	**2 853**	**2 040**	**2 638**	**3 623**	**3 220**	**Amérique du Nord**
United States[1]	4 420	5 239	6 199	6 519	4 044	2 853	2 040	2 638	3 623	3 220	Etats–Unis[1]
America, South	**640**	**415**	**641**	**715**	**1 155**	**890**	**639**	**936**	**988**	**1 040**	**Amérique du Sud**
Brazil	640	415	641	715	1 155	890	639	...	...	...	Brésil
Asia	**24 921**	**29 745**	**45 856**	**54 456**	**57 510**	**49 258**	**44 500**	**51 485**	**61 124**	**61 306**	**Asie**
India	190	141	170	...	...	...	...	...	...	...	Inde
Japan	24 451	29 324	45 590	53 829	57 063	48 478	43 521	49 186	58 270	58 001	Japon
Korea, Republic of	...	...	...	...	280	613	812	2 132	2 687	3 138	Corée, République de
Europe	**27 670**	**29 099**	**26 456**	**32 483**	**26 243**	**20 262**	**19 626**	**19 658**	**23 215**	**19 605**	**Europe**
EEC	***18 903***	***20 597***	***19 668***	***22 175***	***17 147***	***14 267***	***13 713***	***14 518***	***17 713***	***14 065***	***CEE***
Denmark	...	...	...	...	155	146	...	...	...	...	Danemark
Germany, Fed. Rep.[2]	5 038	5 431	6 472	7 556	7 031	5 653	...	...	...	...	Allemagne, Rép. féd.[2]
United Kingdom	13 715	15 016	13 046	14 469	9 961	8 468	6 471	7 020	9 960	...	Royaume–Uni
EFTA	***1 465***	***1 115***	***1 323***	***1 395***	***1 694***	***1 454***	***1 114***	***401***	***337***	***559***	***AELE***
Finland	1 465	1 115	1 323	1 395	1 694	1 454	1 114	401	337	...	Finlande
East Europe	***5 070***	***5 376***	***5 375***	***5 513***	***4 859***	***4 037***	***4 470***	***4 486***	***4 685***	***4 453***	***Europe de l'est***
Czechoslovakia	656	884	593	642	748	784	683	655	572	676	Tchécoslovaquie
German Dem. Rep.	692	713	705	...	...	...	...	...	...	...	Rép. dém. allemande
Hungary	2	0	0	0	4	1	9	1	3	33	Hongrie
Poland	2 475	2 400	2 430	2 508	2 206	1 741	2 306	2 336	2 419	2 144	Pologne
Romania	1 245	1 379	1 647	1 660	1 198	808	769	791	988	897	Roumanie
Other Europe	***2 232***	***2 011***	***90***	***3 400***	***2 543***	***504***	***329***	***253***	***480***	***528***	***Autre Europe***
Yugoslavia	...	...	90	3 400	2 543	504	329	253	480	528	Yougoslavie
USSR	**40 408**	**41 523**	**41 139**	**41 690**	**41 956**	**42 257**	**42 663**	**41 807**	**41 857**	**42 551**	**URSS**
Ukrainian SSR	*9 269*	*9 351*	*9 357*	*9 725*	*9 874*	*10 122*	*9 830*	*9 435*	*9 328*	*10 006*	*RSS d'Ukraine*
Total	**98 059**	**106 021**	**120 291**	**135 863**	**130 908**	**115 520**	**109 468**	**116 524**	**130 807**	**127 722**	**Total**

General note.
Boom, jib and cable types which dig into the soil, above or below machine level, by means of an excavating bucket, grab etc., multi–bucket excavators in which the digging buckets are fitted on endless chains or on rotating wheels, dredgers (bucket or shovel type) other than floating dredgers, railroad ballast excavator–screening machines consisting essentially of a continuous chain of buckets which dig the ballast from under railway tracks. (SITC 71842–2).

[1] Shipments.
[2] Beginning 1982, data are confidential.

Remarque générale.
Pelles mécaniques et excavatrices à godet suspendu, creusant le sol en butte ou en fouille, au moyen d'un godet tranchant ou à griffes etc., excavateurs continus à godets excavateurs disposés en chapelet sur une chaîne sans fin ou la périphérie d'une roue, engins de dragage non flottants (à godet ou à pelle), machines dégarnisseuses et cribleuses de ballast, se composant essentiellement d'un chapelet de godets piocheurs qui reprennent le ballast se trouvant sous la voie. (CTCI 71842–2).

[1] Expéditions.
[2] A partir de 1982, les données sont confidentielles.

Graders and levellers – Niveleuses–régleuses

Unit : Number units — Unité : Nombre

Country or area	1976	1977	1978	1979	1980	1981	1982	1983	1984	1985	Pays ou zone
America, North	**6 262**	**6 706**	**7 372**	**7 257**	**7 165**	**5 947**	**4 006**	**3 443**	**4 816**	**4 936**	**Amérique du Nord**
United States[1]	6 262	6 706	7 372	7 257	7 165	5 947	4 006	3 443	4 816	4 936	Etats–Unis[1]
Asia	**18 298**	**19 647**	**24 662**	**39 690**	**57 837**	**51 537**	**54 243**	**55 070**	**56 761**	**58 761**	**Asie**
India	256	546	...	...	...	...	...	...	...	...	Inde
Japan	18 042	19 101	24 261	39 289	57 436	51 136	53 842	54 669	56 360	58 360	Japon
Europe	**6 137**	**6 565**	**6 267**	**6 495**	**6 264**	**7 184**	**7 904**	**7 924**	**7 252**	**6 225**	**Europe**
EEC	***4 479***	***4 868***	***4 673***	***4 673***	***4 673***	***5 137***	***5 879***	***5 668***	***5 633***	***5 095***	***CEE***
Denmark	0	0	0	0	0	...	1 206	995	960	422	Danemark
United Kingdom	4 479	4 868	...	...	...	...	...	...	...	...	Royaume–Uni
EFTA	***704***	***632***	***720***	***1 007***	***1 111***	***1 426***	***1 471***	***1 804***	***1 189***	***764***	***AELE***
Finland	...	...	...	44	66	84	66	112	77	...	Finlande
Portugal	87	34	140	357	422	755	912	1 202	622	381	Portugal
Sweden	587	560	534	606	623	587	493	490	490	280	Suède
East Europe	***894***	***1 011***	***800***	***711***	***414***	***550***	***476***	***402***	***328***	***254***	***Europe de l'est***
Romania	894	1 011	800	711	414	...	...	...	...	...	Roumanie
Other Europe	***60***	***54***	***74***	***104***	***66***	***71***	***78***	***50***	***102***	***112***	***Autre Europe***
Yugoslavia	60	54	74	104	66	71	78	50	102	112	Yougoslavie
USSR	**8 860**	**9 182**	**8 907**	**7 660**	**8 175**	**7 544**	**7 759**	**7 578**	**6 532**	**6 525**	**URSS**
Oceania	**1 695**	**1 695**	**1 695**	**1 695**	**1 695**	**1 695**	**1 778**	**2 435**	**1 029**	**1 538**	**Océanie**
Australia	...	...	...	...	...	...	1 778	2 435	1 029	1 538	Australie
Total	**41 252**	**43 795**	**48 903**	**62 797**	**81 136**	**73 907**	**75 690**	**76 450**	**76 390**	**77 985**	**Total**

General note.
Machines, usually self–propelled, designed for earth–levelling or smoothing (on flat surfaces or banks) by means of an adjustable grading blade, usually mounted within the wheel base. (SITC 71842–3).

[1] Shipments.

Remarque générale.
Machines, généralement automotrices, conçues pour niveler et régulariser le terrain, même en talus, à l'aide d'une lame réglable et inclinable sur l'horizontale, généralement montée dans l'empattement des rues. (CTCI 71842–3).

[1] Expéditions.

Scrapers – Décapeuses (scrapers)

Unit : Number units

Unité : Nombre

Country or area	1976	1977	1978	1979	1980	1981	1982	1983	1984	1985	Pays ou zone
America, North	**4 186**	**4 915**	**5 112**	**4 215**	**2 571**	**2 484**	**1 226**	**1 290**	**2 740**	**3 523**	**Amérique du Nord**
Cuba	283	0	100	140	0	81	2	2	0	0	Cuba
United States[1]	3 903	4 915	5 012	4 075	2 571	2 403	1 224	1 288	2 740	3 523	Etats–Unis[1]
America, South	**1 576**	**750**	**1 019**	**198**	**1 500**	**810**	**735**	**666**	**598**	**529**	**Amérique du Sud**
Brazil	1 576	750	1 019	[2] 198	1 500	810	...	...	...	...	Brésil
Asia	**46**	**31**	**46**	**58**	**54**	**21**	**71**	**33**	**4**	**28**	**Asie**
India	46	31	46	58	54	21	71	...	4	...	Inde
Europe	**1 208**	**1 032**	**930**	**955**	**1 005**	**1 124**	**893**	**802**	**886**	**877**	**Europe**
EEC	***665***	***704***	***684***	***684***	***684***	***684***	***684***	***684***	***684***	***684***	***CEE***
United Kingdom	665	704	...	...	...	...	...	...	...	...	Royaume–Uni
EFTA	***188***	***214***	***94***	***151***	***135***	***114***	***18***	***15***	***13***	***13***	***AELE***
Sweden	188	214	94	151	135	114	18	15	13	...	Suède
East Europe	***290***	***85***	***70***	***70***	***60***	***152***	***95***	***26***	***75***	***55***	***Europe de l'est***
Bulgaria	15	0	0	0	0	82	70	1	38	42	Bulgarie
Czechoslovakia	275	85	70	70	60	70	25	25	37	13	Tchécoslovaquie
Other Europe	***65***	***29***	***82***	***50***	***126***	***174***	***96***	***77***	***114***	***125***	***Autre Europe***
Yugoslavia	* 65	29	82	50	126	174	96	77	114	125	Yougoslavie
USSR	**14 053**	**12 944**	**11 766**	**11 984**	**11 430**	**11 316**	**9 895**	**11 210**	**11 239**	**10 228**	**URSS**
Byelorussian SSR	*2 002*	*2 022*	*2 013*	*2 004*	*2 010*	*1 900*	*2 050*	*2 059*	*2 131*	*2 166*	*RSS de Biélorussie*
Ukrainian SSR	*10 037*	*8 895*	*8 268*	*8 415*	*8 016*	*7 910*	*6 277*	*7 762*	*7 633*	*6 558*	*RSS d'Ukraine*
Total	**21 069**	**19 672**	**18 873**	**17 410**	**16 560**	**15 755**	**12 820**	**14 001**	**15 467**	**15 185**	**Total**

General note.
Machines incorporating a sharp cutting edge designed to slice off a layer of top soil which is then passed into the scraper body or discharged by a conveyor. Scrapers with incorporated tractor are included. (SITC 71842–4).

[1] Shipments.
[2] Production by establishments employing 5 or more persons.

Remarque générale.
Machines munies d'une lame horizontale coupante travaillant en rabot par découpage d'une couche de terrain, les déblais étant évacués soit dans un chariot de charge incorporé soit au moyen d'un convoyeur à bande. Cette rubrique comprend les scrapers automoteurs. (CTCI 71842–4).

[1] Expéditions.
[2] Production des établissements occupant 5 personnes ou plus.

Concrete mixers for use at construction sites – Bétonnières pour chantiers de construction

Unit : Number units | Unité : Nombre

Country or area	1976	1977	1978	1979	1980	1981	1982	1983	1984	1985	Pays ou zone
America, North	**4 827**	**4 901**	**11 013**	**14 187**	**25 339**	**22 027**	**13 496**	**23 747**	**43 182**	**26 779**	**Amérique du Nord**
United States[1 2]	4 827	4 901	...	...	25 339	22 027	13 496	23 747	43 182	26 779	Etats–Unis[1 2]
America, South	**11 226**	**11 208**	**12 361**	**13 402**	**18 166**	**11 398**	**15 236**	**15 886**	**16 537**	**17 187**	**Amérique du Sud**
Brazil	11 226	11 208	12 361	[3] 13 402	18 166	11 398	...	...	...	...	Brésil
Asia	**12 404**	**8 797**	**4 495**	**3 696**	**1 911**	**1 583**	**1 144**	**1 190**	**1 059**	**1 527**	**Asie**
Japan	11 503	8 188	3 740	2 941	1 156	828	553	516	415	...	Japon
Philippines[1]	545	253	...	...	...	...	...	...	...	...	Philippines[1]
Turkey	...	...	...	...	...	...	192	275	245	713	Turquie
Europe	**284 122**	**301 909**	**325 146**	**417 603**	**392 871**	**351 726**	**310 401**	**302 566**	**254 008**	**241 809**	**Europe**
EEC	***190 620***	***199 997***	***212 525***	***241 211***	***214 237***	***179 331***	***153 086***	***147 370***	***119 419***	***106 445***	***CEE***
Germany, Fed. Rep.	164 553	172 983	181 422	206 895	189 568	155 644	137 783	132 850	109 981	95 594	Allemagne, Rép. féd.
Greece	...	...	...	...	...	2 218	2 630	2 152	1 297	...	Grèce
United Kingdom[4]	23 993	24 940	29 029	32 242	22 595	21 469	12 673	12 368	8 141	...	Royaume–Uni[4]
EFTA	***2 897***	***3 335***	***3 194***	***3 930***	***4 858***	***4 510***	***4 253***	***8 443***	***7 507***	***7 808***	***AELE***
Finland	2 897	3 335	3 194	3 930	4 858	4 510	4 253	8 443	7 507	...	Finlande
East Europe	***53 728***	***57 284***	***64 094***	***68 783***	***72 311***	***71 733***	***64 319***	***63 795***	***61 825***	***56 774***	***Europe de l'est***
Bulgaria	610	578	423	331	390	586	321	201	0	161	Bulgarie
Czechoslovakia	13 421	12 320	17 559	19 210	22 594	22 627	15 899	14 978	15 064	15 787	Tchécoslovaquie
German Dem. Rep.	17 051	19 881	19 928	21 084	23 964	22 936	21 230	21 010	18 665	12 952	Rép. dém. allemande
Hungary	1 986	3 405	3 946	4 616	3 478	3 699	4 984	5 721	6 211	5 989	Hongrie
Poland	20 660	21 100	22 238	23 542	...	...	...	...	...	...	Pologne
Other Europe	***36 877***	***41 293***	***45 333***	***103 679***	***101 465***	***96 152***	***88 743***	***82 958***	***65 257***	***70 782***	***Autre Europe***
Spain	...	...	...	10 687	10 297	9 047	...	...	...	...	Espagne
Yugoslavia	26 867	31 283	35 323	92 992	91 168	87 105	78 733	72 948	55 247	60 772	Yougoslavie
USSR	**32 300**	**31 117**	**32 603**	**32 096**	**29 609**	**29 140**	**28 708**	**28 068**	**21 323**	**21 889**	**URSS**
Ukrainian SSR	*1 585*	*1 543*	*1 881*	*1 862*	*1 732*	*1 721*	*1 688*	*1 704*	*2 078*	*1 954*	*RSS d'Ukraine*
Total	**344 879**	**357 932**	**385 618**	**480 984**	**467 896**	**415 874**	**368 985**	**371 457**	**336 109**	**309 191**	**Total**

General note.
Machines consisting essentially of a container, equipped with paddles or other stirring devices, for mixing concrete or mortar by stirring or agitation. The item is confined to mixers of the types used at construction sites. Mixers permanently mounted on a railway wagon or on a lorry chassis are excluded. (SITC 71851–1).

Remarque générale.
Machines consistant essentiellement en un récipient dans lequel le malaxage du béton et du mortier est effectué à l'aide de palettes ou d'autres dispositifs appropriés. Cette rubrique ne comprend que les bétonnières de tous types utilisées sur les chantiers de construction. Elle ne comprend pas les bétonnières montées de façon permanente sur wagon de chemin de fer ou sur châssis de camion. (CTCI 71851–1).

[1] Shipments.
[2] Including portable truck concrete mixers.
[3] Production by establishments employing 5 or more persons.
[4] Data refer to concrete mixers and placing machinery.

[1] Expéditions.
[2] Y compris les bétonières à chariot mobile.
[3] Production des établissements occupant 5 personnes ou plus.
[4] Données se rapportant aux bétonneuses et au matériel de mise en place.

Typewriters – Machines à écrire

Unit : Thousand units — Unité : En milliers

Country or area	1976	1977	1978	1979	1980	1981	1982	1983	1984	1985	Pays ou zone
America, North	**1 770**	**1 732**	**1 717**	**2 006**	**2 125**	**2 079**	**2 071**	**1 995**	**2 088**	**2 088**	**Amérique du Nord**
Mexico	324	441	424	469	533	600	500	387	442	405	Mexique
United States[1] [2]	1 446	1 291	1 293	1 537	1 592	1 479	...	...	...	...	Etats–Unis[1] [2]
America, South	**489**	**568**	**479**	**609**	**819**	**794**	**864**	**924**	**997**	**1 065**	**Amérique du Sud**
Brazil	461	547	449	[3] 582	794	773	...	...	...	...	Brésil
Colombia	28	21	30	27	25	21	20	10	...	...	Colombie
Asia	**1 627**	**2 032**	**1 938**	**2 056**	**2 712**	**3 141**	**2 937**	**3 390**	**4 873**	**4 681**	**Asie**
India	60	65	83	93	94	90	118	107	113	122	Inde
Japan	1 564	1 963	1 844	1 932	2 588	2 998	2 744	3 190	4 665	4 449	Japon
Korea, Republic of	3	4	11	31	30	53	75	93	95	110	Corée, République de
Europe	**4 107**	**4 068**	**3 805**	**3 747**	**3 728**	**3 521**	**3 033**	**2 907**	**3 270**	**3 408**	**Europe**
EEC	***2 278***	***2 323***	***2 090***	***1 883***	***1 893***	***1 555***	***1 519***	***1 444***	***1 673***	***1 958***	***CEE***
Germany, Fed. Rep.	1 303	1 251	1 190	975	934	740	710	646	723	1 105	Allemagne, Rép. féd.
Italy	582	695	557	537	588	444	438	427	579	482	Italie
United Kingdom	393	377	343	...	...	...	...	...	...	...	Royaume–Uni
EFTA	***153***	***132***	***114***	***124***	***123***	***98***	***79***	***75***	***89***	***58***	***AELE***
Sweden	153	132	114	124	123	98	79	75	89	58	Suède
East Europe	***644***	***515***	***554***	***614***	***679***	***865***	***771***	***786***	***778***	***760***	***Europe de l'est***
Bulgaria	82	119	128	128	158	181	111	91	102	115	Bulgarie
Czechoslovakia	53	54	56	66	75	83	81	88	87	84	Tchécoslovaquie
German Dem. Rep.	407	# [4] 232	[4] 219	[4] 224	[4] 227	[4] 433	[4] 462	[4] 537	[4] 530	[4] 497	Rép. dém. allemande
Hungary	23	33	66	106	142	109	75	26	5	5	Hongrie
Poland	79	77	85	90	77	59	42	44	54	59	Pologne
Other Europe	***1 032***	***1 098***	***1 047***	***1 126***	***1 033***	***1 003***	***664***	***602***	***730***	***632***	***Autre Europe***
Spain	799	858	...	# [5] 871	[5] 769	[5] 703	[5] 373	[5] 336	...	...	Espagne
Yugoslavia	233	240	251	255	264	300	291	266	366	340	Yougoslavie
Total	**7 993**	**8 400**	**7 939**	**8 418**	**9 384**	**9 535**	**8 905**	**9 216**	**11 228**	**11 242**	**Total**

General note.
Manual or electric typewriters except those incorporating calculating mechanisms. Excluding cheque–writing machines. (SITC 71410–1).

[1] Shipments.
[2] Including word processors.
[3] Production by establishments employing 5 or more persons.
[4] Standard typewriters only.
[5] Including calculating machines.

Remarque générale.
Machines à écrire, mécaniques ou électriques, à l'exception de celles comprenant un dispositif de totalisation et des machines à écrire les chèques. (CTCI 71410–1).

[1] Expéditions.
[2] Y compris les systèmes de traitement de textes.
[3] Production des établissements occupant 5 personnes ou plus.
[4] Machines à ecrire ordinaires.
[5] Y compris de machines à calculer.

Calculating machines – Machines à calculer

Unit : Thousand units

Unité : En milliers

Country or area	1976	1977	1978	1979	1980	1981	1982	1983	1984	1985	Pays ou zone
America, North	**12 189**	**13 452**	**15 428**	**12 574**	**15 373**	**10 269**	**3 737**	**2 847**	**3 900**	**2 560**	**Amérique du Nord**
Cuba	0	2	10	11	14	7	...	7	5	2	Cuba
Mexico	157	142	96	80	83	274	293	122	168	352	Mexique
United States	12 032	13 308	15 322	12 483	15 276	9 988	3 438	2 718	...	...	Etats-Unis
America, South	**959**	**753**	**1 236**	**2 043**	**1 951**	**1 633**	**2 501**	**3 861**	**3 088**	**3 381**	**Amérique du Sud**
Brazil[1]	949	736	1 210	1 917	1 922	1 597	...	...	...	...	Brésil[1]
Colombia	9	16	24	23	25	...	...	...	...	...	Colombie
Ecuador	...	1	2	...	4	5	...	# 1 469	...	...	Equateur
Asia	**42 376**	**34 337**	**47 224**	**52 193**	**65 020**	**56 570**	**63 171**	**73 139**	**94 204**	**106 162**	**Asie**
China	...	...	...	...	673	653	1 788	3 708	7 839	17 900	Chine
Japan	40 426	31 835	42 319	45 996	60 356	52 435	58 438	66 547	83 713	86 032	Japon
Korea, Republic of	1 297	1 849	4 252	5 509	3 991	3 482	2 945	2 884	2 652	2 230	Corée, République de
Europe	**1 805**	**1 682**	**1 361**	**1 112**	**838**	**943**	**654**	**588**	**802**	**1 097**	**Europe**
EEC	***905***	***926***	***642***	***293***	***83***	***139***	***75***	***31***	***31***	***31***	***CEE***
Germany, Fed. Rep.[2]	698	723	414	100	31	135	...	...	...	...	Allemagne, Rép. féd.[2]
Italy	207	203	228	193	52	4	0	0	0	0	Italie
EFTA	***174***	***34***	***0***	***0***	***0***	***0***	***23***	***14***	***5***	***34***	***AELE***
Sweden	174	34	0	0	0	0	...	...	...	...	Suède
East Europe	***589***	***608***	***593***	***701***	***625***	***694***	***446***	***433***	***656***	***922***	***Europe de l'est***
Czechoslovakia	42	34	29	30	38	36	36	36	35	17	Tchécoslovaquie
German Dem. Rep.	150	181	223	298	335	407	258	239	446	680	Rép. dém. allemande
Hungary	45	63	34	19	13	11	5	7	5	6	Hongrie
Poland	...	...	...	354	239	...	147	151	170	219	Pologne
Other Europe	***137***	***114***	***126***	***118***	***130***	***111***	***110***	***110***	***110***	***110***	***Autre Europe***
Spain	121	* 98	...	...	...	...	...	...	...	...	Espagne
Yugoslavia	16	16	16	8	20	1	0	0	...	...	Yougoslavie
Total	**57 329**	**50 224**	**65 249**	**67 921**	**83 181**	**69 415**	**70 064**	**80 435**	**101 994**	**113 200**	**Total**

General note.
Calculating machines involving a simple calculating device and usually designed to perform one or more of the four arithmetical operations. Excluding accounting machines and similar machines incorporating a calculating device. (SITC 71420-1).

Remarque générale.
Machines à calculer mettant en jeu un simple dispositif de calcul et généralement conçues pour effectuer une ou plusieurs des quatre opérations arithmétiques. Cette rubrique ne comprend pas les machines comptables ou analogues dans lesquelles un tel dispositif est incorporé. (CTCI 71420-1).

[1] Production by establishments employing 5 or more persons.
[2] Beginning 1982, data are confidential.

[1] Production des établissements occupant 5 personnes ou plus.
[2] A partir de 1982, les données sont confidentielles.

Scales, industrial – Balances et bascules industrielles

Unit : Number units | Unité : Nombre

Country or area	1976	1977	1978	1979	1980	1981	1982	1983	1984	1985	Pays ou zone
America, North											**Amérique du Nord**
Canada	...	3 290	...	...	...	...	...	...	...	...	Canada
America, South											**Amérique du Sud**
Brazil	39 910	51 392	63 128	[1]76 264	47 123	71 657	...	...	...	...	Brésil
Colombia	...	20 358	34 659	15 798	27 531	21 588	26 067	16 421	...	...	Colombie
Asia											**Asie**
Japan	16 541	19 419	19 799	22 206	23 383	21 839	21 664	22 288	23 001	28 329	Japon
Turkey[2]	30 442	30 047	31 179	30 995	...	...	...	...	...	...	Turquie[2]
Europe											**Europe**
EEC											***CEE***
Belgium[3]	...	...	...	...	...	...	...	1 545	...	...	Belgique[3]
France[4 5]	11 959	12 762	9 511	8 396	8 245	7 856	7 591	# 9 535	10 217	19 429	France[4 5]
Germany, Fed. Rep.	217 436	213 854	212 954	207 084	224 959	195 925	179 423	173 932	218 980	237 276	Allemagne, Rép. féd.
EFTA											***AELE***
Austria[3]	1 877	2 034	2 389	2 109	1 596	1 698	1 137	1 065	1 106	1 020	Autriche[3]
Finland	1 981	1 851	1 934	1 921	1 951	1 990	1 995	1 990	1 994	...	Finlande
Portugal	13 135	117 621	64 741	62 189	61 228	54 946	59 749	64 558	...	...	Portugal
East Europe											***Europe de l'est***
Hungary	395	319	260	261	114	142	6 278	4 946	3 419	2 956	Hongrie
Other Europe											***Autre Europe***
Spain	10 822	...	...	5 604	3 758	4 019	4 765	5 967	...	...	Espagne

General note.
Machines for the direct determination of the weight of objects, such as floor scales, bulk material weighers, predetermined weighing and check–weighing scales, and miscellaneous industrial scales. Retail, commercial and household scales and balances are excluded. (SITC 71963–1).

1 Production by establishments employing 5 or more persons.
2 Including other scales.
3 In metric tons.
4 Deliveries.
5 Scales and balances of all types with a capacity of less than 200 kilogrammes.

Remarque générale.
Machines pour la détermination directe du poids des objets, telles que les bascules à plate–forme, les balances pour matières en vrac, les balances vérificatrices indiquant les excédents ou déficits par rapport à un poids prédéterminé et diverses balances industrielles. Cette rubrique ne comprend pas les balances utilisées dans le commerce de détail ou de gros et les balances de ménage. (CTCI 71963–1).

1 Production des établissements occupant 5 personnes ou plus.
2 Y compris les autres balances et bascules.
3 En tonnes métriques.
4 Livraisons.
5 Balances et bascules de tous types, d'une portée inférieure à 200 kilogramme.

Scales, other than industrial – Autres balances et bascules

Unit : Thousand units — Unité : En milliers

Country or area	1976	1977	1978	1979	1980	1981	1982	1983	1984	1985	Pays ou zone
America, North	**416**	**416**	**416**	**416**	**416**	**416**	**416**	**416**	**416**	**416**	**Amérique du Nord**
Canada	...	416	...	...	...	...	...	...	...	...	Canada
America, South	**262**	**115**	**63**	**107**	**131**	**83**	**65**	**55**	**42**	**27**	**Amérique du Sud**
Brazil	[1] 242	[1] 96	[1] 45	[1] 84	* 115	...	...	...	...	...	Brésil
Chile	...	...	...	23	16	11	8	13	15	15	Chili
Europe	**8 377**	**7 784**	**7 735**	**7 623**	**7 721**	**7 189**	**5 148**	**4 793**	**4 792**	**4 439**	**Europe**
EEC	***7 881***	***7 290***	***7 239***	***7 128***	***7 224***	***6 622***	***4 750***	***4 315***	***4 215***	***3 929***	***CEE***
Denmark	137	94	94	52	44	...	...	...	17	8	Danemark
France[2 3]	2 093	2 042	2 693	2 890	3 632	2 888	1 759	# 1 752	2 105	2 244	France[2 3]
Germany, Fed. Rep.[4]	5 603	5 106	4 404	4 138	3 500	3 637	...	...	...	...	Allemagne, Rép. féd.[4]
Greece	...	...	...	...	...	...	...	58	37	...	Grèce
EFTA	***13***	***13***	***13***	***13***	***13***	***13***	***13***	***13***	***13***	***13***	***AELE***
Finland	...	13	...	...	...	...	...	...	...	...	Finlande
East Europe	***9***	***6***	***5***	***4***	***3***	***4***	***3***	***4***	***3***	***3***	***Europe de l'est***
Hungary	9	6	5	4	3	4	3	4	3	3	Hongrie
Other Europe	***475***	***476***	***479***	***479***	***482***	***551***	***382***	***461***	***562***	***494***	***Autre Europe***
Spain	27	...	...	31	35	48	23	50	...	...	Espagne
Yugoslavia	...	...	...	...	...	503	359	411	518	...	Yougoslavie
Total	**9 054**	**8 315**	**8 213**	**8 146**	**8 268**	**7 688**	**5 629**	**5 264**	**5 250**	**4 881**	**Total**

General note.
Machines for the direct determination of the weight of objects such as retail and commercial scales, person–weighing scales and miscellaneous household scales. (SITC 71963–2).

[1] Production by establishments employing 5 or more persons.
[2] Deliveries.
[3] Scales and balances of all types with a capacity of less than 200 kilogrammes.
[4] Beginning 1982, data are confidential.

Remarque générale.
Machines pour la détermination directe du poids des objets, telles que les balances utilisées dans le commerce de gros ou de détail, les bascules pour personnes et diverses balances de ménage. (CTCI 71963–2).

[1] Production des établissements occupant 5 personnes ou plus.
[2] Livraisons.
[3] Balances et bascules de tous types, d'une portée inférieure à 200 kilogramme.
[4] A partir de 1982, les données sont confidentielles.

Ovens, household – Fours pour usages domestiques

Unit : Thousand units — Unité : En milliers

Country or area	1976	1977	1978	1979	1980	1981	1982	1983	1984	1985	Pays ou zone
America, North	**5 777**	**7 066**	**7 342**	**6 527**	**6 862**	**7 360**	**6 578**	**8 932**	**10 520**	**9 902**	**Amérique du Nord**
Canada[1]	17	...	22	16	32	...	...	...	...	...	Canada[1]
United States[1]	...	7 044	7 320	6 511	6 830	7 338	6 556	8 910	10 498	9 880	Etats–Unis[1]
America, South	**20**	**25**	**22**	**29**	**21**	**19**	**40**	**32**	**34**	**28**	**Amérique du Sud**
Argentina	10	13	10	15	14	12	17	17	18	11	Argentine
Colombia	10	12	12	14	7	7	23	15	...	...	Colombie
Asia	**3 114**	**3 482**	**3 368**	**3 383**	**3 234**	**3 774**	**4 133**	**5 831**	**8 021**	**9 721**	**Asie**
Indonesia	236	...	...	...	...	...	...	...	...	...	Indonésie
Iran(Islamic Rep.of)[2]	732	806	750	729	634	629	1 092	1 306	...	...	Iran(Rép.islamique)[2]
Japan	2 129	2 428	2 364	2 398	2 342	2 885	2 777	4 255	6 656	8 294	Japon
Turkey	17	12	...	...	...	...	28	34	27	30	Turquie
Europe	**5 359**	**5 709**	**5 250**	**6 451**	**7 380**	**6 341**	**5 899**	**5 756**	**5 646**	**6 529**	**Europe**
EEC	***4 030***	***4 054***	***3 565***	***4 621***	***5 408***	***4 359***	***4 096***	***3 594***	***3 532***	***4 272***	***CEE***
Denmark	26	37	39	60	60	...	...	...	...	...	Danemark
Germany, Fed. Rep.	3 890	3 924	3 448	4 529	5 310	4 255	3 981	3 478	3 408	4 160	Allemagne, Rép. féd.
Greece	114	93	78	32	38	32	34	26	25	...	Grèce
EFTA	***244***	***449***	***517***	***577***	***681***	***710***	***637***	***715***	***748***	***913***	***AELE***
Austria	77	98	107	183	257	244	164	120	66	83	Autriche
Finland[3]	43	210	244	202	203	204	173	...	...	...	Finlande[3]
Norway	98	114	134	147	160	...	...	...	...	...	Norvège
Portugal	...	11	6	16	13	19	17	19	30	14	Portugal
Sweden	18	16	26	29	48	66	90	136	185	321	Suède
East Europe	***638***	***659***	***579***	***608***	***621***	***581***	***656***	***575***	***573***	***571***	***Europe de l'est***
Czechoslovakia	249	209	156	181	230	256	303	257	239	225	Tchécoslovaquie
Hungary	36	87	55	34	33	32	18	34	38	74	Hongrie
Poland	353	363	368	393	358	293	335	284	296	272	Pologne
Other Europe	***447***	***547***	***589***	***645***	***670***	***691***	***510***	***873***	***793***	***774***	***Autre Europe***
Spain	...	...	...	129	169	172	162	260	...	...	Espagne
Yugoslavia	395	470	487	516	501	519	348	613	539	494	Yougoslavie
Total	**14 270**	**16 282**	**15 983**	**16 390**	**17 497**	**17 494**	**16 649**	**20 551**	**24 221**	**26 181**	**Total**

General note.
Domestic ovens of all types, electric and non–electric, including infra–red ovens and high–frequency induction ovens. (Parts of SITC 6971 and 72505).

Remarque générale.
Fours domestiques de tous types, électriques ou non, y compris les fours à rayons infrarouges et les fours à induction à haute fréquence. (Parties de CTCI 6971 et 72505).

[1] Shipments.
[2] Production by establishments employing 10 or more persons.
[3] Beginning 1983, data are confidential.

[1] Expéditions.
[2] Production des établissements occupant 10 personnes ou plus.
[3] A partir de 1983, les données sont confidentielles.

Stoves, ranges, cookers – Poêles, fourneaux, cuisinières

Unit : Thousand units

Unité : En milliers

Country or area	1976	1977	1978	1979	1980	1981	1982	1983	1984	1985	Pays ou zone
Africa	**194**	**165**	**217**	**291**	**567**	**589**	**493**	**514**	**509**	**418**	**Afrique**
Algeria	...	11	66	94	* 153	[1] 53	[1] 50	[1] 68	[1] 74	...	Algérie
South Africa	111	105	97	139	* 307	* 416	304	295	* 289	251	Afrique du Sud
Tunisia	24	49	54	58	107	120	139	151	146	84	Tunisie
America, North	**6 142**	**6 813**	**6 887**	**6 698**	**5 962**	**11 467**	**11 211**	**11 027**	**11 450**	**11 693**	**Amérique du Nord**
Antigua and Barbuda	...	...	10	12	9	15	6	15	3	...	Antigua–et–Barbuda
Canada[2]	491	519	489	479	378	...	...	...	...	...	Canada[2]
Cuba	128	154	125	143	114	160	139	150	171	229	Cuba
Mexico	836	796	803	874	1 040	1 084	1 079	954	841	957	Mexique
Trinidad and Tobago[1]	19	27	22	15	23	15	23	18	20	19	Trinité–et–Tobago[1]
United States[2]	4 655	5 304	5 438	5 175	4 398	# 9 801	9 599	9 551	10 102	10 195	Etats–Unis[2]
America, South	**2 452**	**3 308**	**3 735**	**4 011**	**3 437**	**3 902**	**3 877**	**3 824**	**4 020**	**4 000**	**Amérique du Sud**
Argentina	321	510	387	508	527	474	464	662	710	609	Argentine
Brazil	[3] 1 789	[3] 2 533	[3] 3 039	[4] 3 213	...	...	...	...	...	...	Brésil
Chile[5]	76	112	161	148	118	180	118	57	50	58	Chili[5]
Colombia	205	80	77	103	145	579	639	458	...	...	Colombie
Ecuador	61	73	71	...	3	25	...	...	...	...	Equateur
Asia	**17 280**	**18 487**	**18 223**	**19 441**	**17 085**	**20 818**	**26 935**	**19 931**	**23 270**	**24 059**	**Asie**
Indonesia	24	...	...	6	54	38	55	42	27	...	Indonésie
Iran(Islamic Rep.of)[6]	434	449	356	366	336	285	977	1 066	...	...	Iran(Rép.islamique)[6]
Israel[7 8]	97	...	...	...	...	...	...	...	...	...	Israël[7 8]
Japan[9]	16 577	17 713	17 563	18 800	16 338	20 010	25 289	18 242	...	...	Japon[9]
Philippines[2]	77	145	...	...	...	...	...	...	...	...	Philippines[2]
Sri Lanka	21	...	27	7	2	11	...	...	...	...	Sri Lanka
Syrian Arab Republic	32	29	34	19	25	57	64	62	46	36	Rép. arabe syrienne
Turkey	18	12	6	35	122	...	337	...	...	...	Turquie
Europe	**12 603**	**12 610**	**12 891**	**13 060**	**13 540**	**12 874**	**13 130**	**15 057**	**14 858**	**15 563**	**Europe**
EEC	***6 201***	***5 780***	***5 801***	***5 917***	***5 681***	***6 113***	***6 362***	***6 780***	***7 046***	***7 380***	***CEE***
Denmark	72	74	66	64	58	...	...	...	...	...	Danemark
France[10 11]	2 363	1 940	1 929	1 929	1 769	1 648	1 979	2 418	2 808	3 213	France[10 11]
Germany, Fed. Rep.	1 845	1 898	1 901	1 997	1 956	2 561	2 609	2 535	2 436	2 508	Allemagne, Rép. féd.
Greece	644	670	701	723	702	662	636	574	494	...	Grèce
Netherlands[12 13]	468	471	446	...	...	...	...	...	...	...	Pays–Bas[12 13]
United Kingdom	809	727	758	742	734	725	625	743	802	602	Royaume–Uni
EFTA	***598***	***836***	***777***	***680***	***773***	***760***	***790***	***822***	***880***	***899***	***AELE***
Austria	130	135	141	149	159	153	137	152	193	195	Autriche
Finland	53	278	221	250	235	249	...	...	...	...	Finlande
Norway	182	165	147	140	154	...	...	...	...	...	Norvège
Sweden	233	258	268	141	...	...	...	...	...	...	Suède
East Europe	***2 028***	***1 978***	***2 055***	***2 009***	***1 922***	***1 746***	***1 596***	***1 708***	***1 748***	***1 881***	***Europe de l'est***
Bulgaria	94	92	116	102	99	127	160	204	210	285	Bulgarie
Czechoslovakia	432	429	408	448	463	440	336	360	400	397	Tchécoslovaquie
German Dem. Rep.[14]	125	157	157	161	168	181	197	212	207	198	Rép. dém. allemande[14]
Hungary	568	462	424	371	334	355	265	256	244	243	Hongrie
Poland[15]	809	838	950	927	858	643	638	676	687	758	Pologne[15]
Other Europe	***3 776***	***4 016***	***4 258***	***4 454***	***5 164***	***4 254***	***4 382***	***5 748***	***5 184***	***5 403***	***Autre Europe***
Spain	3 400	...	...	3 710	4 413	3 519	3 636	5 095	...	...	Espagne
Yugoslavia	376	547	633	744	751	735	746	653	625	688	Yougoslavie
Oceania	**525**	**500**	**438**	**440**	**582**	**578**	**550**	**477**	**523**	**523**	**Océanie**
Australia[16 17]	450	425	392	388	540	523	494	420	456	470	Australie[16 17]
New Zealand	75	75	46	52	42	55	56	57	67	...	Nouvelle–Zélande
Total	**39 197**	**41 882**	**42 390**	**43 941**	**41 173**	**50 227**	**56 196**	**50 831**	**54 630**	**56 256**	**Total**

For general note and footnotes, see end of table.

Voir la fin du tableau pour la remarque générale et les notes.

General note.
Kitchen stoves, ranges and cookers for household use and similar apparatus of larger size suitable for hotels, restaurants etc., burning any type of fuel. Electrically–operated apparatus is included. (Parts of SITC 6971 and 72505).

[1] Gas cookers only.
[2] Shipments.
[3] Production by main establishments only.
[4] Production by establishments employing 5 or more persons.
[5] Stoves only.
[6] Production by establishments employing 50 or more persons.
[7] Marketed local production.
[8] Excluding apparatus operated solely by electricity.
[9] Stoves and ranges only, electric and non–electric.
[10] Deliveries.
[11] Electric or mixed ranges and electric stoves, ovens and dutch ovens.
[12] Industrial sales.
[13] Including gas ovens.
[14] Electric ranges and cookers only.
[15] Gas cookers with ovens only.
[16] Twelve months ending 30 June of year stated.
[17] Including ovens.

Remarque générale.
Poêles, fourneaux de cuisine, cuisinières pour usage ménager et appareils plus grands du même genre convenant aux hôtels, restaurants etc., quel que soit le combustible utilisé. Cette rubrique comprend les appareils fonctionnant à lélectricité. (Parties de CTCI 6971 et 72505).

[1] Cuisinières à gaz seulement.
[2] Expéditions.
[3] Production des principaux établissements seulement.
[4] Production des établissements occupant 5 personnes ou plus.
[5] Poêles seulement.
[6] Production des établissements occupant 50 personnes ou plus.
[7] Production locale commercialisée.
[8] Non compris les appareils fonctionnant uniquement à l'électricité.
[9] Poêles et fourneaux seulement, électriques ou non.
[10] Livraisons.
[11] Cuisinières électriques ou mixtes, réchauds, fours et rôtissoires électriques.
[12] Ventes industrielles.
[13] Y compris les fourneaux à gaz.
[14] Fourneaux et cuisinières électriques seulement.
[15] Cuisinières à gaz avec fours seulement.
[16] Période de douze mois finissant le 30 juin de l'année indiquée.
[17] Y compris les fours.

Drying machines for household use – Machines à sécher, à usage domestique

Unit : Thousand units

Unité : En milliers

Country or area	1976	1977	1978	1979	1980	1981	1982	1983	1984	1985	Pays ou zone
America, North	**3 526**	**3 888**	**3 970**	**3 922**	**3 483**	**3 281**	**2 962**	**3 595**	**3 937**	**4 175**	**Amérique du Nord**
Canada[1]	348	335	333	350	351	316	247	294	289	335	Canada[1]
United States[1]	[2] 3 178	[2] 3 553	[2] 3 637	# 3 572	3 132	2 965	2 715	3 301	3 648	3 840	Etats-Unis[1]
America, South	**434**	**530**	**798**	**931**	**842**	**1 070**	**1 191**	**1 311**	**1 433**	**1 554**	**Amérique du Sud**
Brazil	433	529	797	[3] 929	840	...	...	...	...	...	Brésil
Colombia	...	1	1	2	2	2	2	2	...	...	Colombie
Asia	**148**	**262**	**211**	**290**	**699**	**699**	**545**	**474**	**425**	**393**	**Asie**
Japan	148	262	211	290	699	699	545	474	425	393	Japon
Europe	**370**	**423**	**425**	**481**	**421**	**450**	**480**	**479**	**477**	**645**	**Europe**
EEC	***314***	***369***	***369***	***423***	***360***	***408***	***430***	***429***	***428***	***596***	***CEE***
Denmark	1	0	0	0	0	0	0	0	0	0	Danemark
France[4]	125	129	67	59	56	...	...	...	...	...	France[4]
Germany, Fed. Rep.	188	240	302	364	304	342	372	380	387	563	Allemagne, Rép. féd.
EFTA	***8***	***7***	***7***	***10***	***5***	***5***	***4***	***4***	***4***	***4***	***AELE***
Finland	4	...	...	...	...	...	...	...	...	...	Finlande
Portugal	...	...	...	6	1	1	0	0	0	...	Portugal
Other Europe	***49***	***47***	***49***	***48***	***56***	***37***	***46***	***45***	***45***	***45***	***Autre Europe***
Spain	...	...	...	...	55	35	...	...	...	...	Espagne
Yugoslavia	...	2	4	3	1	* 2	1	0	0	0	Yougoslavie
Oceania	**291**	**259**	**204**	**263**	**181**	**202**	**189**	**176**	**162**	**181**	**Océanie**
Australia	...	143	123	197	...	...	...	...	...	...	Australie
New Zealand	137	116	81	66	27	...	...	...	...	...	Nouvelle-Zélande
Total	**4 770**	**5 362**	**5 608**	**5 887**	**5 626**	**5 702**	**5 367**	**6 035**	**6 434**	**6 948**	**Total**

General note.
Machines designed for the drying of textile fabrics or made-up articles consisting essentially of a closed chamber in which the goods to be dried are subjected to the action of hot air. (SITC 71715-1).

[1] Shipments.
[2] Source: Merchandising Week Magazine, Billboard Publications Inc., (New York).
[3] Production by establishments employing 5 or more persons.
[4] Deliveries.

Remarque générale.
Machines destinées à sécher des tissus ou des ouvrages en matières textiles, se composant essentiellement d'une enceinte fermée dans laquelle les articles à sécher sont soumis à l'action de l'air chaud. (CTCI 71715-1).

[1] Expéditions.
[2] Source: Merchandising Week Magazine, Billboard Publications Inc.,(New York).
[3] Production des établissements occupant 5 personnes ou plus.
[4] Livraisons.

Sewing machines – Machines à coudre

Unit : Thousand units — Unité : En milliers

Country or area	1976	1977	1978	1979	1980	1981	1982	1983	1984	1985	Pays ou zone
Africa	**45**	**61**	**64**	**67**	**207**	**105**	**67**	**48**	**51**	**34**	**Afrique**
Nigeria	40	54	57	60	199	101	61	45	45	29	Nigéria
Tunisia	5	7	7	7	8	4	6	3	6	...	Tunisie
America, South	**1 035**	**1 017**	**1 101**	**1 241**	**1 379**	**1 146**	**1 296**	**1 371**	**1 447**	**1 497**	**Amérique du Sud**
Argentina	75	80	63	74	45	27	23	37	41	32	Argentine
Brazil	855	854	971	[1] 1 092	1 222	1 074	...	...	...	...	Brésil
Chile	15	9	5	5	7	0	...	...	...	...	Chili
Colombia	...	49	41	50	71	21	3	0	...	...	Colombie
Peru	38	25	21	20	34	...	...	...	...	...	Pérou
Asia	**8 901**	**9 518**	**9 502**	**10 466**	**12 295**	**14 568**	**16 727**	**14 537**	**13 012**	**13 151**	**Asie**
China	3 638	4 242	4 865	5 868	7 678	10 391	12 860	10 872	9 349	9 912	Chine
India[2]	361	382	245	336	345	332	319	342	326	322	Inde[2]
Indonesia	164	197	159	353	362	377	496	296	412	* 171	Indonésie
Japan	3 947	3 834	3 431	3 155	3 247	2 873	2 593	2 558	2 463	2 318	Japon
Korea, Republic of	568	552	496	444	350	312	165	127	121	80	Corée, République de
Pakistan[3]	64	58	62	62	67	65	67	64	65	...	Pakistan[3]
Philippines[4]	14	89	...	...	...	...	...	...	...	...	Philippines[4]
Sri Lanka	13	14	32	33	44	...	...	...	...	...	Sri Lanka
Turkey[5]	132	150	160	163	150	129	134	181	175	176	Turquie[5]
Europe	**2 891**	**2 900**	**2 634**	**2 751**	**2 717**	**2 382**	**2 284**	**2 243**	**2 213**	**2 204**	**Europe**
EEC	***1 700***	***1 626***	***1 425***	***1 471***	***1 449***	***1 152***	***1 100***	***986***	***974***	***914***	***CEE***
Denmark	13	12	10	0	0	...	...	...	...	...	Danemark
France	212	179	152	...	...	...	...	...	...	...	France
Germany, Fed. Rep.	620	643	527	541	507	404	390	355	323	295	Allemagne, Rép. féd.
Italy	826	760	709	731	754	553	513	438	461	425	Italie
United Kingdom[6]	29	32	27	18	7	5	...	...	...	...	Royaume-Uni[6]
EFTA	***222***	***206***	***184***	***184***	***174***	***167***	***131***	***155***	***159***	***174***	***AELE***
Sweden[7]	222	206	184	184	174	167	131	155	159	174	Suède[7]
East Europe	***612***	***653***	***652***	***693***	***750***	***741***	***705***	***705***	***715***	***763***	***Europe de l'est***
German Dem. Rep.	206	216	233	239	242	255	272	282	292	310	Rép. dém. allemande
Hungary	2	3	3	4	4	4	5	2	4	2	Hongrie
Poland[7]	334	339	322	364	409	383	350	372	385	419	Pologne[7]
Romania	70	95	94	86	95	99	78	49	34	32	Roumanie
Other Europe	***357***	***415***	***373***	***403***	***344***	***322***	***348***	***397***	***366***	***353***	***Autre Europe***
Spain	244	299	...	264	217	195	215	237	...	...	Espagne
Yugoslavia	113	116	120	139	127	127	133	160	162	158	Yougoslavie
USSR	**1 512**	**1 516**	**1 514**	**1 474**	**1 477**	**1 510**	**1 520**	**1 547**	**1 573**	**1 654**	**URSS**
Byelorussian SSR	*78*	*79*	*80*	*81*	*80*	*82*	*80*	*80*	*80*	*79*	*RSS de Biélorussie*
Ukrainian SSR[8]	*7*	*8*	*8*	*8*	*8*	*9*	*9*	*9*	*10*	*10*	*RSS d'Ukraine[8]*
Total	**14 384**	**15 012**	**14 814**	**15 999**	**18 075**	**19 711**	**21 895**	**19 747**	**18 296**	**18 540**	**Total**

General note.
All types of sewing machines, whether operated by hand or fitted with a built-in electric motor, for household use or for industrial use (tailors, dressmakers, shoe industry etc.). (SITC 71730-0).

1 Production by establishments employing 5 or more persons.
2 Production by large and medium scale establishments only.
3 Twelve months ending 30 June of year stated.
4 Shipments.
5 Excluding industrial sewing machines.
6 Industrial machines only.
7 For household use only.
8 For industrial use only.

Remarque générale.
Machines à coudre de tous types, mues à la main ou par un moteur électrique incorporé, utilisées pour les travaux domestiques ou dans l'industrie (tailleurs, couturières, industrie de la chaussure etc.). (CTCI 71730-0).

1 Production des établissements occupant 5 personnes ou plus.
2 Production des grandes et moyennes entreprises seulement.
3 Période de douze mois finissant le 30 juin de l'année indiquée.
4 Expéditions.
5 Non compris les machines à coudre industrielles.
6 Machines industrielles seulement.
7 Pour usages domestiques seulement.
8 Pour usages industriels seulement.

Air conditioning machines – Groupes pour le conditionnement de l'air

Unit : Thousand units — Unité : En milliers

Country or area	1976	1977	1978	1979	1980	1981	1982	1983	1984	1985	Pays ou zone
Africa											**Afrique**
Egypt	7	8	11	15	19	19	22	22	...	...	Egypte
Gabon	0	0	* 1	2	3	...	...	...	...	...	Gabon
Nigeria	...	...	...	...	...	273	173	187	142	93	Nigéria
South Africa	...	...	...	36	60	63	* 56	48	53	25	Afrique du Sud
America, North											**Amérique du Nord**
Cuba	6	3	4	4	2	5	5	3	2	3	Cuba
Dominican Republic	3	4	4	3	4	3	4	5	7	8	Rép. dominicaine
Mexico	44	84	104	112	135	136	116	87	125	135	Mexique
United States[1 2 3]	5 707	6 482	7 603	7 542	3 914	4 263	3 322	2 498	3 625	3 256	Etats–Unis[1 2 3]
America, South											**Amérique du Sud**
Brazil[4]	267	215	319	[5] 331	323	308	...	...	...	...	Brésil[4]
Colombia	5	32	16	9	9	...	...	...	...	...	Colombie
Asia											**Asie**
Burma[6]	0	0	0	0	0	1	1	1	...	1	Birmanie[6]
India	15	21	21	32	26	32	30	28	29	32	Inde
Indonesia	24	23	27	36	46	46	67	62	70	...	Indonésie
Iran(Islamic Rep.of)[7]	198	243	226	207	157	201	239	...	...	...	Iran(Rép.islamique)[7]
Israel[8]	23	23	37	39	25	29	31	35	26	27	Israël[8]
Japan	4 372	5 099	6 806	8 922	7 947	6 889	8 454	8 291	10 192	11 995	Japon
Korea, Republic of	14	14	37	147	44	48	69	124	188	191	Corée, République de
Philippines[9]	32	36	40	...	...	...	...	...	...	...	Philippines[9]
Singapore	19	26	31	40	33	52	...	...	...	...	Singapour
Thailand	...	...	...	52	49	44	* 40	...	...	...	Thaïlande
Turkey	2	3	4	4	...	...	[10] 0	[10] 0	[10] 1	[10] 1	Turquie
Europe											**Europe**
EEC											***CEE***
Germany, Fed. Rep.[11]	273	273	277	292	318	289	288	286	307	...	Allemagne, Rép. féd.[11]
Greece	5	12	11	7	12	10	11	9	9	...	Grèce
Italy	...	...	65	71	78	57	70	118	154	131	Italie
United Kingdom[12]	31	48	42	46	17	32	...	...	...	...	Royaume–Uni[12]
EFTA											***AELE***
Austria[11]	6	8	7	8	9	9	9	10	10	11	Autriche[11]
Finland	23	...	...	...	14	...	...	...	...	...	Finlande
East Europe											***Europe de l'est***
Hungary	18	18	22	34	33	28	29	26	34	27	Hongrie
Other Europe											***Autre Europe***
Spain	67	106	...	...	...	...	...	...	...	...	Espagne
Yugoslavia	...	10	5	5	5	1	3	5	4	5	Yougoslavie

General note.
Machines equipped with a motor–driven fan or blower, designed to change both the temperature and the humidity of air, self–contained on a common chassis or in a common housing. (SITC 71912–0A).

[1] Excluding air conditioning coils.
[2] Shipments.
[3] Data refer to room air–conditioners only and include dehumidifiers.
[4] Sales.
[5] Production by establishments employing 5 or more persons.
[6] Government production only.
[7] Production by establishments employing 50 or more persons.
[8] Marketed local production.
[9] Excluding central air–conditioning units.
[10] Central air–conditioning units only.
[11] In thousand metric tons.
[12] Air conditioning packages only. Excluding those from 3000 to 9000 kilocalories.

Remarque générale.
Machines comprenant un ventilateur à moteur et des dispositifs montés dans une enveloppe commune ou sur un châssis commun, propres à modifier la température et l'humidité de l'air. (CTCI 71912–0A).

[1] Non compris les serpentins pour appareils de climatisation.
[2] Expéditions.
[3] Données se rapportant aux climatiseurs individuels seulement, y compris les déshumidificateurs.
[4] Ventes.
[5] Production des établissements occupant 5 personnes ou plus.
[6] Production de l'Etat seulement.
[7] Production des établissements occupant 50 personnes ou plus.
[8] Production locale commercialisée.
[9] Non compris les appareils de climatisation centrale.
[10] Les appareils de climatisation centrale.
[11] En milliers de tonnes métriques.
[12] Appareils de climatisation complets seulement. Non compris les appareils d'une capacité de 3000 à 9000 calories.

Industrial refrigerators and freezers – Réfrigérateurs et congélateurs industriels

Unit : Number units — Unité : Nombre

Country or area	1976	1977	1978	1979	1980	1981	1982	1983	1984	1985	Pays ou zone
Africa											**Afrique**
South Africa	47	45	48	60	91	109	58	69	78	51	Afrique du Sud
America, North											**Amérique du Nord**
Canada	7 544	10 477	...	...	...	...	...	...	...	...	Canada
Cuba	...	1 274	523	622	1 032	2 018	2 012	2 199	1 846	1 863	Cuba
United States[1 2]	1 542 000	1 548 000	1 419 000	1 933 400	1 698 900	1 656 500	1 640 500	1 261 500	1 162 000	1 065 000	Etats-Unis[1 2]
America, South											**Amérique du Sud**
Argentina	3 627	7 079	2 227	3 937	3 925	2 037	3 458	5 792	2 374	1 770	Argentine
Brazil[3]	90 680	66 896	87 837	88 949	117 746	72 089	...	...	...	...	Brésil[3]
Chile	1 612	505	512	652	...	...	...	...	...	...	Chili
Colombia	390	310	1 862	707	...	1 195	1 301	1 448	...	...	Colombie
Ecuador[4]	64	...	3 220	...	1 893	90	113	125	...	...	Equateur[4]
Asia											**Asie**
Cyprus	1 780	1 973	3 534	3 607	5 406	7 210	7 410	7 016	8 164	9 050	Chypre
Hong Kong	2 994	1 396	3 663	3 462	5 373	12 659	1 091	3 452	3 714	...	Hong-kong
Japan	887 742	872 228	1 006 073	1 334 999	1 144 546	1 130 045	1 222 360	1 123 241	1 191 489	1 240 666	Japon
Korea, Republic of	...	...	...	...	69 988	65 230	52 309	69 023	119 145	85 040	Corée, République de
Sri Lanka	332	...	338	...	...	...	...	...	...	...	Sri Lanka
Turkey[5]	11 530	11 393	12 145	13 116	...	...	...	2 187	...	...	Turquie[5]
Europe											**Europe**
EEC											***CEE***
Belgium[1 6 7]	16 000	20 000	18 000	19 132	21 317	22 751	25 263	27 754	30 591	43 633	Belgique[1 6 7]
Denmark	22 783	23 419	24 098	12 567	25 968	...	...	...	...	...	Danemark
France	2 192 000	2 311 000	2 042 000	2 354 000	2 765 000	2 593 000	2 423 000	2 484 000	2 288 773	2 731 820	France
Germany, Fed. Rep.	334 606	325 235	317 255	319 765	417 322	316 255	325 490	341 130	296 723	272 782	Allemagne, Rép. féd.
Greece	5 998	5 645	5 702	6 035	8 018	10 904	10 422	9 945	9 258	...	Grèce
United Kingdom	309 308	299 831	...	...	...	...	...	272 700	...	...	Royaume-Uni
EFTA											***AELE***
Austria[6]	...	...	...	...	...	...	...	5 218	...	...	Autriche[6]
Finland	21 605	20 135	21 042	21 061	29 651	...	...	...	...	...	Finlande
Norway	10 099	9 599	7 632	3 425	...	...	...	...	...	...	Norvège
East Europe											***Europe de l'est***
Czechoslovakia	278	249	217	271	209	...	...	...	...	...	Tchécoslovaquie
Hungary	20 184	23 237	22 656	20 147	19 380	19 241	17 355	18 855	16 117	17 423	Hongrie
Poland	...	...	...	...	...	...	...	49 270	...	...	Pologne
Other Europe											***Autre Europe***
Spain	...	...	...	93 016	64 469	64 777	85 771	99 468	...	...	Espagne
USSR	381 904	400 465	395 302	402 802	402 453	404 648	396 569	403 327	412 727	422 393	**URSS**
Ukrainian SSR	*187 020*	*189 361*	*182 749*	*188 669*	*186 150*	*183 959*	*180 850*	*181 871*	*181 875*	*183 310*	*RSS d'Ukraine*
Oceania											**Océanie**
Australia[8]	23 312	23 104	23 429	23 900	24 531	25 687	23 974	22 744	...	31 729	Australie[8]
New Zealand[9]	124 804	85 661	87 018	95 263	75 398	81 731	69 015	...	[10] 5 902	[10] 5 059	Nouvelle-Zélande[9]

General note.
Installations comprising a compressor, a condenser and an evaporator (or a generator and an evaporator not mounted on a common base or in the form of self-contained units, but as separate elements designed to operate together), used industrially for cold-storage plants and for manufacturing operations, for example, for the manufacture of block ice, for quick-freezing food products etc. They may include associated cold brine circulation systems as well as ancillary apparatus such as freezing chambers or cold tables. (SITC 71915-0).

[1] Shipments.
[2] Household freezers only.
[3] Excluding industrial freezers.

Remarque générale.
Installations comprenant un compresseur, un condenseur et un évaporateur (ou un générateur et un évaporateur non montés sur un socle commun ni groupés en un seul corps, mais cependant conçus pour fonctionner ensemble) utilisés pour l'équipement des entrepôts frigorifiques ou à des fins industrielles, par exemple la fabrication de blocs de glace, la surgélation de produits alimentaires etc. Elles peuvent être munies de tuyauteries à saumure et de dispositifs auxiliares tels que chambres de congélation ou tables réfrigérantes. (CTCI 71915-0).

[1] Expéditions.
[2] Congélateurs de ménage seulement.
[3] Non compris congélateurs industriels.

[4] Freezers only.
[5] 1980 and 1981, data are confidential.
[6] In metric tons.
[7] Production by establishments employing 5 or more persons.
[8] Twelve months ending 30 June of year stated.
[9] 1983, data are confidential.
[10] Excluding household freezers.

[4] Congélateurs seulement.
[5] 1980 et 1981, les données sont confidentielles.
[6] En tonnes métriques.
[7] Production des établissements occupant 5 personnes ou plus.
[8] Période de douze mois finissant le 30 juin de l'année indiquée.
[9] 1983, les données sont confidentielles.
[10] Non compris congélateurs de ménage.

Liquid elevators – Elévateurs de liquides

Unit : Thousand units

Unité : En milliers

Country or area	1976	1977	1978	1979	1980	1981	1982	1983	1984	1985	Pays ou zone
America, South											**Amérique du Sud**
Brazil	...	5 035	4 188	[1] 4 545	5 276	...	...	...	...	...	Brésil
Europe											**Europe**
EEC											***CEE***
Belgium[2 3]	14	13	...	...	...	...	...	...	...	...	Belgique[2 3]
Germany, Fed. Rep.[2]	136	...	...	...	...	...	...	...	...	...	Allemagne, Rép. féd.[2]
Netherlands[4]	215	178	195	223	172	86	63	48	...	...	Pays–Bas[4]
EFTA											***AELE***
Austria	32	24	21	23	27	31	33	23	24	20	Autriche
Finland	46	48	57	59	52	44	55	48	44	...	Finlande
Sweden	...	265	245	304	345	305	357	...	...	...	Suède
East Europe											***Europe de l'est***
German Dem. Rep.[5]	371	432	443	458	470	510	526	586	565	518	Rép. dém. allemande[5]

General note.
Chain or cable elevators and elevating wheels with buckets, scoops etc., band elevators, Archimedean screw–type elevators, air lift pumps, as well as delivery pumps equipped with measuring or price–calculating mechanisms. (SITC 71921–1).

1 Production by establishments employing 5 or more persons.
2 In thousand metric tons.
3 Shipments.
4 Industrial sales.
5 Pumps of all kinds.

Remarque générale.
Elévateurs à chaînes ou à câbles, élévateurs du type à vis d'Archimède, élévateurs par émulsion et pompes distributrices comportant un dispositif mesureur et compteur avec ou sans détermination du prix de vente. (CTCI 71921–1).

1 Production des établissements occupant 5 personnes ou plus.
2 En milliers de tonnes métriques.
3 Expéditions.
4 Ventes industrielles.
5 Pompes de tous types.

Pumps for liquids, except liquid elevators –
Pompes pour liquides, non compris élévateurs à liquides

Unit : Thousand units | Unité : En milliers

Country or area	1976	1977	1978	1979	1980	1981	1982	1983	1984	1985	Pays ou zone
Africa	**5**	**2**	**2**	**4**	**4**	**5**	**4**	**4**	**5**	**5**	**Afrique**
Algeria	5	2	2	4	4	5	4	...	...	...	Algérie
America, North	**3 168**	**3 914**	**4 408**	**4 547**	**4 494**	**4 625**	**3 845**	**4 055**	**4 429**	**4 313**	**Amérique du Nord**
Cuba	4	1	1	9	3	7	7	6	5	6	Cuba
United States[1 2]	3 164	3 913	4 407	4 538	4 491	4 618	3 838	4 049	4 424	4 307	Etats–Unis[1 2]
America, South	**414**	**558**	**641**	**537**	**542**	**554**	**578**	**562**	**557**	**559**	**Amérique du Sud**
Brazil	407	550	632	...	...	...	...	...	...	...	Brésil
Colombia	...	8	9	7	12	24	48	32	...	...	Colombie
Asia	**1 874**	**2 448**	**2 912**	**3 513**	**3 696**	**3 777**	**4 456**	**4 974**	**6 157**	**6 240**	**Asie**
Burma[3]	6	5	6	6	4	7	3	4	4	5	Birmanie[3]
China	...	...	...	...	1 096	1 156	1 565	1 851	2 202	2 109	Chine
Cyprus	3	4	4	4	6	10	8	7	8	10	Chypre
India[4]	288	352	372	359	457	349	444	406	477	512	Inde[4]
Japan	1 211	1 430	1 441	1 744	1 661	1 641	1 656	1 699	2 181	2 564	Japon
Korea, Republic of	150	239	405	446	362	499	665	892	1 170	925	Corée, République de
Philippines[1]	61	16	...	...	...	...	...	...	...	...	Philippines[1]
Sri Lanka	...	...	10	5	0	...	...	...	...	...	Sri Lanka
Turkey	62	66	63	95	...	...	...	...	...	...	Turquie
Europe	**12 827**	**12 797**	**13 275**	**14 187**	**14 065**	**12 977**	**12 499**	**12 645**	**15 648**	**16 584**	**Europe**
EEC	***11 327***	***11 284***	***11 728***	***12 839***	***12 666***	***11 582***	***11 096***	***11 246***	***14 226***	***15 142***	***CEE***
Denmark	912	* 762	* 806	...	...	...	...	...	...	...	Danemark
France[5]	323	784	831	1 096	884	814	934	919	# 2 636	2 759	France[5]
Germany, Fed. Rep.	7 556	7 277	7 432	8 192	8 655	7 859	7 170	7 600	8 673	9 657	Allemagne, Rép. féd.
Greece	62	67	71	61	69	64	71	54	57	...	Grèce
Netherlands[6]	59	57	54	38	38	46	32	32	...	...	Pays–Bas[6]
United Kingdom[7]	2 415	2 337	2 534	2 625	2 193	1 972	2 062	1 814	2 007	...	Royaume–Uni[7]
EFTA	***71***	***88***	***74***	***47***	***49***	***47***	***41***	***34***	***33***	***27***	***AELE***
Austria	42	53	40	38	40	37	32	26	25	26	Autriche
Finland	29	35	34	9	9	10	9	8	8	...	Finlande
East Europe	***946***	***979***	***1 028***	***1 090***	***1 136***	***1 118***	***1 136***	***1 138***	***1 167***	***1 195***	***Europe de l'est***
Bulgaria	69	98	109	105	121	132	129	125	145	117	Bulgarie
Czechoslovakia	413	417	388	408	409	430	430	425	412	451	Tchécoslovaquie
Hungary	97	96	116	132	152	145	132	148	168	200	Hongrie
Poland	367	368	415	445	454	411	445	440	442	427	Pologne
Other Europe	***483***	***446***	***445***	***211***	***214***	***230***	***226***	***227***	***222***	***220***	***Autre Europe***
Spain	228	...	...	145	100	118	115	96	...	...	Espagne
Yugoslavia	255	255	272	66	114	112	111	131	157	173	Yougoslavie
USSR	**1 277**	**1 319**	**1 300**	**1 290**	**1 288**	**1 311**	**1 326**	**1 360**	**1 395**	**1 397**	**URSS**
Byelorussian SSR	*11*	*10*	*10*	*11*	*11*	*11*	*12*	*13*	*13*	*13*	*RSS de Biélorussie*
Ukrainian SSR	*155*	*162*	*151*	*150*	*150*	*152*	*156*	*157*	*158*	*164*	*RSS d'Ukraine*
Total	**19 565**	**21 037**	**22 538**	**24 077**	**24 089**	**23 248**	**22 707**	**23 600**	**28 190**	**29 098**	**Total**

General note.
Machines for raising or otherwise continuously displacing volumes of liquids, whether they are operated by hand or by any kind of power unit, integral or otherwise, including reciprocating pumps, rotary pumps, centrifugal pumps, ejector pumps. This item excludes liquid elevators and delivery pumps equipped with measuring or price calculating mechanisms. (SITC 71921–2, 71921–3, 71921–4 and 71921–5).

Remarque générale.
Machines et appareils – qu'ils soient actionnés à la main ou par une force motrice quelconque – destinés à élever ou à mettre en circulation des liquides, visqueux ou non. On y range aussi les machines et appareils de l'espèce avec moteur incorporé (motopompe, turbopompes, électropompes). Y compris pompes alternatives, pompes rotatives volumétriques, pompes centrifuges et turbopompes, et pompes par injection. Cette rubrique ne comprend pas les élévateurs à liquides et les pompes distributrices de liquides comportant un dispositif mesureur et compteur, avec ou sans détermination du prix de vente. (CTCI 71921–2, 71921–3, 71921–4 et 71921–5).

[1] Shipments.
[2] Industrial types only.

[1] Expéditions.
[2] Types industriels seulement.

[3] Government production only.
[4] Production by large and medium scale establishments only.
[5] Deliveries.
[6] Industrial sales.
[7] Excluding hydraulic rams and other liquid elevators.

[3] Production de l'Etat seulement.
[4] Production des grandes et moyennes entreprises seulement.
[5] Livraisons.
[6] Ventes industrielles.
[7] Non compris les béliers hydrauliques et autres élévateurs de liquides.

Unit : Number units

Unité : Nombre

Country or area	1976	1977	1978	1979	1980	1981	1982	1983	1984	1985	Pays ou zone
America, North											**Amérique du Nord**
Mexico	97 296	66 466	53 831	84 189	93 277	104 194	63 306	51 273	0	0	Mexique
United States[1 2 3]	1 656 068	1 912 894	1 812 776	1 913 005	1 820 230	1 837 601	1 664 529	1 973 712	2 319 824	2 290 295	Etats–Unis[1 2 3]
America, South											**Amérique du Sud**
Brazil	45	847	1 295	[4] 2 631	3 426	3 402	...	...	...	...	Brésil
Colombia	914	592	628	613	378	1 764	# 10 066	10 085	...	...	Colombie
Asia											**Asie**
India[5]	6 754	7 937	10 053	12 509	15 899	15 483	27 276	37 620	32 509	23 840	Inde[5]
Japan	189 241	189 945	188 201	212 018	236 497	192 994	192 857	180 929	213 248	247 221	Japon
Korea, Republic of	1 907	2 349	3 308	3 195	2 635	4 143	3 200	3 596	3 821	4 097	Corée, République de
Philippines[1]	6 150	947	...	...	...	...	...	...	...	...	Philippines[1]
Turkey	44 558	85 075	92 643	111 867	...	...	...	...	...	...	Turquie
Europe											**Europe**
EEC											***CEE***
Belgium[1 6]	36 015	32 288	32 564	40 072	41 132	39 119	37 520	32 808	39 301	40 848	Belgique[1 6]
France[6 7]	21 850	20 520	19 260	20 990	30 660	19 012	23 130	25 750	20 070	16 728	France[6 7]
Germany, Fed. Rep.	192 819	219 421	218 988	207 229	...	...	...	...	...	...	Allemagne, Rép. féd.
Greece	...	...	...	...	657	299	191	191	135	...	Grèce
Netherlands[8]	4 310	4 050	3 480	3 170	3 310	...	...	...	...	...	Pays–Bas[8]
United Kingdom	195 068	172 750	162 967	169 203	89 725	89 304	97 537	95 788	110 205	...	Royaume–Uni
EFTA											***AELE***
Finland	1 416	722	1 394	1 702	2 241	2 866	2 602	2 900	2 222	...	Finlande
East Europe											***Europe de l'est***
Bulgaria[9 10]	25 809	24 600	26 509	27 564	31 109	35 995	42 870	48 098	50 829	45 135	Bulgarie[9 10]
Hungary	304 825	310 088	337 341	329 388	353 187	383 353	357 524	392 292	450 761	479 769	Hongrie
Poland	...	...	...	3 899	3 645	3 244	2 949	2 763	3 578	3 138	Pologne
Other Europe											***Autre Europe***
Spain	33 823	...	...	109 834	112 418	140 099	124 916	141 531	...	...	Espagne
Yugoslavia	8 093	8 193	8 443	9 602	9 939	9 615	9 303	13 385	11 725	12 898	Yougoslavie
USSR											***URSS***
Ukrainian SSR	*14 950*	*15 558*	*15 964*	*15 875*	*17 298*	*16 984*	*16 310*	*16 246*	*16 880*	*17 962*	*RSS d'Ukraine*
Oceania											**Océanie**
Australia[11]	704 415	694 747	547 125	648 748	689 308	700 937	564 144	...	292 607	147 034	Australie[11]

General note.

Motor–driven air and gas compressors whether or not stationary which draw air at atmospheric pressure, compress it and deliver it at a higher pressure (that is, pumps, compressors, free–piston generators, and fans and blowers). (SITC 71922–0).

1 Shipments.
2 Excluding air–conditioning and refrigeration compressors.
3 Including vacuum pumps.
4 Production by establishments employing 5 or more persons.
5 Production by large and medium scale establishments only.
6 In metric tons.
7 Deliveries.
8 Industrial sales.
9 Excluding compressors for painters.
10 Including blowers delivering over 100 cubic metres of air per minute, but excluding fans for domestic use.
11 Twelve months ending 30 June of year stated.

Remarque générale.

Machines fixes ou mobiles entraînés par moteur, servant à comprimer l'air ou d'autres gaz, qui aspirent l'air à la pression atmosphérique et le restituent à une pression plus élevée (c'est–à–dire pompes, compresseurs, générateurs à pistons libres et ventilateurs). (CTCI 71922–0).

1 Expéditions.
2 Non compris les compresseurs pour appareils de climatisation et de réfrigération.
3 Y compris les pompes à vides.
4 Production des établissements occupant 5 personnes ou plus.
5 Production des grandes et moyennes entreprises seulement.
6 En tonnes métriques.
7 Livraisons.
8 Ventes industrielles.
9 Non compris les compresseurs pour peintres.
10 Y compris les machines soufflantes d'un débit supérieur à 100 mètres cubes d'air par minute, mais non compris les ventilateurs à usage domestique.
11 Période de douze mois finissant le 30 juin de l'année indiquée.

Cranes – Grues

Unit : Number units

Unité : Nombre

Country or area	1976	1977	1978	1979	1980	1981	1982	1983	1984	1985	Pays ou zone
Africa											**Afrique**
Algeria	180	35	237	243	306	350	357	...	...	...	Algérie
America, North											**Amérique du Nord**
Cuba	76	47	16	0	40	65	91	225	248	274	Cuba
United States	11 170	6 732	7 552	10 126	10 053	10 316	5 037	3 706	3 974	3 801	Etats–Unis
America, South											**Amérique du Sud**
Brazil	4 403	3 648	2 048	[1] 2 344	5 765	...	...	...	...	...	Brésil
Colombia	5	64	...	27	170	216	178	217	...	...	Colombie
Asia											**Asie**
India	18 945	20 110	20 400	18 020	18 422	21 298	...	...	...	...	Inde
Indonesia	...	...	...	35	37	112	68	80	70	...	Indonésie
Japan	5 543	9 015	8 969	10 705	11 813	12 167	9 857	9 285	11 966	13 630	Japon
Turkey	1 081	976	...	...	...	...	...	...	...	...	Turquie
Europe											**Europe**
EEC											***CEE***
France[2 3]	147 459	173 780	177 030	180 090	187 500	190 120	134 730	114 650	83 860	125 000	France[2 3]
Germany, Fed. Rep.[3]	143 376	154 508	144 951	125 043	92 442	152 735	177 773	130 709	102 123	119 558	Allemagne, Rép. féd.[3]
Greece	...	...	...	...	2 755	1 278	1 572	1 329	866	...	Grèce
Netherlands	1 084	962	1 144	1 266	1 101	1 025	748	606	857	...	Pays–Bas
United Kingdom	8 900	8 345	8 246	7 956	6 703	5 076	3 926	3 360	2 851	...	Royaume–Uni
EFTA											***AELE***
Austria[3]	14 620	16 039	17 064	19 355	24 709	27 076	44 354	26 895	23 971	26 851	Autriche[3]
Finland	1 782	1 683	3 164	2 174	3 658	4 579	3 011	3 020	5 045	...	Finlande
Sweden[4]	4 059	2 742	2 059	...	...	...	...	...	...	...	Suède[4]
East Europe											***Europe de l'est***
Bulgaria	1 161	1 118	1 639	1 877	2 056	1 635	1 410	1 272	1 522	1 457	Bulgarie
Czechoslovakia	2 647	2 473	2 454	2 377	2 258	2 596	2 489	2 514	2 293	2 243	Tchécoslovaquie
German Dem. Rep.[5]	1 013	1 041	1 069	1 105	1 195	945	914	906	784	782	Rép. dém. allemande[5]
Hungary	787	663	777	866	678	592	507	530	553	496	Hongrie
Poland	6 845	5 389	5 088	6 246	5 590	5 195	4 275	4 991	5 311	5 059	Pologne
Other Europe											***Autre Europe***
Spain	...	...	...	5 703	4 897	6 493	6 865	6 453	...	...	Espagne
Yugoslavia	1 603	3 136	926	16 603	31 126	29 628	20 334	11 419	8 635	9 499	Yougoslavie

General note.
Fixed or stationary and mobile cranes whether or not self–propelled such as tower cranes, balance cranes, jib or derrick cranes etc. Cranes mounted on transport equipment are excluded. (SITC 71931–1).

[1] Production by establishments employing 5 or more persons.
[2] Deliveries.
[3] In metric tons.
[4] Including truck cranes.
[5] Electrical bridge–cranes only.

Remarque générale.
Grues fixes ou stationnaires et grues mobiles, automobiles ou non, telles que les grues à tour, les grues à contrepoids, les grues à flèche, les derricks etc. Cette rubrique ne comprend pas les grues montées sur matériel de transport. (CTCI 71931–1).

[1] Production des établissements occupant 5 personnes ou plus.
[2] Livraisons.
[3] En tonnes métriques.
[4] Y compris les grues montées sur camion.
[5] Ponts–grues électriques seulement.

Elevators, for lifting goods and persons – Ascenseurs et monte-charge

Unit : Number units | Unité : Nombre

Country or area	1976	1977	1978	1979	1980	1981	1982	1983	1984	1985	Pays ou zone
America, South											**Amérique du Sud**
Brazil	[1] 13 394	[1] 13 176	[1] 12 753	[1] 11 067	18 237	13 208	...	...	...	...	Brésil
Colombia	355	200	887	157	203	94	98	92	...	...	Colombie
Ecuador	...	...	...	...	...	327	180	166	...	...	Equateur
Asia											**Asie**
India	771	696	890	830	862	849	900	921	1 382	1 463	Inde
Iran(Islamic Rep.of)[2]	...	...	...	44	106	65	...	...	...	...	Iran(Rép.islamique)[2]
Japan	10 290	11 340	12 602	15 135	17 143	16 155	16 047	16 576	18 873	20 113	Japon
Korea, Republic of[3]	252	220	816	870	740	628	858	1 520	1 908	1 909	Corée, République de[3]
Turkey	3 112	* 426	362	243	302	193	237	218	140	153	Turquie
Europe											**Europe**
EEC											***CEE***
Denmark	641	623	608	621	474	...	...	...	...	...	Danemark
Germany, Fed. Rep.[4]	30 934	34 153	31 922	31 198	33 035	33 357	29 526	27 858	29 148	29 016	Allemagne, Rép. féd.[4]
Netherlands	3 208	3 548	3 396	4 064	3 680	3 008	2 315	3 433	3 602	...	Pays-Bas
United Kingdom	6 875	5 450	5 088	4 779	5 196	4 261	4 100	3 743	3 651	...	Royaume-Uni
EFTA											***AELE***
Austria[4]	9 918	9 197	8 196	8 787	8 136	7 989	8 682	7 759	8 205	8 717	Autriche[4]
Finland	2 744	2 028	2 010	2 114	2 085	2 150	2 071	2 210	2 253	...	Finlande
Norway	459	...	801	739	677	607	...	...	...	...	Norvège
East Europe											***Europe de l'est***
Bulgaria	2 600	2 753	2 824	2 378	2 356	2 522	2 725	2 854	3 053	3 063	Bulgarie
Hungary	1 564	1 417	1 474	1 634	1 442	1 400	1 449	1 393	1 075	2 088	Hongrie
Poland	5 252	5 688	5 288	4 997	4 933	3 383	2 678	2 875	3 577	5 352	Pologne
Other Europe											***Autre Europe***
Spain	13 044	...	...	17 176	16 248	15 246	13 900	12 650	...	...	Espagne
Yugoslavia	...	...	...	...	...	9 407	6 310	1 485	1 226	...	Yougoslavie
USSR											***URSS***
Byelorussian SSR	*4 893*	*5 302*	*5 732*	*6 856*	*7 201*	*7 855*	*8 344*	*8 570*	*8 770*	*8 835*	*RSS de Biélorussie*

General note.
Electric and hydraulic passenger and freight elevators. Automobile lifts, moving escalators, and other farm and non-farm elevators are excluded. (SITC 71931-2).

Remarque générale.
Ascenseurs pour personnes, et monte-charge à commande électrique ou hydraulique. Cette rubrique ne comprend pas les monte-voitures, les escaliers mécaniques et d'autres appareils de levage agricoles ou non. (CTCI 71931-2).

1 Production by establishments employing 5 or more persons.
2 Production by establishments employing 10 or more persons.
3 Excluding elevators for lifting goods.
4 In metric tons.

1 Production des établissements occupant 5 personnes ou plus.
2 Production des établissements occupant 10 personnes ou plus.
3 Non compris les monte-charges.
4 En tonnes métriques.

Fork–lift trucks – Chariots gerbeurs

Unit : Number units

Unité : Nombre

Country or area	1976	1977	1978	1979	1980	1981	1982	1983	1984	1985	Pays ou zone
America, North	**67 332**	**85 108**	**101 294**	**113 105**	**87 109**	**73 509**	**55 109**	**61 109**	**57 109**	**51 109**	**Amérique du Nord**
Canada	2 332	2 408	3 194	4 505	...	...	...	...	...	...	Canada
United States	65 000	82 700	98 100	108 600	84 000	70 400	52 000	58 000	54 000	48 000	Etats–Unis
Asia	**65 799**	**73 657**	**78 891**	**94 692**	**105 322**	**94 499**	**76 414**	**82 966**	**111 737**	**128 666**	**Asie**
India	434	569	663	...	...	...	...	...	...	...	Inde
Japan	64 572	72 295	77 868	93 374	103 974	93 060	74 919	81 029	109 214	122 292	Japon
Korea, Republic of	...	...	...	...	793	884	940	1 382	1 968	5 819	Corée, République de
Europe	**144 714**	**168 694**	**180 630**	**191 123**	**191 344**	**171 128**	**170 755**	**188 244**	**212 154**	**224 432**	**Europe**
EEC	***76 450***	***93 105***	***97 064***	***102 713***	***103 333***	***82 315***	***79 961***	***87 412***	***96 385***	***103 108***	***CEE***
Denmark	3 250	2 497	3 228	3 141	2 033	1 723	1 989	...	...	2 073	Danemark
France	...	...	...	...	...	...	...	1 558	...	...	France
Germany, Fed. Rep.	54 737	67 026	69 836	76 180	79 214	65 110	61 234	63 052	68 772	79 456	Allemagne, Rép. féd.
United Kingdom	16 905	22 024	22 442	21 834	20 528	13 924	15 180	20 804	24 209	...	Royaume–Uni
EFTA	***10 131***	***9 791***	***11 532***	***12 281***	***13 013***	***10 941***	***10 542***	***11 550***	***13 343***	***14 654***	***AELE***
Finland	35	23	13	26	34	45	39	28	32	...	Finlande
Sweden[1]	10 096	9 768	11 519	12 255	12 979	10 896	10 503	11 522	13 311	14 618	Suède[1]
East Europe	***49 895***	***57 973***	***64 621***	***66 986***	***70 357***	***75 265***	***77 297***	***86 538***	***95 083***	***102 144***	***Europe de l'est***
Bulgaria	...	...	...	...	...	61 745	63 083	71 712	80 438	85 432	Bulgarie
Czechoslovakia	3 186	3 325	3 380	3 541	3 496	3 140	3 145	3 166	3 008	3 114	Tchécoslovaquie
Hungary	5	1	2	4	1	3	0	4	4	31	Hongrie
Poland	19 096	20 628	20 809	16 601	13 609	10 377	11 069	11 656	11 633	13 567	Pologne
Other Europe	***8 238***	***7 825***	***7 413***	***9 143***	***4 641***	***2 607***	***2 955***	***2 744***	***7 343***	***4 526***	***Autre Europe***
Spain	...	...	...	7 939	3 437	2 252	2 548	2 297	...	...	Espagne
Yugoslavia	...	...	...	...	...	355	407	447	3 609	...	Yougoslavie
Oceania	**2 292**	**2 957**	**2 739**	**3 142**	**2 980**	**1 270**	**1 518**	**1 139**	**596**	**691**	**Océanie**
Australia[2]	2 292	2 957	2 739	3 142	2 980	1 270	...	1 139	596	...	Australie[2]
Total	**280 137**	**330 416**	**363 554**	**402 062**	**386 755**	**340 406**	**303 796**	**333 458**	**381 596**	**404 898**	**Total**

General note.
Mechanically–propelled vehicles, generally of small dimensions, used in workshops, mines, warehouses, docks etc., for the handling of short–distance transport of luggage, parcels or other goods. They are not designed for the transport of passengers. (SITC 71932–0).

[1] Limited data.
[2] Twelve months ending 30 June of year stated.

Remarque générale.
Véhicules automobiles de dimensions généralement réduites utilisés dans les ateliers, les mines, les entrepôts, les ports etc., pour la manutention ou le transport sur de courtes distances de bagages, de colis ou de marchandises. Ils ne sont pas conçus pour le transport des personnes. (CTCI 71932–0).

[1] Données limitées.
[2] Période de douze mois finissant le 30 juin de l'année indiquée.

Refrigerators for household use – Réfrigérateurs ménagers

Unit : Thousand units — Unité : En milliers

Country or area	1976	1977	1978	1979	1980	1981	1982	1983	1984	1985	Pays ou zone
Africa	**422**	**423**	**434**	**505**	**545**	**515**	**598**	**725**	**689**	**746**	**Afrique**
Egypt[1]	115	135	146	190	215	236	324	418	...	...	Egypte[1]
Nigeria	...	...	...	...	179	...	...	...	...	...	Nigéria
South Africa[1]	110	76	64	77	95	58	49	58	62	78	Afrique du Sud[1]
Tunisia	18	33	45	59	56	42	46	70	46	47	Tunisie
America, North	**6 107**	**6 914**	**6 809**	**6 931**	**6 346**	**6 670**	**5 736**	**6 918**	**7 174**	**7 314**	**Amérique du Nord**
Antigua and Barbuda	...	...	3	4	3	1	2	2	1	...	Antigua-et-Barbuda
Canada	[2] 605	[2] 608	[2] 622	[2] 538	...	533	366	501	439	510	Canada
Cuba	44	45	45	55	25	39	16	13	22	26	Cuba
Dominican Republic	23	34	36	33	42	31	30	29	16	12	Rép. dominicaine
Mexico	499	490	492	522	572	642	625	451	357	336	Mexique
Trinidad and Tobago	21	26	25	27	29	15	28	20	22	10	Trinité-et-Tobago
United States[2,3]	4 911	5 707	5 586	5 752	5 140	5 409	4 669	5 902	6 317	6 419	Etats-Unis[2,3]
America, South	**1 767**	**1 990**	**2 102**	**2 437**	**3 084**	**2 559**	**2 296**	**2 201**	**2 195**	**2 402**	**Amérique du Sud**
Argentina	191	198	128	233	258	210	198	252	253	162	Argentine
Brazil	1 327	1 469	1 599	1 776	2 377	1 961	* 1 725	* 1 676	* 1 597	...	Brésil
Chile	28	32	43	67	95	86	32	32	42	32	Chili
Colombia	86	120	175	216	188	179	188	155	...	...	Colombie
Ecuador	54	80	83	...	90	42	87	40	...	...	Equateur
Peru	81	91	74	76	76	81	66	46	* 37	* 33	Pérou
Asia	**6 043**	**6 091**	**7 709**	**8 521**	**7 363**	**7 784**	**8 198**	**9 175**	**10 272**	**11 702**	**Asie**
Burma	0	0	0	0	0	1	0	0	0	0	Birmanie
China	52	52	52	52	49	56	100	189	587	1 448	Chine
India	108	143	174	212	278	316	354	449	553	614	Inde
Indonesia	48	43	52	76	86	95	96	115	97	...	Indonésie
Iran(Islamic Rep.of)[4]	513	536	372	560	480	524	559	709	...	...	Iran(Rép.islamique)[4]
Israel[1,5]	57	48	...	...	...	...	...	...	...	...	Israël[1,5]
Japan	3 926	4 025	4 561	4 773	4 282	4 207	4 385	4 541	4 936	5 354	Japon
Korea, Republic of	261	388	1 053	1 445	652	932	985	1 407	1 819	1 864	Corée, République de
Malaysia	...	64	89	88	127	148	193	224	157	149	Malaisie
Philippines	84	111	135	150	222	182	...	602	...	...	Philippines
Singapore	54	57	73	80	93	93	78	66	45	37	Singapour
Sri Lanka[1]	3	3	4	...	...	...	...	...	...	...	Sri Lanka[1]
Syrian Arab Republic	61	72	74	98	139	146	148	141	111	76	Rép. arabe syrienne
Thailand	...	...	...	220	270	288	* 274	...	...	...	Thaïlande
Turkey	549	286	754	711	629	740	580	413	501	488	Turquie
Europe	**15 870**	**16 232**	**15 748**	**15 168**	**15 777**	**15 299**	**14 792**	**15 067**	**14 745**	**14 825**	**Europe**
EEC	***10 278***	***10 616***	***9 981***	***9 304***	***9 867***	***9 420***	***9 394***	***9 687***	***8 872***	***8 907***	***CEE***
Denmark	604	574	577	695	698	668	742	817	814	915	Danemark
France	...	...	...	...	...	...	895	697	469	436	France
Germany, Fed. Rep.	2 982	3 182	2 811	2 931	3 009	2 786	2 787	2 808	2 667	2 788	Allemagne, Rép. féd.
Greece	204	210	168	150	225	218	177	150	118	...	Grèce
Italy	4 493	4 705	4 631	3 922	4 300	4 099	3 713	3 900	3 576	3 358	Italie
United Kingdom	1 371	1 321	1 170	982	1 011	1 025	1 080	1 315	1 228	1 266	Royaume-Uni
EFTA	***1 094***	***1 057***	***1 028***	***1 098***	***1 141***	***1 019***	***928***	***1 005***	***936***	***874***	***AELE***
Finland	125	86	91	83	125	...	...	...	...	...	Finlande
Norway	126	102	60	...	...	...	...	...	...	...	Norvège
Portugal	26	66	90	99	173	205	173	180	227	168	Portugal
Sweden	817	803	787	820	747	617	558	628	513	510	Suède
East Europe	***2 711***	***2 662***	***2 823***	***2 745***	***2 676***	***2 657***	***2 628***	***2 725***	***2 925***	***3 060***	***Europe de l'est***
Bulgaria	142	102	74	83	96	126	133	133	135	135	Bulgarie
Czechoslovakia	385	306	358	370	353	380	383	402	446	480	Tchécoslovaquie
German Dem. Rep.	554	561	609	613	637	655	700	763	895	973	Rép. dém. allemande
Hungary	434	458	441	468	520	543	472	453	473	457	Hongrie
Poland	820	821	890	765	694	553	509	534	543	578	Pologne
Romania	376	414	451	446	376	400	431	440	...	...	Roumanie
Other Europe	***1 787***	***1 897***	***1 916***	***2 021***	***2 093***	***2 203***	***1 842***	***1 650***	***2 012***	***1 984***	***Autre Europe***
Spain	1 063	1 208	...	1 285	1 405	1 518	1 183	1 014	...	...	Espagne

For general note and footnotes, see end of table.

Voir la fin du tableau pour la remarque générale et les notes.

Refrigerators for household use (continued) – Réfrigérateurs ménagers (suite)

Unit : Thousand units

Unité : En milliers

Country or area	1976	1977	1978	1979	1980	1981	1982	1983	1984	1985	Pays ou zone
Yugoslavia[1]	724	689	687	736	688	685	659	636	746	712	Yougoslavie[1]
USSR[6]	**5 827**	**5 798**	**6 069**	**5 961**	**5 932**	**5 944**	**5 816**	**5 700**	**5 667**	**5 860**	**URSS[6]**
Byelorussian SSR	*568*	*603*	*616*	*590*	*614*	*615*	*620*	*621*	*627*	*657*	*RSS de Biélorussie*
Ukrainian SSR	*614*	*663*	*707*	*692*	*702*	*691*	*697*	*695*	*693*	*743*	*RSS d'Ukraine*
Oceania	**473**	**454**	**411**	**442**	**453**	**482**	**494**	**407**	**383**	**355**	**Océanie**
Australia[7]	230	276	249	247	279	328	352	277	265	249	Australie[7]
New Zealand[6 8]	243	178	162	195	174	...	...	...	...	...	Nouvelle-Zélande[6 8]
Total	**36 510**	**37 902**	**39 282**	**39 965**	**39 500**	**39 253**	**37 931**	**40 193**	**41 125**	**43 204**	**Total**

General note.
Refrigerators of the compression type or of the absorption type, of the sizes commonly used in private households. Insulated cabinets to contain an active refrigerating element (block ice) but no machine are excluded. (SITC 71942 and 72501).

[1] Including refrigerators other than domestic.
[2] Shipments.
[3] Electric domestic refrigerators only.
[4] Production by establishments employing 10 or more persons.
[5] Marketed local production.
[6] Including freezers.
[7] Twelve months ending 30 June of year stated.
[8] Beginning 1981, data are confidential.

Remarque générale.
Appareils frigorifiques du type à compression ou à absorption de la taille des appareils communément utilisés dans les ménages. Cette rubrique ne comprend pas les glacières conçues pour contenir un élément frigorifique actif (glace en bloc) mais non un équipement frigorifique. (CTCI 71942 et 72501).

[1] Y compris les réfrigérateurs autres que ménagers.
[2] Expéditions.
[3] Réfrigérateurs électriques de ménage seulement.
[4] Production des établissements occupant 10 personnes ou plus.
[5] Production locale commercialisée.
[6] Y compris les congélateurs.
[7] Période de douze mois finissant le 30 juin de l'année indiquée.
[8] A partir de 1981, les données sont confidentielles.

Washing machines for household use – Machines et appareils à laver, à usage domestique

Unit : Thousand units

Unité : En milliers

Country or area	1976	1977	1978	1979	1980	1981	1982	1983	1984	1985	Pays ou zone
Africa	**139**	**189**	**289**	**346**	**363**	**347**	**319**	**340**	**404**	**419**	**Afrique**
Egypt	71	126	228	273	269	269	252	278	...	...	Egypte
South Africa	68	63	61	73	94	78	67	62	66	54	Afrique du Sud
America, North	**5 373**	**5 917**	**5 995**	**6 089**	**5 578**	**5 520**	**4 991**	**5 490**	**5 688**	**6 185**	**Amérique du Nord**
Canada[1]	487	484	546	569	439	418	322	390	368	407	Canada[1]
Mexico	376	395	425	502	585	621	654	485	314	322	Mexique
United States[1]	4 510	5 038	5 024	5 018	4 554	4 481	4 015	4 615	5 006	5 456	Etats–Unis[1]
America, South	**428**	**475**	**561**	**682**	**777**	**832**	**805**	**866**	**973**	**961**	**Amérique du Sud**
Argentina	118	126	124	144	151	137	133	145	171	103	Argentine
Brazil	214	249	319	[2] 389	431	481	...	...	...	...	Brésil
Chile	44	47	65	80	104	115	43	33	50	43	Chili
Colombia	19	22	29	40	47	58	...	...	...	...	Colombie
Ecuador	6	8	9	...	15	8	5	6	...	...	Equateur
Peru	...	23	15	21	29	33	...	12	11	10	Pérou
Asia	**4 269**	**4 403**	**4 934**	**5 101**	**5 621**	**6 662**	**7 856**	**9 399**	**12 013**	**15 035**	**Asie**
Burma[3 4 5]	...	...	...	...	...	...	...	...	2	0	Birmanie[3 4 5]
China	...	...	...	18	245	1 281	2 533	3 659	5 781	8 872	Chine
Indonesia	...	...	...	1	3	6	9	10	10	...	Indonésie
Israel[6]	14	...	...	15	15	14	13	12	11	11	Israël[6]
Japan	3 919	3 999	4 266	4 360	4 879	4 759	4 787	4 981	5 277	5 092	Japon
Korea, Republic of	65	112	284	343	200	299	247	440	646	635	Corée, République de
Philippines	...	...	...	...	...	...	...	21	...	...	Philippines
Syrian Arab Republic	23	24	22	25	26	44	54	44	52	49	Rép. arabe syrienne
Turkey	207	212	305	317	231	237	191	231	213	345	Turquie
Europe	**11 757**	**11 802**	**11 928**	**12 363**	**12 908**	**12 677**	**11 953**	**12 339**	**12 571**	**12 992**	**Europe**
EEC	***8 579***	***8 242***	***8 225***	***8 475***	***8 833***	***8 590***	***8 004***	***8 027***	***8 040***	***8 417***	***CEE***
Belgium[1 2]	183	171	182	142	179	266	221	237	158	124	Belgique[1 2]
Denmark	22	24	22	30	23	26	6	0	0	0	Danemark
France[7]	1 968	1 749	1 715	1 912	1 955	1 810	1 644	1 418	1 370	1 262	France[7]
Germany, Fed. Rep.	1 766	1 670	1 785	1 785	1 803	1 894	[8] 1 655	[8] 1 606	[8] 1 692	[8] 1 827	Allemagne, Rép. féd.
Greece	97	82	76	95	114	84	77	88	78	...	Grèce
Italy	3 299	3 435	3 247	3 202	3 440	3 393	3 170	3 307	3 393	3 692	Italie
United Kingdom[9]	1 244	1 111	1 198	1 309	1 319	1 117	1 231	1 371	1 349	1 430	Royaume–Uni[9]
EFTA	***140***	***140***	***141***	***141***	***156***	***163***	***152***	***179***	***183***	***183***	***AELE***
Austria	36	36	43	44	56	67	56	72	71	72	Autriche
Finland[10]	43	...	...	...	...	...	...	...	...	...	Finlande[10]
Sweden	61	61	55	54	57	53	53	64	69	68	Suède
East Europe	***2 015***	***2 109***	***2 260***	***2 260***	***2 466***	***2 464***	***2 376***	***2 455***	***2 630***	***2 673***	***Europe de l'est***
Bulgaria	78	71	24	40	65	92	113	130	141	156	Bulgarie
Czechoslovakia	283	307	318	325	355	375	385	399	423	445	Tchécoslovaquie
German Dem. Rep.	390	406	427	433	468	485	485	504	525	502	Rép. dém. allemande
Hungary	382	393	414	414	425	436	398	364	392	385	Hongrie
Poland	683	724	807	754	809	712	623	706	730	739	Pologne
Romania	199	208	270	294	344	364	372	352	...	...	Roumanie
Other Europe	***1 023***	***1 311***	***1 302***	***1 487***	***1 453***	***1 460***	***1 421***	***1 678***	***1 718***	***1 718***	***Autre Europe***
Spain	687	967	...	1 048	1 013	980	998	1 198	...	...	Espagne
Yugoslavia[11]	336	344	398	439	440	480	423	480	533	487	Yougoslavie[11]
USSR	**5 828**	**5 798**	**6 071**	**3 661**	**3 826**	**3 928**	**3 995**	**4 250**	**4 534**	**5 068**	**URSS**
Ukrainian SSR	*249*	*260*	*262*	*262*	*273*	*288*	*290*	*310*	*330*	*372*	*RSS d'Ukraine*
Oceania	**404**	**367**	**335**	**425**	**424**	**429**	**388**	**420**	**425**	**431**	**Océanie**
Australia[12]	321	301	282	358	362	375	338	...	...	...	Australie[12]
New Zealand[13]	83	66	53	67	62	...	...	...	...	...	Nouvelle–Zélande[13]
Total	**28 198**	**28 951**	**30 113**	**28 667**	**29 497**	**30 395**	**30 307**	**33 103**	**36 609**	**41 090**	**Total**

For general note and footnotes, see end of table.

Voir la fin du tableau pour la remarque générale et les notes.

General note.
These machines usually include electrically–driven paddles or rotating cylinders (for keeping the cleaning solution circulating through the fabrics) or alternative devices. Washing machines with attached wringers or centrifugal spin driers, and centrifugal spin driers designed as independent units, are included. (SITC 72502–0).

[1] Shipments.
[2] Production by establishments employing 5 or more persons.
[3] Data refer to assembly.
[4] Government production only.
[5] Twelve months ending 30 September of year stated.
[6] Marketed local production.
[7] Deliveries.
[8] Automatic washing machine only.
[9] Deliveries of U.K. manufactured goods.
[10] Including washing machines other than domestic.
[11] Including drying machines.
[12] Twelve months ending 30 June of year stated.
[13] Beginning 1981, data are confidential.

Remarque générale.
Ces machines comprennent généralement des pales ou des cylindres rotatifs (destinés à assurer le brassage continu du liquide et du linge) ou des dispositifs à mouvements alternés, mus électriquement. Cette rubrique comprend les machines à laver avec essoreuses à rouleau ou essoreuses centrifuges et les essoreuses centrifuges conçues comme des appareils indépendants. (CTCI 72502–0).

[1] Expéditions.
[2] Production des établissements occupant 5 personnes ou plus.
[3] Données se rapportant à l'assemblage.
[4] Production de l'Etat seulement.
[5] Période de douze mois finissant le 30 septembre de l'année indiquée.
[6] Production locale commercialisée.
[7] Livraisons.
[8] Machines à laver automatiques seulement.
[9] Quantités livrées de marchandises fabriquées au Royaume–Uni.
[10] Y compris les machines à laver autres que de ménagè.
[11] Y compris les machines à sécher.
[12] Période de douze mois finissant le 30 juin de l'année indiquée.
[13] A partir de 1981, les données sont confidentielles.

Generators for hydraulic turbines – Génératrices pour entraînement par turbines hydrauliques

Unit : Number units

Unité : Nombre

Country or area	1976	1977	1978	1979	1980	1981	1982	1983	1984	1985	Pays ou zone
America, North	**16**	**20**	**17**	**11**	**12**	**15**	**13**	**6**	**7**	**6**	**Amérique du Nord**
United States[1] [2]	16	20	17	11	12	15	13	6	7	...	Etats–Unis[1] [2]
Asia	**22**	**29**	**35**	**42**	**52**	**57**	**79**	**63**	**78**	**39**	**Asie**
Japan[3]	22	29	35	42	52	57	79	63	78	39	Japon[3]
Europe	**34 845**	**30 952**	**34 735**	**33 749**	**35 523**	**36 909**	**34 741**	**32 114**	**31 026**	**27 134**	**Europe**
EEC	***32 947***	***29 074***	***32 492***	***31 435***	***33 794***	***34 854***	***32 225***	***29 067***	***29 030***	***24 282***	***CEE***
Germany, Fed. Rep.[4]	32 947	29 074	32 492	31 435	33 794	34 854	32 225	29 067	29 030	24 282	Allemagne, Rép. féd.[4]
East Europe	***1 895***	***1 870***	***2 233***	***2 300***	***1 699***	***2 047***	***2 510***	***2 928***	***1 968***	***2 847***	***Europe de l'est***
Bulgaria[5]	1 893	1 861	2 230	2 296	1 694	2 047	2 506	2 926	1 966	2 845	Bulgarie[5]
Czechoslovakia	2	5	3	4	5	0	0	2	2	1	Tchécoslovaquie
Hungary	0	4	0	0	0	0	4	0	0	1	Hongrie
Other Europe	***3***	***8***	***10***	***14***	***30***	***8***	***6***	***119***	***28***	***5***	***Autre Europe***
Yugoslavia	3	8	10	14	30	8	6	119	28	5	Yougoslavie
Total	**34 883**	**31 001**	**34 787**	**33 802**	**35 587**	**36 981**	**34 833**	**32 183**	**31 111**	**27 179**	**Total**

General note.
Machines which transform mechanical power into electrical energy. There are two main classes – direct–current generators (dynamos) and alternating–current generators (alternators). Dynamos used in conjunction with internal–combustion engines or for lighting or signalling equipment on motor vehicles or cycles are excluded. Prime movers associated with the generators are also excluded. (SITC 72210–1A).

[1] Shipments.
[2] Generators for hydraulic turbines of 4000 kW and larger.
[3] A.C. type generators for general use.
[4] Including generators for steam turbines.
[5] Including other generators.

Remarque générale.
Machines qui produisent de l'énergie électrique par transformation de l'énergie mécanique. On appelle dynamos les génératrices de courant continu et alternateurs les génératrices de courant alternatif. Cette rubrique ne comprend pas les dynamos utilisées avec les moteurs à explosion ou à combustion interne, ni les dispositifs d'éclairage et de signalisation des cycles et automobiles. Elle ne comprend pas non plus les machines motrices associées aux génératrices. (CTCI 72210–1A).

[1] Expéditions.
[2] Génératrices pour entraînement par turbines hydrauliques de 4000 kW et plus.
[3] Génératrices à courant alternatif, tous usages.
[4] Y compris les génératrices pour entraînement par turbines à vapeur.
[5] Y compris les autres génératrices.

Generators for hydraulic turbines – Génératrices pour entraînement par turbines hydrauliques

Unit : Thousand kilowatts

Unité : Milliers de kilowatts

Country or area	1976	1977	1978	1979	1980	1981	1982	1983	1984	1985	Pays ou zone
America, North	**832**	**1 540**	**1 361**	**774**	**1 909**	**2 019**	**851**	**125**	**226**	**534**	**Amérique du Nord**
United States	832	1 540	1 361	774	1 909	2 019	851	125	226	...	Etats-Unis
Asia	**1 669**	**3 673**	**6 015**	**4 888**	**4 657**	**4 469**	**6 614**	**4 590**	**5 917**	**742**	**Asie**
Japan[1]	1 669	3 673	6 015	4 888	4 657	4 469	6 614	4 590	5 917	742	Japon[1]
Europe	**815**	**1 226**	**1 145**	**960**	**1 260**	**1 265**	**581**	**373**	**549**	**750**	**Europe**
East Europe	***701***	***909***	***707***	***670***	***779***	***576***	***388***	***223***	***178***	***208***	***Europe de l'est***
Bulgaria[2]	96	67	65	83	71	202	228	85	91	145	Bulgarie[2]
Czechoslovakia	247	564	417	412	449	...	0	24	2	2	Tchécoslovaquie
Hungary	...	...	0	0	0	0	18	0	0	5	Hongrie
Romania	354	274	225	175	259	...	...	...	...	...	Roumanie
Other Europe	***114***	***317***	***438***	***290***	***481***	***689***	***193***	***150***	***371***	***542***	***Autre Europe***
Yugoslavia	114	317	438	290	481	689	193	150	371	542	Yougoslavie
Total	**3 316**	**6 439**	**8 521**	**6 622**	**7 826**	**7 753**	**8 046**	**5 088**	**6 692**	**2 026**	**Total**

General note.
Machines which transform mechanical power into electrical energy. There are two main classes – direct-current generators (dynamos) and alternating-current generators (alternators). Dynamos used in conjunction with internal-combustion engines or for lighting or signalling equipment on motor vehicles or cycles are excluded. Prime movers associated with the generators are also excluded. (SITC 72210-1B).

[1] A.C. type generators for general use.
[2] Including other generators.

Remarque générale.
Machines qui produisent de l'énergie électrique par transformation de l'énergie mécanique. On appelle dynamos les génératrices de courant continu et alternateurs les génératrices de courant alternatif. Cette rubrique ne comprend pas les dynamos utilisées avec les moteurs à explosion ou à combustion interne, ni les dispositifs d'éclairage et de signalisation des cycles et automobiles. Elle ne comprend pas non plus les machines motrices associées aux génératrices. (CTCI 72210-1B).

[1] Génératrices à courant alternatif, tous usages.
[2] Y compris les autres génératrices.

Generators for steam turbines – Génératrices pour entraînement par turbines à vapeur

Unit : Number units | Unité : Nombre

Country or area	1976	1977	1978	1979	1980	1981	1982	1983	1984	1985	Pays ou zone
America, North	**48**	**47**	**45**	**44**	**43**	**47**	**38**	**34**	**36**	**41**	**Amérique du Nord**
United States	...	...	...	...	...	47	38	34	36	41	Etats–Unis
Asia	**156**	**99**	**146**	**80**	**128**	**113**	**197**	**133**	**128**	**127**	**Asie**
Japan[1]	156	99	146	80	128	113	197	133	128	127	Japon[1]
Europe	**228**	**335**	**282**	**178**	**154**	**158**	**122**	**122**	**71**	**40**	**Europe**
EEC	***189***	***301***	***255***	***160***	***130***	***129***	***103***	***78***	***52***	***26***	***CEE***
Greece	189	301	255	160	130	...	...	...	...	...	Grèce
East Europe	***25***	***22***	***21***	***13***	***14***	***26***	***18***	***12***	***14***	***13***	***Europe de l'est***
Czechoslovakia	19	20	18	9	12	19	12	12	13	10	Tchécoslovaquie
Hungary	6	2	3	4	2	7	6	0	1	3	Hongrie
Other Europe	***14***	***12***	***6***	***5***	***10***	***3***	***1***	***32***	***5***	***1***	***Autre Europe***
Yugoslavia	14	12	6	5	10	3	1	32	5	1	Yougoslavie
USSR[2]	**168**	**164**	**163**	**148**	**121**	**122**	**120**	**101**	**85**	**82**	**URSS[2]**
Total	**600**	**645**	**636**	**450**	**446**	**440**	**477**	**390**	**320**	**290**	**Total**

General note.
Machines which transform mechanical power into electrical energy. There are two main classes – direct–current generators (dynamos) and alternating–current generators (alternators). Dynamos used in conjunction with internal–combustion engines or for lighting or signalling equipment on motor vehicles or cycles are excluded. Prime movers associated with the generators are also excluded. (SITC 72210–2A).

[1] A.C. type generators for general use.
[2] Including generators for gas turbines.

Remarque générale.
Machines qui produisent de l'énergie électrique par transformation de l'énergie mécanique. On appelle dynamos les génératrices de courant continu et alternateurs les génératrices de courant alternatif. Cette rubrique ne comprend pas les dynamos utilisées avec les moteurs à explosion ou à combustion interne, ni les dispositifs d'éclairage et de signalisation des cycles et automobiles. Elle ne comprend pas non plus les machines motrices associées aux génératrices. (CTCI 72210–2A).

[1] Génératrices à courant alternatif, tous usages.
[2] Y compris les génératrices à entraînement par turbines à gaz.

Generators for steam turbines – Génératrices pour entraînement par turbines à vapeur

Unit : Thousand kilowatts

Unité : Milliers de kilowatts

Country or area	1976	1977	1978	1979	1980	1981	1982	1983	1984	1985	Pays ou zone
America, North	**17 952**	**16 888**	**15 825**	**14 762**	**13 698**	**13 466**	**9 116**	**11 905**	**10 802**	**7 255**	**Amérique du Nord**
United States	...	...	...	...	...	13 466	9 116	11 905	10 802	7 255	Etats–Unis
Asia	**13 932**	**8 428**	**12 397**	**10 853**	**13 250**	**13 783**	**15 809**	**12 073**	**8 658**	**10 182**	**Asie**
Japan[1]	13 932	8 428	12 397	10 853	13 250	13 783	15 809	12 073	8 658	10 182	Japon[1]
Europe	**7 714**	**8 875**	**6 670**	**6 164**	**4 199**	**6 881**	**4 981**	**4 498**	**4 299**	**3 534**	**Europe**
EEC	***3 835***	***6 375***	***4 715***	***4 390***	***2 580***	***4 265***	***2 715***	***3 070***	***2 557***	***2 237***	***CEE***
United Kingdom[2]	3 835	6 375	4 715	4 390	2 580	4 265	2 715	3 070	...	...	Royaume–Uni[2]
East Europe	***3 512***	***2 168***	***1 755***	***1 720***	***1 403***	***2 098***	***2 150***	***1 255***	***1 480***	***1 105***	***Europe de l'est***
Czechoslovakia	1 528	1 299	1 271	840	430	1 404	1 189	869	862	347	Tchécoslovaquie
Hungary	641	64	23	394	487	161	501	0	305	518	Hongrie
Romania	1 343	805	461	486	486	...	...	...	...	...	Roumanie
Other Europe	***367***	***332***	***200***	***54***	***216***	***518***	***116***	***173***	***262***	***192***	***Autre Europe***
Yugoslavia	367	332	200	54	216	518	116	173	262	192	Yougoslavie
USSR[3]	**16 596**	**17 936**	**18 159**	**17 018**	**16 138**	**13 941**	**12 664**	**12 552**	**13 724**	**13 337**	**URSS[3]**
Ukrainian SSR[3]	*2 744*	*2 444*	*2 336*	*2 958*	*2 263*	*1 584*	*2 084*	*1 953*	*1 700*	*2 000*	*RSS d'Ukraine[3]*
Total	**56 194**	**52 127**	**53 051**	**48 797**	**47 285**	**48 071**	**42 570**	**41 028**	**37 483**	**34 308**	**Total**

General note.
Machines which transform mechanical power into electrical energy. There are two main classes – direct–current generators (dynamos) and alternating–current generators (alternators). Dynamos used in conjunction with internal–combustion engines or for lighting or signalling equipment on motor vehicles or cycles are excluded. Prime movers associated with the generators are also excluded. (SITC 72210–2B).

[1] A.C. type generators for general use.
[2] Deliveries of steam turbo–alternators of 10000 kW and over.
[3] Including generators for gas and hydraulic turbines.

Remarque générale.
Machines qui produisent de l'énergie électrique par transformation de l'énergie mécanique. On appelle dynamos les génératrices de courant continu et alternateurs les génératrices de courant alternatif. Cette rubrique ne comprend pas les dynamos utilisées avec les moteurs à explosion ou à combustion interne, ni les dispositifs d'éclairage et de signalisation des cycles et automobiles. Elle ne comprend pas non plus les machines motrices associées aux génératrices. (CTCI 72210–2B).

[1] Génératrices à courant alternatif, tous usages.
[2] Livraisons de turbo–générateurs à vapeur de 10000 kW et plus.
[3] Y compris les génératrices à entraînement par turbines à gaz et turbines hydrauliques.

Motors, electric, fractional horsepower – Moteurs électriques de moins d'un CV

Unit : Thousand units — Unité : En milliers

Country or area	1976	1977	1978	1979	1980	1981	1982	1983	1984	1985	Pays ou zone
America, North	**192 630**	**223 766**	**239 226**	**243 044**	**201 597**	**204 411**	**181 782**	**214 893**	**236 972**	**235 112**	**Amérique du Nord**
Canada[1 2]	1 437	1 407	1 774	...	...	...	...	...	...	...	Canada[1 2]
Mexico	770	1 200	1 536	2 073	2 511	2 819	2 419	1 288	345	418	Mexique
United States[1]	190 423	221 159	235 916	239 432	197 547	200 053	177 824	212 066	235 088	233 155	Etats–Unis[1]
America, South	**2 977**	**3 054**	**3 918**	**4 111**	**4 928**	**4 473**	**4 013**	**4 919**	**5 167**	**5 415**	**Amérique du Sud**
Brazil	2 977	3 054	3 918	4 111	4 928	4 473	4 013	...	...	...	Brésil
Asia	**14 998**	**15 266**	**17 603**	**19 740**	**20 003**	**18 321**	**19 124**	**20 813**	**25 281**	**25 778**	**Asie**
Japan[3]	14 788	15 024	16 996	19 115	19 446	17 693	18 556	20 026	24 233	24 721	Japon[3]
Pakistan[4]	...	...	22	21	25	28	25	28	28	...	Pakistan[4]
Philippines[1]	7	10	...	...	...	...	...	...	...	...	Philippines[1]
Turkey	183	211	576	595	523	591	534	750	1 011	1 019	Turquie
Europe	**76 128**	**77 439**	**79 569**	**79 587**	**83 060**	**67 689**	**66 811**	**70 594**	**76 926**	**87 601**	**Europe**
EEC	***60 995***	***63 760***	***67 106***	***67 432***	***70 663***	***55 311***	***54 376***	***57 962***	***64 114***	***72 857***	***CEE***
Denmark*	847	889	732	611	514	...	...	...	...	...	Danemark*
Germany, Fed. Rep.	52 934	54 320	57 605	58 739	64 265	50 568	49 630	53 178	59 480	68 018	Allemagne, Rép. féd.
Greece[5]	160	139	116	84	77	5	4	5	4	...	Grèce[5]
United Kingdom	7 054	8 412	8 653	7 998	5 807	4 301	4 399	4 530	4 475	4 774	Royaume–Uni
EFTA	***3 738***	***3 581***	***3 471***	***4 180***	***4 130***	***3 713***	***4 022***	***3 880***	***4 224***	***4 882***	***AELE***
Austria	1 675	1 886	1 717	2 102	1 911	1 648	2 035	1 831	2 004	2 656	Autriche
Sweden	2 063	1 695	1 754	2 078	2 219	2 065	1 987	2 049	2 220	2 226	Suède
East Europe	***3 957***	***4 362***	***4 703***	***4 758***	***4 820***	***4 933***	***4 749***	***4 520***	***4 113***	***4 298***	***Europe de l'est***
Czechoslovakia[6]	2 700	3 008	3 205	3 365	3 433	3 499	3 495	3 247	2 635	2 677	Tchécoslovaquie[6]
Hungary	1 257	1 354	1 498	1 393	1 387	1 434	1 254	1 273	1 478	1 621	Hongrie
Other Europe	***7 438***	***5 736***	***4 289***	***3 217***	***3 447***	***3 732***	***3 664***	***4 232***	***4 475***	***5 563***	***Autre Europe***
Spain	2 841	...	...	649	535	960	448	539	...	...	Espagne
Yugoslavia	4 597	4 271	3 004	2 568	2 912	2 772	3 216	3 693	4 268	5 536	Yougoslavie
USSR[7]	**8 513**	**8 864**	**9 131**	**9 215**	**9 412**	**9 617**	**9 571**	**9 637**	**9 265**	**9 279**	**URSS[7]**
Byelorussian SSR[7]	*696*	*828*	*956*	*1 047*	*1 131*	*1 193*	*1 223*	*1 305*	*1 222*	*1 255*	*RSS de Biélorussie[7]*
Ukrainian SSR[7]	*2 209*	*2 326*	*2 477*	*2 545*	*2 639*	*2 733*	*2 757*	*2 796*	*2 745*	*2 836*	*RSS d'Ukraine[7]*
Oceania	**3 765**	**3 021**	**2 580**	**2 842**	**3 378**	**3 659**	**3 460**	**2 278**	**3 043**	**3 123**	**Océanie**
Australia[8]	3 765	3 021	2 580	2 842	3 378	3 659	3 460	2 278	3 043	3 123	Australie[8]
Total	**299 011**	**331 410**	**352 027**	**358 539**	**322 378**	**308 170**	**284 761**	**323 133**	**356 654**	**366 309**	**Total**

General note.
Machines which transform electrical energy into mechanical power in the form of rotary motion, having a capacity of less than one horsepower. Starter motors for internal–combustion engines are excluded. (SITC 72210–3A).

Remarque générale.
Machines qui transforment l'énergie électrique en énergie mécanique sous forme de mouvement rotatif, dont la puissance est inférieure à un cheval–vapeur. Cette rubrique ne comprend pas les démarreurs des moteurs à explosion ou à combustion interne. (CTCI 72210–3A).

[1] Shipments.
[2] Single–phase and poly–phase induction A.C. motors only.
[3] Single–phase A.C. electric motors, not less than 35 W.
[4] Including electric motors of 1 HP and over.
[5] Electric motors less than 1/4 horsepower.
[6] Electric motors, 1 kW and under.
[7] A.C. electric motors, 0.25–100 kW.
[8] Twelve months ending 30 June of year stated.

[1] Expéditions.
[2] Moteurs d'induction C.A. monophasés et polyphasés seulement.
[3] Moteurs électriques C.A. monophasés d'au moins 35 W.
[4] Y compris les moteurs électriques de 1 ch et plus.
[5] Moteurs électriques de moins de 1/4 ch.
[6] Moteurs électriques de 1 kW et moins.
[7] Alternateurs de 0.25 à 100 kW.
[8] Période de douze mois finissant le 30 juin de l'année indiquée.

Motors, electric, fractional horsepower – Moteurs électriques de moins d'un CV

Unit : Thousand kilowatts

Unité : Milliers de kilowatts

Country or area	1976	1977	1978	1979	1980	1981	1982	1983	1984	1985	Pays ou zone
Asia	**3 397**	**3 675**	**4 406**	**5 375**	**5 125**	**3 881**	**4 416**	**4 943**	**6 774**	**6 770**	**Asie**
Japan[1]	3 397	3 675	4 406	5 375	5 125	3 881	4 416	4 943	6 774	6 770	Japon[1]
Europe	**7 616**	**7 692**	**8 691**	**9 283**	**9 902**	**8 904**	**9 261**	**8 889**	**8 190**	**8 105**	**Europe**
EEC	***5 490***	***5 119***	***5 914***	***6 220***	***6 395***	***5 902***	***5 485***	***4 937***	***5 103***	***5 545***	***CEE***
France[2]	5 490	5 119	5 914	6 220	6 395	5 902	5 485	4 937	5 103	5 545	France[2]
East Europe	***711***	***615***	***664***	***669***	***705***	***774***	***785***	***775***	***736***	***786***	***Europe de l'est***
Czechoslovakia[3]	367	407	443	492	497	525	596	583	511	533	Tchécoslovaquie[3]
Hungary	344	208	221	177	208	249	189	192	225	253	Hongrie
Other Europe	***1 415***	***1 958***	***2 113***	***2 394***	***2 802***	***2 228***	***2 991***	***3 177***	***2 351***	***1 774***	***Autre Europe***
Spain	500	...	...	...	...	...	...	...	...	...	Espagne
Yugoslavia	915	1 458	1 613	1 894	2 302	1 728	2 491	2 677	1 851	1 274	Yougoslavie
USSR[4]	**35 420**	**36 011**	**37 615**	**38 247**	**39 859**	**40 552**	**40 721**	**40 393**	**40 598**	**41 157**	**URSS[4]**
Byelorussian SSR[4]	*2 074*	*2 260*	*2 596*	*2 941*	*3 150*	*3 516*	*3 625*	*3 792*	*3 581*	*3 654*	*RSS de Biélorussie[4]*
Ukrainian SSR[4]	*6 811*	*7 107*	*7 996*	*8 592*	*9 545*	*10 013*	*10 663*	*10 363*	*10 433*	*10 415*	*RSS d'Ukraine[4]*
Total	**46 433**	**47 378**	**50 712**	**52 905**	**54 886**	**53 337**	**54 398**	**54 225**	**55 562**	**56 032**	**Total**

General note.
Machines which transform electrical energy into mechanical power in the form of rotary motion, having a capacity of less than one horsepower. Starter motors for internal–combustion engines are excluded. (SITC 72210–3B).

[1] Single–phase A.C. electric motors, not less than 35 W.
[2] Deliveries.
[3] Electric motors, 1 kW and under.
[4] A.C. electric motors, 0.25–100 kW.

Remarque générale.
Machines qui transforment l'énergie électrique en énergie mécanique sous forme de mouvement rotatif, dont la puissance est inférieure à un cheval–vapeur. Cette rubrique ne comprend pas les démarreurs des moteurs à explosion ou à combustion interne. (CTCI 72210–3B).

[1] Moteurs électriques C.A. monophasés d'au moins 35 W.
[2] Livraisons.
[3] Moteurs électriques de 1 kW et moins.
[4] Alternateurs de 0.25 à 100 kW.

Motors, electric, of one horsepower and over – Moteurs électriques d'un CV et plus

Unit : Thousand units | Unité : En milliers

Country or area	1976	1977	1978	1979	1980	1981	1982	1983	1984	1985	Pays ou zone
Africa	**427**	**409**	**386**	**365**	**384**	**392**	**192**	**245**	**266**	**312**	**Afrique**
South Africa[1]	...	...	...	...	380	388	189	240	* 259	306	Afrique du Sud[1]
Tunisia	2	5	2	1	4	4	3	5	7	...	Tunisie
America, North	**3 851**	**4 668**	**5 167**	**5 526**	**4 275**	**3 878**	**3 698**	**3 993**	**4 327**	**4 105**	**Amérique du Nord**
Canada[2 3]	73	85	78	157	159	...	...	...	...	...	Canada[2 3]
United States[2]	3 778	4 583	5 089	5 369	4 116	3 736	3 545	3 828	4 151	3 917	Etats–Unis[2]
America, South	**821**	**820**	**861**	**955**	**1 107**	**1 103**	**745**	**999**	**1 020**	**1 041**	**Amérique du Sud**
Brazil	653	652	693	787	939	935	577	...	...	...	Brésil
Colombia	168	...	...	...	...	...	...	...	...	...	Colombie
Asia	**6 460**	**7 135**	**8 159**	**9 787**	**7 889**	**7 225**	**7 751**	**8 048**	**10 741**	**11 045**	**Asie**
Burma[4 5]	0	...	1	1	1	1	1	1	1	1	Birmanie[4 5]
India[1]	300	...	...	...	...	...	...	...	...	...	Inde[1]
Japan[6]	5 037	5 305	5 646	6 812	6 063	5 329	5 609	5 717	7 289	7 505	Japon[6]
Korea, Republic of	942	1 226	1 980	2 506	[7] 1 343	[7] 1 427	[7] 1 673	[7] 1 868	[7] 2 840	[7] 3 051	Corée, République de
Syrian Arab Republic	43	53	65	59	65	85	89	91	202	126	Rép. arabe syrienne
Turkey	138	251	167	109	117	83	79	71	109	62	Turquie
Europe	**16 506**	**19 094**	**20 683**	**21 456**	**20 162**	**18 741**	**17 939**	**18 934**	**20 170**	**20 918**	**Europe**
EEC	***3 058***	***3 404***	***3 578***	***3 687***	***3 698***	***3 297***	***3 160***	***3 251***	***3 913***	***4 142***	***CEE***
Denmark	* 23	* 21	* 17	* 21	18	...	...	...	...	...	Danemark
Germany, Fed. Rep.	2 400	2 614	2 699	2 845	3 003	2 643	2 598	2 681	3 340	3 547	Allemagne, Rép. féd.
Greece[8]	38	40	52	38	26	41	43	55	39	...	Grèce[8]
United Kingdom	597	729	810	783	651	596	503	* 500	520	538	Royaume–Uni
EFTA	***290***	***553***	***800***	***1 056***	***1 073***	***895***	***620***	***528***	***540***	***641***	***AELE***
Austria[1]	181	436	685	938	973	* 767	488	406	434	560	Autriche[1]
Portugal[1]	109	117	115	118	100	128	132	122	106	81	Portugal[1]
East Europe	***12 685***	***14 608***	***15 734***	***15 885***	***14 943***	***13 980***	***13 349***	***14 285***	***14 907***	***15 283***	***Europe de l'est***
Bulgaria[1]	1 006	1 207	1 161	1 124	1 251	1 234	1 338	1 375	1 411	1 401	Bulgarie[1]
Czechoslovakia[9]	734	767	808	962	954	967	905	957	1 059	1 070	Tchécoslovaquie[9]
Hungary	315	322	346	411	403	292	270	277	283	307	Hongrie
Poland	10 630	12 312	13 419	13 388	12 335	11 487	10 836	11 676	12 154	12 505	Pologne
Other Europe	***473***	***529***	***571***	***828***	***448***	***569***	***810***	***870***	***810***	***851***	***Autre Europe***
Spain	460	...	...	828	433	553	776	830	...	...	Espagne
Yugoslavia	...	...	...	0	...	...	34	40	4	4	Yougoslavie
USSR[10]	**38**	**39**	**39**	**37**	**38**	**38**	**38**	**37**	**39**	**40**	**URSS[10]**
Ukrainian SSR[10]	*2*	*2*	*1*	*2*	*1*	*1*	*1*	*1*	*0*	*0*	*RSS d'Ukraine[10]*
Oceania	**317**	**298**	**292**	**341**	**364**	**361**	**373**	**262**	**294**	**319**	**Océanie**
Australia[11]	317	298	292	341	364	361	373	262	294	319	Australie[11]
Total	**28 420**	**32 464**	**35 587**	**38 467**	**34 219**	**31 737**	**30 736**	**32 518**	**36 857**	**37 779**	**Total**

General note.
Machines which transform electrical energy into mechanical power in the form of rotary motion. Starter motors for internal–combustion engines are excluded. (SITC 72210–4A).

1 Including fractional–horsepower electric motors.
2 Shipments.
3 Single–phase and poly–phase induction A.C. motors only.
4 Government production only.
5 Twelve months ending 30 September of year stated.
6 Three–phase A.C. electric motors, 200 W and over, for general use.
7 In thousand horsepower.
8 Electric motors over 1/4 horsepower.
9 Electric motors over 1 kW.
10 A.C. electric motors over 100 kW.
11 Twelve months ending 30 June of year stated.

Remarque générale.
Machines qui transforment l'énergie électrique en énergie mécanique sous forme de mouvement rotatif. Cette rubrique ne comprend pas les démarreurs des moteurs à explosion ou à combustion interne. (CTCI 72210–4A).

1 Y compris les moteurs électriques de moins de 1 ch.
2 Expéditions.
3 Moteurs d'induction C.A. monophasés et polyphasés seulement.
4 Production de l'Etat seulement.
5 Période de douze mois finissant le 30 septembre de l'année indiquée.
6 Moteurs électriques C.A. triphasés de 200 W et plus, à usages généraux.
7 En milliers de chevaux–vapeur.
8 Moteurs électriques de plus de 1/4 ch.
9 Moteurs électriques de plus de 1 kW.
10 Moteurs électriques C.A. de plus de 100 kW.
11 Période de douze mois finissant le 30 juin de l'année indiquée.

Motors, electric, of one horsepower and over – Moteurs électriques d'un CV et plus

Unit : Thousand kilowatts — Unité : Milliers de kilowatts

Country or area	1976	1977	1978	1979	1980	1981	1982	1983	1984	1985	Pays ou zone
Africa	**317**	**324**	**331**	**339**	**328**	**350**	**378**	**419**	**331**	**384**	**Afrique**
South Africa	...	...	...	...	* 328	* 350	378	419	331	...	Afrique du Sud
Asia	**46 236**	**46 823**	**53 109**	**59 415**	**49 989**	**44 243**	**47 316**	**51 892**	**57 140**	**62 663**	**Asie**
China	...	26 960	31 950	35 630	25 700	21 260	24 200	28 680	30 510	34 840	Chine
India[1,2]	2 626	2 939	2 934	2 931	2 854	3 382	4 479	4 956	4 940	5 088	Inde[1,2]
Japan[3]	15 031	16 221	17 522	20 151	20 732	18 898	17 934	17 553	20 987	22 032	Japon[3]
Korea, Republic of	703	...	...	...	...	...	...	...	...	...	Corée, République de
Europe	**32 272**	**34 597**	**36 444**	**36 831**	**39 171**	**37 024**	**38 311**	**38 733**	**39 169**	**40 008**	**Europe**
EEC	***814***	***741***	***850***	***781***	***1 388***	***1 390***	***1 365***	***1 406***	***1 214***	***870***	***CEE***
France[4]	814	741	850	781	1 388	1 390	1 365	1 406	1 214	870	France[4]
EFTA	***373***	***435***	***335***	***306***	***391***	***387***	***404***	***333***	***298***	***238***	***AELE***
Portugal[1,5]	* 373	435	335	306	391	387	404	333	298	238	Portugal[1,5]
East Europe	***28 578***	***30 907***	***32 746***	***33 228***	***34 878***	***32 734***	***34 001***	***34 449***	***35 146***	***36 388***	***Europe de l'est***
Bulgaria[1]	5 341	5 822	6 483	6 066	7 111	6 249	6 446	6 358	6 720	6 652	Bulgarie[1]
Czechoslovakia[6]	4 461	4 812	4 870	5 704	6 418	6 451	6 381	6 529	6 228	6 628	Tchécoslovaquie[6]
Hungary	1 540	1 608	1 689	1 514	1 418	1 322	1 241	1 137	1 096	1 286	Hongrie
Poland	10 969	10 987	11 096	10 621	9 864	9 297	9 012	8 830	8 832	8 878	Pologne
Romania[7]	6 267	7 678	8 608	9 323	10 067	9 415	...	...	...	...	Roumanie[7]
Other Europe	***2 507***	***2 514***	***2 513***	***2 516***	***2 514***	***2 513***	***2 541***	***2 545***	***2 511***	***2 512***	***Autre Europe***
Spain	2 500	...	...	...	...	...	...	...	...	...	Espagne
Yugoslavia	7	14	13	...	14	13	41	45	11	12	Yougoslavie
USSR[8]	**7 452**	**7 547**	**7 729**	**7 542**	**7 700**	**7 664**	**7 719**	**7 647**	**8 007**	**8 223**	**URSS[8]**
Ukrainian SSR[8]	*239*	*228*	*210*	*220*	*211*	*216*	*193*	*135*	*51*	*58*	*RSS d'Ukraine[8]*
Total	**86 276**	**89 291**	**97 613**	**104 127**	**97 188**	**89 281**	**93 724**	**98 691**	**104 647**	**111 278**	**Total**

General note.
Machines which transform electrical energy into mechanical power in the form of rotary motion. Starter motors for internal-combustion engines are excluded. (SITC 72210-4B).

[1] Including fractional-horsepower electric motors.
[2] Production by large and medium scale establishments only.
[3] Three-phase A.C. electric motors, 200 W and over, for general use.
[4] Deliveries.
[5] Original data in horsepower.
[6] Electric motors over 1 kW.
[7] Electric motors, 0.6 kW and over.
[8] A.C. electric motors over 100 kW.

Remarque générale.
Machines qui transforment l'énergie électrique en énergie mécanique sous forme de mouvement rotatif. Cette rubrique ne comprend pas les démarreurs des moteurs à explosion ou à combustion interne. (CTCI 72210-4B).

[1] Y compris les moteurs électriques de moins de 1 ch.
[2] Production des grandes et moyennes entreprises seulement.
[3] Moteurs électriques C.A. triphasés de 200 W et plus, à usages généraux.
[4] Livraisons.
[5] Données d'origine exprimées en chevaux-vapeur.
[6] Moteurs électriques de plus de 1 kW.
[7] Moteurs électriques de 0,6 kW et plus.
[8] Moteurs électriques C.A. de plus de 100 kW.

Transformers less than 5 KVA – Transformateurs de moins de 5 kVA

Unit : Thousand units

Unité : En milliers

Country or area	1976	1977	1978	1979	1980	1981	1982	1983	1984	1985	Pays ou zone
Africa											**Afrique**
South Africa	98	61	83	120	139	432	...	...	...	...	Afrique du Sud
America, South											**Amérique du Sud**
Brazil[1]	32	65	47	1 337	1 062	540	1 535	505	544	...	Brésil[1]
Asia											**Asie**
Philippines[2]	73	213	...	...	...	...	...	...	...	...	Philippines[2]
Syrian Arab Republic	19	11	60	33	94	765	551	623	897	1 150	Rép. arabe syrienne
Turkey	969	1 241	966	617	36	10	103	269	1 444	2 378	Turquie
Europe											**Europe**
EEC											***CEE***
Germany, Fed. Rep.[3]	18 829	18 266	21 034	22 284	23 479	19 931	19 259	24 003	32 085	37 353	Allemagne, Rép. féd.[3]
Greece[4]	935	950	1 036	1 212	1 501	1 383	1 407	581	293	...	Grèce[4]
United Kingdom	1 773	2 064	3 125	3 363	1 542	1 209	1 488	1 439	1 548	1 115	Royaume–Uni
EFTA											***AELE***
Austria	90	91	75	135	91	96	94	81	100	102	Autriche
Finland	271	...	...	...	244	210	203	210	212	...	Finlande
Portugal[5]	9	20	15	17	21	34	47	33	24	19	Portugal[5]
Sweden	...	...	349	354	365	333	367	459	632	668	Suède
East Europe											***Europe de l'est***
Czechoslovakia	21	16	18	18	18	18	19	22	23	20	Tchécoslovaquie
Hungary	77	110	103	122	95	136	135	93	54	88	Hongrie
Other Europe											***Autre Europe***
Spain	...	...	...	3 682	2 691	2 451	2 152	2 116	...	...	Espagne
Yugoslavia	75	237	76	69	78	116	120	142	149	164	Yougoslavie

General note.
Electrical appliances which, without any action of moving parts, transform an alternating current system into another system of alternating current of different voltage. (SITC 72210–5A).

[1] Including transformers 5 kVA and over.
[2] Shipments.
[3] Data refer to transformers of less than 16 kVA.
[4] Transformers of all sizes.
[5] Including transformers less than 16 kVA.

Remarque générale.
Appareils électriques qui, sans l'intervention d'organes mobiles, transforment un courant alternatif en un autre courant alternatif d'intensité et de tension différentes. (CTCI 72210–5A).

[1] Y compris les transformateurs de 5 kVA et plus.
[2] Expéditions.
[3] Données se rapportant aux transformateurs de moins de 16 kVA.
[4] Transformateurs de toutes dimensions.
[5] Y compris transformateurs de moins de 16 kVA.

Transformers of 5 KVA and over – Transformateurs de 5 kVA et plus

Unit : Number units

Unité : Nombre

Country or area	1976	1977	1978	1979	1980	1981	1982	1983	1984	1985	Pays ou zone
Africa	**16 090**	**10 190**	**10 762**	**12 036**	**14 364**	**20 657**	**396 506**	**413 384**	**240 603**	**247 092**	**Afrique**
South Africa	14 523	9 515	7 967	9 736	12 257	17 748	[1] 393 858	[1] 411 167	[1] 237 671	[1] 243 987	Afrique du Sud
Tunisia	1 567	675	2 795	2 300	2 107	2 909	2 648	2 217	...	...	Tunisie
America, North	**136 982**	**186 420**	**207 286**	**236 984**	**226 875**	**267 658**	**290 573**	**313 488**	**336 403**	**359 319**	**Amérique du Nord**
Canada[2 3]	136 982	186 420	207 286	236 984	226 875	...	...	...	...	...	Canada[2 3]
America, South	**72 328**	**75 235**	**94 963**	**112 473**	**88 749**	**88 749**	**88 749**	**88 749**	**88 749**	**88 749**	**Amérique du Sud**
Brazil	72 328	75 235	94 963	[4] 112 473	...	...	...	...	...	...	Brésil
Asia	**507 762**	**558 638**	**623 525**	**593 141**	**541 350**	**526 051**	**442 934**	**445 231**	**506 432**	**529 925**	**Asie**
Iran(Islamic Rep.of)[5]	...	...	...	5 477	5 457	7 535	10 957	9 961	...	...	Iran(Rép.islamique)[5]
Japan	493 478	544 515	608 364	577 882	522 272	502 996	420 230	415 255	473 033	480 864	Japon
Philippines	3 995	1 754	...	...	...	...	...	...	...	...	Philippines
Turkey	9 591	10 235	8 717	6 908	10 747	12 646	8 873	17 141	18 341	32 567	Turquie
Europe	**2 257 203**	**1 321 411**	**1 094 978**	**1 090 934**	**1 247 484**	**1 249 888**	**2 042 407**	**1 604 925**	**1 901 899**	**2 013 862**	**Europe**
EEC	***2 147 255***	***1 210 253***	***988 192***	***990 266***	***1 148 110***	***1 146 525***	***1 936 069***	***1 504 545***	***1 799 531***	***1 918 880***	***CEE***
Germany, Fed. Rep.	2 050 255	1 171 253	938 192	944 266	1 117 368	1 121 793	1 909 242	1 470 872	1 748 766	1 869 212	Allemagne, Rép. féd.
United Kingdom	97 000	39 000	50 000	46 000	30 742	24 732	26 827	33 673	50 765	49 668	Royaume–Uni
EFTA	***16 496***	***21 443***	***17 355***	***14 765***	***15 028***	***15 294***	***14 908***	***13 266***	***15 540***	***14 837***	***AELE***
Austria	14 867	18 752	14 660	11 254	11 065	10 531	10 528	10 063	11 735	11 266	Autriche
Portugal[6]	1 629	2 691	2 695	3 511	3 963	4 763	4 380	3 203	3 805	3 571	Portugal[6]
East Europe	***59 776***	***57 069***	***57 225***	***54 570***	***51 830***	***54 213***	***58 185***	***55 138***	***59 249***	***52 099***	***Europe de l'est***
Bulgaria[7]	7 311	8 928	8 495	6 786	7 645	8 427	8 621	8 846	9 522	9 357	Bulgarie[7]
Czechoslovakia	11 292	10 764	12 054	12 169	11 570	13 447	10 954	9 666	10 841	10 389	Tchécoslovaquie
German Dem. Rep.	10 308	10 530	11 186	11 897	12 338	13 143	15 655	12 367	13 952	11 456	Rép. dém. allemande
Hungary	9 809	6 027	6 435	5 476	2 951	4 101	5 658	6 346	7 591	3 571	Hongrie
Poland[8]	21 056	20 820	19 055	18 242	17 326	15 095	17 297	17 913	17 343	17 326	Pologne[8]
Other Europe	***33 676***	***32 646***	***32 206***	***31 333***	***32 516***	***33 856***	***33 245***	***31 976***	***27 579***	***28 046***	***Autre Europe***
Spain	21 504	...	...	17 333	16 323	11 612	13 110	15 444	...	...	Espagne
Yugoslavia[9]	12 172	13 157	13 854	14 000	16 193	22 244	20 135	16 532	16 052	17 657	Yougoslavie[9]
Oceania	**15 025**	**18 358**	**18 888**	**19 311**	**19 565**	**20 747**	**22 589**	**20 627**	**44 514**	**50 365**	**Océanie**
Australia[7 10]	15 025	18 358	18 888	19 311	19 565	20 747	22 589	20 627	44 514	50 365	Australie[7 10]
Total	**3 005 390**	**2 170 252**	**2 050 402**	**2 064 879**	**2 138 387**	**2 173 750**	**3 283 758**	**2 886 404**	**3 118 600**	**3 289 312**	**Total**

General note.
Electrical appliances which, without any action of moving parts, transform an alternating current system into another system of alternating current of different voltage. (SITC 72210–6A).

[1] Including transformers of less than 5 kVA.
[2] Power and distribution transformers.
[3] Shipments.
[4] Production by establishments employing 5 or more persons.
[5] Production by establishments employing 10 or more persons.
[6] Including transformers less than 16 kVA.
[7] Transformers over 1 kVA.
[8] Transformers over 20 kVA.
[9] Including transformers less than 5 kVA.
[10] Twelve months ending 30 June of year stated.

Remarque générale.
Appareils électriques qui, sans l'intervention d'organes mobiles, transforment un courant alternatif en un autre courant alternatif d'intensité et de tension différentes. (CTCI 72210–6A).

[1] Y compris les transformateurs de moins de 5 kVA.
[2] Transformateurs de puissance et de distribution.
[3] Expéditions.
[4] Production des établissements occupant 5 personnes ou plus.
[5] Production des établissements occupant 10 personnes ou plus.
[6] Y compris transformateurs de moins de 16 kVA.
[7] Transformateurs de plus de 1 kVA.
[8] Transformateurs de plus de 20 kVA.
[9] Y compris transformateurs de moins de 5 kVA.
[10] Période de douze mois finissant le 30 juin de l'année indiquée.

Transformers of 5 KVA and over – Transformateurs de 5 kVA et plus

Unit : Thousand kVA — Unité : Milliers de kVA

Country or area	1976	1977	1978	1979	1980	1981	1982	1983	1984	1985	Pays ou zone
America, North	**42 158**	**43 940**	**34 533**	**32 685**	**38 329**	**38 329**	**38 329**	**38 329**	**38 329**	**38 329**	**Amérique du Nord**
Canada[1 2]	42 158	43 940	34 533	32 685	...	...	...	...	...	...	Canada[1 2]
Asia	**131 138**	**158 857**	**197 153**	**205 902**	**201 818**	**176 497**	**178 287**	**166 477**	**184 422**	**226 685**	**Asie**
China	...	35 810	48 620	58 230	44 610	27 340	31 430	42 280	50 300	80 450	Chine
India[3]	13 824	17 250	18 246	19 343	18 807	20 321	20 000	21 600	24 350	26 960	Inde[3]
Japan	79 231	100 821	119 969	114 864	131 111	120 699	113 011	90 119	95 840	103 846	Japon
Korea, Republic of	3 063	4 976	10 318	13 465	7 290	8 137	13 846	12 478	13 932	15 429	Corée, République de
Europe	**118 723**	**125 256**	**118 883**	**130 625**	**127 206**	**132 858**	**129 475**	**119 163**	**116 878**	**120 806**	**Europe**
EEC	***35 712***	***37 404***	***36 002***	***41 757***	***47 566***	***50 138***	***51 707***	***51 890***	***45 564***	***53 908***	***CEE***
France[4 5]	35 712	37 404	36 002	41 757	47 566	50 138	51 707	51 890	45 564	53 908	France[4 5]
EFTA	***1 244***	***2 645***	***3 116***	***2 621***	***3 011***	***3 030***	***3 161***	***2 514***	***2 530***	***2 193***	***AELE***
Portugal[6]	1 244	2 645	3 116	2 621	3 011	3 030	3 161	2 514	2 530	2 193	Portugal[6]
East Europe	***54 318***	***58 656***	***53 424***	***58 694***	***55 779***	***52 933***	***50 005***	***44 690***	***46 321***	***41 975***	***Europe de l'est***
Bulgaria[7]	4 162	4 145	4 138	3 667	4 136	4 894	4 459	4 635	4 442	4 744	Bulgarie[7]
Czechoslovakia	8 499	7 942	6 911	8 005	7 857	7 985	7 555	5 396	6 264	5 638	Tchécoslovaquie
German Dem. Rep.	11 297	11 350	11 946	12 174	12 207	13 389	11 277	9 205	10 350	11 467	Rép. dém. allemande
Hungary	1 786	2 699	3 113	3 648	2 216	1 558	1 268	1 188	2 006	899	Hongrie
Poland[8]	13 140	14 847	13 855	13 779	13 424	11 449	10 860	9 969	9 251	5 508	Pologne[8]
Romania[9]	15 434	17 673	13 461	17 421	15 939	13 658	...	...	...	...	Roumanie[9]
Other Europe	***27 449***	***26 551***	***26 341***	***27 553***	***20 850***	***26 757***	***24 602***	***20 069***	***22 464***	***22 730***	***Autre Europe***
Spain	17 909	...	...	17 053	11 105	13 955	13 365	11 185	...	...	Espagne
Yugoslavia[10]	9 540	9 524	10 240	10 500	9 745	12 802	11 237	8 884	11 917	13 109	Yougoslavie[10]
USSR	**143 698**	**146 287**	**150 165**	**154 961**	**159 254**	**161 134**	**160 888**	**155 061**	**156 192**	**161 096**	**URSS**
Byelorussian SSR	...	...	...	*7 475*	*7 387*	*7 013*	*6 234*	*6 423*	*6 434*	*6 507*	*RSS de Biélorussie*
Ukrainian SSR	...	...	...	*69 760*	*72 109*	*73 206*	*74 182*	*70 522*	*72 973*	*76 874*	*RSS d'Ukraine*
Oceania	**6 498**	**6 195**	**5 508**	**5 101**	**5 738**	**6 847**	**8 740**	**8 222**	**8 664**	**9 076**	**Océanie**
Australia[11]	6 498	6 195	5 508	5 101	5 738	6 847	8 740	8 222	8 664	9 076	Australie[11]
Total	**442 215**	**480 535**	**506 242**	**529 274**	**532 345**	**515 665**	**515 719**	**487 252**	**504 485**	**555 992**	**Total**

General note.
Electrical appliances which, without any action of moving parts, transform an alternating current system into another system of alternating current of different voltage. (SITC 72210–6B).

1 Power and distribution transformers.
2 Shipments.
3 Production by large and medium scale establishments only.
4 Deliveries.
5 Transformers over 25 kVA.
6 Including transformers less than 16 kVA.
7 Transformers over 1 kVA.
8 Transformers over 20 kVA.
9 Transformers over 0.25 kVA.
10 Including transformers less than 5 kVA.
11 Twelve months ending 30 June of year stated.

Remarque générale.
Appareils électriques qui, sans l'intervention d'organes mobiles, transforment un courant alternatif en un autre courant alternatif d'intensité et de tension différentes. (CTCI 72210–6B).

1 Transformateurs de puissance et de distribution.
2 Expéditions.
3 Production des grandes et moyennes entreprises seulement.
4 Livraisons.
5 Transformateurs de plus de 25 kVA.
6 Y compris transformateurs de moins de 16 kVA.
7 Transformateurs de plus de 1 kVA.
8 Transformateurs de plus de 20 kVA.
9 Transformateurs de plus de 0.25 kVA.
10 Y compris transformateurs de moins de 5 kVA.
11 Période de douze mois finissant le 30 juin de l'année indiquée.

Meters, electricity-supply – Compteurs d'électricité

Unit : Thousand units

Unité : En milliers

Country or area	1976	1977	1978	1979	1980	1981	1982	1983	1984	1985	Pays ou zone
Africa	**153**	**154**	**154**	**185**	**137**	**331**	**381**	**359**	**396**	**432**	**Afrique**
Egypt	153	154	154	185	137	331	* 381	...	...	...	Egypte
America, North	**3 783**	**4 394**	**4 969**	**5 111**	**4 685**	**4 746**	**3 850**	**4 520**	**4 725**	**4 660**	**Amérique du Nord**
United States[1]	3 783	4 394	4 969	5 111	4 685	4 746	3 850	4 520	4 725	...	Etats–Unis[1]
America, South	**32**	**26**	**26**	**29**	**35**	**36**	**22**	**19**	**30**	**42**	**Amérique du Sud**
Chile	32	26	26	29	35	36	22	19	30	42	Chili
Asia	**7 336**	**7 581**	**8 924**	**10 489**	**10 659**	**10 011**	**9 196**	**9 552**	**11 156**	**11 442**	**Asie**
India	1 816	1 969	2 386	2 924	3 144	2 753	2 416	2 418	3 361	3 983	Inde
Iran(Islamic Rep.of)[2]	...	...	...	945	743	1 049	...	...	...	...	Iran(Rép.islamique)[2]
Israel	73	58	62	45	17	34	32	36	12	41	Israël
Japan	3 114	3 391	3 931	4 736	4 641	4 060	4 116	4 294	4 615	4 269	Japon
Korea, Republic of	959	801	1 110	1 397	1 702	1 420	1 133	1 404	...	...	Corée, République de
Syrian Arab Republic	101	98	149	133	153	68	48	30	107	10	Rép. arabe syrienne
Turkey	361	352	374	309	259	627	539	458	586	592	Turquie
Europe	**9 430**	**9 112**	**8 022**	**8 656**	**8 366**	**8 576**	**8 763**	**8 753**	**6 550**	**6 435**	**Europe**
EEC	***5 727***	***5 348***	***5 069***	***4 942***	***4 677***	***4 886***	***5 246***	***4 933***	***4 448***	***4 460***	***CEE***
France	2 657	2 710	2 156	2 221	2 095	2 236	2 488	1 849	1 386	968	France
Germany, Fed. Rep	1 424	1 201	1 258	1 215	1 236	1 232	1 129	1 076	1 104	1 086	Allemagne, Rép. féd.
Greece	...	...	...	276	332	373	412	313	346	...	Grèce
United Kingdom	1 356	1 138	1 346	1 230	1 014	1 045	1 217	1 695	1 612	2 031	Royaume–Uni
EFTA	***286***	***300***	***323***	***280***	***276***	***269***	***319***	***310***	***302***	***299***	***AELE***
Austria	231	245	268	225	221	241	255	252	234	244	Autriche
Finland	...	...	...	...	...	28	64	58	68	...	Finlande
East Europe	***812***	***810***	***986***	***1 124***	***1 029***	***1 075***	***1 030***	***1 159***	***682***	***644***	***Europe de l'est***
Bulgaria	361	352	449	526	414	446	450	604	213	113	Bulgarie
Hungary	451	458	537	598	615	629	580	555	469	531	Hongrie
Other Europe	***2 606***	***2 654***	***1 645***	***2 310***	***2 384***	***2 346***	***2 168***	***2 351***	***1 118***	***1 033***	***Autre Europe***
Spain	1 169	1 218	...	684	739	670	452	294	...	...	Espagne
Yugoslavia	1 437	1 436	678	1 626	1 645	1 676	1 716	2 057	922	965	Yougoslavie
Oceania	**254**	**234**	**206**	**237**	**233**	**233**	**233**	**233**	**233**	**233**	**Océanie**
Australia[3]	254	234	206	237	...	...	...	...	...	...	Australie[3]
Total	**20 989**	**21 501**	**22 301**	**24 707**	**24 114**	**23 933**	**22 445**	**23 437**	**23 090**	**23 244**	**Total**

General note.
Meters for measuring the amount of electricity consumed (ampere–hours) or the amount of energy consumed (watt–hours). Apparatus such as voltmeters, ammeters and the like is excluded. (SITC 72951–0).

[1] Shipments.
[2] Production by establishments employing 10 or more persons.
[3] Twelve months ending 30 June of year stated.

Remarque générale.
Compteurs servant à mesurer les quantités d'électricité consommées (ampères–heures) ou l'énergie consommée (watts–heures). Cette rubrique ne comprend pas les voltmètres, ampèremètres etc. (CTCI 72951–0).

[1] Expéditions.
[2] Production des établissements occupant 10 personnes ou plus.
[3] Période de douze mois finissant le 30 juin de l'année indiquée.

Electric furnaces – Fours électriques

Unit : Number units

Unité : Nombre

Country or area	1976	1977	1978	1979	1980	1981	1982	1983	1984	1985	Pays ou zone
America, South	**4 869**	**10 798**	**2 861**	**4 883**	**7 789**	**6 217**	**6 210**	**6 202**	**6 195**	**6 187**	**Amérique du Sud**
Brazil	4 869	10 798	2 861	[1] 4 883	7 789	...	...	...	...	...	Brésil
Asia	**567**	**531**	**522**	**616**	**662**	**719**	**629**	**633**	**790**	**814**	**Asie**
Japan	567	531	522	616	662	719	629	633	790	814	Japon
Europe	**115 080**	**118 380**	**118 668**	**99 347**	**103 291**	**104 904**	**101 929**	**113 610**	**122 896**	**153 699**	**Europe**
EEC	***110 722***	***113 375***	***114 626***	***93 622***	***99 401***	***101 573***	***98 346***	***110 815***	***120 045***	***149 124***	***CEE***
Germany, Fed. Rep.	110 632	113 272	114 511	93 494	99 269	101 454	98 205	110 646	119 755	148 922	Allemagne, Rép. féd.
Greece	...	...	...	...	132	119	141	169	290	...	Grèce
EFTA	***97***	***103***	***275***	***333***	***390***	***342***	***507***	***551***	***604***	***676***	***AELE***
Portugal	97	103	275	333	390	342	507	551	604	...	Portugal
East Europe	***3 870***	***4 486***	***3 302***	***4 925***	***3 027***	***2 510***	***2 610***	***1 746***	***1 768***	***3 398***	***Europe de l'est***
Bulgaria	721	459	330	513	533	569	724	859	853	2 075	Bulgarie
Czechoslovakia	2 258	2 508	1 010	2 195	2 292	1 764	1 714	775	785	1 235	Tchécoslovaquie
Hungary	800	1 375	1 873	2 199	# 169	123	134	102	116	71	Hongrie
Poland	91	144	89	18	33	54	38	10	14	17	Pologne
Other Europe	***391***	***416***	***465***	***467***	***473***	***479***	***466***	***498***	***479***	***501***	***Autre Europe***
Spain	257	...	...	...	...	...	...	...	...	...	Espagne
Yugoslavia	134	159	208	210	216	222	209	241	222	244	Yougoslavie
USSR	**11 944**	**12 991**	**12 641**	**12 673**	**13 035**	**15 342**	**15 330**	**25 809**	**51 241**	**87 758**	**URSS**
Total	**132 460**	**142 700**	**134 692**	**117 519**	**124 777**	**127 182**	**124 098**	**146 254**	**181 122**	**248 458**	**Total**

General note.
Furnaces used for metallurgical and other purposes in which the heat is generated by (a) electric arc, (b) low–frequency or high–frequency electrical induction, or (c) electrical resistance. (SITC 72992–2).

Remarque générale.
Fours utilisés en métallurgie et autres domaines, dans lesquels la chaleur est engendrée par (a) un arc électrique, (b) un courant électrique induit à basse ou haute fréquence, ou (c) des résistances électriques. (CTCI 72992–2).

[1] Production by establishments employing 5 or more persons.

[1] Production des établissements occupant 5 personnes ou plus.

Unit : Thousand units

Unité : En milliers

Country or area	1976	1977	1978	1979	1980	1981	1982	1983	1984	1985	Pays ou zone
Africa	**789**	**639**	**609**	**622**	**1 138**	**1 485**	**1 618**	**1 815**	**1 677**	**1 685**	**Afrique**
Algeria	54	51	60	69	94	145	174	194	225	...	Algérie
Egypt	88	151	174	218	308	440	593	819	...	...	Egypte
Gabon	1	1	1	1	1	* 1	* 1	* 1	...	...	Gabon
Ghana	1	...	...	...	...	...	...	...	...	...	Ghana
Morocco[1]	...	...	...	...	100	95	81	74	72	83	Maroc[1]
Nigeria	14	26	26	26	# 208	309	243	272	88	74	Nigéria
South Africa	472	246	173	134	338	399	425	337	377	273	Afrique du Sud
Tunisia	45	53	69	73	88	95	100	117	124	130	Tunisie
America, North	**9 237**	**9 080**	**10 557**	**10 820**	**11 833**	**12 400**	**11 488**	**12 503**	**12 713**	**14 806**	**Amérique du Nord**
Canada[2]	447	356	336	321	444	...	...	...	...	...	Canada[2]
Cuba	28	33	51	52	40	78	50	91	92	94	Cuba
El Salvador[3]	68	109	76	49	47	74	46	40	...	...	El Salvador[3]
Jamaica	6	5	...	...	...	...	3	...	...	...	Jamaïque
Mexico	729	699	767	847	964	978	788	479	467	588	Mexique
Nicaragua	...	...	...	...	* 1	1	0	1	0	...	Nicaragua
Trinidad and Tobago	13	14	12	11	13	13	18	21	19	21	Trinité-et-Tobago
United States[2]	7 945	7 863	9 309	9 534	10 320	10 883	10 218	11 506	11 738	13 716	Etats-Unis[2]
America, South	**2 618**	**2 911**	**3 169**	**3 483**	**4 229**	**3 538**	**3 150**	**2 571**	**2 553**	**3 163**	**Amérique du Sud**
Argentina	169	254	219	262	454	515	448	335	430	599	Argentine
Brazil	1 916	2 078	2 422	2 747	3 254	2 516	2 354	1 857	1 744	2 190	Brésil
Chile	103	139	70	88	107	80	35	23	31	27	Chili
Colombia	93	102	137	100	103	120	18	87	...	...	Colombie
Ecuador	9	13	12	...	36	27	24	25	...	...	Equateur
Peru	128	125	109	67	75	80	71	44	* 47	* 50	Pérou
Venezuela*	200	...	...	...	...	...	...	...	...	...	Venezuela*
Asia	**19 872**	**20 296**	**21 139**	**24 256**	**28 641**	**32 402**	**29 133**	**32 702**	**40 913**	**48 461**	**Asie**
China	...	285	517	1 329	2 492	5 394	5 920	6 840	10 040	16 677	Chine
Hong Kong	2	11	5	40	108	198	199	368	[4] 602	...	Hong-kong
India	...	...	...	69	88	80	125	101	294	...	Inde
Indonesia	149	372	267	445	607	643	604	517	517	* 773	Indonésie
Iran(Islamic Rep.of)[5]	296	264	277	310	246	346	400	556	...	...	Iran(Rép.islamique)[5]
Iraq	...	...	...	...	...	79	...	...	...	...	Iraq
Israel[6]	48	48	41	26	24	28	26	27	20	36	Israël[6]
Japan	15 103	14 342	13 116	13 577	15 205	14 578	12 796	13 275	15 512	17 727	Japon
Korea, Republic of	2 290	2 990	4 826	5 867	6 819	7 548	6 113	7 641	9 729	7 803	Corée, République de
Malaysia	108	142	150	154	157	159	249	383	443	568	Malaisie
Pakistan	...	96	98	86	74	87	108	111	105	...	Pakistan
Philippines	107	157	180	193	206	219	* 210	291	...	...	Philippines
Singapore	486	560	725	1 390	1 889	2 174	1 516	1 361	1 345	1 501	Singapour
Syrian Arab Republic	58	55	51	71	72	47	59	49	31	4	Rép. arabe syrienne
Thailand	124	160	174	195	248	* 331	* 340	* 500	533	...	Thaïlande
Turkey	618	684	567	425	327	491	389	603	899	1 139	Turquie
Europe	**16 261**	**17 361**	**17 753**	**17 427**	**17 717**	**17 499**	**17 794**	**19 793**	**17 668**	**18 487**	**Europe**
EEC	***10 808***	***11 569***	***12 031***	***11 329***	***11 707***	***11 483***	***11 397***	***12 357***	***11 584***	***11 459***	***CEE***
Belgium[2 7]	558	588	650	608	746	747	666	766	799	833	Belgique[2 7]
Denmark	71	77	86	73	77	93	118	131	124	125	Danemark
France	1 777	1 911	2 101	1 854	1 928	1 960	2 155	2 033	2 000	1 913	France
Germany, Fed. Rep.	3 982	4 370	4 391	4 105	4 425	4 610	4 201	4 705	3 917	[4] 3 738	Allemagne, Rép. féd.
Greece	187	204	168	142	137	179	215	177	158	...	Grèce
Ireland	59	33	...	...	...	...	...	...	...	...	Irlande
Italy	2 068	2 211	2 172	2 031	1 984	1 541	1 719	1 615	1 691	1 663	Italie
United Kingdom	2 106	2 175	2 417	2 470	2 364	2 307	2 277	2 884	2 849	2 972	Royaume-Uni
EFTA	***1 423***	***1 530***	***1 504***	***1 698***	***1 788***	***1 874***	***2 114***	***3 096***	***1 866***	***2 526***	***AELE***
Austria	423	429	375	...	...	...	...	1 645	342	...	Autriche
Finland[8]	274	287	262	302	341	312	356	427	472	...	Finlande[8]
Portugal	359	424	497	465	467	535	633	749	715	717	Portugal
Sweden	367	390	370	332	308	283	308	275	337	320	Suède
East Europe	***2 997***	***2 870***	***2 962***	***3 026***	***2 916***	***2 814***	***2 506***	***2 528***	***2 500***	***2 750***	***Europe de l'est***
Bulgaria	58	65	70	82	91	112	123	127	113	111	Bulgarie

For general note and footnotes, see end of table.

Voir la fin du tableau pour la remarque générale et les notes.

Unit : Thousand units

Unité : En milliers

Country or area	1976	1977	1978	1979	1980	1981	1982	1983	1984	1985	Pays ou zone
Czechoslovakia	456	461	482	450	389	398	391	415	384	432	Tchécoslovaquie
German Dem. Rep.	560	525	487	584	578	618	653	667	640	668	Rép. dém. allemande
Hungary	412	423	435	421	417	424	351	363	370	407	Hongrie
Poland	963	920	972	915	900	764	576	566	587	610	Pologne
Romania	548	476	516	574	541	498	412	390	406	522	Roumanie
Other Europe	***1 033***	***1 392***	***1 256***	***1 374***	***1 306***	***1 328***	***1 777***	***1 812***	***1 718***	***1 752***	***Autre Europe***
Spain	631	965	...	775	763	818	1 288	1 260	...	...	Espagne
Yugoslavia	402	427	451	599	543	510	489	552	481	443	Yougoslavie
USSR	**7 063**	**7 073**	**7 165**	**7 271**	**7 528**	**8 190**	**8 345**	**8 578**	**8 998**	**9 371**	**URSS**
Byelorussian SSR	*539*	*596*	*509*	*448*	*552*	*663*	*712*	*794*	*844*	*886*	*RSS de Biélorussie*
Ukrainian SSR	*2 375*	*2 251*	*2 298*	*2 436*	*2 526*	*2 637*	*2 661*	*2 724*	*2 844*	*3 067*	*RSS d'Ukraine*
Oceania	**688**	**631**	**459**	**410**	**458**	**484**	**507**	**372**	**357**	**392**	**Océanie**
Australia[9]	534	512	368	292	332	358	377	272	255	299	Australie[9]
New Zealand	154	119	91	118	126	126	130	100	102	93	Nouvelle-Zélande
Total	**56 529**	**57 991**	**60 851**	**64 289**	**71 544**	**75 999**	**72 035**	**78 334**	**84 878**	**96 365**	**Total**

General note.
Household television receivers of all kinds (table models, consoles, television sets incorporating a radio receiver or a gramophone). (SITC 72410-0).

1 Including assembly.
2 Shipments.
3 Including radio receivers.
4 Colour television receivers only.
5 Production by establishments employing 50 or more persons.
6 Marketed local production.
7 Production by establishments employing 5 or more persons.
8 Including sets assembled from imported parts.
9 Twelve months ending 30 June of year stated.

Remarque générale.
Récepteurs de télévision de tous genres pour usage privé (récepteurs de table, récepteurs-meubles etc., même avec appareils récepteur de radiodiffusion, phonographe ou tourne-disques incorporés). (CTCI 72410-0).

1 Y compris le montage.
2 Expéditions.
3 Y compris les récepteurs de radio.
4 Récepteurs de télévision en couleur seulement.
5 Production des établissements occupant 50 personnes ou plus.
6 Production locale commercialisée.
7 Production des établissements occupant 5 personnes ou plus.
8 Y compris les appareils constitués d'éléments importés.
9 Période de douze mois finissant le 30 juin de l'année indiquée.

Radio receivers – Récepteurs de radio

Unit : Thousand units

Unité : En milliers

Country or area	1976	1977	1978	1979	1980	1981	1982	1983	1984	1985	Pays ou zone
Africa	**1 594**	**1 569**	**1 693**	**1 802**	**1 886**	**1 897**	**1 641**	**1 836**	**2 155**	**1 870**	**Afrique**
Algeria	21	1	0	6	112	168	166	* 150	...	...	Algérie
Cameroon	67	78	67	71	76	...	...	12	36	16	Cameroun
Central African Rep.	5	11	0	0	0	6	* 4	* 4	0	...	Rép. centrafricaine
Chad	43	* 30	* 35	...	...	...	...	...	...	...	Tchad
Egypt	117	265	368	223	171	182	204	245	...	...	Egypte
Gabon	23	13	5	9	7	...	...	...	...	...	Gabon
Morocco[1]	189	134	42	46	47	23	12	7	34	19	Maroc[1]
Mozambique	...	...	...	...	...	113	106	77	...	...	Mozambique
Nigeria	112	112	92	148	...	...	...	...	...	...	Nigéria
Rwanda	17	3	8	1	0	0	4	7	6	12	Rwanda
South Africa	...	467	657	821	861	905	715	895	1 161	963	Afrique du Sud
Tunisia	89	71	59	37	60	77	80	135	125	76	Tunisie
United Rep. Tanzania	240	257	235	247	223	155	110	...	...	...	Rép.Unie de Tanzanie
Zambia	37	28	26	58	78	61	42	25	14	0	Zambie
America, North	**14 892**	**13 218**	**13 174**	**13 992**	**9 719**	**10 413**	**10 297**	**9 790**	**11 219**	**7 219**	**Amérique du Nord**
Canada[2]	837	852	733	...	...	...	...	...	...	...	Canada[2]
Cuba	92	120	121	143	200	256	239	273	253	236	Cuba
Jamaica	...	...	1	...	...	...	...	...	...	...	Jamaïque
Mexico	1 135	976	1 126	1 290	1 029	893	663	413	363	428	Mexique
Nicaragua*	...	...	...	...	1	1	1	1	0	...	Nicaragua*
Trinidad and Tobago	18	15	10	8	8	9	8	7	2	3	Trinité-et-Tobago
United States[2]	12 807	11 252	11 181	11 741	7 672	8 446	8 577	8 288	9 792	5 743	Etats-Unis[2]
America, South	**862**	**6 107**	**7 430**	**7 026**	**6 835**	**5 707**	**8 273**	**9 019**	**9 769**	**10 517**	**Amérique du Sud**
Brazil	759	6 027	7 387	6 956	6 769	5 639	...	...	...	...	Brésil
Chile	86	68	29	...	...	...	...	...	...	...	Chili
Colombia	16	10	13	7	3	2	* 2	0	...	...	Colombie
Ecuador	1	...	1	...	...	5	...	...	...	...	Equateur
Asia	**104 051**	**100 479**	**89 587**	**94 442**	**138 931**	**133 498**	**96 408**	**107 778**	**109 487**	**99 406**	**Asie**
Burma[3]	25	10	7	12	1	1	0	0	1	...	Birmanie[3]
China[4]	...	10 494	11 677	13 807	30 038	40 572	17 239	19 990	22 203	16 003	Chine[4]
Hong Kong	50 491	53 022	40 902	40 639	67 478	51 758	41 295	47 986	43 372	...	Hong-kong
India[5]	1 676	1 813	1 937	2 030	1 918	1 671	1 563	1 233	1 307	1 209	Inde[5]
Indonesia[6]	1 100	1 000	1 536	1 019	1 530	1 523	1 199	1 045	933	* 1 883	Indonésie[6]
Iran(Islamic Rep.of)[7 8]	242	194	80	80	57	43	36	171	...	...	Iran(Rép.islamique)[7 8]
Israel[9 10]	10	...	...	...	...	...	...	...	...	...	Israël[9 10]
Japan	16 770	17 308	16 278	13 910	15 343	15 196	14 318	13 338	13 589	12 996	Japon
Korea, Republic of	6 717	6 404	4 768	4 772	3 972	5 240	5 925	6 719	7 709	6 392	Corée, République de
Malaysia	...	2	2	3	5	5	4	6	8	9	Malaisie
Philippines	124	149	...	...	...	...	...	544	...	...	Philippines
Singapore[11]	10 737	9 726	11 717	16 748	17 070	16 028	13 461	15 165	18 246	12 824	Singapour[11]
Sri Lanka	55	75	59	44	72	31	...	...	...	...	Sri Lanka
Thailand	132	142	187	968	1 113	1 036	* 880	...	...	...	Thaïlande
Turkey[12]	178	130	155	128	52	112	164	188	244	149	Turquie[12]
Europe	**18 960**	**20 157**	**18 111**	**17 624**	**16 395**	**14 614**	**13 713**	**14 152**	**13 837**	**15 123**	**Europe**
EEC	***13 036***	***13 781***	***11 597***	***11 350***	***10 161***	***8 538***	***8 576***	***9 057***	***8 395***	***9 171***	***CEE***
Belgium[2 13]	1 726	1 894	1 313	1 784	2 246	1 357	974	1 006	976	1 097	Belgique[2 13]
Denmark	144	161	66	105	88	56	44	49	54	42	Danemark
France	3 458	3 570	3 019	2 773	2 141	2 266	2 733	2 489	2 128	2 632	France
Germany, Fed. Rep.	5 443	5 725	4 715	4 387	3 707	2 845	2 864	3 292	3 031	3 376	Allemagne, Rép. féd.
Italy	1 540	...	...	...	...	...	...	...	...	...	Italie
United Kingdom	725	891	# [14] 944	[14] 761	[14] 439	[14] 474	[14] 421	[14] 681	[14] 666	...	Royaume-Uni
EFTA	***859***	***999***	***1 155***	***1 003***	***876***	***784***	***735***	***807***	***808***	***935***	***AELE***
Finland[15]	185	138	287	229	257	238	36	1	1	...	Finlande[15]
Portugal	515	720	757	711	593	521	696	806	807	916	Portugal
Sweden	159	141	111	63	26	25	3	0	0	...	Suède
East Europe	***4 593***	***4 788***	***4 927***	***4 962***	***5 045***	***4 986***	***4 163***	***4 099***	***4 437***	***4 816***	***Europe de l'est***
Bulgaria	169	147	86	53	51	60	54	42	40	42	Bulgarie
Czechoslovakia[16]	223	235	241	270	250	280	310	314	303	277	Tchécoslovaquie[16]
German Dem. Rep.	1 122	1 126	1 103	964	915	965	900	975	1 110	1 132	Rép. dém. allemande

For general note and footnotes, see end of table.

Voir la fin du tableau pour la remarque générale et les notes.

Radio receivers (continued) – Récepteurs de radio (suite)

Unit : Thousand units

Unité : En milliers

Country or area	1976	1977	1978	1979	1980	1981	1982	1983	1984	1985	Pays ou zone
Hungary	250	259	264	257	271	186	125	92	108	104	Hongrie
Poland	2 038	2 291	2 569	2 661	2 695	2 797	2 175	2 134	2 418	2 690	Pologne
Romania	791	730	664	757	863	698	599	542	458	571	Roumanie
Other Europe	***472***	***589***	***432***	***309***	***313***	***306***	***239***	***189***	***197***	***202***	***Autre Europe***
Spain	363	402	...	174	188	146	87	50	...	...	Espagne
Yugoslavia	109	187	172	135	125	160	152	139	173	152	Yougoslavie
USSR	**8 456**	**8 652**	**8 728**	**8 452**	**8 478**	**8 704**	**8 906**	**9 298**	**9 391**	**8 849**	**URSS**
Byelorussian SSR	*436*	*454*	*453*	*474*	*499*	*536*	*595*	*643*	*677*	*712*	*RSS de Biélorussie*
Ukrainian SSR	*299*	*239*	*243*	*256*	*315*	*306*	*283*	*311*	*363*	*291*	*RSS d'Ukraine*
Oceania	**242**	**232**	**359**	**363**	**367**	**307**	**311**	**311**	**260**	**314**	**Océanie**
Australia[17]	84	63	216	163	199	...	143	...	92	...	Australie[17]
New Zealand	158	169	143	200	...	...	...	...	...	...	Nouvelle–Zélande
Total	**149 057**	**150 414**	**139 082**	**143 701**	**182 610**	**175 140**	**139 548**	**152 184**	**156 117**	**143 298**	**Total**

General note.
Complete receiving sets, irrespective of frequencies covered, made for home, automobile and general use, including battery sets. Radio–gramophone combinations are included. (SITC 72420–0).

1 Data refer to assembly.
2 Shipments.
3 Government production only.
4 Portable battery sets only.
5 Production by large and medium scale establishments only.
6 Including radio with tape recording unit.

7 Production by establishments employing 50 or more persons.
8 Including sound reproducers.
9 Sales.
10 Radio receivers for motor vehicles.
11 Including radio with tape recording unit and clock.

12 Excluding radio–phonograph combinations.
13 Production by establishments employing 5 or more persons.
14 Including car tape–players.
15 Including sets assembled from imported parts.
16 Including record players.
17 Twelve months ending 30 June of year stated.

Remarque générale.
Récepteurs complets, quelles que soient les longueurs d'ondes captées, d'appartement, d'automobiles et d'usage général, y compris les postes à piles. Cette rubrique comprend les récepteurs avec phonographes ou tourne–disques incorporés. (CTCI 72420–0).

1 Données se rapportant à l'assemblage.
2 Expéditions.
3 Production de l'Etat seulement.
4 Appareils portatifs à piles seulement.
5 Production des grandes et moyennes entreprises seulement.
6 Y compris les récepteurs de radio avec appareil enregistreur à bande magnétique incorporés.
7 Production des établissements occupant 50 personnes ou plus.
8 Y compris les lecteurs de son.
9 Ventes.
10 Récepteurs de radio pour automobiles.
11 Y compris les récepteurs de radio avec appareil enregistreur à bande magnétique et pendule incorporés.
12 Non compris les radios–phonos.
13 Production des établissements occupant 5 personnes ou plus.
14 Y compris les lecteurs de cassettes pour automobiles.
15 Y compris les appareils constitués d'éléments importés.
16 Y compris les tourne–disques.
17 Période de douze mois finissant le 30 juin de l'année indiquée.

Telephones – Appareils téléphoniques

Unit : Thousand units

Unité : En milliers

Country or area	1976	1977	1978	1979	1980	1981	1982	1983	1984	1985	Pays ou zone
America, North	**17 181**	**21 450**	**24 951**	**24 889**	**22 423**	**22 500**	**20 764**	**20 118**	**20 637**	**24 926**	**Amérique du Nord**
Mexico	565	550	721	824	997	949	938	999	1 051	1 087	Mexique
United States[1]	16 616	20 900	24 230	24 065	21 426	21 551	19 826	19 119	19 586	23 839	Etats–Unis[1]
America, South	**1 269**	**1 072**	**1 164**	**1 089**	**1 738**	**2 310**	**2 169**	**2 384**	**2 545**	**2 746**	**Amérique du Sud**
Brazil	1 262	1 059	1 145	[2] 1 085	1 702	2 253	...	...	...	...	Brésil
Colombia	...	...	...	4	36	57	69	89	...	...	Colombie
Asia	**4 464**	**4 385**	**4 455**	**7 441**	**5 213**	**6 451**	**11 720**	**40 233**	**26 995**	**30 319**	**Asie**
Hong Kong	...	...	...	...	352	925	4 928	27 753	16 328	...	Hong–kong
Iran(Islamic Rep.of)[3]	248	325	376	109	127	182	227	321	...	...	Iran(Rép.islamique)[3]
Japan[4]	3 201	2 797	2 645	3 506	3 573	3 872	3 845	4 671	5 600	8 326	Japon[4]
Korea, Republic of	428	707	813	1 020	921	1 222	2 294	6 936	4 358	5 706	Corée, République de
Syrian Arab Republic	37	0	3	8	47	48	89	56	80	81	Rép. arabe syrienne
Thailand	19	...	22	* 54	* 37	* 29	57	177	32	...	Thaïlande
Turkey	179	182	212	214	156	173	280	319	387	499	Turquie
Europe	**5 662**	**6 203**	**6 433**	**7 647**	**6 981**	**7 056**	**6 298**	**6 679**	**6 255**	**6 280**	**Europe**
EEC	***439***	***519***	***571***	***813***	***980***	***912***	***992***	***1 080***	***1 114***	***1 268***	***CEE***
Denmark	383	416	351	563	737	...	...	...	...	...	Danemark
Greece	56	103	220	250	243	167	162	165	114	...	Grèce
EFTA	***837***	***949***	***1 098***	***1 286***	***1 357***	***1 756***	***1 236***	***1 153***	***940***	***1 026***	***AELE***
Austria	334	346	452	511	785	907	553	416	332	397	Autriche
Finland	253	250	221	252	253	308	254	309	...	...	Finlande
Portugal	250	353	425	523	319	541	429	428	309	322	Portugal
East Europe	***2 038***	***2 228***	***2 455***	***2 583***	***2 668***	***2 739***	***2 846***	***2 875***	***2 941***	***3 005***	***Europe de l'est***
Bulgaria	623	771	850	955	1 005	1 133	1 139	1 195	1 238	1 150	Bulgarie
Hungary	138	60	138	152	143	163	205	203	161	153	Hongrie
Poland	1 277	1 397	1 467	1 476	1 520	1 443	1 502	1 477	1 542	1 702	Pologne
Other Europe	***2 348***	***2 507***	***2 309***	***2 965***	***1 976***	***1 649***	***1 224***	***1 571***	***1 260***	***981***	***Autre Europe***
Spain	2 129	...	...	2 684	1 617	1 318	815	1 146	...	...	Espagne
Yugoslavia	219	228	239	281	359	331	409	425	442	371	Yougoslavie
USSR	**3 766**	**3 915**	...	...	...	...	...	...	...	...	**URSS**
Total	**32 342**	**37 025**	**40 844**	**44 906**	**40 196**	**42 158**	**44 791**	**73 254**	**60 273**	**68 111**	**Total**

General note.
Units composed of a microphone, one or more receivers, a switching device, a bell and possibly a dial selector. (SITC 72491–2).

[1] Shipments.
[2] Production by establishments employing 5 or more persons.
[3] Production by establishments employing 10 or more persons.
[4] Dial–system telephones only.

Remarque générale.
Appareils contenant un microphone, un ou plusieurs récepteurs, un avertisseur, un commutateur–interrupteur et, le cas échéant, un cadran sélecteur. (CTCI 72491–2).

[1] Expéditions.
[2] Production des établissements occupant 5 personnes ou plus.
[3] Production des établissements occupant 10 personnes ou plus.
[4] Téléphones automatiques seulement.

Electronic tubes – Tubes électroniques

Unit : Thousand units

Unité : En milliers

Country or area	1976	1977	1978	1979	1980	1981	1982	1983	1984	1985	Pays ou zone
America, North	**95 574**	**90 400**	**128 647**	**18 733**	**51 427**	**3 729**	**1 799**	**1 756**	**1 863**	**2 504**	**Amérique du Nord**
United States[1]	95 574	90 400	128 647	*[2] 18 733	51 427	3 729	1 799	1 756	1 863	2 504	Etats–Unis[1]
America, South	**92 416**	**45 737**	**9 261**	**2 314**	**3 923**	**2 497**	**1 752**	**2 314**	**2 314**	**2 314**	**Amérique du Sud**
Brazil	92 416	45 737	9 261	[3] 2 314	3 923	2 497	...	...	...	...	Brésil
Asia	**79 908**	**70 915**	**69 016**	**79 738**	**94 507**	**98 581**	**98 399**	**125 139**	**164 205**	**166 898**	**Asie**
Japan[4]	77 683	67 401	63 479	72 776	85 581	89 095	92 171	116 319	151 500	153 639	Japon[4]
Korea, Republic of	2 225	3 514	5 537	6 962	8 926	9 486	6 228	8 820	12 705	13 259	Corée, République de
Europe	**63 577**	**58 431**	**55 132**	**50 671**	**42 496**	**32 077**	**27 895**	**25 670**	**23 316**	**20 642**	**Europe**
EEC	***2 325***	***1 045***	***656***	***602***	***393***	***195***	***149***	***17***	***149***	***149***	***CEE***
Germany, Fed. Rep.[5]	2 325	1 045	656	602	393	195	149	...	...	...	Allemagne, Rép. féd.[5]
EFTA	***0***	***0***	***3***	***0***	***1***	***1***	***1***	***1***	***1***	***1***	***AELE***
Finland	0	0	3	0	...	...	...	...	...	...	Finlande
East Europe	***48 416***	***44 396***	***41 672***	***37 742***	***31 427***	***22 049***	***17 306***	***15 714***	***13 995***	***10 769***	***Europe de l'est***
Czechoslovakia	8 944	8 071	7 222	5 631	4 756	4 215	3 603	3 440	3 386	2 931	Tchécoslovaquie
Hungary	16 769	16 525	17 008	17 251	15 935	9 149	6 286	4 451	3 894	2 349	Hongrie
Poland	22 703	19 800	17 442	14 860	10 736	8 685	7 417	7 823	6 715	5 489	Pologne
Other Europe	***12 836***	***12 990***	***12 801***	***12 327***	***10 675***	***9 832***	***10 439***	***9 938***	***9 171***	***9 723***	***Autre Europe***
Spain	3 648	...	...	...	...	...	...	...	...	...	Espagne
Yugoslavia	9 188	9 342	9 153	8 679	7 027	6 184	6 791	6 290	5 523	6 075	Yougoslavie
Total	**331 475**	**265 483**	**262 056**	**151 456**	**192 353**	**136 884**	**129 845**	**154 879**	**191 698**	**192 358**	**Total**

General note.
Valves and tubes which utilize the effect of electrons emitted from a cathode either in a vacuum or in gas. The envelopes are usually of glass, but sometimes of metal. Cathode–ray tubes and television camera tubes and photocathode valves and tubes are excluded. However, the modified form of cathode–ray tube which is used as a tuning indicator in radio receivers (magic eyes) is included. (SITC 72930–1).

[1] Shipments.
[2] Incomplete coverage.
[3] Production by establishments employing 5 or more persons.
[4] Beginning 1980, scope of series revised.
[5] Beginning 1983, data are confidential.

Remarque générale.
Lampes, tubes et valves utilisant les effets des émissions d'électrons d'une cathode dans le vide ou en atmosphère gazeuse. Les enveloppes sont habituellement en verre, mais parfois aussi en métal. Cette rubrique ne comprend pas les tubes cathodiques et les tubes et valves pour caméras de télevision. Toutefois, les tubes cathodiques sous une forme modifiée qui sont utilisés comme indicateurs d'accord (oeil magique) dans les appareils récepteurs de radio y sont compris. (CTCI 72930–1).

[1] Expéditions.
[2] Couverture incomplète.
[3] Production des établissements occupant 5 personnes ou plus.
[4] A partir de 1980, portée de la série révisée.
[5] A partir de 1983, les données sont confidentielles.

Transistors

Unit : Million units

Unité : En millions

Country or area	1976	1977	1978	1979	1980	1981	1982	1983	1984	1985	Pays ou zone
America, South	**100**	**150**	**208**	**264**	**185**	**312**	**325**	**360**	**395**	**430**	**Amérique du Sud**
Brazil*	100	150	208	[1] 264	185	312	...	...	...	...	Brésil*
Asia	**10 299**	**11 753**	**12 425**	**14 384**	**18 311**	**24 966**	**23 583**	**30 837**	**46 175**	**41 773**	**Asie**
Japan	8 409	9 892	10 567	12 281	16 328	22 661	21 555	28 077	# 42 406	38 283	Japon
Korea, Republic of	1 820	1 772	1 779	2 024	1 904	2 226	1 949	2 681	3 690	3 411	Corée, République de
Philippines[2]	70	89	...	...	...	...	...	...	...	...	Philippines[2]
Europe	**1 560**	**1 665**	**1 655**	**1 907**	**1 778**	**1 795**	**1 888**	**1 819**	**2 239**	**2 582**	**Europe**
EEC	***1 156***	***1 154***	***1 106***	***1 314***	***1 115***	***1 222***	***1 375***	***1 257***	***1 572***	***1 845***	***CEE***
Germany, Fed. Rep.	1 156	1 154	1 106	1 314	1 115	1 222	1 375	1 257	1 572	1 845	Allemagne, Rép. féd.
EFTA	***79***	***89***	***63***	***44***	***42***	***28***	***18***	***20***	***24***	***26***	***AELE***
Portugal	79	89	63	44	42	28	18	20	24	26	Portugal
East Europe	***226***	***267***	***310***	***341***	***341***	***281***	***275***	***286***	***341***	***388***	***Europe de l'est***
Bulgaria	27	38	45	54	40	41	41	...	...	...	Bulgarie
Czechoslovakia	34	34	37	42	41	...	...	...	...	...	Tchécoslovaquie
Hungary	30	36	37	39	26	30	30	25	30	31	Hongrie
Poland	135	159	191	206	234	166	158	165	212	254	Pologne
Other Europe	***99***	***155***	***176***	***208***	***280***	***264***	***220***	***256***	***302***	***323***	***Autre Europe***
Spain	99	...	...	208	280	264	220	256	...	...	Espagne
Oceania	**19**	**19**	**19**	**19**	**19**	**19**	**19**	**19**	**19**	**19**	**Océanie**
Australia[3 4]	19	...	...	...	...	...	...	...	...	...	Australie[3 4]
Total	**11 978**	**13 587**	**14 307**	**16 574**	**20 293**	**27 093**	**25 816**	**33 035**	**48 828**	**44 804**	**Total**

General note.
Semi–conductor crystal, usually of germanium or silicon, and two junctions, usually in an envelope of glass or plastic material. Crystal diodes (crystal plus one junction) are included. (SITC 72930–2).

[1] Production by establishments employing 5 or more persons.
[2] Shipments.
[3] Excluding power transistors.
[4] Twelve months ending 30 June of year stated.

Remarque générale.
Cristal semi–conducteur, généralement de germanium ou de silicium, à deux jonctions, le plus souvent monté dans une enveloppe de verre ou de matière plastique. Cette rubrique comprend les diodes à cristal (cristal à une jonction). (CTCI 72930–2).

[1] Production des établissements occupant 5 personnes ou plus.
[2] Expéditions.
[3] Non compris les transistors de puissance.
[4] Période de douze mois finissant le 30 juin de l'année indiquée.

Sound recorders – Appareils d'enregistrement du son

Unit : Thousand units

Unité : En milliers

Country or area	1976	1977	1978	1979	1980	1981	1982	1983	1984	1985	Pays ou zone
Africa	**1 459**	**1 318**	**1 173**	**1 030**	**890**	**1 158**	**529**	**321**	**156**	**179**	**Afrique**
Gabon	3	4	2	1	* 3	...	...	...	...	...	Gabon
Nigeria	...	...	...	...	...	1 156	528	320	155	178	Nigéria
America, North	**85**	**105**	**206**	**118**	**177**	**99**	**120**	**112**	**116**	**172**	**Amérique du Nord**
Mexico	...	1	2	1	2	8	10	8	9	65	Mexique
United States[1]	84	104	204	117	175	91	110	104	107	107	Etats-Unis[1]
America, South	**91**	**157**	**296**	**633**	**729**	**607**	**689**	**771**	**853**	**935**	**Amérique du Sud**
Brazil	90	156	295	[2] 632	728	...	...	...	...	...	Brésil
Ecuador	...	1	1	...	...	...	...	...	...	...	Equateur
Asia	**49 056**	**48 801**	**52 052**	**58 083**	**72 378**	**80 541**	**70 457**	**85 422**	**108 637**	**103 548**	**Asie**
China	...	...	...	...	743	1 546	3 471	4 977	7 764	13 931	Chine
Indonesia	94	148	133	332	296	556	518	359	678	...	Indonésie
Japan	41 014	40 315	39 742	41 809	54 238	60 540	52 498	60 990	72 889	67 577	Japon
Korea, Republic of	5 324	5 373	8 704	10 038	8 974	9 266	7 281	10 462	15 010	12 517	Corée, République de
Singapore[3]	...	2 206	2 713	4 699	8 060	8 551	6 591	8 521	12 168	8 723	Singapour[3]
Turkey	17	16	17	18	...	...	...	...	...	124	Turquie
Europe	**19 363**	**25 147**	**28 134**	**33 654**	**23 902**	**29 672**	**32 247**	**34 614**	**38 142**	**38 009**	**Europe**
EEC	***18 036***	***23 675***	***26 346***	***31 957***	***22 193***	***28 096***	***30 688***	***32 974***	***35 758***	***36 013***	***CEE***
Denmark	31	28	25	41	28	...	20	26	39	...	Danemark
France	13 209	18 912	21 555	27 150	17 399	...	...	...	...	...	France
Greece	...	...	...	...	...	3 391	4 340	4 966	6 084	...	Grèce
United Kingdom[4 5]	101	40	...	...	...	...	...	...	...	...	Royaume-Uni[4 5]
EFTA	***144***	***175***	***282***	***170***	***144***	***170***	***370***	***314***	***979***	***547***	***AELE***
Finland	143	174	247	155	143	161	182	* 107	822	...	Finlande
Portugal	...	1	35	15	1	9	188	207	157	111	Portugal
East Europe	***1 181***	***1 296***	***1 503***	***1 519***	***1 561***	***1 402***	***1 188***	***1 325***	***1 398***	***1 442***	***Europe de l'est***
Czechoslovakia	200	213	232	222	191	162	134	146	136	133	Tchécoslovaquie
German Dem. Rep.	135	99	86	101	103	116	109	159	184	212	Rép. dém. allemande
Hungary	77	182	273	347	461	556	572	620	648	713	Hongrie
Poland	769	802	912	849	806	568	373	400	430	384	Pologne
Other Europe	***2***	***1***	***3***	***8***	***4***	***4***	***1***	***1***	***7***	***6***	***Autre Europe***
Yugoslavia	2	1	3	8	4	4	1	1	7	6	Yougoslavie
Total	**70 054**	**75 528**	**81 861**	**93 518**	**98 076**	**112 077**	**104 042**	**121 239**	**147 904**	**142 842**	**Total**

General note.
Groove type in which a stylus cuts a groove and magnetic type in which the recording-head is essentially an electro-magnet. (SITC 89111-1).

[1] Shipments.
[2] Production by establishments employing 5 or more persons.
[3] Including those with radio receiving unit.
[4] Combined tape recorders and reproducers.
[5] Deliveries of U.K. manufactured goods.

Remarque générale.
Enregistreurs mécaniques, dans lesquels un graveur creuse un sillon, et enregistreurs magnétiques, dans lesquels la tête d'enregistrement est essentiellement un électro-aimant. (CTCI 89111-1).

[1] Expéditions.
[2] Production des établissements occupant 5 personnes ou plus.
[3] Y compris les appareils avec récepteur de radio incorporé.
[4] Magnétophones.
[5] Quantités livrées de marchandises fabriquées au Royaume-Uni.

Sound reproducers – Appareils de reproduction du son

Unit : Thousand units | Unité : En milliers

Country or area	1976	1977	1978	1979	1980	1981	1982	1983	1984	1985	Pays ou zone
Africa	**137**	**125**	**112**	**103**	**112**	**131**	**58**	**78**	**42**	**48**	**Afrique**
Algeria	3	4	3	9	31	27	12	...	...	...	Algérie
Nigeria	...	...	...	...	...	104	46	51	11	13	Nigéria
Tunisia	3	2	3	0	0	0	0	0	0	...	Tunisie
America, North	**2 621**	**3 323**	**3 204**	**3 118**	**2 544**	**2 004**	**1 627**	**1 196**	**1 493**	**1 169**	**Amérique du Nord**
Canada[1]	...	...	228	...	...	...	...	...	...	...	Canada[1]
Mexico	708	765	779	949	891	592	485	481	332	334	Mexique
United States[2]	1 685	2 330	2 197	1 941	1 425	1 184	914	487	933	607	Etats-Unis[2]
America, South	**50**	**60**	**49**	**38**	**53**	**51**	**51**	**44**	**53**	**56**	**Amérique du Sud**
Chile	39	43	26	6	...	...	...	...	...	...	Chili
Colombia	7	17	14	21	0	2	...	1	...	...	Colombie
Ecuador	...	0	...	...	24	20	19	14	...	...	Equateur
Asia	**11 454**	**11 406**	**12 230**	**10 665**	**11 644**	**13 183**	**10 298**	**13 004**	**12 580**	**11 074**	**Asie**
India	...	99	109	136	122	87	44	28	15	...	Inde
Japan	9 708	9 724	10 686	9 420	10 672	12 072	9 211	11 568	[3] 10 961	9 871	Japon
Korea, Republic of	1 105	1 086	949	617	358	532	551	916	1 112	701	Corée, République de
Philippines	54	60	49	...	...	...	...	...	...	...	Philippines
Turkey	...	...	...	...	...	...	...	...	437	...	Turquie
Europe	**6 969**	**5 690**	**4 974**	**4 194**	**3 319**	**3 292**	**3 269**	**3 003**	**3 182**	**3 719**	**Europe**
EEC	***5 472***	***4 273***	***4 018***	***3 513***	***2 625***	***2 816***	***2 882***	***2 697***	***2 864***	***3 368***	***CEE***
Denmark	89	88	83	85	64	...	59	79	86	72	Danemark
France[4]	998	766	903	893	376	389	334	145	84	346	France[4]
Germany, Fed. Rep.[5]	4 130	3 221	2 893	2 388	2 086	2 227	2 383	2 383	2 621	2 893	Allemagne, Rép. féd.[5]
United Kingdom[6]	255	198	139	147	99	...	...	...	...	...	Royaume-Uni[6]
EFTA	***2***	***2***	***2***	***2***	***6***	***9***	***8***	***14***	***10***	***9***	***AELE***
Finland	1	1	1	1	1	1	1	0	...	...	Finlande
Portugal	...	...	1	1	5	8	7	14	9	9	Portugal
East Europe	***451***	***373***	***300***	***360***	***370***	***312***	***171***	***162***	***198***	***242***	***Europe de l'est***
Poland	451	373	300	360	370	312	171	162	198	242	Pologne
Other Europe	***1 044***	***1 042***	***654***	***319***	***318***	***155***	***208***	***130***	***110***	***100***	***Autre Europe***
Spain	862	901	...	175	190	104	87	91	...	...	Espagne
Yugoslavia	...	141	148	144	128	51	121	39	23	13	Yougoslavie
Oceania	**43**	**23**	**16**	**27**	**27**	**27**	**27**	**27**	**27**	**27**	**Océanie**
Australia	43	23	16	...	...	...	...	...	...	...	Australie
Total	**21 274**	**20 627**	**20 585**	**18 146**	**17 699**	**18 688**	**15 331**	**17 352**	**17 376**	**16 094**	**Total**

General note.
Gramophones, record-players, automatic record changers, electric gramophones and magnetic sound reproducers. (SITC 89111-2).

1 Manufacturers' sales.
2 Shipments.
3 Record players only.
4 Excluding battery-operated.
5 Including sound recorders.
6 Excluding tape reproducers or combined tape recorders and reproducers. Excluding turn-table units.

Remarque générale.
Phonographes, tourne-disques manuels ou automatiques, phonographes électriques et appareils magnétiques de reproduction du son. (CTCI 89111-2).

1 Ventes des fabricants.
2 Expéditions.
3 Tourne-disques seulement.
4 Appareils à piles non compris.
5 Y compris les appareils d'enregistrement sonore.
6 Non compris les appareils de lecture de bandes magnétiques ou les magnétophones. Non compris les tourne-disques.

Gramophone records, blanks – Disques phonographiques

Unit : Thousand units

Unité : En milliers

Country or area	1976	1977	1978	1979	1980	1981	1982	1983	1984	1985	Pays ou zone
Africa	**304**	**171**	**115**	**134**	**117**	**133**	**96**	**76**	**73**	**62**	**Afrique**
Egypt	169	143	87	109	...	111	...	...	...	...	Egypte
Tunisia	135	28	28	25	13	22	...	...	...	...	Tunisie
America, North	**79 451**	**72 179**	**81 051**	**75 907**	**63 364**	**67 129**	**64 157**	**61 699**	**59 289**	**57 325**	**Amérique du Nord**
Barbados[1]	949	1 076	...	...	...	...	...	...	...	...	Barbade[1]
Canada	...	[2] 68 851	[2] 77 682	[2] 72 418	[2] 59 854	...	...	...	...	54 355	Canada
Cuba	...	...	...	...	...	...	...	1 614	1 655	1 609	Cuba
Dominican Republic	849	626	730	850	871	825	326	352	373	...	Rép. dominicaine
America, South	**102 394**	**100 062**	**94 509**	**108 691**	**104 794**	**94 680**	**92 717**	**93 166**	**97 313**	**97 363**	**Amérique du Sud**
Argentina	21 457	18 959	18 057	20 012	15 052	6 706	4 236	4 044	4 788	3 234	Argentine
Brazil	60 087	56 694	53 616	[3] 68 076	67 558	...	...	...	...	...	Brésil
Chile	3 195	4 280	2 663	2 024	...	...	...	...	...	...	Chili
Colombia	10 788	11 361	11 189	11 260	10 493	9 636	7 887	7 959	...	...	Colombie
Ecuador	6 867	8 768	8 984	...	8 650	6 235	5 872	3 822	...	...	Equateur
Asia	**2 354**	**2 478**	**3 718**	**4 949**	**4 179**	**3 150**	**4 375**	**4 860**	**5 260**	**5 703**	**Asie**
Korea, Republic of	1 272	1 705	2 727	4 275	3 739	2 843	...	...	...	...	Corée, République de
Pakistan[4]	1 082	773	991	674	440	307	65	...	...	...	Pakistan[4]
Europe	**575 499**	**595 400**	**658 600**	**614 666**	**543 437**	**566 446**	**561 408**	**570 958**	**531 727**	**565 383**	**Europe**
EEC	***515 960***	***531 182***	***595 494***	***549 517***	***478 145***	***495 035***	***503 138***	***510 499***	***473 932***	***510 303***	***CEE***
Denmark	...	...	...	443	453	...	542	567	704	768	Danemark
France	154 530	166 892	186 543	151 319	107 483	127 959	164 105	156 451	104 436	111 677	France
Germany, Fed. Rep.	178 497	175 098	197 353	187 544	187 508	190 478	178 000	183 878	203 116	236 546	Allemagne, Rép. féd.
Greece	...	...	...	...	...	6 048	6 191	5 511	5 935	...	Grèce
United Kingdom[2 5]	176 769	182 973	205 325	204 290	176 780	170 034	154 300	...	...	...	Royaume–Uni[2 5]
EFTA	***12 560***	***14 947***	***14 248***	***17 104***	***19 299***	***21 617***	***15 573***	***16 139***	***15 322***	***16 377***	***AELE***
Finland	...	...	...	...	1	2	2	2	3	...	Finlande
Portugal	5 908	6 269	6 368	8 372	11 000	12 000	9 000	8 000	7 000	8 000	Portugal
Sweden	6 651	8 677	7 879	8 731	8 298	9 615	6 571	8 137	...	...	Suède
East Europe	***18 000***	***18 749***	***19 824***	***20 796***	***21 434***	***22 152***	***21 593***	***24 920***	***25 297***	***23 315***	***Europe de l'est***
Czechoslovakia	10 350	10 642	11 392	11 818	12 634	13 238	12 882	13 233	13 125	13 193	Tchécoslovaquie
Poland[6]	7 650	8 107	8 432	8 978	8 800	8 914	8 711	11 687	12 172	10 122	Pologne[6]
Other Europe	***28 979***	***30 523***	***29 034***	***27 248***	***24 559***	***27 642***	***21 104***	***19 400***	***17 175***	***15 389***	***Autre Europe***
Spain	15 329	...	...	12 900	11 430	16 524	10 194	9 793	...	...	Espagne
Yugoslavia	13 650	15 710	14 890	14 348	13 129	11 118	10 910	9 607	7 044	5 926	Yougoslavie
USSR	**198 336**	**202 367**	**210 401**	**211 361**	**206 078**	**209 664**	**212 911**	**193 025**	**180 382**	**168 117**	**URSS**
Oceania	**34 590**	**34 435**	**35 049**	**36 637**	**37 427**	**39 787**	**38 647**	**31 863**	**27 747**	**30 164**	**Océanie**
Australia	28 527	28 828	28 536	30 172	31 873	33 886	32 350	25 058	22 130	24 433	Australie
New Zealand[2]	6 063	5 607	6 513	6 465	5 554	5 901	6 297	6 805	5 617	5 731	Nouvelle–Zélande[2]
Total	**992 928**	**1 007 092**	**1 083 443**	**1 052 344**	**959 395**	**980 989**	**974 311**	**955 646**	**901 791**	**924 116**	**Total**

General note.
Commercial records manufactured from shellac or resins mixed with inert materials (chalk, fine sand, slate powder etc.) and colouring (animal black etc.), or made from resins or other plastic materials (particularly in the case of micro–groove, long–playing or stereophonic records). Master records are excluded. (SITC 89120–1).

[1] Data refer to long play and 45 rpm records.
[2] Gramophone records pressed.
[3] Production by establishments employing 5 or more persons.
[4] Twelve months ending 30 June of year stated.
[5] Manufacturers' sales.
[6] Data refer to recorded disks.

Remarque générale.
Disques du commerce faits en gomme laque ou en résine mélangées à des matières inertes (craie, sable fin, poudre d'ardoise etc.), et à des colorants (noir animal etc.), ou composés de résines ou d'autres matières plastiques (particulièrement dans le cas des disques microsillon, des disques de longue durée et des disques stéréophoniques). Cette rubrique ne comprend pas les enregistrements originaux sur disque. (CTCI 89120–1).

[1] Données se rapportant aux disques de longue durée et aux 45 t/m.
[2] Disques phonographiques enregistrés.
[3] Production des établissements occupant 5 personnes ou plus.
[4] Période de douze mois finissant le 30 juin de l'année indiquée.
[5] Ventes des fabricants.
[6] Données se rapportent aux disques enregistrés.

Vacuum cleaners – Aspirateurs

Unit : Thousand units — Unité : En milliers

Country or area	1976	1977	1978	1979	1980	1981	1982	1983	1984	1985	Pays ou zone
America, North	**9 392**	**9 765**	**9 982**	**9 720**	**9 798**	**9 773**	**9 789**	**9 801**	**9 785**	**9 792**	**Amérique du Nord**
Canada[1]	589	538	570	563	626	...	...	...	...	...	Canada[1]
Mexico	36	65	67	66	81	75	81	83	57	55	Mexique
United States[1 2]	8 767	9 162	9 345	...	...	...	...	...	...	...	Etats-Unis[1 2]
America, South	**253**	**333**	**408**	**525**	**735**	**490**	**617**	**648**	**726**	**778**	**Amérique du Sud**
Brazil	219	252	323	[3] 404	588	376	...	...	...	...	Brésil
Chile	25	70	71	101	122	93	48	30	47	44	Chili
Colombia	9	11	14	20	25	21	...	17	...	...	Colombie
Asia	**4 675**	**4 698**	**4 552**	**5 472**	**5 441**	**5 262**	**5 503**	**6 025**	**6 437**	**6 388**	**Asie**
Israel[4]	5	...	...	...	...	...	...	...	...	...	Israël[4]
Japan[5]	4 535	4 526	4 446	5 220	5 265	5 066	5 322	5 769	6 156	5 995	Japon[5]
Turkey	135	167	101	247	171	191	176	251	276	388	Turquie
Europe	**12 714**	**13 181**	**12 634**	**12 940**	**12 901**	**12 149**	**11 861**	**12 809**	**13 989**	**14 845**	**Europe**
EEC	***9 543***	***9 530***	***8 806***	***8 793***	***8 666***	***7 869***	***7 897***	***8 712***	***9 665***	***10 514***	***CEE***
Belgium	...	...	...	...	...	...	...	8	...	...	Belgique
Denmark	221	247	219	250	188	183	171	163	160	181	Danemark
France	1 835	1 752	1 577	1 498	1 636	1 470	1 530	2 031	2 026	2 258	France
Germany, Fed. Rep.	3 303	3 149	2 904	2 930	3 145	3 010	3 055	3 520	4 040	4 480	Allemagne, Rép. féd.
Greece	...	...	...	1	1	0	0	0	...	...	Grèce
Italy	...	...	365	462	433	459	439	392	365	333	Italie
Netherlands[6]	885	941	949	...	...	...	...	...	...	...	Pays-Bas[6]
United Kingdom[7]	2 828	2 980	2 783	2 719	2 330	1 814	1 769	1 673	2 141	2 329	Royaume-Uni[7]
EFTA	***626***	***655***	***617***	***855***	***806***	***656***	***604***	***646***	***672***	***588***	***AELE***
Austria	...	...	...	...	...	...	...	26	...	...	Autriche
Finland	...	24	0	...	0	0	0	0	0	...	Finlande
Sweden	582	605	591	814	780	630	578	620	646	554	Suède
East Europe	***2 188***	***2 456***	***2 461***	***2 500***	***2 641***	***2 749***	***2 637***	***2 685***	***2 881***	***2 976***	***Europe de l'est***
Czechoslovakia	336	409	405	451	478	487	425	455	528	574	Tchécoslovaquie
German Dem. Rep.	840	968	995	1 002	1 048	1 167	1 224	1 206	1 248	1 267	Rép. dém. allemande
Hungary	65	64	45	22	9	43	17	6	20	21	Hongrie
Poland	854	900	901	895	961	891	833	886	927	950	Pologne
Romania	93	115	115	130	145	161	138	132	...	...	Roumanie
Other Europe	***357***	***541***	***750***	***792***	***788***	***875***	***723***	***766***	***771***	***766***	***Autre Europe***
Spain	173	...	...	397	396	283	299	355	...	...	Espagne
Yugoslavia	184	279	471	395	392	592	424	411	387	364	Yougoslavie
USSR	**2 661**	**2 748**	**2 925**	**3 098**	**3 222**	**3 359**	**3 492**	**3 594**	**3 813**	**4 065**	**URSS**
Ukrainian SSR	*714*	*621*	*617*	*634*	*686*	*705*	*735*	*765*	*778*	*789*	*RSS d'Ukraine*
Oceania	**239**	**200**	**175**	**219**	**246**	**236**	**196**	**218**	**218**	**219**	**Océanie**
Australia[8]	239	200	175	219	246	236	196	...	...	...	Australie[8]
Total	**29 934**	**30 925**	**30 676**	**31 974**	**32 343**	**31 269**	**31 458**	**33 095**	**34 968**	**36 087**	**Total**

General note.
Vacuum cleaners of all types, including those with rotating brushes or carpet-beating devices and/or supplementary attachments. (SITC 72503-1).

1 Shipments.
2 Source: Merchandising Week Magazine, Billboard Publications Inc., (New York).
3 Production by establishments employing 5 or more persons.
4 Marketed local production.
5 For household use only.
6 Industrial sales.
7 Deliveries of U.K. manufactured goods.
8 Electric vacuum cleaners only.

Remarque générale.
Aspirateurs de poussières de tous types, y compris les appareils comportant des dispositifs accessoires, tels que brosses rotatives et batteurs de tapis. (CTCI 72503-1).

1 Expéditions.
2 Source: Merchandising Week Magazine, Billboard Publications Inc.,(New York).
3 Production des établissements occupant 5 personnes ou plus.
4 Production locale commercialisée.
5 Pour usages domestiques seulement.
6 Ventes industrielles.
7 Quantités livrées de marchandises fabriquées au Royaume-Uni.
8 Aspirateurs électriques seulement.

Shavers and hair clippers, electric – Rasoirs et tondeuses, électriques

Unit : Thousand units

Unité : En milliers

Country or area	1976	1977	1978	1979	1980	1981	1982	1983	1984	1985	Pays ou zone
America, North	**4 700**	**5 200**	**4 950**	**4 950**	**4 950**	**4 950**	**4 950**	**4 950**	**4 950**	**4 950**	**Amérique du Nord**
United States[1 2]	4 700	5 200	...	...	...	...	...	...	...	...	Etats–Unis[1 2]
America, South	**32**	**39**	**24**	**24**	**1**	**24**	**24**	**24**	**24**	**24**	**Amérique du Sud**
Ecuador	32	39	...	...	1	...	...	...	...	...	Equateur
Asia	**5 670**	**5 925**	**5 919**	**7 227**	**8 586**	**9 004**	**10 286**	**10 144**	**11 631**	**12 773**	**Asie**
Japan[2]	5 670	5 925	5 919	7 227	8 586	9 004	10 286	10 144	11 631	12 773	Japon[2]
Europe	**8 318**	**8 413**	**7 605**	**8 955**	**8 675**	**8 182**	**8 237**	**8 169**	**9 588**	**11 375**	**Europe**
EEC	***6 215***	***6 015***	***5 016***	***6 220***	***6 040***	***5 482***	***5 453***	***5 295***	***6 105***	***7 523***	***CEE***
France[3 4]	1 153	951	487	272	271	259	215	150	194	219	France[3 4]
Germany, Fed. Rep.	5 062	5 064	4 529	5 948	5 769	5 223	5 238	5 145	5 911	7 304	Allemagne, Rép. féd.
EFTA	***1 463***	***1 768***	***1 962***	***2 098***	***2 016***	***2 108***	***2 201***	***2 246***	***2 774***	***3 127***	***AELE***
Austria	1 463	1 768	1 962	2 098	2 016	2 108	2 201	2 246	2 774	3 127	Autriche
Other Europe	***640***	***630***	***627***	***637***	***619***	***592***	***583***	***628***	***709***	***725***	***Autre Europe***
Spain	547	...	...	...	...	...	...	...	...	...	Espagne
Yugoslavia	93	83	80	90	72	45	36	81	162	178	Yougoslavie
Oceania	**222**	**182**	**162**	**126**	**173**	**173**	**173**	**173**	**173**	**173**	**Océanie**
Australia	222	182	162	126	...	...	...	...	...	...	Australie
Total	**18 942**	**19 759**	**18 660**	**21 282**	**22 385**	**22 333**	**23 670**	**23 460**	**26 366**	**29 295**	**Total**

General note.
Shavers and hair clippers which have a built–in electric motor, including those for shearing sheep or for grooming horses, clipping cattle etc. (SITC 72504–0).

1 Shipments.
2 Electric shavers only. Including battery operated shavers.
3 Deliveries.
4 Electric shavers only.

Remarque générale.
Rasoirs et tondeuses entraînés par un moteur électrique incorporé, y compris les appareils utilisés pour tondre les moutons ou pour panser les chevaux, le bétail etc. (CTCI 72504–0).

1 Expéditions.
2 Rasoirs électriques seulement. Y compris les rasoirs à piles.
3 Livraisons.
4 Rasoirs électriques seulement.

Heaters, electric space – Appareils électriques pour le chauffage des locaux

Unit : Thousand units — Unité : En milliers

Country or area	1976	1977	1978	1979	1980	1981	1982	1983	1984	1985	Pays ou zone
Africa	**62**	**41**	**62**	**63**	**62**	**152**	**215**	**260**	**250**	**280**	**Afrique**
Egypt	62	41	62	63	62	152	215	260	...	...	Egypte
America, North	**2 423**	**3 803**	**9 512**	**9 621**	**8 557**	**8 090**	**7 365**	**7 312**	**4 844**	**4 200**	**Amérique du Nord**
United States[1 2]	2 423	3 803	9 512	9 621	8 557	8 090	7 365	7 312	4 844	4 200	Etats-Unis[1 2]
Asia	**1 371**	**1 567**	**1 396**	**1 288**	**1 966**	**1 950**	**1 945**	**1 802**	**2 836**	**2 597**	**Asie**
Japan	1 371	1 567	1 396	1 288	1 966	1 950	1 945	1 802	2 836	2 597	Japon
Europe	**10 947**	**12 094**	**11 097**	**13 532**	**14 631**	**13 969**	**13 335**	**13 144**	**13 154**	**14 993**	**Europe**
EEC	***6 442***	***6 844***	***6 079***	***7 127***	***8 235***	***7 523***	***7 535***	***7 153***	***6 708***	***8 193***	***CEE***
Denmark	104	100	105	102	113	81	...	71	...	...	Danemark
France[3 4]	3 117	3 432	3 073	3 146	3 323	3 788	4 056	4 217	3 814	4 597	France[3 4]
Germany, Fed. Rep.	3 221	3 312	2 901	3 879	4 799	3 654	3 395	2 865	2 819	3 525	Allemagne, Rép. féd.
EFTA	***2 737***	***2 987***	***2 670***	***3 837***	***3 381***	***3 714***	***3 972***	***4 180***	***4 395***	***4 706***	***AELE***
Austria	85	67	51	94	117	120	83	77	56	...	Autriche
Finland[5]	761	812	1 120	2 060	1 409	...	...	...	...	...	Finlande[5]
Norway	1 723	1 863	1 336	1 556	1 690	1 384	...	...	...	...	Norvège
Portugal	168	245	163	127	165	218	252	269	309	396	Portugal
East Europe	***553***	***531***	***495***	***513***	***558***	***576***	***586***	***605***	***614***	***582***	***Europe de l'est***
Bulgaria	433	420	377	397	443	458	460	491	515	462	Bulgarie
Czechoslovakia	45	55	60	59	78	87	93	71	57	58	Tchécoslovaquie
Hungary	75	56	58	57	37	31	33	43	42	62	Hongrie
Other Europe	***1 215***	***1 732***	***1 853***	***2 055***	***2 457***	***2 156***	***1 242***	***1 206***	***1 438***	***1 513***	***Autre Europe***
Spain	1 020	...	...	1 645	2 092	1 786	774	852	...	...	Espagne
Yugoslavia	195	248	407	410	365	370	468	354	225	339	Yougoslavie
Oceania	**679**	**658**	**738**	**758**	**606**	**694**	**604**	**572**	**559**	**493**	**Océanie**
Australia[6]	679	658	738	758	606	694	604	572	559	493	Australie[6]
Total	**15 482**	**18 163**	**22 805**	**25 262**	**25 822**	**24 855**	**23 464**	**23 090**	**21 643**	**22 563**	**Total**

General note.
Electric fires, including portable types with parabolic reflectors, sometimes with built-in fans, convection heaters, and electric heaters in which electric elements heat up oil which circulates in the radiator. (SITC 72505-1).

Remarque générale.
Radiateurs, y compris les appareils portatifs à réflecteur parabolique et parfois ventileur incorporés. Radiateurs par convection et radiateurs à circulation de liquide, dans lesquels les éléments chauffants agissent sur de l'huile que circule dans un radiateur. (CTCI 72505-1).

[1] Portable electric heaters.
[2] Shipments.
[3] Deliveries.
[4] Electric shavers only.
[5] Beginning 1981, data are confidential.
[6] Twelve months ending 30 June of year stated.

[1] Radiateurs électriques portatifs seulement.
[2] Expéditions.
[3] Livraisons.
[4] Rasoirs électriques seulement.
[5] A partir de 1981, les données sont confidentielles.
[6] Période de douze mois finissant le 30 juin de l'année indiquée.

Irons, electric smoothing – Fers à repasser électriques de tous types

Unit : Thousand units

Unité : En milliers

Country or area	1976	1977	1978	1979	1980	1981	1982	1983	1984	1985	Pays ou zone
Africa	**12**	**70**	**70**	**70**	**70**	**70**	**128**	**70**	**70**	**70**	**Afrique**
Algeria	12	...	...	...	...	...	128	...	...	...	Algérie
America, North	**10 885**	**12 509**	**14 679**	**14 479**	**13 976**	**13 706**	**9 383**	**10 086**	**9 584**	**8 494**	**Amérique du Nord**
Canada	...	...	686	...	...	...	...	...	...	...	Canada
Mexico	1 371	1 538	1 594	1 714	1 812	2 007	2 081	2 121	1 055	974	Mexique
United States[1]	8 828	10 285	12 399	12 079	11 478	11 013	6 616	7 279	7 843	6 834	Etats–Unis[1]
America, South	**3 319**	**3 398**	**3 499**	**4 052**	**4 615**	**3 815**	**5 313**	**5 075**	**5 412**	**5 707**	**Amérique du Sud**
Brazil	2 873	2 998	3 145	3 625	4 190	3 484	4 952	...	...	...	Brésil
Chile	...	...	...	80	83	68	48	38	46	46	Chili
Colombia	165	157	186	217	203	116	163	90	...	...	Colombie
Peru	178	148	80	130	139	...	...	158	* 159	* 168	Pérou
Asia	**3 646**	**3 625**	**3 529**	**3 940**	**4 066**	**4 649**	**4 882**	**5 042**	**4 845**	**4 789**	**Asie**
Burma[2 3]	3	8	7	5	12	9	9	4	5	13	Birmanie[2 3]
Indonesia	...	...	20	28	14	47	30	61	33	...	Indonésie
Japan	3 436	3 407	3 305	3 704	3 969	4 441	4 772	4 905	4 756	4 695	Japon
Turkey	195	194	197	203	71	152	71	...	...	...	Turquie
Europe	**15 540**	**16 624**	**16 222**	**17 496**	**15 757**	**15 945**	**15 213**	**15 159**	**15 579**	**15 272**	**Europe**
EEC	***10 928***	***11 046***	***10 749***	***10 346***	***9 853***	***10 811***	***10 490***	***9 735***	***10 180***	***9 844***	***CEE***
France[4]	2 528	2 781	2 404	2 388	2 306	2 615	3 093	2 742	3 138	3 079	France[4]
Germany, Fed. Rep.	4 090	4 293	4 358	4 191	4 206	4 797	4 496	4 516	4 960	4 994	Allemagne, Rép. féd.
Greece	51	115	102	81	91	96	90	57	47	...	Grèce
Italy	...	...	[5] 1 296	[5] 1 241	[5] 1 489	[5] 1 894	[5] 1 424	# 1 264	1 111	1 014	Italie
United Kingdom	2 671	2 313	2 589	2 445	1 761	1 409	...	...	...	...	Royaume–Uni
EFTA	***12***	***19***	***16***	***6***	***5***	***42***	***63***	***141***	***103***	***87***	***AELE***
Portugal	...	6	8	4	2	39	60	137	98	81	Portugal
Sweden	10	13	8	2	3	3	3	4	5	6	Suède
East Europe	***2 945***	***2 869***	***2 838***	***2 820***	***2 892***	***2 908***	***2 955***	***2 988***	***2 931***	***2 961***	***Europe de l'est***
Czechoslovakia	...	...	...	...	...	...	...	1 022	...	...	Tchécoslovaquie
Hungary	205	129	98	80	152	168	215	248	191	221	Hongrie
Poland	...	...	...	...	...	...	...	1 718	...	...	Pologne
Other Europe	***1 655***	***2 690***	***2 619***	***4 324***	***3 007***	***2 184***	***1 705***	***2 295***	***2 365***	***2 380***	***Autre Europe***
Spain	992	...	...	3 524	2 155	1 128	686	1 220	...	...	Espagne
Yugoslavia	* 663	770	794	800	852	1 056	1 019	1 075	1 114	1 225	Yougoslavie
Oceania	**743**	**876**	**774**	**686**	**680**	**639**	**956**	**251**	**516**	**474**	**Océanie**
Australia	743	876	774	686	...	...	956	251	...	...	Australie
Total	**34 145**	**37 102**	**38 773**	**40 723**	**39 164**	**38 824**	**35 875**	**35 682**	**36 005**	**34 807**	**Total**

General note.
Smoothing irons, whether for domestic use or for tailors, dressmakers etc. (SITC 72505–2).

[1] Shipments.
[2] Government production only.
[3] Twelve months ending 30 September of year stated.
[4] Deliveries.
[5] Source: Industrial Statistics, Statistical Office of the European Communities, (Luxembourg).

Remarque générale.
Fers à repasser, pour usage domestique ou servant à des tailleurs, des couturières etc. (CTCI 72505–2).

[1] Expéditions.
[2] Production de l'Etat seulement.
[3] Période de douze mois finissant le 30 septembre de l'année indiquée.
[4] Livraisons.
[5] Source: Statistiques industrielles, Office statistique des Communautés européennes, (Luxembourg).

Fuses, electrical – Coupe–circuits électriques

Unit : Thousand units

Unité : En milliers

Country or area	1976	1977	1978	1979	1980	1981	1982	1983	1984	1985	Pays ou zone
America, South											**Amérique du Sud**
Brazil	17 465	41 303	39 180	45 518	131 891	...	...	...	...	...	Brésil
Colombia	602	411	983	625	526	158	188	134	...	...	Colombie
Asia											**Asie**
Indonesia	82	77	90	57	69	30	...	...	...	...	Indonésie
Iran(Islamic Rep.of) [1 2]	...	...	...	8 897	29 833	22 523	...	...	...	...	Iran(Rép.islamique) [1 2]
Turkey	14 191	[3] 12 721	[3] 14 212	13 665	10 154	14 428	22 686	21 672	19 573	19 294	Turquie
Europe											**Europe**
EEC											***CEE***
Germany, Fed. Rep.	304 567	319 162	...	399 119	375 786	331 846	318 953	337 861	368 447	371 243	Allemagne, Rép. féd.
Greece	3 660	4 283	4 557	3 564	5 716	5 784	6 726	6 653	8 746	...	Grèce
EFTA											***AELE***
Austria	8 855	6 744	6 324	6 424	8 870	9 052	6 491	6 933	2 806	2 969	Autriche
Finland	1 523	1 047	1 873	1 596	1 561	928	465	693	513	...	Finlande
Portugal	...	...	...	...	750	770	723	1 511	1 102	...	Portugal
East Europe											***Europe de l'est***
Hungary	61 340	51 225	51 359	61 232	61 236	50 075	60 928	62 408	60 227	56 408	Hongrie
Other Europe											***Autre Europe***
Spain	...	...	...	2 547	1 836	9 507	13 552	12 436	...	...	Espagne
Yugoslavia	24 769	30 475	23 255	25 000	19 960	20 418	18 732	25 537	20 753	20 370	Yougoslavie

General note.
Cartridge and socket–type non–renewable or renewable fuses for the protection of electrical circuits. (SITC 72220–1).

[1] Production by establishments employing 10 or more persons.
[2] Including electrical switches,
[3] Incomplete coverage.

Remarque générale.
Coupe–circuits à fusible du type à cartouche ou à bouchon, renouvelables ou non, servant à protéger des circuits électriques. (CTCI 72220–1).

[1] Production des établissements occupant 10 personnes ou plus.
[2] Y compris les interrupteurs électriques.
[3] Couverture incomplète.

Switches, electric – Interrupteurs électriques

Unit : Thousand units

Unité : En milliers

Country or area	1976	1977	1978	1979	1980	1981	1982	1983	1984	1985	Pays ou zone
America, North	**787 116**	**819 267**	**924 180**	**889 603**	**852 060**	**908 696**	**888 665**	**1 076 582**	**1 118 969**	**1 052 790**	**Amérique du Nord**
United States[1]	...	...	924 180	889 603	852 060	908 696	888 665	1 076 582	1 118 969	1 052 790	Etats-Unis[1]
Asia	**182 293**	**175 464**	**240 902**	**296 323**	**325 394**	**347 156**	**339 122**	**479 302**	**809 389**	**862 964**	**Asie**
Indonesia	...	30	39	110	216	535	...	...	...	...	Indonésie
Japan	148 339	162 554	215 224	257 742	285 047	305 743	280 342	355 457	680 010	724 421	Japon
Korea, Republic of	...	...	...	...	34 208	33 329	39 862	109 661	120 312	128 311	Corée, République de
Turkey	524	498	514	602	...	...	# 18 767	14 026	8 901	10 057	Turquie
Europe	**81 923**	**97 930**	**107 623**	**114 217**	**143 709**	**194 575**	**131 584**	**151 091**	**224 309**	**324 321**	**Europe**
EEC	***59 442***	***65 694***	***71 519***	***77 316***	***74 653***	***133 959***	***73 260***	***96 166***	***164 622***	***257 477***	***CEE***
Germany, Fed. Rep.	50 556	56 780	63 876	70 036	70 221	128 563	68 518	92 111	160 589	254 796	Allemagne, Rép. féd.
Greece	8 886	8 914	7 643	7 280	4 432	5 396	4 742	4 055	4 033	...	Grèce
EFTA	***4 901***	***8 163***	***7 433***	***8 512***	***10 673***	***12 531***	***10 563***	***10 081***	***11 206***	***14 758***	***AELE***
Austria	2 710	2 232	2 047	2 134	3 943	5 364	4 177	3 118	3 429	6 487	Autriche
Finland	2 177	5 835	5 209	6 119	6 642	6 648	5 567	6 189	7 027	...	Finlande
Portugal	...	...	...	...	88	519	819	774	750	...	Portugal
East Europe	***6 361***	***7 491***	***7 878***	***10 953***	***10 252***	***9 725***	***7 705***	***11 163***	***13 427***	***13 320***	***Europe de l'est***
Hungary	6 361	7 491	7 878	10 953	10 252	9 725	7 705	11 163	13 427	13 320	Hongrie
Other Europe	***11 219***	***16 582***	***20 793***	***17 436***	***48 131***	***38 360***	***40 056***	***33 681***	***35 054***	***38 766***	***Autre Europe***
Spain	...	...	...	5 451	30 797	24 739	25 556	25 725	...	...	Espagne
Yugoslavia	6 284	8 143	8 850	11 985	17 334	13 621	* 14 500	7 956	2 088	2 297	Yougoslavie
Total	**1 051 333**	**1 092 660**	**1 272 706**	**1 300 143**	**1 321 163**	**1 450 427**	**1 359 371**	**1 706 975**	**2 152 667**	**2 240 075**	**Total**

General note.
Apparatus for making and breaking electric circuits of single, double or triple poles. (SITC 72220-2).

[1] Shipments.

Remarque générale.
Appareils unis, bis ou tripolaires servant à établir ou interrompre des circuits électriques. (CTCI 72220-2).

[1] Expéditions.

Wire and cable, insulated – Fils et câbles électriques isolés

Unit : Metric tons

Unité : Tonnes métriques

Country or area	1976	1977	1978	1979	1980	1981	1982	1983	1984	1985	Pays ou zone
Africa											**Afrique**
Algeria	12 274	11 328	10 694	10 700	12 018	11 713	14 066	...	...	...	Algérie
Egypt	23 000	26 000	29 000	31 000	36 000	41 000	48 000	43 000	...	...	Egypte
Tunisia	1 808	2 395	2 314	2 861	4 388	5 569	6 677	6 469	5 990	5 549	Tunisie
America, North											**Amérique du Nord**
Cuba[1]	30 273	21 356	26 313	42 046	38 006	53 539	33 504	41 698	52 139	64 000	Cuba[1]
United States[2 3]	997 737	1 189 292	125 474	1 243 681	1 167 020	1 195 694	1 113 776	1 106 517	1 235 838	1 225 205	Etats-Unis[2 3]
America, South											**Amérique du Sud**
Brazil	74 619	199 702	* 170 087	[4] 239 482	201 413	190 958	...	...	...	...	Brésil
Chile	1 898	2 603	...	...	...	...	...	...	...	...	Chili
Colombia	...	...	...	...	...	9 632	8 693	12 449	...	...	Colombie
Ecuador	...	671	800	...	2 532	...	3 933	2 441	...	...	Equateur
Asia											**Asie**
Hong Kong	597	108	252	989	...	...	...	...	...	...	Hong-kong
India[5]	19 718	20 858	26 043	23 066	25 665	24 809	24 854	24 667	25 560	27 598	Inde[5]
Japan	742 890	659 439	741 155	781 883	765 647	787 351	782 535	...	...	...	Japon
Korea, Republic of	35 312	48 339	87 832	87 787	79 308	96 016	99 058	107 474	120 576	140 471	Corée, République de
Malaysia	...	18 455	18 251	19 242	26 463	30 849	46 458	43 988	27 886	36 135	Malaisie
Turkey[1]	397 805	...	...	...	...	...	268 153	527 539	444 056	2 829 885	Turquie[1]
Europe											**Europe**
EEC											***CEE***
Belgium[4 6]	144 292	121 978	118 067	[2] 131 314	[2] 158 148	[2] 130 807	[2] 157 125	[2] 127 860	[2] 118 849	[2] 113 182	Belgique[4 6]
Germany, Fed. Rep.	805 007	783 372	800 392	868 232	894 401	841 361	793 359	789 501	799 383	822 784	Allemagne, Rép. féd.
Greece	44 794	46 114	41 730	45 540	48 152	48 522	44 966	36 506	36 530	...	Grèce
EFTA											***AELE***
Austria[7]	53 942	56 624	55 417	60 076	59 896	59 862	49 268	51 040	55 103	59 788	Autriche[7]
Finland	...	...	3 689	...	...	...	...	...	...	...	Finlande
Norway	42 856	38 286	40 606	38 504	40 528	42 349	44 427	44 666	47 126	...	Norvège
Portugal	18 970	22 510	24 720	26 750	30 334	32 273	37 809	38 339	35 635	32 045	Portugal
East Europe											***Europe de l'est***
Bulgaria[1]	299 000	338 000	311 000	279 000	293 000	310 000	319 000	338 000	347 000	365 000	Bulgarie[1]
Czechoslovakia	196 781	201 239	201 712	209 126	169 867	166 642	148 841	151 584	154 639	163 747	Tchécoslovaquie
Hungary	56 319	58 356	64 318	61 842	55 000	58 902	63 240	57 576	62 616	60 253	Hongrie
Poland	191 174	197 010	216 825	217 086	203 212	140 453	120 193	148 038	163 377	176 572	Pologne
Romania	446	622	662	702	717	...	...	...	...	...	Roumanie
Other Europe											***Autre Europe***
Spain	109 466	...	...	...	...	...	...	...	...	...	Espagne
Yugoslavia	157 544	176 737	197 149	211 190	221 401	235 754	236 494	240 762	201 941	220 958	Yougoslavie

General note.
Wire, cable, braids, bars, strips etc. covered with an insulating material for use in conducting electric energy, whether or not covered with a metal sheath or fitted with connectors. Enamelled, lacquered or anodized wire and co-axial cable are included. (SITC 72310–1).

[1] In thousand metres.
[2] Shipments.
[3] Data refer to copper content of insulated wires and cables.
[4] Production by establishments employing 5 or more persons.
[5] Production by large and medium scale establishments only.
[6] Including conduits for interior electrical installations.
[7] Excluding multi-polar insulated wire.

Remarque générale.
Fils, câbles, tresses, barres, bandes etc., recouverts de matière isolante et utilisés comme conducteurs électiques, qu'ils soient ou non recouverts d'une gaine en métal ou munis de connecteurs. Cette rubrique comprend les fils émaillés, laqués ou oxydés anodiquement et les câbles coaxiaux. (CTCI 72310–1).

[1] En milliers de mètres.
[2] Expéditions.
[3] Données se rapportant à la teneur en cuivre des fils et câbles isolés.
[4] Production des établissements occupant 5 personnes ou plus.
[5] Production des grandes et moyennes entreprises seulement.
[6] Y compris les canalisations pour installations électriques intérieures.
[7] Non compris les fils isolés multipolaires.

Unit : Million units — Unité : En millions

Country or area	1976	1977	1978	1979	1980	1981	1982	1983	1984	1985	Pays ou zone
Africa											**Afrique**
Algeria	25	0	0	0	0	0	0	...	...	...	Algérie
Cameroon	...	...	...	...	...	...	...	...	22	7	Cameroun
Côte d'Ivoire	55	62	77	86	96	110	91	77	65	...	Côte d'Ivoire
Egypt	128	126	76	81	93	90	101	105	...	...	Egypte
Gabon	...	5	6	4	...	...	...	...	...	...	Gabon
Sudan	...	...	...	...	48	53	59	...	...	...	Soudan
United Rep. Tanzania	58	65	71	71	79	78	73	...	...	...	Rép.Unie de Tanzanie
America, North											**Amérique du Nord**
Canada	74	77	...	...	...	...	...	...	...	...	Canada
Cuba	...	...	25	43	33	53	23	41	52	40	Cuba
Dominican Republic	22	26	28	34	41	35	34	42	49	...	Rép. dominicaine
Mexico	231	283	279	350	399	464	523	381	390	385	Mexique
United States	...	...	...	...	...	...	25 379	...	...	...	Etats–Unis
America, South											**Amérique du Sud**
Brazil	719	631	800	[1] 887	971	841	...	...	...	...	Brésil
Colombia	...	...	...	...	...	262	296	214	...	...	Colombie
Ecuador	18	37	45	...	32	44	51	48	...	...	Equateur
Asia											**Asie**
Burma[2]	12	23	23	17	15	21	19	22	21	19	Birmanie[2]
China	...	...	...	...	323	373	384	423	429	448	Chine
Hong Kong	226	236	170	228	147	320	405	586	680	...	Hong–kong
India	595	622	821	857	993	1 038	1 158	1 043	1 112	1 207	Inde
Indonesia	292	364	399	515	549	582	650	692	756	...	Indonésie
Iran(Islamic Rep.of)[3,4]	162	174	141	151	117	148	139	181	...	...	Iran(Rép.islamique)[3,4]
Japan	1 761	1 882	1 964	2 138	2 439	2 327	2 627	2 854	3 014	2 967	Japon
Jordan	...	...	...	...	...	57	40	36	50	49	Jordanie
Korea, Republic of	128	137	192	253	158	166	204	371	325	311	Corée, République de
Philippines[5]	131	104	...	...	...	...	...	...	...	...	Philippines[5]
Sri Lanka	20	41	26	49	25	25	...	...	...	...	Sri Lanka
Syrian Arab Republic	40	38	41	33	39	28	21	18	9	8	Rép. arabe syrienne
Turkey	257	217	217	266	...	...	140	115	21	22	Turquie
Viet Nam	74	79	71	40	35	38	33	30	45	31	Viet Nam
Europe											**Europe**
EEC											***CEE***
Belgium	...	...	...	...	...	...	...	29	...	...	Belgique
Denmark	...	...	...	...	...	...	...	103	111	...	Danemark
Germany, Fed. Rep.[6]	22 593	21 106	25 860	19 024	21 098	26 437	25 752	30 138	26 525	24 889	Allemagne, Rép. féd.[6]
Italy[6]	13 764	11 510	12 986	12 041	12 794	11 224	11 631	12 431	11 972	10 582	Italie[6]
EFTA											***AELE***
Austria[6]	16 686	10 328	20 677	25 976	27 756	27 756	29 048	28 381	31 514	37 177	Autriche[6]
Portugal	* 28	40	40	63	47	44	72	82	71	56	Portugal
Sweden	52	49	48	52	52	44	0	0	0	...	Suède
East Europe											***Europe de l'est***
Hungary	119	121	123	116	118	126	139	132	148	138	Hongrie
Poland	...	...	...	284	283	219	214	241	231	235	Pologne
Other Europe											***Autre Europe***
Spain	427	...	...	468	442	450	483	468	...	...	Espagne
Yugoslavia	...	...	...	...	...	...	1	2	107	118	Yougoslavie
Oceania											**Océanie**
Australia	3	3	3	3	3	3	3	3	3	...	Australie

General note.
A primary cell consists basically of a container holding a solid or a liquid electrolyte (ammonium chloride) in which are immersed two electrodes. Cells may be grouped together in batteries, either in series or in parallel or a combination of both. The various types of cells include dry cells, wet cells, inert cells and concentration cells. (SITC 72911–0).

Remarque générale.
Une pile consiste essentiellement en un récipient contenant un électrolyte solide ou liquide (chlorure d'ammonium) dans lequel deux électrodes sont immergées. Les piles peuvent être groupées en série ou en parallèle, ou en mixte, pour donner des batteries de piles. Les divers types de piles sonts: les piles sèches, les piles à liquide, les piles amorçables et les piles de concentration. (CTCI 72911–0).

For footnotes, see end of table.

Voir la fin du tableau pour les notes.

1 Production by establishments employing 5 or more persons.
2 Government production only.
3 Twelve months beginning 21 March of year stated.
4 Production by establishments employing 10 or more persons.
5 Shipments.
6 In metric tons.

1 Production des établissements occupant 5 personnes ou plus.
2 Production de l'Etat seulement.
3 Période de douze mois commençant le 21 mars de l'année indiquée.
4 Production des établissements occupant 10 personnes ou plus.
5 Expéditions.
6 En tonnes métriques.

Unit : Thousand units | Unité : En milliers

Country or area	1976	1977	1978	1979	1980	1981	1982	1983	1984	1985	Pays ou zone
Africa	**2 385**	**2 551**	**2 848**	**2 533**	**2 965**	**3 419**	**3 084**	**3 346**	**3 609**	**3 721**	**Afrique**
Algeria	184	211	304	292	315	354	350	* 400	* 500	...	Algérie
Côte d'Ivoire	...	26	0	0	...	...	...	...	...	...	Côte d'Ivoire
Egypt	673	687	696	514	651	978	* 591	...	...	...	Egypte
Madagascar	25	27	27	21	17	8	13	16	13	11	Madagascar
Senegal	20	27	32	29	26	29	26	21	21	18	Sénégal
South Africa	1 266	1 350	1 533	1 437	1 681	...	...	...	...	...	Afrique du Sud
Tunisia	137	140	176	171	187	210	206	190	240	250	Tunisie
Zaire	0	...	...	23	22	51	23	25	...	...	Zaïre
Zambia	71	* 72	65	46	57	53	48	50	50	62	Zambie
America, North	**62 380**	**77 685**	**79 823**	**75 553**	**72 406**	**72 225**	**71 388**	**70 105**	**67 754**	**67 677**	**Amérique du Nord**
Barbados	13	11	14	16	21	21	21	17	14	12	Barbade
Canada[1]	3 514	4 826	...	3 510	4 250	4 459	...	...	...	...	Canada[1]
Cuba	99	97	137	178	302	237	222	302	336	393	Cuba
Dominican Republic	110	109	87	96	116	121	124	115	108	...	Rép. dominicaine
El Salvador	36	40	49	50	54	65	66	64	...	...	El Salvador
Jamaica	47	39	...	...	...	...	...	...	...	...	Jamaïque
Mexico	1 395	1 782	2 141	2 481	3 024	3 518	3 678	3 076	3 340	3 748	Mexique
Nicaragua	...	...	...	68	50	70	50	89	20	...	Nicaragua
United States[1]	57 086	70 705	73 210	69 111	...	...	...	...	59 332	58 684	Etats-Unis[1]
America, South	**6 683**	**9 339**	**4 967**	**5 413**	**5 684**	**4 114**	**4 471**	**4 130**	**3 866**	**3 481**	**Amérique du Sud**
Brazil	...	8 719	4 310	4 696	4 975	3 372	...	...	...	...	Brésil
Chile	181	216	191	211	193	160	* 95	157	198	171	Chili
Colombia	305	370	378	407	388	432	390	380	...	...	Colombie
Ecuador	57	34	88	...	128	150	155	147	...	...	Equateur
Asia	**27 103**	**30 323**	**31 048**	**32 834**	**38 304**	**39 571**	**39 085**	**39 831**	**35 273**	**37 812**	**Asie**
Cyprus	52	74	66	65	70	57	74	81	83	87	Chypre
Democratic Yemen	...	...	...	...	13	14	18	22	25	...	Yémen démocratique
India[2]	1 388	1 656	1 603	1 644	1 683	1 992	1 979	1 936	1 915	1 795	Inde[2]
Indonesia	449	370	245	218	653	854	1 218	1 104	1 652	...	Indonésie
Israel	268	280	309	315	322	328	307	280	291	314	Israël
Japan	22 854	25 522	26 379	27 624	32 113	32 364	31 715	31 771	25 795	27 622	Japon
Jordan	47	51	44	63	66	58	41	37	49	50	Jordanie
Korea, Republic of	593	900	1 166	1 583	2 067	2 156	1 988	2 677	3 332	3 965	Corée, République de
Kuwait	22	22	25	31	21	16	14	13	13	14	Koweït
Malaysia	307	304	323	343	381	511	541	565	...	...	Malaisie
Philippines	403	432	464	...	...	...	...	...	...	...	Philippines
Sri Lanka	...	...	44	95	82	160	...	...	...	...	Sri Lanka
Syrian Arab Republic	134	136	135	159	142	133	172	226	239	258	Rép. arabe syrienne
Turkey	458	447	207	216	237	479	476	578	736	948	Turquie
Europe	**35 881**	**36 729**	**36 678**	**36 602**	**38 565**	**35 222**	**37 584**	**38 812**	**39 305**	**43 469**	**Europe**
EEC	***25 682***	***26 100***	***25 458***	***25 651***	***23 779***	***22 925***	***24 691***	***25 078***	***25 885***	***28 616***	***CEE***
Denmark	697	734	712	789	704	...	...	...	...	...	Danemark
France	7 300	7 300	7 200	7 300	7 000	6 800	7 500	8 400	8 200	9 024	France
Germany, Fed. Rep.	10 655	11 223	10 468	10 805	10 158	10 039	11 234	10 852	11 905	12 792	Allemagne, Rép. féd.
Greece	* 181	199	262	256	304	287	321	323	341	...	Grèce
Netherlands[3]	702	648	617	587	454	397	270	273	276	332	Pays-Bas[3]
United Kingdom	6 147	5 996	6 199	# [4] 5 914	[4] 5 159	[4] 4 654	[4] 4 611	[4] 4 468	[4] 4 395	[4] 5 321	Royaume-Uni
EFTA	***1 758***	***1 939***	***1 953***	***2 034***	***2 326***	***2 153***	***2 221***	***2 137***	***2 067***	***2 376***	***AELE***
Finland	316	367	382	343	401	420	340	298	327	...	Finlande
Portugal[5]	* 441	555	627	759	988	924	969	960	881	989	Portugal[5]
Sweden	1 001	1 017	944	932	...	809	912	879	859	1 046	Suède
East Europe	***2 408***	***2 503***	***2 576***	***2 608***	***2 512***	***2 660***	***2 794***	***2 841***	***2 858***	***2 817***	***Europe de l'est***
Bulgaria	1 041	1 152	1 166	1 183	1 096	1 137	1 116	1 142	1 169	1 186	Bulgarie
Czechoslovakia	...	...	...	...	1 077	...	...	...	...	...	Tchécoslovaquie
Hungary	290	274	333	348	339	446	601	622	612	554	Hongrie
Other Europe	***6 033***	***6 187***	***6 691***	***6 309***	***9 948***	***7 484***	***7 878***	***8 756***	***8 495***	***9 661***	***Autre Europe***
Spain	3 664	...	...	3 409	4 647	4 432	4 540	4 912	...	...	Espagne

For general note and footnotes, see end of table. | Voir la fin du tableau pour la remarque générale et les notes.

Accumulators, electric, for motor vehicles (continued) – Accumulateurs pour véhicules automobiles (suite)

Unit : Thousand units

Unité : En milliers

Country or area	1976	1977	1978	1979	1980	1981	1982	1983	1984	1985	Pays ou zone
Yugoslavia	2 369	2 527	2 839	2 900	5 301	3 052	3 338	3 844	3 492	4 466	Yougoslavie
Oceania	**2 716**	**2 956**	**3 052**	**3 280**	**3 050**	**2 710**	**2 761**	**2 555**	**2 899**	**2 422**	**Océanie**
Australia[6]	2 716	2 956	3 052	3 280	3 050	2 710	2 761	2 555	2 899	2 422	Australie[6]
Total	**137 147**	**159 583**	**158 416**	**156 215**	**160 973**	**157 260**	**158 373**	**158 779**	**152 707**	**158 583**	**Total**

General note.
A battery composed of several cells connected together in series, each of which consist essentially of a container holding the electrolyte in which are immersed two electrodes. A direct current is passed through the accumulator producing certain chemical changes (charging). When the terminals of the accumulator are subsequently connected to an external circuit these chemical changes reverse and produce a direct current in the external circuit (discharging). (SITC 72912-0).

[1] Shipments.
[2] Production by large and medium scale establishments only.
[3] Industrial sales.
[4] Excluding accumulators for motorcycles and scooters.
[5] Excluding recomposed batteries.
[6] Twelve months ending 30 June of year stated.

Remarque générale.
Batteries composées de plusieurs éléments reliés en série, dont chacun consiste essentiellement en un récipient contenant un électrolyte dans lequel plongent deux électrodes. Le passage d'un courant continu dans l'accumulateur produit certaines réactions chimiques (charge). Si l'on connecte ensuite les bornes de l'accumulateur à un circuit extérieur, ces réactions chimiques s'effectuent en sens inverse, engendrant ainsi un courant continu dans le circuit extérieur (décharge). (CTCI 72912-0).

[1] Expéditions.
[2] Production des grandes et moyennes entreprises seulement.
[3] Ventes industrielles.
[4] Non compris les accumulateurs pour motocyclettes et scooters.
[5] Non compris les piles reconstituées.
[6] Période de douze mois finissant le 30 juin de l'année indiquée.

Unit : Million units | Unité : En millions

Country or area	1976	1977	1978	1979	1980	1981	1982	1983	1984	1985	Pays ou zone
Africa	**28**	**29**	**38**	**46**	**46**	**51**	**54**	**56**	**62**	**67**	**Afrique**
Egypt	23	23	33	42	42	46	49	51	...	...	Egypte
Tunisia	5	6	5	4	4	5	5	5	4	...	Tunisie
America, North	**5 602**	**5 506**	**5 546**	**5 803**	**4 658**	**4 050**	**3 763**	**3 498**	**3 500**	**3 163**	**Amérique du Nord**
Canada[1]	222	220	150	155	172	...	...	...	...	...	Canada[1]
Dominican Republic	2	2	2	3	2	2	2	4	3	4	Rép. dominicaine
El Salvador	9	9	10	8	9	7	6	5	...	...	El Salvador
United States	5 369	5 275	5 384	5 637	4 475	3 906	3 637	3 387	3 407	3 086	Etats–Unis
America, South	**398**	**461**	**464**	**530**	**580**	**577**	**606**	**670**	**710**	**737**	**Amérique du Sud**
Argentina[2]	98	106	94	112	107	82	* 83	98	105	93	Argentine[2]
Bolivia	0	0	0	0	0	0	1	1	...	...	Bolivie
Brazil	253	303	315	[3] 354	405	...	...	...	...	...	Brésil
Chile	17	21	20	24	25	24	21	22	21	23	Chili
Colombia	28	28	31	36	38	33	27	40	...	...	Colombie
Ecuador	2	3	4	...	...	6	7	7	...	...	Equateur
Asia	**1 282**	**1 398**	**1 424**	**1 484**	**1 512**	**1 567**	**1 605**	**1 710**	**1 942**	**2 056**	**Asie**
Burma[4]	1	2	2	1	2	3	4	4	3	4	Birmanie[4]
China	50	62	76	85	95	97	107	125	141	153	Chine
India[5]	165	169	193	201	202	245	273	274	278	272	Inde[5]
Indonesia	22	27	27	30	41	44	44	79	51	...	Indonésie
Iran(Islamic Rep.of)[6]	...	...	...	31	22	26	32	44	...	...	Iran(Rép.islamique)[6]
Japan	856	907	920	962	1 022	1 008	970	1 042	1 275	1 363	Japon
Korea, Republic of	78	105	101	67	42	45	...	...	...	...	Corée, République de
Pakistan[7]	17	15	18	21	20	34	41	24	37	...	Pakistan[7]
Philippines[1]	# 14	18	...	...	...	...	...	...	...	...	Philippines[1]
Sri Lanka[8]	...	...	...	6	6	2	...	...	...	...	Sri Lanka[8]
Thailand	12	14	15	14	18	...	...	...	...	...	Thaïlande
Turkey	49	58	31	50	26	29	60	54	61	68	Turquie
Europe	**3 069**	**3 151**	**3 290**	**3 608**	**3 735**	**3 398**	**3 605**	**3 762**	**3 683**	**3 891**	**Europe**
EEC	***1 899***	***1 990***	***2 053***	***2 068***	***2 141***	***1 856***	***2 022***	***2 165***	***2 144***	***2 311***	***CEE***
Denmark	27	31	31	35	37	...	...	41	42	40	Danemark
France[9]	353	351	369	392	375	347	373	394	386	404	France[9]
Germany, Fed. Rep.	716	776	788	799	846	695	796	793	772	832	Allemagne, Rép. féd.
Greece	23	24	27	28	29	30	26	26	20	...	Grèce
Italy	358	401	408	394	461	381	413	567	608	658	Italie
United Kingdom	422	# [10] 407	[10] 430	[10] 420	[10] 393	[10] 366	[10] 376	[10] 344	[10] 316	[10] 352	Royaume–Uni
EFTA	***102***	***109***	***119***	***118***	***123***	***118***	***107***	***112***	***113***	***117***	***AELE***
Austria	35	35	40	44	45	43	47	47	46	52	Autriche
Portugal[8]	23	28	32	30	33	29	30	34	40	40	Portugal[8]
Sweden	44	46	47	44	45	46	30	31	27	25	Suède
East Europe	***785***	***785***	***828***	***1 149***	***1 197***	***1 176***	***1 184***	***1 198***	***1 188***	***1 217***	***Europe de l'est***
Bulgaria	23	28	34	35	40	34	46	43	42	42	Bulgarie
Czechoslovakia	105	103	104	100	91	101	105	115	119	118	Tchécoslovaquie
German Dem. Rep.	182	179	189	188	196	199	216	243	241	247	Rép. dém. allemande
Hungary	357	346	366	367	405	418	431	412	408	408	Hongrie
Poland	118	129	135	459	465	424	386	385	378	402	Pologne
Other Europe	***283***	***267***	***290***	***273***	***274***	***248***	***292***	***287***	***238***	***246***	***Autre Europe***
Spain	190	...	...	138	136	119	170	175	...	...	Espagne
Yugoslavia	93	105	131	135	138	129	122	112	92	102	Yougoslavie
USSR[11]	**2 032**	**2 080**	**2 097**	**2 095**	**2 172**	**2 223**	**2 269**	**2 410**	**2 462**	**2 470**	**URSS[11]**
Byelorussian SSR[11]	*260*	*271*	*260*	*263*	*279*	*287*	*289*	*289*	*294*	*293*	*RSS de Biélorussie[11]*
Ukrainian SSR[11]	*180*	*187*	*192*	*198*	*208*	*236*	*264*	*330*	*384*	*403*	*RSS d'Ukraine[11]*
Total	**12 411**	**12 625**	**12 859**	**13 566**	**12 703**	**11 865**	**11 903**	**12 106**	**12 360**	**12 385**	**Total**

General note.
Electric filament lamps of all shapes and wattages. Fluorescent tubes and special types of electric lamps are excluded. (SITC 72920–1).

Remarque générale.
Lampes électriques à incandescence de toutes formes et de toutes puissances. Cette rubrique ne comprend pas les tubes fluorescents et les types spéciaux de lampes électriques. (CTCI 72920–1).

For footnotes, see end of table.

Voir la fin du tableau pour les notes.

[1] Shipments.
[2] Including special–type electric lamps.
[3] Production by establishments employing 5 or more persons.
[4] Government production only.
[5] Excluding miniature lamps.
[6] Production by establishments employing 10 or more persons.
[7] Twelve months ending 30 June of year stated.
[8] Including fluorescent tubes.
[9] Deliveries.
[10] Excluding lamps not exceeding 28 V for other than motor vehicles.
[11] Including fluorescent tubes and special type electric lamps.

[1] Expéditions.
[2] Y compris les lampes électriques de type spécial.
[3] Production des établissements occupant 5 personnes ou plus.
[4] Production de l'Etat seulement.
[5] Non compris les lampes miniatures.
[6] Production des établissements occupant 10 personnes ou plus.
[7] Période de douze mois finissant le 30 juin de l'année indiquée.
[8] Y compris les tubes fluorescents.
[9] Livraisons.
[10] Non compris les lampes de 28 V ou moins sauf celles qui sont destinées aux véhicules automobiles.
[11] Y compris les tubes fluorescents et les lampes électriques de types spéciaux.

Tubes, fluorescent – Tubes fluorescents

Unit : Thousand units

Unité : En milliers

Country or area	1976	1977	1978	1979	1980	1981	1982	1983	1984	1985	Pays ou zone
America, North	**320 180**	**322 206**	**345 052**	**360 938**	**373 305**	**375 374**	**366 608**	**421 783**	**463 308**	**442 324**	**Amérique du Nord**
Canada[1]	27 173	25 763	30 052	33 922	37 644	...	...	...	...	...	Canada[1]
El Salvador	473	681	692	789	618	732	701	798	...	...	El Salvador
United States	292 534	295 762	314 308	326 227	335 043	335 046	323 416	375 599	414 217	390 310	Etats-Unis
America, South	**28 481**	**33 081**	**29 040**	**35 378**	**42 343**	**40 096**	**43 611**	**47 278**	**50 199**	**51 927**	**Amérique du Sud**
Argentina	5 357	7 182	7 551	8 024	6 992	5 598	* 7 129	7 864	8 333	6 985	Argentine
Brazil	20 131	22 184	17 464	[2] 23 061	30 178	29 997	...	...	...	...	Brésil
Chile	1 148	1 561	1 646	1 871	2 124	1 428	* 1 734	2 145	2 060	2 678	Chili
Colombia	1 808	2 119	2 340	2 385	3 012	3 036	2 988	3 256	...	...	Colombie
Ecuador	...	35	39	...	...	...	...	...	...	...	Equateur
Asia	**247 771**	**284 371**	**286 588**	**315 175**	**317 974**	**321 057**	**341 834**	**397 029**	**418 846**	**433 794**	**Asie**
Burma[3]	738	630	242	41	114	278	323	478	455	421	Birmanie[3]
India	16 893	17 690	21 370	22 972	27 481	31 045	32 210	34 800	36 370	41 696	Inde
Indonesia	3 497	3 366	4 460	4 648	4 964	4 893	8 681	6 967	8 854	...	Indonésie
Japan	199 406	223 051	223 742	244 393	243 388	239 059	255 782	302 678	315 553	324 778	Japon
Korea, Republic of	13 933	21 296	19 144	25 146	24 881	25 187	26 952	33 495	38 400	39 072	Corée, République de
Philippines[1]	# 2 392	4 067	...	...	...	...	...	...	...	...	Philippines[1]
Thailand	...	4 925	6 656	7 703	9 942	11 247	11 050	12 658	14 145	...	Thaïlande
Turkey	6 794	9 346	7 744	7 042	3 974	6 118	...	...	...	132	Turquie
Europe	**158 690**	**165 816**	**240 314**	**230 576**	**252 117**	**223 386**	**213 688**	**197 941**	**230 512**	**253 175**	**Europe**
EEC	***129 605***	***135 975***	***209 299***	***203 340***	***224 615***	***186 720***	***181 675***	***171 300***	***197 494***	***222 068***	***CEE***
Germany, Fed. Rep.	62 315	70 695	128 540	112 398	132 863	108 554	106 503	98 276	101 981	118 544	Allemagne, Rép. féd.
Italy	11 162	13 551	23 406	35 000	39 761	33 140	36 364	33 562	51 802	54 150	Italie
United Kingdom	56 128	51 729	57 353	55 942	51 991	45 026	38 808	39 462	43 711	49 374	Royaume-Uni
EFTA	***2 511***	***2 909***	***2 766***	***2 610***	***2 075***	***1 416***	***2 045***	***2 359***	***2 129***	***2 163***	***AELE***
Sweden[4]	2 511	2 909	2 766	2 610	2 075	1 416	2 045	2 359	2 129	2 163	Suède[4]
East Europe	***13 094***	***14 494***	***15 455***	***16 727***	***14 058***	***14 560***	***17 751***	***16 099***	***20 528***	***18 249***	***Europe de l'est***
Hungary	13 094	14 494	15 455	16 727	14 058	14 560	17 751	16 099	20 528	18 249	Hongrie
Other Europe	***13 480***	***12 438***	***12 794***	***7 899***	***11 369***	***20 690***	***12 217***	***8 183***	***10 361***	***10 695***	***Autre Europe***
Spain	9 201	...	...	1 222	3 935	13 889	6 188	2 447	...	...	Espagne
Yugoslavia	4 279	5 206	5 904	6 677	7 434	6 801	6 029	5 736	5 528	6 204	Yougoslavie
Total	**755 122**	**805 474**	**900 993**	**942 067**	**985 739**	**959 913**	**965 741**	**1 064 031**	**1 162 865**	**1 181 219**	**Total**

General note.
Glass tubes in which a gas becomes luminous under the influence of an electric discharge, and the internal wall of which is coated with substances which transform ultra-violet rays into visible light. (SITC 72920-2A).

[1] Shipments.
[2] Production by establishments employing 5 or more persons.
[3] Government production only.
[4] Fluorescent tubes for lighting only.

Remarque générale.
Tubes en verre contenant un gaz qui devient luminescent sous l'effet d'une décharge électrique et dont la paroi intérieure est enduite de substances qui transforment les rayons ultraviolets en rayonnement visible. (CTCI 72920-2A).

[1] Expéditions.
[2] Production des établissements occupant 5 personnes ou plus.
[3] Production de l'Etat seulement.
[4] Tubes fluorescents pour éclairage seulement.

Tankers, launched – Navires–citernes, mis à flot

Unit : Number units | Unité : Nombre

Country or area	1976	1977	1978	1979	1980	1981	1982	1983	1984	1985	Pays ou zone
Africa	**0**	**0**	**2**	**0**	**1**	**0**	**1**	**1**	**0**	**0**	**Afrique**
Egypt	0	0	2	0	1	0	1	1	0	...	Egypte
America, North	**18**	**15**	**12**	**6**	**7**	**6**	**3**	**5**	**3**	**5**	**Amérique du Nord**
Canada[1]	6	5	5	2	2	2	1	0	0	...	Canada[1]
United States[1]	12	10	7	4	5	4	2	5	3	4	Etats–Unis[1]
America, South	**3**	**2**	**6**	**6**	**8**	**6**	**7**	**0**	**8**	**8**	**Amérique du Sud**
Argentina[1]	0	0	2	2	3	3	5	0	5	...	Argentine[1]
Brazil[1]	2	0	2	4	5	3	1	0	3	3	Brésil[1]
Peru[1]	1	1	0	0	0	0	1	0	0	1	Pérou[1]
Venezuela[1]	0	1	2	0	0	0	...	...	...	...	Venezuela[1]
Asia	**212**	**189**	**202**	**260**	**315**	**276**	**183**	**183**	**207**	**213**	**Asie**
Bangladesh[1]	1	0	0	0	0	0	0	0	0	0	Bangladesh[1]
Hong Kong[1]	0	1	0	0	0	0	0	1	0	...	Hong–kong[1]
India[1]	0	2	0	0	0	1	0	0	0	...	Inde[1]
Indonesia[1]	0	0	4	0	0	0	0	0	3	...	Indonésie[1]
Israel	0	0	0	0	0	1	0	0	0	...	Israël
Japan	201	178	193	255	302	258	170	173	178	191	Japon
Korea, Republic of	[1]6	[1]0	[1]1	1	9	12	10	9	19	16	Corée, République de
Philippines[1]	3	2	1	0	1	1	0	0	0	...	Philippines[1]
Singapore[1]	1	5	1	1	3	2	1	0	6	3	Singapour[1]
Turkey[1]	0	1	2	3	0	1	2	0	1	...	Turquie[1]
Europe	**134**	**89**	**54**	**45**	**43**	**52**	**54**	**48**	**28**	**44**	**Europe**
EEC	***55***	***33***	***22***	***19***	***12***	***20***	***23***	***26***	***10***	***17***	***CEE***
Belgium[1]	1	0	0	0	0	0	...	...	...	...	Belgique[1]
Denmark[1]	7	5	4	3	2	3	1	3	1	7	Danemark[1]
France[1]	3	4	2	1	0	0	2	2	0	...	France[1]
Germany, Fed. Rep.[1]	11	5	3	6	3	5	2	1	0	1	Allemagne, Rép. féd.[1]
Greece[1]	2	2	0	0	0	2	3	4	4	1	Grèce[1]
Italy[1]	8	5	3	2	1	2	5	4	4	6	Italie[1]
Netherlands[1]	9	2	1	1	1	1	3	9	1	1	Pays–Bas[1]
United Kingdom[2]	14	10	9	6	5	7	7	3	0	...	Royaume–Uni[2]
EFTA	***52***	***34***	***20***	***12***	***21***	***20***	***18***	***14***	***7***	***7***	***AELE***
Finland[1]	10	6	9	4	6	11	9	6	3	3	Finlande[1]
Norway[1]	12	4	4	4	9	1	7	5	4	1	Norvège[1]
Portugal[1]	3	0	1	1	1	1	1	1	0	...	Portugal[1]
Sweden[1]	27	24	6	3	5	7	1	2	0	3	Suède[1]
East Europe	***5***	***5***	***1***	***2***	***1***	***3***	***4***	***1***	***3***	***4***	***Europe de l'est***
Bulgaria	2	1	0	1	0	0	0	0	0	1	Bulgarie
Poland[1]	3	4	1	1	1	3	4	1	2	2	Pologne[1]
Romania	0	0	0	0	[1]0	[1]0	[1]0	[1]0	[1]1	[1]1	Roumanie
Other Europe	***22***	***17***	***11***	***12***	***9***	***9***	***9***	***7***	***8***	***16***	***Autre Europe***
Malta[1]	0	1	1	0	1	0	0	0	0	...	Malte[1]
Spain[1]	12	13	3	4	4	7	4	1	1	...	Espagne[1]
Yugoslavia	10	3	7	8	4	2	5	6	7	15	Yougoslavie
Oceania	**1**	**1**	**0**	**0**	**0**	**0**	**0**	**0**	**0**	**0**	**Océanie**
Australia	1	1	0	0	0	0	0	0	0	...	Australie
Total	**368**	**296**	**276**	**317**	**374**	**340**	**248**	**237**	**246**	**270**	**Total**

General note.
Merchant vessels specialized for the transport of liquids (petroleum, wine etc.), of 100 gross tons and over. (SITC 73530–5A).

[1] Source: Lloyd's Register of Shipping, (London).
[2] Excluding vessels under 100 GRT.

Remarque générale.
Navires marchands spécialisés dans le transport de liquides (essence, vins etc.), de 100 tonneaux de jauge brute ou davantage. (CTCI 73530–5A).

[1] Source: Lloyd's Register of Shipping , (Londres).
[2] Non compris les embarcations de moins de 100 tonneaux de jauge brute.

Tankers, launched – Navires-citernes, mis à flot

Unit : Thousand GRT

Unité : Milliers de GRT

Country or area	1976	1977	1978	1979	1980	1981	1982	1983	1984	1985	Pays ou zone
Africa	**1**	**1**	**1**	**1**	**1**	**1**	**0**	**3**	**0**	**1**	**Afrique**
Egypt	...	...	...	...	...	...	0	3	0	...	Egypte
America, North	**753**	**766**	**559**	**403**	**182**	**139**	**55**	**116**	**68**	**67**	**Amérique du Nord**
Canada[1]	98	92	66	37	31	47	8	0	0	...	Canada[1]
United States	655	674	493	366	151	92	47	116	68	59	Etats–Unis
America, South	**101**	**32**	**326**	**178**	**216**	**111**	**155**	**13**	**206**	**178**	**Amérique du Sud**
Argentina[1]	0	0	45	20	45	39	86	0	70	...	Argentine[1]
Brazil[1]	81	0	281	158	171	72	40	0	122	81	Brésil[1]
Peru[1]	20	16	0	0	0	0	17	0	0	17	Pérou[1]
Venezuela[1]	0	16	0	0	0	0	...	...	...	...	Venezuela[1]
Asia	**7 139**	**1 461**	**911**	**1 726**	**3 857**	**3 459**	**2 231**	**1 682**	**1 656**	**2 544**	**Asie**
Bangladesh[1]	1	0	0	0	0	0	0	0	0	0	Bangladesh[1]
Hong Kong[1]	0	1	0	0	0	0	0	1	0	...	Hong–kong[1]
India[1]	0	1	0	0	0	1	0	0	0	...	Inde[1]
Indonesia[1]	0	0	2	0	0	0	0	0	7	...	Indonésie[1]
Israel[1]	0	0	0	0	0	1	0	0	0	...	Israël[1]
Japan	6 654	1 404	901	1 713	3 539	3 228	2 007	1 447	1 289	1 829	Japon
Korea, Republic of	[1] 429	[1] 0	[1] 1	4	316	226	208	234	349	702	Corée, République de
Philippines[1]	3	1	0	0	0	1	0	0	0	...	Philippines[1]
Singapore[1]	52	53	1	2	2	2	0	0	9	4	Singapour[1]
Turkey[1]	0	1	6	7	0	0	16	0	2	...	Turquie[1]
Europe	**8 831**	**5 263**	**2 514**	**1 257**	**1 058**	**1 203**	**1 496**	**1 019**	**685**	**1 314**	**Europe**
EEC	***3 615***	***1 912***	***492***	***582***	***88***	***252***	***592***	***341***	***227***	***280***	***CEE***
Belgium[1]	44	0	0	0	0	0	...	...	...	...	Belgique[1]
Denmark[1]	569	435	118	41	22	24	50	115	28	165	Danemark[1]
France[1]	701	402	2	275	0	0	41	19	0	...	France[1]
Germany, Fed. Rep.[1]	759	185	6	10	52	82	27	1	0	4	Allemagne, Rép. féd.[1]
Greece[1]	2	2	0	0	0	37	55	35	36	17	Grèce[1]
Italy[1]	366	229	36	55	2	24	69	32	126	18	Italie[1]
Netherlands[1]	391	115	0	1	1	1	64	31	1	25	Pays-Bas[1]
United Kingdom[2]	783	544	330	200	11	84	253	73	0	...	Royaume–Uni[2]
EFTA	***3 552***	***2 015***	***1 325***	***308***	***477***	***303***	***223***	***229***	***80***	***172***	***AELE***
Finland[1]	213	217	120	19	33	82	76	44	16	37	Finlande[1]
Norway[1]	408	88	84	35	106	18	127	78	64	24	Norvège[1]
Portugal[1]	232	0	163	163	163	12	13	21	0	...	Portugal[1]
Sweden[1]	2 699	1 710	958	91	175	191	7	86	0	99	Suède[1]
East Europe	***66***	***63***	***1***	***53***	***1***	***74***	***181***	***21***	***81***	***86***	***Europe de l'est***
Bulgaria	64	60	0	52	0	0	0	0	0	5	Bulgarie
Poland[1]	2	3	1	1	1	74	181	21	75	75	Pologne[1]
Romania	0	0	0	0	[1] 0	[1] 0	[1] 0	[1] 0	[1] 6	6	Roumanie
Other Europe	***1 598***	***1 273***	***696***	***314***	***492***	***574***	***500***	***428***	***297***	***776***	***Autre Europe***
Malta[1]	0	4	4	0	4	0	0	0	0	...	Malte[1]
Spain[1]	1 148	1 122	212	191	140	242	131	2	2	...	Espagne[1]
Yugoslavia	450	147	480	123	348	332	369	426	295	772	Yougoslavie
Oceania	**1**	**1**	**0**	**0**	**0**	**0**	**0**	**0**	**0**	**0**	**Océanie**
Australia	1	1	0	0	0	0	0	0	0	...	Australie
Total	**16 826**	**7 524**	**4 311**	**3 565**	**5 314**	**4 913**	**3 938**	**2 833**	**2 615**	**4 104**	**Total**

General note.
Merchant vessels specialized for the transport of liquids (petroleum, wine etc.), of 100 gross tons and over. (SITC 73530–5B).

[1] Source: Lloyd's Register of Shipping, (London).
[2] Excluding vessels under 100 GRT.

Remarque générale.
Navires marchands spécialisés dans le transport de liquides (essence, vins etc.), de 100 tonneaux de jauge brute ou davantage. (CTCI 73530–5B).

[1] Source: Lloyd's Register of Shipping , (Londres).
[2] Non compris les embarcations de moins de 100 tonneaux de jauge brute.

Other sea–going merchant vessels, launched – Autres navires marchands, mis à flot

Unit : Number units

Unité : Nombre

Country or area	1976	1977	1978	1979	1980	1981	1982	1983	1984	1985	Pays ou zone
Africa	**17**	**13**	**8**	**10**	**8**	**7**	**8**	**4**	**5**	**7**	**Afrique**
Egypt[1]	6	7	4	8	1	4	4	1	3	5	Egypte[1]
Kenya[1]	1	0	0	0	0	0	0	0	0	...	Kenya[1]
Mauritius[1]	1	0	0	0	0	0	0	0	0	0	Maurice[1]
Morocco	2	0	0	1	0	0	0	0	...	...	Maroc
South Africa[1]	7	6	4	1	7	3	4	3	2	...	Afrique du Sud[1]
America, North	**157**	**114**	**170**	**202**	**219**	**241**	**256**	**139**	**78**	**72**	**Amérique du Nord**
Canada[1]	22	12	21	26	23	16	21	11	7	11	Canada[1]
Mexico[1]	4	2	2	0	1	15	13	0	0	3	Mexique[1]
Nicaragua[1]	0	0	0	3	0	0	0	0	0	...	Nicaragua[1]
United States[1]	131	100	147	173	195	210	222	128	71	57	Etats–Unis[1]
America, South	**35**	**66**	**43**	**48**	**40**	**30**	**49**	**38**	**34**	**21**	**Amérique du Sud**
Argentina[1]	4	13	13	9	6	3	7	6	8	7	Argentine[1]
Brazil[1 2]	15	26	25	26	27	21	37	29	24	9	Brésil[1 2]
Chile[1]	0	0	0	0	1	4	0	0	0	0	Chili[1]
Guyana[1]	0	0	0	0	0	0	1	1	0	...	Guyana[1]
Peru[1]	16	27	5	11	6	2	4	0	2	...	Pérou[1]
Venezuela[1]	0	0	0	2	0	0	0	2	0	3	Venezuela[1]
Asia	**781**	**972**	**607**	**531**	**592**	**649**	**755**	**681**	**849**	**726**	**Asie**
Hong Kong[1]	2	2	5	10	9	3	9	5	0	2	Hong–kong[1]
India[1]	20	20	11	8	9	15	7	7	6	13	Inde[1]
Indonesia[1]	10	2	7	3	3	0	2	1	6	5	Indonésie[1]
Israel[1]	1	1	1	1	0	0	0	0	0	...	Israël[1]
Japan[3]	644	789	445	393	440	483	557	497	648	575	Japon[3]
Korea, Republic of[1]	27	58	51	40	56	49	61	75	107	90	Corée, République de[1]
Kuwait[1]	2	0	0	0	0	0	0	0	0	0	Koweït[1]
Malaysia[1]	1	6	4	3	4	6	7	10	4	9	Malaisie[1]
Pakistan[1]	2	0	0	0	1	2	1	0	0	...	Pakistan[1]
Philippines[1]	3	13	11	11	10	8	13	2	3	3	Philippines[1]
Singapore[1]	51	49	50	39	45	71	81	61	41	17	Singapour[1]
Thailand[1]	0	0	0	1	0	0	0	0	0	...	Thaïlande[1]
Turkey[1]	16	31	22	22	15	12	17	22	34	11	Turquie[1]
United Arab Emirates[1]	0	1	0	0	0	0	0	1	0	...	Emirats arabes unis[1]
Europe	**907**	**891**	**849**	**790**	**685**	**718**	**738**	**685**	**596**	**605**	**Europe**
EEC	***422***	***431***	***412***	***368***	***338***	***360***	***372***	***368***	***323***	***316***	***CEE***
Belgium[1]	15	12	13	12	12	12	12	12	12	15	Belgique[1]
Denmark[1 3 4]	43	38	45	54	46	45	46	42	43	38	Danemark[1 3 4]
France[1]	32	37	37	28	28	36	38	30	30	25	France[1]
Germany, Fed. Rep.	141	148	124	89	93	77	91	117	112	118	Allemagne, Rép. féd.
Greece[1]	15	19	8	7	7	6	3	4	4	4	Grèce[1]
Ireland[1 5]	2	3	1	3	1	1	1	1	0	...	Irlande[1 5]
Italy[1]	29	35	31	29	39	46	27	29	24	19	Italie[1]
Netherlands[1]	102	88	94	97	84	111	109	98	78	79	Pays–Bas[1]
United Kingdom[4]	43	51	59	49	28	26	45	35	20	18	Royaume–Uni[4]
EFTA	***165***	***189***	***186***	***173***	***124***	***140***	***147***	***98***	***85***	***101***	***AELE***
Austria[1]	0	1	0	0	0	0	0	0	0	...	Autriche[1]
Finland[1]	21	20	22	24	25	31	36	27	21	23	Finlande[1]
Iceland[1]	4	4	1	1	1	5	2	5	2	0	Islande[1]
Norway[1]	110	135	123	109	64	75	78	39	39	53	Norvège[1]
Portugal[1]	13	8	11	8	12	6	11	10	11	7	Portugal[1]
Sweden[1]	17	21	29	31	22	23	20	17	12	18	Suède[1]
East Europe	***148***	***120***	***129***	***137***	***121***	***106***	***96***	***114***	***123***	***125***	***Europe de l'est***
Bulgaria[1]	6	7	9	7	8	8	9	10	10	9	Bulgarie[1]
German Dem. Rep.[1 5]	54	53	51	56	50	54	50	56	54	62	Rép. dém. allemande[1 5]
Hungary	3	0	0	0	0	0	0	0	0	0	Hongrie
Poland[1]	84	60	67	67	62	34	29	42	45	38	Pologne[1]
Romania[1]	...	...	...	7	1	10	8	6	14	16	Roumanie[1]
Other Europe	***172***	***151***	***122***	***112***	***102***	***112***	***123***	***105***	***65***	***63***	***Autre Europe***

For general note and footnotes, see end of table.

Voir la fin du tableau pour la remarque générale et les notes.

Other sea-going merchant vessels, launched (continued) – Autres navires marchands, mis à flot (suite)

Unit : Number units | Unité : Nombre

Country or area	1976	1977	1978	1979	1980	1981	1982	1983	1984	1985	Pays ou zone
Faeroe Islands[1]	0	2	1	2	2	0	1	2	0	2	Iles Féroé[1]
Malta[1]	0	0	0	0	1	0	0	3	0	...	Malte[1]
Spain[1]	156	131	107	94	75	92	115	86	56	42	Espagne[1]
Yugoslavia	16	18	14	16	24	20	7	14	9	18	Yougoslavie
Oceania	**18**	**14**	**16**	**28**	**38**	**45**	**22**	**21**	**38**	**27**	**Océanie**
Australia[1]	16	7	14	25	33	39	19	21	35	27	Australie[1]
Fiji	1	3	2	2	3	5	3	0	2	0	Fidji
New Zealand[1]	1	4	0	1	2	1	0	0	1	...	Nouvelle-Zélande[1]
Total	**1 915**	**2 070**	**1 693**	**1 609**	**1 582**	**1 690**	**1 828**	**1 568**	**1 600**	**1 458**	**Total**

General note.
Passenger vessels, dry cargo vessels and combined cargo-passenger vessels, including refrigerator vessels of 100 gross tons and over. Tankers are excluded. (SITC 73530-6A).

[1] Source: Lloyd's Register of Shipping, (London).
[2] Vessels over 200 DWT.
[3] Excluding wooden vessels.
[4] Excluding vessels under 100 GRT.
[5] Including tankers launched.

Remarque générale.
Paquebots, navires de charge pour le transport de marchandises solides et paquebots mixtes, y compris les navires frigorifiques, de 100 tonneaux de jauge brute ou davantage. Non compris navires-citernes. (CTCI 73530-6A).

[1] Source: Lloyd's Register of Shipping, (Londres).
[2] Navires plus de 200 tonnes de port en lourd.
[3] Non compris les embarcations en bois.
[4] Non compris les embarcations de moins de 100 tonneaux de jauge brute.
[5] Y compris les navires citernes mis à flot.

Other sea–going merchant vessels, launched – Autres navires marchands, mis à flot

Unit : Thousand GRT

Unité : Milliers de GRT

Country or area	1976	1977	1978	1979	1980	1981	1982	1983	1984	1985	Pays ou zone
Africa	**18**	**37**	**18**	**16**	**10**	**12**	**17**	**11**	**46**	**28**	**Afrique**
Egypt[1]	2	18	17	15	5	10	15	10	45	...	Egypte[1]
South Africa[1]	16	19	1	1	5	2	2	1	1	...	Afrique du Sud[1]
America, North	**554**	**464**	**509**	**514**	**456**	**330**	**342**	**223**	**163**	**202**	**Amérique du Nord**
Canada[1]	139	116	99	108	49	74	101	46	45	44	Canada[1]
Mexico[1]	1	1	1	1	0	4	19	0	0	38	Mexique[1]
United States[1]	414	347	409	405	407	252	222	177	118	120	Etats–Unis[1]
America, South	**386**	**933**	**635**	**325**	**682**	**677**	**441**	**380**	**410**	**427**	**Amérique du Sud**
Argentina[1]	35	49	57	29	16	29	22	18	71	96	Argentine[1]
Brazil[1 2 3]	345	878	576	293	648	631	415	359	337	324	Brésil[1 2 3]
Guyana	...	...	0	0	0	0	0	2	0	...	Guyana
Peru[1]	4	4	1	2	17	16	3	0	1	...	Pérou[1]
Venezuela	...	...	...	...	...	...	...	...	...	1	Venezuela
Asia	**7 687**	**8 829**	**4 235**	**2 812**	**4 086**	**6 850**	**7 525**	**6 514**	**10 236**	**9 414**	**Asie**
Hong Kong[1]	2	2	2	8	3	1	3	2	0	1	Hong–kong[1]
India[1]	55	37	60	28	74	62	17	95	35	78	Inde[1]
Indonesia[1]	5	1	1	0	0	0	2	2	9	1	Indonésie[1]
Israel[1]	6	6	6	6	0	0	0	0	0	...	Israël[1]
Japan[4]	7 294	8 210	3 651	2 216	3 528	5 618	6 065	5 286	8 047	7 203	Japon[4]
Korea, Republic of[1]	260	455	424	472	432	1 085	1 310	1 046	2 027	2 075	Corée, République de[1]
Kuwait	1	0	0	0	0	0	0	0	0	0	Koweït
Malaysia[1]	0	0	1	1	3	2	11	11	1	9	Malaisie[1]
Pakistan[1]	10	0	0	0	0	7	13	0	0	...	Pakistan[1]
Philippines[1]	2	6	5	4	5	6	15	2	6	4	Philippines[1]
Singapore[1]	35	64	64	35	27	46	56	35	39	15	Singapour[1]
Turkey	[1]15	[1]47	[1]21	[1]42	[1]14	[1]23	[1]33	[1]34	[1]72	22	Turquie
United Arab Emirates	...	...	0	0	0	0	0	1	0	...	Emirats arabes unis
Europe	**6 675**	**6 709**	**5 994**	**4 552**	**3 859**	**4 909**	**4 390**	**4 925**	**3 740**	**3 045**	**Europe**
EEC	***3 889***	***3 747***	***2 947***	***2 050***	***1 472***	***2 188***	***2 035***	***2 125***	***1 837***	***1 342***	***CEE***
Belgium[1]	142	169	263	152	96	223	123	118	194	25	Belgique[1]
Denmark[1 4 5]	70	139	162	188	169	364	434	410	393	266	Danemark[1 4 5]
France[1]	495	486	638	442	328	252	267	210	229	185	France[1]
Germany, Fed. Rep.	2 059	1 560	890	387	358	661	530	760	451	553	Allemagne, Rép. féd.
Greece[1]	73	83	27	26	2	29	1	2	5	2	Grèce[1]
Ireland[1]	29	41	6	2	7	0	...	40	0	...	Irlande[1]
Italy[1]	296	437	273	176	166	209	209	133	115	20	Italie[1]
Netherlands[1]	183	287	211	276	124	180	113	159	160	165	Pays–Bas[1]
United Kingdom[5]	542	545	477	401	222	270	346	293	290	120	Royaume–Uni[5]
EFTA	***891***	***1 019***	***943***	***806***	***546***	***669***	***622***	***532***	***583***	***494***	***AELE***
Austria[1]	0	2	0	0	0	0	0	0	0	...	Autriche[1]
Finland[1]	177	109	177	211	165	221	179	240	284	213	Finlande[1]
Iceland[1]	1	2	0	1	1	2	1	2	1	0	Islande[1]
Norway[1]	349	435	265	220	213	251	168	81	85	100	Norvège[1]
Portugal[1]	20	18	21	13	4	1	10	3	36	69	Portugal[1]
Sweden[1]	344	453	480	361	163	194	264	206	177	111	Suède[1]
East Europe	***1 043***	***997***	***1 261***	***991***	***917***	***952***	***707***	***990***	***1 015***	***956***	***Europe de l'est***
Bulgaria[1]	108	107	153	150	152	131	154	114	159	137	Bulgarie[1]
German Dem. Rep.[1]	372	381	382	292	340	354	328	343	354	406	Rép. dém. allemande[1]
Poland[1]	532	490	683	489	394	276	123	400	245	218	Pologne[1]
Romania[1]	...	...	...	60	31	191	102	133	257	195	Roumanie[1]
Other Europe	***852***	***946***	***843***	***705***	***924***	***1 100***	***1 026***	***1 278***	***305***	***253***	***Autre Europe***
Faeroe Islands[1]	0	1	1	2	2	0	1	2	0	1	Iles Féroé[1]
Malta[1]	0	0	0	0	0	0	0	2	0	...	Malte[1]
Spain[1]	469	460	450	329	508	590	722	669	148	104	Espagne[1]
Yugoslavia	383	485	392	374	414	510	303	605	157	147	Yougoslavie
Oceania	**68**	**49**	**31**	**5**	**9**	**15**	**8**	**8**	**13**	**11**	**Océanie**

For general note and footnotes, see end of table.

Voir la fin du tableau pour la remarque générale et les notes.

Other sea–going merchant vessels, launched (continued) – Autres navires marchands, mis à flot (suite)

Unit : Thousand GRT

Unité : Milliers de GRT

Country or area	1976	1977	1978	1979	1980	1981	1982	1983	1984	1985	Pays ou zone
Australia[1]	68	48	31	4	8	14	8	8	11	11	Australie[1]
Fiji	0	0	0	0	0	1	0	0	1	0	Fidji
New Zealand[1]	0	1	0	1	1	0	0	0	1	...	Nouvelle–Zélande[1]
Total	**15 388**	**17 021**	**11 422**	**8 224**	**9 102**	**12 793**	**12 723**	**12 061**	**14 608**	**13 127**	**Total**

General note.
Passenger vessels, dry cargo vessels and combined cargo–passenger vessels, including refrigerator vessels of 100 gross tons and over. Tankers are excluded. (SITC 73530–6B).

[1] Source: Lloyd's Register of Shipping, (London).
[2] In thousand DWT.
[3] Vessels over 200 DWT.
[4] Excluding wooden vessels.
[5] Excluding vessels under 100 GRT.

Remarque générale.
Paquebots, navires de charge pour le transport de marchandises solides et paquebots mixtes, y compris les navires frigorifiques, de 100 tonneaux de jauge brute ou davantage. Non compris navires–citernes. (CTCI 73530–6B).

[1] Source: Lloyd's Register of Shipping, (Londres).
[2] En milliers de tonnes de port en lourd.
[3] Navires plus de 200 tonnes de port en lourd.
[4] Non compris les embarcations en bois.
[5] Non compris les embarcations de moins de 100 tonneaux de jauge brute.

Locomotives, electric – Locomotives électriques

Unit : Number units

Unité : Nombre

Country or area	1976	1977	1978	1979	1980	1981	1982	1983	1984	1985	Pays ou zone
Asia	**279**	**285**	**270**	**294**	**337**	**302**	**306**	**291**	**327**	**350**	**Asie**
China	...	...	...	...	...	20	35	56	80	100	Chine
India[1]	183	194	197	189	249	232	202	204	211	214	Inde[1]
Japan	46	56	29	52	25	20	39	1	6	6	Japon
Turkey*	30	...	...	...	...	...	...	...	...	...	Turquie*
Europe	**1 175**	**1 209**	**1 225**	**1 011**	**953**	**1 093**	**977**	**1 110**	**1 120**	**1 136**	**Europe**
EEC	***413***	***447***	***382***	***276***	***305***	***353***	***226***	***277***	***304***	***272***	***CEE***
France	78	108	72	52	67	85	67	38	24	36	France
Germany, Fed. Rep.	169	136	86	60	52	47	34	30	25	17	Allemagne, Rép. féd.
Italy[2]	166	203	224	164	186	221	125	209	255	219	Italie[2]
EFTA	***26***	***38***	***30***	***23***	***38***	***8***	***15***	***40***	***41***	***44***	***AELE***
Austria	24	22	24	22	22	0	15	17	15	13	Autriche
Portugal[2]	0	14	4	0	0	0	0	0	0	...	Portugal[2]
Sweden	2	2	2	1	16	8	0	23	26	30	Suède
East Europe	***671***	***691***	***770***	***695***	***577***	***699***	***710***	***687***	***695***	***746***	***Europe de l'est***
Czechoslovakia[3]	96	114	106	107	102	116	137	148	131	126	Tchécoslovaquie[3]
German Dem. Rep.[2]	422	414	461	...	258	...	...	...	350	385	Rép. dém. allemande[2]
Hungary	31	10	15	0	20	30	26	5	5	12	Hongrie
Poland	85	100	134	123	125	100	91	77	102	108	Pologne
Romania	37	53	54	76	72	79	...	...	...	...	Roumanie
Other Europe	***65***	***33***	***43***	***17***	***33***	***33***	***26***	***106***	***80***	***74***	***Autre Europe***
Spain	35	16	27	1	10	13	17	92	74	...	Espagne
Yugoslavia	30	17	16	16	23	20	9	14	6	12	Yougoslavie
USSR	**410**	**423**	**438**	**413**	**429**	**430**	**451**	**453**	**...**	**...**	**URSS**
Total	**1 864**	**1 917**	**1 933**	**1 718**	**1 719**	**1 825**	**1 734**	**1 854**	**1 901**	**1 945**	**Total**

General note.
An electric locomotive is a railway vehicle equipped with one or more electric motors, deriving current from overhead wires or conductor rails or from accumulators carried on the locomotive. It is used for hauling railway vehicles. A locomotive so equipped which also has an engine (diesel or other) to supply current to the electric motor when it cannot be obtained from an overhead wire or from a conductor rail is classed as an electric locomotive. (SITC 73120-1A).

1 Including diesel and steam locomotives.
2 Including diesel locomotives.
3 Line electric locomotives only.

Remarque générale.
Une locomotive électrique est un véhicule ferroviaire pourvu d'un ou plusieurs moteurs électriques alimentés en énergie électrique par fil ou par rail ou á l'aide d'accumulateurs. La locomotive ainsi équipée, qui serait également pourvue d'une génératrice (diesel ou autre) fournissant du courant au moteur quand celui-ci ne peut s'alimenter à un fil ou à un rail, est classée parmi les locomotives électriques. (CTCI 73120-1A).

1 Y compris les locomotives Diesel et les locomotives à vapeur.
2 Y compris les locomotives Diesel.
3 Locomotives électriques de ligne seulement.

Locomotives, diesel – Locomotives diesel

Unit : Number units | Unité : Nombre

Country or area	1976	1977	1978	1979	1980	1981	1982	1983	1984	1985	Pays ou zone
America, North	**2 181**	**1 961**	**1 312**	**1 892**	**1 700**	**900**	**700**	**640**	**420**	**200**	**Amérique du Nord**
United States	...	...	1 312	1 892	1 700	900	700	...	...	...	Etats–Unis
America, South	**64**	**64**	**64**	**64**	**64**	**64**	**64**	**64**	**64**	**64**	**Amérique du Sud**
Brazil	...	...	...	...	...	64	...	...	...	...	Brésil
Asia	**296**	**241**	**325**	**327**	**555**	**209**	**282**	**472**	**591**	**497**	**Asie**
China	...	129	234	222	456	102	169	209	236	285	Chine
Japan	62	65	55	45	43	68	66	32	10	7	Japon
Korea, Republic of	...	...	...	...	16	14	14	198	295	...	Corée, République de
Turkey	* 20	...	...	...	40	25	...	...	50	...	Turquie
Europe	**1 846**	**1 920**	**1 747**	**1 616**	**1 388**	**1 235**	**1 210**	**1 199**	**1 169**	**987**	**Europe**
EEC	***588***	***564***	***474***	***445***	***355***	***341***	***306***	***323***	***327***	***259***	***CEE***
France	30	29	26	23	19	33	15	40	63	36	France
Germany, Fed. Rep.	356	321	261	280	202	195	199	212	213	193	Allemagne, Rép. féd.
United Kingdom[1]	[2] 202	[2] 214	[2] 187	[2] 142	...	...	...	...	51	...	Royaume–Uni[1]
EFTA	***103***	***112***	***84***	***144***	***135***	***53***	***82***	***68***	***66***	***49***	***AELE***
Austria	35	75	59	116	105	28	58	39	50	27	Autriche
Finland	15	10	13	13	16	10	9	12	3	...	Finlande
Portugal	20	0	0	0	0	0	0	0	0	...	Portugal
Sweden	33	27	12	15	14	15	15	17	13	6	Suède
East Europe	***1 125***	***1 189***	***1 161***	***994***	***814***	***735***	***742***	***727***	***744***	***654***	***Europe de l'est***
Czechoslovakia[3]	448	471	502	499	374	427	482	505	517	530	Tchécoslovaquie[3]
Hungary	21	11	23	41	43	19	47	13	32	4	Hongrie
Poland	409	396	362	168	121	40	30	41	39	29	Pologne
Romania[4]	247	311	274	286	276	249	183	168	156	91	Roumanie[4]
Other Europe	***30***	***55***	***28***	***33***	***84***	***106***	***80***	***81***	***32***	***25***	***Autre Europe***
Spain	22	17	24	29	64	43	10	10	2	...	Espagne
Yugoslavia	8	38	4	4	20	63	* 70	71	30	10	Yougoslavie
USSR	**1 455**	**1 344**	**1 392**	**1 335**	**1 378**	**1 357**	**1 298**	**1 375**	...	...	**URSS**
Ukrainian SSR	*1 389*	*1 278*	*1 327*	*1 269*	*1 311*	*1 295*	*1 234*	*1 306*	...	...	*RSS d'Ukraine*
Total	**5 842**	**5 530**	**4 840**	**5 234**	**5 085**	**3 765**	**3 554**	**3 750**	**3 565**	**3 059**	**Total**

General note.
A diesel locomotive is a railway vehicle in which the source of power is a diesel engine, irrespective of the type of transmission installed. It is used for hauling railway vehicles. However, diesel–electric locomotives equipped to derive power from an overhead wire or from a conductor rail are classed as electric locomotives. (SITC 73130–1A).

[1] Excluding mainline locomotives.
[2] Source: Industrial Statistics, Statistical Office of the European Communities, (Luxembourg).
[3] Locomotives over 800 kW.
[4] Including electric locomotives.

Remarque générale.
Une locomotive diesel est une locomotive actionnée par un moteur Diesel, quel que soit le type de transmission. Toutefois, les locomotives diesel–électrique, équipées pour être actionnées par l'énergie électrique transmise par un fil ou par un rail, sont classées parmi les locomotives électriques. (CTCI 73130–1A).

[1] Non compris les locomotives de grandes lignes.
[2] Source: Statistiques industrielles, Office statistique des Communautés européennes, (Luxembourg).
[3] Locomotives de plus de 800 kW.
[4] Y compris les locomotives électriques.

Locomotives, diesel – Locomotives diesel

Unit : Thousand horsepower

Unité : Milliers de cheval–vapeur

Country or area	1976	1977	1978	1979	1980	1981	1982	1983	1984	1985	Pays ou zone
Europe											**Europe**
East Europe											***Europe de l'est***
Czechoslovakia[1]	616	640	655	666	516	569	635	661	680	696	Tchécoslovaquie[1]
Hungary	18	13	30	52	43	34	46	23	61	4	Hongrie
Poland	315	289	209	135	89	15	12	29	26	24	Pologne
Romania[2]	604	797	760	894	863	855	...	...	...	293	Roumanie[2]
Other Europe											***Autre Europe***
Yugoslavia	6	27	3	0	0	...	...	...	...	...	Yougoslavie
USSR	4 050	3 705	3 846	3 704	3 836	3 754	3 596	3 802	...	...	**URSS**
Ukrainian SSR	***3 850***	***3 503***	***3 649***	***3 504***	***3 633***	***3 567***	***3 401***	***3 593***	...	...	*RSS d'Ukraine*

General note.
A diesel locomotive is a railway vehicle in which the source of power is a diesel engine, irrespective of the type of transmission installed. It is used for hauling railway vehicles. However, diesel–electric locomotives equipped to derive power from an overhead wire or from a conductor rail are classed as electric locomotives. (SITC 73130–1B).

[1] Locomotives over 800 kW.
[2] Including electric locomotives.

Remarque générale.
Une locomotive diesel est une locomotive actionnée par un moteur Diesel, quel que soit le type de transmission. Toutefois, les locomotives diesel–électrique, équipées pour être actionnées par l'énergie électrique transmise par un fil ou par un rail, sont classées parmi les locomotives électriques. (CTCI 73130–1B).

[1] Locomotives de plus de 800 kW.
[2] Y compris les locomotives électriques.

Rail motor passenger vehicles – Automotrices pour transport de passagers

Unit : Number units

Unité : Nombre

Country or area	1976	1977	1978	1979	1980	1981	1982	1983	1984	1985	Pays ou zone
Asia	**1 363**	**1 567**	**1 848**	**1 632**	**1 769**	**1 893**	**1 845**	**1 496**	**1 656**	**1 406**	**Asie**
Japan	1 363	1 567	1 848	1 632	1 769	1 893	1 845	1 496	1 656	1 406	Japon
Europe	**1 481**	**1 571**	**1 437**	**1 457**	**1 337**	**1 533**	**1 585**	**1 475**	**1 406**	**1 419**	**Europe**
EEC	***320***	***378***	***183***	***256***	***221***	***336***	***401***	***314***	***276***	***262***	***CEE***
Denmark	4	10	12	30	...	...	...	30	14	22	Danemark
France	316	368	171	226	205	318	381	284	262	240	France
EFTA	***96***	***98***	***116***	***154***	***95***	***119***	***112***	***122***	***161***	***131***	***AELE***
Austria	35	51	60	73	48	42	22	24	23	34	Autriche
Finland	...	8	6	7	4	12	10	12	16	...	Finlande
Portugal	0	14	4	32	14	0	10	0	38	7	Portugal
Sweden	58	25	46	42	29	65	70	86	84	76	Suède
East Europe	***1 065***	***1 093***	***1 135***	***1 043***	***1 016***	***1 072***	***1 064***	***1 020***	***964***	***1 020***	***Europe de l'est***
Czechoslovakia[1]	966	949	1 005	933	923	985	972	950	901	955	Tchécoslovaquie[1]
Hungary	38	64	53	35	17	27	42	20	30	30	Hongrie
Poland	61	80	77	75	76	60	50	50	33	35	Pologne
Other Europe	***0***	***2***	***3***	***4***	***5***	***6***	***8***	***19***	***5***	***6***	***Autre Europe***
Yugoslavia	0	...	...	...	...	...	8	19	5	6	Yougoslavie
Total	**2 844**	**3 138**	**3 285**	**3 089**	**3 106**	**3 426**	**3 430**	**2 971**	**3 062**	**2 825**	**Total**

General note.
Motor vehicles constructed for the conveyance of passengers by rail, irrespective of the type of power equipment installed. This item includes rail motor vehicles consisting of several articulated vehicles forming an indivisible set. Each of such sets is counted as one unit. (SITC 73140-1A).

[1] Trams only.

Remarque générale.
Véhicles automoteurs aménagés pour le transport sur rail de passagers, quel que soit le mode de propulsion. Cette rubrique comprend les automotrices consistant en plusieurs véhicules articulés formant une rame indivisible. Chaque rame est comptée comme une unité. (CTCI 73140-1A).

[1] Tramways seulement.

Goods wagons and vans – Wagons de marchandises et fourgons

Unit : Number units | Unité : Nombre

Country or area	1976	1977	1978	1979	1980	1981	1982	1983	1984	1985	Pays ou zone
Africa	**175**	**175**	**175**	**175**	**175**	**200**	**250**	**54**	**197**	**175**	**Afrique**
Mozambique[1]	...	...	...	...	...	200	250	54	197	...	Mozambique[1]
America, North	**52 988**	**52 280**	**69 958**	**91 417**	**86 675**	**45 292**	**17 889**	**6 268**	**13 004**	**12 737**	**Amérique du Nord**
Cuba	490	551	468	514	505	392	589	546	608	657	Cuba
United States	52 498	51 729	69 490	90 903	86 170	44 900	17 300	5 722	12 396	12 080	Etats–Unis
America, South	**4 082**	**3 712**	**3 382**	**3 273**	**2 217**	**1 019**	**1 640**	**1 246**	**1 134**	**421**	**Amérique du Sud**
Argentina	438	442	217	742	592	48	297	182	494	83	Argentine
Brazil	3 206	2 682	2 715	[2] 2 381	1 378	912	...	...	...	...	Brésil
Colombia	...	540	412	95	192	4	...	118	...	...	Colombie
Ecuador	80	48	38	...	...	...	...	...	...	...	Equateur
Asia	**24 606**	**24 392**	**34 441**	**31 106**	**24 995**	**28 024**	**28 543**	**33 250**	**34 471**	**29 600**	**Asie**
China	...	6 396	16 950	16 042	10 571	8 779	10 561	15 800	18 100	19 325	Chine
India	11 284	12 671	14 133	11 299	11 395	16 535	14 880	15 880	14 922	8 826	Inde
Japan	1 895	2 525	1 833	2 648	1 967	1 302	139	55	8	63	Japon
Korea, Republic of[3]	930	906	591	831	458	555	2 143	460	465	273	Corée, République de[3]
Turkey	* 1 440	1 894	934	286	604	853	820	1 055	976	1 113	Turquie
Europe	**71 738**	**73 619**	**67 050**	**67 328**	**66 502**	**61 413**	**50 517**	**49 377**	**51 800**	**51 095**	**Europe**
EEC	***17 692***	***21 532***	***17 285***	***19 017***	***18 899***	***20 025***	***14 709***	***15 600***	***16 312***	***14 831***	***CEE***
Denmark	139	50	0	50	55	45	40	12	50	30	Danemark
France	6 922	6 370	3 752	6 063	5 598	6 552	3 825	2 996	2 898	1 680	France
Germany, Fed. Rep.	6 607	6 558	5 893	5 936	6 548	6 282	4 243	5 238	4 707	4 404	Allemagne, Rép. féd.
Italy	1 223	1 884	1 926	1 907	1 637	2 085	1 540	2 293	3 596	3 656	Italie
United Kingdom	2 801	6 670	5 714	...	...	...	...	...	...	...	Royaume–Uni
EFTA	***2 912***	***2 546***	***2 322***	***2 061***	***2 380***	***2 174***	***2 251***	***1 932***	***1 804***	***1 117***	***AELE***
Austria	1 149	503	623	820	1 120	927	863	828	796	468	Autriche
Finland	771	702	363	247	219	331	365	221	223	...	Finlande
Norway	...	...	...	...	...	...	...	...	94	139	Norvège
Portugal	0	0	0	0	0	0	0	0	251	...	Portugal
Sweden[4]	876	1 225	1 220	878	925	800	907	767	440	313	Suède[4]
East Europe	***46 666***	***47 276***	***45 796***	***44 096***	***42 257***	***34 214***	***30 044***	***27 942***	***30 225***	***31 374***	***Europe de l'est***
Bulgaria	2 551	2 750	2 558	2 860	3 000	3 053	2 980	3 095	2 920	2 904	Bulgarie
Czechoslovakia	5 086	5 530	6 198	6 843	7 269	7 437	6 878	5 813	5 809	6 095	Tchécoslovaquie
German Dem. Rep.	5 430	5 587	5 527	5 274	4 455	4 808	3 811	3 145	3 128	3 311	Rép. dém. allemande
Hungary	88	162	60	12	30	3	0	0	10	85	Hongrie
Poland	20 401	18 602	17 869	15 912	15 216	9 141	6 371	6 047	6 362	6 801	Pologne
Romania[5 6]	13 110	14 645	13 584	13 195	12 287	9 772	10 004	9 842	11 996	12 178	Roumanie[5 6]
Other Europe	***4 468***	***2 265***	***1 647***	***2 154***	***2 966***	***5 000***	***3 513***	***3 903***	***3 459***	***3 773***	***Autre Europe***
Spain	1 147	1 037	465	648	1 078	1 848	622	973	958	...	Espagne
Yugoslavia	3 321	1 228	1 182	1 506	1 888	3 152	2 891	2 930	2 501	2 751	Yougoslavie
USSR	**83 330**	**82 618**	**78 691**	**74 263**	**72 619**	**70 579**	**68 487**	...	...	...	**URSS**
Ukrainian SSR	*38 645*	*37 865*	*36 383*	*33 652*	*31 577*	*30 691*	*29 279*	*30 641*	...	...	*RSS d'Ukraine*
Oceania	**2 587**	**2 571**	**3 610**	**2 371**	**2 541**	**2 540**	**2 034**	**2 570**	**1 211**	**1 740**	**Océanie**
Australia	2 587	2 571	3 610	2 371	2 541	2 540	2 034	2 570	1 211	...	Australie
Total	**239 506**	**239 367**	**257 307**	**269 933**	**255 724**	**209 067**	**169 360**	**157 895**	**164 280**	**155 564**	**Total**

General note.
Goods wagons comprise all types of railway vehicles without power equipment, normally intended for the transport of goods. Vans are railway vehicles without power equipment, forming part of a passenger or freight train, used by train crews and possibly for the transport of luggage, mail, parcels, bicycles etc. Freight–train vans (that is, vans used exclusively on freight trains) are included. (Parts of SITC 7315 and 73162).

Remarque générale.
Les wagons de marchandises comprennent tous les types de véhicules ferroviaires sans engin moteur, normalement destinés au seul transport des marchandises. Les fourgons sont des véhicules ferroviaires sans engin moteur, entrant dans la composition des trains de voyageurs ou de marchandises et utilisés par le personnel d'accompagnement et pour le transport éventuel de bagages, de la poste, de colis, de bicyclettes etc. Cette rubrique comprend les fourgons des trains de marchandises (c'est–à–dire ceux qui sont exclusivement utilisés dans ces trains). (Parties de CTCI 7315 et 73162).

For footnotes, see end of table.

Voir la fin du tableau pour les notes.

[1] Including passenger cars.
[2] Production by establishments employing 5 or more persons.
[3] Excluding rail passenger carriages.
[4] Wagons and vans for public railways and tramways only.
[5] Equivalent of four axles.
[6] Goods wagons and vans used in country–wide network.

[1] Y compris les voitures de tourisme.
[2] Production des établissements occupant 5 personnes ou plus.
[3] Non compris les wagons pour passagers.
[4] Wagons et fourgons pour chemins de fer et tramways publics seulement.
[5] En equivalent quatre essieux.
[6] Wagons et fourgons pour grandes voies de communications.

Rail passenger carriages – Voitures de passagers, pour voie ferrée

Unit : Number units

Unité : Nombre

Country or area	1976	1977	1978	1979	1980	1981	1982	1983	1984	1985	Pays ou zone
Africa	**652**	**391**	**439**	**335**	**138**	**644**	**623**	**788**	**895**	**781**	**Afrique**
Algeria	652	391	439	335	138	644	623	* 788	* 895	...	Algérie
America, South	**100**	**90**	**98**	**113**	**15**	**10**	**10**	**66**	**130**	**83**	**Amérique du Sud**
Argentina	90	80	93	93	10	0	0	...	120	73	Argentine
Colombia	...	...	5	20	5	...	...	...	...	...	Colombie
Asia	**2 189**	**2 495**	**3 099**	**2 624**	**2 870**	**3 045**	**2 674**	**2 880**	**3 236**	**3 493**	**Asie**
China	...	538	784	856	1 002	1 159	1 153	1 230	1 200	1 447	Chine
India	816	892	1 050	973	1 005	1 051	1 027	1 168	1 211	1 211	Inde
Indonesia	...	...	...	...	...	...	110	...	605	...	Indonésie
Japan	229	207	679	283	404	271	320	0	30	71	Japon
Korea, Republic of	178	451	179	105	52	157	14	75	140	357	Corée, République de
Turkey*	50	...	...	...	...	...	...	...	...	...	Turquie*
Europe	**5 133**	**5 469**	**5 209**	**5 119**	**4 467**	**4 427**	**4 758**	**4 203**	**4 457**	**4 263**	**Europe**
EEC	***1 738***	***2 104***	***1 733***	***1 196***	***1 135***	***1 183***	***1 514***	***1 466***	***1 750***	***1 469***	***CEE***
Denmark	...	49	22	...	44	56	62	19	...	...	Danemark
France	890	1 144	964	611	445	298	345	365	424	384	France
Germany, Fed. Rep.[1]	553	499	364	291	285	285	485	435	381	319	Allemagne, Rép. féd.[1]
Italy	254	412	383	253	361	544	622	647	903	724	Italie
EFTA	***146***	***256***	***488***	***692***	***311***	***313***	***315***	***267***	***246***	***369***	***AELE***
Austria	97	184	416	622	220	174	179	169	156	286	Autriche
Finland	30	24	31	35	42	38	54	40	35	...	Finlande
Portugal	0	28	16	0	0	37	16	0	0	...	Portugal
Sweden	19	20	25	35	49	64	66	58	55	31	Suède
East Europe	***3 013***	***2 860***	***2 726***	***2 971***	***2 792***	***2 685***	***2 642***	***2 251***	***2 189***	***2 104***	***Europe de l'est***
Bulgaria	102	90	100	90	0	0	0	0	...	...	Bulgarie
Czechoslovakia	245	229	255	287	280	184	195	45	0	44	Tchécoslovaquie
German Dem. Rep.	1 720	1 765	1 521	1 547	1 479	1 612	1 649	1 452	1 506	1 406	Rép. dém. allemande
Hungary	195	151	121	137	104	60	60	0	0	66	Hongrie
Poland[2]	450	420	383	320	328	286	308	350	330	350	Pologne[2]
Romania[3]	301	205	346	590	601	543	430	404	301	191	Roumanie[3]
Other Europe	***236***	***249***	***262***	***260***	***229***	***246***	***287***	***219***	***272***	***321***	***Autre Europe***
Spain	...	...	...	...	...	209	207	148	140	...	Espagne
Yugoslavia	60	73	86	84	53	37	80	71	132	145	Yougoslavie
USSR	**2 078**	**2 110**	**2 124**	**2 060**	**1 990**	**1 915**	**1 939**	**1 916**	**...**	**...**	**URSS**
Total	**10 152**	**10 555**	**10 969**	**10 251**	**9 480**	**10 041**	**10 004**	**9 853**	**10 590**	**10 460**	**Total**

General note.
Railway vehicles without power equipment intended for the conveyance of passengers, even if they comprise one or more compartments or spaces specially reserved for luggage, parcels, mail etc. This item includes special vehicles for the conveyance of passengers, such as sleeping–cars, saloons, dining–cars and ambulance cars. (SITC 73150–2).

[1] Including rail motor passenger vehicles.
[2] Excluding narrow–gauge vehicles.
[3] Goods wagons and vans used in country–wide network.

Remarque générale.
Véhicules ferroviaires sans engin moteur destinés au transport de passagers, même s'il y est réservé un ou plusieurs compartiments pour les bagages, les colis, la poste etc. Cette rubrique comprend les véhicules spéciaux pour le transport de passagers, tels que wagons–lits, wagons–salons, wagons–restaurants et wagons sanitaires. (CTCI 73150–2).

[1] Y compris les automotrices pour le transport de passagers.
[2] Non compris le matériel roulant pour voie étroite.
[3] Wagons et fourgons pour grandes voies de communications.

Engines, internal combustion (compression-ignition), for motor vehicles, diesel engines – Moteurs à combustion interne (à allumage par compression) pour véhicules automobiles, moteurs Diesel

Unit : Thousand units

Unité : En milliers

Country or area	1976	1977	1978	1979	1980	1981	1982	1983	1984	1985	Pays ou zone
America, North	**172**	**226**	**228**	**420**	**559**	**626**	**443**	**422**	**564**	**501**	**Amérique du Nord**
United States	172	226	228	420	559	626	443	422	564	501	Etats-Unis
America, South	**120**	**90**	**125**	**129**	**189**	**196**	**209**	**229**	**248**	**267**	**Amérique du Sud**
Brazil	120	90	125	[1] 129	189	196	...	...	...	...	Brésil
Asia	**5**	**3**	**7**	**2**	**4**	**7**	**6**	**9**	**7**	**8**	**Asie**
India	5	3	7	2	4	7	6	9	7	...	Inde
Europe	**601**	**750**	**870**	**1 107**	**1 168**	**1 314**	**1 250**	**1 151**	**1 257**	**1 507**	**Europe**
EEC	***464***	***604***	***719***	***935***	***991***	***1 144***	***1 079***	***922***	***1 064***	***1 296***	***CEE***
Germany, Fed. Rep.	454	580	680	883	924	1 065	1 005	877	917	1 108	Allemagne, Rép. féd.
United Kingdom[2]	...	...	...	...	...	79	74	45	147	188	Royaume-Uni[2]
EFTA	***58***	***59***	***55***	***69***	***76***	***64***	***60***	***74***	***79***	***90***	***AELE***
Austria	0	0	...	...	...	0	0	19	18	34	Autriche
Finland	6	6	6	7	7	6	6	8	9	...	Finlande
Sweden	52	52	48	59	62	58	54	47	51	48	Suède
East Europe	***25***	***25***	***27***	***27***	***26***	***25***	***24***	***24***	***24***	***26***	***Europe de l'est***
Hungary	25	25	27	27	26	25	24	24	24	26	Hongrie
Other Europe	***53***	***63***	***70***	***76***	***75***	***81***	***87***	***132***	***90***	***95***	***Autre Europe***
Spain	...	...	...	10	10	10	15	72	...	...	Espagne
Yugoslavia	50	56	60	66	66	71	72	60	61	62	Yougoslavie
Total	**898**	**1 069**	**1 230**	**1 660**	**1 920**	**2 143**	**1 909**	**1 811**	**2 076**	**2 284**	**Total**

General note.
Internal combustion (compression-ignition) piston engines for motor vehicles (passenger cars and commercial vehicles) equipped with cylinders, pistons, connecting-rods, crankshafts, flywheels, inlet and exhaust valves etc. Compression-ignition engines employ a somewhat heavier fuel than petrol engines. Included are semi-diesel engines that employ a heat source to heat the cylinder head. (SITC 71150-4A).

[1] Production by establishments employing 5 or more persons.
[2] Deliveries.

Remarque générale.
Moteurs à piston, à combustion interne (à allumage par compression), pour véhicules automobiles destinés au transport de voyageurs ou de marchandises, comportant cylindres, pistons, bielles, vilebrequins, volants, soupapes d'admission et d'échappement etc. Les moteurs à allumage par compression utilisant un carburant un peu plus lourd que l'essence. Sont inclus les moteurs utilisant une source de chaleur pour le réchauffage de la culasse (moteurs semi-diesel). (CTCI 71150-4A).

[1] Production des établissements occupant 5 personnes ou plus.
[2] Livraisons.

Engines, internal-combustion (spark-ignition), for motor vehicles, gasolene fueled – Moteurs à explosion pour véhicules automobiles à essence

Unit : Thousand units

Unité : En milliers

Country or area	1976	1977	1978	1979	1980	1981	1982	1983	1984	1985	Pays ou zone
America, North	**11 498**	**12 700**	**12 899**	**11 480**	**8 010**	**7 265**	**6 404**	**8 925**	**6 155**	**5 323**	**Amérique du Nord**
United States	11 498	12 700	12 899	11 480	8 010	7 265	6 404	8 925	...	...	Etats-Unis
America, South	**15**	**15**	**15**	**15**	**15**	**15**	**14**	**15**	**15**	**15**	**Amérique du Sud**
Colombia	...	...	...	...	...	15	14	15	...	...	Colombie
Asia	**39**	**89**	**164**	**196**	**121**	**133**	**163**	**220**	**270**	**361**	**Asie**
Korea, Republic of	39	89	164	196	121	133	163	220	270	361	Corée, République de
Europe	**5 063**	**5 355**	**5 563**	**5 582**	**4 841**	**4 388**	**4 826**	**5 148**	**5 028**	**5 500**	**Europe**
EEC	***4 094***	***4 447***	***4 626***	***4 589***	***4 059***	***3 653***	***4 083***	***4 030***	***3 800***	***4 202***	***CEE***
Germany, Fed. Rep.[1]	3 620	3 973	4 152	4 115	3 585	3 181	...	...	3 326	3 728	Allemagne, Rép. féd.[1]
United Kingdom	...	...	...	...	...	472	475	...	...	...	Royaume-Uni
EFTA	***275***	***221***	***254***	***320***	***326***	***260***	***328***	***620***	***696***	***770***	***AELE***
Austria	2	3	...	...	...	3	34	269	329	377	Autriche
Sweden	273	218	237	262	227	257	294	351	367	393	Suède
East Europe	***25***	***0***	***0***	***0***	***3***	***0***	***0***	***0***	***0***	***0***	***Europe de l'est***
Hungary	25	0	0	0	3	0	0	0	0	0	Hongrie
Other Europe	***669***	***688***	***684***	***674***	***454***	***475***	***415***	***498***	***532***	***528***	***Autre Europe***
Spain	...	...	...	434	367	403	357	358	352	...	Espagne
Yugoslavia	215	247	257	240	87	72	58	140	180	198	Yougoslavie
Oceania	**359**	**262**	**271**	**341**	**353**	**265**	**345**	**442**	**360**	**400**	**Océanie**
Australia	359	262	271	341	353	265	345	442	360	400	Australie
Total	**16 974**	**18 421**	**18 912**	**17 614**	**13 340**	**12 066**	**11 752**	**14 750**	**11 827**	**11 599**	**Total**

General note.
Internal-combustion piston engines (spark-ignition engines) for motor vehicles (passenger cars and commercial vehicles) equipped with cylinders, pistons, connecting-rods, crankshafts, flywheels, inlet and exhaust valves etc. Spark-ignition motor vehicle engines are usually petrol-fueled but some may employ other fuel, e.g. propane. Rotary engines of the spark-ignition type are included. Motorcycle engines are excluded. (SITC 71150-5A).

[1] 1982–1983, data are confidential.

Remarque générale.
Moteurs à piston, à explosion à allumage par etincelle électrique pour véhicules automobiles destinés au transport de voyageurs ou de marchandises, comportant cylindres, pistons, bielles, vilebrequins, volants, soupapes d'admission et d'échappement etc. Les moteurs de véhicules automobiles à explosion marchent en général à l'essence, mais certains peuvent consommer d'autres carburants, du propane par exemple. Les moteurs à piston rotatif du type à allumage par etincelle sont inclus. Les moteurs de motocycles sont exclus. (CTCI 71150-5A).

[1] 1982–1983, les données sont confidentielles.

Passenger cars, assembled from imported parts – Automobiles destinées au transport de voyageurs, assemblées à partir de pièces importées

Unit : Thousand units

Unité : En milliers

Country or area	1976	1977	1978	1979	1980	1981	1982	1983	1984	1985	Pays ou zone
Africa	**248**	**233**	**310**	**300**	**373**	**454**	**405**	**383**	**386**	**292**	**Afrique**
Côte d'Ivoire	5	7	0	0	2	3	2	2	2	...	Côte d'Ivoire
Egypt	10	14	14	17	16	19	17	25	...	...	Egypte
Morocco	25	21	19	17	17	16	* 17	* 16	14	14	Maroc
Nigeria	38	58	51	55	68	89	75	62	...	* 52	Nigéria
South Africa	169	132	224	207	268	324	292	* 276	273	194	Afrique du Sud
Tunisia	1	1	2	3	1	2	1	1	3	5	Tunisie
Zambia	0	0	0	1	1	1	1	1	1	1	Zambie
America, North	**10**	**12**	**14**	**13**	**10**	**11**	**13**	**18**	**19**	**16**	**Amérique du Nord**
Trinidad and Tobago	10	12	14	13	10	11	13	18	19	* 16	Trinité–et–Tobago
America, South	**150**	**155**	**161**	**151**	**164**	**146**	**149**	**108**	**119**	**121**	**Amérique du Sud**
Chile	5	9	17	18	25	22	8	3	4	5	Chili
Colombia	25	28	32	33	32	25	27	21	34	* 33	Colombie
Ecuador	1	1	1	2	2	4	4	4	...	...	Equateur
Peru	22	18	7	6	11	13	16	8	* 6	* 6	Pérou
Venezuela	97	99	104	92	* 94	82	94	72	70	72	Venezuela
Asia	**304**	**329**	**352**	**298**	**336**	**268**	**241**	**282**	**477**	**329**	**Asie**
Indonesia	30	20	43	40	43	24	30	26	23	24	Indonésie
Iran(Islamic Rep.of)[1 2]	102	132	107	75	73	72	50	54	...	...	Iran(Rép.islamique)[1 2]
Israel	4	4	3	3	2	1	0	0	...	...	Israël
Malaysia[3 4]	44	50	64	61	80	87	84	98	94	70	Malaisie[3 4]
Pakistan[5]	...	...	...	...	...	...	4	8	13	15	Pakistan[5]
Philippines	34	35	48	43	73	22	17	19	* 218	...	Philippines
Thailand	17	20	23	22	24	27	25	34	36	25	Thaïlande
Turkey	63	58	54	44	31	25	31	43	55	60	Turquie
Europe	**1 263**	**1 189**	**1 198**	**1 246**	**1 091**	**1 042**	**1 129**	**1 177**	**1 099**	**1 208**	**Europe**
EEC	***1 170***	***1 109***	***1 119***	***1 160***	***1 005***	***963***	***1 051***	***1 070***	***988***	***1 097***	***CEE***
Belgium[6]	1 051	1 009	1 004	# 1 029	891	859	950	972	887	995	Belgique[6]
Greece	2	1	5	2	2	6	12	12	15	...	Grèce
Ireland[7]	43	50	46	44	45	36	27	24	...	...	Irlande[7]
Netherlands	12	15	4	0	0	0	0	0	0	...	Pays–Bas
United Kingdom	...	34	60	85	67	...	...	...	...	...	Royaume–Uni
EFTA	***40***	***32***	***23***	***22***	***25***	***24***	***24***	***55***	***54***	***60***	***AELE***
Portugal[8]	40	32	23	22	25	24	24	55	54	60	Portugal[8]
Other Europe	***53***	***48***	***56***	***64***	***61***	***55***	***54***	***52***	***57***	***51***	***Autre Europe***
Yugoslavia	53	48	56	64	61	55	54	52	57	51	Yougoslavie
Oceania	**70**	**63**	**52**	**70**	**73**	**95**	**87**	**63**	**90**	**80**	**Océanie**
New Zealand	70	63	52	70	73	95	87	63	90	80	Nouvelle–Zélande
Total	**2 045**	**1 981**	**2 087**	**2 078**	**2 047**	**2 015**	**2 023**	**2 030**	**2 189**	**2 046**	**Total**

General note.

Three– and four–wheeled road motor vehicles, other than motor–cycle combinations, intended for the transport of passengers and seating not more than nine persons (including the driver), which are assembled wholly or mainly from imported parts. (SITC 73210–1).

1 Twelve months beginning 21 March of year stated.
2 Production by establishments employing 10 or more persons.
3 Data refer to Peninsular Malaysia only.
4 Beginning 1982, scope of series revised.
5 Twelve months ending 30 June of year stated.
6 Production by establishments employing 5 or more persons.
7 Beginning 1984, data are confidential.
8 Including production.

Remarque générale.

Véhicules automobiles routiers à trois ou à quatre roues, autres que les motocycles, destinés au transport de voyageurs, dont le nombre de places assises (y compris celle du conducteur) est inférieur à dix, et qui sont montés entièrement ou principalement avec des pièces importées. (CTCI 73210–1).

1 Période de douze mois commençant le 21 mars de l'année indiquée.
2 Production des établissements occupant 10 personnes ou plus.
3 Données se rapportant à la Malaisie péninsulaire seulement.
4 A partir de 1982, portée de la série révisée.
5 Période de douze mois finissant le 30 juin de l'année indiquée.
6 Production des établissements occupant 5 personnes ou plus.
7 A partir de 1984, les données sont confidentielles.
8 Y compris production.

Passenger cars, produced – Automobiles destinées au transport des voyageurs, fabriquées

Unit : Thousand units

Unité : En milliers

Country or area	1976	1977	1978	1979	1980	1981	1982	1983	1984	1985	Pays ou zone
America, North	**9 864**	**10 573**	**10 566**	**9 685**	**7 539**	**7 425**	**6 205**	**7 966**	**8 902**	**9 362**	**Amérique du Nord**
Canada	1 137	1 163	1 140	961	847	803	808	971	1 033	1 075	Canada
Mexico[1]	229	196	249	290	316	369	324	214	247	285	Mexique[1]
United States[2]	* 8 498	9 214	9 177	8 434	6 376	6 253	5 073	6 781	7 622	8 002	Etats-Unis[2]
America, South	**668**	**650**	**694**	**759**	**870**	**743**	**796**	**878**	**816**	**874**	**Amérique du Sud**
Argentina[1]	141	168	135	190	218	138	110	132	143	120	Argentine[1]
Brazil	527	482	559	569	652	605	686	746	673	754	Brésil
Asia	**5 088**	**5 505**	**6 106**	**6 321**	**7 130**	**7 091**	**7 029**	**7 331**	**7 310**	**8 007**	**Asie**
China	...	2	3	4	5	3	5	6	6	9	Chine
India[3]	32	28	35	29	30	42	43	45	64	89	Inde[3]
Japan	5 028	5 431	5 976	6 176	7 038	6 974	6 882	7 152	7 073	7 647	Japon
Korea, Republic of[1]	27	44	92	112	57	72	99	128	167	262	Corée, République de[1]
Europe	**11 721**	**12 330**	**12 595**	**12 644**	**11 814**	**10 931**	**11 298**	**12 081**	**11 690**	**11 997**	**Europe**
EEC	***9 799***	***10 156***	***10 315***	***10 313***	***9 468***	***8 830***	***9 132***	***9 650***	***9 149***	***9 336***	***CEE***
France	3 388	3 559	3 620	3 730	3 488	2 953	3 086	3 228	2 909	2 631	France
Germany, Fed. Rep.	3 548	3 796	3 901	3 943	3 530	3 590	3 771	3 875	3 783	4 165	Allemagne, Rép. féd.
Italy[4]	1 471	1 440	1 509	1 481	1 445	1 254	1 296	1 395	1 439	1 384	Italie[4]
Netherlands[1]	59	45	62	89	81	78	91	107	109	108	Pays-Bas[1]
United Kingdom	1 333	1 316	1 223	1 070	924	955	888	1 045	909	1 048	Royaume-Uni
EFTA	***368***	***288***	***312***	***343***	***297***	***336***	***360***	***413***	***417***	***441***	***AELE***
Austria	0	1	0	3	8	7	7	6	7	7	Autriche
Finland[1]	27	23	22	26	21	23	30	33	32	...	Finlande[1]
Sweden	341	264	290	314	268	306	323	374	378	402	Suède
East Europe	***645***	***697***	***768***	***792***	***815***	***708***	***704***	***740***	***800***	***826***	***Europe de l'est***
Bulgaria[1]	15	15	15	15	15	15	15	15	15	15	Bulgarie[1]
Czechoslovakia	179	159	175	182	184	181	174	178	180	184	Tchécoslovaquie
German Dem. Rep.	164	167	171	171	177	180	183	188	202	210	Rép. dém. allemande
Poland	216	279	326	350	351	240	228	269	278	283	Pologne
Romania	71	77	81	74	88	92	104	90	125	134	Roumanie
Other Europe	***909***	***1 189***	***1 200***	***1 196***	***1 234***	***1 057***	***1 102***	***1 278***	***1 324***	***1 394***	***Autre Europe***
Spain	770	1 010	1 006	990	1 048	877	944	1 110	1 137	* 1 217	Espagne
Yugoslavia	139	179	194	206	186	180	158	168	187	177	Yougoslavie
USSR	**1 239**	**1 280**	**1 312**	**1 314**	**1 327**	**1 324**	**1 307**	**1 315**	**1 327**	**1 332**	**URSS**
Ukrainian SSR	*143*	*150*	*160*	*160*	*161*	*162*	*160*	*162*	*166*	*168*	*RSS d'Ukraine*
Oceania	**369**	**381**	**318**	**357**	**399**	**317**	**375**	**363**	**341**	**365**	**Océanie**
Australia[1 5]	369	381	318	357	399	317	375	363	341	365	Australie[1 5]
Total	**28 949**	**30 719**	**31 591**	**31 080**	**29 079**	**27 831**	**27 010**	**29 934**	**30 386**	**31 937**	**Total**

General note.
Three- and four-wheeled road motor vehicles, other than motor-cycle combinations, intended for the transport of passengers and seating not more than nine persons (including the driver), which are manufactured wholly or mainly from domestically-produced parts. Passenger cars shipped in "knocked-down" form for assembly abroad are included. (SITC 73210-2).

Remarque générale.
Véhicules automobiles routiers à trois ou quatre roues, autres que les motocycles, destinés au transport des voyageurs, dont le nombre de places assises (y compris celle du conducteur) est inférieur à dix, et qui sont construits entièrement ou principalement avec des pièces fabriquées dans le pays. Cette rubrique comprend les voitures destinées au transport des voyageurs exportées en pièces détachées pour être montées à l'étranger. (CTCI 73210-2).

[1] Including assembly.
[2] Factory sales.
[3] Excluding production by ordnance factories.
[4] Excluding production for armed forces.
[5] Twelve months ending 30 June of year stated.

[1] Y compris le montage.
[2] Ventes des fabriques.
[3] Non compris la production des manufactures d'artillerie.
[4] Non compris la production destinée aux forces armées.
[5] Période de douze mois finissant le 30 juin de l'année indiquée.

ISIC–BASED CODE
3843–12

Buses and motor coaches, assembled from imported parts – Autocars et autobus, assemblés à partir de pièces importées

CODE BASE CITI
3843–12

Unit : Number units

Unité : Nombre

Country or area	1976	1977	1978	1979	1980	1981	1982	1983	1984	1985	Pays ou zone
Africa	**11 149**	**6 693**	**8 164**	**9 653**	**11 805**	**13 241**	**17 523**	**15 704**	**13 647**	**11 410**	**Afrique**
Algeria	149	176	450	524	652	577	663	700	731	...	Algérie
Egypt	373	475	468	601	464	622	705	788	...	...	Egypte
South Africa	10 432	5 878	7 031	8 327	10 503	11 641	15 959	13 977	* 11 888	9 344	Afrique du Sud
Tunisia	195	164	215	179	146	347	128	157	146	216	Tunisie
Zambia	0	0	0	22	...	...	...	...	86	124	Zambie
America, North	**1 267**	**1 970**	**1 805**	**2 440**	**1 846**	**1 665**	**1 602**	**1 862**	**2 219**	**2 393**	**Amérique du Nord**
Cuba	1 267	1 970	1 805	2 440	1 846	1 665	1 602	1 862	2 219	2 393	Cuba
Asia	**54 637**	**78 622**	**70 652**	**68 936**	**136 643**	**148 907**	**147 470**	**139 616**	**113 848**	**96 994**	**Asie**
Burma[1]	73	64	203	117	149	187	6	97	62	96	Birmanie[1]
Indonesia[2]	44 398	69 379	65 196	61 015	130 795	142 788	137 000	128 000	100 125	83 784	Indonésie[2]
Israel	100	...	...	...	...	...	...	...	...	...	Israël
Malaysia	457	446	770	599	583	702	...	...	...	...	Malaisie
Pakistan[3]	1 983	1 037	520	1 176	1 176	513	285	765	614	695	Pakistan[3]
Turkey	7 626	7 596	3 863	5 929	3 840	4 617	9 340	9 873	12 125	11 455	Turquie
Europe	**12 737**	**11 167**	**9 739**	**11 956**	**12 867**	**10 469**	**8 622**	**6 248**	**5 940**	**4 800**	**Europe**
EEC	***10 041***	***8 264***	***7 067***	***9 427***	***9 703***	***7 495***	***6 046***	***3 933***	***3 946***	***2 525***	***CEE***
Belgium[4 5]	4 496	4 387	3 692	6 463	6 155	4 959	4 110	2 538	2 962	2 173	Belgique[4 5]
Denmark	162	460	231	224	186	264	332	209	235	69	Danemark
Greece	...	...	...	591	670	553	289	223	138	...	Grèce
Ireland[2 6]	4 200	2 431	2 304	2 064	2 615	...	...	...	...	...	Irlande[2 6]
Netherlands	165	79	43	85	77	52	0	0	0	0	Pays–Bas
EFTA	***562***	***572***	***599***	***453***	***454***	***882***	***480***	***227***	***58***	***63***	***AELE***
Portugal[7]	562	572	599	453	454	882	480	227	58	63	Portugal[7]
East Europe	***84***	***281***	***23***	***26***	***661***	***40***	***39***	***29***	***15***	***8***	***Europe de l'est***
Hungary	84	281	23	26	661	40	39	29	15	8	Hongrie
Other Europe	***2 050***	***2 050***	***2 050***	***2 050***	***2 049***	***2 052***	***2 057***	***2 059***	***1 921***	***2 204***	***Autre Europe***
Malta	3	3	3	3	2	5	10	12	17	...	Malte
Yugoslavia	...	...	...	...	...	...	...	...	1 904	2 190	Yougoslavie
Total	**79 790**	**98 452**	**90 360**	**92 985**	**163 161**	**174 282**	**175 217**	**163 430**	**135 654**	**115 597**	**Total**

General note.
Passenger road motor vehicles (inluding trolley–buses) seating more than nine persons (including the driver), which are assembled wholly or mainly from imported parts. Seating capacity should be measured as the number of seats or berths, including the driver's, available in the vehicle when performing the service for which it is primarily intended. (SITC 73220–1).

Remarque générale.
Véhicules automobiles routiers (y compris les trolleybus) dont le nombre de places assises (y compris celle du conducteur) est supérieur à neuf et qui sont montés entièrement ou principalement avec des pièces importées. Le nombre de places est donné par le nombre de sièges ou de couchettes (y compris la place du conducteur) du véhicule lorsqu'il assure le service auquel il est essentiellement destiné. (CTCI 73220–1).

[1] Government production only.
[2] Including other commercial vehicles.
[3] Twelve months ending 30 June of year stated.
[4] Production by establishments employing 5 or more persons.
[5] Shipments.
[6] Beginning 1981, data are confidential.
[7] Including production.

[1] Production de l'Etat seulement.
[2] Y compris les autres véhicules utilitaires.
[3] Période de douze mois finissant le 30 juin de l'année indiquée.
[4] Production des établissements occupant 5 personnes ou plus.
[5] Expéditions.
[6] A partir de 1981, les données sont confidentielles.
[7] Y compris production.

Buses and motor coaches, produced – Autocars et autobus, fabriqués

Unit : Number units — Unité : Nombre

Country or area	1976	1977	1978	1979	1980	1981	1982	1983	1984	1985	Pays ou zone
America, North	**49 255**	**44 912**	**47 506**	**49 420**	**50 065**	**42 439**	**41 668**	**36 534**	**38 294**	**38 357**	**Amérique du Nord**
Canada	8 817	5 880	4 613	10 298	...	...	...	...	...	...	Canada
Mexico[1]	6 637	7 364	7 551	6 624	8 278	7 742	8 006	2 920	5 446	6 729	Mexique[1]
United States[2 3]	33 801	31 668	35 342	32 498	34 385	27 295	26 260	26 212	...	...	Etats-Unis[2 3]
America, South	**4 582**	**4 774**	**4 878**	**3 285**	**3 178**	**3 575**	**2 460**	**981**	**1 212**	**1 679**	**Amérique du Sud**
Brazil[4]	4 582	4 774	4 878	3 285	3 178	3 575	2 460	981	1 212	1 679	Brésil[4]
Asia	**71 389**	**74 339**	**83 348**	**93 121**	**121 502**	**140 519**	**108 070**	**106 562**	**121 536**	**132 456**	**Asie**
India	14 928	10 954	13 686	14 151	14 322	20 238	14 432	16 263	17 719	19 969	Inde
Iran(Islamic Rep.of)[5]	10 821	9 359	6 239	4 346	3 738	5 037	5 675	9 526	...	...	Iran(Rép.islamique)[5]
Japan	42 139	48 496	56 119	62 561	91 588	102 835	66 990	55 948	72 209	79 591	Japon
Korea, Republic of[1]	3 501	5 530	7 304	12 063	11 854	12 409	20 973	24 825	26 464	28 129	Corée, République de[1]
Europe	**114 264**	**107 742**	**99 121**	**106 112**	**105 396**	**93 977**	**85 926**	**84 515**	**79 335**	**86 741**	**Europe**
EEC	***62 727***	***54 579***	***47 385***	***51 401***	***48 959***	***45 083***	***38 273***	***40 741***	***36 689***	***42 145***	***CEE***
Denmark	...	...	...	...	...	...	...	...	235	231	Danemark
France	3 788	3 080	3 657	3 333	3 084	2 817	2 612	2 562	2 567	2 588	France
Germany, Fed. Rep.	19 899	18 194	14 567	15 224	16 771	18 077	14 537	13 739	10 056	15 181	Allemagne, Rép. féd.
Italy	5 071	4 877	5 308	5 883	6 642	10 887	6 689	7 603	6 588	7 211	Italie
Netherlands	560	562	578	817	657	625	1 095	988	744	907	Pays-Bas
United Kingdom	33 176	27 633	23 042	25 911	21 572	12 444	13 107	15 616	16 499	16 027	Royaume-Uni
EFTA	***6 802***	***5 759***	***5 967***	***7 996***	***8 341***	***7 607***	***6 423***	***4 861***	***5 563***	***6 057***	***AELE***
Austria	296	259	370	...	...	...	...	...	...	...	Autriche
Finland[1]	101	79	78	79	78	72	144	74	44	...	Finlande[1]
Sweden	6 405	5 421	5 519	7 609	7 955	7 227	5 971	4 479	5 211	5 676	Suède
East Europe	***37 174***	***39 015***	***38 106***	***38 307***	***39 473***	***35 176***	***34 504***	***32 602***	***32 143***	***32 619***	***Europe de l'est***
Bulgaria[1]	1 519	1 943	1 957	1 936	2 068	2 070	2 202	2 507	2 501	2 650	Bulgarie[1]
Czechoslovakia	2 786	2 900	3 178	3 401	3 678	3 015	3 662	3 500	3 628	3 798	Tchécoslovaquie
German Dem. Rep.	2 482	2 707	2 784	2 919	2 870	3 041	2 469	1 688	1 691	2 042	Rép. dém. allemande
Hungary	11 502	11 610	13 106	13 360	# 14 032	12 191	13 255	12 806	13 025	13 246	Hongrie
Poland	14 957	15 839	13 465	13 455	13 123	11 528	9 707	9 015	8 334	8 042	Pologne
Romania	3 928	4 016	3 616	3 236	3 702	...	...	...	...	...	Roumanie
Other Europe	***7 561***	***8 389***	***7 663***	***8 408***	***8 623***	***6 111***	***6 726***	***6 311***	***4 940***	***5 920***	***Autre Europe***
Spain	3 462	3 473	3 255	2 982	3 926	3 819	2 863	1 930	1 337	1 497	Espagne
Yugoslavia	4 099	4 916	4 408	5 426	4 697	2 292	3 863	4 381	3 603	4 423	Yougoslavie
USSR	**72 051**	**76 570**	**79 642**	**81 181**	**[4] 2 015**	**[4] 2 219**	**[4] 2 080**	**[4] 2 180**	**[4] 2 350**	**[4] 2 467**	**URSS**
Ukrainian SSR	*13 056*	*13 932*	*14 293*	*15 043*	*15 294*	*15 072*	*15 203*	...	...	...	*RSS d'Ukraine*
Oceania	**2 415**	**1 491**	**1 092**	**1 318**	**1 378**	**1 175**	**734**	**1 104**	**993**	**912**	**Océanie**
Australia[6 7]	2 415	1 491	1 092	1 318	1 378	1 175	734	1 104	993	912	Australie[6 7]
Total	**313 956**	**309 828**	**315 587**	**334 437**	**283 534**	**283 904**	**240 938**	**231 876**	**243 720**	**262 612**	**Total**

General note.
Passenger road motor vehicles (including trolley-buses) seating more than nine persons (including the driver), which are manufactured wholly or mainly from domestically-produced parts. Seating capacity should be measured as the number of seats or berths, including the driver's, available in the vehicle when performing the service for which it is primarily intended. (SITC 73220-2).

Remarque générale.
Véhicules automobiles routiers (y compris les trolleybus) dont le nombre de places assises (y compris celle du conducteur) est supérieur à neuf, et qui sont construits entièrement ou principalement avec des pièces fabriquées dans le pays. Le nombre de places est donné par le nombre de sièges ou de couchettes (y compris la place du conducteur) du véhicule lorsqu'il assure le service auquel il est essentiellement destiné. (CTCI 73220-2).

[1] Including assembly.
[2] Factory sales.
[3] Including school bus chassis.
[4] Buses only.
[5] Production by establishments employing 10 or more persons.
[6] Finished and partly finished.
[7] Twelve months ending 30 June of year stated.

[1] Y compris le montage.
[2] Ventes des fabriques.
[3] Y compris les châssis d'autocars scolaires.
[4] Autobus seulement.
[5] Production des établissements occupant 10 personnes ou plus.
[6] Finis et semi-finis.
[7] Période de douze mois finissant le 30 juin de l'année indiquée.

Lorries (trucks), including articulated vehicles, assembled from imported parts – Camions, y compris les véhicules articulés, assemblés à partir de pièces importées

Unit : Number units | Unité : Nombre

Country or area	1976	1977	1978	1979	1980	1981	1982	1983	1984	1985	Pays ou zone
Africa	**105 161**	**87 056**	**105 894**	**117 524**	**131 878**	**163 213**	**149 943**	**131 511**	**151 695**	**121 758**	**Afrique**
Algeria	3 749	3 659	5 550	6 082	6 464	5 625	5 543	6 500	* 7 344	...	Algérie
Egypt	1 370	1 690	1 173	2 307	1 221	2 227	2 454	2 736	...	...	Egypte
Ghana* [1]	...	...	5 000	...	...	...	...	4 300	...	...	Ghana* [1]
Morocco[1]	11 025	10 658	5 508	4 020	2 557	2 223	2 536	2 217	940	1 719	Maroc[1]
Nigeria	6 321	7 000	...	6 420	11 653	...	* 12 682	2 551	* 1 958	* 2 091	Nigéria
South Africa	72 851	53 536	74 022	84 927	97 136	131 394	111 557	102 903	* 123 070	94 461	Afrique du Sud
Tunisia	3 000	4 007	4 872	7 280	7 420	9 670	9 240	8 464	9 798	7 328	Tunisie
United Rep. Tanzania	...	...	...	524	...	...	* 188	...	...	...	Rép.Unie de Tanzanie
Zaire	1 839	...	1 644	1 314	421	864	1 093	1 484	...	...	Zaïre
America, North	**3 431**	**2 855**	**3 015**	**2 951**	**2 256**	**3 154**	**2 737**	**3 508**	**4 320**	**4 076**	**Amérique du Nord**
Cuba	1 510	193	603	660	552	511	444	415	500	753	Cuba
El Salvador	288	344	0	0	0	0	0	0	...	...	El Salvador
Trinidad and Tobago[1]	1 633	2 318	2 412	2 291	1 704	2 643	2 293	3 093	3 656	3 168	Trinité-et-Tobago[1]
America, South	**91 441**	**83 493**	**99 323**	**89 528**	**83 603**	**96 694**	**78 872**	**50 514**	**38 464**	**36 585**	**Amérique du Sud**
Chile	1 994	2 921	3 502	2 620	4 051	5 281	2 329	1 510	2 556	3 528	Chili
Colombia[1]	11 393	8 908	12 664	15 968	10 553	10 824	9 048	6 768	11 208	5 868	Colombie[1]
Peru[1]	12 054	7 664	4 157	4 940	7 999	8 903	6 237	1 618	* 2 700	* 3 189	Pérou[1]
Venezuela	66 000	64 000	79 000	66 000	* 61 000	* 71 686	* 61 258	* 40 618	22 000	24 000	Venezuela
Asia	**162 560**	**172 275**	**141 632**	**128 924**	**134 253**	**154 855**	**157 783**	**222 836**	**247 554**	**213 850**	**Asie**
Burma[2]	530	357	533	510	462	478	909	736	567	798	Birmanie[2]
Indonesia	...	...	...	298	368	420	580	570	770	...	Indonésie
Iran(Islamic Rep.of)[3 4]	55 224	47 497	33 612	18 466	19 878	30 324	39 145	77 678	...	...	Iran(Rép.islamique)[3 4]
Iraq	...	...	...	...	...	3 115	3 115	...	...	...	Iraq
Israel	3 097	3 485	4 200	5 290	2 329	2 797	2 494	2 936	2 146	1 130	Israël
Malaysia[5 6]	5 660	7 548	9 251	10 803	17 247	16 358	16 044	20 789	26 740	35 772	Malaisie[5 6]
Pakistan[7]	6 291	5 088	4 542	12 530	11 110	11 290	14 245	14 499	14 650	15 722	Pakistan[7]
Philippines	16 761	25 317	23 022	26 000	15 000	13 901	12 149	3 864	* 55 481	...	Philippines
Thailand[1]	32 473	47 310	44 605	30 862	49 341	60 509	52 656	75 314	74 910	58 244	Thaïlande[1]
Turkey	39 399	32 459	18 564	21 050	15 403	15 663	16 446	23 335	23 217	25 025	Turquie
Europe	**105 909**	**107 988**	**132 717**	**87 964**	**108 356**	**101 879**	**106 192**	**85 339**	**66 960**	**72 169**	**Europe**
EEC	***85 322***	***76 111***	***97 646***	***55 586***	***60 582***	***51 406***	***55 187***	***42 841***	***46 456***	***49 427***	***CEE***
Belgium[8]	75 577	65 279	83 948	[9] 43 403	[9] 42 735	[9] 35 960	[9] 42 180	[9] 33 261	[9] 38 951	[9] 37 455	Belgique[8]
Denmark	515	440	432	480	302	...	...	46	109	237	Danemark
Greece	6 997	8 518	11 501	9 838	15 534	13 103	11 332	7 566	4 687	...	Grèce
Netherlands	2 233	1 874	1 765	1 865	2 011	2 057	1 435	1 968	2 709	2 602	Pays-Bas
EFTA	***20 563***	***31 853***	***35 047***	***32 354***	***47 750***	***50 449***	***50 981***	***42 474***	***20 456***	***22 742***	***AELE***
Portugal[10]	20 563	31 853	35 047	32 354	47 750	50 449	50 981	42 474	20 456	22 742	Portugal[10]
Other Europe	***24***	***24***	***24***	***24***	***24***	***24***	***24***	***24***	***48***	***0***	***Autre Europe***
Yugoslavia	...	...	...	...	...	...	...	...	48	0	Yougoslavie
Oceania	**11 507**	**12 555**	**11 091**	**13 816**	**17 366**	**20 133**	**24 217**	**19 030**	**24 997**	**24 185**	**Océanie**
New Zealand[6]	11 507	12 555	11 091	13 816	17 366	20 133	24 217	19 030	24 997	24 185	Nouvelle-Zélande[6]
Total	**480 009**	**466 222**	**493 672**	**440 707**	**477 712**	**539 928**	**519 744**	**512 738**	**533 990**	**472 623**	**Total**

General note.
Road motor vehicles designed for the conveyance of goods, including vehicles specially equipped for the transport of certain goods, which are assembled wholly or mainly from imported parts. Articulated vehicles (that is, units made up of a road motor vehicle and a semi-trailer) are included. Ambulances, prison vans, and special purpose lorries and vans, such as fire-engines, are excluded. (SITC 73230-1).

Remarque générale.
Véhicules automobiles routiers conçus pour le transport des marchandises, y compris les véhicules spécialement équipés pour le transport de certaines marchandises, et qui sont montés entièrement ou principalement avec des pièces importées. Les véhicules articulés (c'est-à-dire les ensembles composés d'un véhicule automobile routier et d'une semi-remorque) sont compris dans cette rubrique. Cette rubrique ne comprend pas les ambulances, les voitures cellulaires et les camions à usages spéciaux, tels que les voitures-pompes à incendie. (CTCI 73230-1).

[1] Including motor coaches and buses.
[2] Government production only.
[3] Production by establishments employing 50 or more persons.

[1] Y compris les autocars et autobus.
[2] Production de l'Etat seulement.
[3] Production des établissements occupant 50 personnes ou plus.

Lorries (trucks), including articulated vehicles, assembled from imported parts (continued) – Camions, y compris les véhicules articulés, assemblés à partir de pièces importées (suite)

4 Twelve months beginning 21 March of year stated.
5 Data refer to Peninsular Malaysia only.
6 Including vans and buses.
7 Twelve months ending 30 June of year stated.
8 Production by establishments employing 5 or more persons.
9 Shipments.
10 Including production.

4 Période de douze mois commençant le 21 mars de l'année indiquée.
5 Données se rapportant à la Malaisie péninsulaire seulement.
6 Y compris les autobus et les camionnettes.
7 Période de douze mois finissant le 30 juin de l'année indiquée.
8 Production des établissements occupant 5 personnes ou plus.
9 Expéditions.
10 Y compris production.

Lorries (trucks), including articulated vehicles, produced –
Camions, y compris les véhicules articulés, fabriqués

Unit : Number units — Unité : Nombre

Country or area	1976	1977	1978	1979	1980	1981	1982	1983	1984	1985	Pays ou zone
America, North	**2 898 221**	**3 905 236**	**4 246 511**	**3 568 217**	**2 199 636**	**2 289 219**	**2 415 480**	**2 923 485**	**3 978 391**	**4 344 998**	**Amérique du Nord**
Canada	493 982	576 807	629 479	615 326	527 522	519 600	468 000	554 400	808 800	855 609	Canada
Mexico[1]	84 961	76 284	123 722	141 572	161 042	210 581	144 471	67 053	94 591	132 389	Mexique[1]
United States[2 3]	2 319 278	3 252 145	3 493 310	2 811 319	1 511 072	1 559 038	1 803 009	2 302 032	3 075 000	3 357 000	Etats-Unis[2 3]
America, South	**458 659**	**470 293**	**523 220**	**585 682**	**561 170**	**361 055**	**170 371**	**160 971**	**197 601**	**216 340**	**Amérique du Sud**
Argentina[1]	38 383	51 014	32 829	46 494	44 204	23 140	18 712	25 052	23 150	17 050	Argentine[1]
Brazil	420 276	419 279	490 391	539 188	516 966	337 915	151 659	135 919	174 451	199 290	Brésil
Asia	**2 863 033**	**3 165 522**	**3 419 375**	**3 626 489**	**4 141 749**	**4 317 004**	**4 005 497**	**4 155 782**	**4 628 913**	**4 961 525**	**Asie**
China	...	75 900	96 100	116 700	135 500	108 300	121 800	137 100	181 800	269 000	Chine
India[4]	27 537	25 531	34 776	44 216	51 394	67 090	68 507	69 509	75 739	85 352	Inde[4]
Japan	2 766 166	3 027 864	3 230 173	3 386 988	3 902 746	4 094 881	3 770 762	3 897 366	4 308 257	4 535 947	Japon
Korea, Republic of[1]	19 358	36 227	58 326	78 585	52 109	46 733	44 428	51 807	63 117	71 226	Corée, République de[1]
Europe	**1 505 809**	**1 564 587**	**1 565 455**	**1 628 324**	**1 699 851**	**1 445 227**	**1 462 387**	**1 441 575**	**1 362 593**	**1 526 246**	**Europe**
EEC	***1 175 866***	***1 209 189***	***1 201 672***	***1 255 107***	***1 331 514***	***1 121 760***	***1 122 214***	***1 115 577***	***1 010 508***	***1 130 792***	***CEE***
France	440 241	437 054	443 160	451 338	492 731	462 681	454 571	451 185	412 757	* 448 692	France
Germany, Fed. Rep.	290 774	276 252	267 306	281 967	317 071	273 899	266 089	268 600	236 876	262 199	Allemagne, Rép. féd.
Italy	107 975	129 993	134 726	140 129	151 790	164 294	145 698	166 543	150 550	171 245	Italie
Netherlands	7 428	7 220	6 856	8 922	9 690	7 696	6 926	6 269	7 360	7 554	Pays-Bas
United Kingdom[5 6]	329 448	358 670	349 624	372 751	360 232	213 190	248 930	222 980	202 965	241 102	Royaume-Uni[5 6]
EFTA	***48 193***	***48 263***	***42 892***	***50 583***	***53 918***	***46 138***	***48 685***	***47 380***	***59 782***	***60 867***	***AELE***
Austria	2 992	2 262	2 042	1 132	1 421	988	1 829	1 722	776	487	Autriche
Finland[1]	23	25	17	17	45	80	56	58	20	...	Finlande[1]
Sweden	45 178	45 976	40 833	49 434	52 452	45 070	* 46 800	* 45 600	* 58 986	* 60 324	Suède
East Europe	***173 367***	***173 693***	***174 225***	***173 182***	***169 078***	***148 580***	***158 904***	***145 008***	***156 624***	***166 015***	***Europe de l'est***
Bulgaria[1]	5 142	4 957	4 907	4 965	4 994	5 329	5 660	5 706	...	...	Bulgarie[1]
Czechoslovakia	33 546	35 539	36 382	39 396	41 480	41 846	42 577	38 454	42 739	44 680	Tchécoslovaquie
German Dem. Rep.	35 919	37 236	36 735	36 719	36 954	39 396	38 763	39 557	43 105	45 305	Rép. dém. allemande
Hungary	1 161	1 518	1 063	1 098	265	120	928	358	201	736	Hongrie
Poland[6]	63 724	59 727	61 261	57 124	53 674	42 689	38 176	42 933	46 903	49 114	Pologne[6]
Romania	33 875	34 716	33 877	33 880	31 711	19 200	32 800	18 000	18 000	20 400	Roumanie
Other Europe	***108 383***	***133 442***	***146 666***	***149 452***	***145 341***	***128 749***	***132 584***	***133 610***	***135 679***	***168 572***	***Autre Europe***
Spain	90 912	117 500	* 131 500	* 131 250	126 902	111 299	116 607	117 172	* 119 901	152 800	Espagne
Yugoslavia	17 471	15 942	15 166	18 202	18 439	17 450	15 977	16 438	15 778	15 772	Yougoslavie
USSR	**715 671**	**733 723**	**762 006**	**779 706**	**[7] 874 169**	**[7] 876 545**	**[7] 866 000**	**[7] 860 400**	**[7] 849 600**	**[7] 900 000**	**URSS**
Ukrainian SSR	*27 085*	*27 727*	*29 301*	*30 160*	*30 206*	*30 317*	...	...	...	...	*RSS d'Ukraine*
Oceania	**86 076**	**86 231**	**72 981**	**86 136**	**55 816**	**46 555**	**40 044**	**20 496**	**10 747**	**16 325**	**Océanie**
Australia[8 9]	86 076	86 231	72 981	86 136	55 816	46 555	40 044	20 496	10 747	16 325	Australie[8 9]
Total	**8 527 469**	**9 925 592**	**10589548**	**10274554**	**9 532 391**	**9 335 605**	**8 959 779**	**9 562 709**	**11027845**	**11965434**	**Total**

General note.
Road motor vehicles designed for the conveyance of goods, including vehicles specially equipped for the transport of certain goods, which are manufactured wholly or mainly from domestically-produced parts. Articulated vehicles (that is, units made up of a road motor vehicle and a semi-trailer) are included. Ambulances, prison vans, and special purpose lorries and vans, such as fire-engines, are excluded. (SITC 73230-2).

Remarque générale.
Véhicules automobiles routiers conçus pour le transport des marchandises, y compris les véhicules spécialement équipés pour le transport de certaines marchandises, et qui sont construits entièrement ou principalement avec des pièces fabriquées dans le pays. Les véhicules articulés (c'est-à-dire les ensembles composés d'un véhicule automobile routier et d'une semi-remorque) sont compris dans cette rubrique. Cette rubrique ne comprend pas les ambulances, les voitures cellulaires et les camions à usages spéciaux, tels que les voitures-pompes à incendie. (CTCI 73230-2).

[1] Including assembly.
[2] Factory sales.
[3] Excluding platform and some other trucks.
[4] Excluding production for armed forces.
[5] Including electrically-powered vehicles.
[6] Including special-purpose vehicles.
[7] Including motor coaches and buses.
[8] Finished and partly finished.
[9] Twelve months ending 30 June of year stated.

[1] Y compris le montage.
[2] Ventes des fabriques.
[3] Non compris les camions plate-forme et certains autres camions.
[4] Non compris la production destinée aux forces armées.
[5] Y compris les véhicules à propulsion électrique.
[6] Y compris véhicules à usages spéciaux.
[7] Y compris les autocars et autobus.
[8] Finis et semi-finis.
[9] Période de douze mois finissant le 30 juin de l'année indiquée.

Road tractors for tractor–trailer combinations, produced – Tracteurs routiers pour les ensembles tracteur–remorque, fabriqués

Unit : Number units

Unité : Nombre

Country or area	1976	1977	1978	1979	1980	1981	1982	1983	1984	1985	Pays ou zone
America, North	**373 349**	**158 753**	**179 790**	**197 356**	**128 629**	**122 513**	**80 101**	**86 186**	**161 729**	**128 603**	**Amérique du Nord**
Mexico[1]	2 011	1 045	2 203	4 467	6 803	7 938	2 915	533	1 798	4 047	Mexique[1]
United States[2 3]	371 338	157 708	177 587	192 889	121 826	114 575	77 186	85 653	159 931	124 556	Etats-Unis[2 3]
Asia	**5 350**	**7 117**	**6 893**	**10 226**	**10 442**	**8 115**	**12 456**	**6 457**	**11 281**	**8 891**	**Asie**
Japan	5 350	7 117	6 893	10 226	10 442	8 115	12 456	6 457	11 281	8 891	Japon
Europe	**93 740**	**102 524**	**102 644**	**104 014**	**109 641**	**112 824**	**112 313**	**105 113**	**104 467**	**102 077**	**Europe**
EEC	***47 715***	***57 269***	***48 134***	***49 494***	***54 370***	***53 411***	***55 081***	***44 114***	***40 232***	***41 498***	***CEE***
France	10 473	9 759	8 510	7 655	9 269	8 712	9 657	7 331	8 422	7 884	France
Germany, Fed. Rep.	17 931	20 544	15 975	20 562	25 216	29 608	30 134	20 866	18 660	18 154	Allemagne, Rép. féd.
Italy	6 323	8 577	7 532	5 373	6 331	7 480	3 301	5 639	2 524	6 083	Italie
Netherlands	3 555	6 424	4 265	6 126	6 188	3 690	5 228	4 360	5 265	5 544	Pays-Bas
United Kingdom	9 433	11 965	11 852	9 778	7 366	3 921	6 761	5 918	5 361	...	Royaume-Uni
EFTA	***19***	***28***	***31***	***55***	***33***	***33***	***33***	***33***	***33***	***33***	***AELE***
Portugal	19	28	31	55	...	...	...	...	...	...	Portugal
East Europe	***3 760***	***3 406***	***4 403***	***4 602***	***4 752***	***4 694***	***5 103***	***5 324***	***4 681***	***4 152***	***Europe de l'est***
Czechoslovakia	3 190	3 059	3 747	3 851	4 208	4 062	4 693	4 740	4 133	3 276	Tchécoslovaquie
Hungary	570	347	656	751	544	632	410	584	548	876	Hongrie
Other Europe	***42 246***	***41 821***	***50 076***	***49 863***	***50 486***	***54 686***	***52 096***	***55 642***	***59 521***	***56 394***	***Autre Europe***
Yugoslavia	42 246	41 821	50 076	49 863	50 486	54 686	52 096	55 642	59 521	56 394	Yougoslavie
Total	**472 439**	**268 394**	**289 327**	**311 596**	**248 712**	**243 452**	**204 870**	**197 756**	**277 477**	**239 571**	**Total**

General note.
Road motor vehicles designed, exclusively or primarily, to haul other road vehicles. (SITC 73250-0).

[1] Including assembly.
[2] Factory sales.
[3] Including platform and some other trucks (40000 in 1973).

Remarque générale.
Véhicules automobiles routiers conçus exclusivement ou principalement pour le remorquage d'autres véhicules routiers. (CTCI 73250-0).

[1] Y compris le montage.
[2] Ventes des fabriques.
[3] Y compris les camions plate-forme et certains autres camions (40000 en 1973).

Trailers and semi–trailers – Remorques et semi–remorques

Unit : Number units

Unité : Nombre

Country or area	1976	1977	1978	1979	1980	1981	1982	1983	1984	1985	Pays ou zone
Africa	**9 842**	**8 645**	**16 303**	**17 765**	**25 026**	**49 043**	**53 271**	**44 554**	**28 438**	**34 283**	**Afrique**
Algeria	1 149	876	1 344	1 481	2 214	2 570	2 982	...	...	...	Algérie
Egypt	2 503	1 951	1 795	2 896	2 272	2 185	3 157	3 696	...	...	Egypte
Mozambique	...	...	...	326	194	121	15	200	106	...	Mozambique
Nigeria	955	810	1 129	1 584	1 488	19 614	25 154	22 717	6 531	13 868	Nigéria
South Africa	4 375	4 329	11 128	10 762	18 153	23 561	20 961	13 643	13 699	11 647	Afrique du Sud
Tunisia	514	367	628	716	705	992	...	...	...	...	Tunisie
America, North	**110 218**	**166 121**	**200 474**	**215 057**	**142 097**	**128 107**	**109 194**	**121 832**	**218 771**	**180 554**	**Amérique du Nord**
Cuba	...	...	...	...	...	5 113	4 806	3 969	4 543	4 696	Cuba
Mexico	687	221	330	476	444	539	524	121	317	706	Mexique
United States[1]	104 146	160 623	194 976	209 522	136 702	122 455	103 864	117 742	213 911	175 152	Etats–Unis[1]
America, South	**26 126**	**23 155**	**25 189**	**23 779**	**28 798**	**25 772**	**24 969**	**24 072**	**25 744**	**25 859**	**Amérique du Sud**
Brazil	23 757	20 282	21 598	[2] 20 834	24 196	...	...	...	...	...	Brésil
Colombia	774	1 278	1 996	1 350	1 736	1 313	1 034	846	...	...	Colombie
Ecuador	...	...	...	...	2 866	1 899	1 233	382	...	...	Equateur
Asia	**10 298**	**12 219**	**13 443**	**21 202**	**15 762**	**15 066**	**18 214**	**19 854**	**19 193**	**22 289**	**Asie**
India	1 836	2 229	2 353	2 469	...	...	...	...	...	...	Inde
Indonesia	17	18	9	18	9	...	...	...	...	...	Indonésie
Iran(Islamic Rep.of)[3]	...	...	...	3 113	1 389	1 536	5 128	6 658	...	...	Iran(Rép.islamique)[3]
Japan	3 309	3 598	5 050	8 777	7 121	3 726	4 031	3 788	5 561	7 996	Japon
Sri Lanka	581	...	794	342	863	3 415	...	...	...	...	Sri Lanka
Turkey	3 161	3 771	3 224	6 483	...	...	...	...	...	...	Turquie
Europe	**417 015**	**463 135**	**424 719**	**437 332**	**416 957**	**396 324**	**329 129**	**344 270**	**309 000**	**289 781**	**Europe**
EEC	***271 694***	***298 531***	***268 107***	***281 940***	***255 049***	***208 532***	***172 663***	***171 567***	***158 758***	***151 374***	***CEE***
Belgium[2]	8 496	13 018	13 266	[1] 14 093	[1] 11 116	[1] 9 099	[1] 9 684	[1] 11 643	...	...	Belgique[2]
Denmark[4]	...	1 010	1 432	1 246	878	...	...	...	...	...	Danemark[4]
Germany, Fed. Rep.	140 873	151 366	153 587	158 490	161 757	137 617	115 872	112 947	108 937	112 412	Allemagne, Rép. féd.
Greece	2 790	2 167	1 997	1 993	3 967	844	1 055	235	75	...	Grèce
Italy	10 691	13 741	12 283	12 912	16 589	16 151	9 381	7 670	10 148	9 183	Italie
Netherlands[5]	4 720	5 830	3 811	3 834	4 037	3 536	4 144	* 4 300	* 5 000	5 100	Pays–Bas[5]
United Kingdom[6]	102 983	111 399	...	89 372	56 705	40 144	31 386	33 631	...	...	Royaume–Uni[6]
EFTA	***8 154***	***14 233***	***11 478***	***15 698***	***24 735***	***29 800***	***30 255***	***25 799***	***20 461***	***23 639***	***AELE***
Austria	3 574	4 486	4 098	4 826	4 763	5 672	6 039	6 080	5 630	9 330	Autriche
Finland	617	874	226	987	1 243	1 540	1 615	1 671	1 177	...	Finlande
Portugal	* 3 963	8 873	7 154	9 885	18 729	22 588	22 601	18 048	13 654	12 541	Portugal
East Europe	***86 213***	***99 078***	***95 753***	***86 507***	***81 892***	***84 316***	***71 948***	***75 831***	***66 334***	***69 132***	***Europe de l'est***
Bulgaria	7 438	8 407	8 326	7 028	7 517	9 622	10 738	11 593	7 979	9 224	Bulgarie
Czechoslovakia	359	644	918	1 047	3 826	3 648	3 810	3 982	4 355	3 741	Tchécoslovaquie
Hungary	14 755	17 494	14 549	16 257	16 084	22 940	12 788	9 357	7 044	7 599	Hongrie
Poland	63 661	72 533	71 960	62 175	54 465	48 106	44 612	50 899	46 956	48 568	Pologne
Other Europe	***50 954***	***51 293***	***49 381***	***53 187***	***55 281***	***73 676***	***54 263***	***71 073***	***63 447***	***45 636***	***Autre Europe***
Spain	...	...	...	19 665	21 310	36 747	12 757	15 987	...	...	Espagne
Yugoslavia	21 768	23 685	23 352	33 522	33 971	36 929	41 506	55 086	46 891	30 659	Yougoslavie
USSR	**158 379**	**163 930**	**166 817**	**171 448**	**177 958**	**176 744**	...	...	...	...	**URSS**
Ukrainian SSR	*20 326*	*22 358*	*22 601*	*22 892*	*23 822*	*24 272*	...	...	...	...	*RSS d'Ukraine*
Oceania	**43 762**	**46 977**	**39 372**	**40 490**	**41 072**	**44 222**	**38 531**	**26 759**	**28 722**	**32 246**	**Océanie**
Australia[7]	43 762	46 977	39 372	40 490	41 072	44 222	38 531	26 759	28 722	32 246	Australie[7]
Total	**775 640**	**884 182**	**886 317**	**927 073**	**847 670**	**835 278**	**756 367**	**768 356**	**820 840**	**779 940**	**Total**

General note.
Road vehicles for the conveyance of goods which are designed to be drawn by a road motor vehicle. Semi–trailers are trailers without a front axle, which are coupled to the hauling vehicle in such a manner that part of the trailer rests on the tractor. Articulated vehicles are included in "lorries". (SITC 73330–1).

Remarque générale.
Véhicules routiers pour le transport des marchandises, conçus pour être remorqués par un véhicule automobile routier. Les semi–remorques sont des remorques sans essieu avant accouplées aux véhicules qui les entraînent de telle manière qu'une partie desdites remorques repose sur le véhicule tracteur. Les véhicules articulés sont classés sous la rubrique "camions". (CTCI 73330–1).

For footnotes, see end of table.

Voir la fin du tableau pour les notes.

[1] Shipments.
[2] Production by establishments employing 5 or more persons.
[3] Production by establishments employing 10 or more persons.
[4] Trailers and semi–trailers over 6 tons (gross weight).
[5] Industrial sales.
[6] Deliveries.
[7] Twelve months ending 30 June of year stated.

[1] Expéditions.
[2] Production des établissements occupant 5 personnes ou plus.
[3] Production des établissements occupant 10 personnes ou plus.
[4] Remorques et semi–remorques de plus de 6 tonnes (poids brut).
[5] Ventes industrielles.
[6] Livraisons.
[7] Période de douze mois finissant le 30 juin de l'année indiquée.

Unit : Thousand units — Unité : En milliers

Country or area	1976	1977	1978	1979	1980	1981	1982	1983	1984	1985	Pays ou zone
Africa	**474**	**450**	**417**	**381**	**381**	**424**	**357**	**222**	**151**	**153**	**Afrique**
Algeria	[1] 20	# 19	27	28	30	37	42	...	...	...	Algérie
Burkina Faso	12	15	15	15	15	9	5	7	6	12	Burkina Faso
Cameroon	7	* 8	9	11	12	...	...	9	8	8	Cameroun
Central African Rep.	5	6	6	5	7	6	7	6	4	5	Rép. centrafricaine
Côte d'Ivoire	0	0	0	0	36	25	21	11	21	...	Côte d'Ivoire
Egypt	19	21	18	20	17	21	23	21	...	...	Egypte
Mali	9	14	11	11	11	6	2	2	...	...	Mali
Nigeria	...	...	...	...	...	306	243	117	37	22	Nigéria
Togo	2	5	...	...	...	...	...	...	...	...	Togo
Zaire	2	2	4	...	1	1	1	1	...	...	Zaïre
America, North	**334**	**345**	**342**	**347**	**357**	**352**	**327**	**327**	**382**	**354**	**Amérique du Nord**
Mexico	222	231	...	...	...	...	...	...	...	...	Mexique
United States	...	...	...	120	130	125	* 100	* 100	155	...	Etats–Unis
America, South	**88**	**116**	**87**	**133**	**201**	**188**	**191**	**231**	**261**	**294**	**Amérique du Sud**
Argentina[2]	9	11	9	15	22	15	9	22	33	47	Argentine[2]
Brazil	51	83	46	[3] 79	128	140	...	...	...	...	Brésil
Colombia	...	14	27	32	39	30	29	39	...	...	Colombie
Ecuador	...	...	5	...	12	3	4	3	...	...	Equateur
Asia	**5 272**	**6 657**	**7 290**	**5 763**	**7 977**	**9 187**	**9 019**	**6 889**	**6 235**	**7 213**	**Asie**
China	...	...	...	...	45	133	194	255	466	917	Chine
India	263	266	298	306	310	312	380	429	477	670	Inde
Indonesia	268	272	331	222	410	492	573	379	303	* 227	Indonésie
Iran(Islamic Rep.of)[4]	114	90	102	107	75	95	96	171	...	...	Iran(Rép.islamique)[4]
Japan	4 235	5 577	6 000	4 476	6 435	7 413	7 063	4 807	4 026	4 536	Japon
Korea, Republic of	17	35	77	101	112	128	124	167	168	172	Corée, République de
Malaysia	...	122	127	117	175	179	208	243	178	182	Malaisie
Pakistan	...	...	37	52	66	53	25	34	54	...	Pakistan
Philippines	27	21	55	46	46	44	* 44	45	...	...	Philippines
Sri Lanka	0	...	...	1	...	...	...	...	...	...	Sri Lanka
Thailand	103	149	191	244	284	305	293	313	321	230	Thaïlande
Turkey	36	30	26	20	18	32	18	45	63	51	Turquie
Europe	**3 490**	**3 718**	**3 582**	**3 254**	**3 559**	**3 056**	**2 741**	**2 494**	**2 352**	**2 347**	**Europe**
EEC	***2 216***	***2 371***	***2 215***	***2 068***	***2 292***	***1 952***	***1 715***	***1 448***	***1 309***	***1 346***	***CEE***
Denmark	1	1	0	0	0	0	0	0	0	0	Danemark
France	898	829	728	657	616	488	504	409	450	440	France
Germany, Fed. Rep.[5]	327	420	333	294	303	219	135	...	119	...	Allemagne, Rép. féd.[5]
Greece	8	7	8	13	7	13	32	17	13	...	Grèce
Italy	921	1 046	1 113	1 081	1 350	1 225	1 039	864	719	800	Italie
Netherlands	61	68	33	23	16	7	5	8	* 8	...	Pays–Bas
EFTA	***304***	***371***	***398***	***293***	***342***	***241***	***204***	***197***	***189***	***201***	***AELE***
Austria	200	266	307	198	247	169	132	133	145	160	Autriche
Finland	14	15	12	15	14	17	11	12	8	...	Finlande
Portugal	* 66	68	64	65	66	39	47	42	27	22	Portugal
Sweden	24	22	15	15	15	16	14	10	9	9	Suède
East Europe	***670***	***641***	***641***	***608***	***621***	***596***	***578***	***595***	***595***	***570***	***Europe de l'est***
Czechoslovakia	128	109	114	131	141	145	148	153	151	163	Tchécoslovaquie
German Dem. Rep.	256	237	250	258	260	267	280	280	289	264	Rép. dém. allemande
Poland	286	295	277	219	220	184	150	162	155	143	Pologne
Other Europe	***300***	***335***	***328***	***285***	***304***	***267***	***244***	***254***	***259***	***230***	***Autre Europe***
Spain	242	268	259	220	233	192	172	180	173	...	Espagne
Yugoslavia	58	67	69	65	71	75	72	74	86	76	Yougoslavie
USSR	**1 060**	**1 090**	**1 099**	**1 078**	**1 090**	**1 095**	**1 110**	**1 127**	**1 151**	**1 148**	**URSS**
Byelorussian SSR	*192*	*195*	*196*	*201*	*217*	*224*	*224*	*230*	*230*	*230*	*RSS de Biélorussie*
Ukrainian SSR	*74*	*78*	*84*	*84*	*85*	*90*	*94*	*96*	*90*	*100*	*RSS d'Ukraine*
Total	**10 718**	**12 376**	**12 816**	**10 955**	**13 564**	**14 301**	**13 744**	**11 288**	**10 532**	**11 509**	**Total**

For general note and footnotes, see end of table.

Voir la fin du tableau pour la remarque générale et les notes.

General note.
Two–wheeled road motor vehicles with or without a side–car, and cycles with auxiliary engines exceeding 50 cc. Motorized delivery tricycles are included, provided their unladen weight does not exceed 400 kilogrammes. (SITC 73291–1).

[1] Including bicycles.
[2] Excluding motor bicycles.
[3] Production by establishments employing 5 or more persons.
[4] Production by establishments employing 10 or more persons.
[5] 1983, data are confidential.

Remarque générale.
Véhicules automobiles routiers à deux roues, avec ou sans side–car, et cycles à moteur auxiliaire d'une cylindrée supérieure à 50 cm^3. Cette rubrique comprend les triporteurs automobiles dont le poids à vide n'excède pas 400 kg. (CTCI 73291–1).

[1] Y compris les bicyclettes.
[2] Non compris les vélomoteurs.
[3] Production des établissements occupant 5 personnes ou plus.
[4] Production des établissements occupant 10 personnes ou plus.
[5] 1983, les données sont confidentielles.

Unit : Thousand units | Unité : En milliers

Country or area	1976	1977	1978	1979	1980	1981	1982	1983	1984	1985	Pays ou zone
Africa	**189**	**226**	**266**	**237**	**215**	**220**	**230**	**240**	**227**	**238**	**Afrique**
Algeria	...	10	15	17	20	21	26	...	...	...	Algérie
Burkina Faso	38	44	49	45	47	44	24	16	17	20	Burkina Faso
Cameroon	14	16	14	17	17	...	...	17	17	16	Cameroun
Central African Rep.	4	5	8	4	4	4	3	3	3	3	Rép. centrafricaine
Côte d'Ivoire	0	0	41	0	15	14	12	8	9	...	Côte d'Ivoire
Egypt	72	91	85	92	80	82	110	128	...	...	Egypte
Mali	10	15	11	12	12	* 13	* 8	8	...	...	Mali
Mozambique	...	...	...	33	5	11	15	13	7	...	Mozambique
Togo	4	6	...	...	...	...	...	...	...	...	Togo
Zaire	9	12	14	...	10	10	10	14	...	...	Zaïre
America, North	**6 989**	**8 089**	**7 966**	**9 544**	**7 756**	**7 389**	**5 759**	**6 859**	**6 489**	**6 381**	**Amérique du Nord**
Canada[1]	...	...	466	544	756	...	...	...	...	...	Canada[1]
United States[1]	6 400	7 500	7 500	9 000	7 000	6 800	5 170	6 270	5 900	...	Etats–Unis[1]
America, South	**2 042**	**2 224**	**2 119**	**2 342**	**3 170**	**2 796**	**3 075**	**3 245**	**3 445**	**3 634**	**Amérique du Sud**
Brazil	1 269	1 452	1 358	[2] 1 533	2 362	2 018	...	...	...	...	Brésil
Chile	43	43	50	98	37	58	* 42	26	27	30	Chili
Colombia	101	118	116	107	151	119	100	112	...	...	Colombie
Ecuador	...	8	14	...	12	12	11	0	...	...	Equateur
Peru	59	47	25	37	52	33	36	...	...	...	Pérou
Venezuela	...	...	...	...	...	...	...	...	556	...	Venezuela
Asia	**16 721**	**18 032**	**19 376**	**15 581**	**25 195**	**30 364**	**36 988**	**41 505**	**42 799**	**46 188**	**Asie**
Bangladesh[3]	29	40	41	43	46	28	30	13	21	15	Bangladesh[3]
Burma[4]	11	12	14	9	10	20	10	13	9	12	Birmanie[4]
China	6 681	7 427	8 540	10 095	13 024	17 543	24 200	27 582	28 614	32 277	Chine
India	2 643	3 058	3 480	3 994	3 893	4 995	4 895	5 465	5 899	5 646	Inde
Indonesia	15	20	23	28	28	26	31	25	22	...	Indonésie
Iran(Islamic Rep.of)[5]	...	...	...	2	...	4	...	...	...	...	Iran(Rép.islamique)[5]
Japan	6 310	6 334	5 869	104	7 083	6 601	6 532	7 039	6 810	6 785	Japon
Korea, Republic of	562	672	980	869	754	748	724	731	779	722	Corée, République de
Pakistan[3]	218	211	245	280	279	327	399	449	448	...	Pakistan[3]
Philippines	27	19	...	...	...	...	...	...	...	...	Philippines
Sri Lanka	138	167	...	...	11	11	...	...	...	...	Sri Lanka
Turkey	84	69	76	52	41	38	59	80	89	111	Turquie
Europe	**15 102**	**16 344**	**16 530**	**16 923**	**19 065**	**17 768**	**16 547**	**16 250**	**16 191**	**15 458**	**Europe**
EEC	***10 302***	***10 983***	***10 986***	***11 044***	***12 751***	***11 625***	***10 535***	***10 302***	***10 002***	***9 017***	***CEE***
Belgium[1,2,6]	368	343	279	288	327	285	271	249	231	201	Belgique[1,2,6]
Denmark	255	289	295	301	308	307	241	244	278	303	Danemark
France	1 915	2 066	2 183	2 277	2 704	2 140	1 989	1 892	1 719	1 435	France
Germany, Fed. Rep.	2 845	3 028	2 923	3 099	3 643	3 441	3 089	3 334	3 024	2 891	Allemagne, Rép. féd.
Greece	80	79	90	31	13	4	0	0	...	...	Grèce
Italy	2 013	2 395	2 123	2 172	2 701	2 397	2 291	1 978	2 188	1 633	Italie
Netherlands	976	1 051	1 019	1 113	1 359	1 311	941	920	* 900	* 920	Pays–Bas
United Kingdom[7,8]	1 850	1 732	2 074	1 763	1 696	...	...	...	...	...	Royaume–Uni[7,8]
EFTA	***803***	***954***	***959***	***1 028***	***1 285***	***1 349***	***1 373***	***1 271***	***1 290***	***1 316***	***AELE***
Austria	214	264	258	303	415	394	377	399	375	354	Autriche
Finland[9]	190	230	216	254	292	332	315	259	220	...	Finlande[9]
Norway	185	196	203	182	238	264	...	...	...	...	Norvège
Portugal	111	64	66	70	96	81	99	74	74	78	Portugal
Sweden	103	200	216	219	244	278	321	263	331	283	Suède
East Europe	***3 155***	***3 386***	***3 479***	***3 566***	***3 564***	***3 207***	***3 150***	***3 105***	***3 273***	***3 432***	***Europe de l'est***
Bulgaria	100	120	126	120	120	124	131	104	94	90	Bulgarie
Czechoslovakia	507	552	570	574	607	619	665	670	738	786	Tchécoslovaquie
German Dem. Rep.	560	576	605	614	614	627	631	651	664	672	Rép. dém. allemande
Hungary[10]	279	322	339	362	372	286	270	260	246	249	Hongrie[10]
Poland	1 469	1 573	1 625	1 691	1 637	1 323	1 192	1 172	1 314	1 402	Pologne
Romania	240	243	214	205	214	228	261	248	217	...	Roumanie
Other Europe	***842***	***1 021***	***1 106***	***1 285***	***1 465***	***1 587***	***1 489***	***1 572***	***1 626***	***1 693***	***Autre Europe***

For general note and footnotes, see end of table.

Voir la fin du tableau pour la remarque générale et les notes.

Unit : Thousand units — Unité : En milliers

Country or area	1976	1977	1978	1979	1980	1981	1982	1983	1984	1985	Pays ou zone
Spain	546	573	583	713	841	884	796	947	1 017	...	Espagne
Yugoslavia	296	448	523	572	624	703	693	625	609	626	Yougoslavie
USSR	**4 354**	**4 518**	**4 686**	**4 649**	**4 736**	**4 837**	**4 978**	**5 060**	**5 281**	**5 362**	**URSS**
Byelorussian SSR	*615*	*637*	*655*	*657*	*695*	*714*	*727*	*729*	*762*	*773*	*RSS de Biélorussie*
Ukrainian SSR	*803*	*830*	*826*	*745*	*739*	*763*	*770*	*778*	*833*	*880*	*RSS d'Ukraine*
Oceania	**188**	**274**	**190**	**203**	**283**	**211**	**145**	**117**	**96**	**108**	**Océanie**
Australia[3]	188	274	190	203	283	211	145	117	96	108	Australie[3]
Total	**45 584**	**49 707**	**51 133**	**49 478**	**60 420**	**63 585**	**67 721**	**73 276**	**74 527**	**77 369**	**Total**

General note.
Two-wheeled road vehicles, fitted with pedals and using human energy as the sole means of propulsion. (SITC 73311-1).

[1] Shipments.
[2] Production by establishments employing 5 or more persons.
[3] Twelve months ending 30 June of year stated.
[4] Government production only.
[5] Production by establishments employing 10 or more persons.
[6] Including motorcycles with engines below 50 cc.
[7] Deliveries.
[8] Including tricycles.
[9] Including delivery tricycles.
[10] Including bath chairs and delivery tricycles.

Remarque générale.
Véhicules routiers à deux roues, munis de pédales et dont le seul moyen de propulsion est l'énergie humaine. (CTCI 73311-1).

[1] Expéditions.
[2] Production des établissements occupant 5 personnes ou plus.
[3] Période de douze mois finissant le 30 juin de l'année indiquée.
[4] Production de l'Etat seulement.
[5] Production des établissements occupant 10 personnes ou plus.
[6] Y compris les motocyclettes ayant un moteur de moins de 50 cc de cylindrée.
[7] Livraisons.
[8] Y compris les tricycles.
[9] Y compris les triporteurs.
[10] Y compris les fauteuils roulants et les triporteurs.

Commercial passenger and cargo planes – Avions commerciaux pour le transport de passagers et de marchandises

Unit : Number units

Unité : Nombre

Country or area	1976	1977	1978	1979	1980	1981	1982	1983	1984	1985	Pays ou zone
America, North	**16 641**	**18 159**	**18 882**	**17 924**	**13 130**	**11 067**	**4 667**	**3 217**	**3 028**	**2 842**	**Amérique du Nord**
United States[1]	16 641	18 159	18 882	17 924	13 130	11 067	4 667	3 217	3 028	2 842	Etats–Unis[1]
America, South	**514**	**556**	**222**	**273**	**417**	**265**	**167**	**128**	**187**	**77**	**Amérique du Sud**
Brazil	514	556	222	273	417	265	167	128	187	...	Brésil
Asia	**33**	**44**	**55**	**44**	**44**	**44**	**44**	**44**	**44**	**44**	**Asie**
Japan	33	44	55	...	...	...	...	...	...	...	Japon
Europe	**1 157**	**1 054**	**881**	**1 091**	**1 223**	**1 147**	**1 278**	**1 046**	**888**	**702**	**Europe**
EEC	***1 082***	***1 054***	***881***	***1 091***	***1 220***	***1 126***	***1 257***	***1 035***	***877***	***700***	***CEE***
France	740	793	621	804	933	839	970	748	590	413	France
United Kingdom[2 3]	342	261	260	...	...	...	...	...	...	...	Royaume–Uni[2 3]
EFTA	***75***	***0***	***0***	***0***	***3***	***21***	***21***	***11***	***11***	***2***	***AELE***
Finland[4]	75	0	0	0	3	21	21	11	11	...	Finlande[4]
Total	**18 345**	**19 813**	**20 040**	**19 332**	**14 814**	**12 523**	**6 156**	**4 435**	**4 147**	**3 665**	**Total**

General note.
Commercial heavier–than–air aircraft which are designed for the transport of passengers or goods for civilian purposes. Helicopters are included. (SITC 73410–1).

[1] Shipments.
[2] Deliveries.
[3] Including military aircraft for the services.
[4] Commercial cargo planes only.

Remarque générale.
Aéronefs commerciaux plus lourds que l'air conçus pour le transport de voyageurs et de marchandises à des fins civiles. Cette rubrique comprend les hélicoptères. (CTCI 73410–1).

[1] Expéditions.
[2] Livraisons.
[3] Y compris les aéronefs militaires opérant pour les forces armées.
[4] Avions commerciaux pour le transport de marchandises seulement.

Perambulators and push-chairs for babies – Landaux et poussettes pour bébés

Unit : Thousand units — Unité : En milliers

Country or area	1976	1977	1978	1979	1980	1981	1982	1983	1984	1985	Pays ou zone
America, South	**176**	**537**	**560**	**683**	**1 600**	**1 257**	**1 441**	**1 626**	**1 811**	**1 996**	**Amérique du Sud**
Brazil	140	487	518	[1] 636	1 555	...	...	...	...	...	Brésil
Colombia	36	50	42	47	45	50	...	...	...	...	Colombie
Asia	**1**	**1**	**1**	**1**	**1**	**1**	**1**	**1**	**1**	**1**	**Asie**
Sri Lanka	...	...	...	...	1	1	...	...	...	...	Sri Lanka
Europe	**2 962**	**2 804**	**2 748**	**2 675**	**2 733**	**2 867**	**2 651**	**2 574**	**3 049**	**2 870**	**Europe**
EEC	***1 010***	***926***	***955***	***1 011***	***925***	***1 461***	***1 316***	***1 139***	***1 788***	***1 797***	***CEE***
Denmark	21	17	18	16	13	...	...	...	...	...	Danemark
France	373	308	321	391	343	# 887	776	620	1 224	1 134	France
Germany, Fed. Rep.	569	538	549	559	526	525	499	484	526	636	Allemagne, Rép. féd.
Greece	47	63	67	45	43	37	31	26	31	...	Grèce
EFTA	***210***	***202***	***184***	***202***	***210***	***226***	***203***	***206***	***241***	***233***	***AELE***
Austria	41	43	35	32	33	38	19	18	34	18	Autriche
Finland	20	23	23	22	21	26	23	8	6	...	Finlande
Norway	30	29	23	28	30	...	...	...	...	...	Norvège
Sweden	119	107	103	120	126	134	133	152	174	177	Suède
East Europe	***621***	***632***	***651***	***634***	***656***	***533***	***532***	***636***	***549***	***496***	***Europe de l'est***
Czechoslovakia	285	258	233	229	232	171	162	122	106	110	Tchécoslovaquie
Hungary	47	50	56	41	64	66	67	81	105	97	Hongrie
Poland	289	324	362	364	360	296	303	433	338	289	Pologne
Other Europe	***1 121***	***1 044***	***958***	***828***	***942***	***647***	***600***	***594***	***471***	***343***	***Autre Europe***
Spain	...	...	...	718	798	489	415	408	...	...	Espagne
Yugoslavia	58	80	94	110	144	158	185	186	204	176	Yougoslavie
USSR	**2 676**	**2 832**	**2 923**	**3 167**	**3 590**	**3 941**	**4 253**	**4 636**	**5 013**	**5 180**	**URSS**
Byelorussian SSR	*53*	*55*	*55*	*62*	*68*	*70*	*81*	*100*	*118*	*123*	*RSS de Biélorussie*
Ukrainian SSR	*675*	*696*	*692*	*645*	*714*	*804*	*855*	*943*	*1 010*	*1 025*	*RSS d'Ukraine*
Oceania	**123**	**123**	**123**	**123**	**123**	**123**	**123**	**123**	**123**	**123**	**Océanie**
Australia[2]	123	...	...	...	...	...	...	...	...	...	Australie[2]
Total	**5 938**	**6 297**	**6 355**	**6 649**	**8 047**	**8 189**	**8 469**	**8 960**	**9 997**	**10 170**	**Total**

General note.
Vehicles used for transporting babies, which have two or more wheels and are designed to be pushed by hand. Perambulators cover those in which the baby can lie down, and push-chairs refer to those in which the baby sits up or reclines at an angle. Either type may be designed so that it can be folded when not in use. Toy perambulators are excluded. (SITC 89410-0).

[1] Production by establishments employing 5 or more persons.
[2] Twelve months ending 30 June of year stated.

Remarque générale.
Véhicules à deux ou plusieurs roues, servant au transport des bébés et conçus pour être poursés à la main. Dans les landaux, le bébé peut être couché alors que dans les poussettes il est assis en position droite ou inclinée. Les deux types peuvent être conçus pous être pliés lorsqu'ils ne sont pas en service. Les jouets en forme de landaux ne sont pas compris dans cette rubrique. (CTCI 89410-0).

[1] Production des établissements occupant 5 personnes ou plus.
[2] Période de douze mois finissant le 30 juin de l'année indiquée.

Binoculars and refracting telescopes – Jumelles et longues-vues

Unit : Thousand units

Unité : En milliers

Country or area	1976	1977	1978	1979	1980	1981	1982	1983	1984	1985	Pays ou zone
America, South	**89**	**89**	**23**	**155**	**89**	**89**	**89**	**89**	**89**	**89**	**Amérique du Sud**
Brazil[1]	...	...	23	155	...	...	...	...	...	...	Brésil[1]
Asia	**1 708**	**2 106**	**1 701**	**1 411**	**1 323**	**1 560**	**1 706**	**1 642**	**1 971**	**1 943**	**Asie**
Japan	866	1 131	836	907	983	1 167	1 233	1 229	1 544	1 576	Japon
Korea, Republic of	842	975	865	504	340	393	473	413	427	367	Corée, République de
Europe	**436**	**431**	**432**	**460**	**447**	**432**	**446**	**414**	**482**	**487**	**Europe**
EEC	***231***	***221***	***210***	***207***	***199***	***184***	***198***	***175***	***179***	***226***	***CEE***
Germany, Fed. Rep.	231	221	210	207	199	184	198	175	179	226	Allemagne, Rép. féd.
East Europe	***205***	***210***	***222***	***253***	***248***	***248***	***248***	***239***	***303***	***261***	***Europe de l'est***
German Dem. Rep.[2]	193	208	222	253	248	248	248	239	241	229	Rép. dém. allemande[2]
Hungary	12	2	0	0	0	0	0	0	62	32	Hongrie
Total	**2 233**	**2 626**	**2 156**	**2 026**	**1 859**	**2 081**	**2 241**	**2 145**	**2 542**	**2 519**	**Total**

General note.
Monocular or binocular instruments normally used for obversation only, such as opera glasses, binoculars for touring or hunting, telescopes for hunting, touring, for use at sea etc. Astronomical telescopes are excluded. Telescopic sights for firearms, periscopes for submarines and telescopes for fitting to other instruments or apparatus are also excluded. (SITC 86131-0).

Remarque générale.
Instruments monoculaires ou binoculaires ne servant normalement qu'à l'observation visuelle, tels que jumelles de spectacle, jumelles de tourisme ou de chasse, longues-vues de chasse, de tourisme, de marine etc. Cette rubrique ne comprend pas les télescopes astronomiques, les lunettes de visée pour armes à feu, les périscopes pour sous-marins et les viseurs destinés à être montés sur d'autres instruments ou appareils. (CTCI 86131-0).

[1] Production by establishments employing 5 or more persons.
[2] Telescopes only.

[1] Production des établissements occupant 5 personnes ou plus.
[2] Télescopes seulement.

Cameras, photographic – Appareils photographiques

Unit : Thousand units — Unité : En milliers

Country or area	1976	1977	1978	1979	1980	1981	1982	1983	1984	1985	Pays ou zone
America, North	**16 258**	**14 382**	**16 258**	**16 258**	**16 258**	**16 258**	**18 134**	**16 258**	**16 258**	**16 258**	**Amérique du Nord**
United States[1]	...	14 382	...	...	...	...	18 134	...	...	...	Etats–Unis[1]
America, South	**953**	**1 466**	**1 648**	**2 151**	**2 288**	**2 743**	**2 956**	**3 268**	**3 636**	**3 961**	**Amérique du Sud**
Brazil	875	1 393	1 563	[2] 2 090	2 182	...	...	...	...	...	Brésil
Colombia	...	...	85	61	106	134	18	0	...	...	Colombie
Asia	**8 745**	**10 981**	**13 035**	**15 141**	**17 863**	**20 387**	**18 638**	**20 870**	**22 769**	**25 698**	**Asie**
China	...	...	179	238	373	623	742	926	1 262	1 790	Chine
Hong Kong	343	972	...	...	...	4 245	3 792	# 5 140	5 389	...	Hong–kong
Japan	8 130	9 670	10 932	12 266	13 987	15 174	13 850	14 184	15 338	17 040	Japon
Korea, Republic of	...	...	...	...	513	345	254	620	780	646	Corée, République de
Europe	**5 121**	**4 674**	**5 483**	**5 534**	**5 599**	**4 648**	**3 267**	**2 521**	**2 225**	**1 943**	**Europe**
EEC	***3 550***	***3 039***	***3 660***	***3 864***	***4 161***	***3 334***	***2 184***	***1 521***	***1 241***	***941***	***CEE***
Denmark	0	0	0	0	0	0	0	6	6	7	Danemark
Germany, Fed. Rep.	3 550	3 039	3 660	3 864	4 161	3 334	2 184	1 515	1 235	934	Allemagne, Rép. féd.
EFTA	***622***	***644***	***829***	***626***	***358***	***252***	***91***	***80***	***120***	***154***	***AELE***
Austria[3]	622	644	829	626	358	252	91	80	120	154	Autriche[3]
East Europe	***916***	***958***	***961***	***1 011***	***1 047***	***1 029***	***959***	***887***	***831***	***815***	***Europe de l'est***
Czechoslovakia	20	26	30	30	25	30	29	6	7	7	Tchécoslovaquie
German Dem. Rep.	844	876	872	921	979	955	899	869	811	808	Rép. dém. allemande
Poland	52	56	59	60	43	44	31	12	13	0	Pologne
Other Europe	***33***	***33***	***33***	***33***	***33***	***33***	***33***	***33***	***33***	***33***	***Autre Europe***
Spain	33	...	...	...	...	...	...	...	...	...	Espagne
USSR[4]	**3 245**	**3 567**	**3 852**	**4 055**	**4 255**	**4 376**	**4 058**	**2 986**	**2 212**	**2 085**	**URSS[4]**
Byelorussian SSR[4]	*840*	*1 052*	*1 255*	*1 270*	*1 412*	*1 485*	*1 150*	*803*	*602*	*504*	*RSS de Biélorussie[4]*
Ukrainian SSR[4]	*378*	*392*	*417*	*443*	*461*	*470*	*482*	*425*	*336*	*263*	*RSS d'Ukraine[4]*
Total	**34 322**	**35 070**	**40 276**	**43 139**	**46 263**	**48 412**	**47 053**	**45 903**	**47 100**	**49 945**	**Total**

General note.
All kinds of photographic cameras other than cinematographic cameras. (SITC 86140–1).

1 Shipments.
2 Production by establishments employing 5 or more persons.
3 Including cinematographic cameras.
4 Excluding industrial still cameras.

Remarque générale.
Appareils photographiques de tous types, autres que les appareils cinématographiques. (CTCI 86140–1).

1 Expéditions.
2 Production des établissements occupant 5 personnes ou plus.
3 Y compris les appareils cinématographiques.
4 Non compris les appareils photographiques industriels.

Watches – Montres

Unit : Thousand units — Unité : En milliers

Country or area	1976	1977	1978	1979	1980	1981	1982	1983	1984	1985	Pays ou zone
Africa	**119**	**86**	**88**	**93**	**97**	**113**	**100**	**100**	**101**	**101**	**Afrique**
Tunisia	119	86	88	93	97	113	...	...	...	...	Tunisie
America, North	**33 813**	**34 475**	**31 081**	**32 998**	**32 581**	**32 881**	**32 845**	**32 809**	**32 772**	**32 736**	**Amérique du Nord**
Canada[1]	3 100	3 671	3 944	3 447	3 030	...	...	...	...	...	Canada[1]
United States	30 713	30 804	27 137	...	...	...	...	...	...	...	Etats-Unis
America, South	**342**	**711**	**532**	**940**	**2 290**	**1 763**	**2 031**	**2 299**	**2 567**	**2 835**	**Amérique du Sud**
Brazil	284	547	481	[2] 849	2 199	...	...	...	...	...	Brésil
Ecuador	58	164	51	...	...	...	...	...	...	...	Equateur
Asia	**67 188**	**101 050**	**116 601**	**159 031**	**259 335**	**340 399**	**363 695**	**624 032**	**613 075**	**703 070**	**Asie**
China	9 114	11 043	13 511	17 070	22 155	28 724	33 010	34 781	38 071	54 471	Chine
Hong Kong	18 156	37 478	42 071	69 780	138 339	195 339	215 995	457 966	410 271	...	Hong-kong
India	1 259	2 660	4 603	4 655	4 641	4 805	5 438	5 375	5 800	3 909	Inde
Indonesia	...	...	...	...	38	30	45	34	22	...	Indonésie
Japan[3]	34 001	44 737	49 192	59 575	86 233	103 388	101 080	116 939	148 507	182 752	Japon[3]
Korea, Republic of	4 601	5 073	7 172	7 904	7 919	8 109	8 121	8 933	10 399	10 476	Corée, République de
Philippines	5	...	...	...	...	...	...	3	...	...	Philippines
Sri Lanka	2	7	...	1	6	0	...	...	...	...	Sri Lanka
Europe	**61 728**	**64 229**	**60 403**	**47 016**	**42 177**	**40 955**	**31 170**	**27 898**	**22 992**	**18 015**	**Europe**
EEC	***14 235***	***14 115***	***15 087***	***12 457***	***9 182***	***8 324***	***6 096***	***5 310***	***4 384***	***3 527***	***CEE***
Germany, Fed. Rep.	8 411	7 084	7 293	6 592	5 895	4 523	3 642	3 170	2 997	2 892	Allemagne, Rép. féd.
United Kingdom	5 824	7 031	7 794	5 865	3 287	3 801	2 454	...	...	...	Royaume-Uni
EFTA	***43 075***	***45 157***	***40 477***	***30 038***	***28 721***	***27 904***	***20 051***	***18 715***	***14 685***	***10 369***	***AELE***
Austria	2 269	2 360	2 190	1 672	2 111	3 428	2 111	3 428	3 905	3 710	Autriche
Switzerland[4]	40 806	42 797	38 287	28 366	26 610	24 476	17 940	15 287	...	...	Suisse[4]
East Europe	***4 418***	***4 932***	***4 813***	***4 486***	***4 217***	***4 656***	***4 966***	***3 814***	***3 843***	***4 030***	***Europe de l'est***
Bulgaria[5]	2	2	22	8	10	8	10	16	4	...	Bulgarie[5]
Czechoslovakia[6]	474	495	489	511	505	531	503	494	443	467	Tchécoslovaquie[6]
German Dem. Rep.[6]	3 942	4 435	4 302	3 967	3 702	4 117	4 441	3 274	3 388	3 551	Rép. dém. allemande[6]
Poland	0	0	0	0	0	0	12	30	8	1	Pologne
Other Europe	***0***	***25***	***26***	***35***	***57***	***71***	***57***	***59***	***80***	***89***	***Autre Europe***
Yugoslavia	0	25	26	35	57	71	57	59	...	...	Yougoslavie
USSR	**57 903**	**60 818**	**63 340**	**64 875**	**66 679**	**68 582**	**69 099**	**69 148**	**67 057**	**67 173**	**URSS**
Byelorussian SSR	*4 198*	*4 746*	*5 408*	*6 092*	*7 289*	*8 167*	*8 662*	*8 710*	*9 134*	*9 640*	*RSS de Biélorussie*
Total	**221 093**	**261 369**	**272 045**	**304 953**	**403 159**	**484 693**	**498 940**	**756 286**	**738 564**	**823 931**	**Total**

General note.
Pocket watches, wrist-watches and other watches including stop-watches. (SITC 86411-0).

1 Shipments.
2 Production by establishments employing 5 or more persons.
3 Excluding stop-watches.
4 Exports.
5 Incomplete coverage.
6 Wrist-watches only.

Remarque générale.
Montres de poche, montres-bracelets et autres montres, y compris les chronomètres. (CTCI 86411-0).

1 Expéditions.
2 Production des établissements occupant 5 personnes ou plus.
3 Non compris les chronomètres.
4 Exportations.
5 Couverture incomplète.
6 Montres-bracelets seulement.

Unit : Thousand units — Unité : En milliers

Country or area	1976	1977	1978	1979	1980	1981	1982	1983	1984	1985	Pays ou zone
Africa	**56**	**56**	**29**	**25**	**46**	**19**	**24**	**19**	**15**	**10**	**Afrique**
Tunisia	56	56	29	25	46	19	...	...	...	...	Tunisie
Asia	**37 009**	**34 421**	**31 863**	**29 271**	**24 518**	**28 020**	**23 040**	**15 110**	**13 701**	**16 452**	**Asie**
China	...	...	...	...	24 246	27 742	22 788	14 925	13 426	16 166	Chine
India	205	218	263	274	269	260	241	167	257	270	Inde
Indonesia	...	3	3	3	3	18	...	18	18	...	Indonésie
Europe	**27 453**	**27 823**	**24 468**	**27 055**	**27 757**	**24 597**	**24 262**	**24 088**	**28 148**	**30 428**	**Europe**
EEC	***21 915***	***22 876***	***19 677***	***22 577***	***23 213***	***19 588***	***19 109***	***19 320***	***22 859***	***25 500***	***CEE***
France[1 2]	2 751	2 708	2 726	2 794	2 347	2 010	1 914	[3] 2 729	[3] 2 611	[3] 1 665	France[1 2]
Germany, Fed. Rep.	19 164	20 168	16 951	19 783	20 866	17 578	17 195	16 591	20 248	23 835	Allemagne, Rép. féd.
East Europe	***4 783***	***4 682***	***4 526***	***4 421***	***4 433***	***4 873***	***4 888***	***4 503***	***5 024***	***4 663***	***Europe de l'est***
German Dem. Rep.	3 870	3 778	3 720	3 940	4 066	4 359	4 256	4 072	4 507	4 173	Rép. dém. allemande
Hungary	913	904	806	481	367	514	632	431	517	490	Hongrie
Other Europe	***755***	***265***	***265***	***57***	***111***	***136***	***265***	***265***	***265***	***265***	***Autre Europe***
Spain	755	...	...	57	111	136	...	...	...	...	Espagne
Total	**64 518**	**62 300**	**56 360**	**56 351**	**52 321**	**52 636**	**47 325**	**39 217**	**41 863**	**46 890**	**Total**

General note.
Clocks equipped with movements regulated by a balance-wheel and hair-spring not more than 12 mm in thickness, other than instrument-panel clocks or clocks of similar type. (SITC 86412-0).

[1] Deliveries.
[2] Mechanical, electric and electronic alarm clocks.
[3] Including other clocks.

Remarque générale.
Pendulettes équipées de mouvements à balancier à ressort spiral de moins de 12 mm d'épaisseur, autres que les montres de tableau de bord ou analogues. (CTCI 86412-0).

[1] Livraisons.
[2] Réveils mécaniques, électriques et électroniques.
[3] Y compris les autres appareils d'horlogerie.

Clocks, instrument-panel and similar type – Montres de tableau de bord, ou similaires

Unit : Thousand units | Unité : En milliers

Country or area	1976	1977	1978	1979	1980	1981	1982	1983	1984	1985	Pays ou zone
America, North	**14 000**	**15 000**	**14 500**	**14 500**	**14 500**	**14 500**	**14 500**	**14 500**	**14 500**	**14 500**	**Amérique du Nord**
United States	14 000	15 000	...	...	...	...	...	...	...	...	Etats-Unis
Europe	**5 134**	**5 018**	**5 043**	**6 320**	**5 623**	**5 669**	**5 361**	**5 575**	**5 350**	**4 985**	**Europe**
EEC	***5 017***	***4 913***	***4 941***	***6 204***	***5 503***	***5 535***	***5 245***	***5 475***	***5 051***	***4 707***	***CEE***
Germany, Fed. Rep.	5 017	4 913	4 941	6 204	5 503	5 535	5 245	5 475	5 051	4 707	Allemagne, Rép. féd.
Other Europe	***117***	***105***	***102***	***116***	***120***	***134***	***116***	***100***	***299***	***278***	***Autre Europe***
Yugoslavia	117	105	102	116	120	134	116	100	299	278	Yougoslavie
Total	**19 134**	**20 018**	**19 543**	**20 820**	**20 123**	**20 169**	**19 861**	**20 075**	**19 850**	**19 485**	**Total**

General note.
Electric and non-electric clocks specially constructed for mounting on the instrument panel of vehicles, aircraft and ships. Vehicle chronographs are included. (SITC 86421-0).

Remarque générale.
Montres, électriques ou non, construites spécialement pour être montées sur les tableaux de bord de véhicules, d'aérodynes ou de bateaux. Cette rubrique comprend les chronographes pour véhicules. (CTCI 86421-0).

Clocks, other, electric and non–electric – Autres appareils d'horlogerie, électriques et non électriques

Unit : Thousand units — Unité : En milliers

Country or area	1976	1977	1978	1979	1980	1981	1982	1983	1984	1985	Pays ou zone
America, North	**18 832**	**22 410**	**20 621**	**20 621**	**20 621**	**20 621**	**20 621**	**20 621**	**20 621**	**20 621**	**Amérique du Nord**
United States[1 2]	18 832	22 410	...	...	...	...	...	...	...	...	Etats–Unis[1 2]
America, South	**2 330**	**2 240**	**4 403**	**3 346**	**4 025**	**4 611**	**5 058**	**5 505**	**5 952**	**6 400**	**Amérique du Sud**
Brazil	2 330	2 240	4 403	[3] 3 346	4 025	...	...	...	...	...	Brésil
Asia	**43 276**	**43 109**	**50 903**	**44 270**	**57 013**	**73 182**	**74 201**	**100 721**	**176 534**	**147 217**	**Asie**
Hong Kong[4 5]	5 072	1 783	9 485	6 537	8 870	18 392	27 676	42 695	101 743	...	Hong–kong[4 5]
Japan	36 965	40 065	39 615	36 056	46 516	52 952	45 153	56 606	73 399	74 602	Japon
Korea, Republic of[6]	1 239	1 261	1 803	1 677	1 627	1 838	1 372	1 420	1 392	1 449	Corée, République de[6]
Europe	**8 823**	**8 108**	**8 085**	**9 507**	**9 302**	**8 126**	**7 984**	**7 736**	**8 043**	**7 937**	**Europe**
EEC	***6 511***	***5 713***	***5 421***	***5 919***	***5 834***	***5 794***	***5 997***	***5 915***	***5 922***	***5 930***	*CEE*
Denmark	0	0	0	1	3	...	...	...	1	1	Danemark
France	735	717	834	798	711	673	876	...	...	...	France
United Kingdom	5 776	4 996	4 587	...	...	...	...	...	...	...	Royaume–Uni
EFTA	***1 341***	***1 259***	***1 403***	***1 988***	***1 910***	***917***	***609***	***383***	***608***	***473***	*AELE*
Finland	...	3	2	8	6	4	5	5	3	...	Finlande
Switzerland[7]	1 337	1 256	1 401	1 980	1 904	913	604	378	...	...	Suisse[7]
Other Europe	***971***	***1 136***	***1 261***	***1 600***	***1 558***	***1 415***	***1 378***	***1 438***	***1 513***	***1 535***	*Autre Europe*
Spain	404	...	...	...	...	...	...	...	...	...	Espagne
Yugoslavia	567	732	857	1 196	1 154	1 011	974	1 034	1 109	1 131	Yougoslavie
Oceania	**81**	**74**	**60**	**60**	**60**	**60**	**60**	**24**	**60**	**60**	**Océanie**
Australia[8]	81	74	...	...	...	...	...	24	...	...	Australie[8]
Total	**73 342**	**75 941**	**84 072**	**77 803**	**91 020**	**106 599**	**107 923**	**134 607**	**211 210**	**182 235**	**Total**

General note.
Clocks having movements other than watch movements, driven by weights, spring or electricity and generally controlled by a pendulum or a balance–wheel and hairspring. Instrument panel and similar–type clocks are excluded. (SITC 86422–0).

1 Shipments.
2 Including clocks with watch movements.
3 Production by establishments employing 5 or more persons.
4 Including clocks with watch movements and instrument–panel and similar type clocks.
5 Beginning 1984, data are not comparable with those of previous years.
6 Wall clocks.
7 Exports.
8 Electric clocks only.

Remarque générale.
Horloges, pendules et pendulettes équipées de mouvements autres que les mouvements de montres, entraînés par des poids, des ressorts ou par l'électricité et contrôlés par un pendule ou un balancier à ressort spiral. Cette rubrique ne comprend pas les montres de tableau de bord ou similaires. (CTCI 86422–0).

1 Expéditions.
2 Y compris les pendulettes à mouvement de montre.
3 Production des établissements occupant 5 personnes ou plus.
4 Y compris les pendulettes á mouvement de montre et montres de tableau de bord ou similaires.
5 A partir de 1984, les données ne sont pas comparables à celles des années antérieures.
6 Pendules murales.
7 Exportations.
8 Horloges électriques seulement.

Unit : Number units

Unité : Nombre

Country or area	1976	1977	1978	1979	1980	1981	1982	1983	1984	1985	Pays ou zone
America, North	**233 849**	**241 147**	**261 343**	**255 607**	**222 725**	**214 486**	**187 596**	**198 008**	**189 769**	**181 530**	**Amérique du Nord**
Canada[1]	7 196	...	...	...	...	...	...	...	...	...	Canada[1]
United States[1]	226 653	233 951	254 147	248 411	...	...	180 400	...	...	...	Etats–Unis[1]
America, South	**4 391**	**3 408**	**3 286**	**3 158**	**3 930**	**3 284**	**3 168**	**3 051**	**2 935**	**2 818**	**Amérique du Sud**
Brazil	4 391	3 408	3 286	[2] 3 158	3 930	...	...	...	...	...	Brésil
Asia	**357 449**	**397 915**	**431 771**	**468 226**	**489 765**	**453 581**	**431 744**	**468 005**	**444 628**	**442 603**	**Asie**
China	...	...	...	...	...	13 096	14 306	15 106	18 101	24 441	Chine
Indonesia	37	37	40	75	0	0	0	...	450	...	Indonésie
Japan[3]	330 537	355 151	364 930	374 704	392 545	360 338	326 675	328 221	298 822	287 195	Japon[3]
Korea, Republic of	15 003	29 852	52 864	78 467	81 197	78 438	89 054	122 782	125 546	129 003	Corée, République de
Philippines	1 730	1 690	...	...	...	...	...	1 707	...	...	Philippines
Europe	**91 369**	**96 070**	**100 426**	**107 035**	**106 755**	**110 620**	**106 304**	**99 921**	**98 381**	**101 243**	**Europe**
EEC	***48 193***	***49 218***	***47 925***	***50 504***	***51 611***	***51 664***	***48 871***	***44 615***	***43 821***	***43 556***	***CEE***
Denmark	500	475	299	234	186	21	...	...	...	...	Danemark
France	2 486	2 652	2 769	3 150	...	...	...	...	...	...	France
Germany, Fed. Rep.	27 695	28 163	28 443	29 836	31 377	31 595	28 747	24 554	23 752	23 487	Allemagne, Rép. féd.
United Kingdom	17 512	17 928	16 414	...	...	...	...	...	...	...	Royaume–Uni
EFTA	***8 768***	***12 363***	***17 085***	***18 394***	***16 485***	***20 090***	***19 337***	***17 907***	***18 386***	***20 542***	***AELE***
Austria	516	557	680	749	800	746	858	683	748	820	Autriche
Finland	4 118	8 880	13 307	14 614	12 834	16 277	15 579	15 445	15 859	...	Finlande
Sweden	4 134	2 926	3 098	3 031	2 851	3 067	2 900	1 779	1 779	660	Suède
East Europe	***34 408***	***34 489***	***35 416***	***38 137***	***38 659***	***38 866***	***38 096***	***37 399***	***36 174***	***37 145***	***Europe de l'est***
German Dem. Rep.	25 118	24 874	25 346	27 817	28 425	28 642	29 077	28 498	27 101	27 682	Rép. dém. allemande
Poland	9 290	9 615	10 070	10 320	10 234	10 224	9 019	8 901	9 073	9 463	Pologne
USSR	**174 978**	**173 856**	**172 585**	**167 410**	**165 691**	**165 266**	**166 993**	**162 825**	**148 364**	**121 343**	**URSS**
Byelorussian SSR	*20 335*	*21 011*	*21 448*	*21 373*	*21 525*	*21 508*	*21 594*	*22 059*	*22 200*	*22 053*	*RSS de Biélorussie*
Ukrainian SSR	*29 406*	*29 442*	*29 125*	*27 188*	*28 944*	*29 106*	*28 882*	*28 085*	*22 392*	*18 336*	*RSS d'Ukraine*
Total	**862 036**	**912 396**	**969 411**	**1 001 436**	**988 866**	**947 237**	**895 805**	**931 810**	**884 077**	**849 537**	**Total**

General note.
Pianos of all types, including grand pianos and upright pianos, but excluding automatic pianos. (SITC 89141–1).

[1] Shipments.
[2] Production by establishments employing 5 or more persons.
[3] Production by establishments employing 20 or more persons.

Remarque générale.
Pianos de tous types, y compris les pianos à queue et les pianos droits, mais non compris les pianos dits automatiques. (CTCI 89141–1).

[1] Expéditions.
[2] Production des établissements occupant 5 personnes ou plus.
[3] Production des établissements occupant 20 personnes ou plus.

Musical instruments, string – Instruments de musique, à cordes

Unit : Thousand units

Unité : En milliers

Country or area	1976	1977	1978	1979	1980	1981	1982	1983	1984	1985	Pays ou zone
America, North	**89**	**89**	**89**	**89**	**89**	**89**	**89**	**87**	**89**	**90**	**Amérique du Nord**
Cuba	...	...	...	...	...	...	...	6	8	9	Cuba
United States	...	...	...	...	...	...	81	...	...	...	Etats–Unis
America, South	**297**	**247**	**385**	**497**	**520**	**598**	**666**	**734**	**805**	**874**	**Amérique du Sud**
Brazil	288	238	376	488	511	...	...	...	...	...	Brésil
Colombia	...	...	...	...	...	10	9	8	...	...	Colombie
Asia	**11**	**11**	**10**	**1**	**30**	**36**	**1**	**1**	**1**	**7**	**Asie**
Indonesia	...	...	...	1	30	36	1	1	1	...	Indonésie
Europe	**560**	**476**	**446**	**486**	**283**	**258**	**253**	**235**	**149**	**96**	**Europe**
EEC	***131***	***112***	***128***	***121***	***115***	***96***	***76***	***60***	***56***	***46***	***CEE***
Denmark	1	0	0	0	0	0	0	0	0	0	Danemark
Germany, Fed. Rep.	129	110	125	119	108	88	75	59	55	43	Allemagne, Rép. féd.
Greece	1	2	3	2	7	8	1	1	1	...	Grèce
EFTA	***73***	***44***	***34***	***33***	***35***	***38***	***30***	***32***	***26***	***19***	***AELE***
Finland	53	27	20	18	26	28	21	25	19	...	Finlande
Sweden	20	17	14	15	9	10	9	7	7	3	Suède
Other Europe	***356***	***320***	***284***	***332***	***133***	***124***	***147***	***143***	***67***	***31***	***Autre Europe***
Spain	...	...	...	332	133	124	147	143	...	...	Espagne
USSR	**1 690**	**1 814**	**1 845**	**1 878**	**1 908**	**1 919**	**2 085**	**2 101**	**2 091**	**2 063**	**URSS**
Ukrainian SSR	*260*	*276*	*277*	*258*	*265*	*286*	*289*	*301*	*312*	*312*	*RSS d'Ukraine*
Total	**2 647**	**2 637**	**2 775**	**2 951**	**2 830**	**2 900**	**3 094**	**3 158**	**3 135**	**3 130**	**Total**

General note.
Instruments in which sound vibrations are produced by running a bow across the strings or by plucking the strings. (SITC 89142–0).

Remarque générale.
Instruments dans lesquels les vibrations sonores sont produites par des cordes sous l'effet de pincements ou du frottement d'un archet. Cette rubrique ne comprend pas les pianos. (CTCI 89142–0).

Unit : Number units

Unité : Nombre

Country or area	1976	1977	1978	1979	1980	1981	1982	1983	1984	1985	Pays ou zone
America, North	**253 000**	**253 000**	**253 000**	**253 000**	**253 000**	**253 000**	**253 000**	**253 000**	**253 000**	**253 000**	**Amérique du Nord**
United States[1]	...	253 000	...	...	...	...	...	...	...	...	Etats–Unis[1]
America, South	**2 107**	**1 655**	**2 466**	**1 869**	**3 246**	**3 012**	**3 260**	**3 508**	**3 756**	**4 003**	**Amérique du Sud**
Brazil	2 107	1 655	2 466	# [2] 1 869	3 246	...	...	...	...	...	Brésil
Asia	**223 818**	**203 109**	**135 962**	**90 421**	**94 540**	**77 831**	**56 534**	**53 684**	**37 229**	**27 922**	**Asie**
Indonesia	...	1 817	2 300	1 918	3 025	3 000	7 000	9 000	8 007	...	Indonésie
Japan[3 4]	216 584	193 845	127 356	80 817	86 245	69 608	44 233	39 691	24 537	16 010	Japon[3 4]
Korea, Republic of	6 352	7 447	6 306	7 686	5 270	5 223	...	...	...	...	Corée, République de
Europe	**310**	**306**	**446**	**486**	**397**	**421**	**478**	**471**	**422**	**389**	**Europe**
EEC	***174***	***174***	***317***	***357***	***277***	***291***	***376***	***374***	***332***	***301***	***CEE***
Denmark	78	77	78	84	66	71	* 70	65	53	60	Danemark
Germany, Fed. Rep.[5]	96	97	239	273	211	220	306	309	279	241	Allemagne, Rép. féd.[5]
EFTA	***136***	***132***	***129***	***129***	***120***	***130***	***102***	***97***	***90***	***88***	***AELE***
Austria	24	15	18	21	10	18	21	19	15	...	Autriche
Finland	33	36	34	29	28	37	9	13	18	...	Finlande
Norway	21	21	21	...	...	...	...	...	...	...	Norvège
Sweden	58	60	56	58	61	54	51	44	36	39	Suède
Total	**479 235**	**458 070**	**391 874**	**345 776**	**351 183**	**334 264**	**313 272**	**310 663**	**294 407**	**285 314**	**Total**

General note.
Keyboard wind instruments with or without pipes (pipe and reed organs, harmonium and similar keyboard instruments and foot–blown accordions). Orchestrions, street organs and similar pipe instruments not fitted with a keyboard are excluded. (SITC 89181–0).

1 Shipments of electronic organs only.
2 Production by establishments employing 5 or more persons.
3 Production by establishments employing 20 or more persons.
4 Excluding electronic organs.
5 Excluding harmoniums and reed organs.

Remarque générale.
Instruments à vent, à clavier, munis ou non de tuyaux (orgues, harmoniums et instruments à clavier similaires, y compris les accordéons à soufflerie à pédale). Cette rubrique ne comprend pas les orchestrions, les orgues de barbarie et instruments à tuyaux similaires dépourvus de clavier. (CTCI 89181–0).

1 Expéditions d'orgues électroniques seulement.
2 Production des établissements occupant 5 personnes ou plus.
3 Production des établissements occupant 20 personnes ou plus.
4 Non compris les orgues électroniques.
5 Non compris les harmoniums.

Unit : Thousand units — Unité : En milliers

Country or area	1976	1977	1978	1979	1980	1981	1982	1983	1984	1985	Pays ou zone
America, North	**2 886**	**634**	**2 886**	**2 886**	**2 886**	**2 886**	**5 138**	**2 886**	**2 886**	**2 886**	**Amérique du Nord**
United States	...	634	...	...	...	...	5 138	...	...	...	Etats–Unis
America, South	**35**	**25**	**21**	**105**	**238**	**177**	**208**	**240**	**271**	**302**	**Amérique du Sud**
Brazil	35	25	21	[1] 105	238	...	...	...	...	...	Brésil
Asia	**199**	**274**	**409**	**214**	**225**	**253**	**251**	**221**	**234**	**233**	**Asie**
Indonesia	...	3	5	3	3	3	5	5	6	...	Indonésie
Japan	196	271	404	211	222	250	246	216	228	227	Japon
Europe	**1 423**	**1 447**	**1 509**	**1 863**	**1 601**	**1 487**	**1 505**	**1 499**	**1 398**	**1 335**	**Europe**
EEC	***1 423***	***1 447***	***1 509***	***1 863***	***1 601***	***1 487***	***1 505***	***1 499***	***1 398***	***1 335***	***CEE***
Germany, Fed. Rep.	1 423	1 447	1 509	1 863	1 601	1 487	1 505	1 499	1 398	1 335	Allemagne, Rép. féd.
USSR	**81**	**93**	**100**	**95**	**99**	**102**	**103**	**106**	**102**	**94**	**URSS**
Ukrainian SSR	*18*	*27*	*33*	*27*	*34*	*35*	*36*	*36*	*34*	*34*	*RSS d'Ukraine*
Total	**4 624**	**2 473**	**4 925**	**5 163**	**5 049**	**4 905**	**7 205**	**4 952**	**4 891**	**4 849**	**Total**

General note.
Wood and brass wind musical instruments, such as flutes, oboes, trumpets, cornets etc., excluding organs and accordions. (SITC 89183–0).

[1] Production by establishments employing 5 or more persons.

Remarque générale.
Instruments de musique à vent, en bois ou en cuivre, tels que les flûtes, les hautbois, les cornets à pistons et les trompettes etc., à l'exclusion des orgues et des accordéons. (CTCI 89183–0).

[1] Production des établissements occupant 5 personnes ou plus.

Fountain pens, ball-point pens, propelling pencils etc. – Porte-plumes réservoirs, stylographes, porte-mines etc.

Unit : Million units

Unité : En million

Country or area	1976	1977	1978	1979	1980	1981	1982	1983	1984	1985	Pays ou zone
America, North	**82.5**	**81.7**	**91.6**	**91.2**	**113.9**	**113.7**	**120.9**	**128.1**	**135.3**	**142.5**	**Amérique du Nord**
Canada[1 2]	82.5	81.7	91.6	91.2	113.9	...	...	...	...	...	Canada[1 2]
America, South	**430.8**	**678.6**	**202.4**	**516.5**	**640.7**	**568.5**	**584.2**	**587.9**	**626.4**	**649.5**	**Amérique du Sud**
Brazil	381.0	614.4	126.9	[3] 473.3	533.1	...	...	...	...	...	Brésil
Chile	18.9	18.7	15.5	19.8	...	...	...	...	...	...	Chili
Colombia	...	43.5	35.8	19.1	89.4	75.8	75.3	62.8	...	...	Colombie
Ecuador	1.2	2.0	24.1	...	0.0	0.0	0.0	0.0	...	...	Equateur
Asia	**1 423.9**	**1 624.3**	**1 745.4**	**2 018.2**	**1 923.7**	**2 409.3**	**2 362.4**	**2 371.0**	**2 555.2**	**2 931.9**	**Asie**
Burma[4]	0.6	0.6	0.4	0.1	0.0	0.0	0.0	0.0	0.0	0.0	Birmanie[4]
China	...	...	...	...	44.4	475.2	426.6	419.8	465.3	499.0	Chine
Indonesia	...	...	...	...	8.4	8.7	22.1	16.3	20.0	...	Indonésie
Iran(Islamic Rep.of)[2 5]	...	...	...	14.5	47.8	86.8	...	...	...	...	Iran(Rép.islamique)[2 5]
Japan[6]	1 148.7	1 334.8	1 328.0	1 550.5	1 562.8	1 546.9	1 636.5	1 619.8	1 777.1	2 093.0	Japon[6]
Korea, Republic of	132.6	152.5	211.8	233.1	212.9	242.0	195.1	205.5	188.9	219.8	Corée, République de
Turkey	39.0	47.4	49.0	49.6	...	...	30.0	57.5	51.8	...	Turquie
Yemen	...	...	4.0	2.4	1.0	...	...	...	...	...	Yémen
Europe	**959.5**	**1 070.5**	**900.2**	**1 080.0**	**1 096.4**	**1 190.0**	**1 170.9**	**1 241.1**	**1 284.4**	**1 319.3**	**Europe**
EEC	***784.2***	***862.1***	***705.5***	***868.8***	***845.7***	***849.4***	***843.5***	***855.8***	***951.9***	***1 056.2***	***CEE***
Germany, Fed. Rep.	523.1	527.1	548.1	620.4	597.9	601.6	600.9	612.3	706.0	813.4	Allemagne, Rép. féd.
Greece	27.5	47.3	30.2	32.2	31.6	31.7	26.4	27.3	29.7	...	Grèce
United Kingdom	233.6	287.7	127.2	...	...	...	...	...	...	...	Royaume-Uni
EFTA	***107.7***	***133.3***	***108.0***	***137.2***	***91.0***	***172.7***	***169.0***	***184.6***	***178.4***	***89.6***	***AELE***
Austria	64.9	85.4	65.7	76.3	56.9	137.2	139.8	158.6	152.6	66.8	Autriche
Portugal	42.8	47.9	42.3	60.9	34.0	35.6	29.2	26.0	25.8	...	Portugal
East Europe	***17.2***	***16.4***	***19.7***	***21.6***	***102.2***	***32.9***	***30.1***	***36.0***	***37.3***	***48.4***	***Europe de l'est***
Hungary	17.2	16.4	19.7	21.6	102.2	32.9	30.1	36.0	37.3	48.4	Hongrie
Other Europe	***50.4***	***58.7***	***67.0***	***52.4***	***57.5***	***134.9***	***128.3***	***164.6***	***116.8***	***125.1***	***Autre Europe***
Spain	...	...	...	52.4	57.5	134.9	128.3	164.6	...	...	Espagne
Oceania	**70.4**	**81.1**	**73.0**	**70.4**	**82.8**	**67.0**	**50.2**	**67.1**	**60.4**	**58.2**	**Océanie**
Australia	70.4	81.1	73.0	70.4	82.8	...	50.2	67.1	...	...	Australie
Total	**2 967.2**	**3 536.1**	**3 012.5**	**3 776.4**	**3 857.4**	**4 348.4**	**4 288.7**	**4 395.2**	**4 661.7**	**5 101.4**	**Total**

General note.
Fountain pens, stylograph pens and pencils (including ball-point pens and pencils) and other pens, pen-holders, pencil holders and similar holders, propelling pencils and sliding pencils. Mathematical drawing pens, pen nibs and nib-points, and pencil leads are excluded. (SITC 89521-0).

Remarque générale.
Porte-plumes réservoirs, stylographes et porte-mines (y compris les tylos à bille) et autres porte-plumes, porte-crayons, porte-mines etc., à l'exclusion des tire-lignes, des plumes et des mines de crayons. (CTCI 89521-0).

[1] Shipments.
[2] Ball-point pens only.
[3] Production by establishments employing 5 or more persons.
[4] Government production only.
[5] Production by establishments employing 10 or more persons.
[6] Production by establishments employing 20 or more persons.

[1] Expéditions.
[2] Stylos à bille seulement.
[3] Production des établissements occupant 5 personnes ou plus.
[4] Production de l'Etat seulement.
[5] Production des établissements occupant 10 personnes ou plus.
[6] Production des établissements occupant 20 personnes ou plus.

Pencils, crayons etc. – Crayons, pastels etc.

Unit : Million units — Unité : En millions

Country or area	1976	1977	1978	1979	1980	1981	1982	1983	1984	1985	Pays ou zone
Africa	**23**	**20**	**10**	**18**	**18**	**18**	**18**	**18**	**18**	**18**	**Afrique**
Egypt[1]	23	20	10	...	...	...	...	...	...	...	Egypte[1]
America, North	**3 000**	**2 296**	**2 904**	**3 136**	**3 090**	**1 274**	**1 516**	**1 665**	**1 437**	**1 227**	**Amérique du Nord**
Canada[1 2]	556	143	153	154	142	...	...	...	...	...	Canada[1 2]
Cuba	7	7	9	9	8	23	3	7	6	2	Cuba
United States[1 3]	2 437	2 146	2 742	2 973	2 940	1 087	1 376	1 549	...	...	Etats–Unis[1 3]
America, South	**698**	**532**	**609**	**713**	**822**	**670**	**674**	**663**	**678**	**680**	**Amérique du Sud**
Brazil	...	401	480	[4] 594	688	...	...	...	...	...	Brésil
Chile	33	28	25	12	...	...	...	...	...	...	Chili
Colombia[1]	109	...	...	...	...	79	82	79	...	...	Colombie[1]
Ecuador	15	16	17	...	22	26	27	18	...	...	Equateur
Asia	**2 193**	**2 344**	**2 291**	**2 325**	**2 076**	**2 040**	**1 948**	**2 136**	**2 124**	**1 990**	**Asie**
China	...	...	...	...	294	322	346	363	362	342	Chine
India[5]	95	179	237	182	178	112	99	84	90	82	Inde[5]
Indonesia	...	...	...	35	34	38	70	80	131	...	Indonésie
Japan[1 6]	1 325	1 318	1 288	1 427	1 123	1 099	1 016	1 085	1 041	943	Japon[1 6]
Korea, Republic of[1]	278	278	206	174	187	180	143	157	...	...	Corée, République de[1]
Syrian Arab Republic	135	189	161	130	184	213	198	324	275	358	Rép. arabe syrienne
Turkey	...	...	...	...	...	...	...	43	110	...	Turquie
Europe	**1 092**	**1 570**	**1 472**	**1 366**	**1 375**	**1 414**	**1 310**	**1 354**	**1 338**	**1 355**	**Europe**
EEC	***884***	***1 342***	***1 226***	***1 074***	***1 107***	***1 112***	***1 004***	***1 043***	***993***	***1 044***	***CEE***
Denmark	21	22	15	17	18	18	16	14	12	12	Danemark
Germany, Fed. Rep.	622	574	563	512	544	549	443	484	436	487	Allemagne, Rép. féd.
United Kingdom	241	746	648	...	...	...	...	...	...	...	Royaume–Uni
EFTA	***11***	***14***	***13***	***13***	***13***	***16***	***9***	***11***	***16***	***13***	***AELE***
Portugal	11	14	...	...	...	16	9	11	16	...	Portugal
East Europe	***101***	***112***	***125***	***161***	***145***	***152***	***156***	***166***	***183***	***145***	***Europe de l'est***
Hungary	101	112	125	161	145	152	156	166	183	145	Hongrie
Other Europe	***96***	***102***	***109***	***118***	***110***	***134***	***141***	***134***	***146***	***152***	***Autre Europe***
Spain	...	...	...	118	110	134	141	134	...	...	Espagne
Total	**7 006**	**6 762**	**7 286**	**7 557**	**7 381**	**5 417**	**5 466**	**5 835**	**5 596**	**5 269**	**Total**

General note.
Pencil leads, slate pencils, crayons and pastels, drawing charcoals, and writing and drawing chalks. Crude chalk and medical or cosmetic pencils are excluded. (SITC 89523–0).

1 Pencils only.
2 Shipments.
3 Including fountain pens, ball–point pens etc.
4 Production by establishments employing 5 or more persons.
5 Production by large and medium scale establishments only.
6 Production by establishments employing 20 or more persons.

Remarque générale.
Mines de crayons, crayons à ardoise, bâtonnets de pastel, fusains et craies pour écrire et dessiner. Cette rubrique ne comprend pas la craie brute et les crayons utilisés à des fins médicales ou cosmétiques. (CTCI 89523–0).

1 Crayons seulement.
2 Expéditions.
3 Y compris porte–plumes réservoirs, stylos à bille etc.
4 Production des établissements occupant 5 personnes ou plus.
5 Production des grandes et moyennes entreprises seulement.
6 Production des établissements occupant 20 personnes ou plus.

Unit : Thousand metres

Unité : Milliers de mètres

Country or area	1976	1977	1978	1979	1980	1981	1982	1983	1984	1985	Pays ou zone
Africa											**Afrique**
Tunisia	1 531	2 741	2 279	2 240	2 735	3 057	...	...	...	...	Tunisie
America, North											**Amérique du Nord**
America, South											**Amérique du Sud**
Brazil	180 131	112 078	131 837	[1] 162 111	100 508	...	...	...	...	...	Brésil
Chile	...	...	...	5 310	4 877	4 728	* 2 600	3 627	3 108	2 753	Chili
Asia											**Asie**
India[2]	1 459	1 323	1 267	1 513	1 393	1 072	1 322	640	570	622	Inde[2]
Indonesia	14 055	15 477	48 395	49 986	46 694	48 932	57 397	46 793	53 454	...	Indonésie
Korea, Republic of[3]	51 477	49 928	89 557	51 955	39 543	40 561	39 203	61 188	76 681	86 934	Corée, République de[3]
Philippines	535	412	...	...	...	...	...	...	...	...	Philippines
Turkey	6 005	6 026	6 766	8 116	...	...	11 289	12 590	14 566	...	Turquie
Europe											**Europe**
EEC											***CEE***
Denmark	...	939	...	...	...	...	...	...	...	...	Danemark
Germany, Fed. Rep.	116 870	97 404	103 579	112 783	108 717	96 387	113 723	106 117	104 354	98 045	Allemagne, Rép. féd.
Greece	10 479	11 703	11 075	11 509	8 857	8 355	8 828	8 951	5 596	...	Grèce
EFTA											***AELE***
Austria	2 658	2 865	2 369	2 294	2 071	994	...	...	...	...	Autriche
Finland	...	33 119	22 503	...	...	31 348	...	...	...	...	Finlande
Sweden[4]	313	262	188	302	264	245	...	106	113	102	Suède[4]
East Europe											***Europe de l'est***
Hungary	13 854	15 311	16 988	20 314	18 075	16 994	18 331	19 189	17 033	17 563	Hongrie
Oceania											**Océanie**
Australia	22 918	21 124	21 372	19 425	20 702	17 926	20 569	14 365	14 984	13 955	Australie

General note.

Zippers of any size and for any purpose (for clothing, footwear, travel goods etc.). (SITC 89953–0).

[1] Production by establishments employing 5 or more persons.
[2] Production by large and medium scale establishments only.
[3] Excluding plastic zippers.
[4] In metric tons.

Remarque générale.

Fermetures à glissière, de toutes dimensions et pour tous usages (habillement, chaussure, bagages etc.). (CTCI 89953–0).

[1] Production des établissements occupant 5 personnes ou plus.
[2] Production des grandes et moyennes entreprises seulement.
[3] Non compris les fermetures à glissière en plastique.
[4] En tonnes métriques.

Electric energy, total gross production (all plants) –
Enérgie électrique, production brute (toutes les centrales) (I + P)

Unit : Million KWH

Unité : Millions de kilowatts-heures

Country or area	1976	1977	1978	1979	1980	1981	1982	1983	1984	1985	Pays ou zone
Africa	**142 885**	**145 094**	**154 660**	**169 827**	**188 677**	**199 971**	**208 750**	**213 736**	**223 968**	**228 198**	**Afrique**
Algeria	4 370	4 412	5 212	6 116	7 123	8 149	9 396	10 216	11 182	12 274	Algérie
Angola	1 300	1 300	1 300	1 400	1 500	1 500	1 600	1 740	1 790	1 790	Angola
Benin	4	5	5	5	5	5	5	5	5	5	Bénin
Botswana	332	348	408	471	473	536	522	463	484	468	Botswana
Burkina Faso	60	70	80	99	97	98	107	110	115	115	Burkina Faso
Burundi	1	1	1	1	1	2	2	2	2	2	Burundi
Cameroon	1 336	1 346	1 303	1 347	1 452	1 908	2 147	1 804	2 230	2 237	Cameroun
Cape Verde	7	6	9	12	16	15	19	21	25	26	Cap-Vert
Central African Rep.	53	58	61	63	67	70	70	71	74	75	Rép. centrafricaine
Chad	55	59	62	63	64	65	65	65	65	65	Tchad
Comoros	5	6	7	9	10	10	10	10	10	10	Comores
Congo	114	123	55	113	156	158	200	233	235	237	Congo
Côte d'Ivoire	1 115	1 243	1 418	1 550	1 752	1 903	1 950	1 966	1 644	1 785	Côte d'Ivoire
Djibouti	82	89	93	102	117	123	126	147	148	150	Djibouti
Egypt	12 256	14 054	15 570	16 875	18 939	21 310	22 576	22 800	22 870	23 220	Egypte
Equatorial Guinea	23	23	21	14	18	15	14	15	15	15	Guinée équatoriale
Ethiopia	614	592	635	653	668	696	763	819	816	831	Ethiopie
Gabon	328	443	436	520	530	535	530	535	539	540	Gabon
Gambia	28	31	34	36	40	40	40	40	42	42	Gambie
Ghana	4 226	4 447	3 771	4 683	5 317	5 382	4 981	2 589	1 838	3 036	Ghana
Guinea	500	500	500	495	500	498	498	499	499	500	Guinée
Guinea-Bissau	14	12	13	13	14	13	13	13	14	14	Guinée-Bissau
Kenya	1 158	1 113	1 381	1 567	1 490	1 754	1 900	2 228	2 253	2 492	Kenya
Liberia	887	852	849	906	910	885	891	887	897	904	Libéria
Libyan Arab Jamah.	2 276	2 833	3 363	4 074	4 833	5 600	6 000	7 150	7 270	8 170	Jamah.arabe libyenne
Madagascar	343	366	376	402	426	427	432	450	452	449	Madagascar
Malawi	318	331	344	392	431	425	446	486	511	514	Malawi
Mali	85	83	99	101	107	106	129	150	164	164	Mali
Mauritania	96	96	97	100	102	102	103	103	102	103	Mauritanie
Mauritius	378	384	416	434	466	463	452	501	510	521	Maurice
Morocco	3 329	3 754	4 100	4 544	4 924	5 716	6 132	6 664	6 877	6 950	Maroc
Mozambique	1 915	4 940	7 800	11 300	14 000	3 800	3 400	6 426	1 945	1 945	Mozambique
Niger	75	87	98	115	130	145	150	47	51	51	Niger
Nigeria	3 930	4 106	4 848	5 964	7 177	7 814	8 568	8 821	8 964	9 000	Nigéria
Réunion	212	242	280	314	344	389	432	487	526	567	Réunion
Rwanda	148	151	153	160	118	108	137	156	163	163	Rwanda
St.Helena and Depend.	1	1	1	2	2	2	2	2	2	2	Ste-Hélène et dépend
Sao Tome – Principe	6	7	8	8	9	9	11	11	15	15	Sao Tomé-et-Principe
Senegal	474	527	580	636	635	673	675	677	695	696	Sénégal
Seychelles	33	37	42	48	50	51	53	56	56	62	Seychelles
Sierra Leone	197	198	213	208	220	243	270	277	280	278	Sierra Leone
Somalia	57	62	67	72	75	75	75	92	140	145	Somalie
South Africa	79 358	74 666	77 320	81 512	89 637	103 637	108 173	108 353	121 599	121 505	Afrique du Sud
Sudan	800	900	950	995	1 000	1 000	1 010	1 010	1 032	1 037	Soudan
Swaziland	197	176	278	269	284	306	264	300	320	320	Swaziland
Togo	47	64	74	70	15	17	24	37	111	34	Togo
Tunisia	1 525	1 725	1 989	2 366	2 797	3 020	3 174	3 552	3 885	4 021	Tunisie
Uganda	711	729	672	633	615	547	543	650	656	653	Ouganda
United Rep. Tanzania	665	687	695	768	766	831	834	867	870	875	Rép.Unie de Tanzanie
Western Sahara	70	70	76	78	77	77	78	78	78	78	Sahara occidental
Zaire	4 088	4 140	4 080	4 133	4 445	4 347	4 566	4 558	4 558	4 615	Zaïre
Zambia	7 046	8 683	7 896	8 785	9 192	9 852	10 058	10 071	9 806	10 090	Zambie
Zimbabwe	5 637	3 916	4 521	4 231	4 541	4 519	4 134	4 426	4 538	4 342	Zimbabwe
America, North	**2 502 583**	**2 628 548**	**2 729 070**	**2 787 493**	**2 844 885**	**2 871 016**	**2 817 677**	**2 907 670**	**3 048 748**	**3 130 685**	**Amérique du Nord**
Antigua and Barbuda	47	51	53	52	60	63	66	73	76	77	Antigua-et-Barbuda
Bahamas	649	687	743	829	853	762	814	871	866	854	Bahamas
Barbados	228	264	287	315	332	349	346	354	360	364	Barbade
Belize	43	45	48	53	54	55	57	58	58	60	Belize
Bermuda	311	327	333	333	332	342	353	368	382	395	Bermudes
British Virgin Islds	15	17	19	20	23	24	25	26	29	30	Iles Vierges brit.
Canada	294 043	326 184	345 165	363 176	377 518	390 937	387 460	408 443	437 990	460 408	Canada
Cayman Islands	37	37	40	40	62	71	83	95	111	124	Iles Caïmanes
Costa Rica	1 701	1 828	1 998	2 000	2 202	2 349	2 457	2 918	3 069	2 826	Costa Rica
Cuba	7 191	7 706	8 481	9 403	9 896	10 559	11 070	11 551	12 292	12 199	Cuba
Dominica	15	17	17	11	11	12	11	18	18	18	Dominique
Dominican Republic	2 580	2 243	2 395	3 268	3 317	3 582	3 206	3 400	4 009	4 020	Rép. dominicaine
El Salvador	1 161	1 303	1 451	1 578	1 543	1 474	1 489	1 600	1 684	1 695	El Salvador
Former Canal Zone	674	543	634	552	...	...	...	...	...	...	Ancien.Zone du Canal
Greenland	145	142	154	158	161	164	170	176	182	185	Groënland
Grenada	19	22	24	25	25	25	25	25	25	25	Grenade

For general note, see end of table.

Voir la fin du tableau pour la remarque générale.

Electric energy, total gross production (all plants) (continued) – Enérgie électrique, production brute (toutes les centrales) (I + P) (suite)

Unit : Million KWH — Unité : Millions de kilowatts–heures

Country or area	1976	1977	1978	1979	1980	1981	1982	1983	1984	1985	Pays ou zone
Guadeloupe	190	220	255	265	310	345	395	410	461	462	Guadeloupe
Guatemala	1 245	1 443	1 554	1 618	1 671	1 668	1 623	1 617	1 690	1 755	Guatemala
Haiti	209	215	246	280	315	325	360	373	375	375	Haïti
Honduras	606	682	756	847	928	1 014	1 090	1 150	1 060	1 065	Honduras
Jamaica	2 378	2 375	2 279	2 218	2 195	2 213	2 252	2 399	2 400	2 400	Jamaïque
Martinique	194	220	242	253	265	270	273	272	273	275	Martinique
Mexico	48 387	52 704	57 257	62 860	66 954	73 559	80 589	82 343	86 971	93 405	Mexique
Montserrat	9	9	10	10	12	12	12	12	12	12	Montserrat
Neth.Antil and Aruba	1 660	1 650	1 834	2 060	2 230	2 275	2 310	2 350	2 380	2 400	Antill.néer.et Aruba
Nicaragua	1 038	1 142	1 136	951	1 068	1 106	1 054	941	973	1 059	Nicaragua
Panama ex.Canal Zone	1 546	1 630	1 564	1 893	...	...	...	...	...	...	Panama ex.zone Canal
Panama	...	...	...	...	1 957	2 037	2 238	2 389	2 360	2 570	Panama
Puerto Rico	12 839	13 554	13 850	13 340	13 206	12 866	11 863	12 066	12 557	12 316	Porto Rico
St.Kitts–Nevis–Angll	26	27	28	30	34	...	...	...	...	...	St.Kitts–Nevis Angll
St.Kitts–Nevis	...	...	...	...	...	34	35	35	35	35	St–Kitts–Nevis
Saint Lucia	45	50	57	61	58	62	61	68	68	73	Sainte–Lucie
St.Pierre–Miquelon	10	11	13	15	17	20	24	26	32	35	St.Pierre–Miquelon
S.Vincent–Grenadines	18	20	23	26	27	27	30	30	30	30	S.Vincent–Grenadines
Trinidad and Tobago	1 412	1 576	1 675	1 818	2 056	2 301	2 683	2 690	2 725	3 035	Trinité–et–Tobago
Turks and Caicos Is.	6	6	7	7	9	11	11	11	11	12	Iles Turques,Caïques
United States	2 123 406	2 211 031	2 285 880	2 318 783	2 354 384	2 359 258	2 302 287	2 367 637	2 472 304	2 525 191	Etats–Unis
U.S. Virgin Islands	720	740	760	790	800	845	855	875	880	900	Iles Vierges amér.
America, South	**180 741**	**199 303**	**217 939**	**243 914**	**272 124**	**278 499**	**295 053**	**312 158**	**335 391**	**352 653**	**Amérique du Sud**
Argentina	30 216	32 413	33 434	37 640	39 676	38 838	39 804	42 998	44 914	45 265	Argentine
Bolivia	1 132	1 260	1 354	1 432	1 564	1 677	1 677	1 668	1 695	1 725	Bolivie
Brazil	89 979	100 822	112 575	124 673	139 485	142 198	151 999	161 969	178 532	192 945	Brésil
Chile	9 276	9 776	10 360	11 133	11 751	11 979	11 872	12 624	13 498	13 893	Chili
Colombia	14 757	15 369	17 358	19 139	22 935	24 195	25 605	26 100	26 500	26 800	Colombie
Ecuador	1 885	2 260	2 565	2 954	3 352	3 730	4 118	4 289	4 207	4 490	Equateur
Falkland I(Malvinas)	3	2	2	2	2	3	3	3	3	3	I Falkland(Malvinas)
French Guiana	65	71	89	102	113	124	138	164	181	190	Guyane française
Guyana	392	431	409	407	414	429	354	400	400	390	Guyana
Paraguay	586	523	516	644	725	747	681	818	920	1 535	Paraguay
Peru	7 911	8 627	8 765	9 265	10 039	10 757	11 350	10 675	11 717	12 115	Pérou
Suriname	1 335	1 421	1 511	1 530	1 577	1 367	1 332	1 107	1 250	1 300	Suriname
Uruguay	2 665	2 876	3 046	2 960	4 559	4 913	6 156	7 343	7 244	6 602	Uruguay
Venezuela	20 539	23 452	25 955	32 033	35 932	37 542	39 964	42 000	44 330	45 400	Venezuela
Asia	**1 037 290**	**1 106 579**	**1 214 240**	**1 300 885**	**1 338 039**	**1 387 180**	**1 449 423**	**1 556 907**	**1 675 733**	**1 786 405**	**Asie**
Afghanistan	712	800	845	908	965	1 018	976	1 025	1 045	1 060	Afghanistan
Bahrain	900	1 110	1 212	1 474	1 660	1 814	2 009	2 026	2 056	2 130	Bahreïn
Bangladesh	1 769	1 934	2 219	2 402	2 653	3 222	3 552	3 758	4 292	4 870	Bangladesh
Bhutan	16	16	12	13	17	20	22	25	27	30	Bhoutan
Brunei Darussalam	264	310	361	410	469	511	570	728	831	949	Brunéi Darussalam
Burma	1 092	1 191	1 243	1 340	1 487	1 415	1 490	1 516	1 726	1 756	Birmanie
China	203 100	223 400	256 550	281 950	300 620	309 270	327 680	351 440	376 990	410 700	Chine
Cyprus	796	860	919	977	1 034	1 060	1 144	1 221	1 250	1 319	Chypre
Democratic Kampuchea.	137	140	155	160	100	65	50	40	70	80	Kampuchea démocrat.
Democratic Yemen	223	233	242	245	248	260	257	280	280	285	Yémen démocratique
Hong Kong	8 342	9 451	10 384	11 391	12 649	13 306	14 504	16 482	17 923	19 235	Hong–kong
India	95 615	98 928	110 130	112 820	119 260	131 125	140 299	150 994	168 646	188 479	Inde
Indonesia	9 278	10 127	11 301	12 747	14 234	12 611	14 647	19 847	27 354	28 933	Indonésie
Iran(Islamic Rep.of)	17 311	18 000	19 847	21 909	22 380	24 906	28 823	33 009	37 168	37 300	Iran(Rép.islamique)
Iraq	5 295	6 429	7 997	10 217	11 426	10 974	13 708	16 200	18 460	18 760	Iraq
Israel	10 361	11 108	11 874	12 436	12 528	13 112	13 826	14 578	14 909	15 698	Israël
Japan	511 793	532 609	563 990	589 644	577 521	583 245	581 383	619 558	649 899	673 412	Japon
Jordan	501	601	704	900	1 070	1 237	1 512	1 918	2 304	2 473	Jordanie
Korea,Dem.Ppl's.Rep.	28 000	30 000	32 000	33 000	35 000	36 000	40 000	41 000	45 000	48 000	Corée,Rép.pop.dém.de
Korea, Republic of	24 454	28 081	33 413	38 271	40 079	44 088	47 164	53 036	58 352	62 716	Corée, République de
Kuwait,part Ntl.Zone	5 667	6 453	7 446	9 039	9 417	10 336	12 016	12 830	14 196	15 689	Koweït et prt.Zne.N.
Lao Peoples Dem.Rep.	400	450	510	1 088	975	1 150	1 200	1 075	990	1 350	Rép. dém. pop. lao
Lebanon	1 450	1 600	1 700	1 800	1 800	1 810	1 290	1 220	1 355	1 355	Liban
Macau	160	181	204	234	262	295	339	404	425	445	Macao
Malaysia	6 446	7 520	8 485	9 203	10 098	10 634	11 433	12 655	13 651	14 995	Malaisie
Maldives	2	2	2	3	4	5	8	8	11	11	Maldives
Mongolia	937	1 101	1 174	1 290	1 566	1 563	1 518	1 768	2 264	2 788	Mongolie
Nepal	154	175	192	211	210	243	307	328	364	408	Népal
Oman	413	550	613	776	957	1 148	1 381	1 623	2 364	2 846	Oman
Pakistan	10 320	10 877	12 375	14 174	14 974	16 062	17 668	19 697	21 873	27 530	Pakistan
Philippines	14 716	15 080	15 542	16 677	18 009	19 824	20 807	20 761	20 800	21 018	Philippines
Qatar	816	1 026	1 364	2 002	2 431	2 772	3 089	3 315	3 425	3 515	Qatar
S.Arabia,pt.Ntrl.Zn.	6 389	7 263	9 713	15 470	18 909	25 061	31 014	29 915	31 150	32 410	Arab.saoud,p.Zn.neut

For general note, see end of table. — Voir la fin du tableau pour la remarque générale.

Electric energy, total gross production (all plants) (continued) – Enérgie électrique, production brute (toutes les centrales) (I + P) (suite)

Unit : Million KWH — Unité : Millions de kilowatts–heures

Country or area	1976	1977	1978	1979	1980	1981	1982	1983	1984	1985	Pays ou zone
Singapore	4 605	5 115	5 898	6 448	6 940	7 442	7 860	8 626	9 401	9 876	Singapour
Sri Lanka	1 202	1 287	1 385	1 525	1 668	1 872	2 066	2 114	2 261	2 464	Sri Lanka
Syrian Arab Republic	1 785	2 043	2 702	3 356	3 837	4 564	5 737	6 312	6 897	7 316	Rép. arabe syrienne
Thailand	10 295	11 691	13 204	14 067	15 112	16 124	17 450	19 770	22 029	24 179	Thaïlande
Turkey	18 231	20 564	21 726	22 522	23 275	24 677	26 552	27 347	30 644	33 313	Turquie
United Arab Emirates	1 941	2 955	3 764	4 991	6 297	6 210	6 470	6 570	6 636	6 690	Emirats arabes unis
Viet Nam	2 957	3 473	3 600	3 600	3 700	4 520	4 680	4 200	4 800	5 000	Viet Nam
Yemen	78	84	118	149	185	228	279	285	295	295	Yémen
Europe	**1 903 873**	**1 965 084**	**2 060 551**	**2 153 756**	**2 176 813**	**2 194 677**	**2 204 825**	**2 279 357**	**2 382 301**	**2 485 554**	**Europe**
EEC	***1 125 791***	***1 147 780***	***1 202 334***	***1 261 184***	***1 259 644***	***1 255 207***	***1 252 123***	***1 276 172***	***1 335 611***	***1 398 346***	***CEE***
Belgium	47 349	47 099	50 580	51 921	53 129	50 606	50 034	51 935	53 699	56 356	Belgique
Denmark	20 928	22 436	20 789	22 204	27 118	19 757	23 733	22 162	22 577	29 001	Danemark
France incl. Monaco	202 438	210 015	225 939	240 347	245 713	263 355	265 396	281 293	307 155	326 400	France y comp.Monaco
Germany, Fed. Rep	332 253	334 062	351 972	370 724	367 532	367 060	365 193	371 967	392 870	406 714	Allemagne, Rép. féd.
Greece	17 861	18 996	21 050	22 102	22 652	23 433	23 272	22 262	24 820	27 740	Grèce
Ireland	8 308	9 019	9 643	10 637	10 563	10 525	10 527	10 781	11 236	11 738	Irlande
Italy and San Marino	161 735	164 953	173 119	179 000	183 464	178 911	181 825	180 109	179 546	182 237	Italie y comp. S.Mrn
Luxembourg	1 112	1 136	1 139	1 096	918	775	528	437	517	502	Luxembourg
Netherlands	58 138	58 285	61 597	64 464	64 806	64 053	60 312	59 650	62 778	62 936	Pays–Bas
United Kingdom	275 669	281 779	286 506	298 689	283 749	276 732	271 303	275 576	280 413	294 722	Royaume–Uni
EFTA	***278 656***	***292 464***	***303 729***	***325 577***	***325 733***	***344 841***	***343 905***	***369 994***	***386 453***	***407 677***	***AELE***
Austria	34 868	37 318	37 510	40 228	41 627	42 385	42 369	42 105	41 827	43 923	Autriche
Finland	27 885	31 563	33 871	37 337	38 710	39 070	39 355	40 347	43 226	47 098	Finlande
Iceland	2 426	2 607	2 679	2 927	3 155	3 329	3 589	3 781	3 848	4 044	Islande
Norway,Svlbd,J.Myn I.	81 985	72 174	80 772	88 725	83 601	92 774	92 600	105 854	106 072	103 190	Norvège,Svalbd,J.May
Portugal	9 776	13 775	14 599	16 715	15 263	13 900	15 267	18 161	20 071	19 007	Portugal
Sweden	86 416	90 018	92 901	95 204	96 316	102 846	99 512	108 869	123 268	136 543	Suède
Switzrld,Liechtenst	35 300	45 009	41 397	44 441	47 061	50 537	51 213	50 877	48 141	53 872	Suisse,Liechtenstein
East Europe	***366 060***	***382 981***	***404 258***	***406 625***	***422 058***	***423 198***	***432 141***	***448 603***	***468 935***	***479 004***	***Europe de l'est***
Albania	2 000	2 150	2 350	2 400	2 450	2 650	2 750	2 885	3 020	3 155	Albanie
Bulgaria	27 747	29 710	31 492	32 368	34 835	36 972	40 459	42 645	44 672	41 633	Bulgarie
Czechoslovakia	62 746	66 501	69 097	68 092	72 732	73 504	74 749	76 275	78 388	80 627	Tchécoslovaquie
German Dem. Rep	89 150	91 996	95 963	96 845	98 808	100 720	102 906	104 928	110 093	113 834	Rép. dém. allemande
Hungary	22 050	23 402	25 543	24 519	23 876	24 219	24 775	25 789	26 303	26 779	Hongrie
Poland	104 101	109 364	115 558	117 468	121 871	114 995	117 580	125 821	134 792	137 708	Pologne
Romania	58 266	59 858	64 255	64 933	67 486	70 138	68 922	70 260	71 667	75 268	Roumanie
Other Europe	***133 366***	***141 859***	***150 230***	***160 370***	***169 378***	***171 431***	***176 656***	***184 588***	***191 302***	***200 527***	***Autre Europe***
Faeroe Islands	113	122	136	150	160	165	170	170	178	178	Iles Féroé
Gibraltar	52	51	52	52	55	58	60	61	61	63	Gibraltar
Malta	382	417	459	501	527	558	597	675	700	784	Malte
Spain	89 246	92 689	98 333	104 701	109 201	110 018	113 505	117 111	118 110	125 560	Espagne
Yugoslavia	43 573	48 580	51 250	54 966	59 435	60 632	62 324	66 571	72 253	73 942	Yougoslavie
USSR	**1 111 420**	**1 150 075**	**1 201 896**	**1 238 196**	**1 293 878**	**1 326 031**	**1 367 000**	**1 419 099**	**1 493 000**	**1 622 117**	**URSS**
Oceania	**101 912**	**108 162**	**112 210**	**116 961**	**122 798**	**128 697**	**133 645**	**135 879**	**143 843**	**152 522**	**Océanie**
American Samoa	62	65	67	70	75	72	72	76	74	75	Samoa américaines
Australia	76 596	82 607	86 295	91 232	96 135	101 480	105 329	106 287	112 947	120 962	Australie
Christmas Isl.(Aust)	28	31	32	32	32	32	32	33	...	...	Ile Christmas (Aust)
Cook Islands	9	10	10	12	11	11	10	10	11	12	Iles Cook
Fiji	265	279	290	306	310	317	324	330	387	395	Fidji
French Polynesia	153	196	215	235	255	280	290	187	203	220	Polynésie française
Guam	980	1 058	1 060	1 100	1 150	1 115	1 100	976	1 000	1 100	Guam
Kiribati	5	4	4	5	5	5	5	5	6	6	Kiribati
Nauru	26	26	26	26	26	26	26	27	28	28	Nauru
New Caledonia	1 584	1 373	1 127	1 184	1 333	1 180	943	737	915	1 120	Nouvelle–Calédonie
New Zealand	20 910	21 265	21 687	21 334	21 982	22 706	23 957	25 525	26 519	26 764	Nouvelle–Zélande
Niue	1	2	2	2	2	3	3	3	3	3	Nioué
Pacific Islds(Trust)	128	130	132	135	140	145	145	148	150	164	I.Pacifique (tutel.)
Papua New Guinea	1 095	1 044	1 184	1 201	1 252	1 230	1 307	1 435	1 495	1 565	Papouasie–Nvl–Guinée
Samoa	29	30	34	39	39	39	44	40	41	42	Samoa
Solomon Islands	18	18	19	19	21	24	25	25	28	29	Iles Salomon
Tonga	6	7	7	9	10	12	12	12	12	12	Tonga
Vanuatu	17	17	19	20	20	20	21	23	24	25	Vanuatu
Total	**6 980 704**	**7 302 845**	**7 690 566**	**8 011 032**	**8 237 214**	**8 386 071**	**8 476 373**	**8 824 806**	**9 302 984**	**9 758 134**	**Total**

For general note, see end of table.

Voir la fin du tableau pour la remarque générale.

Electric energy, total gross production (all plants) (continued) – Enérgie électrique, production brute (toutes les centrales) (I + P) (suite)

General note.
Electric energy generated by both public supply undertakings (that is, enterprises, whatever their legal form, whose primary activity is the production, transmission and distribution of electric energy) and self–producers (that is, enterprises which, in addition to their main activities, themselves produce, individually or in common, electric energy intended in part or in the entirety to meet their own needs). Production is measured gross, that is, including station use and transmission losses. (SITC 35100–0).

Africa
Zambia: Net production.

Zimbabwe: Net production.

America, North
Dominican Republic: Net Production.

United States: Net production.

U.S. Virgin Island: Net Production.

America, South
Mexico: Net production.

Europe
Finland: Net production.

France incl. Monaco: Net production.

Iceland: Net production.

Liechtenstein: Net production.

Switzerland: Net production.

Remarque générale.
Production brute d'énergie électrique, y compris la consommation des centrales et les pertes dues au transport, des entreprises publiques (entreprises, quel que soit leur statut juridique, dont le but essentiel est de produire, de transporter et de distribuer de l'énergie électrique) et des "autoproducteurs" (entreprises qui, subsidiairement à leur activité principale, produisent elles–mêmes, individuellement ou en commun, de l'énergie électrique destinée en totalité ou en partie à satisfaire leurs propres besoins). (CTCI 35100–0).

Afrique
Zambie: Production nette.

Zimbabwe: Production nette.

Amérique du Nord
République dominicaine: Production nette.

Etats–Unis: Production nette.

Iles Vierges amér.: Production nette.

Amérique du Sud
Mexique: Production nette.

Europe
Finlande: Production nette.

France y comp. Monaco: Production nette.

Islande: Production nette.

Liechtenstein: Production nette.

Suisse: Production nette.

Electric energy, gross production by public utilities – Énergie électrique, production brute, services publics (P)

Unit : Million KWH

Unité : Millions de kilowatts–heures

Country or area	1976	1977	1978	1979	1980	1981	1982	1983	1984	1985	Pays ou zone
Africa	**132 249**	**129 482**	**140 110**	**155 334**	**173 053**	**183 626**	**191 082**	**196 334**	**206 048**	**210 362**	**Afrique**
Algeria	3 720	4 141	4 794	5 480	6 220	7 141	8 136	9 106	10 012	11 222	Algérie
Angola	1 205	1 205	1 205	1 300	1 380	1 380	1 460	1 590	1 640	1 640	Angola
Benin	4	5	5	5	5	5	5	5	5	5	Bénin
Botswana	290	302	357	396	387	429	426	395	422	446	Botswana
Burkina Faso	60	70	80	99	97	98	107	110	115	115	Burkina Faso
Burundi	1	1	1	1	1	2	2	2	2	2	Burundi
Cameroon	59	62	71	97	88	99	99	99	110	112	Cameroun
Cape Verde	6	6	9	11	15	14	17	20	24	25	Cap–Vert
Central African Rep.	53	58	61	63	67	70	70	71	74	75	Rép. centrafricaine
Chad	55	59	62	63	64	65	65	65	65	65	Tchad
Comoros	5	6	7	9	10	10	10	10	10	10	Comores
Congo	114	123	55	113	156	158	200	233	235	237	Congo
Côte d'Ivoire	1 115	1 243	1 418	1 550	1 752	1 903	1 950	1 966	1 644	1 785	Côte d'Ivoire
Djibouti	82	89	93	102	117	123	126	147	148	150	Djibouti
Egypt	11 705	13 493	15 084	16 368	18 429	20 747	22 023	22 250	22 310	22 620	Egypte
Equatorial Guinea	23	23	21	14	18	15	14	15	15	15	Guinée équatoriale
Ethiopia	524	548	590	600	614	640	710	764	760	775	Ethiopie
Gabon	328	443	436	520	530	535	530	535	539	540	Gabon
Gambia	23	26	28	30	32	32	32	32	33	33	Gambie
Ghana	4 221	4 445	3 769	4 680	5 314	5 378	4 978	2 586	1 835	3 033	Ghana
Guinea	100	100	100	95	100	98	98	99	99	100	Guinée
Guinea–Bissau	12	10	10	10	11	10	10	10	11	11	Guinée–Bissau
Kenya	1 083	1 043	1 311	1 497	1 420	1 684	1 830	2 158	2 183	2 422	Kenya
Liberia	387	399	406	435	429	404	409	405	415	417	Libéria
Libyan Arab Jamah.	2 276	2 833	3 363	4 074	4 833	5 600	6 000	7 150	7 270	8 170	Jamah.arabe libyenne
Madagascar	248	271	281	312	336	337	342	360	362	359	Madagascar
Malawi	283	297	311	358	393	389	410	450	475	477	Malawi
Mali	65	63	81	83	92	91	114	133	145	146	Mali
Mauritania	96	96	97	100	102	102	103	103	102	103	Mauritanie
Mauritius	245	284	310	329	328	331	319	374	380	390	Maurice
Morocco	3 079	3 392	3 711	4 065	4 431	5 100	5 496	5 909	6 117	6 180	Maroc
Mozambique	1 750	4 775	7 635	11 135	13 835	3 635	3 250	6 276	1 795	1 795	Mozambique
Niger	75	87	98	115	130	145	150	47	51	51	Niger
Nigeria	3 890	4 066	4 808	5 927	7 140	7 777	8 531	8 786	8 929	8 965	Nigéria
Réunion	210	240	278	313	343	387	432	487	526	567	Réunion
Rwanda	47	52	49	64	27	26	44	58	67	67	Rwanda
St.Helena and Depend.	1	1	1	1	1	1	2	2	2	2	Ste–Hélène et dépend
Sao Tome – Principe	6	7	8	8	9	9	11	11	15	15	Sao Tomé–et–Principe
Senegal	469	521	573	628	627	663	665	667	684	685	Sénégal
Seychelles	33	37	42	48	50	51	53	56	56	62	Seychelles
Sierra Leone	125	125	141	133	146	168	192	192	193	195	Sierra Leone
Somalia	57	62	67	72	75	75	75	92	140	145	Somalie
South Africa	77 203	67 050	70 902	75 643	83 362	97 409	101 250	101 333	114 579	114 485	Afrique du Sud
Sudan	710	810	855	900	900	900	910	910	922	922	Soudan
Swaziland	144	123	132	115	128	132	90	120	130	130	Swaziland
Togo	4	8	9	2	15	17	22	28	86	33	Togo
Tunisia	1 339	1 518	1 786	2 082	2 429	2 678	2 739	3 096	3 419	3 571	Tunisie
Uganda	671	689	632	603	585	514	505	615	620	617	Ouganda
United Rep. Tanzania	590	612	620	693	686	745	746	777	780	785	Rép.Unie de Tanzanie
Western Sahara	70	70	76	78	77	77	78	78	78	78	Sahara occidental
Zaire	1 238	1 410	1 355	1 339	1 397	1 373	1 493	1 503	1 508	1 515	Zaïre
Zambia	6 706	8 370	7 589	8 549	8 979	9 520	9 819	9 841	9 571	9 855	Zambie
Zimbabwe	5 444	3 713	4 327	4 027	4 341	4 334	3 934	4 207	4 340	4 142	Zimbabwe
America, North	**2 375 993**	**2 495 227**	**2 601 106**	**2 669 528**	**2 726 980**	**2 754 769**	**2 703 901**	**2 798 174**	**2 940 680**	**3 022 441**	**Amérique du Nord**
Antigua and Barbuda	40	44	46	45	53	56	59	66	69	70	Antigua–et–Barbuda
Bahamas	609	642	693	766	788	702	749	806	801	789	Bahamas
Barbados	228	264	287	315	332	349	346	354	360	364	Barbade
Belize	43	45	48	53	54	55	57	58	58	60	Belize
Bermuda	311	327	333	333	332	342	353	368	382	395	Bermudes
British Virgin Islds	15	17	19	20	23	24	25	26	29	30	Iles Vierges brit.
Canada	263 739	288 488	305 837	326 475	337 991	350 321	347 660	369 456	399 357	421 538	Canada
Cayman Islands	37	37	40	40	62	71	83	95	111	124	Iles Caïmanes
Costa Rica	1 646	1 760	1 926	1 933	2 144	2 291	2 399	2 860	3 011	2 768	Costa Rica
Cuba	5 993	6 445	7 174	8 084	8 680	9 204	9 647	10 107	10 803	10 739	Cuba
Dominica	15	17	17	11	11	12	11	18	18	18	Dominique
Dominican Republic	1 460	1 943	2 102	3 042	3 060	3 301	2 916	3 080	3 432	3 440	Rép. dominicaine
El Salvador	1 108	1 233	1 379	1 496	1 462	1 392	1 439	1 545	1 624	1 635	El Salvador
Former Canal Zone	674	543	634	552	...	...	...	...	...	...	Ancien.Zone du Canal
Greenland	100	98	114	111	116	117	122	127	132	135	Groënland
Grenada	19	22	24	25	25	25	25	25	25	25	Grenade

For general note, see end of table.

Voir la fin du tableau pour la remarque générale.

Unit : Million KWH — Unité : Millions de kilowatts–heures

Country or area	1976	1977	1978	1979	1980	1981	1982	1983	1984	1985	Pays ou zone
Guadeloupe	190	220	255	265	310	345	395	410	461	462	Guadeloupe
Guatemala	1 015	1 202	1 309	1 373	1 466	1 458	1 413	1 407	1 480	1 545	Guatemala
Haiti	184	190	221	255	290	300	335	348	350	350	Haïti
Honduras	560	639	713	804	882	968	1 044	1 100	1 010	1 015	Honduras
Jamaica	1 403	1 400	1 424	1 368	1 345	1 363	1 402	1 549	1 550	1 550	Jamaïque
Martinique	194	220	242	253	265	270	273	272	273	275	Martinique
Mexico	44 632	48 945	52 977	58 070	61 868	67 879	73 237	74 843	79 507	85 352	Mexique
Montserrat	9	9	10	10	12	12	12	12	12	12	Montserrat
Neth.Antil and Aruba	750	750	800	850	850	875	890	900	920	940	Antill.néer.et Aruba
Nicaragua	916	1 021	1 013	869	971	1 011	970	854	895	986	Nicaragua
Panama ex.Canal Zone	1 433	1 510	1 439	1 763	...	...	...	...	...	...	Panama ex.zone Canal
Panama	...	...	...	...	1 811	1 897	2 088	2 239	2 210	2 420	Panama
Puerto Rico	12 509	13 234	13 530	13 030	12 896	12 556	11 563	11 766	12 262	12 026	Porto Rico
St.Kitts–Nevis–Angll	21	22	23	25	27	...	...	...	...	...	St.Kitts–Nevis Angll
St.Kitts–Nevis	...	...	...	...	...	27	28	28	28	28	St–Kitts–Nevis
Saint Lucia	45	50	57	61	58	62	61	68	68	73	Sainte–Lucie
St.Pierre–Miquelon	10	11	13	15	17	20	24	26	32	35	St.Pierre–Miquelon
S.Vincent–Grenadines	18	20	23	26	27	27	30	30	30	30	S.Vincent–Grenadines
Trinidad and Tobago	1 287	1 431	1 528	1 680	1 893	2 169	2 573	2 575	2 600	2 885	Trinité–et–Tobago
Turks and Caicos Is.	3	3	4	4	5	6	6	6	6	6	Iles Turques,Caïques
United States	2 036 487	2 124 078	2 206 515	2 247 411	2 286 439	2 294 812	2 241 211	2 310 285	2 416 304	2 469 841	Etats–Unis
U.S. Virgin Islands	397	400	410	410	415	450	455	465	470	480	Iles Vierges amér.
America, South	**158 796**	**175 980**	**194 148**	**218 399**	**246 124**	**254 085**	**269 940**	**286 294**	**309 083**	**326 208**	**Amérique du Sud**
Argentina	25 218	27 200	28 878	33 020	35 676	35 188	36 164	38 898	40 814	41 465	Argentine
Bolivia	849	971	1 051	1 126	1 260	1 375	1 382	1 399	1 405	1 430	Bolivie
Brazil	84 478	95 083	105 930	117 114	131 041	134 022	143 500	152 816	169 798	184 180	Brésil
Chile	6 604	6 912	7 343	8 035	8 833	9 216	9 182	9 739	10 459	10 893	Chili
Colombia	13 717	14 299	16 258	17 999	21 759	22 971	24 341	24 810	25 210	25 490	Colombie
Ecuador	1 693	2 045	2 370	2 742	3 101	3 410	3 819	4 026	4 193	4 200	Equateur
Falkland I(Malvinas)	3	2	2	2	2	3	3	3	3	3	I Falkland(Malvinas)
French Guiana	65	71	89	102	113	124	138	164	181	190	Guyane française
Guyana	212	233	220	234	181	214	171	220	225	220	Guyana
Paraguay	564	500	492	619	697	721	657	793	895	1 510	Paraguay
Peru	5 032	5 350	5 490	5 961	6 388	7 288	7 638	7 459	8 075	8 379	Pérou
Suriname	58	106	140	189	191	213	145	179	175	175	Suriname
Uruguay	2 562	2 756	2 930	2 847	4 450	4 808	6 079	7 288	7 164	6 523	Uruguay
Venezuela	17 741	20 452	22 955	28 409	32 432	34 532	36 721	38 500	40 486	41 550	Venezuela
Asia	**944 421**	**1 009 798**	**1 112 286**	**1 194 333**	**1 231 624**	**1 284 867**	**1 347 070**	**1 447 514**	**1 552 026**	**1 658 347**	**Asie**
Afghanistan	679	764	840	683	720	726	760	800	813	827	Afghanistan
Bahrain	692	896	992	1 249	1 430	1 584	1 789	1 796	1 826	1 900	Bahreïn
Bangladesh	1 460	1 619	1 913	2 122	2 353	2 662	3 036	3 433	3 967	4 545	Bangladesh
Bhutan	10	9	6	7	8	9	10	10	10	10	Bhoutan
Brunei Darussalam	174	232	265	319	365	413	468	549	633	730	Brunéi Darussalam
Burma	840	931	978	1 080	1 227	1 352	1 415	1 440	1 553	1 580	Birmanie
China	203 100	223 400	256 550	281 950	300 620	309 270	327 680	351 440	376 990	410 700	Chine
Cyprus	783	849	915	977	1 034	1 060	1 141	1 206	1 250	1 319	Chypre
Democratic Kampuchea.	137	140	155	160	100	65	50	40	70	80	Kampuchea démocrat.
Democratic Yemen	153	163	167	170	173	185	182	205	205	210	Yémen démocratique
Hong Kong	8 342	9 451	10 384	11 391	12 649	13 306	14 504	16 482	17 923	19 235	Hong–kong
India	88 333	91 369	102 523	104 627	110 844	122 101	130 263	140 177	156 436	174 696	Inde
Indonesia	3 362	4 489	4 721	5 855	7 188	9 171	10 592	13 185	13 621	15 060	Indonésie
Iran(Islamic Rep.of)	14 211	14 800	17 386	19 441	19 880	22 406	26 323	30 509	34 668	34 800	Iran(Rép.islamique)
Iraq	4 645	5 729	7 247	9 467	10 676	10 374	13 108	15 600	17 810	18 110	Iraq
Israel	10 114	10 864	11 674	12 213	12 326	12 882	13 632	14 384	14 709	15 488	Israël
Japan	448 432	467 993	497 041	521 625	514 050	523 144	522 475	556 686	583 282	605 136	Japon
Jordan	388	481	590	764	939	996	1 322	1 629	1 962	2 119	Jordanie
Korea,Dem.Ppl's.Rep	28 000	30 000	32 000	33 000	35 000	36 000	40 000	41 000	45 000	48 000	Corée,Rép.pop.dém.de
Korea, Republic of	23 117	26 587	31 510	35 600	37 239	40 207	43 122	48 850	53 808	58 007	Corée, République de
Kuwait,part Ntl.Zone	5 202	6 018	6 990	8 616	9 023	10 016	11 699	12 499	13 894	15 417	Koweït et prt.Zne.N.
Lao Peoples Dem.Rep	400	450	510	1 088	975	1 150	1 200	1 075	990	1 350	Rép. dém. pop. lao
Lebanon	1 320	1 450	1 550	1 600	1 600	1 605	1 150	1 100	1 220	1 220	Liban
Macau	160	181	204	234	262	295	339	404	425	445	Macao
Malaysia	6 360	7 139	8 040	8 759	9 607	10 116	10 767	12 085	13 106	14 180	Malaisie
Maldives	2	2	2	3	4	5	8	8	11	11	Maldives
Mongolia	712	837	897	990	1 266	1 263	1 218	1 468	1 964	2 488	Mongolie
Nepal	142	160	177	195	190	218	284	303	337	383	Népal
Oman	266	404	462	600	764	928	1 136	1 366	2 016	2 456	Oman
Pakistan	8 860	9 155	10 283	11 786	12 106	13 199	14 786	16 697	18 318	23 003	Pakistan
Philippines	12 135	12 449	12 703	13 893	15 105	15 952	17 650	18 888	18 637	18 832	Philippines
Qatar	801	1 011	1 349	1 987	2 416	2 757	3 074	3 300	3 410	3 500	Qatar
S.Arabia,pt.Ntrl.Zn	5 839	6 713	9 143	14 880	18 319	24 461	30 364	29 215	30 400	31 600	Arab.saoud,p.Zn.neut

For general note, see end of table. — Voir la fin du tableau pour la remarque générale.

Electric energy, gross production by public utilities (continued) – Enérgie électrique, production brute, services publics (P) (suite)

Unit : Million KWH — Unité : Millions de kilowatts–heures

Country or area	1976	1977	1978	1979	1980	1981	1982	1983	1984	1985	Pays ou zone
Singapore	4 605	5 115	5 898	6 448	6 940	7 442	7 860	8 626	9 401	9 876	Singapour
Sri Lanka	1 132	1 217	1 385	1 525	1 668	1 872	2 066	2 114	2 261	2 464	Sri Lanka
Syrian Arab Republic	1 500	1 889	2 533	3 246	3 714	4 425	5 431	5 942	6 517	6 936	Rép. arabe syrienne
Thailand	9 826	11 175	12 637	13 443	14 426	15 369	16 620	18 857	21 024	23 074	Thaïlande
Turkey	17 208	19 100	20 006	20 553	19 415	20 588	23 243	23 689	26 717	30 244	Turquie
United Arab Emirates	68	132	191	247	320	410	460	470	476	480	Emirats arabes unis
Viet Nam	2 887	3 398	3 520	3 510	3 700	4 520	4 680	4 200	4 800	5 000	Viet Nam
Yemen	63	69	103	134	170	213	264	270	280	280	Yémen
Europe	**1 632 095**	**1 689 663**	**1 779 096**	**1 862 675**	**1 903 159**	**1 945 879**	**1 966 468**	**2 044 972**	**2 142 439**	**2 251 570**	**Europe**
EEC	***957 990***	***980 141***	***1 030 990***	***1 083 284***	***1 093 460***	***1 097 866***	***1 100 593***	***1 129 723***	***1 185 229***	***1 253 566***	***CEE***
Belgium	43 067	43 101	46 647	47 925	49 367	47 113	46 956	49 231	50 817	53 489	Belgique
Denmark	20 510	22 066	20 423	21 838	26 763	19 412	23 388	21 805	22 286	28 725	Danemark
France incl. Monaco	167 326	175 282	189 757	202 690	212 253	233 399	234 264	251 297	276 702	297 100	France y comp.Monaco
Germany, Fed. Rep.	266 560	267 994	282 270	297 078	297 367	300 027	301 960	309 418	326 539	344 487	Allemagne, Rép. féd.
Greece	17 523	18 721	20 764	21 818	22 409	23 211	23 063	22 049	24 554	27 324	Grèce
Ireland	8 142	8 851	9 480	10 473	10 413	10 383	10 388	10 642	11 067	11 569	Irlande
Italy and San Marino	128 831	130 996	140 576	145 044	151 391	147 795	152 980	153 743	154 052	158 365	Italie y comp. S.Mrn
Luxembourg	93	85	108	120	128	188	116	110	127	108	Luxembourg
Netherlands	52 228	52 313	55 357	57 991	58 174	57 610	53 119	52 890	55 151	55 258	Pays–Bas
United Kingdom	253 710	260 732	265 608	278 307	265 195	258 728	254 359	258 538	263 934	277 141	Royaume–Uni
EFTA	***234 203***	***246 360***	***254 776***	***272 865***	***277 248***	***296 754***	***300 035***	***325 825***	***340 957***	***362 007***	***AELE***
Austria	29 909	31 937	32 152	34 816	36 018	36 653	37 034	36 679	36 206	38 260	Autriche
Finland	18 035	23 341	24 324	26 631	31 820	33 180	33 995	35 105	37 244	40 453	Finlande
Iceland	2 421	2 602	2 674	2 922	3 148	3 315	3 575	3 766	3 833	4 029	Islande
Norway,Svlbd,J.Myn I.	64 320	54 952	62 057	68 201	64 455	72 353	72 261	85 227	84 856	83 067	Norvège,Svalbd,J.May
Portugal	9 135	13 137	13 969	15 937	14 381	12 980	14 351	17 156	19 099	17 872	Portugal
Sweden	78 788	79 931	82 659	84 325	84 867	92 418	92 236	101 490	115 744	128 880	Suède
Switzrld,Liechtenst.	31 595	40 460	36 941	40 033	42 559	45 855	46 583	46 402	43 975	49 446	Suisse,Liechtenstein
East Europe	***311 903***	***327 858***	***349 404***	***352 996***	***370 021***	***385 809***	***395 000***	***411 005***	***431 094***	***442 150***	***Europe de l'est***
Albania	1 850	2 000	2 200	2 250	2 300	2 500	2 600	2 725	2 850	2 975	Albanie
Bulgaria	22 981	24 882	26 298	27 788	30 204	32 511	35 896	38 161	40 119	36 944	Bulgarie
Czechoslovakia	51 675	55 709	58 224	57 550	62 491	63 458	64 607	65 826	67 548	70 090	Tchécoslovaquie
German Dem. Rep.	65 069	67 514	72 107	73 615	76 818	91 173	94 016	96 146	101 631	105 691	Rép. dém. allemande
Hungary	20 914	22 253	24 387	23 354	22 664	23 114	23 540	24 594	25 193	25 821	Hongrie
Poland	94 248	98 956	105 307	106 921	111 531	106 458	108 930	116 808	125 688	128 891	Pologne
Romania	55 166	56 544	60 881	61 518	64 013	66 595	65 411	66 745	68 065	71 738	Roumanie
Other Europe	***127 999***	***135 304***	***143 926***	***153 530***	***162 430***	***165 450***	***170 840***	***178 419***	***185 159***	***193 847***	***Autre Europe***
Faeroe Islands	113	122	136	150	160	165	170	170	178	178	Iles Féroé
Gibraltar	52	51	52	52	55	58	60	61	61	63	Gibraltar
Malta	382	417	459	501	527	558	597	675	700	784	Malte
Spain	86 068	88 569	94 601	100 941	105 878	106 598	110 052	113 661	114 747	122 080	Espagne
Yugoslavia	41 384	46 145	48 678	51 886	55 810	58 071	59 961	63 852	69 473	70 742	Yougoslavie
USSR	**1 036 420**	**1 074 075**	**1 124 896**	**1 161 196**	**1 218 478**	**1 249 631**	**1 289 600**	**1 341 699**	**1 415 600**	**1 544 117**	**URSS**
Oceania	**93 523**	**99 783**	**103 583**	**108 245**	**113 809**	**119 769**	**124 811**	**127 178**	**134 473**	**142 843**	**Océanie**
American Samoa	62	65	67	70	75	72	72	76	74	75	Samoa américaines
Australia	69 106	75 084	78 638	83 478	88 141	93 545	97 543	98 667	104 656	112 412	Australie
Cook Islands	9	10	10	12	11	11	10	10	11	12	Iles Cook
Fiji	185	201	211	226	230	237	244	250	307	313	Fidji
French Polynesia	153	196	215	235	255	280	290	187	203	220	Polynésie française
Guam	980	1 058	1 060	1 100	1 150	1 115	1 100	976	1 000	1 100	Guam
Kiribati	5	4	4	5	5	5	5	5	6	6	Kiribati
Nauru	26	26	26	26	26	26	26	27	28	28	Nauru
New Caledonia	1 560	1 347	1 101	1 154	1 303	1 150	920	723	895	1 100	Nouvelle–Calédonie
New Zealand	20 910	21 265	21 687	21 334	21 982	22 706	23 957	25 525	26 519	26 764	Nouvelle–Zélande
Niue	1	2	2	2	2	3	3	3	3	3	Nioué
Pacific Islds(Trust)	121	122	123	125	130	135	135	138	140	156	I.Pacifique (tutel.)
Papua New Guinea	350	344	375	407	426	407	422	510	545	565	Papouasie–Nvl–Guinée
Samoa	22	25	28	32	32	31	36	32	33	34	Samoa
Solomon Islands	15	15	15	15	16	19	20	20	23	24	Iles Salomon
Tonga	6	7	7	9	10	12	12	12	12	12	Tonga
Vanuatu	12	12	14	15	15	15	16	17	18	19	Vanuatu
Total	**6 373 497**	**6 674 008**	**7 055 225**	**7 369 710**	**7 613 227**	**7 792 626**	**7 892 872**	**8 242 165**	**8 700 349**	**9 155 888**	**Total**

For general note, see end of table. — Voir la fin du tableau pour la remarque générale.

Electric energy, gross production by public utilities (continued) – Enérgie électrique, production brute, services publics (P) (suite)

General note.
Electric energy generated by public supply undertakings (that is, enterprises, whatever their legal form, whose primary activity is the production, transmission and distribution of electric energy). Production is measured gross, that is, including station use and transmission losses.(SITC 35100–1).

Africa
Zambia: Net production.

Zimbabwe: Net production.

America, North
Dominican Republic: Net Production.

United States: Net production.

U.S. Virgin Island: Net Production.

America, South
Mexico: Net production.

Europe
Finland: Net production.

France incl. Monaco: Net production.

Iceland: Net production.

Liechtenstein: Net production.

Switzerland: Net production.

Remarque générale.
Production brute d'énergie électrique, y compris la consommation des centrales et les pertes dues au transport, des entreprises publiques (entreprises, quel que soit leur statut juridique, dont le but essentiel est de produire, de transporter et de distribuer de l'énergie électrique). (CTCI 35100–1).

Afrique
Zambie: Production nette.

Zimbabwe: Production nette.

Amérique du Nord
République dominicaine: Production nette.

Etats–Unis: Production nette.

Iles Vierges amér.: Production nette.

Amérique du Sud
Mexique: Production nette.

Europe
Finlande: Production nette.

France y comp. Monaco: Production nette.

Islande: Production nette.

Liechtenstein: Production nette.

Suisse: Production nette.

Gas produced by gas works – Gaz d'usine à gaz

Unit : Terajoules

Unité : Terajoules

Country or area	1976	1977	1978	1979	1980	1981	1982	1983	1984	1985	Pays ou zone
Africa	**27 099**	**27 622**	**27 643**	**29 361**	**30 467**	**30 630**	**31 727**	**33 781**	**32 798**	**33 314**	**Afrique**
Algeria*	167	...	...	...	0	0	0	0	0	0	Algérie*
Egypt*	167	171	167	170	180	200	200	200	200	200	Egypte*
Libyan Arab Jamah.*	33	33	33	35	30	30	30	30	30	30	Jamah.arabe libyenne*
South Africa	26 322	27 000	27 000	28 700	29 786	* 30 000	* 31 000	* 33 000	* 32 000	* 32 500	Afrique du Sud
Tunisia	410	418	443	456	471	* 400	497	551	568	584	Tunisie
America, North	**2 057**	**2 190**	**2 337**	**2 496**	**2 582**	**2 628**	**2 515**	**2 582**	**2 762**	**2 653**	**Amérique du Nord**
Cuba	2 057	2 190	2 337	2 496	2 570	2 613	2 500	2 564	2 744	2 635	Cuba
Panama ex.Canal Zone	62	42	42	20	...	...	...	...	...	...	Panama ex.zone Canal
Panama	...	...	...	...	12	* 15	* 15	* 18	* 18	* 18	Panama
America, South	**15 661**	**16 343**	**17 030**	**18 892**	**18 391**	**18 606**	**18 926**	**19 970**	**20 419**	**20 535**	**Amérique du Sud**
Brazil	10 005	10 482	11 115	11 625	11 738	12 397	13 019	13 716	14 093	14 413	Brésil
Chile	5 196	5 480	5 530	6 878	6 243	5 769	5 480	5 824	5 895	5 728	Chili
Suriname	75	* 0	* 0	* 0	* 0	* 0	* 0	* 0	* 0	* 0	Suriname
Uruguay	385	381	385	389	410	440	427	430	431	394	Uruguay
Asia	**363 395**	**359 115**	**376 467**	**386 087**	**425 872**	**452 812**	**458 213**	**503 561**	**525 011**	**538 290**	**Asie**
Hong Kong	1 892	2 077	2 504	3 021	3 523	4 033	4 858	5 924	6 907	7 979	Hong–kong
India*	375	400	450	425	350	300	15	10	0	0	Inde*
Indonesia	1 072	1 130	* 1 193	* 1 260	* 1 300	* 1 370	1 541	* 1 730	1 315	* 1 078	Indonésie
Japan	356 489	352 122	367 023	375 749	415 008	440 941	445 480	489 462	510 120	521 319	Japon
Korea, Republic of	146	165	184	203	378	969	1 144	1 576	2 152	3 503	Corée, République de
Philippines	356	378	351	351	345	334	313	256	172	154	Philippines
Singapore	1 646	1 755	1 940	2 150	2 211	2 252	2 249	2 179	2 194	2 052	Singapour
Sri Lanka	0	61	123	140	132	106	68	47	19	40	Sri Lanka
Turkey	1 047	670	2 343	2 461	2 286	2 181	2 286	2 181	1 951	1 984	Turquie
Europe	**420 789**	**371 496**	**370 957**	**364 170**	**352 354**	**325 704**	**315 968**	**300 683**	**249 592**	**258 277**	**Europe**
EEC	***221 993***	***177 387***	***172 587***	***164 567***	***158 923***	***140 415***	***129 154***	***106 196***	***48 382***	***57 841***	***CEE***
Belgium	46	49	56	54	53	47	43	39	33	33	Belgique
Denmark	5 617	5 316	5 347	5 358	5 069	4 487	4 186	4 355	4 402	4 044	Danemark
France incl. Monaco	20 586	12 599	6 837	3 611	2 275	1 234	1 108	1 001	842	864	France y comp.Monaco
Germany, Fed. Rep.	138 925	120 678	119 106	123 778	122 663	107 747	97 453	76 315	16 618	32 508	Allemagne, Rép. féd.
Greece	128	126	126	133	128	127	139	144	343	544	Grèce
Ireland	4 520	4 499	4 480	4 613	3 806	3 459	3 113	2 914	2 798	2 441	Irlande
Italy and San Marino	21 898	21 566	22 286	* 22 800	21 236	20 043	20 369	19 001	17 862	11 922	Italie y comp. S.Mrn
United Kingdom	30 273	12 554	14 349	4 220	3 693	3 271	2 743	2 427	5 484	5 485	Royaume–Uni
EFTA	***21 321***	***16 418***	***13 458***	***9 347***	***8 946***	***7 989***	***7 619***	***7 116***	***6 884***	***6 746***	***AELE***
Austria	12 432	8 229	5 593	1 402	1 385	974	990	1 034	1 063	1 005	Autriche
Finland	485	468	410	410	377	360	342	274	257	240	Finlande
Norway,Svlbd,J.Myn I.	452	368	289	280	225	204	133	85	36	0	Norvège,Svalbd,J.May
Portugal	2 335	2 398	2 405	2 406	2 475	2 513	2 615	2 553	2 576	2 554	Portugal
Sweden	4 370	4 169	4 120	4 019	3 684	3 316	3 031	2 660	2 462	2 428	Suède
Switzrld,Liechtenst.	1 247	786	641	830	800	622	508	510	490	519	Suisse,Liechtenstein
East Europe	***158 924***	***158 762***	***166 404***	***170 864***	***164 417***	***159 085***	***160 047***	***168 326***	***175 087***	***174 105***	***Europe de l'est***
Czechoslovakia	51 425	57 410	57 540	56 496	56 963	55 613	50 779	48 261	48 871	46 951	Tchécoslovaquie
German Dem. Rep.	79 450	82 660	88 990	93 557	89 737	87 032	92 148	104 862	111 922	113 070	Rép. dém. allemande
Hungary	12 980	10 157	9 874	9 056	9 638	8 994	8 931	7 714	7 139	6 155	Hongrie
Poland	15 069	8 535	10 000	11 755	8 079	7 446	8 189	7 489	7 155	7 929	Pologne
Other Europe	***18 551***	***18 929***	***18 508***	***19 392***	***20 068***	***18 215***	***19 148***	***19 045***	***19 239***	***19 585***	***Autre Europe***
Spain	14 441	14 764	15 730	16 090	16 481	15 191	15 537	16 095	17 325	17 920	Espagne
Yugoslavia	4 110	4 165	2 778	3 302	3 587	3 024	3 611	2 950	1 914	1 665	Yougoslavie
USSR	**15 885**	**14 479**	**14 056**	**13 419**	**12 864**	*** 10 000**	**9 011**	**8 673**	**7 860**	**6 595**	**URSS**
Oceania	**18 284**	**16 501**	**14 912**	**14 577**	**13 974**	**13 317**	**12 624**	**11 963**	**10 701**	**15 276**	**Océanie**
Australia	16 262	14 529	13 838	13 566	13 054	12 535	12 089	11 518	10 513	15 039	Australie
New Zealand	2 022	1 972	* 1 074	* 1 011	* 920	* 782	* 535	445	188	237	Nouvelle–Zélande
Total	**863 170**	**807 746**	**823 402**	**829 002**	**856 504**	**853 697**	**848 984**	**881 213**	**849 143**	**874 940**	**Total**

For general note and footnotes, see end of table.

Voir la fin du tableau pour la remarque générale et les notes.

General note.
Gas made by establishments belonging to undertakings, whatever their legal form, whose main purpose is the production of manufactured gas, measured at 15 degrees centigrade and standard sea-level atmospheric pressure (760 mm Hg). This item includes gas manufactured in coke ovens situated at gas works and municipal gas plants. Production should include gas consumed for heating furnaces and for other internal uses by the producing establishment. (SITC 34120-2B).

Remarque générale.
Production de gaz (y compris le gaz consommé pour le chauffage des fours et pour d'autres utilisations internes de l'établissement producteur) d'établissements appartenant à des entreprises au statut juridique quelconque dont l'objet principal est de produire du gaz manufacturé, mesurée à la température de 15° C et à la pression atmosphérique normale au niveau de la mer (760 mm de mercure). Cette rubrique comprend le gaz de cokerie produit dans les centrales gazières et les régies municipales. (CTCI 34120-2B).

INDEX OF COMMODITIES IN ORDER OF ISIC CODES
INDICES DES PRODUITS PAR ORDRE DE CODE CITI

INDEX OF COMMODITIES IN ORDER OF ISIC CODES (continued)
INDICES DES PRODUITS PAR ORDRE DE CODE CITI (suite)

Litho in United Nations, New York [illegible] United Nations publication
[illegible]—October [illegible] Sales No. [illegible]
ISSN [illegible] ISBN [illegible]

كيفية الحصول على منشورات الأمم المتحدة

يمكن الحصول على منشورات الأمم المتحدة من المكتبات ودور التوزيع في جميع أنحاء العالم . استعلم عنها من المكتبة التي تتعامل معها أو اكتب إلى : الأمم المتحدة ، قسم البيع في نيويورك أو في جنيف .

如何购取联合国出版物

联合国出版物在全世界各地的书店和经售处均有发售。请向书店询问或写信到纽约或日内瓦的联合国销售组。

HOW TO OBTAIN UNITED NATIONS PUBLICATIONS

United Nations publications may be obtained from bookstores and distributors throughout the world. Consult your bookstore or write to: United Nations, Sales Section, New York or Geneva.

COMMENT SE PROCURER LES PUBLICATIONS DES NATIONS UNIES

Les publications des Nations Unies sont en vente dans les librairies et les agences dépositaires du monde entier. Informez-vous auprès de votre libraire ou adressez-vous à : Nations Unies, Section des ventes, New York ou Genève.

КАК ПОЛУЧИТЬ ИЗДАНИЯ ОРГАНИЗАЦИИ ОБЪЕДИНЕННЫХ НАЦИЙ

Издания Организации Объединенных Наций можно купить в книжных магазинах и агентствах во всех райснах мира. Наводите справки об изданиях в вашем книжном магазине или пишите по адресу: Организация Объединенных Наций, Секция по продаже изданий, Нью-Йорк или Женева.

COMO CONSEGUIR PUBLICACIONES DE LAS NACIONES UNIDAS

Las publicaciones de las Naciones Unidas están en venta en librerías y casas distribuidoras en todas partes del mundo. Consulte a su librero o diríjase a: Naciones Unidas, Sección de Ventas, Nueva York o Ginebra.

Litho in United Nations, New York
40837—October 1987—3,275
ISBN 92-1-061121-7

05000H
(only hardbound edition for sale)
ISBN 92-1-161289-6 (vols.I and II the set)

United Nations publication
Sales No. E/F.87.XVII.9
ST/ESA/STAT/SER.P/24(Vol.II)